A TO Z

OF

BRITISH (and Irish) POPULAR CULTURE

This book is dedicated to the memory of my friend Mark Bytheway (1963-2010)

Mark was the 2007 Brain of Britain, 2008 World Quiz Champion, and 2009 British Quiz Champion. A remarkable man, Mark achieved those astonishing feats despite suffering from oesophageal cancer to which he finally succumbed after an heroic battle. Led by Tim Westcott, the famous Milhous Warriors, which has at various times included world champions Kevin Ashman and Pat Gibson plus an assortment of quizzing stars I refer to as the Swindon Mafia, i.e. Eric Kilby, Sean O'Neill, Brian Wilkins, to name but three, are now a man down.

Many of my happiest quizzing memories have been alongside Mark in hybrid extensions of the Warriors in which we have travelled the country in pursuit of titles and prizes and invariably found success due to the professionalism and sheer brilliance of the team that had Mark as its talisman. Mark is a legend that will not be forgotten. He was a regular guy who lived life to the full and was much admired for his brain but also for his blokeishness. My memories of him include an impromptu Bavarian Ass Slapping Dance after winning a national quiz title with a traditional German-themed finals night, and racing a bicycle alongside him whilst having Trivial Pursuit questions fired at us by Jeremy Beadle. The memory that probably epitomises Mark most clearly though was when I visited him in hospital and he was so poorly he was unable to speak. Kev Ashman, Brian Wilkins and I were discussing Pat Gibson's forthcoming Champion of Champions *Mastermind* subject of Pixar films. We were arguing over how many there were to research (up to spring 2010) and none of us was sure but we settled for nine. I then looked across to Mark's bed and although he was seemingly not with us at all his right hand opened then closed and then opened again to alert us to the fact that the answer was indeed ten! – sheer genius R.I.P. mate.

As with some of my previous books, Mark worked in tandem with his quizzing team-mate, and our mutual friend, Eric Kilby in supplying me with a plethora of trivia across the spectrum of pop culture but in particular biographies of actors; he and Eric splitting their load by one working on actors while the other tackled actresses. This process began seven long years ago and when Mark eventually became too ill to complete his research for me Eric took over his workload quite naturally and without fuss. Eric's ultimate contribution has been immense and I thank him sincerely for not only doing the groundwork for the film section but also for helping in so many other areas, right down to the proofreading function.

ABOUT THE AUTHOR

Trevor was an accountant and BBC question-setter before dedicating himself to producing indispensable works of reference. He was also a veteran of numerous radio and television programmes. In 1997 alone he won a dozen shows, including the grand finals of both Channel 4's *15-to-1* and BBC's *Today's the Day*. He then made his own entry into pop culture history by getting himself temporarily banned by the BBC after being sued by the producers of an opposition quiz show for flouting their appearance rules. Trevor won a Gold Medal at the 1998 Mind Sports Olympiad and the following year founded the British Quiz Association, which held its inaugural championship in 1999 at Olympia in London. Perhaps to show his versatility, in 2000 Trevor gained the bronze medal at the Zest Peugeot National Fitness Challenge in Coventry, from an original field of more than 10,000. The following year saw the first edition of his best-selling *A to Z of almost Everything* which is now in its fifth edition. In 2002 Trevor was placed third in the British Quiz Championships and later that year was part of the *Guardian's* 'Dream Team' that cut a swathe through London's pub quizzes and provided the inspiration for the BBC's *Eggheads*. After hosting the first-ever International quiz, against Belgium, in 2003, Trevor co-presented corporate and charity quizzes with Jeremy Beadle until the great man's death in 2008.

He now presents this, his magnificent opus on every aspect of the popular culture of Britain and Ireland.

ALSO BY TREVOR MONTAGUE

A to Z of almost Everything

A to Z of Sport

A to Z of Britain and Ireland

Introduction to The A to Z of British Popular Culture

In the planning stages of this book I was acutely aware of several potential problem areas that needed to be addressed in order to ensure production of a cohesive text that sat comfortably within my intended parameters. What I didn't want is to stand accused of merely including entries that reflected my own personal preferences and prejudices.
It became clear that I would have to not only define the term "popular culture" but also qualify my definition in order to justify my content.

So what is popular culture?

One generally accepted definition describes it as the regular interactions, needs, desires and cultural exchanges that make up the everyday lives of the mainstream. By dint of this definition it clearly excludes both elitist high cultural art forms, such as opera, historic art, classical music, ballet, theatre and traditional literature as well as formal educational studies such as history, geography, politics, the sciences and nature. What is left is sometimes referred to as popular culture although the lines do begin to blur over time; for example Shakespeare's plays would have been considered as popular culture in England during the seventeenth century, Gilbert and Sullivan operettas likewise in the nineteenth.

Popular culture is therefore an ever-evolving and ever-changing medium which occurs uniquely in time and place. Traditionally the domain of the so-called working classes; the world of pop culture has thrived as class distinctions have become less defined.

In recent years pop culture has had a huge influence on art and one only has to look at the list of Turner Prize-winners to appreciate how the pop-art movement, which began in the late 1950s, has evolved to create a new wave of installation and performance artists devoid of formal training but rich in energy and ambition. This influence has also infiltrated our schools and so-called "dumbing down" techniques are perhaps a direct result of the changing requirements of a working society that values computer literacy, creativity and communication skills above numeracy and grammar.

Conversely, it would be equally true to say that popular culture has itself been influenced quite dramatically by the so-called mass media. Newspapers now feature regular celebrity gossip and pictures of scantily dressed young women; publishers tend to have a disproportionate number of celebrity writers on their books and television has a plethora of lifestyle and reality programmes, to the extent that people are constantly immersed in trivia about celebrity culture.

So in the second decade of the 21st century what topics should I include in an A to Z of Popular Culture?

As always with my projects I have to defer to my natural habitat of the quiz world as the starting point to determine my core subjects. At this point I should probably add that an ever-increasing pop culture bias has infiltrated the world of quiz as much as any other walk of life in recent years. No longer is it possible for the typically elite quizzing animal of the past to dominate even their local pub quiz unless extending their repertoire to a serious study of what is affectionately referred to as trash-trivia.

So my core subjects are those that are touched upon most frequently in pop culture quizzes i.e. popular music, television and radio, cinema and the mass media.

The next problem I wrestled with was whether I should focus on the subjects in-depth or omit the high cultural and historical content and concentrate solely on in vogue areas. Ultimately I decided to give these topics both a contemporary and historical feel.

Within pop music I have listed every UK Top 10 single since the inception of the charts and written biographies of an eclectic array of British and Irish artists within that list, documenting their UK single and album chart successes.

The television and radio section goes back to the early days of broadcasting and is undoubtedly the most comprehensive record of programmes ever published. By way of homage to the world's longest-running soap opera I have included the complete cast of Coronation Street across the 50 years since its birth.

My cinema section not only includes biographies of every major British and Irish film star but also a plethora of directors, producers, costume designers, make-up artists and stuntmen. My cut-off point for these three areas is December 31st 2011 although I could not resist updating up to the time of going to press so there is an abundance of early 2012 material included in the biographies.

The mass media doesn't include many references to the Internet, mobile devices or video games but does include magazines and comics, concentrating on the sort of people featured in tabloid newspapers as a result of their lifestyle. To that end I have written biographies of a host of glamour models, pop artists, reality stars, celebrity sport stars, style icons and comedians.

As is my wont I have included some of the more quirky British infatuations such as 'Rear of the Year', 'Celebrity Mums and Dads of the Year', Beauty Pageant winners, and 'Pipesmokers of the Year'. Alluding back to my definition of popular culture as the sort of trivia that might be discussed by the mainstream (down the pub for instance), I have also included a section on classic cars and motorbikes.

I have endeavoured to accommodate an Irish perspective in all sections but I apologise that limited space prevented me including the Irish Top 10 singles chart alongside the UK chart. The Irish charts started on October 1st 1962 and there is considerable crossover of the UK charts over the past 50 years. I have however mentioned Irish chart success in the pop biography section where relevant.

Finally, I would like to make the observation that some of those featured within the covers of this book have attained no lasting appeal and respect as yet and are merely famous for being famous. Perhaps these people will fade into insignificance in the near future or perhaps their stars will soar. This uncertainty is the nature of popular culture.
It is necessarily youth-driven and fads and trends within it will come and go but true pop icon status is long-lasting and the truly talented will be immortalised by their output and in the fond memories of their fans.

Answers to cover questions
The Chemical Brothers
Tommy Handley
Both banned by the BBC
All Saints

Contents

First published in Great Britain in 2012 by Trevor Montague

Copyright © 2012 Trevor Montague

ISBN 978-0-7481-9997-6

Printed and bound by CPI Group (UK) Ltd, Croydon, CR0 4YY

British (and Irish) Cinema Biographies

Abbott, John (1905-96) Born John Andrew Abbott, 5 June 1905, Wandsworth, London. Actor. John took up acting after switching from studying art. Screen debut: *Madamoiselle Docteur* (1937). He then made *The Return of the Scarlet Pimpernel* (1938*)*, *This Man is News* (1939) and *The Saint in London* (1939*)* in Britain before travelling to Stockholm to work in the British Embassy at the outbreak of WWII. John visited the United States on holiday and decided to stay having gained a part in *The Shanghai Gesture* (1941). He went on to feature in 60 more films including *Mrs Miniver* (1942), *Anna and the King of Siam* (1946), *The Woman in White* (1948), *Omar Khayyam* (1957) and *The Greatest Story Ever Told* (1964). He also had a steady television career in the 1960s and 1970s before becoming a drama coach. He died 24 May 1996, Los Angeles, California.

Acheson, James (1946-) Born 13 March 1946, Leicester. Costume designer. Brought up in Essex, James attended art school in Wimbledon to study theatre design. He worked in the BBC costume department where his work included designing for *Dr Who* between 1973 and 1976. His first film should have been *Flash Gordon* (1980) but after this job fell through he worked on *Time Bandits* (1981). James continued to work with Terry Gilliam on *The Meaning of Life* (1983) and *Brazil* (1985). He then worked with Bernado Bertolucci on *The Last Emperor* (1987), a film featuring 10,000 costumes and won him his first Academy Award for Costume Design. He also collaborated with Bertolucci for *The Sheltering Sky* (1990) and *Little Buddha* (1993). He won further Best Costume Academy Awards for *Dangerous Liaisons* (1988) and *Restoration* (1995) by which time his reputation as a designer for period dramas was second to none. However, he has never forgotten his sci-fi roots and his recent films have seen him interpret the comic book stylings of *Spider-Man* (2002), *Daredevil* (2003) and *Spider-Man 2* (2004). Other films include: *Highlander* (1986), *Wuthering Heights* (1992), *Mary Shelley's Frankenstein* (1994), *The Man in the Iron Mask* (1998) and *The Little Vampire* (2000). James received the Career Achievement for Film Award from the Costume Designers Guild and currently lives in Wellington, New Zealand.

Ackland, Joss (1928-) Born Sidney Edmond Jocelyn Ackland, 29 February 1928, Ladbroke Grove, London. Actor. Graduated from The Central School of Speech and Drama, making his stage debut in *The Hasty Heart* (1945). Screen debut: *Seven Days to Noon* (1950). He spent a few years as a tea planter in Africa during the mid 1950s before returning to acting. Probably best known on film as a villain, especially in *White Mischief* (1987) and *Lethal Weapon II* (1989), Joss is also a prolific stage and television actor. He was Associate Director of the Mermaid Theatre (1962-64) and also played Juan Peron in the original London stage production of *Evita*. In 2001 he admitted that "I do an awful lot of crap", and regretted taking a role in *Bill and Ted's Bogus Journey* (1991). He was awarded the CBE in December 2000. After his wife, Rosemary, died of motor neurone disease in 2002 he took time out to edit the diaries she wrote throughout the 51 years of their marriage. He returned to film acting in a leading role in the British crime thriller *Flawless* (2007). His most recent role is as Rufus in the 2012 film *Katherine of Alexandria*. See also entries in television section for *Lord Raingo, Six Faces,* and *Z Cars*.

Adam, Ronald (1896-1979) Born Ronald George Hinings Adams, 31 December 1896, Bromyard, Worcestershire. Actor and author. Although from a theatrical family Ronald trained as an accountant. He was a member of the Royal Flying Corps and ultimately a POW during WWI. Ronald began acting, directing and producing after the war. Screen debut: *Strange Boarders* (1938). He re-enlisted in the RAF on outbreak of WWII and rose to the rank of wing commander. Films include: *Christopher Columbus* (1949), *The Bad Lord Byron* (1949), *Seven Days to Noon* (1950), *The Lavender Hill Mob* (1951), *Captain Horatio Hornblower* (1951), *Reach for the Sky* (1956) and *Lust for Life* (1956). Ronald was awarded the OBE for his services to film and his secondary career as author and playwright. His novels, *Readiness at Dawn* (1941) and *We Rendezvous at Ten* (1942) were published under the pseudonym 'Blake'. His plays included, *An English Summer* (1948), *A Wind on the Heath* (1949), and

Marriage Settlement (1950), which he also produced. Ronald died 27 March 1979, Uckfield, East Sussex.

Addams, Dawn (1930-85) Born Victoria Dawn Addams, 21 September 1930, Felixstowe, Suffolk. Actress. Educated at RADA. Stage debut: *Charley's Aunt* (1949). Travelled to Hollywood in 1950. Screen debut: *Night into Morning* (1951). In 1953 Dawn appeared in a small role in the ground-breaking film *The Moon is Blue* - the film which helped end religious censorship of Hollywood films. Other films include: *The Robe* (1953), *Return to Treasure Island* (1954), *A King in New York* (1957), *The Two Faces of Dr Jekyll* (1960), *The Vampire Lovers* (1970) and *The Vault of Horror* (1973). She married Prince Vittorio Emanuele Massimo of Arsoli in 1954 but was divorced in 1971. Dawn was an ever-present in the popular sitcom *Father Dear Father* (1968-73) but retired on marrying James White in 1974. She died of cancer, 7 May 1985, Kensington, London. See also entries in the television section for *Father Dear Father, Star Maidens,* and *Triangle.*

Adrian, Max (1903-73) Born Max Bor (aka Max Cavendish), 1 November 1903, Enniskillen, County Fermanagh, Northern Ireland. Actor. Stage debut: *Katja the Dancer* (1926). Screen debut: *The Primrose Path* (1934). Although never a leading man he played a wide variety of roles from classics to revue. Perhaps his two best known roles were as the Dauphin in Olivier's *Henry V* (1945) and as Mr. Max/Lord Hubert Brockhurst in *The Boyfriend* (1971). In the late 1960s he toured his one-man show as George Bernard Shaw and played Ludicrus Sextus, Frankie Howard's master, in the TV series *Up Pompeii*. He also portrayed Frederick Delius in Ken Russell's TV biography *Song of Summer* (1968). Max died of a heart-attack at home in Shamley Green, nr Guildford in Surrey, 19 January 1973.

Agutter, Jenny (1952-) Born Jennifer Ann Agutter, 20 December 1952, Taunton, Somerset. Actress. Her father was an officer in the British army which meant her early years were mostly spent travelling. Trained as a ballerina. Screen debut: *East of Sudan* (1964). Other early films include *Ballerina* (1965) and *Star!* (1967). She appeared as Roberta (Bobbie) in *The Railway Children* on television in 1968 and reprised the role on the big screen in 1970. She next starred in *Walkabout* (1971) before moving to Hollywood. Further roles followed in *Logan's Run* (1976) and *An American Werewolf in London* (1981). Many of her film roles included explicit nude scenes, notably *Equus* (1977), in which she attempts to seduce a stable boy (played by Peter Firth). She returned to England in the early 1990s and continues to appear regularly on television in such series as *Spooks, New Tricks, The Invisibles* and *Monday Monday*. She played the mother in a 2000 TV version of *The Railway Children*. Jenny married Johan Tham, a Swedish hotelier in 1990. See also entries in the television section for *The Good Guys, The Invisibles, It's A Knockout, The Newcomers, The Railway Children, Spooks* and *TECX.*

Aherne, Brian (1902-86) Born William Brian de Lacy Aherne, 2 May 1902, King's Norton, Birmingham. Actor. A child stage actor trained at Italia Conte before taking a job as an architect's clerk in his teenage years but again returning to acting in his early twenties. Stage debut: *Fifinella* (1910). Screen debut: *The Eleventh Commandment* (1924). He moved to the United States in 1933. Major film roles: *Song of Songs* (1933), *Sylvia Scarlett* (1934), *Jaurez* (1939), *I Confess* (1953), *Titanic* (1953), *Prince Valiant* (1954) *and The Swan* (1956). Nominated for Best Supporting Actor Academy Award for his role as Emperor Maximilian in *Juarez* (1939). Brian married twice, Joan Fontaine (1939-1945) - he once commented rather ungallantly that the dates coincided with those of WWII - and Eleanor Labrot (1946-86). Autobiography: *A Proper Job* (1969). His brother Patrick (b. 6 January 1901, King's Norton, Birmingham; died 30 September 1970 Woodland Hills, California) was also an actor. Brian died of heart failure 10 February 1986, Venice, Florida.

Albanesi, Meggie (1899-1923) Born Margherita Cecila Brigida Lucia Maria Albanesi, 8 October 1899, Marylebone, London. Actress. Daughter of Australian-born novelist Effie Maria Henderson Albanesi (aka Effie Adelaide Rowlands). Meggie studied at Sir Herbert Beerbohm Tree's Academy of Dramatic Art. Stage debut: *A Pair of Spectacles* (1917). Screen debut: *The Better 'ole: or, The Romance of Old Bill* (1919). Other films:

Darby and Joan (1919), *Mr Wu* (1919), *The Skin Game* (1921*)*, *The Great Day* (1921*)* and *Det Omringade Huset* (1922). Although the term 'method acting' had not yet been coined, Meggie was undoubtedly a brilliant young actress with a reputation for totally immersing herself in her roles. Unfortunately a life of what was at that time called "gay abandon" led to a tragically early death in Broadstairs, Kent. A memorial to her, designed by Eric Gill, stands in the foyer of St Martin's Theatre, London. It reads: "Remember Meggie Albanesi, an artist who died in the service of the theatre December 9 1923. R.I.P."

Allgood, Sara (1879-1950) Born 15 October 1879, Dublin. Raised, along with her sister Molly (see entry for Maire O'Neill), in an orphanage. Actress. Began acting with the Abbey Theatre in Dublin. Stage debut: *Cathleen Ni Houlihan* (1902). Screen debut: *Just Peggy* (1918). She appeared in *Blackmail* (1929), Alfred Hitchcock's first talkie. Included amongst her many films are: *Juno and the Paycock* (1930), *Sabotage* (1936), *Dr Jekyll and Mr Hyde* (1941), *Jane Eyre* (1944), *The Keys of the Kingdom* (1944) and *Cheaper by the Dozen* (1950). Toured United States in 1940 and decided to stay there, eventually taking US citizenship. Nominated for an Academy Award for Best Supporting Actress for her role as Mrs Morgan in *How Green Was My Valley* (1941). Her husband, stage actor Gerald Henson, and only daughter both died during the Spanish influenza epidemic of 1917. She died of a heart-attack at Woodland Hills, California, 13 September 1950.

Alon, Roy (1943-2006) Born in 1943, Otley, Leeds. Stunt coordinator and Second Unit director (from 1984). Joined the Merchant Navy aged 15 and later worked in a brewery. Continuous falls whilst motorcycle racing eventually led him to take up stunt work in 1968. Initially worked on TV programmes such as *Follyfoot*, *Emmerdale Farm*, *Les Dawson Show* and *The New Avengers*. Made his big screen debut in *A Bridge Too Far* (1977). His stunt work can be seen in many James Bond films beginning with *The Spy Who Loved Me* (1977) and continuing through *Octopussy* (1983), *Never Say Never Again* (1983), *The Living Daylights* (1987), *Goldeneye* (1995), *Tomorrow Never Dies* (1997), *The World is not Enough* (1999) and *Die Another Day* (2002). Other films include: *The Long Good Friday* (1980), *Superman III* (1983), *Indiana Jones and the Temple of Doom* (1984), *Rita, Sue and Bob Too* (1986), *Willow* (1988), *Bullseye!* (1990), *The Three Musketeers* (1993), *Jude* (1996), *Entrapment* (1999), *Troy* (2004) and *The Da Vinci Code* (2006). TV series include *A Touch of Frost* (1992), *No Angels* (2004) and *Max & Paddy's Road to Nowhere* (2004). According to the 2004 edition of The Guinness Book of World Records he is the world's most prolific stuntman at which time his TV, big screen and theatre credits had reached 893. Holds the UK "high fall" record of 138 feet, which he did in an episode of *Taggart*. He died of a heart-attack, 1 February 2006.

Anderson, Lindsay (1923-94) Born Lindsay Gordon Anderson, 17 April 1923, Bangalore, India. Director and writer. Son of a Scottish army officer stationed in India. Educated at Cheltenham and Wadham College, Oxford. Served in India with the Intelligence Corps during WWII (1944-1946). Co-founded the short-lived but influential film magazine *Sequence*. A proponent of the Free Cinema group in the UK who sort to encourage more social and moral awareness amongst British film makers. Began by making public awareness documentaries such as *Meet the Pioneers* (1948) and including *Every Day Except Christmas* (1957) about Covent Garden market and *Thursday's Child* (1953) about teaching deaf children. This film, narrated by Richard Burton, won an Academy Award for Best Documentary Short Subject. Feature screen debut: *This Sporting Life* (1963). He then made two short films *The Singing Lesson* (1967) and *The White Bus* (1967) before embarking on *if....* (1968), the first of three films starring Malcolm McDowell playing a different character but all with the name Mike Travis, the others being *O Lucky Man!* (1973) and *Britannia Hospital* (1982). His other feature films were: *In Celebration* (1975), *Look Back in Anger* (1980), *The Whales of August* (1987) and *Glory! Glory!* (1989). He also directed a documentary about a Wham! concert in China called *Foreign Skies* (1984) and his final documentary was an

autobiographical project for BBC Scotland called *Is That All There Is?* (1993). An occasional screen actor, he had parts in *Inadmissable Evidence* (1968) and *Chariots of Fire* (1981). A director at the Royal Court Theatre in the late 1950s, he continued to be a much sought after theatre director both in the UK and on Broadway. His publications include: *Making a Film* (1952), *About John Ford* (1983) and *Taking the Stage* (1986). Known for his strongly held views which he was always willing to express. Reportedly asked for his epitaph to be "Here I am, still surrounded by idiots". Died at Angouleme, Poitou-Charentes, France, 30 August 1994.

Anderson, Michael (1920-) Born Michael Joseph Anderson, 30 January 1920, Camberwell, London. Director. Worked as an assistant director on such films as *Freedom Radio* (1941) and *In Which We Serve* (1942), in which he also had an acting role. His full directing debut (actually as co-director and co-writer with Peter Ustinov) was *Private Angelo* (1949). His first solo project, and cited as his favourite film, was *The Dam Busters* (1954) and he followed this with further classics *1984* (1956), *Around the World in 80 Days* (1956) and *Yangste Incident* (1957). Over the next two decades his output included *Chase a Crooked Shadow* (1957), *The Wreck of the Mary Deare* (1959 – after Hitchcock had pulled out), *All the Fine Young Cannibals* (1960), *The Naked Edge* (1961), *Operation Crossbow* (1965), *The Quiller Memorandum* (1966), *Pope Joan* (1972), *Doc Savage: The Man of Bronze* (1975) and *Orca: Killer Whale* (1977). He is probably best known for directing the sci-fi classic *Logan's Run* (1976) which also featured his son Michael Anderson Jr (b. 6 August 1943 Hillingdon, London) who made his screen debut in *The Moonraker* (1958), gave Hayley Mills her first screen kiss in *In Search of the Castaways* (1962) and narrated and played Trooper Tim Ryan in *Major Dundee* (1965). Anderson senior subsequently emigrated to Canada, and, like his son has concentrated more on TV work over the past 30 years, notably *The Martian Chronicles* (1980). The 1999 children's fantasy *The New Adventures of Pinocchio* was a rare excursion into film.

Andrews, Harry (1911-89) Born Harry Fleetwood Andrews, 10 November 1911, Tonbridge, Kent. Actor. Stage debut: *The Long Christmas Dinner* (1933) with Liverpool Rep. He joined John Gielgud's company in 1935. Served in the Royal Artillery during WWII, ending as acting major. After the war he joined the Stratford Memorial Theatre and was described by Kenneth Tynan as "the backbone of British theatre." He stayed true to his declared ambition of being "a good actor in good parts." Screen debut: *The Red Beret* (1952). Although perhaps best known for playing military types on screen in such films as *Ice Cold in Alex* (1958), *633 Squadron* (1964) and *The Hill* (1965) he displayed his more natural bent by playing Kath's (played by Beryl Reid) gay brother Ed, in *Entertaining Mr Sloane* (1970). Awarded a CBE in 1966. His last film role was as 'Old Thompson' in the 1986 film *Mesmeris ed* (aka *My Letter to George*). His long term partner was stage actor Basil Hoskins. Died 6 March 1989 Salehurst, East Sussex. See also entries in the television section for *A.J.Wentworth, BA*, *Clayhanger*, *Edward the Seventh*, and *Shades of Greene*.

Andrews, Julie (1935-) Born Julia Elizabeth Wells, 1 October 1935, Walton-on-Thames, Surrey. Actress and singer. Her stage career began as part of her mother Barbara and stepfather Ted Andrew's singing act. The late 1940s and 1950s saw her becoming a well known star in revue and pantomime and a regular radio performer. Stage debut: *Starlight Roof* (1947). On 1 November 1948 she became the youngest solo performer ever to appear in a Royal Command Variety Performance, at the London Palladium. Screen debut: *The Singing Princess* (1952) - voice over for animated film. Starring on Broadway as Polly Browne in *The Boyfriend* (1954) proved her big acting break. Bing Crosby saw her on Broadway and asked her to co-star with him in what is regarded as the first made-for-television movie, *High Tor*. She went on to star in the stage versions (but not the film adaptations of) *My Fair Lady* and *Camelot* before being chosen by Walt Disney for the lead in *Mary Poppins* (1964) for which she won the Best Actress Academy Award. Her most enduring role has been

Maria in *The Sound of Music* (1965) for which she received an Academy Award nomination for Best Actress. She went on to star in such films as *Thoroughly Modern Millie* (1967) and *Star!* (1968). She received another Academy Award Nomination for her role in *Victor/Victoria* (1982). The 1981 film *S.O.B.* (the title was thought to stand for Son Of a Bitch but Blake Edwards has subsequently insisted it meant Standard Operational Bullshit) was notorious for the scene where Andrews bared her breasts. Her most recent screen roles have included *The Princess Diaries* (2001), *The Princess Diaries II: Royal Engagement* (2004) and *Shrek 2* (2004) - voicing the role of Queen Lillian which she reprised for its sequels, *Shrek the Third* (2007) and *Shrek Forever After* (2010). In 2010, Julie also appeared in the comedy film, *Tooth Fairy*, and lent her voice to the comedy animated film, *Despicable Me* (as Marlena, Gru's mother). She is also an author of children's books under the name Julie Edwards - including *Mandy* (1971), *The Last of the Great Whangdoodles (1974)*, *Little Bo* (1999) - plus a series about *Dumpy the Dump Truck* written with her daughter Emma Walton and illustrated by her first husband Tony Walton. She has married twice: Tony Walton (1959-67) and film director Blake Edwards (1969 until his death in 2010). Problems with her throat have led her to severely restrict her singing but in a very busy 2010, Julie made her London comeback after a 21-year absence (her last performance there was a Christmas concert at the Royal Festival Hall in 1989). She performed at the O2 Arena, accompanied by the Royal Philharmonic Orchestra. Julie became a Dame of the British Empire in 2000 and in 2008 she published an autobiography, *Home: A Memoir of My Early Years*.

Angelus, Muriel (1909-2004) Born Muriel Angelus Findlay, 10 March 1909, London. Actress and singer. Stage debut: *A Midsummer Night's Dream* (1924). Screen debut: *The Ringer* (1928). Other films include: *Night Birds* (1930), *Hindle Wakes* (1931), *The Light that Failed* (1939), *The Way of All Flesh* (1940) and *Safari* (1940). She developed from being a music hall soprano at the age of twelve into being a splendid leading lady in stage musicals. She was the first to sing the classic *Falling in Love with Love* on Broadway after she was cast as Adriana in *The Boys from Syracuse* (1938) which in turn led to a contract with Paramount Pictures. Her singing voice was rarely heard on screen and her most memorable role was as Brian Donlevy's secretary in Preston Sturges' first feature film *The Great McGinty (1940)*. She married conductor Paul Lavelle in 1946 and retired from performing. Died 22 August 2004 Harrisonburg, West Virginia.

Annakin, Ken (1914-2009) Born Kenneth Cooper Annakin, 10 August 1914, Beverley, Yorkshire. Director. Initially worked in a tax office before a gambling win enabled him to travel to Australia, New Zealand and the United States. On his return he joined the RAF, only to be invalided out in 1942. He made documentaries in the early 1940s for *Verity Films* before moving on to features, starting with *Holiday Camp* (1947), which spawned the sequels *Here Come the Huggetts* (1948), *Vote for Huggett* (1949) and *The Huggetts Abroad* (1949). He made the Disney films *The Story of Robin Hood and his Merrie Men* (1952), *The Sword and the Rose* (1953), *The Third Man on the Mountain* (1959) and the ever-popular *Swiss Family Robinson* (1960). He also directed two of the better big-budget war films of the period: *The Longest Day* (1962 - one of three co-directors) and *The Battle of the Bulge* (1965). Other films include: *Miranda* (1949), *Hotel Sahara* (1951), *The Planter's Wife* (1952), *The Seekers* (1954), *Three Men in a Boat* (1956), *Nor the Moon by Night* (1958), *Crooks Anonymous* (1962), *The Fast Lady* (1962), *Monte Carlo or Bust* (1969) *Paper Tiger* (1975) and *The New Adventures of Pippi Longstocking* (1988). He gained an Academy Award nomination for co-writing the screenplay to *Those Magnificent Men in their Flying Machines* (1965), which he also directed. It was long thought that his friend George Lucas used his surname to name Anakin Skywalker (aka Darth Vadar) in the *Star Wars* series but after Ken's death on 22 April 2009, Beverly Hills, California, Lucas denied this via his publicist. His publications include *So You Want to be a Director* (2001). Awarded OBE in 2002.

Annis, Francesca (1945-) Born 14 May 1945, Kensington, London. Actress, born to a British father and a Brazilian-French mother. The family moved to Rio De Janeiro soon after Francesca's birth but returned to London when she was aged seven. Screen debut: *The Cat Gang* (1958). Played Eiras in *Cleopatra* (1963) and Estella in a BBC TV production of *Great Expectations* (1967), which brought her to the public's attention. She followed this with roles in Polanski's *Macbeth* (1971) - playing Lady Macbeth, *Krull* (1983) and *Dune* (1984). On television she played Lillie Langtry in the 1975 ITV drama series *Edward the Seventh*, a role she would have further success with in *Lillie* (1978). In recent years she has concentrated more on stage and TV roles but in 1999 starred alongside long-term partner Ralph Fiennes in *Onegin*. She and Fiennes met in 1995 when she played Gertrude in his Hamlet in an award winning Broadway production. They announced their separation in February 2006. Francesca has three children (Charlotte, Taran, Andreas) from a long-term relationship with actor Patrick Wiseman that began in 1976. In Autumn 2007 she starred as Lady Ludlow (an aristocrat opposed to the education of the lower classes) in the BBC1 costume drama series *Cranford*. Her most recent film roles include Valerie in the urban thriller, *Shifty* (2008) and Elizabeth in *The Little House* (2010). See also entries in the television section for *Between the Lines, Cranford, Edward the Seventh, Great Expectations, Jane Eyre, Lillie,* and *Love Story*.

Anthony, Lysette (1963-) Born Lysette Chodźko, 26 September 1963, London. Model and actress. The daughter of actors Michael Anthony (Michael Chodźko) and Bernadette Milnes. Lysette actually made her first screen appearance as baby Roxanne Doyle-Wells in the early days of *Crossroads* in 1964 by courtesy of her father appearing in the popular soap as Colonet St Clair. Lysette was dubbed "The Face of the Eighties" by David Bailey but gave up her modelling career to concentrate on acting at the age of nineteen, making her screen debut proper in the TV film *Ivanhoe* (1982 - as Lady Rowena). Her feature debut followed in the Morecambe and Wise vehicle *Night Train to Murder* (1983). She next starred in the fantasy film *Krull* (1983). Other films include: *Without a Clue* (1988), *Switch* (1991), *Husbands and Wives* (1992), *Face The Music* (1993),*The Hour of the Pig* (1993), *Look Who's Talking Now* (1993), *Save Me* (1994), *Dr. Jekyll and Ms. Hyde* (1995), *Dracula: Dead and Loving It* (1995), *Robinson Crusoe* (1997), *Tale of the Mummy* (1998), *Farewell to Harry* (2002) and *Beneath Loch Ness* (2002). Lysette appeared in Playboy in 1988 and moved to the USA in 1990. Her most famous television role was as Angie in the sitcom *Three Up Two Down* (1985-89). She now runs her own film production company in the UK. Her long-term partner until recently was composer Simon Boswell (b. 15 October 1956). They have a son, Jimi (b. 2004). The couple had an acrimonious court case in December 2011 in which Simon was cleared of domestic violence. Lysette was previously married to Dutch actor Luc Leestermaker (1990-95) and American film director David Price for two years before meeting Simon. Lysette has returned to the small screen in several soaps of late and has just completed filming of her latest film role, as Jilly, in *Strippers vs Werewolves*, due for release in 2012. See also entries in the television section for *The Bill, Casualty, Cluedo, Coronation Street, Crossroads, Doctors, Dombey and Son, Hollyoaks,* and *Three Up, Two Down*.

Apted, Michael (1941-) Born 10 February 1941, Aylesbury, Buckinghamshire. Director. Studied law at Cambridge before working as a researcher on *Coronation Street*. In 1963, working with Paul Almond, he interviewed 14 seven-year-olds from a variety of social backgrounds for the documentary *7 Up*. These were followed at seven-year intervals by *7 Plus 7, 21 Up, 28 Up, 35 Up, 42 Up and 49 Up* (2005) which followed most of the original group as they made their way in life. His directorial feature debut was *The Triple Echo* (1973). This was followed by *Stardust* (1974) and the biopics *Coal Miner's Daughter* (1980), *Gorillas in the Mist* (1988) and *Thunderheart* (1992). His more dramatic works include *Agatha* (1979), *Gorky Park* (1983), *Nell* (1994) the Bond film *The World is Not Enough* (1999) and the 2006 epic *Amazing Grace,* recounting the events that led to the abolition of the slave trade in Britain. Since 2003 he has been president of the Directors Guild of America. His most recent film is *The Chronicles of Narnia: The Voyage of the Dawn Treader* (2010), a sequel to *The Chronicles of Narnia: Prince Caspian*.

Archers, The Production company founded by Michael Powell and Emeric Pressburger in 1942. Although they shared writer-director-producer credit the usual procedure was for Pressburger to write and Powell to direct. They first collaborated on *The Spy in Black* (1939) and during the early years of WWII they also worked together on *Contraband* (1940*)* and *49th Parallel* (1941). They formed Archers Film Productions, with its distinctive archery target logo, in 1942 and their first joint production under this banner was *One of Our Aircraft is Missing* (1942). They then set out their famous five-point "Archers' Manifesto" (basically letting the actors know they were in sole charge) in a letter to Deborah Kerr inviting her to appear in *The Life and Death of Colonel Blimp* (1943).This film was seen as a criticism of the way the war was being fought and Churchill tried to prevent its release. They went on to produce some of the most distinctive British films of the era including *A Canterbury Tale* (1944), *I Know Where I'm Going!* (1945), *A Matter of Life and Death (1946)*, *Black Narcissus* (1947), *The Elusive Pimpernel* (1950), *Gone to Earth* (1950), *Tales of Hoffmann* (1951), *Oh... Rosalinda!!* (1955) and *The Battle of the River Plate* (1956). *The Red Shoes* (1948) was nominated for an Academy Award for Best Picture. Their films always mined a seam of fantasy and romance inside imaginative and unusual situations which did not always prove popular with British audiences but are now regarded as key films in British cinema history. The partnership dissolved in 1957, although they collaborated again on *They're a Weird Mob* (1966) and *The Boy who Turned Yellow* (1972). See also individual entries for Powell and Pressburger.

Arliss, George (1868-1946) Born George Augustus Andrews, 10 April 1868, Bloomsbury, London. Actor. Son of printer William Arliss Andrews. Stage debut: *Vidocq* (1886). Married actress Florence Smith (stage name Florence Montgomery) in Harrow in 1899. Toured the United States with a theatre company in 1902 and decided to stay and ply his trade there. He starred on Broadway before transferring his talents to the screen. Screen debut: *The Devil* (1921), a version of one of his stage successes, as was *Disraeli* (1921). His small success in silent cinema was to blossom once talkies arrived and he is sometimes called "the first gentleman of talking pictures". His forte was playing great historical roles and his portrayal of *Disraeli* (1929*)* won him a Best Actor Academy Award in 1931, making him the first British actor to win an Oscar. In the same year he was also nominated for his role in *The Green Goddess* (1929). One of his films, *The Man Who Played God* (1932*)*, was Bette Davis' first leading role and the two of them also co-starred in *The Working Man* in 1933. Arliss then formed a successful production company at Warners frequently using a preferred cast of actors but also discovering new talent such as James Cagney, Randolph Scott, and Dick Powell. He returned to England in the mid 1930s and after starring in the title role of *Dr Syn* in 1937 he retired when his wife became blind. He published two autobiographies: *Up the Years from Bloomsbury* (1927*)* and *My Ten Years in the Studios* (1940). Died 5 February 1946 in Harrow Weald and is buried in the Rackham Section of Harrow Weald cemetery.

Armstrong, Craig (1959-) Born 29 April 1959, Glasgow. Composer. Studied composition and piano at the Royal Academy of Music. Won the GLAA Young Jazz Musician of the year in 1982. During the 1980s received commissions for compositions for the theatre, the Scottish Arts Council and various classical ensembles. His work as producer and arranger with various popular music artists including U2, Madonna and Massive Attack brought him to the attention of director Baz Luhrmann, who asked him to score *Romeo + Juliet* (1996). Further film work includes songs, arrangements, orchestrations or scores for *Orphans* (1997*)*, *Plunkett & Macleane* (1999), *Cruel Intentions* (1999), *The Bone Collector* (1999), *Moulin Rouge* (2001), *The Quiet American* (2002), *Love Actually* (2003), *Ray* (2004*)*, *Fever Pitch* (2005), *World Trade Center* (2006), *Elizabeth: The Golden Age* (2007), *The Incredible Hulk* (2008), *Wall Street: Money Never Sleeps* (2010), *Neds* (2010) and *In Time* (2011). He has also released the albums *The Space Between Us* (1998), *As If to Nothing* (2002), *Piano Works* (2004*)* and *Film Works 1995-2005* (2005). His rousing music is often featured in the BBC television programme *Top Gear*. In 2008, he co-wrote, with author Ian Rankin, a fifteen minute opera, *Gesualdo*, for Scottish Opera. He was awarded the OBE in the 2010 Queen's New Years Honours List for his services to the music industry.

Armstrong, Vic (1946-) Born Victor Monroe Armstrong, 5 October 1946, Farnham Common, Buckinghamshire. Stuntman, stunt coordinator and director. Set out with the intention of being a jockey but subsequently used his horse riding skills to be a stunt double in *Arabesque* (1966). The following year he worked on *You Only Live Twice* (1967). He went on to double for George Lazenby in *On Her Majesty's Secret Service* (1969), Roger Moore in *Live and Let Die* (1973) and Sean Connery in *Never Say Never Again* (1983). Because of a more than passing resemblance to Harrison Ford he has doubled for him in many films: *Raiders of the Lost Ark* (1981), *Star Wars: Episode VI - Return of the Jedi* (1983), *Indiana Jones and the Temple of Doom* (1984), *Witness* (1985), *The Mosquito Coast* (1986), *Frantic* (1988), *Working Girl* (1988), *Indiana Jones and the Last Crusade* (1989), *Regarding Henry* (1991) and *Patriot Games* (1992). He also doubled for Christopher Reeve on *Superman* (1978), *Superman II* (1980) and *Superman III* (1983) and it was on the first film that he met his future wife Wendy Leech, who was doubling for Margot Kidder as Lois Lane. Has also worked as stunt coordinator on the *Indiana Jones Trilogy*, the first two *Superman* films plus many other films including *Krull* (1983), *Legend* (1985), *Empire of the Sun* (1987), *Total Recall* (1990), *Last Action Hero* (1993), *Starship Troopers* (1997), *Charlie's Angels* (2000) and *Gangs of New York* (2002). His work as second (action) unit director includes *F/X2* (1991), *Rob Roy* (1995), *Entrapment* (1999), *Blade: Trinity* (2004), *War of the Worlds* (2005), *Mission Impossible III* (2006), *I Am Legend* (2007), *The Mummy: Tomb of the Dragon Emperor* (2008), *Robin Hood* (2010) and *The Green Hornet* (2011). He has directed and coordinated the spectacular stunts in *Tomorrow Never Dies* (1997), *The World is not Enough* (1999) and *Die Another Day* (2002). His solo directorial debut was *The Joshua Tree* (1993). Won an Academy Award for Technical Achievement in 2001 for "the refinement and application to the film industry of the Fan Descender for accurately and safely arresting the descent of stunt persons in high freefalls."

Arterton, Gemma (1986-) Born Gemma Christina Arterton, 12 January 1986, Gravesend, Kent. Actress. Made her film debut as head girl, Kelly, in *St Trinian's* (2007). Other films include: *Three and Out* (2008), *Quantum of Solace* (2008 - where the role of "Strawberry Fields" led to her becoming the face of Avon's Bond Girl 007 fragrance), *The Boat That Rocked* (2009) *St. Trinian's II: The Legend of Fritton's Gold* (2009) and the title role in *The Disappearance of Alice Creed* (2009). 2010 was a particularly eventful year for Gemma, playing Io in the remake of *Clash of the Titans*, Princess Tamina in *Prince of Persia: The Sands of Time*, the title role in the Stephen Frear's comedy *Tamara Drewe* and making her West End debut in the UK premiere of *The Little Dog Laughed*. Gemma also found time to marry Stefano Catelli, a sales manager, in June, at a secret ceremony in Zuheros, Andalucia, Spain. She has recently completed filming her role of Gretel in the 2012 film, *Hansel and Gretel: Witch Hunters*. Her television work includes the role of Elizabeth Bennet in the four-part ITV drama *Lost in Austen* (2008). Gemma, who was born with six fingers on each hand, is reported to be a supporter of Charlton Athletic FC and has a tattoo of an angel wing behind her left ear, three facts apparently unrelated!

Arthur, George K (1899-1985) Born Arthur George Brest, 27 January 1899, Littlehampton, West Sussex, but brought up in Brentford, London. Actor and producer. Although appearing in the comedy short *Spring Fever* in 1919 his feature film debut was in *Kipps* (1921). Travelled to the United States in December 1922. Usually a lead in comedies he played a more reflective role as The Boy in Josef von Sternberg's *The Salvation Hunters* (1925). He struck up a comedy partnership with Danish actor Karl Dane and as Dane & Arthur they starred in a series of films 1927-1929 including *Rookies* (1927) and *Circus Rookies* (1928). Arthur retired from acting in 1935 and became a producer, winning an Academy Award for Best (2-Reel) Short Film for *The Bespoke Overcoat* (1956). He also received nominations for Best (2-Reel)

Short Film for *On the Twelfth Day* (1955) and Best (Cartoon) Short Film for *A Place in the Sun* (1960). Died 30 May 1985 New York.

Ashcroft, Peggy (1907-91) Born Edith Margaret Emily Ashcroft, 22 December 1907, Croydon, London. Actress. Graduated from the Central School of Speech and Drama. Stage debut: *Dear Brutus* (1926) but first gained attention playing Naemi in *Jew Suss* in 1929, and Desdemona opposite Paul Robeson's Othello two years later. She was then hailed as the finest Juliet of her generation in playing the role opposite the Romeo's of Olivier and Gielgud in 1934. Screen debut: *The Wandering Jew* (1933). Made an impact in *The 39 Steps* (1935) and *Quiet Wedding* (1940*)* and then concentrated solely on the stage until the late 1950s. Created a Dame Commander of the British Empire in 1956. The Ashcroft Theatre in Croydon was named in her honour in 1962. Won a Best Supporting Actress Academy Award for *A Passage to India* (1984). In the same year, Ashcroft appeared in the role of Barbie Batchelor in the internationally acclaimed British television mini-series *The Jewel in the Crown* for which she won a BAFTA Best Television Actress award. Peggy married publisher Rupert Hart-Davis (1929-1933), theatre director Theodore Komisarjevsky (1934) and her third marriage, to lawyer Jeremy Hutchinson (1940-1965) produced two children. Her granddaughter is the French singer Emily Loizeau. She died 14 June 1991 at the Royal Free Hospital, London. See also entries in the television section for *Edward and Mrs Simpson*, and *The Jewel in the Crown*.

Asher, Jane (1946-) Born 5 April 1946, Marylebone, London. Red-haired Actress. Screen debut: *Mandy* (1951) aged five. Her films include: *Charley Moon* (1956), *The Greengage Summer* (1961 - as Hester Grey), *Girl in the Headlines* (1963), *The Masque of the Red Death* (1964), *Alfie* (1966), *The Winter's Tale* (1967), *Deep End* (1970 - as Susan), *The Buttercup Chain* (1970), *Henry VIII and his Six Wives* (1972), *Runners* (1983 - as Helen), *Success Is the Best Revenge* (1984), *Dreamchild* (1985 as Mrs Liddell), *Paris by Night* (1988), *Closing Numbers* (1993), *Tirante el Blanco* (2006 - as Empress of Visantia) and *Death at a Funeral* (2007 - as Sandra).. Jane was engaged to Paul McCartney 1967-68 but married illustrator Gerald Scarfe in 1981. Her father was the first to identify Munchausen's syndrome and her mother was a professor of oboe at the Guildhall School of Music and Drama and taught George Martin to play the instrument. Her elder brother Peter (b. 22 June 1944) was a well-known child actor and more famous as part of the singing duo Peter and Gordon in the 1960s. Now a successful novelist (*The Longing, The Question* and *Losing It*), cookbook writer and cake shop proprietor, Jane has had numerous television successes. See entries in the television section for *Brideshead Revisited, Chefs, Crossroads, Holby City, Knock on Any Door, Love Story, Maestro, The Mistress, The Old Guys*, and *The Palace*.

Askey, Arthur (1900-1982) See entry in comedy section

Askwith, Robin (1950-) Born 12 October 1950, Southport, Lancashire. Actor. Screen debut: *If* (1968). Appeared in the 1973 film *Carry On Girls* and then made a career in the role of Timothy Lea in a series of comedy soft-core sex films starting with *Confessions of a Window Cleaner* (1974). He went on to confess to being a *...Pop Performer* (1975), *Driving Instructor* (1976) and *...from a Holiday Camp* (1977) before falling out of public favour. Autobiography: *Confessions of Robin Askwith* (1999). Appeared as "British seaman" in *U-571* (2000). In 2007 Robin appeared in *Coronation Street* as a holiday rep and in 2009 played Gary in the popular TV sitcom Benidorm. See also entries in the television section for *Benidorm, Beryl's Lot, Coronation Street, Eastenders*, and *Here Come the Double Deckers*.

Asquith, Anthony (1902-68) Born 9 November 1902, London. Director. Son of the Liberal Prime Minister Herbert Henry Asquith. Educated at Balliol College, Oxford. Founder member of The Film Society. Heavily influenced in his early film-making by continental cinema. Joined British Instructional Films in the early 1920s. Acted as stunt double for the title character in *Boadicea* (1926). Directorial debut: *Shooting Stars* (1928). Other early films include: *Underground* (1928), *A Cottage on Dartmoor* (1929) and *Tell England* (1931). Joined Gainsborough Pictures in 1932 and directed *The Lucky Number* (1932), *Dance, Pretty Lady* (1932) and *Unfinished Symphony* (1934). For London Films he directed *Moscow Nights* (1935). In 1938 he directed *Pygmalion* which gained an Academy Award nomination for Best Picture. There followed a very productive period including: *We Dive at Dawn* (1943), *Fanny by Gaslight* (1944), *The Importance of Being Earnest* (1952), *Carrington V.C.* (1956), *The Millionairess* (1960) and *Orders to Kill* (1962). Worked closely with dramatist Terence Rattigan on: *French Without Tears* (1939), *Quiet Wedding* (1940), *Uncensored* (1942), *The Way to the Stars* (1945), *While the Sun Shines* (1947), *The Winslow Boy* (1948), *The Browning Version* (1951), *The Final Test* (1953), *The V.I.P.s* (1963) and *The Yellow Rolls-Royce* (1964). Considered too arty by some and a talent which perhaps was not properly developed, although he did direct some classic features. Asquith led a very private but controversial life and was implicated in the Profumo Scandal as the 'man in the mask' at an orgy attended by Stephen Ward, Christine Keeler and Mandy Rice-Davies. Nicknamed 'Puff ' or 'Puffin' because of his supposed resemblance to the bird, Asquith was a closet homosexual who never married and died from lymphoma, 20 February 1968 Marylebone, London. Actress Helena Bonham-Carter is his grandniece.

Attenborough, Richard (1923-) Born Richard Samuel Attenborough, 29 August 1923, Cambridge. Actor and director. Studied at RADA. Stage debut in 1941. Screen debut: *In Which We Serve* (1942). Other early films include: *The Hundred Pound Window* (1944), *Journey Together* (1945), *School for Secrets* (1946), *A Matter of Life and Death* (1946), *The Man Within* (1947), *Dancing with Crime* (1947) and *London Belongs to Me* (1948). Richard shot into the public's imagination with his portrayal of the villainous Pinkie in *Brighton Rock* (1947) and followed this up as Jack Read, the title character of *The Guinea Pig* (1948), playing a working-class boy who wins a scholarship to a public school as part of a post-World War Two experiment in bringing boys of different social classes together. In the 1950s his films included: *The Magic Box* (1952), *Gift Horse* (1952), *Father's Doing Fine* (1952), *Eight O'Clock Walk* (1954), *The Ship That Died of Shame* (1955), *Private's Progress* (1956), *The Baby and the Battleship* (1956), *Brothers in Law* (1957), *The Scamp* (1957), *Dunkirk* (1958), *The Man Upstairs* (1958), *Sea of Sand* (1958), *Danger Within* (1959), *I'm All Right Jack* (1959), *Jet Storm* (1959) and *SOS Pacific* (1959).He went on to play a string of character parts in such films as *The League of Gentleman* (1960), *The Angry Silence* (1960), *The Great Escape* (1963) and *10 Rillington Place* (1971), the first two of these four films he also produced. Other films of the 1960s include: *Only Two Can Play* (1962), *All Night Long* (1962), *The Dock Brief* (1962), *The Third Secret* (1964), *Seance on a Wet Afternoon* (1964), *Guns at Batasi* (1965), *The Flight of the Phoenix* (1965), *The Sand Pebbles* (1966), *Doctor Dolittle* (1967), *Only When I Larf* (1968), *The Bliss of Mrs. Blossom* (1968) and *The Magic Christian* (1969). Richard made his directorial debut with *Oh! What a Lovely War* (1969). In the 1970s he appeared in *The Last Grenade* (1970), *Loot* (1972), *And Then There Were None* (1974), *Brannigan* (1975), *Conduct Unbecoming* (1975), *The Chess Players* (1977), *A Bridge Too Far* (1977) and *The Human Factor* (1979) before taking a 14-year sabbatical from acting. After directing *Young Winston* (1972), *A Bridge Too Far* (1977) and *Magic* (1978) he fulfilled a long-held ambition in directing the biopic *Gandhi* (1982), which won him the Academy Award for Best Director, the film also winning Best Picture. After directing *A Chorus Line* (1985), *Cry Freedom* (1987), *Chaplin* (1992) and *Shadowlands* (1993) he returned to acting in *Jurassic Park* (1993), *Miracle on 34th Street* (1994), *Hamlet* (1996), *The Lost World: Jurassic Park* (1997), *Elizabeth* (1998) and *Puckoon* (2002). He has been married to actress Sheila Sim since 1945 and in 1952 they were in the original West End cast of *The Mousetrap*, Richard as Sergeant Trotter and Sheila as Mollie Ralston. He was appointed a CBE in 1967, knighted in 1976 and created a life peer in 1993. Among many positions he holds, he is currently the President of RADA, Chairman of Capital Radio, Chairman of Goldcrest Films and President of the British National Film and Television School. He was formerly President of BAFTA and a director of Chelsea Football Club and is their Life President. His younger brother David (b. 8 May 1926) is a famous naturalist and television presenter.

Atwill, Lionel (1885-1946) Born Lionel Alfred William Atwill, 1 March 1885, Croydon, London. Actor. Originally intended to become an architect. Stage debut: *The Walls of Jericho* (1904). Lionel emigrated to the USA in 1915 to continue his stage career. Screen debut: *Eve's Daughter* (1918). Became typecast as a villain - he said one side of his face was gentle and kind whereas the other side was cruel, predatory and evil - and after he appeared as *Dr X* (1932) his career as a stalwart of horror films was sealed. His most memorable role was as the one-armed police inspector Krogh in *Son of Frankenstein* (1939) where he uttered the immortal line "One doesn't easily forget, Herr Baron, an arm torn out by the roots." which was later hilariously parodied in Mel Brooks' *Young Frankenstein* (1974). Other major roles included *Mystery of the Wax Museum* (1932), *Captain Blood* (1935), *The Three Musketeers* (1939), *The Hound of the Baskervilles* (1939) and *Sherlock Holmes and the Secret Weapon* (1942). He was notorious for throwing wild parties which eventually led to a five-year probationary sentence in 1942 and a virtual blacklisting by the Hays Office (US censorship authority). He married four times, his second marriage being to actress and aviator Elsie Mackay aka Poppy Wyndham and his third to Louise Cromwell Brooks, who had previously been married to Douglas MacArthur. He died 22 April 1946, Pacific Palisades, California whilst filming the serial *Lost City of the Jungle*.

Audley, Maxine (1923-92) Born 29 April 1923, London. Actress. Made her stage debut in 1940 and played Emelia in the 1951 London production of *Othello* which had Orson Welles as the Moor and Peter Finch as Iago. On the opening night she slapped Welles' face after he mistakenly threw coins in her face instead of onto the stage. Screen debut: *The Pleasure Garden* (1952). Always only a supporting actress her most celebrated role was as Anna Massey's blind mother in the controversial *Peeping Tom* (1960). Her many films include *The Vikings* (1958), *The Trials of Oscar Wilde* (1960) and *The King of New York* (1957) in which she played Charlie Chaplin's wife. She was still working on television into the 1990s, appearing on *Casualty* in 1992 just a few weeks before her death on 23 July of that year. See also entries in the television section for *Great Expectations* and *Morgan's Boy*.

Austin, Albert (1882-1953) Born 13 December 1882, Birmingham, West Midlands. Actor. Records appear to differ as to the actual year of Austin's birth and I have cited the year given by the BFI although some sources offer 1881 and 1885. Originally a Music Hall artist, joining Fred Karno's troupe and travelling to the United States with Karno in 1910. Worked mainly with and for Charlie Chaplin and was the only player to appear with Chaplin in all 12 films he made at Mutual. Screen debut: *The Floorwalker* (1916). Other films include: The *Fireman* (1916), *The Vagabond* (1916), *One A.M.* (1916 – a cameo role in this Chaplin film but the only other actor to appear), *The Count* (1916), *The Pawnshop* (1916), *The Rink* (1916), *The Cure* (1917), *The Immigrant* (1917), *The Bond* (1918), *Suds* (1920), *The Kid* (1921), *The Gold Rush* (1925) and *City Lights* (1931). Unfortunately his career did not really survive the coming of the talkies. Directed a handful of films in the 1920s: *Bungalow Troubles* (1920), *My Boy* (1921), *Trouble* (1922), *A Prince of a King* (1923), *The Bronco Express* (1924), *The Misfit* (1924) and *Keep Smiling* (1925). Albert's brother William Austin (12 June 1884 - 15 June 1975) was a lesser known actor but was famous for playing the role of Alfred in the 1943 Batman series films - this portrayal becoming the depiction subsequently used in the comic books. Albert died 17 August 1953 Hollywood, California.

Aylmer, Felix (1889-1979) Born Felix Edward Aylmer-Jones, 21 February 1889, Corsham, Wiltshire. Actor. Educated at Magdelen College School and Exeter College Oxford. Studied under the great Victorian actress Rosina Filippi. Stage debut: *Cook's Man* (1911) at the London Coliseum before joining the Birmingham Repertory Theatre in 1913. Screen debut: *Escape* (1930). Played supporting roles in many popular films including *The Citadel* (1938), *Henry V* (1944), *Hamlet* (1948) and *Quo Vadis* (1951). Felix specialised in playing wise old men, such as Merlin in *Knights of the Round Table* (1953). One of his most memorable roles was as the Archbishop of Canterbury in the film adaptation of *Becket* (1964). His last major screen role was as the Abbot in

the television sitcom *Oh, Brother!* (1968-70). He was President of The British Actors' Equity Association (Equity) 1949-1969. Vice-President of RADA (1953-1955). Appointed an OBE in 1950 and knighted in 1965. Felix was also a notable voice coach and gave elocution lessons to a young Audrey Hepburn in 1950. He died 2 September 1979, nr Cobham, Surrey. See also entry for *The Walrus and the Carpenter* in the television section.

Baddeley, Hermione (1906-86) Born Hermione Youlanda Ruby Clinton-Baddeley, 13 November 1906, Broseley, Shropshire. Actress. Stage debut 1918. Popular stage revue artiste and comedienne, often teamed up with Hermione Gingold. Screen debut: *A Daughter in Revolt* (1927). Became a major supporting actress post WWII in films such as *Brighton Rock* (1947), *Mary Poppins* (1964) and *The Unsinkable Molly Brown* (1964). Gained a Best Supporting Actress Academy Award nomination for her role in *Room at the Top* (1958). Autobiography: *The Unsinkable Hermione Baddeley* (1984). Her sister Angela Baddeley (born Madeleine Angela Clinton-Baddeley, 4 July 1904, West Ham, London; died 22 February 1976 Alton, Hampshire) was also an actress who made her stage debut in *Richard III* (1915) and was best known for her portrayal of Mrs Bridges in TVs *Upstairs, Downstairs* (1971-1975). Hermione died 19 August 1986, Los Angeles, California.

Baker, George (1931-2011) Born 1 April 1931 Varna, Bulgaria. Actor. Son of the honorary British Vice-Consul to Bulgaria and at the outbreak of WWII George was sent back to England. After National Service he took up theatre work full-time. Screen debut: *The Dam Busters* (1954). Made an impression in *The Moonraker* (1958) and other big screen films include: *Goodbye Mr Chips* (1969), *On Her Majesty's Secret Service* (1969) and *The Spy Who Loved Me* (1977). His last feature film was the Bollywood movie, *Parineeta* (2005 – as Sir William Eckhardt). He is, however, much better known for his TV career which includes playing Charles Dodson in *Alice* (1965), Stanley Bowler in *Bowler* (1973), Tiberius in *I, Claudius* (1976), Bruce McGill in *A Woman of Substance* (1985) and Inspector Wexford in *The Ruth Rendell Mysteries* (1987-2000). He has also featured in *Coronation Street* as brewery owner Cecil Newton. George, who was awarded an MBE in 2007, was married three times (Julia Squire (1950-1974), Sally Home (1974-1992) and since 1993 to Louie Ramsay, who played Mrs Wexford on screen. George died of pneumonia on 7 October 2011, shortly after a stroke.

Baker, Stanley (1928-76) Born William Stanley Baker, 28 February 1928, Ferndale, Rhondda Valley, Wales. Actor. Early in his career he appeared alongside Richard Burton on stage. Screen debut: *Undercover* (1943). He was usually cast in, and apparently preferred, roles as villainous, disenchanted, and in many instances, generally unsympathetic characters. Even his role as Victoria Cross-winning John Chard in *Zulu* (1964) was playing the uncompromising British officer against Michael Caine's charmer. His other better known films include: *The Cruel Sea* (1953), *The Guns of Navarone* (1964) and *Accident* (1967). Formed *Oakhurst Productions*, in the 1960s and produced films such as *Zulu* (1964), *Robbery* (1968) and *The Italian Job* (1969). His other films include: *All Over the Town* (1949 – his first as an adult) *Obsession* (1949), *Lilli Marlene* (1950), *Your Witness* (1950), *The Rossiter Case* (1951), *Captain Horatio Hornblower R.N.* (1951), *Whispering Smith Hits London* (1951), *Knights of the Round Table* (1953), *The Red Beret* (1953), *The Good Die Young* (1954), *Richard III* (1955), *Helen of Troy* (1956), *Alexander the Great* (1956), *Checkpoint* (1956), *A Hill in Korea* (1956), *Hell Drivers* (1957), *Campbell's Kingdom* (1957), *Violent Playground* (1958), *Sea Fury* (1958), *The Angry Hills* (1959), *Blind Date* (1959), *Hell Is a City* (1960), *The Criminal* (1960), *Sodom and Gomorrah* (1963), *In the French Style* (1963), *Dingaka* (1965), *Sands of the Kalahari* (1965), *Robbery* (1967), *The Girl with the Pistol* (1968), *Where's Jack?* (1969), *The Last Grenade* (1970), *Perfect Friday* (1970), *The Games* (1970) and his last film, Zorro (1975). After the stock market crash of 1974, his company was declared bankrupt and he went back to work, on television, in the classic mini-series *How Green Was My Valley*. Stanley was knighted in Harold Wilson's Lavender List of 1976. He died of lung cancer, 28 June 1976, Malaga, Andalusia, Spain. See also entries in the television section for *How Green Was My Valley*, and *Jane Eyre*.

Balcon, Jill (1925-2009) Born Jill Angela Henrietta Balcon, 30 January 1925, Westminster, London. Actress. Daughter of film producer Michael Balcon. Screen debut: *Nicholas Nickleby* (1947). Her short early film career included a dormitory fight with Jean Kent in *Good-Time Girl* (1949). Other films include: *Saraband for Dead Lovers* (1948), *The Lost People* (1949) and *Murder in the Cathedral* (1951). She returned to the screen in the 1990s in the Derek Jarman films *Edward II* (1991) and *Wittgenstein* (1993) and her last film *An Ideal Husband* (1999 – as Lady Bracknell). Jill was married to poet laureate Cecil Day-Lewis, from 1951 until his death in 1972. she is the mother of actor Daniel Day-Lewis and documentary film-maker and television chef Tamasin Day-Lewis. A portrait bust of her sculpted by Jacob Epstein is now lost. She died of a brain tumour 18 July 2009, London. See also entries in the television section for *The First Churchills*, and *General Hospital*.

Balcon, Michael (1896-1977) Born Michael Elias Balcon, 19 May 1896, Birmingham. Producer. Educated at George Dixon Grammar School in Edgbaston. Produced over 200 films, including some of the best British films of the mid-20th century. He also oversaw the launching of the career of Alfred Hitchcock. Formed *Victory Motion Pictures* with Victor Saville and Oscar Deutsch. Began producing with *Woman to Woman* (1923). A co-founder of *Gainsborough Pictures* in 1924, he became director of production for *Gaumont-British Pictures Ltd* in 1931 and *Gainsborough* became its production arm. With these companies he produced: *The Rat* (1925), *The Lodger* (1927), *Downhill* (1927), *The Ghost Train* (1931), *Man of Aran* (1934), *Rome Express* (1932), *The 39 Steps* (1935) and *Secret Agent* (1936). He worked briefly for the British arm of *MGM* before taking charge of production at Ealing Studios. Michael produced some classic British features over the next 20 years: *The Proud Valley* (1940), *The Foreman Went to France* (1942), *Went the Day Well?* (1942), *San Demetrio, London* (1943), *Hue and Cry* (1947), *Saraband for Dead Lovers* (1948), *Scott of the Antarctic* (1948), *Passport to Pimlico* (1949), *Whisky Galore!* (1949), *Kind Hearts and Coronets* (1949), *The Blue Lamp* (1950), *The Lavender Hill Mob* (1951), *The Man in the White Suit* (1951), *The Cruel Sea* (1953) and *The Ladykillers* (1955). In 1959 he formed *Bryanston Films* and was chairman of *British Lion* (1964-1965). His final production was *Tom Jones* (1963). Father of actress Jill Balcon. Grandfather of actor Daniel Day-Lewis. Autobiography: *A Lifetime in Films* (1969). He died 17 October 1977, Uckfield, East Sussex.

Bale, Christian (1974-) Born Christian Charles Philip Bale, 30 January 1974, Haverfordwest, Pembrokeshire. Actor. He appeared in adverts for fabric-softener *Lenor*, aged eight, and breakfast cereal *Pac-Man*, aged nine, before making his stage debut in *Nerds* (1984). Christian made his screen debut aged twelve in Spielberg's *Empire of the Sun* (1987) having beaten off a few thousand other hopefuls. He then graduated to more adult roles culminating in playing the serial killer Patrick Bateman in *American Psycho* (2000). Christian married Srbislava Blažić (b. 1970), a former model and personal assistant to Winona Ryder, in 2000. The couple have a daughter, Emmeline (b. 27 March 2005, Santa Monica, California). Christian played the Caped Crusader in *Batman Begins* (2005) *and The Dark Knight* (2008); magician Alfred Borden in *The Prestige* (2005), rancher Dan Evans in the remake of *3.10 to Yuma* (2007), FBI agent Melvin Purvis in *Public Enemies* (2009) and boxing trainer Dicky Eklund in *The Fighter* (2010), a performance for which he won an Academy Award for Best Supporting Actor. In July 2008, Christian had a much-publicised fit of anger on the set of *Terminator Salvation* (2009), while filming in New Mexico. Bale, who plays John Connor, a soldier in the human Resistance against Skynet, in the fourth of the *Terminator* franchise films, accused Shane Hurlbut, director of photography for the film, of continually walking on set during a particularly emotional scene and thereby ruining his concentration. Christian's forthcoming projects include a reprise of his role in Christopher Nolan's final outing as Batman director. *The Dark Knight Rises* (2012), set in Gotham city eight years after

the previous film, also stars Anne Hathaway (Selina Kyle/Catwoman) and Tom Hardy (Bane).

Balfour, Betty (1903-77) Born 27 March 1903, London. Actress. Stage debut in 1913. Screen debut: *Nothing Else Matters* (1920). Starred in a series of films based on her music hall character, a cockney flower girl called "Squibs". Made many films in Europe including *Monte Carlo* (1925), *La Petite Bonne du Palace* (1926), *Croquette* (1927), *Die Sieben Tochter der Frau Gyurkovics* (1927), *Le Diable au Coeur* (1927), *Monkeynuts* (1928) *and Die Regimentstochter* (1929). She also starred in Alfred Hitchcock's *Champagne* (1928). Made only one film in the United States: *The Pearl of Love* (1925). One of Britain's earliest stars of the silent screen, Betty was named by the *Daily Mirror* as Britain's favourite world star in 1927. A blue-eyed, curly-haired blond known as "Britain's Mary Pickford" and "Britain's Queen of Happiness" her career took a downturn with the onset of talkies - mainly because of her broad cockney accent, which did however enable her to make a musical remake of *Squibs* in 1935 and play Cockney Lil opposite Gordon Harker in *My Old Dutch* in 1934. She died 4 November 1977, Weybridge, Surrey.

Banks, Leslie (1890-1952) Born 9 June 1890, West Derby, Merseyside. Actor. Graduated from Keble College, Oxford. Stage debut: *The Merchant of Venice* (1911). Screen debut: *The Hounds of Zaroff (aka The Most Dangerous Game)* (1932). Served with Essex Regiment in WWI and suffered wounds which left one side of his face partially paralysed, a disability which he used to good effect when playing menacing characters on film. Split his time between Britain and USA and established himself as a successful actor on both stage and screen. He appeared in a series of top-notch films during the 1930s and 1940s including *The Man Who Knew Too Much* (1934), *Sanders of the River* (1935), *Fire Over England* (1937), *Jamaica Inn* (1939) and *Henry V* (1945). He was particularly effective as the English squire who is in fact a Nazi sympathiser in *Went the Day Well?* (1942). President of The British Actors' Equity Association (Equity) 1948. Appointed a CBE in 1950. He died 21 April 1952, London.

Bannen, Ian (1928-99) Born 29 June 1928, Airdrie, Lanarkshire. Actor. Educated at Ratcliffe College, Leicester. Stage debut: *Armlet of Jade* (1947). Made his name on the West End stage and was an original member of the Royal Shakespeare Company. Screen debut: *Privates Progress* (1956). Received an Academy Award nomination for Best Supporting Actor for his part in *Flight of the Phoenix* (1965). His other films included *Ghandi* (1982), *Hope and Glory* (1987), *Braveheart* (1995) and *Waking Ned (aka Waking Ned Devine)* (1998). Killed in a car accident 3 November 1999, Knockies Straight, Loch Ness. See also entries in the television section for *Doctor Finlay, Spooner's Patch*, and *Tinker Tailor Soldier Spy*.

Barber, Frances (1958-) Born 13 May 1958, Wolverhampton. Actress. Prolific stage and television performer who made her film debut in Peter Greenaway's *A Zed and Two Noughts* (1985) and followed up in Nicolas Roeg's *Castaway* (1987). She is probably best known to US audiences as Rosie in Stephen Frears's *Sammy and Rosie Get Laid* (1998). Other films include *Still Crazy* (1998), *Shiner* (2000) and *Goal!* (2005). In 2009 she returned to television in the ITV comedy drama *The Fattest Man in Britain*, written by Caroline Aherne and Jeff Pope. Although known to have dated director Danny Boyle and actor Neil Pearson, Frances is currently single. See also entries in the television section for *Bremner, Bird and Fortune, Celeb*, and *Funland*.

Barker, Will (1868-1951) Born William George Barker, 18 January 1868, Edmonton, London. Producer. Founded the *Autoscope Company* in 1900. Built studios at Ealing in 1907. In 1911 he paid Sir Herbert Tree £1,000 a day to appear in *Henry VIII* (1911). He also hired the composer Edward German to write music especially for the film. He followed this lavish extravaganza with *Sixty Years a Queen* (1913) -which cost a British record £12,000 to make - and *East Lynne* (1913) - the first British six-reeler. In contrast with his great rival Cecil Hepworth with his family-centric fare, Barker filled his films with spectacle. His final films were *The Battle of Waterloo* (1913), *Jane Shore* (1915) and *She* (1916). With his films suffering in comparison with those coming out of the US, Barker retired on 12 November 1918. Died 6 November 1951, Wimbledon, London.

Barnes, Ben (1981-) Born Benjamin Thomas Barnes, 20 August 1981, London. Actor. He was educated at the independent King's College School, Wimbledon, before studying Drama and English literature at Kingston University. Ben joined the National Youth Music Theatre as a teenager and gained his first professional job, aged 15, as a drummer in the West End musical adaptation of *Bugsy Malone*. He was then briefly a singer in a boyband, Hyrise, which contested the UK heats for the Eurovision Song Contest in 2004 with the song "Leading Me On"; however, they lost out to James Fox and "Hold Onto Our Love". On stage, in 2006, he starred as the sexually provocative Dakin in the West End production of *The History Boys*. Ben made his screen debut as Craig Irwin in an episode of *Doctors* in 2006. He made his feature-film debut the following year as Young Dunstan in *Stardust* (2007). His most famous role to-date is undoubtedly as Prince Caspian in *The Chronicles of Narnia: Prince Caspian* (2008) and King Caspian in *The Chronicles of Narnia: The Voyage of the Dawn Treader* (2010). Other films include: the TV movie *Split Decision* (2006), *Bigga Than Ben* (2007), Noël Coward's romantic comedy *Easy Virtue* (2008), the title role in *Dorian Gray* (2009) and *Locked In* (2010). Ben's latest film project is *Killing Bono* (2011), in which he plays Neil McCormick, an aspiring rock star who is overshadowed by his friend Bono, the lead singer of U2. He has also just completed filming scenes for the 2012 thriller film, *The Words*.

Barnes, Binnie (1903-98) Born Gitelle Enoyce Gertrude Maude Barnes, 25 March 1903, Finsbury Park, London. Actress. Youngest of 14 children, her father was a policeman. Worked at a variety of jobs before teaming up with Tex McLeod to perform a rope-spinning act. She then went solo as "Texas Binnie" Barnes. She made her "legitimate" stage debut in *The Silver Tassie* (1929). Screen debut: *Phonofilm* (1923). Made an impact when cast by Noël Coward on stage in *Cavalcade* and was lured to the USA. A brief stay in Hollywood was followed by being cast as Catherine Howard in *The Private Lives of Henry VIII* (1933). She also featured in *The Private Life of Don Juan* (1934), *Diamond Jim* (1935), *The Last of the Mohicans* (1938), *The Adventures of Marco Polo* (1938), *The Three Musketeers* (1939) and *The Decameron Nights* (1953). After WWII she moved with her husband to Italy, eventually retiring from acting until making a brief comeback in the late1960s. She died 27 July 1998 Beverly Hills, California.

Barrie, Wendy (1912-78) Born Marguerite Wendy Jenkins, 18 April 1912, Hong Kong. Actress. Goddaughter of J M Barrie, from whom she took her stage name. Educated in England and Switzerland. Screen debut: *The Callbox Mystery (1932)*. Came to greater attention as a coquettish Jane Seymour in *The Private Life of Henry VIII* (1933) which led her to move to the United States, playing opposite Spencer Tracy in *It's a Small World* (1935). Other films include: *The Big Broadcast of 1936* (1935), *The Hound of the Baskervilles* (1939) and *Submarine Alert* (1943). She also featured in the 'B' Picture series *The Saint* and *The Falcon* starring George Sanders. In the late 1940s she made a successful transition into television, hosting the children's programme *The Adventures of Oky Doky* (1948-49) and then her own chat show *The Wendy Barrie Show* (1948-1950). She died 2 February 1978, Englewood, New Jersey.

Bartholomew, Freddie (1924-92) Born Frederick Llewellyn, 28 March 1924, Dublin. Actor. Spent his very early years in Warminster, Wiltshire with his grandparents and aunt Millicent Bartholomew. Screen debut: *Fascination* (1930). Whilst on holiday in New York in 1934 he was spotted by David O. Selznick of *MGM* and cast as *David Copperfield* (1934). Became one of the first millionaire child stars. More films rapidly followed: *Anna Karenina* (1935), *Little Lord Fauntleroy* (1936), *Captains Courageous* (1937), *Kidnapped* (1938) and *Tom Brown's Schooldays* (1940). A series of 27 law suits over who should benefit from his income (Aunt Cissy or his parents) drained his earnings. Aunt Cissy was appointed his legal guardian. The onset of adolescence virtually spelled the end of his career but he went on to be, amongst other things, a chat show host, a director and eventually an advertising executive. Took US citizenship in 1943 on joining the USAAF as an aircraft mechanic. He died 23 January 1992, Sarasota, Florida, USA.

Barton, Mischa (1986-) Born Mischa Anne Barton, 24 January 1986, Hammersmith, London. Actress. Moved to New York at the age of four and attended Professional Children's School in Manhattan. Initially she started acting on the stage. She made her film debut as a child in John Duigan's *Lawn Dogs* (1997), which won awards at film festivals around the World. Since then she has appeared in several films, including *The Sixth Sense* (1999), *Notting Hill* (1999), *Tart* (2001), *Closing the Ring* (2007), and *St Trinians* (2007). The latter as former head girl JJ French. The tag line for *Tart* was "Sex, Drugs and Study Hall" which to a certain extent sums up the types of roles that Mischa has thus far played. It is for her television work that she is best known, first appearing in *All My Children* as a younger Lily Montgomery before taking her signature role of Marissa Cooper in *The OC*. She became a naturalized U.S. citizen in Los Angeles on 3rd February 2006. Mischa's recent films have included: *Assassination of a High School President* (2008), *Walled In* (2009), *Homecoming* (2009), *Don't Fade Away* (2009) and two films released in America in 2012, *Bhopal: Prayer for Rain* (an historical-drama set amidst the real-life Bhopal disaster) and *You and I* (an adaptation of the novel *t.A.T.u. Come Back*) – both of which were distributed in Europe at earlier dates.

Bass, Alfie (1916-87) Born Abraham Basalinsky, 12 April 1916, Bethnal Green, London. Actor. Stage debut: *Plant in the Sun* (1939). Screen debut: *The Bells Go Down* (1943). Other films include: *Brief Encounter* (1945), *Vice Versa* (1948), *The Hasty Heart* (1949), *The Lavender Hill Mob* (1951), *Derby Day* (1952), *The Square Ring* (1953), *The Night my Number Came Up* (1955), *The Bespoke Overcoat* (1956), *The Angel Who Pawned Her Harp* (1956), *Sailor Beware* (1956), *Hell Drivers* (1957), *A Tale of Two Cities* (1958), *I Was Monty's Double* (1958), *The Millionairess* (1960), *Alfie* (1966), *A Funny Thing Happened on the Way to the Forum* (1966), *The Fearless Vampire Killers* (1967), *A Challenge for Robin Hood* (1967), *Up the Junction* (1968), *Moonraker* (1979) and his last film, *High Rise Donkey* (1980). Usually played working class Jewish or cockney (or Jewish cockney) roles, more often than not on the wrong side of the law. Probably most fondly remembered for playing Pte Montague "Excused Boots" Bisley (aka Bootsie) in the TV sitcoms *The Army Game* (1957-1960), *Bootsie and Snudge* (1960) and the spin-off film *I Only Arsked* (1958). His stage work included playing the lead role of Tevye in *Fiddler on the Roof*. He died 15 July 1987, Barnet, London. See also entries in the television section for *The Adventures of Robin Hood, Are You Being Served, The Army Game, Bootsie and Snudge, Dick Turpin* and *Till Death Us Do Part*.

Bates, Alan (1934-2003) Born Alan Arthur Bates, 17 February 1934, Allestree, Derbyshire. Actor. Earned a scholarship to RADA. Stage debut in 1956, the same year he appeared in *Look Back in Anger* at the Royal Court Theatre and established his acting credentials. Screen debut: *The Entertainer* (1960). Apart from *Zorba the Greek* (1964) and *Georgy Girl* (1967) he seemed to avoid commercial projects in favour of pure acting roles. Such films include: *Whistle Down the Wind* (1961), *A Kind of Loving* (1962), *Women in Love* (1969), *A Day in the Death of Joe Egg* (1972) and *The Go-Between* (1974). Gained an Academy Award nomination for Best Actor in 1969 for his role in *The Fixer* (1968). Appointed a CBE in 1996, he was knighted in 2003. He died 27 December 2003, London. See also entries in the television section for *An Englishman Abroad*, and *The Mayor of Casterbridge*.

Bean, Sean (1959-) Born Shaun Mark Bean, 17 April 1959, Sheffield, South Yorkshire. Actor. Amongst other jobs, worked as a welder before training at RADA (1981-83). Stage debut: *Romeo and Juliet* (1983). Screen debut: *Winter Flight* (1984). In contrast to his heroic television role as rifleman Richard Sharpe his film roles tend more towards the villainous, as in *Patriot Games* (1992) and as the turncoat 006 in *Goldeneye* (1995). He seemed to combine the two aspects as Boromir in the *Lord of the Rings Trilogy* (2001-03). Other films include: *Caravaggio* (1986), *Anna Karenina* (1997), *Ronin* (1998), *Don't Say a Word* (2001), *Troy*

(2004), *The Dark* (2006), *Outlaw* (2007) and *Percy Jackson & the Olympians: The Lightning Thief* (2010). Married to childhood sweetheart Debra James (1981-90) and actresses Melanie Hill (1990-97) and Abigail Cruttenden (1997-2000). Georgina Sutcliffe became wife number four in 2008 but the couple announced their separation in August 2010. Sean was scarred by Harrison Ford wielding a boathook in *Patriot Games*. A devoted Sheffield United football fan and club director (he has a tattoo depicting "100% Blade") he played a footballer in *When Saturday Comes* (1996). Sean's most recent screen roles include Eddard Stark in the HBO American TV series *Game of Thrones* and Jones in the 2011 action-thriller film, *Age of Heroes*, based on the real-life events of the formation of Ian Fleming's 30 Commando unit during World War II. See also entries in the television section for *The Bill, Lady Chatterley , Sharpe*, and *Survival*.

Beaton, Cecil (1904-80) Born Cecil Walter Hardy Beaton, 14 January 1904, Hampstead, London. Photographer and designer. Educated at Harrow and St John's College, Cambridge. A self-taught photographer, he set up his own studio on leaving University, specialising in high fashion, society and celebrity subjects. Worked as a staff photographer for *Vanity Fair* and *Vogue*. Became the official photographer to the Royal Family. In the film world his debut as costume designer was *Major Barbara* (1941). Other films on which he worked as costume designer include: *Kipps* (1941), *Young Mr Pitt* (1942), *An Ideal Husband* (1947), *Anna Karenina* (1948) and *The Truth About Women* (1957). He won an Academy Award for Best Costume Design for *Gigi* (1958) and Academy Awards for Best Costume Design and Best Art Direction for the stylish *My Fair Lady* (1964). Published, amongst others, *British Photographers* (1944) and *Persona Grata* (1953). Appointed CBE in 1957 and knighted in 1972. His diaries have also been published. Suffered a stroke in 1974 and died 18 January 1980 at Reddish House, Broad Chalke near Salisbury, Wiltshire.

Beckinsale, Kate (1973-) Born Kathryn Romany Beckinsale, 26 July 1973, London. Actress. Daughter of actress Judy Loe and actor Richard Beckinsale, who died when she was five-years-old in 1979. Won W H Smith Young Writers' competitions twice running in her teens. Studied French and Russian literature at New College, Oxford before turning seriously to an acting career. Screen debut: *One Against the Wind* (1991 - TV movie). Films include: *Much Ado About Nothing* (1993), *Shooting Fish* (1997), *Pearl Harbour* (2001), *Serendipity* (2001), *Underworld* (2003), *Van Helsing* (2004), *Underworld Evolution* (2006), *Nothing But The Truth* (2008) *Fragments - aka Winged Creatures* - (2008), *Whiteout* (2009), *Underworld: Rise of the Lycans* (2009) and *Everybody's Fine* (2009). She played the part of Ava Gardner in the Howard Hughes biopic *The Aviator* (2004). Picked as England's No. 1 Beauty by *Hello* Magazine in 2002. She has a paternal half-sister, Samantha (born in London, 23 July 1966) who is a notable television actress. Kate was the long time partner of actor Michael Sheen but met American director and screenwriter Len Wiseman whist working on the film *Underworld* in 2002 and they married the following year. Kate has recently completed filming scenes for two 2012 films, *Contraband* and the fourth Underworld film, *Underworld: Awakening*.

Bettany, Paul (1971-) Born 27 May 1971, Harlesden, London. Actor. Son of actor Thane Bettany. Trained at The London Drama Centre. Spent a year with the RSC. Made his TV debut playing Prince William of Orange in *Sharpe's Waterloo* (1997). His film debut was *Bent* (1997) and he then made *The Land Girls* (1998) and *After the Rain* (1999). Made an impact in *Gangster No. 1* (2000) playing a younger version of Malcolm McDowell's character. He followed up with *The Suicide Club* (2000), *Kiss Kiss (Bang Bang)* (2000) and *Dead Babies* (2000). Next he played a memorable Geoffrey Chaucer in *A Knight's Tale* (2001) and on the set of *A Beautiful Mind* (2001) he met actress Jennifer Connelly who he was to marry in January 2003. Paul and Jennifer have two children together, a son Stellan, named after actor Stellan Skarsgård, (b. 5 August 2003) and a daughter, Agnes Lark (b. 31 May 2011, New York City). Jennifer also has a son, Kai (b. 1997), from her relationship with photographer David Dugan. After *The Heart of Me* (2002) Paul starred alongside Nicole Kidman in Lars Von Trier's *Dogville* (2003). He played the surgeon Dr Stephen Maturing in *Master and Commander: The Far Side of the World* (2003) and his latest films include a starring role in *Wimbledon* (2004) and *Firewall* (2006) and support roles as Silas in *The Da Vinci Code* (2006) and the voice of Tony Stark/Iron Man's computer J.A.R.V.I.S. in *Iron Man* (2008), *Iron Man II* (2009) and the forthcoming *The Avengers* (2012). Paul has also recently appeared in the 2010 romantic thriller, *The Tourist*; played the Archangel Michael in the apocalyptic supernatural thriller film *Legion* (2010); starred in the title role *Priest* (2011) and was one of a fine ensemble cast in *Margin Call* (2011).

Bird, Norman (1920-2005) Born 30 October 1920, Coalville, Leicestershire. Actor. Trained at RADA. Served in the RAF during WWII. Toured the United States, South Africa and Russia with Gielgud's Shakespeare Company. Screen debut: *An Inspector Calls* (1954). Other films include: *The League of Gentlemen* (1959), *The Angry Silence* (1960), *Whistle Down the Wind* (1961), *Victim* (1961), *The Punch and Judy Man* (1963), *First Men in the Moon* (1964), *The Hill* (1965), *The Wrong Box* (1966), *Oh! What a Lovely War* (1969), *The Raging Moon* (1971), *Young Winston* (1972), *The Medusa Touch* (1978) and *Shadowlands* (1993). Voiced Bilbo Baggins in the animated version of *The Lord of the Rings* (1978). He once described himself as "the man in the cardigan" and he was one of the best known faces on British TV, having made over 200 appearances in total in many of the best small screen dramas and sitcoms including: *Z Cars, The Avengers, Yes, Minister,* and *Boon*. Usually played minor officials or hen-pecked husbands. He died 22 April 2005, Bridgnorth, West Midlands. See also entries in the television section for *Coronation Street, Take The High Road, Whack-O!,* and *Worzel Gummidge*.

Birkin, Jane (1946-) Born Jane Mallory Birkin, 14 December 1946, Marylebone, London. Actress and singer. Probably best remembered for her controversial duet with Serge Gainsbourg, *Je T'Aime..Moi Non Plus* which reached No. 1 in the UK charts in October 1969. She landed several lightweight movie roles in the 1960s, when her looks seemed to symbolize the swinging spirit of the times. She was part of the ensemble cast for *The Knack and How To Get It* (1965) and she played one of the schoolgirls / models in Antonioni's *Blowup* (1966) and subsequently resurfaced as a respected talent in France. She starred opposite Dirk Bogarde in Bertrand Tavernier's *Daddy Nostalgia* (1990). She has been married to John Barry (1965-1968), Gainsbourg (1968-1980) and Jacques Doillon (1981-93). Her mother was actress Judy Campbell. Her daughter with Gainsbourg, Charlotte, is also an actress and her brother is writer-director Andrew Birkin. In 1981, Hermès chief executive Jean-Louis Dumas was seated next to Jane on a flight from Paris to London when he saw her drop the contents of her bag whilst removing it from the overhead hold. She explained that she could not find a suitable bag to enclose her papers securely and three years later the iconic black Birkin Bag was produced by Hermès. Jane has recently starred as Anna in the 2007 French film *Boxes* (French: *Les Boites*) based on her own family life, chronicling three marriages and the three children she bore from these marriages. She also made her directorial debut for this film.

Bisset, Jacqueline (1944-) Born Winnifred Jacqueline Fraser-Bisset, 13 September 1944, Weybridge, Surrey. Actress. Screen debut: *The Knack and How to Get It* (1965). As with many attractive actresses she struggled in a number of middling films but did have a few excellent parts. Her films include: *Bullitt* (1968), *Day for Night* (1973), *Rich and Famous* (1981), *Class* (1983) and *Under the Volcano* (1984). About filming a topless scene in *The Deep* (1977) she said "all they talked about was my tits for the next four years. God, if I was going to do a picture like that, I'd have done it a lot sexier. They looked like two fried eggs on a platter." Jacqueline is Angelina Jolie's godmother. In recent years she has appeared as a very successful television actress, notably in the American drama series *Nip/Tuck* (2006) but still appears in quality films such as *The Fine Art of Love: Mine Ha-Ha* (2006) and *Death In Love* (2008). Jacqueline also won wide acclaim for her role as Mary, mother of Jesus in the 1999 TV film, *Jesus.* She has also appeared in several French productions and was awarded the Légion d'honneur in 2010. Her most recent film, *The Last Film Festival* (2011) was notable for being the last film of the late Dennis Hopper. Although she has never married Jacqueline has had lengthy romances with the actor Michael Sarrazin and dancer-turned-actor Alexander Godunov.

Blair (c1903-14) Born circa 1903, London. Actor. His mother was a bitch and he became a major screen celebrity of early British films. Screen debut: *Rescued by Rover* (1905). Other films include: *The Dog Thief* (1908), *Plucky Little Girl* (1909), *The Dog's Devotion* (1911) and *Lost in the Woods* (1912). *Rescued by Rover* (1905) is now recognised as a major influence on the development of narrative driven film-making and marks a key stage in the development of motion pictures as an art form. Directed by Lewin Fitzhamon, with Blair in the central role of Rover who foils a kidnapping, it uses clever editing to advance the narrative and build tension. This film is believed to have been a great influence on D W Griffith, who built on many of its innovations. Blair apparently survived on a diet of mainly sausages. Died February 1914 Walton-on-Thames, Surrey. On reporting his death *The Bioscope* magazine extolled: "Many....will deplore the death of this old favourite". Blair was in fact a collie and the family pet of the film producer and studio owner Cecil Hepworth.

Blakely, Colin (1930-87) Born Colin George Blakely, 23 September 1930, Bangor, County Down. Actor. Screen debut: *Saturday Night and Sunday Morning* (1960). A versatile actor he appeared in a wide variety of films including: *This Sporting Life* (1963), *A Man for All Seasons* (1966), *The Private Life of Sherlock Holmes* (1970) - as Dr Watson - and *Equus* (1977). Colin was married to actress Margaret Whiting from 1961 until his death, of leukaemia, 7 May 1987 London. See also entries in the television section for *The Beiderbecke Affair*, and *The Hanged Man*.

Blackman, Honor (1925-) Born 22 August 1925, London. Actress. Educated at the Guildhall School of Music and Drama. Stage debut: *The Guinea Pig* (1945). Screen debut: *Fame is the Spur* (1947). As a rank "starlet" she starred in a series of films type cast as an English rose, including *A Night to Remember* (1958). It was only after being cast as Cathy Gale in *The Avengers* TV series in 1960 that she shot to fame. On leaving the series in 1963 she was quickly snapped up to play Pussy Galore in *Goldfinger* (1964). She followed that with roles in *Moment to Moment* (1965), *Life at the Top* (1965) and *The Virgin and the Gypsy* (1970). Other films include: *The Square Peg* (1958 - as Leslie Cartland), *Jason and the Argonauts* (1963 - as Hera and voice of Medea), *Shalako* (1968), *Something Big* (1971), *To the Devil a Daughter* (1976), *The Cat and the Canary* (1979), *Bridget Jones's Diary* (2001), *Jack Brown and the Curse of the Crown* (2001) and *Reuniting the Rubins* (2010). She had a successful stage and TV career and in 1986 had a role in the *Doctor Who* serial *The Trial of a Time Lord* and Honor even had a surprise No 5 UK hit in 1990 with her 1964 recording of *Kinky Boots*. She published *How to Look and Feel Half Your Age for the Rest of Your Life* (1997). Honor has been married twice, to Bill Sankey (1948–56), and the British actor Maurice Kaufmann (1961–75), with whom she appeared in the film *Fright* (1971). They adopted two children, Barnaby and Lottie. See also entries in the television section for *The Avengers*, *Coronation Street*, *The Four Just Men*, *Never the Twain*, *Probation Officer*, *Robin's Nest*, and *The Upper Hand*.

Blessed, Brian (1936-) Born 9 October 1936, Mexborough, Yorkshire. Actor. The son of a coal miner he was trained at the Bristol Old Vic Theatre School. Came to popular attention playing Fancy Smith in *Z Cars* on TV (1962-65) and Porthos in the BBC mini-series *The Three Musketeers* (1966-67) opposite Jeremy Brett's D'Artagnan. His other most famous TV role was as the Roman Emperor Augustus in *I, Claudius* (1976). Screen debut: *The Christmas Tree* (1966). He has many films to his credit including *Flash Gordon* (1980 – as Prince Vultan), *Henry V* (1989), *Robin Hood: Prince of Thieves* (1991 - as Lord Locksley) and *Alexander* (2004). Known for his booming voice (which since October 2010 can be heard on Tom Tom satnav systems) and larger than life style he has in recent years set his sights on climbing Mount Everest. He has attempted the climb three times. Brian has written about his early life in his autobiography, *Dynamite Kid* (1992). He has been married to actress Hildegarde Neil since 1978 and has a daughter, Rosalind, with her, who is

also an actress. See also entries in the television section for *Arthur of the Britons*, *The Blackadder*, *Churchill's People*, *Great Railway Journeys*, *I Claudius*, *Love Story*, and *Z Cars*.

Blethyn, Brenda (1946-) Born Brenda Ann Bottle, 20 February 1946, Ramsgate, Kent. Actress. One of nine children to a working-class Roman Catholic family. She started her career at British Rail in the 1960s. Saving money during her time there, she took a risk and enrolled herself at The Guildford School of Acting in Surrey and therafter the National Theatre Company in 1975. She won the London Critics' Circle Theatre Award for Best Supporting Actress in 1980 for the play *Steaming* before moving on to television roles. For many the first glimpse of Brenda was as Alison Little in the Michael Mills' comedy *Chance in a Million* (1984) although her most memorable television role came a decade later as Mim in Richard Harris's cricketing play *Outside Edge*. Brenda made her big screen debut in *The Witches* (1990). She followed this by playing Brad Pitt's mother in *A River Runs Through It* (1992) and has been a mainstay of (mostly) British films ever since. She won a BAFTA for her performance as Cynthia Rose Purley in Mike Leigh's *Secrets and Lies* (1996) for which she was also nominated for an Academy Award for Best Actress. Brenda received a further nomination, this time for Best Supporting Actress, for her role as Jane Horrock's mother in *Little Voice* (1998). She was awarded the OBE in 2003 and since then has appeared in *Beyond The Sea* (2004), *Pride and Prejudice* (2005), *Atonement* (2007), *London River* (2009) and *Dead Man Running* (2009), co-starring Danny Dyer, in which Brenda plays the mother of Nick (Tamer Hassan) who finds himself indebted to Thigo (Curtis '50 Cent' Jackson). Footballers Ashley Cole and Rio Ferdinand served as executive producers. Her most recent leading role in TV drama is the title role in the ITV police series *Vera* (2011), playing Detective Chief Inspector Vera Stanhope. See also entries in the television section for *The Buddha of Suburbia*, *Chance in a Million*, and *Outside Edge*.

Bloom, Claire (1931-) Born Patricia Claire Blume, 15 February 1931, Finchley, London. Actress. After spending some time in the USA during WWII she returned to London to attend the Central School of Speech Training and Dramatic Art. She made her stage debut in *Pink String and Sealing Wax* (1946). Screen debut: *The Blind Goddess* (1948). Had a huge international break when Charlie Chaplin cast her as a ballerina in *Limelight* (1952). Her other major films include *Richard III* (1956), *Look Back in Anger* (1959), *The Haunting* (1963), *The Spy Who Came in from the Cold* (1965) and *A Doll's House* (1973). In recent years Claire has concentrated on stage and television roles, notably as a Time Lord in *Dr Who* (2009). Married to Rod Steiger (1959-69), producer Hillard Elkins (1969-72) and novelist Philip Roth (1990-95). Autobiographies: *Limelight and After* (1987) and *Leaving a Doll's House* (1996). Claire made a film come-back in the multi-award-winning *The King's Speech* (2010 – as Queen Mary). See also entry for *The Camomile Lawn* in the television section.

Bloom, Orlando (1977-) Born Orlando Jonathan Blanchard Bloom, 13 January 1977, Canterbury, Kent. Actor. Joined the National Youth Theatre and then attended the British American Drama Academy and the Guildhall School of Music and Drama. Screen debut: *Wilde* (1997). Recovered from a broken back following a fall in 1998 and first came to prominence playing the elf Legolas in the *Lord of the Rings Trilogy* and Will Turner in the *Pirates of the Caribbean* franchise. Films include: *The Lord of the Rings: Fellowship of the Ring* (2001), *Black Hawk Down* (2001), *The Lord of the Rings: The Two Towers* (2002), *Ned Kelly* (2003), *Pirates of the Caribbean: The Curse of the Black Pearl* (2003), *The Lord of the Rings: The Return of the King* (2003), *The Calcium Kid* (2004), *Troy* (2004), *Haven* (2004), *Kingdom of Heaven* (2005), *Elizabethtown* (2005), *Pirates of the Caribbean: Dead Man's Chest* (2006), *Pirates of the Caribbean: At World's End* (2007), *New York, I Love You* (2009), *Sympathy for Delicious* (2009), *Main Street* (2010), *The Good Doctor* (2011), *The Three Musketeers* (2011 - as the Duke of Buckingham) and reprising his role of Legolas in the 2012 film, *The Hobbit: An Unexpected Journey* . In 2010 Orlando married Australian model Miranda Kerr. See also entry for *Extras* in the television section.

10

Blore, Eric (1887-1959) Born 23 December 1887, Finchley, London. Actor. After working in the insurance business he took up acting in his early twenties. Stage debut: *The Girl from Kay's* (1908). Screen debut: *A Night Out and a Day In* (1920). After WWI he performed in West End musical comedies and in 1933 he travelled to the USA with Fred Astaire's production of *The Gay Divorce*. He had a part in *Flying Down to Rio* (1933) which led to him becoming a fixture in Astaire-Rogers musicals including *The Gay Divorcee* (1934), *Top Hat* (1935) and *Swing Time* (1936). He followed an appearance in *Road to Zanzibar* (1941) with parts in two Preston Sturges comedies *The Lady Eve* (1941) and *Sullivan's Travels* (1942). He specialised in playing a butler, valet or dissipated nobleman, usually with an insolent or snide edge but always humourously. This was in the days before Hollywood saw every well-spoken Englishman as a villain. His film career had ended by the mid 1950s. Eric died 2 March 1959 Hollywood, California and was buried in Forest Lawn Memorial Park.

Blunt, Emily (1983-) Born Emily Olivia Leah Blunt, 23 February 1983, Roehampton, London. Actress. Emily made her professional debut in the stage musical *Bliss*, at the 2000 Edinburgh Fringe, while still studying for her A-levels. Her debut film role was a small part as Isolda in *Boudica* (2003) before gaining a major role in the British film *My Summer of Love* (2004). She then appeared in *The Devil Wears Prada* (2006) for which she was nominated for a Golden Globe and a BAFTA. She has since appeared in a number of American and British productions, including *Charlie Wilson's War* (2007), *The Jane Austen Book Club* (2007), *The Young Victoria* (2009 – as the young queen), *The Wolfman* (2010), *Gulliver's Travels* (2010), *Gnomeo & Juliet* (2011 - voice of Juliet), *The Adjustment Bureau* (2011), *Salmon Fishing in the Yemen* (2011) and *The Muppets* (2011). In 2007, Emily won a Golden Globe Award for her performance in the 2005 BBC TV film, *Gideon's Daughter*. Emily had a relationship with singer Michael Bublé from 2005 but eventually married American actor / director John Krasinski (now famous for playing Jim Halpert – based on Tim Canterbury - in the American version of *The Office*) on 10 July 2010 in Italy.

Bogarde, Dirk (1921-99) Born Derek Jules Gaspard Ulric Niven van den Bogaerde, 28 March 1921 Hampstead, London. Actor. A scene designer and commercial artist whilst studying acting. Worked for army Air Photographic Intelligence during WWII and was present at the liberation of Belsen. Stage debut: *When We are Married* (1939). Screen debut: *Esther Waters* (1947). A Rank contract employee he was the cockney criminal who shot George Dixon in *The Blue Lamp* (1950) and he went on to be especially popular for his role of Dr Simon Sparrow in the series of Doctor films: *Doctor in the House* (1954), *Doctor at Large* (1957) and *Doctor in Distress* (1963). Nerves forced him to abandon his stage career in 1951. After a brief and disappointing spell in Hollywood he moved on to more challenging roles including that of the homosexual blackmail victim Melville Farr in *Victim* (1961). Other films include: *The Servant* (1963), *Accident* (1967), *The Damned* (1969), *The Night Porter* (1974) and *Death in Venice* (1977). He was the only major cast member of *A Bridge Too Far* (1977) to have actually served in the battles portrayed in the film. Dirk wrote a series of eight autobiographies including: *A Postillion Struck by Lightning (1977)*, *Snakes and Ladders (1979)* and *An Orderly Man (1983)*. Also a novelist, he wrote *A Gentle Occupation*, *Jericho*, *West of Sunset*, *Voices in the Garden* and *Closing Ranks*. Lived in Italy and France before returning to London in 1987. Known during the 1950s as *The Idol of the Odeons*. Appointed Chevalier de l'Ordre des Artes et des Lettres in 1982. Knighted 1992. His long-time partner was British actor Gareth Forwood (1945–2007), the only son of actors Glynis Johns and Anthony Forwood. Dirk died 8 May 1999, Chelsea, London.

Bonham Carter, Helena (1966-) Born 26 May 1966, Golders Green, London. Actress. Great-granddaughter of Prime Minister Herbert Henry Asquith and great niece of film director Anthony Asquith. She is also a great-niece of the late Baroness Liliane de Rothschild (1916-2003) of the Rothschild banking family. TV debut: *A Pattern of Roses* (1982). Screen debut: *Lady Jane* (1985). She went on to feature in a number of costume dramas including *A Room With a View* (1985), *Hamlet* (1990), *Twelfth Night* (1996) and *The Wings of the Dove* (1997), for her part in which as Kate Croy she was nominated for an Academy Award as Best Actress.

She finally escaped into modern dress for *Mighty Aphrodite* (1995) - playing Woody Allen's wife - *Fight Club* (1999) then into heavy prosthetics for *Planet of the Apes* (2001). Many of her recent outings have been with her boyfriend, film director Tim Burton: *Planet of the Apes* (2001), *Big Fish* (2003), *Charlie and the Chocolate Factory* (2005), *Corpse Bride* (2005), *Sweeney Todd: The Demon Barber of Fleet Street* (2007) and *Alice in Wonderland* (2010) are all joint ventures. They have one son, Billy-Ray Burton (b. 4 October 2003). Helena plays Death Eater Bellatrix Lestrange in the Harry Potter films and was nominated for an Academy Award for her role as Queen Elizabeth in *The King's Speech* (2010). She was appointed Commander of the Order of the British Empire (CBE) in the 2012 New Year Honours.

Bonneville, Hugh (1963-) Born Hugh Richard Bonneville, 10 November 1963, London. Actor. Hugh read theology at Corpus Christi College, Cambridge, before training for the stage at the Webber Douglas Academy of Dramatic Art in London. He initially worked at the Open Air Theatre, Regents Park before joining the National Theatre and, in 1991, the RSC. His first screen appearance was as Jas in an episode of the ITV series *Chancer*, in 1990. Hugh's film debut came in the TV movie *Stalag Luft* (1993) and his feature debut was as Schiller in *Frankenstein* (1994). Other films include: *Tomorrow Never Dies* (1997), *Notting Hill* (1999 - as Bernie), *Mansfield Park* (1999 - as Mr Rushworth), *High Heels and Low Lifes* (2001), *The Emperor's New Clothes* (2001), *Iris* (2001 – as John Bayley), *Conspiracy of Silence* (2003), *Stage Beauty* (2004 - as Samuel Pepys), *Man to Man* (2005), *Asylum* (2005), *Piccadilly Jim* (2006), *Scenes of a Sexual Nature* (2006), *Four Last Songs* (2007), *French Film* (2008 - as Jed), *Glorious 39* (2009 - as Gilbert), *From Time to Time* (2009), *Critical Eye* (2010), *Third Star* (2010) and *Burke and Hare* (2010 - as Lord Harrington). Although in his early roles he was pigeon-holed as a mild-mannered bumbling character he has appeared in several TV films in more hard-edged roles, notably as the domineering Henleigh Grandcourt in *Daniel Deronda* (2002) and the psychopathic killer James Lampton in *The Commander* (2003). He has been married to Lulu Evans since 1998. A fine television actor - see entries in the television section for *Bonekickers*, *Downton Abbey*, *Freezing*, *The Robinsons*, *The Silence*, *Tipping the Velvet* and *The Vet*.

Boorman, John (1933-) Born 18 January 1933, Shepperton, Middlesex. Director. Worked at various jobs until he began working for the BBC and in 1962 became head of the BBC Bristol documentary unit. Screen directorial debut: *Catch us if You Can* (1965). In Hollywood he directed *Point Blank* (1967) and *Hell in the Pacific* (1968). Back in the UK during the 1970s he directed *Leo the Last* (1970) and *Zardoz* (1974). He was nominated for an Academy Award for Best Director for the film *Deliverance* (1972). He went on to direct *Excalibur* (1981), *The Emerald Forest* (1985) and the autobiographical *Hope and Glory* (1987) for which he was also nominated for an Academy Award for Best Director and Best Screenplay. More recent films include *The General* (1998), *The Tailor of Panama* (2001), *In My Country* (2004) and *The Tiger's Tail* (2006). Autobiographies: *Money into Light: The Emerald Forest: A Diary* (1985) and *Bright Dreams, Hard Knocks: A Journal for 1991* (1992). Made Chevalier de l'Ordre des Artes et Lettres in 1993 by the French government, John has lived in Annamoe, County Wicklow, Ireland, for many years. Actor and television presenter Charley Boorman is one of John's seven children.

Booth, Douglas (1992-) Born 9 July 1992, Greenwich, London. Actor. After a tough childhood in various Kent schools due to his dyslexia, Douglas modelled for British fashion brand Burberry for two years while acting with the National Youth Theatre. Douglas made his film debut in *Hunters of the Kahri* when he was sixteen and followed this up in Julian Fellowes' haunting ghost story, *From Time to Time* (2009 – as Sefton). He rose to prominence following his portrayal of Boy George in the BBC Two television drama *Worried About the Boy* (2010) and again garnered rave reviews for his portrayal of Pip in BBC1's hit version of *Great Expectations* (2011). He has recently completed filming on his latest film *LOL: Laughing Out Loud* (2012 – as Kyle) co-starring Miley Cyrus and Demi Moore.

Bouchier, Chili (1909-99) Born Dorothy Irene Boucher, 12 September 1909, London. Actress. A winner of a *Daily Mirror* beauty contest in 1925 she moved from working at Harrods to modelling and then to acting in rapid succession. Screen debut: *Shooting Stars* (1927). Changed her name from Boucher to Bouchier because it sounded more glamorous and reverted from her nickname Chili back to Dorothy on the advent of talkies before changing back in 1936. She starred in numerous films including *Chick* (1928), *Carnival* (1931), *The Blue Danube* (1932), *The Ghost Goes West* (1936), *Gypsy* (1936), *The Dark Stairway* (1938) and *Everything Happens to Me* (1938). She spent more time on the stage in the 1940s and 1950s and her final film was *Dead Lucky* (1960). She continued appearing on the stage into her eighties, including a run with James Stewart in *Harvey* in London (1975). Known as Britain's "It Girl" she was reputedly the final surviving British silent movie star at the time of her death. Autobiographies: *For Dogs and Angels* (1968), *Shooting Star* (1995). Died 9 September 1999, Marylebone, London.

Boulting Brothers John Boulting (b. Joseph Edward Boulting) and Roy Boulting (b. Roy Alfred Clarence Boulting) born 13 November 1913 Bray, Berkshire. Directors and producers. Twin brothers who spent their working lives in partnership. John volunteered as an ambulance driver in the Spanish Civil War. Formed *Charter Productions* in 1938. At first John acted as producer and Roy as director but after WWII they took turns in swapping the roles. Directorial / production debut: *Trunk Crime* (1939). During WWII John served in the RAF and Roy in the army whilst also making documentaries. Other films include dramas such as *Brighton Rock* (1947), *Seven Days to Noon* (1950), *Run for the Sun* (1956) and *The Family Way* (1966) and a string of comedies including *Private's Progress* (1956) and *Lucky Jim* (1957). Their comedies tended to poke fun at targets such as the legal system - *Brothers in Law* (1957), the trade union movement - *I'm All Right Jack* (1959) and religion - *Heaven's Above* (1963). They once remarked that they began by making low budget films with a high mind and ended making high budget films with a low mind. Roy was married five times including to Hayley Mills (1971-76). John died 17 June 1985, Sunningdale, Berkshire and Roy died 5 November 2001, Eynsham, Oxfordshire.

Bowie, David See entry in the music section

Box, Betty (1915-99) Born Betty Evelyn Box, 25 September 1915, Beckenham, Kent. Producer. In 1942 joined her brother Sydney Box at *Verity Films* and helped produce over 200 shorts during the war. Appointed Head of Production for *Gainsborough Studios* in 1946. Films produced during this period include: *When the Bough Breaks* (1947), *Here Come the Huggetts* (1948), *Miranda* (1948*)*, *Vote for Huggett* (1949) and *The Huggetts Abroad* (1949). Moved with her brother to Rank's *Pinewood Studios* and began a long collaboration with director Ralph Thomas with *The Clouded Yellow* (1950). Along with Thomas she is best remembered for the popular series of seven Doctor films which began with *Doctor in the House* (1954) and ended with *Doctor in Trouble* (1970). Other films include: *A Tale of Two Cities* (1958), *The 39 Steps* (1959), *Some Girls Do* (1969) and *The Olive Tree* (1975). Her second husband was fellow producer Peter Rogers (best known for the *Carry On* films). Awarded the OBE in 1958. Posthumous autobiography: *Lifting the Lid* (2000). Died 15 January 1999, Beaconsfield, Buckinghamshire.

Box, John (1920-2005) Born John Allan Hyatt Box, 27 January 1920, Hampstead, London. Production designer and art director. Raised in Sri Lanka, where his father was an engineer. His architectural studies were interrupted by WWII during which he served in the Tank Corps. Having completed his studies he began working as a draughtsman for *London Films* at Denham. Art directorial debut: *The Million Pound Note* (1953). An early success was building a walled Chinese city on Snowdonia for *The Inn of the Sixth Happiness* (1958) when the plans to shoot in China had to be abandoned. Worked regularly with Carol Reed and David Lean. He had the sand painted white and bordered in black for Omar Sharif's stunning entrance from the mirage in *Lawrence of Arabia* (1962) for which he won his first Academy

Award for Best Art Direction. Won further Academy Awards for Best Art Direction for *Doctor Zhivago* (1965), *Oliver!* (1968) and *Nicholas and Alexandra* (1971). He also received Best Art Direction nominations for *Travels with my Aunt* (1972) and *A Passage to India* (1984). Other films include: *The Cockleshell Heroes* (1955), *Of Human Bondage* (1964), *A Man for All Seasons* (1966), *Rollerball* (1975) - for which he helped devise the game, *Sorcerer* (1977), *A Passage to India* (1984) and *First Knight* (1995). Known in the industry as 'The Magician', no doubt partly for making Wales look like China and Spain look like a snowy Russia. Died 7 March 2005, Leatherhead, Surrey.

Box, Muriel (1905-91) Born Violette Muriel Baker, September 1905, New Malden, Surrey. Director and writer. She is one of the few English women to have been a successful screenwriter, director and producer of films. Initially worked as a continuity and script girl. With her journalist husband Sydney, to whom she was married from 1935 to 1969, she wrote several British films and after co-writing several plays, helped him in setting up and running *Verity Films*. Began by making short propaganda films. Directorial debut: *The Lost People* (1949). Screenwriting debut: *Alibi Inn* (1935). Co-wrote the Academy Award winning best original screenplay for *The Seventh Veil* (1945) with husband Sydney. Ran the scenario department of *Gainsborough Pictures* before following Sydney in his new venture, *London Independent Producers*, in 1951. In a long career as director and script-writer, often in collaboration with Sydney, she ploughed a lonely furrow as a woman director in a predominantly male industry, which on occasion lost her directing opportunities. For example, during WWII, she was replaced by Ken Annakin as director of a road safety film for children as it was felt to be an unfit subject for a woman to helm. Other films she wrote and directed include: *A Passionate Stranger* (1957), *The Truth about Women* (1957) and *Too Young to Love* (1960). She also wrote amongst others: *Daybreak* (1947), *Holiday Camp* (1948) and *Here Come the Huggetts* (1948). Other films directed include: *Street Corner* (1953), *The Beachcomber* (1954), *Simon and Laura* (1955) and *Rattle of a Simple Man* (1964). After retiring from the film industry in the mid-1960s she took up writing and set up the publishing house *Femina*. Muriel divorced Sidney in 1969 and the following year married Gerald Austin Gardiner, Lord Chancellor (1964-1970), who was created Baron Gardiner of Kittisford. Wrote a biography of her second husband *Rebel Advocate* (1983). Autobiography: *Odd Woman Out: An Autobiography* (1974). Died 18 May 1991, London.

Box, Sydney (1907-83) Born Frank Sydney Box, 29 April 1907, Beckenham, Kent. Producer and writer. After writing many one act plays for the theatre he formed *Verity Films*. Husband of Muriel Box, with whom he won an Academy Award for Best Original Screenplay for *The Seventh Veil* (1946). Head of *Gainsborough Pictures* 1946-49. Producing debut: *O.H.M.S.* (1939). Other films include: *On Approval* (1944), *A Girl in a Million* (1946), *Holiday Camp* (1948), *My Brother's Keeper* (1948), *So Long at the Fair* (1950), *The Beachcomber* (1954), *The Truth About Women* (1957) and *Deadlier than the Male* (1966). Turned from the big screen to television in 1958 and was part of a consortium that launched *Tyne Tees Television* in 1959. In 1963 he acquired *British Lion* and *London Weekend Television*. Autobiography: *The Lion that Lost its Way: and other Cautionary Tales of the Show Business Jungle*. Retired from the industry through ill-health in 1967. Died 25 May 1983 Perth, Western Australia.

Boyd, Billy (1968-) Born William Boyd, 28 August 1968, Glasgow. Actor. Raised by his grandmother after being orphaned at 12-years-old. Worked for six years as a bookbinder. Left work to study at the Royal Scottish Academy of Music and Drama. Stage debut: *The Secret Life of Adrian Mole* (1994). Screen debut: *Soldiers Leap* (1998). Played the Hobbit Peregrin Took (Pippin) in *The Lord of the Rings Trilogy of films* (2001-03). Also featured in *Master and Commander* (2003), *The Flying Scotsman* (2006), *Stone of Destiny* (2008), *Pimp* (2010) and Irvine Welsh's *Ecstasy* (2011). Topped a list of the 100 most eligible men in Scotland (2002). Currently, he is the lead singer and co-songwriter in the band, *Beecake*. Billy has a tattoo of the word "nine" written in the Tengwar (Elvish) script, a reference to the fact that his character was one of the nine members of the Fellowship of the Ring. The other actors of "The Fellowship" (Elijah Wood, Sean Astin, Sean Bean, Ian McKellen, Dominic Monaghan, Viggo Mortensen, and Orlando Bloom) got the same tattoo with the exception of John Rhys-Davies whose stunt double got the tattoo instead. Billy and his long time girlfriend, Alison McKinnon were married in a small ceremony at Oran Mor in Glasgow's West End on 29 December 2010.

Boyd, Stephen (1928-77) Born William Millar, 4 July 1931, Glengormley, County Antrim. Actor. Joined Ulster Theatre Company whilst working in an insurance office. Moved to London and eventually joined the Midland Theatre Company and worked extensively in television. Screen debut: *An Alligator Named Daisy* (1955). Signed to *20th Century Fox* in 1956. His most famous role was as Messala in *Ben Hur* (1959) and he went on to feature in the epics *The Fall of the Roman Empire* (1964), *Genghis Khan* (1964) and *The Bible* (1966). He was originally cast as Mark Anthony in *Cleopatra* (1963) but had to withdraw in Richard Burton's favour after filming was delayed by Elizabeth Taylor's illness. Other films include: *The Man Who Never Was* (1956), *The Oscar* (1966), *Fantastic Voyage* (1966) and *Slaves* (1969). Died 2 June 1977 whilst playing golf at the Porter Valley Country Club, Granada Hills, California. Buried Tarzana, California.

Boyle, Danny (1956-) Born Daniel Boyle, 20 October 1956, Bury, Greater Manchester. Director, producer and writer. Studied at University of Wales, Bangor. Worked with the Joint Stock Theatre Company. Artistic director at the Royal Court Theatre Upstairs (1982-85) and deputy director of the Royal Court (1985-87). Began by directing television programmes, including an episode of *Inspector Morse* in 1987 and the mini-series *Mr Wroe's Virgins* (1993). Made his big screen debut with the low-budget but successful *Shallow Grave* (1994). In this project he collaborated with producer Andrew McDonald and writer John Hodge, who both joined him, along with Ewan McGregor, on the adaptation of Irvine Welsh's novel *Trainspotting* (1996). This popular success brought Boyle international recognition. McGregor also starred in Boyle's next film, *A Life Less Ordinary* (1997), which was a comparative flop. The adaptation of Alex Garland's *The Beach* (2000) was also poorly received. He returned to form with the post-apocalyptic zombie film *28 Days Later* (2002), the comedy drama *Millions* (2004) and the science fiction film *Sunshine* (2007), before producing the sequel *28 Weeks Later* (2007). Danny won an Academy Award for Best Director for the film *Slumdog Millionaire* (2008) and his latest film is *127 Hours* (2010), the true story of mountain climber Aron Ralston, who was forced to amputate his arm after becoming trapped by a boulder in Robbers Roost, Utah, for more than five days in 2003. More recently, Danny has been chosen as the artistic director for the 2012 Olympic games opening ceremony.

Branagh, Kenneth (1960-) Born Kenneth Charles Branagh, 10 December 1960, Belfast. Actor and director. Moved with his family to Reading, Berkshire in 1970. Graduated from RADA in 1981. Stage debut: *Another Country* (1981). Joined the Royal Shakespeare Company in 1983 but soon went on to form his own company, the Renaissance Theatre Company. Screen debut: *A Month in the Country* (1987). Received Best Actor and Best Director Academy Award Nominations for *Henry V* (1989). Directed the short film *Swan Song* (1992) which was nominated for an Academy Award for Best Short Film. Nominated for an Academy Award for Best Adapted Screenplay for *Hamlet* (1996). Other films he has acted in include *Dead Again* (1991), *Peters Friends* (1992), *Much Ado About Nothing* (1993), *Mary Shelley's Frankenstein* (1994), *Wild, Wild, West* (1999), *Love's Labour's Lost* (2000), *Rabbit Proof Fence* (2002) and *Harry Potter and the Chamber of Secrets* (2002). More recently Kenneth has directed the remake of *Sleuth* (2007) and starred in *Valkyrie* (2008), a film depicting the plot by German army officers to assassinate Adolf Hitler, and was one of an ensemble cast in *The Boat That Rocked* (2009). On television Kenneth has appeared in two episodes of the medical drama *Maybury* (1983), the TV mini-series *The Fortunes of War* (1987) and since 2008 has concentrated on his role as *Wallender*. In response to being proclaimed the "New Olivier" on numerous occasions he is reported to have said he'd "rather be known as the new Daffy Duck". Despite this Kenneth starred as Olivier in the 2011 film, *My Week With Marilyn*. Married Emma Thompson (1989-95) and Lindsay Brunnock (2003-present), to whom he was introduced by former lover Helena Bonham Carter. Autobiography: *Beginning* (1989).

Bray Studios Founded at Down Place, Bray, Berkshire in 1949. Closely associated with *Hammer Film Productions*. Films made by Hammer at Bray include: *The Hound of the Baskervilles* (1959), *The Mummy* (1959), *The Damned* (1963) and *Kiss of the Vampire* (1964). After the demise of Hammer, films made at Bray include: *The Music Lovers* (1970), *Sunday Bloody Sunday* (1971), *The Hireling* (1973), *The Rocky Horror Picture Show* (1975) and *Edward II* (1991). Bray Studios continues to host television, film work and band rehearsals although is now under threat of redevelopment into a residential area.

Brent, George (1904-79) Born George Brendan Nolan, 15 March 1904, Shannonbridge, County Offaly. Actor. Member of the Abbey Theatre, Dublin where he became involved in the Easter Uprising and eventually he fled to the United States. Screen debut: *Under Suspicion* (1930). A rather uninspiring leading man on screen, although apparently he was more dynamic in reality. Nevertheless he played the love interest opposite a succession of glamorous leading ladies such as Bette Davis in 12 films including *Jezebel* (1938) and *Dark Victory* (1939), Kay Francis in six films, Barbara Stanwyck in four films and Ruth Chatterton also in four films. George played opposite Greta Garbo in *The Painted Veil* (1934) and Myrna Loy in *Stamboul Quest* (1934) and *The Rains Came* (1939). The suggestion is that his very ordinariness was desirable to the studios as it made the performances of his actress co-stars appear more starry. Married five times including: Ruth Chatterton (1932-34), Constance Worth (1937) and Ann Sheridan (1942-43). Died 26 May 1979, Solana Beach, California.

Bresslaw, Bernard (1934-93) Born 25 February 1934, Stepney, London. Actor. Won a scholarship to RADA, where he won the Emile Littler Award for Most Promising Actor and caught the attention of Laurence Olivier who cast him in his stage debut: *The MacRory Whirl*. Screen debut: *Men of Sherwood Forest* (1954). He played Private 'Popeye' Popplewell in TVs *The Army Game* (1957-62) and the movie spin-off with a title based on his catch-phrase *I Only Arsked* (1957). Scored a top ten pop hit with *Mad Passionate Love* in 1958. He became a regular in the *Carry On* series of films after being cast as Little Heap in *Carry On Cowboy* (1965). He went on to feature in 14 Carry Ons in total. He was also a fine Shakespearian actor and it was whilst waiting to take the stage as Grumio in *The Taming of the Shrew* at Regents Park Open Air Theatre in London that he collapsed and died on 11 June 1993. See also entries in the television section for *The Army Game*, *Carry On Laughing*, and *Our House*.

Broadbent, Jim (1949-) Born 24 May 1949, Lincoln, Lincolnshire. Actor. Studied at London Academy of Music and Dramatic Art (LAMDA). Screen debut: *The Shout* (1978). Has appeared in over 60 films of increasing popularity and critical acclaim. His early films included *Time Bandits* (1981) and *Brazil* (1985), directed by Terry Gilliam. Collaboration with the director Mike Leigh saw him appear in *Life is Sweet* (1990) and *Topsy-Turvy* (1999) in which he portrayed W S Gilbert. In 2001 he appeared in three successful films: *Bridget Jones's Diary* (2001), *Moulin Rouge!* (2001) and *Iris* (2001) for which he won an Academy Award for Best Supporting Actor as Iris Murdoch's husband John Bayley. Other films include: *The Crying Game* (1992), *Bullets Over Broadway* (1994), *The Borrowers* (1997), *Nicholas Nickleby* (2002), *Gangs of New York* (2002), *Bright Young Things* (2003), *Vanity Fair* (2004), *Bridget Jones: The Edge of Reason* (2004), *The Chronicles of Narnia: The Lion, the Witch and the Wardrobe* (2005), *Robots* (2005 – voice of Madame Gasket), *And When Did You Last See Your Father?* (2007), *Indiana Jones and the Kingdom of the Crystal Skull* (2008), *The Damned United* (2009), *Harry Potter and the Half-Blood Prince* (2009), playing Horace E. F. Slughorn, the long-serving Potions teacher and Head of Slytherin House at Hogwarts, *Perrier's Bounty* (2009), *Another Year* (2010), *Animals United* (2010 - voice of Winston the Giant Tortoise), *Harry Potter and the Deathly Hallows – Part II* (2011), *Arthur Christmas* (2011 - voice of Santa) and *The Iron Lady* (2011 - as Denis Thatcher). Television appearances include Roy Slater in *Only Fools and Horses* and his much acclaimed role of Alfred Salteena in the 2003 TV film, *The Young Visiters*. He is one half of The National Theatre of Brent, along with Patrick Barlow. They mainly perform reduced histories such as *The Greatest Story Ever Told*. See also entries in the television section for *Happy Families, The Peter Principle, The Staggering Stories of Ferdinand De Bargos,* and *The Street*.

Bron, Eleanor (1934-) Born 14 March 1934, Stanmore, Middlesex. Actress. Educated at Newnham College, Cambridge. She made her debut in the Beatles second film *Help!* (1965) directed by Richard Lester. She made other film appearances notably *Alfie* (1966) and *Women in Love* (1969) but has mostly been a light character player. She began her career with *The Establishment* revue in London and toured with the group in the US for two years in the early 1960s. Ideal for middle class roles she has portrayed Lady Bareacres in the *Vanity Fair* (1998) mini-series and played Paul Bettany's mother in *Wimbledon* (2004). She also featured in the TV comedy *Absolutely Fabulous* as Patsy's mother. She will perhaps be best remembered for turning down the role of Emma Peel in the 1960's TV cult classic *The Avengers*. See also entries in the television section for *Not So Much A Programme*, and *Oh in Colour*.

Brook, Clive (1887-1974) Born Clifford Hardman Brook, 1 June 1887, Tufnell Park, London. Actor. Rose to the rank of Major during WWI, after which he took up acting. Stage debut: *Fair and Warmer* (1918). Screen debut: *Trent's Last Case* (1920). Signed for Paramount in Hollywood. Starred in, amongst others, *The Sheik* (1922), *A Tale of Two Cities* (1922), *The Four Feathers* (1929), *Shanghai Express* (1932) and *Cavalcade* (1933). Also played in Paramount's first talkie, *Interference* (1928). Clive portrayed the Baker Street sleuth in *The Return of Sherlock Holmes* (1929) and *Sherlock Holmes* (1932). Returning to England in 1936 he continued to perform on stage, film and eventually television. Final film: *The List of Adrian Messenger* (1963). Mainly called upon to play English gentlemen and cads, which was something he came to resent. Married actress Mildred Evelyn (b. Charlotte Elizabeth Mildred Evelyn, 26 September 1898, York, d. 30 December 1989. Hillingdon, London). Father of playwright Lyndon Brook and actress Faith Brook (b. 16 February 1922, York). Clive wrote an unpublished autobiography. Died 17 November 1974 Ealing, London.

Brosnan, Pierce (1953-) Born Pierce Brendan Brosnan, 16 May 1953, Drogheda, County Louth. Actor. Joined his mother in London at age 11, flying to the UK on the day that Ian Fleming died, 12 August 1964. Stage debut in 1971. Screen debut: *The Long Good Friday* (1980). Travelled to USA in 1982 and landed the title role in the TV series *Remington Steele*. Was touted as the new James Bond in 1986 but could not get released from his TV contract. Finally landed the role in 1995 and appeared in four Bond films: *Goldeneye* (1995), *Tomorrow Never Dies* (1997), *The World is not Enough* (1999) and *Die Another Day* (2002). Interestingly, Pierce owns Ian Fleming's typewriter. Other major films *Mrs Doubtfire* (1993), *Dante's Peak* (1997), *The Thomas Crown Affair* (1999), *The Tailor of Panama* (2000), *Laws of Attraction* (2004) *After the Sunset* (2004), *The Matador* (2005), *Mamma Mia!* (2008), *The Greatest* (2009), *The Ghost Writer* (2010), *Percy Jackson & the Olympians: The Lightning Thief* (2010), *Remember Me* (2010), *Salvation Boulevard* (2011) and *I Don't Know How She Does It* (2011). His first marriage, in 1980, to Australian actress Cassandra Harris (15 December 1948 – 28 December 1991) ended in tragedy with Cassandra succumbing to ovarian cancer. Pierce married American author and television presenter Keely Shaye Smith (born September 25, 1963) in 2001. He became a naturalised US citizen in 2004.

Brown, Pamela (1917-75) Born Pamela Mary Brown, 8 July 1917, London. Actress. Studied at RADA. Stage debut: *Romeo and Juliet* (1936). Although mainly a stage actress she appeared in many Powell and Pressburger productions such as *One of Our Aircraft is Missing* (1942) - her screen debut, *I Know Where I'm Going!* (1945*)* and *The Tales of Hoffmann* (1951). Michael Powell

said of her that "She was a witch. Women adored her, men feared her, and for the same reason - she fascinated them." Pamela suffered from arthritis from the age of 16. She died 18 September 1975, and was buried at Avening, Gloucestershire next to Michael Powell with whom she lived during her last years.

Browne, Coral (1913-91) Born Coral Edith Browne, 23 July 1913, Melbourne, Australia. Actress. Arrived in Britain aged 21, quickly establishing an excellent reputation as a stage actress. Screen debut: *Charing Cross Road* (1935). Other films include: *Let George Do It* (1940), *Piccadilly Incident* (1946), *The Courtneys of Curzon Street* (1947), *Auntie Mame* (1958), *The Roman Spring of Mrs Stone* (1961), *Dr Crippen* (1962) - as Belle Crippen, *The Killing of Sister George* (1968), *The Ruling Class* (1972) and *Dreamchild* (1985). She met Vincent Price whilst being murdered by him in *Theatre of Blood* (1973) and married him a year later. She met the spy Guy Burgess whilst touring Russia and this encounter was recreated, with Coral playing herself 25 years earlier, in the award winning TV production *An Englishman Abroad* (1983). Died 29 May 1991, Los Angeles, California.

Bruce, Nigel (1895-1953) Born William Nigel Bruce, 14 February 1895, Ensenada, Mexico. Actor. Born when his parents were on holiday. Son of Sir William Waller Bruce. Served in France during WWI before being invalided out in 1915. Stage debut: *Why Marry?* (1920). Screen debut: *Red Acres* (1929). Settled in Hollywood in 1934 although he did appear in several further British films. Cast as Dr Watson alongside his friend Basil Rathbone as Sherlock Holmes in 15 films starting with *The Hound of the Baskervilles* (1939). Before the Holmes films he had appeared in *Treasure Island* (1934), *Becky Sharp* (1935), *She* (1935), *The Scarlet Pimpernel* (1935), *The Charge of the Light Brigade* (1936) and *Lassie Come Home* (1943). He perfected the role of a slightly befuddled, bumbling Englishman. Married to actress Violet Campbell. Unpublished memoirs: *Games, Gossip and Greasepaint*. He died 8 October 1953, Santa Monica, California. See also entry for Basil Rathbone.

Bryan, Dora (1924-) Born Dora Mary Broadbent, 7 February 1924, Southport, Lancashire. Actress. Stage debut 1936 in pantomime. Screen debut: *Odd Man Out* (1946). She was mainly on cinema screens in the 1950s and 1960s, although began her career in the familiar role of a lady of easy virtue in *The Fallen Idol* (1948). Dora also played opposite Robert Donat in *The Cure for Love* (1949) and won a BAFTA for her role in *A Taste of Honey* (1961). Other films include: *The Blue Lamp* (1950), *You Know What Sailors Are* (1954), *Carry on Sergeant* (1958) and *The Great St Trinians Train Robbery* (1966). Dora also appeared in several stage musicals; *Gentleman Prefer Blondes* (1962), *Hello, Dolly!* (1966-68), *Pygmalion* (1987) and *Follies* (1987), probably the best known. An accomplished theatre actress, Dora's credits in this sphere include, Mistress Quickly in *The Merry Wives of Windsor* (1984), Mrs. Malaprop in *She Stoops to Conquer* (1985), and in 1996 Dora won a Laurence Olivier Award for her role in the West End production of the Harold Pinter play, The Birthday Party. Dora was an ever-present on British television in the 1960s, her comic timing making her a popular guest on chat shows. In 2000 she began playing Ros Utterthwaite in *Last of the Summer Wine* but was forced to leave in 2005 when she began to forget her lines. Dora was married to former Lancashire County Cricketer Bill Lawton until his death as a result of Alzheimer's disease in August 2008. She currently resides in a Hove rest home. Autobiography: *According to Dora* (1987). See also entries in the radio and television section for *Last of the Summer Wine, Much Binding in the Marsh*, and *On the Up*.

Bryan, John (1911-69) Born 1911, London. Production designer. Started his career as a stage designer before joining *London Film Productions* in 1932 and working as assistant art director on *Things to Come* (1936). His work as art director on Gainsborough melodramas such as *Fanny by Gaslight* (1944) reflected the essence of the film rather than any attempt at realistic Victoriana. Some of his sets were particularly sumptuous as in *Caesar and Cleopatra* (1945), for which he was nominated for an Academy Award for Best Art Direction. He won the Academy Award in the following year for *Great Expectations* (1946). John was production designer on *Blanche Fury* (1947) and *Oliver Twist* (1948) and he was again nominated for an Academy Award for Best Art Direction for *Becket* (1964). He formed *Knightsbridge Films* with Ronald Neame in 1957. John also produced films during the 1950s and 1960s including: *The Card* (1952), *The Spanish Gardener* (1956), *Tamahine* (1963) and *The Touchables* (1968). Died 10 June 1969.

Buchanan, Jack (1890-1957) Born Walter John Buchanan, 2 April 1890, Helensburgh, Argyll & Bute. Actor and dancer. Began his working life in his father's business as an auctioneer. Stage debut: *The Grass Widows* (1912). Screen debut: *Auld Lang Syne* (1917). Spent a short time in Hollywood making *Paris* (1929) and *Monte Carlo* (1930) with Jeanette MacDonald but returned to the UK until making *The Band Wagon* (1953) with Fred Astaire, with whom he duetted on *I Guess I'll Have to Change my Plans*. Other films include: *Man of Mayfair* (1932), *Brewster's Millions* (1933) and *The Gang's All Here* (1939). He directed *That's a Good Girl* (1935). Jack featured in the first TV outside broadcast made by John Logie Baird, who was also from Helensburgh, on 12 June 1928, having helped finance the invention. He starred in Preston Sturges' last film *Las Carnets du Major Thompson* (1956). An outstanding comedian and a consummate song and dance man he died 20 October 1957, Marylebone, London after suffering from spinal arthritis.

Burke, Kathy (1964-) Born Katherine Lucy Bridget Burke, 13 June 1964, Camden, London. Actress, comedienne, playwright and theatre director. Kathy's first television role was in the shortlived ITV children's comedy drama series *Educating Marmalade* (1982) and the following year she featured more prominently as Glennis in *Scrubbers* (1983), a sort of female version of the 1979 film, *Scum*. Film roles didn't follow automatically and Kathy concentrated on mainly television roles with character parts in *Doctor Who* (1983), *Bleak House* (1985) and *A Very Peculiar Practice* (1986). Kathy also showed her comedic talents at this time by making regular appearances on Channel 4's *An Hour With Jonathan Ross Show*, playing the character 'Tina Bishop', a perpetually pregnant household goddess offering advice on household chores, always with disastrous results. Undoubtedly her big break came when she played Waynetta Slob in the *Harry Enfield's Television Programme* between 1990 and 1992. Meatier roles soon came her way and she starred as Magda in *Absolutely Fabulous* (1992-96) and several characters, notably Perry the Schoolboy and Lulu the Toddler in *Harry Enfield and Chums* (1994-97). The film *Nil By Mouth* (1997) showed the depth of Kathy's acting talents and although she played Mary I in *Elizabeth* (1998) and made two films in 2000, *Love, Honour and Obey* and *Kevin & Perry Go Large*, Kathy decided to remain in television and won many plaudits for her role of Linda La Hughes in *Gimme Gimme Gimme* (1999-2001). In 2002 Kathy starred in *Once Upon a Time in the Midlands* and *Anita and Me*, but then apart from the odd television performance such as *A Bucket o' French & Saunders* in 2007, has been reluctant to perform before the camera preferring theatre directing. In 2009, Kathy made her television directorial debut with the BBC3 sketch show series *Horne & Corden*. In 2011 Kathy made her film comeback in *Tinker Tailor Soldier Spy*, as Connie Sachs, a part played by another iconic British actress, Beryl Reid, in the television series. See also entries in the television section for *Absolutely Fabulous, The Bill, Common as Muck, Gimme Gimme Gimme,* and *Harry Enfield's Television Programme.*

Burrows, Saffron (1972-) Born Saffron Dominique Burrows, 22 October 1972, London, England. Actress and model. The six-foot Saffron was discovered by a modeling talent scout, aged 15. She made her screen debut in the film short *The Body Beautiful* (1991), not being too stretched to play a model. Saffron progressed to full feature with a small role in *In the Name of the Father* (1993) before gaining favourable reviews as the ambitious Irish woman, Nan Mahon, in *Circle of Friends* (1995). The prolific actress made four films in 1997, *Lovelife, Nevada, One Night Stand* and *The Matchmaker* and four more in 1999, *Wing Commander, The Loss of Sexual Innocence, Deep Blue Sea* and the title role in *Miss Julie*. Other films include: *Timecode* (2000), *Gangster No. 1* (2000), *Enigma* (2001), *Hotel* (2001), *Frida*

(2002), *Peter Pan* (2003), *Troy* (2004), *Perfect Creature* (2005), *Fay Grim* (2006), *Reign Over Me* (2007), *Dangerous Parking* (2007), *The Guitar* (2008), *The Bank Job* (2008) and *Shrink* (2009). She has recently completed filming her roles in *Small Apartments* and *Knife Fight*, two films scheduled for 2012. Saffron has also become a fine stage actress appearing in *Earthly Paradise* at the Almeida Theatre in January 2005 and later that year being part of an ensemble cast performing at the Old Vic theatre in London in a 24-hour play, *Night Sky*. On television she played Sandra Sollars in the mini-series' *Cold Lazarus* (1996) and its prequel *Karaoke* (1996), the last two works of Dennis Potter. More recently she has starred as Lorraine Weller in the American series *Boston Legal* (2007-08) and has just begun the role of Detective Serena Stevens in *Law & Order: Criminal Intent* (2010). Saffron modelled for M&S for their most recent campaign for Autumn 2010. Saffron is bisexual and among her previous male lovers are actor Alan Cumming and director Mike Figgis (in whose films she has often starred). She is currently in a close friendship with Irish actress Fiona Shaw.

Burton, Richard (1925-84) Born Richard Walter Jenkins, 10 November 1925, Pontrhydyfen, Neath. Actor. Burton was the twelfth of thirteen children and was brought up by his sister Cecilia (Cis) after the death of his mother. He was tutored in acting by his schoolteacher Philip Burton, who became his legal guardian and whose surname he took. An RAF trainee during WWII, Richard's stage debut was *The Druid's Rest* (1944) and his screen debut *The Last Days of Dolwyn* (1948). One of Britain's finest Shakespearean actors he was from very early on in his career dividing his time between playing Hamlet and Henry V on the stage and appearing in a series of Hollywood films such as: *My Cousin Rachel* (1952), *The Robe* (1953) and *Alexander the Great* (1956). Richard moved to Celigny, Switzerland in 1957. He met Elizabeth Taylor on the set of *Cleopatra* (1963) and started an affair which fascinated the World's press and led both of them to divorce their current spouses and get married (1964). He made two or three films a year including *Who's Afraid of Virginia Woolf* (1966).and *The Taming of the Shrew* (1967) with Taylor. He gained an undenied reputation for taking film roles simply for the money, which meant he made many forgettable movies. However, in amongst those he gained seven Academy Award nominations: Best Supporting Actor for *My Cousin Rachel* (1952) and Best Actor for *The Robe* (1953), *Becket* (1964), *The Spy Who Came in from the Cold* (1965), *Who's Afraid of Virginia Woolf* (1966), *Anne of the Thousand Days* (1969) and *Equus* (1977). He never won an Academy Award and he shares this unenviable record (seven nominations but no win) with Peter O'Toole, which says more about the selection process than his prodigious ability. In the late 1960s and early 1970s Burton and Taylor were so famous they would make regular appearances on American television shows as themselves, *Here's Lucy, Batman* and *The Fall Guy*, to mention but three. Appointed Commander of the British Empire in 1970, he divorced (1974), remarried (1975) and divorced (1976) Taylor and then married Susan Hunt, the ex-wife of F1 World Champion James Hunt, in 1976. They were divorced in turn in 1982 and he married for the final time to Sally Hay (1983). Burton was a hard drinking, heavy smoker and this eventually took its toll. He died 5 August 1984 in Celigny, Switzerland, his last film being *Nineteen Eighty-Four* (1984).

Butler, Gerard (1969-) Born 13 November 1969, Paisley, Scotland. Actor. Graduate of the School of Law at Glasgow University. Film debut *Mrs Brown* (1997). Other films include: *Tale of the Mummy* (1998), *Fast Food* (1998), *The Cherry Orchard* (1999), *Dracula 2000* (2000), *Harrison's Flowers* (2000), *Shooters* (2002), *Reign of Fire* (2002), *Lara Croft Tomb Raider: The Cradle of Life* (2003), *Timeline* (2003), *The Phantom of the Opera* (2004), *Beowulf & Grendel* (2005), *Dear Frankie* (2005), *300* (2007), *Butterfly On A Wheel* (2007), *PS, I Love You* (2007), *Nim's Island* (2008), *RocknRolla* (2008), *The Ugly Truth* (2009), *Gamer* (2009) and *Law Abiding Citizen* (2009). The media have fervently been engaging in speculation as to a romantic link between Gerard and Jennifer Aniston since they began work on the 2010 film *The Bounty Hunter* but they have both denied these rumours. Gerard's recent films include *Coriolanus* (2011) and Machine Gun Preacher (2011) and in 2012 he has several films due to be released including *Movie 43, Of*

Men and Mavericks, Playing the Field and *How to Train Your Dragon 2*

Byrne, Gabriel (1950-) Born 12 May 1950, Dublin. Actor. Educated at Dublin University. Became an actor at the age of 29 after being variously employed as a teacher, a cook and a teddy bear eye attacher. Gabriel came to prominence on the final season of the Irish television show *The Riordans*, subsequently starring in his own spin-off series, *Bracken*. Screen debut: *Excalibur* (1981) - as Uther Pendragon. Major films: *Miller's Crossing* (1990), *Into the West* (1992), *Little Women* (1994), *The Usual Suspects* (1995), *Man in the Iron Mask* (1998), *The Bridge of San Luis Rey* (2004), *Assault on Precinct 13* (2005), *Wah-Wah* (2005) and *Perrier's Bounty* (2009). In 1999 he played both a priest - *Stigmata* (1999) - and the devil - *End of Days* (1999). Gabriel also does some producing and writing. Autobiography: *Pictures in My Head* (1998). Gabriel was married to actress Ellen Barkin (1988-99) and now holds both Irish and US citizenship. He starred as therapist Dr. Paul Weston in the HBO primetime weeknight series *In Treatment* between 2008 and 2010.

Byron, Kathleen (1923-2009) Born 11 January 1923, London. Actress. Trained at the Old Vic. Screen debut: *Young Mr Pitt* (1941). A star of the Powell and Pressburger films *A Matter of Life and Death* (1946), *Black Narcissus* (1947) and *The Small Back Room* (1948). She made *Young Bess* (1953) in Hollywood before sinking into 'B' moviedom. She revived her career somewhat with appearances in *Emma* (1996), *Les Miserables* (1998) and *Saving Private Ryan* (1998). She died 18 January 2009 in Northwood, London. See also entry for *Who Is Sylvia?* In the television section.

Caine, Michael (1933-) Born Maurice Joseph Micklewhite, 14 March 1933, Bermondsey, London. Actor. Served in the army in Korea. Took the name Michael Scott until settling on the surname Caine - taken from the film *The Caine Mutiny* (1954). Screen debut: *Sailor Beware!* (1956). After playing bit parts in many British films, mainly as cockneys, he came to international attention playing the upper-class officer Gonville Bromhead in *Zulu* (1964). Played the spy Harry Palmer in five films: *The Ipcress File* (1965), *Funeral in Berlin* (1966), *Billion Dollar Brain* (1967), *Midnight in St. Petersburgh* (1995) and *Bullet to Beijing* (1995). Gained an Academy Award Nomination for Best Actor playing Alfie Elkins in *Alfie* (1966). He received other Academy Award Best Actor nominations for his two-hander with Laurence Olivier *Sleuth* (1972), *Educating Rita* (1983) and *The Quiet American* (2002). He won Academy Awards for Best Supporting Actor for his parts in *Hannah and her Sisters* (1986) and *The Cider House Rules* (1999). Other major films: *The Italian Job* (1969), *Get Carter* (1971), *The Man Who Would be King* (1975), *California Suite* (1978), *Dressed to Kill* (1980), *Mona Lisa* (1986), *Dirty Rotten Scoundrels* (1988), *Little Voice* (1998), *Miss Congeniality* (2000), *Bewitched* (2005), *Batman Begins* (2005), *The Weatherman* (2005), *The Prestige* (2006), *Sleuth* (2007 - a remake of the earlier film, with Caine taking the role originally played by Laurence Olivier, and Jude Law taking Caine's role), *The Dark Knight* (2008), *Harry Brown* (2010), *Inception* (2010), *Gnomeo & Juliet* (2011 - voice of Lord Redbrick) and *Cars 2* (2011 - voice of Finn McMissile). Responsible for more repeatable movie quotes than most, including: "You were only supposed to blow the bloody doors off! (*The Italian Job*) and "You're a big man, but you're in bad shape" (*Get Carter*). Ironically this second famous film quote was said to Cliff Brumby (played by ex-Corrie actor Bryan Mosley), a character Michael portrayed in the less-successful remake of *Get Carter* in 2000. Michael has been married twice; to actress Patricia Haines (1955-58) and, former Miss Guyana, Shakira Baksh (1973-present). Michael met Shakira after he saw her in a Maxwell House coffee commercial and a friend gave him her telephone number. Autobiographies: *What's it all about?* (1992) and *The Elephant to Hollywood* (2011). Appointed CBE in 1993 and knighted (as Sir Maurice Micklewhite) in 2000. Some time after his mother died, Michael and his younger brother, Stanley, learned they had an elder half-brother, David, who suffered from severe epilepsy and had been kept in Cane Hill Mental Hospital his entire life. Although their mother regularly visited David, even her husband did not know the child existed. David died in 1992. See also entries in the television section for *Harry Enfield's Television Programme* and *Stella Street*.

Callow, Simon (1949-) Born Simon Phillip Hugh Callow, 15 June 1949, Streatham, London. Actor. Stage debut: *The Plumber's Progress* (1975). Screen debut: *Amadeus* (1984). Appeared in three Merchant-Ivory adaptations of E M Forster novels: *A Room with a View* (1986), *Maurice* (1987) and *Howard's End* (1992). He also made an impact as Gareth in *Four Weddings and a Funeral* (1994). Other films include: *Jefferson in Paris* (1995), *Shakespeare in Love* (1998), *Thunderpants* (2002), *Merci Docteur Rey* (2002), *Bright Young Things* (2003), *The Phantom of the Opera* (2004), *The Civilization of Maxwell Bright* (2005), *Bob the Butler* (2005), *Chemical Wedding* (2007) and *No Ordinary Trifle* (2011 - aka *Love's Kitchen*). Simon also directed *The Ballad of the Sad Cafe* (1991). His recent stage work includes the one-man play *The Mystery of Charles Dickens*. He has also written biographies of Oscar Wilde, Orson Welles and Charles Laughton. Appointed CBE in 1999. Simon is also an excellent television actor who made his name in this sphere starring as Tom Chance in *Chance In A Million* (1984). He was one of the first actors publicly to declare his homosexuality, doing so in his 1984 book *Being An Actor*. See also entries in the television section for *Chance in a Million* and *David Copperfield*

Calthrop, Donald (1888-1940) Born Donald Esme C Calthrop, 11 April 1888, Chelsea, London. Actor. Nephew of theatre director Dion Boucicault. His brother Dion Clayton Calthrop (b. 2 May 1878, d. 7 March 1937) was an artist, designer, novelist and playwright. Stage debut: *A Wire Entanglement* (1906). Screen debut: *Wanted: a Widow* (1916). Films include: *Masks and Faces* (1917), *Shooting Stars* (1927), *Blackmail* (1929 - Tracy, the blackmailer), *Juno and the Paycock* (1929), *The Ghost Train* (1931), *Rome Express* (1932) and *Fire Over England* (1937). Worked for the BBC in the 1920s. A versatile actor who usually played villains although he did play Bob Crachit in *Scrooge* (1935) and featured in *Let George Do It* (1940 - with George Formby) and *Charley's Big-Hearted Aunt* (1940 - with Arthur Askey). A young actress called Nita Foy (b. Ann Foy Tipping, 1909, Middlesbrough, d. 31 March 1930) was sitting in his dressing room at Twickenham Studios whilst filming *Spanish Eyes* (1930). Her costume was caught by an electric fire and she died from her burns in Richmond Hospital that same day. Calthrop was himself burned in attempting to save her life and his later roles were limited due to a drinking problem probably resulting from the trauma of the accident. Calthrop died whilst filming *Major Barbara* on 15 July 1940 Denham, England.

Calvert, Phyllis (1915-2002) Born Phyllis Hannah Bickle, 18 February 1915, Chelsea, London. Actress. Trained at the Margaret Morris Dance School but an injury meant she became an actress rather than a dancer. Stage debut: *Crossings* (1925). Screen debut: *The Arcadians* (1927). She moved from playing light roles opposite the likes of George Formby in *Let George Do It* (1940) and Arthur Askey in *Charley's Big-Hearted Aunt* (1940), to featuring with Robert Donat in *The Young Mr Pitt* (1942). Her other films include: *Kipps* (1941), *The Man in Grey* (1943), *Fanny by Gaslight* (1944), *They Were Sisters* (1945) and *The Magic Bow* (1946). She went to Hollywood in 1947 but apart from *Mandy* (1952) her career there was disappointing. She later said "I hated America and they hated me." Later films include: *Oscar Wilde* (1960) and *Mrs Dalloway* (1997). One of the four leading ladies of Gainsborough Pictures - the others being Jean Kent, Margaret Lockwood and Patricia Roc. She was also a successful stage actress, tending to play weightier roles than she did on screen. In her later years she concentrated on TV work including her own series *Kate* (1970). Died 8 October 2002 Sutton, Surrey. See also entries in the television section for *Kate* and *Love Story*.

Cammell, Donald (1934-96) Born Donald Seton Cammell, 17 January 1934, Edinburgh. Writer and director. His father Charles was a poet, writer and heir to the Cammell ship-building business, the fortunes of which had plummeted during the Depression. Donald attended the Royal College of Art and began a successful career as a portrait artist and book illustrator. During the 1960s he decided to turn his hand to screenwriting. His script for *The Touchables* (1968) was rewritten by Ian La Frenais and he followed this with *Duffy* (1968). He also wrote his directorial debut: *Performance (1970)* - which he co-directed with Nicolas Roeg. A story of sex, drugs and power starring James Fox and Mick Jagger it survived intense controversy to become a cult classic. Surprisingly he only directed three further films. The first was a sci-fi tale called *Demon Seed* (1977). Then a proposed collaboration with Marlon Brando failed to get off the ground although a manuscript version of the screenplay has been published by Cammell's widow as *Fan Tan* (2005). His final films were *White of the Eye* (1987) and *Wild Side* (1996). This last named film was removed from Cammell's control by the production company and cut without his permission. The resulting film went straight to video with Franklin Brauner credited as director. It is believed that the distress caused by this episode resulted in Cammell committing suicide by gunshot 24 April 1996, Hollywood, California. The film has since been re-cut by his widow, China Kong (b. 1960) and long-time associate Frank Mazzola and issued to critical acclaim as *Donald Cammell's Wild Side*.

Campbell, Eric (1880-1917) Born Alfred Eric Stuart Campbell, 26 April 1880, Dunoon, Strathclyde. Actor. He made only eleven films in a career that lasted barely two years: *The Floorwalker* (1916), *The Fireman* (1916), *The Vagabond* (1916), *The Count* (1916), *The Pawnshop* (1916), *Behind the Screen* (1916), *The Rink* (1916), *Easy Street* (1917), *The Cure* (1917), *The Immigrant* (1917) and *The Adventurer* (1917). However, this 6' 4" giant of a man with the intimidating expression is always recognisable as the villain in films Charlie Chaplin made for *Mutual*. Like Chaplin he had been part of Fred Karno's troupe and he followed them to the United States in 1914. In 1915 Chaplin signed him up. Unlike his film persona he was in fact a kindly and sociable man. The loss of his first wife in a car crash seems to have affected him badly and alcohol problems brought a swift end to a hasty second marriage. He was killed 20 December 1917 in a car crash on Wilshire Boulevard following a cast party for a film he was making with Mary Pickford. Buried Angelus-Rosedale Cemetery, Los Angeles, California.

Campbell, Judy (1916-2004) Born Judy Mary Campbell, 31 May 1916, Grantham, Lincolnshire. Actress and playwright. Daughter of the manager of the Theatre Royal, Grantham, where she made her stage debut in *Last of Mrs Cheney* (1935). Judy had a very successful professional relationship with Noël Coward. Screen debut: *Convoy* (1940). She spent most of her career as a stage actress with starring roles in *The Reluctant Debutante*, *Heartbreak House*, *Mr Whatnot* (1964) and *Relatively Speaking* (1967). Judy also made about a dozen films including *Breach of Promise* (1942), *Green for Danger* (1946) and *Mr Forbush and the Penguins* (1971). A versatile performer, Judy also wrote the plays *Sing Cuckoo* (1950) and *The Bright One* (1958). The mother of actress Jane Birkin, she was still acting until shortly before her death on 6 June 2004, Westminster, London.

Cardiff, Jack (1914-2009) Born 18 September 1914, Great Yarmouth. Director and cinematographer. His father played football for Watford before taking up the stage as a dancer and later a comic. Jack appeared as a child actor in *My Son, My Son* (1918). He began as a camera operator on such films as Rene Clare's *The Ghost Goes West* (1935). Joined *British Technicolor* in 1936 and worked on the first full-colour British film *Wings of the Morning* (1937). Other work as cinematographer include: *Western Isles* (1941), *Caesar and Cleopatra* (1945*)*, *A Matter of Life and Death* (1946), *The Red Shoes* (1948), *Under Capricorn* (1949), *The Magic Box* (1951), *The African Queen* (1951), *War and Peace* (1956), *The Prince and the Showgirl* (1957), *The Vikings* (1958), *Death on the Nile* (1978), *The Dogs of War* (1980), *Conan the Destroyer* (1984), *The Dance of Shiva* (1998) and *The Tell-Tale Heart* (2004). During WWII he worked for the Ministry of Information on documentaries such as *Western Approaches* (1944). As a director he began with an Errol Flynn vehicle, *William Tell*, which was never completed. His other directorial outings include *Intent to Kill* (1958), *My Geisha* (1962), *The Long Ships* (1963), *Girl on a Motorcycle* (1968) and *Dr of Evil* (1973). His 1960 film *Scent of Mystery* (UK title

Holiday in Spain) was shot in Smell-O-Vision. He was nominated for a Best Director Academy Award for *Sons and Lovers* (1960). He won an Academy Award for Best Cinematography for *Black Narcissus* (1947) and received an honorary Academy Award in 2001. Received the OBE in 2001. Autobiography: *Magic Hour (1996)*. Jack died, aged 94, on 22 April 2009, the same day as Ken Annakin, with whom he had worked on *The Fifth Musketeer* (1979).

Carey, Joyce (1898-1993) Born Joyce Lilian Lawrence, 30 March 1898, Kensington, London. Actress. Daughter of actress Lilian Braithwaite and actor Gerald Lawrence. Screen debut: *God and the Man* (1918). Made an impact in *In Which We Serve* (1942) and *Brief Encounter* (1945). Other films: *The Way to the Stars* (1945), *Cry, the Beloved Country* (1952), *Libel* (1959) and *A Nice Girl Like Me* (1969). Wrote plays under the name Jay Mallory including *Sweet Aloes*. A close friend of Noël Coward, when the 'master' received his knighthood in 1970, Joyce, along with costume designer Gladys Calthrop, accompanied him to the ceremony at Buckingham Palace. Awarded the OBE in 1982. Died 28 February 1993, Westminster, London. See also entry for *Father Dear Father* in the television section.

Carlyle, Robert (1961-) Born 14 April 1961, Maryhill, Glasgow. Actor. Worked in his father's trade as a painter and decorator before training at the Royal Scottish Academy of Music and Drama. Founded his own theatre company called *Rain Dog*. Stage debut: *The Golden Mask of Agamemnon*. Screen debut: *Silent Scream* (1990). Had a breakthrough role in Ken Loach's *Riff Raff* (1990). Made an impact on television as a killer in *Cracker* (1993) and a policeman in *Hamish Macbeth* (1995-97). From the mid-1990s he had a series of strong roles in films such as *Trainspotting* (1996) and *Carla's Song* (1996) but also displayed perhaps a more populist side in *The Full Monty* (1997), *Plunkett and Macleane* (1999) and as a Bond villain in *The World is not Enough* (1999). Other films include *Angela's Ashes* (1999), *The 51st State* (2001), *Once Upon a Time in the Midlands* (2002), *Marilyn Hotchkiss' Ballroom Dancing & Charm School* (2005), *Eragon* (2006), *28 Weeks Later* (2007), *Stone of Destiny* (2008), *Summer* (2008), *I Know You Know* (2009) and *The Tournament* (2009). Awarded the OBE in 1999. Robert has been married to makeup artist Anastasia Shirley since 1997 and the couple have three children: Ava (b. 2002), Harvey (b. 2004) and Pearce Joseph (b. 2006).See also entries in the television section for *The Bill*, *Hamish Macbeth*, and *99 - 1*.

Carmichael, Ian (1920-2010) Born 18 June 1920, Kingston-upon-Hull, East Riding of Yorkshire. Actor. Studied at RADA. Stage debut in 1939. Screen debut: *Bond Street (1947)*. Spotted by the Boulting Brothers, he was given the part of Stanley Windrush in *Privates Progress* (1955), a part he reprised in *I'm All Right Jack* (1959). Other films include: *Brothers in Law* (1956), *Lucky Jim* (1957), *Left, Right and Centre* (1959), *School for Scoundrels* (1959) and *Heavens Above!* (1963). Epitomised satirical but amiable British comedy films in the 1950s. Went on to TV success in *The World of Wooster* (1966-1967) and *Lord Peter Wimsey* (1972-1975). Appointed to the Order of the British Empire in 2003. Autobiography: *Will the Real Ian Carmichael?* (1979). Ian continued to act until shortly before his death on 5 February 2010. See also entries in the radio and television section for *Bachelor Father, Jeeves and Wooster, Just A Minute, Lord Peter Wimsey,* and *The World of Wooster.*

Carroll, Leo G (1886-1972) Born Leo Grattan Carroll, 25 October 1886, Weedon, Northamptonshire. Actor. Son of a British Army officer. Made his stage debut in 1912 performing in both the West End and on Broadway. Leo based himself in America from 1934. Screen debut: *Sadie McKee* (1934). Early films include *Stamboul Quest* (1934), *The Barretts of Wimpole Street* (1934), *Clive of India* (1935), *Captains Courageous* (1937), *A Christmas Carol* (1938 - as Marley's ghost), *The Private Lives of Elizabeth and Essex* (1939), *Wuthering Heights* (1939) and *The Tower of London* (1939). A favourite of Alfred Hitchcock, he featured in that director's *Rebecca* (1940), *Suspicion* (1941), *Spellbound* (1945), *The Paradine Case* (1947), *Strangers on a Train* (1951) and *North by Northwest* (1959). His later films include *Father of the Bride* (1950), *The Bad and the Beautiful* (1952), *The Parent Trap* (1961) and *From Nashville with Music* (1969). On American television he starred as Cosmo Topper in

Topper (1953-56*)* but is best remembered in the UK for playing Alexander Waverly in *The Man from U.N.C.L.E.* (1964-1968) and the spin-off films. Died 16 October 1972 Los Angeles, California.

Carroll, Madeleine (1906-87) Born Marie-Madeleine Bernadette O'Carroll, 26 February 1906, West Bromwich, West Midlands. Actress. She studied French at Birmingham University and worked as a French teacher before taking up acting full-time in 1927. Stage debut: *The Lash* (1927). Screen debut: *The First Born* (1928). After starring in two Alfred Hitchcock films as Pamela in *The Thirty-Nine Steps* (1935) and Elsa in *Secret Agent* (1936) she moved to America and enjoyed more success in *The General Died at Dawn* (1937) and as Princess Flavia in *The Prisoner of Zenda* (1937). She went on to feature in light comedies including *My Favourite Blonde* (1942), opposite Bob Hope. She became an American citizen in 1943 after her marriage to actor Sterling Hayden (1942-45). She virtually put an end to her acting career when taking up full-time war relief after the death of her sister Margueritte in the London blitz. She was awarded the Legion d'Honneur in 1946 and then made her last film *The Fan* (1949). Remarried in 1950 (her 4th husband) and eventually retired to France and subsequently Spain. Died 2 October 1987, Marbella, Spain and buried in Fuengirola.

Castle, Roy (1932-94) Born 31 August 1932, Scholes, nr Holmfirth, Yorkshire. Entertainer. Best known as one of a dying breed of brilliant all-round entertainers (comedian, singer, musician, dancer) and as the presenter of *Record Breakers* on TV. He made a few films including playing Captain Keene in *Carry on Up the Khyber* (1968) and as a reluctant companion to Peter Cushing's Time Lord in *Dr Who and the Daleks* (1965). Roy was a supremely fit man who held several Guinness World Records himself. I had the great pleasure of playing squash with Roy in Gerrards Cross whilst working there as an accountant in 1988 and being 22 years younger and having won many fitness competitions myself, I thought I was in for an easy ride. Suffice to say he thrashed me. His death on 2 September 1994, Gerrards Cross, Buckinghamshire from lung cancer was particularly sad as Roy never smoked a cigarette in his life but probably contracted the disease as a result of his many years of performing in smoky clubs, for several years playing Hutton Conyers, one of the chain-smoking Jimmy James' stooges. See also entries in the television section for *The Good Old Days*, *Record Breakers*, and *Seven of One*.

Cattrall, Kim (1956-) Born Kim Victoria Cattrall, 21 August 1956, Liverpool. Actress. Her family emigrated to Canada when she was only three months old but she is still often claimed as a British actress. Aged eleven she returned to England to learn to act, studying at LAMDA, before moving on to the American Academy of Dramatic Arts in New York. As a prize in her final year she won a part in Otto Preminger's *Rosebud* (1975). Initially a jobbing actress on numerous American series in the late 1970s and early 1980s, her first starring roles were in *Police Academy* (1984), as Cadet Karen Thompson and *Mannequin* (1987), in the title role. Her career never really took off until the hit series *Sex and the City* (1998 - 2004). In this she played the sexually aggressive Samantha Jones. For this series she won Emmy nominations every year between 2000 and 2004, and also a Golden Globe in 2003. As part of her revived film career she has played various roles including Britney Spears' mother in *Crossroads* (2002). In 2008 Kim reprised her role as Samantha in *Sex and the City: The Movie*. Her recent films include *The Ghost Writer* (2009) and *Sex and the City 2* (2010). Kim has been married three times, her third marriage lasting the same time span as the *Sex and the City* television series. Kim also once dated former Canadian Prime Minister, Pierre Trudeau. Despite having dual British and Canadian citizenship, Kim became an American citizen in 2008.

Cavill, Henry (1983-) Born Henry William Dalgliesh Cavill, 5 May 1983, Jersey. Henry's first acting break came in the film *The Count of Monte Cristo* (2002), playing Albert Mondego. He followed this with relatively small parts in the nouveau film *I Capture the Castle* (2003) and an experimental High-Definition film *Red Riding Hood* (2004). Henry then began to develop further, starring in *Hellraiser: Hellworld* (2005) and having a supporting role in *Tristan & Isolde* (2006). In 2005, Henry made the final three (with Daniel Craig and Sam Worthington) for the role of James Bond in *Casino Royale* but the producers ultimately thought him too young for the role and for a time he was dubbed 'the unluckiest man in Hollywood'. Henry's fortunes soon changed when he landed the part of Humphrey in the all-star cast of *Stardust* (2007) and later in the year played the meaty role of Charles Brandon, 1st Duke of Suffolk in the Showtime series *The Tudors* (2007-10). Henry's more recent films include, *Blood Creek* (2009), *Whatever Works* (2009) and *Immortals* (2011 – as Theseus). He has also just completed filming for his role of Will Shaw in the forthcoming *The Cold Light of Day* and has recently been cast to play Superman in the 2013 film *The Man of Steel*.

Chaplin, Charlie (1889-1977) Born Charles Spencer Chaplin, 16 April 1889, Lambeth, London. Actor, writer and director. The son of music hall entertainers. After a spell in Lambeth Workhouse he joined a juvenile troupe "The Eight Lancashire Lads". Stage debut: *Jim, A Romance of Cockayne* (1903). Joined Fred Karno's Comedians in 1908 and toured the US (1910-13). Stayed in the US to join the *Keystone Film Company*. Screen debut: *Making a Living* (1914). First featured in his tramp guise in *Kid Auto Races at Venice* (1914). Moved to *Essanay Company* in 1915 to be replaced at Keystone by his brother Sydney. For Essanay he made 14 films, including *The Tramp* (1915). He then moved swiftly on to the *Mutual Film Corporation* (1916) before setting up his own studio in 1918. Charlie formed *United Artists* with Mary Pickford, Douglas Fairbanks and David Wark Griffith in 1919. His major films of the 1920s and 1930s were *The Kid* (1921), *The Idle Class* (1921), *Woman of Paris* (1923), *The Gold Rush* (1925), *The Circus* (1928), *City Lights* (1931), *Modern Times* (1936) and *The Great Dictator* (1940). He was awarded an Honorary Academy Award for *The Circus* in 1928 and nominated as Best Director for *Modern Times* in 1940. After travelling to Europe in 1952 he found that his re-entry permit had been rescinded. He had never given up his British citizenship and was considered to have Communist leanings. Thereafter he settled in Corsier sur Vevey, Switzerland. Later films: *Monsieur Verdoux* (1947), *Limelight* (1952), *A King in New York* (1957), *A Countess from Hong Kong* (1967). Awarded a special Academy Award in 1972. Autobiographies: *My Trip Abroad* (1922), *My Wonderful Visit* (1930), *My Autobiography* (1964) and *My Life in Pictures* (1974). Charlie was the younger half-brother of actor Sydney Chaplin. He was married to Mildred Harris (1918-1921), Lita Grey (1924-1927), Paulette Goddard (1936-1942) and Oona O'Neill (1943-1977). Charlie's fourth and final marriage to the daughter of playwright Eugene O'Neill was a happy one. They had eight children, Annette, Jane, Victoria, Josephine, Eugene, Christopher, Michael, and actress Geraldine (b. July 31, 1944). Knighted in 1975. Died 25 December 1977 Corsier sur Vevey. On 3 March 1978, his body was stolen in a failed attempt to extort money from his family. The body was recovered shortly afterwards in a field near Lake Geneva.

Chaplin, Sydney (1885-1965) Born Sidney John Hill, 16 March 1885, Walworth, London. Actor. The Sydney and Sidney are apparently interchangeable as he corresponded using both spellings. His mother Hannah Hill married Charles Chaplin in June 1885 and his half-brother Charlie was born in 1889. A story that his father was a bookmaker called Sydney Hawkes and that he was born in South Africa has never been substantiated. Sydney joined the Union Castle Mail Steamship Company in 1901 and worked aboard ship until 1905, with one break where he toured with Charlie. He joined Fred Karno's troupe in 1906 with his brother joining in 1908. He stayed in the UK with Karno until 1914 when he signed with the *Keystone Studios*. Screen debut: *Fatty's Wine Party* (1914). He starred in a series of films as a character called Gussle including: *A Lover's Lost Control* (1915), *Gussle, The Golfer* (1915), *Gussle's Wayward Path* (1915), *Gussle Rivals Jonah* (1915) and *Gussle's Backward Way* (1915). He played alongside Charlie in *A Dog's Life* (1918), *Shoulder Arms* (1918), *Pay Day* (1922) and *The Pilgrim* (1923). His other films include: *Hello, 'Frisco* (1924), *Charley's Aunt* (1925), *The*

Better 'Ole (1926) and *A Little Bit of Fluff* (1928). Described by Darryl F Zanuck as "the greatest ladies man in Hollywood history - better even than Errol Flynn." This particular piece of Hollywood hyperbole might well be true given that *The Mumming Birds*, the film he was making after the success of *A Little Bit of Fluff*, was cancelled following a sex scandal involving actress Molly Wright. He never made another film but is felt by many to have been the driving force behind his brother's career. Died 16 April 1965 Nice, France.

Chapman, Edward (1901-77) Born Edward Arnold Chapman, 13 October 1901, Harrogate, Yorkshire. Actor. Worked as a bank clerk before taking up acting. Stage debut: *Trilby* (1924). Screen debut: *Caste* (1930). Other films include: *Juno and the Paycock* (1930), *Murder* (1930), *The Skin Game* (1931), *Things to Come* (1936), *The Man Who Could Work Miracles* (1936), *The Citadel* (1938), *The Four Just Men* (1939), *The Proud Valley* (1940), *The History of Mr Polly* (1949), *The Magic Box* (1951), *Bhowani Junction* (1956), *Doctor at Large* (1957), *The Bulldog Breed* (1960), *Oscar Wilde* (1960), *School for Scoundrels* (1960) and *The Man Who Haunted Himself* (1970). In spite of a long and distinguished career as a character actor he is perhaps best remembered as playing alongside Norman Wisdom in such films as *The Square Peg* (1958), *A Stitch in Time* (1963) and *The Early Bird* (1965). Died 9 August 1977, Brighton, East Sussex. All together now: "Mr Grimsdale!"

Charleson, Ian (1949-90) Born 11 August 1949, Edinburgh. Actor. An architectural student at Edinburgh University but then switched to the London Academy of Music and Dramatic Art. Best known for his portrayal of Olympic gold medallist Eric Liddell in *Chariots of Fire* (1981). His other films include: *Gandhi* (1982), *Greystoke: The Legend of Tarzan* (1985) and *Opera* (1987). An award for young actors is named in his honour. Died 6 January 1990, London, from an AIDS-related illness whilst appearing as Hamlet at the Olivier Theatre. See also entries in the television section for *Churchill's People, It's A Knockout, Oxbridge Blues,* and *Reilly - Ace of Spies.*

Christie, Julie (1941-) Born Julie Frances Christie, 14 April 1941, Assam, India. Actress. Daughter of a tea planter. Trained at London Central School of Music and Drama before getting her big break in the 1961 science fiction series *A for Andromeda*. Screen debut: *Crooks Anonymous* (1962). Played Tom Courtenay's girlfriend in *Billy Liar* (1963) and quickly rose to stardom. She gained an Academy Award for Best Actress for her role as Diana Scott (a prime example of the 60s female for whom "Fidelity means not having more than one man at the same time") in *Darling* (1965). Her other films in the 1960s include *Dr Zhivago* (1965), *Fahrenheit 451* (1966), *Far from the Madding Crowd* (1967) and *Petulia* (1968). She has continued to adorn films through the decades, receiving Academy Award Best Actress nominations for *McCabe and Mrs Miller* (1971) and *Afterglow* (1997) and Bafta Best Supporting Actress nomination for *Finding Neverland* (2004). Her other films include: *The Go-Between* (1971), *Don't Look Now* (1973), *Shampoo* (1975), *Heaven Can Wait* (1978), *Return of the Soldier* (1982), *Hamlet* (1996), *Harry Potter and the Prisoner of Azkaban* (2004), *Troy* (2004), *Away From Her* (2006), *New York, I Love You* (2009), *Glorious 39* (2009) and *Red Riding Hood* (2011 - as Grandmother). Julie was a leading figure in the glamorous London nightspots of the 1960s, and had a high profile relationship with Warren Beatty between 1967 and 1974, maintaining a life-long friendship with Beatty's sister Shirley MacLaine. Fluent in French and Italian, Julie has made several foreign language films, notably *Les Quarantièmes rugissants* (1982) *Belphégor - Le fantôme du Louvre* (2001 – starring alongside Sophie Marceau) and *The Secret Life of Words* (2005). Julie's partner since 1979 has been *Guardian* journalist Duncan Campbell. Despite repeated admissions that she would never marry, "Men don't want any responsibility and neither do I", Julie did in fact marry Duncan in a quiet ceremony in November 2007. Al Pacino once called Julie "the most poetic of all actresses".

Churchill, Sarah (1914-82) Born Sarah Millicent Hermione Churchill, 7 October 1914, St Martins, London. Actress. Daughter of Sir Winston Churchill. Became a professional dancer. Stage debut: *Follow the Sun*. Screen debut: *Who's Your Lady Friend* (1937). Served in the WAAF during WWII. Her films include:

Spring Meeting (1941), *He Found a Star* (1941), *Daniele Cortis* (1947), *All Over the Town* (1949) and *Fabian of the Yard* (1954). Made her US stage debut in *The Philadelphia Story* in 1949 which led her to be cast as Fred Astaire's love interest in *Royal Wedding* (1950). Sarah did some TV work during the 1950s and her final film was *Serious Charge* (1959). Married to Vic Oliver (1936-45), Anthony Beauchamp (1949-57) and Henry, Lord Audley (1962-63). She died 24 September 1982, Westminster, London.

Clark, Petula (1932-) Born Petula Sally Olwen Clark, 15 November 1932, Epsom, Surrey. Singer and actress. During WWII she became popular as a child singer on the BBC in London concert halls, and at the age of 11 began playing child roles in British films. Screen debut: *Strawberry Roan* (1940). She remained on the screen through adolescence and early maturity, mostly in syrupy roles in films of little consequence such as playing Pet Huggett in the series of films about the Huggett family. She then left for Paris in her early 20s when she married pop promoter Claude Woolf and achieved great popularity in the 1950s and 1960s as a concert and recording artist, her first UK singles success being *The Little Shoemaker* (No 7 in June 1954). Her popularity spread into the English-speaking world after a string of top-ten pop hits including, *Suddenly There's A Valley* (No 7, Nov 1955), *With All My Heart* (No 4, July 1957), *Alone* (No 8, Nov 1957), *Romeo* (No 3, July 1961), *My Friend The Sea* (No 7, Nov 1961), *Downtown* (No 2, Nov 1964), *My Love* (No 4, Feb 1966) and *I Couldn't Live without your Love* (No 6, June 1966). One of her most enduring songs, *Don't Sleep In The Subway* only managed No 12 in May 1967. She gained No. 1 UK chart hits with *Sailor* (1961) and *This is My Song* (1967) and also topped the US Charts with *Downtown* and *My Love*. Pet (as she has always been known) then starred in two musical films, firstly as Sharon McLonergan in *Finian's Rainbow* (1968) and then as Katherine Bridges in *Goodbye Mr. Chips* (1969) and also filmed a number of specials on American TV. Though regarded as more of a singer than an actress (she was the first British solo artist to win a Grammy Award and the first British female pop singer to have a number one hit single in the United States), she continued to act and in 1981, opened in *The Sound of Music* in London's West End. Awarded the CBE in 1998 and in 2010 became the President of the Hastings Musical Festival.

Clarke, Alan (1935-90) Born Alan John Clarke, 28 October 1935, Birkenhead, Cheshire. Director. Initially worked as an insurance clerk and, following National Service, emigrated to Canada to be a gold miner. In 1958 he enrolled on a course in Radio and TV Arts in Toronto. Returned to England in the early 1960s and joined the BBC in 1969. Worked as a director on the acclaimed series *The Wednesday Play* and *Play for Today*. His directorial debut was: *Shelter* (1967) and he also directed *Sovereign's Company* (1970), *To Encourage the Others* (1972), *Penda's Fen* (1974), *Contact* (1985) and *Elephant* (1989). These last two dealt with the Northern Ireland issue. His film for the BBC, *Scum* (1977) was banned before it could be shown but in 1979 it was remade as a feature. This bleak and violent film, set in a Borstal was to be followed by the equally powerful television plays *Made in Britain* (1982) and *The Firm* (1988) which seemed to chart the progress of Clarke's vision of Thatcher's Britain. Although these social realism films make for uncomfortable viewing, they are, like many films of the genre, at times also very funny. The majority of his output was for television but he did make three films for the cinema: the aforementioned *Scum* (1979), the unfathomable box office flop *Billy the Kid and the Green Baize Vampire* (1985) and the much more successful *Rita, Sue and Bob Too* (1986). Died 24 July 1990 Islington, London.

Clarke, Noel (1975-) Born Noel Anthony Clarke, 6 December 1975, London, England. Actor, writer and director. On television Noel is best known for playing Wyman Norris in *Auf Wiedersehen Pet* (2002–04) and Mickey Smith in *Doctor Who* (2005–06). An accomplished stage actor, he won the Laurence Olivier Award for "Most Promising Newcomer" in 2003 for his performance in the play *Where Do We Live* at the Royal Court Theatre. Noel made his film debut as Cyril in *I'll Sleep When I'm Dead* (2004) but then went on to write, and star in, his second film *Kidulthood* (2006), which was very well received by critics and the viewing public. Noel went one better in his next film, *Adulthood* (2008), by adding the director's role to his writing and acting duties. This sequel to *Kidulthood*, takes up the story of newly-released Sam Peel (Clarke) six years after being sent down for murder. Noel's recent films include *Heartless* (2009), *Doghouse* (2009), *Centurion* (2009) *Sex & Drugs & Rock & Roll* (2010) and *4.3.2.1.* (2010), a crime thriller he wrote, appears in, and co-directed with Mark Davis. In 2009, Noel won a BAFTA award in the category: Orange Rising Star Award.

Clarke, T E B (1907-89) Born Thomas Ernest Bennett Clarke, 7 June 1907, Watford, Hertfordshire. Writer. Known as Tibby. Educated at Charterhouse and Cambridge. After an abortive attempt at settling in Australia he worked as a journalist and policeman. His book *What's Yours?*, about pubs and pub life, was used as a reference when Ealing Studios were making *Saloon Bar* (1940) and he was subsequently hired as a screenwriter. He wrote 15 films between 1943 and 1957, the first being the popular *Hue and Cry* (1947). He was nominated for an Academy Award for Best Story and Screenplay for *Passport to Pimlico* (1949) which he was inspired to write after reading an article about how the Dutch royal succession had to be secured by the heir being born on Dutch soil. During WWII a room in Ottawa was so declared in order that the rule could be obeyed. Clarke won an Academy Award for Best Story and Screenplay for *The Lavender Hill Mob* (1951). His other Ealing films include: *The Blue Lamp* (1950), *The Titfield Thunderbolt* (1953), *The Rainbow Jacket* (1954) and *Barnacle Bill* (1957). His post-Ealing films include: *A Tale of Two Cities* (1958), *Gideon's Day* (1958), *A Man Could Get Killed* (1966) and *High Rise Donkey* (1980). He was nominated for an Academy Award for Best Adapted Screenplay for *Sons and Lovers* (1960). He also wrote novels such as *Murder at Buckingham Palace* and *The Wrong Turning*, and the play *A Little Temptation*. Awarded OBE in 1952. Autobiography: *This is Where I Came In* (1974). Died 11 February 1989, Southwark, London.

Clayton, Jack (1921-95) Born 1 March 1921, Brighton, East Sussex. Director and producer. Worked at Denham Studios where he worked his way up from tea boy to assistant director and editor. Served in the RAF during WWII, during which time he was asked to direct a short documentary called *Naples is a Battlefield* (1944). Continued to work for Korda post-war and also for John Huston. Was associate producer on: *The Queen of Spades* (1949), *Moulin Rouge* (1952), *Beat the Devil* (1953), *The Good Die Young* (1954), *I am a Camera* (1955) and *Moby Dick* (1956). He also produced several films including: *Three Men in a Boat* (1956), *Sailor Beware* (1956) and *The Story of Esther Costello* (1957). In 1955 Jack made his commercial directorial debut with the Academy Award winning short film *The Bespoke Overcoat*. His first feature as director was *Room at the Top* (1959) which gained him a Best Director Academy Award nomination as well as being nominated for Best Film. His output over the next 30 years was not extensive. There followed further literary adaptations including: *The Innocents* (1961 - based on *The Turn of the Screw*), *The Pumpkin Eater* (1964) and *Our Mother's House* (1967). Seven years later he directed the disappointing *The Great Gatsby* (1974) and another nine years passed before he made *Something Wicked this Way Comes* (1983), during which time he had suffered a stroke. His final films both featured Maggie Smith: the critically acclaimed *The Lonely Passion of Judith Hearne* (1987) and the TV film *Momento Mori* (1992). He died 26 February 1995, Slough, Berkshire.

Cleese, John See entry in comedy section

Clive, Colin (1900-37) Born Colin Glenn Clive-Greig, 20 January 1900, St Malo, France. Actor. Son of a British colonel. Educated at the Royal Military College Sandhurst. Left the military and trained for the stage at RADA. Stage debut: *The Eclipse* (1919). Made his screen debut in *Journey's End* (1930) in a repeat of a stage success both of which were directed by James Whale. Whale cast him again in what became his signature role as Dr Henry Frankenstein in *Frankenstein* (1931) and he repeated the success in *Bride of Frankenstein* (1935). His other films include: *The Key* (1934), *One More River* (1934), *Clive of India* (1935), *The Hands of Orlac* (1935), *The Man who Broke the Bank at Monte Carlo* (1935), *The Widow from Monte Carlo* (1935) and

The Woman I Love (1937). Colin also played Edward Rochester in the first talkie version of *Jane Eyre* (1934). He died 25 June 1937, Los Angeles, California, after being unable to fight off his lung problems because of his alcohol consumption.

Close, Ivy (1890-1968) Born Ivy Lillian Close, 15 June 1890, Stockton-on-Tees, England. Actress. Daughter of a jeweler. In 1908 her father submitted her photograph for a competition being run by the *Daily Mirror* to find "The Most Beautiful Woman in the World", which she duly won. Ivy married photographer Elwin Neame in 1910. Together with Neame she formed *Ivy Close Films*, a production company whose films were distributed by Cecil Hepworth. Neame also directed several films in which she starred including her screen debut *Dream Paintings* (1912), *Mifanwy: a Tragedy* (1913), *The Girl from the Sky* (1914) and *The Haunting of Silas P Gould* (1915). She went on to feature in a series of *Ivy Close* productions until in 1919 she was signed up to star in Abel Gance's highly influential *La Roue (The Wheel)* (1922), which was made in France over a two year period. Her performance was well received but her star had already begun to fade, a fact not helped by the death of Neame in a motorcycle accident in 1923. She made two further films in Germany before finally retiring in 1929. Mother of director and cinematographer Ronald Neame and writer Derek Neame. She subsequently married Australian make-up artist Curly Batson (1938-57) and died 4 December 1968, Goring, Oxfordshire.

Clyde, Andy (1892-1967) Born Andrew Allan Clyde, 25 March 1892, Rattray, Perthshire. Actor. Son of a draper turned actor. Travelled to the United States and joined Mack Sennett's ensemble. Screen debut: *A Small Town Idol* (1921). Made as many as 250 films including: *Million Dollar Legs* (1932), *Annie Oakley* (1955), *Three Men from Texas* (1940) and *Abiline Trail* (1951). He spent much of his career playing the role of sidekick to the cowboy hero. He played Hopalong Cassidy's companion California Carlson in almost 40 films. His brother David Clyde (b. 27 May 1887 Gorbals, Glasgow; d. 16 May 1945 California) and sister Jean Clyde (b. Jeannie Clyde, 17 March 1889, Gorbals, Glasgow; died 1962) were also actors. Andy Clyde died 18 May 1967, Los Angeles, California and is interred in Forest Lawn.

Coates, Anne (1925-) Born Anne Voase Coates, 12 December 1925, Reigate, Surrey. Editor. She originally started out as a nurse working with the famous plastic surgeon Sir Archibald McIndoe in East Grinstead. Anne began to fulfil her long-held ambition to be a film director with a company called *Religious Films*. The work consisted of patching up prints of devotional shorts before sending them out to Britain's churches. This lead to her working uncredited on *The Red Shoes* (1948) and *The Pickwick Papers* (1952). She was to become a talented, prolific editor who is still at the top of the male-dominated profession well into her eighties. Anne won an Academy Award for her work on David Lean's classic *Lawrence of Arabia* (1962) and also acted as a consultant on the restoration of the film in 1989. She has also received Academy Award nominations for Best Film Editing for *Becket* (1964), *The Elephant Man* (1980), *In the Line of Fire* (1993) and *Out of Sight* (1999). Her other more recent films include: *Erin Brockovich* (2000), *Taking Lives* (2004), *The Golden Compass* (2007) and *Extraordinary Measures* (2010). In February 2007, she was awarded BAFTA's highest honour, The Academy Fellowship.

Cole, George (1925-) Born George Edward Cole, 22 April 1925, Tooting, London. Actor. Stage debut: *White Horse Inn* (1939). Served in the RAF 1943-1947. Screen debut: *Cottage to Let* (1941). George featured in a string of British films in the 1950s, usually playing a chirpy cockney, including: *Laughter in Paradise* (1951), *Scrooge* (1951 - as the young Scrooge), *The Green Man* (1956) and *Too Many Crooks* (1958). His most popular role was as the spiv Flash Harry in the *St Trinian's* films: *The Belles of St Trinian's* (1954), *Blue Murder at St Trinian's* (1957), *The Pure Hell of St Trinian's* (1961) and *The Great St Trinian's Train Robbery* (1966). Many of these films were played opposite Alastair Sim, George's great friend and acting mentor. George lived in the Sim household for 14 years between 1940 and 1954. George later played Arthur Daley - a sort of elder statesman version of Flash Harry - in the popular TV series *Minder* (1979-

85). Although George found his London accent helped to authenticate these parts he was equally at home playing upper-class characters, such as Sir Giles Lynchwood in the TV adaptation of Tom Sharpe's novel *Blott on the Landscape*. Indeed George is known to have distinct middle-class tendencies, right down to finishing the *Times* crossword every day. He was awarded the Order of the British Empire in 1992. George has been married to two actresses, Eileen Moore (1954-62) and Penny Morrell (1964-present). See also entries in the television section for *Blott on the Landscape*, *The Bounder*, *Comrade Dad*, *A Life of Bliss*, and *Minder*.

Coleman, Charlotte (1968-2001) Born Charlotte Ninon Coleman, 3 April 1968, Westminster, London. Actress. The daughter of actress Ann Beach. She did some early television work mainly on the series *Worzel Gummidge*. Her major acting breakthrough came in the television film *Oranges Are Not the Only Fruit* (1990). Here she played the older Jess in a powerful drama about sexuality and religion. The rebellious side portrayed by Jess was mirrored by Charlotte in reality as she had been expelled from high school for smoking and drinking. More television work followed until she made her feature film debut in *Map of the Human Heart* (1993). Her next film was her most memorable, playing the "dippy" Scarlett in *Four Weddings and A Funeral* (1994). Her final film was a short drama entitled *A Loving Act* (2001). After filming she died of an asthma attack, aged only 33, on 14 November 2001, Islington, London. Her sister Lisa Coleman (b. 10 July 1970, Charing Cross, London) is a popular television actress. See also entries in the television section for *How Do You Want Me?* and *Worzel Gummidge*.

Collier, Constance (1878-1955) Born Laura Constance Hardie, 22 January 1878, Windsor, Berkshire. Actress. Born into a theatrical family she made an early stage appearance at the age of three as a fairy in *A Midsummer Nights Dream*. Going on to become a distinguished dramatic actress on the British and American stage, she began as a chorus girl in musical revues when she joined the Gaiety Girls in in 1893. Joined Sir Beerbohm Tree's company in 1901 as a leading lady and during the next twenty years she spent much time touring Europe and the United States. She married fellow actor Julian L'Estrange (an Irishman with the real name Julian Boyle) in 1905 but he died in New York in 1918 during the influenza epidemic. During a tour in 1916 she made four films including her film debut in an uncredited appearance in D.W. Griffith's *Intolerance* (1916) and playing Lady Macbeth in "The Scottish Play". She continued making infrequent but impressive appearances in Hollywood films of the 1930s and 1940s, typically playing stately ladies with grand manners in such films as *Anna Karenina* (1935), *Little Lord Fauntleroy* (1936), *Stage Door* (1937), *The Perils of Pauline* (1947), *An Ideal Husband* (1947), *Rope* (1948) and *Whirlpool* (1949). She authored several plays including collaborating with the young Ivor Novello on the very successful *The Rat* (1924). After her retirement from acting she was in great demand as a voice and drama coach, at one time including Marilyn Monroe amongst her pupils. Autobiography: *Harlequinade* (1929). She died 25 April 1955, in New York.

Collins, Joan (1933-) Born Joan Henrietta Collins, 23 May 1933, Paddington, London. Actress. Stage debut: *The Dolls House* (1942). Studied at RADA. Signed to Rank Organisation 1950. Screen debut: *Lady Godiva Rides Again* (1951). A leading lady in many 1950s and early 1960s films including: *The Land of the Pharaohs* (1954), *The Girl in the Red Velvet Swing* (1955), *The Opposite Sex* (1956), *The Bravados* (1958) and *The Road to Hong Kong* (1962). Joan played Edith Keeler in a much-loved episode of *Star Trek*, *The City on the Edge of Forever* (1966). In 1978, Joan appeared alongside Leonard Rossiter in a series of Cinzano television commercials in which the drink was inevitably spilt down her character's dress. This helped Joan have a second coming and she went on to box office success playing Fontaine Khaled in both *The Stud* (1978) and *The Bitch* (1979) based on novels written by her sister Jackie. Her TV career took off around the same time with her portrayal of Alexis Colby (born Morell and formerly Carrington, Dexter, and Rowan) in *Dynasty* (1981-89). In reality, Joan went one better than Alexis by marrying five times: Maxwell Reed (1952-56), Anthony Newley (1963-70), Ronald Kass (1972-83), Peter Holm (1985-87) and Percy Gibson

(2002-present). Tara Newley (b. 1963, New York) is the only child of Joan's that has entered showbusiness (as singer and presenter). As well as autobiographies: *Past Imperfect* (1978) and *Second Act* (1996), Joan has written several bestselling novels including *Prime Time*, *Love & Desire & Hate*, *Infamous*, *Star Quality*, and *Misfortune's Daughters*. Joan was presented with the OBE in 1997. See also entries in the television section for *Footballers' Wives*, *The Human Jungle*, and *Saturday Live*.

Collins, Pauline (1940-) Born 3 September 1940, Exmouth, Devon. Actress. Worked as a teacher whilst acting part-time. Pauline's first television role was as a nurse in the long-running medical soap *Emergency Ward 10* (1960) Screen debut: *Secrets of a Windmill Girl* (1965). Although appearing in many drama series and sitcoms of the 1960s, Pauline came to public attention as Sarah Moffat in the TV series *Upstairs, Downstairs* (1971-75) and its spin-off *Thomas and Sarah* (1979). Other films include: *City of Joy* (1992) and *Paradise Road* (1997). Nominated for an Academy Award for Best Actress for her portrayal of the title role in *Shirley Valentine* (1989). Awarded the Order of the British Empire in 2001. Married to actor John Alderton (1969-present). Her later career has seen her move in to more character-driven roles as personified by her turn as Mrs Flight in the BBC production of *Bleak House* (2005) and Thyrza Grey in the television film *Marple: The Pale Horse* (2010). In 1967 Pauline appeared as Samantha Briggs in the *Doctor Who* story *The Faceless Ones* and in 2006 became only the third actor to have appeared in both the classic and new series of *Doctor Who* when she appeared in the episode *Tooth and Claw* as Queen Victoria. In 2011, Pauline returned to the big screen in the film *Albert Nobbs*. See also entries in the television section for *Ambassador*, *Bleak House*, *Forever Green*, *The Liver Birds*, *No Honestly*, *Thomas and Sarah*, and *Upstairs Downstairs*.

Colman, Ronald (1891-1958) Born Ronald Charles Colman, 9 February 1891, Richmond, Surrey. Actor. Worked as a shipping clerk for the British Steamship Company whilst dabbling in amateur dramatics. During WWI he was wounded at the Battle of Messines and invalided out of the army. Stage debut: *The Maharani of Arakam* (1916). Screen debut: *The Live Wire* (1917). Travelled to America in 1920 and struggled to make a living in New York until spotted by Lilian Gish and cast in the film *The White Sister* (1923). Went on to make amongst others *Her Night of Romance* (1924), *The Dark Angel* (1925), *Stella Dallas* (1925) and *Lady Windermere's Fan* (1925) before making a big impact as *Beau Geste* (1926). Went on to greater success once the talkies arrived. Nominated for a Best Actor Academy Award for both *Bulldog Drummond* (1929) and *Condemned* (1929). The mid 1930s saw him star in the classic films *Clive of India* (1935), *A Tale of Two Cities* (1935), *Under Two Flags* (1936), *Prisoner of Zenda* (1937) and *Lost Horizon* (1937). After starring alongside Cary Grant in *The Talk of the Town* (1942) he gained his third Academy Award Nomination for Best Actor for his work opposite Greer Garson in *Random Harvest* (1942). He finally won a Best Actor Academy Award for *A Double Life* (1948), which turned out to be his last major film. He married actresses Thelma Raye (1920-34) and Benita Hume (1938-58). He spent the 1950s mostly appearing on radio and television. Died 19 May 1958 Santa Barbara, California.

Coltrane, Robbie (1950-) Born Robert MacMillan, 30 March 1950, Rutherglen, Glasgow. Actor and comedian. Attended Glasgow Art School. Directed documentary *Young Mental Health* (1973) which was voted Film of the Year by the Scottish Education Council. Took his surname from the jazz musician. Robbie performed stand-up and improvisational comedy whilst also pursuing his acting career. Screen debut: *Death Watch* (1980). Films include: *Britannia Hospital* (1982), *Scrubbers* (1983), *Krull* (1983), *Defence of the Realm* (1985), *Absolute Beginners* (1986), *Mona Lisa* (1986), *Henry V* (1989 - as Falstaff, *Nuns on the Run* (1990), *Let It Ride* (1989), *The Pope Must Die* (1991) and *From Hell* (2001). Played Valentin Zukovsky in two Bond films: *Goldeneye* (1995) and *The World is not Enough* (1999) and the giant Rubius Hagrid in Harry Potter films: *The Philosopher's Stone (2001)*, *The Chamber of Secrets (2002)*, *The Prisoner of Azkaban (2004)*, *The Goblet of Fire (2005)*, *Order of the Phoenix* (2007), *Half-Blood Prince* (2009) and *Deathly Hallows: Part I* (2010) and *Part II* (2011). He is also in great demand as a voice actor in films such as *Van Helsing* (2004 - as Mr Hyde), *The Tale of Despereaux* (2008 - as Gregory), the title role of the teddy bear *Gooby* (2009) and the upcoming American 3D computer-animated fantasy adventure film, *Brave* (2012 – as Lord Dingwall). Robbie is of course also well known for his role of 'Fitz' in the popular detective series, *Cracker* (1993-96; 2006). See also entries in the television section for *Alfresco, Blackadder the Third, The Comic Strip Presents, Cracker, A Kick Up the Eighties, Saturday Live, Tutti Frutti,* and *The Young Ones.*

Compton, Fay (1894-1978) Born Virginia Lilian Emmeline Compton Mackenzie, 18 September 1894, West Kensington, London. Actress. Born into a theatrical family. Stage debut: *The Follies* (1911). Screen debut: *She Stoops to Conquer* (1914). In general her stage work - J M Barrie wrote *Mary Rose* for her - took precedence over her films but that did not prevent her having a film career spanning 56 years. Her films include: *A Woman of No Importance* (1922), *The Loves of Mary Queen of Scots* (1923), *The Mill on the Floss* (1937), *Nicholas Nickleby* (1947), *Odd Man Out* (1947), *Othello* (1952), *The Haunting* (1963) and *The Virgin and the Gypsy* (1970). Fay was the sister of novelist Sir Compton Mackenzie. She died 12 December 1978, London.

Connery, Sean (1930-) Born Thomas Sean Connery, 25 August 1930, Edinburgh. Actor. Spent three years in the Merchant Navy (1947-50) and in various other jobs (including coffin polisher) before taking up bodybuilding and modelling. After appearing in the *Mr Universe* contest in London he landed a job in the chorus of *South Pacific* (1950). Screen debut: *Lilacs in Spring* (1954). Featured in *Tarzan's Greatest Adventure* (1959), *Darby O'Gill and the Little People* (1959) and *The Longest Day* (1962) before being spotted by Harry Salzman for the part of James Bond in *Dr No* (1962). Sean went on to play 007 in *From Russia with Love* (1963), *Goldfinger* (1964), *Thunderball* (1965), *You Only Live Twice* (1967) and *Diamonds are Forever* (1971). After saying he would never play Bond again he succumbed once more, remaking *Thunderball* as *Never Say Never Again* (1983). Whilst playing Bond he also starred in *Marnie* (1964), *The Hill* (1965), *Shalako* (1968) and *The Molly Maguires* (1970). Once away from 007 Sean branched out a bit more in films such as *The Man Who Would be King* (1975), *The Wind and the Lion* (1975) and *Outland* (1979). As he matures he gets more popular, being regularly voted among the sexiest men in films. He also continues to capture major roles. After *Highlander* (1986) and *The Name of the Rose* (1986) he gained a Best Supporting Actor Academy Award for his role as the tough Chicago cop in *The Untouchables* (1987). His later films include: *The Presidio* (1988), *Indiana Jones and the Last Crusade* (1989), *The Hunt for Red October* (1990), *Medicine Man* (1992), *Rising Sun* (1993), *First Knight* (1995), *The Rock* (1996), *Entrapment* (1999), *Finding Forrester* (2000) and *The League of Extraordinary Gentlemen* (2003). Married to Diane Cilento (1962-73) and Micheline Roquebrune (1975-present). His son Jason Connery (b. Jason Joseph Connery, 11 January 1963, London) is also a film and television actor. Sean was knighted in 2000 after reportedly being snubbed in 1998 because of his views on Scottish independence. In 2005 he announced his retirement from film acting although he has recently performed a voice over for the animated film *Sir Billi The Vet* (2010). Sean's autobiography, *Being a Scot* (2008), was co-written with Murray Grigor.

Connolly, Billy (1942-) See entry in comedy section

Connor, Kenneth (1918-93) Born 6 June 1918, Islington, London. Actor. Performed in revue with his brother when a youngster before studying at the Central School of Music and Drama. Screen debut: *Poison Pen* (1939). Featured in 17 Carry On films starting with the very first *Carry On Sergeant* (1958) all the way through to *Carry On Emmanuelle* (1978). He usually played a nervous and shy romantic lead in the early Carry Ons before being supplanted by Jim Dale. Other films include: *Don't Say Die* (1950) and *Dentist in the Chair* (1960). A favourite on both radio and television he appeared in sitcoms such as *'Allo 'Allo.* Awarded the MBE in 1991. Died 28 November 1993, Harrow, London. See also entries in the television section for *'Allo 'Allo, Carry On Laughing, Four Feather Falls, Hi-De-Hi, The*

Idiot Weekly, Price 2d, A Show Called Fred, and *Torchy the Battery Boy.*

Considine, Paddy (1973-) Born Patrick George Considine, 5 September 1973, Burton-on-Trent, Staffordshire. Actor, director and screenwriter. Took a drama course at Burton College where he met film-maker Shane Meadows. Studied photography at Brighton University. Screen debut: *A Room for Romeo Brass* (1999). Other films include: *Last Resort* (2000), *Happy Now* (2001), *The Martins* (2001), *24 Hour Party People* (2002), *Doctor Sleep* (2002), *In America* (2002), *Dead Man's Shoes* (2004 – a film Paddy co-wrote), *My Summer of Love* (2004), *Cinderella Man* (2005) *Stoned* (2005), *Hot Fuzz* (2007), *The Bourne Ultimatum* (2007), *The Cry of the Owl* (2009), *Le Donk & Scorzay-zee* (2009), *Submarine* (2010), *Blitz* (2011 and *Tyrannosaur* (2011 – a film in which he played an extra but wrote and directed). Paddy's directorial debut, the short film *Dog Altogether* (2007), won a number of awards including the 2008 BAFTA Award for Best Short Film.

Conti, Tom (1941-) Born Thomas Conti, 22 November 1941, Paisley, Scotland. Actor. A Scot of Italian extraction. Trained at Royal Scottish Academy of Music and Drama. Screen debut: *Galileo* (1975). Other films include: *The Duellists* (1977), *Merry Christmas, Mr Lawrence* (1983), *American Dreamer* (1984), *Saving Grace* (1985), *Heavenly Pursuits* (1985), *Miracles* (1986), *Beyond Therapy* (1987), *Shirley Valentine* (1989), *Someone Else's America* (1995), *Something to Believe In* (1998), *Don't Go Breaking My Heart* (1999), *O Jerusalem* (2006), *A Closed book* (2010) and *The Dark Knight Rises* (2012). Nominated for a Best Actor Academy Award for *Reuben, Reuben* (1983). Tom has been married to Scottish actress Kara Wilson (b. 1974, Hampstead, London) since 1967 and their daughter Nina is an actress and ventriloquist. See also entries in the television section for *Adam Smith, Andy Pandy, Churchill's People, Donovan,* and *The Glittering Prizes.*

Conway, Tom (1904-67) Born Thomas Charles Sanders, 15 September 1904, St Petersburg, Russia. Actor. His family left Russia during the Revolution and settled in Brighton. Educated at Brighton College. Settled for a time in then Northern Rhodesia as a miner and rancher before returning to England. Member of the Manchester Repertory Company before joining his brother George Sanders in Hollywood. Screen debut: *The Great Meddler* (1940). Other early films include: *The Trial of Mary Dugan* (1941), *The People vs Dr Kildare* (1941), *Rio Rita* (1942) and *Mrs Miniver* (1942). In *The Falcon's Brother* (1942) he played the title role and took over as *The Falcon* from George, who had tired of the role and asked to be written out - George had played Gay Lawrence and Tom went on to play his brother Tom Lawrence in 10 films, ending with *The Falcon's adventure* (1946). Tom also played the lead in the television detective series *Mark Saber* (1951-54). His later films include: *Prince Valiant* (1954), *Death of a Scoundrel* (1956) and *What a Way to Go!* (1964). Became a naturalised US citizen in 1946. Failing eyesight and alcohol problems blighted his later life and he died 22 April 1967 Los Angeles, California.

Coogan, Steve (1965-) Born Stephen J Coogan, 14 October 1965, Middleton, Manchester. Actor and comedian. Trained at Manchester Polytechnic of Theatre. Began as a stand-up comedian and impressionist. His early television included providing voices for *Spitting Image* and acting on the observation round of *The Krypton Factor.* Perrier Award winner in 1992. Steve created the personae of Alan Partridge, Paul and Paula Calf and Tony Ferrino, initially on radio. These were later to become highly successful transfers to TV in series including: *Knowing Me, Knowing You with Alan Partridge* (1994), *Coogan's Run* (1995), *I'm Alan Partridge* (1997 and 2002) and *Anglian Lives: Alan Partridge* (2003). After a brief big screen debut in *Resurrected* (1989) his other films include: *The Indian in the Cupboard* (1995), *The Wind in the Willows* (1996 – as Mole), *The Parole Officer* (2001), *24 Hour Party People* (2002), *Around the World in 80 Days* (2004 - as Phileas Fogg), *Happy Endings* (2005), *A Cock and Bull Story* (2006), *Night at the Museum* (2006), *Marie Antoinette* (2006), *Hot Fuzz* (2007), *Finding*

Amanda (2008), *Tropic Thunder* (2008), *Hamlet 2* (2008), *What Goes Up* (2009), *In the Loop* (2009*), Night at the Museum 2: Battle of the Smithsonian* (2009), *Percy Jackson & the Olympians: The Lightning Thief* (2010), *The Other Guys* (2010), *Marmaduke* (2010) and *Our Idiot Brother* (2011). He also played Samuel Pepys in the TV drama *The Private Life of Samuel Pepys* (2003). Steve became a prominent figure in the News International phone hacking scandal in 2011, as one of the celebrities who took action against the *News of the World* and ultimately forced the closure of the paper. See also entries in the television section for *Coogan's Run, Marion and Geoff, Nighty Night,* and *Saxondale.*

Cook, Peter See entry in comedy section.

Cooper, Dominic (1978-) Born Dominic Edward Cooper, 2 June 1978, Greenwich, London. Actor. Trained at the London Academy of Music and Dramatic Art (LAMDA), graduating in 2000 and making his film debut in *Anazapta* (2001) with a small role as a clerk. A succession of films followed: *From Hell* (2001), *The Final Curtain* (2002), *I'll Be There* (2003), *Boudica* (2003), *Breakfast on Pluto* (2005), *Starter for 10* (2006), *The History Boys* (2006) and *The Escapist* (2008) – all of which listed Dominic's name low down in the credits. His big break came as Sky, Sophie's fiancé in the musical film Mamma Mia! (2008). Dominic next starred opposite Keira Knightley in *The Duchess* (2008) replaced Orlando Bloom, as Danny, in *An Education* (2009) and then co-starred, with Gemma Arterton, in *Tamara Drewe* (2010). More recent films include a starring role in *The Devil's Double* (2011 - as Latif Yahia/Uday Hussein) and smaller roles as Howard Stark in *Captain America: The First Avenger* (2011) and as fashion photographer Milton H. Greene in *My Week with Marilyn* (2011) . Dominic was in a steady relationship with *Mamma Mia!* co-star Amanda Seyfried but they announced their split in May 2010. He is a good friend of James Corden.

Cooper, Gladys (1888-1971) Born Gladys Constance Cooper, 18 December 1888, Chiswick, London. Actress. Made her stage début in 1905 in *Bluebell in Fairyland* and her film debut in *The Eleventh Commandment* (1913). It was not until 1922, however, that she found major success, in Arthur Wing Pinero's *The Second Mrs. Tanqueray*. Her last major success on the stage was in the role of "Mrs. St. Maugham" in Enid Bagnold's *The Chalk Garden*, a role she created in London and on Broadway. She found success in Hollywood in mainly character roles and was most frequently cast as a disapproving, aristocratic society woman. She appeared in *Rebecca* (1940) and was nominated three times for an Academy Award for Best Supporting Actress for her performances as Bette Davis's repressive mother Mrs. Henry Windle Vale in *Now, Voyager* (1942); as a sceptical nun Sister Marie Therese Vauzous in *The Song of Bernadette* (1943); and as Mrs. Higgins in *My Fair Lady* (1964). Gladys had three children from her first two marriages. Gladys Cooper's elder daughter Joan Buckmaster (1910-2005) married the actor Robert Morley. Her younger daughter, Sally Pearson (aka Sally Cooper) married the actor Robert Hardy. As an actress her work spanned six decades and she was made a Dame Commander of the Order of the British Empire in 1967. Gladys died on 17 November 1971 from pneumonia at the age of 82, Henly-on-Thames. Gladys's sister Doris was a small-part actress. According to a very famous anecdote, in 1928 Doris appeared in the play *Excelsior* and had a speaking part. On opening night, she was reduced to tears backstage after her first appearance, which was greeted by a low hiss from the audience. A friend reassured her. "They're all just whispering to each other, "She's Doris Cooper. She's Gladys Cooper's sister. Gladys Cooper's sister"".

Cooper, Melville (1896-1973) Born George Melville Cooper, 15 October 1896, Birmingham, Warwickshire. Actor. An accomplished stage actor he made his screen debut in *All Riot on the Western Front* (1930) and making his mark as Leporello in *The Private Life of Don Juan* (1934). Moved to America in 1934. Other screen roles include the Sheriff of Nottingham in *The Adventures of Robin Hood* (1938), Mr Collins in *Pride and Prejudice* (1940), W S Gilbert in *The Return of Gilbert and Sullivan* (1950) and Mr Tringle in *Father of the Bride* (1950). Other films include *The Dawn Patrol* (1938), *Rebecca* (1940), *The Lady Eve* (1941), *Random Harvest* (1942), *Around the World in Eighty Days* (1956) and *From Earth to the Moon* (1958).

Mainly a comic actor he was often cast as weak, incompetent, officious types. He retired from the screen in 1958 but continued to appear on Broadway in plays such as *My Fair Lady* and *Charley's Aunt* (1970). Died 31 March 1973, Woodland Hills, California.

Corri, Adrienne (1930-) Born Adrienne Riccoboni, 13 November 1930, Glasgow. Actress. Trained at RADA. Screen debut: *The Romantic Age* (1949). Other films include: *The River* (1951), *The Kidnappers* (1953), *Lease of Life* (1954), *Dr. Zhivago* (1965 – as Lara's mother), *Revenge of the Pink Panther* (1978), and a series of sci-fi and horror flicks such as *Devil Girl from Mars* (1954), *Corridors of Blood* (1958), *The Hellfire Club* (1961) and *Vampire Circus* (1971). Probably best remembered for playing Mrs Alexander, the victim of Alex and the Droogs gang rape in *A Clockwork Orange* (1971). Adrienne often played the vamp both on film and television and is often described with such adjectives as red-haired, fiery and tempestuous. She married twice, to actors Derek Fowlds and Daniel Massey (1961-67). Author of a book on Thomas Gainsborough: *The Search for Thomas Gainsborough* (1984) which details her attempt to provenance a painting of David Garrick. See also entries in the television section for *Armchair Theatre, Sword Of Freedom*, and *You're Only Young Twice.*

Cossart, Ernest (1876-1951) Born Emil von Holst 24 September 1876 Cheltenham. Actor. Films include *The Great Ziegfeld* (1936), *Tom Brown's School Days* (1940), *Charley's Aunt* (1941), *Kings Row* (1942) and *The Jolson Story* (1946). Well-known actor of his day but probably most famous for being the brother of composer Gustav Holst. Died 21 January 1951, New York.

Court, Hazel (1926-2008) Born 10 February 1926, Sutton Coldfield, West Midlands. Actress. Screen debut: *Champagne Charlie* (1944). A green-eyed, red-haired graduate of the Rank Charm School who went on to appear in Hammer Horrors and Roger Corman classics such as *Devil Girl from Mars* (1954), *The Curse of Frankenstein* (1957), *The Man Who Could Cheat Death* (1959), *The Raven* (1963) and *The Masque of the Red Death* (1964). She also had a long TV career both in the UK and the US, making appearances in series such as *The Buccaneers* (1957), *Alfred Hitchcock Presents* (1958-1961), *Danger Man* (1960-1961), *Dr Kildare* (1965) and *Macmillan and Wife* (1972). Married to actors Dermot Walsh (1949-63) and Don Taylor (1964-1998), Hazel gave up acting in 1964 to concentrate on family life, although making a brief appearance in *Omen: The Final Conflict* (1981). Died 15 April 2008, Lake Tahoe, California.

Courtenay, Tom (1937-) Born Thomas Daniel Courtenay, 25 February 1937, Kingston-Upon-Hull, Humberside. Actor. Trained at RADA. Stage debut: *The Seagull* (1960). Made an immediate impact in his screen debut: *The Loneliness of the Long Distance Runner* (1962) and went on to star in *Billy Liar* (1963) and *King and Country* (1964). Nominated for An Academy Award for Best Supporting Actor for his portrayal of Pasha in *Dr Zhivago* (1965) and again eighteen years later for his title role of Norman in *The Dresser* (1983). Concentrates mainly on stage work but other films include: *Operation Crossbow* (1965), *King Rat* (1966), *The Night of the Generals* (1967), *One Day in the Life of Ivan Denisovich* (1987), *Let Him Have It* (1991), *Last Orders* (2001) and *The Golden Compass* (2007). He has recently completed scenes for his role of 'The Major' in the 2012 American/British comedy film, *Gambit*. Tom was married to actress Cheryl Kennedy (1973-82) and then stage manager Isabel Crossley (1988-present). Knighted in 2001. Autobiography: *Dear Tom: Letters from Home* (2000).

Courtneidge, Cicely (1893-1980) Born Cicely Esmerelda Courtneidge, 1 April 1893 Sydney, New South Wales, Australia. Actress. Daughter of actor-manager Robert Courtneidge. Stage debut: *A Midsummer Night's Dream*. Married and formed an act with entertainer Jack Hulbert (see separate entry) in 1916. Screen debut: *Elstree Calling* (1930). Other films include *The Ghost Train* (1931), *Jack's the Boy* (1932), *Things are Looking Up* (1935), *Everybody Dance* (1936) and *Under Your Hat* (1940). Made a rare screen appearance as an ageing lesbian entertainer in *The L-Shaped Room* (1962). Awarded the CBE in 1951 and created a Dame in 1972 for her services to entertainment. One of her last roles was as Reg Varney's mum (Mrs Butler) in the first series of the sitcom *On the Buses* (1969). Died 26 April 1980, Wandsworth, London.

Coward, Noël (1899-1973) Born Noël Peirce Coward, 16 December 1899, Teddington, Middlesex (now Greater London). Actor, playwright and songwriter. Son of a music publisher's clerk. Known as 'The Master', to describe Noël Coward as an occasional actor, and writer of light comedies and humorous songs would be a gross understatement. Stage debut: *The Goldfish* (1911). Screen debut: *Hearts of the World* (1917). Following a miserable time after being called up towards the end of WWI he turned to writing plays. He made a brief sojourn to America in the early 1920s and returned to the UK to produce a string of successful plays including *The Vortex* (1924), *Hay Fever* (1925), *Private Lives* (1930), *Cavalcade* (1931), *Present Laughter* (1942), *This Happy Breed* (1942) and *Blithe Spirit* (1942). In *Private Lives*, Noël starred alongside his most famous stage partner, Gertrude Lawrence, together with the young Laurence Olivier. He also wrote, *Bitter Sweet*, an operetta in three acts, first produced in 1929 at Her Majesty's Theatre in London. It ran for 967 performances. Noël's experience of WWII was far more satisfying than the Great War, initially running the British propaganda office in Paris and ultimately working with the Secret Service. In the 1950s Noël found critical acclaim as a cabaret performer of his own songs, such as "Mad Dogs and Englishmen", "London Pride" and "I Went to a Marvellous Party". In the world of cinema he appeared in *The Scoundrel* (1935), *The Astonished Heart* (1949), *Around the World in 80 Days* (1956), *Our Man in Havana* (1959), *Surprise Package* (1960), *Paris - When it Sizzles* (1964), *Bunny Lake is Missing* (1965), *Boom* (1968) and *The Italian Job* (1969). He received an Academy Award Nomination as Best Writer for *In Which We Serve* (1942) which he also produced, co-directed and starred in. Noël's short play, *Still Life*, (one of ten that make up *Tonight at 8:30*), was made into the film *Brief Encounter* (1945). Post WWII he moved firstly to Bermuda and then Jamaica. He continued to write and appear in plays until the mid-1960s. His carefully manufactured, and much imitated, image was of a man wearing a dressing-gown, smoking cigarettes in an elongated holder and invariably saying 'Darling, how wonderful'. Autobiographies: *Present Indicative* (1937), *Future Indefinite* (1954) and *Past Conditional* (1986 - unfinished at the time of his death and published posthumously). Noël never admitted his homosexuality during his lifetime but his life parther, actor and singer Graham Payn (25 April 1918 - 4 November 2005), openly discussed details of their life together after his death, on 26 March 1973 at his home Firefly Hill in Kingston, Jamaica. See also references to him in the television section under *Goodnight Sweetheart*, and *Willo the Wisp*.

Cox, Brian (1946-) Born Brian Denis Cox, 1 June 1946, Dundee. Actor. Graduated from LAMDA. Stage debut: *As You Like It* (1967). Screen debut: *Nicholas and Alexandra* (1971 – playing Trotsky). Brian was the first actor to portray Hannibal Lector on screen in *Manhunter* (1986). He usually plays unsympathetic characters, often devious politicians or government officials in films such as *The Long Kiss Goodnight* (1996), *Rushmore* (1998), *Adaptation* (2002), *The Bourne Identity* (2002), *X-Men 2* (2003), *The Bourne Supremacy* (2004), *Troy* (2004), *The Flying Scotsman* (2006), *Zodiac* (2007), *The Escapist* (2008), *Fantastic Mr Fox* (2009), *Red* (2010). His recent films include: *Coriolanus* (2011), *Ironclad* (2011), *Rise Of The Planet Of The Apes* (2011) and *The Veteran* (2011).Brian has written the books: *The Lear Diaries* and *From Salem to Moscow* about some of his acting experiences. His son Alan Cox (b. 1970) is also an actor. See also entries in the television section for *Churchill's People*, *Hammer House of Horror*, *Sharpe*, and *Survival*.

Craig, Daniel (1968-) Born Daniel Wroughton Craig, 2 March 1968, Chester. Actor. Studied at the Guildhall School of Music and Drama. Screen debut: *The Power of One* (1992). His big break came as Geordie in the TV series *Our Friends in the North* (1996). Films include: *Elizabeth* (1998), *I Dreamed of Africa* (1999), *Lara Croft: Tomb Raider* (2001), *Road to Perdition* (2002 - as Connor Rooney, the son of Paul Newman's character), *The Mother* (2003), *Sylvia* (2003 - as Ted Hughes), *Layer Cake*

(2004), *Enduring Love* (2004) and *The Jacket* (2005). His other TV roles include *The Ice House* (1997). In October 2005 he was chosen to replace Pierce Brosnan as James Bond and star in *Casino Royale* (2006). His first major role after this success was as Lord Asriel in *The Golden Compass* (2007) and he has since reprised his Bond role in *Quantum of Solace* (2008) and starred in *Flashbacks of a Fool* (2008), a film in which he was also credited as executive director. David lent his voice and likeness as James Bond for both the Nintendo Wii game *GoldenEye 007*, an enhanced remake of the 1997 game for the Nintendo 64, and *Blood Stone*, an original game for Xbox 360, PlayStation 3, Nintendo DS, and Microsoft Windows. David's latest roles in 2011 include crusading journalist Mikael Blomkvist in David Fincher's adaptation of Stieg Larsson's best-selling novel *The Girl with the Dragon Tattoo*; Jake Lonergan, a wanted outlaw with amnesia, in *Cowboys & Aliens*; and Ivan Ivanovitch Sakharine / Red Rackham, in Spielberg's *The Adventures of Tintin: The Secret of the Unicorn*. He is currently filming the next Bond movie, *Skyfall*, due for release in 2012. Daniel married Scottish actress Fiona Loudon in 1992, with whom he has a daughter, Ella (b. 1993). After his divorce in 1994 he dated German actress Heike Makatsch until 2001 and then film producer Satsuki Mitchell from 2004 until 2010. Whilst working on *Dream House* (2011) he rekindled his relationship with Rachel Weisz and the couple subsequently married on 22 June 2011.

Craig, Michael (1928-) Born Michael Francis Gregson, 27 January 1928, Poona, Maharashtra, India. Actor. Son of a British Army officer. Made his stage debut in 1949. Screen debut: *Passport to Pimlico* (1949). Other films include: *House of Secrets* (1956), *Yield to the Night* (1956), *Sapphire* (1959), *The Angry Silence* (1960), *Mysterious Island* (1961), *Life for Ruth* (1962), *Life at the Top* (1965), *Star!* (1968), *The Royal Hunt of the Sun* (1969), *The Vault of Horror* (1973), *Turkey Shoot* (1982), *Appointment with Death* (1988) and *Fat Pizza: The Movie* (2003). Began his career as the handsome leading man in the *Rank* star system but fortunately managed to progress to more challenging character parts. Michael came to England with his family in 1931 but moved to Canada in 1938. He has lived in Australia since 1971 and appeared as the senior doctor in the Australian TV series *G.P.* (1989-95). Michael co-wrote the Academy Award nominated screenplay for *The Angry Silence* (1960) together with his brother Richard Gregson and Bryan Forbes. Autobiography: *The Smallest Giant: An Actors Tale* (2005). Michael is the father of novelist Jessica Gregson (b. 24 June 1978). See also entries in the television section for *Love Story*, and *Triangle*.

Crawford, Michael (1942-) Born Michael Patrick Dumble-Smith, 19 January 1942, Salisbury, Wiltshire. Actor and singer. Performed as a boy soprano in Benjamin Britten's *Let's Make an Opera*. He featured as a child actor in films. Screen debut: *Soapbox Derby* (1950). Other films include: *Blow Your Own Trumpet* (1954), *The Knack and How to Get It* (1964), *A Funny Thing Happened on the Way to the Forum* (1965), *How I Won the War* (1967), *Hello Dolly* (1969), *The Games* (1970) and *Alice's Adventures In Wonderland* (1972 –as the White Rabbit). Now mainly known for the TV sitcom *Some Mother's do 'Ave 'Em* and his numerous musical theatre successes such as *Barnum* and *Phantom of the Opera*. Whilst playing the morbidly obese Count Fosco in Andrew Lloyd Webber's musical *The Woman in White* at the Palace Theatre, London, in December 2004, Michael was taken ill, initially thought to be suffering from dehydration caused by wearing the very heavy fat costume but eventually being diagnosed with myalgic encephalopathy (ME) which debilitated him for two years. Now fully fit again Michael played the role of the Wizard in Andrew Lloyd Webber's musical version of *The Wizard of Oz* at the London Palladium from its opening in March 2011 to February 2012. Awarded the OBE in 1986. Autobiography: *Parcel Arrived Safely: Tied with String* (1999). See also entries in the television section for *Billy Bunter of Greyfriars School*, *Not So Much A Programme*, *Sir Francis Drake*, and *Some Mothers do 'Ave 'Em*.

Crazy Gang, The A collection of seven British comics made up of three duos - Nervo and Knox, Flanagan and Allen and

Naughton and Gold - plus Monsewer Eddie Gray. The Gang were originally brought together for the *Crazy Month* revues at the London Palladium in June 1932 - these also featured a husband and wife team called Caryll and Mundy who left shortly after Flanagan and Allen joined. One of these revues was transferred to film: *Okay for Sound* (1937). There followed *Alf's Button Afloat* (1938), *The Frozen Limits* (1939), *Gasbags* (1940) and *Life is a Circus* (1958). They played their last ever performance together in May 1962 at the Victoria Palace, London. Jimmy Nervo (b. James Henry Holloway, 2 January 1897, Hackney, London; died 5 December 1975 London). Son of a circus owner he was in a high-wire act with his brothers (The Four Holloways) by the age of eight. Nicknamed Nervo after a comic-strip character he was fond of, he formed an acrobatic dancing act with Teddy Knox in 1919 and they successfully toured the USA in the 1920s. Their best known routine was a slow-motion wrestling act. Recognised by many as the driving force behind the Crazy Gang. Teddy Knox (b. Albert Edward Cromwell, 12 July 1896, Gateshead; died 1 December 1974, Salcombe, Devon). The son of George Thomas Cromwell, an actor and music-hall agent. Teddy's family appear to have adopted the surname Knox sometime after 1901. Teddy formed a juggling act called The Cromwells with his brothers. An injury during WWI prevented him from continuing juggling and he then joined forces with Jimmy Nervo. Married actress, and notable principal boy, Clarice Mayne in 1934. His sister Rosie (b. Rose Elizabeth Cromwell, 1887 Camberwell, London) married Sax Rohmer (b. Arthur Henry Ward, 15 February 1883, Birmingham), the creator of Doctor Fu Manchu in 1909. Bud Flanagan (b. Reuben Chaim Weintrop - later anglicised to Robert Winthrop, 14 October 1896, Whitechapel, London; died 20 October 1968, Kingston, Surrey). He began as Fargo the Boy Wizard before forming a double act with Dale Burgess and touring America, Australia and South Africa. Bud served with the Royal Artillery during WWI, meeting Chesney Allen briefly and taking his new stage surname from a detested Sergeant-Major Flanagan. At a low point in his career he took up taxi driving before forming his long-lasting duo with Allen in 1924. Flanagan and Allen wrote and performed many of the most popular British songs of the 1930s and 1940s including *Underneath the Arches*, *Strollin'*, *The Umbrella Man*, *Run, Rabbit, Run* and *We're Gonna Hang Out the Washing on the Siegfried Line*. Always dressed in a tatty racoon coat and a battered boater, Flanagan is best known to modern audiences for his rendition of the theme song to the TV sitcom *Dad's Army* 'Who do You Think You are Kidding Mr Hitler?'. Autobiography: *My Crazy Life* (1961). Chesney Allen (b. William Ernest Allen, 5 April 1894, London; died 13 November 1982 Midhurst, Sussex). Son of a Brighton builder. Known as the best straight man in the business, he was in a double act called Stanford and Allen. When Stanford moved on in 1924 he was replaced by Bud Flanagan who, down on his luck, had walked from London to Glasgow in search of a job. Known for his business sense he was already Florrie Forde's business manager by the time Flanagan joined him. He suffered from arthritis for much of his life which meant he retired from performing in 1945 and became the Gang's agent. Charlie Naughton (b. Charles John Naughton, 15 December 1886, Tradeston, Glasgow; died 7 October 1976, Streatham, London). In 1908 he joined fellow Glaswegian Jimmy Gold in a slapstick act involving painters and decorators, which they had both been before taking to the music-hall stage. This act was famously recreated by Bruce Forsyth and Norman Wisdom on a special edition of Sunday Night at the London Palladium. Naughton and Gold went on to become the longest-running double act in the history of variety (53 years). Charlie Naughton was the grandfather of ice-skater Sally Stapleford. Jimmy Gold (b. James McGonigal, 21 April 1886, Anderston, Glasgow; died 11 February 1967, London). Possessed of a remarkable memory which meant he could remember every joke he ever heard. However, in later life he suffered from a form of epilepsy which affected his performance so much that he had to withdraw from the last two series of *Crazy Gang* shows when he was understudied by Peter Glaze. Eddie Gray (b. Edward Earl Gray, 10 January 1898, Pimlico, London; died 15 September 1969, Brighton, Sussex). Son of a florist named Earl Gray, Eddie formed a juggling act with his brother Danny. An innovative juggler he is credited with introducing the juggling apple trick where he ate one of the apples while still juggling. His act was accompanied by a running commentary in a strange cross between cockney and French which led to him being billed as "Monsewer" Eddie Gray. Eddie is known to have never signed a contract with any management. He was a great friend of the poet John Betjeman who wrote *To the Crazy Gang* to commemorate the Gang's last performance. Eddie was known as The Black Swan. He, and the other six members of the gang, received the OBE in 1959. Eddie died the day after an impromptu performance at the Eastbourne Hippodrome aged 71.

Crichton, Charles (1910-99) Born Charles Ainslie Crichton, 7 August 1910, Wallasey, Cheshire. Director. Educated at Oundle and Oxford. In 1932 he met Zoltan Korda who offered him a job as an assistant editor. By 1935 he was an editor, his debut being: *Sanders of the River* (1935). His other films as an editor for Korda include: *Things to Come* (1936), *Elephant Boy* (1937) and *The Thief of Bagdad* (1940). He moved to *Ealing Studios* in 1940 and worked on *The Big Blockade* (1941) and *Nine Men* (1942) before making his directorial debut with *For Those in Peril* (1944). There followed the series of Ealing comedies for which Crichton is best remembered: *Hue and Cry* (1947), *The Lavender Hill Mob* (1951) and *The Titfield Thunderbolt* (1953). These were interspersed with dramas such as: *Against the Wind* (1948), *Dance Hall* (1950), *Hunted* (1952) - for *Rank* - and *The Divided Heart* (1954). After *Ealing* closed as a film studio he directed *The Battle of the Sexes* (1959), *The Third Secret* (1964) and *He Who Rides the Tiger* (1965) and was also replaced as director of *Birdman of Alcatraz* (1962) after clashing with Burt Lancaster. He then moved into television, directing such series as *Danger Man* (1964), *Man in a Suitcase* (1967), *The Protectors* (1972) and *Space:1999* (1975). A meeting with John Cleese, for whom he was shooting a series of corporate videos ended with him agreeing to direct *A Fish Called Wanda* (1988). The result was a hugely successful film and an Academy Award nomination for Best Director. He then retired in comfort. Died 14 September 1999 South Kensington, London.

Cricklewood Studios (1920-38) Started by Sir Oswald Stoll and his *Stoll Picture Productions* from a former aeroplane factory. Possibly Britain's first colour picture *The Glorious Adventure* (1922) starring Lady Diana Manners and Victor McLaglen was filmed at Cricklewood. Other films of the 1920s and 1930s: *Becket* (1923), *Don Quixote* (1923), *Blink Eyes* (1926), *Dick Turpin* (1933) and the *Old Mother Riley* series of films starring Arthur Lucan and Kitty McShane. The studio was sustained by the production of "quota quickies" - whereby American studios had to produce a number of films in Britain to comply with the *Films Act* - until it was finally closed in 1938.

Crisp, Donald (1882-1974) Born George William Crisp, 27 July 1882, Bow, London. Actor and director. Despite having a plaque put up for him in Aberfeldy, Perthshire, by the Scottish Film Council and constantly playing soft spoken celts on film, recent research has established that he was in fact a Londoner. One of the best loved character actors of Hollywood's golden era he appeared in over 150 films and directed 70 more. He travelled to the United States in 1906. Screen debut: *The French Maid* (1908). His second film was *Through the Breakers* (1909), directed by D W Griffith, for whom Crisp acted in a further 40 of the more than 70 films he featured in up to 1919, culminating in *The Birth of a Nation* (1915 - as Ulysses S Grant), *Intolerance* (1916) and *Broken Blossoms* (1919). After WWI he divided his time between acting in such films as *Don Q, Son of Zorro* (1925) and *Trent's Last Case* (1929) and directing the likes of Douglas Fairbanks and Buster Keaton - the latter in *The Navigator* (1924). His last film as director was *The Runaway Bride* (1930). Over the next decade he featured in many classic Hollywood films, including *Mutiny on the Bounty* (1935), *The Charge of the Light Brigade* (1936), *Jezebel* (1938), *Wuthering Heights* (1939), *The Private Lives of Elizabeth and Essex* (1939) and *The Sea Hawk* (1940). Won a Best Supporting Actor Award for his role as Gwilym Morgan in *How Green was my Valley* (1941). In contrast to his early silent films where he often played a villain, in his later films he usually played kindly, sympathetic characters, particularly in films such as *Lassie Come Home* (1943), *National Velvet* (1944 - as Velvet Brown's father), *Pollyanna* (1960) and *Greyfriars Bobby* (1961).

His final film was *Spencer's Mountain* (1963). He also worked as an advisor to Bank of America and was an astute businessman. He died 25 May 1974, Van Nuys, California.

Crook, Mackenzie (1971-) Born Paul Mackenzie Crook, 29 September 1971, Maidstone, Kent. Actor. Mackenzie began his professional career as a stand-up comedian in the guise of Charlie Cheese, "the cheeky chirpy chappy from Chorley" and on occasion Mr. Bagshaw, a hideous school teacher he based on a variety of obnoxious, overbearing science teachers he had encountered during his school days. Although appearing in the comedy short *The Man who Fell in Love with a Traffic Cone* in 1996, his break came appearing in the Channel 4 comedy sketch show *11 O'Clock Show* (1998). Having worked with the likes of Ricky Gervais on this show probably helped his chances when auditioning for the role of Gareth Keenan in *The Office* in 2001. The success of this series gained him the role of Ragetti, a pirate with a ridiculously ill-fitting wooden false eye, in *Pirates of the Caribbean: The Curse of the Black Pearl* (2003), *Pirates of the Caribbean: Dead Man's Chest* (2006) and *Pirates of the Caribbean: At Worlds End* (2007). Other films include: *The Life and Death of Peter Sellers* (2004), *Finding Neverland* (2004), *The Brothers Grimm* (2005), *I Want Candy* (2007), *Three and Out* (2008), *City of Ember* (2008), *Solomon Kane* (2009), *Sex & Drugs & Rock & Roll* (2010), *Ironclad* (2011) and *The Adventures of Tintin* (2011 – as Tom). Interestingly, Mackenzie lives in Peter Sellers' former home in Muswell Hill. Married, with two children to-date, Mackenzie's hobbies include breeding chelonians (turtles). See also entries in the television section for *Demons, The 11 O'Clock Show, Love Soup,* and *The Office.*

Crowden, Graham (1922-2010) Born 30 November 1922, Edinburgh. Actor. Screen debut: *Why Bother to Knock?* (1961). Directed by Lindsay Anderson in *If* (1969), *O Lucky Man!* (1973) and *Britannia Hospital* (1982). Other films include: *The Ruling Class* (1973), *Jabberwocky* (1981), *For Your Eyes Only* (1982), *The Company of Wolves* (1984), *Out of Africa* (1985), *A Handful of Dust* (1988), *The Innocent Sleep* (1996), *The Sea Change* (1998), *The 10th Kingdom* (1999), *Possession* (2002) and *Calendar Girls* (2003). Known for playing eccentrics, his TV credits include *A Very Peculiar Practice* (1986-88) and *Waiting for God* (1990-94). Died 19 October 2010 in Edinburgh. See also entries in the television section for *Harpers West One, A Very Peculiar Practice,* and *Waiting For God.*

Culver, Roland (1900-84) Born Roland Joseph Culver, 21 August 1900, Crouch End, London. Actor. Initially followed his father working for an optical company. Served in the RAF during WWI and subsequently studied at RADA. Stage debut in 1924. Screen debut: *Fascination* (1931). Other films include: *Accused* (1936), *French Without Tears* (1940), *One of Our Aircraft is Missing* (1942), *The Life and Death of Colonel Blimp* (1943), *The Ship that Died of Shame* (1955), *The Yellow Rolls-Royce* (1964), *Thunderball* (1965) and *Britannia Hospital* (1982). In general played typical English gentlemen. Autobiography: *Not Quite a Gentleman* (1979). Died 29 February 1984, Henley-on-Thames, Oxfordshire. See also entries in the television section for *The Caesars,* and *The Pallisers.*

Cumberbatch, Benedict (1976-) Born Benedict Timothy Carlton Cumberbatch, 19 July 1976, London, England. Actor. Benedict is the son of actor Timothy Carlton (b. Timothy Carlton Cumberbatch) and television actress Wanda Ventham (b. 5 August 1935, Brighton, East Sussex). A gifted stage actor, Benedict has appeared in many West End plays since 2001 and also on television in *Heartbeat* (2002 and 2004), *Tipping the Velvet* (2002 – as Freddie), *Cambridge Spies* (2003 – as Edward Hand) and *Fortysomething* (2003 – as Rory). He has also featured in *Spooks* and *Silent Witness*. His most acclaimed television roles include: Stephen Hawking in the BBC drama *Hawking* (2004) and Sherlock Holmes in the modern BBC adaptation series *Sherlock* (2010). His film debut was a minor role as a Royalist in *To Kill a King* (2003) before having a more substantial role in *Starter for 10* (2006 - as Patrick Watts). He next won critical acclaim as William Pitt in the historical film *Amazing Grace* (2006) and subsequently appeared in major roles in *Atonement* (2007), *The Other Boleyn Girl* (2008), *Creation* (2009), The Whistleblower (2010), *War Horse* (2011 – as Major Stewart) and *Tinker Tailor Soldier Spy* (2011 - as Peter Guillam). Benedict lives with his long-time partner, actress Olivia Poulet (b. 1978, London).

Cumming, Alan (1965-) Born 27 January 1965, Aberfeldy, Perthshire, Scotland. Actor. He made his screen debut as wood-cutter Jim Hunter in *Take the High Road* in 1980. In 1981 he worked for just over a year as a sub-editor at D.C. Thompson Publishers in Dundee, where he worked on the launch of a new magazine, *Tops,* and was also the "Young Alan" who answered readers' letters.The following year he began a three-year course at the Royal Scottish Academy of Music and Drama in Glasgow. He graduated in 1985 with a B.A. (Dramatic Studies). By this time he had formed a very successful cabaret double act with fellow student Forbes Masson called Victor and Barry. His film debut was in the TV movie *Conquest of the South Pole* (1989) and his feature debut in *Prague* (1992 – as Alexander Novak). Alan co-wrote, co-directed, co-produced, and co-starred in the ensemble film *The Anniversary Party* with friend and former *Cabaret* co-star Jennifer Jason Leigh, in 2001. He also produced and starred in *Gray Matters* (2007). Other films include: *Second Best* (1994), *Black Beauty* (1994), *Circle of Friends* (1995), *GoldenEye* (1995 - as Boris Ivanovich Grishenko), *Emma* (1996), *Romy and Michele's High School Reunion* (1997), *Spice World* (1997), *Buddy* (1997), *Titus* (1999), *Plunkett & Macleane* (1999), *Eyes Wide Shut* (1999), *Annie* (1999), *Urbania* (2000), *The Flintstones in Viva Rock Vegas* (2000 - as Mick Jagged / Gazoo), *Get Carter* (2000), *Investigating Sex* (2001), *Josie and the Pussycats* (2001), *Spy Kids* (2001 - as Fegan Floop), *Company Man* (2001), *Spy Kids 2: The Island of Lost Dreams* (2002), *Nicholas Nickleby* (2002), *X2* (2003 - as Kurt Wagner / Nightcrawler), *Spy Kids 3-D: Game Over* (2003), *Garfield: The Movie* (2004 - voice of Persnikitty), *Eighteen* (2004), *Son of the Mask* (2005 - as Loki), *Reefer Madness* (2005), *Ripley Under Ground* (2005), *Neverwas* (2005), *Sweet Land* (2005), *Suffering Man's Charity* (aka *Ghost Writer*) (2007), *Boogie Woogie* (2009), *Dare* (2009), *The Tempest* (2010), *Riverworld* (2010) and *Burlesque* (2010). His latest project has been to voice the role of Gutsy Smurf in *The Smurfs* (2011). On television he starred as the devil opposite James Garner's portrayal of God in the American series *God, the Devil and Bob* (2000-01). He has also written a novel, *Tommy's Tale,* had a cable talk show, *Eavesdropping with Alan Cumming,* and produced a line of perfumed products labelled "Cumming". Although retaining his British citizenship, he became a U.S. citizen in November 2008. Alan was married to actress Hilary Lyon from 1985 to 1993 and is now in a civil relationship with graphic artist Grant Shaffer. The couple live in New York with their dogs, Honey and Leon. See also entries in the television section for *The High Life, Shoebox Zoo, Take The High Road,* and *Who Do You Think You Are?*

Cummins, Peggy (1925-) Born Augusta M D Fuller, 18 December 1925, Prestatyn, Denbighshire. Actress. Screen debut: *Dr O'Dowd* (1940). She moved to the United States to make *Forever Amber* but was replaced in the lead role by Linda Darnell. However, she made an impact as the bank robber Annie Laurie Starr in *Deadly is the Female* (1949 - aka *Gun Crazy*). Other films include *Night of the Demon* (1957) and *Hell Drivers* (1957). Peggy had several high profile suitors whilst in Hollywood including Howard Hughes and the future American president John F. Kennedy. Her later film career included British comedies such as *Carry on Admiral* (1957), *The Captain's Table* (1959), *Dentist in the Chair* (1960) and *In the Doghouse* (1961), after which she retired to Hampshire, although since her husband's death in 2000 has lived in London.

Currie, Finlay (1878-1968) Born William Finlay Currie (many sources incorrectly state Finlay Jefferson Currie) 20 January 1878, Edinburgh. Actor. Originally a music hall performer, latterly with his wife Maude Courtney. Sometimes worked under the name *Harry Calvo* the double-voiced vocalist. "Legitimate" stage debut: *Cramond Brig* (1898). Spent over ten years in Australia working as a comedian before returning to the UK in 1930. He made his screen debut as late as 1932 in *The Old Man*. Despite his early career he nearly always played figures of authority, including saints and popes and he was particularly impressive in epic and historical films such as *Quo Vadis* (1951), *Ivanhoe* (1952), *Saint Joan* (1957), *Ben Hur* (1959), *Solomon and Sheba* (1959), *Francis of Assisi* (1961) and *The Fall of the Roman Empire* (1965). However, it was as the escaped convict Abel Magwitch in *Great Expectations* (1946) that he made his most memorable screen appearance. Died 9 May 1968, Gerrards Cross, Buckinghamshire.

Curry, Tim (1946-) Born Timothy James Curry, 19 April 1946, Grappenhall, Cheshire. Actor. Stage debut: *Hair* (1968). Most noted for his portrayal of the transvestite scientist Dr Frank 'N Furter in *The Rocky Horror Show* which he recreated on screen in *The Rocky Horror Picture Show* (1975). Other films include: *Annie* (1982), *Legend* (1985), *The Hunt for Red October* (1990), *Oscar* (1991), *Home Alone 2* (1992), *The Three Musketeers* (1993), *Congo* (1995), *Kinsey* (2004), *Bailey's Billion$* (2005), *Christmas in Wonderland* (2007), *The Secret of Moonacre* (2008) and *Burke and Hare* (2010). Says that his speciality roles are "louche, brio and bravura". Between 2004 and 2007 Tim played King Arthur in *Spamalot*, firstly on Broadway and then in London's West End. Tim's voice can be heard in many video games, notably as Melek in *Wing Commander III: Heart of the Tiger* (1994), Doctor Victor Frankenstein in *Frankenstein: Through the Eyes of the Monster* (1995), Count Nefarious in *Toonstruck* (1996), Stratos in *Sacrifice* (2000), Mastermind in *Scooby-Doo! Night of 100 Frights* (2002), Lemony Snicket in *Lemony Snicket's A Series Of Unfortunate Events* (2004), Professor Finbarr Calamitous in *Nicktoons Unite!* (2005) and *Nicktoons: Attack of the Toybots* (2007), Premier Anatoly Cherdenko in *Command & Conquer: Red Alert 3* (2008), Emperor Doviculus in *Brütal Legend* (2009) and Arl Rendon Howe in *Dragon Age: Origins* (2009).

Cusack, Cyril (1910-93) Born 26 November 1910 Durban, South Africa. Actor. Raised in Ireland by his mother. Stage debut: *East Lynne* (1917 - aged 6). Screen Debut: *Knocknagow* (1918 - aged 7). Made his screen breakthrough as Pat in *Odd Man Out* (1947). An acclaimed stage actor he also made over 100 films including: *Gone to Earth* (1950), *The Spy Who Came in from the Cold* (1965), *Fahrenheit 451* (1966), *Taming of the Shrew* (1967), *Nineteen Eighty-Four* (1984), *My Left Foot* (1989) and *Far and Away* (1992). Intended to become a barrister but joined the Abbey Theatre Dublin in 1932. Reportedly his London stage career was interrupted for 20 years after he upset Laurence Olivier and Vivien Leigh by being "tired and emotional" during a performance of *The Doctors Dilemma* in 1942. Father of Sorcha, Sinead, Niamh, Catherine, Paul and Padraig. All four daughters became actresses. Died 7 October 1993 London. See entry for *Glenroe* in the television section.

Cusack, Sinéad (1948-) Born Sinéad Mary Cusack 18 February 1948, Dalkey, nr Dublin. Actress. Daughter of actor Cyril Cusack. Stage debut: *The Trial* (1959). Screen Debut: *Alfred the Great* (1969). Other films include: *Hoffman* (1970), *Waterland* (1993), *Stealing Beauty* (1996), *I Capture the Castle* (2003), *Mathilde* (2004), *V for Vendetta* (2006), *The Tiger's Tail* (2006), *Eastern Promises* (2007) and *Cracks* (2009). Sinéad is also a talented television and stage actress. She has received two Tony Award nominations: once for Best Leading Actress in *Much Ado About Nothing* (1985), and again for Best Featured Actress in *Rock 'n' Roll* (2008). She has been married to actor Jeremy Irons since 1978. See also entry for *Home Again* in the television section.

Cushing, Peter (1913-94) Born Peter Wilton Cushing, 26 May 1913, Kenley, Surrey. Actor. Son of a quantity surveyor he worked as a surveyor's assistant until studying at the Guildhall School of Music and Drama. Stage debut: *The Middle Watch* (1935). Went to Hollywood in 1939. Screen debut: *The Man in the Iron Mask* (1939). Following a few more films, including *A Chump at Oxford* (1940) he returned to Britain to join the Entertainment National Services Association (ENSA) during the remainder of WWII. Apart from a few films such as *Hamlet* (1948) and *Moulin Rouge* (1952) most of his early post-war work was on television. In the late 1950s he began his association with *Hammer Film Productions* in *The Curse of Frankenstein* (1957), *Dracula* (1958), *The Hound of the Baskervilles* (1959) and *The Brides of Dracula* (1960). Teamed up with Christopher Lee in

over 20 films including: *Dr Terror's House of Horrors* (1965), *The Skull* (1965), *Scream and Scream Again* (1970), *I, Monster* (1972) and *The Creeping Flesh* (1973). Peter's name is synonymous with horror films in the same vein as Lee, Vincent Price and Boris Karloff although he did have brief respite by playing, quite magnificently, Dr Who in *Doctor Who* (1963) and *Dr Who and the Daleks* (1965). Peter became an ever-present in the Morecambe and Wise Christmas specials on television, invariably never being paid for his efforts as the running joke. He featured in *Star Wars* (1977) as Grand Moff Wilhuff Tarkin. Peter retired in 1986 to pursue his hobbies of bird watching and painting. He received the OBE in 1989. Autobiographies: *An Autobiography* (1986) and *Past Forgetting* (1988). He died 11 August 1994, Canterbury, Kent. See also entries in the television section for *Dr Who*, *Epitaph for a Spy*, *Hammer House of Horror*, *Pride and Prejudice*, *Sherlock Holmes*, *The Spread of the Eagle* and *Story Parade*.

Dale, Jim (1935-) Born James Smith, 15 August 1935, Rothwell, Northamptonshire. Actor and singer. Served in the RAF (1953-55). Screen debut: *Raising the Wind* (1961). In his early career he was a stand-up comedian and a pop singer. He reached No.2 with *Be My Girl* in 1957 and had three further Top 30 hits in 1958 before turning to acting. He performed in 11 Carry On films starting with bit parts in *Carry On Cabby* (1963), *Carry On Spying* (1964) and *Carry On Jack* (1964) before progressing to romantic lead in *Carry On Cleo* (1964) and perhaps most memorably as Marshall P Knutt, the plumber turned reluctant lawman, in *Carry On Cowboy* (1965). He played Dr Kilmore in *Carry on Doctor* (1968) - during which he broke his arm performing his own stunt on a runaway hospital trolley - and Dr Nookey in *Carry On Again Doctor* (1969). He returned in the title role in the last of the series *Carry On Columbus* (1992). Other roles include playing Spike Milligan in *Adolf Hitler - My Part in His Downfall* (1972). He received an Academy Award Nomination for the lyrics to *Georgy Girl* (1966). Jim became the host of the revamped *Sunday Night at the London Palladium* on ITV in 1973 although his greatest successes have in fact been on the stage in both the West End and Broadway. Jim created the role of *Barnum* in the original Broadway production. His last major starring role was as Charlie Baxter in the Sherman Brothers' musical, *Busker Alley*, alongside Glenn Close in 2006. He has lived in New York since marrying his second wife, Julie Schafler, in 1980.In recent years Jim has specialized in voice-over work and is the narrator of the *Harry Potter* audio books and the popular American comedy series *Pushing Daisies* (2007-09). He was awarded the MBE in 2003. See also entries in the television section for *Six-Five Special*, *Sunday Night at the London Palladium*, and *Thank Your Lucky Stars*.

Dalton, Timothy (1946-) Born 21 March 1946, Colwyn Bay, Conwy, Wales. Actor. Studied at RADA (1964-66). Screen debut: *The Lion in Winter* (1968 - as King Philip of France. Followed with more costume dramas: *Cromwell* (1970), *Wuthering Heights* (1970) and *Mary Queen of Scots* (1971). Concentrated on stage work and made few films in the 1970s before featuring in *Sextette* (1978), *Agatha* (1979), *Flash Gordon* (1980) and *The Doctor and the Devils* (1985). Chosen to replace Roger Moore as James Bond for *The Living Daylights* (1987) and played 007 again in *Licence to Kill* (1989) before relinquishing the role. Further films include: *La Putain du Roi* (1990), *The Rocketeer* (1991), *The Beautician and the Beast* (1997), *The Reef* (1999), *Time Share* (2000), *Looney Tunes: Back in Action* (2003) and *Hot Fuzz* (2007). More recently he has concentrated on TV and stage work although he did voice the character Mr. Pricklepants in *Toy Story 3* (2010) and the film shorts *Hawaiian Vacation* (2011) and *Small Fry* (2011). He also voiced Lord Milori in *Tinker Bell: Secret of the Wings* (2011) and played Chief Inspector Jones in *The Tourist* (2011). Timothy had a long-term relationship with actress Vanessa Redgrave but his one child, a son, Alexander (b. 7 August 1997) is by Russian model Oksana Grigorieva. See also entry for *Sat'day While Sunday* in the television section.

Dance, Charles (1946-) Born Walter Charles Dance, 10 October 1946, Redditch, Worcestershire. Actor. Joined the Royal Shakespeare Company in 1975 and has extensive stage and television experience including a breakthrough part as Guy Perron in TV's *The Jewel in the Crown* (1984). TV debut: *Edward the*

King (1975). Screen debut: *For Your Eyes Only* (1981). Other films include: *Plenty* (1985), *The Golden Child* (1986), *White Mischief* (1987), *Last Action Hero* (1993), *Michael Collins* (1996), *Hilary and Jackie* (1998), *Gosford Park* (2001), *Dark Blue World* (2001), *Black and White* (2002), *Swimming Pool* (2002), *Ali G In Da House* (2002), *Dolls* (2006), *Scoop* (2006), *The Contractor* (2007), *Paris Connections* (2010) and the fourth installment in the Underworld film series, *Underworld: Awakening* (2012 - as Thomas the vampire elder). His debut film as a screenwriter and director was *Ladies in Lavender* (2004), which starred Dame Judi Dench and Dame Maggie Smith. He was married to Joanna Haythorn, from 1970 to 2004, and they have two children, Oliver (b. 1974) and Rebecca (b. 1980). He became engaged to sculptor Eleanor Boorman in September 2010 and they are soon to have their first child together. Appointed an Officer of the Order of the British Empire (OBE) on 17 June 2006. Charles says of himself: "I hate the suave debonair tag. I am neither." See also entries in the television section for *Bleak House*, *Fingersmith*, *First Born*, and *The Jewel in the Crown*.

Daniell, Henry (1894-1963) Born Charles Henry Daniel, 5 March 1894, London. Actor. Educated at St Paul's School. A much respected stage actor he travelled to the United States in the 1920s to further his career. Stage debut: *Ann* (1913). Screen debut: *The Awful Truth* (1929). Casting Englishmen as villains is not altogether a modern Hollywood phenomenon. Daniell usually played the villain and played it well, whether a conniving Elizabethan politician as in *The Private Lives of Elizabeth and Essex* (1939) and *The Sea Hawk* (1940) or a high-ranking Nazi as in *The Great Dictator* (1940), *Mission to Moscow* (1943) and *Watch on the Rhine* (1943) or as the dastardly Professor Moriarty in *The Woman in Green* (1942). Other films include: *Jealousy* (1929), *Camille* (1936), *Marie Antoinette* (1938), *The Philadelphia Story* (1940), *Dressed to Kill* (1941), *Jane Eyre* (1944), *The Body Snatcher* (1945), *The Egyptian* (1954), *Lust for Life* (1956), *Voyage to the Bottom of the Sea* (1961) and *Mutiny on the Bounty* (1962). Henry was a favourite actor and friend of director George Cukor. Not noted for his agility he was replaced by a stunt double for his climactic duel with Errol Flynn in the *Sea Hawk* after the initial rushes were described as "more of a walk" than a fight. His style and voice were perfectly mimicked by Christopher Guest when playing Count Rugen in *The Princess Bride* (1987). He died 31 October 1963 Santa Monica, California shortly after completing his scenes for *My Fair Lady* (1964).

Davies, John Howard (1939-2011) Born 9 March 1939, London. Actor and television producer and director. The son of scriptwriter Jack Davies, his screen credits as a child actor consisted of the title role in David Lean's *Oliver Twist* (1948), Paul Grahame in *The Rocking Horse Winner* (1949), the title role in *Tom Brown's Schooldays* (1951), Maurice Friese-Greene in *The Magic Box* (1952) and two episodes of the television series *William Tell* (1958). Following National Service in the Royal Navy, he started working for a City finance company. He then trained as a carpet salesman but quit after six months to travel the world. Eventually he became a production assistant at the BBC in 1968 and immediately made an impact by taking over production of the popular sitcom, *The Very Merry Widow*. He then produced and directed the Spike Milligan vehicles *The World of Beachcomber* and *Oh in Colour* plus the early episodes of *Monty Python's Flying Circus*. His other production credits include: *All Gas and Gaiters*, *Misleading Cases*, *Steptoe and Son*, *Fawlty Towers* (series 1), *The Goodies*, *The Fall and Rise of Reginald Perrin*, *The Good Life*, *No Job for a Lady* and *Mr. Bean*. He also directed several episodes of *The Vicar of Dibley*. John became the BBC's Head of Comedy from 1977-82, Managing Director of EMI Television Productions and the Head of Light Entertainment at Thames Television, where he was described by the popular press as 'the man who sacked Benny Hill' when the station decided not to renew his contract after 20 years service. He died from cancer on 22 August 2011, Blewbury, Oxfordshire.

Davies, Terence (1945-) Born 10 November 1945, Liverpool. Director and screenwriter. Spent 10 years working in a shipping office and accountancy firm before enrolling at Coventry Drama School in 1971. For the next 12 years he worked on the three short films which formed *The Terence Davies Trilogy* (1984). *They are Children* (1974), *Madonna and Child* (1980) - his graduation film from the British Film School - and *Death and Transfiguration* (1983). *The Trilogy* plus *Distant Voices, Still Lives* (1988) and *The Long Day Closes* (1992) trace a thinly veiled picture of his own childhood growing up in a Catholic working-class household in Liverpool during the 1940s and 1950s and being burdened with a violent father and the discovery of his own homosexuality. The films are notable for not being remorselessly stark and for the interweaving of popular songs from the period. His other films are: *The Neon Bible* (1995), *The House of Mirth* (2000) and *Of Time and the City* (2008), a documentary in the vein of his earlier films recalling his life growing up in Liverpool. His most recent film is *The Deep Blue Sea* (2011) an adaptation of the 1952 Terence Rattigan play about the wife of a Judge who engages in an affair with an RAF pilot. Terence has also written a novel: *Hallelujah Now* (1984).

Davis, Sammi (1964-) Born Samantha Davis, 21 June 1964, Kidderminster, West Midlands. Actress. Sammi's first film was as a heroin addict in Neil Jordan's *Mona Lisa* (1986). She followed this with roles in John Boorman's *Hope and Glory* (1987) and two Ken Russell films *The Lair of the White Worm* (1988) and *The Rainbow* (1989). Since then she has worked mainly in television and smaller features. Her last film was the little known *Soft Toilet Seats* (1999). Fans of the ABC science fiction series, *Lost* (2004-10) will remember Sammi as Megan Pace the mother of Charlie Pace, Dominic Monaghan's character. In 1991 she married film director Kurt Voss, but they are now divorced.

Davis, Warwick (1970-) Born Warwick Ashley Davis, 3 February 1970, Epsom, Surrey. Actor. He made his stage debut as Sleepy in *Snow White and the Seven Dwarfs* (1988) but he already had a burgeoning screen career having played the Ewok Wicket Wysrti Warrick in *Star Wars: Episode VI - Return of the Jedi* (1983). He also featured in the spin-off TV movies *An Ewok Adventure* (1984) and *Ewoks: The Battle for Endor* (1985) plus *Labyrinth* (1986) before rejoining George Lucas to star as Willow Ufgood in *Willow* (1988). He then starred as the bad leprechaun in *Leprechaun* (1993) and its five sequels. Plays Professor Filius Flitwick in all the *Harry Potter* films. Other films include *Star Wars: Episode I - The Phantom Menace* (1999), *Ray* (2004), *The Hitchhiker's Guide to the Galaxy* (2005), *The Chronicles of Narnia: Prince Caspian* (2008) and *Invasion of the Not Quite Dead* (2008). He currently stars in the BBC2 sitcom *Life's Too Short*, written and directed by Ricky Gervais and Stephen Merchant. Standing 3ft 6in (1.07 m) tall, Warwick runs an agency for short actors.

Dawson, Richard (1932-) Born Colin Lionel Emm, 20 November ,1932 Gosport, Hampshire. Actor, comedian and game show host. Served in the Merchant Navy 1946-49 and also tried his hand at boxing. Married to Diana Dors 1959-66. A short film career includes: *The Longest Day* (1962), *Promises! Promises!* (1963), *King Rat* (1965), *The Devil's Brigade* (1968) and *The Running Man* (1987 – in which he parodied himself as the egotistical game show host Damon Killian). He became better known as Corporal Newkirk in *Hogan's Heroes* (1965-71), which he followed with regular appearances on *Rowan and Martin's Laugh-In* (1971-73)and then as host of the American equivalent of *Family Fortunes* entitled *Family Feud* (1976-85; 1994-95). Dickie Dawson, the name he worked under as an aspiring comedian in the 1950s, became a US citizen in 1984. Known as *The Kissing Bandit* after his habit of kissing all the attractive contestants on *Family Feud*, one of whom, Gretchen Johnson, became his second wife in 1991. After a promise made to Gretchen, Richard decided to dispense with the kissing for the final two series of *Family Feud*.

Day Lewis, Daniel (1957-) Born Daniel Michael Blake Day-Lewis, 29 April 1957, Kensington, London. Actor. Son of Poet Laureate Cecil Day-Lewis (who also wrote as Nicholas Blake) and actress Jill Balcon. A love of woodworking failed to be converted into full-time work so he turned to his other love, acting. Screen debut: *Sunday, Bloody Sunday* (1971). Other films include: *Gandhi* (1982), *My Beautiful Launderette* (1985), *A Room with a View* (1985), *The Unbearable Lightness of Being* (1988), *The Last of the Mohicans* (1992), *The Age of Innocence* (1993), *The Crucible* (1996), *The Boxer* (1997), *The Ballad of Jack and Rose* (2005 - written and directed by his wife) and *Nine* (2009). Won Best Actor Academy Awards for his portrayal of Christy Brown in *My Left Foot* (1989) and Daniel Plainview in *There Will Be Blood* (2007). Nominated for Best Actor Academy Awards for *In the Name of the Father* (1993) and *Gangs of New York* (2002). Has not appeared on stage since 1989. Assumed Irish citizenship in 1993 and is one of a select band of actors who have appeared on Irish stamps (as Christy Brown in the 1996 Centenary of Irish Cinema). In addition to being a skilled woodworker he is also an accomplished cobbler. Daniel is known for his discerning choice of film roles and complete submersion into every role he sporadically accepts. Married to film director Rebecca Miller, the daughter of playwright Arthur Miller, since 1996. They have two sons, Ronan Cal Day-Lewis (b. June 1998) and Cashel Blake Day-Lewis (b. May 2002). Daniel also has another son Gabriel-Kane Day-Lewis (b. 1995) with French actress Isabelle Adjani, the fruit of a six-year relationship that ended just before Gabriel's birth. Daniel has recently completed filming his title role of Abraham Lincoln in the forthcoming Steven Spielberg film biopic, *Lincoln*, due to be released in 2012.

Dean, Basil (1888-1978) Born Basil Herbert Dean, 27 September 1888, Croydon, Surrey. Actor, dramatist, impresario, director and producer. Stage debut: *The School for Scandal* (1906). Worked at the Gaiety Theatre Manchester 1907-11. Director of Liverpool Repertory Theatre 1911-13. Joined Cheshire Regiment 1914. Appointed Head of Entertainment branch of the Navy and Army Canteen Board. Formed theatrical partnership Reandea**N** (1919-1926) with Alec Rea, and this partnership made an outstanding contribution to the British theatre in the 1920s. Directorial debut: *The Constant Nymph* (1929) - a filmed version of his own stage play. Other films he directed include: *The Return of Sherlock Holmes* (1929), *Lorna Doone (1935), Whom the Gods Love (1936)* and *21 Days (1940)*. He also produced these films as well as many others including *Three Men in a Boat* (1933) and *Penny Paradise* (1938). General European Representative for RKO 1930-31. First Chairman of Associated Talking Pictures (later Ealing Studios). An important influence on the film careers of both Gracie Fields - he produced *Sally in Our Alley (1931)* and directed *Sing As We Go (1934)* - and George Formby for whom he produced *No Limit (1936), Keep Your Seats, Please (1936), Keep Fit (1937), Feather Your Nest (1937)* and *It's in the Air (1937)*. Ousted from Ealing in 1939, he returned his attention to the theatre. Appointed Director of Entertainment for NAAFI in early 1939. Created, and was the first director general of, ENSA (Entertainments National Service Association) in 1939. Author of *The Theatre at War* (1955), *The Changing Theatre* (1965) and *Minds Eye* (1973). Appointed MBE in 1918 and created CBE in 1947. Basil's wives included Lady Mercy Greville and Esther Van Gruisen but his most famous marriage was to British stage and film actress, Victoria Hopper between 1934 and 1939. Basil died 22 April 1978, Westminster, London.

Dearden, Basil (1911-71) Born Basil Clive Dear, 1 January 1911, Westcliff-on-Sea, Essex. Director, screenwriter and producer. Worked for an insurance company before joining the studios at The Grand Theatre, Fulham. Then began working with Basil Dean at Associated Talking Pictures (Ealing). He changed his name to Dearden to avoid confusion with Dean. Stayed on at Ealing after Dean's departure. After co-directing credits on the Will Hay features *The Black Sheep of Whitehall* (1941), *The Goose Steps Out* (1942) and *My Learned Friend* (1943) his solo directorial debut was *The Bells Go Down* (1944) working with Michael Relph as art director. This forged a partnership with Relph as producer and Dearden as director which lasted for nearly 30 years. They went on to make some of the best-known British films from the 1940s to the 1960s with a mixture of comedy and social drama including: *Frieda* (1947), *Saraband for Dead Lovers* (1948), *The Blue Lamp* (1950), *The Ship that Died of Shame* (1955), *The Smallest Show on Earth* (1957), *The League of Gentlemen* (1959), *Sapphire* (1959) and *Victim* (1961). His later films were big budget efforts such as *Masquerade* (1965) and *Khartoum* (1966). His work has received something of a critical bruising since his

death and he is regarded by many as a technically proficient but unimaginative director. However, there is no denying that his contribution to British cinema is notable. Killed in a road accident 23 March 1971, Hillingdon, London.

De Banzie, Brenda (1915-81) Born 28 July 1915, Manchester. Actress. Brenda was a leading lady and character actress of British stage (from 1935), films (from 1951), and television. Amongst her most memorable roles are Maggie Hobson in *Hobson's Choice* (1954) and Phoebe Rice in *The Entertainer* (1960). For the same play in the theatre she was nominated for aTony Award in 1958 as Best Supporting Actress. Other films include: *The Man Who Knew Too Much* (1956) and *The Pink Panther* (1963). Brenda was the aunt of actress, Lois De Banzie. She died 5 March 1981, Sussex.

De Banzie, Lois (1930-) Born 4 May 1930, Glasgow. Actress. A naturalized American citizen she made her film debut in *So Fine* (1981) and has had minor parts in numerous television series interspersing this career with film projects such as *Tootsie* (1982), *Mass Appeal* (1984), *Big Business* (1988), *Arachnophobia* (1990), *Sister Act* (1992), *Addams Family Values* (1993) and *Dunston Checks In* (1996). Mainly a theatre actress she was nominated for Broadway's 1980 Tony Award as Best Actress (Featured Role - Play) for a revival of *Morning's at Seven*. She is the niece of actress Brenda de Banzie.

De Brulier, Nigel (1877-1948) Born Francis George Packer, 8 August 1877, Frenchay, Gloucestershire. Actor. He began life as a servant in Frenchay House before emigrating to the United States. Screen debut: *The Pursuit of the Phantom* (1914). Other early silent films include: *Ghosts* (1915), *Intolerance* (1916), *Sahara* (1919), *The Virgin of Stamboul* (1920), *The Four Horsemen of the Apocalypse* (1921), *The Hunchback of Notre Dame* (1923) and *Ben-Hur* (1925). His career in the talkies centred around parts as priests, monks and bishops in such films as: *Rasputin and the Empress* (1932), *The Robin Hood of El Dorado* (1936), *Marie Antoinette* (1938) and *Tower of London* (1939). Nigel seems to have cornered the market in playing Cardinal Richelieu, portraying the *eminence gris* no less than four times: *The Three Musketeers* (1921), *The Iron Mask* (1929), *The Three Musketeers* (1935) and *The Man in the Iron Mask* (1939). He also featured in the series *Zorro Rides Again* and *Adventures of Captain Marvel*. His last film was *Tonight we Raid Calais* (1943). Died 30 January 1948, Los Angeles, California.

Delgado, Roger (1918-73) Born Roger Caesar Marius Bernard de Delgado Torres Castillo Roberto, 1 March 1918, Whitechapel, London. Actor. Born to a Spanish father and French mother but proud of being a true Cockney (as he was born within the sound of the Bow Bells). Roger worked in a bank until quitting to become an actor. Stage debut: *You Can't Take it with You* (1935). Screen debut: *The Captain's Paradise* (1953). Films include: *Storm Over the Nile* (1955), *The Battle of the River Plate* (1956), *The Terror of the Tongs* (1961), *The Road to Hong Kong* (1962), *Masquerade* (1965) and *Star!* (1968). Worked extensively for the BBC from the mid-1950s in classic series such as Quatermass II (1955) and Sir Francis Drake (1961-62). He mostly played the bad guy and he is probably best known as the villainous Time Lord *The Master* in the sci-fi BBC TV series *Dr Who*, a role he first played in 1971. Died 18 June 1973 when his chauffeur-driven hire car plunged into a ravine near Nevsehir, Turkey where he was shooting a film. See also entries in the television section for *The Buccaneers, Dr Who, Quatermass*, and *Sir Francis Drake*.

Dench, Judi (1934-) Born Judith Olivia Dench, 9 December 1934, York. Actress. Attended the Central School of Speech and Drama, London. She made her professional debut as Ophelia in *Hamlet* in Liverpool in 1957, and in 1961 joined the RSC. Her film debut was in Charles Crichton's *The Third Secret* (1964). In 1971 she married British actor Michael Williams (b. 9 July 1935; d. 11 January 2001) and they had their only child, Tara Cressida Williams (aka Finty), on 24 September 1972. In the 1980s Judi starred with her husband in the sitcom *A Fine Romance* as Laura Dalton and in the 1990s opposite Geoffrey Palmer as Jean Pargetter / Hardcastle in *As Time Goes By*. Dame Judi, as she now is, has become one of the most honoured actresses in British stage and cinematic history, her tally stands (as at the end of 2011) at ten BAFTAs, seven Laurence Olivier Awards, two Screen Actors Guild Awards, two Golden Globes, an Academy Award, and a

Tony Award. Her film credits include *Mrs. Brown* (1997), *Shakespeare in Love* (1998), *Chocolat* (2000) and *Iris* (2002), for all of which she gained Academy Award nominations, winning Best Supporting Actress for her portrayal of Elizabeth I in *Shakespeare in Love*. More recently she has starred in *Mrs Henderson Presents* (2005), *Pride & Prejudice* (2005) and *Notes on a Scandal* (2006), the latter gaining her yet another Academy Award nomination. Other even more recent films include: *Rage* (2009), *Nine* (2009), *Jane Eyre* (2011 - as Mrs Fairfax), *Pirates of the Caribbean: On Stranger Tides* (2011), *My Week with Marilyn* (2011 - as Dame Sybil Thorndike) and *J. Edgar* (2011). Her Tony award was for *Amy's View* (1999). Dame Judi is no stranger to being honoured by her country. She was awarded the OBE in 1970, made a Dame Commander of the Order of the British Empire (DBE) in 1988 and in 2005 a Companion of Honour. She is now known and established as "M" in the Bond films having first played the role in *Goldeneye* (1995). Her brother Jeffrey Dench and her daughter Finty Williams are also actors. Dame Judi's husband was mainly a stage and television actor. His film roles included *Dead Cert* (1974), *Enigma* (1983), *Educating Rita* (1983), *Henry V* (1989) and *Tea with Mussolini* (1999). In 1981 he became President of the Roman Catholic Actors' Guild and shortly before his death from lung cancer at the age of 65, was awarded a Knighthood of St. Gregory by Pope John Paul II. See also entries in the radio and television section for *As Time Goes By, Cranford, Desert Island Discs, A Fine Romance,* and *Going Gently*.

Denham, Maurice (1909-2002) Born William Maurice Denham, 23 December 1909, Beckenham, Kent. Actor. Worked as a lift engineer before taking up acting. Stage debut: *The Marquise (1934)*. Well-known in the 1940s as a "man of a thousand voices" he voiced the parts of charlady Mrs Tickle and the Russian inventor Vodkin in the radio comedy *ITMA (It's That Man Again)* and various RAF officers and villagers in *Much Binding in the Marsh*. Screen debut: *The Man Within* (1947). Appeared in over 100 films including: *Fame is the Spur* (1947), *Oliver Twist* (1948), *The Purple Plain* (1954), *Our Man in Havana* (1959), *Sink the Bismarck* (1960), *The Virgin and the Gypsy* (1970), *Sunday Bloody Sunday* (1971), *The Day of the Jackal* (1973) and *84 Charing Cross Road* (1987). Maurice provided the voices for all the animals in the animated version of *Animal Farm* (1955). He usually played gentleman, both straight and shifty, but could turn his hand to more varied roles. Appeared as disgraced Judge Rawley in the TV sitcom *Porridge*. Awarded the OBE in 1992. Died 24 July 2002, Denville Hall, Northwood, London. See also entries in the radio and television section for *ITMA, Knock on Any Door, The Lotus Eaters, Much Binding in the Marsh, The Old Men at the Zoo,* and *Porridge*.

Denham Studios (1936-51) Forever associated with Alexander Korda. Flush from the financial success of his *London Films* production *The Private Life of Henry VIII* (1933) Korda acquired the finance to build a new studio at The Fishery near Denham village, Buckinghamshire, which was opened in 1936. It was the largest film studio in Britain. The first film completed there was *Southern Roses* (1936). Other major productions made at Denham include: *Rembrandt* (1936), *Elephant Boy* (1937), *Fire over England* (1937), *Knight without Armour* (1937), *The Citadel* (1938), *The Four Feathers* (1939), *Goodbye Mr Chips* (1939), *In Which We Serve* (1942), *This Happy Breed* (1944), *Henry V* (1944), *The Way Ahead* (1944), *Brief Encounter* (1945), *Caesar and Cleopatra* (1945), *A Matter of Life and Death* (1946), *Odd Man Out* (1946), *Vice Versa* (1947), *Hamlet* (1948) and *The History of Mr Polly* (1948). The ownership of the studios passed from Korda to the *J. Arthur Rank Organisation* in 1939 which set up *D & P Ltd* to oversee *Denham* and *Pinewood*. At the end of the 1940s, with *Rank* in real financial difficulties they decided to safeguard the future of *Pinewood* by winding down *Denham*. The final film made at *Denham* was *Robin Hood* (1951). For a short time the site was leased to the United States Air Force and then housed *Rank Xerox* equipment. The main buildings were eventually demolished for an industrial park.

Denison, Michael (1915-98) Born John Michael Terrence Wellesley Denison, 1 November 1915, Doncaster, Yorkshire. Actor. Son of a paint manufacturer. Educated at Harrow and Magdelene, Oxford from where he graduated with a degree in modern languages. Stage debut: *Charley's Aunt* (1938). Screen debut: *Inspector Hornleigh on Holiday* (1939). Served in the Royal Signals and Intelligence Service during WWII. Films include: *My Brother Johnathan* (1948), *The Glass Mountain* (1949), *The Importance of Being Ernest* (1952) and, after a gap of 30 years, *Shadowlands* (1993). Married to actress Dulcie Gray (see separate entry). He and Dulcie were in the cast of what is believed to be the first soap opera broadcast by the BBC. *The Robinsons* (aka *Front Line Family*) was a WWII radio soap broadcast to North America to highlight the life of a British family during wartime. It first aired in 1942 and outlasted the war by three years, eventually ending in 1948. Michael also starred in *Boyd QC* (1956-64) and *Howard's Way* (1985-90) on television. He died 22 July 1998, Amersham, Buckinghamshire.

Denny, Reginald (1891-1967) Born Reginald Leigh Dugmore, 20 November 1891, Richmond, Surrey. Actor and inventor. Son of actor William Henry Denny. A child actor, he made his stage debut, aged eight, in *A Royal Family* (1899). Toured in the United States, India and the Far East 1911-14. Served in the Royal Flying Corps 1917-19. Returned to the United States in 1919 and established his film career which had begun with *The Melting Pot* (1912). A versatile actor who played in action dramas and comedies in the silent era, including as a boxer in a series called *The Leather Pushers* (1922). His films from the late 1920s onwards include: *The Lost Patrol* (1934), *Anna Karenina* (1935), *Rebecca* (1940), *My Favourite Brunette* (1948), *The Secret Life of Walter Mitty* (1947), *Mr Blandings Builds his Dream House* (1947), *Around the World in Eighty Days* (1956), *Cat Ballou* (1965) and *Batman* (1966). He also played Algy Longworth in eight *Bulldog Drummond* films and was well-known for playing English dim-wits. However, his film career is only half the story and his film persona nowhere near true to life. Interested in aeroplanes since his days in the RFC he opened a model shop on Hollywood Boulevard and began Reginald Denny Industries in 1934. He pioneered and developed the first pilotless radio-controlled aircraft to fly in the United States. Reg then won a US Army contract to develop the Radioplane as a target drone for anti-aircraft practice. He was Vice President of The Radioplane Company (1940-48). It was whilst a "women doing war work" photoshoot was taking place at the Radioplane plant in Burbank on 26 June 1945 that Marilyn Monroe (then known as Norma Jeane Dougherty and working as a model plane assembler) was first discovered by photographer David Conover. Conover had been sent there by his commanding officer, Denny's friend Captain Ronald Reagan no less. Reg died 16 June 1967, Richmond, Surrey, whilst visiting relatives.

Desmonde, Jerry (1908-67) Born James Robert Sadler, 20 July 1908, Middlesbrough, Cleveland. Actor. Part of a family act called *The Four Sadlers*, originally replacing his sister Elsie and dressing as a girl. He developed into being the perfect straight man to a series of comedians including Arthur Askey and Sid Field with whom he appeared in *London Town* (1946) and *Cardboard Cavalier* (1949). He was the butt of Norman Wisdom's antics in a string of films during the 1950s and 1960s including: *Trouble in Store* (1953), *Man of the Moment* (1955), *A Stitch in Time* (1963) and *The Early Bird* (1965). He presented the TV quiz *The 64,000 Question* (1956-1958) which unlike its American counterpart dealt in increments of sixpence to a maximum of £1,600. He committed suicide 11 February 1967, Marylebone, London.

Deutsch, Oscar (1893-1941) Born September 1893, Balsall Heath, Birmingham, West Midlands. Distributor. Son of a Hungarian scrap metal dealer. Formed *Victory Motion Pictures* with school friends Michael Balcon and Victor Saville. Whilst his colleagues went into production Deutsch was more interested in distribution. Opened his first Odeon Cinema in Perry Barr, Birmingham in 1930 and by 1937 he had built or acquired 258 cinemas throughout Britain. The name odeon came from the

Greek odeion, meaning an open air theatre and had already been used for some cinemas in France, however, the idea put forward, possibly by Deutsch's company *Odeon Cinema Holdings Ltd*, that it was actually an acronym for Oscar Deutsch Entertains Our Nation has stuck. The later Odeons were notable for their art deco design and beautiful interiors. On Deutsch's death in 1941 (in Kensington, London) the chain was acquired by *The Rank Organisation*.

Dickinson, Thorold (1903-84) Born Thorold Barron Dickinson, 16 November 1903, Bristol. Director and writer. His Christian name apparently comes from the horse-holding dwarf depicted on the Bayeux Tapestry, from whom he claimed descent (along with Lady Godiva). Educated at Keble College, Oxford, but failed to graduate, preferring to work in the theatre and in film. Worked as a film editor during the early 1930s on such films as: *Tilly of Bloomsbury* (1931) and *Sing As We Go!* (1934). He co-founded the short-lived *Fanfare Pictures* in 1936 and made his directorial debut: *The High Command* (1937). In 1938 he visited Spain and made documentaries during the Civil War. His best known film is probably *Gaslight* (1940) but he also directed seven further films: *The Arsenal Stadium Mystery* (1940), *The Prime Minister* (1941), *Next of Kin* (1942), *Men of Two Worlds* (1946), *The Queen of Spades* (1949), *The Secret People* (1952) and the Israeli feature *Giv'a 24 Eina Ona - Hill 24 Doesn't Answer* (1955). Thorold was Chief of Film Services for UNESCO (1956-60). He established a film studies department at *Slade School of Fine Art* in 1960 and was Britain's first Professor of Film (1967-71). Wrote *A Discovery of Cinema* (1971). Died 14 April 1984, Kingsclere, Hampshire.

Dickson, W K L (1860-1935) Born William Kennedy Laurie Dickson, 3 August 1860, Minihic-sur-Ranse, France. "The Father of Film". The son of a French mother and a Scottish father. Despite being initially rejected by Thomas Edison, who was not interested in Dickson's obsession with capturing motion on film he travelled to the United States and did eventually join Edison's company in 1883. At first he worked on projects in electrical engineering and iron-ore milling until in 1889 he was asked by Edison to investigate any progress taking place in motion capture. As a result he developed the Kinetograph camera and the Kinetoscope peep-show viewer, which were patented in 1891. The prototype used 19mm single sprocket film but Dickson's insistence on replacing this with 35mm double sprocket Eastman film set a standard which remains to this day. In 1893 he built the first film studio at Edison's West Orange factory in New Jersey - nicknamed The Black Maria because of its resemblance to a police van. Dickson produced many films lasting only 20 seconds each in 1894 including: *French Dancers*, *Buffalo Bill*, *Carmencita* and *Annie Oakley*. In 1895 in an attempt to break away from the peep-show style of viewing films favoured by Edison he brought out a camera and projector system. Dickson left Edison's employ and co-founded the *American Mutoscope and Biograph Company* in New York (later just called *The Biograph Company*), which was the first company entirely devoted to film production. The first film released was *Empire State Express* (1896). Dickson returned to England in 1897 to form a British subsidiary of *Biograph*. He toured Europe filming the heads of state, including capturing the first film of a Pope (Leo XIII) in 1898. He also filmed in South Africa during the Boer War, after which he wrote *The Biograph in Battle* (1901). He left the film world in the early 1900s to concentrate on being an electrical engineer. Died 28 September 1935, Twickenham, Middlesex.

Donat, Robert (1905-58) Born Friedrich Robert Donat, 18 March 1905, Withington, Manchester. Actor. The son of a Polish clerk he became an actor after taking elocution lessons to cure a stammer. Stage debut: *Julius Caesar* (1921). Screen debut: *That Night in London* (1932). A true international movie star he suffered from asthma all his life which limited his screen appearances to 20 films including some of the best loved of the period. Spotted by Alexander Korda, he featured in *The Private Life of Henry VIII* (1933). A brief spell in Hollywood to play *The Count of Monte Cristo* (1934) proved unsatisfactory. Robert played an innocent man on the run in the Hitchcock classic version of John Buchan's *The 39 Steps* (1935), the ghost in *The Ghost Goes West* (1935) and a secret agent in *Knight Without Armour* (1937). He gained a Best Actor Academy Award Nomination for *The Citadel* (1938)

and he went on to win an Academy Award for Best Actor for his role of Mr Chipping in *Goodbye Mr Chips* (1939), in which he had to age from 25 to 83 on screen - beating Clark Gable's record whilst playing Rhett Butler in the process. Robert produced, directed and starred in *The Cure for Love* (1949). Other films include: *The Young Mr Pitt* (1942), *Perfect Strangers* (1945), *Captain Boycott* (1947), *The Winslow Boy* (1948) and *Lease of Life* (1954). He also played film pioneer William Friese-Greene in *The Magic Box* (1951). His ironic final words on screen in his last film *The Inn of the Sixth Happiness* (1958) were "We shall not see each other again, I think. Farewell." Robert died after a chronic asthma attack, 9 June 1958, Finchley, London.

Donohoe, Amanda (1962-) Born 29 June 1962, London. Actress. She attended the *Central School of Speech and Drama*. Her debut film appearance was as Susan Partridge in the British rom-com *Foreign Body* (1986) but Amanda's second appearance, in the film version of Lucy Irvine's book *Castaway* (1986), gave her career a boost. After a number of low-budget films memorable amongst which is her turn as Lady Sylvia Marsh in *The Lair of the White Worm* (1988), she became a global actress in the TV series *L.A. Law* as the bisexual Cara Jean "C.J." Lamb. Other films include: *The Rainbow* (1989 - as Winifred Inger), *Paper Mask* (1990 - as Christine Taylor), *The Madness of King George* (1995 - as Lady Pembroke), *Liar Liar* (1997 - as Miranda), *Glory Glory* (2000 - as Widow) and *Starship Troopers 3* (2008 - as Admiral Enolo Phid). Amanda has also played Mrs Robinson on the London stage in *The Graduate* (replacing Jerry Hall in 2000). In the past she has been romantically linked with Adam Ant, appearing in a number of his videos in the 1980s, and the documentary director Nick Broomfield. Her current partner is the multidisciplinary artist Russell Haswell (b 1970, Coventry). Amanda recently joined the cast of *Emmerdale* as Natasha Wylde (2009–2010) before resuming her stage career in *Star Quality*. See also entries in the television section for *Bad Girls, Emmerdale,* and *Murder City*.

Dors, Diana (1931-1984) Born Diana Mary Fluck, 23 October 1931, Swindon, Wiltshire. Actress. She Trained at LAMDA and made her screen debut in *The Shop at Sly Corner* (1947) and went on to make over 70 films in her career. Throughout the 1950s and 1960s she was seen by many as Britain's answer to Marilyn Monroe. She loved the good life that fame brought her and in 1951 was the youngest registered owner of a Rolls Royce in the country. She was the archetypal "blonde bombshell" and was billed as such in J. Lee Thompson's *Yield To the Night* (1956). She relished the role and once described herself as "the only sex symbol Britain [had] produced since Lady Godiva". *The Beatles* obviously agreed as in 1967 they put her on the cover of their *Sgt. Pepper's Lonely Hearts Club Band* album. Other films include: *Here Come the Huggetts* (1948), *Oliver Twist* (1948), *Vote for Huggett* (1949), *Lady Godiva Rides Again* (1951), *A Kid for Two Farthings* (1955), *On the Double* (1961), *The Sandwich Man* (1966), *Steptoe and Son Ride Again* (1973), *Theatre of Blood* (1973) and *Adventures of a Taxi Driver* (1976). The 1970s and 1980s saw Diana turn in more of a celebrity appearing on TV game shows and even a famous appearance in Adam Ant's video for *Prince Charming* in 1981. With the passing of years Diana began to put on weight and became a fine character actress in television series such as *Queenie's Castle* (1970-72) and *Just William* (1977-78 – as Mrs Bott).Her last film released in 1985, the year after her death, was Joseph Losey's *Steaming* based on the play by Nell Dunn. She is still much loved and revered as both an actress and an icon. The Smiths used her on the cover of their 1995 compilation album, *Singles* and a bronze statue of Diana can be seen outside the cinema in West Swindon. The "Hurricane in Mink" died 4 May 1984 of stomach cancer, Windsor, Berkshire. See also entries in the radio and television section for *Life With the Lyons*, and *Queenie's Castle*.

Down, Lesley-Anne (1954-) Born Lesley Anne Down, 17 March 1954, Wandsworth, London. Actress. She is probably best remembered for her television roles as Lady Georgina Worsley in the TV series *Upstairs Downstairs* (1973-75), her controversial role as stripper Phyllis Dixey in *The One and Only Phyllis Dixey* (1978) and her brief appearance as Cliff Barnes' PR guru Stephanie Rogers in *Dallas* (1990). She was, and still is, a beautiful woman and in 1970 was voted "Most Beautiful

Teenager" in Britain. She began modelling before her teens and moved on to acting at the same early age. She has been married three times, to film director Enrique Gabriel (1980-81), William Friedkin (1982-85) and finally camerman (and director) Don E. FauntLeroy since 1985 when they both worked on the mini-series *North and South*. Films include: *School for Untamed Girls* (1969), *Countess Dracula* (1971), *Brannigan* (1975), *The Pink Panther Strikes Again* (1976 - as Olga Bariosova), *Hanover Street* (1979), *Sphinx* (1981), *The Hunchback of Notre Dame* (1982 - as Esmeralda), *Saving Grace* (1996), *13th Child* (2002), *Today You Die* (2005) and *Rosewood Lane* (2011). Has appeared on the US TV soap operas *Days of Our Lives* (2001) and since 2003, *The Bold and the Beautiful*.

Drake, Charlie See entry in comedy section

Drew, Ben See entry in pop music section

Dudley-Ward, Penelope (1919-82) Born Penelope Ann Rachel Dudley Ward, 4 August 1914, Marylebone, London. Actress. Mainly known as a refined leading lady in British films of the 1930s and 1940s. Screen debut: *Escape Me Never* (1935). She only made 11 films including *The Citadel* (1938), *Hells Cargo* (1940), *Major Barbara* (1941), *In Which we Serve* (1942), *The Way Ahead* (1944) and *English Without Tears* (1944), announcing her retirement in 1948. Married first to Anthony Pelissier (1939-44) and then to Sir Carol Reed (1948-76). She died 22 January 1982, Kensington, London.

Duncan, Lindsay (1950-) Born 7 November 1950, Edinburgh. Actress. Lindsay had an inauspicious start to her career playing the role of Scrubba in *Further Up Pompeii* (1975) on television. Mostly a stage actress she has appeared in a number of film and television roles usually in the more aristocratic roles, Servilia of the Junii in *Rome* (2005) and Lady Bellaston in *The History of Tom Jones, a Foundling* (1997) are typical. Other films include: *Samson and Delilah* (1985), *Prick Up Your Ears* (1987), *A Midsummer Might's Dream* (1996), *Mansfield Park* (1999), *Afterlife* (2003), *The Queen of Sheba's Pearls* (2004) and *Starter for 10* (2006). Lindsay's most recent role is as Alice's mother in Tim Burton's 2010 film *Alice in Wonderland*. She has won numerous stage awards including a Laurence Olivier Theatre Award in 1987 for Best Actress in a New Play for *Les Liaisons Dangereuses* (which also garnered a Tony nomination), the London Critics Circle Theatre Award (Drama) for Best Actress for her performance in *Mouth to Mouth* (2001) and a Tony and an Olivier for *Private Lives* (2002). On television her dulcet tones can be heard as narrator of the Matt Lucas and David Walliams BBC fly-on-the-wall mockumentary series *Come Fly with Me* (2010). Lindsay is married to fellow Scottish actor Hilton McRae (b. 28 December 1949, Dundee). They have one son, Cal McRae (b. September 1991). She was appointed Commander of the Order of the British Empire (CBE) in the 2009 Birthday Honours. See also entries in the television section for *Criminal Justice, GBH, Muck and Brass, Rome,* and *A Year in Provence*.

Duprez, June (1918-84) Born 14 May 1918, Teddington, Middlesex (now Greater London). Actress. Daughter of comedian Fred Duprez. Made her stage debut in Coventry in 1935. Screen debut: *The Crimson Circle* (1936). Featured in many Alexander Korda films including: *The Four Feathers* (1939), *The Spy in Black* (1939), and *The Thief of Baghdad* (1940). Moved to Hollywood but appeared in only a few more films before retiring in 1948 after getting married for the second time. Her best Hollywood movie was opposite Cary Grant in *None but the Lonely Heart* (1944). She died 30 October 1984, Kensington, London.

Dyall, Valentine (1908-85) Born 7 May 1908 Wandsworth, London. Actor. Son of actor Franklin Dyall and actress Phyllis Logan. Educated at Harrow and Oxford. Stage debut in 1930. Screen debut: *Much Too Shy* (1941). His many films include: *The Life and Death of Colonel Blimp* (1943), *Henry V* (1944), *Caesar and Cleopatra* (1945), *Brief Encounter* (1945) and *Ivanhoe* (1952). He was on various occasions understudy to Laurence Olivier, Spike Milligan (in Son of Oblomov) and even replaced an ill Peter Sellers in one episode of *The Goons*. He seemed to enjoy his supporting player status. Best remembered as *The Man in Black* from the long-running radio series *Appointment with Fear* (1941-1953). His sepulchral tones meant he was used as narrator or as a disembodied voice for many films including *Knights of the Round Table* (1953), *First Men in the Moon* (1964) and *Casino Royale* (1967). Late in life he made guest appearances in such diverse TV shows as *Dr Who* and *Blackadder*. Died 24 June 1985, London. See also entries in the television section for *The Idiot Weekly, Price 2d, A Show Called Fred,* and *Treasure Island*.

Dyer, Danny (1977-) Born 24 July 1977, Custom House, Newham, London. Actor. Keen amateur footballer, supporter of West Ham United and chairman of non-League Greenwich Borough FC. Television roles include *Prime Suspect* (his first – 1993), *Cadfael* (1994), *A Touch of Frost* (1995), *Loved Up* (1995), *Thief Takers* (1996) and *Soldier Soldier* (1997). Wide screen debut *Human Traffic* (1999). Other films include: *The Trench* (1999), *Borstal Boy* (2000), *Greenfingers* (2000), *Goodbye Charlie Bright* (2001), *High Heels and Low Lifes* (2001), *Mean Machine* (2002), *Wasp* (2003), *The Football Factory* (2004), *The Business* (2005), *The Other Half* (2006), *Severance* (2006), *The Great Ecstasy of Robert Carmichael* (2006), *Outlaw* (2007), *Straightheads* (2007), *The All Together* (2007) *Tattoos: A Scarred History* (2008 – documentary film), *Adulthood* (2008), *7 Lives* (2008), *City Rats* (2009), *Doghouse* (2009), *Dead Man Running* (2009), *Jack Said* (2009), *Pimp* (2009), *The Devil's Playground* (2010), *The Last Seven* (2010), *Age of Heroes* (2011), *Freerunner* (2011) and *7lives* (2011). Danny is also the voice of Kent Paul in the video games *Grand Theft Auto: Vice City* (2002) and *Grand Theft Auto: San Andreas* (2004). Known for playing hardman characters, Danny recently had the misfortune to have two luxury cars (a black Porsche Cayenne and a Mercedes A-Class) stolen from his drive-way at his Loughton home.

Ealing Studios (1907-) Showman Will Barker bought a mansion in Ealing in 1907 and built three stages for film production. One of Barker's early productions was *Henry VIII* (1911) starring Sir Herbert Tree as Cardinal Wolsey. This was the first British film to have a recognised composer, Edward German, create the music. Barker produced many lavish productions at Ealing including: *Hamlet* (1912) and *Jane Shore* (1915). Barker retired in 1921 and the studios passed through a few hands until they were bought by *Associated Radio Pictures* who built a new studio on the site at Ealing Green. The company was run by Sir Gerald Du Maurier, Reginald Baker, Stephen Courtauld and Basil Dean. It became *Associated Talking Pictures* (ATP) in 1933 and claimed to be Britain's first purpose built sound studio. Dean was the creative mind behind the studio and guided the development of Gracie Fields and George Formby as screen performers. However, Dean was not able to control the budgets of his films with the result that in 1939 he was ousted in favour of Michael Balcon as head of the studios, now renamed *Ealing Studios*. The films made over the next sixteen years were distinct in style and are amongst the best-loved of British cinema output. They include war-time dramas such as *Went the Day Well?* (1943), costume dramas such as *Saraband for Dead Lovers* (1948) and classics such as *Nicholas Nickleby* (1947). Best remembered are the post-war comedies: *Hue and Cry* (1947), *Passport to Pimlico* (1949), *Whisky Galore!* (1949), *Kind Hearts and Coronets* (1949), *The Lavender Hill Mob* (1951), *The Man in the White Suit* (1951), *The Titfield Thunderbolt* (1953) and *The Ladykillers* (1955). Falling cinema audiences saw the company fall into financial difficulties and the studios were sold to the BBC in 1955 and then purchased by the *National Film & Television School* in 1995.

Eaton, Shirley (1937-) Born 12 January 1937, London. Actress. Best remembered for her role as Jill Masterson in *Goldfinger* (1964), Shirley was by then a film veteran who had also appeared on television from the early days of ITV. Her first screen appearance was in the six-part BBC drama *Parent-Craft* (1951) and her later television credits include the very first episode of *The Saint* (1962). Her film debut was *A Day To Remember* (1953) and she went on to appear in a string of British comedies mostly in the Doctor and Carry On franchises: *Doctor In The House (1954), Doctor At Large* (1957), Carry *On Sergeant* (1958), *Carry*

On Nurse (1959), and *Carry On Constable* (1960). More films followed the success in Goldfinger, notably *Ten Little Indians* (1965) and *Around the World Under the Sea* (1966) but in 1969 she retired from acting to bring up her family. Autobiography: *Golden Girl* (1999).

Eccleston, Christopher (1964-) Born 16 February 1964, Salford, Lancashire. Actor. Trained at the Central School of Speech and Drama. Screen debut: *Let Him Have It* (1991 - as Derek Bentley). Other films include: *Death and the Compass* (1992), *Shallow Grave* (1994), *Jude* (1996), *Elizabeth* (1998), *eXistenZ* (1999), *Gone in Sixty Seconds* (2000), *The Others* (2001), *24 Hour Party People* (2002), *Revengers Tragedy* (2002), *28 Days Later* (2002), *The Seeker: The Dark Is Rising* (2007), *G.I. Joe: The Rise of Cobra* (2009) and *Amelia* (2009). A well-known face on British TV, having starred in such series as *Cracker* (1993), *Our Friends in the North* (1996) and the two-part ITV drama *The Second Coming* (2003). Christopher played the ninth incarnation of *Dr Who* (2005) although deciding not to film more than one series. See also entries in the television section for *Clocking Off, Cracker, Dr Who,* and *Our Friends In The North.*

Edwards, Henry (1883-1952) Born Arthur Harold Ethelbert Edwards, 18 September 1883, Weston-Super-Mare, Somerset. Actor and director. Son of an architect. An actor and director who often featured in his own films playing the romantic lead. Made his stage debut in 1900 and toured in provincial theatres 1900-11. Screen debut: *A Welsh Singer* (1915). Other films in which he acted: *Far From the Madding Crowd* (1915), *East is East* (1916), *Her Savings Saved* (1918), *Aylwin* (1920), *Simple Simon* (1922), *The Flag Lieutenant* (1926), *The Fake* (1927), *The Flag Lieutenant* (1933), *Green for Danger* (1946), *The Magic Bow* (1946), *London Belongs to Me* (1948), *Trio* (1950), *The Magic Box* (1951), *The Long Memory* (1952) and *Trent's Last Case* (1952). Directorial debut: *A Welsh Singer* (1915). Other films as director: *The Failure* (1917), *The Kinsman* (1919), *Lily of the Alley* (1920), *Stranglehold* (1930), *Anne One Hundred* (1933), *The Lash* (1934), *Scrooge* (1935), *The Private Secretary* (1935), *Juggernaut* (1936) and *Beauty and the Barge* (1937). In both his acting and directing he was noted for an element of sophistication often missing from other British films of the period. Formed a production company at *Twickenham Studios* called *W P Film Company* with Julius Hagen in 1927. Married actress Chrissie White in January 1924 and as a couple they were celebrated as Britain's answer to Fairbanks and Pickford. They made 22 films together. Chairman of *Twickenham Film Studios* and Joint Managing Director of *Teddington Film Studios.* Died 2 November 1952, Chobham, Surrey.

Egerton, Tamsin (1988-) Born Tamsin Olivia Egerton-Dick, 26 November 1988, Petersfield, Hampshire. Actress and model. Tamsin's film debut in *Keeping Mum* (2005 - as Holly Goodfellow) was controversial as she appeared topless when only sixteen. She next had a small role in *Driving Lessons* (2006 - as Sarah) before landing the role of Chelsea Parker (the Posh Totty) in the 2007 film *St Trinian's* and the sequel *St. Trinian's II: The Legend of Fritton's Gold* (2009). Her other films to-date include *Knife Edge* (2008), *4.3.2.1.* (2010) and *Chalet Girl* (2011). Tamsin currently lives in Hampstead with theatre producer Jamie Hendry. See also entry in the television section for *Camelot.*

Eggar, Samantha (1939-) Born Victoria Louise Samantha Marie Elizabeth Therese Eggar, 5 March 1939, Hampstead, London. Actress. Her father was English and her mother of Dutch and Portuguese descent. She began her acting career in several Shakespearean companies, and debuted in film in 1962 in *The Wild and the Willing* alongside Ian McShane and John Hurt. She received an Academy Award nomination as Best Actress for her performance as Miranda Grey in *The Collector* (1965). Samantha has appeared in such films as *Walk, Don't Run* (1966), *Doctor Dolittle* (1967), *The Molly Maguires* (1970), *Hercules* (1997 – voice of Hera) and *The Astronaut's Wife* (1999). In 1972, she played the governess opposite Yul Brynner for the American television series *Anna and the King.* Recently she has been providing the voice of "M" in the *James Bond – 007* Video Games. In 1964, Samantha married actor Tom Stern, with whom she has two children, film producer Nicholas Stern and actress Jenna Stern. The couple divorced in 1971.

Ehle, Jennifer (1969-) Born 29 December 1969, Winston-Salem, North Carolina, United States. Actress. American-born but unquestionably English. She attended the *Central School of Speech and Drama* in London. She is the daughter of Rosemary Harris (see separate entry) and starred with her in Peter Hall's adaptation of Mary Wesley's *The Camomile Lawn* (1992) as the Young Calypso. She made her film debut in *Backbeat* (1994) but her next breakthrough was as Miss Elizabeth Bennet in the hugely popular BBC mini-series *Pride and Prejudice* (1995), adapted by Simon Langton and Andrew Davies (the doyen of costume drama). Since then she has made surprisingly few films. She usually plays beautiful, independent and often haughty young woman. She played Empress Zita of Austria in *The Adventures of Young Indiana Jones: Adventures in the Secret Service* (TV 1992, video 1999) and in 1997 she played Constance Lloyd Wilde, Oscar Wildes' wife in *Wilde.* Her other films include *This Year's Love* (1999), *Possession* (2002), *The River King* (2005 - as Betsy Chase), *Pride and Glory* (2008 - as Abby Tierney) and the multi-award-winning *The King's Speech* (2010 as Myrtle Logue). Jennifer has appeared in three films in 2011, a cameo in *The Adjustment Bureau,* and meatier parts in *Contagion* and the George Clooney-directed *The Ides of March.* She has won a number of major awards, including a BAFTA for Best Actress for the mini-series *Pride and Prejudice* (1995). Off-screen she has won a Tony and an Olivier Award for *The Real Thing* in 2000. In 2001 she shared the International Press Academy's Golden Satellite Award for *Sunshine* (1999) with her mother. In 2005 she played the leading female role of Tracy Lord in the revival of *The Philadelphia Story* in London's West End opposite Kevin Spacey. Jennifer was in a relationship with Colin Firth in the 1990s but has been married to writer Michael Ryan since 2001 and the couple have two children. See also entries in the television section for *The Camomile Lawn,* and *Pride and Prejudice.*

Ekland, Britt (1942-) Born Britt-Marie Eklund, 6 October 1942, Stockholm, Sweden. Actress. Grew up to be the archetypal beautiful, blue-eyed Scandinavian blonde. Although Scandinavian most of her best films were British and she was married to one of Britain's greatest comedy actors Peter Sellers. She appeared in *After the Fox* (1966), *Get Carter* (1971), *The Wicker Man* (1973) and *The Man With the Golden Gun* (1974). Known as much for her off screen life, she remained married to Sellers for just four years (1964-68) thereafter, in June 1973, she had a son, Nic, with record producer Lou Adler before embarking on a two year romance with singer Rod Stewart and then married the *Stray Cats's* "Slim Jim" Phantom (real name James McDonnell) in 1984. They divorced in 1992. In 2010 Britt took part in the reality TV show *I'm a Celebrity...Get Me Out of Here!* To paraphrase her 1980 autobiography, whilst she may not be English she will always be a *True Brit.*

Elliott, Denholm (1922-92) Born Denholm Mitchell Elliott, 31 May 1922, Ealing, London. Actor. Advised by a psychoanalyst to enter for RADA as therapy for his confused sexuality. Formed a drama group whilst a POW in Stalag 8B Silesia during WWII, having been radio operator in a bomber shot down over Denmark in 1942. Stage debut: 1946. Screen debut: *Dear Mr Prohack* (1949). "I can make two lines seem like Hamlet" he once said and most of his career was spent in supporting roles in films such as *The Cruel Sea* (1955), *King Rat* (1966), *Alfie* (1968) and *The Night They Raided Minsky's* (1973). He was nominated for an Academy Award as Best Supporting Actor in *A Room With a View* (1985). Gained greatest popularity at the end of his career in box-office triumphs *Raiders of the Lost Ark* (1981), *Trading Places* (1983) and *Indiana Jones and the Last Crusade* (1989). Awarded the CBE in 1988. He married twice: to actresses Virginia McKenna (1954) and Susan Robinson (1962-92), with whom he had two children a son, Mark, and a daughter, Jennifer (1964–2003) who committed suicide by hanging herself. The bisexual actor shared an open marriage for the last 30 years of his life and was diagnosed with HIV in 1987, and died of AIDS-related tuberculosis at his home on Ibiza, Spain, 6 October 1992. See also entries in the television section for *Bleak House, Clayhanger, Love Story, The Man in Room 17,* and *Shades of Greene.*

Elphick, Michael (1946-2002) Born Michael J Elphick, 19 September 1946, Chichester, West Sussex. Actor. Screen debut:

Fraulein Doktor (1969). Other films include: *Where's Jack* (1969), *Hamlet* (1969), *O Lucky Man!* (1973), *The Odd Job* (1978), *The Quiz Kid* (1979), *Quadrophenia* (1979), *The Elephant Man* (1980), *Privates on Parade* (1982), *Curse of the Pink Panther* (1983), *Gorky Park* (1984), *Memed my Hawk* (1984), *Withnail & I* (1987), *Little Dorrit* (1988), *The Krays* (1990) and *Let Him Have It* (1991). The hard-drinking actor made an impression on television as the star of *Boon* and *Private Schultz*. Michael was appearing as Harry Slater in *Eastenders* at the time of his death from a heart attack on 7 September 2002, Willesden, London. See also entries in the television section for *Adam Smith*, *Auf Wiedersehen Pet*, *Boon*, *Coronation Street*, *David Copperfield*, *Eastenders*, *Oxbridge Blues*, *Private Schulz*, *Roger Doesn't Live Here Anymore*, and *Three Up, Two Down*.

Elsom, Isobel (1893-1981) Born Isabella Reed, 16 March 1893, Chesterton, Cambridge. Actress. Took her brother's Christian name as her stage surname. She is perhaps best remembered as Mrs. Eynsford-Hill in her last but one screen outing *My Fair Lady* (1964). She had however made over 80 films before this starting with the silent *A Prehistoric Love Story* (1915). A mention of her name conjures up a picture of outraged minor royalty, particularly in those films starring opposite Jerry Lewis in his solo pictures of the late 1950s and early 1960s. A sort of "cut-price" Margaret Dumont if you will, her last film was *The Pleasure Seekers* (1964). Married to director Maurice Elvey and actor Carl Harbord. Died 12 January 1981, Woodland Hills, Los Angeles, California.

Elstree Studios The Elstree film studio complex known as "The British Hollywood" is located in Elstree and Borehamwood, Hertfordshire. The history of the various main branches are described as follows: **BBC Elstree Centre, Clarendon Road** - The first studio was built on this site by *Neptune Studio* (1914-17) at Eldon Avenue producing patriotic wartime features. In 1924 they were leased to the *Ludwig Blatter Film Corporation* (aka *British Phototone Sound Productions*). From 1931-38 they were leased to American producer Joe Rock, who produced such films as *The Man Behind the Mask* (1936) and *The Edge of the World* (1937). They were acquired by Lady Yule in 1940 and renamed *British National Studios*. Productions in the 1940s include: *Gaslight* (1940), *Love on the Dole* (1941), *The Ghosts of Berkeley Square* (1947) and *My Brother Jonathan* (1947). After Lady Yule's death in 1950, for a short period the studios were leased by Douglas Fairbanks Jnr. who began making TV films there. From this point onward these studios have been used solely for TV production and have been bought by *ATV* (1962) and the *BBC* (1984) and are probably most famous nowadays for being the home of *EastEnders*. **Elstree Studios, Shenley Road** - Built as British National Studios in 1925 in Shenley Road, Borehamwood, Hertfordshire. They were fully acquired by John Maxwell's *British International Pictures* (BIP) in 1927. The first film completed by *BIP* was *The White Sheik* (1927). Maxwell engaged Alfred Hitchcock to direct *The Ring* (1927) and *The Farmer's Wife* (1928). He also took on Walter Mycroft, known as "The Czar of all the Rushes", as head of the studio. Films produced at Elstree during this period include: *Blackmail* (1929), *Atlantic* (1929), *Blossom Time* (1934), *Mimi* (1935), *St Martin's Lane* (1938) and *Jamaica Inn* (1939). Maxwell died in 1940 and the renamed *Associated British Picture Corporation* (ABPC) was bought by Warner Bros. The studios were closed during WWII and the first post-war film was *Man on the Run* (1947). Films made during the late 1940s and 1950s include: *The Hasty Heart* (1949), *Stagefright* (1950), *Captain Horatio Hornblower RN* (1951), *Moby Dick* (1956), *The Dam Busters* (1954) and *Ice Cold in Alex* (1958). From 1955, and the introduction of commercial television onwards, the studio produced both films and television programmes, including *Look Back in Anger* (1959), *The Roman Spring of Mrs Stone* (1961), *The Trials of Oscar Wilde* (1960) and *The Avengers* TV series. The studios also played host to a series of pop star film vehicles such as *The Young Ones* (1961) and *Summer Holiday* (1962) as well as horror genre films including *The Masque of the Red Death* (1964) and the *Fearless Vampire Killers* (1967). *ABPC* was acquired by *Electrical & Musical Industries* (EMI) in 1969 and Bryan Forbes became Head of Production. Notable films of this period include *The Railway Children* (1970) and *The Go-Between* (1970). The studio struggled through the early 1970s despite the star-studded *Murder on the Orient Express* (1974), but fortunes changed by 1976 when *Star Wars* was made at Elstree-EMI, followed by the remainder of the original trilogy plus the *Indiana Jones* franchise and some other blockbusters. The studio changed hands in the 1980s, being bought by the *Cannon Organisation* and then *Brent Walker* who rechristened it *Goldcrest Studios* before selling a large chunk of it to become a Tesco Superstore. Hertsmere Borough Council bought the remaining studio in February 1996 and appointed a management company, Elstree Film & Television Studios Ltd., to run the studios. Elstree Studios is now home to two of the top shows on British television today; ITV's *Dancing on Ice* and *Who Wants to be a Millionaire?* It was also the home of Channel 4's *Big Brother* until its demise in 2010. The **British and Dominion Film Corporation** was begun by Herbert Wilcox in the late 1920s on a site adjoining the *BIP* studios. Known as *Imperial Studios* or *British and Dominion Studios*. The company virtually moved straight into talkies and the first completed film was *Wolves* (1930). Some of the best costume dramas of the early 1930s were shot on these stages including *The Private Life of Henry VIII* (1933), *The Private Life of Don Juan* (1934), *The Scarlet Pimpernel* (1934) and *Nell Gwyn* (1934). The studios were destroyed by fire in February 1936. **Amalgamated Studios Ltd** were completed in Shenley Road by 1937 but the company immediately fell into financial difficulty and sold them to *J Arthur Rank* who in turn sold them after WWII to the *Prudential* who then sold them to *MGM British* in 1948. Films produced during this period include: *Edward, My Son* (1949), *Ivanhoe* (1952), *Knights of the Round Table* (1953), *Beau Brummel* (1954), *Quentin Durward* (1955) and *The Inn of the Sixth Happiness* (1958), *The VIPs* (1963), *The Yellow Rolls Royce* (1964), *2001: A Space Odyssey* (1968), *Where Eagles Dare* (1969) and a musical version of *Goodbye Mr Chips* (1969). The studios were closed in 1970 and *MGM* briefly joined *EMI* at the adjoining studios.

Elvey, Maurice (1887-1967) Born William S Folkard, 11 November 1887, Stockton-on-Tees, County Durham. Director. His early life saw him working as a hotel page boy before becoming a stage hand and actor. Acted in two films: *The Fallen Idol* (1913) and *The Cup Final Mystery* (1914). Directorial debut: *Maria Marten, or: The Murder in the Red Barn* (1913). Maurice mixed making melodramas and comedies with directing biographical films such as: *Florence Nightingale* (1915) and *Nelson* (1918). Post WWI he worked for *Stoll* on a series of short films based on the Sherlock Holmes stories and also spent 1922 in the United States before returning to England. He directed some of the most popular films of the late 1920s: *Hindle Wakes* (1927), *Roses of Picardy* (1927), *Palaise de Dance* (1928) and *High Treason* (1928). He became caught up in the production of "quota quickies" in the 1930s. Maurice worked with Gracie Fields on her first feature *Sally in Our Alley* (1931) and subsequently on *This Week of Grace* (1933) and *Love, Life and Laughter* (1934). He directed over 300 films, including shorts, over a period of 44 years, which makes him the most prolific of British directors, something which perhaps has worked against his reputation. His film made in 1918, *The Life Story of David Lloyd George*, was never released, all prints having been seized by the Liberal Party, which felt it portrayed the Prime Minister in a poor light and might influence the forthcoming election. It was believed lost but a copy was discovered at the home of Lloyd George's grandson, Lord Tenby, in 1996. In the film Lloyd George's daughter was played by Alfred Hitchcock's future wife, Alma Reville. Its premier in 1999 was a critical success and has led to a reassessment of Elvey's place in British cinematic history. Suffering from failing eyesight, he directed his last film in 1957. He died 28 August 1967, Brighton, East Sussex.

Emery, Dick (1915-1983) See entry in comedy section

Entwistle, Peg (1908-32) Born Lillian Millicent Entwistle, 1 July 1908, Port Talbot, Wales. Actress. Moved to the United States in 1922 with her widowed father, who was himself killed in an accident shortly afterwards. Peg made her stage debut in 1927, the year she married actor Robert Keith (who later turned out to be a bigamist). After moving to Los Angeles in 1932 she became obsessed with the idea of being an actress on film, turning her back on the stage. Peg realised her dream, playing the role of Hazel in *Thirteen Women* (1932). This was to be her only film. Dropped by her studio on 18 September 1932, she partook in a night of drinking and feeling rather depressed about her plight, climbed the 50 foot "H" on the Hollywood sign on Mount Lee (then actually HOLLYWOODLAND) and jumped. Her suicide note read "I am afraid I am a coward. I am sorry for everything. If I had done this a long time ago, it would have saved a lot of pain. P.E." She will be forever known as "The Hollywood Sign Girl" and, not unexpectedly, she is said to haunt the sign.

Evans, Edith (1888-1976) Born Edith Mary Evans, 8 February 1888, London. Actress. Edith's countless stage appearances have included numerous works by Shakespeare, Congreve, Ibsen, Wycherley, Wilde, and contemporary playwrights including Shaw, Enid Bagnold, Christopher Fry and Coward. She began her film career in *A Welsh Singer* (1915), but was always considered a stage actress during the silent era – one of the finest. Edith was married to George Booth for 19 years until his death in 1935 and was appointed DBE in 1946. She appeared in her first talking picture aged 61 in *The Last Days of Dolwyn* (1949). From then until 1977, she made several acclaimed films, including *Tom Jones* (1963)and *The Chalk Garden* (1964) both of which gained her Academy Award nominations as Best Supporting Actress. For *The Whisperers* (1966) she received an Academy Award nomination as Best Actress and a Golden Bear for the Best Actress at the Berlin Film Festival. One of her most quoted comments was when she said "As a young actress I always had a rule. If I didn't understand a line I always said it as though it were improper". She died 14 October 1976, Cranbrook, Kent.

Eve, Alice (1982-) Born Alice Sophie Eve, 6 February 1982, London. Actress. Alice initially followed her illustrious parents, Trevor Eve and Sharon Maughan, into television dramas including the BBC's *Hawking* (2004), *The Rotters' Club* (2005) and *Poirot* (2005) before making her film debut as Miss Frayne in *Stage Beauty* (2004). Other films include: *Starter for 10* (2006), *Big Nothing* (2006) and *Crossing Over* (2008). She made her professional stage debut in the summer of 2006 in Trevor Nunn and Tom Stoppard's production, *Rock 'n' Roll,* at the Royal Court Theatre, and reprised her role when the play transferred to Broadway in 2007. In 2009, Alice played Roxanne in a production of *Cyrano de Bergerac* at the Chichester Festival Theatre. In 2010 Alice starred in the romantic comedy film *She's Out of My League* and also as Charlotte's Irish nanny, Erin in *Sex and the City 2.* Her most recent film is the British romantic thriller *The Decoy Bride* (2011) opposite David Tennant, and she has recently completed filming for the 2012 films *The Raven* and *Men in Black III.* Alice shares a distinction with David Bowie, being a fellow heterochromia sufferer (she has one green eye and one blue eye).

Everett, Rupert (1959-) Born Rupert James Hector Everett, 29 May 1959, Fakenham, Norfolk. Actor. After leaving the *Central School of Speech and Drama* following clashes with his tutors he joined the *Glasgow Citizen's Theatre.* Whilst a struggling young actor Rupert worked as a model and as a male prostitute in order to support himself, and furnish his drug-fuelled lifestyle. His break came on stage in 1981 playing gay schoolboy Guy Bennett opposite Kenneth Branagh in *Another Country,* initially at the Greenwich Theatre but later transferring to the West End. Rupert was to reprise this role for his feature film debut in 1984, although before *Another Country* he had also appeared on screen in the comedy short *A Shocking Accident* (1982) and the TV mini-series *Princess Daisy* (1983 - as Ram Valenski). Other films include: *Dance with a Stranger* (1985), *The Comfort of Strangers* (1990), *Pret-a-Porter* (1994), *Shakespeare in Love* (1998), *A Midsummer Night's Dream* (1999), *The Importance of Being Ernest* (2002), *To Kill a King* (2003 - as Charles I), *Stage Beauty* (2004 - as Charles II), *Shrek 2* (2004 – voice of Prince Charming), *A Different Loyalty* (2004), *Separate Lies* (2005), *The Chronicles of Narnia: The Lion, the Witch and the Wardrobe* (2005 - voice of Mr Fox), *Stardust* (2007), *Shrek the Third* (2007 - voice of Prince Charming), *St. Trinian's* (2007), *St. Trinian's II: The Legend of Fritton's Gold* (2009), *Wild Target* (2010) and *Hysteria,* a 2011

film about the invention of the vibrator. The immensely honest but outspoken actor has made few bad films, the Bob Dylan vehicle *Hearts of Fire* (1987) being one of few flops. This box-office and critical disaster prompted Rupert to embark on a short-lived pop career recording the unsuccessful album *Generation Of Loneliness.* Many years later Rupert provided backing vocals on Madonna's cover of 'American Pie' and on the track 'They Can't Take That Away from Me' on Robbie Williams' *Swing When You're Winning* in 2001. On moving to Paris in 1989 Rupert wrote a novel, *Hello, Darling, Are You Working?* and then announced his homosexuality, although fearing this would damage his career. Indeed, through the early 1990s film work was scarce but his performances in *My Best Friend's Wedding* (1997 – as George Downes), opposite Julia Roberts' and in *The Next Best Thing* (2000 –as Robert Whittaker), opposite Madonna, should have allayed his fears. In both films Rupert played the gay friend of the heroines to rave reviews. Rupert's portrayal of headmistress Camilla Fritton in the two St Trinian's films has been favourably compared to the original Alastair Sim characterisation, itself vaunted as a comedy masterpiece. See also entry for *The Far Pavilions* in the television section.

Faith, Adam (1940-2003) Born Terence Nelhams, 23 June 1940, Acton, London. Singer and actor. Screen debut: *Beat Girl* (1960). Other films: *Never Let Go* (1960), *What a Whopper!* (1961), *Mix me a Person* (1962), *Stardust* (1974), *Yesterday's Hero* (1979), *Foxes* (1980) and *McVicar* (1980). After a singing career including 35 singles - two of which reached No. 1 - and 7 albums, Adam moved on to concentrate solely on his other great love, acting. He found success on both stage and television - *Budgie* and *Love Hurts* - and combined this with some acute entrepreneurship and pop management. He died 8 March 2003, Stoke-on-Trent, Staffordshire. See also entry in pop music section and entries in the television section for *Budgie, Drumbeat, Face to Face, Love Hurts,* and *Six-Five Special.*

Farrar, David (1908-95) Born 21 August 1908, Forest Gate, London. Actor. Worked as a publisher whilst taking part in amateur productions. Screen debut: *Return of a Stranger* (1937). Featured in British films including *Went the Day Well?* (1942), *Meet Sexton Blake* (1944 - as Blake), *Black Narcissus* (1947), *Frieda* (1947), *Mr Perrin and Mr Traill* (1948), *The Small Back Room* (1949) and *Gone to Earth* (1950). He then moved to Hollywood. Unfortunately he found himself typecast as a villain in such films as *The Golden Horde* (1951), *The Black Shield of Falworth* (1954), *Escape to Burma* (1955) and *The Sea Chase* (1955). After playing the heroine's father in *Beat Girl* (1960) he decided to retire from the cinema in 1962. Autobiography: *No Royal Road* (1947). He died 31 August 1995, Durban, South Africa.

Farrell, Colin (1976-) Born Colin James Farrell, 31 May 1976, Castlenock, Dublin. Actor. Studied at the Gaiety School of Drama, Dublin. Screen debut: *Drinking Crude* (1997). Other films include: *The War Zone* (1999), *Ordinary Decent Criminal* (2000), *Tigerland* (2000), *American Outlaws* (2001), *Hart's War* (2002), *Minority Report* (2002), *Phone Booth* (2002), *The Recruit* (2003), *Daredevil* (2003), *Veronica Guerin* (2003), *S.W.A.T.* (2003), *Intermission* (2003), *A Home at the End of the World* (2004), *Alexander* (2004 - as Alexander the Great), *The New World* (2005), *Ask the Dust* (2006), *Miami Vice* (2006 - as Det. James "Sonny" Crockett), *Pride and Glory* (2008), *Triage* (2009), *Crazy Heart* (2009 – as Tommy Sweet), *The Way Back* (2010), *London Boulevard* (2010), *Horrible Bosses* (2011) and *Fright Night* (2011). Colin won a Golden Globe Award for 'Best Actor – Motion Picture Musical or Comedy' for his portrayal of the novice hitman, Ray, in *In Bruges* (2008) and an Irish Film & Television Award for Best Actor for his role of Syracuse, the Irish fisherman, in *Ondine* (2010). He was cast as (alongside Johnny Depp and Jude Law) the third transformation of Heath Ledger's character, Tony, in *The Imaginarium of Doctor Parnassus* (2009) after the death of the American actor. Colin made a meteoric rise in the film world in a few short years after failing an audition for the Irish group Boyzone and then appearing as Danny Byrne in the BBC television serial *Ballykissangel* in the 1990s. Colin's off-screen antics are as famous as on and in particular his love-life. He was married to English actress Amelia Warner from July to November 2001, and has a son, James Padraig (b. 12 September

2003), with US model Kim Bordenave. In 2005 he was alleged to have propositioned actress Dame Eileen Atkins, who was 70 at the time, for "sex with no strings". In July 2006, he filed a lawsuit against his former girlfriend, Playboy model Nicole Narain and the Internet Commerce Group (ICG) over the unauthorised public distribution of a 14-minute sex tape that he made with Narain in 2003. His most recent partner, since 2009, was Polish actress and singer Alicja Bachleda-Curuś, his *Ondine* co-star. The couple have a son, Henry Tadeusz Farrell (b. 7 October 2009). On 15 October 2010 it was reported that Colin and Alicja had split up. Colin has recently completed filming for his roles as Marty in the black comedy *Seven Psychopaths* and Doug Quaid in the remake of *Total Recall*, both due for 2012 releases.

Fassbender, Michael (1977-) Born 2 April 1977, Heidelberg, Baden-Württemberg, West Germany. Actor born of a Northern Irish mother and German father and brought up in Killarney, County Kerry. Michael first came to prominence as Sergeant Burton "Pat" Christenson in the HBO mini-series, *Band of Brothers*, in 2001. After various television and radio roles he appeared at the 2006 Edinburgh Festival Fringe, playing Michael Collins in *Allegiance*, a play by Mary Kenny based on the meeting between Winston Churchill and Collins, of whom Fassbender's mother is a great-niece. Michael's film debut was as the young Spartan soldier, Stelios, in *300* (2007). Other films include: *Angel* (2007), *Hunger* (2008), *Eden Lake* (2008), *Blood Creek* (2009), *Fish Tank* (2009), *Inglourious Basterds* (2009 - as Lt. Archie Hicox), *Centurion* (2010), *Jonah Hex* (2010), *Jane Eyre* (2011 - as Edward Rochester), *X-Men: First Class* (2011 - as Erik Lensherr / Magneto), *A Dangerous Method* (2011 - as Carl Jung) and the sexually provocative Steve McQueen film, *Shame* (2011). Michael stars in the Steven Soderbergh action thriller *Haywire* (released in early 2012) plus science fiction film, *Prometheus*, directed by Ridley Scott, and scheduled for release in June 2012. Michael is also set to take on the role of Harry Flashman in a film adaptation of the books by George MacDonald Fraser.

Feldman, Marty (1934-82) Born Martin A Feldman, 8 July 1934, Canning Town, London. Actor and comedian. A comedy writer, along with Barry Took he scripted, amongst other shows, *Educating Archie* and *Round the Horne* for radio and *The Army Game* and *Bootsie and Snudge* for television. He suffered from a hyperthyroid condition in 1961 which brought on his "bug-eyed" look. Screen debut: *The Bed-Sitting Room* (1969). After a series of successful television series including *At Last the 1948 Show* (1967-68) and *Marty* (1968) which won the Golden Rose Award at Montreux, and a starring role in his second film *Every Home Should Have One* (1970), he moved to Hollywood. Marty appeared successfully in *Young Frankenstein* (1974), *The Adventure of Sherlock Holmes' Smarter Brother* (1975) and *Silent Movie* (1976), However, his two directorial projects, in which he also starred, *The Last Remake of Beau Geste* (1977) *and In God we Trust* (1980) were not so popularly received, neither was his last completed film *Slapstick of Another Kind* (1982). Marty was married to Lauretta Sullivan (b. 29 September 1935; d. 12 March 2010) from 1959 until his death, of a heart attack on 2 December 1982, in Mexico City, whilst filming *Yellowbeard* (1983). He is buried in Hollywood, California. See also entries in the radio and television section for *The Army Game, At Last The 1948 Show, Bootsie and Snudge, Broaden Your Mind, Educating Archie, The Frost Report, Marty, No - That's Me Over Here!,* and *The Walrus and the Carpenter*.

Fellowes, Julian (1949-) Born Julian Alexander Fellowes, 17 August 1949 Cairo, Egypt. Actor and writer. Julian specialised in playing aristocratic roles on television for several years before making his film debut in *Priest of Love* (1981). Other films include: *Baby: The Secret of the Lost Legend* (1985), *Damage* (1992), *Shadowlands* (1993), *Jane Eyre* (1996), *Savage Hearts* (1997), *Regeneration* (1997), *Tomorrow Never Dies* (1997), *Place Vendôme* (1998) and *Shergar* (1999). He wrote the screenplay for *Gosford Park* (2001) for which he won the Academy Award for Best Original Screenplay. He has also written the screenplay for *Piccadilly Jim* (2004), *Vanity Fair* (2004), *Separate Lies* (2005), for which he made his debut as director, and *Young Victoria*

(2009). Julian also co-wrote the screenplays for *The Tourist* (2010) and *From Time to Time* (2009), which he also directed. He has recently written a new Titanic mini-series (to coincide with the 100th anniversary of the tragedy) that is being produced by ITV1 and is to be aired in April 2012. Julian has also written romantic novels under various pseudonyms, the most famous being Rebecca Greville, however in 2004 he wrote about the social nuances of the upper class under his own name in *Snobs*. On television Julian played Lord Kilwillie in the series *Monarch of the Glen* (2000-05) but is most famous for creating the period drama *Downton Abbey* (2010-). He married Emma Joy Kitchener, LVO (a Lady-in-Waiting to Princess Michael of Kent), the great-great-niece of the 1st Earl Kitchener, in 1990, and subsequently changed his name to Kitchener-Fellowes. They have one son, Peregrine (b. 1991). Julian became Baron Fellowes of West Stafford in the New Years Honours List 2010/11. See also entries in the television section for *Downton Abbey, Monarch of the Glen, Our Friends In The North,* and *University Challenge*.

Felton, Tom (1987-) Born Thomas Andrew Felton, 22 September 1987, Kensington, London. Actor. Made his screen debut as Peagreen Clock in *The Borrowers* (1997) and then played Louis, the son of Anna Leonowens in *Anna and the King* (1999). To date his best known role is as Draco Malfoy in all eight of the *Harry Potter* films. Other films include: *The Disappeared* (2009), *Get Him to the Greek* (2010), *13Hrs* (2010), *Rise of the Planet of the Apes* (2011) and *The Apparition* (2011). A keen fisherman, Tom and his brother Chris started the World Junior Carp Tournament, in New York – described as a competition for anglers aged eleven to eighteen in a family-friendly environment.

Field, Shirley Anne (1938-) Born Shirley Broomfield, 27 June 1938, Bolton, Lancashire. Actress. Shirley was brought up in an orphanage and began modelling as a way out. She made her first film aged, 17 in 1955, as an extra in *Simon and Laura*. As an attractive brunette and former model who had appeared in *Titbits* and *Reveille*, Shirley gained small parts in *Lost* (1956), *The Flesh Is Weak* (1957), *Horrors of the Black Museum* (1959), *Upstairs and Downstairs* (1959), *Man in the Moon* (1960), *Beat Girl* (1960), *Once More, With Feeling!* (1960) and *Peeping Tom* (1960) before being chosen by Laurence Olivier to star opposite him in *The Entertainer* (1960), the same year gaining her best-known role as Doreen, the would-be girlfriend of Arthur Seaton (played by Albert Finney) in *Saturday Night and Sunday Morning*. Shirley's other films include: *The Damned* (1961), *The War Lover* (1962), *Kings of the Sun* (1963), *Doctor in Clover* (1966), *Alfie* (1966), *My Beautiful Laundrette* (1986), *Shag* (1989) and *Hear My Song* (1991). When parts dried up after *Alfie*, she worked mainly in the theatre and television. In recent years Shirley has played more character driven roles in episodes of television series such as *Dalziel and Pascoe, Waking the Dead, Last of the Summer Wine* and *Monarch of the Glen*. Autobiography *A Time for Love* (1991). Shirley made a rare film appearance in *The Kid* (2010 – as Margaret). See also entries in the television section for *Buccaneer, Lady Chatterley,* and *Where the Heart Is*.

Field, Sid (1904-50) Born Sidney Arthur Field, 1 April 1904, Ladywood, Birmingham. Comedian and actor. Bob Hope is said to have remarked that Sid Field was "probably the best comedian of them all". Sid made his stage debut in 1916 as a member of the Kino Juveniles. Sadly for him, he spent over 20 years treading the boards in the provinces before hitting the big time in 1943 with the West End revue *Strike a New Note*. He made just three films: *That's the Ticket* (1940), *London Town* (1946) and *Cardboard Cavalier* (1949). None of these films capture his appeal to a live audience. Catchphrase: "What a performance!" He died 3 February 1950, Richmond, Surrey, the day after appearing as Elwood P Dowd in *Harvey* at the Prince of Wales Theatre, London.

Fielding, Fenella (1927-) Born Fenella Feldman, 17 November 1927, London. Actress. Educated at North London Collegiate School. After early work as a secretary she toyed with the theatre, her first role being in a fringe play *In the Lap of the Gods* (1953). With her remarkable voice (very similar to that of Joan

Greenwood) she was usually cast in aristocratic roles. Her first film was *Follow A Star* (1959) as Lady Finchington. She appeared mostly in comedy films and is probably best remembered for her role as Valeria Watt in *Carry On Screaming!* (1966) and her earlier role of vampish Penny Panting in *Carry On Regardless* (1961). Other films include: *Foxhole in Cairo* (1960), *No Love for Johnnie* (1961), *Doctor in Distress* (1963), *The Old Dark House* (1963), *Doctor in Clover* (1966), *Lock Up Your Daughters* (1969), *The Zany Adventures of Robin Hood* (1984), *Guest House Paradiso* (1999), *The All Together* (2007) and *Radio Mania* (2009). With her distinctive tones Fenella has done quite a bit of voice work providing the voice of the camp loudspeaker in the cult television series *The Prisoner*, the voice of the Blue Queen in *Dougal and the Blue Cat* (1970) and was also an announcer on the "yoof" TV series *The Word*. She also voiced 'MOOD', the quirky supercomputer in the video game Martian Gothic (released in 2000). Trivia-wise it should be noted there are two portraits of her in the National Portrait Gallery (one by Cecil Beaton) and although she is the younger sister of Lord Feldman of Frognal she most certainly is not, as often stated, the sister of Marty Feldman.

Fields, Gracie (1898-1979) Born Grace Stansfield, 9 January 1898, Rochdale, Lancashire. Singer and actress. Gracie started out as a music-hall entertainer as a child. In 1923 she married comedian and impresario Archie Pitt who had been guiding her career for some years prior. Gracie actually made very few films, sixteen in total with twelve of those in the 1930s. Her most famous song, which became her theme, 'Sally,' was worked into the title of her first film, *Sally in Our Alley* (1931). Her other pre-WWII films were: *Looking on the Bright Side* (1932), *This Week of Grace* (1933), *Love, Life and Laughter* (1933), *Sing As We Go* (1934), *Look Up and Laugh* (1935), *Queen of Hearts* (1936), *The Show Goes On* (1937), *We're Going to Be Rich* (1938), *Young and Beautiful* (1938), *Keep Smiling* (1938) and *Shipyard Sally* (1939). In March 1940, Gracie married Italian-born film director Monty Banks, following her divorce from Pitt, and in May they moved to their home in Santa Monica. During these inter war years the indomitable spirit she portrayed resonated with audiences and Gracie became the top box-office draw and the highest-paid actress in Britain for most of the decade. Indeed her popularity was such that Parliament was once adjourned early so that members could go home to listen to one of her radio broadcasts. Gracie remained an English phenomenon and did not take America by storm as she had in the UK. Her next film was a cameo role in *Stage Door Canteen* (1943) followed by two Hollywood films, *Holy Matrimony* (1943) and *Molly and Me* (1945) and her final British film *Paris Underground* (1945). During WWII Gracie travelled to France to entertain the troops in the midst of air-raids, performing on the backs of open lorries and in war-torn areas. She was the first artist to play behind enemy lines in Berlin. Gracie gave up film acting (returning only briefly for a cameo in the 1956 film *Around th' World in Eighty Days*) as she found the process boring. She thrived on a live audience and sang her most famous songs 'Sally', 'Sing As We Go', 'Wish Me Luck As You Wave Me Goodbye', 'The Isle of Capri', 'The Biggest Aspidistra in the World' and 'Walter', Walter, Lead Me to the Altar' at almost every performance. She once quipped that she wanted to "Drown blasted Sally with Walter with the Aspidastra on top!". In 1951, Gracie opened the Festival of Britain celebrations but after that she lived in semi-retirement on the Mediteranean island of Capri with her third husband, Boris Alperovici, a Romanian radio repairman, who she married two years after the death of Monty Banks (he died in 1950 of a heart attack whilst travelling on the Orient Express). Gracie died on Capri, 27 September 1979 from pneumonia, soon after being created Dame Commander of the Order of the British Empire.

Fiennes, Joseph (1970-) Born Joseph Alberic Twisleton-Wykeham Fiennes, 27 May 1970, Salisbury, Wiltshire. Actor. Trained at Guildhall School of Music and Drama. Screen debut: *Stealing Beauty* (1996). Other films include: *Martha, Meet Frank, Daniel and Laurence* (1998), *Elizabeth* (1998), *Shakespeare in Love* (1999 - as William Shakespeare), *Rancid Aluminium* (2000), *Enemy at the Gates* (2001), *Killing Me Softly* (2002), *Luther* (2003), *The Merchant of Venice* (2004), *Man to Man* (2005), *The Great Raid* (2005), *Running with Scissors* (2006), *The Darwin Awards* (2006), *Goodbye Bafana* (2007 aka The Color Of

Freedom), *The Escapist* (2008) and *The Red Baron* (2008). Joseph has recently starred as Mark Benford in the American television drama series *FlashForward* (2009-10) and also as Merlin in the Channel 4 mini-series, *Camelot* (2011). He is the younger brother of Ralph Fiennes, a cousin of Sir Ranulph Fiennes, Bt. and eighth cousin of HRH The Prince of Wales. Joseph married María Dolores Diéguez (b. 1982), a Swiss model of Spanish descent, in August, 2009. Their first child, a daughter, was born on 8 March 2010 and their second daughter, Isabel, was born on 29 December 2011.

Fiennes, Ralph (1962-) Born Ralph Nathaniel Twisleton-Wykeham Fiennes, 22 December 1962, Ipswich, Suffolk. Actor. He is the son of novelist Jennifer Lash and photographer Mark Fiennes, and the elder brother of Joseph Fiennes. Educated at RADA after dropping out of Chelsea College of Art and Design. Made his stage debut in 1986 and joined the Royal Shakespeare Company in 1989. Screen debut: *Wuthering Heights* (1992 - as Heathcliff). Other films include: *The Baby of Macon* (1993), *Quiz Show* (1994), *Oscar and Lucinda* (1997), *The Avengers* (1998 - as John Steed), *Onegin* (1999), *Spider* (2002), *Red Dragon* (2002), *Maid in Manhattan* (2002), *Chromophobia* (2005), *Harry Potter and the Goblet of Fire* (2005 - as Lord Voldemort), *The Constant Gardener* (2005), *The White Countess* (2006), *Harry Potter and the Order of the Phoenix* (2007), *Bernard and Doris* (2007), *In Bruges* (2008), *The Duchess* (2008), *The Reader* (2008), *The Hurt Locker* (2009), *Cemetery Junction* (2010), *Clash of the Titans* (2010 - as Hades), *Nanny McPhee and the Big Bang* (2010), *Harry Potter and the Deathly Hallows: Part 1* (2010) and *Harry Potter and the Deathly Hallows: Part II* (2011) in which he reprises his role of the evil Lord Voldemort for the fourth time. In 2011, Ralph made his directorial debut with his film adaptation of Shakespeare's tragedy *Coriolanus*, in which he also played the title character. Nominated for Academy Awards for Best Actor for *The English Patient* (1996) and Best Supporting Actor for his role as the sadistic Nazi Amon Goeth in *Schindler's List* (1993). He was married to actress Alex Kingston (1993-97) and was the long-term partner of Francesca Annis, whom he met in 1995 when she played Gertrude to his Hamlet. The couple announced a split in early 2006. In February 2007, 38-year-old flight attendant Lisa Robertson confessed to having sex in the lavatory with Fiennes during a Qantas flight from Sydney, Australia, to Mumbai, India. Ralph was en route to Mumbai, as a participant in AIDS awareness efforts for UNICEF. Although the organisation retained Fiennes as an ambassador; Qantas fired Robertson!

Figgis, Mike (1948-) Born Michael Lawrence Dundus Figgis, 28 February 1948, Carlisle, Cumbria. Director, writer and composer. Spent his childhood in Kenya before his family moved to Newcastle when he was eight. He played in the same band (*Gas Board*) as Brian Ferry when a teenager and later joined a performance art group *People Show*. Mike next formed his own theatre group, the *Mike Figgis Group*, in 1980. Channel 4 financed his first film *The House* (1984). He followed this with *Stormy Monday* (1988), the corrupt cop story *Internal Affairs* (1990), the dark thriller *Liebestraum* (1991), which starred Kim Novac, *Mr Jones* (1993) and *The Browning Version* (1993). His next project *Leaving Las Vegas* (1995) earned him Academy Award nominations for Best Director and Best Adapted Screenplay. His later films include: *The Loss of Sexual Innocence* (1999), *Cold Creek Manor* (2003), *Co/Ma* (2004) and *Love Live Long* (2008), an experimental film centred around the Gumball 3000 rally - starring Sophie Winkleman (b. 5 August 1980, the half-sister to Claudia Winkleman). Mike also writes and composes the scores for most of his films. He increasingly uses experimental techniques in his films, as in *Timecode* (2000), which features a screen split into quarters with a different but connected narrative being seen in each part. A similar effect was used in Mike's contribution to the 2002 film, *Ten Minutes Older*, a project consisting of two compilation feature films entitled *The Trumpet* and *The Cello*. Mike was the founding patron of the independent filmmakers online community Shooting People. He is cousin to Irish filmmakers Jonathan Figgis and Jason Figgis who run the film production company October Eleven Pictures in Ireland. His sons Arlen Figgis and Louis Figgis have also followed their father in to the film industry, as editor and producer respectively. Mike is currently professor of film studies at the

European Graduate School in Saas-Fee, Switzerland. See also entry for Saffron Burrows.

Finch, Peter (1916-77) Born Peter George Frederick Ingle Finch, 28 September 1916, South Kensington, London. Actor. Son of Professor George Ingle-Finch. Peter was brought up in France, India and Australia, working in a variety of jobs. Stage debut: *While Parents Sleep* (1935). Screen debut: *The Magic Shoes* (1935). Made a few films in Australia before moving to the UK in 1949 with his mentor Laurence Olivier. Became a regular screen leading man in such films as: *Eureka Stockade* (1949), *The Wooden Horse* (1950), *The Heart of the Matter* (1953), *Elephant Walk* (1954), *Father Brown* (1954), *A Town Like Alice* (1956), *The Battle of the River Plate* (1956), *The Nun's Story* (1959), *The Trials of Oscar Wilde* (1960), *No Love for Johnnie* (1961), *Far From the Madding Crowd* (1967), *A Bequest to the Nation* (1973) and *The Abdication* (1974). He was nominated for a Best Actor Academy Award for *Sunday, Bloody, Sunday* (1971) and won the award posthumously for his role as disillusioned television anchorman Howard Beale in the film *Network* (1976). Infamous as a hard-drinking hell-raiser, Peter married three times; first to Russian ballerina Tamara Rechemcinc (aka Tamara Tchinarova), secondly to South African actress Yolande Eileen Turnbull, and thirdly to Mavis "Eletha" Barrett. He also had relationships with actresses Kay Kendall, Vivien Leigh and Mai Zetterling, as well as singer Dame Shirley Bassey. Peter died from a heart attack, 14 January 1977, Beverly Hills, California.

Finlay, Frank (1926-) Born Francis Finlay, 6 August 1926, Farnworth, Lancashire. Actor. Graduated from RADA. Screen debut: *Private Potter* (1962). *Other films include: The Longest Day* (1962), *A Study in Terror* (1965), *Inspector Clouseau* (1968), *The Molly Maguires* (1970), *Cromwell* (1970), *Sitting Target* (1972), *The Three Musketeers* (1973), *The Four Musketeers* (1974), *The Wild Geese* (1978), *Murder by Decree* (1979), *The Ploughman's Lunch* (1983), *The Return of the Musketeers* (1989), *Gospa* (1995), *Dreaming of Joseph Lees* (1999), *The Ghosthunter* (2000), *The Pianist* (2002), *The Statement* (2003), *Lighthouse Hill* (2004) and *The Waiting Room* (2007). Nominated for an Academy Award as Best Supporting Actor for *Othello* (1965). Appointed a CBE in 1984. Frank has recently been starring as Alex Combe in the American mini-series *The Four Seasons*. See also entries in the television section for *Bouquet of Barbed Wire, Casanova*, *Common as Muck, How Do you Want Me, Life Begins, Merlin, Prime Suspect* and *The Sins*.

Finlayson, James (1887-1953) Born James Henderson Finlayson, 27 August 1887, Larbert, Falkirk, Stirling. Actor. The son of a blacksmith. Studied engineering at Edinburgh University. Screen debut: *The Foolish Age* (1919). Travelled to the United States in 1911. He joined the *Roach Studios* in 1923. Although he made over 200 films his career will for ever be defined by the films he made with Laurel and Hardy, including: *Liberty* (1929), *Night Owls* (1930), *Another Fine Mess* (1930), *Pardon Us* (1931), *Pack Up Your Troubles* (1932), *Bonnie Scotland* (1935), *The Bohemian Girl* (1935), *Our Relations* (1936), *Way Out West* (1937), *Blockheads* (1938), *The Flying Deuces* (1939), *A Chump at Oxford* (1940*)* and *Saps at Sea* (1940). Noted for his bald head and large (false) moustache. Died 9 October 1953, Los Angeles, California.

Finney, Albert (1936-) Born 9 May 1936, Salford, Lancashire. Actor. Graduated from RADA. Screen debut: *The Entertainer* (1960). Other films include: *Saturday Night and Sunday Morning* (1960), *Charlie Bubbles* (1967), *Scrooge* (1970), *Gumshoe* (1971), *The Duellists* (1977), *Shoot the Moon* (1982), *Annie* (1982), *Miller's Crossing* (1990), *The Browning Version* (1994), *Washington Square* (1997), *Traffic* (2000), *Big Fish* (2003), *Ocean's Twelve* (2004), *A Good Year* (2006), *Amazing Grace* (2006), The Bourne Ultimatum (2007) and *Before the Devil Knows You're Dead* (2007). Received Academy Award nominations for Best Actor for *Tom Jones* (1963), *Murder on the Orient Express* (1974), *The Dresser* (1983) and *Under the Volcano* (1984). Received Academy Award nominations for Best Supporting Actor for *Erin Brockovich* (2000). Albert starred in Dennis Potter's final plays: *Karaoke* (1996) and *Cold Lazarus*

(1996). He also played Winston Churchill in the TV film *The Gathering Storm* (2002). Called "a second Olivier" during his early career, he was married to British actress Jane Wenham (b. 26 November 1927, Southampton) between 1957 and 1961, and French actress Anouk Aimée (b. 27 April 1932, Paris) between 1970 and 1978. He has been married to Pene Delmage since 2006. Albert reportedly has declined both a CBE and a Knighthood.

Firth, Colin (1960-) Born Colin Andrew Firth, 10 September 1960, Grayshott, Hampshire. Actor. Spent his early childhood in Nigeria. Trained at the London Drama Centre. Stage debut: *Another Country* (1983 – as Guy Bennett). Screen debut: *Another Country* (1984 – as Tommy Judd, opposite Rupert Everett as Bennett). Other films include: *A Month in the Country* (1987), *Valmont* (1989), *The Hour of the Pig* (1993), *Circle of Friends* (1995), *The English Patient* (1996), *Fever Pitch* (1997), *Shakespeare in Love* (1998), *Bridget Jones's Diary* (2001), *Londinium* (2001), *The Importance of Being Earnest* (2002), *Girl with a Pearl Earring* (2003), *Love Actually* (2003), *Bridget Jones: The Edge of Reason* (2004), *Where the Truth Lies* (2005), *The Last Legion* (2007), *And When Did You Last See Your Father?* (2007), *Then She Found Me* (2007), *St. Trinian's* (2007 - as Geoffrey Thwaites), *The Accidental Husband* (2008), *Mamma Mia!* (2008 - as Harry Bright), *Easy Virtue* (2008), *Genova* (2008), *A Christmas Carol* (2009), *Dorian Gray* (2009), *St. Trinian's II: The Legend of Fritton's Gold* (2009) and *Main Street* (2010). Colin won a BAFTA Award for Best Actor in a Leading Role for his performance as middle-aged English college professor George Falconer in *A Single Man* (2009), and was also nominated for an Academy Award for Best Actor for this role. He went one better for his outstanding performance as King George VI in *The King's Speech* (2010), winning the BAFTA, Oscar and the Golden Globe Award for Best Actor - Motion Picture Drama and the 2010 Screen Actors Guild Award for Outstanding Performance by a Male Actor in a Leading Role. *The King's Speech* also won Oscars for Best Picture, Director, and Original Screenplay. Colin's latest role is as Bill Hayden ('Tailor') in *Tinker Tailor Soldier Spy* (2011). On television he received rave notices for his portrayal of Mr Darcy in *Pride and Prejudice* (1995) which kick-started his film career. Colin's partner between 1989 and 1994 was American actress Meg Tilly (b. 14 February 1960). They have a son, William Joseph Firth. Since 1997 he has been married to Italian film producer Livia Giuggioli (b. 1969). They have two sons, Luca (b. 2001) and Matteo (b. 2003). Colin's first published work, "The Department of Nothing", appeared in *Speaking with the Angel* (2000), a collection of short stories edited by Nick Hornby.

Firth, Peter (1953-) Born 27 October 1953, Bradford, Yorkshire. Actor. Screen debut: *Brother Sun, Sister Moon* (1972). Other films include: *King Arthur, the Young Warlord* (1975), *Aces High* (1976), *Joseph Andrews* (1977), *Tess* (1979), *White Elephant* (1983), *Letter to Brezhnev* (1985), *Trouble in Paradise* (1989), *The Hunt for Red October* (1990), *Shadowlands* (1993), *An Awfully Big Adventure* (1995), *Amistad* (1997), *Chill Factor* (1999), *Pearl Harbor* (2001) and *The Greatest Game Ever Played* (2005). His big break came when playing a horse-obsessed teenager in the stage production of *Equus* (1973). He repeated the performance in the film version of *Equus* (1977) and earned an Academy Award nomination for Best Supporting Actor. In recent years Peter has concentrated more on television work and played senior MI5 officer Harry Pearce in the BBC's popular spy drama series *Spooks* (2002-11), and Fred Hoyle in *Hawking* (2004), a BBC dramatisation of the early career of Stephen Hawking. See also entries in the television section for *The Broker's Man, The Flaxton Boys* and *Here Come the Double Deckers* and *Spooks*.

Fisher, Terence (1904-80) Born Terence Roland Fisher, 23 February 1904, Maida Vale, London. Director. After a short stint in the merchant marine he eventually started work in the film industry in 1933 as a clapper boy. He joined *Rank* films as a film editor and then as a director, making his debut with: *Colonel Bogey* (1948). Early films include: *To the Public Danger* (1948), *The Astonished Heart* (1949), *So Long at the Fair* (1949) and *Kill* *me Tomorrow* (1957). In 1957 he directed *The Curse of Frankenstein* for Hammer Films, which proved incredibly popular and led him to be commissioned by Hammer to direct a string of follow ups including: *Dracula* (1958), *The Revenge of Frankenstein* (1958), *The Mummy* (1959), *The Brides of Dracula* (1960), *The Two Faces of Dr Jekyll* (1960), *The Curse of the Werewolf* (1961), *The Phantom of the Opera* (1962), *Dracula: Prince of Darkness* (1966), *Frankenstein Created Woman* (1967), *Frankenstein Must be Destroyed* (1969) and *Frankenstein and the Monster from Hell* (1974). These lurid films usually featured Peter Cushing and Christopher Lee and were often a not-so-subtle mix of sex and violence. A non-Hammer film he directed, *The Devil Rides Out* (1968) also stands out as a classic of the horror genre. During the 1970s Fisher became increasingly unreliable because of alcohol-related problems and he died 18 June 1980, Twickenham, London.

Fitzgerald, Barry (1888-1961) Born William Joseph Shields, 10 March 1888, Dublin. Actor. Worked as a civil servant before he joined the Abbey Theatre Dublin full-time in 1929. Screen debut: *Juno and the Paycock* (1930), directed by Alfred Hitchcock. He travelled to the United States to reprise on screen his stage success as Fluther in *The Plough and the Stars* (1936), directed by John Ford. Barry stayed in the USA and worked with success in films such as: *Bringing Up Baby* (1938), *How Green Was My Valley* (1941), *The Sea Wolf* (1941), *Tarzan's Secret Treasure* (1941), *The Amazing Mrs Holliday* (1943), *None but the Lonely Heart* (1944), *Incendiary Blonde* (1945), *And Then There Were None* (1945), *Two Years before the Mast* (1946), *The Naked City* (1948) and *The Story of Seabiscuit* (1949). Despite being a protestant he won an Academy Award for Best Supporting Actor for his role as Roman Catholic Father Fitzgibbon in *Going My Way* (1944) and was uniquely nominated as Best Actor for the same role. He apparently broke the head off his Academy Award whilst practicing his golf swing. Barry's final feature film was *Broth of a Boy* (1959 - as Patrick Farrell). His brother Arthur Shields (b. 15 February 1896; d. 27 April 1970) was also an actor and appeared with him in many films including, *The Plough and the Stars (1936), The Long Voyage Home* (1940), and *The Quiet Man (1952)*. Returning to Ireland in 1959, he died 14 January 1961, Dublin.

Fitzgerald, Geraldine (1914-2005) Born 24 November 1914, Greystones, County Wicklow, just south of Dublin. Actress. Geraldine made her theatrical debut at the Gate Theatre aged 18. Her first film was *Open All Night* (1934). She continued in English films such as *The Mill on the Floss* (1937), before moving to New York in 1937. Her Broadway debut in 1938 was in the Mercury Theatre production *Heartbreak House* with fellow former Gate Theatre performer, Orson Welles. Geraldine received a Best Supporting Actress Academy Award nomination for her first American film role, that of Isabella, wife to Olivier's Heathcliff, in *Wuthering Heights* (1939), losing out to Hattie McDaniel (*Gone with the Wind*) in one of the Academy's most competitive years. Geraldine had roles in some other quality films of the time such as *Dark Victory* (1939), *Watch on the Rhine* (1943) and *Wilson* (1944) but she lost the role of Brigid O'Shaughnessy, the villainess of *The Maltese Falcon* (1941) due to disagreements with Jack Warner, the part eventually going to Mary Astor. In fact, Geraldine was later suspended by Warner Bros for refusing to take roles she felt unsuitable. About this time her first marriage, to Edward Lindsay-Hogg, 4th Bt ended and she married Stuart Scheftel, this lasting nearly 50 years until his death in 1994. During WWII she became an American citizen. After the war she returned to Britain to film *So Evil My Love* (1948) and received critical acclaim for her performance as an alcoholic adultress. In 1951 she appeared in *The Late Edwina Black* and then returned to America. By now Geraldine had matured into a fine character actress, appearing in a wide variety of quality movies, including *Ten North Frederick* (1958), *The Pawnbroker* (1965), *Rachel, Rachel* (1968) and *Harry and Tonto* (1974). Her other films include *The Mango Tree* (1977), *Arthur* (1981), *Poltergeist II: The Other Side* (1986) and *Arthur 2: On the Rocks* 1988). Geraldine also received a Tony Award nomination for *Mass Appeal,* a play about Catholic priests. Away from the screen she was a successful cabaret singer and also received the Handel Medallion, New York City's highest cultural award, for her civic

work, particularly with her street theatre company. Her last film was *Bump in the Night* (1991). Geraldine was the mother of director Michael Lindsay-Hogg (b. 5 May 1940), who helmed the *Beatles'* documentary film *Let It Be* and also several episodes of *Brideshead Revisited*. She was also the great-aunt of Tara Fitzgerald, and cousin of the novelist Nevil Shute. Geraldine died 17 July 2005, in New York City from complications of Alzheimer's Disease.

Fitzgerald, Tara (1967-) Born Tara Anne Cassandra Callaby-Fitzgerald, 18 September 1967, Cuckfield, Sussex. Actress. Grand-niece of actress Geraldine Fitzgerald. Her first film was as Nancy Doyle in Peter Chelsom's quirky *Hear My Song* (1991) and this role of a fun-loving sexually adventurous young woman became her trademark and was further established in Channel 4's 1992 television adaptation of *The Camomile Lawn* (1992) where she played the part of young Polly. Following her film debut Tara starred opposite Hugh Grant in *Sirens* (1993) and *The Englishman Who Went Up a Hill But Came Down a Mountain* (1995) and in between these films played Adele Rice in the Irish film *A Man of No Importance* (1994). Other films include: *Brassed Off* (1996), *Conquest* (1998), *Rancid Aluminium* (2000) and *Dark Blue World* (2001). Tara then moved into her "mother" period of her film career, playing matriarchs in such films as *I Capture the Castle* (2003), *Five Children and It* (2004) and *In a Dark Place* (2006). Tara is also an excellent stage and television actress. In 1995 she played Ophelia opposite Ralph Fiennes in Hamlet and in 2004 she completed a very successful tour of the UK playing the role of Nora Helmer in *A Doll's House*. On television her most enduring role was as forensic pathologist Dr Eve Lockhart in the BBC series *Waking The Dead* (2007-11). Tara was married to American actor-director John Sharian between 2001 and 2003 but her present partner is actor Richard Clothier.

Fleetwood, Susan (1944-95) Born Susan Maureen Fleetwood, 21 September 1944, St Andrews, Fife. Actress. Sister of Mick Fleetwood, of the rock group *Fleetwood Mac*. Trained at RADA. Susan made her film debut in *Hamlet* (1970) as Ophelia and later appeared in such films as *Clash of the Titans* (1981 - as Athena), *Heat and Dust* (1983), *White Mischief* (1987) and *The Krays* (1990). Susan also starred in the television series *The Buddha of Suburbia* (1993). She died after completing *Persuasion* (1995) on 29 September 1995, Salisbury, Wiltshire, of ovarian cancer. Her partner at the time of her death was theatre director Sebastian Graham-Jones.

Fleming, Lucy (1947-) Born Eve Lucinda Fleming, 15 May 1947 Nettlebed, Oxfordshire. Actress. Lucy is the daughter of Dame Celia Johnson and Peter Fleming (brother of *James Bond* novelist Ian Fleming). Mainly a television actress she has played Lydia Bennet in the 1967 version of *Pride and Prejudice* and Helen Wycliffe in *Wycliffe*. Her film debut was as the uncredited 'wide eyes' in the 1966 film *Rasputin: The Mad Monk*. Her next film credit was as Mrs Roberts in *The Boat That Rocked* (2009), a period comedy about an illegal radio station in the North Sea in the 1960s. Recent films include: the horror movie *Out of the Night* (2009) starring alongside her husband, and *Emulsion* (2011). Lucy married Joe Laycock in 1971, and the couple produced two sons and a daughter, Flora. Tragically, Joe and Flora were both drowned in a boating accident on the Thames in 1980. Lucy married actor Simon Williams in 1986. See also entry in the television section for *Survivors*.

Fletcher, Dexter (1966-) Born 31 January 1966, Enfield, London. Actor. Trained at the Anna Scher Theatre drama club. Screen debut: *Bugsy Malone* (1976 - as Babyface). Other films include: *The Long Good Friday* (1980), *The Elephant Man* (1980), *Revolution* (1985), *Caravaggio* (1986), *The Rachel Papers* (1989), *Jude* (1996), *The Man Who Knew Too Little* (1997), *Lock, Stock and Two Smoking Barrels* (1998), *Topsy-Turvy* (1999), *Below* (2002), *Layer Cake* (2004), *Doom* (2005), *Tristan & Isolde* (2006), *Stardust* (2007), *Kick-Ass* (2010), *Hong Kong Confidential* (2010 aka as *Amaya* in Latvia) and *Jack Falls* (2011). A child actor who has made a successful transition to adult roles, Dexter has appeared in the HBO drama, *Band of Brothers* and also in the BBC1 series *Hotel Babylon* (2006-09) and the BBC3 sitcom *White Van Man* (2011). Dexter had relationships with Julia Sawalha (see entry in radio and television section for *Press Gang* in which they both starred) and actress

Liza Walker (b. 7 July 1972) but eventually married Lithuanian director and playwright Dalia Ibelhauptaite in Westminster, London, in 1997.

Fontanne, Lynn (1887 -1983) Born Lillie Louise Fontanne, 6 December 1887, Woodford, Essex. Actress. Lynn became famous as an acting pair with her husband, Alfred Lunt (1892-1977), whom she married in 1922. The two were more famous for their stage performances than for their film roles. So inseperable were they that they both received a Special Tony Award in 1970 and nearly 30 years later appeared on a 33 cent US stamp. Lynn only made three films *The Second Youth* (1924), *The Man Who Found Himself* (1925) and *The Guardsman* (1931), for which she was nominated for the Academy Award for Best Actress, and one film for television *Peter Pan* (1960). Ironically Lynn lost out to her life-long friend Helen Hayes at the 1933 Oscar ceremony. Helen had fallen in love with Alfred Lunt while they were working together in 1920 but on that occasion Lynn won the heart of Alfred. Lynn died on 30 July 1983, Genesee Depot, Wisconsin, of pneumonia and is interred next to her husband Alfred in Forest Home Cemetery in West Milwaukee, Wisconsin.

Forbes, Bryan (1926-) Born John Theobald Clarke, 22 July 1926, Stratford, London. Actor and director. Stage debut: *The Gathering Storm* (1948). Screen debut: *The Small Back Room* (1949). Other films as an actor include: *The Wooden Horse* (1950), *Green Grow the Rushes* (1951), *The Million Pound Note* (1953), *An Inspector Calls* (1954), *The Colditz Story* (1955), *I was Monty's Double* (1958), *The League of Gentlemen* (1959), *The Angry Silence* (1960), *The Guns of Navarone* (1961), *A Shot in the Dark* (1964), *Of Human Bondage* (1964), *International Velvet* (1978) and *Restless Natives* (1985). A stalwart supporting actor in some of the best British films of the 1950s he turned his hand very successfully to writing and directing. Credits as both screenwriter and director include: *The L-Shaped Room* (1962), *Seance on a Wet Afternoon* (1964), *King Rat* (1965), *The Whisperers* (1967), *The Raging Moon* (1971) and *The Naked Face* (1984). As a director his debut was *Whistle Down the Wind* (1961) and he went on to direct *The Wrong Box* (1966), *The Madwoman of Chaillot* (1969) and *The Stepford Wives* (1975). He also wrote the screenplays for: *The Cockleshell Heroes* (1955), *The League of Gentlemen* (1959), *Man in the Moon* (1960), T*he Angry Silence* (1960), *Only Two Can Play* (1962), *Station Six Sahara* (1962), *International Velvet* (1978) and *Chaplin* (1992). Bryan formed *Beaver Films* production company with Richard Attenborough in 1959 and was head of production and managing director of *Associated British Films* (EMI) at Elstree (1969-71). He was made a CBE in 2004 for his services to the arts. Bryan married Constance Smith in 1951 and following their divorce married actress Nanette Newman in 1955. The couple have two daughters, television presenter Emma Forbes (b. 14 May 1965) and Sarah Standing (b. 21 May 1959), the wife of actor John Standing. Autobiographies: *Notes for a Life* (1974) and *A Divided Life* (1992). Bryan was diagnosed with multiple sclerosis in 1975.

Formby, George (1904-61) Born George Hoy Booth, 26 May 1904 Wigan, Lancashire. Actor. Son of a music hall comedian George Formby Snr (b. 1875 aka James Booth), known as the 'Wigan Nightingale'. George tried to become a jockey but outgrew the possibility. He took up his father's act after his death in 1921. Stage debut: Hippodrome, Earlstown (1921). Originally called himself George Hoy (his mother's maiden name) and initially struggled. First worked as George Formby Jr in 1924 and took up the banjo ukelele (banjulele) in 1925 after which his music hall career took off under the management of his wife Beryl (nee Ingham), a dancer he had married the year before. His best-known songs were "Leaning on a Lamp Post", written by Noel Gay and "When I'm Cleaning Windows". Screen debut: *By the Shortest of Heads* (1915) whilst still a stable boy. Films included: *Boots! Boots!* (1934 - his first sound film), *Feather Your Nest* (1937), *Trouble Brewing* (1939), *Let George Do It* (1940), *Turned Out Nice Again* (1941), which was George's catchphrase, and *Bell-Bottom George* (1943). George was as famous in Russia as Norman Wisdom was to become, over a decade later, with the long-suffering proletarians of Albania. George remains the only

British person to be awarded the Order of Lenin, which was conferred on him in 1943. He was also awarded the OBE in 1946 for services to the armed forces during WWII. George died 6 March 1961, Preston, Lancashire, whilst preparing to marry Pat Howson, to whom he had become engaged just a few weeks after Beryl's death on 24 December 1960. He was buried in the family plot in Warrington Cemetery, and an estimated 100,000 lined the route of his funeral procession.

Forsyth, Bill (1946-) Born William David Forsyth, 29 July 1946, Glasgow. Director. Made experimental documentaries before ultimately becoming a successful writer and director. Directorial/writing debut: *That Sinking Feeling* (1980). Bill made a breakthrough with the enchanting *Gregory's Girl* (1981) and went on to write and direct the critically and popularly well received *Local Hero* (1983). Later films include: *Comfort and Joy* (1984), *Housekeeping* (1987), *Breaking In* (1989), *Being Human* (1993) and *Gregory's Two Girls* (1999). His films are generally characterised by being small-scale and low-key.

Foster, Julia (1943-) Born 2 August 1943, Lewes, Sussex. Actress. Julia made her first screen appearance on the popular soap *Emergency Ward 10* in 1960. Her film debut was as a fresh-faced teenager in *The Loneliness of the Long Distance Runner* (1962) and she became somewhat typecast with "peaches and cream" roles. Julia appeared in *The System* (1964), *Alfie* (1966), *Half a Sixpence* (1967), and on television in the series *Wilde Alliance* (1978), always playing the delicate girl next door. Her other films include *Percy* (1971), *The Great McGonagall* (1974) and the title role in the 1975 TV film, *Moll Flanders*. Julia also starred in *Je t'aime John Wayne* (2000) a film short with Kris Marshall taking on the Jean-Paul Belmondo role in Godard's classic *A Bout de Souffle*. Julia's first husband was Lionel Morton, leader of the 1960's pop group *The Four Pennies* and her second Bruce Fogle, a celebrity veterinarian. She currently runs an antique shop specialising in 18th and 19th century Swedish furniture. Julia is the mother of BBC "Castaway" Ben Fogle (b. 3 November 1973) who is now a television presenter and who, along with Olympian James Cracknell, won their class in the pairs division of the Atlantic Rowing Race 2005-06. Julia made a rare film appearance in the 2008 camp horror movie, *Flick*, co-starring Faye Dunaway.

Fowler, Harry (1926-2012) Born 10 December 1926, Lambeth, London. Actor. Harry's working life began as a newsboy. His screen debut was in *Those Kids from Town* (1942) released a few weeks before Went the Day Well? (1942). Harry also appeared in *Salute John Citizen* (1942), but was uncredited for his role as an office boy. His early career saw him playing juvenile leads (usually cockney), most memorably in *Hue and Cry* (1947). Other films include: *Now Barabbas was a Robber* (1949), *The Pickwick Papers* (1952 - as Sam Weller), *Lucky Jim* (1957), *I Was Monty's Double* (1958), *Idol on Parade* (1959), *The Longest Day* (1962), *Lawrence of Arabia* (1962), *Crooks Anonymous* (1962), *Life at the Top* (1965), *Sir Henry at Rawlinson End* (1980) and *Chicago Joe and the Showgirl* (1990). Harry achieved national acclaim in his role of Corporal "Flogger" Hoskins in the television sitcom *The Army Game* (1959-1961). He was awarded the MBE in 1970. Harry died 4 January 2012. See also entries in the television section for *The Army Game, Our Man At St Mark's, Spooner's Patch, Tales From Dickens,* and *World's End.*

Fox, Edward (1937-) Born Edward Charles Morrice Fox, 13 April 1937, Chelsea, London. Actor. As with his brother Edward was educated at Harrow and served in the Coldsteam Guards. Trained at RADA. Screen debut: as an extra in *The Loneliness of the Long Distance Runner* (1962) followed by another non-speaking role as a waiter in *This Sporting Life* (1963). Other films include: *The Mind Benders* (1963), *Life at the Top* (1965), *The Naked Runner* (1967), *Oh! What a Lovely War* (1969), *Battle of Britain* (1969), *The Go Between* (1970), *The Day of the Jackal* (1973), *A Doll's House* (1973), *Galileo* (1975), *A Bridge Too Far* (1977 – as Lt General Horrocks), for which he won the Best Supporting Actor award at the British Academy Film Awards. *The Duellists* (1977), *The Big Sleep* (1978), *Force 10 from Navarone* (1978), *The Cat and the Canary* (1979), *The Mirror Crack'd*

(1980), *Gandhi* (1982), *Never Say Never Again* (1983 - as 'M'), *The Shooting Party* (1985), *Shaka Zulu* (1986), *Return from the River Kwai* (1989), *Robin Hood* (1991), *Sherwood's Travels* (1994), *A Feast at Midnight* (1994), *Prince Valiant* (1997), *Lost in Space* (1998), *The Importance of Being Earnest* (2002), *Nicholas Nickleby* (2002), *Stage Beauty* (2004) *Lassie* (2005) and *Oliver Twist* (2007). Probably more typecast as the haughty aristocrat than his brother although proved his versatility as the malign criminal mastermind in *The Day of the Jackal*. Edward has recently appeared in *Marple: The Secret of Chimneys* (2010), as Lord Caterham. He has been married twice: to Tracy Reed (1958–1961) and Joanna David (2004–present). Edward was awarded the OBE in 2002. See also entries for James Fox and Emilia Fox and entries in the television section for *Churchill's People, Edward and Mrs Simpson*, and *The Good Guys*.

Fox, Emilia (1974-) Born Emilia Lydia Rose Fox, 31 July 1974, London. Actress. Emilia (she is known as 'Millie' to her friends) comes from a theatrical family. Her father is Edward Fox and her mother Joanna David. Her cousin Lawrence and uncle James are also actors. In her early twenties Emilia came to be known mostly in TV mini-series/costume dramas. Her first outing was as Georgiana Darcy in Simon Langton's *Pride and Prejudice* (1995). In this she starred with her mother, Colin Firth and Jennifer Ehle. Nowadays she is probably best known for her role as forensic pathologist Dr. Nikki Alexander in BBC crime drama *Silent Witness*, having joined the cast in 2004 following the departure of Amanda Burton. Other mini-series she has starred in include *Rebecca* (1997), *The Scarlet Pimpernel* (1999), *David Copperfield* (1999), *Henry VIII* (2003), *Gunpowder, Treason & Plot* (2004), *The Virgin Queen* (2005), *Fallen Angel* (2007), *Merlin* (2009-11) and *Upstairs Downstairs* (2012). Emilia was cast as Lynne Frederick in the 2004 film *The Life and Death of Peter Sellers* but her scenes were cut. She has made few feature films, the first being *The Pianist* (2002 – as Dorota). Other films include *The Republic of Love* (2003), *Things To Do Before You're 30* (2004), *Keeping Mum* (2005), Cashback (2006), *Flashbacks of a Fool* (2008), *Dorian Gray* (2009) and *Ways to Live Forever* (2010). Romantically linked at various times to Orlando Bloom and British artist and designer Toby Mott (b. 12 January 1964), Emily was engaged to comedian Vic Reeves for a short time at the turn of the new millennium. In July 2005, she married British actor Jared Harris (born 24 August 1961), the son of the Irish actor Richard Harris. Following their divorce in June 2010 she was in a relationship with actor Jeremy Gilley (b. 1969), and their first child, a daughter, Rose, was born in November 2010. The couple split up in 2011. See also entries in the television section for *David Copperfield, Randall and Hopkirk (Deceased)*, and *Silent Witness*.

Fox, James (1939-) Born William F Fox, 19 May 1939, Chelsea, London. Actor. Trained at the Central School of Speech and Drama. Billed as William Fox whilst a child actor, he then changed his name to avoid confusion with another actor. Educated at Harrow, James served in the Coldsteam Guards. Screen debut: *The Miniver Story* (1950). Other films include: *The Loneliness of the Long Distance Runner* (1962), *The Servant* (1963), *King Rat* (1965), *Those Magnificent Men in Their Flying Machines* (1965), *Thoroughly Modern Millie* (1967), *Isadora* (1968), *Greystoke: The Legend of Tarzan, Lord of the Apes* (1984), *A Passage to India* (1984), *Absolute Beginners* (1986), *The Russia House* (1990), *Patriot Games* (1992), *The Remains of the Day* (1993), *Anna Karenina* (1997), *Mickey Blue Eyes* (1999), *Sexy Beast* (2000), *The Prince & Me* (2004) *Charlie and the Chocolate Factory* (2005), *Suez: A Very British Crisis* (2006 - as Anthony Eden), *Mister Lonely* (2007 - as The Pope) and *Sherlock Holmes* (2009). His most recent roles have been as King George V in the Madonna-directed film *W.E.* (2011 – a film also starring Laurence Fox as Bertie) and alongside Sean Bean in the terrorist thriller *Cleanskin* (2012). In the 1960s, James had a relationship with actress Sarah Miles and began to lead a very unconventional lifestyle, including experimentation with psychedelic drugs. After starring in *Performance* (1970) he took a break from acting throughout the rest of the 1970s in order to sort his life out. This he did successfully and he went on to carry out evangelical Christian work; the only film in which he appeared during this time was *No Longer Alone* (1978), the story of a suicidal woman

saved by Christianity. James is part of a theatrical dynasty; he is the brother of actor Edward Fox and film producer Robert Fox; the actress Emilia Fox is his niece and the actor Laurence Fox (b. 1978), best known for his role of Detective Sergeant James Hathaway in the television drama series *Lewis*, is his son. The playwright Frederick Lonsdale was his grandfather. James appeared opposite Laurence in an episode of *Lewis*. James married Mary Elizabeth Piper in 1973 and the couple have four other children in addition to Laurence; three boys and a girl, Lydia. Both Laurence and Lydia were married to fellow actors in 2007, making James the father-in-law of both Billie Piper and Richard Ayoade. He is also the grandfather of Winston James Fox, by Laurence and Billie. Autobiography: *Comeback: An Actor's Direction* (1983). See also entries in the television section for *Harley Street*, and *Parent-Craft*.

Fox, Laurence (1978-) See entry for James Fox and for *Lewis* in the television section.

Francis, Freddie (1917-2007) Born Frederick W Francis, 22 December 1917, Islington, London. Director and cinematographer. Freddie started his career as a photographer and joined *Gaumont-British* in 1936 as a clapper boy. He served in the Army Kinematograph Unit during WWII. Freddie made his debut as cinematographer on *A Hill in Korea* (1956). His other early films as cinematographer include: *The Battle of the Sexes* (1959), *Room at the Top* (1959), *Saturday Night and Sunday Morning* (1960) and *Night Must Fall* (1964). During the rest of the 1960s and 1970s he turned his attention to directing, mainly in the horror genre with *Hammer Films, Amicus Pictures* and *Tyburn Films*, this last company set up by his son Kevin. His directorial debut was *Two and Two Make Six* (1962). He followed up with film such as *Paranoiac* (1963), *The Evil of Frankenstein* (1964), *Dr Terror's House of Horrors* (1965), *The Psycopath* (1966), *Mumsy, Nanny, Sonny and Girly* (1969), *Trog* (1970), *The Creeping Flesh* (1973) and *The Ghoul* (1975). Freddie returned to cinematography with *The Elephant Man* (1980). Since then his films have included: *The French Lieutenant's Woman* (1981), *The Executioner's Song* (1982), *Memed My Hawk* (1984), *Dune* (1984), *Her Alibi* (1989), *Cape Fear* (1991), *Princess Caraboo* (1999) and *The Straight Story* (1999). He won Academy Awards for Best Cinematography for *Sons and Lovers* (1960) and *Glory* (1988). He died 17 March 2007, Isleworth, Greater London.

Franklin, Pamela (1950-) Born 3 February 1950, Yokahama, Japan. Actress. Trained as a ballet dancer, she entered British films, aged eleven, in *The Innocents* (1961), an adaptation of Henry James's *Turn of the Screw*. Pamela gradually matured on the screen from juvenile roles to ingénue leads. She impressed as a wide-eyed youngster in the creepy thriller *The Nanny* (1965) and aged 19 she became one of Maggie Smith's "gels" in the school drama *The Prime of Miss Jean Brodie* (1969 – as Sandy). Probably her stand-out performance was as a sexually repressed psychic in *The Legend of Hell House* (1973), a remake of *The Haunting*. Pamela made her last film, *The Food of the Gods,* in 1976. She then appeared in bit parts in, mainly, American TV shows such as *Police Woman, Fantasy Island, The Love Boat* and *Barnaby Jones* before retiring from the screen in 1981. Pamela married actor Harvey Jason in 1971, and they live in Hollywood with their two children.

Fraser, Bill (1907-87) Born William Simpson Fraser, 5 June 1908, Perth, Scotland. Actor. Began life in the banking profession but switched to the theatre. Ran a repertory company during the 1930s. Screen debut: *East of Piccadilly* (1941). His other films include: *The Common Touch* (1941), *Helter Skelter* (1949), *The Captain's Paradise* (1953), *The Barefoot Contessa* (1954), *Another Time, Another Place* (1958), *I've Gotta Horse* (1965), *The Best House in London* (1969), *Doctor in Love* (1960), *The Fast Lady* (1962), *Not Now Darling* (1973), *Love Thy Neighbour* (1973), *Dead Cert* (1974), *Moments* (1974), *The Amorous Milkman* (1975), *Eye of the Needle* (1981) *Pirates* (1986) and his last film *Little Dorrit* (1988). Bill featured in all three Frankie Howerd vehicles: *Up Pompeii* (1971), *Up the Chastity Belt* (1971) and *Up the Front* (1972). Probably best remembered for playing Claude Snudge in the TV sitcoms *The Army Game* (1957-1960) and *Bootsie and Snudge* (1960). Bill was married to character actress Pamela Cundell from 1981 until his death from emphysema, 9 September 1987, Hertfordshire. See also entries in the television section for *The Army Game, Bootsie and Snudge, Rumpole of the Bailey, That's Your Funeral,* and *The Secret Diary of Adrian Mole Aged 13 3/4.*

Fraser, Liz (1933-) Born Elizabeth Winch, 14 August 1930, London. Actress. The star of over 50 British films she started out in small roles such as the 'Girl On Bridge' in her film debut *Touch and Go* (1955). Other films include: *The Smallest Show on Earth* (1957), *Dunkirk* (1957), *Davy* (1958), *Wonderful Things!* (1958), *Alive and Kicking* (1959), *Top Floor Girl* (1959), *I'm All Right Jack* (1959), *Desert Mice* (1959), *The Night We Dropped a Clanger* (1959), *Two-Way Stretch* (1960), *Doctor in Love* (1960), *The Bulldog Breed* (1960), *The Pure Hell of St Trinian's* (1960), *The Night We Got the Bird* (1961), *The Rebel* (1961), *Fury at Smugglers' Bay* (1961), *Carry On Regardless* (1961), *Double Bunk* (1961), *Raising the Wind* (1961), *On the Fiddle* (1961), *Watch it, Sailor!* (1961), *A Pair of Briefs* (1962), *The Painted Smile* (1962), *Live Now - Pay Later* (1962), *Carry On Cruising* (1962), *The Amorous Prawn* (1962), *Carry On Cabby* (1963), *The Americanization of Emily* (1964), *Every Day's a Holiday* (1965), *The Family Way* (1966), *Up the Junction* (1968), *Dad's Army* (1971), *Carry On Behind* (1975), *Under the Doctor* (1976), *Adventures of a Taxi Driver* (1976), *Confessions of a Driving Instructor* (1976), *Confessions from a Holiday Camp* (1977), *Adventures of a Private Eye* (1977), *Rosie Dixon - Night Nurse* (1978), *The Great Rock 'n' Roll Swindle* (1980) and *Chicago Joe and the Showgirl* (1990). Liz usually played the desirable girl in film comedies, a characterisation she perfected on television in comedy serials such as *Hancock's Half-Hour* and the Sid James vehicle *Citizen James.* In recent years she has appeared in *Doctors* (2006), *Foyle's War* (2007) and *Holby City* (2007). Liz is also an accomplished bridge player featuring in a number of high-profile tournaments.

Fraser, Ronald (1930-97) Born Ronald Gordon Fraser, 11 April 1930, Ashton-under-Lyne, Greater Manchester. Actor. Screen debut: *The Sundowners* (1960) Other films include: *The Long and the Short and the Tall* (1961), *The Punch and Judy Man* (1963), *The V.I.P.s* (1963), *Crooks in Cloisters* (1964), *The Flight of the Phoenix* (1965), *The Killing of Sister George* (1968), *Too Late the Hero* (1969), *The Rise and Rise of Michael Rimmer* (1970), *Percy's Progress* (1974), *Swallows and Amazons* (1974), *Paper Tiger* (1975), *Hardcore* (1977), *Come Play with Me* (1977), *The Wild Geese* (1978), *Absolute Beginners* (1986), *Scandal* (1989) and *The Mystery of Edwin Drood* (1993). A brilliant character actor he was described after his death as not under-employed but certainly under-used. His career certainly took a dip during the 1970s before being revived somewhat on TV by appearances in such series as *Pennies From Heaven, Brideshead Revisited, Minder,* and *Moll Flanders.* Usually played pompous, priggish parts or loveable rogues. Had a reputation for hard-drinking alongside his friends Richard Burton, Richard Harris and Peter O'Toole. He died 13 March 1997 Camden, London. The pallbearers at his funeral were Sean Connery, Peter O'Toole, Simon Ward (who had played his son in *The Misfit*) and Chris Evans (Ronald made his last screen appearance on Chris's *TFI Friday*). See also entries in the radio and television section for *Fortunes of War, The Misfit, The Practice,* and *Spooner's Patch.*

Frears, Stephen (1941-) Born Stephen Arthur Frears 20 June 1941, Leicester, Leicestershire. Director. Graduated in law from Trinity College, Cambridge. Joined the Royal Court Theatre and worked with Lindsay Anderson and Karel Reisz. Directorial debut: *The Burning* (1968). Early feature films include: *Gumshoe* (1971), *Bloody Kids* (1979) and *The Hit* (1984). The made for TV film *My Beautiful Launderette* (1985) proved to be a breakthrough after it received theatrical distribution. He followed this with *Prick Up Your Ears* (1987), *Sammy and Rosie Get Laid* (1987), *Dangerous Liaisons* (1988) and *The Grifters* (1990) - which won him a Best Director Academy Award nomination. His later films include: *Accidental Hero* (1992), *Mary Reilly* (1996), *The Van* (1996), *The Hi-Lo Country* (1998), *High Fidelity* (2000), *Liam* (2000), *Dirty Pretty Things* (2002), *Mrs Henderson Presents* (2005), *The Queen* (2006) - which won him his second Best Director Academy Award nomination, *Cheri* (2009) and *Tamara*

Drewe (2010). He has a great record in directing for TV including such diverse projects as *Follyfoot* (1971), *Three Men in a Boat* (1975), the Alan Bennett TV plays *Me! I'm Afraid of Virginia Woolf* (1978), *Doris and Doreen* (1978), *Afternoon Off* (1979) and *One Fine Day* (1979), *Saigon: Year of the Cat* (1983), *The Snapper* (1993), *Fail Safe* (2000) and *The Deal* (2003). His film *Walter* (1982) was the first film produced for Film on Four. Stephen was married to American editor and journalist Mary-Kay Wilmers (b. 19 July 1938) in 1968 and they had two sons, Sam and Will, a stage and film director himself. The couple divorced in the early 1970s. Stephen is currently married to the painter Anne Rothenstein. They have two children, Frankie and Lola. His latest project is the soon-to-be-released film *Lay the Favourite.* After working with the Liverpool-based pop group Scaffold in the 1960s Stephen was immortalised in their 1968 hit, *Lily the Pink,* "Mr Frears had sticky out ears".

Frederick, Lynne (1954-94) Born Lynn Wagner Hardin Frederick, 25 July 1954, Uxbridge, Middlesex. Actress. Made her film debut aged sixteen in Cornel Wilde's *No Blade of Grass* (1970). Other films include: *Nicholas and Alexandra* (1971), *Henry VIII and His Six Wives* (1972), *The Amazing Mr. Blunden* (1972) and *A Long Return* (1975). Her roles consisted mainly of royalty, duchesses and the general upper class. Her last film was the *Prisoner of Zenda* (1979 - as Princess Flavia). She is perhaps better known for her marriages than for her films. In 1977 she married Peter Sellers (1977-80) and thereafter David Frost (1981-82) and Barry Unger (1982-91). There was bitter acrimony when Sellers died. He was in the process of excluding Lynne from his will a week before he died of a heart attack on July 24 1980, but because the divorce decree had not been finalized she inherited almost his entire estate worth an estimated £4.5 million. In 1982 she won over $1 million against the makers of *Trail of the Pink Panther* arguing that it insulted the memory of Peter Sellers. Lynne suffered from severe depression throughout her thirties and became an alcoholic. She died, of a seizure in her sleep, 27 April 1994, Los Angeles, California.

Freeman, Martin (1971-) Born Martin John C. Freeman, 8 September 1971, Aldershot, Hampshire. Actor. Martin trained at the Central School of Speech and Drama in London. He began his television career with small parts in *The Bill* and *This Life* in 1997 and made his wide screen debut in the film short *I Just Want to Kiss You* (1998). The short theme is soon to be continued as Martin has recently been cast in the role of Bilbo Baggins in the 2012 two-part Peter Jackson prequel to *The Lord of the Rings* film trilogy, entitled *The Hobbit.* Following a few minor roles Martin's stock improved after his celebrated television role as Tim Canterbury in *The Office.* He played Ricky C in *Ali G Indahouse* (2002) and John in *Love Actually* (2003), followed by a cameo performance in *Shaun of the Dead* (2004 - as Declan) and the starring role in *The Hitchhiker's Guide to the Galaxy* (2005 - as Arthur Dent). Other films include *Confetti* (2006), *Breaking and Entering* (2006), *Hot Fuzz* (2007), *The All Together* (2007), *Nightwatching* (2007 - as Rembrandt), *Nativity!* (2009), *Wild Target* (2010) and *What's your Number?* (2011). Martin is married to actress and comedian Amanda Abbington (b. October 1974). The couple have a son, Joe (b. 2005), and a daughter, Grace (b. 2009). See also entries in the radio and television section for *Hardware, The Office,* and *Sherlock.*

Fricker, Brenda (1945-) Born 17 February 1945, Dublin. Actress. She began her feature film career with a small uncredited part in the 1964 film *Of Human Bondage* based on the 1915 novel by William Somerset Maugham. In the years that followed she appeared in numerous TV staples, *Coronation Street* (as Staff Nurse Maloney), *Z-Cars, Juliet Bravo* and *Angels.* After 25 years of performing she became an overnight star when she won the Academy Award for Best Supporting Actress for *My Left Foot* (1989) opposite Daniel Day Lewis. Prior to winning the award she was better known to most people as Megan Roach from the TV series *Casualty,* a series to which she returned in August 2010 for a short time to follow a plot-line to kill off her character. For the most part she has played character roles in her films, usually set in Ireland, these include *The Ballroom of Romance* (1982 - as

Bridie), *The Field* (1990 - as Maggie McCabe), *A Man of No Importance* (1994 - as Lily Byrne), *Conspiracy of Silence* (2003 - as Annie McLaughlin), *Veronica Guerin* (2003 - as Bernie Guerin), *Omagh* (2004 – as Police Ombudsman Nuala O'Loan), *Inside I'm Dancing* (2004 - as Eileen), *Tara Road* (2005 – as Mona), *How About You* (2007 - as Heather Nightingale), *Closing the Ring* (2007 - as Grandma Reilly) and *Albert Nobbs* (2011 – as Polly) . Other films include: *Home Alone 2: Lost in New York* (1992) *So I Married an Axe Murderer* (1993), as Mike Myers' mother, *A Time to Kill* (1996), *Masterminds* (1997), *Painted Angels* (1998), *Stone of Destiny* (2008), *Locked In* (2010), *Cloudburst* (2011).

Friel, Anna (1976-) Born Anna Louise Friel, 12 July 1976, Rochdale, Lancashire. Actress. Of Irish descent. She first appeared on TV in Alan Bleasdale's *G.B.H.* (1991) thereafter she played Poppy Bruce in *Emmerdale* before her breakthrough part as Beth Jordache in *Brookside*. Here she was part of a number of sensational plot lines involving incest, lesbianism and murder. Her lesbian on-screen kiss was the first in British soap history. Anna's feature film debut was as Prue in The Land Girls (1998) although she made her television film debut a few months earlier in the controversial *The Tribe*, Anna's character being involved in a much discussed ménage à trois sex scene. She next played Hermia in *A Midsummer Night's Dream* (1999) and Nick Leeson's wife Lisa in *Rogue Trader* (1999) opposite Ewan McGregor. Other films include: *Timeline* (2003), *Goal!* (2005), *Irish Jam* (2006), *Niagara Motel* (2006), *Goal! 2: Living the Dream* (2007), *Bathory* (2008), *Land of the Lost* (2009), *London Boulevard* (2010), *You Will Meet a Tall Dark Stranger* (2010) and *Limitless* (2011). In 2001, Anna began a relationship with actor David Thewlis, whom she met on a flight to Cannes. She gave birth to her first child, a daughter, Grace Ellen Mary Friel (b. 9 July 2005) but the couple announced their separation in December 2010. Anna began dating fellow actor Rhys Ifans, with whom she acted in the SyFy (US digital channel) mini series, *Neverland*, in 2011.

Friend, Rupert (1981-) Born 1 October 1981, Stonesfield, Oxfordshire. Actor. Rupert trained at the Webber Douglas Academy of Dramatic Art in London. His film debut was as Billy Downs in *The Libertine* (2004), a role for which he was named "outstanding new talent" at the 2005 Satellite Awards. He is probably best known for his second film role, as Mr. Wickham in the 2005 film *Pride and Prejudice*. Other films include: *Mrs. Palfrey at the Claremont* (2005), *The Last Legion* (2007), *Outlaw* (2007), *Virgin Territory* (2007), *Jolene* (2008), *The Boy in the Striped Pajamas* (2008 - as Lt Kotler), *Cheri* (2009), *The Young Victoria* (2009 - as Prince Albert), *The Kid* (2010) and *5 Days of War* (2011). Rupert was in a relationship with Keira Knightly from 2005 but the couple announced their split in December 2010.

Friese-Greene, William (1855-1921) Born William Edward Green, 7 September 1855, Bristol. Pioneer film-maker. In 1869 he was apprenticed to photographer Maurice Guttenberg. He married Helena Friese in 1874 and changed his name to what he considered to be the more "artistic" sounding Friese-Greene. By 1877 he had set up his own shops and studios in Bath, Bristol and Plymouth. In 1880 he met John Arthur Roebuck Rudge who had developed a "biophantic lantern" which projected seven slides in rapid succession to produce the illusion of movement. This spurred Friese-Green on to produce, with Rudge, the Biophantoscope (using glass plates) and then to experiment using celluloid for motion picture cameras. He moved to London in 1885, opening two shops and expanded his operations over the next few years. In 1889 he designed a sequence camera with Mortimer Evans and, after exposing some film at Hyde Park, he gave a public demonstration. However, the low frame rate meant that the results were ultimately disappointing. This was patented as a chronophotographic camera. In 1891 he was made bankrupt, sold his patent and fell behind others in the field of producing moving pictures. By 1905 he had moved to Brighton and was working on colour photography, developing his Biocolour process and eventually succeeding in a court challenge to Charles Urban and G A Smith over their Kinemacolor process. The rest of his life saw him have both financial success and failure including a second bankruptcy and even a period of imprisonment. A highly romanticised version of his life was made for the Festival of Britain with Robert Donat as Friese Greene in *The Magic Box*

(1951). His son Claude Friese-Greene was a successful cinematographer. He died 5 May 1921, St Giles, London, during a meeting to discuss the state of the British film industry. His funeral was marked by a two minutes silence in all British cinemas. His Lutyens-designed memorial in Highgate Cemetery reads "The inventor of Kinematography".

Frost, Nick (1972-) Born Nicholas John Frost, 28 March 1972, Dagenham, Essex. Actor, comedian and screenwriter. Nick's first screen role was as 'Fatso' in a 1994 episode of *Casualty*. He appeared in corporate training videos before gaining the role of Mike Watt in the Channel 4 comedy series *Spaced* (1999-2001). His film debut came in the romantic zombie comedy *Shaun of the Dead* (2004 - as Ed). Other films include: *Kinky Boots* (2005), *Penelope* (2006), *Grindhouse* (2007), *Hot Fuzz* (2007), *Wild Child* (2008), *The Boat that Rocked* (2009), *Attack the Block* (2011) and *Paul* (2011 - as Clive Gollings), a science fiction comedy film co-written with his long-time friend Simon Pegg who also co-stars with him as Graeme Willy. Nick and Simon also appeared together as Thomson and Thompson in *The Adventures of Tintin: The Secret of the Unicorn* (2011). On television in 2001, Nick played an armed robber who appeared to have shot dead *Acorn Antiques'* main star, Mrs Overall (Julie Walters). He also starred in the BBC2 sitcom *Hyperdrive* (2006-07) and narrated the Channel 4 reality show *Supernanny* for three series.

Frost, Sadie (1965-) Born Sadie Liza Vaughan, 19 June 1965, London. Actress. Sadie is the daughter of psychedelic artist David Vaughan and actress Mary Davidson. She had a strange upbringing with several half-brothers and sisters plus a step-father, rock photographer Robert Davidson, who was a follower of the Bhagwan cult. Sadie's first screen role was in a television advert for Jelly Tots. She attended the Italia Conti Theatre School from the age of eleven and started her career at Manchester's Royal Exchange Theatre where she appeared in *Mumbo Jumbo* at the age of 19. Her first film was *Empire State* (1987). Other films include: *Diamond Skulls* (1989), *Paper Marriage* (1992), *Splitting Heirs* (1993), *Magic Hunter* (1994), *A Pyromaniac's Love Story* (1995), *Crimetime* (1996), *Flypaper* (1997), *Bent* (1997), *An Ideal Husband* (1998), *Final Cut* (1998), *Presence of Mind* (1999), *Captain Jack* (1999), *Love, Honour and Obey* (2000), *Rancid Aluminium* (2000), *Soul Patrol* (2000), *Uprising* (2001), *The Heavy* (2008), *Shoot on Sight* (2008) and *Beyond the Rave* (2008). Her first marriage was to Gary Kemp of Spandau Ballet (1988-95). The couple had a son Finlay Munro (b. 20 September 1990). During this time she worked with Gary on the film *The Krays* (1990). It was during the filming of Paul W.S. Anderson's *Shopping* (1994) that she first worked with Jude Law, a man who would become her second husband three years later (1997-2003). The couple had three children, a son, Rafferty (b. 6 October 1996), a daughter Iris (b. 25 October 2000) and second son Rudy Indiana Otis (b. 10 September 2002). In 1997 Sadie co-founded the production company Natural Nylon along with Jonny Lee Miller, Ewan McGregor, Sean Pertwee, and her then husband Jude Law. The first film to be produced by Natural Nylon was David Cronenberg's *eXistenZ* (1999) and the last, *Sky Captain and the World of Tomorrow* (2004), a vehicle for Jude Law and Angelina Jolie. The company lasting as long as Sadie's marriage. In 1999, she co-founded the successful fashion label FrostFrench with her friend, Jemima French. In September 2006, Saide posed nude for Canadian photographer Bryan Adams for a PETA anti-fur advert to coincide with London Fashion Week. She is perhaps best remembered for her American debut performance as Lucy Westenra in Francis Ford Coppola's *Bram Stoker's Dracula* (1992) and as the star of Pulp's video for *Common People*. Sadie's younger sister Holly Davidson (b. 1980) is also an actress.

Fry, Stephen (1957-) Born Stephen John Fry, 24 August 1957, Hampstead, London. Actor, comedian and writer. After being convicted of credit card fraud Stephen spent three months in Pucklechurch Prison on remand. He then gained a degree in English literature at Queen's College, Cambridge, and made his first appearance on television on *University Challenge*. In a 1984 episode of *The Young Ones,* entitled Bambi, he appeared as Lord Snot in the Footlights College team against The Young Ones in a *University Challenge* spoof. Stephen did in fact become a member of the Cambridge Footlights Revue alongside Hugh Laurie, with whom he then began a fruitful comedy partnership. His adaption of *Me and My Girl* for the 1980s stage garnered him both financial and critical rewards. Although he made an uncredited appearance in *Chariots of Fire* (1981), his film debut-proper was *The Good Father* (1985). Other films include: *A Handful of Dust* (1988), *A Fish Called Wanda* (1988), *Peter's Friends* (1992), *I.Q.* (1994), *Wilde* (1997), *Spice World* (1997), *Whatever Happened to Harold Smith?* (1999), *Best* (2000), *Relative Values* (2000), *Sabotage!* (2000), *Gosford Park* (2001), *The Discovery of Heaven* (2001), *Four Play* (2001),*Thunderpants* (2002), *Bright Young Things* (2003 - Stephen's sister, Jo Crocker, was assistant director), *Le Divorce* (2003), *Tooth* (2004), *The Life and Death of Peter Sellers* (2004), *MirrorMask* (2005), *The Hitchhiker's Guide to the Galaxy* (2005), *A Cock and Bull Story* (2005), *V for Vendetta* (2006), *Alex Rider: Stormbreaker* (2006), *Eichmann* (2007), *St. Trinian's* (2007), *Tales of the Riverbank* (2008), *House of Boys* (2009), *Alice in Wonderland* (2010 - voice of Cheshire Cat) and *Animals United* (2010 - voice of socrates). Whilst appearing on stage in *Cell Mates* in 1995 he suffered such a serious attack of stage fright that he ran away to Belgium. Also a novelist, he has written *The Liar* (1992), *The Hippopotamus* (1994), *Making History* (1997) and *The Stars' Tennis Balls (aka Revenge)* (2000) as well as *The Ode Less Travelled: Unlocking the Poet Within* (2005), a guide to writing poetry. Much in demand for voice-over work he is the narrator of all seven of the audio versions of the *Harry Potter* books and has also been featured in a number of video games, including an appearance as Reaver, a main character in Lionhead Studios games *Fable II* and *Fable III*, and as the narrator in *LittleBigPlanet* on PlayStation 3 and PlayStation Portable. Autobiography: *Moab is my Washpot* (1997) and *The Fry Chronicles* (2010). Stephen has recently become a director of Norwich City Football Club and he also has over two million followers on Twitter which from time-to-time has meant him having to make public apologies for outspoken comments. Stephen was in a 14-year relationship with Daniel Cohen, which ended in 2010, and prior to that he claims to have been celibate for 16 years. Stephen is also a successful television performer in such as the TV film *Longitude* (2000) and the American crime series *Bones* (2007-09). Stephen's use of the word "luvvie" in *The Guardian* on 2 April 1988 is cited by the Oxford English Dictionary as the earliest recorded use of the word. A man of undoubted intellect and breeding, Stephen's latest role of Sherlock Holmes' smarter elder brother Mycroft in *Sherlock Holmes: A Game of Shadows* (2011) is probably the definitive example of perfect casting. See also entries in the radio and television section for *Absolute Power*, *Alfresco*, *A Bit of Fry and Laurie*, *Blackadder Goes Forth*, *Blackadder II*, *Blackadder the Third*, *Gormenghast*, *Happy Families*, *I'm Sorry I Haven't A Clue*, *Jeeves and Wooster*, *Just A Minute*, *Kingdom*, *Mastermind*, *Pocoyo*, *QI*, *Saturday Live*, *University Challenge*, *Walk on the Wild Side*, *Who Do You Think You Are?*, *Whose Line Is It Anyway?*, *Woof!*, and *The Young Ones*.

Gainsborough Pictures (1924-1951) Founded by Michael Balcon in 1924, quickly becoming linked with *Gaumont-British*. In its early days its links with German cinema influenced directors such as Alfred Hitchcock. In the 1930s, with social and political changes affecting all aspects of German society, several German film stars fled to Britain, including Conrad Veidt. From the late 1930s *Gainsborough* came under the control of *The Rank Organisation* and its output became dominated by what in literary terms might be called "bodice rippers". In fact these morally ambivalent costume melodramas such as *The Man in Grey* (1943) and *The Wicked Lady* (1945) were incredibly popular and boosted the careers of stars such as Margaret Lockwood and James Mason. In tandem with these films *Gainsborough* also produced modern-dress versions such as *Love Story* (1944) and *They Were Sisters* (1945). Apart from Sydney Box and his sister Betty, the only female producer in Britain, most of the creative talent departed and *Gainsborough Pictures* disappeared from the screens in 1951.

Gambon, Sir Michael (1940-) Born 19 October 1940, Dublin. Actor. His family moved to London after WWII and Michael's father successfully applied for British citizenship for his son.

Michael worked as an engineer before moving into acting whilst studying at RADA. His stage debut was in *Othello* (1962) and his film debut was also in: *Othello* (1965). Other films include: *The Beast Must Die* (1974), *Turtle Diary* (1985), *The Cook, The Thief, His Wife and Her Lover* (1989), *The Rachel Papers* (1989), *Mobsters* (1991), *Toys* (1992), *The Browning Version* (1994), *Bullet to Beijing* (1995), a TV film with Michael Caine reprising his role of Harry Palmer, *Mary Reilly* (1996), *The Wings of the Dove* (1997), *The Gambler* (1997 - as Fyoder Dostoyevsky), *Dancing at Lughnasa* (1998), *The Insider* (1999), *Longitude* (2000 - as John Harrison in the made-for-television film), *Gosford Park* (2001), *Christmas Carol: The Movie* (2001), *Charlotte Gray (2001)*, *Ali G Indahouse* (2002), *Open Range* (2003), *Sylvia* (2003), *Harry Potter and the Prisoner of Azkaban* (2004), replacing the late Richard Harris as Albus Dumbledore, *Sky Captain and the World of Tomorrow* (2004), *Being Julia* (2004), *Layer Cake* (2004), *The Life Aquatic with Steve Zissou* (2004), *Harry Potter and the Goblet of Fire* (2005), *The Omen* (2006), *The Good Shepherd* (2006), directed by Robert De Niro, *Amazing Grace* (2006), *The Good Night* (2007), *Harry Potter and the Order of the Phoenix* (2007), *Brideshead Revisited* (2008 - as Lord Marchmain), *Harry Potter and the Half-Blood Prince* (2009), *Fantastic Mr. Fox* (2009 - as voice of Franklin Bean), *The Book of Eli* (2010), *Harry Potter and the Deathly Hallows Part 1* (2010), *The King's Speech* (2010), *Harry Potter and the Deathly Hallows – Part II* (2011) and *Page Eight* (2011). His work as the action hero of the TV series *The Borderers* (1968-1970) led to him being considered as a replacement for George Lazenby as James Bond. One of his most popular and critically acclaimed television roles was as Philip E Marlow in Dennis Potter's *The Singing Detective* (1986). More recently he was the narrator in the BBC2 sword and sorcery series *Kröd Mändoon and the Flaming Sword of Fire* (2009). Michael was the obvious replacement for Richard Harris in the Harry Potter series having already replaced him as *Maigret* (1992-93) on television, after Richard had made the pilot episode. Michael was made a CBE in 1992 and knighted in 1998. He married Ann Miller in 1962 but separated in 1999. They have one child, Fergus, an expert on the BBC's *Antiques Roadshow*. He is currently living with film-set decorator Philippa Hart who he met while making the film *Sylvia*. The couple have two children, Michael (b. May 2007) and William (b. June 2009). See also entries in the television section for *The Borderers*, *Cranford*, *Emma*, *Kröd Mändoon and the Flaming Sword of Fire*, *Love Story*, *Maigret*, and *The Singing Detective*.

Garai, Romola (1982-) Born Romola Sadie Garai, 6 August 1982, Hong Kong. Actress. Romola's family moved to Singapore when she was five, and then to Wiltshire, England, three years later. Whilst still at school she was spotted for her first role, as the younger Elizabeth (Judi Dench's character) in the TV film *Last of the Blonde Bombshells* (2000). Her feature film debut came in *Nicholas Nickleby* (2002) and since then she has had major roles in Tim Fywell's adaptation of Dodie Smith's *I Capture the Castle* (2003), *Vanity Fair* (2004 - as Amelia Sedley) and the New Zealand based mini-series *Mary Byrant* (2005), as the title character. Other films include *Dirty Dancing: Havana Nights* (2004), *Inside I'm Dancing* (2004), *Scoop* (2006), *As You Like It* (2006), *Amazing Grace* (2006), *Angel* (2007), *Atonement* (2007), *The Other Man* (2008), *Glorious 39* (2009) and *One Day* (2011 – as Sylvie). In 2009, she played the title role in a television adaptation of Jane Austen's *Emma*, co-starring Jonny Lee Miller and Sir Michael Gambon. In 2011 she starred in the BBC mini-series' *The Hour* (as Bel Rowley) and *The Crimson Petal and the White* (as Sugar).

Garfield, Andrew (1983-) Born Andrew Russell Garfield, 20 August 1983, Los Angeles, California, to a British mother and an American father. His family moved to England when he was three-years-old. Andrew graduated from the Central School of Speech and Drama in 2004 and made his first screen appearance in the film short *Mumbo Jumbo* (2005) and followed this with the role of Tom in the Emmy Award-winning television series *Sugar Rush* (2005). His feature debut was in the Robert Redford-directed *Lions for Lambs* (2007 - as Todd Hayes) and the following month starred as Jack Burridge in the Channel 4 TV film *Boy A* (2007, for which he won the 2008 BAFTA for Best Actor. His subsequent films include *The Other Boleyn Girl* (2008), *The Imaginarium of Doctor Parnassus* (2009), *Never Let Me Go* (2010) and *The Social Network* (2010). Andrew has recently completed filming his new role of Spider-Man opposite Emma Stone in Marc Webb's *The Amazing Spider-Man* (2012).

Garson, Greer (1904-96) Born Eileen Evelyn Greer Garson, 29 September 1904, Manor Park, Greater London. Actress. She was educated at King's College London, where she gained degrees in French and 18th century literature, and at the University of Grenoble, France. Greer's first thoughts were of teaching but via local theatrical productions she moved into acting. She was discovered by Louis B. Mayer who was taken with her beauty and stunning red hair. During her relatively short film career (she made fewer than 30 films) she was nominated seven times for a Best Actress Academy Award, winning on just one occasion for *Mrs Minniver* (1942). Her other nominations were her debut film *Goodbye, Mr. Chips* (1939), *Blossoms In the Dust* (1941), *Madame Curie* (1943), *Mrs. Parkington* (1944), *The Valley of Decision* (1945) and for playing Eleanor Roosevelt in *Sunrise at Campobello* (1960). Possibly her most famous role was as Elizabeth Bennet in the 1940 film *Pride and Prejudice*. Although often cited as being an Irish actress (her mother was Irish), in 1951, she became a naturalized citizen of the United States. Her other films include: *When Ladies Meet* (1941), *Random Harvest* (1942), *Adventure* (1945), *Julia Misbehaves* (1948), *That Forsyte Woman* (1949), *The Miniver Story* (1950), *The Law and the Lady* (1951), *Scandal at Scourie* (1953), *Julius Caesar* (1953 - as Calpurnia), *Her Twelve Men* (1954), *The Singing Nun* (1966) and her last feature, *The Happiest Millionaire* (1967). Greer made rare appearances subsequently although she did narrate the children's television special The Little Drummer in 1968 and appeared as Aunt Kathryn March in the 1978 TV film *Little Women*. The story that she rambled on for an hour during the 1943 Academy Award show when accepting her Best Actress Academy Award for Mrs Minniver is apocryphal and more reasonable accounts estimate a mere five to six minutes. An interesting piece of trivia is that Greer twice later picked up Best Actress Academy Awards, but only for other people, in 1952 and 1962 when Vivien Leigh and Sophia Loren couldn't attend. Greer was married three times, firstly to Edward Alec Abbot Snelson (1904–92), later Sir Edward, a British civil servant who became a noted judge and expert in Indian and Pakistani affairs. The actual marriage reportedly lasted only a few weeks, but was not formally dissolved until 1940. After the filming of *Mrs Minniver* she married her co-star Richard Ney (1916-2004), who had played her son in the film. The marriage lasted four years but they divorced in 1947 after it became clear that the twelve-year age gap was an insurmountable problem. She finally married millionaire Texas oilman and horse breeder, E. E. 'Buddy' Fogelson (1900–87), in 1949, and in 1967 the couple retired to their "Forked Lightning Ranch" in New Mexico. Nicknamed "Eggy" and "Duchess" Garson was a beautiful aristocratic actress who dominated the screen during the war years. On 6 April 1996 she died in Dallas, Texas of heart failure.

Gaumont-British Picture Corporation Originally a subsidiary of the French production company *Gaumont* and based at Shepherd's Bush. From 1922 it became a wholly British company run by the Ostrer brothers, David, Isidore, Harry, Mark and Maurice. By the late 1920s it controlled 280 cinemas and had a production arm run by Michael Balcon. In 1928 *Gainsborough Pictures* was acquired and re-built studios were opened in 1932. Films produced during this period include: *I was a Spy* (1933), *Cuckoo in the Nest* (1933), *Soldiers of the King* (1933), *Jew Suss* (1934) and *The Passing of the Third Floor Back* (1935). Balcon moved on to *MGM-British* in 1936 and the company headed into financial difficulties but was given financial support by the *Rank Corporation* which insisted all production was switched to *Pinewood* in 1937. The company was fully acquired by *Rank* in 1941. Other branches included *G-B Instructional*, which made educational documentaries, *Gaumont-British News*, which made newsreels and *G-B Animation*.

George, Susan (1950-) Born Susan Melody George, 26 July 1950, London. Actress. She trained at the Corona Theatre School.

A child actress, Susan first appeared on television in the *Dickie Henderson Show* in 1962 and followed this with a starring role as Kitty Walker in the BBC children's series *Swallows and Amazons* (1963). Her film debut role came as Vicky Davis in *Cup Fever* (1965). Her other early films include: *Davy Jones' Locker* (1966), *The Sorcerers* (1967), *Billion Dollar Brain* (1967), *Up the Junction* (1968), *The Strange Affair* (1968), *All Neat in Black Stockings* (1969), *The Looking Glass War* (1969), *Twinky* (1970), *Spring and Port Wine* (1970), *Eyewitness* (1970) and *Die Screaming, Marianne* (1971). Susan was usually cast as the vulnerable, blond leading lady, sometimes in a feisty or slightly dippy role. Her next two roles either side of *Fright* (1972) were probably her strongest. In *Straw Dogs* (1971) she played Amy Summer, Dustin Hoffman's victimised wife and in *Dirty Mary Crazy Larry* (1974) she played Mary Coombs, opposite Peter Fonda. Her subsequent films include: *Mandingo* (1975), *A Small Town in Texas* (1976), *Tomorrow Never Comes* (1978), *Enter the Ninja* (1981), *Venom* (1981), *Kiss My Grits* (1982), *The House Where Evil Dwells* (1982), *The Jigsaw Man* (1984), *Lightning, the White Stallion* (1986), *That Summer of White Roses* (1989), *In Your Dreams* (2008) and *City of Life* (2009). Despite her very successful film career Susan has been an ever-present on television in quality series such as *ITV Television Playhouse* (1963), *The Human Jungle* (1964), *Armchair Theatre* (1967), *Mystery and Imagination* (1968), *Doctor in the House* (1970), *The Persuaders!* (1971), *Tales of the Unexpected* (1979; 1980), *The Kenny Everett Television Show* (1982), *Hammer House of Mystery and Suspense* (1985), *Hotel* (1986), *Cluedo* (1992 - as Mrs Peacock), *Stay Lucky* (1993), *Tales of Mystery and Imagination* (1995) and *Eastenders* (2001). In her personal life, after dating such celebrities as Jack Jones, Andy Gibb and even the Prince of Wales, Susan eventually married actor Simon MacCorkindale (12 February 1952 – 14 October 2010) on 5 October 1984. In 1988, the couple co-produced the film *Stealing Heaven*. Susan currently runs a stud farm called Georgian Arabians in Northamptonshire and is also firm believer in homeopathy, selling a range of therapeutic products for horses. See also entries in the television section for *Cluedo, Eastenders, Stay Lucky,* and *Weaver's Green*.

Gervais, Ricky (1961-) See entry in comedy section

Gielgud, John (1904-2000) Born Arthur John Gielgud, 14 April 1904, South Kensington, London. Actor. Great-nephew of actress Ellen Terry. Educated at Westminster School, Lady Benson's Acting School and RADA. Stage debut: *Henry V* (1921) - just the one line "Here is the number of the slaughtered French". He went on to become one of the finest actors of the Twentieth Century and apparently only spent four weeks out of work until his death. Screen debut: *Who is the Man?* (1924). Other films include: *The Clue of the New Pin* (1929), *Insult* (1932), *The Good Companions* (1933), *Secret Agent* (1936), *Hamlet* (1948) - as the voice of Old Hamlet's ghost - *Julius Caesar* (1953) - as Cassius - *Richard III* (1955) - as Clarence - *Saint Joan* (1957), *The Charge of the Light Brigade* (1968), *Oh! What a Lovely War* (1969), *Julius Caesar* (1970) - as Caesar - *Murder on the Orient Express* (1974), *The Elephant Man* (1980), *Chariots of Fire* (1981), *Gandhi* (1982), *Prospero's Books* (1991) - as Prospero, a part which called for him to appear naked - *Shine* (1996) and *Elizabeth* (1998). He was nominated for a Best Supporting Actor Academy Award for *Becket* (1964) and won the Best Supporting Actor Academy Award for his role as Dudley Moore's butler Hobson in the comedy *Arthur* (1981). Only one of a few people to receive an Academy Award, a Grammy, an Emmy and a Tony. He was also an award winning stage director. John received a knighthood in 1953 and shortly after he was convicted of "persistently importuning for immoral purposes" having been arrested for trying to pick up a man in a public lavatory. John's career was not unduly affected by his humiliation and he continued to impress with his performances both on stage and film. John became a Companion of Honour in 1977, and was admitted to the Order of Merit in 1996. The Globe Theatre in London's West End was renamed in his honour in 1994. He wrote two autobiographies: *Early Stages* (1939) and *An Actor and his Time* (1979). He died 21 May 2000, Aylesbury, Buckinghamshire. See also entries in the television section for *Brideshead Revisited, Edward the Seventh, The Far Pavilions,* and *Shades of Greene.*

Gilliam, Terry (1940-) Born Terence Vance Gilliam, 22 November 1940, Medicine Lake, Minnesota. Director, writer, actor and animator. Worked in New York as a comic editor and in advertising before moving to London in 1967 and taking British citizenship the following year. He joined the team of *Monty Python's Flying Circus* in 1969. His animation skills added greatly to the show's appeal and he also played the odd part when required. Made his big screen debut when, alongside Terry Jones, he directed *Monty Python and the Holy Grail* (1975). His first solo effort *Jabberwocky* (1977) set a visual style which he continued into the popular *Time Bandits* (1981). Terry followed this with a short film about piratical accountants *The Crimson Permanent Assurance* (1983) and his next effort was *Brazil* (1985). This visually intriguing film with its theme of the individual battling bureaucracy and censorship also led to a dispute with the studio about the not-so-happy ending. It gained him an Academy Award nomination for Best Original Screenplay but was not a box-office success. Neither, unfortunately, was the grandiose *The Adventures of Baron Munchausen* (1988) which ran vastly over budget. He gained redemption in Hollywood with *The Fisher King* (1991) and, after trying to develop a few other projects, *The Twelve Monkeys* (1995) and *Fear and Loathing in Las Vegas* (1998). For the next few years his career centred around the ongoing trials and tribulations surrounding the attempt to get *The Man Who Killed Don Quixote* onto the screen, which in turn spawned the documentary *Lost in La Mancha* (2002). His latest directing projects include *The Brothers Grimm* (2005), *Tideland* (2005) and *The Imaginarium of Doctor Parnassus* (2009), all of which he also co-wrote. In January 2006 Terry renounced his American citizenship. He has been married to the British make-up and costume designer Maggie Weston since 1973. They have three children, Amy (b. 1978), Holly (b. 1980), and Harry (b. 1988), who have also appeared in several of Gilliam's films. See also entries in the television section for *Do Not Adjust Your Set, Hark at Barker, Marty,* and *Monty Python's Flying Circus.*

Gilliat, Sidney (1908-94) Born Sidney Gilliatt, 15 February 1908, Edgeley, Stockport, Cheshire. Director, writer and producer. Began his career in the film industry as a writer of inter-titles for silent films. Began screenwriting with Frank Launder on *Under the Greenwood Tree* (1929) and the partnership lasted for over 35 years. Sidney joined *Gaumont-British* in 1931. Other screenwriting credits include some of the best of British cinema: *Rome Express* (1932), *Facing the Music* (1933), *Friday the Thirteenth* (1933), *Seven Sinners* (1936), *The Man who Changed his Mind* (1936), *A Yank at Oxford* (1938), *The Lady Vanishes* (1938), *Jamaica Inn* (1939), *Night Train to Munich* (1940), *Kipps* (1941), *The Young Mr Pitt* (1942), *Millions Like Us* (1943), *London Belongs to Me* (1948), *The Green Man* (1956) and *Endless Night* (1971). Sidney was also a director, and always of films he had a hand in writing. Directing credits include: *Partners in Crime* (1942), *Waterloo Road* (1945), *The Rake's Progress* (1945), *Green for Danger* (1946), *State Secret* (1950), *Only Two Can Play* (1962) and *Endless Night* (1971). Launder and Gilliat are best remembered for their collaboration on the films featuring the outrageously behaved schoolgirls of St Trinian's: *The Belles of St Trinian's* (1954), *Blue Murder at St Trinian's* (1957), *The Pure Hell of St Trinian's* (1960) and *The Great St Trinian's Train Robbery* (1966). They formed their own production company in 1945 called *Individual Pictures* which formed part of *Independent Producers*, a group financed by the *Rank Organisation*. In 1950 they joined Korda's *London Films*. After they took management positions at British Lion in 1958 their on-screen output was severely diminished. Sidney resigned from *British Lion* in 1972 and effectively retired. At his death on 31 May 1994, Devizes, Wiltshire, he was working on a comic crime novel called *Catch Me Who Can.*

Gingold, Hermione (1897-1987) Born Hermione Ferdinanda Gingold, 9 December 1897, Marylebone, London. Actress. The daughter of a Viennese stock broker. Stage debut: *Pinkie and the Fairies* (1908). A star of revue specialising in rather grotesque characters, she was always closely linked with fellow revue artiste Hermione Baddeley and they were known unimaginatively as "The Two Hermiones" and perhaps less flatteringly as "The Gorgeous Gargoyles". Her screen debut was an uncredited appearance in *Dance Pretty Lady* (1932). Other films in this period include *Someone at the Door* (1936), also uncredited, *Merry Comes to Town* (1937), her first credited feature, *Meet Mr. Penny* (1938) and *The Butler's Dilemma* (1943). During the 1950s she spent most of her time in the USA and featured in films such as *Around the World in 80 Days* (1956), *Bell, Book and Candle* (1958) and *The Music Man* (1961). Her most celebrated screen role was as Madame Alavrez in *Gigi* (1958), in which she duetted with Maurice Chevalier on the classic song "I Remember it Well". Her final film appearance was as Elizabeth Rennick in *Garbo Talks!* (1984). Hermione wrote several autobiographies: *The World Is Square* (1946), *My Own Unaided Work* (1952), *Sirens Should Be Seen and Not Heard* (1963) and *How to Grow Old Disgracefully* (1988), published posthumously. Her many quotable sayings include: "I'll try anything once - except country dancing and incest" and "The trouble with men is that there aren't enough of them." Hermione was married twice, to Michael Joseph (1918–26) and British entertainer Eric Maschwitz (1926–45). She died 24 May 1987, New York, USA.

Gleeson, Brendan (1955-) Born 29 March 1955, Dublin. Actor. Trained at RADA. Brendan worked as an English and Drama secondary school teacher for several years before joining the RSC and then making his big screen debut in *The Field* (1990). He featured in several films with an Irish base such as *Into the West* (1992) and *Far and Away* (1992) and played Michael Collins in the TV drama *The Treaty* (1991). Brendan made his breakthrough playing Hamish Campbell alongside Mel Gibson's William Wallace in Gibson's version of Scottish history, *Braveheart* (1995). He then starred as Martin Cahill in *The General* (1998). Brendan has appeared in big-budget fare such as *Michael Collins* (1996), *Mission Impossible II* (2000), *Artificial Intelligence A.I.* (2001), *Gangs of New York* (2002), *Cold Mountain* (2003), *Troy* (2004), *Kingdom of Heaven* (2005), *Beowulf* (2007), and as Alastor "MadEye" Moody in *Harry Potter and the Goblet of Fire* (2005), *Harry Potter and the Order of the Phoenix* (2007) and *Harry Potter and the Deathly Hallows: Part 1* (2010). Other films include: *I Went Down* (1997), *Lake Placid* (1999), *Wild About Harry* (2002), *28 Days Later* (2002), *Breakfast on Pluto* (2005), *The Tiger's Tail* (2006), *Black Irish* (2007), *In Bruges* (2008), *Perrier's Bounty* (2009) and *Green Zone* (2010). Brendan also starred in the film short *Six Shooter* in 2006, which won an Academy Award for Best Live Action Short. Perhaps his most acclaimed role was his portrayal of Winston Churchill in the HBO (Home Box Office) film *Into the Storm*, for which he won an Emmy award in 2009. Brendan lives with his wife Mary, whom he married in 1982, in Malahide, Dublin. Their sons Brian and Domhnall are also actors, the last named appearing as Bill Weasley in the seventh Harry Potter film. Brendan is also an accomplished fiddle player and has played at traditional music seisiúins in Hughes' pub in Chancery Street, Dublin 7. In 2011 he appeared in two highly-acclaimed Irish films, *The Guard* (as Sergeant Gerry Boyle) and *Albert Nobbs* (as Dr. Holloran). Brendan will soon be making his directorial debut in a film adaptation of Flann O'Brien's novel *At Swim Two Birds.*

Glover, Brian (1934-97) Born 2 April 1934, in Sheffield, South Yorkshire. Actor. Brian worked as a professional wrestler, billed as "Leon Aris the Man from Paris" and also taught English and French. His screen debut was in *Kes* (1969) - as Mr Sugden the games teacher - a part he got after being recommended by a work colleague who happened to have written the book on which the film was based (*A Kestrel for a Knave* by Barry Hines). Other films include: *O! Lucky Man* (1972), *Sweeney!* (1976), *An American Werewolf in London* (1981), *The Company of Wolves* (1984), *Alien 3* (1992) and *Leon The Pig Farmer* (1993). His last film was John Godber's rugby league comedy *Up 'n' Under* (1998). He also made many stage and television appearances and will always be remembered as the voice of the "gaffer" of the "Tetley Tea Folk" in a long-running series of television advertisements for Tetley tea. He is quoted as saying: "You play to your strengths in this game. My strength is as a bald-headed, rough-looking Yorkshireman". Brian was married twice, secondly to television producer Tara Prem, the daughter of television actor Bakhshi Prem. He died, of a brain tumour, 24 July 1997 Lambeth, London. See also entries in the television section for *Campion, Coronation Street, Don't Ask Me*, and *Porridge*.

Glover, Julian (1935-) Born Julian Wyatt Glover, 27 March 1935, Hampstead, London. Actor. Trained at the National Youth Theatre. Attended RADA and became a member of the Royal Shakespeare Company. Screen debut: *Tom Jones* (1963). Other films include: *Girl with Green Eyes* (1965), *The Alphabet Murders* (1965), *Alfred the Great* (1969), *Wuthering Heights* (1970), *Anthony and Cleopatra* (1972), *Juggernaut* (1974), *Star Wars: Episode V - The Empire Strikes Back* (1980), *For Your Eyes Only* (1981), *Heat and Dust* (1983), *Cry Freedom* (1987), *Indiana Jones and the Last Crusade* (1989), *King Ralph* (1991), *Two Men Went to War* (2002), *Harry Potter and the Chamber of Secrets* (2002), *Troy* (2004), *Strings* (2004), *Scoop* (2006), *Mirrors* (2008) and *The Young Victoria* (2009 - as the Duke of Wellington). He has recently starred in the HBO mini-series *Game of Thrones* (2010) and will appear in the upcoming horror movie, *Airborne* (2012). A fine Shakespearean actor, nevertheless he may be the only actor to have appeared in the popular film series' *James Bond* - as Aris Kristatos, *Indiana Jones* - as Walter Donovan, *Star Wars* - as General Veers and *Harry Potter* - as the voice of the giant spider Aragog. His Hollywood career has tended to centre around the liking for casting excellent English actors as villains. On television he has appeared in episodes of numerous top notch British drama series since 1960. Julian was married to actress Eileen Atkins (1957-66) and has been married to actress Isla Blair since 1968. See also entries in the television section for *By the Sword Divided, Dombey and Son, The Hanged Man* , and *Wish Me Luck*.

Goddard, Willoughby (1926-2008) Born Willoughby Wittenham Rees Goddard, 4 July 1926, Bicester, Oxfordshire. Actor. His screen debut was as John Hartley in the little-known film, *Bait* (1950). Willougby's other films include: *The Million Pound Note* (1954), *The Green Man* (1956), *Inn for Trouble* (1960), *The Millionairess* (1960), *The Wrong Box* (1966), *The Charge of the Light Brigade* (1968), *Laughter in the Dark* (1969), *The Canterbury Tales* (1971), *Gawain and the Green Knight* (1973), *Young Sherlock Holmes* (1985) and his last film, *God's Outlaw* (1986). He was the voice of the polar bear which advertised "cool, clear and minty" Fox's Glacier Mints on television in the 1970s and 1980s. Despite lending his voice to this famous advert Willoughby was far better known for his very distinct looks rather than his voice. His most famous role was undoubtedly as Gessler in the much-repeated adventure series, *William Tell*. He died 11 April 2008. See entries in the television section for *Ace of Wands, The Man in Room 17, The Mind of Mr. J.G. Reeder, Oliver Twist, Porterhouse Blue*, and *The Adventures of William Tell*.

Goldcrest Films (1977-1987) A production founded by Jake Eberts in 1977 as a finance company for film projects. It helped finance *Black Jack* (1979) but the breakthrough came with the award winning *Chariots of Fire* (1981) after which the company became closely identified with the revival of British film-making. Goldcrest financed, to varying degrees: *Gandhi* (1982), *Local Hero* (1983), *The Killing Fields* (1984), *Dance with a Stranger* (1984), *A Room with a View* (1985) and *Hope and Glory* (1987). Unfortunately large investment in *Revolution* (1985), *The Mission* (1985) and *Absolute Beginners* (1986) brought the company to the edge of bankruptcy and it was sold to *Brent Walker* in 1987.

Goode, Matthew (1978-) Born 3 April 1978, Exeter, Devon. Actor. First seen on our screens as a television actor; an early role was as the brother of Inspector Lynley in the 2003 BBC production *Inspector Lynley Mysteries: A Suitable Vengeance*. His film roles include Charles Ryder in the 2008 film *Brideshead Revisited*, Adrian Veidt in Zack Snyder's 2009 film *Watchmen*, and Jim, the gay lover of George Falconer in the highly acclaimed 2009 film *A Single Man*. His recent films include, *Leap Year* (2010 - as Declan) and *Cemetery Junction* (2010 - as Mike Ramsay). He is currently the face of Hackett, the English Gentleman's outfitters. Matthew and his long-term girlfriend, Sophie Dymoke, have a daughter, Matilda Eve (b. March 2009). His half sister is television presenter Sally Meen (b. 1966).

Gordon, Mary (1882-1963) Born Mary Clark Gilmour 16 May 1882, Glasgow. Actress. One of five children, she worked in a confectioners shop before treading the boards. She arrived in the US with a touring stage company and from the mid-1920s played character roles in numerous Hollywood films, most memorably in the role of Mrs. Hudson, housekeeper for Sherlock Holmes, on the screen as well as in the radio series. From her first film *The Homemaker* (1925) to her last *West of Wyoming* (1950) she made over two hundred film appearances. She died 23 August 1963, Pasadena, California.

Goring, Marius (1912-98) Born 23 May 1912, Newport, Isle of Wight. Actor. Marius made his stage debut in 1927. He studied at the Old Vic dramatic school and was stage manager at the Old Vic 1932-34 before fulfilling a childhood ambition and joining *La Compagnie des Quinze*, touring France and Netherlands in classical roles. A distinguished Shakespearean actor his film and television roles never really reflected this. His screen debut was *Consider Your Verdict* (1936). His most memorable films were those directed by Powell and Pressburger: *A Matter of Life and Death* (1946), *The Red Shoes* (1948) and *Ill Met by Moonlight* (1956). A strong supporter of Equity, of which he was a founder member, he battled against it's politicisation in the 1970s. He was appointed Commander of the British Empire in 1991. Marius married Mary Westwood Steel (1931-41), German actress Lucie Mannheim, from 1941 to her death in 1976, and director Prudence Fitzgerald, from 1977 to his death on 30 September 1998, Eastbourne, East Sussex. See also entries in the television section for *Edward and Mrs Simpson, The Expert,* and *The Adventures of the Scarlet Pimpernel*.

Goulding, Edmund (1891-1959) Born Edmund George Goulding, 20 March 1891, Feltham, Middlesex. Actor, director and writer. Son of a butcher. Stage debut: *Alice in Wonderland* (1909). Screen acting debut: *Henry VIII* (1911). Edmund settled in the United States in 1915. Screenwriting debut: *The Quest for Life* (1916). He was hired as a director/screenwriter by *MGM* in 1925 where he directed such screen stars as Joan Crawford in *Sally, Irene and Mary* (1926); Greta Garbo in *Anna Karenina* (1927); Gloria Swanson in *The Trespasser* (1929) and Garbo again in *Grand Hotel* (1932). After his move to *Warner Bros* in 1936 he directed Bette Davis, with whom he reportedly had a stormy professional relationship, in *That Certain Woman* (1937), *Dark Victory* (1939), *The Old Maid* (1939) and *The Great Lie* (1941). Other films he directed include: *The Dawn Patrol* (1938), *We Are Not Alone* (1939), *The Constant Nymph* (1943), *Of Human Bondage* (1946), *Nightmare Alley* (1948), *Mister 880* (1950), *Teenage Rebel* (1956) and *Mardi Gras* (1958). He wrote over 60 films including: *Dangerous Toys* (1921), *Broadway Rose* (1922), *Till We Meet Again* (1922), *Dark Secrets* (1923), *Dante's Inferno* (1924), *Havoc* (1925), *Broadway Melody* (1929), *The Grand Parade* (1930), *Flesh* (1932), *That Certain Woman* (1937), *Flight from Folly* (1945) and *Teenage Rebel* (1956). Edmund was author of plays including: *Out of the Fog* (1912), *God Save the King* (1914), *Dancing Mothers* (1924) and *The Ryan Girl* (1945). He also wrote a novel: *Fury* (1922), which was filmed in 1923. A man of great versatility and eccentricity, he was also a composer, songwriter and poet. He died 24 December 1959, Los Angeles, California.

Graham, Sheilah (1904-88) Born Lily Sheil, 15 September 1904, Leeds, Yorkshire. Gossip columnist and author. Daughter of Ukrainian immigrants who moved to the East End of London. She spent some of her early years in an orphanage after the death of her father and her mother finding herself in straightened circumstances. After working in a department store she married a much older man and enrolled at RADA, before eventually becoming one of C B Cochran's chorus girls. She then began writing and moved from the stage to the page as a freelance journalist and emigrated to the United States in 1933. She then relocated to Hollywood in 1936 as a nationally syndicated columnist, writing *Hollywood Today*, vying with Hedda Hopper and Louella Parsons as top Hollywood gossip columnist. From 1937, until his death in 1940, she was in a relationship with F Scott Fitzgerald, and as she herself put it "I was never a mistress. I was a woman who loved F Scott Fitzgerald for better or worse until he died." During this period he "educated" her and in particular improved her appreciation of literature as documented in her book *College of One* (1966). She was the inspiration for the character Kathleen in his unfinished novel *The Last Tycoon*. She wrote a book about her life and her love affair called *Beloved Infidel* (1957), named after one of Fitzgerald's poems. The book was turned into a disappointing film of the same name in 1959 with Gregory Peck as Fitzgerald and Deborah Kerr as Graham. She was still writing columns into the early 1970s and also wrote several books. Her daughter Wendy Fairey wrote *One of the Family* (1992) about her mother and father, the British philosopher A J Ayer. She died 17 November 1988, Palm Beach, Florida.

Graham, Stephen (1973-) Born 3 August 1973, Kirkby, Liverpool. Actor. He made his wide screen debut in *Dancin' thru the Dark* (1990) but is best known for his roles as Tommy in the movie *Snatch* (2000), Shang in *Gangs of New York* (2002), Combo in *This Is England* (2006), Harry Beechman in the Madonna-directed *Filth and Wisdom*, bank robber Baby Face Nelson in *Public Enemies* (2009) and his portrayal of Billy Bremner in the 2009 film *The Damned United*. His television roles include Sgt. Myron 'Mike' Ranney in *Band of Brothers* (2001) and he has recently starred as Al Capone in the HBO series *Boardwalk Empire* (2010-present) and had a small cameo in the Channel 4 series *This Is England '88* (2011), reprising his role of Combo. His most recent films include *London Boulevard* (2010), *Season of the Witch* (2011), *Pirates of the Caribbean: On Stranger Tides* (2011), *Texas Killing Fields* (2011 - as Rhino) and *Tinker Tailor Soldier Spy* (2011 - as Jerry Westaby). See also entries in the television section for *Coronation Street*, *The Passion*, and *The Street*.

Grahame, Margot (1911-82) Born Margaret Clark, 20 February 1911, Canterbury, Kent. Actress. Margot was born into an acting family which was touring in South Africa at the outbreak of WWI and decided to stay there. Billed during her early career as Britain's answer to Jean Harlow and she gained the unlikely appellation "The Aluminium Blonde". She made her stage debut in South Africa in 1926 before returning to Britain. She hit the big screen in *Rookery Nook* (1930). By 1932 she was reputedly Britain's highest paid film actress. She met actor Francis Lister and impulsively followed him to the United States, where they were married in 1934. Lister travelled to Hollywood for a part in *Mutiny on the Bounty* (1935) and Margot accompanied him. She was spotted by John Ford and cast as Katie Madden, a prostitute and girl friend of *The Informer* (1935) played by Victor McLaglen. She went on to play Milady de Winter in *The Three Musketeers* (1935) but, according to *RKO*, whereas her looks were more suited to playing a gangster's moll her English accent betrayed her as someone more ladylike. The result was that she began to slip down the billing to second lead. She was impressive as Annette de Remy in *The Buccaneer* (1938) after which she returned to the stage. Her career was then interrupted by WWII and when she returned to the screen it was as a redhead in *The Fabulous Joe* (1947). A number of British films followed plus a stage tour in *Blithe Spirit* alongside Kay Kendall and Irene Handl. Her final film was a small part in *Saint Joan* (1957). She married three times: actor Francis Lister (1934-36), oil man Allan McMartin (1938-46) and literary agent Augustus Peters (1958-72). It was after her last wedding that she decided to retire. She died 1 January 1982, Knightsbridge. London.

Granger, Stewart (1913-93) Born James Lablache Stewart, 6 May 1913, Kensington, London. Actor. He was the great-great grandson of the opera singer Luigi Lablache and the grandson of the actor Luigi Lablache. Studied at the Webber-Douglas School. Although known throughout his life as Jim by family and friends he was obliged to change his name to avoid being confused with the American actor James Stewart. He flipped his surname and chose his Scottish grandmother's maiden name of Granger. Stage debut: *The Cardinal* (1935). Screen debut: *A Southern Maid* (1933). His first credited film role was as Laurence in *So This is London* (1939). Other films include: *The Man in Grey* (1943), *Fanny by Gaslight* (1944), *Waterloo Road* (1945), *Caesar and Cleopatra* (1945), *Captain Boycott* (1947), *Saraband for Dead Lovers* (1948), *King Solomon's Mines* (1950), *Scaramouche*

(1952), *The Prisoner of Zenda* (1952), *Young Bess* (1953), *Beau Brummell* (1954), *Moonfleet* (1955), *Bhowani Junction* (1956), *North to Alaska* (1960), *The Crooked Road* (1965), *The Trygon Factor* (1966), *The Wild Geese* (1978), *Hell Hunters* (1988), and his final film *Fine Gold* (1989). His final screen appearance was in the American detective series *Pros and Cons* in 1991. A great example of the suave leading man in costume dramas. In later life he said "I haven't aged into a character actor, I'm still an old leading man". Although Stewart became an American citizen in 1956 we claimed him as our own in the same vein as Bob Hope, Cary Grant and Charlie Chaplin; indeed his stock was of that ilk. Stewart married three times, firstly to actress Elspeth March (1938-48), two children, Jamie and Lindsay, secondly to actress Jean Simmons (1950-60), one daughter Tracy, and finally to Caroline LeCerf (1964-69), one daughter Samantha. He wrote an autobiography: *Sparks Fly Upward* (1983). Stewart died 16 August 1993, Santa Monica, California.

Grant, Cary (1904-86) Born Archibald Alexander Leach, 18 January 1904, Bristol. Actor. At the age of nine his mother suffered a breakdown and was institutionalized unbeknown to Cary, whose father told him that she had merely gone away on a "long holiday". They were reunited in 1935. He worked backstage at the Bristol Empire and Bristol Hippodrome which sparked an interest in the theatre and he eventually joined Bob Penders troupe of young performers and toured the UK, he specialising in stilt-walking. He travelled with the troupe to America in 1920 and remained behind when the tour was over. His legitimate stage debut came in *Golden Dawn* (1927) and his screen debut in *Singapore Sue* (1931). Cary was then contracted to Paramount, who had earlier rejected him. His early films include: *This is the Night* (1932), *Blonde Venus* (1932) - opposite Marlene Dietrich - and *She Done him Wrong* (1933) - opposite Mae West. He went on to make *I'm No Angel* (1933), *Sylvia Scarlett* (1935), *The Toast of New York* (1937), *Topper* (1937) and *The Awful Truth* (1937), a film where he established his template persona of fast-talking suave charmer. From this point on he became one of Hollywood's most bankable stars and featured in some of the best loved comedies of the period: *Bringing up Baby* (1938), *The Philadelphia Story* (1940), *His Girl Friday* (1940), *My Favourite Wife* (1940), *The Talk of the Town* (1942), *Arsenic and Old Lace* (1944), *Mr Blandings Builds His Dream House* (1948), *I Was a Male War Bride* (1949), *Monkey Business* (1952), *Dream Wife* (1953), *Indiscreet* (1958), *Operation Petticoat* (1959) alongside Tony Curtis, a notable mimic of Grant's mid-Atlantic tones, *The Grass Is Greener* (1960), *That Touch of Mink* (1962), *Father Goose* (1964) and his last feature film, *Walk, Don't Run* (1966). He also teamed up with Alfred Hitchcock in a series of thrillers: *Suspicion* (1941), *Notorious* (1946), *To Catch a Thief* (1955) and *North by North West* (1959). Hitchcock described him as "the only actor I ever loved in my whole life". Other films include: *Gunga Din* (1939), *An Affair to Remember* (1957), *The Pride and the Passion* (1957) and *Charade* (1963).He retired from the screen in 1969. Nominated for Best Actor Academy Awards for *Penny Serenade* (1941) and *None but the Lonely Heart* (1944), in which he played a rare British role as cockney Ernie Mott. Cary did however receive an honorary Academy Award in 1971 "for his unique mastery of the art of screen acting with the respect and affection of his colleagues". Cary was a great innovator, being the first actor to "go independent" by not renewing his studio contract and he also formed his own production company, Grantley Productions, in the 1950s. He was also a great raconteur and wit. After receiving a telegram from a magazine editor asking "HOW OLD CARY GRANT?" Cary was reported to have responded with "OLD CARY GRANT FINE. HOW YOU?" Although he was married five times: Virginia Cherrill (1934-35), Barbara Hutton (1942-45), Betsy Drake (1949-62), Dyan Cannon (1965-67), with whom he had his only child, a daughter Jennifer Diane Grant (b. 26 February 1966) and Barbara Harris (1981-86) he is also believed to have had a long-term relationship with actor Randolph Scott with whom he co-habited at various times, although Cary himself always denied being homosexual. He died

29 November 1986, Davenport, Iowa whilst touring his *A Conversation with Cary Grant* show.

Grant, Hugh (1960-) Born Hugh John Mungo Grant, 9 September 1960, Hammersmith, London. Actor and film producer. Educated at New College Oxford. Performed with a comedy revue called The Jockeys of Norfolk. His screen debut was in *Privileged* (1982 – credited as Hughie Grant), a film in which Imogen Stubbs (born 20 February 1961, Northumberland) also made her screen debut. He then had a variety of jobs including assistant groundsman at Fulham Football Club, before appearing in the ITV mini-series *Last Place On Earth* (1985) and an episode of *A Very Peculiar Practice* (1986). Hugh then continued his film career with: *Maurice* (1987), *White Mischief* (1987), *The Big Man* (1990), *Impromptu* (1991 – as Frederic Chopin) and *Remains of the Day* (1993). His big break came in, *Four Weddings and a Funeral* (1994), which became the highest-grossing British film to date. Hugh won a Golden Globe and a BAFTA Award for this film and he now became an international star. His subsequent films include: *Sirens* (1994), *The Englishman Who Went Up a Hill But Came Down a Mountain* (1995), *An Awfully Big Adventure* (1995), *Nine Months* (1995), *Sense and Sensibility* (1995), *Notting Hill* (1999), *Mickey Blue Eyes* (1999), *Small Time Crooks* (2000), *Bridget Jones Diary* (2001), *About a Boy* (2002), *Two Weeks Notice* (2002), *Love Actually* (2003), *Bridget Jones: The Edge of Reason* (2004), *American Dreamz* (2006), *Music and Lyrics* (2007) and *Did You Hear About the Morgans?* (2009). Hugh's private life has spawned much media comment. He began a relationship with actress Liz Hurley in 1987 and they formed the production company *Simian Films* (apparently so called because Hurley thinks Grant looks like a monkey) in 1994. On 27 June 1995, he was arrested in a Los Angeles Vice police operation in the vicinity of Sunset Boulevard, for the misdemeanour 'lewd conduct in a public place' with Hollywood prostitute Divine Brown. He pleaded no contest and was fined $1,180, placed on two years' summary probation, and ordered to complete an AIDS education program. He eventually split with Liz Hurley in 2000 and then dated Jemima Khan between 2004 and 2007. In September 2011, Hugh became a father to a baby girl by 32-year-old Chinese actress Tinglan Hong. Reported to be a scratch golfer, Hugh has been touted as the modern day successor to his namesake Cary, with the ability to carry off the bumbling charmer with aplomb but well able to play the cad if called upon to do so.

Grant, Richard E (1957-) Born Richard Grant Esterhuysen, 5 May 1957, Mbabane, Swaziland. Actor, screenwriter and director. Educated at the University of Capetown. Arrived in England in 1982. Made an immediate impression with his screen debut in *Withnail & I* (1987). Other films include: *How to Get Ahead in Advertising* (1989), *L.A. Story* (1991), *Hudson Hawk* (1991), *Dracula* (1992), *The Age of Innocence* (1993), *Pret-a-Porter* (1994), *Jack and Sarah* (1995), *Twelfth Night* (1996), *Spice World* (1997), *The Little Vampire* (2000), *Gosford Park* (2001), *Bright Young Things* (2003) *Tooth* (2004), *Penelope* (2006), *Filth and Wisdom* (2008), notable for being the directorial debut for Madonna, *Love Hurts* (2009), *Cuckoo* (2010), *Jackboots on Whitehall* (2010), *The Nutcracker in 3D* (2010), *Horrid Henry: The Movie* (2011) and *The Iron Lady* (2011 - as Michael Heseltine).. His TV credits include: *Hard Times* (1994), *A Royal Scandal* (1996), *The Scarlet Pimpernel* (1999), *The Hound of the Baskervilles* (2002), *Posh Nosh* (2003). *Above and Beyond* (2006), *Dalziel and Pascoe* (2007) and *Mumbai Calling* (2007). Nicknamed Reg; in 2005 he wrote and directed *Wah-Wah* a semi-autobiographical film. Autobiography: *With Nails - The Film Diaries of Richard E Grant* (1996). See also entry for *Dr Who* in the television section.

Graves, Rupert (1963-) Born 30 June 1963, Weston-Super-Mare, Somerset. Actor. Briefly worked as a circus clown and joined a troupe called Silly Billy Pickles and the Peanut Street Gang. Rupert made his television debut in *The Return of the Saint* (1978), his stage debut in *The Killing of Mr Toad* (1983) and his feature film debut in *A Room with a View* (1985). Other films include: *Maurice* (1987), *A Handful of Dust* (1988), *Damage* (1992), *The Madness of King George* (1994), *Different for Girls* (1996), *The Innocent Sleep* (1996), *Intimate Relations* (1996), *Mrs Dalloway* (1997), *Dreaming of Joseph Lees* (1999), *Extreme Ops*

(2002), *V for Vendetta* (2006). *Death at a Funeral* (2007), *The Waiting Room* (2008) and *Made in Dagenham* (2010). Rupert is also an ever-present on British television appearing in such series as *Ashes to Ashes, Waking the Dead, Wallander, Lewis, Law & Order: UK, Single Father* and *New Tricks*. He has been married to Susie Lewis since 2001. See also entries in the television section for *The Forsyte Saga, Fortunes of War*, and *Sherlock*.

Gray, Charles (1928-2000) Born Donald Marshall Gray, 29 August 1928, Bournemouth, Dorset. Actor. Worked as an estate agent before taking up acting full time. Stage debut: *As You Like It* (1952) as Charles the Wrestler - he went on to take Charles as his stage Christian name. Screen debut: *The Black Whip* (1956). Other films include: *I Accuse!* (1958), *The Entertainer* (1960), *Masquerade* (1965), *The Night of the Generals* (1967), *You Only Live Twice* (1967 - as Dikko Henderson), *The Devil Rides Out* (1968), *Cromwell* (1970), *The Rocky Horror Picture Show* (1975), *The Seven-per-cent-Solution* (1976 - as Mycroft Holmes), *The Mirror Crack'd* (1980), *The Jigsaw Man* (1984) and his last film, *The Tichborne Claimant* (1998). His most memorable role was as Ernst Stavro Blofeld in *Diamonds Are Forever* (1971). He also dubbed the voice of Jack Hawkins after that actor's throat surgery. He died 7 March 2000, Brompton Hospital, London. See also entries in the television section for *Churchill's People, Love Story, The New Statesman, Porterhouse Blue, The Rivals of Sherlock Holmes, The Adventures of Sherlock Holmes*, and *The Upper Crusts*.

Gray, Dulcie (1915-2011) Born Dulcie Winifred Catherine Savage Bailey, 20 November 1915 Kuala Lumpur, Malaysia. Actress. Educated in England before returning to Malaya to run a girl's boarding school whilst still in her teens. It was during this time that she wrote the legendary song *You Tickle Me Spitless, Baby*. Dulcie returned to England and, after working as an artist's model, enrolled at the Webber-Douglas Drama School where she met her future husband Michael Denison. After playing in *Brighton Rock* on the stage she was signed by *Gainsborough Pictures* where by her own account she got to be the dull one next to Phylis Calvert and Patricia Roc. However, that didn't stop her making an impact in *2,000 Women* (1944 – her feature debut), *Madonna of the Seven Moons* (1945) and *They Were Sisters* (1945). After a few more films including *My Brother Jonathan* (1948), *The Glass Mountain* (1949), and *Angels One Five* (1953) she virtually disappeared from the big screen (the 1966 film *Welcome, Mr. Beddoes* being her only other feature) to join her husband in a fantastically popular theatre career which saw them together in thirty West End productions. In the mid 1980s she returned to grace the small screen as Kate Harvey in *Howard's Way*. Awarded the CBE in 1983, she was also a successful author, having penned 24 books, including seventeen detective stories featuring Inspector Cardiff such as *Death in Denims* and *Died in the Red*. Married to Michael Denison from 1939 until his death in 1998, she was still treading the boards in plays such as *The Lady Vanishes* well into the new Millennium. Dulcie died from bronchial pneumonia in the actors' residential care home, Denville Hall, Northwood, Middlesex, on 15 November 2011.

Gray, Sally (1916-2006) Born Constance Vera Stevens, 14 February 1916, Holloway, London. Actress. Made her stage debut in 1928 and her screen debut in *School for Scandal* (1930). Described as a voluptuous blonde, she made 20 films between 1935 and 1941, which apparently led to a breakdown through nervous exhaustion. Some of those films were *The Dictator* (1935), *Sword of Honour* (1938), *The Lambeth Walk* (1940) and *Dangerous Moonlight* (1941). She returned to the screen in 1946 with *Green for Danger, The Mark of Cain* (1947), *Obsession* (1949) and *Escape Route* (1952). In 1950 she married Dominick Geoffrey Edward Browne, 4th Baron Oranmore and Browne, and retired happily. Dominick died in 2002 and Sally died on 24 September 2006.

Green, Hughie (1920-97) Born Hughie Hughes Green, 2 February 1920 Marylebone, London. Actor and television presenter. Raised in Canada, Hughie returned to England in 1932 and became a child actor. Screen debut: *Midshipman Easy* (1935). Other films include: *Melody and Romance* (1937), *Music Hall Parade* (1939), *Down Our Alley* (1939), *Tom Brown's School Days* (1940) and *Men of the Sea* (1951). He joined the Royal Canadian Air Force during WWII and worked in America during the early 1950s in order to pay off debts incurred after a failed law suit against the BBC - he claimed they were conspiring to prevent the screening of *Opportunity Knocks*, which he had hosted on BBC radio and Radio Luxembourg. Hughie hosted many successful game shows during the 1960s, 1970s and 1980s including *Double Your Money* and *The Sky's the Limit*. After his death it was revealed that he was the biological father of TV presenter Paula Yates. Autobiography: *Opportunity Knocked* (1965). He died 3 May 1997, Kensington, London. See also entries in the television section for *Sunday Night at the London Palladium*, and *Take Your Pick*.

Greenaway, Peter (1942-) Born Peter J Greenaway, 5 April 1942, Newport, Gwent. Director, installation artist and writer. Studied at Walthamstow College of Art. Peter worked as a film editor for the Central Office of Information (1965-76) and whilst there began making his own experimental short films including *Train* (1966), *Intervals* (1969), *Windows* (1974), *Goole by Numbers* (1976) and *A Walk Through H* (1978). His first feature film was *The Falls* (1980). His big breakthrough came with *The Draughtsman's Contract* (1982). He followed this with *A Zed and Two Noughts* (1985), *The Belly of an Architect* (1987) and *Drowning by Numbers* (1988). The controversial and critically acclaimed *The Cook, the Thief, his Wife and her Lover* (1989) brought him to wider attention. His reworking of *The Tempest*, *Prospero's Books* (1991) saw him make some innovative visual experiments. His later films include: *The Baby of Macon* (1993), *The Pillow Book* (1996), *8 1/2 Women* (1999) and *The Man in the Bath* (2001). In 2004 he completed a trilogy entitled *The Tulse Luper Suitcases*. Whilst living in The Netherlands in 2006 he began a series of digital video installations, *Nine Classical Paintings Revisited*, with his exploration of Rembrandt's *Night Watch* in the Rijksmuseum, Amsterdam. On 30 June 2008, he staged a 'remixing' of da Vinci's *The Last Supper* in the refectory of Santa Maria delle Grazie in Milan and as part of the 2009 Venice Biennial he offered a 50-minute presentation of *The Wedding at Cana* by Paolo Veronese, set to a soundtrack, incorporating closeup images of the 126 faces engaging in small talk and banal chatter that culminates in reaction to the miraculous transformation of water into wine. He is currently professor of cinema studies at the European Graduate School in Saas-Fee, Switzerland. Peter has recently completed shooting his latest project, *Goltzius and the Pelican Company*, an upcoming film about Hendrik Goltzius, a late 16th century Dutch printer and engraver of erotic prints.

Greene, Richard (1918-85) Born Richard Marius Joseph Greene, 25 August 1918, Plymouth, Devon. Actor. His father, Richard Abraham Greene and his mother, Kathleen Gerrard, were both actors with the Plymouth Repertory Theatre and his aunt was the musical theatre actress Evie Greene. Richard began his stage career as a spear-carrier in Shakespeare's *Julius Caesar* in 1933 but by 1938 he had joined *20th Century Fox* as a rival to *MGM's* Robert Taylor. He made his film debut in John Ford's *Four Men and a Prayer* (1938), although he did have an uncredited walk-on in the Gracie Fields vehicle *Sing As We Go* (1934). Films of this period include: *Submarine Patrol* (1938), *Kentucky* (1938), *The Little Princess* (1939), *The Hound of the Baskervilles* (1939) and *Stanley and Livingstone* (1939). Richard interrupted his acting career to serve in World War II in the Royal Armoured Corps of the Twenty Seventh Lancers where he distinguished himself and reached the rank of Captain. He was relieved from duty to appear in the British propaganda films *Flying Fortress* and *Unpublished Story*, in 1942, and appeared in *The Yellow Canary* while on furlough in 1943. He later toured in Shaw's *Arms and the Man* entertaining the forces before being discharged in December 1944. After the war his popularity diminished somewhat and *Forever Amber* (1947) was his last substantial role before embarking on several swashbuckling ventures interspersed with the odd romantic lead in such films as *The Fighting O'Flynn* (1949), *The Fan* (1949), *Now Barabbas* (1949), *Shadow of the Eagle* (1950), *The Desert Hawk* (1950), *The Bandits of Corsica* (1953), *Rogue's March* (1953) and *Captain Scarlett* (1953). This eventually led to his career being resurrected as a television actor

in the *Adventures of Robin Hood*, where he played the definitive Robin Hood for those of a certain age, in the same manner as Errol Flynn had done so for the previous generation. His final films include: *Beyond the Curtain* (1960), *Sword of Sherwood Forest* (1961), *Island of the Lost* (1968), *The Blood of Fu Manchu* (1968), *The Castle of Fu Manchu* (1968 – as Nayland Smith) and his final film *Tales from the Crypt* (1972). Richard then retired to breed horses in County Wexford, Ireland. His two marriages were to British actress Patricia Medina (1941-51) and Brasilian heiress Beatriz Summers (1960-80). Richard underwent surgery in 1982 for a brain tumor and never fully recovered. He died of cardiac arrest on 1 June 1985, Norfolk, England.

Greenstreet, Sydney (1879-1954) Born Sydney Hughes Greenstreet, 27 December 1879, Sandwich, Kent. Actor. Worked at various jobs, including tea planting in Ceylon before plumping for acting. He studied at Ben Greet Academy of Acting and made his stage debut in *Sherlock Holmes* (1902). Sydney concentrated on the stage both in Britain and the United States until making a memorable screen debut as Kaspar Gutman in *The Maltese Falcon* (1941) at the age of 61. He gained an Academy Award Nomination as Best Supporting Actor for this performance. After playing Lt. General Winfield Scott in *They Died with their Boots On* (1941) he took the role of Senor Ferrari in *Casablanca* (1942). His other films include: *The Mask of Dimitrios* (1944), *Christmas in Connecticut* (1945), *The Verdict* (1946), *Three Strangers* (1946) and *The Woman in White* (1948). Weighing in at almost 300 pounds, his huge stature contributed to his death from the complications of diabetes and Bright's Disease on 18 January 1954, Hollywood, California.

Greenwood, Joan (1921-87) Born 4 March 1921, Chelsea, London. Actress. Studied at RADA in London. With her demeanour, looks and husky voice, Joan always seemed to be playing a Lady either titled or otherwise, indeed finding a role which didn't have the prefix Lady may prove troublesome. Lady Warren, Lady Ashwood, Lady Caroline Lamb, Lady Mary Fairchild, Lady Dodo Fitzadam...the list goes on. Her first big screen outing was *My Wife's Family* (1941), after which she appeared in many classic British comedies of the 1940s and 1950s, including *The Gentle Sex* (1943), *Latin Quarter* (1945), *The October Man* (1947), *Saraband for Dead Lovers* (1948), *Whisky Galore!* (1949), *Kind Hearts and Coronets* (1949), *The Man in the White Suit* (1951) and the screen version of Oscar Wilde's *The Importance of Being Earnest* (1952). Her subsequent films include: *Monsieur Ripois* (1954), *Father Brown* (1954), *Moonfleet* (1955), *Stage Struck* (1958), *Mysterious Island* (1961), *Tom Jones* (1963), *The Moon-Spinners* (1964), *Barbarella* (1968 – voice only), *The Water Babies* (1978), *The Hound of the Baskervilles* (1978) and *At Bertram's Hotel* (1987). Her last film released after her death was *Little Dorritt* (1988), in which she played Mrs Clenham. Joan did very little television but towards the end of her career she appeared in the comedy series *Girls On Top* (1985), as Lady Chloe Carlton. From 1959 until his death in 1978 she was married to the actor Andre Morrell. She died 27 February 1987, Chelsea, London.

Gregg, Everley (1903-59) Born 26 October 1903, Bishop Stoke, Hampshire. Actress. Not much is recorded of her off-screen life but on the screen she made her debut as Katherine Parr in *The Private Life of Henry VIII* (1933). Her other films include *Pygmalion* (1938) as Mrs Eynsford-Hill, *In Which We Serve* (1942), *Brief Encounter* (1945 - as Dolly Messiter), *Great Expectations* (1946 - as Sarah Pocket), *The Magic Box* (1951), *Carry on Admiral* (1957) and *Room at the Top* (1959). She died 9 June 1959, Beaconsfield, Buckinghamshire.

Gregson, John (1919-75) Born Harold Thomas Gregson, 15 March 1919, Liverpool. Actor. Screen debut: *Saraband for Dead Lovers* (1948). Other films include: *Scott of the Antarctic* (1948), *Whisky Galore* (1949), *Treasure Island* (1950), *The Lavender Hill Mob* (1951), *The Titfield Thunderbolt* (1953 – as Squire Gordon Chesterford), *The Battle of the River Plate* (1956), *The Captain's Table* (1959), *SOS Pacific* (1959), *Hand in Hand* (1960), *Faces in the Dark* (1960), *The Frightened City* (1961), *The Treasure of Monte Cristo* (1961), *The Longest Day* (1962), *Tomorrow at Ten*

(1964), *The Night of the Generals* (1967) and his final film, *Fright* (1971). His best known film role was as Alan McKim in *Genevieve* (1953) but he will always be remembered for playing the title role in the TV police series *Gideon's Way* (1965-66). John died 8 January 1975, Porlock Weir, Somerset, whilst on holiday. He left a widow, actress Thea Gregory, and six children. See also entries in the television section for *Gideon's Way, Love Story,* and *Shirley's World.*

Grenfell, Joyce (1910-79) Born Joyce Irene Phipps, 10 February 1910, London. Actress and comedienne. Daughter of architect Paul Phipps and an eccentric American mother, Nora Langhorne (herself the daughter of an American railroad millionaire and sister of Nancy Astor). A former journalist and radio critic of *The Observer,* Joyce made her stage debut in 1939, presenting her own monologues in a London revue. In 1942 she wrote what became her signature song, "I'm Going to See You Today." A year earlier she made her film debut in *A Letter from Home* (1941) and although she made another 20 films, nearly all comedies, she is perhaps best remembered as a comedienne and queen of the monologues and comic songs. She was also an avid letter writer and her friendship with Virginia Graham lasted for 62 years until her death. From film she will be forever remembered as Sergeant Ruby Gates failing to contend (time-after-time) with the girls of St Trinians in *The Belles of St Trinian's* (1954), *Blue Murder at St Trinian's* (1957) and *The Pure Hell of St Trinian's* (1960). Other films include: *The Happiest Days of Your Life* (1950), *The Magic Box* (1951), *The Pickwick Papers* (1952), *The Million Pound Note* (1953), *Genevieve* (1953) and *The Good Companions* (1957). In 1957 she was elected president of England's Society of Women Writers and Journalists and seven years later made her last film appearance in *The Yellow Rolls Royce* (1964), coincidentally, given her family background, playing a character called Hortense Astor. She was married to Reggie Grenfell from 1929 until her death on 30 November 1979 in Chelsea, London. See also entries in the television section for *Face the Music,* and *The World of Beachcomber.*

Grierson, John (1898-1972) Born 26 April 1898 Deanston, Kilmadock, Perthshire. Director and producer. John served on minesweepers during WWI and subsequently graduated in philosophy from Glasgow University. He was a Rockefeller research fellow 1923-27, during which time he visited Hollywood. John focused on the influence of mass media, including the tabloid press and public opinion. He joined the *Empire Marketing Board* (*EMB*), an organisation which promoted British products and workers, as an Assistant Films Officer and in 1929 directed *Drifters,* a documentary about the North Sea herring fleet. It was premiered in London on the same bill as Eisenstein's *Battleship Pontemkin.* John actively encouraged the development of government-funded film-making and in particular for youth. The *EMB* was disbanded in 1933 and the unit moved virtually wholesale to the *General Post Office* (*GPO*) with Grierson as *Films Officer.* He next produced *Night Mail* (1936), which was directed by Harry Watt from a script by W H Auden and a score by Benjamin Britten. After resigning from the *GPO* in 1937 he formed the *Film Centre* and became production advisor to *Films of Scotland* and during WWII served as film commissioner at the *National Film Board of Canada.* In 1946-48 he served as UNESCO's first Director of Mass Communications and Public Information. From 1948-50 he worked in the films division of the *Central Office of Information* but, frustrated by public spending cuts, he joined the production arm of the *National Film Finance.* He next hosted a Scottish television programme *This Wonderful World* (1957-67) before completing his working life as a teacher at a Canadian university. John is considered by many to be the father of modern documentary. In a review he wrote of Robert Flaherty's *Moana* he is believed to be the first writer to coin the word 'documentary'. Examples of other documentaries he produced include: *Song of Ceylon* (1934), *Coal Face* (1935), *Housing Problems* (1935), *Song of Ceylon* (1934) and *Brandy for the Parson* (1952). He died 19 February 1972, Bath, Somerset.

Griffith, Hugh (1912-80) Born Hugh Emrys Griffith, 30 May 1912, Marian Glas, Anglesey. Actor. Began his working life as a bank clerk. Trained at RADA, where he graduated a gold medallist, top of his class of 300. Stage debut in 1939. His screen debut was in the TV film *Johnson Was No Gentleman* (1939). He then had an uncredited role in *Neutral Port* (1940). He served in India and Burma during WWII. After the war his first full credited feature role was as Packman in Silver Darlings (1947). Other films include: *The Three Weird Sisters* (1948), *London Belongs to Me* (1948), *Kind Hearts and Coronets* (1949), *Laughter in Paradise* (1951), *The Beggar's Opera* (1953), *The Titfield Thunderbolt* (1953), *The Million Pound Note* (1954), *Lucky Jim* (1957), *The Good Companions* (1957), *Exodus* (1960), *Mutiny on the Bounty* (1962), *Oliver!* (1968), *Wuthering Heights* (1970), *Take me High* (1973), *The Passover Plot* (1976), *Joseph Andrews* (1977), *The Last Remake of Beau Geste* (1977) and his final film, *A Nightingale Sang in Berkeley Square* (1979). Hugh was nominated for a Best Supporting Actor Academy Award for playing the lusty Squire Western in *Tom Jones* (1963). He did however earlier win a Best Supporting Actor Academy Award for his portrayal of the shrewd horse-loving chariot owner Sheik Iilderim in *Ben-Hur* (1959). A scene-stealing character actor par excellence. He died 14 May 1980, Kensington, London. See also entry for *The Walrus and the Carpenter* in the television section.

Griffiths, Richard (1947-) Born 31 July 1947, Stockton-on-Tees, Cleveland. Actor. Both Richard's parents were deaf and he learned sign language at an early age in order to communicate with them. He studied drama at Stockton & Billingham College and spent ten years with the RSC (1974-84) playing roles as diverse as Bottom and Henry VIII. Rather aptly perhaps, his first screen role was as an interpreter in an episode of the long-running television series *Crown Court* (1974). His feature debut came in *It Shouldn't Happen to a Vet* (1977). Other films include: *Breaking Glass* (1980), *Superman II* (1980), *Breaking Glass* (1980), *Ragtime* (1981), *The French Lieutenant's Woman* (1981), *Chariots of Fire* (1981), *Gandhi* (1982), *Gorky Park* (1983), *A Private Function* (1984), *Greystoke - The Legend of Tarzan, Lord of the Apes* (1984), *Shanghai Surprise* (1986), *Withnail & I* (1987 - as Uncle Monty), *The Naked Gun 2½: The Smell of Fear* (1991), *King Ralph* (1991), *Blame It on the Bellboy* (1992), *Guarding Tess* (1994), *Funny Bones* (1995), *Sleepy Hollow* (1999), *Vatel* (2000), *Harry Potter and the Philosopher's Stone* (2001), *Harry Potter and the Chamber of Secrets* (2002), *Stage Beauty* (2004), *Harry Potter and the Prisoner of Azkaban* (2004), *The Hitchhiker's Guide to the Galaxy* (2005), *Venus* (2006), *The History Boys* (2006), winning numerous awards for his portrayal of 'Hector', the general studies teacher, *Harry Potter and the Order of the Phoenix* (2007), *Bedtime Stories* (2008), *Jackboots on Whitehall* (2009), *Harry Potter and the Deathly Hallows* (2010), *Pirates of the Caribbean: On Stranger Tides* (2011) and *Hugo* (2011). After years of stage work with the RSC he became best known for playing a gourmet chef detective in the TV series *Pie in the Sky* (1994-97) before reaching even dizzier heights as Harry Potter's unpleasant Uncle Vernon Dursley in the Harry Potter series. Richard has recently appeared in *Episodes,* a British/American series featuring Matt Le Blanc as himself. He was appointed Officer of the Order of the British Empire (OBE) in the 2008 New Year Honours. He has been married to Heather Gibson since 1980. See also entries in the television section for *Bleak House, The Cleopatras, Gormenghast, Hope and Glory, Nobody's Perfect,* and *Whoops! Apocalypse.*

Grint, Rupert (1988-) Born Rupert Alexander Lloyd Grint, 24 August 1988, Harlow, Essex. Actor. Rupert grew up in Watton-at-Stone, Hertfordshire, and performed in school plays and with his local theatre group, Top Hat Stage School, before auditioning for, and being cast as, Ron Weasley in *Harry Potter and the Philosopher's Stone* (2001), a role he reprised in all seven subsequent Harry Potter films, *Harry Potter and the Chamber of Secrets, Harry Potter and the Prisoner of Azkaban, Harry Potter and the Goblet of Fire, Harry Potter and the Order of the Phoenix, Harry Potter and the Half-Blood Prince and Harry Potter and the Deathly Hallows Parts I and II.* His other film roles to date include: *Thunderpants* (2002 - as Alan A. Allen), *Driving Lessons* (2006 - as Ben Marshall), *Cherrybomb* (2009 - as Malachy) and *Wild Target* (2010 - as Tony). He is scheduled to play the title role of ski-jumper Eddie Edwards in the forthcoming film *Eddie the Eagle.* Rupert has also worked on radio and television, starring as Nigel Molesworth in the *Baggy Trousers* series for BBC Radio 4 (2003) and voicing Peter Pan in a BBC documentary.

Gruffudd, Iaon (1973-) Born 6 October 1973, Cardiff. Actor. As a teenage he played Gareth Wyn Harries In the Welsh language soap opera *Pobol Y Cwm (People of the Valley)* (1987-94). Iaon attended RADA (1992-95). Screen debut: *Wilde* (1997). Other films include: *Titanic* (1997), *102 Dalmations* (2000), *Black Hawk Down* (2001), *This Girl's Life* (2003), *King Arthur* (2004 - as Lancelot), *Fantastic Four* (2005 - as Reed Richards aka Mr Fantastic), *The TV Set* (2006), *Amazing Grace* (2006), *4: Rise of the Silver Surfer* (2007), *Agent Crush* (2008 - voice of the title character), *Fireflies in the Garden* (2008), *The Secret of Moonacre* (2008), *W.* (2008 - as Tony Blair), *The Kid* (2010), *Horrible Bosses* (2011) and *Sanctum* (2011). His TV films include: *A Relative Stranger* (1995), *Poldark* (1996), Great Expectations (1999), *Very Annie Mary* (2001), *Man and Boy* (2002) and *The Meant to Be's* (2008). Iaon also played Horatio Hornblower in the popular TV series *Hornblower* (1998-2003) and starred in the music video of Westlife's version of "Uptown Girl" (2001), alongside Claudia Schiffer. Iaon married actress Alice Evans (b. 2 August 1971, Bristol) in 2007.

Guinness, Alec (1914-2000) Born Alec Guiness de Cuffe, 2 April 1914, Maida Vale, London. Actor. Alec had a peripatetic childhood. Worked in an advertising agency whilst waiting to apply for RADA. He was recommended by Johh Gielgud to go to Martita Hunt for acting lessons and made his stage debut at the Albery Theatre in 1936 playing the role of Osric in John Gielgud's successful production of Hamlet. Alec served in the Royal Navy Volunteer Reserve during World War II and took part in the invasion of Sicily and Elba, later ferrying supplies to the Yugoslav partisans. Alec's screen debut came in the film *Great Expectations* (1946), playing the sympathetic role of Herbert Pocket. He then had starring roles in *Oliver Twist* (1948 – as Fagin) and *Kind Hearts & Coronets* (1949), playing the eight members of the D'Ascoyne family. Other films include: *The Mudlark* (1950 - as Benjamin Disraeli), *The Man in the White Suit* (1951), *The Captain's Paradise* (1953), *Father Brown* (1954), *The Ladykillers* (1955), *Our Man in Havana* (1959), *Tunes of Glory* (1960), *Lawrence of Arabia* (1962 – as Prince Faisal), *The Fall of the Roman Empire* (1964), *Dr Zhivago* (1965), *The Comedians* (1967), *Cromwell* (1970), *Scrooge* (1970 – as Jacob Marley's ghost), *Brother Sun, Sister Moon* (1972 - as Pope Innocent III), *Hitler: The Last Ten Days* (1973), *Raise the Titanic* (1980*), Little Lord Fauntleroy* (1980), *A Passage to India* (1984), *A Foreign Field* (1993), *Mute Witness* (1994), his final feature film, and the TV film *Eskimo Day* (1996), his final screen appearance. He won a Best Actor Academy Award for his portrayal of stubborn Colonel Nicholson in *The Bridge on the River Kwai* (1957). He was nominated for Academy Awards for *The Lavender Hill Mob* (1951) - actor, *The Horse's Mouth* (1958) - screenplay, *Star Wars* (1977) - supporting actor and *Little Dorritt* (1988) - supporting actor. He received a special Academy Award in 1980 for his contribution to film. He became well-known to a younger audience and a much richer man into the bargain having struck a 2% of the profits contract when he played Obi-Wan (Ben) Kenobi in the original *Star Wars Trilogy* (1977 - 1983). On television he won British Academy Television Awards for Best Actor for the role of George Smiley in *Tinker, Tailor, Soldier, Spy* (1979) and *Smiley's People* (1982). Alec was appointed CBE in 1955, knighted in 1959 and created a Companion of Honour in 1994. One of the all-time great British screen actors. Autobiographies: *My Name Escapes Me: Blessings in Disguise* (1985), *My Name Escapes Me: The Diary of a Retiring Actor* (1997), *A Positively Final Appearance* (1999). He married the artist, playwright, and actress Merula Sylvia Salaman (16 October 1914 – 18 October 2000) in 1938; in 1940, they had a son, Matthew Guinness, who later became an actor. Alec died 5 August 2000, Midhurst, Hampshire.

Guyler, Deryck (1914-99) Born Derrick B Guyler, 29 April 1914, Wallasey, Liverpool. Actor. Tried his hand at helping in his father's jewellery business and training as an Anglican priest (he subsequently converted to Catholicism) before joining the Liverpool Repertory Company in 1935. He served in the RAF during WWII before being invalided out and joining ENSA. After the war, he became a regular on the immensely popular radio series, *It's That Man Again (ITMA)* until the series was cancelled in 1949 upon the death of the main star Tommy Handley. Deryck became a well-known face on television in such comedies as *Sykes* - as PC Corky Turnbull and *Please Sir!* - as janitor Norman Hesquith Potter. His film debut came in *A Day to Remember* (1953). Other films include: *Mad About Men* (1954), *The Fast Lady* (1962), *Nurse on Wheels* (1963), *A Hard Day's Night* (1964), *Ferry Cross the Mersey* (1965), *Carry On Doctor* (1968), *Please Sir!* (1971), *No Sex Please, We're British* (1973), *Barry Mackenzie Holds his Own* (1974) and *One of Our Dinosaurs is Missing* (1976). He married Paddy Lennox from the three-sister music hall act The Lennox Theatre, and they had two sons, Peter and Christopher. Deryck specialised in playing officious jobsworths both on television and film. He was a founding member of the Society of Ancients, a group of wargamers specialising in the classical era, being elected its first president in 1966. Deryck was also a dab-hand at playing the washboard. He retired to Australia in the early 1990s and died 7 October 1999, Brisbane, Australia. See also entries in the television section for *It's A Square World*, *The Love of Mike*, *Please Sir*, *Sykes*, *Sykes and A..,* and *That's My Boy.*

Gwenn, Edmund (1877-1959) Born Edmund John Kellaway, 26 September 1877, Wandsworth, London. Actor. Son of a Customs Officer from Bodmin, Cornwall. Educated at St Olaves and King's College. Stage debut: *Rogues and Vagabonds* (1895). Screen debut: *The Real Thing at Last* (1916). Films made in Britain include: *The Skin Game* (1921), *Hindle Wakes* (1931), *The Skin Game* (1931), *Tell me Tonight* (1932), *The Good Companions* (1933), *Friday the Thirteenth* (1933) and *The Admiral's Secret* (1934). In 1935 he travelled to Hollywood. His later films include: *Sylvia Scarlett* (1935), *Anthony Adverse* (1936), *A Yank at Oxford* (1938), *The Doctor Takes a Wife* (1940), *Pride and Prejudice* (1940 - as Mr Bennet), *The Devil and Miss Jones* (1941), *Charley's Aunt* (1941), *The Keys of the Kingdom* (1944), *Of Human Bondage* (1946), *Life with Father* (1947), *A Woman of Distinction* (1950), *Les Miserables* (1952), *The Student Prince* (1954), *Them!* (1954), *The Trouble with Harry* (1955), *It's a Dog's Life* (1955) and *Calabuch* (1956). Edmund usually portrayed mild-mannered, cheery characters but could also use his elfin looks to hide a mischievous or even menacing demeanour - he played an assassin in *Foreign Correspondent* (1940). He won an Academy Award nomination for Best Supporting Actor for his role as a counterfeiter in *Mister 880* (1950). He won a Best Supporting Actor Academy Award for what is his best-loved role as Kris Kringle in *Miracle on 34th Street* (1947). His acceptance speech at the Oscars ceremony included the immortal, if somewhat predictable line, "There is a Santa Claus!". He was married to Minnie Terry for a matter of a few hours in 1901. His brother was actor Arthur Chesney (b. Arthur Kellaway 1882, Wandsworth, London; d. 27 August 1949 London). Edmund died 6 September 1959, Woodland Hills, California, and on his deathbed he was asked if dying was tough. His response: "Not as tough as comedy."

Gwillim, Jack (1909-2001) Born Jack William Frederick Gwillim, 15 December 1909, Canterbury, Kent. Actor. Joined the Royal Navy, aged 17, and remained in the service until invalided out with the rank of commander in 1946. He then enrolled in the Central School of Speech and Drama. A fine stage actor, he worked with Shakespeare Memorial Theatre and the Old Vic before emigrating to the United States in 1969. Screen debut: *The Battle of the River Plate* (1956). Other films include: *The One That Got Away* (1957), *Solomon and Sheba* (1959), *Sink the Bismarck!* (1960), *Lawrence of Arabia* (1962), *Jason and the Argonauts* (1963), *Thunderball* (1965), *A Man for All Seasons* (1966), *Battle of Britain* (1969), *Cromwell* (1970), *Patton* (1970), *Clash of the Titans* (1981), *Blind Date* (1987), *The Monster Squad* (1987) and his final film, *Blue Shark Harsh* (2000). Jack was married to Peggy Bollard, until 1958, and Olivia Selby, from 1969 until his death. He had two children from his first marriage, Sarah-Jane Gwillim and David Gwillim, and a third, Jaxon Duff Gwillim, from his second marriage. His children also became actors, and he acted onstage with them in 1995 in a production of *On Borrowed Time*, his final stage performance.He died 2 July 2001, Los Angeles, California.

Haigh, Kenneth (1931-) Born 25 March 1931, Mexborough, Yorkshire. Actor. Trained at the Central School of Speech and Dramatic Art before joining the English Stage Company. His feature film debut was as John Kendall in *Companions in Crime* (1954) but it was his subsequent stage appearance in the very first production of John Osborne's seminal play *Look Back in Anger* in 1956 that earnt him the soubriquet "angry young man". Kenneth's performance as Jimmy Porter in a 1958 Broadway theatre production of that play so moved one young lady in the audience that she climbed the stage and slapped him in mid-performance. Unfortunately, for the film version produced that year, he was passed over in favour of Richard Burton. Other films include: *Saint Joan* (1957), *High Flight* (1957), *Cleopatra* (1963), *A Hard Day's Night* (1964), *Weekend at Dunkirk* (1964), *The Deadly Affair* (1966), *A Lovely Way to Die* (1968), *Eagle in a Cage* (1972 - as Napoleon Bonaparte), *Man at the Top* (1973 - as Joe Lampton), reprising an earlier television role, *Robin and Marian* (1976), *The Bitch* (1979), *Night Train to Murder* (1983), *Wild Geese II* (1985), *A State of Emergency* (1986), *Shuttlecock* (1991) and the film short *Mr Blue* (2004). Richard Burton influenced Kenneth's life in several ways. Apart from missing out to him on the film role of Jimmy Porter, he played Brutus opposite Burton's Mark Antony in *Cleopatra* and also played the great Welsh actor's namesake Sir Richard Burton in the BBC mini-series *The Search for the Nile* (1971). Kenneth was undoubtedly one of Britain's greatest actors both on stage and television, making numerous appearances in one-off dramas and TV films. There was always a feeling he never really fulfilled his potential after his star burgeoned so brightly early on in his career. In 1960 he made a huge impact in the American television series *The Twilight Zone* as Flight Lieutenant William Terrance Decker in the episode "The Last Flight" but Kenneth chose to work on the stage and television plays for the remainder of the decade. His performance as social climber Joe Lampton in the television series *Man at the Top* (1970-72) vies with that of Edward Woodward in *Callan* as a role made so indelibly his own that one might easily forget that Laurence Harvey had already won a nomination for the Academy Award for Best Actor, for playing the role of Lampton in the 1959 film *Room at the Top*. See also entries in the television section for *Man at the Top,* and *The Search for the Nile.*

Hall, Rebecca (1982-) Born Rebecca Maria Hall, 19 May 1982, London. Actress. Rebecca hails from a theatrical family, her father being film and theatre director Peter Hall and her mother American opera singer Maria Ewing. A good student, Rebecca was head girl at Roedean but dropped out of her English Literature studies at Cambridge University in 2002 to appear as Vivie in her father's production of *Mrs Warren's Profession* at the Strand Theatre in London. In fact, Rebecca had made her television acting debut some ten years earlier when she appeared as young Sophy in her father's television adaptation of Mary Wesley's *The Camomile Lawn*. Her feature film debut came in 2006 as Rebecca Epstein in the film adaptation of David Nicholls's *Starter for Ten*. Rebecca made a breakthrough with the role of Sarah Borden in Christopher Nolan's film *The Prestige*. She next appeared in several television films, including: *Wide Sargasso Sea* (2006), *Rubberheart* (2007) and Stephen Poliakoff's *Joe's Palace* (2007). Rebecca was nominated for a Golden Globe for Best Actress in a Motion Picture – Musical or Comedy, for her role as Vicky in the Woody Allen film *Vicky Cristina Barcelona* (2008) and also won acclaim for her portrayal of David Frost's girlfriend in *Frost/Nixon* (2008). Other films include: *Dorian Gray* (2009), *Please Give* (2010), *The Town* (2010), *Everything Must Go* (2010) and *The Awakening* (2011). See also entry for Sam Mendes.

Hall-Davis, Lillian (1898-1933) Born Lilian Davis, 23 June 1898, Mile End, London. Actress. Screen debut: *La P'tite du Sixieme* (1917). Other films include: *The Admirable Crichton* (1918), *The Better 'ole: or The Romance of Old Bill* (1919), *The Game of Life* (1922), *The Eleventh Commandment* (1924), *Quo Vadis?* (1925), *If Youth but Knew* (1926), *Roses of Picardy* (1927), *Blighty* (1927), *The Ring* (1927), *Boadicea* (1928), *The Farmer's Wife* (1928) and *Her Reputation* (1931). An elegant blonde who was a beautiful presence in British films during the 1920s. Her star waned with the onset of the talkies. Out of work and suffering from insecurity and depression, she committed suicide 25 October 1933, Golders Green, London.

Hamer, Robert (1911-63) Born Robert James Hamer, 31 March 1911, Kiddermister, Worcestershire. Director, writer and editor. Sent down from Cambridge for his involvement in a homosexual scandal. Began his film career working in the cutting rooms at *Gaumont-British* before moving on to *London Films* at Denham and then *Mayflower Pictures*, where he worked as a film editor. Films he edited include: *Vessel of Wrath* (1938), *Jamaica Inn* (1939) and *The Foreman Went to France* (1942). In 1939 he joined the GPO unit under John Grierson before then joining Alberto Cavalcanti at *Ealing Studios*. He made his directorial debut by helming *San Demetrio London* (1943), which he also wrote. He directed a segment of *Dead of Night* (1945) called *The Haunted Mirror* and then directed his first full feature *Pink String and Sealing Wax* (1946). After this he directed *It Always Rains on Sunday* (1948). He wrote the screenplay for *Kind Hearts and Coronets* (1949) based on the novel *Israel Rank*. The fact that he directed this classic British film came in time to weigh on him as he said that "people get the impression it's the only picture I've ever made.". He made *The Spider and the Fly* (1950) for Mayflower before directing *His Excellency* (1951) back at Ealing. However, a disagreement with Michael Balcon over future projects saw him leave Ealing in 1951. After this he directed *The Long Memory* (1952), starring John Mills, and the popular *Father Brown* (1954), *To Paris with Love* (1955) and *The Scapegoat* (1958), which all starred Alec Guinness. By this time his personal life was in disarray and he had become an alcoholic. He had stayed sober during *The Scapegoat* but its subsequent mangling in the cutting room pushed him back to the bottle. He collapsed on the set of his next project, *School for Scoundrels* (1960) and he was removed from the picture. He was declared bankrupt in 1961. He died 4 December 1963, St Thomas's Hospital, London.

Hammond, Kay (1909-80) Born Dorothy Katherine Standing, 18 February 1909, London. Actress. Daughter of Sir Guy Standing. Made her stage debut in 1927 and her screen debut in *Children of Chance* (1930). Other films include: *Carnival* (1931), *Bitter Sweet* (1933), *Britannia of Billingsgate* (1933) and *Jeannie* (1941). A favourite during the 1930s, she briefly retired whilst married to her first husband but made a popular comeback as Elvira Condomine in *Blithe Spirit* (1945). Her final films include: *Call of the Blood* (1949), *Henry V* (1953) and her last film, *Five Golden Hours* (1961). Kay's first husband was baronet Sir Ronald George Leon. Their son is the popular stage and television actor John Standing (b. John Leon, 16 August 1934, London). Following their divorce in 1946 Kay married the stage actor Sir John Clements (25 April 1910 – 6 April 1988) and they remained wed until Kay's death, 4 May 1980, Brighton, East Sussex.

Hampshire, Susan (1937-) Born 12 May 1937, Kensington, London. Actress. Susan's first screen appearance was as a child actress in *The Woman in the Hall* (1947). Her early films included small parts in the BBC TV film *Expresso Bongo* (1960), *During One Night* (1960) and *The Long Shadow* (1961). On television she found fame playing Andromeda in the sequel to *A for Andromeda*, and as the lead in a 1962 BBC adaptation of *What Katy Did* called *Katy*. Susan's roles were often of the typical "English rose" variety. Susan was taken up by Walt Disney and starred in *The Three Lives of Thomasina* (1964), opposite Patrick McGoohan, and *The Fighting Prince of Donegal* (1966). She also appeared opposite McGoohan in two linked episodes of *Danger Man* (1965). Her other major films were *Monte Carlo or Bust* (1969) and *Living Free* (1972 - as Joy Adamson). Other films include: *The Trygon Factor* (1966), the TV film *David Copperfield* (1969 – as Agnes Wickfield), *Neither the Sea Nor the Sand* (1972), the TV film *Dr. Jekyll and Mr. Hyde* (1973), *A Time for Loving* (1975), the TV film The *Story of David* (1976 - as Michal) and *Bang!* (1977). Susan will always be remembered for her television roles rather than the impact she made in films. In 1966, she was introduced to American TV viewers in the pilot episode of *The Time Tunnel*, guest starring as a young passenger of the ill-fated Titanic that befriends Dr. Tony Neuman after he appears on the ship. She then starred in the hugely popular drama series *The Forsyte Saga* as Fleur Mont née Forsyte (1967), as Sarah

Churchill in *The First Churchills (1969),* and as Lady Glencora Palliser in *The Pallisers* (1974). Younger viewers may know her best as Molly MacDonald in *Monarch of the Glen* (2000-05) and as Elizabeth Middleditch in *The Royal* (2009). A sufferer from dyslexia, in her autobiography, *Susan's Story* (1983), she publicised her experiences, and her work on behalf of dyslexics eventually led to her being awarded the OBE in 1995. She has also published books on gardening and children's books including the *Lucy Jane* series. A many times told story about her is that when in 1973 at a show-business dinner she met the Prince of Wales whilst wearing an extremely low-cut dress. The Prince told her, "My father told me that if I ever met a lady in a dress like yours, I must look her straight in the eyes". Married to Sir Eddie Kulukundis since 1981 she was from 1967 to 1974 the wife of French film producer Pierre Granier-Deferre. See also entries in the television section for *A for Andromeda, The First Churchills, The Forsyte Saga, Monarch of the Glen, The Pallisers, The Royal,* and *Sir Francis Drake.*

Hancock, Tony See entry in comedy section

Handl, Irene (1901-87) Born 27 December 1901, Maida Vale London. Actress. The daughter of an Austrian banker father and an aristocratic French mother. Irene took up acting in her mid thirties on the advice of her father. Stage debut: *George and Margaret* (1935). Screen debut: *Missing believed Married* (1937). Although Irene had minor roles in classic films such as *Night Train to Munich* (1940), *Spellbound* (1941), *Brief Encounter* (1945) and *The History of Mr. Polly* (1949), she found fame in the Peter Sellers' vehicles *I'm All Right Jack* (1959 – as Mrs Kite), *Two Way Stretch* (1960 – as Mrs Price) and *Heavens Above!* (1963 – as Rene Smith), perfecting the role of a downtrodden, slightly eccentric, but typically working class mother that many could identify with and even more laugh at. Irene's presence was always enough to guarantee laughter. She also played Mrs Cravatte, Tony Hancock's landlady, in *The Rebel* (1961) and in a rare straight role, Mrs Hudson in *The Private Life of Sherlock Holmes* (1971). Other films include: *Dear Octopus* (1943), *The Shop at Sly Corner* (1947), *Woman Hater* (1948), *Adam and Evelyne* (1949), *Stage Fright* (1950), *The Belles of St Trinian's* (1954), *A Kid for Two Farthings* (1955), *It's Never Too Late* (1956), *The Silken Affair* (1956), *Brothers in Law* (1957), *Upstairs and Downstairs* (1959), *Carry On Nurse* (1959), *Inn for Trouble* (1960), *Carry On Constable* (1960), *Doctor in Love* (1960), *School for Scoundrels* (1960), *Make Mine Mink* (1960), *The Pure Hell of St Trinian's* (1960), *You Must Be Joking!* (1965), *Morgan, a Suitable Case for Treatment* (1966), *The Wrong Box* (1966), *The Italian Job* (1969), *Doctor in Trouble* (1970), *For the Love of Ada* (1972), *Confessions of a Driving Instructor* (1976), *Adventures of a Private Eye* (1977), *Come Play with Me* (1977), *The Last Remake of Beau Geste* (1977), *The Hound of the Baskervilles* (1978), *The Great Rock & Roll Swindle* (1979), *Riding High* (1981) and her last film, *Absolute Beginners* (1986). Although Irene was one of the best-loved comedy actresses of her day both on television and in film, as an example of her stage versatility she played Lady Bracknell in *The Importance of Being Earnest* in 1975, directed by Jonathan Miller. An accomplished author, her novels *The Sioux* (1965) and *The Gold Tipped Phitzer* (1966) were very well received. She also included presidency of the Lewisham Branch of the Elvis Presley Fan Club amongst her interests. She died 29 November 1987, Kensington, London. See also entries in the radio and television section for *Angels, Educating Archie, For the Love of Ada, Hancock's Half Hour, Maggie and Her, Metal Mickey,* and *The Rag Trade.*

Handley, Tommy (1892-1949) Born Thomas Reginald Handley, 17 January 1892, Toxteth Park, Liverpool. Comedian. A huge star of radio and the stage, Tommy began his young professional life as a magician and occasional singer before he realised an aptitude for comedy. In 1934 he teamed up with Ronald Frankau to form a successful double act as Mr Murgatroyd (Frankau) and Mr Winterbottom (Handley). They made several early film shorts for the BBC usually meeting on park benches or the like, the bespectacled, cloth-capped Winterbottom puffing on a cigar, walking stick in hand, while the monacled, bowler-hatted

Murgatroyd clutched his umbrella while they pontificated on life's absurdity. The scripts were sharp and witty and contained more jokes than an evening with Ken Dodd. Tommy made his film debut in *Elstree Calling* (1930) and followed this with the film short *Tommy Handley in Making a Christmas Pudding* (1933), *The Disorderly Room* (1937: TV Series), *Two Men in a Box* (1938), the film version of *It's that Man Again* (1943) and *Time Flies* (1944). He died 9 January 1949, Paddington, London. Tommy's abiding memory is of his iconic radio show *ITMA,* for which you can see further details in the radio and television section.

Hanley, Jimmy (1918-70) Born Jimmy Douglas Hanley, 22 October 1918, Norwich, Norfolk. Actor. A product of the *Rank Studios* contract system who later became a household name on television. Screen debut: *Those Were the Days* (1933). Other films include: *Boys will be Boys* (1935), *There Ain't no Justice* (1939), *The Way Ahead* (1944), *Henry V* (1944), *The Captive Heart* (1946), *Holiday Camp* (1948), *Here Come the Huggetts* (1948), *The Huggetts Abroad* (1949), *The Blue Lamp* (1950), *Radio Cab Murder* (1954) and *The Lost Continent* (1968). A familiar face on TV in the late 1950s and early 1960s, especially in an advertising magazine programme *Jim's Inn,* the format of which - people plugging their new products - was later banned by the IBA. Jim was married to Dinah Sheridan (1942-52) and Maggie Avery (1955-70). Daughter Jenny Hanley (b. 15 August 1947, Gerrards Cross, Buckinghamshire) was a film actress before presenting children's television show, *Magpie* (1974-80) and is now a regular radio presenter. His son Jeremy Hanley was chairman of the Conservative Party. Jimmy died 13 January 1970 Leatherhead, Surrey. See also entries in the television section for *Crossroads, Dotto, Five O'Clock Club, Jim's Inn,* and *Small Time.*

Hannah, John (1962-) Born John David Hannah, 23 April 1962, East Kilbride. Actor. Worked as an apprentice electrician for four years before attending the Royal Scottish Academy of Music and Drama. His film debut came in the limited release *Harbour Beat* (1990) but John then came to the public's attention in *Four Weddings and a Funeral* (1994 – as Matthew). He cemented his popularity in *Sliding Doors* (1998) and as Jonathan Carnahan, the charming, rather cowardly, but ultimately heroic brother of the heroine in *The Mummy* (1999), *The Mummy Returns* (2001) and *The Mummy: Tomb of the Dragon Emperor* (2008). Other films include: *The James Gang* (1997), *Resurrection Man* (1998), *The Hurricane* (1999), *Pandaemonium* (2000 - as William Wordsworth), *I'm with Lucy* (2002), *I Accuse* (2003), *Ghost Son* (2007) and *The Last Legion* (2007 - as Nestor). He also played a starring role in the ITN crime drama Cold Blood (2007-08). On Christmas Eve 1997, John founded the production company *Clerkenwell Films* with *Scottish Films* producer Murray Ferguson. *Clerkenwell Films* first venture was to produce the television detective series *Rebus,* in which John starred for the first two series. He married actress Joanna Roth on 20 January 1996. They have twins, a boy named Gabriel and a girl named Astrid (b. 11 February 2004). John has recently been the voice of The Co-operative Group adverts in the UK and also appeared in the American min-series *Spartacus: Blood and Sand* (2010) and its sequel *Spartacus: Gods of the Arena* (2011). . See also entries in the television section for *McCallum, Out of the Blue* and *Rebus.*

Hardwicke, Cedric (1893-1964) Born Cedric Webster Hardwicke, 19 February 1893, Lye, near Stourbridge, West Midlands. Actor. Studied at RADA. Stage debut: The Monk and the Woman *(1912).* Screen debut: *Riches and Rogues* (1913). Took leading roles in *Dreyfus* (1931 - as Dreyfus), *Nell Gwynn* (1934 - as Charles II), *King Solomon's Mines* (1937 - as Allan Quartermain) and *Stanley and Livingstone* (1939 - as Livingstone). His post-WWII work included: *Nicholas Nickleby* (1947), *The Winslow Boy* (1948), *A Connecticut Yankee at King Arthur's Court* (1949 - as King Arthur), in which he sang *Busy Doing Nothing* with Bing Crosby, *Richard III* (1955) and *The Pumpkin Eater* (1964). He wrote an autobiography: *Let's Pretend: Recollections of a Lucky Actor* (1932) - reissued as *A Victorian in Orbit* (1960). Cedric specialised in figures of authority but sometimes with either a humourous or villainous edge.

Apparently he was George Bernard Shaw's fifth favourite actor - the first four being the Marx Brothers. Knighted in 1934, at the age of 41, and at a time when few actors received such an honour. He died 6 August 1964, New York.

Harker, Gordon (1885-1967) Born William Gordon Harker, 7 August 1885, Wandsworth, London. He was the son of Joseph Harker, a scenic artist and sculptor and he pursued the same career as his father for a time. Stage debut: *Much Ado About Nothing* (1903). He served with the Hampshire Regiment during WWI. Screen debut: *General John Regan* (1921). Featured in early Alfred Hitchcock films: *The Ring* (1927), *Champagne* (1928) and *The Farmer's Wife* (1928). Other films include: *The Ringer* (1931), *Rome Express* (1932), *Squibs* (1935), *Boys will be Boys* (1935), *Once a Crook* (1941), *Derby Day* (1952), *Bang, You're Dead* (1954) and *Left, Right and Centre* (1959). A stalwart of British films for thirty years from the late 1920s, he specialised in East End characters. Gordon also played the lead in *Inspector Hornleigh* (1939) and the two sequels: *Inspector Hornleigh on Holiday* (1939) and *Inspector Hornleigh Goes to It* (1941). He died 2 March 1967, Chelsea, London.

Harmer, Dani (1989-) Born Danielle Jane Harmer, 8 February 1989, Bracknell, Berkshire. Actress. She started at the Redroof Drama School in Bracknell and after some early television work in minor roles she got the part for which she is known to children across Britain, the lead character in *The Story of Tracy Beaker* in the BBC adaptation of Jacqueline Wilson's stories. Dani hasn't yet made a feature film but justifies her place in the cinema section as she starred in the BBC TV film *Tracy Beaker's Movie of Me*, broadcast in 2004 - and she is a children's television superstar. See also entries in the television section for *After You've Gone*, *Dani's House* and *The Story Of Tracy Beaker*.

Harris, Naomie (1976-) Born Naomie Melanie Harris, 6 September 1976, London. Actress. After graduating in 1998 from Pembroke College, Cambridge with an undergraduate degree in social and political science, Naomi trained at the Bristol Old Vic Theatre School. Her first screen appearance was in an episode of the children's television series *Simon and the Witch* in 1987. Naomie's film debut was in the role of Ginny in *Living in Hope* (2002) closely followed by roles in *Anansi* (2002 –as Carla) and her breakthrough film *28 Days Later...* (2002 - as Selena), in which she starred opposite Cillian Murphy. In the same year, she starred in the television adaptation of Zadie Smith's White Teeth and in the American fantasy series Dinotopia (2002–as Romana). Since then Naomie has become known for her supporting role as Tia Dalma in the second and third *Pirates of the Caribbean* films, *Pirates of the Caribbean: Dead Man's Chest* (2006) and *Pirates of the Caribbean: At World's End* (2007 – also playing Calypso). Her other films include: *Trauma* (2004 - as Elisa), *After the Sunset* (2004 - as Sophie), *Miami Vice* (2006 - as Det. Trudy Joplin), *A Cock and Bull Story* (2006 - as Jennie), *Street Kings* (2008 - as Linda Washington), *August* (2008 - as Sarah), *Morris: A Life with Bells On* (2009 - as Sonja), *Ninja Assassin* (2009 - as Mika Coretti), *Sex & Drugs & Rock & Roll* (2009 - as Denise), *My Last Five Girlfriends* (2009 - as Gemma) and *The First Grader* (2010 - as Jane Obinchu). Naomie has recently been playing Elizabeth Lavenza in Danny Boyle's production of Nick Dear's adaptation of *Frankenstein* for the National Theatre. In November 2011, it was announced that she would appear in the next James Bond movie, *Skyfall*. See also entries in the television section for *Poppy Shakespeare*, *Runaway Bay*, *Simon and the Witch*, and *The Tomorrow People*.

Harris, Richard (1933-2002) Born Richard St John Harris, 1 October 1930, Limerick, Ireland. Actor. The fifth of nine children, whose early aspirations as a rugby player were dealt a cruel blow by a bout of tuberculosis. He was thereafter lured into a life of acting. Trained at the London Academy of Music and Dramatic Art and then joined Joan Littlewood's Theatre Workshop. Stage debut: *The Quare Fellow* (1956). He made his screen debut in the TV film *The Iron Harp* (1959) and his feature debut in *Alive and Kicking* (1959). There followed a career of ups and downs. His next few films included fairly minor roles in, *Shake Hands with the Devil* (1959), *The Wreck of the Mary Deare* (1959), *A Terrible Beauty* (1960), *The Guns of Navarone* (1961), *The Long and the Short and the Tall* (1961) and *Mutiny on the Bounty* (1962) before he won the lead role as rugby league player Frank Machin in *This*

Sporting Life (1963), based on a novel of the same name by David Storey. This role won Richard a BAFTA and a nomination for a Best Actor Academy Award. His next few films included *Il Deserto Rosso* (1964), which was Antonioni's first colour film, *The Heroes of Telemark* (1965), *Major Dundee* (1965), *The Bible* (aka *The Bible... In the Beginning* 1966 - as Cain), Hawaii (1966) and Caprice (1966) before again scoring a huge hit as King Arthur in the film musical *Camelot* (1967), for which he won a Golden Globe. Richard continued his career with strong performances in *The Molly Maguires* (1970), *A Man Called Horse* (1970), *Cromwell* (1970 - as Cromwell) and *Bloomfield* (1972) before embarking on some disappointing choices of films including: *Man in the Wilderness* (1971), *The Deadly Trackers* (1973), *Call Harry Crown* (aka *99 and 44/100% Dead* 1974), *Echoes of a Summer* (1976), *Robin and Marian* (1976 - as King Richard), *The Cassandra Crossing* (1976), *Gulliver's Travels* (1977 - as Gulliver), *Orca* (1977), *Golden Rendezvous* (1977), *Ravagers* (1979), *A Game for Vultures* (1979), *Tarzan, the Ape Man* (1981), *Triumphs of a Man Called Horse* (1982), *Highpoint* (1984), *Strike Commando 2* (aka *Trappola Diabolica* 1988), *King of the Wind* (1989 - as King George II) and *Mack the Knife* (1990). During this period he did make at least three meritorious films, *Juggernaut* (1974), *The Return of a Man Called Horse* (1976) and *The Wild Geese* (1978) but the rest of the 1970s were a disappointment. In 1973 he did however publish a widely-acclaimed book of poetry, *I, In The Membership Of My Days*, and during the 1980s he concentrated on rescuing his career through stage work. He was back on top form with *The Field* (1990), for which he was nominated for a Best Actor Academy Award, and from then on his final years were particularly successful. His later films include: *Unforgiven* (1992 - as the gunfighter "English Bob"), *Patriot Games* (1992), *Wrestling Ernest Hemingway* (1993), *Silent Tongue* (1994), the TV film *Abraham* (1984 - as Abraham), *Cry, the Beloved Country* (1995), *Trojan Eddie* (1996), *Smilla's Sense of Snow* (1997), *This Is the Sea* (1997), *The Barber of Siberia* (1998), *To Walk with Lions* (1999 - as George Adamson), *Grizzly Falls* (1999), *Gladiator* (2000 - as Roman Emperor Marcus Aurelius), *My Kingdom* (2001), *Harry Potter and the Philosopher's Stone* (2001), *The Count of Monty Christo* (2002) and *Harry Potter and the Chamber of Secrets (2002),* reprising his role of the headmaster of Hogwarts school, Albus Dumbledore. He also scored an unlikely UK No 4 chart record with *MacArthur Park* in 1968. Notorious as a hard-drinking hellraiser. The critic Kenneth Tynan once bracketed him with Albert Finney and Peter O'Toole as one of the three best young actors on the British stage. Richard was married twice, in 1957, to Welsh socialite Elizabeth Rees-Williams (b. 1 May 1936). Their three children are the actor Jared Harris (b. 24 August 1961), once married to Emilia Fox, the actor Jamie Harris (b. 15 May 1963), and the director Damian Harris (born 2 August 1958), once married to Annabel Brooks and partner of Peta Wilson. Harris and Rees-Williams divorced in 1969, after which Elizabeth married Sir Rex Harrison. His maternal niece is actress Annabelle Wallis. His second marriage, in 1974, was to American actress and model Ann Turkel (b. 16 July 1946). They divorced in 1982. For years, whenever he was in London, Richard resided at the Savoy Hotel. According to the hotel archivist, as he was being taken from the hotel on a stretcher, shortly before his death, he warned the diners, "It was the food!" Richard died 25 October 2002, University College Hospital, London.

Harris, Rosemary (1927-) Born Rosemary Ann Harris, 19 September 1927, Ashby, Suffolk. Actress. Graduated from RADA in 1952 and immediately gained the role of Tansy Clampett in the TV film, *A Cradle of Willow* (1952). Her feature debut came in *Beau Brummell* (1954), which starred Stewart Granger and Peter Ustinov. Rosemary next played Desdemona in the TV film *Othello* (1955), Viola in the TV film *Twelfth Night* (1957), Yelena in the feature *Uncle Vanya* (1963) and Elvira Condomine in the TV film Blithe Spirit. Other films include: *A Flea in Her Ear* (1968), *The Boys from Brazil* (1978), *The Ploughman's Lunch* (1983), *Crossing Delancey* (1988), *The Delinquents* (1989), *The Bridge* (1992), *Hamlet* (1996), *My Life So Far* (1999), *The Gift* (2000), *Blow Dry* (2001), *Being Julia* (2004), *Before the Devil Knows You're Dead* (2007), *Is Anybody There?* (2008) and *Radio Free Albemuth* (2010). Rosemary is best known to younger filmgoers for her role as May Parker, Peter's aunt, in *Spider-Man* (2002), *Spider-Man 2* (2004) and *Spider-Man 3* (2007). Rarely a leading character she was however nominated for a Best Supporting Actress Academy Award for *Tom and Viv* (1994) in which she played Rose Haigh-Wood. Rosemary was married to American actor Ellis Rabb (1959-1967) and is currently married to American writer John Ehle (1967-present). Apart from her film roles she is perhaps best known as the mother of actress Jennifer Ehle. In the 1992 TV mini-series *The Camomile Lawn* they played the younger and older versions of the character of Calypso. A similar role-sharing happened in the 1999 film *Sunshine*. Equally at home on stage, Rosemary has won a Tony Award as Best Actress (Dramatic) for originating the part of Eleanor of Aquitaine in *The Lion in Winter* (1996) and she has been nominated for several other Tony Awards, indeed, her consecutive Tony Award nominations in 1984, 1985 and 1986 is a unique achievement. In 2000 both she and her daughter received Tony Award nominations, with Jennifer winning. See also entry in the television section for *The Camomile Lawn*.

Harrison, Kathleen (1892-1995) Born 23 February 1892, Blackburn. Actress. Studied at RADA. Stage debut: *The Constant Flirt* (1926). Screen debut: *Our Boys* (1915). From 1931 onwards, when she took a part in *Hobson's Choice* (1931), she played in a number of the best British films of the era, including the Dickensian classics *Oliver Twist* (1948), *Scrooge* (1951 - as Scrooge's housekeeper) and *The Pickwick Papers* (1952). She is perhaps best remembered by those around at the time for her co-starring role with Jack Warner as Ma and Pa Huggett in a series of films starting with *Holiday Camp* (1947) and leading on to *Here Come the Huggetts* (1948), *Vote for Huggett* (1949) and *The Huggetts Abroad* (1949). A Lancastrian, her family moved to Southwark in London when she was nine-years-old and that is where she picked up the accent and ended up playing loveable cockney servant girls, cleaning ladies, housekeepers and the like, most notably in the ITV television series *Mrs Thursday* (1966-67). Kathleen spent the early 1920s in Argentina with her husband before returning to the UK. She was married to John Henry Back from 1916 until his death in 1960. Kathleen died 6 December 1995, Merton, London, aged 103. See also entries in the radio and television section for *Meet the Huggetts*, and *Mrs Thursday*.

Harrison, Rex (1908-90) Born Reginald Carey Harrison, 5 March 1908, Huyton, Liverpool. Actor. After a bout of childhood measles, Rex lost most of the sight in his left eye. He joined the Liverpool Repertory Company as a young lad in 1918 and made his stage debut locally in 1924. Rex made his screen debut in a walk-on uncredited role in *School for Scandal* (1930), his first credited role soon following, as George, in *The Great Game* (1930). Other early films include *School for Husbands* (1937), *The Citadel* (1938), *Over the Moon* (1939), *The Silent Battle* (1939), *Night Train to Munich* (1940) and *Major Barbara* (1941). After WWII, in which he served in the Royal Air Force, reaching the rank of Flight Lieutenant, he starred in *The Rake's Progress* (1945), *Blithe Spirit* (1945 – as Charles Condomine), *Anna and the King* (1946 - as King Mongkut), *The Ghost and Mrs Muir* (1947*)*, *The Foxes of Harrow* (1947), and *Unfaithfully Yours* (1948). In 1947, while married to Lilli Palmer, Harrison began an affair with actress Carole Landis. Landis committed suicide in 1948 after spending the night with him and the resultant scandal surrounding Landis' death briefly damaged his career and his contract with Fox was ended by mutual consent. For the next fifteen years he hardly made a notable film, *The Long Dark Hall* (1951), *King Richard and the Crusaders* (1954), *The Constant Husband* (1955 aka *Marriage a la Mode*) and *The Reluctant Debutante* (1958), probably the pick of them. Back on track, he was nominated for a Best Actor Academy Award for playing Julius Caesar in *Cleopatra* (1963) and in the following year he was a winner in that category for his portrayal of Professor Henry Higgins in *My Fair Lady* (1964). His later films include: *The Yellow Rolls-Royce* (1964), *The Agony and the Ecstasy* (1965 – as Pope Julius II), *Doctor Doolittle* (1967), *Shalimar* (1978), *Ashanti* (1979), *The Fifth Musketeer* (1979), and his last film, *A Time to Die* (1983). On 25 July 1989 Rex was knighted by Queen Elizabeth II at Buckingham Palace and an orchestra played the music of songs from *My Fair Lady* during the ceremony. He wrote two autobiographies, *Rex: An Autobiography* (1974) and *A Damned Serious Business: My Life in Comedy*, published posthumously in 1991. Rex was married six times. In 1934 he married Colette Thomas, with whom he had a son, Noel Harrison (see entry in pop biography section). In 1942 he divorced Colette and married actress Lilli Palmer the following year; the two later appeared together in numerous plays and films, including *The Fourposter* (1952). Lilli had a son, novelist/playwright Carey Harrison (b. 1944), with Rex. Harrison and Palmer divorced in 1957 explicitly so Rex could marry actress Kay Kendall (see separate entry), who was diagnosed with myeloid leukemia. The intention was to remarry after Kay's death but subsequently Lilli fell in love and married Argentian actor Carlos Thompson. He was subsequently married to Welsh-born Rachel Roberts from 1962 to 1971 (Roberts committed suicide in 1980) and Elizabeth Rees-Williams, from 1971 to 1975, before his final marriage to Mercia Tinker, from 1978 until his death from pancreatic cancer on 2 June 1990, Manhattan, New York. In *Fatal Charm: The Life of Rex Harrison*, his biographer Alexander Walker alludes to the fact that Rex could be an obnoxious egotist, noted off-screen for an unpleasant demeanour - especially with his relatives. Indeed he adopted the name Rex as a child actor because he knew it meant King. Rex undoubtedly lived up to his reputation as a cad, as his unfaithfulness to six wives and numerous lovers plus the devastation caused when both his lover Carole Landis and fourth wife Rachel Roberts, each committed suicide when he left them, bears witness, but there is no doubting his energy and stubborn determination to succeed in a business where only the strong survive.

Hart, Ian (1964-) Born Ian Davies, 8 October 1964, Liverpool. Actor. His first screen appearance was in an episode of *Play For Today* in 1982 and his feature debut in *No Surrender* (1985). Other films include: *Land and Freedom* (1995), *The Englishman Who Went Up a Hill and Came Down a Mountain* (1995), *Clockwork Mice* (1995), *Hollow Reed* (1996), *Michael Collins* (1996), *The Butcher Boy* (1997), the title role in *Robinson Crusoe* (1997), *Enemy of the State* (1998), *Frogs for Snakes* (1998), *This Year's Love* (1999), *Wonderland* (1999), *The End of the Affair* (1999), *Liam* (2000), *Best* (2000 - as Nobby Stiles), *Harry Potter and the Philosopher's Stone* (2001 - as Professor Quirrell), *Finding Neverland* (2004 - as Sir Arthur Conan Doyle), *A Cock and Bull Story* (2005), *Breakfast on Pluto* (2005), *Intervention* (2007), *Morris: A Life with Bells On* (2009), *A Boy Called Dad* (2009) and *Within the Whirlwind* (2009). Another acclaimed role was as William Cecil, Lord Burghley in the 2006 TV film *The Virgin Queen*. Ian also played Dr Watson on screen twice: in the Christmas TV specials *The Hound of the Baskervilles* (2002) and *Sherlock Holmes and the Case of the Silk Stocking* (2004); and fellow Liverpudlian John Lennon on the wide-screen twice: *The Hours the Times* (1991) and *Backbeat* (1994). Ian's most recent film role was a cameo in *Harry Potter and the Deathly Hallows: Part II* (2011 - as Professor Quirrell). See also entries in the television section for *Father and Son*, *Five Daughters* and *One Summer*.

Hartnell, William (1908-75) Born William Henry Hartnell, 8 January 1908, St Pancras, London. Actor. After touring England and abroad with various repertory companies and gaining a reputation as a farceur he embarked on a long career in films. Screen debut: *Say it with Music* (1932). Other films include: *I'm an Explosive* (1933), *While Parents Sleep* (1935), *They Drive by Night* (1938), *Flying Fortress* (1942), *The Goose Steps Out* (1942), *Brighton Rock* (1947), *Odd Man Out* (1947), *The Pickwick Papers* (1952), *Private's Progress* (1956), *The Yangtse Incident* (1957), *This Sporting Life* (1963) and *Heavens Above!* (1963). He was invalided out of the Royal Armoured Corps during WWII. Usually billed as Billy Hartnell until his role in *The Way Ahead* (1944) which saw him switch from mainly comedy roles to more serious parts. Best known as the first television *Dr Who* (1963-1966). He was also *the* sergeant in the first Carry On film, *Carry On Sergeant* (1958), having only just finished playing the very similar part of Sergeant Major Bullimore in TV's *The Army Game*. He died 23 April 1975, Marden, Kent. See also entries in the television section for *The Army Game*, and *Dr Who*.

Harvey, Laurence (1928-73)
Born Zvi Mosheh Skikne, 1 October 1928, Joniskis, Lithuania. Actor. Although Laurence claimed his birth name was Laruschka Mischa Skikne, legal documents appear to suggest otherwise. He was raised in South Africa from the age of five and known as 'Harry'. After WWII he travelled to England and enrolled at RADA before quickly joining a repertory company in Manchester and was now known as 'Larry'. His great friend Sid James followed him to England from South Africa in 1946. Laurence made his screen debut as Francis Merryman in *House of Darkness* (1948). Other films include: *Man on the Run* (1948), *The Man from Yesterday* (1949), *I Believe in You* (1952), *The Good Die Young* (1954), *Romeo and Juliet* (1954 - as Romeo), *King Richard and the Crusaders* (1954), *I Am a Camera* (1955), *Storm Over the Nile* (1955), *Three Men in a Boat* (1956), *The Truth About Women* (1957), *The Silent Enemy* (1958), *Expresso Bongo* (1960), *Butterfield 8* (1960), *The Long and the Short and the Tall* (1960), *Walk on the Wild Side* (1962), *The Running Man* (1963), *Of Human Bondage* (1964), *Darling* (1965), *The Spy with a Cold Nose* (1966), *The Winter's Tale* (1967 - as King Leontes), *A Dandy in Aspic* (1968), *Appointment in Beirut* (1969), *The Magic Christian* (1969 – in which he recited Hamlet's soliloquy, semi-nude), *The Deep* (1970), *Escape to the Sun* (1972), *Night Watch* (1973) and his last film, *Welcome to Arrow Beach* (1974). Laurence played Joe Lampton in *Room at the Top* (1959) - for which he received an Academy Award Best Actor nomination - and *Life at the Top* (1965), Colonel Travis leading the defence of *The Alamo* (1960) and, in possibly his best performance, the brainwashed assassin in *The Manchurian Candidate* (1962). Laurence had the distinction of appearing opposite three actresses who won the Academy Award for their performances: Simone Signoret in *Room at the Top*, Elizabeth Taylor in *Butterfield 8*, and Julie Christie in *Darling*. In all three roles, he established a screen persona of being a thoroughly disreputable character. In his late teens, Laurence became involved with Hermione Baddeley, an actress more than twice his age. He was subsequently married three times, to actress Margaret Leighton in 1957, whom he divorced in 1961, and to Joan Perry Cohn in 1968, the very rich widow of movie mogul Harry Cohn of Columbia Pictures, and finally to Pauline Stone. Harvey had met Stone on the set of *A Dandy in Aspic*, and while still married to Cohn he became a father for the first time when Stone gave birth to a daughter, Domino, in 1969. Eventually, Harvey divorced Cohn and married Stone in 1972. His daughter Domino Harvey started as a model before becoming a bounty hunter. She died 27 June 2005, aged 35. Despite his marriages Laurence was known to be bisexual and his partner for many years was his manager James Woolf. After James died in 1966 Laurence went into serious decline. He died from stomach cancer at the age of 45, on 25 November 1973, Hampstead, London.

Hassall, Imogen (1942-80) Born 25 August 1942, Woking, Surrey. Actress. Studied at the London Academy of Music and Dramatic Art. Imogen's first film role was as a secretary in the Norman Wisdom vehicle *The Early Bird* (1965). Her other films include: *Press for Time* (1966), *Bedtime* (1967), *The Long Duel* (1967), *Mumsy, Nanny, Sonny & Girly* (1970), *The Virgin and the Gypsy* (1970), *When Dinosaurs Ruled the Earth* (1970), *Carry on Loving* (1970), *Incense for the Damned* (1972), *White Cargo* (1973) and her last film, *Licensed to Love and Kill* (1980). Imogen was an ever-present on television in light drama series such as *The Saint, The Avengers, The Champions* and the *Persuaders*. She is often referred to as the "Countess of Cleavage", and is perhaps better known for her looks rather than her acting roles as such. Imogen was married twice, to actor Kenneth Ives and then a very brief second marriage to Andrew Knox in the early months of 1979. Frustrated at her lack of success and typecast forever as the buxom starlet, she took her own life with an overdose of sleeping pills on 16 November 1980, Wimbledon, London. She was due to go on holiday that day with her actress friend Suzanna Leigh.

Hassan, Tamer (1968-) Born 18 March 1968, London. Actor. Tamer was born into a Turkish-Cypriot family and was a keen boxer as a youth. His first screen role was in an episode of *Judge John Deed* in 2002. Tamer's wide-screen debut was The Calcium Kid (2004). Other films include: *Spivs* (2004), *The Football Factory* (2004), *Layer Cake* (2004), *Unleashed* (2005), *Batman Begins* (2005), *The Business* (2005), *The Ferryman* (2007), *Eastern Promises* (2007), *Sucker Punch* (2008), *Cass* (2008), *K* (2009), *City Rats* (2009), *Dead Man Running* (2009), *Jack Falls* (2010), *Kick-Ass* (2010), *Clash of the Titans* (2010 - as Ares), *The Last Seven* (2010), *Bonded By Blood* (2010), *Jack Falls* (2011), *Freerunner* (2011), *The Hike* (2011), *The Reverend* (2011) and *The Double* (2011). He has also appeared in two episodes of the soap opera Eastenders (2008 – as Ahmet). Tamer is the owner, chairman and player/coach of Greenwich Borough FC and his son, Taser is on the books of Huddersfield Town FC. He also owns Eltham Boxing Gym. Tamer by name but not fully tamed as an incident in early 2010 with fellow 'hard man' actor Vinnie Jones bears witness. A testosterone-fuelled "handbags at dawn" incident between the two at the Chateau Marmont hotel, Hollywood, left both of them sporting cuts and bruises.

Hawkins, Jack (1910-73) Born John Edward Hawkins, 14 September 1910, Wood Green, London. Actor. Studied at Italia Conti. He made his stage debut when barely a teenager, in *Where the Rainbow Ends* at the Holborn Empire on 26 December 1923, a production that also included the young Noël Coward. Jack learned his craft on the London stage and then appeared on Broadway in 1929 before making his screen debut in *Birds of Prey* (1930). He established his acting credentials in such films as: *The Lodger* (1932), *The Good Companions* (1933), *The Lost Chord* (1933), *I Lived with You* (1933), *The Jewel* (1933), *A Shot in the Dark* (1933), *Autumn Crocus* (1934), *Lorna Doone* (1934), *Death at Broadcasting House* (1934), *Peg of Old Drury* (1935), *Beauty and the Barge* (1937), *The Frog* (1937), *Who Goes Next?* (1938), *A Royal Divorce* (1938), *Murder Will Out* (1940), *The Flying Squad* (1940) and *The Next of Kin* (1942). After the fall of France in 1940, Jack volunteered for service with the Royal Welsh Fusiliers. He was posted to India and put in charge of troop entertainment and, by July 1944, he was a colonel commanding the administration of the Entertainments National Service Association (ENSA) for India and Southeast Asia. After the war he signed a three-year film contract with Alexander Korda and later switched to Rank, ceasing to appear on the stage after 1951. During this period he found great success in *The Fallen Idol* (1948), *Bonnie Prince Charlie* (1948), *The Elusive Pimpernel* (1950), Angels One Five (1952), *Mandy* (1952) and *The Cruel Sea* (1953). He went on to appear in a series of epics: *Land of the Pharaohs* (1955), *The Bridge on the River Kwai* (1957), *Ben-Hur* (1959), *Lawrence of Arabia* (1962) and *Zulu* (1964). He lost his voice after surgery for cancer of the larynx in 1966 but this did not prevent him from continuing his career. His voice was dubbed (by Charles Gray or Robert Rietti) in films such as *Shalako* (1968), *Oh! What a Lovely War* (1969), *Monte Carlo or Bust* (1969), *Jane Eyre* (1970), *Kidnapped* (1971), *Nicholas and Alexandra* (1971), *Young Winston* (1972), *Theatre of Blood* (1973) and his last film, *Tales that Witness Madness* (1973). Other films include: *The Planter's Wife* (1952), *The Malta Story* (1953), *Twice Upon a Time* (1953), *The Seekers* (1954), *Front Page Story* (1954), *The Prisoner* (1955), *Touch and Go* (1955), *The Long Arm* (1956), *Fortune is a Woman* (1957), *Man in the Sky* (1957), *The Two-Headed Spy* (1958), *Gideon's Day* (1958), *Two Loves* (1961), *Lafayette* (1961), *Five Finger Exercise* (1962), *Rampage* (1963), *Guns at Batasi* (1964), *The Third Secret* (1964), *Lord Jim* (1965), *Masquerade* (1965), *Judith* (1966), *Danger Grows Wild* (1966), *Great Catherine* (1968), *The Beloved* (1970), *The Adventures of Gerard* (1970), *Twinky* (1970), *When Eight Bells Toll* (1971), *The Last Lion* (1972) and *Escape to the Sun* (1972). Jack also became a television star with his performance as Ben Manfred in the classic crime series *The Four Just Men* (1959-60). A personification of the firm but fair Englishman. Married to actresses Jessica Tandy (1932-40), with whom he had a daughter, Susan; and from 31 October 1947 until his death, to Doreen Lawrence, with whom he had a daughter, Caroline and two sons, Nick and Andrew. Jack's autobiography: *Anything for a Quiet Life* (1973), was published posthumously. He died 18 July 1973, Fulham, London, after complications during surgery to have an artificial voice box inserted. See also entries in the television section for *The Four Just Men* and *Gideon's Way*.

Hawkins, Sally (1976-) Born Sally Cecilia Hawkins, 27 April 1976, Dulwich, London. Actress. Sally trained at RADA and graduated in 1998. Her first screen appearance was in an episode of *Casualty* (1999) and her film debut, in the role of Samantha, was *All or Nothing* (2002). Her subsequent films include: *Vera Drake* (2004 - as Susan), *Layer Cake* (2004 - as Slasher), *Cassandra's Dream* (2007 - as Kate), before her performance as Poppy in the 2008 film *Happy-Go-Lucky* won her the Golden Globe Award for Best Actress – Motion Picture Musical or Comedy. Her recent films include: *An Education* (2009 - as Sarah), *Happy Ever Afters* (2009 -as Maura), *Never Let Me Go* (2010 -as Miss Lucy), *It's a Wonderful Afterlife* (2010), *Made in Dagenham* (2010 - as Rita O'Grady), *Submarine* (2010 - as Jill), *Jane Eyre* (2011) and *Love Birds* (2011). See also entries for *Fingersmith* and *Tipping the Velvet* in the television section.

Hawthorne, Nigel (1929-2001) Born Nigel Barnard Hawthorne, 5 April 1929, Coventry, Warwickshire. Actor. Raised in South Africa and after an unsuccessful foray in the UK in 1951 he returned for another try in 1963. Screen debut: *Young Winston* (1972). An award winning actor on both stage and television. He came to general popularity as Sir Humphrey Appleby in *Yes, Minister* (1980-84) and *Yes, Prime Minister* (1986-88). Nominated for an Academy Award for Best Actor for reprising his stage role as King George III in *The Madness of King George* (1994) after which his big screen presence increased considerably. Other films include: *Sweeney 2* (1978), *History of the World: Part 1* (1981), *Firefox* (1982), *Gandhi* (1982), *Turtle Diary* (1985), *Demolition Man* (1993), *Richard III* (1995 - as Clarence), *Twelfth Night* (1996 - as Malvolio), *Amistad* (1997 - as Martin van Buren), *Madeline* (1998), *The Winslow Boy* (1999) and *The Clandestine Marriage* (1999). Appointed CBE in 1987 and knighted in 1999. He died 26 December 2001, Thundridge, Hertfordshire, and was survived by his partner of 22 years, screenwriter Trevor Bentham. See also entries in the television section for *Bill Brand, Edward and Mrs Simpson,* and *Yes Minister / Prime Minister.*

Hawtrey, Charles (1914-88) Born George Frederick Joffre Hartree, 30 November 1914, Hounslow, Middlesex. Actor. The son of a motor mechanic, he trained at the Italia Conti School and took his stage name from the recently deceased Edwardian actor-manager Sir Charles Hawtrey. Stage debut: *The Windmill Man (1925).* Charles made his screen debut with an uncredited role in the silent film *Tell your Children* (1922) and appeared similarly uncredited in *This Freedom* (1923). His first credited feature role, and indeed his first talkie, was as Billy Hart in *Marry Me* (1932). He then appeared as the young schoolboy foil to Will Hay's blundering old fool in the comedy films *Good Morning, Boys* (1937), *Where's That Fire?* (1940), *The Ghost of St Michael's* (1941) and *The Goose Steps Out* (1942). A role in the popular television sitcom *The Army Game* led to him being cast in *Carry On Sergeant (1958).* In all he appeared in 23 of the Carry On series, the others being: *Carry On Nurse* (1959), *Carry On Teacher* (1959), *Carry On Constable* (1960), *Carry On Regardless* (1961), *Carry On Cabby* (1963), *Carry On Jack* (1963), *Carry On Spying* (1964), *Carry On Cleo* (1964), *Carry On Cowboy* (1965), *Carry On Screaming* (1966), *Don't Lose Your Head* (1966), *Follow That Camel* (1967), *Carry On Doctor* (1967), *Carry On... Up the Khyber* (1968), *Carry On Camping* (1969), *Carry On Again Doctor* (1969), *Carry On Loving* (1970), *Carry On Henry* (1970), *Carry On Up the Jungle* (1970), *Carry On at Your Convenience* (1971), *Carry On Matron* (1972) and *Carry On Abroad* (1972), after which he was dropped because of his heavy drinking. His other films include: *Passport to Pimlico* (1949), *Man of the Moment* (1955), *Inn for Trouble* (1960), *What a Whopper* (1961), *Dentist on the Job* (1961) and his last film, *Zeta One* (1973 - as Swyne), often cited as one of the worst films of all time. Charles' final sreen performance was as Clarence, Duke of Claridge, in an episode of *Supergran*, in 1987. A master of comedy timing and a very talented actor and director (he once directed Dame Flora Robson), alas, in his private life Charles was known to be abrasive and eccentric. Openly homosexual, in August 1984 he was embarrassed when having to be rescued from a fire at his home after he left a cigarette burning whilst in bed with a teenaged boy. He died 27 October 1988, Deal, Kent. See also entries in the television section for *The Army Game,* and *Our House.*

Hay, Will (1888-1949) Born William Thomson Hay, 6 December 1888, Stockton-on-Tees, Durham. Actor and comedian. Will was a superb linguist who, after an early career following in his fathers' footsteps as an engineer, became an interpreter. He numbered French, German, Italian, Afrikaans and Norwegian amongst his languages. At the same time he was also trying to be a stand-up comedian, developing a series of sketches based on his sisters' experiences as a teacher. He eventually gave up the day job and after a time in Fred Karno's troupe as a juggler became a much-loved music hall performer. Screen debut: *Those were the Days* (1934). His best-known films are *Oh, Mr Porter!* (1937), *Good Morning, Boys* (1937), *Convict 99* (1938), *Ask A Policeman* (1939), *Where's That Fire?* (1940), *The Black Sheep of Whitehall* (1941) and *The Goose Steps Out* (1942). Most of his films were farces based on his character's incompetence and usually included two "stooges", Graham Moffatt and Moore Marriott, although Edgar Kennedy partnered him in *Hey, Hey, U.S.A* (1938), Claude Hulbert in *The Ghost of St Michael's* (1941) and Charles Hawtrey was the schoolboy foil in several films. His final film, *My Learned Friend* (1943), again co-starring Hulbert, is often considered his finest work. A keen amateur astronomer he discovered a white spot on Saturn in 1933 and published a book *Through my Telescope* (1935). He was made a fellow of the Royal Astronomical Society. During WWII he was a navigation and astronomy instructor to the Naval Cadet Corp. A man of many talents, he was one of Britain's first private pilots and gave flying lessons to Amy Johnson. His party piece was to write gibberish on a blackboard before turning it upside down to display a perfectly written paragraph. He married Gladys Perkins in 1907 but legally separated on 18 November 1935. They had two daughters and a son: Gladys Elspeth Hay (b. 1909), William E. Hay (b. 1913) and Joan A. Hay (b. 1917). Hay was diagnosed with cancer in 1943 but was in remission when he died from a heart attack on 18 April 1949, Chelsea, London.

Hayter, James (1907-83) Born 23 April 1907, Lonavala, Maharashtra Province, India. Actor. Raised in Scotland. Studied at RADA. Screen debut: *Sensation* (1936). Other pre-WWII films include: *Marigold* (1938), *Murder in Solo* (1939), *Come on George!* (1939) and *Sailors Three* (1940). Served in the Royal Armoured Corps during WWII. Made over 70 films in the next 30 years including: *Vice Versa* (1948), *My Brother Jonathan* (1948), *Passport to Pimlico* (1949), *The Blue Lagoon* (1949), *Morning Departure* (1950), *Tom Brown's Schooldays* (1951), *The Crimson Pirate* (1952), *Beau Brummell* (1954), *Land of the Pharaohs* (1955), *I Was Monty's Double* (1958), *The 39 Steps* (1959) and his last film role, *The Bawdy Adventures of Tom Jones* (1976). Had some signature roles which he will always be identified with. He played Friar Tuck in *The Story of Robin Hood and his Merrie Men* (1952) and reprised the role in *A Challenge for Robin Hood* (1967) and was Samuel Pickwick in *The Pickwick Papers* (1952). A man who could have been sketched by Phiz, he featured in other Dickensian adaptations: *Nicholas Nickleby* (1947) as Ned and Charles Cheeryble, *Oliver!* (1968) and the television adaptation of *David Copperfield* (1969). James was a famous face from the early days of television, starring in *Pinwright's Progress* (1946), often considered the first British TV sitcom. He also appeared in episodes of *The Forsyte Saga* and *The Onedin Line*. Despite his long and varied career James will always be exceedingly well remembered for his voice-overs for the Mr Kipling's Cakes adverts. He died 27 March 1983 in Spain. See also entries in the television section for *Are You Being Served, The Flaxton Boys, Pinwright's Progress* and *Under the Same Sun.*

Hemmings, David (1941-2003) Born 18 November 1941, Guildford, Surrey. Actor and director. David was educated at Alleyn's School, the Glyn Grammar School (now the Glyn Technology School) and the Epsom School of Art. He was a boy soprano of some note before becoming a child actor and featured in several works by the composer Benjamin Britten, who formed a close friendship with him at this time. Most notably, David created the role of Miles in the opera *Turn of the Screw* (1954). Screen debut: *The Rainbow Jacket* (1954). Other films as an actor include: *In the Wake of a Stranger* (1958), *Live it Up* (1963), *Blow-Up* (1966), *Camelot* (1967), *The Charge of the Light Brigade* (1968), *Barbarella* (1968), *Alfred the Great* (1969), *Unman, Wittering and Zigo* (1971), *Juggernaut* (1974), *The Squeeze* (1977), *Murder by Decree* (1979), *Harlequin* (1980), *The Rainbow* (1989), *Gladiator* (2000), *Last Orders* (2001), *Mean Machine* (2001), *Gangs of New York* (2002), *The League of Extraordinary Gentlemen* (2003) and his final film, *Blessed* (2004). Also a director. Directorial debut: *Running Scared* (1972). Other films directed: *The 14* (1973), which won the Silver Bear at the 23rd Berlin International Film Festival, *Just a Gigolo* (1979), *The Survivor* (1981), *Race for the Yankee Zephyr* (1981) and *Dark Horse* (1992). He also worked as a director on several television series such as *Magnum P.I.*, *The A Team*, *Airwolf* and *Quantum Leap*. David starred as Bertie Wooster in the short-lived Andrew Lloyd Webber musical, *Jeeves* (1975). David was co-founder of the film production company HemDale Corporation in 1967 with his manager, John Daly. Married four times: Genista Ouvry (1960-67); Gayle Hunnicutt (1968-75), who is the mother of his son, British actor Nolan Hemmings (b. 1970); Baroness Prudence de Casembroot (1976-97) and Lucy Williams (2002-03). His autobiography *Blow Up... and Other Exaggerations – The Autobiography of David Hemmings* (2004), was published posthumously. He died 3 December 2003 Bucharest, Romania. on the film set of *Blessed*. See also entry in the television section for *Billy Bunter of Greyfriars School*.

Hendry, Ian (1931-84) Born Ian Mackendrick Hendry, 13 January 1931, Ipswich, Suffolk. Actor. Early jobs included an estate agent and a stunt motorcyclist before attending the Central School of Speech and Drama. Screen debut: *Room at the Top* (1959). Other films include: *Sink the Bismarck!* (1960), *Live Now - Pay Later* (1962), *Girl in the Headlines* (1963), *Children of the Damned* (1963), *The Beauty Jungle* (1964), *Repulsion* (1965), *The Hill* (1965), *Cry Wolf* (1968), *Doppelganger* (1969), *Get Carter* (1971), *Tales from the Crypt* (1972), *Theatre of Blood* (1973), *The Internecine Project* (1974), *Damien: Omen II* (1978), *The Bitch* (1979) and *McVicar* (1980). A fine and generally underrated actor, he also starred in several popular television series. His final role was as Davey Jones in *Brookside* in 1984. Ian married actress Janet Munro in 1963, and they had two daughters, Sally and Corrie, but their turbulent life together ended in divorce in 1971. He then married Sandra Jones and had another daughter, Emma. He died 24 December 1984, Camden, London. See also entries in the television section for *The Avengers*, *Brookside*, *Churchill's People* *The Adventures of Don Quick*, *The Informer*, and *The Lotus Eaters*.

Henley, Georgie (1995-) Born Georgina Helen Henley, 9 July 1995, Ilkley, West Yorkshire Actress. Georgie attends Bradford Grammar School, and is part of the Ilkley Upstagers' Theatre Group. She appeared in the stage version of *Babes In The Wood* in early 2006. Her film debut, and indeed her screen debut, was as Lucy Pevensie in *The Chronicles of Narnia: The Lion, the Witch and the Wardrobe* (2005). Georgie subsequently went on to star in the sequels *The Chronicles of Narnia: Prince Caspian* (2008) and *The Chronicles of Narnia: The Voyage of the Dawn Treader* (2010). She also appeared as the young Jane Eyre in the 2006 BBC adaptation of *Jane Eyre*. Georgie has two older sisters, Rachael and Laura Henley. Rachael played the older Lucy in the first film. While filming *The Lion, the Witch, and the Wardrobe*, Georgie wrote two books, *The Snow Stag*, and *A Pillar of Secrets*. See also entry for *Jane Eyre* in the television section.

Henshall, Douglas (1965-) Born Douglas James Henshall, 19 November 1965, Glasgow. Actor. While at school he joined the Scottish Youth Theatre in Glasgow. Screen debut: *The Big Man* (1990). Other films include: *Rose Red* (1994), *Angels and Insects* (1995), *Orphans* (1997), *Kull the Conqueror* (1997), *This Year's Love* (1999), *The Lawless Heart* (2001), *Silent Cry* (2002), *It's All About Love* (2003), *Unscrew* (2003), *Ripley Under Ground* (2005), *Dead Long Enough* (2006), *Flying Lessons* (2007), *French Film* (2008) and *Dorian Gray* (2009). His most recent film role was Cradoc in the epic set in Roman Britain, *The Eagle* (2011). Douglas also has some sound television credits to his name, most recently in the BBC mini-series, *South Riding*, but also in episodes of *Taggart* (1990), *Van Der Valk* (1992), *Common as Muck* (1994) and *Dalziel and Pascoe* (2005). He married Croatian playwright Tena Štivičić (b. 1977) in 2010. See also entries in the television section for *Sea of Souls*, *The Silence* and as Nick Cutter in *Primeval*, the last named by far his most famous role.

Henson, Nicky (1945-) Born Nicholas Victor Leslie Henson, 12 May 1945, Marylebone, London. Actor. Son of actor and comedian Leslie Henson. Screen debut: *Father Came Too!* (1963). Other films include: *Here We Go Round the Mulberry Bush* (1967), *Witchfinder General* (1968), *Mosquito Squadron* (1969), *There's a Girl in My Soup* (1970). Rarely off our televisionscreens since the early 1970s with appearances in such series as *Fawlty Towers* (1979 - as ladies' man Mr. Johnson in *The Psychiatrist* episode), *Minder* (1979), *Boon* (1989), *Lovejoy* (1991), *A Touch of Frost* (2000) and *Bad Girls* (2005). He joined the Royal Shakespeare Company in 1977 and has numerous stage credits to his name. He has also appeared in the films *Vera Drake* (2004), *Syriana* (2005) and *Blitz* (2009). Nicky was married to actress Una Stubbs (1969-75), with whom he had two sons, composers Joe and Christian Henson. He is currently married to former ballet dancer Marguerite Porter, with whom he has a third son, Keaton. See also entries in the television section for *After You've Gone*, *Eastenders*, *The Frost Report*, *Preston Front*, *Shine On Harvey Moon*, and *The Upper Hand*.

Hepburn, Audrey (1929-93) Born Audrey Kathleen Ruston, 4 May 1929, Ixelles, Belgium. Actress. Audrey was the only child of English banker Joseph Victor Anthony Ruston (1889–1980) and his second wife Ella, baroness van Heemstra (1900–84), a Dutch aristocrat. Audrey had British citizenship through her father and after her parents divorced in 1935 she attended school in Kent until the outbreak of war when she relocated to her grandfather's home in Arnhem, Holland. After the Germans invaded the Netherlands in 1940, Audrey adopted the name Edda van Heemstra. After the war she moved to London with her mother and continued her training as a dancer at the Ballet Rambert while working as a photographer's model. Although showing considerable promise as a ballerina, Audrey graduated towards musical theatre and, after taking elocution lessons from the actor Felix Aylmer, made her film debut as a stewardess in *Nederlan in 7 Lessen* (1948). Other early films include: *One Wild Oat* (1951), *Laughter in Paradise* (1951), *The Lavender Hill Mob* (1951 - as Chiquita) and *The Secret People* (1952). During the filming of *Monte Carlo Baby* (1951), French novelist Colette appeared on set, choosing Hepburn to play the title character in the Broadway play Gigi. Audrey then went to Hollywood and found instant fame in her first role, as Princess Ann in *Roman Holiday* (1953), opposite Gregory Peck, for which she won an Academy Award for Best Actress. After *Sabrina* (1954), for which many of her costumes were designed by Hubert de Givenchy, Audrey became a style icon and her slender, elfin, but beautifully regal look was much sought after and imitated. Her most famous subsequent films include: *War and Peace* (1956 - as Natasha Rostova), *Funny Face* (1957), *The Nun's Story* (1959 - as Sister Luke, Gabrielle van der Mal), *The Unforgiven* (1960), *The Children's Hour* (1961), *Charade* (1963), *Paris When It Sizzles* (1964), *How to Steal a Million* (1966), *Wait Until Dark* (1967), *Robin and Marian* (1976 - as Marian), *They All Laughed* (1981) and her last film, *Always* (1989). Possibly her most famous role was as Holly Golightly in *Breakfast at Tiffany's* (1961), her little black Givenchy dress becoming one of cinema's most iconic costumes. Although Audrey had starred in Funny Face she was a controversial choice to play Eliza Doolittle in *My Fair Lady* (1964) as Julie Andrews had made the part her own on Broadway, however with the help of Marni Nixon's singing voice the film was a great success. Ironically, Julie won the Best Actress Oscar that year for her performance in *Mary Poppins*. By the end of the 1960s Audrey had all but retired from making movies to concentrate on her family and the last years of her life were spent working as a Goodwill Ambassador for UNICEF. Audrey was married twice, to American actor Mel Ferrer (1954–68), by whom she had a son, Sean (b. 17 July 1960), whose godfather was the novelist A. J. Cronin, and Italian psychiatrist Andrea Dotti (1969–82), by whom she had a son, Luca (b. 8 February 1970). She lived with Dutch actor Robert Wolders from 1980 until her death, from appendiceal cancer, 20 January 1993, Tolochenaz, Vaud, Switzerland.

Hepworth, Cecil (1873-1953) Born Cecil Milton Hepworth, 19 March 1874, Lewisham, London. Director and producer. One of the founders of the British film industry. His father was a magic lantern showman. Although Cecil was an occasional actor he spent most of his efforts in producing and directing. He converted his house in Walton-on-Thames into a film studio in 1899. Began by making short (45 second) films of everyday events such as *Express Train on a Railway Cutting* (1898) and *Thames River Scene* (1899). These he developed into comedy shorts with early special effects such as *How it Feels to be Run Over* (1900) and *Explosion of a Motor Car* (1900). A breakthrough came with *Rescued by Rover* (1905) which was a narrative short film with innovative editing. He developed something of a star system within his studio, making household names of Alma Taylor and Chrissie White in the *Tilly the Tomboy* series of films. Despite producing and directing the very popular *Alf's Button* (1920), over-expansion, old-fashioned perceptions and competition from the United States ended in bankruptcy in 1924. Disastrously for the history of the British film industry all 2,000 of the studio's original negatives were melted down to reclaim the silver. He wrote the first British books on cinema including: *Animated Photography*. Autobiography: *Came the Dawn* (1951). He died 9 February 1953, Greenford, London.

Herbert, Percy (1920-92) Born 31 July 1920, London. Actor. Percy was a soldier and prisoner of war during World War II, captured by the Japanese when they took Singapore. Discovered by Sybil Thorndike, he was a jobbing character actor who made numerous appearances on stage and screen before making his feature debut in *The Young Lovers* (1954). Other films include: *The Cockleshell Heroes* (1955), *A Hill in Korea* (1956), *Quatermass 2* (1957), *The Bridge on the River Kwai* (1957), *Serious Charge* (1959), *The Devil's Disciple* (1959), *There Was a Crooked Man* (1960), *Tunes of Glory* (1960), *The Guns of Navarone* (1961), *Mysterious Island* (1961), *Mutiny on the Bounty* (1962), *Call Me Bwana* (1963), *The Cracksman* (1963), *Carry On Jack* (1963), *Becket* (1964), *Carry On Cowboy* (1965), *One Million Years B.C.* (1966), *Casino Royale* (1967), *Tobruk* (1967), *The Royal Hunt of the Sun* (1969), *The Mackintosh Man* (1973), *One of Our Dinosaurs Is Missing* (1975), *Valentino* (1977), *The Wild Geese* (1978), *The Sea Wolves* (1980) and his last film, *The Love Child* (1988). Percy is best known for playing scotsman McGregor in the classic 1960s western series *Cimarron Strip*, opposite Stuart Whitman and Jill Townsend. On British television he played Mr Preston in the Reg Varney vehicle *Down the Gate* (1975) and Mr Whittaker in *The Worker* (1965). Percy died, of a heart-attack, 6 December 1992, Kent, England.

Heywood, Anne (1932-) Born Violet Pretty, 11 December 1932, Handsworth, Birmingham. Actress. Not surprisingly, given her surname, she started out as a model and was Miss Great Britain in 1950. She was credited as Violet Pretty when playing a beauty contest contestant in her first film *Lady Godiva Rides Again* (1951), a film which also saw the debut of Joan Collins as a fellow contestant. By the time of her second, *Find the Lady* (1956*)*, she was a Rank starlet and renamed Anne Heywood. Her career spanned more than 30 years and saw her make films in amongst other countries Germany, Italy and France. A foray to the United States saw her nominated for a Golden Globe for *The Fox* (1967). Other films include: *Doctor at Large* (1957), *Violent Playground* (1958), *Upstairs and Downstairs* (1959), *Petticoat Pirates* (1961), *The Most Dangerous Man in the World* (1969) and her final film, *What Waits Below* (1985). She was married to producer Raymond Stross (1979-88). Anne's career declined in the 1980s, and after a character role in the TV series *The Equalizer*, in 1985, she retired from acting and now resides in the United States.

Highmore, Freddie (1992-) Born Alfred Thomas Highmore, 14 February 1992, Camden, London. Actor. His mother, Sue Latimer, is a talent agent whose clients include actors Daniel Radcliffe and Imelda Staunton, and his father, Edward Highmore, is an actor. Freddie's screen debut was in the role of Sam in *Women Talking Dirty* (1999) which also featured his brother Bertie. He then played the Young King Arthur in the TV mini-series *Mists of Avalon* (2001) and also featured in another American mini-series *Jack and the Beanstalk: the Real Story* (2001), where his father was played by his actual father Edward Highmore. After *Two Brothers* (2004 – as the young Raoul) he gained great recognition, and several awards, for his role of Peter Llewellyn Davies in *Finding Neverland* (2004). Freddie then starred in *Five Children and It* (2004- as Robert) and then took the title role of Charlie Bucket in *Charlie and the Chocolate Factory* (2005). Other films include: *A Good Year* (2006 - as Max), *Arthur and the Invisibles* (2007 - as Arthur), *August Rush* (2007 - as Evan Taylor / August Rush), *The Golden Compass* (2007 - voice of Pantalaimon), *The Spiderwick Chronicles* (2008 - as Jared and Simon Grace), *A Fox's Tale* (2008 - voice of Little Jack), *Astro Boy* (2009 - voice of Astro Boy), *Arthur and the Revenge of Maltazard* (2009), *Arthur and the War of Two Worlds* (2010) *Master Harold...and the Boys* (2010 - as Hally) and *The Art of Getting By* (2011) starring alongside Emma Roberts in the romantic comedy. Several of the films that he has been cast in have accompanying video games (*Astro Boy, The Spiderwick Chronicles, The Golden Compass, Arthur and the Invisibles, Charlie and the Chocolate Factory*) and he has lent his voice to all of these projects.On television he took the main role in *Toast* a BBC autobiographical film about Nigel Slater, the chef, which was shown in December 2010. Freddie has been quoted as saying he will not continue acting into adulthood. In 2010 he became a student at Emmanuel College, Cambridge, studying Spanish and Arabic.

Hill, Benny (1924-92) See entry in comedy section

Hill, Bernard (1944-) Born 17 December 1944, Manchester. Actor. Screen debut: *It Could Happen to You* (1975). Other films include: *Trial by Combat* (1976), *Gandhi* (1982), *Runners* (1983), *The Bounty* (1984), *Bellman and True* (1987), *Drowning by Numbers* (1988), *Shirley Valentine* (1989), *The Mill on the Floss* (1997), *Titanic* (1997 – as Captain Smith). *True Crime* (1999), *A Midsummer Night's Dream* (1999), *The Scorpion King* (2002), *The Lord of the Rings: The Two Towers* (2002 – as King Théoden), *Gothika* (2003), *The Lord of the Rings: The Return of the King* (2003), *Wimbledon* (2004), *The League of Gentlemen's Apocalypse* (2005), *Joy Division* (2006), *The Heart of the Earth* (2007), *Exodus* (2007), *Save Angel Hope* (2007), *Franklyn* (2008), *Valkyrie* (2008) and *The Kid* (2010). He has been in three different versions of "A Midsummer Night's Dream". In the animated mini series *Shakespeare: The Animated Tales*, he voiced Nick Bottom. In the 1999 live action movie, he played Egeus, and in the English version of the 2005 animated Spanish film, *Midsummer Dream*, he was the voice of Theseus. Bernard came to popular attention playing Yosser Hughes on television in *The Black Stuff* (1980) and *Boys from the Blackstuff* (1982) and subsequently starred in several TV films in the Screen Two series shown between 1985 and 1994. Other TV film roles include: the Duke of York in *Henry VI (Parts 1, 2 and 3)* (1983), the title role in *John Lennon: A Journey in the Life* (1985 – a role he first played on stage in *John, Paul, George, Ringo... and Bert*, in 1974) and Abel Magwitch in *Great Expectations* (1999), as well as playing Uncle Fred in the Dennis Potter mini-series *Lipstick on Your Collar* (1993). Bernard once had a relationship with actress Kathy Bates but he is now married and is guarded about his private life. See also entries in the television section for *A Very Social Secretary, Between The Lines, Boys From the Blackstuff, Fox, I Claudius,* and *Once Upon a Time in the North.*

Hiller, Wendy (1912-2003) Born Wendy Margaret Hiller ,15 August 1912, Bramhall, Stockport. Actress. The daughter of Frank Watkin Hiller and Marie Stone, her professional debut as an actress was in repertory at Manchester in the early 1930s. She first found success as Sally Hardcastle in the stage version of *Love on the Dole* in 1934, and married the play's author Ronald Gow (1 November 1897 – 27 April 1993) in 1937. It was also in this year that she made her film debut in a small film *Lancashire Luck*, also scripted by Gow. The popularity of *Love on the Dole*, took the production to New York, where her performance attracted the attention of George Bernard Shaw. Shaw cast her in several of his plays, including *Saint Joan*, *Pygmalion* and *Major Barbara*. Unlike other stage actresses of her generation, she did relatively little Shakespeare, preferring the more modern dramatists and new plays adapted from the novels of Henry James and Thomas Hardy amongst others. Her impressive major film debut opposite Leslie Howerd in *Pygmalion* (1938) earned her an Academy Award nomination for Best Actress for her role as Eliza Doolittle. After a TV film, *The Fame of Grace Darling* (1939) she returned to Shaw for his film adaptation of *Major Barbara* (1941 – as Major Barbara Undershaft). She won the Best Supporting Actress Academy Award for the film *Separate Tables* (1958), as a lonely hotel manageress and was nominated again for her performance as the wife of Sir Thomas More in *A Man for All Seasons* (1966). *Toys in the Attic* (1963) earned her a Golden Globes nomination. Other films include: *Outcast of the Islands* (1952), *How to Murder a Rich Uncle* (1957), *Sons and Lovers* (1960), *Murder on the Orient Express* (1974), *Voyage of the Damned* (1976), *The Cat and the Canary* (1978), *The Elephant Man* (1980) and *The Lonely Passion of Judith Hearne* (1987). Wendy was equally at home on stage or screen and in 1958 was nominated for Broadway's Tony Award as Best Dramatic Actress for her performance in Eugene O'Neill's *A Moon for the Misbegotten*. Apart from Shaw, Synge, James and many other comtemporary playwrights she developed an affinity for the plays of Henrik Ibsen, appearing in *When We Dead Awaken* (1968), *Ghosts* (1972) and *John Gabriel Borkman* (1975). She was awarded an OBE in 1971, and made a Dame Commander of the Most Excellent Order of the British Empire in 1975. Her final West End performance was the title role in *Driving Miss Daisy* (1988) and her final film was *The Countess Alice* (1992), where she played Countess Alice von Holzendorf. She eventually retired from acting in 1992. She died at her home in Beaconsfield, Buckinghamshire 14 May 2003.

Hinds, Ciarán (1953-) Born 9 February 1953, Belfast. Actor. Trained at RADA and joined the Glasgow Citizen's Theatre and made his stage debut in 1976. Screen debut: *Excalibur* (1981). Other films include: *The Cook, the Thief, his Wife and her Lover* (1989), *December Bride* (1990), *Circle of Friends* (1995), *Rules of Engagement* (1995), *Persuasion* (1995), *Mary Reilly* (1996), *Some Mother's Son* (1996), *The Life of Stuff* (1997), *Oscar and Lucinda* (1997), *Titanic Town* (1998), *The Sum of All Fears* (2002), *Road to Perdition* (2002), *Veronica Guerin* (2003), *Calendar Girls* (2003), *The Phantom of the Opera* (2004), *Mickybo and Me* (2005), *Munich* (2005), *Miami Vice* (2006), *Amazing Grace* (2006), *The Tiger's Tail* (2006), *The Nativity Story* (2006 - as Herod), *Hallam Foe* (2007), *Margot at the Wedding* (2007), *There Will Be Blood* (2007), *In Bruges* (2008), *Stop-Loss* (2008), *Ca$h* (2008), *The Tale of Despereaux* (2008 - voice of Botticelli), *Race to Witch Mountain* (2009), *The Eclipse* (2009), *The Debt* (2010), *The Rite* (2011), *Salvation Boulevard* (2011) and *Tinker Tailor Soldier Spy* (2011 - as Roy Bland). Ciarán has recently been seen as Aberforth Dumbledore in *Harry Potter and the Deathly Hallows: Part I* (2010) and *Part II* (2011). A leading man who can also be an effective supporting player, Ciarán has an impressive set of television credits including the mini-series' *Cold Lazarus* (1996 – as Fyodor), *Ivanhoe* (1997 - as Brian de Bois-Gilbert) and *Rome* (2005 – as Julius Caesar); as well as the TV films *Jane Eyre* (1997 - as Mr Rochester) and *The Mayor of Casterbridge* (2003 – as Michael Henchard). Ciarán lives in Paris with his long-time partner, Hélène Patarot; they met in 1987 while in the cast of Peter Brook's production of *The Mahabharata*. They have a daughter, Aoife (b. 1991)

Hird, Thora (1911-2003) Born 28 May 1911, Morecambe, Lancashire. Actress. Thora was one of Britain's greatest character actresses. Quintessentially English, and within that northern, so it is probably surprising that her first film role in *The Big Blockade* (1940) called on her to play a German barmaid. She was never the beautiful young starlet, indeed in *Corridor of Mirrors* (1948) she played 'Old Woman Visiting Tussauds' when she was only 37. A succession of housekeepers, maids, aunts (later grandmothers) and landladies followed. She was in more than 80 films, including: *The Foreman Went to France* (1942), *Went the Day Well?* (1942),

The Courtneys of Curzon Street (1947), *The Weaker Sex* (1948), *Once a Jolly Swagman* (1949), *The Magic Box* (1952), *Time, Gentlemen, Please!* (1952),*The Quatermass Experiment* (1955), *Sailor Beware* (1956), *The Good Companions* (1957), *Further Up the Creek* (1958), *The Entertainer* (1960), *A Kind of Loving* (1962), *Bitter Harvest* (1963), *Rattle of a Simple Man* (1964), *Some Will, Some Won't* (1970), *The Nightcomers* (1971), her last feature film, *Consuming Passions* (1988) and her final TV film, *The Nearly Complete and Utter History of Everything* (1999). In 1978 she appeared on stage in *Me! I'm Afraid of Virginia Woolf* directed by Stephen Frears from Alan Bennet's play. This was an association that would flourish on the small screen in years to come when, in 1988, Thora played Doris in an episode of the mini-series *Talking Heads*, entitled *A Cream Cracker Under the Settee*, and ten years on played Violet in the second series of *Talking Heads*, in an episode entitled, *Waiting for the Telegram*. Despite her many films Thora will always be remembered for her television. She was married to James Scott from 1937 until his death in 1994; their daughter is the actress Janette Scott (see separate entry). Thora was made a Dame in 1993. She was also a committed Christian, hosting the religious programme *Praise Be!*, a spin-off from *Songs of Praise* on the BBC. A national treasure, Thora was rarely off our screens, due mainly to her long-running advertisements for Churchill stairlifts. She died 15 March 2003 Twickenham, Middlesex following a stroke. She wrote an autobiography, *Scene and Hird* (1976). See also entries in the radio and television section for *The First Lady, Hallelujah!, In Loving Memory, Just A Minute, Last of the Summer Wine,* and *Meet the Wife.*

Hitchcock, Alfred (1899-1980) Born Alfred Joseph Hitchcock, 13 August 1899 Leytonstone, London. Director. Joined the *Islington Film Studios* in 1920. Directorial debut: *The Pleasure Garden* (1925). Pre-Hollywood films include: *The Lodger* (1926), *Blackmail* (1929 - Britain's first full-length "talkie"), *The 39 Steps* (1935), *Secret Agent* (1936), *Sabotage* (1936), *The Lady Vanishes* (1938) and *Jamaica Inn* (1939). He moved to the United States in 1939 to direct *Rebecca* (1940), which subsequently won the Academy Award for Best Picture. Known as "The Master of Suspense" he made a series of brilliant thrillers including *Suspicion* (1941), *Spellbound* (1945), *Notorious* (1946), *Rope* (1948), *Strangers on a Train* (1951), *Dial M for Murder* (1954), *To Catch a Thief* (1955), *Vertigo* (1958), *North by Northwest* (1959), *The Birds* (1963), *Marnie* (1964), *Torn Curtain* (1966), *Frenzy* (1972) and *Family Plot* (1976). Other films include: *Foreign Correspondent* (1940), *Mr & Mrs Smith* (1941), *Shadow of a Doubt* (1943), *The Paradine Case* (1947), *The Trouble with Harry* (1955), *The Man Who Knew Too Much* (1956) and *Topaz* (1969). Alfred also received Academy Award nominations for Best Director for *Rebecca* (1940), *Lifeboat* (1944), *Spellbound* (1945), *Rear Window* (1954) and *Psycho* (1960). He received the Irving G Thalberg Memorial Award at the 1967 Academy Awards - his acceptance speech was only two words: "Thank you". Known around the world for his profile and voice but within the industry as one of the greatest innovators and most talented of directors. He made fleeting appearances in most of his own films. On television he hosted his own successful series: *Alfred Hitchcock Presents* (see entry in television section). Alfred renounced his British citizenship in 1955. Created an Honorary KBE in 1980. He was married to Alma Reville from 1926 until his death on 29 April 1980, Bel Air, Los Angeles, California. His tombstone reads "I'm in on a plot".

Hobson, Valerie (1917-98) Born Valerie Babette Louise Hobson, 14 April 1917, Larne, County Antrim, Northern Ireland. Actress. Studied dancing at RADA but grew too tall to take it up professionally. Stage debut: *Ball at the Savoy* (1932). Screen debut: *Eyes of Fate* (1933). Signed to *Universal Pictures* she starred in *The Bride of Frankenstein* (1935) - as the wife of Henry Frankenstein, not of Frankenstein's monster. She returned to pre-war Britain for such films as: *The Drum* (1938), *Q Planes* (1939) and *The Spy in Black* (1939). After the war her career took off with her role as Estella in *Great Expectations* (1946) and she followed up with starring parts in *Blanche Fury* (1947), *Kind Hearts and Coronets* (1949) and *The Rocking Horse Winner* (1949). She married film producer Anthony Havelock-Allen in 1939 and after their divorce in 1952 Valerie married John

Profumo (30 January 1915 – 9 March 2006) in 1954. She stood by her husband following revelations he had lied to the House of Commons about his affair with Christine Keeler, - later filmed as *Scandal* (1989) - which saw his resignation in 1963 as Minister for War and as an MP, and which ultimately brought down the government of the day. She remained married to Profumo until her death on 13 November 1998, Westminster, London.

Hodge, Patricia (1946-) Born Patricia Ann Hodge, 29 September 1946, Cleethorpes, Lincolnshire. Actress. Trained at LAMDA, being awarded on graduation the Eveline Evans Award for Best Actress. Patricia is a successful stage and television actress whose stately bearing has graced a number of films. Her screen debut was in an episode of the BBC series *Menace* in 1973. She made her small screen film debut in the BBC TV film *The Girls of Slender Means* (1975) and her feature debut in *The Disappearance* (1977). Other films include: *Rosie Dixon - Night Nurse* (1978), *The Elephant Man* (1980), *Heavy Metal* (1981), *Betrayal* (1983), *Hud* (1986), *Just Ask for Diamond* (1988) and *Before you Go* (2002). She also starred as Margaret Thatcher in the BBC4 offering *The Falklands Play* (2002). Patricia married music publisher Peter Douglas Owen in 1976. The couple have two children: Alexander Richard Charles (b. March 1989); and Edward Frederick James (b. January 1992). Despite her stage success, Patricia is probably best known for her numerous television appearances. See entries in the television section for *The Fall and Rise of Reginald Perrin, Jemima Shore Investigates, The Life and Loves of a She Devil, Menace,Miranda, Nanny, The Other 'Arf, Rich Tea and Sympathy* and *Rumpole of the Bailey*.

Hodges, Mike (1932-) Born Michael Tommy Hodges, 29 July 1932, Bristol. Director, writer and producer. Qualified as a chartered accountant. After National Service he entered television and directed and produced the documentary series *World in Action* (1963-64) and the arts series *Tempo* (1965-66). After directing the thrillers *Suspect* (1969) and *Rumour* (1970) for television he made his big screen debut with *Get Carter* (1971), which he also wrote. Now seen as a classic, at the time it suffered by being considered too violent and by being poorly distributed. Neither of his next two films *Pulp* (1972) and *The Terminal Man* (1974) were box-office successes but he ended the 1970s with the popular *Flash Gordon* (1980). After the poor *Morons from Outer Space* (1985), the mangled in the cutting room *A Prayer for the Dying* (1987) and the well-received but rarely seen *Black Rainbow* (1989) he didn't direct again until *Croupier* (1998). This film was initially a failure in the UK but was re-released in 2001 after it became a box-office hit in the US. This was followed by *Murder by Numbers* (2001) and *I'll Sleep When I'm Dead* (2003). His first novel, *Watching The Wheels Come Off*, was published in 2010.

Holden, Fay (1893-1973) Born Dorothy Fay Hammerton, 26 September 1893, Birmingham. Actress. On the British stage from the age of nine, initially as a dancer, it was over 30 years before she made her Hollywood debut. She did so in a low budget B-movie called *The Pace That Kills* (aka *The Cocaine Fiends*) (1935). In her early films up to 1937 she is credited as Gaby Fay, which was her stage name. She played many supporting roles in films, usually in a matronly role until she landed the role of Andy Hardy's (played by Mickey Rooney) mother in *You're Only Young Once* (1937). Fay continued to play this role in another fourteen films, and indeed her last film was *Andy Hardy Comes Home* (1958) as Mrs Emily Hardy. Other notable films include: *Bulldog Drummond Escapes* (1937 - her first film billed as Fay Holden), *Bitter Sweet* (1940) and Samson and Delilah (1949). From 1914 until his death in 1945 she was married to David Clyde, the actor brother of screen comedian Andy Clyde. She herself died of cancer on 23 June 1973 in Los Angeles, California.

Holloway, Stanley (1890-1982) Born Stanley Augustus Holloway, 1 October 1890, Manor Park, London. Actor. Operatically trained, he began as a musical entertainer. Served in the Connaught Rangers during WWI. Screen debut: *The Rotters* (1921). Stanley had a few roles in the 1920s and 1930s including in *The Co-Optimists* (1929) based on a successful stage show. Other films included opportunities to deliver his famous comic monologues, the most famous of which were based on colourful 'Northern England' characters named Albert and the Ramsbottoms (by George Marriott Edgar) and 'Sam Small' (whom Holloway created). Apart from speaking the monologues, Holloway would sometimes sing the verses, carefully sticking to the words and heavily characterising them. Edgar's Albert and the Lion (whom Edgar named Wallace) became a huge hit for Stanley. Another popular song of Stanley's from the 1930s was *My Word, You Do Look Queer*. During the 1940s he often appeared alongside the Crazy Gang and even acted as a temporary replacement for Bud Flanagan from time to time when Flanagan had to pull out for contractual reasons. After *Major Barbara* (1941) he featured in *The Way Ahead* (1944), *This Happy Breed* (1944) and *Brief Encounter* (1945). He followed playing Vincent Crummles in *Nicholas Nickleby* (1947) and the gravedigger in *Hamlet* (1948) by starring in the Ealing comedies *Passport to Pimlico* (1949) and *The Lavender Hill Mob* (1951), *The Titfield Thunderbolt* (1952) and *Meet Mr Lucifer* (1953). He gained an Academy Award Nomination for Best Supporting Actor for his role of Alfred P. Doolittle in *My Fair Lady* (1964). Autobiography: *Wiv a Little Bit of Luck* (1969). He died 30 January 1982, Littlehampton, West Sussex.

Holm, Ian (1931-) Born Ian Holm Cuthbert, 12 September 1931, Goodmayes, Ilford, Essex. Actor. Attended RADA and joined the RSC in 1954. A fine actor on stage and on film and TV. Stage debut: *Othello* (1954). Screen debut: *The Fixer* (1968). Other films include: *The Bofors Gun* (1968), *Oh! What a Lovely War* (1969), *Mary, Queen of Scots* (1971), *Nicholas and Alexandra* (1971), *Young Winston* (1972), *Juggernaut* (1974), *Robin and Marian* (1976), *Alien* (1979), *Time Bandits* (1981), *Greystoke: The Legend of Tarzan, The Lord of the Apes* (1984), *Brazil* (1985), *Henry V* (1989), *Hamlet* (1990), *Frankenstein* (1994), *The Madness of King George* (1994), *The Fifth Element* (1997), *eXistenZ* (1999), *From Hell* (2001), *The Lord of the Rings: The Fellowship of the Ring* (2001 – as Bilbo Baggins), *The Lord of the Rings: The Return of the King* (2003), *Garden State* (2004), *The Day After Tomorrow* (2004), *The Aviator* (2004), *Chromophobia* (2005), *Lord of War* (2005), *Renaissance* (2006), *O Jerusalem* (2006) and *Ratatouille* (2007). Nominated for an Academy Award for Best Supporting Actor for playing Sam Mussabini in *Chariots of Fire* (1982). Ian has been married to Lynn Mary Shaw (1955-65), Sophie Baker (1982-86), actress Penelope Wilton (1991-2001) and, since 2003, artist Sophie de Stempel, a protégée and life model of Lucian Freud. He has five children; his eldest two, from his first marriage, are Jessica, a presenter of the Crufts Dog Show and Sarah-Jane Holm, who played Jenny Rodenhurst Simcock in *A Bit of a Do*. Two are by Bee Gilbert (Barnaby Holm, who acted as a child but now lives in Los Angeles as a Hollywood club owner, and Melissa Holm, who is a casting director) and his youngest child, Harry Holm, from his second marriage, is a filmmaker most notable for his music videos, and is engaged to Samantha Morton. Appointed CBE in 1990 and knighted 1998.

Hooper, Tom (1972-) Born Thomas George Hooper, 1972, London, to a British father and Australian mother. Director. He began directing plays and television commercials while at Oxford University and made his first film short *Painted Faces* in 1992. He next concentrated on television and directed episodes of *Byker Grove, Eastenders*, and *Cold Feet*, before moving on to serials such as *Love in a Cold Climate* (2001), *Daniel Deronda* (2002), and *Prime Suspect 6: The Last Witness* (2003). His feature film debut came with *Red Dust* (2004), starring Hilary Swank. Back on television he directed the two-part serial *Elizabeth I* (2005), the TV film *Longford* (2006) and the seven-part miniseries John Adams (2008). His stock rose when he directed his next feature *The Damned United* (2009) and positively soared after winning the Academy Award for Best Director for *The King's Speech* (2010). In his acceptance speech Tom praised his mother, Meredith, for suggesting he make the film. Tom is currently directing the forthcoming musical film *Les Miserables* starring Hugh Jackman as Jean Valjean and Russell Crowe as Inspector Javert.

Hope, Bob See entry in comedy section

Hopkins, Anthony (1937-) Born Philip Anthony Hopkins, 31 December 1937, Margam, Port Talbot, Wales. Actor. Trained at the Welsh College of Music and Drama in Cardiff and RADA. Stage debut: *Have a Cigarette* (1960). Joined the National Theatre in 1965. He made his screen debut in an episode of the ITV crime series, *The Man In Room 17*, in 1965. His film debut came in the 1967 TV movie *A Flea in Her Ear* and his feature debut, as Brechtian, in *The White Bus* (1967). Other films include: *The Lion in Winter* (1968), *The Looking Glass War* (1969), *Hamlet* (1969), *When Eight Bells Toll* (1971), *Young Winston* (1972), *All Creature Great and Small* (1974), *Juggernaut* (1974), *A Bridge too Far* (1976), *Magic* (1978), *The Bounty* (1984), *84 Charing Cross Road* (1987), *Howard's End* (1992), *Dracula* (1992), *Chaplin* (1992), *Shadowlands* (1993), *Legends of the Fall* (1994), *The Mask of Zorro* (1998), *Meet Joe Black* (1998), *Titus* (1999), *Alexander* (2004), *The World's Fastest Indian* (2005), *All the King's Men* (2006), *Fracture* (2007), *Beowulf* (2007), *The City of Your Final Destination* (2009), *The Wolfman* (2010), *You Will Meet a Tall Dark Stranger* (2010), *Bare Knuckles* (2010), *The Rite* (2011) and *Thor* (2011 – as Odin). Won a Best Actor Academy Award for playing Hannibal Lecter in *The Silence of the Lambs* (1991), a role he repeated in *Hannibal* (2001) and *Red Dragon* (2002). Nominated for Academy Awards as Best Actor for *The Remains of the Day* (1993) and *Nixon* (1995). He was also nominated as Best Supporting Actor for *Amistad* (1997). Anthony has been married three times. His first two wives were Petronella Barker (1967–72) and Jennifer Lynton (1973–2002). Since 2003 he has been married to Colombian-born actress and producer Stella Arroyave. He has a daughter from his first marriage, Abigail Hopkins (b. 20 August 1968), who is an actress and singer. His wife produced the film *Slipstream* (2007), in which Sir Anthony not only starred, but also wrote, scored and directed. Away from the cameras he is patron of the Tommy Cooper Society and frequently mimics the great comedian. Appointed CBE in 1987 and knighted in 1993. Became an American citizen in 2000. According to Richard Attenborough he is "the greatest actor of his generation". He has certainly gone a long way to emulating his fellow Port Talbot thespian, Richard Burton. See also entries in the television section for *The Edwardians*, *Face to Face*, and *The Man in Room 17*.

Hordern, Michael (1911-95) Born Michael Murray Hordern, 4 October 1911, Berkhamsted, Hertfordshire. Actor. In a screen career lasting almost 60 years he made his screen debut in *A Girl Must Live* (1939). He had small parts in films including: *A Girl in a Million* (1946), *Passport to Pimlico* (1949), *Tom Brown's Schooldays* (1951), *The Magic Box* (1951), *Scrooge* (1951 - as Jacob Marley) and *The Heart of the Matter* (1953). From the mid-1950s he began to play more significant roles in films such as: *The Night my Number Came Up* (1955), *The Spanish Gardener* (1956), *Alexander the Great* (1956), *I Was Monty's Double* (1958), *Sink the Bismarck!* (1960) and *Macbeth* (1960). During the 1960s he featured in *El Cid* (1961), *Cleopatra* (1963), *Genghis Khan* (1965), *The Spy who Came in from the Cold* (1965), *Khartoum* (1966), *The Taming of the Shrew (1967)*, *How I Won the War* (1967), *Where Eagles Dare* (1968), *The Bed-Sitting Room* (1969) and *Anne of a Thousand Days* (1969). Michael could also produce excellent comedy performances in such films as: *A Funny Thing Happened on the Way to the Forum* (1966), *Futtocks End* (1970) and *Up Pompeii* (1971). He showed no sign of slowing down in the 1970s and 1980s although he spent more time on television projects. His later films include: *Theatre of Blood* (1973), *Juggernaut* (1974), *The Old Curiosity Shop* (1975), *The Slipper and the Rose* (1976), *The Missionary* (1982), *Gandhi* (1982), *Lady Jane* (1986) and his last film, *The Fool* (1990). Autobiography: *A World Elsewhere* (1993). A keen angler, Michael bought a house close to the river Lambourn in Newbury, Berkshire, in 1956, so he could indulge his passion for fishing for trout and grayling, often joined by his great friend, dramatist Tom Stoppard. Michael was married to Eve Mortimer from 1943 until her death in 1986. He was knighted in 1983. He died 2 May 1995, Oxford. See also entries in the television section for *Edward the Seventh*, *The History Man*, *Middlemarch*, *Paddington*, and *The Wind in the Willows*.

Hoskins, Bob (1942-) Born Robert William Hoskins, 26 October 1942, Bury St Edmunds, Suffolk. Actor. Attended the Central School of Speech and Drama. Screen and film debut: *Up the Front* (1972). Made his screen acting breakthrough in *Pennies from Heaven* on television in 1978 and his first major film role in *The Long Good Friday* (1980). Other films include: *The National Health* (1973), *Inserts* (1975), *Royal Flash* (1975), *Zulu Dawn* (1979), *Pink Floyd The Wall (1982)*, *The Honorary Consul* (1983), *Lassiter* (1984), *The Cotton Club* (1984), *Brazil* (1985), *Sweet Liberty* (1986), *The Lonely Passion of Judith Hearne* (1987), *A Prayer for the Dying* (1987), *Who Framed Roger Rabbit* (1988), *Mermaids* (1990), *Heart Condition* (1990), *Shattered* (1991), *Hook* (1991), *The Favour, the Watch and the Very Big Fish* (1991), *The Inner Circle* (1991), *Passed Away* (1992), *Blue Ice* (1992), *The Big Freeze* (1993), *Super Mario Bros.*(1993), *Rainbow* (1995), *Nixon* (1995), *Michael* (1996), *Spice World* (1997), *Cousin Bette* (1998), *Parting Shots* (1999), *Felicia's Journey* (1999), *Captain Jack* (1999), *The White River Kid* (1999), *Live Virgin* (2000), *Enemy at the Gates* (2001 - as a young Khrushchev), *Last Orders* (2001), *Where Eskimos Live* (2002), *Maid in Manhattan* (2002), *The Sleeping Dictionary* (2003), *Den of Lions* (2003), *Vanity Fair* (2004), *Son of the Mask* (2005 - as Odin), *Stay* (2005), *Mrs Henderson Presents* (2005), *Paris, Je T'Aime* (2006), *Hollywoodland* (2006), the TV film *The Wind in the Willows* (2006 - as Badger), *Sparkle* (2007), *Outlaw* (2007), *Ruby Blue* (2007), *Go Go Tales* (2007), *Doomsday* (2008), the TV film *Pinocchio* (2008 - as Geppetto), *A Christmas Carol* (2009), and *Made in Dagenham* (2010). Bob was famously on standby as replacement in the film *The Untouchables* if star Robert De Niro had not decided to play Al Capone. When De Niro took the part, director Brian De Palma mailed Bob a cheque for £20,000 with a Thank You note, which prompted Hoskins to call up De Palma and ask him if there were any more movies he didn't want him to be in. He gained a Golden Globe award and an Academy Award nomination for Best Actor for *Mona Lisa* (1986). Bob has always taken time to appear in smaller budget independent projects such as *The Raggedy Rawney* (1988) - which he also wrote and directed - *Twenty Four Seven* (1997) and *A Room for Romeo Brass* (1999). His latest films include: *Will* (2011) and the upcoming *Outside Bet* (2012). He has been married twice: to Linda Banwell (1967-78; divorced; 2 children) and Jane Livesey (1982-present; 2 children). See also entries in the television section for *Big Jim and the Figaro Club*, *On the Move*, *Pennies From Heaven*, *Rock Follies of '77*, and *The Street*.

Hoult, Nicholas (1989-) Born Nicholas Caradoc Hoult, 7 December 1989, Wokingham. Actor. He attended the Sylvia Young Stage School. He made his film debut, as Bobby, in *Intimate Relations* (1996) but it was his second film *About a Boy* (2002), in which he played a nerdy teenager named Marcus, that established him as an actor. Other films include: *Wah-Wah* (2005), *The Weather Man* (2006), *Kidulthood* (2006), *A Single Man* (2009) and *Clash of the Titans* (2010 - as Eusebios). Most famously cast as Tony Stonem in the E4 television series *Skins* (2007-08). His great aunt was Dame Anna Neagle. Nicholas has recently been cast in the role of Hank McCoy / Beast in the X-Men prequel, *X-Men: First Class*, (2011), directed by Matthew Vaughn, and is currently in a relationship with actress Jennifer Lawrence whom he met on the set.

Houston, Penelope (1927-) Born 9 September 1927, Kensington, London. Writer and critic. Educated at Somerville College, Oxford (history). She is the author of *The Contemporary Cinema* (1963), a seminal work in the development of the new film culture in late 1950s and early 1960s, and a formidable, longtime (1956-90) editor of the *British Film Institute*'s journal, *Sight and Sound*. Penelope also wrote *Went the Day Well* (1992) and *Keepers of the Frame: the Film Archives* (1994). One of the very few intelligent women film critics who happens to be English. Awarded the OBE in 1981.

Howard, Leslie (1893-1943) Born Leslie Howard Steiner, 3 April 1893, Lewisham, London. Actor. Born to Hungarian parents who later changed their name to Stainer. Educated at Dulwich College. Worked as a bank clerk before serving briefly in WWI until he was invalided out with shell shock. Stage debut: *Peg o' My Heart* (1917). A fine stage actor who early in his career appeared more in the theatre than on film. Screen debut: *The Heroine of Mons*

(1914). Other films include: *Outward Bound* (1930), *Secrets* (1933), *Of Human Bondage* (1934), *British Agent* (1934), *The Scarlet Pimpernel* (1934), *Petrified Forest* (1936), *Intermezzo* (1939), *Pimpernel Smith* (1941), *In Which We Serve* (1942), *The First of the Few* (1942) and *The Gentle Sex* (1943). He played Ashley Wilkes in *Gone with the Wind* (1939) and was nominated for Best Actor Academy Awards for *Berkeley Square* (1933) and *Pygmalion* (1938). Leslie was the on-screen embodiment of the sophisticated Englishman. He married Ruth Martin in 1916 and they had two children. His son Ronald Howard (1918–96) became an actor and is noted for portraying the title character in a television series *Sherlock Holmes* (1954). Arthur, Howard's younger brother, was also an actor, primarily in British comedies. A sister, Irene, was a costume designer. A much-publicised ladies' man Leslie reportedly had clandestine affairs with actresses Tallulah Bankhead, Merle Oberon, Conchita Montenegro, Norma Shearer and Myrna Loy. However, towards the end of his life, with the full knowledge of his wife, he did take a mistress, Violette Cunningham. Leslie died 1 June 1943. He was flying on a DC-3 Dakota returning from Portugal which was shot down by the Luftwaffe apparently in the belief that Winston Churchill was on board.

Howard, Trevor (1913-88) Born Trevor Wallace Howard-Smith 29 September 1913, Cliftonville, Margate, Kent. Actor. Attended RADA. Stage debut: *Revolt in the Reformatory* (1934). Screen debut: *The Way Ahead* (1944). Best known early role was as Dr Alec Harvey opposite Celia Johnson in *Brief Encounter* (1945). Won an Academy Award Nomination for Best Actor for *Sons and Lovers* (1960). Also starred as Captain Bligh in *Mutiny on the Bounty* (1962) opposite Marlon Brando, whom he described as "unprofessional and utterly ridiculous". Others of his 75 films include: *The Way to the Stars* (1945), *I See a Dark Stranger* (1946), *Green for Danger* (1946), *They Made Me a Fugitive* (1947), *So Well Remembered* (1947), *The Passionate Friends* (1949) *The Third Man* (1949), *Odette* (1950), *Golden Salamander* (1950), *The Clouded Yellow* (1950), *Lady Godiva Rides Again* (1951), *Outcast of the Islands* (1952), *The Gift Horse* (1952), *The Heart of the Matter* (1953), *Cockleshell Heroes* (1955), *Run for the Sun* (1956), *Around the World in Eighty Days* (1956), *Interpol* (1957), *The Key* (1958 – for which he won a BAFTA), *The Roots of Heaven* (1958), *Moment of Danger* (1960), *The Lion* (1962), *Man in the Middle* (1963), *Father Goose* (1964), *Operation Crossbow* (1965), *Von Ryan's Express* (1965), *The Liquidator* (1965), *The Poppy Is Also a Flower* (1966), *Triple Cross* (1966), *Pretty Polly* (1967), *The Long Duel* (1967), *The Charge of the Light Brigade* (1968), *Battle of Britain* (1969), *Ryan's Daughter* (1970), *Twinky* (1970), *Kidnapped* (1971), *The Night Visitor* (1971), *To Catch a Spy* (1971), *Mary, Queen of Scots* (1972), *Pope Joan* (1972), *11 Harrowhouse* (1974), *Aces High* (1976), *The Bawdy Adventures of Tom Jones* (1976), *The Last Remake of Beau Geste* (1977), *Stevie* (1978), *Superman* (1978), *Hurricane* (1979), *The Sea Wolves* (1980), *Sir Henry at Rawlinson End* (1980), *Windwalker* (1980 - in the role of a Cheyenne Indian), *The Great Muppet Caper* (1981), *The Missionary* (1982), *Gandhi* (1982), *Sword of the Valiant* (1984), *Dust* (1985), *Time After Time* (1986), *Shaka Zulu* (1986), *White Mischief* (1988), *The Unholy* (1988) and his last film, *The Dawning* (1988). Throughout his film career Howard insisted that all of his contracts held a clause excusing him from work whenever a cricket Test Match was being played. Known for his hell-raising behaviour off-screen which he himself described as "eccentric", he was married to actress Helen Cherry from 1944 until his death on 7 January 1988, Bushey, Hertfordshire.

Howerd, Frankie See entry in comedy section

Howes, Sally Ann (1930-) Born 20 July 1930, St John's Wood, London. Actress. Daughter of comedian Bobby Howes. As a child actor, she made her screen debut, aged 13, in *Thursday's Child* (1943) and before she was twenty she had appeared in films such as *Nicholas Nickleby* (1947), *Anna Karenina* (1948) and *The History of Mr Polly* (1949). During the 1950s she starred in a series of stage musicals, including replacing Julie Andrews in *My Fair Lady* on Broadway in 1958. However, it is for the role of Truly Scrumptious in the popular musical *Chitty, Chitty, Bang, Bang* (1968) that she is best known. After that she returned to the stage and has made rare screen appearances. She is now a naturalised US citizen. She has been married three times, to Maxwell Koker (1950–53), Richard Adler (1958–66) and Douglas Rae (1972–present).

Hudson, Hugh (1936-) Born 25 August 1936, Marylebone, London. Director. Educated at Eton and Harvard. Began his career in advertising before becoming a film editor. Directed documentaries and television commercials. Formed *Hudson Films* in 1975. His directorial debut was *Chariots of Fire* (1981) which won a Best Picture Academy Award and gained Hugh a nomination as Best Director. His follow-up was *Greystoke: The Legend of Tarzan, Lord of the Apes* (1984). In 1985 he directed *Revolution* which ran vastly over budget, was savaged by the critics and ignored at the box office. In 2008 he re-edited Revolution, giving the film a narration by Al Pacino. His latest films are Lost Angels (1989), My Life So Far (1999) and I Dreamed of Africa (2000). In 1988 Hugh directed a 2½-minute advert for British Rail, a parody of the Post Office Film Unit's 25-minute documentary, Night Mail, made in 1936. Poet W. H. Auden had written verse specifically to fit the original 1936 film's footage, which showed the enormous scale of BR's daily operation and the structure of the 'sectorised' business. The opening sequence of Hudson's British Rail advert features the northbound Travelling Post Office with Auden's original verse, narrated by Sir Tom Courtenay. Among other acclaimed adverts he directed were the famous Cinzano "Airplane" adverts, featuring the British actors Leonard Rossiter and Joan Collins. Hugh's first marriage in 1977, was to painter Susan Michie, with whom he had a son, Tom (b. 1978). Following his divorce, he married actress Maryam d'Abo (b. 27 December 1960) in November 2003.

Hughes, Gareth (1894-1965) Born William John Hughes, 23 August 1894, Llanelli, Carmarthenshire. Actor. Joined The Welsh Players theatre company and travelled to the United States in 1914. Deciding to stay after the end of the tour, he made an immediate impression on Broadway. Screen debut: *And the Children Pay* (1918). Other early films include: *Mrs Wigg of the Cabbage Patch* (1919), *Eyes of Youth* (1919), *The Chorus Girl's Romance* (1920), *Sentimental Tommy* (1921), *Forget Me Not* (1922), *The Christian* (1923) and *The Spanish Dancer* (1923). After the mid-1920s his career took a downturn and his last two pictures were his only talkies: *Mister Antonio* (1929) and *Scareheads* (1931). Following a successful return to stage work his life took a new direction in 1944 when he became a lay missionary to the Paiute tribe on their reservation at Nixon, Nevada. His last work in film was as Welsh dialect coach to Bette Davis for *The Corn is Green* (1945). He worked in Nevada until 1958 and he then became unofficial chaplain at the Motion Picture Country Home in California, officiating at Edmund Gwenn's funeral in 1959. He died 1 October 1965, Woodland Hills, California.

Hulbert, Claude (1900-64) Born Claude Noel Hulbert, 25 December 1900, Fulham, London. Actor. Educated at Cambridge. Leading member of the Footlights Revue. Screen debut: *Champagne* (1928). Other films include: *Their Night Out* (1933), *Hello Sweetheart* (1935), *Wolf's Clothing* (1936) and *Honeymoon-Go-Round* (1940). He replaced Moore Marriott and Graham Moffatt alongside Will Hay in *The Ghost of St Michael's* (1941) and *My Learned Friend* (1943). His final films were *The Ghosts of Berkeley Square* (1947), *Cardboard Cavalier* (1949), *Fun at St Fanny's* (1956) and *Not a Hope in Hell* (1960). Brother of Jack Hulbert and married to actress Enid Trevor, the great-grand niece of David Garrick. He died 23 January 1964, Sydney, Australia.

Hulbert, Jack (1892-1978) Born John Norman Hulbert, 24 April 1892, Ely, Cambridgeshire. Actor. Educated at Cambridge. Studied at Central School of Speech and Drama. Brother of Claude Hulbert. Stage debut: *The Pearl Girl* (1913). In 1916 he married actress Cicely Courtneidge (1 April 1893 – 26 April 1980). Jack's screen debut: *Elstree Calling* (1930), was opposite his wife. Other films include *The Ghost Train* (1931), *Love on*

Wheels (1932) and Bulldog Jack (1935). By now he had formed a very successful light comedy, song and dance act with Cicely. They moved away from films after WWII and concentrated more on radio and stage work. Jack did make the odd cameo performance in a few films, notably, *The Magic Box* (1951) and *Not Now Darling* (1973). His last film role was as Sir Hugh Fawcett in *The Cherry Picker* (1974). Jack's autobiography was entitled, *The Little Woman's Always Right* (1975). He died 25 March 1978, Westminster, London.

Hunter, Ian (1900-75) Born Ian Basil Hunter, 13 June 1900, Capetown, South Africa. Actor. Moved to England and served in France during WWI. Made his stage debut in 1919 and his screen debut in a career lasting forty years in *Not For Sale* (1924). His early films include *The Ring* (1927), *The Physician* (1928), *Sally in Our Alley* (1931) and *The Sign of Four* (1932 - as Dr Watson). He moved to Hollywood in 1934. Played Theseus in *A Midsummer Night's Dream* (1935), Richard the Lionheart in *The Adventures of Robin Hood* (1938) and Captain Crewe in *The Little Princess* (1939). His other films include *Tower of London* (1939), *Bitter Sweet* (1940), *Billy the Kid* (1941) and *A Yank at Eton* (1942). Ian returned to England for war service and stayed on afterwards to feature in films such as *Edward, My Son* (1949), *The Battle of the River Plate* (1956), *North West Frontier* (1959), *The Bulldog Breed* (1960), *Guns of Darkness* (1962) and *Il Mistero del Tempio Indiano* (1963). He died 23 September 1975, Ealing, London.

Hunter, Russell (1925-2004) Born Russell Ellis, 18 February 1925 ,Glasgow. Actor. Began his professional life at the very first Edinburgh Festival Fringe in Sean O'Casey's *The Plough and the Stars* in 1947. Made his film debut in *Lilli Marlene* (1950) and later that year appeared with Archie Duncan in *The Gorbals Story*, a film which also featured his first wife, Marjorie Thomson. He followed these by playing a pilot in the Battle of Britain drama *Angels One Five* in 1951. Other films include: *The Brave Don't Cry* (1952), *Taste the Blood of Dracula* (1970), *Up Pompeii* (1971), *Callan* (1974), *American Cousins* (2003) and his last film *Skagerrak* (2003). In 1958 the Saturday evening radio series *The McFlannels* transferred to BBC television and Russell and Marjorie took the lead roles. For all his promise in theatre and film Russell will forever be remembered for his iconic portrayal of Lonely, the grubby, smelly informant, in the TV espionage series *Callan*, starring Edward Woodward. Russell's second wife was the actress Caroline Blakiston and his third, the popular pantomime actress Una McLean to whom he was married from 1991 until his death on 26 February 2004 in Edinburgh. See also entries in the radio and television section for *Ace of Wands, Callan, The Gaffer,* and *The McFlannels.*

Hurley, Liz (1965-) Born Elizabeth Jane Hurley, 10 June 1965, Basingstoke, Hampshire. Actress and model. Trained at the London Studio Centre. Screen debut: *Aria* (1987). After television appearances in *Inspector Morse* (1988), *Rumpole of the Bailey* (1988) and the *Young Indiana Jones Chronicles* (1992) she made her Hollywood debut in *Passenger 57* (1992). More television work followed in the TV films *Sharpe's Enemy* (1994), *Harrison: Cry of the City* (1996) and *Samson and Delilah* (1996 - as Delilah). In the meantime she had set up *Simian Films* with her then partner Hugh Grant. Their first production was *Extreme Measures* (1996) and this was followed by *Mickey Blue Eyes* (1999) - both of which starred Grant. Liz then filmed *Method* (2004) and the TV series *Project Catwalk* (2006). Her film career saw her appearing as Vanessa Kensington in *Austin Powers: International Man of Mystery* (1997) and the sequel *Austin Powers: The Spy Who Shagged Me* (1999). Other films include: *Bedazzled* (2000 - as The Devil), *Double Whammy* (2001), *Bad Boy* (2002), *Serving Sara* (2002) and *Method* (2004). Other films include: *Passenger 57* (1992 - as Sabrina Ritchie), *Beyond Bedlam* (1994 - as Stephanie Lyell), *Mad Dogs and Englishmen* (1995 - as Antonia Dyer), *Dangerous Ground* (1997 - as Karen), *Permanent Midnight* (1998 - as Sandra), *My Favorite Martian* (1999 - as Brace Channing), *Edtv* (1999 - as Jill), *The Weight of Water* (2000 - as Adaline Gunne) and *Dawg* (2002 - as Anna Lockheart). Away from the screen she became a bit of a media darling after appearing alongside Grant at the premiere of *Four Weddings and a Funeral* (1994) in a Versace-designed dress which appeared to be barely held together by a row of golden

safety pins. She has also had a long association with the cosmetics company Estée Lauder. She met Hugh Grant whilst they were making *Rowing with the Wind* (1988) and their relationship lasted until 2000. In recent years Liz has taken a break from film work and has concentrated on modelling work. She has her own beachwear line and is signed to the Independent Modeling Agency in London. On 4 April 2002, she gave birth to a son, Damian Charles Hurley. The baby's father, Steve Bing, denied paternity by alleging that he and Hurley had a brief, non-exclusive relationship in 2001. A DNA test, however, established Bing as the child's father. Liz is godmother to Patsy Kensit's son Lennon and two of David Beckham and Victoria Beckham's sons (Brooklyn and Romeo). In 2002, Liz began dating Indian textile heir and software director Arun Nayar, and the couple eventually married on 2 March 2007, at Sudeley Castle, Gloucs, before having a second traditional Hindu wedding at Umaid Bhawan Palace in Jodhpur, India. She announced their separation on Twitter in December 2010 and has subsequently been romantically linked to Australian cricketer Shane Warne. Liz has recently been filming for her latest role as Veronica Cale in the NBC television series, *Wonder Woman* (2011).

Hurt, John (1940-) Born John Vincent Hurt, 22 January 1940, Chesterfield, Derbyshire. Actor. Son of a clergyman. Studied art at Grimsby Art School and St Martin's School for Art in London. John abandoned painting after winner a scholarship to RADA in 1960. His screen debut was in an episode of the ITV series *Probation Officer* (1961). His feature debut was in *The Wild and the Willing* (1962). Other films include: *A Man for All Seasons* (1966), *Sinful Davey* (1969), *Mr Forbush and the Penguins* (1971), *10 Rillington Place* (1971), *Alien* (1979), *History of the World: Part I* (1981), *Nineteen Eighty-Four* (1984), *The Hit* (1984), *Space Balls* (1987), *King Ralph* (1991), *Rob Roy* (1995), *Captain Corelli's Mandolin* (2001), *Harry Potter and the Philosopher's Stone* (2001), *Hellboy* (2004), *The Skeleton Key* (2005), *The Proposition* (2005), *V for Vendetta* (2006), *Boxes* (2007), *The Oxford Murders* (2008), *Outlander* (2008), *Indiana Jones and the Kingdom of the Crystal Skull* (2008), *Hellboy II: The Golden Army* (2008), *Lecture 21* (2008), *New York, I Love You* (2009), *The Limits of Control* (2009), *44 Inch Chest* (2009), *Ultramarines: A Warhammer 40,000 Movie* (2010), *Lou* (2010), *Brighton Rock* (2010), *Harry Potter and the Deathly Hallows: Part I* (2010 - as Ollivander) and *Part II* (2011), *Melancholia* (2011), *Tinker Tailor Soldier Spy* (2011) and *Immortals* (2011). Gained Academy Award nominations for Best Actor for *Midnight Express* (1978) and *The Elephant Man* (1980). A supremely versatile actor, John also made an impact on television in the series *I Claudius* (1976) and the TV film *The Naked Civil Servant* (1975). It would have been easy to cast an actor such as Charles Hawtrey in the role of the homosexual Quentin Crisp but the light and shade that John brings to all his roles undoubtedly helped to create a more tolerant society. He later reprised his role of Crisp in the 2009 film, *An Englishman in New York*. John has also undertaken many voice only film roles including: *Watership Down* (1978 - voice of Hazel), *The Lord of the Rings* (1978 – voice of Aragorn), *Vincent* (1987 – voice of Vincent Van Gogh), *Dogville* (2003 - narrator) and *Perfume: The Story of a Murderer* (2006 - narrator). Appointed CBE in 2004. John has been married four times: Annette Robertson (1962–64), Donna Peacock (1984–90), Jo Dalton (1990–96) and Ann Rees Meyers (2005–present). John had two sons: Sasha John Vincent Hurt (b. 6 February 1990) and Nick Hurt (b. 5 February 1993) by Jo Dalton. In 1967 he began a relationship, with French model Marie-Lise Volpeliere-Pierrot, the sister of fashion photographer Jean-Claude Volpeliere-Pierrot, whose son Ben would later become a teen idol singing in the pop band *Curiosity Killed the Cat*. The couple had planned to get married after fifteen years together, when, on 26 January 1983, John and Marie-Lise went horse riding early in the morning near their house in Ascott-under-Wychwood, Oxfordshire. Tragically, Marie-Lise lost her stirrup and was thrown off the horse, landing on her head in the middle of the lane. She went into a coma and died later that day. See also entries in the television section for *I Claudius, Merlin, The Naked Civil Servant, Probation Officer,* and *Who Do You Think You Are?*

Hyde-White, Wilfrid (1903-91) Born 12 May 1903, Bourton-on-the-Water, Gloucestershire. Actor. The son of a canon of

Gloucester Cathedral, he was educated at Marlborough before moving on to RADA. Wilfrid made his stage debut as Maitland in the Evans-Valentine hit comedy *Tons of Money* (1922) at Ryde, Isle of Wight, and his London debut as a juror in *Beggar on Horseback* (1925) at the Queen's. He made his feature film debut as Brooks in *Josser on the Farm* (1934), billed as Hyde White. Other films include: *Admirals All* (1935), *Murder by Rope* (1936), *Rembrandt* (1936), *Elephant Boy* (1937), *Bulldog Drummond at Bay* (1937), *I've Got a Horse* (1938), *Keep Smiling* (1938), *Over the Moon* (1939), *Poison Pen* (1939), *Turned Out Nice Again* (1941), *Asking for Trouble* (1942), *Night Boat to Dublin* (1946), *The Ghosts of Berkeley Square* (1947), *The Winslow Boy* (1948), *Quartet* (1948), *Adam and Evelyne* (1949), *The Third Man* (1949), *The Mudlark* (1950), *The Browning Version* (1951), *The Story of Gilbert and Sullivan* (1953), *The Adventures of Quentin Durward* (1955), *See How They Run* (1955), *The Silken Affair* (1956), *The March Hare* (1956), *Tarzan and the Lost Safari* (1957), *Up the Creek* (1958), *Carry On Nurse* (1959), *Life in Emergency Ward 10* (1959) and *North West Frontier* (1959). After a successful stage career in the UK he went to Hollywood in 1960 to take a part in *Let's Make Love* which saw him remain in the States being cast as the perfect Englishman. He appeared in over 100 films, many taken to clear gambling and tax debts, which made his role as multi-millionaire Roderick Montpelier in *The Million Pound Note* (1954), somewhat ironic as the wager he makes with his brother in the film was purely for honour only. Wilfrid's most famous films were yet to come and include: *Two Way Stretch* (1960 – as Soapy Stevens), *Let's Make Love* (1960), *My Fair Lady* (1964 - as Colonel Pickering), *On the Double* (1961), *On the Fiddle* (1961), *In Search of the Castaways* (1962), *Crooks Anonymous* (1962 - as Montague), *You Must Be Joking!* (1965), *Ten Little Indians* (1965), *The Liquidator* (1965), *The Sandwich Man* (1966), *The Magic Christian* (1969), *The Cat and the Canary* (1979), *Xanadu* (1980) and his last film role as Mr John Barville in *Sex, Lies and Renaissance* (aka *Fanny Hill*) (1983). He was once described as "a player who could give lessons in relaxation to a sleepy cat." In 1927 Wilfrid married Blanche Hope Aitken, an actress known professionally as Blanche Glynne (b. 1893). The couple had one son. Following Blanche's death in 1948, Hyde-White (he had added the hyphen for effect) married American actress Ethel Korenman (stage name Ethel Drew) in 1957. They had two children: a son, actor Alex Punch Hyde-White (b. 30 January 1959), and a daughter, Juliet. Wilfrid died 6 May 1991, Woodland Hills, Los Angeles, California.

Hynes, Jessica (1972-) Born Jessica Stevenson, 15 November 1972, Lewisham, London. Actress and writer. Jessica's screen debut was as Helga in *Swing Kids* (1993). Other films include: *The Baby of Mâcon* (1993), *Born Romantic* (2000), *Pure* (2002), *Shaun of the Dead* (2004 - as Yvonne), *Bridget Jones: The Edge of Reason* (2004 - as Magda), *Confetti* (2006 - as Sam), *Four Last Songs* (2007 - as Miranda), *Son of Rambow* (2007), *Magicians* (2007), *Harry Potter and the Order of the Phoenix* (2007 - voice of Mafalda Hopkirk), *Faintheart* (2008) and *Burke and Hare* (2010 - as Lucky). She is possibly best known as one of the creators, writers and stars of the British sitcom *Spaced*. Jessica has won two British Comedy Awards for her performances in Spaced: Best Female Comedy Newcomer in 1999 and Best TV Comedy Actress in 2001. She was also nominated for a TV BAFTA for her performance in the largely improvised TV feature *Tomorrow La Scala* (2000), and for an Olivier Award for her role in the play *The Night Heron* (2003). She married Adam Hynes in 2002 and has worked under her married name since 2007. See also entries in the television section for *According to Bex, Crown Prosecutor, The Royle Family, Six Pairs of Pants, Spaced* and Staying *Alive*.

Idle, Eric See entry in comedy section

Ifans, Rhys (1967-) Born Rhys Owain Evans, 22 July 1967, Haverfordwest, Pembrokeshire, Wales. Actor. Rhys was brought up in Ruthin, Denbighshire and educated at the Guildhall School of Music and Drama. After making his Welsh television debut on S4C as presenter of the anarchic children's quiz programme *Sdwnsh* (Welsh for "Mash") in 1990 he made his national television debut as Dave in the Thames Television comedy series

Spatz (1991). Rhys made his film debut in the BBC TV film *Streetlife* (1995). Other films include: *August* (1996), *Dancing at Lughnasa* (1998), *Rancid Aluminium* (2000), *Kevin & Perry Go Large* (2000), *Love, Honour and Obey* (2000), *Little Nicky* (2000), *Human Nature* (2001), *The Shipping News* (2001), *The 51st State* (2001), *Danny Deckchair* (2003), *Vanity Fair* (2004), *Enduring Love* (2004 – as Jed Parry), *Chromophobia* (2005), *Garfield 2* (2006 - voice of McBunny), *Four Last Songs* (2007), *Hannibal Rising* (2007), *Elizabeth: The Golden Age* (2007), *The Informers* (2008), *The Boat That Rocked* (2009), *Mr Nobody* (2009), *Greenberg* (2010), *Mr Nice* (2010), *Nanny McPhee and the Big Bang* (2010), *Harry Potter and the Deathly Hallows: Part 1* (2010 - as Xenophilius Lovegood), the Banksy-directed *Exit Through the Gift Shop* (2010) and *Anonymous* (2011). Best remembered so far as Hugh Grant's ill-kempt housemate, Spike, in *Notting Hill* (1999) and his portrayal of Peter Cook in the TV film *Not Only But Always* (2004), for which he won a BAFTA. His brother Llŷr Evans is also an actor and appeared as his twin in the film *Twin Town* (1997). Although it is an urban myth that in his teens Rhys sang lead vocals for the Welsh rock band Super Furry Animals he did in fact unite with the band's drummer Dafydd Ieuan to form psychedelic rock band Y Peth (The Thing) in 2008 and even penned a song *Stonefinger* about his break-up with actress Sienna Miller in May of that year. The split was something of a surprise as they had only been engaged a few months and Rhys had expressed his love by having a swallow tattoo etched on his right wrist to match hers.

Imrie, Celia (1952-) Born Celia Diana Savile Imrie, 15 July 1952, Guildford, Surrey. Actress. Celia trained at the Guildford School of Acting. She made her screen debut in an episode of *The Fenn Street Gang* (1971) and her feature debut in *Assassin* (1973). Other films include: *Death on the Nile* (1978), *The Wicked Lady* (1983), *Highlander* (1986), *Blue Black Permanent* (1992), *Frankenstein* (1994), *In the Bleak Midwinter* (1995), *The Borrowers* (1997 - as Homily Clock), *Hilary and Jackie* (1998 – as Iris du Pré), *Star Wars: Episode I - The Phantom Menace* (1999 - as Fighter Pilot Bravo 5), *Bridget Jones's Diary* (2001), *Revelation* (2001), *Thunderpants* (2002), *Heartlands* (2002), *Calendar Girls* (2003 - as Celia), *Out of Bounds* (2003), *Wimbledon* (2004), *Bridget Jones: The Edge of Reason* (2004), *Wah-Wah* (2005), *Imagine Me & You* (2005), *Nanny McPhee* (2005 - as Selma Quickly), *St. Trinian's* (2007), *St Trinian's 2: The Legend of Fritton's Gold* (2009) and *You Will Meet a Tall Dark Stranger* (2010). Celia is perhaps best known for her portrayal of Miss Babs, owner of *Acorn Antiques*, a parody of the low budget British soap opera Crossroads. First seen on *Victoria Wood As Seen on TV* in 1985, *Acorn Antiques* had its own spin-off series the following year, and in 2005 became a West End musical in which Celia won an Olivier Award for her performance. Celia gave birth to a son, Angus (b. August 1994), by fellow actor Benjamin Whitrow. The birth was a planned arrangement with her friend on condition that he had no control over the child's life. See also entries in the television section for *After You've Gone, Bergerac, Blackhearts in Battersea, Cranford, dinnerladies, Gormenghast, Kingdom,* and *Victoria Wood As Seen On TV*.

Ingram, Rex (1893-1950) Born Reginald Ingram Montgomery Hitchcock, 15 January 1893 Dublin. Director, actor and writer. Son of the Reverend Francis Ryan Montgomery Hitchcock who wrote several books about the early Christian church and Irish genealogy. He was rector of Kinnitty in Offaly when Rex was born and later became vicar of Tiptree, Essex. Rex emigrated to the United States in 1911. An accomplished artist and sculptor, he studied at the Yale School of Fine Art where he met Thomas Edison's son Charles and began his career in the film world. Screen acting debut: *Beau Brummel* (1913). He acted for only a couple of years before making his directing debut with *The Great Problem* (1916). He spent some part of WWI in the Royal Flying Corps but never got nearer to Europe than Canada. Rex both wrote and directed several other films including: *Broken Fetters* (1915), *The Chalice of Sorrow* (1916), *Black Orchids* (1917) and *The Little Terror* (1917). His films are noted for their bold visual style. In 1921 he directed *The Four Horsemen of the Apocalypse* which featured his future wife Alice and made a star of Rudolf Valentino. He followed this with *The Conquering Power* (1921), *The Prisoner of Zenda* (1922), *Scaramouche* (1923) and *The Arab* (1924). Married to actresses Doris Prawn (1917-20) and Alice Terry (1921-50). He was a friend of Erich von Stroheim and shared his wish to have complete artistic control over his work, which usually ended with budget over-runs and severe post-production editing. Fed up with studio interference he moved with Alice to France and acquired the Victorine Studios in Nice. He directed some sequences on *Ben-Hur* (1925), which were filmed in Italy, plus *Mare Nostrum* (1927) and *The Magician* (1927). His fascination with North Africa and Arab culture led him to film *The Garden of Allah* (1927*)* and his only talkie *Baroud* (1933), in which he also acted, although he was never a fan of talking pictures. The family adopted an Arab boy but reports that Ingram converted to Islam were refuted during his lifetime. He retired from film-making and, returning to California, went back to spending his time sculpting and writing. He died 21 July 1950 Los Angeles, California.

Ireland, Jill (1936-90) Born Jill Dorothy Ireland, 24 April 1936, Brentford, London. Actress. Jill was a professional dancer who made her screen debut in 1955 in *The Woman For Joe*. Her early films include: *Three Men in a Boat* (1956), *Hell Drivers* (1957), *Carry on Nurse* (1959), *Raising the Wind* (1961), *The Battleaxe* (1962) and *Twice Round the Daffodils* (1962). Jill then took a prolonged break from film acting and starred in episodes of many popular television series on both sides of the Atlantic, including *The Cheaters* (1962), *Richard the Lionheart* (1963), the medical drama *Ben Casey* (1964), *The Third Man* (1964), *Voyage to the Bottom of the Sea* (1964), *My Favorite Martian* (1965), *Shane* (1966), *Star Trek* (1967) and several episodes of The Man from U.N.C.L.E. (1967), opposite her then husband David McCallum. Jill married David in 1957. They had three sons, Paul, Valentine, and their adopted son, Jason McCallum, who died of a drug overdose in 1989, six months before Jill's own death. The couple divorced in 1967.

Jill then married actor Charles Bronson in 1968. She had first met him when he and David were filming The Great Escape in 1962. Together they had a daughter, Zuleika, and adopted a daughter, Katrina. They remained married until Jill's death in 1990. Jill now returned to film-acting and featured alongside Bronson in her next 15 films: *Twinky* (1970), *Le passager de la pluie* (aka *Rider in the Rain*)(1970), *Violent City* (1970), *Cold Sweat* (1970), *Two Minds for Murder* (1971), *The Valachi Papers* (1972), *The Mechanic* (1972), *Valdez the Halfbreed* (1973), *Breakout* (1975), *The Streetfighter* (1975), *Showdown at Breakheart Pass* (1975), *From Noon Till Three* (1976), *Love and Bullets* (1979), *Death Wish II* (1982) and *Assassination* (1987). This became such a recognised feature of her work that she said "I'm in so many Charles Bronson films because no other actress will work with him". Her last film, *Caught* (1987), was the only film she made without Bronson during their marriage. A beautiful woman and fine actress but the closest that she ever came to acting honours was presenting the Best Supporting Actress and Best Actress Academy Awards in 1974 and 1976. She died in Malibu, California, 18 May 1990, from breast cancer. She was cremated and Charles had her ashes inserted into a cane which he carried with him for the rest of his life. It was later buried with him. In 1991, Jill Clayburgh portrayed Jill in the made-for-television film *Reason for Living: The Jill Ireland Story*, which told of her later years, including her fight with cancer. Ironically, Clayburgh herself would die of the disease in November 2010.

Irons, Jeremy (1948-) Born Jeremy John Irons, 19 September 1948, Cowes, Isle of Wight. Actor. He trained at the Bristol Old Vic Drama School. Made his stage breakthrough playing John the Baptist in *Godspell*. Jeremy began on television with a small role in an episode of the London Weekend Television production of *The Rivals of Sherlock Holmes* (1971). Another early appearance was a much-shown clip singing and playing his guitar on the children's programme *Play Away*. His film debut was *Nijinsky* (1980 – as Mikhail Fokine). Other films include: *The French Lieutenant's Woman* (1981), *Moonlighting* (1982), *Betrayal* (1983), *The Mission* (1986), *Dead Ringers* (1988), *A Chorus of Disapproval* (1989), *Damage* (1992), *Waterland* (1992), *Die Hard with a Vengeance* (1995), *Lolita* (1997 – as Humbert Humbert), *The Man in the Iron Mask* (1998), *Dungeons and Dragons* (2000), *The Time Machine* (2002), *Mathilde* (2004), *The Merchant of Venice* (2004), *Casanova* (2005), opposite Heath Ledger in the title role, *Kingdom of Heaven* (2005), *Inland Empire* (2006), *Eragon* (2006), *Appaloosa* (2008), *The Pink Panther 2* (2009) and *Margin Call* (2011). Jeremy won an Academy Award for Best Actor for *Reversal of Fortune* (1990 – as Claus von Bülow). In 2006, Jeremy starred opposite Helen Mirren in television miniseries *Elizabeth I*, for which he received a Golden Globe Award and an Emmy Award for Best Supporting Actor. He has been married to actress Sinead Cusack since 1978. They have two sons, Samuel James Brefni Irons (b. 16 September 1978), who works as a photographer, and Maximilian Paul Diarmuid Irons (b. 17 October 1985), also an actor, who appeared in the 2006 Burberry fashion campaign. Both sons have appeared in films with their father, Sam in *Danny, Champion of the World* (1989) and Max in *Being Julia* (2004). Jeremy has also had much television success and is currently starring as Pope Alexander VI in the American Showtime series, *The Borgias*. See entries in the television section for *Brideshead Revisited*, *Churchill's People*, *Love for Lydia*, *The Pallisers*, *Play Away*, *The Rivals of Sherlock Holmes*, and *Who Do You Think You Are?*

Irvine, Jeremy See entry for Mike Newell

Isaacs, Jason (1963-) Born 6 June 1963, Liverpool, Merseyside. Actor. Jason's Jewish parents sent him to a cheder twice a week as a young adult to learn about Jewish ways. He then attended the Haberdashers' Aske's Boys' School before studying law at Bristol University but ultimately choosing to train to be an actor at the London Central School of Speech and Drama. He made his screen debut in *The Tall Guy* (1989) and then featured in the TV drama series *Capital City* (1989). Other early films include: *Dragonheart* (1996), *Event Horizon* (1997), *Armageddon* (1998), *Divorcing Jack* (1998) and *The End of the Affair* (1999). Made a breakthrough as the resident English bad guy Colonel William Tavington in Mel Gibson's version of the American Revolution, *The Patriot* (2000) and has since appeared in films such as *Black Hawk Down* (2001), *Reign of Fire* (2002), *Windtalkers* (2002), *Peter Pan* (2003), *Tennis, Anyone... ?* (2005), *Friends with Money* (2006), *Good* (2008), *La Conjura de El Escorial* (2008), *Green Zone* (2010) and *Abduction* (2011). Jason also plays the evil Lucius Malfoy in *Harry Potter and the Chamber of Secrets* (2002), *Harry Potter and the Goblet of Fire* (2005), *Harry Potter and the Order of the Phoenix* (2007), *Harry Potter and the Half Blood Prince* (2009), where he is seen in a moving portrait, *Harry Potter and the Deathly Hallows: Part 1* (2010) and *Harry Potter and the Deathly Hallows: Part II* (2011). As a voice actor Jason has lent his talents to the films *Batman: Under The Red Hood* (2010), *Green Lantern: Emerald Knights* (2011) and *Cars 2* (2011). On the stage Jason played Ben, opposite Lee Evans (Gus), in the critically-acclaimed 50th-anniversary production of Harold Pinter's *The Dumb Waiter*, at *Trafalgar Studios*, in London (2007). On television he was nominated at the British Academy Television Awards for Best Actor for his role as Harry H. Corbett in the BBC 4 drama *The Curse of Steptoe* (2009), opposite Phil Davis as Wilfrid Brambell. Jason and his partner, BBC documentary film-maker Emma Hewitt, whom he began dating at the Central School, have lived together since 1988 and have two daughters: Lily (b. 23 March 2002) and Ruby (b. 26 August 2005). See also enry for *Capity City* in the television section.

Isleworth Studios (1914-52) Founded by George Berthold "Bertie" Samuelson, who bought Worton Hall in Hounslow, Middlesex, for £200 in 1914. The first film completed was *A Study in Scarlet* (1914). Within months the outbreak of WWI meant a shift in output. Fictitious newsreels called *The Great European War Day-By-Day* and *Incidents of the Great European War* were based on the daily headlines and proved a roaring success. The studio was enlarged in 1916 and turned out quality two-reel adaptations of classic books. In 1922 the studio was bought out by *British Super Films*, partly owned by Samuelson. The films produced in this period include: *Stable Companions* (1922), *The Game of Life* (1922), *The Faithful Heart* (1922), *Brown Sugar* (1922) and *A Royal Divorce* (1923). The making of *She* (1925) caused financial problems, especially after a law suit involving the star Betty Blythe, and the studios were sold to *British Screen Productions* in 1928. By 1936 they were owned by

Douglas Fairbanks Jnr's *Criterion Film Productions*. Alexander Korda produced *The Ghost Goes West* (1935) and *The Man Who Could Work Miracles* (1936). *Criterion* produced *Accused* (1936), *Crime Over London* (1936) and *Jump for Glory* (1937). The studios were commandeered and closed during WWII and purchased by *British Lion Film Corporation* in 1944. Among films made in the post-war period were: *The Shop at Sly Corner* (1946), *White Cradle Inn* (1947), *The Last Days of Dolwyn* (1949), *The Small Back Room* (1949) and *The Happiest Days of Your Life* (1950). The studios were sold to the *National Coal Board*'s Central Research Establishment in 1952 when *British Lion* found itself unable to repay its loans from the *National Film Finance Corporation*.

Islington Studios (1919-49) Built at Poole Street, Islington, London, in 1919 and sold to Michael Balcon and his *Gainsborough Pictures* in 1924. The first film produced was *The Passionate Adventure* (1924). Other early films released before *Gainsborough* merged with *Gaumont-British* were *The Rat* (1925) and *The Constant Nymph* (1928). The studios served as a production facility for *Gaumont-British* during which time *The Ghost Train* (1931), *Tudor Rose* (1936) and *The Man Who Changed His Mind* (1936) were made at Islington. Balcon left in 1936 and *Gaumont-British* was bought by *J Arthur Rank Organisation* in 1937. The Will Hay vehicles *Oh, Mr Porter* (1937) and *Good Morning Boys* (1937), the Crazy Gang's *O-Kay for Sound* (1937) and Hitchcock's *The Lady Vanishes* (1938) were among the films made before the studio was virtually shut down for the duration of WWII. With the *Rank Organisation* then in difficulties the studio was closed in 1949.

Ivory, James (1928-) Born James Francis Ivory, 7 June 1928 Berkeley, California. Director. Educated at the University of Oregon and the University of Southern California but of Irish and French descent. His directorial debut was *Venice: Themes and Variations* (1957), made whilst he was still at University. After *The Sword and the Flute* (1959) he teamed up with Ismail Merchant to form *Merchant Ivory Productions* to make "English language films in India aimed at the international market". His first film for *MIP* was *The Housholder* (1963) based on a story by Ruth Prawer Jhabvala, a fellow member of the *MIP* triumvirate. He followed this by directing more than 25 films for *MIP* including: *Shakespeare Wallah* (1965), *Savages* (1972), *Autobiography of a Princess* (1975), *Roseland* (1977), *The Europeans* (1979), *Heat and Dust* (1983), *Maurice* (1987), *Jefferson in Paris* (1995), *Surviving Picasso* (1996), *The White Countess* (2005) and *The City of Your Final Destination* (2008). He directed the beautifully photographed, elegant and well observed *A Room with a View* (1985), *Howards End* (1992) and *The Remains of the Day* (1993), for all three of which he received nominations for an Academy Award for Best Director.

Izzard, Eddie (1962-) Born Edward John Izzard, 7 February 1962, Aden, Yemen. Comedian and actor. Father worked for BP which meant he was brought up in Aden, Bangor, Northern Ireland, Skewn near Swansea, Wales and Bexhill, East Sussex. He attended Sheffield University to gain an accountancy degree but ended up forming a double act with close friend Rob Ballard as street comics. After their split he became a stand-up comedian and constantly toured. Eddie received a Perrier Award nomination at the 1991 Edinburgh Festival. He made his West End debut in 1993 and then won the Top Stand-Up Comedian British Comedy Award. Eddie's act consists of a stream of consciousness description of sometimes mundane events but often taking a new spin on the great events in history. He speaks French and German and liberally uses this to comic effect. Acting stage debut: *The Cryptogram* (1994). Made his acting screen debut as Rich in the TV film *Open Fire* (1994). He next appeared, as Socrates, in another TV film *Aristophanes: The Gods Are Laughing* (1995) before making his feature debut in *The Secret Agent* (1996). Eddie received a second British Comedy Award for his one-man show *Definite Article* (1996) and followed this up with the *Glorious* (1997) tour and *Dress to Kill* (1999), supporting his friend Robin Williams. This won him two Emmy awards. Other films include: *Velvet Goldmine* (1998), *The Avengers* (1998), *Mystery Men*

(1999), *The Criminal* (1999), *Circus* (2000), *Shadow of the Vampire* (2000), *The Cat's Meow* (2001 – as Charlie Chaplin), *Revengers Tragedy* (2002), *Five Children and It* (2004 – as voice of It), *Oceans Twelve* (2004 - as Roman Nagel), *The Aristocrats* (2005 - as Himself), *The Wild* (2006), *My Super Ex-Girlfriend* (2006 - as Professor Bedlam), *Ocean's Thirteen* (2007), *Across the Universe* (2007 - as Mr. Kite), *The Chronicles of Narnia: Prince Caspian* (2008 - as voice of Reepicheep), *Igor* (2008 - as voice of Dr Schadenfreude), *Valkyrie* (2008 - as Erich Fellgiebel), *Rage* (2009 - as Tiny Diamonds), *Every Day* (2010 - as Garrett), *Cars 2* (2011 – voice of Miles Axelrod), *Lost Christmas* (2011 - as Anthony) and the upcoming *Snow White & the Huntsman* (2012 - as Tiberius). Eddie also portrayed comedian Lenny Bruce in the 1999 production of Julian Barry's 1971 play Lenny. His other one-man shows include: *Unrepeatable* (1994), the extremely irreverent *Circle* (2000), *Sexie* (2003) and *Stripped* (2008). In 2009, Eddie completed 43 marathons in 51 days for Sport Relief. His career has not been without controversy. In 1999, after complaints that his act recycled jokes appearing on his DVDs, the BBC's consumer programme *Watchdog* investigated his live act and he was issued a warning by the Department of Trade and Industry despite explaining that like most comedy performers, he used some of his most successful routines in each show. Eddie is 5ft 7ins in his stockinged feet but invariably dresses in womens' clothing both on and off stage, and depending on his choice of boots he can literally feel 6ft tall at times! Although it is often assumed that he is homosexual because of the camp nature of his routine and appearance, Eddie describes himself as a "straight transvestite or a male lesbian". He has also described himself as "a lesbian trapped in a man's body". See also entries in the radio and television section for *The Day of the Triffids*, and *Just A Minute*.

Jackson, Glenda (1936-) Glenda May Jackson, 9 May 1936, Birkenhead, Cheshire. Actress and politician. The daughter of a bricklayer. It is appropriate that she turned to acting as she is named after American actress Glenda Farrell. Although she came from a working class background and once worked for Boots the Chemist, she attended RADA. Although Glenda first worked as an extra on the film *The Extra Day* (1956) she made her screen debut proper with a small appearance in *This Sporting Life* (1963). She first attracted attention as a stage actress, notably as Charlotte Corday in the London and New York productions of Peter Brook's *Marat/Sade*, a role that she reprised in the 1967 film version. Other films include: *Tell Me Lies* (1968), *Negatives* (1968), *The Music Lovers* (1970), *The Boy Friend* (1971), *Mary, Queen of Scots* (1971 - as Queen Elizabeth), *The Triple Echo* (1972), *Bequest to the Nation* (1973), *The Tempter* (1974), *The Maids* (1975), *The Romantic Englishwoman* (1975), *Hedda* (1976 - as Hedda Gabler), *The Incredible Sarah* (1976 - as Sarah Bernhardt), *Nasty Habits* (1977), *House Calls* (1978), *Stevie* (1978 - as Stevie Smith), *The Class of Miss MacMichael* (1979), *Lost and Found* (1979), *HealtH* (1980), *Hopscotch* (1980), *Giro City* (1982), *The Return of the Soldier* (1983), *Turtle Diary* (1985), *Beyond Therapy* (1987), *Salome's Last Dance* (1988), *Doombeach* (1988), *The Rainbow* (1989 - as Anna Brangwen), *Business as Usual* (1989) and her last feature film, *King of the Wind* (1990 - as Queen Caroline). Glenda also played the title roles in the TV films, *The Patricia Neal Story* (1981) and *A Wave of Passion: The Life of Alexandra Kollontai* (1994), which was a voice-only narrative. Glenda won two Best Actress Academy Awards, for her roles in Ken Russell's adaptation of D H Lawrence's *Women in Love* (1969) and Melvin Frank's *A Touch of Class* (1973). She was also nominated twice more, for *Sunday Bloody Sunday* (1971) and for *Hedda* (1975). Apart from the film awards and nominations she was four times nominated for a Tony Award, but never won. She is also well remembered by many for her starring role in the television series *Elizabeth R* (1971), for which she shaved her head for her art. Awarded the CBE in 1978. In 1990 she announced that she was to give up acting and in 1992 she became MP for Hampstead and Highgate. After constituency changes for the 2010 general election, Glenda became MP for Hampstead and Kilburn, her majority of 42 votes was one of the closest results of the entire election, but still no mean feat given the anti-Labour trends throughout Britain. She is the first British Member of Parliament ever to have won an Academy Award. Glenda was married to Roy Hodges from 1958 until their divorce in 1976. They had a son, Dan (b. 1969), who is a Labour advisor and commentator.

Jackson, Gordon (1923-90) Born Gordon Cameron Jackson, 19 December 1923, Glasgow. Actor. His first acting parts were taken whilst he was working full-time for Rolls-Royce as a draughtsman. Screen debut: *The Foreman went to France* (1942). Stage debut: *George and Margaret* (1943). Before achieving fame in the TV series *Upstairs, Downstairs* (as Mr Hudson) and *The Professionals* (as Cowley) he was an established screen actor in such films as *Millions Like Us* (1943), *Whiskey Galore* (1948), *Bitter Springs* (1950), *The Lady with the Lamp* (1951), *Death Goes to School* (1953), *Meet Mr. Lucifer* (1953), *Windfall* (1955), *The Quatermass Xperiment* (1955), *Sailor Beware!* (1956), *Rockets Galore!* (1957), *Hell Drivers* (1957), *Three Crooked Men* (1958), *The Navy Lark* (1959), *The Bridal Path* (1959), *Tunes of Glory* (1960), *Greyfriars Bobby: The True Story of a Dog* (1961), *Mutiny on the Bounty* (1962), *The Great Escape* (1963) *The Long Ships* (1964), *Those Magnificent Men in Their Flying Machines* (1965), *The Ipcress File* (1965), *Cast a Giant Shadow* (1966), *The Fighting Prince of Donegal* (1966), *The Night of the Generals* (1967), *Hamlet* (1969), *Scrooge* (1970), *Kidnapped* (1971), *Madame Sin* (1972), *Russian Roulette* (1975), *Golden Rendezvous* (1977), *The Medusa Touch* (1978), *The Shooting Party* (1985), *Shaka Zulu* (1986) and his last feature, *The Whistle Blower* (1987). Appointed an OBE in 1979. Gordon starred opposite Scottish actress Rona Anderson (b. August 1928) in *Floodtide* (1949) and was married to her from 1951 until his death, from bone cancer, 15 January 1990, Chelsea, London. They had two sons, Graham and Roddy. He starred with his wife in several productions, notably the film *The Prime of Miss Jean Brodie* (1969). See also entries in the television section for *The Professionals, Stars On Sunday,* and *Upstairs Downstairs.*

Jacobi, Derek (1938-) Born Derek George Jacobi, 22 October 1938, Leytonstone, London. Actor. Studied at Cambridge and trained at the Birmingham Repertory Company before joining the National Theatre as one of the eight founding members. Screen debut: *Othello* (1965). Other films include: *The Day of the Jackal* (1973), *The Odessa File* (1974), *The Medusa Touch* (1978), *Enigma* (1983), *Little Dorrit* (1988), *Henry V* (1989), *Dead Again* (1991), *Hamlet* (1996), *Gladiator* (2000), *Gosford Park* (2001), *Revengers Tragedy* (2002), *Bye Bye Blackbird* (2005), *Nanny McPhee* (2005 - as Mr Wheen), *Underworld: Evolution* (2006), *Arritmia* (2007), *The Riddle* (2007), *The Golden Compass* (2007), *Adam Resurrected* (2008), *Morris: A Life with Bells On* (2009), *Endgame* (2009), *The King's Speech* (2010 - as Archbishop Cosmo Lang), a cameo playing himself in the Clint Eastwood film *Hereafter* (2010), *Anonymous* (2011) and *My Week with Marilyn* (2011 - as Sir Owen Morshead). Derek is currently appearing as Cardinal Orsini in the American Showtime mini-series, *The Borgias.* On television he came to prominence with his portrayal of the Emperor Claudius in the award winning *I, Claudius* (1976). In the 1990s he starred as the sleuthing monk in *Cadfael* (1994-98). Derek is also one of Britain's most accomplished stage performers who is notable for the diversity of his roles. Appointed CBE in 1985 and knighted in 1994. Derek in fact has the distinction of holding two knighthoods as he was awarded the Order of the Dannebrog (knighthood) by Denmark in 1989. In March 2006, Derek registered his civil partnership with Richard Clifford, four months after civil partnerships were introduced in the UK. They live in north London. See also entries in the television section for *Cadfael, Dr Who, I Claudius, In The Night Garden, The Long Firm, The Pallisers,* and *The Rivals of Sherlock Holmes.*

Jacques, Hattie (1922-80) Born Josephina Edwina Jacques, 7 February 1922, Sandgate, Kent. Actress. Hattie's first film was Sidney Giliat's *Green For Danger* (1940). She then served as a nurse in the Voluntary Aid Detachment during the Second World War, and was employed as a welder in a factory in North London. After the war she appeared in *Oliver Twist* (1948), *Trottie True* (1949), *Waterfront* (1950), *Chance of a Lifetime* (1950), *Scrooge* (1951 - as Mrs Fezziwig), *As Long as They're Happy* (1955) and *The Square Peg* (1958). From 1958 to 1974 she appeared in 14

Carry On films: *Carry On Sergeant* (1958 - Captain Clark), *Carry on Nurse* (1959 - Matron), *Carry On Teacher* (1959 - Grace Short), *Carry On Constable* (1960 - Sergeant Laura Moon), *Carry On Regardless* (1961 - Sister), *Carry On Cabby* (1963 - Peggy), *Carry On Doctor* (1967 - Matron), *Carry On Camping* (1969 - Miss Haggerd), *Carry On Again Doctor* (1969 - Matron), *Carry On Loving* (1970 - Sophie Bliss), *Carry On at Your Convenience* (1971 - Beatrice Plummer), *Carry On Matron* (1971 - Matron), *Carry On Abroad* (1972 - Floella) and *Carry On Dick* (1974 - Martha Hoggett). Hattie usually was the butt of the jokes as the straight-laced authority figure or the battle-axe matron. During this time she received the nickname Mother Superior from the rest of the usual cast. She was married to actor John Le Mesurier in 1949 and they had two sons, Robin (b. 1953) and Kim (b. 1956). When they divorced in 1965, the media were given the impression that the fault was on Le Mesurier's side. It was later revealed that Jacques had been having an affair with John Schofield, a younger man (died 2003, Torbay). The 2007 book *Hattie: the Authorised Biography* claims that Schofield, a cockney used-car dealer, moved into the master bedroom while Le Mesurier retreated to the attic. Schofield eventually ran off with an Italian heiress and Hattie, who had had a weight problem since her teens began eating comfort food and her weight ballooned to almost 127 kg (20st). Le Mesurier went along with the charade of the marriage breakdown being his fault so as not to damage Hattie's career. Other films include: *The Navy Lark* (1959), *Follow a Star* (1959), *Make Mine Mink* (1960), *School for Scoundrels* (1960), *In the Doghouse* (1961), *The Punch and Judy Man* (1963), *Rhubarb* (1969), *Crooks and Coronets* (1969), *Monte Carlo or Bust* (1969), *The Magic Christian* (1969), *Three for All* (1975) and her last film, released in the year she died, was one of Eric Sykes's comedy shorts *Rhubarb Rhubarb*. On television she is best known as Eric Sykes's sister Hattie. She died, from a heart attack, 6 October 1980, Kensington. See also entries in the radio and television section for *Educating Archie, Hancock's Half Hour, Happy Holidays, ITMA, Our House, Sykes, Sykes and A..and The World of Beachcomber.*

James, Sid (1913-76) Born Solomon Joel Cohen, 8 May 1913, Hillbrow, Johannesburg, South Africa. Actor. Son of stand-up comedian Laurie Cohen (billed as Lou James). He initially worked in his mother's hairdressing salon before setting up a dance school. On marrying Berthe Sadie 'Toots' Delmont in 1936 his new father-in-law handed him the 'keys' to become boss of a new hairdressing salon. Within a year he had joined the Johannesburg Repertory Players which led to radio work with the South African Broadcasting Corporation. He divorced Toots in 1940 and, after a serious breakdown in relations with his ex-father-in-law decided to join the army, eventually reaching the rank of lieutenant in the South African Tank Corps before being recruited for the Entertainment Unit in 1941. He married Meg Sergei née Williams (born 1913) in 1943 and at the end of 1946 followed his friend Larry Skikne (aka Laurence Harvey) to England. Almost immediately made his screen debut as a gangster in *Black Memory* (1947- credited as Sydney James). Other early films include: *Nightbeat* (1947 – now credited as Sidney James), *Once a Jolly Swagman* (1948), *No Orchids for Miss Blandish* (1948), *It Always Rains on Sunday* (1948), *The Small Back Room* (1949), *The Magic Box* (1951), *Lady Godiva Rides Again* (1951), and *The Lavender Hill Mob* (1951). This last film led to Galton and Simpson casting him in *Hancock's Half Hour* on radio. The popularity of this and the subsequent television series brought Sid to a wider audience. He divorced his second wife in 1952 and immediately married actress Valerie Assan (who worked under the name Valerie Ashton). Sid continued to make films in the 1950s, in fact over 50, including: *Miss Robin Hood* (1952), *The Yellow Balloon* (1953 - as Sydney James), *The Titfield Thunderbolt* (1953), *The Square Ring* (1953), *Orders are Orders* (1954), *Father Brown* (1954), *The Belles of St Trinian's* (1954), *A Kid for Two Farthings* (1955), *Trapeze* (1956), *The Iron Petticoat* (1956), *Interpol* (1957), *The Smallest Show on Earth* (1957), *Quatermass 2* (1957 - as Sydney James), *Hell Drivers* (1957), *Campbell's Kingdom* (1957), *The Silent Enemy* (1958), *I Was Monty's Double* (1958), *The Sheriff of Fractured Jaw* (1958), *Tommy the Toreador* (1959), *Idol on Parade* (1959), *Upstairs and Downstairs* (1959), *Too Many Crooks* (1959) and *The 39 Steps*

(1959). In 1960 he made his first *Carry On* film, *Carry On Constable* as Sgt Frank Wilkins, and went on to star in: *Carry on Regardless* (1961 - as Bert Handy), *Carry on Cruising* (1962 - as Capt Wellington Crowther), *Carry on Cabby* (1963 - as Charlie Hawkins), *Carry on Cleo* (1964 - as Mark Antony), *Carry on Cowboy* (1966 - as Johnny Finger, the Rumpo Kid), *Don't Lose Your Head* (1966 - as Sir Rodney Ffing / The Black Fingernail), *Carry on Doctor* (1967 - as Charlie Roper), *Carry On... Up the Khyber* (1968 - as Sir Sidney Ruff-Diamond), *Carry on Camping* (1969 - as Sid Boggle), *Carry on Again Doctor* (1969 - as Gladstone Screwer), *Carry on Up the Jungle* (1970 - as Bill Boosey), *Carry on Loving* (1970 - as Sidney Bliss), *Carry on Henry* (1971 - as King Henry VIII), *Carry on at Your Convenience* (1971 - as Sid Plummer), *Carry on Matron* (1972 - as Sid Carter), *Carry on Abroad* (1972 - as Vic Flange), *Carry on Girls* (1973 - as Sidney Fiddler) and, his last film *Carry on Dick* (1974 - as Big Dick Turpin / Reverend Flasher) – a total of 19, in seventeen of which he took top-billing. It was in these films that Sid cemented his place in British popular culture. Sid should have appeared in 20 *Carry Ons* but, in 1967, he was about to begin filming his role of Sergeant Nocker in *Follow That Camel*, but suffered a massive heart attack and was replaced by the American comic actor Phil Silvers. During his Carry On era Sid continued to work in other film projects, notably, *A Weekend with Lulu* (1961), *The Green Helmet* (1961), *Watch Your Stern* (1961), *Raising the Wind* (1961), *What a Carve Up!* (1961), *What a Whopper* (1961), *Tokoloshe* (1965) and *Bless This House* (1972). After several more heart scares Sid collapsed during a performance of *The Mating Season*, 26 April 1976, at the Sunderland Empire and died within an hour. Sid's ashes were scattered at Golders Green Crematorium. His ghost reportedly haunts his last dressing room. Sid was known for his filthy laugh, his gambling, and his womanising (including a much-publicised affair with *Carry On* co-star Barbara Windsor) and yet he was one of the best-loved screen actors of all time. He was probably even better known for his television work. See entries in the radio and television section for *Bless this House*, *Carry On Laughing*, *Citizen James*, *Educating Archie*, *George and the Dragon*, *Hancock's Half Hour*, *Taxi*, and *Two In Clover*.

Jarman, Derek (1942-94) Born Michael Derek Elworthy Jarman, 31 January 1942, Northwood, Middlesex (now Greater London). Director, writer, editor and cinematographer. Father was in the RAF. Derek was educated at King's College, London and the Slade School of Art. He worked as a set designer on *The Devils* (1971) and *Savage Messiah* (1972) before he began making films using a super-8 camera, a system he continued with throughout his career. His directorial feature debut was the controversial *Sebastiane* (1976), based on the martyrdom of the saint, with dialogue in Latin. He followed this with *Jubilee* (1977) which featured a time-travelling Elizabeth I surveying a decayed future London populated with punks. In 1979 he made an adaptation of *The Tempest* and over the next few years made a series of short films and a feature based around Shakespeares' sonnets, *Angelic Conversation* (1985). With funding help from the BFI he released *Carravagio* (1986), a film based on the life of the artist which featured Jarman's usual mixture of brilliant visuals, anachronisms and homosexual love. Diagnosed HIV Positive in 1986. He wrote and directed *The Last of England* (1987) and directed *War Requiem* (1989), based on the music of Benjamin Britten and the poetry of Wilfred Owen. His other major films in the final years of his life were an excellent interpretation of Marlowe's *Edward II* (1991) and a biography of *Wittgenstein* (1993). The last film released before his death was *Blue* (1993), which projected an unchanging blue screen for over an hour with Jarman talking with John Quentin, Nigel Terry and Tilda Swinton. *Glitterbug* (1994) was issued posthumously. Towards the end of his life he lived at Prospect Cottage, Dungeness and created an extraordinary beach garden. He also wrote: *Chroma* (1994) and *Derek Jarman's Garden* (1995), plus several autobiographical memoirs: *Dancing Ledge* (1984), *Modern Nature* (1991), *At Your Own Risk* (1992), *Smiling in Slow Motion* (2000). He died 19 February 1994, St Bartholomew's Hospital, London.

Jean-Baptiste, Marianne (1967-) Born Marianne Raigipcien Jean-Baptiste, 26 April 1967, London. Actress. Trained at RADA. Marianne is of Antiguan and St. Lucian heritage. She joined the *Cheek by Jowl Theatre Company* and had a sound stage career before becoming the proverbial overnight sensation in her first feature film, Mike Leigh's social drama *Secrets & Lies* (1996), for which she became the first black British actress to be nominated for an Academy Award (for Best Supporting Actress) for her role as Hortense Cumberbatch. She also received a Golden Globe nomination for the same film. Her other films include: the TV film, *London Kills Me* (1991), *Mr. Jealousy* (1997), *How to Make the Cruelest Month* (1998), *Nowhere to Go* (1998), *A Murder of Crows* (1999), *The 24 Hour Woman* (1999), *28 Days* (2000), *New Year's Day* (2000), *The Cell* (2000), *Women in Film* (2000), *Spy Game* (2001), *Don't Explain* (2002), *Welcome to California* (2005), *Jam* (2006), *Takers* (2010) and *Breaking Waves* (2010). Marianne is also a gifted musician who has composed a musical score, *Career Girls* (1997), and recorded an album of blues songs. She recently starred in the US TV series *Without a Trace* as FBI agent Vivian Johnson. On British television she appeared in an episode of the popular detective series *Cracker* in 1994 as Marcia Reid. She has been married to British ballet dancer Evan Williams since 1997, and they have two daughters.

Jeffrey, Peter (1929-99) Born 18 April 1929, Bristol. Actor. Educated at Harrow and Pembroke College, Cambridge and was a member of the Cambridge Footlights. His debut film was an uncredited part in the film short *Sports Day* (1944), famous for also being the debut of Jean Simmons. After 20 years of treading the boards, Peter made his feature debut as a local baron in no less a film than *Becket* (1964). Other films include: *If...* (1968), *Ring of Bright Water* (1969), *Anne of the Thousand Days* (1970), *O Lucky Man* (1973), *The Odessa File* (1974), *The Return of the Pink Panther* (1975), *Midnight Express* (1978), *Britannia Hospital* (1982), his last feature film *The Adventures of Baron Munchausen* (1988) and the TV film *A Village Affair* (1994). Peter is probably best remembered as Inspector Trout in *The Abominable Dr. Phibes* (1971) and *Dr. Phibes Rises Again* (1972). An excellent, classically trained actor with an instantly recognisable face he featured in episodes of many much-loved drama series including *No Hiding Place*, *The Saint*, *Public Eye*, *Cluff*, *Adam Adamant Lives!*, *Dixon of Dock Green*, *Softly, Softly: Task Force*, *The Avengers*, *The Troubleshooters*, *The Onedin Line*, *Special Branch*, *The Protectors*, *The Sweeney*, *Porridge*, *Some Mothers Do 'Ave 'Em*, *The New Avengers*, *Rumpole of the Bailey*, *Crown Court*, *Rising Damp*, *Doctor Who*, *Minder*, *Nanny*, *Tales of the Unexpected*, *Juliet Bravo*, *Yes Minister*, *Bergerac*, *Lovejoy*, *Heartbeat*, *Kavanagh QC*, *Where the Heart Is*, and his last screen appearance as Marquis de Rochambeau in *The Scarlet Pimpernel* (1999). He died, of prostate cancer, 25 December 1999 Stratford-upon-Avon, Warwickshire. See also entries in the television section for *Bognor*, *By the Sword Divided*, *Elizabeth R*, *Knight School*, *Lipstick on your Collar*, *Middlemarch*, *One By One*, *Our Friends in the North*, *The Plane Makers*, *The Prince and the Pauper*, and *The Spread of the Eagle*.

Jeffries, Lionel (1926-2010) Born Lionel Charles Jeffries, 10 June 1926, Lewisham, London. Actor and director. Trained at RADA. Lionel's screen debut was rather aptly as an uncredited bald RADA student in the Hitchcock thriller *Stage Fright* (1950). His first credited role was as Mr Frobisher in *Will Any Gentleman?* (1953). Other films include: *The Colditz Story* (1955), *The Quatermass Experiment* (1955), *Bhowani Junction* (1956), *Lust For Life* (1956), *Barnacle Bill* (1957), *Doctor at Large* (1957), *Blue Murder at St. Trinian's* (1957), *Up the Creek* (1958), *The Revenge of Frankenstein* (1958), *Idol on Parade* (1959), *The Nun's Story* (1959),*The Trial of Oscar Wilde* (1960), *Two Way Stretch* (1960 – as Chief P.O. Sidney Crout), *Tarzan the Magnificent* (1960), *The Long Ships* (1963), *The Wrong Arm of the Law* (1963 – as Inspector Fred 'Nosey' Parker), *Call Me Bwana* (1963), *First Men in the Moon* (1964), *Drop Dead Darling* (1966), *The Spy with a Cold Nose* (1966), *Oh Dad, Poor Dad, Mama's Hung You in the Closet and I'm Feeling So Sad* (1967), *Rocket to the Moon* (1967), *Camelot* (1967 – as King Pellinore),

Chitty Chitty Bang Bang (1968 - playing Dick van Dyke's father even though he was 6 months his junior), *Twinky* (1970), *Eyewitness* (1970), *Whoever Slew Auntie Roo?* (1972), *Royal Flash* (1975), *The Prisoner of Zenda* (1979), *Better Late Than Never* (1983) and his last feature film, *A Chorus of Disapproval* (1989). Also wrote and directed the much-loved *The Railway Children* (1970), *The Amazing Mr Blunden* (1972) and *Wombling Free* (1977). A superb character actor with a special talent for playing eccentrics, bumbling bureaucrats and absent-minded professors. Lionel was married to Eileen Mary Walsh from 1951 until his death on 19 February 2010, in a nursing home in Poole, Dorset. On television Lionel gained early exposure, along with a fine crop of other British actors, in the American series *Assignment Foreign Legion* (1956-57) and starred in many one-off episodes of classic series as well as having longer stints in - See entries in the television section for *Rich Tea and Sympathy, Room at the Bottom, Shillingbury Tales, Tom, Dick and Harriet,* and *Woof!*

Jenkins, Megs (1917-98) Born Muguette Mary Jenkins, 21 April 1917, Birkenhead, Cheshire. Actress. Trained as a ballet dancer. Made her stage debut, aged 16, and her film debut in *The Silent Battle* (1939). A stalwart of British film and television often playing landladies, barmaids or nurses. Other films include *Millions Like Us* (1943), *Green for Danger* (1946), *The History of Mr Polly* (1949), *A Boy, a Girl and a Bike* (1949), *Ivanhoe* (1952), *The Cruel Sea* (1953), *Trouble in Store* (1953), *The Man in the Sky* (1957), *The Story of Esther Costello* (1957), *Indiscreet* (1958), *Tiger Bay* (1959), *Life for Ruth* (1962), *The Wild and the Willing* (1962), *Murder Most Foul* (1964), *Bunny Lake is Missing* (1965), *Stranger in the House* (1967), *Oliver!* (1968), *The Smashing Bird I Used to Know* (1970), *Asylum* (1972), and her last feature film, *The Amorous Milkman* (1975). On American television she featured in the TV film *David Copperfield* (1969) as Clara Peggotty in an all-star British cast including Laurence Olivier as Mr Creakle, Richard Attenborough as Mr Tungay, Michael Redgrave as Dan Peggotty, Ralph Richardson as Mr Micawber, and the little-known Robin Phillips as David Copperfield. She died 5 October 1998, Ipswich, Suffolk. See also entries in the television section for *Jane Eyre, Nathaniel Titlark, The Newcomers, Oh No It's Selwyn Froggitt, Weaver's Green, A Woman of Substance, Worzel Gummidge,* and *Young At Heart.*

Jensen, Ashley (1969-) Born Ashley Samantha Jensen, 11 August 1969, Annan, Dumfries and Galloway. Actress. Ashley trained at Queen Margaret University, Edinburgh and was a member of the National Youth Theatre. After making her screen debut in an episode of the television sitcom, *City Lights*, Ashley made her film debut in *Tickets for the Zoo* (1991). Her other films include: *Topsy-Turvy* (1999 - as Miss Tringham), *A Cock and Bull Story* (2005 - as Lindsey), *Nativity!* (2009 - as Jennifer Lore), *How to Train Your Dragon* (2010 - voice of Phlegma the Fierce), *Gnomeo & Juliet* (2011 - voice of Nanette), *Arthur Christmas* (2011 - voice of Bryony) and *Hysteria* (2011). In 1996 she played Clare Donnelly, the daughter of Glasgow criminal Jo-Jo Donnelly (played by Billy Connolly) in *Down Among the Big Boys*, one of the BBC's *Screen One* TV films. Ashley rose to fame playing Maggie Jacobs in *Extras* in 2005 and the following year gained the role of Christina McKinney on the ABC series *Ugly Betty*. In September 2009, until its cancellation in May 2010, she co-starred alongside Jenna Elfman in the American sitcom *Accidentally on Purpose* as Olivia. Ashley married English actor Terence Beesley in a ceremony in the woods of Big Sur, California on 29 January 2007. They have a son together, Francis Jonathan Beesley (b. 20 October 2009). See also entries in the television section for *Bad Boys, City Central, City Lights, Clocking Off, Eastenders, Eleventh Hour, Extras, May to December, Roughnecks* and *Two Thousand Acres of Sky*

Joffé, Roland (1945-) Born 17 November 1945, London. Director and producer. A founder of the Young Vic. He cut his screen directorial teeth with *Coronation Street* and continued in television until making a brilliant big screen debut with *The Killing Fields* (1984), for which he was nominated for an Academy Award for Best Director. He repeated the trick with his next feature *The Mission* (1986), gaining a further Best Director nomination. His subsequent films include: *Fat Man and Little Boy* (1989), *City of Joy* (1992), *Super Mario Bros.* (uncredited, 1993),

The Scarlet Letter (1995), *Goodbye Lover* (1999), *Vatel* (2000), *Captivity* (2007), *You and I* (2010), *There Be Dragons* (2010) and the soon to be released *Singularity* (2012). Roland was married to actress Jane Lapotaire from 1971 to 1980; they had one son, the screenwriter and director Rowan Joffé (b. 1972). He was then in a relationship with actress Cherie Lunghi, with whom he had a daughter, actress Nathalie Lunghi (born Natalie Kathlene Lunghi-Joffé, 26 August 1986).

John, Rosamund (1913-98) Born Nora Rosamund Jones, 19 October 1913, Edmonton, London. Actress. She made her first film *Secret of the Loch* in 1934, after this it was another eight years until she ventured on to the screen again. Most of her films were made during WWII and the early post-war years. She made her last film *Operation Murder* in 1957. By now she was married to Labour MP, John Silkin (later to be Secretary of State for Agriculture in the Labour government of the 1970s) and acting was not at the top of her agenda. Her first marriage to film editor Russell Lloyd in 1943 ended in divorce six years later and her second to Silkin, in 1950 on his death in 1987. Her other films include: *The First of the Few* (1942), *The Gentle Sex* (1943), *The Lamp Still Burns* (1943), *Tawny Pipit* (1944), *The Way to the Stars* (1945), *Green for Danger* (1946), *The Upturned Glass* (1947), *Fame is the Spur* (1947), *When the Bough Breaks* (1947), *No Place for Jennifer* (1949), *She Shall Have Murder* (1950), *Never Look Back* (1952) and *Street Corner* (1953). She died 27 October 1998, Lambeth, London.

Johns, Glynis (1923-) Born 5 October 1923, Pretoria, South Africa. Welsh Actress. Daughter of Alys Maude (née Steele-Payne), a concert pianist, and Welsh actor Mervyn Johns, with whom she appeared in the film *Halfway House* (1944). Glynis was born whilst her parents were on tour. She trained as a dancer and got her stage break in 1935, performing in the West End the following year, aged 13. She made her screen debut in *South Riding* (1938). Glynis gained great popularity after playing the mermaid Miranda Trewella in *Miranda* (1948), a role she repeated in *Mad About Men* (1954). With her spirited performances and instantly recognisable husky-voice she was cast in a variety of roles including comedies such as *Josephine and Men* (1955) and *The Court Jester* (1956), costume films such as *The Sword and the Rose* (1953) and *Rob Roy, the Highland Rogue* (1953) and dramas like *The Weak and the Wicked* (1954). She was nominated for an Academy Award for Best Supporting Actress for *The Sundowners* (1960). She also had her own US TV show *Glynis* (1963) and played Lady Penelope Peasouper in the 1960s TV version of *Batman*. Although an accomplished stage actress (in 1973, she won a Tony Award for Best Actress in a Musical for her role in *A Little Night Music*), she is probably best-known for her role as Mrs. Winifred Banks, the mother of Jane and Michael (Karen Dotrice and Matthew Garber) in Robert Stevenson's film version of *Mary Poppins* (1964). With her Welsh ancestry she also enjoyed appearing in the film of *Under Milk Wood* (1972) with Richard Burton. Because of her unusual looks she was billed as "The Girl with the Upside-Down Eyes" early in her career. Her other films include: *On the Night of the Fire* (1939), *The Thief of Bagdad* (1940), *49th Parallel* (1941), *The Adventures of Tartu* (1943), *Perfect Strangers* (1945), *This Man Is Mine* (1946), *Frieda* (1947), *An Ideal Husband* (1947), *The Blue Lamp* (1950), *The Magic Box* (1951), *Appointment with Venus* (1951), *The Card* (1952), *Personal Affair* (1953), *The Beachcomber* (1954), *Around the World in Eighty Days* (1956), *Another Time, Another Place* (1958), *Shake Hands with the Devil* (1959), *Dear Brigitte* (1965), *Lock Up Your Daughters!* (1969), *The Vault of Horror* (1973), *The Ref* (1994), *While You Were Sleeping* (1995), and her last film to-date, *Superstar* (1999). Glynis was married four times, firstly to actor Anthony Forwood (1942-48), with whom she had her only son, Gareth, who was the long-time partner of fellow actor Dirk Bogarde. She was subsequently married to David Foster, Cecil Henderson, and Elliott Arnold.

Johnson, Aaron (1990-) Born Aaron Perry Johnson, 13 June 1990, High Wycombe, Buckinghamshire. Actor. Began acting, aged six, and appeared in episodes of *Casualty* and *The Bill*. Aaron's film debut was as identical twins in *Tom & Thomas* (2002). In *Shanghai Knights* (2003) he played a young Charlie Chaplin but his big screen breakthrough was playing John Lennon in the biopic of Lennon's early life before The Beatles, *Nowhere*

Boy (2009). This film was also the directorial debut of Sam Taylor-Wood (b. 1967, Croydon), former wife of art dealer Jay Jopling. Aaron and Sam are currently engaged and have two daughters: Wylda Rae (b. 7 July 2010) and Romy Hero (b. 18 January 2012). Other films include: *Dead Cool* (2004), *The Thief Lord* (2006), *The Illusionist* (2006 - as Young Eisenheim), *Angus, Thongs and Perfect Snogging* (2008), *The Greatest* (2009) and *Chatroom* (2010). Aaron's latest starring roles are as budding super hero Dave Lizewski in *Kick Ass* (2010) and young alcoholic Joe Mackins alongside Glenn Close in the title role of *Albert Nobbs* (2011).

Johnson, Celia (1908-82) Born Celia Elizabeth Johnson, 18 December 1908, Richmond, Surrey. Actress. Educated at St Paul's Girls School in London and trained at RADA. Stage début: *Major Barbara* (1928). By 1931, she was starring as Ophelia in a New York production of *Hamlet*. Celia made her screen debut in the TV film *A Night at the Hardcastles* (1939). She followed this up with the film short *A Letter From Home* (1941) before making her feature debut in the 1942 film *In Which We Serve*. Celia became famous and received an Academy Award nomination as Best Actress for her role as Laura Jesson in *Brief Encounter* (1945) opposite Trevor Howard. Although primarily a stage actress, Celia appeared in such noted British films as *This Happy Breed* (1944), *The Captain's Paradise* (1953), *A Kid For Two Farthings* (1955), *The Good Companions* (1957) and her last film, *The Prime of Miss Jean Brodie* (1969). She was married to Ian Fleming's elder brother Peter (from 1936 until his death in 1971), a travel writer, literary editor of *The Spectator* and Head of Strategic Deception in SEAC (South East Asia Command) during WWII. She is the mother of actress Lucy Fleming (see separate entry). She was appointed a CBE in 1958 and a Dame of the British Empire in 1981. Her final screen appearance was as Mrs Gladstone in the ITV television series, *Number 10*. She died 25 April 1982, Nettlebed, Oxfordshire.

Johnson, Katie (1878-1957) Born Bessie Kate Johnson, 18 November 1878, Pyecombe, West Sussex. Actress. A stage actress from the age of twenty, she made her first film *After Office Hours* (1932) when she was 54. A short review of Katie's filmography will list numerous characters called "old lady" or "Miss x" and indeed it was that Katie was nearly always the spinster or maiden aunt or grandmother in such films as *Gaslight* (1940), *He Snoops to Conquer* (1944), *Tawny Pipit* (1944), *Meet Me at Dawn* (1947) and *The Shop at Sly Corner* (1947). Until her seminal role in 1955 she had always been a supporting player and in *The Ladykillers* she had more reason than any to be overshadowed, given the crop of British acting talent on display. However, cast as usual as 'The Old Lady', well actually Mrs Louisa Alexandra Wilberforce, Katie almost steals the show, at times upstaging Sellers, Guinness and co. For the part of this genial but seemingly invulnerable geriatric Katie won a BAFTA Best Actress award. She only made one more film, *How to Murder a Rich Uncle* (1957) before her death on 4 May 1957, Elham, near Folkestone, Kent aged 78.

Johnson, Richard (1927-) Born 30 July 1927, Upminster, Essex. Actor. Son of a paint manufacturer. Trained at RADA. Made his screen debut in *Calling Bulldog Drummond* (1951) and followed this with *Captain Horatio Hornblower R.N.* (1951). Spent most of the 1950s in the theatre working with Peter Brook and at the Shakespeare Memorial Theatre. Returned to the big screen with *Never So Few* (1959), *80,000 Suspects* (1963), *The Haunting* (1963), *The Pumpkin Eater* (1964) and *Operation Crossbow* (1965). He met Kim Novak, to whom he was briefly married (1965-66) on the set of *The Amorous Adventures of Moll Flanders* (1965). Richard's other films include: *Khartoum* (1966), *Oedipus the King* (1967), *Lady Hamilton* (1968), *Julius Caesar* (1970), *Anthony and Cleopatra* (1972), *Aces High* (1976), *Zombie Flesh-Eaters* (1979), *The Monster Club* (1981) and *Lady Jane* (1986). During the 1990s he concentrated on television and stage work before making *Milk* (1999), *Lara Croft: Tomb Raider* (2001), *The Birthday* (2002), *Scoop* (2006), *Two Families* (2007), *Jump!* (2008) *and his last film to-date, The Boy in the Striped Pyjamas* (2008). He also played Hugh "Bulldog" Drummond in *Deadlier*

than the Male (1967) and *Some Girls Do* (1969). Founder of United British Artists with Peter Shaw (1983-87) under whose auspices he produced *Turtle Diary* (1985) and *The Lonely Passion of Judith Hearne* (1987). He has also had a long and distinguished television career, his TV film roles include: Marc Antony in *Antony and Cleopatra* (1974), the title role in *Cymbeline* (1982), The Duke of Norfolk in *A Man for All Seasons* (1988), Squire Trelawney in *Treasure Island* (1990), Dr Watson in *The Crucifer of Blood* (1991), Dilwyn 'Dilly' Knox in *Breaking the Code* (1996), Sir Alastair Montgomery in *The Whistle-Blower* (2001), Lord Mountbatten in *Whatever Love Means* (2005) and Stanley Baldwin in *Wallis & Edward* (2005). See also entries in the television section for *The Camomile Lawn, Churchill's People, Pride and Prejudice, The Robinsons,* and *Spooks.*

Jones, Freddie (1927-) Born 12 September 1927, Stoke-on-Trent, Staffordshire. Actor. Spent 10 years as a laboratory assistant whilst pursuing amateur dramatics. Trained at the Rose Bruford College of Speech and Drama. Freddie made his screen debut in *Accident* (1967) which was released in England before *Marat/Sade* (1967). Other films include: *The Bliss of Mrs Blossom* (1968), *Frankenstein Must be Destroyed* (1969), *Doctor in Trouble* (1970), *Kidnapped* (1971), *Anthony and Cleopatra* (1972), *All Creatures Great and Small* (1974), *Juggernaut* (1974), *Zulu Dawn* (1979), *Erik the Viking* (1989), *Prince of Jutland* (1994), *Seeing Things* (1997), *My Life So Far* (1999), *The Count of Monte Cristo* (2002), *Caught in the Act* (2008) and *Come on Eileen* (2010).Has made an impact on the international scene in such films as: *The Elephant Man* (1980), *Firefox* (1982), *Krull* (1983), *E la Neve Va* (1983), *Dune* (1984) and *Wild at Heart* (1990). Freddie married Jennifer Heslewood and had three sons - actor Toby Jones (see separate entry), with whom he appeared in the film, *Ladies in Lavender* (2004), Rupert Jones, a director, and Casper Jones, who works in Brighton. Freddie is a much-loved character actor, sometimes bordering on caricature, who has also made his mark on the small screen. See entries in the television section for *The Caesars, District Nurse, Emmerdale, The Ghosts of Motley Hall, In Loving Memory, Love and Mr Lewisham* and *Pennies From Heaven.*

Jones, Peter (1920-2000) Born 12 June 1920, Wem, Shropshire. Actor. Best known for his radio and television work but also had a long stage and film career, mainly in comedies. Stage debut: *The Composite Man* (1936). Screen debut: *Fanny by Gaslight* (1944). Other films include: *Chance of a Lifetime* (1950), *The Magic Box* (1951), *The Browning Version* (1951), *Albert R.N.* (1953), *Yellow Balloon* (1953), *Blue Murder at St Trinian's* (1957), *The Bulldog Breed* (1960), *School for Scoundrels* (1960), *A Stitch in Time* (1963), *The Sandwich Man* (1966), *Carry On Doctor* (1968), *The Return of the Pink Panther* (1975), *Confessions of a Pop Performer* (1975), *Carry On England* (1976), *Chariots of Fire* (1981), *In Your Eye* (1994) and his last film, *Milk* (1999). Peter was married to Jeri Sauvenet until her death in 1999. Their daughter, Selena Carey-Jones, is an actress and one of his two sons, Bill Dare, is a writer, and producer of BBC Radio's *Dead Ringers*. Peter died 10 April 2000, Westminster, London. See also entries in the radio and television section for *Beggar My Neighbour, The Hitch-Hiker's Guide to the Galaxy, I Thought You'd Gone, In All Directions, Just A Minute, Mr Big, Mr Digby Darling, Night Train to Surbiton, One-Upmanship, The Rag Trade, Treasure Island,* and *Whoops! Apocalypse.*

Jones, Toby (1966-) Born Toby Edward Heslewood Jones, 7 September 1966, Hammersmith, London. Actor. Toby attended Abingdon School in Oxfordshire in the early 1980s, at the same time as actor Tom Hollander and the members of Radiohead. He studied Drama at The University of Manchester from 1986-89 and made his screen debut in the film *Orlando* (1992). Toby had small roles in *Naked* (1993), *Les Misérables* (1998), *Cousin Bette* (1998), *EverAfter* (1998), *Simon Magus* (1999), *Joan of Arc* (1999), *The Nine Lives of Tomas Katz* (2000) and *Hotel Splendide* (2000) before voicing the role of Dobby the House Elf in *Harry Potter and the Chamber of Secrets* (2002), a role he reprised in *Harry Potter and the Deathly Hallows: Part 1* (2010). His other films include: *Finding Neverland* (2004 - as Smee), *Mrs*

Henderson Presents (2005), *Infamous* (2006 - as Truman Capote), *Amazing Grace* (2006 - as the Duke of Clarence), *The Painted Veil* (2006), *Nightwatching* (2007), *The Mist* (2007), *St. Trinian's* (2007), *City of Ember* (2008), *Frost/Nixon* (2008 - as Swifty Lazar), *W.* (2008 - as Karl Rove), *Creation* (2009 - as Thomas Huxley), *St Trinian's 2: The Legend of Fritton's Gold* (2009), *Sex & Drugs & Rock & Roll* (2010), *What's Wrong with Virginia* (2010), *The Rite* (2011), *Your Highness* (2011), *Tinker Tailor Soldier Spy* (2011 - as Percy Alleline), *My Week with Marilyn* (2011 - as Arthur Jacobs), *The Adventures of Tintin: The Secret of the Unicorn* (2011 - as pickpocket Aristides Silk) and *Captain America: The First Avenger* (2011 - as Arnim Zola). On television he appeared in *Midsomer Murders* (1999-2000), played Robert Cecil, 1st Earl of Salisbury, in the HBO/Channel 4 production *Elizabeth I* (2005), opposite Helen Mirren and more recently he appeared in a 2010 episode of *Doctor Who* as the 'Dream Lord'.

Jones, Vinnie (1965-) Born Vincent Peter Jones, 5 January 1965, Watford, Hertfordshire. Footballer and actor. As a part-time footballer with Alliance Premier League side Wealdstone (1984-86) Vinnie earned a living as a hod carrier and groundsman. After a brief spell with Swedish club IFK Holmsund (1986) he began a long spell of top tier football in the English leagues with Wimbledon (1986–89; 1992-98), Leeds United (1989–90), Sheffield United (1990–91), Chelsea (1991–92) and Queens Park Rangers (1998–99). He reached the pinnacle of his career captaining the Welsh national football team, having qualified via his Welsh maternal grandfather. He was a member of the immensely physical "Crazy Gang" that won the 1988 FA Cup Final for Wimbledon and despite his limited ability was always popular with the fans for his uncompromising behaviour on behalf of his team. He made his feature film debut in Guy Ritchie's *Lock, Stock and Two Smoking Barrels* (1998 – as Big Chris) and then starred in Guy Ritchie's next blockbuster *Snatch* (2000 - as Bullet-Tooth Tony). Other early films include: *Gone in 60 Seconds* (2000 - as The Sphinx), *Swordfish* (2001), *Mean Machine* (2001 - aka *The Longest Yard*), *Night at the Golden Eagle* (2002), *The Big Bounce* (2004), *EuroTrip* (2004 - as Mad Maynard the Manchester Utd fan*), Slipstream* (2005), *Submerged* (2005), *Johnny Was* (2006) and She's the Man (2006). His next blockbuster was X-Men 3: The Last Stand (2006 – as Cain Marko / Juggernaut). Vinnie then starred alongside Stone Cold Steve Austin in the WWE-produced *The Condemned* (2007) as Ewan McStarley an ex-SAS psychopath. Recent films include: *The Bleeding* (2009 - alongside Michael Madsen), *Year One* (2009), *Kill the Irishman* (2011 - as Keith Ritson) and *Blood Out* (2011 - as Zed). Vinnie was a housemate on the reality television show *Celebrity Big Brother 2010* and finished third. A controversial character whose exploits in his private life have caused him to be described as a thug and a bully, Vinnie has managed to sometimes use this in a positive way, for example, a recent British Heart Foundation television advert promoting Hands-only CPR to the rhythm of the famous Bee Gees single "Stayin' Alive". On other occasions Vinnie's image has tarnished his reputation among his fans. He has a string of brushes with the law, the most famous being after a 2008 bar fight at Wiley's Tavern in Sioux Falls, South Dakota, in which the pool cue-wielding Vinnie required numerous stitches to his face (see also entry for Tamer Hassan). Vinnie married Tanya Terry (b. 1966) in 1994 in Watford. She has a daughter, Kaley Jay Terry (b. 1987, Watford), by her first husband, footballer Steve Terry. Tanya had a heart transplant straight after the birth and is also a cervical cancer survivor. Vinnie also has a son, Aaron Elliston Jones (b. 1991, Sheffield) by Mylene Elliston. His son currently serves in the Life Guards.

Jordan, Neil (1950-) Born Neil Patrick Jordan, 25 February 1950, Sligo, Ireland. Director, producer and novelist. Educated at University College, Dublin. Neil worked as a script consultant on *Excalibur* (1981) before writing and directing *Angel* (1982), starring Stephen Rea as a musician who becomes a murder witness during The Troubles. Originally intended as a Channel 4 TV film, *Angel,* was eventually distributed as a feature, to high acclaim, many critics believing this film to be Neil's finest work. His next film was a re-telling of Little Red Riding Hood as *The Company of Wolves* (1984). The popularity of his film noir *Mona Lisa* (1986) led to him directing the comedies *High Spirits* (1988) and the remake, *We're No Angels* (1989) neither of which could

match his earlier success. After directing *The Miracle* (1991) he teamed up again with Stephen Rea to make *The Crying Game* (1992). This proved to be a huge international success and gained him an Academy Award for Best Screenplay and a nomination for Best Director. Neil's eclectic approach led him to return to the horror genre with the big-budget *Interview with the Vampire* (1994). His next two films were the biography *Michael Collins* (1996) and the tale of a young murderer *The Butcher Boy* (1997) which featured Sinead O'Connor as the Virgin Mary conjured in the mind of the young protaganist. Recently he has written and directed: *In Dreams* (1999), *The End of the Affair* (1999), *The Good Thief* (2002), *Breakfast on Pluto* (2005), *The Brave One* (2007) and *Ondine* (2009). He won the Guardian Fiction Prize in 1976 with a book of short stories called *Night in Tunisia*. Neil has also written several novels including: *The Past* (1979), *The Dream of a Beast* (1983), *Sunrise with Sea Monster* (1994), *Shade* (2004) and *Mistaken* (2011). His latest creation is the American Showtime mini-series, *The Borgias*. He has been married to Brenda Rawn since 2004.

Judd, Edward (1932-2009) Born 4 October 1932, Shanghai, China. Actor. Edward was born of an English father and Russian mother. They fled Shanghai in 1937 following a Japanese attack, and settled in England. Edward's screen debut was in an uncredited role in *The Guinea Pig* (1948) and other early films include: *Once a Jolly Swagman* (1949), *The Small Voice* (1949), Carry on Sergeant (1958), and I Was Monty's Double (1958). In the mid-1950s Edward starred on television in *Sixpenny Corner*, Britain's first daily soap opera, but by the 1960s he was closely associated with British science fiction films such as *First Men in the Moon* (1964), *Island of Terror* (1966), *Invasion* (1966), *The Vengeance of She* (1968), *O Lucky Man!* (1973), *The Boys in Blue* (1982) and his last feature film, *The Kitchen Toto* (1987). His last film role was in the TV film, *Jack the Ripper* (1988) and his final screen appearance was in an episode of *Van Der Valk* in 1992. He was married to actress Gene Anderson (b. Jean Anderson 28 March 1931, London; died 5 May 1965 Merton, London) who appeared with him in *The Day the Earth Caught Fire* (1961). His second wife was actress Norma Ronald (d. 1993), with whom he had two daughters. Edward's voice was used in the 1975 "Think Once, Think Twice, Think Bike" campaign on making motorists aware of the risks faced on the road by motorcyclists. He died 24 February 2009. Mitcham, Surrey. See also entries in the radio and television section for *Coronation Street, Intrigue,* and *Sixpenny Corner.*

Justice, James Robertson (1907-75) Born James Norval Harold Justice, 15 June 1907, Lewisham, London. Actor. James was a larger-than-life character in his films and in reality he lived life to the full and ultimately died penniless. Educated at Marlborough College and Bonn University. James returned from Germany in 1927 and then worked for a time as a journalist with Reuters before emigrating to Canada in 1928 and eventually becoming a lumberjack and mining unsuccessfully for gold. He came home to Britain in 1930 and played ice hockey goaltender for London Lions during 1931/32 season. Then, after being injured, refereed before serving as assistant secretary to the British Ice Hockey Association. James managed the Great Britain ice hockey team which finished 7th in the 1932 European Championships. He fought for The International Brigade against the fascists during the Spanish Civil War and it was at this time that he grew his trademark full bushy beard. During WWII he served in the Royal Navy until being invalided out. Spotted deputising for Leonard Sachs as chairman in a music hall night at the Players' Club in London, which led to his screen debut in *For Those in Peril* (1944). His first leading role was as headmaster in the film *Vice Versa* (1948), written and directed by Peter Ustinov, who cast him partly because he'd been "a collaborator of my father's at Reuters." Other films include: *Fiddlers Three* (1944), *Champagne Charlie* (1944), *Appointment with Crime* (1946), *Hungry Hill* (1947), *Scott of the Antarctic* (1948), *My Brother Johnathan* (1948), *Whisky Galore!* (1949), *Captain Horatio Hornblower R N* (1951), *The Story of Robin Hood and his Merrie Men* (1952), *Les Misérables* (1952), *Miss Robin Hood* (1952), *The Sword and the Rose* (1953), *Rob Roy, the Highland Rogue* (1954), *Above us the Waves* (1955), *Land of the Pharaohs* (1955), *An Alligator Named Daisy* (1955), *The Iron Petticoat* (1956), *Moby Dick* (1956),

Campbell's Kingdom (1957), Upstairs and Downstairs (1959), Raising the Wind (1961), Murder, She Said (1961), Very Important Person (1961), The Guns of Navarone (1961), The Fast Lady (1962), Crooks Anonymous (1962), Father Came Too! (1964), Up from the Beach (1965), The Face of Fu Manchu (1965), You Must Be Joking! (1965), Those Magnificent Men in Their Flying Machines (1965), Chitty Chitty Bang Bang (1968), Some Will, Some Won't (1970), The Massacre of Glencoe (1971) and his last film, Zeta One (1973), in which a race of topless, large-breasted women from the planet Angvia, in another dimension, come to earth to kidnap women to repopulate their planet. With his imposing physique, domineering personality and rich, booming voice, it was inevitable that James was going to be typecast as authoritarian figures and he is probably best known for playing Sir Lancelot Spratt in the series of Doctor films beginning with Doctor in the House (1954) and including Doctor at Sea (1955), Doctor at Large (1957), Doctor in Love (1960), Doctor in Distress (1963), Doctor in Clover (1966) and ending with a cameo appearance in Doctor in Trouble (1970). An accomplished linguist, he could converse in over 20 languages. One of the founders of the Wildfowl Trust along with Sir Peter Scott. He was part of a team which invented a device to catch wildfowl for marking. James was also an expert falconer and, amongst others, instructed HRH Prince Charles in the art. He was also a keen amateur motor racing driver who once had a trial at Brooklands. The son of an Aberdeen-born geologist, James was obsessively proud of his Scottish heritage. He stood unsuccessfully as a Labour Party candidate in the 1950 General Election, contesting the North Angus and Mearns constituency. In 1957 he helped launch the TV station Scottish Television, hosting the channel's first show, This is Scotland. From 1957 to 1960, and again from 1963 to 1966, he was Rector of the University of Edinburgh. A series of strokes severely restricted his performances during the late 1960s. James' first marriage, in 1941, was to nurse Dilys Hayden, with whom he had a son, James Norval. Young James was drowned, aged four, at their watermill home in Whitchurch, Hampshire, in 1949, and this put a strain on an already rocky marriage. They eventually separated and divorced in 1968. James met German actress Irene von Meyendorff on the set of The Ambassadress (1960) and she became his second wife three days before he died, on 2 July 1975, King's Somborne, Hampshire.

Justin, John (1917-2002) Born John Justinian de Ledesma, 24 November 1917, Knightsbridge, London. Actor. Spent his early years in Argentina, where his father hailed from. Performed with Plymouth and Liverpool Reps and was briefly at RADA. Made a stunning screen debut as the dashing Prince Ahmad in Alexander Korda's sumptious The Thief of Bagdad (1940). Other films include: The Gentle Sex (1943), Journey Together (1944), The Angel with the Trumpet (1950), King of the Khyber Rifles (1953), The Tekman Mystery (1954), The Man who Loved Redheads (1955), Safari (1956), Island in the Sun (1957), The Spider's Web (1960), Savage Messiah (1972), Lisztomania (1975), Valentino (1977), The Big Sleep (1978) and his last film, Trenchcoat (1983). An accomplished pilot he gained his licence, aged 12, and served as an RAF spitfire pilot instructor during WWII. In 1952 he took the role of test pilot Philip Peel for The Sound Barrier. He once dismissed his film career as "a mistake" and always concentrated on his first love, the theatre. He was married three times, to dancer Pola Nirenska (1935-49), actress Barbara Murray (1952-64), with whom he had three daughters, and theatre actress Alison McMurdo from 1970 until his death on 29 November 2002, Petersfield, Hampshire. See also entries in the television section for Churchill's People, Ladykillers, Lillie, and The Widow of Bath.

Karloff, Boris (1887-1969) Born William Henry Pratt, 23 November 1887, East Dulwich, London. Actor. Great-nephew of Anna Leonowens of Anna and the King of Siam fame. He was the youngest of nine children, and following his mother's death was raised by his elder siblings. Educated at Merchant Taylor's School and Uppingham. Son of a diplomat, he was expected to follow in his fathers' footsteps, as indeed did his brother, Sir John Thomas Pratt. Emigrated to Montreal, Canada, in 1909 against the wishes of hs family. Made his stage debut in 1910 in Kamloops, British Columbia. Screen debut: The Dumb Girl of Portici (1916). He took a variety of jobs whilst also working in the movies. Made over 170 films in total. Early films include: The Lightning Raider (1919), The Prince and Betty (1919), The Last of the Mohicans (1920), The Hope Diamond Mystery (1921), Omar, the Tentmaker (1922), The Prisoner (1923), The Golden Web (1926), Tarzan and the Golden Lion (1927 – as Owaza), opposite James Pierce as Tarzan, The Unholy Night (1929), The Mad Genius (1931), The Criminal Code (1931) and Scarface (1932), where he was memorably gunned down in a bowling alley. Bela Lugosi turned down the part of Frankenstein's monster in Frankenstein (1931) and James Whale cast Karloff in his stead, billing him as "?" in the credits. From this point on his name was forever linked with the horror movie genre, his lisp often giving a cruel ironic edge to his dialogue. Of the many horror films he made over the next 30 years, some of the most famous include: The Mask of Fu Manchu (1932 – as Fu Manchu), The Mummy (1932 – as Imhotep), The Ghoul (1934), Bride of Frankenstein (1935), The Raven (1935), Devil's Island (1939), Son of Frankenstein (1939), The Man with Nine Lives (1940), House of Frankenstein (1944), The Body Snatcher (1945), Isle of the Dead (1945), Abbott and Costello Meet Dr Jeckyll and Mr Hyde (1953 – memorable for the wrong reasons unfortunately), Voodoo Island (1957), Grip of the Strangler (1958), Frankenstein - 1970 (1958) and his last film, The Incredible Invasion (1971). His career was revived somewhat in the 1960s by director Roger Corman for whom he featured in The Raven (1963), The Terror (1963), Tre volti della paura, I (1963) and Die, Monster, Die! (1965). His final Hollywood film was Targets (1968). He was married six times, to Grace Harding, Olive de Wilton, Montana Laurena Williams, Helene Vivian Soule, Dorothy Stine, and Evelyn Hope Helmore. Known for being a well-read, cultured and thoroughly pleasant gentleman off-screen. He died 2 February 1969, Midhurst, Sussex. See also entries in the television section for Colonel March of Scotland Yard, and Out of this World.

Kendall, Kay (1926-59) Born Justine Kay Kendall-McCarthy, 21 May 1926, Withernsea, Yorkshire. Actress. Daughter of a dancing father and a singing mother. Began her career in her early teens as a chorus girl and quickly moved to the front of the stage. Made her screen debut in Fiddlers Three (1944) and, after appearing in some largely forgettable fare, the pick of the bunch being Champagne Charlie (1944), Caesar and Cleopatra (1945), London Town (1946), Lady Godiva Rides Again (1951), It Started in Paradise (1952) and Curtain Up (1952), she made a huge impact in the popular Genevieve (1953 – as Rosalind Peters). She met her future husband Rex Harrison whilst playing one of his wives in the bigamist comedy The Constant Husband (1955). Her other films include:The Square Ring (1953), Meet Mr. Lucifer (1953), Fast and Loose (1954), Doctor in the House (1954), Simon and Laura (1955), The Adventures of Quentin Durward (1955), Les Girls (1957) - for which she won a Golden Globe, The Reluctant Debutante (1958) and her last film, Once More, with Feeling! (1960) which was released after her death. A delight to watch, with a rare mixture of charm, beauty and comedic exuberance she could easily have been a sort of British Carole Lombard but for her early death. She was diagnosed with myeloid leukemia in 1957, although there is some dispute as to whether she was actually told this as she is said to have believed she was suffering from iron deficiency. Married to Rex Harrison (1957-59), who divorced his then wife Lilli Palmer by mutual agreement so that he could take care of her. Kay's sister Kim contributed to the biography The Brief, Madcap Life of Kay Kendall (2002). She died on 6 September 1959, Marylebone, London.

Kensit, Patsy (1968-) Born Patricia Jude Francis Kensit, 4 March 1968, Hounslow, London. Actress. Patsy's mother was Irish while her father James, nicknamed "Jimmy the Dip", was an associate of the Kray twins (her brother's godfather was Reggie Kray) and their rivals, the Richardsons. She attended Corona Theatre School and the Italia Conti Academy stage school. As a four-year-old child actress she appeared in a television commercial for Birds Eye frozen peas and made her big screen debut in the film spin-off from the popular TV series *For the Love of Ada* (1972), although this was uncredited. Other films she appeared in as a child include: *Gold* (1974), *Hennessy* (1975), *Alfie Darling* (1976), *The Blue Bird* (1976), *Lady Oscar* (1979), *Hanover Street* (1979) and *Quincy's Quest* (1979). Her adult break came when she was chosen to play Crepes Suzette in Absolute *Beginners* (1986), during which time she was also lead singer with the band *Eighth Wonder* (1984-88) that had UK chart hits with I'm Not Scared (7) written and produced by the Pet Shop Boys, and Cross My Heart (13). Her other films include *A Chorus of Disapproval* (1988), *Lethal Weapon 2* (1989), *Chicago Joe and the Showgirl* (1990), *Don Bosco* (1990), *Bullseye!* (1990), *Timebomb* (1991), *Twenty-One* (1991), *Blue Tornado* (1991), *Beltenebros* (1991), *Blame it on the Bellboy* (1992), *The Turn of the Screw* (1992), *Bitter Harvest* (1993), *Kleptomania* (1995), *Angels and Insects* (1995), *Tunnel Vision* (1995), *Grace of My Heart* (1996), *Speedway Junky* (1999), *Best* (2000), *Things Behind the Sun* (2001), *Bad Karma* (2002), *The One and Only* (2002), *Darkness Falling* (2003), *Shelter Island* (2003), *The Pavilion* (2004) and *Played* (2006). On television Patsy's most popular role has been Sadie King in *Emmerdale*. Her first credited big screen role was as Mia Farrow's daughter, Pamela Buchanan, in *The Great Gatsby* (1974) and Patsy subsequently played Mia Farrow herself in the TV film *Love and Betrayal* (1995). She competed in the 2010 series of *Strictly Come Dancing*, partnered by Robin Windsor, they finished in 7th place. Patsy famously had breast implants which took her bust measurement from a 32B to a 35C. She also has tattoos on her back, above the blade of her left foot and on her ankle. The Gaelic words on her foot and her pop career give a clue to Patsy's passions. She has a predilection for marrying musicians with Irish descent - Don Donovan (*Big Audio Dynamite*) (1988-91), Jim Kerr (*Simple Minds*) (1992-96), Liam Gallagher (*Oasis*) (1997-2000; with whom she had a son, Lennon) and Jeremy Healy (Haysi Fantayzee) (2009). Patsy and Jeremy announced their split in February 2010. See also entries for the television section for *Bo' Selecta!*, *Emmerdale*, *Great Expectations*, *Hannah*, *Holby City*, *Luna*, and *Who Do You Think You Are?*

Kent, Jean (1921-) Born Joan Mildred Summerfield, 29 June 1921, Brixton, London. Actress. From a theatrical family, aged only 13 she used a cousin's birth certificate (Jean Carr) to gain a place as a chorus girl at the Windmill Theatre. At the same time, billed as Joan Kent, she made her screen debut in *Who's Your Father* (1935). During the rest of the 1930s she mostly stuck to revue work, including a stint as a stooge to Max Miller, which gained her a contract with *Gainsborough*. As a Gainsborough Girl she featured prominently in a series of the best costume melodramas to hit the screen including *Fanny by Gaslight* (1944), *2,000 Women* (1944), *The Wicked Lady* (1945), *The Magic Bow* (1946), *Caravan* (1946) and *Trottie True* (1949). After *The Browning Version* (1951) she turned more to television work, her last film to-date being *Shout at the Devil* (1976). Jean was typecast early in her career as a strawberry-blonde seductress both on stage and in film but became a fine character actress late in her career. Her last screen appearance was in an episode of Lovejoy in 1991. See also entries in the television section for *Love Story*, *Sir Francis Drake*, *Thicker Than Water*, and *Time of My Life*.

Kenyon, James (1850-1925) Born 26 May 1850, Blackburn, Lancashire. Cinematographer. Began working as a furniture dealer before making penny slot machines. In 1897 he formed a partnership with Sagar Mitchell and they released films under the trade name *Norden*. For more details see the entry under Sagar Mitchell. Kenyon died 6 February 1925, Blackburn, Lancashire.

Kerr, Deborah (1921-2007) Born Deborah Jane Kerr-Trimmer, 30 September 1921, Glasgow, Scotland. Actress. Lived in Helensburgh, Argyll & Bute, until she was three-years-old. Educated at Rossholme School in Weston-super-Mare. Actress. Graceful, elegant and beautiful she originally trained as a ballet dancer, first appearing on stage at Sadler's Wells in 1938. Her aunt, the radio star Phyllis Smale, ran the Hicks-Smale Drama School in Bristol and managed to get the young budding actress some stage work and this very quickly led to film. Her first role was in Michael Powell's *Contraband* (1940) but her scenes were cut and her first film appearance was in *Major Barbara* (1941 – as Jenny Hill). During the remainder of the 1940s she played a variety of parts with her roles growing steadily. These included:

Love on the Dole (1941 – as Sally), *Hatter's Castle* (1942 - as Mary Brodie), *The Day Will Dawn* (1942 - as Kari Alstad), *Perfect Strangers* (1945 - as Catherine Wilson), *I See a Dark Stranger* (1946 - as Bridie Quilty), *The Hucksters* (1947 - as Kay Dorrance), *If Winter Comes* (1947 - as Nona Tybar) and *Edward, My Son* (1949 - as Evelyn Boult). Deborah also continued the association with Michael Powell appearing in *The Life and Death of Colonel Blimp* (1943) and *Black Narcissus* (1947). For two of her best-known roles *From Here to Eternity* (1953 – as Karen Holmes) and *The King and I* (1956 – as Anna Leonowens) she was not the first choice, only getting the roles when Joan Crawford and Maureen O'Hara respectively had turned them down. Her singing voice in *The King and I* was dubbed by the ubiquitous Marni Nixon. Deborah received six Academy Award nominations for Best Actress but won none! These were for *Edward, My Son*, *From Here to Eternity*, *The King and I*, *Heaven Knows, Mr Allison* (1957 – as Sister Angela), *Separate Tables* (1958 – as Sibyl Railton-Bell) and *The Sundowners* (1960 – as Ida Carmody). Her other films include: *King Solomon's Mines* (1950), *Quo Vadis* (1951), *The Prisoner of Zenda* (1952), *Young Bess* (1953 - as Catherine Parr), *Julius Caesar* (1953 - as Portia), *The End of the Affair* (1955 - as Sarah miles), *Tea and Sympathy* (1956), *An Affair to Remember* (1957), *The Grass Is Greener* (1960*), The Naked Edge* (1961), *The Chalk Garden* (1964), *The Night of the Iguana* (1964), *Casino Royale* (1966), *The Gypsy Moths* (1969) and her last feature film, *The Assam Garden* (1985). Her final screen appearance as an actress was in the 1986 TV film *Hold the Dream* based on the Barbara Taylor Bradford book of the same name, where she played Emma Harte, a character she had played earlier on television. In 1998 she was appointed a Commander of the British Empire. In 1994 she received an honorary Academy Award, the citation reading: "An artist of impeccable grace and beauty, a dedicated actress whose motion picture career has always stood for perfection, discipline and elegance". Deborah was married twice. Her first marriage, in 1945, was to Royal Air Force Squadron Leader Anthony Bartley. They had two daughters, Melanie Jane (b. 27 December 1947) and Francesca Ann (b. 20 December 1951), who married the actor John Shrapnel. Following her divorce in 1959, Deborah married author Peter Viertel in July 1960. Although she long resided in Klosters, Switzerland and Marbella, Spain, Deborah moved back to Britain to be closer to her own children as her health began to deteriorate. Her husband, however, continued to live in Marbella. Deborah died from the effects of Parkinson's disease on 16 October 2007, Botesdale, Suffolk. See also entry for *A Woman of Substance* in the television section.

Kidron, Beeban (1961-) Born 2 May 1961, St Pancras, London. Director. Trained as a camera woman at the National Film and Television School (NFTS). A prize-winning photographer while still a teenager, Beeban began her career directing documentaries such as *Carry Greenham Home* (1983), about a women's peace camp, and worked for *British TV* before directing the BAFTA award-winning BBC series *Oranges Are Not the Only Fruit* (1990). This controversial series based on Jeanette Winterson's novel about a young girl discovering her sexuality in a fanatically religious household starred a young Charlotte Coleman and put Beeban on the map. In the meantime she had made her first feature film *Vroom* (1988), which starred Clive Owen in his debut movie. Beeban's next work was *Antonia & Jane* (1991) again looking at the relationships between women. Her first American feature was *Used People* (1992), an ensemble drama about a recently widowed Jewish woman (Shirley MacLaine) courted by an Italian stranger (Marcello Mastroianni) who claims to have been watching her from afar for many years. In 1994 she made *To Wong Foo Thanks for Everything, Julie Newmar*, a drag queen road movie starring Wesley Snipes and Patrick Swayze, in which the former television catwoman also makes a cameo appearance. It was whilst filming this that Beeban and her then partner Spencer Style gave birth to their first child Noah Kidron-Style. Her second child, Blaze Kidron-Style (b. February 1997) was born during filming of *Amy Foster, (Swept from the Sea)* starring Rachel Weisz and Ian McKellen. Following the TV films, *Texarkana* (1998 - NBC), *Cinderella* (2000 –C4), and *Murder* (2002 -BBC), for which she was nominated for a second Bafta, Beeban found more mainstream appeal when helming the box-office hit *Bridget Jones: The Edge of Reason* (2004), which became one of the most successful films in British film history. Her next project was the Channel 4 documentary, *Anthony Gormley: Making Space* (2007) about the Turner Prize-winning sculptor. Beeban and her husband, playwright and author Lee Hall (b. 1966, Newcastle upon Tyne), best known for his screenplay for the 2000 film *Billy Elliot*, then began work on *Hippie Hippie Shake,* a film about the OZ magazine trials. The film was shot in 2009 with Sienna Miller and Cillian Murphy, however Lee and then Beeban left during post production citing artistic differences with the producers. In 2006, Beeban and Lindsey Makie started FILMCLUB, an educational charity which sets up after-school film clubs in schools in England and Wales.

King, Dennis (1897-1971) Born Dennis John Pratt, 2 November 1897, Coventry, West Midlands. Actor and singer. Stage debut in 1915. Emigrated to the United States in 1920. Stage debut on Broadway: *Claire de Lune* (1921). Played Francois Villon in the original stage production of *The Vagabond King* (1925-26) and went on to make his screen debut in the same role in *The Vagabond King* (1930) opposite Jeanette MacDonald. He was primarily a stage actor but he made the following films: *Paramount on Parade* (1930), *The Devil's Brother* (1933), *Between Two Worlds* (1944), *The Miracle* (1959) and *Some Kind of a Nut* (1969). Both a successful classical and musical actor his stage credits on Broadway include *Romeo and Juliet* (1923), *Antony and Cleopatra* (1924), *Rose Marie* (1924-25), *The Three Musketeers* (1928), *Show Boat* (1932), *A Doll's House* (1937-38), *The Devil's Disciple* (1950), *Billy Budd* (1951), *The Greatest Man Alive* (1957) and *A Patriot for Me* (1969). He died 21 May 1971, New York, United States.

Kingsley, Ben (1943-) Born Krishna Pandit Bhanji, 31 December 1943, Snainton, near Scarborough, North Yorkshire. Actor. The son of a doctor, he was brought up in Pendlebury, near Salford and educated at Manchester Grammar School, where one of his classmates was the actor Robert Powell. Stage debut: *A Smashing Day* (1966). His screen debut was as Roy in the *Coronation Street* spin-off *Pardon the Expression* (1966) and later in the year began a two-year stint in *Corrie* itself, as Ron Jenkins. He joined the RSC in 1967 and after several theatre runs made his feature film debut in *Fear is the Key* (1973). Concentrating on stage and television work, it was ten years before he made his next film, but, for the title role of *Gandhi* (1982) he won an Academy Award for Best Actor. Other films include: *Maurice* (1987), *Without a Clue* (1988 - as Dr Watson), *Testimony* (1988 - as Dmitri Shostakovich), *Sneakers* (1992), *Dave* (1993), *Schindler's List* (1993), *Death and the Maiden* (1994), *Twelfth Night* (1996 - as Feste), *The Confession* (1999), *Rules of Engagement* (2000), *Thunderbirds* (2004 - as The Hood), *Mrs Harris* (2005), *Oliver Twist* (2005 – as Fagin), *BloodRayne* (2005), *You Kill Me* (2007), *The Last Legion* (2007), *Transsiberian* (2008), *The Wackness* (2008), *Elegy* (2008), *War, Inc.* (2008), *The Love Guru* (2008), *Fifty Dead Men Walking* (2008), *Shutter Island* (2010), *Teen Patti* (2010), *Prince of Persia: The Sands of Time* (2010) and Hugo (2011 – as Georges Méliès, the toy shop owner). Received Academy Award nominations for Best Actor for *House of Sand and Fog* (2003) and for Best Supporting Actor for *Bugsy* (1991) and *Sexy Beast* (2001) - in both films playing a gangster. Knighted in 2002, he initially insisted on being billed as Sir Ben Kingsley but since a BBC documentary showed this in a somewhat negative light he seems to have altered his stance on this. He has been married four times, to actress Angela Morant (1966–72), with whom he had two children, Thomas Bhanji and artist Jasmin Bhanji; theatre director Alison Sutcliffe (1978–92), with whom he also had two children, Edmund Kingsley and Ferdinand Kingsley, both of whom became actors; German-born Alexandra Christmann (2003–05) and Brazilian actress Daniela Lavender (2007–present). See also entries in the television section for *Coronation Street, Love School, Orlando,* and *Oxbridge Blues.*

Kinnear, Roy (1934-88) Born Roy Mitchell Kinnear, 8 January 1934, Wigan, Lancashire. Actor. His father, Roy Muir Kinnear, was a dual Scottish international at both codes of rugby and scored 81 tries in 184 games for Wigan. He collapsed and died while playing rugby union with the RAF in 1942, at age 38. Roy was educated at George Herriot School, Edinburgh. His training at RADA was interrupted by National Service. Screen debut: *Oh... Rosalinda!!* (1955). Worked in rep during the 1950s and joined Joan Littlewood's Theatre Wokshop in 1959. Came to the public's attention as a member of the satirical TV show *That Was the Week That Was* (1962). His films include: *The Millionairess* (1960), *Sparrows Can't Sing* (1963), *Heavens Above!* (1963), *The Hill* (1965), *Help!* (1965), *How I Won the War* (1967), *The Bed-Sitting Room* (1969), *Lock Up Your Daughters!* (1969), *Scrooge* (1970), *Willy Wonka and the Chocolate Factory* (1971), *Juggernaut* (1974), *Royal Flash* (1975), *The Adventures of Sherlock Holmes' Smarter Brother* (1979), *Herbie Goes to Monte Carlo* (1977), *The Last Remake of Beau Geste* (1977), *The Boys in Blue* (1982) and *Just Ask for Diamond* (1988). His TV credits include his own sitcom *A World of his Own* (1965) and his several guest appearances on *The Avengers*. Roy played D'Artagnan's put-upon servant Planchet in *The Three Musketeers* (1973) and *The Four Musketeers* (1974). He died 20 September 1988, Madrid, Spain after falling from a horse whilst reprising the role in *The Return of the Musketeers* (1989). A fine comic actor who is sorely missed. Director Richard Lester decided to quit the film business as a direct result of his death. Roy was married to actress Carmel Cryan (b. 1949) and they had three children, including actor Rory and casting director Kirsty. Their eldest daughter, Karina, was born with cerebral palsy. The Roy Kinnear Foundation was founded in 1994 in his memory to fund a house for disabled young adults. See also entries in the television section for *Inside George Webley, Mother Nature's Bloomers, N.U.T.S., Shades of Greene, A Slight Case Of, Superted, That Was The Week That Was,* and *World of His Own.*

Kirwan, Dervla (1971-) Born 24 October 1971, Churchtown, Co. Dublin. Actress. The name Dervla means 'Daughter of the Poet'. She initially went to convent school, but left after deciding she wanted to act. Dervla made her screen debut as Viola O'Neill in the TV film, *Troubles* (1988) and her feature debut followed the year after, as Fiona, in *The Fantasist* (1989). Her big break came in the controversial television mini-series *A Time To Dance* (1992) as Bernadette Kennedy. Her film roles have been few and far between but include: *December Bride* (1991), *War of the Buttons* (1994), *Pete's Meteor* (1998), *With or Without You* (1999), *School For Seduction* (2004), *Dangerous Parking* (2007), *Ondine* (2009), in which she played Maura, the alcoholic bitter ex-girlfriend of Colin Farrell's character Syracuse, and *Luna* (2011). Dervla is however far better known for playing two extremely popular characters on television; Phoebe Bamford in *Goodnight Sweetheart* (1993-96) and Assumpta Fitzgerald in *Ballykissangel* (1996-98), thereafter having an off-screen relationship with her co-star Stephen Tompkinson. She met actor Rupert Penry-Jones (b. 22 September 1970, London, the son of actress Angela Thorne) in 2001 while appearing in *Dangerous Corner* and they married in 2007 after a three-year engagement. They have two children, Florence and Peter. She also co-owns the production company Aphra Productions with actress Sarah Parish. Her latest television role was as Jane Travers in the ITV mini-series *Injustice* (2011). See also entries in the television section for *Ballykissangel, Casanova, Eureka Street, 55 Degrees North, Goodnight Sweetheart, Hearts and Bones, Material Girl, Shades, The Silence, A Time to Dance, True Dare Kiss, The Vicar Of Dibley* and *Who Do You Think You Are?*

Knight, Esmond (1906-87) Born Esmond Pennington Knight, 4 May 1906, East Sheen, Surrey. Actor. Stage debut: *Wild Duck* (1925). Screen debut: *The Blue Peter* (1928). Served in the Royal Navy during WWII. Lost one eye and was virtually blinded in the other whilst serving on the Prince of Wales during an encounter with the Bismarck. He later played the captain of the Prince of Wales in *Sink the Bismarck!* (1960). He partially recovered his sight and returned to acting. Several of his films were with Powell and Pressburger, including: *77 Park Lane* (1931), *What Men Live By* (1939), *A Canterbury Tale* (1944), *Black Narcissus* (1947), *The Red Shoes* (1948), *Gone to Earth* (1950), *The Wild Heart* (1952), *Peeping Tom* (1960) and *The Boy who Turned Yellow*

(1972). Other films include: *The Ringer* (1931), *The Bermondsey Kid* (1933), *Father and Son* (1934 - as Michael Bolton), *This England* (1941), *Hamlet* (1948 - as Bernardo), *Richard III* (1955), *Decision at Midnight* (1963), *The Winter's Tale* (1967 - as Camillo), *Anne of the Thousand Days* (1969), *Yellow Dog* (1976) and his last feature film, *The Element of Crime* (1984). He played everything from the classics to farce and also performed his own one-man play *Agincourt -The Archers Tale* (1973). Esmond didn't let his blindness stop him being a painter, mainly of military scenes. Autobiography: *Seeking the Bubble* (1942). He was married twice, to Frances Clare (1929-46) and actress Nora Swinburne (b. Leonora Mary Johnson, 24 July 1902, Bath; d. 1 May 2000, London), from 1946 until his death on 23 February 1987, Chelsea, London, shortly after returning from filming in Egypt. His daughter by his first wife is the actress Rosalind Knight (b. 3 December 1933, Marylebone, London). See also entries in the television section for *A for Andromeda*, and *Elizabeth R*.

Knightley, Keira (1985-) Born Keira Christina Knightley, 26 March 1985, Teddington, London. Actress. Keira comes from an acting family, her mother is actress turned playwright Sharman Macdonald and her father stage and television actor Will Knightley. She also has a brother, composer Caleb Knightley. Keira became a child star appearing in *Royal Celebration* (1993), one of the BBC films released under the banner of *Screen One*. After appearing as Natasha Jordan in another TV film, *A Village Affair* (1995), she made her feature debut, as Young Celia, in *Innocent Lies* (1995). She came to the attention of American audiences in her next feature as Sabé the Queen's decoy in *Star Wars: Episode I - The Phantom Menace* (1999). Keira's first starring role followed in 2001, when she played the daughter of Robin Hood in the made-for-television *Walt Disney Productions* feature, *Princess of Thieves*. Her next outing as Frances 'Frankie' Almond Smith in *The Hole* (2001) had a luke-warm reception but her co-starring role, as Juliette 'Jules' Paxton, in *Bend It Like Beckham* (2002) was highly acclaimed by film critics and the British public. Keira has developed into one of the hottest properties in Hollywood. Often cast as the "English Rose" but with a feisty edge, whether in a corset, as Elizabeth Swann, for *Pirates of the Caribbean: The Curse of the Black Pearl* (2003) and its sequels; a leather jacket, as in *Domino* (2005), or seemingly both in *Pride and Prejudice* (2005). She also played Guinevere as a warrior queen in *King Arthur* (2004). Her other films include: *Thunderpants* (2002), *Pure* (2002), *Love Actually* (2003 - as Juliet), *Stories of Lost Souls* (2005 - as Leah), *The Jacket* (2005 - as Jackie Price), *Pirates of the Caribbean: Dead Man's Chest* (2006), *Pirates of the Caribbean: At World's End* (2007), *Atonement* (2007 – as Cecilia Tallis), *Silk* (2007 - as Hélène Joncour), *The Edge of Love* (2008 – as Vera Phillips), *The Duchess* (2008 - as Georgina Cavendish), *Never Let Me Go* (2010 – as Ruth), *Last Night* (2010 – as Joanna Reed) and *London Boulevard* (2010 – as Charlotte). She has also recently played Tinkerbell in the TV film *Neverland* (2011) and Sabina Spielrein in *A Dangerous Method*, a film looking at the intense relationship between Carl Jung and Sigmund Freud. In October 2004, Keira received her first major accolade, the Hollywood Film Award for Best Breakthrough Actor – Female, and in 2006 was nominated for a Golden Globe and a Best Actress Academy Award for *Pride and Prejudice*. On television Keira has starred, as Lara, in a mini-series adaptation of *Doctor Zhivago* that first aired in 2002 and also appeared in an episode of *The Bill* in 1995 (as Sheena Rose). Keira had a long-term relationship with her *Pride and Prejudice* co-star Rupert Friend from 2005 until the couple separated in December 2010. She has been dating Klaxons member James Righton since late February 2011.See also entry for *Oliver Twist* in the television section.

Knowles, Patric (1911-95) Born Reginald Lawrence Knowles, 11 November 1911, Horsforth, Yorkshire. Actor. Screen debut: *Men of Tomorrow* (1933). Moved to Hollywood in 1934 and embarked on a film career which lasted forty years, more often than not in a supporting role. He played opposite Errol Flynn in some of the best adventure films of the period including playing Flynn's younger brother who wins the hand of Olivia De Haviland in *The Charge of the Light Brigade* (1936) and Will Scarlett in *The Adventures of Robin Hood* (1938). He then transferred from Warner Bros to Universal where he got leads in B pictures such as*The Wolf Man* (1941), *The Strange Case of Dr Rx* (1942) and *Frankenstein Meets the Wolfman* (1943). Other films include: *How Green was my Valley* (1941), *Of Human Bondage* (1946), *Tarzan's Savage Fury* (1952), *Auntie Mame* (1958), *The Devil's Brigade* (1968 - as Lord Louis Mountbatten), *Chisum* (1970) and his last film, *Arnold* (1973). He also wrote the novel *Even Steven* (1960). Patric died 23 December 1995, Woodland Hills, California.

Korda, Alexander (1893-1956) Born Sándor László Kellner, 16 September 1893, Pusztatúrpásztó, Hungary. Director and producer. Worked as a journalist and film critic in Hungary before joining a film company. Directorial debut: *Orhaz a Karpatokban* (1914). Established a studio in Bucharest in 1917 and eventually left Hungary in 1919. He continued directing in Vienna (1919-22) and Berlin (1922-26) before moving to the United States (1927-30) and directing *The Private Life of Helen of Troy* (1927), *Love and the Devil* (1929) and *The Princess and the Plumber* (1930). Korda then went to France where he directed *Marius* (1931) before settling in England later that year and founding *London Films* (with its famous Big Ben logo) in 1932. The early films produced by the company include *Wedding Rehearsal* (1932) and *Cash* (1933) and were not too notable but then he directed *The Private Life of Henry VIII* (1933), which became an international hit and gained a nomination for Academy Award for Best Picture. The boost to his fortunes enabled Korda to establish a studio complex at Denham, Buckinghamshire. Initially combining directing with production, as the 1930s went on he began to direct fewer projects, among the more memorable being, *The Private Life of Don Juan* (1934), *Rembrandt* (1936), *Lady Hamilton* (1941) and *Perfect Strangers* (1945). His final directorial outing was *An Ideal Husband* (1947). Financial problems forced the ownership of Denham Studios to pass from Korda to the J. *Arthur Rank Organisation* in 1939. His productions proved to be some of the best of the era and include: *The Scarlet Pimpernel* (1934), *Sanders of the River* (1935), *The Ghost Goes West* (1935), *Things to Come* (1936), *Fire Over England* (1937), *Elephant Boy* (1937), *The Drum* (1938), *Q Planes* (1939), *The Four Feathers* (1939), *The Thief of Bagdad* (1940), *To Be or Not to Be* (1942), *Jungle Book* (1942), *Anna Karenina* (1948) and *Storm Over the Nile* (1955). In 1946, *London Films* bought a controlling interest in *British Lion Films*, which was involved in such productions as *The Third Man* (1949). Alexander became the first film industry person to be knighted when he received the accolade in 1942. He was married to Hungarian actress Maria Corda (1919-30), film star Merle Oberon (1939-45) and finally to Alexandra Boycun, from 1953 to his death on 23 January 1956, Kensington, London. His brothers Zoltán and Vincent worked as a director and art director respectively.

Korda, Vincent (1897-1979) Born Vincent Kellner, 22 June 1897, Pusztatúrpásztó, Hungary. Production Designer. Trained as a painter at the Budapest Academy of Art and also studied in Vienna, Florence and Paris. Eventually teamed up with his brothers Alexander and Zoltán at *London Films* to work as an art and production designer beginning with *The Private Life of Henry VIII* (1933). His work helped to make the films produced by the company some of the most stylish of the period. His films include: *The Scarlet Pimpernel* (1934), *The Ghost Goes West* (1935), *The Four Feathers* (1939), *The Third Man* (1949), *Summer Madness* (1955) and *Scent of Mystery* (1960). As well as winning an Academy Award for Best Colour Set Design for the sumptuous *The Thief of Bagdad* (1940) he received further nominations for Best Art Direction for *Lady Hamilton* (1941), *Jungle Book* (1942*)* and *The Longest Day* (1962). He died 4 January 1979, Chelsea, London.

Korda, Zoltan (1895-1961) Born Zoltán Kellner, 3 May 1895, Pusztatúrpásztó, Hungary. Director. Served as a cavalry officer during WWI. Directed films in Hungary and Germany: *Karoly Bakak* (1918), *A Csodagyerek* (1920) and *Elf Teufel, Die* (1927*)* and also worked as an editor and cameraman. He joined his brother Alexander in the United States as a writer before following him to England to work with him at *London Films*. His English language directorial debut: *Men of Tomorrow* (1933). At his best when helming action films such as *Sanders of the River* (1935), *Revolt in the Desert* (1937), *Elephant Boy* (1937), *The*

Drum (1938), *Jungle Book* (1942) and *Sahara* (1943). He also directed the more melodramatic *The Macomber Affair* (1947) and *A Woman's Vengeance* (1948). His last films were *Cry, the Beloved Country* (1951) and *Storm Over the Nile* (1955), a remake of his own classic *The Four Feathers* (1939). Zoltán suffered from tuberculosis during his middle-age. Having returned to Hollywood in the early 1940s he settled there when his brothers returned to England. He died 13 October 1961, Los Angeles, California.

Kubrick, Stanley (1928-99) Born 26 July 1928, Bronx, New York, United States. Director, producer and writer. Worked as a photographer for *Look* magazine (1946-51). Began by making short documentaries such as *Day of the Fight* (1951), *Flying Padre* (1951) and *The Seafarers* (1953). He wrote, produced and directed his first feature: *Fear and Desire* (1953) which was financed by money raised from his family, as was his next feature *Killer's Kiss* (1955). Another low-budget thriller *The Killing* (1956) was followed by his first major studio film *Paths of Glory* (1957), a powerful anti-war story starring Kirk Douglas which was both a commercial and critical success. He replaced Anthony Mann as director of the epic *Spartacus* (1960), which also starred Douglas. Kubrick moved to England to make *Lolita* (1962) and settled there. Having made a war film, an epic and a literary adaptation he then made the black comedy *Dr Strangelove or: How I Learned to Stop Worrying and Love the Bomb* (1964) which gained an Academy Award nomination for Best Film and Kubrick a nomination for Best Director and Best Adapted Screenplay. He gained further Academy Award nominations for Best Director and Best Original Screenplay for his stunning *2001: A Space Odyssey* (1968), which won the Academy Award for Best Special Visual Effects. This was followed by the controversial *A Clockwork Orange* (1971) and further Academy Award nominations for Best Picture, Best Director and Best Adapted Screenplay. The historical costume drama *Barry Lyndon* (1975) gained him the self-same trio of Academy Award nominations. His horror film *The Shining* followed in 1980 but it was another seven years before the release of the Vietnam War film *Full Metal Jacket* (1987). This gained Kubrick his final Academy Award nomination for Best Adapted Screenplay. During the 1990s there was an on-off saga regarding a project to bring *Artificial Intelligence: AI* to the screen, which was eventually realised by Steven Spielberg. Stanley was married three times, to Toba Metz (1948–51), Austrian actress Ruth Sobotka (1954–57) and German actress Christiane Harlan, from 1958 until his death, on 7 March 1999 Harpenden, Hertfordshire, shortly after the release of his last film, *Eyes Wide Shut* (1999). He was buried next to his favourite tree in Childwickbury Manor, Hertfordshire, England.

Lanchester, Elsa (1902-86) Born Elsa Sullivan Lanchester, 28 October 1902, Lewisham, London. Actress. Her parents, James Sullivan and Edith Lanchester, were unconventional and never married. The young Elsa trained as a dancer under Isadora Duncan before turning to acting. Few can say that their first feature film was one of the best, but Elsa certainly can as she began her career, as Kitty, in *One Of the Best* (1927). Elsa is perhaps best known for two things – being the long-suffering wife of Charles Laughton for 33 years until his death in 1962, and for playing the dual roles of Mary Wollstonecraft Shelley and The Monster's Mate in *Bride of Frankenstein* (1935). Unconventionally beautiful she never really made the top flight but forever she will be remembered hissing her way on to the screen in this film. This may seem a little unfair for a woman whose screen career spanned seven decades. She also appeared in *The Private Life of Henry VIII* (1933 - as Anne of Cleves), *Rembrandt* (1936 - as Hendrickje Stoffels), *Lassie Come Home* (1943 - as Mrs Carraclough), *The Bishop's Wife* (1947), *The Secret Garden* (1949 - as Martha), *The Inspector General* (1949), *Les Miserables* (1952), *Androcles and the Lion* (1952 - as Megaera), *Witness for the Prosecution* (1957 - as Miss Plimsoll) and *Mary Poppins* (1964 - as Katie Nanna). Her last film was *Die Laughing* (1980), although she did have an uncredited part in *National Lampoon's Vacation* (1983). She died 26 December 1986, Woodland Hills, California.

Lansbury, Angela (1925-) Born Angela Brigid Lansbury, 16 October 1925 St Pancras, London. Actress. She is the granddaughter of Labour Party leader George Lansbury. Educated at Feagin School of Dramatic Arts, New York. Travelled to the US in the early 1940s to avoid the London Blitz. Contracted to *MGM*. Screen debut: *Gaslight* (1944) for which she gained her first Academy Award Nomination as Best Supporting Actress. Angela next played Elizabeth Taylor's sister in *National Velvet* (1944). She quickly earned a second Academy Award Nomination as Best Supporting Actress for her role in *The Picture of Dorian Gray* (1945). Her next film roles were in the musicals *Till the Clouds Roll By* (1946) and *The Harvey Girls* (1946). After *State of the Union* (1948) she began to be type-cast as beautiful but rather hard-hearted, iron-willed, manipulative women (or "bitches" as she herself put it), a persona she perfected for *The Manchurian Candidate* (1961), to earn her a final Academy Award Nomination as Best Supporting Actress. In between she had appeared in *The Three Musketeers* (1948 - as Queen Ann of France), *Samson and Delilah* (1949), *The Court Jester* (1956) and *Blue Hawaii* (1961 - as Elvis Presley's mother). Her films for Disney include *Bedknobs and Broomsticks* (1971) and as voice characterisations in *Beauty and the Beast* (1991) and *Anastasia* (1996). Other films include: *The World of Henry Orient* (1964), *The Amorous Adventures of Moll Flanders* (1965), *Harlow* (1965), *The Lady Vanishes* (1979) and *The Pirates of Penzance* (1983). Her stage debut was in *Hotel Paradiso* (1957) and she went on to star in the musicals *Mame* (1966), *Dear World* (1969), *Gypsy* (1974), for which she won Tony Awards, and *Sweeny Todd* (1979). She played Miss Marple in *The Mirror Crack'd* (1980) - again opposite Elizabeth Taylor - and to most younger audiences she is known primarily as another female sleuth, Jessica Fletcher, in the highly successful TV series *Murder, She Wrote* (1984-1996). Still working, now in her eighth decade, she was recently in *Nanny McPhee* (2005 - as Great Aunt Adelaide), *Heidi 4 Paws* (2008 - voice of Grandmamma) and *Mr Popper's Penguins* (2011 - as Selma Van Gundy). Angela married actor Richard Cromwell (b. 8 January 1910; d. 11 October 1960) in 1945 but divorced him the following year when she found out he was bi-sexual. In 1948 she wed Irish-born actor and businessman Peter Shaw, to whom she was married until his death in 2003. She became a naturalised American citizen in 1951. Angela's half-sister, Isolde, was married to Peter Ustinov for some years but divorced in 1946. Angela and Peter appeared together professionally only once, in *Death on the Nile* (1978).

Laughton, Charles (1899-1962) Born 1 July 1899, Scarborough, Yorkshire. Actor. His parents ran the Victoria Hotel in Scarborough and he was sent to train at Claridges hotel. He enlisted during WWI and was eventually invalided home in 1918. Charles continued in the hotelier trade in Scarborough before fulfilling his ambition and enrolling at RADA in 1925. Stage debut: *The Government Inspector* (1926). Screen debut: *Daydreams* (1928). Early films: *Piccadilly* (1929), *The Sign of the Cross* (1932), *If I had a Million* (1932), *Island of Lost Souls* (1933), *White Woman* (1933), and *The Barretts of Wimpole Street* (1934). He starred in a series of biopics, epics and classic stories: *Les Miserables* (1935), *St Martin's Lane* (1938), *Jamaica Inn* (1939), *The Hunchback of Notre Dame* (1939), *The Canterville Ghost* (1944), *Captain Kidd* (1945), *Young Bess* (1953), *Salome* (1953), *Hobson's Choice* (1954), *Spartacus* (1960) and *Advise and Consent* (1962). Awarded a Best Actor Academy Award for his starring role in *The Private Life of Henry VIII* (1933). He received a Best Actor nomination for playing Captain Bligh in *Mutiny on the Bounty* (1935). Formed a film production company, *Mayflower Pictures Corp.* in 1937. Began filming the title role in *I, Claudius* (1937) before the production was cancelled. Directed only one film, the critically acclaimed *Night of the Hunter* (1955). Married actress Elsa Lanchester in 1929. Charles appeared opposite his wife in several films, including *Rembrandt* (1936), *Tales of Manhattan* (1942) and *The Big Clock* (1948). Elsa wittily portrayed Anne of Cleves, Henry VIII's fourth wife, as a playful half-wit opposite Laughton in The Private Life of Henry VIII. They both received Academy Award nominations for their performances in *Witness for the Prosecution* (1957) – Laughton for Best Actor, and Lanchester for Best Supporting Actress – but neither won. They took US Citizenship in 1950. Charles once described his face as "like the behind of an elephant." He died 15 December 1962, Hollywood, California.His wife subsequently wrote a book alleging that the reason they never had children was because he was homosexual.

Launder, Frank (1906-97) Born 28 January 1906 Hitchin, Hertfordshire. Director, writer and producer. Began working in the office of the Official Receiver. He acted with the Brighton Repertory Company. Joined the scenario department of *British International Pictures* (BIP) in 1928. Began screenwriting with Sidney Gilliat on *Under the Greenwood Tree* (1929) and the partnership lasted for over 35 years. Joined *Gaumont-British* in 1931. Other screenwriting credits include: *Facing the Music* (1933), *Seven Sinners* (1936), *Oh! Mr Porter* (1937), *The Lady Vanishes* (1938), *Night Train to Munich* (1940), *Kipps* (1941), *Partners in Crime* (1942), *The Young Mr Pitt* (1942), *Millions Like Us* (1943), *2,000 Women* (1944), *The Green Man* (1956) and *Joey Boy* (1965). Also a director, always of films he had a hand in writing. Directing credits include: *The Last Coupon* (1932), *Partners in Crime* (1942), *Captain Boycott* (1947), *The Blue Lagoon* (1949), *The Happiest Days of Your Life* (1950), *Geordie* (1955) and *The Bridal Path* (1959). President of the Screenwriter's Association (1946), which he had helped to found along with Gilliat in 1937. They formed their own production company in 1945 called *Individual Pictures* which formed part of *Independent Producers*, a group financed by the *Rank Organisation*. In 1950 they joined Korda's *London Films*. After they took management positions at *British Lion* in 1958 their on-screen output was severely diminished. He resigned from *British Lion* in 1972 and moved to France. Launder and Gilliat are best-remembered for their collaboration on the films featuring the outrageously behaved schoolgirls of St Trinian's: *The Belles of St Trinian's* (1954), *Blue Murder at St Trinian's* (1957), *The Pure Hell of St Trinian's* (1960) and *The Great St Trinian's Train Robbery* (1966). Frank also penned and directed *The Wildcats of St Trinian's* (1980) by himself. Apparently Gilliat's only input was to advise him not to do it. He was married to actress Bernadette O'Farrell from 1950 until his death on 23 February 1997, Monte Carlo, Monaco.

Laurel, Stan (1890-1965) See entry in comedy section

Laurie, Hugh (1959-) Born James Hugh Calum Laurie, 11 June 1959, Oxford, Oxfordshire. Actor. Son of William "Ran" Laurie who won an Olympic gold medal for rowing in the coxless pairs at the 1948 games. Hugh was educated at Eton and Selwyn College, Cambridge. He rowed at No. 4 in the losing Cambridge boat during the 1980 University Boat Race. Forced to abandon rowing during a bout of glandular fever, he joined the Cambridge Footlights, where he met Emma Thompson, with whom he had a romantic relationship; the two remaining good friends. Emma introduced him to his future comedy partner, Stephen Fry. Hugh was president of the Cambridge Footlights which won the first Perrier Award at the Edinburgh Festival in 1981 with *The Cellar Tapes*. His feature film debut was *Plenty* (1985). Other films include: *Peter's Friends* (1992), *Sense and Sensibility* (1995), *101 Dalmations* (1996), *The Borrowers* (1997), *Spice World* (1997), *The Man in the Iron Mask* (1998), *Stuart Little* (1999), *Maybe Baby* (2000), *Stuart Little 2* (2002), *The Flight of the Phoenix* (2004), *Valiant* (2005 - voice of Gutsy), *Street Kings* (2008), *Monsters vs Aliens* (2009 - voice of Dr Cockroach PhD), *Hop* (2011 - voice of Mr Bunny), *The Oranges* (2011 - as David Walling) and *Arthur Christmas* (2011 - voice of Steve). In 2004 he began playing the misanthropic Dr Gregory House in the critically acclaimed American drama *House*, for which he received two Golden Globe awards and four Emmy nominations. He is currently the highest paid actor in a drama on American television, reputed to earn $400,000 per episode. Hugh married theatre administrator Jo Green in June 1989 in Camden, London. They live part of the year in North London with sons Charles Archibald "Charlie" (b. November 1988, Camden), William Albert "Bill" (b. January 1991, Camden) and daughter Rebecca Augusta (b. September 1993, Westminster) and part of the year in Los Angeles. He was awarded an OBE in 2007. Hugh released a blues album 'Let Them Talk' in May 2011 (which peaked at No 2 in the UK album chart) and performed tracks live on various music shows. In the UK he remains best-known for his television work, particularly with Stephen Fry. See entries in the television section for *Alfresco, The Bill, A Bit of Fry and Laurie, Blackadder Goes Forth, Blackadder II, Blackadder the Third, Fortysomething, Happy Families, Jeeves and Wooster, Saturday Live*, and *The Young Ones*.

Laurie, John (1897-1980) Born John Paton Laurie, 25 March 1897, Dumfries, Scotland. Actor. John abandoned a career in architecture to serve in WWI but was eventually invalided out. He trained at the Central School of Speech Training. Stage debut: *What Every Woman Knows* (1921). A fine Shakespearean actor, his film career began with *Juno and the Paycock* (1930), directed by Alfred Hitchcock. Other films include: *The 39 Steps* (1935), *As You Like It* (1936), *Edge of the World* (1937), *Q Planes* (1939), *The Life and Death of Colonel Blimp* (1943), *Henry V* (1944), *Caesar and Cleopatra* (1946), *Treasure Island* (1950), *Richard III* (1954), *Hobson's Choice* (1954), *Kidnapped* (1960), *Dad's Army* (1971), *One of Dinosaurs is Missing* (1976), *Return to the Edge of the World* (1978) and his last film, *The Prisoner of Zenda* (1979). Best known, somewhat to his irritation at the time, for playing Pte James Fraser in the TV sitcom *Dad's Army* - during the Second World War, John actually served in the Home Guard, the only Dad's Army cast member to do so. John was finally doomed, 23 June 1980, Chalfont St Peter, Buckinghamshire.

Law, Jude (1972-) Born David Jude Heyworth Law, 29 December 1972, Lewisham, London. Actor. Attended the National Youth Music Theatre and joined the cast of the TV soap opera *Families* in 1990. His screen debut was in the TV movie *The Tailor of Gloucester* (1989). Following appearances in the TV films *The Ragged Child* (1989) and *The Marshal* (1993) and the film short *The Crane* (1994), he made his feature debut in *Shopping* (1994). Other films include: *Wilde* (1997), *Gattaca* (1997), *Midnight in the Garden of Good and Evil* (1997), *eXistenZ* (1999), *Enemy at the Gates* (2001), *Artificial Intelligence: AI* (2001), *Road to Perdition* (2002), *I Heart Huckabees* (2004), *Sky Captain and the World of Tomorrow* (2004), *Alfie* (2004), *Closer* (2004), *The Aviator* (2004 - as Errol Flynn), *Lemony Snicket's A Series of Unfortunate Events* (2004 – voice of Lemony Snicket), *All the King's Men* (2006), *Breaking and Entering* (2006), *The Holiday* (2006), *My Blueberry Nights* (2007), *Sleuth* (2007 - as Milo) opposite Michael Caine, *Rage* (2009), *The Imaginarium of Doctor Parnassus* (2009 - as Imaginarium Tony 2), *Sherlock Holmes* (2009 - as Dr John Watson), *Repo Men* (2010 - as Remy), *Contagion* (2011 - as Alan Krumwiede), *Hugo* (2011 - as Hugo's father) and reprising his role in the Guy Ritchie film *Sherlock Holmes: A Game of Shadows* (2011). Jude was nominated for an Academy Award for Best Supporting Actor for his performance in *The Talented Mr Ripley* (1999) and nominated for an Academy Award for Best Actor for *Cold Mountain* (2003). In May 2009, he played the title role in Shakespeare's *Hamlet* at the Donmar Warehouse West End season at Wyndham's Theatre, London. Jude was named the "Sexiest Man Alive" by *People* magazine in 2004. He is currently the face of the male perfume of Dior, *Dior Homme Sport* and in 2008 he became the international face of Dunhill and appears in their worldwide advertising campaigns. Jude met actress Sadie Frost while working on the film *Shopping* and they subsequently married in 1997 and divorced in 2003. He is the father of a stepson, Finlay Munro (b. 20 September 1990), and three biological children with Sadie: Rafferty (b. 6 October 1996), Iris (b. 25 October 2000) and Rudy (b. 10 September 2002). Jude became a father for the fourth time (Sophia - b. 22 September 2009, New York) following a brief relationship with New Zealand model Samantha Burke. He has also had a much-publicised on-off relation ship with actress Sienna Miller since 2003 but as of the end of December 2011 it is off!

Law, Phyllida (1932-) Born Phyllida Ann Law, 8 May 1932, Glasgow. Actress. Probably better known as the mother of Emma Thompson, she made her film debut in *Otley* (1968). She has acted in film, theatre and television, teaming up with her daughter in the films *Peter's Friends* (1992), *Much Ado About Nothing* (1993), *The Winter Guest* (1997) and *Nanny McPhee* (2005). Other films include: *Hitler: The Last Ten Days* (1973), *Tree of Hands* (1989), *Before the Rain* (1994), *Junior* (1994), *Emma*

(1996), *Leo Tolstoy's Anna Karenina* (1997), *Judas Kiss* (1998), *Milk* (1999), *Saving Grace* (2000), *The Time Machine* (2002), *Day of Wrath* (2006), *Copying Beethoven* (2006), *Mia Sarah* (2006), *Miss Potter* (2006), *The Waiting Room* (2007), *Lecture 21* (2008), *Ways to Live Forever* (2010) and voicing Sadako for the UK version of the Japanese animated film, *Arriety* (2010). She was married to Eric Thompson, the narrator of the *Magic Roundabout*, from 1957 until his death, at the end of 1982. A prolific television actress who has appeared in episodes of countless drama series. See also entries in the television section for *House of Eliott, Kingdom, Play School,* and *Stig of the Dump.*

Lawford, Peter (1923-84) Born Peter Sydney Ernest Vaughn Aylen, 7 September 1923, Mayfair, London. Actor. His mother married Sir Sydney Lawford, the putative father of her son to whom she had given birth whilst married to Ernest Aleyn. Peter was brought up in France Screen debut: *Poor Old Bill* (1930). At the age of 14, Peter badly damaged his right arm when he accidentally pushed it through a glass door. This injury prevented him signing up for war duty but enhanced his career as he was available for countless MGM films during this period as its major stars such as James Stewart and Clark Gable were enlisted. His other films include: *A Gentleman of Paris* (1931), *The Boy from Barnardo's* (1938), *Lord Jeff* (1938), *A Yank at Eton* (1942), *Mrs Miniver* (1942), *Eagle Squadron* (1942), *Random Harvest* (1942), *The Canterville Ghost* (1944), *The Picture of Dorian Gray* (1945), *Son of Lassie* (1945), *Two Sisters from Boston* (1946), *It Happened in Brooklyn* (1947), *Easter Parade* (1948), *Little Women* (1949), *Kangaroo* (1952), *It Should Happen to You* (1954), *Exodus* (1960), *Ocean's Eleven* (1960 – as Jimmy Foster), *Exodus* (1960), *The Longest Day* (1962), *Advise & Consent* (1962), *Sergeants 3* (1962), *Harlow* (1965), *The Oscar* (1966, *A Man Called Adam* (1966), *Buona Sera, Mrs. Campbell* (1968), *The April Fools* (1969), *They Only Kill Their Masters* (1972), *Rosebud* (1975), *Won Ton Ton, the Dog who Saved Hollywood* (1976) Angels' Brigade (1979), Gypsy Angels (1980), Body and Soul (1981) and his last screen appearance, as Montague Chippendale in the film *Where Is Parsifal?*, which was screened at the 1984 Cannes Film Festival but was withdrawn prior to its official release date in the UK, although eventually being released in France in 1988. In 1961, he and his manager Milt Ebbins formed *Chrislaw Productions*, which was named after his son Christopher Lawford. Peter also made two comedy detective films with Sammy Davis Jr, the Richard Donner film *Salt and Pepper* (1968) and the Jerry Lewis film *One More Time* (1970), Peter playing Christopher Pepper and Sammy playing Charles Salt, two cool nightclub owners with a rather unconventional approach to crime detection. Both these films were produced by *Chrislaw*. In 1959 Frank Sinatra invited Peter to join "The Rat Pack" after marrying Patricia Kennedy, sister of John F Kennedy, in 1954, he eventually had the distinction of also being a member of "The Court of Camelot". Peter was supposedly the last person to speak to Marilyn Monroe on the night of her death. He was married four times: Patricia Kennedy (1954–66), with whom he had a son, Christopher, and three daughters, Sydney, Victoria and Robin; Mary Rowan (1971–75), the daughter of comedian Dan Rowan; Deborah Gould (1976–77) and Patricia Seaton, whom he married a few months before his death on 24 December 1984, Los Angeles, California.

Lawrence, Gertrude (1898-1952) Born Gertrud Alexandra Dagma Klasen, 4 July 1898, Southwark, London. Actress. Daughter of a Danish music hall performer. Trained at Italia Conti. Stage debut: *Babes in the Wood* (1908). Had long successful professional relationships with Noël Coward and Andre Charlot. One of the greats of musical theatre her screen career was sparse, beginning with *The Battle of Paris* (1929) and including *Mimi* (1935), *Rembrandt* (1936) and *The Glass Menagerie* (1950). In 1923, Noël Coward developed his first musical revue, *London Calling!*, specifically for Gertrude. One of Coward's surviving songs was "Parisian Pierrot," a tune that was to be identified closely with Lawrence throughout her career. In November 1926, she became the first British performer to star in an American musical on Broadway when she opened in *Oh, Kay!,*

with music by George Gershwin and lyrics by his brother Ira. In 1931 Lawrence and Coward triumphed in his play *Private Lives*, first in the UK and then on Broadway. In 1948, Gertrude starred in *September Tide*, a play written specifically for her by Daphne du Maurier. Her role was that of a middle-aged Cornish woman whose son-in-law, a bohemian artist, falls in love with her. The two women shared a close friendship and various subsequent biographies have suggested the possibility of a sexual relationship. Gertrude's life was portrayed in the film *Star!* (1968), with Julie Andrews as Lawrence. She wrote an autobiography: *A Star Danced* (1945). Gertrude was married twice, to dance director Francis Gordon-Howley (1917-27) and theatre manager Richard Aldrich, from 1940 until her death on 6 September 1952, New York. She was buried in the pink dress she wore for the *Shall We Dance* number from *The King and I*, which Rogers and Hammerstein wrote for her and in which she starred in the months before her death. Three years after Gertrude died, her daughter Pamela gave birth to Benn Clatworthy, Lawrence's only grandchild. He is now a tenor saxophonist based in Los Angeles.

Lawson, Denis (1947-) Born Denis Stamper Lawson, 27 September 1947 Crieff, Perth and Kinross. Actor. Attended the Royal Scottish Academy of Music and Drama. His sister, Carol, is the mother of actor Ewan McGregor. His screen debut came on television in a 1969 episode of *Dr Finlay's Casebook*. His film debut was as Launcelot Gobbo in the 1973 TV movie *The Merchant of Venice*. After success on the television series *Rock Follies*, he made his feature film debut in *Providence* (1977). His next role was as Wedge Antilles, the pilot of Red Two X-Wing fighter, in *Star Wars: A New Hope* (1977), a role he reprised in *Star Wars: The Empire Strikes Back* (1980) and *Star Wars: The Return of the Jedi* (1983). He is also well-known for playing Gordon Urquhart in *Local Hero* (1983). Other films include: *Holocaust 2000* (1977), the film shorts *Bitter Cherry* (1983), *The Zip* (1988) and *Leonard* (2001), *High Speed* (2002), *The Ride* (2003) and *Perfect Sense* (2011) alongside his nephew. His television credits include *That Uncertain Feeling* (1985) - on the set of which he met Sheila Gish (23 April 1942 – 9 March 2005), his partner of twenty years, whom he married a year before her death. Denis has spent the majority of his acting career as a stage performer but see entries in the television section for *Ambassador, Bleak House, Bob Martin, Holby City, Kit Curran Radio Show, The Passion, Rock Follies, Sensitive Skin,* and *That Uncertain Feeling.*

Lawton, Frank (1904-69) Born Frank Lawton Mokeley, 30 September 1904, St Giles, London. Actor. Born into a theatrical family. Stage debut: *Yes!* (1923). Screen debut: *Birds of Prey* (1930). His main career was in the theatre but his films include: *Young Woodley* (1930), *The Skin Game* (1931), *Cavalcade* (1933), *The Mill on the Floss* (1937), *The Four Just Men* (1939), *Went the Day Well?* (1942), *The Winslow Boy* (1948), *Gideon's Day* (1958) and *The Queen's Guards* (1961). He also played the title role in *David Copperfield* (1935) and Bruce Ismay, the MD of the White Star Line, in *A Night to Remember* (1958). He was married to actress Evelyn Laye, from 1934 until his death on 10 June 1969, Marylebone, London.

Laye, Dilys (1934-2009) Born Dilys Lay, 11 March 1934, Muswell Hill, London. Actress. During World War II Dilys and her brother were evacuated to Devon, where they purportedly suffered physical abuse. After training at the Aida Foster Stage School, she made her stage debut in 1948, aged 13, as a boy in a play called *The Burning Bush* at the New Lindsey Theatre and her film debut a year later as a younger version of Jean Kent in *Trottie True* (1949). Dilys was a pretty actress with a flair for comedy and featured in *Blue Murder at St Trinians* (1957) and *Doctor at Large* (1957). She is probably best known for her appearances as Flo Castle in *Carry On Cruising* (1962), Lila in *Carry On Spying* (1964), Mavis Winkle in *Carry on Doctor* (1967) and Anthea Meeks in *Carry On Camping* (1969). Dilys only began in *Carry Ons* because Joan Sims was taken ill while filming *Carry On Cruising* and was replaced by her. Other films include: *Idol on Parade* (1959), *The Bridal Path* (1959), *Upstairs and Downstairs* (1959), *Petticoat Pirates* (1961), *On the Beat* (1962), *The*

Countess from Hong Kong (1967) and her final film, Dog Eat Dog (2001). On television Dilys played Maxine Palmer in Eastenders (1994-95) and Isabel Stephens in Coronation Street (2000-01). She was married three times, firstly to stunt man Frank Maher and secondly, to actor Garfield Morgan. In 1972, she married her third husband, Alan Downer, who wrote scripts for Coronation Street and Emmerdale Farm on television and Waggoner's Walk on radio. He died in 1995 after years of ill-health following a stroke. They had a son, Andrew, who is an agent for film crews. She died of cancer, 13 February 2009. See also entries in the television section for *The Amazing Mrs Pritchard, The Bed-Sit Girl, Coronation Street, Eastenders, The Strange World of Gurney Slade, Village Hall* and *Whodunnit?*

Laye, Evelyn (1900-96) Born Elsie Evelyn Lay, 10 July 1900, Bloomsbury, London. Actress and singer. Made her stage debut in 1915 and is best known as a theatre actress, particularly in musical comedies. Known as "Boo" Laye, her film credits are few but include her debut in *Luck of the Navy* (1927) plus *One Heavenly Night* (1931), *Waltz Time* (1933), *Princess Charming* (1934), *Make Mine a Million* (1959), *Theatre of Death* (1966) and *Never Never Land* (1980). Her first marriage was to actor Sonnie Hale (1926-30) but divorced him when he began a relationship with Jessie Matthews. Her second marriage was to Frank Lawton (see separate entry).In 1973 she was awarded the OBE. She died 17 February 1996, Westminster. London.

Le Mesurier, John (1912-83) Born John Elton Halliley, 5 April 1912, Bedford, Bedfordshire. Actor. He was brought up in Bury St Edmunds in Suffolk and educated at Sherborne School in Dorset. Worked as an articled clerk in a firm of solicitors until deciding to be an actor in 1933 and signing up at the Fay Compton Studio of Dramatic Art. His mother was from Alderney, one of the Channel Islands, and he adopted her maiden name as his stage name. His first screen roles were in the early BBC TV films *The Marvellous History of St. Bernard* (1938) and *Richard of Bordeaux* (1938). He was commissioned into the Royal Tank Regiment in 1941 and served in the UK and India during the Second World War, reaching the rank of captain. After the war he appeared in the TV film *They Flew Through Sand* (1946), the film shorts *Death in Hand* (1948) and *Escape from Broadmoor* (1948) before making his feature debut in *Old Mother Riley's New Venture* (1949). Other films include: *Private's Progress* (1956), *The Battle of the River Plate* (1956), *The Good Companions* (1957), *Law and Disorder* (1958), *I was Monty's Double* (1958), *The Moonraker* (1958 - as Oliver Cromwell), *Jack the Ripper* (1959), *I'm All Right Jack* (1959), *Ben-Hur* (1959), *Too Many Crooks* (1959), *Carlton-Browne of the F.O.* (1959), *School for Scoundrels* (1960), *Doctor in Love* (1960 - as Dr Mincing), *The Rebel* (1961), *Very Important Person* (1961), *Only Two Can Play* (1962), *The Wrong Arm of the Law* (1963), *The Punch and Judy Man* (1963 - as The Sandman), *The Liquidator* (1965), *The Early Bird* (1965), The Wrong Box (1966), *Casino Royale* (1967), *Salt and Pepper* (1968), *The Italian Job* (1969), *Doctor in Trouble* (1970), *Dad's Army* (1971) *Au Pair Girls* (1972), *The Alf Garnett Saga* (1972), *Jabberwocky* (1977) and his last film, *Facelift* (1984). Autobiography: *A Jobbing Actor* (1985). A well-known voice on radio and face on TV he is perhaps best known for being the kindly Sergeant Arthur Wilson in the TV sitcom *Dad's Army* (1968-1977). His close friendship with the comedian Tony Hancock was seriously tested early in his third marriage, when his wife Joan left him for Hancock, only to return a year later. John was married three times in all, to June Melville (1939-47), Hattie Jacques (1949-65) and Joan Malin, from 1965 until his death on 15 November 1983, Ramsgate, Kent. His last words are reported to have been: "It's all been rather lovely." At his request the notice of his death in *The Times* read: "John Le Mesurier wishes it to be known that he 'conked out' on November 15th. He sadly misses family and friends". See also entry for Hattie Jacques and entries in the television section for *Dad's Army, George and the Dragon,* and *Happy Holidays.*

Lean, David (1908-91) Born 25 March 1908, Croydon, Surrey (now Greater London). Director. His parents were Quakers and he was a pupil at the Quaker-founded Leighton Park School, Reading. His younger brother, Edward Tangye Lean (1911–74), founded the original Inklings literary club when a student at Oxford University. David worked in his father's accountancy office before joining *Gaumont* in 1927 and working his way up from tea boy to film editor. Directorial debut: *In Which we Serve* (1942) and his next films were also Noël Coward projects: *This Happy Breed* (1944), *Blithe Spirit* (1945) and *Brief Encounter* (1945). He followed these up with *Great Expectations* (1946) and *Oliver Twist* (1948). Apart from *Brief Encounter* and *Great Expectations* he also received Academy Award nominations for Best Director for *Summertime* (1955), *Doctor Zhivago* (1965) and his last film, *A Passage to India* (1984). He won the Academy Award for Best Director for *The Bridge on the River Kwai* (1957) and *Lawrence of Arabia* (1962). Other films: *The Passionate Friends* (1949), *Madeleine* (1950), *The Sound Barrier* (1952), *Hobson's Choice* (1954) and *Ryan's Daughter* (1970). David was one of the founding members of the British Film Academy (later the British Academy of Film and Television Arts, or BAFTA) and was appointed its first chairman in 1947. David was married six times, to his first cousin Isabel Lean (1930-36), with whom he had a son, Peter; actress Kay Walsh (1940-49); actress Ann Todd (1949-57), Leila Matkar (1960-78), Sandra Hotz (1981-84) and Sandra Cooke, from 1990 until his death on 16 April 1991, East London whilst preparing to film Joseph Conrad's *Nostromo*.

Lee, Anna (1913-2004) Born Joan Boniface Winnifrith, 2 January 1913, Ightham, Kent. Actress. The god-daughter of Sir Arthur Conan Doyle and Dame Sybil Thorndyke. Studied at the Central School of Speech Training and Dramatic Art in London. Screen debut: *His Lordship* (1932). Featured in many British films in the 1930s such as *The Passing of the Third Floor Back* (1935), *The Man who Changed his Mind* (1936) and *King Solomon's Mines* (1937). She moved to Hollywood at the outbreak of WWII deciding to stay and featured regularly in John Ford films such as *How Green was my Valley* (1941), *Fort Apache* (1948), *The Horse Soldiers* (1959) and *The Man Who Shot Liberty Valance* (1962). Anna played a singing nun in *The Sound of Music* (1965). She was married three times, to director Robert Stevenson (1934–44), George Stafford (1944–64) and to poet and playwright Robert Nathan (his 7th wife), from 1970 until his death in 1985. She has five children, including actors Venetia Stevenson (once married to Don Everly of the Everly Brothers and before that to actor Russ Tamblyn) and Jeffrey Byron (by Stafford). Anna was paralysed from the waist down in a car accident in 1978, a year after joining the US TV soap opera *General Hospital* as Lila Quartermaine. She continued in the part for more than twenty years, in a wheelchair. Awarded the MBE in 1982. she died 14 May 2004, Beverly Hills, Los Angeles, California.

Lee, Belinda (1935-61) Born 15 June 1935, Budleigh Salterton, Devon. Actress. Blonde bombshell who studied at RADA. Screen debut: *The Runaway Bus* (1954). Other early films include: *Murder by Proxy* (1954), *Life with the Lyons* (1954), *Meet Mr Callaghan* (1954) and *The Belles of St. Trinian's* (1954). Signed up by *Rank* she found herself being repeatedly cast as the "sexy blonde girl" in such films as *Who Done It?* (1956), *Miracle in Soho* (1957) and *Dangerous Exile* (1957). She eventually moved to Italy where she starred in a series of "pulp" films as various goddesses and historical characters such as Lucretia Borgia and Messalina. She divorced *Rank Studio* photographer Cornel Lucas in 1959 having married him in 1954. Her final film was *Sold Into Egypt* (1962). She died 13 March 1961 in a car accident whilst on holiday in San Bernadino, California, purportedly as part of a suicide pact with her Italian prince lover.

Lee, Bernard (1908-81) Born John Bernard Lee, 10 January 1908, Brentford, Middlesex (now Greater London). Actor. Trained at RADA. Stage debut at age six. Attended RADA. Screen debut: *The Double Event* (1934). Other films include: *Murder in Soho* (1939), *The Courtneys of Curzon Street* (1947), *The Fallen Idol* (1948), *The Third Man* (1949), *The Blue Lamp* (1950), *Odette* (1950), *Gift Horse* (1952), *The Yellow Balloon* (1953), *Beat the Devil* (1953), *Father Brown* (1954), *The Battle of the River Plate* (1956), *Dunkirk* (1958), *Kidnapped* (1960), *The Angry Silence* (1960), *Whistle Down the Wind* (1961), *Ring of Spies* (1963), *The Spy Who Came in from the Cold* (1965), *OK Connery* (1967), *Raging Moon* (1971) and the TV film, *Dangerous Davies* (1981), his last screen appearance. Best known for playing "M" (Admiral Sir Miles Messervy) in eleven of the series of James Bond films: *Dr No* (1962) *From Russia with Love* (1963), *Goldfinger* (1964), *Thunderball* (1965), *You Only Live*

Twice (1967), *On Her Majesty's Secret Service* (1969), *Diamonds Are Forever* (1971), *Live and Let Die* (1973), *The Man with the Golden Gun* (1974), *The Spy Who Loved Me* (1977) and *Moonraker* (1979), his last feature film. Bernard also portrays M, along with Lois Maxwell as Moneypenny, in the 1975 French comedy *Bons baisers de Hong Kong*. He was married to Gladys Emily Merredew (1934-72) and had a daughter, Ann Gladys Lee, the mother of actor Jonny Lee Miller. He died 16 January 1981, Camden, London.

Lee, Christopher (1922-) Born Christopher Frank Carandini Lee, 27 May 1922, Belgravia, London. Actor. Son of Lieutenant Colonel Jeffrey Lee and Contessa Estelle Marie Carandini di Sarzano. After his parents divorced his mother married Harcourt Rose, the uncle of Ian Fleming. Christopher won a scholarship to Wellington College. He served in the RAF during WWII, reaching the rank of Flight Lieutenant. A product of the Rank Company of Youth - otherwise known as the Rank Charm School. Screen debut: *Corridor of Mirrors* (1948). Other early films, in many of which he seemed to play a series of Spaniards, Germans and Arabs, include: *One Night with You* (1948), *A Song for Tomorrow* (1948), *Penny and the Pownall Case* (1948), *Hamlet* (1948) which was his first of many collaborations with Peter Cushing, *Saraband for Dead Lovers* (1948), *Scott of the Antarctic* (1948), *Captain Horatio Hornblower* (1951), *Babes in Bagdad* (1952), *Storm over the Nile* (1955) and *The Battle of the River Plate* (1956). He made his breakthrough as Frankenstein's monster in *The Curse of Frankenstein* (1957) which was swiftly followed by his first of many portrayals of the neck-biting count in *Dracula* (1958). His films after this include: *The Mummy* (1959), *The Two Faces of Dr. Jekyll* (1960), *The Pirates of Blood River* (1962), *Dr Terror's House of Horrors* (1965), *She* (1965), *Theatre of Death* (1966), *Dracula: Prince of Darkness* (1966) which was famous for Christopher having no dialogue, *Circus of Fear* (1966), *The Devil Rides Out* (1968), *Dracula Has Risen from the Grave* (1968), *The Magic Christian* (1969 - as the ship's vampire of course), *Scream and Scream Again* (1970), *Count Dracula* (1970), *Taste the Blood of Dracula* (1970), *Scars of Dracula* (1970), *Dracula A.D. 1972* (1972), *The Creeping Flesh* (1973), *The Satanic Rites of Dracula* (1973), *To the Devil a Daughter* (1976), *Gremlins 2: The New Batch* (1990), *Police Academy: Mission to Moscow* (1994), *Tale of the Mummy* (1998), *Sleepy Hollow* (1999) and *Charlie and the Chocolate Factory* (2005). Christopher also played Dr Fu Manchu in *The Face of Fu Manchu* (1965), *The Brides of Fu Manchu* (1966), *The Vengeance of Fu Manchu* (1967) and *The Blood of Fu Manchu* (1968). Other stand-outs include his Lord Summerisle in *Wicker Man* (1973), Scaramanga in *The Man with the Golden Gun* (1974) and Rochefort in *The Three Musketeers* (1973), *The Four Musketeers* (1974) and *The Return of the Musketeers* (1989). He also starred as Mohammed Ali Jinnah, the founder of modern Pakistan, in *Jinnah* (1998), a film that Christopher considers his most important. He is still going strong in blockbusters such as *The Lord of the Rings* trilogy, playing the evil Saruman, and *Star Wars Episodes 2 and 3* plus *Star Wars: The Clone Wars* (2008) as Count Dooku / Darth Tyranus. He was the only member of the Lord of the Rings cast to have actually met J R R Tolkein. His most recent films include: *The Golden Compass* (2007), *Boogie Woogie* (2009), *Triage* (2009), *Glorious 39* (2009), *The Heavy* (2010), *Alice in Wonderland* (2010 - voice of Jabberwocky), *Burke and Hare* (2010), *Season of the Witch* (2011), *The Resident* (2011), *The Wicker Tree* (2011) and *Hugo* (2011). Christopher has appeared in almost 300 films, giving him an entry in the *Guinness Book of Records* for most film acting roles ever. He was appointed CBE in 2001, and knighted in 2009. Christopher has been married to Danish model Birgit "Gitte" Kroencke Lee since 1961. They have a daughter, Christina Erika Carandini Lee. He is also the uncle of the British actress Harriet Walter, who is the daughter of Christopher's elder sister Xandra Lee. At 6ft 5ins and given the nature of his roles, his autobiography is perhaps rather aptly entitled, *Tall, Dark and Gruesome*. See also entries in the television section for *The Far Pavilions*, and *Gormenghast*.

Leigh, Mike (1943-) Born 20 February 1943, Brocket Hall, Welwyn, Hertfordshire. Director. Brought up in Salford, Greater Manchester. His grandfather was a portrait miniaturist from Russia and his father was a doctor. The family name was originally Lieberman. Attended RADA, the Camberwell School of Art, the London International School of Film Technique and the Central School of Art and Design. His feature directorial debut was based on his own stage play *Bleak Moments* (1971). He then concentrated on television work until writing and directing *High Hopes* (1988). Other films include: *Life is Sweet* (1990) and *Naked* (1993). Mike was nominated for Academy Awards for Best Director and Best Original Screenplay for *Secrets and Lies* (1996); for Best Original Screenplay for *Topsy-Turvy* (1999), Best Director and Best Original Screenplay for *Vera Drake* (2004), and Best Original Screenplay for both *Happy-Go-Lucky* (2007) and *Another Year* (2010). His best known TV work is probably from the 1970's *Play for Today* series and includes: *Hard Labour* (1973), *Nuts in May* (1976), *Kiss of Death* (1977), *Who's Who* (1979) and, of course, the remarkable *Abigail's Party* (1977), again based on his original stage play. Mike develops his largely improvised scripts in collaboration with his cast before setting the dialogue in place. He was married to Alison Steadman (1973-2001) and they have two sons, Toby (b. February 1978) and Leo (b. August 1981). He now lives in Camden with costume designer Charlotte Holdich. Awarded the OBE in 1993.

Leigh, Vivien (1913-67) Born Vivian Mary Hartley, 5 November 1913, Darjeeling, India. Actress. A quintessentially British actress born to Ernest Hartley, a British Officer in the Indian Cavalry, and Gertrude Robinson Yackje. She remained in India for the first six years of her life before the family moved back to England. Her father took her travelling through Europe in her teenage years and she changed schools frequently, eventually returning to England in 1931. At the end of her education, she met and married barrister Herbert Leigh Holman in 1932 and they had a daughter, Suzanne (b. 12 October 1933). Married and with a two year old child she was however determined to be an actress and made her debut, as an uncredited schoolgirl, in *Things Are Looking Up* (1935). Later in 1935 she appeared in the low key films *Gentlemen's Agreement*, *Look Up and Laugh* and the Reginald Denham comedy *The Village Squire*. At this time, her agent, John Gliddon, suggested "April Morn" as her stage name but she eventually opted for "Vivian Leigh". Gliddon then recommended her to Alexander Korda as a possible film actress, but Korda initially rejected her as lacking potential but after attending her opening night performance in the critically acclaimed stage play *The Mask of Virtue* (1935), changed his mind, and her name subtly, to Vivien Leigh, before signing her. Bigger and better roles followed beginning with *Fire Over England* (1937 - as Cynthia). *Dark Journey* (1937 - as Madeleine Goddard) and *Storm in a Teacup* (1937 - as Vickie Gow) followed and she was then perfectly cast as Elsa Craddock in *A Yank at Oxford* (1938) opposite Maureen O'Sullivan her friend and classmate from school (Convent of the Sacred Heart, Roehampton). After *Sidewalks of London* (1938 - as Liberty) she was cast as Scarlett O'Hara in *Gone With the Wind* (1939) and although this role rewarded her with an Academy Award for Best Actress (the first Englishwoman to win one) and made her a worldwide name she only made another nine films after this. Among these were *That Hamilton Woman* (1941 - as Emma Hamilton), *Caesar and Cleopatra* (1945 - as Cleopatra) the title role in *Anna Karenina* (1948) and *A Streetcar Named Desire* (1951 - as Blanche DuBois), for which she won her second Best Actress Academy Award. Her other films were: *21 Days* (1940), *Waterloo Bridge* (1940), *The Deep Blue Sea* (1955), *The Roman Spring of Mrs. Stone* (1961) and her last film *Ship of Fools* (1965). After the success of *Gone With the Wind* she divorced her first husband (they had been separated for a number of years) and married Laurence Olivier in Santa Barbara, California, in a ceremony attended only by their witnesses, Katharine Hepburn and Garson Kanin. This marriage lasted from 1940 until they finally divorced in 1960, however, Vivien's continued bouts of bi-polar disorder which had blighted much of her private life had put considerable strain on their relationship. By 1958, Vivien considered herself single and began a relationship with actor John Merivale which she maintained until her death, from tuberculosis, on 7 July 1967, Westminster, London. She was a beautiful and talented actress often portraying women who were troubled and self-destructive, which in some ways mirrored her off-screen life.

Leighton, Margaret (1922-76) Born 26 February 1922, Barnt Green, Worcestershire. Actress. Primarily a stage actress, making her debut in *Laugh With Me* (1938), but with some significant credits in film. On stage she was with the Old Vic Company and made her Broadway debut in *Henry IV* (both parts) in May 1946. She went on to gain four Tony Award nominations, winning twice, for *Separate Tables* (1956) and *The Night of the Iguana* (1962), playing the effervescent Hannah Jelkes (a role played by Deborah Kerr on film) opposite Bette Davis's Maxine Faulk. On screen her debut was also in *Laugh With Me* (1938) where she reprised her role of Dorothy, from her stage performance earlier in the year. Her feature debut was *The Winslow Boy* (1944). Her other films include *Bonnie Prince Charlie* (1948 - as Flora MacDonald), *The Astonished Heart* (1949), *Under Capricorn* (1949), *The Constant Husband* (1955), *Carrington VC* (1955), *The Sound and the Fury* (1959), *Seven Women* (1966), *Lady Caroline Lamb* (1972) and *Trial by Combat* (1976). She gained an Academy Award nomination for Best Supporting Actress for *The Go-Between* (1970). Margaret married three times, to publisher Max Reinhardt (1947-55), actor Laurence Harvey (1957-61) and to actor Michael Wilding, from 1964 until her death, from multiple sclerosis, on 13 January 1976, Chichester, West Sussex. See also entry for *The Upper Crusts* in the television section.

Lester, Adrian (1968-) Born 14 August 1968, Birmingham. Actor. Adrian is the son of Jamaican immigrants. He graduated from RADA. His screen debut was a walk on part in Crossroads in the mid-1980s. His film debut came in the TV movie *Touch and Die* (1991) and his feature debut in the French comedy *Les Soeurs Soleil* (1997). Other films include: *Primary Colors* (1998), *Love's Labour's Lost* (2000), *Best* (2000), *Maybe Baby* (2000), the TV film *Jason and the Argonauts* (2000 – as Orpheus), *The Final Curtain* (2002), *The Day After Tomorrow* (2004), *As You Like It* (2006), *Scenes of a Sexual Nature* (2006), *Starting Out in the Evening* (2007), *Doomsday* (2008) and *Case 39* (2009). Has built an award winning stage career playing, amongst others, Rosalind in an all-male production of *As You Like It* (1991 and 1994), Bobby in *Company* (1995), *Hamlet* (2000), *Henry V* (2003) for the National Theatre and, in 2010 he played the part of Brick in Tennessee Williams' play *Cat on a Hot Tin Roof* at the Novello Theatre in London. He has come to greater attention by playing Michael "Mickey Bricks" Stone in the TV series *Hustle* (2004-2006; 2009-11). Adrian is married to actress Lolita Chakrabarti (b. 1 June 1969, Yorkshire). They have two daughters, both born in Lambeth, Lila Harvey Chakrabarti (b. 2001) and Jasmine Harvey Chakrabarti (b. 2004). See also entries in the television section for *Bonekickers*, and *Hustle*.

Lester, Richard (1932-) Born 19 January 1932, Philadelphia, Pennsylvania, United States. Director. Graduated in clinical psychology from the University of Pennsylvania. Worked in US television before settling in England in 1956. After meeting Peter Sellers he directed a television version of *The Goons*, *The Idiot Weekly, Price 2d* and the follow-on series *A Show Called Fred* (1956) and *Son of Fred* (1956). He collaborated with Sellers and Spike Milligan on his big screen debut, the film short *The Running, Jumping & Standing Still Film* (1959). Richard seemed to dial into the emerging 1960's youth boom in Britain with his feature debut *It's Trad Dad!* (1962) and *The Knack* (1965) but particularly with the films he directed for The Beatles: *A Hard Day's Night* (1964) and *Help!* (1965). However, films such as *How I Won the War* (1967) and *The Bed Sitting Room* (1969) did have a darker tone amongst the surrealism. In the 1970s he directed a single film, closely based on the Dumas classic but it was released as two films *The Three Musketeers* (1973) and *The Four Musketeers* (1974). He also directed the successful *Superman II* (1980) and *Superman III* (1983). Other films include: *The Mouse on the Moon* (1963) which was the sequel to the *Mouse That Roared*, *A Funny Thing Happened on the Way to the Forum* (1966), *Petulia* (1968), *Juggernaut* (1974), *Royal Flash* (1975) which was based on the George McDonald Fraser novel, *Robin and Marian* (1976), *The Ritz* (1976), *Cuba* (1979), *Butch*

and Sundance: The Early Years (1979) and *Finders Keepers* (1984). He returned to Dumas for *The Return of the Musketeers* (1989) but the film was marred by the accidental death of Roy Kinnear and apart from a documentary of a Paul McCartney tour, *Get Back* (1991) he then retired.

Lewis, Damian (1971-) Born Damian Watcyn Lewis, 11 February 1971, St John's Wood, London. His maternal grandfather was Lord Mayor of London Ian Frank Bowater. Damian made his screen debut, as Clive in the TV film *Micky Love* (1993). His feature debut came in *Robinson Crusoe* (1997). Other films include: *Dreamcatcher* (2003), *Keane* (2004), *Brides* (2004), *Chromophobia* (2005), *An Unfinished Life* (2005), *Alex Rider: Stormbreaker* (2006), *The Situation* (2006), *The Baker* (2007 - directed by his brother, Gareth Lewis), *The Escapist* (2008), *Your Highness* (2011) and *Will* (2011). While appearing in Jonathan Kent's production of Hamlet, playing Laertes opposite Ralph Fiennes' Hamlet, he was spotted by Steven Spielberg, who subsequently cast him as Major Richard Winters in the American World War II television mini-series *Band of Brothers* (2001). Damian also starred as Detective Charlie Crews in the NBC drama *Life* (2007-09). On British television he played Jeffrey Archer in the satirical BBC TV film *Jeffrey Archer: The Truth* (2002) and Tony Blair in the ITV TV film Confessions of a Diary Secretary (2007). Damian has been married to actress Helen McCrory (see separate entry) since 2007. They have two children: a daughter, Manon (b. 8 September 2006), and a son, Gulliver (b. 2 November 2007). They live in Tufnell Park, London and Los Angeles. See also entries in the television section for *The Forsyte Saga*, and *Hearts and Bones*.

Livesey, Roger (1906-76) Born 25 June 1906, Barry, Vale of Glamorgan, Wales. Actor. Born into a theatrical family. Educated at Westminster School and Italia Conti. Stage debut: *Loyalty* (1917). Screen debut: *The Four Feathers* (1921). He concentrated almost exclusively on stage work in his early career but his other films over the next twenty years include: *Where the Rainbow Ends* (1921), *Midshipman Easy* (1935), *Lorna Doone* (1935), *Rembrandt* (1936) and *The Drum* (1938). Roger was working in an aircraft factory during WWII when he was chosen to play the lead in the Powell and Pressburger classic *The Life and Death of Colonel Blimp* (1943). He next played the impoverished highland laird Torquil MacNeil in *I Know Where I'm Going* (1945) and his final film for The Archers was *A Matter of Life and Death* (1946). Further films include: *Vice Versa* (1948), *Green Grow the Rushes* (1951), *The Master of Ballantrae* (1953), *The League of Gentlemen* (1959), *The Entertainer* (1960), *Of Human Bondage* (1964), *The Amorous Adventures of Moll Flanders* (1965), *Hamlet* (1969*)* and his last film, *Futtocks End* (1970). Roger was married to actress Ursula Jeans, from 1936 until her death, from cancer, in 1973. He too suffered from cancer during the early 1950s and, after her death had a recurrence and died 4 February 1976, Watford, Hertfordshire. See also entry for *The Pallisers* in the television section.

Llewelyn, Desmond (1914-99) Born Desmond Wilkinson Llewelyn, 12 September 1914, Newport, Gwent. Actor. Trained at RADA. Desmond made his screen debut in an early BBC TV film *Campbell of Kilmhor* (1939 – as Captain Sandeman). His feature debut was in *Ask a Policeman* (1939). He served in the Royal Welch Fusiliers during WWII and was held as a POW 1940-45. After the war his films include: *The Lavender Hill Mob* (1951), *Further Up the Creek* (1958), *The Pirates of Blood River* (1962), *Cleopatra* (1963) and *Chitty, Chitty Bang Bang* (1968). TV credits include *Follyfoot* (1971-73). Best known for his portrayal of "Q" (Major Boothroyd) in 17 of the series of James Bond films - more than anyone else - beginning with *From Russia with Love* (1963) and ending with his last film appearance, in *The World is not Enough* (1999) - but excluding *Live and Let Die* (1973), in which "Q" did not make an appearance. The part of "Q" in the 1st Bond film *Dr No* (1962) was played by Peter Barton, who was unavailable for the next production. Autobiography: *Q, the Autobiography of Desmond Llewelyn* (1999). He was married to Pamela Mary Pantlin, from 1938 until his death on 19 December 1999, in a car crash nr Berwick, East Sussex on the way back from promoting his autobiography.

Lloyd, Emily (1970-) Born Emily Alice Lloyd Pack, 29 September 1970, Islington, London. Actress. She is the daughter of actor Roger Lloyd Pack (or Trigger from *Only Fools and Horses* as he will always be remembered) and grand-daughter of actor Charles Lloyd Pack. She attended the Italia Conti School in London. Her first film *Wish You Were Here* (1987) based on the early life of Cynthia Payne, received rave reviews and she was nominated for a BAFTA and was touted as the next great British actress. However, *Cookie* (1989), *In Country* (1989) and *Chicago Joe and the Showgirl* (1990) soon dispelled the hype. Since then she has turned in creditable performances in *A River Runs Through It* (1992) and *When Saturday Comes* (1996) mainly in supporting roles. Other films include: *Scorchers* (1991), *Under the Hula Moon* (1995), *Livers Ain't Cheap* (1996), *Dead Girl* (1997), *Welcome to Sarajevo* (1997), *Boogie Boy* (1998), *Woundings* (1998), *The Honeytrap* (2002) and *Hey Mr DJ* (2003). Her role as a leading lady is currently on hold although she does continue to act. Emily's latest screen appearance was in the film short *The Conservatory* (2008), directed by director Reed Van Dyk. There is no doubt Emily is a talented actress but she has been dogged by problems both on-set and off. Since 1992 she has fought depression and anxiety and at various times has been diagnosed as suffering from Obsessive Compulsive Disorder, Tourette's Syndrome and mild schizophrenia.

Lloyd, Frank (1886-1960) Born 2 February 1886, Glasgow, Scotland. Actor, director, producer and writer. Travelled to the United States in 1908 and became a citizen in 1911. Screen acting debut: *Shadows of Life* (1913). He went on to act in more than 60 films in three years, his last film being *The Stronger Love* (1916). Frank began directing with *Mexican's Last Raid* (1914). Other early directing features include literary adaptations such as *A Tale of Two Cities* (1917), *Les Miserables* (1917), *Riders of the Purple Sage* (1918), *Madame X* (1920), *Oliver Twist* (1922) and *The Sea Hawk* (1924). He won an Academy Award for directing the silent film *The Divine Lady* (1929) - he was also considered that year for directing the talkies *Drag* (1929) and *Weary River* (1929). Uniquely, *Divine Lady* was not considered in the Best Film category. He won another Academy Award for *Calvacade* (1933) which was also Best Picture. Frank also received an Academy Award nomination for the big-budget star-studded *Mutiny on the Bounty* (1935), which won the Best Picture Oscar. The three male leads in *Mutiny* - Clark Gable, Charles Laughton and Franchot Tone - all received nominations, which is a record for a single film. Later films include: *Under Two Flags* (1936), *Wells Fargo* (1937), *If I Were King* (1938) and *The Last Command* (1955). In all directed over 130 films between 1914 and 1955. Frank also produced several films, notably, *Saboteur* (1942). He died 10 August 1960, Santa Monica, California.

Loach, Ken (1936-) Born 17 June 1936, Nuneaton, Warwickshire. Director and writer. Studied law at St Peter's College, Oxford. Briefly acted before joining Northampton Repertory Theatre as assistant director. Became a trainee TV director at the BBC. Directed some episodes of *Z-Cars* before, along with producer Tony Garnett, he was responsible for directing some of the most impact-making single dramas of the 1960s such as *Up The Junction* (1965) and *Cathy Come Home* (1966) from the *Wednesday Play* series. His big screen debut *Poor Cow* (1967) followed on from these in both style - realistic and documentary - and issues. Next came *Kes* (1969) based on the novel by Barry Hines, which proved both a critical and commercial success. He concentrated more on television work over the next two decades and his few theatrical releases such as *Family Life* (1971), *The Gamekeeper* (1980) and *Fatherland* (1986) failed to see him regain his earlier success. Several of his television documentaries were also aborted or shelved because of perceived controversial political content. However, the 1990s saw a welcome return to the big screen with films such as *Hidden Agenda* (1990), *Riff-Raff* (1990), *Ladybird Ladybird* (1994), *Land and Freedom* (1995), *Carla's Song* (1996) and *My Name is Joe* (1998). His latest films have been *Sweet Sixteen* (2002), *AE Fond Kiss...* (2004), *Tickets* (2005), *It's a Free World...* (2007), *Looking for Eric* (2009) and *Route Irish* (2010). Ken values having a strong, creative partnership with scriptwriters, most recently with Paul Laverty, who has written nine feature films for him,

including *The Wind That Shakes the Barley* (2006), which won the Palme d'Or at the 2006 Cannes Film Festival. A fierce socialist, as one would expect on close inspection of his work, Ken turned down an OBE in 1977.

Lockwood, Margaret (1916-90) Born Margaret Mary Lockwood Day, 15 September 1916, Karachi, then part of India and now a part of Pakistan. Actress. After her mother brought her back to South London in 1920 she attended the Italia Conti School and later RADA, making her satge debut in 1932. She started out on stage using the name Margie Day briefly before making her film debut in *Lorna Doone* (1934 - as Annie Ridd). Early films include: *The Case of Gabriel Perry* (1935), *Man of the Moment* (1935), *Midshipman Easy* (1935), *The Amateur Gentleman* (1936) and *Irish for Luck* (1936). She showed a deft touch for comedy suspense alongside Michael Redgrave in *The Lady Vanishes* (1938) and went on to star with some of the leading actors of the time, Randolph Scott, Douglas Fairbanks Jr and Rex Harrison to name but a few. A brief Hollywood foray in 1939, however, proved unsuccessful, and she returned to her roots with quality British films such as Carol Reed's *Night Train to Munich* (1940), Anthony Asquith's *Quiet Wedding* (1941) and Leslie Arliss's *The Man in Grey* (1943), opposite James Mason, in which she murders her best friend played by Phylis Calvert. She was the arch villainess amongst the "Gainsborough Girls". In probably her most famous film *The Wicked Lady* (1945) she reunited with director Leslie Arliss and leading man James Mason, to play Barbara Worth, a seductress, drinker, gambler, and highwayman. Margaret retired from films in the mid-1950s but resurfaced two decades later to play Cinderella's stepmother in her last film *The Slipper and the Rose* (1976). During this period she had, in 1965, made a TV appearance in *The Flying Swan* with her actress daughter Julia Lockwood (b. 23 August 1941, Ringwood, Hampshire), the offspring from her marriage to Rupert Leon (1937-49). Margaret rediscovered fame in the long-running television series, *Justice,* playing opposite John Stone, her partner of 17 years. Margaret was created a Dame in 1980 and died 15 July 1990, Kensington, London from cirrhosis of the liver. See also entries in the television section for *The Flying Swan, The Human Jungle,* and *Justice.*

Lodge, David (1921-2003) Born David William Frederick Lodge, 19 August 1921, Strood, Kent. Actor. Worked for the Post Office before joining the RAF at the start of WWII. By the end of the war he was part of Ralph Reader's Gang Show, together with Dick Emery and Peter Sellers. He and Sellers were to become life-long friends and he featured alongside Sellers in such films as *I'm All Right Jack* (1959), *Two Way Stretch* (1960), *A Shot in the Dark* (1964) and *Return of the Pink Panther* (1975). He was best man at Peter Sellers wedding to Britt Ekland in 1964. After WWII he worked as a circus clown and a ringmaster to make ends meet. Eventually made his screen debut in *Orders Are Orders* (1954), although his first credited role was in *Cockleshell Heroes* (1955). He was equally at home in war films such as *Ice-Cold in Alex* (1958) or comedies such as *Private's Progress* (1956). David appeared in five *Carry Ons, Carry On Regardless* (1961), *Carry On Girls* (1973), *Carry On Dick* (1974), *Carry On Behind* (1975) and *Carry on England* (1976). Other films include: *I Was Monty's Double* (1958), *I Only Arsked!* (1958), *Life in Emergency Ward 10* (1959), *The League of Gentlemen* (1960), *The Bulldog Breed* (1960), *The Hellfire Club* (1961), *Go to Blazes* (1962), *The Pirates of Blood River* (1962), *Guns at Batasi* (1964), *The Intelligence Men* (1965), *The Alphabet Murders* (1965), *The Sandwich Man* (1966), *Press for Time* (1966), *Oh! What a Lovely War* (1969), *The Magic Christian* (1969), *The Railway Children* (1970), *On the Buses* (1971), *Mutiny on the Buses* (1972), *Sahara* (1983) and his last film, *Edge of Sanity* (1989). A regular on TV featuring both as a heavy in series such as *The Saint* and in sitcoms such as *Bless This House*. A notorious corpser, particularly in the on-screen company of Spike Milligan and Peter Sellers. He died 18 October 2003, Hillingdon, London. See also entries in the television section for *Carry On Laughing, Here Come the Double Deckers, Q,* and *United!*

Lom, Herbert (1917-) Born Herbert Charles Angelo Kuchacevich von Schluderpacheru, 9 January 1917, Prague, Bohemia (now Czech Republic). Actor. A successful stage actor he made his screen debut in the Czech film Žena pod křížem (1937) and emigrated to England in 1938. His first film in Britain was *The Young Mr Pitt* (1942) in which he played Napoleon, a role he later repeated in *War and Peace* (1956). After playing a psychologist in the melodramatic *Seventh Veil* (1945), he played twin trapeze artists in *Dual Alibi* (1946) and then settled into playing roles tending towards the dark side in films such as *Night and the City* (1950), *State Secret* (1950) and *The Ladykillers* (1955). He played Captain Nemo in *Mysterious Island* (1961) and also featured in the epics *Spartacus* (1960) and *El Cid* (1961). After playing the lead in *The Phantom of the Opera* (1962) he began a stint in horror films in such as *Count Dracula* (1970 - as van Helsing), *Murders in the Rue Morgue* (1971), *Asylum* (1972), *And Now the Screaming Starts!* (1973) and *Dark Places* (1974). He also starred in *The Mark of the Devil* (1969), a German film refused a certificate in the UK because of its bloodthirsty content. He is best known to television viewers of a certain age for his role of Dr Roger Corder in the 1960s series *The Human Jungle*. In film, he is best known for playing the increasingly put-upon Commissioner Charles Dreyfus in the Inspector Clouseau series of films starting with *A Shot in the Dark* (1964) and continuing through *The Return of the Pink Panther* (1975), *The Pink Panther Strikes Again* (1976), *Revenge of the Pink Panther* (1978), *Trail of the Pink Panther* (1982), *Curse of the Pink Panther* (1983) and finally *Son of the Pink Panther* (1993). Other films include: *And Then There Were None* (1974), *The Lady Vanishes* (1979), *The Dead Zone* (1983), *Whoops Apocalypse* (1988), *Ten Little Indians* (1989), *The Sect* (1991) and *The Pope Must Die* (1991). He wrote the historical novels *Enter a Spy: The Double Life of Christopher Marlowe* (1971) and *Dr Guillotine: the Eccentric Exploits of an Early Scientist* (1993).

Lowe, Arthur (1915-82) Born 22 September 1915, Hayfield, Derbyshire. Actor. Worked as a stagehand at the Manchester Palace of Varieties prior to serving in the Middle East during WWII, with the Duke of Lancaster's Own Yeomanry, where he began to take part in shows put on for the troops. He left the Army at the end of the war with the rank of Sergeant Major. Arthur made his screen debut as an uncredited commuter on a train in *London Belongs to Me* (1948), his first credited role, as The Titbits Reporter, came in *Kind Hearts and Coronets* (1949). Other films include: *Final Appointment* (1954), *The Green Man* (1956), *Go to Blazes* (1962), *This Sporting Life* (1963), *You Must Be Joking!* (1965), *The White Bus* (1967), *If...* (1968), *The Bed Sitting Room* (1969), *Spring and Port Wine* (1970), *Dad's Army* (1971), *The Ruling Class* (1972), *Theatre of Blood* (1973), *No Sex, Please - We're British* (1973), *O! Lucky Man* (1973), *Man About the House* (1974), *The Bawdy Adventures of Tom Jones* (1976), *The Lady Vanishes* (1979), *Sweet William* (1980) and his last film *Britannia Hospital* (1982). Probably best known for two parts on TV: Mr Swindley in *Coronation Street* - which garnered the only spin-off from that programme, *Pardon the Expression* - and Captain George Mainwaring in *Dad's Army*. His career was apparently hampered by his devotion to his wife Joan Cooper Lowe (23 August 1922 – 1 July 1989), whom he married in 1948 and insisted on appearing in his projects whenever possible. For example, she played Dolly, Private Godfrey's sister in some episodes of *Dad's Army*. Arthur died 15 April 1982, at the Alexandra Theatre, Birmingham whilst waiting to go on stage. Apparently the show and his widow went on. Arthur and Joan had a son, Stephen (b. 1953, Hammersmith), who wrote a biography of his father. See also entries in the television section for *A.J.Wentworth, BA, Bill Brand, Bless Me Father, Churchill's People, Coronation Street, Dad's Army, David Copperfield, Pardon The Expression, Potter,* and *Shades of Greene*.

Lucan, Arthur See entry in comedy section

Lupino, Ida (1918-95) Born 4 February 1918, Camberwell, London. Actress, director, producer and screenwriter. Daughter of comedian Stanley Lupino. Studied at RADA. Screen debut: *The Love Race* (1931). Other films include: *Her First Affaire* (1933) and after emigrating to America in 1933, *Paris in Spring* (1935), *Anything Goes* (1936) and *The Gay Desperado* (1936). She had been cast as a fragile ingenue until she played a fiery part in *The*

Light that Failed (1939) after which, despite continually refusing parts which had been turned down by the American star, she became, in her own words "the poor man's Bette Davis". Her later films include: *They Drive by Night* (1940), *The Sea Wolf* (1941), *High Sierra* (1941), *The Hard Way* (1943), *The Man I Love* (1947), *The Bigamist* (1953), *Women's Prison* (1955), *While the City Sleeps* (1956), *Junior Bonner* (1972) and her last film, *My Boys are Good Boys* (1978). She became an American citizen in 1948. In 1949 she took up directing, which at the time was a male-dominated profession, and formed an independent company, *The Filmakers*, with her then husband Collier Young, and began to direct, produce and write low budget films. In fact her directorial debut on *Not Wanted* (1949) was unintentional. The original director Elmer Clifton suffered a heart attack and could not finish the film and Ida stepped in as it was her production company. Other films include: *Never Fear* (1949), *Outrage* (1950), *Hard, Fast and Beautiful* (1951), *The Hitchhiker* (1953), making her the first woman to direct a film noir, and *The Bigamist* (1953). Ida now joked that if she had been the "poor man's Bette Davis" as an actress, then she had become the "poor man's Don Siegel" as a director. In 1952 Ida become the "fourth star" in *Four Star Productions* with Dick Powell, David Niven, and Charles Boyer, a television production company that was responsible for numerous hit series. Ida herself directed several episodes of popular television series' such as *The Untouchables, The Virginian, The Fugitive, Bewitched, Gilligan's Island, Alfred Hitchcock Presents, The Twilight Zone, Have Gun – Will Travel, 77 Sunset Strip, The Ghost & Mrs. Muir, The Rifleman, Batman, Sam Benedict, Bonanza,* and *Columbo*. Nicknamed Little Scout, she was married three times: to British actor Louis Hayward (1938–1945), film producer Collier Young (1948–1951) and American actor Howard Duff (1951–1984), with whom she had a daughter Bridget Duff (b. 23 April 1952). Ida died 3 August 1995, Los Angeles, California.

Lyne, Adrian (1941-) Born 4 March 1941, Peterborough, Cambridgeshire. Director. Began by directing television adverts. Big screen debut: *Foxes* (1980). In 1983 he directed the popular film about the welder who wants to be a dancer *Flashdance* (1983) and he followed that with the erotic drama *9½ Weeks* (1986). His most successful film to date has been another erotic thriller *Fatal Attraction* (1987) which gained him an Academy Award nomination for Best Director even though the version issued theatrically had an ending at odds with the one Lyne favoured. He eventually issued a director's cut. *Jacob's Ladder* (1990) proved a disappointment at the box office but his next project, *Indecent Proposal* (1993) was more successful. He subsequently directed a new adaptation of *Lolita* (1997) and remade the 1969 Claude Chabrol film *La Femme Infidele* as *Unfaithful* (2002) with Richard Gere and Diane Lane, who gained a Best Actress Academy Award nomination. Adrian is known as a visual stylist. His latest project, due for release in 2012, is *Back Roads*, a film about a young man stuck in the Pennsylvania backwoods caring for his three younger sisters after the shooting death of his abusive father and the arrest of his mother.

Macdonald, Kelly (1976-) Born 23 February 1976, Glasgow. Actress. Her film career began after she attended an open audition for *Trainspotting* (1996) whilst she was working as a barmaid before applying for drama school. As it was she got the part of Diane, Ewan McGregor's teenage seducer and her first feature film was released on her 20th birthday. Kelly has subsequently played a series of memorable roles including the lead as Stella in *Stella Does Tricks* (1996), Hortense Hulot in *Cousin Bette* (1998), Isabel Knollys in *Elizabeth* (1998), Laura in *Some Voices* (2000), Mary Maceachran in *Gosford Park* (2001) and Peter Pan in *Finding Neverland* (2004). She had a busy year in 2005 which saw the release of five films in which she featured: *The Hitchhiker's Guide to the Galaxy, A Cock and Bull Story, All the Invisible Children, Nanny McPhee,* and *Lassie*. She was nominated for a Best Supporting Actress BAFTA for her portrayal of Carla Jean Moss in *No Country for Old Men* (2007) and she followed this with roles in *The Merry Gentleman* (2008), *Choke* (2008) and *In the Electric Mist* (2009). Her other big screen appearances are: *My Life So Far* (1999), *Splendor* (1999), *The Loss of Sexual Innocence* (1999), *Entropy* (1999), *House!* (2000), *Two Family House* (2000), *Strictly Sinatra* (2001), *Intermission*

(2003), *The Decoy Bride* (2011) and *Harry Potter and the Deathly Hallows: Part II* (2011), in which she played the Grey Lady. In 2009 she appeared in the TV film *Skellig* based on the popular children's book by David Almond. Her other television work includes the min-series *State of Play* (2003) and the TV film *The Girl in the Café* (2005) plus the US series *Boardwalk Empire* (2010). She has been married to Dougie Payne from the group *Travis* since 2003. They have a son, Freddie Peter Payne (b. 9 March 2008).

MacKendrick, Alexander (1912-93) Born 8 September 1912, Boston, Massachusetts, United States. Director. On the death of his father in 1919 he was sent to Scotland to live with his grandfather. Studied at the Glasgow School of Art. Moved to London to work as an artist in advertising for J Walter Thomson, where he stayed throughout the 1930s. During WWII he worked on animated propaganda films for the Army Psychological Warfare Branch. In 1946 he formed *Merlin Productions* with his cousin Roger MacDougall but the company quickly fell into financial difficulties and he consequently found work at *Ealing Studios* as a production designer and scriptwriter. In the latter capacity he wrote the screenplay for *Saraband for Dead Lovers* (1948). His directorial debut was *Whisky Galore!* (1949). His next film *The Man in the White Suit* (1951) earned him an Academy Award nomination for Best Screenplay. The success of his next films *Mandy* (1952) about a deaf-mute girl, *The Maggie* (1954) set on the Clyde, and the classic black comedy *The Ladykillers* (1955) and the closure of Ealing Studios resulted in him being hired by *Hecht-Hill-Lancaster* to direct *Sweet Smell of Success* (1957). Although this film is now seen as his masterwork, and he elicited stunning performances from Burt Lancaster and Tony Curtis, at the time it was a box-office and critical disaster, being seen by many as un-American. After this he suffered more setbacks when he was removed from directing duties on both *The Devil's Disciple* (1959) and *The Guns of Navarone* (1961). His final films were *Sammy Going South* (1963), *A High Wind in Jamaica* (1965) and *Don't Make Waves* (1967). Alexander effectively retired from active film making to become Dean of the Film and Video School at the California Institute of Art (1969-78) and then professor (1978 until shortly before his death). He was married to Eileen Ashcroft (1934-43) and Hilary Lloyd, from 1948 until his death on 22 December 1993, Los Angeles, California.

Macnee, Patrick (1922-) Born Daniel Patrick Macnee, 6 February 1922, Paddington, London. Actor. Son of race-horse trainer Daniel "Shrimp" Macnee and great grandson of Scottish artist Sir Daniel Macnee. Raised by his mother Dorothea and her lesbian partner, who Patrick knew as "uncle Evelyn". He was educated at Eton and then trained at the Webber Douglas School of Dramatic Art. Stage debut: *Little Women* (1941). Served in Royal Navy during WWII. Appeared as an extra in *Pygmalion* (1938) and *The Life and Death of Colonel Blimp* (1943) before making his acting screen debut in *The Fatal Night* (1948). His early films in England include: *The Elusive Pimpernel* (1950), *Scrooge* (1951) as the young Jacob Marley, *The Battle of the River Plate* (1956) and *Les Girls* (1957). During this period he also spent a great deal of time pioneering the early days of Canadian television, appearing in more than 30 television plays. After spending time in Hollywood, he returned to the UK to star as John Steed in *The Avengers* (1960-1969), the series which made him a household name. A further series, *The New Avengers*, was made in 1976-77. He has made numerous television appearances on both sides of the Atlantic since the 1970s and has also featured in films including *King Solomon's Treasure* (1979), *The Sea Wolves* (1980), *Sweet Sixteen* (1983), *This is Spinal Tap* (1984), the Bond film *A View to a Kill* (1985), *Waxwork* (1988), *Transformations* (1988), *Masque of the Red Death* (1989), the wonderfully titled 1950s sci-fi film spoof *Lobster Man from Mars* (1979) where he played Professor Plocostomos, *Eye of the Widow* (1981), *Chill Factor* (1992) and *Waxwork II: Lost in Time* (1992). Patrick "appeared" as Invisible Jones in the disappointing big screen version of *The Avengers* (1998) and his latest film was *Low Budget Time Machine* (2003). Patrick, a passionate nudist, married three times, to: Barbara Douglas (1942-56), Katherine Woodville (1965-69) and Baba Nagyzsenye (1988-2007). The epitome of the English gentleman, he became a US citizen in 1959. His autobiography is *Blind in One Ear* (1988).

Magee, Patrick (1922-82) Born Patrick Joseph Gerard McGee, 31 March 1922, Armagh, County Armagh. Actor. Attended St Patrick's College, Armagh. Began acting in the 1950s and settled in London after arriving with a company run by Tyrone Guthrie. Joined the Royal Shakespeare Company in 1964. Screen debut: *The Criminal* (1960). A favourite actor of Samuel Beckett, he always concentrated more on his stage career than his celluloid one. Beckett wrote *Krapp's Last Tape* specifically for Magee, having heard him on the radio. Considered amongst Patrick's major screen successes were *The Servant* (1963), *Zulu* (1964), *Marat/Sade* (1967), *The Birthday Party* (1968), *King Lear* (1970), *A Clockwork Orange* (1971), *Barry Lyndon* (1975) and *Chariots of Fire* (1981). In many of his other films, which included more than a few in the horror genre, he played a villain. He also appeared in *Rag Doll* (1961), *Never Back Losers* (1961), *The Boys* (1962), *A Prize of Arms* (1962), *The Young Racers* (1963), *Operacija Ticijan* (1963), *Ricochet* (1963), *The Very Edge* (1963), *The Haunted and the Hunted* (1963), *Séance on a Wet Afternoon* (1964), *The Masque of the Red Death* (1964), *Portrait in Terror* (1965), *The Skull* (1965), *Die, Monster, Die!* (1965), *Anzio* (1968), *Decline and Fall of a Birdwatcher* (1968) *Hard Contract* (1969), *Cromwell* (1970), *You Can't Win 'Em All* (1970), *The Trojan Women* (1971), *The Fiend* (1971), *Tales from the Crypt* (1972), *Young Winston* (1972), *Asylum* (1972), *Pope Joan* (1972), *Demons of the Mind* (1972), *And Now the Screaming Starts!* (1973), *Lady Ice* (1973), *The Final Programme* (1975), *Telefon* (1977), *The Bronte Sisters* (1979), *The Monster Club* (1980), *Hawk the Slayer* (1980), *Rough Cut* (1980), *Sir Henry at Rawlinson End* (1980), *Dr. Jekyll and His Women* (1981) and his last film, *The Sleep of Death* (1981). Patrick died, after a heart-attack, on 14 August 1982 in Hammersmith, London. He was survived by his wife, Belle Sherry, also a native of County Armagh, and their two children, twins Mark and Caroline (b. February 1961, London).

Malleson, Miles (1888-1969) Born William Miles Malleson, 25 May 1888, Croydon, Surrey. Actor, playwright and screenwriter. He was educated at Brighton College and Emmanuel College, Cambridge, and trained at RADA. Miles appeared in almost 100 films, including some of the classics of British cinema. An excellent character actor, he specialised in eccentric and befuddled authority figures such as judges and academics. Stage debut: *Justice* (1911). Screen debut: *The Headmaster* (1921). Other films include: *The Sign of Four* (1932), *The 39 Steps* (1935), *Major Barbara* (1941), *Dead of Night* (1945), *Saraband for Dead Lovers* (1949), *The History of Mr Polly* (1949), *Kind Hearts and Coronets* (1949), *The Magic Box* (1951), *The Man in the White Suit* (1951), *Scrooge* (1951), *The Importance of Being Earnest* (1952), *Folly to be Wise* (1953), *King's Rhapsody* (1955), *Private's Progress* (1956), *Brothers in Law* (1957), *The Admirable Crichton* (1957), *I'm All Right Jack* (1959), *Kidnapped* (1960), *Peeping Tom* (1960), *Heavens Above!* (1963) and his last film, *You Must be Joking!* (1965). He eventually retired due to failing eyesight. In addition, his screenwriting credits include: *Nell Gwynne* (1934), *Peg of Old Drury* (1935), *Tudor Rose* (1936), *Victoria the Great* (1937), *Sixty Glorious Years* (1938) and *The Thief of Bagdad* (1940). He appeared in all these films and in particular he was a memorable sultan obsessed with mechanical toys in *The Thief of Bagdad*. Miles was also a prolific playwright, in many cases updating and adapting the plays of Moliere. He was a member of *Masses Stage and Film Guild* established by the Independent Labour Party in 1929 and his output included a play about the Tolpuddle Martyrs and others about WWI called *D Company* and *Black 'Ell*. He was married three times: actress Lady Constance Annesley (aka Colette O'Neil) (1915-23); doctor Joan Graeme Billson (1923-46) and Tatiana Lieven, from 1946 until his death on 15 March 1969 in Westminster, London.

Manville, Lesley (1956-) Born 12 March 1956, Brighton, East Sussex. Actress. Lesley trained as a soprano and apparently showed talent as a dancer too as she turned down an invitation to join Arlene Phillips' Hot Gossip dance troupe as she felt it was too risque. One of her earliest televison acting appearances was as Rosemary Kendall in *Emmerdale Farm* between 1974 and 1976. In the late 1970s and early 1980s she concentrated on stage work with first the Royal Shakespeare Company and then at the Royal Court and consequently had to wait until the mid 1980s for her big screen debut in *Dance with a Stranger* (1985). Her other films in this period were *High Season* (1987) and *Sammy and Rosie Get Laid* (1987). In 1980 she appeared in *Grown Ups* for the BBC and this began her long association with director Mike Leigh, with whom she has made the films *High Hopes* (1988), *Secrets & Lies* (1996), *Topsy-Turvy* (1999), *All or Nothing* (2002), *Vera Drake* (2004) and *Another Year* (2010), for which she received a BAFTA nomination for Best Supporting Actress. Her other big screen appearances are *Milk* (1999), *The Great Ecstasy of Robert Carmichael* (2005), *Richard Is My Boyfriend* (2005), *Sparkle* (2007) and *Womb* (2010). She also voiced Mrs Cratchit in the animated *A Christmas Carol* (2009). On television her most recent roles were as Margaret Thatcher in the Channel 4 docudrama, The Queen (2009) and as Phoebe Archbold in an episode of *Midsomer Murders*: "Fit for Murder" (2011). Lesley was married to actor Gary Oldman (1988-90), with whom she had a son, Alfie (b.1989), and actor Joe Dixon (1999-2002) but is currently single.

March, Jane (1973-) Born Jane March Horwood, 20 March 1973, Edgware, London. Actress. Initially a model she turned to acting, aged 19, and made a stunning star turn as the Young Girl in director Jean-Jacques Annaud's adaptation of Marguerite Duras' autobiographical novel *The Lover* (1992), after which, and thanks to some steamy sex scenes, she was thereafter dubbed "the sinner from Pinner". In 1993 she married Carmine Zozzora (a stalwart of Bruce Willis actioners and 14 years her senior). Willis was best man and Demi Moore was maid of honour, but alas they divorced in 2001. Her subsequent films include: *Color of Night* (1994), where she had the dubious distinction of being nominated for a Golden Raspberry (Razzie) for both Worst Actress and Worst Supporting Actress for the same movie in which she plays a triple role, *Never Ever* (1996), *Provocateur* (1998), *Tarzan and the Lost City* (1998), *Beauty and the Beast* (2003), *The Stone Merchant* (2006), *My Last Five Girlfriends* (2009), *Exposé* (2010), *Clash of the Titans* (2010), *Stalker* (2010) and *Will* (2011).

Margolyes, Miriam (1941-) Born 18 May 1941, Oxford, Oxfordshire. Actress. A character actress of more than 50 films she is remarkable both for her stature, just 5ft tall, and her range of voices that she brings to her parts. One of her first screen parts was in the TV mini-series *Fall of Eagles* (1974). Because of her non-Hollywood looks (she is quoted as saying "I'm not the sort of woman men boast of having slept with") she has never really been a leading actress always being brought in to add depth of character or a touch of class to proceedings. For the 1993 film *The Age of Innocence* she won a BAFTA for Best Supporting Actress. As with most British character actors she has had a role in the Harry Potter series playing Professor Sprout in *Harry Potter and the Chamber of Secrets* (2002) and *Harry Potter and the Deathly Hallows: Part II* (2011). A major fan of Charles Dickens she appeared in Peter Ackroyd's TV *Dickens* (2002) as his wife Catherine and also presented the four-part series *Dickens in America* in 2005. Her other films include: *On the Game* (1974), *Rime of the Ancient Mariner* (1975), *The Battle of Billy's Pond* (1976), *Stand Up, Virgin Soldiers* (1977), *On a Paving Stone Mounted* (1978), *Star Rock* (1980), *The Awakening* (1980), *Reds* (1981), *Crystal Gazing* (1982), *Scrubbers* (1983), *Yentl* (1983), *Electric Dreams* (1984), *Morons from Outer Space* (1985), *The Good Father* (1985), *Little Shop of Horrors* (1986), *Body Contact* (1987), *Little Dorrit* (1988), *I Love You to Death* (1990), *Pacific Heights* (1990), *The Fool* (1990), *Dead Again* (1991), *The Butcher's Wife* (1991), *As You Like It* (1992), *Bon Appetit, Mama* (1993), *The Age of Innocence* (1993), *Immortal Beloved* (1994), *Different for Girls* (1996), *Romeo + Juliet* (1996), *Left Luggage* (1998), *Candy* (1998), *Dreaming of Joseph Lees* (1999), *End of Days* (1999), *Magnolia* (1999), *Sunshine* (1999), *House!* (2000), *Cats & Dogs* (2001), *Not Afraid, Not Afraid* (2001), *Alone* (2002),

Plotz with a View (2002), *Being Julia* (2004), *Chasing Liberty* (2004), *Ladies in Lavender* (2004), *Modigliani* (2004), *The Life and Death of Peter Sellers* (2004), *The Dukes* (2007), *How to Lose Friends & Alienate People* (2008) and *A Closed Book* (2010). She has also lent her voice to the following films: *The Princess and the Cobbler* (1993), *Babe* (1995), *Balto* (1995), *James and the Giant Peach* (1996), *Mulan* (1998), *Babe: Pig in the City* (1998), *Flushed Away* (2006), *Happy Feet* (2006) and *Legend of the Guardians: The Owls of Ga'Hoole* (2010). Openly gay, Miriam has been with her partner for over 40 years. She is also one of those select band of celebrities who has appeared on the television quiz show *University Challenge*, whilst at Cambridge University in 1963. See also entries in the television section for *Blackadder II, The Blackadder, The History Man, A Kick Up the Eighties, The Life and Loves of a She Devil,* and *University Challenge.*

Marriott, Moore (1885-1949) Born George Thomas Moore Marriott, 14 September 1885, West Drayton, Middlesex. Actor. Born into a theatrical family from Birmingham. Made his first stage appearances as a child. Recordings of his early films are lost along with Cecil Hepworths' negatives but his known screen debut is *By the Shortest of Heads* (1915). Other early films include *Lawyer Quince* (1924), *Every Mother's Son* (1926) and *Sweeney Todd* (1928). In *The Gold Cure* (1925) he played Janbois who was a sort of prototype for the old man character roles he played so well during the 1930s and 1940s in such films as *The Flying Scotsman* (1929), *Turn of the Tide* (1935), *Green for Danger* (1946) and *The Root of All Evil* (1947). He is best known for playing the marvellous cunning toothless old codger Jeremiah Harbottle, who was first introduced in the Will Hay comedy *Windbag the Sailor* (1936) alongside Hay and Graham Moffatt as Young Albert. The trio were reunited in *Oh, Mr Porter!* (1937), *Old Bones of the River* (1938), *Ask a Policeman* (1939), *Convict 99* (1939) and *Where's That Fire?* (1940) before Hay went his own way for good. Moore went on to support other comedians including Arthur Askey and The Crazy Gang. His final films include: *Millions Like Us* (1943), *The Hills of Donegal* (1947), *The History of Mr Polly* (1949) and his last film, *High Jinks in Society* (1949). He died 11 December 1949 Chichester, West Sussex.

Marshall, Herbert (1890-1966) Born Herbert Brough Falcon Marshall, 23 May 1890, Regent's Park, London. Actor. Son of Percy Marshall, an actor and grandson of painter Thomas Falcon Marshall. Began working as an accountant before taking up acting. Stage debut: *The Adventure of Lady Ursula* (1911). Herbert served during WWI, losing his right leg in action and having a prosthetic limb fitted. Screen debut: *Mumsie* (1927). His polished style combined with his cultured tones saw him feature in films covering everything from comedy, such as *Trouble in Paradise* (1932), to thriller, *Foreign Correspondent* (1940), drama, *The Little Foxes* (1941), Western, *Duel in the Sun* (1946), historical, *The Virgin Queen* (1955), and science fiction with *The Fly* (1958). In a career spanning 40 years he developed from a romantic lead into a distinguished character actor. His other films include: *The Letter* (1929), *Murder!* (1930), *Michael and Mary* (1931), *Secrets of a Secretary* (1931), *The Calendar* (1931), *Blonde Venus* (1932), *Evenings for Sale* (1932), *The Faithful Heart* (1932), *I Was a Spy* (1933), *The Solitaire Man* (1933), *Four Frightened People* (1934), *Outcast Lady* (1934), *Riptide* (1934), *The Painted Veil* (1934), *Accent on Youth* (1935), *If You Could Only Cook* (1935), *The Dark Angel* (1935), *The Flame Within* (1935), *The Good Fairy* (1935), *A Woman Rebels* (1936), *Girls' Dormitory* (1936), *Make Way for a Lady* (1936), *The Lady Consents* (1936), *Till We Meet Again* (1936), *Forgotten Faces* (1936), *Angel* (1937), *Breakfast for Two* (1937), *Always Goodbye* (1938), *Mad About Music* (1938), *Woman Against Woman* (1938), *Zaza* (1938), *Bill of Divorcement* (1940), *The Letter* (1940), *Female Correspondent* (1941), *Kathleen* (1941), *When Ladies Meet* (1941), *The Moon and Sixpence* (1942), *Flight for Freedom* (1943), *Forever and a Day* (1943), *Young Ideas* (1943), *Andy Hardy's Blonde Trouble* (1944), *The Enchanted Cottage* (1945), *The Picture of Dorian Gray* (1945), *The Unseen* (1945), *Crack-Up* (1946), *Monuments of the Past* (1946), *The Razor's Edge* (1946), *High Wall* (1947), *Ivy* (1947), *The Secret Garden* (1949), *Black Jack* (1950), *The Underworld Story* (1950), *Anne of the*

Indies (1951), *Angel Face* (1952), *Gog* (1954), *Riders to the Stars* (1954), *The Black Shield of Falworth* (1954), *Wicked as They Come* (1956), *The Weapon* (1957), *Stage Struck* (1958), *College Confidential* (1960), *Midnight Lace* (1960), *A Fever in the Blood* (1961), *Five Weeks in a Balloon* (1962), *Borderlines* (1963), *The List of Adrian Messenger* (1963) and his last film, *The Third Day* (1965). Herbert's lack of a right leg didn't seem to hamper either his professional career or his personal life as he was married five times: Mollie Maitland (1915-28), British actress Edna Best (1928-40), Lee Russell (1940-47), American actress Patricia 'Boots' Mallory (1947-58) and Dee Anne Kaufmann, from 1960 until his death on 22 January 1966, Beverly Hills, California.

Mason, James (1909-84) Born James Neville Mason, 15 May 1909, Huddersfield, West Yorkshire. Actor. Gained a first class degree in architecture from Peterhouse, Cambridge, before taking up an acting profession, initially at the Old Vic and the Gate Theatre, Dublin. Stage debut: *The Rascal* (1931). Screen debut: *Late Extra* (1935). Made over 100 films. Other early films include: *Twice Branded* (1936), *Blind Man's Bluff* (1936), *The Mill on the Floss* (1937), *The Return of the Scarlet Pimpernel* (1938) and *Hatter's Castle* (1941). He eventually made his mark in films - almost literally on Margaret Lockwood - in *The Man in Grey* (1943) and followed this up by playing brutish characters in other costume dramas: *Fanny by Gaslight* (1944) and *The Wicked Lady* (1945). Excellent performances in *The Seventh Veil* (1945) and *Odd Man Out* (1947) lead to him moving to Hollywood. Here his films include: *The Desert Fox* (1951) - as Rommel - *The Prisoner of Zenda* (1952) – as Rupert of Hentzau - *Julius Caesar* (1953) - as Brutus - *The Desert Rats* (1953) - again as Rommel and *Bigger than Life* (1956). He starred in two adaptations of Jules Verne: *20,000 Leagues Under the Sea* (1954) and *Journey to the Centre of the Earth* (1959). His later films include: *North by Northwest* (1959), *Lolita* (1962), *Tiara Tahiti* (1962), *The Pumpkin Eater* (1964), *Genghis Khan* (1965), *Mayerling* (1968), *Spring and Port Wine* (1970), *Murder by Decree* (1979), *The Shooting Party* (1984) and his last feature film *The Assisi Underground* (1985). His last screen appearance was in the title role in the BBC TV film, *Dr Fischer of Geneva*, broadcast in October 2005. James was nominated for a Best Actor Academy Award for *A Star is Born* (1954) and for Best Supporting Actor Academy Awards for *Georgy Girl* (1966) and *The Verdict* (1982). Autobiography: *Before I Forget* (1981). He was married twice, firstly to Pamela Ostrer (1941-64), the daughter of Isidore Ostrer,who was one time head of the *Gaumont-British Picture Corporation*. They had a daughter, Portland Mason Schuyler (1948–2004), and a son, Morgan (b. 26 June 1955), a former Acting Chief of Protocol of the United States who married singer Belinda Carlisle in 1986. James' second marriage was to Australian actress Clarissa Knipe (1931-94 – worked as Clarissa Kaye), from 1971 until his death on 27 July 1984, Lausanne, Switzerland. James ashes are buried in Vevey in the Vaud canton of Switzerland, a few tombs away from his old friend Charlie Chaplin. See also entries in the television section for *Jesus of Nazareth, The Search for the Nile,* and *Stars On Sunday.*

Massey, Anna (1937-2011) Born Anna Raymond Massey, 11 August 1937, Thakeham, West Sussex. Actress. Anna was the daughter of British actress Adrianne Allen (1907-93) and Canadian-born Hollywood actor Raymond Massey. Her brother, Daniel Massey, was also an actor. She was the niece of Vincent Massey (1887-1967), a former Governor General of Canada. Her father returned to the United States whilst she was a child, leaving her to be raised in England by her mother. Stage debut: *The Reluctant Debutante* (1955). Made her screen debut in *Gideon's Day* (1958) before playing Helen Stephens in the controversial *Peeping Tom* (1960). Her other films include: *The Trip to Biarritz* (1963), *Bunny Lake Is Missing* (1965), *De Sade* (1969), *The Looking Glass War* (1969), *Frenzy* (1972), *The Vault of Horror* (1973), *A Doll's House* (1973), *A Little Romance* (1979), *Sweet William* (1980), *Five Days One Summer* (1982), *Another Country* (1984), *The Chain* (1984), *The Little Drummer Girl* (1984), *Sacred Hearts* (1985), *Foreign Body* (1986), *La Couleur du Vent* (1988), *The Tall Guy* (1989), *Killing Dad or How to Love Your*

Mother (1990), *Mountains of the Moon* (1990), *Impromptu* (1991), *Emily's Ghost* (1992), *Angels and Insects* (1995), *Haunted* (1995), *The Grotesque* (1995), *Sweet Angel Mine* (1996), *Déjà Vu* (1997), *Driftwood* (1997), *The Slab Boys* (1997), *Captain Jack* (1999), *Mad Cows* (1999), *Room to Rent* (2000), *Dark Blue World* (2001), *Possession* (2002), *The Importance of Being Earnest* (2002), *The Machinist* (2004), *Mrs Palfrey at The Claremont* (2005), *The Gigolos* (2006), *The Oxford Murders* (2008) and her last film, *Affinity* (2008). Equally adept on stage or film she also has a long list of television film credits including classics such as *A Midsummer Night's Dream* (1964 - as Titania), *David Copperfield* (1969 - as Jane Murdstone), *Rebecca* (1979 - as Mrs Danvers), *The Cherry Orchard* (1981 – as Charlotte), *Mansfield Park* (1983 – as Aunt Norris) and *Anna Karenina* (1985 – as Betsy). Perhaps her finest TV performance was as Edith Hope in *Hotel du Lac* (1986). Her most recent project was narrating the radio series *This Sceptered Isle.* Anna was awarded the CBE in 2005 and wrote an autobiography, *Telling Some Tales* (2006). Married to actor Jeremy Brett (1958-1962) and Russian professor of metallurgy Uri Andres, from 1990 until her death, from cancer, on 3 July 2011, London. See also entries in the television section for *Churchill's People, Love Story, The Mayor of Casterbridge, The Pallisers,* and *The Robinsons.*

Massey, Daniel (1933-98) Born Daniel Raymond Massey, 10 October 1933, Westminster, London. Actor. Educated at Eton and Kings College, Cambridge. His screen debut was as Bobby Kinross, the son of Noël Coward's character in *In Which We Serve* (1942). He went on to play Coward in the Gertrude Lawrence bio-pic *Star!* (1968) for which he was nominated for an Academy Award as Best Supporting Actor. His other films were *Girls at Sea* (1958), *Operation Bullshine* (1959), *Upstairs and Downstairs* (1959), *The Entertainer* (1960), *The Queen's Guards* (1961), *Go to Blazes* (1962), *The Amorous Adventures of Moll Flanders* (1965), *The Jokers* (1967), *Mary, Queen of Scots* (1971), *The Vault of Horror* (1973), *The Incredible Sarah* (1976), *The Devil's Advocate* (1977), *The Cat and the Canary* (1978), *Warlords of Atlantis* (1978), *Bad Timing* (1980), *Escape to Victory* (1981), *Scandal* (1989), *In the Name of the Father* (1993) and his last film, released two years after his death, *The Miracle Maker* (2000). Daniel was also an accomplished stage actor, particularly in musical theatre. Married to actresses Adrienne Corri (1961-67) and Penelope Wilton (1975-84) and also Penelope's sister Linda Wilton, from 1984 until his death on 25 March 1998, Kensington, London. See also entry for Anna Massey.

Matthews, A E (1869-1960) Born Alfred Edward Matthews, 22 November 1869, Bridlington, Yorkshire. Actor. Great-nephew of Tom Matthews, *The Clown of Drury Lane.* His father William Matthews was a member of the Matthews Brothers troupe. He was known as "Matty" to his friends. Stage debut: *The Noble Vagabond* (1886). He shared the role of Mr Darling in the original staging of *Peter Pan* (1904) and did not seriously concentrate on film work until the 1930s. Screen debut: *Wanted: a Widow* (1916). His other films include: *The Real Thing at Last* (1916), *The Lifeguardsman* (1916), *Once Upon a Time* (1918), *Castle of Dreams* (1919), *The Lackey and the Lady* (1919), *The Iron Duke* (1934), *Men Are Not Gods* (1936), *'Pimpernel' Smith* (1941), *Quiet Wedding* (1941), *This England* (1941), *The Great Mr Handel* (1942), *Thunder Rock* (1942), *Escape to Danger* (1943), *The Life and Death of Colonel Blimp* (1943), *The Man in Grey* (1943), *Love Story* (1944), *The Way Ahead* (1944), *They Came to a City* (1944), *Flight from Folly* (1945), *Twilight Hour* (1945), *Piccadilly Incident* (1946), *Just William's Luck* (1947), *The Ghosts of Berkeley Square* (1947), *William Comes to Town* (1948), *Britannia Mews* (1949), *Edward, My Son* (1949), *Landfall* (1949), *The Chiltern Hundreds* (1949), *Whisky Galore* (1949), *Laughter in Paradise* (1951), *Mister Drake's Duck* (1951), *The Galloping Major* (1951), *Penny Princess* (1952), *Something Money Can't Buy* (1952), *The Magic Box* (1952), *Who Goes There!* (1952), *Castle in the Air* (1952), *Made in Heaven* (1953), *Skid Kids* (1953), *Aunt Clara* (1954), *Happy Ever After* (1954), *The Million Pound Note* (1954), *The Weak and the Wicked* (1954), *Miss Tulip Stays the Night* (1955), *Around the World in Eighty*

Days (1956), *Jumping for Joy* (1956), *Loser Takes All* (1956), *Three Men in a Boat* (1956), *Carry on Admiral* (1957), *Doctor at Large* (1957) and his last film, *Inn for Trouble* (1960). He featured in a BBC television sitcom *The Skylarks* (1958) some of which was shot on location on the *HMS Ark Royal*. As usual he played a character noted for their irascibility. He worked into his nineties, once saying, and often repeated by numerous showbiz personalities ever since, "I always wait for *The Times* each morning. I look at the obituary column and if I'm not in it, I go to work." In 1958 he staged a sit-down protest outside his house to prevent the local council from putting up a concrete lamp-post. The incident inspired an episode of *The Goon Show: The Evils of Bushey Spon* (1958) in which Matthews made an unforgettable appearance in the final few minutes in which he literally lost the plot and went off on an unscripted tangent about himself and his plight. Cary Grant once said he patterned his early persona on a combination of Matthews, Noël Coward and Jack Buchanan. He was managing director of the *British Actor's Film Company* (1917-18). Awarded the OBE in 1951. Autobiography: *Matty* (1953). He died 25 July 1960, Bushey Heath, Hertfordshire.

Matthews, Jessie (1907-81) Born Jessie Margaret Matthews, 11 March 1907, Soho, London. Actress and singer. Her early career included dancing in the street to a barrel-organ. Stage debut: *The Music Box Revue* (1923). Screen debut: *The Beloved Vagabond* (1923). Apart from a couple of films such as *This England* (1923) and *Straws in the Wind* (1924) she spent the 1920s on the stage, building a career in musical revues where she became the first performer of numerous popular songs of the period, including *A Room with a View* and *London Calling!* by Noël Coward and *Let's Do It, Let's Fall in Love* by Cole Porter. She eventually made a return to the screen in *Out of the Blue* (1931) and became one of the top box-office draws during the 1930s in such films as *There Goes the Bride* (1932), *The Good Companions* (1933) and *Friday the Thirteenth* (1933). Her best known films are probably *Evergreen* (1934), *First a Girl* (1935) - later remade as *Victor/Victoria* (1982) - and *Head Over Heels* (1937). Jessie's other films were: *The Midshipmaid* (1932), *The Man from Toronto* (1933), *Waltzes from Vienna* (1933), *It's Love Again* (1936), *Gangway* (1937), *Climbing High* (1938), *Sailing Along* (1938), *Forever and a Day* (1943), *Candles at Nine* (1944), *Tom Thumb* (1958) and her last film, *The Hound of the Baskervilles* (1978). Her screen career drifted away with the onset of the 1940s and she eventually found a new career on radio playing Mrs Dale in *Mrs Dale's Diary* (1963-69). Married three times, to Lord Henry Lytton (1926-29), actor Sonnie Hale (1931-43), and Brian Lewis (1945-59). She was known as "The Dancing Divinity" and was awarded the OBE in 1970. Autobiography: *Over My Shoulder* (1974). Jessie died 19 August 1981, Hillingdon, London. See also entries in the radio and television section for *Edward and Mrs Simpson*, and *Mrs Dale's Diary*.

McAnally, Ray (1926-89) Born 30 March 1926, Buncrana, County Donegal, Ireland. Actor. The son of a bank manager, he was educated at St. Eunan's College in Letterkenny where he wrote, produced and staged a musical, *Madame Screwball*, when he was 16. He entered a seminary at the age of 18, but left shortly after when he realised that the priesthood was not his vocation. He joined the Abbey Theatre in 1947. After years of repertory theatre he made his feature debut in *Professor Tim* (1957). Other early films include: *She Didn't Say No!* (1958), *Sea of Sand* (1958), *Shake Hands with the Devil* (1959), *Murder in Eden* (1961), *The Naked Edge* (1961), *Billy Budd* (1962) and *He Who Rides a Tiger* (1965). On television he was already a familiar face, having appeared in episodes of glossy thriller series like *Gideon's Way*, *The Avengers*, *The Human Jungle* and *Man in a Suitcase*. In 1968 he won many plaudits for his role of gangland boss Alec Spindoe in the ITV series *Spindoe*. He followed this with the film *The Looking Glass War* (1969) but although his film career now looked assured Ray decided to concentrate on the theatre throughout the 1970s and early 1980s with a sprinkling of television appearances in the popular fare of the day such as *The Strange Report*, *Paul Temple*, *The Troubleshooters*, *The Mind of Mr. J.G. Reeder*, *Me Mammy*, *Barlow*, *Dial M for Murder*, *Public Eye*, *Crown Court*, and *Dick Turpin*. Whilst at the Abbey, Ray met actress Ronnie Masterson (b. 4 April 1926, Dublin, Ireland) and they married in 1951 and later formed Old Quay Productions

to present an assortment of classic plays throughout this period. Ray's role as Cardinal Altamirano in the highly acclaimed film *The Mission* (1986) won him a BAFTA, and began a second career for him as a film star. His subsequent films include: *White Mischief* (1987), *The Fourth Protocol* (1987), *The Sicilian* (1987), *My Left Foot* (1989), for which he won a posthumous BAFTA, and his last film, *We're No Angels* (1989). Ray was then due to play "Bull McCabe" in Jim Sheridan's 1990 film *The Field*, but died suddenly of a heart attack on 15 June 1989, at the home he shared with Irish actress Britta Smith in County Wicklow, he and his wife now living apart. Ray had four children with his wife; Conor, Aongus, Máire and Niamh, two of which work in showbusiness and one daughter became a nun. Ray was possibly an even bigger star on television. See entries in the television section for *The Fellows*, *The Man in Room 17*, *Me Mammy*, *A Perfect Spy*, *Pollyanna*, *Spindoe*, and *A Very British Coup*.

McAvoy, James (1979-) Born 21 April 1979, Scotstoun, Glasgow. Actor. Graduated from the Royal Scottish Academy of Music and Drama in 2000. Stage debut: *The Tempest*. Screen debut: *The Near Room* (1995). His other big screen efforts to date are: *Regeneration* (1997), *Swimming Pool* (2001), *Bollywood Queen* (2002), *Bright Young Things* (2003), *Inside I'm Dancing* (2004), *Strings* (2004), *Wimbledon* (2004), *The Chronicles of Narnia: The Lion, the Witch and the Wardrobe* (2005), *Penelope* (2006), *Starter for 10* (2006), *The Last King of Scotland* (2006), *Atonement* (2007), *Becoming Jane* (2007), *Wanted* (2008), *The Last Station* (2009), *The Conspirator* (2010), *Gnomeo & Juliet* (2011), *X-Men: First Class* (2011 - as Professor Charles Xavier / Professor X) and the voice of the title role in *Arthur Christmas* (2011). He won the BAFTA for Rising Star in 2006 and was nominated Best Actor in a Supporting Role in 2007 for *The Last King of Scotland* and for Best Actor in a Lead Role in 2008 for *Atonement*. He has been married to actress Anne-Marie Duff since 2006, and they have a son, Andrew (b. 2010). See also entries in the television section for *Early Doors*, *Shameless*, and *State of Play*.

McCallum, David (1933-) Born David Keith McCallum, 19 September 1933, Glasgow. Actor. His father, David McCallum Sr., was first violinist for the London Philharmonic and his mother, Dorothy Dorman, was a cellist, so it is not surprising that he was originally headed for a career as an oboeist, studying briefly at the Royal Academy of Music before training to be an actor at RADA. David worked in the props department of the Glyndebourne Opera for a season. He served with the Royal West African Frontier Force in Ghana (1951-53). He was signed up by the Rank Organisation in 1957 after acting in provincial repertory. Screen debut: *Ill Met by Moonlight* (1957), as an uncredited sailor. His other early films include his first credited role as Mike Wilson in, *The Secret Place* (1957), *Hell Drivers* (1957), *Robbery Under Arms* (1957), *These Dangerous Years* (1957), *A Night to Remember* (1958), *Violent Playground* (1958), *Jungle Street* (1961), *Karolina Rijecka* (1961), *The Long and the Short and the Tall* (1961), *Billy Budd* (1962), *Freud* (1962) and *The Great Escape* (1963). In 1964 he was picked for the televisin role by which he is best known to older audiences, Illya Nickovetch Kuryakin in *The Man from U.N.C.L.E.* (1964-68) and he went on to play him in the spin-off films *To Trap a Spy* (1964), *The Spy with My Face* (1965), *The Spy in the Green Hat* (1966), *One Spy too Many* (1966), *One of Our Spies is Missing* (1966), *The Karate Killers* (1967), *How to Steal the World* (1968) and *The Helicopter Spies* (1968). He also played Judas Iscariot in *The Greatest Story Ever Told* (1965) and Squadron Leader Munroe in *Mosquito Squadron* (1969). His other films to date are: *Around the World Under the Sea* (1966), *Three Bites of the Apple* (1967), *The Heroin Gang* (1968), *Dogs* (1976), *The Kingfisher Caper* (1976), *King Solomon's Treasure* (1979), *The Watcher in the Woods* (1980), *Terminal Choice* (1985), *The Haunting of Morella* (1990), *Hear My Song* (1991), *Dirty Weekend* (1993), *Fatal Inheritance* (1993), *Healer* (1994) and *Cherry* (1999). Along with an active theatre career he has tended to concentrate on television work since the 1960s. His recent work includes Dr Donald "Ducky" Mallard in *NCIS* (2003-present) and he supplied the voice of Paradox in the children's animation *Ben 10* (2008-10). He reprised the role of Kuryakin in *The Return of the Man from U.N.C.L.E.* (1983). Married to actress Jill Ireland (1957-67) (see separate entry) and Katherine Carpenter (1967-present). See also entries in the television section for *Cluedo*, *Colditz*, *The Invisible Man*, *Mother Love*, *Our Mutual Friend*, *Sapphire and Steel*, *Sir Francis Drake*, and *Trainer*.

McClure, Vicky (1983-) Born 8 May 1983, Nottingham. Actress. Vicky made her screen debut as Ladine Brass in the Shane Meadows film *A Room for Romeo Brass* (1999). Her character was the sister of the eponymous hero, played by Andrew Shim. After appearing in the TV film *Tough Love* (2002 – as Zoe Love), opposite Ray Winstone, she again teamed up with Shane Meadows and Andrew Shim in the highly-acclaimed feature *This is England* (2006 – as Lol). Her next film role was as Juliette in the comedy feature *Filth and Wisdom* (2008), famous for being the directorial debut of pop legend Madonna. More recently, Vicky has reprised her role as Lol in the four-episode Channel 4 spin-off *This is England '86*, set three years later, but this time Vicky taking the lead, although Andrew Shim (Milky), Thomas Turgoose (Shaun) and Stephen Graham (Combo) also reappear. For this role she won the Best Actress Award at the 2011 BAFTAs. Another three-episode sequel, *This is England '88*, were shown on channel 4 in 2011. Vicky has also featured in several of *Plan B*'s music videos, notably "She Said", one of the UK's top-selling singles of 2010. See also entries in the television section for *Five Daughters* and *This is England '86*.

McCrory, Helen (1968-) Born 17 August 1968, London. Actress. Studied drama at the University of the Arts, London. Helen made her screen debut in the TV series *Full Stretch* (1993) and her feature film debut in *Interview with the Vampire: The Vampire Chronicles* (1994). Other films include: *Uncovered* (1995), *Streetlife* (1995), *The James Gang* (1997), *Dad Savage* (1998), *Hotel Splendide* (2000), *Charlotte Gray* (2001), *The Count of Monte Cristo* (2002), *Enduring Love* (2004), *Casanova* (2005 - as Casanova's mother), *Becoming Jane* (2007), *Flashbacks of a Fool* (2008), *Fantastic Mr. Fox* (2009 - voice of Mrs Bean), *4.3.2.1.* (2010) and *Hugo* (2011). She has recently completed filming her role as Clair Dowar in the forthcoming Bond movie, *Skyfall* (2012). Helen portrayed Cherie Blair in both the 2006 film *The Queen* and the 2010 film *The Special Relationship*. She also portrayed Narcissa Malfoy in *Harry Potter and the Half-Blood Prince* (2009), *Harry Potter and the Deathly Hallows: Part I* (2010) and *Harry Potter and the Deathly Hallows: Part II* (2011). Helen was originally cast as Bellatrix Lestrange in *Harry Potter and the Order of the Phoenix* (2007) but had to pull out due to pregnancy. In 2002, she was nominated for a London Evening Standard Theatre Award for Best Actress for playing Elena in Chekhov's *Uncle Vanya* at the Donmar Warehouse. See also entry for her husband Damian Lewis and entries in the television section for *Full Stretch*, and *North Square*.

McDowall, Roddy (1928-1998) Born Roderick Andrew Anthony Jude McDowall, 17 September 1928, Herne Hill, London. Actor and director. A child star who progressed successfully into adult roles. His screen debut was as an uncredited bit part player in *Sarah Siddons* (1938). His first credited role was as Peter Osborne in *Murder in the Family* (1938). His pre-Hollywood films were: *Yellow Sands* (1938), *Scruffy* (1938), *Hey! Hey! USA* (1938), *I See Ice* (1938), *John Halifax* (1938), *Convict 99* (1938), *Dirt* (1939), *The Outsider* (1939), *Dead Man's Shoes* (1939), *Poison Pen* (1940), *His Brother's Keeper* (1940), *Murder Will Out* (1940), *Just William* (1940), *Saloon Bar* (1940), *You Will Remember* (1941), *Man Hunt* (1941) *and This England* (1941). Roddy travelled to America, aged 12, to appear in *How Green was my Valley* (1941) and remained there to play in: *Confirm or Deny* (1941), *Son of Fury: The Story of Benjamin Blake* (1942), *On the Sunny Side* (1942), *The Pied Piper* (1942), *My Friend Flicka* (1943), *Lassie Come Home* (1943), *The White Cliffs of Dover* (1944) and *The Keys of the Kingdom* (1944). His other films in this period were: *Thunderhead, Son of Flicka* (1945), *Molly and Me* (1945), *Holiday in Mexico* (1946), *Rocky* (1948), *Macbeth* (1948), *Kidnapped* (1948), *Tuna Clipper* (1949), *Black Midnight* (1949), *Killer Shark* (1950), *and The Steel Fist* (1952). Roddy concentrated more on stage and television work in the 1950s before returning to the big screen with *The Subterraneans* (1960)

and *Midnight Lace* (1960). He played Octavian in *Cleopatra* (1963) and during breaks in production took a part in another Fox production *The Longest Day* (1962). He apparently lost out on an Academy Award nomination as Best Supporting Actor for *Cleopatra* because 20th Century Fox had listed him as a leading player. He famously played the chimpanzees Cornelius and Caesar in the series of films based upon *Planet of the Apes* (1968) – *Beneath the Planet of the Apes* (1970), *Escape from the Planet of the Apes* (1971), *Conquest of the Planet of the Apes* (1972) *and Battle for the Planet of the Apes* (1973). He played Galen in the subsequent television series. Amongst a heavy workload of television work his later films were: *Shock Treatment* (1964), *The Greatest Story Ever Told* (1965), *The Third Day* (1965), *The Loved One* (1965), *That Darn Cat!* (1965), *Inside Daisy Clover* (1965), *Lord Love a Duck* (1966), *The Defector* (1966), *It!* (1966), *The Adventures of Bullwhip Griffin* (1967), *The Cool Ones* (1967), *5 Card Stud* (1968), *Midas Run* (1969), *Hello Down There* (1969), *Angel, Angel, Down We Go* (1969), *Pretty Maids All in a Row* (1971), *Bedknobs and Broomsticks* (1971), *The Poseidon Adventure* (1972), *The Life and Times of Judge Roy Bean* (1972), *The Legend of Hell House* (1973), *Arnold* (1973), *Dirty Mary, Crazy Larry* (1974), *Funny Lady* (1975), *Mean Johnny Barrows* (1976), *Embryo* (1976), *Sixth and Main* (1977), *Laserblast* (1978), *Rabbit Test* (1978), *The Cat from Outer Space* (1978), *Circle of Iron* (1978), *Scavenger Hunt* (1979), *Charlie Chan and the Curse of the Dragon Queen* (1981), *Evil Under the Sun* (1982), *Class of 1984* (1982), *Fright Night* (1985), *Dead of Winter* (1987), *Overboard* (1987), *Doin' Time on Planet Earth* (1988), *Fright Night II* (1988), *Heroes Stand Alone* (1989), *Cutting Class* (1989), *The Big Picture* (1989), *Shakma* (1990), *Going Under* (1990), *The Naked Target* (1992), *Double Trouble* (1992), *The Evil Inside Me* (1993), *Angel 4: Undercover* (1993), *The Color of Evening* (1994), *Mirror, Mirror 2: Raven Dance* (1994), *Star Hunter* (1995), *The Grass Harp* (1995), *Last Summer in the Hamptons* (1995), *It's My Party* (1996), *The Second Jungle Book: Mowgli & Baloo* (1997) *and Something to Believe In* (1998). His last role was as the voice of Mr Soil in *A Bug's Life* (1998). He was also a director, making his debut in *Tam-Lin* (1970) starring Ava Gardner, and a very accomplished, published photographer. The Academy of Motion Picture Arts and Sciences has named it's photo archive in his honour. Roddy was involved in several Batman ventures. He played a 'guest' villain, the Bookworm, in the 1960s TV series *Batman* and had a recurring role as The Mad Hatter in *Batman: The Animated Series* as well as lending his voice to the audio adaptation of the 1989 *Batman* film. Roddy died 3 October 1998, Los Angeles, California. He never married.

McDowell, Malcolm (1943-) Born Malcolm John Taylor, 13 June 1943, Horsforth, Leeds. Actor. Attended Tunbridge Boarding School and the London Academy of Music and Art. He worked at a variety of jobs, including selling coffee and messenger boy, before taking up acting as a profession. His first screen role was as Crispin Ryder in *Crossroads* (1964). What should have been his big screen debut as Billy in *Poor Cow* (1967) was left on the cutting room floor. The result was that he burst onto the screen as Mick Travis in the Lindsay Anderson directed *if....* (1968). He was to play different characters also called Mick Travis in two later Anderson films *O Lucky Man!* (1973) and *Britannia Hospital* (1982). From this auspicious start he went on to star as Alex DeLarge in Stanley Kubrick's controversial classic *A Clockwork Orange* (1971). His next films *Royal Flash* (1975), *Aces High* (1976) and *Voyage of the Damned* (1976) failed to raise the same spark as his early work. He then played the title role in *Caligula* (1979) which had been turned into a soft-porn epic by the time it reached the screen. In 1979 he starred as H G Wells in a time-travelling Jack the Ripper romance called *Time After Time*, which also starred his future wife Mary Steenburgen, but this venture failed to create much interest at the box-office. His other early films were: *Figures in a Landscape* (1970), *The Raging Moon* (1971), *The Passage* (1979), *Cat People* (1982), *Blue Thunder* (1983), *Cross Creek* (1983), *Get Crazy* (1983), *The Caller* (1987), *Buy & Cell* (1987), *Sunset* (1988), *Mortacci* (1989). By the middle of the 1980s his lifestyle seems suddenly to have caught up with him and he fell away from the attention of mainstream film makers. He made *Assassin of the Tsar* (1991) in Russia and *Bopha!* (1993) in South Africa before returning to big budget villainy as Soran, the man who killed Captain Kirk, in *Star Trek: Generations* (1994). His films since 1990 include: *Jezebel's Kiss* (1990), *Schweitzer* (1990), *In the Eye of the Snake* (1990), *Class of 1999* (1990), *Moon 44* (1990), *Disturbed* (1990), *Chain of Desire* (1992), *Il Maestro* (1992), *Vent d'est* (1993), *Happily Ever After* (1993), *Milk Money* (1994), *Cyborg 3* (1995), *Dangerous Indiscretion* (1995), *Exquisite Tenderness* (1995), *Tank Girl* (1995), *Fist of the North Star* (1995), *Ringer* (1996), *Night Train to Venice* (1996), *Where Truth Lies* (1996), *Kids of the Round Table* (1997), *Asylum* (1997), *2103: The Deadly Wake* (1997), *Hugo Pool* (1997), *Mr. Magoo* (1997), *The Gardener* (1998), *Fatal Pursuit* (1998), *The First 9½ Weeks* (1998), *Southern Cross* (1999), *Love Lies Bleeding* (1999), *My Life So Far* (1999), *Y2K* (1999), *Gangster No. 1* (2001), *Just Visiting* (2001), *I Spy* (2002), *The Barber* (2002), *Between Strangers* (2002), *Beings* (2002), *Tempo* (2003), *The Company* (2003), *Inhabited* (2003), *I'll Sleep When I'm Dead* (2003), *Hidalgo* (2004), *Evilenko* (2004), *Bobby Jones: A Stroke of Genius* (2004), *Tempesta* (2004), *Pinocchio 3000* (2004), *In Good Company* (2004), *Rag Tale* (2005), *Dinotopia: Quest for the Ruby Sunstone* (2005), *Mirror Wars: Reflection One* (2005), *Cut Off* (2006), *Bye Bye Benjamin* (2006), *The List* (2007), *Exitz* (2007), *Halloween* (2007), *Red Roses and Petrol* (2008), *Doomsday* (2008), *Delgo* (2008), *Bolt* (2008), *The Evening Journey* (2008), *Halloween II* (2009), *Suck* (2009), *The Book of Eli* (2010), *Barry Munday* (2010), *Pound of Flesh* (2010), *Golf in the Kingdom* (2010), *Easy A* (2010), *Suing the Devil* (2011 – as Satan), *L.A., I Hate You* (2011 - as Harold Weintraub) and the multi-award-winning *The Artist* (2011 - as the butler). Younger viewers on both sides of the Atlantic will know him as Daniel Linderman in the hit TV series, Heroes (2007-08). Malcolm was married to Margot Bennett (1975-80), Mary Steenburgen (1980-90), with whom he had two children, Lily Amanda (b. 21 January 1981) and Charles Malcolm (b. 10 July 1983), and Kelley Kuhr (1991-present), with whom he has three children, Beckett Taylor (b. 29 January 2004), Finnian Anderson (b. 23 December 2006), and Seamus Hudson (b. 7 January 2009). He is the maternal uncle of actor Alexander Siddig, who appeared in *Star Trek: Deep Space Nine, Kingdom of Heaven, Syriana, 24,* and the current fourth season of the UK and BBC America hit series *Primeval.* See also entries in the television section for Crossroads, *Knock on Any Door, Love Story, Our Friends In The North*, and *Sat'day While Sunday.*

McElhone, Natascha (1971-) Born Natasha Abigail Taylor, 23 March 1971, Hampstead, London. She eventually switched to using her mother's maiden name as her stage surname. Trained at the London Academy of Music and Dramatic Art. She featured in episodes of several television series including *Ruth Rendell Mysteries, Bergerac, Absolutely Fabulous, Cadfael* and *Minder* before making her big screen debut in *Surviving Picasso* (1996). Her other films to date are: *The Devil's Own* (1997), *Mrs Dalloway* (1997), *The Truman Show* (1998), *What Rats Won't Do* (1998), *Ronin* (1998), *Contagion* (2000), *Love's Labour's Lost* (2000), *City of Ghosts* (2002), *FeardotCom* (2002), *Killing Me Softly* (2002), *Laurel Canyon* (2002), *Solaris* (2002), *Ladies in Lavender* (2004), *Guy X* (2005), *Big Nothing* (2006), *The Secret of Moonacre* (2008), *Blessed* (2008), *The Kid* (2010) and *Thorne: Sleepyhead* (2010). She also stars in the US television series *Californication* (2007-). She married Dr Martin Kelly in 1998 and, following his sudden death in 2008, she continued to write her diary and letters to Martin and published *After You: Letters of Love, and Loss, to a Husband and Father* (2010).

McGregor, Ewan (1971-) Born Ewan Gordon McGregor, 31 March 1971, Crieff, Perthshire. Actor. Nephew of actor Denis Lawson. Studied at the Guildhall School of Music and Drama (1989-92). He made his television debut in *Lipstick on your Collar* (1993) and his big screen debut the following year in *Being Human* (1994). He followed this up with eye-catching performances in *Shallow Grave* (1994) and *Trainspotting* (1996). He has mixed appearing in British films such as *Brassed Off* (1996), *Young Adam* (2003) and *Scenes of a Sexual Nature* (2006), with blockbusters such as the Star Wars prequels where he

played the young Obi-Wan Kenobi in *Star Wars Episode I: The Phantom Menace* (1999), *Star Wars Episode II: Attack of the Clones* (2002) and *Star Wars Episode III: Revenge of the Sith* (2005). Ewan's other films to date are: *Blue Juice* (1995), *The Pillow Book* (1996), *Emma* (1996), *Nightwatch* (1997), *The Serpent's Kiss* (1997), *A Life Less Ordinary* (1997), *Velvet Goldmine* (1998), *Little Voice* (1998), *Desserts* (1999), *Rogue Trader* (1999), *Eye of the Beholder* (1999), *Nora* (2000), *Moulin Rouge!* (2001), *Black Hawk Down* (2001), *Solid Geometry* (2002), *Down with Love* (2003), *Faster* (2003), *Big Fish* (2003), *Robots* (2005), *Valiant* (2005), *The Island* (2005), *Stay* (2005), *Stormbreaker* (2006), *Miss Potter* (2006), *Cassandra's Dream* (2007), *Incendiary* (2008), *Deception* (2008), *I Love You Phillip Morris* (2009), *Angels & Demons* (2009), *The Men Who Stare at Goats* (2009), *Amelia* (2009), *The Ghost Writer* (2010), *Nanny McPhee and the Big Bang* (2010), *Beginners* (2010), *Perfect Sense* (2011), *Haywire* (2011), *The Impossible* (2011) and *Salmon Fishing in the Yemen* (2011). Ewan formed the production company *Natural Nylon* with Sean Pertwee, Jonny Lee Miller and Jude Law. In 1995 he married Eve Mavrakis, a French production designer, whom he met while filming a guest appearance on the British television series *Kavanagh QC* in 1994. They have four daughters. Ewan has a heart and dagger tattoo of the names of his wife and daughters on his right arm. He has been a keen motorcyclist since his youth - see entries in the television section for *Charley Boorman: Ireland to Sydney, Long Way Down,* and *Long Way Round.*

McKellen, Ian (1939-) Born Ian Murray McKellen, 25 May 1939 Burnley, Lancashire. Actor. One of Britain's most respected contemporary stage actors and a staunch supporter of gay rights. Won a scholarship to St Catharine's College Cambridge, where he studied English Literature and joined the amateur dramatics society and performed alongside Derek Jacobi, Trevor Nunn and David Frost. Stage debut: *A Man for All Seasons* (1961). Worked in repertory at Coventry (1961-62), Ipswich (1962-63) and Nottingham (1963-64) before joining the National Theatre in 1965. He formed *The Actor's Company* with Edward Petherbridge in 1972 and joined the RSC in 1974. Screen debut: *A Touch of Love* (1969). He was nominated for a Best Actor Academy Award for portraying director James Whale in *Gods and Monsters* (1998) and the 2000s saw him appear in such blockbusters as the *Lord of the Rings* trilogy - *The Lord of the Rings: The Fellowship of the Ring* (2001), *The Lord of the Rings: The Two Towers* (2002) and *The Lord of the Rings: The Return of the King* (2003) – the *X-Men* trilogy - *X-Men* (2000), *X2* (2003) and *X-Men: The Last Stand* (2006) – *The Da Vinci Code* (2006), *Stardust* (2007) and *The Golden Compass* (2007). He was nominated for a Best Supporting Actor Academy Award for his role as Gandalf in *The Lord of the Rings: The Fellowship of the Ring* (2001). His other films to date are: *Alfred the Great* (1969), *The Promise* (1969), *Priest of Love* (1981), *The Keep* (1983), *Plenty* (1985), *Zina* (1985), *Scandal* (1989), *Six Degrees of Separation* (1993), *The Ballad of Little Jo* (1993), *Last Action Hero* (1993), *To Die For* (1994), *The Shadow* (1994), *I'll Do Anything* (1994), *Restoration* (1995), *Richard III* (1995), *Jack and Sarah* (1995), *Bent* (1997), *Amy Foster* (1997), *Apt Pupil* (1998), *Emile* (2003), *Neverwas* (2005), *Asylum* (2005), *The Magic Roundabout* (2005), *Eighteen* (2005), *Flushed Away* (2006) and *The Academy* (2009). Ian appeared as Mel Hutchwright in *Coronation Street* in 2005. He was appointed CBE in 1979 and knighted in 1990. Ian has had two long-term relationships, Brian Taylor (1964–72) and Sean Mathias (1978–88) but it was not until after the second was over that he came out publicly as being gay. See also entries in the television section for *Coronation Street, David Copperfield, Extras,* and *The Prisoner.*

McKenna, Virginia (1931-) Born 7 June 1931, Marylebone, London. Actress. Trained at the Central School of Speech and Drama. Screen debut: *The Second Mrs Tanqeray* (1952). She featured in *The Cruel Sea* (1953), *The Ship that Died of Shame* (1955) and *The Smallest Show on Earth* (1957). She won a Best Actress BAFTA for *A Town Like Alice* (1956). She is particularly remembered for portraying Violette Szabo in *Carve her Name with Pride* (1958). She starred in *Born Free* (1966) with her husband Bill Travers and from then on they both became active in protecting the rights of wild animals. They also appeared together in *An Elephant Called Slowly* (1969) and *Ring of Bright Water*

(1969). Her other films to date are: *Father's Doing Fine* (1952), *The Oracle* (1953), *Simba* (1955), *The Barretts of Wimpole Street* (1957), *Passionate Summer* (1958), *The Wreck of the Mary Deare* (1959), *Two Living, One Dead* (1961), *Waterloo* (1970), *Swallows and Amazons* (1976), *Holocaust 2000* (1977), *The Disappearance* (1977), *Blood Link* (1982), *Staggered* (1984), *Sliding Doors* (1998) and *Love/Loss* (2010). In 1984 the *Zoo Check Campaign* was begun and in 1991 the *Born Free Foundation* was established. As well as Bill Travers, to whom she was married from 1957 until his death in 1994, she was also briefly married to Denholm Eliott in 1954. She was awarded the OBE in 2004 for her services to the arts and animal conservation.

McKern, Leo (1920-2002) Born Reginald McKern, 16 March 1920, Sydney, New South Wales, Australia. Actor. He worked as commercial artist and served in the Australian Army Engineering Corps before moving to England in 1946. Joined the Old Vic and subsequently the Royal Shakespeare Company. Screen debut: *Murder in the Cathedral* (1952). He featured in *Help!* (1965 - as Clang), in *A Man for All Seasons* (1966 - as Thomas Cromwell), in *Ryan's Daughter* (1970 - as Ryan) and in *The Adventures of Sherlock Holmes' Smarter Brother* (1975 - as Moriarty). Other films include: *All for Mary* (1955), *X: The Unknown* (1956), *Time Without Pity* (1957), *A Tale of Two Cities* (1958), *Beyond This Place* (1959), *The Running Jumping & Standing Still Film* (1959), *The Mouse That Roared* (1959), *Yesterday's Enemy* (1959), the Smell-o-Visioned *Scent of Mystery (aka Holiday in Spain)* (1960), *Jazz Boat* (1960), *Mr Topaze* (1961), *The Day the Earth Caught Fire* (1961), *The Inspector* (1962), *Doctor in Distress* (1963), *A Jolly Bad Fellow* (1964), *Hot Enough for June* (1964), *King & Country* (1964), *The Amorous Adventures of Moll Flanders* (1965), *Assignment K* (1968), *Decline and Fall... of a Birdwatcher* (1968), *Nobody Runs Forever* (1968), *The Shoes of the Fisherman* (1968), *Massacre in Rome* (1973), *The Omen* (1976), *Candleshoe* (1977), *Damien: Omen II* (1978), *The Blue Lagoon* (1980), *The French Lieutenant's Woman* (1981), *The Chain* (1984), *Ladyhawke* (1985), *Travelling North* (1987), *Dad and Dave: On Our Selection* (1995) and his last film, *Molokai: The Story of Father Damien* (1999). He overcame the loss of an eye as a teenager which necessitated him having a glass one fitted. He was appointed Officer of the Order of Australia in 1983. Leo was married to Jane Holland from 1946 until his death on 23 July 2002, Bath, Bath & North East Somerset. He was survived by his wife and two daughters, Abigail and Harriet. For all his success on both stage and screen Leo will always be remembered fondly as the television character *Rumpole of the Bailey*. See also entries in the television section for *Churchill's People, Love Story, March of the Peasants, The Prisoner, Reilly - Ace of Spies,* and *Shades of Greene.*

McLaglen, Victor (1886-1959) Born Victor Andrew De Bier McLaglen, 10 December 1886, Mile End, London. Actor. Son of Andrew Charles Alfred McLaglen a Bishop of the Free Protestant Episcopal Church who had been born in Cape Colony (South Africa). His father became Bishop of Claremont and Colonial Missionary to Cape Colony and this is where Victor grew up. He spent the pre-war years travelling and holding down a variety of jobs. Whilst earning money as a professional boxer he purportedly fought exhibition bouts against heavyweight champions Jack Johnson (in Vancouver, 1909), Bob Fitzsimmons (in Australia, 1909) and Jess Willard (in Missouri, 1911). He served with the Middlesex Regiment during WWI and some sources claim that he was a one point Provost Marshal of Baghdad. Although this cannot be confirmed, his military record puts him in Basrah in 1916 so it could have some foundation. He returned to England after the war and carried on boxing until being cast in *The Call of the Road* (1920). Victor went on to make over 100 films including: *The Sport of Kings* (1921), *A Romance of Old Baghdad* (1922), *The Glorious Adventure* (1922), *The Romany* (1923), *The Beloved Brute* (1924), *The Gay Corinthian* (1924), *The Unholy Three* (1925), *Beau Geste* (1926), *The Loves of Carmen* (1927), *A Girl in Every Port* (1928), *The River Pirate* (1928), *Captain Lash* (1929), *King of the Khyber Rifles* (1929), *A Devil with Women* (1930), *Three Rogues* (1931), *The Gay Caballero* (1932),

Laughing at Life (1933), *The Lost Patrol* (1934), *Dick Turpin* (1935), *Under Two Flags* (1936), *Wee Willie Winkie* (1937), *Battle of Broadway* (1938), *Captain Fury* (1939), *Gunga Din* (1939), *South of Pago Pago* (1940), *Broadway Limited* (1941), *Call Out the Marines* (1942), *Forever and a Day* (1943), *The Last Gangster* (1944), *The Princess and the Pirate* (1944), *Love, Honor and Goodbye* (1945), *Men of the Deep* (1945), *Whistle Stop* (1946), *Calendar Girl* (1947), *The Foxes of Harrow* (1947). *The Michigan Kid* (1947), *Fair Wind to Java* (1953), *Prince Valiant* (1954), *Trouble in the Glen* (1954), *Bengazi* (1955), *City of Shadows* (1955), *Lady Godiva of Coventry* (1955), *Many Rivers to Cross* (1955), *Around the World in Eighty Days* (1956), *The Abductors* (1957), *The Italians They Are Crazy* (1958) and his last film, *Sea Fury* (1958). He won an Academy Award for Best Actor for his portrayal of Gypo Nolan in *The Informer* (1935) and was nominated as Best Supporting Actor for *The Quiet Man* (1952). These were two of many films he featured in which were directed by John Ford. Amongst others were the horse soldier trilogy alongside John Wayne: *Fort Apache* (1948), *She Wore a Yellow River* (1949) and *Rio Grande* (1950). He became an American citizen in 1933 and in 1936 formed his own "private army" - The Light Horse Troop - seen mistakenly by many as pro-fascist. His brothers Arthur, Clifford, Cyril and Leopold were also actors. His son Andrew Victor McLaglen was a successful director. Autobiography: *Express to Hollywood* (1934). He died 7 November 1959, Newport Beach, California.

McTeer, Janet (1961-) Born 8 May 1961, Newcastle, Tyne & Wear. Actress. Graduated from RADA. She first appeared on film in Bob Swaim's 1986 film *Half Moon Street*. A striking actress, she is 6' 1'' tall and blind in one eye, she has been more succesful on the stage than on screen. For her performance in *A Doll's House* she won a 1996 London Critics Circle Theatre Award (Drama Theatre) for Best Actress, a Tony Award in 1997 and a Laurence Olivier Theatre Award. She has however been nominated for an Academy Award for Best Actress in 2000 for her performance in *Tumbleweeds* (1999). Her other films to date are: *Hawks* (1988), *Wuthering Heights* (1992), *Carrington* (1995), *Saint-Ex* (1996), *Velvet Goldmine* (1998), *Songcatcher* (2000), *The King Is Alive* (2000), *Waking the Dead* (2000), *The Intended* (2002), *Tideland* (2005), *As You Like It* (2006) and *Cat Run* (2011). for her most recent role as Hubert Page (a cross-dressing lesbian in 1890s Ireland) in the critically-acclaimed *Albert Nobbs* (2011) she has been nominated for several awards. See also entries in the television section for *Gems, Les Girls, Portrait of a Marriage, The Governor,* and *The Amazing Mrs Pritchard.*

Meadows, Shane (1972-) Born 26 December 1972, Uttoxeter, Staffordshire. Director, actor and writer. Shane moved to Nottingham when he was twenty and after a brief spell of ducking and diving he enrolled on a Performing Arts course at Burton College, where he first met friend and future collaborator Paddy Considine. Amongst other things, they formed the band She Talks To Angels (inspired by a Black Crowes song of the same name), with Shane as vocalist and Paddy as drummer. Whilst on the dole he borrowed a video camera and made 25 short films including *Where's the Money Ronnie?* (1996) which won a National Film Theatre competition. He made a sixty-minute comedy drama *Smalltime* (1996) and then embarked on The Midlands Trilogy of features: *Twenty Four Seven* (1997) - funded by the BBC and starring Bob Hoskins, *A Room for Romeo Brass* (1999) and *Once Upon a Time in the Midlands* (2002) - his homage to the Spaghetti Western, featuring Rhys Ifans, Robert Carlyle and Kathy Burke. He also took small acting parts in all these features. Shane finances his projects by making commercials. His other films to date are *Dead Man's Shoes* (2004), *Northern Soul* (short) (2004), *The Stairwell* (short) (2004), *This Is England* (2006), *Somers Town* (2008) and *Le Donk & Scor-zay-zee* (2009). He also wrote four episodes of *This is England '86* (2010) for television and directed two of the episodes.

Meaney, Colm (1953-) Born 30 May 1953, Dublin. Actor. Trained at the Abbey Theatre School of Acting and later joined the Irish National Theatre Company. Screen debut: *Nailed* (1981). He appeared in the pilot episode of the TV series *Star Trek: The*

Next Generation (1987) which eventually led to him playing the recurring character of Miles O'Brien in both that series and in *Star Trek: Deep Space Nine* (1993). During this time his film career also began to flourish, with appearances in *Dick Tracy* (1990) and *Die Hard 2* (1990) before he made a bigger impact in *The Commitments* (1991). He also starred in the other parts of the Barrytown Trilogy *The Snapper* (1993) and *The Van* (1996). Apart from being cast in a series of films with an Irish background such as *Into the West* (1992), *Far and Away* (1992) and *The War of the Buttons* (1994) he is also notable in *The Englishman Who Went Up a Hill and Came Down a Mountain* (1995), *Con Air* (1997) and *The Damned United* (2009) – where he played the Leeds and England football manager Don Revie. His other films to date are: *Omega Syndrome* (1987), *Come See the Paradise* (1990), *The Last of the Mohicans* (1992), *Under Siege* (1992), *The Road to Wellville* (1994), *The Last of the High Kings* (1996), *Claire Dolan* (1998), *October 22* (1998), *Owd Bob* (1998), *Snitch* (1998), *This Is My Father* (1998), *Chapter Zero* (1999), *Four Days* (1999), *Most Important* (1999), *Mystery, Alaska* (1999), *How Harry Became a Tree* (2001), *Intermission* (2003), *The Boys from County Clare* (2003), *Blueberry* (2004), *Layer Cake* (2004), *New France* (2004), *Turning Green* (2005), *A Lobster Tale* (2006), *Five Fingers* (2006), *The Metrosexual* (2007), *Kings* (2007), *Clean Break* (2008), *Three and Out* (2008), *Law Abiding Citizen* (2009), *The Race* (2009), *Alleged* (2010), *Get Him to the Greek* (2010), *The Conspirator* (2010), *Parked* (2010), *The Flight of the Swan* (2011) and *The Hot Potato* (2011). Colm was married to Irish actress Bairbre Dowling (1977–94) and since 2007, to Ines Glorian.

Medina, Patricia (1919-) Born Patricia Paz Maria Medina, 19 July 1919, Liverpool. Actress. Her father was Spanish and her mother English, which no doubt accounted for her exotic looks. She made her film debut as an uncredited bit part actor in *Dinner at the Ritz* (1937) and made her credited debut in *Mr Satan* (1938). Her other films are *Double or Quits* (1938), *Simply Terrific* (1938), *This Man Is News* (1938), *Crook's Tour* (1941), *The Day Will Dawn* (1942), *They Met in the Dark* (1943), *Don't Take It to Heart* (1944), *Hotel Reserve* (1944), *Kiss the Bride Goodbye* (1945), *Waltz Time* (1945), *The Secret Heart* (1946), *Moss Rose* (1947), *The Beginning or the End* (1947), *The Foxes of Harrow* (1947), *The Three Musketeers* (1948), *Children of Chance* (1949), *The Fighting O'Flynn* (1949), *Abbott and Costello in the Foreign Legion* (1950), *Fortunes of Captain Blood* (1950), *Francis* (1950), *The Jackpot* (1950), *Dick Turpin's Ride* (1951), *The Magic Carpet* (1951), *Valentino* (1951), *Aladdin and His Lamp* (1952), *Captain Blood, Fugitive* (1952), *Desperate Search* (1952), *Lady in the Iron Mask* (1952), *Botany Bay* (1953), *Plunder of the Sun* (1953), *Sangaree* (1953), *Siren of Bagdad* (1953), *Drums of Tahiti* (1954), *Phantom of the Rue Morgue* (1954), *The Black Knight* (1954), *Confidential Report* (1955), *Duel on the Mississippi* (1955), *Pirates of Tripoli* (1955), *Miami Expose* (1956), *Stranger at My Door* (1956), *The Beast of Hollow Mountain* (1956), *Uranium Boom* (1956), *The Buckskin Lady* (1957), *Battle of the V-1* (1958), *Count Your Blessings* (1959), *The Killing of Sister George* (1968), *Timber Tramps* (1975) and her last film, *El llanto de los pobres* (1978). Patricia's two marriages were to British actor Richard Greene (1941-51) and American actor Joseph Cotton, from 1960 until his death in 1994. She published an autobiography entitled *Laid Back in Hollywood: Remembering* (1998).

Medwin, Michael (1923-) Born Michael Hugh Medwin, 18 July 1923, London. Actor and producer. Educated in Switzerland. Screen debut: *Piccadilly Incident* (1946). Spent much of the 1950s playing cockney characters in films such as *Genevieve* (1953), *Doctor at Sea* (1955) and *Carry on Nurse* (1959). He made more of an impact as Cpl Springer in the TV sitcom *The Army Game* and the film spin-off *I Only Arsked!* (1958). With Bernard Bresslaw, Leslie Fyson and Alfie Bass, he took the theme tune from *The Army Game* into the UK Singles Chart in 1958, where it peaked at No 5. Other films include: *An Ideal Husband* (1947), *Black Memory* (1947), *Just William's Luck* (1947), *Night Beat* (1947), *Root of All Evil* (1947), *The Courtneys of Curzon Street* (1947), *Anna Karenina* (1948), *Another Shore* (1948), *Look Before I Love* (1948), *My Sister and I* (1948), *Operation Diamond* (1948), *William Comes to Town* (1948), *Woman Hater* (1948), *Boys in Brown* (1949), *Call of the Blood* (1949), *For Them That Trespass* (1949), *Forbidden* (1949), *Helter Skelter* (1949), *The Queen of Spades* (1949), *Trottie True* (1949), *Shadow of the Past* (1950), *Someone at the Door* (1950), *The Lady Craved Excitement* (1950), *Trio* (1950), *The Long Dark Hall* (1951), *Curtain Up* (1952), *Hindle Wakes* (1952), *Love's a Luxury* (1952), *Miss Robin Hood* (1952), *Top Secret* (1952), *Malta Story* (1953), *Spaceways* (1953), *Street Corner* (1953), *The Intruder* (1953), *The Oracle* (1953), *Bang! You're Dead* (1954), *The Green Scarf* (1954), *The Teckman Mystery* (1954), *Above Us the Waves* (1955), *A Hill in Korea* (1956), *Charley Moon* (1956), *Checkpoint* (1956), *Doctor at Large* (1957), *The Steel Bayonet* (1957), *The Duke Wore Jeans* (1958), *The Wind Cannot Read* (1958), *The Heart of a Man* (1961), *Crooks Anonymous* (1962), *The Longest Day* (1962), *It's All Happening* (1963), *Night Must Fall* (1964), *Rattle of a Simple Man* (1964), *Twenty-Four Hours to Kill* (1965), *I've Gotta Horse* (1966), *The Sandwich Man* (1966), *A Countess from Hong Kong* (1967), *Scrooge* (1970), *O Lucky Man!* (1973), *Law and Disorder* (1974), *The Sea Wolves* (1980), *Britannia Hospital* (1982), *Never Say Never Again* (1983), *The Jigsaw Man* (1984), *Sleepwalker* (1985), *Hôtel du Paradis* (1986), *Just Ask for Diamond* (1990), *The Fool* (1990), *Staggered* (1994), *Fanny and Elvis* (1999), *Framed* (2008) and *The Duchess* (2008). Michael formed a production company in the 1960s and made *Charlie Bubbles* (1967), *Spring and Port Wine* (1970), *Gumshoe* (1971) and *Memoirs of a Survivor* (1981). He was a friend of Lindsay Anderson and produced two of the Mick Travis Trilogy *if....* (1968) and *O Lucky Man!* (1973). Michael received the OBE in 2005 for services to drama. A superb comic actor (his popularity was unsurpassed in the late 1950s), and despite his superb achievements in film production, one can't help thinking the viewing public were denied his considerable acting talents for long periods. See also entries in the television section for *The Army Game, Call Me Mister, Colin's Sandwich, The Love of Mike,* and *Shoestring*.

Mendes, Sam (1965-) Born Samuel Alexander Mendes, 1 August 1965, Reading, Berkshire. Director and producer. Joined the Chichester Festival Theatre in 1987. After spending some time with the Royal Shakespeare Company (1990-92) he became artistic director of the Donmar Warehouse. He won Laurence Olivier Awards for Best Director of a Play in both 1996 and 2003. His screen directorial debut was *American Beauty* (1999) which won an Academy Award for Best Picture and gained Mendes an Academy Award for Best Director. He next both produced and directed *Road to Perdition* (2002) a gangster film based on a graphic novel and starring Tom Hanks and Paul Newman. He has also produced and directed *Jarhead* (2005) about the Gulf War. Sam then directed *Revolutionary Road* (2008) and *Away We Go* (2009). He is slated to direct, *Skyfall,* the next film in the James Bond franchise due for release in 2012. He married actress Kate Winslet in 2003 but the couple separated in 2010. Sam is currently dating actress Rebecca Hall (see separate entry)

Menges, Chris (1940-) Born Christopher J Menges, 15 September 1940, Kington, Herefordshire. Cinematographer and director. Son of musical director Herbert Menges. Chris initially had a job in an estate agency before working as an assistant editor. He was a cameraman on the current affair series *World in Action* during the 1960s and made his name accompanying director Adrian Cowell on dangerous assignments in places such as Tibet and Burma. For the big screen he worked as camera operator on *Poor Cow* (1967) and *if....* (1968). His debut as a cinematographer was *Abel Gance: The Charm of Dynamite* (1968). He followed this with *Kes* (1969), *Gumshoe* (1971), *The Gamekeeper* (1980) and *Local Hero* (1983). He won Academy Awards for Best Cinematography for both *The Killing Fields* (1984) and *The Mission* (1986). He gained an Academy Award nomination for Best Cinematography for *Michael Collins* (1996) *and for Best Achievement in Cinematography for The Reader* (2008). His other films as cinematographer to date are *Loving Memory* (1971), *A Sense of Freedom* (1979), *Black Jack* (1979), *Bloody Kids* (1979), *Babylon* (1981), *Looks and Smiles* (1981), *Warlords of the 21st Century* (1982), *Angel* (1982), *Comfort and Joy* (1984), *Which Side Are You On?* (1985), *Fatherland* (1986), *Winter Flight* (1986), *High Season* (1987), *Dirty Pretty Things* (2002), *The Good Thief* (2002), *Concert for George* (2003), *North Country*

(2005), *Tickets* (2005), *The Yellow Handkerchief* (2008), *London Boulevard* (2010), *Route Irish* (2010) and *Extremely Loud and Incredibly Close* (2011). He was also director of photography on *Black Beauty* (1971), *Marie* (1985), *Shy People* (1987), *The Boxer* (1997), *The Pledge* (2001), *Criminal* (2004), *The Three Burials of Melquiades Estrada* (2005), *Notes on a Scandal* (2006), *Stop-Loss* (2008) and *The Reader* (2008). His directorial debut was the critically acclaimed *World's Apart* (1988). His other films as a director to date are: *Criss Cross* (1992), *Second Best* (1994) and *The Lost Son* (1999).

Merchant, Ismail (1936-2005) Born Ismail Noormohamed Abdul Rehman, 25 December 1936, Bombay (now Mumbai), India. Producer and director. Educated in New York. His producing debut was *The Creation of Woman* (1960) which was nominated for an Academy Award as Best Short Subject. He subsequently met director James Ivory and they embarked on one of the longest partnerships in screen history. Their company, *Merchant Ivory Productions*, was responsible for more than 40 films, including *The Householder* (1963), *Shakespeare Wallah* (1965), *Savages* (1972), *Autobiography of a Princess* (1975), *The Europeans* (1979), *Jane Austen in Manhattan* (1980), *Heat and Dust* (1983), *Maurice* (1987), *Jefferson in Paris* (1995) and *The White Countess* (2005). He produced *A Room with a View* (1985), *Howards End* (1992) and *The Remains of the Day* (1993), all three of which received nominations for an Academy Award for Best Picture. He also did some directing, starting with *Mahatma and the Mad Boy* (1974) and including *In Custody* (1993) and *Cotton Mary* (1999). Many of the *MIP* films were based on the works of Henry James, E M Forster and, in particular, their screenwriting partner, the author Ruth Prawer Jhabvala. He also published several cookery books including *Ismail Merchant's Indian Cuisine* and a memoir entitled, *My Passage From India: A Filmmaker's Journey from Bombay to Hollywood and Beyond*. He died 25 May 2005, London and is buried in Mumbai.

Merrow, Jane (1941-) Born Jane Meirowsky, 26 August 1941, Hemel Hempstead, Hertfordshire. Actress. Studied at RADA. Her first film in 1961 was a minor part in Cyril Frankel's *Don't Bother To Knock*. Similar size roles followed until she played the lead in the television adaptation of *Lorna Doone* (1963). More established now, she won the part of Alais in *The Lion in Winter* (1968) and was nominated for a Golden Globe for her role as the king's mistress. Jane narrowly missed out on being Diana Rigg's replacement in *The Avengers*, but was consoled by playing James Hadleigh's love interest Anne Hepton in the second season of *Hadleigh* (1971). Having moved to the United States Jane made regular appearances in such television series as *Mission:Impossible, Alias Smith and Jones, Cannon,* and *The Incredible Hulk* but since the early 1980s her film and television roles have been sparse with her last being in 1997 in *Sharpe's Waterloo* as the Duchess of Richmond. Her other film appearances to date are: *The Phantom of the Opera* (1962), *The Wild and the Willing* (1962), *The System* (1964), *Catacombs* (1965), *Night of the Big Heat* (1967), *Assignment K* (1968), *Adam's Woman* (1970), *Hands of the Ripper* (1971), *A Time for Love* (1974) and *The Appointment* (1981). See also entries in the television section for *Deadline Midnight, Hadleigh, Lorna Doone, Love Story, Oliver Twist,* and *The Prisoner*.

Miles, Bernard (1907-91) Born Bernard James Miles, 27 September 1907, Uxbridge, Middlesex. Actor and director. Graduated from Pembroke College, Oxford. He initially worked as a teacher before joining the New Theatre in London. Screen debut: *Channel Crossing* (1933). Appeared in many supporting roles before starring in *In Which We Serve* (1942). Other well-known roles were as Joe Gargery in *Great Expectations* (1946) and Newman Noggs in *The Life and Adventures of Nicholas Nickleby* (1947). As well as appearing in many of the best-loved British films of the war years and the 1950s he also featured in more big-budget films such as *The Man Who Knew Too Much* (1956) and *Moby Dick* (1956). His other films were: *The Love Test* (1935), *The Guv'nor* (1935), *Twelve Good Men* (1936), *Everything Is Thunder* (1936), *Crown v Stevens* (1936), *Midnight at Madame Tussaud's* (1936), *The Rebel Son* (1938), *Strange Boarders* (1938), *Convict 99* (1938), *13 Men and a Gun* (1938), *The Challenge* (1938), *The Citadel* (1938), *They Drive by Night* (1938), *The Spy in Black* (1939), *The Lion Has Wings* (1939), *Band Waggon* (1940), *Contraband* (1940), *Pastor Hall* (1940), *Freedom Radio* (1941), *Quiet Wedding* (1941), *The Common Touch* (1941), *The Big Blockade* (1942), *This Was Paris* (1942), *One of Our Aircraft Is Missing* (1942), *The Day Will Dawn* (1942), *The First of the Few* (1942), *Carnival* (1946), *Fame Is the Spur* (1947), *The Guinea Pig* (1948), *The Magic Box* (1952), *Never Let Me Go* (1953), *Tiger in the Smoke* (1956), *Zarak* (1956), *Waiting* (1957), *Fortune Is a Woman* (1957), *Doctor at Large* (1957), *The Smallest Show on Earth* (1957), *Saint Joan* (1957), *Tom Thumb* (1958), *Sapphire* (1959), *Heavens Above!* (1963) and his last film, *Run Wild, Run Free* (1969). He both directed and acted in two films: *Tawny Pipit* (1944) and *Chance of a Lifetime* (1950). From the early 1950s onwards most of his energies were concentrated on making a success of The Mermaid Theatre, Blackfriars, London. The first stage was built in a converted hall in 1951 and the completed theatre, the first to be built in the City of London for 300 years, was opened in 1959. Bernard was married to his co-founder of the Mermaid, actress Josephine Wilson. They had three children. Their daughters are the actress Sally Miles and the artist Bridget Miles. Their son John Miles (b. 14 June 1943, Islington, London) was a motor racing driver who had a brief F1 grand prix career (12 starts, 2 points) with Lotus 1969-70 before becoming a journalist and engineer. Bernard was knighted in 1969 for his services to the theatre and became Lord Miles of Blackfriars in 1979. He wrote *The British Theatre* (1948) and *Beautiful Britain* (1984) and also co-wrote with J C Trewin: *Curtain Calls* (1981). He died 14 June 1991, Knaresborough, Yorkshire, the year after the death of his wife. See also entries in the television section for *Nathaniel Titlark,* and *Treasure Island*.

Miles, Sarah (1941-) Born 31 December 1941, Ingatestone, Essex. Actress. Daughter of a merchant. At the age of 15 she enrolled at RADA. Sarah made her screen debut in an episode of the ITV drama series *Deadline Midnight* (1961), set in a busy newspaper office. Her film debut came the following year, as precocious schoolgirl Shirley Taylor in *Term of Trial* (1962), opposite Laurence Olivier. In the years that followed she became a popular actress of British New Wave with her roles in Joseph Losey's *The Servant* (1963) and in Michelangelo Antonioni's *Blow Up* (1966). After having been out of sight for several years doing stage work, she produced an outstanding performance in the lead role of David Lean's *Ryan's Daughter* (1970), which earned her an Academy Award nomination for Best Actress. Her other films to date are: *The Ceremony* (1963), *Those Magnificent Men in Their Flying Machines or How I Flew from London to Paris in 25 hours 11 minutes* (1965), *I Was Happy Here* (1966), *The Hireling* (1973), *Pepita Jiménez* (1975), *The Sailor Who Fell from Grace with the Sea* (1976), *The Big Sleep* (1978), *Priest of Love* (1981), *Venom* (1981), *Ordeal by Innocence* (1985), *Steaming* (1985), *White Mischief* (1987), *Hope and Glory* (1987), *The Silent Touch* (1992), *Days of Grace* (2001), *The Accidental Detective* (2003) and *Jurij* (2004). During the filming of *The Man Who Loved Cat Dancing* (1973) in which she co-starred with Burt Reynolds, her young manager David Whiting died under mysterious circumstances which cast a shadow over her career for some time although neither she nor Reynolds were charged with any wrongdoing. Sarah is known for her eccentricity, her advocacy of urine therapy, and her erstwhile use of anglo-saxon expletives. Her brother is film director, producer and screenwriter Christopher Miles (b. 19 April 1939). She was twice married to the British playwright Robert Bolt, (1967-75) and (1988-1995) who wrote the screenplay for the film *Lady Caroline Lamb* (1973) in which she starred.

Milland, Ray (1905-86) Born Reginald Alfred John Truscott-Jones, 3 January 1907, Neath, Wales. Actor and director. According to his autobiography he took his stage name from the "mill lands" area of Neath. He served as a guardsman with the Household Cavalry for three years and went on to make more than 100 films. He made his screen debut in *The Plaything* (1929) before travelling to Hollywood and featuring as the romantic lead in light comedies. His early films include: *The Flying Scotsman* (1929), *Just a Gigolo* (1931), *We're Not Dressing* (1934), *Bolero* (1934), *The Big Broadcast of 1937* (1936) and *Ebb Tide* (1937). He entertained with perhaps more interesting roles in *Beau Geste* (1939), *French Without Tears* (1939), *Reap the Wild Wind* (1942) and *Forever and a Day* (1943). Ray won a Best Actor Academy Award for his cast against usual type performance as the alcoholic in *The Lost Weekend* (1945). His later films never seemed to really give him the chance to extend himself in the same way but he gave typically strong performances in *The Big Clock* (1948), *Alias Nick Beal* (1949), *The Thief* (1952), *Dial M for Murder* (1954) and *The Girl in the Red Velvet Swing* (1955). He also directed a few films in the 1950s including *A Man Alone* (1955), *Lisbon* (1956) and *The Safecracker* (1958). Ray starred in two Roger Corman directed horror / sci-fi efforts in the early 1960s: *Premature Burial* (1962) and *The Man with X-Ray Eyes* (aka *X*) (1963). After this he mainly concentrated on television during the 1960s until he featured in *Love Story* (1970) and its sequel *Oliver's Story* (1978). During the 1970s he was in *Gold* (1974) and *The Last Tycoon* (1976) as well as some low-budget horror films such as *Frogs* (1972), *The Thing with Two Heads* (1972), *Terror in the Wax Museum* (1973), *The House in Nightmare Park* (1977), *The Uncanny* (1977), *Survival Run* (1978) and *The Attic* (1980). His other late films were: *Panic in Year Zero!* (1962), *The Confession* (1964), *Hostile Witness* (1968), *Embassy* (1973), *Control Factor* (1974), *Escape to Witch Mountain* (1975), *Aces High* (1976), *The Swiss Conspiracy* (1976), *Blackout* (1978), *Slavers* (1978), *Game for Vultures* (1978) and his final feature film, *Serpiente de mar* (1984). His autobiography was entitled *Wide-eyed in Babylon* (1974). Ray was married to Malvina Webber from 1932 until his death on 10 March 1986, Torrance, California.

Miller, Jonny Lee (1972-) Born Jonathan Lee Miller, 15 November 1972, Kingston, Surrey. Actor. Grandson of actor Bernard Lee. After appearing on television in episodes of series such as *Mansfield Park* (1983), *Prime Suspect* (1993) and *Eastenders* (1993), he made his big screen debut in *Hackers* (1995), opposite Angelina Jolie. Jonny made his breakthrough in his next film, playing Sick Boy in *Trainspotting* (1996). He followed this with *Afterglow* (1997) and *Regeneration* (1997) but unfortunately *Plunkett & Macleane* (1999), *Mansfield Park* (1999), *Complicity* (2000), *Love, Honour & Obey* (2000), *Dracula 2000* (2000) and *The Escapist* (2002) all failed to bring success at the box office. His other films to date include the title role of the TV film : *Lord Byron* (2003), *Mindhunters* (2004), *Melinda and Melinda* (2004), *Æon Flux* (2005), and *Endgame* (2009). Undoubtedly his greatest performance so far was as the obsessive cyclist Graeme Obree in *The Flying Scotsman* (2006). It has only come to light since the film was released that Graeme was in fact a closet homosexual which accounted for some of his frustrations. This film opened doors for Jonny and in recent years he has appeared in US television series such as the lead character in *Eli Stone* (2008-2009) and in *Dexter* (2010). He formed the production company *Natural Nylon* with his friends Ewan McGregor, Jude Law, Sadie Frost and Sean Pertwee. His latest highly acclaimed stage project, at the National Theatre, has been to switch roles on alternate nights playing both Dr Frankenstein and his creature, opposite Benedict Cumberbatch. Jonny was married to actress Angelina Jolie (1996-99) and, since 2008, to Michelle Hicks. They have a son, Buster Timothy Miller (b. 3 December 2008, Los Angeles, California). See also entries in the television section for *The Canterbury Tales*, *Eastenders*, and *Emma*.

Miller, Max See entry in comedy section

Miller, Sienna (1981-) Born Sienna Rose Miller, 28 December 1981, New York, USA. Actress and model. The daughter of Jo Miller, a former model and administrator of Lee Strasberg's London studio. Sienna came to Britain when she was a year old and was taught at Heathfield School in Ascot, Berkshire and has been quoted as saying "I'm English, definitely. I don't feel like I'm American in any way." Prior to commencing her professional acting career, Sienna worked as a photographic model, signing with Tandy Anderson of Select Model Management London. She initially modelled for Coca-Cola, and Italian Vogue, and also posed topless in the 2003 Pirelli Calendar. She has appeared in a small number of films since her debut in *South Kensington* (2001), in which her role of Sharon was credited as Sienna Rose, with *Layer Cake* (2004) and *Alfie* (2004) being the pick of the bunch. In *Alfie* she played opposite her soon-to-be boyfriend Jude Law. Since then her private life has been rather more prominent than her film career, and her relationship with Law being an exceptionally on-off story. In 2005, she made her professional stage debut as Celia in a West End production of Shakespeare's As You Like It. Her other films to date are: *High Speed* (2002), *The Ride* (2003), *Casanova* (2005), *Factory Girl* (2006 – as Edie Sedgwick), *Interview* (2007), *Stardust* (2007), *Camille* (2008), *The Mysteries of Pittsburgh* (2008), *A Fox's Tale* (2008), *The Edge of Love* (2008) and *G.I. Joe: The Rise of Cobra* (2009). She has recently completed filming for several forthcoming films including, *Hippie Hippie Shake*, *Two Jacks*, and *Just Like a Woman*, all of which have been delayed for various reasons. Sienna has been closely associated with the style of fashion that has become known as boho chic, a style also adopted by model Kate Moss. She signed a two-year contract with Pepe Jeans London in 2006 and in 2009, Hugo Boss Fragrances made her new ambassador for their women's BOSS Orange women's perfume.

Millington, Mary (1945-79) Born Mary Ruth Quilter, 30 November 1945, Kenton, Greater London. Actress and model. She married Robert Maxted in 1964, her husband until her death 15 years later and early in her film career was billed as Mary Maxted. At 4ft 11ins, Mary was too short to make it on the catwalk and her career took off when she met photographer John Jesnor Lindsay a blue-movie pioneer of films such as *Dr Sex* (1971) and *I'm Not Feeling Myself Tonight* (1976). In 1974 she met David Sullivan and he turned her into one of the most recognisable nude models in the UK, he also arranged for her to appear in her most well known film *Come Play with Me* (1977). Charitably this film can be regarded as very amateur, but despite its shortcomings the film ran for 201 weeks at one London cinema and broke box office records throughout the country. After *Come Play with Me* she made only five more films, the last of which was *The Great Rock 'n' Roll Swindle* (1980) as the girlfriend of "the Crook" (Steve Jones). The film was released a year after Mary had committed suicide with a cocktail of paracetamol and alcohol on 19 August 1979, Walton-on-the-Hill, Surrey. Films, books and television programmes have subsequently attempted to put Mary's tragic life into context but all that is known for sure is that by the end of her life she struggled with depression and cocaine addiction and was an inveterate shoplifter who felt persecuted by authority figures such as police and taxmen.

Mills, Hayley (1946-) Born Catherine Hayley Rose Vivien Mills, 18 April 1946, Marylebone, London. Actress. She is the daughter of John Mills and Mary Hayley Bell. Hayley is the god-daughter of both Noël Coward and Sir Laurence Olivier. Although it is widely thought that her first film was J.Lee Thompson's *Tiger Bay* (1959) she did in fact have an uncredited part alongside her father in *So Well Remembered* (1947) as a baby. She is the younger sister of Juliet, who also started out as a baby in one of her father's films, *In Which We Serve* (1942). Hayley followed *Tiger Bay* by signing to Disney and making a series of films for them, *Pollyanna* (1960), *The Parent Trap* (1961), *In Search of the Castaways* (1962), *Summer Magic* (1963) and *The Moon-Spinners* (1964). In 1961 she had a UK No 17 single with Let's Get Together, a song from *The Parent Trap*. After completing *That Darn Cat!* (1965), she left Disney and branched out into older roles. Her other films in this period were *Whistle Down the Wind* (1961) – based on a novel written by her mother, *The Chalk Garden* (1964), *The Truth About Spring* (1965) – playing alongside her father, *Sky West and Crooked* (1966) – again written by her mother, *The Trouble With Angels* (1966) and the animation *The Daydreamer* (1966) She shocked her fans in the comedy *The Family Way* (1966), but a larger off-screen shock was due as she began a relationship with the director of the film, Roy Boulting, 33-years her senior (and only five years younger than her father). They married in 1971 but eventually divorced five years later. Her child from this marriage is Crispian Mills (b. 18 January 1973, Hammersmith, London) lead singer and founding member of Kula Shaker. Hayley also had another son, Jason, with future Mr

Twiggy, actor Leigh Lawson. Her films following *The Family Way* were *Pretty Polly* (1967), *Twisted Nerve* (1968), *Take a Girl Like You* (1970), *Mr. Forbush and the Penguins* (1971), *Endless Night* (1972), *What Changed Charley Farthing?* (1976), *Deadly Strangers* (1976), *The Kingfisher Caper* (1976), *Appointment with Death* (1988), *After Midnight* (1990) *A Troll in Central Park* (1994) and a trio of TV films back with Disney *The Parent Trap II* (1986), *Parent Trap III* (1989) and *Parent Trap: Hawaiian Honeymoon* (1989). She also played Tilly in the television series *Flame Trees of Thika* (1981). After a long lay off she returned to the screen with *2BperfectlyHonest* (2004), *Stricken* (2005), *Mandie and the Cherokee Treasure* (2010) and *Foster* (2011). Since 2007 she has played Caroline de Plessis in the televison series *Wild at Heart*. Hayley's current partner is Indian-American actor Firdous Bamji (b. 3 May 1966, Bombay – now Mumbai)

Mills, John (1908-2005) Born Lewis Ernest Watts Mills, 22 February 1908, at the Watts Naval Training College, North Elmham, Norfolk. Actor. Studied at RADA. He began his career as a song and dance man. Stage debut: *The Five O'Clock Revue* (1929). John was spotted by Noël Coward whilst touring in Singapore and was recruited for the London stage. He made his screen debut in *The Midshipmaid* (1932). His other early films were: *The Ghost Camera* (1933), *Britannia of Billingsgate* (1933), *The River Wolves* (1934), *The Lash* (1934), *Blind Justice* (1934), *A Political Party* (1934), *Those Were the Days* (1934), *Doctor's Orders* (1934), *Car of Dreams* (1935), *Charing Cross Road* (1935), *Royal Cavalcade* (1935), *Brown on Resolution* (1935), *The First Offence* (1936), *Tudor Rose* (1936), *O.H.M.S.* (1937) and *The Green Cockatoo* (1937). His first venture to Hollywood saw him in *Goodbye, Mr Chips* (1939). He then appeared in *Old Bill and Son* (1941), *Cottage to Let* (1941), *The Black Sheep of Whitehall* (1942), *The Young Mr. Pitt* (1942) and *Waterloo Road* (1945). He featured in several war films during WWII such as *The Big Blockade* (1942), *In Which We Serve* (1942), *We Dive at Dawn* (1943), *This Happy Breed* (1944) and *The Way to the Stars* (1945). The immediate post-war years saw him in some classic British films including playing Pip in *Great Expectations* (1946), Captain Scott in *Scott of the Antarctic* (1948) and Alfred Polly in *The History of Mr Polly* (1949). In the 1950s he played a string of military roles including *The Colditz Story* (1955), *Above Us the Waves* (1955), *I Was Monty's Double* (1958), *Dunkirk* (1958) plus the acclaimed *Ice-Cold in Alex* (1958) and *Tunes of Glory* (1960). He also featured in *So Well Remembered* (1947), *The October Man* (1947), *The Rocking Horse Winner* (1949), *Morning Departure* (1950), *Mr. Denning Drives North* (1952), *The Gentle Gunman* (1952), *The Long Memory* (1953), *Hobson's Choice* (1954), *The End of the Affair* (1955), *The Baby and the Battleship* (1956), *War and Peace* (1956), *Around the World in Eighty Days* (1956), *It's Great to be Young!* (1956), *Town on Trial* (1957), *Escapade* (1957), *The Vicious Circle* (1957), *Tiger Bay* (1959), *Summer of the Seventeenth Doll* (1960) and *Swiss Family Robinson* (1960). He took on more character roles in such films as *Tiara Tahiti* (1962), *The Chalk Garden* (1964), *King Rat* (1965), *The Wrong Box* (1966) and *Oh! What a Lovely War* (1969) and his other films during the decade were *The Singer Not the Song* (1961), *The Parent Trap* (1961), *Flame in the Streets* (1961), *The Valiant* (1962), *Operation Crossbow* (1965), *The Truth About Spring* (1965), *The Family Way* (1966), *Africa: Texas Style* (1967), *Chuka* (1967), *Emma Hamilton* (1968), *Run Wild, Run Free* (1969) and *Adam's Woman* (1970). He ended the 1960s by playing the role of the mentally damaged Michael in *Ryan's Daughter* (1970), a portrayal that gained him an Academy Award for Best Supporting Actor. Despite failing health and deteriorating eyesight his later films were *Dulcima* (1971), *Young Winston* (1972), *Lady Caroline Lamb* (1973), *Oklahoma Crude* (1973), *The 'Human' Factor* (1975), *Trial by Combat* (1976), *The Devil's Advocate* (1977), *The Big Sleep* (1978), *The Thirty Nine Steps* (1978), *The Quatermass Conclusion* (1979), *Zulu Dawn* (1979), *Gandhi* (1982), *Sahara* (1983), *When the Wind Blows* (1986), *Who's That Girl* (1987), *The Big Freeze* (1993), *Deadly Advice* (1994), *The Grotesque* (1995), *Hamlet* (1996), *Bean* (1997) and

his last film, *Bright Young Things* (2003). In parallel with his screen career he was also a highly popular and accomplished stage actor. He was the father of actresses Juliet and Hayley Mills. John was made a CBE in 1960 and knighted in 1976. His autobiography was entitled *Up in the Clouds, Gentleman Please* (1981). Married to Aileen Raymond (1927-41) and Mary Hayley Bell, from 1941 until his death on 23 April 2005, Denham, Buckinghamshire. His wife (b. 22 January 1911, Chiltern, Buckinghamshire) died later that year on 1 December. See also entries in the television section for *Muffin the Mule, Quatermass, Stars On Sunday, A Woman of Substance, Young At Heart*, and *The Zoo Gang*.

Mills, Juliet (1941-) Born Juliet Maryon Mills, 21 November 1941, Islington, London. Actress. She is the daughter of John Mills and Mary Hayley Bell and the elder sister of Hayley Mills. Her godmother was actress Vivien Leigh, and her godfather was playwright Noël Coward. She made her first screen appearance as a baby in *In Which We Serve* (1942) alongside her father and she appeared in three more films with her father before she was in her teens: *So Well Remembered* (1947), *The October Man* (1947) and *The History of Mr. Polly* (1949). At the age of sixteen she appeared on the London stage in Peter Shaffer's *Five Finger Exercise* which then transferred to Broadway where she was nominated for a Tony Award in 1960 as Best Featured Actress. Her first films as an adult were the very British comedies *No My Darling Daughter* (1961), *Twice Round the Daffodils* (1962), *Nurse on Wheels* (1963) and *Carry on Jack* (1963). Her other films to date are: *The Rare Breed* (1966) – a James Stewart western, *Oh! What a Lovely War* (1969), *Avanti!* (1972) – opposite Jack Lemmon for which she received a Golden Globe nomination, *Jonathan Livingston Seagull* (1973), *The Devil Within Her* (1974), *Waxwork II: Lost in Time* (1992) and *The Other Sister* (1999). The vast majority of her screen appearances have been for television where she has made many one-off guest appearances on US shows such as *Fantasy Island, The Love Boat, Murder, She Wrote* and *Saved by the Bell*. An early television success was as Nanny in the comedy *Nanny and the Professor* (1970-71) and she played the witch Tabitha Lennox in the daytime soap opera *Passions* from 1999 until 2008. Back on British television she also appeared in eight episodes of *Wild At Heart* in 2009 playing alongside her sister Hayley. She has married three times: Russell Alquist (1961-64), Michael Miklenda (1975–80) and British actor Maxwell Caulfield (1980-present). She has a son, Sean, by her first marriage, and a daughter, Melissa, by her second.

Milner, Bill (1995-) Born William Henry Milner, 4 March 1995, Richmond upon Thames, Surrey. He made an immediate impression on his screen debut in *Son of Rambow* (2007) which he followed up with two television films *Who Killed Mrs De Ropp?* (2007) and *My Boy Jack* (2007). He then starred alongside Michael Caine in *Is Anybody There?* (2008). After appearing in the TV film, *Skellig* (2009), he played Ian Dury's son in the biopic *Sex & Drugs & Rock & Roll* (2010) and the Young Magneto in *X-Men: First Class* (2011).

Minghella, Anthony (1954-2008) Born 6 January 1954 Ryde, Isle of Wight. Director, producer and writer. On an ice-cream manufacturer. Educated at University of Hull and lectured there until 1981. Initially he concentrated on writing and worked as a script editor on television series *Grange Hill* (1983-88) and *Eastenders* (1983-88) and a writer of episodes of *Boon* (1986) and *Inspector Morse* (1987). He collaborated with Jim Henson on *The Storyteller* (1988). His directorial debut was the award winning *Truly, Madly Deeply* (1991), which he also wrote. He followed this with the romantic comedy *Mr Wonderful* (1993). Having written the screenplay based on Michael Ondaatje's 1992 Booker Prize winning novel, he also directed *The English Patient* (1996). The film won an Academy Award for Best Picture and Minghella won the award for Best Director. He was also nominated for Best Adapted Screenplay. His next adaptation was from Patricia Highsmith's *The Talented Mr Ripley* (1999) which in the USA went under the complete title of *The Mysterious Yearning Secretive Sad Lonely Troubled Confused Loving Musical Gifted*

Intelligent Beautiful Tender Sensitive Haunted Passionate Talented Mr Ripley. This gained him another Academy Award nomination for Best Adapted Screenplay. He also directed the American Civil War drama Cold Mountain (2003) and the romantic drama Breaking and Entering (2006), which he also produced. His other productions were Iris (2001), Heaven (2002), The Quiet American (2002), The Interpreter (2005), Catch a Fire (2006), Michael Clayton (2007) and The Reader (2008). His final television project was The No. 1 Ladies' Detective Agency (2008) both as director and producer. He married Carolyn Choa in 1985. He was appointed CBE in 2001 and he was Chairman of the Board of Governors at the British Film Institute between 2003 and 2007. Anthony died on 18 March 2008, in London.

Mirren, Helen (1945-) Born Ilyena Lydia Mironoff, 26 July 1945, Chiswick, London. Actress. Daughter of a Russian-noble father who emigrated there in response to the Russian Revolution, and an English mother. Her great-great-great-great-grandfather was field-marshal Kamensky, one of the Russian heroes of the Napoleonic wars. She studied at the National Youth Theatre, the Royal Shakespeare Company and Peter Brook's International Centre for Theatre Research, Paris. She is particularly well-known for her role as the female detective Jane Tennison in the Prime Suspect series of TV dramas. Her early films include an uncredited appearance in the Norman Wisdom classic Press for Time (1966), but her first credited film was Don Levy's mysterious and neglected classic Herostratus (1967). She also played Hermia in A Midsummer Nights Dream (1968). She has played a combination of classic and contemporary roles, from Miss Julie (1972), Ophelia and Gertrude in Hamlet (1976), Morgana in Excalibur (1981) to Marcella in the gritty Irish love story Cal (1984), Georgina Spica in The Cook the Thief His Wife & Her Lover (1989), a sadistic teacher who gets her comeuppance in Teaching Mrs Tingle (1999) and one of the Calendar Girls (2003). Her other films in this period are Savage Messiah (1972), O Lucky Man! (1973), Caligula (1979), The Quiz Kid (1979), Hussy (1980), The Fiendish Plot of Dr. Fu Manchu (1980), The Long Good Friday (1980), 2010 (1984), Cal (1984), White Nights (1985), The Mosquito Coast (1986), Heavenly Pursuits (1987), Pascali's Island (1988), When the Whales Came (1989), Bethune: The Making of a Hero (1990), The Comfort of Strangers (1990), Where Angels Fear to Tread (1991), The Hawk (1993), Prince of Jutland (1994), The Snow Queen (1995), Some Mother's Son (1996), Critical Care (1997), The Prince of Egypt (1998), Greenfingers (2000), Last Orders (2001), No Such Thing (2001), The Pledge (2001), Raising Helen (2004) and The Clearing (2004). In 2005 she played the Queen in the costume drama Elizabeth I, provided the voice for Deep Thought in the film adaptation of Douglas Adams' The Hitchhiker's Guide to the Galaxy (2005) and played the dying female assassin, Rose, in Shadowboxer (2005). She won an Academy Award for Best Actress in a leading role for her portrayal of Elizabeth II in The Queen (2006). She received an Academy Award nomination for The Last Station (2010) and she was also nominated for an Academy Award for Best Actress in a Supporting Role for playing Queen Charlotte in The Madness of King George (1994) and Mrs Wilson in Gosford Park (2001). Her other recent films include: National Treasure: Book of Secrets (2007), Inkheart (2008), State of Play (2009), Love Ranch (2010), The Tempest (2010 – as Prospera), Brighton Rock (2010), Legend of the Guardians: The Owls of Ga'Hoole (2010), Red (2010) – a rare "action hero" role, The Debt (2011), and the film remake of Arthur (2011) where she takes on the John Gielgud role of Hudson. She has also written an autobiography, In the Frame: My Life in Words and Pictures (2007). In 1997 she married her long term partner, director, Taylor Hackford. She was invested as a Dame Commander of the British Empire (DBE) in 2003.

Mistry, Jimi (1973-) Born 1 January 1973, Scarborough, North Yorkshire. Actor. Son of an Indian Hindu father and an Irish Roman Catholic mother. He first came to prominence as a television actor playing Dr Federico Fonseca, on EastEnders (1998-2000), but began to gain supporting roles in films such as East Is East (1999), Born Romantic (2000), The Mystic Masseur (2001) and My Kingdom (2001) before playing the title role of dance teacher Ramu Gupta in The Guru (2002) - a role that no doubt stood him in good stead for his stint on the 2010 BBC television series Strictly Come Dancing. His other films to date are: Hamlet (1996), Anxiety (2000), Touch of Pink (2004), Ella Enchanted (2004), Things to Do Before You're 30 (2005), The Truth About Love (2005), Dead Fish (2005), Blood Diamond (2006), Partition (2007), RocknRolla (2008), Exam (2009), 2012 (2009), It's a Wonderful Afterlife (2010), Basement (2010), West Is West (2010) and Festival of Lights (2010). Jimi was married to Meg Leonard from 2001 until their divorce in March 2010. They have a daughter Elin (b.13 May 2001). He is an accomplished DJ, a passion he explains in the 2009 documentary film about the music scene on Ibiza, And the Beat Goes On.

Mitchell, Sagar (1866-1952) Born Sagar James Mitchell, 1866, Blackburn, Lancashire. Cinematographer. Son of a hotel keeper from Howarth, Yorkshire. An apprentice cabinet maker he went on to make photographic apparatus. In 1897 he formed a partnership with James Kenyon and they released films under the trade name Norden. They primarily produced short films of local interest, including processions, street scenes, sporting events and workers at factory gates. They also produced films purporting to be action from the Boer War but in fact filmed in the Lancashire countryside. Their fiction output included Diving Lucy (1903), Black Diamonds (1904) and The Interrupted Picnic (1906). Their film Arrest of Goudie (1901) depicted the recent crimes and arrest of bank embezzler Thomas Goudie in Liverpool, shot at the actual locations and first shown within days of the actual events. They also filmed the bowling action of well-known Lancashire cricketer Arthur Mold to try to disprove the rumours that he was a "chucker". They are also responsible for the first known film of Manchester United in action in their match against Burnley at Turf Moor on 6 December 1902. The films were usually shown at fairgrounds or in local halls and were sometimes commissioned by fairground showmen. The firm's output appears to have declined by the immediate pre-WWI period. Eight hundred of the original negatives of their films were discovered in milk churns in the cellar of their old shop in 1994 and these were preserved and restored by the British Film Insitute. After the partnership dissolved in 1922 Mitchell returned to being a portrait photographer. He died 2 October 1952, Chorley, Lancashire.

Moffatt, Graham (1919-65) Born Graham Victor Harold Moffatt, 6 December 1919, Hammersmith, London. Actor. Began working at Gaumont Studios and was picked out to play a choirboy in A Cup of Kindness (1934). After appearing in Clairvoyant (1934) and Stormy Weather (1935) he appeared alongside Will Hay in Where There's a Will (1936). His next film saw him in the guise of Young Albert teamed with Hay and Moore Marriott in Windbag the Sailor (1936). He was to play the character on numerous occassions including in Oh, Mr Porter! (1937), Good Morning, Boys (1937), Old Bones of the River (1938), Ask a Policeman (1939), Convict 99 (1939) and Where's That Fire? (1940). He played along with the Crazy Gang in Okay for Sound (1937) and with Arthur Askey in Charleys (Big-Hearted) Aunt (1940) and I Thank You (1941). His other films were Gangway (1937), Doctor Syn (1937), Owd Bob (1938), The Drum (1938), Cheer Boys Cheer (1939), Hi Gang! (1941), Back-Room Boy (1942), Dear Octopus (1943), Time Flies (1944), Welcome, Mr. Washington (1944), A Canterbury Tale (1944), I Know Where I'm Going! (1945), The Voyage of Peter Joe (1946), Woman Hater (1948), Three Bags Full (1949), The Second Mate (1950) and The Dragon of Pendragon Castle (1950). After Mother Riley Meets the Vampire (1952) he retired from acting to become a publican, at first in Market Harborough and later in Bath. He did make two further minor appearances on the big screen in Inn for Trouble (1960) and his last film, 80,000 Suspects (1963). He married Joyce Hazeldine in 1948. Graham died 2 July 1965, Bath, Bath and North East Somerset.

Molina, Alfred (1953-) Born Alfredo Molina, 24 May 1953, Paddington, London. Actor. Studied at the Guildhall School of Music and Drama. Made a brief screen debut as Satipo, Indiana Jones' treacherous companion at the start of Raiders of the Lost Ark (1981). He played a Russian sailor in Letter to Brezhnev (1985) and he made a real breakthrough as Kenneth Halliwell in Prick Up Your Ears (1987). A familiar face on TV during the early 1990s including playing Tony Hancock in Hancock (1991) and George Melly in The Trials of Oz (1991). His other big screen outings during this period were: Ladyhawke (1985), Water (1985),

Eleni (1985), *Letter to Brezhnev* (1985), *Manifesto* (1988), *Not Without My Daughter* (1991), *American Friends* (1991), *Enchanted April* (1992), *The Trial* (1993), *When Pigs Fly* (1993), *Cabin Boy* (1994), *White Fang 2: Myth of the White Wolf* (1994), *Maverick* (1994), *Hideaway* (1995), *The Steal* (1995), *The Perez Family* (1995), *Dead Man* (1995), *Species* (1995), *Nervous Energy* (1995), *Before and After* (1996), *Mojave Moon* (1996), *Scorpion Spring* (1996), *Leo Tolstoy's Anna Karenina* (1997) and *A Further Gesture* (1997). Alfred has since gone on to appear in big budget films such as *Boogie Nights* (1997), *Magnolia* (1999), *Chocolat* (2000) and *Frida* (2002). He played the villain Doctor Octopus (Doc Ock) in *Spiderman 2* (2004) and Bishop Aringarosa in *The Da Vinci Code* (2006). He has also had a successful stage career including playing Tevye in *Fiddler on the Roof*. His other films to date are *The Man Who Knew Too Little* (1997), *The Impostors* (1998), *The Treat* (1998), *Pete's Meteor* (1998), *Dudley Do-Right* (1999), *The Miracle Maker* (2000), *Texas Rangers* (2001), *Plotz with a View* (2002), *My Life Without Me* (2003), *Identity* (2003), *Luther* (2003), *Coffee and Cigarettes* (2003), *Chronicles* (2004), *Steamboy* (2004), *As You Like It* (2006), *The Hoax* (2006), *The Moon and the Stars* (2007), *Silk* (2007), *The Little Traitor* (2007), *The Ten Commandments* (2007), *Nothing Like the Holidays* (2008), *The Lodger* (2009), *An Education* (2009), *The Pink Panther 2* (2009), *Prince of Persia: The Sands of Time* (2010), *The Sorcerer's Apprentice* (2010), *The Tempest* (2010), *Abduction* (2011) and the animation *Rango* (2011). His television credits include *Roger and Val Have Just Got In* (2010-). He has been married to actress Jill Gascoine since 1986. He has a daughter, Rachel (b. 1980), from a previous relationship, and two stepsons, Adam and Sean, from Jill's first marriage.

Mollo, John (1931-) Born 18 March 1931, Lambeth, London. Costume designer. A military enthusiast and writer and illustrator of books on military uniforms he acted as technical advisor on *The Charge of the Light Brigade* (1968). He worked as historical and military advisor on *Nicholas and Alexandra* (1971) and *Barry Lyndon* (1975). His debut as costume designer came on *Star Wars: A New Hope* (1977) where he produced the designs for the storm-trooper and Darth Vader costumes and for which he won an Academy Award for Best Costume Design. He followed this with designs for *Alien* (1979), *Star Wars: The Empire Strikes Back* (1980) and *Outland* (1981). He won another Academy Award for Best Costume Design for *Gandhi* (1982). His other films to date are: *The Lords of Discipline* (1983), *Greystoke: The Legend of Tarzan, Lord of the Apes* (1984), *King David* (1985), *Revolution* (1985), *Cry Freedom* (1987), *Hanna's War* (1988), *White Hunter Black Heart* (1990), *Air America* (1990), *Chaplin* (1992), *The Three Musketeers* (1993), *The Jungle Book* (1994) and *Event Horizon* (1997). He returned to the military sphere, acting as costume designer on the television series *Sharpe* (1993) and *Hornblower* (1998)

Monaghan, Dominic (1976-) Born Dominic Bernard Patrick Luke Monaghan, 8 December 1976, Berlin, Germany. Actor. His family returned to England in 1989. He joined the Manchester Youth Theatre and was picked to play Geoffrey Shawcross in the television series *Hetty Wainthrop Investigates* (1996-98). His other early television credits include the TV film *Hostile Waters* (1997) and the four-part mini-series *Monsignor Renard* (2000). He is best known for playing Meriadoc Brandybuck (Merry) in *The Lord of the Rings: The Fellowship of the Ring* (2001), *The Lord of the Rings: The Two Towers* (2002) and *The Lord of the Rings: The Return of the King* (2003). He has since featured in *Spivs* (2004), *The Purifiers* (2004), *Shooting Livien* (2005), *I Sell the Dead* (2008) and *X-Men Origins: Wolverine* (2009). He returned to the TV screen, playing Charlie Pace in the popular American series *Lost* (2004-10) and Simon Campos in *FlashForward* (2009-10). He has recently completed filming for his latest movies *Soldiers of Fortune* and *The Day*. Dominic dated his *Lost* co-star Evangeline Lilly from 2004 until they split in 2009. A keen nature lover, Dominic owns a small forest in India. Among other tattoos he has the Elvish word "nine" written in Quenya-mode Tengwar on his right arm, a reference to his involvement in the *Lord of the Rings* and the fact that his character was one of the nine members of the Fellowship of the Ring.

Moody, Ron (1924-) Born Ronald Moodnick, 8 January 1924, Edmonton, London. Actor. He was educated at the London School of Economics with a view to becoming an economist or sociologist and he only became a fully-fledged actor in his late twenties, making his stage debut in the revue *Intimacy at Eight* (1952). He continued in revue until the late 1950s. Screen debut: *Davy* (1957). His other early films were *Follow a Star* (1959), *Make Mine Mink* (1960), *Five Golden Hours* (1961), *A Pair of Briefs* (1962), *Ladies Who Do* (1963), *Summer Holiday* (1963), *The Mouse on the Moon* (1963), *Murder Most Foul* (1964), *Every Day's a Holiday* (1965), *San Ferry Ann* (1965), and *The Sandwich Man* (1966). He had played Fagin to universal acclaim in the original production of Lionel Bart's stage musical *Oliver!* at the New Theatre, London (1960-62) and he was called upon to reprise the role in Carol Reed's film version in 1968. His portrayal gained him an Academy Award nomination for Best Actor. Whilst never scaling such heights again he has continued to be a familiar face on both television and the big screen. He has played Merlin in *The Spaceman and King Arthur* (1979) and *A Kid in King Arthur's Court* (1995). His other films to date are *The Twelve Chairs* (1970), *Flight of the Doves* (1971), *Dogpound Shuffle* (1975), *Legend of the Werewolf* (1975), *The Strange Case of the End of Civilization as We Know It* (1977), *Dominique* (1980), *The Man with the Deadly Lens* (1982), *Where Is Parsifal?* (1988), *Asterix and the Big Fight* (1989), *How's Business* (1991), *Emily's Ghost* (1992), *The 3 Kings* (2000), *Revelation* (2001), *Paradise Grove* (2003), *Lost Dogs* (2005) and *Moussaka & Chips* (2005). See also entries in the television section for *The Animals of Farthing Wood, Eastenders, The Edwardians, Hideaway, Into the Labyrinth, Midnight is a Place, Shirley's World, The Telebugs,* and *Village Hall.*

Moore, Dudley (1935-2002) Born Dudley Stuart John Moore, 19 April 1935, Charing Cross Hospital, London. Actor, comedian, composer and musician. Dudley was brought up in Dagenham and had a difficult childhood having been born with club feet necessitating several hospital stays and also being of diminutive stature, never reaching more than 5 ft 2½ in (1.588 m) in height. He attended Dagenham County High School where he received musical tuition from a dedicated teacher, Peter Cork. He blossomed into a talented pianist and organist and was playing the pipe organ at church weddings by the time he was a teenager. While studying music at Magdalen College, Oxford, he performed with Alan Bennett in the *Oxford Revue*. Alan then recommended him to the producer putting together *Beyond the Fringe*, a comedy revue, where he was to first meet Peter Cook. *Beyond the Fringe* was the precursor of the 1960s satire boom and after success in Britain, it transferred to the United States where it was also a hit. Dudley was working as a member of the John Dankworth Jazz Band at this time but left to pursue other avenues, eventually forming his own jazz trio with drummer Chris Karan and bassists Pete McGurk and later Peter Morgan. His partnership with Peter Cook was reformed after Dudley was offered his own television show, *Not Only...But Also*. Dudley decided to engage Peter, who was already an established comedy star after his appearances as E.L. Whisty in *On the Braden's Beat* (1964) and the chemistry was perfect. Dudley's screen debut came in the film *The Third Alibi* (1961) where he appeared as a background pianist. He next appeared with Peter Cook in *The Wrong Box* (1966), *Bedazzled* (1967), *Monte Carlo or Bust!* (1969), *The Bed Sitting Room* (1969) and *The Hound of the Baskervilles* (1978). In the late 1970s, Pete and Dud made their infamous obscene comedy recordings made under the pseudonyms Derek and Clive. Dudley then moved to Hollywood, where he appeared in *Foul Play* (1978) opposite Goldie Hawn, and Blake Edwards's *10* (1979 – as George Webber) opposite Bo Derek. He followed this up with the less successful *Wholly Moses!* (1980) but was nominated for an Oscar for his role of Arthur Bach in *Arthur* (1981) opposite Liza Minnelli. His other films include: *30 Is a Dangerous Age, Cynthia* (1968) on the set of which he met his first wife, *Six Weeks* (1982), *Lovesick* (1983), *Romantic Comedy* (1983), *Unfaithfully Yours*

(1984), *Best Defense* (1984), *Micki + Maude* (1984), *Santa Claus: The Movie* (1985 - as Patch), *Like Father Like Son* (1987), *Arthur 2: On the Rocks* (1988), *Crazy People* (1990), and his last feature film, *Blame It on the Bellboy* (1992). Dudley also composed the soundtracks for the films *Bedazzle* and *Six Weeks* among others. In 1991, he collaborated with the conductor Sir Georg Solti to create a television series, *Orchestra!*, which introduced audiences to the subtleties of the symphony orchestra. Dudley was married four times, to actresses Suzy Kendall (1968-72), Tuesday Weld (1975-80 - one son, Patrick, b. 1976), Brogan Lane (1988-91) and Nicole Rothschild (1994-98 - one son, Nicholas, b. 1995). He also had a relationship with American actress and singer Susan Anton. He died on 27 March 2002, Plainfield, New Jersey. His final words were reported to be, "I can hear the music all around me." See also entries in the television section for *The Goon Show, Love Story,* and *Not Only But Also.*

Moore, Owen (1886-1939) Born 12 December 1886, County Meath, Ireland. Actor. His family emigrated to the United States in the mid 1890s. He featured in over 270 films between 1908 and 1937 and he made his screen debut in 1908 in *The Guerilla* for the Biograph company. His other films include: *The Cricket on the Hearth* (1909), *The Lonely Villa* (1909), *Home Sweet Home* (1914), *Little Meena's Romance* (1916), *A Divorce of Convenience* (1921), *Code of the West* (1925), *The Road to Mandalay* (1926) and *Becky* (1927). Whilst they were both working for Biograph he met and married Mary Pickford (1911-20) with whom he starred in films such as *Cinderella* (1914 - as Prince Charming) and *Mistress Nell* (1915 - as King Charles II). With her career eventually outshining his, the marriage faltered. A matinee idol during the silent era, as with so many, after the coming of the talkies his career declined and his final films include *She Done him Wrong* (1933) and *A Star is Born* (1937). After he and Pickford divorced he married actress Katherine Perry with whom he starred in *The Chicken in the Case* (1921), *Love is an Awful Thing* (1922) and *Side Street* (1929). This last is also the only film in which he played alongside his actor brothers Tom (b. 1 May 1883, d. 12 February 1955) and Matt (b. 8 January 1888, d. 20 January 1960). A further brother, Joseph, and sister Mary were also screen actors. Owen Moore died of a heart attack 9 June 1939, Beverly Hills, California.

Moore, Roger (1927-) Born Roger George Moore, 14 October 1927, Stockwell, London. Actor. Studied at RADA. Screen debut: *Caesar and Cleopatra* (1945). He served in the army 1946-48 and moved to the US in 1953 under contract to MGM, making films such as *The Last Time I Saw Paris* (1954) and *The King's Thief* (1955). His other early films were: *Perfect Strangers* (1945), *Gaiety George* (1946), *Piccadilly Incident* (1946), *Paper Orchid* (1949), *Trottie True* (1949), *The Interrupted Journey* (1949), *Honeymoon Deferred* (1950), *One Wild Oat* (1951), *Interrupted Melody* (1955), *Diane* (1956), *The Miracle* (1959), *The Sins of Rachel Cade* (1961), *Gold of the Seven Saints* (1961) plus two Italian-made films *Il ratto delle sabine* (1961) and *Un branco di vigliacchi* (1962). After a successful television career he accepted the role of James Bond for *Live and Let Die* (1973) and played him six more times in *The Man with the Golden Gun* (1974), *The Spy who Loved Me* (1977), *Moonraker* (1979), *For Your Eyes Only* (1981), *Octopussy* (1983) and *A View to a Kill* (1985). His other films to date are *Crossplot* (1969), *The Man Who Haunted Himself* (1970), *Gold* (1974), *That Lucky Touch* (1975), *The Sicilian Cross* (1976), *Shout at the Devil* (1976), *The Wild Geese* (1978), *Escape to Athena* (1979), *North Sea Hijack* (1980), *The Sea Wolves* (1980), *Sunday Lovers* (1980), *The Cannonball Run* (1981), *Curse of the Pink Panther* (1983), *The Naked Face* (1984), *The Magic Snowman* (1987), *Fire, Ice & Dynamite* (1990), *Bullseye!* (1990), *Bed & Breakfast* (1991), *The Quest* (1996), *The Saint* (1997 – as a voice on a car radio), *Spice World* (1997), *The Enemy* (2001), *Boat Trip* (2002) and *A Princess for Christmas* (2011). He has also recently lent his voice to the following films: *Agent Crush* (2008), *Gnomes and Trolls: The Forest Trial* (2010) and *Cats & Dogs: The Revenge of Kitty Galore* (2010). Roger has been married to ice skater Doorn van Steyn (1946-53), singer Dorothy Squires (1953-68), actress Luisa Mattioli (1969-96) and Christina Tholstrup (2002-present). He was appointed CBE in 1999 and knighted in 2003. Roger's autobiography, *My Word is My Bond*, was published in 2008.

Roger made his mark on television on both sides of the Atlantic as Beauregarde Maverick in the popular American western *Maverick* (1960-61), but the role that made him a true international star was as Simon Templar in *The Saint* (1962-69). See also entries in the television section for *Ivanhoe, The Persuaders, Return of the Saint, The Saint, Stella Street,* and *Sunday Night at the London Palladium.*

More, Kenneth (1914-82) Born Kenneth Gilbert More, 20 September 1914, Gerrards Cross, Buckinghamshire. Actor. A stalwart of British films of the 1950s. He briefly worked as a fur trapper in Canada before returning to England to act as stagehand and eventually stage manager at the Windmill Theatre (1935). He served in the Naval Reserve during WWII. Screen debut: *Look Up and Laugh* (1935). His other early films were *Carry on London* (1937), *School for Secrets* (1946), *Scott of the Antarctic* (1948 - as Teddy Evans), *Man on the Run* (1949), *Now Barabbas* (1949), *Stop Press Girl* (1949), *Chance of a Lifetime* (1950), *Morning Departure* (1950), *The Clouded Yellow* (1950), *Appointment with Venus* (1951), *No Highway* (1951), *The Franchise Affair* (1951), *The Galloping Major* (1951) and *Brandy for the Parson* (1952), Following *Genevieve* (1953) he appeared in a string of the best loved British films of the 1950s: *Doctor in the House* (1954), *Our Girl Friday* (1954), *The Deep Blue Sea* (1955), *Reach for the Sky* (1956 - as Douglas Bader), *The Admirable Crichton* (1957), *The Sheriff of Fractured Jaw* (1958), *A Night to Remember* (1959), *North West Frontier* (1959) and *The Thirty-Nine Steps* (1959). His other films include: *The Yellow Balloon* (1953), *Raising a Riot* (1955), *The Man Who Loved Redheads* (1955), *Next to No Time* (1958), *Man in the Moon* (1960), *Sink the Bismarck!* (1960), *The Greengage Summer* (1961), *Some People* (1962), *The Longest Day* (1962), *We Joined the Navy* (1963), *The Comedy Man* (1964), *The Collector* (1965), *The Mercenaries* (1968), *Battle of Britain* (1969), *Fräulein Doktor* (1969), *Oh! What a Lovely War* (1969), *Scrooge* (1970), *The Slipper and the Rose: The Story of Cinderella* (1976), *Leopard in the Snow* (1978) and his last film, *The Spaceman and King Arthur* (1979). There is a Kenneth More Theatre in Ilford, Essex. His autobiography, *More or Less* was published in 1979. Kenneth was married three times – to actress Mary Beryl Johnstone (1940-46), Mabel Edith Barkby (1952-67) and actress Angela Douglas (b. 29 October 1940, Gerrards Cross, Buckinghamshire), from 1968 until his death on 12 July 1982, Fulham, London. See also entries in the television section for *Father Brown, The Forsyte Saga, Lord Raingo,* and *Six Faces.*

Morgan, Terence (1921-2005) Born Terence Ivan Grant Morgan, 8 December 1921, Lewisham, London. Actor. He worked as an insurance clerk before landing a scholarship to RADA. His army service was cut short when he was invalided out after two years. Stage debut: *The Astonished Ostrich.* Discovered by Laurence Olivier in 1945 he made his screen debut as Laertes in Olivier's adapation of *Hamlet* (1948). He then featured in *Captian Horatio Hornblower* (1951) playing the capable but ill-fated Mr Gerard, alongside Gregory Peck and Virginia Mayo. Despite being the cliched tall, dark and handsome man, he spent much of his big screen career playing villains. A list of his roles reveals he played a cad in *Encore* (1952), an insensitve father in *Mandy* (1952), a bounder in *Street Corner* (1953), a burglar in *Turn the Key Softly* (1953), a smuggler in *Forbidden Cargo* (1954), an unscrupulous father in *Dance, Little Lady* (1955), a murderer in *Tread Softly Stranger* (1958), a blackmailer in *The Shakedown* (1959) and a petty thief in *Piccadilly Third Stop* (1960). His other films in the 1950s were *Shadow of the Past* (1950), *It Started in Paradise* (1952), *The Steel Key* (1953), *Always a Bride* (1953), *The Face That Launched a Thousand Ships* (1954), *Svengali* (1954), *They Can't Hang Me* (1955), *The March Hare* (1956), *It's a Wonderful World* (1956), *The Scamp* (1957) and *The Flaming Sword* (1958). He was also in the BBC television series *More Than Robbery* (1958). Then in 1961 he landed the leading role in the ITV series *The Adventures of Sir Francis Drake* (1961-62). His few big screen parts after this were *The Curse of the Mummy's Tomb* (1964), *The Fighting Corsair* (1966), *The Penthouse* (1967), *Hide and Seek* (1972) and his last film, *The Lifetaker* (1975). Thereafter, he retired from acting, ran a hotel in Hove and became a property developer, although he did make a cameo appearance in an episode of the ITV crime series, *King and Castle* in 1986.

He was married to actress Georgina Symondson Jumel, from 1947 until his death on 25 August 2005, Brighton, East Sussex.

Morley, Robert (1908-1992) Born Robert Adolph Wilton Morley, 26 May 1908, Semley, Wiltshire. Actor. Trained at RADA. Stage debut: *Dr Syn* (1928). Screen debut: *Marie Antoinette* (1938 – as Louis XVI), for which he received an Academy Award nomination for Best Supporting Actor. His other films were: *Major Barbara* (1941), *You Will Remember* (1941), *The Big Blockade* (1942), *The Foreman Went to France* (1942), *The Young Mr. Pitt* (1942), *This Was Paris* (1942), *I Live in Grosvenor Square* (1945), *The Ghosts of Berkeley Square* (1947), *The Small Back Room* (1949), *The African Queen* (1951), *Curtain Up* (1952), *Outcast of the Islands* (1952), *Beat the Devil* (1953), *Melba* (1953), *The Story of Gilbert and Sullivan* (1953 – as W S Gilbert), *Beau Brummell* (1954) – as George III, *The Final Test* (1954), *The Good Die Young* (1954), *The Rainbow Jacket* (1954), *The Adventures of Quentin Durward* (1955 – as Louis XI), *Around the World in Eighty Days* (1956), *Loser Takes All* (1956), *Law and Disorder* (1958), *The Doctor's Dilemma* (1958), *The Sheriff of Fractured Jaw* (1958), *Libel* (1959), *The Battle of the Sexes* (1959), *The Journey* (1959), *Oscar Wilde* (1960), *The Young Ones* (1961 – as Cliff Richard's father), *Go to Blazes* (1962), *Sold Into Egypt* (1962), *The Boys* (1962), *The Road to Hong Kong* (1962), *Ladies Who Do* (1963), *Murder at the Gallop* (1963), *Nine Hours to Rama* (1963), *Take Her, She's Mine* (1963), *The Old Dark House* (1963), *Hot Enough for June* (1964), *Of Human Bondage* (1964), *Topkapi* (1964), *A Study in Terror* (1965), *Life at the Top* (1965), *The Alphabet Murders* (1965), *The Loved One* (1965), *Those Magnificent Men in Their Flying Machines or How I Flew from London to Paris in 25 hours 11 minutes* (1965), *Finders Keepers* (1966), *Hotel Paradiso* (1966), *The Trygon Factor* (1966), *Way... Way Out* (1966), *Woman Times Seven* (1967), *Hot Millions* (1968), *Sinful Davey* (1969), *Some Girls Do* (1969), *Cromwell* (1970), *Doctor in Trouble* (1970), *Song of Norway* (1970), *Twinky* (1970), *When Eight Bells Toll* (1971), *Theatre of Blood* (1973), *The Blue Bird* (1976), *Too Many Chefs* (1978), *Scavenger Hunt* (1979), *The Human Factor* (1979), *Oh Heavenly Dog* (1980), *Loophole* (1981), *The Great Muppet Caper* (1981), *High Road to China* (1983), *Second Time Lucky* (1984), *The Trouble With Spies* (1987), *Little Dorrit* (1988) and *Istanbul* (1989). He usually played pompous, or rather eccentric types, frequently aristocrats, Pope Leo X in the TV film *Luther* (1968) and the Emperor of China in *Genghis Khan* (1965). He was appointed a CBE in 1957. He married Joan Buckmaster in 1940 and he was the father of critic Sheridan Morley. His autobiography: *Robert Morley: Responsible Gentleman* was published in 1966. Robert died 3 June 1992, Wargrave, Berkshire. See also entries in the television section for *Call My Bluff, Ladykillers, The Old Men at the Zoo, Parent-Craft, Sunday Night at the London Palladium,* and *Tales From Dickens*

Mortimer, Emily (1971-) Born Emily Kathleen Mortimer, 1 December 1971, Finsbury Park, London. Actress. Educated at the St Paul's Girls School (a contemporary of actress Rachel Weisz) and Lincoln College, Oxford, Emily is the daughter of Sir John Mortimer, QC (creator of Rumpole of the Bailey) and his second wife, Penelope Gollop. She has a younger sister, Rosie; two older half-siblings, Sally Silverman and Jeremy, by her father's first marriage, to author Penelope Fletcher; and a half-brother, Ross Bentley, by her father's liaison with actress Wendy Craig (b. 20 June 1934, Sacriston, County Durham). Emily made her screen debut as Angela in the 1994 seven-part drama series *Under the Hammer*, which was written by her father. Other early television work include roles in *Sharpe's Sword, Ruth Rendell Mysteries, Silent Witness,* and *Midsomer Murders*. She made her feature film debut in *The Ghost and the Darkness* (1996 – as Helena Patterson). Other films include: *The Last of the High Kings* (1996 – as Romy Thomas), *The Saint* (1997), *Elizabeth* (1998 - as Kat Ashley), *Notting Hill* (1999), *Scream 3* (2000), *The Miracle Maker* (2000 - voice of Mary of Nazareth), *The Kid* (2000), *Lovely & Amazing* (2001), *The 51st State* (2001 - as Dakota Parker), *A Foreign Affair* (2003), *Nobody Needs to Know* (2003), *The Sleeping Dictionary* (2003 - as Cecil), *Bright Young Things* (2003 - as Nina Blount), *Young Adam* (2003 - as Cathie Dimly), *Dear Frankie* (2004), *Howl's Moving Castle* (2004 - voice of Young Sophie, English version), *Match Point* (2005 - as Chloe Hewett Wilton), *The Pink Panther* (2006 - as Nicole Durant), *Paris, Je T'Aime* (2006), *Lars and the Real Girl* (2007), *Chaos Theory* (2008), *Transsiberian* (2008 - as Jessie), *Redbelt* (2008 - as Laura Black), *The Pink Panther 2* (2009), *City Island* (2009 - as Molly), *Harry Brown* (2009 - as D.I. Alice Frampton), *Shutter Island* (2010 - as Rachel 1), *Leonie* (2010), *Our Idiot Brother* (2011), *Cars 2* (2011 - voice of Holly Shiftwell) and *Hugo* (2011 - as Lisette). During the making of *Love's Labour's Lost* (2000), Emily met actor Alessandro Nivola and they subsequently married in 2003. The couple have two children, Samuel (b. 26 September 2003, London) and May (b. 15 January 2010, New York).

Morton, Samantha (1977-) Born Samantha-Jane Morton, 13 May 1977, Nottingham, Nottinghamshire. Actress and film director. Samantha had a troubled childhood growing up in a broken home with a brother and sister and six half-siblings. Under the effects of drugs, she threatened an older girl who had been bullying her and served 18 weeks in an attendance centre. After leaving care, she lived in a hostel for the homeless and worked on a Youth Training Scheme in hairdressing. Samantha began acting at an early age and by 13 had left school and made her screen debut in the televison series *Soldier Soldier* (1991). Samantha gained further minor television roles in series such as *Boon* (1991), *Cracker* (1994), *Peak Practice* (1994) and *The Vet* (1995), before having a more substantial role, as Tracy Richards, in *Band of Gold* (1995). This exposure led to her first film roles in the made-for-televison movies *Emma* (1996 – as Harriet Smith) and the title role in *Jane Eyre* (1997). Her feature debut came in the Irish film *This is the Sea* (1997) and this was closely followed by her acclaimed performances as Iris Kelly in the film *Under the Skin* (1997) and as Sophia Western in the mini-series *The History of Tom Jones, a Foundling* (1997). She then received her first nomination for the Academy Award for Best Supporting Actress, for Woody Allen's *Sweet and Lowdown* (1999). She came to the attention of mainstream America when starring opposite Tom Cruise in the 2002 Sci-Fi thriller *Minority Report*. She received a second nomination for the Academy Award for Best Actress for *In America* (2003). Samantha has an eclectic taste in roles, turning down the major roles of Iris in *Iris* (2001) and Lisa in *Girl Interrupted* (1999) but appearing as the mermaid in the U2 music video *Electrical Storm,* released in 2002. Other films include: *Jesus' Son* (1999), *Dreaming of Joseph Lees* (1999), *Pandaemonium* (2000), *Morvern Callar* (2002), *Code 46* (2003), *Enduring Love* (2004), *The Libertine* (2004), *River Queen* (2005), *Lassie* (2005), *Free Jimmy* (2006), *Control* (2007), a black-and-white biographical film about Joy Division singer Ian Curtis, *Elizabeth: The Golden Age* (2007 - as Mary, Queen of Scots), *Mister Lonely* (2007 - as Marilyn Monroe), *Expired* (2007), *Synecdoche, New York* (2008), *The Daisy Chain* (2008) and *The Messenger* (2009). Samantha also starred in the television film *Longford* (2007), for which she won a Golden Globe for her portrayal of Moors Murderer Myra Hindley. Her directorial debut came in the semi-autobiographical Channel 4 drama *The Unloved* (2009), which won a BAFTA. Samantha lives in Spitalfields, East London, with her fiancé Harry Holm, the son of actor Ian Holm. She has two daughters, Esme (b. 5 February 2000, London), with actor Charlie Creed-Miles, and Edie (b. 4 January 2008, London), with filmmaker Holm. In 2006 Samantha apparently suffered a stroke after sustaining head injuries when part of the ceiling in her home fell down on her. Recently Samantha penned an open letter to her step-father in *Port*, the new men's style magazine. In the page-long letter she apologises for her wayward youth and expresses her love for the man who was married to her mother between 1983 and 1992, Frank Braidwood. Tragically, Frank died in 2007.

Mount, Peggy (1915-2001) Born Margaret Rose Mount, 2 May 1915, Leigh-on-Sea, Essex. Actress. Peggy first worked as a secretary while taking acting lessons from a drama tutor, Phyllis Reader, in her spare time. She progressed through amateur ranks and wartime concert party productions and, in 1944, gained her first professional stage part, in *Hindle Wakes* at the Hippodrome, Keighley, West Yorkshire. Peggy then joined the Harry Hanson Court Players for three years and toured in repertory theatre. Her first screen role was as Polly Sutherland in the short-lived BBC drama series, *The Cabin in the Clearing* (1954). Her first film role was in the TV film, *The Embezzler* (1954), coincidentally playing a character named Mrs Larkin, a quite different role from the one she later made famous in the popular television series, *The Larkins*. Peggy's feature debut came with a starring role as battle-axe Emma Hornett in *Sailor Beware* (1956), a role she had already played to rave reviews on stage in the West End. Emma's domineering personality tempered with a deep-down vulnerability being a recurrent feature of most of Peggy's characterisations. Ironically, off-set Peggy had the sweetest of dispositions, and indeed it was often this heart of gold that shone through among all the bluster and great booming voice that endeared her to millions of fans. Her other films include: *Dry Rot* (1956), *The Naked Truth* (1957), the TV film, *The Adventures of Mr. Pastry* (1958), *Inn for Trouble* (1960), *Ladies Who Do* (1963), *One Way Pendulum* (1964), *Hotel Paradiso* (1966), *Finders Keepers* (1966) and her last film appearance *Oliver!* (1968 – as Mrs Bumble), although she did lend her voice to *The Princess and the Goblin* (1991 - voice of the Goblin Queen). She was awarded an OBE in 1996. In her later years she lost her sight and suffered a series of strokes, forcing her home to retire. She died at Denville Hall, the actors' retirement home in North London, 13 November 2001. She never married. Despite her numerous stage successes and popularity in films, Peggy was possibly best known for her television work. See also entries in the television section for *George and the Dragon, John Browne's Body, The Larkins, Lollipop, The Tomorrow People, Winning Windows,* and *You're Only Young Twice.*

Mullard, Arthur (1910-1995) Born Arthur Ernest Mullord, 19 September 1910, Islington, London. Actor. Arthur spent his early life boxing and as a rag and bone man. He appeared in over 100 films, although he rarely made it onto the list of credits until the 1960s. Screen debut: *Inspector Hornleigh* (1939). His other films include: *Bonnie Prince Charlie* (1948), *The Case of Charles Peace* (1949), *The Blue Lamp* (1950), *The Lavender Hill Mob* (1951), *The Pickwick Papers* (1952), *Time Bomb* (1953), *The Belles of St. Trinian's* (1954), *The Colditz Story* (1955), *The Ladykillers* (1955), *My Teenage Daughter* (1956), *Happy Is the Bride* (1958), *The Man Who Liked Funerals* (1959), *Two Way Stretch* (1960), *On the Fiddle* (1961), *It's Trad, Dad!* (1962), *Postman's Knock* (1962), *Crooks Anonymous* (1962), *The Loneliness of the Long Distance Runner* (1962), *Sparrows Can't Sing* (1963), *The Wrong Arm of the Law* (1963), *Heavens Above!* (1963), *Band of Thieves* (1963), *Ladies Who Do* (1963), *Father Came Too!* (1964), *Allez France!* (1964), *Gonks Go Beat* (1965), *Morgan: A Suitable Case for Treatment* (1966), *The Great St. Trinian's Train Robbery* (1968), *Cuckoo Patrol* (1967), *Smashing Time* (1967), *Chitty Chitty Bang Bang* (1968), *Lock Up Your Daughters!* (1969), *Crooks and Coronets* (1969), *The Vault of Horror* (1973), *Steptoe and Son* (1973), *Holiday on the Buses* (1973), *Three for All* (1975) and *Adventures of a Plumber's Mate* (1978). Known for his large frame, distinctive voice and London accent he was always in demand as the stupid tough guy and he also proved an effective foil to a series of comedians including Tony Hancock and Tommy Cooper. Autobiography: *Oh, Yus, It's Arthur Mullard.* Arthur died 11 December 1995, Islington, London. See also entries in the television section for *The Army Game, Churchill's People, Oh in Colour, Romany Jones, The World of Beachcomber* and *Yus, My Dear.*

Mulligan, Carey (1985-) Born Carey Hannah Mulligan, 28 May 1985, Westminster, London. Actress. She made her screen debut in *Pride and Prejudice* (2005) as Kitty Bennet and then took the role of Ada Clare in a television adaptation of *Bleak House* (2005). She played Emily Pritchard in *The Amazing Mrs Pritchard* (2006) and then had roles in episodes of *Waking the Dead* and *Trial and Retribution*. She played Isabella Thorpe in another Austen adaptation, this time a television version of *Northanger Abbey* (2007) but came to more prominence after her portrayal of Sally Sparrow in the *Dr Who* episode *Blink* (2007). Her other screen roles in 2007 were on the big screen in *And When Did You Last See Your Father?* and on television in *My Boy Jack*. She also made a successful stage appearance in *The Seagull*

in London, which transferred to Broadway in 2008. Her next film was *The Greatest* (2009) but it was her first lead role as Jenny in *An Education* (2009) which gained her a BAFTA together with an Academy Award nomination for Best Actress. Her other films to date are *Public Enemies* (2009), *Brothers* (2009), *Wall Street: Money Never Sleeps* (2010), *Never Let Me Go* (2010), *Drive* (2011) and *Shame* (2011). In August 2011, she became engaged to Mumford & Sons lead singer Marcus Mumford and they eventually married on 21 April 2012.

Munro, Janet (1934-72) Born Janet Neilson Horsburgh, 28 September 1934, Blackpool, Lancashire. Actress. She was the daughter of Scottish comedian Alex Horsburgh, who took Munro as his stage name. Screen debut: *Small Hotel* (1957). She caught the eye of Walt Disney who cast her in *Darby O'Gill and the Little People* (1959) opposite a young Sean Connery, *Third Man on the Mountain* (1959) and *Swiss Family Robinson* (1960). She also starred with Tommy Steele in *Tommy the Toreador* (1959). Her attempts at more "adult" roles had one or two successes such as *The Day the Earth Caught Fire* (1961) and *Life for Ruth* (1962) but her career began to falter and she developed a drink problem. Her other films were: *The Young and the Guilty* (1958), *The Trollenberg Terror* (1958), *Bitter Harvest* (1963), *Hide and Seek* (1964), *A Jolly Bad Fellow* (1964), *Daylight Robbery* (1964), *Sebastian* (1968) and her last film, *Cry Wolf* (1972). Janet married actors Tony Wright (1956-59) and Ian Hendry (1963-71). She died, from a heart problem, 6 December 1972, Islington, London.

Napier, Alan (1903-88) Born Alan William Napier-Clavering, 7 January 1903, King's Norton, West Midlands. Actor. Nephew of British Prime Minister Neville Chamberlain. Studied at RADA. Stage debut: *Dandy Dick* (1924). Screen debut: *Caste* (1930). Other films include: *The Four Just Men* (1939), *The Invisible Man Return* (1940), *A Yank at Eton* (1942), *Random Harvest* (1942), *Cat People* (1942), *Lassie Come Home* (1943), *The Song of Bernadette* (1943), *The Uninvited* (1943), *Thirty Seconds over Tokyo* (1944), *House of Horror* (1946), *Forever Amber* (1947), *Sinbad the Sailor* (1947), *Macbeth* (1948), *Johnny Belinda* (1948), *Joan of Arc* (1948), *A Connecticut Yankee in King Arthur's Court* (1949), *Tarzan's Magic Fountain* (1949), *The Great Caruso* (1951), *Big Jim McLain* (1952), *Young Bess* (1953), *Julius Caesar* (1953), *The Court Jester* (1955), *Journey to the Centre of the Earth* (1959), *Tender is the Night* (1962), *Marnie* (1964), *Batman: the Movie* (1966) and his last feature, *Come Die with Me* (1974). Alan continued to make numerous appearances on television and his last screen role was in the TV film, *The Monkey Mission* (1981). He is of course best known for playing Bruce Wayne's butler Alfred Pennyworth in the American television series *Batman* (1966-68). Alan's second wife was Aileen Dickens Hawklsey, known as Gypsy (1907–1961). She was the great granddaughter of Charles Dickens. Alan was the step-grandfather of actor Brian Forster (b. 1960), best known for portraying the second Chris Partridge in the television series, *The Partridge Family.* He is also the great-grandfather of James Napier (b. 1982), best known for playing Connor McKnight on Power Rangers Dino Thunder. Alan died, 8 August 1988, Santa Monica , California.

Neagle, Anna (1904-86) Born Florence Marjorie Robertson, 20 October 1904, Forest Gate, London. Actress. She trained as ballerina and made her stage debut in 1917, as a dancer. Her first film role was an uncredited bit part in *Those Who Love* (1929); her first credited role was as Charlotte in *The Chinese Bungalow* (1930). In 1932 she appeared in *Good Night, Vienna*, directed by Herbert Wilcox, who was to mould her into one of Britain's leading screen heroines, and eventually marry her in 1943. For this film she used her stage name, Anna Neagle; the surname taken from her mother's maiden name. Anna's first major hit was in the title role of *Nell Gwyn* (1934) and she became famous for her biopic roles such as Irish actress Peg Woffington in *Peg of Old Drury* (1935); Queen Victoria in *Victoria the Great* (1937) and *Sixty Glorious Years* (1938); Edith Cavell in *Nurse Edith Cavell* (1939), her first Hollywood film; Amy Johnson in *They Flew Alone* (1942); Odette Sansom in *Odette* (1950; Florence Nightingale in *The Lady With the Lamp* (1950) and both Nell Gwyn and Queen Victoria in *Lilacs in the Spring* (1954). She also starred alongside Michael Wilding in the series of incredibly popular post-war films set in London: *Piccadilly Incident* (1946),

The Courtneys of Curzon Street (1947), Spring in Park Lane (1948) and Maytime in Mayfair (1949). Other films include: Bitter Sweet (1933), Limelight (1937), No, No, Nanette (1940 - in which she sang "Tea For Two"), Yellow Canary (1943), Forever and a Day (1943 – her final Hollywood film), I Live in Grosvenor Square (1945), Derby Day (1952), King's Rhapsody (1955), My Teenage Daughter (1956), The Man Who Wouldn't Talk (1958) and her final film, The Lady Is a Square (1959), opposite Frankie Vaughan. All these films were directed by Wilcox and the only film she made without him at the helm since, The Flag Lieutenant (1932 - directed by Henry Edwards) was No Time for Tears (1957 - directed by Cyril Frankel). Anna also produced, but did not star, in three films starring Frankie Vaughan: These Dangerous Years (1957), Wonderful Things (1957), and The Heart of a Man (1959). After WWII, she was voted the favourite English actress in seven consecutive years. Anna was equally at home on the stage and had an entry in the Guinness Book of World Records for her 2,062 consecutive performances in the stage play Charlie Girl which ran from 1965 to 1971. She was made a Dame in 1969 and died on 3 June 1986, West Byfleet, Surrey, from complications of Parkinson's disease. She was buried alongside her husband in the City of London Cemetery.

Neame, Elwin (1886-1923) Born Stuart Elwin Neame, 5 March 1886, Portishead, Bristol. Director. Studied art before taking up photography. Moved to London and established a successful photographic studio on Bond Street. In 1908 he was asked by the Daily Mirror to take portrait photographs of the finalists of their "Most Beautiful Woman in the World" competition. While doing this he met the winner, Ivy Close and they married in Hendon in late 1910. The pair established a film production company, Ivy Close Films in 1912, boasting that they would pursue the conviction that "films are art". He directed and she starred in a number of films including Dream Paintings (1912), Pygmalion and Galatea (1912), Mifanwy: a Tragedy (1913), Ghosts (1914), The Girl from the Sky (1914) and The Haunting of Silas P Gould (1915). Elwin was the father of director and cinematographer Ronald Neame and writer Derek Neame. He died 13 August 1923, in central London when his motorbike was in collision with a poorly parked car.

Neame, Ronald (1911-2010) Born Ronald Elwin Neame, 23 April 1911, Hendon, London. Director and cinematographer. Son of actress Ivy Close and director Elwin Neame. Educated at University College School and Hurstpierpoint College. Began his career in the cinema at Elstree Studios as assistant cameraman on Hitchcock's Blackmail (1928). He worked as a cinematographer during the 1930s on such films as Happy (1933), Drake of England (1935), Catch as Catch Can (1937) and Brief Ecstasy (1937). He also worked on George Formby vehicles such as It's in the Air (1938), I See Ice (1938), Trouble Brewing (1939),Come on George! (1939) and Let George Do It (1940). Ronald gained an Academy Award nomination for Best Special Effects for One of Our Aircraft is Missing (1942). He met David Lean whilst working on Major Barbara (1941) and, along with Anthony Havelock-Allan, they formed Cineguild. Together they received Academy Award nominations for Best Screenplay for Brief Encounter (1945) and Great Expectations (1946). Ronald also worked with Noël Coward on In Which We Serve (1942) and This Happy Breed (1944). His directorial debut was Take My Life (1947) and he followed this with The Golden Salamander (1949). He directed Alec Guinness in The Card (1952) and Gregory Peck in The Million Pound Note (1953). He worked on The Seventh Sin (1957) in Hollywood before returning to Britain for Windom's Way (1957). He formed Knightsbridge Films with John Bryan and then directed Alec Guiness in two of his best films The Horse's Mouth (1958) and Tunes of Glory (1960). In the 1960s he directed, amongst others, Judy Garland in her last film I Could Go on Singing (1963), Michael Caine in Gambit (1966) and Maggie Smith in her Academy Award winning performance in The Prime of Miss Jean Brodie (1969). After Scrooge (1970) he directed the blockbusting disaster movie The Poseidon Adventure (1972). His final films include The Odessa File (1974), Hopscotch (1980), First Monday in October (1981), his last feature film, Foreign

Body (1986) and the film short The Magic Balloon (1990). Autobiography: Direct from the Horse's Mouth (2003). He married Beryl Heanly in 1933. They separated in 1971 and divorced in 1992. The couple had one son, Christopher Elwin Neame (b. 1942), a writer / producer. Ronald's grandson, Gareth Neame (b. 1967) is a successful television producer. In 1993 Ronald married film researcher and television producer Donna Bernice Friedberg – who worked on his 1979 film Meteor. Ronald was appointed CBE in 1996 for his contribution to the film industry. He died, 16 June 2010, Los Angeles, California, after suffering complications from a broken leg.

Neeson, Liam (1952-) Born William John Neeson, 7 June 1952, Ballymena, County Antrim. Actor. Liam was Ulster amateur senior boxing champion. He studied briefly at the University of Belfast before working for Guinness, whilst pursuing amateur dramatics. Following a stint of teacher training in Newcastle he returned to Belfast. Stage debut: The Risen People (1976) at Belfast's Lyric Theatre. Screen debut: Pilgrim's Progress (1979). His first major role was as Gawain in John Boorman's Excalibur (1981). Other early films include Krull (1983), The Bounty (1984) and The Mission (1986). After moving to Hollywood in 1987, he starred alongside Cher and Dennis Quaid in Suspect. He won critical acclaim and after The Dead Pool (1988) and High Spirits (1988), he won his first lead role, in Darkman (1990), a comic-book sci-fi tale of a scientist who invents fake flesh to hide his disfigurement. He next featured in Woody Allen's Husbands and Wives (1992) and the Steve Martin vehicle Leap of Faith (1992) before taking the lead in an adapatation of Edith Wharton's Ethan Frome (1993). He was chosen by Steven Spielberg to play Oskar Schindler in Schindler's List (1993), which gained him an Academy Award nomination for Best Actor. Liam followed this success with Nell (1994) before taking the lead roles in Rob Roy (1995) and Michael Collins (1996), and as Jean Valjean in Les Miserables (1998). The following year he played Jedi Master Qui-Gon Jinn in Star Wars: Episode I - The Phantom Menace (1999) and then featured in The Haunting (1999) and Gun Shy (2000), but a serious motorbike crash, involving a deer, meant he was off the big screen until he returned with K19: The Widowmaker (2002). He took very different roles in The Gangs of New York (2002) and Love Actually (2003) before starring as Dr Alfred Kinsey in Kinsey (2004), a role which won him the Irish Film Awards – Best Actor Film. More recently he has featured in the Kingdom of Heaven (2005), Batman Begins (2005), The Chronicles of Narnia: The Lion, the Witch and the Wardrobe (2005 - as the voice of Aslan); Breakfast On Pluto (2005) Seraphim Falls (2006), Taken (2008), The Chronicles of Narnia: Prince Caspian (2008), Ponyo (2008 - voice of Fujimoto), The Other Man (2008), Five Minutes of Heaven (2009), Chloe (2009), After.Life (2009), Clash of the Titans (2010 - as Zeus), The A-Team (2010 - as Colonel Hannibal Smith), The Next Three Days (2010), The Chronicles of Narnia: The Voyage of the Dawn Treader (2010), and Unknown (2011). His voice is also featured in the video game Fallout 3 (released in October 2008) as the main character's father, James. Liam was married to actress Natasha Richardson from 3 July 1994 until her death on 18 March 2009, when she suffered a severe head injury in a skiing accident at the Mont Tremblant Resort in the Canadian province of Quebec. Natasha had just completed filming of the docudrama, The Wildest Dream, for which Liam offered the narration. Liam and Natasha have two sons: Michael and Daniel. Liam currently lives in Millbrook, New York. A staunch Catholic all his life although newspaper reports suggest he has recently been pondering conversion to Islam. He was awarded an OBE in 1999. See also entry for A Woman of Substance in the television section.

Neill, Sam (1947-) Born Nigel Neill 14 September 1947, Omagh, County Tyrone, Northern Ireland. Actor and director. Son of a New Zealand-born British army officer stationed in Northern Ireland. The family returned to New Zealand in 1954 and his father joined the family wholesale drink business. Educated at Canterbury University. Sam worked for the New Zealand National Film Unit in Wellington where he directed documentaries such as Telephone Etiquette (1974) and Architect

Athfield (1977) and made his acting debut in the feature films *Landfall* (1975) and *Ashes* (1975). He next took the lead role in *Sleeping Dogs* (1977) and this in turn led him to leave the Unit to star in *My Brilliant Career* (1979). After having a brief stint in the classic Australian soap, *The Sullivans*, he moved to England to make *Omen III: The Final Conflict* (1981) and followed this with *Possession* (1981), *From a Far Country* (1981) and *Enigma* (1983). He then starred in the British television series *Reilly: Ace of Spies* (1983) which brought him to wider public appreciation. He made *A Cry in the Dark* (1988) before playing in *Dead Calm* (1989) and *The Hunt for Red October* (1990). After *Memoirs of an Invisible Man* (1992) with Steve Martin he returned to New Zealand to film *The Sinking of the Rainbow Warrior* (1992) and *The Piano* (1993). He then had one of the lead roles, as palaeontologist Dr Alan Grant, in *Jurassic Park* (1994). Other films in the late 1990s include *The Jungle Book* (1994), *Restoration* (1995), the sci-fi thriller *Event Horizon* (1997), *The Horse Whisperer* (1998) and *Bicentennial Man* (1999). He also played the wizard in *Merlin* (1998), a four-part mini-series shown on the Hallmark television channel. He returned to the role of Dr Grant for *Jurassic Park III* (2001) and his later big screen roles include *Dirty Deeds* (2002), *Wimbledon* (2004), *Little Fish* (2005), *Angel* (2007), *My Talks with Dean Spanley* (2008), *I Am You* (2009), *Under the Mountain* (2009), *Daybreakers* (2009), *Legend of the Guardians: The Owls of Ga'Hoole* (2010) and *The Hunter* (2011). Sam was married firstly, to Australian actress Lisa Harrow, with whom he has a son, Tim (b. 1983) and, since 1989 to make-up artist Noriko Watanabe, with whom he has a daughter, Elena (b. 1991). Sam owns a vineyard in the Gibbston Valley, Otago, New Zealand. He received the OBE in 1991 for services to acting.

Nesbitt, Cathleen (1889-1982) Born Kathleen Mary Nesbitt, 24 November 1888, Cheshire. Actress. Stage debut: *The Cabinet Minister* (1910). Appeared on Broadway 1911 and 1915-1918. Screen debut: *A Star Over Night* (1919). Mainly a stage actress, she still found the time to make more than 70 TV and film appearances including in more than 60 years: *Pygmalion* (1938), *Fanny by Gaslight* (1944), *Caesar and Cleopatra* (1945), *Three Coins in the Fountain* (1954), *Separate Tables* (1958), *Villain* (1971), *Family Plot* (1976) and *Never Never Land* (1980). Engaged to poet Rupert Brook from 1912 until his death in 1915, she was married to actor Cecil Ramage, from 1920 until her death, on 2 August 1982, Kensington, London.

Newell, Mike (1942-) Born Michael Cormac Newell, 28 March 1942, St Albans, Hertfordshire. Director. Studied at Cambridge. Began his directorial career with Granada TV with *Sharon* (1964) and the majority of his output has been on the small screen. He learned his craft on TV series such as *Big Breadwinner Hog* (1969), *Budgie* (1971), *Wessex Tales* (1973) and *Play for Today* (1975). His TV movie debut was *The Man in the Iron Mask* (1977). His big screen debut was the horror film *The Awakening* (1980), which he followed with *Bad Blood* (1981). His next was the successful *Dance with a Stranger* (1985) about Ruth Ellis, the last woman executed in the UK. During the late 1980s he directed *The Good Father* (1985), *Amazing Grace and Chuck* (1987) and *Soursweet* (1988). In 1992 he made the Irish fable *Into the West* with Gabriel Byrne. After *Enchanted April* (1992) he made one of the most successful British films of the decade, *Four Weddings and a Funeral* (1994). Following this he teamed up with Hugh Grant again for *An Awfully Big Adventure* (1995) and then switched genres for the mafia mob based *Donnie Brasco* (1997). He directed Billy Bob Thornton and John Cusack in a film about rival air-traffic controllers *Pushing Tin* (1999). After *Mona Lisa Smile* (2003) with Julia Roberts he was asked to helm part four of the Harry Potter series, *Harry Potter and the Goblet of Fire* (2005). The success of this film meant that Newell became the third most commercially successful British director in recent years, behind Christopher Nolan and David Yates. His recent films include: *Love in the Time of Cholera* (2007) and *Prince of Persia: The Sands of Time* (2010). He has just completed helming *Great Expectations*, a film starring the young diabetic actor Jeremy Irvine (born Jeremy Smith, 1990, Gamlingay, Cambridgeshire) in the lead role of Pip.

Newley, Anthony (1931-99) Born Anthony George Newley, 24 September 1931, Hackney, London. Actor, singer and songwriter. Although his father's name was George Kirby, his mum and dad never married and the young Anthony was brought up by his Jewish mother, Frances Grace Newley. He was evacuated during the Blitz and was tutored during this time by George Pescud, a former British music hall entertainer who managed to get him work as an extra on *Henry V* (1944). By the age of fourteen he was working as an office boy for an insurance company when he read an ad placed by the Italia Conti Stage School in the *Daily Telegraph*, headed "Boy Actors Urgently Wanted". He applied, and although the fees were too high, after a brief audition, he was offered a job as an office boy on a salary of 30 shillings (£1.50) per week, with tuition thrown in free of charge. Tony made his stage debut in *Winds of Heaven* (1946). His first credited role was in the title role of *The Adventures of Dusty Bates* (1947) in the five-part film short series. His feature debut came as Dick Bultitude in *Vice Versa* (1948). Other films include: *Oliver Twist* (1948 - as the Artful Dodger), *The Guinea Pig* (1948), *Vote for Huggett* (1949), *A Boy, a Girl and a Bike* (1949), *Top of the Form* (1953), *Above us the Waves* (1955), *The Cockleshell Heroes* (1955), *The Battle of the River Plate* (1956), *The Good Companions* (1957), *Idol on Parade* (1959), *Let's Get Married* (1960), *The Small World of Sammy Lee* (1963), *Doctor Doolittle* (1967), the semi-autobiographical *Can Hieronymous Merkin ever Forget Mercy Humppe and Find True Happiness?* (1969), *The Old Curiosity Shop* (1975 - as Daniel Quilp), and his last film, *Boris and Natasha* (1992). A fine writer of musicals, he was responsible, in collaboration with Leslie Bricusse, for *Stop the World: I Want to Get Off* (1961), *The Roar of the Greasepaint - The Smell of the Crowd* (1965), *The Good Old Bad Old Days* (1972). They also wrote the songs for the films *Doctor Doolittle* (1967) - for which they received an Academy Award nomination - and *Willy Wonka and the Chocolate Factory* (1971). Tony was also a successful pop singer, with two No 1 hits in the UK - *Why* (1960) and *Do You Mind* (1960) and other hits such as *Strawberry Fair* (No 3 in 1960) and *Pop Goes the Weasel* (No 12 in 1961) which clearly influenced the early singing style of David Bowie. He was married three times, to Elizabeth Ann Lynn (1956-63), Joan Collins (1963-70), with whom he had two children, singer and broadcaster Tara Newley and portrait artist Sacha Newley; and former air hostess Dareth Rich (1971-89), with whom he also had two children, Shelby and Christopher. In 2007, the former *Dr Who* actress Anneke Wills published a memoir that detailed her relationship with Tony just before he took up with Joan Collins, producing a daughter named Polly who subsequently died in a car accident. His signature tune was *What Kind of Fool am I?* and he was inducted into the Songwriters' Hall of Fame in 1989. Made a TV appearance as Vince Watson in *Eastenders* shortly before he died, in the arms of his companion, the designer Gina Fratini, on 14 April 1999, Jensen Beach, Florida. See also entries in the television section for *Eastenders, The Strange World of Gurney Slade,* and *Wogan.*

Newman, Nanette (1934-) Born 29 May 1934, Northampton, Northamptonshire. Actress. Trained at the Italia Conti Academy of Theatre Arts and RADA. Nanette is not only known for advertising Fairy Liquid and being married to Bryan Forbes. She has appeared in over 30 films. As a child she appeared in the film short *Here We Come Gathering: A Story of the Kentish Orchards* (1945). Her first feature film was Anthony Pelissier's *Personal Affair* in 1953. Other films include: *The League of Gentlemen* (1959), *The Rebel* (1961), *Twice Round the Daffodils* (1962), *The Wrong Arm of the Law* (1963), *Séance on a Wet Afternoon* (1964), *Of Human Bondage* (1964), *The Wrong Box* (1966),*The L-Shaped Room* (1962), *Oh! What A Lovely War* (1969), *Man at the Top* (1973), *The Stepford Wives* (1975) and *International Velvet* (1978 - as Velvet Brown). Her last film was *The Mystery of Edwin Drood* (1993). See also entry for Bryan Forbes and entries in the television section for *Let There Be Love,* and *Sir Francis Drake.*

Newton, Robert (1905-56) Born 1 June 1905, Shaftsbury, Dorset. Actor. His grandfather was artist Henry Charles Newton who co-founded the Winsor & Newton artists supply company. Educated at Newbury and in Switzerland. Stage debut: *Henry IV, Part I* (1920). His screen debut was in the silent film *The Tremarne Case* (1924), his first talkie being *Reunion* (1932). He managed the Grand Theatre Fulham (1932-34). Other films include: *Fire Over England* (1937), *Jamaica Inn* (1939), *Major Barbara*

(1941), *This Happy Breed* (1944), *Henry V* (1944), *Tom Brown's Schooldays* (1951), *Blackbeard the Pirate* (1952), *Androcles and the Lion* (1952), *The Desert Rats* (1953) and his last film, *Around the World in 80 Days* (1956). Robert played a splendidly villainous Bill Sikes in *Oliver Twist* (1948) but is probably best remembered for his portrayal of the unscrupulous one-legged cook Long John Silver in *Treasure Island* (1950). He reprised the role on film in *Long John Silver* (1954) and on television in *The Adventures of Long John Silver* in the mid-1950s. Before Johnny Depp's turn as Captain Jack Sparrow in *Pirates of the Caribbean* (2003) he is probably everyone's idea of a screen pirate, all rolling eyes and west country accent - "Shiver me timbers, a landlubber I'll never be." In addition he was a fine Shakespearean actor who featured in many successful London and New York stage productions during the 1930s. Served on a minesweeper during WWII but was given special leave to work on patriotic films such as *Henry V*. Robert was married four times, to Petronella Walton, Annie McLean, Natalie Newhouse and Vera Budnik. His career was blighted due to alcoholism which ultimately led to his early death on 25 March 1956, Beverly Hills, California. See also entry in the television section for *The Adventures of Long John Silver*.

Newton, Thandie (1972-) Born Thandiwe Nashita Newton, 6 November 1972, London, England. Actress. Biographies of Thandie (pronounced Tandy) reported her birthplace as Lusaka, Zambia, but in a 2008 interview she stated she was born in London, during a two week trip by her parents, a Zimbabwean mother of the Shona Tribe and a British father. She lived in Zambia until moving back to the UK, where she was brought up in Cornwall. She studied modern dance at London's Arts Educational School, but moved on to acting after an accident. Her first film role was in John Duigan's *Flirting* (1991). After some minor work in LA she returned to Cambridge University to study, eventually receiving a 2:1 in anthropology. Her full name, Thandiwe, means "beloved." Apparently coincidentally, in her first film she played a character called Thandiwe Adjewa and later appeared in a film called *Beloved* (1998)! Because of her striking looks perhaps, her early career consisted of mainly vacuous roles *Interview with the Vampire: The Vampire Chronicles* (1994), *Mission: Impossible II* (2000) and *The Chronicles of Riddick* (2004) being three examples. In 2006 however, she won a Best Supporting Actress BAFTA for her role in Paul Haggis's ensemble piece *Crash* (2005*)* and this success has merited more challenging roles in *The Pursuit of Happyness* (2006), *Run Fat Boy Run* (2007), *Norbit* (2007), *RocknRolla* (2008), *W.* (2008 - as Condoleezza Rice), *2012* (2009) *Huge* (2010), *Vanishing on 7th Street* (2010), *For Colored Girls* (2010) and *Retreat* (2011). Thandie married English director Ol Parker in 1998 and the couple have two daughters, Ripley (b. 2000) and Nico (b. 2004), named after the character Ripley in the *Alien* films and Nico from The Velvet Underground.

Nighy, Bill (1949-) Born William Francis Nighy, 12 December 1949, Caterham, Surrey. Actor. Trained at The Guildford School of Dance and Drama (now the Guildford School of Acting). His first screen appearance was in an episode of *Softly, Softly: Task Force* (1976) and his feature debut came as an uncredited flower delivery man in *The Bitch* (1979). For 25 years he only had small character roles in films such as *Little Lord Fauntleroy* (1980), *Eye of the Needle* (1981), *Curse of the Pink Panther* (1983), *The Phantom of the Opera* (1989), *Mack the Knife* (1989), *Being Human* (1994), *True Blue* (1996), *Indian Summer* (1996), *Still Crazy* (1998), *Guest House Paradiso* (1999), *Blow Dry* (2001), *Lawless Heart* (2001), *Lucky Break* (2001) and *AKA* (2002). In 2003 he won a BAFTA for his role of Billy Mack, the middle-aged pop star in the box-office hit *Love Actually*, and in the same year played James Mortmain, the eccentric husband struggling to keep his family afloat in a decaying English castle, in *I Capture the Castle*. Subsequently he has been in great demand and his recent films include: *Underworld* (2003 - as Viktor), *Shaun of the Dead* (2004), *Enduring Love* (2004), *The Magic Roundabout* (2005 - voice of Dylan), *The Hitchhiker's Guide to the Galaxy* (2005 - as Slartibartfast), *The Constant Gardener* (2005), *Underworld: Evolution* (2006), *Pirates of the Caribbean: Dead Man's Chest* (2006 - as Davy Jones), *Alex Rider: Stormbreaker* (2006), *Flushed Away* (2006 - voice of Whitey), *Notes on a Scandal* (2006), *Hot Fuzz* (2007), *Pirates of the Caribbean: At World's End* (2007), *A Fox's Tale* (2008 - voice of Ringmaster), *Valkyrie* (2008), *Underworld: Rise of the Lycans* (2009), *The Boat That Rocked* (2009), *G-Force* (2009), *Glorious 39* (2009), *Astro Boy* (2009 - voice of Dr Elefun and Robotsky), *Wild Target* (2010), *Harry Potter and the Deathly Hallows: Part 1* (2010 - as Minister Rufus Scrimgeour), *Rango* (2011 – voice of Rattlesnake Jake), *Chalet Girl* (2011) and *Arthur Christmas* (2011 – voice of Grandsanta). Bill suffers from Dupuytren's contracture, a condition which causes the ring and little finger of each hand to be permanently bent inwards towards the palm. He had a 27-year-relationship with English actress Diana Quick, with whom he has a daughter, actress Mary Nighy (b. 17 July 1984). The couple split in 2008. See also entries in the television section for *Agony, Auf Wiedersehen Pet, The Canterbury Tales, Grumpy Old Men / Women, Last Place On Earth,* and *State of Play.*

Niven, David (1910-83) Born James David Graham Niven, 1 March 1910, Belgravia, London. Actor and author. Educated at Stowe. Trained at Sandhurst and joined the Highland Light Infantry before resigning his commission and travelling around Canada and the United States. He registered with Central Casting in Hollywood as "Anglo Saxon Type Number 2008" and made a series of appearances as an extra (usually of Mexican origin) before his screen debut proper in *There Goes the Bride* (1932). Other early films include: *Cleopatra* (1934), *Barbary Coast* (1934), *Mutiny on the Bounty* (1935) and *Thank you, Jeeves* (1936). His first major role was in the Errol Flynn vehicle *The Charge of the Light Brigade* (1936). He played support to Ronald Colman in *The Prisoner of Zenda* (1937), teamed up with Flynn again in *The Dawn Patrol* (1938) and played opposite Laurence Olivier in *Wuthering Heights* (1939). His first headline role was with Ginger Rogers in *Bachelor Mother* (1939), which he followed with the title role as the gentleman thief in *Raffles* (1939). David joined the Rifle Brigade during WWII, rising to the rank of Lt Colonel, with Peter Ustinov as his batman, although this was mainly a ploy for them to collaborate as actor and scriptwriter. He was given leave to make *The First of the Few* (1942) and *The Way Ahead* (1945). After the war he starred as the RAF pilot who should have died but didn't in the Powell and Pressburger classic *A Matter of Life and Death* (1946). His other post-war films include: *The Bishop's Wife* (1947), *Bonnie Prince Charlie* (1948), *The Elusive Pimpernel* (1950), *The Moon is Blue* (1953), *Happy Ever After* (1954) and *Carrington VC* (1955). In the early 1950s he formed a production company *Four Star Television* with fellow actors Charles Boyer and Dick Powell. He played Phileas Fogg in the star-studded *Around the World in 80 Days* (1956) and his career reached a peak when he won a Best Actor Academy Award for *Separate Tables* (1958). He still featured in some very popular films during the last decades of his life including *The Guns of Navarone* (1961), *55 Days at Peking* (1963), *The Pink Panther* (1963 – as Sir Charles Lytton, aka. "the Phantom,"), *Casino Royale* (1967 - as Sir James Bond), *Paper Tiger* (1975), *Candleshoe* (1977), *Death on the Nile* (1978), *The Sea Wolves* (1980) and his last film, *Curse of the Pink Panther* (1983) in which his voice had to be dubbed by impressionist Rich Little as David's health deteriorated. In 1979, he appeared in the film *Escape to Athena*, which was produced by his son David Niven Jr. On screen he was always at his best as the witty and debonair English gentleman in light comedy. He wrote two novels: *Round the Rugged Rocks* (1951) and *Go Slowly, Come Back Quickly* (1981); and two autobiographies: *Bring on the Empty Horses* (1975) and *The Moon's a Balloon* (1981). David's first marriage was to Primula Susan Rollo, in 1940. The couple had two sons, David Jr. and Jamie. "Primmie", died at age 28, of a fractured skull following a fall at the home of Tyrone Power. While playing hide and seek, she walked through a door believing it led to a closet. Instead, it led to a stone staircase to the basement. His second marriage was to Swedish fashion model Hjordis Paulina Tersmeden, from 1948 until his death, from motor neurone disease (more specifically Amyotrophic lateral sclerosis, or Lou Gehrig's disease), on 29 July 1983, Chateaux-d'Oex, Switzerland. Raymond Massey, David's friend and co-star in *The Prisoner of Zenda* and *A Matter of Life and Death* coincidentally died on the same day. David and Hjordis adopted two girls, Kristina and Fiona, although Kristina is thought to be David's biological daughter following an affair with 18-year-old Swedish fashion model, Mona Gunnarson.

Norwood, Eille (1861-1948) Born Anthony Edward Brett, 11 October 1861, York. Actor. Son of a brewer. Educated at St John's College, Cambridge. A noted stage actor and producer. Stage debut: *Romeo and Juliet* (1884). He was forced to retire from the stage 1884-1901 through illness. Made his screen debut aged 50 in *Princess Clementina* (1911). Joined *Stoll Picture Productions* in 1920 and became famous for portraying Sherlock Holmes in 45 short (20 minute) films and two feature versions of the Conan Doyle stories. This means he is the actor who has played Holmes the most times on screen. The first short films were all made in 1921. There were 15 in all, called *The Adventures of Sherlock Holmes* and directed by Maurice Elvey. In 1922 George Ridgewell directed the next fifteen, which were called *The Further Adventures of Sherlock Holmes*. The final 15, all made in 1923 by Ridgewell, were not unexpectedly entitled *The Last Adventures of Sherlock Holmes*. Elvey directed both the full-length films *The Hound of the Baskervilles* (1920) and *The Sign of Four* (1923). Basing his look closely on the Sidney Paget drawings, Conan Doyle said of Norwood's portrayal: "His wonderful impersonation of Holmes has amazed me". Hubert Willis played Dr Watson in all these productions bar the last, in which he was replaced by Arthur Cullin. Norwood was noted for being, like Holmes, something of a master of disguise, a fact which helped him land the role. He went on to play Holmes on stage after the film series ended. His other films include: *The Charlatan* (1916), *The Tavern Knight* (1920) and *The Yellow Face* (1921). Eille returned exclusively to the stage after 1923. He also wrote plays such as: *Chalk and Cheese*, *The Noble Art* and *One Good Turn*, and composed songs. A lover of words and language, he compiled more than 2,000 crosswords for the *Daily Express*. He died 24 December 1948, Chelsea, London.

Novello, Ivor (1893-1951) Born David Ivor Davies, 15 January 1893, Cardiff. Actor, writer and composer. Son of singing teacher Clara Novello Davies. Educated at Magdalen College Choir School, Oxford. After leaving school, he gave piano lessons in Cardiff, and then moved to London in 1913, taking a flat above the Strand Theatre, which became his London home for the rest of his life. He came to prominence when he wrote *Keep the Home Fires Burning* at the outbreak of WWI in 1914 and became an established song writer after a spell in the Royal Naval Air Service. Ivor then turned to acting and made his screen debut in *L'Appel du Sang (The Call of the Blood)* (1921) and his stage debut in *Deburau* (1921) using his mother's maiden name, "Novello" as his professional surname, although he did not change it legally until 1927. He then wrote the successful play *The Rat* in 1924 with Constance Collier, which was later turned into a film, and continued to write and star in plays such as *Glamorous Night* (1935), *Careless Rapture* (1936), *The Dancing Years* (1939), *King's Rhapsody* (1949) and *Gay's the Word* (1951) throughout his life. His film career lasted through the 1920s into the early 1930s and included: *Carnival* (1921), *The White Rose* (1923), *Bonnie Prince Charlie* (1923), *The Rat* (1925 - as Pierre "The Rat" Boucheron), *The Triumph of the Rat* (1926), *The Return of the Rat* (1928), *The Vortex* (1928), *The Constant Nymph* (1928) and *Autumn Crocus* (1934). He starred in *The Lodger* (1926), Alfred Hitchcock's first major film, and in the sound remake in 1932. At one point considered to be the "New Valentino". He was jailed for a month during WWII for fiddling petrol coupons for his Rolls-Royce. His other best remembered songs are *And Mother Came Too* and *We'll Gather Lilacs*. The British Academy of Composers inaugurated the Ivor Novello Awards which are given annually to songwriters, composers and arrangers. Ivor, who was fairly openly gay, met British stage actor Bobbie Andrews (1895-1976) in 1916 and he remained his partner until his death on 6 March 1951, Aldwych, London.

Nunn, Trevor (1940-) Born Trevor Robert Nunn, 14 January 1940, Ipswich, Suffolk. Theatre and film director and writer. Educated at Downing College, Cambridge. Trevor began his career as a trainee director at the Belgrade Theatre in Coventry before being appointed Artistic Director of the Royal Shakespeare Company in 1968, a position he held until 1986 when he took up a similar position at the Royal National Theatre, replacing Sir Peter Hall. His film credits are few. He directed Glenda Jackson in the 1976 film *Hedda* and it was fully ten years before his next film project *Lady Jane* (1986), with Helena Bonham Carter in the title role. A decade later he again directed Helena's portrayal of Olivia in *Twelfth Night* (1996), a film which also starred his wife Imogen Stubbs as Viola. Trevor also wrote the screenplay for this film. A prolific theatre director of everything from Shakespearean tragedies to opera to light musicals. In 2010 he directed a revival of the Andrew Lloyd Webber musical *Aspects of Love* at the Menier Chocolate Factory and the play *Birdsong* (based on Sebastian Faulks novel) at the Comedy Theatre). He was knighted in 2002. He has been married three times, to actress Janet Suzman (1969-86), Sharon Lee-Hill (1986-91) and actress Imogen Stubbs (1994-present), with whom he has two children, Ellie and Jesse. In April 2011 Imogen announced that she and Sir Trevor had separated. She admitted she was involved in a new relationship while he was on holiday with the Italian-American lawyer and television presenter Nancy Dell'Olio, the former girlfriend of England football coach Sven-Goran Eriksson. See also entry for Hugh Grant.

Oberon, Merle (1911-79) Born Estelle Merle Thompson, 18 February 1911, Bombay (now Mumbai), British India. Actress. Daughter of an Anglo-Welsh-Irish father and an Anglo-Sinhalese mother, Constance Selby, who gave birth to Merle at the age of 15 and allowed her to be raised as her sister. Merle was given "Queenie" as a nickname, in honour of Queen Mary, who visited India along with King George V in 1911. Known for her sultry looks, the origins of which would be hidden by her for the rest of her life. Merle came to England for the first time aged 17 in 1928 and made her screen debut in *The Three Passions* (1929), a film famous for a scene where George Bernard Shaw and Harpo Marx, who were friends of the director Rex Ingram, appeared as extras shooting pool. Initially Merle worked as a club hostess under the name Queenie O'Brien and played in minor and unbilled roles in various films such as *Alf's Button* (1930), *Never Trouble Trouble* (1931), *Aren't We All?* (1932) and *Strange Evidence* (1933). Her first major film roles were as Anne Boleyn in *The Private Life of Henry VIII* (1933) opposite Charles Laughton, and Lady Marguerite Blakeney in *The Scarlet Pimpernel* (1934) opposite Leslie Howard, whom she later dated. Her career reached greater heights partly as a result of her relationship with director Alexander Korda, who had persuaded her to take the name under which she became famous. She received her only Academy Award nomination (for Best Actress) for the role of Kitty Vane in *The Dark Angel* (1935) and around this time she had a passionate affair with David Niven. She next starred in Korda's film *I, Claudius* (1937 - as Messalina), but a serious car accident resulted in filming being abandoned. Although facially scarred for life, skilled lighting technicians prevented her injuries being spotted by cinema audiences. She went on to appear as Cathy in *Wuthering Heights* (1939), as George Sand in *A Song to Remember* (1945) and as Empress Josephine in *Désirée* (1954). After *The Price of Fear* (1956) she concentrated on American television work and only made three more films, *Of Love and Desire* (1963), *Hotel* (1967) and her last film, *Interval* in 1973. During her time as a film star she went to great lengths to disguise her mixed-race background and when her dark-skinned mother moved in with her in Hollywood, she masqueraded as Merle's maid. Merle was married four times, to Sir Alexander Korda (1939-1945), American cinematographer Lucien Ballard (1945-49), Italian-born industrialist Bruno Pagliai (1957-73) and Dutch television actor Robert Wolders, from 1975 until her death on 23 November 1979, Malibu, California.

O'Connell, Jack (1990-) Born 1 August 1990, Alvaston, Derby. Actor. Jack made his screen debut as Connor Yates in an episode of *Doctors* in 2005 and later that year had a recurring role as Ross Trescott in *The Bill*. His feature film debut came in *This is England* (2006 – as Pukey Nicholls). He followed this up with the horror film *Eden Lake* (2008 – as Brett) and in between garnered television roles in *Waterloo Road*, *Wire in the Blood* and *Holby City*. After a small role as a shepherd boy in the television film,

Wuthering Heights (2009) he had a more substantial role, opposite Michael Caine, in the feature film *Harry Brown* (2009 – as Marky). More recently he has appeared in the television series *Skins* (2010 – as James Cook) and *The Runaway* (2011 – as Eamonn) and in the films *United* (2011 – as Bobby Charlton) and *Weekender* (2011 – as Dylan). He is currently dating former N-Dubz star Tulisa.

O'Connor, T P (1848-1929) Born Thomas Power O'Connor, 5 October 1848, Athlone, County Westmeath, Ireland. Film censor. Educated at Queen's College, Galway. Worked as a journalist, eventually with the *Daily Telegraph* and *The New York Herald* in London. Founder of several newspapers including *The Star* (1887), *Weekly Sun* (1891) and *The Sun* (1893). He was elected Nationalist MP for Galway (1880-85) and MP for Liverpool Scotland Division (1885-1929) and was in fact Father of the House (1918-1929). He served as president of the British Board of Film Censors (1916-1929) and took an active role in film censorship saying in 1923: "So long as decorum is maintained, so long as the subject is not one that should be reserved for the study hall or the dissecting hall or a special theatre, I deem it my duty to fight for the liberty of this new form of artistic expression.". In 1916 he drew up a list of rules describing grounds for deletion for British film makers known as "O'Connor's 43". He also wrote *Lord Beaconsfield* (1879), *The Parnell Movement* (1886) and *Memoirs of an Old Parliamentarian* (1928). Also known as Tay Pay, he died 18 November 1929 London.

O'Hara, Maureen (1920-) Born Maureen FitzSimons, 17 August 1920, Ranelagh, Dublin. Actress. After elocution lessons she was accepted by the Abbey Theatre aged 14. Discovered by Charles Laughton in 1938 whilst in London for a screen test at Elstree, she made her screen debut in *Kicking the Moon Around* (1938). Laughton played opposite Maureen in Hitchcock's *Jamaica Inn* (1939) and again in *The Hunchback of Notre Dame* (1939 – as Esmeralda). Her looks and red hair meant that she became known as "The Queen of Technicolor" and she was described by John Ford as "the best bloody actress in Hollywood". He directed her in five films: *How Green Was My Valley* (1941), *Rio Grande* (1950), the classic *The Quiet Man* (1952), *The Long Gray Line* (1955) and *The Wings of Eagles* (1957). She also made five films with John Wayne, *Rio Grande* (1950), *The Quiet Man* (1952), *The Wings of Eagles* (1957), *McLintock!* (1963) and *Big Jake* (1971). The most versatile of actresses, equally at home as the love interest in westerns, a pirate in *The Black Swan* (1942), *The Spanish Main* (1945) and *Sinbad the Sailor* (1947), or more quietly as a mother in films such as *Miracle on 34th Street* (1947), *Against All Flags* (1952) and *The Parent Trap* (1961). Other films include: *Buffalo Bill* (1944), *Sentimental Journey* (1946), *The Foxes of Harrow* (1947), *Flame of Araby* (1951), *Sons of the Musketeers* (1952), *Kangaroo* (1952), *The Redhead from Wyoming* (1953), *The Brave and the Beautiful* (1955), *Lady Godiva of Coventry* (1955 - as Lady Godiva), *Our Man in Havana* (1959), *Mr. Hobbs Takes a Vacation* (1962), *Spencer's Mountain* (1963) and *The Rare Breed* (1966). Maureen had the most beautiful soprano voice and was a regular on American television shows although this talent was never realized in feature films. Married three times, to film producer George H Brown (1939-41), film director Will Price (1941-53) with whom she had a daughter, Bronwyn FitzSimons Price (b. 1944).and aviator General Charles F Blair (1968-78). During her last marriage her acting took a back seat until her husband was killed in a plane crash in 1978. Her last big screen outing (her first since *Big Jake*) was in *Only the Lonely* (1991) playing John Candy's obstinate mother. Her last film to-date was the TV movie *The Last Dance* (2000). Autobiography: *'Tis Herself* (2004).

O'Herlihy, Dan (1919-2005) Born Daniel Peter O'Herlihy, 1 May 1919, Wexford, Ireland. Actor. Briefly studied with a view to following in his architect father's footsteps before turning to acting with the Gate and Abbey Theatres in Dublin. Spotted by director Carol Reed, who cast him in *Odd Man Out* (1947), a film released a few months after his debut in *Hungry Hill* (1947). Through a long career he featured in such films as *Macbeth* (1948 - as Macduff), *Kidnapped* (1948), *At Sword's Point* (1952), *The*

Black Shield of Falworth (1955), *Imitation of Life* (1959), *Fail Safe* (1964), *Waterloo* (1970 – as Marshal Ney), *MacArthur* (1977 - as FD Roosevelt, *The Last Starfighter* (1984), *The Dead* (1987), *RoboCop* (1987) and *RoboCop 2* (1990). His last feature film was *Love, Cheat and Steal* (1993) and his last screen appearance in the TV film The Rat Pack (1998 – as Joe Kennedy). The pinnacle of his career was being nominated for an Academy Award for Best Actor for his virtual solo lead performance in *The Adventures of Robinson Crusoe* (1954). His brother Michael O'Herlihy (1928-97) was a television and film director. Dan died 17 February 2005, Malibu, California. See also entry in the television section for *Colditz*.

Okonedo, Sophie (1969-) Born 1 January 1969, London. Actress. Daughter of a caucasian Jewish mother and a Nigerian father. Her father left the family a few years after her birth, and Sophie was raised in poverty by her single mother. She trained at RADA. Her first film was *Young Soul Rebels* in 1991 after which she appeared in a number of television roles. She came to mass attention in 2003 with *Scream of the Shalka* — a webcast based on the BBC television series *Doctor Who* as Alison Cheney, a companion of the Doctor. A year later she was nominated for an Academy Award in the category of Best Supporting Actress for her role as Tatiana Rusesabagina in *Hotel Rwanda* (2004). Other films include: *Ace Ventura: When Nature Calls* (1995 - as The Wachati Princess), *The Jackal* (1997), *This Year's Love* (1999), *Mad Cows* (1999), *Peaches* (2000), *Dirty Pretty Things* (2002), *Cross My Heart* (2003), *Æon Flux* (2005), *Alex Rider: Stormbreaker* (2006), *Scenes of a Sexual Nature* (2006), *The Secret Life of Bees* (2008) and *Skin* (2008). Sophie has a daughter, Aoife (b. 1997), from a previous relationship with Irish film editor Eoin Martin. She was appointed Officer of the Order of the British Empire (OBE) in the 2010 Queen's Birthday Honours. Most recently Sophie has concentrated on television roles and has appeared as Aisha in the Australian drama series *The Slap* (2011). See also entries in the television section for *Father & Son*, and *The Governor*.

Oldman, Gary (1958-) Born Gary Leonard Oldman, 21 March 1958, New Cross, London. Actor and director. After many jobs he won a scholarship to the Rose Bruford College of Speech and Drama. Worked in repertory in York and Colchester before joining the Glasgow Citizen's Theatre. Screen debut: *Remembrance* (1982). Made his big screen breakthrough playing Sid Vicious in *Sid and Nancy* (1986) and swiftly followed this with a stirring portrayal of Joe Orton in *Prick Up Your Ears* (1987). He then starred as Rosencrantz in *Rosencrantz and Guildenstern are Dead* (1990) alongside Tim Roth and followed this with *State of Grace* (1990). Gary moved to the United States in the early 1990s and along with the likes of Roth, Colin Firth, Rupert Everett, Miranda Richardson and Daniel Day Lewis, is often referred to as a member of the 'Brit Pack' in Hollywood circles. His ability with accents and physical transformation means that he has played a wide variety of roles including Lee Harvey Oswald in *JFK* (1991) and Beethoven in *Immortal Beloved* (1994). In between these two films he sandwiched a portrayal of the Prince of Darkness in *Dracula* (1992), a pimp in *True Romance* (1993) and corrupt cops in *Romeo is Bleeding* (1993) and *Leon* (1994). He then made *Murder in the First* (1995) and *The Scarlet Letter* (1995) before embarking on his only directorial project to date, the gritty south London set *Nil by Mouth* (1997). He followed this with a series of appearances in big budget films such as *The Fifth Element* (1997), *Air Force One* (1997), *Lost in Space* (1998), *The Contender* (2000) and *Hannibal* (2001). His films since then include the Harry Potter films *The Prisoner of Azkaban* (2004), *The Goblet of Fire* (2005), *The Order of the Phoenix* (2007) and *Harry Potter and the Deathly Hallows Part II* (2011– as Sirius Black), the London gangster film *Dead Fish* (2004), the caped crusader films *Batman Begins* (2005) and *The Dark Knight* (2008 – as Commissioner James Gordon), *The Unborn* (2009), *Rain Fall* (2009), *A Christmas Carol* (2009), *Planet 51* (2009), *The Book of Eli* (2010), *Red Riding Hood* (2011 - as Father Solomon), *Kung Fu Panda 2* (2011 - voice of Lord Shen), *Tinker Tailor Soldier Spy* (2011 - as George Smiley) and *Guns, Girls and Gambling* (2011 - as Elvis). Gary will reprise his role of Commisioner Gordon in *The Dark Knight Rises* (2012). He seems to excel in parts calling for evil, psychotic characters. Gary has been married four times, to actresses Lesley Manville (1987-90) and Uma Thurman (1990-92), photographer Donya Fiorentino (1997-2001) and, since 2008, jazz singer Alexandra Edenborough. He has three sons: Alfie (b. 1988), from his marriage to Manville, and Gulliver Flynn (b. 20 August 1997) and Charlie John (b. 11 February 1999), from his marriage to Fiorentino. His sister Maureen (aka Laila Morse) plays Big Mo Slater in *Eastenders*. Laila (b. 1 August 1945, Dorking, Surrey) played Janet in *Nil By Mouth*, and Interestingly, her stage name is an anagram of an Italian phrase for "my sister" (Mia Sorella) - a name she got from Gary's then girlfriend Isabella Rossellini.

Olivier, Laurence (1907-89) Born Laurence Kerr Olivier, 22 May 1907, Dorking, Surrey. Actor and director. Son of a clergyman. Educated at St Edward's School, Oxford and the Central School of Speech and Drama. Stage debut: *The Ghost Train* (1925). Worked with the Birmingham Repertory Company (1926-28). His stage breakthrough came in *Private Lives* (1930). In 1935 he alternated with John Gielgud as Romeo and Mercutio in *Romeo and Juliet* which was a major step in his distinguished classical theatrical career. Screen debut: *Too Many Crooks* (1930). A stint on Broadway led to him being cast in *Friends and Lovers* (1931) and *The Yellow Ticket* (1931) but he returned to Britain after losing out to John Gilbert as the male lead in *Queen Christina* (1933). In 1937 he left his first wife, Jill Esmond, by whom he had a son, Simon Tarquin (b. 21 August 1936), and began an affair with Vivien Leigh, his co-star in *Fire Over England* (1937). They eventually married in 1940. Meanwhile he gained his first Academy Award nomination for Best Actor for his portrayal of Heathcliff in *Wuthering Heights* (1939). Laurence gained a further nomination the following year as George de Winter in *Rebecca* (1940). He starred as Darcy in *Pride and Prejudice* (1940) and joined Leigh again in *21 Days* (1940) and *That Hamilton Woman* (1941). After serving in the Fleet Air Arm during WWII (1941-1942) he starred in, produced and directed *Henry V* (1944), a cinematic tour de force which won an Academy Award nomination for Best Picture, and for him a nomination for Best Actor and an award for Outstanding Achievement. He topped this with *Hamlet* (1948) which gained him an Academy Award nomination for Best Director but won him a Best Actor Academy Award and became the first British film to win an Academy Award for Best Film. He is one of only two people - the other is Roberto Benigni - to direct himself in an Academy Award winning performance. Laurence next played a cameo as a police constable in the star-studded Festival of Britain film *The Magic Box* (1951). After *The Beggar's Opera* (1953) he directed and starred in *Richard III* (1955), which saw him gain another Academy Award nomination for Best Actor. After appearing with Marilyn Monroe in *The Prince and the Showgirl* (1956) he took the part of Archie Rice in *The Entertainer* (1960), receiving another Academy Award nomination for Best Actor and he received a further nomination for playing the Moor in *Othello* (1965). During the 1960s his other films include *Spartacus* (1960), *Khartoum* (1966), *Battle of Britain* (1969) and *Oh! What a Lovely War* (1969). During the last few years of his life he was accused of taking roles which were "beneath" him in order to provide for his young family. However, he was still able to pull out outstanding performances such as Andrew Wyke in *Sleuth* (1972) and Ezra Lieberman in *The Boys from Brazil* (1978), both of which gained him Best Actor Academy Award nominations. He also received a Best Supporting Actor Academy Award for his role of sadistic Nazi dentist Christian Szell in *Marathon Man* (1976). His other films include: *Lady Caroline Lamb* (1972), *The Seven-Per-Cent Solution* (1976), *A Bridge too Far* (1977), *The Jazz Singer* (1979), *Clash of the Titans* (1981), *The Bounty* (1984) and his last film, *War Requiem* (1989). In all he received no fewer than 14 individual Academy Award nominations/wins. In the theatre he was co-director of the Old Vic Theatre Company (1944-49), founding director of the Chichester Festival Theatre (1962-66) and also of the National Theatre Company (1962-73). Widely regarded as the greatest actor in the English speaking world during the twentieth century. Knighted in 1947. Became the first theatrical Lord to be elevated to a Baronetcy in 1970 when he became Baron Olivier of Brighton. Britain's premier theatre awards are named in his honour. Married three times, to actresses Jill Esmond (1930-40), Vivien Leigh (1940-60) and Joan Plowright (1961-89), with whom he had a son and two daughters. Autobiography: *Confessions of an Actor* (1984). He died 11 July 1989, Steyning, West Sussex and is one of the few actors (along with Ben Johnson, David Garrick, Henry Irving and Dame Sybil Thorndike) to have his ashes interred in Westminster Abbey. See also entries in the television section for *Brideshead Revisited, Jesus of Nazareth*, and *World at War*.

O'Neill, Maire (1885-1952) Born Mary Allgood (known as "Molly") 12 January 1885, Dublin, Ireland. Actress. Screen Debut: *Juno and the Paycock* (1930) alongside her sister, Sara Allgood. Other films include: *Sing As We Go* (1934), *The Arsenal Stadium Mystery* (1940), *Love on the Dole* (1941), *Scrooge* (1951) and her last film, The Oracle (1953). Maire, whose career did not reach the heights of her more illustrious sister, had been engaged to Irish playwright John Millington Synge before his untimely death on 24 March 1909. She died in Park Prewett Hospital, Basingstoke, on 2 November 1952, after being badly burned in a fire at her London home.

Ormond, Julia (1965-) Born Julia Karin Ormond, 4 January 1965, Epsom, Surrey. Actress. Brought up in relatively privileged surroundings as the daughter of a well-to-do laboratory technician. She is said to be a distant niece of the Welsh rebel and prince Owain Glyndwr through her paternal grandmother. She was the second of five children and her parents divorced when she was young. She then attended Cranleigh, a private school, and although initially attending art school she transferred to Webber-Douglas Academy of Dramatic Art, where she graduated in 1988 after receiving the London Drama Critics Award for best newcomer. Her screen debut came in the Channel 4 mini-series, *Traffik* (1989) and her film debut in the TV movie *Young Catherine* (1991 – as Catherine). After starring in another TV film, *Stalin* (1992) she made her feature film debut in Peter Greenaway's *The Baby of Mâcon* (1993). Other films include: *Nostradamus* (1994), *Legends of the Fall* (1994), *First Knight* (1995 - as Guinevere), *Sabrina* (1995), *Smilla's Feeling for Snow* (1997), *The Barber of Siberia* (1998), *The Prime Gig* (2000), *Resistance* (2003), *Inland Empire* (2006), *I Know Who Killed Me* (2007), *Surveillance* (2008), *Che* (2008), *Kit Kittredge: An American Girl* (2008), *The Curious Case of Benjamin Button* (2008), *Albatross* (2010) and *My Week with Marilyn* (2011 - as Vivien Leigh). Julia has an independent production company, Indican Productions, based in New York City. She has married twice: actor Rory Edwards in 1989 (divorcing in 1994) after they had met whilst both performing in *Wuthering Heights*, and political activist Jon Rubin in 1999. The couple's first child, daughter Sophie, was born in the autumn of 2004 although Julia has now split from Rubin. See also entry for *Traffik* in the television section.

O'Shea, Milo (1926-) Born 2 June 1926, Dublin. Actor. Joined the Abbey Players in 1945. Made his screen debut in *Talk of a Million* (1951) but spent the 1950s in the theatre until reappearing in *This Other Eden* (1959). His best known screen work was probably in the 1960s when he starred as Leopold Bloom in *Ulysses* (1967), played Friar Laurence in *Romeo and Juliet* (1968) and Duran Duran in *Barbarella* (1968). Other films include: *Theatre of Blood* (1973), *The Verdict* (1982), *The Purple Rose of Cairo* (1985), *The Dream Team* (1989), *The Playboys* (1992), *The Butcher Boy* (1997), *Moonglow* (2000), *Puckoon* (2002) and *Mystics* (2003). His most recent role on television has been as Chief Justice Roy Ashland in *The West Wing* in 2004. He is currently married to the Irish actress Kitty Sullivan, with whom he has occasionally acted, most notably in a 1981 Broadway revival of *My Fair Lady*. He has two sons, Colm and Steven by his previous marriage to Irish actress Maureen Toal. See also entries in the television section for *Me Mammy*, and *Out of this World*.

O'Sullivan, Maureen (1911-98) Born Maureen Paula O'Sullivan 17 May 1911 Boyle, County Roscommon. Actress. Daughter of the Lord Mayor of Cork. At school she was a classmate of Vivien Leigh at the Convent of the Sacred Heart at Roehampton. Her film debut was in a Will Rogers comedy *So This Is London* (1930) followed three months later by *Song o' My Heart* (1930) directed by Frank Borzage who invited her to Hollywood and Irving Thalberg then signed her to play Jane Parker in six MGM Tarzan films, *Tarzan the Ape Man* (1932), *Tarzan and His Mate* (1934), *Tarzan Escapes* (1936), *Tarzan Finds a Son!* (1939), *Tarzan's Secret Treasure* (1941) and *Tarzan's New York Adventure* (1942), all opposite Johnny Weissmuller, with whom she had a brief affair during the early 1930s. She married writer and director John Farrow (co-director of *Tarzan Escapes*) in 1936, a marriage that was to last until his death in 1963 and produce seven children, one of which was actress, Mia Farrow. Although she will always be remembered for her six ape-man films she had a number of supporting roles, always turning in good solid performances. Some of the more noteworthy are *David Copperfield* (1935), *Anna Karenina* (1935), the Marx Brothers' *A Day at the Races* (1937), as the beautiful Molly Beaumont in *A Yank at Oxford* (1938), Jane Bennett in *Pride and Prejudice* (1940) and supporting Ann Sothern in Maisie Was a Lady (1941). After taking time off to start a family she returned to the screen in *The Big Clock* (1948), directed by her husband. Other films include: *Where Danger Lives* (1950), *No Resting Place* (1951), *All I Desire* (1953), *Bonzo Goes to College* (1953), *Men Behind Bars* (1954), *The Tall T* (1957), *Wild Heritage* (1958) and *Never Too Late* (1965). Apart from the occasional TV movie Maureen again retired but made a brief comeback in such films as, *Too Scared to Scream* (1985), *Hannah and Her Sisters* (1986), *Peggy Sue Got Married* (1986), *Stranded* (1987) and her last feature film, *Good Old Boy: A Delta Boyhood* (1988). In 1983 she married again this time to James Cushing, a marriage that lasted until her death from complications during heart surgery on 23 June 1998, Scottsdale, Arizona. Maureen was a beautiful actress, who was often the bridesmaid and rarely the bride, ironic since outside of film she operated a bridal consulting service called Wediquette International. In *Love and Betrayal: The Mia Farrow Story* (1995) she was portrayed by actress Frances Helm.

O'Sullivan, Richard (1944-) Born 7 May 1944, Chiswick, London. Actor. After enrolling at the Corona Theatre School he became a child star and made his screen debut in *The Yellow Balloon* (1953) as a boy soprano. His first credited role in a feature was in *The Stranger's Hand* (1954) and other early films include *Make me an Offer* (1955), *It's Great to be Young* (1956), *Carry on Teacher* (1959) and *Spare the Rod* (1961). He played Pharoah Ptolemy in *Cleopatra* (1963) and also featured in two Cliff Richard films *The Young Ones* (1961) and *Wonderful Life* (1964). Other films include *Every Day's a Holiday* (1965), *A Dandy in Aspic* (1968), *Futtocks End* (1970) and his last film *Holed* (1996). Richard had a relationship with actress Sally Thomsett for three years after meeting her on the set of *Man About the House*. In 1977 he co-starred with Tessa Wyatt in *Robin's Nest* and in 1978 she left her husband, DJ Tony Blackburn, to live with him although seven years later they parted. Richard eventually married Christine Smart but had a turbulent marriage. In 2002 he broke his leg which gave him a permanent disability and the following year he had a stroke and chose to enter Brinsworth House, a retirement home for actors and performers in Twickenham. Best known for his numerous television appearances, particularly in comedies. See entries in the television section for *Alcock and Gander, Dick Turpin, Doctor in the House, Great Expectations, Love Story, Man About the House, Me and My Girl, Now Look Here, The Adventures of Robin Hood,* and *Robin's Nest*.

O'Toole, Peter (1932-) Peter Seamus Lorcan O'Toole was born in 1932. He himself is not certain of his birthplace or date, noting in his autobiography that, while he considers 2 August as his birthdate, he has an Irish birth certificate giving a June 1932 date and birthplace as Connemara, County Galway, Ireland. He also has an English birth certificate citing Leeds as his birthplace on 2 August 1932. The anglo-Irish actor was undoubtedly raised in Leeds and began his working life as a journalist before turning to acting. Peter served in the Royal Navy before studying at RADA (1952-54). Stage debut: *Midsummer Night's Dream* (1954). He spent most of the 1950s doing stage work at the Bristol Old Vic before making his screen debut in an episode of *The Scarlet Pimpernel* in 1956. After appearing in the TV film *The Castiglioni Brothers* (1958) he made his feature debut in

Kidnapped (1960 - as Robin MacGregor). After a minor role in *The Savage Innocents* (1960) he came to international fame after he was chosen by David Lean to play the lead in the epic *Lawrence of Arabia* (1962) which gained him his first Academy Award nomination for Best Actor. He gained a further nomination for his portrayal of Henry II in *Becket* (1964) and again for playing him in *The Lion in Winter* (1968) and thereby joins Paul Newman (Eddie Felson), Bing Crosby (Father O'Malley) and Al Pacino (Michael Corleone) in receiving two separate nominations for playing the same character. The following year saw his fourth Academy Award Best Actor nomination for playing Arthur Chipping in a musical version of *Goodbye Mr Chips* (1969). After *Murphy's War* (1971) he was nominated for Best Actor by the Academy for *The Ruling Class* (1972). During the 1970s he had serious health problems, not helped by his hard-drinking lifestyle, but he overcame these to receive two more Academy Award Best Actor nominations for *The Stunt Man* (1980) and *My Favourite Year* (1982). His later films include *Supergirl* (1984), *The Last Emperor* (1987), *High Spirits* (1988), *King Ralph* (1991), *Phantoms* (1998), *Molokai* (1999), *Fine Young Things* (2003), *Troy* (2004 – as King Priam), *Lassie* (2005), *One Night with the King* (2006), *Ratatouille* (2007 - voice of Anton Ego), *Stardust* (2007), *My Talks with Dean Spanley* (2008), *Christmas Cottage* (2008) and *Eager to Die* (2010). He was once again nominated for the Best Actor Academy Award for his portrayal of Maurice in the 2006 film *Venus,* directed by Roger Michell, his eighth such nomination. In 2003 he was awarded an Honorary Academy Award for being someone "whose remarkable talents have provided cinema history with some of its most memorable characters." He has managed to combine his screen career with a busy stage career including *Jeffrey Barnard is Unwell* (1989-91). Autobiography: *Loitering with Intent* (1992). See also entries in the television section for *Casanova, The Adventures of the Scarlet Pimpernel,* and *The Tudors*. Married to actress Siân Phillips (1959-79) with whom he had two daughters: award-winning actress Kate O'Toole (b. 1960, Stratford-on-Avon) and Patricia. Peter and his then girlfriend, model Karen Brown, had a son, Lorcan Patrick O'Toole (b. 14 March 1983) who is now an actor. Kate's first film role, as a child actor, was as Amelia More in *Laughter in the Dark* (1969). Her adult debut was in John Huston's last film *The Dead* (1987). Other film credits include *Dancing at Lughnasa* (1998), *Nora* (2000), *Possession* (2002), *The League of Gentlemen's Apocalypse* (2005) *32a* (2007) and *Eden* (2008). In November 2008 she was convicted of driving whilst drunk and disqualified from driving for three years.

Owen, Bill (1914-99) Born William John Owen Rowbotham, 14 March 1914, Acton, Greater London. Actor, songwriter and playwright. Bill initially had a variety jobs including band vocalist and drummer. He took acting classes before joining the Unity Theatre. He served with the Royal Army Ordinance Corps during WWII before being invalided out. His screen debut was in the Ministry of Information film short, *Tank Patrol* (1941) and his feature debut in *The Way to the Stars* (1945). He was credited as Bill Rowbotham in his early films until joining the *Rank Organisation* and changing to Bill Owen for *When the Bough Breaks* (1947). At this point in his career he was better known as an accomplished stage actor, appearing as *Touchstone* in *As You Like It* (1950) in a production starring Katharine Hepburn. During the 1950s he appeared in films such as *A Day to Remember* (1953), *The Ship that Died of Shame* (1955) and *Carve her Name with Pride* (1958) usually playing cockney roles. He appeared in four *Carry On* films *....Sergeant* (1958), *....Nurse* (1959), *....Regardless* (1961) and *....Cabby* (1963). His later films include *Georgy Girl* (1966), *O Lucky Man!* (1973) and his last film, *The Handmaids Tale* (1990). After appearing in *Coronation Street* as Charlie Dickinson (1971) his next television role was as the woollen-hatted scruff William "Compo" Simmonite in *The Last of the Summer Wine*. He went on to play this character for 27 years (1973-99) and become something of a national institution. After his death his son Tom Owen (b. 12 July 1949) joined the cast as Compo's son. Bill was also a songwriter and Cliff Richard had a number 22 hit with his song *Marianne* in 1968. His stage musical

The Matchgirl was staged in the West End in the mid-1960s. He was awarded the MBE in 1976 for his work for the National Association of Boys Clubs. Bill was also chairman of the Performing Arts Advisory Panel. He died 12 July 1999, Highgate, London and is buried in Holmfirth, Yorkshire where *Last of the Summer Wine* is shot. See also entries in the television section for *Angels, Coronation Street, Last of the Summer Wine, The Likely Lads, Love Story,* and *Taxi.*

Owen, Clive (1964-) Born 3 October 1964, Keresley, Coventry. Actor. Studied at RADA before joining the Young Vic Theatre Company. His screen debut came in an episode of *Rockliffe's Babies* in 1987. His film debut was in the TV movie *Precious Bane* (1989). Having played John Ridd in a television film version of *Lorna Doone* (1990) he made a great impact in the ITV drama series *Chancer* (1990). His feature debut came in the road movie *Vroom* (1990). His early films include the controversial *Close My Eyes* (1991), *Century* (1993) and the made-for-television movie *The Turnaround* (1994 – as Nick Sharman) which was extended into a four-part ITV drama series in 1995 under the name of *Sharman.* Clive returned to the big screen with his first major Hollywood film *The Rich Man's Wife* (1996), then played Max in the concentration camp drama *Bent* (1997) before making a breakthrough in America with *Croupier* (1998). This Mike Hodges film was initially a failure in the UK but was re-released in 2001 after it became a box-office hit in the US. His subsequent films have all further raised his profile including *Gosford Park* (2001), *The Bourne Identity* (2002) and *I'll Sleep When I'm Dead* (2003). He played the title role in *King Arthur* (2004) and was nominated for a Best Supporting Actor Academy Award for *Closer* (2004), repeating a role he had played on stage in 1997. In 2005 he starred in the graphic novel adaptation *Sin City.* His recent films include: *Derailed* (2005), *Inside Man* (2006), *The Pink Panther* (2006), *Children of Men* (2006), Shoot 'Em Up (2007), Elizabeth: *The Golden Age* (2007 - as Sir Walter Raleigh), *The International* (2009), *Duplicity* (2009), *The Boys Are Back* (2009), *Trust* (2010), *Killer Elite* (2011) and *Intruders* (2011). Clive married actress Sarah-Jane Fenton in 1995 and they have two daughters – Hannah and Eve.

Owen, Reginald (1887-1972) Born John Reginald Owen, 5 August 1887, Wheathampstead, Hertfordshire. Actor. Son of a builder and decorator. Trained at Sir Herbert Tree's Academy of Dramatic Arts. Made his stage debut in 1905. Made his screen debut as Thomas Cromwell in *Henry VIII* (1911). He worked on Broadway from 1924 and in Hollywood from 1929 when he featured in *The Letter* (1929). Reginald made no less than 60 films during the 1930s and although mainly a supporting player he also had some lead roles. He played Doctor Watson in *Sherlock Holmes* (1932) and Sherlock Holmes in *A Study in Scarlet* (1933). He also played Louis XV three times, in *Voltaire* (1933), *Madame DuBarry* (1934) and *Monsieur Beaucaire* (1946). He starred as Ebenezer Scrooge in *A Christmas Carol* (1938). Other major films include *Queen Christina* (1933), *Anna Karenina* (1935), *A Tale of Two Cities* (1935), *The Great Ziegfeld* (1936), *Kidnapped* (1938), *Mrs Miniver* (1942), *Random Harvest* (1942), *The Canterville Ghost* (1944), *National Velvet* (1944), *The Three Musketeers* (1948), *Master of Lassie* (1948), *The Secret Garden* (1949), *Challenge to Lassie* (1949), *The Miniver Story* (1950), *Five Weeks in a Balloon* (1962), *Tammy and the Doctor* (1963), *Mary Poppins* (1964 - as Admiral Boom) and his last film, *Bedknobs and Broomsticks* (1971). Shortly before his death he was back on Broadway in *A Funny Thing Happened to me on the Way to the Forum* (1972). He died 5 November 1972, Boise, Idaho.

Oz, Frank (1944-) Born Richard Frank Oznowicz, 25 May 1944, Hereford, Herefordshire. Director, actor and puppeteer. Parents moved to California in 1949. Joined Jim Henson's team of puppeteers in 1963 and one of his first jobs was as manipulator of Rowlf the Dog in *The Jimmy Dean Show* (1963). Creator of characters such as Grover, Cookie Monster and Bert on *Sesame Street* (1969-2000) and Miss Piggy, Fozzie Bear and Sam the Eagle on *The Muppet Show* (1977-1981). His films with The Muppets include *The Muppet Movie* (1979), *The Great Muppet Caper* (1981), *The Muppets Take Manhattan* (1984), *The Muppet Christmas Carol* (1992), *Muppets Treasure Island* (1996) and *Muppets from Space* (1999). After the Muppets his most famous creation is Yoda, the diminutive Jedi Master with speech patterns, strange, they are. Frank performed the voice and puppet for Yoda in *The Empire Strikes Back* (1980), *Return of the Jedi* and *The Phantom Menace,* and provided the voice of the computer-generated imagery (CGI) Yoda in *Attack of the Clones* and *Revenge of the Sith.* His directorial career began with co-directing *The Dark Crystal* (1983) and then going solo with *The Muppets Take Manhattan* (1984). His other films as director include: *The Little Shop of Horrors* (1986), *Dirty Rotten Scoundrels* (1988), *What About Bob?* (1991), *House Sitter* (1992), *The Indian in the Cupboard* (1995), *In & Out* (1997), *Bowfinger* (1999), *The Stepford Wives* (2004) and the British version of *Death at a Funeral* (2007). As a non-puppet related actor, mainly in cameo roles, he debuted as a Corrections Officer in *The Blues Brothers* (1980), had a minor role in *An American Werewolf in London* (1981), went on to be a corrupt cop in *Trading Places* (1983) and also appeared in *Spies Like Us* (1985), *Innocent Blood* (1992), *Blues Brothers 2000* (1998) and the Pixar film *Monsters, Inc.*(2001) as Randall's scare assistant, Fungus.

Park, Nick (1958-) Born Nicholas Wulstan Park, 6 December 1958, Preston, Lancashire. Animator. Experimented with various types of animation techniques whilst a schoolboy. Graduated from Sheffield Hallam University (then Sheffield Polytechnic) before studying animation at the National Film and Television School where he began work on *A Grand Day Out.* He joined Peter Lord (the man behind Morph) and David Sproxton at Aardman Animations in Bristol in 1985, developing his stop-motion animation techniques. His next project was animating parts of the Peter Gabriel video *Sledgehammer* (1987). Nick completed *Wallace and Gromit: A Grand Day Out* (1989) at around the same time as he worked on *Creature Comforts* (1989) for Channel 4. In 1991 both gained nominations for an Academy Award as Best Short Animation, with *Creature Comforts* winning and going on to form the basis of a successful TV advertising campaign. He then produced *Wallace and Gromit: The Wrong Trousers* (1993) which won him a second Academy Award for Best Short Animation. He followed this with the equally successful *Wallace and Gromit: A Close Shave* (1995) which garnered him a futher Academy Award for Best Animated Short. He briefly moved away from Wallace and Gromit to make the feature-length *Great Escape* homage *Chicken Run* (2000) and a further series of *Creature Comforts* (2003) before making *Wallace and Gromit: The Curse of the Were-Rabbit* (2005) which won the Academy Award for Best Animated Feature. On 10 October 2005, a fire gutted Aardman Animations' archive warehouse resulting in the loss of most of Park's creations although the master prints survived. In 2007 the first series of *Shaun the Sheep* aired on CBBC and in 2008 the TV short *Wallace and Gromit in 'A Matter of Loaf and Death'* was broadcast on BBC1 in the UK. Nick is a fan of *The Beano* comic, and guest-edited the 70th anniversary issue dated 2 August 2008.

Parker, Alan (1944-) Born Alan William Parker, 14 February 1944, Islington, London. Director and writer. Worked as an advertising copywiter. Wrote the screenplay for *S.W.A.L.K.(* aka *Melody)* (1971). David Puttnam was the producer of this film and he would later produce a number of Parker's films including the highly acclaimed *Midnight Express* (1978), set in a Turkish prison, for which Alan earned a Best Director Academy Award nomination. His directorial debut was the film short *Our Cissy* (1974) and his full feature debut *Bugsy Malone* (1976). He followed this success with the musical *Fame* (1980), *Shoot the Moon* (1982), the film of the Pink Floyd album *The Wall* (1982), *Birdy* (1984) and the psychological horror *Angel Heart* (1987). He received another Academy Award nomination for Best Director for *Mississippi Burning* (1988) based on a civil rights murder case. During the 1990s he made *The Commitments* (1991), *The Road to Wellville* (1994), *Evita* (1996) and *Angela's Ashes* (1999). His latest film was *The Life of David Gale* (2003). Appointed CBE 1995 and knighted 2002.

Parker, Cecil (1897-1971) Born Cecil Schwabe, 3 September 1897, Hastings, East Sussex. Actor. The son of a German-born hotel manager. Educated at St Francis Xavier College and in Bruges, Belgium. Stage debut: *The Merchant of Venice* (1922). Screen debut: *The Golden Cage* (1933). Although known as an excellent supporting player, for a short period he played major roles in such films as: *Captain Boycott* (1947 - as Captain

Boycott), *Dear Mr Prohack* (1949), *The Chiltern Hundreds* (1949) and *Tony Draws a Horse* (1950). Other early films include: *Me and Marlborough* (1935), *The Man who Changed his Mind* (1936), *The Lady Vanishes* (1938), *The Stars Look Down* (1940), *Dangerous Moonlight* (1941), *Caesar and Cleopatra* (1945), *The Magic Box* (1951), *Father Brown* (1954), *The Court Jester* (1956) and *The Admirable Crichton* (1957). In the early 1950s he featured in a series of Ealing Studio classics such as: *The Man in the White Suit* (1951), *His Excellency* (1952), *I Believe in You* (1952) and *The Ladykillers* (1955). By the 1960s he had settled into playing character roles in sturdy British comedies such as *Petticoat Pirates* (1961), *The Amorous Prawn* (1962), *Heavens Above!* (1963), *Carry on Jack* (1963) and *The Magnificent Two* (1967). His final film was *Oh! What a Lovely War* (1969). He died 21 April 1977, Brighton, East Sussex.

Parkinson, Katherine (1978-) Born Laura Katherine Parkinson, 9 March 1978, Cambridge. Actress and comedian. Katherine was educated at Tiffin Girls' School in Kingston upon Thames, and then read Classics at St Hilda's College, Oxford (where she first befriended Katy Brand) before studying at the London Academy of Music and Dramatic Art (where she first befriended Chris O'Dowd). She made her screen debut in the TV film *Ahead of the Class* (2005 – as Vicky Foley) opposite Julie Walters. Her feature film debut came in *Easy Virtue* (2008 - as Marion Whittaker) and other films include: *How to Lose Friends & Alienate People* (2008), *The Boat That Rocked* (2009) and *St Trinian's 2: The Legend of Fritton's* Gold (2009). In 2007, she appeared on stage in Chekhov's *The Seagull* at the Royal Court Theatre in London, alongside Kristin Scott Thomas and Mackenzie Crook. Later that year she announced her engagement to fellow comedian Harry Peacock whom she now refers to as her husband although no announcement of the nuptials are on record. On television she has appeared in *Katy Brand's Big Ass Show* on ITV2 and *Psychoville* on BBC, but is best known for her role of Jen Barber in *The IT Crowd*. See also entries in the television section for *Doc Martin, The It Crowd, The Old Guys*, and *Whites*.

Patel, Dev (1990-) Born 23 April 1990, Harrow, Greater London. Actor. His parents are from Gujarati Indian descent and both were born in Nairobi, Kenya. As a youth, Dev was a nationally-ranked martial artist and trained at the Rayners Lane Academy of Taekwon-do from the age of ten. He had his first acting role as Sir Andrew Aguecheek in the school's production of *Twelfth Night* and made his mind up to pursue an acting career at that time. Dev auditioned for the E4 teen drama television series *Skins* in 2006 and was cast as Anwar Kharral, a British Pakistani Muslim teenager (although he himself was brought up Hindu). He made his feature film debut when he was cast in the role of Jamal Malik, the central character in Danny Boyle's multi-award-winning film *Slumdog Millionaire* (2008). His most recent film is *The Last Airbender* (2010) an adventure fantasy film combining live action and computer animation. In 2012, Dev has two films to look forward to, *The Best Exotic Marigold Hotel*, playing the role of Sonny Kapoor in an ensemble cast; and *Cherry*, the directorial debut of Stephen Elliott. Dev has been dating his *Slumdog Millionaire* co-star Freida Pinto (b. 18 October 1984, Mumbai) since 2009. See also entry for *Mister Eleven* in the television section.

Pattinson, Robert (1986 -) Born Robert Douglas Thomas Pattinson, 13 May 1986, London. Actor, model, musician and producer. Initially working as a model Robert gained acting fame playing Cedric Diggory in *Harry Potter and the Goblet of Fire* (2005) before being propelled to superstardom as Edward Cullen in the film *Twilight* (2008) and the sequels *The Twilight Saga: New Moon* (2009), *The Twilight Saga: Eclipse* (2010), *The Twilight Saga: Breaking Dawn – Part 1* (2011) and the upcoming *The Twilight Saga: Breaking Dawn – Part 2* (2012), all adaptations of the Twilight novels by Stephenie Meyer. Robert also played Art in the British comedy *How to Be* (2008) and Salvador Dali in *Little Ashes* (2009). The 2010 film *Remember Me*, marked Robert's debut as a producer as well as taking the lead role of Tyler Hawkins. In 2011, he starred in *Water for Elephants*, a film adaptation of the Sara Gruen romantic novel of the same name. In 2012, he will play Georges Duroy in a film adaptation of the 1885 novel *Bel Ami*, opposite Uma Thurman. Robert is a talented musician (guitar and piano) and composer. Rpatts is his nickname although Spunk Ransom has gained some momentum since Robert gave an interview to MTV denouncing the nickname Rpattz and declaring he would rather it be Ransom Spunk or Spunk Ransom! Since meeting on the set of *Twilight*, he has been romantically linked to co-star Kristen Stewart although they have never explicitly confirmed a relationship. Robert is one of the hottest properties both on and off set and invariably tops lists of "world's sexiest" or "best dressed"…

Peake, Maxine (1974 -) Born 14 July 1974, Bolton, Greater Manchester. Actress. Trained at RADA. Started her career at age 13, when she joined Bolton's Octagon Youth Theatre Club. Maxine made her screen debut in an episode of Hetty Wainthropp Investigates in 1996. From there she appeared in episodes of *Clocking Off* (2000) and *Holby City* (2002) but is probably best known for playing the dippy Twinkle in *Dinnerladies* (1998-2000) and thereafter Veronica Fisher, the next-door-neighbour and part time exotic dancer in *Shameless* (2004). Her feature debut was as Sharon in *Girls' Night* (1998) and her next feature was *All or Nothing* (2002). A talented and versatile actress, she took on a controversial role as Myra Hindley in the television film *See No Evil: The Moors Murders* (2006) opposite Sean Harris as Ian Brady. Her recent work includes her first major feature film role, as Angela in *Clubbed* (2008) and the second part of Channel 4's Red Riding trilogy *Red Riding: In the Year of Our Lord 1980* (2009). See also entries in the television section for *Coronation Street, Criminal Justice, dinnerladies, Early Doors, Shameless, Silk*, and *The Street*.

Pearce, Guy (1967-) Born Guy Edward Pearce, 5 October 1967, Ely, Cambridgeshire. Actor. His mother was English and his father a New Zealand-born air force test pilot who died when Guy was nine. The family emigrated to Australia in 1971. Guy was involved with the Geelong Society of Operatic and Dramatic Arts from an early age. He was also a competive amateur bodybuilder who won Mr Junior Victoria. Guy made his small screen debut in the role which brought him to the attention of the UK public as Mike Young in the soap opera *Neighbours* (1986-1989). His big screen debut, *Friday on my Mind* (1990), was followed by *Heaven Tonight* (1990) and *Hunting* (1991). He then played David Croft in another Australian soap *Home and Away* (1991-1992). He also starred as Errol Flynn in a biopic, *Flynn*, which was eventually released in 1997. Guy then surprised many of his fans by playing drag queen Felicia Jollygoodfellow in *The Adventures of Priscilla, Queen of the Desert* (1994). After the body-switch tale *Dating the Enemy* (1996) he was cast as straight-as-a-die LAPD cop Ed Exley in *L.A. Confidential* (1997) opposite Russell Crowe and Kevin Spacey. This proved both a critical and audience-pleasing performance but his next projects were the relatively low key *Woundings* (1998), *A Slipping-Down Life* (1999) and *Ravenous* (1999). He followed *Rules of Engagement* (2000) with the innovative *Memento* (2000) playing Leonard Shelby, a man with no short-term memory investigating his wife's death. He then starred in two adaptations of 19th century classics *The Count of Monte Cristo* (2002) and the big-budget *The Time Machine* (2002). Guy returned to Australia to make *The Hard Word* (2002) and has since featured in *Till Human Voices Wake Us* (2002), *Two Brothers* (2004), *The Proposition* (2005), *First Snow* (2006), *Factory Girl* (2006 - as Andy Warhol), *Death Defying Acts* (2007 - as Harry Houdini), *Fragments* (2008), *Traitor* (2008), *The Hurt Locker* (2008), *Bedtime Stories* (2008), *I Am You* (2009), *The Road* (2009), *Animal Kingdom* (2010), *The King's Speech* (2010 – as King Edward VIII aka David), *Don't Be Afraid of the Dark* (2011), *33 Postcards* (2011) and *Seeking Justice* (2011). He has been married to Kate Mestitz, a psychologist, since March 1997.

Pearson, George (1875-1973) Born George William Pearson, 19 March 1875, Bermondsey, London. Director, producer and writer. Son of a silk cutter. Educated at Culham College, Oxford. Became a school teacher and eventually a headmaster. In 1913 he decided on a complete career change and joined *Pathe* in London before quickly moving on to *Gaumont* at Lime Grove via George

Samuelson at Worton Hall. Directorial debut: *A Study in Scarlet* (1914), the first screen adaptation of a Sherlock Holmes story. At the height of WWI in 1916 he created the character of Ultus, an avenger of injustice who appeared in *Ultus, the Man from the Dead* (1916), *Ultus and the Secret of the Night* (1916), *Ultus and the Grey Lady* (1916) and *Ultus and the Three-Button Mystery* (1917). In 1918 he formed *Welsh-Pearson* with Thomas Welsh and directed *The Better 'Ole* (1919) and then developed the popular cockney character Squibs played by Betty Balfour in *Squibs* (1921), *Squibs Wins the Calcutta Sweep* (1922), *Squibs M.P.* (1923) and *Squibs' Honeymoon* (1923). He also directed *Nothing Else Matters* (1920), *Love, Life and Laughter* (1923), *Reveille* (1924) and *The Little People* (1926). In 1930 he travelled to Hollywood to supervise the production of *Journey's End* (1930). *Welsh-Pearson* dissolved in 1934 and he found himself making quota quickies. His final film as a director was *The Fatal Hour* (1937) and as a writer *Command Performance* (1937). During WWII he joined the GPO Film Unit before becoming Director-in-Chief of the Colonial Film Unit and his career came full circle as he became a teacher of young Commonwealth film makers. Founder of the London Film Society and was President of the Association of British Film Directors. One of Britain's best director's of silent films. Received an OBE in 1951 for his services to the film industry. Autobiography: *Flashback: an Autobiography of a British Film Maker* (1957). He retired in 1955 and died 6 February 1973, Malvern, Worcestershire.

Peck, Bob (1945-99) Born 23 August 1945, Leeds, Yorkshire. Actor. Graduated from Leeds College of Art. Bob was in amateur dramatics when spotted by Alan Ayckbourn and spent time in repertory in Birmingham, Scarborough and Exeter (1969-74). Member of the Royal Shakespeare Company (1975-84). Big screen debut: *Royal Flash* (1975). Featured as Macduff in a TV adaptation of *Macbeth* (1979). He is probably best remembered for his brooding portrayal of policeman Ron Craven in the acclaimed TV drama series *Edge of Darkness* (1985). The success of this series brought him roles in *On the Black Hill* (1987) and *The Kitchen Toto* (1987). After a string of television roles in dramas such as *After Pilkington* (1987) and *The Black Velvet Gown* (1991) he landed the role of game warden Robert Muldoon in *Jurassic Park* (1993) which brought him international recognition. His final films include *Surviving Picasso* (1996), *Smilla's Sense of Snow* (1997) and *Fairy Tale: A True Story* (1997). His last film credit was *The Miracle Maker* (2000 - voice of Joseph of Arimathea). After battling cancer for several years, he died 4 April 1999, Kingston-upon-Thames, London. He is survived by his wife, actress Jill Baker (b. 1952), whom he married in 1982, and their three children Hannah, George and Milly.

Pegg, Simon (1970-) Born Simon John Beckingham, 14 February 1970, Brockworth, Gloucestershire. Actor, comedian, writer, film producer and director. Simon is the son of Gillian Rosemary Smith and John Henry Beckingham. After his parents divorced when he was seven he took on the surname "Pegg" when his mother re-married. He studied drama at the University of Bristol. Following a stint as a stand-up comedian, Simon made his screen debut in the comedy sketch series *Six Pairs of Pants* in 1995 and then appeared in the surreal comedies *Asylum* (1996) and *We Know Where You Live* (1997), both shown on the Paramount Comedy Channel. He made his feature debut in *Guest House Paradiso* (1999) and followed this up with *The Parole Officer* (2001), *24 Hour Party People* (2002) and *The Reckoning* (2003). He then co-wrote and starred as the title character in the zombie rom-com *Shaun of the Dead* (2004), which became a cult-hit. Subsequent films include: *The League of Gentlemen's Apocalypse* (2005), *Land of the Dead* (2005), *Free Jimmy* (2006), *Mission: Impossible III* (2006 – as Benji Dunn), *Big Nothing* (2006), *The Good Night* (2007), *Hot Fuzz* (2007 - as Nicholas Angel), *Grindhouse* (2007), *Run Fatboy Run* (2007 - as Dennis), *How to Lose Friends & Alienate People* (2008), *Star Trek* (2009 - as Scotty), *Ice Age: Dawn of the Dinosaurs* (2009 - voice of Buck), *Burke and Hare* (2010 - as William Burke), *The Chronicles of Narnia: The Voyage of the Dawn Treader* (2010 - voice of Reepicheep), *Paul* (2011), *The Adventures of Tintin* (2011 - as Thompson) and *Mission: Impossible IV – Ghost Protocol* (2011). He married Maureen McCann on 23 July 2005, in Glasgow. Nick

Frost was the best man at his wedding. Simon is the godfather of Chris Martin and Gwyneth Paltrow's daughter, Apple, and in turn they are the godparents of his daughter, Matilda, born in July 2009. On television he was originally slated to play Rose Tyler's father in the first series of the re-vamped *Dr Who* (2005), but due to a scheduling conflict took the role of The Editor in a later episode that year. He has also appeared in the American World War II mini-series *Band of Brothers*, and made guest appearances on *Black Books*, *Brass Eye*, and *I'm Alan Partridge*. See also entries in the television section for *Big Train*, *Danger! 50,000 Volts!*, *Faith in the Future*, *Hippies*, *I Am Not an Animal*, *The 99p Challenge*, *Six Pairs of Pants*, and *Spaced*.

Pertwee, Jon (1919-96) Born John Devon Roland Pertwee, 7 July 1919, Chelsea, London. Actor. His father, Roland, was a playwright and novelist. After having problems at his school, Sherborne, and RADA, from both of which he was expelled, he eventually settled into repertory. Jon served in the Royal Navy during WWII. His screen debut was in *A Yank at Oxford* (1938). Other films include: *The Four Just Men* (1939), *Helter Skelter* (1949), *Miss Pilgrim's Progress* (1950), *A Yank in Ermine* (1955), *It's a Wonderful World* (1956), *The Ugly Duckling* (1959), *Carry on Cleo* (1964), *You Must Be Joking!* (1965), *I've Gotta Horse* (1965), *Carry on Cowboy* (1965), *Carry on Screaming!* (1966), *A Funny Thing Happened on the Way to the Forum* (1966), *The House That Dripped Blood* (1971), *One of Our Dinosaurs Is Missing* (1975), *Adventures of a Private Eye* (1977), *The Water Babies* (1978), *The Boys in Blue* (1982) and his last feature film, *Carry on Columbus* (1992). Subsequently he made the film short *Cloud Cuckoo* (1994) and the TV movie *The Young Indiana Jones Chronicles* (1995). Jon, with his soft lisp and gift for mimicry, was a well-known voice on radio in such programmes as *The Navy Lark* but is best known for two television roles. He was the third reincarnation of *Dr Who* which he played as a sort of Victorian adventurer, all velvet and ruffles, but then went to the other extreme and played the scarecrow *Worzel Gummidge*. Jon wrote two autobiographies: *Moon Boots and Dinner Suits* (1984) and the posthumously published *Doctor Who: I Am the Doctor – Jon Pertwee's Final Memoir* (1996). He was married to actress Jean Marsh (1955-60) and Ingeborg Rhoesa from 1960 until his death, from a heart attack on 20 May 1996, Litchfield, Connecticut. He had two children with Ingeborg, a son Sean (b. 1964) and a daughter Dariel (b. 1961) both of which are actors. See also entries in the radio and television section for *Dr Who*, *The Navy Lark*, *Six-Five Special*, *Superted*, *Whodunnit?* and *Worzel Gummidge*.

Phillips, Leslie (1924-) Born Leslie Samuel Phillips, 20 April 1924, Tottenham, London. Actor. Educated at Italia Conti where he was given elocution lessons to drop his Cockney brogue. Leslie made his West End stage debut in Dear Octopus in 1938 and his film debut soon followed, in *Lassie from Lancashire* (1938). After WWII, during which he served in the Durham Light Infantry, reaching the rank of Second Lieutenant, he featured in such well-remembered British films as *The Sound Barrier* (1952), *The Barretts of Wimpole Street* (1957), *The Smallest Show on Earth* (1957) and *I was Monty's Double* (1958). He came to national attention as Lt. Pouter in the radio series *The Navy Lark* which was turned into a film in 1959. Leslie played Jack Bell in *Carry On Nurse* (1959) and gave the world his catchphrase "Ding Dong". He also featured in *Carry On Teacher* (1959), *Carry On Constable* (1960) and, over 30 years later, *Carry On Columbus* (1992). He was also a regular in the *Doctor in...* series, appearing in *Doctor in Love* (1960), *Doctor in Clover* (1966) and *Doctor in Trouble* (1970). The 1970s saw him appear in some unappealing fare such as *Not Now Darling* (1973), *Not Now, Comrade* (1976), *Don't Just Lie There, Say Something!* (1976) and *Spanish Fly* (1976) but he made a comeback in the 1980s when featuring in big-budget films such as *Out of Africa* (1985), *Empire of the Sun* (1987) and *Scandal* (1989). Since then he has appeared in numerous television series and dramas and in films such as *King Ralph* (1991), *The Jackal* (1997), *Lara Croft: Tomb Raider* (2001), *Thunderpants* (2002), *Colour Me Kubrick* (2005), *Venus* (2006) and *Is Anybody There?* (2008). He also features as the voice of The Sorting Hat in *Harry Potter and the Philosopher's Stone* (2001), *Harry Potter and the Chamber of Secrets* (2002) and *Harry Potter and the Deathly Hallows – Part II* (2011). His trademark is his suave voice when he delivers his catchphrases "Ding Dong", "Lummy" and "Hello", also the name of his autobiography published in 2006. Leslie married his first wife, actress Penelope Bartley, in 1948. They had four children, Caroline, Claudia, Andrew and Roger. The couple divorced in 1965, after Leslie's affair with Caroline Mortimer, daughter of writer Penelope Mortimer and stepdaughter of Sir John Mortimer. Leslie eventually married former Bond Girl Angela Scoular (b. 1945) in 1982 and the couple remained together until her death in April 2011. See also entries in the radio and television section for *Casanova '73, Chancer, The Navy Lark,* and *Our Man At St Mark's.*

Piggott-Smith, Tim (1946-) Born 13 May 1946, Rugby, Warwickshire. Actor. Educated at University of Bristol. Made his stage debut in 1969. Tim made his screen debut in the TV film *Boswell's Life of Johnson* (1971) and his feature debut in *Aces High* (1976). Other films include: *Joseph Andrews* (1977), *Clash of the Titans* (1981), *The Remains of the Day* (1993), *Bloody Sunday* (2002), *The Four Feathers* (2002), *Gangs of New York* (2002), *Johnny English* (2003), *Alexander* (2004), *V for Vendetta* (2006), *Flyboys* (2006), *L'entente cordiale* (2006), *Quantum of Solace* (2008) and *Alice in Wonderland* (2010). His television credits include playing two different members of the Hale family in BBC adaptations of Elizabeth Gaskell's love story *North and South* in 1975 and 2004. He has also appeared in episodes of *Dr Who, The Glittering Prizes, Wings, Danger UXB, Winston Churchill: The Wilderness Years,* and *The Inspector Lynley Mysteries.* Formed, and was artistic director of, Compass theatre company (1989-1992). See also entries in the television section for his main television roles in *The Chief, Hannah, HolbyBlue, The Jewel in the Crown,* and *The Vice.*

Pike, Rosamund (1979-) Born Rosamund Mary Pike, 27 January 1979, London. Actress. Rosamund is the only child of opera singers Caroline and Julian Pike. She read English Literature at Wadham College, Oxford and graduated with an Upper Second class degree in 2001. Her first professional roles were gained while at university and included small roles in the television series *A Rather English Marriage* (1998), *Wives and Daughters* (1999) and *Trial & Retribution IV* (2000) before playing the part of Fanny in the mini-series *Love in a Cold Climate* (2001). Her feature film debut was as Bond Girl Miranda Frost in *Die Another Day* (2002). Alternating between stage and screen, Rosamund had increasingly meaty parts in the feature films *The Libertine* (2004), *Pride & Prejudice* (2005), *Doom* (2005), *Fracture* (2007), *Fugitive Pieces* (2007), *An Education* (2009) and *Surrogates* (2009). Undoubtedly 2010 was the year when her acting talents were universally recognised, the release of *Burning Palms* being followed by her critically acclaimed role of Miriam in *Barney's Version* and an equally solid performance as Lisa in *Made in Dagenham.* Her final film role of a successful year was voicing Daisy in *Jackboots on Whitehall,* a satirical film featuring animatronic puppets. Her most recent films are the spoof spy film *Johnny English Reborn* (2011 – as Kate Sumner) and the American comedy film, *The Big Year* (2011 – as Jessica). She has recently completed filming her role of Andromeda in the upcoming blockbuster, *Wrath of the Titans.* Rosamund is a fine cellist, and speaks fluent French and German, acquiring these skills whilst travelling Europe extensively with her concert musician parents. Currently single, Rosamund dated actor Simon Woods while at Oxford and got engaged to film director Joe Wright in 2007, but the planned marriage for 2008 was subsequently cancelled. She has been dating businessman Robie Uniacke since 2009 and is due to have their first child in 2012.

Pilbeam, Nova (1919-) Born Nova Margery Pilbeam, 15 November 1919, Wimbledon, Surrey. Actress. She started acting just as the silent movies ended and the talkies began. Her first film was *Little Friend* (1934) after which she was cast in Hitchcock's *The Man Who Knew Too Much* (1934) which found her lauded as a future great, at only 15 years of age, and *Gaumont-British* promptly signed her to a seven year contract. She played Lady Jane Grey in *Tudor Rose* (1936) and Erica Burgoyne in *Young and Innocent (*1937). However, on the very brink of major

success, failure beckoned. She was considered for *The Lady Vanishes* and *Rebecca* but didn't get either role. Her film contract soon lapsed and she drifted from one project to another. In 1939 she married young director Pen Tennyson who was killed in a plane crash during 1941. A few war and crime pot-boilers later she made her last films, *Three Weird Sisters* and *Counterblast* in 1948 and retired on marrying BBC Radio journalist Alexander Whyte (d. 1972) in 1950. Their daughter, Sarah Jane, was born in 1952.

Pinewood Studios (1936-) Built by J Arthur Rank and Charles Boot on the estate of Heatherden Hall, Iver, Buckinghamshire and opened in 1936. The first film wholly completed film was *Talk of the Devil* (1936). Other pre-WWII films include: *Young and Innocent* (1937) and *Pygmalion* (1938). The studios were closed 1940-46. Immediate post-war films made at Pinewood include: *Great Expectations* (1946), *Oliver Twist* (1948), *The Red Shoes* (1948) and *Kind Hearts and Coronets* (1949). Rank closed Islington and Denham in 1949 and concentrated production at Pinewood after which a series of first-class British films was made there including: *The Browning Version* (1951), *The Importance of Being Earnest* (1952) and *Genevieve* (1953). The 1950s also saw *Reach for the Sky (1956), The Prince and the Showgirl* (1957) and *Carve her Name with Pride* (1958) produced at Pinewood, and an abortive attempt at *Cleopatra* (1963) before the production was transferred to Italy. During the next few years, in addition to popular television series such as *The Avengers* and *The Persuaders,* films such as *Sleuth* (1972) and *Frenzy* (1972) were made and since 1980 films include: *Aliens* (1986), *Memphis Belle* (1990), *The Secret Garden* (1993), *Interview with a Vampire* (1994), *First Knight* (1995), *The Fifth Element* (1997), *Tomb Raider* (2000), *The Hours* (2002), *Charlie and the Chocolate Factory* (2005), *The Da Vinci Code* (2006), *Stardust* (2007), *Sweeney Todd: The Demon Barber of Fleet Street* (2007), *The Bourne Ultimatum* (2007), *Mamma Mia!* (2008), *The Dark Knight* (2008), *Prince of Persia: The Sands of Time* (2010), *The Wolfman* (2010), *Kick-Ass* (2010), *Harry Potter and the Deathly Hallows: Part I* (2010) and *Part II* (2011) and the forthcoming blockbuster *Wrath of the Titans* and Bond film *Skyfall.* The Doctor, Carry On, James Bond and Superman franchises were all based at Pinewood. The studios were bought from Rank by a management team in 2000. Pinewood Studios acquired Shepperton Studios in 2001 and Teddington Studios was added in 2005.

Pleasence, Donald (1919-95) Born Donald Henry Pleasence, 5 October 1919, Worksop, Nottinghamshire. Actor. Son of a station master he worked in the railway industry before taking up acting. Unable to take up his scholarship at RADA he became assistant stage manager at the Jersey Playhouse. London stage debut: *Wuthering Heights* (1939). Initially a conscientious objector before serving in the RAF during WWII. He was shot down over France and was a POW for two years. After the war he toured with the Olivier company. His feature debut was in *The Beachcomber* (1954) and he followed this with *1984* (1956), *Look Back in Anger* (1958), *The Battle of the Sexes* (1959), *Circus of Horrors* (1960) and *Sons and Lovers* (1960). He played one of his best remembered roles as Colin "The Forger" Blythe in *The Great Escape* (1963). During the 1960s and 1970s he also featured in *The Caretaker* (1964), *The Night of the Generals* (1967), *Will Penny* (1968), *Henry VIII and his Six Wives* (1973) *and Escape to Witch Mountain* (1975). He also featured in George Lucas' first film *THX 1138* (1971) and played Dr Sam Loomis in *Halloween* (1978) and its sequels *Halloween II* (1981), *Halloween 4: The Return of Michael Myers* (1988), *Halloween 5* (1989) and *Halloween: The Curse of Michael Myers* (1995). Donald also played characters called Loomis in *Innocent Bystanders* (1972) and *Prince of Darkness* (1997). His other films include *Dracula* (1979), *Race for the Yankee Zephyr* (1981), *Phenomena* (1985), *The House of Usher* (1988), *River of Death* (1989), *Buried Alive* (1991), *Shadows and Fog* (1992) and his last film, *Fatal Frames* (1996). His roles mainly focused in a range between simply villainous to just plain evil - from Blofeld in *You only Live Twice* (1967) - where he was called in to replace Jan Werich who couldn't complete the filming - to *Dr Crippen* (1962), to Heinrich

Himmler in *The Eagle has Landed* (1976), to the Devil in *The Greatest Story Ever Told* (1965). To demonstrate his lighter side he wrote the children's books *Scouse the Mouse* (1971) and *Scouse in America* (1977). Awarded the OBE in 1993. Donald was married four times, to Miriam Raymond (1941–58), Josephine Crombie (1959–70), Meira Shore (1970–88) and Linda J. Kentwood from 1988 until his death on 2 February 1995, St Paul de Vence, Alpe Maritimes, France. He has five daughters, the best known being Angela Pleasance (b. 1941). See also entries in the television section for *The Adventures of Robin Hood, Jesus of Nazareth,* and *The Rivals of Sherlock Holmes.*

Plowright, Joan (1929-) Born Joan Ann Plowright, 28 October 1929, Brigg, Lincolnshire. Actress. Made her stage debut in 1951 and her uncredited big screen debut in *Moby Dick* (1956). Other early films include *Time Without Pity* (1957), *The Entertainer* (1960) and *Uncle Vanya* (1963). Primarily known as a premier division stage actress she has made increasingly more frequent forays into TV and film since the 1980s in such projects as *Britannia Hospital* (1982), *Drowning by Numbers* (1988), *I Love you to Death* (1990), *Last Action Hero* (1993), *The Scarlet Letter* (1995), *Jane Eyre* (1996), *101 Dalmations* (1996), *Tea with Mussolini* (1999), *Bringing Down the House* (2003), *Mrs Palfrey and Claremont* (2005), *Curious George* (2006), *The Spiderwick Chronicles* (2008), *Knife Edge* (2009) and *Goose on the Loose* (2011). She was nominated for an Academy Award for Best Supporting Actress for *Enchanted April* (1992). Married to actor Roger Gage (1953-61) and actor Laurence Olivier, from 1961 until his death in 1989. Together the couple had three children, Richard Kerr, Tamsin Agnes Margaret and Julie-Kate. Both daughters are actresses. Awarded the CBE in 1970 and made a DBE in 2004 for her services to drama. Autobiography: *And That's Not All - The Memoirs of Joan Plowright* (2001).

Popplewell, Anna (1988-) Born Anna Katherine Popplewell, 6 December 1988, Lambeth, London. Actress. She began attending drama classes at Allsorts Drama School at the age of six. Her screen debut was in the TV film *Frenchman's Creek* (1998) and her feature debut, as Betsey, in *Mansfield Park* (1999). She then appeared in supporting roles in films like *The Little Vampire* (2000), *Me Without You* (2001), *Thunderpants* (2002) and *Girl with a Pearl Earring* (2003). In 2001 she appeared as Victoria in the BBC mini-series *Love in a Cold Climate*. In 2005 she made a big screen leap to leading role as Susan Pevensie in *The Chronicles of Narnia: The Lion, the Witch and the Wardrobe* and reprised her role in the sequel, The *Chronicles of Narnia: Prince Caspian* (2008) and also made a cameo appearance in the third Narnia film, *The Chronicles of Narnia: The Voyage of the Dawn Treader* (2010) despite her character's absence from the book on which it is based. Anna attended North London Collegiate School and was Head Girl 2006–07 before becoming a student of English at Magdalen College, Oxford. Her sister Lulu Popplewell (b. Laura Francesca Popplewell, 15 January 1991, Lambeth, London) and brother Freddie Popplewell (b. Frederick Arthur L Popplewell, 1994 Lambeth, London) are both actors; Freddie played Michael Darling in *Peter Pan* (2003).

Portman, Eric (1903-69) Born 13 July 1903, Akroydon, Halifax, Yorkshire. Actor. Made his stage debut in Sunderland (1924). Screen debut: *The Girl from Maxim's* (1933). Other early films include: *Maria Marten, or Murder in the Red Barn* (1935), *The Prince and the Pauper* (1937) and *Moonlight Sonata* (1938). Eric featured in several early BBC films in the late 1930s, including: *The Constant Nymph* (1938), *A Hundred Years Old* (1938), *The Rivals* (1938), *The Gamblers* (1939), *She Stoops to Conquer* (1939) and *A Night at the Hardcastles* (1939). He often played characters with something to hide and his roles are often described as psychotic or obsessive. Made an impact in Powell and Pressburger's *49th Parallel* (1941) and worked for them again on *One of Our Aircraft is Missing* (1942) and *A Canterbury Tale* (1944). He also starred in *Squadron Leader X* (1941) and *We Dive at Dawn* (1943). Eric played a murderer in both *Wanted for Murder* (1946) and *Dear Murderer* (1947). During the 1950s his films include: *The Magic Box* (1951), *The Colditz Story* (1955), *The Deep Blue Sea* (1955) and *The Good Companions* (1957). He featured in two Bryan Forbes' films *The Whisperers* (1967) and *Deadfall* (1968) before making his last film, *Assignment to Kill*

(1968). He died 7 December 1969, St Veep, Cornwall. See also entries in the television section for *Love Story,* and *The Prisoner.*

Postlethwaite, Pete (1946-2011) Born Peter William Postlethwaite, 7 February 1946, Warrington. Actor. Initially worked as a drama teacher, he trained at the Bristol Old Vic Drama School before appearing at the Liverpool Everyman, Manchester Royal Exchange and joining the RSC. Pete made his screen debut in the film short *The Racer* (1975) and his feature debut in *The Duellists* (1977). He appeared in numerous television roles and also in films such as *A Private Function* (1984) and *Number 27* (1988) before he made an impact as an abusive husband and father in *Distant Voices, Still Lives* (1988). He followed this up by taking the roles of the Player King in *Hamlet* (1990), Paulsen in *Alien 3* (1992), Captain Beams in *The Last of the Mohicans* (1992) and Henry Crick in *Waterland* (1992). He gained an Academy Award nomination for Best Supporting Actor for playing the wrongly-convicted Giuseppe Conlon in *In the Name of the Father* (1993). Two excellent TV roles followed, as the evil Obadiah Hakeswill in *Sharpe* (1994) and as Tigg Montague in the BBC mini-series *Martin Chuzzlewitt* (1994). He then played the inscrutable lawyer Kobayashi in *The Usual Suspects* (1995). Later films include: *When Saturday Comes* (1996), *James and the Giant Peach* (1996), *DragonHeart* (1996), *Romeo + Juliet* (1996 – as Father Lawrence), *Crimetime* (1996), *Brassed Off* (1996), *Amistad* (1997), *Wayward Son* (1999), *Rat* (2000), *The Shipping News* (2001), *Between Strangers* (2002), *The Limit* (2003), *Strange Bedfellows* (2004), *Dark Water* (2005) *The Constant Gardener* (2005), *Æon Flux* (2005), *Valley of the Heart's Delight* (2006), *The Omen* (2006), *Ghost Son* (2007), *Closing The Ring* (2007), *Solomon Kane* (2009), *The Age of Stupid* (2009), *Clash of the Titans* (2010), *Inception* (2010), *The Town* (2010) and his last film role, as Karl in *Killing Bono* (2011). Steven Spielberg called Pete "the best actor in the world" after working with him on *The Lost World: Jurassic Park* (1997). Awarded an OBE in 2004. Pete was married to former BBC producer Jacqueline Morrish, from 2003 until his death, from pancreatic cancer, on 2 January 2011, Shrewsbury, Shropshire. They have two children, William John (b. 1989, Shropshire), a drama student at LAMDA, and daughter Lily Kathleen (b. 1995, Shropshire). See also entries in the television section for *Boys From the Blackstuff, Coronation Street, Criminal Justice, Sharpe,* and *The Sins.*

Poulter, Will (1993-) Born William Jack Poulter, 28 January 1993, Hammersmith, London. Actor. Educated at Harrodian School, London. He made his screen debut, as spiky-haired delinquent Lee Carter, in the Garth Jennings' film *Son of Rambow* (2007). Will then starred in the Channel 4 *Comedy Lab* pilot *School of Comedy* (2008) in which a cast of teenagers parody the world of adults. The pilot was made into a six-part series the following year and shown on E4. He next played Eustace Clarence Scrubb in the third film in the Narnia franchise *The Chronicles of Narnia: The Voyage of the Dawn Treader* (2010). Will has recently appeared in the British independent film, *Wild Bill* (2011) directed by Dexter Fletcher.

Powell, Anthony (1935-) Born 2 June 1935, Chorlton-cum-Hardy, Greater Manchester. Costume designer. Trained at the Central School of Art in London. Worked at Oxford Playhouse and was primarily a costume designer for the stage, winning a Tony award for *School for Scandal* in 1963. First big screen project: *The Royal Hunt of the Sun* (1969). He won an Academy Award for Best Costume Design for *Travels with my Aunt* (1972). His next films were *Papillon* (1973), *That Lucky Touch* (1975), *Buffalo Bill and the Indians* (1976) and *Sorcerer* (1977). He won a second Academy Award for Best Costume Design for *Death on the Nile* (1978) and then made it a hat-trick of wins with *Tess* (1979). After *Priest of Love* (1981), *Evil Under the Sun* (1982) and *Indiana Jones and the Temple of Doom* (1984) he gained an Academy Award nomination for Best Costume Design for *Pirates* (1986). He designed for *Ishtar* (1987), *Frantic* (1988) and *Indiana Jones and the Last Crusade* (1989) and then gained a further Academy Award nomination for Best Costume Design for *Hook* (1991). He worked on *101 Dalmations* (1996), *The Avengers* (1998) and *The Ninth Gate* (1999). He then gained a further Academy Award nomination for Best Costume Design for *102 Dalmations* (2000). His most recent film is *Miss Potter* (2006) in which for the scene when Miss Potter and Norman Warne say goodbye at the train station, the script said "exterior rain" and Anthony insisted the actors be heavily sprayed down for the scene to look authentic. Anthony won the Career Achievement Award from The Costume Designers Guild in 2000. He has also designed for opera, industry, menswear and architectural projects such as Paul Getty's mansion.

Powell, Dilys (1901-95) Born Elizabeth Dilys Powell, 20 July 1901, Bridgnorth, Shropshire. Film critic and writer. Graduated from Somerville College, Oxford. Married to archaeologist Humfrey Payne from 1926 until his death in 1936 and to Leonard Russell from 1943 until his death in 1974. She was the highly-respected and popular film critic of the *Sunday Times* from 1939 until 1976. Thereafter she contributed to *Punch* and *Sight and Sound*. Her published works on film include *The Golden Screen: Fifty Years at the Films* (1989) and *The Dilys Powell Film Reader* (1991). Awarded the CBE in 1974. She died 3 June 1995, Kensington, London.

Powell, Michael (1905-90) Born Michael Latham Powell, 30 September 1905, Bekesbourne, Canterbury, Kent. Director, producer and writer. Educated at King's School, Canterbury and Dulwich College. Worked in a bank (1922-25) but was determined to work in the film industry. In 1925 he joined Rex Ingram at his studio in Nice and worked there until 1928, when he returned to England. He then took jobs as a cameraman, editor, scenarist at *Denham* and *Pinewood Studios* including working as a stills photographer for Alfred Hitchcock. Finally he directed many low-budget films during the 1930s starting with *Two Crowded Hours* (1931) and including *Rynox* (1932), *Born Lucky* (1933), *Red Ensign* (1934), *The Brown Wallet* (1936) and *The Edge of the World* (1937). Alexander Korda suggested he team up with Emerich Pressburger on the thriller *The Spy in Black* (1938). Powell and Pressburger founded The Archers production company in 1942 and together they wrote, directed and produced some of the best British films of the era. These include: *The Life and Death of Colonel Blimp* (1943), *A Canterbury Tale* (1944), *I Know Where I'm Going!* (1945), *A Matter of Life and Death* (1946), *Black Narcissus* (1946), *The Small Back Room* (1949), *The Elusive Pimpernel* (1950), *The Tales of Hoffmann* (1951), *Oh... Rosalinda!* (1955), *The Battle of the River Plate* (1956) and *Ill Met by Moonlight* (1957). *The Red Shoes* (1948) gained an Academy Award nomination for Best Picture. In addition to his work with Pressburger he also co-directed *The Thief of Bagdad* (1940). His best known work after The Archers folded was the controversial and critically panned psychosexual thriller *Peeping Tom* (1960). Michael eventually lectured at Dartmouth College in the US and worked at Francis Ford Copolla's *Zoetrope Studios*. Autobiographies: *A Life in Movies* (1985) and *Million Dollar Movie* (1995). He was married to American dancer Gloria Mary Rouger for a few short weeks in 1927, Frankie Reidy, from 1943 until her death in 1983 and American film editor Thelma Schoonmaker, from 1984 until his death on 19 February 1990 Avening, Gloucestershire. He was buried next to actress Pamela Brown with whom he lived for many years until her death in 1975.

Powell, Robert (1944-) Born Robert Thomas Powell, 1 June 1944, Salford, Manchester. Actor. Studied at Manchester University before joining a repertory company in Stoke-on-Trent. Robert made his screen debut in an episode of the BBC series *The Hunchback of Notre Dame* (1967) and his feature film debut in *Robbery* (1967). He had a more meaty role in *The Italian Job* (1969) but he really came to the public's attention as the ultimately doomed himself Toby Wren in the television series *Doomwatch* which in turn led to lead roles in single TV dramas such as *Jude the Obscure* (1971),and *Mahler* (1974). His early big screen experience includes *Asylum* (1972), *The Asphyx* (1973) and *Tommy* (1975). He played Richard Hannay in *The Thirty-Nine Steps* (1978) and reprised the role in a later TV series *Hannay* (1988). He is probably best known for playing Jesus in the two-part TV film *Jesus of Nazareth* (1977). Other film credits include *Shaka Zulu* (1987), *Hey Mr DJ* (2003) and *Colour Me Kubrick: A True...ish Story* (2005). In recent years he has continued to concentrate more on television roles including playing alongside Jasper Carrott in the comedy series *The Detectives* and more recently as Mark Williams in *Holby City* (2005-11). He married ex-Pans People dancer Babs Lord (b. Barbara M Load) in 1975. They have a son, Barney (b. 1977) and a daughter, Kate (b. 1979). See also entries in the television section for *The Detectives, Doomwatch, Holby City, Jesus of Nazareth,* and *Survival.*

Powell, Sandy (1960-) Born 7 April 1960, London. Costume designer. Attended the Central School of Art, London, studying theatre design. After theatre work she began her film costume design career working with Derek Jarman on *Caravaggio* (1986). She also collaborated with Jarman on *The Last of England* (1987), *Edward II* (1991) and *Wittgenstein* (1993). Jarman gave her a role as a seamstress in *Edward II*. Sandy has also worked extensively with Neil Jordan on *The Miracle* (1991), *The Crying Game* (1992), *Interview with the Vampire* (1994), *Michael Collins* (1996), *The Butcher Boy* (1997) and *The End of the Affair* (1999). Sandy has gained seven unsuccessful Academy Award nominations for Best Costume Design, for the adaptation of Virginia Woolf's *Orlando* (1992), *The Wings of the Dove* (1997), *Velvet Goldmine* (1998), *Gangs of New York* (2002), *Mrs Henderson Presents* (2005), *The Tempest* (2010) and *Hugo* (2011). She also gained a further three successful nominations for, *Shakespeare in Love* (1998), *The Aviator* (2004) and *The Young Victoria* (2009). Her other films include: *Rob Roy* (1995), *Hilary and Jackie* (1998), *Far From Heaven* (2002), *Sylvia* (2003), *The Departed* (2006), *The Other Boleyn Girl* (2008) and *Shutter Island* (2010). She was awarded an OBE in 2011.

Press, Natalie (1980-) Born Nathalie Press, 15 August 1980. Actress. Studied Fine Art at university, and worked as an office temp and as a video store clerk on the Fulham Road after training at the Tony Greco & Oxford School of Speech & Drama. Now credited as Natalie, she made her screen debut in an episode of *Holby City* in 2001 and her feature film debut in *The Gathering* (2003). Natalie won the London Film Critic's award for Best British Newcomer, playing Mona in Pawel Pawlikowski's *My Summer of Love* (2004). She had already starred in Andrea Arnold's *Wasp* (2003) which won the Academy Award for Best Live Action Short Film in 2005. Other films include: *Chromophobia* (2005), *Animal* (2005), *Song of Songs* (2005), *Red Road* (2006), *Nightwatching* (2007), *In Tranzit* (2008), *Cass* (2008), *Fifty Dead Men Walking* (2008), *Knife Edge* (2009), and *Island* (2011). See also entries in the television section for *Bleak House,* and *Five Daughters.*

Pressburger, Emerich (1902-1988) Born Imre Jozsef Emmerich Pressburger, 5 December 1902, Miskolc, Hungary. Director, producer and writer. Son of a land agent. Studied in Prague and Stuttgart before running a business selling radios in Budapest. Moved to Berlin in 1927 and eventually began writing film scripts for Universum-Film Aktien-Gesellschaft (UFA). Left Berlin for Paris in 1933, where he lived until moving to England in 1935. Alexander Korda suggested he team up with Michael Powell on the thriller *The Spy in Black* (1938). Powell and Pressburger founded The Archers production company in 1942 and together they wrote, directed and produced some of the best British films of the era. (See entry for Michael Powell). His early contributions to the team were mainly in a writing capacity and he won an Academy Award for Best Original Screenplay for *One of Our Aircraft is Missing* (1942) and he was also nominated for *49th Parallel* (1941) and *The Red Shoes* (1948). According to Powell their usual working method was for Pressburger to write a script and then Powell would re-write it in order to present Pressburger's storyline in an effective way on the screen. Pressburger had one solo outing as a director with *Twice Upon a Time* (1953). Emerich wrote the novels *Miracle of St Anthony's Lane* (1934) - filmed as *Miracle in Soho* (1957), *Killing a Mouse on Sunday* (1961) - filmed as *Behold a Pale Horse* (1964) and *The Glass Pearls* (1966). Married to Agi Donath (1938-41) and Wendy Green (b Gwynneth May Zillah Orme) (1947-71). He died 5 February 1988, Saxtead, Woodbridge, Suffolk.

Price, Dennis (1915-73) Born Dennistoun John Franklin Rose Price, 23 June 1915, Ruscombe, Berkshire. Actor. Son of

Brigadier-General T Rose-Price. Educated at Radley College, Berkshire and Worcester College, Oxford, where he joined the Oxford University Dramatic Society. Studied at the Embassy Theatre School of Acting. Stage debut: *Behind Your Back* (1937). Screen debut: *No Parking* (1938). Served with the Royal Artillery (1940-42) until being invalided out and then featured in films such as *A Canterbury Tale* (1944), *The Magic Bow* (1946) and *The Dancing Years* (1948). Then took the title role in *The Bad Lord Byron* (1949), which was a critical flop. He is best known for playing the deliciously and deviously suave serial murderer Louis Mazzini in *Kind Hearts and Coronets* (1949). Alcohol problems meant that his career never reached the heights his early success had promised. His next films include *The Magic Box* (1951) and *Oh... Rosalinda!* (1955) and he had a brief resurgence of popularity with comedies such as *Private's Progress* (1955), *The Naked Truth* (1957), *I'm All Right, Jack* (1959) and *School for Scoundrels* (1960). He also had television success in the 1960s, playing Jeeves in *The World of Wooster* opposite Ian Carmichael. However, by the 1970s he was reduced to appearing in such low-budget horrors as *Vampyros Lesbos* (1971) and *The Erotic Rites of Frankenstein* (1972). He made one more memorable cameo as Hector Snipe in *Theatre of Blood* (1973) before his final film appearance in *Lovers of Devil's Island* (1974). Experiencing severe financial problems he moved to the Channel Islands and died 6 October 1973 on Guernsey. His obituary in *The Times* highlighted his adeptness at portraying "both suave villainy and polished comedy." but his opinion of himself was that he lacked "the essential spark" that would have made him a star. See also entries in the radio and television section for *Jason King, The Navy Lark*, and *The World of Wooster*.

Pryce, Jonathan (1947-) Born Jonathan Price, 1 June 1947, Holywell, Flintshire. Actor. Studied at RADA and a member of the Royal Shakespeare Company. Made his screen debut on television, in an episode of *Doomwatch* in 1972 and his feature film debut in *Voyage of the Damned* (1976). Appeared in *Breaking Glass* (1980), *Loophole* (1981), *Something Wicked this Way Comes* (1983) and *The Ploughman's Lunch* (1983) before making an impact as Sam Lowry, the protagonist of Terry Gilliam's *Brazil* (1985). He has also featured in Gilliam's *The Adventures of Baron Munchausen* (1989) and *The Brothers Grimm* (2005). His other major film roles include Juan Peron in *Evita* (1996), the villain Elliot Carver in *Tomorrow Never Dies* (1997) and Governor Weatherby Swann in *Pirates of the Caribbean: The Curse of the Black Pearl* (2003), *Pirates of the Caribbean: Dead Man's Chest* (2006) and *Pirates of the Caribbean: At World's End* (2007). Jonathan's most recent films include *Bedtime Stories* (2008), *Echelon Conspiracy* (2009), *G.I. Joe: The Rise of Cobra* (2009) and *Hysteria* (2011). His TV film credits include *The Day Christ Died* (1980 - as Herod), *Timon of Athens* (1981 - as Timon), *Martin Luther, Heretic* (1983 - as Luther), *Mr Wroe's Virgins* (1993 - as Mr Wroe), *Victoria & Albert* (2001 - as King Leopold I of Belgium) and *Sherlock Holmes and the Baker Street Irregulars* (2007 – as Holmes). He is also an award winning stage actor in musicals such as *Miss Saigon* and *My Fair Lady*. Married to actress Kate Fahy since 1974. He was awarded an OBE in 2009. See also entries in the television section for *Bill Brand, Cranford*, and *Roger Doesn't Live Here Anymore*.

Purcell, Noel (1900-85) Born 23 December 1900, Dublin. Actor. Worked as a carpenter before becoming a vaudeville artist and then a legitimate stage actor. Noel lost the tip of his right index finger while making cigarette vending machines in his youth and this was later exploited for dramatic effect in his role of Seaman William McCoy in the Marlon Brando film *Mutiny on the Bounty* (1962). He made his screen debut in *Blarney* (1926) and then did not appear again until *Jimmy Boy* (1935). An unmistakeable character actor being 6ft 4ins tall with a white bushy beard and thick Irish brogue, he played an assortment of sailors, bartenders and churchmen. He appeared in such films as *Captain Boycott* (1947), *Odd Man Out* (1947), *The Blue Lagoon* (1949), *The Pickwick Papers* (1952), *The Crimson Pirate* (1952), *Svengali* (1954), *Doctor at Sea* (1955), *Moby Dick* (1956), *Lust for Life* (1956), *Doctor at Large* (1957), *The Millionairess* (1960), *The List of Adrian Messenger* (1963), *Lord Jim* (1965), *Doctor in Clover* (1966), *Drop Dead Darling* (1966), *Where's Jack* (1969)

and his last film, *The Mackintosh Man* (1973). His final screen appearance was as O'Reilly in an episode of *The Irish R.M.* in 1984. Noel received the Freedom of the City of Dublin in June 1984 and died in that city on 3 March 1985.

Puttnam, David (1941-) Born David Terence Puttnam, 25 February 1941, Edmonton, London. Film producer. Started out as a photographers' agent in the 1960s. Began producing films with *Peacemaking 1919* (1971) and the feature *Melody (aka S.W.A.L.K.)* (1971). Other early films include the David Essex vehicles *That'll Be the Day* (1973) and *Stardust* (1974) and the Ken Russell films *Mahler* (1974) and *Lisztomania* (1975). He then produced the successful *Bugsy Malone* (1976) and *Midnight Express* (1978), both of which were directed by Alan Parker, with the latter gaining an Academy Award nomination for Best Picture. Even more successful was *Chariots of Fire* (1981) which won the Best Picture Academy Award. After *Local Hero* (1983) his productions of *The Killing Fields* (1984) and *The Mission* (1986) gained further Best Picture Academy Award nominations. He was chairman and chief executive of *Columbia Pictures* (1986-88) but his forthright opinions and independent outlook failed to provoke anything other than a backlash and his tenure was short-lived. Since then he has been producer of *Memphis Belle* (1990), *Meeting Venus* (1991), *Being Human* (1993), *War of the Buttons* (1994), *The Confessional* (1995) and *My Life So Far* (1999). His latest film on which he had some input is the documentary *We Are the People We've Been Waiting For* (2009), for which he was executive producer. Appointed CBE in 1982 and became a life peer in 1997 as Lord Puttnam of Queensgate. In 1998 he was named in a list of the biggest private financial donors to the Labour Party. Lord Puttnam was the first chancellor of the University of Sunderland from 1997 until 13 July 2007. He was appointed as chancellor of the Open University in 2006 and was for 10 years chairman of the National Film and Television School.

Quayle, Anthony (1913-89) Born John Anthony Quayle, 7 September 1913, Ainsdale, Southport, Lancashire. Actor. Attended Rugby School and trained at RADA. Stage debut: *The Ghost Train* (1931). He then joined the Old Vic in 1932. Served in the Special Operations Executive during WWII rising to the rank of major. His screen debut was *Moscow Nights* (1935) but after *Pygmalion* (1938), the war and then stage commitments saw him off the big screen until playing Marcellus in Olivier's adaptation of *Hamlet* (1948). Following *Saraband for Dead Lovers* (1948) he was again off screen whilst acting and directing at The Shakespeare Memorial Theatre. He returned with *Oh... Rosalinda* (1955), *The Battle of the River Plate* (1956), *The Wrong Man* (1956) and *Woman in a Dressing Gown* (1957). He is probably best known for his military roles in such films as *Ice-Cold in Alex* (1958), *The Guns of Navarone* (1961) and *Lawrence of Arabia* (1962). He received an Academy Award nomination for Best Supporting Actor for playing Cardinal Wolsey in *Anne of the Thousand Days* (1969). Other films include: *Serious Charge* (1959), *The Fall of the Roman Empire* (1964), *East of Sudan* (1964), *A Study in Terror* (1965), *Operation Crossbow* (1965), *Mackenna's Gold* (1969), *Everything You Always Wanted to Know About Sex* (*But Were Afraid to Ask*) (1972), *The Tamarind Seed* (1974), *The Eagle has Landed* (1976), *Murder by Decree* (1979), *Buster* (1988) and his last film, *King of the Wind* (1989). Anthony made regular appearances on television in dramas such as *QB VII* (1974), *Masada* (1981) and *The Bourne Identity* (1988). He wrote the novels *Eight Hours from England* (1945) and *On Such a Night* (1951) and an autobiography *A Time to Speak* (1990). Appointed CBE in 1952 and knighted in 1985. Anthony was married twice. His first wife was actress Hermione Hannen (1913–83) and his widow and second wife was Dorothy Hyson (1914–96). He and Dorothy had two daughters, Jenny and Rosanna, and a son, Christopher. He died 20 October 1989, Kensington, London. See also entries in the television section for *The Six Wives of Henry VI I I* and *The Strange Report*.

Radcliffe, Daniel (1989-) Born Daniel Jacob Radcliffe, 23 July 1989, Hammersmith, London. Actor. Made his screen debut as the young *David Copperfield* in the 1999 BBC television adaptation and his feature debut in *The Tailor of Panama* (2001). He gained possibly the biggest young role on offer so far in the 21st Century when he was cast as the young wizard Harry Potter in *Harry Potter and the Philosopher's Stone* (2001). He has followed these with *Harry Potter and the Chamber of Secrets* (2002), *Harry Potter and the Prisoner of Azkaban* (2004), *Harry Potter and the Goblet of Fire* (2005), *Harry Potter and the Order of the Phoenix* (2007), *Harry Potter and the Half-Blood Prince* (2009), *Harry Potter and the Deathly Hallows* Part 1 (2010) and *Harry Potter and the Deathly Hallows Part II* (2011). Daniel has had few screen roles outside the Harry Potter films. In 2007, he played Maps in the Australian coming-of-age film, *December Boys*, and John 'Jack' Kipling in the TV film My Boy Jack. He also played himself in an episode of the Ricky Gervais comedy series *Extras* (2006). On the stage he appeared in a 2007 revival of Peter Shaffer's play *Equus*, as Alan Strang, a stable boy who has an obsession with horses, and in 2011 he appeared in the Broadway revival of the musical *How to Succeed in Business Without Really Trying*. At the age of 16, Daniel became the youngest non-royal ever to have an individual portrait in Britain's National Portrait Gallery. In November 2007, he published several poems under the pen name Jacob Gershon. He has recently completed filming his role of Arthur Kipps in the upcoming horror movie, *The Woman In Black*, based on the Susan Hill novel.

Radford, Basil (1897-1952) Born Arthur Basil Radford, 25 June 1897, Chester, Cheshire. Actor. Son of a clergyman. Studied at RADA. Stage debut: *Bulldog Drummond* (1922). He toured Australia, New Zealand, United States and Canada 1927-31. Whilst touring the US he made his screen debut in *Barnum was Right* (1929). Alfred Hitchcock cast him as Charters, who, along with his companion Caldicott (played by Naunton Wayne), provided some light relief in *The Lady Vanishes* (1938) as two Englishmen more interested in the Test Match score than in the fate of the missing Miss Froy. The pairing proved so popular that they reprised the roles in *Night Train to Munich* (1940), *Crook's Tour* (1941) and *Millions Like Us* (1943). They also appeared together in *Next of Kin* (1942), as Parratt and Potter in *Dead of Night* (1945), as Prendergast and Fotheringham in *A Girl in a Million* (1946), in *Stop Press Girl* (1949), as Bright and Early in *It's Not Cricket* (1949), in *Quartet (1949)* and in *Passport to Pimlico* (1949). The pair were also successful on radio as Charters and Caldicott until a contractual dispute with the creators Launder and Gilliat meant they could no longer appear under those names. The result was that the BBC then commissioned the actors in a number of series in which they appeared variously as Woolcott and Spencer, Berkeley and Bulstrode, Hargreaves and Hunter and Fanshaw and Fothergill. The character of Charters was played by Arthur Lowe in the remake of the *Lady Vanishes* (1979) and by Robin Bailey in a television series in 1985. Radford also appeared in *Young and Innocent* (1937), *Jamaica Inn* (1939), *Just William* (1940), *The Way to the Stars* (1945), *Whisky Galore!* (1949), *The Blue Lamp* (1950) and *The Galloping Major* (1951). He died 20 October 1952, Westminster, London whilst rehearsing a radio show with Wayne.

Rains, Claude (1889-1967) Born William Claude Rains, 10 November 1889, Camberwell, London. Actor. Stage debut: *Sweet Nell of Old Drury* (1900) at the Haymarket Theatre where he rose from call-boy to assistant stage manager by 1911. After serving in WWI 1915-19 he taught at RADA and gained a small role in a silent film, *Build Thy House* (1920). Claude toured in America in 1927 and remained there, finally making his screen talkie debut in his forties in *The Invisible Man* (1933). Other films include: *The Clairvoyant* (1935), *Mystery of Edwin Drood* (1935), *Anthony Adverse* (1936), *The Prince and the Pauper* (1937), *Four Daughters* (1938), *The Adventures of Robin Hood* (1938 - as Prince John), *Four Wives* (1939), *The Sea Hawk* (1940), *Four Mothers* (1941), *Kings Row* (1942), *Now Voyager* (1942), *Phantom of the Opera* (1943), *Caesar and Cleopatra* (1945 – as Julius Caesar), *Notorious* (1946), *Angel on My Shoulder* (1946), *The White Tower* (1950), *The Man Who Watched Trains Go By* (1952), *This Earth Is Mine* (1959), *The Lost World* (1960 - as Prof. George Edward Challenger), *Lawrence of Arabia* (1962) and his last film *The Greatest Story Ever Told* (1965 – as King Herod). He was nominated as Best Supporting Actor four times, for *Mr Smith Goes to Washington* (1939), *Casablanca* (1942 – as Capt Renault), *Mr Skeffington* (1944) and *Notorious* (1946). He

married six times: to actress Isabel Jeans (1913-16), Marie Hemingway (1920), Beatrix Thomson (1924-35), Frances Propper (1935-56), Hungarian concert pianist Agi Jambor (1959-60) and Rosemary McGroarty Clark Schrode (1960-her death in 1964). All his marriages ended in divorce except the last. His only child, Jessica Rains (b. 24 January 1938), was born to him and Frances Proper. Claude died 30 May 1967, Laconia, New Hampshire.

Rampling, Charlotte (1946-) Born Tessa Charlotte Rampling, 5 February 1946, Sturmer, Essex. Actress. Educated at Jeanne d'Arc Académie pour Jeunes Filles in Versailles and St. Hilda's School in Bushey, HertfordshireSt. Hilda's school in Bushey, Hertfordshire. After an initial stint of modelling she had an uncredited role as a water-skier in Richard Lester's The Knack ...and *How to Get It* (1965) following this up with her credited feature debut in *Rotten to the Core* (1965 - as Sara Capell) and the typically 1960s *Georgy Girl* (1966). With her upbringing she seemed ideal for international fare and she moved on to *Sequestro di Persona* (1968), Luchino Visconti's *La Caduta Degli Dei* (1969) and the film for which she is perhaps best known *Il Portiere di Notte (The Night Porter)* (1974) by Liliana Cavani. Other films include: *The Long Duel* (1967), *Vanishing Point* (1971), *Henry VIII and His Six Wives* (1972 - as Anne Boleyn), *Corky* (1972), *Zardoz* (1974), *Farewell, My Lovely* (1975), *Stardust Memories* (1980), *The Verdict* (1982), *Angel Heart* (1987), *D.O.A.* (1988), *Rebus* (1990), *Asphalt Tango* (1996), *The Wings of the Dove* (1997), *The Cherry Orchard* (1999), *The Fourth Angel* (2001), *I'll Sleep When I'm Dead* (2003), *Swimming Pool* (2003), *The Keys to the House* (2004), *Basic Instinct 2* (2006 - as Milena Gardosh), *Twice Upon a Time* (2006), *Angel* (2007), *The Duchess* (2008), *Boogie Woogie* (2009), *Never Let Me Go* (2010), *Rio Sex Comedy* (2010), *The Mill and the Cross* (2010), *Melancholia* (2011), *Cars 2* (2011 - narrator), *The Eye of the Storm* (2011) and the forthcoming *Cleanskin* (2012). She was awarded the OBE in 2000. As a piece of trivia her father, Godfrey (14 May 1909 - 20 June 2009), won silver and gold medals at the 1932 and 1936 Olympics respectively in the 4 x 400m relay. Charlotte has been married twice: to actor and publicist Bryan Southcombe (1972-76), with whom she had a son Barnaby, who is now a successful television director; and French composer Jean Michel Jarre (1978-98), with whom she also had a son, magician David Jarre. She also raised stepdaughter Émilie Jarre, now a fashion designer. She has been engaged to Jean-Noël Tassez, a French communications tycoon, since 1998.

Rank, J Arthur (1888-1972) Born Joseph Arthur Rank, 23 December 1888 Kingston-upon-Hull, Yorkshire. Film executive. Son of a highly successful flour miller, whose opinion of his son was that the only way he'd get on was "in the mill." An attempt to start his own company, *Peterkins Self-Raising Flour*, proved a failure and he returned to work for his father. A devout Methodist, he taught Sunday School and began showing religious films, swiftly realising that this medium was an excellent method of spreading the word. He helped form the *Religious Film Society* and produced *Mastership* (1934). This developed into a production company called the *British National Films Company*. First film: *Turn of the Tide* (1935). Over the next few years he formed the *Rank Organisation* took control of *Pinewood Film Studios*, *Denham Studios*, *Elstree Studios*, *Shepherd's Bush Studios*, the *Odeon* cinema chain, *Gaumont-British* and the *Paramount* cinema chain. The result was a vertically integrated company covering production, distribution and exhibition to rival anything in the United States. The Organisation was also known for its Company of Youth (aka The Rank Charm School) which fostered the early careers of such as Christopher Lee, Joan Collins and Diana Dors. Known by the *Rank* filmmakers as "Uncle Arthur" he encouraged the creative arm of the organisation and under his aegis the likes of Powell and Pressburger, David Lean and Launder and Gilliat produced some of their best work. However, creative people aren't necessarily the best for running a business and a few lavish, over-budget flops such as *Caesar and Cleopatra* (1945) nearly brought the organisation to the point of collapse. After the death of his elder brother Jimmy (b. James Voase Rank, 1882) in 1952 he went back to running the flour business. He stayed on as chairman of the *Rank Organisation* for a further ten years but left the running of the company to accountant John Davis. Davis was much disliked, especially by the creative branch, who swiftly upped stakes and joined Alexander Korda virtually to a man, but the new output of cheaply-made but still popular films starring the likes of Norman Wisdom saved the company. In 1953 *Rank* created the charity later known as *The Rank Foundation*. Created Baron Rank of Sutton Scotney in 1957. He died 29 March 1972 Winchester, Hampshire.

Rathbone, Basil (1892-1967) Born Philip St John Basil Rathbone, 13 June 1892, Johannesburg, South Africa. Actor. Educated at Repton College. Worked for an insurance company before turning to acting. Stage debut: *The Taming of the Shrew* (1911). Served with the London Scottish and Liverpool Scottish during WWI. He received the Military Cross in September 1918 for conspicuous daring and resource on patrol. Screen debut: *The Fruitful Vine* (1921). Other films include: *The Loves of Mary, Queen of Scots* (1923), *A Notorious Affair* (1930), *After the Ball* (1933), *Anna Karenina* (1935), *David Copperfield* (1935), *The Last Days of Pompeii* (1935), *A Tale of Two Cities* (1935), *Captain Blood* (1935), *The Adventures of Robin Hood* (1938), *Son of Frankenstein* (1939), *Tower of London* (1939), *The Mark of Zorro* (1940), *Frenchman's Creek* (1944), *The Court Jester* (1956), *Hillbillys in a Haunted House* (1967)and his last film, *Autopsia De Un Fantasma* (1967). Remembered for his fencing duels with the likes of Errol Flynn, Tyrone Power and Danny Kaye, Basil was considered to be the most accomplished fencer in Hollywood. Although he played the villain in many films he remains best known for portraying Sherlock Holmes, opposite Nigel Bruce as Watson, in 15 films: *The Hound of The Baskervilles* (1939), *The Adventures of Sherlock Holmes* (1939), *Sherlock Holmes and the Voice of Terror* (1942), *Sherlock Holmes and the Secret Weapon* (1943), *Sherlock Holmes in Washington* (1943), *Sherlock Holmes Faces Death* (1943), *Crazy House* (1943), *The Spider Woman* (1944), *The Scarlet Claw* (1944), *The Pearl of Death* (1944), *The House of Fear* (1945), *The Woman in Green* (1945), *Pursuit to Algiers* (1945), *Terror by Night* (1946) and *Dressed to Kill* (1946). Rathbone and Bruce reprised their film roles in a radio series, *The New Adventures of Sherlock Holmes*, which began in October 1939. Basil remained in the radio series for the duration of the film series but after the films lapsed in 1946, he yielded his radio part to Tom Conway. Conway and Bruce carried on with the series for two seasons, until both dropped out in July 1947. Basil received Best Supporting Actor nominations for *Romeo and Juliet* (1936) and *If I Were King* (1938), losing out to Walter Brennan on both occasions. Autobiography: *In and Out of Character: An Autobiography* (1956). Basil was married twice, to actress Ethel Marion Foreman, from 1914 until their divorce in 1926, and American actress and screenwriter Ouida Bergère, from 1927 until his death on 21 July 1967, New York. He had a son Rodion Rathbone (1915–1996), who had a brief Hollywood career under the name John Rodion. See also entry for *Tales From Dickens* in the television section.

Ray, Ted See entry in comedy section

Rea, Stephen (1946-) Born Graham Rea, 31 October 1946, Belfast. Actor. Educated at Belfast High School and Queen's University, Belfast. Trained for acting at the Abbey Theatre School, Dublin. He made his screen debut in *Crossroads* (1964) and after appearing in episodes of *Z Cars* and *Softly Softly* he made his big screen debut in *Cry of the Banshee* (1970). Spent most of the 1970s on stage with a few television appearances until he made *Angel* (1982) under Neil Jordan's direction. He collaborated with Jordan again on *The Company of Wolves* (1984). Stephen then made *The Doctor and the Devils* (1985) and *Life is Sweet* (1990) before hooking up with Jordan again and gaining an Academy Award nomination for Best Actor for his portrayal of Fergus in *The Crying Game* (1992). This success saw him move on to a wide variety of projects such as *Bad Behaviour* (1993), *Angie* (1994) and *Princess Caraboo* (1994) plus *Interview with the Vampire* (1994) again with Neil Jordan and *Pret-a-Porter* (1994) for Robert Altman. More Jordan collaborations include *Michael Collins* (1996), *The Butcher Boy* (1997), *In Dreams* (1999), *The End of the Affair* (1999), *Breakfast on Pluto* (2005) and *Ondine* (2009). His other films include *Fever Pitch* (1997), *Still Crazy* (1998), *The Musketeer* (2001 - as Cardinal Richelieu), *Bloom* (2003 - as Leopold Bloom), *The Good Shepherd* (2004), *Tara Road* (2005), *V for Vendetta* (2006), *Sisters* (2006), *Sixty Six* (2006), *Until Death* (2007), *The Reaping* (2007), *Stuck* (2007), *Heidi 4 Paws* (2008), *The Devil's Mercy* (2008), *Kisses* (2008), *Spy(ies)* (2009), *Child of the Dead End* (2009), *Nothing Personal* (2009), *The Heavy* (2010), *Blackthorn* (2011) and *The Shadow Line* (2011). Formed the Field Day Theatre Company in 1980 with Brian Friel, Tom Paulin, Seamus Heaney and Seamus Deane. Stephen was married to former Provisional Irish Republican Army hunger striker and now staunch critic of Sinn Féin, Dolours Price, from 1983 to 2003. They have two children. See also entries in the television section for *Crossroads, Father & Son, I Didn't Know You Cared,* and *Not With A Bang*.

Redgrave, Corin (1939-2010) Born Corin William Redgrave, 16 July 1939, Marylebone, London. Actor. Son of Sir Michael Redgarve and Rachel Kempson, brother of Vanessa and Lynn Redgrave. Studied at Westminster School and Cambridge. Stage debut: *Midsummer Night's Dream* (1961). Screen debut: *Crooks in Cloisters* (1964). Featured in such films as *A Man for All Seasons* (1966), *The Charge of the Light Brigade* (1968), *Oh! What a Lovely War* (1969), *When Eight Bells Toll* (1971) and *Excalibur* (1981). Played a corrupt policeman in *In the Name of the Father* (1993), Hamish in *Four Weddings and a Funeral* (1994) and Sir Walter Elliot in *Persuasion* (1995). His latest films include *Enigma* (2001), *To Kill a King* (2003), *Enduring Love* (2004), *The Trial of the King Killers* (2005), *The Calling* (2009), *Glorious 39* (2009) and his last film, *Eva* (2010). In addition to his extensive stage work his many TV films include *David Copperfield* (1969), *Antony and Cleopatra (1974), Shackleton (2002), Sunday* (2002), *The Relief of Belsen* (2007) and *The Turn of the Screw* (2009). In 1994 he established the Moving Theatre stage company with his sister Vanessa. Corin has written a biography of his father *Michael Redgrave: My Father* (1995). He was a lifelong activist in left-wing politics. With his elder sister Vanessa, he was a prominent member of the Workers' Revolutionary Party. Corin was married twice, to Deirdre Hamilton-Hill (1962-75) and actress Kika Markham, from 1985 until his death on 6 April 2010 in St George's Hospital, Tooting, South West London. See also entry for *The Forsyte Saga* in the television section.

Redgrave, Lynn (1943-2010) Born Lynn Rachel Redgrave, 8 March 1943, Marylebone, London. Actress. Daughter of Sir Michael Redgrave and Rachel Kempson, sister of Vanessa and Corin Redgrave, aunt of Natasha Richardson, Joely Richardson and Jemma Redgrave. Attended Central School of Speech and Drama. Her screen debut was an uncredited bit part in Michael Winner's *Shoot to Kill* (1960). Following a small role in *Tom Jones* (1963) and a somewhat more substantial part in *Girl with Green Eyes* (1964), Lynn was nominated for an Academy Award for Best Actress for her title role in *Georgy Girl* (1966), losing out to Elizabeth Taylor. Her only other Academy Award nomination (this time Best Supporting Actress) has come for *Gods and Monsters* (1998). She has also been twice nominated for Tony Awards and is the 1977 and 1995 winner of the Sarah Siddons Award for her work in Chicago theatre. She also starred in the US TV series *House Calls* (1979-81). Lynn was awarded the OBE in 2001 but subsequently became a naturalised American citizen. Her other films include: *The Deadly Affair* (1966), *Smashing Time* (1967), *The Virgin Soldiers* (1969), *Every Little Crook and Nanny* (1972), *Every Thing You Always Wanted to Know About Sex * But Were Afraid to Ask* (1972), *The National Health* (1973), *The Happy Hooker* (1975 - as Xaviera Hollander), *The Big Bus* (1976), *Getting It Right* (1989), *Midnight* (1989), *Shine* (1996), *Strike!* (1998), *Touched* (1999), *The Annihilation of Fish* (1999), *Lion of Oz* (2000), *The Simian Line* (2000), *Venus and Mars* (2001), *Unconditional Love* (2002), *Anita and Me* (2002), *Charlie's War* (2003), *Peter Pan* (2003), *Kinsey* (2004), *The White Countess* (2005), *The Jane Austen Book Club* (2007 - as Mama Sky), *Confessions of a Shopaholic* (2009) and her last film, *My Dog Tulip* (2009). She is well known for her numerous American TV shows and *Weight Watchers* commercials, her last screen appearance being in an episode of *Ugly Betty* in 2009. In 1967 she married British actor, director and writer John Clark.

117

They had three children: airline pilot Benjamin Clark (b. 1968), singer-songwriter Kelly 'Pema' Clark (b. 1970), and author and photographer Annabel Lucy Clark (b. 1981). The marriage ended in 2000 after Clark revealed that he had fathered a child with Lynn's personal assistant, who later married (and subsequently divorced) their son Benjamin. In 2004, jointly with her daughter Annabel she published *Our Journal* in *The New York Times*, detailing the ups and downs of her recovery from a mastectomy in 2003. Lynn finally succumbed to breast cancer on 2 May 2010, Kent, Connecticut, and was buried at Saint Peter's Episcopal Cemetery in Lithgow, New York, alongside her mother Rachel Kempson and niece Natasha Richardson. See also entry for *Love Story* in the television section.

Redgrave, Michael (1908-85) Born Michael Scudamore Redgrave, 20 March 1908, Bristol. Actor. Son of Australian actor Roy Redgrave and actress Margaret Scudamore. Educated at Clifton College and Magdalene College, Cambridge and afterwards took up teaching at Cranleigh School, Surrey. Made his stage debut in 1934. His screen debut was in Hitchcock's *Secret Agent* (1936) and he shot to prominence with his performance as Gilbert Redman in *The Lady Vanishes* (1938) opposite Margaret Lockwood. His other early films include: *A Stolen Life* (1939), *The Stars Look Down* (1939), *Kipps* (1941) and *Jeannie* (1941). He owned White Roding Windmill from 1937 to 1946. Michael served in the navy during WWII. After the war he had successful collaborations with director Anthony Asquith on *The Way to the Stars* (1945), *The Browning Version* (1951) and *The Importance of Being Earnest* (1952). He played a demented ventriloquist in *Dead of Night* (1946). A spell in Hollywood saw him receive a Best Actor Academy Award nomination for *Mourning Becomes Electra* (1947). Other major films during the 1940s and 1950s include *Fame is the Spur* (1946), *The Magic Box* (1951), *The Sea Shall Not Have Them* (1954), *The Dam Busters* (1954 - as Barnes Wallis), *The Night My Number Came Up* (1955), *1984* (1956), *Time without Pity* (1957) and *The Quiet American* (1958). He had a very successful stage career in both classical and modern roles for the Shakespeare Memorial Theatre and the National Theatre. His later films include *The Loneliness of the Long Distance Runner* (1962), *Uncle Vanya* (1963), *Battle of Britain* (1969), *Goodbye, Mr Chips* (1969), *Oh! What a Lovely War* (1969), *The Go-Between* (1970) and his last film, *Rime of the Ancient Mariner* (1975). Suffered from Parkinsons Disease during later life. He married actress Rachel Kempson in 1935. Father of Corin, Lynn and Vanessa Redgrave. Michael was bisexual and had a long-term relationship with Bob Michell although this was kept private. Appointed CBE in 1952 and knighted in 1959. Wrote the books *The Actor's Ways and Means* (1955), *Mask or Face* (1958) and *The Mountebank Tale* (1959) plus the play *The Aspern Papers*. Autobiography: *In My Mind's Eye* (1983). He died 21 March 1985, Denham, Buckinghamshire. See also entries in the television section for *The Great War*, and *The World of Beachcomber*.

Redgrave, Vanessa (1937-) Born 30 January 1937, Greenwich, London. Actress. Vanessa is part of a theatrical dynasty. She is the daughter of Michael Redgrave and Rachel Kempson, sister of Lynn and Corin Redgrave, mother to Joely and the late Natasha Richardson, aunt to Jemma Redgrave, mother-in-law of Liam Neeson and from 1962-67 was married to director Tony Richardson. She attended the Central School of Speech and Drama. She made her stage debut in 1958. Vanessa's screen debut came in the BBC film short *Men, Women and Clothes: Sense and Nonsense in Fashion* (1956). Her feature debut in *Behind the Mask* (1958) was opposite her father. She has established herself as one of the foremost actresses of her generation and has an imposing screen presence, usually playing strong-willed, independent figures. Some examples are Guinevere in *Camelot* (1967), Isadora Duncan in *Isadora* (1968) and Sister Jeanne in *The Devils* (1971). Her trophy cabinet must be creaking. Among some of the awards that she has won are: two individual Acting Awards at Cannes (the first person to do so), a Tony Award for *Long Day's Journey Into Night* (2003), Laurence Olivier Theatre Award for *The Aspern Papers* (1985), London Critics Circle Theatre Award for *The Seagull* (1985) and *A Touch of the Poet* (1988), London Evening Standard Theatre Award for *When She Danced* (1991) and last but not least an Academy Award for Best Supporting Actress for *Julia* (1977) (she is the only person in the Academy Awards history to win a Best Supporting Actress Award for playing the title role). However, she has also missed out several times, having been nominated for Academy Awards a further five times, three times for Best Actress for *Morgan: A Suitable Case for Treatment* (1966), *Isadora* (1968) and *Mary, Queen of Scots* (1971) plus twice more for Best Supporting Actress for *The Bostonians* (1984) and *Howards End* (1992). Other films include: *A Man For All Seasons* (1966 - as Anne Boleyn), *Blowup* (1966), *The Charge of the Light Brigade* (1968), *Oh! What a Lovely War* (1969 - as Sylvia Pankhurst), *Murder on the Orient Express* (1974), *Agatha* (1979 - as Agatha Christie), *Yanks* (1979), *Steaming* (1985), *Prick Up Your Ears* (1987), *Consuming Passions* (1988), *The Ballad of the Sad Cafe* (1991), *Mission: Impossible* (1996), *Wilde* (1997), *Déjà Vu* (1997) and *Deep Impact* (1998). Her recent films include: *The Keeper: The Legend of Omar Khayyam* (2005), *The White Countess* (2005), *How About You* (2007), *Evening* (2007), *Atonement* (2007 - as Older Briony Tallis), *Letters to Juliet* (2010), *The Whistleblower* (2010), *Miral* (2010), *Animals United* (2010 - voice of Winnie for the English version), *Coriolanus* (2011 - as Volumnia), *Cars 2* (2011 - voice of Mama Topolino / The Queen) and *Anonymous* (2011 - as Elizabeth I). A long-time member of Britain's Workers Revolutionary Party, she is known off screen for her strong political views. On accepting her Academy Award in 1978 for *Julia* she was openly booed as she referred to Zionist hoodlums. In December, 2002, Vanessa paid £50,000 bail for Chechen separatist Akhmed Zakayev and in 2004 she and her brother Corin announced the launch of the Peace and Progress Party which would campaign against the Iraq War and for human rights. She was awarded the CBE in 1967 but declined a damehood in 1999. After divorcing Tony Richardson, Vanessa had a long-term relationship with actor Timothy Dalton between 1971 and 1986. She then had an even longer relationship with actor Franco Nero, whom she first met on the set of *Camelot*. They eventually married in 2006. Vanessa has lost several family members in recent years. See entries for Natasha Richardson, Corin Redgrave and Lynn Redgrave. See also entries in the television section for *The Day of the Triffids*, and *Love Story*.

Reed, Carol (1906-76) Born Carol Pinney, 30 December 1906, Putney, London. Director. Illegitimate son of actor-manager Sir Herbert Beerbohm Tree. Educated at King's School, Canterbury. Stage debut: *Heraclius* (1924). He acted 1924-31 before taking up stage directing. Worked closely with writer Edgar Wallace on staging and subsequently filming his work. Appointed dialogue director by *Associated Talking Pictures* in 1932 and worked as an assistant director 1933-34. Directorial debut: *Midshipman Easy* (1935). Other films during the 1930s and early 1940s include: *Laburnum Grove* (1936), *Bank Holiday* (1938), *A Girl Must Live* (1939), *The Stars Look Down* (1940), *Night Train to Munich* (1940), *Kipps* (1941) and *The Young Mr Pitt* (1942). He then made *The New Lot* (1943) for the Army Kinema Corporation, which he subsequently turned into the feature length *The Way Ahead* (1944), written by Peter Ustinov. After the drama *Odd Man Out* (1947) he began a collaboration with writer Graham Greene. He received Academy Award nominations for his work with Greene on *The Fallen Idol* (1948) and *The Third Man* (1949). During the 1950s he directed *Outcast of the Islands* (1952), *The Man Between* (1953), *A Kid for Two Farthings* (1955), *Trapeze* (1956), *The Key* (1958) and another Greene collaboration *Our Man in Havana* (1959). While working on *Mutiny on the Bounty* (1962) he quit because of repeated clashes with Marlon Brando. He then directed *The Running Man* (1963) and the big budget *The Agony and the Ecstasy* (1965). Carol won a Best Director Academy Award for the screen adaptation of Lionel Bart's musical *Oliver!* (1968), which was also the winner of an Academy Award for Best Film. His final films were *The Last Warrior* (1970) and *Follow Me!* (1972). Carol was a strong believer in tackling a mixture of subjects and genres; some of his films, particularly those in the late 1940s, are distinguished by tilted camera angles and odd spatial compositions. Uncle of actor Oliver Reed. Knighted 1952, the first British director to receive this accolade. Married to actresses Diana Wynyard (1943-47) and Penelope Dudley-Ward, from 1948 until his death on 25 April 1976, Chelsea, London.

Reed, Oliver (1938-99) Born Robert Oliver Reed, 13 February 1938, Wimbledon, London. Actor. Took a variety of jobs including nightclub bouncer before taking up acting. Screen debut: *The Square Peg* (1958). Along with horror genre films *The Two Faces of Dr Jekyll* (1960) and a starring role in *The Curse of the Werewolf* (1961), his other early films include: *The League of Gentlemen* (1959), *The Bulldog Breed* (1960), *The Rebel* (1961), *The Pirates of Blood River* (1962), *The Crimson Blade* (1963) and *The Brigand of Kandahar* (1965). During the 1960s he worked closely with director Michael Winner on *The System* (1964), *The Jokers* (1967), *I'll Never Forget What's 'is Name* (1967), *Hannibal Brooks* (1969) and later, *The Big Sleep* (1978 – as Eddie Mars) and *Parting Shots* (1999). With director Ken Russell he starred in *Women in Love* (1969), *The Devils* (1971), *Lisztomania* (1975) and *Tommy* (1975). He also worked with Richard Lester, playing Athos in *The Three Musketeers* (1973), *The Four Musketeers* (1974) and *The Return of the Musketeers* (1989) and Otto von Bismarck in *Royal Flash* (1975). Other films include *The Assassination Bureau* (1969), *And Then There Were None* (1974), *The Brood* (1979), the title role in *Dr. Heckyl and Mr. Hype* (1980), *Fanny Hill* (1983), *Castaway* (1986 - as Gerald Kingsland), *The House of Usher* (1988), *The Adventures of Baron Munchausen* (1988), *Funny Bones* (1995) and *Orpheus & Eurydice* (2000 – as the narrator). The "bad boy" of British films, infamous for his hell-raising life-style and drunkenness when interviewed on chat shows; the *Michael Aspel Show* in 1986 is particularly well-remembered for Oliver's rendition of "The Wild One" after walking on stage with a jug of vodka and orange. The nephew of director Carol Reed for whom he played a memorable Bill Sykes in *Oliver!* (1968), Oliver was undoubtedly one of the finest actors of his generation. Autobiography: *Reed All About Me* (1979). Oliver was married twice, to Kate Byrne (1959–69) and Josephine Burge, from 1985 until his death on 2 May 1999, Valetta, Malta whilst filming *Gladiator* (2000). His role of Proximo was completed using body doubles and CGI. Oliver was buried in Churchtown, County Cork, near his favourite pub.

Reid, Beryl (1919-96) Born Beryl Elizabeth Reid, 17 June 1919, Hereford. Actress and comedienne. Raised in Manchester. She featured as a comedienne of British revues and stage from the age of 17. Her film debut had to wait a little longer and she was in her thirties when she appeared in *The Belles of St. Trinian's* (1954). She was well-known during the 1950s for her appearances on *The Benny Hill Show* and her "turns" as the schoolgirl Monica and the Brummie Marlene on the radio programme *Educating Archie*. She made a number of film appearances, usually in comic roles. For example in *Father Dear Father* (1972), *Dr Phibes Rises Again* (1972), *No Sex Please: We're British* (1975) and *Carry On Emmannuelle* (1978). She was, however, much more versatile and some of her later work stretched her out of the more usual areas. She appeared on Broadway in *The Killing of Sister George* (1966), later reprising her role in the 1968 film. Other films include: *Two Way Stretch* (1960), *The Dock Brief* (1962), *Inspector Clouseau* (1968), *Star!* (1968), *Entertaining Mr. Sloane* (1970), *Joseph Andrews* (1977), *Rosie Dixon - Night Nurse* (1978), *Yellowbeard* (1983) and her last feature film, *The Doctor and the Devils* (1985) On television she was especially memorable as Connie Sachs in *Tinker, Tailor, Soldier, Spy* (1979) and *Smiley's People* (1982), for which she won a Best Actress BAFTA. One of her final roles was as Fitz's mother in *Cracker* (1993). She died, of pneumonia, on 13 October 1996, Wraysbury, Berkshire. See also entries in the radio and television section for *Alcock and Gander, The Beiderbecke Affair, Bold As Brass, Educating Archie, The Irish RM, Just A Minute, Love Story, Secret Diary of Adrian Mole, Aged 13 3/4, Tinker Tailor Soldier Spy* and *Wink To Me Only*.

Reilly, Kelly (1977-) Born 18 July 1977, Chessington, Surrey. Actress. With no formal acting training, she landed a part in *Prime Suspect 4: Inner Circles* (1995) and has become a sought after actress on both stage and screen. On stage she has starred in *The Graduate* as Elaine Robinson, *Look Back in Anger* as Alison Porter, *Sexual Perversity in Chicago* and *After Miss Julie* (2003), which netted her a Laurence Olivier award nomination for Best Actress - the youngest person ever nominated for that award. On TV she featured in *Poldark* (1996), *Rebecca* (1997), *The History of Tom Jones, a Foundling* (1997) and *Children of the New Forest* (1998) before making her feature film debut in *Maybe Baby* (2000). Her other early films include *Peaches* (2000), *Last Orders* (2001) as a young version of Helen Mirren's character, and *Dead Bodies* (2003). In 2004 she featured in *The Libertine* before moving on to more substantial roles in *Les Poupees Russe* (2005 – aka The Russian Dolls) and *Mrs Henderson Presents* (2005). She also played Caroline Bingley in *Pride and Prejudice* (2005). In 2006 she was chosen to play Christine / Andromeda in a television film remake of *A for Andromeda*, the role which launched Julie Christie's career in 1961. Following *Puffball* (2007) she had her first starring role in *Eden Lake* (2008). Subsequently Kelly has appeared in more high profile films such as *Me and Orson Welles* (2008), *Triage* (2009), *Sherlock Holmes* (2009), *Meant to Be* (2010), *Ti presento un amico* (2010) and *Sherlock Holmes: A Game of Shadows* (2011). Kelly was once engaged to Israeli actor Jonah Lotan and more recently has dated Guy Ritchie.

Relph, Michael (1915-2004) Born Michael Leighton George Relph, 16 February 1915, Broadstone, Dorset. Producer, director and designer. Son of the actor George Relph. He worked as apprentice to Alfred Junge for *Gaumont-British Art Department* (1932-36) and then *Warner Brothers* (1937-42). Michael also designed for the stage with his debut being *Indoor Fireworks* (1934) and he continued this aspect of his career with success in parallel with his screen work. His art directorial debut for the screen was *Who Killed John Savage?* (1937), which he followed with *Thy Drive by Night* (1938). He joined *Ealing Studios* in 1942 and began a creative partnership with Basil Dearden as a production team. He was art director on such Ealing films as *My Learned Friend* (1943), *The Bells Go Down* (1943) and *They Came to a City* (1945). He was production designer for *Champagne Charlie* (1944), *Dead of Night* (1945) and *Nicholas Nickleby* (1947). His other collaborations as producer, director or writer with Dearden have been on some classics of British cinema including *The Captive Heart* (1946), *Frieda* (1947), *Saraband for Dead Lovers* (1948), *The Blue Lamp* (1950), *I Believe in You* (1952) and *The Ship that Died of Shame* (1955). Moving from Ealing to MGM at Elstree they made *The Smallest Show on Earth* (1957), *The League of Gentlemen* (1959), *Sapphire* (1959), *Victim* (1961), *Life for Ruth* (1961), *Woman of Straw* (1964), *Masquerade* (1965), *The Assassination Bureau* (1969) and *The Man who Haunted Himself* (1970). He gained an Academy Award nomination for Best Art Direction for his sumptuous designs for *Saraband for Dead Lovers* (1948). He also produced *Kind Hearts and Coronets* (1949) without Dearden. After Dearden's death in 1971 he produced *Scum* (1979), *An Unsuitable Job for a Woman* (1981) and *Heavenly Pursuits* (1986). Michael was chairman of the Film Production Association of Great Britain (1971-76) and chairman of the British Film Institute Production Board (1972-79). Father of Simon Relph. He died 30 September 2004, Selsey, West Sussex.

Relph, Simon (1940-) Born Simon George Michael Relph, 13 April 1940 Chelsea, London. Producer and director. Graduate of King's College, Cambridge. Worked as an assistant director on several films including Doctor in *Distress* (1963), *Anne of a Thousand Days* (1969), *Sunday Bloody Sunday* (1971), *A Touch of Class* (1973) and *Zardoz* (1974) before joining the National Theatre (1974-78), ending as production administrator. He returned as assistant director for *Yanks* (1979) and *Reds* (1981), on which he was also executive director. Simon next became an independent producer of such films as *The Return of the Soldier* (1982), *The Ploughman's Lunch* (1983) and *Comrades* (1987). He was chief executive of British Screen Finance Limited (1985-90) which co-financed more than 50 films. During the 1990s he was producer or executive producer of amongst others *Damage* (1992), *The Land Girls* (1998), *Hideous Kinky* (1998), *Bugs!* (2003) and *Get the Picture* (2004). Simon wrote "The Relph Report" on the financing of low budget British films and is a former chairman of BAFTA. Son of Michael Relph. Appointed CBE in 2003 for his services to the British Film Industry.

Rennie, Michael (1909-71) Born Eric Alexander Rennie, 25 August 1909, Bradford, Yorkshire. Actor. Graduated from Cambridge. Worked as a car salesman and also managed a rope factory before joining the York Repertory company. He made his screen debut in Hitchcock's *The Secret Agent* (1936). Early films include: *The Squeaker* (1937), *Bank Holiday* (1938), *Dangerous Moonlight* (1941 – his first credited role) and *Turned Out Nice Again* (1941). Served in the RAF during WWII. After the war his career took off as he starred in *The Wicked Lady* (1945) and *I'll Be Your Sweetheart* (1945) before leaving Britain for Hollywood. After *The Black Rose* (1950) he starred as the alien Klaatu in the classic science fiction film *The Day the Earth Stood Still* (1951) and also featured in *The 13th Letter* (1951), *Phone Call from a Stranger* (1952), *Les Miserables* (1952) and *5 Fingers* (1952). He then starred in epics and adventure films such as *The Robe* (1953), *King of the Khyber Rifles* (1953), *Prince Valiant* (1954), *Princess of the Nile* (1954) and *Demetrius and the Gladiators* (1954). His TV career included roles as Harry Lime in the popular BBC series *The Third Man* (1959-65) plus guest appearances in American series such as *Batman* - as The Sandman, *Lost in Space* and *The Man from U.N.C.L.E.*. His other films include *Desiree* (1954), *Omar Khayyam* (1957), *The Lost World* (1960), *Cyborg 2087* (1966), *The Devil's Brigade* (1968), *Dracula Versus Frankenstein* (1970 - as Dr Odo Warnoff) and his last film, *The Last Generation* (1971). Michael was married twice, to Joan England (1938–45) and actress Maggie McGrath (1947–60); their son, David Rennie, is an English circuit judge in Lewes, Sussex. Michael settled in Switzerland but died 10 June 1971, Harrogate, Yorkshire, whilst visiting relatives.

Rhys-Davies, John (1944-) Born 5 May 1944, Ammanford, Carmarthenshire, Wales. Actor. His young years were spent in Tanzania, Wiltshire and Wales at various times. He graduated from the University of East Anglia. Trained at RADA, he initially worked as a teacher then joined the Madder-Market Theatre in Norwich and eventually the Royal Shakespeare Company. He made his screen debut in the television series *Crossroads* in 1964 and his feature film debut a decade later in *The Black Windmill* (1974). After appearing in several British television series he gained international recognition as Portuguese navigator Vasco Rodrigues in the 1980 American television mini-series *Shogun*, based on the novel by James Clavell. In 1989 John starred in another American mini-series based on a James Clavell novel, *Noble House*, set in Hong Kong, in which he played Ian Dunross' corporate enemy, Quillian Gornt. Early films include: *Penny Gold* (1974), *A Nightingale Sang in Berkeley Square* (1979) and *Sphinx* (1981), however, he made a far bigger impression as Sallah, Indiana Jones' sidekick in *Raiders of the Lost Ark* (1981) and *Indiana Jones and the Last Crusade* (1989). His films during the 1980s include *Victor/Victoria* (1982), *Sahara* (1983), *Sword of the Valiant* (1984), *King Solomon's Mines* (1985), *In the Shadow of Kilimanjaro* (1986), *Firewalker* (1986) and *The Living Daylights* (1987). On television he played Front de Boeuf in the TV film *Ivanhoe* (1982) and Joe Gargery in Disney's *Great Expectations* (1989). During the 1990s he concentrated more on television work in America and had a lead role as Professor Maximillian Arturo in the sci-fi series *Sliders* (1995-1997). In 1992 he played Professor challenger in the film *The Lost World* and the sequel *Return to the Lost World* but most of his other films of this period are fairly unmemorable. He was then cast as Gimli the Dwarf in *The Lord of the Rings: The Fellowship of the Ring* (2001), *The Lord of the Rings: The Two Towers* (2002) - in which he also provided the voice of Treebeard - and *The Lord of the Rings: The Return of the King* (2003). His other films include: *Scorcher* (2002), *The Jungle Book 2* (2003), *The Medallion* (2003), *The Lost Angel* (2005), *The King Maker* (2005), *The Game of Their Lives* (2005), *The Shadow Dancer* (2005), *The Legend of Sasquatch* (2006), *The Reef* (2006), *One Night with the King* (2006), *In the Name of the King: A Dungeon Siege Tale* (2007), *The Ferryman* (2007) and *31 North 62 East* (2009). John married Suzanne Wilkinson, a translator, in 1966. They have two sons, Ben and Tom. Although he separated from Suzanne (who was diagnosed with Alzheimer's in 1995) he remained close to her until her death in August 2010. He has lived with television presenter Lisa Manning since 2004. See also entries in the television section for *Budgie, Crossroads, I, Claudius, Kröd Mändoon and the Flaming Sword of Fire* and *Robin of Sherwood*.

Rhys Meyers, Jonathan (1977-) Born Jonathan Michael Francis O'Keeffe, 27 July 1977, Dublin. Actor and Model. His stage name is derived from his mother's maiden name, Meyers. Jonny's family moved to County Cork when he was a baby, and his father left the family home when he was three-years-old, leaving his mother to care for him and his three younger brothers Jamie, Paul and Alan. He was discovered in a local pool hall by Hubbard Casting, who were talent-spotting for the David Puttnam production of *War of the Buttons* (1994) and although he failed to gain a part in that film he was soon to make his screen debut in *A Man of No Importance* (1994). His first lead role was in the film *The Disappearance of Finbar* (1996) and this was followed by the role of Collins' assassin in Neil Jordan's *Michael Collins* (1996). His other films include: *The Maker* (1997), *Telling Lies in America* (1997), *The Tribe* (1998), *The Governess* (1998), *B. Monkey* (1998), *Titus* (1999), *Ride with the Devil* (1999), *The Loss of Sexual Innocence* (1999), *Happy Now* (2001), *Prozac Nation* (2001), *Tangled* (2001), *Bend It Like Beckham* (2002), *I'll Sleep When I'm Dead* (2003), *Vanity Fair* (2004), *Alexander* (2004), *Match Point* (2005), *Mission: Impossible III* (2006), *August Rush* (2007), *The Children of Huang Shi* (2008), *A Film with Me in It* (2008), *Shelter* (2010), *From Paris with Love* (2010) and *Albert Nobbs* (2011). He is also a talented singer and musician, having performed his own vocals in the film *Velvet Goldmine* (1998 – as Brian Slade). On television he has starred as Elvis Presley in the 2005 CBS mini-series *Elvis*, which earned him a Golden Globe for Best Actor, and as King Henry VIII in the historical drama *The Tudors*. Jonny was the Face of the *Versace* men's collection of Autumn/Winter 2006 and Spring 2007 as well as of the new fragrances of *Hugo Boss,* from 2006 until May 2011. Having already been banned for life from flying on United Airlines for aggressive conduct and having checked in to rehab on several occasions, Jonny seems to be living the stereotypical 'bad boy' lifestyle. See also entries in the television section for *Gormenghast,* and *The Tudors*.

Richard, Cliff See entry in the music section

Richardson, Ian (1934-2007) Born Ian William Richardson, 7 April 1934, Edinburgh. Actor. Educated at George Heriot's School. Trained at the College of Dramatic Arts, Glasgow. Joined Birmingham Repertory before becoming a member of the RSC. His screen debut came as Le Beau in the TV film *As You Like It* in 1963. Ian created the role of Jean Paul Marat in *Marat/Sade* on stage both in the UK and on Broadway (1965-66) and this was to be his feature film debut in 1967. His other films include *A Midsummer Night's Dream* (1968 - as Oberon), *Eyeless in Gaza* (1971), *The Darwin Adventure* (1972 - as Captain Fitzroy), *Man of La Mancha* (1972), *Brazil* (1985), *The Fourth Protocol* (1987), *Cry Freedom* (1987), *Rosencrantz & Guildernstern are Dead* (1990 - as Polonius), *M. Butterfly* (1993), *B*A*P*S* (1997), *Dark City* (1998),*102 Dalmatians* (2000), *From Hell* (2001), *Joyeux Noel* (2005), *Greyfriars Bobby* (2005), *Twice Upon a Time* (2006) and his last film, *Becoming Jane* (2007). Probably better known for his many television films, including Sherlock Holmes in both *The Hound of the Baskervilles* (1983) and *The Sign of Four* (1985), Anthony Blunt in *Blunt* (1987), General Burgoyne in *The Devil's Disciple* (1987), Simon de Canterville in *The Canterville Ghost* (1997) and Dr Joseph Bell in *Murder Rooms* (2001). His most celebrated TV role is the Machiavellian politician Francis Urquhart in *House of Cards* (1990), *To Play the King* (1993) and *The Final Cut* (1995). Appointed CBE in 1989. Ian was married to actress Maroussia Frank, from 1961 until his death, from a heart-attack on 9 February 2007, London. See also entries in the television section for *Bleak House, Gormenghast, House of Cards, Number 10, Porterhouse Blue, Private Schulz,* and *Tinker Tailor Soldier Spy*.

Richardson, Joely (1965-) Born Joely Kim Richardson, 9 January 1965, Marylebone, London. Actress. Born into an acting family; she is the daughter of Tony Richardson and Vanessa Redgrave, and sister of Natasha. Joely spent two years at a tennis academy in Florida before turning to acting and training at RADA. Apart from a very early appearance in *The Charge of the Light Brigade* (1968), her screen debut proper was in 1984's *The Hotel New Hampshire* based on John Irving's novel. Both films were directed by her father. Some television drama and a couple of adaptations of David Hare plays followed, *Wetherby* (1985) and *Heading Home* (1991). Joely had a much publicised affair with Archie Stirling, the then husband of actress Diana Rigg, before marrying co-founder of *Working Title*, Tim Bevan in 1992 and having a child, Daisy (b. 1992). About this time she made the steamy BBC romp *Lady Chatterley* (1993) with Sean Bean as Mellors. A variety of roles have followed. On film she has played the owner of Pongo and Perdita in *101 Dalmatians* (1996), leader of the tribe in Stephen Poliakoff's *The Tribe* (1998) and Wallis Simpson in the TV movie *Wallis & Edward* (2005). On television she has appeared opposite her real-life mother, Vanessa Redgrave, (playing her mother) as Julia McNamara in the American drama series *Nip/Tuck* (2003-10) and played Catherine Parr in the Showtime series *The Tudors* (2010) reuniting herself with ex-husband Tim Bevan, a producer on the show. Her other films include: *King Ralph* (1991), *The Patriot* (2000), *The Affair of the Necklace* (2001 - as Marie Antoinette), *The Last Mimzy* (2007), *The Christmas Miracle of Jonathan Toomey* (2007), *Anonymous* (2011), and the film adaptation of Stieg Larsson's *The Girl with the Dragon Tattoo* (2011 – as Anita Vanger). See also entries in the television section for *The Day of the Triffids*, *Lady Chatterley*, and *The Tudors*.

Richardson, Miranda (1958-) Born Miranda Jane Richardson, 3 March 1958, Southport, Lancashire. Actress. Attended Bristol University where she studied drama. She had originally intended to study veterinary medicine. She began her career in regional theatre, on British TV and minor films. Her debut was in the film short *The First Day* (1980). Quickly however she moved on to greater things making a stunning impression in her feature film debut as brassy blonde night-club hostess Ruth Ellis, the last woman to be hanged in Britain, in Mike Newell's haunting *Dance With a Stranger* (1985). Miranda will however never escape the shadow of her portrayal of "Queenie" (Queen Elizabeth I) in TV's *Blackadder II* (1986). She almost always plays emotional roles of off-kilter personalities. On television she was Bettina, the obsessive compulsive interior decorator, in *Absolutely Fabulous*, on film an IRA gangster in *The Crying Game* (1992), Lady Van Tassel in *Sleepy Hollow* (1999), The Wicked Stepmother, Queen Elspeth in *Snow White: The Fairest of Them All* (2001), Vanessa Bell in *The Hours* (2002) and the emotionally repressed Queen Mary in the TV film *The Lost Prince* (2003). For *Enchanted April* (1992), again by Newell, she won a Best Actress Golden Globe and two years later won a second Golden Globe (Best Supporting Actress) for her role of Charlie Maguire in the TV film *Fatherland* (1994). She has twice been nominated for Academy Awards, for Best Supporting Actress in *Damage* (1992) and for Best Actress for *Tom & Viv* (1994). For her role of Pamela Flitton in *A Dance to the Music of Time* (1997) she was nominated for a BAFTA TV award. As with most British actors and actresses she will now perhaps be known to a new generation of filmgoers, as Rita Skeeter, the toxic *Daily Prophet* journalist, due to her appearances in *Harry Potter and the Goblet of Fire* (2005) and *Harry Potter and the Deathly Hallows: Part 1* (2010). For trivia fans she also played Queen Asphyxia XIX in *Blackadder's Christmas Carol* (1988) as well as Elizabeth - and apparently has a pet axolotl. She is one of the finest British actresses of her day bringing power and depth of character to her many and varied roles, even when cast in potentially "cartoon" roles she still manages to imbue them with meaning and be thought provoking. Other films include: *Empire of the Sun* (1987), *The Evening Star* (1996), *The Apostle* (1997), *St. Ives* (1998), *The King and I* (1999 - voice of Anna Leonowens), *Alice in Wonderland* (1999 - as Queen of Hearts / Society Woman), *Get Carter* (2000), *The Miracle Maker* (2000 - voice of Mary Magdalene), *Chicken Run* (2000 - voice of Mrs Tweedy), *The Actors* (2003), *Falling Angels* (2003), *The Prince & Me* (2004), *Churchill: The Hollywood Years*

(2004 - as Eva Braun), *The Phantom of the Opera* (2004), *Wah-Wah* (2005), *Provoked: A True Story* (2006), *Paris, Je T'Aime* (2006), *Southland Tales* (2006), *Puffball* (2007), *Fred Claus* (2007), *Spinning Into Butter* (2008), *A Fox's Tale* (2008 - voice of Anna Conda), *The Young Victoria* (2009 - as The Duchess of Kent) and *Made in Dagenham* (2010 - as Barbara Castle). See also entries in the television section for *Absolutely Fabulous*, *Blackadder Goes Forth*, *Blackadder II*, *Blackadder the Third*, *The Life and Times of Vivienne Vyle*, and *A Woman of Substance*.

Richardson, Natasha (1963-2009) Born Natasha Jane Richardson, 11 May 1963, Marylebone, London. Actress. Daughter of Vanessa Redgrave and Tony Richardson and sister of Joely. Attended the Central School of Speech and Drama, London. Although she is now a naturalised United States citizen she is undoubtedly an English actress. As with her sister she made her screen debut as a child in *The Charge of the Light Brigade* (1968). Her next big-screen outing was in *La Polizia Incrimina la Legge Assolve* (1973). Her feature debut as an adult came in her third screen appearance *Every Picture Tells a Story* (1983 - as Miss Bridle), but the role that brought her to the attention of the public was as Mary Shelley in Ken Russell's *Gothic* (1986). She played the title role in *Patty Hearst* (1988), Kate / Offred in *The Handmaid's Tale* (1990) and Zelda Sayre Fitzgerald in *Zelda* (1993) opposite Timothy Hutton as F. Scott Fitzgerald. For her performance in *The Handmaid's Tale* and *The Comfort of Strangers* (1990), she earned The London Evening Standard Award for Best Actress of 1990; for *Widows' Peak* (1994) she received the Best Actress Award at the 1994 Karlovy Vary Festival. On the stage she has also won awards. In 1986, she won the London Drama Critics' Most Promising Newcomer Award for her performance as Nina in *The Seagull* and for her role in *Anna Christie* (1992) she won the London Drama Critics' Best Actress Award and as Sally Bowles in Sam Mendes' production of *Cabaret*, she won the 1998 Tony. Her other films include: *A Month in the Country* (1987), *The Favour, the Watch and the Very Big Fish* (1991), *The Parent Trap* (1998), *Blow Dry* (2001), *Chelsea Walls* (2001), *Waking Up in Reno* (2002), *Maid in Manhattan* (2002), *Asylum* (2005), *The White Countess* (2005), *Evening* (2007), her last film appearance, *Wild Child* (2008) and her last film *The Wildest Dream* (2010 - voice of Ruth Mallory). She has been married twice, to film-maker Robert Fox (1990–92) and to actor Liam Neeson from 1994 until her death on 18 March 2009, New York. On 16 March, Natasha sustained a head injury whilst taking a beginner's skiing lesson at the Mont Tremblant Resort in Quebec. Initially it was thought that Natasha was nothing more than shaken but several hours later she complained of a headache and was rushed to hospital in Montreal. The following day she was flown to Lenox Hill Hospital in New York City, where she died of an "epidural haematoma due to blunt impact to the head". Natasha was buried near her grandmother Rachel Kempson and aunt Lynn Redgrave in the church cemetery of St. Peter's Episcopal Church near Millbrook, New York. Natasha and Liam have two sons: Micheál (b. 1995) and Daniel (b. 1996).

Richardson, Ralph (1902-83) Born Ralph David Richardson, 19 December 1902, Cheltenham, Gloucestershire. Actor. Son of an art teacher. Worked in insurance and tried his hand at art and journalism before taking up acting. Made his stage debut in *The Merchant of Venice* (1921). He joined the Birmingham Repertory Company in 1926 and then the Old Vic. His screen debut came in *The Ghoul* (1933). Other early films include: *Friday the Thirteenth* (1933), *The King of Paris* (1934), the title role in *The Return of Bulldog Drummond* (1934), *Things to Come* (1936), *The Man who Could Work Miracles* (1937), *The Citadel* (1938), *Q Planes* (1939) and *The Four Feathers* (1939), in all of which he gave superb performances. Ralph served in the Fleet Air Arm during WWII. After the war he became a co-director of the Old Vic, along with Laurence Olivier, and carved out a stage career every bit as worthy as Olivier's and his later friend and collaborator John Gielgud. On film he played Alexei Karenin in *Anna Karenina* (1948) and after *The Fallen Idol* (1948) he received an Academy Award nomination for Best Supporting Actor for *The Heiress* (1949). Some of his best screen performances during the 1950s include Lingard in *Outcast of the Islands* (1952), Ridgefield in *The Sound Barrier* (1952), Reverend

Gregory in *The Holly and the Ivy* (1952), Buckingham in *Richard III* (1955) and Carson in *Oscar Wilde* (1959). His later films include *Exodus* (1960), *The 300 Spartans* (1962), *Long Day's Journey into Night* (1962), big budget productions such as *Doctor Zhivago* (1965), *Khartoum* (1966) and *Battle of Britain* (1969) plus *Oh! What a Lovely War* (1969), *Alice's Adventures in Wonderland* (1972 - as The Caterpillar), *O Lucky Man!* (1973), *Time Bandits* (1981), *Invitation to the Wedding* (1983) and his last film, *Give My Regards to Broad Street* (1984). He received a second Academy Award nomination for Best Supporting Actor for his penultimate film, *Greystoke: The Legend of Tarzan, Lord of the Apes* (1984). On a rare small screen outing, Ralph played Lord Emsworth on BBC television in dramatisations of P. G. Wodehouse's *Blandings Castle* stories, with his real-life wife Meriel Forbes playing his domineering sister Connie, and his friend Stanley Holloway as his butler Beach. Noted for his eccentricity, Ralph collected motorcycles and rode until well into his seventies. He was knighted in 1947. Ralph was married twice, in 1924 to Muriel "Kit" Hewitt, a seventeen-year-old student actress, who died in 1942 after a long illness (sleeping sickness); and from 1944 to actress Meriel "Mu" Forbes (1913-2000), until his death on 10 October 1983, Marylebone, London (buried in Highgate Cemetery). They had one son, David (1945–1998). See also entries in the television section for *Blandings Castle*, *Jesus of Nazareth*, and *The Great War*.

Richardson, Tony (1928-91) Born Cecil Antonio Richardson, 5 June 1928, Shipley, Yorkshire. Director. Educated at Wadham College, Oxford. Trained at the BBC. Founded the English Stage Company at the Royal Court Theatre and directed the first stage productions of *Look Back in Anger* (1956) and *The Entertainer* (1957). He co-directed the documentary *Momma Don't Allow* (1955) with Karel Reisz. Founded *Woodfall Films* with John Osborne to film both *Look Back in Anger* (1958) and *The Entertainer* (1960). He helped form the Free Cinema Group with Reisz to advance British New Wave cinema such as *A Taste of Honey* (1961) and *The Loneliness of the Long Distance Runner* (1962). He gained Hollywood backing for his next film, an adaptation of Fielding's *Tom Jones* (1963), which won Best Picture and Best Director Academy Awards. Tony then directed an adaptation of Evelyn Waugh's *The Loved One* (1965) and two projects with Jeanne Moreau, *Mademoiselle* (1966) and *The Sailor from Gibraltar* (1967). After the critically disappointing *The Charge of the Light Brigade* (1968) he directed *Hamlet* (1969), *Nijinsky* (1970) and *Ned Kelly* (1970). During the 1970s his films include *A Delicate Balance* (1973), *Dead Cert* (1974), based on a Dick Francis novel, and an attempt to recapture earlier success with an adaptation of Fielding's *Joseph Andrews* (1977). His last three features were *The Border* (1982), *The Hotel New Hampshire* (1984) and *Blue Sky* (1994). Married to Vanessa Redgrave (1962-67). Father of Natasha Richardson and Joely Richardson. Autobiography: *Long Distance Runner: A Memoir* (1993). Tony was bisexual, but never acknowledged it publicly until after he contracted AIDS. He died of complications from AIDS on 14 November 1991, Los Angeles, California.

Rickman, Alan (1946-) Born Alan Sidney Patrick Rickman, 21 February 1946, Hammersmith, London. Actor and director. Educated at Latymer School. Initially wanted to be a graphic artist and studied at the Chelsea College of Art and Design and the Royal College of Art. Whilst working for a design company he continued in amateur dramatics and entered RADA in 1972 and during his two-year apprenticeship he became a dresser for Sir Nigel Hawthorne and Sir Ralph Richardson. Alan subsequently performed in a variety of roles including musicals and pantomime. He formed something of a creative partnership with future comedienne Ruby Wax at the RSC (1978-79) before returning to repertory. Alan made his screen debut in the TV film *Romeo and Juliet* (1978 – as Tybalt) before appearing as Vidal in the television mini-series *Thérèse Raquin* (1980) and went on to give well-received performances in *Smiley's People* (1982) and *The Barchester Chronicles* (1982). He rejoined the RSC in 1985 and created the stage role of Vicomte de Valmont in *Les Liaisons Dangereuse* in both London and on Broadway (1985-87), which landed him his big screen debut as the German criminal Hans Gruber in *Die Hard* (1988). He followed this with *January Man* (1989), *Quigley Down Under* (1990) and *Closet Land* (1991). His role as the dead cellist in *Truly Madly Deeply* (1991) brought him many critical plaudits and his magnificently over the top Sheriff of Nottingham in *Robin Hood: Prince of Thieves* (1991) brought him popular acclaim. He was in the controversial *Close my Eyes* (1991) and his next films include *An Awfully Big Adventure* (1995), *Sense and Sensibility* (1995) and *Michael Collins* (1996) in which he played Eamon de Valera. He featured in *Dogma* (1999 – as Metatron), sent himself up in the comedy *Galaxy Quest* (1999) and then landed the role of Professor Severus Snape in all eight Harry Potter films. He also provided the voice of Marvin the Paranoid Android in *The Hitchhiker's Guide to the Galaxy* (2005). Other films include: the title role in *The Search for John Gissing* (2001), *Snow Cake* (2006), *Perfume: The Story of a Murderer* (2006), *Nobel Son* (2007), *Sweeney Todd: The Demon Barber of Fleet Street* (2007) and *Bottle Shock* (2008). Alan continues to be much in demand in the theatre and on film where he can turn his hand to a wide variety of roles. In 2010 he lent his voice to Noel Odell in *The Wildest Dream* and Absolem the Blue Caterpillar in *Alice in Wonderland*. Alan also directed *The Winter Guest* at London's Almeida Theatre in 1995 and made his directorial film debut with the film version of the same play in 1996 starring Emma Thompson and her real life mother Phyllida Law. In late 2010, he starred in the titles role in Ibsen's *John Gabriel Borkman* at the Abbey Theatre, Dublin alongside Lindsay Duncan and Fiona Shaw. See also entry in the television section for *Girls on Top*.

Rigg, Diana (1938-) Born Enid Diana Elizabeth Rigg, 20 July 1938, Doncaster, South Yorkshire. Actress. Trained at RADA. Her first screen appearance was in the film *Our Man in the Caribbean* (1962). Diana's second screen appearance was in an episode of *The Sentimental Agent* (1963), which was a spin-off from episode six of *Man of the World*, which in turn formed the basis of *Our Man in the Caribbean*. A strikingly beautiful woman who established her reputation in Shakespearean roles but gained international fame and popularity as the karate-skilled secret agent Emma Peel in *The Avengers* from 1965 to 1968. From there she created history by becoming the only woman to wed James Bond, marrying him as Contessa Teresa 'Tracy' Di Vicenzo in *On Her Majesty's Secret Service* (1969), although she was summarily assassinated of course. She later briefly starred in her own American TV show *Diana* (1973) as Diana Smythe, a fashion co-ordinator at a Fifth Avenue department store. Her other films include: *A Midsummer Night's Dream* (1968 - as Helena), *The Assassination Bureau* (1969), *Julius Caesar* (1970), *A Little Night Music* (1977), *The Great Muppet Caper* (1981), *Evil Under the Sun* (1982), *Snow White* (1987), *A Good Man in Africa* (1994), *Parting Shots* (1999), *Heidi* (2005) and *The Painted Veil* (2006). In 1992 she replaced the then-ailing Vincent Price as host of the American television series *Mystery!*. Vincent was an actor with whom she had worked with on the film *Theatre of Blood* (1973), co-starring as his daughter, Edwina. In 1971, a nude scene with Keith Michell in *Abelard and Heloise* led to a notorious description of her as 'built like a brick basilica with insufficient flying buttresses', by American theatre critic John Simon. One can only assume that Mr Simon is not enamoured of the female form. A magnificent actress who brings depth and humour to her work, she was awarded a CBE in 1988 and made a Dame in 1994. Diana has been married twice, to Israeli painter Menachem Gueffen (1973–76) and theatrical producer Archibald Stirling (1982–90). Coincidentally Diana was Chancellor of Stirling University in Scotland until her ten year term of office ended in 2008 (succeeded by James Naughtie). Her second marriage broke up when Stirling had an affair with actress Joely Richardson. Diana has a daughter, actress Rachael Atlanta Stirling (b. 30 May 1977, London), a talented stage, television and film actress with a remarkable resemblance to her mother. Rachael's film credits include: *Still Crazy* (1998), *Maybe Baby* (2000), *Complicity* (2000), *Another Life* (2001), *The Triumph of Love* (2001), *Freeze Frame* (2004), *The Young Victoria* (2009) and *Centurion* (2010), although she remains best known for her performance as Nancy Astley in the BBC drama *Tipping the Velvet*. For Diana's television credits see entries in the television section for *The Avengers, Bleak House, Extras, Face to Face, Mother Love, Mrs Bradley Mysteries, The Sentimental Agent*, and *Survival*.

Ritchie, Guy (1968-) Born Guy Stuart Ritchie, 10 September 1968, Hatfield, Hertfordshire. Director and writer. Educated at Stanbridge Earls, a specialist school for dyslexia sufferers. Began his career as a runner before directing music videos. His directorial debut was the self-penned short film *Hard Case* (1995). His feature debut was the hugely successful tale of London's gangland *Lock, Stock and Two Smoking Barrels* (1998). The follow-up *Snatch* (2000) featured bigger stars and a bigger budget without really moving on much from Lock, Stock... Next he directed the critically mauled *Swept Away* (2002) starring his wife Madonna, whom he married in 2000. His *Revolver* (2005) returned to his well-trodden themes as did *RocknRolla* (2008). His latest films are *Sherlock Holmes* (2009), with Robert Downey, Jr. as Holmes and Jude Law as Watson, and its sequel *Sherlock Holmes: A Game of Shadows* (2011). Following his divorce from Madonna in 2008, Guy has been dating model Jacqui Ainsley (b. 28 November 1981) since April 2010. He has a son, Rocco (b. 11 August 2000, Los Angeles, California) by Madonna and the couple also adopted a Malawian baby boy named David. He also has a son born to Jacqui in September 2011.

Roberts, Rachel (1927-80) Born 20 September 1927, Llanelli, Carmarthenshire. Actress. True to her roots Rachel's film debut was in the Welsh film, *Valley of Song* (1953 – as Bessie Lewis). She next played a barmaid in *The Limping Man* (1953) and a pregnant inmate in J. Lee Thompson's *The Weak and the Wicked* (1953). Rachel worked on stage and television for the remainder of the 1950s although she did have small film roles in *The Good Companions* (1957) and *Our Man in Havana* (1959). It was for the part of Brenda in *Saturday Night and Sunday Morning* (1960) that she became well-known, starring opposite Albert Finney. She married actor Alan Dobie in 1955 and following their divorce in 1961 her second marriage was to actor Rex Harrison (1962-71). She next starred in *This Sporting Life* (1963), for which she was nominated for the Academy Award for Best Actress. Other films include *A Flea in Her Ear* (1968), *Doctors' Wives* (1971), *Wild Rovers* (1972), *O Lucky Man!* (1973), *Murder on the Orient Express* (1974), *Picnic at Hanging Rock* (1975), *Foul Play* (1978), *Yanks* (1979) and her last film, *Charlie Chan and the Curse of the Dragon Queen* (1981). Rachel was a powerful actress, swift-tongued, seductive, sexy, but with great comic instinct. Aged only 53, Rachel, who had suffered depression and alcoholism for several years, committed suicide by barbiturate poisoning on 26 November 1980 Los Angeles, California. Her gardener found her lying in her negligee on her kitchen floor amongst shards of glass, having fallen through a decorative glass screen when the overdose took effect. See also entry for *Our Mutual Friend* in television section.

Robey, George (1869-1954) See entry in comedy section.

Robson, Flora (1902-84) Born Flora McKenzie Robson, 28 March 1902, South Shields, Tyne and Wear. Actress. Although she was to appear in over 50 films and become one of the great character players she came relatively late to the big screen, making her debut in *A Gentleman of Paris* (1931) aged 29. She is best remembered as one of Britain's theatrical grandes dames. She made her professional stage debut in 1921 after graduating from RADA with a bronze medal but because of the uncertainty of theatre work she also worked as a factory welfare officer in London. Her route to character roles was perhaps necessitated as she lacked the usual glamorous looks of a leading lady and at 5ft 10ins often dwarfed her co-stars. Among her most notable films are *Fire over England* (1937) and *The Sea Hawk* (1940) both as Queen Elizabeth I, *The Rise of Catherine the Great* (1934) and *Black Narcissus* (1947). She also appeared in the very popular Huggett films after the war, starting with *Holiday Camp* (1947). Her only Academy Award nomination came for Best Supporting Actress as Ingrid Bergman's fiercely protective servant Angelique in *Saratoga Trunk* (1945). Other films include: her first credited role, *Dance Pretty Lady* (1932 - as Mrs Raeburn), *I, Claudius* (1937 - as Livia), *Wuthering Heights* (1939), *We Are Not Alone* (1939), *Caesar and Cleopatra* (1945), *Frieda* (1947), *Saraband*

for Dead Lovers (1948), *Malta Story* (1953), *The Gypsy and the Gentleman* (1958), *55 Days at Peking* (1963), *Murder at the Gallop* (1963), *Guns at Batasi* (1964), *Those Magnificent Men in Their Flying Machines or How I Flew from London to Paris in 25 hours 11 minutes* (1965 - as Mother Superior), *Alice's Adventures in Wonderland* (1972 - as Queen of Hearts), *Dominique* (1980) and her last film, *Clash of the Titans* (1981). After being made a CBE in 1952 she became a Dame in 1960. Dame Flora never married and died 7 July 1984, Brighton, East Sussex.

Roc, Patricia (1915-2003) Born Felicia Miriam Ursula Herold 7 June 1915, Hampstead, London. Actress. The adopted daughter of André Riese, a Dutch-Belgian stockbroker, and a half-French mother, she was educated at private schools in London and Paris, before joining RADA in 1937. She did not learn that she was adopted until 1949. Stage debut: *Nuts in May* (1937), in which she was spotted by Alexander Korda and given her first film role as a Polish princess in *The Rebel Son* (1939). At the onset of WWII she was swiftly placed in patriotic fare such as *We'll Meet Again* (1942) and *Millions Like Us* (1943). She played alongside her fellow Gainsborough Girls in *2,000 Women* (1944). As the perpetual "nice" girl she crossed swords with the wicked Margaret Lockwood in *Love Story* (1944), *The Wicked Lady* (1945) and *Jassy* (1947). After *When the Bough Breaks* (1947) and *One Night with You* (1948) she moved to France with her second husband and made a few more films after his death in 1954 notably, *The Hypnotist* (1957), *The House in the Woods* (1957), *La vedova X* (1959) and her last film, *Bluebeard's Ten Honeymoons* (1960). She completely retired on her third marriage in 1962. She married Dr Murray Laing (1939-44), André Thomas (1949-54) and Walter Reif (1962-86). Known as "The Goddess of the Odeons". She died 30 December 2003, Locarno, Switzerland. See also entry for Anthony Steel.

Roeg, Nicolas (1928-) Born Nicolas Jack Roeg, 15 August 1928, Marylebone, London. Director and cinematographer. Worked his way up from clapper-boy to camera operator at Marylebone studios. Worked on such films as *Tarzan's Great Adventure* (1959), *The Trials of Oscar Wilde* (1960) and *The Sundowners* (1960) before being cinematographer on *The Masque of the Red Death* (1964), *Fahrenheit 451* (1966) and *Far from the Madding Crowd* (1967). Whilst the showing of his co-direction project with Donald Cammell *Performance* (1970) was delayed because of studio problems with it's content Roeg went to Australia to helm *Walkabout* (1971), which was well-received by critics and public alike. He followed this up with the even more successful adaptation of a Daphne du Maurier short story *Don't Look Now* (1973). His next films were an adpatation of the sci-fi novel *The Man who Fell to Earth* (1976) starring David Bowie, *Bad Timing* (1980) and the big-budget *Eureka* (1984). *Insignificance* (1985) imagined a meeting between Marilyn Monroe, Albert Einstein, Jo DiMaggio and Joe McCarthy and *Castaway* (1986) starred Oliver Reed. His later films include an adaptation of Roald Dahl's *The Witches* (1990), *Cold Heaven* (1991), *Hotel Paradise* (1995), *Two Deaths* (1995) and *Puffball* (2007). Nicolas was married to actress Susan Stephen (1957-77). They had four children, including the producer Luc Roeg, who also starred in Roeg's first film, *Walkabout*, as Lucien John. His second marriage, in 1982, was to American actress Theresa Russell, with whom he collaborated on five films. They had two children, actor Max Roeg, and Statten Roeg. Following their divorce, Nicolas married Harriet Harper in 2004.

Rogers, Peter (1914-2009) Born 20 February 1914, Rochester, Kent. Producer. Educated at Kings School, Rochester. Worked as a journalist and a writer of radio plays. Wrote the five minute religious shorts called *Thought of the Week* for J Arthur Rank. After co-producing with his future wife Betty on films such as *Appointment with Venus* (1951) he made his solo production debut with the children's film *The Dog and the Diamonds* (1953). He formed a partnership with director Gerald Thomas and their first films together include *Circus Friends* (1956), *The Vicious Circle* (1957), *Chain of Events* (1957) and *Time Lock* (1957). Peter held the rights to an R F Delderfield story called *The Bull Boys* about a ballet dancer whose boyfriend is called up on their marriage day. Building on the popularity of the TV series *The Army Game*, Rogers and Thomas switched the focus of the story to the barracks, made it a comedy and called it *Carry On Sergeant*

(1958). Peter subsequently produced all 31 Carry On films. He was married to producer Betty Box, from 1948 until her death on 15 January 1999. He died on 14 April 2009, Buckinghamshire.

Rome, Stewart (1886-1965) Born Septimus William Ryott, 30 January 1886, Newbury Berkshire. Actor. During 150 films spanning nearly 40 years he moved from being a leading man in the silent era to a character actor in the talkies. Screen debut: *The Whirr of the Spinning Wheel* (1914). Other films include: *The Heart of Midlothian* (1914), *Coward!* (1915), *Trelawny of the Wells* (1916), *The Great Gay Road* (1920), *Dicky Monteith* (1922), *Reveille* (1924), *The Desert Sheik* (1924), *The Passing of Mr Quinn* (1928), *Lest We Forget* (1934), *One of Our Aircraft is Missing* (1942) and his last film, *Let's Have a Murder* (1950). In 1915 he was voted runner-up to Charlie Chaplin in *Pictures* magazine popularity poll. Given the name Stewart Rome by Cecil Hepworth although Hepworth insisted that he could no longer use that name when he left his employment. In a landmark case in 1919 Rome successfully sued Hepworth and was granted the rights to his stage name. Stewart played Dr Goodfellow, who presented *A Sunday Thought for the Coming Week* in a series of short films during the 1940s. He died 26 February 1965, Newbury, Berkshire.

Rose, George (1920-88) Born 19 February 1920, Bicester, Oxfordshire. Actor. Studied at Central School of Speech and Drama. Worked briefly as a farmer. Made his stage debut in 1944. Screen debut: *Midnight Frolics* (1949). A fine stage actor he played Common Man in the original stage production of *A Man for All Seasons* (1961-1963). He was also a much loved Gilbert and Sullivan player. Performed in more than twenty Broadway productions including *Henry IV* (1946), *Much Ado About Nothing* (1959), *My Fair Lady* (1976-1977), *Peter Pan* (1979-1981), *The Pirates of Penzance* (1981-1982) and *The Mystery of Edwin Drood* (1985-1987). His films include, his debut, *Midnight Frolics* (1949, *The Pickwick Papers* (1952), *The Square Ring* (1953), *The Sea Shall Not Have Them* (1954), *The Night my Number Came Up* (1955), *Track the Man Down* (1955), *The Good Companions* (1957), *Barnacle Bill* (1957), *A Night to Remember* (1958), *Jack the Ripper* (1959), *Hawaii* (1966), *A New Leaf* (1971) and his last film, *The Pirates of Penzance* (1983). He worked a lot in America and appeared in the CBS series, *Beacon Hill* (1975) and the TV film *The Saint in Manhattan* (1987). George was gay but had no permanent partner or family. He bought a holiday home in Sousa, Dominican Republic in 1984 and took in a 14 year old boy whom he planned to leave his estate. He eventually adopted the boy in January 1988. On 5 May 1988, during a break from his tour of *Drood*, George was beaten to death by his adopted son and three other men. The assailants, including the boy's biological father and uncle, tried to make the death look like an accident, but soon confessed to the killing. Though all four men were charged and spent time in prison, no trial was ever held, and eventually all were released.

Rossington, Norman (1928-99) Born Norman Arthur Rossington, 24 December 1928, Liverpool. Actor. After a string of jobs he trained as a draughtsman before taking up amateur dramatics. Trained for the stage at the Bristol Old Vic. Norman's screen debut was in *Keep it Clean* (1956), closely followed by a small role in *Three Men in a Boat* (1956). After appearing as a soldier in *Saint Joan* (1957) he gained wide popularity in the TV comedy *The Army Game* and reprised his role of 'Cupcake' in the big screen spin-off *I Only Arsked!* (1958). He then again appeared as a conscript squaddie in *Carry On Sergeant* (1958). His comedy film credits include *Carry On Nurse* (1959), *Carry On Regardless* (1961), *Crooks Anonymous* (1962), *Nurse on Wheels* (1963), *Those Magnificent Men in Their Flying Machines or How I Flew from London to Paris in 25 hours 11 minutes* (1965), and *The Wrong Box* (1966). He also featured in a dramatic role in *Saturday Night and Sunday Morning* (1960) and had minor roles in epics such as *Lawrence of Arabia* (1962) and *The Longest Day* (1962). His other films include: *The Long Haul* (1957), *A Night to Remember* (1958), *The League of Gentlemen* (1960), *Go to Blazes* (1962) *The Charge of the Light Brigade* (1968), *Young Winston* (1972), *Joseph Andrews* (1977), *The Krays* (1990) and his last

film, *Let Him Have It* (1991). Norman also played the Beatle's road manager in *A Hard Day's Night (1964)* and also appeared with Elvis Presley in *Double Trouble* (1967), apparently a unique distinction. Norman was also a stage actor, particularly in musicals such as *My Fair Lady*, *Guys and Dolls* and *Beauty and the Beast*. A stalwart of British television, featuring in episodes of numerous series, his final appearances before his death were as Sergeant Horatio Havercamp in Sharpe's Regiment (1996) and Bertie Mould in *Heartbeat* (1996). He was married twice. His second marriage, on 19 January 1999, to Cindy Barnes, lasted until his death four months later on 20 May 1999 Manchester. See also entries in the television section for *The Army Game, Big Jim and the Figaro Club, The Big Noise, Casanova, Curry and Chips, Our House, The Search for the Nile*, and *Spooner's Patch*.

Rossiter, Leonard (1926-84) Born 21 October 1926, Wavertree, Liverpool, Merseyside. Actor. Son of a barber who was killed during an air raid whilst a volunteer ambulanceman. Leonard joined the Education Corps in Germany in the immediate post-war period. Worked in insurance alongside another future actor, Michael Williams, and got interested in amateur dramatics. He joined Preston Repertory Company (1954-55) and Wolverhampton Repertory Company (1955-58). Stage debut: *The Gay Dog* (1954). TV debut: *Story Conference* (1956). Big screen debut: *A Kind of Loving* (1962), which he followed with *This Sporting Life* (1963) and *Billy Liar* (1963). On television he played Detective Inspector Bamber in *Z Cars* and appeared in an episode of *Steptoe and Son* (1964) - returning in a further much-loved episode as an escaped criminal in 1972. His role as Major McCoy in the prison camp film drama *King Rat* (1965) was followed by appearances in *Deadlier than the Male* (1966), *The Wrong Box* (1966), *Hotel Paradiso* (1966), *The Witches* (1966) and *The Whisperers* (1967). Leonard played Dr Andrei Smyskov in *2001: A Space Odyssey* (1968) and the undertaker Mr Sowerberry in *Oliver!* (1969). On stage he scored a huge success as the title character in Bertolt Brecht's *The Resistable Rise of Arturo Ui* (1967-69) and then played *Richard III* and Davies in *The Caretaker* before he was chosen to play the miserly, bigotted landlord Rooksby in a play by Eric Chappell called *The Banana Box* (1973). The play was turned into the exceptionally popular TV sitcom *Rising Damp,* with Rossiter now playing the renamed landlord Rigsby. In addition to *Rising Damp* he is also best remembered for his lead role in *The Fall and Rise of Reginald Perrin*. He also featured in the classic Cinzano television commercials (1978-83) in which he engaged in a comic drink-spilling partnership with Joan Collins. His later films include *Luther* (1973), *Barry Lyndon* (1974), *The Pink Panther Strikes Again* (1976), *Le Petomane* (1979) – a classic film short in which Leonard played Monsieur Joseph Pujol who had the ability to extricate wind from his behind in quite tuneful tones, *Britannia Hospital* (1982), *Trail of the Pink Panther* (1982) and his last film, *Water* (1985). He also starred in the feature film *Rising Damp* (1980). He wrote *Devil's Bedside Book - A Cynic's Survival Guide* (1980) and *The Lowest Form of Wit* (1981). Leonard was a county standard squash player who enjoyed regular charity matches against other top celebrity players such as tommy Steele and Roy Castle. He was married to Josephine Tewson (1959-61) and Gillian Raine from 1964 until his death, in his dressing room at the Lyric Theatre, Shaftesbury Avenue, London on 5 October 1984 whilst appearing in *Loot*. See also entries in the television section for *The Fall and Rise of Reginald Perrin, Rising Damp, Tripper's Day*, and *Z Cars*.

Roth, Tim (1961-) Born Simon Timothy Roth, 14 May 1961, Dulwich, London. Actor and director. His American father was born with the surname Smith but changed it to Roth after WWII. Tim studied sculpture at the Camberwell School of Art before turning to acting. In his TV debut he played Trevor the Skinhead in *Made in Britain* (1982) and then featured in Mike Leigh's *Meantime* (1984). Big screen debut: *The Hit* (1984). After a lean spell he featured in *The Cook the Thief his Wife and her Lover* (1989) and then starred as Vincent van Gogh in *Vincent and Theo* (1990) and as Guildenstern in *Rosencrantz and Guildenstern are Dead* (1990). His next role was as the very bloody Mr Orange (aka Freddy Newandyke) in *Reservoir Dogs* (1992) and he starred for Quentin Tarantino again in *Pulp Fiction* (1994). Tim played yet another hit man in *Little Odessa* (1994) and then gained an Academy Award nomination for Best Supporting Actor for his role as the sadistic Archibald Cunningham in *Rob Roy* (1995). His next films include *No Way Home* (1996), singing in Woody Allen's *Everyone Says I Love You* (1996), *Gridlock'd* (1997), opposite Tupac Shakur, *Hoodlum* (1997) and *Liar* (1997). He played the part of Danny Boodmann T.D. Lemon Nineteen Hundred (aka 1900), a piano playing prodigy raised in the depths of a cruise liner in *The Legend of 1900* (1998). He then directed a stark family drama *War Zone* (1999). His latest films include *Planet of the Apes* (2001), *The Musketeer* (2001), *To Kill a King* (2003 - as Oliver Cromwell), *Silver City* (2004), *Dark Water* (2005), *Even Money* (2006), *Youth Without Youth* (2007), *Funny Games U.S.* (2007), *Virgin Territory* (2007), *The Incredible Hulk* (2008 - as Emil Blonsky), *King Conqueror* (2009), Skellig (2009 – aka Skellig the Owl Man) and *Pete Smalls Is Dead* (2010). Between 2009 and 2011 he played body-language expert Dr Cal Lightman in the American series *Lie to Me*. Tim married Nikki Butler in 1993 and they have two sons, Timothy Hunter (b. 1995) and Michael Cormac (b. 1996). Tim also has a son, Jack, born to Lori Baker in 1984. See also entry in the television section for *King of the Ghetto*

Russell, Ken (1927-2011) Born Henry Kenneth Alfred Russell, 3 July 1927 Southampton, Hampshire. Director, writer, actor and producer. Served in the Merchant Navy and the RAF. Ken dabbled in dance, acting and photography before directing the short films *Peepshow* (1956) and *Amelia and the Angel* (1957) which led him to film documentaries for the BBC arts series *Monitor* (1958-65), including well-received films on *Elgar* (1962), *Bartok* (1964) and *Debussy* (1965). He directed his first feature, *French Dressing*, in 1964 and subsequently made *Billion Dollar Brain* (1967) and, after a brief stint on the BBC arts series *Omnibus* (1968), he made his big screen breakthrough with a film adaptation of D H Lawrence's *Women in Love* (1969) which proved both a critical and box-office success and gained him an Academy Award nomination for Best Director. He followed this up with a controversial film about Tchaikovsky, *The Music Lovers* (1970) and the even more notorious *The Devils* (1971). Taking a break from notoriety he helmed the musical *The Boy Friend* (1971) before returning with a run of dramatised biographies *Savage Messiah* (1972), *Mahler* (1974), *Lisztomania* (1975) and *Valentino* (1977). In the midst of these he directed an over-the-top version of The Who's already pretty overblown rock opera *Tommy* (1975). He made *Altered States* (1980) and *Crimes of Passion* (1984) before directing *Gothic* (1986) and the *Lair of the White Worm* (1988). He then directed his second D H Lawrence adaptation, *The Rainbow* (1989) and his later films include *Whore* (1991), *Lion's Mouth* (2000) and *The Fall of the Louse of Usher* (2002). His films have always displayed imagination and visual creativity. Ken is also a prolific writer having written half a dozen novels, various books on film-making and an autobiography *A British Picture: An Autobiography* (1989) which was later published in the US under the title *Altered States: The Autobiography of Ken Russell* (1991). He married four times: to costume designer Shirley Kingdon (1956-78), Vivian Jolly (1983-91), actress Hetty Baynes (1992-99) and Lisi Tribble, from 2001 until his death on 28 November 2011. Younger viewers will remember him for his short, but very interesting, appearance on *Celebrity Big Brother* in January 2007, where he left voluntarily after an altercation with Jade Goody. See also entry for *Lady Chatterley* in the television section.

Russell, Shirley (1935-2002) Born Shirley Ann Kingdon, 11 March 1935, West Ham, London. Costume Designer. Shirley met Ken Russell at art school and worked with him on many of his films including *Amelia and the Angel* (1957), *French Dressing* (1964), *Billion Dollar Brain* (1967), *Dante's Inferno* (1967), *Song of Summer* (1968), *Women in Love* (1969), *The Music Lovers* (1970), *The Devils* (1971), *The Boy Friend* (1971), *Savage Messiah* (1972), *Mahler* (1974), *Tommy* (1975), *Lisztomania* (1975), *Valentino* (1977) and *Clouds of Glory* (1978). They were married from 1956 to 1978. After they divorced her first film was *Agatha* (1979) for which she gained an Academy Award nomination for Best Costume Design. After *Cuba* (1979) and *Lady Chatterley's Lover* (1979) she gained a further Academy Award nomination for Best Costume Design for *Reds* (1981). Her later films include *The Return of the Soldier* (1982), *Greystoke: The Legend of Tarzan, Lord of the Apes* (1984), *Fairy Tale: A True Story* (1997) and *Enigma* (2001). Her last project was the television programme *Shackleton* (2002). She died 4 March 2002, Westminster, London.

Rutherford, Margaret (1892-1972) Born Margaret Taylor Rutherford, 11 May 1892, Balham, London. Actress. Margaret was the only child of William Rutherford Benn and his wife Florence, née Nicholson. Her first cousin once removed was British politician Tony Benn. Margaret's father suffered a nervous breakdown on his honeymoon, and on being given leave from an asylum on 4 March 1883, he murdered his father, the Reverend Julius Benn, by bludgeoning him to death with a chamberpot. William was confined to the Broadmoor Criminal Lunatic Asylum for several years but was eventually released, apparently cured, and, after returning to his wife, changed his surname to Rutherford. Soon after Margaret's birth, the family moved to India but she returned to Britain when she was three to live with an aunt, Bessie Nicholson, in Wimbledon, after her mother committed suicide by hanging herself from a tree. Her father was again confined to Broadmoor in 1904 and died in 1921. Margaret was educated at Ravens Croft School, Seaford, the independent Wimbledon High School, and RADA. Margaret taught speech and piano before serving her theatrical apprenticeship at the Old Vic. She made her stage debut, aged 33, in *Little Jack Horner* (1925). Her career continued in the theatre and it was eleven more years before she made the transition to film, eventually doing so as an uncredited bit player in *Troubled Waters* (1936). Her first credited role was as Evelyn Summers (aka Miss Butterby) an old gang moll in *Dusty Ermine* (1936). Other films include: *Catch As Catch Can* (1937), *Yellow Canary* (1943), *English Without Tears* (1944), *Blithe Spirit* (1945 - as Madame Arcati) *Meet Me at Dawn* (1947), *Miranda* (1948), *Passport to Pimlico* (1949), *The Happiest Days of Your Life* (1950), *The Magic Box* (1951), *Miss Robin Hood* (1952), *Trouble in Store* (1953), *The Runaway Bus* (1954), *The Smallest Show on Earth* (1957), *Just My Luck* (1957), *I'm All Right Jack* (1959), *On the Double* (1961), *The Mouse on the Moon* (1963), *Chimes at Midnight* (1965 - as Mistress Quickly), *A Countess from Hong Kong* (1967), *Arabella* (1967), and her final film, *The Wacky World of Mother Goose* (1967 - voice of mother Goose). Margaret won a Golden Globe and an Academy Award for Best Supporting Actress for *The VIPs* (1963) as The Duchess of Brighton. She also gave an entertaining interpretation of Jane Marple in five Agatha Christie adaptations: *Murder, She Said* (1961), *Murder at the Gallop* (1963), *Murder Most Foul* (1964), *Murder Ahoy!* (1964) and *The Alphabet Murders* (1965). Margaret married her long-term partner, the character actor Stringer Davis (4 June 1899 - 29 August 1973), in 1945 and they appeared in many productions together, notably *The Importance of Being Earnest* (1946 – she as Lady Bracknell). Margaret also appeared in the 1952 feature film of the Oscar Wilde play but Edith Evans now played Lady Bracknell while Margaret played Miss Letitia Prism. In the 1950s, Margaret and her husband unofficially adopted the writer Gordon Langley Hall, then in his twenties. He later had gender reassignment surgery and became Dawn Langley Simmons, under which name she wrote a biography of Rutherford in 1983. In 1961 Margaret was awarded an OBE, and in 1967 was made a Dame Commander of the British Empire. Margaret's on-screen persona was that of everyones favourite eccentric aunt but tragically she was blighted by her parents genes and suffered from bouts of depression often involving stays in mental hospitals which were kept hidden from the press. She suffered from Alzheimer's disease in later life and died in Chalfont St. Peter, Buckinghamshire on 22 May 1972, just a few days after her 80th birthday, following complications from a hip injury.

Sabu (1924-63) Born Sabu Dastagir 27 January 1924, Karapur, Mysore, then a Princely State of British India. Actor. Sabu was the son of an Indian mahout (elephant driver) and worked in the stables of the Maharajah of Mysore. He made his screen debut in Robert Flaherty's semi-documentary *Elephant Boy* (1937), aptly playing a mahout, and followed up by starring in two Alexander Korda classic feature films *The Drum* (1938) and *The Thief of*

Bagdad (1940). He then played Mowgli in Korda's The Jungle Book (1942). Sabu then moved to Universal Pictures and featured in Arabian Nights (1942), White Savage (1943) and Cobra Woman (1944). He became a US citizen in 1944 and joined the USAAF during the latter part of WWII, serving with distinction as a tail-gunner. He made two films with Powell and Pressburger: Black Narcissus (1947) and The End of the River (1947) before returning to the United States. Sabu, he was only ever known by his first name, grew from being the young boy women wanted to mother into a handsome man they lusted after. He married actress Marilyn Cooper in 1948, and they had two children. Their son Paul founded the rock band Sabu in the 1980s, their daughter Jasmine was an animal trainer on various films. She died in 2001. Sabu's later films include Song of India (1949), Jungle Hell (1956), Jaguar (1956) and his final film A Tiger Walks (1964). He died of a heart-attack, 2 December 1963, Los Angeles, California.

Samuelson, G. B. (1889-1947) Born George Berthold Samuelson, 1889 Southport, Merseyside. Director, producer and distributor. Son of Prussian immigrants who ran a tobacconist shop. George began the first film distribution service in the country, in Southport, before transferring the operation to Birmingham in 1912. He then began film production, with his first effort being A Study in Scarlet (1914), the first screen adaptation of a Sherlock Holmes story, using James Bragington, his accountant as Holmes in his only screen role. He bought Worton Hall in Hounslow, Middlesex for £200 in 1914, establishing Isleworth Studios. Other productions made between 1914 and 1928, when the studios were sold, include literary adaptations such as Little Women (1917 & 1918) and She (1925) plus A Royal Divorce (1923), Little Dolly Daydream (1925) and Land of Hope and Glory (1927). George was also an occasional director, beginning with In Another Girl's Shoes (1917) and including The Admirable Crichton (1918), Spanish Eyes (1930) and The Crucifix (1934). He was the father of Sir Sydney Wylie Samuelson, CBE (b. 7 December 1925) appointed as the first British Film Commissioner in 1991. George died 24 April 1947, Wednesbury, West Midlands.

Sanders, George (1906-72) Born George Henry Sanders, 3 July 1906, St Petersburg, Russia, of English parents. Actor. His family left Russia during the Revolution and settled in Brighton. George was educated at Brighton College and had a variety of jobs including working alongside Greer Garson in an advertising company. It was she who suggested he might try acting. Screen debut: Love, Life and Laughter (1934). George moved to the United States in 1936 and made over 100 films. His early films include: Lloyds of London (1936), Lancer Spy (1937) and Four Men and a Prayer (1938). He featured prominently in Rebecca (1940), The Moon and Sixpence (1942), Appointment in Berlin (1943), The Lodger (1944), The Picture of Dorian Gray (1945), Forever Amber (1947), The Ghost and Mrs Muir (1947) and Samson and Delilah (1949). He then won a Best Supporting Actor Academy Award for his performance as the acid-tongued Broadway critic Addison DeWitt in All About Eve (1950). Whether it was the curse of the Oscar or merely bad judgement, his later films, never seemed to be of the same calibre as his early ones although hugely successful. These include: Ivanhoe (1952), King Richard and the Crusaders (1954), Call Me Madam (1953), The King's Thief (1955), Solomon and Sheba (1959), A Shot in the Dark (1964), The Quiller Memorandum (1966), Doomwatch (1972) and his final film Psychomania (1972). He played the lead in two series of popular B films: Simon Templar as The Saint (1939-1941) and Gay Lawrence as The Falcon (1941-1942). His brother Tom Conway (b. 15 September 1904, St Petersburg) took over as The Falcon after George gave up the role. George was famously (ask any quiz player) the voice of Shere Khan in The Jungle Book (1967), which built on his trademark silky, insinuating voice which appeared to disguise a definite malice. George was also a fine television actor and made stylish appearances in episodes of The Man From Uncle and Batman in the 1960s. He married four times: Susan Larson (1940-49), Zsa Zsa Gabor (1949-54), Benita Hume Colman (1959-67), Magda Gabor (1970-71). Although three of his marriages ended in divorce, his third marriage, to actress Benita Colman (14 October

1906 – 1 November 1967), ended when the actress, who had previously been married to Ronald Colman, died of bone cancer. George wrote an autobiography: Memoirs of a Professional Cad (1960). George committed suicide 25 April 1972, Castelldefels, Barcelona, Spain. His partner of four years before his death was Lorraine Chanel.

Sands, Julian (1958-) Born 4 January 1958 Otley, Yorkshire. Actor. Studied at the Central School of Speech and Drama. Screen debut: Privates on Parade (1983). After making an impression in The Killing Fields (1984) and A Room with a View (1985), Julian made a series of horror films including Gothic (1986 - as Percy Shelley), Warlock (1989), Arachnophobia (1990), Tale of a Vampire (1992) and Warlock: Armageddon (1993). He played Franz Liszt in Impromptu (1991) and also featured in Naked Lunch (1991), Boxing Helena (1993) and The Turn of the Screw (1994). Julian then worked with Mike Figgis on The Browning Version (1994), Leaving Las Vegas (1995), One Night Stand (1997) and The Loss of Sexual Innocence (1999). Other films include Il Fantasma dell'Opera (1998 - as the Phantom), Timecode (2000), Vatel (2000), The Medallion (2003), Romasanta (2004), Her Name is Carla (2005), Ocean's Thirteen (2007), Cat City (2008), Blood and Bone (2009), Assisting Venus (2010), Golf in the Kingdom (2010) and The Girl with the Dragon Tattoo (2011 - as Young Henrik Vanger). On television Julian starred in the made-for-TV films The Sun Also Rises (1984), A Married Man (1983), Murder on the Moon (1989), Blood Royal: William the Conqueror (1990), Crazy in Love (1992), The Great Elephant Escape (1995), The Tomorrow Man (1996), End of Summer (1997), Curse of the Ring (2004), Kenneth Tynan: In Praise of Hardcore (2005 - as Sir Laurence Olivier), The Haunted Airman (2006), Marple: Towards Zero (2007) and Beyond Sherwood Forest (2009). Julian is also well known for his role of Vladimir Bierko in the hugely popular concept drama 24 (2006) and more recently for playing the role of Jor-El, Superman's biological father, in the science fiction series, Smallville (2009-10). Julian has been married twice: to journalist Sarah Harvey, with whom he has a son, Henry (b. 1985), and, following their divorce in 1987, he married writer Evgenia Citkowitz in 1990, and lives in Los Angeles with her and their two young daughters, Natalya Morley Sands (b. 16 August 1996) and Imogen Morley Sands (b. 31 December 1999).

Saville, Victor (1897-1979) Born Victor Myer Salberg, 25 September 1897, King's Norton, West Midlands. Director and producer. Served in the London Regiment and invalided out during WWI. Victor became a film salesman, which led him into film production. He started Victory Motion Pictures with fellow Brummies Michael Balcon and Oscar Deutsch and then joined Balcon in forming Gainsborough Pictures in 1924. His early productions include Woman to Woman (1923), Roses of Picardy (1927) and Hindle Wakes (1927). He moved into direction with The Arcadians (1927) and set up his own company, Burlington. His early directing projects include Kitty (1929), talkie versions of Woman to Woman (1929) and Hindle Wakes (1931), A Warm Corner (1930), The Sport of Kings (1931) and The W Plan (1931). He next developed a successful collaboration with rising star Jessie Matthews in a series of classy musicals such as Friday the Thirteenth (1933), The Good Companions (1933), Evergreen (1934), First a Girl (1935) and It's Love Again (1936). Victor moved on to making thrillers for Alexander Korda, such as Storm in a Teacup (1937) and South Riding (1938). He then relocated to the US to produce for MGM and had success with The Citadel (1938) and Goodbye Mr Chips (1939), which were both nominated for Academy Awards for Best Picture. During WWII he remained in the US, initially courting controversy by producing anti-German material such as The Mortal Storm (1940) in a still uncommitted country. He returned to directing after the war with films such as The Green Years (1946), If Winter Comes (1947), Conspirator (1949), Kim (1950) and The Silver Chalice (1954). He finished his film career as a producer with Kiss Me Deadly (1955), My Gun is Quick (1957), The Greengage Summer (1961) and Mix me a Person (1962). He published an autobiography:

Evergreen: Victor Saville in His Own Words (1974), written with Ron Moseley. Victor died 8 May 1979, Westminster, London.

Scacchi, Greta (1960-) Born Greta Gracco, 18 February 1960, Milan, Italy. Actress. Daughter of an English dancer mother and Italian painter father. She grew up in Milan and moved to London with her mother, aged four, following her parent's divorce. In 1975, her family (her mother had now remarried) moved to Australia, and Greta worked as a cowgirl and an Italian interpreter. In 1977 Greta returned to England to pursue an acting career, studying at the Bristol Old Vic Theatre School. An accomplished linguist, not surprising perhaps given her mixed background, she learned German for her first film role *Das Zweite Gesicht* (1982). Other films include: *Heat and Dust* (1983), *The Ebony Tower* (1984), *The Coca Cola Kid* (1985), *White Mischief* (1987), *Presumed Innocent* (1990), *Fires Within* (1991), *Desire* (1992), *The Player* (1992), *Country Life* (1994), *The Browning Version* (1994), *Emma* (1996), *The Serpent's Kiss* (1997), *Love and Rage* (1998), *The Red Violin* (1998), *Ladies Room* (1999), *Cotton Mary* (1999), *Tom's Midnight Garden* (1999), *One of the Hollywood Ten* (2000), *Looking for Alibrandi* (2000), *Flightplan* (2005), *The Book of Revelation* (2006), *Hidden Love* (2007), *Brideshead Revisited* (2008), *Shoot on Sight* (2008) and *Ways to Live Forever* (2010). Given the fact that she is renowned for almost always taking her clothes off during a film it is surprising that she turned down the lead in the 1992 film *Basic Instinct*. As Spitting Image once said of her in a sketch "If the role demanded it would you ever consider leaving your clothes on?" In 1996 she won an Emmy Award for her role as Empress Alexandra Fyodorovna of Russia in the television film *Rasputin: Dark Servant of Destiny*. Greta has a daughter Leila (b. March 1992) from her relationship with actor Vincent D'Onofrio and a son Matteo Mantegazza (b. September 1997) by her Italian first cousin, Carlo Mantegazza. Despite having an English mother and living in Sussex for many years of her life Greta was refused British citizenship but is content with dual Italian / Australian nationality.

Schlesinger, John (1926-2003) Born John Richard Schlesinger, 16 February 1926, Hampstead, London. Director, actor and producer. Son of a Harley Street doctor, he studied at Uppingham School and Balliol College, Oxford. John served in the Royal Engineers during WWII and subsequently joined the Colchester Repertory Company and the Ngaio Marsh Touring Company. His acting screen debut was in *Single-Handed* (1953). Other films as an actor include: *The Divided Heart* (1954), *Oh... Rosalinda!* (1955), *The Battle of the River Plate* (1956) and *Brothers in Law* (1957). He then joined the BBC and directed episodes of the arts programme *Monitor* (1958) and the award-winning documentary *Terminus* (1961) about Waterloo railway station. Producer Joseph Janni then chose him to direct an adaptation of Stan Barstow's *A Kind of Loving* (1962). He collaborated with Janni again on *Billy Liar* (1963) and then gained an Academy Award nomination for Best Director for *Darling* (1965), starring Julie Christie. She also starred in his next film, an adaptation of Thomas Hardy's *Far from the Madding Crowd* (1967). His first film made in the United States was *Midnight Cowboy* (1969) for which he won an Academy Award for Best Director and was the first X-rated film to win an Academy Award for Best Picture. He received a further Best Director Academy Award nomination for *Sunday Bloody Sunday* (1971). During the 1970s he split his time between directing for the screen and for the stage, becoming associate director of the National Theatre. His later films include *Marathon Man* (1976), *Yanks* (1979), *Honky Tonk Freeway* (1981), *The Falcon and the Snowman* (1985), the self-penned *Madama Sousatzka* (1988), *Pacific Heights* (1990), *Cold Comfort Farm* (1995) and *The Next Best Thing* (2000). For television he directed *Separate Tables* (1983), *An Englishman Abroad* (1983), *A Question of Attribution* (1992) and *The Tale of Sweeney Todd* (1998). He was appointed CBE in 1970. John's life partner for more than 30 years was photographer Michael Childers, who took the decision to turn off life support at Desert Regional Medical Center in Palm Springs, California, on 24 July 2003, after John suffered a series of strokes.

Scofield, Paul (1922-2008) Born David Paul Scofield, 21 January 1922, King's Norton, West Midlands. Actor. Raised in Hurstpierpoint, West Sussex, and educated at the Varndean School, Brighton. Stage debut: *The Only Way* (1935). Trained at Croydon Repertory School (1939) and the London Mask School (1940). During WWII he toured with ENSA before joining Birmingham Repertory Theatre in 1944. Concentrated on theatre work and did not make his screen debut until *That Lady* (1955) and only featured in *Carve Her Name with Pride* (1958) and *The Train* (1964) over the following decade. Paul played Sir Thomas Moore in *A Man for All Seasons* in both London and on Broadway (1960-62) and his screen version of the role in 1965 gained him an Academy Award for Best Actor. He continued to appear in films but always chose his films carefully. These choices include *Nijinsky* (1970), *Bartleby* (1970), *King Lear* (1971), *A Delicate Balance* (1973), *Scorpio* (1973), *1919* (1985), *Henry V* (1989), *Hamlet* (1990), *Utz* (1992), *The Crucible* (1996) and *Animal Farm* (1999 - as voice of Boxer). He gained an Academy Award nomination for Best Supporting Actor for playing Mark Van Doren in *Quiz Show* (1994). TV credits include *Anna Karenina* (1985), *When the Whales Came* (1989), and *Martin Chuzzlewit* (1994). Considered by many to be the greatest classical actor of his generation. His portrayal of King Lear in the 1962 RSC production was voted the greatest performance ever given in a Shakespeare play in a poll of members of the RSC. Co-director of the RSC (1966-68) and director of the National Theatre (1970). Appointed CBE in 1956. Made a Companion of Honour for services to drama in 2001 having consistently rejected offers of a knighthood. Paul married actress Joy Parker in 1943. The couple had two children; Martin (b. 1945) and Sarah (b. 1951). He died 19 March 2008, Sussex, England.

Scott, Janette (1938-) Born Thora Janette Scott, 14 December 1938, Morecambe, Lancashire. Actress. She is the daughter of actors Jimmy Scott and Thora Hird (see separate entry). She began her film career as a child actress in *Went the Day Well?* (1942) and her autobiography, *Act One*, was published in 1953 when she was 14-years-old. Her other films include: *The Lamp Still Burns* (1943), *Two Thousand Men* (1944), *Medal for the General* (1944), *Conspirator* (1949), *No Place for Jennifer* (1950), *The Galloping Major* (1951), *The Magic Box* (1952), *Background* (1953), *As Long as They're Happy* (1955), *Helen of Troy* (1956), *The Good Companions* (1957), *Happy is the Bride* (1958), *The Devil's Disciple* (1959), *School for Scoundrels* (1960), *Siege of the Saxons* (1963), *The Beauty Jungle* (1964), *Bikini Paradise* (1967), and after a break of over 40 years, *How to Lose Friends & Alienate People* (2008). Janette is famously mentioned in the opening title song of *The Rocky Horror Picture Show* with reference to her appearance in *The Day of the Triffids* (1962) - "And I really got hot When I saw Janette Scott fight a triffid that spits poison and kills." Even more famously, Janette has been married three times: to Canadian entertainer Jackie Rae (1959-65); American vocalist Mel Tormé (1966-77), with whom she had two children, including jazz singer James Tormé; and finally to William Rademaekers since 1981. See also entry for *Ready Steady Go* in the television section.

Scott, Ridley (1937-) Born 30 November 1937, South Shields, Tyne and Wear. Producer and director. Studied at the West Hartlepool College of Art and Royal College of Art, where he made a short film *Boy and Bicycle* (1962), starring his younger brother Tony and their father. Ridley worked as a set designer for the BBC before making his directorial debut with episodes of *Z Cars* and went on to helm TV series such as *The Troubleshooters* (1965) and *Adam Adamant Lives!* (1966). He left the BBC in 1968 and established a production company with Tony, *Ridley Scott Associates* (RSA), working with Alan Parker, Hugh Hudson, and Hugh Johnson. After making various television commercials, including the 1974 Hovis advert, "Bike Round" (Dvořák's New World Symphony), which was filmed in Shaftesbury, Dorset, he moved to Hollywood, where he produced and directed a number of top box office films, making his big screen feature debut with *The Duelists* (1977) before scoring an international hit with the sci-fi classic *Alien* (1979). He then made *Blade Runner* (1982), which was initially not as successful but proved immensely popular on video and in a director's cut (1993). His next films were the fantasy *Legend* (1985) and the cop drama *Black Rain* (1989), set in Japan. He then directed the very successful *Thelma and Louise* (1991) which gained him his first Academy Award nomination for Best Director. Following the commercial failure of

1492: Conquest of Paradise (1992) he put his directing career in abeyance for four years until, together with Tony he formed *Scott Free Productions* (1995) in Los Angeles, and produced *White Squall* (1996) and *G.I. Jane* (1997). He then directed the hugely successful *Gladiator* (2000) which revived the epic genre and for which he was nominated for an Academy Award as Best Director. He followed this success with an adaptation of Thomas Harris' *Hannibal* (2001) and the action film *Black Hawk Down* (2001), which gained him a further Academy Award nomination for Best Director. Latest films include *Matchstick Men* (2003), the epic centred on the Crusades, *Kingdom of Heaven* (2005), *A Good Year* (2006), *American Gangster* (2007), *Body of Lies* (2008) and *Robin Hood* (2010). The Scott brothers acquired *Shepperton Studios* in 1995 which were then bought by *Pinewood Studios* in 2001. Ridley has been married twice: to Felicity Heywood (1964–75), producing two sons, Jake (b. 1965) and Luke (b.1968); and to Sandy Watson (1979–89), producing a daughter, Jordan (b. 1978). All three of his children have followed him into the directing profession.

Scott Thomas, Kristin (1960-) Born 24 May 1960, Redruth, Cornwall. Actress. Kristin studied acting at the École Nationale des Arts et Technique de Théâtre, in Paris. She made her TV debut in *Mistral's Daughter* (1984) a mini-series based on a Judith Krantz novel. Her first film was a French short called *Charly* (1985) and her first full length film *Under the Cherry Moon* (1986) co-starred pop star Prince, who also directed it. Later in 1986 she was nominated for "Worst New Star" at the Golden Raspberry Awards. In numerous films she has played an upper class English rose of which *Bitter Moon* (1992), *Four Weddings and a Funeral* (1994), for which she won a BAFTA for Best Actress in a Supporting Role, and *Angels & Insects* (1995) are all examples, but the most memorable is her turn as Katharine Clifton in the *The English Patient* (1996). For this she was nominated for an Academy Award as Best Actress. Other films include: *Mission: Impossible* (1996), *The Pompatus of Love* (1996), *Sweet Revenge* (1998), *The Horse Whisperer* (1998), *Random Hearts* (1999), *Life as a House* (2001), *Gosford Park* (2001), *Arsène Lupin* (2004),*Keeping Mum* (2005), *Tell No One* (French: *Ne le dis à personne*) (2006), *The Valet* (French: *La doublure*) (2006), *The Walker* (2007), *The Golden Compass* (2007), *I've Loved You So Long* (French: *Il y a longtemps que je t'aime*) (2008), The Other Boleyn Girl (2008), *Easy Virtue* (2008), *Largo Winch* (2008), *Confessions of a Shopaholic* (2009), *Leaving* (French: *Partir*) (2009), *Nowhere Boy* (2009 - as John Lennon's Aunt Mimi), *Sarah's Key* (French: *Elle s'appelait Sarah*) (2010), *The Woman in the Fifth* (2011) and *Salmon Fishing in the Yemen* (2011). In 2012, Kristin is scheduled to star in the upcoming film, *Bel Ami*. She is equally admired by the French as the English and indeed can be said to have a foot in both camps. She speaks French fluently, having dubbed herself for *Four Weddings and a Funeral*, has lived in France since she was nineteen, was married to a Frenchman, Dr. François Olivennes (between 1987 and 2005), with whom she has three children Hannah (b. 1988), Joseph (b. 1991) and George (b. 2000), and in 2005 was awarded the Legion d'Honneur by the French government. Although she considers herself more French than English, Kristin was made an OBE in 2003. Around this time she was reported to have begun dating actor Tobias Menzies (b. 7 March 1974, London). Her younger sister Serena Scott Thomas (b. 21 September 1961, Nether Compton, Dorset) is also an actress and has starred in films such as *Let Him Have It* (1991 – her debut), *The World Is Not Enough* (1999 - as Dr Molly Warmflash) and *Hostage* (2005).

Scott, Tony (1944-) Born 21 June 1944, Stockton-on-Tees, Durham. Producer and director. Studied at the West Hartlepool College of Art and Royal College of Art. Starred in his brother Ridley's short film *Boy and Bicycle* (1962). Initial intention to be a painter before joining Ridley in his advertising company. After his big screen directorial debut *The Hunger* (1983) proved unsuccessful at the box-office he returned to making commercials until he came back with the very successful *Top Gun* (1986). He next helmed *Beverly Hills Cop II* (1987) and *Revenge* (1990).

Tony directed Tom Cruise again in *Days of Thunder* (1990) and directed Bruce Willis in the action film *The Last Boy Scout* (1991). His next film was the Quentin Tarantino-scripted hit *True Romance* (1993) and was followed by the popular *Crimson Tide* (1995). *The Fan* (1996) failed to spark the same sort of enthusiasm but he was redeemed by *Enemy of the State* (1998). His latest films include *Spy Game* (2001), *Man on Fire* (2004), *Agent Orange* (2004), *Domino* (2005), *Déjà Vu* (2006), *The Taking of Pelham 1 2 3* (2009) and *Unstoppable* (2010). Formed Scott Free Productions with Ridley in 1995. He has been married three times, to his last wife, Donna, since 1994.

Seagrove, Jenny (1957-) Born Jennifer Ann Seagrove, 4 July 1957, Kuala Lumpur, Malaya (now Malaysia). Actress. After training at the Bristol Old Vic, Jenny pursued a stage career although has also made an impact in several television mini-series such as *The Woman in White* (1982 - as Laura Fairlie) and *Diana* (1984 - as Diana Gayelorde-Sutton). Her film debut came in *Local Hero* (1983 – as Marina). Her next film roles as Fay Hubbard in *A Chorus of Disapproval,* and as Dr Sarah King in *Appointment with Death* were not until 1988, both films directed by her long-time boyfriend, Michael Winner. Her other films include *The Guardian* (1990), *Miss Beatty's Children* (1992), *Don't Go Breaking My Heart* (1999) and *Zoe* (2001). Her recent television work has included roles in *Judge John Deed* (2002-07) and *Identity* (2010). Jenny, a high profile animal rights activist, has been married once, to actor Madhav Sharma (1984-88) but is currently in a relationship with West End theatre producer Bill Kenwright and has starred in many of his productions on the stage. See also entry for *A Woman of Substance* in the television section.

Seidler, David (1937-) Born in 1937, London. Playwright and film and television writer. David was raised in an upper-middle class Jewish family, his father, Bernard, was a fur broker who had an office in New York City. Bernard's parents were killed in the Holocaust. When the Seidler family's home in London was bombed during the Blitz in World War II, they initially relocated to Lingfield in Surrey before moving to Long Island, New York. From a young age David developed a pronounced stammer which blighted his life. David used to listen to George Vi's wartime speeches and found great encouragement when his parent's assured him that the king's stammer was far worse than his and yet he found a way to overcome the problem. David passed out of Cornell University in 1959 and initially wrote for television series before co-penning the TV film *Malice in Wonderland* (1985). His feature debut as writer was *Tucker: The Man and His Dream* (1988), starring Jeff Bridges. His other credits include: *Onassis: The Richest Man in the World* (1988), *Goldrush: A Real Life Alaskan Adventure* (1988), *Quest for Camelot* (1998), *The King and I* (1999), *Come On, Get Happy: The Partridge Family Story* (1999) and *Son of the Dragon* (2008) but David had always wanted to write the story of George VI and began his research in the 1970s. He met Dr. Valentine Logue, a retired brain surgeon, and son of Lionel Logue, who was keen to help but only on condition that he received written permission from the Queen Mother first. David wrote to Her Majesty and received a reply from her private secretary, asking him not to pursue the project during her lifetime. Consequently David abandoned the project in 1982 and it was shelved for more than 20 years. The story had a happy ending when David received an Academy Award for Best Original Screenplay for *The King's Speech* (2010).

Sellers, Peter See entry in comedy section

Selway, Mary (1936-2004) Born Mary J Selway, 14 March 1936, Norwich, Norfolk. Casting director. Her original intention was to be an actress but after studying at Italia Conti she realised she would be more suited to casting than acting. Began primarily as a casting director for stage and television. First big screen project was *If It's Tuesday, This Must be Belgium* (1969). She quickly established a good reputation and subsequently worked with Roman Polanski on *Tess* (1979), Ridley Scott on *Alien* (1979), Stephen Spielberg on *Raiders of the Lost Ark* (1981) and *Indiana Jones and the Temple of Doom* (1984), George Lucas on *Star Wars: Episode VI - Return of the Jedi* (1983), James Cameron on

Aliens (1986) and Michael Apted on *Gorillas in the Mist* (1988). Other major casting projects include *Superman* (1978), *Flash Gordon* (1980), *Out of Africa* (1985), *Emma* (1996), *Lost in Space* (1998), *Notting Hill* (1999), *Captain Corelli's Mandolin* (2001), *Gosford Park* (2001), *Master and Commander: The Far Side of the World* (2003), *Vanity Fair* (2004) and *Harry Potter and the Goblet of Fire* (2005). Considered to be the "grand dame of British casting agents". Mary was presented with the Michael Balcon Award for outstanding contribution to British cinema at the 2001 BAFTA award ceremony. In 2005 it was announced that the Orange Rising Star Award to be presented at subsequent BAFTA ceremonies would be named in her honour. She died 21 April 2004 London.

Serkis, Andy (1964-) Born 20 April 1964, Ruislip. London. Actor. Andrew's mother was English and his father Iraqi. He studied visual arts at Lancaster University, where he decided upon an acting career, initially working with a number of touring companies. After a few television roles he made his big screen debut in *Prince of Jutland* (1994), which he followed with films such as *Stella Does Tricks* (1996), *Insomnia* (1998) and *Clueless* (1998). In 1999 he featured as choreographer John D'Auban in *Topsy-Turvy* and starred as Bill Sikes in a TV adaptation of *Oliver Twist*. He was then handed the plum role of Sméagol / Gollum in *The Lord of the Rings: The Fellowship of the Ring* (2001), *The Lord of the Rings: The Two Towers* (2002) and *The Lord of the Rings: The Return of the King* (2003). His performance was achieved by Serkis providing motion capture reference points for the character, which was then realised using CGI. Other films include: *Shiner* (2000), *Pandaemonium* (2000), *The Jolly Boys' Last Stand* (2000), *The Escapist* (2001), *24 Hour Party People* (2002), *Deathwatch* (2002), *13 Going on 30* (2004), *Blessed* (2004), *King Kong* (2005), playing both Lumpy the Cook and the giant ape, his performance for the latter rendered by the same process as with Gollum, *Stormbreaker* (2006), *The Prestige* (2006), *Flushed Away* (2006), *Extraordinary Rendition* (2007), *Sugarhouse* (2007), *The Cottage* (2008), *Inkheart* (2008 - as Capricorn), *Sex & Drugs & Rock & Roll* (2009 - as Ian Dury), *Burke and Hare* (2010 - as William Burke), *Death of a Superhero* (2010), *Brighton Rock* (2011), *Rise of the Planet of the Apes* (2011 - as Caesar), *Arthur Christmas* (2011 - as General Elf), *Wild Bill* (2011) and *The Adventures of Tintin* (2011 - as Captain Haddock / Sir Francis Haddock). He also played Ian Brady in the British television film *Longford* (2006) and is contracted to reprise the role of Gollum in the forthcoming *Hobbit* films. Andy lives in Crouch End, North London with his wife since 2002, actress Lorraine Ashbourne, and their three children: Ruby (b. 1998), Sonny (b. 2000) and Louis (b. 2004). See also entry for *Oliver Twist* in the television section.

Shaw, Fiona (1958-) Born Fiona Mary Wilson, 10 July 1958, County Cork, Ireland. Actress. She trained at RADA and immediately showed a stage presence and comedic timing in her first role as Julia in the National Theatre production of Richard Sheridan's *The Rivals* (1983). Fiona is principally one of the finest home-grown stage actors working in the theatre today and famously played the lead in Richard II, directed by Deborah Warner in 1995. Her first film role was as Young Deidre in the 1985 TV film *Love Song*. Her feature debut was as Sister Felicity in *Sacred Hearts* (1985). Other films include: *My Left Foot* (1989), *Mountains of the Moon* (1990), *3 Men and a Little Lady* (1990), *London Kills Me* (1991), *Super Mario Bros.* (1993), *Undercover Blues* (1993), *Persuasion* (1995), *Jane Eyre* (1996), *Leo Tolstoy's Anna Karenina* (1997), *The Butcher Boy* (1997), *The Avengers* (1998 - as 'Father'), *The Last September* (1999), *Doctor Sleep* (2002), *The Triumph of Love* (2002), *Midsummer Dream* (2005), *The Black Dahlia* (2006), *Catch and Release* (2006), *Fracture* (2007), *Dorian Gray* (2009), *Noi credevamo* (2010) and *Tree of Life* (2011). Despite the quality of her work Fiona is probably best-known globally for her minor role as Petunia Dursley in *Harry Potter and the Philosopher's Stone* (2001), *Harry Potter and the Chamber of Secrets* (2002), *Harry Potter and the Prisoner of Azkaban* (2004), *Harry Potter and the Order of the Phoenix* (2007) and *Harry Potter and the Deathly Hallows: Part 1* (2010). In 2008, Fiona directed her first opera, *Riders to the Sea* by Vaughan Williams at the ENO. See also

entries for Saffron Burrows and *Gormenghast* in the television section.

Shaw, Robert (1927-78) Born Robert Archibald Shaw, 9 August 1927, Westhoughton, Lancashire. Actor. He trained at RADA and made his stage debut in 1949. His screen debut was *The Lavender Hill Mob* (1951 - uncredited). After films such as *The Dambusters* (1954 - first credited role), *A Hill in Korea* (1956) and *Doublecross* (1956) he came to more prominence as Captain Dan Tempest in the swashbuckling TV series *The Buccaneers* (1956-1957). His films after this series include *Man from Tangier* (1957), *Sea Fury* (1958), *Libel* (1959), *The Valiant* (1962), *The Cracksman* (1963) and *The Caretaker* (1963). He then played the ruthless killer Red Grant in *From Russia with Love* (1963), the German tank commander Hessler in *Battle of the Bulge* (1965), George Armstrong Custer in *Custer of the West* (1967), Squadron Leader Skipper in *Battle of Britain* (1969), Francisco Pizarro in *The Royal Hunt of the Sun* (1969), Lord Randolf Churchill in *Young Winston* (1972), Doyle Lonnegan in *The Sting* (1973) and Mr Blue in *The Taking of Pelham One Two Three* (1974). Perhaps his most popular performance was as Quint in *Jaws* (1975). His later films include *Robin and Marian* (1976 - as the Sheriff of Nottingham), *The Scarlet Buccaneer* (1976), *Black Sunday* (1977), *The Deep* (1977), *Force 10 from Navarone* (1978) and and his last film, *Avalanche Express* (1979). He was nominated for a Best Supporting Actor Academy Award for his portrayal of Henry VIII in *A Man for All Seasons* (1966). Robert was an extremely intelligent man whose roles sometimes belied this. He wrote the novel and play *The Man in the Glass Booth* (1967) and the novel *The Hiding Place*, which was filmed as *Situation Hopeless - But Not Serious* (1965). Other novels include: *A Card from Morocco* (1969) and *The Flag* (1968). Other plays include: *Cato Street*. He was married three times: Jennifer Bourke (1952-63) with whom he fathered four daughters; actress Mary Ure (1963-75) with whom he had two sons and two daughters, including actor Ian Shaw (b. 18 December 1969); and Virginia Jansen (1976-78) with whom he fathered a son and also adopted Virginia's son from a previous relationship. He died 28 August 1978, Tourmakeady, Ireland.

Shaw, Susan (1929-78) Born Patricia G Sloots, 29 August 1929, Norwood, London. Actress. Briefly worked for the Ministry of Information before trying out modelling and acting. A graduate of the Rank Charm School. Screen debut: *Walking on Air* (1946). She was a minor cast member in the film *Holiday Camp* (1948), which featured a family called the Huggetts. Strangely she then found herself cast as the eldest Huggett daughter Susan in the sequels: *Here Come the Huggetts* (1948), *Vote for Huggett* (1949) and *The Huggetts Abroad* (1949). Other films include: *It Always Rains on Sundays* (1948), *Pool of London* (1951), *Time is my Enemy* (1954) and *Fire Maidens from Outer Space* (1956). She married German actor Albert Lieven (1949-53) and in 1954, American actor Bonar Colleano (b. Bonar Sullivan). After Colleano's death in a car crash in Liverpool in 1958 both her professional and personal life seems to have gone down hill. She appeared in a few more films such as *Carry on Nurse* (1959), *Stranglehold* (1962) and her final film, *The Switch* (1963), but then disappeared from the screen to battle alcohol problems. Her son Mark Colleano (b. Mark Sullivan, 4 March 1955) was raised by his paternal grandmother and enjoyed some success as a child actor. Susan died penniless 27 November 1978, London.

Sheard, Michael (1938-2005) Born Michael Lawson Sheard, 18 June 1938, Aberdeen. Actor. Trained at RADA before doing National Service in the RAF. Joined the Perth Repertory Company. Screen debut: *Nobody Runs Forever* (1968). Other films include: *The McKenzie Break* (1970), *England Made Me* (1973), *Holiday on the Buses* (1973), *Erotic Inferno* (1975), *Force 10 from Navarone* (1978), *The Riddle of the Sands* (1979), *Escape to Athena* (1979), *High Road to China* (1983), *Doombeach* (1989), *Another Life* (2001) and *The Green Door* (2005). Best known for his film role as Admiral Ozzel, who is telekinetically strangled by Darth Vadar in *Star Wars: Episode V - The Empire Strikes Back* (1980) and for playing Mr Bronson in the chidren's TV series *Grange Hill* (1985-89). He also played Heinrich Himmler on screen three times and Adolf Hitler four times - in *Rogue Male* (1976), *The Dirty Dozen: The Next Mission* (1985), *Indiana Jones and the Last Crusade* (1989) and *Hitler of the*

Andes (2003). On television Michael made numerous appearances in *Dr Who* over the years. Autobiographies: *Yes, Mr Bronson - Memoirs of a Bum Actor* (1997), *Yes, Admiral - SciFi and Further Memories* (1999), *Yes, School's Out! - SciFi Conventions, Parties and Much, Much More* (2001) and *Yes, It's Photographic!* (2004). He died 31 August 2005, Newport, Isle of Wight. See also entries for *Coronation Street* and *Take The High Road* in the television section.

Shearer, Moira (1926-2006) Born Moira Shearer King, 17 January 1926, Dunfermline, Fife. Ballerina and actress. Her early years were spent in Northern Rhodesia (now Zambia) and Scotland. She studied ballet under Flora Fairbairn, Nicholas Legat and Nadine Nicolayeva and joined Sadler's Wells Ballet School in 1940, making her professional debut in 1941. By 1944 she was a principal of the Sadler's Wells Ballet Company. Whilst continuing with a stellar ballet career she entered films playing ballerina Vicky Page in the Powell and Pressburger classic *The Red Shoes* (1948). The success of this film led to her taking roles in *The Tales of Hoffmann* (1951), *The Story of Three Loves* (1953), *The Man who Loved Redheads* (1955), *Les Collants Noirs (Black Tights)* (1960) and her last film, the controversial Powell film *Peeping Tom* (1960). In the theatre, she had virtually retired from dancing by 1952 and turned her hand equally successfully to mainstream drama. Another of film history's beautiful red-headed stars, she was also a successful literary reviewer and author, including a biography of *Ellen Terry* (1998) and choreographer *George Balanchine* (1986). In 1972, she was chosen by the BBC to present the Eurovision Song Contest when it was staged at the Usher Hall in Edinburgh. Moira was married to Ludovic Kennedy from 1950 until her death on 31 January 2006 Oxford, Oxfordshire'

Sheen, Michael (1969-) Born Michael Christopher Sheen, 5 February 1969, Newport, Wales. Actor. Studied acting at the National Youth Theatre of Wales in Cardiff and then trained at RADA. His television screen debut came in the BBC drama serial, *Gallowglass* (1993), based on the novel by Ruth Rendell. His film debut was in Oliver Parker's *Othello* (1995). Other films include: *Mary Reilly* (1996), *Wilde* (1997), *Heartlands* (2002), *Bright Young Things* (2003), *Timeline* (2003), *Laws of Attraction* (2004), *Kingdom of Heaven* (2005), *The League of Gentlemen's Apocalypse* (2005), *The Queen* (2006 - as Tony Blair), *Blood Diamond* (2006), *Music Within* (2007), *Frost/Nixon* (2008 - as David Frost), *The Damned United* (2009 - as Brian Clough), *My Last Five Girlfriends* (2009), *The Twilight Saga: New Moon* (2009), *Unthinkable* (2010), *Alice in Wonderland* (2010 - voice of The White Rabbit), *Tinker Bell and the Great Fairy Rescue* (2010 - voice of Dr Griffiths), *Tron: Legacy* (2010), *Resistance* (2011 - as Tommy Atkins), and *The Twilight Saga: Breaking Dawn - Part 2* (2011 - as Aro). Michael also played Tony Blair in the made-for-television films, *The Deal* (2003), opposite David Morrissey's portrayal of Gordon Brown, and *The Special Relationship* (2010), opposite Dennis Quaid as Bill Clinton. Michael has become known for his portrayals of well-known public figures and apart from those mentioned above he also played the title role in *Kenneth Williams: Fantabulosa!* (2006) on BBC4. Mimicking is definitely in Michael's genes, his father being a part-time professional Jack Nicholson look-alike. Michael has also played the Lycan Lucian in all three of the Underworld films, *Underworld* (2003), *Underworld: Evolution* (2006) and *Underworld: Rise of the Lycans* (2009). On television he won many plaudits for his role of a man with obsessive-compulsive disorder and Tourette syndrome in the ITV drama, *Dirty Filthy Love* (2004). Michael had a long-term relationship with actress Kate Beckinsale and they have a daughter, Lily Mo Sheen (b. 31 January 1999). During the filming of *Underworld*, Beckinsale left him for the film's director, Len Wiseman, whom she subsequently married. Michael then had a lengthy relationship with ballet dancer Lorraine Stewart from 2003 until 2010 but is currently dating Canadian actress Rachel McAdams whom he met on the set of Woody Allen's *Midnight in Paris* (2011). He was appointed Officer of the Order of the British Empire (OBE) in the 2009 New Year Honours.

Shepherd's Bush Studios (1915-49) Built at Lime Grove, Hammersmith, London by brothers A. C. and R. C. Bromhead in 1915 at a cost of £30,000. They were British agents for the French firm of *Gaumont* and bought out the French interests in forming *Gaumont-British* in 1922. This was expanded after financial backing by the Ostrer brothers to become the *Gaumont-British Picture Corporation* in 1926. Early films made at Shepherd's Bush include: *Bonnie Prince Charlie* (1923), *Mademoiselle From Armentieres* (1926) and *Roses of Picardy* (1927). With the onset of the talkies the studios were rebuilt in *1929*. Michael Balcon was Head of Production 1928-36. Films made include: *Rome Express* (1932) and *The Thirty-Nine Steps* (1935). The studio was in financial trouble at the end of the 1930s but during WWII production was transferred from Islington Studios. Wartime productions include: *Kipps* (1941), *The Man in Grey* (1943) and *The Wicked Lady* (1945). In the late 1940s films include: *Holiday Camp* (1947), *The Man Within* (1947) and *The Bad Lord Byron* (1949). The studios were sold to the BBC in 1949. See also entry for *Gainsborough Pictures* (1924-1951).

Shepperton Studios (1932-) Founded by Norman Loudon at Littleton Park, Shepperton, Surrey, in 1932. Known as Sound City. Early films: *Watch Beverley* (1932), *French Without Tears* (1939) and *Quiet Wedding* (1939). The studios were requisitioned by the War Office during WWII. Sound City was bought by British Lion in 1946. Films during this period include: *An Ideal Husband* (1947), *Spring in Park Lane* (1948) and *The Third Man* (1949). The 1950s saw the making of *The Sound Barrier* (1952), *Moulin Rouge* (1952), *Hobson's Choice* (1953), *Richard III* (1955) and *I'm Alright Jack* (1959). The 1960s began with *The Entertainer* (1960), *The Angry Silence* (1960) and *The L-Shaped Room* (1962) and finished with *A Man for All Seasons* (1966) and *Cromwell* (1970). Later films made at Shepperton include *Young Winston* (1972), *The Elephant Man* (1980), *Gandhi* (1982), *The Company of Wolves* (1984), *Cry Freedom* (1987), *Henry V* (1989), *The Crying Game* (1992) and *The Madness of King George* (1994). The studios were acquired by Ridley and Tony Scott in 1995 and then bought by Pinewood studios in 2001.

Sheridan, Dinah (1920-) Born Dinah Nadyejda Ginsburg, 17 September 1920, Hampstead, London. Actress. Dinah was born to a Russian father and German mother who were photographers to the Royal Family. The family changed their name by deed poll to Sheridan. Dinah's stage debut was as a child actor in *Where the Rainbow Ends* (1932). Her screen debut was opposite her future husband Jimmy Hanley in *Landslide* (1937). Other early films include: *Behind Your Back* (1937), *Father Steps Out* (1937), *Merely Mr. Hawkins* (1938), *Irish and Proud of It* (1938), *Full Speed Ahead* (1940) and *Salute John Citizen* (1942). Her early film career also includes a George Formby film *Get Cracking* (1943), a Huggett family film *The Huggetts Abroad* (1949), *Blackout* (1950), *Where No Vultures Fly* (1951), *The Sound Barrier* (1952), *The Story of Gilbert and Sullivan* (1952), *Appointment in London* (1953) and what should have been her breakthrough into the bigtime, the highly successful *Genevieve* (1953 - as Wendy McKim). However Dinah's first marriage, to actor Jimmy Hanley (1942-52) was now over and she then married the head of the *Rank Organisation* Sir John Davis (1954-65) with a condition of the marriage being that she gave up acting. After their divorce in 1965 she went back on the stage before making a big screen return, after 17 years, as Mrs Waterbury, the mother, in the ever popular *Railway Children* (1970), her only other screen appearance since *Genevieve* being a solitary episode of *Armchair Theatre* in 1968. Retaining her beauty and elegance she has since appeared in various TV series, the last being *Jonathan Creek* in 1999. She has married twice more. Firstly to actor John (Jack) Merivale, from 1986 until his death in 1990, and Aubrey Ison, from 1992 until his death in 2007. Dinah had three children with Jimmy Hanley (see separate entry), including Sir Jeremy Hanley MP and actress Jenny Hanley. See also entries in the television section for *All Night Long, Don't Wait Up* and *Jim's Inn*.

Sheridan, Jim (1949-) Born 6 February 1949, Dublin. Producer, director and writer. Worked in children's theatre and co-founded

Project Art Centre. Jim emigrated to Canada and then moved to New York and spent some time as artistic director of the Irish Arts Center. His directorial screen debut was the acclaimed *My Left Foot* (1989), which he also wrote, and gained him Academy Award nominations for Best Screenplay and Best Director. His follow-up was *The Field* (1990) and the screenplay for *Into the West* (1992). He produced, directed and wrote *In the Name of the Father* (1993) which gained him Academy Award nominations for Best Picture, Best Director and Best Screenplay. He then wrote and produced *Some Mother's Son* (1996) and wrote, produced and directed *The Boxer* (1997). He gained a further Best Screenplay Academy Award nomination for *In America* (2002). His next directorial project, starring rapper 50 Cent, *Get Rich or Die Trying* (2005) was his first without any reference to Ireland. Jim helmed the 2009 film *Brothers*, starring Tobey Maguire and Jake Gyllenhaal, which was shot in New Mexico and his most recent offering is the thriller *Dream House* (2011), which stars Daniel Craig and Rachel Weisz. He is also an accomplished playwright with credits including *The Immigrant* and *Where All Your Dreams Come True*. Jim has three daughters, including director and screenwriter Kirsten Sheridan (b. July 14, 1976, Dublin).

Sim, Alastair (1900-76) Born Alastair George Bell Sim, 9 October 1900, Edinburgh. Actor. Son of a tailor. Educated at Gillespie's School. Studied to be an analytical chemist and then taught elocution in Edinburgh (1925-30). Stage debut: *Othello* (1930). Screen debut: *The Riverside Murder* (1935), followed closely by *The Case of Gabriel Perry* (1935), *The Private Secretary* (1935), *Late Extra* (1935) and *A Fire Has Been Arranged* (1935). Other early films include: *The Big Noise* (1936), *Gangway* (1937), *The Squeaker* (1937) and *Alf's Button Afloat* (1938). During WWII he toured with ENSA. His career took off after the war with classic films such as *Green for Danger* (1946), *Hue & Cry* (1947) and *London Belongs to Me* (1948), his performance as Mr Squales in this film impressed Alec Guinness so much that he based his own performance in *The Ladykillers* (1955) on it, and is often mistaken for Sim as a consequence. Into the 1950s his films include: *The Happiest Days of Your Life* (1950), *Laughter in Paradise* (1951), *An Inspector Calls* (1954), *Geordie* (1955), *The Green Man* (1956), *The Doctor's Dilemma* (1959), *School for Scoundrels* (1960) and *The Millionairess* (1960). He played Sergeant Bingham, Inspector Hornleigh's comic side-kick in a series of films (1939-41) and Headmistress of St Trinian's, Miss Fritton in *The Belles of St Trinian's* (1954) and *Blue Murder at St Trinian's* (1957). Probably his best-loved role was as Ebenezer Scrooge in *A Christmas Carol* (1951). His later films include *The Ruling Class* (1972), *Royal Flash* (1975) and his last film, *Escape from the Dark* (1976). On television he played Magistrate Mr Swallow in *Misleading Cases* (1967). His stage career included spells at the Old Vic during the 1930s and a recurring role playing Captain Hook six times in *Peter Pan* between 1941 and 1968. He became a CBE in 1953 but refused a knighthood offered to him by Edward Heath. Alastair was married to Naomi Plaskitt from 1932 until his death on 19 August 1976, University College Hospital, London. Alastair was 25 years older than the 15 year old George Cole when he entered his household in 1940 and George remained with the couple for 14 years, serving a rich acting apprenticeship under Alastair's guidance.

Simmons, Jean (1929-2010) Born Jean Merilyn Simmons, 31 January 1929, Islington, London. Actress. Began acting while still in her teens. Her debut film was an uncredited part in the film short *Sports Day* (1944) and her feature debut followed soon after when, as a 14-year-old dance student she was plucked from school to play Margaret Lockwood's precocious sister in Give Us the Moon (1944). In her early film roles she is often credited as Simmonds not Simmons. Her first major film was *Great Expectations* (1946), in which she played the young Estella. She was nominated for an Academy Award as Best Supporting Actress for her performance as Ophelia in Laurence Olivier's *Hamlet* (1948). In 1950, she married Stewart Granger, with whom she appeared in several films, successfully making the transition to Hollywood. The marriage lasted ten years and they had one daughter, Tracy (b. September 1956). Among her best-known leading roles are *Guys and Dolls* (1955), *Elmer Gantry* (1960), directed by her second husband Richard Brooks (whom she

married in 1960 and divorced in 1977, producing a daughter, Kate Brooks - b. July 1961), and *Spartacus* (1960). She gained a second Best Actress Academy Award nomination for *The Happy Ending* (1969), which was again directed by Brooks. For her appearance in the mini-series, *The Thorn Birds*, she won an Emmy Award. In 1989, she again starred in a mini-series version of *Great Expectations*, where she played Miss Havisham. Her other films include: *Black Narcissus* (1947), *The Blue Lagoon* (1949), *Adam and Evelyne* (1949), *Androcles and the Lion* (1952), *Young Bess* (1953), *The Dawning* (1988) and her final film, *Shadows in the Sun* (2009). Towards the end of her career Jean provided the voices for characters in Anime films, notably *Final Fantasy: The Spirits Within* (2001), *Howl's Moving Castle* (2004) and *Thru the Moebius Strip* (2005). She died 22 January 2010, Santa Monica, California.

Sims, Joan (1930-2001) Born Irene Joan Marion Sims, 9 May 1930, Laindon, Essex. Actress. She graduated from RADA in 1950 and her screen debut was as a parlourmaid in the television film John of the Fair (1951). Her feature debut was as Bunty in *The Square Ring* (1953). She followed this up with *Will Any Gentleman...?* (1953), opposite George Cole, and the Norman Wisdom vehicle Trouble in Store (1953). It was here that she found her niche, comedy. Over the next 25 years she appeared in numerous British films, almost all comedies, including: *Meet Mr. Lucifer* (1953), *Doctor in the House* (1954), as the sexually repressed Nurse Rigor Mortis, *What Every Woman Wants* (1954), *The Young Lovers* (1954), *The Belles of St. Trinian's* (1954), *To Dorothy a Son* (1954), *The Sea Shall Not Have Them* (1954), *Doctor at Sea* (1955), *Stars in Your Eyes* (1956), *Keep It Clean* (1956), *Carry on Admiral* (1957), not part of the *Carry On* series, *Just My Luck* (1957), *The Naked Truth* (1957), *Passport to Shame* (1958), *Please Turn Over* (1959), *Carry on Nurse* (1959), *The Captain's Table* (1959), *Life in Emergency Ward 10* (1959), *Upstairs and Downstairs* (1959), *Carry on Teacher* (1959), *Watch Your Stern* (1960), *Carry on Constable* (1960), *Doctor in Love* (1960), *Carry on Regardless* (1961), *No My Darling Daughter* (1961), *The Iron Maiden* (1962), *A Pair of Briefs* (1962), *Twice Round the Daffodils* (1962), *Nurse on Wheels* (1963), *Strictly for the Birds* (1963), *Carry on Cleo* (1964), *The Big Job* (1965), *Doctor in Clover* (1966), *Carry on Cowboy* (1966), *Carry on Screaming!* (1966), *Don't Lose Your Head* (1966), *Follow That Camel* (1967), *Carry on Doctor* (1967), *Carry On... Up the Khyber* (1968), *Carry on Camping* (1969), *Carry on Again Doctor* (1969), *Carry on Up the Jungle* (1970), *Doctor in Trouble* (1970), *Carry on Loving* (1970), *Carry on Henry* (1971), *The Magnificent Seven Deadly Sins* (1971), *Carry on at Your Convenience* (1971), *Carry on Matron* (1972), *The Alf Garnett Saga* (1972), *Carry on Abroad* (1972), *Don't Just Lie There, Say Something!* (1973), *Not Now Darling* (1973), *Carry on Girls* (1973), *Carry on Dick* (1974), *One of Our Dinosaurs Is Missing* (1975), *Carry on Behind* (1975), *Carry on England* (1976) and *Carry on Emmannuelle* (1978). In total, Joan starred in 24 Carry On....films, and it would have been at least one more as she was taken ill during filming of *Carry On Cruising* and had to be replaced by Dilys Laye. Her final screen appearance was in the 2000 television film, *The Last of the Blonde Bombshells*. She died, having never been married, 28 June 2001 Kensington, London. Her autobiography was entitled *High Spirits* (2000). See also entries in the television section for *As Time Goes By, Cluedo, Farrington of the F.O., On the Up, Our House, Sykes,* and *Worzel Gummidge.*

Sinden, Sir Donald (1923-) Born Donald Alfred Sinden, 9 October 1923, Plymouth, Devon. Actor. Initially considered becoming an architect. Trained at the Webber Douglas Academy of Dramatic Arts. Joined Shakespeare Memorial Theatre (1946) and later the Bristol Old Vic. Screen debut: *Portrait from Life* (1948). Made his breakthrough in *The Cruel Sea* (1953) after which he was rarely off screen for the next few years. Working for *Rank*, he usually starred in comedies such as *You Know What Sailors Are* (1954), *Doctor in the House* (1954), *An Alligator Named Daisy* (1955), *Doctor at Large* (1957) and *Rockets Galore!* (1957) but was also cast as a killer in *Eyewitness* (1956). On his return to the stage in 1957, at the end of his *Rank* contract, his ability as both a comic player and a versatile Shakespearian actor enabled him to take on stage roles as diverse as Lord

Foppington in *The Relapse* (1967), *King Lear* (1977) and *Othello* (1979). He joined the RSC in 1963. His later films include *Villain* (1971), *The National Health* (1973), *The Day of the Jackal* (1973) and *The Accidental Detective* (2003). A founder of the British Theatre Museum. Appointed CBE in 1979 and knighted in 1997. Donald's most recent performances have been on the television series *Midsomer Murders* (2008) and the television film *Marple: The Blue Geranium* (2010). He is soon to make a cameo appearance in the ensemble film, *Run For Your Wife*. donald has written two autobiographies: *A Touch of the Memoirs* (1982) and *Laughter in the Second Act* (1985). He was married to actress Diana Mahony from 1948 until her death in 2004. The couple had two sons: actor Jeremy Sinden (14 June 1950 – 29 May 1996), who died of lung cancer, and Marc Sinden (b. 9 May 1954) who is a West End theatre producer. See also entries in the television section for *Judge John Deed*, *Never the Twain*, *Our Man At St Mark's* and *Two's Company*.

Slaughter, Tod (1885-1956) Born Norman Carter Slaughter, 19 March 1885 Gosforth, Northumbria. Actor and director. His father worked in the advertising industry. He worked for a time for a wine merchant. Stage debut: *A Wrecker of Men* (1905). Served in the RFC and RAF during WWI. An actor-manager of the old school, he ran both the Theatre Royal Chatham and The Elephant and Castle Theatre (1923-27) where he successfully revived the Victorian melodramas *Maria Marten* and *Sweeney Todd*. It was in 1925 that Norman changed his name to Tod Slaughter. He finally made it to the screen at the age of fifty playing the aristocratic killer Squire William Corder, a role he had played many times on stage, in *Maria Marten: or, The Murder in the Red Barn* (1935), which like so many of his subsequent films was produced on a shoe string at *Shepperton Studios* by George King. His next role was another familiar one as *Sweeney Todd: The Demon Barber of Fleet Street* (1936). He played a robber turned murderer in both *The Crimes of Stephen Hawke* (1936) and *The Ticket of Leave Man* (1937) and, after a couple of non-horror outings in *Song of the Road* (1937) and *Darby and Joan* (1937), he was back to his wicked ways in the rather ironically titled *It's Never too Late to Mend* (1937). He played a crime boss "The Snake" in the more mainstream *Sexton Blake and the Hooded Terror* (1938). After returning to murderous melodrama in *The Face at the Window* (1939) and *Crimes at the Dark House* (1940) he was off the screen for six years because George King had outgrown this type of production. He returned in *The Curse of the Wraydons* (1946). Tod also played master criminal Terence Reilly in *Murder at Scotland Yard* (1952) and *King of the Underworld* (1952). His style remained to the end ham theatrical, all staring eyes, twirled moustache and lustful leering after a young lady usually labelled "a delightful little baggage" but it did the job it was intended to do - put bums on seats in the cinema. He died 19 February 1956, Derby, Derbyshire, and was survived by his actress wife, Jenny Lynn.

Smith, C Aubrey (1863-1948) Born Charles Aubrey Smith, 21 July 1863, City of London. Actor. Educated at Charterhouse and Cambridge. A fine cricketer he gained a Blue at Cambridge and played for Sussex CCC and Transvaal. He played one Test match for England against South Africa in 1889, when he was also captain. Known as "Round the Corner Smith" because of his strange bowling run-up. In first-class cricket he scored 2,986 runs and took 346 wickets and in his Test for England he scored 3 runs and took 5 wickets for 19 runs in the first innings and 2 for 42 in the second. He remained in South Africa for a few years in a stockbroking partnership with fellow cricketer Monty Bowden before returning to London and taking up acting. However, he did not forget his first love and established the Hollywood CC in 1932, having a pitch sown with English grass at Griffith Park, Los Angeles. Team sheets included such names as Bruce, Colman, Flynn, Karloff (wicket-keeper), Niven, Olivier, Rathbone and Wodehouse. Stage debut: *The Idler* (1892). Screen debut: *The Builder of Bridges* (1915). Other films include: *Red Pottage* (1918), *The Temptation of Carlton Earle* (1923), *Surrender* (1931), *Just a Gigolo* (1931), *Trouble in Paradise* (1932), *Queen Christina* (1933), *Cleopatra* (1934), *The Scarlet Empress* (1934),

The House of Rothschild (1934), *Little Lord Fauntleroy* (1936), *The Prisoner of Zenda* (1937), *Victoria the Great* (1937), *Wee Willie Winkie* (1937), *Kidnapped* (1938), *Sixty Glorious Years* (1938), *The Four Feathers* (1939), *Rebecca* (1940), *Dr. Jekyll and Mr. Hyde* (1941), *Madame Curie* (1943), *And Then There Were None* (1945), in which he played General Mandrake, *An Ideal Husband* (1947) and *Little Women* (1949). He generally played the archetypical English gentleman. Awarded the CBE in 1938 and knighted in 1944 for services to Anglo-American amity. He died 20 December 1948, Beverly Hills, California, and his ashes were returned to England and interred in his mother's grave at St Leonard's churchyard in Hove, East Sussex.

Smith, George (1864-1959) Born George Albert Smith, 4 January 1864, City of London. Cinema pioneer. Moved to Brighton with his widowed mother and began to work the music halls as a stage hypnotist. He worked a "second sight" telepathy act with his partner Douglas Blackburn that many thought was genuine. He was Secretary to the Honorary Secretary of the Society for Psychical Research (1883-88) and co-author of *Experiments in Thought Transference*. George purchased St Ann' Well Garden, Hove in 1892 and turned it into a pleasure garden including magic lantern exhibitions. He bought a film camera from Brighton engineer Alfred Darling in 1896, built a glasshouse studio and developed a commercial film production and processing business with close ties to Charles Urban's *Warwick Trading Company*. George then made films such as *Santa Claus* (1898), *The Mesmerist* (1898), *The Kiss in the Tunnel* (1899), *Grandma's Reading Glass* (1900), *The House that Jack Built* (1900), *Let Me Dream Again* (1900) and *Mary Jane's Mishap* (1903), the last featuring his wife, actress Laura Eugenia Bayley. Using techniques he had learned from his magic lantern exhibition, he was an early pioneer of continuity editing to provide a narrative action sequence. He then moved to his "laboratory lodge" in Southwick where he developed a two-colour process with Urban called Kinemacolor which was launched in Paris and London in 1908. Urban and Smith formed the Natural Colour Kinemacolor Company. However, After the success of a patent suit brought by Friese-Green in 1914 Smith's business interests suffered and he retired from the film business. He became a Fellow of the Royal Astronomical Society. Michael Balcon called him "The father of the British Film Industry". He died 17 May 1959 Brighton, East Sussex.

Smith, Madeline (1949-) Born 2 August 1949, Hartfield, Sussex. Actress. Began her professional life as a model and gained her first screen role as Samantha in *The Mini-Affair* (1967). Her subsequent films include: *Some Like It Sexy* (1969), *Taste the Blood of Dracula* (1970), *The Vampire Lovers* (1970), *The Magnificent Seven Deadly Sins* (1971), *Up the Front* (1972 - as Fanny), *Carry on Matron* (1972 - as Miss Pullitt), *Anyone for Sex?* (1973), *Theatre of Blood* (1973), *Take Me High* (1973), *Frankenstein and the Monster from Hell* (1974), *Percy's Progress* (1974) and *The Bawdy Adventures of Tom Jones* (1976). The titles of her films tend to contain clues as to the parts she was considered for. In numerous films she was either chased by a vampire (and usually caught), or played the sexy nurse. Madeline was the definitive "Hammer Heroine". An actress who suffered from her looks, she never really had the opportunity to be anything other than a pretty minor character, as she herself said '"When you've got a bosom like mine, there's a very narrow margin between being sexy and ridiculous". Sources tell us that her bust was 32B until the age of 21, and then blossomed to a 34DD. Two of her best-remembered roles are as Erotica in *Up Pompeii* (1971) and Bond Girl Miss Caruso in *Live and Let Die* (1973). Here playing an Italian (why not) she has her dress removed by the "sheer magnetism" of Roger Moore. See also entry in the television section for *Eureka!*

Smith, Maggie (1934-) Born Margaret Natalie Smith, 28 December 1934, Ilford, Essex. Actress. A British film, stage, and television actress who has received numerous honours throughout her career, culminating in a DBE in 1990. She started at the Oxford Playhouse Theatre with Frank Shelley in 1952, and made her film debut, as an uncredited party guest, in *Child in the House*

(1956), her first credited film role was as Bridget Howard in *Nowhere to Go* (1958). She was nominated for a Best Actress Academy Award for playing Desdemona in *Othello* (1965) and went on to win the Academy Award for Best Actress for her role in *The Prime of Miss Jean Brodie* (1969). Her third Best Actress Academy Award nomination arrived for *Travels with My Aunt* (1972) and her fourth, which was duly converted, this time for Best Supporting Actress, was for her role in *California Suite* (1978). A further brace of Best Supporting Actress Academy Award nominations were gained for *A Room with a View* (1985) and *Gosford Park* (2001). Other films include: *Go to Blazes* (1962), *The V.I.P.s* (1963), *The Pumpkin Eater* (1964), *Young Cassidy* (1965), *The Honey Pot* (1967), *Oh! What a Lovely War* (1969), *Love and Pain and the Whole Damn Thing* (1973), *Murder by Death* (1976), *Death on the Nile* (1978), *Quartet* (1981), *Clash of the Titans* (1981 - as Thetis), *Evil Under the Sun* (1982), *The Missionary* (1982), *A Private Function* (1984), *The Lonely Passion of Judith Hearne* (1985), *Hook* (1991), *Sister Act* (1992), *The Secret Garden* (1993), *Sister Act 2: Back in the Habit* (1993), *Richard III* (1995), *The First Wives Club* (1996), *Washington Square* (1997), *Curtain Call* (1998), *Tea with Mussolini* (1999), *Divine Secrets of the Ya-Ya Sisterhood* (2002), *Ladies in Lavender* (2004), *Keeping Mum* (2005), *Becoming Jane* (2007), *From Time to Time* (2009), *Nanny McPhee and the Big Bang* (2010), *Gnomeo & Juliet* (2011 - voice of Lady Bluebury) and *The Best Exotic Marigold Hotel* (2011 - as Muriel). She is probably best known to the latest generation of cinema-goers as Professor Minerva McGonagall in seven of the eight *Harry Potter* films (all bar *Harry Potter and the Deathly Hallows: Part 1*) and to television viewers as Violet Crawley, the Dowager Countess of Grantham in *Downton Abbey* (2010-present). In a career spanning almost sixty years Maggie has won five BAFTA Awards, two Academy Awards, two Golden Globes, two Emmy Awards, two Laurence Olivier Awards, two SAG Awards, and a Tony Award. She has been married twice, to Sir Robert Stephens (see separate entry) and playwright Beverley Cross (13 April 1931 – 20 March 1998), to whom she was married from 1975 until his death. She has two children from her first marriage, Chris Larkin and the actor Toby Stephens. See also entry for *Downton Abbey* in the television section.

Spall, Timothy (1957-) Born Timothy Leonard Spall, 27 February 1957, Battersea, London. Actor. Trained at the National Youth Theatre and RADA. Joined the RSC (1979-81) and later joined the National Theatre. Screen debut: *Quadrophenia* (1979). Other early films include *The Missionary* (1982), *Gothic* (1986) and *To Kill a Priest* (1988). Tim began a long and successful collaboration with director Mike Leigh in *Home Sweet Home* (1982) on television and went on to feature in Leigh's *Life is Sweet* (1990), *Secrets & Lies* (1996) and in particular as the singer Richard Temple in *Topsy-Turvy* (1999). Other major films include: *White Hunter, Black Heart* (1990), *The Sheltering Sky* (1990), *Hamlet* (1996), *Still Crazy* (1998), *Love's Labour's Lost* (2000), *Chicken Run* (2000), *Intimacy* (2001), *Vanilla Sky* (2001), *Nicholas Nickleby* (2002), *The Last Samurai* (2003), *Harry Potter and the Prisoner of Azkaban* (2004 – as Peter Pettigrew), *Lemony Snicket's A Series of Unfortunate Events* (2004), *Harry Potter and the Goblet of Fire* (2005), *Pierrepoint* (2005), *Sweeney Todd: The Demon Barber of Fleet Street* (2007 - as Beadle Bamford), *Appaloosa* (2008), *The Damned United* (2009 - as Peter Taylor), *Harry Potter and the Half-Blood Prince* (2009), *Heartless* (2009), *Reuniting the Rubins* (2010), *Alice in Wonderland* (2010) and *Harry Potter and the Deathly Hallows – Part 1* (2010) and *Part II* (2011). In the 2006 video game *Grand Theft Auto: Vice City Stories*, Tim voiced Phil Collins' manager, Barry Mickelthwaite. In 2010 he portrayed Winston Churchill in the multi-award-winning film *The King's Speech* for which as a member of the ensemble he was jointly awarded the Screen Actors Guild Award for Outstanding Performance by a Cast in a Motion Picture. He had previously played Churchill on film in *Jackboots on Whitehall* (2010). Tim has made a full recovery from Leukemia diagnosed in 1996. His performances, whether comic or dramatic are always memorable. Awarded OBE in 1999. He married his wife, Shane, in 1981 and has three children: Pascale (b. 1976), Rafe (b. 1983), who is also an actor, and Mercedes (b. 1985). Tim is probably best known as a television star - see entries in the television section for *Auf Wiedersehen Pet, The Fattest Man in Britain, Frank Stubbs Promotes, Outside Edge, Saturday Live,* and *The Street.*

Stamp, Terence (1938-) Born Terence H Stamp, 22 July 1938, Bow, London. Actor. Trained at the Webber Douglas Academy of Dramatic Arts. His screen debut was as the title character in *Billy Budd* (1962) for which he received an Academy Award nomination for Best Supporting Actor. He followed this up with *The Collector* (1965), *Modesty Blaise* (1966), *Poor Cow* (1967) and *Far from the Madding Crowd* (1967). Terence became one of the "faces of the 1960s" and he had much-publicised relationships with actresses Julie Christie (immortalised in the Kinks' lyric "Terry and Julie" from *Waterloo Sunset*) and Brigitte Bardot as well as supermodel Jean Shrimpton. Things however, turned sour for him at the end of the decade and he went into retreat in Spain and later in India. Apart from a couple of small roles he was not seen on the big screen again until playing Kryptonian General Zod, briefly in *Superman* (1978) and then in a memorable performance in *Superman II* (1979). The 1980s saw him playing small parts in Hollywood films such as *The Hit* (1984), *Legal Eagles* (1986), *The Sicilian* (1987), *Wall Street* (1987) and *Young Guns* (1988). He made another memorable appearance as Ralph/Bernadette Bassenger in the international hit *The Adventures of Priscilla, Queen of the Desert* (1994) and ended the 1990s playing Wilson in the excellent *The Limey* (1999) and Supreme Chancellor Valorum in *Star Wars: Episode 1 - The Phantom Menace* (1999). His latest films include: *Bowfinger* (1999), *Revelation* (2001), *My Boss's Daughter* (2003), *The Haunted Mansion* (2003), *Dead Fish* (2004), *Elektra* (2005), *These Foolish Things* (2005), *September Dawn* (2007 - as Brigham Young), *Wanted* (2008), *Get Smart* (2008), *Yes Man* (2008), *Valkyrie* (2008), based on the true story of Colonel Claus von Stauffenberg's failed attempt to assassinate Hitler, *Ultramarines:The Movie* (2010) and *The Adjustment Bureau* (2011 - as Thompson). His recent projects include the video game *Elder Scrolls IV: Oblivion*, in which he lends his voice to the villainous cult leader Mankar Camoran. Terence has also written a novel: *The Night* (1993), a cook book, and has a food range called *The Stamp Collection* which caters for people with food intolerances. Autobiographies: *Stamp Album* (1987), *Coming Attractions* (1988) and *Double Feature* (1989). On New Year's Eve 2002, at the age of 64, Terence married for the first time. His 29-year-old bride was Elizabeth O'Rourke, whom Stamp first met during the mid-1990s at a pharmacy in Bondi, New South Wales. The couple divorced in April 2008.

Standing, Gordon (1887-1927) Born Gordon Hope Standing, 24 November 1887, London. Actor. Son of opera singer Frank Celli (born Francis Standing) and nephew of Sir Guy Standing. Emigrated to the United States in 1910. Screen debut: *Three Black Eyes* (1919). Made only eleven films before he died 21 March 1927 when, whilst filming *King of the Jungle* (1927), he was mauled to death by a lion on the set at Selig Zoo Studios, Los Angeles, California.

Standing, Guy (1873-1937) Born 1 September 1873, Shepherds Bush, London. Actor. Son of actor Herbert Standing and brother of Wyndham Standing. Stage debut: *Wild Oats (1889).* A successful stage actor in both the West End and appeared on Broadway from 1896 until 1936 in plays including *Sue* (1896), *A Man and his Wife* (1900), *Gypsy* (1903), *Hedda Gabler* (1907), *Jenny* (1929-1930) and *Jefferson Davis* (1936). Made his screen debut at the age of 57 in *Such is the Law* (1930) and made 18 more films including *The Eagle and the Hawk* (1933), *Hell and High Water* (1933), *Palm Springs* (1936), *Lloyd's of London* (1936) and *Bulldog Drummond Escapes* (1937). His best remembered role was as Colonel Stone in *Lives of a Bengal Lancer* (1935). Guy is the father of actress Kay Hammond (18 February 1909 - 4 May 1980). He served in the Royal Navy Volunteer Reserve during WWI. Knighted in 1918 in connection with his services as a member of the British War Mission to the United States. He died 24 February 1937, Hollywood Hills, California from a heart attack brought on by a rattlesnake bite.

Standing, Herbert (1846-1923) Born 13 November 1846, Peckham, London. Actor. Stage debut: *Still Waters Run Deep* (1867). Appeared on Broadway 1900-12. Made his screen debut at the age of 67 in *Twickenham Ferry* (1913). Herbert made over

80 films in the next 13 years including *Peer Gynt* (1915), *Davy Crockett* (1916), *David Garrick* (1916), *A Misfit Earl* (1919), *The Trap* (1922) and *The Brown Derby* (1926). Father of Sir Guy Standing and Wyndham Standing. He died 5 December 1923, Los Angeles, California.

Standing, Wyndham (1880-1963) Born Cecil Wyndham Standing, 24 August 1880, St Johns Wood, London. Actor. Son of Herbert Standing and brother of Sir Guy Standing. He emigrated to the United States in 1907. Screen debut: *Extravagance* (1915). Made over 100 films including *The Bugle Call* (1916), *The Iron Trail* (1921), *White Heat* (1926), *The Eternal Triangle* (1930), *A Study in Scarlet* (1933), *Clive of India* (1935), *The Man in the Iron Mask* (1939), *Mr Smith Goes to Washington* (1939), *Waterloo Bridge* (1940), *Pride and Prejudice* (1940), *Meet John Doe* (1941), *Counter-Espionage* (1942) and *B.F.'s Daughter* (1948). He died 1 February 1963, Los Angeles, California.

Statham, Jason (1972-) Born 12 September 1972, Sydenham, London. Actor. Member of the British Diving Team at the 1992 World Championships, finishing 12th. Also worked as a model with French Connection. Made his screen debut as Bacon in *Lock, Stock and Two Smoking Barrels* (1998) after being spotted by director Guy Ritchie. He also featured in Ritchie's *Snatch* (2000) and followed up with *Turn it Up* (2000), *Ghosts of Mars* (2001), *The One* (2001) and *Mean Machine* (2001). He gained his first starring role as Frank Martin in *Transporter* (2002). Jason then played Handsome Rob in the remake of *The Italian Job* (2003) and featured in *Collateral* (2004) and *Cellular* (2004) before starring in *Transporter 2* (2005) and returning to Guy Ritchie's direction in *Revolver* (2005). Other films include: *Chaos* (2005), *London* (2006), *The Pink Panther* (2006), *Crank* (2006), *War* (2007), *The Bank Job* (2008), *In the Name of the King: A Dungeon Siege Tale* (2008), *Death Race* (2008), *Transporter 3* (2008), *Crank: High Voltage* (2009), *13* (2010), *The Expendables* (2010), *The Mechanic* (2011), *Gnomeo & Juliet* (2011 - voice of Tybalt), *Blitz* (2011) and *Killer Elite* (2011). Jason was in a seven year relationship with model Kelly Brook, until 2004, and since April 2010, he has been dating model and actress Rosie Huntington-Whiteley.

Staunton, Imelda (1956-) Born Imelda Mary Philomena Bernadette Staunton, 9 January 1956, Islington, London. Actress. As is indicated by her full name, Imelda is of Irish extraction, with her parents hailing from County Mayo. She trained at RADA, graduating in 1976, and spent six years in English repertory, including a period at the Northcott Theatre, Exeter, before joining the Royal Shakespeare Company, and in 1982 moving on to the National Theatre. Imelda made her television debut in an episode of the BBC2 *Playhouse* series in 1982 and then appeared as Nurse White in the TV adaptation of *The Singing Detective* (1986) opposite her husband Jim Carter (b. 19 August 1948, Harrogate, Yorkshire), whom she married in 1985. Her first big-screen outing was in a tale of the Tolpuddle Martyrs *Comrades* (1987) playing Betsy Loveless. At 5 foot tall and not classically beautiful in the "Hollywood" sense of the word, she has tended to be offered (or at least played) more character-driven roles, often to good effect and usually very memorably. She was Gwynneth Paltrow's nurse in *Shakespeare in Love* (1998), voiced Bunty in *Chicken Run* (2000) and played Queen Elizabeth II in *Cambridge Spies* (2003). For *Shakespeare in Love* she shared a Screen Actors Guild Award for Best Performance by a Cast. In 2004, Staunton received the Best Actress honours at the European Film Awards, the BAFTAs, and the Venice Film Festival for her performance in *Vera Drake* (2004). For the same role, she received Best Actress nominations for the 2005 Golden Globes and Academy Awards. Off screen she has also been rewarded. She is a three-time recipient of Britain's highest theatre honour, the Olivier Award, for roles in *A Chorus of Disapproval* (1985), *The Corn Is Green* (1985) and *Into the Woods* (1991). As with many of her contemporary leading British actresses Imelda has garnered the inevitable Harry Potter role by taking on the part of Dolores Jane Umbridge in David Yates's adaptation of *Harry Potter and the Order of the Phoenix* (2007) and *Harry Potter and the Deathly Hallows: Part 1* (2010). Other films include: *Peter's Friends* (1992), *Much Ado About Nothing* (1993), *Deadly Advice* (1994), *The Snow Queen* (1995), *The Snow Queen's Revenge* (1996), *Twelfth Night* (1996), *The Ugly Duckling* (1997), *Rat* (2000), *Another Life* (2001), *Bright Young Things* (2003), *Nanny McPhee* (2005), *Guilty Hearts* (2006), *Freedom Writers* (2007), *Three and Out* (2008), *A Bunch of Amateurs* (2008), *Taking Woodstock* (2009), *The Mr Men Movie* (2010), *Alice in Wonderland* (2010) *Another Year* (2010), *The Awakening* (2011) and *Arthur Christmas* (2011 - as Mrs Santa). Imelda was awarded the OBE in 2006. She has a daughter, Bessie (b. 1993) by Jim Carter and currently lives in West Hampstead. All three of the family appeared in the BBC series *Cranford*. See also entries in the television section for *Big & Small*, *Cranford*, and *Fingersmith*.

Steel, Anthony (1920-2001) Born Anthony Maitland Steel, 21 May 1920, Chelsea, London. Actor. Studied at Cambridge. Served in the Grenadier Guards during WWII. After the war he enrolled in the Rank Charm School where he made his screen debut in *Saraband for Dead Lovers* (1948), although he was uncredited. Also that year he appeared in *A Piece of Cake* (also uncredited), before making his credited debut in *Portrait from Life* (1948). Anthony then made another uncredited appearance in *The Blue Lamp* (1950) but made his breakthrough in *The Wooden Horse* (1950), which depicted the true events of an escape attempt made by British POWs in the German POW camp Stalag Luft III. He then vied with Dirk Bogarde as Britain's highest paid actor and starred in films including: *The Mudlark* (1950), *Laughter in Paradise* (1951), *Where No Vultures Fly* (1951), *The Planter's Wife* (1952), *Malta Story* (1953), *Albert R.N.* (1953), *The Master of Ballantrae* (1953), the film where Errol Flynn ran his epee through Anthony's hand, *The Sea Shall Not Have Them* (1954), *West of Zanzibar* (1954), the title song giving Anthony a UK No 11 hit single, and *Storm Over the Nile* (1955), a remake of *The Four Feathers*. He then embarked on a stormy marriage to actress Anita Ekberg (1956-59) which led to a brief and unhappy transfer to Hollywood which in retrospect did not aid his career as it antagonised some powerful British film magnates. He returned to Europe in 1958 and featured in films made all over the continent including *Revenge of the Barbarians* (1960), *Tiger of the Seven Seas* (1963) and some exploitation films such as *The Story of O* (1975), *Let's Get Laid* (1977) and *Hardcore* (1977). His later films included: *The World Is Full of Married Men* (1979), *The Mirror Crack'd* (1980) and his final film, *The Monster Club* (1981). Anthony made guest appearances on several television series and did some stage tours in the 1980s before he disappeared into obscurity. Anthony made his final screen appearance, after a break of twelve years, as Dr Harman in, 'Kith and Kin', an episode of the BBC drama series, *The Broker's Man* (1997) before entering a theatrical retirement home. Apart from his marriage to Ekberg, Anthony had previously been wed to Juanita Forbes (1949-54), and subsequently to Johanna Melcher from 1964 until his death on 21 March 2001, Northwood, Middlesex. In 1952, Anthony had a much-publicised affair with actress Patricia Roc while they were co-starring in *Something Money Can't Buy*, resulting in a son, Michael. At the time Roc was married to André Thomas but they were unable to have children so Thomas agreed to raise Michael as his own. See also entries in the television section for *The Broker's Man*, and *Crossroads*.

Steele, Tommy See entry in the music section

Stephens, Robert (1931-95) Born Robert Graham Stephens, 14 July 1931, Bristol. Actor. Trained at the Northern Theatre School, Bradford. Member of the Royal Court English Stage Company (1956-63) and joined the National Theatre in 1963. His screen debut was an uncredited role in *War and Peace* (1956), his first credited film being *A Circle of Deception* (1960). Other films include: *A Taste of Honey* (1961), *Cleopatra* (1963), *Morgan: A Suitable Case for Treatment* (1966), *The Prime of Miss Jean Brodie* (1969), *The Private Life of Sherlock Holmes* (1970), *Travels with My Aunt* (1972), *Luther* (1973), *Empire of the Sun* (1987), *Henry V* (1989), *The Bonfire of the Vanities* (1990), *The Pope Must Die* (1991), *Chaplin* (1992), *Searching for Bobby Fischer* (1993) and his last film *England, My England* (1995). One of the most respected actors of his generation, who vied for a time with Paul Scoffield as a candidate to succeed Olivier as the master of stage-craft, however he suffered a slump in his career during the 1970s and 1980s, not helped by bouts of heavy drinking, but he recovered to perform somewhere near his peak during his later life. Married four times: Nora Ann Simmonds (1951-52), one son, Michael Stephens; Tarn Bassett (1956-67), one daughter; actress Maggie Smith (1967-74), two sons, actors Toby Stephens (b. 21 April 1969) and Chris Larkins (b. 19 June 1967); and actress Patricia Quinn (1995), who appeared with him in *Fortunes of War* (1987) and the BBC adaptation of *The Box of Delights* (1984). Knighted in 1995, he died eleven months later on 12 November 1995, Camden, London. See also entries in the television section for *Fortunes of War, 99 - 1*, and *The Rivals of Sherlock Holmes*.

Stephenson, Henry (1871-1956) Born Henry Stephenson Garroway, 16 April 1871, Granada, West Indies. Actor. Educated at Rugby School. After his stage debut in 1896 he had a very successful stage career both in Britain and on Broadway. He made his screen debut in *The Spreading Dawn* (1917) but didn't concentrate on films until the talkies arrived. He reprised a successful stage performance in *Cynara* (1932) and other early films include *Little Women* (1933), *One More River* (1934) and *Mutiny on the Bounty* (1935). A familiar face in the cast of Errol Flynn adventures such as *Captain Blood* (1935), *The Charge of the Light Brigade* (1936), *The Prince and the Pauper (1937)* and *The Private Lives of Elizabeth and Essex* (1939), usually playing an aristocrat or commanding officer. Later films include *Down Argentine Way* (1940), *Mantrap* (1943), *Of Human Bondage* (1946), *Oliver Twist* (1948) and his final film, *Challenge to Lassie* (1949). He died 24 April 1956, San Francisco, California, leaving behind his widow, actress Ann Shoemaker (b. 10 January 1891, Brooklyn, New York; d. 18 September 1978, Los Angeles, California).

Stephenson, James (1889-1941) Born James Albert Stephenson, 14 April 1888 Selby, Yorkshire. Actor. Made his screen debut at the age of 49 in *You Live and Learn* (1937). Over the next four years as a Warner Brothers contract player he appeared in supporting roles, often as a villain, in nearly forty films including *Take It From Me* (1937), *Boy Meets Girl* (1938), *Devil's Island* (1939), *Beau Geste* (1939), *We Are Not Alone* (1939), and the Errol Flynn adventures *The Private Lives of Elizabeth and Essex* (1939) and *The Sea Hawk* (1940). He featured as the sympathetic attorney Howard Joyce in *The Letter* (1940), a role which gained him an Academy Award nomination for Best Supporting Actor. His career appeared to be on the up as he starred as Philo Vance in *Calling Philo Vance* (1940) and *Shining Victory* (1941). His last film was *International Squadron* (1941) before he died after a heart-attack on 29 July 1941, Pacific Palisades, California.

Stewart, Patrick (1940-) Born Patrick Hewes Stewart, 13 July 1940, Mirfield, Kirklees, West Yorkshire. Actor. While working as a newspaper reporter, Patrick began to study acting at the Bristol Old Vic and eventually joined the Royal Shakespeare Company in 1966. He made his screen debut in a 1964 episode of the BBC2 series *Story Parade*. His film debut came as Enobarbus in the ITC-produced 1974 TV film *Antony and Cleopatra* and his feature debut followed as Tilney in *Hennessy* (1975). Other films include: *Hedda* (1976), *Little Lord Fauntleroy* (1980), *Excalibur* (1981), *Dune* (1984), *Wild Geese II* (1986), *Lady Jane* (1986), *L.A. Story* (1991), *Gunmen* (1993 - as Loomis), *Robin Hood: Men in Tights* (1993 - as King Richard), *Jeffrey* (1995 – as Sterling), *Masterminds* (1997), *Dad Savage* (1998), and *The Game of Their Lives* (2005). He has also lent his distinctive voice to films such as *The Plague Dogs* (1982 - Major), *Nausicaä of the Valley of the Wind* (1984 - Lord Yupa), *The Pagemaster* (1994 - Adventure), *The Prince of Egypt* (1998 - Seti), *Animal Farm* (1999 - Napoleon), *Jimmy Neutron: Boy Genius* (2001 - King Goobot), *Boo, Zino & the Snurks* (2004 - Albert Drollinger), *Steamboy* (2004 - Dr Lloyd Steam), *Chicken Little* (2005 - Mr Woolensworth), *The Snow Queen* (2005 - The Raven), *Bambi II* (2006 - The Great Prince), *TMNT* (2007 - Winters) and *Gnomeo & Juliet* (2011 - Bill Shakespeare). His TV films include: *Hamlet, Prince of Denmark* (1980 - as Claudius), *Pope John Paul II* (1984 - as Party Secretary Wladyslaw Gomulka), *In Search of Dr Seuss* (1994 - as Sgt Mulvaney), *The Canterville Ghost* (1996), *A Christmas Carol* (1999 - as Ebenezer Scrooge), *The Lion in*

Winter (2003 - as King Henry II), *Mysterious Island* (2005 - as Nemo), *Hamlet* (2009 - as Claudius / Ghost) and the title role in *Macbeth* (2010). On film Patrick is best known for his role of Professor Charles Xavier / Professor X in *X-Men* (2000) and its sequels: *X-Men 2* (2003), *X-Men: The Last Stand* (2006) and *X-Men Origins: Wolverine* (2009). He has also since voiced the role in three video games, *X-Men Legends*, *X-Men Legends II* and *X-Men: Next Dimension*. A fine Shakespearean actor he has also won much acclaim for his performances on stage in *Waiting For Godot* and *The Master Builder*. Patrick has been married twice, to Sheila Falconer (1966–90) and American film producer Wendy Neuss (2000–03). His son Daniel is a television actor, and has appeared alongside his father in the 1993 made for television film *Death Train*, and the 1992 Star Trek episode "The Inner Light" playing his son. Patrick is currently the Chancellor and Professor of Performing Arts of the University of Huddersfield. In 2001 he was awarded the OBE and in 2010 he was knighted. On the 8th June 2010 Patrick was invited to present the gong for Film Actress of the Year to *Avatar*'s Zoe Saldana at the Glamour Awards in London. Before doing so he criticised host James Corden for standing at the back with his hands in his pocket, commenting "From where I was sitting, I could see your belly. And that was from right over there at the back of the room". The pair have since made up. On television Patrick is best known for his role of Captain Jean-Luc Picard / Locutus of Borg in *Star Trek: The Next Generation* (1987-94) and more recently as the voice of Avery Bullock in the American animated sitcom *American Dad!*. See also entries in the television section for *Churchill's People*, *Coronation Street*, *Eleventh Hour*, *Extras*, *I Claudius*, *Maybury*, *Story Parade*, and *Tinker Tailor Soldier Spy*.

Sting See entry in the music section

Stone, Marianne (1922-2009) Born Mary Haydon Stone, 23 August 1922, London. Actress. Although perhaps not a familiar name, Marianne has in fact appeared in more than 200 films, notably, nine Carry Ons: *Carry On Nurse* (1959 – Alice Able), *Carry On Jack* (1963 - Peg), *Carry On Screaming* (1966 – Mrs Parker), *Carry On Don't Lose Your Head* (1966 - Landlady), *Carry On Doctor* (1967 - Mother), *Carry On at Your Convenience* (1971 - Maud), *Carry On Girls* (1973 – Miss Drew), *Carry On Dick* (1974 - Maggie) and *Carry On Behind* (1975 – Mrs Rowan). On television she also appeared in an episode of *Carry On Laughing* (*The Case of the Screaming Winkles* as Madame Petra) in 1975 and in a more dramatic role played Lena Van Broecken in three episodes of the BBC's *Secret Army* between 1977 and 1978. Other films included: *Miss London Ltd* (1943 – her first film role), (*Brighton Rock* (1947), *Seven Days to Noon* (1950), *Time Gentlemen, Please!* (1952), *Woman in a Dressing Gown* (1957), *Hell Drivers* (1957), *Just My Luck* (1957), *The 39 Steps* (1959), *The Angry Silence* (1960), *Lolita* (1962), *The Fast Lady* (1962), *Doctor in Distress* (1963), *The Wrong Arm of the Law* (1963), *Ladies Who Do* (1963), *The Curse of the Mummy's Tomb* (1964), *To Sir, with Love* (1967), *Oh! What a Lovely War* (1969), *Doctor in Trouble* (1970), *Bless This House* (1972), *The Creeping Flesh* (1973), *Confessions of a Window Cleaner* (1974), *Percy's Progress* (1974), *The Wicked Lady* (1983) and her last film *Terry on the Fence* (1986). Marianne (sometimes credited as Mary and Marian in early roles) also appeared in two Quatermass films: *The Quatermass Xperiment* (1955) and *Quatermass 2* (1957). Never more than a character actress making fleeting appearances in film and television dramas (such as *Dixon of Dock Green, No Hiding Place, Crown Court, Public Eye, The Informer, Edgar Wallace Mysteries* and *Bless This House*) sometimes uncredited, Marianne made her final screen appearance in Eric Sykes' *The Nineteenth Hole* in 1989. Mugsie, as she was known, was married for fifty years, from 1947 to 1997, to actor turned theatre critic and film historian Peter Noble, with whom she had two children, one of whom is DJ Kara Noble. She died on 21 December 2009.

Strong, Mark (1963-) Born Marco Giuseppe Salussolia, 30 August 1963, London. Actor. Mark has an Italian father and an Austrian mother and was raised a Catholic. His English name is not a stage name but was in fact changed by deed poll when he was a boy to help him fit in to the English way of life. He speaks fluent German and some Italian. Mark intended to pursue a career in law after studying in Munich for a year but returned to the Royal Holloway University of London to study English and

Drama before training at the Bristol Old Vic Theatre School. His first screen appearance was as Roger in an episode of the television version of *After Henry* (1989). He appeared, uncredited, as a German soldier in the 1991 TV film *One Against the Wind* before making his feature debut with a small part as a policeman in *Century* (1993). In 1996 he made an impact as the villainous Colonel Brand in *Sharpe's Mission* (1996) and the romantic lead, Mr Knightley, in the ITV adaptation of Jane Austen's novel *Emma*. Mark then returned to film with a highly acclaimed performance as Steve in *Fever Pitch* (1997). Other films include: *Sunshine* (1999), *To End All Wars* (2001), *Hotel* (2001), *The Martins* (2001), *Heartlands* (2002), *It's All About Love* (2003), *Revolver* (2005) playing the unforgettable role of Sorter, the bespectacled professional hit-man "who never misses", *Oliver Twist* (2005), *Syriana* (2005), *Tristan + Isolde* (2006), *Scenes of a Sexual Nature* (2006), *Sunshine* (2007), *Stardust* (2007), *Miss Pettigrew Lives for a Day* (2008), *Flashbacks of a Fool* (2008), *Babylon A.D.* (2008), *RocknRolla* (2008) playing the compelling role of henchman Archy, a fixer, and also the film's narrator, *Body of Lies* (2008), *Good* (2008), *The Young Victoria* (2009), *Sherlock Holmes* (2009), *Kick-Ass* (2010), *Robin Hood* (2010), *The Way Back* (2010), *The Eagle* (2011), *Green Lantern* (2011 - as Thaal Sinestro), *The Secret World of Arrietty* (2011 - voice of Pod in the English version), *Tinker Tailor Soldier Spy* (2011 - as Jim Prideaux), *Black Gold* (2011) and *John Carter* (2012 - as Matai Shang). In his stage career, Mark was nominated in 2003 for the Laurence Olivier Award for Best Performance in a Supporting Role for his role in Shakespeare's *Twelfth Night* at the Donmar Warehouse. Mark lives in north-west London with his wife Liza Marshall and sons Gabriel and Roman (b. 5 October 2007), whose godfather is actor Daniel Craig. See also entries in the television section for *The Long Firm*, *Our Friends In The North*, *Prime Suspect* and *Who Do You Think You Are?*.

Studdy, George (1878-1948) Born George Ernest Studdy, 23 June 1878, Devonport, Devon. Animator. Son of a lieutenant in the Argyll and Sutherland Highlanders. Educated at Clifton College, Bristol and Dulwich College, London. An accident with a pitchfork ended any hopes of following his father's career. He briefly worked as an apprentice engineer and then a stockbroker, eventually taking evening classes in art and becoming a freelance artist. George contributed to *Comic Cuts*, *Boys Own* and *Tatler* and also for Valentine's Postcards of Dundee. From 1912 he worked regularly for *The Sketch* magazine, producing a weekly full-page drawing. Unfit for war service he was commissioned by *Gaumont-British* to make a series of three short cartoon films called *Studdy's War Studies*. In 1921 he introduced the highly successful "Studdy Dog" in *The Sketch*, illustrating a puppy that soon became known as Bonzo. This puppy developed into a hugely popular image, appearing on many products including cards, games and china. In 1924 and 1925 Studdy, with ten assistants, produced 26 ten-minute animated films for *New Era Films* including *Bonzo* (1924), *Detective Bonzo and the Black Hand Gang* (1924), *Bonzo Broadcasted* (1925) and *Topical Bonzette* (1925). The cartoon *A Sausage Sensation* (1924) was seen by King George V and Queen Mary in their first visit to a public cinema. In 1927 Bonzo was replaced in *The Sketch* by Ooloo the Studdy Cat. After WWII he began producing postcards in a similar style to Donald McGill and signed Cheero. He died 25 July 1948, Kensington, London.

Sullivan, Francis L (1903-56) Born Francis Loftus Sullivan, 6 January 1903, Wandsworth, London. Actor. Educated at Stonyhurst College and Neuchatel, Switzerland. Stage debut: *Richard III* (1921). Francis had a very successful classical stage career before making his screen debut in *The Missing Rembrandt* (1932). He featured in many of the best British films of the late 1930s and 1940s including *The Drum* (1938), *The Citadel* (1938), *The Four Just Men* (1939), *Pimpernel Smith* (1941), *The Day Will Dawn* (1942), *The Foreman Went to France* (1942), *Caesar and Cleopatra* (1945) and *Joan of Arc* (1948). Francis was well known for his Dickensian roles Mr Jaggers in *Great Expectations* in both the 1934 and 1946 productions, Mr Crisparkle in *The Mystery of Edwin Drood* (1935) and Mr Bumble in *Oliver Twist*

(1948). His later films made in the US include *My Favourite Spy* (1951) and *The Prodigal* (1955), his last film. A friend of Agatha Christie, he played Hercule Poirot on stage. Often unfairly dubbed "the poor man's Sidney Greenstreet" because of his size, he became a naturalised US citizen in 1954. He died, of a heart-attack, 19 November 1956 New York.

Sutherland, Edward (1897-1973) Born Albert Edward Sutherland, 5 January 1897, London. Actor and director. His parents were from Boston Massachusetts and both were in the entertainment industry. The family returned to the US in 1905. Acting screen debut: *The Hazards of Helen* (1914). Other films as an actor include: *Caught in the End* (1917), *The Paliser Case* (1920), *The Witching Hour* (1921) and *The Dramatic Life of Abraham Lincoln* (1924). He then supervised Charlie Chaplin's sequences when Chaplin was on screen in *The Gold Rush* (1925) before making his solo directorial debut with *Coming Through* (1925). Whilst directing *It's the Old Army Game* (1927) he began a life-long friendship with W C Fields, whom he also directed in *Tillie's Puctured Romance* (1927), *International House* (1933) and *Mississippi* (1935). Other films include: *Diamond Jim* (1935), *The Flying Deuces* (1939), *The Boys from Syracuse* (1940), *Sing Your Worries Away* (1942) and *Dixie* (1943). A disastrous production and directing performance on *Abie's Irish Rose* (1946) saw him abandon Hollywood and spend the 1950s in Britain working in television. He married three times, including to actress Louise Brooks (1926-28). Edward died 31 December 1973, Palm Springs, California.

Swinton, Tilda (1960-) Born Katherine Matilda Swinton, 5 November 1960, Westminster, London. Actress. Tilda was born to a Scottish father and Australian mother. She attended the West Heath Girls' School (the same class as Diana, Princess of Wales), and also Fettes College, before graduating from New Hall, Cambridge with a degree in Social and Political Sciences. Her first screen role was in Derek Jarman's *Caravaggio* (1986), and this set the scene for many of her subsequent roles, quirky, offbeat, artistic…different. Most of her earlier film roles were in arthouse films, which sometimes required a little "deciphering". Indeed she made a number of films with the auteur Jarman: *Caravaggio* (1986), *Aria* (1987), *The Last of England* (1988), War Requiem (1989), *The Garden* (1990), *Edward II* (1991), *Wittgenstein* (1993) and *Blue* (1993). A tall willowy actress she has a delicacy and androgynous beauty that perhaps suggests the otherworldly. This characteristic has been used to good effect on a number of occasions in *Orlando* (1992*)* where she vacillates between sexes, *Constantine* (2005) where she plays the archangel Gabriel and as Jadis, the White Witch in *The Chronicles of Narnia: The Lion, the Witch and the Wardrobe* (2005), *The Chronicles of Narnia: Prince Caspian* (2008) and *The Chronicles of Narnia: The Voyage of the Dawn Treader* (2010). In 2008 Tilda won both a BAFTA and an Oscar for Best Supporting Actress for her performance as ruthless Karen Crowder, the legal counsel for U-North, in *Michael Clayton* (2007). Her other films, many of which are more mainstream than earlier, include: *Conceiving Ada* (1997), the TV film *Love Is the Devil: Study for a Portrait of Francis Bacon* (1998), *The Protagonists* (1998), *The War Zone* (1999), *Possible Worlds* (2000), *The Beach* (2000), *Vanilla Sky* (2001), *The Deep End* (2001), *Adaptation* (2002), *Teknolust* (2002), *The Statement* (2003), *Young Adam* (2003), *Broken Flowers* (2005), *Thumbsucker* (2005), *Stephanie Daley* (2006), *The Man from London* (2007), *Julia* (2008), *Burn After Reading* (2008), *The Curious Case of Benjamin Button* (2008), *The Limits of Control* (2009), *I Am Love* (2009), *We Need to Talk about Kevin* (2011 - as Eva Khatchadourian) and the upcoming *Moonrise Kingdom* (2012). Tilda's personal life is as intriguing as her screen persona. She was in a fifteen-year relationship with Scottish playwright and artist John Byrne (b. 6 January 1940) and still lives in Nairn, in the Scottish Highlands, near him and and their twin children: a son, Xavier, and a daughter, Honor, although since 2004 she has been in a relationship with Sandro Kopp, a German/New Zealand painter. This relationship apparently having John's blessing. Tilda herself dabbled in artistic projects outside of film; her most well known video-art installation/performance piece is *The Maybe*, in which she slept in a glass case for eight hours a day at the Serpentine Gallery in London. She also appeared in Orbital's music video for *The Box*.

Sykes, Eric See entry in comedy section.

Syms, Sylvia (1934-) Born 6 January 1934, Greenwich, London. Actress. Sylvia was educated at convent schools before receiving dramatic training at the Royal Academy of Dramatic Art. She was a repertory player by the time she was discovered for films by Anna Neagle and her husband Herbert Wilcox. Her screen debut came in the TV film, *The Romantic Young Lady* (1955) and her feature debut the following year in *My Teenage Daughter* (1956). Her career continued with roles such as Georgie Harlow in *Woman in a Dressing Gown* (1957) and as the army nurse Sister Diana Murdoch opposite John Mills and Anthony Quayle in the classic British war film *Ice-Cold in Alex* (1958). Other early films include: *The Moonraker* (1958), *No Trees in the Street* (1959), *Conspiracy of Hearts* (1960), *Expresso Bongo* (1960), *The World of Suzie Wong* (1960), *Flame in the Streets* (1961), *Victim* (1961), *The Quare Fellow* (1962), *The Punch and Judy Man* (1963), *East of Sudan* (1964), *Operation Crossbow* (1965), Her screen roles over the next 20 years were few and far between although she had great reviews for her role of Margaret Stephenson in *The Tamarind Seed* (1974). Sylvia was as well known on television as in film and starred in episodes of many of the leading dramas of the day. After her 50th birthday she developed from the fresh-faced beauty into a fine character actress. Her later films include: *Absolute Beginners* (1986), *A Chorus of Disapproval* (1989), *Shirley Valentine* (1989), *Dirty Weekend* (1993), *Staggered* (1994), *The House of Angelo* (1997), *Food of Love* (1997), *What a Girl Wants* (2003), *I'll Sleep When I'm Dead* (2003) and *Is Anybody There?* (2008). She also played Margaret Thatcher in both *Thatcher: The Final Days* (1991) and *Half the Picture* (1996) and HRH The Queen Mother in *The Queen* (2006). Her TV films include: *Intimate Contact* (1987), *The Chemistry Lesson* (1995), *Neville's Island* (1998), *Doctor Zhivago* (2002), *The Poseidon Adventure* (2005) and *Child of Mine* (2005). Sylvia has two feature films to look forward to in 2012, the comedy *Booked Out* and Ray Cooney's farce *Run For Your Wife*. Sylvia was married to Alan Edney between 1956 and 1989. Her daughter Beatie Edney (b. 23 October 1962) is a fine television actress and played Joan Sims in the 2006 BBC4 play *Kenneth Williams: Fantabulosa!* See also entries in the television section for *At Home with the Braithwaites, Doctors, My Good Woman,* and *Peak Practice*.

Tafler, Sydney (1916-79) Born 31 July 1916, Hackney, London. Actor. Trained at RADA. Sydney's screen debut was an uncredited appearance as an RAF officer in *Cottage to Let* (1941). It was six years before he made his next film Busman's Honeymoon (1947), an early BBC made-for-television production. His next film was *It Always Rains on Sunday* (1947), playing Morry Hyams, the first of several Jewish characterizations. Other films include: *Uneasy Terms* (1948), *London Belongs to Me* (1948), the Ealing comedies *Passport to Pimlico* (1949) and *The Lavender Hill Mob* (1951), *Wide Boy* (1952), *The Square Ring* (1953), *The Sea Shall Not Have Them* (1954), *A Kid for Two Farthings* (1955), *The Cockleshell Heroes* (1955), *Reach for the Sky* (1956), *Carve Her Name With Pride* (1958), *Too Many Crooks* (1959), *Tommy the Toreador* (1959 - as Ramon - uncredited), *Follow a Star* (1959), *Sink the Bismark!* (1960), *The Bulldog Breed* (1960), *Carry on Regardless* (1961), *A Weekend with Lulu* (1961), *Alfie* (1966), *The Sandwich Man* (1966), *Berserk!* (1967), *The Birthday Party* (1968), *The Adventurers* (1970) and his final film, *The Spy Who Loved Me* (1977). On television he appeared alongside Sid James in *Citizen James* (1960-62). An accomplished character actor, in early films he played wide boys and shiftless, shady characters. He was an ever-present television personality who appeared in one-off episodes of the most popular drama series of the day as well as guesting on comedy shows with Tony Hancock and Alfred Marks. Syd was married to Joy Shelton from 1941 until his death on 8 November 1979, Richmond, Surrey. They had three children - two sons Jeremy and Jonathan (also an actor) and a daughter, Jennifer, who appeared in some films with her father. See also entry for *Citizen James Love Story* and *Village Hall* in the television section.

Tandy, Jessica (1909-94) Born Jessie Alice Tandy, 7 June 1909 Hackney, London. Actress. Studied at the *Ben Greet Academy of Acting*. Jessica was sixteen when she made her professional debut as Sara Manderson in the play *The Manderson Girls* and subsequently joined the *Birmingham Repertory Theatre*. In 1929 she appeared in her first West End play *The Rumour* and three years later made her first cinematic outing in *The Indiscretions of Eve* (1932) as a maid. On the stage her roles grew in size enacting a succession of Shakespeare's most famous women (Cordelia, Titania, Viola, and Ophelia). Jessica's film roles were relatively scarce in her early days. In 1947 she played Nan Britton in *Forever Amber*, In 1951 she played Lucie Marie Mollin, later married to James Mason's Field Marshal Erwin Johannes Rommel, in *The Desert Fox* and in 1963 she played Lydia Brenner in Alfred Hitchcock's classic *The Birds*. Apart from these few highlights however she stayed mostly off screen, her only film after The Birds and before 1980 was the Harold Pinter-directed *Butley* (1976). She won Tony Awards in 1948, 1978 and 1983 for *A Street Car Named Desire*, *The Gin Game* and *Foxfire* respectively, was nominated in 1971 and 1986 and won a special joint award with husband Hume Cronyn in 1994. Other films include: *Honky Tonk Freeway* (1981), *The World According to Garp* (1982), *The Bostonians* (1984), and the two most famous films she appeared in opposite her husband, *Cocoon* (1985) and *Cocoon: The Return* (1988). She is perhaps best known to audiences for her Best Actress Academy Award winning film *Driving Miss Daisy* (1989) playing Daisy Werthan, chauffeured around by Hoke (played by Morgan freeman, who also won an Academy Award). She was also nominated two years later for *Fried Green Tomatoes* (1991) in the Best Supporting Actress category, but lost out to Mercedes Ruehl (for *The Fisher King*). Her last film was Robert Benton's *Nobody's Fool* in 1994. She was married to actor Jack Hawkins from 1932 until 1940 but her second marriage to Hume Cronyn lasted from 1942 until her death, from cancer on 11 September 1994, Fairfield, Connecticut. Her daughter from her second marriage, Tandy Cronyn is also an actress.

Taylor, Alma (1895-1974) Born Alma Louise Taylor, 3 January 1895, London. Actress. Screen debut: *The Story of a Picture* (1909). For most of her career she worked with director and producer Cecil Hepworth as a member of the *Hepworth Picture Players* and was particularly popular at the time for her comedy films with Chrissie White as the unruly Tilly Girls in such films as *Tilly the Tom Boy Visits the Poor* (1910), *Tilly's Party* (1911), *Tilly's Breaking Up Party* (1913), *Tilly at the Football Match* (1914) and finally *Tilly and the Nut* (1915). She was one of Britain's top female film stars of the early 1920s. Her film career lasted through nearly 50 years with a gap between 1936 and 1955. Her other films include two versions of *Comin' Thro' the Rye* (1916 and 1923), *Alf's Button* (1920), *Everybody Dance* (1936), *Lilacs in the Spring* (1955), *The Man who Knew Too Much* (1956), *Blue Murder at St Trinian's* (1957) and *A Night to Remember* (1958). The singer Alma Cogan was named after her. She died 23 January 1974, Wandsworth, London.

Taylor, Elizabeth (1932-2011) Born Elizabeth Rosemond Taylor, 27 February 1932, Hampstead, London. Actress. Elizabeth was the second child of Francis Lenn Taylor (1897–1968) and Sara Viola Warmbrodt (1895–1994), who were Kansans living in London. This gave Elizabeth dual nationality. She undoubtedly got the acting bug from her mother, an actress whose stage name was 'Sara Sothern'. Elizabeth's first film was *There's One Born Every Minute* (1942), after which she was dropped by Universal, the studio's production chief, Edward Muhl famously commenting: "She can't sing, she can't dance, she can't perform. What's more, her mother has to be one of the most unbearable women it has been my displeasure to meet." MGM immediately signed Elizabeth for her role as Priscilla in Lassie Come Home (1943). Two uncredited roles in *Jane Eyre* and The *White Cliffs of Dover* followed in early 1944 until, aged just 12, she starred as Velvet Brown in *National Velvet* (1944). Now a star, she played Amy in *Little Women* (1949) and got married in *Father of the Bride* (1950). She developed into a beautiful and talented actress and both *Giant* (1956) and *Cat On A Hot Tin Roof* (1958) gave her a chance to show her range. She was nominated for a Best Actress Academy Award in four consecutive years; losing for

Raintree County (1957), Cat On A Hot Tin Roof (1958) and Suddenly, Last Summer (1959) before finally winning for the Daniel Mann film Butterfield 8 (1960). She moved from these roles to more and more extreme characters, whether playing Cleopatra (1963), Laura Reynolds in The Sandpiper (1965), Martha in Who's Afraid of Virginia Woolf (1966), for which role she won her second Best Actress Academy Award, or Helen of Troy in Doctor Faustus (1967). Many of her films during the 1960s and 1970s were co-starring vehicles with husband Richard Burton. As time moved on she became less of an actress and more of a parody of herself, famous for being "Liz". In this way she voiced Maggie Simpson's first words in The Simpsons and also took on the role of Pearl Slaghoople in The Flintstones (1994 – her last feature role). Other films include: Courage of Lassie (1946), A Place in the Sun (1951), Quo Vadis (1951), Ivanhoe (1952), Beau Brummell (1954), The Last Time I Saw Paris (1954), The V.I.P.s (1963), The Taming of the Shrew (1967), The Comedians (1967), Anne of the Thousand Days (1969 - as an uncredited courtesan), Under Milk Wood (1972 - as Rosie Probert), The Blue Bird (1976), A Little Night Music (1977), The Mirror Crack'd (1980), Young Toscanini (1988) and her last film, the 2001 TV movie These Old Broads. She was in her time one of the most beautiful women in the world and a very very fine actress. In 1999 she was made a Dame in the Millennium honours. Her off-screen life has been as colourful as her on, she was eight times married, Conrad Hilton, Jr. (1950–51), Michael Wilding (1952–57), Mike Todd (1957–58), Eddie Fisher (1959–64), Richard Burton (1964–74, 1975–76), John Warner (1976–82) and Larry Fortensky (1991–96). Her children are Michael Howard Wilding (b. 6 January 1953), Christopher Edward Wilding (b. 27 February 1955), Elizabeth Frances "Liza" Todd (b. 6 August 1957) and, Maria Burton (b. 1 August 1961; adopted 1964). All her marriages ended in divorce except her third, to Mike Todd, who died. Her most recent companion was Jason Winters. Elizabeth worked vigorously at promoting various AIDS charities and events despite her numerous health scares. She died of heart failure on 23 March 2011, surrounded by her four children, at Cedars-Sinai Medical Center, Los Angeles, California.

Taylor, William Desmond (1872-1922) Born William Cunningham Deane Tanner, 26 April 1872, Carlow, Ireland. Actor and director. A man with a colourful life and a much discussed death. The young William emigrated to the United States in the 1890s, becoming an actor and then an antique dealer before suddenly leaving his wife and daughter, Ethel Daisy, in New York in 1908 and four years later re-appearing in Hollywood, now calling himself William Taylor. His screen debut was The Counterfeiter (1913). After a short screen acting career in films such as Granddad (1913) and Captain Alvarez (1914) he decided to move into directing, his debut being The Crucible (1914). Other films include Davy Crockett (1916), Tom Sawyer (1917), Captain Kidd Jr (1919), Anne of Green Gables (1919), Huckleberry Finn (1920), The Green Temptation (1922) and The Top of New York (1922). He was elected head of the Motion Picture Director's Association in 1917 and then enlisted in the Canadian Army (1918-19). On 1 February 1922, at his home in Los Angeles, California, he was shot dead. A celebrated case, the crime was never solved although the police had a number of suspects. His murder spelled the end of the career for actress Mary Miles Minter, with whom he was involved, and severely harmed that of Mabel Normand who was the last person to see him alive. In the 1950 film Sunset Boulevard, the character Norma Desmond is a reference to both William's middle name and the surname of his actress friend, Mabel Normand.

Teddington Studios (1912-) The grounds of Weir House, Teddington were used for filming from 1914 and the house itself was converted into studios during the post-WWI period. Films were made by Ec-Ko Films (1912-16), Master Films (1918-27), Ideal Films (1927-29). Henry Edwards and E G Norman formed Teddington Film Studios Ltd in 1931 and shortly afterwards the studios were purchased, and extended by Warner Bros in order to make "quota quickies". Films produced in the pre-WWII period include: Murder on the Second Floor (1932), Murder at Monte Carlo (1934) and They Drive by Night (1938). The studio remained open during WWII despite being bombed, and some employees being killed. The partly-destroyed studios were rebuilt after the war and formally re-opened in 1948. However, they were closed again between 1950 and 1952 and the only major film made in that period was The Crimson Pirate (1952). The studios were purchased by ABC TV in 1955 and have concentrated on TV production ever since. In 2005 they were acquired by Pinewood Shepperton Studios Group. The site has eight studios in total, as well as post production editing facilities. Studio 1 is by far the largest at almost 8,900 square feet (827m2). It is a fully digital widescreen studio, with audience seating for 500. Many of the late Tommy Cooper and Morecambe and Wise shows were recorded in Studio 1 as was the long-running reality show This is Your Life.

Tennant, David (1971-) Born David John MacDonald, 18 April 1971, Bathgate, West Lothian. Actor. Son of a Church of Scotland minister. Educated at Paisley Grammar School. He trained at the Royal Scottish Academy of Music and Drama. David' stage roles include Touchstone, Antipholus and Romeo for the RSC, Edgar in King Lear at the Royal Exchange and Jimmy Porter in a touring Look Back in Anger. He made his television debut as Jim in an anti-smoking public service advertisement for the Glasgow Health Board, in 1987. Other early TV roles include Campbell Bain in Takin' Over the Asylum (1994), a six part BBC Scotland television drama about a hospital radio station in a Glasgow psychiatric hospital. His feature film debut came in Jude (1996), in which he shared a scene with Christopher Eccleston. Other films include the film shorts Bite (1997), Sweetnightgoodheart (2001), One Eyed Jacques (2001), and Nine 1/2 Minutes (2002), plus features Being Considered (2000), Nine 1/2 Minutes (2002), Bright Young Things (2003), as the quaintly named Ginger Littlejohn, Old Street (2004), Traffic Warden (2004), Harry Potter and the Goblet of Fire (2005), as Barty Crouch Junior, Free Jimmy (2006), Glorious 39 (2009), St. Trinian's II: The Legend of Fritton's Gold (2009), How to Train Your Dragon (2010), The Decoy Bride (2011), Fright Night (2011), The Pirates! In an Adventure with Scientists (2012 - voice of Charles Darwin) and Nativity 2: The Second Coming (2012). In 2012 His television credits include the one-off plays The Deputy (2004) and He Knew He Was Right (2004); the comedy series Blackpool (2004) and the title role of Casanova in the 2005 BBC mini-series. In 2005 he was also chosen to be the tenth incarnation of Dr Who after Christopher Eccleston announced his decision not to film a further series. David married actress Georgia Moffett (b. 25 December 1984), the daughter of actors Peter Davison and Sandra Dickinson, in December 2011. Georgia, who played the Doctor's daughter on the show in 2008, gave birth to baby Olive in March 2011. David adopted Georgia's son, Tyler, in March 2012. See also entries in the television section for Blackpool, Casanova, Dr Who, and Who Do You Think You Are?

Terry-Thomas (1911-90) Born Thomas Terry Hoar-Stevens, 14 July 1911, Finchley London. Actor. Worked as a clerk for the Union Cold Storage Company before working as a film extra and supporting himself as a professional ballroom dancer. Originally known as Thomas Terry he changed his name to stop being asked if he was related to Ellen Terry. Stage debut: Rhythm in the Air (1930). He came to the fore as a forces entertainer during WWII and had popular radio and television shows to his credit. Terry made his screen debut in Private's Progress (1956) as a silly ass CO, Major Hitchcock, whose men were "an absolute shower". This remark had become Terry's catchphrase by the time he reprised the role of Hitchcock in I'm All Right Jack (1959). His most successful films were Brothers-in-Law (1957), It's A Mad, Mad, Mad, Mad World (1962), How to Murder Your Wife (1965), Those Magnificant Men in Their Flying Machines (1965), Monte Carlo or Bust (1969) and The Abominable Dr Phibes (1971). Other films include Lucky Jim (1957), Blue Murder at St Trinian's (1957), tom thumb (1958), The Wonderful World of the Brothers Grimm (1962), The Mouse on the Moon (1963), You Must Be Joking! (1965), The Sandwich Man (1966), Munster, Go Home! (1966), Jules Verne's Rocket to the Moon (1967), The Perils of

Pauline (1967), *Where Were You When the Lights Went Out?* (1968), *How Sweet It Is!* (1968), *Dr. Phibes Rises Again* (1972), *The Cherry Picker* (1972*), Robin Hood* (1973), inevitably cast as the voice of Sir Hiss (who had a gap between his teeth similar to Terry), *Side by Side* (1975), *Spanish Fly* (1975), *The Bawdy Adventures of Tom Jones* (1976), *The Last Remake of Beau Geste* (1977) and *The Hound of the Baskervilles* (1978), his last film role. He also starred in Italian and French films, notably as an RAF airman travelling through occupied France (nicknamed "Big Moustache") in the 1966 French film La Grande Vadrouille, which for over forty years remained the most successful film in the history of French cinema. Terry regularly played upper-class bounders and cads to perfection and was very much a loveable rogue always known for his gap-toothed smile. He co-starred opposite Max Miller in a 1959 BBC TV special, *Around the Town*, where he showed his full range of talents as a mimic and comedian. He was a gifted voice-artist and actor Ivan Owen based his voice for Basil Brush on Terry-Thomas's distinctive tones. In the 1970s Terry was diagnosed with Parkinson's Disease and his career and lifestyle went into decline. He was married twice, firstly to Ida Patlansky (1938-62) and then to Belinda Cunningham from 1963 until his death on 8 January 1990, Godalming, Surrey. He had two sons. His autobiography, *Terry-Thomas Tells Tales*, was published posthumously in 1992. Terry was a second cousin of actor Richard Briers, who because of Terry-Thomas's Parkinson's disease, became President of Parkinson's UK.

Thatcher, Heather (1896-1987) Born Heather Mary Thatcher, 3 September 1896, Pimlico, London. Actress. Stage debut: *The Girl from Ciro's* (1916). Screen debut: *The Prisoner of Zenda* (1915), as an uncredited extra, her first credited role being Alice Vaughan in *Altar Chains* (1916). After a rapid rise to top billing she put her film career on hold in 1920 to make a name for herself on the musical comedy stage, where she was reknowned for her Egyptian-style dancing. She returned to the big screen with the onset of the talkies in *The Plaything* (1929). Heather travelled to Hollywood in 1931 to attend the wedding of actor James Gleason and was contracted by MGM. As her career progressed she began to specialise in roles of quirky, eccentric aristocratic ladies beginning with Lady Joan Culver in *But the Flesh is Weak* (1932) and continuing as a Lady at the court of King Christian VII of Denmark in *The Dictator* (1935), Lady Kartegann in *Tovarich* (1937), The Queen in *If I Were King* (1938) and Lady Patricia Brandon in *Beau Geste* (1939). Heather also played the actress Anna Dora in the 1934 British comedy film *The Private Life of Don Juan*. During WWII she returned to England and toured Europe and Far East with ENSA. Towards the end of the war she played Lady Dalroy in *Gaslight* (1944) and then in peacetime, Countess Lydia Ivanova in *Anna Karenina* (1948), Mrs Whittle in *Will Any Gentleman...?* (1953) and, in her final film before her retirement, Lady Dawson in *The Deep Blue Sea* (1955). She died 15 February 1987, Hillingdon, London.

Thesiger, Ernest (1879-1961) Born Ernest Frederic Graham Thesiger, 15 January 1879, Chelsea, London. Actor. Son of Sir Edward Pierson Thesiger and grandson of the first Baron of Chelmsford. He was also the nephew of General Frederic Augustus Thesiger, 2nd Baron Chelmsford, who, exactly a week after Ernest's birth, famously led his troops in battle against the Zulu army at the Battle of Isandlwana. Ernest was educated at Marlborough College and the Slade School of Art and began life as a painter. Stage debut: Colonel Smith (1909). Having enlisted in the vain hope of being able to wear a kilt he was invalided out of the army in 1915. Screen debut: *The Real Thing at Last* (1916). At this time he was mainly a stage actor and was unequalled in drag roles. Ernest made two films in Hollywood with his friend, director James Whale: *The Old Dark House* (1932) and *Bride of Frankenstein* (1935 - as Dr. Septimus Pretorius) and featured opposite Will Hay in *My Learned Friend* (1943) and *Don't Take it to Heart* (1944). An outstanding character actor, especially in films with something of a macabre feel, he was capable of stealing a scene without apparently even trying. Other films include: *Nelson* (1918), *The Adventures of Mr Pickwick* (1921), *The Man Who Could Work Miracles* (1936), *They Drive by Night* (1938), *Henry V* (1944), *Caesar and Cleopatra* (1945), *The Ghosts of Berkeley Square* (1947), *The Winslow Boy* (1948), *Last Holiday*

(1950), *The Magic Box* (1951), *Laughter in Paradise* (1951), *The Man in the White Suit* (1951), *Scrooge* (1951), *The Robe* (1953), *Meet Mr. Lucifer* (1953), *The Million Pound Note* (1953), *Father Brown* (1954), *The Adventures of Quentin Durward* (1955), *Three Men in a Boat* (1956), *Doctor at Large* (1957), *The Truth About Women* (1958), *The Horse's Mouth* (1958), *Sons and Lovers* (1960), *The Roman Spring of Mrs Stone* (1961) and his last film appearance *Invitation to Murder* (1962). With an appearance perhaps best described as cadaverous he was famous for his eccentricities. An accomplished artist and embroiderer - he is said to have taken his handiwork with him into the trenches during WWI and been the crochet partner of Queen Mary. He had a book *Adventures in Embroidery* published in 1945. Autobiography: *Practically True* (1927). Appointed CBE in 1960. He died 14 January 1962, Kensington, London.

Thewlis, David (1963-) Born David Wheeler, 20 March 1963, Blackpool, Lancashire. Actor. Thewlis is his mother's maiden name. David trained at the Guildhall School of Music and Drama. Screen debut: *Road* (1987). He then featured in Mike Leigh's *Life is Sweet* (1990), *Afraid of the Dark* (1991), *Swords at Teatime* (1992), *Damage* (1992) and *The Trial* (1993) before making a breakthrough in Mike Leigh's *Naked* (1993). He has appeared in a wide variety of films which have emphasised his versatility including *Black Beauty* (1994), *Total Eclipse* (1995), *Restoration* (1995), *James and the Giant Peach* (1996), *Dragonheart* (1996), *The Island of Dr Moreau* (1996), *Seven Years in Tibet* (1997), *The Big Lebowski* (1998), *Divorcing Jack* (1998), *Gangster No.1* (2000), *Timeline* (2003), *Harry Potter and the Prisoner of Azkaban* (2004 – as Remus Lupin), *Kingdom of Heaven* (2005), *All the Invisible Children* (2005), *The New World* (2005), *Basic Instinct 2* (2006), *The Omen* (2006), *Harry Potter and the Order of the Phoenix* (2007), *The Boy in the Striped Pyjamas* (2008 - as Ralf), *Harry Potter and the Half-Blood Prince* (2009), *Veronika Decides to Die* (2009), *Mr. Nice* (2010), *London Boulevard* (2010), *Harry Potter and the Deathly Hallows: Part 1* (2010) and *Part II* (2011), *The Lady* (2011), *Anonymous* (2011 - as William Cecil, 1st Baron Burghley) and *War Horse* (2011 - as Lyons). He also wrote and directed *Hello, Hello, Hello* (1995) and *Cheeky* (2003) plus a novel: *The Late Hector Kipling* (2007). His television credits include *Oranges are not the Only Fruit* (1990), *Prime Suspect 3* (1993) and the American mini-series in which sentient dinosaurs and humans coexist *Dinotopia* (2002). David married Welsh actress and director Sara Sugarman in 1992 but they divorced in 1993. He has also had relationships with Bill Oddie's daughter Kate Hardie and actress Anna Friel, with whom he has a daughter Gracie Ellen Mary Friel (b. 9 July 2005). Although David and Anna were together throughout the first decade of the new millennium they have recently split up. See also entries in the television section for *A Bit of a Do*, and *The Street*.

Thomas, Gerald (1920-93) Born Gerald Cyril Thomas, 10 December 1920, Hull, Yorkshire. Director. Gerald studied to be a doctor but his training was interrupted by WWII, during which he served with the Royal Sussex Regiment. He then decided not to pursue a medical career and worked as assistant editor and then editor at Denham Studios alongside his brother Ralph. He next developed a working partnership with Peter Rogers. Their first film together was *Circus Friends* (1956) for The Children's Film Foundation. He went on to direct *The Vicious Circle* (1957), *Chain of Events* (1957), *Time Lock* (1957), *The Solitary Child* (1958) and *The Duke Wore Jeans* (1958), which starred Tommy Steele. In 1958 a drama named *The Bull Boys* based on a novel by R F Delderfield was rewritten as a comedy and renamed *Carry On Sergeant* (1958). Gerald went on to direct a further 29 of this formulaic but incredibly popular series. Made on a shoe-string and usually in only six weeks they tapped into a rich vein of British humour. His non-Carry On films include *Please Turn Over* (1959), *Twice Round the Daffodils* (1962), *The Iron Maiden* (1962), *The Big Job* (1965), *Bless This House* (1972) and *The Second Victory* (1986). He also provided the voice of Oddbod Junior in *Carry on Screaming!* (1966) and the voice of the Mynah bird in *Carry on Behind* (1975). Gerald was nicknamed 'The Headmaster' and on occasion 'The Ringmaster'. He died 9 November 1993, Beaconsfield, Buckinghamshire.

Thomas, Jeremy (1949-) Born Jeremy Jack Thomas, 26 July 1949, Ealing, London. Producer. Jeremey began as an editor but made his producing debut in 1976 with *Mad Dog Morgan*. Other early films include: *The Shout* (1978), *Bad Timing* (1980) and *Merry Christmas Mr Lawrence* (1983). He produced *The Last Emperor* (1987) which won an Academy Award for Best Picture. Other films include: *Let Him Have It* (1991), *Stealing Beauty* (1996), *Crash* (1996), *Sexy Beast* (2000), *Rabbit-Proof Fence* (2002), *Promised Land* (2004), *Dreaming Lhasa* (2005), *Heimat 3* (2004), *Tideland* (2005), *Thirteen Assassins* (2009), *Essential Killing* (2010), *A Dangerous Method* (2011) and Terry Gilliam's much-delayed *The Man Who Killed Don Quixote*. Jeremy directed and produced *All the Little Animals* (1998). He was chairman of the BFI (1993-97) and is the son of Ralph Thomas and nephew of Gerald Thomas.

Thomas, Ralph (1915-2001) Born Ralph Philip Thomas, 10 August 1915, Hull, Yorkshire. Director. Educated at Middlesex University College. Progressed from clapperboy to camera assistant and then editor (1932-39). Ralph served in 9th Lancers during WWII, being awarded the Military Cross. He joined the Rank Organisation at Gainsborough. Directorial debut: *Once Upon a Dream* (1947). Other early films include: *Traveller's Joy* (1949), *The Clouded Yellow* (1951) and *Appointment with Venus* (1951). He developed a successful collaboration with producer Betty Box. His direction of the very popular comedy *Doctor in the House* (1954) led to a series comprising *Doctor at Sea* (1955), *Doctor at Large* (1957), *Doctor in Love* (1960), *Doctor in Distress* (1963), *Doctor in Clover* (1966) and *Doctor in Trouble* (1970). Other films include: *Above Us the Waves* (1955), *The Iron Petticoat* (1956), *Campbell's Kingdom* (1957), *A Tale of Two Cities* (1958), *The 39 Steps* (1959), *Conspiracy of Hearts* (1960), *No Love for Johnnie* (1961), *The Wild and the Willing* (1962), *Quest for Love* (1971), *Percy* (1971), and *A Nightingale Sang in Berkeley Square* (1979). Father of Jeremy Thomas and brother of Gerald Thomas, he was also a nephew of producer Victor Saville. He died 17 March 2001, Westminster, London.

Thompson, Emma (1959-) Born 15 April 1959, Paddington, London. Actress. The daughter of English actor Eric Thompson (of *The Magic Roundabout* fame) and Scottish actress Phyllida Law. Her sister is actress Sophie Thompson. She read English Literature at Newnham College, Cambridge where she was a member of the *Footlights* comedy club. After Cambridge she sprung to fame with a leading role in the BBC drama serial *Fortunes of War* (1987), based on the novels of Olivia Manning, in which she played opposite Kenneth Branagh, whom she later married (1989). Her film debut was as Catherine of Valois in *Henry V* (1989) again opposite Brannagh, whom she appeared with in a number of productions before they divorced in 1995. Other films include: *The Tall Guy* (1989), *Dead Again* (1991), *Impromptu* (1991), *Peter's Friends* (1992), *The Remains of the Day* (1993), *In the Name of the Father* (1993), *Junior* (1994), *Carrington* (1995), Alan Rickman's directorial debut *The Winter Guest* (1997) opposite her mother, *Primary Colors* (1998), *Judas Kiss* (1998), *Maybe Baby* (2000), *Treasure Planet* (2002), *Imagining Argentina* (2003), *Love Actually* (2003), as Professor Sybil Trelawney in *Harry Potter and the Prisoner of Azkaban* (2004) and *Harry Potter and the Order of the Phoenix* (2007), an uncredited cameo in *I Am Legend* (2007 - as Dr Alice Krippin), a modern day Mary Poppins as *Nanny McPhee* (2005) and *Nanny McPhee and the Big Bang* (2010), *Brideshead Revisited* (2008), *Last Chance Harvey* (2008), *An Education* (2009), *The Boat That Rocked* (2009) and *Harry Potter and the Deathly Hallows Part II* (2011). Emma also voices the role of Queen Elinor in the upcoming American 3D computer-animated fantasy adventure film *Brave* (2012) and plays Agent O in the third *Men in Black* film due to be released in the summer. A very versatile lady both in front of and behind the camera she remains the only person to have won Academy Awards for both acting and writing, doing so with a Best Actress for *Howard's End* (1992) and a Best Adapted Screenplay for *Sense and Sensibility* (1995). Emma married actor Greg Wise in 2003 and they have one daughter Gaia Romilly Wise (b. 1999). In 2003, the couple unofficially adopted a 16-year-old Rwandan refugee, Tindyebwa Agaba. See also entries in the television section for *Alfresco, Fortunes of War, Saturday Live, Tutti Frutti*, and *The Young Ones*.

Thompson, J Lee (1914-2002) Born John Lee Thompson, 1 August 1914, Bristol. Director and writer. Educated at Dover College. As a member of Croydon Repertory had his first play *Murder Happens* staged in 1934. On the scenario staff of *Associated British Pictures* for five years. Screen writing debut: *The Price of Folly* (1937), followed by *The Middle Watch* (1940) and *East of Picadilly* (1941). He served in the RAF during WWII. After the war he wrote *No Place for Jennifer* (1950) and then made his directorial debut with an adaptation of his own play *Murder without Crime* (1950). His next projects were the self-penned dramas *The Yellow Balloon* (1953) and *The Weak and the Wicked* (1953) and two comedies *For Better, For Worse* (1954) and *An Alligator Named Daisy* (1955), followed by the crime drama *Yield to the Night* (1956), in which Diana Dors gave a strong performance. He directed a remake of *The Good Companions* (1957) and the highly acclaimed domestic dramas *Woman in a Dressing Gown* (1957), *No Trees in the Street* (1958) and *Tiger Bay* (1959) as well as the classic war movie *Ice Cold in Alex* (1958) and the colonial adventure story *North West Frontier* (1959). The success of this last led to his being picked to helm the international box office smash *The Guns of Navarone* (1961) which gained him an Academy Award nomination for Best Director. He followed this with the chilling *Cape Fear* (1962) and the epic *Taras Bulba* (1962). His other major films include *What a Way to Go!* (1964), *John Goldfarb, Please Come Home* (1965), *Return from the Ashes* (1965), *Eye of the Devil* (1967), *McKenna's Gold* (1969), *Conquest of the Planet of the Apes* (1972), *Battle for the Planet of the Apes* (1973), the musical film Huckleberry Finn (1974), *The Greek Tycoon* (1978), *King Solomon's Mines* (1985), *Death Wish 4: The Crackdown* (1987) and his final film *Kinjite: Forbidden Subjects* (1989). Nicknamed "Mighty Mouse" by Gregory Peck, he died 30 August 2002, Sooke, British Colombia, Canada.

Thompson, Sophie (1962 -) Born 20 January 1962, Hampstead, London. Actress. The younger sister of Emma Thompson. She began with small television roles before her film debut as an uncredited mission girl in *The Missionary* (1982). Sophie's next film was *Twenty-One* (1991 - as Francesca), followed by *Four Weddings and a Funeral* (1994) - as one of the brides, *Emma* (1996), Dancing at Lughnasa (1998), *Relative Values* (2000), *Gosford Park* (2001), *Nicholas Nickleby* (2002), *Fat Slags* (2004 – as Tracy), *Morris: A Life with Bells On* (2009), *Eat Pray Love* (2010) and *Harry Potter and the Deathly Hallows Part I* (2010 - as Mafalda Hopkirk). In 1999 she won the Laurence Olivier Theatre Award for Best Actress in a Musical for her performance in *Into the Woods*. Sophie is perhaps best known for her role of child abuser Stella Crawford in the BBC1 soap opera *EastEnders* (2006-07). She has been married to actor Richard Lumsden since 1995. They have two sons, Ernie James (b. 1997) and Walter Eric (b. 2000) and live in London.

Thorndike, Sybil (1882-1976) Born Agnes Sybil Thorndike, 24 October 1882, Gainsborough, Lincolnshire. Actress. Daughter of a clergyman. The grand dame of the British stage. She began as a pianist but her nerves caused piano cramp and she was forced to divert her attention to acting. Stage debut: *The Merry Wives of Windsor* (1904). She spent much of her early stage career touring Europe, North America and the Commonwealth before joining the Old Vic during WWI. G B Shaw wrote *Saint Joan* especially for her in 1924 and she played the role until 1941. Although known more for her theatre successes she made her screen debut in *Moth and Rust* (1921) and played Esmeralda in *The Hunchback of Notre Dame* (1922). Other early screen roles include Lady Macbeth in *Macbeth* (1922), Portia in *The Merchant of Venice* (1922), the title role in *Jane Shore* (1922) and, of course, *Saint Joan* (1927). Other films include *Dawn* (1928) - playing Nurse Edith Cavell, *Hindle Wakes* (1931), *Major Barbara* (1941), *Nicholas Nickleby* (1947), *The Prince and the Showgirl* (1957), *Alive and Kicking* (1959) and her final film *Uncle Vanya* (1963). On television Dame Sybil appeared in *A Passage To India* (1965) as Mrs Moore and made her final screen appearance in the Ned Sherrin-directed TV film The Great Inimitable Mr Dickens (1970). Her last stage performance was at The Thorndike Theatre in Leatherhead, Surrey, in *There Was an Old Woman* in 1969. Dame Sybil was married to actor and director Lewis Casson from 1908 until his death in 1969. They had four children. When once asked if she ever considered leaving her husband, she famously replied "Divorce, never! Murder, often!" She was made a Dame of the Order of the British Empire in 1931 and a Companion of Honour in 1970. The Thorndike Theatre in Leatherhead was named in her honour and opened in 1969, when she made her farewell stage appearance. She died 9 June 1976, Chelsea, London. Her ashes are buried in Westminster Abbey. In the upcoming film *My Week with Marilyn*, she will be played by Dame Judi Dench.

Todd, Ann (1909-93) Born 24 January 1909, Hartford, Cheshire. Actress. She made her screen debut in *These Charming People* (1931) and her other early films include *The Ghost Train* (1931), *Things to Come* (1936) and *South Riding* (1938) but it wasn't until after WWII that she became a star. In 1947 she played emotionally fragile pianist Francesca Cunningham in *The Seventh Veil* opposite a sadistic James Mason and this role made her reputation. Unfortunately her next few films, including Hitchcock's *The Paradine Case* (1947) made in Hollywood, did little to enhance it. She married director David Lean (1949-57) and he directed her in *The Passionate Friends* (1949), *Madeleine* (1950) and *The Sound Barrier* (1952). Ann was previously married to Victor Malcolm, a grandson of Lillie Langtry, and her second marriage was to author Nigel Tangye 1945-49, Lean's cousin. Ann's other films include: *The Green Scarf* (1954), *Time Without Pity* (1957), *Taste of Fear* (1961), *Ninety Degrees in the Shade* (1965), *The Fiend* (1972), *The Human Factor* (1979) and *Maelstrom* (1985). Ann was known as the "pocket Garbo" for her diminutive, blond beauty. She joined the Old Vic in the 1950s before eventually turning her hand to directing travelogues. She made a few television appearances after this including her last in an episode of *Maigret* in 1992. Autobiography: *The Eighth Veil* (1980). She died 6 May 1993, Kensington, London. See also entry in the television section for *Love Story*.

Todd, Richard (1919-2009) Born Richard Andrew Palethorpe Todd, 11 June 1919, Dublin. Actor. Son of an army doctor he spent his childhood in India and then Devon. Educated at Shrewsbury Public School. Richard trained for a military career at Sandhurst before deciding on an acting career with hopes of becoming a playwright, initially training at the Italia Conti Academy before founding the Dundee Repertory Theatre in 1939. He served with the Yorkshire Light Infantry and then the 7th Battalion (LI) Parachute Regiment during WWII and was involved in the fight at Pegasus Bridge during D-Day, a scenario he also acted in during both *D Day The 6th of June* (1956) and *The Longest Day* (1962). He returned to the stage immediately after the war and made his screen debut in *The Hasty Heart* (1949), picking up an Academy Award nomination for Best Actor for reprising a role he had played with success on stage. After Hitchcock's *Stage Fright* (1950) he starred in many costume dramas and swashbucklers including *The Story of Robin Hood and his Merrie Men* (1952 – as Robin), *The Sword and the Rose* (1953 – as Charles Brandon), *Rob Roy, The Highland Rogue* (1954 – as Rob Roy), *The Virgin Queen* (1955 – as Sir Walter Raleigh) and *Saint Joan* (1957 – as Dunois). He also starred in possibly his most popular role as Wing Commander Guy Gibson in *The Dam Busters* (1954). Other films include *Yangtse Incident* (1957), *Danger Within* (1959), *The Long and the Short and the Tall* (1960), *Don't Bother to Knock* (1961), *The Very Edge* (1962), *Operation Crossbow* (1965), *Blood Bath* (1966), *Dorian Gray* (1970), *The Big Sleep* (1978), *House of the Long Shadows* (1983) and *Murder One* (1988), his final film. Richard's last screen roles include Mr Barnes in the ITV mini-series Last Place On Earth (1985) and Harold Beecham in an episode of Heartbeat in 2007. He wrote an autobiography: *Caught in the Act* (1986) and was awarded an OBE in 1993. Richard was married to actress Catherine Grant-Bogle in 1949 and they had a son Peter (1952–2005) and a daughter Fiona. He divorced Catherine in 1970 and married model Virginia Mailer, with whom he had two sons, Andrew and Seumas (1977–1997). Richard had his fair share of

grief. His estranged mother committed suicide when he was 19 (said to be severely depressed at her son's choice of career) and in 1997, Seumus shot himself in the head in the family home in Lincolnshire and on 21 September 2005, Peter killed himself with a shotgun in East Malling, Kent, following marital difficulties, before he himself died in his sleep at his Little Humby home on 3 December 2009, after a long battle with cancer. See also entry in the television section for *Last Place On Earth*.

Tomlinson, David (1917-2000) Born David Cecil Tomlinson, 7 May 1917, Henley-on-Thames, Oxfordshire. Actor. Son of a solicitor. Educated at Tonbridge School. Served briefly in the Grenadier Guards and as a clerk before taking to the stage. Screen debut: *Quiet Wedding* (1940). After *Pimpernel Smith* (1941) he joined the RAF for the duration of WWII and after the war famously crashed a Tiger Moth plane near his backyard much to the annoyance of his neighbours. Other films include: *The Way to the Stars* (1945), *Sleeping Car to Trieste* (1948), *My Brother's Keeper* (1948), *Miranda* (1948), *So Long at the Fair* (1950), *The Wooden Horse* (1950), *The Magic Box* (1951), *All For Mary* (1955), *Three Men in a Boat* (1956), *Up the Creek* (1958), *Further Up the Creek* (1958) and *Tom Jones* (1963). He starred in a series of films for Disney including his best loved role as Mr George Banks in *Mary Poppins* (1964), Peter Thorndyke in *The Love Bug* (1968) and Emelius Browne in *Bedknobs and Broomsticks* (1971). His last film was *The Fiendish Plot of Dr Fu Manchu* (1980). He wrote an autobiography: *Luckier Than Most: An Autobiography* (1992). David's first marriage, to Mary Lindsay Hiddingh lasted for two months in 1943 but his second, to actress Audrey Freeman lasted from 17 May 1953 until his death on 24 June 2000 Winslow, Buckinghamshire.

Torrence, David (1864-1951) Born David Bryce Thomson, 17 January 1864, South Leith, Edinburgh. Actor. Educated in Edinburgh, England and Germany. The son of a banker, he worked as an apprentice salesman before taking up acting. David made his stage debut in the United States in 1892 and was on Broadway from 1900. He made his screen debut as Michael of Strelsau in *Prisoner of Zenda* (1913) and after *Tess of the D'Urbervilles* (1913) he returned to the stage and for a while retired to a ranch in Mexico. David returned to the screen with *The Inside of the Cup* (1921) and appeared in more than 100 films over the next 18 years including *Annie Laurie* (1927), *Disreali* (1929), *A Successful Calamity* (1932), *Bonnie Scotland* (1935), *Mutiny on the Bounty* (1935), *Captain Blood* (1935), *Lost Horizon* (1937), *Stanley and Livingstone* (1939) and *Rulers of the Sea* (1939). After a 14-year hiatus David made his final film appearance as the prison governor in *Botany Bay* (1953). During his career David moved from playing leads in the silent era to more character parts in talkies. He was the elder brother of Ernest Torrence. David died 26 December 1951, Los Angeles, California.

Torrence, Ernest (1878-1933) Born Ernest Torrance Thomson, 26 June 1878, Edinburgh. Actor and vocalist. Ernest was the younger brother of actor David Torrence. Educated at Edinburgh Academy, Stuttgart Conservatorium and the Royal Academy of Music, London. Stage debut: *The Emerald Isle* (1901). He was a member of the D'Oyly Carte Opera Company. In 1911 Ernest traveled to America to act on Broadway but returned to Britain during WWI. He made his screen debut in *A Dangerous Affair* (1919) before again returning to Broadway. Ernest's career took a change of direction when he was cast as the evil Luke Hatburn in his first Hollywood film *Tol'able David* (1922). After that he was often to be seen in the role of the heavy (he was 6' 4" tall and solid) but usually with a touch of compassion or humour. Films include: *The Trail of the Lonesome Pine* (1923), *The Hunchback of Notre Dame* (1923), *The Covered Wagon* (1923), *Peter Pan* (1924 - as Captain Hook), *Mantrap* (1926), *The King of Kings* (1927), *Steamboat Bill Jr* (1928), *Fighting Caravans* (1931) and *Sherlock Holmes* (1932 - as Professor Moriarty). Also a composer, song writer and accomplished pianist, Ernest had just completed what turned out to be his final film role in *I Cover the Water Front* (1933), in which he starred (as a smuggler) opposite Claudette Colbert, when he suffered an acute attack of gall stones while en route to Europe by ship, and was rushed back to a New York hospital but died later of complications following surgery on 15 May 1933. According to *The Times* "There was certainly no man more popular.... than Mr Torrence, who revelled in villainy on the screen but was kindness personified in private life.".

Towb, Harry (1925-2009) Born 27 July 1925 Larne, County Antrim. Actor. Harry took up acting as a teenager and moved to London after WWII. Screen debut: *The Quiet Woman* (1950). Other films include *Above the Waves* (1955), *The 39 Steps* (1959), *The Scarlet Blade* (1963), *The Blue Max* (1966), *Prudence and the Pill* (1968), *Patton* (1970), *Barry Lyndon* (1975), *Rosie Dixon - Night Nurse* (1978), *Lamb* (1985), *Moll Flanders* (1996), *The Most Fertile Man in Ireland* (1999), *Conspiracy of Silence* (2003) and *Cheeky* (2003). A well known face on television, his credits include *The Army Game, The Avengers, Callan, Casualty, The Bill, Minder, Doctor Who, Heartbeat, Emmerdale Farm,* and *Brighton Belles*. An accomplished writer with over twenty radio short stories and radio plays to his credit including *A Candle for Casey* (2003). Harry was married to actress Diana Hoddinott (b. 1945) from 1965 until his death from cancer, 24 July 2009, London. See also entries in the television section for *Home James,* and *So You Think You've Got Troubles*.

Townsend, Stuart (1972-) Born 15 December 1972, Howth, County Dublin. Actor and director. Son of professional golfer Peter Townsend (member of the Great Britain and Ireland Ryder Cup team in 1969 and 1971). Trained at the Gaiety School of Acting, Dublin. Stuart made his screen debut in a couple of shorts before his first feature *Trojan Eddie* (1996). He gained wider recognition in *Shooting Fish* (1997) alongside Kate Beckinsale, and followed this with *Under the Skin* (1997), *Resurrection Man* (1998), *Simon Magus* (1999), *Wonderland* (1999), *The Venice Project* (1999), *Mauvaise Passe* (1999) and *About Adam* (2000). He was then cast as Aragorn in the *Lord of the Rings* trilogy but replaced by the much older Viggo Mortensen after a few days. He recovered from this disappointment by taking the role of Lestat de Lioncourt in an adaptation of Anne Rice's *Queen of the Damned* (2002). His next projects were *Trapped* (2002), *Shade* (2003) and then played Dorian Gray in *The League of Extraordinary Gentlemen* (2003). In 2004 he featured alongside his then fiancé Charlize Theron in *Head in the Clouds* (2004). At this time Stuart starred in the short-lived ABC television series *Night Stalker* (2005). Recent films include *The Best Man* (2005), *Chaos Theory* (2007) and *Maggie Hill* (2009). Stuart made his directorial debut with the 2008 film *Battle in Seattle*, which again starred Charlize Theron, whom he met on the set of *Trapped* and subsequently lived with until they split in January 2010.

Travers, Bill (1922-94) Born William Inglis Lindon-Travers, 3 January 1922, Newcastle-upon-Tyne, Tyne & Weir. Actor. Bill was the younger brother of actress Linden Travers. He made his stage debut in 1947 and his screen debut came in *The Wooden Horse* (1950). Other early films include *Hindle Wakes* (1952), *The Story of Robin Hood and his Merrie Men* (1952), *The Planter's Wife* (1952), *Mantrap* (1953) and *Romeo and Juliet* (1954). Bill came to prominence as the hammer thrower *Geordie* (1955). He starred with his second wife Virginia McKenna (married from 1957 until his death) in a number of films : *The Barretts of Wimpole Street* (1957), *The Smallest Show on Earth* (1957), *Passionate Summer* (1958), *Two Living, One Dead* (1961), the highly popular *Born Free* (1966), *Ring of Bright Water* (1969) and *An Elephant Called Slowly* (1969).Together they founded *Zoo Check*, in 1984, which focuses on the plight of animals in both zoos and circuses, and in 1991 the *Born Free Foundation* which extended the remit to cover animals in their natural habitats. His last film was *The Belstone Fox* (1973). Bill wrote, directed and produced *The Lion at World's End* (1971). He died 29 March 1994, Dorking, Surrey. Bill had five children, one with his first wife Pat Rains and four with Virginia McKenna. See also entry for *Lorna Doone* in the television section.

Travers, Henry (1874-1965) Born Travers John Heagerty, 5 March 1874, Prudhoe, Northumberland. Actor. Stage debut: *The Famine* (1895). Settled in the United States from 1901. Had a long stage career before making his screen debut recreating a stage role in *Reunion in Vienna* (1933). A much loved character actor whose films include *The Invisible Man* (1933), *After Office Hours* (1935), *Escapade* (1935), *Dodge City* (1939), *Dark Victory* (1939), *High Sierra* (1941), *Random Harvest* (1942), *Madame Curie* (1943), *The Bell's of St Mary's* (1945) and *The Girl from Jones Beach* (1949). His best known roles are as Professor Jerome in *Ball of Fire* (1941), Mr Ballard in *Mrs Miniver* (1942) for which he gained an Academy Award nomination for Best Supporting Actor, Joseph Newton in Hitchcock's *Shadow of a Doubt* (1943) and, of course, as guardian angel second class Clarence Oddbody in *It's a Wonderful Life* (1946). He died 18 October 1965 Hollywood, California.

Travers, Linden (1913-2001) Born Florence Lindon-Travers, 27 May 1913, Houghton-le-Spring, Tyne & Weir. Actress. Educated at Convent de la Sagesse. Stage debut: *Cynara* (1933). Screen debut: *Children of the Fog* (1935). Her other films include *Brief Ecstasy* (1937), *Bank Holiday* (1938), *The Lady Vanishes* (1938) - as Cecil Parker's mistress "Mrs" Todhunter - *The Stars Look Down* (1940), *Jassy* (1947), *Quartet* (1948), *The Bad Lord Byron* (1949) and, her last, *Christopher Columbus* (1949). She also starred as Miss Blandish in *No Orchids for Miss Blandish* (1948), a film which was described as a "sickening exhibition of brutality, perversion, sex and sadism" and was banned for some years - a sort of 1940's "video nasty". A far cry from her turns opposite Tommy Trinder in *Almost a Honeymoon* (1938), Arthur Askey in *The Ghost Train* (1941) and George Formby in *South American George* (1941). She married Guy Leon and then James Holman from 1948 until his death in 1974. She retired from acting in 1949 although did come back temporarily on television to make a final screen appearance as Martha Loring in the hugely popular series *Sea Hunt* (1960). Linden was the elder sister of actor Bill Travers. She died 23 October 2001, Penzance, Cornwall.

Trevelyan, John (1903-86) Born 11 July 1903, Bromley, Kent. Censor. A teacher who went on to work in local government as an educational administrator. Joined the British Board of Film Censors in 1951 as an examiner and became Secretary in 1958. Responsible for extensive liberalisation of film censorship, insisting that artistic integrity should be taken into account when applying the examination rules. Under his regime several controversial films were passed by the BBFC virtually uncut. John retired from the BBFC in 1971. Autobiography: *What the Censor Saw* (1973). He died 15 August 1986, Croydon, Greater London.

Trinder, Tommy (1909-89) Born Thomas Edward Trinder, 24 March 1909, Streatham, London. Comedian and actor. Son of a tram driver. On the stage by the age of twelve after winning a talent show as a singer at the Collins Music Hall, Islington. Tommy joined Caseys Court until his voice broke, forcing him to become an errand boy for a time before going back to the halls as a comedian and touring for many years. He featured in the revues *Tune In* (1937) and *In Town Tonight* (1937) which brought him enough recognition to make a screen debut in *Save a Little Sunshine* (1938). Early films include: *Almost a Honeymoon* (1938) and *She Couldn't Say No* (1938). He starred in *Sailors Three* (1940) alongside Claude Hulbert and Michael Wilding. Tommy went on to star or feature in a series of Ealing films: *The Foreman Went to France* (1942), *Went the Day Well?* (1942), *The Bells Go Down* (1943), *Fiddlers Three* (1944), *Champagne Charlie* (1944) and *Bitter Springs* (1950). After that his screen career took a back seat as his stage and television career took off. Fast-talking and quick-thinking, Tommy's cheeky avuncular patter, had only been seen spasmodically on television until he began a long run (complete with trademark pork pie hat and wagging finger) as the first compere of the ATV variety show *Val Parnell's Sunday Night At The London Palladium* in 1955. He was the perfect host for such a show as he always gave the impression he had seen it all and done even more, which of course he had done, having started his professional career in 1922. He made one subsequent television series, the Denis Goodwin written *Trinder Box* (1959). Tommy was a lifelong devoted supporter of Fulham Football Club and was chairman of the club between 1959 and 1976. Tommy's final films include *You Lucky People* (1955 – his catchphrase), *The Beauty Jungle* (1964) and *Barry McKenzie Holds his Own* (1974). He was appointed CBE in 1975 and died 10 July 1989, Chertsey, Surrey. See also entries in the radio and television section for *Just A Minute*, and *Sunday Night at the London Palladium*.

Turgoose, Thomas (1992-) Born 11 February 1992, Grimsby, Lincolnshire. Actor. Thomas is the youngest of four brothers. His parents Rob Eggleston and Sharon Turgoose separated when he was one year old and Thomas was brought up by his mother, using her maiden name. Due to Sharon's chronic illness Thomas lost much of his schooling and was placed on a scheme for troubled children, The Space Project, where he was spotted by a casting director. Thomas famously demanded, and received, a £5 fee for his first audition, although he later explained that it was mainly because he was convinced he wouldn't get the part. In his first film role in 2006, he played the lead character, Shaun, in *This Is England*, written and directed by Shane Meadows. His almost disturbingly real performance won him the British Independent Film Award for Most Promising Newcomer. Thomas again co-starred with Stephen Graham in *The Innocence Project* on television before playing Tomo in another Shane Meadows film *Somers Town* (2008), set in Somers Town, an area of the London Borough of Camden, south of Camden Town. His other films to-date are the thriller *Eden Lake* (2008 – as Cooper) and Tom Harper's directorial debut film, *The Scouting Book For Boys* (2010). Thomas reprised his role of Shaun in the television sequels *This is England '86* and *This is England '88*. See also entry in television section for *The Innocence Project* and *This is England '86*.

Tushingham, Rita (1942-) Born 14 March 1942, Garston, Liverpool. Actress. Educated at Convent de la Sagesse. Easily recognisable by her soulful "doe eyes" she made her stage debut in 1960. Her screen debut followed shortly afterwards as Jo in the kitchen-sink drama *A Taste of Honey* (1961), which brought her overnight fame. Her other films include *A Place to Go* (1963), *Girl with Green Eyes* (1963), *The Leather Boys* (1964), *The Knack ...and How to Get It* (1965), *Doctor Zhivago* (1965), *The Trap* (1966), *Smashing Time* (1967), *The Bed Sitting Room* (1969), *Straight on Till Morning* (1972) and *The 'Human' Factor* (1975). Rita married the photographer Terry Bicknell in 1962. They had two daughters, Dodonna and Aisha. After their divorce Rita worked in Europe initially but married Iraqi cinematographer Ousama Rawi in 1981, and spent eight years in Canada with him and her two children. After her second divorce she returned to the screen in England, initially starring on television as Celia Higgins in the popular comedy series, *Bread* (1988). *An Awfully Big Adventure* (1995) was her next film and she has since made several appearances including *Under the Skin* (1997), *Being Julia* (2004), the film short *Loneliness and the Modern Pentathlon* (2005), *Telstar: The Joe Meek Story* (2008), *The Calling* (2009) and the upcoming *Outside Bet* (2012). Rita now divides her time between Germany and London, with her partner since the mid-1990s, writer Hans-Heinrich Ziemann.

Twickenham Studios (1913-) Converted from an ice-rink in St Margaret's, Twickenham in 1913 by the *London Film Company*. First film: *The House of Temperley* (1913). Acquired by the short-lived *Alliance Company* (1918-22) before being leased to various companies (1923-28). Films made during this period include: *The Flag Lieutenant* (1926) and *The Only Way* (1925). The studio was bought by the newly formed *Twickenham Film Studios Limited* in 1928, a company which included actor Henry Edwards as one of its directors. Films made before WWII include: *The Crooked Staircase* (1928), *The Call of the Sea* (1930), *The Man Who Changed his Name* (1934), *Squibs* (1935), *Scrooge* (1935), *Juggernaut* (1937) and *The Man in the Mirror* (1936). The studios ran into financial difficulty and closed in 1938, just after completion of Carol Reed's *The Stars Look Down* (1939). Following bomb damage during WWII, Twickenham re-opened in 1946, and concentrated on short films and television programmes until 1960 when *Saturday Night and Sunday Morning* was made at Twickenham and after this the cinematic output of the studios increased. In addition to the Beatle's *Hard Day's Night* (1964), *Help!* (1965) and *Let it Be* (1970), films made at Twickenham include: *Alfie* (1966), *The Italian Job* (1969), *Juggernaut* (1974), *The Eagle has Landed* (1976), *The Mirror Crack'd* (1980), *An American Werewolf in London* (1981), *Reds* (1981), *The French Lieutenant's Woman* (1981), *1984* (1984), *A Fish Called Wanda* (1988), *Shirley Valentine* (1989), *Interview with the Vampire: The*

Vampire Chronicles (1994), *Sweet Revenge* (1998), *Layer Cake* (2004), *Burke and Hare* (2010) and *Bel Ami* (2011). In the field of television, series ranging from *Poirot* to *Horrible Histories* have headed up a wide-ranging array of drama, comedy and children's programmes. The studios are set to close in June 2012.

Tyson, Cathy (1965-) Born 12 June 1965, Kingston-upon-Thames, London. Actress. The daughter of a black barrister from Trinidad and a white English social worker mother, the family moved to Liverpool when Cathy was two-years-old. She dropped out of college aged 17 to pursue acting at Liverpool's Everyman's Youth Theatre. This was perhaps a natural persuasion as Cathy is the niece of actress Cicely Tyson. After appearing in the Liverpool-based TV series *Scully* (1984), she became an overnight success in her first film *Mona Lisa* (1986) playing Simone, a high-class call girl. Since then she has starred in the Wes Craven horror film *The Serpent and the Rainbow* (1988) and appeared with Craig Charles in *Business as Usual* (1989). Her other rare film appearances include *Turbulence* (1991), *Priest* (1994), *The Old Man Who Read Love Stories* (2001) and *Ollie Kepler's Expanding Purple World* (2010). Better known for her television roles she has played Carol Johnson in *Band of Gold* (1995-97) and the sequel *Gold* (1997), Miss Gayle in *Grange Hill* (2005-07) and more recently, one-off appearances in *Emmerdale*, *Doctors* and *Lewis*. Off screen she was married to actor Craig Charles (1984-89) and the couple have one son, Jack (b. May 1988).

Unsworth, Geoffrey (1914-78) Born Geoffrey Gilyard Unsworth, 1914, Leigh, Lancashire. Cinematographer. Worked for *Gaumont-British* (1932-37). Whilst employed by Technicolor he worked as a camera operator on *The Life and Death of Colonel Blimp* (1943) and *A Matter of Life and Death* (1946). Having moved to the *Rank Organisation* in 1946, his full feature debut as cinematographer was *The Laughing Lady* (1946) and he followed this by working on a series of *Gainsborough Pictures* costume dramas including *The Man Within* (1947) and *Jassy* (1947). Other films during this period include *A Town Like Alice* (1956), *Hell Drivers* (1957), *The World of Suzie Wong* (1960) and *Tamahine* (1963). From the early 1960s he worked on epic productions such as *The 300 Spartans* (1962), *Genghis Khan* (1965), *2001: A Space Odyssey* (1968), *Cromwell* (1970) and *A Bridge Too Far* (1977). He gained an Academy Award nomination for Best Cinematography for his work on *Becket* (1964) and won for *Cabaret* (1972). A further Academy Award nomination for Best Cinematography followed for *Murder on the Orient Express* (1974). Richard Donner puts much of the success of *Superman* (1977) down to Unsworth's development of blue screen techniques used for the flying sequences. Geoffrey was awarded the OBE in 1976. He died 28 October 1978, Brittany, France whilst filming *Tess* (1979) for which he was awarded a posthumous Academy Award for Best Cinematography (shared with Ghislain Cloquet).

Urban, Charles (1867-1942) Born Carl Urban, 15 April 1867, Cincinnati, Ohio. Anglo-American film director and producer. Started his working career as a book-seller before he began selling tyrpewriters and phonographs in Detroit. He then managed a Kinetoscope and Phonograph parlour and his connections to the Edison company led to him becoming selling agent for the Edison Vitascope. In 1897 he became manager of the London branch of Maguire and Baucus, agents for Edison films in Europe. Charles reformed the company as *Warwick Trading Company* and marketed his own Bioscope projector. He was then joined by Cecil Hepworth for a brief period, who invented an automatic developing system. Charles worked with G A Smith, James Williamson and engineer Alfred Darling, in Brighton and with cameramen and cinematographers all around the world including George Melies, Joe Rosenthal and Lumiere. In 1903, he created a sixty-second- long, science film, *The Cheese Mites*, consisting of cheese mites crawling all over a piece of Stilton. The following year he recorded a twelve-minute silent documentary, *Living London*, featuring Londoners going about their business on a typical day. Charles then published a manifesto stating his belief in film as an educative force: *The Cinematograph in Science, Education and Matters of State* (1907). In 1908 he opened Urbana House, thus establishing the first film business in Wardour Street. He famously lost a court case brought against his company by

Friese-Green in respect of their respective colour film processes and in 1908, he developed a two-colour process with George Albert Smith (1864–1959) called Kinemacolor and formed his own company, the *Charles Urban Trading Company* (*Urbanora*). His most famous Kinemacolor film was a two and a half hour epic, *With Our King and Queen Through India* (1912), also known as *The Durbar in Delhi*, depicting the December 1911 Delhi Durbar celebrating the coronation of George V. Charles became a figurehead of the pre-WWI British film industry and during the war produced propaganda films such as *Britain Prepared* and *Fight for the Dardanelles* (1915) and he edited the classic documentary *The Battle of the Somme* (1916). Charles then returned to the United States to re-establish himself. He published cine-magazines and opened a studio at Irvington-on-Hudson, founding the *Urban Motion Picture Industries Inc.* He next made the films *The Four Seasons* (1921), *Permanent Peace* (1921) and *Evolution* (1925) before his company went bankrupt. Charles returned to Britain in 1929 and retired from the film business. He died 29 August 1942, Brighton, East Sussex.

Ure, Mary (1933-75) Born Mary Eileen Ure, 18 February 1933, Glasgow. Actress. Studied at the Glasgow School of Drama and then the Central School of Speech and Drama in London. Her first film was Alexander Korda's *Storm Over the Nile* (1955), a remake of *The Four Feathers*. Known for her outstanding beauty, Mary began performing on the London stage and quickly developed a reputation for her abilities as a dramatic actress. In 1956 while starring in John Osborne's play, *Look Back in Anger*, she began a relationship with the married Osborne and after he obtained a divorce they married in 1957. Mary travelled to New York in 1958 to star in the Broadway production of *Look Back in Anger* and earned a Tony Award nomination. That same year Mary starred in the film version of the play. In 1960, she appeared as Clara Dawes in the film version of Lawrence's *Sons and Lovers* for which she was nominated for both the Golden Globe Award and the Academy Award for Best Supporting Actress. In 1963 she divorced Osborne and married Robert Shaw. Her other films include, *Windom's Way* (1957), *The Mind Benders* (1963), *The Luck of Ginger Coffey* (1964), *Custer of the West* (1967), *Where Eagles Dare* (1968) and her ninth, and final, film *Reflection of Fear* (1973). Alcohol-induced depression blighted Mary's late career and she was fired from the 1974 pre-Broadway production of Love for Love and replaced by her understudy Glenn Close. Mary died from an overdose of tranquillisers and whisky on 3 April 1975, Westminster, London. At the time of her death she was appearing in the Don Taylor play *The Exorcism* on the London stage.

Ustinov, Peter (1921-2004) Born Peter Alexander Ustinov, 16 April 1921, Swiss Cottage, London. Actor, director, producer, writer. Educated at Westminster School. Studied at the London Theatre Studio. Stage debut: *Swinging the Gate* (1940). During WWII he briefly served as batman to David Niven. Peter spent most of the war working for the *Army Film Unit*, whilst also making his screen debut in *One of Our Aircraft is Missing* (1942). In the same year he also appeared in *The Goose Steps Out* (1942). He wrote and appeared in *The Way Ahead* (1944); wrote, directed and produced *School for Secrets* (1946), about the new radar devices, and *Vice Versa* (1948) and wrote, directed, produced and featured in *Private Angelo* (1949). Peter gained an Academy Award nomination for Best Supporting Actor for his role of Nero in *Quo Vadis* (1951), the director Mervyn LeRoy having given him the advice "The way I see Nero, this is the kinda guy who plays with himself nights". Peter played The Prince of Wales in *Beau Brummell* (1954) before winning a Best Supporting Actor Academy Award for his role as the slave trader Lentulus Batiatus in *Spartacus* (1960). He then wrote, produced, directed and appeared in *Romanoff and Juliet* (1961) based on his own play, and *Billy Budd* (1962). He won a second Academy Award for Best Supporting Actor for *Topkapi* (1964). His other films include *Odette* (1950), *Hotel Sahara* (1951), *We're No Angels* (1955), *Lola Montes* (1955), *The Sundowners* (1960), *Blackbeard's Ghost* (1968), *Logan's Run* (1976), *The Last Remake of Beau Geste* (1977), *Memed My Hawk* (1984) - which he also wrote and

directed, *Lorenzo's Oil* (1992) and *Luther* (2003). He starred on film as Hercule Poirot in *Death on the Nile* (1978), *Evil Under the Sun* (1982) and *Appointment with Death* (1988) and also on television. Peter wrote his first play *House of Regrets* (1941) at the age of 19 and this was followed by *Blow Your Own Trumpet* (1943), *The Banbury Nose* (1944),*The Tragedy of Good Intentions* (1945), *The Indifferent Shepherd* (1948), *Frenzy* (1948), *The Man in the Raincoat* (1949), *The Love of Four Colonels* (1949), *The Moment of Truth* (1951), *High Balcony* (1952), *No Sign of the Dove* (1953), *Photo Finish* (1962), *The Life in My Hands* (1964), *Halfway Up the Tree* (1967), *The Unknown Soldier and his Wife* (1968) and *Beethoven's Tenth* (1983). He was also nominated for an Academy Award for Best Original Screenplay for *Hot Millions* (1968). Peter became a CBE in 1975 and was knighted in 1990. He was also a Goodwill Ambassador for UNICEF (1969-2004). Just for good measure this outrageously talented actor and raconteur wrote the novels *The Loser* (1961) and *Krumnagel* (1971) and the autobiography: *Dear Me* (1977). Peter was married three times, firstly to Isolde Denham (1940–1950), the half-sister of Angela Lansbury. Their daughter is Tamara Ustinov. His second marriage was to Suzanne Cloutier (1954–1971). They had three children, two daughters, Pavla Ustinov and Andrea Ustinov, and a son Igor Ustinov. His third and final marriage was to Helene du Lau d Allemans, which lasted from 1972 until his death on 28 March 2004, Genolier, Vaud, Switzerland. See also entries in the radio and television section for *In All Directions* and *Jesus of Nazareth*

Vaughan, Peter (1923-) Born Peter E Ohm, 4 April 1923, Wem, Shropshire. Actor. An accomplished stage actor he made his screen debut in *Sapphire* (1959) which was closely followed by an appearance in *The 39 Steps* (1959). In both films he played a policeman (uncredited) but went on to more villainous roles in such films as *Village of the Damned* (1960), *Make Mine Mink* (1960), *The Devil's Agent* (1961), *I Thank a Fool* (1962) and *The Victors* (1963). On television he made an appearance in *Coronation Street* (1966) and played Mr Jaggers in *Great Expectations* (1967). His other films in the 1960s and 1970s include *The Bofors Gun* (1968), *Taste of Excitement* (1969), *Alfred the Great* (1969), *Eyewitness* (1970), *Straw Dogs* (1971), *The MacKintosh Man* (1973), *11 Harrowhouse* (1974) and *Zulu Dawn* (1979). Back on television he appeared in *The Pallisers* (1974), *Fall of Eagles* (1974), *The Crucible* (1980) and starred as patriarch Billy Fox in the 13-part serial Fox (1980), but is probably best known for his TV sitcom appearances as Mr Johnson in *Citizen Smith* (1977) and as 'Genial' Harry Grout in *Porridge* (1974-77). His later films include the Terry Gilliam productions *Time Bandits* (1981) and *Brazil* (1985), *The Remains of the Day* (1993), playing Anthony Hopkins father, *The Crucible* (1996), *Face* (1997), *The Legend of 1900* (1998), *An Ideal Husband* (1999), *Kiss Kiss (Bang Bang)* (2000), *Hotel Splendide* (2000), *The Mother* (2003), *The Life and Death of Peter Sellers* (2004), *The Queen of Sheba's Pearls* (2004), *Death at a Funeral* (2007), *Is Anybody There?* (2008), *Albatross* (2010) and *Game of Thrones* (2011). He has continued to appear regularly on TV in such series as *Sins* (1986), *Countdown to War* (1989) - as Hermann Goring, *Our Friends in the North* (1996), *Our Mutual Friend* (1998), *Longitude* (2000), *Lorna Doone* (2000) and *Malice Aforethought* (2005) and *Silk* (2011). Peter was married to Billie Whitelaw in 1952 but the couple divorced in 1966. He is now married to actress Lillias Walker, with whom he lives in the village of Mannings Heath, in West Sussex, having previously lived in Crawley, West Sussex for many years. In between Peter moved to Scotland temporarily to be near his step-daughter, Victoria, who is married to comedy actor Gregor Fisher, but the call of work has brought him back down south at the age of 87. See also entries in the television section for *Bleak House, Chancer, Citizen Smith, Coronation Street, Fox, Great Expectations, Knock on Any Door, Lark Rise To Candleford, Oliver Twist, Our Man At St Mark's, Our Friends In The North , Porridge, The Rivals of Sherlock Holmes,* and *The Tomorrow People.*

Veidt, Conrad (1893-1943) Born Hans Walter Conrad Weidt, 22 January 1893, Berlin, Germany. Actor. Joined Max Reinhardt's *Deutsches Theatre* in 1913. His screen debut was *Der Weg des Todes (The Road to Death)* (1916) and he subsequently appeared in many films purporting to cover social and moral issues but were often criticised in their day for the level of general debauchery brought to the screen. These include *The Diary of a Lost Woman* (1918), *Sinning Mother* (1918), *Prostitution* (1919) and *Prostitution II* (1919). He made a breakthrough as the homicidal somnambulist Cesare in *Das Kabinett des Doktor Caligari (The Cabinet of Dr Caligari)* (1920). To a certain extent this typecast him in horror genre films such as *The Hands of Orlac* (1924) and *Waxworks* (1924) but he also appeared in several historical biopics, as Nelson in *Lady Hamilton* (1921), Cesare Borgia in *Lucrezia Borgia* (1922) and Gessler in *William Tell* (1923). After further success in the faustian tale *The Student of Prague* (1926) he was invited to Hollywood to make *The Beloved Rogue* (1927) and stayed on to make *The Man who Laughs* (1928) – Veldt's character later becoming the inspiration for the depiction of the iconic supervillain The Joker, and *The Last Performance* (1929) before returning to Germany. The advent of the talkies, which meant death to the careers of so many silent screen stars, actually enabled Veidt to expand his repertoire to include suave characters rather than the standard fare of grotesque and sinister roles he had previously been playing. His command of English also meant that Michael Balcon invited him to England to film *Rome Express* (1932). He left Germany in April 1933 with his new wife Lily Preger, a Jewish woman, and, apart from a brief return in the autumn of that year to reprise his role as Gessler in *William Tell* (1934), he never returned. Conrad fervently opposed the Nazi regime, and played the lead roles in *The Wandering Jew* (1933) and *Jew Suss* (1934). After making *The Passing of the Third Floor Back* (1935) he moved from Gaumont to join Alexander Korda for *Dark Journey* (1937) and became a British citizen in 1938. Powell and Pressburger cast him in *The Spy in Black* (1939) and *Contraband* (1940) but it was his role as the evil grand vizier Jaffar in the spectacular and sumptuous *The Thief of Bagdad* (1940) which sticks in the memory. It was also his only colour film. On the outbreak of WWII he turned over his personal fortune to the UK government to aid the war effort and travelled to America to raise further funds. Whilst there he took a leading role in *Escape* (1940) which he followed with *A Woman's Face* (1941), *Nazi Agent* (1942) and culminated by playing Major Strasser in *Casablanca* (1942). His final film was *Above Suspicion* (1943). He died of a heart attack, 3 April 1943, whilst playing golf at the Riviera Country Club, Los Angeles, California. In 1998, his ashes were interred at the Golders Green Crematorium in London.

Walbrook, Anton (1900-66) Born Adolph Anton Wilhelm Wohlbruck, 19 November 1900, Vienna, Austria. Actor. Son of Adolph Wohlbruck, a famous circus clown. Trained under Max Reinhardt. Made his stage debut in 1920. Made his screen debut in *Mater Dolorosa* (1924) but didn't really concentrate on film work until the 1930s with such films as *Viktor und Viktoria* (1933), *Maskerade* (1934), *Michel Strogoff* (1935) and *The Student of Prague* (1935), where he took the role of Balduin which had catapulted Conrad Viedt to success some ten years earlier. He then went to Hollywood to remake *Michel Strogoff* as *The Soldier and the Lady* (1937) for RKO, now being billed as Anton Walbrook rather than Adolph. Disliking the experience he then chose to settle in Britain rather than return to Germany and joined Herbert Wilcox, playing Prince Albert in both *Victoria the Great* (1937) and *Sixty Glorious Years* (1938). Having played Ivor Novello's creation *The Rat* (1937) he cemented his popularity with British audiences when he took the role of the chilling Paul Mallen in *Gaslight* (1940). Despite being vehemently anti-Nazi he refused to take on predictable nasty German roles but this probably helped him in featuring in some of the best films of the war years in *Dangerous Moonlight* (1941), *49th Parallel* (1941) and *The Life and Death of Colonel Blimp* (1943). Anton became a naturalised British subject in 1947. He had known Emerich Pressburger through Universum-Film Aktien-Gesellschaft (UFA) and he played possibly his best role as Lermontov in the *Archers* production *The Red Shoes* (1948). After the war he began working more in Europe on films such as *La Ronde* (1950), *Wiener Walzer* (1951), *L'Affaire Maurizius* (1954), *Lola Montes* (1955) billed once again as Adolph Anton Wilhelm Wohlbruck. He also appeared in the British made *Oh... Rosalinda!* (1955), *Saint Joan* (1957) and *I Accuse!* (1958). Died 9 August 1967 Garatshausen, Bavaria, Germany.

Walls, Tom (1883-1949) Born Tom Kirby Walls, 18 February 1883, Kingsthorpe, Northamptonshire. Actor and director. Son of a plumber and builder. Had a variety of jobs including carpenter, jockey and policeman before he made his stage debut in *Aladdin* (1905) in Glasgow. Toured North America (1906-07) and Australia (1910-11) with music hall comedy routines. From 1924 he began an association with the Aldwych Theatre as actor-manager and between then and 1933 he starred in and directed the series of Ben Travers farces which also featured Yvonne Arnaud, Ralph Lynn and J Robertson Hare. At the beginning of the 1930s Walls was contracted by Herbert Wilcox at *British and Dominion* to film the farces starting with *On Approval* (1930), *Canaries Sometimes Sing* (1930), the best known *Rookery Nook* (1930), *Plunder* (1931), *A Night Like This* (1931) and *Thark* (1932). The contract moved to Michael Balcon at *Gaumont-British* with *Turkey Time* (1933) and continued throughout the pre-war period including *A Cuckoo in the Nest* (1933), *Leave it to Smith* (1933), *Foreign Affaires* (1935), *Second Best Bed* (1938) and *Old Iron* (1938). Tom starred and directed all of these, which were basically films of the stage productions but they made him and his co-stars very popular and well-known faces. He carried on acting after the farces as a character actor in films including *Undercover* (1943), *Love Story* (1944), *While I Live* (1947), *Spring in Park Lane* (1948), *Maytime in Mayfair* (1949) and *The Interrupted Journey* (1949). In addition to his thespian career he was also a race horse trainer from his small stables in Looe Park, Ewell, nr Epsom, Surrey. In 1932 he reached the pinnacle of any horse-race trainer's career by training the winner of the Epsom Derby, *April the Fifth*, which he also owned. No Epsom trained horse has won the Derby since. Walls died 27 November 1949 Ewell, Surrey.

Walker, Polly (1966-) Born Polly Alexandra Walker, 19 May 1966, Warrington, Cheshire. Actress. Polly began her career as a dancer, graduating from the Ballet Rambert School in Twickenham, aged 16. A leg injury forced a change of tack at the age of 18 and Polly attended the *London Drama Centre* moving from there to the RSC, eventually graduating to television, playing the title role in *Lorna Doone* (1990). Her film debut in *Shogun Mayeda* (1991) was unremarkable but the following year this very striking actress gained a part in *Patriot Games* (1992) with Harrison Ford. Her other films include: *Enchanted April* (1992), *Sliver* (1993), *The Trial* (1993), *Restoration* (1995), *Emma* (1996), *Roseanna's Grave* (1997), *Dark Harbor* (1998), *Talk of Angels* (1998), *8½ Women* (1999), *D-Tox* (2002), *Savage Messiah* (2002), *Scenes of a Sexual Nature* (2006) and *Clash of the Titans* (2010 – as Cassiopeia). Polly has also starred in several television film dramas, notably playing Atia of the Julii, the niece of Julius Caesar and mother of Octavian/Augustus and Octavia, in the British-Italian historical drama television series *Rome* (2005-07). On 23 October 2008, Polly married actor Laurence Penry-Jones, most famous for his role as Dr Oliver Berg in the BBC soap, *Doctors*. Polly has two children from two previous relationships, Giorgio (b. 1993) and Delilah (b. 2000). She currently lives in the United States.

Walsh, Kay (1914-2005) Born Kathleen Walsh, 27 August 1914, London. Actress. Started her working life as a chorus girl, graduating to solo dancer she made her screen debut in *How's Chances?* (1934). Her early work saw her co-star with George Formby in *Keep Fit* (1937) and *I See Ice* (1938). She featured in the classic WWII films *In Which We Serve* (1942) and *This Happy Breed* (1944) as she moved into playing more character parts. She played Nancy in her then husband's *Oliver Twist* (1948) to which she also contributed the ideas for the film's atmospheric opening montage of Oliver's birth. She had already written the closing adaptation of *Great Expectations* (1946). Other films include *Vice Versa* (1948), *Stage Fright* (1950), *Young Bess* (1953), *Cast a Dark Shadow* (1957), *The Horse's Mouth* (1958), *Tunes of Glory* (1960) and playing a Jack the Ripper victim in *A Study in Terror* (1965). She retired in 1981 after her last film *Night Crossing*. Well-known for her life-long held left-wing views, Noël Coward dubbing her "Red Emma". Described by James Mason as "witty, bright and petite". Married to director David Lean (1940-49) and to psychologist Elliott Jacques (1949-56). Died 16 April 2005 London, a few days before Sir John Mills, with whom she often co-starred.

Walters, Julie (1950-) Born Julia Mary Walters, 22 February 1950, Smethwick, West Midlands. Actress. Julie began her working life as an insurance clerk before serving an 18-month stint as a nurse at the Queen Elizabeth Hospital, Birmingham. Aged 19, Julie decided to leave nursing to study English and Drama at Manchester Polytechnic (now Manchester Metropolitan University) in pursuit of her then boyfriend (a shaggy red-headed chap Julie refers to as 'DT' in her autobiography). Julie worked for the Everyman Theatre Company in Liverpool in the mid 1970s and in 1978 became friendly with Victoria Wood, who was then dating Geoffrey Durham (The Great Soprendo), an old friend of Julie's. Their first collaboration was in the theatre but they became something of a double act by the time their first series, *Wood and Walters*, appeared on television in 1982. One of Julie's best-known roles is as "Mrs Overall" in Wood's spoof soap opera, *Acorn Antiques* which was transferred to the London stage as a musical in 2005 with Julie reprising her dual role of Bo Beaumont / Mrs Overall. Julie's film career has been varied, she started with a superb performance in *Educating Rita* (1983) for which she won a BAFTA and received an Academy Award Best Actress nomination, before embarking on a number of less well received pieces such as *She'll Be Wearing Pink Pajamas* (1984) and *Car Trouble* (1985). Alternating between comedy and serious character parts she has become one of England's best known and best loved actresses. She has done much of her work in the theatre and on the small screen from the superb *Boys From the Blackstuff* (1982) to *Talking Heads 2* (1998) and *The Canterbury Tales* (2003) and is usually the name read out at the BAFTAs. Her other major films include *Personal Services* (1987), *Prick Up Your Ears* (1987), *Buster*, (1988), *Stepping Out* (1991), *Just Like a Woman* (1992), *Sister My Sister* (1994), *Intimate Relations* (1996), *Titanic Town* (1998), *Billy Elliot* (2000) - for which she was nominated for an Academy Award as Best Supporting Actress, *Before You Go* (2002), *Calendar Girls* (2003) *Wah-Wah* (2005), *Driving Lessons* (2006), *Becoming Jane* (2007), *Mamma Mia!* (2008) and *Gnomeo and Juliet* (2011 - voice of Miss Montague). She is perhaps best known to a younger generation of cinema goers as Mrs Molly Weasley in seven of the eight *Harry Potter* films (she did not appear in *Harry Potter and the Goblet of Fire*). Julie's long-term partner is former AA patrol man Grant Roffey. The couple have a daughter, Maisie Mae Roffey (b. 1988, City of Westminster, London). Julie and Grant married in 1997 and they live on an organic farm run by Roffey in West Sussex. Julie has written three books: *Baby Talk: The Secret Diary of a Pregnant Woman* (1990), the novel *Maggie's Tree* (2007) and an autobiography, *That's Another Story* (2008). See also entries in the television section for *Boys From the Blackstuff, The Canterbury Tales, dinnerladies, GBH, Secret Diary of Adrian Mole, Aged 13 3/4, Victoria Wood As Seen On TV*, and *Wood and Walters*.

Walton-on-Thames Studios (1899-1961) In 1899 Cecil Hepworth leased a house at Walton-on-Thames and turned it into a film studio. His early output included a trick film *The Egg-Laying Man* and a slow-motion *The Eccentric Dancer*. He expanded the studio in 1905, produced *Rescued by Rover* and ran a family-based company whilst at the same time developing a star system with actors such as Chrissie White, Alma Taylor and Stewart Rome being billed as the *Hepworth Picture Players*. Films produced include a series of Dicken's adaptations and propaganda shorts during WWI. After initial success in the post-war period which included *Sheba* (1919) and *Comin' Thro' the Rye* (1922), the company was declared bankrupt in 1924. The resulting destruction of 25 years of negatives was a bitter blow to the history of British cinema. The studios were bought by Archibald Nettlefold and subsequently turned out "quota quickies" during the 1930s. Closed during WWII, the post-war period saw a steady stream of films including: *The Sleeping Tiger*

(1954) and *Dance Little Lady* (1954). The studios were closed and demolished in 1961.

Warde, Frederick (1851-1935) Born Frederick Barkham Warde, 23 February 1851, Deddington, Oxfordshire. Actor. Educated at City of London School. Stage debut: *Macbeth* (1867). Settled in the US in 1874, touring with Edwin Booth, brother of John Wilkes Booth. His stage career had many ups and downs resulting in bankruptcy in 1904 and eventually he took up lecturing on Shakespeare rather than performing. However, he made his screen debut at the age of 61 as the king in *Richard III* (1912) for the *Shakespeare Film Company*, which cost $30,000 to make. This hand-tinted film was rediscovered and preserved and is now thought to be the United States' oldest surviving feature film. His other films include *Silas Marner* (1916), *King Lear* (1916), *The Vicar of Wakefield* (1917), *Under False Colors* (1917) and *The Unveiling Hand* (1919). He published *The Fools of Shakespeare* and an autobiography: *Fifty Years of Make-Believe* (1923). He died 7 February 1935, Brooklyn, New York.

Warner, David (1941-) Born 29 July 1941, Manchester. Actor. Studied at RADA. Joined the RSC in 1962 and in 1965 he played a controversial but critically acclaimed *Hamlet*. After making an uncredited screen debut in *We Joined the Navy* (1962) David had a jobbing part in *Z Cars* before enjoying early screen success as Mr Blifil in *Tom Jones* (1963) before starring in *Morgan: A Suitable Case for Treatment* (1966). Other early films include *The Bofors Gun* (1968), *The Ballad of Cable Hogue* (1970) and *Straw Dogs* (1971). At this time he stopped appearing on stage. After *The Omen* (1976) and *Age of Innocence* (1977), he cultivated a stereotype appearing as villains in films such as *The Thirty-Nine Steps* (1978), *Holocaust* (1978), *Time After Time* (1979), *The Island* (1980), *Masada* (1981), *Time Bandits* (1981), *Tron* (1982) and *The Man with Two Brains* (1983). Since then he has appeared in more than 100 television series and films including *Star Trek V* (1989) and *Star Trek VI* (1991) (as different characters), *Titanic* (1997), *Scream 2* (1997), *Planet of the Apes* (2001), *Ladies in Lavender* (2004), *The League of Gentlemen's Apocalypse* (2005), *Black Death* (2010) and *A Thousand Kisses Deep* (2011). David has also starred in sci-fi roles on television including *Star Trek: The Next Generation* (1992), *Babylon 5* (1994) and *Spiderman* (1995-97). In recent years he has appeared in television series such as *Wild At Heart* (2007) and as the voice of Lord Azlok in *Doctor Who*. David has been twice married: to Harriet Lindgren (1969-72) and Sheilah Kent (1981-2005). See also entries in the television section for *Hold the Back Page, Hornblower*, and *Wallander*.

Warner, H B (1875-1958) Born Harry Byron Warner, 26 October 1875, St John's Wood, London. Actor. Son of actor Charles J Warner. Studied medicine but decided to follow in his father's footsteps and indeed spent many years touring with him. Settled in the United States in 1905. Made his screen debut in *The Harp of Tara* (1914) and went on to appear in more than 130 films over the next 44 years. The highlight of his silent screen career was his portrayal of Christ in Cecil B DeMille's *King of Kings* (1927) and his career carried on unabated into the talkies. He became more of a character actor during the 1930s and 1940s and was a particular favourite of Frank Capra for whom he featured in *Mr Deeds Goes to Town* (1936), *Lost Horizon* (1937) - where he gained an Academy Award nomination for Best Supporting Actor as Chang, *You Can't Take it With You* (1938), *Mr Smith Goes to Washington* (1939) and his best remembered and most out of character role as Mr Gower in *It's a Wonderful Life* (1946) - where he apparently appreciated playing a drunk for a change. He also played Colonel Nielson in a series of *Bulldog Drummond* films (1938-39). Other films include: *Sorrell and Son* (1927 and 1933), *A Tale of Two Cities* (1935), *Victoria the Great* (1937), *The Girl of the Golden West* (1938), *The Corsican Brothers* (1941), *The Prince of Thieves* (1948) and his final film saw him back with DeMille in *The Ten Commandments* (1956). Died 21 December 1958, Woodland Hills, California.

Warner, Jack (1895-1981) Born Horace John Waters, 24 October 1895, Bromley-by-Bow, London. Actor. As a teenager he worked as a car mechanic and an undertaker. Joined the Royal

Flying Corps during WWI. He returned to car mechanics and motor racing before taking up acting in his late thirties. Screen debut: *The Dummy Talks* (1943). Jack played the dad in the series of films about the Huggett family: *Holiday Camp* (1947), *Here Come the Huggetts* (1948), *Vote for Huggett* (1949) and *The Huggetts Abroad* (1949). His short role in *The Blue Lamp* (1949) led to him being cast as PC (later Sergeant) George Dixon in the long running TV series *Dixon of Dock Green* (1955-1976). Although he is best remembered for this role, he was also adept at playing the villain in such films as *Hue & Cry* (1947), *Against the Wind* (1947) and *My Brother's Keeper* (1948). Other films include: *Scrooge* (1951), *Albert R N* (1953), *The Cruel Sea* (1953), *The Ladykillers* (1955), *Carve her Name with Pride* (1958) and *Dominique* (1978). His sisters Elsie and Doris Waters (see entry in comedy section) were a much loved radio act known as Gert and Daisy. Autobiographies: *Jack of All Trades* (1975) and *'Evening All* (1979). Died 24 May 1981, Ravenscourt Park, London. See also entries in the radio and television section for *Dixon of Dock Green, Jim's Inn*, and *Meet the Huggetts*.

Waterman, Dennis (1948-) Born 24 February 1948, Clapham, London. Actor and singer. Dennis was a product of Rona Knight's Corona Stage Academy (now known as Corona Theatre School, situated in Kew). Dennis was a fine child actor. At the age of 13, he played the part of Winthrop Paroo in the Adelphi Theatre production of The Music Man. A year later, he starred as William Brown in the BBC TV series William based on the *Just William* books of Richmal Crompton and also became a regular in the American *CBS* comedy *Fair Exchange*, playing teenage son Neville Finch. His film career began in 1960 with two low budget offerings *Night Train for Inverness* and *Snowball*. 1962 brought small roles in the classic films *Crooks Anonymous* and *The Pirates of Blood River*. Dennis then had a major role in *Up the Junction* (1968) before embarking on a varied fare of sex, horror and comedy films such as *The Smashing Bird I Used to Know* (1969), *This That and The Other!* (1970), *My Lover My Son* (1970), *Scars of Dracula* (1970), *Fright* (1971), *Man in the Wilderness* (1971), *Alice's Adventures in Wonderland* (1972 – as the two of spades) and *The Belstone Fox* (1973). Then followed his best films *Sweeney!* (1977) and *Sweeney 2* (1978) which were extensions of the very popular television detective series. Dennis's next film project was *The World Cup: A Captain's Tale* (1982), telling the story of West Auckland F.C. a team of part time footballers who represented England in the Sir Thomas Lipton Trophy, unofficially considered the first 'World Cup', in 1909 and 1911. Dennis kept with the sporting theme to make *The First Kangaroos* (1988), a film about the first-ever rugby league tour of England by the Australian national team. His more recent films have included *Vol-au-vent* (1996), *Arthur's Dyke* (2001) and *Back in Business* (2007). Dennis is also a gifted singer and had a UK No 3 hit in 1980 with *I Could Be So Good For You*, the theme to *Minder*. He has been married four times: to Penny Dixon (1967–76), actress Patricia Maynard (1977–87), actress Rula Lenska (1987–98) and former model and actress Pam Flint (2011-present). Dennis only told the world of his fourth marriage during a televised interview with Piers Morgan which aired on ITV in May 2012. He also admitted an affair with his fellow New Tricks actor Amanda Redman in the 1980s and also being driven to violence towards Rula Lenska on at least two occasions. Dennis has two daughters by his second wife, one of whom, Hannah Waterman, (b. 22 July 1975) is also an actor and played Laura Beale in the BBC1 soap opera *EastEnders* from 2000 until 2004. Dennis' older brother Peter was a British welterweight boxing champion. Mainly a television actor - see entries in the radio and television section for *The Life and Loves of a She Devil, Little Britain, Minder, New Tricks, On the Up, Stay Lucky, Survival* and *The Sweeney*.

Watson, Emily (1967-) Born Emily Margaret Watson, 14 January 1967, Islington, London. Actress. The daughter of an architect and an English professor. Although three times refused a place at a drama school, in 1992, she entered the Royal Shakespeare Company. Here she met Jack Waters, whom she married in 1995 and later appeared with in *The Boxer* (1997). Emily was a virtual unknown until controversial director Lars von Trier chose her to star in his film *Breaking the Waves* (1996) after first choice, Helena Bonham Carter, dropped out due to the amount of nudity involved. Her performance as Bess McNeill, her first in front of a camera, was hailed by critics. She won the Los Angeles, London and New York Critics Circle Awards, the US National Society of Film Critics Award for Best Actress and ultimately an Academy Award nomination. She came to public notice again in another controversial role; playing cellist Jacqueline du Pre in *Hilary and Jackie* (1998) and received another Academy Award Best Actress nomination for that performance despite the fact that many of du Pre's friends and fans decried it as an inaccurate and unfair portrayal. Emily was again lauded for her performance as Elsie in *Gosford Park* (2001) and then demonstrated her great range playing Reba McClane in the adaptation of Thomas Harris's *Silence of the Lambs* prequel, *Red Dragon* (2002) and Adam Sandler's romantic interest in Paul Thomas Anderson's strange, disturbing, quirky black comedy *Punch-Drunk Love* (2002). In 2003 Emily took a break from film, preferring a return to the theatre to play two roles in Sam Mendes' productions of *Uncle Vanya* and *Twelfth Night*, for which she received an Olivier Award nomination. In 2004 she received a Golden Globe nomination for her role as Peter Sellers's first wife, Anne Howe, in *The Life and Death of Peter Sellers* opposite Geoffrey Rush. In 2005 she appeared in *Wah-Wah*, Richard E. Grant's autobiographical directorial debut; *Separate Lies*, directed by Gosford Park writer Julian Fellowes, and Tim Burton's animated film *Corpse Bride*. Since then her films have included: *Miss Potter* (2006), *Crusade in Jeans* (2006), *The Water Horse: Legend of the Deep* (2007), *Fireflies in the Garden* (2008), *Synecdoche, New York* (2008- a film more strange, disturbing and quirky than *Punch-Drunk Love*) *Cold Souls* (2009), *Cemetery Junction* (2010), *Oranges and Sunshine* (2010) and Steven Spielberg's *War Horse* (2011 – as Rose Narracott). Emily has often had as much publicity for the roles she didn't get as in those she did. Most notably, director Jean-Pierre Jeunet wrote the character "Amélie" especially for her (Amélie was originally named Emily) but she eventually turned the role down due to difficulties working in French and a desire not to be away from home. The role went on to make an international star of Audrey Tautou. She was also the first choice to play Elizabeth I in *Elizabeth* (1998), the role that ultimately made a star of Cate Blanchett. Emily was also intended to be the lead in *Miss Potter*, but ended up with a supporting role.

Watson, Emma (1990-) Born Emma Charlotte Duerre Watson, 15 April 1990, Paris, France. Actress. Emma is the daughter of Jacqueline Luesby and Chris Watson, both British lawyers. Her grandmother is French and Emma lived in Paris until moving to Oxfordshire with her mother and younger brother at the age of five following her parents' divorce. Although enrolling in a stage school, Emma rose to fame, aged eleven, playing Hermione Granger in the *Harry Potter* film series, having never acted professionally. Emma has appeared in all the Potter films and her first non-Potter role was playing Pauline Fossil in the 2007 TV film *Ballet Shoes* and her second voicing the character of Princess Pea in the children's comedy film, *The Tale of Despereaux* (2008). Emma made her modelling debut for Burberry's Autumn/Winter campaign in 2009 and also appeared in their 2010 Spring/Summer campaign. In 2011 Emma played the role of Lucy, a wardrobe assistant, in *My Week with Marilyn*, a British film depicting the making of the 1957 film *The Prince and the Showgirl* which starred Marilyn Monroe and Laurence Olivier.

Wattis, Richard (1912-75) Born Richard C Wattis, 25 February 1912, Wednesbury, Staffordshire. Actor. Initially worked in the family electrical engineering business before training in drama at the Croydon Repertory Theatre. Stage debut: *The Little Minister* (1935). Screen debut: *A Yank at Oxford* (1938). Other films include: *The Happiest Days of Your Life* (1950), *Top Secret* (1952), *The Importance of Being Earnest* (1952), *Hobson's Choice* (1954), *The Colditz Story* (1955), *The Inn of the Sixth Happiness* (1958), *The Longest Day* (1962), *Casino Royale* (1967), *Chitty Chitty Bang Bang* (1968) and *Confessions of a Window Cleaner* (1974) plus various *Carry Ons* and *St Trinian's* films. On television he had a long association with comedian Eric Sykes and appeared as his snobby neighbour Charles Brown in both *Sykes and a...* (1960-61) and in *Sykes* (1972-74). Died 1 February 1975, Belgravia, London.

Watts, Naomi (1968-) Born 28 September 1968, Shoreham-by-Sea, West Sussex. Actress. Following the break-up of her parent's marriage, when she was eight-years-old, Naomi lived in Wales and thereafter Australia. Her father was a sound engineer with Pink Floyd. It was in Sydney that she attended several acting schools. Naomi then worked as a model in both Australia and Japan before returning to acting, initially in commercials, her feature film debut being *For Love Alone* (1986). She then worked in television and won the part of Julie Gibson in the TV soap *Home and Away* (1991). A number of small film roles followed - *Flirting* (1991), *Wide Sargasso Sea* (1993) and *Matinee* (1993) - until she played Jet Girl in *Tank Girl* (1995) with Lori Petty. Although *Tank Girl* established Naomi as a bankable actress her next three films *Children of the Corn IV: The Gathering* (1996), *Under the Lighthouse Dancing* (1997) and *Dangerous Beauty* (1998) did not advance her reputation. It was her performance as Betty Elms/Diane Selwyn in David Lynch's psychological thriller *Mulholland Drive* (2001) that won her many plaudits and many awards. Naomi was the main lead in *The Ring* (2002), the Gore Verbinski American remake of "Ringu", itself based on Kôji Suzuki's novel *Ring*. She then received an Academy Award nomination for Best Actress for her performance in the Alejandro González Iñárritu film *21 Grams* (2003). Three films in 2004, *We Don't Live Here Anymore*, *I Heart Huckabees*, and *The Assassination of Richard Nixon*, were fairly well received before she reprised her role of Rachel Keller in *The Ring Two* (2005). Naomi's next role as femme fatale Ann Darrow in Peter Jackson's remake of *King Kong* (2005) will ensure her place in cinematic history as the second woman to play this role following Fay Wray in the original 1933 production. For those film buffs wishing to take issue with this perhaps I should add that Jessica Lange's character in the 1976 remake of *King Kong* was known as 'Dwan'. In fact Ann Darrow has been depicted in one other film based on *King Kong*, the unauthorized 1998 animated musical film, *The Mighty Kong*, where she is voiced by Jodi Benson. Naomi's subsequent films include: *The Painted Veil* (2006), *Eastern Promises* (2007), *Funny Games* (2008), *The International* (2009), the 2010 releases *Mother and Child, You Will Meet a Tall Dark Stranger,* and *Fair Game* plus the psychological thriller *Dream House* (2011) and the Clint Eastwood film *J Edgar* (2011). Naomi had relationships with director Stephen Hopkins in the 1990s and actor Heath Ledger in the early 2000s but has been the partner of American actor Liev Schreiber since 2005. They have two sons, Alexander "Sasha" Pete (b. 25 July 2007, Los Angeles) and Samuel "Sammy" Kai (b. 13 December 2008, New York City).

Wayne, Naunton (1901-70) Born Henry Wayne Davies, 22 June 1901, Llanwonno, Glamorganshire. Actor. Made his stage debut in 1920 as a member of *The Tweenies* concert party and spent the next ten years touring as a compere, comedian and cabaret artist. Legitimate stage debut: *Wise Tomorrow* (1937). Screen debut: *The First Mrs Fraser* (1932). Alfred Hitchcock cast him as Caldicott who, along with his companion Charters (played by Basil Radford), provided some light relief in *The Lady Vanishes* (1938) as two Englishmen more interested in the Test Match score than in the fate of the missing Miss Froy. (See entry for Basil Radford for further information on this pairing). After Radford's death in 1952 Naunton appeared in *The Titfield Thunderbolt* (1953), *You Know What Sailors Are* (1954) and *Double Bunk* (1961). His final screen role was as Fitzroy in the seven-part ITV drama series *John Browne's Body* (1969). Died 17 November 1970, Surbiton, Surrey.

Weeks, Honeysuckle (1979-) Born Honeysuckle Hero Susan Weeks, 1 August 1979, Cardiff. Actress. She is so named because the scent of honeysuckle was very strong at the time she was born. Honeysuckle has a younger sister Perdita (b. Perdita Rose Weeks, 25 December 1985, Cardiff) and a younger brother Rollo (b. Rollo Percival Weeks, 20 March 1987, Chichester, West Sussex), both of whom have followed her into acting and have successful careers of their own. Honeysuckle first appeared on television in an adaptation of Anne Fine's *Goggle Eyes* (1993) (along with her brother and sister) aged 13. She has appeared in a number of TV adaptations, notably *Lorna Doone* (2000) and *Ruth Rendell* and *Poirot* mysteries. She has also appeared in Midsomer Murders, The Inspector Lynley Mysteries and Ladies & Their Gentlemen (2002-06) but is perhaps best known for her role in the long-running WWII drama *Foyle's War* (2002-10) where she played Samantha Stewart. To-date Honeysuckle has only had three roles in feature films, as Sarah in *My Brother Tom* (2001), Clarissa in *Red Mercury* (2005) and Lolly in *The Wicker Tree* (2011). Honeysuckle was engaged to young British musician Anno Birkin (b. 9 December 1980; d. 8 November 2001) for a short period just before his death in a car crash in Italy while recording in Milan with other members of his band Kicks joy Darkness (KjD). Honeysuckle subsequently married Lorne Stormonth-Darling, a hypnotherapist 16 years her senior.

Weisz, Rachel (1970-) Born Rachel Hannah Weisz, 7 March 1970, Westminster, London, to Edith, an Austrian psychoanalyst and George, an Hungarian inventor, best known for the respirators that supply their own oxygen and machines that sense land mines. Actress and fashion model. Educated at the St Paul's Girls School in London, Rachel was a model when she was 14 and began acting during her studies at Trinity Hall, Cambridge, where she co-founded the theatrical group *Cambridge Talking Tongues*. Her first screen role was as Sarah Thompson in the three-part television series *Advocates II* (1992), the sequel to a 1991 series made by Scottish television. After further television roles in series such as *Inspector Morse* (1993 - as Arabella Baydon), Rachel made her feature film debut as an unnamed junior executive in *Death Machine* (1994). Other films include: *Stealing Beauty* (1996), *Chain Reaction* (1996), *Going All the Way* (1997), *Bent* (1997), *Amy Foster* (1997), *The Land Girls* (1998 - as Agapanthus), *I Want You* (1998), *The Mummy* (1999 - as Evy Carnahan), *Sunshine* (1999), *This Is Not an Exit: The Fictional World of Bret Easton Ellis* (2000 - as Lauren Hynde), *Beautiful Creatures* (2000), *Enemy at the Gates* (2001), *The Mummy Returns* (2001 - as Evy and Princess Nefertiti), *About a Boy* (2002 - as Rachel), *The Shape of Things* (2003 - as Evelyn Ann Thompson), *Confidence: After Dark* (2003), *Runaway Jury* (2003 - as Marlee), *Envy* (2004 - as Debbie Dingman), *Constantine* (2005 - as Angela Dodson / Isabel Dodson), *The Fountain* (2006 - as Isabel / Izzi Creo), *Eragon* (2006 - voice of Saphira), *My Blueberry Nights* (2007 - as Sue Lynne), *Fred Claus* (2007 - as Wanda), *Definitely, Maybe* (2008 - as Summer Hartley), *The Brothers Bloom* (2008 - as Penelope), *Agora* (2009 - as Hypatia), *The Lovely Bones* (2009 - as Abigail Salmon), *The Whistleblower* (2010 - as Kathryn Bolkovac), 360 (2011 - as Rose) and *The Deep Blue Sea* (2011 - as Hester Collyer). For her role of Tessa Quayle in the 2005 film, *The Constant Gardener*, she won both an Oscar and Golden Globe as Best Supporting Actress for her performance. Rachel is also a talented theatre actress. As a fashion model she became the face of Revlon in 2005 and replaced Kate Moss as the new face of the Burberry campaign. She was in a relationship with American film director Darren Aronofsky for eight years and the couple have a son, Henry (b. 2006). Whilst working on *Dream House* (2011) she rekindled her relationship with Daniel Craig and the couple subsequently married on 22 June 2011.

Welland, Colin (1934-) Born Colin Williams, 4 July 1934, Leigh, Lancashire. Actor and writer. Studied at Goldsmith's College and was an art teacher (1958-62) before making his television debut as PC David Graham in *Z Cars* (1962-65). Colin made his big screen debut as English teacher Mr Farthing in *Kes* (1969). He also appeared on TV in such series as *The Wild Wild West* (1975), *Cowboys* (1980) and *Bramwell* (1998) as well as single dramas such as Dennis Potter's award- winning *Blue Remembered Hills* (1979), *United Kingdom* (1981), *The Fix* (1997) and *Trial and Retribution* (1997). His film career continued with *Villain* (1971), *Straw Dogs* (1971) and ended with *Sweeney!* (1977) after which he began to concentrate more on his writing. He began writing for the screen with TV projects *Roll on Four O'Clock* (1970), *The Hallelujah Handshake* (1970), *Jack Point* (1973), *Kisses at Fifty* (1973), *Leeds United* (1974),*Your Man from 6 Counties* (1976) and *Bambino Mio* (1994). His first film as a writer was *Yanks*

(1979). His next was *Chariots of Fire* (1981) which won an Academy Award for Best Picture and gained Welland an Academy Award for Best Original Screenplay. He is probably best remembered for his acceptance speech, during which he held his Academy Award aloft and shouted "The British are Coming". He has since written *Twice in a Lifetime* (1985), *A Dry White Season* (1989) and *War of the Buttons* (1994). See also entries in the television section for *Don't Ask Me, Village Hall*, and *Z Cars*.

Westmore, George (1879-1931) Born 27 June 1879, Newport, Isle of Wight, Hampshire. Make-up artist and founder of a dynasty. Son of a coalman. Originally a hairdresser, he moved with his wife and family to the United States in 1913 and took up dye-making and wig-making. In 1917 George set up the first film make-up department. Films he worked on include *The Education of Elizabeth* (1921), *The Three Musketeers* (1921), *Robin Hood* (1922), *The Thief of Bagdad* (1924), *Ben Hur: A Tale of the Christ* (1925), *Don Q Son of Zorro* (1925) and *The Black Pirate* (1926). George committed suicide by swallowing mercury on 12 July 1931, Hollywood, California. His son Percival Harry Westmore (b. 29 October 1904, Canterbury, Kent; d. 30 September 1970, Los Angeles, California) was a make-up artist on no fewer than 333 films from 1925 to 1970 and developed cosmetics which looked similar under diverse lighting conditions and when using different film types. George's other sons Montague George Westmore (b. 22 July 1902, Bedford, Bedfordshire; d. 30 March 1940. Los Angeles, California), Ernest Henry Westmore - Percival's twin (b. 29 October 1904, Canterbury, Kent; d. 1 February 1967, Los Angeles, California), Walter James Westmore (b. 13 February 1906, Canterbury, Kent; d. 3 July 1973, Los Angeles, California), George Hamilton (Bud) Westmore (b. 13 January 1918, Louisiana; d. 23 June 1973, Los Angeles, California) and Frank Courtney Westmore (b. 13 April 1923, California; d. 14 May 1985, Los Angeles, California) were all involved in the make-up business.

Whale, James (1889-1957) Born 22 July 1889, Dudley, West Midlands. Director. Worked as a cobbler and in a sheet metal factory to raise the fees to study at Dudley School of Arts and Crafts. Trained as an artist he was originally a cartoonist for *The Bystander*. He served in the Worcestershire Regiment in WWI until captured in France in 1917. Began acting whilst a POW. Stage debut: *Abraham Lincoln* (1919). Worked in repertory in Birmingham until he directed *Journey's End*, which he took to the West End with great success, starring Laurence Olivier. James travelled with this production to America and whilst awaiting to direct a screen version he was hired as a dialogue coach on the films *The Love Doctor* (1929) and *Hell's Angels* (1930). Screen directorial debut: *Journey's End* (1930). Contracted to *Universal Studios,* he next directed *Waterloo Bridge* (1931) but it was his next project, an adaptation of Mary Shelley's *Frankenstein* (1931) which cemented his reputation. He was quickly stereotyped by the studio as a horror film maestro but he made the best of what he considered an unfortunate assumption to rope in some respected British thespians to help out. For *The Old Dark House* (1932) he used Charles Laughton and Ernest Thesiger, for *The Invisible Man* (1933) he used Claude Rains and for the classic *The Bride of Frankenstein* (1935) he cast Elsa Lanchester. James did manage to direct some non-horror films including *A Kiss Before the Mirror* (1933), *One More River* (1934) and *Remember Last Night?* (1935). In 1936 he directed the musical *Showboat* (1936). He was disappointed after *The Road Back* (1937) was recut by the studio and he never reached his previous level of success with films such as *The Great Garrick* (1937), *Port of the Seven Seas* (1938) and *The Man in the Iron Mask* (1939). Disenchanted by his lack of independence he walked off the set of *They Dare Not Love* (1941) and never directed a feature again. On retirement he returned to painting and took up set design. James never concealed his homosexuality and was the long-time partner of American producer David Lewis between 1930 and 1952. Debilitated by a series of strokes, he committed suicide by drowning in his swimming pool, 29 May 1957, Los Angeles, California. His later life is dramatised in the film *Gods and Monsters* (1998) starring Ian McKellen.

Whalley, Joanne (1964-) Born 25 August 1964, Salford, Lancashire. Actress. The daughter of a plumber and nothing in her background can explain her sultry Latin colouring and looks. At Harrytown's Girls School in 1982 she fronted a band called *Cindy and the Saffrons* and in the same year appeared as a groupie in Alan Parker's *The Wall*. Despite early forays into television with the almost obligatory cameos in *Coronation Street* and *Emmerdale*, she first appeared on TV "proper" in 1985's *Edge of Darkness* a classy thriller with Bob Peck. A year later she took on one of her best remembered roles, Nurse Mills in *The Singing Detective* (1986). In 1988 she played Christine Keeler in Michael Caton-Jones' *Scandal* before leaving the UK to film *Willow* (1988). On the set of *Willow* she met Val Kilmer and they married (28 February 1988) and moved to New Mexico to raise a family. During this period the Kilmer was added to her name but when they divorced in February 1996, this was removed. The divorce was unpleasant with Whalley filing the papers in Kilmer's absence after he had left to work on *The Island of Dr. Moreau* (1996). Despite a hiatus in the early 1990s, after playing Scarlett O'Hara in the Gone With the Wind made-for-TV sequel *Scarlett* (1994), she revived her career and began performing more often in film, TV and on the stage including playing Jackie Kennedy Onassis in a TV mini series in 2000. Other films include *Dance with a Stranger* (1985), *Scandal* (1989 – as Christine Keeler), *The Man Who Knew Too Little* (1997), *The Guilty* (2000), and more recently *44 Inch Chest* (2009) and *Diverted* (2009). She is currently appearing in the American Showtime mini-series, The Borgias. See also entries in the television section for *Coronation Street, Edge of Darkness, Emmerdale,* and *The Singing Detective*.

Whishaw, Ben (1980-) Born Benjamin John Whishaw, 14 October 1980, Clifton, Bedfordshire. Actor. Ben trained at RADA. His film debut was as Private James Deamis in *The Trench* (1999). Working mainly on stage and television for the following four years, he gave a highly acclaimed performance as the title character in Trevor Nunn's 2004 production of *Hamlet* at the Old Vic. He then made the films *Enduring Love* (2004 - as Spud), *Layer Cake* (2004 - as Sidney) and *Stoned* (2005 - as Keith Richards) before gaining the lead role of Jean-Baptiste Grenouille in the quirky, but charming, film *Perfume: The Story of a Murderer* (2006). His more recent films include the role of Arthur in the Bob Dylan-inspired *I'm Not There* (2007), poet John Keats in *Bright Star* (2009) and Ariel in *The Tempest* (2010). Ben is slated to make his debut as Q in the forthcoming Bond movie, *Skyfall* (2012). See also entries in the television section for *Criminal Justice,* and *Nathan Barley*.

White, Carol (1943-91) Born 1 April 1943, Hammersmith, London. Actress. Attended the Corona theatre school. Screen debut: *Circus Friends (1956)*. She came to prominence in the TV dramas *Up the Junction* (1965) and *Cathy Come Home* (1966). Her film roles included *Poor Cow* (1967) and *Dulcima* (1971). Autobiography: *Carol Comes Home* (1982). A move to Hollywood in the late 1960s proved to be a mistake which led to over-indulgence in drink and drugs which brought on her early death through liver failure on 16 September 1991, Miami, Florida, USA.

White, Chrissie (1895-1989) Born Ada Constance White, 23 May 1895, Brentford, London. Actress. Stage debut: Bluebell in Fairyland. Screen debut: *The Cabman's Good Fairy* (1909). Teamed up with Alma Taylor to make a series of sentimental comedies featuring The Tilly Girls - with White as Sally, including *Tilly the Tomboy Visits the Poor* (1910), *Tilly's Party* (1911) and *Tilly and the Dogs* (1911). A blue-eyed blond, she appeared in nearly 100 films between 1909 and 1924 before she married actor and director Henry Edwards and virtually retired from the screen, although she did make a brief comeback in the talkies with: *The Call of the Sea* (1930) and *General John Regan* (1933) both directed by Edwards. As a couple they were celebrated as Britains answer to Fairbanks and Pickford. Died 18 August 1989 Petersfield, Hampshire.

Whitlock, Albert (1915-99) Born Albert J Whitlock, 15 September 1915, Wandsworth, London. Special effects expert. Trained as a sign painter. Initially worked as a set-builder for *British Gaumont*. His first screen work was as a scenic artist on Hitchcock's *The 39 Steps* (1935) and he continued a close relationship with Hitchcock for many years, working with him on *The Man Who Knew Too Much* (1934), *The Lady Vanishes* (1938) and on his final film *Family Plot* (1976). Whitlock's abilities as a matte artist attracted the attention of Walt Disney, who persuaded him to move to the United States in 1954. His work for Disney includes *20,000 Leagues Under the Sea* (1954). He moved to *Universal Studios* in 1961 and became head of the matte department. Films include: *Robinson Crusoe on Mars* (1964), *Beau Geste* (1966), *Diamonds are Forever* (1971), *The Sting* (1973), *The Man Who Would be King* (1975), *High Anxiety* (1977), *The Blues Brothers* (1980), *Coming to America* (1988) and *Chaplin* (1992). Albert was considered to be the master of matte painting, a technique whereby a painted representation of a landscape gave the impression of reality. He was nominated for an Academy Award for his Special Effects for *Tobruk* (1967) and was awarded Special Achievement Academy Awards for his work on *Earthquake* (1974) and *The Hindenburg* (1975). Died 26 October 1999, Santa Barbara, California.

Whitty, May (1865-1948) Born Mary Louise Whitty, 19 June 1865, Liverpool. Actress. Made her first stage appearance in Liverpool in 1881 before moving to London to appear in the West End. She married the actor-manager Ben Webster (b, 2 June 1864, London; d. 26 February 1947, Hollywood) in 1892 and in 1895 they visited the United States where Whitty appeared on Broadway. Whilst continuing her stage career she made her first film *Enoch Arden* (1914) based on an Alfred Lord Tennyson poem with her husband as one of her co-stars. In 1918 she was made Dame of the British Empire (DBE) in recognition of her charitable work during WWI and for her contributions to acting. She made her first major Hollywood film appearance, recreating her stage role in the film *Night Must Fall* (1937) an adaptation of the Emlyn Williams' play for which she received an Academy Award nomination for Best Supporting Actress. From the mid 1930s until her death she made at least one film every year, usually in a major supporting role. She is probably best remembered as Miss Foy the eponymous character in *The Lady Vanishes* (1938). A brief glance at her character names will give some idea of the parts that she was offered, Lady Kitty Melrose in *Raffles* (1940), Lady Beldon in *Mrs. Miniver* (1942), Lady Stackhouse *Thunder Birds* (1942). It was for *Mrs. Minniver* that she received her second Best Supporting Actress Academy Award nomination. Her last films were the Glenn Ford vehicle *The Return of October* (1948) and *The Sign of the Ram* (1948), both made in the months before she died on 29 May 1948 in Beverly Hills from cancer, just a year after her husband had passed away. Their only child, daughter Margaret Webster (b. 1905, New York; d. 1972, Chilmark, Massachusetts), was a stage actress, theatrical producer, author and lecturer. She wrote biographies about her parents called *The Same Only Different* (1969) and *Don't Put Your Daughter on the Stage* (1972).

Wilcox, Herbert (1890-1977) Born Herbert Sydney Wilcox, 19 April 1890, Norwood, London. Director and producer. A little uncertain as to his own origins, official records point to him being a Londoner rather than a native of Cork as is sometimes claimed, although his mother was Irish. He was brought up and educated in Brighton. A professional billiards player in his youth before turning to film production and direction. Directorial debut: *Chu Chin Chow* (1923). Other films he directed include: *Nell Gwynne* (1926), *Goodnight Vienna* (1932), *Limelight* (1936), *No, No, Nanette* (1940), *Trent's Last Case* (1952) and *The Heart of a Man* (1959). He produced *Black Waters* (1929) which was filmed on a sound stage in Hollywood and flown back to Britain to be shown to the film trade weeks before Britain's first official "talkie" *Blackmail* (1929) was shown to the public. Herbert founded *Elstree Studios* and became head of production of *The British and Dominions Film Corporation*. One of Britain's most successful film makers of the middle decades of the 20th century. Married four times, including to Anna Neagle (1943-70) who starred in over 30 of his films including biographies such as: *Nell Gwyn* (1934), *Victoria the Great* (1937), *Sixty Glorious Years* (1938), *Nurse Edith Cavell* (1939), *They Flew Alone* (1942 – a biopic of Amy Johnstone, *Odette* (1950) and *The Lady with the Lamp* (1951); as well as the series of post-war films set in London: *I Live in Grosvenor Square* (1945), *Picadilly Incident* (1946), *The Courtneys of Curzon Street* (1947), *Spring in Park Lane* (1948) and *Maytime in Mayfair* (1949). Autobiography: *Twenty-five*

Thousand Sunsets (1967). He died 15 May 1977, Marylebone, London.

Wilcoxon, Henry (1905-84) Born 8 September 1905, Dominica, Leeward Islands, West Indies. Actor. British parents. Educated in Barbados before moving to England. Began his working life as a commercial traveller in the corn trade. Stage debut: *The Hundredth Chance* (1927). Member of Birmingham Repertory Company (1928-32). Screen debut: *The Perfect Lady* (1931). After *The Flying Squad* (1932) and *Lord of the Manor* (1933) he went to America after being cast by Cecil B DeMille as Marc Anthony in *Cleopatra* (1934). This was the beginning of a long personal friendship and professional relationship with DeMille, who next cast him as Richard the Lionheart in *The Crusades* (1935). Henry went on to play many second leads and supporting characters in such films as *The Last of the Mohicans* (1936), *That Hamilton Woman* (1941 - as Hardy), *Mrs Miniver* (1942), *A Connecticut Yankee at King Arthur's Court* (1949 - as Lancelot), *Samson and Delilah* (1949) and *Scaramouche* (1952). He featured in, and was DeMille's associate producer on, *The Greatest Show on Earth* (1952) and *The Ten Commandments* (1956). After DeMille's death in 1959 his screen appearances were fewer but his later films include *The War Lord* (1965), *Won Ton Ton, the Dog who Saved Hollywood* (1976), *F.I.S.T.* (1978), *Caddyshack* (1980) and *Sweet Sixteen* (1983). An imposing presence and chiselled features meant he was often cast as military men or aristocrats. Autobiography: *Lionheart in Hollywood* (1991). Died 6 March 1984, Los Angeles, California.

Wild, Jack (1952-2006) Born 30 September 1952, Royton, Lancashire. Actor. Child actor who played Oliver Twist in the London stage production of the Lionel Bart musical *Oliver!* He subsequently played the Artful Dodger in the film version in 1968 and gained an Academy Award nomination for Best Supporting Actor. This success led to him moving to America to take the lead role in a children's TV show *H R Pufnstuf* (1969) and the spin-off film in 1970. Other films include: *Melody (aka S.W.A.L.K.)* (1971), *Flight of the Doves* (1971), *The Pied Piper* (1972) and *The 14* (1973). He was also making pop records at this period. Unfortunately the Hollywood lifestyle and problems making the transition from child actor to adult roles resulted in personal problems including alcoholism. As a consequence of this, and heavy smoking, his health has suffered with the result that he has rarely been seen on screen. Since 1990 he has had two small film roles: *Robin Hood: Prince of Thieves* (1991) and *Basil* (1998). Having apparently beaten his alcoholism in 1989 he was subsequently diagnosed with oral cancer, resulting in major surgery during 2005. He died 1 March 2006, London.

Wilding, Michael (1912-79) Born Michael Charles Gaunlet Wilding, 23 July 1912, Westcliff-on-Sea, Essex. Actor. Initially worked as an artist. Stage debut: *The Ringer* (1934). Screen debut: *Bitter Sweet* (1933). Other films include: *Late Extra* (1935), *There Ain't No Justice* (1939), *Tilly of Bloomsbury* (1940), *The Farmer's Wife* (1941), *Kipps* (1941), *In Which We Serve* (1942), *Carnival* (1946), *Stage Fright* (1950), *Ivanhoe* (1952), *Trent's Last Case* (1952), *Danger Within* (1959), *The World of Suzie Wong* (1960), *Waterloo* (1970) and *Lady Caroline Lamb* (1972). Michael starred in six films with Anna Neagle: *Picadilly Incident* (1946), *The Courtneys of Curzon Street* (1947), *Spring in Park Lane* (1948), *Maytime in Mayfair* (1949), *The Lady with the Lamp* (1951) and *Derby Day* (1952). Married four times: Kay Young (1937-51), Elizabeth Taylor (1952-57), Susan Nell (1958-62) and Margaret Leighton (1964-76). A matinee idol whose acting talents were hidden behind his good looks. Autobiography: *Apple Sauce: The Story of My Life* (1982). He died 8 July 1979, Chichester, Sussex, after a fall during an epileptic seizure.

Wilkinson, Tom (1948-) Born 12 December 1948, Leeds, Yorkshire. Actor. Lived in Canada during his early years before the family moved back to Yorkshire. Educated at University of Kent at Canterbury. Graduated from RADA. An extremely successful stage actor he spent time with the Nottingham Theatre, Oxford Playhouse, the Royal Court and the RSC. Made his screen debut in *The Shadow Line* (1976). His next film was *Bones* (1984), which was followed by *Sylvia* (1984) and *Wetherby*

(1985). He featured in *In the Name of the Father* (1993), a Hamlet adaptation *Prince of Jutland* (1994) and starred in *Priest* (1994). Tom made a brief appearance in *Sense and Sensibility* (1995) as the dying Mr Dashwood and then featured in *The Ghost and the Darkness* (1996) and *Smilla's Sense of Snow* (1997) before landing the part of Gerald in *The Full Monty* (1997) which gave his screen career an extra boost. He followed this success by playing the Marquess of Queensbury in *Wilde* (1997) and then *Oscar and Lucinda* (1997) and *The Governess* (1998). He appeared as the villain in the big budget Jackie Chan vehicle *Rush Hour* (1998) before playing the play backer Hugh Fennyman in *Shakespeare in Love* (1998). His next projects were the American Civil War film *Ride with the Devil* (1999) and the American War of Independence themed *The Patriot* (2000). After *Essex Boys* (2000) and *Chain of Fools* (2000) he gained an Academy Award nomination for Best Actor for his role in *In The Bedroom* (2001). His more recent films include, *Black Knight* (2001), *Girl with a Pearl Earring* (2003), *Eternal Sunshine of the Spotless Mind* (2004), *Batman Begins* (2005), *The Exorcism of Emily Rose* (2005), *Michael Clayton* (2007 – for which he received an Academy Award nomination), *Duplicity* (2009), *Burke and Hare* (2010), *The Green Hornet* (2011), the Robert Redford film *The Conspirator* (2011), *The Debt* (2011) and *Mission: Impossible – Ghost Protocol* (2011). Tom has been married to actress Diana Hardcastle since 1998.

Williams, Emlyn (1905-87) Born George Emlyn Williams, 26 November 1905, Pen-y-Fford, Mostyn, Flintshire. Actor and writer. Studied in Geneva, Switzerland and at Christ Church, Oxford. Stage debut: *And So to Bed* (1927). Screen debut: *Sally Bishop* (1932). His other films include: *The Frightened Lady* (1932), *Friday the Thirteenth* (1933), *The Iron Duke* (1934), *They Drive by Night* (1938), *The Citadel* (1938), *Jamaica Inn* (1939), *The Stars Look Down* (1940), *Major Barbara* (1941), *The Magic Box* (1951), *The Wreck of the Mary Deare* (1959) and *The Walking Stick* (1970). He played the hero's squire Wamba in *Ivanhoe* (1952) and Emile Zola in *I Accuse!* (1958). Emlyn would have played Caligula in the ill-fated production of *I, Claudius* (1937) which never made it to the screen. He wrote, directed and acted in *The Last Days of Dolwyn* (1949), which was Richard Burton's debut film. He also wrote Burton's stage debut *Druid's Rest* (1944). Emlyn played Mr Dick in the 1969 TV adaptation of *David Copperfield* and he had a one-man stage show *Emlyn Williams as Charles Dickens* which was shown on television in 1983. His last performance on screen was in *Past Caring* (1985). He wrote over 20 plays including *Full Moon* (1927), *Night Must Fall* (1935) and *The Corn is Green* (1938). He also wrote the novel *Headlong* (1980) - upon which the film *King Ralph* (1991) was based. His book *Beyond Belief* (1967) was a controversial account of the Moors Murders. Autobiographies: *George* (1961) and *Emlyn* (1967). Although openly homosexual, Emlyn was married in 1935 to actress Molly Shan, who died in 1970. They had two sons, Alan, a writer, and Brook, an actor. Emlyn died of cancer at his flat in Dovehouse Street, Chelsea, 25 September 1987. See also entry in the television section for *The Great War*.

Williams, Hugh (1904-69) Born Hugh Anthony Glanmor Williams, 6 March 1904, Bexhill-on-Sea, Sussex. Actor. Studied at RADA. Stage debut: *The Charm School* (1921). Screen debut: *Charley's Aunt* (1930). Other films include: *White Face* (1932), *Rome Express* (1932), *David Copperfield* (1935 - as Steerforth), *Wuthering Heights* (1939), *The Day will Dawn* (1942), *One of Our Aircraft is Missing* (1942), *An Ideal Husband* (1947), *Gift Horse* (1952), *Khartoum* (1966) and *Doctor Faustus* (1967). A poised and debonair leading man of British films of the 1930s. Known as Tam. Co-author with his wife Margaret Vyner of several plays including *The Grass is Greener* and *Charlie Girl*. Father of actor Simon Williams and poet Hugo Williams. Died 7 December 1969, Paddington, London.

Williams, Kenneth See entry in comedy section

Williams, Michael See entry for Judi Dench

Williams, Olivia (1968-) Born Olivia Haigh Williams, 26 July 1968, Camden Town, London. Actress. Both Olivia's parents are barristers. After graduating from Newnham College, Cambridge with a degree in English literature, Olivia studied drama at the Bristol Old Vic Theatre School for two years before spending another three years at the Royal Shakespeare Company. Her first screen roles were small cameos in television series such as *Van Der Valk* and *The Ruth Rendell Mysteries* in 1992. Her first leading role was as Jane Fairfax in the TV film *Emma* (1996) and her feature debut was as Nicky in *Gaston's War* (1997). Other films include *The Postman* (1997), *Rushmore* (1998), *The Sixth Sense* (1999), *Lucky Break* (2001), *The Body* (2001), *The Heart of Me* (2002), *Peter Pan* (2003), *Broken Lines* (2008), *An Education* (2009), *Sex & Drugs & Rock & Roll* (2010), *Collaborator* (2011) and *Hanna* (2011). She was uncredited for her role as Dr Moira MacTaggert in the 2006 film *X-Men: The Last Stand*. Olivia married American actor and playwright Rhashan Stone on 2 November 2003. The couple have two children, Esmé Ruby (b. 6 April 2004) and Roxana May (b. 7 April 2007). Olivia was once in a long-term relationship with the current Polish Minister of Foreign Affairs Radosław Sikorski

Williamson, James (1855-1933) Born 8 November 1855, Kirkcaldy, Fife. Cinema pioneer. Raised in Edinburgh but moved to London in 1868 and trained to be a chemist. Lived in Eastry in Kent until 1886 when he set up a pharmacy in Hove, Sussex - a centre for early cinematography. Began selling photographic supplies and started making films in 1894. A pioneer of film narrative, beginning by faking newsreel footage, a popular film-making device of the period. Founded the *Williamson Kinematographic Company*. His early films include *Attack on a China Mission* (1901), *Fire!* (1901), *A Big Swallow* (1901) and *Stop Thief* (1901). Built a glasshouse studio and made a trilogy of films about the hardships of war *The Soldier's Return* (1902), *A Reservist Before and After the War* (1902) and *Wait Till Jack Comes Home* (1903). A keen exhibitor, he developed a service for exhibitors including the manufacture of intertitles. Directed his last film in 1908, moved to London in 1910 and began film equipment manufacture including specialist cameras such as those used for horse-race photo-finishes. Died 18 August 1933, Richmond, Surrey.

Williamson, Nicol (1938-2011) Born 14 September 1938, Hamilton, South Lanarkshire. Actor. Trained at the Birmingham School of Speech & Drama. Member of the Dundee Repertory Company and the Arts Theatre Cambridge before joining the RSC. Although making an uncredited first appearance in the 1956 Bob Hope film *The Iron Petticoat* (as a man lighting the distorted cigarette of the great comedian), Nicol's screen debut proper was in *Six-sided Triangle* (1963). Other early films such as *Inadmissable Evidence* (1968) and *Hamlet* (1969) were filmed versions of his earlier stage successes, a medium in which Nicol was unrivalled in his generation. Most of his screen performances could be said to be idiosynchratic as he brings his own style and interpretation to roles such as Little John in *Robin and Marian* (1976), Sherlock Holmes in *The Seven-Per-Cent Solution* (1976) and Merlin in *Excalibur* (1981). His other films include: *The Bofors Gun* (1968), *The Reckoning* (1969), *Le Moine* (1973), *Venom* (1982), *Return to Oz* (1985), *Black Widow* (1987), *The Exorcist III* (1990), *The Hour of the Pig* (1993), *The Wind in the Willows* (1996 – as Badger) and his last film, *Spawn* (1997). Nicol also played the title role in the highly acclaimed 1986 mini-series *Lord Mountbatten: The Last Viceroy*. A talented television and film actor who undoubtedly excelled in the theatre, Nicol perhaps failed to live up to the extreme hype of his potential in the 1960s and the prickly personality which manifests in so many of the perfectionist actors probably didn't help his career. He married actress Jill Townsend (star of *Poldark* and *The Cimarron Strip*) in 1971 but they divorced six years later. Nicol died on 16 December 2011, after a two-year struggle with esophageal cancer.

Windsor, Barbara (1937-) Born Barbara Ann Deeks, 6 August 1937, Shoreditch, London. Actress. Her first film was *The Belles of St. Trinian's* (1954) as one of the indomitable schoolgirls. Improved roles followed culminating in her leading role in Joan Littlewood's *Sparrows Can't Sing* (1963). She had also become a household name as Judy in the very popular TV series *The Rag Trade*. In 1964 she joined the *Carry On* team and thereafter she was a victim of Jack the Ripper in *A Study in Terror* (1965), but usually her work was limited to more *Carry On*'s and comedies usually focusing on her shapeliness rather than her acting ability. In total Barbara appeared in nine Carry Ons: *Carry On Spying* (1964 – as Daphne Honeybutt), *Carry On Doctor* (1967 - as Nurse Sandra May), *Carry On Camping* (1969 - as Babs), *Carry On*

Again Doctor (1969 - as Goldie Locks), *Carry On Henry* (1971 - as Bettina), *Carry On Matron* (1972 - as Nurse Susan Ball), *Carry On Abroad* (1972 - as Sadie Tomkins), *Carry On Girls* (1973 - as Hope Springs) and *Carry On Dick* (1974 - as Harriet). Other films include *A Kid for Two Farthings* (1955), *Crooks in Cloisters* (1964), *Chitty Chitty Bang Bang* (1968), *The Boy Friend* (1971), *Not Now, Darling* (1973), *It Couldn't Happen Here* (1987) and *Alice in Wonderland* (2010 – voice of Mallymkun, the Dormouse). Typecast, her work showed little variety until her appearance in *Eastenders* (1994-2010) as the matriarch of the Queen Vic, Peggy Mitchell. Barbara has married three times: to gangster Ronnie Knight (married 2 March 1964; divorced January 1985), Stephen Hollings (married 12 April 1986 in Jamaica; divorced 1995) and Scott Mitchell (married 8 April 2000-present). Autobiography, *All of Me: My Extraordinary Life* (2001). See also entries in the television section for *Carry On Laughing, Eastenders, The Rag Trade, Who Do You Think You Are?, Worzel Gummidge,* and *You Rang M'Lord.*

Winner, Michael (1935-) Born Robert Michael Winner, 30 October 1935, Hampstead, London. Director, producer and writer. Studied law at Downing College, Cambridge. His early career was at the BBC before he directed the B-feature *Shoot to Kill* (1960) and the nudist film *Some Like it Cool* (1961). His first main feature was *Play it Cool* (1962), starring Billy Fury and his first real success was *West 11* (1963). His films *The System* (1964), *The Jokers* (1967) and *I'll Never Forget What's 'is Name* (1967) were reflective of 1960s London and all starred Oliver Reed, as did *Hannibal Brooks* (1969). His move to Hollywood saw him make the westerns *Lawman* (1971) and *Chato's Land* (1972) and an adaptation of Henry James's Turn of the Screw, *The Nightcomers* (1972) before he moved on to the violent action thrillers which were to become something of a trademark. These include *The Mechanic* (1972), *The Stone Killer* (1973), *Death Wish* (1974) and the inferior sequels *Death Wish II* (1982) and *Death Wish 3* (1985). His other films include *Won Ton Ton, the Dog who Saved Hollywood* (1976), remakes of *The Big Sleep* (1978) and *The Wicked Lady* (1983), *A Chorus of Disapproval* (1988), the revenge film *Dirty Weekend* (1993) and the comedy revenge film *Parting Shots* (1999). Michael often edits his films under the name Arnold Crust. Nowadays he writes restaurant reviews and appears in TV adverts. Michael had a long-term relationship with actress Jenny Seagrove but after being a life-long bachelor married Geraldine Lynton Edwards in Chelsea, London on 19 September 2011.

Winslet, Kate (1975-) Born Kate Elizabeth Winslet, 5 October 1975, Reading, Berkshire. Actress. She is best remembered as Rose DeWitt Bukater in the 1997 blockbuster film *Titanic*. Her career began on television, with a co-starring role in the BBC children's science-fiction serial *Dark Season* (1991), followed by an appearance in an episode of the BBC television medical drama *Casualty* in 1993. Kate's film career took off in 1994 when she performed her first leading role as Juliet Hulme in Peter Jackson's *Heavenly Creatures*. Her high quality performances have thus far earned her six Academy Award nominations for *Sense and Sensibility* (1995), *Titanic* (1997), *Iris* (2001), *Eternal Sunshine of the Spotless Mind* (2004), *Little Children* (2006) and *The Reader* (2008)- her performance as Hanna Schmitz in the last named film winning the Academy Award for Best Actress. In 2000 she won a Grammy Award for Best Spoken Word Album for Children for *Listen To the Storyteller*. Some of her other major roles have been in *Quills* (2000), *Finding Neverland* (2004), *The Holiday* (2006), *Flushed Away* (2006), and *Revolutionary Road* (2008), a film directed by Sam Mendes and co-starring Leonardo De Caprio. Her most recent films have been *Contagion* (2011) and *Carnage* (2011). She won a Golden Globe for her title role of Mildred Pierce in the HBO mini series in 2011. Kate has also enjoyed a brief taste of success as a singer, with her single *What If* from the *Christmas Carol: The Movie* (2001) soundtrack. *What If* debuted at No 1 on the Irish Singles Chart in December 2001 and peaked at No 6 on the UK Singles Chart. She has married twice: to director Jim Threapleton (1998–2001) with whom she has a daughter, Mia Honey (b. 12 October 2000), and in 2003 to

director Sam Mendes with whom she has a son, Joe Alfie Winslet-Mendes (b. 22 December 2003). The couple announced their separation in March 2010. Her sisters Anna (b. Anna Melissa Winslet, 1972 Reading, Berkshire) and Beth (b. Beth Amelia Winslet, 1978 Reading, Berkshire) are both actresses. Kate's home town of Reading has named a street - Winslet Place - in her honour. See also entries in the television section for *Dark Season*, and *Extras*.

Winstone, Jaime (1985-) Born Jaime Margaret Winstone, 6 May 1985, Camden, London. Actress. Daughter of actor Ray Winstone and his wife Elaine McCausland. Made her film debut as Becky in *Bullet Boy* (2004). Other films include *Daddy's Girl* (2006), *Kidulthood* (2006), *Donkey Punch* (2008), *Boogie Woogie* (2009), *Made in Dagenham* (2010) and *Anuvahood* (2011). She also starred in the Channel 4 television series *Goldplated* (2006) and in an episode of *Vincent* (2005), alongside her father. Jaime made her modelling debut in 2008, for Vivienne Westwood and in February 2009 she appeared on the front cover of Arena. See also entries in the television section for *Five Daughters*, and *Goldplated.*

Winstone, Ray (1957-) Born Raymond Andrew Winstone, 19 February 1957, Hackney, London. Actor. An amateur boxer who was London Schoolboy Champion and boxed for England. Studied acting at Corona School. Ray made his television acting debut in *Scum* (1977) which was shelved and then reshot as a feature film in 1979. This was swiftly followed by *Quadrophenia* (1979) and *That Summer* (1979). On television he featured as Will Scarlet in *Robin of Sherwood* (1984). His next films were *Ladybird Ladybird* (1994), *Yellow* (1996) and *Masculine Mescaline* (1996) before making an award-winning impact in *Nil by Mouth* (1997). He was in increasing demand as a tough guy in films such as *War Zone* (1999) but also in more gentle roles in films like *Fanny and Elvis* (1999). He starred in *Sexy Beast* (2001), *Last Orders* (2001) and *Ripleys Game* (2002) before being cast as the larger than life king in *Henry VIII* (2003) on television. Recent films include *King Arthur* (2004), *The Proposition* (2005), voice characterisations in *The Magic Roundabout* (2005) and *The Lion the Witch and the Wardrobe* (2005), *The Departed* (2006), *Beowulf* (2007), *Indiana Jones and the Kingdom of the Crystal Skull* (2008), *44 Inch Chest* (2009), *Sex & Drugs & Rock & Roll* (2010), *Percy Jackson & the Olympians: The Lightning Thief* (2010 - as Ares), *Edge of Darkness* (2010), *London Boulevard* (2010), *Tracker* (2010), *Rango* (2011 - voice of Bad Bill) and *Hugo* (2011). He also starred on television in *Vincent* (2005) and in the title role of *Sweeney Todd* (2006). Obviously liking the Sweeney theme, Ray is currently filming the forthcoming series of *The Sweeney*, taking on the role of Jack Regan opposite Ben Drew (Plan B) as George Carter. Ray married Elaine McCausland in 1979 and they have three children. Their eldest Lois Winstone (b. 1982), is a part-time actress, part time model and part-time pop star, currently part of electro pop band *This Year's Model*. Lois was the face and body of the Ann Summers Spring Summer 2009 Enchantment lingerie collection. See separate entry for Jaime Winstone. See also entries in the television section for *Fox, Robin of Sherwood*, and *Vincent.*

Winterbottom, Michael (1961-) Born 29 March 1961, Blackburn, Lancashire. Director. Studied English at Oxford and film-making at Bristol University. Worked as an editor for *Thames Television* and the *BBC*. His directorial screen debut was the documentary *Ingmar Bergman - The Director* (1988). His work for TV includes an episode of *Cracker* (1993) and *Family* (1994). Michael formed *Revolution Films* with producer Andrew Eaton in March 1994 and made his feature debut with *Butterfly Kiss* (1995), a lesbian road movie. His next film, *Jude* (1996), an adaptation of Thomas Hardy's *Jude the Obscure*, starring Christopher Eccleston and Kate Winslet. *Welcome to Sarajevo* (1997) was based on war correspondent Michael Nicholson's book *Natasha's Story*. After the romantic dramas *I Want You* (1998) and *Wonderland* (1998) he directed his first big-budget project *The Claim* (2000), a loose adaptation of Thomas Hardy's *The Mayor of Casterbridge* transposed to the Sierra Nevada. *24 Hour Party People* (2002) documented the 1980s "Madchester" music scene using Winterbottom's normal techniques of montage, jump cuts and a mixture of fictional and archive footage. His *In this World* (2002) is about an Afghan refugee seeking asylum in Britain and he followed this with a foray into science fiction with *Code 46* (2003). He courted controversy with the explicitness of the sex scenes in *9 Songs* (2004) and his latest films are *Tristram Shandy: A Cock and Bull Story* (2006), *The Road to Guantanamo* (2006), *A Mighty Heart* (2007), *Genova* (2008), *The Shock Doctrine* (2009) and *The Killer Inside Me* (2010). Michael also directed the 2010 television sitcom series, *The Trip,* starring Steve Coogan and Rob Brydon.

Wisdom, Norman See entry in comedy section

Withers, Googie (1917-2011) Born Georgette Lizette Withers, 12 March 1917, Karachi, Sindh Province, British India (now part of Pakistan). Actress. "Googie" apparently means "little pigeon" in Hindi, although a mispronunciation of Georgette might also explain the epithet. Originally a dancer she made her stage debut as a child in *The Windmill Man* (1929) and by 1935 had landed a lead role on stage in *Happy Weekend* and on screen in *The Girl in the Crowd*, both times being promoted from understudying after original actresses were sacked. Her career then followed much the same course as that of other British actresses of the era. She played a friend of Margaret Lockwood in *The Lady Vanishes* (1938*)* and starred opposite Will Hay in *Convict 99* (1939) and George Formby in *Trouble Brewing* (1939). Her dramatic break came when Michael Powell cast her in *One of Our Aircraft is Missing* (1942). At the same time she appeared in J B Priestley's *They Came to a City* in the West End, a role she reprised on film in 1945. She had some good roles in the late 1940s and early 1950s in such films as *Dead of Night* (1945), *Pink String and Sealing Wax* (1946), *It Always Rains on Sunday* (1948) and *Miranda* (1948). After *Port of Escape* (1956) she disappeared from our screens and moved to Australia with her husband, Australian actor and director John McCallum (b.14 March 1918; d. 3 February 2010) who she had met on the set of *The Loves of Joanna Godden* (1947). They were married in 1948 and the marriage produced three children including actress Joanna McCallum (b. 27 June 1950). Googie continued stage work alongside her husband and finally returned to screen acting during the 1970s, most memorably as prison governess Faye Boswell in the TV drama *Within These Walls* (1974-75). Her subsequent films were *Time after Time* (1986), *Country Life* (1994) and, her last film, *Shine* (1996). She was awarded the CBE in 2002. Granada Television was forced to issue an apology for Googie's premature 'death' in 2004 after the character Norris Cole quipped, in an episode of Coronation Street, "Googie Withers would turn in her grave". Googie did however die on 15 July 2011, Sydney, Australia. See also entries in the television section for *Trainer,* and *Within These Walls.*

Wolfit, Donald (1902-68) Born Donald Woolfitt, 20 April 1902, Balderton, Nottinghamshire. Actor. Donald took up acting in 1920 after having elocution lessons. Screen debut: *Death at Broadcasting House* (1934). Other films during the 1930s include: *Hyde Park Corner* (1935), *Drake of England* (1935) and *Calling the Tune* (1936). He formed his own theatre company in 1937, *The Donald Wolfit Shakespeare Company* which specialised in abridged versions of Shakespeare. He continued to perform during the Blitz in WWII. Appointed CBE in 1950 and knighted in 1957 for his services to the theatre. Donald returned to the screen as Sergeant Buzfuz in *The Pickwick Papers* (1952). Other films include: *Svengali* (1954), *I Accuse!* (1958), *Room at the Top* (1959), *The Hands of Orlac* (1961), *Dr Crippen* (1962), *Lawrence of Arabia* (1962), *Becket* (1964), *Life at the Top* (1965), *The Charge of the Light Brigade* (1968) and *Decline and Fall... of a Birdwatcher* (1968). Donald toured with his own company during the late 1950s and he caused some resentment in 1962 when he sided with the management during an *Actor's Equity* strike. On television he starred as Sir Andrew Wilson in *Ghost Squad* (1961-63). Ronald Harwood was once Donald's dresser and he based his award winning play *The Dresser* (later turned into a film) on his relationship with Wolfit. He died 17 February 1968, Hammersmith, London. See also entries in the television section for *Ghost Squad,* and *Hour of Mystery.*

Woodward, Edward (1930-2009) Born Edward Albert Arthur Woodward, 1 June 1930, Croydon, Surrey. Actor. Studied at RADA. Stage debut: *A Kiss for Cinderella* (1946). Edward spent years in repertory before appearing on the London stage in 1955 in *Where There's a Will*, which also became his screen debut the following year when it was adapted as a feature film. Edward next had a small role in the film adaptation of the very popular *Larkins* television serial, *Inn for Trouble* (1960) and an even smaller role in *Becket* (1964) before gaining larger parts in *File of the Golden Goose* (1969), *Incense for the Damned* (1970), *Sitting Target* (1972) and *Young Winston* (1972). On television he was in series such as *Emergency Ward 10* (1957) and *Sword of Honour* (1967) before he starred as David Callan in the series *Callan* (1967-72) winning great acclaim with his portrayal of the brooding, world-weary spy. Principally a television actor, Edward showed his versatility as the repressed Scottish policeman, Howie, in the cult horror film *The Wicker Man* (1973) after which he starred in the film version of *Callan* (1974) and the British comedy films *Three for All* (1975) and *Stand Up, Virgin Soldiers* (1977). His next screen role was as the title character in the Australian story of the court-martial of *Breaker Morant* (1980). During the 1980s his television work included *Winston Churchill: The Wilderness Years* (1981) and *Arthur the King* (1985) but he once again struck a popular chord, on both sides of the Atlantic, with his role of Robert McCall in *The Equalizer* (1985-89). His later films include *Who Dares Wins* (1982), *Champions* (1984 – as trainer Josh Gifford), *King David* (1985), *Mister Johnson* (1990), *Deadly Advice* (1993), *The House of Angelo* (1997), *The Abduction Club* (2002), *Hot Fuzz* (2007) and his last film role as the Reverend Frederick Densham in *A Congregation of Ghosts* (2009). In parallel with his screen career he also featured in stage musicals such as *Blithe Spirit* and *Two Cities* and appeared in television singing specials such as *The Edward Woodward Hour* (1971) as well as releasing several albums. Awarded an OBE in 1978, Edward married twice, to actress Venetia Barrett (1952-86) and then to actress Michele Dotrice from 1987 until his death on 16 November 2009, Truro, Cornwall. He is survived by his wife, and their daughter, Emily Beth Woodward (b. 1983), and the three children of his first marriage, actors Tim Woodward (b. 1953), Peter Woodward (b. 1956) and Sarah Woodward (b. 1963). See also entries in the television section for *Callan, Common as Muck, Eastenders, The Equalizer, Shadow Squad, Winston Churchill - The Wilderness Years* and *Whodunnit?*

Wymark, Patrick (1926-70) Born Patrick Cheeseman, 11 July 1926, Cleethorpes, Lincolnshire. Actor. Studied at University College London. Trained for the stage at the Old Vic Theatre School. Stage debut: *Othello* (1951). Toured South Africa in 1952 and directed at the drama department Stanford University, California in 1953-54. Member of the Shakespeare Memorial Theatre (1955-58) and The RSC (1960-62). Screen debut: *The League of Gentlemen* (1960). Other films include: *The Criminal* (1960), *West 11* (1963), *Children of the Damned* (1964), *Repulsion* (1965), *Witchfinder General* (1968 - as Oliver Cromwell), *Where Eagles Dare* (1968), *Battle of Britain* (1969), *Cromwell* (1970 - as The Earl of Strafford) and *Blood on Satan's Claw* (1970). Patrick appeared as Winston Churchill in *Operation Crossbow* (1965), having previously performed voice over impersonations of the great statesman for various documentaries. Although a fine film actor, Patrick is probably best known for his television roles, notably as the rather unpleasant managing director Sir John Wilder in *The Plane Makers* (1963-65) and its sequel *The Power Game* (1965-69). Married to American playwright Olwen Wymark (from whom he took his stage name) from 1953 until his death, the couple had four children including television actress Jane Wymark (b.31 October 1952). Patrick died of a heart attack 20 October 1970, Melbourne, Australia, and is buried in Highgate Cemetery.

Wynter, Dana (1931-2011) Born Dagmar Winter, 8 June 1931, the daughter of Hungarian-born Jutta Oarda and Dr Peter Wynter, a noted British surgeon. Actress. Brought up in England she moved to Southern Rhodesia with her father when she was 16-years-old and eventually enrolled at Rhodes University in South Africa and began studying medicine. She then abandoned her studies and moved back to England in 1950 and took up acting seriously after performing in amateur productions in Africa. During a performance at the Hammersmith Apollo she was spotted by an American agent and a series of bit parts in films soon followed. Her debut came in *Night Without Stars* (1951) and her early films included *White Corridors* (1951), *Lady Godiva Rides Again* (1951), *The Crimson Pirate* (1952) and *It Started in Paradise* (1952), all credited as Dagmar Wynter. In November 1953, having changer her name to Dana Wynter, she moved to Hollywood (via New York) and initially carved out a career in television before gaining the role of Becky Driscoll in the original film version of *Invasion of the Body Snatchers* (1956). Dana went on to star opposite Robert Taylor in *D-Day the Sixth of June* (1956), Rock Hudson and Sidney Poitier in *Something of Value* (1957), Mel Ferrer in *Fräulein* (1958), Robert Wagner in *In Love and War* (1958), James Cagney in *Shake Hands with the Devil* (1959), Kenneth More in *Sink the Bismarck!* (1960), Danny Kaye in *On the Double* (1961), and George C. Scott in *The List of Adrian Messenger* (1963), before concentrating mainly on American television roles, although also appearing in Irish soap opera, *Bracken* (she owned a home in Glendalough, County Wicklow) between 1978 and 1980. Other films include: *Airport* (1970), *Santee* (1973) and her last feature film, *Call Me Savage* (1975). Dana also played Queen Elizabeth II in the TV movie *The Royal Romance of Charles and Diana* (1982). Her last screen appearance was as Raymond Burr's wife in *The Return of Ironside* (1993). She was married to celebrity attorney Greg Bautzer between 1956 and 1981. They had one son, Mark Ragan Bautzer (b. 29 January 1960). Dana died on 5 May 2011, from congestive heart failure, at the Ojai Valley Community Hospital's Continuing Care Center, California.

Wynyard, Diana (1906-64) Born Dorothy Isobel Cox, 16 January 1906, Lewisham, London. Actress. A successful stage actress whose first feature was *Rasputin and the Empress* (1932), a film famous as the only one where all three Barrymore siblings appeared together. She was nominated in 1933 for the Academy Award for Best Actress for the film that won the Best Film Award *Cavalcade* (1933), losing to Katherine Hepburn for *Morning Glory* (1933). Thereafter she returned to the stage for the remainder of the decade. Diana's other films include *On the Night of the Fire* (1940), *Gaslight* (1940), *An Ideal Husband* (1947), *Tom Brown's Schooldays* (1951) and her final film *Island in the Sun* (1957). She was married to film director Sir Carol Reed from 1943 to 1947. Diana joined the National Theatre in its inaugural year of 1963 but died from a kidney ailment shortly afterwards on 13 May 1964, Holborn, London.

Yates, Peter (1929-2011) Born Peter J Yates, 24 July 1929, Aldershot, Hampshire. Director and producer. Educated at Charterhouse and RADA. Acted in repertory before taking up racing driving as an amateur and working with a team featuring Stirling Moss. Worked in dubbing and editing before becoming assistant director on *The Inn of the Sixth Happiness* (1958). Also worked as assistant director on *The Entertainer* (1960), *The Guns of Navarone* (1961), *A Taste of Honey* (1961) and *The Roman Spring of Mrs Stone* (1961). His first solo directing job was on the TV series *The Saint* (1962) before he made his big screen directorial debut with *Summer Holiday* (1963), starring Cliff Richard. His followed this with an adaptation of the play *One Way Pendulum* (1964) which he had also directed at the Royal Court Theatre. Returning to TV to work on *Danger Man* he did not direct for cinema again until *Robbery* (1967). The car chase in this film led to him being signed up to direct *Bullitt* (1968) in Hollywood, which features one of the most famous car chases in cinematic history. His films in the 1970s include *Murphy's War* (1971), *The Hot Rock* (1972), *The Friends of Eddie Coyle* (1973), *Mother, Jugs and Speed* (1976) and *The Deep* (1977). His next film, which he also produced, was *Breaking Away* (1979). Noted for its quiet charm it was an unlikely hit and gained Academy Award nominations for Best Picture and Best Director. He produced and directed another stage adaptation *The Dresser* (1983), which gained the same two Academy Award nominations as *Breaking Away*. Other films include: the thriller *Eyewitness* (1981), the comic-book based *Krull* (1983), *Suspect* (1987), *The House on Carroll Street* (1988), *Roommates* (1995), *Curtain Call* (1999) and the TV films *Don Quixote* (2000) and *A Separate Peace* (2004). Peter is notable for the way he has covered so many

genres from coming of age to comic book to thriller to action. He died in London on 9 January 2011 and left a widow Virginia Pope (m. 1960) and two children.

York, Michael (1942-) Born Michael Hugh Johnson, 27 March 1942, Fulmer, Buckinghamshire. Actor. Educated at Bromley Grammar School and University College, Oxford. A member of the National Youth Theatre and the Oxford University Dramatic Society. Worked at Dundee Repertory Company and then joined the National Theatre Company in 1965. Screen debut: *Red and Blue* (1967). Played Lucentio in *The Taming of the Shrew* (1967) and Tybalt in *Romeo and Juliet* (1968) both directed by Franco Zeffirelli. He was later to take the role of John the Baptist in Zeffirelli's TV series *Jesus of Nazareth* (1977). Michael was already a television star, having made a breakthrough as Jolyon Forsyte in the acclaimed 1967 production of the *Forsyte Saga*. He went on to achieve success in *Cabaret* (1972), as D'Artagnan in *The Three Musketeers* (1973) and *The Four Musketeers* (1974), *Murder on the Orient Express* (1974), as Logan 5 in *Logan's Run* (1976) and as Beau Geste in *The Last Remake of Beau Geste* (1977). Michael was a continuous screen presence on television during the 1980s including a stint in *Knots Landing* (1987-88) before again taking up his sword as D'Artagnan for *The Return of the Musketeers* (1989). He has continued to mix television, film and stage work, with his most notable big screen roles being Basil Exposition in *Austin Powers: International Man of Mystery* (1997), *Austin Powers: The Spy Who Shagged Me* (1999) and Austin Powers in *Goldmember* (2002) and as Stone Alexander in *The Omega Code* (1999) and *Megiddo: The Omega Code 2* (2001). He has also buckled on his sword belt to reprise D'Artagnan yet one more time for the TV series *La Femme Musketeer* (2004). Michael is also in great demand as a narrator for audio books. He wrote *A Shakespearean Actor Prepares* (2001) and *Dispatches from Armageddon: Making the Movie Megiddo* (2002), plus an autobiography: *Travelling Player* (1993). Appointed an OBE. Became a US citizen in October 2004. Married to photographer Pat McCallum since 1968, Michael's step-son is *Star Wars* producer Rick McCallum. Michael's latest film role was as Nicholas Jonghelinck in *The Mill and the Cross* (2011), was inspired by Peter Bruegel's painting, Christ Carrying A Cross. See also entries in the television section for *The Forsyte Saga*, and *Jesus of Nazareth*.

York, Susannah (1942-2011) Born Susannah Yolande Fletcher, 9 January 1939, London. Actress. Susannah studied at the RADA in London. Her first screen outing was *Tunes of Glory* (1960) and followed this with a starring role in *The Greengage Summer* (1961). She first gained international prominence as the winsome object of Albert Finney's affection in *Tom Jones* (1963). Other major films followed including *A Man for All Seasons* (1966), *The Killing of Sister George* (1968) and *Battle of Britain* (1969). She was nominated for a Best Supporting Actress Academy Award for *They Shoot Horses, Don't They?* (1969). Susannah co-starred with George C. Scott (as Edward Rochester) playing the title role in an American television movie of *Jane Eyre* (1970). In 1972 she won the Best Actress award at the Cannes Film Festival for her role in *Images* (1972). Susannah played Superman's mother Lara on the doomed planet Krypton in *Superman* (1978) and its sequels, *Superman II* (1980) and *Superman IV: The Quest for Peace* (1987), although never commanding the mega-fees of her screen husband, played by Marlon Brando. She has also written books for children, including *In Search of Unicorns (1973)* and *Lark's Castle (1975)*. In 1960 she married Michael Wells. The couple had two children, Orlando and Sasha, but they divorced in 1976. In the 1984 TV adaptation of *A Christmas Carol*, she played Mrs Cratchit and both of her children co-starred as offspring of the Cratchit's. Susannah again worked with George C. Scott (who played Ebenezer Scrooge) in this production. In recent years Susannah concentrated on stage and television work. She was the quintessential English rose in her early films and played the vulnerable sensuous blonde in an understated manner but with great conviction. Susannah died of cancer at the Royal Marsden Hospital in London, 15 January 2011, six days after her 72nd birthday. See also entries in the television section for *Holby City*, *Trainer*, and *We'll Meet Again*.

Young, Freddie (1902-98) Born Frederick Archibald Young, 9 October 1902, Marylebone, London. Cinematographer. After a year working in a munitions factory he began work at the Gaumont Studios at Shepherd's Bush in 1917, initially in the laboratory before becoming assistant cameraman on *Rob Roy* (1922). He worked on *The Flag Lieutenant* (1926) and *The Somme* (1927) before becoming chief cameraman on *Victory* (1928). Joined Herbert Wilcox at The *British and Dominions Film Corporation* in 1929 and filmed many Anna Neagle vehicles such as *Nell Gwyn* (1934) and *Victoria the Great* (1937). After shooting *Goodbye Mr Chips* (1939) Freddie spent a brief period in Hollywood with Wilcox and Neagle on *Nurse Edith Cavell* (1939) before returning to England to join the Army Film Unit during WWII. He was also able to work on *49th Parallel* (1941) and *The Young Mr Pitt* (1942) at this time. After the war he worked as an independent and was able to apply his lush colour camerawork to films such as *Caesar and Cleopatra* (1945). He gained an Academy Award nomination for Best Colour Cinematography for *Ivanhoe* (1952). During the 1950s his films include *Lust for Life* (1956) and *The Inn of the Sixth Happiness* (1958). At the top of his profession during the 1960s, winning no less than three Academy Awards for Best Cinematography for the David Lean films *Lawrence of Arabia* (1962), *Dr Zhivago* (1965) and *Ryan's Daughter* (1970). He gained another Academy Award nomination for Best Cinematography for his work on *Nicholas and Alexandra* (1970). His later films include *Luther* (1973), *Bloodline* (1979) and *Invitation to the Wedding* (1985). In 1985, at the age of 82, he made his directorial debut with *Arthur's Hallowed Ground*. In his final years he turned to painting rather than the camera. Undoubtedly one of the world's greatest cameramen. Appointed OBE in 1970. Autobiography: *Seventy Light Years: A Life in Movies* (1999). Died 1 December 1998, Roehampton, Surrey.

Young, Roland (1887-1953) Born Roland Keith Young, 11 November 1887, Brentford, Middlesex (now Greater London). Actor. Trained at RADA. Stage debut in 1908 and on Broadway by 1912, after which he decided to remain in the United States. Made his screen debut as Dr Watson opposite John Barrymore's portrayal of the Baker Street sleuth in *Sherlock Holmes* (1922). Other films include: *The Prodigal* (1931), *Wedding Rehearsal* (1933), *The Man Who Could Work Miracles* (1936), *King Solomon's Mines* (1937), *No, No, Nanette* (1940), *Tales of Manhattan* (1942), *Let's Dance* (1950), *St Benny the Dip* (1951) and *The Man from Tangier* (1953). His best known roles were as Uriah Heep in *David Copperfield* (1935), the Earl of Burnfield in *Ruggles of Red Gap* (1935), Uncle Willie in *The Philadelphia Story* (1940) and as Cosmo Topper in *Topper* (1937) for which he was nominated for an Academy Award for Best Supporting Actor and spawned the ghostly sequels *Topper Takes a Trip* (1938) and *Topper Returns* (1941). Roland also wrote *Actors and Others* (1925), a collection of 92 black-and-white caricatures of luminaries in film, literature, and other sectors of our culture. Died 5 June 1953 New York, New York State.

Young, Terence (1915-94) Born 20 June 1915, Shanghai, China. Director, producer and writer. Studied at St Catherine's College, Cambridge. Began his film career as a writer on films such as *Dangerous Moonlight* (1941), *On Approval* (1944) and *The Bad Lord Byron* (1949). Directorial feature debut: *Corridor of Mirrors* (1948). His WWII experiences as a member of the Parachute Regiment had encouraged him to write and direct a documentary called *Men of Arnhem* (1946) and he also directed the wartime based feature films *They were not Divided* (1950) and *The Red Beret* (1953). His other films from the 1950s include *Storm Over the Nile* (1955), *Sahara* (1956), *Action of the Tiger* (1957) and Cliff Richard's debut *Serious Charge* (1959). Terence is probably best remembered for helming three early James Bond films: *Dr No* (1962), *From Russia with Love* (1963) and *Thunderball* (1965), which helped establish the series as a hit franchise. His later films include *The Amorous Adventures of Moll Flanders* (1965), *Wait Until Dark* (1967), *Mayerling* (1968), *Inchon* (1981), *The Jigsaw Man* (1983) and *Run for Your Life* (1988). Died 7 September 1994, Cannes, Alpes-Maritimes, France.

Yule, Joe (1892-1950) Born Ninnian Yule, 30 April 1892, Hutchesontown, Glasgow. Comic and actor. Son of a boilermaker.

His family moved to the United States in 1893. Had a long career as a vaudevillian before his screen debut in *Idiot's Delight* (1939). His film career was relatively undistinguished, including appearances in *Strike Up the Band* (1940), *Go West* (1940), *For Me and My Gal* (1942), *Kismet* (1944) and *The Thin Man Goes Home* (1945). In his final films he played the character Jiggs in a series of four films based on a popular cartoon strip: *Jiggs and Maggie in Society* (1947), *Jiggs and Maggie in Court* (1948), *Jiggs and Maggie in Jackpot Jitters* (1949) and *Jiggs and Maggie Out West* (1950). Joe is the father of film star Mickey Rooney (aka Joe Yule Jr b. 23 September 1920 Brooklyn, New York) with whom he appeared in *Babes on Broadway* (1941). Died 30 March 1950, Hollywood, California.

Catherine Zeta-Jones (1969-) Born Catherine Jones, 25 September 1969, Swansea, West Glamorgan. Actress. Her name stems from those of her grandmothers; one named Catherine, and the other Zeta (named after a ship which her great-grandfather had sailed on). Her stage career began in childhood as she sang and danced her way to local stardom as part of a Catholic congregation's performing troupe before she was ten-years-old. By 1987 she was starring in *Forty-Second Street* as Peggy Sawyer in the West End. Once the show closed she travelled to France (she is fluent in French), where she received the lead role in her feature film debut, Phillippe De Broca's *1001 Nights* (1990). *The Darling Buds of May* TV series soon followed in 1991 and she captivated many a male heart as Mariette Jane Larkin. More challenging roles ensued, particularly that of Chloe opposite Ewan McGregor and Sean Pertwee in *Blue Juice* (1995), but it was not until *The Mask of Zorro* (1998) with Antonio Banderas and *Entrapment* (1999) with Sean Connery that she became a bankable star in the United States. Danny DeVito introduced Catherine to American actor Michael Douglas at the Deauville Film Festival in France in August 1998, although they did not begin a relationship until March 1999, eventually becoming engaged on New Years Eve and marrying at the Plaza Hotel in New York City on 18 November 2000. They have two children. Their son, Dylan was born on 8 August 2000, with Catherine's pregnancy incorporated into her most-acclaimed film role to that point, Helena Ayala in *Traffic* (2000). Their daughter Carys Zeta was born on 20 April 2003. Despite being exactly 25 years younger (they share the same birthday) the marriage has been a success, sometimes in the face of adversity. In 2004, the couple took legal action against stalker Dawnette Knight, who was found guilty of sending violent letters that contained graphic threats on Catherine's life. Knight was sentenced to three years imprisonment. More recently Michael has fought cancer, apparently successfully. Catherine's next film *America's Sweethearts* (2001) was a moderate hit but her performance as Velma Kelly in the musical *Chicago* (2002) won Catherine box office acclaim as well as an Academy Award for Best Supporting Actress (presented to her by Sean Connery). Other films include the DreamWorks animation *Sinbad: Legend of the Seven Seas* (2003 - voice of Marina), *Intolerable Cruelty* (2003 - as Marylin Rexroth), *The Terminal* (2004 - as Amelia Warren), *Ocean's Twelve* (2004 - as Isabel Lahiri), a reprisal of her role as Elena in *The Legend of Zorro* (2005), *No Reservations* (2007 - as Kate Armstrong), *Death Defying Acts* (2008 - as Mary McGarvie) and *The Rebound* (2009 - as Sandy). Most of the aforementioned films being romantic comedies, a genre Catherine suits admirably. She is currently the global spokeswoman for cosmetics giant Elizabeth Arden and performs a similar duty for Di Modolo jewellery. Catherine was appointed Commander of the Order of the British Empire (CBE) in the 2010 Birthday Honours. She has recently completed filming for three films due for release in 2012: Playing the Field, Lay the Favourite and Rock of Ages. See also entries in the television section for *The Darling Buds of May*, and *Star Stories*.

Zetterling, Mai (1925-94) Born Mai Elisabet Zetterling 24 May 1925, Vasteras, Sweden. Actress, director and writer. Included here as she became a stalwart of the British film and theatre scene from the 1940s onwards. As a teenager Zetterling joined a children's theatre club and trained at the Royal Dramatic Theatre School, Stockholm. She met Alf Sjöberg, who took her under his wing and directed her first film *Frenzy (aka Torment)* (1944). Her almost obligatory collaboration with Ingmar Bergman came with

Night Is My Future (aka Music in Darkness) (1948). She came to England to feature in Frieda (1947) and spent the 1950s co-starring with such stars as Richard Widmark, Tyrone Power and Danny Kaye in mostly unremarkable vehicles. In 1961 she co-starred with Peter Sellers in the more successful Only Two Can Play. In 1964 she made her directorial debut with the typically Swedish Alaskande Par (Loving Couples), and then followed this up two years later with Nattlek (Night Games). Both of these showed touches of Bergman and were introspective and anxiety-ridden. She notes in her autobiography All Those Tomorrows (1985) that when the reviews of her first full-length film came out, they said that she "directs like a man". In 1983 she made her most well known film Scrubbers and in the 1990s, shortly before her death, she returned to film acting with The Witches (1990) and Ken Loach's Hidden Agenda (1990). Her final film was Morfars resa (Grandpa's Journey) (1993). She died of cancer on 17th March 1994, Westminster, London.

Zucco, George (1886-1960) Born George D Zucco, 11 January 1886, Manchester. Actor. Educated at Borden Grammar School. Worked as a clerk in a stockbroker's office before moving with his family to Canada. Stage debut: What Happened to Jones (1908) in Regina, Saskatchewan. He returned to England in 1914 to join up during WWI and met film director James Whale. He was wounded in the right arm whilst fighting in France. Screen debut: The Dreyfus Case (1931). Other early films include The Midshipmaid (1932) and Autumn Crocus (1934) before he moved to the US after appearing on Broadway. First Hollywood films include After the Thin Man (1936), Parnell (1937) and Marie Antoinette (1938). Found a niche as an arch-villain. Played Rolf Alferson "The Stinger" in Arrest Bulldog Drummond (1939), the Royal Procurator in The Hunchback of Notre Dame (1939) and Professor Moriarty in The Adventures of Sherlock Holmes (1939). A recurring role was Andoheb, The High Priest of Karnak in The Mummy's Hand (1940), The Mummy's Tomb (1942) and The Mummy's Ghost (1944). George played a string of doctors, scientists and professors in such films as My Favourite Blonde (1942), The Mad Ghoul (1943), House of Frankenstein (1944), Hold that Blonde (1945) and Scared to Death (1947). His final films include Joan of Arc (1948), Flame of Stamboul (1951) and David and Bathsheba (1951). He suffered a stroke and was in declining health throughout the last years of his life. George played the mad scientist to perfection and brought a touch of class to even the meanest of roles. Sometimes called "The Boris Karloff of the 'B' feature". Father of actress Frances M Zucco (b. 30 May 1931, Hampton Court, London; d. 14 March 1962, Los Angeles, California). George died 27 May 1960 Los Angeles, California.

The BFI Top 100 British Films (up to 1998)

1. The Third Man
2. Brief Encounter
3. Lawrence of Arabia
4. The 39 Steps
5. Great Expectations
6. Kind Hearts and Coronets
7. Kes
8. Don't Look Now
9. The Red Shoes
10. Trainspotting
11. The Bridge on the River Kwai
12. if....
13. The Ladykillers
14. Saturday Night and Sunday Morning
15. Brighton Rock
16. Get Carter
17. The Lavender Hill Mob
18. Henry V
19. Chariots of Fire
20. A Matter of Life and Death
21. The Long Good Friday
22. The Servant
23. Four Weddings and a Funeral
24. Whisky Galore!
25. The Full Monty
26. The Crying Game
27. Doctor Zhivago
28. Monty Python's Life of Brian
29. Withnail and I
30. Gregory's Girl
31. Zulu
32. Room at the Top
33. Alfie
34. Gandhi
35. The Lady Vanishes
36. The Italian Job
37. Local Hero
38. The Commitments
39. A Fish Called Wanda
40. Secrets & Lies
41. Dr. No
42. The Madness of King George
43. A Man for All Seasons
44. Black Narcissus
45. The Life and Death of Colonel Blimp
46. Oliver Twist
47. I'm All Right Jack
48. Performance
49. Shakespeare in Love
50. My Beautiful Laundrette
51. Tom Jones
52. This Sporting Life
53. My Left Foot
54. Brazil
55. The English Patient
56. A Taste of Honey
57. The Go-Between
58. The Man in the White Suit
59. The Ipcress File
60. Blowup
61. The Loneliness of the Long Distance Runner
62. Sense and Sensibility
63. Passport to Pimlico
64. The Remains of the Day
65. Sunday Bloody Sunday
66. The Railway Children
67. Mona Lisa
68. The Dam Busters
69. Hamlet
70. Goldfinger
71. Elizabeth
72. Goodbye, Mr. Chips
73. A Room with a View
74. The Day of the Jackal
75. The Cruel Sea
76. Billy Liar
77. Oliver!
78. Peeping Tom
79. Far from the Madding Crowd
80. The Draughtsman's Contract
81. A Clockwork Orange
82. Distant Voices, Still Lives
83. Darling
84. Educating Rita
85. Brassed Off
86. Genevieve
87. Women in Love
88. A Hard Day's Night
89. Fires Were Started
90. Hope and Glory
91. My Name Is Joe
92. In Which We Serve
93. Caravaggio
94. The Belles of St Trinian's
95. Life is Sweet
96. The Wicker Man
97. Nil by Mouth
98. Small Faces
99. Carry On... Up the Khyber
100. The Killing Fields

British (and Irish) Films

There is almost as much debate as to the definition of a British film as there is to the definition of popular culture itself. At the turn of the new millennium the British Film Institute published a list of the top 100 greatest British Films of the 20th century as voted by a target audience of 1,000 people, mostly from the world of British film and television. The BFI drew up the shortlist of films which they considered to be 'culturally' British irrespective of nationality of the films' stars, directors, production company or distributor. The top-ranked film was *The Third Man* - an anglo-American production, but certainly British enough for it to be adapted for American audiences.

I have included a brief synopsis of all 100 films below (complete table overleaf) and also added almost 2,000 that have ranked highly in other surveys during the aforementioned period plus those of the past decade which might well have been considered if released earlier. In certain instances I have had to make a reasoned decision as to the Britishness of the film. For instance, *The African Queen* (1952) was not considered eligible for the BFI survey although this film was at least intended to be culturally British. The two leading stars were originally playing British characters invented by the film's British writer and much of the film was shot in England by a British production company. That said, unfortunately, Humphrey Bogart struggled with the cockney accent of his character Charlie Allnut and eventually it was decided that he play the part as a Canadian. This worked splendidly well as Mr Bogart was awarded a Best Actor Oscar, however the film cannot be said to be culturally British by any stretch of the imagination so does not feature here. Conversely, the 2007 fantasy film, *Stardust*, was distributed by an American production company and starred several American leading actors, however the overall feel of the film was undoubtedly British, as was intended by Neil Gaiman's novel of the same name. I apologise now for all those instances where I have breached my own rule of thumb and included films that have tenuous British links.

In compiling these films I have noticed a tenuous genre timeline beginning in the 1930s with an abundance of espionage and farce which inevitably became war-themed throughout the 1940s. The 1950s continued in a similar vein although by mid-decade the war theme had been exhausted to some degree and a host of gritty realism and gangster-oriented films prevailed. On the comedy front, the Ealing comedies had replaced the George Formby / Will Hay / Crazy Gang output and in turn were themselves replaced by the Carry On, Norman Wisdom and Doctor series as the staple diet. The 1960s were epitomised by a number of 'swinging London' films, kitchen sink and coming-of-age sagas, spy spoofs and costume dramas. It was also the decade which brought us James Bond and the Hammer Horror series. The 1970s ushered in a period of television spin-offs and soft porn films of the comedic and sometimes tragic variety. The 1980s onwards have seen a plethora of literary costume dramas and art house fare. Throughout the whole period British cinema has been admired around the world for producing the likes of Alfred Hitchcock, St Trinians, The Goons (notably Peter Sellers at the cinema), James Bond, The Beatles, Monty Python and into the new millennium by Harry Potter – all of which influenced and inspired world cinema in their own genres.

Abdulla the Great (1955) Gregory Ratoff (Abdulla), Kay Kendall (Ronnie), Marina Berti (Aziza), Sydney Chaplin (Ahmed), Alexander D'Arcy (Marco), Mary Costes (The Countess), Marti Stevens (Singer). A Middle Eastern potentate in the 1950s is surrounded by wealth, women and a growing opposition to him in his country. The story is a thinly veiled parody of the life of King Farouk of Egypt and the events preceding his overthrow in 1952. *Dir.* Gregory Ratoff

Abominable Dr Phibes, The (1971) Vincent Price (Dr Anton Phibes), Joseph Cotten (Dr Vesalius), Peter Jeffrey (Insp Harry Trout), Virginia North (Vulnavia), Terry-Thomas (Dr Longstreet), Susan Travers (Nurse Allen), David Hutcheson (Dr Hedgepath), Edward Burnham (Dr Dunwoody), Alex Scott (Dr Hargreaves), Peter Gilmore (Dr Kitaj), Maurice Kaufmann (Dr Whitcombe), Sean Bury (Lem Vesalius), Caroline Munro (Phibe's wife - uncredited). Beginning in 1925, doctors are being murdered by bizarre methods, representing the ten Biblical plagues of Egypt. Professor Thornton is stung to death by bees, Dr Dunwoody is mauled to death by bats, Dr Hargreaves's is crushed by a mechanical frog mask, Dr Longstreet has all the blood drained out of his body, Dr Hedgepath is frozen to death by an ice machine, Dr Kitaj's plane goes down when attacked by rats, Dr Whitcombe is impaled by a brass unicorn head and Nurse Allen is eaten by a swarm of locusts. The crimes are orchestrated by a demented organ player, Dr Phibes, with the help of his mute assistant, Vulnavia. Inspector Trout is initially stumped until he finds that all of the doctors being killed assisted a Dr. Vesalius on an unsuccessful operation involving the wife of Dr Phibes, the problem being he was reportedly killed in a car crash upon learning of his wife's death in 1921. The disfigured Phibes then kidnaps and attempts to kill Dr Vesalius's son, Lem, before injecting himself with embalming fluid, apparently joining his wife in death. *Dir.* Robert Fuest. See also *Dr Phibes Rises Again* (1972).

Abominable Snowman, The (1957) Forrest Tucker (Dr Tom Friend), Peter Cushing (Dr John Rollason), Maureen Connell (Helen Rollason), Richard Wattis (Peter Fox), Robert Brown (Ed Shelley), Michael Brill (Andrew McNee), Wolfe Morris (Kusang), Arnold Marle (Lhama), Anthony Chinn (Major-Domo). English anthropologist John Rollason joins an American expedition as they search the Himalayas for the legendary Yeti (aka the abominable snowman). The film was adapted from an earlier television play by Nigel Kneale, Peter Cushing reprising his role but American actor Forrest Tucker replacing Welsh actor Stanley Baker as Tom Friend. The film was an early horror production from Hammer Film Productions, previously known for detective thrillers. *Dir.* Val Guest.

About a Boy (2002) Hugh Grant (Will Freeman), Nicholas Hoult (Marcus Brewer), Toni Collette (Fiona Brewer), Rachel Weisz (Rachel), Nat Gastiain Tena (Ellie), Victoria Smurfit (Suzie). Will Freeman is a layabout whose days are filled by conning young women into bed and reading about pop culture (a worthy pastime methinks!). His lush London lifestyle is subsidised by the royalties left to him from a successful Christmas song that his father composed. Will decides that a rich source of available women would be found at the local SPAT (Single Parents Alone Together) meetings so he goes along under the pretence of having a two-year-old son, Ned. Will immediately targets Suzie and while at a picnic he meets Marcus, the 12-year-old son of Suzie's friend, Fiona. The relationship between Will and Marcus is cemented when he defends the lad for accidentally killing a duck with a loaf of stale bread. The two become supportive of each other through their struggles in love, Will with Rachel and Marcus with Ellie. Marcus is a chronic victim of bullying due to his propensity to sing at inappropriate times and has a depressive mother. Will is a shit. Together they help each other to overcome these problems. Based on a Nick Hornby novel the film was a US / UK co-production between Robert DeNiro's Tribeca Grind and Tim Bevan's Working Title Films. The soundtrack was composed by singer / songwriter Badly Drawn Boy. *Dirs.* Chris and Paul Weitz.

Above Us the Waves (1955) John Mills (Cmdr Donald Fraser), John Gregson (Lt Alec Duffy), Donald Sinden (Lt Tom Corbett), James Robertson Justice (Admiral Ryder), Michael Medwin (Steward Smart), William Franklyn (No 1, X2), Anthony Newley (Engineer, X2), O.E. Hasse (Captain of the Tirpitz), Theodore Bikel (German officer). The true story of the British X class midget submarine attacks on the German battleship *Tirpitz* anchored in a Norwegian fjord in September 1943. Although the *Tirpitz* was not sunk (by RAF Avro Lancaster heavy bombers) until November 1944, the attacks severely damaged the ship and put it out of action for several months. *Dir.* Ralph Thomas.

Absolute Beginners (1986) Eddie O'Connell (Colin), Patsy Kensit (Suzette), David Bowie (Vendice Partners) Ray Davies (Arthur - Colin's father), James Fox (Henley of Mayfair, Dressmaker to the Queen), Steven Berkoff ('The Fanatic'), Mandy Rice Davies (Flora), Robbie Coltrane (Mario), Irene Handl (Mrs Larkin), Eric Sykes (arcade attendant), Lionel Blair (Harry Charms - a record producer), Sade (Athene Duncannon), Gary Beadle (Johnny Wonder), Alan Freeman ('Call-Me-Cobber'), Edward Tudor-Pole (Ed the Ted), Eve Ferret (Big Jill), Tony Hippolyte (Mr Cool), Graham Fletcher-Cook (Wizard), Zoot Money (Chez Nobody - a barman), Sandie Shaw (Baby Boom's mum), Bruno Tonioli (Maltese lodger), Sylvia Syms (Cynthia Eve), Jess Conrad (Cappuccino Man), Smiley Culture (D.J. Entertainer), Ronald Fraser (Amberley Drove). A musical adaptation of Colin MacInnes' novel about life in London in 1958. Nineteen-year-old photographer Colin is in love with model 'Crepe' Suzette, but her relationships depend on her progressing in the fashion world. Colin decides to get involved with a pop promoter and attempts to crack the big time. The sub-plot concerns the racial tension brewing on Colin's Notting Hill housing estate. *Dir.* Julien Temple

Accident (1967) Dirk Bogarde (Stephen), Stanley Baker (Charley), Jacqueline Sassard (Anna), Michael York (William), Vivien Merchant (Rosalind - Stephen's wife), Delphine Seyrig (Francesca - The Provost's daughter), Alexander Knox (The University Provost), Anne Firbank (Laura - Charley's wife), Brian Phelan (Police Sergeant), Terence Rigby (Plain clothed policeman), Freddie Jones (Man in Bell's office), Harold Pinter (Bell), Nicholas Mosley (Hedges). Stephen is a middle aged philosophy tutor at Oxford. He is married with two children and one on the way. Stephen becomes hopelessly infatuated with Anna, a foreign exchange student. Charley is Stephen's best friend. He is a middle aged professor, married with three kids, but is sleeping with Anna. William is one of Stephen's pupils. He is an aristocratic young man who is also in love with Anna. The film opens with the sound of a car crash in the distance, while the camera focuses on Stephen's house. He runs out to see what has happened and finds William and Anna in the car. William is obviously dead while Anna has just superficial injuries. The remainder of the film is a flashback of how they all met and what led up to the accident. A memorable scene is when we see a dazed Anna crushing her dying fiancé beneath her spike-heeled foot as she stomps on his face while desperately trying to escape from the overturned car. The screenplay by Harold Pinter is based on the novel by Nicholas Mosley (son of Sir Oswald Mosley, founder of the British Union of Fascists). *Dir.* Joseph Losey.

Accused (1936) Douglas Fairbanks Jr (Tony Seymour), Dolores del Rio (Gaby Ramarios / Seymour), Florence Desmond (Yvette Delange), Edward Rigby (Alphonse de la Riveire), Googie Withers (Ninette Duval - a chorus girl). Tony and Gaby are a dance team who perform the aggressive Apache speciality act which ends with Gaby apparently stabbing Tony. Gaby is an expert knife thrower and the act becomes popular. The couple hide the fact they are married while auditioning for parts in a revue at the Parisian Alhambra. The star of the show, Yvette Delange, asks assistant producer Alphonse de la Riviere, to invite Tony to her dressing room. Tony accepts but Yvette is found murdered, stabbed with a knife belonging to Gaby. Gaby is duly charged with murder. Tony seeks to find the real killer and his list of suspects is long. *Dir.* Thornton Freeland

Aces High (1976) Malcolm McDowell (Maj. John Gresham), Christopher Plummer (Capt. "Uncle" Sinclair), Simon Ward (Lt. Crawford), Peter Firth (Lt. Stephen Croft), David Wood (Lt. 'Tommy' Thompson), John Gielgud (Headmaster), Trevor Howard (Lieutenant Colonel Silkin), Richard Johnson (Major Lyle), Ray Milland (Brigadier General Whale), Christopher Blake (Lieutenant Roberts), David Daker (Mess Corporal Bennett), Barry Jackson (Corporal Albert Joyce), Ron Pember (Lance Corporal Eliot), Tim Pigott-Smith (Major Stoppard). A young pilot in WWI has to learn combat skills at a time when the turnover in pilots is increasing. Based on both the play *Journey's*

End by R. C. Sherriff and the memoir *Sagittarius Rising* by Cecil Lewis. *Dir.* Jack Gold.

Across the Bridge (1957) Rod Steiger (Carl Schaffner), David Knight (Johnny), Noel Willman (Chief of Police), Marla Landi (Mary), Dolores (Dolores), Bernard Lee (Chief Inspector Hadden), Eric Pohlmann (Police Sergeant), Alan Gifford (Cooper), Ingeborg von Kusserow (Mrs. Scarff), Bill Nagy (Paul Scarff), Faith Brook (Kay), Marianne Deeming (Anna), Stanley Maxted (Milton), Mark Baker (Baggage Man), Jack Lester (Sam), Jon Farrell (Stationmaster), Betty Cooper (Miss Hilton), Stratford Johns (Detective). Embezzler Schaffner drugs a fellow train passenger as he flees from New York to Mexico, throws him from the train and assumes his identity. However, on arrival in Mexico he is arrested as the man whose identity he has stolen is a wanted murderer. Based on a short story of the same name by Graham Greene. *Dir.* Ken Annakin.

Adam and Evelyne (1949) Stewart Granger (Adam Black), Jean Simmons (Evelyne Kirby), Edwin Styles (Bill Murray), Raymond Young (Roddy Black), Helen Cherry (Moira), Beatrice Varley (Mrs. Parker), Joan Swinstead (Molly), Wilfrid Hyde-White (Colonel Bradley), Fred Johnson (Chris Kirby), Geoffrey Denton (Police Inspector Collins), Peter Reynolds (David), Dora Bryan (Blonde Sales Assistant), Larry Dann (Boy), Francis De Wolff (Man at Bar), Irene Handl (Mrs. Crouch). Gambler Adam promises Evelyne's estranged father on his deathbed that he will look after her. However, Evelyne believes Adam is actually her father. *Dir.* Harold French.

Admirable Crichton, The (1957) Kenneth More (William Crichton), Diane Cilento (Eliza Tweeny), Cecil Parker (Lord Henry Loam), Sally Ann Howes (Lady Mary), Martita Hunt (Lady Brocklehurst), Jack Watling (John Treherne), Peter Graves (George Brocklehurst), Gerald Harper (Ernest Woolley). Lord Loam has modern ideas about his household; he believes in treating his servants as his equals - at least when it suits him. His ultra-efficient butler, Crichton, believes that members of the serving class should know their place. When the Loam family is shipwrecked on a desert island with their butler Crichton and lady's maid Tweeny, a role reversal takes place with the class system meaning little. The film was based on J. M. Barrie's 1902 stage comedy of the same name. *Dir.* Lewis Gilbert.

Adolf Hitler: My Part in his Downfall (1972) Spike Milligan (Leo - Spike's father), Jim Dale (Spike Milligan), Pat Coombs (Spike's Mother), Arthur Lowe (Major Drysdale), Bill Maynard (Sgt. Ellis), Tony Selby (Bill), Geoffrey Hughes (Larry), Jim Norton (Pongo), John Forgeham (Wally), Robert Longden (Heavenly), Tony Hughes (Edwards), Paul Antrim (Anderson), Lionel Guyett (Sutton), David Fennell (Neville), Windsor Davies (Sgt. MacKay), Stephen Yardley (Lt. Martin), Bob Todd (Referee), Anthony Booth (Tommy Brettell). Based on the first volume of Milligan's war memoirs, the action begins in London soon after the start of WWII. Young aspiring jazz musician Terence "Spike" Milligan reluctantly obeys his call-up and joins the Royal Artillery regiment at Bexhill, where he begins training to take part in the War. Along the way Spike and his friends get involved in some hilarious - and some quite harrowing - escapades. The future comedy genius's father was played by Spike himself. *Dir.* Norman Cohen.

Adulthood (2008) Noel Clarke (Sam Peel), Adam Deacon (Jay - Sam's former friend), Scarlett Alice Johnson (Lexi - Sam's new love interest), Femi Oyeniran (Moony), Red Madrell (Alisa), Jacob Anderson (Omen), Ben Drew (Dabs), Wil Johnson (Big Man), Nathan Constance (Zac), Adjoa Andoh (Mrs Peel), Madeleine Fairley (Claire - Sam's former girlfriend who is now with Jay), Lindsey Jordan (Devo), Kiera Booth (Tramp), Danny Dyer (Hayden), Arnold Ochien (Henry), Don Klass (Blammy).. Directed and written by Noel Clarke, this film is a sequel to the 2006 film *Kidulthood*, and takes up the story of newly-released Sam Peel six years after being sent down for killing Trife. *Dir.* Noel Clarke

Adventure of Sherlock Holmes' Smarter Brother, The (1975) Gene Wilder (Sigerson Holmes), Madeline Kahn (Jenny Hill), Marty Feldman (Sgt. Orville Stanley Sacker), Dom DeLuise

(Eduardo Gambetti), Leo McKern (Professor Moriarty), Roy Kinnear (Moriarty's assistant), Douglas Wilmer (Sherlock Holmes), Thorley Walters (Dr. Watson), George Silver (Bruner), Nicholas Smith (Hunkston), John Hollis (Moriarty's Gunman), Aubrey Morris (Coach Driver), Tommy Godfrey (Fred), Susan Field (Queen Victoria). A Holmes spoof in which Sherlock's younger brother tries to solve a case. *Dir*. Mel Brooks.

Adventures of a Plumber's Mate (1978) Christopher Neil (Sid South), Elaine Paige (Daisy), Arthur Mullard (Blackie), Anna Quayle (Loretta Proudfoot), Stephen Lewis (Crapper), Nina West (Sally), Willie Rushton (Dodger), Prudence Drage (Janice), Jonathan Adams (Rent Collector), Christopher Biggins (Robin), Richard Caldicot (Wallings). The third and final *Adventures of* film, notable only for the presence of Elaine Paige as Sid's very prim and well-behaved girlfriend, played with not a hint of any salaciousness. *Dir*. Stanley A Long.

Adventures of a Private Eye (1977) Christopher Neil (Bob West), Suzy Kendall (Laura Sutton), Harry H. Corbett (Sydney), Diana Dors (Mrs. Horne), Fred Emney (Sir Basil), Liz Fraser (Violet), Irene Handl (Miss Friggin), Ian Lavender (Derek), Julian Orchard (Police Cyclist), Jon Pertwee (Judd Blake), Adrienne Posta (Lisa Moroni), Anna Quayle (Medea), Willie Rushton (Wilfred), Jonathan Adams (Inspector Hogg), Richard Caldicot (Craddock), Angela Scoular (Jane Hogg), Linda Regan (Clarissa). Barry Evans had bailed out after one film to be replaced by Christopher Neil. One of the film's working titles was *Adventures of a Private Dick* but they eventually pulled out from using it. *Dir*. Stanley A Long.

Adventures of a Taxi Driver (1976) Barry Evans (Joe North), Judy Geeson (Nikki), Adrienne Posta (Carol), Diana Dors (Mrs. North), Liz Fraser (Maisie), Jane Hayden (Linda), Ian Lavender (Ronald), Stephen Lewis (Doorman), Robert Lindsay (Tom), Henry McGee (Inspector Rogers), Angela Scoular (Marion), Brian Wilde (Harold), Marc Harrison (Peter), Graham Ashley (Gerry), Dave Carter (Bill), Gloria Maley (Dora), Anna Bergman (Helga), Prudence Drage (Mrs. DeVere Barker), Natasha Staiteh-Masri (Alice), Charles Pemberton (Sergeant Jeeves). The first in a rival series to the more successful *Confessions* franchise starring Robin Askwith. *Dir*. Stanley A Long.

Adventures of Gerard, The (1970) Peter McEnery (Colonel Gerard), Claudia Cardinale (Theresa), Eli Wallach (Napoleon I), Jack Hawkins (Millefleurs), Mark Burns (Colonel Russell), Norman Rossington (Sergeant Papilette), John Neville (Wellington), Paolo Stoppa (Santarem), Ivan Desny (Gen. Lassalle), Leopoldo Trieste (Marshal Massena). Etienne Gerard is a hussar in the army of Napoleon Bonaparte. Based on *The Exploits of Brigadier Gerard* by Sir Arthur Conan Doyle. *Dir*. Jerzy Skolimowski.

Adventures of Tartu, The (1943) Robert Donat (Captain Terence Stevenson/Jan Tartu), Valerie Hobson (Maruschuka Lanova), Walter Rilla (Inspector Otto Vogel), Glynis Johns (Paula Palacek), Phyllis Morris (Anna Palacek), Martin Miller (Doctor Novotny), Anthony Eustrel (German Officer), Percy Walsh (Dr. Willendorf), David Ward (Bronte), Friedrich Richter (General Weymouth), John Penrose (Lieutenant Krantz), Hubert Leslie (Peter Valek), Mabel Terry-Lewis (Mrs. Stevenson), Charles Carson (Arthur Wakefield), Aubrey Mallalieu (ARP Warden), Lawrence O'Madden (Colonel Perry), Maurice Rhodes (Danny), John Salew (Heinrich Müller). A member of a UXB squad who speaks German and Romanian is recruited for a mission involving being dropped into Romania, assuming a new identity and infiltrating a factory believed to be producing poison gas. *Dir*. Harold S. Bucquet.

Ae Fond Kiss... (2004) Atta Yaqub (Casim), Eva Birthistle (Roisin), Ahmad Riaz (Tariq), Shamshad Akhtar (Sadia). Casim Khan is a Glaswegian DJ of Pakistani origin. His devout Muslim parents, Tariq and Sadia, have arranged for him to marry his first cousin, Jasmine, but Casim subsequently falls in love with Roisin Hanlon, an Irish teacher working at his sister's Catholic school. Casim and Roisin have to decide whether their love can overcome the lack of tolerance of their respective communities. *Dir*. Ken Loach.

After the Ball (1957) Patricia Kirkwood (Vesta Tilley), Laurence Harvey (Walter de Frece), Jerry Stovin (Frank Tanhill), Jerry Verno (Harry Ball), Clive Morton (Henry de Frece), Marjorie Rhodes (Bessie), Leonard Sachs (Richard Warner), Ballard Berkeley (Andrews), Margaret Sawyer (Vesta Tilley as a Child). A biopic of music hall performer Vesta Tilley. *Dir*. Compton Benn.

After the Fox (1966) Peter Sellers (Aldo Vanucci), Victor Mature (Tony Powell), Britt Ekland (Gina Romantica), Martin Balsam (Harry), Akim Tamiroff (Okra), Paolo Stoppa (Polio), Tino Buazzelli (Siepi), Mac Ronay (Carlo), Lydia Brazzi (Mamma Vanucci), Lando Buzzanca (Police Chief), Maria Grazia Buccella (Bikini Girl), Maurice Denham (Chief of Interpol). Master criminal Vanucci (The Fox) escapes from prison and devises a plan to smuggle the "gold of Cairo" into Italy by assembling a film crew and pretending to shoot a film in a village on the coast. The "film" stars an ageing matinee idol (Mature plays a knowing parody of himself). A British-Italian comedy which was Neil Simon's first screenplay. *Dir*. Vittorio De Sica.

Against the Wind (1948) Robert Beatty (Father Philip Elliot), Simone Signoret (Michèle Denis), Jack Warner (Max Cronk), Gordon Jackson (Scotty Duncan), Paul Dupuis (Jacques Picquart), James Robertson Justice (Ackerman), André Morell (Abbott), Eugene Deckers (Marcel van Hecke), John Slater (Emile Meyer), Peter Illing (Andrew), Sybille Binder (Florence Malou), Andrew Blackett (Frankie), Arthur Lawrence (Capt. Verreker). The training and deployment of Special Operations Executive agents in occupied Belgium during WWII is compromised when one of them is discovered to be a double agent. *Dir*. Charles Crichton.

Agatha (1979) Vanessa Redgrave (Agatha Christie), Dustin Hoffman (Wally Stanton), Timothy Dalton (Col. Archibald Christie). Agatha Christie disappeared in December 1926, leaving her car abandoned nr Dorking in Surrey. She turned up in Harrogate eleven days later, and to this day no one knows the details of what she did during that time, although many theories have been indulged. This film, written by Kathleen Tynan, offers one such theory. When her husband Archie announces his affair and demands a divorce, Agatha informs him she fears for her life and promptly vanishes. She signs into a Harrogate hotel under the name of Archie's lover and secretly plots a revenge that can only be averted by Wally Stanton, an ambitious American journalist who falls in love with her. *Dir*. Michael Apted.

Airman's Letter to His Mother, An (1941) A documentary-style British propaganda short based on an actual letter from be Flying Officer Vivian Rosewarne to his mother published in *The Times* in June 1940. Rosewarne had been killed over Dunkirk in May 1940. The letter is read out by John Gielgud in a voiceover. *Dir*. Michael Powell.

AKA (2002) Matthew Leitch (Dean Page), Diana Quick (Lady Gryffoyn), George Asprey (David), Lindsey Coulson (Georgie), Blake Ritson (Alexander Gryffoyn), Peter Youngblood Hills (Benjamin), Geoff Bell (Brian Page), Hannah Yelland (Camille Sturton), Daniel Lee (Jamie Page), Bill Nighy (Uncle Louis Gryffoyn), David Kendall (Lee Page), Fenella Woolgar (Sarah), Sean Gilder (Tim Lyttleton), Robin Soans (Neil Frost) and Stephen Boxer (Dermot). Set in the late 1970s the film is largely an autobiographical account of the director Duncan Roy's early life. It deals with the story of Dean Page, an 18-year-old boy who assumes another identity in order to enter high society where he then meets David, an older gay man who desires him and Benjamin, a young Texan hustler. The film is presented as a row of three frames, showing three perspectives. *Dir*. Duncan Roy.

Akenfield (1974) Stanley Baxter (Blacksmith), Ronald Blythe (The Vicar), Ethel Branton (Mrs. Quantrill), Lyn Brooks (Charlotte Rouse), Peggy Cole (Dulcie Rouse), Reg Hall (Policeman), Mary Hammond (Young Dulcie Rouse), Garrow Shand (Tom Rouse). The film takes place on the day of the funeral of 'Old' Tom, who apart from fighting in the First World War, never left the village in which he was born, although not for lack of trying. His grandson Tom Rouse is living alone in a cottage with his widowed mother Dulcie and, seen through his eyes, the film tells the story of the day, with frequent encounters between the 'Young' Tom and his grandfather. On the day of the funeral Tom has to decide if he is going to accept the tied cottage which is now available to him, marry his girlfriend and probably spend the rest of his life in Akenfield or to take the risk of leaving the village and seek his fortune elsewhere. The film was inspired by a short script written by Ronald Blythe, based on his classic book *Akenfield: Portrait of an English Village* written in 1969. Many of the cast lived in and around the village and extemporised their dialogue, drawing on their own experiences. *Dir*. Peter Hall.

Albert R.N. (1953) Anthony Steel (Lt. Geoffrey Ainsworth), Jack Warner (Capt. Maddox), Robert Beatty (Lt. Jim Reed), William Sylvester (Lt. 'Texas' Norton), Michael Balfour (Lt. Henry Adams), Guy Middleton (Capt. Barton), Paul Carpenter (Lt. Erickson), Geoffrey Hibbert (Lt. Craig), Peter Jones (Lt. Browne), Frederick Valk (Camp Kommandant), Anton Diffring (Capt. Schultz). POWs build a life-like dummy to cover the absence of escapers during roll call. The film is based on a true story wherein John Worsley constructed a dummy in Marlag O, a prisoner of war camp for naval officers. It was used on two separate occasions to cover an escape. US title: *Break to Freedom*. *Dir*. Lewis Gilbert.

Alf Garnett Saga, The (1972) Warren Mitchell (Alf Garnett), Dandy Nichols (Else Garnett), Paul Angelis (Mike Rawlins), Adrienne Posta (Rita), John Le Mesurier (Frewin), John Bird (Willis), Roy Hudd (Milkman), Roy Kinnear (Wally), Joan Sims (Gran). A big screen version of the television sitcom *Till Death Us Do Part*. The parts played on television by Una Stubbs and Tony Booth were played by Adrienne Posta and Paul Angelis respectively in this film. *Dir*. Bob Kellett.

Alfie (1966) Michael Caine (Alfie), Shelley Winters (Ruby), Millicent Martin (Siddie), Julia Foster (Gilda), Jane Asher (Annie), Shirley Anne Field (Carla), Vivien Merchant (Lily), Eleanor Bron (The Doctor), Denholm Elliot (The Abortionist), Alfie Bass (Harry Clamcraft). Donig his bit to make sure the 1960s swing, Alfie is a young working class Londoner on the prowl. He is determined not to get involved with his series of "conquests" but life doesn't make that easy. He sees the mother of his natural son (Gilda) marry and his child being raised by another man. A decision to settle down goes awry when his intended (Ruby) dumps him for a younger man and he also has to arrange for an abortion (for Lily). He is left wondering "What's it all about". The film features Alfie talking directly to the camera and sometimes justifying his actions to the audience. The title song was written by Burt Bacharach and Hal David but did not feature on the British release. It was recorded by Cher in the US and by Cilla Black in the UK. *Dir*. Lewis Gilbert

Alfie (2004) Jude Law (Alfie), Marisa Tomei (Julie), Susan Sarandon (Liz), Renée Taylor (Lu Schnitman), Jane Krakowski (Dorie), Jeff Harding (Phil), Kevin Rahm (Terry), Omar Epps (Marlon), Sienna Miller (Nikki). Not so much a remake of the 1960s film, more a reinvention of it with a still Cockney Alfie now bed-hopping his way around New York and working as a driver for the local limousine service. After various episodes, some similar to the earlier film, and including a cancer scare he also finds himself questioning what his life is all about. *Dir*. Charles Shyer.

Alfie Darling (1975) Alan Price (Alfie Elkins), Jill Townsend (Abby Summers), Paul Copley (Bakey), Joan Collins (Fay), Sheila White (Norma), Annie Ross (Claire), Hannah Gordon (Dora), Rula Lenska (Louise), Minah Bird (Gloria), Derek Smith (Harold), Vicki Michelle (Bird, hitchhiker), Brian Wilde (Doctor). Alan Price takes over the Michael Caine role as well as contributing the music. Alfie is now working as a London-France HGV driver and taking his opportunities to rediscover his 1960s lifestyle. Unfortunately a decision to finally settle down ends in tragedy. *Dir*. Ken Hughes.

Alfred the Great (1969) David Hemmings (Alfred), Michael York (Guthrum), Prunella Ransome (Aelhswith), Colin Blakely (Asher), Ian McKellen (Roger), Peter Vaughan (Burrud), Alan Dobie (Ethelred), Julian Glover (Shrdlu), Vivien Merchant (Freda), Julian Chagrin (Ivar), Jim Norton (Thanet), John Rees (Cuthbert), Christopher Timothy (Cerdic), Peter Blythe (Eafa), Sinéad Cusack (Edith), Barry Evans (Ingild), Barry Jackson (Wulfstan), Henry Woolf (Wenda), Andy Bradford (Edwin), Keith Buckley (Hadric), Michael Billington (Offa), David Glaisyer (Olaf), Robin Askwith (Shepherd Boy). Alfred puts aside his religious vows to lead the West Saxon English against the invading Danes. *Dir*. Clive Donner.

Alf's Button (1930) Tubby Edlin (Alf Higgins), Alf Goddard (Bill Grant), Nora Swinburne (Lady Isobel Fitzpeter), Polly Ward (Liz), Humberston Wright (Eustace the genie). Based on a 1920 novel of the same by W.A. Darlington. In the trenches of WWI Alf gets a new uniform jacket which has a button made from Aladdin's Lamp. Encounters with the genie of the button ensue until the button is lost in the Flanders mud. *Dir*. W.P. Kellino.

Alf's Button Afloat (1938) Bud Flanagan (Alf Higgins), Chesney Allen (Ches), Jimmy Nervo (Cecil), Teddy Knox (Teddy), Charlie Naughton (Charlie), Jimmy Gold (Jimmy), Alastair Sim (Eustace the genie). The Crazy Gang parody the 1920 novel and 1930 film with Alf's button being on his pyjamas. *Dir*. Marcel Varnel.

Ali G Indahouse (2002) Sacha Baron Cohen (Alistair "Ali G" Graham/Borat Sagdiyev), Michael Gambon (Prime Minister), Charles Dance (David Carlton), Kellie Bright (Julie), Martin Freeman (Richard "Ricky C" Cunningham), Rhona Mitra (Kate Hedges), Barbara New (Nan). Ali G is the leader of Da West Staines Massiv (a group of wannabe gangsters) who becomes a national hero after becoming an MP. *Dir*. Mark Mylod.

Alibi (1931) Austin Trevor (Hercule Poirot), Franklin Dyall (Sir Roger Ackroyd), Elizabeth Allan (Ursula Browne), J.H. Roberts (Dr. Sheppard), John Deverell (Lord Halliford), Ronald Ward (Ralph Ackroyd). Adapted from the 1928 play *Alibi* which in turn was based on the Agatha Christie novel *The Murder of Roger Ackroyd*. *Dir*. Leslie Hiscott

Alibi (1942) Margaret Lockwood (Helene Ardouin), Hugh Sinclair (Inspector Calas), James Mason (Andre Laurent), Raymond Lovell (Prof. Winkler), Enid Stamp-Taylor (Dany), Hartley Power (Gordon), Jane Carr (Delia). Based on the novel *L'Alibi* by Marcel Achard. *Dir*. Brian Desmond Hurst

Alice's Adventures in Wonderland (1972) Fiona Fullerton (Alice), Michael Jayston (Lewis Carroll (Charles Dodgson)), Hywel Bennett (Duckworth), Michael Crawford (White Rabbit), Davy Kaye (Mouse), William Ellis (Dodo), Julian Chagrin (Bill the Lizard), Ralph Richardson (The Caterpillar), Patsy Rowlands (Cook), Roy Kinnear (Cheshire Cat), Robert Helpmann (The Mad Hatter), Peter Sellers (The March Hare), Dudley Moore (Dormouse), Dennis Waterman (2 of Spades), Ray Brooks (5 of Spades), Dennis Price (King of Hearts), Flora Robson (Queen of Hearts), Rodney Bewes (Knave of Hearts), Spike Milligan (Gryphon), Michael Hordern (Mock Turtle). An adaptation of Lewis Carroll's book with music by John Barry. *Dir*. William Sterling.

Alien (1979) Tom Skerritt (Dallas), Sigourney Weaver (Ripley), Veronica Cartwright (Lambert), Harry Dean Stanton (Brett), John Hurt (Kane), Ian Holm (Ash), Yaphet Kotto (Parker). A science fiction horror film. When commercial towing vehicle Nostromo, heading back to Earth, intercepts an S. O. S. signal from a nearby planet, the crew are under obligation to investigate. After a bad landing on the planet, some crew members leave the ship to explore the area. At the same time as they discover a hive colony of some unknown creatures, the ship's computer deciphers the message to be a warning, not a call for help. When one of the eggs is disturbed, the crew do not know the danger they are in until it is too late. Tagline: "In space no one can hear you scream". *Dir*. Ridley Scott.

Alien Autopsy (2006) Declan Donnelly (Ray Santilli), Anthony McPartlin (Gary Shoefield), Bill Pullman (Morgan Banner), Götz Otto (Laszlo Voros), Morwenna Banks (Jasmine), Omid Djalili (Melik), Harry Dean Stanton (Harvey), Jimmy Carr (Gary's manager). Ray and Gary are offered a film showing the autopsy of an alien supposedly killed in a UFO crash in Roswell, New Mexico. *Dir*. Johnny Campbell.

All at Sea (1939) Sandy Powell (Sandy Skipton), Kay Walsh (Diana), John Warwick (Brown), Gus McNaughton (Nobby), George Merritt (Bull), Leslie Perrins (Williams), Franklin Dyall (Dr. Stolk), Robert Rendel (Sir Herbert), Aubrey Mallalieu (Prof. Myles). When a factory worker is sent off to deliver a message, he inadvertently enlists in the navy. *Dir*. Herbert Smith

All Creatures Great and Small (1974) Simon Ward (James Herriot), Anthony Hopkins (Siegfried Farnon), Brian Stirner (Tristan Farnon), Lisa Harrow (Helen). Television film sponsored by *Reader's Digest* based on the books by James Herriot. The story of a young vet's apprenticeship to a somewhat eccentric older vet in Yorkshire and his courtship of the daughter of a local farmer. *Dir.* Claude Whatham.

All Night Long (1962) Patrick McGoohan (Johnny Cousin), Keith Michell (Cass Michaels), Betsy Blair (Emily), Paul Harris (Aurelius Rex), Marti Stevens (Delia Lane), Richard Attenborough (Rod Hamilton), Bernard Braden (Lou Berger), Harry Towb (Phales), María Velasco (Benny), Dave Brubeck (Himself), John Dankworth (Himself), Charles Mingus (Himself). An updated version of *Othello* featuring performances by top jazz musicians. *Dir.* Basil Dearden

All or Nothing (2002) Timothy Spall (Phil), Lesley Manville (Penny), James Corden (Rory), Alison Garland (Rachel), Ruth Sheen (Maureen), Marion Bailey (Carol), Paul Jesson (Ron), Sam Kelly (Sid). Set on a London housing estate over a long weekend the film tells the story of taxi-driver Phil, his wife Penny, children Rory and Rachel and their neighbours. *Dir.* Mike Leigh.

All the Right Noises (1971) Olivia Hussey (Val), Tom Bell (Len Lewin), Judy Carne (Joy Lewin), John Standing (Bernie), Yootha Joyce (Mrs. Bird), Robert Keegan (Mr. Lewin), Lesley-Anne Down (Laura). A married man has an affair with a teenage girl. *Dir.* Gerry O'Hara.

Alligator Named Daisy, An (1955) Donald Sinden (Peter Weston), Jeannie Carson (Moira O'Shannon), James Robertson Justice (Sir James Colbrooke), Diana Dors (Vanessa Colbrooke), Roland Culver (Mr Weston), Stanley Holloway (The General), Avice Landone (Mrs Weston), Richard Wattis (Hoskins), Stephen Boyd (Albert O'Shannon), Ernest Thesiger (Notcher), Margaret Rutherford (Prudence Croquet), Joan Hickson (Piano Customer), Jimmy Edwards (Alligator owner), Frankie Howerd (Comedian). Peter Weston is left a pet alligator by a fellow train passenger in Ireland who abandons it to him. Keeping the pet, called Daisy, causes him many headaches along the way. *Dir.* J. Lee Thompson

Almost a Gentleman (1938) Billy Bennett (Bill Barker), Kathleen Harrison (Mrs Barker), Gibb McLaughlin (Bartholomew Quist), Marcelle Rogez (Mimi), Mervyn Johns (Percival Clicker), Basil Langton (Andrew Sinker), Harry Terry (Jim), Dorothy Vernon (Mrs Garrett). A night watchman is mistaken for a wealthy financier. *Dir.* Oswald Mitchell.

Almost a Honeymoon (1930) Clifford Mollison (Basil Dibley), Dodo Watts (Rosalie Quilter), Lamont Dickson (Cuthbert de Gray), Donald Calthrop (Charles, the butler), C.M. Hallard (Sir James Jephson). A young man takes a job in the colonial service but has only 24 hours to find a woman and persuade her to marry him as there is a stipulation that he needs to be married to keep the job. *Dir.* Monty Banks

Amazing Mr Blunden, The (1972) Laurence Naismith (Frederick Percival Blunden), Lynne Frederick (Lucy Allen), Garry Miller (Jamie Allen), Rosalyn Landor (Sara Latimer), Marc Granger (Georgie Latimer), Diana Dors (Mrs. Wickens), Dorothy Alison (Mrs. Allen), James Villiers (Uncle Bertie), Madeline Smith (Arabella Wickens), David Lodge (Mr. Wickens), Graham Crowden (Mr. Clutterbug), Erik Chitty (Mr. Claverton), Paul Eddington (Vicar). A mysterious, very old solicitor Mr Blunden visits Mrs Allen and her young children Lucy and Jamie in her tiny Camden Town flat and makes her an offer she cannot refuse. The family become the housekeepers to a derelict country mansion in the charge of the solicitors. One day the children meet the spirits of two other children who died in the mansion nearly a hundred years previously. The children prepare a magic potion that allows them to travel backwards in time to the era of the ghost children. Will the children be able to help their new friends and what will happen to them if they do? *Dir.* Lionel Jeffries

American Friends (1991) Michael Palin (Rev. Francis Ashby), Trini Alvarado (Elinor Hartley), Connie Booth (Caroline Hartley), Alfred Molina (Oliver Syme), Bryan Pringle (Haskell), Roger Lloyd-Pack (Dr. Butler), Alun Armstrong (Dr. Victor Weeks), Jimmy Jewel (Ashby Senior). Based on a real-life incident involving Palin's great-grandfather, Edward Palin. Francis Ashby, a senior Oxford professor is on holiday in the Swiss Alps where he meets and befriends Caroline Hartley and her ward Elinor. Ashby is surprised when they later arrive in Oxford and rent a house. As women are not allowed in the College, nor are Fellows allowed to marry, he is in an embarrassing situation which his

rival for the post of College President, Oliver Syme, tries to take advantage of. *Dir.* Tristran Powell

American Gothic (1988) Rod Steiger (Pa), Yvonne De Carlo (Ma), Sarah Torgov (Cynthia), Janet Wright (Fanny), Michael J. Pollard (Woody), William Hootkins (Teddy). Cynthia, traumatised by the accidental death of her child, decides to go on vacation with five of her friends. Their plane is forced to land on an apparently deserted island. However, they find a cottage occupied by what turns out to be a crazed, homicidal family, with predictable consequences. The film poster and all other related media art were based on Grant Wood's famous painting by the same name. *Dir.* John Hough

American Werewolf in London, An (1981) David Naughton (David Kessler), Jenny Agutter (Nurse Alex Price), Griffin Dunne (Jack Goodman), John Woodvine (Dr. J.S. Hirsch), Lila Kaye (Barmaid), Frank Oz (Mr. Collins), John Landis (Man gets smashed in window). Two American students are on a walking tour of England and are attacked by a Werewolf. Jack is killed and David is mauled. The Werewolf is killed, but reverts to its human form, and the townspeople are able to deny it's existence. David begins to have nightmares of hunting, on four feet at first, but then finds that Jack and other recent victims appear to him, demanding that he find a way to die to release them from their curse, trapped between worlds because of their unnatural death. *Dir.* John Landis.

Among Giants (1998) Pete Postlethwaite (Ray), Rachel Griffiths (Gerry), James Thornton (Steve), Lennie James (Shovel), Andy Serkis (Bob), Rob Jarvis (Weasel), Alan Williams (Frank). Ray and his crew are employed, cash-in-hand, to paint all the power towers (the giants) in a 15-mile stretch of high-tension wires outside Sheffield. They are joined by Gerry, a spirited Australian backpacker with mountain climbing skills who Ray hires despite the others objecting. Eventually they fall in love and Ray asks her to marry him, which sparks unforeseen consequences for the pair and a jealous Steve. *Dir.* Sam Miller.

Amorous Prawn, The (1962) Ian Carmichael (Corporal Sidney Green), Joan Greenwood (Lady Dodo Fitzadam), Cecil Parker (General Sir Hamish Fitzadam), Dennis Price (Mr Vernon – Prawn), Robert Beatty (Lady Hoffman), Liz Fraser (Private Suzie Tidmarsh), Finlay Currie (Lochaye), Robert Nichols (Sam Goulansky), Bridget Armstrong (Private Biddy O'Hara), Harry Locke (Albert Huggin), Derek Nimmo (Private Willie Maltravers), Roddy McMillan (Private McTavish), Sandra Dorne (Busty Babs), Michael Ripper (Angus), Geoffrey Bayldon (2nd Telephone Operator). When General Fitzadam is posted to the Scottish Highlands his wife decides to run their home as a hotel for American tourists. *Dir.* Anthony Kimmins.

Amsterdam Affair (1968) Wolfgang Kieling (Van Der Valk), William Marlowe (Martin Ray), Catherine Schell (Sophie Ray), Pamela Ann Davy (Elsa de Charmoy). Based on the novel *Love in Amsterdam* by Nicholas Freeling, policeman Van Der Valk investigates a novelist who is accused of murdering his mistress. *Dir.* Gerry O'Hara

Anchoress (1993) Natalie Morse (Christine Carpenter), Gene Bervoets (Reeve), Toyah Willcox (Pauline Carpenter),Pete Postlethwaite (William Carpenter), Christopher Eccleston (Priest), Michael Pas (Drover), Brenda Bertin (Meg Carpenter), Annette Badland (Mary), Veronica Quilligan (Daisy), Julie T. Wallace (Bertha). Set in 14th century England, a girl has visions of the Virgin Mary and becomes a walled-in recluse. *Dir.* Chris Newby.

And Now For Something Completely Different (1971) Graham Chapman, John Cleese, Terry Gilliam (animations), Eric Idle, Terry Jones, Michael Palin, Carol Cleveland, Connie Booth. A compilation of the best sketches from the television series *Monty Python's Flying Circus*. *Dir.* Ian MacNaughton.

And Soon The Darkness (1970) Pamela Franklin (Jane), Michele Dotrice (Cathy), Sandor Elès (Paul), John Nettleton (Gendarme), Clare Kelly (Schoolmistress), Hana Maria Pravda (Madame Lassal), John Franklyn (Old Man), Claude Bertrand (Lassal), Jean Carmet (Renier). Two English girls take a cycling holiday in France. However, they become separated on an infamous stretch of road, where a mad killer abducts and kills Cathy. Jane meanwhile, is left isolated and frightened and doesn't know who to trust. *Dir.* Robert Fuest.

And Then There Were None (1974) Charles Aznavour (Michel Raven), Stéphane Audran (Ilona Morgan), Elke Sommer (Vera Clyde), Gert Fröbe (Wilhelm Blore), Herbert Lom (Dr Edward Armstrong), Oliver Reed (Hugh Lombard), Richard Attenborough (Judge Arthur Cannon), Orson Welles (the Voice on the Tape), Maria Rohm (Elsa Martino), Alberto de Mendoza (Otto Martino), Adolfo Celi (General André Salvé). Updated version of the Agatha Christie book *And Then There Were None*. In this version, the group is invited, under false pretenses, to an isolated hotel in the Iranian desert. After dinner, a cassette tape accuses them all of crimes that they have gotten away with. One by one they begin to die, in accordance with the Ten Little Indians nursery rhyme. After a search is made of the hotel, they realize that the murderer is one of them. US title: *Ten Little Indians*. The writer Peter Welbeck is in fact Harry Alan Towers, who has made a living out of remaking this film. *Dir.* Peter Collinson.

And When Did You Last See Your Father? (2007) Jim Broadbent (Arthur Morrison), Colin Firth (Blake Morrison), Juliet Stevenson (Kim Morrison), Gina McKee (Kathy Morrison), Claire Skinner (Gillian), Sarah Lancashire (Beaty), Matthew Beard (younger Blake), Elaine Cassidy (Sandra), Justin McDonald (Steve), Carey Mulligan (Rachel). Screenplay by David Nicholls based on the 1993 memoir of the same title by Blake Morrison. As his father Arthur lays on his deathbed, Blake's family life to that point is shown in a series of flashbacks. *Dir.* Anand Tucker

Androcles and the Lion (1952) Jean Simmons (Lavinia), Victor Mature (Captain), Alan Young (Androcles), Robert Newton (Ferrovius), Maurice Evans (Caesar), Elsa Lanchester (Megaera), Reginald Gardiner (Lentulus), Gene Lockhart (Menagerie Keeper), Alan Mowbray (Editor of Gladiators), Noel Willman (Spintho), John Hoyt (Cato), Jim Backus (Centurion), Woody Strode (The Lion), Sylvia Lewis (Queen of the Vestal Virgins). Escaped and on the run, slave Androcles does a wounded lion a good deed. Based on the George Bernard Shaw play of the same name. *Dirs.* Chester Erskine and Nicholas Ray.

Angela's Ashes (1999) Emily Watson (Angela McCourt), Robert Carlyle (Malachy McCourt), Devon Murray (Middle Malachy), Joe Breen (Young Frank), Ciaran Owens (Middle Frank), Michael Legge (Older Frank), Kerry Condon (Theresa Carmondy), Ronnie Masterson (Grandma Sheehan), Pauline McLynn (Aunt Aggie), Liam Carney (Uncle Pa Keating), Eanna MacLiam (Uncle Pat), Susan Fitzgerald (Sister Rita), Eamonn Owens (Quasimodo), Martin Benson (Christian brother), Andrew Bennett (Narrator), Alan Parker (Dr Campbell). Based on Frank McCourt's bestseller about the life of a Roman Catholic writer brought up in poverty-stricken Limerick. Ultimately fails to capture the spirit and sense of identity of the Irish people but a touching story of triumph over adversity. *Dir.* Alan Parker.

Angelic Conversation, The (1985) Judi Dench (Narrator). Slow moving photographic images of homosexuality and landscapes set to Shakespeare's sonnets. *Dir.* Derek Jarman.

Angels One Five (1952) Jack Hawkins (Group Captain 'Tiger' Small), Michael Denison (Squadron Leader Peter Moon), Dulcie Gray (Nadine Clinton), John Gregson (Pilot Officer 'Septic' Baird), Cyril Raymond (Squadron Leader Barry Clinton), Veronica Hurst (Betty Carfax), Harold Goodwin (A.C. 2 Wailes), Norman Pierce ('Bonzo'), Geoffrey Keen (Company Sergeant Major), Harry Locke (Look Out), Philip Stainton (Police Constable), Vida Hope (W.A.A.F.), Amy Veness (Aunt Tabitha), Ronald Adam (Group Controller), Joan Sterndale-Bennett (W.A.A.F.). Based on the book *What Are Your Angels Now?* by Pelham Groom. The plot centres on a young fighter pilot "Septic" Baird immediately before and during the Battle of Britain. *Dir.* George More O'Ferrall

Angry Silence, The (1960) Richard Attenborough (Tom Curtis), Pier Angeli (Anna Curtis), Michael Craig (Joe Wallace), Bernard Lee (Bert Connolly), Alfred Burke (Travers), Geoffrey Keen (Davis), Laurence Naismith (Martindale), Russell Napier (Thompson), Penelope Horner (Pat), Brian Bedford (Eddie), Brian Murray (Gladys), Norman Bird (Roberts), Beckett Bould (Arkwright), Oliver Reed (Mick), Edna Petrie (Harpy), Lloyd Pearson (Howarth), Norman Shelley (Seagrave), Daniel Farson (Himself), Alan Whicker (Himself), Ronald Hines (Ball), Bernard Horsfall (Pryce-Evans), Roger Maxwell (Collins), George Murcell (Jones), Gerald Sim (Masters). A young factory worker decides to stand up against his work-mates and fellow union members when they want to hold a wildcat strike. *Dir.* Guy Green

Angus, Thongs and Perfect Snogging (2008) Georgia Groome (Georgia Nicolson), Aaron Johnson (Robbie), Karen Taylor (Connie Nicolson), Alan Davies (Bob Nicolson), Eleanor Tomlinson (Jas), Georgia Henshaw (Rosie Barnes), Manjeeven Grewal (Ellen), Kimberley Nixon (Wet Lindsay), Sean Bourke (Tom), Tommy Bastow (Dave the Laugh), Liam Hess (Peter Dyer), Eva Drew (Libby), Steve Jones (Jem). A film based on two teenage novels by Louise Rennison: *Angus, Thongs and Full-Frontal Snogging* and *It's OK, I'm Wearing Really Big Knickers*. It follows fourteen-year-old Georgia as she tries to find a boyfriend and throw her fifteenth birthday party whilst worrying about her mum having an affair whilst her dad is looking at a job abroad. *Dir.* Gurinder Chadha

Animal Farm (1954) Gordon Heath (Narrator), Maurice Denham (all animals - voice). Animated film by Halas and Batchelor, based on the book of the same name by George Orwell. *Dirs.* John Halas and Joy Batchelor

Anita and Me (2002) Chandeep Uppal (Meena Kumar), Max Beesley (Hairy Neddy), Sanjeev Bhaskar (Mr. Kumar), Anna Brewster (Anita Rutter), Kathy Burke (Mrs. Rutter), Ayesha Dharker (Mrs. Daljeet Kumar), Omid Djalili (Uncle Amman), Alex Freeborn (Sam Lowbridge), Lynn Redgrave (Mrs. Ormerod), Zohra Sehgal (Nanima), Meera Syal (Auntie Shaila), Christine Tremarco (Sandy), Kabir Bedi (Yeti), Mark Williams (The Reverend 'Uncle' Alan), Lucy Pargeter (Brenda). Based on the book of the same name by Meera Syal. Twelve year old Meena's life in a mining village changes with the arrival of the blonde and beautiful fourteen-year-old Anita and her family. *Dir.* Metin Hüseyin

Anna Karenina (1948) Vivien Leigh (Anna Karenina), Ralph Richardson (Alexei Karenin), Kieron Moore (Count Vronsky), Hugh Dempster (Stefan Oblonsky), Mary Kerridge (Dolly Oblonsky), Marie Lohr (Princess Scherbatsky), Frank Tickle (Prince Scherbatsky), Sally Ann Howes (Kitty Scherbatsky), Niall MacGinnis (Konstantin Levin), Michael Gough (Nicholai), Martita Hunt (Princess Betty Tversky), Heather Thatcher (Countess Lydia Ivanova). Based on the classic novel by Leo Tolstoy. *Dir.* Julien Duvivier

Anne of the Thousand Days (1969) Richard Burton (Henry VIII), Geneviève Bujold (Anne Boleyn), Irene Papas (Catherine of Aragon), Anthony Quayle (Cardinal Thomas Wolsey), John Colicos (Thomas Cromwell), Michael Hordern (Thomas Boleyn), Katharine Blake (Elizabeth Boleyn), Valerie Gearon (Mary Boleyn), Michael Johnson (George Boleyn), Peter Jeffrey (Thomas Howard), Joseph O'Conor (Bishop Fisher), William Squire (Sir Thomas More), Esmond Knight (Kingston). The story of Anne Boleyn's brief reign as queen of England and her downfall and execution. Highly acclaimed film with many Oscar nominations but no awards. *Dir.* Charles Jarrott.

Anniversary, The (1968) Bette Davis (Mrs. Taggart), James Cossins (Henry Taggart), Jack Hedley (Terry Taggart), Christian Roberts (Tom Taggart), Sheila Hancock (Karen Taggart), Elaine Taylor (Shirley Blair). Black comedy centred on manipulative one-eyed Mrs Taggart, who still celebrates her wedding anniversary ten years after being widowed. *Dir.* Roy Ward Baker

Another Country (1984) Rupert Everett (Guy Bennett), Colin Firth (Tommy Judd), Michael Jenn (Barclay), Robert Addie (Delahay), Rupert Wainwright (Donald Devenish), Tristan Oliver (Fowler), Cary Elwes (James Harcourt), Frederick Alexander (Jim Menzies), Anna Massey (Imogen Bennett). A biographical film by Julian Mitchell adapted from his play of the same title. It is set in an English Public School in the 1930s and is loosely based on the early life of Guy Burgess, who later became a Russian spy. *Dir.* Marek Kanievska,

Another Man's Poison (1951) Bette Davis (Janet Frobisher), Gary Merrill (George Bates), Emlyn Williams (Dr. Henderson),

Anthony Steel (Larry Stevens), Barbara Murray (Chris Dale), Reginald Beckwith (Mr. Bigley), Edna Morris (Mrs. Bunting). Based on the play *Intent to Murder* by Leslie Sands. Janet Frobisher is a mystery novelist who decides to deal with the return of her estranged husband by murdering him. *Dir.* Irving Rapper

Another Shore (1948) Robert Beatty (Gulliver), Moira Lister (Jennifer), Stanley Holloway (Alastair McNeil), Michael Medwin (Yellow Bingham), Sheila Manahan (Nora), Fred O'Donovan (Coghlan), Maureen Delaney (Mrs Gleeson), Dermot Kelly (Boxer), Irene Worth (Bucsy Vere-Brown), Bill Shine (Bats Vere-Brown), Muriel Aked (Little Old Lady), Wilfrid Brambell (Arthur Moore). Dubliner Gulliver Shields dreams of living in the South Seas but eventually has to choose between this dream coming true and a girl. *Dir.* Charles Crichton.

Another Time, Another Place (1958) Lana Turner (Sara Scott), Barry Sullivan (Carter Reynolds), Raymond Burr (Walt Radak), Glynis Johns (Kay Trevor), Sean Connery (Mark Trevor), Terence Longdon (Alan Thompson), Sid James (Jake Klein), Martin Stephens (Brian Trevor), Doris Hare (Mrs. Bunker), John Le Mesurier (Doctor Aldridge), Cameron Hall (Alfy), Robin Bailey (Captain Barnes). Sarah Scott is a journalist who had an affair with married man Mark Trevor. During the shoot Connery was confronted by Turner's gangster boyfriend Johnny Stompanato, who brandished a gun and warned him to stay away from Turner. Shortly afterward Stompanato was infamously killed by Turner's daughter Cheryl Crane. The killing was ruled a justifiable homicide. *Dir.* Lewis Allen

Another Year (2010) Lesley Manville (Mary), Jim Broadbent (Tom Hepple), Ruth Sheen (Gerri Hepple), Peter Wight (Ken), Oliver Maltman (Joe Hepple), David Bradley (Ronnie Hepple), Karina Fernandez (Katie), Martin Savage (Carl Hepple), Michele Austin (Tanya), Philip Davis (Jack), Stuart McQuarrie (Tom's colleague), Imelda Staunton (Janet). The film follows Tom Hepple and his wife Gerri and their family and friends, in particular divorcee Mary, over the course of the four seasons of a year. *Dir.* Mike Leigh

Antonio's Breakfast (2005) George Irving (Father), Doreen Mantle (Lady with Rubbish). Won the BAFTA for Best Short Film. Dir. Daniel Mulloy

Antony and Cleopatra (1972) Charlton Heston (Marc Antony), Hildegard Neil (Cleopatra), Eric Porter (Enobarbus), John Castle (Octavius Caesar), Fernando Rey (Lepidus), Juan Luis Galiardo (Alexas), Carmen Sevilla (Octavia), Freddie Jones (Pompey), Warren Clarke (Scarus), Roger Delgado (Soothsayer), Julian Glover (Proculeius). Film adaptation of the Shakespearean play. *Dir.* Charlton Heston

Appointment in London (1952) Dirk Bogarde (Wing Commander Tim Mason), Ian Hunter (Group Captain Logan), Dinah Sheridan (Eve Canyon), Bryan Forbes (Pilot Officer Peter Greeno), Walter Fitzgerald (Dr. Mulvaney), Bill Kerr (Flight Lieutenant Bill Brown), William Sylvester (Mac), Anne Leon (Pam Greeno), Charles Victor (Dobbie), Richard Wattis (Pascal), Carl Jaffe (German General), Sam Kydd (Ackroyd). Second World War drama centred on a Lancaster bomber squadron on nightly raids over Germany. *Dir.* Philip Leacock.

Appointment with Crime (1946) William Hartnell (Leo Martin), Raymond Lovell (Gus Loman), Robert Beatty (Detective Inspector Rogers), Herbert Lom (Gregory Lang), Joyce Howard (Carol Dane), Alan Wheatley (Noel Penn), Cyril Smith (Detective Sergeant Charlie Weeks), Elsie Wagstaff (Mrs. Wilkins), Ian Fleming (Prison governor), Wally Patch (Joe Fisher), Ian McLean (Detective Mason). Leo is a crook who decides to gain revenge on his gang boss for leaving him at a crime scene. *Dir.* John Harlow

Appointment with Venus (1951) David Niven (Major Valentine Morland), Glynis Johns (Nicola Fallaize), George Coulouris (Captain Weiss), Barry Jones (Provost), Kenneth More (Lionel Fallaize), Noel Purcell (Trawler Langley), Bernard Lee (Brigadier), Jeremy Spenser (Georges), Patric Doonan (Sergeant Forbes), Martin Boddey (Sergeant Vogel), John Horsley (Naval Officer Kent), George Benson (Senior clerk), Richard Wattis (Carruthers), David Horne (Magistrate), Philip Stainton (Constable). At the outbreak of WWII the British realise they can't prevent the invasion of the Channel Islands. However, someone realises that a prize cow (the Venus in the title) is on the islands and the Nazis mustn't get hold of her. This is the intrepid story of

the cow-napping from under the noses of the Nazi's. US title: *Island Rescue. Dir.* Ralph Thomas.

Arabian Adventure (1979) Christopher Lee (Alquazar), Oliver Tobias (Prince Hasan), Milo O'Shea (Khasim), Emma Samms (Princess Zuleira), Puneet Sira (Majeed), Peter Cushing (Wazir Al Wuzara), Capucine (Vahishta), Mickey Rooney (Daad El Shur), John Wyman (Bahloul), John Ratzenberger (Achmed), Shane Rimmer (Abu), Hal Galili (Asaf), Art Malik (Mamhoud), Suzanne Danielle (Dancer). As the title suggests, a film with an Arabian Nights setting featuring an evil caliph, a prince, a princess, a young peasant boy and a magic carpet. *Dir.* Kevin Connor.

Aria (1987) Theresa Russell, Nicola Swain, Jack Kyle, Marion Peters, Beverley D'Angelo, Elizabeth Hurley, John Hurt, Bridget Fonda. An anthology film consisting of ten episodes each with a different director and based on a different opera. *Dirs:* Nicolas Roeg, Jean-Luc Godard, Charles Sturridge, Julien Temple, Bruce Beresford, Robert Altman, Franc Roddam, Ken Russell, Derek Jarman, Bill Bryden.

Arsenal Stadium Mystery, The (1939) Leslie Banks (Insp. Anthony Slade), Greta Gynt (Gwen Lee), Ian McLean (Sgt. Clinton), Liane Linden (Inga Larson), Anthony Bushell (John Doyce), Esmond Knight (Raille), Brian Worth (Phillip Morring), Richard Norris (Setchley), Wyndham Goldie (Kindilett), Alastair MacIntyre (Carter), George Allison (Himself – Arsenal FC Manager). During a friendly match between Arsenal and The Trojans at Highbury one of the Trojans' players drops dead during the match. When it is discovered that he has been poisoned, Inspector Slade is called in to investigate. The football action sequences were filmed at the Arsenal against Brentford 1st Division match on 6 May 1939 with the away team playing in a special striped kit to match The Trojans. *Dir.* Thorold Dickinson.

Arsène Lupin (2004) Romain Duris (Arsène Lupin), Kristin Scott Thomas (Joséphine, comtesse de Cagliostro), Pascal Greggory (Beaumagnan), Eva Green (Clarisse de Dreux-Soubise), Robin Renucci (Le duc de Dreux-Soubise), Patrick Toomey (Léonard), Mathieu Carrière (Le duc d'Orléans). A co-production of France, Spain, Italy and the United Kingdom based around the classic Arsène Lupin stories of Maurice Leblanc. *Dir.* Jean-Paul Salomé.

Arthur Christmas (2011) The voice talents of James McAvoy (Arthur), Hugh Laurie (Steve), Bill Nighy (Grandsanta), Jim Broadbent (Santa), Imelda Staunton (Mrs. Santa), Ashley Jensen (Bryony), Marc Wootton (Peter), Laura Linney (North Pole Computer), Eva Longoria (Chief De Silva), Ramona Marquez (Gwen), Michael Palin (Ernie Clicker), Sanjeev Bhaskar (Lead Elf), Robbie Coltrane, (Lead Elf), Joan Cusack (Lead Elf), Rhys Darby (Lead Elf). Animated film in which Santa's son Arthur Christmas must complete a mission before Christmas morning. *Dir.* Sarah Smith.

As You Like It (1936) Laurence Olivier (Orlando), Elisabeth Bergner (Rosalind), Henry Ainley (Exiled Duke), Felix Aylmer (Duke Frederick), Stuart Robertson (Amiens), Mackenzie Ward (Touchstone), Leon Quartermaine (Jacques), Austin Trevor (Le Beau), Lionel Braham (Charles, the Wrestler), John Laurie (Oliver), Fisher White (Adam), Aubrey Mather (Corin), Richard Ainley (Sylvius), Peter Bull (William), Sophie Stewart (Celia). Film adaptation of the Shakespearean play. *Dir.* Paul Czinner.

Ascendancy (1982) Julie Covington (Connie Wintour), Ian Charleson (Lt. Ryder), John Phillips (Wintour), Susan Engel (Nurse), Philip Locke (Dr Strickland). Connie is a British landowner in Ireland during WWI and becomes embroiled in movement for Irish independence. *Dir.* Edward Bennett.

Ashes to Ashes (1999) Wayne Gerard Trotman (Gabriel Darbeaux), Gary Cameron (Muhammed Armen), Jason Ninh Cao (Nelson Kong), Keith McCoy (Michael Trent), Tessa Brown (Arabella Simone), Cecil Cheng (Dennis Cheng), Olivia Carruthers (Felicity Wood), Chris Gabriel (Valentino Tarontola), John Garcia (Enrico Tarontola). A British martial arts film which references the 1970s martial arts film boom. *Dir.* Wayne Gerard Trotman.

Ask a Policeman (1938) Will Hay (Sergeant Samuel Dudfoot), Graham Moffatt (Albert Brown), Moore Marriott (Jerry Harbottle/Harbottle Senior), Glennis Lorimer (Emily Martin), Peter Gawthorne (Chief Constable), Charles Oliver (The Squire), Herbert Lomas (The Coastguard), Dave O'Toole (Dudfoot's witness), Noel Dainton (Revenue Officer), Cyril Chamberlain

163

(Radio Announcer), Brian Worth (Broadcasting Engineer), Patrick Aherne (First motorist), Desmond Llewelyn (Headless Horsemen). Turnbottom Round prides itself as the village without crime; there has not been an arrest recorded by the local police for years. Unfortunately, this is more to do with the inability of Sgt Dudfoot and his constables Albert and Harbottle to so much as recognise a crime. With their jobs on the line, the trio attempt to stage a crime of their own, only to inadvertently uncover a smuggling ring and a headless horseman. A classic comedy written by Val Guest and remade by him in 1983 as the somewhat less popular *The Boys in Blue* starring Cannon and Ball. *Dir*. Marcel Varnel.

Asking for Trouble (1942) Max Miller (Dick Smith), Carole Lynne (Jane Smythe), Mark Lester (General Smythe), Wilfrid Hyde-White (Pettifer), Aubrey Mallalieu (General Fortescue), Esma Cannon (Ada), Raymond Glendenning (Commentator). "Cheeky Chappie" Max Miller's last big screen outing. *Dir*. Oswald Mitchell.

Asphyx, The (1973) Robert Stephens (Sir Hugo Cunningham), Robert Powell (Giles Cunningham), Jane Lapotaire (Christina Cunningham), Alex Scott (Sir Edward Barrett), Ralph Arliss (Clive Cunningham). A horror film in which scientist Hugo Cunningham believes he has discovered an ancient Greek spirit known as an "asphyx", which according to legends appears only at the moment of a person's death. *Dir*. Peter Newbrook.

Assam Garden, The (1985) Deborah Kerr (Helen), Madhur Jaffrey (Ruxmani), Alec McCowen (Mr. Philpott), Zia Mohyeddin (Mr. Lal), Anton Lesser (Mr. Sutton), Iain Cuthbertson (Arthur). In Miss Kerr's last big screen appearance she plays an elderly woman in the west of England whose husband has just died. As a young married couple in India they had run a tea plantation and on their return home, they created an elaborate, Indian-style garden. She is visited by Ruxmani, an Indian lady from the nearby housing estate. *Dir*. Mary McMurray.

Assassination Bureau, The (1969) Oliver Reed (Ivan Dragomiloff), Diana Rigg (Sonya Winter), Telly Savalas (Lord Bostwick), Curd Jürgens (Gen. von Pinck), Philippe Noiret (Monsieur Lucoville), Warren Mitchell (Herr Weiss), Beryl Reid (Madame Otero), Clive Revill (Cesare Spado), Kenneth Griffith (Monsieur Popescu), Vernon Dobtcheff (Baron Muntzof), Annabella Incontrera (Eleanora Spado), Jess Conrad (Angelo), George Coulouris (Swiss Peasant). In 1906, a woman journalist breaks up an international gang of professional killers by falling in love with their leader. *Dir*. Basil Dearden.

Assassination of Trotsky, The (1972) Richard Burton (Leon Trotsky), Alain Delon (Frank Jackson), Romy Schneider (Gita Samuels), Valentina Cortese (Natalia Sedowa Trotsky), Enrico Maria Salerno (Salazar), Luigi Vannucchi (Ruiz), Jean Desailly (Alfred Rosmer), Simone Valère (Marguerite Rosmer). The last days of Trotsky in Mexico. *Dir*. Joseph Losey.

Assault (1971) Suzy Kendall (Julie West), Frank Finlay (Det. Chief Supt. Velyan), Freddie Jones (Reporter), James Laurenson (Greg Lomax), Lesley-Anne Down (Tessa Hurst), Tony Beckley (Leslie Sanford), Anthony Ainley (Mr. Bartell), Dilys Hamlett (Mrs. Sanford), James Cosmo (Det. Sgt. Beale), Patrick Jordan (Sgt. Milton), Allan Cuthbertson (Coroner). The police chase a rapist and murderer. *Dir*. Sidney Hayers.

Astonished Heart, The (1950) Celia Johnson (Barbara Faber), Noel Coward (Dr. Christian Faber), Margaret Leighton (Leonora Vail), Joyce Carey (Susan Birch), Graham Payn (Tim Verney), Amy Veness (Alice Smith), Ralph Michael (Philip Lucas), Michael Hordern (Ernest), Patricia Glyn (Helen), Alan Webb (Sir Reginald), Everley Gregg (Miss Harper), John Salew (Mr. Bowman), Gerald Anderson (Waiter), John Warren (Barman), Jacqueline Byrne (Mary), Frank Duncan (Soames), Bill Owen (Mr. Burton). Told in flashback. A psychiatrist becomes obsessed with an old friend of his wife, with tragic consequences. Adapted from a Noel Coward play. *Dir*. Terence Fisher.

Asylum (1972) Peter Cushing (Mr. Smith), Britt Ekland (Lucy), Herbert Lom (Dr. Byron), Patrick Magee (Dr. Lionel Rutherford), Barry Morse (Bruno), Barbara Parkins (Bonnie), Robert Powell (Dr. Martin), Charlotte Rampling (Barbara), Sylvia Syms (Ruth),

Richard Todd (Walter), James Villiers (George), Geoffrey Bayldon (Max Reynolds), Ann Firbank (Anna), Megs Jenkins (Nurse Higgins), John Franklyn-Robbins (Mr. Stebbins). A horror portmanteau film in four segments within a framing story - Dr Martin is asked to interview four inmates of an asylum in order to ascertain his suitability for a post there. *Dir*. Roy Ward Baker.

Asylum (2005) Natasha Richardson (Stella Raphael), Marton Csokas (Edgar Stark), Ian McKellen (Dr. Peter Cleave), Hugh Bonneville (Dr. Max Raphael), Sean Harris (Nick), Judy Parfitt (Brenda Raphael), Gus Lewis (Charlie), Wanda Ventham (Mrs. Straffen), Joss Ackland (Dr. Jack Straffen). Based on the novel of the same name by Patrick McGrath. Dr Stella Raphael starts an affair with Edgar Stark, an inmate at her asylum, who murdered his wife. *Dir*. David Mackenzie.

At the Earth's Core (1976) Doug McClure (David Innes), Peter Cushing (Dr. Abner Perry), Caroline Munro (Princess Dia), Cy Grant (Ra), Godfrey James (Ghak), Keith Barron (Dowsett), Sean Lynch (Hoojah), Helen Gill (Maisie), Anthony Verner (Gadsby), Robert Gillespie (Photographer), Michael Crane (Jubal), Bobby Parr (Sagoth Chief). Whilst testing a drilling machine Innes and Dr Perry end up in an underground world where they are captured by a reptiles using humans as slaves. Based on the novel of the same name by Edgar Rice Burroughs. *Dir*. Kevin Connor.

At the Villa Rose (1930) Norah Baring (Celia Harland), Richard Cooper (Inspector Hanaud), Austin Trevor (Ricardo), Barbara Gott (Madame D'Auvray), Francis Lister (Weathermill), Amy Brandon Thomas (Mrs Starling), Violet Farebrother (Helen). Based on the 1910 novel At the Villa Rose by A.E.W. Mason, featuring his fictional detective Inspector Hanuad. A further version of the story was made in 1940 when the title role was played by Kenneth Kent. *Dir*. Leslie Hiscott.

Atlantic Ferry (1941) Michael Redgrave (Charles MacIver), Valerie Hobson (Mary Ann Morison), Griffith Jones (David MacIver), Hartley Power (Samuel Cunard), Margaretta Scott (Susan Donaldson), Bessie Love (Begonia Baggot), Milton Rosmer (George Burns), Frederick Leister (James Morison), Henry Oscar (Josiah Eagles), Edmund Willard (Robert Napier), Charles Victor (Tim Grogan), Frank Tickle (Mr. Donaldson), Leslie Bradley (Horatio Stubbs), Felix Aylmer (Bank president), Joss Ambler (Dr. Lardner). The MacIver brothers compete on a transatlantic voyage by steamship. *Dir*. Walter Forde.

Atonement (2007) Keira Knightley (Cecilia Tallis), James McAvoy (Robbie Turner), Saoirse Ronan (Briony Tallis - Age 13), Romola Garai (Briony Tallis - age 18), Vanessa Redgrave (Older Briony), Brenda Blethyn (Grace Turner), Harriet Walter (Emily Tallis), Patrick Kennedy (Leon Tallis), Juno Temple (Lola Quincey). A young fledgling writer, Briony Tallis, irrevocably changes the course of several lives when she accuses her older sister's lover of a crime he did not commit. The film comprises four parts, corresponding to the four parts of the novel. Some scenes are shown several times from different perspectives. Screenplay by Christopher Hampton based on the British romance novel by Ian McEwan. *Dir*. Joe Wright.

Attack on the Iron Coast (1968) Lloyd Bridges (Major James Wilson), Andrew Keir (Captain Owen Franklin), Sue Lloyd (Sue Wilson), Mark Eden (Lieutenant Commander Donald Kimberly), Maurice Denham (Rear Admiral Sir Frederick Grafton), Glyn Owen (Forrester), Howard Pays (Lieutenant Graham), Walter Gotell (Van Horst), John Welsh (Admiral of the Fleet Lord William Cansley), George Mikell (Captain Strasser), Ernest Clark (Air Vice Marshall Woodbridge). Canadian Commando Major Jamie Wilson plans an Allied raid on the Axis held French port of La Plagé during World War II. Loosely based on the actual St Nazaire raid of 1942. *Dir*. Paul Wendkos.

Attack the Block (2011) John Boyega (Moses), Jodie Whittaker (Sam), Alex Esmail (Pest), Franz Drameh (Dennis), Leeon Jones (Jerome), Simon Howard (Biggz), Luke Treadaway (Brewis), Jumayn Hunter (Hi-Hatz), Danielle Vitalis (Tia), Paige Meade (Dimples), Michael Ajao (Mayhem), Sammy Williams (Probs), Nick Frost (Ron). A science fiction film written and directed by comedian and television presenter Joe Cornish. Set on a council estate in South London on Bonfire night, the film follows members of a street gang who have to defend themselves from alien invaders falling from the sky. *Dir.* Joe Cornish.

Aunt Clara (1954) Ronald Shiner (Henry Martin), Margaret Rutherford (Clara Hilton), A.E. Matthews (Simon Hilton), Fay Compton (Gladys Smith), Nigel Stock (Charles Willis), Jill Bennett (Julie Mason), Reginald Beckwith (Alfie Pearce), Raymond Huntley (Rev. Maurice Hilton), Eddie Byrne (Fosdick), Sid James (Honest Sid), Diana Beaumont (Dorrie). Based on the novel of the same name by Noel Streatfeild (author of Ballet Shoes). Clara Hilton comes into an inheritance but finds that it includes several less than legal businesses including a brothel and a gambling den. Her attempts at cleaning them up run into problems. *Dir.* Anthony Kimmins.

Autumn Crocus (1934) Ivor Novello (Andreas Steiner), Fay Compton (Jenny Grey), Muriel Aked (Miss Mayne), Esme Church (Edith), Frederick Ranalow (Herr Feldmann), Jack Hawkins (Alaric), Diana Beaumont (Audrey), Mignon O'Doherty (Frau Feldmann), George Zucco (Reverend Mayne), Gertrude Gould (Frau Steiner), Alyce Sandor (Minna), Pamela Blake (Lenchen). Whilst on holiday in Austria a young English woman falls in love with the married owner of the inn in which she is staying. Based on the play of the same name by Dodie Smith. *Dir.* Basil Dean.

Aventure malgache (1944) Paul Bonifas (Michel), Paul Clarus (Paul Clarus), Jean Dattas (Man behind Michel), Andre Frere (Pierre), Guy Le Feuvre (General), Paulette Preney (Yvonne). An actor tells the rest of his company about the time he outwitted the Nazis as part of the French Resistance. A short British propaganda film in French. *Dir.* Alfred Hitchcock.

Awakening of Emily, The (1976) Koo Stark (Emily Foster), Sarah Brackett (Margaret Foster), Victor Spinetti (Richard Walker), Jane Hayden (Rachel), Constantine Gregory (Rupert Wain), Ina Skriver (Augustine Wain), Richard Oldfield (James Wise), David Auker (Billy), Jeremy Child (Gerald), Jack Haig (Taxi Driver), Pamela Cundell (Mrs. Prince), Jeannie Collings (Rosalind). A film mostly notable for the presence of Koo Stark in a state of undress a few years before she embarked on a much publicized romance with HRH Prince Andrew. *Dir.* Henry Herbert.

Awakening, The (1980) Charlton Heston (Matthew Corbeck), Susannah York (Jane Turner), Stephanie Zimbalist (Margaret Corbeck), Jill Townsend (Anne Corbeck), Patrick Drury (Paul Whittier), Bruce Myers (Dr Khalid), Nadim Sawalha (Dr El Sadek), Ian McDiarmid (Dr Richter), Ahmed Osman (Yussef), Miriam Margolyes (Dr Kadira). Based on Bram Stoker's novel *Jewel of the Seven Stars*. An archaeologist believes the spirit of an Egyptian queen has entered the soul of his daughter. *Dir.* Mike Newell.

Awaydays (2009) Nicky Bell (Paul Carty), Liam Boyle (Elvis), Stephen Graham (Godden), Oliver Lee (Baby Millan), Lee Battle (Billy), Michael Ryan (Marty), Sean Ward (Robbie), Anthony Borrows (Pee Wee), David Barlow (Eddie). Based on the novel of the same name by Kevin Sampson which follows Paul Carty, who joins The Pack, a gang of football hooligans in the early 1980s. *Dir.* Pat Holden.

Awfully Big Adventure, An (1994) Alan Rickman (P.L. O'Hara), Hugh Grant (Meredith Potter), Georgina Cates (Stella Bradshaw), Alun Armstrong (Uncle Vernon), Peter Firth (Bunny), Carol Drinkwater (Dawn Allenby), Rita Tushingham (Aunt Lily), Prunella Scales (Rose Lipton), Edward Petherbridge (Richard St. Ives), Nicola Pagett (Dotty Blundell), Clive Merrison (Desmond Fairchild), Alan Cox (Geoffrey), James Frain (John Harbour). Romance in a Liverpool repertory theatre in 1947 during a Christmas production of *Peter Pan*. An adaptation of the Booker Prize-nominated novel of the same name by Beryl Bainbridge. *Dir.* Mike Newell.

Baby Love (1968) Ann Lynn (Amy Quayle), Keith Barron (Robert Quayle), Linda Hayden (Luci Thompson), Diana Dors (Liz Thompson), Derek Lamden (Nicholas 'Nick' Quayle), Patience Collier (Mrs. Carmichael), Dick Emery (Harry Pearson), Sheila Steafel (Tessa Pearson), Sally Stephens (Margo Pearson), Timothy Carlton (Jeremy), Christopher Witty (Jonathan), Marianne Stone (Shop manageress), Lewis Wilson (Priest), Terence Brady (Man in Shop). After her sluttish mother's suicide, teenager Luci is brought into the home of Amy and Robert Quayle. Plunged into middle class life and attitudes she begins to break the family apart, using both sex and violence to get her way. *Dir.* Alastair Reid.

Baby of Mâcon, The (1993) Julia Ormond (The Daughter), Ralph Fiennes (The Bishop's Son), Philip Stone (The Bishop), Jonathan Lacey (Cosimo Medici), Don Henderson (The Father Confessor), Celia Gregory (Mother Superior), Jeff Nuttall (The Majordomo), Jessica Hynes (The First Midwife), Kathryn Hunter (The Second Midwife), Gabrielle Reidy (The Third Midwife), Frank Egerton (The Prompter), Phelim McDermott (The First Tutor), Tony Vogel (The Father), Diana Van Kolck (The Mother). In a town riven by famine, an aged woman gives birth to a baby but her daughter then claims it as hers, claiming a virgin birth. *Dir.* Peter Greenaway.

Babylon (1980) Brinsley Forde (David, "Blue"), Karl Howman (Ronnie), Trevor Laird ("Beefy"), Brian Bovell ("Spark"), Victor Romero Evans ("Lover"), David N Haynes (Errol), Archie Pool ("Dreadhead"), T-Bone Wilson (Wesley), Mel Smith (Alan), Beverly Michaels (Elaine), Maggie Steed (Woman at Lockup Garage), Bill Moody (Man on Balcony), Stefan Kalipha (Fat Larry), Beverley Dublin (Sandra), Granville Garner (Sandra's Father), Mark Monero (Carlton), David Cunningham (Sir Watts), Cosmo Laidlaw (Rastaman), Terence Dackombe (Thug), Mikey Campbell (Promoter). The struggles of a black musician in London, who faces racism at every turn. Forde was a founder member of the group Aswad and a child actor in children's television series, *Here Come the Double Deckers*. *Dir.* Franco Rosso.

Backbeat (1994) Stephen Dorff (Stuart Sutcliffe), Sheryl Lee (Astrid Kirchherr), Ian Hart (John Lennon), Gary Bakewell (Paul McCartney), Chris O'Neill (George Harrison), Paul Duckworth (Ringo Starr), Scot Williams (Pete Best), Kai Wiesinger (Klaus Voorman), Jennifer Ehle (Cynthia Powell), Wolf Kahler (Bert Kaempfert), James Doherty (Tony Sheridan). A chronicle of the early days of The Beatles in Hamburg focusing on the relationship between Stuart Sutcliffe, John Lennon and Sutcliffe's German girlfriend Astrid Kirchherr. *Dir.* Iain Softley.

Background (1953) Valerie Hobson (Barbie Lomax), Philip Friend (John Lomax), Norman Wooland (Bill Ogden), Janette Scott (Jess Lomax), Mandy Miller (Linda Lomax), Jeremy Spenser (Adrian Lomax), Lily Kann (Brownie), Helen Shingler (Mary Wallace), Thora Hird (Mrs. Humphries), Louise Hampton (Miss Russell), Jack Melford (Mackay), Richard Wattis (David Wallace), Joss Ambler (Judge), Lloyd Lamble (Defence Counsel), Barbara Hicks (Mrs Young). The story of a divorce. *Dir.* Daniel Birt.

Back-Room Boy (1942) Arthur Askey (Arthur Pilbeam), Moore Marriott (Jerry), Graham Moffatt (Albert), Googie Withers (Bobbie), Vera Frances (Jane), Joyce Howard (Betty), John Salew (Steve Mason), George Merritt (Uncle), Eileen Bennett (Bit), Philip Friend (Damon Ravel), Aubrey Mallalieu (West). Meteorologist Arthur gets himself posted to an isolated Scottish lighthouse station where a shipwreck means he is not as lonely as he expected to be. *Dir.* Herbert Mason.

Bad Lord Byron, The (1949) Dennis Price (Lord Byron), Mai Zetterling (Teresa Guiccioli), Joan Greenwood (Lady Caroline Lamb), Linden Travers (Augusta Leigh), Sonia Holm (Annabella Milbanke), Raymond Lovell (John Hobhouse), Leslie Dwyer (Fletcher), Denis O'Dea (Prosecuting Counsel), Irene Browne (Lady Melbourne), Virgilio Teixeira (Pietro Gamba), Ernest Thesiger (Count Guiccioli), Gerard Heinz (Austrian Officer), Cyril Chamberlain (Defending Counsel), Wilfrid Hyde-White (Mr. Hopton), Henry Oscar (Count Gamba), Richard Molinas (Gondolier), Robert Harris (Dallas), Ronald Adam (Judge), Archie Duncan (John Murray), Barry Jones (Colonel Stonhope), Natalie Moya (Lady Milbanke), John Stone (Lord Clark), Nora Swinburne (Lady Jersey), John Salew (Samuel Rogers), Lena Lanare (La Fornarina), Betty Lynne (Signora Segati), Bernard Rebel (Doctor Bruno), Liam Gaffney (Tom Moore), Aubrey Mallalieu (Old club member). A dying Lord Byron looks back at his life, his poetry and loves. *Dir.* David MacDonald.

Bad Timing (1980) Art Garfunkel (Alex Linden), Theresa Russell (Milena Flaherty), Harvey Keitel (Inspector Netusil), Denholm Elliott (Stefan Vognic), Daniel Massey (Foppish Man), Dana Gillespie (Amy Miller), William Hootkins (Col. Taylor), Robert Walker (Konrad), Ania Marson (Dr. Schneider), Ellan

Fartt (Ulla). In Vienna, as a woman struggles to live after a failed suicide attempt we see in flashback the events leading up to this, in particular her intense sexual relationship with professor of psychology Alex Linden. *Dir*. Nicolas Roeg.

Badger's Green (1934) Valerie Hobson (Molly Butler), Bruce Lester (Dickie Wetherby), David Horne (Major Forrester), Sebastian Smith (Mr. Twigg), John Turnbull (Thomas Butler), Wally Patch (Mr. Rogers), Elsie Irving (Mrs. Wetherby). A developer decides the future of a threatened village on the result of a cricket match. Based on the play of the same name by R C Sheriff. *Dir*. Adrian Brunel.

Band Waggon (1940) Arthur Askey (Arthur Askey), Richard Murdoch (Stinker Murdoch), Patricia Kirkwood (Pat), Moore Marriott (Jasper), Michael Standing (himself), Peter Gawthorne (Claude Pilkington), Donald Calthrop (Hobday), Wally Patch (Commissionaire). A spin-off from the popular radio series of the time where Askey and Murdoch live on the roof of BBC Broadcasting House. However, in this film they are evicted and find accommodation in a haunted castle. *Dir*. Marcel Varnel

Bang! You're Dead (1954) Jack Warner (Bonsell), Anthony Richmond (Cliff Bonsell), Sean Barrett (Willy Maxted), Derek Farr (Detective Gray), Veronica Hurst (Hilda), Michael Medwin (Bob Carter), Gordon Harker (Mr. Hare), Beatrice Varley (Mrs. Maxted), Philip Saville (Ben Jones), John Warwick (Sgt. Gurney), Toke Townley (Jimmy Knuckle). When a young boy accidently shoots someone dead, another man is wrongly suspected by the police. *Dir*. Lance Comfort.

Bank Holiday (1938) John Lodge (Stephen Howard), Margaret Lockwood (Catherine Lawrence), Hugh Williams (Geoffrey), René Ray (Doreen Richards), Merle Tottenham (Milly), Linden Travers (Ann Howard), Wally Patch (Arthur), Kathleen Harrison (May), Garry Marsh ('Follies' manager), Jeanne Stuart (Miss Mayfair), Wilfrid Lawson (Police sergeant), Felix Aylmer (Surgeon), Leonard Sharp (Jack). The stories of a variety of people on a bank holiday weekend at the seaside. *Dir*. Carol Reed.

Bargee, The (1964) Harry H. Corbett (Hemel Pike), Hugh Griffith (Joe Turnbull), Eric Sykes (The Mariner), Ronnie Barker (Ronnie), Julia Foster (Christine Turnbull), Miriam Karlin (Nellie Marsh), Eric Barker (Mr Parkes), Derek Nimmo (Dr. Scott), Norman Bird (Albert Williams), Richard Briers (Tomkins), Ronnie Brody (Ted Croxley), George A. Cooper (Mr Williams), Ed Devereaux (Boat Man), Wally Patch (Bargee), Michael Robbins (Bargee), Jo Rowbottom (Cynthia), Una Stubbs (Bridesmaid), Rita Webb (Onlooker), Patricia Hayes (Onlooker), Brian Wilde (Policeman), Godfrey Winn (Announcer). Bargee Hemel has a girl at most stops along his regular canal routes but his freewheeling lifestyle is brought to a halt when one of them tells him she is pregnant. *Dir*. Duncan Wood.

Barnacle Bill (1957) Alec Guinness (Captain William Horatio Ambrose), Irene Brown (Mrs Barrington), Maurice Denham (Mayor Crowley), Percy Herbert (Tommy), Victor Maddern (Figg), Allan Cuthbertson (Chailey), Harold Goodwin (Duckworth), Richard Wattis (Registrar of Shipping), Lionel Jeffries (Garrod), Joan Hickson (Mrs Kent), Miles Malleson (Angler), Charles Lloyd Pack (Tritton), Warren Mitchell (Artie White). An Ealing Comedy (Guiness's last) in which Captain Ambrose, a seasick naval officer, buys a seaside pier on his retirement and runs into conflict with the local council. Guiness also portrays six of Ambrose's sea-faring ancestors in a series of vignettes. *Dir*. Charles Frend.

Barretts of Wimpole Street, The (1936) Norma Shearer (Elizabeth Barrett), Fredric March (Robert Browning), Charles Laughton (Edward Moulton-Barrett), Maureen O'Sullivan (Henrietta Barrett), Katharine Alexander (Arabel Barrett), Vernon Downing (Octavius Barrett), Ralph Forbes (Captain Surtees Cook), Marion Clayton (Bella Hedley), Ian Wolfe (Harry Bevan), Ferdinand Munier (Dr Chambers), Una O'Connor (Wilson), Leo G. Carroll (Dr Waterlow). Elizabeth Barrett's life is severely restricted by her domineering father. Then the poet Robert Browning arrives on the scene. *Dir*. Sidney Franklin.

Barretts of Wimpole Street, The (1957) Jennifer Jones (Elizabeth Barrett), John Gielgud (Edward Moulton-Barrett), Bill Travers (Robert Browning), Virginia McKenna (Henrietta Barrett), Susan Stephen (Bella), Vernon Gray (Captain Surtees Cook), Jean Anderson (Wilson), Maxine Audley (Arabel), Leslie Phillips (Harry Bevan), Laurence Naismith (Dr. Chambers), Moultrie Kelsall (Dr. Ford-Waterlow), Michael Brill (George), Kenneth Fortescue (Octavius), Nicholas Hawtrey (Henry), Richard Thorp (Alfred), Keith Baxter (Charles), Brian Smith (Septimus). A remake, with the same director, of the 1936 film. *Dir*. Sidney Franklin.

Barry Lyndon (1975) Ryan O'Neal (Barry Lyndon/Redmond Barry), Marisa Berenson (Lady Honoria Lyndon), Patrick Magee (Chevalier de Balibari), Hardy Krüger (Captain Potzdorf), Steven Berkoff (Lord Ludd), Gay Hamilton (Nora Brady), Marie Kean (Barry's Mother), Diana Körner (Lischen), Murray Melvin (Reverend Samuel Runt), Frank Middlemass (Sir Charles Lyndon), André Morell (Lord Gustavus Adolphus Wendover), Arthur O'Sullivan (Captain Feeny, the Highwayman), Godfrey Quigley (Captain Grogan), Leonard Rossiter (Captain John Quin), Philip Stone (Graham). A gentlemanly rogue travels the battlefields and parlors of 18th century Europe determined to make for himself the life of a nobleman through seduction, gambling and dueling in this methodical film showing the rhythm and life of the period. The film is divided into two halves each headed with a title card: Act I - By What Means Redmond Barry Acquired the Style and Title of Barry Lyndon, and Act II - Containing an Account of the Misfortunes and Disasters Which Befell Barry Lyndon. In line with other Kubrick projects, the film has some technical innovations, in particular scenes filmed in "candlelight" to attempt to reproduce the lighting of the period. Adapted from *The Luck of Barry Lyndon* by William Makepeace Thackeray, *Dir*. Stanley Kubrick.

Battle Beneath the Earth (1967) Kerwin Mathews (Cmdr. Jonathan Shaw), Viviane Ventura (Tila Yung), Robert Ayres (Adm. Felix Hillebrand), Peter Arne (Arnold Kramer), Al Mulock (Sgt. Marvin Mulberry), Martin Benson (Gen. Chan Lu), Peter Elliott (Dr. Kengh Lee), Earl Cameron (Sgt. Seth Hawkins), John Brandon (Maj. Frank Cannon), Ed Bishop (Lt. Cmdr. Vance Cassidy), Carl Jaffe (Dr. Galissi), Norma West (Susan Kramer), Larry Cross (Broadcaster), Bessie Love (Matron), Bill Hutchinson (Lanchek). A Cold War sci-fi espionage film. The Americans discover that the Chinese are digging tunnels from China under the Pacific and across the US in order to plant strategically placed atomic bombs. US Special forces are dispatched to deal with the problem. *Dir*. Montgomery Tully.

Battle of Britain (1969) Laurence Olivier (Air Chief Marshal Sir Hugh Dowding), Trevor Howard (Air Vice-Marshal Sir Keith Park), Patrick Wymark (Air Vice-Marshal Trafford Leigh-Mallory), Christopher Plummer (Squadron Leader Colin Harvey), Michael Caine (Squadron Leader Canfield), Ralph Richardson (Sir David Kelly), Robert Shaw (Squadron Leader - "Skipper"), Susannah York (Section Officer Maggie Harvey), Ian McShane (Sergeant Pilot Andy), Kenneth More (Group Captain Barker), Edward Fox (Pilot Officer Archie), Michael Redgrave (Air Vice-Marshal Evill), Harry Andrews (Military Envoy), Curd Jürgens (Baron von Richter), Hein Riess (Reichsmarschall Hermann Göring), Manfred Reddemann (Major Falke), Wilfried von Aacken (Gen. Osterkamp), Karl-Otto Alberty (Gen. Jeschonnek), Helmut Kircher (Boehm), Alexander Allerson (Major Brandt), Paul Neuhaus (Major Föehn), Dietrich Frauboes (Field Marshal Milch), Malte Petzel (Colonel Beppo Schmidt), Alf Jungermann (Brandt's navigator), Peter Hager (Field Marshal Albert Kesselring), Wolf Harnisch (General Fink), Rolf Stiefel (Adolf Hitler), Nigel Patrick (Group Capt. Hope), Michael Bates (Warrant Officer Warwick), Robert Flemyng (Wing Cmdr. Willoughby), Isla Blair (Mrs. Andy), Barry Foster (Squadron Leader Edwards), W.G. Foxley (Squadron Leader Evans), James Cosmo (Jamie), David Griffin (Sgt. Pilot Chris), Jack Gwillim (Senior Air Staff Officer), Duncan Lamont (Flight Sgt. Arthur), Reinhard Horras (Bruno). A star-studded film version of the events of the Battle of Britain in 1940. *Dir*. Guy Hamilton.

Battle of the River Plate, The (1956) Peter Finch (Captain Langsdorff), John Gregson (Captain Bell), Anthony Quayle

(Commodore Harwood), Ian Hunter (Captain Woodhouse), Jack Gwillim (Captain Parry), Bernard Lee (Captain Dove), Lionel Murton (Mike Fowler), Anthony Bushell (Mr. Millington Drake), Peter Illing (Dr. Guani), Michael Goodliffe (Captain McCall), Patrick Macnee (Lieutenant Commander Medley), John Chandos (Dr. Langmann), Douglas Wilmer (M. Desmoulins), William Squire (Ray Martin), Roger Delgado (Captain Varela), Andrew Cruickshank (Captain Stubbs), Christopher Lee (Manolo). Set during the early years of World War II, where a Royal Navy force of three lightly armed cruisers (Ajax, Achilles and Exeter) force the German pocket battleship Admiral Graf Spee to dock in the neutral port of Montevideo on the River Plate despite being comprehensively outgunned. Political and naval machinations ensue. Powell and Pressburger make this more than a run of the mill war film with, in particular, the German captain Hans Langsdorff being portrayed as an honourable man. The US title was *Pursuit of the Graf Spee*. Dirs. Michael Powell and Emeric Pressburger.

Battle of the Sexes, The (1959) Peter Sellers (Mr. Martin), Robert Morley (Robert Macpherson), Constance Cummings (Angela Barrows), Jameson Clark (Andrew Darling), Ernest Thesiger (Old Macpherson), Donald Pleasence (Irwin Hoffman), Moultrie Kelsall (Graham), Alex Mackenzie (Robertson), Roddy McMillan (Macleod), Michael Goodliffe (Detective), Noel Howlett (Mr. White), William Mervyn (Detective's friend), Patricia Hayes (Jeannie Macdougall). Based on the short story *The Catbird Seat* by James Thurber. An American female efficiency expert battles with Mr Martin to revolutionise a traditional British textile company. Dir. Charles Crichton.

Be My Guest (1965) David Hemmings (Dave Martin), Steve Marriott (Ricky), John Pike (Phil), Andrea Monet (Erica Page), Ivor Salter (Herbert Martin), Diana King (Margaret Martin), Avril Angers (Mrs. Pucil), Joyce Blair (Wanda), David Healy (Milton Bass), Tony Wager (Artie Clough), David Lander (Routledge), Robin Stewart (Jim Matthews), Monica Evans (Dyllis), Pamela Ann Davy (Zena), Douglas Ives (Steward), Jerry Lee Lewis (Himself). The owners of a seaside hotel strike it lucky when their musician son's group becomes successful. Dir. Lance Comfort.

Beach, The (2000) Leonardo DiCaprio (Richard), Tilda Swinton (Sal), Virginie Ledoyen (Françoise), Guillaume Canet (Étienne), Paterson Joseph (Keaty), Lars Arentz-Hansen (Bugs), Robert Carlyle (Daffy), Peter Youngblood Hills (Zeph), Jerry Swindall (Sammy), Zelda Tinska (Sonja), Victoria Smurfit (Weathergirl), Daniel Caltagirone (Unhygienix), Peter Gevisser (Gregorio), Lidija Zovkic (Mirjana), Samuel Gough (Guitarman), Staffan Kihlbom (Christo), Jukka Hiltunen (Karl), Magnus Lindgren (Sten), Abhijati 'Meuk' Jusakul (Senior Farmer), Emma Renae Griffiths (Waitress). Travelling in South East Asia, Richard acquires a map to a "beach paradise" and persuades Francoise and Etienne to join him in finding it. Based on the novel of the same name by Alex Garland. Dir. Danny Boyle.

Beachcomber, The (1954) Glynis Johns (Martha Jones), Robert Newton (Edward 'Honorable Ted' Wilson), Donald Sinden (Ewart Gray), Paul Rogers (Rev. Owen Jones), Donald Pleasence (Tromp), Walter Crisham (Vederala), Michael Hordern (The Headman), Auric Lorand (Alfred, Major Domo), Tony Quinn (Ship Captain), Ah Chong Choy (Wang the Barkeep), Ronald Lewis (Headman's Son), Jean Rollins (Amao), Lizabeth Rollins (Girl at Maputiti), Michael Mellinger (Medical Orderly), Ronald Adam (Sir Henry Johnstone). The residents of the Welcome Islands face a difficult time when cholera threatens the population. Dir. Muriel Box.

Bean (1997) Rowan Atkinson (Mr. Bean), Peter MacNicol (David Langley), Burt Reynolds (Gen. Newton), Pamela Reed (Alison Langley), Richard Gant (Lt. Brutus), Andrew Lawrence (Kevin Langley), Tricia Vessey (Jennifer Langley), Johnny Galecki (Stingo Wheelie), Sandra Oh (Bernice Schimmel), Harris Yulin (George Grierson), Larry Drake (Elmer), Tom McGowan (Walter Merchandise), June Brown (Delilah), Chris Ellis (Det. Butler), Robert Curtis Brown (Dr. Frowning). A spin-off film from the television series *Mr Bean*. The bumbling Mr. Bean is entrusted to oversee the transfer of *Whistler's Mother* from a gallery in London to a museum in Los Angeles. Dir. Mel Smith.

Beast Must Die, The (1974) Peter Cushing (Dr. Christopher Lundgren), Calvin Lockhart (Tom Newcliffe), Anton Diffring (Pavel), Charles Gray (Arthur Bennington), Ciaran Madden (Davina Gilmore), Marlene Clark (Caroline Newcliffe), Michael Gambon (Jan Jarmokowski), Peter Cushing (Dr. Christopher Lundgren), Tom Chadbon (Paul Foote), Sam Mansary (Butler), Andrew Lodge (Pilot). Tom Newcliffe invites six guests to his estate and then tells them that one of them is a werewolf. He will discover which one by the end of the weekend….and the beast must die. Based on the short story *There Shall Be No Darkness* by James Blish. Dir. Paul Annett.

Beat the Devil (1953) Humphrey Bogart (Billy Dannreuther), Jennifer Jones (Mrs. Gwendolen Chelm), Gina Lollobrigida (Maria Dannreuther), Robert Morley (Peterson), Peter Lorre (Julius O'Hara), Edward Underdown (Harry Chelm), Ivor Barnard (Maj. Jack Ross), Marco Tulli (Ravello), Bernard Lee (Insp. Jack Clayton). The Dannreuthers are joined by four crooks as they wait in Italy for their steamer to be repaired before they all head off to Africa with the prospect of acquiring land containing uranium. Dir. John Huston.

Beau Brummell (1954) Stewart Granger (Beau Brummell), Elizabeth Taylor (Lady Patricia), Peter Ustinov (Prince of Wales), Robert Morley (King George III), James Donald (Lord Edwin Mercer), James Hayter (Mortimer), Rosemary Harris (Mrs. Fitzherbert), Paul Rogers (William Pitt), Noel Willman (Lord Byron), Peter Dyneley (Midger), Charles Carson (Sir Geoffrey Baker), Ernest Clark (Doctor Warren), Peter Bull (Mr. Fox), Mark Dignam (Mr. Burke), Desmond Roberts (Colonel), David Horne (Thurlow), Ralph Truman (Sir Ralph Sidley), George De Warfaz (Doctor Dubois), Henry Oscar (Doctor Willis), Yvonne Andre (Madame Binard), Elwyn Brook-Jones (Mr. Tupp), John Chandos (Silva), D.A. Clarke-Smith (Sir John Wyatt), Finlay Currie (McIver), Geoffrey Dunn (St. Clair), Thomas Gallagher (Bruiser), Alexander Gauge (Newspaper Man), Ann Hanslip (Lady Manley), Maurice Kaufmann (Lord Alvanley), Andrew Osborn (Lord Mindon), Gordon Phillott (Roper Sr.), Gordon Whiting (Squerry), Margaret Withers (Countess Marie Duvarre). Brummell becomes the Prince Of Wales' arbiter of fashion but an insult could prove his undoing. Based on the play by Clyde Fitch. Dir. Curtis Bernhardt.

Becket (1964) Richard Burton (Thomas Becket), Peter O'Toole (King Henry II), John Gielgud (King Louis VII), Paolo Stoppa (Pope Alexander III), Donald Wolfit (Gilbert Foliot, Bishop of London), David Weston (Brother John), Martita Hunt (Empress Matilda), Pamela Brown (Queen Eleanor of Aquitaine), Siân Phillips (Gwendolen), Felix Aylmer (Theobald of Bec). The story of the events leading to the murder of Archbishop of Canterbury Thomas Becket. At the heart of the film is the personal dispute between Henry II, who felt betrayed by his friend, and Becket, who mistrusted the motives of the king and took his role as archbishop much more seriously than Henry had expected. This leads to the famous "Who will rid me of this turbulent priest?" An adaptation of the play *Becket or the Honour of God* by Jean Anouilh. Dir. Peter Glenville.

Becoming Jane (2007) Anne Hathaway (Jane Austen), James McAvoy (Thomas Lefroy), Julie Walters (Mrs. Austen), James Cromwell (Mr. Austen), Maggie Smith (Lady Gresham), Joe Anderson (Henry Austen), Lucy Cohu (Eliza de Feuillide), Laurence Fox (Mr. Wisley), Anna Maxwell Martin (Cassandra Austen), Leo Bill (John Warren), Jessica Ashworth (Lucy Lefroy), Christopher McHallem (Mr. Curtis), Ian Richardson (Judge Langlois), Alan Smyth (The Showman), Sophie Vavasseur (Jane Lefroy), Faye Sewell (Recital Lady). An imagining of the early life of Jane Austen and her possible relationships with Thomas Lefroy and Mr Wisley. Much of the possible narrative is taken from ideas in the book *Becoming Jane Austen* by Jon Spence, who was the historical consultant on the film. Dir. Julian Jarrold.

Bedazzled (1967) Peter Cook (George Spiggott/The Devil), Dudley Moore (Stanley Moon), Eleanor Bron (Margaret), Raquel Welch (Lust/Lilian Lust), Alba (Vanity), Robert Russell (Anger), Barry Humphries (Envy), Parnell McGarry (Gluttony), Danièle Noël (Avarice), Howard Goorney (Sloth), Michael Bates (Inspector Clarke), Bernard Spear (Irving Moses), Robin Hawdon (Randolph), Michael Trubshawe (Lord Dowdy), Evelyn Moore (Mrs. Wisby), Charles Lloyd Pack (Vicar), Lockwood West (St. Peter), Betty Cooper (Sister Phoebe). Stanley's suicide attempt is interrupted by the Devil, who is in contest with God to be the first to collect 100 billion souls. He offers Stanley seven wishes in return for his soul but Stanley's efforts to use the wishes to woo Margaret come to nought because of the Devil's willful misinterpretation. Remade in the US in 2000 with Liz Hurley in the Peter Cook role. *Dir*. Stanly Donen.

Bedford Incident, The (1965) Richard Widmark (Captain Eric Finlander), Sidney Poitier (Ben Munceford), James MacArthur (Ensign Ralston), Martin Balsam (Chester Potter), Wally Cox (Seaman Merlin Queffle), Eric Portman (Commodore Wolfgang Schrepke), Ed Bishop (Lieutenant Hacker), Donald Sutherland (Hospitalman Nerney). A Cold War story where the captain of the destroyer USS *Bedford* ruthlessly harries a Russian submarine he discovers off coast of Greenland. Based on the book of the same name by Mark Rascovich. *Dir*. James B Harris.

Bed-Sitting Room, The (1969) Rita Tushingham (Penelope), Michael Hordern (Bules Martin), Richard Warwick (Alan), Mona Washbourne (Mother), Arthur Lowe (Father), Dudley Moore (Police Sergeant), Harry Secombe (Shelter Man), Roy Kinnear (Plastic Mac Man), Spike Milligan (Mate), Jimmy Edwards (Nigel), Peter Cook (Police Inspector), Ralph Richardson (Lord Fortnum of Alamein), Frank Thornton (The BBC), Dandy Nichols (Mrs Ethel Shroake), Jack Shepherd (Underwater Vicar), Marty Feldman (Nurse Arthur). In a post nuclear war London, pregnant Penelope lives on the Circle Line with her parents and Lord Fortnum fears he may be changing into a bed-sitting room. Bizarre! *Dir*. Richard Lester.

Bees in Paradise (1944) Arthur Askey (Arthur Tucker), Anne Shelton (Rouana), Peter Graves (Peter Lovell), Max Bacon (Max Adler), Ronald Shiner (Ronald Wild), Jean Kent (Jani), Antoinette Cellier (The Queen), Joy Shelton (Almura), Beatrice Varley (Moagga), Koringa (Crocodile charmer). Musical comedy. The crew of a bomber has to bail out and land on Paradise Island, a place ruled by women where men are used merely as breeding stock. *Dir*. Val Guest.

Beggar's Opera, The (1953) Laurence Olivier (Captain MacHeath), Hugh Griffith (The Beggar), George Rose (1st Turnkey), Stuart Burge (1st Prisoner), Cyril Conway (2nd Prisoner), Gerald Lawson (3rd Prisoner), Dorothy Tutin (Polly Peachum), George Devine (Peachum), Mary Clare (Mrs. Peachum), Edward Pryor (Filch), Athene Seyler (Mrs. Trapes), Stanley Holloway (Mr. Lockit), Daphne Anderson (Lucy Lockit), Eric Pohlmann (Inn Keeper), Yvonne Furneaux (Jenny Diver), Kenneth Williams (Jack the Pot Boy), Sandra Dorne (Sukey Tawdrey), Laurence Naismith (Matt of the Mint). A film version of John Gay's 1728 opera. *Dir*. Peter Brook.

Belles of St Trinian's, The (1954) Alastair Sim (Headmistress Millicent Fritton/Clarence Fritton), Joyce Grenfell (Sergeant Ruby Gates), George Cole (Flash Harry), Hermione Baddeley (Miss Drownder), Betty Ann Davies (Miss Waters), Renee Houston (Miss Brimmer), Beryl Reid (Miss Wilson), Irene Handl (Miss Gale), Mary Merrall (Miss Buckland), Joan Sims (Miss Dawn), Balbina (Mlle de St. Emilion), Jane Henderson (Miss Holland), Lloyd Lamble (Superintendent Kemp Bird), Richard Wattis (Manton Bassett), Eric Pohlmann (The Sultan of Makyad), Sid James (Benny), Windsor Cottage (the Horse "Arab Boy"), Uncredited - Roger Delgado (Sultan's Aide), Shirley Eaton (Sixth Former), Raymond Glendenning (Commentator), Dilys Laye (Sixth Former), Arthur Mullard (Henchman), Ronald Searle (Visiting Parent), Carol White (Schoolgirl), Barbara Windsor (Schoolgirl). Inspired by the cartoons of Ronald Searle. The plot revolves around gambling on the horse Arab Boy to resolve the problem of the school finances, the disappearance of several school inspectors and the planting of sergeant Ruby Gates as a teacher at the school by the local police. *Dir*. Frank Launder.

Bells Go Down, The (1943) Tommy Trinder (Tommy Turk), James Mason (Ted Robbins), Philip Friend (Bob), Mervyn Johns (Sam), William Hartnell (Brookes), Finlay Currie (District Officer McFarlane), Philippa Hiatt (Nan), Meriel Forbes (Susie), Beatrice Varley (Ma Turk), Norman Pierce (Pa Robbins), Muriel George (Ma Robbins), Julian Vedey (Lou Freeman), Richard George (P.C. O'Brien), H Victor Weske (Peters), Leslie Harcourt (Alfie

Parrot), Leo Genn (Narrator – voice). A tribute to the work of the British Auxiliary Fire Service (AFS) during the Blitz. *Dir*. Basil Dearden.

Belly of an Architect, The (1987) Brian Dennehy (Stourley Kracklite), Chloe Webb (Louisa Kracklite), Lambert Wilson (Caspasian Speckler), Sergio Fantoni (Io Speckler), Stefania Casini (Flavia Speckler), Vanni Corbellini (Frederico), Alfredo Varelli (Julio), Geoffrey Copleston (Caspetti), Francesco Carnelutti (Pastarri), Marino Masé (Trettorio), Marne Maitland (Battistino). An architect appointed to construct an exhibition in honour of French architect, Boullée, suffers stomach pains and begins to think he is being poisoned. *Dir*. Peter Greenaway.

Bend It Like Beckham (2002) Parminder Nagra (Jesminder Kaur "Jess" Bhamra), Jonathan Rhys Meyers (Joe), Keira Knightley (Juliette "Jules" Paxton), Archie Panjabi ("Pinky" Bhamra), Shaznay Lewis (Marlena "Mel" Goines), Anupam Kher (Mohaan Singh Bhamra), Shaheen Khan (Mrs. Bhamra), Juliet Stevenson (Paula Paxton), Frank Harper (Alan Paxton). Jess is not allowed to play football by her parents but is spotted by Jules and joins the local woman's team, the Hounslow Harriers. *Dir*. Gurinder Chadha.

Bermondsey Kid, The (1933) Esmond Knight (Eddie Martin), Ellis Irving (Joe Dougherty), Pat Peterson (Mary), Ernest Sefton (Lou Rodman), Clifford McLaglen (Bates), Eve Gray (Toots), Syd Crossley (Porky), Winifred Oughton (Mrs Bodge), Len Harvey (Himself), Henry Mason (Himself). A newspaper seller enters a boxing competition but finds his opponent is a sick friend. *Dir*. Ralph Dawson.

Berserk! (1967) Joan Crawford (Monica Rivers), Ty Hardin (Frank Hawkins), Diana Dors (Matilda), Michael Gough (Albert Dorando), Judy Geeson (Angela Rivers), Robert Hardy (Detective Supt. Brooks), Geoffrey Keen (Commissioner Dalby), Sydney Tafler (Harrison Liston), George Claydon (Bruno Fontana), Philip Madoc (Lazlo), Ambrosine Phillpotts (Miss Burrows), Thomas Cimarro (Gaspar), Peter Burton (Gustavo), Golda Casimir (Bearded Lady), Ted Lune (Skeleton Man), Milton Reid (Strong Man), Marianne Stone (Wanda), Miki Iveria (Gypsy Fortune-Teller), Howard Goorney (Emil), Reginald Marsh (Sergeant Hutchins), Bryan Pringle (Constable Bradford). Death visits the travelling circus owned by Monica Rivers but the box office takings just keep on rising. *Dir*. Jim O'Connolly.

Bespoke Overcoat, The (1956) Alfie Bass (Fender - Ghost), David Kossoff (Morrie), Alan Tilvern (Ranting). An adaptation of Gogol's short story *The Overcoat* with the action relocated from Russia to the East End of London. Working in a clothing warehouse, Fender is refused an overcoat by his boss Ranting and asks his friend, Morrie, to make him one instead. Unfortunately Fender dies of cold before he gets it but returns as a ghost to fulfil his desire. The film won an Academy Award for Best Short Subject (Two-Reel). *Dir*. Jack Clayton.

Best Exotic Marigold Hotel, The (2012) Judi Dench (Evelyn), Bill Nighy (Douglas), Dev Patel (Sonny), Tom Wilkinson (Graham), Maggie Smith (Muriel), Ronald Pickup (Norman), Celia Imrie (Madge), Penelope Wilton (Jean), Diana Hardcastle (Carol), Ramona Marquez (Grandchild), Liza Tarbuck (Head Nurse Karen), Lillete Dubey (Mrs. Kapoor), Tena Desae (Sunaina). A group of British pensioners are enticed by an advert to travel to India to spend their retirement at the Marigold Hotel. *Dir*. John Madden.

Beyond Bedlam (1994) Craig Fairbrass (Detective Terry Hamilton), Elizabeth Hurley (Dr Stephanie Lyell), Keith Allen (Marc Gilmour), Anita Dobson (Judith), Jesse Birdsall (Scott), Craig Kelly (Matthew Hamilton), Faith Kent (Miss Coope), Georgina Hale (Sister Romulus), Samantha Spiro (WPC Foster), Steven Brand (Turnball), Zoe Heyes (Josie), Annette Badland (Nurse Wrekin). Dr Lyell is treating serial killer Gilmour with a mind altering drug which seems to be having unexpected side effects. *Dir*. Vadim Jean.

Beyond this Place (1959) Van Johnson (Paul Mathry), Vera Miles (Lena Anderson), Emlyn Williams (Enoch Oswald), Bernard Lee (Patrick Mathry), Jean Kent (Louise Burt), Moultrie Kelsall (Chief Inspector Dale), Leo McKern (McEvoy), Ralph

Truman (Sir Matthew Sprott), Geoffrey Keen (Prison Governor), Jameson Clark (Swann), Rosalie Crutchley (Ella Mathry), Oliver Johnston (Prusty), Joyce Heron (Lady Catherine Sprott), Anthony Newlands (Dunn), Vincent Winter (Paul Mathry, Aged 6), Henry Oscar (Alderman Sharpe), John Glyn-Jones (Magistrate), Hope Jackman (Mrs. Hanley), Eira Heath (Mona Spurling), Thomas Baptiste (Haydock), Michael Collins (Detective Sergeant Trevor), Lynda King (Miss Williams), Danny Green (Roach). On returning to Liverpool, having emigrated to Canada 20 years earlier, Paul discovers that the father whom he had thought had died a war hero is actually in prison for murder. He decides to try and prove his father's innocence. *Dir.* Jack Cardiff.

Bhaji on the Beach (1993) Kim Vithana (Ginder), Jimmi Harkishin (Ranjit), Sarita Khajuria (Hashida), Akbar Kurtha (Manjit), Mo Sesay (Oliver), Lalita Ahmed (Asha), Shaheen Khan (Simi), Zohra Sehgal (Pushpa), Amer Chadha-Patel (Amrik), Nisha Nayar (Ladhu), Renu Kochar (Madhu), Surendra Kochar (Bina), Souad Faress (Rekha), Tanveer Ghani (Balbir), Peter Cellier (Ambrose Waddington). A group of British women of South Asian descent go on a day trip to Blackpool. *Dir.* Gurinder Chadha.

Bhowani Junction (1956) Ava Gardner (Victoria Jones), Stewart Granger (Col. Rodney Savage), Bill Travers (Patrick Taylor), Abraham Sofaer (Surabhai), Francis Matthews (Ranjit Kasel), Marne Maitland (Govindaswami), Peter Illing (Ghanshyam), Edward Chapman (Thomas Jones), Freda Jackson (The Sandani), Lionel Jeffries (Lt. Graham McDaniel), Alan Tilvern (Ted Dunphy), Ronald Adam (General Ackerby), Anthony Bushell (Lanson), Eric Corrie (Man-at-Arms), George Cukor (Man on Train), Dharma Emmanuel (Sentry), Raymond Francis (Captain Cumberly).
Anglo-Indian WAC Victoria is aware that as British rule of India ends, her race will become a problem as neither the British nor the Indians seem to have much respect for Anglo-Indians. When she returns to Bhowani for a holiday she soon finds herself accidently involved in a terrorist plot which she cannot reveal to the British Army officer to whom she has become attracted. Based on the novel of the same name by John Masters. *Dir.* George Cukor.

Big Blockade, The (1942) Leslie Banks (Taylor), Michael Redgrave (Russian), Will Hay (Skipper), John Mills (Tom), Frank Cellier (Schneider), Robert Morley (Von Geiselbrecht), Alfred Drayton (Direktor), Bernard Miles (Mate), Marius Goring (Propaganda Officer), Austin Trevor (U-boat Captain), Michael Rennie (George), Morland Graham (Civil Service), Albert Lieven (Gunter), John Stuart (Naval officer), Joss Ambler (Stoltenhoff), Michael Wilding (Captain), David Evans (David, an RAF Officer), George Woodbridge (Quisling), Ronald Adam (German businessman), Cyril Chamberlain (Press), Thora Hird (German barmaid), Lawrence Kingston (Quisling), Charles Minor (Quisling), Ronald Shiner (Shipping clerk). A propaganda piece in the form of what would probably now be called a humorous docudrama which praises the success of the wartime economic blockade of Germany. *Dir.* Charles Frend.

Big Job, The (1965) Sid James (George 'the Brain'), Sylvia Syms (Myrtle Robbins), Dick Emery (Frederick 'Booky' Binns), Joan Sims (Mildred Gamely), Lance Percival (Timothy 'Dipper' Day), Jim Dale (Harold), Deryck Guyler (Police Sergeant), Edina Ronay (Sally Gamely), Reginald Beckwith (Register Office Official), Michael Ward (Undertaker), Brian Rawlinson (Henry Blobbitt), David Horne (Judge), Frank Forsyth (Bank Cashier), Frank Thornton (Bank Official), Wanda Ventham (Dot Franklin). Resembling a *Carry On* film in terms of cast and crew. A gang of crooks are released from prison 15 years after the bank robbery for which they were arrested only to find that the hollow tree where they stashed the loot is now in the grounds of a police station. *Dir.* Gerald Thomas.

Big Sleep, The (1978) Robert Mitchum (Philip Marlowe), Sarah Miles (Charlotte Sternwood Regan), Richard Boone (Lash Canino), Candy Clark (Camilla Sternwood), Joan Collins (Agnes Lozelle), Edward Fox (Joe Brody), John Mills (Inspector Jim Carson), James Stewart (General Sternwood), Oliver Reed (Eddie Mars), Harry Andrews (Norris), Colin Blakely (Harry Jones), Richard Todd (Commander Barker), Diana Quick (Mona Grant), James Donald (Inspector Gregory), John Justin (Arthur Geiger), Simon Fisher-Turner (Karl Lundgren), Martin Potter (Owen

Taylor), David Savile (Rusty Regan), Dudley Sutton (Lanny), Don Henderson (Lou). Private detective Philip Marlowe is engaged by General Sternwood to settle a problem with a blackmail threat. He also encounters the General's two daughters, who will lead him even further into a tangled web of intrigue. An adaptation of Raymond Chandler's novel of the same name but set in England rather than Los Angeles. *Dir.* Michael Winner.

Big Switch, The (1968) Sebastian Breaks (John), Virginia Wetherell (Karen), Jack Allen (Hornsby-Smith), Derek Aylward (Karl Mendez), Erika Raffael (Samantha), Douglas Blackwell (Bruno Miglio), Julie Shaw (Cathy), Jane Howard (Jane), Roy Sone (Al), Nicholas Hawtrey (Gerry), Brian Weske (Mike), Gilly Grant (Sally), Desmond Cullum-Jones (Chief Inspector), Patrick Allen (Narrator - voice). Low budget gangster thriller. Playboy John Carter finds himself the victim of an extortion racket after a one-night stand. *Dir.* Pete Walker.

Billion Dollar Brain (1967) Michael Caine (Harry Palmer), Karl Malden (Leo Newbigen), Ed Begley (Gen. Midwinter), Oskar Homolka (Col. Stok), Françoise Dorléac (Anya), Guy Doleman (Col. Ross), (Vladek Sheybal (Dr. Eiwort), Milo Sperber (Basil), Mark Elwes (Birkenshaw), Stanley Caine (G.P.O. Special Delivery Boy), John Brandon (Jim), Tony Harwood (Macey), Donald Sutherland (Scientist at Computer), George Roubicek (Edgar), Susan George (Russian Girl on Train). Now a private investigator, ex-MI5 agent Harry Palmer accepts an assignment which shoves him back into the world of espionage and the Cold War. Based on the novel of the same name by Len Deighton. *Dir.* Ken Russell.

Billy Budd (1962) Terence Stamp (Billy Budd), Robert Ryan (John Claggart), Peter Ustinov (Edwin Fairfax Vere), Melvyn Douglas (The Dansker), Paul Rogers (Philip Seymour), John Neville (Julian Radcliffe), David McCallum (Steven Wyatt), Ronald Lewis (Enoch Jenkins), Lee Montague (Squeak), Thomas Heathcote (Alan Payne), Ray McAnally (William O'Daniel), Robert Brown (Talbot), John Meillon (Neil Kincaid), Cyril Luckham (Hallam), Niall MacGinnis (Captain Nathaniel Graveling). Set in 1797 aboard HMS *Avenger*, simple crewman Billy Budd falls foul of the cruel Master at Arms John Claggart. Adapted from the stage play version of Herman Melville's short novel of the same name. *Dir.* Peter Ustinov

Billy Elliot (2000) Jamie Bell (Billy Elliot), Julie Walters (Georgia Wilkinson), Gary Lewis (Jackie Elliot), Jamie Draven (Tony Elliot), Jean Heywood (Grandma), Stuart Wells (Michael Caffrey), Nicola Blackwell (Debbie Wilkinson), Colin Maclachlan (Tom Wilkinson), Billy Fane (Mr. Braithwaite), Janine Blirkett (Jenny Elliot), Adam Cooper (Billy Elliot, age 25), Merryn Owen (Michael Caffrey, age 25), Stephen Mangan (Dr. Crane). Set against the background of the 1984 Miner's Strike, Billy Elliot is an 11 year old boy who stumbles out of the boxing ring and onto the ballet floor. He faces many trials and triumphs as he strives to conquer his family's set ways, inner conflict, and standing on his toes! *Dir.* Stephen Daldry.

Billy Liar (1963) Tom Courtenay (William Terrence 'Billy' Fisher), Wilfred Pickles (Geoffrey Fisher), Mona Washbourne (Alice Fisher), Ethel Griffies (Florence, Billy's grandmother), Finlay Currie (Duxbury), Gwendolyn Watts (Rita), Helen Fraser (Barbara), Julie Christie (Liz), Leonard Rossiter (Emanuel Shadrack), Rodney Bewes (Arthur Crabtree). Billy works in an undertaker's office but spends most of his time daydreaming about a land (Ambrosia) where he is a hero. A number of minor indiscretions cause Billy to lie in order to avoid the penalties. As these events start catching up with him, he finds himself telling bigger lies to cover his tracks. Finally, when his life is a total mess, and nobody believes a word he says, an opportunity to just run away and leave it all behind presents itself. Billy has a difficult decision to make. Based on the novel of the same name by Keith Waterhouse. *Dir.* John Schlesinger.

Billy the Kid and the Green Baize Vampire (1985) Phil Daniels (Billy the Kid), Bruce Payne (T.O.), Richard Ridings (Egypt), Alun Armstrong (Maxwell Randall), Don Henderson (The Wednesday Man), Louise Gold (Miss Sullivan), Zoot Money (Supersonic Sam), Eve Ferret (Mrs Randall), Neil McCaul (Big Jack Jay), Johnny Dennis (Referee), Ralph Morse (Guitarist). Cocky cockney snooker player Billy Kid accepts the challenge of a grudge match from Maxwell Randall (the Green Baize

Vampire), six times world champion; the loser will never play professional snooker again. *Dir*. Alan Clarke.

Bitch, The (1979) Joan Collins (Fontaine Khaled), Antonio Cantafora (Nico Cantafora), Kenneth Haigh (Arnold Rinstead), Ian Hendry (Thrush Feather), Pamela Salem (Lynn), Sue Lloyd (Vanessa Grant), Mark Burns (Leonard Grant), John Ratzenberger (Hal Leonard), Carolyn Seymour (Polly Logan), Doug Fisher (Sammy), Sharon Fussey (Denise), Peter Wight (Ricky), George Sweeney (Sandy Roots), Bill Nighy (Flower Delivery Boy). Fontaine has to run a high class discotheque, fend off the Mafia, wear basques and have sex in interesting places. A film from the same stable as *The Stud* (1978) and likewise based on a novel by Jackie Collins. *Dir*. Gerry O'Hara.

Bitter Harvest (1963) Janet Munro (Jennie), John Stride (Bob Williams), Anne Cunningham (Ella), Alan Badel (Karl Denny), Vanda Godsell (Mrs. Pitt), Norman Bird (Mr. Pitt), Terence Alexander (Andy), Richard Thorp (Rex), Barbara Ferris (Violet), William Lucas (David Medwin), Daphne Anderson (Nancy Medwin), Derek Francis (Mr. Jones), Mary Merrall (Aunt Louise), May Hallatt (Aunt Sarah), Colin Gordon (Charles), Thora Hird (Mrs. Jessup), Allan Cuthbertson (Mr. Eccles), Nigel Davenport (Police Inspector), Jane Hylton (Carole), Francis Matthews (Michael). Country girl Jennie Jones finds that although bright lights, big city may be an alluring idea, in actuality the streets of London are paved with troubles. Based on the book *20,000 Streets Under the Sky* by Patrick Hamilton. *Dir*. Peter Graham Scott.

Black Knight, The (1954) Alan Ladd (John), Patricia Medina (Linet), André Morell (Sir Ontzlake), Harry Andrews (Earl Of Yeonil), Peter Cushing (Sir Palamides), Anthony Bushell (King Arthur), Laurence Naismith (Major Domo), Patrick Troughton (King Mark), Bill Brandon (Bernard), Ronald Adam (The Abbot), Basil Appleby (Sir Hal), Tommy Moore (The Apprentice), Jean Lodge (Queen Guenevere), Pauline Jameson (Lady Yeonil), John Kelly (The Woodchopper), John Laurie (James), Olwen Brookes (Lady Ontzlake), David Paltenghi (High Priest), Elton Hayes (Minstrel).
Blacksmith John makes himself a suit of armour in order to win the hand of the fair Linet and also thwart a threat to King Arthur. *Dir*. Tay Garnett.

Black Narcissus (1947) Deborah Kerr (Sister Clodagh), Flora Robson (Sister Philippa), Jean Simmons (Kanchi), David Farrar (Mr. Dean), Sabu (The Young General), Esmond Knight (The Old General), Kathleen Byron (Sister Ruth), Jenny Laird (Sister Honey), Judith Furse (Sister Briony), May Hallatt (Angu Ayah). Five young British nuns of the Saint Faith Order move to the mountain top former house of the concubines of an old general in the Himalayas in order to open a convent, a school and an infirmary for the locals. The isolation and the disturbing presence of Mr Dean awake long suppressed emotions amongst the nuns. This film won two Academy Awards: Best Art Direction and Best Cinematography. *Dirs*. Michael Powell and Emeric Pressburger.

Black Pond (2011) Simon Amstell (Eric Sacks), Arnab Chanda (Edward), Helen Cripps (Jess Thompson), Sophia Di Martino (Rachel), Amanda Hadingue (Sophie Thompson), Colin Hurley (Blake), Chris Langham (Tom Thompson), Anna O'Grady (Katie Thompson), Bernadette Russell (Mad Rita), Arthur Tatsuki Sharpe (Hal), Will Sharpe (Tim Tanaka), Elisabeth Vriend (Eve), Robert Harper (Pompous Reporter). A black comedy in which a family is accused of murder when a visitor dies whilst having dinner. *Dirs*. Tom Kingsley and Will Sharpe.

Black Rose, The (1950) Tyrone Power (Walter of Gurnie), Orson Welles (Bayan), Cécile Aubry (Maryam), Jack Hawkins (Tristram Griffin), Michael Rennie (King Edward), Finlay Currie (Alfgar), Herbert Lom (Anthemus), Mary Clare (Countess Eleanor Lessford), Robert Blake (Mahmoud), Alfonso Bedoya (Lu Chung), Gibb McLaughlin (Wilderkin), James Robertson Justice (Simeon Beautrie), Henry Oscar (Friar Roger Bacon), Laurence Harvey (Edmond), Rufus Cruikshank (Dickon), Peter Drury (Young man), Valéry Inkijinoff (Chinese Minister), Carl Jaffe (Officer), Ley On (Chinese Captain), Madame Phang (Empress of China), Hilary Pritchard (Hal, the Miller), Peter Sellers (Alfonso

Bedoya - voice), Torin Thatcher (Harry). Set in the 13th Century, a disgraced Anglo-Saxon nobleman leaves England and travels as far as China to seek his fortune; on the way he falls in love with a beautiful woman known as "The Black Rose". Based on the novel of the same name by Thomas B. Costain. *Dir*. Henry Hathaway.

Black Sheep of Whitehall, The (1942) Will Hay (Davis), John Mills (Bobby Jessop), Basil Sydney (Costello), Henry Hewitt (Professor Davys), Felix Aylmer (Crabtree), Owen Reynolds (Harman), Frank Cellier (Dr Innsbach), Joss Ambler (Sir John), Frank Allenby (Onslowe), Thora Hird (Joyce), Margaret Halstan (Matron), Barbara Valerie (Sister Spooner), Leslie Mitchell (Radio interviewer), George Woodbridge (Male Nurse), George Merritt (Stationmaster), Aubrey Mallalieu (Ticket Collector), Ronald Shiner (Porter). A case of at least two mistaken identities as correspondence school teacher is taken to be an expert economist during World War II. *Dir*. Basil Dearden and Will Hay

Black Torment, The (1964) John Turner (Sir Richard Fordyke), Heather Sears (Lady Elizabeth Fordyke), Ann Lynn (Diane), Peter Arne (Seymour), Norman Bird (Harris), Raymond Huntley (Colonel John Wentworth), Joseph Tomelty (Sir Giles Fordyke), Francis de Wolff (Black John), Patrick Troughton (Regis), Derek Newark (Tom), Edina Ronay (Lucy Judd), Annette Whiteley (Mary), Kathy McDonald (Kate), Roger Croucher (Brian), Charles Houston (Jenkins). Set in Devon in the 18th century. When Sir Richard returns home from London with his new wife strange things seem to be afoot. A young girl has been raped and murdered recently with his name on her dying breath and there have been sightings of him at night being pursued by his first wife who is calling him a murderer. Despite having been in London when the murder occurred, the locals believe he was involved. *Dir*. Robert Hartford-Davis.

Black Windmill, The (1974) Michael Caine (Major John Tarrant), Donald Pleasence (Cedric Harper), Joseph O'Conor (Sir Edward Julyan), John Vernon (McKee), Janet Suzman (Alex Tarrant), Delphine Seyrig (Ceil Burrows), Joss Ackland (Chief Superintendent Wray), Clive Revill (Alf Chestermann), Catherine Schell (Lady Melissa Julyan), Denis Quilley (Bateson), Edward Hardwicke (Mike McCarthy), Paul Moss (David Tarrant), Maureen Pryor (Mrs Harper), Molly Urquhart (Margaret), Hermione Baddeley (Hetty), Patrick Barr (General St John), Russell Napier (Admiral Ballantyne), Robert Dorning (Jeweller), John Rhys-Davies (Fake military policeman). Intelligence officer John Tarrant is investigating arms smuggling when his son is kidnapped and held for ransom. Based on Clive Egleton's novel *Seven Days to a Killing*. *Dir*. Don Siegel.

Blackball (2003) Paul Kaye (Cliff Starkey), James Cromwell (Ray Speight), Mark Little (Mark Doohan), Mark Dymond (Kyle Doohan), Alice Evans (Kerry), Bernard Cribbins (Mutley), Johnny Vegas (Trevor), Vince Vaughn (Rick), Imelda Staunton (Bridget), James Fleet (Alan the Pipe), David Ryall (Giles Wilton), Ian McNeice (Hugh The Sideburns), Kenneth Cranham (Chairman Collins), Terry Alderton (Bouncer Jonno), Emma Amos (Local News Reporter), Paul Bentall (Gate Guard), Josie D'Arby (Herself), Angus Loughran (Himself), Jeff Rawle (Dennis), Tony Slattery (Flash Referee), Jon Snow (Himself). After being banned from playing by Ray, head of his local bowls association, Cliff is re-branded as the "Bad Boy of Bowls". Together with Ray he takes on the Australian Doohan brothers in a grudge Ashes match. *Dir*. Mel Smith.

Blackmail (1929) Anny Ondra (Alice White), Sara Allgood (Mrs. White), Charles Paton (Mr. White), John Longden (Det. Frank Webber), Donald Calthrop (Tracy), Cyril Ritchard (Mr. Crewe), Hannah Jones (Mrs. Humphries), Harvey Braban (The Chief Inspector – sound version), Sam Livesey (The Chief Inspector - silent version), Ex-Det. Sergt. Bishop (The Detective Sergeant). Alice kills a man trying to rape her and is blackmailed by a petty crook who saw them together. The film began production as a silent film but Hitchcock was permitted to film a portion of the movie in sound. However, he in fact surreptitiously filmed almost the entire feature in sound along with a silent version for cinemas not yet equipped for talking pictures and it was marketed as one of Britain's earliest "all-talkie" feature films. Anny Ondra proved a problem as she had a heavy Czech accent so Joan Barry was hired to actually speak the dialogue off-camera while Anny lip-synched them for the man. Hitchcock's cameo in this film is as a man bothered by a young boy on the Underground as he is trying to read a book. *Dir.* Alfred Hitchcock.

Blanche Fury (1948) Valerie Hobson (Blanche Fury), Stewart Granger (Philip Thorn), Michael Gough (Laurence Fury), Walter Fitzgerald (Simon Fury), Susanne Gibbs (Lavinia), Maurice Denham (Maj. Fraser), Sybille Binder (Louisa), Ernest Jay (Calamy), Townsend Whitling (Banks), J.H. Roberts (Doctor), Allan Jeayes (Mr. Weatherby), Edward Lexy (Col. Jenkins), Arthur Wontner (Lord Rudford), Amy Veness (Mrs. Winterbourne), Cherry London (Molly), George Woodbridge (Aimes), Lionel Grose (Jordon), Bryan Herbert (Elliot), Margaret Withers (Mrs. Hawkes), Norman Pierce (Coroner), Wilfrid Caithness (Clerk of Court), James Dale (Judge), Cecil Ramage (Prosecuting Counsel). In Victorian England Blanche Fullerton plots to become lady of the manor after she becomes governess to her relatives, the Fury family. Unfortunately the scheme may involve murder. Based on a novel by Joseph Shearing. *Dir.* Marc Allégret.

Bless This House (1972) Sid James (Sid Abbot), Diana Coupland (Jean Abbot), Sally Geeson (Sally Abbot), Robin Askwith (Mike Abbot), Terry Scott (Ronald Baines), June Whitfield (Vera Baines), Carol Hawkins (Kate Baines), Peter Butterworth (Trevor Lewis), Patsy Rowlands (Betty Lewis), Bill Maynard (Oldham), Marianne Stone (Muriel), Janet Brown (Annie Hobbs), Julian Orchard (Tom Hobbs), Tommy Godfrey (Murray), Wendy Richard (Carol), Patricia Franklin (Mary), Molly Weir (Mary's Mother), Ed Devereaux (Jim), Johnny Briggs (Truck Driver), Frank Thornton (Mr Jones), Norman Mitchell (Police Sergeant), Michael Nightingale (Vicar). A big screen spin-off from the television sitcom of the same name. *Dir.* Gerald Thomas.

Blind Corner (1963) William Sylvester (Paul Gregory), Barbara Shelley (Anne Gregory), Alexander Davion (Rickie Seldon), Elizabeth Shepherd (Joan Marshall), Mark Eden (Mike Williams), Ronnie Carroll (Himself), Barry Alldis (Compere), Edward Evans (Chauffeur), Frank Forsyth (Policeman). A blind musician discovers his wife is having an affair but then forms an alliance with her lover against his scheming spouse. *Dir.* Lance Comfort.

Blind Date (1959) Hardy Krüger (Jan), Stanley Baker (Inspector Morgan), Micheline Presle (Jacqueline Cousteau), John Van Eyssen (Inspector Westover), Gordon Jackson (Sergeant), Robert Flemyng (Sir Brian Lewis), Jack McGowran (Postman), Redmond Phillips (Police Doctor), George Roubicek (Police Constable), Lee Montague (Sergeant Farrow). When Jacqueline is murdered, painter Jan Van Rooyer is the prime suspect but Inspector Morgan begins to suspect there is more to the case. *Dir.* Joseph Losey.

Bliss of Mrs. Blossom, The (1968) Shirley MacLaine (Harriet Blossom), Richard Attenborough (Robert Blossom), James Booth (Ambrose Tuttle), Freddie Jones (Det. Sgt. Dylan), Bob Monkhouse (Dr. Taylor), Patricia Routledge (Miss Reece), William Rushton (Dylan's assistant), John Bluthal (Judge), Harry Towb (Doctor), Sheila Steafel (Pet shop saleslady), Frank Thornton (Factory manager), Barry Humphries (Art dealer), John Cleese (Post Office clerk), Leslie Dwyer (Bookshop assistant), Marianne Stone (Factory tea lady), Clive Dunn (Dr. Zimmerman), Geraldine Sherman (Dr. Krunhauser), Carol Cleveland (Bra Model). Harriet is married to a workaholic and takes a lover in the shape of Ambrose Tuttle, who moves into the attic of the Blossom house in order that they can continue the affair more conveniently. However, his disappearance is reported to the police. Seemingly based on the story of Walburga Oesterreich and her lover, although with a much happier ending. *Dir.* Joseph McGrath.

Blithe Spirit (1945) Rex Harrison (Charles Condomine), Constance Cummings (Ruth Condomine), Kay Hammond (Elvira Condomine), Margaret Rutherford (Madame Arcati), Hugh Wakefield (Dr. George Bradman), Joyce Carey (Violet Bradman), Jacqueline Clarke (Edith). Charles' first wife Elvira returns from beyond the grave after Charles and his second wife Ruth light-heartedly arrange for local mystic Madame Arcati to give a séance. *Dir.* David Lean.

Blockhouse, The (1973) Peter Sellers (Rouquet), Charles Aznavour (Visconti), Jeremy Kemp (Grabinski), Per Oscarsson (Lund), Peter Vaughan (Aufret), Nicholas Jones (Kromer), Leon Lissek (Kozhek), Alfred Lynch (Larshen). On D-Day, forced labourers are buried underground by shelling. Luckily they have enough food to last them for years. Based on a novel by Jean-Paul Clébert. *Dir.* Clive Rees.

Blood Beast Terror, The (1968) Peter Cushing (Inspector Quennell), Robert Flemyng (Dr. Carl Mallinger), Wanda Ventham (Clare Mallinger), Vanessa Howard (Meg Quennell), Glynn Edwards (Sgt. Allan), William Wilde (Frederick Britewell), Kevin Stoney (Granger), David Griffin (William Warrender), John Paul (Mr. Warrender), Leslie Anderson (Joe Trigger), Simon Cain (Clem Warren), Norman Pitt (Police Doctor), Roy Hudd (Smiler), Russell Napier (Landlord), Robert Cawdron (Chief Constable), Kenneth Colley (James), Beryl Cooke (Housekeeper), Roy Evans (Second Porter), Joan Ingram (Cook), John Scott Martin (Snaflebum), Malcolm Rogers (Dr. Elliott), Drew Russell (PC Smith), Honor Shepherd (Senior Housemaid), Robin Wentworth (Starkadder). One minute she's a beautiful woman, the next she's a giant Death's Head Moth – the daughter of a professor of entomology is apparently a were-moth terrorising the local area, killing young men and draining them of their blood. *Dir.* Vernon Sewell.

Blood from the Mummy's Tomb (1971) Andrew Keir (Julian Fuchs), Valerie Leon (Margaret Fuchs/Princess Tera), James Villiers (Corbeck), Hugh Burden (Geoffrey Dandridge), George Coulouris (Berigan), Mark Edwards (Tod Browning), Rosalie Crutchley (Helen Dickerson), Aubrey Morris (Doctor Putnam), David Markham (Doctor Burgess), Joan Young (Mrs. Caporal), James Cossins (Older Male Nurse). A curse of the Mummy film where the production was famously troubled. Peter Cushing had to leave the cast after only one day when his wife became ill and director Seth Holt died during filming, actually on the set. Professor Fuchs finds the tomb of ancient Egyptian Princess Tera and takes the perfectly preserved body and sarcophagus back to his home in England. His daughter Margaret then falls under the influence of the Princess' evil spirit. Adapted from Bram Stoker's novel *The Jewel of Seven Stars*. *Dir.* Seth Holt.

Blood of the Vampire (1958) Donald Wolfit (Doctor Callistratus), Vincent Ball (Dr. John Pierre), Barbara Shelley (Madeleine Duval), Victor Maddern (Carl), William Devlin (Kurt Urach), Andrew Faulds (Chief Guard Wetzler), John Le Mesurier (Judge), Bryan Coleman (Monsieur Auron), Cameron Hall (Drunken Doctor), George Murcell (First Guard), Julian Strange (Second Guard), Bruce Wightman (Third Guard), Barbara Burke (Housekeeper), Bernard Bresslaw (Tall Sneak Thief), Hal Osmond (Small Sneak Thief), Henri Vidon (Professor Bernhardt Meinster), John Stuart (Uncle Phillippe), Colin Tapley (Commissioner of Prisons), Muriel Allen (Gypsy Dancer), Max Brimmell (Warder), Denis Shaw (Blacksmith), Otto Diamant (Gravedigger), Milton Reid (Executioner), Richard Golding (Official), Gordon Honeycombe (Stretcher Bearer), Patricia Phoenix (Woman). A scientist who has been "resurrected" conducts experiments on the blood of the inmates of a prison for the criminally insane. *Dir.* Henry Cass.

Blood on Satan's Claw (1971) Patrick Wymark (The Judge), Linda Hayden (Angel Blake), Barry Andrews (Ralph Gower), Michele Dotrice (Margaret), Wendy Padbury (Cathy Vespers), Anthony Ainley (Reverend Fallowfield), Charlotte Mitchell (Ellen), Tamara Ustinov (Rosalind Barton), Simon Williams (Peter Edmonton), James Hayter (Squire Middleton), Howard Goorney (The Doctor), Avice Landone (Isobel Banham), Robin Davies (Mark Vespers), Godfrey James (Angel's Father), Roberta Tovey (Coven member). Set in the 17th century, the uncovering of a strange skull slowly begins to have an evil effect on the children of the village. *Dir.* Piers Haggard.

Blow-Up (1966) Vanessa Redgrave (Jane), Sarah Miles (Patricia), David Hemmings (Thomas), John Castle (Bill), Jane Birkin (The Blonde), Gillian Hills (The Brunette), Peter Bowles (Ron), Veruschka von Lehndorff (Verushka), Julian Chagrin (Mime), Claude Chagrin (Mime). A London fashion photographer uncovers what may be a crime when he blows up the details of a photograph he takes in a park. Thomas's Rolls Royce actually belonged to Jimmy Savile and although originally white, it was painted black for the film. *Dir.* Michelangelo Antonioni.

Blue (1993) Voice cast: John Quentin, Nigel Terry, Derek Jarman, Tilda Swinton. The film consists of a blue screen with a soundtrack of voices, sound effects and music which convey a portrait of Derek Jarman's experiences with AIDS. It was his last film, released a few months before his death. *Dir*. Derek Jarman.

Blue Juice (1995) Catherine Zeta-Jones (Chloe), Sean Pertwee (J.C.), Ewan McGregor (Dean Raymond), Steven MacKintosh (Josh Tambini), Peter Gunn (Terry Colcott), Heathcote Williams (Shaper), Colette Brown (Junior), Michelle Chadwick (Sarah), Keith Allen (Mike), Robin Soans (Young Bob), Jenny Agutter (Guinevere/Mary Fenton), Guy Leverton (Crab), Mark Frost (Moose), Paul Reynolds (Recording Engineer), Edwin Starr (Ossie Sands). The arrival of some old friends spells problems for J.C. and his girlfriend Chloe. *Dir*. Carl Prechezer

Blue Lagoon, The (1949) Jean Simmons (Emmeline Foster), Donald Houston (Michael Reynolds), Susan Stranks (Emmeline, as child), Peter Rudolph Jones (Michael, as child), Noel Purcell (Paddy Button), James Hayter (Doctor Murdoch), Cyril Cusack (James Carter), Nora Nicholson (Mrs. Stannard), Maurice Denham (Ship Captain), Philip Stainton (Mr. Ansty), Patrick Barr (Second Mate), Lyn Evans (Trotter), Russell Waters (Craggs), John Boxer (Nick Corbett), Bill Raymond (Marsden). Two young children are shipwrecked and marooned on a desert island. After the only adult dies, they must face the adventure of growing up together. *Dir*. Frank Launder.

Blue Lamp, The (1950) Jack Warner (PC George Dixon), Jimmy Hanley (PC Andy Mitchell), Dirk Bogarde (Tom Riley), Robert Flemyng (Police Sgt. Roberts), Bernard Lee (Inspector Cherry), Peggy Evans (Diana Lewis), Patric Doonan (Spud), Bruce Seton (PC Campbell), Meredith Edwards (PC Hughes), Clive Morton (Police Sgt. Brooks), Frederick Piper (Alf Lewis), Dora Bryan (Maisie), Gladys Henson (Mrs Dixon), Tessie O'Shea (Herself). Two London bobbies, veteran George Dixon and rookie Andy Mitchell go about their daily routine in Paddington Green and cross paths with two young gangsters Tom and Spud. Although Dixon is famously shot and killed by Tom Riley he was of course resurrected for the long-running TV series, *Dixon of Dock Green*. *Dir*. Basil Dearden.

Blue Max, The (1966) George Peppard (Lt. Bruno Stachel), James Mason (General Count von Klugermann), Ursula Andress (Countess Kaeti von Klugermann), Jeremy Kemp (Willi von Klugermann), Karl Michael Vogler (Colonel Otto Heidemann), Anton Diffring (Holbach), Harry Towb (Kettering), Peter Woodthorpe (Corporal Rupp), Derek Newark (Ziegel), Derren Nesbitt (Fabian), Loni von Friedl (Elfi Heidemann), Friedrich von Ledebur (The Field Marshal), Carl Schell (Von Richthofen), Roger Ostime (The Crown Prince). During WWI a German soldier from the trenches becomes a pilot and aims to claim the country's highest military decoration for valour, the Pour le Mérite - nicknamed the Blue Max. To do this he must shoot down 20 enemy planes but also overcome the prejudice of his more aristocratic fellow pilots. Based on Jack D. Hunter's novel. *Dir*. John Guillermin.

Blue Murder at St Trinian's (1957) Terry-Thomas (Captain Romney Carlton-Ricketts), George Cole ('Flash' Harry), Joyce Grenfell (Sergeant Ruby Gates), Alastair Sim (Miss Amelia Fritton), Sabrina (Virginia), Lionel Jeffries (Joe Mangan), Terry Scott (Police sergeant), Ferdy Mayne (Italian police inspector), Thorley Walters (Major), Judith Furse (Dame Maud Hackshaw), Michael Ripper (Eric - the liftman), Kenneth Griffith (Charlie Bull), Richard Wattis (Manton Bassett), Peter Jones (Prestwick), Charles Lloyd Pack (Henry Roberts), Dilys Laye (Bridget Strong), Nicola Braithwaite (Daphne), Eric Barker (Culpepper Brown), Carol White (Schoolgirl). Miss Fritton is in prison but the schoolgirls win a trip to Europe in a competition. Throw a marriage agency managed by Flash Harry and a missing diamond into the mix and the result is classic comedy mayhem. *Dir*. Frank Launder.

Boat That Rocked, The (2009) Philip Seymour Hoffman (The Count), Tom Sturridge (Carl), Bill Nighy (Quentin), Will Adamsdale ("News" John Mayford), Rhys Darby (Angus "The Nut" Nutsford), Nick Frost (DJ "Doctor" Dave), Katherine Parkinson (Felicity), Chris O'Dowd ("Simple" Simon Swafford), Ike Hamilton (Harold), Kenneth Branagh (Sir Alistair Dormandy),

Sinead Matthews (Miss C), Tom Wisdom ("Midnight" Mark), Gemma Arterton (Desiree), Jack Davenport (Twatt), Ralph Brown ("Smooth" Bob Silver), Rhys Ifans (Gavin Kavanagh), Talulah Riley (Marianne), January Jones (Elenore), Emma Thompson (Charlotte), Ian Mercer (Transfer Boatman), Tom Brooke (Thick Kevin), Rhys Darby (Angus), Stephen Moore (Prime Minister), Michael Thomas (Sandford), Bohdan Poraj (Fredericks), Olegar Fedoro (Rock Boat Captain). Quentin runs "Radio Rock", a pirate radio station anchored in the North Sea and broadcasting rock and pop music to the mainland. This comedy tells the story of the crew of DJs, their love lives and the machinations of the government which is trying to shut the station down. *Dir*. Richard Curtis.

Bobo, The (1967) Peter Sellers (Juan), Britt Ekland (Olimpia), Rossano Brazzi (Carlos Matabosch), Adolfo Celi (Francisco Carbonell), Hattie Jacques (Trinity Martinez), Ferdy Mayne (Silvestre Flores), Kenneth Griffith (Pepe Gamazo), Al Lettieri (Eugenio Gomez), Marne Maitland (Luis Castillo), John Wells (Pompadour Major Domo), Don Lurio (Ramon Gonzales). Unsuccessful singing matador Juan Bautista is guaranteed a spot at a theatre if he manages to seduce the notorious Olimpia Segura, who is known for leaving broken hearts in her wake. Based on the novel *Olimpia* by Burt Cole. *Dir*. Robert Parrish.

Bonnie Prince Charlie (1948) David Niven (Prince Charles Edward Stuart), Margaret Leighton (Flora MacDonald), Judy Campbell (Clementine Walkinshaw), Jack Hawkins (Lord George Murray), Morland Graham (Donald), Finlay Currie (Marquis of Tullibardine), Elwyn Brook-Jones (Duke of Cumberland), John Laurie (Blind Jimmie), Hector Ross (Glenalandale), Franklin Dyall (Macdonald), Ronald Adam (Macleod), James Hayter (Kingsburgh). A romanticised version of the Jacobite Rebellion of 1745. *Dir*. Anthony Kimmins.

Boom! (1968) Elizabeth Taylor (Flora 'Sissy' Goforth), Richard Burton (Chris Flanders), Noel Coward (The Witch of Capri), Joanna Shimkus (Miss Black), Michael Dunn (Rudi), Romolo Valli (Doctor Luilo), Fernando Piazza (Etti), Veronica Wells (Simonetta), Howard Taylor (Journalist). Sissy is terminally ill but into her life comes a man who may or may not bring death closer. Adapted from Tennessee Williams' play *The Milk Train Doesn't Stop Here Anymore*. *Dir*. Joseph Losey.

Boots! Boots! (1934) George Formby (John Willie), Beryl Formby (Snooky), Arthur Kingsley (Hotel Manager), Tonie Forde (Chambermaid), Lilian Keyes (Lady Royston), Donald Read (Sir Alfred Royston), Constance Fletcher (Mrs Clifford), Betty Driver (Betty), Wallace Bosco (Mr Clifford). This musical was Formby's first film (as an adult), and it could be seen as a dedication to his father, George senior, who played John Willie in *No Fool Like An Old Fool* (1914). *Dir*. Bert Tracy.

Born Free (1966) Virginia McKenna (Joy Adamson), Bill Travers (George Adamson), Geoffrey Keen (John Kendall), Peter Lukoye (Nuru), Surya Patel (Doctor), Geoffrey Best (Watson), Bill Godden (Sam), Omar Chambati (Makkede), Bryan Epsom (Baker), Robert Cheetham (Ken), Robert S. Young (James). Joy and George Adamson raise Elsa the Lioness, an orphaned lion cub, to adulthood, and release her into the wilds of Kenya. Based on a true story and Joy Adamson's book of the same name. The film won two Academy Awards: Best Music, Original Music Score (John Barry) and Best Music, Original Song (sung by Matt Monro). *Dir*. James Hill.

Borrowers, The (1997) John Goodman (Ocious P. Potter), Mark Williams (Exterminator Jeff), Jim Broadbent (Pod Clock), Celia Imrie (Homily Clock), Flora Newbigin (Arrietty 'Ett' Clock), Tom Felton (Peagreen Clock), Raymond Pickard (Spud Spiller), Bradley Pierce (Pete Lender), Aden Gillett (Joe Lender), Doon Mackichan (Victoria Lender), Hugh Laurie (Police Officer Steady), Ruby Wax (Town Hall Clerk). The four-inch-tall Clock family secretly share a house with the normal-sized Lender family, "borrowing" such items as thread, safety pins, batteries and scraps of food. However, their peaceful co-existence is disturbed when evil lawyer Ocious P. Potter steals the will granting title to the house, which he plans to demolish in order to build apartments. The Lenders are forced to move, and the Clocks face the risk of being exposed to the normal-sized world. Very loosely based on the children's book of the same name by Mary Norton. *Dir.* Peter Hewitt.

Bostonians, The (1984) Christopher Reeve (Basil Ransom), Vanessa Redgrave (Olive Chancellor), Jessica Tandy (Miss Birdseye), Madeleine Potter (Verena Tarrant), Nancy Marchand (Mrs. Burrage), Wesley Addy (Dr. Tarrant), Barbara Bryne (Mrs. Tarrant), Linda Hunt (Dr. Prance), Charles McCaughan (Music Hall Police Officer), Nancy New (Adeline), John Van Ness Philip (Henry Burrage), Wallace Shawn (Mr. Pardon). Based on Henry James's novel of the same name. *Dir.* James Ivory.

Bottoms Up (1960) Jimmy Edwards (Professor Jim Edwards), Arthur Howard (Oliver Pettigrew), Martita Hunt (Lady Gore-Willoughby), Sydney Tafler (Sid Biggs), Raymond Huntley (Garrick Jones), Reginald Beckwith (Bishop Wendover), Vanda Hudson (Matron), Melvyn Hayes (Cecil Biggs), John Mitchell (Peregrine Wendover), Donald Hewlett (Hamley), Richard Briers (Colbourne), Neil Wilson (Hackforth), Gordon Phillott (Dinwiddie), John Wilder (Roebuck), Graham Tonbridge (Pelbrook), Paul Castaldini (Prince Hassid). A spin-off from Edwards' television series *Whack-O!*. *Dir.* Mario Zampi.

Bounty, The (1984) Anthony Hopkins (William Bligh), Mel Gibson (Fletcher Christian), Laurence Olivier (Admiral Hood), Edward Fox (Captain Greetham), Daniel Day-Lewis (John Fryer), Bernard Hill (William Cole), Phil Davis (Edward "Ned" Young), Liam Neeson (Charles Churchill, Ship's Corporal), Wi Kuki Kaa (King Tynah), Tevaite Vernette (Mauatua), Philip Martin Brown (Able Seaman John Adams), Simon Chandler (David Nelson), Malcolm Terris (Dr. Thomas Huggan), Simon Adams (Peter Heywood), John Sessions (John Smith), Andrew Wilde (William McCoy), Neil Morrissey (Matthew Quintal), Richard Graham (John Mills), Dexter Fletcher (Thomas Ellison), Pete Lee-Wilson (William Purcell), Jon Gadsby (John Norton), Brendan Conroy (Robert Lamb), Barry Dransfield (Michael Byrne), Steve Fletcher (James Valentine). A re-telling of the story of the mutiny on HMS *Bounty* in the Pacific in 1788. The screenplay was by Robert Bolt and it was based on the book *Captain Bligh and Mr. Christian* by Richard Hough. *Dir.* Roger Donaldson.

Boxer, The (1997) Daniel Day-Lewis (Danny Flynn), Emily Watson (Maggie), Brian Cox (Joe Hamill), Ken Stott (Ike Weir), Gerard McSorley (Harry), Ian McElhinney (Reggie Bell). Danny is released from prison in Belfast after fourteen years for his part in IRA activities. He determines to avoid the bloodshed that was inherent in his political past and to build a new life in his old home. He starts a gym to train young boxers like himself, with no political or sectarian ties, and renews his relationship with Maggie, the woman he left behind when imprisoned. *Dir.* Jim Sheridan.

Boy Friend, The (1971) Twiggy (Polly Browne), Christopher Gable (Tony Brockhurst), Max Adrian (Max Mandeville/Lord Hubert Brockhurst), Bryan Pringle (Percy Parkhill/Percy Browne), Murray Melvin (Alphonse), Moyra Fraser (Moyra Parkhill/Madame Dubonnet), Georgina Hale (Fay), Sally Bryant (Nancy), Vladek Sheybal (De Thrill), Tommy Tune (Tommy), Brian Murphy (Peter), Graham Armitage (Michael), Antonia Ellis (Maisie), Caryl Little (Dulcie), Anne Jameson (Mrs. Peter), Catherine Willmer (Catherine Max/Lady Catherine Brockhurst), Robert La Bassier (Chauffer), Barbara Windsor (Rosie/Hortense), Glenda Jackson (Rita). Film adapted from the musical of the same name by Sandy Wilson. Filmed as a "play within a play", Polly Browne, the assistant stage manager of a small theatre company, is forced to take the place of the leading lady for a performance of *The Boy Friend* attended by a film producer. *Dir.* Ken Russell.

Boy in the Striped Pyjamas, The (2008) Asa Butterfield (Bruno), Zac Mattoon O'Brien (Leon), Domonkos Németh (Martin), Henry Kingsmill (Karl), Vera Farmiga (Elsa, Mother), David Thewlis (Ralf, Father), Amber Beattie (Gretel), Richard Johnson (Grandpa), Sheila Hancock (Grandma), Cara Horgan (Maria), Zsuzsa Holl (Berlin Cook), László Áron (Lars), Charlie Baker (Palm Court Singer), Iván Verebély (Meinberg), Béla Fesztbaum (Schultz), Attila Egyed (Heinz), Rupert Friend (Lieutenant Kotler), David Hayman (Pavel), Jim Norton (Herr Liszt), Jack Scanlon (Shmuel), László Nádási (Isaak). During WWII, the son of a concentration camp commandant befriends a Jewish boy in the camp. Based on John Boyne's novel of the same name. *Dir.* Mark Herman.

Boys from Brazil, The (1978) Gregory Peck (Dr. Josef Mengele), Laurence Olivier (Ezra Lieberman), James Mason (Eduard Seibert), Lilli Palmer (Esther Lieberman), Uta Hagen (Frieda Maloney), Steve Guttenberg (Barry Kohler), Denholm Elliott (Sidney Beynon), Rosemary Harris (Frau Doring), John Dehner (Henry Wheelock), John Rubinstein (David Bennett), Anne Meara (Mrs. Curry), Jeremy Black (Jack Curry/Simon Harrington/Erich Doring/Bobby Wheelock), Bruno Ganz (Dr. Bruckner), Walter Gotell (Mundt), David Hurst (Strasser), Wolfgang Preiss (Lofquist), Michael Gough (Mr. Harrington), Joachim Hansen (Fassler), Sky du Mont (Hessen), Carl Duering (Trausteiner), Linda Hayden (Nancy), Richard Marner (Doring), Georg Marischka (Gunther), Günter Meisner (Farnbach), Prunella Scales (Mrs. Harrington), Wolf Kahler (Schwimmer). Nazi hunter Lieberman is on the trail of Josef Mengele, who has a plan to clone Hitler and bring into being the Fourth Reich. *Dir.* Franklin J. Schaffner.

Boys in Blue, The (1982) Tommy Cannon (Sergeant Cannon), Bobby Ball (PC Ball), Suzanne Danielle (Kim), Roy Kinnear (Lloyd), Eric Sykes (Chief Constable), Jack Douglas (Chief Superintendent), Edward Judd (Hilling), Jon Pertwee (Coastguard), Arthur English (Man on Motorbike). *Dir.* Val Guest. See also *Ask a Policeman*.

Boys Will Be Boys (1935) Will Hay (Dr. Alec Smart), Gordon Harker (Faker Brown), Jimmy Hanley (Cyril Brown), Davy Burnaby (Colonel Crableigh), Norma Varden (Lady Dorking), Claude Dampier (Theo P. Finch), Charles Farrell (Louis Brown), Percy Walsh (Prison Governor). Dr Smart is a teacher in a prison and then manages to be made headmaster of Narkover, the local public school which prides itself on the pupils' criminal activities. Hay tries out the schoolmaster persona which he would successfully develop over a number of films. *Dir.* William Beaudine.

Brannigan (1975) John Wayne (Lt. James Brannigan), Richard Attenborough (Commander Swann), Mel Ferrer (Mel Fields), Judy Geeson (Jennifer), John Vernon (Ben Larkin), Daniel Pilon (Gorman), Ralph Meeker (Captain Moretti), Lesley Anne Down (Luana), Barry Dennen (Julian), John Stride (Insp. Michael Traven), James Booth (Charlie-the-Handle), Arthur Batanides (Angell), Pauline Delany (Mrs. Cooper), Del Henney (Drexel), Brian Glover (Jimmy-the-Bet), Don Henderson (Geef). A rare outing for The Duke in a British film as tough Chicago cop Jim Brannigan who is sent to London to extradite a gangster. *Dir.* Douglas Hickox.

Brassed Off (1996) Pete Postlethwaite (Danny), Tara Fitzgerald (Gloria), Ewan McGregor (Andy), Stephen Tompkinson (Phil), Jim Carter (Harry), Philip Jackson (Jim), Peter Martin (Ernie), Sue Johnston (Vera), Mary Healey (Ida), Melanie Hill (Sandra). Set against the proposed closure of the local colliery, the film centres on the personnel of the colliery brass band led by Danny. *Dir.* Mark Herman.

Brazil (1985) Jonathan Pryce (Sam Lowry), Robert De Niro (Archibald 'Harry' Tuttle), Katherine Helmond (Mrs. Ida Lowry), Ian Holm (Mr. M. Kurtzmann), Bob Hoskins (Spoor), Michael Palin (Jack Lint), Ian Richardson (Mr. Warrenn), Peter Vaughan (Mr. Helpmann), Kim Greist (Jill Layton), Jim Broadbent (Dr. Jaffe). A fantasy black comedy set in a dystopian society completely overwhelmed by its red-tape and over-reliance on technology. Sam, a daydreaming government employee, falls foul of the implacable bureaucracy when he attempts to rectify an error which resulted in the arrest and death of a man called Buttle, rather than a "terrorist" named Tuttle because of the interference of a fly. The film went through various working titles but was eventually named after the song *Aquarela do Brasil* which Sam is humming in the final scene. *Dir.* Terry Gilliam.

Bread and Roses (2000) Pilar Padilla (Maya), Adrien Brody (Sam Shapiro), Elpidia Carrillo (Rosa), Jack McGee (Bert), Monica Rivas (Simona), Frank Davila (Luis), Lillian Hurst (Anna), Mayron Payes (Ben), Maria Orellana (Berta), Melody Garrett (Cynthia), Gigi Jackman (Dolores), Beverly Reynolds (Ella), Eloy Mendez (Juan), Elena Antonenko (Maria), Olga Gorelik (Olga), George Lopez (Perez). Two Los Angeles office-cleaning sisters fight for the right to be unionised. *Dir.* Ken Loach.

Breakfast on Pluto (2005) Cillian Murphy (Patrick/Patricia "Kitten" Braden), Liam Neeson (Father Liam), Stephen Rea (Bertie Vaughan), Brendan Gleeson (John Joe Kenny), Gavin Friday (Billy Hatchett), Ruth Negga (Charlie), Laurence Kinlan (Irwin), Seamus Reilly (Lawrence), Eva Birthistle (Eily Bergin), Ian Hart (PC Wallis), Steven Waddington (Inspector Routledge), Ruth McCabe (Ma Braden), Liam Cunningham (1st Biker), Patrick McCabe (Schoolmaster Peepers Egan), Bryan Ferry (Mr Silky String). Growing up in an Irish town in the 1950s and 1960s, foundling Patrick Braden discovers his transgender nature and then sets out to find his biological mother. *Dir.* Neil Jordan.

Breaking Glass (1980) Phil Daniels (Danny), Hazel O'Connor (Kate), Jon Finch (Woods), Jonathan Pryce (Ken), Peter-Hugo Daly (Mick), Mark Wingett (Tony), Gary Tibbs (Dave), Charles Wegner (Campbell), Mark Wing-Davey (Fordyce), Hugh Thomas (Davis), Derek Thompson (Andy), Nigel Humphreys (Brian), Ken Campbell (Publican), Lowri Ann Richards (Jane), Peter Tilbury (CID Officer), Zoot Money (Promotions Man), Jim Broadbent (Station Porter), Richard Griffiths (Studio Engineer), Janine Duvitski (Jackie), Michael Kitchen (Larner), Jonathan Lynn (Radio DJ). The rise and fall of Kate, a young singer and keyboard player with the group Breaking Glass. *Dir.* Brian Gibson.

Brewster's Millions (1935) Jack Buchanan (Jack Brewster), Lili Damita (Rosalie), Nancy O'Neil (Cynthia), Sydney Fairbrother (Miss Plimsole), Ian Maclean (McLeod), Fred Emney (Freddy), Alan Aynesworth (Rawles), Laurence Hanray (Grant), Dennis Hoey (Mario), Henry Wenman (Pedro), Amy Veness (Mrs Barry), Jean Gillie (Miss Tompkins). One of many film versions, this time a musical set in Britain, of the novel of the same name by George Barr McCutcheon. In this version the title character has to spend £500,000 in 60 days in order to inherit £6 million. *Dir.* Thornton Freeland.

Brick Lane (2007) Tannishtha Chatterjee (Nazneen Ahmed), Satish Kaushik (Chanu Ahmed), Christopher Simpson (Karim), Naeema Begum (Rukshana 'Shahna' Ahmed), Lana Rahman (Bibi Ahmed), Lalita Ahmed (Mrs. Islam), Harvey Virdi (Razia), Zafreen (Hasina), Harsh Nayyar (Dr. Azad), Abdul Nlephaz Ali (Tariq), Bijal Chandaria (Shefali), Jean Carnell (Tattooed Woman), Debjani Deb (Young Nazneen), Kusumika Nagar (Young Hasina), Bidyut Das (Abba - Nazneen's father), Dola Chakraborty (Amma - Nazneen's mother). Nazneen moves to London from Bangladesh with her much older husband from an arranged marriage. Sixteen years later she becomes attracted to Karim. Adapted from the novel of the same name by Monica Ali. *Dir.* Sarah Gavron.

Bridal Path, The (1959) Bill Travers (Ewan MacEwan), George Cole (Police Sgt. Bruce), Bernadette O'Farrell (Siona), Duncan Macrae (H.Q. Police Sgt.), Alex Mackenzie (Finlay), Patricia Bredin (Margaret), Fiona Clyne (Katie), Dilys Laye (Isobel), Eddie Byrne (Mike Flanagan), Terry Scott (P.C. Donald), Gordon Jackson (P.C. Alec), Roddy McMillan (Murdo), Joan Benham (Barmaid), Nell Ballantyne (Jessie), Jameson Clark (P.C. at Crossroads), Jack Lambert (Hector), Vincent Winter (Neil), Elizabeth Campbell (Kirsty), John Rae (Angus), Jefferson Clifford (Wallace), Eric Woodburn (Archie), Andrew Downie (P.C. Hamish), John Dunbar (Sgt. MacConnochie), Robert James (Inspector), Joan Fitzpatrick (Sarah), Pekoe Ainley (Craigie), Annette Crosbie (1st Waitress), Molly Weir (2nd Waitress), Graham Crowden (Man giving directions). Ewan MacEwan leaves the Hebridean island of Eorsa in search of the perfect wife. Based on the novel of the same name by Nigel Tranter. *Dir.* Frank Launder.

Brides of Dracula, The (1960) Peter Cushing (Doctor Van Helsing), Martita Hunt (Baroness Meinster), Freda Jackson (Greta), Yvonne Monlaur (Marianne), David Peel (Baron Meinster), Miles Malleson (Dr. Tobler), Henry Oscar (Herr Lang), Mona Washbourne (Frau Lang), Victor Brooks (Hans), Michael Ripper (Coachman), Andree Melly (Gin). Hammer Horror. Abandoned by her coachdriver in a village in Transylvania, young teacher Marianne accepts the offer to stay in the local castle for the night - will they never learn? The Count himself does not make an appearance. *Dir.* Terence Fisher.

Bridge on the River Kwai, The (1957) William Holden (US Navy Commander/Seaman Shears), Alec Guinness (Lieutenant Colonel Nicholson), Jack Hawkins (Major Warden), Sessue Hayakawa (Colonel Saito), James Donald (Major Clipton), Geoffrey Horne (Lieutenant Joyce), André Morell (Colonel Hornsby), Peter Williams (Captain Reeves), John Boxer (Major Hughes), Percy Herbert (Private Grogan), Harold Goodwin (Private Baker). The Japanese are using POWs to build a bridge over the River Kwai. The clash of wills between Saito, the prison camp commander, and Nicholson, commanding the prisoners, ends with Nicholson agreeing to build the bridge to raise morale. As Nicholson becomes obsessed with the construction, a team of commandos guided by Shears, an American escapee, is tasked with destroying the bridge. The film won 7 Oscars: Best Actor in a Leading Role (Alec Guinness), Best Cinematography (Jack Hildyard), Best Director, Best Film Editing, Best Music, Scoring (Malcolm Arnold), Best Picture and Best Writing. *Dir.* David Lean.

Bridge Too Far, A (1977) Dirk Bogarde (Lieutenant-General Frederick "Boy" Browning), James Caan (Staff Sergeant Eddie Dohun), Michael Caine (Lieutenant-Colonel J.O.E. Vandeleur), Michael Byrne (Lt. Col. Giles Vandeleur), Sean Connery (Major General Roy Urquhart), Edward Fox (Lt. Gen. Brian Horrocks), Elliot Gould (Col. Robert Stout), Gene Hackman (Maj. Gen. Stanisław Sosabowski), Anthony Hopkins (Lt. Col. John Frost), Ryan O'Neal (Brig. Gen. James Gavin), Robert Redford (Maj. Julian Cook), Denholm Elliott (RAF meteorologist officer), Peter Faber (Capt. Arie D. "Harry" Bestebreurtje), Christopher Good (Maj. Carlyle), Frank Grimes (Maj. Fuller), Jeremy Kemp (RAF briefing officer), Nicholas Campbell (Capt. Glass), Paul Copley (Pte Wicks), Donald Douglas (Brigadier Gerald Lathbury), Keith Drinkel (Lieutenant Cornish), Colin Farrell (Corporal Hancock), Richard Kane (Col. Weaver), Paul Maxwell (Maj. Gen. Maxwell Taylor), Stephen Moore (Maj. Robert Steele), Donald Pickering (Lt. Col. C.B. Mackenzie), Gerald Sim (Col. Sims), John Stride (Grenadier Guards major), Alun Armstrong (Cpl. Davies), Philip Raymond (Grenadier Guards Colonel), Michael Graham Cox (Capt. Jimmy Cleminson), John Ratzenberger (Lt James Megellas), Hardy Krüger (SS-Brigadeführer Ludwig), Maximilian Schell (SS-Obergruppenführer Wilhelm Bittrich), Wolfgang Preiss (Generalfeldmarschall Gerd von Rundstedt), Walter Kohut (Generalfeldmarschall Walter Model), Hans von Borsody (General der Infanterie Günther Blumentritt), Fred Williams (SS-Hauptsturmführer Viktor Eberhard Gräbner), Laurence Olivier (Dr. Jan Spaander), Liv Ullmann (Kate ter Horst), Erik Chitty (Organist). Star-studded epic World War II film based on the 1974 book of the same name by Cornelius Ryan. The story of the ultimately ill-fated Operation Market Garden aimed at crossing into Germany by dropping paratroops behind enemy lines in order to capture bridges over the Meuse (Maas) and the Rhine. *Dir.* Richard Attenborough.

Bridget Jones: The Edge of Reason (2004) Renée Zellweger (Bridget Jones), Hugh Grant (Daniel Cleaver), Colin Firth (Mark Darcy), Gemma Jones (Mrs. Jones), Jim Broadbent (Mr. Jones), Celia Imrie (Una Alconbury), James Faulkner (Uncle Geoffrey), Jacinda Barrett (Rebecca Gillies), Sally Phillips (Shazzer), Shirley Henderson (Jude), James Callis (Tom), Jeremy Paxman (Himself), Ian McNeice (Quizmaster), Jessica Stevenson (Magda). Bridget's lack of confidence in her relationships continues and this time she also ends up in a foreign jail through no fault of her own. The sequel to *Bridget Jones's Diary* (2001) based on Helen Fielding's novel of the same name. Andrew Davies, who adapted Jane Austen's *Pride and Prejudice* for the BBC in 1995 which starred Colin Firth as Mr Darcy, also co-wrote, with Richard Curtis, the screenplays for both Bridget Jones' films. *Dir.* Beeban Kidron.

Bridget Jones's Diary (2001) Renée Zellweger (Bridget Jones), Hugh Grant (Daniel Cleaver), Colin Firth (Mark Darcy), Jim Broadbent (Mr. Jones), Gemma Jones (Mrs. Jones), Celia Imrie (Una Alconbury), James Faulkner (Uncle Geoffrey), Shirley

Henderson (Jude), James Callis (Tom), Lisa Barbuscia (Lara), Charmian May (Mrs. Darcy), Paul Brooke (Mr. Fitzherbert), Sally Phillips (Shazzer), Embeth Davidtz (Natasha Glenville), Patrick Barlow (Julian), Felicity Montagu (Perpetua). Based on Helen Fielding's novel of the same name. Bridget is a thirty something woman worried about the usual stuff - her weight, her smoking and the men in her life, or lack of them. She is also accident prone, leading to the many slapstick moments in the film. *Dir*. Sharon Maguire

Brief Encounter (1945) Celia Johnson (Laura Jesson) Trevor Howard (Dr Alec Harvey) Stanley Holloway (Albert Godby), Joyce Carey (Myrtle Bagot), Cyril Raymond (Fred Jesson), Valentine Dyall (Stephen Lynn), Everley Gregg (Dolly Messiter), Marjorie Mars (Mary Norton), Alfie Bass (Waiter at *The Royal*), Irene Handl (Cellist and Organist). Both married, Laura and Alec meet by chance in a railway station cafe when he removes a piece of grit from her eye. Their relationship develops beyond just friendship over a series of meetings until a decision has to be reached about the future. Based on Noël Coward's one-act play *Still Life*. The Theme Music was Rachmaninov's *Piano Concerto No 2*. The northern railway station was located at Carnforth in Lancashire. *Dir*. David Lean.

Brighton Rock (1947) Richard Attenborough (Pinkie), Carol Marsh (Rose Brown), Hermoine Baddeley (Ida Arnold), William Hartnell (Dallow), Nigel Stock (Cubit), Wylie Watson (Spicer), Alan Wheatley (Fred Hale), Harcourt Williams (Lawyer Prewitt), George Carney (Phil Corkery), Victoria Winter (Judy). The film centres on the activities of a gang of criminals, particularly their leader Pinkie Brown, a teenage sociopath, and the consequences of the murder of Charles "Fred" Hale. Based on the 1938 novel of the same name by Graham Greene. *Dir*. John Boulting.

Brighton Rock (2010) Sam Riley (Pinkie), Andrea Riseborough (Rose), Helen Mirren (Ida), John Hurt (Phil Corkery), Philip Davis (Spicer), Nonso Anozie (Dallow), Craig Parkinson (Cubitt), Andy Serkis (Colleoni), Sean Harris (Hale), Geoff Bell (Kite), Steven Robertson (Crab), Maurice Roëves (Chief Inspector). Remake updated from pre-war Brighton to the Mods and Rockers era of the 1960s. *Dir*. Rowan Joffe.

Bring Me the Head of Mavis Davis (1997) Rik Mayall (Marty Starr), Jane Horrocks (Mavis Davis/Marla Dorland), Danny Aiello (Mr. Rathbone), Paul Keating (Paul), Ross Boatman (Rock Star), Marc Warren (Clint), Mem Ferda (S.Bon), Daniel Abineri (Bruce), Hamish Clark (John), Joanne Farrell (Kirsty), Rob Freeman (Brendan), Ricky Grover (Gary Belter), Mark Heap (Duncan), Steven O'Donnell (Lenny), Ronald Pickup (Percy Stone), Corrina Preece (Sarah), Ben Richards (Mark), Jaclyn Mendoza (Cynthia), Michael Wildman (Hilary), Heathcote Williams (Jeff), Stewart Harwood (Villain). When debt-ridden music producer Marty Starr discovers his major star Marla Dorland (Mavis Dorland) is losing her popularity he decides her death would boost her fame and fill his pockets. *Dir*. John Henderson.

Britannia Hospital (1982) Leonard Rossiter (Vincent Potter), Malcolm McDowell (Mick Travis), Mark Hamill (Red), Brian Pettifer (Biles), Richard Griffiths (Cheerful Bernie), John Moffatt (Greville Figg), Fulton Mackay (Chief Superintendent Johns), Alan Bates (Macready), Vivian Pickles (Matron), Barbara Hicks (Miss Tinker), Graham Crowden (Professor Millar), Jill Bennett (Dr. MacMillan), Peter Jeffrey (Sir Geoffrey), Joan Plowright (Phyllis Grimshaw), Robin Askwith (Ben Keating), Dave Atkins (Sharkey), Arthur Lowe (hospital patient), Dandy Nichols (Florrie), Betty Marsden (Hermione), Liz Smith (Maisie), T.P. McKenna (Theatre Surgeon), Michael Medwin (Theatre Surgeon), Valentine Dyall (Mr Rochester), Robert Pugh (Picket). A documentary maker, a visit from a member of the Royal family, striking ancillary workers, demonstrations against a VIP patient and Frankensteinian experiments in the science wing. All in a day's work for hospital administrator Vincent Potter in this black comedy. *Dir*. Lindsay Anderson.

Britannia Mews (1949) Dana Andrews (Henry Lambert/Gilbert Lauderdale), Maureen O'Hara (Adelaide 'Addie' Culver), Sybil Thorndike (Mrs. 'The Sow' Mounsey), Fay Compton (Mrs. Culver), A.E. Matthews (Mr. Bly), Diane Hart (The Blazer), Anne Butchart (Alice Hambro), Wilfrid Hyde-White (Mr. Culver), Anthony Tancred (Treff Culver), Herbert C. Walton (The Old

'Un), Mary Martlew (Milly Lauderdale), June Allen (Adelaide Culver – child), Susanne Gibbs (Alice Hambro – child), Heather Latham (The Blazer – child). The life and loves of a young woman in Victorian London. Also known as *The Forbidden Street*. *Dir*. Jean Negulesco.

Broken Blossoms (1936) Emlyn Williams (Chen), Dolly Haas (Lucy Burrows), Arthur Margetson (Battling Burrows), C. V. France (High Priest), Basil Radford (Mr. Reed), Edith Sharpe (Mrs. Reed), Ernest Jay (Alf), Bertha Belmore (Daisy), Gibb McLaughlin (Evil Eye), Ernest Sefton (Manager), Donald Calthrop (Old Chinaman), Kathleen Harrison (Mrs. Lossy), Kenneth Villiers (Missionary), Jerry Verno (Bert).
Peace-loving Chinaman Chen rescues Lucy from her brutal boxing father but the father plots his revenge. A remake of the D W Griffith film of 1919. Released in the US as *Limehouse Murder*. *Dir*. John Brahm.

Broken Journey (1948) Phyllis Calvert (Mary Johnstone), James Donald (Bill Haverton), Margot Grahame (Joanna Dane), Francis L. Sullivan (Perami), Raymond Huntley (Edward Marshall), Derek Bond (Richard Faber), Guy Rolfe (Fox), Sonia Holm (Anne Stephens), Grey Blake (John Barber), David Tomlinson (Jimmy Marshall), Andrew Crawford (Kid Cormack), Charles Victor (Harry Gunn), Gerard Heinz (Joseph Romer), Sybille Binder (Lilli Romer), Amy Frank (Frau Romer), Michael Allan (Lt. Albert), Stuart Lindsell (Mr. Barber), Mary Hinton (Mrs. Barber), Jan Van Loewen (Opera House Director), Arthur Goullet (1st Guide), Leo Bieber (2nd Guide), Ferdy Mayne (Pelotti). An airliner crashes on a mountain side but there are survivors. *Dirs*. Ken Annakin and Michael C. Chorlton.

Brothers in Law (1957) Richard Attenborough (Henry Marshall), Ian Carmichael (Roger Thursby), Terry-Thomas (Alfred Green), Jill Adams (Sally Smith), Miles Malleson (Kendall Grimes), Raymond Huntley (Tatlock), Eric Barker (Alec Blair), Nicholas Parsons (Charles Poole), Kynaston Reeves (Judge Lawson), John Le Mesurier (Judge Ryman), Irene Handl (Mrs. Potter), Olive Sloane (Mrs. Newen), Edith Sharpe (Mrs. Thursby), Leslie Phillips (Shopkeeper), Brian Oulton (Client). Roger is a keen young barrister in his first year in chambers. Based on the novel *Brothers in Law* by Henry Cecil which was also adapted by Frank Muir and Denis Norden as a television series featuring Richard Briers in the leading role. *Dir*. Roy Boulting.

Brothers, The (1947) Patricia Roc (Mary Lawson), Will Fyffe (Aeneas McGrath), Maxwell Reed (Fergus Macrae), Finlay Currie (Hector Macrae), John Laurie (Dugald), Andrew Crawford (Willie McFarish), Duncan Macrae (John Macrae), Morland Graham (Angus McFarish), Megs Jenkins (Angustina McFarish), James Woodburn (Priest), David McAlister (George McFarish), Patrick Boxill (The Informer). On a remote Scottish island the feud between the Macrae and the McFarish clans is reignited by the arrival of Mary Lawson. She also causes bad blood between the Macrae brothers. *Dir*. David MacDonald.

Browning Version, The (1951) Michael Redgrave (Andrew Crocker-Harris), Jean Kent (Millie Crocker-Harris), Nigel Patrick (Frank Hunter), Ronald Howard (Gilbert), Wilfrid Hyde-White (the Headmaster), Brian Smith (Taplow), Bill Travers (Fletcher), Judith Furse (Mrs. Williamson), Peter Jones (Carstairs), Sarah Lawson (Betty Carstairs). The story of an embittered schoolmaster's final few days in his post. The title refers to Robert Browning's translation of the *Agamemnon* by Aeschylus which is given to him as a gift by a pupil. Based on the 1948 play of the same name by Terence Rattigan. *Dir*. Anthony Asquith.

Browning Version, The (1994) Albert Finney (Andrew Crocker-Harris), Greta Scacchi (Laura Crocker-Harris), Matthew Modine (Frank Hunter), Julian Sands (Tom Gilbert), Michael Gambon (Dr. Frobisher), Ben Silverstone (Taplow), Jim Sturgess (Bryant), Joseph Beattie (Wilson), David Lever (David Fletcher), Maryam d'Abo (Diana). Another adaptation of the Rattigan's play. *Dir*. Mike Figgis.

Brylcreem Boys, The (1998) Billy Campbell (Miles Keogh), Chris 'Kit' Ryan (Colin Parker), Jean Butler (Mattie Guerin), Gabriel Byrne (Commandant O'Brien), Hal Fowler (Bunty Winthrop), Anders Jillybo (Sten Larsen), Alistair McLeod (Sergeant Marshall), Tim Hayes (Sergeant Walsh), Joe McGann (Captain Deegan), Anthony Madigan (Policeman), Angus Macfadyen (Rudolph von Stegenbek), B.J. Hogg (Sean), Trevor

Nelson (Seamus), John Gordon Sinclair (Richard Lewis), Hugh Vyvyan (Henshaw), Jérôme Pradon (Ricard), William McNamara (Sam Gunn), Marc Sinden (Senior Allied Officer White), Oliver Tobias (Hans Jorg Wolff), Peter Woodward (Ernst Stossel). During WWII neutral Ireland detained military personnel from the warring nations who were caught on Irish soil. In this film a Canadian pilot and a German airman, imprisoned in the same camp, both fall in love with the same girl. *Dir.* Terence Ryan.

Bugsy Malone (1976) Scott Baio (Bugsy Malone), Florrie Dugger (Blousey Brown), John Cassisi (Fat Sam), Jodie Foster (Tallulah), Martin Lev (Dandy Dan), Paul Murphy (Leroy Smith), Albin Humpty Jenkins (Fizzy), Sheridan Russell (Knuckles), Dexter Fletcher (Baby Face), Bonnie Langford (Lena Marelli). A gangster movie musical where all the parts are played by children. The story tells of the rise of Bugsy Malone and the battle for power between rival gang bosses Fat Sam and Dandy Dan. Instead of "real" weapons the combatants use "splurge guns" that cover the victim in cream, with the final "shoot out" being a particularly messy affair. *Dir.* Alan Parker.

Bulldog Breed, The (1960) Norman Wisdom (Ordinary Seaman Norman Puckle), Penny Morrell (Marlene), Ian Hunter (Admiral Sir Bryanston Blyth), David Lodge (Chief Petty Officer Knowles), Robert Urquhart (Commander Clayton), Edward Chapman (Mr. Philpots), Eddie Byrne (Petty Officer Filkins), Peter Jones (Diving instructor), John Le Mesurier (Prosecuting counsel), Terence Alexander (Defending counsel), Sydney Tafler (Speedboat owner), Brian Oulton (Bert Ainsworth), Harold Goodwin (Streaky Hopkinson), Johnny Briggs (Johnny Nolan), Frank Williams (Mr. Carruthers), Joe Robinson (Tall sailor), Liz Fraser (NAAFI girl), Penny Morrell (Marlene Barlow), Claire Gordon (Peggy), Julie Shearing (WRN Smith), Leonard Sachs (Yachtsman), Glyn Houston (Gym instructor), Michael Caine (Sailor), Oliver Reed (Teddy boy). Having lost out in love, Norman joins the Royal Navy but ends up in outer space – as you do!. *Dir.* Robert Asher.

Bulldog Sees It Through (1940) Jack Buchanan (Bill Watson), Greta Gynt (Jane Sinclair), Sebastian Shaw (Derek Sinclair), David Hutcheson (Freddie Caryll), Googie Withers (Toots), Robert Newton (Watkins), Arthur Hambling (Inspector Horn), Wylie Watson (Dancing Professor), Polly Ward (Miss Fortescue), Nadine March (Gladys), Ronald Shiner (Pug), Aubrey Mallalieu (Magistrate), Raymond Huntley (Tramp Steamer Officer). "Bulldog" Watson and his friend Derek investigate sabotage at a munitions factory. *Dir.* Harold Huth.

Bullet Boy (2004) Ashley Walters (Ricky), Luke Fraser (Curtis), Leon Black (Wisdom), Claire Perkins (Beverley), Sharea-mounira Samuels (Shea), Curtis Walker (Leon), Rio Tison (Rio), Clark Lawson (Godfrey), Jadiel Vitalis (Meadow), Sylvester Williams (Neville), Jaime Winstone (Natalie), Louise Delamere (Probation Officer). Ricky and his friend Wisdom's involvement in gun crime has inevitable consequences for themselves and Ricky's younger brother Curtis. *Dir.* Saul Dibb.

Bullshot (1983) Alan Shearman (Capt. Hugh "Bullshot" Crummond), Diz White (Rosemary Fenton), Ronald E. House (Bruno), Frances Tomelty (Fräulein Lenya von Bruno), Ron Pember (Dobbs), Mel Smith (Crouch), Michael Aldridge (Prof. Rupert Fenton), Christopher Good (Lord Binky Brancaster), Billy Connolly (Hawkeye McGillicuddy), Geoffrey Bayldon (Col. Hinchcliff), Christopher Godwin (Maitre d'), Bryan Pringle (Waiter), Angela Thorne (Hotel Manageress), Peter Bayliss (Chairman of the Institute), John Wells (American Scientist), Nicholas Lyndhurst (Nobby Clark), Ray Cooper (Len Cunningham), Derek Deadman (Reg Erskine), 'Legs' Larry Smith (Dusty Miller), John Du Prez (Ginger Johnson), Zoot Money (Chalky White), Ted Moult (Station Porter), Ballard Berkeley (Hotel Guest). Bullshot Crummond is a man of many talents including amateur detective, fighter ace, Olympic athlete and racing driver. Now, he must save the world from the dastardly Count Otto van Bruno. Based on the stage play *Bullshot Crummond. Dir.* Dick Clement.

Bunker, The (2001) Jason Flemyng (Cpl. Baumann), Andrew Tiernan (Cpl. Schenke), Christopher Fairbank (Sgt. Heydrich),

Simon Kunz (Lt. Krupp), Andrew-Lee Potts (Pvt. Neumann), John Carlisle (Pvt. Mirus), Eddie Marsan (Pfc. Kreuzmann), Jack Davenport (Cpl. Ebert), Charley Boorman (Pfc. Franke). Surrounded whilst defending a bunker towards the end of WWII, a group of German soldiers explore tunnels beneath the bunker and begin to have strange and uncomfortable experiences. *Dir.* Rob Green.

Bunny Lake is Missing (1965) Laurence Olivier (Superintendent Newhouse), Carol Lynley (Ann Lake), Keir Dullea (Steven Lake), Martita Hunt (Ada Ford), Anna Massey (Elvira), Clive Revill (Andrews), Finlay Currie (Doll Maker), Lucie Mannheim (Cook), Noel Coward (Horatio Wilson), Adrienne Corri (Dorothy), Megs Jenkins (Sister), Delphi Lawrence (1st Mother), Jill Melford (Teacher), Suzanne Neve (2nd Mother), Damaris Hayman (Daphne), Jane Evers (Policewoman), Kika Markham (Nurse), Suky Appleby (Felicia 'Bunny' Lake), Richard Wattis (Clerk in Shipping Office), Victor Maddern (Taxi Driver), Percy Herbert (Policeman at Station), Fred Emney (Man in Soho), Norman Mitchell (Mover), Tim Brinton (Newscaster), Michael Wynne (Rogers), John Forbes-Robertson (Hospital Attendant). On arriving at school at the end of her daughter's first day, Ann Lake, recently arrived in Britain from America to stay with her brother Steve, discovers that her little girl, Bunny, is not there and everyone denies any knowledge of ever seeing her. Based on the novel of the same name by Merriam Modell. *Dir.* Otto Preminger.

But Not in Vain (1948) Raymond Lovell (Jan Alting), Carol van Derman (Elly Alting), Martin Benson (Mark Meyer), Agnes Bernelle (Mary Meyer), Scott Forbes (Willem Bakker), Bruce Lester (Fred Van Nespen), Ben van Eysselsteijn (Sergeant Eeslyn), Jordan Lawrence (Anton), Harry Croizet (Skipper), Victor Colane (Ludwig), Henry Almar (Koba), Gerhard Alexander (Ross). Set in the Nazi occupied Netherlands during the winter of 1944 when famine was rife in the country. The owner of a farm who is harbouring fugitives from the Nazis is faced with a dilemma when his collaborator son returns home and demands he turns them over to the authorities. A British-Dutch production. *Dir.* Edmond T. Gréville.

Cabinet of Caligari, The (1962) Glynis Johns (Jane), Dan O'Herlihy (Paul/Caligari), Dick Davalos (Mark Lindstrom), Lawrence Dobkin (Dr Frank David), Constance Ford (Christine), Estelle Winwood (Ruth), J. Pat O'Malley (Martin), Vicki Trickett (Jeanie the Maid), Doreen Lang (Vivian), Charles E. Fredericks (Bob), Phyllis Teagardin (Little Girl). When Jane's car breaks down she seeks out help from a nearby estate. Unfortunately she soon finds herself the prisoner of Caligari. *Dir.* Roger Kay.

Caesar and Cleopatra (1945) Claude Rains (Julius Caesar), Vivien Leigh (Cleopatra), Stewart Granger (Apollodorus), Flora Robson (Ftatateeta), Francis L. Sullivan (Pothinus), Basil Sydney (Rufio), Cecil Parker (Britannus), Stanley Holloway (Belzanor), Raymond Lovell (Lucius Septimus), Ernest Thesiger (Theodotus), Anthony Harvey (Ptolemy), Jean Simmons (Harpist), Michael Rennie (Quayside Centurion), Ronald Shiner (Second Porter). Adapted from a 1901 play by George Bernard Shaw. *Dir.* Gabriel Pascal

Cage of Gold (1950) Jean Simmons (Judith Moray), David Farrar (Bill Glennan), James Donald (Dr Alan Keam), Herbert Lom (Rahman), Madeleine Lebeau (Marie Jouvet), Maria Mauban (Antoinette Duport), Bernard Lee (Inspector Grey), Grégoire Aslan (Duport), Gladys Henson (Nanny), Harcourt Williams (Dr Kearn Sr), Léo Ferré (Victor), George Benson (Assistant Registrar), Martin Boddey (Police Sgt. Adams), Arthur Hambling (Jenkins), Campbell Singer (Constable), Guy Verney (George), Tony Britton (Nicky), Sam Kydd (Waiter), Arthur Lowe (Short Man). When her husband, who left her when he realised she had no money, is reported dead, Judith marries the doctor she had previously been engaged to. Then her "dead" husband reappears and demands money from her. *Dir.* Basil Dearden.

Cairo Road (1950) Eric Portman (Col. Youssef Bey), Laurence Harvey (Lt. Mourad), Maria Mauban (Marie), Camelia (Anna Michelis), Harold Lang (Rico Pavlis/Humble), Grégoire Aslan (Lombardi), Karel Stepanek (Edouardo Pavlis), John Bailey (Doctor), Martin Boddey (Maj. Ahmed Mustafa), John Gregson

(Coast Guardsman), Marne Maitland .(Gohari), John Harvey (Maj. Maggoury), Oscar Quitak (Bedouin boy), Abraham Sofaer (Commandant), Ferdy Mayne (Doctor at Port Said), Peter Jones (Ship's Lieutenant), Eric Pohlmann (Ship's captain), Reginald Dyson (Prison governor), Arnold Diamond (Police major), Thomas Gallagher (Farghali). An Egyptian Narcotics Bureau unit tries to catch a hashish smuggler and murderer. *Dir.* David MacDonald.

Cal (1984) Helen Mirren (Marcella), John Lynch (Cal), Donal McCann (Shamie), Ray McAnally (Cyril Dunlop), John Kavanagh (Skeffington), Stevan Rimkus (Crilly), Catherine Gibson (Mrs Morton), Louis Rolston (Dermot Ryan), Tom Hickey (Preacher), Gerard Mannix Flynn (Arty), Seamus Forde (Mr Morton), Edward Byrne (Skeffington Sr), Audrey Johnson (Luc), Brian Munn (Robert Morton). Burdened with guilt over the murder of a member of the RUC whilst he worked as a driver for the IRA, Cal seeks out the dead constable's widow. Based on the novella *Cal* written by Bernard MacLaverty. *Dir.* Pat O'Connor.

Calcium Kid, The (2004) Orlando Bloom (Jimmy), Michael Peña (José Mendez), Billie Piper (Angel), Rafe Spall (Stan Parlour), Tamer Hassan (Pete Wright), Omid Djalili (Herbie Bush), David Kelly (Paddy O'Flanagan), Mark Heap (Sebastian Gore-Brown), Michael Lerner (Artie Cohen), John Joyce (Jon Wright), Cathy Dunning (Joyce Wright), Frank Harper (Clive Connelly), Ronni Ancona (Pat Connelly), Peter Serafinowicz (Radio DJ). A mockumentary following the career of Jimmy Connelly, a milkman and amateur boxer. *Dir.* Alex De Rakoff.

Calendar Girls (2003) Helen Mirren (Chris), Julie Walters (Annie), John Alderton (John), Linda Bassett (Cora), Annette Crosbie (Jessie), Philip Glenister (Lawrence), Ciarán Hinds (Rod), Celia Imrie (Celia), Geraldine James (Marie), Penelope Wilton (Ruth), George Costigan (Eddie), Graham Crowden (Richard), John Fortune (Frank), Georgie Glen (Kathy), Angela Curran (May), Rosalind March (Trudy), John-Paul Macleod (Jem), Marc Pickering (Gaz), John Sharian (Danny), Belinda Everett (Maya), Harriet Thorpe (Brenda Mooney), Gillian Wright (Eddie's Woman), Ian Embleton (Andy), Janet Howd (Julia), Lesley Staples (Jenny), Richard Braine (Policeman), Ted Robbins (Bike Man). Annie's husband dies and her friend Chris decides to raise some money to buy a sofa for the hospital by producing a calendar featuring some of the members of her local Women's Institute tastefully posing nude while engaged in everyday activities. What starts as a little local idea eventually becomes an international phenomenon. *Dir.* Nigel Cole.

Call Me Bwana (1963) Bob Hope (Matt), Anita Ekberg (Luba), Edie Adams (Frederica), Lionel Jeffries (Ezra), Paul Carpenter (Col. Spencer), Orlando Martins (Chief), Percy Herbert (First Henchman), Al Mulock (Second Henchman), Bari Jonson (Uta), Peter Dyneley (Williams), Mai Ling (Hyacinth), Mark Heath (Koba), Robert Nichols (American Major), Neville Monroe (Reporter), Mike Moyer (Reporter). Because of his unwarranted reputation as a big game hunter and expertise on Africa, Matt is hired by NASA to locate a missing secret space probe before it is found by anyone else. Dir. Gordon Douglas.

Camp on Blood Island, The (1958) Carl Möhner (Piet van Elst), André Morell (Col. Lambert), Edward Underdown (Major Dawes), Walter Fitzgerald (Cyril Beattie), Phil Brown (Lt. Peter Bellamy), Barbara Shelley (Kate Keiller), Michael Goodliffe (Father Paul Anjou), Michael Gwynn (Tom Shields), Ronald Radd (Commander Yamamitsu), Marne Maitland (Captain Sakamura), Richard Wordsworth (Dr. Robert Keiller), Mary Merrall (Helen Beattie), Wolfe Morris (Interpreter), Michael Ripper (Japanese Driver), Edwin Richfield (Sergeant-Major), Geoffrey Bayldon (Foster), Lee Montague (Japanese Officer), Jan Holden (Nurse). As the war comes to an end the prisoners in a Japanese POW camp decide they must take action as the commandant has vowed to kill them all should Japan surrender. *Dir.* Val Guest.

Can Hieronymus Merkin Ever Forget Mercy Humppe and Find True Happiness? (1969) Anthony Newley (Heironymus Merkin), Joan Collins (Polyester Poontang), Alexander Newley (Thaxted), Tara Newley (Thumbelina), Milton Berle (Goodtime Eddie Filth), Connie Kreski (Mercy Humppe), George Jessel (The Presence), Bruce Forsyth (Uncle Limelight), Patricia Hayes (Grandma), Stubby Kaye (Fat Writer), Ronald Rubin (Skinny Writer), Louis Negin (Producer Peter), Tom Stern (Producer Ron), Ronald Radd (Critic Bentley), Rosalind Knight (Critic Penelope), Victor Spinetti (Critic Sharpnose), Julian Orchard (Red Cardinal), Judy Cornwell (Filigree Fondle), Desmond Walter-Ellis (Philip Bluster), Bernard Stone (Icicle Ike), Margaret Nolan (Little Assistance), Yolanda (Trampolena Whambang), Sally Douglas (Automation Bunny), Roy Desmond (The Mask), Lynda Baron (Baby Boobala Salesgirl), Joyce Blair (Oat-O-Rinos Girl), Muriel Young (Liz Harper). A musical in which Merkin re-tells his life story, focusing on his relationships with a variety of women and being "advised" by Goodtime Eddie Filth and "The Presence". *Dir.* Anthony Newley.

Canaries Sometimes Sing (1930) Tom Walls (Geoffrey Lymes), Cathleen Nesbitt (Anne Lymes), Athole Stewart (Ernest Melton), Yvonne Arnaud (Elma Melton). Two disaffected spouses attempt to throw their respective partners into each other's arms. Adaptation of the play of the same name by Frederick Lonsdale. *Dir.* Tom Walls.

Candlelight in Algeria (1944) James Mason (Alan Thurston), Carla Lehmann (Susan Foster), Raymond Lovell (Von Alven), Enid Stamp-Taylor (Maritza), Walter Rilla (Dr. Muller), Pamela Stirling (Yvette), Leslie Bradley (Henri de Lange), Harold Berens (Toni), Cot D'Ordan (Hotel Manager), Richard George (Capt. Matthews), Meinhart Maur (Schultz), Bart Norman (Gen. Mark Clark). A German agent attempts to find out the details of a top-level Allied meeting in Algeria. *Dir.* George King.

Canterbury Tale, A (1944) John Sweet (Bob), Dennis Price (Peter), Sheila Sim (Alison), Eric Portman (Thomas Colpeper), Charles Hawtrey (Thomas Duckett), Esmond Knight (Narrator/Seven-Sisters Soldier/Village Idiot), Kim Hunter (Johnson's Girl in US release), Raymond Massey (Narrator US version). Alison Smith, a 'Land Girl', Bob Johnson, an American GI, and Peter Gibbs, a British soldier, find themselves in a small Kent town on the road to Canterbury and together go about investigating the mysterious "glue-man", who pours glue on the hair of girls dating soldiers after dark. *Dirs.* Michael Powell and Emeric Pressburger.

Captain Horatio Hornblower R.N. (1951) Gregory Peck (Capt. Horatio Hornblower R.N), Virginia Mayo (Lady Barbara Wellesley), Robert Beatty (Lt. William Bush), Moultrie Kelsall (Lt. Crystal), Terence Morgan (2nd Lt. Gerard), James Kenney (Midshipman Longley), James Robertson Justice (Seaman Quist), Denis O'Dea (Sir Rodney Leighton), Richard Hearne (Polwheal), Michael Dolan (Surgeon Gundarson), Stanley Baker (Mr. Harrison), Alan Tilvern (Hernandez), Alec Mango (El Supremo), Christopher Lee (Spanish Captain), John Witty (Capt. Entenza), Michael Goodliffe (Col. Caillard), Eugene Deckers (French Commandant), Ingeborg von Kusserow (Hebe), Amy Veness (Mrs. McPhee), Kynaston Reeves (Lord Hood), Ronald Adam (McCartney), Basil Bartlett (Capt. Elliott), Diane Cilento (Maria Hornblower - voice), Anthony Forwood (Lt. Woodford), Arthur Gomez (French Corvette Captain), Richard Johnson (Macrae), Sam Kydd (Seaman Garvin). Adventures on the high seas during the Napoleonic Wars. Captain Hornblower sails into the Pacific to supply "El Supremo" during his rebellion against the Spanish, unaware that Britain and Spain have signed an alliance during the months the HMS *Lydia* has been at sea. Matters are complicated when Hornblower is forced to take on the Duke of Wellington's sister (in reality the Duke had no sister) as a passenger as she is fleeing a yellow fever epidemic. An excellent swashbuckler with some tender moments and the American stars are well supported by a largely British cast. Based on three of C. S. Forester's novels: *The Happy Return*, *A Ship of the Line* and *Flying Colours*. *Dir.* Raoul Walsh.

Captain Kronos: Vampire Hunter (1974) Horst Janson (Captain Kronos), John Cater (Professor Hieronymus Grost), Caroline Munro (Carla), John Carson (Dr. Marcus), Shane Briant (Paul Durward), Lois Daine (Sara Durward), Wanda Ventham (Lady Durward), William Hobbs (Hagen), Ian Hendry (Kerro). Captain Kronos and his hunchbacked assistant Grost hunt vampires – "it does what it says on the tin". *Dir.* Brian Clemens.

Captain's Paradise, The (1953) Alec Guinness (Captain Henry St. James), Yvonne De Carlo (Nita St. James), Celia Johnson (Maud St. James), Charles Goldner (Chief Officer Ricco), Miles Malleson (Lawrence St. James), Walter Crisham (Bob), Nicholas

Phipps (The Major), Bill Fraser (Absalom), Ferdy Mayne (The Sheikh), Sebastian Cabot (Ali), Claudia Grey (Susan Dailey), Ann Hefferman (Daphne Bligh), Arthur Gomez (Chief steward), George Benson (Mr. Salmon), Joss Ambler (Prof. Ebbart), Victor Fairley (Customs official 1), Michael Balfour (Customs official 2), Robert Adair (Customs official 3), Tutte Lemkow (Principal dancer), Henry B. Longhurst (Prof. Killick), Ambrosine Phillpotts (Majorie), Roger Delgado (Kalikan policeman). Captain St James is commander of a ship which sails between Gibraltar and Morocco and he has a wife in both ports of call. As time passes he finds it more and more difficult to maintain the deception. *Dir.* Anthony Kimmins.

Captive Heart, The (1946) Michael Redgrave (Capt. Karel Hasek/Geoffrey Mitchell), Rachel Kempson (Celia Mitchell), Frederick Leister (Mr. Mowbray), Mervyn Johns (Pte. Evans), Rachel Thomas (Mrs. Evans), Jack Warner (Cpl. Horsfall), Gladys Henson (Mrs. Horsfall), James Harcourt (Doctor), Gordon Jackson (Lieut. Lennox), Elliott Mason (Mrs. Lennox), Margot Fitzsimons (Elspeth McDougall), David Keir (Mr. McDougall), Derek Bond (Lieut. Harley), Jane Barrett (Caroline Harley), Meriel Forbes (Beryl Curtiss), Robert Wyndham (Lt.Cdr.Robert Marsden R.N.V.R.), Basil Radford (Major Ossy Dalrymple), Guy Middleton (Capt. Jim Grayson), Jimmy Hanley (Pte. Mathews), Ralph Michael (Capt. Thurston R.A.M.C.), Jack Lambert (Padre), Karel Stepanek (Forster), Friedrich Richter (Camp Kommandant), Frederick Schiller (German M.O.), Jill Gibbs (Janet), David Walbridge (Desmond), Sam Kydd (POW in Top Bunk), Torin Thatcher (Repatriation Official). Hasek escapes from a concentration camp during WWII and assumes the identity of a British officer named Mitchell, only then to be captured and imprisoned in a POW camp. In order to maintain the fiction of his new identity he begins a correspondence with Mitchell's wife. *Dir.* Basil Dearden.

Caravaggio (1986) Nigel Terry (Caravaggio), Dexter Fletcher (Young Caravaggio), Noam Almaz (Boy Caravaggio), Dawn Archibald (Pipo), Sean Bean (Ranuccio), Tilda Swinton (Lena), Michael Gough (Cardinal Del Monte), Jack Birkett (The Pope), Robbie Coltrane (Scipione Borghese), Nigel Davenport (Giustiniani), Lol Coxhill (Old Priest), Sadie Corre (Princess Collona), Terry Downes (Bodyguard), Jonathan Hyde (Baglione), Cindy Oswin (Lady Elizabeth), Simon Fisher Turner (Fra Fillipo). A fictionalised re-telling of the life of painter Michelangelo Merisi da Caravaggio. *Dir.* Derek Jarman.

Caravan (1946) Stewart Granger (Richard Darrell), Jean Kent (Rosal), Anne Crawford (Oriana Camperdene), Dennis Price (Sir Francis Castleton), Robert Helpmann (Wycroft), Gerard Heinz (Don Carlos), Arthur Goullet (Suiza), John Salew (Diego), Julian Somers (Mandel), Pete Murray (Juan), Josef Ramart (José), Joseph O'Donohue (Bandit), Sylvia St. Clair (Marie), Patricia Laffan (Betty), Henry Morrell (Cumbermere), Merle Tottenham (Tweeny), Victoria Campbell (Fanny), Enid Stamp-Taylor (Bertha), David Horne (Charles Camperdene). A Gainsborough melodrama set in the 19th century. When Richard Darrell is assaulted by the henchman of Sir Francis Castleton he suffers memory loss and later marries a gypsy girl; meanwhile, his love, Oriana, thinking Richard is dead, has married the dastardly Sir Francis. *Dir.* Arthur Crabtree.

Card, The (1952) Alec Guinness (Denry Machin), Valerie Hobson (Countess of Chell), Petula Clark (Nellie Cotterill), Glynis Johns (Ruth Earp), Edward Rigby (Herbert Duncalf), Veronica Turleigh (Mrs Machin), Joan Hickson (Mrs Codleyn), George Devine (Herbert Calvert), Wilfrid Hyde-White (Lord at Liverpool Docks). The adventures of Denry Machin, a man from a poor background, as he tries to climb the social ladder by fair means or foul. *Dir.* Ronald Neame.

Cardboard Cavalier (1949) Sid Field (Sidcup Buttermeadow), Margaret Lockwood (Nell Gwynne), Jerry Desmonde (Col. Lovelace), Jack McNaughton (Uriah Group), Brian Worth (Tom Pride), Edmund Willard (Oliver Cromwell), Mary Clare (Milady Doverhouse), Alf Dean (Murdercasket), Anthony Hulme (Charles II), Miles Malleson (Judge Gorebucket), Irene Handl (Lady Agnes), Joan Young (Maggie), Claude Hulbert (Sylvester

Clutterbuck), Michael Brennan (Brother Barebones), Francis De Wolff (Soldier). The love story of Nell Gwynne and Lord Lovelace. *Dir.* Walter Forde.

Caretaker, The (1963) Alan Bates (Mick), Donald Pleasence (Mac Davies/Bernard Jenkins), Robert Shaw (Aston), Harold Pinter (Man). Aston takes in a tramp and makes him caretaker of his house but his brother Mick makes the tramp's life difficult. Based on Harold Pinter's play of the same name. *Dir.* Clive Donner.

Carla's Song (1996) Robert Carlyle (George), Oyanka Cabezas (Carla), Scott Glenn (Bradley), Salvador Espinoza (Rafael), Louise Goodall (Maureen), Richard Loza (Antonio), Gary Lewis (Sammy), Subash Singh Pall (Victor), Margaret McAdam (George's Mother). Bus driver George Lennox travels from Glasgow with Carla as she returns to her home land in war-torn Nicaragua to search for her family and boyfriend. *Dir.* Ken Loach.

Carlton-Browne of the F.O. (1959) Terry-Thomas (Cadogen De Vere Carlton-Browne), Peter Sellers (Prime Minister Amphibulos), Luciana Paluzzi (Princess Ilyena), Ian Bannen (young king), Thorley Walters (Colonel Bellingham), Raymond Huntley (Foreign Office Minister), Miles Malleson (Davidson), John Le Mesurier (Grand Duke), Marie Lohr (Lady Carlton-Browne), Kynaston Reeves (Sir Arthur Carlton-Browne), Ronald Adam (Sir John Farthing), John Van Eyssen (Hewitt), Nicholas Parsons (Rodgers), Irene Handl (Mrs. Carter), Harry Locke (Gaillardian commentator), Basil Dignam (Security Officer), Sam Kydd (Signaller). The death of the king of the small Pacific island of Gaillardia prompts the Foreign Office to send the incompetent Carlton-Browne to try and re-establish relations. *Dirs.* Roy Boulting and Jeffrey Dell

Carrington (1995) Emma Thompson (Dora Carrington), Jonathan Pryce (Lytton Strachey), Steven Waddington (Ralph Partridge), Samuel West (Gerald Brenan), Rufus Sewell (Mark Gertler), Penelope Wilton (Lady Ottoline Morrell), Janet McTeer (Vanessa Bell), Peter Blythe (Phillip Morrell), Jeremy Northam (Beacus Penrose), Alex Kingston (Frances Partridge). A biographical film about the life of the English painter Dora Carrington (1893–1932). Split into six chapters, the film focuses on her relationship with the author Lytton Strachey and the other members of the Bloomsbury Group. The film's musical score was composed by Michael Nyman. *Dir.* Christopher Hampton

Carrington V.C. (1955) David Niven (Major Charles 'Copper' Carrington VC), Margaret Leighton (Valerie Carrington), Noelle Middleton (Captain Alison L. Graham), Allan Cuthbertson (Colonel Henniker), Victor Maddern (Sergeant Owen), Raymond Francis (Major Jim Mitchell), Geoffrey Keen (Brigadier Ayers Meadmore), Newton Blick (A. Tesker Terry), Mark Dignam (Major Morse), Maurice Denham (Lieutenant Colonel B.R. Reeve), Laurence Naismith (Major R.E. Panton), Clive Morton (Lieutenant Colonel T.B. Huxford), Michael Bates (Major A.T.M. Broke-Smith), Stuart Saunders (Sergeant Crane), John Chandos (John Rawlinson), John Glyn-Jones (Reporter). Victoria Cross winner Carrington appears in his own defence when he is court-martialled for embezzlement. Adapted from the play of the same name by Campbell and Dorothy Christie. *Dir.* Anthony Asquith

Carry On Abroad (1972) Sid James (Vic Flange), Kenneth Williams (Stuart Farquhar), Charles Hawtrey (Eustace Tuttle), Joan Sims (Cora Flange), Peter Butterworth (Pepe), Kenneth Connor (Stanley Blunt), Hattie Jacques (Floella), Bernard Bresslaw (Brother Bernard), Barbara Windsor (Sadie Tomkins), Jimmy Logan (Bert Conway), June Whitfield (Evelyn Blunt), Sally Geeson (Lily), Carol Hawkins (Marge), Gail Grainger (Moira Plunkett), Ray Brooks (Georgio), John Clive (Robin Tweet), David Kernan (Nicholas Phipps), Patsy Rowlands (Miss Dobbs), Derek Francis (Brother Martin), Jack Douglas (Harry). The island of Els Bels proves not to be quite the paradise that the British holidaymakers expected. The last time all the regular cast members are in the same film together. *Dir.* Gerald Thomas.

Carry on Admiral (1957) David Tomlinson (Tom Baker), Peggy Cummins (Susan Lashwood), Brian Reece (Peter Fraser), Eunice Gayson (Jane Godfrey), A.E. Matthews (Adm. Sir Maximillian Godfrey), Joan Sims (Mary), Lionel Murton (Psychiatrist),

178

Reginald Beckwith (Receptionist), Desmond Walter-Ellis (Willy Oughton-Formby), Ronald Shiner (Salty Simpson), Peter Coke (Lt. Lashwood), Derek Blomfield (Lt. Dodson), Tom Gill (Petty Officer), Howard Williams (Sub Lieutenant), Joan Hickson (Mother), Toke Townley (Steward), Arthur Lovegrove (Orderly), Ronald Adam (First Sea Lord), Sam Kydd (Attendant), Philip Ashley (First Officer), Donald Pickering (Second Officer), Alfie Bass (Orderly), George Moon (Casey), Everley Gregg (Housekeeper), David Hannaford (Alfie), Jimmy Ray (Bert), James Hayter (M. P.). Old friends Tom and Peter get drunk and switch clothes and jobs, with hilarious results (apparently). NOT a film in the "Carry On" series, which it predates. Based on the stage play *Off the Record*. *Dir.* Val Guest.

Carry On Again Doctor (1969) Sid James (Gladstone Screwer), Jim Dale (Doctor James Nookey), Kenneth Williams (Doctor Frederick Carver), Charles Hawtrey (Doctor Ernest Stoppidge), Joan Sims (Ellen Moore), Barbara Windsor (Goldie Locks), Hattie Jacques (Matron), Patsy Rowlands (Miss Fosdick), Peter Butterworth (Patient), Wilfrid Brambell (Mr Pullen), Elizabeth Knight (Nurse Willing), Peter Gilmore (Henry), Pat Coombs (New Matron), William Mervyn (Lord Paragon), Patricia Hayes (Mrs Beasley), Valerie Leon (Nurse), Eric Rogers (Bandleader), Bob Todd (Patient), Yutte Stensgaard (Trolley Nurse), Scrubba (Shakira Baksh Caine). Dr Nookey is sent off in disgrace to a tropical island only to discover that one of the residents (Gladstone) has discovered a slimming potion. He returns to England determined to cash in on the discovery. *Dir.* Gerald Thomas.

Carry On at Your Convenience (1971) Sid James (Sid Plummer), Kenneth Williams (WC Boggs), Charles Hawtrey (Charles Coote), Hattie Jacques (Beattie Plummer), Joan Sims (Chloe Moore), Bernard Bresslaw (Bernie Hulke), Kenneth Cope (Vic Spanner), Jacki Piper (Myrtle Plummer), Richard O'Callaghan (Lewis Boggs), Patsy Rowlands (Hortence Withering), Davy Kaye (Benny), Bill Maynard (Fred Moore), Renee Houston (Agatha Spanner), Geoffrey Hughes (Willie), Leon Greene (Chef), Harry Towb (Film doctor), Shirley Stelfox (Bunny waitress), Julian Holloway (Roger), Anouska Hempel (New canteen girl), Bill Pertwee (Pub landlord). The toiletware manufacturer WC Boggs & Son is having difficulties both financially and because of wildcat strikes called by union rep Vic for any minor reason. Factory foreman Sid is trying to keep both management and workers happy. The film is an above average Carry On which includes a running gag about Sid's budgie (Joey) who can pick horserace winners, and the enjoyable finale of the works outing. *Dir.* Gerald Thomas.

Carry On Behind (1975) Kenneth Williams (Professor Roland Crump), Elke Sommer (Professor Anna Vrooshka), Bernard Bresslaw (Arthur Upmore), Kenneth Connor (Major Leep), Jack Douglas (Ernie Bragg), Joan Sims (Daphne Barnes), Windsor Davies (Fred Ramsden), Peter Butterworth (Henry Barnes), Liz Fraser (Sylvia Ramsden), Patsy Rowlands (Linda Upmore), Ian Lavender (Joe Baxter), Adrienne Posta (Norma Baxter), Patricia Franklin (Vera Bragg), Donald Hewlett (Dean), Carol Hawkins (Sandra), Sherrie Hewson (Carol), David Lodge (Landlord), George Layton (Doctor), Larry Martyn (Electrician), Sam Kelly (Projectionist), Johnny Briggs (Plasterer). A caravan site, an archaeological dig (with European beauty Sommer as an archaeologist), a pair of husbands with wandering eyes (Fred and Ernie) and several "dolly birds" in evidence. *Dir.* Gerald Thomas.

Carry On Cabby (1963) Sid James (Charlie Hawkins), Hattie Jacques (Peggy Hawkins), Charles Hawtrey (Terry "Pintpot" Tankard), Kenneth Connor (Ted Watson), Esma Cannon (Flo Sims), Liz Fraser (Sally), Bill Owen (Smiley), Milo O'Shea (Len), Jim Dale (Expectant father), Judith Furse (Battleaxe), Renee Houston (Molly), Ambrosine Phillpotts (Aristocratic lady), Amanda Barrie (Anthea), Carole Shelley (Dumb driver), Cyril Chamberlain (Sarge), Norman Chappell (Allbright), Peter Gilmore (Dancy), Noel Dyson (District nurse), Norman Mitchell (Bespectacled businessman). Charlie runs Speedy Cabs and so neglects his wife Peggy that she secretly sets up a rival firm, GlamCabs, with an all female staff. The first appearance of Jim Dale in a Carry On as an expectant father. *Dir.* Gerald Thomas.

Carry On Camping (1969) Sid James (Sid Boggle), Kenneth Williams (Doctor Kenneth Soaper), Joan Sims (Joan Fussey),

Dilys Laye (Anthea Meeks), Charles Hawtrey (Charlie Muggins), Terry Scott (Peter Potter), Barbara Windsor (Babs), Bernard Bresslaw (Bernie Lugg), Hattie Jacques (Miss Haggard), Peter Butterworth (Josh Fiddler), Julian Holloway (Jim Tanner), Betty Marsden (Harriet Potter), Trisha Noble (Sally), Amelia Bayntun (Mrs Fussey), Brian Oulton (Store manager), Patricia Franklin (Farmer's daughter), Derek Francis (Farmer), Anna Karen (Hefty girl), Valerie Leon (Store assistant), Michael Nightingale (Man in cinema), Sandra Caron (Fanny), George Moon (Scrawny man), Georgina Moon (Joy), Valerie Shute (Pat), Elizabeth Knight (Jane), Vivien Lloyd (Verna), Jennifer Pyle (Hilda), Lesley Duff (Norma), Jackie Pool (Betty), Gilly Grant (Sally G-string). Sid and Bernie take their girlfriends Joan and Anthea to the *Paradise* camp site believing it to be a nudist camp. Unfortunately for them, it is not. The camp site is also the holiday venue for the girls from the *Chayste Place* finishing school with their teachers Dr Soaper and Miss Haggard. One of the best Carry Ons and most often remembered for Barbara Windsor's bra flinging performance in the exercise scene. *Dir.* Gerald Thomas.

Carry On Cleo (1964) Sid James (Mark Anthony), Kenneth Williams (Julius Caesar), Amanda Barrie (Cleopatra), Kenneth Connor (Hengist Pod), Jim Dale (Horsa), Charles Hawtrey (Seneca), Joan Sims (Calpurnia), Victor Maddern (Sergeant Major), Julie Stevens (Gloria), Sheila Hancock (Senna Pod), Jon Pertwee (Soothsayer), Brian Oulton (Brutus), Michael Ward (Archimedes), Francis de Wolff (Agrippa), Tom Clegg (Sosages), Tanya Binning (Virginia), David Davenport (Bilius), Peter Gilmore (Galley master), Gertan Klauber (Marcus), Warren Mitchell (Spencius), Sally Douglas (Antony's dusky maiden), Wanda Ventham (Pretty bidder), Peggy Ann Clifford (Willa Claudia), E.V.H. Emmett (Narrator). Hengist and Horsa are Britons captured by Mark Anthony and taken back to Rome for sale, where by mischance Hengist becomes Caesar's bodyguard. Meanwhile, Mark Anthony falls for Cleopatra and determines to do away with his rival, Caesar. Spectacularly historically inaccurate apart from the sets used in the film, which were taken from the Burton and Taylor epic *Cleopatra* after that production moved on to Rome. Probably one of the best of the Carry On series. It is best remembered for its classic lines such as "Infamy, infamy - they've all got it in for me!" and the performance of Amanda Barrie, who some might say portrayed a much more seductive Cleo than Miss Taylor ever did. *Dir.* Gerald Thomas.

Carry On Columbus (1992) Jim Dale (Christopher Columbus), Bernard Cribbins (Mordecai Mendoza), Leslie Phillips (King Ferdinand), June Whitfield (Queen Isabella), Jon Pertwee (Duke of Costa Brava), Jack Douglas (Marco the Cereal Killer), Maureen Lipman (Countess Esmerelda), Alexei Sayle (Achmed), Rik Mayall (The Sultan), Sara Crowe (Fatima), Julian Clary (Don Juan Diego), Keith Allen (Pepi the Poisoner), Richard Wilson (Don Juan Felipe), Rebecca Lacey (Chiquita), Nigel Planer (The Wazir), Burt Kwouk (Wang), Tony Slattery (Baba the Messenger), Martin Clunes (Martin), Sara Stockbridge (Nina the model), Holly Aird (Maria), Don Maclean (Inquisitor), James Pertwee (Inquisitor), Lynda Baron (Meg), Don Henderson (The Bosun), Peter Gilmore (Governor of the Canaries), Chris Langham (Hubba), Peter Gordeno (The Shaman). The series was revived 14 years after the previous film (Emmannuelle) with an historical effort to coincide with the 500th anniversary of Columbus "discovering" the New World. Some of the old crew were still aboard but not enough to make it feel like a true Carry On. *Dir.* Gerald Thomas.

Carry On Constable (1960) Sid James (Sergeant Frank Wilkins), Eric Barker (Inspector Mills), Kenneth Connor (Constable Charlie Constable), Charles Hawtrey (Special Constable Timothy Gorse), Kenneth Williams (Constable Stanley Benson), Leslie Phillips (Constable Tom Potter), Joan Sims (WPC Gloria Passworthy), Hattie Jacques (Sergeant Laura Moon), Shirley Eaton (Sally Barry), Cyril Chamberlain (Constable Thurston), Joan Hickson (Mrs May), Irene Handl (Distraught Mother), Terence Longdon (Herbert Hall), Jill Adams (WPC Harrison), Freddie Mills (Jewel Thief), Brian Oulton (Store Manager), Victor Maddern (Detective Sergeant Liddell), Esma Cannon (Deaf old lady), Noel Dyson (Vague woman). Short of constables due to a flu epidemic, Inspector Mills is lumbered with four trainees who make a series of blunders before coming good. The first appearance of Sid James in a Carry On film. *Dir.* Gerald Thomas.

Carry On Cowboy (1965) Sid James (The Rumpo Kid), Kenneth Williams (Judge Burke), Jim Dale (Marshal P Knutt), Charles Hawtrey (Big Heap), Bernard Bresslaw (Little Heap), Angela Douglas (Annie Oakley), Joan Sims (Belle), Peter Butterworth (Doc), Jon Pertwee (Sheriff Albert Earp), Percy Herbert (Charlie), Sydney Bromley (Sam Houston), Edina Ronay (Delores), Lionel Murton (Clerk), Peter Gilmore (Curly), Davy Kaye (Josh), Sally Douglas (Kitkata), Margaret Nolan (Miss Jones), Tom Clegg (Blacksmith), Richard O'Brien (Rider), Eric Rogers (Pianist). An excursion into the Wild West with saloon girls and gunfights. "Sanitation engineer" Marshal P Knutt arrives in Stodge City and is mistaken for a US Marshal but is helped in tackling The Rumpo Kid by sharpshooting Annie Oakley. *Dir.* Gerald Thomas.

Carry On Cruising (1962) Sid James (Captain Wellington Crowther), Kenneth Williams (First Officer Leonard Marjoribanks), Kenneth Connor (Dr Arthur Binn), Liz Fraser (Glad Trimble), Dilys Laye (Flo Castle), Esma Cannon (Bridget Madderley), Lance Percival (Wilfred Haynes), Jimmy Thompson (Sam Turner), Ronnie Stevens (Drunk), Vincent Ball (Jenkins), Cyril Chamberlain (Tom Tree), Willoughby Goddard (fat man), Ed Devereaux (Young officer), Brian Rawlinson (Steward), Anton Rodgers (young man). The first Carry On filmed in colour. Wellington Crowther, captain of the cruise ship SS *Happy Wanderer*, finds himself lumbered with a set of green officers. Highlights include chef Lance Percival's multi-flavoured cake and the performance of Ronnie Stevens who gravitates to the cocktail bar whenever the ship hits port. *Dir.* Gerald Thomas.

Carry On Dick (1974) Sid James (The Reverend Flasher/Dick Turpin), Kenneth Williams (Captain Desmond Fancey), Barbara Windsor (Harriett), Hattie Jacques (Martha Hoggett), Bernard Bresslaw (Sir Roger Daley), Joan Sims (Madame Desiree), Peter Butterworth (Tom), Kenneth Connor (Constable), Jack Douglas (Sergeant Jock Strapp), Patsy Rowlands (Mrs Giles), Bill Maynard (Bodkin), Margaret Nolan (Lady Daley), John Clive (Isaak), David Lodge (Bullock), Marianne Stone (Maggie), Patrick Durkin (William), Sam Kelly (Sir Roger's coachman), George Moon (Mr Giles), Michael Nightingale (Squire Trelawney), Max Faulkner (Highwayman), Jeremy Connor (Footpad), Nosher Powell (Footpad), Penny Irving (Bird of Paradise), Eva Reuber-Staier (Bird of Paradise). The gang's take on the legend of Dick Turpin (or " Big Dick" as he is known to his friends) was the last for Sid James, Hattie Jacques and Barbara Windsor. *Dir.* Gerald Thomas.

Carry On Doctor (1967) Frankie Howerd (Francis Bigger), Kenneth Williams (Doctor Kenneth Tinkle), Sid James (Charlie Roper), Charles Hawtrey (Mr Barron), Jim Dale (Doctor Jim Kilmore), Hattie Jacques (Matron), Peter Butterworth (Mr Smith), Bernard Bresslaw (Ken Biddle), Barbara Windsor (Nurse Sandra May), Joan Sims (Chloe Gibson), Anita Harris (Nurse Clarke), June Jago (Sister Hoggett), Derek Francis (Sir Edmund Francis), Dandy Nichols (Mrs Roper), Peter Jones (Chaplain), Deryck Guyler (Surgeon Hardcastle), Gwendolyn Watts (Mrs Barron), Dilys Laye (Mavis Winkle), Peter Gilmore (Henry), Valerie Van Ost (Nurse Parkin), Julian Orchard (Fred), Brian Wilde (Cox & Carter man), Pat Coombs (Patient), Gertan Klauber (Wash orderly), Julian Holloway (Simmons), Patrick Allen (Narrator). Francis Bigger is and the rest of The plot revolves around the unrequited love between Nurse Clarke and the clumsy Dr Kilmore and Matron and Doctor Tinkle plus a faith healer (Francis Bigger) who can't heal himself. *Dir.* Gerald Thomas.

Carry On Don't Lose Your Head (1966) Sid James (Sir Rodney Ffing/The Black Fingernail), Kenneth Williams (Citizen Camembert), Jim Dale (Lord Darcy de Pue), Charles Hawtrey (Duke de Pommefrites), Joan Sims (Desiree Dubarry), Peter Butterworth (Citizen Bidet), Dany Robin (Jacqueline), Peter Gilmore (Citizen Robespierre), Marianne Stone (Landlady), Michael Ward (Henri), Leon Green (Malabonce), Hugh Futcher (Guard), Richard Shaw (Captain), David Davenport (Sergeant), Jennifer Clulow (1st lady), Valerie Van Ost (2nd lady), Jacqueline Pearce (3rd lady), Nikki van der Zyl (Messenger), Julian Orchard (Rake), Elspeth March (Lady Binder), Patrick Allen (Narrator). The Carry On version of the French Revolution and the Scarlet Pimpernel legend. The Black Fingernail saves French aristos and bamboozles Citizen Camembert, the head of the secret police. *Dir.* Gerald Thomas.

Carry On Emmannuelle (1978) Kenneth Williams (Emile Prevert), Suzanne Danielle (Emmannuelle Prevert), Kenneth Connor (Leyland), Jack Douglas (Lyons), Joan Sims (Mrs Dangle), Peter Butterworth (Richmond), Larry Dann (Theodore Valentine), Beryl Reid (Mrs Valentine), Tricia Newby (Nurse in surgery), Albert Moses (Doctor), Henry McGee (Harold Hump), Howard Nelson (Harry Hernia), Claire Davenport (Blonde in pub), Tim Brinton (BBC newscaster), Corbett Woodall (ITN newscaster), Robert Dorning (Prime Minister), Bruce Boa (US Ambassador), Eric Barker (Ancient General), Victor Maddern (Man in launderette), Norman Mitchell (Drunken husband), Dino Shafeek (Immigration officer), Gertan Klauber (German soldier). A spoof of the *Emmannuelle* soft porn films which brought the curtain down on the original Carry On series on a rather unsatisfactory note with double entendre in general replaced with just single entendre. *Dir.* Gerald Thomas.

Carry On England (1976) Kenneth Connor (Captain S Melly), Windsor Davies (Sergeant Major "Tiger" Bloomer), Patrick Mower (Sergeant Len Able), Judy Geeson (Sergeant Tilly Willing), Jack Douglas (Bombardier Ready), Peter Jones (Brigadier), Diane Langton (Private Alice Easy), Melvyn Hayes (Gunner Shorthouse), Peter Butterworth (Major Carstairs), Joan Sims (Private Jennifer Ffoukes-Sharpe), Julian Holloway (Major Butcher), David Lodge (Captain Bull), Larry Dann (Gunner Shaw), Brian Osborne (Gunner Owen), Johnny Briggs (Melly's driver), Patricia Franklin (Corporal Cook). Set on a mixed anti-aircraft battery during WWII, but missing most of the regulars and most of the regular laughs. *Dir.* Gerald Thomas.

Carry On Follow That Camel (1967) Phil Silvers (Sergeant Ernie Knocker), Jim Dale (Bertram Oliphant "Bo" West), Peter Butterworth (Simpson), Kenneth Williams (Commandant Burger), Charles Hawtrey (Captain Le Pice), Joan Sims (Zig-Zig), Angela Douglas (Lady Jane Ponsonby), Bernard Bresslaw (Sheikh Abdul Abulbul), Anita Harris (Corktip), John Bluthal (Corporal Clotski), Peter Gilmore (Captain Bagshaw), William Mervyn (Sir Cyril Ponsonby), Julian Holloway (Ticket collector), William Hurndell (Riff), Julian Orchard (Doctor), Gertan Klauber (Spiv), Michael Nightingale (Nightingale), Sally Douglas (Harem girl). A Foreign Legion saga borrowing a little from Beau Geste. Disgraced Bo joins the Foreign Legion. When the love of his life Lady Jane is set to become the 13th wife of the Riff chief Abdul Abulbul, Bo and his fellow legionnaires are called upon to defend the isolated Fort Zuassantneuf. Anita Harris plays a belly dancer named Corktip – apparently a nod to the Foreign Legion film from the 1930s *Under Two Flags*, in which Claudette Colbert's character was called Cigarette. *Dir.* Gerald Thomas.

Carry On Girls (1973) Sid James (Sidney Fiddler), Barbara Windsor (Hope Springs), Joan Sims (Connie Philpotts), Kenneth Connor (Mayor Frederick Bumble), Bernard Bresslaw (Peter Potter), Peter Butterworth (Admiral), June Whitfield (Augusta Prodworthy), Jack Douglas (William), Patsy Rowlands (Mildred Bumble), Joan Hickson (Mrs Dukes), David Lodge (Police Inspector), Valerie Leon (Paula Perkins), Margaret Nolan (Dawn Brakes), Angela Grant (Miss Bangor), Sally Geeson (Debra), Wendy Richard (Ida Downe), Jimmy Logan (Cecil Gaybody), Arnold Ridley (Alderman Pratt), Robin Askwith (Larry), Patricia Franklin (Rosemary), Bill Pertwee (Fire chief), Michael Nightingale (City gent). Councillor Fiddler decides to hold a beauty contest to attract more tourists to the town of Fircombe but this runs against the wishes of feminist Councillor Prodworthy. *Dir.* Gerald Thomas.

Carry On Henry (1971) Sid James (King Henry VIII), Kenneth Williams (Thomas Cromwell), Charles Hawtrey (Sir Roger de Lodgerley), Joan Sims (Queen Marie of Normandy), Terry Scott (Cardinal Wolsey), Barbara Windsor (Bettina), Kenneth Connor (Lord Hampton of Wick), Julian Holloway (Sir Thomas), Peter Gilmore (Francis, King of France), Peter Butterworth (Charles,

Earl of Essex), Julian Orchard (Duc de Poncenay), Gertan Klauber (Bidet), David Davenport (Major-domo), Margaret Nolan (Buxom lass), William Mervyn (Physician), Norman Chappell (1st plotter), Derek Francis (Farmer), Bill Maynard (Guy Fawkes), Leon Greene (Torturer), David Prowse (Torturer), Monica Dietrich (Katherine Howerd), Patsy Rowlands (Queen), John Bluthal (Royal tailor). The other two wives of Henry VIII (Marie of Normandy and Bettina) are revealed at last in a new manuscript written by William Cobbler. Perhaps not historically accurate but probably more so than either *Braveheart* or *The Patriot* and definitely more fun. Highlights are the constant putting of Sir Roger to the rack to extract and retract confessions and the increasingly large scrolls which Wolsey has to secrete in a certain part of his anatomy. *Dir*. Gerald Thomas.

Carry On Jack (1963) Kenneth Williams (Captain Fearless), Bernard Cribbins (Midshipman Albert Poop-Decker), Juliet Mills (Sally), Charles Hawtrey (Walter Sweetley), Percy Herbert (Mr Angel), Donald Houston (First Officer Jonathan Howett), Jim Dale (Carrier), Cecil Parker (First Sealord), Patrick Cargill (Spanish Governor), Peter Gilmore (Patch), Anton Rodgers (Hardy), Michael Nightingale (Town Crier), Frank Forsyth (Second Sealord), Marianne Stone (Girl at Dirty Dicks), Sally Douglas (Girl at Dirty Dicks). Midshipman Poop-Decker finds his position on board the HMS *Venus* taken by a disguised Sally who is searching for her boyfriend Roger (the Lodger). The latter part of the film seems to spoof the Gregory Peck film *Horatio Hornblower R.N..Dir*. Gerald Thomas.

Carry On Loving (1970) Sid James (Sidney Bliss), Hattie Jacques (Sophie Bliss), Kenneth Williams (Percival Snooper), Charles Hawtrey (James Bedsop), Joan Sims (Esme Crowfoot), Bernard Bresslaw (Gripper Burke), Terry Scott (Terry Philpott), Jacki Piper (Sally Martin), Richard O'Callaghan (Bertrum Muffet), Imogen Hassall (Jenny Grubb), Patsy Rowlands (Miss Dempsey), Peter Butterworth (Sinister client), Joan Hickson (Mrs Grubb), Julian Holloway (Adrian), Bill Maynard (Mr Dreery), Derek Francis (Bishop), Patricia Franklin (Mrs Dreery), Anna Karen (Wife), Lauri Lupino Lane (Husband), Kenny Lynch (Bus conductor). Sidney and Sophie run the Wedded Bliss computer dating agency and the film follows their matches and mismatches which are actually randomly chosen by Sophie without the use of technology. *Dir*. Gerald Thomas.

Carry On Matron (1972) Sid James (Sid Carter), Kenneth Williams (Sir Bernard Cutting), Charles Hawtrey (Doctor Francis A Goode), Hattie Jacques (Matron), Joan Sims (Mrs Tidey), Kenneth Connor (Mr Tidey), Bernard Bresslaw (Ernie Bragg), Barbara Windsor (Nurse Susan Ball), Terry Scott (Doctor Prod), Kenneth Cope (Cyril Carter), Jacki Piper (Sister), Bill Maynard (Freddy), Patsy Rowlands (Evelyn Banks), Derek Francis (Arthur), Amelia Bayntun (Mrs Jenkins), Valerie Leon (Jane Darling), Gwendolyn Watts (Frances Kemp), Margaret Nolan (Mrs Tucker), Michael Nightingale (Pearson), Wendy Richard (Miss Willing), Bill Kenwright (Reporter), Robin Hunter (Mr Darling), Jack Douglas (Twitching father), Madeline Smith (Mrs Pullitt). Despite the title this is actually a crime caper with Sid and his gang after the hospital stock of contraceptive pills. *Dir*. Gerald Thomas.

Carry On Nurse (1959) Kenneth Connor (Bernie Bishop), Kenneth Williams (Oliver Reckitt), Shirley Eaton (Dorothy Denton), Charles Hawtrey (Mr Hinton), Joan Sims (Stella Dawson), Hattie Jacques (Matron), Terence Longdon (Ted York), Bill Owen (Percy Hickson), Irene Handl (Mrs Madge Hickson), Leslie Phillips (Jack Bell), Joan Hickson (Sister), Jill Ireland (Jill Thompson), Wilfrid Hyde-White (The Colonel), Harry Locke (Mick the Orderly), Rosalind Knight (Student Nurse Nightingale), Cyril Chamberlain (Bert Able), June Whitfield (Meg), Michael Medwin (Ginger), Norman Rossington (Norm), Susan Shaw (Mrs Jane Bishop). The film focuses on the patients of one ward and their interaction with the staff, especially Ted and Dorothy's romance. Highlights include the Colonel's temperature being taken rectally using a daffodil and a patients' mutiny. Hattie Jacques makes her first appearance as a matron. Based on the play *Ring for Catty*. Gerald Thomas directed *Twice Round the Daffodils* in 1962 which was based on the same play and included some of the same cast (Kenneth Williams, Joan Sims and Jill Ireland). *Dir*. Gerald Thomas.

Carry On Regardless (1961) Sid James (Bert Handy), Kenneth Connor (Sam Twist), Charles Hawtrey (Gabriel Dimple), Kenneth Williams (Francis Courtenay), "Professor" Stanley Unwin (Landlord), Joan Sims (Lily Duveen), Liz Fraser (Delia King), Terence Longdon (Montgomery Infield-Hopping), Bill Owen (Mike Weston), Esma Cannon (Miss Cooling), Freddie Mills ('Lefty' Vincent), Fenella Fielding (Penny Panting), Hattie Jacques (Sister), Joan Hickson (Matron), David Lodge (Connoisseur), Jerry Desmonde (Martin Paul), Ambrosine Phillpotts (Yoki's Owner), Nicholas Parsons (Wolf). Bert Handy sets up the "Helping Hands" agency and recruits candidates from the local labour exchange. The film is essentially a set of vignettes showing the series of jobs they are assigned and includes a fine turn by Stanley Unwin as the gobbledygook speaking landlord. Hattie Jacques and Joan Hickson swap the matron/sister roles they had in *Carry on Nurse*. *Dir*. Gerald Thomas.

Carry On Screaming! (1966) Harry H. Corbett (Detective Sergeant Sidney Bung), Kenneth Williams (Doctor Orlando Watt), Fenella Fielding (Valeria Watt), Jim Dale (Albert Potter), Angela Douglas (Doris Mann), Charles Hawtrey (Dan Dann), Joan Sims (Emily Bung), Bernard Bresslaw (Sockett), Peter Butterworth (Detective Constable Slobotham), Jon Pertwee (Doctor Fettle), Michael Ward (Mr Vivian), Tom Clegg (Oddbod), Billy Cornelius (Oddbod Junior), Norman Mitchell (Cabby), Frank Thornton (Mr. Jones), Frank Forsyth (Desk Sergeant), Anthony Sagar (Policeman), Sally Douglas (Girl), Marianne Stone (Mrs. Parker). Dr Watt (his uncle is Dr Who) is turning pretty girls into wax mannequins with the help of his sister Valeria and his home grown (literally) henchman Oddbod. A worthy send up of the then popular British Hammer Horror films, with all the horror greats from Dracula to the Mummy making an appearance. Fenella Fielding has a field day vamping it up seducing detective Sid Bung ("Do you mind if I smoke?") and Kenneth Williams has a memorable exit ("Frying tonight!). Unusually for a Carry On it features a title song, which was performed by Ray Pilgrim. *Dir*. Gerald Thomas.

Carry On Sergeant (1958) William Hartnell (Sergeant Grimshawe), Bob Monkhouse (Charlie Sage), Shirley Eaton (Mary Sage), Eric Barker (Captain Potts), Dora Bryan (Nora), Bill Owen (Corporal Copping), Charles Hawtrey (Peter Golightly), Kenneth Connor (Horace Strong), Kenneth Williams (James Bailey), Terence Longdon (Miles Heywood), Norman Rossington (Herbert Brown), Gerald Campion (Andy Galloway), Hattie Jacques (Captain Clark), Cyril Chamberlain (Gun Sergeant), Terry Scott (Sergeant O'Brien). The first in the series and it introduces us to the now so familiar stereotypes – Hawtrey is fey, Connor is the opposite of his name and Williams is a questioning intellectual – all dedicated to making soon to retire Sergeant Grimshaw's life a misery, largely through no fault of their own. Likewise, Hattie Jacques' first casting in the series is as a Medical Officer. Very loosely based on *The Bull Boys* by R F Delderfield. *Dir*. Gerald Thomas.

Carry On Spying (1964) Kenneth Williams (Desmond Simkins), Barbara Windsor (Daphne Honeybutt), Charles Hawtrey (Charlie Bind), Bernard Cribbins (Harold Crump), Jim Dale (Carstairs), Eric Barker (The Chief), Richard Wattis (Cobley), Dilys Laye (Lila), Eric Pohlmann (The Fat Man), Victor Maddern (Milchmann), Judith Furse (Dr Crow), John Bluthal (The head waiter), Renee Houston (Madame), Tom Clegg (Doorman), Gertan Klauber (Code clerk), Norman Mitchell (Native policeman), Frank Forsyth (Professor Stark), Sally Douglas (Amazon guard). Barbara Windsor made her first Carry On appearance in this Bond spoof. *Dir*. Gerald Thomas.

Carry On Teacher (1959) Ted Ray (William Wakefield), Kenneth Connor (Gregory Adams), Charles Hawtrey (Michael Bean), Leslie Phillips (Alistair Grigg), Kenneth Williams (Edwin Milton), Hattie Jacques (Grace Short), Joan Sims (Sarah Allcock), Rosalind Knight (Felicity Wheeler), Cyril Chamberlain (Alf), Richard O'Sullivan (Robin Stevens), George Howell (Billy Haig), Roy Hines (Harry Bird), Diana Beevers (Penny Lee), Jacqueline Lewis (Pat Gordon), Carol White (Sheila Gale). Acting Headmaster William Wakefield's chances of a getting a job as head at a new school are sabotaged by his pupils who want him to stay. *Dir*. Gerald Thomas.

Carry On Up the Jungle (1970) Frankie Howerd (Professor Inigo Tinkle), Sid James (Bill Boosey), Charles Hawtrey (Walter Bagley/King Tonka), Joan Sims (Lady Evelyn Bagley), Kenneth Connor (Claude Chumley), Bernard Bresslaw (Upsidasi), Terry Scott (Ug the Jungle Boy/Cecil Bagley), Jacki Piper (June), Valerie Leon (Leda), Edwina Carroll (Nerda), Danny Daniels (Nosha Chief), Nina Baden-Semper (Girl Nosha). Lady Evelyn is in search of her long-lost husband and son. She finances an expedition into the jungle led by Bill and Upsidasi, joined by Professor Tinkle and his assistant Chumley who are on the path of the oozlum bird. *Dir.* Gerald Thomas.

Carry On... Up the Khyber (1968) Sid James (Sir Sidney Ruff-Diamond), Joan Sims (Lady Joan Ruff-Diamond), Charles Hawtrey (Private James Widdle), Roy Castle (Captain Keene), Kenneth Williams (Randi Lal, the Khasi of Kalabar), Angela Douglas (Princess Jelhi), Bernard Bresslaw (Bunghit Din), Peter Butterworth (Brother Belcher), Terry Scott (Sergeant Major MacNutt), Cardew Robinson (The Fakir), Peter Gilmore (Private Ginger Hale), Julian Holloway (Major Shorthouse), Leon Thau (Stinghi), Michael Mellinger (Chindi), Alexandra Dane (Busti), Wanda Ventham (Khasi's First Wife), Patrick Allen (Narrator - voice), Johnny Briggs (Sporran Soldier), Valerie Leon (Hospitality Girl). The local tribe (the Burpa) is reluctant to rebel against the British because the Khyber Pass is guarded by the kilted Third Foot and Mouth or "the devils in skirts" as they are known. That is until they discover that, contrary to orders, Private Widdle wears underpants. Sir Sidney's wife defects to the Khasi with an even more incriminating photograph and trouble brews. One of the best of the series; highlights include the procession of wives of the Khasi who have "tiffin" with Sir Sidney in order to "right the wrong" caused by his wives running off (apart from number 5), the unfortunate fakir who loses his head, the escape of the rescue party dressed as dancing girls and the attack on the British residence during a formal banquet. *Dir.* Gerald Thomas.

Carve Her Name With Pride (1958) Virginia McKenna (Violette Szabo), Paul Scofield (Tony Fraser), Jack Warner (Mr. Charles Bushell), Denise Grey (Mrs. Bushell), Alain Saury (Etienne Szabo), Maurice Ronet (Jacques), Anne Leon (Lilian Rolfe), Sydney Tafler (Potter), Avice Landone (Vera Atkins), Nicole Stéphane (Denise Bloch), Noel Willman (Interrogator), Bill Owen (NCO Instructor), Billie Whitelaw (Winnie), William Mervyn (Colonel Maurice Buckmaster), Michael Goodliffe (Coding expert), André Maranne (Garage Man), Harold Lang (Commandant Suhren). Violette Bushell meets and marries a French officer in London but is soon widowed. She joins the Special Operations Executive and is sent on a mission to occupied France. The film is based on the true story of the heroism of SOE agent Violette Szabo and is adapted from the book of the same name by R.J. Minney. *Dir.* Lewis Gilbert.

Case of the Frightened Lady, The (1940) Marius Goring (Lord Lebanon), Penelope Dudley-Ward (Isla Crane), Ronald Shiner (Sergeant Totty), Helen Haye (Lady Lebanon), Felix Aylmer (Dr. Amersham), George Merritt (Det. Inspector Tanner), Patrick Barr (Richard Ferraby), Roy Emerton (Gilder), George Hayes (Brooks), John Warwick (Studd), Elizabeth Scott (Mrs. Tilling), Torin Thatcher (Jim Tilling). A thriller centring on Mark's Priory, the family seat of the Lebanons, who are served by a couple of sinister butlers and a menacing doctor. *Dir.* George King.

Case of the Mukkinese Battle Horn, The (1956) Peter Sellers (Narrator/Supt. Quilt/Asst. Commissioner Sir Jervis Fruit/Henry Crun), Spike Milligan (Sgt. Brown/Eccles), Dick Emery (Mr. Nodule). Short film. Quilt of the Yard attempts to retrieve a 'Mukkinese Battlehorn' stolen from a London museum. *Dir.* Joseph Sterling.

Casino Royale (1967) David Niven (Sir James Bond 007), Peter Sellers (Evelyn Tremble), Ursula Andress (Vesper Lynd), Orson Welles (Le Chiffre), Woody Allen (Dr.Noah/Jimmy Bond), Barbara Bouchet (Miss Moneypenny), Deborah Kerr (Agent Mimi/Lady Fiona McTarry), Jacqueline Bisset (Miss Goodthighs), Joanna Pettet (Mata Bond), Daliah Lavi (The Detainer), Terence Cooper (Coop), Bernard Cribbins (Carlton Towers), Ronnie Corbett (Polo), John Huston (M/McTarry),

William Holden (Ransome), Charles Boyer (Le Grand), Jean-Paul Belmondo (French Legionnaire), Alexandra Bastedo (Meg), John Bluthal (M.I.5 Man), Geoffrey Bayldon (Q), John Wells (Fordyce), Graham Stark (Casino Cashier), Chic Murray (Chic), Jonathan Routh (John), Richard Wattis (British Army Officer), Peter O'Toole (a piper), Stirling Moss (driver). A star-studded but rather chaotic comedy spy film which largely spoofs the James Bond films of that time but is still loosely based on the Ian Fleming novel of the same name. Sir James Bond is forced out of retirement in order to deal with SMERSH and Dr Noah. *Dirs.* Ken Hughes, John Huston, Joseph McGrath, Robert Parrish, Val Guest, Richard Talmadge.

Casino Royale (2006) Daniel Craig (James Bond), Eva Green (Vesper Lynd), Mads Mikkelsen (Le Chiffre), Judi Dench (M), Jeffrey Wright (Felix Leiter), Giancarlo Giannini (René Mathis), Simon Abkarian (Alex Dimitrios), Caterina Murino (Solange Dimitrios), Ivana Milicević (Valenka), Isaac de Bankolé (Steven Obanno), Jesper Christensen (Mr. White). Craig's first outing as 007 in what is seen by many as a rebooting of the franchise to match actioners such as the Bourne films. Based on the Ian Fleming novel of the same name which sees Bond take on Le Chiffre, a villain who bank rolls terrorist organisations. Some of the plot continues into *Quantum of Solace*. In this film Bond drives an Aston Martin DBS and an Aston Martin DB5. The theme song is *You Know My Name* performed by Chris Cornell. *Dir.* Martin Campbell.

Cassandra Crossing, The (1976) Sophia Loren (Jennifer Rispoli Chamberlain), Richard Harris (Dr. Jonathan Chamberlain), Burt Lancaster (Col. Stephen MacKenzie), Martin Sheen (Robby Navarro), Lee Strasberg (Herman Kaplan), Ava Gardner (Nicole Dressler), O. J. Simpson (Haley), Lionel Stander (Max), Ingrid Thulin (Dr. Elena Stradner), Alida Valli (Mrs. Chadwick), John Phillip Law (Major Stark), Ann Turkel (Susan), Ray Lovelock (Tom), Thomas Hunter (Captain Scott), Fausta Avelli (Katherine), Angela Goodwin (Nun), Lou Castel (Terrorist), Stefano Patrizi (Terrorist). A terrorist infected with a deadly plague escapes from custody and boards a train which is then diverted by the authorities towards an unstable bridge known as the Cassandra Crossing. *Dir.* George Pan Cosmatos.

Cast a Dark Shadow (1955) Dirk Bogarde (Edward Bare), Margaret Lockwood (Freda Jeffries), Kay Walsh (Charlotte Young), Kathleen Harrison (Emmie), Robert Flemyng (Phillip Mortimer), Mona Washbourne (Monica Bare), Philip Stainton (Charlie Mann), Walter Hudd (The Coroner), Lita Roza (Singer), Myrtle Reed (Waitress). After getting away with murdering one wife, Edward Bare moves on to the next but finds she may be alive to his intentions. Based on the play *Murder Mistaken* by Janet Green. *Dir.* Lewis Gilbert.

Cat and the Canary, The (1979) Honor Blackman (Susan Sillsby), Michael Callan (Paul Jones), Edward Fox (Hendricks), Wendy Hiller (Allison Crosby), Olivia Hussey (Cicily Young), Beatrix Lehmann (Mrs. Pleasant), Carol Lynley (Annabelle West), Daniel Massey (Harry Blythe), Peter McEnery (Charlie Wilder), Wilfrid Hyde-White (Cyrus West). The potential heirs to a fortune must stay in an isolated mansion overnight. One of many film adaptations of John Willard's 1922 black comedy play of the same name. *Dir.* Radley Metzger.

Catch Us If You Can (1965) Dave Clark (Steve), Barbara Ferris (Dinah), Lenny Davidson (Lenny), Rick Huxley (Rick), Mike Smith (Mike), Denis West Payton (Denis), Clive Swift (Duffie), Hugh Walters (Grey), Robin Bailey (Guy), Yootha Joyce (Nan), David de Keyser (Zissell), Robert Lang (Whiting), Michael Blakemore (Officer), Marianne Stone (Mrs. Vera Stone), Julian Holloway (Asst. Director). A film vehicle for pop band The Dave Clark Five and named after their hit song, it is basically a road movie. Steve and Dinah abscond during the filming of a meat commercial and are pursued across southern England. Unlike *A Hard Day's Night* in that the band are playing parts rather than themselves. Clark had been a stuntman in many films before hitting the big time in music so his knowledge of the industry probably helped in the making of the film. *Dir.* John Boorman - his first film as a director.

Catherine the Great (1934) Douglas Fairbanks Jr. (Grand Duke Peter), Elisabeth Bergner (Catherine), Flora Robson (Empress Elisabeth), Gerald du Maurier (Lecocq), Irene Vanbrugh (Princess Anhalt-Zerbst), Joan Gardner (Katushienka), Dorothy Hale (Countess Olga), Diana Napier (Countess Vorontzova). A biopic charting the rise to power of Catherine, a young German-born princess after her marriage to the mentally unstable Peter, the heir to the Russian throne. *Dir*. Paul Czinner.

Cemetery Junction (2010) Christian Cooke (Freddie Taylor), Ricky Gervais (Len Taylor), Julia Davis (Mrs. Taylor), Felicity Jones (Julie), Tom Hughes (Bruce Pearson), Jack Doolan (Paul/Snork), Albert Welling (Mr. Waring), Katy Murphy (Mrs. Waring), Ralph Fiennes (Mr. Kendrick), Emily Watson (Mrs. Kendrick), Burn Gorman (Renwick), Matthew Goode (Mike Ramsay), Matthew Holness (Bandleader), Kirk Yeomans (Voice of Bandleader), Steve Speirs (Sgt. Wyn Davies), Anne Reid (Freddie's Gran), Stephen Merchant (Dougie). Set in the early 1970s, three young friends from Reading (Cemetery Junction) face decisions about the future. *Dirs*. Ricky Gervais and Stephen Merchant.

Challenge, The (1960) Jayne Mansfield (Billy), Anthony Quayle (Jim), Carl Möhner (Kristy), Peter Reynolds (Buddy), Barbara Mullen (Ma Piper), Robert Brown (Bob Crowther), Dermot Walsh (Detective Sergeant Willis), Patrick Holt (Max), Edward Judd (Detective Sergeant Gittens), John Bennett (Spider), Lorraine Clewes (Mrs. Rick), Percy Herbert (Shop Steward), John Stratton (Rick), Peter Pike (Joey). When Jim gets out of prison both his old gang members and the police are interested in where he stashed the loot from his last job. Released in the US as *It Takes a Thief*. *Dir*. John Gilling.

Champagne Charlie (1944) Tommy Trinder (George Leybourne), Stanley Holloway (The Great Vance), Betty Warren (Bessie Bellwood), Jean Kent (Dolly Bellwood), Austin Trevor (Duke), Peter De Greef (Lord Petersfield), Leslie Clarke (Fred Saunders), Eddie Phillips (Tom Sayers), Robert Wyndham (Duckworth), Harry Fowler (Horace), Aubrey Mallalieu (Butler). The story of the rivalry between two real stars of the British music halls - George Leybourne, who first performed the song of that name, and Alfred Vance. *Dir*. Alberto Cavalcanti.

Champions (1983) John Hurt (Bob Champion), Edward Woodward (Josh Gifford), Jan Francis (Jo Beswick), Ben Johnson (Burly Cocks), Ann Bell (Valda Embiricos), Peter Barkworth (Nick Embiricos), Alison Steadman (Mary Hussey), Kirstie Alley (Barbara), Judy Parfitt (Dr. Merrow), Carolyn Pickles (Sally), Andrew Fell (Doctor), Noel Dyson (Mrs. Champion), John Woodnutt (Mr. Champion), John Buckingham (Valet), Richard Adams (Nicky Hussey), Julie Adams (Emma Hussey), Michael Byrne (Richard Hussey), Jonathan Newth (Mr. Griffith Jones), Aldaniti (Himself). The true story of jockey Bob Champion who recovered from testicular cancer to win the 1981 Grand National aboard Aldaniti. *Dir*. John Irvin

Chance of a Lifetime (1950) Basil Radford (Dickinson), Niall MacGinnis (Baxter), Bernard Miles (Stevens), Julien Mitchell (Morris), Kenneth More (Adam), Geoffrey Keen (Bolger), Josephine Wilson (Miss Cooper), John Harvey (Bland), Russell Waters (Palmer), Patrick Troughton (Kettle), Hattie Jacques (Alice), Peter Jones (Doctor), Bernard Rebel and Eric Pohlmann (Xenobian trade delegation), Amy Veness (Lady Davis), Stanley Van Beers (Calvert), Norman Pierce (Franklin), Gordon McLeod (Garrett), Compton Mackenzie (Sir Robert Dysart), Nigel Fitzgerald (Pennington), Alastair Hunter (Groves), Molly Palmer (Millie), George Street and Stanley Rose (Trade Union Men), Erik Chitty (Silas Pike). In post WWII Britain a factory is handed over to the workers to run. *Dir*. Bernard Miles.

Chaplin (1992) Robert Downey, Jr. (Charlie Chaplin), Geraldine Chaplin (Hannah Chaplin), Paul Rhys (Sydney Chaplin), John Thaw (Fred Karno), Moira Kelly (Hetty Kelly/Oona O'Neill), Anthony Hopkins (George Hayden), Dan Aykroyd (Mack Sennett), Marisa Tomei (Mabel Normand), Penelope Ann Miller (Edna Purviance), Kevin Kline (Douglas Fairbanks), Matthew Cottle (Stan Laurel), Maria Pitillo (Mary Pickford), Milla Jovovich (Mildred Harris), Kevin Dunn (J. Edgar Hoover), Deborah Moore (Lita Grey), Diane Lane (Paulette Goddard), Nancy Travis (Joan Barry), James Woods (Joseph Scott), David Duchovny (Roland Totheroh), Hugh Downer (Charlie Age 5), Nicholas Gatt (Sydney Age 9), Bill Paterson (Stage Manager), Thomas Bradford (Charlie Age 14), Gerald Sim (Doctor), Jack Ritschel (William Randolph Hearst), Heather McNair (Marion Davies). A biopic of Charlie Chaplin told in flashbacks as he recollects moments and relationships from his life whilst talking to his (fictional) biographer. *Dir*. Richard Attenborough.

Charge Of The Light Brigade, The (1968) Trevor Howard (Lord Cardigan), Vanessa Redgrave (Mrs. Clarissa Morris), John Gielgud (Lord Raglan), Harry Andrews (Lord Lucan), Jill Bennett (Mrs. Fanny Duberly), David Hemmings (Capt. Louis Edward Nolan), Ben Aris (Capt. Fitz Maxse), Mickey Baker (Trooper Metcalfe), Peter Bowles (Paymaster Capt. Henry Duberly), Leo Britt (Gen. Scarlett), Mark Burns (Capt. William Morris), Helen Cherry (Lady Scarlett), Alan Dobie (Riding Master Mogg), Clive Endersby (Trooper), Andrew Faulds (Quaker preacher), Willoughby Goddard (Squire), Rachel Kempson (Mrs. Codrington), T.P. McKenna (William Russel), Corin Redgrave (Capt. Featherstonhaugh), Norman Rossington (S.M. Corbett), Dino Shafeek (Indian servant), Donald Wolfit (Macbeth in 'Macbeth'), Laurence Harvey (Russian Prince), Joely Richardson (extra), Natasha Richardson (Flower girl at wedding). A critique of the events leading up to the infamous Charge of the Light Brigade during the Crimean War highlighting the general incompetence of the British high command. The film innovatively used graphics to explain the background to the film. *Dir*. Tony Richardson.

Chariots of Fire (1981) Ben Cross (Harold Abrahams), Ian Charleson (Eric Liddell), Nicholas Farrell (Aubrey Montague), Nigel Havers (Lord Andrew Lindsay), Ian Holm (Sam Mussabini), John Gielgud (Master of Trinity College), Lindsay Anderson (Master of Caius College), Cheryl Campbell (Jennie Liddell), Alice Krige (Sybil Gordon), Struan Rodger (Sandy McGrath), Nigel Davenport (Lord Birkenhead), Patrick Magee (Lord Cadogan), David Yelland (Prince of Wales), Peter Egan (Duke of Sutherland), Daniel Gerroll (Henry Stallard), Dennis Christopher (Charlie Paddock), Brad Davis (Jackson Scholz). A film based around the events of the 1924 Olympic Games in Paris where two very contrasting young British sprinters (Abrahams and Liddell) are competing. The film was nominated for seven Academy Awards and won four, Best Picture, Best Music, Best Costume Design and Original Screenplay. The film's title is taken from the line, "bring me my chariot of fire" from the hymn *Jerusalem* which was adapted from a William Blake poem. *Dir*. Hugh Hudson.

Charley's (Big-Hearted) Aunt (1940) Arthur Askey (Arthur Linden-Jones), Richard Murdoch ('Stinker' Burton), Graham Moffatt (Albert Brown), Moore Marriott (Jerry), J.H. Roberts (Dean of Bowgate), Felix Aylmer (The Proctor), Wally Patch (The Buller), Phyllis Calvert (Betty Forsythe), Jeanne De Casalis (Aunt Lucy), Elliott Mason (Dame Luckton), Donald Calthrop (Guide). Based on the farce *Charley's Aunt*. *Dir*. Walter Forde.

Charlie and the Chocolate Factory (2005) Johnny Depp (Willy Wonka), Freddie Highmore (Charlie Bucket), David Kelly (Grandpa Joe), Jordan Fry (Mike Teavee), Julia Winter (Veruca Salt), AnnaSophia Robb (Violet Beauregarde), Philip Wiegratz (Augustus Gloop), Helena Bonham Carter (Mrs. Bucket), Noah Taylor (Mr. Bucket), Missi Pyle (Mrs. Beauregarde), James Fox (Mr. Salt), Deep Roy (Oompa-Loompas - vocals by Danny Elfman), Christopher Lee (Dr. Wilbur Wonka), Adam Godley (Mr. Teavee), Franziska Troegner (Mrs. Gloop), Blair Dunlop (Young Willy Wonka), Liz Smith (Grandma Georgina), Eileen Essell (Grandma Josephine), David Morris (Grandpa George). Owner of a world famous chocolate factory, Willy Wonka announces a contest in which five Golden Tickets have been placed in five random Wonka Bars worldwide and anyone finding one of them will be given a full tour of the factory plus a lifetime supply of chocolate. An adaptation of the book of the same name by Roald Dahl. *Dir*. Tim Burton.

Charlie Bubbles (1967) Albert Finney (Charlie Bubbles), Colin Blakely (Smokey Pickles), Billie Whitelaw (Lottie Bubbles), Liza Minnelli (Eliza), Timothy Garland (Jack Bubbles), Richard Pearson (Accountant), Nicholas Phipps (Agent), Peter Sallis (Solicitor), Charles Hill (Head Waiter), Charles Lamb (Mr. Noseworthy), Margery Mason (Mrs. Noseworthy), Diana Coupland (Maud), George Innes (Garage Attendant), Arthur

Pentelow (Man With Car), Alan Lake (Airman), Yootha Joyce (Woman in Café), Wendy Padbury (Woman in Café), Susan Engel (Nanny), Rex Boyd (Receptionist), Joe Gladwin (Waiter), Jean Marsh (Waitress). A successful writer returns home in an attempt to reconnect with the environment which helped him create his original work. Notable for the presence in the cast of a young Liza Minelli playing Charlie's secretary Eliza. *Dir.* Albert Finney.

Charlotte Gray (2001) Cate Blanchett (Charlotte Gray), James Fleet (Richard Cannerly), Abigail Cruttenden (Daisy), Charlotte McDougall (Sally), Rupert Penry-Jones (Peter Gregory), Billy Crudup (Julien Levade), Michael Gambon (Levade), Anton Lesser as Renech Robert Hands (Borowski), Hugh Ross (Psychiatrist). During WWII, a young woman joins the Special Operations Executive and is sent into occupied France. Based on the novel of the same name by Sebastian Faulks. *Dirs.* Gillian Armstrong and Danny Boyle.

Chase a Crooked Shadow (1958) Richard Todd (Ward Prescott), Anne Baxter (Kimberley), Herbert Lom (Police Commissar Vargas), Alexander Knox (Chandler Brisson), Faith Brook (Elaine Whitman), Alan Tilvern (Carlos), Thelma D'Aguilar (Maria). Two years after her brother died in a car accident, a man claiming to be him turns up and is accepted as such by everyone except Kimberley Prescott. *Dir.* Michael Anderson.

Chicago Joe and the Showgirl (1990) Emily Lloyd (Betty Jones), Kiefer Sutherland (Karl Hulten), Liz Fraser (Mrs. Evans), Harry Fowler (Morry), Keith Allen (Lenny Bexley), John Lahr (Radio commentator), Patsy Kensit (Joyce Cook), John Surman (Mr. Cook), Janet Dale (Mrs. Cook), John Dair (John), Stephen Hancock (Doctor), Hugh Millais (U.S. colonel), Harry Jones (Taxi driver), Alexandra Pigg (Violet), John Junkin (George Heath), Gerard Horan (John Wilkins), Colin Bruce (Robert De Mott), Ralph Nossek (Insp. Tansill), Roger Ashton-Griffiths (Insp. Tarr), Angela Morant (Customer). The film was inspired by a real-life murder case of 1944, known as the Cleft Chin Murder in which waitress Elizabeth Jones met an American army deserter called Karl Hulten and in the course of six days killed a nurse and a taxi driver. *Dir.* Bernard Rose.

Chicken Run (2000) Voices of: Julia Sawalha (Ginger), Mel Gibson (Rocky), Miranda Richardson (Mrs. Melisha Tweedy), Benjamin Whitrow (Fowler), Timothy Spall (Nick), Phil Daniels (Fetcher), Jane Horrocks (Babs), Imelda Staunton (Bunty), Lynn Ferguson (Mac), Tony Haygarth (Mr. Willard Tweedy). After their farm is converted into a pie factory a flock of chickens plot their escape with the help of Rocky, a "flying" rooster. Stop animation. *Dir.* Nick Park

Children of Men (2006) Clive Owen (Theo Faron), Julianne Moore (Julian Taylor), Michael Caine (Jasper Palmer), Claire-Hope Ashitey (Kee), Chiwetel Ejiofor (Luke), Pam Ferris (Miriam), Peter Mullan (Syd), Charlie Hunnam (Patric), Danny Huston (Nigel), Oana Pellea (Marichka), Paul Sharma (Ian), Jacek Koman (Tomasz), Miriam Karlin (Elderly German). Set in a 2027 where the human race has become infertile, Theo agrees to escort a pregnant woman to a group of scientists who are trying to find a cure. Based on P. D. James' novel *The Children of Men*. *Dir.* Alfonso Cuarón.

Children of the Damned (1963) Ian Hendry (Col. Tom Lewellin), Alan Badel (Dr. David Neville), Barbara Ferris (Susan Eliot), Alfred Burke (Colin Webster), Sheila Allen (Diana Looran), Ralph Michael (Defense Minister), Patrick Wymark (Commander), Martin Miller (Prof. Gruber), Harold Goldblatt (Harib), Patrick White (Mr. Davidson), André Mikhelson (Russian official), Bessie Love (Mrs. Robbins), Clive Powell (Paul), Yoke-Moon Lee (Mi Ling), Roberta Rex (Nina). Six children with incredible psychic abilities are brought from various countries to London to be studied. However, they escape from their embassies and meet in a derelict church in South London. A sequel to *Village of the Damned* (1960). *Dir.* Anton Leader.

Chitty Chitty Bang Bang (1968) Dick Van Dyke (Caractacus Potts), Sally Ann Howes (Truly Scrumptious), Adrian Hall (Jeremy), Heather Ripley (Jemima), Lionel Jeffries (Grandpa Potts), Gert Fröbe (Baron Bomburst), Anna Quayle (Baroness Bomburst), Benny Hill (Toymaker), James Robertson Justice (Lord Scrumptious), Robert Helpmann (Child Catcher), Desmond Llewelyn (Mr. Coggins), Alexander Doré (Herman, First Spy), Bernard Spear (Sherman, Second Spy), Peter Arne (Captain of Bomburst's Army), Victor Maddern (Customer Junkman), Arthur Mullard (Cyril), Barbara Windsor (Blonde at Fair), Heather Ripley (Jemima Potts), Adrian Hall (Jeremy Potts), Davy Kaye (Admiral), Stanley Unwin (Chancellor), Ross Parker (Chef), Gerald Campion (1st Minister), Felix Felton (2nd Minister), Monti DeLyle (3rd Minister), Totti Truman Taylor (Duchess), Larry Taylor (Lieutenant), Max Wall (Inventor), Michael Audreson (Peter), Phil Collins (Vulgarian child), Richard Wattis (Secretary at Sweet Factory). Widowed inventor Caractacus Potts restores an old racing car and turns it into a flying machine. When he invents a new sweet he meets the daughter of the sweet factory owner, Truly Scrumptious. On a picnic, he tells Truly and his children a story about the country of Vulgaria, where children are imprisoned. Musical based on the novel *Chitty Chitty Bang Bang: The Magical Car* by Ian Fleming. *Dir.* Ken Hughes.

Christopher Columbus (1949) Fredric March (Christopher Columbus), Florence Eldridge (Queen Isabella), Francis L. Sullivan (Francisco de Bobadilla), Kathleen Ryan (Beatriz Enriquez de Arana), Derek Bond (Diego de Arana), Nora Swinburne (Joanna de Torres), Abraham Sofaer (Luis de Santangel), Linden Travers (Beatriz de Peraza), James Robertson Justice (Martin Alonso Pinzon), Dennis Vance (Francisco Pinzon), Richard Aherne (Vicente Yañez Pinzon), Felix Aylmer (Father Perez), Francis Lister (King Ferdinand), Edward Rigby (Pedro), Niall MacGinnis (Juan de la Cosa), Ralph Truman (Captain), Ronald Adam (Talavera), Guy Le Feuvre (Admiral), Lyn Evans (Lope), David Cole (Diego Columbus), Hugh Pryse (Almoner), Stuart Lindsell (Prior), Valentine Dyall (Narrator - voice), William Monroe Cypert (Antonio Camino), Thelma Grigg (Lady in waiting), Anthony Steel (Messenger). Biopic of the famous explorer. *Dir.* David MacDonald.

Chronicles of Narnia: The Lion, the Witch and the Wardrobe, The (2005) William Moseley (Peter Pevensie), Anna Popplewell (Susan Pevensie), Skandar Keynes (Edmund Pevensie), Georgie Henley (Lucy Pevensie), Tilda Swinton (Jadis, the White Witch), Liam Neeson (Aslan – voice), James McAvoy (Mr. Tumnus), Ray Winstone (Mr. Beaver – voice), Dawn French (Mrs. Beaver – voice), Kiran Shah (Ginarrbrik), Jim Broadbent (Professor Digory Kirke), Elizabeth Hawthorne (Mrs. Macready), James Cosmo (Father Christmas), Michael Madsen (Maugrim – voice), Patrick Kake (Oreius), Shane Rangi (General Otmin), Morris Cupton (Train Guard), Judy McIntosh (Helen Pevensie), Rupert Everett (fox – voice), Cameron Rhodes (Gryphon – voice), Noah Huntley (Peter Pevensie – adult), Sophie Winkleman (Susan Pevensie – adult), Mark Wells (Edmund Pevensie – adult), Rachael Henley (Lucy Pevensie – adult). During WWII the four Pevensie children are evacuated to a country estate. One day when they are playing hide and seek Lucy hides in a wardrobe and the adventure begins. The film won one Academy Award: Best Achievement in Makeup. Based on the children's book by C. S. Lewis. *Dir.* Andrew Adamson.

Circus of Horrors (1960) Anton Diffring (Dr. Schuler), Erika Remberg (Elissa Caro), Yvonne Monlaur (Nicole Vanet), Donald Pleasence (Vanet), Jane Hylton (Angela), Kenneth Griffith (Martin), Conrad Phillips (Inspector Arthur Ames), Jack Gwillim (Superintendent Andrews), Vanda Hudson (Magda von Meck), Yvonne Romain (Melina), Colette Wilde (Evelyn Morley Finsbury), William Mervyn (Doctor Morley), John Merivale (Edward Finsbury), Peter Swanwick (German Police Inspector Knopf). A disgraced plastic surgeon eventually becomes the owner of a circus which he uses as a means to perform more of his work. *Dir.* Sidney Hayers.

Citadel, The (1938) Robert Donat (Dr. Andrew Manson), Rosalind Russell (Christine Barlow), Ralph Richardson (Dr. Philip Denny), Rex Harrison (Freddie Hampton), Emlyn Williams (Mr. Owen), Penelope Dudley Ward (Toppy LeRoy), Francis L. Sullivan (Ben Chenkin), Mary Clare (Mrs. Orlando), Cecil Parker (Charles Every), Nora Swinburne (Mrs. Thornton), Edward

Chapman (Joe Morgan), Athene Seyler (Lady Raebank), Felix Aylmer (Mr. Boon). An earnest young doctor starts out treating Welsh miners but on moving to London finds that his higher aims are brought down by the possibilities of a more lucrative but less morally rewarding life. Based on the 1937 novel of the same name by A. J. Cronin. *Dir.* King Vidor.

City of the Dead, The (1960) Dennis Lotis (Richard Barlow), Christopher Lee (Prof. Alan Driscoll), Patricia Jessel (Elizabeth Selwyn/Mrs. Newless), Tom Naylor (Bill Maitland), Betta St. John (Patricia Russell), Venetia Stevenson (Nan Barlow), Valentine Dyall (Jethrow Keane), Ann Beach (Lottie), Norman Macowan (Reverend Russell), Fred Johnson (The Elder), James Dyrenforth (Garage attendant), Maxine Holden (Sue), William Abney (Policeman). A student travels to the Massachusetts town of Whitewood to research into witchcraft and finds that she has arrived amidst a coven of immortal witches who choose her as a virgin sacrifice. Released in the US as *Horror Hotel*. *Dir.* John Llewellyn Moxey.

City Under the Sea, The (1965) Vincent Price (Sir Hugh, The Captain), David Tomlinson (Harold Tufnell-Jones), Tab Hunter (Ben Harris), Susan Hart (Jill Tregillis), John Le Mesurier (Rev. Jonathan Ives), Henry Oscar (Mumford), Derek Newark (Dan), Roy Patrick (Simon). An underwater city is discovered off the coast of Cornwall where the residents have extended lifespans. Also known as *War-Gods of the Deep*. *Dir.* Jacques Tourneur.

Claim, The (2000) Peter Mullan (Daniel Dillon), Milla Jovovich (Lucia), Wes Bentley (Donald Dalglish), Nastassja Kinski (Elena Dillon/Burn/Dillon), Sarah Polley (Hope Dillon/Burn), Julian Richings (Frank Bellanger), Shirley Henderson (Annie), Sean McGinley (Sweetley), Tom McCamus (Burn), Karolina Muller (Young Elena), Barry Ward (Young Dillon), Duncan Frasier (Crocker). In 1867 Daniel Dillon is a prosperous owner in the gold-mining town of Kingdom Come. However, in 1849 he had sold his wife and daughter to another miner in exchange for his claim and now the woman and teenage girl have arrived in his town looking for him. The film is loosely based on *The Mayor of Casterbridge* by Thomas Hardy. *Dir.* Michael Winterbottom.

Clash of the Titans (2010) Sam Worthington (Perseus), Gemma Arterton (Io), Mads Mikkelsen (Draco), Alexa Davalos (Andromeda), Jason Flemyng (Acrisius/Calibos), Tine Stapelfeldt (Danaë), Nicholas Hoult (Eusebius), Hans Matheson (Ixas), Liam Cunningham (Solon), Liam Neeson (Zeus), Ralph Fiennes (Hades), Jamie Sives (Commander), Ian Whyte (Sheikh Sulieman), Pete Postlethwaite (Spyros), Foster Father (Perseus), Elizabeth McGovern (Marmara), Polly Walker (Cassiopeia), Vincent Regan (Kepheus), David Kennedy (Kepheus's General), Kaya Scodelario (Peshet), Luke Treadaway (Prokopion), Danny Huston (Poseidon), Izabella Miko (Athena), Tamer Hassan (Ares), Luke Evans (Apollo), Nathalie Cox (Artemis), Nina Young (Hera), Agyness Deyn (Aphrodite), Paul Kynman (Hephaestus), Alexander Siddig (Hermes), Charlotte Comer (Demeter), Jane March (Hestia), Natalia Vodianova (Medusa), Mouloud Achour (Kucuk), Ross Mullan (Pemphredo), Ashraf Barhom (Ozal). The story of the mythological Greek hero (demi-god) Perseus and his quest to save the Princess Andromeda from being sacrificed. A remake of the 1981 film of the same name. *Dir.* Louis Leterrier.

Clockwise (1986) John Cleese (Brian Stimpson), Stephen Moore (Mr. Jolly), Alison Steadman (Gwenda Stimpson), Mark Burdis (Glen Scully), Nadia Sawalha (Mandy Kostakis), Sharon Maiden (Laura Wisely), Joan Hickson (Mrs. Trellis), Penelope Wilton (Pat), Sheila Keith (Pat's Mother), Constance Chapman (Mrs. Wheel), Ann Way (Mrs. Way), Pat Keen (Mrs. Wisely), Geoffrey Hutchings (Mr. Wisely), Tony Haygarth (Ivan), Michael Aldridge (Prior), Leslie Schofield (Policeman), Benjamin Whitrow (Headmaster), Geoffrey Palmer (Headmaster), Peter Cellier (Headmaster), Patrick Godfrey (Headmaster), Nick Stringer (Det. Sgt. Rice). Things go from bad to worse for obsessively punctual headmaster Brian Stimpson as he travels to a conference. *Dir.* Christopher Morahan.

Clockwork Orange, A (1971) Malcolm McDowell (Alex/Narrator), James Marcus (Georgie), Warren Clarke (Dim), Michael Tarn (Pete), Patrick Magee (Mr. Frank Alexander), Adrienne Corri (Mrs. Mary Alexander), Michael Bates (Chief Guard Barnes), John Clive (Stage actor), Carl Duering (Dr. Brodsky), Paul Farrell (Tramp), Richard Connaught (Billyboy), Clive Francis (Joe the Lodger), Michael Gover (Prison Governor), Miriam Karlin (Miss Weathers), John Savident (Conspirator), Margaret Tyzack (Conspirator Rubinstein), Steven Berkoff (Detective Constable Tom), David Prowse (Julian). Based on the novel of the same name by Anthony Burgess. Set in a futuristic London, the film follows Alex and his gang (the Droogs) as they cause mayhem (including beatings and rape) until Alex is arrested when his gang turn on him and abandon him. In prison he volunteers to undergo treatment to "cure" him of his violent tendencies. Always controversial, in 1973 the film was withdrawn from distribution in the UK by Warner Brothers at the request of Kubrick after a sustained hate campaign by the tabloids (including insinuating it was responsible for "inspiring" several crimes) led to his family receiving death threats. It was finally screened again in the UK shortly after Kubrick's death in 1999. *Dir.* Stanley Kubrick.

Close My Eyes (1991) Alan Rickman (Sinclair), Clive Owen (Richard), Saskia Reeves (Natalie), Karl Johnson (Colin), Lesley Sharp (Jessica), Kate Garside (Paula), Niall Buggy (Geof), Karen Knight (Philippa), Campbell Morrison (Scotsman), Annie Hayes (Receptionist), Maxwell Hutcheon (Interviewee), Geraldine Somerville (Natalie's Boss), Helen FitzGerald (Scottish Girl). A film with incest, AIDS and town planning as its main themes. *Dir.* Stephen Poliakoff.

Close Shave, A (1995) Voice cast: Peter Sallis (Wallace), Anne Reid (Wendolene). Wallace and Gromit have a window cleaning business. Wallace falls for wool shop owner Wendolene but her evil dog Preston is running a sheep rustling operation. The first official screen appearance of Shaun the Sheep, now a children's television favourite. The film won an Academy Award for Best Animated Short Film. *Dir.* Nick Park.

Clouded Yellow, The (1951) Jean Simmons (Sophie Malraux), Trevor Howard (Maj. David Somers), Sonia Dresdel (Jess Fenton), Barry Jones (Nicholas Fenton), Kenneth More (Willy Shepley), Geoffrey Keen (Police Inspector), André Morell (Secret Service Chief Chubb), Michael Brennan (Superintendent Ross), Gerard Heinz (Dr. Karl Cesare), Lily Kann (Minna Cesare), Eric Pohlmann (Greek taxidermist), Richard Wattis (Employment Agent), Sandra Dorne (Kyra), Maire O'Neill (Nora), Maxwell Reed (Hick), Cyril Chamberlain (Passport Official), Glyn Houston (Lancastrian Bus Conductor), Sam Kydd (Police Radio Operator), Dandy Nichols (Ernie's Mother on Train), Marianne Stone (Young Woman at Nora's House). Sophie and David go on the run from the police after she is wrongly accused of murder. *Dir.* Ralph Thomas.

Cockleshell Heroes, The (1955) José Ferrer (Major Stringer), Trevor Howard (Captain Thompson), Dora Bryan (Myrtie), Victor Maddern (Sgt Craig), Walter Fitzgerald (Gestapo Comdt.), Karel Stepanek (Assistant Gestapo Officer), Beatrice Campbell (Mrs Ruddock), Sydney Tafler (Policeman), Gladys Henson (Barmaid), Jacques B. Brunius (French Fisherman), Andreas Malandrinos (French Fisherman), Judith Furse (W.V.S. Woman), Christopher Lee (Submarine Cmdr Alan Grieves) and Marines: Anthony Newley (Clarke), David Lodge (Ruddock), Peter Arne (Stevens), Percy Herbert (Lomas), Graham Stewart (Booth), John Fabian (Cooney), John Van Eyssen (Bradley), Robert Desmond (Todd). A fictionalised account of Operation Frankton, a raid by canoe-borne (cockleshells) British Marine commandos on Bordeaux during WWII. *Dir.* José Ferrer.

Colditz Story, The (1955) John Mills (Pat Reid), Christopher Rhodes (Mac McGill), Lionel Jeffries (Harry Tyler), Bryan Forbes (Jimmy Winslow), Guido Lorraine (Polish officer), Anton Diffring (Fischer), Richard Wattis (Richard Gordon), Ian Carmichael (Robin Cartwright), Eric Portman (Colonel Richmond), Frederick Valk (Kommandant). Based on the book by Major Pat Reid recounting his time as escape officer in the reportedly escape-proof German prison, Colditz Castle. *Dir.* Guy Hamilton.

Collector, The (1965) Terence Stamp (Freddie Clegg), Samantha Eggar (Miranda Grey), Mona Washbourne (Aunt Annie), Maurice Dallimore (Neighbour), Allyson Ames (First victim), William Bickley (Crutchley), Gordon Barclay (Clerk), David Haviland (Clerk), Edina Ronay (The Nurse). Butterfly-collector Freddie Clegg kidnaps art student Miranda Grey, keeping her in the cellar

185

of his house. Based on the novel of the same name by John Fowles. *Dir.* William Wyler.

Come On George! (1939) George Formby (George), Patricia Kirkwood (Ann Johnson), Joss Ambler (Sir Charles Bailey), Meriel Forbes (Monica Bailey), Cyril Raymond (Jimmy Taylor), George Hayes (Bannerman), George Carney (Sergeant Johnson), Ronald Shiner (Nat), Gibb McLaughlin (Dr MacGregor), Hal Gordon (Stableboy), Davy Burnaby (Col. Bollinger), C. Denier Warren (Banker), James Hayter (Barker), Syd Crossley (Police Constable Cronley). Stableboy George puts his ability to calm a nervous racehorse to good use. *Dir.* Anthony Kimmins.

Come Play With Me (1977) Mary Millington (Sue), George Harrison Marks (Cornelius Clapworthy), Alfie Bass (Kelly), Irene Handl (Lady Bovington), Ronald Fraser (Slasher), Tommy Godfrey (Blitt), Ken Parry (Podsnap), Jerry Lorden (Rodney), Sue Longhurst (Christina), Cardew Robinson (McIvar), Suzy Mandel (Rena), Rita Webb (Rita), Queenie Watts (Cafe Girl), Talfryn Thomas (Nosegay), Bob Todd (Vicar), Henry McGee (Deputy Prime Minister), Derek Aylward (Sir Geoffrey), Norman Vaughan (Stage Performer), Valentine Dyall (Minister of Finance), Josephine Harrison Marks (Brownie), Toni Harrison Marks (Miss Dingle). Two elderly forgers are hiding out in a mansion in the Scottish highlands when a troupe of dancing girls arrives. A British sex comedy very much of its time, featuring a sprinkling of old character actors who perhaps should have known better. *Dir.* George Harrison Marks.

Comfort and Joy (1984) Bill Paterson (Alan Bird), Eleanor David (Maddy), Clare Grogan (Charlotte), Alex Norton (Trevor), Patrick Malahide (Colin), Rikki Fulton (Hilary), Roberto Bernardi ("Mr. McCool"), George Rossi (Bruno), Peter Rossi (Paolo), Billy McElhaney (Renato), Gilly Gilchrist (Rufus), Caroline Guthrie (Gloria), Ona McCracken (Nancy), Elizabeth Sinclair (Fiona), Katy Black (Sarah), Robin Black (Lily), Ron Donachie (George), Arnold Brown (Psychiatrist), Iain McColl (Archie), Billy Johnstone (Amos). After Alan's long-time girlfriend leaves him he is accidentally drawn into a Glasgow ice-cream war. *Dir.* Bill Forsyth.

Comfort of Strangers, The (1990) Christopher Walken (Robert), Rupert Everett (Colin), Natasha Richardson (Mary), Helen Mirren (Caroline), Manfredi Aliquo (Concierge), David Ford (Waiter), Daniel Franco (Waiter), Rossana Canghiari (Hotel Maid), Fabrizio Castellani (Bar Manager), Mario Cotone (Detective), Giancarlo Previati (First Policeman), Antonio Serrano (Second Policeman). Colin and Mary holiday in Venice in an attempt to repair their relationship. They are befriended by Robert and Caroline a rather mysterious couple. The screenplay by Harold Pinter is adapted from the novel of the same name by Ian McEwan. *Dir.* Paul Schrader.

Commitments, The (1991) Robert Arkins (Jimmy Rabbitte), Colm Meaney (Jimmy Rabbitte, Sr.), Anne Kent (Mrs. Rabbitte), Andrea Corr (Sharon Rabbitte), Gerard Cassoni (Darren Rabbitte), Ruth Fairclough (Rabbitte Twin), Lindsay Fairclough (Rabbitte Twin), Michael Aherne (Steven Clifford), Andrew Strong (Deco Cuffe), Angeline Ball (Imelda Quirke), Maria Doyle Kennedy (Natalie Murphy), Dave Finnegan (Mickah Wallace), Bronagh Gallagher (Bernie McGloughlin), Félim Gormley (Dean Fay), Glen Hansard (Outspan Foster), Dick Massey (Billy Mooney), Johnny Murphy (Joey 'The Lips' Fagan), Ken McCluskey (Derek Scully), Michael O'Reilly (Greg), Liam Carney (Duffy), Ger Ryan (Pawnbroker), Mark O'Regan (Father Molloy), Phelim Drew (Roddy Craig), Sean Hughes (Dave Machin), Philip Bredin (Ray), Aoife Lawless (Imelda's Sister), Alan Parker(Eejit Record Producer), Jim Corr (Avant-Garde-A-Clue Band), Caroline Corr (Extra), Sharon Corr (Fiddle Player). Part of the *Barrytown Trilogy* (with *The Snapper* and *The Van*) written by Roddy Doyle. Teenager Jimmy Rabbitte puts together a soul band in Barrytown, Dublin using friends and neighbours, a singer he spots at a wedding and an advert which brings many hopefuls to his door as well as attracting the attention of an old trumpet player. The film follows the bands early travails finding instruments and places to practice and gigs to play. Eventually

local success is threatened by the tensions within the band. *Dir.* Alan Parker.

Company of Wolves, The (1984) Angela Lansbury (Granny), Sarah Patterson (Rosaleen), David Warner (Father), Tusse Silberg (Mother), Graham Crowden (Old Priest), Brian Glover (Amorous Boy's Father), Kathryn Pogson (Young Bride), Stephen Rea (Young Groom), Micha Bergese (Huntsman), Georgia Slowe (Alice), Shane Johnstone (Amorous Boy), Susan Porrett (Amorous Boy's Mother), Dawn Archibald (Witch Woman). A dark and seductive interpretation of the fairy story of *Little Red Riding-Hood* with emphasis on the type of narrative which includes a grandmother being eaten by a wolf and red riding-hood getting her kit off. Based on *The Bloody Chamber and other Stories* by Angela Carter. *Dir.* Neil Jordan.

Comrades (1986) Robin Soans (George Loveless), William Gaminara (James Loveless), Stephen Bateman (Old Tom Stanfield), Philip Davis (Young John Stanfield), Jeremy Flynn (James Brine), Keith Allen (James Hammett), Alex Norton (Lanternist/Sergeant Bell/ Diorama Showman/Laughing Cavalier), Michael Clark (Sailor), Arthur Dignam (Fop), James Fox (William Norfolk), John Hargreaves (Convict), Michael Hordern (Mr Pitt), Freddie Jones (Vicar of Tolpuddle), Murray Melvin (Frampton's Clerk), Vanessa Redgrave (Mrs Violet Carlyle), Robert Stephens (James Frampton), Barbara Windsor (Mrs Wetham), Imelda Staunton (Betsy Loveless), Katy Behean (Sarah Loveless), Amber Wilkinson (Hetty Loveless), Patricia Healey (Mrs Brine), Shane Downe (Joseph Brine), Sandra Voe (Diana Stanfield), Valerie Whittington (Elvi Stanfield), Harriet Doyle (Charity Stanfield), Patrick Field (John Hammett), Heather Page (Bridget Hammett), Joanna David (Mrs Frampton). Historical drama about the Tolpuddle Martyrs. *Dir.* Bill Douglas.

Cone of Silence (1960) Michael Craig (Captain Hugh Dallas), Peter Cushing (Captain Clive Judd), Bernard Lee (Captain George Gort), Elizabeth Seal (Charlotte Gort), George Sanders (Sir Arnold Hobbes), André Morell (Captain Edward Manningham), Gordon Jackson (Captain Bateson), Charles Tingwell (Captain Braddock), Noel Willman (Nigel Pickering), Delphi Lawrence (Joyce Mitchell), Marne Maitland (Mr. Robinson), William Abney (First Officer), Jack Hedley (First Officer), Simon Lack (Navigator). A pilot is blamed for a crash but then similar crashes occur. Also known as *Trouble in the Sky*. Based on a David Beaty novel. *Dir.* Charles Frend.

Confessions from a Holiday Camp (1977) Robin Askwith (Timmy Lea), Antony Booth (Sidney Noggett), Bill Maynard (Mr. Lea), Doris Hare (Mrs. Lea), Sheila White (Rosie Noggett), Linda Hayden (Brigitte), Lance Percival (Lionel), John Junkin (Mr. Whitemonk), Liz Fraser (Mrs. Antonia Whitemonk), Colin Crompton (Roughage), Nicholas Bond-Owen (Kevin), Mike Savage (Kevin's Dad), Janet Edis (Kevin's Mum), Nicola Blackman (Blackbird), Caroline Ellis (Gladys), Sue Upton (Renee), Penny Meredith (Married Woman), Margo Field (Mrs. Dimwiddy), Marianne Stone (Waitress), Leonard Woodrow (Chaplain), Lauri Lupino Lane (Mayor). Tim and Sid are threatened with the sack by the new owner of the holiday camp where they work, until they decide to hold a beauty contest. The last of the *Confessions* series as the British sex-comedy era started to wind down. *Dir.* Norman Cohen.

Confessions from the David Galaxy Affair (1979) Alan Lake (David Galaxy), Diana Dors (Jenny Stride), Mary Millington (Millicent Cumming), Antony Booth (Steve), Glynn Edwards (Chief Inspector Evans), John Moulder-Brown (Sergeant Johnson), Milton Reid (Eddie), Bernie Winters (Mr. Pringle), Kenny Lynch (Joe), Sally Faulkner (Amanda), Rosemary England (Sandra), Queenie Watts (David Galaxy's Mother), Cindy Truman (Anne), Vicki Scott (Charlotte), Alec Mango (Pembleton), Maria Parkinson (Susan), George Lewis (George), John M. East (Willie), Ballard Berkeley (Judge). A sex comedy about an astrologer. *Dir.* Willy Roe.

Confessions of a Driving Instructor (1976) Robin Askwith (Timothy Lea), Antony Booth (Sidney Noggett), Sheila White (Rosie Noggett), Doris Hare (Mrs Lea), Bill Maynard (Walter Lea), Windsor Davies (Mr Truscott), Lynda Bellingham (Mary

Truscott), Liz Fraser (Mrs Chalmers), Irene Handl (Miss Slenderparts), Suzy Mandel (Mrs Hargreaves), George Layton (Tony Bender), Ballard Berkeley (Lord Snodley), Chrissy Iddon (Lady Snodley), Lewis Collins (Rugby Player). British sex comedy where Timothy gets in the fast lane with several of his clients as well as his landlady. The rivalry with another firm of instructors provides the sub-plot. *Dir*. Norman Cohen.

Confessions of a Pop Performer (1975) Robin Askwith (Timothy Lea), Antony Booth (Sidney Noggett), Sheila White (Rosie Noggett), Doris Hare (Mrs. Lea), Bill Maynard (Mr. Lea), Peter Cleall (Nutter Normington), Richard Warwick (Petal), Bob Todd (Mr Barnwell), Jill Gascoine (Mrs Barnwell), Peter Jones (Maxy Naus), Carol Hawkins (Jill Brown), Diane Langton (Ruby Climax), Linda Regan (Brenda Climax), Rita Webb (Fanny's Mother), Andee Cromarty (Fanny), Sally Harrison (Patsie), Helli Louise (Eva), Ian Lavender (Rodney), Bill Pertwee (Husband), David Prowse (Man at Cinema), Rula Lenska (Receptionist), David Hamilton (TV interviewer). Tim and Sid become managers of a local band and then Tim becomes a member of the group. An appearance on *Opportunity Knockers* ensues as do numerous sexual encounters. *Dir*. Norman Cohen.

Confessions of a Window Cleaner (1974) Robin Askwith (Timothy Lea), Antony Booth (Sidney Noggett), Linda Hayden (Elizabeth Radlett), Sheila White (Rosie Noggett), Dandy Nichols (Mrs. Lea), Bill Maynard (Mr. Lea), John Le Mesurier (Inspector Radlett), Joan Hickson (Mrs. Radlett), Sue Longhurst (Jacqui Brown), Katya Wyeth (Carole), Richard Wattis (Carole's Father), Melissa Stribling (Mrs. Villiers), Anita Graham (Ingrid), Sam Kydd (1st Removal Man), Brian Hall (2nd Removal Man), Christine Donna (Lil Lamour), Olivia Munday (Brenda), Judy Matheson (Elvie), Elaine Baillie (Ronnie), Christopher Owen (Vicar), Peter Dennis (Waiter), Marianne Stone (Woman in Cinema). Brother-in-law Sid employs Tim in his window-cleaning business and as George Formby once sang "You should see what I can see when I'm cleaning windows", although in this case it involves a good deal of doing as well as seeing. The first in the successful *Confessions* series. Based on the book of the same name by Christopher Wood. *Dir*. Val Guest.

Confetti (2006) Jimmy Carr (Antoni Clarke), Felicity Montagu (Vivienne), Jessica Stevenson (Sam), Martin Freeman (Matt), Meredith MacNeill (Isabelle), Stephen Mangan (Josef), Olivia Colman (Joanna), Robert Webb (Michael), Vincent Franklin (Archie), Jason Watkins (Gregory), Marc Wootton (Snoopy), Alison Steadman (Sam's mother), Sarah Hadland (Sam's sister), Selina Cadell (Joanna's mother), Ron Cook (Sam's father), Jesús de Miguel (Tennis coach), Julia Davis (Marriage counsellor), Mark Heap (Registrar), Kate Smallwood (Sophie). A mockumentary comedy about three couples competing for a bridal magazine's prize for the most original wedding. *Dir*. Debbie Isitt.

Constant Gardner, The (2005) Ralph Fiennes (Justin Quayle), Rachel Weisz (Tessa Quayle), Hubert Koundé (Dr. Arnold Bluhm), Danny Huston (Sandy Woodrow), Daniele Harford (Miriam), Bill Nighy (Sir Bernard Pellegrin), Keith Pearson (Porter Coleridge), Bernard Otieno Oduor (Jomo), Damaris Itenyo Agweyu (Jomo's Wife), John Sibi-Okumu (Dr. Joshua Ngaba), Packson Ngugi (Officer in Morgue), Pete Postlethwaite (Lorbeer). Justin Quayle – the constant gardener of the title – sets out to investigate the murder in Kenya of his wife Tessa. The film follows the development of their relationship through flashbacks. *Dir*. Fernando Meirelles.

Constant Husband, The (1955) Rex Harrison (William Egerton), Margaret Leighton (Miss Chesterman), Kay Kendall (Monica Hathaway), Cecil Parker (Llewellyn), Nicole Maurey (Lola), Raymond Huntley (J.F. Hassett), Michael Hordern (Judge), Robert Coote (Jack Carter), George Cole (Luigi Sopranelli), Eric Pohlmann (Papa Sopranelli), Marie Burke (Mama Sopranelli), Valerie French (Bridget), Jill Adams (Miss Brent), Muriel Young (Clara). A man wakes up in a Wales with no recollection of who he is or how he got there. With the help of a local psychiatrist he gradually discovers that he has been rather over-enthusiastic matrimonially. *Dir*. Sidney Gilliat.

Constant Nymph, The (1933) Victoria Hopper (Tess), Brian Aherne (Lewis), Leonora Corbett (Florence), Lyn Harding (Albert Sanger), Mary Clare (Linda Sanger), Jane Baxter (Antonia Sanger), Fritz Schulz (Jacob Birnbaum), Tony De Lungo

(Roberto), Jane Cornell (Kate Sanger), Peggy Blythe (Lena Sanger), Athole Stewart (Charles Churchill), Beryl Laverick (Susan Sanger), Jim Gérald (Trigorin). Sickly teenager Tess Sanger is in love with composer Lewis Dodd but he marries her cousin Florence. Adapted from the novel of the same name by Margaret Kennedy. *Dir*. Basil Dean.

Consuming Passions (1988) Tyler Butterworth (Ian Littleton), Jonathan Pryce (Mr.Farris), Freddie Jones (Graham Chumley), Vanessa Redgrave (Mrs.Garza), Prunella Scales (Ethel), Sammi Davis (Felicity), Thora Hird (Mrs.Gordon), John Wells (Dr.Forrester), Timothy West (Dr.Rees), Bryan Pringle (Gateman), Andrew Sachs (Jason), William Rushton (Big Teddy), Wincey Willis (TV Presenter), Linda Lusardi (French Beauty). When Ian accidentally knocks some fellow workers into the mixing vat, it has unexpected consequences for the sales figures of the chocolate makers where he works. *Dir*. Giles Foster.

Contraband (1940) Conrad Veidt (Capt. Andersen), Valerie Hobson (Mrs.Sorensen), Hay Petrie (Axel Skold/Erik Skold), Joss Ambler (Lt. Cmdr. Ashton, RNR), Raymond Lovell (Van Dyne), Esmond Knight (Mr.Pidgeon), Charles Victor (Hendrick), Phoebe Kershaw (Miss Lang), Harold Warrender (Lt. Cmdr. Ellis, RN), John Longden (Passport Officer), Eric Maturin (Passport Officer), Paddy Browne (Singer in 'Regency'), Leo Genn (First Brother Grimm), Stuart Latham (Second Brother Grimm), Peter Bull (Third Brother Grimm), Dennis Arundell (Lieman), Molly Hamley-Clifford (Baroness Hekla), Eric Berry (Mr. Abo), Olga Edwardes (Mrs. Abo), Toni Gable (Miss Karoly), Deborah Kerr (Cigarette Girl), Esma Cannon (Erik Skold's Niece), Erik Chitty (Cloakroom Attendant), Bernard Miles (Man Lighting Pipe), Milo O'Shea (Air Raid Warden), Torin Thatcher (Sailor). A Danish captain has his shore passes stolen whilst in a British port in the first year of WWII. His attempts to follow the thieves lead him into a German spy ring. *Dir*. Michael Powell.

Control (2007) Sam Riley (Ian Curtis), Samantha Morton (Debbie Curtis), Alexandra Maria Lara (Annik Honore), Joe Anderson (Hooky), James Anthony Pearson (Bernard Sumner), Harry Treadaway (Steve Morris), Craig Parkinson (Tony Wilson), Toby Kebbell (Rob Gretton), Andrew Sheridan (Terry), Robert Shelly (Twinny), Richard Bremmer (Ian's Father), Tanya Myers (Ian's Mother), Martha Myers Lowe (Ian's Sister), Matthew McNulty (Nick). Based on the memoir *Touching from a Distance* by Deborah Curtis. The story of Ian Curtis, his personal life and the band Joy Division. *Dir*. Anton Corbijn.

Convict 99 (1939) Will Hay (Dr. Benjamin Twist), Moore Marriott (Jerry the Mole), Graham Moffatt (Albert Brown), Googie Withers (Lottie), Peter Gawthorne (Sir Cyril), Basil Radford (Deputy Governor), Dennis Wyndham (Head Warder), Wilfred Walter (Max Slessor), Alf Goddard (Sykes), Garry Marsh (Johnson), Graham Soutten (Raymond), Teddy Brown (Slim Charlie), Kathleen Harrison (Mabel), Roy Emerton (Colonial). Hay, Marriott and Moffatt team up for another case of mistaken identity. This time a disgraced school teacher is mistaken for a prison governor. *Dir*. Marcel Varnel.

Cook, the Thief, His Wife and Her Lover, The (1989) Richard Bohringer (Richard Borst, the cook), Michael Gambon (Albert Spica, the thief), Helen Mirren (Georgina Spica, his wife), Alan Howard (Michael, her lover), Tim Roth (Mitchel), Ciarán Hinds (Cory), Gary Olsen (Spangler), Ewan Stewart (Harris), Roger Ashton-Griffiths (Turpin), Ron Cook (Mews), Liz Smith (Grace). A gangster's wife has an affair under the nose of her husband in a restaurant. The film includes episodes of torture, murder and cannibalism. *Dir*. Peter Greenaway.

Cool Mikado, The (1963) Frankie Howerd (Ko-Ko Flintridge), Stubby Kaye (Judge Herbert Mikado/Charlie Hotfleisch), Mike Winters (Mike), Bernie Winters (Bernie),Tommy Cooper (Pooh-Bah, Private Detective), Dennis Price (Ronald Fortescue), Peter Barkworth (Fanshaw), Jacqueline Jones (Katie Shaw), Kevin Scott (Hank Mikado), Jill Mai Meredith (Yum-Yum), Burt Kwouk (Art School Teacher), Lionel Blair (Nanki), Pete Murray (Man No. 1 in Boudoir), Ed Bishop (Man No. 2 in Boudoir), Tsai Chin (Pitti-Sing), Glen Mason (Harry), Dermot Walsh (Elmer), Carole Shelley (Mrs. Smith), C. Denier Warren (Mr. Smith), Yvonne Shima (Peep-Bo), Kenji Takaki (Ho Ho). The plot of Gilbert & Sullivan's Mikado set in (then) modern day Japan and recast as a gangster story. Described by Frankie Howerd as "the worst film ever made." *Dir*. Michael Winner.

Coriolanus (2011) Ralph Fiennes (Caius Martius Coriolanus), Gerard Butler (Tullus Aufidius), Brian Cox (Menenius), Vanessa Redgrave (Volumnia), Jessica Chastain (Virgilia), James Nesbitt (Tribune Sicinius), Paul Jesson (Tribune Brutus), Harry Fenn (Young Martius), Lubna Azabal (First Citizen), Ashraf Barhom (Second Citizen), John Kani (General Cominius), Dan Tana (1st Senator), Jon Snow (TV Anchorman), David Yelland (TV Pundit), Nikki Amuka-Bird (TV Pundit). A modern day adaptation of William Shakespeare's play. *Dir*. Ralph Fiennes

Corridors of Blood (1958) Boris Karloff (Dr. Thomas Bolton), Betta St. John (Susan), Finlay Currie (Supt. Matheson), Francis Matthews (Jonathan Bolton), Adrienne Corri (Rachel), Francis de Wolff (Black Ben), Basil Dignam (Chairman of Hospital), Frank Pettingell (Mr. Blount), Christopher Lee (Resurrection Joe), Nigel Green (Inspector Donovan), Yvonne Romain (Rosa), Howard Lang (Chief Inspector), Marian Spencer (Mrs Matheson), Carl Bernard (Ned, The Crow), John Gabriel (Baker), Julian D'Albie (Bald Man), Roddy Hughes (Man with Watch), Robert Raglan (Wilkes), Charles Lloyd Pack (Hardcastle), Bernard Archard (Hospital Official), Frank Sieman (Evans, Hospital Night Porter), Desmond Llewelyn (Assistant at Operations), Marianne Stone (Arrested Woman), Brian Wilde (Man in Operating Theatre Audience). Set in the 1840s, Doctor Boton develops an anaesthetic to help his patients but becomes addicted to it. To help feed his addiction he becomes involved with a gang of "resurrection men". *Dir*. Robert Day.

Cosh Boy (1953) James Kenney (Roy Walsh), Joan Collins (Rene Collins), Betty Ann Davies (Elsie Walsh), Robert Ayres (Bob Stevens), Hermione Baddeley (Mrs. Collins), Hermione Gingold (Queenie), Nancy Roberts (Gran Walsh), Laurence Naismith (Inspector Donaldson), Ian Whittaker (Alfie Collins), Stanley Escane (Pete), Michael McKeag (Brian), Sean Lynch (Darky), Johnny Briggs (Skinny Johnson), Edward Evans (Sgt. Woods), Cameron Hall (Mr. Beverley), Sid James (Police Sergeant), Nosher Powell (Instructor). The story of a juvenile delinquent in post WWII London. *Dir*. Lewis Gilbert.

Count Five and Die (1957) Jeffrey Hunter (Captain Bill Ranson), Annemarie Düringer (Rolande Hertog), Nigel Patrick (Major Julien Howard), David Kossoff (Dr. Mulder), Rolf Lefebvre (Hans Faber), Larry Burns (Martins), Claude Kingston (Willem Mulder), Robert Raglan (Lt. Miller), Peter Prouse (Sgt. Bill Parrish), Philip Bond (Piet van Wijt), Otto Diamant (Mr. Hendrijk), Marianne Walla (Mrs. Hendrijk), Beth Rogan (Mary Ann Lennig), Arthur Gross (Jan Guldt), Wolf Frees (Brauner). British Intelligence tries to disseminate misinformation about the upcoming D-Day landings. *Dir*. Victor Vicas.

Counterblast (1948) Robert Beatty (Dr. Paul Rankin), Mervyn Johns (Dr. Bruckner the Beast of Ravensbruck), Nova Pilbeam (Tracy Hart), Margaretta Scott (Sister 'Johnnie' Johnson), Sybille Binder (Martha Lert), Marie Lohr (Mrs. Coles), Karel Stepanek (Prof. Inman), Alan Wheatley (M.W. Kennedy), Gladys Henson (Mrs. Plum), John Salew (Padre Latham), Anthony Eustrel (Dr. Richard Forrester), Carl Jaffe (Heinz), Ronald Adam (Col Ingram), Martin Miller (Van Hessian), Aubrey Mallalieu (Maj. Walsh), Horace Kenney (Taxi Driver). After WWII a Nazi doctor in disguise plans to unleash biological warfare whilst immunising the German population. *Dir*. Paul L Stein.

Countess Dracula (1971) Ingrid Pitt (Countess Elisabeth Nadasdy), Nigel Green (Captain Dobi), Sandor Elès (Lt. Imre Toth), Maurice Denham (Grand Master Fabio), Patience Collier (Julia Szentes), Lesley-Anne Down (Countess Ilona Nadasdy), Peter Jeffrey (Captain Balogh), Leon Lissek (Sergeant of Bailiffs), Jessie Evans (Rosa), Andrea Lawrence (Ziza), Marianne Stone (Kitchen Maid), Charles Farrell (The Seller), Anne Stallybrass (Pregnant Woman), Susan Brodrick (Teri), Ian Trigger (Clown), Nike Arrighi (Fortune Teller), Peter May (Janco), John Moore (Priest). The Countess discovers that bathing in the blood of virgins helps her maintain a youthful appearance, so decides she needs a steady supply. *Dir*. Peter Sasdy.

Countess from Hong Kong, A (1967) Marlon Brando (Ogden Mears), Sophia Loren (Natasha), Sydney Chaplin (Harvey), Tippi Hedren (Martha), Patrick Cargill (Hudson), Oliver Johnston (Clark), Michael Medwin (John Felix), John Paul (Captain), Margaret Rutherford (Miss Gaulswallow), Angela Scoular (Society girl), Geraldine Chaplin (Girl at dance), Dilys Laye (Saleswoman), Geraldine Chaplin (Girl at dance), Josephine Chaplin (Young girl), Victoria Chaplin (Young girl), Marianne Stone (Reporter), Carol Cleveland (Nurse), Charles Chaplin (An old steward). A Russian Countess becomes a stowaway aboard a diplomat's yacht, causing him countless problems. The film was famous as Chaplin's last film role and also for the theme music, written by Chaplin, which became the hit song *This Is My Song* for Petula Clark. *Dir*. Charlie Chaplin.

Cracksman, The (1963) Charlie Drake (Ernest Wright), Nyree Dawn Porter (Muriel), George Sanders (Guv'nor), Dennis Price (Grantley), Percy Herbert (Nosher), Eddie Byrne (Domino), Finlay Currie (Feathers), Geoffrey Keen (Magistrate), George A. Cooper (Fred), Patrick Cargill (Museum Guide), Norman Bird (Policeman), Neil McCarthy (Van Gogh), Christopher Rhodes (Mr. King), Ronnie Barker (Yossle), Wanda Ventham (Sandra), Richard Leech (Detective Sergeant), Robert Shaw (Moke). A locksmith is jailed after getting conned into cracking a safe and gains an unwanted reputation as an expert thief. *Dir*. Peter Graham Scott.

Creeping Flesh, The (1973) Christopher Lee (Dr. James Hildern), Peter Cushing (Prof. Emmanuel Hildern), Lorna Heilbron (Penelope Hildern), Jenny Runacre (Marguerite Hildern), George Benson (Prof. Waterlow), Kenneth J. Warren (Charles Lenny), Duncan Lamont (Inspector), Harry Locke (Barman), Hedger Wallace (Dr. Perry), Michael Ripper (Carter), Catherine Finn (Emily), Robert Swann (Young Aristocrat), David Bailie (Young Doctor), Maurice Bush (Karl), Tony Wright (Sailor), Marianne Stone (Female Assistant). Told in flashback from the insane asylum in which he has been confined, Professor Hildern explains how the skeleton he brought back from New Guinea turns into a monster when immersed in water. *Dir*. Freddie Francis.

Crimes at the Dark House (1940) Tod Slaughter (The False Sir Percival Glyde), Sylvia Marriott (Laurie Fairlie/Anne Catherick), Hay Petrie (Dr. Isidor Fosco), Hilary Eaves (Marian Fairlie), Geoffrey Wardwell (Paul Hartwright), Margarde Yarde (Mrs. Bullen), Rita Grant (Jessica), David Horne (Frederick Fairlie), Elsie Wagstaff (Mrs. Catherick), David Keir (Lawyer Mr. Merriman), Grace Arnold (Maid), Vincent Holman (Asylum Doctor). The murderer of Sir Percival Glyde assumes his identity and seeks to eliminate all those who might suspect that he is an imposter. *Dir*. George King.

Criminal, The (1960) Stanley Baker (Johnny Bannion), Sam Wanamaker (Mike Carter), Grégoire Aslan (Frank Saffrion), Margit Saad (Suzanne), Jill Bennett (Maggie), Rupert Davies (Edwards), Laurence Naismith (Mr Town), John Van Eyssen (Formby), Noel Willman (Prison Governor), Derek Francis (Priest), Redmond Phillips (Prison Doctor), Kenneth J. Warren (Clobber), Patrick Magee (Barrows), Robert Adams (Judas), Kenneth Cope (Kelly), Patrick Wymark (Sol), Jack Rodney (Scout), John Molloy (Snipe), Brian Phelan (Pauly Larkin), Paul Stassino (Alfredo Fanucci), Jerold Wells (Warder Brown), Tom Bell (Flynn), Neil McCarthy (O'Hara), Keith Smith (Hanson), Nigel Green (Ted), Tom Gerard (Quantock), Larry Taylor (Charles), Murray Melvin (Antlers), Edward Judd (Young warder), Charles Lamb (Mr. Able). Ex-con Johnny Bannion finds himself back in prison where he is pressured into revealing where he stashed the loot from his last job. Released in the United States as *The Concrete Jungle*. *Dir*. Joseph Losey.

Cromwell (1970) Richard Harris (Oliver Cromwell), Alec Guinness (King Charles I), Robert Morley (The Earl of Manchester), Dorothy Tutin (Queen Henrietta Maria), Frank Finlay (John Carter), Timothy Dalton (Prince Rupert), Patrick Wymark (The Earl of Strafford), Patrick Magee (Hugh Peters), Nigel Stock (Sir Edward Hyde), Charles Gray (The Earl of Essex), Michael Jayston (Henry Ireton), Douglas Wilmer (Sir

Thomas Fairfax), Geoffrey Keen (John Pym), Anthony May (Richard Cromwell), Stratford Johns (President Bradshaw), Ian McCulloch (John Hampden), Patrick O'Connell (John Lilburne), Jack Gwillim (General Byron), Richard Cornish (Oliver Cromwell II), Anna Cropper (Ruth Carter), Michael Goodliffe (Solicitor General), Basil Henson (Hacker), Patrick Holt (Captain Lundsford), John Paul (General Digby), Bryan Pringle (Trooper Hawkins), Llewellyn Rees (The Speaker), Robin Stewart (The Prince of Wales), Andre Van Gyseghem (Archbishop Rinucinni), Zena Walker (Mrs. Cromwell), John Welsh (Bishop Juxon), Anthony Kemp (Henry Cromwell), Stacy Dorning (Mary Cromwell), Mel Churcher (Bridget Cromwell), George Merritt (William), Gerald Rowland (Drummer Boy), Josephine Gillick (Elizabeth Cromwell). An historical epic re-telling the events of the English Civil War with Alec Guiness as a very Scottish sounding Charles I and Richard Harris as a not too warty Oliver Cromwell. The film won an Academy Award for Best Costume Design. *Dir.* Ken Hughes.

Crooks Anonymous (1962) Leslie Phillips ("Dandy" Forsdyke), Stanley Baxter (Brother Widdowes), Wilfrid Hyde-White (Montague), Julie Christie (Babette), James Robertson Justice (Sir Harvey Russelrod), Michael Medwin (Ronnie), Pauline Jameson (Prunella), Robertson Hare (Grimsdale), Raymond Huntley (Wagstaffe), Dermot Kelly (Stanley), Norman Rossington (Bert), Harry Fowler (Woods), Charles Lloyd Pack (Fletcher), Harold Goodwin (George), Harry Locke (Fred), Colin Gordon (Drunk), Jeremy Lloyd (M.C. at the Peekaboo Club), Dennis Waterman (Boy in park), Brian Coleman (Holding), Arthur Mullard (Grogan), Joyce Blair (Carol), Timothy Bateson (Partrige), John Bennett (Thomas), Julian Orchard (1st Jeweller), Patrick Newell (2nd Jeweller), Alfred Burke (Caulfield), Arthur Lovegrove (Jones), Cardew Robinson (Wiseman), Dick Emery (Reginald Cundell). Babette signs up her habitual criminal boyfriend Dandy for Crooks Anonymous, an organisation which promises to wean him away from a life of crime. *Dir.* Ken Annakin.

Crooks in Cloisters (1963) Ronald Fraser (Walter Dodd), Barbara Windsor (Bikini), Bernard Cribbins (Squirts McGinty), Davy Kaye (Specs), Wilfrid Brambell (Phineas), Melvyn Hayes (Willy), Grégoire Aslan (Lorenzo), Joseph O'Conor (Father Septimus), Corin Redgrave (Brother Lucius), Francesca Annis (June), Norman Chappell (Benson), Arnold Ridley (Newsagent), Patricia Laffan (Lady Florence), Alister Williamson (Superintendent Mungo), Russell Waters (Ship's Chandler), Howard Douglas (Publican), Max Bacon (Bookmaker), George Tovey (Tick Tack Man), Brian Dent (Journalist), Karen Kaufman (Strip Girl), Barbara Roscoe (Kate). After a robbery a group of crooks hide out in a disused monastery on an island. As they settle in to the slow pattern of life they begin to appreciate its advantages over that of the criminal. *Dir.* Jeremy Summers.

Crossroads to Crime (1960) Anthony Oliver (Don Ross), Patricia Heneghan (Joan Ross), Miriam Karlin (Connie Williams), George Murcell (Diamond), Ferdy Mayne (Miles), David Graham (Johnny), Arthur Rigby (Sergeant Pearson), Victor Maddern (Len), Geoffrey Benton (Butler), Terence Brook (Harry), Peter Diamond (Escort), William Kerwin (Martin), J. Mark Roberts (Phillips), David Sale (Youth), Terry Sale (Youth), Bill Sawyer (Lorry Driver), Donald Tandy (Basher), Harry Towb (Paddy). A policeman infiltrates a gang of lorry highjackers. A rare live action film from the "supermarionation" stable of Gerry Anderson. *Dir.* Gerry Anderson.

Crosstrap (1962) Laurence Payne (Duke), Jill Adams (Sally), Gary Cockrell (Geoff), Zena Marshall (Rina), Bill Nagy (Gaunt), Robert Cawdron (Joe), Larry Taylor (Peron), Max Faulkner (Ricky), Derek Sydney (Juan), Michael Turner (Hoagy). A couple find themselves caught amidst two rival sets of gangsters. *Dir.* Robert Hartford-Davis.

Crucible of Terror (1971) Mike Raven (Victor Clare), Mary Maude (Millie), James Bolam (John 'Jack' Davies), Ronald Lacey (Michael Clare), Betty Alberge (Dorothy Clare), John Arnatt (Bill), Beth Morris (Jane Clare), Judy Matheson (Marcia), Melissa Stribling (Joanna Brent), Kenneth Keeling (George Brent), Me Me Lai (Chi-San). The source of a sculptor's lifelike statues of young women becomes clear. *Dir.* Ted Hooker.

Cruel Sea, The (1953) Jack Hawkins (Ericson), Donald Sinden (Lockhart), John Stratton (Ferraby), Denholm Elliott (Morell),

John Warner (Baker), Stanley Baker (Bennett), Bruce Seton (Tallow), Liam Redmond (Watts), Virginia McKenna (Julie Hallam), Moira Lister (Elaine Morell), June Thorburn (Doris Ferraby), Megs Jenkins (Tallow's sister), Meredith Edwards (Yeoman Wells), Glyn Houston (Phillips), Sam Kydd (Carslake), Andrew Cruickshank (Scott Brown). The WWII story of the crew of convoy escort HMS *Compass Rose*. Based on the best-selling novel *The Cruel Sea* by Nicholas Monsarrat *Dir.* Charles Frend.

Cry Freedom (1987) Kevin Kline (Donald Woods), Denzel Washington (Steve Biko), Penelope Wilton (Wendy Woods), Kate Hardie (Jane Woods), Graeme Taylor (Dillon Woods), Adam Stuart Walker (Duncan Woods), Hamish Stuart Walker (Gavin Woods), Spring Stuart Walker (Mary Woods), Kevin McNally (Ken), Albert Ndinda (Alec), Andrew Whaley (Sub-Editor), Shelley Borkum (Woods' receptionist), Josette Simon (Dr. Ramphele), Wabei Siyolwe (Tenjy), John Matshikiza (Mapetla), Juanita Waterman (Ntsiki Biko), Timothy West (Captain De Wet), Zakes Mokae (Father Kani), John Thaw (Kruger), Peggy Marsh (Helen Suzman), Gwyneth Strong (Girl at funeral), Julian Glover (Don Card), Michael Turner (Judge Boshoff), Ian Richardson (State Prosecutor), Hilary Minster (1st Passport Control officer), Judy Cornwell (Receptionist), Alec McCowen (Acting High Commissioner). A film set in South Africa in 1977, during apartheid. After Steve Biko, leader of the black consciousness movement, dies in police custody, his friend Donald Woods, editor of the *Daily Dispatch*, writes a book which he can only get published if he can get out of South Africa. *Dir.* Richard Attenborough.

Cry of the Banshee (1970) Vincent Price (Lord Edward Whitman), Elisabeth Bergner (Oona), Essy Persson (Lady Patricia Whitman), Hugh Griffith (Mickey), Sally Geeson (Sarah), Patrick Mower (Roderick), Hilary Heath (Maureen Whitman), Carl Rigg (Harry Whitman), Stephan Chase (Sean Whitman), Marshall Jones (Father Tom), Andrew McCulloch (Bully Boy), Michael Elphick (Burke), Pamela Fairbrother (Margaret Donald), Quinn O'Hara (Maggie), Jan Rossini (Bess), Richard Everett (Timothy), Louis Selwyn (Apprentice), Mickey Baker (Rider), Ann Barrass (Elga). In the 17th Century, when evil witchfinder Lord Whitman wipes out a coven he earns the undying enmity of its leader Oona. She swears vengeance against his family and unleashes a supernatural spirit to destroy them all. *Dir.* Gordon Hessler.

Cry, The Beloved Country (1952) Sidney Poitier (Reverend Msimangu), Joyce Carey (Margaret Jarvis), Geoffrey Keen (Father Vincent), Canada Lee (Stephen Kumalo), Charles Carson (James Jarvis), Michael Goodliffe (Martens, Probation Official), Edric Connor (John Kumalo), Lionel Ngakane (Absolom Kumalo), Vivien Clinton (Mary), Albertina Temba (Mrs. Kumalo), Bruce Anderson (Frank Smith). Based on the novel of the same name by Alan Paton. Set in South Africa during apartheid, the stories of a black priest and a white farmer are drawn together by tragedy. *Dir.* Zoltán Korda.

Crying Game, The (1992) Forest Whitaker (Jody), Stephen Rea (Fergus), Jaye Davidson (Dil), Miranda Richardson (Jude), Adrian Dunbar (Maguire), Breffni McKenna (Tinker), Joe Savino (Eddie), Birdy Sweeney (Tommy), Andrée Bernard (Jane), Jim Broadbent (Col), Ralph Brown (Dave), Tony Slattery (Deveroux). Fergus, an IRA man, kidnaps British soldier Jody and, while he awaits instructions, he begins to talk to Jody about Dil, his hairdresser girlfriend in London. *Dir* Neil Jordan.

Cul-de-sac (1966) Donald Pleasence (George), Françoise Dorléac (Teresa), Lionel Stander (Richard), Jack MacGowran (Albie), Iain Quarrier (Christopher), Geoffrey Sumner (Christopher's father), Renee Houston (Christopher's mother), Robert Dorning (Philip Fairweather), Marie Kean (Marion Fairweather), William Franklyn (Cecil), Jacqueline Bisset (Jacqueline), Trevor Delaney (Nicholas). A wounded crook and his dying partner hide out with an odd couple in a seaside castle. *Dir.* Roman Polanski.

Curse of Frankenstein, The (1957) Peter Cushing (Victor Frankenstein), Christopher Lee (Creature), Robert Urquhart (Paul Krempe), Hazel Court (Elizabeth), Valerie Gaunt (Justine), Paul Hardtmuth (Professor Bernstein), Noel Hood (Aunt), Fred Johnson (Grandpa), Claude Kingston (Little Boy), Alex Gallier (Priest), Michael Mulcaster (Warder), Andrew Leigh (Burgomaster), Ann Blake (Wife), Melvyn Hayes (Young Victor), Sally Walsh (Young Elizabeth), Middleton Woods (Lecturer),

Raymond Ray (Uncle). Whilst in prison awaiting execution Baron Victor Frankenstein recounts the tale of how he had managed to resurrect a dead body, with murderous consequences for all those around him. *Dir.* Terence Fisher.

Curse of the Crimson Altar (1968) Christopher Lee (Morley), Boris Karloff (Professor Marshe), Mark Eden (Robert Manning), Barbara Steele (Lavinia Morley), Michael Gough (Elder), Virginia Wetherell (Eve Morley), Rosemarie Reede (Esther), Derek Tansley (Judge), Michael Warren (Chauffeur), Ron Pember (Petrol attendant), Denys Peek (Peter Manning), Rupert Davies (The Vicar), Roger Avon (Sergeant Tyson). Robert Manning visits remote Craxford Lodge looking for his missing brother and although told that his brother is not there he feels there is a menace about the place. Released as *The Crimson Cult* in the United States. *Dir.* Vernon Sewell.

Curse of the Fly (1965) Brian Donlevy (Henri Delambre), George Baker (Martin Delambre), Carole Gray (Patricia Stanley), Yvette Rees (Wan), Burt Kwouk (Tai), Michael Graham (Albert Delambre), Jeremy Wilkins (Inspector Ronet), Charles Carson (Inspector Charas), Mary Manson (Judith Delambre), Rachel Kempson (Madame Fournier), Warren Stanhope (Hotel Manager), Mia Anderson (Nurse), Arnold Bell (Hotel Porter). An escapee from a mental asylum marries a man with recessive fly genes. He also carries out experiments in teleportation which sometimes go horribly wrong. His disfigured first wife is locked up in his stables. Sequel to the American film *The Fly* (1958). *Dir.* Don Sharp.

Curse of the Pink Panther (1983) Ted Wass (Sgt. Clifton Sleigh), Herbert Lom (Chief Inspector Charles Dreyfus), Robert Loggia (Bruno Langlois), David Niven (Sir Charles Litton - voiced by Rich Little), Joanna Lumley (Countess Chandra), Capucine (Lady Simone Litton), Robert Wagner (George Litton), Burt Kwouk (Cato Fong), Andre Maranne (Sgt. Francios Duval), Peter Arne (General Bufoni), Ed Parker (Mr. Chong), Bill Nighy (ENT Doctor), Roger Moore/Turk Thrust II (Jacques Clouseau), Harvey Korman (Prof. Auguste Balls). A pretty unwise, some might say desperate, attempt to keep the franchise going after the death of Peter Sellers in 1980 with Ted Wass as an incompetent detective assigned by Dreyfus to find the apparently missing Inspector Clouseau. David Niven (in his last film), Capucine and Robert Wagner all reprise their roles from the first Pink Panther film of 1963. *Dir.* Blake Edwards.

Curse of the Werewolf, The (1961) Clifford Evans (Don Alfredo Corledo), Oliver Reed (Leon Corledo), Yvonne Romain (Servant girl), Catherine Feller (Cristina), Anthony Dawson (Marques Siniestro), Josephine Llewelyn (Marquesa), Richard Wordsworth (Beggar), Hira Talfrey (Teresa), John Gabriel (The priest), Warren Mitchell (Pepe Valiente), Anne Blake (Rosa Valiente), George Woodbridge (Dominique), Michael Ripper (Old Soak), Ewen Solon (Don Fernando), Peter Sallis (Don Enrique), Denis Shaw (Gaoler), Charles Lamb (Marques' Chef), Desmond Llewelyn (Marques's servant), Serafina Di Leo (Senora Zumara), Sheila Brennan (Vera), Joy Webster (Isabel), Renny Lister (Yvonne). A girl who has been raped by a beggar dies in childbirth and her son is raised by Don Alfredo and his housekeeper Teresa. Unfortunately, as you might suspect from the film's title, the boy suffers from the werewolf's curse. Based on the novel *The Werewolf of Paris* by Guy Endore. *Dir.* Terence Fisher.

Curtain Up (1952) Robert Morley (W.H. 'Harry' Derwent Blacker), Margaret Rutherford (Catherine Beckwith/Jeremy St. Claire), Kay Kendall (Sandra Beverley), Michael Medwin (Jerry Winterton), Olive Sloane (Maud Baron), Liam Gaffney (Norwood Beverley), Lloyd Lamble (Jackson), Charlotte Mitchell (Daphne Ray), Charles Lamb (George), Constance Lorne (Sarah Stebbins), Maggie Hanley (Mary), Stringer Davis (Vicar), Joan Hickson (Harry's Landlady), John Cazabon (Mr Stebbins), Diana Calderwood (Set Painter), Joan Rice (Avis), Sam Kydd (Ambulanceman). The lives and loves of the members of a regional repertory company as they struggle to put on a second-rate play. *Dir.* Ralph Smart.

Dad Savage (1998) Patrick Stewart (Dad Savage), Kevin McKidd (H), Helen McCrory (Chris), Joe McFadden (Bob), Marc Warren (Vic), Jake Wood (Sav). Local gangster and East Anglian tulip farmer Dad Savage is targeted by Vic and Bob, who decide to relieve him of his money. *Dir.* Betsan Morris Evans.

Dad's Army (1971) Arthur Lowe (Captain Mainwaring), John Le Mesurier (Sergeant Wilson), Clive Dunn (Lance Corporal Jones), John Laurie (Private Frazer), James Beck (Private Walker), Arnold Ridley (Private Godfrey), Ian Lavender (Private Pike), Liz Fraser (Mrs. Pike), Bernard Archard (Major General Fullard), Derek Newark (Regimental Sergeant Major), Bill Pertwee (Hodges), Frank Williams (Vicar), Edward Sinclair (Verger), Anthony Sagar (Police Sergeant), Pat Coombs (Mrs. Hall), Roger Maxwell (Peppery Old Gent), Paul Dawkins (Nazi General), Sam Kydd (Nazi Orderly), Michael Knowles (Staff Captain), Fred Griffiths (Bert King), John Baskcomb (Mayor), Colin Bean (Private Sponge), Alvar Liddell (Newsreader - voice. Big screen spin-off from the popular television series. *Dir.* Norman Cohen.

Daleks – Invasion Earth: 2150 A.D. (1966) Peter Cushing (Dr. Who), Roberta Tovey (Susan), Bernard Cribbins (PC Tom Campbell), Ray Brooks (David), Andrew Keir (Wyler), Jill Curzon (Louise), Roger Avon (Wells), Geoffrey Cheshire (Roboman), Keith Marsh (Conway), Philip Madoc (Brockley), Steve Peters (Leader Roboman), Eddie Powell (Thompson), Godfrey Quigley (Dortmun), Sheila Steafel (Young woman). The time travelling Doctor must foil the Dalek's fiendish plans for Earth with the help of his grand-daughter Susan, his niece Louise and PC Campbell. The second and last incarnation of Peter Cushing's Doctor (see also *Dr Who and the Daleks*). *Dir.* Gordon Flemyng.

Dam Busters, The (1955) Richard Todd (Wing Commander Guy Gibson), Michael Redgrave (Dr Barnes Wallis), Ursula Jeans (Mrs Molly Wallis), Basil Sydney (Air Chief Marshal Sir Arthur Harris), Patrick Barr (Captain Joseph "Mutt" Summers), Ernest Clark (Air Vice-Marshal Ralph Cochrane), Derek Farr (Group Captain John Whitworth), Charles Carson (Doctor), Stanley Van Beers (David Pye), Colin Tapley (Dr William Glanville), Frederick Leister (Committee Member), Eric Messiter (Committee Member), Laidman Browne (Committee Member), Raymond Huntley (National Physical Laboratory Official), Hugh Manning (Ministry of Aircraft Production Official), Laurence Naismith (Farmer), Nigel Stock (Flying Officer Frederick Spafford), Brian Nissen (Flight Lieutenant Torger Taerum), Robert Shaw (Flight Sergeant John Pulford), Peter Assinder (Pilot Officer Andrew Deering, Bill Kerr (Flight Lieutenant H. B. "Micky" Martin), George Baker (Flight Lieutenant David Maltby), Ronald Wilson (Flight Lieutenant Dave Shannon), Denys Graham (Flying Officer Les Knight), Harold Goodwin (Gibson's Batman), Gerald Harper (uncredited), Philip Latham (uncredited), Patrick McGoohan (uncredited). The story of Operation Chastise, the May 1943 attack on the Ruhr dams using the innovative "bouncing bomb" designed by Barnes Wallis. The film shows both the development of the bomb and the raid. Based on the books *The Dam Busters* by Paul Brickhill and *Enemy Coast Ahead* by Guy Gibson. The famous theme music *The Dam Busters March* was composed by Eric Coates. *Dir.* Michael Anderson.

Damage (1992) Jeremy Irons (Dr. Stephen Fleming), Juliette Binoche (Anna Barton), Miranda Richardson (Ingrid Fleming), Rupert Graves (Martyn Fleming), Leslie Caron (Elizabeth Prideaux), Ian Bannen (Edward Lloyd), Peter Stormare (Peter Wetzler), David Thewlis (Detective), Gemma Clarke (Sally Fleming), Ray Gravell (Raymond), Julian Fellowes (Donald Lyndsay, MP), Tony Doyle (Prime Minister), Susan Engel (Miss Snow), Jeff Nuttall (Trevor Leigh Davies MP), Roger Llewellyn (Palmer), Barry Stearn (Prime Minister's Aide), Linda Delapena (Beth), Francine Stock (TV Interviewer), Henry Power (Henry). A cabinet minister starts an affair with his son's fiancé and his obsession threatens his career. Based on the novel of the same name by Josephine Hart. *Dir.* Louis Malle.

Damned United, The (2009) Michael Sheen (Brian Clough), Timothy Spall (Peter Taylor), Colm Meaney (Don Revie),

Elizabeth Carling (Barbara Clough), Oliver Stokes (Nigel Clough), Ryan Day (Simon Clough), Jim Broadbent (Sam Longson), Brian McCardie (Dave Mackay), Martin Compston (John O'Hare), Colin Harris (John McGovern), Maurice Roëves (Jimmy Gordon), Henry Goodman (Manny Cussins), Jimmy Reddington (Keith Archer), Liam Thomas (Les Cocker), Peter McDonald (Johnny Giles), Stephen Graham (Billy Bremner), Danny Tomlinson (David Harvey), Lesley Maylett (Paul Reaney), Chris Moore (Paul Madeley), John Savage (Gordon McQueen), Mark Cameron (Norman Hunter), Tom Ramsbottom (Trevor Cherry), Matthew Storton (Peter Lorimer), Bill Bradshaw (Terry Yorath), Stuart Gray (Eddie Gray), Alex Harker (Allan Clarke), Craig Williams (Joe Jordan), Joe Dempsie (Duncan McKenzie), Giles Alderson (Colin Todd), Stewart Robertson (Archie Gemmill), Laurie Rea (Terry Hennessey), Tomasz Kocinski (Roy McFarland), Peter Quinn (Bob Matthewson), A highly fictional version of Brian Clough's 44 day tenure as manager of Leeds United in 1974. Adapted from David Peace's novel of the same name. *Dir.* Tom Hooper.

Damned, The (1963) Macdonald Carey (Simon Wells), Shirley Anne Field (Joan), Viveca Lindfors (Freya Neilson), Alexander Knox (Bernard), Oliver Reed (King), Walter Gotell (Major Holland), James Villiers (Captain Gregory), Tom Kempinski (Ted), Kenneth Cope (Sid), Brian Oulton (Mr. Dingle), Barbara Everest (Miss Lamont), James Maxwell (Mr. Talbot), Nicholas Clay (Richard), Kit Williams (Henry), Rachel Clay (Victoria), Caroline Sheldon (Elizabeth), David Palmer (George), John Thompson (Charles), Christopher Witty (William), Rebecca Dignam (Anne), Siobhan Taylor (Mary). Whilst trying to elude a biker gang, Simon and Joan discover children confined beneath a military base. The children are cold to the touch and only usually approached by men in radiation suits. Based on H.L. Lawrence's novel *The Children of Light. Dir.* Joseph Losey.

Dance Hall (1950) Donald Houston (Phil), Bonar Colleano (Alec), Petula Clark (Georgie Wilson), Natasha Parry (Eve), Jane Hylton (Mary), Diana Dors (Carole), Gladys Henson (Mrs Wilson), Sydney Tafler (Jim Fairfax), Douglas Barr (Peter), Fred Johnson (Mr Wilson), James Carney (Mike), Kay Kendall (Doreen), Eunice Gayson (Mona), Dandy Nichols (Mrs Crabtree), Grace Arnold (Mrs Bennett), Alec Finter (Palais instructor), Harry Fowler (Amorous youth), Harold Goodwin (Jack), Thomas Heathcote (Fred), Tonie MacMillan (Mrs. Hepple), Michael Trubshawe (Colonel), Alma Cogan (Dancer), Doris Hare (Blonde), Geraldo (Himself), Ted Heath (Himself). Four young women factory workers escape from their everyday lives by regularly visiting the local Palais de Dance. *Dir.* Charles Crichton.

Dancing Years, The (1950) Dennis Price (Rudi Kleiber), Gisèle Préville (Maria Zeitler), Patricia Dainton (Grete), Anthony Nicholls (Prince Reinaldt), Grey Blake (Franzl), Muriel George (Hatti), Olive Gilbert (Frau Kurt), Martin Ross (Tenor), Gerald Case (Rudi's Secretary), Carl Jaffe (Headwaiter), Jeremy Spenser (Maria's Son). A musical about a composer in old Vienna and the two loves of his life. *Dir.* Harold French.

Dandy Dick (1935) Will Hay (Vicar the Rev. Richard Jedd), Nancy Burne (Pamela Jedd), Esmond Knight (Tony Mardon), Davy Burnaby (Sir William Mardon), Mignon O'Doherty (Georgiana Jedd), Syd Crossley (Wilkins), Robert Nainby (Bale), John Singer (Freddie), Antonia Brough (Mrs. Hannah Topping), Jimmy Godden (Creecher), Hal Gordon (Mullins), Kathleen Harrison (Jane), Moore Marriott (Stableboy), Prince Monolulu (Racing Tipster), Wally Patch (Police Constable Topping). A vicar tries various schemes to raise money to fix his church's crooked steeple and eventually turns to gambling on a racehorse. Based on the play of the same name by Arthur Wing Pinero. *Dir.* William Beaudine.

Dandy in Aspic, A (1968) Laurence Harvey (Eberlin), Tom Courtenay (Gatiss), Mia Farrow (Caroline), Harry Andrews (Fraser), Peter Cook (Prentiss), Lionel Stander (Sobakevich), Per Oscarsson (Pavel), Barbara Murray (Miss Vogler), John Bird (Henderson), Norman Bird (Copperfield), Geoffrey Bayldon (Lake), Calvin Lockhart (Brogue), James Cossins (Heston-Stevas), Michael Trubshawe (Flowers), Geoffrey Lumsden (Ridley), Elspeth March (Lady Hetherington), Richard O'Sullivan (Nevil), Mike Pratt (Greff), George Murcell (Sergeant Harris), Vernon Dobtcheff (Stein). Double agent Eberlin is given a mission which it is impossible for him to carry out – to eliminate himself! Will his partner on the assignment discover the truth? Based on the novel of the same name by Derek Marlowe. *Dir.* Anthony Mann.

Danger Within (1959) Richard Todd (Lt. Col. David Baird), Bernard Lee (Lt. Col. Huxley), Michael Wilding (Major Charles Marquand), Richard Attenborough (Capt. 'Bunter' Phillips), Dennis Price (Capt. Rupert Callender), Donald Houston (Capt. Roger Byfold), William Franklyn (Capt. Tony Long), Vincent Ball (Capt. Pat Foster), Peter Arne (Capitano Benucci), Peter Jones (Capt. Alfred Piker), Ronnie Stevens (Lt. Meynell, 'The Sewer Rat'), Terence Alexander (Lt. Gibbs), Andrew Faulds (Lt. Comdr. 'Dopey' Gibbon, R.N.), Steve Norbert (Lt. Pierre Dessin), Cyril Shaps (Lt. Cyriakos Coutoules), Eric Lander (Lt. Tim O'Brien), John Dearth (Lt. Robson), Robert Bruce ('Doc' Simmonds, R.A.M.C.), Harold Siddons (Capt. 'Tag' Burchnall), Ian Whittaker (2nd. Lt. Betts-Hanger), David Williams (Lt. Parsons), David Graham (Lt. Moxhay), Howard Williams (Lt. Bush), Dino Galvani (Commandante Arletti), Michael Caine (Prisoner with Pin-Up), Max Faulkner (Hamlet Play POW), John Leyton (Prisoner). A WWII POW escape drama, this time set in Italy. *Dir.* Don Chaffey.

Dark Crystal, The (1982) Voices of: Stephen Garlick (Jen), Lisa Maxwell (Kira), Billie Whitelaw (Aughra), Percy Edwards (Fizzgig), Barry Dennen (SkekSil/The Chamberlain), Michael Kilgarriff (SkekUng/The Garthim Master), Jerry Nelson (SkekZok/The Ritual Master and SkekSo/The Emperor), Thick Wilson (SkekAyuk/The Gourmand), Brian Muehl (SkekEkt/The Ornamentalist), John Baddeley (SkekOk/The Scroll Keeper), David Buck (SkekNa/The Slave Master), Charles Collingwood (SkekShod/The Treasurer), Steve Whitmire (SkekTek/The Scientist), Sean Barrett (UrSu/The Master and UrZah/The Ritual Guardian), Joseph O'Conor (the narrator and UngIm). A fantasy film made using animatronics. On the planet Thra, Jen, apparently the last of the Gelflings, is tasked with restoring order and fulfilling his destiny by healing the Crystal of Truth. *Dirs.* Jim Henson and Frank Oz.

Dark Eyes of London (1939) Bela Lugosi (Dr. Feodor Orloff/Prof. John Dearborn), Hugh Williams (Det. Insp. Larry Holt), Greta Gynt (Diana Stuart), Edmon Ryan (Lieutenant Patrick O'Reilly), Wilfred Walter (Jake), Alexander Field (Fred Grogan). A series of deaths in London are linked to a home for the blind run by Prof. John Dearborn and to an insurance agent called Feodor Orloff. Adapted from a novel of the same name by Edgar Wallace. *Dir.* Walter Summers.

Darklands (1997) Craig Fairbrass (Frazer Truick), Jon Finch (David Keller), Rowena King (Rachel Morris), Roger Nott (Dennis Cox), Dave Duffy (Carver), Richard Lynch (Salvy), Bob Blythe (McCullen), Nicola Branson (Becky), Hubert Rees (Bill Sawyer), Philip Babot (Chainsaw), Morega Polser (May Queen), Ian Deveraux (Green Man), William Thomas (Detective Jarvis), Beth Morris (Doctor Morgan), Ray Gravell (Bearded Gypsy), Kim Ryan (Scared Gypsy). Whilst investigating a death, journalist Frazer Truick finds himself involved with a religious cult which practises devil worship. *Dir.* Julian Richards.

Darling (1965) Laurence Harvey (Miles Brand), Dirk Bogarde (Robert Gold), Julie Christie (Diana Scott), José Luis de Vilallonga (Prince Cesare della Romita), Roland Curram (Malcolm), Basil Henson (Alec Prosser-Jones), Helen Lindsay (Felicity Prosser-Jones), Tyler Butterworth (William Prosser-Jones), Alex Scott (Sean Martin), Brian Wilde (Basil Willett), Pauline Yates (Estelle Gold), Trevor Bowen (Tony Bridges), Carlo Palmucci (Curzio), Peter Bayliss (Lord Alex Grant), Georgina Cookson (Carlotta Hale), Hugo Dyson (Walter Southgate), John Woodvine (Customs Officer). Model Diana Scott uses her relationships to help build her career. The film won three Academy Awards; Best Actress (Julie Christie), Best Costume (Julie Harris) and Best Writing, Story and Screenplay - Written Directly for the Screen (Frederic Raphael). *Dir.* John Schlesinger.

Date with a Dream, A (1948) Terry-Thomas (Terry), Jeannie Carson (Jean), Len Lowe (Len), Bill Lowe (Bill), Wally Patch (Uncle), Vic Lewis (Vic), Ida Patlanski (Bedelia), Joey Porter (Max Imshy). A year after being demobbed, four wartime entertainers decide to reform. *Dir.* Dicky Leeman.

Davy (1957) Harry Secombe (Davy Morgan), Alexander Knox (Sir Giles Manning), Ron Randell (George), George Relph (Uncle Pat Morgan), Susan Shaw (Gwen), Bill Owen (Eric), Isabel Dean (Miss Helen Carstairs), Adele Leigh (Joanna Reeves), Peter Frampton (Tim), Joan Sims (Tea Lady), Gladys Henson (Beatrice, Tea Lady), George Moon (Jerry), Clarkson Rose (Mrs. Magillicuddy), Kenneth Connor (Herbie), Liz Fraser (Tea Lady), Charles Lamb (Henry), Arnold Marlé (Mr. Winkler), Campbell Singer (Stage Doorkeeper). Davy, the star of his family's music hall act, is given the chance to go solo. The last of the Ealing Comedies. *Dir*. Michael Relph.

Day of the Jackal, The (1973) Edward Fox (The Jackal), Adrien Cayla-Legrand (President Charles de Gaulle), Michael Lonsdale (Claude Lebel Commissioner), Cyril Cusack (The Gunsmith), Terence Alexander (Lloyd), Alan Badel (The Minister), Tony Britton (Inspector Thomas), Maurice Denham (General Colbert), Delphine Seyrig (Colette de Montpellier), Philippe Léotard (Policeman), Michel Auclair (Colonel Rolland), Denis Carey (Casson), Vernon Dobtcheff (The Interrogator), Jacques François (Pascal), Olga Georges-Picot (Denise), Raymond Gérôme (Flavigny), Edward Hardwicke (Charles Calthrop), Barrie Ingham (St. Clair), Derek Jacobi (Caron), Jean Martin (Wolenski), Ronald Pickup (The Forger), Eric Porter (Col. Rodin), Anton Rodgers (Bernard), Donald Sinden (Mallinson), David Swift (Montclair), Timothy West (Berthier). "The Jackal", a killer for hire, is paid $500,000 to kill President Charles de Gaulle. The film follows his preparations and the attempts of the French police to thwart him. Based on the novel of the same name by Frederick Forsyth. *Dir*. Fred Zinnemann.

Day of the Triffids, The (1962) Howard Keel (Bill Masen), Nicole Maurey (Christine Durrant), Janette Scott (Karen Goodwin), Kieron Moore (Tom Goodwin), Mervyn Johns (Mr. Coker), Ewan Roberts (Dr. Soames), Alison Leggatt (Miss Coker), Geoffrey Matthews (Luis de la Vega), Janina Faye (Susan), Gilgi Hauser (Teresa de la Vega), John Tate (Captain, SS Midland), Carole Ann Ford (Bettina), Arthur Gross (Flight 356 Radioman), Colette Wilde (Nurse Jamieson), Ian Wilson (Greenhouse Watchman), Victor Brooks (Poiret). Unluckily for Bill Masen he misses a beautiful meteor shower display because he was in hospital with his eyes bandaged. Luckily for him it means he is not struck down with blindness as is 99% of the rest of the Earth's population. However, the meteor shower also brought spores to a deadly man-killing plant – the triffid. Loosely based on John Wyndham's science fiction novel of the same name. *Dir*. Steve Sekely.

Day the Earth Caught Fire, The (1961) Janet Munro (Jeannie Craig), Leo McKern (Bill Maguire), Edward Judd (Peter Stenning), Michael Goodliffe ('Jacko', Night editor), Bernard Braden (News editor), Reginald Beckwith (Harry), Gene Anderson (May), Renée Asherson (Angela), Arthur Christiansen (Jeff Jefferson the Editor), Austin Trevor (Sir John Kelly), Edward Underdown (Sanderson), Ian Ellis (Michael Stenning), John Barron (1st Sub-Editor), Timothy Bateson (printer), Peter Blythe (Copy Desk), Peter Butterworth (2nd Sub-Editor), Norman Chappell (hotel receptionist), Geoffrey Chater (Pat Holroyd), Pamela Green (nurse), Carmel McSharry (woman lost in fog), Charles Morgan (Foreign Editor), Marianne Stone (Miss Evans). As an unscheduled solar eclipse occurs and a series of climatic and natural disasters hit around the world it emerges that the super-powers have set off H-bombs simultaneously on different sides of the world and may have tilted the Earth's access. Told in flashback through the investigations of journalists working for the *Daily Express*, the world discovers that the truth is far worse even than this. Filmed in a documentary style. Arthur Christiansen had been the editor of the *Daily Express* from 1933 to 1957. *Dir*. Val Guest.

Day the Fish Came Out, The (1967) Tom Courtenay (The Navigator), Colin Blakely (The Pilot), Sam Wanamaker (Elias), Candice Bergen (Electra Brown), Ian Ogilvy (Peter), Dimitris Nikolaidis (The Dentist), Nicolas Alexios (Goatherd), Patricia Burke (Mrs Mavroyannis), Paris Alexander (Fred), Arthur Mitchell (Frank), Tom Klunis (Mr French). Comedy. A NATO plane is forced to jettison its nuclear payload and the mysterious "Container Q" over the Greek island of Karos. *Dir*. Michael Cacoyannis.

Day They Robbed the Bank of England, The (1960) Aldo Ray (Charles Norgate), Elizabeth Sellars (Iris Muldoon), Peter O'Toole (Capt. Monty Fitch), Kieron Moore (Walsh), Albert Sharpe (Albert Tosher Sparrow), Joseph Tomelty (Cohoun), Wolf Frees (Dr. Hagen), John Le Mesurier (Green), Miles Malleson (Assistant Curator), Colin Gordon (Benge), Andrew Keir (Sergeant of the Guard), Hugh Griffith (O'Shea), Geoffrey Bayldon (The Bombardier bartender), Erik Chitty (Gudgeon), Charles Lloyd Pack (Mr. Peabody), Arthur Lowe (Bank Official), Anita Sharp-Bolster (Maid). In 1901, three IRA men plan to rob the Bank of England via a disused sewer. *Dir*. John Guillermin.

Day Will Dawn, The (1942) Hugh Williams (Colin Metcalfe), Griffith Jones (Police Inspector Gunter), Deborah Kerr (Kari Alstad), Ralph Richardson (Frank Lockwood), Francis L. Sullivan (Commandant Ulrich Wettau), Roland Culver (Cmdr. Pittwaters), Finlay Currie (Capt. Alstad), Niall MacGinnis (Olaf), Elizabeth Mann (Gerda), Raymond Huntley (Norwegian Under Secretary), Patricia Medina (Ingrid), Roland Pertwee (Capt. Waverley), Henry Oscar (Newspaper Editor), David Horne (Evans, Foreign Editor), Henry Hewitt (Jack, News Editor), John Warwick (Milligan, Reporter in Fleet Street Pub), Brefni O'Rorke (Political Journalist), Bernard Miles (McAllister), Beckett Bould (Bergen), George Carney (Harry), Meriel Forbes (Milly, the Barmaid), H Victor Weske (Heinrich), Albert Chevalier (Receptionist), Valentine Dyall (German Guard), Jack Watling (Lieutenant). Journalist Colin Metcalfe is made foreign correspondent in neutral Norway as the Germans invade Poland in 1939. Despite warnings of German intentions towards Norway he is brought back to England only to return again when the Germans invade. *Dir*. Harold French.

Daybreak (1948) Ann Todd (Frankie), Eric Portman (Eddie), Maxwell Reed (Olaf), Edward Rigby (Bill Shackle), Bill Owen (Ron), Eliot Makeham (Mr. Bigley), Jane Hylton (Doris), Margaret Withers (Mrs.Bigley), John Turnbull (Superintendent), Maurice Denham (Inspector), Milton Rosmer (Governor), Lyn Evans (Waterman). Film noir in which one of England's official hangmen marries and sets up home on a Thames barge, although his new wife is unaware of his secret occupation. *Dir*. Compton Bennett.

Dead Man's Shoes (2004) Paddy Considine (Richard), Toby Kebbell (Anthony), Gary Stretch (Sonny), Emily Aston (Patti), Neil Bell (Soz), Jo Hartley (Jo), Craig Considine (Craig), Matt Considine (Matt), Andrew Shim (Elvis). Disaffected soldier Richard returns to his home town in order to wreak revenge on the thugs who terrorized his brother. *Dirs*. Shane Meadows and Paddy Considine.

Dead of Night (1945) Mervyn Johns (Walter Craig), Anthony Baird (Hugh Grainger), Michael Redgrave (Maxwell Frere), Roland Culver (Eliot Foley), Renée Gadd (Mrs. Craig), Sally Ann Howes (Sally O'Hara), Barbara Leake (Mrs O'Hara), Mary Merrall (Mrs Foley), Frederick Valk (Dr. van Straaten), Googie Withers (Joan Cortland), Judy Kelly (Joyce Grainger), Miles Malleson (Hearse Driver/Bus Conductor/Jailer), Robert Wyndham (Dr. Albury), Michael Allan (Jimmy Watson), Sally Ann Howes (Sally O'Hara), Barbara Leake (Mrs O'Hara), Ralph Michael (Peter Cortland), Esmé Percy (Mr. Rutherford), Peggy Bryan (Mary Lee), Basil Radford (George Parratt), Naunton Wayne (Larry Potter), Allan Jeayes (Maurice Olcott), Magda Kun (Mitzi), Garry Marsh (Harry Parker), Hartley Power (Sylvester Kee), Elisabeth Welch (Beulah). Guests at a country house dinner party entertain each other with various tales of uncanny or supernatural events including the story of an unbalanced ventriloquist (Michael Redgrave) who believes his dummy is truly alive. A portmanteau horror film made by Ealing Studios, with its various episodes directed by Alberto Cavalcanti (Ventriloquist's Dummy and Christmas Party sequences), Charles Crichton (Golfing Story), Basil Dearden (linking narrative and Hearse Driver sequence) and Robert Hamer (Haunted Mirror).

Dead, The (1987) Anjelica Huston (Gretta Conroy), Donal McCann (Gabriel Conroy), Dan O'Herlihy (Mr. Browne), Donal Donnelly (Freddy Malins), Helena Carroll (Aunt Kate), Cathleen Delany (Aunt Julia), Ingrid Craigie (Mary Jane), Rachael Dowling (Lily), Marie Kean (Mrs. Malins), Frank Patterson (Bartell D'Arcy), Maria McDermottroe (Molly Ivors), Sean McClory (Mr. Grace), Colm Meaney (Mr. Bergin). Set during an Epiphany party held by two elderly sisters in Dublin in 1904. Adapted from the short story *The Dead* by James Joyce (from his short works collection *Dubliners*). *Dir.* John Huston (his last film).

Deadfall (1968) Michael Caine (Henry Stuart Clarke), Giovanna Ralli (Fé Moreau), Eric Portman (Richard Moreau), David Buck (Salinas), Leonard Rossiter (Fillmore), Geraldine Sherman (Delgado's Receptionist), Carlos Pierre (Antonio), Vladek Sheybal (Dr. Delgado), John Barry (Symphony Orchestra Conductor), Philip Madoc (Bank Manager). Cat burglar Henry Clarke gets involved with a couple of fellow crooks with tragic results. *Dir.* Bryan Forbes.

Deadlier than the Male (1967) Richard Johnson (Hugh 'Bulldog' Drummond), Elke Sommer (Irma Eckman), Sylva Koscina (Penelope), Nigel Green (Carl Petersen), Suzanna Leigh (Grace), Steve Carlson (Robert Drummond), Virginia North (Brenda), Justine Lord (Miss Peggy Ashenden), Leonard Rossiter (Henry Bridgenorth), Laurence Naismith (Sir John Bledlow), Zia Mohyeddin (King Fedra), Lee Montague (Boxer), Milton Reid (Chang), Yasuko Nagazumi (Mitsouko), Didi Sydow (Anna), George Pastell (Carloggio), Dervis Ward (Henry Keller), John Stone (David Wyngarde), William Mervyn (Chairman of the Phoenician Board), George Sewell (Car Park Assassin). Detective Bulldog Drummond, with the help of his American Nephew Robert, is on the trail of two beautiful female assassins. Based on the Bulldog Drummond series of books created by "Sapper", a pseudonym of Herman Cyril McNeile. *Dir.* Ralph Thomas.

Deadly Affair, The (1966) James Mason (Charles Dobbs), Simone Signoret (Elsa Fennan), Maximilian Schell (Dieter Frey), Harriet Andersson (Ann Dobbs), Harry Andrews (Inspector Mendel), Kenneth Haigh (Bill Appleby), Roy Kinnear (Adam Scarr), Max Adrian (Adviser), Lynn Redgrave (Virgin), Robert Flemyng (Samuel Fennan), Leslie Sands (Inspector), Corin Redgrave (David). A spy investigates the suicide of a colleague. Based on John le Carré's novel *Call for the Dead*. For the film George Smiley, who is the central character in the book, is renamed as Charles Dobbs. *Dir.* Sidney Lumet

Deadly Bees, The (1966) Suzanna Leigh (Vicki Robbins), Frank Finlay (H.W. Manfred), Guy Doleman (Ralph Hargrove), Catherine Finn (Mary Hargrove), John Harvey (Thompson), Michael Ripper (David Hawkins), Anthony Bailey (Compere), Tim Barrett (Harcourt), James Cossins (Coroner), Frank Forsyth (Doctor), Percy Edwards (Tess the Dog - voice), Ronnie Wood (Member of The Birds). A farmer trains his swarm of bees to attack "the smell of fear". Based on H.F. Heard's novel *A Taste for Honey*. *Dir.* Freddie Francis.

Dean Spanley (2008) Jeremy Northam (Fisk Junior), Peter O'Toole (Fisk Senior), Sam Neill (the Dean), Bryan Brown (Wrather), Judy Parfitt (Mrs Brimley), Dudley Sutton (Mariott), Charlotte Graham (woman in the park), Eva Sayer (a girl), James Lever (the cricketer), Ramon Tikaram (the Nawab of Ranjiput). A joint New Zealand and British comedy-drama. The film explores the relationship between Fisk Snr and Jnr which has become strained since the loss of Fisk Snr's wife and other son. They attend a lecture by a swami about the transmigration of souls which leads to a meeting with Dean Spanley, who has odd experiences when drinking Tokay. Based on Lord Dunsany's novel *My Talks with Dean Spanley*. *Dir.* Toa Fraser.

Dear Murderer (1947) Eric Portman (Lee Warren), Greta Gynt (Vivien Warren), Dennis Price (Richard Fenton), Jack Warner (Insp. Penbury), Maxwell Reed (Jimmy Martin), Hazel Court (Avis Fenton), Jane Hylton (Rita), Andrew Crawford (Sgt. Fox), Charles Rolfe (Prison Warder), Hélène Burls (Charwoman), Ernest Butcher (Hall Porter), Judith Carol (American Secretary), Valerie Ward (Warren's Secretary), John Blythe (Ernie), Vic Hagan (American Barman), Howard Douglas (Doctor). A man kills his wife's lover and makes it look like he committed suicide because she dumped him. However, he then discovers that the couple had parted months before and she has taken another lover. *Dir.* Arthur Crabtree.

Death on the Nile (1978) Peter Ustinov (Hercule Poirot), Lois Chiles (Linnet Ridgeway Doyle), Simon MacCorkindale (Simon Doyle), Mia Farrow (Jacqueline De Bellefort), Jane Birkin (Louise Bourget), George Kennedy (Andrew Pennington), Bette Davis (Marie Van Schuyler), Maggie Smith (Miss Bowers), Angela Lansbury (Salome Otterbourne), Olivia Hussey (Rosalie Otterbourne), David Niven (Colonel Johnny Race), Jon Finch (Mr. James Ferguson), Jack Warden (Dr. Bessner), Celia Imrie (Maid), Harry Andrews (Barnstable), Sam Wanamaker (Rockford), I. S. Johar (Mr. Choudry). Whilst travelling down the Nile, Poirot is called upon to solve the murder of wealthy heiress Linnet Ridgeway. Which member of the all-star cast, if any, is responsible? The film won an Oscar for Best Costume Design. Based on the Agatha Christie mystery novel of the same name. *Dir.* John Guillermin.

Deathwatch (2002) Jamie Bell (Private Charlie Shakespeare), Ruaidhri Conroy (Private Colin Chevasse), Mike Downey (Captain Martin Plummer), Laurence Fox (Captain Bramwell Jennings), Dean Lennox Kelly (Private Willie McNess), Torben Liebrecht (Friedrich), Kris Marshall (Private Barry Starinski), Hans Matheson (Private Jack Hawkstone), Hugh O'Conor (Private Anthony Bradford), Matthew Rhys (Corporal "Doc" Fairweather), Andy Serkis (Private Thomas Quinn), Hugo Speer (Sergeant David Tate). After going over the top, a group of British WWI soldiers pass through some thick fog and find themselves in German trenches. However, all does not seem as it should. *Dir.* Michael J. Bassett.

Deep Blue Sea, The (1955) Vivien Leigh (Hester Collyer), Kenneth More (Freddie Page), Eric Portman (Miller), Emlyn Williams (Sir William Collyer), Moira Lister (Dawn Maxwell), Alec McCowen (Ken Thompson), Dandy Nichols (Mrs. Elton), Arthur Hill (Jackie Jackson), Jimmy Hanley (Dicer Durston), Miriam Karlin (Barmaid), Heather Thatcher (Lady Dawson), Bill Shine (Golfer), Brian Oulton (Drunk), Gibb McLaughlin (Clerk), Sid James (Man outside bar). Hester Collyer leaves her husband, a High Court Judge, for a troubled former RAF pilot. Britain's first film in CinemaScope and DeLuxe colour. Based on Terence Rattigan's 1952 play. *Dir.* Anatole Litvak.

Deep Blue Sea, The (2011) Rachel Weisz (Hester Collyer), Tom Hiddleston (Freddie Page), Simon Russell Beale (William Collyer), Harry Hadden-Paton (Jackie Jackson), Ann Mitchell (Mrs Elton). Based on Terence Rattigan's 1952 play. *Dir.* Terence Davies.

Deep End (1970) Jane Asher (Susan), John Moulder-Brown (Mike), Karl Michael Vogler (Swimming instructor), Christopher Sandford (Chris), Diana Dors (Lady client), Louise Martini (Prostitute), Anita Lochner (Kathy), Cheryl Hall (Hot Dog Girl), Gerald Rowland (Mike's Friend), Burt Kwouk (Hot Dog Salesman), Uli Steigberg (Mike's Father), Erika Wackernagel (Mike's Mother), Jerzy Skolimowski (Passenger). Mike, a 15 year old, becomes obsessed with Susan a co-worker at the local swimming baths. His obsession will have tragic results. *Dir.* Jerzy Skolimowski.

Defence of the Realm (1985) Gabriel Byrne (Nick Mullen), Greta Scacchi (Nina Beckman), Denholm Elliott (Vernon Bayliss), Ian Bannen (Dennis Markham), Fulton Mackay (Victor Kingsbrook), Bill Paterson (Jack Macleod), David Calder (Harry Champion), Frederick Treves (Arnold Reece), Robbie Coltrane (Leo McAskey), Annabel Leventon (Trudy Markham), Graham Fletcher-Cook (Micky Parker), Steven Woodcock (Steven Dyce), Alexei Jawdokimov (Dietrich Kleist), Danny Webb (Danny Royce), Prentis Hancock (Frank Longman), Michael Johnson (Humphrey Channing), Mark Tandy (Philip Henderson), Laurance Rudic (Charlie), James Fleet (Ministry Man). Journalist Nick Mullen investigates the events which prompt the resignation of an MP opposed to nuclear armament. *Dir.* David Drury.

Demi-Paradise, The (1943) Laurence Olivier (Ivan Kouznetsoff), Penelope Dudley-Ward (Ann Tisdall), Marjorie Fielding (Mrs. Tisdall), Margaret Rutherford (Rowena Ventnor), Felix Aylmer (Mr. Runalow), George Thorpe (Herbert Tisdall), Leslie Henson (Himself), Guy Middleton (Dick Christian), Michael Shepley (Mr. Walford), Edie Martin (Miss Winifred Tisdall), Muriel Aked (Mrs. Tisdall-Stanton), Joyce Grenfell (Sybil Paulson), Everley

Gregg (Mrs. Flannel), Jack Watling (Tom), David Keir (Jordan), Miles Malleson (Theatre Cashier), Aubrey Mallalieu (Toomes, the Butler), John Laurie (Wounded Sailor), Brian Nissen (George Tisdall), John Boxer (British Sailor), Johnnie Schofield (Ernie), George Cole (Percy), Harry Fowler (Small Boy), Wilfrid Hyde-White (Nightclub Waiter). A Russian engineer arrives in Britain in the late 1930s and finds out more about the British way of life and attitudes and in the process falls in love with an English girl. The film was released when Britain and the Soviet Union were allies during WWII. *Dir.* Anthony Asquith.

Demons of the Mind (1972) Robert Hardy (Baron Zorn), Shane Briant (Emil), Gillian Hills (Elizabeth), Yvonne Mitchell (Hilda), Paul Jones (Carl Richter), Patrick Magee (Falkenberg), Kenneth J. Warren (Klaus), Michael Hordern (Priest), Robert Brown (Fischinger), Virginia Wetherell (Inge), Deirdre Costello (Magda), Barry Stanton (Ernst), Sidonie Bond (Zorn's Wife), Thomas Heathcote (Coachman), Sheila Raynor (Crone). A Baron imprisons his teenage children in the belief that they will become mentally unstable as did their mother. The locals are worried about a spate of murders in the area and then a doctor arrives who says that he can cure the children of their "bad blood". *Dir.* Peter Sykes.

Dentist in the Chair (1960) Bob Monkhouse (David Cookson), Peggy Cummins (Peggy Travers), Kenneth Connor (Sam Field), Eric Barker (The Dean), Ronnie Stevens (Brian Dexter), Vincent Ball (Michaels), Eleanor Summerfield (Ethel), Reginald Beckwith (Mr. Watling), Stuart Saunders (Inspector Richardson), Ian Wallace (Dentist), Peggy Simpson (Miss Brent), Jean St. Clair (Lucy), Rosie Lee as Maggie), Sheree Winton (Jayne). The misadventures of two student dentists. *Dir.* Don Chaffey.

Dentist on the Job (1961) Bob Monkhouse (David Cookson), Kenneth Connor (Sam Field), Ronnie Stevens (Brian Dexter), Shirley Eaton (Jill Venner), Eric Barker (Colonel J.J. Proudfoot/The Dean), Reginald Beckwith (Mr. Duff), Richard Wattis (Macreedy), Charles Hawtrey (Mr. Roper), Richard Caldicot (Prison Governor), Cyril Chamberlain (Director), David Horne (Admiral Southbound), Graham Stark (Sourfaced Man), Alec Dane (Gong Man), Alf Dean (Bruiser), David Glover (Mr. Bull), Mercy Haystead (Miss Figg), Valerie Holman (Carol Potter), Patrick Holt (Newsreader), Bettine Le Beau (Judith Dobbin), Sheena Marshe (Lolita Roughage), Charlotte Mitchell (Mrs. Burke), Valerie Pitts (Pat Horrocks), Ian Whittaker (Mr. Fuller), Julian Holloway (Man on Phone in Factory), Keith Fordyce (Himself), Michael Miles (Himself). Two young dentists are chosen by a big pharmaceutical company to front an advertising campaign for a tooth-paste called "Dreem". A sequel to *Dentist in the Chair*. *Dir.* C.M. Pennington-Richards.

Derby Day (1952) Anna Neagle (Lady Helen Forbes), Michael Wilding (David Scott), Googie Withers (Betty Molloy), John McCallum (Tommy Dillon), Peter Graves (Gerald Berkeley), Suzanne Cloutier (Michele Jolivet), Gordon Harker (Joe Jenkins), Edwin Styles (Sir George Forbes), Gladys Henson (Gladys Jenkins), Nigel Stock (Jim Molloy), Ralph Reader (Bill Hammond), Tom Walls Jr. (Gilpin), Josephine Fitzgerald (O'Shaughnessy), Alfie Bass (Spider Wilkes), Toni Edgar-Bruce (Mrs. Harbottle-Smith), Ewan Roberts (Studio Driver), Leslie Weston (Capt. Goggs), Sam Kydd (Harry Bunn), Michael Ripper (1st Newspaper Reporter), Richard Wattis (Editor), Brian Johnston (Interviewer), Raymond Glendenning (Narration and Commentary), Prince Monolulu (Himself), The stories of various characters on their way to the races at Epsom on Derby Day. One of a number of Neagle/Wilding films directed by Neagle's husband. The father of actor Tom Walls junior (Tom Kirby Walls), was a well-known character actor but also trained racehorses and trained *April the Fifth* to win the 1932 Epsom Derby. *Dir.* Herbert Wilcox.

Descent, The (2005) Shauna Macdonald (Sarah), Natalie Mendoza (Juno), Alex Reid (Beth), Saskia Mulder (Rebecca), MyAnna Buring (Sam), Nora-Jane Noone (Holly), Oliver Milburn (Paul), Molly Kayll (Jessica), Craig Conway, Leslie Simpson, Mark Cronfield, Stephen Lamb, Catherine Dyson, Julie Ellis, Sophie Trott, Tristan Matthiae, Stuart Luis, Justin Hackney,

(Crawlers). Six women go pot-holing in the Appalachians and are attacked and hunted in the dark. *Dir.* Neil Marshall.

Devil Girl from Mars (1954) Patricia Laffan (Nyah), Hugh McDermott (Michael Carter), Hazel Court (Ellen Prestwick), Peter Reynolds (Robert Justin/Albert Simpson), Adrienne Corri (Doris), Joseph Tomelty (Prof. Arnold Hennessey), John Laurie (Mr. Jamieson), Sophie Stewart (Mrs. Jamieson), Anthony Richmond (Tommy), James Edmund (David), Stewart Hibberd (News Reader). A female alien crash lands in Scotland armed with a ray gun and accompanied by a powerful robot; her mission is to harvest men for breeding stock on her planet. *Dir.* David MacDonald.

Devil Rides Out, The (1968) Christopher Lee (Duc de Richleau), Charles Gray (Mocata), Nike Arrighi (Tanith Carlisle), Leon Greene (Rex van Ryn), Patrick Mower (Simon Aron), Sarah Lawson (Marie Eaton), Paul Eddington (Richard Eaton), Gwen Ffrangcon-Davies (Countess), Rosalyn Landor (Peggy Eaton), Russell Waters (Malin). The Duc de Richleau rescues Simon from a devil-worshipping cult but finds he has to do battle against Mocata, the leader of the Satanists. Released in the United States as *The Devil's Bride*. Based on Dennis Wheatley's novel. *Dir.* Terence Fisher.

Devil's Disciple, The (1959) Burt Lancaster (The Rev. Anthony Anderson), Kirk Douglas (Richard Dudgeon), Laurence Olivier (Gen. Burgoyne), Janette Scott (Judith Anderson), Eva Le Gallienne (Mrs. Dudgeon), Harry Andrews (Maj. Swindon), Basil Sydney (Lawyer Hawkins), George Rose (British Sergeant), Neil McCallum (Christie Dudgeon), Mervyn Johns (Rev. Maindeck Parshotter), David Horne (Uncle William), Erik Chitty (Uncle Titus), Allan Cuthbertson (British Captain), Percy Herbert (British Lieutenant), Phyllis Morris (Wife of Titus), Brian Oulton (Mr. Brudenell), Steven Berkoff (British Corporal). An adaptation of the George Bernard Shaw play of the same name. *Dirs.* Guy Hamilton and Alexander MacKendrick.

Devils, The (1971) Oliver Reed (Urbain Grandier), Vanessa Redgrave (Sister Jeanne), Christopher Logue (Cardinal Richelieu), Kenneth Colley (Legrand), Graham Armitage (Louis XIII), Dudley Sutton (Baron de Laubardemont), Max Adrian (Ibert), Gemma Jones (Madeleine), Murray Melvin (Mignon), Judith Paris (Sister Judith), Catherine Willmer (Sister Catherine), John Woodvine (Trincant), Brian Murphy (Adam), Georgina Hale (Philippe), Andrew Faulds (Rangier), Michael Gothard (Father Barre). 17th century political and religious rivalries explode in the French town of Loudun. Sex, violence, nuns, nudity, nude nuns, various lascivious activities involving holy relics, possession by the devil, accusations of witchcraft and a burning at the stake. Based on *The Devils of Loudun* by Aldous Huxley and the play *The Devils* by John Whiting, also based on Huxley's book. *Dir.* Ken Russell.

Diamond City (1949) David Farrar (Stafford Parker), Honor Blackman (Mary Hart), Diana Dors (Dora Bracken), Niall MacGinnis (Hans Muller), Andrew Crawford (David Raymond), Mervyn Johns (Hart), Phyllis Monkman (Ma Bracken), Hal Osmond (Brandy Bill), Bill Owen (Pinto), Philo Hauser (Piet Quieman), John Blythe (Izzy Cohen), Dennis Vance (John Albert Rogers), Norris Smith (Jan Bloem), John Salew (Dr. Woods), Tony Quinn (Vanderbyl), Ronald Adam (Robert Southey), Reginald Tate (Longdon), Slim Harris (Hartje), Julian Somers (van Niekerk), Harry Quashie (Klaas), Arthur Lane (Timothy Maxie), John Warren (Town Crier), Ernest Butcher (Tom the Carpenter), Valentine Dyall (Opening narration). Set in a shanty town around a diamond mine in South Africa. Beleaguered lawman, Stafford Parker is the romantic interest for both Salvation Army girl Mary Hart and saloon girl Dora Bracken. *Dir.* David MacDonald.

Diamonds Are Forever (1971) Sean Connery (James Bond), Jill St. John (Tiffany Case), Charles Gray (Ernst Stavro Blofeld), Jimmy Dean (Willard Whyte), Bruce Glover (Mr. Wint), Putter Smith (Mr. Kidd), Norman Burton (Felix Leiter), Joseph Furst (Doctor Metz), Lana Wood (Plenty O'Toole), Bruce Cabot ('Bert' Saxby), Bernard Lee (M), Lois Maxwell (Miss Moneypenny), Desmond Llewelyn (Q), Joe Robinson (Peter Franks), Leonard

Barr (Shady Tree), Laurence Naismith (Sir Donald Munger), David Bauer (Morton Slumber), Ed Bishop (Klaus Hergerscheimer), David de Keyser (Doctor), Lola Larson and Trina Parks (Bambi and Thumper). Sean Connery's final outing as 007 (before his return in *Never Say Never Again*). Bond infiltrates a diamond smuggling ring and discovers that Blofeld is using diamonds to build a giant laser in a satellite orbiting Earth. Bond encounters both the camp assassins Mr Wint and Mr Kidd and the female duo Bambi and Thumper in his attempts to thwart Blofeld's dastardly plan. Bond drives a moon buggy and a Ford Mustang Mach 1. Title song performed by Shirley Bassey. *Dir.* Guy Hamilton.

Dick Turpin (1933) Victor McLaglen (Dick Turpin), Jane Carr (Eleanor Mowbray), Frank Vosper (Tom King), James Finlayson (Jeremy), Cecil Humphreys (Sir Luke Rookwood), Gillian Lind (Nan), Gibb McLaughlin (Governor of Newgate), Alexander Field (Weazel Jones), Roy Findlay (Dan Smollet), Helen Ferrers (Lady Rookwood), Lewis Gilbert (Jem). A re-telling of the life of the legendary 18th Century highwayman. *Dirs.* John Stafford and Victor Hanbury.

Dictator, The (1935) Clive Brook (Dr. Struensee), Madeleine Carroll (Queen Caroline Matilde of Danmark), Emlyn Williams (King Christian VII of Danmark), Helen Haye (Queen Mother Juliana), Frank Cellier (Sir Murray Keith), Isabel Jeans (Von Eyben), Alfred Drayton (Count Brandt), Nicholas Hannen (Prime Minister Guldberg of Danmark), Ruby Miller (Hilda), Heather Thatcher (Lady). Drama set in 18th century Denmark (Danish: Danmark), featuring a dissolute King, a not very impressed new Queen and multiple opportunities for dalliance. *Dir.* Victor Saville.

Die Another Day (2002) Pierce Brosnan (James Bond), Halle Berry (Giacinta 'Jinx' Johnson), Toby Stephens (Gustav Graves), Rick Yune (Zao), Rosamund Pike (Miranda Frost), Judi Dench (M), Will Yun Lee (Colonel Moon), Kenneth Tsang (General Moon), John Cleese (Q), Ho Yi (Mr. Chang), Rachel Grant (Peaceful Fountains of Desire), Emilio Echevarría (Raoul), Samantha Bond (Miss Moneypenny), Michael Gorevoy (Vladimir Popov), Lawrence Makoare (Mr. Kil), Michael Madsen (Damian Falco), Madonna (Verity). Brosnan's last outing as 007. The film opens with Bond being captured and interrogated in North Korea. He is exchanged over a year later and determines to discover who betrayed him. The main villain is billionaire Gustav Graves who is not whom he appears to be at first. Bond drives an Aston Martin V12 Vanquish and a Ford Fairlane. Title song performed by Madonna. *Dir.* Lee Tamahori.

Die Screaming, Marianne (1971) Susan George (Marianne), Barry Evans (Eli Frome), Christopher Sandford (Sebastian), Judy Huxtable (Hildegarde), Leo Genn (The Judge), Kenneth Hendel (Rodriguez), Paul Stassino (Portuguese Police Sergeant), Alan Curtis (Disco Manager), Anthony Sharp (Registrar). When Marianne turns 21 she will inherit a fortune plus some papers which will incriminate her father, a crooked judge. He is determined that she'll never make it to that birthday. *Dir.* Pete Walker.

Digby, the Biggest Dog in the World (1973) Jim Dale (Jeff Eldon), Spike Milligan (Dr. Harz), Angela Douglas (Janine), John Bluthal (Jerry), Norman Rossington (Tom), Milo O'Shea (Dr. Jameson), Richard Beaumont (Billy White), Dinsdale Landen (Colonel Masters), Garfield Morgan (Rogerson), Victor Spinetti (Professor Ribart), Harry Towb (Ringmaster), Kenneth J. Warren (General Frank), Bob Todd (The Great Manzini), Margaret Stuart (Assistant), Molly Urquhart (Aunt Ina), Victor Maddern (Dog Home Manager), Frank Thornton (Estate Agent), Sheila Steafel (Control Operator), Clovissa Newcombe (Bunny Girl), Henry McGee (TV Announcer). When Old English Sheepdog Digby accidentally drinks a liquid growth formula he just keeps on getting bigger and bigger and bigger. *Dir.* Joseph McGrath.

Dirty Pretty Things (2002) Chiwetel Ejiofor (Okwe), Audrey Tautou (Senay), Sophie Okonedo (Juliette), Sergi López (Sneaky), David Hoggard (Asian businessman), Jeffery Kissoon (Cab Controller), Zlatko Buric (Ivan), Benedict Wong (Guo Yi). Okwe, a former doctor in Nigeria, is now a cab driver in London and develops a friendship with Senay, a Turkish woman being chased by immigration. *Dir.* Stephen Frears

Disappearance of Alice Creed, The (2009) Gemma Arterton (Alice Creed), Martin Compston (Danny), Eddie Marsan (Vic). Danny and Vic kidnap Alice but is this just a simple abduction for gain? Written and directed by J Blakeson.

Distant Voices, Still Lives (1988) Pete Postlethwaite (Father), Freda Dowie (Mother), Lorraine Ashbourne (Maisie), Angela Walsh (Eileen), Dean Williams (Tony), Jean Boht (Aunty Nell), Michael Starke (Dave), Andrew Schofield (Les), Debi Jones (Micky), Chris Darwin (Red), Vincent Maguire (George), Pauline Quirke (Doreen), Antonia Mallen (Rose), Carl Chase (Uncle Ted), Sally Davies (Eileen as a child), Frances Dell (Margie), Anne Dyson (Granny), Susan Flanagan (Maisie as a child). This story of a working-class family in Liverpool during the war years and into the 1950s is in fact two separate films which were shot two years apart. The first section, *Distant Voices*, sees the family living under a heavy-handed patriarch, whilst part 2, *Still Lives*, sees the children grown up in the 1950s. The second film in director Terence Davies' autobiographical series (see also *Trilogy* and *The Long Day Closes*).

Divided Heart, The (1954) Michel Ray (Toni aged 10), Martin Keller (Toni aged 3), Cornell Borchers (Inga), Yvonne Mitchell (Sonja), Armin Dahlen (Franz), Geoffrey Keen (Marks), Alexander Knox (Chief Justice), Liam Redmond (First Justice), Eddie Byrne (Second Justice), Theodore Bikel (Josip), Pamela Stirling (Mlle. Poncet), Martin Stephens (Hans), André Mikhelson (Professor Miran). A three-year old boy is found wandering alone in Germany during WWII and is presumed to be an orphan. He is adopted but when he is ten years old his mother is discovered in Yugoslavia and comes to claim him. A court must decide his future. Based on a true story. *Dir.* Charles Crichton.

Divorce of Lady X, The (1938) Merle Oberon (Leslie Steele), Laurence Olivier (Everard Logan), Binnie Barnes (Lady Claire Mere), Ralph Richardson (Lord Mere), Morton Selten (Lord Steele). Staid solicitor Everard Logan mistakenly believes that the woman he innocently spent the night with must be the wife of his latest client who is looking for a divorce. Based on the play *Counsel's Opinion* by Gilbert Wakefield. *Dir.* Tim Whelan.

Divorcing Jack (1998) David Thewlis (Dan Starkey), Alan McKee (Mouse), Laine Megaw (Patricia Starkey), Robert Lindsay (Michael Brinn), Richard Gant (Charles Parker), Rachel Griffiths (Lee Cooper), Jason Isaacs (Cow Pat Keegan), Laura Fraser (Margaret), Kitty Aldridge (Agnes Brinn), Adam Black (Young Starkey), Simon Magill (Starkey's Brother), George Shane (Woods), Sean Caffrey (Joe), Ian McElhinney (Alfie Stewart), B.J. Hogg (Billy McCoubrey), Dale Kirkpatrick (Robert Brinn), Jonathan Collier (Robert Brinn - voice), Thomas Hourican (Sod), Frank Mannion (Finbar Kelly), Colin Murphy (Giblet O'Gibber), Paddy Rocks (Mad Dog), Derek Halligan (Frankie), John Keegan (Father Flynn). Black comedy. Cynical Northern Irish journalist Dan Starkey, with problems in both his personal and professional life, finds himself embroiled in murderous political and criminal shenanigans. Based on Colin Bateman's novel. *Dir.* David Caffrey.

Doctor at Large (1957) Dirk Bogarde (Dr. Simon Sparrow), Muriel Pavlow (Joy Gibson), Donald Sinden (Benskin), James Robertson Justice (Sir Lancelot Spratt), Shirley Eaton (Nan), Derek Farr (Dr. Potter-Shine), Michael Medwin (Bingham), Martin Benson (Maharajah), Edward Chapman (Wilkins), George Coulouris (Pascoe), Lionel Jeffries (Dr. Hatchet), Mervyn Johns (Smith), Ernest Thesiger (First Examiner), Geoffrey Keen (Second Examiner), Dilys Laye (Mrs. Jasmine Hatchet), Terence Longdon (George - House Surgeon), A.E. Matthews (Duke of Skye and Lewes), Guy Middleton (Major Porter), Barbara Murray (Kitty), Dandy Nichols (Lady in Outpatients Dept.), Athene Seyler (Lady Hawkins), Michael Trubshawe (Colonel Graves). A newly graduated Dr Sparrow tries his hand at being a GP. The third installment of the series which began with *Doctor in the House* sees the double entendre count rising (Doctor to patient: "Big breaths"; Patient: "Yes, and I'm only sixteen"). *Dir.* Ralph Thomas.

Doctor at Sea (1955) Dirk Bogarde (Dr. Simon Sparrow), Brigitte Bardot (Hélène Colbert), James Robertson Justice (Captain Hogg), Brenda De Banzie (Muriel Mallet), Maurice Denham (Steward Easter), Geoffrey Keen (Chief Officer Hornbeam), Hubert Gregg (Second Officer Archer), Michael

Medwin (Third Officer Trail), James Kenney (Fellowes), Raymond Huntley (Capt. Beamish), George Coulouris (Ship's Carpenter), Noel Purcell (Corbie), Jill Adams (Jill), Joan Sims (Wendy). Dr Sparrow signs on as medical officer on a cargo ship SS *Lotus* and becomes romantically involved with a French night club singer he meets in South America. Notable for the presence of Bardot in the cast and for James Robertson Justice playing a role other than Sir Lancelot Spratt. *Dir.* Ralph Thomas.

Doctor in Clover (1966) Leslie Phillips (Dr Gaston Grimsdyke), James Robertson Justice (Sir Lancelot Spratt), Shirley Anne Field (Nurse Bancroft), John Fraser (Dr Miles Grimsdyke), Joan Sims (Matron Sweet), Arthur Haynes (Tarquin Wendover), Fenella Fielding (Tatiana Rubikov), Jeremy Lloyd (Lambert Symington), Noel Purcell (O'Malley), Eric Barker (Professor Halfbeck), Norman Vaughan (TV Commentator), Terry Scott (Robert), Alfie Bass (Flemyng), Harry Fowler (Grafton), Peter Gilmore (Choreographer), Bill Kerr (Digger), Nicky Henson (Salesman), Justine Lord (New Matron), Alexandra Bastedo (Nurse at Party), Ronnie Stevens (TV Producer), Wendy Richard (Nurse), Jack Smethurst (Patient). Fun and games at St Swithins involving mistaken intentions and a "re-juvenating serum". *Dir.* Ralph Thomas.

Doctor in Distress (1963) Dirk Bogarde (Dr. Simon Sparrow), James Robertson Justice (Sir Lancelot Spratt), Samantha Eggar (Delia Mallory), Barbara Murray (Iris Marchant), Mylène Demongeot (Sonia), Donald Houston (Major Tommy Ffrench), Jessie Evans (Mrs. Parry), Ann Lynn (Mrs. Whittaker), Leo McKern (Harry), Dennis Price (Dr. Blacker), Rodney Cardiff (Dr. Stewart), Fenella Fielding (Train Passenger), Jill Adams (Genevieve), Michael Flanders (Bradby), Amanda Barrie (Rona), Bill Kerr (Australian Sailor), Ronnie Stevens (Hotel Manager), Peter Butterworth (Ambulance Driver), Derek Fowlds (Gillibrand), Ronnie Barker (Man at Railway Station), John Bluthal (Railway Porter), Marianne Stone (Cafe Waitress), Denise Coffey (Food seller), Frank Finlay (Corsetiere). Dirk Bogarde returns to the series as both Sparrow and Spratt have woman trouble. *Dir.* Ralph Thomas.

Doctor in Love (1960) James Robertson Justice (Sir Lancelot Spratt), Michael Craig (Dr. Richard Hare), Leslie Phillips (Dr. Tony Burke), Moira Redmond (Sally Nightingale), Virginia Maskell (Dr. Nicola Barrington), Joan Sims (Dawn), Liz Fraser (Leonora), Carole Lesley (Kitten Strudwick), Reginald Beckwith (Wildewinde), Nicholas Phipps (Dr. Clive Cardew), Ambrosine Phillpotts (Lady Spratt), Irene Handl (Professor MacRitchie), Fenella Fielding (Mrs. Tadwich), Nicholas Parsons (Dr. Hinxman), Ronnie Stevens (Harold Green), John Le Mesurier (Dr. Mincing), Esma Cannon (Raffia Lady), Patrick Cargill (Car Salesman), Bill Fraser (Police Sergeant), Joan Hickson (Nurse), John Junkin (Policeman), Sheila Hancock (Librarian), Robin Ray (Doctor), Norman Rossington (Doorman), Peter Sallis (Love-struck Patient), Marianne Stone (Nurse), Sally Douglas (Stripper). Richard is in love with first Sally and then Nicola. He also has to contend with a philandering practice partner and having to operate on Sir Lancelot. *Dir.* Ralph Thomas.

Doctor in the House (1954) Dirk Bogarde (Simon Sparrow), Donald Houston (Taffy Evans), Kenneth More (Richard Grimsdyke), Donald Sinden (Tony Benskin), Muriel Pavlow (Joy Gibson), Kay Kendall (Isobel), James Robertson Justice (Lancelot Spratt), Suzanne Cloutier (Stella), George Coulouris (Briggs), Jean Taylor Smith (Sister Virtue), Joan Sims ("Rigor Mortis"), Gudrun Ure (May), Shirley Eaton (Milly Groaker), Joan Hickson (Mrs. Groaker), Mona Washbourne (Midwifery sister), Richard Gordon (Anaethetist), Richard Wattis (Medical book salesman). The story follows the antics, successes and failures of students in medical training at the fictitious St Swithins in the 1950s all under the ever-present figure of chief surgeon Sir Lancelot Spratt. The first in the "Doctor" series based on the books by Richard Gordon which, in general, featured the cream of British character and comedy actors, in particular James Robertson Justice, who starred in all seven films. Kenneth More won the BAFTA for Best British Actor for his performance as Grimsdyke. The films were produced by Betty Box, the wife of Peter Rogers whose name was synonymous with the Carry On films. *Dir.* Ralph Thomas.

Doctor in Trouble (1970) Leslie Phillips (Doctor Anthony Burke), Harry Secombe (Llewellyn Wendover), Robert Morley (Captain George Spratt), James Robertson Justice (Sir Lancelot Spratt), Simon Dee (Basil Beauchamp), Angela Scoular (Ophelia O'Brien), Irene Handl (Mrs. Dailey), Janet Mahoney (Dawn Dailey), Freddie Jones (Master-at-Arms), Joan Sims (Russian Captain), John Le Mesurier (Purser), Graham Stark (Saterjee), Graham Chapman (Roddie), Jacki Piper (Girl in taxi), Fred Emney (Father), Yuri Borionko (Model), Gerald Sim (1st Doctor), Yutte Stensgaard (Eve), Marianne Stone (Spinster), John Bluthal (TV Doctor). The last in the Doctor series sees Dr Burke accidentally stowing away on a cruise ship captained by Sir Lancelot Spratt's brother George. *Dir.* Ralph Thomas.

Doctor's Dilemma, The (1958) Leslie Caron (Mrs. Dubedat), Dirk Bogarde (Louis Dubedat), Alastair Sim (Cutler Walpole), Robert Morley (Sir Ralph Bloomfield-Bonington), John Robinson (Sir Colenso Ridgeon), Felix Aylmer (Sir Patrick Cullen), Michael Gwynn (Dr. Blenkinsop), Maureen Delaney (Emmy), Alec McCowen (Redpenny), Colin Gordon (Newspaper Man), Gwenda Ewen (Minnie), Terence Alexander (Mr. Lanchester), Derek Prentice (Head Waiter), Peter Sallis (Secretary at Picture Gallery), Clifford Buckton (Butcher), Mary Reynolds (Young girl). Based on George Bernard Shaw's play involving the dilemma of a doctor in saving a patient suffering from TB. *Dir.* Anthony Asquith.

Dog Eat Dog (2002) Mark Tonderai (Rooster), Nathan Constance (Jess), David Oyelowo (CJ), Crunski (Chang), Alan Davies (Phil), Melanie Blatt (Ex-girlfriend), Gary Kemp (Jesus), Steve Toussaint (Darcy), Ricky Gervais (Bouncer), Rebecca Hazlewood (Mina), Stewart Wright (Eastwood). Four friends try to raise the cash they need in order to make it as DJs. *Dir.* Moody Shoaibi.

Dog Soldiers (2002) Kevin McKidd (Private Lawrence Cooper), Sean Pertwee (Sergeant Harry Wells), Emma Cleasby (Megan), Liam Cunningham (Captain Richard Ryan), Darren Morfitt (Private Phil "Spoon" Witherspoon), Chris Robson (Private Joe Kirkley), Leslie Simpson (Private Terry Milburn), Thomas Lockyer (Corporal Bruce Campbell). Five squaddies on an exercise in the Scottish Highlands find themselves besieged by a pack of werewolves. *Dir.* Neil Marshall.

Dogs of War, The (1980) Christopher Walken (Jamie Shannon), Tom Berenger (Drew Blakeley), Colin Blakely (Alan North), Hugh Millais (Roy Endean), Paul Freeman (Derek Godwin), Jean-Francois Stevenin (Michel Claude), JoBeth Williams (Jessie Shannon), Robert Urquhart (Capt. Lockhart), Winston Ntshona (Dr. Okoye), George Harris (Col. Sekou Bobi), Alan Beckwith (The Mercenary), Eddie Tagoe (Jinja), Ed O'Neill (Terry), Harlan Cary Poe (Richard), Olu Jacobs (Customs Officer). A group of mercenaries are hired to overthrow an African President and pave the way for a businessman to acquire rich platinum mining rights. Based upon the novel of the same name by Frederick Forsyth. *Dir.* John Irvin.

Don't Bother to Knock (1961) Richard Todd (Bill Ferguson), Nicole Maurey (Lucille), Elke Sommer (Ingrid), June Thorburn (Stella), Rik Battaglia (Guilio), Judith Anderson (Maggie Shoemaker), Dawn Beret (Harry), Scott Finch (Perry), Eleanor Summerfield (Mother), John Le Mesurier (Father), Colin Gordon (Rolsom), Kenneth Fortescue (Ian), Ronald Fraser (Fred), Tommy Duggan (Al), Michael Shepley (Colonel), Joan Sterndale-Bennett (Spinster), Kynaston Reeves (Neighbour), John Laurie (Taxi driver), Warren Mitchell (Waiter), Amanda Barrie (Girl in art gallery), Angela Douglas (Girl in art gallery), Graham Crowden (Scoutmaster), A philandering travel agent has to juggle with the various women in his life, having stupidly given each one a key to his flat. *Dir.* Cyril Frankel.

Don't Ever Leave Me (1949) Jimmy Hanley (Jack Denton), Petula Clark (Sheila Farlaine), Linden Travers (Mary Lamont), Hugh Sinclair (Michael Farlaine), Edward Rigby (Harry Denton), Anthony Newley (Jimmy Knowles), Barbara Murray (Joan Robbins), Brenda Bruce (Miss Smith), Maurice Denham (Mr. Knowles), Frederick Piper (Max Marshall), Sandra Dorne (Ruby

Baines), Russell Waters (Mr. Robbins), Anthony Steel (Harris), Michael Balfour (Jim Kennedy), James Hayter (Man with Summons), Dandy Nichols (Mrs. Marshall), Cyril Chamberlain (News Reporter), Philip Stainton (Detective Inspector), John Salew (Farlaine's Manager), Barbara Leake (Mrs. Brand), Arthur Hambling (Policeman), Martin Miller (Leon Stoltz), Ben Williams (Superintendent in Cells), Dora Bryan (Beautician), Joan Hickson (Mrs. Pearson). In an attempt to prove he still has what it takes to be a criminal Harry Denton decides to kidnap Sheila Farlaine. When he begins to waver, the girl takes control in order to give her egotistical actor father a lesson. *Dir.* Arthur Crabtree.

Don't Look Now (1973) Julie Christie (Laura Baxter), Donald Sutherland (John Baxter), Hilary Mason (Heather), Clelia Matania (Wendy), Massimo Serato (Bishop Barbarrigo), Renato Scarpa (Inspector Longhi), Giorgio Trestini (Workman), Leopoldo Trieste (Hotel Manager), David Tree (Anthony Babbage), Ann Rye (Mandy Babbage). After John and Laura Baxters' daughter accidently drowns in their garden pond they travel to Venice to try and recover from the tragedy. They meet two elderly sisters, one of whom claims to be psychic and is able to see the spirit of the Baxters' daughter with them. John is sceptical but, after Laura has to return to England to look after their son, he begins to have strange visions, including seeing a girl in a red cloak like the one his daughter once wore. Meanwhile, there is a serial killer on the loose in the city. Adapted from the short story by Daphne du Maurier. *Dir.* Nicolas Roeg.

Doppelgänger (1969) Roy Thinnes (Colonel Glenn Ross), Ian Hendry (John Kane), Patrick Wymark (Jason Webb), Lynn Loring (Sharon Ross), Loni von Friedl (Lisa Hartmann), Franco De Rosa (Paulo Landi), George Sewell (Mark Neuman), Ed Bishop (David Poulson (as Edward Bishop), Philip Madoc (Dr. Pontini), Vladek Sheybal (Psychiatrist), Herbert Lom (Doctor Hassler), Nicholas Courtney (Medical Data Analyst), Cy Grant (Dr. Gordon), Annette Kerr (Nurse). In 2069 a new planet is discovered on the far side of the Sun and a mission is sent by the West (the film was made in the Cold War/Space Race era) in order to beat the East. On arrival it eventually becomes clear that the new planet is actually a parallel Earth where everything is identical but reversed. Also known as *Journey to the Far Side of the Sun*. Produced by Gerry Anderson, some of the cast and props went on to the television series *UFO*. *Dir.* Robert Parrish.

Double Bunk (1961) Ian Carmichael (Jack), Janette Scott (Peggy), Sid James (Sid), Liz Fraser (Sandra), Dennis Price (Watson), Reginald Beckwith (Harper), Irene Handl (Mrs. Harper), Noel Purcell (O'Malley), Naunton Wayne (1st Thames Conservancy Officer), Bill Shine (2nd Thames Conservancy Officer), Michael Shepley (Granville-Carter), Toby Perkins (Pukka Type), Miles Malleson (Reverend Thomas), Jacques Cey (French Official), Hedger Wallace (1st River Policeman), Terry Scott (2nd River Policeman), Desmond Roberts (Freighter Captain), Peter Swanwick (Freighter Pilot), Gerald Campion (Charlie), John Harvey (Johnnie), Graham Stark (Flowerman), Gladys Henson (Madame de Sola), Willoughby Goddard (Prospective Purchaser), Marianne Stone (Prospective Purchaser's Wife). After being tricked into buying a run-down houseboat Jack and Peggy take some friends on a trip to the coast but end up in France. *Dir.* C.M. Pennington-Richards.

Down Among the Z Men (1952) Harry Secombe (Harry Jones), Michael Bentine (Prof. Osrick Purehart), Spike Milligan (Pvt. Eccles), Peter Sellers (Major Bloodnok), Carole Carr (Carole Gayley), Clifford Stanton (Stanton), Andrew Timothy (Captain Evans), Graham Stark (Spider), Elizabeth Kearns (Girl in Shop), Miriam Karlin (Woman in Shop), Sidney Vivian (Isaiah Crabb). The Goons make the big screen. Harry discovers that Professor Osrick has left a secret formula in his shop and tries to return it to him but is mistakenly enlisted into the "z" men. *Dir.* MacLean Rogers.

Dr. Crippen (1964) Donald Pleasence (Dr. Hawley Harvey Crippen), Coral Browne (Belle Crippen), Samantha Eggar (Ethel Le Neve), Donald Wolfit (R.D. Muir), James Robertson Justice (Captain McKenzie), John Arnatt (Chief Inspector Dew), Oliver Johnston (Lord Chief Justice), John Lee (Harry), Olga Lindo (Mrs. Arditti), Elspeth March (Mrs. Jackson), Geoffrey Toone (Mr. Tobin), Edward Underdown (The Governor), Douglas

Bradley-Smith (Dr. Pepper), Hamilton Dyce (Dr. Rogers), Basil Henson (Mr. Arditti), Totti Truman Taylor (Miss Curnow), Edward Cast (Harding), Colin Rix (Chemist). The story of the notorious murderer Dr. Crippen, although this film does leave the question of his guilt open. *Dir.* Robert Lynn.

Dr. Jekyll and Sister Hyde (1971) Ralph Bates (Dr. Henry Jekyll), Martine Beswick (Mrs. Edwina Hyde), Gerald Sim (Professor Roberston), Lewis Fiander (Howard Spencer), Susan Brodrick (Susan Spencer), Dorothy Alison (Mrs. Spencer), Ivor Dean (William Burke), Tony Calvin (William Hare), Philip Madoc (Ryker), Paul Whitsun-Jones (Sergeant Danvers), Virginia Wetherell (Betsy). Based on Robert Louis Stevenson's short story *The Strange Case of Dr Jekyll and Mr Hyde* but with a twist which the title of the film rather telegraphed. The story also includes body snatchers Burke and Hare. *Dir.* Roy Ward Baker.

Dr. No (1962) Sean Connery (James Bond), Ursula Andress (Honey Ryder), Joseph Wiseman (Dr. Julius No), Jack Lord (Felix Leiter), Bernard Lee (M), Anthony Dawson (Professor R. J. Dent), John Kitzmiller (Quarrel), Zena Marshall (Miss Taro), Eunice Gayson (Sylvia Trench), Lois Maxwell (Miss Moneypenny), Peter Burton (Major Boothroyd), Timothy Moxon (John Strangways), Reggie Carter (Mr. Jones). The first James Bond film, based on the 1958 Ian Fleming novel of the same name. British Secret Service agent, James Bond (007), is sent out to the West Indies to investigate the murder of fellow agent John Strangways. His attention is drawn by scientist Julius No (who is a member of SPECTRE (SPecial Executive for Counter-intelligence, Terrorism, Revenge, and Extortion) who it transpires has a fiendish plan involving a rocket launch and a radio beam. Bond drives a Sunbeam Alpine and Ursula Andress begins the long line of "Bond Girls", although in the film she is preceded by Zena Marshall and Eunice Gayson, who is also the first person to elicit the response "Bond, James Bond". The James Bond theme composed by Monty Norman and arranged by John Barry was played over the title sequence. *Dir.* Terence Young.

Dr. Phibes Rises Again! (1972) Vincent Price (Dr. Anton Phibes), Robert Quarry (Darrus Biederbeck), Valli Kemp (Vulnavia), Peter Jeffrey (Inspector Trout), Fiona Lewis (Diana Trowbridge), Hugh Griffith (Harry Ambrose), Peter Cushing (Captain), Beryl Reid (Miss Ambrose), Terry-Thomas (Lombardo), John Cater (Superintendent Waverley), Gerald Sim (Hackett), Lewis Fiander (Baker), John Thaw (Shavers), Keith Buckley (Stewart), Milton Reid (Butler), Caroline Munro (Victoria Regina Phibes). The moon rises at a predestined angle and awakens the sleeping Dr. Phibes three years after the events of the preceding film (*The Abominable Dr. Phibes*). With the aim of awakening his dead wife Victoria he travels to Egypt to regain the scrolls he needs, which have been stolen from him. Once he traces the thieves he begins to whittle away at their number in a variety of imaginative ways. *Dir.* Robert Fuest.

Dr. Strangelove Or: How I Learned To Stop Worrying And Love The Bomb (1964) Peter Sellers (Group Captain Lionel Mandrake/President Merkin Muffley/Dr. Strangelove), George C. Scott (General Buck Turgidson), Sterling Hayden (Brigadier General Jack D. Ripper), Keenan Wynn (Colonel Bat Guano), Slim Pickens (Major T. J. Kong), Peter Bull (Soviet Ambassador Alexei de Sadeski), James Earl Jones (Lieutenant Lothar Zogg), Tracy Reed (Miss Scott). A black comedy which satirises the nuclear tensions of the early 1960s. When a rogue USAF general orders a nuclear first strike against the Soviet Union, the US President and his advisors in the "War Room" try to prevent World War III from breaking out. Sellers plays three parts (he was originally contracted to play four): an RAF officer, the President of the US and wheelchair-bound Dr Strangelove, who has a false arm with Nazi tendencies. Highlights include the line "Gentlemen. You can't fight in here. This is the War Room!" *Dir.* Stanley Kubrick.

Dr. Syn (1937) George Arliss (Doctor Syn), Margaret Lockwood (Imogene Clegg), John Loder (Denis Cobtree), Roy Emerton (Captain Howard Collyer), Graham Moffatt (Jerry Jerk), George Merritt (Mipps), Athole Stewart (Squire Cobtree), Frederick Burtwell (Rash), Wilson Coleman (Dr. Pepper), Wally Patch (Bo'sun), Muriel George (Mrs. Waggetts), Meinhart Maur (Mulatto). In 18th century Kent the revenue men arrive in the coastal town of Dymchurch bent on rooting out the source of the local smuggling operation. They are welcomed by the local vicar Doctor Syn. Based on the Doctor Syn novels of Russell Thorndike. *Dir*. Roy William Neill.

Dr. Terror's House of Horrors (1964) Peter Cushing ('Dr. Terror'/Dr. W. R. Schreck), Neil McCallum(Jim Dawson - segment 1 "Werewolf"), Peter Madden (Caleb - segment 1 "Werewolf"), Ursula Howells (Mrs. Deirdre Biddulph - segment 1 "Werewolf"), Katy Wild (Valda - segment 1 "Werewolf"), Edward Underdown (Tod - segment 1 "Werewolf"), Ann Bell (Ann Rogers - segment 2 "Creeping Vine"), Bernard Lee (Hopkins - segment 2 "Creeping Vine"), Alan Freeman (Bill Rogers - segment 2 "Creeping Vine"), Jeremy Kemp (Jerry Drake - segment 2 "Creeping Vine"), Phoebe Nicholls (Carol Rogers - segment 2 "Creeping Vine"), Roy Castle (Biff Bailey - segment 3 "Voodoo"), Kenny Lynch (Sammy Coin - segment 3 "Voodoo"), Harold Lang (Roy Shine - segment 3 "Voodoo"), Christopher Carlos (Vrim - segment 3 "Voodoo"), Thomas Baptiste (Dambala - segment 3 "Voodoo"), Valerie St. Clair (Cigarette Girl - segment 3 "Voodoo"), Christopher Lee (Franklyn Marsh - segment 4 "Disembodied Hand"), Michael Gough (Eric Landor - segment 4 "Disembodied Hand"), Isla Blair (Pretty Girl - segment 4 "Disembodied Hand"), Judy Cornwell (Nurse - segment 4 "Disembodied Hand"), Hedger Wallace (Surgeon - segment 4 "Disembodied Hand"), Brian Hawkins (George - segment 4 "Disembodied Hand"), John Martin (Second Male Friend - segment 4 "Disembodied Hand"), Faith Kent (Lady in Art Gallery - segment 4 "Disembodied Hand"), Kenneth Kove (Third Male Friend - segment 4 "Disembodied Hand"), Frank Forsyth (Toastmaster - segment 4 "Disembodied Hand"), Walter Sparrow (Second Ambulance Man - segment 4 "Disembodied Hand"), Max Adrian (Dr. Blake - segment 5 "Vampire"), Jennifer Jayne (Nicolle Carroll - segment 5 "Vampire"), Donald Sutherland (Dr. Bob Carroll - segment 5 "Vampire"), Al Mulock (Detective - segment 5 "Vampire"), Laurie Leigh (Nurse - segment 5 "Vampire"), Frank Barry (Johnny Ellis - segment 5 "Vampire"), Irene Richmond (Mrs. Ellis - segment 5 "Vampire"). A portmanteau film consisting of five stories within a framing story whereby five train passengers are joined by Dr Schreck who reads their tarot cards and tells five horror stories. *Dir*. Freddie Francis.

Dr. Who and the Daleks (1965) Peter Cushing (Dr. Who), Roy Castle (Ian), Jennie Linden (Barbara), Roberta Tovey (Susan), Barrie Ingham (Alydon), Geoffrey Toone (Temmosus), Michael Coles (Ganatus), John Bown (Antodus), Yvonne Antrobus (Dyoni). A retelling of the original Dalek story featured in the first season of Dr Who on BBC television which was first broadcast in seven weekly parts from December 1963 to February 1964. The Tardis lands on a planet where the Doctor and his companions, granddaughters Susan and Barbara plus Barbara's boyfriend Ian (in the television series Ian and Barbara were Susan's teachers) become caught up in the conflict between two tribes – the Thals and the Daleks. *Dir*. Gordon Flemyng.

Dr. Zhivago (1965) Omar Sharif (Dr. Yuri Zhivago), Julie Christie (Larissa "Lara" Antipova), Tom Courtenay (Pasha Antipov), Rod Steiger (Victor Komarovsky), Alec Guinness (General Yevgraf Zhivago), Geraldine Chaplin (Tonya Gromeko), Siobhán McKenna (Anna Gromeko), Ralph Richardson (Sasha Gromeko), Rita Tushingham (Tonya Komarovskaya), Klaus Kinski (Kostoyed Amoursky), Gerard Tichy (Liberius), Noel Willman (Commissar Razin), Geoffrey Keen (Professor Boris Kurt), Bernard Kay (Kuril), Jack MacGowran (Petya), Adrienne Corri (Amelia). Set in Russia during the period which saw WWI, the Bolshevik Revolution, the overthrow of the Tsar and the Russian Civil War (1912-23). As a framing device the film uses the narration of Yevgraf Zhivago, who at the start is on the point of meeting Tonya, the possible daughter of his brother Yuri and Lara. Yevgraf tells Tonya the story of Yuri's life, the vicissitudes of life in Russia during that period and his love for Lara. The film won five Oscars: Best Art Direction, Music, Cinematography, Costume Design, and Best Writing. It is loosely based on the novel of the same name by Boris Pasternak. *Dir*. David Lean.

Dracula (1958) Christopher Lee (Count Dracula), Peter Cushing (Doctor Van Helsing), John Van Eyssen (Jonathan Harker),

Melissa Stribling (Mina Harker), Michael Gough (Arthur Holmwood), Carol Marsh (Lucy Holmwood), Olga Dickie (Gerda), Valerie Gaunt (Vampire Woman), Janina Faye (Tania), Barbara Archer (Inga), Charles Lloyd-Pack (Doctor Seward), George Merritt (Policeman), George Woodbridge (Landlord), George Benson (Official), Miles Malleson (Undertaker), Geoffrey Bayldon (Porter). A Hammer Horror inspired by the novel of the same name by Bram Stoker. Jonathan Harker arrives at Dracula's castle with intent to kill but all does not go to plan. *Dir*. Terence Fisher.

Dracula AD 1972 (1972) Christopher Lee (Count Dracula), Peter Cushing (Lorrimer Van Helsing/Lawrence Van Helsing, Stephanie Beacham (Jessica Van Helsing), Christopher Neame (Johnny Alucard), Michael Coles (Inspector Murray), Marsha Hunt (Gaynor Keating), Caroline Munro (Laura Bellows), Janet Key (Anna Bryant), William Ellis (Joe Mitcham), Philip Miller (Bob), Michael Kitchen (Greg), David Andrews (Detective Sergeant), Lally Bowers (Matron Party Hostess), Constance Luttrell (Mrs. Donnelly), Michael Daly (Charles), Artro Morris (Police Surgeon), Jo Richardson (Crying Matron), Penny Brahms (Hippy Girl), Flanagan (Go Go Dancer). A modern day disciple of Count Dracula (Johnny Alucard) raises him from the grave and together they are determined to wreak vengeance on the descendants of Van Helsing. *Dir*. Alan Gibson.

Dracula Has Risen From the Grave (1967) Christopher Lee (Count Dracula), Rupert Davies (Monsignor Ernest Muller), Veronica Carlson (Maria Muller), Barry Andrews (Paul), Barbara Ewing (Zena), Ewan Hooper (Priest), Marion Mathie (Anna), Michael Ripper (Max), John D. Collins (Student), George A. Cooper (Landlord). As Monsignor Muller exorcises Castle Dracula, the dead Count is accidently resurrected. Dracula makes the Monsignor's niece his target. *Dir*. Freddie Francis.

Dracula, Prince of Darkness (1965) Christopher Lee (Count Dracula), Andrew Keir (Father Sandor), Barbara Shelley (Helen Kent), Francis Matthews (Charles Kent), Suzan Farmer (Diana Kent), Charles Tingwell (Alan Kent), Thorley Walters (Ludwig), Philip Latham (Klove), Walter Brown (Brother Mark), George Woodbridge (Landlord), Jack Lambert (Brother Peter), Philip Ray (Priest), Joyce Hemson (Mother), John Maxim (Coach Driver). The sequel to *Dracula* (1958). Four British tourists (the Kents) are lured to Castle Dracula, where Dracula's servant Klove kills one of them and uses the blood to bring the Count back to life. Dracula then attempts to make sure the rest of the family join the ranks of the undead. *Dir*. Terence Fisher.

Drake of England (1935) Matheson Lang (Francis Drake), Athene Seyler (Queen Elizabeth), Jane Baxter (Elizabeth Sydenham), Henry Mollison (John Doughty), Ben Webster (Lord Burghley), Donald Wolfit (Thomas Doughty), George Merritt (Tom Moore), Amy Veness (Mother Moore), Sam Livesey (Sir George Sydenham), Margaret Halstan (Lady Sydenham), Charles Quatermaine (Parson Fletcher), Allan Jeayes (Don Bernardino), Gibb McLaughlin (Don Enriquez), Helen Haye (Lady Lennox), Moore Marriott (Bright). A re-telling of Sir Francis Drake and the defeat of the Spanish Armada. *Dir*. Arthur B. Woods.

Draughtsman's Contract, The (1982) Anthony Higgins (Mr Neville), Janet Suzman (Mrs Herbert), Anne-Louise Lambert (Mrs. Talmann), Hugh Fraser (Mr. Talmann), Neil Cunningham (Mr. Noyes), Dave Hill (Mr. Herbert), David Gant (Mr. Seymour), David Meyer (The Poulencs), Tony Meyer (The Poulencs), Nicolas Amer (Mr. Parkes), Suzan Crowley (Mrs. Pierpont), Lynda La Plante (Mrs. Clement), Michael Feast (The Statue), Alastair Cumming (Philip), Steve Ubels (Mr Van Hoyten). Set in the late 17th century, Mr Neville, an arrogant young artist, is contracted by Mrs Herbert to produce a set of twelve drawings of her husband's estate. However, according to the contract the artist is entitled to more than just pecuniary reward. As he completes the sketches the body of Mr Herbert is found in the moat. *Dir*. Peter Greenaway.

Dream Demon (1988) Jemma Redgrave (Diana), Kathleen Wilhoite (Jenny Hoffman), Timothy Spall (Peck), Jimmy Nail (Paul), Mark Greenstreet (Oliver), Susan Fleetwood (Deborah), Annabelle Lanyon (Little Jenny), Nickolas Grace (Jenny's Father),

Patrick O'Connell (Detective), Andrew Jones (Designer), Richard Warner (Minister). As her wedding approaches Diane begins to have nightmares which feature terrifying demons. *Dir.* Harley Cokeliss.

Dresser, The (1983) Albert Finney (Sir), Tom Courtenay (Norman), Edward Fox (Oxenby), Zena Walker (Her Ladyship), Eileen Atkins (Madge), Michael Gough (Frank Carrington), Cathryn Harrison (Irene), Betty Marsden (Violet Manning), Sheila Reid (Lydia Gibson), Lockwood West (Geoffrey Thornton), Donald Eccles (Mr. Godstone), Llewellyn Rees (Horace Brown), Guy Manning (Benton), Anne Mannion (Beryl), Kevin Stoney (C. Rivers Lane), Ann Way (Miss White), John Sharp (Mr. Bottomley), Kathy Staff (Bombazine Woman), Roger Avon (Charles). A dresser, Norman, tries his best to support the star of the ensemble (Sir) during a performance of King Lear. *Dir.* Peter Yates.

Dressmaker, The (1988) Joan Plowright (Nellie), Billie Whitelaw (Margo), Pete Postlethwaite (Jack), Jane Horrocks (Rita), Tim Ransom (Wesley), Pippa Hinchley (Val), Rosemary Martin (Mrs Manders), Tony Haygarth (Mr Manders), Michael James Reed (Chuck), Sam Douglas (Corporal Zawadski), Bert Parnaby (Mr. Barnes), Lorraine Ashbourne (Factory Girl), Mandy Walsh (Factory Girl), Margi Clarke (Shopwoman). During World War II, a dressmaker and her sister struggle to look after their teenage niece. An adaptation of Beryl Bainbridge's novel. *Dir.* Jim O'Brien.

Dreyfus (1931) Cedric Hardwicke (Capt. Alfred Dreyfus), Charles Carson (Col. Picquart), George Merritt (Émile Zola), Sam Livesey (Labori), Beatrix Thomson (Lucille Dreyfus), Garry Marsh (Maj. Esterhazy), Randle Ayrton (Court-martial president), Henry Caine (Col. Henry), Reginald Dance (President, Zola trial), George Skillan (Maj. Paty du Clam), Leonard Shepherd (Georges Clemenceau), Arthur Hardy (Gen. Mercier), Alexander Sarner (Matthieu Dreyfus), Frederick Leister (Demange), J. Fisher White (Pellieux), Abraham Sofaer (Dubois), J. Leslie Frith (Bertillon), George Zucco (Cavaignac), Nigel Barrie (Lauth), Violet Howard (Marguerite). Based on the play of the same name by Wilhelm Herzog and Hans Rehfisch and essentially a remake of the 1930 German film also called *Dreyfus*. *Dirs.* F.W. Kraemer and Milton Rosmer.

Drowning by Numbers (1988) Joan Plowright (Cissie Colpitts), Juliet Stevenson (Cissie Colpitts), Joely Richardson (Cissie Colpitts), Bernard Hill (Madgett), Jason Edwards (Smut), Bryan Pringle (Jake), Trevor Cooper (Hardy), David Morrissey (Bellamy), John Rogan (Gregory), Paul Mooney (Teigan), Jane Gurnett (Nancy), Kenny Ireland (Jonah Bognor), Michael Percival (Moses Bognor), Joanna Dickens (Mrs. Hardy), Janine Duvitski (Marina Bellamy). With the complicity of the local coroner, three women all named Cissie Colpitts drown their husbands. The film has overtones of a folk tale and the numbers 1 to 100 appear or are spoken progressively during the film. *Dir.* Peter Greenaway.

Drum, The (1938) Sabu Dastagir (Prince Azim), Raymond Massey (Prince Ghul), Roger Livesey (Captain Carruthers), Valerie Hobson (Mrs. Carruthers), David Tree (Lieutenant Escott), Desmond Tester (Bill Holder), Francis L. Sullivan (Governor), Archibald Batty (Major Bond), Frederick Culley (Dr. Murphy), Amid Taftazani (Mohammed Khan), Lawrence Baskcomb (Zarullah), Roy Emerton (Wafadar), Michael Martin Harvey (Mullah), Martin Walker (Herrick), Ronald Adams (Major Gregoff). Set in the North West Frontier of India during the British Raj, Prince Azim's life is in danger after his brother Prince Ghul murders their father and usurps the throne of Tokot. Based on the book by A. E. W. Mason. *Dir.* Zoltan Korda.

Duchess, The (2008) Keira Knightley (Georgiana Cavendish), Ralph Fiennes (William Cavendish), Hayley Atwell (Lady Elizabeth 'Bess' Foster), Charlotte Rampling (Countess Spencer), Dominic Cooper (Charles Grey), Aidan McArdle (Richard Brinsley Sheridan), Simon McBurney (Charles James Fox), Sebastian Applewhite (Augustus Clifford), Calvin Dean (Devonshire House Servant), Emily Jewell (Nanny), Richard McCabe (Sir James Hare), Bruce Mackinnon and Georgia King (actor and actress in The School for Scandal), Alistair Petrie (Heaton), Paul Daley (George Augustus Henry Cavendish). A historical biopic based on Amanda Foreman's biography of the 18th-century aristocrat Georgiana Cavendish, Duchess of Devonshire. *Dir.* Saul Dibb.

Duellists, The (1977) Keith Carradine (D'Hubert), Harvey Keitel (Feraud), Albert Finney (Fouche), Edward Fox (Colonel), Cristina Raines (Adele), Robert Stephens (Gen. Treillard), Tom Conti (Dr. Jacquin), John McEnery (Chevalier), Diana Quick (Laura), Alun Armstrong (Lacourbe), Maurice Colbourne (Second), Gay Hamilton (Maid), Meg Wynn Owen (Leonie), Jenny Runacre (Mme. de Lionne), Alan Webb (Chevalier). During the Napoleonic Wars a quarrel between two French army officers develops into a feud which lasts many years. Based on the Joseph Conrad short story *The Duel*. Ridley Scott's first feature film as director.

Duke Wore Jeans, The (1958) Tommy Steele (Tony Whitecliffe/Tommy Hudson), June Laverick (Princess Maria), Michael Medwin (Cooper), Eric Pohlmann (Bastini - Prime Minister), Alan Wheatley (King of Ritallia), Noel Hood (Lady Marguerite), Mary Kerridge (Queen), Elwyn Brook-Jones (Bartolomeo), Ambrosine Phillpotts (Duchess Cynthia Whitecliffe), Clive Morton (Lord Edward Whitecliffe), Cyril Chamberlain (Barman). Tommy Steele plays a dual role as a Prince of Ritallia and a commoner who swap places. *Dir.* Gerald Thomas.

Dunkirk (1958) John Mills (Cpl. 'Tubby' Bins), Robert Urquhart (Pvt. Mike), Ray Jackson (Pvt. Barlow), Meredith Edwards (Pvt. Dave Bellman), Anthony Nicholls (Military spokesman), Bernard Lee (Charles Foreman), Michael Shillo (Jouvet), Richard Attenborough (John Holden), Sean Barrett (Frankie), Victor Maddern (Merchant seaman in pub), Maxine Audley (Diana Foreman), Kenneth Cope (Lt. Lumpkin), Denys Graham (Pvt. Fraser), Barry Foster (Don R), Warwick Ashton (Battery sergeant major in France), Peter Halliday (Battery major in France), Ronald Hines (Pvt. Miles), Roland Curram (Pvt. Harper), John Welsh (Staff colonel), Lloyd Lamble (Staff colonel), Cyril Raymond (Gen. Viscount Gort, VC), Nicholas Hannen (Vice-Adm. Ramsey at Dover), Eddie Byrne (Commander), Patricia Plunkett (Grace Holden), Michael Gwynn (Commander at Sheerness), Michael Bates (Froome), Rodney Diak (Pannet), Fred Griffiths (Old Sweet), Dan Gressy (Joe), Lionel Jeffries (Medical colonel), Harry Landis (Dr. Lt. Levy), John Horsley (Padre), Patrick Allen (Sergeant on parade ground), Joss Ambler (Small Boat Owner), Bernard Cribbins (Thirsty Sailor), Liz Fraser (Worker in Holden's Factory), Harold Siddons (Doctor), William Squire (Captain), Charles 'Bud' Tingwell (Sergeant in Cookhouse), Mona Washbourne (Worker Who Speaks to Holden). A realistic account of the evacuation of British and allied troops from the beaches of Dunkirk in 1940. *Dir.* Leslie Norman.

Eagle has Landed, The (1976) Michael Caine (Oberst Kurt Steiner), Donald Sutherland (Liam Devlin), Robert Duvall (Oberst Max Radl), Jenny Agutter (Molly Prior), Donald Pleasence (Heinrich Himmler), Anthony Quayle (Adm. Wilhelm Canaris), Jean Marsh (Joanna Grey), Sven-Bertil Taube (Hauptmann Ritter von Neustadt), Siegfried Rauch (Sergeant Major Otto Brandt), John Standing (Father Philip Verecker), Judy Geeson (Pamela Verecker), Treat Williams (Capt. Harry Clark), Kent Williams (Mallory), Roy Marsden (Sturmbannführer Toberg), Wolf Kahler (Hauptsturmführer Fleischer), Larry Hagman (Col. Clarence E. Pitts), Maurice Roëves (Maj. Corcoran). The Nazi's decide to kidnap Winston Churchill whilst he is visiting an airfield in Norfolk. Based on a Jack Higgins' novel. *Dir.* John Sturges.

Eagle, The (2011) Channing Tatum (Marcus Flavius Aquila), Jamie Bell (Esca), Donald Sutherland (Aquila's Uncle), Aladár Laklóth (Flavius Aquila), Mark Strong (Guern/Lucius Caius Metellus), Douglas Henshall (Cradoc), Denis O'Hare (Lutorius), Dakin Matthews (Senator Claudius), Pip Carter (Legate Placidus), Ned Dennehy (Chief of the Seal People), Tahar Rahim (Prince of the Seal People), James Hayes (Stephanos), István Göz (Cohort Centurion), Bence Gerö (Young Marcus), Paul Ritter (Galba), Zsolt László (Paulus), Julian Lewis Jones (Cassius), Lukács Bicskey (Druid). Accompanied by his British slave, Esca, young centurion Marcus Flavius Aquila determines to recover the lost Eagle of the Ninth Legion, which had disappeared along with his father twenty years earlier. Based on the novel *The Eagle of the Ninth* by Rosemary Sutcliffe. *Dir.* Kevin Macdonald

Early Bird, The (1965) Norman Wisdom (Norman Pitkin), Edward Chapman (Mr. Thomas Grimsdale), Jerry Desmonde (Mr. Walter Hunter), Paddie O'Neil (Mrs. Gladwys Hoskins), Bryan Pringle (Austin), Richard Vernon (Sir Roger Wedgewood), John Le Mesurier (Colonel Foster), Peter Jeffrey (Fire Chief), Penny Morrell (Miss Curry), Marjie Lawrence (Woman in negligee), Frank Thornton (Drunken doctor), Dandy Nichols (Woman flooded by milk), Harry Locke (Commissionaire), Michael Bilton (Nervous Man), Imogen Hassall (Sir Roger's Secretary). Norman works for Grimsdale Dairies which is in competition with the larger Consolidated Dairies run by Walter Hunter. The first Norman Wisdom film in colour. *Dir.* Robert Asher.

Earth Dies Screaming, The (1964) Willard Parker (Jeff Nolan), Virginia Field (Peggy), Dennis Price (Quinn Taggart), Thorley Walters (Edgar Otis), Vanda Godsell (Violet Courtland), David Spenser (Mel), Anna Palk (Lorna). Earth devastated – few survivors – alien killer robots – great title. *Dir.* Terence Fisher.

East is East (1999) Om Puri (Zahir "George" Khan), Linda Bassett (Ella Khan), Ian Aspinall (Nazir "Nigel" Khan), Raji James (Abdul "Arthur" Khan), Jimi Mistry (Tariq "Tony" Khan), Emil Marwa (Maneer "Gandhi" Khan), Chris Bisson (Saleem "Picasso" Khan), Archie Panjabi (Meenah Khan), Jordan Routledge (Sajid "Spaz" Khan), Emma Rydal (Stella Moorhouse), John Bardon (Mr. Moorhouse), Gary Damer (Earnest "Pongo" Moorhouse), Ruth Jones (Peggy), Madhav Sharma (Mr Shah), Lesley Nicol (Auntie Annie). Set in the early 1970s, Salford fish-and-chip shop owner George Khan struggles to control his children, who with an English mother, begin to reject their father's rules on dress, food, religion, and in particular who they should fall in love with. Based on the play of the same name by Ayub Khan-Din, the film won the Alexander Korda Award for Best British Film at the BAFTA Awards. A sequel, *West is West,* premiered in 2010. *Dir.* Damien O'Donnell.

East of Piccadilly (1941) Judy Campbell (Penny Sutton), Sebastian Shaw (Tamsie Green), Niall MacGinnis (Joe), Henry Edwards (Inspector), George Pughe (Oscar Kuloff), Martita Hunt (Ma), George Hayes (Mark Struberg), Cameron Hall (George), Edana Romney (Sadie Jones), Bunty Payne (Tania), Charles Victor (Editor), Frederick Piper (Ginger Harris), Bill Fraser (Maxie). A female reporter is on the trail of a serial killer in London. *Dir.* Harold Huth.

East of Sudan (1964) Anthony Quayle (Richard Baker), Sylvia Syms (Margaret Woodville), Derek Fowlds (Murchison), Johnny Sekka (Kimrasi), Jenny Agutter (Asua), Derek Blomfield (Second Major). During the Mahdist insurrection in the Anglo-Egyptian Sudan, veteran colonial private Baker teams up with freshly arrived gentleman Murchison, trying to evacuate from southern Barash the emir's daughter Asua and her English governess, Miss Woodville. They are soon joined on their perilous journey by king Gondoko's missionary-raised brother Kimrasi. All of the action scenes were taken from the 1939 film *The Four Feathers,* and the 1956 films *Odongo* and *Safari*. *Dir.* Nathan Juran

Eastern Promises (2007) Viggo Mortensen (Nikolai Luzhin), Naomi Watts (Anna), Vincent Cassel (Kirill), Armin Mueller-Stahl (Semyon), Jerzy Skolimowski (Stepan), Sinéad Cusack (Helen), Mina E. Mina (Azim), Josef Altin (Ekrem), Donald Sumpter (Yuri), Raza Jaffrey (Dr. Aziz), Sarah-Jeanne Labrosse (Tatiana), Tamer Hassan (Chechen), Olegar Fedoro (Tattooist). Anna Khitrova, a British-Russian midwife determines to reunite a baby girl with her dead mother's family but is then caught up in the murky dealings of a Russian gang boss and his son. *Dir.* David Cronenberg

Easy Money (1948) Jack Warner (Philip Stafford), Marjorie Fielding (Ruth Stafford), Yvonne Owen (Carol Stafford), Jack Watling (Dennis Stafford), Petula Clark (Jackie Stafford), Mabel Constanduros (Grandma Stafford), David Tomlinson (Martin Latham), Maurice Denham (Detective-Inspector Kirby), Mervyn Johns (Herbert Atkins), Joan Young (Agnes Watkins), Gordon McLeod (Cameron), Grey Blake (Wilson), Ernest Butcher (Clerk), Greta Gynt (Pat Parsons), Dennis Price (Joe Henty), Bill Owen (Mr. Lee), Hugh Pryse (Martin), Jack Raine (Managing Director), Richard Molinas (Johnny), Edward Rigby (Edward

'Teddy' Ball), Guy Rolfe (Archie), Raymond Lovell (Mr. Cyprus), Frank Cellier (Director of Orchestra). Four stories about how the football pools affect a family, a clerk, a musician and a worker at the pools company. *Dir.* Bernard Knowles.

Eat the Rich (1988) Al Pillay (Alex), Nosher Powell (Nosher), Adrian Edmondson (Charles), Dawn French (Debbie Draws), Kathy Burke (Kathy), Robbie Coltrane (Jeremy), Miranda Richardson (DHSS Blonde), Sean Chapman (Mark), Rik Mayall (Micky), Fiona Richmond (Fiona), Jimmy Fagg (Jimmy), Paul McCartney (Banquet guest), Lemmy (Spider), Jools Holland (Sun reporter), Ron Tarr (Ron), Les Bubb (Waiter), Kevin Allen (Waiter), Ronald Allen (Cmdr. Fortune), Dave Beard (Gen. Karpov), Rowena Bently (Indecisive Girlfriend), Angela Bowie (Henry's Wife), Alex (as Lanah Pellay), Nigel Planer (DHSS Manager), Peter Richardson (Henry), Rowland Rivron (Star reporter), Jennifer Saunders (Lady Caroline), Sandie Shaw (Edgeley's Girlfriend), Koo Stark (Hazel), Bill Wyman (Toilet Victim). A film made by The Comic Strip Presents company. *Dir.* Peter Richardson.

Eden Lake (2008) Kelly Reilly (Jenny), Michael Fassbender (Steve), Jack O'Connell (Brett), James Gandhi (Adam), Thomas Turgoose (Cooper), Bronson Webb (Reece), Shaun Dooley (Jon), Finn Atkins (Paige), Thomas Gill (Ricky), James Burrows (Harry). A couple escape for a romantic weekend at a remote lake but are terrorised by a gang of youths. *Dir.* James Watkins.

Edge of Darkness (2010) Mel Gibson (Thomas Craven), Ray Winstone (Darius Jedburgh), Danny Huston (Jack Bennett), Bojana Novakovic (Emma Craven), Shawn Roberts (Burnham), David Aaron Baker (Millroy), Jay O. Sanders (Whitehouse), Denis O'Hare (Moore), Damian Young (Senator Jim Pine), Caterina Scorsone (Melissa), Frank Grillo (Agent One), Wayne Duvall (Chief of Police), Gbenga Akinnagbe (Detective Darcy Jones), Gabrielle Popa (Young Emma), Paul Sparks (Northampton Police Detective), Christy Scott Cashman (Detective Vicki Hurd), Dossy Peabody (Annie), Gordon Peterson (Interviewer), Tom Kemp (Paul Honeywell), Timothy Sawyer (Doctor), Amelia Broome (Tina), Celeste Oliva (Janet), Scott Winters (Northmoor Doctor). Homicide detective Tom Craven gets on the case when his activist daughter is murdered. He begins to uncover a web of intrigue centred on a research and development company called Northmoor, which is running a facility under contract to the U.S. government. An adaptation of the 1985 BBC television series of the same name with the action moved from England to Boston. *Dir.* Martin Campbell.

Edge of the World, The (1937) John Laurie (Peter Manson), Belle Chrystall (Ruth Manson), Eric Berry (Robbie Manson), Kitty Kirwan (Jean Manson), Finlay Currie (James Gray), Niall MacGinnis (Andrew Gray), Grant Sutherland (John), Campbell Robson (Mr. Dunbar), George Summers (Trawler Skipper), James Garrioch (Doctor), Michael Powell (Mr. Graham). As a remote Scottish island becomes de-populated the remaining inhabitants must decide whether to stay or leave for the mainland. Filmed on the very isolated Shetland island of Foula. *Dir.* Michael Powell.

Educating Rita (1983) Michael Caine (Dr. Frank Bryant), Julie Walters (Rita, aka Susan), Michael Williams (Brian), Maureen Lipman (Trish), Jeananne Crowley (Julia), Malcolm Douglas (Denny), Godfrey Quigley (Rita's Father), Dearbhla Molloy (Elaine), Patrick Daly (Bursar), Kim Fortune (Collins), Philip Hurd-Wood (Tiger), Hilary Reynolds (Lesley), Jack Walsh (Price), Christopher Casson (Professor), Rosamund Burton (Denise). Hairdresser Rita decides to take an Open University course in literature and thus crosses the path of Frank, an alcoholic English professor. Caine and Walters were both nominated for Academy Awards, along with writer Willy Russell, upon whose play the film was based. *Dir.* Lewis Gilbert.

Education, An (2009) Carey Mulligan (Jenny Miller), Peter Sarsgaard (David Goldman), Dominic Cooper (Danny), Rosamund Pike (Helen), Emma Thompson (Miss Walters), Alfred Molina (Jack Miller), Olivia Williams (Miss Stubbs), Cara Seymour (Marjorie Miller). Written by Nick Hornby and Lynn Barber and set in England in 1961. Schoolgirl Jenny is given a lift home by David, an older man, and the two strike up a relationship. *Dir.* Lone Scherfig.

Edward II (1991) Steven Waddington (Edward II), Tilda Swinton (Isabella), Andrew Tiernan (Piers Gaveston), Nigel Terry (Mortimer), John Lynch (Spencer), Dudley Sutton (Bishop of Winchester), Jerome Flynn (Kent), Annie Lennox (The Singer), Jody Graber (Prince Edward). Based on Christopher Marlowe's play. The story of King Edward II of England, his infatuation with Piers Gaveston and the plot to overthrow him by his wife Isabella and her lover Sir Roger Mortimer. *Dir.* Derek Jarman

84 Charing Cross Road (1987) Anne Bancroft (Helene Hanff), Anthony Hopkins (Frank Doel), Judi Dench (Nora Doel), Maurice Denham (George Martin), Eleanor David (Cecily Farr), Mercedes Ruehl (Kay), Daniel Gerroll (Brian), Wendy Morgan (Megan Wells), Ian McNeice (Bill Humphries), J. Smith-Cameron (Ginny), Connie Booth (The Lady from Delaware). A moving long term friendship develops between American Helene Hanff and bookshop manager Frank Doel through correspondence between 1949 and 1970. *Dir.* David Hugh Jones.

Elephant Boy (1937) Sabu (Toomai), W. E. Holloway (Father), Walter Hudd (Petersen), Allan Jeayes (Machua Appa), Bruce Gordon (Rham Lahl), D. J. Williams (Hunter),Wilfrid Hyde-White (Commissioner). A young boy helps his father and a hunter track down a herd of elephants. Based on short story *Toomai of the Elephants* from Rudyard Kipling's *The Jungle Book*. Produced by Alexander Korda. *Dirs.* Robert J. Flaherty and Zoltan Korda

Elizabeth (1998) Cate Blanchett (Elizabeth I of England), Geoffrey Rush (Sir Francis Walsingham), Christopher Eccleston (Thomas Howard), Joseph Fiennes (Robert Dudley), Richard Attenborough (William Cecil), Kathy Burke (Mary I of England), George Yiasoumi (Philip II of Spain), Emily Mortimer (Kat Ashley), Edward Hardwicke (Henry FitzAlan), Daniel Craig (John Ballard), James Frain (Alvaro de la Quadra), Kelly Macdonald (Isabel Knollys), Kenny Doughty (Sir Thomas Elyott), Angus Deayton (Waad), John Gielgud (The Pope), Fanny Ardant (Mary of Guise), Vincent Cassel (Henri, Duc d'Anjou), Eric Cantona as Monsieur de Foix, Lily Allen (Lady in Waiting), Wayne Sleep (Dance tutor). The film charts the early years of the reign of Elizabeth I, when she faces threats to her throne both internal and external. The film won six BAFTAs: Alexander Korda Award for Best British Film, Best Actress (Cate Blanchett), Best Supporting Actor (Geoffrey Rush), Anthony Asquith Award for Film Music (David Hirschfelder), Best Cinematography (Remi Adefarasin) and Best Makeup/Hair (Jenny Shircore) and one Academy Award for Best Makeup plus Cate Blanchett was nominated for Best Actress. This was Sir John Gielgud's final film and the first film where ex-footballer Eric Cantona had an English-speaking role. *Dir.* Shekhar Kapur.

Elizabeth: the Golden Age (2007) Cate Blanchett (Elizabeth I), Geoffrey Rush (Sir Francis Walsingham), Clive Owen (Sir Walter Raleigh), Abbie Cornish (Elizabeth Throckmorton), Samantha Morton (Mary, Queen of Scots), Susan Lynch (Annette Fleming), Jordi Mollà (Philip II of Spain), Rhys Ifans (Robert Reston), Eddie Redmayne (Anthony Babington), Tom Hollander (Sir Amyas Paulet), David Threlfall (Dr. John Dee), Adam Godley (William Walsingham), Laurence Fox (Christopher Hatton), William Houston (Don Gerau De Spes), Christian Brassington (Archduke Charles of Austria), John Shrapnel (Charles Howard), Tom Hollander (Sir Amyas Paulet). The sequel to *Elizabeth* which sees an older Elizabeth facing the twin threats of her cousin Mary and also the Spanish Armada. The film won an Academy Award for Best Costume Design. Cate Blanchett's nomination for a Best Actress Academy Award means she is, to date, the first actress to receive another Academy Award nomination for the reprisal of the same role. *Dir.* Shekhar Kapur

Elusive Pimpernel, The (1950) David Niven (Sir Percy Blakeney/The Scarlet Pimpernel), Margaret Leighton (Marguerite Blakeney), Jack Hawkins (Prince of Wales), Cyril Cusack (Chauvelin), Robert Coote (Sir Andrew ffoulkes), Arlette Marchal (Contesses de Tournai), Gérard Nery (Philippe de Tournai), Danielle Godet (Suzanne de Tournai), Edmond Audran (Armand St. Juste), Charles Victor (Colonel Winterbotham), Eugene Deckers (Captain Merieres), David Oxley (Captain Duroc), Raymond Rollett (Bibot), Philip Stainton (Jellyband), John Longden (The Abbot), Robert Griffiths (Trubshaw), Patrick Macnee (Hon. John Bristow). Sir Percy Blakeney must outwit Citizen Chauvelin as he attempts to rescue aristocrats from the guillotine under the guise of the Scarlet Pimpernel. Based on novel *The Scarlet Pimpernel* by Baroness Emmuska Orczy. *Dirs.* Michael Powell and Emeric Pressburger.

Emerald Forest, The (1985) Powers Boothe (Bill Markham), Meg Foster (Jean Markham), Yara Vaneau (Young Heather), William Rodriguez (Young Tommy), Estee Chandler (Heather Markham), Charley Boorman (Tomme), Dira Paes (Kachiri), Eduardo Conde (Werner), Ariel Coelho (Padre Leduc), Peter Marinker (Perreira), Mario Borges (Costa), Átila Iório (Trader), Gabriel Archanjo (Trader's Henchman), Gracindo Júnior (Carlos), Arthur Muhlenberg (Rico). The green eyed Tommy Markham is kidnapped by the Invisible People from the Brazilian rain forest. Ten years later his engineer father finally tracks him down. *Dir.* John Boorman.

Emergency Call (1952) Jack Warner (Inspector Lane), Anthony Steel (Dr. Carter), Joy Shelton (Laura Bishop), Sid James (Danny Marks), Earl Cameron (George Robinson), John Robinson (Dr. Braithwaite), Thora Hird (Mrs. Cornelius), Eric Pohlmann (Flash Harry), Sydney Tafler (Brett), Geoffrey Hibbert (Jackson), Henry Hewitt (Mr. Wilberforce), Vida Hope (Brenda), Avis Scott (Marie), Freddie Mills (Tim Mahoney), Peggy Bryan (Ward Sister), Bruce Seton (Sgt. Bellamy), Anna Turner (Mrs. Jackson), Nosher Powell (Boy Booth), Campbell Singer (Sgt. Phillips), Nigel Clarke (Supt Travers), Michael Brennan (Police Constable), Anthony Oliver (Police Constable), Duncan Lamont (Police Constable), Arthur Lovegrove (Gunner Terry), Richard Gale (Matthews), Dandy Nichols (Barmaid), Jennifer Tafler (Penny Bishop), Carmen Manley (Mrs. Robinson), Michael Ward (Roberto), Iris Vandeleur (Mrs. Flint), Philip Ray (Captain Wilcox), Peter Swanwick (Police Sergeant), Graham Stark (Posh Charlie). In a race against time – three rare-type blood donors need to be found in order to save a little girl's life. *Dir.* Lewis Gilbert.

Emma (1996) Gwyneth Paltrow (Emma Woodhouse), Greta Scacchi (Mrs Weston), James Cosmo (Mr Weston), Jeremy Northam (Mr Knightley), Toni Collette (Miss Harriet Smith), Alan Cumming (Mr Elton), Juliet Stevenson (Mrs Elton), Ewan McGregor (Mr Frank Churchill), Polly Walker (Miss Jane Fairfax), Phyllida Law (Mrs Bates), Sophie Thompson (Miss Bates), Edward Woodall (Mr Robert Martin). Young Emma Woodhouse is an inveterate match-maker who manages to upset friends, family and neighbours. Based on Jane Austen's novel. *Dir.* Douglas McGrath

End of the Affair, The (1955) Deborah Kerr (Sarah Miles), Van Johnson (Maurice Bendrix), John Mills (Albert Parkis), Peter Cushing (Henry Miles), Michael Goodliffe (Smythe), Stephen Murray (Father Crompton), Charles Goldner (Savage), Nora Swinburne (Mrs. Bertram), Frederick Leister (Dr Collingwood), Mary Williams (Maid), O'Donovan Shiell (Doctor), Elsie Wagstaff (Bendrix Landlady), Christopher Warbey (Lancelot Parkis), Nan Munro (Mrs. Tomkins), Joyce Carey (Miss Palmer), Josephine Wilson (Miss Smythe), Victor Maddern (Orator). Towards the end of WWII, Sarah abruptly ends her affair with Maurice. Two years later he meets her husband Henry who says he believes she is being unfaithful. Maurice decides to find out the truth. Based on Graham Greene's novel. *Dir.* Edward Dmytryk.

End of the Affair, The (1999) Ralph Fiennes (Maurice Bendrix), Stephen Rea (Henry Miles), Julianne Moore (Sarah Miles). James Bolam (Mr. Savage), Ian Hart (Mr. Parkis), Sam Bould (Lance Parkis), Cyril Shaps (Waiter), Penny Morrell (Bendrix's Landlady), Simon Fisher Turner (Doctor Gilbert), Jason Isaacs (Father Richard Smythe), Deborah Findlay (Miss Smythe), Nicholas Hewetson (Chief Warden), Jack McKenzie (Chief Engineer), Nic Main (Commanding Officer), Heather-Jay Jones (Henry's Maid). A remake of the 1955 film. *Dir.* Neil Jordan.

End of the River, The (1947) Sabu (Manoel), Bibi Ferreira (Teresa), Esmond Knight (Dantos), Antoinette Cellier (Conceicao), Robert Douglas (Jones), Torin Thatcher (Lisboa), Orlando Martins (Harrigan), Raymond Lovell (Porpino), James Hayter (Chico), Nicolette Bernard (Dona Serafina), Minto Cato (Dona Paula), Maurice Denham (Defending Counsel), Eva Hudson (Maria Gonsalves), Alan Wheatley (Irygoyen), Charles Hawtrey (Raphael), Zena Marshall (Sante), Dennis Arundell

(Continho), Milton Rosmer (The Judge), Peter Illing (Ship's Agent), Nino Rossini (Feliciano), Basil Appleby (Ship's Officer), Milton Sperber (Ze), Andreas Malandrinos (Officer of the Indian Protection Society), Arthur Goullet (The Pedlar), Russell Napier (The Padre). Set, and made, in Brazil, a young boy leaves the rainforest for the city but is then accused of murder. *Dir*. Derek N. Twist.

English Patient, The (1996) Ralph Fiennes (Count Laszlo de Almásy), Juliette Binoche (Hana), Willem Dafoe (David Caravaggio), Kristin Scott Thomas (Katharine Clifton), Naveen Andrews (Kip), Colin Firth (Geoffrey Clifton), Julian Wadham (Madox), Jürgen Prochnow (Major Muller), Kevin Whately (Sgt. Hardy), Clive Merrison (Fenelon-Barnes), Nino Castelnuovo (D'Agostino), Hichem Rostom (Fouad), Peter Rühring (Bermann), Geordie Johnson (Oliver), Torri Higginson (Mary), Liisa Repo-Martell (Jan), Raymond Coulthard (Rupert Douglas), Philip Whitchurch (Corporal Dade). Told mainly in flashback as Count Laszlo lies dying from terrible burns suffered in a plane crash, the film recounts his time in the late 1930s as co-leader of a Royal Geographical Society archaeological and surveying expedition in Egypt and Libya. He falls in love with Katherine, a fellow expedition member, but the onset of WWII sees his life torn apart. The chronology then moves on to the last months of WWII in Italy where the Count is a patient in an old villa and is being looked after by his other love, Hana. Based on Michael Ondaatje's novel. The film won nine Academy Awards: Best Picture, Best Actress (Juliette Binoche), Best Art Direction, Best Cinematography, Best Costume Design, Best Director, Best Film Editing, Best Music and Best Sound. *Dir*. Anthony Minghella.

Englishman Who Went Up A Hill And Came Down A Mountain, The (1995) Hugh Grant (Reginald Anson), Tara Fitzgerald (Elizabeth), Colm Meaney (Morgan the Goat), Ian McNeice (George Garrad), Ian Hart (Johnny Shellshocked Jones), Kenneth Griffith (Reverend Jones), Tudor Vaughan (Thomas Twp), Hugh Vaughan (Thomas Twp Too), Robert Pugh (Williams the Petroleum), Robert Blythe (Ivor), Garfield Morgan (Davies the School), Lisa Palfrey (Blod Jones), Dafydd Wyn Roberts (Tommy Twostroke), Ieuan Rhys (Sgt. Thomas), Anwen Williams (Mavis). Set in 1917, two English cartographers arrive in a Welsh village in order to measure its "mountain" – only to find that it is slightly short of the required 1,000 feet and is therefore only a hill. *Dir*. Christopher Monger.

Enigma (2001) Dougray Scott (Tom Jericho), Kate Winslet (Hester Wallace), Saffron Burrows (Claire Romilly), Jeremy Northam (Mr. Wigram), Nikolaj Coster Waldau (Jozef 'Puck' Pukowski), Tom Hollander (Logie), Donald Sumpter (Leveret), Matthew Macfadyen (Cave), Corin Redgrave (Admiral Trowbridge), Nicholas Rowe (Villiers), Edward Hardwicke (Heaviside), Anne-Marie Duff (Kay), Tim Bentinck (U-boat Commander). Set during WWII, a cryptoanalyst tries to crack the new code used by German U-Boats whilst at the same time tracking down an ex-lover who has disappeared. The screenplay by Tom Stoppard was based on the Robert Harris novel. The final film to be scored by John Barry. *Dir*. Michael Apted.

Entertainer, The (1960) Laurence Olivier (Archie Rice), Brenda De Banzie (Phoebe Rice), Roger Livesey (Billy Rice), Joan Plowright (Jean Rice), Alan Bates (Frank Rice), Daniel Massey (Graham), Shirley Anne Field (Tina Lapford), Thora Hird (Mrs Lapford), Albert Finney (Mick Rice), Miriam Karlin (Soubrette), Geoffrey Toone (Harold Hubbard), MacDonald Hobley (Himself). An undischarged bankrupt and music hall comedian finds both his career and family life are on a downward spiral. An adaptation of John Osborne's stage play. *Dir*. Tony Richardson.

Entertaining Mr Sloane (1970) Beryl Reid (Kath), Peter McEnery (Sloane), Harry Andrews (Ed), Alan Webb (Kemp). When the amoral Mr Sloane becomes a lodger he manipulates the household for his own entertainment but eventually the roles are reversed. Based on a Joe Orton play. *Dir*. Douglas Hickox.

Equus (1977) Richard Burton (Martin Dysart), Peter Firth (Alan Strang), Colin Blakely (Frank Strang), Joan Plowright (Dora Strang), Harry Andrews (Harry Dalton), Eileen Atkins (Hesther Saloman), Jenny Agutter (Jill Mason), Kate Reid (Margaret Dysart), John Wyman (Horseman), Elva Mai Hoover (Miss Raintree), Ken James (Mr Pearce). When stableboy Alan Strang blinds six horses he is examined by psychiatrist Martin Dysart. Peter Shaffer wrote the screenplay based on his own play of the same name. *Dir*. Sidney Lumet

Erik the Viking (1989) Tim Robbins (Erik), Mickey Rooney (Erik's Grandfather), Eartha Kitt (Freya), Terry Jones (King Arnulf), Imogen Stubbs (Princess Aud), John Cleese (Halfdan the Black), Antony Sher (Loki), Gary Cady (Keitel Blacksmith), Tim McInnerny (Sven the Berserk), Charles McKeown (Sven's Dad), John Gordon Sinclair (Ivar the Boneless), Richard Ridings (Thorfinn Skullsplitter), Freddie Jones (Harald the Missionary), Samantha Bond (Helga), Jim Broadbent (Ernest the Viking), Jim Carter (Jennifer the Viking), Neil Innes (Hy-Brasilian), Tsutomu Sekine (Slavemaster), Danny Schiller (Snorri the Miserable), Matyelok Gibbs (Erik's Mum), Tilly Vosburgh (Unn-the-Thrown-At), Jay Simpson (Leif the Lucky), John Scott Martin (Ingemund the Old), Sian Thomas (Thorhild the Sarcastic), Simon Evans (Odin), Matthew Baker (Thor). A viking saga inspired by Terry Jones' book for children *The Saga of Erik the Viking*. Erik discovers he is the antithesis of a true Viking warrior – he doesn't really like raping and pillaging and has guilty feelings – and so starts a quest to find Valhalla in order to end Ragnarok. *Dir*. Terry Jones.

Escape (1948) Rex Harrison (Matt Denant), Peggy Cummins (Dora Winton), William Hartnell (Inspector Harris), Norman Wooland (Minister), Jill Esmond (Grace Winton), Frederick Piper (Brownie), Marjorie Rhodes (Mrs. Pinkem), Betty Ann Davies (Girl in Park), Cyril Cusack (Rodgers), John Slater (Salesman), Frank Pettingell (Constable Beames), Michael Golden (Detective Penter), Frederick Leister (Judge), Walter Hudd (Defense Counsel), Maurice Denham (Crown Counsel), Jacqueline Clarke (Phyllis), Frank Tickle (Mr. Pinkem), Peter Croft (Titch), Stuart Lindsell (Sir James Winton), Patrick Troughton (Jim). An RAF pilot is jailed for manslaughter after accidently causing the death of a policeman. He escapes on Dartmoor and is helped by Dora as the police close in. Based on a play by John Galsworthy. *Dir*. Joseph L. Mankiewicz.

Escape Me Never (1935) Elisabeth Bergner (Gemma Jones), Hugh Sinclair (Sebastian Sanger), Griffith Jones (Caryl Sanger), Penelope Dudley-Ward (Fenella McClean), Irene Vanbrugh (Lady Helen McClean), Leon Quartermaine (Sir Ivor McClean), Lyn Harding (Herr Heinrich), Rosalinde Fuller (Teremtcherva). The relationship between a composer and an unmarried mother. An adaptation of the play of the same name by Margaret Kennedy. *Dir*. by Paul Czinner.

Escape to Athena (1979) Roger Moore (Major Otto Hecht), Telly Savalas (Zeno), David Niven (Prof Blake), Stefanie Powers (Dottie Del Mar), Elliott Gould (Charlie), Claudia Cardinale (Eleana), Richard Roundtree (Nat Judson), Sonny Bono (Bruno Rotelli), Anthony Valentine (Sturmbannführer Volkmann), Siegfried Rauch (Obersturmführer Braun), Richard Wren (SS Obersturmführer Reistoffer), Michael Sheard (Feldwebel Mann), William Holden (Prisoner smoking a cigar). A POW camp escape film with a difference in that some of the inmates are entertainers and are being used to dig for archaeological treasures. *Dir*. George Pan Cosmatos.

Eskimo Nell (1975) Michael Armstrong (Dennis Morrison), Terence Edmond (Clive Potter), Christopher Timothy (Harris Tweedle), Roy Kinnear (Benny U. Murdoch), Rosalind Knight (Lady Longhorn), Lloyd Lamble (The Bishop), Jonathan Adams (Lord Coltwind), Christopher Biggins (Jeremy), Katy Manning (Hermione), Diane Langton (Gladys Armitage), Gordon Tanner (Big Dick), Beth Porter (Billie Harris), Max Mason (Dave), Christopher Neil (Brendan), Richard Caldicot (Ambrose Cream). A writer, a producer and a director are hired to make a film based on the bawdy poem *The Ballad of Eskimo Nell*. *Dir*. Martin Campbell.

Esther Waters (1948) Kathleen Ryan (Esther Waters), Dirk Bogarde (William Latch), Cyril Cusack (Fred), Ivor Barnard (John Randall), Fay Compton (Mrs. Barfield), Margaret Diamond (Sarah), George Hayes (Journeyman), Morland Graham (Ketley),

Mary Clare (Mrs. Latch), Pauline Jameson (Hospital Nurse), Shelagh Fraser (Margaret), Margaret Withers (Grover), Julian D'Albie (Squire Barfield), Nuna Davey (Matron), Beryl Measor (Mrs. Spires), Barbara Shaw (Mistress), Archie Harradine (Singer), Duncan Lewis (Butcher), A. Parker (Jockey Fred Archer), F. Lane (Jockey Webb), Billy Rees (The Demon). Victorian melodrama in which young Esther leaves home, becomes a servant, gets seduced and dumped by the footman and ends up in the Workhouse. However, she meets the footman again years later and they settle down to a life of bliss but will it end happily? An adaptation of George Moore's novel. *Dirs.* Ian Dalrymple and Peter Proud.

Europeans, The (1979) Lee Remick (Eugenia Young), Robin Ellis (Robert Acton), Wesley Addy (Mr. Wentworth), Tim Choate (Clifford), Lisa Eichhorn (Gertrude), Kristin Griffith (Lizzie Acton), Nancy New (Charlotte), Norman Snow (Mr. Brand), Helen Stenborg (Mrs. Acton), Tim Woodward (Felix Young). Eugenia and Felix, the daughter and son of his half sister, arrive from Europe at the home of Mr Wentworth in Boston, Massachusetts. Based upon a Henry James novel. *Dir.* James Ivory.

Event Horizon (1997) Laurence Fishburne (Capt. Miller), Sam Neill (Dr. William Weir), Kathleen Quinlan (Lt. Peters), Joely Richardson (Lt. Starck), Richard T. Jones (Lt. Cooper), Jack Noseworthy (Ensign Justin), Jason Isaacs (Lt. Cmdr. D.J.), Sean Pertwee (Lt. Smith), Peter Marinker (Captain John Kilpack), Holley Chant (Claire Weir), Barclay Wright (Denny Peters), Noah Huntley (Burning Man/Edward Corrick), Robert Jezek (Rescue Technician), Emily Booth (Girl on monitor), Teresa May (Vanessa). A sci-fi horror film set in the year 2047. A distress signal is received from the starship *Event Horizon* seven years after its disappearance on a voyage to Proxima Centauri. The *Lewis and Clark* is sent out on a mission to investigate. *Dir.* Paul W.S. Anderson.

Evergreen (1934) Jessie Matthews (Harriet Green/Harriet Hawkes), Sonnie Hale (Leslie Benn), Betty Balfour (Maudie), Barry MacKay (Tommy Thompson), Ivor McLaren (Marquis of Staines), Hartley Power (George Treadwell), Patrick Ludlow (Lord Shropshire), Betty Shale (Mrs. Hawkes), Marjorie Brooks (Marjorie Moore). Harriet Greene is a popular music hall singer but she has a secret illegitimate daughter. She moves to South Africa to avoid a blackmail threat and many years later her daughter returns to Britain and is persuaded to masquerade as her own mother. *Dir.* Victor Saville.

Every Home Should Have One (1970) Marty Feldman (Teddy Brown), Judy Cornwell (Liz Brown), Julie Ege (Inga Giltenburg), Patrick Cargill (Wallace Trufitt), Jack Watson (McLaughlin), Patience Collier (Mrs. Monty Levin), Penelope Keith (Lotte von Gelbstein), Dinsdale Landen (Vicar Geoffrey Mellish), Annabel Leventon (Chandler's secretary), Sarah Badel (Joanna Snow), Michael Bates (Magistrate), Shelley Berman (Nat Kaplan), Frances de la Tour (Maud Crape), Hy Hazell (Mrs. Kaplan), John Wells (Tolworth), Sheila Gish (Mother in TV Commercial), Marianne Stone (TV Production Assistant). Advertising man Teddy has to come up with a sexy image for frozen porridge, whilst his wife is a clean-up campaigner. *Dir.* Jim Clark.

Evil of Frankenstein, The (1964) Peter Cushing (Baron Victor Frankenstein), Peter Woodthorpe (Zoltan), Duncan Lamont (Chief of Police), Sandor Eles (Hans), Katy Wild (Rena), David Hutcheson (Burgomaster of Karlstaad), James Maxwell (Priest), Howard Goorney (Drunk), Anthony Blackshaw (Policeman), David Conville (Policeman), Caron Gardner (Burgomaster's Wife), Kiwi Kingston (Creature). Returning to his old home Baron Frankenstein is hounded out by the locals but manages to revive his original creature having found it frozen in a glacier. However, he needs the services of Zoltan the hypnotist in order to control it. *Dir.* Freddie Francis.

Evil Under the Sun (1982) Peter Ustinov (Hercule Poirot), Colin Blakely (Sir Horace Blatt), Jane Birkin (Christine Redfern), Nicholas Clay (Patrick Redfern), Maggie Smith (Daphne Castle), Roddy McDowall (Rex Brewster), Sylvia Miles (Myra Gardener), James Mason (Odell Gardener), Denis Quilley (Kenneth Marshall), Diana Rigg (Arlena Marshall), Emily Hone (Linda Marshall), Richard Vernon (Flewitt), Barbara Hicks (Flewitt's Secretary). Poirot investigates the case of a missing blue diamond and the murder of a glamorous actress on a holiday island. Ustinov's second outing as Poirot. Based on an Agatha Christie novel. *Dir.* Guy Hamilton.

Exposé (1976) Udo Kier (Paul Martin), Linda Hayden (Linda), Fiona Richmond (Suzanne), Patsy Smart (Mrs. Aston), Karl Howman (Big Youth), Vic Armstrong (Small Youth). Sex, violence, more sex, much more violence. Little wonder that this was the only British film on the Department of Public Prosecutions' list of banned titles – otherwise known as the "video nasties". *Dir.* James Kenelm Clarke.

Expresso Bongo (1959) Laurence Harvey (Johnny Jackson), Sylvia Syms (Maisie King), Yolande Donlan (Dixie Collins), Cliff Richard (Bert Rudge/Bongo Herbert), Meier Tzelniker (Mayer), Ambrosine Phillpotts (Lady Rosemary), Eric Pohlmann (Leon), Gilbert Harding (Himself), Hermione Baddeley (Penelope), Reginald Beckwith (Reverend Tobias Craven), Avis Bunnage (Mrs. Rudge), Esma Cannon (Night Club Cleaner), Kenneth Griffith (Charlie), Susan Hampshire (Cynthia). Talent agent Johnny Jackson spots Bert Rudge singing in a coffee bar and decides he is ripe for exploitation. *Dir.* Val Guest.

Eyewitness (1956) Donald Sinden (Wade), Muriel Pavlow (Lucy), Belinda Lee (Penny), Michael Craig (Jay), Nigel Stock (Barney), Susan Beaumont (Probationary Nurse), David Knight (Mike), Ada Reeve (Mrs. Hudson), Avice Landone (Night Sister), Richard Wattis (Anesthetist), George Woodbridge (Patrolman), Gillian Harrison (Molly), Nicholas Parsons (House Surgeon), Leslie Dwyer (Henry Cammon), Anna Turner (Mrs. Hays), Anthony Oliver (Podge), John Stuart (Chief Constable), Harry Towb (Sugdon), Charles Victor (Sergeant), Cyril Chamberlain (Cinema Patron), Allan Cuthbertson (Det Insp), Marianne Stone (Cinema Usherette). A woman witnesses a theft in a cinema. She is knocked down by a bus as the thieves chase her but they find out what hospital she has been taken to. *Dir.* Muriel Box.

Face (1997) Robert Carlyle (Ray), Ray Winstone (Dave), Steven Waddington (Stevie), Philip Davis (Julian), Damon Albarn (Jason), Lena Headey (Connie), Andrew Tiernan (Chris), Peter Vaughan (Sonny), Sue Johnston (Alice), Steve Sweeney (Weasel). A raid on a security depot ends with a murderous fall out among the thieves. *Dir.* Antonia Bird.

Face at the Window, The (1939) Tod Slaughter (Chevalier Lucio del Gardo), Marjorie Taylor (Cecile de Brisson), John Warwick (Lucien Cortier), Leonard Henry (Gaston, the Cook), Aubrey Mallalieu (M. de Brisson), Robert Adair (Police Inspector Gouffert), Wallace Evennett (Prof. LeBlanc), Kay Lewis (Babette, the Maid), Bill Shine (Pierre, Babette's Beau), Margaret Yarde (La Pinan), Harry Terry (The Face at the Window). Classic horror where victims see a drooling face at the window before their demise. Is a wolfman on the loose in 1880s France? *Dir.* George King.

Face of Fu Manchu, The (1965) Christopher Lee (Fu Manchu), Nigel Green (Nayland Smith), Joachim Fuchsberger (Carl Jannsen), Karin Dor (Maria Muller), James Robertson Justice (Sir Charles), Howard Marion-Crawford (Dr. Petrie), Tsai Chin (Lin Tang), Walter Rilla (Muller), Harry Brogan (Gaskell), Poulet Tu (Lotus), Archie O'Sullivan (Chamberlain), Edwin Richfield (Chief Magistrate), Joe Lynch (Custodian), Peter Mosbacher (Hanumon), Ric Young (Grand Lama). Scotland Yard detective Nayland Smith believes he has seen his arch nemesis, the fiendish Fu Manchu, executed but evidence of crimes in London seem to indicate otherwise. The first in a series starring Lee as Fu Manchu, others being *The Brides of Fu Manchu* (1966), *The Vengeance of Fu Manchu* (1967), *The Blood of Fu Manchu* (1968), and *The Castle of Fu Manchu* (1969). *Dir.* Don Sharp.

Faces in the Dark (1960) John Gregson (Richard Hammond), Mai Zetterling (Christiane Hammond), John Ireland (Max Hammond), Michael Denison (David Merton), Tony Wright (Clem), Nanette Newman (Janet), Valerie Taylor (Miss Hopkins). An inventor is blinded in a lab accident and is cared for by his wife and brother in a country house. Based on the novel *Les Visages de l'ombre* by Boileau-Narcejac. *Dir.* David Eady.

Fahrenheit 451 (1966) Oskar Werner (Guy Montag), Julie Christie (Clarisse/Linda Montag), Cyril Cusack (The Captain), Anton Diffring (Fabian/Headmistress), Jeremy Spenser (Man with the Apple), Bee Duffell (Book Woman), Alex Scott (Book Person: 'The Life of Henry Brulard'), Michael Balfour (Book

Person: Machiavelli's 'The Prince'), Ann Bell (Doris), Yvonne Blake (Book Person: 'The Jewish Question'), Arthur Cox (Male Nurse), Frank Cox (Book Person: 'Prejudice'), Fred Cox (Book Person: 'Pride'), Arthur Haynes (Man on Commuter Train), Mark Lester (Second Schoolboy). Set in the future when all literature is burned by "Firemen". Clarisse meets Guy who then begins to read the books he has confiscated. This leads to conflict with his wife, Linda, who is aspires to be a member of "The Family" (an interactive television program that refers to its viewers as "Cousins"). Based on the novel of the same name by Ray Bradbury. *Dir.* François Truffaut.

FairyTale: A True Story (1997) Peter O'Toole (Sir Arthur Conan Doyle), Florence Hoath (Elsie Wright), Elizabeth Earl (Frances Griffiths), Harvey Keitel (Harry Houdini), Paul McGann (Arthur Wright), Bill Nighy (Edward Gardner), Phoebe Nicholls (Polly Wright), Anna Chancellor (Peter Pan), Mel Gibson (Frances' father – uncredited). Young Elsie and Frances take photographs of themselves with fairies, sparking a controversy involving Conan Doyle and Harry Houdini. Based on the true story of the Cottingley Fairies. *Dir.* Charles Sturridge.

Fallen Idol, The (1948) Ralph Richardson (Baines), Michèle Morgan (Julie), Sonia Dresdel (Mrs. Baines), Bobby Henrey (Phillipe), Denis O'Dea (Inspector Crowe), Jack Hawkins (Detective Ames), Walter Fitzgerald (Dr. Fenton), Dandy Nichols (Mrs. Patterson), Joan Young (Mrs. Barrow), Karel Stepanek (First Secretary), Gerard Heinz (Ambassador), Torin Thatcher (Police Officer), James Hayter (Perry), Geoffrey Keen (Detective Davis), Bernard Lee (Detective Hart), Dora Bryan (Rose). Philippe, a diplomat's son is left in the charge of his father's butler, a man he idolises. When Baines' wife is found dead Philippe believes Baines must have killed her but his attempts at helping his friend only cause him more problems. Based on Graham Greene's short story *The Basement Room. Dir.* Carol Reed.

Family Way, The (1966) Hayley Mills (Jenny Piper Fitton), Hywel Bennett (Arthur Fitton), John Mills (Ezra Fitton), Marjorie Rhodes (Lucy Fitton), Avril Angers (Liz Piper), John Comer (Leslie Piper), Barry Foster (Joe Thompson), Wilfred Pickles (Uncle Fred), Liz Fraser (Molly Thompson), Diana Coupland (Mrs. Rose), Colin Gordon (Mr. Hutton), Murray Head (Geoffrey Fitton), Thorley Walters (The Vicar), Windsor Davies (Man in crowd), Kathy Staff (Neighbour). A newlywed couple has trouble consummating their marriage. Based on Bill Naughton's play *All in Good Time. Dir.* Roy Boulting.

Fanny By Gaslight (1944) Phyllis Calvert (Fanny Hooper), James Mason (Lord Manderstoke), Wilfrid Lawson (Chunks), Stewart Granger (Harry Somerford), Jean Kent (Lucy Beckett), Margaretta Scott (Alicia), Nora Swinburne (Mrs. Hopwood), Cathleen Nesbitt (Kate Somerford), Helen Haye (Mrs. Somerford), John Laurie (William Hopwood), Stuart Lindsell (Clive Seymour), Amy Veness (Mrs. Heaviside), Ann Wilton (Carver), Guy Le Feuvre (Doctor Lowenthal), Esma Cannon (Gossiping maid), Peter Jones (New client). A Gainsborough Pictures melodrama, typical of that studios 1940s output. After the death of her foster father, Fanny is employed by her Cabinet Minister real father as a servant. *Dir.* Anthony Asquith.

Fanny Hill (1983) Lisa Foster (Fanny Hill), Oliver Reed (Edward Widdlecome), Wilfrid Hyde-White (Barville), Shelley Winters (Mrs Cole), Alfred Marks (Lecher), Paddie O'Neil (Mrs Brown), Barry Stokes (Charles), Maria Harper (Phoebe), Fanny Carby (Old Wench), Harry Fowler (Beggar), Gordon Rollings (Beggar), Vicki Scott (Polly), Liz Smith (Mrs. Jones). A comedy adapted from the notorious 18th Century novel of the same name by John Cleland. *Dir.* Gerry O'Hara

Far From the Madding Crowd (1967) Julie Christie (Bathsheba Everdene), Terence Stamp (Sgt. Francis 'Frank' Troy), Peter Finch (William Boldwood), Alan Bates (Gabriel Oak), Fiona Walker (Liddy), Prunella Ransome (Fanny Robin), Alison Leggatt (Mrs. Hurst), Paul Dawkins (Henery Fray), Julian Somers (Jan Coggan), John Barrett (Joseph Poorgrass). Freddie Jones (Cainy Ball), Brian Rawlinson (Matthew Moon), Denise Coffey (Soberness), Dave Swarbrick (Fiddler at Barn Dance). The story of headstrong Bathsheba Everdene and her three suitors: shepherd Gabriel Oak, farmer William Boldwood and Dragoon Sergeant Francis Troy. Adapted from the book of the same name by Thomas Hardy. *Dir.* John Schlesinger.

Fast and Loose (1954) Stanley Holloway (Major George Crabb), Kay Kendall (Carol Hankin), Brian Reece (Peter Wickham), Joan Young (Mrs. Gullett), Fabia Drake (Mrs. Crabb), June Thorburn (Barbara Wickham), Dora Bryan (Mary Rawlings), Vida Hope (Gladys), Charles Victor (Lumper), Reginald Beckwith (Reverend Tripp-Johnson), Alexander Gauge (Hankin), Aubrey Mather (Noony), Toke Townley (Alfred). A farce in which an unmarried couple face the problem of staying in a guest house with only one free room – well, it was made in the 1950s! *Dir.* Gordon Parry.

Fast Lady, The (1962) James Robertson Justice (Charles Chingford), Leslie Phillips (Freddie Fox), Stanley Baxter (Murdoch), Julie Christie (Claire Chingford), Kathleen Harrison (Mrs Staggers), Eric Barker (Wentworth), Oliver Johnston (Bulmer), Allan Cuthbertson (Bodley), Esma Cannon (Lady on Zebra Crossing), Dick Emery (Shingler), Deryck Guyler (Doctor Blake), Victor Brooks (Policeman), Terence Alexander (Policeman on Motorcycle), Trevor Reid (Examiner), Allan Cuthbertson (Bodley), Fred Emney (1st Golfer), Monsewer Eddie Gray (2nd Golfer), Frankie Howerd (Road Workman in Hole), Clive Dunn (Old Gentleman in Burning House), Gerald Campion (Actor in Scottish TV show), Campbell Singer (Kingscombe), Ann Beach (Miss Timpkins), Marianne Stone (Miss Oldham), Eddie Leslie (Bandit), Michael Balfour (Bandit), Bernard Cribbins (Man on Stretcher). Shy cycling Scotsman Murdoch Troon falls for Claire, the daughter of a sportscar magnate. He buys a 1927 vintage 4.5 litre engined Bentley named The Fast Lady and takes driving lessons in order to impress her. *Dir.* Ken Annakin.

Father Brown (1954) Alec Guinness (Father Brown), Joan Greenwood (Lady Warren), Peter Finch (Flambeau), Cecil Parker (The Bishop), Bernard Lee (Inspector Valentine), Sid James (Bert Parkinson), Gérard Oury (Inspector Dubois), Ernest Clark (Bishop's Secretary), Aubrey Woods (Charlie), Sam Kydd (Scotland Yard sergeant). The Catholic priest and amateur sleuth pits his wits against master art thief Flambeau. Based on characters created by G K Chesterton. *Dir.* Robert Hamer.

Father, Dear Father (1973) Patrick Cargill (Patrick Glover), Noel Dyson (Nanny), Natasha Pyne (Anna), Ann Holloway (Karen), Ursula Howells (Barbara), Jack Watling (Bill), Donald Sinden (Phillip), Jill Melford (Georgie Thompson), Beryl Reid (Mrs Stoppard), Joseph O'Conor (Vicar), Richard O'Sullivan (Richard), Joyce Carey (Patrick's Mother), Elizabeth Adare (Maggie), Clifton Jones (Larry), A big-screen version of the ITV sitcom. *Dir.* William G. Stewart.

Fatherland (1986) Gerulf Pannach (Klaus Dittemann), Fabienne Babe (Emma de Baen), Cristine Rose (Lucy Bernstein), Sigfrit Steiner (Drittemann), Robert Dietl (Lawyer), Heike Schroetter (Marita), Stephan Samuel (Max), Thomas Öhlke (Young Drittemann). A singer-songwriter in East Berlin moves to the West but finds the commercial music industry equally as oppressive. *Dir.* Ken Loach.

Fathom (1967) Raquel Welch (Fathom Harvill), Anthony Franciosa (Peter Merriwether), Ronald Fraser (Col. Douglas Campbell), Richard Briers (Flight Lt. Timothy Webb), Greta Chi (Maj. Jo-May Soon), Tom Adams (Mike), Elizabeth Ercy (Ulla), Ann Lancaster (Mrs. Trivers), Clive Revill (Sergi Serapkin), Tutte Lemkow Mehmed (Serapkin's servant), Reg Lye (Mr. Trivers). An American skydiver is asked to parachute into a Chinese compound and retrieve a lost nuclear device. *Dir.* Leslie H. Martinson.

Feather Your Nest (1937) George Formby (Willie Piper), Polly Ward (Mary Taylor), Enid Stamp-Taylor (Daphne Randall), Val Rosing (Rex Randall), Moore Marriott (Mr Jenkins). A comedy musical set in a gramophone factory. *Dir.* William Beaudine.

Ferry Cross the Mersey (1965) Gerry Marsden (Gerry), Freddie Marsden (Fred), Leslie Maguire (Les), Les Chadwick (Chad), Julie Samuel (Dodie Dawson), T.P. McKenna (Jack Hanson), Mona Washbourne (Aunt Lil), Eric Barker (Col. Dawson),

George A. Cooper (Mr. Lumsden), Mischa De La Motte (Dawson's Butler), Donald Gee (Art Student), Margaret Nolan (Norah), Deryck Guyler (Trasler), Andy Ho (Chinese Restaurant Manager), Patricia Lawrence (Miss Kneave) and as themselves, Cilla Black, The Fourmost, Gerry and the Pacemakers, George Martin and Jimmy Savile. A story that showcases the Mersey Beat scene. *Dir*. Jeremy Summers.

Festival (2005) Lyndsey Marshal (Faith Myers), Daniela Nardini (Joan Gerard), Chris O'Dowd (Tommy O'Dwyer), Clive Russell (Brother Mike), Stephen Mangan (Sean Sullivan), Raquel Cassidy (Petra Loewenberg), Lucy Punch (Nicky Romanowski), Amelia Bullmore (Micheline Menzies), Jonah Lotan (Rick), Billy Carter (Conor Kelly), Jimmy Chisholm (Radio Producer), Kevin Masson (The P), Gabriel Quigley (Receptionist), Deirdre O'Kane (Frida Finucane), Stuart Milligan (Arnold Weiss), Dorothy Paul (Micheline's Mother), Richard Ayoade (Dwight Swan), Sanjeev Kohli (Ahmed Khan), Mark McDonnell (Comedy Award Presenter), Denys McNair (The Priest), Paddy Bonner (Man on Street). A black comedy set during the Edinburgh Festival. *Dir*. Annie Griffin.

Fever Pitch (1996) Colin Firth (Paul), Ruth Gemmell (Sarah Hughes), Mark Strong (Steve), Neil Pearson (Mr. Ashworth), Lorraine Ashbourne (Mrs. Ashworth), Holly Aird (Jo), Stephen Rea (Ray), Emily Conway (Sasha), Luke Aikman (Young Paul), Bea Guard (Paul's Sister), Richard Claxton (Robert Parker), Ken Stott (Ted), Mark Strong (Steve). Teacher Paul Ashworth's love of Arsenal FC is tested when he meets Sarah. Based on the Nick Hornby novel. *Dir*. David Evans.

Fiddlers Three (1944) Tommy Trinder (Tommy Taylor), Frances Day (Poppaea), Sonnie Hale (The Professor), Francis L. Sullivan (Nero), Diana Decker (Lydia), Elisabeth Welch (Nora), Mary Clare (Volumnia), Ernest Milton (Titus), Frederick Piper (Auctioneer), Robert Wyndham (Lionkeeper), Russell Thorndike (High Priest), Danny Green (Lictor), James Robertson Justice (Centurion), Kay Kendall (Girl). Comedy in which two sailors and a Wren are struck by lightning and transported back to Ancient Rome at the time of Nero. *Dir*. Harry Watt.

Fierce Creatures (1997) John Cleese (Rollo Lee), Jamie Lee Curtis (Willa Weston), Kevin Kline (Vince McCain/Rod McCain), Michael Palin (Adrian 'Bugsy' Malone), Robert Lindsay (Sydney Lotterby), Ronnie Corbett (Reggie Sea Lions), Carey Lowell (Cub Felines), Bille Brown (Neville), Derek Griffiths (Garry Ungulates), Cynthia Cleese (Pip Small Mammals), Richard Ridings (Hugh Primates), Maria Aitken (Di Harding), Susie Blake (Woman in Red Dress), Gareth Hunt (Inspector Masefield), Tom Georgeson (Sea Lion Spectator), Jack Davenport (Student Zoo Keeper). Under pressure from a new owner, zoo manager Rollo Lee institutes a "fierce creatures" policy where only potentially lethal animals will be kept in the zoo in order to attract more visitors. From much the same team responsible for the successful *A Fish Called Wanda* but with the actors playing different roles and credited as an "equal" rather than a sequel to that film. *Dirs*. Fred Schepisi and Robert Young.

51st State, The (2001) Samuel L. Jackson (Elmo), Robert Carlyle (Felix DeSouza), Emily Mortimer (Dawn "Dakota" Parker), Meat Loaf (The Lizard), Ricky Tomlinson (Leopold Durant), Sean Pertwee (Detective Virgil Kane), Rhys Ifans (Iki), Ade (Omar), Stephen Walters (Blowfish), James Roach (Grimtooth), Anna Keaveney (Shirley DeSouza), Robert Fyfe (Hector Dougal McElroy), Jake Abraham (Konokko), Mac McDonald (Mr. Davidson), Aaron Swartz (Mr. Yuri), David Webber (Mr. Jones), Michael J. Reynolds (Mr. Escobar), Junix Inocian (Mr. Ho-Fat), Paul Barber (Frederick), Christopher Hunter (Lawrence), Ade (Omar), Nick Bartlett (Trevor), Angus MacInnes (Pudsey Smith). American chemist Elmo McElroy tries to break away from the drug lord who employs him (The Lizard) and, after blowing up the entire gang except the boss, flees the States and heads to Liverpool where he seals a deal for the production of his new drug POS 51. Meanwhile, the Lizard has set a contract killer on Elmo's trail. Action comedy film. *Dir*. Ronny Yu.

Filth and the Fury, The (2000) A rockumentary film about the Sex Pistols which tells the story from the viewpoint of the band members and acts as a rebuttal to the same director's *The Great Rock and Roll Swindle* (1980). *Dir*. Julien Temple.

Final Cut (1998) Ray Winstone (Ray), Jude Law (Jude), Sadie Frost (Sadie), John Beckett (John), William Scully (Bill), Mark Burdis (Mark), Perry Benson (Tony), Lisa Marsh (Lisa), Ray Burdis (Burdis), Dominic Anciano (Dominic), Holly Davidson (Holly). After Jude's funeral his gathering of friends is shown secret videos he took of them in compromising and unsavoury situations. *Dirs*. Dominic Anciano and Ray Burdis.

Finding Neverland (2004) Johnny Depp (J. M. Barrie), Kate Winslet (Sylvia Llewelyn Davies), Dustin Hoffman (Charles Frohman), Julie Christie (Mrs Emma du Maurier), Radha Mitchell (Mary Ansell Barrie), Freddie Highmore (Peter Llewelyn Davies), Nick Roud (George Llewelyn Davies), Joe Prospero (Jack Llewelyn Davies), Luke Spill (Michael Llewelyn Davies), Ian Hart (Arthur Conan Doyle), Oliver Fox (Gilbert Cannan), Mackenzie Crook (Mr Jaspers), Kelly Macdonald (Peter Pan), Angus Barnett (Nana/Mr. Reilly), Toby Jones (Smee), Kate Maberly (Wendy Darling), Matt Green (John Darling), Catrin Rhys (Michael Darling), Tim Potter (Capt Hook /George Darling), Jane Booker (Mary Darling), Eileen Essell (Mrs Snow), Jimmy Gardner (Mr Snow), Paul Whitehouse (Stage Manager). Story of J. M. Barrie's love for the family who inspired him to create Peter Pan. *Dir*. Marc Forster.

Fire Over England (1937) Laurence Olivier (Michael), Vivien Leigh (Cynthia), Flora Robson (Elizabeth I of England), Raymond Massey (Philip II of Spain), Leslie Banks (Earl of Leicester), Morton Selten (Lord Burleigh), Tamara Desni (Elena), Lyn Harding (Sir Richard Ingolby), George Thirlwell (Mr. Lawrence Gregory), Henry Oscar (Spanish Ambassador), Robert Rendel (Don Miguel), Robert Newton (Don Pedro), Donald Calthrop (Don Escobal), Charles Carson (Valdez), James Mason (English traitor). The story of Michael Ingolby and his love life against a background of the impending Spanish Armada. Leigh's performance helped her to be cast as Scarlett O'Hara in *Gone with the Wind*. *Dir*. William K. Howard.

Fires Were Started (1943) A documentary style film covering a day and night with the National Fire Service during the London Blitz of WWII. The firefighting scenes are reconstructions, not actual events. *Dir*. Humphrey Jennings.

First A Girl (1935) Jessie Matthews (Elizabeth), Sonnie Hale (Victor), Anna Lee (Princess Mironoff), Griffith Jones (Robert), Alfred Drayton (Mr. McLintock), Constance Godridge (Beryl), 'Monsewer' Eddie Gray (Goose Trainer), Martita Hunt (Madame Seraphina). A young woman posing as a man posing as a woman. Adapted from the 1933 German film *Viktor und Viktoria* and remade as *Victor Victoria* starring Julie Andrews in 1982. *Dir*. Victor Saville.

First Gentleman, The (1948) Jean-Pierre Aumont (Prince Leopold), Joan Hopkins (Princess Charlotte), Cecil Parker (The Prince Regent), Margaretta Scott (Lady Hartford), Jack Livesey (Edward), Ronald Squire (Mr. Brougham), Athene Seyler (Miss Knight), Anthony Hawtrey (Sir Richard Croft), Hugh Griffith (Bishop of Salisbury), Gerard Heinz (Dr. Stockmar), George Curzon (Duke of York), Betty Huntley-Wright (Princess Elizabeth), Tom Gill (Prince William), Lydia Sherwood (Princess Augusta), Frances Waring (Queen Charlotte), Amy Frank (Princess Caroline). The life and loves of the Prince Regent. *Dir*. Alberto Cavalcanti.

First Great Train Robbery, The (1979) Sean Connery (Edward), Donald Sutherland (Agar), Lesley-Anne Down (Miriam), Alan Webb (Trent), Malcolm Terris (Henry Fowler), Robert Lang (Sharp), Michael Elphick (Burgess), Wayne Sleep (Clean Willy), Pamela Salem (Emily Trent), Gabrielle Lloyd (Elizabeth Trent), George Downing (Barlow), James Cossins (Harranby), Janine Duvitski (Maggie), André Morell (Judge), Donald Churchill (Prosecutor), Brian Glover (Captain Jimmy), Noel Johnson (Connaught), Peter Butterworth (Putnam). During the Crimean War, Edward Pierce plans to rob the train from London to Folkestone carrying gold needed to pay the troops. Based on Michael Crichton's novel *The Great Train Robbery*. *Dir*. Michael Crichton.

First Man into Space (1959) Marshall Thompson (Cmdr. Charles Ernest Prescott), Marla Landi (Tia Francesca), Bill Edwards (Lt. Dan Milton Prescott), Robert Ayres (Capt. Ben Richards), Bill Nagy (Police Chief Wilson), Carl Jaffe (Dr. Paul von Essen), Roger Delgado (Ramon de Guerrera), John McLaren (Harold

Atkins), Richard Shaw (Witney), Bill Nick (Clancy), Helen Forrest (Secretary), Roland Brand (Truck Driver), Barry Shawzin (Sanchez), Mark Sheldon (Doctor), Michael Bell (State Trooper), Sheree Winton (Nurse), Franklyn Fox (Larson), Larry Taylor (Taylor). Dan Prescott pilots the Y-13 experimental rocket and after taking it out of Earth's atmosphere against orders he passes through a cloud of metallic dust and is forced to eject. The spacecraft returns to Earth in New Mexico with no sign of Dan. Then local cattle are killed and a blood bank broken into. *Dir*. Robert Day.

First Men in the Moon (1964) Edward Judd (Bedford), Martha Hyer (Kate), Lionel Jeffries (Cavor), Miles Malleson (Dymchurch registrar), Norman Bird (Stuart), Gladys Henson (Mental hospital matron), Hugh McDermott (Richard Challis), Betty McDowall (Margaret Hoy), Hugh Thomas (Announcer), Erik Chitty (Gibbs), Peter Finch (Bailiff's man). A United Nations rocket lands on the Moon and the crew discover a British flag on the surface and a note naming Katherine Callender, claiming the Moon for Queen Victoria. Katherine's husband is tracked down and he tells the story of Professor Cavor who in the 1890s invented an anti-gravity substance which he named cavorite, the use of which prompted a Moon landing. Adaptation by Nigel Kneale of the H. G. Wells novel *The First Men in the Moon*. *Dir*. Nathan Juran.

First of the Few, The (1942) Leslie Howard (R.J. Mitchell), David Niven (Geoffrey Crisp), Rosamund John (Diana Mitchell), Roland Culver (Commander Bride), Anne Firth (Miss Harper), David Horne (Mr. Higgins), J.H. Roberts (Sir Robert McLean), Derrick De Marney (Squadron Leader Jefferson), Rosalyn Boulter (Mabel Lovesay), Herbert Cameron (MacPherson), Toni Edgar-Bruce (Lady Houston), Gordon McLeod (Major Buchan), George Skillan (Mr. Royce), Erik Freund (Messerschmitt), Fritz Wendhausen (Von Straben), John Chandos (Krantz), Victor Beaumont (Von Crantz), Suzanne Clair (Madeleine), Filippo Del Giudice (Bertorelli), Brefni O'Rorke (The Specialist), Gerry Wilmot (Radio Announcer), Jack Peach (Radio Announcer), Robert Beatty (American Airman), Miles Malleson (Vickers Rep), Bernard Miles (Lady Houston's Agent). A biopic of aero designer R J Mitchell who was responsible for designing the Supermarine Spitfire, which, along with the Hawker Hurricane, helped win the Battle of Britain in 1940. *Dir*. Leslie Howard.

Fish Called Wanda, A (1988) John Cleese (Archie), Jamie Lee Curtis (Wanda Gershwitz), Kevin Kline (Otto), Michael Palin (Ken), Maria Aitken (Wendy Leach), Tom Georgeson (George Thomason), Patricia Hayes (Mrs. Coady), Geoffrey Palmer (Judge), Cynthia Caylor (Portia Leach), Ken Campbell (Bartlett), Stephen Fry (Hutchison). A crime caper where thieves (Wanda and Otto from America with their British accomplices George and Ken) attempt multiple double-crosses in the aftermath of a successful diamond robbery. In the process they involve barrister Archie Leach in their machinations. Kevin Kline won an Academy Award for Best Supporting Actor as insanely jealous weapons man Otto West and Michael Palin won the BAFTA Award for Best Actor in a Supporting Role as stammering Ken Pile. Palin based the role on his own father who suffered from stammering all his life and in 1993 the Michael Palin Centre for Stammering Children was officially opened as a joint initiative between the Association for Research into Stammering in Childhood (ARSC) and the then Camden & Islington Community Health Services NHS Trust. The creative team behind the film also made *Fierce Creatures*. *Dirs*. Charles Crichton and John Cleese (Uncredited).

Fish Tank (2009) Katie Jarvis (Mia Williams), Michael Fassbender (Connor O'Reily), Kierston Wareing (Joanne Williams), Rebecca Griffiths (Tyler Williams), Harry Treadaway (Billy), Sydney Mary Nash (Keira), Sarah Bayes (Keeley), Grant Wild (Keeley's Dad), Carrie-Ann Savill (Tyler's Friend), Toyin Ogidi (Tyler's Friend), Harry Treadaway (Billy), Jason Maza (Billy's Brother), Jack Gordon (Billy's Brother), Michael Prior (Connor's Friend). The story of aggressive and volatile 15 year-old Mia and her relationship with Connor, her mother's boyfriend. Won the 2010 BAFTA for Best British Film. *Dir*. Andrea Arnold.

Flash Gordon (1980) Sam J. Jones (Flash Gordon), Melody Anderson (Dale Arden), Topol (Dr. Hans Zarkov), Timothy Dalton (Prince Barin), Max von Sydow (Emperor Ming the Merciless), Ornella Muti (Princess Aura), Brian Blessed (Prince Vultan), Peter Wyngarde (General Klytus), Mariangela Melato (General Kala), Richard O'Brien (Fico), John Hallam (General Luro), Robbie Coltrane (Man at airfield), William Hootkins (Munson), George Harris (Prince Thun), John Osborne (Arborian Priest), Philip Stone (Zogi), Suzanne Danielle (Serving Girl), Peter Duncan (Young Treeman), Graeme Crowther (Battle Room Controller), Tony Scannell (Ming's Officer), Colin Taylor (King of Frigia), Doretta Dunkley (Queen of Frigia), Sally Nicholson (Queen of Azuria), Deep Roy (Princess Aura's Pet). Colourful version of the 1930s cinema serial and comic strip created by Alex Raymond. Flash Gordon saves the Earth from the clutches of Ming the Merciless, Emperor of Mongo to a backdrop of music by rock legends, Queen. *Dir*. Mike Hodges.

Flesh and Blood Show, The (1972) Ray Brooks (Mike), Jenny Hanley (Julia Dawson), Luan Peters (Carol Edwards), Robin Askwith (Simon), Candace Glendenning (Sarah), Tristan Rogers (Tony Weller), Judy Matheson (Jane), David Howey (John), Elizabeth Bradley (Mrs. Saunders), Rodney Diak (Warner), Penny Meredith (Angela), Sally Lahee (Iris Vokins), Raymond Young (Insp. Walsh), Alan Curtis (Jack Phipps), Brian Tully (Willesden), Jane Cardew (Lady Pamela), Tom Mennard (Fred), Stewart Bevan (Harry Mulligan), Michael Knowles (Curran), Patrick Barr (Major Bell/Sir Arnold Gates). As a group of young actors are rehearsing a new play in a derelict theatre they begin to be bumped off one by one. *Dir*. Pete Walker.

Flesh and the Fiends, The (1958) Peter Cushing (Dr. Robert Knox), June Laverick (Martha Knox), Donald Pleasence (William Hare), George Rose (William Burke), Renee Houston (Helen Burke), Dermot Walsh (Dr. Geoffrey Mitchell), Billie Whitelaw (Mary Patterson), John Cairney (Chris Jackson), Melvyn Hayes (Daft Jamie), June Powell (Maggie O'Hara), Andrew Faulds (Inspector McCulloch). A retelling of the story of infamous "resurrection men" Burke and Hare. *Dir*. John Gilling.

Flight from Folly (1945) Patricia Kirkwood (Sue), Hugh Sinclair (Clinton), Sydney Howard (Dr. Wylie), Tamara Desni (Nina), Jean Gillie (Millicent), A.E. Matthews (Neville), Marian Spencer (Harriet), Leslie Bradley (Bamber), Charles Goldner (Ramon), Edmundo Ros (Himself). Showgirl Sue Brown poses as a nurse for composer and playwright Clinton Clay. *Dir*. Herbert Mason.

Follow a Star (1959) Norman Wisdom (Norman Truscott), June Laverick (Judy), Jerry Desmonde (Carew), Hattie Jacques (Dymphna Dobson), Richard Wattis (Dr. Chatterway), Eddie Leslie (Harold Franklin), John Le Mesurier (Birkett), Sydney Tafler (Pendlebury), Fenella Fielding (Lady Finchington), Charles Heslop (The General), Joe Melia (Stage Manager), Ron Moody (Violinist). Fading singing star Vernon Carew passes off Norman's voice as his own. *Dir*. Robert Asher.

Folly to Be Wise (1953) Alastair Sim (Capt. William Paris), Elizabeth Allan (Angela Prout), Roland Culver (George Prout), Colin Gordon (Prof. James Mutch), Martita Hunt (Lady Dodds), Janet Brown (Jessie Killegrew), Peter Martyn (Walter), Miles Malleson (Dr. Hector McAdam), Edward Chapman (Joseph Byres M.P.), Cyril Chamberlain (Drill Sergeant), Michael Ripper (Drill Corporal), Robin Bailey (Intellectual Corporal), Michael Kelly (Staff Sergeant), George Cole (Soldier). An army padre organises a Brains Trust in order to entertain the troops but the local worthies he engages for the panel have scores to settle with each other. *Dir*. Frank Launder.

For Better, for Worse (1954) Dirk Bogarde (Tony Howard), Susan Stephen (Anne Purves), Cecil Parker (Anne's Father), Eileen Herlie (Anne's Mother), Athene Seyler (Miss Mainbrace), Dennis Price (Debenham), Pia Terri (Mrs. Debenham), James Hayter (The Plumber), Thora Hird (Mrs. Doyle), George Woodbridge (Alf), Charles Victor (Fred), Sid James (The Foreman), Peter Jones (Car Salesman), Edwin Styles (Anne's Boss). The trials and tribulations of newlyweds Tony and Anne. *Dir*. J. Lee Thompson

For Queen and Country (1988) Denzel Washington (Reuben James), Dorian Healy (Tony aka Fish), Amanda Redman (Stacey), Geff Francis (Lynford), Sean Chapman (Bob Harper), Graham McTavish (Lieutenant), Frank Harper (Mickey), Craig Fairbrass (Challoner), Michael Bray (Bryant), George Baker (Kilcoyne), Bruce Payne (Colin), Stella Gonet (Debbie), Colin Thomas (Feargal), Brian McDermott (Harry), Lisa O'Connor (Haley), Anselm Peters (Oscar), Carlton Dixon (Stylee), Mike Smart (Peelhead), Peter McNamara (Pete), Chris Pitt (Chris), Paul McKenzie (Sean), Jo Martin (Pearl), Linda Henry (Kim), Ken Stott (Civil Servant). A returning Falklands war hero finds the East End unchanged from before his enlistment and finds his war record does not help him find a respectable job. *Dir*. Martin Stellman.

For Those in Peril (1944) David Farrar (Flt.Lt Murray), Ralph Michael (P/O Rawlings), Robert Wyndham (Sqr.Ldr Leverett), John Slater (Wilkie), Robert Griffith (Coxswain), John Batten (Wireless Officer), William Rodwell (Air Gunner), Tony Bazell (Lt Overton R.N.), Leslie Clarke (Pearson), Peter Arne (Junior officer), James Robertson Justice (Operations Room Officer). Rawlings fails to make the grade in the RAF so joins the Air and Sea Rescue Service. A WWII propaganda film developed from a short story by Richard Hillary, an RAF pilot killed in action in January 1943. *Dir*. Charles Crichton.

For You Alone (1945) Lesley Brook (Katherine Britton), Jimmy Hanley (Dennis Britton), Dinah Sheridan (Stella White), G.H. Mulcaster (Rev. Peter Britton), Robert Griffiths (John Bradshaw), Olive Walter (Lady Markham), Manning Whiley (Max Borrow), Irene Handl (Miss Trotter), George Merritt (Police Constable Blundell), Muriel George (Mrs. Johns), Aubrey Mallalieu (Eye Specialist). The story of a young naval officer in WWII and the girl he falls in love with after a lunchtime concert at Westminster Central Hall. *Dir*. Geoffrey Faithfull.

For Your Eyes Only (1981) Roger Moore (James Bond), Carole Bouquet (Melina Havelock), Julian Glover (Aristotle Kristatos), Chaim Topol (Milos Columbo), Lynn-Holly Johnson (Bibi Dahl), Michael Gothard (Emile Leopold Locque), Cassandra Harris (Countess Lisl von Schlaf), John Wyman (Erich Kriegler), Desmond Llewelyn (Q), Jill Bennett (Jacoba Brink), Jack Hedley (Sir Timothy Havelock), Lois Maxwell (Miss Moneypenny), Geoffrey Keen (Fredrick Gray), James Villiers (Bill Tanner), John Moreno (Luigi Ferrara), Walter Gotell (General Gogol), Jack Klaff (Apostis), Stefan Kalipha (Hector Gonzales), Charles Dance (Claus), Janet Brown (Margaret Thatcher). Bond's mission is to find the lost Automatic Targeting Attack Communicator (ATAC) used by the Ministry of Defence to communicate with Polaris submarines, and prevent it from falling into enemy hands. In this film Bond drives a Lotus Esprit Turbo and Citroen 2CV. The title song is sung by Sheena Easton, who also appears in the title sequence. *Dir*. John Glen.

Forbidden (1949) Douglass Montgomery (Jim), Hazel Court (Jane Thompson), Patricia Burke (Diana), Garry Marsh (Jerry Burns), Ronald Shiner (Dan Collins), Kenneth Griffith (Johnny), Eliot Makeham (Pop Thompson), Frederick Leister (Dr. Franklin), Richard Bird (Jennings), Michael Medwin (Cabby), Andrew Cruickshank (Insp Baxter), Peggy Ann Clifford (Millie), William Douglas (Lawson), Dennis Harkin (Bert), Peter Jones (Pete), Dora Sevening (Mrs Franklin), Erik Chitty (Schofield), Audrey Teasdale (Ethel), Mark Stone (Critic), Sam Kydd (Joe), Bill Fraser (Railway Porter). Jim Harding begins an affair with Jane and when his wife, Diana finds out he decides that the only way out is to kill her. *Dir*. George King.

Forbidden Cargo (1954) Jack Warner (Maj. Alec White), Nigel Patrick (Insp. Michael Kenyon), Elizabeth Sellars (Rita Compton), Terence Morgan (Roger Compton), Greta Gynt (Mme. Simonetta), Theodore Bikel (Max), Joyce Grenfell (Lady Flavia Queensway), James Gilbert (Agent Larkins), Eric Pohlmann (Steven Lasovich), Martin Boddey (Sub-Director Holt), Michael Hordern (Director of Customs), Hal Osmond (The Baggage Room Clerk), Jacques B. Brunius (Det. Pierre Valance), Ballard Berkeley (Cooper), Cyril Chamberlain (Customs Officer), Campbell Singer (Sgt. - River Police), Brian Wilde (Smuggler at Airfield). Customs & Excise are on the trail of an illegal drug shipment. *Dir*. Harold French.

Force 10 from Navarone (1978) Robert Shaw (Major Keith Mallory), Harrison Ford (Lieutenant Colonel Mike Barnsby), Barbara Bach (Maritza Petrović), Edward Fox (Staff Sergeant John Miller), Franco Nero (Captain Nikolai Lescovar/Colonel von Ingorslebon), Carl Weathers (Sergeant Weaver), Richard Kiel (Captain Dražak), Alan Badel (Major Petrović), Michael Byrne (Major Schroeder), Philip Latham (Cmdr. James Jensen), Angus MacInnes (1st Lieutenant Doug Reynolds), Michael Sheard (Sergeant Bauer), Petar Buntic (Marko). Following the destruction of the guns at Navarone, Mallory and Miller team up with Force 10 on a mission to eliminate a German spy. Unfortunately they are shot down over the Balkans and captured by allies of the Germans. A sequel to the *The Guns of Navarone* (1961), loosely based on Alistair MacLean's novel of the same name. *Dir*. Guy Hamilton.

Fortune is a Woman (1957) Jack Hawkins (Oliver Branwell), Arlene Dahl (Sarah Moreton Branwell), Dennis Price (Tracey Moreton), Violet Farebrother (Mrs Moreton), Ian Hunter (Clive Fisher), Malcolm Keen (Old Abercrombie), Geoffrey Keen (Young Abercrombie), Patrick Holt (Fred Connor), John Robinson (Berkeley Reckitt), Michael Goodliffe (Det Insp Barnes), Martin Lane (Det Con Watson), Bernard Miles (Mr Jerome), Christopher Lee (Charles Highbury), Greta Gynt (Vere Litchen), John Phillips (Willis Croft), Patricia Marmont (Ambrosine). An insurance inspector meets an old flame who manages to light more than just his fire. *Dir*. Sidney Gilliat.

44 Inch Chest (2009) Ray Winstone (Colin Diamond), Ian McShane (Meredith), John Hurt (Old Man Peanut), Tom Wilkinson (Archie), Stephen Dillane (Mal), Joanne Whalley (Liz Diamond), Melvil Poupaud (Loverboy), Steven Berkoff (Tippi Gordon), Edna Doré (Archie's Mum), Andy de la Tour (Biggy Walpole), Derek Lea (Bumface). When Colin discovers his wife is having an affair, his friends encourage him to exact retribution against her lover. *Dir*. Malcolm Venville.

49th Parallel (1941) Richard George (Kommandant Bernsdorff), Eric Portman (Lieutenant Hirth), Raymond Lovell (Lieutenant Kuhnecke), Niall MacGinnis (Vogel), Peter Moore (Kranz), John Chandos (Lohrmann), Basil Appleby (Jahner), Laurence Olivier (Johnnie), Finlay Currie (The Factor), Ley On (Nick), Anton Walbrook (Peter), Glynis Johns (Anna), Charles Victor (Andreas), Frederick Piper (David), Tawera Moana (George), Eric Clavering (Art), Charles Rolfe (Bob), Raymond Massey (Andy Brock), Leslie Howard (Philip Armstrong Scott). Six German sailors come ashore in Canada after the sinking of their U-boat and attempt to reach the neutral United States. Released in the United States as *The Invaders*, it was intended in Powell's words to "scare the pants off the Americans", who were yet to come into the war. *Dirs*. Michael Powell and Emeric Pressburger.

Four Feathers, The (1939) John Clements (Harry Faversham), Ralph Richardson (Captain John Durrance), C. Aubrey Smith (General Burroughs), June Duprez (Ethne Burroughs), Allan Jeayes (General Faversham), Jack Allen (Lieutenant Willoughby), Donald Gray (Peter Burroughs), Frederick Culley (Dr Sutton), Clive Baxter (Young Harry Faversham), Robert Rendel (Colonel), Archibald Batty (Adjutant), Derek Elphinstone (Lieutenant Parker), Hal Walters (Joe), Norman Pierce (Sergeant Brown), Henry Oscar (Dr. Harraz), John Laurie (The Khalifa). Resigning his commission on the eve of his regiment's departure for a campaign in Egypt and the Sudan, Harry Faversham is given white feathers by his friends and fiancé to indicate that he is a coward. He decides to go to Egypt in order to restore his reputation. Based on the 1902 novel by A.E.W. Mason. *Dir*. Zoltan Korda.

Four in the Morning (1965) Ann Lynn (Girl), Judi Dench (Wife), Norman Rodway (Husband), Brian Phelan (Boy), Joe Melia (Friend). Tragedy unites two couples. *Dir*. Malcolm Simmons

Four Just Men, The (1939) Hugh Sinclair (Humphrey Mansfield), Griffith Jones (James Brodie), Francis L. Sullivan (Leon Poiccard), Frank Lawton (Terry), Anna Lee (Arm Lodge), Alan Napier (Sir Hamar Ryman M.P.), Basil Sydney (Frank Snell), Lydia Sherwood (Myra Hastings), Edward Chapman (B.J. Burrell), Athole Stewart (Police Commissioner), George Merritt (Inspector Falmouth), Garry Marsh (Bill Grant), Ellaline Terriss (Lady Willoughby), Roland Pertwee (Mr Hastings), Eliot

Makeham (Simmons), Frederick Piper (Pickpocket), Henrietta Watson (Mrs. Truscott), Jon Pertwee (Rally campaigner), Liam Gaffney (Taxi driver). Four young, handsome, wealthy vigilantes kill dastardly people who are beyond the reach of the law in the name of justice. Based on the Edgar Wallace novel. *Dir.* Walter Forde.

Four Lions (2010) Riz Ahmed (Omar), Kayvan Novak (Waj), Nigel Lindsay (Barry), Adeel Akhtar (Faisal), Arsher Ali (Hassan), Craig Parkinson (Matt), Preeya Kalidas (Sofia), Julia Davis (Alice), Benedict Cumberbatch (Negotiator). Controversial comedy about a group of radical Muslim men from Sheffield who aspire to become suicide bombers and plan an attack on the London Marathon. *Dir.* Chris Morris.

Four Musketeers, The (1974) Michael York (D'Artagnan), Oliver Reed (Athos), Frank Finlay (Porthos), Richard Chamberlain (Aramis), Jean-Pierre Cassel (Louis XIII), Richard Briers (Louis XIII -voice), Geraldine Chaplin (Anne of Austria), Charlton Heston (Cardinal Richelieu), Faye Dunaway (Milady de Winter), Christopher Lee (Count De Rochefort), Raquel Welch (Constance Bonacieux), Roy Kinnear (Planchet), Michael Gothard (Felton), Ángel del Pozo .(Jussac), Simon Ward (Duke of Buckingham), Sybil Danning (Eugenie), Gitty Djamal (Beatrice), Jack Watson (Busigny), Bob Todd (Firing Squad Officer), Tom Buchanan (Firing Squad Sergeant), Leon Greene (Swiss Officer), Lucy Tiller (Mother Superior). Richelieu assigns Rochefort to kidnap Constance whilst Milady distracts D'Artagnan. Sequel to *The Three Musketeers,* filmed at the same time and only produced once the makers realised they actually had enough material for two films. *Dir.* Richard Lester.

4.3.2.1 (2010) Ophelia Lovibond (Shannon), Shanika Warren-Markland (Kerrys), Emma Roberts (Joanne), Tamsin Egerton (Cassandra), Freddie Stroma (Cool Brett), Andrew Harwood Mills (Driving Instructor), Adam Deacon (Dillon), Ashley "Bashy" Thomas (Smoothy), Noel Clarke (Tee), Linzey Cocker (Gwen), Jacob Anderson (Angelo), Michelle Ryan (Kelly), Ben Miller (Mr Philips), Susannah Fielding (Jas), Kevin Smith (Big Larry), Eve (Latisha), Mandy Patinkin (Jago Larofsky), Ben Drew (Terry). Four friends (Shannon, Kerrys, Jo and Cassandra) become involved with the theft of 15 diamonds. *Dir.* Noel Clarke.

Four Weddings and a Funeral (1994) Hugh Grant (Charles), Andie MacDowell (Carrie), James Fleet (Tom), Simon Callow (Gareth), John Hannah (Matthew), Kristin Scott Thomas (Fiona), David Bower (David), Charlotte Coleman (Scarlett), Timothy Walker (Angus), Sara Crowe (Laura), Rowan Atkinson (Father Gerald), David Haig (Bernard), Sophie Thompson (Lydia), Corin Redgrave (Sir Hamish Banks), Anna Chancellor (Henrietta "Duckface"), Jeremy Kemp (Sir John Delaney). Rom-com charting the love life of Charles and Carrie, whom he repeatedly meets as he attends the titular functions. The poem read at the funeral is *Funeral Blues* by W.H. Auden. Dir. Mike Newell.

Fourth Protocol, The (1987) Michael Caine (John), Pierce Brosnan (Valeri Petrofsky/James Ross), Ned Beatty (Borisov), Joanna Cassidy (Irina Vassilievna), Julian Glover (Brian Harcourt-Smith), Michael Gough (Sir Bernard Hemmings), Ray McAnally (General Karpov), Ian Richardson (Sir Nigel Irvine), Anton Rodgers (George Berenson), Caroline Blakiston (Angela Berenson), Joseph Brady (Carmichael), Matt Frewer (Tom McWhirter), Alan North (Govershin), Ronald Pickup (Wynne-Evans), Michael Bilton (Kim Philby), Betsy Brantley (Eileen McWhirter), Sean Chapman (Captain Lyndhurst), Matt Frewer (Tom McWhirter), Jerry Harte (Professor Krilov), Michael J. Jackson (Major Pavlov), Aaron Swartz (Gregoriev), Julia Verdin (Jill Dunkley), Sarah Bullen (Dorothy), Gordon Honeycombe (Television Announcer), Frederick Forsyth (Radio Newsreader – voice). A Cold War thriller in which MI5 agent John Preston must foil a Soviet plot to smuggle the parts of a nuclear bomb into Britain. Based on Frederick Forsyth's novel. *Dir.* John Mackenzie.

Frankenstein and the Monster From Hell (1973) Peter Cushing (Baron Victor Frankenstein), Shane Briant (Dr Simon Helder), Madeline Smith (Sarah, "the Angel"), David Prowse (Monster), John Stratton (Asylum director), Michael Ward (Transient), Elsie Wagstaff (Wild one), Norman Mitchell (Police Sergeant), Clifford Mollison (Judge), Chris Cunningham (Hans), Patrick Troughton (Bodysnatcher), Philip Voss (Ernst), Charles Lloyd-Pack (Prof Durendel), Lucy Griffiths (Old hag), Bernard Lee (Tarmut), Peter Madden (Coach driver). The film finds Dr Frankenstein building another monster, this time from body parts gleaned from murdering fellow patients in an insane asylum. The last Hammer Horror Frankenstein of the original series. *Dir.* Terence Fisher.

Frankenstein Created Woman (1967) Peter Cushing (Baron Victor Frankenstein), Susan Denberg (Christina), Thorley Walters (Doctor Hertz), Robert Morris (Hans), Peter Blythe (Anton), Derek Fowlds (Johann), Duncan Lamont (The Prisoner), Barry Warren (Karl), Alan MacNaughtan (Kleve), Peter Madden (Chief of Police), Philip Ray (Mayor), Ivan Beavis (Landlord), Colin Jeavons (Priest), Bartlett Mullins (Bystander), Alec Mango (Spokesman). Dr Frankenstein believes he has devised a method of transferring the soul from one recently deceased person to another and thus resurrecting the latter. He manages to do so with the soul of Hans, who was executed for a murder he did not commit, and resurrects Han's girlfriend Christina, who had committed suicide on hearing of his death. A cut above the usual Hammer Horror in terms of the thought placed on the metaphysical aspects of Dr Frankenstein's experiments. *Dir.* Terence Fisher.

Frankenstein Must Be Destroyed (1969) Peter Cushing (Baron Victor Frankenstein), Veronica Carlson (Anna Spengler), Freddie Jones (Professor Richter/the Creature), Simon Ward (Dr. Karl Holst), Thorley Walters (Inspector Frisch), Windsor Davies (Police Sergeant), Maxine Audley (Ella Brandt), George Pravda (Dr. Frederick Brandt), Geoffrey Bayldon (Police Doctor), Colette O'Neil (Madwoman), Frank Middlemass (Guest), Norman Shelley (Guest). One of the best of the Hammer Dr Frankenstein series. Frankenstein blackmails young Dr Horst into helping him perform the first brain transplant on Professor Richter, a fellow scientist. *Dir.* Terence Fisher.

French Lieutenant's Woman, The (1981) Meryl Streep (Sarah Woodruff/Anna), Jeremy Irons (Charles Henry Smithson/Mike), Hilton McRae (Sam), Emily Morgan (Mary), Charlotte Mitchell (Mrs. Tranter), Lynsey Baxter (Ernestina), Jean Faulds (Cook), Peter Vaughan (Mr. Freeman), Colin Jeavons (Vicar), Liz Smith (Mrs. Fairley), Patience Collier (Mrs. Poulteney), Leo McKern (Dr. Grogan), Arabella Weir (Girl on Undercliff), Ben Forster (Boy on Undercliff), Richard Griffiths (Sir Tom), Toni Palmer (Mrs. Endicott), Cecily Hobbs (Betty Anne), Doreen Mantle (Lady on Train), David Warner (Murphy), Alun Armstrong (Grimes), Penelope Wilton (Sonia). Set in Lyme Regis, across two time frames, telling the story of Victorians Sarah and Charles and also the story of Anna and Mike, the actors playing them in the present day. Meryl Streep won a BAFTA for Best Actress in a leading role. Adapted by Harold Pinter, based on John Fowles' novel. *Dir.* Karel Reisz

French Without Tears (1940) Ray Milland (Alan Howard), Ellen Drew (Diana Lake), Janine Darcey (Jacqueline Maingot), David Tree (Chris Neilan), Roland Culver (Cmdr. Bill Rogers), Guy Middleton (Brian Curtis), Kenneth Morgan (Kenneth Lake), Margaret Yarde (Marianne), Toni Gable (Chi-Chi), Jim Gérald (Professor Maingot), Mantovani (Himself). Based on Terence Rattigan's play. *Dir.* Anthony Asquith.

Frenzy (1972) Jon Finch (Dick Blaney), Alec McCowen (Chief Inspector Oxford), Barry Foster (Bob Rusk), Billie Whitelaw (Hetty Porter), Anna Massey (Babs Milligan), Barbara Leigh-Hunt (Brenda Blaney), Bernard Cribbins (Felix Forsythe), Vivien Merchant (Mrs. Oxford), Michael Bates (Sergeant Spearman), Jean Marsh (Monica Barling), Clive Swift (Johnny Porter), Madge Ryan (Mrs. Davison), Elsie Randolph (Gladys), Gerald Sim (Mr. Usher), John Boxer (Sir George), George Tovey (Neville Salt), Jimmy Gardner (Hotel Porter), Noel Johnson (Doctor in Pub), Michael Sheard (Jim), Rita Webb (Mrs. Rusk). Alfred Hitchcock returned to London to film this thriller in which a serial killer is raping and then strangling women with a neck-tie. Hitchcock's cameo is as a spectator wearing a bowler hat in a crowd scene. Based on the novel *Goodbye Piccadilly,*

Farewell Leicester Square by Arthur La Bern. *Dir.* Alfred Hitchcock.

Frequently Asked Questions About Time Travel (2009) Chris O'Dowd (Ray), Marc Wootton (Toby), Dean Lennox Kelly (Pete), Anna Faris (Cassie), Meredith MacNeill (Millie), Ray Gardner (Mellor), Nick Ewans (Barry), Arthur Nightingale (Old Man). Three men in a pub find themselves at the centre of a time-travel puzzle when a girl from the future appears. *Dir.* Gareth Carrivick.

Frightened City, The (1961) Herbert Lom (Waldo Zhernikov), John Gregson (Det Insp Sayers), Sean Connery (Paddy Damion), Alfred Marks (Harry Foulcher), Yvonne Romain (Anya Bergodin), Olive McFarland (Sadie), Frederick Piper (Sgt Bob Ogle), John Stone (Hood), David Davies (Alf Peters), Tom Bowman (Tanky Thomas), Robert Cawdron (Nero), George Pastell (Sanchetti), Patrick Holt (Supt Dave Carter), Kenneth Griffith (Wally Smith), Robert Percival (Wingrove), Marianne Stone ('Riviera' barmaid), Vanda Godsell (Sophie Peters), Yvonne Ball (Myrna), Tony Hawes (Lord Buncholme), Penelope Service (Clarissa). London is in the grip of rival racketeers. The Shadows had a hit with the main theme. *Dir.* John Lemont.

Frightmare (1974) Rupert Davies (Edmund Yates), Sheila Keith (Dorothy Yates), Deborah Fairfax (Jackie), Paul Greenwood (Graham), Kim Butcher (Debbie), Fiona Curzon (Merle), Jon Yule (Robin), Trisha Mortimer (Lillian), Pamela Fairbrother (Delia), Edward Kalinski (Alec), Victor Winding (Detective Inspector), Anthony Hennessey (Detective Sergeant), Noel Johnson (The Judge), Michael Sharvell-Martin (Barman). Dorothy Yates, a killer and cannibal, is released, along with her innocent husband Edmund. After being incarcerated in an insane asylum for many years she begins to kill and kill again. *Dir.* Pete Walker.

From Beyond the Grave (1974) Peter Cushing (Antique Shop Proprietor), Donald Pleasence (Jim Underwood), Angela Pleasence (Emily Underwood), Ian Bannen (Christopher Lowe), Diana Dors (Mabel Lowe), John O'Farrell (Stephen Lowe), Nyree Dawn Porter (Susan Warren), David Warner (Edward Charlton), Marcel Steiner (Mirror Demon), Ian Ogilvy (William Seaton), Ian Carmichael (Reggie Warren), Lesley-Anne Down (Rosemary Seaton), Jack Watson (Sir Michael Sinclair), Margaret Leighton (Madame Orloff), Wendy Allnutt (Pamela), Rosalind Ayres (Prostitute), Tommy Godfrey (Mr Jeffries). Four-part horror anthology: The Gatecrasher, An Act of Kindness, The Elemental and The Door - all linked by an antiques shop. *Dir.* Kevin Connor.

From Russia with Love (1963) Sean Connery (James Bond), Daniela Bianchi (Tatiana Romanova (voiced by Barbara Jefford), Pedro Armendáriz (Ali Kerim Bey), Lotte Lenya (Rosa Klebb), Robert Shaw (Red Grant), Bernard Lee (M), Walter Gotell (Morzeny), Vladek Sheybal (Kronsteen), Anthony Dawson (body) and Eric Pohlmann (voice) ("?" - Ernst Stavro Blofeld), Lois Maxwell (Miss Moneypenny), Desmond Llewelyn (Major Boothroyd: Head of 'Q' Section), Eunice Gayson (Sylvia Trench), Francis de Wolff (Vavra), George Pastell (Train Conductor), Fred Haggerty (Krilencu), Aliza Gur and Martine Beswick (Vida and Zora), Nadja Regin (Kerim Bey's girlfriend). Bond is lured into a trap involving a beautiful Russian agent and a cipher machine (lektor) by SPECTRE, who hope to gain revenge for the death of Dr No. Bond drives a Bentley Mark IV and the title song is sung by Matt Monro. Based on the 1957 novel of the same name by Ian Fleming. *Dir.* Terence Young.

Frost/Nixon (2009) Frank Langella (Richard Nixon), Michael Sheen (David Frost), Kevin Bacon (Jack Brennan), Oliver Platt (Bob Zelnick), Sam Rockwell (James Reston Jr.), Matthew Macfadyen (John Birt), Rebecca Hall (Caroline Cushing), Patty McCormack (Pat Nixon), Toby Jones (Swifty Lazar), Andy Milder (Frank Gannon), Keith MacKechnie (Marvin Minoff), Clint Howard (Lloyd Davis), Rance Howard (Ollie), Kaine Bennett Charleston (Sydney News Director), Gabriel Jarret (Ken Khachigian), Kate Jennings Grant (Diane Sawyer), Geoffrey Blake (Interview Director). A dramatisation of the interviews of Richard Nixon by David Frost in 1977. Based on the play of the same name by Peter Morgan. *Dir.* Ron Howard.

Full Monty, The (1997) Robert Carlyle (Gaz), Mark Addy (Dave), William Snape (Nathan), Steve Huison (Lomper), Tom Wilkinson (Gerald), Paul Barber (Horse), Hugo Speer (Guy), Lesley Sharp (Jean), Emily Woof (Mandy), Deirdre Costello (Linda), Paul Butterworth (Barry), Dave Hill (Alan), Bruce Jones (Reg), Andrew Livingston (Terry), Vinny Dhillon (Sharon). The closure of the Sheffield steel mills forces a group of local men to join forces and put together a "Chippendales" style dance and striptease act with the added allure for the local women that they will go "full monty", totally nude. The film follows the comedy of putting together the act through to the first performance but also addresses the more serious problem of middle age unemployment. The film won an Academy Award for Best Music, Original Musical or Comedy Score and BAFTAs for Best Film, Best Performance by an Actor in a Leading Role (Robert Carlyle), and Best Performance by an Actor in a Supporting Role (Tom Wilkinson). *Dir.* Peter Cattaneo.

Funeral In Berlin (1966) Michael Caine (Harry Palmer), Paul Hubschmid (Johnny Vulkan), Oskar Homolka (Colonel Stok), Eva Renzi (Samantha Steel), Guy Doleman (Colonel Ross), Hugh Burden (Hallam), Heinz Schubert (Aaron Levine), Wolfgang Völz (Werner), Thomas Holtzmann (Reinhardt), Günter Meisner (Kreutzman), Herbert Fux (Artur), Rainer Brandt (Benjamin), Rachel Gurney (Mrs. Ross), John Abineri (Otto Rukel), David Glover (Chico), Sarah Brackett (Babcock), Ira Hagen (Monica). A plan to help a Russian colonel defect goes badly wrong and Palmer finds himself at the centre of a series of double-crosses. A spy film based on the novel of the same name by Len Deighton. It is the second of three films where Michael Caine played Harry Palmer, the others being *The Ipcress File* (1965) and *Billion Dollar Brain* (1967). *Dir.* Guy Hamilton.

Funny Bones (1994) Oliver Platt (Tommy Fawkes), Jerry Lewis (George Fawkes), Lee Evans (Jack Parker), Leslie Caron (Katie Parker), Richard Griffiths (Jim Minty), Sadie Corre (Poodle Woman), Oliver Reed (Dolly Hopkins), George Carl (Thomas Parker), Freddie Davies (Bruno Parker), Ian McNeice (Stanley Sharkey), Christopher Greet (Lawrence Berger), Peter Gunn (Nicky), Gavin Millar (Steve Campbell), Terence Rigby (Billy Man), Ruta Lee (Laura Fawkes), Mouss (Poquelin), Peter McNamara (Canavan). After failing as a comedian in Las Vegas, Tommy, son of comedy legend George Fawkes, returns home to Blackpool (which he left aged six) in order to find the best comedy acts to take back to America. He comes across the talented but troubled Jack Parker. The story also involves a corrupt policeman, smugglers and mystical wax eggs. *Dir.* Peter Chelsom.

Further up the Creek (1958) David Tomlinson (Lt. Fairweather), Frankie Howerd (Bos'n), Shirley Eaton (Jane), Thora Hird (Mrs. Galloway), Lionel Jeffries (Steady Barker), Lionel Murton (Perkins), Sam Kydd (Bates), John Warren (Cooky), David Lodge (Scouse), Ian Whittaker (Lofty), Esma Cannon (Maudie), Tom Gill (Philippe), Jack Le White (Kentoni Brother), Max Day (Kentoni Brother), Eric Pohlmann (President), Michael Goodliffe (Lt. Commander), Wolfe Morris (Algeroccan Major), John Singer (Dispatch Rider), Larry Noble (Postman), Ballard Berkeley (Whacker Payne), Judith Furse (Chief Wren), Michael Ripper (Ticket Collector), Desmond Llewelyn (Chief Yeoman), Basil Dignam (Flagship Commander), Jess Conrad (Signalman), Charles Lloyd Pack (El Diabolo), Stanley Unwin (Porter). A hasty sequel to *Up the Creek* (1958) with Tomlinson reprising his role as the incompetent Fairweather and Howerd replacing Peter Sellers as the most nefarious member of the crew. *Dir.* Val Guest.

Fury at Smugglers' Bay (1961) Peter Cushing (Squire Trevenyan), Bernard Lee (Black John), Michèle Mercier (Louise Lejeune), John Fraser (Christopher Trevenyan), William Franklyn (The Captain), George Coulouris (François Lejeune), Liz Fraser (Betty), June Thorburn (Jenny Trevenyan), Katherine Kath (Maman), Maitland Moss (Tom), Tommy Duggan (Red Friars), Christopher Carlos (The Tiger), Miles Malleson (Duke of Avon), Alan Browning (2nd Highwayman), Patrick Desmond (Watchman), Alfred Pim (Jasper), Ken Buckle (The Fox), Valentine Dyall (Narrator - voice), Juma (Juma), Maitland Moss (Tom), Humphrey Heathgate (Roger Treherne), (Humphrey Heathcote), Bob Simmons (Carlos), James Liggat (Sergeant). The Squire's son is dismayed by the wrecking and smuggling being carried out on the Cornish coast. *Dir.* John Gilling.

Futtock's End (1970) Ronnie Barker (Gen. Futtock), Roger Livesey (The Artist), Julian Orchard (The Twit), Kika Markham

(The Niece), Mary Merrall (The Aunt), Hilary Pritchard (The Bird), Peggy Ann Clifford (The Cook), Richard O'Sullivan (The Boots), Jennifer Cox (The Maid), Suzanne Togni (Tweenie), Sammie Winmill (Tweenie), Kim Kee Lim (The Japanese Businessman). A silent film but for the incoherent mutterings of the characters and some sound effects. The story revolves around a weekend at the country estate of the eccentric General Futtock. *Dir.* Bob Kellett.

Gandhi (1982) Ben Kingsley (Gandhi), Rohini Hattangadi (Kasturba Gandhi), Roshan Seth (Pandit Jawaharlal Nehru), Saeed Jaffrey (Sardar Vallabhbhai Patel), Alyque Padamsee (Muhammad Ali Jinnah), Virendra Razdan (Maulana Azad), Candice Bergen (Margaret Bourke-White), Edward Fox (Gen. Reginald Dyer), John Gielgud (Lord Irwin), Trevor Howard (Judge Broomfield), John Mills (Lord Chelmsford), Martin Sheen (Vince Walker), Ian Charleson (Rev. Charlie Andrews), Athol Fugard (Gen. Jan Christiaan Smuts), Günther Maria Halmer (Dr. Herman Kallenbach), Geraldine James (Mirabehn), Amrish Puri (Khan), Dilsher Singh (Khan Abdul Ghaffar Khan), Ian Bannen (Senior Officer Fields), Richard Griffiths (Collins), Nigel Hawthorne (Kinnoch), Richard Vernon (Sir Edward Gait), Michael Hordern (Sir George Hodge), Shreeram Lagoo (Gopal Krishna Gokhale), Harsh Nayyar (Nathuran Godse), Terrence Hardiman (Ramsay MacDonald), Om Puri (Nahari), Shane Rimmer (Commentator), Bernard Hill (Sergeant Putnam), Daniel Day-Lewis (Colin), John Ratzenberger (Driver for Bourke-White). A biopic of Mohandas Karamchand (Mahatma) Gandhi which opens with his assassination and funeral in 1948 and then flashes back to 1893 in South Africa. From there it concentrates on his fight to achieve Indian independence from Britain using non-violent means. A film with a long gestation (at least 20 years for Richard Attenborough alone) which won 8 Academy Awards: Best Picture, Best Director (Richard Attenborough), Best Actor in a Leading Role (Ben Kingsley), Best Original Screenplay (John Briley), Best Film Editing (John Bloom), Best Art Direction, Best Cinematography, Best Costume Design. As many as 300,000 extras appeared in the funeral sequence. *Dir.* Richard Attenborough

Gang's All Here, The (1939) Jack Buchanan (John Forrest), Googie Withers (Alice Forrest), Edward Everett Horton (Treadwell), Syd Walker (Younce), Otto Kruger (Mike Chadwick), Jack La Rue (Alberni), Walter Rilla (Prince Homouska), David Burns (Beretti), Charles Carson (Charles Cartwright), Leslie Perrins (Harper), Ronald Shiner (Spider Ferris), Robb Wilton (Barman). A comedy thriller about a husband and wife team who hunt down a gang of jewel thieves. *Dir.* Thornton Freeland.

Gangster No 1 (2000) Malcolm McDowell (Gangster 55), David Thewlis (Freddie Mays), Paul Bettany (Young Gangster), Saffron Burrows (Karen), Kenneth Cranham (Tommy), Jamie Foreman (Lennie Taylor), Eddie Marsan (Eddie Miller), Andrew Lincoln (Maxie King), Doug Allen (Mad John), Razaaq Adoti (Roland), Cavan Clerkin (Billy), David Kennedy (Fat Charlie), Johnny Harris (Derek), Anton Saunders (Trevor). The rise and fall of a criminal who aspires to be the top gangster in London. *Dir.* Paul McGuigan.

Gangway (1937) Jessie Matthews (Pat Wayne), Barry MacKay (Bob Deering), Nat Pendleton (Smiles Hogan), Alastair Sim (Detective Taggett), Olive Blakeney (Nedda Beaumont), Noel Madison (Mike Otterman), Patrick Ludlow (Carl Freemason), Liane Ordeyne (Greta Brand), Graham Moffatt (Joe), Danny Green (Shorty), Edmon Ryan (Red Mike), Lawrence Anderson (Tracy), Blake Dorn (Benny the Gent), Henry Hallett (Smithers), Michael Rennie (Ship's Officer). A woman journalist, a Scotland Yard detective and a gangster all board a transatlantic ocean liner. The detective and gangster are on the trail of the jewel thief and the journalist becomes a suspect. *Dir.* Sonnie Hale.

Garden, The (1990) A virtually wordless narrative used by Jarman to put across his views on Christianity and homosexuality set against his garden on the foreshore at Dungeness in Kent. *Dir.* Derek Jarman.

Gasbags (1941) Bud Flanagan (Bud), Chesney Allen (Ches), Jimmy Nervo (Cecil), Teddy Knox (Knoxy), Charlie Naughton (Charlie), Jimmy Gold (Goldy), Moore Marriott (Jerry Jenkins), Wally Patch (Sergeant-Major), Peter Gawthorne (Commanding Officer), Frederick Valk (Sturmfuehrer), Eric Clavering (Scharffuehrer), Anthony Eustrel (Gestapo Officer), Carl Jaffe (Gestapo Chief), Manning Whiley (Colonel), Torin Thatcher (SS Man), Irene Handl (Wife). When the Crazy Gang's mobile fish and chip shop floats to Germany attached to a barrage balloon they find themselves taking on (and beating) the Nazis. *Dir.* Walter Forde.

Gaslight (1940) Anton Walbrook (Paul Mallen), Diana Wynyard (Bella Mallen), Frank Pettingell (B.G. Rough), Cathleen Cordell (Nancy the Parlour Maid), Robert Newton (Vincent Ullswater), Minnie Rayner (Elizabeth, the Cook), Jimmy Hanley (Cobb), Marie Wright (Alice Barlow), Aubrey Dexter (House Agent), Mary Hinton (Lady Winterbourne), Angus Morrison (Pianist), Jack Barty (Chairman of Music Hall). Years after the murder of a woman, her house is finally re-occupied, this time by a married couple. After a while the wife begins to believe she is losing her mind. Based on Patrick Hamilton's play. *Dir.* Thorold Dickinson.

Gay Love (1934) Florence Desmond (Gloria Fellowes), Sophie Tucker (Herself), Sydney Fairbrother (Dukie), Enid Stamp-Taylor (Marie Hopkins), Ivor McLaren (Lord Tony Eaton), Garry Marsh (Freddie Milton), Leslie Perrins (Gerald Sparkes), Ben Welden (Ben), Finlay Currie (Highams). One of two Music Hall performing sisters falls for the other sister's fiancé. *Dir.* Leslie S Hiscott.

Genevieve (1953) Kenneth More (Ambrose Claverhouse), John Gregson (Alan McKim), Dinah Sheridan (Wendy McKim, Kay Kendall (Rosalind Peters), Geoffrey Keen (Policeman), Reginald Beckwith (J.C. Callahan), Arthur Wontner (Old Gentleman), Joyce Grenfell (Hotel proprietress), Leslie Mitchell (Himself), Michael Medwin (Father to be). Classic British comedy set against the annual London to Brighton antique car rally where friends and rivals Alan and Ambrose decide to have a wager on who will be the first back to London. The film's theme music is composed by Larry Adler, although his name was originally kept off the credits in the United States due to blacklisting. The film won the BAFTA Award for Best British Film. *Dir.* Henry Cornelius.

Genghis Khan (1965) Omar Sharif (Temujin-Genghis Khan), Stephen Boyd (Jamuga), James Mason (Kam Ling), Eli Wallach (Shah of Khwarezm), Françoise Dorléac (Bortei), Telly Savalas (Shan), Robert Morley (The Emperor of China), Michael Hordern (Geen), Yvonne Mitchell (Katke), Woody Strode (Sengal), Kenneth Cope (Subodai), Roger Croucher (Kassar), Don Borisenko (Jebai), Patrick Holt (Kuchluk), Susanne Hsiao (Chin Yu). Biopic of the Mongol emperor. *Dir.* Henry Levin.

Gentle Sex, The (1943) Joan Gates (Gwen Hayden), Jean Gillie (Dot Hopkins), Joan Greenwood (Betty Miller), Joyce Howard (Anne Lawrence), Rosamund John (Maggie Fraser), Lilli Palmer (Erna Debruski), Barbara Waring (Joan Simpson), John Justin (Flying Officer David Sheridan), Elliott Mason (Mrs. Fraser), Tony Bazell (Ted), Frederick Leister (Colonel Lawrence), Everley Gregg (Miss Simpson), John Laurie (Scots Corporal), Mary Jerrold (Mrs. Sheridan), Meriel Forbes (Junior Commander Davis), Noreen Craven (Convoy Sergeant), Miles Malleson (Guard), Jimmy Hanley (1st Soldier), Frederick Peisley (2nd Soldier), Ronald Shiner (Racegoer), Harry Welchman (Captain Ferrier), Rosalyn Boulter (Telephonist), Leslie Howard (Narrator - voice). The film follows seven women from different backgrounds who meet at an Auxiliary Territorial Service training camp. It was the last film on which Leslie Howard worked before his death. *Dirs.* Leslie Howard and Maurice Elvey.

Geordie (1955) Alastair Sim (The Laird), Bill Travers (Geordie), Norah Gorsen (Jean), Molly Urquhart (Geordie's mother), Jameson Clark (Geordie's father), Miles Malleson (Lord Paunceton), Francis de Wolff (Samson), Jack Radcliffe (The Minister), Brian Reece (Olympic Selector), Raymond Huntley (Olympic Selector), Doris Goddard (Helga), Stanley Baxter (Postman), Duncan Macrae (Schoolmaster), Paul Young (Young

Geordie), Anna Ferguson (Young Jean), Margaret Boyd (Laird's maid), Michael Ripper (Australian journalist). A Scottish hammer thrower gains a place at the 1956 Melbourne Olympic Games. *Dir.* Frank Launder.

Georgy Girl (1966) Lynn Redgrave (Georgy), James Mason (James Leamington), Alan Bates (Jos Jones), Charlotte Rampling (Meredith), Bill Owen (Ted), Clare Kelly (Doris), Rachel Kempson (Ellen Leamington), Denise Coffey (Peg), Peggy Thorpe-Bates (Hospital Sister), Dandy Nichols (Hospital Nurse), Dorothy Alison (Health Visitor), Terence Soall (Salesman). Twenty-something Georgy is offered a contract to be the mistress of her father's employer James Leamington. Meanwhile, she lives with self-absorbed Meredith, who finds herself pregnant. Based on a novel by Margaret Forster. The title song, performed by The Seekers, reached No. 3 in the UK hit parade. *Dir.* Silvio Narizzano.

Get Carter (1971) Michael Caine (Carter), Ian Hendry (Eric), Britt Eckland (Anna), John Osborne (Cyril Kinnear), Tony Beckley (Peter), George Sewell (Con), Geraldine Moffat (Glenda), Dorothy White (Margaret), Rosemarie Dunham (Edna), Petra Markham (Doreen), Bryan Mosley (Cliff Brumby), Glynn Edwards (Albert Swift), Terence Rigby (Gerald Fletcher), Alun Armstrong (Keith), Bernard Hepton (Thorpe), Geraldine Moffat (Glenda), Dorothy White (Margaret), Rosemarie Dunham (Edna Garfoot), John Bindon (Sid Fletcher), Kevin Brennan (Harry), Maxwell Deas (Vicar), Liz McKenzie (Mrs Brumby), Carl Howard ("J"). Newcastle born gangster Jack Carter returns home for his brother Frank's funeral and, suspecting the death was not the drunk driving accident he was told it was, sets out to find the truth. Based on the novel *Jack's Return Home* by Ted Lewis. *Dir.* Mike Hodges

Get Cracking (1943) George Formby (George Singleton), Dinah Sheridan (Mary Pemberton), Edward Rigby (Sam Elliott), Frank Pettingell (Alf Pemberton), Ronald Shiner (Everett Manley), Wally Patch (Sergeant Joe Preston), Mike Johnson (Josh), Irene Handl (Maggie Turner), Vera Frances (Irene). Comedy based around George's antics as a member of the Home Guard. *Dir.* Marcel Varnel.

Ghost Goes West, The (1935) Robert Donat (Murdoch/Donald Glourie), Jean Parker (Peggy Martin), Eugene Pallette (Mr Martin), Elsa Lanchester (Miss Shepperton), Everley Gregg (Mrs Martin), Patricia Hilliard (Shepherdess), Ralph Bunker (Ed Bigelow), Hay Petrie (The McLaggen), Morton Selten (The Glourie), Chili Bouchier (Cleopatra), Elliott Mason (Mrs MacNiff). Murdoch Glourie dies a cowardly death on an 18th century battlefield and must haunt a castle until he can exact restitution from his clan's great rivals, the McLaggens. This means going with the castle to America after it is purchased and moved there brick by brick. *Dir.* Rene Clair.

Ghost of St. Michael's, The (1941) Will Hay (William Lamb), Claude Hulbert (Hilary Teasdale), Charles Hawtrey (Percy Thorne), Raymond Huntley (Mr Humphries), Felix Aylmer (Dr Winter), Eliott Mason (Mrs Wigmore), John Laurie (Jamie), Hay Petrie (Procurator Fiscal), Roddy Hughes (Amberley), Derek Blomfield (Sunshine), Brefni O'Rorke (Sgt Macfarlane). A Will Hay wartime comedy thriller which involves an incompetent teacher, a castle, a curse, murders and a Nazi spy. *Dir.* Marcel Varnel.

Ghost Ship (1952) Dermot Walsh (Guy Thornton), Hazel Court (Margaret Thornton), Hugh Burden (Dr. Fawcett), John Robinson (Mansel Martineau), Joss Ambler (Yacht Port Manager), Hugh Latimer (Peter), Mignon O'Doherty (Mrs. Manley), Laidman Browne (Coroner), Meadows White (Mr Leech), Pat McGrath (Bert), Joss Ackland (Ron), Ian Carmichael (Bernard). A couple hire a ghost hunter after finding their yacht is haunted. *Dir.* Vernon Sewell.

Ghost Story (1974) Anthony Bate (Dr. Borden), Larry Dann (Talbot), Marianne Faithfull (Sophy Kwykwer), Sally Grace (Girl), Penelope Keith (Rennie), Leigh Lawson (Robert), Vivian MacKerrell (Duller), Murray Melvin (McFayden), Barbara Shelley (Matron). A group of friends from university meet up in a country house and it soon becomes clear that all is not what it seems. *Dir.* Stephen Weeks.

Ghost Train, The (1931) Jack Hulbert (Teddy Deakin), Cicely Courtneidge (Miss Bourne), Ann Todd (Peggy Murdock), Cyril

Raymond (Richard Winthrop), Allan Jeayes (Dr. Sterling), Donald Calthrop (Saul Hodgkin), Angela Baddeley (Julia Price), Henry Caine (Herbert Price). Passengers find themselves stranded in the waiting room of an isolated station on a stormy night but are discouraged from staying by the station master, who tells them of the local legend of a ghost train which dooms all who set eyes on it to death. Based on the play of the same name by Arnold Ridley (best known as Private Godfrey in *Dad's Army*). *Dir.* Walter Forde.

Ghost Train, The (1941) Arthur Askey (Tommy Gander), Richard Murdoch (Teddy Deakin), Kathleen Harrison (Miss Bourne), Peter Murray-Hill (Richard G. Winthrop), Carole Lynne (Jackie Winthrop), Morland Graham (Dr. Sterling), Betty Jardine (Edna), Stuart Latham (Herbert), Herbert Lomas (Saul Hodgkin), Raymond Huntley (John Price), Linden Travers (Julia Price), D.J. Williams (Ben Isaacs). A remake of the 1931 film, introducing some wartime elements. *Dir.* Walter Forde.

Ghost, The (2010) Ewan McGregor (unnamed ghostwriter), Pierce Brosnan (Adam Lang), Olivia Williams (Ruth Lang), Kim Cattrall (Amelia Bly), Timothy Hutton (Sidney Kroll), Tom Wilkinson (Paul Emmett), Jon Bernthal (Rick Ricardelli), James Belushi (John Maddox), Robert Pugh (Richard Rycart), Tim Preece (Roy), David Rintoul (The Stranger), Eli Wallach (The Old Man at the Vineyard). After the ghostwriter of a British ex-Prime Minister's memoirs dies in an accident a new man is taken on and begins work. He soon discovers that perhaps his predecessor's demise might not have been accidental. *Dir.* Roman Polanski.

Ghosts of Berkeley Square, The (1947) Robert Morley (Gen. "Jumbo" Burlap/Nawab of Bagwash), Felix Aylmer (Col. H. "Bulldog" Kelsoe), Yvonne Arnaud (Millie), Claude Hulbert (Merryweather), Abraham Sofaer (Benjamin Disraeli), Ernest Thesiger (Dr. Cruickshank of Psychical Research Society), Marie Lohr (Lottie), Martita Hunt (Lady Mary), A.E. Matthews (Gen. Bristow), John Longden (Mortimer Digby), Ronald Frankau (Tex Farnum), Wilfrid Hyde-White (Staff Captain), Martin Miller (Professor), Wally Patch (Foreman), Esme Percy (Vizier), Mary Jerrold (Lettie), James Hayter (Capt. Dodds), Aubrey Mallalieu (Butler), Tom Walls Jr. (Provost Marshal). A comedy in which two 18th Century soldiers accidently kill themselves in a house in Berkeley Square and are then condemned by Queen Anne to haunt the place until a monarch visits the house. They eventually begin to plan a way of engineering a royal visit by manipulating the residents of the house. An adaptation of the novel *No Nightingales* by Caryl Brahms and S. J. Simon about 50 Berkeley Square – apparently the most haunted house in London. *Dir.* Vernon Sewell.

Ghoul, The (1933) Boris Karloff (Prof. Henry Morlant), Cedric Hardwicke (Broughton), Ernest Thesiger (Laing), Dorothy Hyson (Betty Harlon), Anthony Bushell (Ralph Morlant), Kathleen Harrison (Kaney), Harold Huth (Aga Ben Dragore), D.A. Clarke-Smith (Mahmoud), Ralph Richardson (Nigel Hartley). An Egyptologist believes that if he is buried with a jewel called "The Eternal Light", he will be granted eternal life. When the jewel is stolen, he apparently rises from the grave in order to track down the culprit. *Dir.* T. Hayes Hunter.

Gideon's Day (1958) Jack Hawkins (Insp. George Gideon), Dianne Foster (Joanna Delafield), Cyril Cusack (Herbert 'Birdie' Sparrow), Andrew Ray (PC Simon Farnaby-Green), James Hayter (Robert Mason), Ronald Howard (Paul Delafield), Howard Marion-Crawford (Chief of Scotland Yard), Laurence Naismith (Arthur Sayer), Derek Bond (Det. Sgt. Eric Kirby), Grizelda Harvey (Mrs. Kirby), Frank Lawton (Det. Sgt. Frank Liggott), Anna Lee (Mrs. Kate Gideon), John Loder (Ponsford), Doreen Madden (Miss Courtney), Miles Malleson (Judge at Old Bailey), Marjorie Rhodes (Mrs. Rosie Saparelli), Michael Shepley (Sir Rupert Bellamy), Michael Trubshawe (Sgt. Golly), Jack Watling (Rev. Julian Small), Anna Massey (Sally Gideon), John Le Mesurier (Prosecuting Barrister), Henry B. Longhurst (Rev. Mr. Courtney), Billie Whitelaw (Christine). Gideon of the Yard investigates the death of a policeman he had just suspended for corruption. An adaptation of John Creasey's novel of the same name. *Dir.* John Ford.

Girl from Maxim's, The (1933) Frances Day (La Mome), Lady Tree (Madame Petypon), Leslie Henson (Dr. Petypon), George

211

Grossmith (The general), Desmond Jeans (Etienne), Evan Thomas (Corignon), Stanley Holloway (Mongicourt), Gertrude Musgrove (Clementine). An adaptation of the Feydeau farce in which a respectable doctor gets involved with a coquette. *Dir.* Alexander Korda.

Girl on the Boat, The (1961) Norman Wisdom (Sam Marlowe), Millicent Martin (Billie Bennett), Richard Briers (Eustace Hignett), Philip Locke (Bream Mortimer), Sheila Hancock (Jane), Athene Seyler (Mrs Hignett), Bernard Cribbins (Peters), Noel Willman (Webster), Reginald Beckwith (Barman). Norman Wisdom stars in a film based on the story of the same name by P.G. Wodehouse. *Dir.* Henry Kaplan.

Girl with a Pearl Earring, The (2003) Colin Firth (Johannes Vermeer), Scarlett Johansson (Griet), Tom Wilkinson (Pieter van Ruijven), Cillian Murphy (Pieter), Judy Parfitt (Maria Thins), Essie Davis (Catharina Bolnes), Anna Popplewell (Maertge), Alakina Mann (Cornelia). Based on the novel of the same name by Tracy Chevalier which itself references a painting by Johannes Vermeer. A servant girl in the house of the artist Vermeer becomes the subject of one of his paintings. *Dir.* Peter Webber

Girl with Green Eyes (1964) Peter Finch (Eugene Gaillard), Rita Tushingham (Kate Brady), Lynn Redgrave (Baba Brennan), Marie Kean (Josie Hannigan), Arthur O'Sullivan (James Brady), Julian Glover (Malachi Sullivan), T. P. McKenna (The Priest), Liselotte Goettinger (Joanna), Pat Laffan (Bertie Counham), Eileen Crowe (Mrs. Byrne), May Craig (Aunt), Joe Lynch (Andy Devlin), Yolande Turner (Mary Maguire), Harry Brogan (Jack Holland). A young girl in Dublin becomes involved with an older married man. Adapted from Edna O'Brien's novel *The Lonely Girl*. *Dir.* Desmond Davis.

Girls at Sea (1958) Guy Rolfe (Captain Alwin Maitland), Ronald Shiner (Marine Ogg), Michael Hordern (Admiral Reginald Victor Hewitt), Anne Kimbell (Mary Carlton), Nadine Tallier (Antoinette), Fabia Drake (Lady Kitty Hewitt), Mary Steele (Jill Eaton), Richard Coleman (Captain Robert 'Bobby' Randall), Lionel Jeffries (Harry), Teddy Johnson (Singer), Daniel Massey (Flag Lieutenant Courtney), David Lodge (Corporal Duckett), Warren Mitchell (Arthur), Michael Ripper (Jumper, Marine), Mercy Haystead (Claudine), Brian Wilde (Bill), Harold Goodwin (Wal), David Aylmer (Navigating Officer), Richard Briers ('Popeye' Lewis). Two beautiful girls stow away on a warship. *Dir.* Gilbert Gunn.

Give Us The Moon (1944) Margaret Lockwood (Nina), Jean Simmons (Heidi), Vic Oliver (Sascha), Peter Graves (Peter Pyke), Roland Culver (Ferdinand), Max Bacon (Jacobus), Frank Cellier (Pyke), Eliot Makeham (Dumka), Iris Lang (Tania), George Relph (Otto), Gibb McLaughlin (Marcel), Irene Handl (Miss Haddock), Henry Hewitt (Announcer), Alan Keith (Raphael), Harry Fowler (Bellboy). A lazy young man attaches himself to the "White Elephants", a group who are happy with any situation which requires them to do no work. Based on the book *The Elephant is White* by Caryl Brahms and S.J. Simon. *Dir.* Val Guest.

Give Us This Day (1949) Sam Wanamaker (Geremio), Lea Padovani (Annuziata), Kathleen Ryan (Kathleen), Charles Goldner (Luigi), Bonar Colleano (Julio), William Sylvester (Giovanni), George Pastell (The lucy), Philo Hauser (Head of Pig), Sid James (Murdin), Karel Stepanek (Jaroslav), Ina De La Haye (Dame Katarina), Rosalie Crutchley (Julio's wife), Ronan O'Casey (Bastian), Robert Rietty (Pietro), Charles Moffat (Pasquale). A rather grim film depicting a bricklayer and his family trying to survive in Brooklyn during the Great Depression. Based on the novel *Christ in Concrete* by Pietro Di Donato and released in the United States under that name. *Dir.* Edward Dmytryk.

Gladiator (2000) Russell Crowe (Maximus Decimus Meridius), Joaquin Phoenix (Commodus), Connie Nielsen (Lucilla), Djimon Hounsou (Juba), Oliver Reed (Antonius Proximo), Derek Jacobi (Senator Gracchus), Ralf Möeller (Hagen), Spencer Treat Clark (Lucius Verus), Richard Harris (Marcus Aurelius), Tommy Flanagan (Cicero), Tomas Arana (General Quintus), John Shrapnel (Gaius), David Schofield (Senator Falco), Sven-Ole Thorsen (Tigris of Gaul), David Hemmings (Cassius), Giannina

Facio (Maximus' wife), Giorgio Cantarini (Maximus' son). Successful Roman General Maximus Decimus Meridius falls foul of the unstable Commodus, who murders his father, the Emperor Marcus Aurelius, before it can be announced that Maximus is his preferred successor in power. As the new Emperor, Commodus then orders the death of Maximus and his family. Although Maximus escapes he is too late to save his family and thus becomes "father to a murdered son, husband to a murdered wife". He will have his vengeance, "in this life or the next". Found by slave traders he is trained as a gladiator and embarks on the path which eventually will bring him face to face with his mortal enemy. The film won five Academy Awards: Best Picture, Best Actor in a Leading Role (Russell Crowe), Best Costume Design, Best Effects, Visual Effects, and Best Sound. The film shares several plot points with *The Fall of the Roman Empire* (1964) in that it deals with the death of Marcus Aurelius and the reign of Commodus. *Dir.* Ridley Scott.

Glass Mountain, The (1949) Michael Denison (Richard Wilder), Dulcie Gray (Anne Wilder), Valentina Cortese (Alida Morrosini), Sebastian Shaw (Bruce McLeod), F. Terschack (Sandro), Antonio Centa (Gino), Arnold Marlé (Manager of Teatro La Fenice), Sidney King (Charles), Tito Gobbi (Himself), Elena Rizzieri (Herself). An RAF pilot an aspiring composer is shot down over Italy and is then rescued by a local girl. When he returns to his wife in England he finds he is inspired to write an opera. The theme music by Nino Rota is memorable. *Dir.* Henry Cass.

Go-Between, The (1970) Julie Christie (Marian - Lady Trimingham), Edward Fox (Hugh), Alan Bates (Ted), Margaret Leighton (Mrs. Maudsley), Michael Redgrave (Old Leo), Dominic Guard (Young Leo), Michael Gough (Mr Maudsley), Richard Gibson (Marcus Maudsley), Simon Hume-Kendall (Denys), Roger Lloyd-Pack (Charles), Amaryllis Garnett (Kate). In the summer of 1900, Leo colston, who is visiting his friend Marcus, is asked by Marcus' sister Marion to become a "go-between" and deliver letters between herself and local farmer Ted Burgess even though she is about to become engaged to Hugh Trimingham. An adaptation by Harold Pinter of the book of the same name by L. P. Hartley. *Dir.* Joseph Losey.

Gold (1974) Roger Moore (Rod Slater), Susannah York (Terry Steyner), Ray Milland (Hurry Hirschfeld), Bradford Dillman (Manfred Steyner), John Gielgud (Farrell), Tony Beckley (Stephen Marais), Simon Sabela (Big King), Marc Smith (Tex Kiernan), John Hussey (Plummer), Bernard Horsfall (Dave Kowalski), Bill Brewer (Aristide), George Jackson (Mine Doctor), Ken Hare (Jackson), Ralph Loubser (Mine Captain). Rod Slater becomes manager of a South African gold mine unaware that there is a plot to sabotage it. He is, however fully aware of the attractions offered by Terry, the mine owners wife. *Dir.* Peter R Hunt.

Golden Bowl, The (2000) Kate Beckinsale (Maggie), Nick Nolte (Adam Verver), Uma Thurman (Charlotte Stant), Jeremy Northam (Prince Amerigo), Anjelica Huston (Fanny Assingham), James Fox (Colonel Bob Assingham), Madeleine Potter (Lady Castledean), Nicholas Day (Lord Castledean), Peter Eyre (A.R. Jarvis). Prince Amerigo marries rich heiress Maggie Verver even though he is the lover of her poor but beautiful friend Charlotte. Meanwhile Maggie's aunt Fanny begins to matchmake between her widowed father and Charlotte. Screenplay by Ruth Prawer Jhabvala based on the 1904 novel by Henry James. *Dir.* James Ivory.

Golden Compass, The (2007) Nicole Kidman (Marisa Coulter), Daniel Craig (Lord Asriel), Dakota Blue Richards (Lyra 'Silvertongue' Belacqua), Ben Walker (Roger), Freddie Highmore (Pantalaimon - voice), Ian McKellen (Iorek Byrnison - voice), Eva Green (Serafina Pekkala), Jim Carter (John Faa), Tom Courtenay (Farder Coram), Ian McShane (Ragnar Sturlusson - voice), Sam Elliott (Lee Scoresby), Christopher Lee (First High Councilor), Kristin Scott Thomas (Stelmaria - voice), Edward de Souza (Second High Councilor), Kathy Bates (Hester - voice), Simon McBurney (Fra Pavel), Jack Shepherd (Master), Magda Szubanski (Mrs. Lonsdale), Derek Jacobi (Magisterial Emissary), Clare Higgins (Ma Costa), Charlie Rowe (Billy Costa), Steven

Loton (Tony Costa), Michael Antoniou (Kerim Costa), Mark Mottram (Jaxer Costa), Paul Antony-Barber (Bolvangar Doctor), Jason Watkins (Bolvangar Official), Jody Halse (Bolvangar Orderly), Hattie Morahan (Sister Clara), John Bett (Thorold). The story depicts the adventures of Lyra Belacqua, an orphan living in a parallel universe where a dogmatic ruling power called the Magisterium is conspiring to end tolerance and free inquiry. Lyra discovers that poor orphan children are disappearing at the hands of a group called the Gobblers and goes on a trip to the far north in search of the missing children. The film won an Academy Award for Best Achievement in Visual Effects. Based on *Northern Lights* (published as *The Golden Compass* in the U.S.), the first novel in Philip Pullman's trilogy *His Dark Materials*. *Dir.* Chris Weitz.

Golden Salamander (1950) Trevor Howard (David Redfern), Anouk Aimée (Anna), Herbert Lom (Rankl), Walter Rilla (Serafis), Miles Malleson (Douvet), Jacques Sernas (Max), Wilfrid Hyde-White (Agno), Peter Copley (Aribi), Marcel Poncin (Dommic), Kathleen Boutall (Mme. Guillard), Eugene Deckers (Police Chief), Percy Walsh (Guillard), Sybille Binder (Mme. Labree), Valentine Dyall (Ben Ahrim). An archaeologist in North Africa falls foul of a criminal gang. *Dir.* Ronald Neame.

Golden Voyage of Sinbad, The (1974) John Phillip Law (Sinbad), Tom Baker (Koura), Takis Emmanuel (Achmed), Caroline Munro (Margiana), Douglas Wilmer (The Vizier), Kurt Christian (Haroun), Martin Shaw (Rachid), Robert Shaw (Oracle of All Knowledge), Grégoire Aslan (Hakim), David Garfield (Abdul), Aldo Sambrell (Omar). A golden piece of a puzzle is dropped onto Sinbad's ship by a winged creature. He then meets a Vizier who has another piece who reveals that if they find the third and final piece it will lead them to a fountain of youth. *Dir.* Gordon Hessler.

GoldenEye (1995) Pierce Brosnan (James Bond), Sean Bean (Alec Trevelyan (006)/Janus), Izabella Scorupco (Natalya Simonova), Famke Janssen (Xenia Onatopp), Joe Don Baker (Jack Wade), Judi Dench (M), Gottfried John (General Ourumov), Robbie Coltrane (Valentin Dmitrovich Zukovsky), Alan Cumming (Boris Grishenko), Tchéky Karyo (Dmitri Mishkin), Desmond Llewelyn (Q), Samantha Bond (Miss Moneypenny), Minnie Driver (Irina). A rogue Russian general steals the control disc of the GoldenEye satellite weapon system and Bond discovers he was working for Alec Trevelyan (Janus), a fellow agent whom he had left for dead nine years earlier. Helped by beautiful Russian programmer Natalya he pursues the general, Janus and henchwoman Onatopp. Bond drives a BMW Z3 Roadster and an Aston Martin DB5. The title song was written by Bono and The Edge and performed by Tina Turner. *Dir.* Martin Campbell.

Goldfinger (1964) Sean Connery (James Bond), Honor Blackman (Pussy Galore), Gert Fröbe (Auric Goldfinger), Shirley Eaton (Jill), Tania Mallet (Tilly), Harold Sakata (Oddjob), Bernard Lee (M), Martin Benson (Martin Solo), Cec Linder (Felix Leiter), Austin Willis (Simmons), Desmond Llewelyn (Q), Lois Maxwell (Miss Moneypenny), Michael Mellinger (Kisch), Burt Kwouk (Mr. Ling), Richard Vernon (Colonel Smithers), Margaret Nolan (Dink). Bond must stop tycoon Auric Goldfinger from initiating "Operation Grand Slam," a scheme to raid Fort Knox and obliterate the world economy. In the process he loses sisters Jill (famously painted gold) and Tilly Masterson but is introduced to Pussy Galore. Harold Sakata won a silver medal for the United States in weightlifting at the 1948 Summer Olympics in London. Bond drives the iconic 007 car – the Aston Martin DB5 with its various accoutrements - revolving licence plates, spinner hubcaps that doubled as tyre slashers, passenger ejector seat, rear bulletproof shield, forward machine guns concealed behind the headlights and rearward defenses including smoke and oil slick sprayers. The title song is sung by Shirley Bassey. Based on the novel of the same name by Ian Fleming. *Dir.* by Guy Hamilton.

Gone to Earth (1950) Jennifer Jones (Hazel Woodus), David Farrar (John 'Jack' Reddin), Cyril Cusack (Edward Marston), Sybil Thorndike (Mrs. Marston), Edward Chapman (Mr. James), Esmond Knight (Abel Woodus), Hugh Griffith (Andrew Vessons), George Cole (Cousin Albert), Beatrice Varley (Aunt Prowde), Frances Clare (Amelia Clomber), Raymond Rollett (Landlord), Gerald Lawson (Roadmender), Bartlett Mullins

(Dress shop owner), Ann Tetheradge (Miss James), Louis Phillip (Policeman), Valentine Dunn (Martha), Richmond Nairne (Mathias Booker), Owen Holder (Narrator), Daniel Stephens (Master of fox hounds). A beautiful free spirited nature loving girl marries a vicar but this does not put off the attentions of the local squire. Based on the novel of the same name by Mary Webb. *Dirs.* Michael Powell and Emeric Pressburger.

Gonks Go Beat (1965) Kenneth Connor (Wilco Roger), Frank Thornton (Mr. A & R), Barbara Brown (Helen), Iain Gregory (Steve), Terry Scott (PM), Reginald Beckwith (Professor), Jerry Desmonde (Great Galaxian), Arthur Mullard (Drum Master), Pamela Donald (Tutor), Gillian French (Beatland Prime Minister), Babs Lord (Beat Girl), Lulu (Herself), The Nashville Teens (Themselves), Ginger Baker (Himself), Jack Bruce (Himself), Graham Bond (Himself), Dick Heckstall-Smith (Himself), John McLaughlin (Himself), Derek Thompson (Singer), Dick Heckstall-Smith (Himself). A sci-fi musical fantasy which could probably only have been made in the 1960s. On a future Earth the world is split between beat lovers (in Beatland) and ballad lovers (on Ballad Isle), who despise each other. Can a clandestine romance between a beat boy and a ballad girl bring about reconciliation? Gonks were small, furry, soft toys popular at the time. *Dir.* Robert Hartford-Davis.

Good Companions, The (1933) Jessie Matthews (Susie Dean), Edmund Gwenn (Jess Oakroyd), John Gielgud (Inigo Jollifant), Mary Glynne (Miss Elizabeth Trant), Percy Parsons (Morton Mitcham), A. W. Baskcomb (Jimmy), Florence Gregson (Mrs. Oakroyd), Frank Pettingell (Sam Oglethorpe), Laurence Hanray (Mr. Tarvin), Annie Esmond (Mrs. Tarvin), George Zucco (Fauntley), Frederick Piper (Ted Oglethorpe), Cyril Smith (Leonard Oakroyd), Tom Shale (Gatford Hotel landlord), Dennis Hoey (Joe Brundit). Musical based on JB Priestley's novel about three musicians joining together to save "The Dinky Doos", a failing concert party during the inter-war years. *Dir.* Victor Saville.

Good Companions, The (1956) Janette Scott (Susie Dean), Eric Portman (Jess Oakroyd), John Fraser (Inigo Jollifant), Celia Johnson (Miss Trant), Hugh Griffith (Morton Mitcham), Bobby Howes (Jimmy Nunn), Joyce Grenfell (Lady Parlitt), Rachel Roberts (Elsie and Effie Longstaff), John Salew (Mr.Joe), Mona Washbourne (Mrs.Joe), Paddy Stone (Jerry Jerningham). A remake of the 1933 film. *Dir.* J Lee Thompson.

Good Die Young (1954), The Laurence Harvey ('Rave'), Stanley Baker (Mike Morgan), Richard Basehart (Joe Halsey), John Ireland (Eddie Blaine), Joan Collins (Mary Halsey), Gloria Grahame (Denise Blaine), Freda Jackson (Mrs Freeman), Margaret Leighton (Eve), Robert Morley (Sir Francis), Rene Ray (Angela Morgan), James Kenney (Dave), Susan Shaw (Doris), Lee Patterson (Tod Maslin), Sandra Dorne (Pretty Girl), Leslie Dwyer (Stookey), Patricia McCarron (Carole), George Rose (Bunny), Walter Hudd (Dr. Reed). The film tells in flashback how four men (Rave, Mike, Joe and Eddie) come to be on the point of robbing a postal van. *Dir.* Lewis Gilbert.

Good Morning, Boys (1937) Will Hay (Dr Benjamin Twist), Martita Hunt (Lady Bagshott), Peter Gawthorne (Col. Willoughby-Gore), Graham Moffatt (Albert), Fewlass Llewellyn (The Dean), Mark Daly (Arty Jones), Peter Godfrey (Cliquot), C. Denier Warren (Minister of Education), Lilli Palmer (Yvette), Charles Hawtrey (Septimus). An incompetent head master and his pupils fraudulently earn a trip to Paris where they cross paths with thieves trying to steal the Mona Lisa. Elements of this plot seem to have been recycled for *St Trinian's* (2007). *Dir.* Marcel Varnel.

Good Time Girl (1948) Jean Kent (Gwen Rawlings), Dennis Price (Michael 'Red' Farrell), Herbert Lom (Max Vine), Bonar Colleano (Micky Malone), Peter Glenville (Jimmy Rosso), Flora Robson (Miss Thorpe), George Carney (Mr. Rawlings), Beatrice Varley (Mrs. Rawlings), Hugh McDermott (Al Schwartz), Griffith Jones (Danny Martin), Amy Veness (Mrs. Chalk), Diana Dors (Lyla Lawrence), Elwyn Brook-Jones (Mr. Pottinger), Orlando Martins (Kolly), Renee Gadd (Mrs. Parsons), Jill Balcon (Roberta), Joan Young (Mrs. Bond), Margaret Barton (Agnes), Jack Raine (Detective Inspector Girton), Nora Swinburne (Miss Mills), George Merritt (Police Sergeant), Michael Hordern (Seddon), Garry Marsh (Mr. Hawkins), Harry Ross (Fruity Lee), Dorothy Vernon (Mrs. Chudd), Vera Frances (Edie Rawlings),

June Byford (Joan Rawlings), John Blythe (Art Moody), Edward Lexy (Mr. Morgan), Phyl French (Sonia), Danny Green (Smiling Billy), Noel Howlett (Clerk), Zena Marshall (Annie Farrell), Ilena Sylva (Ida), Betty Nelson (Connie), Rosalind Atkinson (Doctor), Jane Hylton (Doris), Wally Patch (Bookie), Phyllis Stanley (Ida). Told in flashback as Juvenile Court magistrate Miss Thorpe relates to young runaway Lyla the cautionary tale of Gwen Rawlings who moved from one bad situation to another, spending time in reform school and eventually being given a long prison sentence. Based on Arthur La Bern's novel *Night Darkens the Street*. *Dir*. David MacDonald.

Goodbye Mr Chips (1939) Robert Donat (Charles Edward Chipping – "Mr. Chips"), Greer Garson (Katherine Chipping), Terry Kilburn (John Colley/Peter Colley I/Peter Colley II/ Peter Colley III), John Mills (Peter Colley, Paul Henreid (Max Staefel), Judith Furse (Flora), Lyn Harding (Wetherby), Milton Rosmer (Chatteris), Frederick Leister (Marsham), Louise Hampton (Mrs. Wickett). In old age a classics master who has worked at the same boy's public school for over 60 years looks back over his life. In particular he remembers his holiday to Austria where he meets a much younger English woman who transforms both his life and his career. Robert Donat won the Academy Award for Best Actor in a Leading Role beating Clark Gable for *Gone with the Wind*. Based on the novel of the same name by James Hilton, who modelled Mr Chips on W.H. Balgarnie, his old classics master who taught for over 50 years at The Leys public school in Cambridge. *Dir*. Sam Wood.

Goose Steps Out, The (1942) Will Hay (William Potts/Muller), Charles Hawtrey (Max), Frank Pettingell (Prof Hoffman), Julien Mitchell (Gen Von Glotz), Peter Ustinov (Krauss), Barry Morse (Kurt), Leslie Harcourt (Vagel), Peter Croft (Hans), Ann Firth (Lena), Ray Lovell (Schmidt), Jeremy Hawk (ADC), Aubrey Mallalieu (Rector), John Williams (Maj Bishop), Lawrence O'Madden (Col Truscott), William Hartnell (German Officer). Mr Potts, a teacher, is the double of a captured Nazi spy and is sent to Germany to uncover the plans of a secret weapon. *Dirs*. Will Hay and Basil Dearden.

Gorgon, The (1964) Christopher Lee (Professor Karl Meister), Peter Cushing (Dr. Namaroff), Richard Pasco (Paul Heitz), Barbara Shelley (Carla Hoffman), Michael Goodliffe (Professor Jules Heitz), Patrick Troughton (Inspector Kanof), Joseph O'Conor (Coroner), Prudence Hyman (The Gorgon), Jack Watson (Ratoff), Redmond Phillips (Hans), Jeremy Longhurst (Bruno Heitz), Toni Gilpin (Sascha Cass), Joyce Hemson (Martha), Alister Williamson (Janus Cass), Michael Peake (Constable), Sally Nesbitt (Nurse). The last of the snake-haired Gorgons is living in a castle in the middle of Europe in the early 20th Century and still turning people to stone. *Dir*. Terence Fisher.

Gosford Park (2001) Maggie Smith (Constance Trentham), Michael Gambon (William McCordle), Kristin Scott Thomas (Sylvia McCordle), Camilla Rutherford (Isobel McCordle), Charles Dance (Lord Raymond Stockbridge), Geraldine Somerville (Louisa Stockbridge), Tom Hollander (Anthony Meredith), Natasha Wightman (Lavinia Meredith), Jeremy Northam (Ivor Novello), Bob Balaban (Morris Weissman), James Wilby (Freddie Nesbitt), Claudie Blakley (Mabel Nesbitt), Laurence Fox (Rupert Standish), Trent Ford (Jeremy Blond), Ryan Phillippe (Henry Denton), Stephen Fry (Inspector Thompson), Ron Webster (Constable Dexter), Kelly Macdonald (Mary Maceachran), Clive Owen (Robert Parks), Helen Mirren (Mrs. Wilson), Eileen Atkins (Mrs. Croft), Emily Watson (Elsie), Alan Bates (Jennings), Derek Jacobi (Probert), Richard E. Grant (George), Frank Thornton (Mr. Burkett). A murder occurs during a shooting weekend at an English country house. A study of the class system in England during the 1930s. *Dir*. Robert Altman.

Grand Day Out, A (1990) The first Wallace and Gromit stop-motion animation. Wallace decides to take a trip to the Moon to picnic in a place where cheese is plentiful. *Dir*. Nick Park.

Great Escape, The (1963) Steve McQueen (Captain Virgil Hilts), James Garner (Flight Lieutenant Bob Hendley), Richard Attenborough (Squadron Leader Roger Bartlett), James Donald (Group Captain Ramsey), Charles Bronson (Flight Lieutenant Danny Velinski), Donald Pleasence (Flight Lieutenant Colin Blythe), James Coburn (Flying Officer Louis Sedgwick), Hannes Messemer (Oberst von Luger), David McCallum (Lieutenant-Commander Eric Ashley-Pitt), Gordon Jackson (Flight Lieutenant Andy 'Mac' MacDonald), John Leyton (Flight Lieutenant William 'Willie' Dickes), Angus Lennie (Flying Officer Archibald 'Archie' Ives), Nigel Stock (Flight Lieutenant Denis Cavendish), Robert Graf (Werner), Jud Taylor (First Lieutenant Goff), Hans Reiser (Kuhn), Harry Riebauer (Hauptfeldwebel Strachwitz), William Russell (Flight Lieutenant Sorren), Robert Freitag (Hauptmann Posen), Ulrich Beiger (Preissen), George Mikell (SS-Oberstürmführer Dietrich), Lawrence Montaigne (Flying Officer Haynes), Robert Desmond (Flying Officer 'Griff' Griffith), Til Kiwe (Frick), Heinz Weiss (Kramer), Tom Adams (Flight Lieutenant 'Dai' Nimmo), Karl-Otto Alberty (SS-Oberstürmführer Steinach). Possibly the greatest of all war films. Based on a true story. Interned together in an 'escape proof' camp, POWs plan the biggest mass escape yet attempted– using tunnels nicknamed Tom, Dick and Harry. The first half of the film covers the preparations for the escape and the second half follows the journeys of the escapees and the final consequences of the escape. Adapted from the book by Paul Brickhill, who had been a prisoner at Stalag Luft III during World War II. *Dir*. John Sturges.

Great Expectations (1946) John Mills (Pip, as a young man), Anthony Wager (Phillip 'Pip' Pirrip, as a boy), Valerie Hobson (Estella, as an adult), Jean Simmons (Young Estella), Bernard Miles (Joe Gargery), Alec Guinness (Herbert Pocket), Francis L. Sullivan (Mr. Jaggers), Finlay Currie (Abel Magwitch), Martita Hunt (Miss Havisham), Ivor Barnard (Mr. Wemmick), John Forrest (Herbert Pocket, as a boy), Freda Jackson (Mrs. Joe Gargery), Torin Thatcher (Bentley Drummle), O. B. Clarence (The Aged Parent), Eileen Erskine (Biddy), George Hayes (Convict), Hay Petrie (Uncle Pumblechook), John Forrest (The Pale Young Gentleman), John Burch (Mr. Wopsle), Richard George (The Sergeant), Grace Denbigh Russell (Mrs. Wopsle), Everley Gregg (Sarah Pocket), Anne Holland (Relation), Frank Atkinson (Mike), Gordon Begg (Night Porter), Edie Martin (Mrs. Whimple), Walford Hyden (The Dancing Master), Roy Arthur (Galley Steersman). Adapted from Charles Dickens' novel of the same name, this is probably the classic film version of a classic novel. Orphan Pip's life is changed forever when he becomes the beneficiary of the largesse of a mysterious benefactor. The film won two Academy Awards: Best Art Direction and Best Cinematography. *Dir*. David Lean.

Great Game, The (1953) James Hayter (Joe Lawson), Thora Hird (Miss Rawlings), Diana Dors (Lulu Smith), Sheila Shand Gibbs (Mavis Pink), John Laurie ('Mac' Wells), Glyn Houston (Ned Rutter), Geoffrey Toone (Jack Bannerman), Jack Lambert (Ralph Blake), Meredith Edwards (Skid Evans), Alexander Gauge (Ben Woodhall), Frank Pettingell (Sir Julius), Glenn Melvyn (Heckler), Roddy Hughes (Mr. Broderick), Charles Leno (Rovers Supporter), Sidney Vivian (Club Chairman). A football club chairman is caught making illegal approaches to the star player of a rival team. *Dir*. Maurice Elvey.

Great McGonagall, The (1974) Spike Milligan (William McGonagall), Peter Sellers (Queen Victoria), Julia Foster (Mrs McGonagall), John Bluthal (Mr Giles + other roles), Victor Spinetti (Mr Stewart + other roles), Valentine Dyall (Lord Tennyson + other roles), Julian Chagrin (Prince Albert + other roles), Clifton Jones (King Theebaw + other roles), Charlie Atom (Postman + other roles). A humorous look at the life and works of the Scottish poet. *Dir*. Joseph McGrath.

Great Muppet Caper, The The Muppets plus: Charles Grodin (Nicky Holiday), Diana Rigg (Lady Holiday), John Cleese (Neville), Joan Sanderson (Dorcas), Jack Warden (Mike Tarkenian), Robert Morley (British gentlemen), Peter Ustinov (Truck driver), Peter Falk (Tramp), Michael Robbins (Henderson). Identical twins Kermit the Frog and Fozzie Bear are reporters for the *Daily Chronicle* and are assigned to investigate the theft of valuable jewels from fashion designer Lady Holliday. *Dir*. Jim Henson.

Great Rock'n'Roll Swindle, The (1980) A mockumentary about the British punk rock band the Sex Pistols. *Dir.* Julien Temple. See also *The Filth and the Fury*.

Great St Trinian's Train Robbery, The (1966) Frankie Howerd ("Alphonse of Monte Carlo"/Alfred Askett), Dora Bryan (Amber Spottiswood), George Cole (Flash Harry), Reg Varney (Gilbert), Raymond Huntley (Sir Horace), Richard Wattis (Manton Bassett), Terry Scott (Policeman), Eric Barker (Culpepper Brown), Godfrey Winn (Truelove), Colin Gordon (Noakes), Desmond Walter-Ellis (Leonard Edwards), Arthur Mullard (Big Jim), Norman Mitchell (William), Cyril Chamberlain (Maxie), Larry Martyn (Chips), Peter Gilmore (Butters), Michael Ripper (The Liftman), Stratford Johns (The Governor – voice only), Jeremy Clyde (Monty), George Benson (Gore-Blackwood), William Kendall (Mr Parker), Maureen Crombie (Marcia Askett), Barbara Couper (Mabel Radnage), Elspeth Duxbury (Veronica Bledlow), Carole Ann Ford (Albertine), Margaret Nolan (Susie Naphill), Maggie Rennie (Magda O'Riley), Jean St. Clair (Drunken Dolly). After pulling off a robbery and hiding the loot in a deserted mansion, a gang is dismayed to find that when they go back to collect it the house is the new home of the notorious St Trinians School for Girls. Alphonse, who runs the gang under the instruction of "The Governor" decides to use his delinquent daughters to infiltrate the school. The film ends with a hectic train chase. *Dirs.* Sidney Gilliat and Frank Launder.

Greed of William Hart, The (1948) Tod Slaughter (William Hart), Henry Oscar (Mr. Moore), Jenny Lynn (Helen Moore), Winifred Melville (Meg Hart), Aubrey Woods ('Daft Jamie' Wilson), Patrick Addison (Hugh Alston), Arnold Bell (Dr. Cox), Mary Love (Mary Patterson), Ann Trego (Janet Brown), Edward Malin (David Patterson), Hubert Woodward (Innkeeper Swanson), Dennis Wyndham (Sergeant Fisher). A horror film based on the story of Burke and Hare. *Dir.* Oswald Mitchell.

Green for Danger (1946) Alastair Sim (Inspector Cockrill), Leo Genn (Mr. Eden), Henry Edwards (Mr. Purdy), Trevor Howard (Dr. Barney Barnes), Ronald Adam (Dr. White), Judy Campbell (Sister Bates), Wendy Thompson (Sister Carter), Rosamund John (Nurse Esther Sanson), Sally Gray (Nurse Frederica 'Freddi' Linley), Megs Jenkins (Nurse Woods), John Rae (The Porter), Moore Marriott (Joseph Higgins), Frank Ling (Rescue Worker), George Woodbridge (Det.-Sgt. Hendricks), Hattie Jacques (Radio Announcer - voice). After a second patient dies on the operating table, a nurse cries murder and is then herself killed. Inspector Cockrill arrives at the hospital to investigate. *Dir.* Sidney Gilliat.

Green Man, The (1956) Alastair Sim (Hawkins), George Cole (William), Jill Adams (Ann Vincent), Terry-Thomas (Charles Boughtflower), Raymond Huntley (Sir Gregory), Colin Gordon (Reginald Willoughby-Cruft), Avril Angers (Marigold), Eileen Moore (Joan Wood), Dora Bryan (Lily), John Chandos (McKechnie), Cyril Chamberlain (Sgt Bassett), Richard Wattis (Doctor), Vivien Wood (Leader of Trio), Marie Burke (Felicity), Lucy Griffiths (Annabel), Arthur Brough (Landlord), Arthur Lowe (Radio salesman), Alexander Gauge (Chairman), Peter Bull (Gen Niva), Willoughby Goddard (Statesman), Michael Ripper (Waiter), Leslie Weston (Porter), Doris Yorke (Mrs Bostock), Terence Alexander (Man in Radio Studio). Watchmaker and killer Hawkins is tasked with blowing up Sir Gregory Upshott, but he has vacuum cleaner salesman William Blake to deal with. *Dirs.* Robert Day and Basil Dearden.

Greengage Summer, The (1961) Kenneth More (Eliot), Danielle Darrieux (Madame Zisi), Susannah York (Joss Grey), Claude Nollier (Madame Corbet), Jane Asher (Hester), Elizabeth Dear (Vicky), Richard Williams (Wilmouse), David Saire (Paul), Raymond Gérôme (Renard), Maurice Denham (Mr. Bullock), André Maranne (M. Dutour), Harold Kasket (M. Prideaux), Jacques B. Brunius (M. Joubert), Joy Shelton (Mrs. Grey), Balbina (Mauricette), Will Stampe (Monsieur Armand), Jean Ozenne (Champagne Director). Set in Epernay in France, this is a coming-of-age story which also encompasses jealousy and jewel theft. Released in the US as *Loss of Innocence*. Based on the novel by Rumer Godden. *Dir.* Lewis Gilbert.

Gregory's Girl (1980) John Gordon Sinclair (Gregory), Dee Hepburn (Dorothy), Clare Grogan (Susan), Jake D'Arcy (Phil), Robert Buchanan (Andy), Billy Greenless (Steve), Alan Love (Eric), Caroline Guthrie (Carol), Carol Macartney (Margo), Douglas Sannachan (Billy), Graham Thompson (Charlie), Allison Forster (Madeline Underwood), Chic Murray (Headmaster). In this gentle romantic comedy set in the Abronhill district of Cumbernauld, Scotland, teenaged Gregory Underwood falls for Dorothy, the latest member of the school football team. His first date with her does not go to plan but still ends up very much to his satisfaction. *Dir.* Bill Forsyth.

Gregory's Two Girls (1999) John Gordon Sinclair (Gregory), John Murtagh (Headmaster), Carly McKinnon (Frances), Hugh McCue (Douglas), Dougray Scott (Fraser Rowan), Alexander Morton (Norman), Martin Schwab (Dimitri), Maria Doyle Kennedy (Bel), William Harkness (Courier), Albert Coulson (Bus driver), Paul Birchard (US executive), Simon Huh (Asian executive), Dawn Steele (Jan), Kevin Anderson (Jon), Fiona Bell (Maddy Underwood), Constanzo Cacace (Italian restaurateur), Gary Lewis (Mr. McCance), Anne Kidd (Headmaster's secretary), Matt Costello (Det Gorrie), Jane Stabler (Detective Ritchie), Stewart Preston (Asst headmaster), Anne Marie Timoney (Joyce), Dougie Robertson (Policeman), Jonathan Hackett (Deere), Bruce Byron (Telfor). Sequel to Gregory's Girl set 18 years after the events of that film. Gregory is now teaching English at his old school. *Dir.* Bill Forsyth.

Greystoke: The Legend of Tarzan, Lord of the Apes (1984) Christopher Lambert (John Clayton/Tarzan), Ralph Richardson (Earl of Greystoke), Ian Holm (Captain D'Arnot), James Fox (Lord Charles Esker), Andie MacDowell (Jane Porter), Cheryl Campbell (Lady Alice Clayton), Ian Charleson (Jeffson Brown), Nigel Davenport (Maj Jack Downing), Nicholas Farrell (Sir Hugh Belcher), Paul Geoffrey (Lord John 'Jack' Clayton), Richard Griffiths (Captain Billings), Hilton McRae (Willy), David Suchet (Buller), John Wells (Sir Evelyn Blount), Eric Langlois (Tarzan aged 12), Danny Potts (Tarzan aged 5), Peter Kyriakou (Tarzan aged one), Tali McGregor (Infant Tarzan), Paul Brooke (Rev. Stimson), Tristram Jellinek (Chalky White), Roddy Maude-Roxby (Olivestone), Peter Elliott (Silverbeard, Primate Father), Ailsa Berk (Kala, Primate Mother), John Alexander (White Eyes, Primate Leader), Christopher Beck (Droopy Ears, Tarzan's Childhood Friend), Glenn Close (Jane Porter - voice). After his parents are stranded in Africa and then die, the newborn baby heir of Greystoke is taken under the care of a chimp. Through the years he grows to become the lead male of the chimps until he is discovered by Philippe D'Arnot who convinces him to return to England with him to reunite with his family. A re-telling of the Tarzan legend which goes back to source material rather than cinematic record, with Tarzan being articulate rather than a "Me Tarzan, you Jane" type character. Based on Edgar Rice Burroughs' novel *Tarzan of the Apes*. *Dir.* Hugh Hudson.

Guinea Pig, The (1948) Richard Attenborough (Jack Read), Sheila Sim (Lynne Hartley), Bernard Miles (Mr. Read), Cecil Trouncer (Lloyd Hartley), Robert Flemyng (Nigel Lorraine), Edith Sharpe (Mrs. Hartley), Joan Hickson (Mrs. Read), Timothy Bateson (Tracey), Clive Baxter (Gregory), Basil Cunard (Buckton), John Forrest (Fitch), Maureen Glynne (Bessie), Brenda Hogan (Lorna Beckett), Herbert Lomas (Sir James Corfield), Anthony Newley (Miles Minor), Anthony Nicholls (Mr. Stringer), Wally Patch (Uncle Percy), Hay Petrie (Peck), Oscar Quitak (David Tracey), Kynaston Reeves (The Bishop), Peter Reynolds (Grimmett), Olive Sloane (Aunt Mabel), Tony Wager (Bert), Percy Walsh (Alec Stevens), Norman Watson (Fanshaw). As an experiment a 14-year-old working-class boy is given a scholarship to an exclusive public school – God forbid!. *Dir.* Roy Boulting.

Gumshoe (1971) Albert Finney (Eddie), Billie Whitelaw (Ellen), Frank Finlay (William), Janice Rule (Mrs Blankerscoon), Carolyn Seymour (Alison), Fulton Mackay (Straker), George Innes (Bookshop Proprietor), George Silver (De Fries), Bill Dean (Tommy), Wendy Richard (Anne Scott), Maureen Lipman (Naomi), Neville Smith (Arthur), Oscar James (Azinge), Joe Kenyon (Joey), Bert King (Mal), Christopher Cunningham (Clifford), Ken Jones (Labour Exchange Clerk), Tom Kempinski (Psychiatrist). Binger-caller Eddie Ginley has always wanted to be a private detective so on his thirty-first birthday places an ad in the local paper and soon gets contacted by a man with a case for him to handle. *Dir.* Stephen Frears.

Guns at Batasi (1964) Richard Attenborough (Regimental Sergeant Major Lauderdale), Jack Hawkins (Colonel Deal), Flora

Robson (Miss Barker-Wise MP), John Leyton (Private Wilkes), Mia Farrow (Karen Eriksson), Cecil Parker (Fletcher), Errol John (Lieutenant Boniface), Graham Stark (Sergeant 'Dodger' Brown), Earl Cameron (Captain Abraham), Percy Herbert (Colour Sergeant Ben Parkin), David Lodge (Sergeant 'Muscles' Dunn), Bernard Horsfall (Sergeant 'Schoolie' Prideaux), John Meillon (Sergeant 'Aussie' Drake), Patrick Holt (Captain), Alan Browning (Adjutant), Richard Bidlake (Lieutenant), Horace James (Corporal Abou), Joseph Layode (Archibong Shaw), Ric Hutton (Russell). A group of British sergeants, commanded by a martinet RSM are caught between rival factions in a post-colonial African state. Based on the novel *The Siege of Battersea* by Robert Holles. *Dir*. John Guillermin.

Guns of Darkness (1962) Leslie Caron (Claire Jordan), David Niven (Tom Jordan), David Opatoshu (President Rivera), James Robertson Justice (Hugo Bryant), Eleanor Summerfield (Mrs Bastian), Ian Hunter (Dr Swann), Derek Godfrey (Hernandez), Richard Pearson (Bastian), Sandor Elès (Lt Gomez), Steven Scott (Gabriel), Tutte Lemkow (Gabriel's Cousin), Dorita Sensier (Nightclub Singer), John Carson (1st Officer), Ali Nagi (Indian Boy), Barry Shawzin (Gen Zoreno), Peter Allenby (Sergeant), Roger Delgado (Hernandez - voice). A married couple are caught up in the middle of a coup d'état in South America. *Dir*. Anthony Asquith.

Guns of Navarone, The (1961) Gregory Peck (Capt Keith Mallory), David Niven (Cpl John Anthony Miller), Anthony Quinn (Col Andrea Stavrou), Stanley Baker (Pvt 'Butcher' Brown), Anthony Quayle (Maj Roy Franklin), James Darren (Pvt Spyros Pappadimos), Peter Grant (British Commando), Irene Papas (Maria Pappadimos), Gia Scala (Anna), James Robertson Justice (Cmdre James Jensen), Richard Harris (Sq Leader Howard Barnsby), Bryan Forbes (Cohn), Allan Cuthbertson (Maj Baker), Michael Trubshawe (Weaver), Percy Herbert (Sgt Grogan), George Mikell (Hauptsturmführer Sessler), Walter Gotell (Oberleutnant Muesel), Tutte Lemkow (Nikolai), Albert Lieven (Commandant), Norman Wooland (Group Capt Aldo Raine), Cleo Scouloudi (Bride). A team of saboteurs is sent to Navarone to destroy the guns which threaten a rescue of Allied soldiers. Based on Alistair MacLean's novel about the real-life 1943 Battle of Leros. *Dir*. J. Lee Thompson.

H.M.S. Defiant (1962) Alec Guinness (Capt Crawford), Dirk Bogarde (Lt Scott-Padget), Maurice Denham (Mr Goss), Nigel Stock (Senior Midshipman Kilpatrick), Richard Carpenter (Lt Ponsonby), Peter Gill (Lt D'Arblay), David Robinson (Midshipman Harvey Crawford), Robin Stewart (Midshipman Pardoe), Ray Brooks (Hayes), Peter Greenspan (Johnson), Anthony Quayle (Vizard), Tom Bell (Evans), Murray Melvin (Percival Wagstaffe), Victor Maddern (Bosun Dawlish), Bryan Pringle (Marine Sgt Kneebone), Johnny Briggs (Wheatley), Brian Phelan (Grimshaw), Toke Townley (Silly Billy), Declan Mulholland (Morrison), Walter Fitzgerald (Adm Jackson), Joy Shelton (Mrs Crawford), Anthony Oliver (Tavern Leader), Russell Napier (Flag Capt), Michael Coles (Flag Lt), Andre Maranne (Col Giraud). Set during the Napoleonic wars, the HMS *Defiant* has a mutinous crew and a captain and second-in-command at constant loggerheads. *Dir*. Lewis Gilbert.

Half a Sixpence (1967) Tommy Steele (Arthur Kipps), Julia Foster (Ann), Cyril Ritchard (Harry Chitterlow), Penelope Horner (Helen), Elaine Taylor (Victoria), Grover Dale (Pearce), Hilton Edwards (Shalford), Julia Sutton (Flo), Leslie Meadows (Buggins), Sheila Falconer (Kate), Pamela Brown (Mrs Washington), James Villiers (Hubert), Christopher Sandford (Sid), Jean Anderson (Lady Botting), Allan Cuthbertson (Wilkins), Marti Webb (Ann's singing voice), Bartlett Mullins (Carshott). The changes in fortune of draper's assistant Arthur Kipps. Musical film based on *Kipps: The Story of a Simple Soul* by H.G. Wells. *Dir*. George Sidney.

Halfway House, The (1944) Mervyn Johns (Rhys), Glynis Johns (Gwyneth), Sally Ann Howes (Joanna French), Richard Bird (Richard French), Valerie White (Jill French), Françoise Rosay (Alice Meadows), Tom Walls (Captain Harry Meadows), Guy Middleton (Captain Fortescue), Alfred Drayton (William Oakley),

Esmond Knight (David Davies), Philippa Hiatt (Margaret), Pat McGrath (Terence), John Boxer (John), Roland Pertwee (Prison governor), Eliot Makeham (George), C.V. France (Mr. Truscott), Rachel Thomas (Miss Morgan), Joss Ambler (Pinsent). On a stormy night a group of travellers, all with problems, seek shelter in a remote Welsh Inn. The innkeeper and his daughter are welcoming but as time passes it is clear all is not as it should be – the newspapers are all a year old and the daughter casts no shadow. An early Ealing Studios morality tale based on *The Peaceful Inn*, a play by Denis Ogden. *Dirs*. Basil Dearden and Alberto Cavalcanti.

Hallam Foe (2007) Jamie Bell (Hallam), Sophia Myles (Kate Breck), Ciarán Hinds (Julius Foe), Jamie Sives (Alasdair), Maurice Roëves (Raymond), Ewen Bremner (Andy), Claire Forlani (Verity Foe), John Paul Lawler (Carl), Ruth Milne (Jenny), Lucy Holt (Lucy). Hallam Foe spends much of his time spying on people. He is suspicious that his mother's death by drowning might not have been an accident and suspects his stepmother. On moving to Edinburgh he gets a job in a hotel and begins spying on a colleague. Based on Peter Jinks' novel. *Dir*. David Mackenzie.

Hamlet (1948) Laurence Olivier (Hamlet), Jean Simmons (Ophelia), Basil Sydney (King Claudius), Eileen Herlie (Queen Gertrude), Norman Wooland (Horatio), Felix Aylmer (Polonius), Terence Morgan (Laertes), John Laurie (Francisco), Esmond Knight (Bernardo), Anthony Quayle (Marcellus), Niall MacGinnis ('Sea Captain'), Harcourt Williams (First Player), Patrick Troughton (Player King), Tony Tarver (Player Queen), Peter Cushing (Osric), Stanley Holloway (Gravedigger), Russell Thorndike (Priest). Version of the Shakespearean tragedy, wherein Hamlet struggles to revenge the murder of his father. The film won four Academy Awards: Best Picture, Best Actor, Best Art Direction and Best Costume Design with Olivier being the first actor to direct themselves to the Best Actor Oscar. Olivier was 11 years older than Eileen Herlie who played his mother in the film.

Hamlet (1969) Nicol Williamson (Hamlet), Judy Parfitt (Gertrude), Anthony Hopkins (Claudius), Marianne Faithfull (Ophelia), Mark Dignam (Polonius), Michael Pennington (Laertes), Gordon Jackson (Horatio), Ben Aris (Rosencrantz), Clive Graham (Guildenstern), Peter Gale (Osric), Roger Livesey (Lucianus/Gravedigger), John J. Carney (Player King), Richard Everett (Player Queen), Robin Chadwick (Francisco), Ian Collier (Priest), Michael Elphick (Captain), David Griffith (Messenger), Anjelica Huston (Court Lady), Bill Jarvis (Courtier), Roger Lloyd-Pack (Reynaldo), John Railton (1st Sailor), John Trenaman (Barnardo). The first colour film version of the Shakespearean tragedy. *Dir*. Tony Richardson.

Hamlet (1996) Kenneth Branagh (Prince Hamlet), Derek Jacobi (King Claudius), Julie Christie (Gertrude), Richard Briers (Polonius), Kate Winslet (Ophelia), Nicholas Farrell (Horatio), Michael Maloney (Laertes), Rufus Sewell (Fortinbras), Robin Williams (Osric), Gérard Depardieu (Reynaldo), Timothy Spall (Rosencrantz), Reece Dinsdale (Guildenstern), Jack Lemmon (Marcellus), Ian McElhinney (Barnardo), Ray Fearon (Francisco), Brian Blessed (Ghost of Hamlet's Father), Billy Crystal (First Gravedigger), Simon Russell Beale (Second Gravedigger), Don Warrington (Voltimand), Ravil Isyanov (Cornelius), Charlton Heston (Player King), Rosemary Harris (Player Queen), Richard Attenborough (English Ambassador), John Gielgud (Priam), Judi Dench (Hecuba), John Mills (Old King Norway), Ken Dodd (Yorick). A full text adaptation of Shakespeare's play with a running time (uncut) of 242 minutes. *Dir*. Kenneth Branagh.

Hammer the Toff (1952) John Bentley (The Hon Richard Rollison), Patricia Dainton (Susan Lancaster), Valentine Dyall (Inspector Grice), John Robinson (Linnett), Wally Patch (Bert Ebbutt), Katharine Blake (Janet Lord), Roddy Hughes (Jolly), Basil Dignam (Superintendent), Lockwood West (Kennedy), Charles Hawtrey (Cashier), Max Brent (Bill Merrick), Vivienne Burgess (Miss Parkinson), Ian Fleming (Dr. Lancaster), Andreas Malandrinos (Benson), Patricia Page (Ethel Kent), John Powe (Flatty), Vi Stevens (Emily Ebbutt), Ben Williams (Sgt. Barrow).

Susan's uncle, a scientist with a secret formula, has disappeared. Enter Det. Richard Rollison ("The Toff"). Based on the novel by John Creasey. *Dir*. Maclean Rogers.

Hand in Hand (1960) Philip Needs (Michael O'Malley), Loretta Parry (Rachel Mathias), Kathleen Byron (Mrs. O'Malley), Finlay Currie (Mr. Pritchard), Arnold Diamond (Mr. Mathias), Denis Gilmore (Tom), John Gregson (Father Timothy), Barbara Hicks (Miss Roberts), Miriam Karlin (Mrs. Mathias), Barry Keegan (Mr. O'Malley), Martin Lawrence (The Cantor), Peter Pike (Harry), Susan Reid (Priscilla), Madge Ryan (George's Wife), Derek Sydney (Rabbi Benjamin), Donald Tandy (George), Sybil Thorndike (Lady Caroline). Told in flashback by Michael, this is the story of a friendship between a young catholic boy and a jewish girl. The film won a Golden Globe for Best Film Promoting International Understanding. *Dir*. Philip Leacock.

Hannibal Brooks (1969) Oliver Reed (Stephen Brooks), Michael J. Pollard (Packy), Wolfgang Preiss (Col von Haller), Helmuth Lohner (Willi), Peter Carsten (Kurt), Karin Baal (Vronia), Aida (The Elephant Lucy), Ralf Wolter (Doctor Mendel), John Alderton (Bernard), Jürgen Draeger (Sami), Ernst Fritz Fürbringer (Elephant keeper Kellerman), Erik Jelde (Zoo director Stern), James Donald (Padre), Maria Brockerhoff (Anna), Til Kiwe (Sergeant), Fred Haltiner (Josef), John Porter-Davison (Geordie), Terence Sewards (Twilight). British POW working in Munich Zoo during WWII attempts to escape to Switzerland with an elephant. *Dir*. Michael Winner.

Hanover Street (1979) Harrison Ford (Lt Halloran), Lesley-Anne Down (Margaret), Christopher Plummer (Paul Sellinger), Alec McCowen (Major Trumbo), Michael Sacks (2nd Lt. Martin Hyer), Patsy Kensit (Sarah Sellinger), Max Wall (Harry Pike), Shane Rimmer (Col. Ronald Bart), Richard Masur (2nd Lieut. Jerry Cimino), Keith Buckley (Lieut. Wells), Sherrie Hewson (Phyllis), Cindy O'Callaghan (Paula), John Ratzenberger (Sgt. John Lucas), Eddie Kidd (Motorcycle Jump Performer). In London during WWII American flyer David Halloran falls for nurse Margaret Sellinger but she decides not to tell him she is married. Within weeks her husband and her lover find themselves stranded together in occupied France. *Dir*. Peter Hyams.

Happiest Days of your Life, The (1950) Alastair Sim (Wetherby Pond), Margaret Rutherford (Miss Whitchurch), Guy Middleton (Victor Hyde-Brown), Joyce Grenfell (Miss Gossage), Edward Rigby (Rainbow), Muriel Aked (Miss Jezzard), Richard Wattis (Arnold Billings), John Bentley (Richard Tassell), Bernadette O'Farrell (Miss Harper), Richard Wattis (Arnold Billings), Gladys Henson (Mrs. Hampstead), Myrette Morven (Miss Chapel), Laurence Naismith (Dr. Collett), Margaret Anderson (Alice). The life of Nutbourne College, a boys boarding school, is turned upside down when St Swithin's Girls School is accidentally billeted on it. Alastair Sim and Margaret Rutherford lock horns as the head teachers and Joyce Grenfell does her jolly hockey sticks schtick. *Dir*. Frank Launder.

Happy Ever After (1954) David Niven (Jasper O'Leary), Yvonne De Carlo (Serena McGluskey), Barry Fitzgerald (Thady O'Heggarty), George Cole (Terence), A.E. Matthews (Gen O'Leary), Noelle Middleton (Kathy McGluskey), Robert Urquhart (Dr. Michael Flynn), Michael Shepley (Maj McGluskey), Joseph Tomelty (Dooley), Eddie Byrne (Lannigan), Liam Redmond (Regan), Anthony Nicholls (Solicitor), Tommy Duggan (Toastmaster), Fred Johnson (Father Cormac), Denis Martin (Singer), Patrick McAlinney (O'Connor), Ronan O'Casey (Reporter), Brian O'Higgins (Milligan), Bill Shine (Saxby), Patrick Westwood (Murphy). When an Irish landowner dies his son is called on to take over the running of his estate. *Dir*. Mario Zampi.

Happy Family, The (1952) Stanley Holloway (Henry Lord), Kathleen Harrison (Lillian Lord), Naunton Wayne (Mr. Filch), Dandy Nichols (Ada), John Stratton (David), Eileen Moore (Joan), Shirley Mitchell (Marina), Margaret Barton (Anne), George Cole (Cyril), Tom Gill (Maurice Hennessey), Miles Malleson (Mr Thwaites), Geoffrey Sumner (Sir Charles Spanniell), Laurence Naismith (Councillor), Edward Lexy (Alderman), Cameron Hall (Mayor), Hal Osmond (Shop Steward), John Salew (Mr. Granite), Michael Ward (BBC Announcer), Richard Wattis (M.P.), David Keir (Process Server), Campbell Singer (PC), Arthur Hambling (Granger), Eileen Way

(Mrs Potter). A family that runs a grocery shop refuses to move when the property hinders construction needed for the 1951 Festival of Britain. *Dir*. Muriel Box.

Happy Go Lovely (1951) David Niven (B.G. Bruno), Vera-Ellen (Janet), Cesar Romero (John Frost), Bobby Howes (Charlie), Diane Hart (Mae), Gordon Jackson (Paul Tracy), Barbara Couper (Madame Amanda), Henry Hewitt (Dodds), Gladys Henson (Mrs. Urquhart), Hugh Dempster (Bates), Sandra Dorne (Betty), Joyce Carey (Bruno's Secretary), John Laurie (Jonskill), Wylie Watson (Stage Door Keeper), Joan Heal (Phyllis Gardiner), Hector Ross (Harold), Ambrosine Phillpotts (Lady Martin), Molly Urquhart (Madame Amanda's Assistant), Archie Duncan (Police Inspector), Kay Kendall (Secretary). Set during the Edinburgh Festival, millionaire B G Bruno falls for chorus girl Janet Jones and her show's impresario decides to try and take advantage of the situation. *Dir*. H. Bruce Humberstone.

Happy is the Bride (1958) Ian Carmichael (David Chaytor), Janette Scott (Janet Royd), Cecil Parker (Arthur Royd), Terry-Thomas (Policeman), Joyce Grenfell (Aunt Florence), Eric Barker (Vicar), Edith Sharpe (Mildred Royd), Elvi Hale (Petula), Miles Malleson (1st Magistrate), Athene Seyler (Aunt Harriet), Irene Handl (Mme. Edna), John Le Mesurier (Chaytor), Thorley Walters (Jim), Nicholas Parsons (John Royd), Virginia Maskell (Marcia), Brian Oulton (2nd Magistrate), Joan Hickson (Mrs. Bowels), Cardew Robinson (George the Verger). When a young couple decides it is time to get married their hopes for a quiet wedding are ignored. Based on the play *Quiet Wedding* by Esther McCracken. *Dir*. Roy Boulting.

Happy-Go-Lucky (2008) Sally Hawkins (Pauline "Poppy" Cross), Eddie Marsan (Scott), Alexis Zegerman (Zoe), Andrea Riseborough (Dawn), Sinead Matthews (Alice), Sylvestra Le Touzel (Heather), Samuel Roukin (Tim), Caroline Martin (Helen), Oliver Maltman (Jamie), Sarah Niles (Tash), Joseph Kloska (Suzy's Boyfriend), Nonso Anozie (Ezra), Jack MacGeachin (Nick), Charlie Duffield (Charlie), Ayotunde Williams (Ayotunde), Karina Fernandez (Flamenco teacher), Philip Arditti, Viss Elliot Safavi, Rebekah Staton (Flamenco Students), Elliot Cowan (Bookshop Assistant), Anna Reynolds (Receptionist), Trevor Cooper (Patient), Stanley Townsend (Tramp). The film follows teacher Poppy Cross, who is almost pathologically happy and optimistic. Despite friends and relatives telling her its time she took life more seriously, she just carries on being happy-go-lucky. *Dir*. Mike Leigh.

Hard Day's Night, A (1964) John Lennon (John), Paul McCartney (Paul), George Harrison (George), Ringo Starr (Ringo), Wilfrid Brambell (Grandfather), Norman Rossington (Norm), John Junkin (Shake), Victor Spinetti (T.V. director), Anna Quayle (Millie), Deryck Guyler (Police Inspector), Richard Vernon (Man on Train), Edward Malin (Hotel Waiter), Robin Ray (T.V. Floor Manager), Lionel Blair (T.V. Choreographer), Alison Seebohm (Secretary), David Janson (Young Boy), John Bluthal (Car Thief), Pattie Boyd (Schoolgirl on Train), Kenneth Haigh (Simon Marshall), Susan Hampshire (Dancer at Disco), Julian Holloway (Adrian), Derek Nimmo (Leslie Jackson), Gordon Rollings (Man with Sandwich in Pub), Marianne Stone (Society Reporter), Michael Trubshawe (Casino Manager). The film follows The Beatles for a day as they travel from Liverpool to London to perform in a television programme at the height of Beatlemania – so lots of screaming, running and general larking about all backed up with some classic Beatles songs. A mockumentary before anyone had thought of that word and ultimately very influential film. *Dir*. Richard Lester.

Hardware (1989) Dylan McDermott (Moses "Hard Mo" Baxter), Stacey Travis (Jill Berkowski), John Lynch (Shades), William Hootkins (Lincoln Wineberg Jr), Iggy Pop (Angry Bob), Carl McCoy (Nomad), Mark Northover (Alvy), Paul McKenzie (Vernon), Lemmy (Water taxi driver). In post apocalyptic earth the unearthing of robot spare parts brings only disaster to the discoverer and his friends. *Dir*. Richard Stanley.

Harry Brown (2009) Michael Caine (Harry Brown), Emily Mortimer (Detective Inspector Alice Frampton), Charlie Creed Miles (Detective Sergeant Terry Hicock), David Bradley (Len Attwell), Ben Drew "Plan B" (Noel Winters), Sean Harris (Stretch), Jack O'Connell (Marky), Jamie Downey (Carl), Lee Oakes (Dean Saunders), Joseph Gilgun (Kenny), Liam

Cunningham (Sid Rourke), Iain Glen (Superintendent Childs), Klariza Clayton (Sharon), Liz Daniels (Kath Brown), Radoslaw Kaim (Doctor), Claire Hackett (Jean Winters), Ashley McGuire (Community WPC), Raza Jaffrey (Father Bracken), Grace Vallorani (Linda), Forbes KB (Troy Martindale). When his friend Len is terrorised and murdered by a gang of local youths, previously law-abiding ex-Royal Marine Harry Brown decides to take matters into his own hands and clean up his estate. *Dir.* Daniel Barber.

Harry Potter and the Chamber of Secrets (2002) Daniel Radcliffe (Harry Potter), Rupert Grint (Ron Weasley), Emma Watson (Hermione Granger), Robbie Coltrane (Rubeus Hagrid), Alan Rickman (Severus Snape), Matthew Lewis (Neville Longbottom), Devon Murray (Seamus Finnigan), Tom Felton (Draco Malfoy), Josh Herdman (Gregory Goyle), Bonnie Wright (Ginny Weasley), James Phelps (Fred Weasley), Oliver Phelps (George Weasley), Geraldine Somerville (Lily Potter), Richard Harris (Professor Albus Dumbledore), Maggie Smith (Professor Minerva McGonagall), Warwick Davis (Professor Flitwick), David Bradley (Argus Filch), Kenneth Branagh (Professor Gilderoy Lockhart), Miriam Margolyes (Professor Pomona Sprout), Gemma Jones (Madam Pomfrey), Sally Mortemore (Madam Irma Pince), Alfred Burke (Professor Armando Dippet), Christian Coulson (Tom Marvolo Riddle), Jamie Waylett (Vincent Crabbe), Charlotte Skeoch (Hannah Abbott), David Churchyard (Slytherin Keeper), Emily Dale (Katie Bell), Helen Stuart (Millicent Bulstrode), Gemma Padley (Penelope Clearwater), Hugh Mitchell (Colin Creevey), Rochelle Douglas (Alicia Spinnet), Danielle Tabor (Angelina Johnson), Jamie Yeates (Marcus Flint), Sean Biggerstaff (Oliver Wood), Scot Fearn (Adrian Pucey), Edward Randell (Justin Finch-Fletchley), Louis Doyle (Ernie MacMillan), Eleanor Columbus (Susan Bones), Luke Youngblood (Lee Jordan), Jason Isaacs (Lucius Malfoy), Toby Jones (Dobby the House Elf (voice)), Robert Hardy (Cornelius Fudge), Martin Bayfield (Young Rubeus Hagrid), Richard Griffiths (Uncle Vernon Dursley), Fiona Shaw (Aunt Petunia Dursley), Harry Melling (Dudley Dursley), Julie Walters (Molly Weasley), Mark Williams (Arthur Weasley), Chris Rankin (Percy Weasley), Adrian Rawlins (James Potter), Harry Taylor (Station Guard), Jim Norton (Mr. Mason), Veronica Clifford (Mrs. Mason), Tom Knight (Mr. Granger), Heather Bleasdale (Mrs. Granger), Leslie Phillips (The Sorting Hat (voice)), John Cleese (Nearly Headless Nick), Shirley Henderson (Moaning Myrtle), Peter Taylor (Man - Moving Picture), Daisy Bates (Brunette Lady - Moving Picture), David Tysall (Count - Moving Picture), Julian Glover (Aragog (voice)). Harry is visited at the Dursley's by Dobby, who warns him not to go back to Hogwarts. He ignores the warning and shortly after the start of term it becomes clear that the Heir of Slytherin has opened the Chamber of Secrets and a monster has been unleashed. Based on J K Rowling's book of the same name, the second in the seven book series. *Dir.* Chris Columbus.

Harry Potter and the Deathly Hallows – Part 1 (2010) Daniel Radcliffe (Harry Potter), Rupert Grint (Ron Weasley), Emma Watson (Hermione Granger), Robbie Coltrane (Rubeus Hagrid), Alan Rickman (Severus Snape), Matthew Lewis (Neville Longbottom), Devon Murray (Seamus Finnigan), Tom Felton (Draco Malfoy), Josh Herdman (Gregory Goyle), Bonnie Wright (Ginny Weasley), James Phelps (Fred Weasley), Oliver Phelps (George Weasley), Geraldine Somerville (Lily Potter), Michael Gambon (Professor Albus Dumbledore), Toby Regbo (Young Albus Dumbledore), Carolyn Pickles (Charity Burbage), Brendan Gleeson (Professor Alastor 'Mad-Eye' Moody), Shefali Chowdhury (Parvati Patel), Afshan Azad (Padma Patil), Katie Leung (Cho Chang), William Melling (Nigel), Evanna Lynch (Luna Lovegood), Jessie Cave (Lavender Brown), Georgina Leonidas (Katie Bell), Isabella Laughland (Leanne), Freddie Stroma (Cormac McLaggen), Scarlett Byrne (Pansy Parkinson), Anna Shaffer (Romilda Vane), Louis Cordice (Blaise Zabini), Julie Walters (Molly Weasley), Mark Williams (Arthur Weasley), Chris Rankin (Percy Weasley), Domhnall Gleeson (Bill Weasley), Matyelok Gibbs (Auntie Muriel Weasley), Adrian Rawlins (James Potter), Ralph Fiennes (Lord Voldemort), Helena Bonham Carter (Bellatrix Lestrange), Imelda Staunton (Dolores Umbridge), David Thewlis (Remus Lupin), Bill Nighy (Minister Rufus Scrimgeour), Timothy Spall (Wormtail/Peter Pettigrew), Jason Isaacs (Lucius Malfoy), Helen McCrory (Narcissa Malfoy), Tom Moorcroft (Regulus Black), Ralph Ineson (Amycus Carrow), Suzanne Toase (Alecto Carrow), Dave Legeno (Fenrir Greyback), Rod Hunt (Thorfinn Rowle), Natalia Tena (Nymphadora Tonks), Miranda Richardson (Rita Skeeter), Eva Alexander (Waitress), Paul Ritter (Eldred Worple), Richard Griffiths (Uncle Vernon Dursley), Fiona Shaw (Aunt Petunia Dursley), Harry Melling (Dudley Dursley), Ian Kelly (Mr. Granger), Michelle Fairley (Mrs. Granger), Guy Henry (Pius Thicknesse), Arben Bajraktaraj (Antonin Dolohov), David Ryall (Elphias Doge), George Harris (Kingsley Shacklebolt), Andy Linden (Mundungus Fletcher), Clémence Poésy (Fleur Delacour), John Hurt (Ollivander), Warwick Davis (Griphook), Frances de la Tour (Madame Maxime), Rhys Ifans (Xenophilius Lovegood), Eva Alexander (Waitress), Simon McBurney (Kreacher (voice)), Amber Evans (Twin Girl 1), Ruby Evans (Twin Girl 2), David O'Hara (Albert Runcorn), Steffan Rhodri (Reg Cattermole), Nick Moran (Scabior), Toby Jones (Dobby (voice)), Sophie Thompson (Mafalda Hopkirk), Ned Dennehy (Scared Man), Kate Fleetwood (Mary Cattermole), Rade Serbedzija (Gregorovitch), Jamie Campbell Bower (Young Gellert Grindelwald), Michael Byrne (Old Gellert Grindelwald), Hazel Douglas (Bathilda Bagshot). Realising they cannot return to Hogwarts, Harry, Ron and Hermione decide to finish the hunt for Voldemort's remaining Horcruxes. They also learn of the Deathly Hallows - three sacred objects - the Elder Wand, the Resurrection Stone and the Cloak of Invisibility. Based on J K Rowling's book of the same name, the first part of the last in the seven book series. *Dir.* David Yates.

Harry Potter and the Deathly Hallows – Part 2 (2011) Daniel Radcliffe (Harry Potter), Rupert Grint (Ron Weasley), Emma Watson (Hermione Granger), Robbie Coltrane (Rubeus Hagrid), Alan Rickman (Severus Snape), Matthew Lewis (Neville Longbottom), Devon Murray (Seamus Finnigan), Tom Felton (Draco Malfoy), Josh Herdman (Gregory Goyle), Bonnie Wright (Ginny Weasley), James Phelps (Fred Weasley), Oliver Phelps (George Weasley), Geraldine Somerville (Lily Potter), Michael Gambon (Professor Albus Dumbledore), Ciarán Hinds (Aberforth Dumbledore), Hebe Beardsall (Ariana Dumbledore), Maggie Smith (Professor Minerva McGonagall), Warwick Davis (Griphook/Professor Filius Flitwick), Jim Broadbent (Professor Horace Slughorn), Miriam Margolyes (Professor Pomona Sprout), Gemma Jones (Madam Pomfrey), Emma Thompson (Professor Sybil Trelawney), David Bradley (Argus Filch), Kelly Macdonald (Helena Ravenclaw), Shefali Chowdhury (Parvati Patel), Afshan Azad (Padma Patil), Katie Leung (Cho Chang), William Melling (Nigel), Evanna Lynch (Luna Lovegood), Jessie Cave (Lavender Brown), Georgina Leonidas (Katie Bell), Isabella Laughland (Leanne), Freddie Stroma (Cormac McLaggen), Scarlett Byrne (Pansy Parkinson), Anna Shaffer (Romilda Vane), Louis Cordice (Blaise Zabini), Alfie Enoch (Dean Thomas), Julie Walters (Molly Weasley), Mark Williams (Arthur Weasley), Chris Rankin (Percy Weasley), Domhnall Gleeson (Bill Weasley), Adrian Rawlins (James Potter), Ralph Fiennes (Lord Voldemort), Helena Bonham Carter (Bellatrix Lestrange), Gary Oldman (Sirius Black), David Thewlis (Remus Lupin), Bill Nighy (Minister Rufus Scrimgeour), Timothy Spall (Wormtail/Peter Pettigrew), Jason Isaacs (Lucius Malfoy), Helen McCrory (Narcissa Malfoy), Tom Moorcroft (Regulus Black), Ralph Ineson (Amycus Carrow), Suzanne Toase (Alecto Carrow), Dave Legeno (Fenrir Greyback), Rod Hunt (Thorfinn Rowle), Natalia Tena (Nymphadora Tonks), Guy Henry (Pius Thicknesse), George Harris (Kingsley Shacklebolt), Clémence Poésy (Fleur Delacour), John Hurt (Ollivander), Amber Evans (Twin Girl 1), Ruby Evans (Twin Girl 2), Nick Moran (Scabior), Jon Key (Bogrod), Anthony Allgood (Gringotts Guard), Rusty Goffe (Gringotts Goblin), Sian Grace Phillips (Screaming Girl), Ellie Darcey-Alden (Young Lily Potter), Ariella Paradise (Young Petunia Dursley), Benedict Clarke (Young Severus Snape), Alfie McIlwain (Young James Potter), Rohan

Gotobed (Young Sirius Black), Toby Papworth (Baby Harry Potter), Arthur Bowen (Albus Severus Potter - 19 years later), Daphne de Beistegui (Lily Luna Potter - 19 years later), Will Dunn (James Sirius Potter - 19 years later), Jade Gordon (Astoria Malfoy -19 years later), Bertie Gilbert (Scorpius Malfoy - 19 years later), Helena Barlow (Rose Weasley - 19 years later), Ryan Turner (Hugo Weasley - 19 years later). The series reaches its climax with the battle for Hogwarts. Based on J K Rowling's book of the same name, the second part of the last in the seven book series. *Dir.* David Yates.

Harry Potter and the Goblet of Fire (2005) Daniel Radcliffe (Harry Potter), Rupert Grint (Ron Weasley), Emma Watson (Hermione Granger), Robbie Coltrane (Rubeus Hagrid), Alan Rickman (Severus Snape), Matthew Lewis (Neville Longbottom), Devon Murray (Seamus Finnigan), Tom Felton (Draco Malfoy), Josh Herdman (Gregory Goyle), Bonnie Wright (Ginny Weasley), James Phelps (Fred Weasley), Oliver Phelps (George Weasley), Geraldine Somerville (Lily Potter), Michael Gambon (Professor Albus Dumbledore), Maggie Smith (Professor Minerva McGonagall), Warwick Davis (Filius Flitwick), David Bradley (Argus Filch), Brendan Gleeson (Professor Alastor 'Mad-Eye' Moody), Robert Pattinson (Cedric Diggory), Jamie Waylett (Vincent Crabbe), Shefali Chowdhury (Parvati Patel), Afshan Azad (Padma Patil), Tiana Benjamin (Angelina Johnson), Charlotte Skeoch (Hannah Abbott), Katie Leung (Cho Chang), Henry Lloyd-Hughes (Roger Davies), William Melling (Nigel), Stanislav Ianevski (Viktor Krum), Frances de la Tour (Madame Olympe Maxime), Angelica Mandy (Gabrielle Delacour), Clémence Poésy (Fleur Delacour), Predrag Bjelac (Igor Karkaroff), Tolga Safer (Karkaroff's Aide), Louis Doyle (Ernie MacMillan), Alan Watts (Assistant Judge), Mark Williams (Arthur Weasley), Adrian Rawlins (James Potter), Ralph Fiennes (Lord Voldemort), Gary Oldman (Sirius Black), Timothy Spall (Wormtail/Peter Pettigrew), Robert Hardy (Cornelius Fudge), David Tennant (Bartemius 'Barty' Crouch Junior), Roger Lloyd-Pack (Bartemius 'Barty' Crouch), Jeff Rawle (Amos Diggory), Jason Isaacs (Lucius Malfoy), Miranda Richardson (Rita Skeeter), Robert Wilfort (Photographer), Eric Sykes (Frank Bryce), Shirley Henderson (Moaning Myrtle), Margery Mason (Food Trolley Lady), Jarvis Cocker (Band Lead Singer), Jonny Greenwood (Band Lead Guitar), Phil Selway (Band Drums), Steve Mackey (Band Bass Guitar), Jason Buckle (Band Rhythm Guitar), Steve Claydon (Band Keyboards). Harry is chosen for the Triwizard Tournament despite being underage. Based on J K Rowling's book of the same name, the fourth in the seven book series. *Dir.* Mike Newell.

Harry Potter and the Half-Blood Prince (2009) Daniel Radcliffe (Harry Potter), Rupert Grint (Ron Weasley), Emma Watson (Hermione Granger), Robbie Coltrane (Rubeus Hagrid), Alan Rickman (Severus Snape), Matthew Lewis (Neville Longbottom), Devon Murray (Seamus Finnigan), Tom Felton (Draco Malfoy), Josh Herdman (Gregory Goyle), Bonnie Wright (Ginny Weasley), James Phelps (Fred Weasley), Oliver Phelps (George Weasley), Geraldine Somerville (Lily Potter), Michael Gambon (Professor Albus Dumbledore), Maggie Smith (Professor Minerva McGonagall), Warwick Davis (Filius Flitwick), David Bradley (Argus Filch), Gemma Jones (Madam Pomfrey), Jim Broadbent (Professor Horace Slughorn), Jamie Waylett (Vincent Crabbe), Shefali Chowdhury (Parvati Patel), Afshan Azad (Padma Patil), Katie Leung (Cho Chang), William Melling (Nigel), Evanna Lynch (Luna Lovegood), Robert Knox (Marcus Belby), Jessie Cave (Lavender Brown), Georgina Leonidas (Katie Bell), Isabella Laughland (Leanne), Freddie Stroma (Cormac McLaggen), Scarlett Byrne (Pansy Parkinson), Anna Shaffer (Romilda Vane), Louis Cordice (Blaise Zabini), Alfie Enoch (Dean Thomas), Amelda Brown (Mrs. Cole), Julie Walters (Molly Weasley), Mark Williams (Arthur Weasley), Chris Rankin (Percy Weasley), Ralph Fiennes (Lord Voldemort), Hero Fiennes-Tiffin (Tom Riddle (11 Years)), Frank Dillane (Tom Riddle (16 Years)), Helena Bonham Carter (Bellatrix Lestrange), David Thewlis (Remus Lupin), Timothy Spall (Wormtail/Peter Pettigrew), Sian Thomas (Amelia Bones), Jason Isaacs (Lucius Malfoy), Helen McCrory (Narcissa Malfoy), Tom Moorcroft (Regulus Black), Ralph Ineson (Amycus Carrow), Suzanne Toase (Alecto Carrow), Dave Legeno (Fenrir Greyback), Rod Hunt (Rowle), Natalia Tena (Nymphadora Tonks), Elarica Gallacher (Waitress), Paul Ritter (Eldred Worple), Amber Evans (Twin Girl 1), Ruby Evans (Twin Girl 2). As Lord Voldemort's grip tightens Harry learns of the existence of the horcruxes, the destroying of which could be the means to defeat him. Based on J K Rowling's book of the same name, the sixth in the seven book series. *Dir.* David Yates.

Harry Potter and the Order of the Phoenix (2007) Daniel Radcliffe (Harry Potter), Rupert Grint (Ron Weasley), Emma Watson (Hermione Granger), Robbie Coltrane (Rubeus Hagrid), Alan Rickman (Severus Snape), Matthew Lewis (Neville Longbottom), Devon Murray (Seamus Finnigan), Tom Felton (Draco Malfoy), Josh Herdman (Gregory Goyle), Bonnie Wright (Ginny Weasley), James Phelps (Fred Weasley), Oliver Phelps (George Weasley), Geraldine Somerville (Lily Potter), Michael Gambon (Professor Albus Dumbledore), Maggie Smith (Professor Minerva McGonagall), Warwick Davis (Filius Flitwick), David Bradley (Argus Filch), Brendan Gleeson (Professor Alastor 'Mad-Eye' Moody), Emma Thompson (Sybil Trelawney), Imelda Staunton (Dolores Umbridge), Apple Brook (Wilhelmina Grubbly-Plank), Robert Pattinson (Cedric Diggory), Jamie Waylett (Vincent Crabbe), Shefali Chowdhury (Parvati Patel), Afshan Azad (Padma Patil), Katie Leung (Cho Chang), William Melling (Nigel), Sian Thomas (Amelia Bones), Evanna Lynch (Luna Lovegood), Alfie Enoch (Dean Thomas), Richard Griffiths (Uncle Vernon Dursley), Fiona Shaw (Aunt Petunia Dursley), Harry Melling (Dudley Dursley), Julie Walters (Molly Weasley), Mark Williams (Arthur Weasley), Chris Rankin (Percy Weasley), Adrian Rawlins (James Potter), Ralph Fiennes (Lord Voldemort), Helena Bonham Carter (Bellatrix Lestrange), Gary Oldman (Sirius Black), John Atterbury (Phineas Nigellus Black), David Thewlis (Remus Lupin), Timothy Spall (Wormtail/Peter Pettigrew), Jim McManus (Aberforth Dumbledore), Robert Hardy (Cornelius Fudge), Sian Thomas (Amelia Bones), Jason Isaacs (Lucius Malfoy), John Atterbury (Phineas Nigellus), Jason Boyd (Piers), Richard Macklin (Malcolm), Kathryn Hunter (Mrs. Arabella Figg), Miles Jupp (TV Weatherman), Jessica Hynes (Mafalda Hopkirk (voice)), Alec Hopkins (Young Severus Snape), Robbie Jarvis (Young James Potter), James Walters (Young Sirius Black), Charles Hughes (Young Peter Pettigrew), James Utechin (Young Remus Lupin), James Payton (Frank Longbottom), Natalia Tena (Nymphadora Tonks), George Harris (Kingsley Shacklebolt), Peter Cartwright (Elphias Doge), Brigitte Millar (Emmeline Vance), Timothy Bateson (Kreacher), Jamie Wolpert (Newspaper Vendor), Nicholas Blane (Bob), Nick Shirm (Zacharias Smith), Sam Beazley (Everard), Richard Leaf (John Dawlish), Tony Maudsley (Grawp), Jason Piper (Centaur), Michael Wildman (Centaur). The *Daily Prophet* runs a smear campaign against Harry and Dumbledore, the Ministry of Magic is in denial about the return of Voldemort and Dolores Umbridge is the new Defense Against the Dark Arts teacher at Hogwarts. Meanwhile, Voldemort is searching for a prophecy concerning himself and Harry. Based on J K Rowling's book of the same name, the fifth in the seven book series. *Dir.* David Yates.

Harry Potter and the Philosopher's Stone (2001) Daniel Radcliffe (Harry Potter), Rupert Grint (Ron Weasley), Emma Watson (Hermione Granger), Robbie Coltrane (Rubeus Hagrid), Alan Rickman (Severus Snape), Matthew Lewis (Neville Longbottom), Devon Murray (Seamus Finnigan), Tom Felton (Draco Malfoy), Josh Herdman (Gregory Goyle), Bonnie Wright (Ginny Weasley), James Phelps (Fred Weasley), Oliver Phelps (George Weasley), Geraldine Somerville (Lily Potter), Richard Harris (Professor Albus Dumbledore), Maggie Smith (Professor Minerva McGonagall), Warwick Davis (Goblin Bank Teller/Professor Flitwick), David Bradley (Argus Filch), Ian Hart (Professor Quirinus Quirrell), Zoë Wanamaker (Madame Hooch), Jamie Waylett (Vincent Crabbe), Richard Griffiths (Uncle Vernon Dursley), Fiona Shaw (Aunt Petunia Dursley), Harry Melling (Dudley Dursley), Julie Walters (Molly Weasley), Chris Rankin (Percy Weasley), Adrian Rawlins (James Potter), Saunders Triplets (Baby Harry Potter), Harry Taylor (Station Guard), Verne Troyer (Griphook the Goblin), John Hurt (Mr. Ollivander), Derek Deadman (Tom - Bartender in Leaky Cauldron), Ben Borowiecki (Diagon Alley Boy), Jean Southern (Food Trolley Woman on Train), Leslie Phillips (The Sorting Hat (voice)), John Cleese (Nearly Headless Nick), Terence Bayler (The Bloody Baron),

Simon Fisher-Becker (Fat Friar), Nina Young (The Grey Lady), Elizabeth Spriggs (Fat Lady), Alfie Enoch (Dean Thomas), Eleanor Columbus (Susan Bones), Luke Youngblood (Lee Jordan), Sean Biggerstaff (Oliver Wood), Richard Bremmer (He Who Must Not Be Named). Eleven-year-old Harry is treated terribly by his relatives but discovers he is a wizard with a place waiting for him at Hogwarts School of Witchcraft and Wizardry which is entered via platform 9 ¾ at King's Cross Station. On the train to the school he meets Ron and Hermione and the three begin a journey which will be both amazing and dangerous. The main plot covers the mystery of Nicholas Flamel and the search for the philosopher's stone. Based on J K Rowling's book of the same name, the first in the seven book series. *Dir.* Chris Columbus.

Harry Potter and the Prisoner of Azkaban (2004) Daniel Radcliffe (Harry Potter), Rupert Grint (Ron Weasley), Emma Watson (Hermione Granger), Robbie Coltrane (Rubeus Hagrid), Alan Rickman (Severus Snape), Matthew Lewis (Neville Longbottom), Devon Murray (Seamus Finnigan), Tom Felton (Draco Malfoy), Josh Herdman (Gregory Goyle), Bonnie Wright (Ginny Weasley), James Phelps (Fred Weasley), Oliver Phelps (George Weasley), Geraldine Somerville (Lily Potter), Michael Gambon (Professor Albus Dumbledore), Maggie Smith (Professor Minerva McGonagall), Warwick Davis (Wizard/Professor Flitwick), David Bradley (Argus Filch), David Thewlis (Professor Lupin), Emma Thompson (Professor Sybil Trelawney), Jamie Waylett (Vincent Crabbe), Sitara Shah (Parvati Patel), Genevieve Gaunt (Pansy Parkinson), Danielle Tabor (Angelina Johnson), Jennifer Smith (Lavender Brown), Richard Griffiths (Uncle Vernon Dursley), Fiona Shaw (Aunt Petunia Dursley), Harry Melling (Dudley Dursley), Pam Ferris (Aunt Marge Dursley), Julie Walters (Molly Weasley), Mark Williams (Arthur Weasley), Chris Rankin (Percy Weasley), Adrian Rawlins (James Potter), Gary Oldman (Sirius Black), Timothy Spall (Peter Pettigrew), Robert Hardy (Cornelius Fudge), Peter Best (The Executioner), Jim Tavaré (Tom - Bartender in Leaky Cauldron), Lee Ingleby (Stan Shunpike), Julie Christie (Madame Rosmerta), Jimmy Gardner (Ernie the Bus Driver), Paul Whitehouse (Sir Cadogan), Dawn French (Fat Lady), Alfie Enoch (Dean Thomas), Lenny Henry (Shrunken Head), Abby Ford (Young Witch Maid), Annalisa Bugliani (Mother in Portrait), Tess Bu Cuarón (Baby in Portrait), Violet Columbus (Girl With Flowers), Freddie Davies (Old Man in Portrait). Voldemort's supporter Sirius Black escapes from the Prison of Azkaban and it is believed he intends to kill Harry. Based on J K Rowling's book of the same name, the third in the seven book series. *Dir.* Alfonso Cuarón.

Hasty Heart, The (1949) Ronald Reagan (Yank), Patricia Neal (Sister Margaret Parker), Richard Todd (Cpl. Lachlan 'Lachie' MacLachlan), Anthony Nicholls (Lt Colonel Dunn), Howard Marion-Crawford (Tommy), Ralph Michael (Kiwi), John Sherman (Digger), Alfie Bass (Orderly), Orlando Martins (Blossom), Robert Douglas (Off-Screen Narrator - voice), Clive Dunn (MacDougall), John Gregson (Raw recruit), Sam Kydd (Driver). As WWII ends in Burma, a soldier, unaware that he is dying, spurns the friendship offered by his fellow hospital patients. *Dir.* Vincent Sherman.

Hatter's Castle (1942) Robert Newton (James Brodie), Deborah Kerr (Mary Brodie), James Mason (Dr. Renwick), Emlyn Williams (Dennis), Henry Oscar (Grierson), Enid Stamp-Taylor (Nancy), Beatrice Varley (Mrs. Brodie), Tony Bateman (Angus Brodie), June Holden (Janet), George Merritt (Gibson), Laurence Hanray (Dr. Lawrie), Claude Bailey (Paxton), Ian Fleming (Sir John Latta), Mary Hinton (Lady Winton), Roddy Hughes (Gordon), David Keir (Perry), Stuart Lindsell (Lord Winton), Aubrey Mallalieu (Clergyman), Brefni O'Rorke (Foyle), John Slater (Card Player). A Scottish hatmaker is convinced he is a member of the nobility. Based on the novel of the same name by A. J. Cronin. *Dir.* Lance Comfort.

Haunted House of Horror, The (1968) Frankie Avalon (Chris), Jill Haworth (Sheila), Dennis Price (Inspector), Mark Wynter (Gary), George Sewell (Kellett), Gina Warwick (Sylvia), Carol Dilworth (Dorothy), Julian Barnes (Richard), Veronica Doran (Madge), Robin Stewart (Henry), Jan Holden (Peggy), Clifford Earl (Police Sgt), Robert Raglan (Bradley), Richard O'Sullivan (Peter). A group of youngsters decide to spend the night in a haunted mansion – oh dear. An early "teen slasher". *Dir.* Michael Armstrong.

He Snoops To Conquer (1945) George Formby (George Gribble), Robertson Hare (Sir Timothy Strawbridge), Elizabeth Allan (Jane Strawbridge), Claude Bailey (Councillor Oxbold), James Harcourt (Councillor Hopkins), Aubrey Mallalieu (Councillor Stubbins), Gordon McLeod (Angus McGluee), Vincent Holman (Butler), Katie Johnson (Ma). George gets mixed up with corrupt local councilors. *Dir.* Marcel Varnel.

He Who Rides a Tiger (1965) Tom Bell (Peter Rayston), Judi Dench (Joanne), Paul Rogers (Superintendent Taylor), Kay Walsh (Mrs. Woodley), Ray McAnally (Orphanage Superintendent), Jeremy Spenser (The Panda), Peter Madden (Peepers Woodley), Inigo Jackson (Detective Sergeant Scott), Annette Andre (Julie), Edina Ronay (Anna), Nicolette Pendrell (Ellen), Ralph Michael (Carter), Frederick Piper (Mr. Steed), Rita Webb (Flower seller), Robin Hughes (Detective Sergeant Crowley), Jimmy Gardner (Waiter), Howard Lang (Prison Governor), Naomi Chance (Lady Cleveland). Habitual burglar Peter Rayston just can't stop thieving, even though he has spent much of his life in prison. *Dir.* Charles Crichton.

Hear My Song (1990) Adrian Dunbar (Micky O'Neill), Ned Beatty (Josef Locke), Vernon Midgley (Josef Locke (voice)), Tara Fitzgerald (Nancy Doyle), David McCallum (Jim Abbott), Shirley Anne Field (Cathleen Doyle), James Nesbitt (Fintan O'Donnell), Brian Flanagan (Young Micky O'Neill), Constance Cowley (Nurse), Marie Mullen (Micky's Mum), Phil Kelly (Ronnie Lavelle), Jean Blanchflower (Ronnie's Mum), John Dair (Derek), Norman Vaughan (Himself), Aiden Grennell (Compere), Anna Manahan (Mrs. McGlinchy), Harold Berens (Benny Rose), Tommy Lack (Old Musician), Agnes Bernelle (Receptionist), Mary MacLeod (Librarian). Micky O'Neill tries to revive the fortunes of his Liverpool nightclub by promising his patrons that he will produce the singer Josef Locke, who had left Britain to avoid tax. *Dir.* Peter Chelsom.

Heart of a Man, The (1959) Frankie Vaughan (Frankie Martin), Anne Heywood (Julie), Tony Britton (Tony), Peter Sinclair (Bud), Michael Medwin (Sid), Anthony Newley (Johnnie), Harry Fowler (Razor), George Rose (Charlie), Harold Kasket (Oscar), Vanda Hudson (Cha Cha), Leslie Mitchell (Himself), Kent Walton (Himself), Barry Cryer (Boxing Second), Marianne Stone (Counter Girl), Richard Vernon (Manager). A millionaire disguised as a tramp helps an aspiring singer. *Dir.* Herbert Wilcox.

Heart of the Matter, The (1953) Trevor Howard (Harry), Elizabeth Allan (Louise Scobie), Maria Schell (Helen Rolt), Denholm Elliott (Wilson), Gérard Oury (Yusef), Peter Finch (Father Rank), George Coulouris (Portuguese Captain), Michael Hordern (Commissioner). Harry Scobie, a policeman in Sierra Leone, is wracked with guilt over his affair with Helen. Based on the book by Graham Greene. *Dir.* George More O'Ferrall.

Heat and Dust (1983) Christopher Cazenove (Douglas Rivers), Greta Scacchi (Olivia), Julian Glover (Crawford), Susan Fleetwood (Mrs. Crawford), Patrick Godfrey (Saunders), Jennifer Kendal (Mrs. Saunders), Shashi Kapoor (The Nawab), Madhur Jaffrey (Begum Mussarat Jahan), Nickolas Grace (Harry Hamilton-Paul), Barry Foster (Major Minnies), Julie Christie (Anne), Zakir Hussain (Inder Lal), Ratna Pathak (Ritu), Tarla Mehta (Inder Lal's mother), Charles McCaughan (Chid), Sajid Khan (Dacoit Chief), Amanda Walker (Lady Mackleworth), Praveen Paul (Maji), Jayant Kripalani (Dr. Gopal), Sudha Chopra (Chief Princess). In India in 1982, Anne begins to investigate the story of her great aunt Olivia, who had lived there 60 years earlier (the narrative covers both time periods). The screenplay was written by Ruth Prawer Jhabvala based upon her own novel. *Dir.* James Ivory.

Heaven Is Round the Corner (1944) Will Fyffe (Dougal), Leni Lynn (Joan Sedley), Austin Trevor (John Cardew), Magda Kun (Musette), Peter Glenville (Donald McKay), Barbara Waring

(Dorothy Trevor), Leslie Perrins (Robert Sedley), Barbara Couper (Mrs. Trevor), Toni Edgar-Bruce (Mrs. Harcourt), Hugh Dempster (Captain Crowe), Paul Bonifas (Rostond), Jan Van Loewen (Titoni), Rosamund Greenwood (Maid), Elsa Tee (Nora Thompson), Marcel de Haes (Louis), Neville Brook (Mr. Harcourt), Louise Lord (Audrey), Suzy Marquis (Cabaret Artiste), Christine Silver (Hospital Matron). Musical. A country girl goes to Paris to sing professionally, where she falls in love with a member of the British Embassy. *Dir*. Maclean Rogers.

Heavenly Pursuits (1986) Tom Conti (Vic Mathews), Helen Mirren (Ruth Chancellor), David Hayman (Jeff Jeffries), Brian Pettifer (Father Cobb), Jennifer Black (Sister), Dave Anderson (Headmaster), Ewen Bremner (Stevie Deans), Tom Busby (Brusse), Bill Denniston (Bishop), James Gibb (MacArthur), Sam Graham (Doctor Knox), Phillip J. Maxwell (Wee Mike), David McCormack (James), Jenny McCrindle (Carole Adams), John Mitchell (Gibbons), Paul Nolan (Robbie). A teacher in a Scottish Catholic school has his lack of faith tested by a series of apparent "miracles". Also known as *The Gospel According to Vic*. *Dir*. Charles Gormley

Heavens Above! (1963) Peter Sellers (Rev John Smallwood), Cecil Parker (Archdeacon Aspinall), Isabel Jeans (Lady Despard), Ian Carmichael (The Other Smallwood), Bernard Miles (Simpson), Brock Peters (Matthew Robinson), Eric Sykes (Harry Smith), Irene Handl (Rene Smith), Miriam Karlin (Winnie Smith), William Hartnell (Maj Fowler), Joan Miller (Mrs. Smith-Gould), Miles Malleson (Rockeby), Eric Barker (Bank Manager), Roy Kinnear (Fred Smith), Joan Hickson (Housewife), Kenneth Griffith (Rev Owen Smith), Mark Eden (Sir Geoffrey Despard), John Comer (Butcher), Basil Dignam (Prisoner Governor), Franklyn Engelman (TV Commentator), Colin Gordon (Prime Minister). Smallwood is a prison chaplain who is accidently assigned to a parish where his attempts to promote the true spirit of Christianity do not go down too well with the locals. *Dirs*. John and Roy Boulting.

Hell Below Zero (1954) Alan Ladd (Duncan), Joan Tetzel (Judie Nordhal), Basil Sydney (Bland), Stanley Baker (Erik Bland), Joseph Tomelty (Capt. McPhee), Niall MacGinnis (Dr. Howe), Jill Bennett (Gerda Petersen), Peter Dyneley (Miller), Susan Rayne (Kathleen), Philo Hauser (Sandeborg), Ivan Craig (Larsen), Paddy Ryan (Manders), Cyril Chamberlain (Factory Ship Radio Operator), Paul Homer (Kista Dan Radio Operator), Edward Hardwicke (Ulvik), John Witty (Martens), Brandon Toomey (Christiansen), Genine Graham (Stewardess), Basil Cunard (Office Manager), Fred Griffiths (Drunken Sailor), John Warren (Hotel Receptionist), Philip Ray (Capt Petersen), Paul Connell (Svensen), Glyn Houston (Borg). Capt. Nordhal falls overboard from a whaling ship. His daughter Judie suspects he was murdered. American Duncan Craig signs on her ship and helps solve the mystery, which seems to involve fellow whaling captain Erik Bland. Based on the Hammond Innes' novel *The White South*. *Dir*. Mark Hobson.

Hell Drivers (1957) Stanley Baker (Tom Yately), Herbert Lom (Gino Rossi), Peggy Cummins (Lucy), Patrick McGoohan (C. 'Red' Redman), William Hartnell (Cartley), Wilfrid Lawson (Ed), Sid James (Dusty), Jill Ireland (Jill), Alfie Bass (Tinker), Gordon Jackson (Scottie), David McCallum (Jimmy Yately), Sean Connery (Johnny Kates), Wensley Pithey (Pop), George Murcell (Tub), Marjorie Rhodes (Ma West), Vera Day (Blonde at dance), Beatrice Varley (Mrs. Yately), Robin Bailey (Assistant Manager), Jerry Stovin (Chick Keithley), John Horsley (Doctor), Marianne Stone (Nurse), Ronald Clarke (Barber Joe). Tom, an ex-convict, joins a gravel haulage company and tries to expose his boss's racket. *Dir*. Cy Endfield.

Hell Is a City (1960) Stanley Baker (Insp Harry Martineau), John Crawford (Don Starling), Donald Pleasence (Gus Hawkins), Maxine Audley (Julia Martineau), Billie Whitelaw (Chloe Hawkins), Joseph Tomelty (Furnisher Steele), George A. Cooper (Doug Savage), Geoffrey Frederick (Det Devery), Vanda Godsell (Lucky Luske), Charles Houston (Clogger Roach), Joby Blanshard (Tawny Jakes), Charles Morgan (Laurie Lovett), Peter Madden (Bert Darwin), Dickie Owen (Bragg), Lois Daine (Cecily Wainwright), Warren Mitchell (Commercial Traveller), Sarah Branch (Silver Steele), Doris Speed (Older Nursing Sister). Harry

Martineau pursues a jailbreaker. Based on the novel by Maurice Proctor. *Dir*. Val Guest.

Hellbound: Hellraiser II (1988) Doug Bradley (Pinhead/Captain Elliot Spencer), Ashley Laurence (Kirsty Cotton), Imogen Boorman (Tiffany), Kenneth Cranham (Dr. Philip Channard/Channard Cenobite), Clare Higgins (Julia Cotton), William Hope (Kyle MacRae), Barbie Wilde (Female Cenobite), Simon Bamford (Butterball Cenobite), Nicholas Vince (Chatterer/Chatterer II), Deborah Joel ("Skinless" Julia), Angus MacInnes (Homicide Detective Bronson), Oliver Smith (Mr. Browning/"Skinless" Frank), Sean Chapman (Uncle Frank Cotton), James Tillitt (Officer Cortez), Bradley Lavelle (Officer Kucich). Sequel to *Hellraiser* (1987) with many of the same cast in attendance. Firstly we see how Elliot became Pinhead and then the story moves to the present and focuses on Kirsty and Tiffany, and Dr Channard, who runs the psychiatric hospital in which they are both patients. *Dir*. Tony Randel.

Hellraiser (1987) Andrew Robinson (Larry Cotton/Frank Cotton), Clare Higgins (Julia Cotton), Ashley Laurence (Kirsty Cotton), Oliver Smith ("Skinless" Frank/Frank The Monster), Doug Bradley (Lead Cenobite - Pinhead), Sean Chapman (Frank Cotton - original), Robert Hines (Steve), Sean Chapman (Frank Cotton), Anthony Allen (Victim 1), Leon Davis (Victim 2), Michael Cassidy (Victim 3), Frank Baker (Derelict), Kenneth Nelson (Bill), Gay Baynes (Evelyn), Nicholas Vince (Chattering Cenobite). Cult British horror. Frank Cotton buys a puzzle box in Morocco. When he gets home he goes into the attic of his house and manages to solve the box. Unfortunately, it rips him apart and releases monsters (Pinhead and the Cenobites) which take his body and reset the box. Frank's brother Larry and his wife Julia (Frank's mistress) then move into the house, unaware of the story so far. When Larry cuts his hand in the attic he begins a chain of events involving a restored Frank and Julia, who set about murdering men - including Larry - in order to replenish Frank's body. Meanwhile Larry's daughter Kirsty becomes suspicious. Based upon the novella *The Hellbound Heart* by Clive Barker, who also wrote the screenplay and directed the film.

Help! (1965) The Beatles (John Lennon, Paul McCartney, George Harrison, Ringo Starr), Leo McKern (Clang), Eleanor Bron (Ahme), Victor Spinetti (Foot), Roy Kinnear (Algernon), Patrick Cargill (Superintendent), John Bluthal (Bhuta), Alfie Bass (Doorman), Warren Mitchell (Abdul), Peter Copley (Jeweller), Bruce Lacey (Lawnmower), Deborah DeLacey (High Priestess), Durra (Belly Dancer), Eve Eden (High Priestess), Mal Evans (Channel Swimmer), Gretchen Franklin (Neighbour), Jeremy Lloyd (Man in Restaurant), Zienia Merton (Marie-Lise), Dandy Nichols (Neighbour), Zorenah Osborne (High Priestess). Ringo is sent the sacred sacrificial ring of an eastern cult whose members then resolve to retrieve it. A comedy musical featuring the music of The Beatles. *Dir*. Richard Lester.

Henry V (1944) Laurence Olivier (King Henry V), Renée Asherson (Princess Katherine), George Robey (Sir John Falstaff), Michael Warre (Duke of Gloucester), Nicholas Hannen (Duke of Exeter), Morland Graham (Sir Thomas Erpingham), Griffith Jones (Earl of Salisbury), Gerald Case (Earl of Westmoreland), Robert Helpmann (Bishop of Ely), Felix Aylmer (Archbishop of Canterbury), Leslie Banks (Chorus), Vernon Greeves (English herald), Ralph Truman (Mountjoy - The French Herald), Harcourt Williams (King Charles VI of France), Russell Thorndike (Duke of Bourbon), Leo Genn (The Constable of France), Francis Lister (Duke of Orleans), Max Adrian (The Dauphin), Ernest Thesiger (Duke of Berri - French Ambassador), Ivy St. Helier (Alice), Janet Burnell (Queen Isabel of France), Valentine Dyall (Duke of Burgundy), Frederick Cooper (Corporal Nym), Roy Emerton (Lieutenant Bardolph), Robert Newton (Ancient Pistol), Freda Jackson (Mistress Quickly), George Cole (Boy), Esmond Knight (Fluellen), Jonathan Field (The French Messenger), Michael Shepley (Gower), John Laurie (Jamy), Niall MacGinnis (Macmorris), Frank Tickle (The Governor of Harfleur), Brian Nissen (Court), Arthur Hambling (Bates), Jimmy Hanley (Williams), Ernest Hare (A Priest). An adaptation of Shakespeare's play which had particular resonance as it was produced and released during WWII. The film begins and ends as a stage production at a re-imagined Globe Theatre on 1 May 1600 with the campaign and Battle of Agincourt being shown "in reality". Olivier won a Special Academy Award for his "Outstanding achievement as actor, producer and director in bringing Henry V to the screen". The poetry, the sumptuous technicolour and the brilliant score by William Walton all combine to make the film a remarkable spectacle, even today. *Dir.* Laurence Olivier.

Henry V (1989) Kenneth Branagh (King Henry V), Emma Thompson (Princess Katherine de Valois), Robbie Coltrane (Sir John Falstaff), Simon Shepherd (Duke Humphrey of Gloucester), Brian Blessed (Duke Thomas Beaufort of Exeter), Edward Jewesbury (Sir Thomas Erpingham), James Larkin (Duke John of Bedford), James Simmons (Duke Edward of York), Paul Gregory (Westmoreland), Fabian Cartwright (Earl Richard of Cambridge), Stephen Simms (Lord Henry Scroop), Jay Villiers (Sir Thomas Grey), Charles Kay (Archbishop of Canterbury), Alec McCowen (Bishop of Ely), Derek Jacobi (Chorus), David Parfitt (Messenger), Paul Scofield (King Charles VI of France), Michael Maloney (Louis the Dauphin), Harold Innocent (Duke Philippe of Burgundy), Richard Clifford (Duke Charles of Orleans), Colin Hurley (Grandpré), Richard Easton (Constable Charles Delabreth), Christopher Ravenscroft (Montjoy), David Lloyd Meredith (Governor of Harfleur), Nicholas Ferguson (Earl Richard Beauchamp of Warwick), Tom Whitehouse (Sir John Talbot), Nigel Greaves (Duke Jean of Berri), Julian Gartside (Duke Jean of Bretagne), Ian Holm (Captain Fluellen), Danny Webb (Gower), Jimmy Yuill (Jamy), John Sessions (Macmorris), Shaun Prendergast (Bates), Patrick Doyle (Court), Michael Williams (Williams), Richard Briers (Lieutenant Bardolph), Geoffrey Hutchings (Corporal Nym), Robert Stephens (Auncient Pistol), Christian Bale (Robin the Luggage-Boy), Geraldine McEwan (Alice), Judi Dench (Mistress Nell Quickly), Mark Inman (1st Soldier), Chris Armstrong (2nd Soldier). A much grittier adaptation than the 1944 Olivier version and includes scenes of the Cambridge, Scroop and Grey conspiracy and the hanging of Bardolph which were omitted from that production. The film won an Academy Award for Costume Design. *Dir.* Kenneth Brannagh.

Henry VIII and His Six Wives (1972) Keith Michell (Henry VIII), Frances Cuka (Katherine of Aragon), Charlotte Rampling (Anne Boleyn), Jane Asher (Jane Seymour), Jenny Bos (Anne of Cleves), Lynne Frederick (Catherine Howard), Barbara Leigh-Hunt (Catherine Parr), Donald Pleasence (Thomas Cromwell), Michael Gough (Norfolk), Brian Blessed (Suffolk), Michael Goodliffe (Thomas More), Bernard Hepton (Cranmer), Garfield Morgan (Cardiner), John Bryans (Wolsey), John Bennett (Wriothesley), Peter Madden (Fisher). A film version of the BBC television series *The Six Wives of Henry VIII. Dir.* Waris Hussein.

Here Come the Huggetts (1948) Jack Warner (Joe Huggett), Kathleen Harrison (Ethel Huggett), Jane Hylton (Jane Huggett), Susan Shaw (Susan Huggett), Petula Clark (Pet Huggett), Jimmy Hanley (Jimmy Gardner), David Tomlinson (Harold Hinchley), Diana Dors (Diana Hopkins), Peter Hammond (Peter Hawtrey), John Blythe (Gowan), Amy Veness (Grandma Huggett), Clive Morton (Mr. Campbell), Maurice Denham (1st Engineer), Doris Hare (Mrs. Fisher), Esma Cannon (Youth Leader), Alison Leggatt (Miss Perks), Dandy Nichols (Aunt Edie), Hal Osmond (2nd Engineer), Peter Scott (Office Boy), Keith Shepherd (Vicar), Edmundo Ros (Himself), Cyril Chamberlain (Policeman at Crash Site). A film about a family first introduced in *Holiday Camp* (1947) and seen again in the sequels to this film *Vote for Huggett* (1949) and *The Huggetts Abroad* (1949). The Huggetts have a telephone installed – a big deal in Britain in 1948. *Dir.* Ken Annakin.

Here we Go Round the Mulberry Bush (1967) Barry Evans (Jamie McGregor), Judy Geeson (Mary Gloucester), Angela Scoular (Caroline Beauchamp), Sheila White (Paula), Adrienne Posta (Linda), Vanessa Howard (Audrey), Diane Keen (Claire), Moyra Fraser (Mrs. McGregor), Michael Bates (Mr. McGregor), Maxine Audley (Mrs. Beauchamp), Denholm Elliott (Mr. Beauchamp), Christopher Timothy (Spike), Nicky Henson (Craig Foster), Allan Warren (Joe McGregor), Roy Holder (Arthur). What in swinging 1960s England passed for a coming-of-age film

– Jamie McGregor wants to have sex and there seem to be plenty of mini-skirted dolly birds in his immediate vicinity. Based on the novel of the same name by Hunter Davies. *Dir.* Clive Donner.

Heroes of Telemark, The (1965) Kirk Douglas (Rolf), Richard Harris (Knut), Ulla Jacobsson (Anna), Michael Redgrave (Uncle), David Weston (Arne), Sebastian Breaks (Gunnar), John Golightly (Freddy), Alan Howard (Oli), Patrick Jordan (Henrik), William Marlowe (Claus), Brook Williams (Einar), Roy Dotrice (Jensen), Anton Diffring (Major Frick), Ralph Michael (Nilssen), Eric Porter (Terboven), Wolf Frees (Knippelberg), Karel Stepanek (Hartmuller), Gerard Heinz (Erhardt), Mervyn Johns (Col. Wilkinson), Barry Jones (Professor Logan), Geoffrey Keen (General Bolt), Robert Ayres (General Courts), Jennifer Hilary (Sigrid), Maurice Denham (Doctor), David Davies (Captain of 'Galtesund'), Elvi Hale (Mrs. Sandersen), Russell Waters (Mr. Sandersen), Brian Jackson (Norwegian Naval Attaché). The factual story of how the Norwegian resistance sabotaged the Vemork Norsk Hydro plant in the county of Telemark, Norway, which the Nazis were using to produce heavy water to make a nuclear bomb. *Dir.* Anthony Mann.

Hey! Hey! USA! (1938) Will Hay (Benjamin Twist/Professor Phineas Tavistock), Edgar Kennedy (Bugs Leary), David Burns (Tony Ricardo), Eddie Ryan (Ace Marco), Arthur Goullet (Glove Johnson), Gibb McLaughlin (Steward), Eddie Pola (Broadcast Announcer), Roddy McDowall (Boy). Teacher and part time ship's porter Ben Twist gets involved in a kidnap plot. *Dir.* Marcel Varnel.

Hide and Seek (1964) Ian Carmichael (David), Curd Jürgens (Hubert Marek), Janet Munro (Maggie), George Pravda (Frank Melnicker), Kieron Moore (Paul), Hugh Griffith (Wilkins), Esma Cannon (Tea Lady), Kynaston Reeves (Hunter), Edward Chapman (McPherson). Mild-mannered astronomer David Garrett becomes involved in Cold War espionage. *Dir.* Cy Endfield.

Hideous Kinky (1998) Kate Winslet (Julia), Bella Riza (Bea), Carrie Mullan (Lucy), Saïd Taghmaoui (Bilal), Pierre Clémenti (Santoni), Sira Stampe (Eva), Abigail Cruttenden (Charlotte), Ahmed Boulane (Ben Said), Sira Stampe (Eva), Amidou (Sufi Sheikh), Michelle Fairley (Patricia), Kevin McKidd (Henning), Peter Youngblood Hills (Hippy). Told from the perspective of the youngest daughter, an Englishwoman travels to Morocco with her two young daughters. Based on the novel of the same name by Esther Freud. *Dir.* Gillies MacKinnon.

High Bright Sun, The (1964) Dirk Bogarde (Maj. McGuire), George Chakiris (Haghios), Susan Strasberg (Juno Kozani), Denholm Elliott (Baker), Grégoire Aslan (Gen. Stavros Skyros), Colin Campbell (Emile Andros), Joseph Fürst (Dr. Andros), Katherine Kath (Mrs. Andros), George Pastell (Prinos), Paul Stassino (Alkis), Nigel Stock (Col. Park). Set in Cyprus during the EOKA uprising against British rule of the 1950s. Based on a novel by Ian Stuart Black. *Dir.* Ralph Thomas.

High Hopes (1988) Philip Davis (Cyril Bender), Ruth Sheen (Shirley), Edna Doré (Mrs. Bender), Philip Jackson (Martin Burke), Heather Tobias (Valerie Burke), Lesley Manville (Laetitia Boothe-Brain), David Bamber (Rupert Boothe-Braine), Jason Watkins (Wayne), Judith Scott (Suzi), Cheryl Prime (Martin's Girl Friend), Diane-Louise Jordan (Chemist Shop Assistant). The life of Cyril and Shirley, their family, friends and neighbours in London. *Dir.* Mike Leigh.

High Spirits (1988) Daryl Hannah (Mary Plunkett), Peter O'Toole (Peter Plunkett), Steve Guttenberg (Jack), Beverly D'Angelo (Sharon), Liam Neeson (Martin Brogan), Jennifer Tilly (Miranda), Peter Gallagher (Brother Tony), Ray McAnally (Plunkett Senior), Martin Ferrero (Malcolm), Connie Booth (Marge), Donal McCann (Eamon), Liz Smith (Mrs. Plunkett), Mary Coughlan (Katie), Ruby Buchanan (Great Aunt Nan), Isolde Cazelet (Julia), Aimée Delamain (Great Granny Plunkett), Tom Hickey (Sampson), Krista Hornish (Wendy), Little John (Gateman), Preston Lockwood (Great Uncle Peter). Finding his castle, which he has turned into a B&B, to be losing money hand over fist, and in debt to an American businessman, Peter Plunkett decides to advertise it as "The most haunted castle in Europe" and gets the locals to pretend to be ghosts. The mock hauntings aren't going well until some real spirits decide to join in. *Dir.* Neil Jordan.

High Treason (1951) Liam Redmond (Cmdr. Robert Brennan), André Morell (Supt. Folland), Anthony Bushell (Maj. Elliott), Kenneth Griffith (Jimmy Ellis), Patric Doonan (George Ellis), Joan Hickson (Mrs. Ellis), Anthony Nicholls (Grant Mansfield), Mary Morris (Anna Braun), Geoffrey Keen (Morgan Williams), Stuart Lindsell (Commissioner), John Bailey (Stringer), Dora Bryan (Mrs. Bowers), Charles Lloyd Pack (Percy Ward), Laurence Naismith (Reginald Gordon-Wells), John Harvey (Scotland Yard Man), Jean Anderson (Woman in Street), Alfie Bass (Albert Brewer), Harry Fowler (Street Photographer), Everley Gregg (Mrs. Finch-Harvey), Glyn Houston (Railway Shunter), Douglas Ives (Mr. Mathews), Peter Jones (Announcer at Music Club), Moultrie Kelsall (Ships Captain), Sam Kydd (Sam), Harry Locke (Andy), Victor Maddern (Anarchist), Jack McNaughton (Benson), Julien Mitchell (Mr. Philips), Dandy Nichols (Woman Scrubbing), Marianne Stone (Alfie's Mother), John Warwick (Inspector Hewitt). The police are on the track of communist saboteurs who are targeting industrial facilities. The hunt culminates in a shoot out in Battersea Power Station. *Dir.* Roy Boulting.

High Wind in Jamaica, A (1965) Anthony Quinn (Chavez), James Coburn (Zac), Dennis Price (Mathias), Isabel Dean (Mrs Thornton), Lila Kedrova (Rosa), Nigel Davenport (Mr Thornton), Henry Beltran (Harry), Philip Madoc (Guardia Civile). Kenneth J. Warren (Capt Marpole), Ben Carruthers (Alberto), Gert Fröbe (Dutch Captain), Brian Phelan (Curtis), Vivienne Ventura (Margaret Fernandez) and the Thornton children, Deborah Baxter (Emily), Roberta Tovey (Rachel), Martin Amis (John), Jeffrey Chandler (Edward), Karen Flack (Laura), Set in 19th century Jamaica, the Thorntons decide to send their five children home to England, but the ship is intercepted by pirates. Based on the Richard Hughes' novel. *Dir.* Alexander Mackendrick

Hilary and Jackie (1998) Emily Watson (Jacqueline du Pré), Rachel Griffiths (Hilary du Pré), James Frain (Daniel Barenboim), David Morrissey (Christopher Finzi), Charles Dance (Derek du Pré), Celia Imrie (Iris du Pré), Rupert Penry-Jones (Piers du Pré), Bill Paterson (William Pleeth), Auriol Evans (Young Jackie), Keeley Flanders (Young Hilary), Nyree Dawn Porter (Dame Margot Fonteyn), Vernon Dobtcheff (Prof Bentley). Biopic of the tragic life of the international concert cellist, the film being divided into two sections, the first telling events from her sister Hilary's point of view and the second from Jacqueline's. *Dir.* Anand Tucker.

Hill in Korea, A (1956) George Baker (Lt Butler), Harry Andrews (Sgt Payne), Stanley Baker (Cpl Ryker), Michael Medwin (Pvt Docker), Ronald Lewis (Pvt Wyatt), Stephen Boyd (Pvt Sims), Victor Maddern (Pvt Lindop), Harry Landis (Pvt Rabin), Robert Brown (Pvt O'Brien), Barry Lowe (Pvt Neill), Robert Shaw (LCpl Hodge), Charles Laurence (Pvt Kim), Percy Herbert (Pvt Moon), Eric Corrie (Pvt Matthews), David Morrell (Pvt Henson), Michael Caine (Pvt Lockyer). As you might expect from the title, the struggles of British troops as they fight for a hill during the Korean War. Based on the novel by Max Chatto. Also known as *Hell in Korea*. *Dir.* Julian Amyes.

Hill, The (1965) Sean Connery (Joe Roberts), Harry Andrews (RSM Wilson), Ian Bannen (Harris), Alfred Lynch (George Stevens), Ossie Davis (Jacko King), Roy Kinnear (Monty Bartlett), Jack Watson (Jock McGrath), Ian Hendry (Staff Sgt Williams), Michael Redgrave (Medical Officer), Norman Bird (Commandant), Neil McCarthy (Burton), Howard Goorney (Walters), Tony Caunter (Martin). Set in a British disciplinary camp in the Libyan desert during WWII. Punishment includes forcing prisoners to repeatedly climb a man-made hill in the centre of the camp but when a new inmate dies recriminations amongst the officers are apparent. *Dir.* Sidney Lumet.

Hindle Wakes (1952) Leslie Dwyer (Chris Hawthorn), Lisa Daniely (Jenny Hawthorn), Brian Worth (Alan Jeffcote), Sandra Dorne (Mary Hollins), Ronald Adam (Mr. Jeffcote), Joan Hickson (Mrs. Hawthorn), Michael Medwin (George Ackroyd), Mary Clare (Mrs. Jeffcote), Bill Travers (Bob), Beatrice Varley (Mrs. Hollins), Tim Turner (Tommy Dykes), Diana Hope (Betty Farrer), Lloyd Pearson (Tim Farrer), Judy Vann (Jeffcote's Secretary), Cyril Smith (Hotel Porter), Rita Webb (Mrs. Slaughter), Ian Wilson (Mr. Slaughter), Alastair Hunter (Police Sergeant), Edward Evans (Chauffeur), Ben Williams (Jimmy), Roy Russell (Sparks). A liaison between a factory girl and the mill owner's son is revealed by a tragic accident. The last big screen remake (to date) of the play of the same name by Stanley Houghton – other versions appeared in 1918, 1927 and 1931. *Dir.* Arthur Crabtree.

History Boys, The (2006) Richard Griffiths (Hector), Clive Merrison (Felix, the Headmaster), Frances de la Tour (Mrs. Lintott), Stephen Campbell Moore (Irwin), Samuel Anderson (Chris Crowther), Samuel Barnett (David Posner), Dominic Cooper (Stuart Dakin), James Corden (Richard Timms), Sacha Dhawan (Adi Akthar), Andrew Knott (James Lockwood), Russell Tovey (Peter Rudge), Jamie Parker (Donald Scripps), Georgia Taylor (Fiona), Penelope Wilton (Mrs. Bibby), James Lombard (Mr. Wilkins), Adrian Scarborough (Wilkes), Set in Sheffield in 1983, where eight grammar school boys are being prepared for Oxbridge entrance exams by their teachers Hector, Miss Lintott and newly appointed Irwin. Adapted by Alan Bennett from his play of the same name. *Dir.* Nicholas Hytner.

History of Mr Polly, The (1949) John Mills (Alfred Polly), Betty Ann Davies (Miriam Larkins Polly), Megs Jenkins (The Innkeeper), Finlay Currie (Uncle Jim), Gladys Henson (Aunt Larkins), Diana Churchill (Annie Larkins), Shelagh Fraser (Minnie Larkins), Edward Chapman (Mr. Johnson), Dandy Nichols (Mrs. Johnson), Sally Ann Howes (Christabel), Juliet Mills (Little Polly), Laurence Baskcomb (Mr. Rumbold), Edie Martin (Lady on roof), Moore Marriott (Uncle Pentstemon), David Horne (Mr. Garvace), Ernest Jay (Mr. Hinks), Cyril Smith (Mr. Voules), Wylie Watson (Mr. Rusper), Irene Handl (Lady on left), Doris Hare (May Pant), Wally Patch (Customer), Miles Malleson (Old gentleman), Grace Arnold (Mrs. Rusper), Peggy Ann Clifford (Mother), William Murray (Father), Cameron Hall (Mr. Podger), Jay Laurier (Mr. Boomer), Richard Levin (Student), Frank Ling (Mr. Chuffles), Frederick Piper (Mr. Wintershed), Victor Platt (Mr. Gambell), Michael Ripper (Store Employee), Muriel Russell (Betsy), Ian Wilson (Mr. Clamp). The adventures of Alfred Polly, who is unhappy in both his marriage and his shop business. Eventually he leaves his wife, travels into the countryside and is employed as a handyman at an inn. Although this quiet life is what he has always craved, he still has to cope with drunkard Uncle Jim – a confrontation with whom will lead to unforeseen circumstances. Based on the novel by H G Wells. *Dir.* Anthony Pelissier.

Hitchhiker's Guide to the Galaxy, The (2005) Stephen Fry (Narrator/The Guide - voice), Martin Freeman (Arthur Dent), Zooey Deschanel (Tricia McMillan/Trillian), Mos Def (Ford Prefect), Sam Rockwell (Zaphod Beeblebrox), Bill Nighy (Slartibartfast), Anna Chancellor (Questular Rontok), John Malkovich (Humma Kavula), Warwick Davis (Marvin the Paranoid Android), Alan Rickman (Marvin - voice), Kelly Macdonald (Reporter), Richard Griffiths (Jeltz – voice), Bill Bailey (The Whale - voice), Helen Mirren (Deep Thought - voice), Steve Pemberton (Mr. Prosser), Mark Gatiss (Additional Vogon Voices), Reece Shearsmith (Additional Vogon Voices). Arthur Dent is helped by his friend Ford Prefect to escape from Earth moments before it is destroyed in order to make way for a hyperspace expressway. Based on the radio series and book of the same name by Douglas Adams. *Dir.* Garth Jennings.

Hobson's Choice (1931) James Harcourt (Henry Hobson), Viola Lyel (Maggie Hobson), Frank Pettingell (Will Mossup), Belle Chrystall (Vicky Hobson), Jay Laurier (Tubby Wadlow), Joan Maude (Alice Hobson), Amy Veness (Mrs. Hepworth), Reginald Bach (Albert Prosser), Basil Moss (Freddy Beenstock), Herbert Lomas (Jim Heeler), Kathleen Harrison (Ada Figgins). For plot see the 1954 film. *Dir.* Thomas Bentley.

Hobson's Choice (1954) Charles Laughton (Henry Horatio Hobson), John Mills (Will Mossop), Brenda De Banzie (Maggie Hobson), Daphne Anderson (Alice Hobson), Prunella Scales (Vicky Hobson), Richard Wattis (Albert Prosser), Derek Blomfield (Freddy Beenstock), Helen Haye (Mrs. Hepworth), Jack Howarth (Tubby Wadlow), Joseph Tomelty (Jim Heeler), Julien Mitchell (Sam Minns), Gibb McLaughlin (Tudsbury), Philip Stainton (Denton), John Laurie (Dr. MacFarlane), Dorothy Gordon (Ada Figgins). Successful bootmaker Henry Hobson is widowed with three daughters who all work for him for no wages.

Therefore he has no wish to see them get married and leave his employ. Although the two younger daughters have their eyes on likely partners, all seems well until he locks horns with his eldest daughter Maggie. Based on the play by Harold Brighouse. *Dir.* David Lean.

Hole, The (2001) Thora Birch (Liz Dunn), Keira Knightley (Frankie Almond Smith), Desmond Harrington (Mike Steel), Laurence Fox (Geoff Bingham), Daniel Brocklebank (Martyn Taylor), Embeth Davidtz (Dr. Philippa Horwood), Steven Waddington (DCS Tom Howard), Kelly Hunter (DI Chapman), Anastasia Hille (Forensic Pathologist Gillian). Hoping to escape from a school trip, four teenagers hide in an old war bunker for three days and discover that the fifth teenager, who locked them in, doesn't return. They begin to turn on each other. Based on the novel *After the Hole* by Guy Burt. *Dir.* Nick Hamm.

Holiday Camp (1947) Flora Robson (Esther Harman), Dennis Price (Sq. Ldr. Hardwick), Jack Warner (Joe Huggett), Hazel Court (Joan Huggett), Emrys Jones (Michael Halliday), Kathleen Harrison (Mrs Ethel Huggett), Yvonne Owen (Angela Kirby), Esmond Knight (Camp Announcer), Jimmy Hanley (Jimmy Gardner), Peter Hammond (Harry Huggett), Esma Cannon (Elsie Dawson), John Blythe (Steve), Jeannette Tregarthen (Valerie Thompson), Beatrice Varley (Valerie's Aunt), Dennis Harkin (Charlie), Susan Shaw (Patsy Crawford), Maurice Denham (Camp Doctor), Jane Hylton (Receptionist), Jack Raine and John Stone (Detectives), Alfie Bass (Redcoat), Diana Dors (Dancer) and as themselves, Patricia Roc and Charlie Chester. Various Brits experience a holiday camp for the first time. *Dir.* Ken Annakin. See also *Here Come the Huggetts* (1948) *Vote for Huggett* (1949) and *The Huggetts Abroad* (1949).

Holiday on the Buses (1973) Reg Varney (Stan Butler), Doris Hare (Mum), Michael Robbins (Arthur Rudge), Anna Karen (Olive Rudge), Stephen Lewis (Inspector 'Blakey' Blake), Bob Grant (Jack Harper), Wilfrid Brambell (Bert Thomsson), Kate Williams (Nurse), Arthur Mullard (Wally Briggs), Queenie Watts (Mrs Briggs), Henry McGee (Holiday Camp Manager), Adam Rhodes (Little Arthur), Michael Sheard (Depot manager). After being sacked, Stan and Jack get jobs as bus crew at a holiday camp, only to find that Blakey, who was also given the boot, is the new security inspector. The third spin-off film from the ITV sitcom *On the Buses*. *Dir.* Bryan Izzard.

Home at Seven (1952) Ralph Richardson (David Preston), Margaret Leighton (Janet Preston), Jack Hawkins (Dr Sparling), Campbell Singer (Insp Hemingway), Michael Shepley (Maj Watson), Margaret Withers (Mrs Watson), Frederick Piper (Mr Petherbridge), Meriel Forbes (Peggy Dobson), Gerald Case (Sgt Evans), Diana Beaumont (Ellen), Johnnie Schofield (Joe Dobson), Archie Duncan (Station Sergeant). A bank official cannot account for a "lost" 24 hours, during which time he has been accused of a robbery. Based on the play by R. C. Sherriff. *Dir.* Ralph Richardson.

Home of Your Own, A (1964) Ronnie Barker (The Cement Mixer), Richard Briers (The Husband), Peter Butterworth (The Carpenter), Bernard Cribbins (The Stonemason), Bill Fraser (The Shop Steward), Norman Mitchell (The Foreman), Ronnie Stevens (The Architect), Fred Emney (The Mayor), George Benson (Gatekeeper), Tony Tanner (Workman with radio), Thorley Walters (Estate agent). Other cast members include: Janet Brown, Gerald Campion and Aubrey Woods. Wordless film (with sound effects) about a young couple building a house. *Dir.* Jay Lewis.

Hope and Glory (1987) Sebastian Rice-Edwards (Bill Rowan), Geraldine Muir (Sue Rowan), Sarah Miles (Grace Rowan), David Hayman (Clive Rowan), Sammi Davis (Dawn Rowan), Derrick O'Connor (Mac), Susan Wooldridge (Molly), Jean-Marc Barr (Cpl. Bruce Carrey), Ian Bannen (Grandfather George), Annie Leon (Grandma), Jill Baker (Faith), Amelda Brown (Hope), Katrine Boorman (Charity), Colin Higgins (Clive's Pal), Shelagh Fraser (WVS Woman), Gerald James (Headmaster), Nicky Taylor (Roger), Charley Boorman (Luftwaffe Pilot). A semi-autobiographical project by John Boorman which charts the wartime story of the Rowan family in London – particularly through the experiences of young Bill Rowan. *Dir.* John Boorman.

Horror of Frankenstein, The (1970) Ralph Bates (Baron Victor Frankenstein), Kate O'Mara (Alys), Veronica Carlson (Elizabeth Heiss), Dennis Price (The Graverobber), Joan Rice (Graverobber's wife), Jon Finch (Lieutenant Becker), Bernard Archard (Professor Heiss), Graham James (Wilhelm Kassner), James Hayter (Bailiff), Stephen Turner (Stephan), Neil Wilson (Schoolmaster), James Cossins (Dean), Glenys O'Brien (Maggie), Geoffrey Lumsden (Instructor), Chris Lethbridge-Baker (Priest), Terry Duggan (First Bandit), George Belbin (Baron Frankenstein), Hal Jeayes (Woodsman), Carol Jeayes (Woodsman's Daughter), Michael Goldie (Workman), David Prowse (The Monster). A brilliant but wayward doctor builds a creature from harvested body parts and resurrects it only to find it is not overly bright and not amenable to taking orders. Basically a remake of the 1957 film *The Curse of Frankenstein*. *Dir.* Jimmy Sangster.

Horrors of the Black Museum (1959) Michael Gough (Edmond Bancroft), Graham Curnow (Rick), June Cunningham (Joan Berkley), Shirley Anne Field (Angela Banks), Geoffrey Keen (Superintendent Graham), Gerald Anderson (Dr. Ballan), John Warwick (Inspector Lodge), Beatrice Varley (Aggie), Austin Trevor (Commissioner Wayne), Vanda Godsell (Miss Ashton), Gerald Case (Bookshop Manager), Garard Green (Fingerprint Expert), Sydney Bromley (Neighbour), John Harvey (Man in Bookshop), Marianne Stone (Neighbour). A thriller writer hypnotises his assistant into performing crimes which he can then write about. The film was promoted as being shown in "hypnovista" whereby a "real hypnotist" hypnotises the audience before the start of the film, giving them "hypnovision". *Dir.* Arthur Crabtree

Horse's Mouth, The (1958) Alec Guinness (Gulley), Kay Walsh (Dee Coker), Renee Houston (Sara Monday), Mike Morgan (Nosey), Robert Coote (Sir William Beeder), Arthur Macrae (A.W. Alabaster), Veronica Turleigh (Lady Beeder), Michael Gough (Abel), Reginald Beckwith (Capt Jones), Ernest Thesiger (Hickson), Gillian Vaughan (Lollie), Richard Caldicot (Roberts), Clive Revill (Art Student). Artist Gulley Jimson is searching for the perfect wall on which to paint a mural. The paintings featured in the film were the work of John Bratby. Based on the novel by Joyce Cary. *Dir.* Ronald Neame.

Hot Fuzz (2007) Simon Pegg (PC/Sgt./Insp. Nicholas Angel), Nick Frost (PC/Sgt. Danny Butterman), Jim Broadbent (Insp. Frank Butterman), Paddy Considine (DS Andy Wainwright), Rafe Spall (DC Andy Cartwright), Kevin Eldon (Sgt. Tony Fisher), Olivia Colman (PC Doris Thatcher), Karl Johnson (PC Bob Walker), Bill Bailey (Sergeant Turner), Timothy Dalton (Simon Skinner), Edward Woodward (Tom Weaver), Billie Whitelaw (Joyce Cooper), Eric Mason (Bernard Cooper), Stuart Wilson (Dr. Robin Hatcher), Paul Freeman (Rev. Philip Shooter), Kenneth Cranham (James Reaper), Peter Wight (Roy Porter), Julia Deakin (Mary Porter), Patricia Franklin (Annette Roper), Lorraine Hilton (Amanda Paver), Tim Barlow (Mr. Treacher), Rory McCann (Michael Armstrong), Martin Freeman (Sergeant), Steve Coogan (Inspector), Bill Nighy (Chief Inspector Kenneth), Cate Blanchett (Janine), Chris Waitt (Dave), Joe Cornish (Bob), Robert Popper ("Not Janine"), Stephen Merchant (Peter Ian Staker), Alice Lowe (Tina), David Bradley (Arthur Webley), Anne Reid (Leslie Tiller), Ben McKay (Peter Cocker), Adam Buxton (Tim Messenger), David Threlfall (Martin Blower), Lucy Punch (Eve Draper), Ron Cook (George Merchant), Edgar Wright (Shelf Stacker), Joseph McManners (Gabriel), Graham Low (The Living Statue), Alexander King (Aaron A Aaronson). Dedicated PC Nick Angel is transferred to rural Sandford from London because his arrest record was making his colleagues look bad. Sandford is apparently a no-crime zone and Angel is reduced to mundane policing duties alongside partner Danny Butterman, the son of the local police inspector. That is until there is a series of gruesome deaths in the village. *Dir.* Edgar Wright.

Hot Millions (1968) Peter Ustinov (Marcus Pendleton/Caesar Smith), Maggie Smith (Patty Terwilliger Smith), Karl Malden (Carlton J. Klemper), Bob Newhart (Willard C. Gnatpole), Robert

Morley (Caesar Smith), Cesar Romero (Customs Inspector), Lynda Baron (Louise), Elizabeth Counsell (Miss Glyn), Margaret Courtenay (Mrs. Hubbard), Raymond Huntley (Bayswater), Peter Jones (Prison Governor), William Mervyn (Sir Charles Wilson), Bob Todd (British Commissionaire). Comedy crime caper in which a conman assumes the identity of insurance company computer programmer Caesar Smith and begins to fleece the company by sending himself claim cheques under various different identities. *Dir.* Eric Till.

Hound of the Baskervilles, The (1921) Eille Norwood (Sherlock Holmes), Hubert Willis (Dr. Watson), Catina Campbell (Beryl Stapleton), Rex McDougall (Sir Henry Baskerville), Lewis Gilbert (Roger Stapleton Baskerville), Allan Jeayes (Dr. James Mortimer), Fred Raynham (Barrymore), Robert Vallis (Selden). Holmes is summoned to investigate a mysterious death on Dartmoor. Norwood was the first English big screen Holmes. Based on Arthur Conan Doyle's novel. *Dir.* Maurice Elvey.

Hound of the Baskervilles, The (1932) Robert Rendel (Sherlock Holmes), Frederick Lloyd (Dr. Watson), Heather Angel (Beryl Stapleton), John Stuart (Sir Henry Baskerville), Reginald Bach (Stapleton), Wilfred Shine (Dr. Mortimer), Sam Livesey (Sir Hugo Baskerville), Henry Hallett (Barrymore). *Dir.* Gareth Gundrey. See the 1921 film for plot summary.

Hound of the Baskervilles, The (1959) Peter Cushing (Sherlock Holmes), André Morell (Dr Watson), Christopher Lee (Sir Henry Baskerville), Marla Landi (Cecile Stapleton), David Oxley (Sir Hugo Baskerville), Francis de Wolff (Doctor Richard Mortimer), Miles Malleson (Bishop Frankland), Ewen Solon (Stapleton), John Le Mesurier (Barrymore), Helen Goss (Mrs. Barrymore), Sam Kydd (Perkins), Michael Hawkins (Lord Caphill). *Dir.* Terence Fisher. See the 1921 film for plot summary.

Hound of the Baskervilles, The (1978) Peter Cook (Sherlock Holmes), Dudley Moore (Doctor Watson/Mr. Spiggot/Mrs. Ada Holmes/Piano Player), Denholm Elliott (Stapleton), Joan Greenwood (Beryl Stapleton), Hugh Griffith (Frankland), Irene Handl (Mrs. Barrymore), Terry-Thomas (Dr. Mortimer), Max Wall (Arthur Barrymore), Kenneth Williams (Sir Henry Baskerville), Roy Kinnear (Ethel Seldon), Dana Gillespie (Mary Frankland), Lucy Griffiths (Iris), Penelope Keith (Massage-Parlour Receptionist), Jessie Matthews (Mrs. Tinsdale), Prunella Scales (Glynis), Josephine Tewson (Nun), Rita Webb (Elder Masseuse), Henry Woolf (Shopkeeper), Spike Milligan (Policeman). A spoof of the classic Sherlock Holmes story featuring a cast of some of the best known British comedy actors of the time. *Dir.* Paul Morrissey.

Hours, The (2002) Nicole Kidman (Virginia Woolf), Stephen Dillane (Leonard Woolf), Miranda Richardson (Vanessa Bell), Lyndsey Marshal (Lottie Hope), Linda Bassett (Nelly Boxall), Julianne Moore (Laura Brown), John C. Reilly (Dan Brown), Jack Rovello (Richie Brown), Toni Collette (Kitty), Margo Martindale (Mrs. Latch), Meryl Streep (Clarissa Vaughan), Ed Harris (Richard "Richie" Brown), Allison Janney (Sally Lester), Claire Danes (Julia Vaughan), Jeff Daniels (Louis Waters). The film follows one day in three separate time periods – in 1923 Virginia Woolf is writing her novel *Mrs. Dalloway*; in 1951 pregnant housewife Laura Brown is preoccupied with reading Woolf's novel, whilst preparing for her husband's birthday; and in 2001 Clarissa Vaughn is planning an award party for her friend, an author dying of AIDS. Nicole Kidman won a Best Actress Oscar. *Dir.* Stephen Daldry

House Across the Lake, The (1954) Alex Nicol (Mark Kendrick), Hillary Brooke (Carol Forrest), Sid James (Beverly Forrest), Susan Stephen (Andrea Forrest), Paul Carpenter (Vincent Gordon), Alan Wheatley (Insp MacLennan), Peter Illing (Harry Stevens), Gordon McLeod (Dr Emery), Joan Hickson (Mrs Hardcastle), John Sharp (Mr Hardcastle), Hugh Dempster (Frank), Monti DeLyle (Head Waiter). A beautiful woman murders her husband and seduces her pulp novelist neighbour across the lake into corroborating her story that he died accidently. Aka *Heat Wave*. *Dir.* Ken Hughes.

House in the Square, The (1951) Tyrone Power (Peter Standish), Ann Blyth (Helen Pettigrew/Martha Forsyth), Michael Rennie (Roger Forsyth), Dennis Price (Tom Pettigrew), Beatrice Campbell (Kate Pettigrew), Kathleen Byron (Duchess of Devonshire), Raymond Huntley (Mr. Throstle), Irene Browne (Lady Anne Pettigrew), Ronald Adam (Ronson), Robert Atkins (Dr. Samuel Johnson), Felix Aylmer (Sir William), Hamlyn Benson (Magistrate), Richard Carrickford (Bow Street Runner), Arthur Denton (Loonies' Driver), Peter Drury (Policeman), Alec Finter (Throstle's Coachman), Tom Gill (Macaroni), Diane Hart (Dolly), Victor Maddern (Geiger Man), Alex McCrindle (James Boswell), Gibb McLaughlin (Jacob), Ronald Simpson (Sir Joshua Reynolds). An American scientist is struck by lightning and transported back to 1784 where he has switched bodies with the first Peter Standish. His speech, knowledge and ideas lead him to be considered mad by all except the sister of the woman he is due to marry. The film uses black and white and technicolour to delineate the different time periods. Remake of the American film *Berkeley Square* (1933) starring Leslie Howard and based on the stage play by John L Balderston. Aka *I'll Never Forget You*. *Dir.* Roy Ward Baker.

House of Mirth, The (2000) Gillian Anderson (Lily), Dan Aykroyd (Gus Trenor), Laura Linney (Bertha Dorset), Anthony LaPaglia (Sim Rosedale), Eric Stoltz (Lawrence Selden), Terry Kinney (George Dorset), Eleanor Bron (Julia Peniston), Jodhi May (Grace Stepney), Elizabeth McGovern (Carry Fisher), Penny Downie (Judy Trenor), Pearce Quigley (Percy Gryce), Lorelei King (Mrs Hatch), Morag Siller (Mary Lee). Lily Bart's life begins to unravel. Based on Edith Wharton's novel. *Dir.* Terence Davies.

House of the Long Shadows (1983) Vincent Price (Lionel Grisbane), Desi Arnaz Jr. (Kenneth Magee), Christopher Lee (Corrigan), Peter Cushing (Sebastian Grisbane), John Carradine (Lord Elijah Grisbane), Sheila Keith (Victoria Grisbane), Julie Peasgood (Mary Norton), Richard Todd (Sam Allyson), Louise English (Diana Caulder), Richard Hunter (Andrew Caulder), Norman Rossington (Station Master). Kenneth goes to a remote, deserted Welsh manor after he takes a $20,000 bet that he can write a Wuthering Heights-calibre novel in just 24 hours. However he discovers that the mansion is not actually empty and then more people keep arriving. Based on the novel *Seven Keys to Baldpate* by Earl Derr Biggers. *Dir.* Pete Walker.

House of Whipcord (1974) Barbara Markham (Mrs. Wakehurst), Patrick Barr (Justice Bailey), Robert Tayman (Mark E. Desade), Ray Brooks (Tony), Penny Irving (Ann-Marie Di Verney), Ann Michelle (Julia), Sheila Keith (Walker), Dorothy Gordon (Bates), Ivor Salter (Jack), Karan David (Karen), Celia Quicke (Denise), Ron Smerczak (Ted), Tony Sympson (Henry), Judy Robinson (Claire), Jane Hayward (Estelle), Celia Imrie (Barbara), Barry Martin (Al), Rose Hill (Henry's Wife). The immorality of the 1970s prompts a judge and some other worthies to set up their own court and prison in an abandoned school. The title and the presence of a character named Mark E Desade provide a clue as to the film's content. *Dir.* Pete Walker.

House That Dripped Blood, The (1970) John Bennett (Detective Inspector Holloway - *Framework* segment), John Bryans (A.J. Stoker - *Framework* segment), John Malcolm (Sergeant Martin - *Framework* segment), Denholm Elliott (Charles Hillyer - *Method For Murder* segment), Joanna Dunham (Alice Hillyer - *Method For Murder* segment), Tom Adams (Richard/Dominic - *Method For Murder* segment), Robert Lang (Dr. Andrews - *Method For Murder* segment), Judy Pace (Armenia McCormick - *Method For Murder* segment), Peter Cushing (Philip Grayson – *Waxworks* segment), Joss Ackland (Neville Rogers – *Waxworks* segment), Wolfe Morris (Waxworks Proprietor – *Waxworks* segment), Christopher Lee (John Reid - *Sweets to the Sweet* segment), Nyree Dawn Porter (Ann Norton - *Sweets to the Sweet* segment), Chloe Franks (Jane Reid - *Sweets to the Sweet* segment), Hugh Manning (Mark - *Sweets to the Sweet* segment), Jon Pertwee (Paul Henderson – *The Cloak* segment), Ingrid Pitt (Carla Lynde – *The Cloak* segment), Geoffrey Bayldon (Theo von Hartmann – *The Cloak* segment). A film split into four segments and framing scenes. A police inspector is investigating the disappearance of a film star from the old house he had been renting whilst shooting a horror film. A local policeman and an estate agent tell him stories of the house's history. *Dir.* Peter Duffell.

How I Won the War (1967) Michael Crawford (Lt Earnest Goodbody), John Lennon (Gripweed), Roy Kinnear (Clapper), Lee Montague (Sgt Transom), Jack MacGowran (Juniper), Michael Hordern (Grapple), Jack Hedley (Melancholy

Musketeer), Karl Michael Vogler (Odlebog), Ronald Lacey (Spool), James Cossins (Drogue), Ewan Hooper (Dooley), Alexander Knox (American General), Robert Hardy (British General), Sheila Hancock (Mrs Clapper's Friend). An anti-war black comedy where the 3rd Troop and the 4th Musketeers fight their way across North Africa and Europe whilst trying to rid themselves of their incompetent C/O. *Dir*. Richard Lester.

How to Get Ahead in Advertising (1989) Richard E. Grant (Denis Dimbleby Bagley), Rachel Ward (Julia Bagley), Richard Wilson (John Bristol), Jacqueline Tong (Penny Wheelstock), John Shrapnel (Psychiatrist), Susan Wooldridge (Monica), Hugh Armstrong (Harry Wax), Mick Ford (Richard), Jacqueline Pearce (Maud), Pip Torrens (Jonathan), Tony Slattery (Basil), Rachel Fielding (Jennifer), Roddy Maude-Roxby (Dr. Gatty), Sean Bean (Larry Frisk), Terry Jones (Man on Train), Bruce Robinson (The Boil - voice). Whilst making an advert for pimple cream Denis has a mental breakdown and then a boil on his neck develops into another head. *Dir*. Bruce Robinson.

Howards End (1992) Anthony Hopkins (Henry Wilcox), Emma Thompson (Margaret Schlegel), Helena Bonham Carter (Helen Schlegel), Vanessa Redgrave (Ruth Wilcox), Joseph Bennett (Paul Wilcox), Prunella Scales (Aunt Juley), Adrian Ross Magenty (Tibby Schlegel), Jo Kendall (Annie), James Wilby (Charles Wilcox), Jemma Redgrave (Evie Wilcox), Samuel West (Leonard Bast), Nicola Duffett (Jacky Bast), Simon Callow (Music and Meaning Lecturer), Crispin Bonham Carter (Albert Fussell). The shifting class structure in Edwardian England played out through the changes endured by three families of different standing – the middle class Basts, the bourgoise Schlegels and the industrialist Wilcoxes (the owners of Howards End). Won three Academy Awards: Best Actress in a Leading Role (Emma Thompson), Best Writing, Screenplay Based on Material Previously Produced or Published (Ruth Prawer Jhabvala), Best Art Direction-Set Decoration. Based upon the novel of the same name by E. M. Forster. *Dir*. James Ivory.

Hue and Cry (1947) Alastair Sim (Felix H. Wilkinson), Harry Fowler (Joe Kirby), Douglas Barr (Alec), Joan Dowling (Clarry), Jack Warner (Nightingale), Valerie White (Rhona), Jack Lambert (Ford), Ian Dawson (Norman), Gerald Fox (Dicky), David Simpson (Arthur), Albert Hughes (Wally), John Hudson (Stan), David Knox (Dusty), Jeffrey Sirett (Bill), James Crabbe (Terry), Stanley Escane (Roy), Frederick Piper (Mr. Kirby), Vida Hope (Mrs. Kirby). Joe realises that his favourite comic strip is being used to plan robberies but fails to convince the police. With the help of a street gang and the eccentric author of the strip he hopes to foil the thieves. Although actually more of a thriller in plot line, the film is generally considered to be the first of the "Ealing comedies". *Dir*. Charles Crichton.

Huggetts Abroad, The (1949) Jack Warner (Joe Huggett), Kathleen Harrison (Ethel Huggett), Dinah Sheridan (Jane Huggett), Susan Shaw (Susan Huggett), Petula Clark (Pet Huggett), Jimmy Hanley (Jimmy Gardner), Peter Hammond (Peter Hawtrey), Hugh McDermott (Bob McCoy), Amy Veness (Grandma Huggett), John Blythe (Gowan), Everley Gregg (Miss Phipps), Esma Cannon (Brown Owl), Brian Oulton (Travel Clerk), Olaf Pooley (Straker), Martin Miller (Customer), Meinhart Maur (Jeweller), Philo Hauser (Egyptian), Peter Illing (Algerian Detective), Frith Banbury (French Doctor), Marcel Poncin (Commander of the Fort), Cyril Chamberlain (Hopkinson), Eunice Gayson (Peggy), Ferdy Mayne (Gendarme), Clive Morton (Campbell), Mona Washbourne (Lugubrious Housewife). In the final film of the series, the family decides to emigrate to South Africa via a land route and get involved with a diamond smuggler. *Dir*. Ken Annakin. See also *Holiday Camp* (1947), *Here Come the Huggetts* (1948) and *Vote for Huggett* (1949).

Hunger (2008) Michael Fassbender (Bobby Sands), Liam Cunningham (Father Dominic Moran), Liam McMahon (Gerry Campbell), Stuart Graham (Raymond Lohan), Brian Milligan (Davey Gillen), Laine Megaw (Mrs. Lohan), Karen Hassan (Gerry's Girlfriend), Frank McCusker (The Governor), Lalor Roddy (William), Helen Madden (Mrs. Sands), Des McAleer (Mr. Sands). The story of Bobby Sands, a member of the Provisional IRA who led a hunger strike at the Maze Prison in 1981. *Dir*. Steve McQueen.

Hungry Hill (1947) Margaret Lockwood (Fanny Rosa), Dennis Price (Greyhound John Brodrick), Cecil Parker (Copper John Brodrick), Dermot Walsh (Wild Johnnie Brodrick), Michael Denison (Henry Brodrick), F.J. McCormick (Old Tim), Arthur Sinclair (Morty Donovan), Jean Simmons (Jane Brodrick), Eileen Crowe (Bridget), Eileen Herlie (Katherine), Barbara Waring (Barbara Brodrick), Michael Golden (Sam Donovan), Shamus Locke (Young Tim), Siobhan McKenna (Kate Donovan), Dan O'Herlihy (Harry Brodrick), Tony Quinn (Denny Donovan), Tony Wager (Young Wild Johnnie), Hector MacGregor (Nicholson), Henry Mollison (Dr. Armstrong), Pete Murray (Lieutenant Fox), Ingrid Forrest (Nora), Ann Wilton (Cousin Eliza), Dock Mathieson (Micky Sullivan), Patrick Holt (Ward), Guy Rolfe (Miner), Shelah Richards (Mary Donovan), Eddie Byrne (Hennessy), Maureen Moore (Mrs. Morty Donovan). The story of a feud spanning generations between two families in Ireland. Based on a novel by Daphne du Maurier. *Dir*. Brian Desmond Hurst.

Hunky Dory (2011) Minnie Driver (Vivienne), Aneurin Barnard (Davey), Danielle Branch (Stella), Robert Pugh (Headmaster), Haydn Gwynne (Mrs Valentine), Steve Speirs (Mr Cafferty), Aled Pugh (Tim), Julia Perez (Sylvie), Kimberley Nixon (Vicki Munro), Tom Harries (Evan), Kristian Gwilliam (Hoople/Andy Dixon), Kayleigh Bennett (Dena Davies), Jodie Davis (Mandy), George MacKay (Jake Zeppi), Adam Byard (Lewis Munro), David Garner (Mac). During the hot summer of 1976 a school in Swansea puts on a performance of Shakespeare's *The Tempest* using contemporary (1970s) music. *Dir*. Marc Evans.

Hunted (1952) Dirk Bogarde (Chris Lloyd), Jon Whiteley (Robbie), Elizabeth Sellars (Magda Lloyd), Kay Walsh (Mrs. Sykes), Frederick Piper (Mr Sykes), Julian Somers (Jack Lloyd), Jane Aird (Mrs Campbell), Jack Stewart (Mr Campbell), Geoffrey Keen (Det Insp Deakin), Douglas Blackwell (Det Sgt Grayson), Leonard White (Police Station Sgt), Gerald Anderson (Asst Commissioner), Denis Webb (Chief Supt), Gerald Case (Dep Asst Commissioner), John Bushelle (Chief Insp), Ewen Solon (Radio Operator), Katharine Blake (Waitress), Molly Urquhart (Barmaid), Sam Kydd (Potman), Joe Linnane (Pawnbroker), Howard Lane (Policeman), Grace Arnold (Woman in Courtyard), Alec Finter (McDougall). A man on the run from the police and a young boy in fear of his foster parents travel from London to Scotland in the hope of escaping their lives. *Dir*. Charles Crichton.

I Am a Camera (1955) Julie Harris (Sally Bowles), Laurence Harvey (Christopher Isherwood), Shelley Winters (Natalia Landauer), Ron Randell (Clive), Lea Seidl (Fräulein Schneider), Anton Diffring (Fritz Wendel), Ina De La Haye (Herr Landauer), Jean Gargoet (Pierre), Stanley Maxted (Editor), Alexis Bobrinskoy (Proprietor), André Mikhelson (Head Waiter), Frederick Valk (Doctor), Tutte Lemkow (Electro-Therapist), Patrick McGoohan (Swedish Water Therapist), Julia Arnall (Model), Zoe Newton (Cigarette Girl), Richard Wattis (Bespectacled Man). Fictionalised account of Christopher Isherwood's life in Berlin in the 1930s as the Nazis rise to power – later turned into the much better known musical *Cabaret*. Based on *The Berlin Stories* by Christopher Isherwood and the play *I Am a Camera* by John Van Druten. *Dir*. Henry Cornelius.

I Believe in You (1952) Celia Johnson (Matty Matheson), Cecil Parker (Henry Phipps), Godfrey Tearle (Judge Pyke), Harry Fowler (Charlie Hooker), George Relph (Mr Dove), Joan Collins (Norma Hart), Laurence Harvey (Jordie Bennett), Ernest Jay (Judge Quayle), Ursula Howells (Hon Ursula), Sid James (Sgt. Body), Katie Johnson (Miss Mackline), Ada Reeve (Mrs Crockett), Brenda De Banzie (Mrs Hooker), Alex McCrindle (Tom Haines), Laurence Naismith (Sgt Braxton), Gladys Henson (Mrs Stevens), Stanley Escane (Buck Wilson), Fred Griffiths (Fred Crump), Richard Hart (Eric Stevens), Glyn Houston (Passerby), Mandy Miller (Child). Various stories about parole officers and parolees. *Dirs*. Basil Dearden and Michael Relph.

I Could Go On Singing (1963) Judy Garland (Jenny Bowman), Dirk Bogarde (David Donne), Jack Klugman (George Kogan), Gregory Phillips (Matt), Aline MacMahon (Ida), Pauline Jameson (Miss Plimpton), Jeremy Burnham (Hospital surgeon), Lorna Luft (Girl on boat), Joey Luft (Boy on boat), Gerald Sim (Assistant Manager at Palladium). A singing superstar returns to London to perform at the Palladium and to take the opportunity to visit the son she has not seen for 15 years. Judy Garland's final film role. *Dir.* Ronald Neame.

I Didn't Do It! (1945) George Formby (George Trotter), Billy Caryll (Tiger Tubbs), Hilda Mundy (Ma Tubbs), Gaston Palmer (Le Grand Gaston), Jack Daley (Terry O'Rourke), Carl Jaffe (Hilary Vance), Marjorie Browne (Betty Dickson), Wally Patch (Sgt. Carp), Ian Fleming (Chief Insp. Twyning), Vincent Holman (Erasmus Montague), Dennis Wyndham (Tom Driscoll), Jack Raine (J.B. Cato), Georgina Cookson (Willow Thane), Merle Tottenham (Tessie), Gordon McLeod (Supt. Belstock). A murder takes place in a theatrical boarding house and George is the chief suspect. *Dir.* Marcel Varnel.

I Know Where I'm Going! (1945) Wendy Hiller (Joan Webster), Roger Livesey (Torquil MacNeil), Pamela Brown (Catriona), Finlay Currie (Ruairidh Mhór), George Carney (Mr. Webster), Nancy Price (Mrs. Crozier), Catherine Lacey (Mrs. Robinson), Jean Cadell (Postmistress), John Laurie (John Campbell), Valentine Dyall (Mr. Robinson), Norman Shelley (Sir Robert Bellinger - voice), Margot Fitzsimons (Bridie), Murdo Morrison (Kenny), C.W.R. Knight (Colonel Barnstaple), Walter Hudd (Hunter), Ian Sadler (Iain), Donald Strachan (Shepherd), John Rae (Old Shepherd), Anthony Eustrel (Hooper), Petula Clark (Cheril), Alec Faversham (Martin), Herbert Lomas (Mr. Campbell), Kitty Kirwan (Mrs. Campbell), Graham Moffatt (RAF. Sergeant). Joan Webster knows where she's going – to the Hebrides to marry Sir Robert Bellinger. However, on her way there she meets Torquil MacNeil. *Dirs.* Michael Powell and Emeric Pressburger.

I See a Dark Stranger (1946) Deborah Kerr (Bridie Quilty), Trevor Howard (Lt. David Baynes), Raymond Huntley (J. Miller), Michael Howard (Hawkins), Norman Shelley (Man in Straw Hat), Liam Redmond (Uncle Timothy), Brefni O'Rorke (Michael O'Callaghan), James Harcourt (Grandfather), George Woodbridge (Walter), Garry Marsh (Capt. Goodhusband), Olga Lindo (Mrs. Edwards), Tom Macaulay (Lt. Spanswick), David Ward (Oscar Pryce), Harry Hutchinson (Chief Mourner), Harry Webster (Uncle Joe), Eddie Golden (Terence Delaney), Marie Ault (Mrs. O'Mara), Humphrey Heathcote (Sgt. Harris), David Tomlinson (Intelligence Officer), Kenneth Buckley (Radio-Telephone Operator), Torin Thatcher (Police Constable), Gerald Case (Col. Dennington), William G. O'Gorman (Danny Quilty), Brenda Bruce (American Waitress), Leslie Dwyer (Soldier in Café), Kathleen Harrison (Waitress), Joan Hickson (Manx Hotel Manager), Peter Jones (Soldier in Pub), Katie Johnson (Old Lady on Train). An English-hating Irish girl fails to join the IRA but is recruited by the Nazis. Then she begins to have doubts about her commitment. Also known as *The Adventuress*. *Dir.* Frank Launder.

I See Ice (1938) George Formby (George Bright), Kay Walsh (Judy Gaye), Betty Stockfeld (Mrs. Hunter), Cyril Ritchard (Paul Martine), Garry Marsh (Galloway), Frederick Burtwell (Detective), Ernest Sefton (Outhwaite), Gavin Gordon (Night Club Singer). George is a keen amateur photographer who has invented a hidden camera. The ice in the title refers to his work at an ice rink. *Dir.* Anthony Kimmins.

I Thank a Fool (1962) Susan Hayward (Christine Allison), Peter Finch (Stephen Dane), Diane Cilento (Liane Dane), Cyril Cusack (Capt Ferris), Kieron Moore (Roscoe), Richard Wattis (Ebblington), Athene Seyler (Aunt Heather), Miriam Karlin (Woman in Black Maria), Laurence Naismith (O'Grady), JG Devlin (Coroner), Clive Morton (Judge), Richard Leech (Irish Doctor), Brenda De Banzie (Nurse Drew), Joan Hickson (Landlady), Peter Sallis (Sleazy Doctor), Yolande Turner (Polly), Peter Vaughan (Police Insp). Doctor is struck off for aiding a suicide but is then employed by the prosecutor at her trial to look after his sick wife. *Dir.* Robert Stevens.

I Want Candy (2007) Tom Riley (Joe Clarke), Tom Burke (John 'Baggy' Bagley), Carmen Electra (Candy Fiveways), Eddie Marsan (Doug Perry), Michelle Ryan (Lila Owens), Mackenzie Crook (Dulberg), Felicity Montagu (Mum), Philip Jackson (Dad), Jimmy Carr (Video Store Guy), John Standing (Michael de Vere), Felicity Montagu (Val), Philip Jackson (Stephen), Carl Prekopp (Vlad), Rasmus Hardiker (Christi), Colin Michael Carmichael (Gabi), Stephanie Blacker (Tiffany Thomas), Giles Alderson (Carl), Sid Mitchell (Robby), Martin Savage (Priest), Nick Nevern (Angry Mourner), Miranda Hart (Working Title Receptionist). Film students Joe and Baggy are struggling to finance their graduation film but then an adult film producer offers to put up the money as long as they use porn actress Candy Fiveways in the film. *Dir.* Stephen Surjik.

I Was Monty's Double (1958) John Mills (Major Harvey), Cecil Parker (Col. Logan), M.E. Clifton James (Himself/General Montgomery), Patrick Allen (Col. Mathers), Patrick Holt (Col. Dawson), Leslie Phillips (Major Tennant), Michael Hordern (Governor of Gibraltar), Marius Goring (Nielson), Barbara Hicks (Hester), Duncan Lamont (Wing Cdr. Bates), Anthony Sagar (Guard Sergeant), John Gale (Flight Lt. Osborne), Kenneth J. Warren (Davies), James Hayter (Sgt. Adams), Sid James (Porter Y.M.C.A.), Brian Weske (Despatch Rider), Bill Nagy (American Captain), Edward Judd (Soldier), Victor Maddern (Orderly Sergeant), Bryan Forbes (Young Lieutenant), Victor Beaumont (Gottmann), Alfie Bass (The Small Man), Ronald Wilson (American Driver), John Le Mesurier (Adjutant R.A.P.C.), Walter Gotell (German Colonel), David Lodge (Sergeant R.A.P.C.), MacDonald Parke (American General), Marne Maitland (Arab Proprietor), Vera Day (Angela), Maureen Connell (Peggy), Sam Kydd (Go-Between), Allan Cuthbertson (Guards Officer), Harry Fowler (Civilian), Martin Shaban (War Correspondent), Ronnie Stevens (M.I.5. Tail), Desmond Roberts (Brigadier), George Eugeniou (Garcia), Diana Beaumont (Barmaid). In an attempt to spread misinformation about the forthcoming D-Day landings, British intelligence recruit a Royal Army Pay Corp lieutenant and peacetime actor M E Clifton James (playing himself in the film) to impersonate Field Marshall Bernard Montgomery and visit the troops in North Africa. Based on the autobiography of M E Clifton James. *Dir.* John Guillermin.

I, Claudius (1937) Charles Laughton (Claudius), Merle Oberon (Messalina), Emlyn Williams (Caligula), Flora Robson (Livia), Alan Aynesworth (Asiaticus), John Clements (Valente), Leonora Corbett (Caesonia), Roy Emerton (Octavius), Gina Evans (Vestal Virgin), Frank Forbes-Robertson (Lupus), Basil Gill (Xenophon), Morland Graham (Halotus), Everley Gregg (Domita), Lyn Harding (Vespasian), Allan Jeayes (Musa), Robert Newton (Cassius). The "film that never was". With some of the film already shot, Merle Oberon was injured in a car crash and the director Josef von Sternberg abandoned the film. The BBC used the existing footage in a 70-minute documentary *The Epic That Never Was* (1965), hosted by Dirk Bogarde.

I, Monster (1971) Christopher Lee (Dr. Charles Marlowe/Edward Blake), Peter Cushing (Frederick Utterson), Mike Raven (Enfield), Richard Hurndall (Dr. Lanyon), George Merritt (Poole), Kenneth J. Warren (Mr. Deane), Susan Jameson (Diane Thomas), Marjie Lawrence (Annie), Aimée Delamain (Landlady), Michael Des Barres (Boy in Alley), Lesley Judd (Woman in Alley), Ian McCulloch (Man at Bar). Plot follows that of the classic Jekyll and Hyde tale. *Dir.* Stephen Weeks.

i.d. (1995) Reece Dinsdale (John), Richard Graham (Trevor), Perry Fenwick (Eddie), Philip Glenister (Charlie), Warren Clarke (Bob), Claire Skinner (Marie), Saskia Reeves (Lynda), Sean Pertwee (Martin), Charles De'Ath (Nik), Lee Ross (Gumbo), Terry Cole (Puff), Steve Sweeney (Viny), Nicholas R. Bailey (Mickey), Nick Bartlett (David Daley), Peter Blythe (DC Evans), Ian Redford (DI Schofield), Philip Davis (Duty Sgt). Set in the 1980s, four policemen go undercover to investigate football gangs but one of them becomes inexorably drawn into the culture and lifestyle of the yob. *Dir.* Philip Davis.

Ice Cold in Alex (1958) John Mills (Captain Anson), Sylvia Syms (Sister Diana Murdoch), Anthony Quayle (Capt van der Poel/Hauptmann Otto Lutz), Harry Andrews (MSM Tom Pugh), Diane Clare (Sister Denise Norton), Richard Leech (Capt Crosbie), Liam Redmond (Brigadier, Deputy Director Medical Services), Allan Cuthbertson (Brigadier's Staff Officer), David Lodge (CMP Captain), Michael Nightingale (CMP Captain), Basil Hoskins (CMP Lieutenant), Walter Gotell (1st German Officer), Frederick Jaeger (2nd German Officer), Richard Marner (German

Guard), Peter Arne (British officer), Paul Stassino (Barman). During the evacuation of Tobruk in WWII two Brits (Anson and Pugh) and two nurses pick up a South African army officer, set off across the desert towards the British lines and dream of having an ice cold beer at the end of the journey in Alexandria. *Dir*. J. Lee Thompson.

Ideal Husband, An (1947) Paulette Goddard (Mrs. Laura Cheveley), Michael Wilding (Viscount Arthur Goring), Diana Wynyard (Lady Gertrude Chiltern), Hugh Williams (Sir Robert Chiltern), C. Aubrey Smith (Earl of Caversham), Glynis Johns (Miss Mabel Chiltern), Constance Collier (Lady Markby), Christine Norden (Mrs. Margaret Marchmont), Harriette Johns (Olivia, Countess of Basildon), Michael Medwin (Duke of Nonesuch). Adaptation of Oscar Wilde's play. The career and marriage of Government minister Sir Robert Chiltern are threatened when Mrs Cheveley appears in London with evidence of a past wrongdoing. *Dir*. Alexander Korda.

Ideal Husband, An (1999) Cate Blanchett (Lady Gertrude Chiltern), Minnie Driver (Miss Mabel Chiltern), Rupert Everett (Lord Arthur Goring), Julianne Moore (Mrs. Laura Cheveley), Jeremy Northam (Sir Robert Chiltern), John Wood (Lord Caversham), Peter Vaughan (Phipps), Ben Pullen (Tommy Trafford), Marsha Fitzalan (Countess), Lindsay Duncan (Lady Markby), Neville Phillips (Mason), Nickolas Grace (Vicomte de Nanjac), Simon Russell Beale (Sir Edward). Adaptation of Oscar Wilde's play. *Dir*. Oliver Parker.

Ideal Husband, An (2000) James Wilby (Sir Robert Chiltern), Sadie Frost (Mrs. Laura Cheveley), Jonathan Firth (Lord Arthur Goring), Trevyn McDowell (Lady Gertrude Chiltern), Robert Hardy (Lord Caversham), Karen Hayley (Mabel Chiltern), Prunella Scales (Lady Markby), Tyler Butterworth (Phipps, Arthur's Valet), Tamara Beckwith (Margaret Marchmont), Tara Palmer-Tomkinson (Olivia Basildon). Adaptation of Oscar Wilde's play. *Dir*. William P Cartlidge.

Idol on Parade (1959) Anthony Newley (Jeep Jackson), William Bendix (Sgt. Lush), Anne Aubrey (Caroline), Lionel Jeffries (Bertie), Sid James (Herbie), David Lodge (Shorty), Dilys Laye (Renee), William Kendall (Commanding Officer), Bernie Winters (Joseph Jackson), Harry Fowler (Ron), Norman Atkyns (Stage manager), Percy Herbert (Sgt. Hebrides), Sean Kelly (Ernie), Gordon Needham (Cpl. Nerking), Susan Hampshire (Martha), Rupert Davies (Sergeant). A pop singer is called up to serve in the British army. *Dir*. John Gilling.

If ... (1968) Malcolm McDowell (Mick Travis), David Wood (Johnny), Richard Warwick (Wallace), Christine Noonan (The Girl), Rupert Webster (Bobby Phillips), Robert Swann (Rowntree), Hugh Thomas (Denson), Michael Cadman (Fortinbras), Peter Sproule (Barnes), Peter Jeffrey (Headmaster), Arthur Lowe (Housemaster), Mona Washbourne (Matron), Ben Aris (John Thomas), Robin Askwith (Keating), Charles Sturridge (Markland), Graham Crowden (History master), Charles Lloyd Pack (Classics master), Richard Everett (Pussy Graves). Mick Travis leads a bloody revolt at his public school. McDowell went on to play a character called Mick Travis (although not necessarily the same "person") in O Lucky Man! (1973) and Britannia Hospital (1982). *Dir*. Lindsay Anderson.

Ill Met by Moonlight (1957) Dirk Bogarde (Major Patrick Leigh Fermor/Philedem), Marius Goring (Major General Kreipe), David Oxley (Captain W. Stanley Moss), Dimitri Andreas (Niko), Cyril Cusack (Sandy), Laurence Payne (Manoli), Wolfe Morris (George), Michael Gough (Andoni Zoidakis), John Cairney (Elias), Brian Worth (Stratis Saviolkis), Roland Bartrop (Micky Akoumianakis), George Eugeniou (Charis Zographakis), Paul Stassino (Yani Katsias), Adeeb Assaly (Zahari), Theo Moreas (Village Priest), Takis Frangofinos (Michali), Christopher Lee (German officer), Peter Augustine (Dentist), Richard Marner (German Officer), David McCallum (Sailor).
Two members of the British Special Operations Executive land on Crete with the mission to capture the German commander of the island. Based on the book *Ill Met by Moonlight: The Abduction of General Kreipe* by W. Stanley Moss. Also known as *Night Ambush*. *Dirs*. Michael Powell and Emeric Pressburger.

I'll Never Forget What's 'Isname (1967) Orson Welles (Jonathan Lute), Oliver Reed (Andrew Quint), Carol White (Georgina Elben), Harry Andrews (Gerald Sater), Michael Hordern (Headmaster), Wendy Craig (Louise Quint), Norman Rodway (Nicholas), Marianne Faithfull (Josie), Frank Finlay (Chaplain), Ann Lynn (Carla), Harvey Hall (Charles Maccabee), Lyn Ashley (Susannah), Edward Fox (Walter), Mark Burns (Michael Cornwall), Mark Eden (Kellaway), Stuart Cooper (Lewis Force), Veronica Clifford (Anna), Roland Curram (Eldrich), Peter Graves (Bankman), Robert Mill (Galloway). Successful advertising agent Andrew Quint wants to ditch his lifestyle and start all over again. *Dir*. Michael Winner.

I'll Sleep When I'm Dead (2004) Clive Owen (Will), Charlotte Rampling (Helen), Jonathan Rhys Meyers (Davey), Malcolm McDowell (Boad), Jamie Foreman (Mickser), Ken Stott (Turner), Sylvia Syms (Mrs. Bartz), Alexander Morton (Victor), John Surman (Pathologist), Paul Mohan (Coroner), Damian Dibben (David Myers), Amber Batty (Sheridan), Daisy Beaumont (Stella), Lidija Zovkic (Philippa), Geoff Bell (Arnie Ryan), Desmond Bayliss (Cannibal), Kirris Riviere (Big John), Brian Croucher (Al Shaw), Noel Clarke (Cyril). Will, an ex-gangster, returns to London to investigate the death of his brother Davey. *Dir*. Mike Hodges

I'm All Right Jack (1959) Ian Carmichael (Stanley Windrush), Terry-Thomas (Major Hitchcock), Peter Sellers (Fred Kite/Sir John Kennaway), Richard Attenborough (Sidney De Vere Cox), Dennis Price (Bertram Tracepurcel), Margaret Rutherford (Aunt Dolly), Irene Handl (Mrs. Kite), Liz Fraser (Cynthia Kite), Miles Malleson (Windrush Snr.), Marne Maitland (Mr. Mohammed), John Le Mesurier (Waters), Raymond Huntley (Magistrate), Victor Maddern (Knowles), Kenneth Griffith (Dai), John Comer (Shop Steward), Sam Kydd (Shop Steward), Cardew Robinson (Shop Steward), John Glyn-Jones (Detto Executive), Terry Scott (Crawley), David Lodge (Card Player), Wally Patch (Worker). Comedy highlighting the problems in management and the workplace in the post-war world. University graduate Stanley Windrush gets talked into taking an unskilled job, unaware that he is a pawn in a money-making scheme of his uncle Bertram's which includes upsetting the unions. Ian Carmichael, Dennis Price, Richard Attenborough, Terry-Thomas and Miles Malleson all reprise their characters from *Private's Progress* (1956). Based on the novel *Private Life* by Alan Hackney. *Dir*. John Boulting.

Imaginarium of Doctor Parnassus, The (2009) Heath Ledger (Tony), Johnny Depp (Tony), Colin Farrell (Tony), Jude Law (Tony), Christopher Plummer (Doctor Parnassus), Andrew Garfield (Anton), Verne Troyer (Percy), Lily Cole (Valentina), Tom Waits (Mr. Nick), Peter Stormare (President), Maggie Steed (Louis Vuitton Woman), Mark Benton (Dad), Simon Day (Uncle Bob), Paloma Faith (Sally), Richard Riddell (Martin), Montserrat Lombard (Sally's friend), Bruce Crawford (Face Changed Martin), Katie Lyons (Martin's Girlfriend), Richard Shanks (Martin's friend), Lorraine Cheshire (Mum), Mark Benton (Dad), Lewis Gott (Diego), Sian Scott (Linda), Simon Day (Uncle Bob), Vitaly Kravchenko (Piotr), Ray Cooper (Vladimir), Emil Hostina (Serge), Igor Ingelsman (Gregor), Cassandra Sawtell (Olga), Donna Lysell (President's Wife), Ryan Grantham (Little Anton). The apparently 1000 year-old Doctor Parnassus runs a street theatre troupe and has an "Imaginarium" through which people's dreams can come true. However, his life-long adversary Mr Nick has come to collect the soul of the Doctor's daughter Valentina when she turns 16 in a few days time. The troupe rescues a hanging man, Tony, and he joins them. When Heath Ledger died part way through filming the role was recast with Johnny Depp, Jude Law, and Colin Farrell portraying transformations of Ledger's character as he travels through a dream world. *Dir*. Terry Gilliam.

Importance of Being Earnest, The (1952) Michael Denison (Algernon Moncrieff), Michael Redgrave (Jack Worthing), Edith Evans (Lady Bracknell), Joan Greenwood (Gwendolen Fairfax), Dorothy Tutin (Cecily Cardew), Margaret Rutherford (Miss Prism), Miles Malleson (Canon Chasuble), Aubrey Mather (Merriman), Richard Wattis (Seton), Walter Hudd (Lane). When two young gentlemen use the name Ernest to disguise their activities and themselves, the deceptions cause confusion for everyone around them. Edith Evans's delivery of the line "A handbag?" is a highlight. Adaptation of the play by Oscar Wilde. *Dir.* Anthony Asquith.

Importance of Being Earnest, The (2002) Rupert Everett (Algernon "Algy" Moncrieff), Colin Firth (John "Jack" Worthing/Ernest), Judi Dench (Lady Bracknell), Frances O'Connor (Gwendolen Fairfax), Reese Witherspoon (Cecily Cardew), Tom Wilkinson (Dr Chasuble), Anna Massey (Miss Prism), Edward Fox (Lane), Patrick Godfrey (Merriman), Charles Kay (Gribsby), Cyril Shaps (Pew Opener), Marsha Fitzalan (Dowager), Finty Williams (Young Augusta Bracknell), Guy Bensley (Young Lord Bracknell). Adaptation of Oscar Wilde's play of the same name. *Dir.* Oliver Parker.

In Bruges (2008) Colin Farrell (Ray), Brendan Gleeson (Ken), Ralph Fiennes (Harry), Clémence Poésy (Chloë Villette), Jordan Prentice (Jimmy), Thekla Reuten (Marie), Jérémie Renier (Eirik), Anna Madeley (Denise), Elizabeth Berrington (Natalie), Eric Godon (Yuri), Mark Donovan (Fat Man), Željko Ivanek (Canadian Guy), Theo Stevenson (Boy in Church), Cinsyla Key (Hotel guest), Ciarán Hinds (Priest), Matt Smith (Young Harry). After accidently killing a boy on his first assignment, hit man Ray is told by his boss Harry Waters to hide out in Bruges along with his partner Ken while he decides what to do about Ray. *Dir.* Martin McDonagh

In the Loop (2009) Peter Capaldi (Malcolm Tucker), Tom Hollander (Simon Foster MP), Chris Addison (Toby Wright), Gina McKee (Judy Molloy), Mimi Kennedy (Karen Clark), Anna Chlumsky (Liza Weld), James Gandolfini (Lt. Gen. Miller), David Rasche (Linton Barwick), Paul Higgins (Jamie MacDonald), James Smith (Michael Rodgers), Olivia Poulet (Suzy), Steve Coogan (Paul Michaelson), Zach Woods (Chad), Alex MacQueen (Sir Jonathan Tutt). Pro and anti war factions manouevre with luckless Simon Foster as piggy in the middle. A feature film spin-off from the BBC Television series *The Thick of It. Dir.* Armando Iannucci.

In the Name of the Father (1993) Daniel Day-Lewis (Gerry Conlon), Pete Postlethwaite (Guiseppe Conlon), John Lynch (Paul Hill), Mark Sheppard (Paddy Armstrong), Beatie Edney (Carole Richardson), Emma Thompson (Gareth Peirce), Don Baker (Joe McAndrew), Corin Redgrave (Inspector Robert Dixon), Eileen Atkins (Cheryl Conlon), Joan Cusack (Jennifer Smalls), Gerard McSorley (Detective Pavis), Kathleen Turner (Elaine McAndrew), Frank Harper (Ronnie Smalls), Fiona Shaw (Marlene Dixon), Robert Englund (Michael Peirce), Jamie Harris (Deptford Jim), Jessica Tandy (Brooke Armstrong), Natasha Richardson (Susan Hill), Tom Wilkinson (Grant Richardson). Anna Meegan (Granny Conlon), Marie Jones (Sarah Conlon), Leah McCullagh (Bridie Conlon), Joanna Irvine (Ann Conlon), Anthony Brophy (Danny), Frankie McCafferty (Tommo), Saffron Burrows (Girl in Commune), Mark Sheppard (Paddy Armstrong), Britta Smith (Annie Maguire), Don Baker (Joe McAndrew), Barbara Mulcahy (Marian), Joe McPartland (Charlie Burke), Gerard McSorley (Detective Pavis). The story of the conviction and eventual release of the Guildford Four. Adapted from the autobiography *Proved Innocent: The Story of Gerry Conlon of the Guildford Four* by Gerry Conlon. *Dir.* Jim Sheridan.

In This World (2002) Jamal Udin Torabi (Jamal), Enayatullah (Enayat), Nabil Elouahabi (Yusif), Imran Paracha (Travel Agent), Hiddayatullah (Enayat's Brother), Jamau (Enayat's Father), Wakeel Khan (Enayat's Uncle), Lal Zarin (Enayat's Uncle). A docudrama which follows two refugees from Afghanistan as they attempt by any means they can to reach London. *Dir.* Michael Winterbottom.

In Which We Serve (1942) Noel Coward (Capt. Edward V. Kinross), John Mills (Ordinary Seaman Shorty Blake), Bernard Miles (CPO Walter Hardy), Celia Johnson (Alix Kinross), Ann Stephens (Lavinia Kinross), Daniel Massey (Bobby Kinross), Joyce Carey (Kath Hardy), Dora Gregory (Mrs. Lemmon), Kay Walsh (Freda Lewis), Derek Elphinstone (First Lieutenant, the 'Torrin'). Michael Wilding (Flags), Leslie Dwyer (Parkinson), James Donald (Doc), Richard Attenborough (Young Stoker), Kathleen Harrison (Mrs. Blake), Daniel Massey (Bobby Kinross), Juliet Mills (Freda's baby), Wally Patch (Uncle Fred). The story

of *HMS Torrin* told mainly in flashback from its construction until it's sinking during the Battle for Crete in 1941 and including its part in the Norwegian campaign and the Dunkirk evacuation. The film also touches on the lives of the crew's loved ones suffering during the London blitz. A patriotic drama made during the Second World War with the assistance of the Ministry of Information. *Dirs.* Noel Coward and David Lean.

Inbetweeners Movie, The (2011) Simon Bird (Will McKenzie), James Buckley (Jay Cartwright), Blake Harrison (Neil Sutherland), Joe Thomas (Simon Cooper), Emily Head (Carli D'Amato), Laura Haddock (Alison), Tamla Kari (Lucy), Jessica Knappett (Lisa), Lydia Rose Bewley (Jane), Theo James (James), Theo Barklem-Biggs (Richard), Anthony Head (Mr. McKenzie), Belinda Stewart-Wilson (Polly McKenzie), Martin Trenaman (Alan Cooper), Robin Weaver (Pamela Cooper), David Schaal (Terry Cartwright), Victoria Willing (Mrs Cartwright), Alex MacQueen (Kevin Sutherland), Greg Davies (Mr. Gilbert), Henry Lloyd-Hughes (Mark Donovan), Lauren O'Rourke (Nicole). At the end of their final year at school, four friends go on holiday to Crete to try and get over recent misfortunes. A big screen version of the popular E4 sitcom *The Inbetweeners. Dir.* Ben Palmer.

Incense for the Damned (1970) Patrick Macnee (Derek Longbow), Peter Cushing (Dr Walter Goodrich), Edward Woodward (Dr Holstrom), Alexander Davion (Tony Seymore), Johnny Sekka (Bob Kirby), Madeleine Hinde (Penelope), William Mervyn (Marc Honeydew), Patrick Mower (Richard Fountain), David Lodge (Colonel), Imogen Hassall (Chriseis), John Barron (Diplomat). A student goes missing in Greece and his friends find he has come under the influence of a vampire. *Dir.* Robert Hartford-Davis.

Indiscreet (1958) Cary Grant (Philip Adams), Ingrid Bergman (Anna Kalman), Cecil Parker (Alfred Munson), Phyllis Calvert (Mrs. Margaret Munson), David Kossoff (Carl Banks), Megs Jenkins (Doris Banks), Michael Anthony (Oscar), Martin Boddey (Albert), David Coote (Charles), Richard Vernon (Guide). Actress Anna falls for suave, debonair, charming Philip (well it is Cary Grant) but believes him to be a married man. Based on the play *Kind Sir* by Norman Krasna. *Dir.* Stanley Donen.

Infidel, The (2010) Omid Djalili (Mahmud Nasir/Solly Shimshillewitz), Yigal Naor (Arshad Al-Masri), Matt Lucas (Rabbi), Archie Panjabi (Saamiya Nasir), Richard Schiff (Lenny Goldberg), Miranda Hart (Mrs. Keyes), David Schneider (Monty), Tracy-Ann Oberman (Monty's wife), Mina Anwar (Muna), James Floyd (Gary Page), Shobu Kapoor (Kashmina), Sartaj Garewal (Wasif), Ricky Sekhon (Hazeem). Muslim Mahmud Nasir discovers he was born Solly Shimshillewitz to a Jewish family and adopted as a child. Written by David Baddiel. *Dir.* Josh Appignanesi.

Inkheart (2008) Brendan Fraser (Mortimer Folchart), Eliza Bennett (Meggie Folchart), Paul Bettany (Dustfinger), Andy Serkis (Capricorn), Jim Broadbent (Fenoglio), Helen Mirren (Elinor Loredan), Rafi Gavron (Farid), Sienna Guillory (Teresa "Resa" Folchart), Lesley Sharp (Mortola), Jamie Foreman (Basta), Matt King (Cockerell), John Thomson (Darius), Jennifer Connelly (Roxanne), Marnix Van Den Broeke (The Shadow), Steve Speirs (Flatnose), Jessie Cave (Nymph), Adam Bond (Prince Charming), Tereza Srbova (Rapunzel), Emily Eby (Guinevere), Richard Strange (Antiquarian Bookshop Owner), Stephen Graham (Fulvio), Mirabel O'Keefe (Young Meggie), Roger Allam (Narrator - voice). "Silver tongue" Mortimer has the ability to make the characters in the books he reads aloud come to life. Unfortunately this ability has led to tragedy. One day, with his daughter Meggie he finds a book he has been looking for, *Inkheart*. Based on the novel with the same name by Cornelia Funke. *Dir.* Iain Softley.

Innocents, The (1961) Deborah Kerr (Miss Giddens), Peter Wyngarde (Peter Quint), Megs Jenkins (Mrs. Grose), Michael Redgrave (The Uncle), Martin Stephens (Miles), Pamela Franklin (Flora), Clytie Jessop (Miss Jessel), Isla Cameron (Anna), Eric Woodburn (Coachman). Miss Giddens is employed to look after orphaned children Miles and Flora. A series of apparently supernatural happenings leads her to believe that the children are possessed by the spirits of the previous governess and valet Peter Quint. Based on *The Turn of the Screw* by Henry James. *Dir.* Jack Clayton.

Inside I'm Dancing (2004) James McAvoy (Rory Gerard O'Shea), Steven Robertson (Michael Connolly), Romola Garai (Siobhán), Brenda Fricker (Eileen), Gerard McSorley (Fergus Connolly), Tom Hickey (Con O'Shea), Alan King (Tommy), Ruth McCabe (Annie), Anna Healy (Alice). Two young disabled men in a residential home decide to try to become more independent. *Dir*. Damien O'Donnell.

Inspector Calls, An (1954) Alastair Sim (Insp Poole), Jane Wenham (Eva Smith), Brian Worth (Gerald Croft), Eileen Moore (Sheila Birling), Olga Lindo (Sybil Birling), Arthur Young (Arthur Birling), Bryan Forbes (Eric Birling), Norman Bird (Foreman Jones-Collins), Charles Saynor (Police Sgt Arnold Ransom), John Welsh (Mr Timmon), Barbara Everest (Mrs Lefson), George Woodbridge (Stanley), George Cole (Tram conductor). Inspector Poole calls on the Birling family whilst they are at dinner and informs them of the suicide of a young woman. He then proceeds to explain to each of them how they may have contributed to her death. Based on the play by J.B. Priestley. *Dir*. Guy Hamilton.

Intelligence Men, The (1965) Eric Morecambe (Eric), Ernie Wise (Ernie Sage), William Franklyn (Colonel Grant), April Olrich (Madame Petrovna), Gloria Paul (Gina Carlotti), Richard Vernon (Sir Edward Seabrook), David Lodge (Stage Manager), Jacqueline Jones (Karin), Terence Alexander (Reed), Francis Matthews (Thomas), Warren Mitchell (Prozoroff), Peter Bull (Philippe), Tutte Lemkow (Seedy Schlecht Agent), Brian Oulton (Laundry Basket Man), Johnny Briggs (Boy in cinema), Joe Melia (Conductor). Coffee shop manager Eric helps MI5 office worker Ernie stumble across an assassination plot. The comic denouement takes place during a performance of *Swan Lake*. *Dir*. Robert Asher.

Intent to Kill (1958) Richard Todd (Dr. Bob McLaurin), Betsy Drake (Dr. Nancy Ferguson), Herbert Lom (Juan Menda), Warren Stevens (Finch), Carlo Giustini (Francisco Flores), Paul Carpenter (O'Brien), Alexander Knox (Dr. McNeill), Lisa Gastoni (Carla Menda), Peter Arne (Kral), Catherine Boyle (Margaret McLaurin), John Crawford (Boyd), Kay Callard (Carol's Friend), Jackie Collins (Carol Freeman), John McLaren (Anaesthetist), Maggie Rennie (Night Nurse), Brenda Dunrich (Day Nurse), Natalie Lynn (McNeill's Secretary), Kathryn Sadler (Night Receptionist), Nancy Lewis (Day Receptionist), Ann Stephens (Nurse), Hedger Wallace (Autopsy Doctor), Mark Baker (Autopsy Orderly), William Sherwood (Mr. Hardy), Stella Bonheur (Mrs. Hardy). Whilst a trio of assassins stalks the hospital corridors, Dr McLaurin has to operate on a South American. *Dir*. Jack Cardiff.

Interrupted Journey, The (1949) Valerie Hobson (Carol North), Richard Todd (John North), Christine Norden (Susan Wilding), Tom Walls (Mr Clayton), Alexander Gauge (Jerves Wilding), Ralph Truman (Insp Waterson), Vida Hope (Miss Marchmont), Vincent Ball (1st Workman), Jack Vyvian (2nd Workman), Dora Bryan (Waitress), Cyril Smith (Publican), Elsie Wagstaff (Wilding's Maid), Dora Sevening (Mrs Wilding Snr), Nigel Neilson (Sgt Sanger), Arthur Lane (PC Cowley), Roger Moore (Soldier in Paddington Café), Arnold Ridley (Mr Saunders). John is travelling on a train with his mistress but feels they are being followed. He pulls the communication chord and jumps from the train, which has stopped near his home. The stopped train is then wrecked in a crash with many dead. *Dir*. Daniel Birt.

Intimate Stranger, The (1956) Richard Basehart (Reginald 'Reggie' Wilson), Mary Murphy (Evelyn Stewart), Constance Cummings (Kay Wallace), Roger Livesey (Ben Case), Faith Brook (Lesley Wilson), Mervyn Johns (Ernest Chaple), Vernon Greeves (George Mearns), André Mikhelson (Steve Vadney), David Lodge (Police Sgt. Brown), Basil Dignam (Dr. Gray), Grace Denbigh Russell (Mrs. Lynton), Joseph Losey (Director), Marianne Stone (Miss Cedrick). A film editor is harassed by a woman who claims they had an affair but whom he can't remember. *Dir*. Joseph Losey.

Into the Blue (1950) Michael Wilding (Nicholas Foster), Odile Versois (Jackie), Jack Hulbert (John Fergusson), Constance Cummings (Mrs. Kate Fergusson), Edward Rigby (Bill), Betty Paul (Singer). When a couple decides to sail a yacht to Norway

little did they think they would become involved with smugglers and end up in Paris. *Dir*. Herbert Wilcox.

Into the West (1992) Gabriel Byrne (Papa Riley), Ellen Barkin (Kathleen), Ciarán Fitzgerald (Ozzie), Rúaidhrí Conroy (Tito), David Kelly (Grandfather), Johnny Murphy (Tracker), Colm Meaney (Barreller), John Kavanagh (Hartnett), Brendan Gleeson (Inspector Bolger), Jim Norton (Superintendent O'Mara), Anita Reeves (Mrs. Murphy), Ray McBride (Mr. Murphy), Dave Duffy (Morrissey), Stuart Dannell-Foran (Conor Murphy), Becca Hollinshead (Birdy Murphy). When their storytelling grandfather gives them a beautiful white horse called Tír na nÓg, Ozzie and Tito decide to keep it in the flat of the Dublin tower block they live in. When the horse is stolen the adventure begins. *Dir*. Mike Newell.

Invasion (1965) Edward Judd (Dr. Mike Vernon), Yoko Tani (Leader of the Lystrians), Valerie Gearon (Dr. Claire Harland), Lyndon Brook (Brian Carter), Ric Young (Lystrian), Tsai Chin (Nurse Lim), Barrie Ingham (Major Muncaster), Anthony Sharp (Lawrence Blackburn), Glyn Houston (Police Sergeant Draycott), John Tate (Dundy), Jean Lodge (Barbara Gough), Tony Wall (Ted), Peter Thomas (Harry), Cali Raia (Lystrian), Mark Kingston (Morgan), Emrys Leyshon (Sergeant Williams), Leonard Cracknell (Lloyd), Stephanie Bidmead (Elaine), Norman Mitchell (Lorry driver). A spaceship crashes to earth and survivors are taken to a rural hospital. The facility is then surrounded by a forcefield. *Dir*. Alan Bridges.

Ipcress File, The (1965) Michael Caine (Harry Palmer), Nigel Green (Major Dalby), Guy Doleman (Colonel Ross), Sue Lloyd (Jean Courtney), Gordon Jackson (Carswell), Aubrey Richards (Dr. Radcliffe), Frank Gatliff (Bluejay), Thomas Baptiste (Barney), Oliver MacGreevy (Housemartin), Freda Bamford (Alice), Pauline Winter (Charlady), Stanley Meadows (Inspector Keightley), Glynn Edwards (Police Station Sergeant), Harry Andrews (Man on Train). British Intelligence Officer Harry Palmer is assigned to investigate the kidnapping and brainwashing of Western scientists. IPCRESS stands for Induction of Psychoneuroses by Conditioned Reflex Under Stress. A downbeat view of Cold War espionage, in stark contrast to the James Bond films. Based on Len Deighton's novel. *Dir*. Sidney J. Furie.

Iris (2001) Kate Winslet (Young Iris Murdoch), Hugh Bonneville (Young John Bayley), Judi Dench (Iris Murdoch), Jim Broadbent (John Bayley), Juliet Aubrey (Young Janet Stone), Charlotte Arkwright (Young Phillida Stone), Harriet Arkwright (Young Emma Stone), Penelope Wilton (Janet Stone), Saira Todd (Phillida Stone), Juliet Howland (Emma Stone), Matilda Allsopp (Little Stone), Samuel West (Young Maurice), Timothy West (Older Maurice), Eleanor Bron (Principal), Angela Morant (Hostess), Siobhan Hayes (Check-Out Girl), Joan Bakewell (BBC Presenter), Nancy Carroll (BBC PA), Kris Marshall (Dr. Gudgeon), Tom Mannion (Neurologist), Pauline McLynn (Maureen), Gabrielle Reidy (Tricia). A biopic of the author Iris Murdoch as seen through the eyes of her husband John. The film follows the seemingly mismatched couple in excerpts of their lives from a first meeting at university through to the struggles in later life as Iris begins to suffer from dementia. The film won an Academy Award: Best Actor in a Supporting Role (Jim Broadbent). It is based on Bayley's memoir *Elegy for Iris*. *Dir*. Richard Eyre.

Iron Duke, The (1934) George Arliss (Duke of Wellington), Ellaline Terriss (Kitty, Duchess of Wellington), Gladys Cooper (Duchess d'Angoulême), A.E. Matthews (Lord Hill), Peter Gawthorne (Duke of Richmond), Felix Aylmer (Lord Uxbridge), Lesley Wareing (Lady Frances Webster), Alan Aynesworth (Louis XVIII), Emlyn Williams (Bates), Edmund Willard (Marshal Ney), Norma Varden (Duchess of Richmond), Gerald Lawrence (Lord Castelreagh), Gibb McLaughlin (Talleyrand), Farren Soutar (Metternich), Walter Sondes (Wedderburn Webster), Frederick Leister (King of Prussia), Gyles Isham (Czar of Russia), Annie Esmond (Denise), Franklin Dyall (Blücher), Campbell Gullan (D'Artois), Norman Shelley (Pozzo d Borgo), Peter Gawthorne (Duke of Richmond), The life and career of the

Duke of Wellington from 1810 until the Battle of Waterloo in 1815. *Dir*. Victor Saville.

Iron Maiden, The (1963) Michael Craig (Jack Hopkins), Anne Helm (Kathy Fisher), Jeff Donnell (Miriam Fisher), Alan Hale Jr. (Paul Fisher), Noel Purcell (Admiral Sir Digby Trevelyan), Cecil Parker (Sir Giles Thompson), Roland Culver (Lord Upshott), Joan Sims (Nellie Trotter), John Standing (Humphrey Gore-Brown), Brian Oulton (Vicar), Sam Kydd (Fred Trotter), Judith Furse (Mrs. Webb), Richard Thorp (Harry Markham), Jim Dale (Bill), George Woodbridge (Sid Ludge), Brian Rawlinson (Albert), Raymond Glendenning (Commentator - voice), Anton Rodgers (Member of hotel staff). An aircraft designer must persuade an American millionaire to place an order for a new supersonic jet. The action centres on Jack Hopkin's traction engine *The Iron Maiden* and his attempt to win a rally with the help of millionaire Fisher and Fisher's daughter. *Dir*. Gerald Thomas.

Iron, Lady, The (2011) Meryl Streep (Margaret Thatcher), Jim Broadbent (Denis Thatcher), Alexandra Roach (Young Margaret Thatcher), Harry Lloyd (Young Denis Thatcher), Olivia Colman (Carol Thatcher), Anthony Head (Geoffrey Howe), Nicholas Farrell (Airey Neave), Richard E. Grant (Michael Heseltine), Paul Bentley (Douglas Hurd), Robin Kermode (John Major), John Sessions (Edward Heath), Roger Allam (Gordon Reece), Michael Pennington (Michael Foot), Angus Wright (John Nott), Julian Wadham (Francis Pym), Reginald Green (Ronald Reagan). A biopic of British Prime Minister Margaret Thatcher told mainly in flashback depicting the great lady (rather controversially) as suffering from advanced dementia in the present day. The film won two Academy Awards: Best Makeup (Mark Coulier and J. Roy Helland) and Best Actress (Meryl Streep). *Dir*. Phyllida Lloyd.

Isadora (1968) Vanessa Redgrave (Isadora Duncan), John Fraser (Roger), James Fox (Gordon Craig), Jason Robards (Singer), Zvonimir Crnko (Sergey Esenin), Vladimir Leskovar (Bugatti), Cynthia Harris (Mary Desti), Bessie Love (Mrs. Duncan), Tony Vogel (Raymond Duncan), Libby Glenn (Elizabeth Duncan), Ronnie Gilbert (Miss Chase), Wallas Eaton (Archer), Nicholas Pennell (Bedford), John Quentin (Pim), Christian Duvaleix (Armand), Stefan Gryff (Russian Party Interpreter). A biopic of dancer Isadora Duncan. *Dir*. Karel Reisz.

Island of Terror (1966) Peter Cushing (Dr Brian Stanley), Edward Judd (Dr David West), Carole Gray (Toni Merrill), Eddie Byrne (Dr Reginald Landers), Sam Kydd (Constable John Harris), Niall MacGinnis (Roger Campbell), James Caffrey (Peter Argyle), Liam Gaffney (Ian Bellows), Roger Heathcote (Dunley), Keith Bell (Halsey), Margaret Lacey (Old Woman), Shay Gorman (Morton), Peter Forbes-Robertson (Dr Lawrence Phillips), Richard Bidlake (Carson), Joyce Hemson (Mrs Bellows). Scientists seeking a cure for cancer on Petrie's Island accidently create creatures which kill by dissolving the bones of their victims. *Dir*. Terence Fisher.

It Always Rains on Sunday (1947) Googie Withers (Rose Sandigate), Edward Chapman (George Sandigate), Susan Shaw (Vi Sandigate), Patricia Plunkett (Doris Sandigate), David Lines (Alfie Sandigate), Sydney Tafler (Morry Hyams), Betty Ann Davies (Sadie Hyams), John Slater (Lou Hyams), Jane Hylton (Bessie Hyams), Meier Tzelniker (Solly Hyams), John McCallum (Tommy Swann), Jimmy Hanley (Whitey), John Carol (Freddie), Alfie Bass (Dicey Perkins), Jack Warner (Det. Sergt. Fothergill), Frederick Piper (Det. Sergt. Leech), Michael Howard (Slopey Collins), Hermione Baddeley (Mrs. Spry), Nigel Stock (Ted Edwards), John Salew (Caleb Neesley), Gladys Henson (Mrs. Neesley), Edie Martin (Mrs. Watson), Betty Bascomb (Barmaid of the 'Two Compasses'), Gilbert Davis (Governor of the 'Two Compasses'), Al Millen (Bill Hawkins), Vida Hope (Mrs. Wallis), Arthur Hambling (Yardmaster), Grace Arnold (Ted's Landlady), John Vere (Rev. Black), Patrick Jones (Chuck Evans), Joe E. Carr (Joe), Fred Griffiths (Sam), Francis O'Rawe (Bertie Potts), Sid James (Bandleader). A gritty, realistic film concerning the events of one Sunday in Bethnal Green. A housewife is persuaded to hide a former lover who is on the run from the police. *Dir*. Robert Hamer.

It Happened Here (1966) Pauline Murray (Pauline), Sebastian Shaw (Doctor Richard Fletcher), Bart Allison (Skipworth), Reginald Marsh (Immediate Action Medical Officer), Frank Bennett (IA Political Leader), Nicolette Bernard (IA Woman Commandant), Nicholas Moore (IA Group Leader Moorfield), Rex Collett (IA NCO), Peter Dineley (German Officer), Honor Fearson (Honor Hutton), Bertha Russell (Matron), Miles Halliwell (IA Political Lecturer), Carole James (IA Girl), Bill Thomas (IA Group Leader), Stella Kemball (Nurse Drayton), Ralph Wilson (Dr. Walton), Fiona Leland (Helen Fletcher), Alfred Ziemen (German Officer). A film which takes the proposition that the Nazis successfully invaded Britain in 1940. Set in 1944-45 as allied forces begin to menace occupied Britain, apolitical Irish nurse Pauline is at some points a collaborator although her allegiances are never firm one way or another. *Dirs*. Kevin Brownlow and Andrew Mollo.

It Happened One Sunday (1944) Robert Beatty (Tom Stevens), Barbara White (Moya Malone), Marjorie Rhodes (Mrs Buckland), Ernest Butcher (Mr Buckland), Judy Kelly (Violet), Kathleen Harrison (Mrs Purkiss), Irene Vanbrugh (Mrs Bellamy), Moore Marriott (Porter), C.V. France (Magistrate), Marie Ault (Madame), Brefni O'Rorke (Engineer), Charles Victor (Frisco Kid), Paul Demel (Cassio), Philip Green (Bandleader), Robert Adams (Gorilla Jim), Kathryn Beaumont (Jill Buckland), On one Sunday in Liverpool a nurse meets and falls in love with a serviceman. *Dir*. Karel Lamac.

It Started in Paradise (1952) Jane Hylton (Martha Watkins), Ian Hunter (Arthur Turner), Terence Morgan (Edouard), Muriel Pavlow (Alison), Martita Hunt (Mme. Alice), Brian Worth (Michael), Ronald Squire (Mary Jane), Kay Kendall (Lady Caroline Frencham), Joyce Barbour (Lady Burridge), Harold Lang (Mr. Louis), Margaret Withers (Miss Madge), Lucienne Hill (Madame Lucienne), Diana Decker (Crystal Leroy), Arthur Lane (Sydney Bruce), Dana Wynter (Barbara), June Brown (Announcer), Conrad Phillips (1st Photographer), Bill Travers (2nd Photographer). Set in the world of *haute couture* this film gained the reputation of being the *All About Eve* of the fashion world. Over a period of thirteen years between 1938 and 1951 fashion designers are ousted by younger assistants as fashions change. Thus Martha replaces Alice only to be replaced in her turn by Alison. *Dir*. Compton Bennett.

It's All Happening (1963) Tommy Steele (Billy Bowles), Michael Medwin (Max Catlin), Angela Douglas (Julie Singleton), Jean Harvey (Delia), Bernard Bresslaw (Parsons), Walter Hudd (J.B. Magdeburg), John Tate (Julian Singleton), Janet Henfrey (April), Richard Goolden (Lord Sweatstone), Keith Faulkner (Mick), Edward Cast (Hugh), Anthony Dawes (Cyril Bong), Barbara Clegg (Miss Ventnor), Iris Russell (Nellie), Abril Ward (Penny), Michael Thompson (Pete), Jeffrey Chandler (Herbert), Robert Dean (Geoff Munday), Bryan Parker (Archie), Anthony Pelly (Norman Winten). Musical. Billy works in a recording studio and arranges a charity pop concert to raise funds for the orphanage where he was brought up. *Dir*. Don Sharp.

Italian Job, The (1969) Michael Caine (Charlie Croker), Noel Coward (Mr Bridger), Benny Hill (Prof Simon Peach), Raf Vallone (Altabani), Tony Beckley ('Camp' Freddie), Rossano Brazzi (Roger Beckerman), Margaret Blye (Lorna), Irene Handle (Miss Peach), John Le Mesurier (Governor), Fred Emney (Birkinshaw), Robert Powell (Yellow), Simon Dee (Shirtmaker), Henry McGee (Tailor). Charlie Croker has a plan to steal $4 million of gold from Italy and breaks into prison to persuade Mr Bridger to finance it. The film is noted for its unforgettable lines (Croker's "You're only supposed to blow the bloody doors off!" was voted the most memorable line from any film in a 2003 poll), the red, white and blue Minis careering through the streets, buildings, rivers, sewers and rooftops of Turin, plus its literal cliffhanger ending. Dir. Peter Collinson.

It's a Wonderful Afterlife (2010) Shabana Azmi (Mrs. Sethi), Goldy Notay (Roopi), Sendhil Ramamurthy (Raj), Sally Hawkins (Linda/Geetali), Zoë Wanamaker (Mrs. Goldsmith), Sanjeev Bhaskar (The Curry Man), Catherine Balavage (Waitress), Shaheen Khan (Manjeet Kahl/The Kebab Woman), Adlyn Ross (Mrs. Chakra/The Rolling Pin Woman), Ash Varrez (Mr. Chakra/The Naan Man), Mark Addy (D.I. Smythe), Jimi Mistry (Dev), Ray Panthaki (Jazz). Mrs Sethi starts killing her daughter's failed suitors by using poisoned curry. *Dir*. Gurinder Chadha

It's in the Air (1938) George Formby (George Brown), Polly Ward (Peggy), Jack Hobbs (Cpl. Craig), Julien Mitchell (The

Sergeant Major), Garry Marsh (Commanding Officer Hill), Ilena Sylva (Anne Brown), Frank Leighton (Pvt. Bob Bullock), C. Denier Warren (Sir Philip), Michael Shepley (Adjutant), Hal Gordon (Nobby Clark), Joe Cunningham (Flight Sergeant), Jack Melford (Lt. Terry). George has been rejected by the RAF, however a couple of excursions on a motorbike and an aeroplane might just change their mind. *Dir.* Anthony Kimmins.

It's Not Cricket (1949) Basil Radford (Maj. Bright), Naunton Wayne (Capt. Early), Susan Shaw (Primrose Brown), Maurice Denham (Otto Fisch), Nigel Buchanan (Gerald Lawson), Alan Wheatley (Felix), Jane Carr (Virginia Briscoe), Patrick Waddington (Valentine Christmas), Edward Lexy (Brig. Falcon), Leslie Dwyer (Batman), Frederick Piper (Yokel), Diana Dors (Blonde), Mary Hinton (Lady Lawson), Margaret Withers (Mrs. Falcon), Brian Oulton (Simon Herbage), John Boxer (MP 1), Cyril Chamberlain (MP 2), Charles Cullum (Sir Leslie Lawson), Hal Osmond (Stage manager), Sheila Huntington (Shoe shop assistant), John Warren (Orderly), Arthur Hambling (Barman), Hamilton Keene (Intelligence sergeant). Demobbed because of incompetence ex-army officers Messrs Bright and Early decide to go into the detecting business. More by luck than judgement they manage to solve a diamond theft during a cricket match. Wayne and Radford had first appeared together in Hitchcock's *The Lady Vanishes* in 1938 as cricket mad pair Charters and Caldicott. *Dirs.* Roy Rich and Alfred Roome.

Jabberwocky (1977) Michael Palin (Dennis), Harry H. Corbett (The Squire), Warren Mitchell (Mr. Fishfinger), John Le Mesurier (Passelewe, the Chamberlain), Annette Badland (Griselda Fishfinger), Max Wall (King Bruno the Questionable/Voice of Red Herring), Deborah Fallender (The Princess), Rodney Bewes (The Other Squire), John Bird (1st Herald), Neil Innes (2nd Herald), Bernard Bresslaw (Landlord), Alexandra Dane (Landlord's Wife), Brian Glover (Armourer), Derrick O'Connor (Flying Hogfish Peasant), Peter Cellier (First Merchant), Derek Francis (Bishop), Gorden Kaye (Sister Jessica), Ted Milton (The Puppeteer), David Prowse (Red Herring and Black Knights), Terry Gilliam (Man with Rock), Terry Jones (Poacher). Fantasy black comedy. When Dennis Cooper goes to town he finds he must defend the realm against the monster threatening it. *Dir* Terry Gilliam

Jack and Sarah (1995) Richard E. Grant (Jack), Samantha Mathis (Amy), Judi Dench (Margaret), Eileen Atkins (Phil), Cherie Lunghi (Anna), Imogen Stubbs (Sarah), Ian McKellen (William), David Swift (Michael), Kate Hardie (Pamela), Laurent Grévill (Alain), Niven Boyd (Nathaniel), Tracy Thorne (Susan), Lorraine Ashbourne (Jackie), Deborah Findlay (Miss Cartwright), Claire Toeman (Health Visitor), Geff Francis (Rob). When Jack's wife Sarah dies in childbirth he is forced by his in-laws to overcome his grief and take care of his new baby daughter, also called Sarah. One day he meets Amy in a café and decides to take her on as Sarah's nanny. *Dir.* Tim Sullivan.

Jack the Ripper (1959) Lee Patterson (Sam Lowry), Eddie Byrne (Insp O'Neill), Betty McDowall (Anne Ford), Ewen Solon (Sir David Rogers), John Le Mesurier (Dr Tranter), George Rose (Clarke), Philip Leaver (Music Hall Manager), Barbara Burke (Kitty Knowles), Anne Sharp (Helen), Denis Shaw (Simes), Jack Allen (Asst. Commissioner Hodges), Jane Taylor (Hazel), Dorinda Stevens (Margaret), Hal Osmond (Snakey the pickpocket), George Street (Station Sgt), Olwen Brookes (Lady Almoner), Endre Muller (Louis Benz), Esma Cannon (Nelly), George Woodbridge (Blake), Bill Shine (Lord Tom Sopwith), Marianne Stone (Drunken Woman), Garard Green (Dr Urquhart), Charles Lamb (Harry), Jennifer White (Beth), Cameron Hall (Hospital Porter), Alan Robinson (Coroner), Anthony Sagar (Drunk), John Mott (Singer), Lucy Griffiths (Salvation Army Woman), Jack the Ripper is on his 1888 killing spree but in this film is brought to justice thanks to the help of an American detective. *Dirs.* Robert S. Baker and Monty Berman.

Jackboots on Whitehall (2010) Voice cast: Ewan McGregor (Chris), Rosamund Pike (Daisy), Richard E. Grant (The Vicar), Timothy Spall (Winston Churchill), Tom Wilkinson (Albert and Joseph Goebbels), Dominic West (Fiske), Alan Cumming (Adolf Hitler and Braveheart), Sanjeev Bhaskar (Major Rupee), Richard Griffiths (Hermann Göring), Richard O'Brien (Heinrich Himmler), Stephen Merchant (Tom), Pam Ferris (Matron Rutty), Hugh Fraser (Gaston and the Newsreader), Tobias Menzies (Captain English), Neil Newbon (Zeppelin Captain). An animation using puppets. The film posits an alternative history when, after the Nazis have successfully invaded using a channel tunnel, the defence of Britain takes place on Hadrian's Wall. *Dirs.* Edward McHenry and Rory McHenry.

Jamaica Inn (1939) Charles Laughton (Sir Humphrey Pengallan), Leslie Banks (Joss Merlyn), Emlyn Williams (Harry the pedlar), Robert Newton (James 'Jem' Trehearne), Marie Ney (Patience Merlyn), Maureen O'Hara (Mary Yellen), Horace Hodges (Butler), Hay Petrie (Groom), Frederick Piper (Agent), Herbert Lomas (Tenant), Clare Greet (Tenant), William Devlin (Tenant), Jeanne De Casalis (Sir Humphrey's friend), Mabel Terry-Lewis (Lady Beston), A. Bromley Davenport (Ringwood), George Curzon (Captain Murray), Basil Radford (Lord George). In the early 19th century a gang of wreckers (smugglers who lure ships onto rocks in order to rob them) are based at Jamaica Inn in Cornwall. Jem and Mary try to stop them. Adapted from Daphne du Maurier's novel of the same name. *Dir.* Alfred Hitchcock.

Jason and the Argonauts (1963) Todd Armstrong (Jason), Nancy Kovack (Medea), Gary Raymond (Acastus), Laurence Naismith (Argos), Niall MacGinnis (Zeus), Michael Gwynn (Hermes), Douglas Wilmer (Pelias), Jack Gwillim (King Aeetes), Honor Blackman (Hera), John Cairney (Hylas), Patrick Troughton (Phineas), Andrew Faulds (Phalerus), Nigel Green (Hercules). The classic story of Jason and his quest for the Golden Fleece, with equally classic stop-motion monsters created by Ray Harryhausen, including the army of skeletons. *Dir.* Don Chaffey.

Jassy (1947) Margaret Lockwood (Jassy Woodroofe), Patricia Roc (Dilys Helmar), Dennis Price (Christopher Hatton), Basil Sydney (Nick Helmar), Dermot Walsh (Barney Hatton), Esma Cannon (Lindy Wicks), Cathleen Nesbitt (Elizabeth Twisdale), Linden Travers (Beatrice Helmar), Nora Swinburne (Mrs. Hatton), Ernest Thesiger (Sir Edward Follesmark), Jean Cadell (Meggie), Grace Arnold (Housemaid), John Laurie (Tom Woodroofe), Grey Blake (Stephen Fennell), Bryan Coleman (Sedley), Clive Morton (Sir William Fennell), Torin Thatcher (Bob Wicks), Beatrice Varley (Mrs. Wicks), Eliot Makeham (Moult), Maurice Denham (Jim Stoner), Joan Haythorne (Kathleen Hamilton), Alan Wheatley (Sir Edward Walker), Hugh Pryse (Sir John Penty), Alfie Bass (Witness), Noel Howlett (Court Usher), Brefni O'Rorke (Fielding), Stewart Rome (Judge), Susan Shaw (Cecily). A Gainsborough melodrama set in the 19th century which centres on gypsy girl Jassy Woodroofe, the Mordelaine Estate, her love for Barney, who was once heir to that estate and the murder of Nick, who won the estate from Barney's father in a card game. *Dir.* Bernard Knowles.

Jew Suss (1934) Conrad Veidt (Josef 'Jew Süss' Oppenheimer), Benita Hume (Marie Auguste), Frank Vosper (Duke Karl Alexander), Cedric Hardwicke (Rabbi Gabriel), Gerald du Maurier (Weissensee), Paul Graetz (Landauer), Pamela Mason (Naomi Oppenheimer). Although set in 18th Wurtenburg, the film was intended to be a commentary on the rise of anti-Semitism in 1930s Germany. An adaptation of Lion Feuchtwanger's novel of the same name. *Dir.* Lothar Mendes.

Joe Macbeth (1955) Paul Douglas (Joe MacBeth), Ruth Roman (Lily MacBeth), Bonar Colleano (Lennie), Grégoire Aslan (Mr. del Duca), Sid James (Banky), Harry Green (Big Dutch), Walter Crisham (Angus), Kay Callard (Ruth), Robert Arden (Ross), George Margo (Second Assassin), Minerva Pious (Rosie), Philip Vickers (Tommy), Mark Baker (Benny), Bill Nagy (Marty), Al Mulock (First Assassin), Victor Baring (Chef), Shirley Douglas (Patsy). Modern retelling of Shakespeare's *Macbeth*, this time set amongst gangsters in America. *Dir.* Ken Hughes.

Johnny English (2003) Rowan Atkinson (Johnny English), Ben Miller (Angus Bough), Natalie Imbruglia (Lorna Campbell), John Malkovich (Pascal Sauvage), Oliver Ford Davies (Archbishop of Canterbury), Tim Pigott-Smith (Pegasus), Kevin McNally (Prime Minister), Douglas McFerran (Klaus/Carlos Vendetta), Greg Wise

(Agent One), Tim Berrington (Roger), Tasha de Vasconcelos (Countess Alexandra), Steve Nicolson (Dieter Klein), Jenny Galloway (Foreign Secretary), Chris Tarrant (Radio announcer – voice), Trevor McDonald (Newscaster - voice). Secret agent spoof. Inept Johnny English finds himself as top British agent after all the others are killed. He must foil the dastardly plan of Frenchman Sauvage to claim the British throne, helped by the beautiful and competent Lorna. *Dir*. Peter Howitt.

Johnny English Reborn (2011) Rowan Atkinson (Johnny English), Gillian Anderson (Pamela Thornton), Rosamund Pike (Kate Sumner), Dominic West (Simon Ambrose), Daniel Kaluuya (Agent Tucker), Richard Schiff (Titus Fisher), Tim McInnerny (Patch Quartermain), Mark Ivanir (Artem Karlenko), Burn Gorman (Slater), Joséphine Baume (Madeleine), Pik-Sen Lim (Killer Cleaner), Togo Igawa (Ting Wang), Stephen Campbell Moore (British Prime Minister), Roger Barclay (Agent Two), Eric Carte (Agent One). Johnny must foil a plot to assassinate the premier of China. Comedy spy thriller sequel to *Johnny English*. *Dir*. Oliver Parker.

Johnny Frenchman (1945) Françoise Rosay (Lanec Florrie), Tom Walls (Nat Pomeroy), Patricia Roc (Sue Pomeroy), Ralph Michael (Bob Tremayne), Paul Dupuis (Yan Kervarec), Frederick Piper (Zacky Penrose), Arthur Hambling (Steven Matthews), Richard George (Charlie West), Bill Blewitt (Dick Trewhiddle), James Harcourt (Joe Pender), Richard Harrison (Tim Bassett), Stan Paskin (Sam Olds), James Knight (Tom Hocking), Leslie Harcourt (Jack Nicholas), John Stone (Sam Harvey), George Hirste (Dave Pascoe), Carol O'Connor (Mr Harper), Franklyn Bennett (Sgt), Bernard Fishwick (Exciseman), Herbert Thomas (Spargoe), Denver Hall (Billy Pomeroy), Vincent Holman (Truscott), Alfie Bass (Cpl), Grace Arnold (Mrs Matthews), Beatrice Varley (Mrs Tremayne), Judith Furse (June Matthews), Drusilla Wills (Miss Bennett), Paul Bonifas (Jerome), Henri Bollinger (Alain), Jean-Marie Balcon (Malo), Louis Gournay (Yves), Charles Jezequel (Bob), Jean-Marie Nacry (Grandpere), Joseph Menou (Mattieu). Rivalries between Cornish and Breton fishermen subside as World War II breaks out. *Dir*. Charles Frend.

Jokers, The (1967) Michael Crawford (Michael), Oliver Reed (David), Harry Andrews (Supt Marryatt), James Donald (Col Gurney-Simms), Daniel Massey (Riggs), Michael Hordern (Sir Matthew), Gabriella Licudi (Eve), Lotte Tarp (Inge), Frank Finlay (Harassed man), Warren Mitchell (Lennie), Rachel Kempson (Mrs Tremayne), Peter Graves (Mr Tremayne), Ingrid Boulting (Sarah), Brian Wilde (Sgt Catchpole), Edward Fox (Lt Sprague), Michael Goodliffe (Lt Colonel Paling). Brothers Michael and David Tremayne plan to steal the Crown Jewels. *Dir*. Michael Winner.

Jubilee (1978) Jenny Runacre (Queen Elizabeth I/Bod), Nell Campbell (Crabs), Toyah Willcox (Mad), Jordan (Amyl Nitrite), Hermine Demoriane (Chaos), Ian Charleson (Angel), Karl Johnson (Sphinx), Linda Spurrier (Viv), Neil Kennedy (Max), Jack Birkett (Borgia Ginz), Jayne County (Lounge Lizard), Richard O'Brien (John Dee), David Brandon Ariel (as David Haughton), Helen Wellington-Lloyd (Lady in Waiting), Adam Ant (Kid), Claire Davenport (First Customs Lady), Donald Dunham (Policeman), Iris Fry (Bingo lady), Quinn Hawkins (Boy), Barney James (Policeman), Lindsay Kemp (Cabaret performer), Ulla Larson-Styles (Waitress), Howard Malin (Schmeitzer), Luciana Martínez (Escort to Borgia), William Merrow (Maurice), Gene October (Happy Days), Prudence Walters (Escort to Borgia), Joyce Windsor (Bingo Lady). When alchemist John Dee transports Elizabeth I into the late 1970s she finds a broken Britain. *Dir*. Derek Jarman.

Jude (1996) Christopher Eccleston (Jude Fawley), Kate Winslet (Sue Bridehead), Liam Cunningham (Phillotson), Rachel Griffiths (Arabella), June Whitfield (Aunt Drusilla), Berwick Kaler (Farmer Troutham), David Tennant (Drunk Undergraduate), Ross Colvin Turnbull (Little Jude), James Daley (Jude as a boy), James Nesbitt (Uncle Joe), Mark Lambert (Tinker Taylor), Paul Bown (Uncle Jim), Paul Copley (Mr. Willis), Dexter Fletcher (Priest). Jude and Sue leave their respective spouses and embark on a life of struggle and, ultimately, tragedy. Based on Thomas Hardy's novel *Jude the Obscure*. *Dir*. Michael Winterbottom.

Juggernaut (1936) Boris Karloff (Dr Victor Sartorius), Joan Wyndham (Nurse Eve Rowe), Arthur Margetson (Roger Clifford), Mona Goya (Lady Yvonne Clifford), Anthony Ireland (Capt Arthur Halliday), Morton Selten (Sir Charles Clifford), Nina Boucicault (Miss Mary Clifford), Gibb McLaughlin (Jacques), J.H. Roberts (Chalmers), Victor Rietti (Dr Bousquet). A dying doctor in need of funds to complete his research, accepts £20,000 from Lady Clifford to poison her ageing husband. *Dir*. Henry Edwards.

Juggernaut (1974) Richard Harris (Lt. Cmdr. Anthony Fallon), Omar Sharif (Captain Alex Brunel), David Hemmings (Charlie Braddock), Anthony Hopkins (Supt. John McLeod), Shirley Knight (Barbara Bannister), Ian Holm (Nicholas Porter), Clifton James (Corrigan), Roy Kinnear (Social Director Curtain), Caroline Mortimer (Susan McLeod), Mark Burns (Hollingsworth), John Stride (Hughes), Freddie Jones (Sidney Buckland), Julian Glover (Commander Marder), Jack Watson (Chief Engineer Mallicent), Roshan Seth (Azad), Kenneth Colley (Detective Brown), Andy Bradford (3rd Officer Jim Hardy), Paul Antrim (Digby), Ben Aris (The Walker), John Bindon (Driscoll), Adam Bridge (David McLeod), Rebecca Bridge (Nancy McLeod), Tom Chadbon (Juggernaut's Contact), Kenneth Cope (Bridgeman), Michael Egan (Mr. Fowlers), Simon MacCorkindale (No.1 Helmsman), Gareth Thomas (Liverpool Joiner), Cyril Cusack (Major O'Neill), Michael Hordern (Mr. Baker). Whilst his ship, the SS *Britannic*, is crossing the Atlantic, the owner is informed that unless he pays £500,000, seven bombs on board the ship will explode. A team of bomb disposal experts is parachuted aboard in an attempt to defuse the devices. *Dir*. Richard Lester.

Jules Verne's Rocket to the Moon (1967) Burl Ives (Phineas T. Barnum), Jimmy Clitheroe (Gen Tom Thumb), Terry-Thomas (Capt Sir Harry Washington Smythe), Graham Stark (Bertram Grundle), Gert Fröbe (Prof Siegfried von Bulow), Lionel Jeffries (Sir Charles Dillworthy), Dennis Price (Duke of Barset), Troy Donahue (Gaylord Sullivan), Daliah Lavi (Madelaine), Edward de Souza (Henri), Hermione Gingold (Angelica), Judy Cornwell (Lady Electra), Renate von Holt (Anna Lindstrom), Joachim Teege (Joachim Bulgeroff), Stratford Johns (Warrant Officer), Derek Francis (Puddleby), Anthony Woodruff (Announcer), Hugh Walters (Carruthers), Allan Cuthbertson (Colonel Scuttling), Donald Bisset (Jack Flood), Cecil Nash (Chambers), Vernon Hayden (Mr Brown), John Franklyn (Railway Guard), Harry Brogan (Prof Dingle), Derek Young (French Officer), Joan Sterndale-Bennett (Queen Victoria), Dan Cressy (Kaiser), Sinéad Cusack (Vera), Maurice Denham (Narrator). Sci-fi comedy. Showman Barnum aims to send a rocket to the moon using a huge gun barrel. Loosely based on Verne's *From the Earth to the Moon*. *Dir*. Don Sharp.

Jumping for Joy (1956) Frankie Howerd (Willie Joy), Stanley Holloway (Captain Jack Montague), A.E. Matthews (Lord Reginald Cranfield), Tony Wright (Vincent), Alfie Bass (Blagg), Joan Hickson (Lady Emily Cranfield), Lionel Jeffries (Bert Benton), Susan Beaumont (Susan Storer), Terence Longdon (John Wyndham), Colin Gordon (Max, 1st Commentator), Richard Wattis (Carruthers), Danny Green (Plug Ugly), Barbara Archer (Marlene), William Kendall (Blenkinsop), Ewen Solon (Haines), Reginald Beckwith (Smithers), Gerald Campion (Man with Ice Cream), Andrew Faulds (Drunk's Friend), Bill Fraser (Drunk in Pool Hall), Charles Hawtrey (Punter at Bar), Arthur Mullard (Bruiser). A comedy surrounding greyhound racing and race-fixing. *Dir*. John Paddy Carstairs.

Juno and the Paycock (1930) Barry Fitzgerald (The Orator), Edward Chapman (Captain Boyle), Sidney Morgan ("Joxer" Daly), Sara Allgood (Mrs Boyle, "Juno"), John Laurie (Johnny Boyle), Dave Morris (Jerry Devine), Kathleen O'Regan (Mary Boyle), John Longden (Charles Bentham), Maire O'Neill (Maisie Madigan), Dennis Wyndham (The Mobiliser), Fred Schwartz (Mr Kelly). Juno calls her husband Paycock because he struts around like a peacock but does nothing else. Set in Dublin during the Irish Civil War, the family is told they are due an inheritance and start spending straight away. Based on Sean O'Casey's play. *Dir*. Alfred Hitchcock.

Just My Luck (1957) Norman Wisdom (Norman Hackett), Margaret Rutherford (Mrs Dooley), Jill Dixon (Anne), Leslie Phillips (Hon Richard Lumb), Delphi Lawrence (Miss Daviot),

Joan Sims (Phoebe), Edward Chapman (Mr Stoneway), Peter Copley (Gilbert Weaver), Vic Wise (Eddie Diamond), Marjorie Rhodes (Mrs Hackett), Michael Ward (Cranley), Marianne Stone (Tea Bar Attendant), Felix Felton (Man in Cinema), Michael Brennan (Masseur), Cyril Chamberlain (Goodwood Official), Eddie Leslie (Gas Man), Freda Bamford (Mrs Crossley), Robin Bailey (Steward), Campbell Cotts (Steward), Sam Kydd (Craftsman), Raymond Francis (Ritchie), Sylvia Childs (Kathie), Ballard Berkeley (Starter at Goodwood), Peggy Ann Clifford (Lady on Tube), Stringer Davis (Goodwood Steward), Jerry Desmonde (Racegoer), Bill Fraser (Powell), Sabrina (Herself). Norman puts £1 on a six horse accumulator in the hope of winning enough to buy an engagement ring. When the first five come in his bookmaker panics. *Dir*. John Paddy Carstairs.

Just William (1940) Richard Lupino (William Brown), Fred Emney (Mr Brown), Iris Hoey (Mrs Brown), Basil Radford (Mr Sidway), Amy Veness (Mrs Bott), Roddy McDowall (Ginger), Norman Robinson (Douglas), Peter Miles (Henry), David Tree (Marmaduke Bott), Jenny Laird (Ethel Brown), Simon Lack (Robert Brown), Aubrey Mather (Fletcher). Based on the books by Richmal Crompton. *Dir*. Graham Cutts.

Kaleidoscope (1966) Warren Beatty (Barney), Susannah York (Angel McGinnis), Clive Revill (Insp McGinnis), Eric Porter (Harry Dominion), Murray Melvin (Aimes), George Sewell (Billy), Stanley Meadows (Dominion Captain), John Junkin (Dominion Porter), Larry Taylor (Dominion Chauffeur), Yootha Joyce (Museum Receptionist), Jane Birkin (Exquisite Thing), George Murcell (Johnny), Anthony Newlands (Leeds), Michael Balfour (Poker Player), Stephen Lewis (Truck Driver). Gambler Barney Lincoln hits on a scheme to mark all the cards used in European casinos at the source – the factory in Switzerland where they are made. *Dir*. Jack Smight.

Keep Fit (1937) George Formby (George Green), Kay Walsh (Joan Allen), Guy Middleton (Hector Kent), George Benson (Ernie Gill), Edmund Breon (Sir Augustus Marks), Leo Franklyn (Racing Tough), Hal Gordon (Reporter), Aubrey Mallalieu (Magistrate), Gus McNaughton (Tom), Evelyn Roberts (Barker), Hal Walters (Racing Tough), C. Denier Warren (Editor). Weedy George decides to take up boxing in order to impress a girl. *Dir*. Anthony Kimmins.

Keep Smiling (1938) Gracie Fields (Gracie Gray), Roger Livesey (Bert Wattle), Mary Maguire (Avis Maguire), Peter Coke (Rene Sigani), Jack Donohue (Denis Wilson), Hay Petrie (Jack), Mike Johnson (Charlie), Eddie Gray (Silvo), Tommy Fields, Gladys Dehl, Nino Rossini (The Three Bolas), Edward Rigby (Silas Gray), Joe Mott (Bill Sneed), Philip Leaver (De Courcy), Gus McNaughton (Eddie Perkins). A group of performers club together to buy a bus and travel around the country doing shows. *Dir*. Monty Banks.

Keep Your Seats Please (1936) George Formby (George Withers), Florence Desmond (Florrie), Gus McNaughton (Max), Alastair Sim (A. S. Drayton), Harry Tate (Auctioneer), Enid Stamp-Taylor (Madame Louise), Hal Gordon (Sailor), Tom Payne (Man from Child Welfare), Beatrix Fielden-Kaye (Woman from Child Welfare), Clifford Heatherley (Dr. G. Wilberforce), Binkie Stuart (Binkie). A prospective heir searches for his fortune in a set of chairs. Based on the play *The Twelve Chairs* by Ilya Ilf and Yevgeni Petrov. *Dir*. Monty Banks.

Keeping Mum (2005) Rowan Atkinson (Reverend Walter Goodfellow), Kristin Scott Thomas (Gloria Goodfellow), Maggie Smith ("Grace Hawkins"), Patrick Swayze (Lance), Tamsin Egerton (Holly Goodfellow), Toby Parkes (Petey Goodfellow), Liz Smith (Mrs. Parker), Emilia Fox (Rosie Jones), James Booth (Mr. Brown), Patrick Monckton (Bob), Rowley Irlam (Ted), Vivienne Moore (Mrs. Martin). The reverend Goodfellow is blissfully unaware of his family problems as he prepares a sermon for a bible conference. When the new housekeeper, Grace, arrives all these problems begin to disappear in a rather disturbing way. *Dir*. Niall Johnson.

Kes (1969) David Bradley (Billy Casper), Freddie Fletcher (Jud Casper), Lynne Perrie (Mrs Casper), Colin Welland (Mr Farthing, English Teacher), Brian Glover (Mr Sugden, Games Teacher),

Bob Bowes (Mr Gryce, Headmaster), Bernard Atha (Youth Employment Officer), Joe Miller (Reg, Mother's Friend), Geoffrey Banks (Maths Teacher), Duggie Brown (Milkman), Joey Kaye (Pub comedian), Bill Dean (Fish and Chip Shop Man), Harry Markham (Newsagent). Deprived and bullied at home and school, Billy's future looks to be as grim until the discovery of a young kestrel – which he names Kes – draws encouragement from teachers and schoolmates. Brian Glover is best remembered for the school football match that he both referees and plays in as "the fair-haired and slightly balding Charlton". Based on the novel *A Kestrel for a Knave* by Barry Hines. *Dir*. Ken Loach.

Kevin & Perry Go Large (2000) Harry Enfield (Kevin), Kathy Burke (Perry), Rhys Ifans (Eyeball Paul), James Fleet (Dad), Louisa Rix (Mum), Laura Fraser (Candice), Tabitha Wady (Gemma), Steve O'Donnell (Big Baz), Paul Whitehouse (Bouncer 1), Steve McFadden (Bouncer 2), Natasha Little (Anne Boleyn), Anna Shillinglaw (Bikini Girl), Badi Uzzaman (Norma Baxter), Kenneth Cranham (Vicar), Sam Parks (Police Officer), Frank Harper (Robber), Mark Tonderai (Music Store Boss), Amelia Curtis (Sharon). Teenagers Kevin and Perry accidentally foil a bank raid and with the reward decide to go to Ibiza, become top DJs and lose their virginity. Kevin's mum and dad agree they can go on holiday together as long as they can come along too. Based on characters from *Harry Enfield's Television Programme* and *Harry Enfield and Chums*. *Dir*. Ed Bye.

Key, The (1958) William Holden (Capt David Ross), Sophia Loren (Stella), Trevor Howard (Capt Chris Ford), Oskar Homolka (Capt Van Dam), Kieron Moore (Kane), Bernard Lee (Cmdr Wadlow), Beatrix Lehmann (Housekeeper), Noel Purcell (Hotel Porter), Bryan Forbes (Weaver), Sidney Vivian (Grogan), Rupert Davies (Baker), Russell Waters (Sparks), Irene Handl (Clerk), John Crawford (US Captain), Jameson Clark (English Captain), Carl Möhner (Van Barger). Centres on the commanders of the poorly armed tugboats which are used to rescue ships disabled by enemy action during WWII. The key of the title is the key to Stella's apartment which is handed from one tugboat captain to the next as each man faces his possible death. Based on the novel *Stella* by Jan de Hartog. *Dir*. Carol Reed.

Khartoum (1966) Charlton Heston (General Charles Gordon), Laurence Olivier (The Mahdi), Richard Johnson (Colonel Stewart), Ralph Richardson (William Ewart Gladstone), Alexander Knox (Sir Evelyn Baring), Johnny Sekka (Khaleel), Nigel Green (General Wolseley), Michael Hordern (Lord Granville), Peter Arne (Major Kitchener), Hugh Williams (Lord Hartington), Zia Mohyeddin (Zobeir Pasha), Ralph Michael (Charles Duke), Douglas Wilmer (Khalifa Abdullah), Edward Underdown (William Hicks), Alan Tilvern (Awaan), Marne Maitland (Sheikh Osman), Leo Genn (Narrator), Ronald Leigh-Hunt (Lord Northbrook). An epic re-telling of the siege of Khartoum by the forces of the Mahdi and the death of General Charles "Chinese" Gordon. *Dir*. Basil Dearden.

Kick-Ass (2010) Aaron Johnson (David "Dave" Lizewski/Kick-Ass), Nicolas Cage (Damon Macready/Big Daddy), Chloë Grace Moretz (Mindy Macready/Hit-Girl), Christopher Mintz-Plasse (Chris D'Amico/Red Mist), Mark Strong (Frank D'Amico), Lyndsy Fonseca (Katie Deauxma), Michael Rispoli (Big Joe), Kofi Natei (Rasul), Yancy Butler (Angie D'Amico), Jason Flemyng (Lobby Goon), Elizabeth McGovern (Alice Lizewski), Garrett M. Brown (Mr. Lizewski), Sophie Wu (Erika Cho), Dexter Fletcher (Cody), Clark Duke (Marty), Evan Peters (Todd), Xander Berkeley (Detective Victor "Vic" Gigante), Omari Hardwick (Sergeant Marcus Williams), Deborah Twiss (Mrs. Zane), Stu "Large" Riley (Huge Goon), Craig Ferguson (Himself), John Romita, Jr. (Atomic Comics barista), Hubert Boorder (Oscar Juarez), Christopher McGuire (Diner Fight Guy 1), Max White (Diner Fight Guy 2), Dean Copkov (Diner Fight Guy 3), Jacob Cartwright (Running Teenager), Tamer Hassan (Matthew), Tim Plester (Danil), Omar A. Soriano (Leroy), Val Jobara (Nervous Goon), Joe Bacino (Posh Goon), Kenneth Simmons (Scary Goon), Corey Johnson (Sporty Goon), Anthony Desio (Baby Goon), Adrian Martinez (Ginger Goon), Johnny Hopkins (1st Gang Kid), Ohene Cornelius (2nd Gang Kid), Carlos Besse Peres (Buttons),

234

Randall Batinkoff (Tre Fernandez), Russell Bentley (Medic), Quinn Smith (Big Mean Boy). Comic book fan Dave decides to don a costume and become a super-hero in order to right wrongs. His first mission ends with him being stabbed and run over by a car. However, the nerve damage and reconstructive surgery make him stronger and more impervious to pain. He then becomes an internet hero as Kick-Ass but also attracts the attention of gangster Frank D'Amico. Based on the comic book of the same name by Mark Millar and John Romita, Jr. *Dir.* Matthew Vaughn.

Kid for Two Farthings, A (1955) Celia Johnson (Joanna), Diana Dors (Sonia), David Kossoff (Avrom Kandinsky), Joe Robinson (Sam Heppner), Jonathan Ashmore (Joe), Brenda De Banzie ('Lady' Ruby), Primo Carnera (Python Macklin), Lou Jacobi (Blackie Isaacs), Irene Handl (Mrs Abramowitz), Danny Green (Bully Bason), Sydney Tafler (Madam Rita), Sid James (Ice Berg), Vera Day (Mimi), Daphne Anderson (Dora), Joseph Tomelty (Vagrant), Harold Berens (Oliver), Alfie Bass (Alf the Bird Man), Spike Milligan (Indian with Grey Beard), Barbara Windsor (Blonde with crush on Sam). A little boy buys a kid goat with a small horn believing it to be a unicorn, in order that the wishes of his friends and neighbours can come true. *Dir.* Carol Reed.

Kidnappers, The (1953) Duncan Macrae (Jim MacKenzie, Granddaddy), Jean Anderson (Grandma MacKenzie), Adrienne Corri (Kirsty), Theodore Bikel (Dr Willem Bloem), Jon Whiteley (Harry, Jim's Grandson), Vincent Winter (Davy, Jim's Grandson), Francis De Wolff (Jan Hooft Sr), James Sutherland (Arron McNab), John Rae (Andy McCleod), Jack Stewart (Dominie), Jameson Clark (Tom Cameron), Eric Woodburn (Sam Howie), Christopher Beeny (Jan Hooft Jr), Howard Connell (Archibald Jenkins), Danny (Rover), Anthony Michael Heathcoat (Baby Girl), Alex McCrindle (Minister). Charming tale of two young orphan boys in Nova Scotia in the early 20th century being brought up by their rather dour and stern grandfather. After being told that they cannot have a pet dog they decide to take care of an untended baby and "kidnap" it. Aka *The Little Kidnappers*. *Dir.* Philip Leacock.

Kidulthood (2006) Aml Ameen (Trevor/'Trife'), Red Madrell (Alisa), Adam Deacon (Jay), Noel Clarke (Sam), Jaime Winstone (Becky), Femi Oyeniran (Moony), Madeleine Fairley (Claire), Cornell John (Curtis), Rafe Spall (Lenny), Nicholas Hoult (Blake), Rebecca Martin (Katie), James Witherspoon (Kilpo), Ortis Deley (Derek), Stephanie Di Rubbo (Shaneek). The film follows two days in the lives of a group of 15-year olds living in the Ladbroke Grove and Latimer Road area of west London - which mainly involves sex, drugs and violence. *Dir.* Menhaj Huda.

Kill or Cure (1962) Terry-Thomas (Jerry Barker-Rynde), Eric Sykes (Rumbelow), Dennis Price (Dr Julian Crossley), Lionel Jeffries (Insp Hook), Moira Redmond (Francis Roitman), Katya Douglas (Rita), David Lodge (Richards), Ronnie Barker (Burton), Derren Nesbitt (Roger Forrester), Hazel Terry (Mrs Rachel Crossley), Arthur Howard (Desk Clerk), Harry Locke (Riggins), Tristram Jellinek (Asst Clerk), Patricia Hayes (Lily), Peter Butterworth (Barman), Julian Orchard (PC Lofthouse). Incompetent policeman investigates the Green Glades health club. *Dir.* George Pollock.

Killers of Kilimanjaro (1959) Robert Taylor (Robert Adamson), Anthony Newley (Hooky Hook), Anne Aubrey (Jane Carlton), Grégoire Aslan (Ben Ahmed), Allan Cuthbertson (Sexton), Martin Benson (Ali), Orlando Martins (Chief), Donald Pleasence (Captain), John Dimech (Pasha), Martin Boddey (Gunther), Earl Cameron (Witchdoctor), Harry Baird (Boraga), Anthony Jacobs (Mustaph). Adamson is on the trail of two missing engineers in order to complete a railway in Africa. On his trek he encounters the inevitable wild animals, cannibals and slave traders. Based on J A Hunter's book *African Bush Adventures*. *Dir.* Richard Thorpe.

Killing Fields, The (1984) Sam Waterston (Sydney Schanberg), Haing S. Ngor (Dith Pran), John Malkovich (Alan 'Al' Rockoff, Photographer), Julian Sands (Jon Swain), Craig T. Nelson (Major Reeves, Military Attaché), Spalding Gray (United States consul), Bill Paterson (Dr. MacEntire), Athol Fugard (Dr. Sundesval), Graham Kennedy (Dougal), Katherine Krapum Chey (Ser Moeum: Dith Pran's wife). Based on the experiences of two journalists covering the civil war in Cambodia: Cambodian Dith

Pran and American Sydney Schanberg. Before the Khmer Rouge arrives in Phnom Penh, Pran manages to get his family evacuated to the United States and shortly afterwards Schanberg also returns home. Pran is left to cope under the new totalitarian regime. This film won three Academy Awards: Best Actor in a Supporting Role (Haing S. Ngor), Best Cinematography and Best Film Editing. Ngor had been a gynaecologist in Cambodia prior to the victory of Pol Pot in the Cambodian Civil War. He was murdered in 1996. *Dir.* Roland Joffé.

Killing Time (1998) Craig Fairbrass (Det. Robert Bryant), Nigel Leach (Jacob Reilly), Kendra Torgan (Maria), Peter Harding (Madison), Rick Warden (Smithy), Neil Armstrong (John), Ian McLaughlin (George), Stephen Thirkeld (Charlie), Phil Dixon (Frank), David Cosgrove (Jonah), Gordon Griffin (Mr. Blake), Anthony Hardaker (Mr. Jenkins), Tony Leary (Mr. Thomas). The gangster who killed Bryant's partner is acquitted so he decides to hire an assassin to dispense summary justice. *Dir.* Bharat Nalluri

Kind Hearts and Coronets (1949) Alec Guinness (Duke Etherel/The Banker/Rev Lord Henry d'Ascoyne/General Lord Rufus D'Ascoyne/Admiral Horatio d'Ascoyne/Young Henry d'Ascoyne/Lady Agatha d'Ascoyne/Lord Ascoyne d'Ascoyne), Dennis Price (Duke Louis Mazzini/Mazzini Sr.), Valerie Hobson (Edith D'Ascoyne), Joan Greenwood (Sibella Holland), Audrey Fildes (Louisa d'Ascoyne Mazzini, Louis' mother), Miles Malleson (Mr Elliott the Hangman), Clive Morton (Prison Governor), John Penrose (Lionel Holland), Cecil Ramage (Crown Counsel), Hugh Griffith (Lord High Steward), John Salew (Mr Perkins), Peggy Ann Clifford (Maud Redpole), Arthur Lowe (Tit-Bits magazine representative). Shown in flashback, Louis Mazzini, in prison awaiting execution, describes the implementation of his murderous (but ingenious) plan to gain the title to which he believes he is entitled. Considered one of the best of the Ealing comedies. Guiness gives a bravura display playing eight members of the D'Ascoyne family. The film's title derives from Tennyson's poem *Lady Clara Vere de Vere*: "Kind hearts are more than coronets, And simple faith than Norman blood". *Dir.* Robert Hamer.

Kind of Loving, A (1962) Alan Bates (Vic Brown), June Ritchie (Ingrid Rothwell), Thora Hird (Mrs Rothwell), Bert Palmer (Mr Geoffrey Brown), Pat Keen (Christine Harris), James Bolam (Jeff), Jack Smethurst (Conroy), Gwen Nelson (Mrs Brown), John Ronane (Draughtsman), David Mahlowe (David Harris), Patsy Rowlands (Dorothy), Michael Deacon (Les), Annette Robertson (Phoebe), Fred Ferris (Althorpe), Leonard Rossiter (Whymper), Kathy Staff (Neighbour). Early kitchen sink drama. Having got a co-worker pregnant, Vic "does the right thing" and marries her. They move in with her mother. Based on Stan Barstow's novel. *Dir.* John Schlesinger.

King and Country (1964) Dirk Bogarde (Capt Hargreaves), Tom Courtenay (Pte Arthur Hamp), Leo McKern (Capt O'Sullivan), Barry Foster (Lt Webb), Peter Copley (Colonel), James Villiers (Capt Midgley), Jeremy Spenser (Pte Sparrow), Barry Justice (Lt Prescott), Vivian Matalon (Padre), Keith Buckley (Cpl of the Guard), Derek Partridge (Capt Court Martial), Brian Tipping (Lt Court Martial). British infantryman is court-martialled for desertion and is defended by an initially unsympathetic officer. *Dir.* Joseph Losey.

King in New York, A (1957) Charles Chaplin (King Shahdov), Maxine Audley (Queen Irene), Jerry Desmonde (Prime Minister Voudel), Oliver Johnston (Ambassador Jaume), Dawn Addams (Ann Kay), Sid James (Johnson), Joan Ingram (Mona Cromwell), Michael Chaplin (Rupert Macabee), John McLaren (Macabee Senior), Phil Brown (Headmaster), Harry Green (Lawyer), Robert Arden (Liftboy), Alan Gifford (School Supt), Robert Cawdron (Ulrich), George Woodbridge, Clifford Buckton, Vincent Lawson (Members of Atomic Commission), Shani Wallis, Joy Nichols (Singers), Lauri Lupino Lane, George Truzzi (Comedians), Tubby Hayes (Nightclub Saxophonist). A recently deposed European monarch is living in exile in New York. In an effort to raise money he takes part in television commercials. After he meets the child of communist parents he is brought before the House of Un-American Activities Committee and accused of being a communist himself. Chaplin used the film to further discredit and satirise this body, having himself been forced to leave the US in

1952. The film did not receive a US release until 1967. *Dir*. Charlie Chaplin.

King of the Damned (1936) Conrad Veidt (Convict 83), Helen Vinson (Anna Courvin), Noah Beery (Mooche), Cecil Ramage (Maj Ramon Montez), Edmund Willard (The Greek), Percy Parsons (Lumberjack), Peter Croft ('Boy' Convict), Raymond Lovell (Capt Torres), C.M. Hallard (Commandant Courvin), Allan Jeayes (Dr Prada), Percy Walsh (Capt Perez). Convict 83 leads a revolt against a repressive regime on a prison island. Spanish names were used in order not to upset the French who were sensitive to any references which might refer to Devil's Island. *Dir*. Walter Forde.

King Ralph (1991) John Goodman (Ralph Hampton Gainesworth Jones), Peter O'Toole (Sir Cedric Charles Willingham), John Hurt (Lord Percival Graves), Camille Coduri (Miranda Greene), Ann Beach (Miranda's Mother), Jack Smethurst (Miranda's Father), Richard Griffiths (Duncan Phillips), Leslie Phillips (Gordon Halliwell), James Villiers (Prime Minister Geoffrey Haile), Joely Richardson (Princess Anna), Niall O'Brien (Tommy McGuire), Julian Glover (King Gustav of Finland), Judy Parfitt (Queen Katherine), Leo Jean (Grampy), Ed Stobart (Dysentery), Gedren Heller (Punk Girl), Rudolph Walker (King Mulambon of Zambezi), Michael Johnson (Hamilton), Ann Beach (Miranda's Mother), Jack Smethurst (Miranda's Father), Tim Seely (King of England), Alison McGuire (Queen of England). When the entire British Royal Family dies by being electrocuted in a freak accident while standing for a family photograph apparently the only living relative is uncouth American Ralph Jones. Whilst he sets about getting to grips with his new duties a rival is plotting his downfall. *Dir*. David S. Ward.

King's Rhapsody (1955) Anna Neagle (Marta Karillos), Errol Flynn (Richard, King of Laurentia), Patrice Wymore (Princess Cristiane), Martita Hunt (Queen Mother), Finlay Currie (King Paul), Francis De Wolff (The Prime Minister), Joan Benham (Countess Astrid), Reginald Tate (King Peter), Miles Malleson (Jules), Edmund Hockridge (The Serenader - voice), Brian Franklin (Boy King), Patrick Allen (Richard's Companion), Lionel Blair (Dancer). An exiled European monarch marries an innocent princess but maintains a mistress as well. Based on the musical of the same name by Ivor Novello. *Dir*. Herbert Wilcox.

King's Speech, The (2010) Colin Firth (King George VI), Geoffrey Rush (Lionel Logue), Helena Bonham Carter (Queen Elizabeth), Guy Pearce (King Edward VIII), Michael Gambon (King George V), Timothy Spall (Winston Churchill), Jennifer Ehle (Myrtle Logue), Derek Jacobi (Archbishop Cosmo Lang), Anthony Andrews (Stanley Baldwin), Eve Best (Wallis Simpson), Freya Wilson (Princess Elizabeth), Ramona Marquez (Princess Margaret), Claire Bloom (Queen Mary), Tim Downie (Duke of Gloucester), Claire Bloom (Queen Mary), Orlando Wells (George - Duke of Kent), Anthony Andrews (Stanley Baldwin), Roger Parrott (Neville Chamberlain), Calum Gittins (Laurie Logue), Dominic Applewhite (Valentine Logue), Ben Wimsett (Anthony Logue), Roger Hammond (Dr. Blandine Bentham), David Bamber (Theatre Director), Jake Hathaway (Willie), Patrick Ryecart (Lord Wigram), Teresa Gallagher (Nurse), Simon Chandler (Lord Dawson), Dick Ward (Butler), Robert Portal (Equerry), Richard Dixon (Private Secretary), Paul Trussell (Chauffeur), Adrian Scarborough (BBC Radio Announcer), Andrew Havill (Robert Wood), Charles Armstrong (BBC Technician). The story of Prince Albert, Duke of York, the second son of King George V, who battles against his stammer with the help of his wife and speech therapist Lionel Logue. Beginning with the 1925 British Empire Exhibition, the film moves through Abdication Crisis of 1936, when Albert becomes King George VI, and on to the approach of war in 1939. The film won four Academy Awards: Best Motion Picture of the Year, Best Achievement in Directing (Tom Hooper), Best Performance by an Actor in a Leading Role (Colin Firth), Best Writing, Original Screenplay (David Seidler). *Dir*. Tom Hooper.

Kinky Boots (2005) Joel Edgerton (Charlie Price), Chiwetel Ejiofor (Simon/Lola), Sarah-Jane Potts (Lauren), Nick Frost (Don), Linda Bassett (Melanie), Jemima Rooper (Nicola), Robert Pugh (Harold Price), Ewan Hooper (George), Stephen Marcus (Big Mike), Mona Hammond (Pat), Kellie Bright (Jeannie), Joanna Scanlan (Trish), Geoffrey Streatfield (Richard Bailey), Leo Bill (Harry Sampson), Gwenllian Davies (Mrs. Cobb), Sebastian Hurst-Palmer (Young Charlie), Courtney Phillips (Young Lola), Ilario Bisi-Pedro (Lola's Dad), Joe Grossi (Organiser), Barry McCarthy (Bernie), Josh Cole (Tramp). A failing Northampton shoemaker turns to producing fetish footwear in order to save the family business. *Dir*. Julian Jarrold.

Kiss of the Vampire, The (1963) Clifford Evans (Professor Zimmer), Edward de Souza (Gerald Harcourt), Noel Willman (Dr. Ravna), Jennifer Daniel (Marianne Harcourt), Barry Warren (Carl Ravna), Brian Oulton (1st disciple), Noel Howlett (Father Xavier), Jacquie Wallis (Sabena Ravna), Peter Madden (Bruno), Isobel Black (Tania), Vera Cook (Anna), John Harvey (Police Sergeant). A honey-mooning couple have car trouble in Bavaria. They are invited to a nearby castle. Sound familiar? *Dir*. Don Sharp.

Kiss the Bride Goodbye (1945) Patricia Medina (Joan Dodd), Jimmy Hanley (Jack Fowler), Frederick Leister (Captain Blood), Marie Lohr (Emma Blood), Claud Allister (Adolphus Pickering), Ellen Pollock (Gladys Dodd), Wylie Watson (David Dodd), Jean Simmons (Molly Dodd), Muriel George (Mrs. Fowler), Irene Handl (Mrs. Victory), Aubrey Mallalieu (Reverend Glory), Hay Petrie (Fraser), C. Denier Warren (Reporter), Julie Suedo (Part-time Worker). After her boyfriend Jack is called up, Joan's parents pressure her to marry Adolphus instead. She finally agrees but then unexpectedly Jack returns home. *Dir*. Paul L. Stein.

Knack ...and How to Get It, The (1965) Rita Tushingham (Nancy Jones), Ray Brooks (Tolen), Michael Crawford (Colin), Donal Donnelly (Tom), John Bluthal (Angry Father), Wensley Pithey (Teacher), Timothy Bateson (Junkyard Owner), Peter Copley (Picture Owner), William Dexter (Dress Shop Owner), Bruce Lacey (Surveyor's Assistant), Dandy Nichols (Tom's Landlady), Kenneth Farrington (Guardsman), Lucy Bartlett (Water Skier), Jane Birkin (Girl on Motorbike), Pattie Boyd (Girl Perfuming Ankle). Three friends become rivals when Nancy arrives in London at the height of the Swinging Sixties. *Dir*. Richard Lester.

Knight Without Armour (1937) Marlene Dietrich (Alexandra Adraxine, née Vladinoff), Robert Donat (A.J. Fothergill/"Peter Ouranoff"), Irene Vanbrugh (Duchess), Herbert Lomas (General Gregor Vladinoff), Austin Trevor (Colonel Adraxine), Basil Gill (Axelstein), David Tree (Maronin), John Clements (Poushkoff), Frederick Culley (Stanfield), Laurence Hanray (Colonel Forester), Dorice Fordred (the Maid), Franklin Kelsey (Tomsky), Laurence Baskcomb (Commissar), Hay Petrie (Station Master), Miles Malleson (Drunken Red Commissar). Recruited by the British Government to spy on Russia, Fothergill is sent to Siberia in 1913 when he is mistaken for a revolutionary. When the Russian Revolution takes place and then the Civil War breaks out he tries to save Alexandra. *Dir*. Jacques Feyder.

Krays, The (1990) Billie Whitelaw (Violet Kray), Alfred Lynch (Charlie Kray, Snr), Gary Kemp (Ronnie Kray), Martin Kemp (Reggie Kray), Roger Monk (Charlie Kray, Jnr.), Susan Fleetwood (Rose), Charlotte Cornwell (May), Kate Hardie (Frances), Avis Bunnage (Helen), Tom Bell (Jack 'The Hat' McVitie), Steven Berkoff (George Cornell), Gary Love (Steve), Jimmy Jewel (Cannonball Lee), Gary Love (Steve), Barbara Ferris (Mrs. Lawson), Victor Spinetti (Mr. Lawson), John McEnery (Eddie Pellam), Philip Bloomfield (Charlie Pellam), Norman Rossington (Shopkeeper), Patti Love (Iris), Sadie Frost (Sharon Pellam), Stephen Lewis (Policeman), John H. Stracey (Boxer). A biopic of the Kray twins (Ronnie and Reggie), the notorious East London gangsters. *Dir*. Peter Medak.

Ladies in Lavender (2004) Judi Dench (Ursula Widdington), Maggie Smith (Janet Widdington), Daniel Brühl (Andrea Marowski), Natascha McElhone (Olga Danilof), Miriam Margolyes (Dorcas), David Warner (Dr Francis Mead), Freddie Jones (Jan Pendered), Gregor Henderson-Begg (Luke Pendered), Clive Russell (Adam Penruddocke), Richard Pears (Barry), Iain Marshall (Fisherman), Toby Jones (Hedley), Joanna Dickens (Mrs

Pendered), Geoffrey Bayldon (Mr Penhaligan), Timothy Bateson (Mr Hallett), Rebecca Hulbert (Fiancée), Finty Williams (Pretty Local Girl), Roger Booth (Arthur), Jimmy Yuill (PC Timmins). Sisters take care of a mysterious foreigner who washes up on the beach near their village. *Dir.* Charles Dance.

Lady Godiva Rides Again (1951) Dennis Price (Simon Abott), John McCallum (Larry Burns), Stanley Holloway (Mr Clark), Pauline Stroud (Marjorie Clark), Gladys Henson (Mrs Clark), Bernadette O'Farrell (Janie), George Cole (Johnny), Diana Dors (Dolores August), Eddie Byrne (Eddie Mooney), Kay Kendall (Sylvia), Renee Houston (Beattie), Dora Bryan (Publicity Lady), Sid James (Lew Beeson), Tommy Duggan (Compere), Eddy Leslie (Comic), Walford Hyden (Conductor), Edward Forsyth (Singer), Lisa Lee (Singer), Cyril Chamberlain (Harry), Lyn Evans (Vic Kennedy), Peter Martyn (Photographer), Fred Berger (Mr Green), Henry B. Longhurst (Soap director), Felix Felton, Arthur Brander, Sidney Vivian (Councillors), Arthur Howard, Clive Baxter, Paul Connell (Soap PR men), John Harvey (Buller), Rowena Gregory (Waitress), Tom Gill (Receptionist), Patricia Goddard (Susan), Richard Wattis (Otto Mann), Michael Ripper (Joe), Charlotte Mitchell (Lucille), Toke Townley (Lucille's husband), Dana Wynter (Myrtle Shaw), Joan Collins and Ruth Ellis (Beauty Queen Contestants), Trevor Howard (Guest at Theatre), Leslie Mitchell (TV Interviewer), Alastair Sim (Hawtrey Murington), Jimmy Young (Singer at Dance). Marjorie Clark appears as Lady Godiva in a Festival of Britain pageant and then enters a beauty contest. Notable for being the first film for Joan Collins and the presence of Ruth Ellis (hanged in 1955 for the murder of David Blakely) as contestants in the beauty contest. Aka *Bikini Baby*. *Dir.* Frank Launder.

Lady is a Square, The (1958) Anna Neagle (Frances Baring), Frankie Vaughan (Johnny Burns), Janette Scott (Joanna Baring), Anthony Newley (Freddy), Wilfrid Hyde-White (Charles), Christopher Rhodes (Greenslade), Kenneth Cope (Derek), Josephine Fitzgerald (Mrs. Eady), Harold Kasket (Spolenski), John Le Mesurier (Fergusson), Ted Lune (Harry Shuttleworth), Mary Peach (Mrs. Freddy). An aspiring singer becomes a butler in a household where popular music is disapproved of. As he becomes successful he has to hide his career from the family. *Dir.* Herbert Wilcox.

Lady Is Willing, The (1934) Leslie Howard (Albert Latour), Cedric Hardwicke (Gustav Dupont), Binnie Barnes (Helene Dupont), Nigel Playfair (Prof Menard), Nigel Bruce (Welton), Claud Allister (Brevin), W. Graham Brown (Pignolet), Kendall Lee (Valerie), Arthur Howard (Dr. Germont), Virginia Field (Maid), John Turnbull (Butler). Comedy thriller in which a French detective kidnaps the wife of a crooked businessman in order to spoil his plans. *Dir.* Gilbert Miller.

Lady Jane (1986) Helena Bonham Carter (Jane Grey), Cary Elwes (Lord Guilford Dudley), Jane Lapotaire (Queen Mary), Patrick Stewart (Henry Grey, 1st Duke of Suffolk), Sara Kestelman (Lady Frances Brandon), Michael Hordern (Dr Feckenham), John Wood (John Dudley, 1st Duke of Northumberland), Jill Bennett (Mrs. Ellen, Lady-in-Waiting), Adele Anderson (Lady Warwick), Warren Saire (Edward VI), Joss Ackland (Sir John Bridges), Ian Hogg (Sir John Gates), Lee Montague (Renard, the Spanish Ambassador), Richard Vernon (The Marquess of Winchester), David Waller (Archbishop Cranmer), Richard Johnson (The Earl of Arundel), Pip Torrens (Thomas), Matthew Guinness (Dr Owen), Guy Henry (Robert Dudley), Andrew Bicknell (John Dudley), Clyde Pollitt (Peasant Leader), William Morgan Sheppard (Executioner), Zelah Clarke (Lady Anne Wharton), Laura Clipsham (Katherine Grey), Adèle Anderson (Lady Warwick), Anna Gilbert (Lady Robert Dudley). Story of Lady Jane Grey, the tragic "nine days queen". *Dir.* Trevor Nunn.

Lady L (1965) Sophia Loren (Lady Louise Lendale/Lady L), Paul Newman (Armand Denis), David Niven (Dicky, Lord Lendale), Marcel Dalio (Sapper), Cecil Parker (Sir Percy), Philippe Noiret (Ambroise Gérôme), Jacques Dufilho (Bealu), Eugene Deckers (Koenigstein), Daniel Emilfork (Kobeleff), Hella Petri (Madam), Jean Wiener (Krajewski), Michel Piccoli (Lecoeur), Claude Dauphin (Inspector Mercier), Peter Ustinov (Prince Otto of Bavaria). An elderly Corsican lady recalls the loves of her life. *Dir.* Peter Ustinov.

Lady Vanishes, The (1938) Margaret Lockwood (Iris Henderson), Michael Redgrave (Gilbert Redman), Paul Lukas (Dr Hartz of Prague), Dame May Whitty (Miss Froy, Governess), Cecil Parker (Eric Todhunter), Linden Travers ('Mrs.' Margaret Todhunter), Naunton Wayne (Caldicott), Basil Radford (Charters), Mary Clare (Baroness Isabel Nisatona), Emile Boreo (Boris the Hotel Manager), Googie Withers (Blanche), Sally Stewart (Julie), Philip Leaver (Signor Doppo), Selma Vaz Dias (Signora Doppo), Catherine Lacey (Nun), Josephine Wilson (Madame Kummer), Charles Oliver (The Officer), Kathleen Tremaine (Anna). Iris makes friends with Miss Froy aboard a train travelling through Europe. After Iris wakes up, having earlier accidently been hit on the head, she cannot find the old lady and others aboard the train deny any knowledge of her. Iris enlists the help of Gilbert to find her friend. Hitchcock makes his cameo at a London railway station. Charters and Caldicott proved to be such popular characters that they were teamed up in other films, including *Night Train to Munich* and *It's Not Cricket*. The film was adapted from the novel *The Wheel Spins* by Ethel Lina White. *Dir.* Alfred Hitchcock.

Lady Vanishes, The (1979) Elliot Gould (Robert), Cybill Shepherd (Amanda), Angela Lansbury (Miss Froy), Herbert Lom (Doctor Hartz), Arthur Lowe (Charters), Ian Carmichael (Caldicott), Gerald Harper (Mr Todhunter), Jenny Runacre ("Mrs" Todhunter), Jean Anderson (Baroness), Madlena Nedeva (Nun), Madge Ryan (Rose Flood Porter), Rosalind Knight (Evelyn Barnes), Vladek Sheybal (Trainmaster), Wolf Kahler (Helmut), Barbara Markham (Frau Kummer), Jonathan Hachett (Dining Car Waiter), Gary McDermott (Baroness's Manservant), Jacki Harding (Baroness's Maid). A remake of the 1938 film. *Dir.* Anthony Page.

Ladykillers, The (1955) Alec Guinness (Prof Marcus), Cecil Parker (Claude aka Maj Courtney), Herbert Lom (Louis aka Mr Harvey), Peter Sellers (Harry aka Mr Robinson), Danny Green (One-Round aka Mr Lawson), Jack Warner (Supt), Katie Johnson (Mrs Wilberforce, The Old Lady), Philip Stainton (The Sergeant), Frankie Howerd (Barrow boy), Kenneth Connor (Taxi driver), Stratford Johns (Security van guard). British black comedy par excellence. A gang of crooks led by "Professor" Marcus, pose as a string quartet and lodge with a little old lady because the house is strategically placed. *Dir.* Alexander Mackendrick.

Lair of the White Worm, The (1988) Hugh Grant (Lord James D'Ampton), Amanda Donohoe (Lady Sylvia Marsh), Catherine Oxenberg (Eve Trent), Peter Capaldi (Angus Flint), Sammi Davis (Mary Trent), Paul Brooke (Erny), Stratford Johns (Peters), Imogen Claire (Dorothy Trent), Chris Pitt (Kevin), Gina McKee (Nurse Gladwell), Christopher Gable (Joe Trent), Lloyd Peters (Jesus Christ). When an archaeologist unearths the skull of a large snake at the site of a former convent he links it to the legend of the D'Ampton worm. James, the ancestor of the supposed slayer of the worm, believes the creature may still be lurking in nearby caverns. *Dir.* Ken Russell.

Lamp Still Burns, The (1943) Rosamund John (Hilary Clarke), Stewart Granger (Laurence Rains), Godfrey Tearle (Sir Marshall Freyne), Sophie Stewart (Christine Morris), Cathleen Nesbitt (Matron), Margaret Vyner (Pamela Siddell), John Laurie (Mr Hervey), Joan Maude (Sister Catley), Mignon O'Doherty (Sister Tutor), Leslie Dwyer (Siddons), Wylie Watson (Diabetic Patient), Eric Micklewood (Mr Trevor), Joyce Grenfell (Dr Barrett), Ernest Thesiger (Chairman), Brefni O'Rorke (Mr Lorrimer), Patric Curwen (Mr Lavery), Jenny Laird (Ginger Watkins), Megs Jenkins (Nurse), Aubrey Mallalieu (Rev Ashton). The adventures of wartime probationary nurses. Based on the book *One Pair of Feet* by Monica Dickens. *Dir.* Maurice Elvey.

Land and Freedom (1995) Ian Hart (David), Rosana Pastor (Blanca), Frederic Pierrot (Bernard), Tom Gilroy (Lawrence), Iciar Bollain (Maite), Marc Martínez (Juan Vidal), Frédéric Pierrot (Bernard Goujon), Suzanne Maddock (Kim), Mandy Walsh (Dot), Angela Clarke (Kitty). Told in flashback by his granddaughter Kim after his death, the film tells the story of David Carr, an unemployed worker from Liverpool in the 1930s who decides to fight for the republican side in the Spanish Civil War. *Dir.* Ken Loach.

Land Girls, The (1998) Catherine McCormack (Stella), Rachel Weisz (Agapanthus), Anna Friel (Prudence), Steven Mackintosh

(Joe Lawrence), Tom Georgeson (Mr Lawrence), Maureen O'Brien (Mrs Lawrence), Lucy Akhurst (Janet), Gerald Down (Ratty), Paul Bettany (Philip), Nick Mollo (Barry Hampton), Michael Mantas (Desmond), Nicholas Le Prevost (Agricultural Officer), Ann Bell (Philip's Mother), Edmund Moriarty (Harry), Celia Bannerman (District Commissioner), Nigel Planer (Gerald), Shirley Newbery (WAAF at Dance), Russell Barr (Jamie), John Gill (Doctor), Crispin Layfield (German Pilot), Grace Leland (Baby Barry), Alan Bennett (Rev Alan Bennett), Charlie Higson (Subaltern). In 1941 three girls from very different backgrounds arrive to work on a farm in Dorset as "Land Girls". *Dir.* David Leland.

Land That Time Forgot, The (1974) Doug McClure (Bowen Tyler), John McEnery (Captain Von Schoenvorts), Susan Penhaligon (Lisa Clayton), Keith Barron (Bradley), Anthony Ainley (Dietz), Godfrey James (Borg), Bobby Parr (Ahm), Declan Mulholland (Olson), Colin Farrell (Whiteley), Ben Howard (Benson), Roy Holder (Plesser), Andrew McCulloch (Sinclair), Ron Pember (Jones), Grahame Mallard (Deusett), Andrew Lodge (Reuther), Brian Hall (Schwartz), Stanley McGeagh (Hiller), Peter Sproule (Hindle), Steve James (First Sto-Lu). The crew of a British merchant ship seize the German U-boat which sank its ship. They find the uncharted sub-continent of Caprona where dinosaurs still roam along with a tribe of primitive man. Based upon the novel by Edgar Rice Burroughs. *Dir.* Kevin Connor.

Last Days of Dolwyn, The (1949) Edith Evans (Merri), Emlyn Williams (Rob), Richard Burton (Gareth), Anthony James (Defydd), Alan Aynesworth (Lord Lancashire), Barbara Couper (Lady Dolwyn), Andrea Lea (Margaret), Hugh Griffith (The Minister), Maurice Browning (Huw), Rita Crailey (Hen Ann), Eileen Dale (Mrs Ellis), David Davies (Septimus), Frank Dunlop (Ephrain), Kenneth Evans (Jabbez), Patricia Glyn (Dorcas). In 1897, the village of Dolwyn is threatened with destruction by the building of a reservoir to supply water to Liverpool. *Dirs.* Russell Lloyd and Emlyn Williams.

Last Holiday (1950) Alec Guinness (George Bird), Beatrice Campbell (Sheila Rockingham), Jean Colin (Daisy Clarence), Kay Walsh (Mrs Poole), Grégoire Aslan (Gambini), Muriel George (Lady Oswington), Brian Worth (Derek Rockingham), Campbell Cotts (Bellinghurst), Esma Cannon (Miss Fox), Bernard Lee (Insp Wilton), Sid James (Joe Clarence), Moultrie Kelsall (Sir Robert Kyle), Madam Kirkwood-Hackett (Miss Hatfield), Wilfrid Hyde-White (Chalfont), Eric Maturin (Wrexham), Helen Cherry (Miss Mellows), Harry Hutchinson (Michael the Waiter), Hal Osmond (Trade Unionist), Brian Oulton (Prescott), Heather Wilde (Maggie the Maid), Ernest Thesiger (Sir Trevor Lampington), Ronald Simpson (Dr Pevensey), Arthur Howard (Burden), Meier Tzelniker (Baltin), Leslie Weston (William the Waiter), Lockwood West (Dinsdale), David McCallum Sr (Blind Fiddler), Peter Jones (Travel Agent), Charles Lloyd Pack (Bank Cashier). An agricultural machinery salesman is told he only has a few weeks to live so moves into a high-class hotel and begins to live a life he had not previously considered. *Dir.* Henry Cass.

Last King of Scotland, The (2006) Forest Whitaker (Idi Amin), James McAvoy (Dr. Nicholas Garrigan), Kerry Washington (Kay Amin), Gillian Anderson (Sarah Merrit), Simon McBurney (Stone), David Oyelowo (Dr. Junju), Stephen Rwangyezi (Jonah Wasswa), Abby Mukiibi Nkaaga (Masanga), Adam Kotz (Dr. Merrit), Sam Okelo (Bonny), Sarah Nagayi (Tolu), Chris Wilson (Perkins), Dick Stockley (Times Journalist), Barbara Rafferty (Mrs. Garrigan), David Ashton (Dr. Garrigan – Senior), Apollo Okwenje Omamo (Mackenzie Amin), Louis Asea (Campbell Amin). Newly graduated doctor is working in a mission in Uganda when he meets the new leader of the country, Idi Amin. Forest Whitaker won the Academy Award: Best Performance by an Actor in a Leading Role. Based on Giles Foden's novel. *Dir.* Kevin Macdonald.

Last of England, The (1988) Tilda Swinton, Gay Gaynor, Matthew Hawkins, Spencer Leigh, Gerrard McArthur, Jonny Phillips, Tilda Swinton, Nigel Terry. Derek Jarman's view of the state of Britain in the late 1980s. It is named after a painting by the Pre-Raphaelite artist Ford Madox Brown. *Dir.* Derek Jarman.

Last Orders (2001) Michael Caine (Jack Dodds), Tom Courtenay (Vic Tucker), David Hemmings (Lenny), Bob Hoskins (Ray Johnson), Helen Mirren (Amy Dodds), Ray Winstone (Vince Dodds), JJ Feild (Young Jack), Cameron Fitch (Young Vic), Nolan Hemmings (Young Lenny), Anatol Yusef (Young Ray), Kelly Reilly (Young Amy), Stephen McCole (Young Vince), Laura Morelli (June Dodds), George Innes (Bernie), Laura Morelli (June), Sally Hurst (Mandy), Denise Black (Carol), Sue James (Pam), Meg Wynn Owen (Joan), Kitty Leigh (Young Carol), Alex Reid (Young Pam), Tracey Murphy (Young Joan), Claire Harman (Young Sally), John Baker (11 Year Old Vince), Emma Deigman (10 Year Old Sally), Tom Baker (7 Year Old Vince), Laura Deigman (5 Year Old Sally), Simon Oats (Andy), Patricia Valentine (Sue), Lois Winstone (Kath). When butcher Jack Dodds dies his friends fulfill his last request to have his ashes scattered off the end of Margate Pier. As they make the trip they reminisce about the events of the past 50 years. Based on the Booker Prize-winning novel by Graham Swift. *Dir.* Fred Schepisi.

Last Resort (2000) Dina Korzun (Tanya), Artyom Strelnikov (Artyom), Paddy Considine (Alfie), Steve Perry (Les), Perry Benson (Immigration Officer), Katie (Katie), Dave Bean (Frank). Asylum seeker Tanya and her son are confined in a seaside resort whilst their case is considered. *Dir.* Paweł Pawlikowski.

Last Valley, The (1970) Michael Caine (The Captain), Omar Sharif (Vogel), Florinda Bolkan (Erica), Nigel Davenport (Gruber), Per Oscarsson (Father Sebastian), Arthur O'Connell (Hoffman), Madeleine Hinde (Inge), Yorgo Voyagis (Pirelli), Miguel Alejandro (Julio), Christian Roberts (Andreas), Brian Blessed (Korski), Ian Hogg (Graf), Michael Gothard (Hansen), George Innes (Vornez), Ralph Arliss (Claus), Claudia Butenuth (Helga), Paul Challen (Zollner), Chris Chittell (Svenson), Kurt Christian (Tsarus), Dave Crowley (Pastori), Mark Edwards (Sernen), John Hallam (Geddes), Frazer Hines (Corg). Set during the Thirty Years War. A band of mercenaries come across a valley which has not been devastated by the war. The captain is convinced to preserve the peace and stay in the valley for the winter. *Dir.* James Clavell.

Late Edwina Black, The (1951) David Farrar (Gregory Black), Geraldine Fitzgerald (Elizabeth Grahame), Roland Culver (Insp Martin), Jean Cadell (Ellen), Mary Merrall (Lady Southdale), Harcourt Williams (Dr Septimus Prendergast), Charles Heslop (Vicar), Ronald Adam (Head-Master), Sydney Moncton (Horace). An autopsy reveals that Lady Edwina Black was poisoned and Inspector Martin investigates. *Dir.* Maurice Elvey.

Latin Quarter (1945) Derrick De Marney (Charles), Frederick Valk (Dr Ivan Krasner), Beresford Egan (Anton Minetti), Joan Greenwood (Christine), Joan Seton (Lucille Lindbeck), Lily Kann (Maria), Martin Miller (Morgue Keeper), Valentine Dyall (Prefecture of Police), Gerhard Kempinski (Sergeant of Police), Espinosa (Ballet Master), Margaret Clarke (Ballet Mistress), Bruce Winston (Jo-Jo), Anthony Hawtrey (The Specialist), Rachel Brodbrar (Country Girl), Sybille Binder (Mme. Cordova), Billy Holland (Cave Man), Cleo Nordi (Suzanne). Sculptor Charles Garrie has an affair with married Christine Minetti. However, Christine goes missing and her mentally unstable husband is suspected of having something to do with it. An adaptation of the play *L'Angoisse* by Pierre Mills and C. Vylars. *Dir.* Vernon Sewell.

Laughing Anne (1953) Wendell Corey (Capt Davidson), Margaret Lockwood (Laughing Anne), Forrest Tucker (Jem Farrell), Ronald Shiner (Nobby Clark), Robert Harris (Joseph Conrad), Jacques B. Brunius (Frenchie), Daphne Anderson (Blonde singer), Helen Shingler (Susan Davidson), Danny Green (Nicholas), Harold Lang (Jacques), Edgar Norfolk (Conrad's companion), Sean Lynch (David), Gerard Lohan (Davy), Andy Ho (Chinese merchant), Maurice Bush (Battling Brunius). A singer and her washed-up boxer boyfriend end up in Java, where she meets Captain Davidson. Adapted from the short story *Because of the Dollars* by Joseph Conrad. *Dir.* Herbert Wilcox.

Laughing Lady, The (1946) Anne Ziegler (Denise Tremayne), Webster Booth (Andre), Francis L. Sullivan (Sir Williams

Tremayne), Peter Graves (Prince of Wales), Chili Bouchier (Louise), Felix Aylmer (Sir Felix Mountroyal), Ralph Truman (Lord Mandeville), Charles Goldner (Robespierre), Jack Melford (Lord Barrymore), Paul Dupuis (Poerre), John Ruddock (Gilliatt), George De Warfaz (Tinville), Mary Martlew (Lady Langley), Frederick Burtwell (Jenkins), Hay Petrie (Tom), James Hayter (Ostler).

Musical set during the French Revolution. In order to save his mother from the guillotine a young aristocrat makes a deal with Robespierre. *Dir.* Paul L. Stein.

Laughter in Paradise (1951) Alastair Sim (Captain James Deniston Russell), Fay Compton (Agnes Russell), Guy Middleton (Simon Russell), George Cole (Herbert Russell), Hugh Griffith (Henry Augustus Russell), Ernest Thesiger (Lawyer Endicott), Audrey Hepburn (Frieda - Cigarette girl), Beatrice Campbell (Lucille Grayson), Mackenzie Ward (Benson), A.E. Matthews (Sir Charles Robson), Joyce Grenfell (Elizabeth "Fluffy" Robson), Eleanor Summerfield (Sheila Wilcott), John Laurie (Gordon Webb), Veronica Hurst (Joan Webb), Anthony Steel (Roger Godfrey), Charlotte Mitchell (Ethel), Leslie Dwyer (Police sergeant), Colin Gordon (Station constable), Ronald Adam (Mr. Wagstaffe), Michael Pertwee (Stewart), Mary Germaine (Susan Heath), Noel Howlett (Clerk of the Court), Ian Fleming (Doctor). When practical joker Henry dies his will specifies that the beneficiaries can only claim their inheritances if they perform allotted tasks which are completely out of keeping with their normal behaviour. Audrey Hepburn makes a brief first appearance in an English film as a cigarette girl in a night club. *Dir.* Mario Zampi.

Lavender Hill Mob, The (1951) Alec Guinness (Henry Holland), Stanley Holloway (Alfred Pendlebury), Sid James (Lackery), Alfie Bass (Shorty), Marjorie Fielding (Mrs Chalk), Edie Martin (Miss Evesham), John Salew (Parkin), Ronald Adam (Turner), Arthur Hambling (Wallis), Gibb McLaughlin (Godwin), John Gregson (Farrow), Clive Morton (Station Sergeant), Sydney Tafler (Clayton), Marie Burke (Senora Gallardo), Audrey Hepburn (Chiquita), Richard Wattis (MP). Sitting in a restaurant in Rio de Janeiro, mild mannered bank transfer agent Henry Holland relates to his companion how, together with Alfred, Lackery and Shorty he set about stealing a shipment of gold bullion disguised as Eiffel Tower paperweights. The film won one Academy Award: Best Writing, Story and Screenplay. *Dir.* Charles Crichton.

Lawrence of Arabia (1962) Peter O'Toole (T.E. Lawrence), Alec Guinness (Prince Feisal), Anthony Quinn (Auda abu Tayi), Jack Hawkins (General Lord Edmund Allenby), Omar Sharif (Sherif Ali), Jose Ferrer (Turkish Bey), Anthony Quayle (Colonel Brighton), Claude Rains (Mr. Dryden), Arthur Kennedy (Jackson Bentley), Donald Wolfit (General Sir Archibald Murray), I.S. Johar as Gasim, Gamil Ratib (Majid Ratib), Fernando Sancho (Turkish sergeant), Kenneth Fortescue (Allenby's aide), Harry Fowler (Corporal Potter), Howard Marion-Crawford (Medical Officer), John Ruddock (Elder Harith), Norman Rossington (Corporal Jenkins), Jack Hedley (Reporter), Henry Oscar (Silliam), Peter Burton (Damascus Sheik), Jack Gwillim (Club Secretary), Robert Bolt (Officer Gazing at Lawrence), Noel Howlett (Vicar), David Lean (Motorcyclist), George Plimpton (Bedouin), Bryan Pringle (Driver). The film, noted for its striking visuals, tells the epic story of British army officer Thomas Edward Lawrence whose liaison role during the Arab Revolt against Ottoman Turkish rule during the latter years of WWI (1916-18) earned him international fame as Lawrence of Arabia. The film won seven Academy Awards: Best Picture, Best Director, Best Art Direction-Set Decoration, Colour, Best Cinematography, Colour, Best Film Editing, Best Music, Score - Substantially Original (Maurice Jarre), Best Sound. Famously among quiz fans this is the Oscar winning film which has no women in speaking roles. *Dir.* David Lean.

Layer Cake (2004) Daniel Craig (XXXX), Colm Meaney (Gene), Kenneth Cranham (Jimmy Price), George Harris (Morty), Jamie Foreman (The Duke), Sienna Miller (Tammy), Michael Gambon (Eddie Temple), Marcel Iureş (Slavo), Tom Hardy (Clarkie), Tamer Hassan (Terry), Ben Whishaw (Sidney), Burn Gorman (Gazza), Sally Hawkins (Slasher), Dexter Fletcher (Cody), Steve John Shepherd (Tiptoes), Louis Emerick (Trevor), Stephen

Walters (Shanks), Paul Orchard (Lucky), Dragan Mićanović (Dragan), Nick Thomas-Webster (Dragan's henchman), Nathalie Lunghi (Charlie), Jason Flemyng (Crazy Larry). Gangster X's plans to retire are put on hold when both his friends and his enemies conspire against him. A crime thriller based on the novel by J. J. Connolly. *Dir.* Matthew Vaughn.

League of Gentlemen, The (1960) Jack Hawkins (Lt Col Norman Hyde), Nigel Patrick (Maj Peter Race), Roger Livesey (Capt "Padre" Mycroft), Richard Attenborough (Lt Edward Lexy), Bryan Forbes (Capt Martin Porthill), Kieron Moore (Capt Stevens), Terence Alexander (Maj Rupert Rutland-Smith), Norman Bird (Capt Frank Weaver), Robert Coote (Brigadier "Bunny" Warren), Melissa Stribling (Peggy), Nanette Newman (Elizabeth Rutland-Smith), Lydia Sherwood (Hilda), Doris Hare (Molly Weaver), David Lodge (C.S.M.), Patrick Wymark (Wylie), Gerald Harper (Capt Saunders), Brian Murray (Pte "Chunky" Grogan), Dinsdale Landen (Young man in gym), Ronald Leigh-Hunt (Police Supt), Oliver Reed (Chorus Boy), Norman Rossington (Staff Sgt Hall), Basil Dearden (Blackmailer). Hyde assembles a group of disgraced or unhappy ex-servicemen in order to pull off a bank robbery. Based on the novel by John Boland. *Dir.* Basil Dearden.

League of Gentlemen's Apocalypse, The (2005) Mark Gatiss (Himself/Matthew Chinnery/Hilary Briss/Mickey/Sir Nicholas Sheet-Lightning), Steve Pemberton (Himself/Tubbs/Pauline/Herr Lipp/Lemuel Blizzard), Reece Shearsmith (Himself/Edward/Papa Lazarou/Geoff/Bernice/Father Halfhearte/Red Devil), Michael Sheen (Jeremy Dyson), Emily Woof (Lindsay), Danielle Tilley (Dahlia), Bruno Langley (Damon), Alan Morrissey (Johnny), Liana O'Cleirigh (Claire), Victoria Wood (Queen Mary II), David Warner (Dr. Erasmus Pea), Bernard Hill (King William III), Simon Pegg (Peter Cow), Peter Kay (Simon Pig). When the creators of the population of Royston Vasey decide to stop writing about them, they have to break out of their world and convince the writers to carry on. A big screen spin-off of the television comedy series *The League of Gentlemen*. *Dir.* Steve Bendelack.

Lease of Life (1954) Robert Donat (Rev. William Thorne), Kay Walsh (Mrs. Vera Thorne), Denholm Elliott (Martin Blake), Adrienne Corri (Susan Thorne), Walter Fitzgerald (The Dean), Reginald Beckwith (Journalist Foley), Vida Hope (Mrs. Sproatley), Cyril Raymond (Headmaster), Jean Anderson (Miss Calthorp), Russell Waters (Russell), Richard Wattis (Solicitor), Beckett Bould (Mr. Sproatley), Robert Sandford (Boy with book), Frank Atkinson (Verger), Alan Webb (Dr. Pembury), Frederick Piper (Jeweller), Richard Leech (Carter), Edie Martin (Miss Calthorp's Friend), Mark Daly (Spooner), Mark Dignam (Mr. Black). The story of a Yorkshire country vicar, his wife and musically gifted daughter. *Dir.* Charles Frend.

Leather Boys, The (1964) Rita Tushingham (Dot), Colin Campbell (Reggie), Dudley Sutton (Pete), Gladys Henson (Gran), Avice Landone (Reggie's Mother), Lockwood West (Reggie's Father), Betty Marsden (Dot's Mother), Martin Matthews (Uncle Arthur), Johnny Briggs (Boy Friend), James Chase (Les), Geoffrey Dunn (Mr. Lunnis), Dandy Nichols (Mrs. Stanley), Valerie Varnam (Brenda), Jill Mai Meredith (June), Carmel McSharry (Bus Conductor), Joyce Hemson (Publican's Wife). Reggie marries Dot when they are both young and does not discover his true feelings until he meets biker Pete. Based on the book by Gillian Freeman. *Dir.* Sidney J. Furie.

Leaving Lenin (1993) Sharon Morgan (Eileen), Wyn Bowen Harries (Mostyn), Ifan Huw Dafydd (Mervyn), Steffan Trefor (Spike), Catrin Mai (Rhian), Ivan Shvedoff (Sasha), Richard Harrington (Charlie), Shelley Rees (Sharon), Nerys Thomas (Elin), Helen Rosser Davies (Lisa), Geraint Francis (Izzy), Mikhail Maizel (Sergei). A Welsh language film about a school trip to Russia. *Dir.* Endaf Emlyn.

Left Right and Centre (1959) Ian Carmichael (Robert Wilcot), Alastair Sim (Lord Wilcot), Patricia Bredin (Stella Stoker), Richard Wattis (Harding-Pratt), Eric Barker (Bert Glimmer), Moyra Fraser (Annabel), Jack Hedley (Bill Hemmingway), Gordon Harker (Hardy), William Kendall (Pottle), Anthony Sharp (Peterson), George Benson (Egerton), Leslie Dwyer (Alf Stoker), Moultrie Kelsall (Grimsby Armfield), Russell Waters (Mr Bray), Olwen Brookes (Mrs Samson), John Salew (Mayor), Bill Shine (Basingstoke), Erik Chitty (Deputy returning officer), Redmond

Phillips (Mr Smithson), Irene Handl (Mrs Maggs), Hattie Jacques (Woman in car), Eamonn Andrews and Gilbert Harding (themselves). Political comedy which follows the events of a by-election in a small English town, where the rival candidates begin to fall in love with each other, much to the disgust of their political party agents. *Dir*. Sidney Gilliat.

Legend of Hell House, The (1973) Pamela Franklin (Florence Tanner), Roddy McDowall (Benjamin Franklin Fischer), Clive Revill (Dr. Barrett), Gayle Hunnicutt (Ann Barrett), Roland Culver (Rudolph Deutsch), Peter Bowles (Hanley), Michael Gough (Emeric Belasco). A physicist, his wife and two mediums are invited by a millionaire to investigate the truth or otherwise of the multiple haunting of the notorious Belasco House, which he has just bought. The house was once owned by a sadistic murderer. Based on the novel *Hell House* by Richard Matheson. *Dir*. John Hough.

Legend of the Seven Golden Vampires, The (1973) Peter Cushing (Prof Lawrence Van Helsing), Robin Stewart (Leyland Van Helsing), Julie Ege (Vanessa Buren), David Chiang (Hsi Ching), John Forbes-Robertson (Count Dracula), Shih Szu (Mei Kwei), Robert Hanna (British Consul), Shen Chan (Kah), James Ma (Hsi Ta), Hui-Ling Liu (Hsi Hong), Chia Yung Liu (Hsi Kwei), Han Chen Wang (Leung Hon), Tien Lung Chen (Hsi San), Hark-On Fung (Hsi Sung). Professor Van Helsing is taken to a remote Chinese village which is being terrorised by the Seven Golden Vampires. Unbeknownst to him they are led by Count Dracula. A kung-fu vampire film with the tag line "Black Belt vs Black Magic". *Dirs*. Roy Ward Baker and Chang Cheh.

Leo the Last (1970) Marcello Mastroianni (Prince Leo), Billie Whitelaw (Margaret), Calvin Lockhart (Roscoe), Keefe West (Jasper), Glenna Forster-Jones (Salambo Mardi), Louis Gossett Jr. (Roscoe), Graham Crowden(Max), Gwen Ffrangcon Davies (Hilda), Vladek Sheybal (Laszlo), Kenneth J. Warren (Kowalski), David de Keyser (David), Thomas Bucson (Mr Mardi), Ishaq Bux (Supermarket Manager), Doris Clark (Singing Lady), Brinsley Forde (Bip), Ram John Holder (Black Preacher), Lucita Lijertwood (Wailing Lady). A scion of a long deposed monarchy returns to his father's London home to find the area is now run-down. *Dir*. John Boorman.

Leon the Pig Farmer (1993) Mark Frankel (Leon Geller), Janet Suzman (Judith Geller), Brian Glover (Brian Chadwick), Connie Booth (Yvonne Chadwick), David de Keyser (Sidney Geller), Maryam d'Abo (Madeleine), Gina Bellman (Lisa), Vincent Riotta (Elliot Cohen), Jean Anderson (Mrs. Samuels), John Woodvine (Vitelli), Annette Crosbie (Dr. Johnson), Stephen Greif (Doctor), Neil Mullarkey (Waiter), Barry Stanton (Peter), Burt Kwouk (Art Collector), Sean Pertwee (Keith Chadwick), Bernard Bresslaw (Rabbi Hartmann), Peter Whitman (Rabbi Jobson), Gordon Reid (Man), Jack Raymond (Gordon), Claudia Morris (Lawyer), Stanley Davis Jr. (Gutterman), Cyril Varley (Mr Goldman), Frank Lee (Mr Samuels), Stan Pretty (Uncle Louis), Thelma Ruby (Mrs Bernstein), Robbie Gringras (Harvey Geller), Danny Scheinmann (Nat Geller), Edward Halsted (Uncle Benny), Lesley Rubenson (Uncle Ernest), Ray McVay (Band Leader at Wedding). A Jewish estate agent discovers that his father is actually a Yorkshire pig farmer. *Dirs*. Vadim Jean and Gary Sinyor.

Les Bicyclettes de Belsize (1969) Anthony May (The Boy), Judy Huxtable (The Girl), Leslie Goddard (Little Girl), Barny Reisz (Little Boy), Danny Green (Man at Bus Stop), Dermot Kelly (Tramp at Bus Stop). A young man crashes into a billboard whilst out cycling and falls in love with the model depicted on it. Short film. *Dir*. Douglas Hickox

Lesbian Vampire Killers (2009) Mathew Horne (Jimmy), James Corden (Fletch), Paul McGann (Vicar), MyAnna Buring (Lotte), Louise Dylan (Anke), Ashley Mulheron (Trudi), Tiffany Mulheron (Heidi), Silvia Colloca (Carmilla), Vera Filatova (Eva), Lucy Gaskell (Judy), Travis Oliver (Steve), Emer Kenny (Rebecca), Emma Clifford (Ms Rossi), Susie Amy (Blonde), John Pierce Jones (Landlord), Margarita Hall (Daughter of Darkness 1), Sianad Gregory (Daughter of Darkness 2), Jessica Powell, Mary Liddell, Michelle Carter, Nellie McQuinn, Kimberley Payne, Stacy Franklin, Kelly Franklin, Suzanne Perkins, Rossana

Stocchino, Lucy Emes, Josephine McGrail, Sirle Von Schihver (Lesbian Vampires), Natalie Totham (Main Title Dancing Girl), Steve Clark-Hall (Sidney Goatherder No.7/The Storyteller). The village of Cragwich has been put under a curse that every female resident will turn into a lesbian vampire on her eighteenth birthday. Jimmy and Fletch decide to go camping and find themselves lodged in a cottage in the woods outside the village together with four beautiful female students of folklore. *Dir*. Phil Claydon.

Let George Do It (1940) George Formby (George Hepplewhite), Phyllis Calvert (Mary Wilson), Garry Marsh (Mendez), Romney Brent (Slim Selwyn), Bernard Lee (Oscar), Coral Browne (Iris), Helena Pickard (Oscar's Wife), Percy Walsh (Schwartz), Diana Beaumont (Greta), Torin Thatcher (U-Boat commander), Donald Calthrop (Frederick Strickland), Bill Shine (Untipped steward), Ronald Shiner (Musician), Ian Fleming (Col. Harcourt). George, a ukulele player for the Dinky Do concert party is engaged to play on board a ship and ends up taking on Nazi spies on the way to Bergen in Norway. *Dir*. Marcel Varnel.

Let Him Have It (1991) Christopher Eccleston (Derek Bentley), Paul Reynolds (Chris Craig), Tom Courtenay (William Bentley), Eileen Atkins (Lilian Bentley), Clare Holman (Iris Bentley), Ben Brazier (Denis Bentley), Rebecca Eccleston (Iris aged 10), Peter Eccleston (Bentley aged 8), Craig Turner (Bentley aged 14), Edward Hardwicke (Approved School Principal), Serena Scott Thomas (Stella), Rudolph Walker (West Indian Driver), Ronald Fraser (Niven's Judge), Niven Boyd (PC McDonald), Robert Morgan (PC Miles), Steve Nicolson (PC Harrison), Linda Bassett (Mrs Miles), Tom Bell (Fairfax), Iain Cuthbertson (Sir David Maxwell-Fyfe), Michael Gough (Lord Goddard), James Villiers (Cassels), Norman Rossington (Postman), Michael Elphick (Prison Officer Jack), Clive Revill (Pierrepoint), Walter Sparrow (Nightwatchman). Based on the true story of the case against Derek Bentley, who was hanged for the murder of PC Sidney Miles despite the fact he did not pull the trigger. The title of the film is taken from Bentley's alleged cry of "Let him have it, Chris!" shortly before Christopher Craig shot and wounded the first policeman on the scene. It was variously interpreted as meaning either "Go ahead and shoot him," or "Give him the gun". *Dir*. Peter Medak.

Let's Get Laid (1978) Fiona Richmond (Maxine Lupercal), Robin Askwith (Gordon Laid/Jimsy Deveroo), Anthony Steel (Moncrieff Dovecraft), Graham Stark (Inspector Nugent), Linda Hayden (Gloria), Roland Curram (Rupert Dorchester), Tony Haygarth (Sgt. Costello), Fanny Carby (Lady in Phone Booth), Patrick Holt (The Commissioner), Zuleika Robson (Thelma), Shelagh Dey (Helen), Ron Eagleton (Wilbur), Frank Ellis (Mortician), Elise Relnah (Old Lady), Daryl Fahey (Coutourier), Clive Moss (Corporal), John Clive (Piers Horrabin). Set in 1947, shy and retiring Gordon Laid is demobbed from the army but quickly gets involved in espionage and murder. Soon the police are shouting "Let's get Laid!". Typical 1970s sex comedy based on a stage revue of the same name. *Dir*. James Kenelm Clarke.

Letter to Brezhnev (1985) Alfred Molina (Sergei), Peter Firth (Peter), Tracy Marshak-Nash (Tracy), Alexandra Pigg (Elaine), Margi Clarke (Teresa), Susan Dempsey (Girl in Pub), Ted Wood (Mick), Sharon Power (Charlie's Girl), Robbie Dee (Charlie), Eddie Ross (Rayner), Syd Newman (Dmitri), Eileen Walsh (Mother), Angela Clarke (Josie), Joey Kaye (Father), Frank Clarke (Vinny), Iggy Navarro (President of Russia), Thelma Dee (Miss Jones), D.J. Swan (Postman), Ken Campbell (Reporter), Neil Cunningham (Foreign Office Man). Two Soviet sailors spend a night in Liverpool and meet and have fun with two girls. After they return to the ship and sail away one of the girls writes a letter to Soviet Premier Leonid Brezhnev asking if she can be reunited with her love. *Dir*. Chris Bernard.

Libel (1959) Dirk Bogarde (Sir Mark Sebastian Loddon/Frank Welney), Olivia de Havilland (Lady Margaret Loddon), Paul Massie (Jeffrey Buckenham), Robert Morley (Sir Wilfred), Wilfrid Hyde-White (Hubert Foxley), Anthony Dawson (Gerald Loddon), Richard Wattis (The Judge), Richard Dimbleby (Himself), Martin Miller (Dr Schrott), Millicent Martin (Maisie),

Toke Townley (Associate), Deering Wells (Editor), Bill Shine (Guide), Ivan Samson (Adm Loddon), Sebastian Saville (Michael Loddon), Richard Pearson (Butler), Joyce Carey (Miss Sykes), Robert Shaw (1st Photographer), Geoffrey Bayldon (2nd Photographer), Gordon Sterne (Maddox), Arthur Howard (Car Salesman), Josephine Middleton (Mrs Squire), Kenneth Griffith (Fitch). A Canadian pilot who escaped from a POW camp with Mark Loddon and Frank Welney claims that the Sir Mark he has seen on TV is actually Welney. Sir Mark's wife insists he sues for libel. *Dir.* Anthony Asquith.

Libertine, The (2004) Johnny Depp (John Wilmot), John Malkovich (King Charles II), Samantha Morton (Elizabeth Barry), Rosamund Pike (Elizabeth Wilmot), Tom Hollander (Sir George Etherege), Johnny Vegas (Charles Sackville), Richard Coyle (Alcock), Rupert Friend (Billy Downs), Jack Davenport (Harris), Kelly Reilly (Jane), Clare Higgins (Molly Luscombe), Francesca Annis (Countess), Paul Ritter (Chiffinch), Stanley Townsend (Keown), Tom Burke (Vaughan), Hugh Sachs (Ratcliffe), Trudi Jackson (Rose), Freddie Jones (Betterton), Robert Wilfort (Huysmans), Jake Curran (Sackville's Servant), Paul Chahidi (Barrillon), Kevin Doyle (Constable), Morgan Walters (Trooper), Niall Buggy (Chaplain), Peter Howell (Bishop), T.P. McKenna (Black Rod). The story of the short life of the notoriously debauched John Wilmot, 2nd Earl of Rochester, a writer of satirical and bawdy poetry during the reign of Charles II. *Dir.* Laurence Dunmore.

Licence to Kill (1989) Timothy Dalton (James Bond), Carey Lowell (Pam Bouvier), Robert Davi (Franz Sanchez), Talisa Soto (Lupe Lamora), Anthony Zerbe (Milton Krest), Frank McRae (Sharkey), Everett McGill (Ed Killifer), Wayne Newton (Professor Joe Butcher), Benicio del Toro (Dario), Anthony Starke (Truman-Lodge), Pedro Armendáriz, Jr. (President Hector Lopez), Desmond Llewelyn (Q), David Hedison (Felix Leiter), Priscilla Barnes (Della Churchill), Robert Brown (M), Caroline Bliss (Miss Moneypenny), Don Stroud (Colonel Heller), Grand L. Bush (Hawkins), Cary-Hiroyuki Tagawa (Kwang), Christopher Neame (Fallon), Diana Lee Hsu (Loti). After Felix Leiter is badly injured and his wife murdered on the night of their wedding Bond vows revenge on the man responsible – drug lord Franz Sanchez. He refuses the assignment when M orders him to go to Istanbul, has his licence to kill revoked and goes rogue. *Licence Revoked* was the original intended title for the film. The first film in the series not to use at least the title of an Ian Fleming novel. Bond drives a Kenworth W900B Truck and a Lincoln Mark VII LSC. The theme song was sung by Gladys Knight. *Dir.* John Glen

Life and Adventures of Nicholas Nickleby, The (1947) Derek Bond (Nicholas), Cedric Hardwicke (Ralph Nickleby), Mary Merrall (Mrs Nickleby), Sally Ann Howes (Kate Nickleby), Bernard Miles (Newman Noggs), Athene Seyler (Miss La Creevy), Alfred Drayton (Wackford Squeers), Sybil Thorndike (Mrs Squeers), Vida Hope (Fanny Squeers), Roy Hermitage (Wackford Squeers Jnr), Aubrey Woods (Smike), Patricia Hayes (Phoebe), Cyril Fletcher (Mr Mantalini), Fay Compton (Madame Mantalini), Cathleen Nesbitt (Miss Knag), Stanley Holloway (Vincent Crummles), Vera Pearce (Mrs Crummles), Una Bart (Infant Phenomenon), June Elvin (Miss Snevellicci), Drusilla Wills (Mrs Grudden), James Hayter (Ned and Charles Cheeryble), Emrys Jones (Frank Cheeryble), Roddy Hughes (Tim Linkinwater), George Relph (Mr Bray), Jill Balcon (Madeline Bray), Michael Shepley (Mr Gregsbury MP), Cecil Ramage (Sir Mulberry Hawk), Tim Bateson (Lord Verisopht), Laurence Hanray (Mr Gride), Frederick Burtwell (Sheriffs Mercury), John Salew (Mr Lillyvick), Arthur Brander (Mr Snawley), Eliot Makeham (Postman), John Chandos (Employment agent), Hattie Jacques (Mrs Kenwick), Dandy Nichols (Mantalini's employee). Adaptation of the Dickens novel. *Dir.* Alberto Cavalcanti.

Life and Death of Colonel Blimp, The (1943) Roger Livesey (Clive Candy), Deborah Kerr (Edith Hunter/Barbara Wynne/Angela "Johnny" Cannon), Anton Walbrook (Theo Kretschmar-Schuldorff), Ursula Jeans (Frau von Kalteneck), James McKechnie (Spud Wilson), David Hutcheson (Hoppy), Frith Banbury (Baby-Face Fitzroy), Muriel Aked (Aunt Margaret), John Laurie (Murdoch), Neville Mapp (Stuffy Graves), Spencer Trevor (Period Blimp), Roland Culver (as Colonel Betteridge), Valentine Dyall (von Schönborn), A. E. Matthews (President of Tribunal), Carl Jaffe (von Reumann), Albert Lieven (von Ritter), Eric Maturin (Colonel Goodhead), Yvonne Andre (The Nun), Marjorie Gresley (The Matron), Felix Aylmer (The Bishop). Framed by scenes in the modern day (1943 in wartime Britain) the film tells the story of Clive Wynne-Candy. After winning a Victoria Cross in the Boer War he travels to Germany to protest anti-British propaganda. Whilst there he both insults and then makes friends with a German officer. The film then recounts his experiences from 1902 until returning to the present. During production it was felt by some in the war department that the film might depict the British high command as "blimpish" (from the David Low cartoon character Colonel Blimp – a pompous and jingoistic character who issued commands whilst in a Turkish Bath) would somehow damage the war effort. In fact Clive Candy is a sympathetic character whose main problem is in not seeing that war was no longer a contest between "honourable" people. *Dirs.* Michael Powell and Emeric Pressburger.

Life at the Top (1965) Laurence Harvey (Joe Lampton), Jean Simmons (Susan Lampton), Honor Blackman (Norah Hauxley), Michael Craig (Mark), Donald Wolfit (Abe Brown), Robert Morley (Tiffield), Margaret Johnston (Sybil), Ambrosine Phillpotts (Mrs. Brown), Allan Cuthbertson (George Aisgill), Paul A. Martin (Harry), Frances Cosslett (Barbara), Ian Shand (Hethersett), George A. Cooper (Graffham), Nigel Davenport (Mottram), Andrew Laurence (McLelland), Geoffrey Bayldon (Industrial Psychologist), Denis Quilley (Ben). Having married the boss' daughter Joe thinks he has reached the top but finds both his career and personal life are not what he really expected? A sequel to *Room at the Top* (1958). *Dir.* Ted Kotcheff.

Life is Sweet (1990) Alison Steadman (Wendy), Jim Broadbent (Andy), Claire Skinner (Natalie), Jane Horrocks (Nicola), Stephen Rea (Patsy), Timothy Spall (Aubrey, Regret Rien Owner), David Thewlis (Nicola's Lover), Moya Brady (Paula, Aubrey's Cook), David Neilson (Steve the Plumber), Harriet Thorpe (Bunnikins' Customer), Paul Trussel (Chef), Jack Thorpe-Baker (Nigel). Follows the fortunes of a London family – good-natured Wendy, chef Andy and their twin daughters Natalie, a plumber and Nicola, a bulimic - over a few weeks one summer. *Dir.* Mike Leigh.

Lilacs in the Spring (1955) Errol Flynn (John 'Beau' Beaumont), Anna Neagle (Carole Beaumont/Lillian Grey/Nell Gwynn/Queen Victoria), David Farrar (Charles King/King Charles II), Kathleen Harrison (Kate), Peter Graves (Albert Gutman/Prince Albert), Helen Haye (Lady Drayton), Scott Sanders (Old George), Alma Taylor (1st Woman), Hetty King (2nd Woman), Alan Gifford (Hollywood Director), Jennifer Mitchell (Young Carole), Gillian Harrison (Very Young Carole), George Margo (Reporter), Stephen Boyd (Beaumont's Poolside Companion). Neagle plays an actress knocked out by a bomb, who in a delirious state dreams she is Queen Victoria, Nell Gwyn and also her own mother. Also known as *Let's Make Up*. Based on the play *The Glorious Days*. *Dir.* Herbert Wilcox.

Limping Man, The (1953) Lloyd Bridges (Frank Prior), Moira Lister (Pauline French), Alan Wheatley (Inspector Braddock), Leslie Phillips (Detective Cameron), Hélène Cordet (Helene Castle), Andre Van Gyseghem (George), Tom Gill (Stage Manager), Bruce Beeby (Kendal Brown), Rachel Roberts (Barmaid), Lionel Blair (Dancer), Robert Harbin (Harper LeStrade), Charles Bottrill (The Xylophonist), Verne Morgan (Henry Stone), Marjorie Hume (Landlady), Raymond Rollett (Jones), Jean Marsh (Landlady's Daughter), Maxwell Gardner (Airport Official), Irissa Cooper (Cynthia), Olive Lucius (Sandwich Lady). On his arrival in London to visit an ex-girlfriend Frank Prior, a sniper kills the man standing next to him. Police begin looking for a limping man who was at the scene. It transpires that his ex-girlfriend was a lover of the man who was shot. *Dir.* Cy Endfield.

Linda (1960) Carol White (Linda), Alan Rothwell (Phil), Cavan Malone (Chief), Edward Cast (Vicar), Vivienne Lacey (Rosie), Lois Daine (Clara), Larry Dann (Len), Keith Faulkner (Joe), Harry Pringle (Fred), Richard Palmer (Teddy), Tony Lyons (Dave), Pearson Todd (Jack). Phil falls for Linda and she tries to lead him away from the gang he spends his time with. *Dir.* Don Sharp.

Lion in Winter, The (1968) Peter O'Toole (King Henry II), Katharine Hepburn (Queen Eleanor), Anthony Hopkins (Richard),

John Castle (Geoffrey), Nigel Terry (John), Timothy Dalton (King Philip II), Jane Merrow (Alais), Nigel Stock (Capt William Marshall), Kenneth Ives (Queen Eleanor's guard), O.Z. Whitehead (Hugh de Puiset). At Christmas 1183, Henry II brings together all the parties of interest in his succession plans - his estranged and imprisoned wife, a French Princess who is his mistress, his three sons (Richard, Geoffrey and John) and the brother of his mistress who just happens to be King of France. Machiavellian intrigue, double-dealing and back-stabbing ensues. The film won three Academy Awards: Best Actress in a Leading Role (Katharine Hepburn), Best Music, Original Score for a Motion Picture (not a Musical) (John Barry), Best Writing, Screenplay Based on Material from Another Medium. Based on the play by James Goldman. Anthony Hopkins and Timothy Dalton both made their big screen debuts in this film. *Dir*. Anthony Harvey.

Liquidator, The (1965) Rod Taylor ("Boysie" Oakes), Trevor Howard (Maj/Col Mostyn), Jill St. John (Iris), Wilfrid Hyde-White (Chief), David Tomlinson (Quadrant), Akim Tamiroff (Sheriek), Eric Sykes (Griffen), Gabriella Licudi (Corale), John Le Mesurier (Chekhov), Derek Nimmo (Fly), Jeremy Lloyd (Young Man), Jennifer Jayne (Janice Benedict), Heller Toren (Assistant), Betty McDowall (Frances Anne), Jo Rowbottom (Betty), Colin Gordon (Vicar), Louise Dunn (Jessie), Henri Cogan (Yakov), Daniel Emilfork (Gregory), Scott Finch (Operations Officer), Ronald Leigh-Hunt (Mac), Richard Wattis (Flying Instructor), David Langton (Station Commander), Tony Wright (Flying Control), Suzy Kendall (Judith). Twenty years after saving Mostyn's life during WWII, Oakes is hired by him as a "liquidator" to eliminate security leaks. Based on the first of a series of Boysie Oakes novels by John Gardner. *Dir*. Jack Cardiff.

Lisztomania (1975) Roger Daltrey (Franz Liszt), Sara Kestelman (Princess Carolyn), Paul Nicholas (Richard Wagner), Ringo Starr (The Pope), Rick Wakeman (Thor), John Justin (Count d'Agoult), Fiona Lewis (Marie d'Agoult), Veronica Quilligan (Cosima), Nell Campbell (Olga Janina), Andrew Reilly (Hans Von Buelow), David English (Captain), Imogen Claire (George Sand), Rikki Howard (Countess), David Corti (Daniel), Anulka Dziubinska (Lola Montez), Lucy Willers (Blondine), Felicity Devonshire (Governess), Murray Melvin (Hector Berlioz), Aubrey Morris (Manager), Andrew Faulds (Strauss), Ken Parry (Rossini), Kenneth Colley (Frederic Chopin), Otto Diamant (Felix Mendelsohn), Oliver Reed (Princess Carolyn's Servant). An irreverent biopic of composer Franz Liszt (Russell had already tackled Elgar, Tchaikovsky and Mahler) which depicts him as the first classical pop star. *Dir*. Ken Russell.

Little Dorrit (1987) Derek Jacobi (Arthur Clennam), Joan Greenwood (Mrs Clennam), Max Wall (Jeremiah Flintwinch), Patricia Hayes (Affery Flintwinch), Luke Duckett (Young Arthur), Alec Guinness (William Dorrit), Cyril Cusack (Frederick Dorrit), Sarah Pickering (Little Dorrit), Amelda Brown (Fanny Dorrit), Daniel Chatto (Tip Dorrit), Miriam Margolyes (Flora Finching), Bill Fraser (Mr Casby), Roshan Seth (Mr Pancks), Mollie Maureen (Mr F's Aunt), Diana Malin (Mr Casby's Maid), Pauline Quirke (Maggy), Janice Cramer (Young Flora), Roger Hammond (Mr. Meagles), Sophie Ward (Minnie Meagles), Kathy Staff (Mrs Tickit), Julia Lang (Henry Gowan's Mother), Pip Torrens (Henry Gowan), Graham Seed (William Barnacle), Beth Ellis (Mrs Wiliam Barnacle), Ian Gelder (Reverend Samuel Barnacle), Lee Fox (Richard Barnacle), Robert Mill (Hugh Stilstalking), Morwenna Banks (Georgina), John Savident (Tite Barnacle), Brian Pettifer (Clarence Barnacle), John Harding (Ferdinand Barnacle), Ken Morley (Mr Wobbler), David Thewlis (George Braddle), Gerald Campion (Mr Tetterby), Rita Treisman (Mrs Tetterby), Betty Turner (Mrs Kidgerbury), Johnnie Clayton (Fiddler), Moya Brady (Fiddler's Daughter), John Fahey (Furniture Seller), Joanna Maude (Furniture Seller's Wife), Iris Sadler (Shirtmaker), Joanna Brookes (Shirtmaker's Daughter), Nat Pearn (Mr Strong), Cyril Epstein (Mr Strong's Friend), Alan Bungay (Principal Messenger), Howard Goorney (Bob - the Turnkey), Liz Smith (Mrs Bangham, Midwife), Gwenda Hughes (Mrs Dorrit), Celia Bannerman (Milliner), Murray Melvin (Dancing Master), Eleanor Bron (Mrs Merdle), Michael Elphick

(Mr Merdle), Simon Dormandy (Sparkler), Ian Hogg (Butler), Robert Morley (Lord Decimus Barnacle), Alan Bennett (Bishop), Brenda Bruce (Duchess), Rosalie Crutchley (Wife), Betty Marsden (Mrs Phoebe Barnacle). The lives of successful businessman Arthur Clennam and Little Dorrit continually cross. Adaptation of the Dickens novel. *Dir*. Christine Edzard.

Little Voice (1998) Brenda Blethyn (Mari Hoff), Jane Horrocks (Laura 'Little Voice' Hoff), Michael Caine (Ray Say), Ewan McGregor (Billy), Jim Broadbent (Mr. Boo), Philip Jackson (George), Annette Badland (Sadie), Fred Feast (Arthur), Graham Turner (LV's Dad), Fred Gaunt (Wild Trigger Smith). Ray, a talent agent and one of her blousey mother's boyfriends hears reclusive and intensely shy Laura impersonating the singers from her late father's collection of old records and decides she could be the answer to boosting his own career. Based on the play *The Rise and Fall of Little Voice* by Jim Cartwright. *Dir*. Mark Herman.

Live and Let Die (1973) Roger Moore (James Bond), Yaphet Kotto (Mr. Big), Jane Seymour (Solitaire), Julius Harris (Tee Hee Johnson), David Hedison (Felix Leiter), Gloria Hendry (Rosie Carver), Clifton James (Sheriff J.W. Pepper), Geoffrey Holder (Baron Samedi), Bernard Lee (M), Roy Stewart (Quarrel Jr.), Earl Jolly Brown (Whisper), Tommy Lane (Adam), Lois Maxwell (Miss Moneypenny), Madeline Smith (Miss Caruso). The plot revolves around the plan by Dr Kananga (aka Mr Big), the dictator of Caribbean island St Monique to release tons of heroin on to the market for free and thus put his rival drug dealers out of business and increase the number of addicts. Solitaire is a tarot card wielding virgin (at least at the start of the film). Bond drives a double-decker bus and a white Coronado. The theme song was written by Paul and Linda McCartney and performed by Wings. Adapted from the novel by Ian Fleming. *Dir*. Guy Hamilton.

Live It Up! (1963) David Hemmings (Dave Martin), Jennifer Moss (Jill), Veronica Hurst (Kay), Heinz Burt (Ron), Joan Newell (Margaret Martin), David Bauer (Mark Watson), Steve Marriott (Ricky), Mitch Mitchell (Andrews). Music by Kenny Ball and his Jazzmen, Patsy Ann Noble, Gene Vincent, Sounds Incorporated and The Outlaws. Dave Martin is a despatch rider with big dreams of making it in the music industry with his band of co-workers. His father does not want to see him waste his life so offers him an ultimatum: if the music business does not want him after one month, he must pack it in. The producer and writer of many of the songs in the film was the legendary Joe Meek, here still riding high just prior to The Beatles and the Stones making this type of film a last Hurrah. *Dir*. Lance Comfort.

Living Daylights, The (1987) Timothy Dalton (James Bond), Maryam d'Abo (Kara Milovy), Jeroen Krabbé (General Georgi Koskov), Joe Don Baker (Brad Whitaker), John Rhys-Davies (General Leonid Pushkin), Art Malik (Kamran Shah), Andreas Wisniewski (Necros), Thomas Wheatley (Saunders), Robert Brown (M), Desmond Llewelyn (Q), Geoffrey Keen (Frederick Gray), Caroline Bliss (Miss Moneypenny), John Terry (Felix Leiter), Walter Gotell (General Gogol), Julie T. Wallace (Rosika Miklos). Bond is sent to Bratislava to aid the defection of a KGB officer, General Georgi Koskov and in the process crosses paths with beautiful Russian sniper and cellist Kara Milovy. Bond drives an Aston Martin DBS V8 Vantage and an Audi 200 Quattro. The theme song was sung by A-ha. *Dir*. John Glen.

Local Hero (1983) Burt Lancaster (Felix Happer), Peter Riegert (Mac), Fulton Mackay (Ben), Denis Lawson (Urquhart), Norman Chancer (Moritz), Peter Capaldi (Oldsen), Rikki Fulton (Geddes), Alex Norton (Watt), Jenny Seagrove (Marina), Jennifer Black (Stella), Christopher Rozycki (Victor), Gyearbuor Asante (Rev Macpherson), John M. Jackson (Cal), John Gordon Sinclair (Ricky). Texan oil magnate sends Mac to a remote Scottish village to secure the property rights for a refinery they want to build. Mac teams up with Danny and at first the negotiations with the locals go well. However, it turns out that Ben, a local hermit, owns the beach. The film spawned a very popular soundtrack scored by Mark Knopfler. *Dir*. Bill Forsyth.

Lock, Stock and Two Smoking Barrels (1998) Jason Flemyng (Tom), Dexter Fletcher (Soap), Nick Moran (Eddy), Jason Statham (Bacon), Steven Mackintosh (Winston), Vinnie Jones

(Big Chris), Nicholas Rowe (J), Nick Marcq (Charles), Lenny McLean (Barry "the Baptist"), Steve Sweeney (Plank), Peter McNicholl (Little Chris), Suzy Ratner (Gloria), P. H. Moriarty ("Hatchet" Harry Lonsdale), Stephen Marcus (Nick "the Greek"), Vas Blackwood (Rory Breaker), Frank Harper (Diamond Dog), Huggy Leaver (Paul), Alan Ford (Alan/Narrator), Victor McGuire (Gary), Jake Abraham (Dean), Sting (JD), Rob Brydon (Traffic Warden), Danny John-Jules (Barman). Four young friends lose big to "Hatchet" Harry in a crooked card game and have a week to pay off the debt. Their plan to relieve a neighbouring gang of thieves of its ill-gotten gains is only the first of a bewildering series of schemes mainly surrounding a pair of antique shot guns. *Dir*. Guy Ritchie.

Lodger, The (1932) Ivor Novello (Michel Angeloff), Elizabeth Allan (Daisy Bunting), A.W. Baskcomb (George Bunting), Barbara Everest (Mrs Bunting), Jack Hawkins (Joe Martin), Shayle Gardner (Detective Snell), Peter Gawthorne (Lord Southcliff), Kynaston Reeves (Bob Mitchell), Drusilla Wills (Mrs Coles), Anthony Holles (Silvano), George Merritt (Commissioner). A remake of Hitchcock's 1926 film *The Lodger: A Story of the London Fog* with the same star. *Dir*. Maurice Elvey.

Lodger: A Story of the London Fog, The (1926) Ivor Novello (The Lodger), Marie Ault (Mrs. Bunting), Arthur Chesney (Mr. Bunting), June (Daisy Bunting), Malcolm Keen (Joe), Reginald Gardiner (Dancer at Ball), Eve Gray (Showgirl Victim), Alma Reville (Woman Listening to Wireless). A Jack the Ripper style killer known as "The Avenger" is stalking the streets of London murdering blonde women. Is Mrs Bunting's new lodger a suspect? Hitchcock can be seen seated at desk in a newsroom, and later he's one of the onlookers watching the arrest of the lodger. A 1926 film that did not go on general release until February 1927. Based on a story by Marie Belloc Lowndes and a play *Who Is He?*. *Dir*. Alfred Hitchcock.

Lola (1969) Charles Bronson (Scott Wardman), Susan George (Lola/Twinky/Sybil Londonderry), Orson Bean (Hal), Honor Blackman (Mummy), Michael Craig (Daddy), Paul Ford (Mr Wardman), Jack Hawkins (Judge Millington-Draper), Trevor Howard (Lola's Grandfather), Lionel Jeffries (Solicitor), Kay Medford (Mrs Wardman), Robert Morley (Judge Roxborough), Peggy Aitchison (Mrs Finchley), Eric Barker (Scottish Clerk), Erik Chitty (Lawyer's Elderly Client), Anthony Kemp (Peter), Sue Lloyd (Ursula). An American writer of pornography marries a 16 year old in London and they move to the US, where the bride has to attend school. The age-gap begins to cause problems. *Dir*. Richard Donner.

Lolita (1962) James Mason (Prof. Humbert Humbert), Shelley Winters (Charlotte Haze), Sue Lyon (Lolita), Gary Cockrell (Richard T. Schiller), Jerry Stovin (John Farlow), Diana Decker (Jean Farlow), Lois Maxwell (Nurse Mary Lore), Cec Linder (Physician), Bill Greene (George Swine), Shirley Douglas (Mrs. Starch), Marianne Stone (Vivian Darkbloom), Marion Mathie (Miss Lebone), James Dyrenforth (Frederick Beale Sr.), Maxine Holden (Miss Fromkiss), John Harrison (Tom), Colin Maitland (Charlie Sedgewick), Terry Kilburn (Man), C. Denier Warren (Potts), Roland Brand (Bill Crest), Peter Sellers (Clare Quilty), Ed Bishop (Ambulance Attendant). Waiting to take up a teaching position, Prof Humbert takes a room for the summer with Charlotte Haze and her daughter Dolores, known as "Lolita". Based on the Vladimir Nabokov novel. *Dir*. Stanley Kubrick.

London Belongs to Me (1948) Richard Attenborough (Percy Boon), Alastair Sim (Mr. Squales), Fay Compton (Mrs. Josser), Stephen Murray (Uncle Henry), Wylie Watson (Mr. Josser), Susan Shaw (Doris Josser), Joyce Carey (Mrs. Vizzard), Ivy St. Helier (Connie Coke), Andrew Crawford (Bill), Hugh Griffith (Headlam Fynne), Eleanor Summerfield (The Blonde), Gladys Henson (Mrs. Boon), Maurice Denham (Jack Rufus), Ivor Barnard (Mr. Justice Plymme), Cecil Trouncer (Mr. Henry Wassall), Arthur Howard (Mr. Chinkwell), John Salew (Mr. Barks), Cyril Chamberlain (Detective Sergeant Wilson), Aubrey Dexter (Mr. Battlebury), Jack McNaughton (Jimmy), Henry Hewitt (Verriter), Fabia Drake (Mrs. Jan Byl), Sydney Tafler (Nightclub Receptionist), George Cross (Inspector Cartwright), Edward Evans (Detective Sergeant Taylor), Kenneth Downey (Mr. Veezey Blaize K.C.), Leo Genn (Narrator, introduction), Arthur Lowe (Commuter on Train). The inter-related stories of the families living in a large London terrace house, and in particular Percy, who ends up being accused of murder. Based on the novel by Norman Collins. Also known as *Dulcimer Street*. *Dir*. Sidney Gilliat.

London to Brighton (2006) Lorraine Stanley (Kelly), Georgia Groome (Joanne), Johnny Harris (Derek), Nathan Constance (Chum), Sam Spruell (Stuart Allen), Alexander Morton (Duncan Allen), David Keeling (Charlie), Jamie Kenna (Tony), Chloe Bale (Karen), Claudie Blakley (Tracey), Tim Matthews (Shane), Louise Appel (Debbie), Su Douglas (Gran), David Barker (David). Prostitute Kelly and young Joanne are on the run from London after the death of a client. Their first stop is Brighton but Kelly's pimp is on her trail. *Dir*. Paul Andrew Williams.

London Town (1946) Sid Field (Jerry Sanford), Greta Gynt (Mrs. Eve Barry), Petula Clark (Peggy Sanford), Kay Kendall (Patsy), Sonnie Hale (Charlie de Haven), Claude Hulbert (Belgrave), Mary Clare (Mrs. Gates), Tessie O'Shea (Herself), Jerry Desmonde (George), Beryl Davis (Paula), Scotty McHarg (Bill), W.G. Fay (Mike), Reginald Purdell (Stage Manager), Alf Dean (Heckler), Charles Paton (Novelty Shopkeeper), Pamela Carroll (Street Singer), Jack Parnell (Drummer), Wally Patch (Constable). A rare big budget British technicolour musical which, unfortunately "took a bath" at the box office. An ageing Music Hall performer is slated to be an understudy to the lead in a new musical revue in the West End. His daughter decides to sabotage the star and give her father a last chance of fame. A much cut version of the film was released in the US in 1953 as *My Heart Goes Crazy*, one of the songs in the film's score. *Dir*. Wesley Ruggles.

Loneliness of the Long Distance Runner, The (1962) Michael Redgrave (Ruxton Towers Reformatory governor), Tom Courtenay (Colin Smith), Avis Bunnage (Mrs. Smith), Alec McCowen (Brown, House Master), James Bolam (Mike), Joe Robinson (Roach), Dervis Ward (Detective), Topsy Jane (Audrey), Julia Foster (Gladys), John Brooking (Green). After being sent to a borstal for theft Colin discovers he has a talent for running, much to the delight of the governor. Based on the Alan Sillitoe short story. *Dir*. Tony Richardson.

Lonely Passion of Judith Hearne, The (1987) Maggie Smith (Judith Hearne), Bob Hoskins (James Madden), Wendy Hiller (Aunt D'Arcy), Marie Kean (Mrs. Rice), Ian McNeice (Bernard Rice), Alan Devlin (Father Quigley), Rudi Davies (Mary), Prunella Scales (Moira O'Neill), Aine Ni Mhuiri (Edie Marinan), Sheila Reid (Miss Friel), Niall Buggy (Mr. Lenehan), Kate Binchy (Sister Ignatius), Martina Stanley (Sister Mary-Paul), Veronica Quilligan (Mrs. Mullen), Frank Egerton (The Major), Leonard Maguire (Doctor Bowe), Kevin Flood (Owen O'Neill), Catherine Cusack (Una O'Neill), Peter Gilmore (Kevin O'Neill), James Holland (Shaun O'Neill), Aiden Murphy (Youth at Liquor Store), Emma Jane Lavin (Young Judith), Dick Sullivan (Priest), Alan Radcliffe (Young Priest). A middle-aged spinster piano teacher falls for hotel owner James Madden. Based on the novel *Judith Hearne* by Brian Moore. *Dir*. Jack Clayton.

Long and the Short and the Tall, The (1961) Laurence Harvey (Pvt. 'Bammo' Bamforth), Richard Todd (Sgt. 'Mitch' Mitchem), Richard Harris (Cpl. Johnstone), David McCallum (Pvt. Sammy Whitaker), Ronald Fraser (LCpl. 'Mac' Macleish), John Meillon (Pvt. 'Smudger' Smith), John Rees (Pvt. Evans), Kenji Takaki (Tojo), Anthony Chinn (Japanese Sniper). In 1942 a group of British soldiers are holed up in a hut in the Burmese jungle with no means of communication with base. Then a lone Japanese soldier stumbles into the hut and is taken prisoner. Based on the play by Willis Hall. *Dir*. Leslie Norman

Long Arm, The (1956) Jack Hawkins (Supt Tom Halliday), John Stratton (Sgt Ward), Dorothy Alison (Mary Halliday), Michael Brooke (Tony Halliday), Sam Kydd (Police Operator), Glyn Houston (Sergeant), Richard Leech (Gilson), Newton Blick (Det Comdr Harris), Geoffrey Keen (Chief Supt Malcolm), Sydney Tafler (Mr Stone), Peter Burton (Mr. Creasey), George Rose (Slob), Arthur Rigby (Det Insp), Ralph Truman (Col Blenkinsop), Ian Bannen (Hit and Run Victim), Joss Ambler (Shipping office cashier), Harry Locke (Junk Dealer), Nicholas Parsons (PC Bates), Ursula Howells (Mrs Elliott), Meredith Edwards (Thomas), Maureen Delaney (Mrs Stevens), Jameson Clark (Det Ogilvie), William Mervyn (Manager of the Royal Festival Hall),

Stratford Johns (PC), David Lodge (Detective). Superintendent Tom Halliday is on the trail of a safe cracker who is targeting companies with the same model of safe. *Dir*. Charles Frend.

Long Day Closes, The (1992) Marjorie Yates (Mother), Leigh McCormack (Bud), Anthony Watson (Kevin), Nicholas Lamont (John), Ayse Owens (Helen), Tina Malone (Edna), Jimmy Wilde (Curly), Robin Polley (Mr. Nicholls), Peter Ivatts (Mr. Bushell), Joy Blakeman (Frances), Denise Thomas (Jean), Patricia Morrison (Amy), Gavin Mawdslay (Billy), Kirk McLaughlin (Labourer/Christ), Marcus Heath (Black Man), Victoria Davies (Nun), Brenda Peters (Nurse), Kerl Skeggs (Albie). Set in Liverpool in the 1950s. After moving to a new school Bud uses the local cinema as a retreat from life. *Dir*. Terence Davies.

Long Good Friday, The (1980) Bob Hoskins (Harold Shand), Helen Mirren (Victoria), Dave King (Parky), Bryan Marshall (Harris), Derek Thompson (Jeff), Eddie Constantine (Charlie), Paul Freeman (Colin), Leo Dolan (Phil), Kevin McNally (Irish Youth) Patti Love (Carol), P.H. Moriarty (Razors), Pierce Brosnan (1st Irishman), Daragh O'Malley (2nd Irishman), Karl Howman (David), Brian Hall (Alan), Alan Ford (Jack), Paul Barber (Erroll), Dexter Fletcher (Kid), Gillian Taylforth (Sherry). Old-time gangster Harold is thinking of going legit as he sees an opportunity in the East End property market because of an upcoming London Olympics (such prescience) but his plans are suddenly disrupted by a series of bombings on his manor. Classic Harold quotes from the film include: "The Mafia? I've shit 'em", "You don't crucify people! Not on Good Friday!" and "Nothing unusual, he says! Eric's been blown to smithereens, Colin's been carved up, and I've got a bomb in me casino, and you say nothing unusual?" *Dir*. John Mackenzie.

Long Memory, The (1952) John Mills (Phillip Davidson), John McCallum (Supt. Bob Lowther), Elizabeth Sellars (Fay Lowther), Eva Bergh (Ilse), Geoffrey Keen (Craig), Michael Martin Harvey (Jackson), John Chandos (Boyd), John Slater (Pewsey), Thora Hird (Mrs. Pewsley), Vida Hope (Alice Gedge), Harold Lang (Boyd's Chauffeur), Mary Mackenzie (Gladys), John Glyn-Jones (Gedge), John Horsley (Bletchley), Fred Johnson (Driver), Laurence Naismith (Hasbury), Peter Jones (Fisher), Christopher Beeny (Mickie), Arthur Mullard (Policeman). Davidson is released from prison 12 years after having been framed for murder and sets out to revenge himself on those responsible. *Dir*. Robert Hamer.

Long Ships, The (1964) Richard Widmark (Rolfe), Sidney Poitier (Aly Mansuh), Russ Tamblyn (Orm), Rosanna Schiaffino (Aminah), Oskar Homolka (Krok), Edward Judd (Sven), Lionel Jeffries (Aziz), Beba Loncar (Gerda), Clifford Evans (King Harald), Gordon Jackson (Vahlin), Colin Blakely (Rhykka), David Lodge (Olla), Henry Oscar (Auctioneer), Paul Stassino (Raschid), Jeanne Moody (Ylva). Rolfe steals King Harald's funeral ship in an attempt to find the legendary giant solid gold bell known as the "Mother of Voices". However, he also has to overcome the Moors led by Aly Mansuh. Based on the novel by Frans G. Bengtsson. *Dir*. Jack Cardiff.

Long Time Dead (2002) Joe Absolom (Rob), Lara Belmont (Stella), Melanie Gutteridge (Annie), Lukas Haas (Webster), James Hillier (Spencer), Alec Newman (Liam), Mel Raido (Joe), Marsha Thomason (Lucy), Tom Bell (Becker), Michael Feast (Paul Brennan), Cyril Nri (Dr Wilson), Tameka Empson (student), Peter Gevisser (Lucy's neighbour), Derek Lea (Guard), Joel Pitts (Young Liam), Pete Valente (Djinn). At the end of a drunken night out, a group of students using a Ouija board unleash an evil spirit which could spell their doom. *Dir*. Marcus Adams.

Look Back in Anger (1959) Richard Burton (Jimmy Porter), Claire Bloom (Helena Charles), Mary Ure (Alison Porter), Edith Evans (Mrs. Tanner), Gary Raymond (Cliff Lewis), Glen Byam Shaw (Colonel Redfern), Phyllis Neilson-Terry (Mrs. Redfern), Donald Pleasence (Hurst), Jane Eccles (Miss Drury), S.P. Kapoor (Kapoor), George Devine (Doctor), Walter Hudd (Actor), Anne Dickins (Girl A.S.M.), John Dearth (Pet Stall Man), Nigel Davenport (1st Commercial Traveller), Alfred Lynch (2nd Commercial Traveller), Toke Townley (Spectacled Man), Bernice

Swanson (Sally), Michael Balfour (Picky Shopper). The original "angry young man" and "kitchen sink drama". Based on John Osborne's play. *Dir*. Tony Richardson.

Look Before you Love (1948) Margaret Lockwood (Ann Markham), Griffith Jones (Charles Kent), Norman Wooland (Ashley Morehouse), Phyllis Stanley (Bettina Colby), Maurice Denham (Fosser), Frederick Piper (Miller), Bruce Seton (Johns), Michael Medwin (Emile Garat), Violet Farebrother (Dowager), Dorothy Bramhall (Amy). A woman working at the British Embassy in Rio marries a fraudster. *Dir*. Harold Huth.

Look Up and Laugh (1935) Gracie Fields (Gracie Pearson), Alfred Drayton (Belfer), Douglas Wakefield (Joe Chirk), Billy Nelson (Alf Chirk), Harry Tate (Turnpenny), Huntley Wright (Ketley), Vivien Leigh (Marjorie Belfer), Helen Ferrers (Lady Buster), Tommy Fields (Sidney Pearson), Maud Gill (Miss Canvey), Morris Harvey (Rosenbloom), Jack Melford (Journalist), Norman Walker (Brierley), D.J. Williams (Malpas). Singer Gracie sets out to save a market from being demolished. *Dir*. Basil Dean.

Looking for Eric (2009) Steve Evets (Eric Bishop), Eric Cantona (Himself), Stephanie Bishop (Lily), Gerard Kearns (Ryan), Stefan Gumbs (Jess), Lucy-Jo Hudson (Sam), Cole and Dylan Williams (Daisy), Matthew McNulty (Young Eric), Laura Ainsworth (Young Lily), Max Beesley (Eric's Father), Kelly Bowland (Ryan's Girlfriend), Julie Brown (Nurse), John Henshaw (Meatballs), Justin Moorhouse (Spleen), Des Sharples (Jack), Greg Cook (Monk), Mick Ferry (Judge), Smug Roberts (Smug), Johnny Travis (Travis), Steve Marsh (Zac), Cleveland Campbell (Buzz), Ryan Pope (Fenner). A postman with family problems takes sage advice from his hero, footballer Eric Cantona. *Dir*. Ken Loach.

Looking Glass War, The (1969) Christopher Jones (Leiser), Pia Degermark (The Girl), Ralph Richardson (LeClerc), Paul Rogers (Haldane), Anthony Hopkins (John Avery), Susan George (Susan), Ray McAnally (Undersecretary of State), Robert Urquhart (Johnson), Anna Massey (Avery's Wife), Vivian Pickles (Mrs King), Maxine Audley (Mrs LeClerc), Cyril Shaps (East German Detective), Michael Robbins (Truck Driver), Timothy West (Taylor), Guy Deghy (Fritsche). An agent is reactivated and sent into East Germany to investigate new missile emplacements. *Dir*. Frank Pierson.

Looking on the Bright Side (1932) Gracie Fields (Gracie), Richard Dolman (Laurie), Julian Rose (Oscar Schultz), Wyn Richmond (Josie Joy), Tony De Lungo (Delmonico), Betty Shale (Hetty Hunt), Viola Compton (Police Sergeant), Bettina Montahners (Bettina), Charles Farrell (Released criminal). Gracie and Laurie's double act is in trouble when he falls for a beautiful actress. *Dirs*. Basil Dean and Graham Cutts.

Loot (1970) Richard Attenborough (Insp Truscott), Lee Remick (Nurse Fay McMahon), Hywel Bennett (Dennis), Milo O'Shea (Mr. McLeavy), Roy Holder (Hal), Dick Emery (Mr. Bateman), Joe Lynch (Father O'Shaughnessy), John Cater (Meadows), Aubrey Woods (Undertaker), Enid Lowe (W.V.A. Leader), Harold Innocent (Bank Manager), Kevin Brennan (Vicar). Hal and Dennis rob a bank and hide the money in Hal's mum's coffin. Based Joe Orton's play. *Dir*. Silvio Narizzano.

Lord Jim (1965) Peter O'Toole (Lord Jim/James Burke), James Mason ("Gentleman" Brown), Curd Jürgens (Cornelius), Eli Wallach (The General), Jack Hawkins (Marlow), Paul Lukas (Stein), Daliah Lavi (The Girl), Akim Tamiroff (Schomberg), Juzo Itami (Waris), Tatsuo Saito (Du-Ramin), Andrew Keir (Brierly), Jack MacGowran (Robinson), Eric Young (Malay), Noel Purcell (Capt Chester), Walter Gotell (Captain of Patna). After an exhibition of cowardice, Jim takes on a dangerous mission in order to try and gain some redemption. An adaptation of the novel of the same name by Joseph Conrad. *Dir*. Richard Brooks.

Lord of the Flies (1963) James Aubrey (Ralph), Tom Chapin (Jack), Hugh Edwards (Piggy), Roger Elwin (Roger), Tom Gaman (Simon), David Surtees (Sam), Simon Surtees (Eric), Roger Allan (Piers), David Brunjes (Donald), Peter Davy (Peter), Kent Fletcher (Percival Wemys Madison), Nicholas Hammond (Robert), Christopher Harris (Bill), Alan Heaps (Neville),

Jonathan Heaps (Howard), Burnes Hollyman (Douglas), Andrew Horne (Matthew), Richard Horne (Lance), Timothy Horne (Leslie), Peter Ksiezopolski (Francis), Anthony McCall-Judson (Morris), Malcolm Rodker (Harold), David St. Clair (George), Rene Sanfiorenzo Jr. (Charles), Jeremy Scuse (Rowland), John Stableford (Digby), Nicholas Valkenburg (Rupert), Patrick Valkenburg (Robin), Edward Valencia (Frederick), John Walsh (Michael), David Walsh (Percy), Jeremy Willis (Henry). After their airline is brought down a group of schoolchildren find themselves on a deserted island and revert to savagery. An adaptation of William Golding's novel. *Dir.* Peter Brook.

Love Actually (2003) Alan Rickman (Harry), Emma Thompson (Karen), Heike Makatsch (Mia), Hugh Grant (David), Martine McCutcheon (Natalie), Keira Knightley (Juliet), Chiwetel Ejiofor (Peter), Andrew Lincoln (Mark), Colin Firth (Jamie), Lúcia Moniz (Aurélia), Liam Neeson (Daniel), Thomas Sangster (Sam), Bill Nighy (Billy Mack), Gregor Fisher (Joe), Laura Linney (Sarah), Rodrigo Santoro (Karl), Kris Marshall (Colin), Abdul Salis (Tony), Martin Freeman (John), Joanna Page (Judy), Olivia Olson (Joanna), Billy Bob Thornton (US President), Rowan Atkinson (Rufus), Claudia Schiffer (Carol), Nina Sosanya (Annie), Ivana Miličević (Stacey), January Jones (Jeannie), Elisha Cuthbert (Carol-Anne), Shannon Elizabeth (Harriet), Denise Richards (Carla), Lulu Popplewell (Daisy), Marcus Brigstocke (Mikey), Julia Davis (Nancy), Sienna Guillory (Jamie's Girlfriend). The film explores the relationships between various couples as Christmas approaches. *Dir.* Richard Curtis.

Love Lottery, The (1954) David Niven (Rex Allerton), Peggy Cummins (Sally), Anne Vernon (Jane Dubois), Herbert Lom (André Amico), Charles Victor (Jennings), Gordon Jackson (Ralph), Felix Aylmer (Winant), Hugh McDermott (Rodney Wheeler), Stanley Maxted (Oliver Stanton), June Clyde (Viola), John Chandos (Gulliver Kee), Theodore Bikel (Parsimonious), Sebastian Cabot (Suarez), Eugene Deckers (Vernet), Andreas Malandrinos (Fodor), Hattie Jacques (Chambermaid), Jean Marsh (Dancer). A Hollywood heart-throb becomes a lottery prize. *Dir.* Charles Crichton.

Love on the Dole (1941) Deborah Kerr (Sally Hardcastle), Clifford Evans (Larry Meath), George Carney (Mr. Hardcastle), Mary Merrall (Mrs. Hardcastle), Geoffrey Hibbert (Harry), Joyce Howard (Helen), Frank Cellier (Sam Grundy), Martin Walker (Ned Narkey), Maire O'Neill (Mrs. Dorbell), Iris Vandeleur (Mrs. Nattle), Marie Ault (Mrs. Jike), Marjorie Rhodes (Mrs. Bull), Kenneth Griffith (Harry's Pal), Brefni O'Rorke (Dole Officer). Sally has to choose between socialist Larry and illicit bookmaker Sam, who could help her family during difficult financial times. Adapted from the novel by Walter Greenwood. *Dir.* John Baxter.

Love, Honour and Obey (2000) Jonny Lee Miller (Jonny), Jude Law (Jude), Ray Winstone (Ray Kreed), Sadie Frost (Sadie), Sean Pertwee (Sean), Ray Burdis (Ray), Dominic Anciano (Dominic), Kathy Burke (Kathy), Denise van Outen (Maureen), Rhys Ifans (Matthew), John Beckett (John), Trevor Laird (Trev), William Scully (Bill), Perry Benson (Perry "Fat Alan"), Mark Burdis (Mark), Laila Morse (Laila). A courier decides he'd like to be a gangster. *Dirs.* Dominic Anciano and Ray Burdis.

Love's Labours Lost (2000) Alessandro Nivola (King Ferdinand of Navarre), Alicia Silverstone (The Princess of France), Natascha McElhone (Rosaline), Kenneth Branagh (Berowne), Carmen Ejogo (Maria), Matthew Lillard (Longaville), Adrian Lester (Dumaine), Emily Mortimer (Katherine), Richard Briers (Nathaniel), Geraldine McEwan (Holofernes), Stefania Rocca (Jaquenetta), Jimmy Yuill (Dull), Nathan Lane (Costard), Timothy Spall (Don Armado), Tony O'Donnell (Moth), Daniel Hill (Marcade), Richard Clifford (Boyet). An adaptation of Shakespeare's play as a Hollywood musical with sets and music from the 1930s. *Dir.* Kenneth Branagh.

Loves of Madame Dubarry, The (1935) Gitta Alpar (Jeanne, Madame du Barry), Patrick Waddington (René), Owen Nares (Louis XV), Arthur Margetson (Count Du Barry), Margaret Bannerman (Marechale), Hugh Miller (Choiseul), Gibb McLaughlin (De Brissac). Jeanne falls for René, but decides to marry the Count du Barry and becomes the mistress of Louis XV. *Dir.* Marcel Varnel.

L-Shaped Room, The (1962) Leslie Caron (Jane Fosset), Tom Bell (Toby), Brock Peters (Johnny), Cicely Courtneidge (Mavis), Bernard Lee (Charlie), Patricia Phoenix (Sonia), Emlyn Williams (Dr. Weaver), Avis Bunnage (Doris), Gerry Duggan (Bert), Mark Eden (Terry), Anthony Booth (Youth in Street), Harry Locke (Newsagent), Gerald Sim (Doctor in Hospital). A pregnant girl moves into an L-shaped room in a boarding house. Adapted from the novel by Lynne Reid Banks. *Dir.* Bryan Forbes.

Lucky Jim (1957) Ian Carmichael (Jim Dixon), Terry-Thomas (Bertrand Welch), Hugh Griffith (Professor Welch), Sharon Acker (Christine Callaghan), Jean Anderson (Mrs Welch), Maureen Connell (Margaret Peel), Clive Morton (Sir Hector Gore-Urquhart), John Welsh (The Principal), Reginald Beckwith (University Porter), Kenneth Griffith (Cyril Johns), Jeremy Hawk (Bill Atkinson), Ronald Cardew (Registrar), Penny Morrell (Miss Wilson), John Cairney (Roberts), Ian Wilson (Glee Singer), Charles Lamb (Contractor), Henry B. Longhurst (Prof Hutchinson). Jim is clinging on to a life in academia as a lecturer in Medieval history at a provincial university although he is not happy with either his lot – he is ending an unsuccessful probationary year - or his love life with the manipulative Margaret. Then one weekend he spies the girl of his dreams on the arm of his boss' son. An adaptation of the Kingsley Amis novel. *Dir.* John Boulting.

Lust for a Vampire (1971) Yutte Stensgaard (Mircalla Herritzen/Carmilla Karnstein), Michael Johnson (Richard Lestrange), Ralph Bates (Giles Barton), Barbara Jefford (Countess Herritzen), Suzanna Leigh (Janet Playfair), Helen Christie (Miss Simpson), Pippa Steel (Susan Pelley), David Healy (Raymond Pelley), Harvey Hall (Inspector Heinrich), Mike Raven (Count Karnstein), Michael Brennan (Landlord), Jack Melford (Bishop), Christopher Cunningham (Coachman), Judy Matheson (Amanda), Christopher Neame (Hans), Sue Longhurst (Schoolgirl), Kirsten Lindholm (Peasant girl). At a finishing school the pupils begin to die. Are the vampiric Karnsteins once again striking by night? The second film in the "Karnstein Trilogy" (with *The Vampire Lovers* and *Twins of Evil*) and loosely based on the J. Sheridan Le Fanu novella *Carmilla. Dir.* Jimmy Sangster.

Mackintosh Man, The (1973) Paul Newman (Joseph Rearden), Dominique Sanda (Mrs Smith), Ian Bannen (Slade), James Mason (Sir George Wheeler MP), Michael Horden (Brown), Harry Andrews (Mackintosh), Nigel Patrick (Soames-Trevelyan), Peter Vaughan (Inspector Brunskill), Jenny Runacre (Gerda), Andre Trottier (Jobs), Roland Culver (Judge), Percy Herbert (Taafe), Robert Lang (Jack Summers), Noel Purcell (O'Donovan), John Bindon (Buster), Hugh Manning (Prosecutor). British intelligence agent Rearden gets himself deliberately imprisoned as part of a plan to infiltrate a spy ring and expose a traitor. Based on the novel *The Freedom Trap* by Desmond Bagley. *Dir.* John Huston.

Mad about Men (1954) Glynis Johns (Caroline Trewella/Miranda Trewella), Donald Sinden (Jeff Saunders), Anne Crawford (Barbara Davenport), Margaret Rutherford (Nurse Carey), Dora Bryan (Berengaria), Nicholas Phipps (Colonel Barclay Sutton), Peter Martyn (Ronald Baker), Noell Purcell (Percy), Joan Hickson (Mrs Forster), Judith Furse (Viola), Irene Handl (Mme. Blanche), David Hurst (Signor Mantalini), Martin Miller (Dr. Fergus), Deryck Guyler (Editor), Anthony Oliver (Pawnbroker). Sequel to *Miranda* with Glynis Johns now also playing Miranda's schoolteacher "relative" Caroline, who discovers Miranda in the family house on the Cornish coast. Miranda swaps places with her and as usual flirts outrageously with every man in sight, sparking much female jealousy. *Dir.* Ralph Thomas.

Madame Louise (1951) Richard Hearne (Mr Pastry), Petula Clark (Miss Penny), Garry Marsh (Mr Trout), Richard Gale (Lt Edwards), Doris Rogers (Mrs Trout), Hilda Bayley (Mme. Louise), Charles Farrell (Felling), Vic Wise (Curly), Harry Fowler (Trout's clerk). Mr Pastry is the inventor of a new style dress that helps Miss Penny against a bookie who has taken over her employer's dress shop. *Dir.* Maclean Rogers.

Made in Dagenham (2010) Sally Hawkins (Rita O'Grady), Daniel Mays (Eddie O'Grady), Miranda Richardson (Barbara Castle), Rosamund Pike (Lisa), Jaime Winstone (Sandra), Bob Hoskins (Albert), Richard Schiff (Robert Tooley), John Sessions (Harold Wilson), Rupert Graves (Peter Hopkins), Kenneth Cranham (Monty Taylor), Andrea Riseborough (Brenda), Geraldine James (Connie), Matt King (Trevor Innes), Roger

Lloyd-Pack (George), Joseph Mawle (Gordon), Phil Cornwell (Dave), Andrew Lincoln (Mr. Clarke). Based on the true story of a strike by women workers for equal pay and conditions in 1968, which led to the Equal Pay Act of 1970. *Dir*. Nigel Cole

Madeleine (1950) Ann Todd (Madeleine Smith), Norman Wooland (William Minnoch), Ivan Desny (Emile L'Anglier), Leslie Banks (James Smith), Barbara Everest (Mrs. Smith), Susan Stranks (Janet Smith), Patricia Raine (Bessie Smith), Elizabeth Sellars (Christina Hackett), Edward Chapman (Dr. Thompson), Jean Cadell (Mrs. Jenkins), Eugene Deckers (Thuau), Ivor Barnard (Mr. Murdoch), David Horne (Lord Justice-Clerk), Henry Edwards (Clerk of the Court), Barry Jones (Lord Advocate), André Morell (Dean of Faculty), Amy Veness (Miss Aiken), Kynaston Reeves (Dr. Penny), Cameron Hall (Dr. Yeoman), Douglas Barr (William the Boot Boy), Irene Browne (Mrs. Grant), Moyra Fraser (Highland Dancer), Albert Chevalier (Policeman), John Laurie (Scots Divine), Anthony Newley (Chemist's Assistant). The true story of Madeleine Smith, a Glaswegian socialite who was tried for the murder in 1857. *Dir*. David Lean.

Mademoiselle (1966) Jeanne Moreau (Mademoiselle), Ettore Manni (Manou), Keith Skinner (Bruno), Umberto Orsini (Antonio), Georges Aubert (René), Jane Beretta (Annette), Paul Barge (Young Policeman), Pierre Collet (Marcel), Gérard Darrieu (Boulet), Jean Gras (Roger), Gabriel Gobin (Police Sergeant), Rosine Luguet (Lisa), Antoine Marin (Armand), Georges Douking (The Priest), Jacques Monod (Mayor), Mony Reh (Vievotte). The schoolmistress of the French village school is actually a raving nutter responsible for arson attacks and flooding the village although the chief suspect is an Italian woodcutter. *Dir*. Tony Richardson.

Madness of King George, The (1994) Nigel Hawthorne (George III), Helen Mirren (Queen Charlotte), Ian Holm (Dr Willis), Rupert Graves (Greville), Amanda Donohoe (Lady Pembroke), Rupert Everett (Prince of Wales), Julian Rhind-Tutt (Duke of York), Julian Wadham (Pitt), Jim Carter (Fox), Geoffrey Palmer (Warren), Anthony Calf (Fitzroy), John Wood (Thurlow, Lord Chancellor), Cyril Shaps (Dr Pepys), Selina Cadell (Mrs Cordwell), Matthew Lloyd Davies (Arthur Papendiek). The story surrounding the temporary mental decline of George III, which led to the Regency Crisis of 1788. The king's illness is now thought to be caused by intermittent porphyria, a blood disorder. The film won the Oscar for Best Art Direction. *Dir*. Nicholas Hytner.

Madness of the Heart (1949) Margaret Lockwood (Lydia Garth), Paul Dupuis (Paul de Vandiere), Kathleen Byron (Verite Faimont), Maxwell Reed (Joseph Rondolet), Thora Hird (Rosa), Raymond Lovell (Comte de Vandiere), Maurice Denham (Dr. Simon Blake), David Hutcheson (Max Ffoliott), Cathleen Nesbitt (Mother Superior), Peter Illing (Dr. Matthieu), Jack McNaughton (Attendant), Pamela Stirling (Felicite), Marie Burke (Comtesse de Vandiere), Marie Ault (Nun), Joy Harington (Sister Agnes), Kynaston Reeves (Sir Robert Hammond), Cynthia Teale (Gwennie), Muriel Russell (Millie), George De Warfaz (Georges), Gordon Littmann (Henri), Gillian Maude (Mignon), Fletcher Lightfoot (Abbé Merrand), Sam Kydd (Soldier at airport). Costume melodrama in which Lydia loses her sight and her eventual marriage to Paul is threatened by a rival. *Dir*. Charles Bennett.

Madonna of the Seven Moons (1944) Phyllis Calvert (Maddalena), Stewart Granger (Nino), Patricia Roc (Angela), Peter Glenville (Sandro), John Stuart (Guiseppe), Reginald Tate (Ackroyd), Peter Murray-Hill (Logan), Dulcie Gray (Nesta), Alan Haines (Evelyn), Hilda Bayley (Mrs. Fiske), Evelyn Darvell (Millie), Nancy Price (Mama Barucci), Jean Kent (Vittoria), Amy Veness (Tessa), Robert Speaight (Priest), Eliot Makeham (Bossi), Danny Green (Scorpi), Helen Haye (Mother Superior), Thea Wells (Convent sister). A Gainsborough melodrama. After a teenage trauma Maddalena has bouts of amnesia and believes she is not a respectable married woman but rather a free-spirited gypsy. *Dir*. Arthur Crabtree.

Magdalene Sisters, The (2002) Anne-Marie Duff (Margaret McGuire), Nora Jane Noone (Bernadette Harvey), Dorothy Duffy (Rose/Patricia Dunne), Eileen Walsh (Harriet/Crispina), Geraldine McEwan (Sister Bridget), Daniel Costello (Father Fitzroy), Mary Murray (Una O'Connor), Frances Healy (Sister Jude), Eithne McGuinness (Sister Clementine), Phyllis MacMahon (Sister Augusta), Britta Smith (Katy), Rebecca Walsh (Josephine), Eamonn Owens (Eamonn), Chris Patrick-Simpson (Brendan), Sean Colgan (Seamus), Lisa Branney (Orphan). In the early 1960s, four Irish teenage girls (Margaret, Bernadette, Rose and Harriet) are sent to a Magdalene Asylum, which is maintained by the Roman Catholic Church for "fallen" women and run by the sadistic Mother Superior, Sister Bridget. *Dir*. Peter Mullan

Maggie, The (1954) Paul Douglas (Calvin B. Marshall), Alex Mackenzie (Mactaggart), James Copeland (Mate), Abe Barker (Engineer), Tommy Kearins (Dougie), Hubert Gregg (Pusey), Geoffrey Keen (Campbell), Dorothy Alison (Miss Peters), Andrew Keir (Reporter), Meg Buchanan (Sarah), Mark Dignam (The Laird), Jameson Clark (Dirty Dan), Moultrie Kelsall (C.S.S. skipper), Fiona Clyne (Sheena), Sheila Shand Gibbs (Barmaid), Betty Henderson (Campbell's Secretary). Calvin Marshall is tricked by Mactaggart into using his unseaworthy ship *The Maggie* to transport his personal furniture to a Scottish island. *Dir*. Alexander Mackendrick

Magic Box, The (1951) Robert Donat (William Friese-Greene), Margaret Johnston (Edith Harrison Friese-Greene), Maria Schell (Helena Friese-Greene), Renée Asherson (Miss Tagg), Richard Attenborough (Jack Carter), Robert Beatty (Lord Beaverbrook), Martin Boddey (Sitter in Bath Studio), Edward Chapman (Father in Family Group), John Charlesworth (Graham Friese-Greene), Maurice Colbourne (Bride's Father in wedding group), Roland Culver (1st Company Promoter), John Howard Davies (Maurice Friese-Greene), Janette Scott (Ethel Friese-Greene), David Oake (Claude Friese-Greene), Michael Denison (Reporter), Joan Dowling (Maggie), Mary Ellis (Mrs Nell Collings), Marjorie Fielding (Elderly Viscountess), Leo Genn (Maida Vale Doctor), Marius Goring (House Agent), Joyce Grenfell (Mrs Claire), Robertson Hare (Sitter in Bath Studio), Kathleen Harrison (Mother in Family Group), William Hartnell (Recruiting Sergeant), Joan Hickson (Mrs Stukely), Thora Hird (Doctor's Housekeeper), Stanley Holloway (Broker's Man), Michael Hordern (Official Receiver), Jack Hulbert (1st Holborn Policeman), Sid James (Sgt in Storeroom), Glynis Johns (May Jones), Mervyn Johns (Goitz), Peter Jones (Industry Man), Miles Malleson (Orchestra Conductor), Muir Mathieson (Sir Arthur Sullivan), A.E. Matthews (Old Gentleman), John McCallum (Sitter in Bath Studio), Bernard Miles (Cousin Alfred), Richard Murdoch (Sitter in Bath Studio), Laurence Olivier (PC 94-B), Cecil Parker (1st Platform Man), Eric Portman (Arthur Collings), Dennis Price (Harold), Michael Redgrave (Mr Lege), Margaret Rutherford (Lady Pond), Ronald Shiner (Fairground Barker), Sheila Sim (Nursemaid), Marianne Stone (Bride-wedding group), Basil Sydney (William Fox-Talbot), Ernest Thesiger (Earl), Sybil Thorndike (Sitter in Bath Studio), David Tomlinson (Assistant in Laboratory), Michael Trubshawe (Sitter in Bath Studio), Peter Ustinov (Industry Man), Kay Walsh (Hotel Receptionist), Emlyn Williams (Bank Manager), Googie Withers (Sitter in Bath Studio). All-star biopic of William Friese-Greene, a candidate for the inventor of the moving picture camera. *Dir*. John Boulting.

Magic Christian, The (1969) Peter Sellers (Sir Guy Grand), Ringo Starr (Youngman Grand), Isabel Jeans (Dame Agnes Grand), Caroline Blakiston (Hon. Esther Grand), Spike Milligan (Traffic warden No 27), Richard Attenborough (Oxford coach), Leonard Frey (Laurence Faggot), John Cleese (Mr. Dugdale), Patrick Cargill (Auctioneer), Joan Benham (Socialite), Ferdy Mayne (Edouard), Graham Stark (Waiter), Laurence Harvey (Hamlet), Dennis Price (Winthrop), Wilfrid Hyde-White (Capt. Reginald K. Klaus), Christopher Lee (Ship's vampire), Roman Polanski (Solitary drinker), Raquel Welch (Priestess of the Whip), Victor Maddern (Hot dog vendor), Terence Alexander (Mad Major), Clive Dunn (Sommelier), Fred Emney (Fitzgibbon), David Hutcheson (Lord Barry), Hattie Jacques (Ginger Horton), Edward Underdown (Prince Henry), Jeremy Lloyd (Lord Hampton), Peter Myers (Lord Kilgallon), Roland Culver (Sir

Herbert), Michael Trubshawe (Sir Lionel), David Lodge (Ship's guide), Peter Graves (Lord at ship's bar), Robert Raglan (Maltravers), Frank Thornton (Police Inspector), Michael Aspel, Michael Barratt, Harry Carpenter, John Snagge and Alan Whicker (TV commentators), Graham Chapman (Oxford crewman), Yul Brynner (Transvestite cabaret singer), John Le Mesurier (Sir John). A black comedy which explores the idea that people will do absolutely anything as long as they are offered enough money. Billionaire Guy Grand uses his money to bribe people to satisfy his whims, play practical jokes and make people act against their normal inclinations. He adopts a vagrant (Youngman) and decides to teach him the ways of his world. The cast list includes well-known actors and celebrities playing minor and cameo roles. The soundtrack featured the hits songs "Come And Get It" (written by Paul McCartney and performed by Badfinger) and Thunderclap Newman's "Something in the Air". Loosely adapted from the novel by Terry Southern. *Dir.* Joseph McGrath.

Magnet, The (1950) Stephen Murray (Dr Brent), Kay Walsh (Mrs Brent), James Fox (Johnny Brent), Meredith Edwards (Harper), Gladys Henson (Nanny), Thora Hird (Nanny's friend), Michael Brooke (Kit), Wylie Watson (Pickering), Julien Mitchell (Mayor), Anthony Oliver (Policeman), Molly Hamley-Clifford (Mrs. Dean), Harold Goodwin (Pin table man), Edward Davies (Delinquent youth), Keith Robinson (Spike), Thomas Johnston (Perce), David Boyd (Mike), Geoffrey Yin (Choppo), Joan Hickson (Mrs Ward), Grace Arnold (Mrs Mercer), Jane Bough (Sally Mercer), Bryan Michie (Announcer), Joss Ambler (Businessman), Sam Kydd (Postman), Russell Waters (Doctor), Thea Gregson (Nurse), James Robertson Justice (Tramp). The young son of a pair of psychologists swaps his "invisible watch" for a large magnet belonging to a younger boy. This transaction sets off a series of events which involve an iron lung. *Dir.* Charles Frend.

Magnificent Seven Deadly Sins, The (1971) Bruce Forsyth (Clayton – Avarice segment), Paul Whitsun-Jones (Elsinore – Avarice segment), Bernard Bresslaw (Mr. Violet – Avarice segment), Joan Sims (Policewoman – Avarice segment), Roy Hudd (Fisherman – Avarice segment), Julie Samuel (Petrol Station Attendant – Avarice segment), Cheryl Hall (Vanessa – Avarice segment), Suzanne Heath as Chloe – Avarice segment), Harry Secombe (Stanley – Envy segment), Geoffrey Bayldon (Vernon – Envy segment), June Whitfield (Mildred – Envy segment), Carmel Cryan (Vera – Envy segment), Leslie Phillips (Dickie – Gluttony segment), Julie Ege (Ingrid – Gluttony segment), Patrick Newell (Doctor – Gluttony segment), Rosemarie Reed (Woman – Gluttony segment), Sarah Golding (Secretary – Gluttony segment), Bob Guccione (Photographer – Gluttony segment), Tina McDowell (Penthouse Pet – Gluttony segment), Harry H. Corbett (Ambrose Twombly – Lust segment), Cheryl Kennedy (Greta – Lust segment), Bill Pertwee (Cockney Man – Lust segment), Mary Baxter (Charlady – Lust segment), Anouska Hempel (Blonde – Lust segment), Kenneth Earle (Boy Friend – Lust segment), Nicole Yerna (Thin Girl – Lust segment), Sue Bond (Girl with Glasses – Lust segment), Yvonne Paul (Receptionist – Lust segment), Ian Carmichael (Mr. Ferris – Pride segment), Alfie Bass (Mr. Spencer – Pride segment), Audrey Nicholson (Mrs. Ferris – Pride segment), Sheila Bernette (Mrs. Spencer – Pride segment), Robert Gillespie (A.A. Patrol Man – Pride segment), Keith Smith (R.A.C. Patrol Man – Pride segment), Ivor Dean (Policeman – Pride segment), Spike Milligan (Tramp – Sloth segment), Melvyn Hayes (Porter – Sloth segment), Ronnie Brody (Costermonger – Sloth segment), Ronnie Barker, Peter Butterworth, Marty Feldman, Davy Kaye, David Lodge, Cardew Robinson, Madeline Smith (actors on screen – Sloth segment), Ronald Fraser (George – Wrath segment), Stephen Lewis (Jarvis, the park keeper - – Wrath segment), Arthur Howard (Kenneth – Wrath segment). The film is made up of seven segments, each portraying a different deadly sin (avarice, envy, gluttony, lust, pride, sloth and wrath). It features some of the top British comedy performers and writers (Graham Chapman, Barry Cryer, John Esmonde, Marty Feldman, Dave Freeman, Ray Galton, Bob Larbey, Spike Milligan, Alan Simpson and Graham Stark) of the period. *Dir.* Graham Stark.

Magnificent Two, The (1967) Eric Morecambe (Eric), Ernie Wise (Ernie), Margit Saad (Carla), Virgilio Teixeira (Carillo),

Cecil Parker (British ambassador), Isobel Black (Juanita), Martin Benson (President Diaz), Tyler Butterworth (Miguel), Sandor Elès (Armandez), Andreas Malandrinos (Juan), Victor Maddern (Drunken soldier), Michael Gover (Doctor), Charles Laurence (Assassin), Michael Gover (Dr Pablo), David Charlesworth (Torres), Larry Taylor (Paco), Bettine Le Beau (Telephonist). Two travelling salesmen find themselves in the middle of a revolution in a South American country and one of them just happens to look like the rebel leader. *Dir.* Cliff Owen.

Mahler (1974) Robert Powell (Gustav Mahler), Georgina Hale (Alma Mahler), Lee Montague (Bernhard Mahler), Miriam Karlin (Aunt Rosa), Rosalie Crutchley (Marie Mahler), Gary Rich (Young Gustav), Richard Morant (Max), Angela Down (Justine Mahler), Antonia Ellis (Cosima Wagner), Ronald Pickup (Nick), Peter Eyre (Otto Mahler), Dana Gillespie (Anna von Mildenburg), George Coulouris (Doctor Roth), David Collings (Hugo Wolf), Arnold Yarrow (Grandfather), David Trevena (Doctor Richter), Elaine Delmar (Princess), Benny Lee (Uncle Arnold), Andrew Faulds (Doctor on Train), Otto Diamant (Professor Sladky), Michael Southgate (Alois Mahler), Ken Colley (Siegfried Krenek), Sarah McClellan (Putzi), Claire McClellan (Glucki). A look at the life, loves, music and religion of composer Gustav Mahler, mainly shown in flashback and containing fantasy elements. *Dir.* Ken Russell.

Major Barbara (1941) Wendy Hiller (Major Barbara Undershaft), Rex Harrison (Adolphus Cusins), Robert Morley (Andrew Undershaft), Robert Newton (Bill Walker), Sybil Thorndike (The General), Emlyn Williams (Snobby Price), Marie Lohr (Lady Britomart), Penelope Dudley-Ward (Sarah Undershaft), Walter Hudd (Stephen Undershaft), David Tree (Charles Lomax), Deborah Kerr (Jenny Hill), Donald Calthrop (Peter Shirley), Marie Ault (Rummy Mitchens), Cathleen Cordell (Mog Habbijam), Torin Thatcher (Todger Fairmile), Miles Malleson (Morrison), Felix Aylmer (James), Stanley Holloway (Policeman), S.I. Hsiung (Ling), Kathleen Harrison (Mrs. Price), Mary Morris (A Girl), Charles Victor (Bilton), O.B. Clarence (Pettigrew). Based on George Bernard Shaw's play centring on a Salvation Army major and the relationship with her father. *Dir.* Gabriel Pascal.

Make Mine Mink (1960) Terry-Thomas (Major Rayne), Athene Seyler (Dame Beatrice), Hattie Jacques (Nanette Parry), Elspeth Duxbury (Pinkie), Billie Whitelaw (Lily), Jack Hedley (Jim Benham), Raymond Huntley (Inspector Pape), Irene Handl (Madame Spolinski), Sydney Tafler (Mr. Spanager), Joan Heal (Mrs. Spanager), Penny Morrell (Gertrude), Freddie Frinton (Drunk), Michael Balfour (Doorman), Noel Purcell (Burglar), Kenneth Williams (Freddie Warrington). A group of lodgers hatch a plan to steal fur coats and sell them for money which can be donated to charities. Based on the play *Breath of Spring* by Peter Coke. *Dir.* Robert Asher.

Malaga (1954) Maureen O'Hara (Joanna Dana), Macdonald Carey (Van Logan), Binnie Barnes (Frisco), Guy Middleton (Soames Howard), Hugh McDermott (Richard Farrell), James O'Hara (Danny Boy), Harry Lane (Augie), Leonard Sachs (Paul Dupont), Ferdy Mayne (Mustapha), Eric Corrie (Pebbles), Bruce Beeby (Potts), Gérard Tichy (Cronkhite), Derek Sydney (Signor Amato), Jacques Cey (Monsieur Ducloir), Mike Brendall (Rodrigo), Meinhart Maur (Jakie), Antonio Casas (Aziz). Former O.S.S. operative Joanna Dane is sent to Tangier to investigate a smuggling ring. Released in the US as *Fire Over Africa*. *Dir.* Richard Sale.

Malta Story (1953) Alec Guinness (Flight Lt. Peter Ross), Jack Hawkins (Air CO Frank), Anthony Steel (Wing Cmdr Bartlett), Muriel Pavlow (Maria Gonzar), Renée Asherson (Joan Rivers), Hugh Burden (Eden), Nigel Stock (Giuseppe Gonzar), Reginald Tate (Vice Adm Payne), Ralph Truman (Vice Adm Willie Banks), Flora Robson (Melita Gonzar), Ronald Adam (British Officer), Michael Craig (British Officer), Rosalie Crutchley (Carmella Gonzar), Maurice Denham (British Officer), Jerry Desmonde (General), Gordon Jackson (British Soldier), Dermot Kelly (British Soldier), Sam Kydd (Soldier), Victor Maddern (Soldier), Michael Medwin (Ramsey). The story of the defence of Malta during 1942 as the RAF protects Allied supplied lines. The sub-plot is a love story between pilot Peter Ross and local girl Maria Gonzar. *Dir.* Brian Desmond Hurst.

Mamma Mia! The Movie (2008) Meryl Streep (Donna Sheridan), Amanda Seyfried (Sophie Sheridan), Pierce Brosnan (Sam Carmichael), Colin Firth (Harry Bright), Stellan Skarsgård (Bill Anderson), Dominic Cooper (Sky), Julie Walters (Rosie Mulligan), Christine Baranski (Tanya Chesham-Leigh), Philip Michael (Pepper), Ashley Lilley (Ali), Rachel McDowall (Lisa), Enzo Squillino (Gregoris), Niall Buggy (Father Alex). Sophie sends wedding invitations to three men, one of whom she believes to be her father. Adapted from the stage musical based around the songs of ABBA. *Dir.* Phyllida Lloyd

Man About the House (1974) Richard O'Sullivan (Robin Tripp), Paula Wilcox (Chrissy), Sally Thomsett (Jo), Brian Murphy (George Roper), Yootha Joyce (Mildred Roper), Doug Fisher (Larry Simmonds), Peter Cellier (Morris Pluthero), Patrick Newell (Sir Edmund Weir), Aimi MacDonald (Hazel Lovett), Melvyn Hayes (Nigel), Michael Ward (Mr. Gideon), Bill Grundy (Himself), Berry Cornish (P.A.), Norman Mitchell (Arthur Mulgrove), Michael Robbins (Second Doorman), Johnny Briggs (Milkman), Bill Pertwee (Postman), Bill Sawyer (Chauffeur), Aubrey Morris (Lecturer), Arthur Lowe (Spiros), Andrea Lawrence (Miss Bird), Julian Orchard (Producer), Bill Maynard (Chef). When a property developer who wants to demolish the street comes around offering money, George Roper is tempted but his wife and the lodgers are not. A spin-off from the television sitcom. *Dir.* John Robins.

Man About the House, A (1947) Margaret Johnston (Agnes Isit), Dulcie Gray (Ellen Isit), Kieron Moore (Salvatore), Guy Middleton (Sir Benjamin "Ben" Dench), Felix Aylmer (Richard Sanctuary), Lilian Braithwaite (Mrs. Armitage), Jone Salinas (Maria), Marisa Finiani (Assunta), Wilfrid Caithness (Solicitor), Fulvia De Priamo (Gita), Nicola Esposito (Antonina), Reginald Purdell (Higgs). Two English sisters inherit a villa and estate in Italy. One of them falls for, and then marries, Salvatore, the majordomo of the villa. When she falls ill her sister begins to suspect foul play. Adapted from the novel by Francis Brett Young. *Dir.* Leslie Arliss.

Man for All Seasons, A (1966) Paul Scofield (Sir Thomas More), Wendy Hiller (Alice More), Robert Shaw (King Henry VIII), Leo McKern (Thomas Cromwell), Orson Welles (Cardinal Wolsey), Susannah York (Margaret More), Nigel Davenport (Duke of Norfolk), John Hurt (Richard Rich), Corin Redgrave (William Roper), Colin Blakely (Matthew), Cyril Luckham (Archbishop Thomas Cranmer), Jack Gwillim (Chief Justice), Vanessa Redgrave (Anne Boleyn). Henry VIII contemplates abandoning Catholicism once the Pope turns down his request to divorce Catherine of Aragon in favour of Anne Boleyn. His Chancellor, Sir Thomas More, faces the dilemma of choosing between his King and his faith. The film won six Academy Awards: Best Picture, Best Actor in Leading Role (Paul Scofield), Best Director, Best Writing, based on Material from Another Medium, Best Cinematography, Colour, Best Costume Design, Colour. Based on Robert Bolt's play. *Dir.* Fred Zinnemann.

Man in Grey, The (1943) Margaret Lockwood (Hesther Snow), Phyllis Calvert (Clarissa in 1943 and 19th century), James Mason (Lord Rohan), Stewart Granger (Rokeby in 1943 and 19th century), Harry Scott (Toby), Martita Hunt (Miss Patchett), Helen Haye (Lady Rohan), Beatrice Varley (Gipsy), Raymond Lovell (The Prince Regent), Nora Swinburne (Mrs. Fitzherbert). Framed by the meeting of Clarissa and Rokeby in 1943, the film flashes back to the Regency period where Clarissa's ancestor meets Hesther, with whom her destiny and that of Rokeby are intertwined. The first of Gainsborough Pictures popular (with the public) melodramas was based on the novel of the same name by Lady Eleanor Smith. *Dir.* Leslie Arliss.

Man in the White Suit, The (1951) Alec Guinness (Sidney Stratton), Joan Greenwood (Daphne Birnley), Cecil Parker (Alan Birnley), Michael Gough (Michael Corland), Ernest Thesiger (Sir John Kierlaw), Howard Marion-Crawford (Cranford), Henry Mollison (Hoskins), Vida Hope (Bertha), Patric Doonan (Frank), Duncan Lamont (Harry), Harold Goodwin (Wilkins), Colin Gordon (Hill), Joan Harben (Miss Johnson), Arthur Howard (Roberts), Roddy Hughes (Green), Stuart Latham (Harrison), Miles Malleson (The Tailor), Edie Martin (Mrs Watson), Mandy Miller (Gladdie), Charlotte Mitchell (Mill Girl). Sidney Stratton invents a revolutionary fabric which never gets dirty or wears out. The unions and the mill owners soon realise that such a fabric could be disastrous for long-term business. *Dir.* Alexander Mackendrick.

Man of No Importance, A (1994) Albert Finney (Alfred Byrne), Brenda Fricker (Lily Byrne), Michael Gambon (Ivor J. Garney), David Kelly (Baldy), Tara FitzGerald (Adele Rice), Rufus Sewell (Robbie Fay), Patrick Malahide (Insp Carson), Mick Lally (Father Ignatius Kenny), Anna Manahan (Mrs Grace), Joe Pilkington (Ernie Lally), Brendan Conroy (Rasher Flynn), Joan O'Hara (Mrs Crowe), Eileen Reid (Mrs Rock), Eileen Conroy (Mrs Curtin), Maureen Egan (Mrs Dunne), Jonathan Rhys-Meyers (First young man), Enda Oates (The Garda). In 1960s Dublin, a homosexual bus driver fends of his sister's attempts to find him the "right girl" and spends his spare time putting on amateur theatre productions of Oscar Wilde plays. *Dir.* Suri Krishnamma.

Man of the Moment (1955) Norman Wisdom (Norman), Lana Morris (Penny), Belinda Lee (Sonia), Jerry Desmonde (Jackson), Karel Stepanek (Lom), Garry Marsh (British Delegate), Inia Te Wiata (King of Tawaki), Evelyn Roberts (Sir Horace), Violet Farebrother (Queen of Tawaki), Martin Miller (Swiss Tailor), Eugene Deckers (Day Lift Man), Hugh Morton (Mitchell), Cyril Chamberlain (British Delegate), Lisa Gastoni (Chambermaid), Harold Kasket (Enrico), Beverley Brooks (Air Hostess), Michael Ward (Photographer), Derek Sydney (Lesnevitch), Peter Taylor (Gritter), Josef Behrmann (Rietz), Peggy Ann Clifford (Second Chambermaid), Charles Hawtrey (Play Director), Marianne Stone (Florrie the Cleaner). Foreign Office clerk causes consternation as a delegate at a UN conference in Geneva by supporting the people of the small Pacific island of Tawaki. *Dir.* John Paddy Carstairs.

Man on Wire (2008) A documentary which tells the story of Philippe Petit's 1974 high-wire walk between the Twin Towers of New York's World Trade Center. The film won one Academy Award: Best Documentary Feature. It is based on Petit's book *To Reach the Clouds*. *Dir.* James Marsh

Man Who Changed His Mind, The (1936) Boris Karloff (Dr. Laurience), Anna Lee (Dr. Clare Wyatt), John Loder (Dick Haslewood), Frank Cellier (Lord Haslewood), Donald Calthrop (Clayton), Cecil Parker (Dr. Gratton), Lyn Harding (Prof. Holloway), Clive Morton (Journalist).
Dr Laurience was once a respected scientist but his researches into the origin of the mind and soul have led to his ostracism from the scientific community. He begins to use his work for his own nefarious purposes. *Dir.* Robert Stevenson.

Man Who Could Cheat Death, The (1959) Anton Diffring (Dr. Georges Bonner), Hazel Court (Janine Du Bois), Christopher Lee (Dr. Pierre Gerrard), Arnold Marlé (Dr. Ludwig Weiss), Delphi Lawrence (Margo Philippe), Francis De Wolff (Inspector Legris). Charles Lloyd Pack (Man At Private View), Michael Ripper (Morgue Attendant). Set in Paris in the 1890s, Dr Georges Bonner is 104 years old but only looks about 40. His secret is taking an elixir made from the glands of youthful female victims. Based on the play *The Man in Half Moon Street* by Barré Lyndon. *Dir.* Terence Fisher.

Man Who Could Work Miracles, The (1936) Roland Young (George), Ralph Richardson (Col Winstanley), Edward Chapman (Maj Grigsby), Ernest Thesiger (Mr Maydig), Joan Gardner (Ada Price), Sophie Stewart (Maggie Hooper), Robert Cochran (Bill Stoker), Lady Tree (Mr Maydig's Housekeeper), Laurence Hanray (Mr Bamfylde), George Zucco (Moody), Wallace Lupino (PC Winch), Joan Hickson (Effie Brickman), Wally Patch (Police Supt Smithelle), Mark Daly (Toddy Beamish), George Sanders (Indifference). After two angels give haberdasher's clerk George McWhirter Fotheringay the power to perform miracles, he discovers this gift is not all it might appear. A version of H.G. Wells' story of the same name. *Dir.* Lothar Mendes.

Man Who Fell to Earth, The (1976) David Bowie (Thomas Jerome Newton), Buck Henry (Oliver Farnsworth), Rip Torn (Nathan Bryce), Candy Clark (Mary-Lou), Tony Mascia (Arthur), Rick Riccardo (Trevor), Bernie Casey (Mr. Peters), Jackson D.

Kane (Professor Canutti), Linda Hutton (Elaine), Hilary Holland (Jill), Adrienne Larussa (Helen), Jim Lovell (Himself), Terry Southern (Reporter). An alien comes to earth on a mission to save his own dying planet. He uses his advanced technology to amass wealth. Based on the novel by Walter Tevis. *Dir*. Nicolas Roeg.

Man Who Haunted Himself, The (1970) Roger Moore (Harold Pelham), Hildegarde Neil (Eve Pelham), Alastair Mackenzie (Michael Pelham), Hugh Mackenzie (James Pelham), Kevork Malikyan (Luigi), Thorley Walters (Frank Bellamy), Anton Rodgers (Tony Alexander), Olga Georges-Picot (Julie Anderson), Freddie Jones (Dr. Harris – Psychiatrist), John Welsh (Sir Charles Freeman), Edward Chapman (Barton), Laurence Hardy (Mason), Charles Lloyd Pack (Jameson), Gerald Sim (Morrison), Anthony Nicholls (Sir Arthur Richardson), John Carson (Ashton). Harold Pelham appears to have a doppelganger. Tagline "Harold Pelham hasn't been himself lately....but someone who looks exactly like him has". Based on the novel *The Strange Case of Mr Pelham* by Anthony Armstrong. *Dir*. Basil Dearden.

Man Who Knew Too Much, The (1934) Leslie Banks (Bob), Edna Best (Jill), Peter Lorre (Abbott), Frank Vosper (Ramon), Hugh Wakefield (Clive), Nova Pilbeam (Betty Lawrence), Pierre Fresnay (Louis), Cicely Oates (Nurse Agnes), D. A. Clarke Smith (Binstead), George Curzon (Gibson), Clare Greet (Mrs Brockett). Bob and Jill witness a murder and come into possession of information about a planned assassination. Their daughter is kidnapped in order to guarantee their silence. *Dir*. Alfred Hitchcock.- who remade the film in 1956 with James Stewart and Doris Day

Man Who Never Was, The (1956) Clifton Webb (Lt. Cmdr. Ewen Montagu), Gloria Grahame (Lucy Sherwood), Robert Flemyng (Lt. George Acres), Josephine Griffin (Pam), Stephen Boyd (Patrick O'Reilly), Laurence Naismith (Adm. Cross), Geoffrey Keen (Gen. Nye), Moultrie Kelsall (The Father), Cyril Cusack (Taxi Driver), André Morell (Sir Bernard Spilsbury), Michael Hordern (Gen. Coburn), Allan Cuthbertson (Vice-Admiral), Joan Hickson (Landlady), Terence Longdon (Larry), Miles Malleson (Scientist), William Russell (Joe), William Squire (Lt. Jewell), Richard Wattis (Shop Assistant). A fictionalised telling of the story behind WWII Operation Mincemeat, where the Allies used fake papers on a dead body put into the sea near Huelva, Spain in an attempt to convince the Axis that Operation Husky, the Allied invasion of Sicily, would take place elsewhere. *Dir*. Ronald Neame

Man Who Would Be King, The (1975) Sean Connery (Daniel Dravot), Michael Caine (Peachy Carnehan), Christopher Plummer (Rudyard Kipling), Saeed Jaffrey (Billy Fish), Doghmi Larbi (Ootah), Jack May (District Commissioner), Karroom Ben Bouih (Kafu Selim), Mohammad Shamsi (Babu), Albert Moses (Ghulam), Paul Antrim (Mulvaney), Graham Acres (Officer), Shakira Caine (Roxanne). Adapted from the Rudyard Kipling short story of the same name. Set during the Indian Raj, ex-soldiers Danny and Peachy travel to Kafiristan in the Hindu Kush to make their fortune. Danny is mistaken for a god and the son of Alexander the Great and is made king. The story is shown in flashback. *Dir*. John Huston.

Man with the Golden Gun, The (1974) Roger Moore (James Bond), Christopher Lee (Francisco Scaramanga), Britt Ekland (Mary Goodnight), Maud Adams (Andrea Anders), Hervé Villechaize (Nick Nack), Soon-Tek Oh (Lieutenant Hip), Clifton James (Sheriff J.W. Pepper), Bernard Lee (M), Marc Lawrence (Rodney), Desmond Llewelyn (Q), Marne Maitland (Lazar), Lois Maxwell (Miss Moneypenny), James Cossins (Colthorpe), Carmen du Sautoy (Saida). Bond is assigned to retrieve the Solex agitator, a vital part for a solar power station, and in the process kill Scaramanga, the triple-nippled famous assassin whose trademark is his golden gun. Bond drives a red AMC Hornet. The theme song is sung by Lulu. The film is loosely adapted from Ian Fleming's novel of same name. *Dir*. Guy Hamilton.

Man Without a Body, The (1957) Robert Hutton (Dr. Phil R. Merritt), George Coulouris (Karl Brussard), Julia Arnall (Jean Cramer), Nadja Regin (Odette Vernet), Sheldon Lawrence (Dr. Lew Waldenhouse), Peter Copley (Leslie), Michael Golden (Michel de Notre Dame), Norman Shelley (Dr. Alexander), Stanley Van Beers (Madame Tussaud's Guide), Tony Quinn (Dr. Brandon), Maurice Kaufmann (Chauffeur), William Sherwood (Dr.

Charot). A man with a brain tumour finds a scientist doing head transplants – what are the odds? The head of the long dead prophet Nostradamus becomes an object of attention. *Dir*. Charles Saunders.

Mandy (1952) Phyllis Calvert (Christine Garland), Jack Hawkins (Dick Searle), Terence Morgan (Harry Garland), Godfrey Tearle (Mr Garland), Mandy Miller (Mandy Garland), Marjorie Fielding (Mrs Garland), Nancy Price (Jane Ellis), Edward Chapman (Ackland), Patricia Plunkett (Miss Crocker), Eleanor Summerfield (Lily Tabor), Colin Gordon (Woollard Junior), Dorothy Alison (Miss Stockton), Julian Amyes (Jimmy Tabor), Gabrielle Brune (The Secretary), John Cazabon (Davey), Gwen Bacon (Mrs Paul), W.E. Holloway (Woollard Senior), Phyllis Morris (Miss Tucker), Gabrielle Blunt (Miss Larner), Jean Shepherd (Mrs Jackson), Jane Asher (Nina). Young Mandy is a deaf-mute. Her parents enroll her in a special school in the hope that she may one day be able to speak. *Dir*. Alexander Mackendrick

Manuela (1957) Trevor Howard (James Prothero), Elsa Martinelli (Manuela Hunt), Pedro Armendáriz (Mario Constanza), Donald Pleasence (Evans), Warren Mitchell (Moss), Jack MacGowran (Tommy), Harcourt Curacao (Wellington Jones), Barry Lowe (Murphy), Juan Carolilla (Official), John Rae (Ferguson), Roger Delgado (Stranger), Harold Kasket (Pereira), Max Butterfield (Bliss), Andy Ho (Cook), Peter Illing (Agent), Armand Guinle (Patron). When the mate of a tramp steamer smuggles a girl aboard it appears she comes from cold, morally upright but occasionally drunk Captain Prothero can't resist her wild charms. Billed as *Half Savage-All Woman* and released as *Stowaway Girl* in the US. *Dir*. Guy Hamilton.

March Hare, The (1956) Peggy Cummins (Pat McGuire), Terence Morgan (Sir Charles Hare), Martita Hunt (Lady Anne), Cyril Cusack (Lazy Mangan), Wilfrid Hyde-White (Col. Keene), Derrick De Marney (Capt. Marlow), Charles Hawtrey (Fisher), Maureen Delaney (Bridget), Ivan Samson (Hardwicke), MacDonald Parke (Maguire), Peter Swanwick (Nils Svenson), Charles Wade (Tim Doughty), John Gilbert (Connor), Fred Johnson (Joe Duffy), Bernard Rook (Slater), Reginald Beckwith (Insurance Broker), Stringer Davis (Doctor). Aristocrat Sir Charles Hare gambles away his family fortune and property but is mistaken for a stable lad by the new owner of his Irish estate. He helps her race a colt to run in the Derby. Based on *Gamblers Sometimes Win*, a novel by Captain Field. *Dir*. George More O'Ferrall.

Maria Marten, or The Murder in the Red Barn (1935) Tod Slaughter (Squire William Corder), Sophie Stewart (Maria Marten), D. J. Williams (Farmer Thomas Marten), Eric Portman (Carlos), Clare Greet (Mrs Marten), Gerard Tyrell (Timothy Winterbottom), Ann Trevor (Nan, the maid), Stella Rho (Gypsy Crone), Dennis Hoey (Gambling Winner), Antonia Brough (Maud Sennett), Quentin McPhearson (Matthew Sennett), Noel Dainton (Officer Steele). Film version of the popular 19th century melodrama. *Dir*. Milton Rosmer.

Maroc 7 (1967) Gene Barry (Simon Grant), Elsa Martinelli (Claudia), Leslie Phillips (Raymond Lowe), Cyd Charisse (Louise Henderson), Denholm Elliot (Inspector Barrada), Alexandra Stewart (Michelle Craig), Angela Douglas (Freddie), Eric Barker (Professor Bannen), Tracy Reed (Vivienne), Maggie London (Suzie), Ann Norman (Alexa), Penny Riley (Penny). An international jewel thief plans to steal a valuable artefact in Morocco. *Dir*. Gerry O'Hara.

Masque of the Red Death, The (1964) Vincent Price (Prince Prospero), Hazel Court (Juliana), Jane Asher (Francesca), David Weston (Gino), Nigel Green (Ludovico), John Westbrook (The Red Death), Patrick Magee (Alfredo), Paul Whitsun-Jones (Scarlatti), Skip Martin (Hop Toad), Robert Brown (Guard), Julian Burton (Señor Veronese), Gaye Brown (Señora Escobar), Verina Greenlaw (Esmeralda), Doreen Dawn (Anna-Marie), Brian Hewlett (Senor Lampredi), Sarah Brackett (Grandmother). As the Red Death plague ravages the land Satanist Prince Prospero takes refuge in his castle with some of the local nobility. *Dir*. Roger Corman.

Match Point (2005) Jonathan Rhys Meyers (Chris), Matthew Goode (Tom Hewett), Emily Mortimer (Chloe Hewett Wilton), Scarlett Johansson (Nola Rice), James Nesbitt (Detective Banner), Margaret Tyzack (Mrs. Eastby), Brian Cox (Alec Hewett),

Penelope Wilton (Eleanor Hewett), Rupert Penry-Jones (Henry), Ewen Bremner (Inspector Dowd), Alexander Armstrong (Mr. Townsend), Paul Kaye (Estate Agent), John Fortune (John the Chauffeur), Mark Gatiss (Ping-Pong Player), Simon Kunz (Rod Carver), Geoffrey Streatfield (Alan Sinclair), Miranda Raison (Heather), Rose Keegan (Carol), Zoe Telford (Samantha), Selina Cadell (Margaret), Colin Salmon (Ian). Former tennis pro Chris Wilton marries Chloe but makes Nola his mistress. Eventually the situation forces him to make a choice. *Dir*. Woody Allen.

Matter of Life and Death, A (1946) David Niven (Sq Leader Peter D. Carter), Kim Hunter (June), Robert Coote (F/O Bob Trubshawe), Kathleen Byron (An Angel), Richard Attenborough (An English Pilot), Bonar Colleano (An American Pilot), Joan Maude (Chief Recorder), Marius Goring (Conductor 71), Roger Livesey (Doctor Frank Reeves), Robert Atkins (The Vicar). A mix-up in Heaven means that pilot Peter Carter does not die at his allotted time after his plane is damaged and his parachute ripped to shreds during a sortie in World War II. By the time his "Conductor" from heaven catches up with him 20 hours later, Peter has fallen for June, a young American woman working for the RAF whom he talked to in what they both thought were his last moments on Earth. This changes everything, and since it happened through no fault of his own, Peter believes that heaven owes him a second chance. Heaven agrees to a trial to decide his fate. The scenes on Earth are shot in technicolour and those in Heaven in monochrome. Robert Coote's character is called "Bob" in the credits, but referred to in the dialogue as "Trubshawe", after Niven's friend Michael Trubshawe, the source of numerous references and/or character names in Niven's films. *Dirs*. Michael Powell and Emeric Pressburger.

Maurice (1987) James Wilby (Maurice Hall), Hugh Grant (Clive Durham), Rupert Graves (Alec Scudder), Denholm Elliott (Dr Barry), Simon Callow (Mr Ducie), Billie Whitelaw (Mrs Hall), Barry Foster (Dean Cornwallis), Judy Parfitt (Mrs Durham), Phoebe Nicholls (Anne Durham), Ben Kingsley (Lasker-Jones), Patrick Godfrey (Simcox), Mark Tandy (Risley), Kitty Aldridge (Kitty Hall), Catherine Rabett (Pippa Durham), Helena Michell (Ada Hall), Peter Eyre (Rev Borenius). Homosexual Maurice is disappointed when his friend from university gets married but hopes to find love in the arms of the gamekeeper? Based on E. M. Forster's novel. *Dir*. James Ivory.

Mayerling (1968) Omar Sharif (Archduke Rudolf), Catherine Deneuve (Maria Vetsera), James Mason (Emperor Franz-Josef), Ava Gardner (Empress Elizabeth), James Robertson Justice (Prince of Wales), Geneviève Page (Countess Larish), Andréa Parisy (Princess Stephanie), Ivan Desny (Count Hoyos), Maurice Teynac (Moritz Szeps), Mony Dalmès (Baroness Vetsera), Moustache (Bratfisch), Fabienne Dali (Mizzi Kaspar), Roger Pigaut (Count Karolyi), Bernard La Jarrige (Loschek), Véronique Vendell (Lisl Stockau), Jacques Berthier (Prince Salvator), Charles Millot (Count Taafe), Lyne Chardonnet (Hanna Vetsera), Jacqueline Lavielle (Marinka), Roger Lumont (Insp Losch), Jean-Michel Rouzière (Police Supt), Irene von Meyendorff (Countess Stockau), Jean-Claude Bercq (Duke Michael of Braganza). Based upon the supposed manner of the suicides of Crown Prince Rudolf of Austria and his mistress Baroness Maria Vetsera at the Imperial hunting lodge of Mayerling in January 1889. *Dir*. Terence Young.

Mayfair Melody (1937) Keith Falkner (Mark), Chili Bouchier (Carmen), Bruce Lester (Dickie), Joyce Kirby (Brenda), Glen Alyn (Daphne), Aubrey Mallalieu (Dighton), George Galleon (Lord Chester), Louis Goodrich (Ludborough), Ian McLean (Collecchi), Vivienne Chatterton (Mme. Collecchi), Aubrey Mallalieu (Dighton). Factory worker Mark is discovered to be a singer and embarks on a stage career. *Dir*. Arthur B. Woods.

Maytime in Mayfair (1949) Anna Neagle (Eileen Grahame), Michael Wilding (Michael Gore-Brown), Peter Graves (D'Arcy Davenport), Nicholas Phipps (Sir Henry Hazelrigg), Thora Hird (Janet), Michael Shepley (Shepherd), Tom Walls (Inspector), Max Kirby (Mr Keats), Desmond Walter-Ellis (Mr Shelley), Tom Walls Jr. (Policeman), Doris Rogers (Lady Manbury-Logan-Manbury), Mona Washbourne (Lady Leveson). Michael inherits the haute couture dress salon run by Eileen but finds that he has a rival for both the shop and her affections. Sequel to *Spring in Park Lane* (1948). *Dir*. Herbert Wilcox.

McKenzie Break, The (1970) Brian Keith (Capt Jack Connor), Helmut Griem (Kapitän zur See Willi Schlüter), Ian Hendry (Maj Perry), Jack Watson (Maj Gen Ben Kerr), Patrick O'Connell (Sgt Maj Cox), Horst Janson (Lt Neuchl), Alexander Allerson (Lt Wolff), John Abineri (Capt Kranz), Constantine Gregory (Lt Hall), Tom Kempinski (Lt Schmidt), Eric Allan (Lt Hochbauer), Caroline Mortimer (A.T.S. Sgt. Bell), Mary Larkin (Cpl Jean Watt), Gregg Palmer (Lt Berger), Michael Sheard (Ingenieur-Offizier Unger), Ingo Mogendorf (Lt Fullgrabe), Lamont Johnson (PT Boat Captain), David Kelly (Adjutant). German prisoners plan an escape from the McKenzie POW camp in Scotland. *Dir*. Lamont Johnson.

McVicar (1980) Roger Daltrey (John McVicar), Adam Faith (Walter Probyn), Cheryl Campbell (Sheila McVicar), Billy Murray (Joey David), Georgina Hale (Kate), Steven Berkoff (Ronnie Harrison), Brian Hall (Terry Stokes), Peter Jonfield (Bobby Harris), Matthew Scurfield (Streaky Jeffries), Leonard Gregory (Jimmy Collins), Joe Turner (Panda), Ian Hendry (Hitchens), Tony Haygarth (Rabies). Biopic of armed robber and public enemy No. 1 John McVicar. *Dir*. Tom Clegg.

Me Without You (2001) Michelle Williams (Holly), Anna Friel (Marina), Oliver Milburn (Nat), Ella Jones (Young Holly), Anna Popplewell (Young Marina), Cameron Powrie (Young Nat), Trudie Styler (Linda), Allan Corduner (Max), Deborah Findlay (Judith), Nicky Henson (Ray), Hannah Bourne (Carolyn). Told in chronological sequence, the film follows the changes in the friendship between Holly and Marina from their teens in the 1970s up until the present (2001). *Dir*. Sandra Goldbacher.

Meet Me Tonight (1952) Segment *Ways and Means*: Valerie Hobson (Stella Cartwright), Nigel Patrick (Toby Cartwright), Jack Warner (Murdoch), Jessie Royce Landis (Olive Lloyd Ransome), Michael Trubshawe (Prof 'Chaps' Chapsworth), Mary Jerrold (Nanny), Yvonne Furneaux (Elena), Jacques Cey (The Fence). Segment *Red Peppers*: Kay Walsh (Lily Pepper), Ted Ray (George Pepper), Martita Hunt (Mabel Grace), Frank Pettingell (Mr. Edwards), Bill Fraser (Bert Bentley), Toke Townley (Stage Manager), Ian Wilson (Call Boy). Segment *Fumed Oak*: Stanley Holloway (Henry Gow), Betty Ann Davies (Doris Gow), Mary Merrall (Grandma Rockett), Dorothy Gordon (Elsie). An omnibus film adapted from three one-act plays by Noël Coward that are part of his *Tonight at 8:30* cycle. Dir. Anthony Pelissier.

Meet Mr. Lucifer (1953) Stanley Holloway (Sam Hollingsworth/Mr Lucifer), Peggy Cummins (Kitty Norton), Jack Watling (Jim Norton), Barbara Murray (Patricia Pedelty), Joseph Tomelty (Mr Pedelty), Kay Kendall (Lonely Hearts Singer), Gordon Jackson (Hector McPhee), Charles Victor (Mr Elder), Humphrey Lestocq (Arthur), Jean Cadell (Mrs Macdonald), Raymond Huntley (Mr Patterson), Ernest Thesiger (Mr Macdonald), Frank Pettingell (Mr Roberts), Olive Sloane (Mrs Stannard), Gilbert Harding (Himself), Olga Gwynne (Principal Boy), Joan Sims (Fairy Queen), Ian Carmichael (Man Friday), Irene Handl (Lady with Dog), Roddy Hughes (Billings), Eliot Makeham (Edwards), Bill Fraser (Bandleader), Dandy Nichols (Mrs. Clarke), Molly Hamley-Clifford (Mrs Ensor), Toke Townley (Trumpet Player), Fred Griffiths (Removal Man), Philip Harben (Himself), MacDonald Hobley (Himself). A thinly veiled attack on the "new" medium of television. The devil curses a television set which is passed between neighbours bringing only unhappiness. Based on the play *Beggar My Neighbour* by Arnold Ridley. *Dir*. Anthony Pelissier.

Memoirs of a Survivor (1981) Julie Christie ('D'), Christopher Guard (Gerald), Leonie Mellinger (Emily Cartwright), Debbie Hutchings (June), Nigel Hawthorne (Victorian Father), Pat Keen (Victorian Mother), Georgina Griffiths (Victorian Emily), Christopher Tsangarides (Victorian Son), Mark Dignam (Newsvendor), Alison Dowling (Janet White), John Franklyn-Robbins (Prof. White), Rowena Cooper (Mrs. White), Barbara Hicks (Woman on Waste Ground), John Comer (Man Delivering Emily), Adrienne Byrne (Maureen), Marion Owen Smith (Sandra), Tara MacGowran (Jill). In a dystopian future "D", who can travel in time through the wall of her flat, takes custody of Emily. Based on the novel by Doris Lessing. *Dir*. David Gladwell.

Memphis Belle (1990) Matthew Modine (Capt Dennis Dearborn), Eric Stoltz (Sgt Danny Boy Daly), Tate Donovan (1st Lt Luke Sinclair), D.B. Sweeney (Lt Phil Lowenthal), Billy Zane (Lt Valentine Kozlowski), Sean Astin (Sgt Richard "Rascal" Moore), Harry Connick Jr (Sgt Clay Busby), Reed Diamond (Sgt Virgil Hoogesteger), Courtney Gains (Sgt Eugene McVey), Neil Giuntoli (Sgt Jack Bocci), David Strathairn (Col Craig Harriman), John Lithgow (Lt Col Bruce Derringer), Jane Horrocks (Faith), Mac McDonald (Les), Jodie Wilson (Singer), Keith Edwards (S-2), Steven Mackintosh (Stan the Rookie), Greg Charles (Adjutant), Bradley Lavelle (Sergeant), Ben Browder (Rookie Captain), Mitch Webb (Group Navigator). Fiction version of a 1943 documentary *Memphis Belle: A Story of a Flying Fortress* directed by William Wyler. In May 1943 the crew of the *Memphis Belle* are preparing for its 25th and final mission of its tour of duty. *Dir*. Michael Caton-Jones.

Men of Sherwood Forest, The (1954) Don Taylor (Robin Hood), Reginald Beckwith (Friar Tuck), Eileen Moore (Lady Alys), David King-Wood (Sir Guy Belton), Douglas Wilmer (Sir Nigel Saltire), Harold Lang (Hubert), Ballard Berkeley (Walter), Patrick Holt (King Richard), Wensley Pithey (Hugo), Leslie Linder (Little John), John Van Eyssen (Will Scarlett), Vera Pearce (Elvira), John Stuart (Moraine), John Kerr (Brian of Eskdale), Raymond Rollett (Abbot St. Jude), Leonard Sachs (Sheriff of Nottingham), Bernard Bresslaw (Garth), Tom Bowman, Michael Godfrey, Dennis Wyndham, Jack McNaughton, Edward Hardwicke (Outlaws). Robin travels to the Continent disguised as a troubadour in search of the kidnapped King Richard but returns to Sherwood to foil an ambush. *Dir*. Val Guest.

Men of Tomorrow (1932) Maurice Braddell (Allan Shepherd), Joan Gardner (Jane Anderson), Emlyn Williams (Horners), Robert Donat (Julian Angell), Merle Oberon (Ysobel d'Aunay), John Traynor (Mr. Waters), Esther Kiss (Maggie), Annie Esmond (Mrs. Oliphant), Charles Carson (Senior Proctor), Gerald Cooper (Tutor). Allan leaves his wife when she gets a teaching job. *Dirs*. Zoltan Korda and Leontine Sagan.

Merry Christmas, Mr. Lawrence (1983) David Bowie (Maj Jack 'Strafer' Celliers), Tom Conti (Col John Lawrence), Ryuichi Sakamoto (Capt Yonoi), Takeshi Kitano (Sgt Gengo Hara), Jack Thompson (Group Capt Hicksley), Johnny Okura (Kanemoto), Alistair Browning (De Jong), James Malcolm (Celliers' brother), Chris Broun (Celliers aged 12), Yuya Uchida (Commandant), Ryunosuke Kaneda (President of the Court), Takashi Naitô (Lt Iwata), Tamio Ishikura (Prosecutor), Rokko Toura (Interpreter), Kan Mikami (Lt Ito). Explores the complex relationships which develop between four men, two prisoners and the Japanese commandant and sergeant in a POW camp during WWII. Based on Laurens van der Post's works *The Seed and the Sower* (1963) and *The Night of the New Moon* (1970). *Dir*. Nagisa Oshima.

Michael Collins (1996) Liam Neeson (Michael Collins), Aidan Quinn (Harry Boland), Stephen Rea (Ned Broy), Alan Rickman (Éamon de Valera), Julia Roberts (Kitty Kiernan), Brendan Gleeson (Liam Tobin), Ian Hart (Joe O'Reilly), Charles Dance (Soames), Owen O'Neill (Rory O'Connor), Gerard McSorley (Cathal Brugha), Jonathan Rhys Meyers (Collins' assassin), Ian McElhinney (Belfast Detective), Richard Ingram (British Officer), John Kenny (Patrick Pearse), Ronan McCairbre (Thomas MacDonagh), Jer O'Leary (Thomas Clarke), Michael Dwyer (James Connolly), Martin Murphy (Captain Lee-Wilson), Owen Roe (Arthur Griffith), Sean McGinley (Smith), Gary Whelan (Hoey), Frank O'Sullivan (Kavanagh), Frank Laverty (Sean McKeoin), Stuart Graham (Tom Cullen), Liam De Staic (Austin Stack), Paul Bennett (Cosgrave), Tom Murphy (Vinny Byrne), David Gorry (Charlie Dalton). Biopic of Irish soldier and politician Michael Collins told in flashback from the Easter Rising of 1916 until his assassination in 1922. *Dir*. Neil Jordan.

Middle Watch, The (1930) Owen Nares (Capt Maitland), Jacqueline Logan (Mary Carlton), Jack Raine (Cmdr Baddeley), Dodo Watts (Fay Eaton), Frederick Volpe (Adm Sir Herbert Hewitt), Henry Wenman (Marine Ogg), Reginald Purdell (Cpl Duckett), Margaret Halstan (Lady Agatha Hewitt), Phyllis Loring (Nancy Hewitt), Hamilton Keene (Capt Randall), Muriel Aked (Charlotte Hopkinson), George Carr (Ah Fong). Two beautiful women stowaway on a battleship. *Dir*. Norman Walker.

Middle Watch, The (1940) Jack Buchanan (Captain Maitland), Greta Gynt (Mary Carlton), Fred Emney (Adm. Sir Reginald Hewett), Kay Walsh (Fay Eaton), David Hutcheson (Cmdr. Baddeley), Leslie Fuller (Marine Ogg), Bruce Seton (Captain Randall), Martita Hunt (Lady Elizabeth Hewett), Louise Hampton (Charlotte Hopkinson), Romney Brent (Ah Fong), Jean Gillie (Betty Hewett), Ronald Shiner (Engineer), Reginald Purdell (Cpl Duckett A remake of the 1930 film. *Dir*. Thomas Bentley.

Midnight Express (1978) Brad Davis (Billy Hayes), Irene Miracle (Susan), Bo Hopkins ('Tex'), Paolo Bonacelli (Rifki), Paul L. Smith (Hamidou), Randy Quaid (Jimmy Booth), Norbert Weisser (Erich), John Hurt (Max), Kevork Malikyan (Prosecutor), Yashaw Adem (Airport police chief), Mike Kellin (Mr Hayes), Franco Diogene (Yesil), Michael Ensign (Stanley Daniels), Vic Tablian (Star), Peter Jeffrey (Ahmet Ahmed), El Shenawi (Negdir), Alan Parker (Long-Haired Man at Airport). When Billy is arrested at Istanbul airport with hashish taped to his body he is sentenced to four years in prison but is eventually found guilty of smuggling and his term increased to 30 years. Life in the Turkish prison is awful and he must find a way to escape ("take the Midnight Express"). Based on Billy Hayes's book. *Dir*. Alan Parker.

Midshipman Easy (1935) Hughie Green (Midshipman Easy), Margaret Lockwood (Donna Agnes), Harry Tate (Mr Biggs), Robert Adams (Mesty), Roger Livesey (Captain Wilson), Dennis Wyndham (Don Silvio), Lewis Casson (Mr Easy), Tom Gill (Gascoine), Frederick Burtwell (Mr. Easthupp), Desmond Tester (Gossett), Dorothy Holmes-Gore (Mrs. Easy). Set during the Napoleonic Wars, young Easy joins the navy and has adventures on the high seas. Based on the novel *Mr Midshipman Easy* by Frederick Marryat. *Dir*. Carol Reed.

Mike Bassett: England Manager (2001) Ricky Tomlinson (Mike Bassett), Amanda Redman (Karine Bassett), Bradley Walsh (Dave Dodds), Philip Jackson (Lonnie Urquart), Phill Jupitus (Tommo Thompson), Dean Lennox Kelly (Kevin Tonkinson), Martin Bashir (Interviewer), Robbie Gee (Rufus Smalls), Robert Putt (Jack Marshall), Malcolm Terris (Phil Cope), Danny Tennant (Jason Bassett), Geoff Bell (Gary Wackett), Chris McQuarry (Alan Massey), Geoffrey Hutchings (Geoffrey Lightfoot), Angela Curran (Margaret), Scott Mean (Parksey), Julian Ballantine (Robbo), Dean Holness (Danny), John Alford (Deano), Terry Kiely (Harpsey), Peter McGillycuddy (Gorgeous), Toby Redwood (Berksey), Andy Ansah (Super), Thomas Kenyon (Macca), Robert Campion (Smudger), Alex Lawler (Sexy), Dion Osborne (Ossie), Danny Husbands (Normal), Declan Perkins (Perky). Ulrich Thomsen (Dr Hans Shoegaarten), Clive Tyldesley and Martin Tyler (Commentators), Natasha Kaplinsky (Sky News Reader), Kevin Piper (Norwich newsreader) and Pelé, Sue Barker, Dickie Bird, Keith Allen, Gabby Logan, Barry Venison, Ronaldo, Richard Guest, Jenny Frost, Liz McClarnon (Themselves). Mockumentary following the World Cup campaign of Mike Bassett. After the sudden death of the incumbent, the management of the England international football team devolves, because no-one else wants the job - enter Mike Bassett, manager of Norwich City. Having luckily qualified for the World Cup Finals, Bassett suffers the abuse of both the media and the fans as the campaign goes from bad to worse both on and off the field. *Dir*. Steve Barron.

Mill on the Floss, The (1937) James Mason (Tom Tulliver), Geraldine Fitzgerald (Maggie Tulliver), Frank Lawton (Philip Wakem), Victoria Hopper (Lucy Deane), Fay Compton (Mrs Tulliver), Griffith Jones (Stephen Guest), Mary Clare (Mrs Moss), Athene Seyler (Mrs Pullet), Sam Livesey (Mr Tulliver), Amy Veness (Mrs Deane), Felix Aylmer (Mr Wakem), Eliot Makeham (Mr Pullet), William Devlin (Bob Jakin), Ivor Barnard (Mr Moss), David Horne (Mr Deane). The ultimately tragic story of Tom and Maggie Tulliver. Based on the classic novel by George Eliot. *Dir*. Tim Whelan.

Million Pound Note, The (1953) Gregory Peck (Henry Adams), Ronald Squire (Oliver Montpelier), Wilfrid Hyde-White (Roderick Montpelier), Joyce Grenfell (Duchess of Cromarty), A. E. Matthews (Duke of Frognal), Jane Griffiths (Portia Lansdowne), Maurice Denham (Mr Reid), Reginald Beckwith

(Rock), Brian Oulton (Lloyd), John Slater (Parsons), Wilbur Evans (US ambassador), Hartley Power (Hastings), George Devine (Restaurant proprietor), Bryan Forbes (Todd), Gudrun Ure (Renie), Hugh Wakefield (Duke of Cromarty). Henry Adams is an American sailor stranded without money in England. He becomes involved with two wealthy men who have a wager over the use of a million pound bank note – do you need to actually spend it or is its mere possession sufficient to enable you to live in luxury? Based on the Mark Twain short story *The Million Pound Bank Note*. *Dir*. Ronald Neame.

Millionairess, The (1960) Sophia Loren (Epifania Parerga), Peter Sellers (Dr. Ahmed el Kabir), Alastair Sim (Julius Sagamore), Vittorio De Sica (Joe), Dennis Price (Dr. Adrian Bland), Gary Raymond (Alastair), Alfie Bass (Fish Curer), Miriam Karlin (Mrs. Maria Joe), Noel Purcell (Prof. Merton), Virginia Vernon (Polly Smith), Graham Stark (Butler), Diana Coupland (Nurse), Pauline Jameson (Muriel Pilkington), Eleanor Summerfield (Mrs. Willoughby), Willoughby Goddard (President), Basil Hoskins (First Secretary), Gordon Sterne (Second Secretary), Tempe Adam (Gloria), Wally Patch (Whelk-Seller), Charles Hill (Corelli), Davy Kaye (Tommy True), Roy Kinnear (Man Carrying Crate), Derek Nimmo (Assistant Butler). An Italian heiress falls for a poor Indian doctor. A song which was not used in the film "Goodness Gracious Me", sung in character by Loren and Sellers was a No 4 UK single. Loosely adapted from George Bernard Shaw's play. *Dir*. Anthony Asquith.

Millions (2004) Alex Etel (Damian Cunningham), Lewis McGibbon (Anthony Cunningham), James Nesbitt (Ronald Cunningham), Daisy Donovan (Dorothy), Christopher Fulford (Poor Man), Pearce Quigley (Community Policeman), Jane Hogarth (Mum), Alun Armstrong (Saint Peter), Enzo Cilenti (Saint Francis of Assisi), Nasser Memarzia (St Joseph), Kathryn Pogson (St Clare), Harry Kirkham (St Nicholas), Cornelius Macarthy (Gonzaga), Kolade Agboke (Ambrosio), Leslie Phillips (Himself). Two young brothers find a bag full of money. One of them decides to spend it whilst the other decides to give his share to the poor. Adaptation by Frank Cottrell Boyce of his own novel. *Dir*. Danny Boyle.

Millions Like Us (1943) Patricia Roc (Celia), Gordon Jackson (Fred), Anne Crawford (Jennifer), Moore Marriott (Jim), Basil Radford (Charters), Naunton Wayne (Caldicott), Joy Shelton (Phyllis), John Boxer (Tom), Valentine Dunn (Elsie), Megs Jenkins (Gwen), Terry Randall (Annie), Amy Veness (Mrs. Blythe), John Salew (Doctor), Beatrice Varley (Miss Wells), Bertha Willmott (The Singer), Eric Portman (Charlie), Brenda Bruce (Brenda), Albert Chevalier (Roof Spotter), Irene Handl (Landlady), Tommy Trinder (Station Announcer). The story of a family which represents life on the British Home Front during the early years of WWII. Whilst her younger sister joins the ATS, Celia moves into a hostel and works at an aircraft engineering factory. She is married and widowed within a short space of time but is bolstered by her friends and family. *Dirs*. Sidney Gilliat and Frank Launder.

Mimi (1935) Douglas Fairbanks Jr. (Rodolphe), Gertrude Lawrence (Mimi), Diana Napier (Mme. Sidonie), Harold Warrender (Marcel), Carol Goodner (Musette), Richard Bird (Colline), Martin Walker (Schaunard), Austin Trevor (Lamotte), Laurence Hanray (Barbemouche), Paul Graetz (Durand), Jack Raine (Duke). A film based on the libretto of Puccini's opera *La Boheme*. *Dir*. Paul L Stein.

Mind Benders, The (1963) Dirk Bogarde (Dr. Henry Laidlaw Longman), Mary Ure (Oonagh Longman), John Clements (Maj Hall), Michael Bryant (Dr Danny Tate), Wendy Craig (Annabella), Harold Goldblatt (Prof Sharpey), Geoffrey Keen (Calder), Terry Palmer (Norman), Norman Bird (Aubrey), Terence Alexander (Coach), Timothy Beaton (Paul Longman), Elizabeth Counsell (Student on Station), Roger Delgado (Dr Jean Bonvoulois), Terence Edmond (Student at Party), Christopher Ellis (Peers Longman), Edward Fox (Stewart), Georgina Moon (Persephone Longman). A scientist indulges in some experimenting in brainwashing. *Dir*. Basil Dearden.

Mine Own Executioner (1947) Burgess Meredith (Felix Milne), Dulcie Gray (Patricia Milne), Michael Shepley (Peter Edge), Christine Norden (Barbara 'Babs' Edge), Kieron Moore (Adam Lucian), Barbara White (Molly Lucian), Walter Fitzgerald (Dr. Norris Pile), Edgar Norfolk (Sir George Freethorne), John Laurie (Dr James Garsten), Martin Miller (Dr Hans Tautz), Clive Morton (Robert Paston), Joss Ambler (Julian Briant), Jack Raine (Insp Pierce), Laurence Hanray (Dr Lefage), Helen Haye (Lady Maresfield), John Stuart (Dr John Hayling), Ronald Simpson (Mr Grandison), Gwynne Whitby (Miss English), Malcolm Dalmayne (Charlie Oakes), Michael Hordern (Co-counsel at Felix's Hearing). A psychiatrist with marital problems pushes his treatment of a WWII Japanese POW camp survivor too far. *Dir*. Anthony Kimmins.

Miracle, The (1991) Beverly D'Angelo (Renee Baker), Donal McCann (Sam), Niall Byrne (Jimmy), Lorraine Pilkington (Rose), J. G. Devlin (Mr. Beausang), Cathleen Delaney (Miss Strange), Tom Hickey (Tommy), Shane Connaughton (Rose's Father), Mikkel Gaup (Jonner). Jimmy and Rose while away the hours by making up stories about the people they see in the small seaside town of Bray in Ireland. One day they spot Renee at the train station. *Dir*. Neil Jordan.

Miranda (1948) Glynis Johns (Miranda Trewella), Griffith Jones (Paul Martin), Googie Withers (Clare Martin), John McCallum (Nigel), David Tomlinson (Charles), Margaret Rutherford (Nurse Carey), Yvonne Owen (Betty), Sonia Holm (Isobel), Brian Oulton (Manell), Zena Marshall (Secretary), Lyn Evans (Inn Landlord), Stringer Davis (Museum Attendant), Hal Osmond (Railway Carman), Maurice Denham (Cockle Vendor), Gerald Campion (Lift Boy). Whilst on a fishing trip Paul snags a mermaid (Miranda) and is pulled underwater. She keeps him in a cave until he agrees to take her to London. *Dir*. Ken Annakin. See also *Mad About Men*

Miss Potter (2006) Renée Zellweger (Beatrix Potter), Ewan McGregor (Norman Warne), Emily Watson (Amelia "Millie" Warne), Barbara Flynn (Helen Potter), Bill Paterson (Rupert Potter), Matyelok Gibbs (Miss Wiggin), Lloyd Owen (William Heelis), Anton Lesser (Harold Warne), David Bamber (Fruing Warne), Phyllida Law (Mrs. Warne), Patricia Kerrigan (Fiona), Lucy Boynton (Young Beatrix), Oliver Jenkins (Young Bertram), Justin McDonald (Young Heelis), Judith Barker (Hilda), Jennifer Castle (Jane), Chris Middleton (Saunders), Lynn Farleigh (Lady Sybil), Geoffrey Beevers (Mr Copperthwaite), John Woodvine (Sir Nigel), Jane How (Lady Armitage), Bridget McConnell (Lady Stokely), Joseph Grieves (Lionel Stokely), Clare Clifford (Mrs Haddon-Bell), Andy McSorley (Harry Haddon-Bell), Sarah Crowden (Lady Clifford), Richard Mulholland (Ashton Clifford), Marc Finn (Mr Cannon). Biopic of children's author and illustrator Beatrix Potter and in particular her relationship with Norman Warne, her publisher. Combines live action with animated sequences featuring characters from her stories. *Dir*. Chris Noonan.

Miss Robin Hood (1952) Margaret Rutherford (Miss Honey), Richard Hearne (Henry Wrigley), James Robertson Justice (The Macalister), Dora Bryan (Pearl), Michael Medwin (Ernest), Peter Jones (Cyril Lidstone), Sid James (Sidney), Eric Berry (Lord Otterbourne), Edward Lexy (Wilson), Fanny Rowe (Marion), Eunice Gayson (Pam), Russell Waters (Bunyan), Reg Varney (Dennis), Susanne Gibbs (Sue), Francis De Wolff (Accident Policeman), Ian Carmichael (Office Junior), Kenneth Connor and Stringer Davis (Board Members). Henry Wrigley produces a comic strip, *Miss Robin Hood*, for a children's magazine and is embroiled in a plot by Miss Honey to retrieve a secret whisky formula from a safe belonging to Macalister. *Dir*. John Guillermin.

Mission, The (1986) Robert De Niro (Rodrigo Mendoza), Jeremy Irons (Father Gabriel), Ray McAnally (Cardinal Altamirano), Aidan Quinn (Felipe Mendoza), Cherie Lunghi (Carlotta), Ronald Pickup (Hontar), Chuck Low (Cabeza), Liam Neeson (Fielding), Bercelio Moya (Indian Boy), Sigifredo Ismare (Witch Doctor), Asuncion Ontiveros (Indian Chief), Alejandrino Moya (Chief's Lieutenant), Daniel Berrigan (Sebastian), Rolf Gray (Young

Jesuit), Álvaro Guerrero (Jesuit). The experiences of a Jesuit missionary in 18th century South America where the Jesuits are trying to protect the natives from falling into the clutches of Portuguese slavers. The film won an Academy Award for Best Cinematography (Chris Menges). *Dir*. Roland Joffé.

Missionary, The (1982) Michael Palin (Rev Charles Fortescue), Maggie Smith (Lady Isabel Ames), Trevor Howard (Lord Henry Ames), Denholm Elliott (The Bishop), Michael Hordern (Slatterthwaite/Narrator), Graham Crowden (The Reverend Fitzbanks), David Suchet (Corbett), Phoebe Nicholls (Deborah Fitzbanks), Tricia George (Ada), Valerie Whittington (Emmeline), Roland Culver (Lord Fermleigh), Rosamund Greenwood (Lady Fermleigh), Timothy Spall (Parswell), Neil Innes (Singer). When Fortescue returns from Africa he finds his new mission is to minister to the prostitutes of London. His fiancé is a total innocent and Lady Ames, who is funding his mission, has more carnal desires. *Dir*. Richard Loncraine.

Mister Drake's Duck (1951) Douglas Fairbanks Jr. (Donald 'Don' Drake), Yolande Donlan (Penny Drake), Jon Pertwee (Reuben), Wilfrid Hyde-White (Mr May), Reginald Beckwith (Mr Boothby), Howard Marion-Crawford (Maj Travers), Peter Butterworth (Higgins), A.E. Matthews (Brig Matthews), Tom Gill (Capt White), John Boxer (Sergeant), Gilbert Davis (Sgt Maj), Ballard Berkeley (Maj Deans), Roger Maxwell (Col Maitland), Harry Fowler (Corporal), Bruce Belfrage (Air Vice Marshal), Raymond Rollett (Admiral), Frederick Bradshaw (Wing Comdr), Frank Phillips (BBC announcer), Richard Littledale (MP), George Merritt (Home Secretary), Arthur Hill (American Vice Consul). The quiet life of Farmer Drake is turned upside down when one of his ducks lays a Uranium egg. *Dir*. Val Guest.

Mix Me a Person (1962) Anne Baxter (Dr. Anne Dyson), Donald Sinden (Philip Bellamy, QC), Adam Faith (Harry Jukes), David Kernan (Socko), Frank Jarvis (Nobby), Peter Kriss (Dirty Neck), Carole Ann Ford (Jenny), Anthony Booth (Gravy), Topsy Jane (Mona), Jack MacGowran (Terence), Walter Brown (Max Taplow), Glyn Houston (Sam), Dilys Hamlett (Doris), Meredith Edwards (Johnson), Alfred Burke (Lumley), Russell Napier (PC Jarrold), Ray Barrett (Insp. Wagstaffe), Ed Devereaux (Supt. Malley). A psychiatrist believes a young man sentenced to be hanged for murder is in fact innocent. *Dir*. Leslie Norman.

Modesty Blaise (1966) Monica Vitti (Modesty Blaise), Terence Stamp (Willie Garvin), Dirk Bogarde (Gabriel), Harry Andrews (Sir Gerald Tarrant), Michael Craig (Paul Hagan), Clive Revill (McWhirter/Sheik Abu Tahir), Alexander Knox (Minister), Rossella Falk (Mrs Fothergill), Scilla Gabel (Melina), Michael Chow (Weng), Joe Melia (Crevier), Saro Urzì (Basilio), Tina Aumont (Nicole), Jon Bluming (Hans), Lex Schoorel (Walter), Max Turilli (Strauss), Giuseppe Paganelli (Friar), Wolfgang Hillinger (Handsome), Roberto Bisacco (Enrico), John Karlsen (Oleg), Aldo Silvani (Pacco). Modesty is employed by the British government to thwart a diamond robbery masterminded by Gabriel. High-tech spy spoof of a type popular in the mid 1960s. Based on the comic strip *Modesty Blaise* by Peter O'Donnell. *Dir*. Joseph Losey.

Mona Lisa (1986) Bob Hoskins (George), Cathy Tyson (Simone), Michael Caine (Denny Mortwell), Robbie Coltrane (Thomas), Clarke Peters (Anderson), Kate Hardie (Cathy), Zoë Nathenson (Jeannie), Sammi Davis (May), Rod Bedall (Terry), Joe Brown (Dudley), Pauline Melville (George's Wife), Hossein Karimbeik (Raschid), John Darling (Hotel Security), Bryan Coleman (Gentleman in Mirror Room), Robert Dorning (Hotel Bedroom Man). Petty criminal George gets out of prison and takes a job as driver for Simone, a beautiful high-priced call girl. *Dir* Neil Jordan.

Month in the Country, A (1987) Colin Firth (Tom Birkin), Kenneth Branagh (James Moon), Patrick Malahide (Reverend Keach), Natasha Richardson (Alice Keach), Jim Carter (Ellerbeck), Richard Vernon (Colonel Hebron), Tim Barker (Mossop), Vicki Arundale (Kathy Ellerbeck), Martin O'Neil (Edgar Ellerbeck), Eileen O'Brien (Mrs. Ellerbeck), Tony Haygarth (Douthwaite), Elizabeth Anson (Lucy Sykes), Barbara Marten (Mrs. Sykes), Kenneth Kitson (Mr. Sykes), Judy Gridley (Mrs. Clough), Lisa Taylor (Emily Clough), Andrew Wilde (Shop Assistant), David Gillies (Milburn), David Garth (Old Birkin), John Atkinsons (Old Man on Train). A veteran of WWI, still suffering from the after effects of that conflict, spends time in the country restoring a Medieval church and begins to come to terms with himself. Adaptation of the novel by J. L. Carr. *Dir*. Pat O'Connor.

Monty Python and the Holy Grail (1974) Main roles: Graham Chapman (King Arthur), John Cleese (Sir Lancelot), Terry Gilliam (Patsy), Eric Idle (Sir Robin), Terry Jones (Sir Bedevere), Michael Palin (Sir Galahad), Neil Innes (Sir Robin's Minstrel), Connie Booth (The Witch), Carol Cleveland (Zoot), Bee Duffell (Old crone), John Young (Historian), Rita Davies (Historian's Wife), Sally Kinghorn (Dr Winston), Avril Stewart (Piglet), Mark Zycon (Prisoner). King Arthur of the Britons gathers his knights and goes on a quest to find the Holy Grail. In the course of the film they encounter the Black Knight, a French-controlled castle, the dreaded Knights who say Ni, the Three-Headed Giant, the predatory women of Castle Anthrax, the Rabbit of Caerbannog (also called The Killer Rabbit), the Legendary Black Beast of Aaaaarrrrrrggghhh, and finally the Bridge of Death. The first non-sketch based Monty Python film. *Dirs*. Terry Gilliam and Terry Jones.

Monty Python's Life of Brian (1979) Graham Chapman (Wise Man No 2/Brian Cohen/Biggus Dickus), John Cleese (Wise Man No 1/Reg/Jewish Official/Centurion/Deadly Dirk/Arthur), Terry Gilliam (Man Even Further Forward/Revolutionary/Jailer/Blood & Thunder Prophet/Frank/Audience member/Crucifee), Eric Idle (Mr Cheeky/Stan (Loretta)/Harry the Haggler/Culprit Woman/Warris/Intensely Dull Youth/Jailer's Assistant/Otto/Lead Singer Crucifee), Terry Jones (Mandy Cohen/Colin/Simon the Holy Man/Bob Hoskins/Saintly Passer-by/Alarmed Crucifixion Assistant), Michael Palin (Wise Man No 3/Mr. Big Nose/Francis/Mrs. A/Ex-Leper/Announcer/Ben/Pontius Pilate/Boring Prophet/Eddie/Shoe Follower/Nisus Wettus), Terence Bayler (Gregory), Carol Cleveland (Mrs. Gregory), Kenneth Colley (Jesus Christ), Neil Innes (A weedy Samaritan), Gwen Taylor (Mrs Big Nose/ Woman with sick donkey/young girl), Charles McKeown (Man further forward (at Mount)/Stig/Blind Man/False Prophet/Giggling Guard), Chris Langham (Alfonso/Giggling Guard), Sue Jones-Davies (Judith Iscariot), John Young (Matthias), Bernard McKenna (Stoner's Helper, Parvus), Spike Milligan (Spike), George Harrison (Mr Papadopoulos). A biopic of Brian Cohen who is born on the same day as, and in a stable next door to, Jesus Christ, and is subsequently mistaken for the Messiah. Irreverent? Maybe – but very funny. *Dir* Terry Jones.

Monty Python's The Meaning of Life (1983) Various roles: Graham Chapman, John Cleese, Terry Gilliam, Eric Idle, Terry Jones, Michael Palin, Carol Cleveland, Patricia Quinn, Mark Holmes, Simon Jones, Matt Frewer. A return to the sketch format – designed to take the viewer through the stages of life. A highlight of the film is the scene in Part VI where the incredibly overweight Mr. Creosote (Terry Jones) waddles into a decorous restaurant, swears at the French waiter (John Cleese), and vomits copiously on all and sundry. Having made room, he eats an enormous meal, and finally, despite protestations that he is now full, he is persuaded to eat one last "waffeur-thin" mint, whereupon he explodes, showering the restaurant with human entrails. *Dir*. Terry Jones.

Moon (2009) Sam Rockwell (Sam Bell), Kevin Spacey (GERTY – voice), Dominique McElligott (Tess Bell), Kaya Scodelario (Eve Bell), Benedict Wong (Lunar Industries' Thompson), Matt Berry (Lunar Industries' Overmeyers), Malcolm Stewart ('The Technician'), Robin Chalk (Sam Bell Clone No 6). Towards the end of his solitary three year shift on a lunar mining station Sam Bell begins to have hallucinations. *Dir*. Duncan Jones.

Moon Zero Two (1969) James Olson (Capt. William H. Kemp), Catherine Schell (Clementine Taplin), Warren Mitchell (J.J. Hubbard), Adrienne Corri (Elizabeth Murphy), Ori Levy (Korminski), Dudley Foster (Whitsun), Bernard Bresslaw (Harry), Neil McCallum (Space Captain), Joby Blanshard (Smith), Michael Ripper (1st Card Player), Sam Kydd (Len the Barman), Carol Cleveland (Hostess), Roy Evans (Workman), Chrissie Shrimpton (Boutique Attendant). Set on the newly colonised Moon in 2021. A gang has a plan involving an asteroid made of sapphire and a mining claim on the far side of the Moon. *Dir*. Roy Ward Baker.

Moonraker (1979) Roger Moore (James Bond), Lois Chiles (Holly Goodhead), Michael Lonsdale (Sir Hugo Drax), Toshiro Suga (Chang), Richard Kiel (Jaws), Corinne Clery (Corinne Dufour), Bernard Lee (M), Geoffrey Keen (Frederick Gray), Desmond Llewelyn (Q), Lois Maxwell (Miss Moneypenny), Emily Bolton (Manuela), Michael Marshall (Col Scott), Walter Gotell (Gen Gogol), Blanche Ravalec (Dolly). Drax Industries is building space shuttles and Bond discovers a devilish plot to exterminate life on Earth by launching a deadly toxin into the Earth's atmosphere from a space station. In the process he also crosses paths with beautiful astronaut Holly Goodhead. Jaws makes his second and final appearance and also finds a love interest. Bond drives a 1930 Bentley 4½ Litre, a 1953 Bentley Mark VI and an MP Roadster. The theme song is performed by Shirley Bassey. *Dir.* Lewis Gilbert.

Morgan: A Suitable Case for Treatment (1966) David Warner (Morgan Delt), Vanessa Redgrave (Leonie Delt), Robert Stephens (Charles Napier), Irene Handl (Mrs. Delt), Bernard Bresslaw (Policeman), Arthur Mullard (Wally), Newton Blick (Mr. Henderson), Nan Munro (Mrs. Henderson), Peter Collingwood (Geoffrey), Graham Crowden (Counsel), John Garrie (Tipstatt), John Rae (Judge), Angus MacKay (Best Man), Marvis Edwards (Maid). Morgan has a breakdown when his wife asks for a divorce and kidnaps her with the help of his friend Wally. *Dir.* Karel Reisz.

Morning Departure (1950) John Mills (Lt. Cmdr. Armstrong), Nigel Patrick (Lt. Manson), Peter Hammond (Sub-Lt. Oakley), Andrew Crawford (Sub-Lt. J. McFee), Michael Brennan (CPO Barlow), George Cole (ERA Marks), Victor Maddern (Leading Telegraphist Hillbrook), Roddy McMillan (Leading Seaman Andrews), Frank Coburn (Leading Seaman Brough), Jack Stewart (Leading Seaman Kelly), James Hayter (Able Seaman Higgins), Wylie Watson (Able Seaman Nobby Clark), Richard Attenborough (Stoker Snipe), George Thorpe (Capt. Fenton), Bernard Lee (Cmdr. Gates), Kenneth More (Lt. Cmdr. James), Alastair Hunter (Capt. Jenner), Helen Cherry (Helen Armstong), Lana Morris (Rose Snipe), Zena Marshall (WREN). The British submarine *Trojan* is severely damaged by a magnetic mine whilst on a routine patrol after WWII. Many crewmen are killed and the captain manages to get more out using rescue equipment. However, he and several others remain in the submarine as it rests on the seabed and the rescue mission on the surface begins to run into problems. *Dir.* Roy Ward Baker

Morons from Outer Space (1985) Mel Smith (Bernard), Griff Rhys Jones (Graham Sweetley), Joanne Pearce (Sandra Brock), Jimmy Nail (Desmond Brock), Paul Bown (Julian Tope), James Sikking (Col. Raymond Laribee), Dinsdale Landen (Comdr Grenville), Matteson, Tristram Jellinek (Simpson), George Innes (Stanley Benson), John Joyce (Chief Inspector Miller), Mark Lewis Jones (Godfrey), Leonard Fenton (Commissionaire), André Maranne (Prof. Trousseau), Joanna Dickens (Lady Farmer), R.J. Bell (Klutz), Peter Whitman (Friborg), Olivier Pierre (Jabowlski), Edward Wiley (Laribee's Aide), Robert Austin (Newscaster), John Barcroft (McKenzie), Bill Stewart (Walters). Three aliens crash land on Earth and become celebrities whilst forgetting about the fourth member of their party. *Dir.* Mike Hodges.

Morvern Callar (2002) Samantha Morton (Morvern Callar), Kathleen McDermott (Lanna), Linda McGuire (Vanessa), Paul Popplewell (Cat in the Hat), Ruby Milton (Couris Jean), Dolly Wells (Susan), Duncan McHardy (Red Hanna), Andrew Townley (Creeping Jesus), Dan Cadan (Dazzer), Carolyn Calder (Sheila Tequila), Bryan Dick (Guy with Hat's Mate), Andrew Flanagan (Overdose), Danny Schofield (Dave), James Wilson (Tom Boddington), Des Hamilton (Him). After her boyfriend commits suicide Morvern passes off his manuscript for a novel as her own. Based on Alan Warner's novel of the same name. *Dir.* Lynne Ramsay.

Moscow Nights (1935) Laurence Olivier (Capt Ivan Ignatoff), Penelope Dudley-Ward (Natasha), Harry Baur (Peter Brioukow), Athene Seyler (Madame Anna Sabine), Lilian Braithwaite (Countess), Morton Selten (Gen Kovrin), Sam Livesey (Fedor), Robert Cochran (Polonsky), Hay Petrie (Spy), Walter Hudd (Doctor), Kate Cutler (Madame Kovrin), C.M. Hallard (President of Court Martial), Charles Carson (Officer of Defense), Edmund Willard (Officer of Prosecution), Morland Graham (Brioukow's Servant), Anthony Quayle (Vanya). When Captain Ignatoff is wounded in WWI he falls in love with his nurse but she is promised to another. *Dir.* Anthony Asquith.

Moulin Rouge (1952) José Ferrer (Henri de Toulouse-Lautrec/The Comte de Toulouse-Lautrec), Colette Marchand (Marie Charlet), Zsa Zsa Gabor (Jane Avril), Suzanne Flon (Myriamme Hayam), Claude Nollier (Countess de Toulouse-Lautrec), Katherine Kath (La Goulue), Muriel Smith (Aicha), Mary Clare (Madame Louet), Walter Crisham (Valentin Dessosse), Harold Kasket (Zidler), Georges Lannes (Police Sgt. Patou), Lee Montague (Maurice Joyant), Maureen Swanson (Denise de Frontiac), Tutte Lemkow (Aicha's Partner), Jill Bennett (Sarah), Theodore Bikel (King Milo IV of Serbia), Peter Cushing (Marcel de la Voisier), Charles Carson (Mr. Paquin), Walter Cross (Babare), Michael Balfour (Dodo), Francis De Wolff (Victor), Christopher Lee (Georges Seurat). A partial biopic of the artist Toulouse-Lautrec, mainly concentrating on his time at the Moulin Rouge in Paris, where he sketches and paints the can-can dancers. The film also depicts his tortured love life and shows some of his early years as the son of a Comte. *Dir.* John Huston.

Mouse on the Moon, The(1963) Margaret Rutherford (Grand Duchess Gloriana XIII), Ron Moody (Prime Minister Rupert Mountjoy), Bernard Cribbins (Vincent Mountjoy), David Kossoff (Prof Kokintz), Terry-Thomas (Maurice Spender), June Ritchie (Cynthia), John Le Mesurier (British Delegate), John Phillips (Bracewell - U.S. Delegate), Eric Barker (M.I.5. Man), Roddy McMillan (Benter), Tom Aldredge (Wendover), Michael Trubshawe (British Aide), Peter Sallis (Russian Delegate), Clive Dunn (Bandleader), Hugh Lloyd (Plumber), Graham Stark (Standard Bearer), Mario Fabrizi (Mario), Jan Conrad (Russian Aide), John Bluthal (Von Neidel), Richard Marner (Russian Air Force General), Allan Cuthbertson (Member of Whitehall Conference), Robin Bailey (Member of Whitehall Conference), George Chisholm (Wine Waiter), Frank Duncan (News Announcer), Ed Bishop (US Astronaut), Frankie Howerd (Himself). In a satire on the Space Race and Cold War, the Duchy of Grand Fenwick, tricks both the US and Russia into providing aid for its plumbing needs under the guise of building a rocket. Sequel to *The Mouse That Roared* (1959). Based on the Leonard Wibberley novel. *Dir.* Richard Lester.

Mouse That Roared, The (1959) Peter Sellers (Grand Duchess Gloriana XII/Prime Minister Count Rupert of Mountjoy/Tully Bascombe), Jean Seberg (Helen Kokintz), William Hartnell (Will Buckley), David Kossoff (Dr Alfred Kokintz), Leo McKern (Benter), MacDonald Parke (Gen Snippet), Austin Willis (US Secretary of Defense), Timothy Bateson (Roger), Monte Landis (Cobbley), Colin Gordon (BBC Announcer), Harold Kasket (Pedro). The little Duchy of Grand Fenwick decides to declare war on the US and lose, thus qualifying for state aid. However, by a series of mischances the little army arrives in New York and manages to capture a scientist who has invented an "ultimate" weapon. Based on the Leonard Wibberley novel. *Dir.* Jack Arnold.

Mr. Bean's Holiday (2007) Rowan Atkinson (Mr. Bean), Max Baldry (Stepan Dachevsky), Karel Roden (Emil Dachevsky), Willem Dafoe (Carson Clay), Emma de Caunes (Sabine), Steve Pemberton (Vicar), Lily Atkinson (Lily at the stereo), Preston Nyman (Boy with train), Sharlit Deyzac (Buffet attendant), Francois Touch (Busker), Arsène Mosca (Traffic controller), Stéphane Debac (Traffic controller), Philippe Spall (French journalist), Antoine de Caunes (TV presenter). Mr Bean wins a holiday to Cannes in a raffle. Misadventure abounds at every turn. *Dir.* Steve Bendelack.

Mr. Topaze (1961) Peter Sellers (Auguste Topaze), Nadia Gray (Suzy), Herbert Lom (Castel Benac), Leo McKern (Muche), Martita Hunt (Baroness), Michael Gough (Tamise), Anne Leon (Mrs. Tamise), Billie Whitelaw (Ernestine), Joan Sims (Colette), John Neville (Roger), John Le Mesurier (Blackmailer), Michael Sellers (Gaston), Pauline Shepherd (Lilette), Thomas Gallagher

(Policeman). An honest man is fired from his schoolteaching job for not giving a poor student a pass mark in order to favour a Baroness' wishes. He is then hired by a crook as a front for his business and begins to turn into an avaricious schemer. *Dir.* Peter Sellers.

Mrs Henderson Presents (2005) Judi Dench (Laura Henderson), Bob Hoskins (Vivian Van Damm), Will Young (Bertie), Christopher Guest (Lord Cromer), Kelly Reilly (Maureen), Thelma Barlow (Lady Conway), Anna Brewster (Doris), Rosalind Halstead (Frances), Sarah Solemani (Vera), Natalia Tena (Peggy), Thomas Allen (Eric Woodburn), Richard Syms (Ambrose), Ralph Nossek (Leslie Pearkes), Camille O'Sullivan (Jane), Doraly Rosen (Maggie), Matthew Hart (Frank Lawson), Tony De La Fou (Victor Thornton), Dorian Ford (Christian), Lloyd Hutchinson (Harry), Toby Jones (Gordon), Christopher Logan (Ken), Michael Culkin (Lord Cromer's Secretary), Samuel Barnett (Paul), Richard Dormer (Comic), Joseph Long (Harry), Patti Love (Natalie Van Damm). In 1931, wealthy and eccentric widow Laura Henderson purchases the Palais de Luxe building and turns it into the Windmill Theatre. She hires Vivian Van Damm and they produce the "Revudeville", a programme of continuous variety which after initial success begins to lose money. Then an example from the Continent, which causes consternation in the Lord Chamberlain's office (the then theatrical censors), might prove to be the theatre's life line. Based on the true story of the Windmill Theatre. *Dir.* Stephen Frears.

Mrs. Brown (1997) Judi Dench (Queen Victoria), Billy Connolly (John Brown), Geoffrey Palmer (Henry Ponsonby), Antony Sher (Benjamin Disraeli), Gerard Butler (Archie Brown), David Westhead (Bertie/Prince of Wales), Bridget McConnell (Lady Ely), Georgie Glen (Lady Churchill), Catherine O'Donnell (Lady in waiting), Sara Stewart (Princess Alexandra), Finty Williams (Princess Helena), Claire Nicolson (Princess Louise), Hattie Ladbury (Princess Alice), Oliver Kent (Prince Alfred), Alex Menzies (Prince Arthur), Simon McKerrell (Prince Leopold), Jason Morell (Lord Stanley), Cherith Mellor (Mary Anne Disraeli), George Hall (Speaker of the House of Commons), Oliver Ford Davies (Dean of Windsor), James Vaughan (Sir Charles Dilke). The film tells of the relationship which developed between Queen Victoria and her Scottish servant John Brown in the years following the death of her husband Prince Albert. *Dir.* John Madden.

Much Ado About Nothing (1993) Emma Thompson (Beatrice), Kenneth Branagh (Benedick), Denzel Washington (Don Pedro), Keanu Reeves (Don John), Kate Beckinsale (Hero), Richard Briers (Leonato), Imelda Staunton (Margaret), Brian Blessed (Antonio), Andy Hockley (George Seacole), Chris Barnes (Francis Seacole), Conrad Nelson (Hugh Oatcake), Phyllida Law (Ursula), Alex Lowe (Messenger), Richard Clifford (Conrade), Gerard Horan (Borachio), Jimmy Yuill (Friar Francis), Robert Sean Leonard (Claudio), Patrick Doyle (Balthazar), Alex Scott (The Boy), Michael Keaton (Dogberry), Ben Elton (Verges), Edward Jewesbury (Sexton). An adaptation of the Shakespearean play. *Dir.* Kenneth Branagh.

Much Too Shy (1942) George Formby (George Andy), Kathleen Harrison (Amelia Peabody), Hilda Bayley (Lady Driscoll), Eileen Bennett (Jackie Somers), Joss Ambler (Sir George Driscoll), Jimmy Clitheroe (Jimmy), Frederick Burtwell (Mr. Harefield), Brefni O'Rorke (Mr. Somers), Eric Clavering (Robert Latimer), Gibb McLaughlin (Rev. Sheepshanks), Peter Gawthorne (Counsel), Valentine Dyall (Defence Counsel), Charles Hawtrey (Student of Modern Art), Wally Patch (Police Constable), Jack Vyvian (Commissionaire at Art School). Amateur artist George gets into bother when some portraits of local ladies are sold to an advertising company with nude bodies attached. *Dir.* Marcel Varnel.

Mudlark, The (1950) Irene Dunne (Queen Victoria), Alec Guinness (Benjamin Disraeli), Andrew Ray (Wheeler - the Mudlark), Beatrice Campbell (Lady Emily Prior), Finlay Currie (John Brown), Anthony Steel (Lt Charles McHatten), Ronan O'Casey (Slattery), Raymond Lovell (Sgt Footman Naseby), Marjorie Fielding (Lady Margaret Prior), Constance Smith (Kate Noonan), Edward Rigby (The Watchman), Ernest Clark (Hammond), Howard Douglas (Broom), Paul Garrard (Petey), Marjorie Gresley (Meg Bowles), Bob Head (Dandy Fritch),

Wilfrid Hyde-White (Tucker), Leonard Morris (Hooker Morgan), Barry Jones (Speaker), Alan Judd (Sentry), Vi Kaley (Mrs Feeney), Eric Messiter (Police Lt Ash), Richard Nairne (Didbit), Kynaston Reeves (Gen Sir Ponsonby). A young mudlark – someone who scavenges on the banks of the Thames – finds a locket containing the likeness of Queen Victoria. He decides to travel to Windsor to see her and in the process prompts a national debate. Based on the novel by Theodore Bonnet. *Dir.* Jean Negulesco.

Mummy, The (1959) Peter Cushing (John Banning), (Christopher Lee (Kharis, the Mummy), Yvonne Furneaux (Isobel Banning/Princess Ananka), Eddie Byrne (Insp Mulrooney), Felix Aylmer (Stephen Banning), Raymond Huntley (Joseph Whemple), George Pastell (Mehemet Bey), Michael Ripper (Poacher), George Woodbridge (PC), Harold Goodwin (Pat), Denis Shaw (Mike), Gerald Lawson (Irish Customer), Willoughby Gray (Dr Reilly), John Stuart (Coroner), David Browning (Police Sgt), Frank Sieman (Bill), Stanley Meadows (James), Frank Singuineau (Head Porter). An Egyptologist accidently brings back to life Kharis, the mummified high priest of Karnak who was sentenced to be entombed alive to serve as the guardian of Princess Ananka's tomb. Mehemet Bey brings the mummy to England to wreak vengeance on the men who opened the Princess's tomb. *Dir.* Terence Fisher.

Mumsy, Nanny, Sonny and Girly (1970) Ursula Howells (Mumsy), Pat Heywood (Nanny), Howard Trevor (Sonny), Vanessa Howard (Girly), Michael Bryant (New Friend), Robert Swann (Soldier), Imogen Hassall (Girlfriend), Michael Ripper (Zoo attendant), Hugh Armstrong (Friend in No 5). The title characters live in a secluded manor house and play "The Game", which usually ends in the murder of the person they play it with. Then they invite a "new friend" to join them! *Dir.* Freddie Francis.

Murder Ahoy! (1964) Margaret Rutherford (Miss Marple), Lionel Jeffries (Capt Sydney De Courcy Rhumstone), Charles 'Bud' Tingwell (Chief Insp Craddock), William Mervyn (Comm. Breeze-Connington), Joan Benham (Matron Alice Fanbraid), Stringer Davis (Mr Jim Stringer), Nicholas Parsons (Dr Crump), Miles Malleson (Bishop), Henry Oscar (Lord Rudkin), Derek Nimmo (Sub-Lt Eric Humbert), Gerald Cross (Brewer), Norma Foster (Asst Matron Shirley Boston), Terence Edmond (Sgt Bacon), Francis Matthews (Lt Compton), Lucy Griffiths (Millie), Bernard Adams (Dusty Miller), Tony Quinn (Kelly, a Tramp), Edna Petrie (Miss Pringle), Roy Holder (Petty Officer). Miss Marple, Mr Stringer and Chief Inspector Craddock investigate a murder surrounding the trust which runs HMS Battledore, a ship used to train wayward youths. *Dir.* George Pollock.

Murder at the Gallop (1963) Margaret Rutherford (Miss Marple), Stringer Davis (Mr. Stringer), Robert Morley (Hector Enderby), Flora Robson (Miss Milchrest), Bud Tingwell (Insp Craddock), Gordon Harris (Sergeant Bacon), Robert Urquhart (George Crossfield), Katya Douglas (Rosamund Shane), James Villiers (Michael Shane), Noel Howlett (Mr. Trundell), Finlay Currie (Old Enderby), Duncan Lamont (Hillman), Kevin Stoney (Doctor Markwell), Frank Atkinson (Hotel Night Porter), Roger Avon (Police Photographer). Miss Marple, Mr Stringer and Inspector Craddock investigate the death of a man apparently scared to death. Based on the novels *After the Funeral* and *At Bertram's Hotel* by Agatha Christie. *Dir.* George Pollock.

Murder by Decree (1979) Christopher Plummer (Sherlock Holmes), James Mason (Dr. John Watson), David Hemmings (Inspector Foxborough), Susan Clark (Mary Kelly), Frank Finlay (Inspector Lestrade), Anthony Quayle (Sir Charles Warren), Donald Sutherland (Robert Lees), Geneviève Bujold (Annie Crook), John Gielgud (Prime Minister Lord Salisbury), Chris Wiggins (Doctor Hardy), Tedde Moore (Mrs. Lees), Peter Jonfield (William Slade), Roy Lansford (Sir Thomas Spivey), Catherine Kessler (Carrie), Ron Pember (Makins), June Brown (Anne Chapman), Terry Duggan (Danny), Hilary Sesta (Catherine Eddowes), Anthony May (Lanier), Betty Woolfe (Mrs. Dobson), Iris Fry (Elizabeth Stride), Geoffrey Russell (Home Secretary Henry Matthews), Michael Cashman (Constable Watkins). Holmes and Watson are on the trail of Jack the Ripper. *Dir.* Bob Clark.

Murder Most Foul (1964) Margaret Rutherford (Jane Marple), Ron Moody (H. Driffold Cosgood), Charles 'Bud' Tingwell (Insp Craddock), Andrew Cruickshank (Justice Crosby), Megs Jenkins (Mrs Gladys Thomas), Dennis Price (Harris Tumbrill), Ralph Michael (Ralph Summers), James Bolam (Bill Hanson), Stringer Davis (Jim Stringer), Francesca Annis (Sheila Upward), Alison Seebohm (Eva McGonigall), Terry Scott (PC Wells), Pauline Jameson (Maureen Summers), Maurice Good (George Rowton), Annette Kerr (Dorothy), Windsor Davies (Sgt Brick), Neil Stacy (Arthur), Stella Tanner (Mrs Florrie Harris). Miss Marple, Mr Stringer and Inspector Craddock investigate murders amongst a theatre troupe. Loosely based on the novel *Mrs McGinty's Dead* by Agatha Christie. *Dir*. George Pollock.

Murder on the Orient Express (1974) Albert Finney (Hercule Poirot), Lauren Bacall (Mrs Harriet Hubbard), Sean Connery (Col Arbuthnott), Ingrid Bergman (Greta Ohlsson), Michael York (Count Rudolf Andrenyi), Vanessa Redgrave (Mary Debenham), Jacqueline Bisset (Countess Elena Andrenyi), Richard Widmark (Mr Ratchett), John Gielgud (Edward Beddoes), Anthony Perkins (Hector McQueen), Martin Balsam (Bianchi), Rachel Roberts (Hildegarde Schmidt), Wendy Hiller (Princess Dragomiroff), Denis Quilley (Antonio Foscarelli), Colin Blakely (Cyrus B. "Dick" Hardman), Jean-Pierre Cassel (Pierre Michel), George Coulouris (Dr Constantine). Hercule Poirot is asked to investigate the murder of an American business tycoon, Mr. Ratchett, aboard the Orient Express train. Everyone is a suspect. Based on the novel by Agatha Christie. *Dir*. Sidney Lumet.

Murder Will Out (1939) John Loder (Dr. Paul Raymond), Jane Baxter (Pamela Raymond), Jack Hawkins (Stamp), Hartley Power (Campbell), Peter Croft (Nigel), Frederick Burtwell (Morgan), William Hartnell (Dick), Ian McLean (Inspector). A piece of jade brings trouble to everyone connected with it. *Dir*. Roy William Neill.

Murder! (1930) Herbert Marshall (Sir John Menier), Norah Baring (Diana Baring), Phyllis Konstam (Doucie Markham), Edward Chapman (Ted Markham), Miles Mander (Gordon Druce), Esme Percy (Handel Fane), Donald Calthrop (Ion Stewart), Esme V. Chaplin (Prosecuting Counsel), Amy Brandon Thomas (Defending Counsel), Joynson Powell (Judge), S.J. Warmington (Bennett), Marie Wright (Miss Mitcham), Hannah Jones (Mrs Didsome), Una O'Connor (Mrs Grogram), R.E. Jeffrey (Foreman of the Jury). When Diana is convicted of murder and sentenced to be hanged, one of the jurors begins to have doubts and investigates further. Hitchcock's cameo is as a passer-by on the street. Based on *Enter Sir John* by Clemence Dane and Helen Simpson. *Dir*. Alfred Hitchcock.

Murder, She Said (1961) Margaret Rutherford (Miss Marple), Arthur Kennedy (Quimper), Muriel Pavlow (Emma), James Robertson Justice (Ackenthorpe), Thorley Walters (Cedric), Charles 'Bud' Tingwell (Craddock), Conrad Phillips (Harold), Ronald Howard (Eastley), Joan Hickson (Mrs Kidder), Stringer Davis (Stringer), Ronnie Raymond (Alexander), Gerald Cross (Albert), Michael Golden (Hillman), Barbara Leake (Mrs Stainton), Gordon Harris (Bacon), Peter Butterworth (Ticket Collector), Richard Briers (Mrs Binster), Lucy Griffiths (Lucy), Nadia Pavlova (Dr Quimper's Wife). Miss Marple, Mr Stringer and Inspector Craddock investigate the murder of a young woman on a train which was only witnessed by Miss Marple from another train. Based on the novel by Agatha Christie. *Dir*. George Pollock.

Murphy's War (1971) Peter O'Toole (Murphy), Siân Phillips (Dr. Hayden), Philippe Noiret (Louis Brezon), Horst Janson (Commander Lauchs), John Hallam (Lieutenant Ellis), Ingo Mogendorf (Lieutenant Voght). When the crew of his merchant ship is massacred by a German U-Boat, Murphy manages to survive. After reaching shore in Venezuela he vows vengeance. *Dir*. Peter Yates.

Music Lovers, The (1970) Richard Chamberlain (Tchaikovsky), Glenda Jackson (Antonina Miliukova), Izabella Telezynska (Nadezhda von Meck), Max Adrian (Nikolai Rubinstein), Christopher Gable (Count Anton Chiluvsky), Kenneth Colley (Modest Ilyich Tchaikovsky), Maureen Pryor (Nina's Mother), Sabina Maydelle (Sasha Tchaikovsky), Andrew Faulds (Davidov),

Bruce Robinson (Alexei Sofronov), Ben Aris (Young Lieutenant), Dennis Myers (Von Meck, twin), John Myers (Von Meck, twin), Joanne Brown (Olga Bredska), Alexei Jawdokimov (Dmitri Shubelov), Clive Cazes (Doctor), Georgina Parkinson (Odile in Swan Lake), Graham Armitage (Prince Balukin), Alan Dubreuil (Prince in Swan Lake), Consuela Chapman (Tchaikovsky's Mother), Alexander Russell (Von Meck child), James Russell (Bobyek), Xavier Russell (Koyola), Victoria Russell (Tatiana), Alex Brewer (Young Tchaikovsky). A biopic of Russian composer Pyotr Ilyich Tchaikovsky mainly told in flashback and dream sequences and paying particular attention to the composer's sexual leanings, latent or otherwise. *Dir*. Ken Russell.

Mutiny on the Buses (1972) Reg Varney (Stan Butler), Doris Hare (Mum), Michael Robbins (Arthur Rudge), Anna Karen (Olive Rudge), Stephen Lewis (Insp 'Blakey' Blake), Bob Grant (Jack Harper), Janet Mahoney (Susy), Pat Ashton (Norah), Bob Todd (New Inspector), Kevin Brennan (Mr Jenkins), David Lodge (Safari Guard), Tex Fuller (Harry), Caroline Dowdeswell (Sandra), Damaris Hayman (Mrs. Jenkins), Michael Nightingale (Airline pilot). The installation of a new radio control system in the buses causes a mutiny at the depot. Second big screen version of the ITV comedy. *Dir*. Harry Booth.

My Ain Folk (1973) Stephen Archibald (Jamie), Hughie Restorick (Tommy), Paul Kermack (Jamie's Father), Bernard McKenna (Tommy's Father), Jean Taylor Smith (Grandmother), Mr. Munro (Jamie's Grandad), Helena Gloag (Father's Mother), Jessie Combe (Father's Wife), William Carroll (Father's Son), Anne McLeod (Father's Girlfriend), Robert Hendry (Soldier), Miss Cameron (teacher), John Downie (Undertaker). When Jamie's maternal grandmother dies, he and his brother Tommy are separated. Whilst Tommy is sent to a care home, Jamie goes to live with his paternal grandmother and uncle. The second part of director Bill Douglas's semi-autobiographical trilogy (*My Childhood*, *My Ain Folk* and *My Way Home*).

My Beautiful Laundrette (1985) Daniel Day-Lewis (Johnny), Gordon Warnecke (Omar), Saeed Jaffrey (Nasser), Roshan Seth (Papa), Derrick Branche (Salim), Rita Wolf (Tania), Souad Faress (Cherry), Richard Graham (Genghis), Shirley Anne Field (Rachel), Stephen Marcus (Moose), Winston Graham (Jamaican One). Set in the Thatcherite 1980s and touching on economic realities, homosexuality and racism, Omar is offered a job by his entrepreneurial uncle Nasser and then persuades him to let him manage his rundown launderette. He then ropes in his old friend Johnny to help him run it. *Dir* Stephen Frears.

My Brother Jonathan (1948) Michael Denison (Jonathan), Dulcie Gray (Rachel Hammond), Ronald Howard (Harold), Stephen Murray (Dr. Craig), Mary Clare (Mrs. Dakers), Finlay Currie (Dr. Hammond), Beatrice Campbell (Edie Martyn), Arthur Young (Sir Joseph Higgins), James Robertson Justice (Eugene Dakers), James Hayter (Tom Morse), Pete Murray (Tony Dakers), Jessica Spencer (Connie), Stuart Lindsell (Mr. Martyn), Avice Landone (Mrs. Martyn), Beatrice Varley (Mrs. Hodgkiss), Felix Deebank (Alec Martyn), Eric Messiter (Surgeon Moore), John Salew (Wilburn), Kathleen Boutall (Mrs. Gaige), Wilfrid Hyde-White (Mr. Gaige), Eunice Gayson (Young Girl), Thora Hird (Ada), Hazel Adair (Mary), Ray Cooney (Ralph Hingston). Told in flashback, the story of the relationship between Jonathan Dakers and his brother Harold and the two women they fall in love with. *Dir*. Harold French.

My Brother's Keeper (1948) Jack Warner (George Martin), George Cole (Willie Stannard), Jane Hylton (Nora Lawrence), David Tomlinson (Ronnie Waring), Bill Owen (Syd Evans), Yvonne Owen (Meg Waring), Raymond Lovell (Bill Wainwright), Brenda Bruce (Winnie Foreman), Susan Shaw (Beryl), Beatrice Varley (Mrs. Jenny Martin), Garry Marsh (Brewster), Maurice Denham (Supt. Trent), Frederick Piper (Gordon), Wilfrid Hyde-White (Harding), John Boxer (Police Sgt Bert Foreman), Amy Veness (Mrs Gully), Arthur Hambling (Edward Hodges), Valentine Dyall (Insp at Milton Wells), George Merritt (PC at Milton Wells), Jack Raine (Chief Constable Col. Heatherly), Reginald Beckwith (1st Barber), Cyril Chamberlain (Archer), Arthur Mullard (Policeman). Martin escapes whilst being transported to prison but is handcuffed to young Willie. He takes Willie on a trek to the West of England where he knows he can get aid from his mistress but the police are hot on the trail. In the course of the journey Martin manages to kill a man in a tussle just before he breaks the handcuffs and leaves Willie to fend for himself. *Dir.* Alfred Roome.

My Childhood (1972) Stephen Archibald (Jamie), Hughie Restorick (Tommy), Jean Taylor Smith (Grandmother), Karl Fieseler (Helmuth), Bernard McKenna (Tommy's Father), Paul Kermack (Jamie's Father), Helena Gloag (Father's Mother), Ann Smith (Jamie's Mother). Cinema is the only escape for an eight-year-old living in a Scottish mining village. The first part of Bill Douglas's semi-autobiographical trilogy (*My Childhood*, *My Ain Folk* and *My Way Home*). *Dir.* Bill Douglas.

My Learned Friend (1943) Will Hay (William Fitch), Claude Hulbert (Claude Babbington), Mervyn Johns (Grimshaw), Laurence Hanray (Sir Norman), Aubrey Mallalieu (Magistrate), Charles Victor ('Safety' Wilson), Derna Hazell (Gloria), Leslie Harcourt (Barman), Eddie Phillips ('Basher' Blake), G.H. Mulcaster (Dr Scudamore), Ernest Thesiger (Ferris), Lloyd Pearson (Colonel Chudleigh), Gibb McLaughlin (Butler), Maudie Edwards (Ethel 'Aladdin' Redfern), Ronald Shiner (Man in Wilson's Bar). A black comedy in which a murderer is working his way through a list of those who have "done him wrong", which includes incompetent solicitor William Fitch. The film ends with a set piece of William dangling from the hands of the clock face on the Clock Tower of the Palace of Westminster (Big Ben) a scenario also used in later films. This was Will Hay's last film. *Dirs.* Basil Dearden and Will Hay.

My Left Foot (1989) Daniel Day-Lewis (Christy Brown), Brenda Fricker (Bridget Brown), Ray McAnally (Paddy Brown), Alison Whelan (Sheila Brown), Kirsten Sheridan (Sharon Brown), Declan Croghan (Tom Brown), Eanna MacLiam (Benny Brown), Marie Conmee (Sadie Brown), Fiona Shaw (Dr. Eileen Cole), Cyril Cusack (Lord Castlewelland), Phelim Drew (Brian), Ruth McCabe (Mary Carr), Hugh O'Conor (young Christy Brown). The biopic of Christy Brown, an Irish author, painter and poet who had cerebral palsy which left him only able to write or type with the toes of his left foot. The story is told through flashbacks, and shows how he overcomes his disabilities through his own determination and the help of his mother. The film won two Academy Awards: Best Actor in a Leading Role (Daniel Day-Lewis) and Best Actress in a Supporting Role (Brenda Fricker). *Dir* Jim Sheridan.

My Little Eye (2002) Sean Cw Johnson (Matt), Kris Lemche (Rex), Stephen O'Reilly (Danny), Laura Regan (Emma), Jennifer Sky (Charlie), Bradley Cooper (Travis Patterson), Nick Mennell (The Cop). Five participants in a reality show are nearing the end of their stay in the house when an outsider arrives and death ensues. *Dir.* Marc Evans.

My Name is Joe (1998) Peter Mullan (Joe), Louise Goodall (Sarah Downie), David McKay (Liam), Anne-Marie Kennedy (Sabine), David Hayman (McGowan), Gary Lewis (Shanks), Lorraine McIntosh (Maggie), Scott Hannah (Scott), David Peacock (Hooligan), Gordon McMurray (Scrag). Ex-alcoholic Joe Kavanagh begins a relationship with health visitor Sarah but his friendship with Liam is a problem! *Dir* Ken Loach.

My Summer of Love (2004) Natalie Press (Mona), Emily Blunt (Tamsin), Paddy Considine (Phil), Dean Andrews (Ricky), Michelle Byrne (Ricky's wife), Paul-Anthony Barber (Tamsin's father), Lynette Edwards (Tamsin's mother), Kathryn Sumner (Sadie). Explores the relationship which develops one summer between two girls from very different backgrounds. Based on the Helen Cross novel. *Dir.* Paweł Pawlikowski.

My Way Home (1978) Stephen Archibald (Jamie), Paul Kermack (Jamie's father), Jessie Combe (Father's wife), William Carrol (Archie), Morag McNee (Father's girl friend), Lennox Milne (Grandmother), Gerald James (Mr Bridge), Joseph Blatchley (Robert), Radir (Egyptian boy). Jamie leaves the care home but fails to settle anywhere for long. He ends up in Egypt on his National Service in the RAF, where he meets Robert. The final part of director Bill Douglas's semi-autobiographical trilogy (*My Childhood*, *My Ain Folk* and *My Way Home*).

My Week With Marilyn (2011) Michelle Williams (Marilyn Monroe), Kenneth Branagh (Sir Laurence Olivier), Eddie Redmayne (Colin Clark), Judi Dench (Dame Sybil Thorndike), Emma Watson (Lucy), Zoë Wanamaker (Paula Strasberg), Dougray Scott (Arthur Miller), Dominic Cooper (Milton H. Greene), Julia Ormond (Vivien Leigh), Derek Jacobi (Sir Owen Morshead), Richard Clifford (Richard Wattis), Philip Jackson (Roger Smith), Simon Russell Beale (Admiral Cotes-Preedy). Marilyn Monroe, accompanied by her new husband Arthur Miller, is in London to shoot the film *The Prince and the Showgirl*. When Miller returns to America, Colin Clark becomes her escort for a week. Based on books by Colin Clark. *Dir.* Simon Curtis.

Mysterious Island (1961) Michael Craig (Capt. Cyrus Harding), Joan Greenwood (Lady Mary Fairchild), Michael Callan (Herbert Brown), Gary Merrill (Gideon Spilitt), Herbert Lom (Captain Nemo), Beth Rogan (Elena Fairchild), Percy Herbert (Sgt. Pencroft), Dan Jackson (Cpl. Neb Nugent). During the American Civil War some Union POWs use a gas balloon to escape from prison but end up being blown to a Pacific island inhabited by monstrously sized animals. Loosely based on the novel *The Mysterious Island* (*L'Île Mystérieuse*) by Jules Verne. *Dir.* Cy Endfield.

Mystery of the Marie Celeste, The (1935) Béla Lugosi (Anton Lorenzen), Shirley Grey (Sarah Briggs), Arthur Margetson (Capt Benjamin Briggs), Edmund Willard (Toby Bilson), Dennis Hoey (Tom Goodschard), George Mozart (Tommy Duggan), Johnnie Schofield (Peter Tooley), Gunner Moir (Ponta Katz), Ben Welden ('Sailor' Hoffman), Clifford McLaglen (Capt Jim Morehead), Tom Bastable (Olly Deveau), Matt Ramage (Andy Gilling), Terence De Marney (Charlie Kaye), Edgar Pierce (Arian Harbens), Herbert Cameron (Volkerk Grot), Wilfred Essex (Horatio Sprague), James Carew (James Winchester), Monti DeLyle (Portunato), Alec Fraser (Comdr Mahon). An attempt to explain the story behind the Mary Celeste, which was found adrift in the Atlantic in 1872 without crew. An early Hammer production. *Dir.* Denison Clift.

Naked (1993) David Thewlis (Johnny), Lesley Sharp (Louise Clancy), Katrin Cartlidge (Sophie), Greg Cruttwell (Jeremy Smart), Claire Skinner (Sandra), Peter Wight (Brian), Ewen Bremner (Archie), Gina McKee (The Cafe Girl). Embittered, aggressive and possibly mentally ill Johnny flees Manchester after raping a woman and moves in with an old girlfriend in London. He then spends much of his time wandering the city and telling anyone and everyone what he thinks. *Dir.* Mike Leigh.

Naked Edge, The (1961) Gary Cooper (George Radcliffe), Deborah Kerr (Martha Radcliffe), Eric Portman (Jeremy Gray), Diane Cilento (Mrs Heath), Hermione Gingold (Lilly Harris), Peter Cushing (Mr. Evan Wrack), Michael Wilding (Morris Brooke), Ronald Howard (Mr Claridge), Ray McAnally (Donald Heath), Sandor Elès (Manfridi St John), Wilfrid Lawson (Mr Pom), Helen Cherry (Miss Osborne), Joyce Carey (Victoria Hicks), Diane Clare (Betty), Frederick Leister (Judge). After George Radcliffe's testimony puts Donald Heath in prison for murder and robbery, he invests a large amount of money. His wife begins to wonder where the money came from. Gary Cooper's last film. *Dir.* Michael Anderson.

Naked Truth, The (1957) Terry-Thomas (Lord Henry Mayley), Peter Sellers (Sonny MacGregor), Peggy Mount (Flora Ransom), Shirley Eaton (Melissa Right), Dennis Price (Nigel Dennis), Georgina Cookson (Lady Lucy Mayley), Joan Sims (Ethel Ransom), Miles Malleson (Rev. Cedric Bastable), Kenneth Griffith (Porter), Moultrie Kelsall (Mactavish), Bill Edwards (Bill Murphy), Wally Patch (Fred), Henry Hewitt (Gunsmith), John Stuart (Police Inspector), David Lodge (Constable Johnson), Joan Hurley (Authoress), Peter Noble (T.V. Announcer), Victor Rietti (Doctor), Michael Ripper (J.E. Freeman). The victims of a blackmailer who produces the scandal sheet *The Naked Truth* gang up on him. *Dir.* Mario Zampi.

Nanny McPhee (2005) Emma Thompson (Nanny McPhee), Colin Firth (Cedric), Thomas Sangster (Simon Brown), Eliza Bennett (Tora Brown), Jennifer Rae Daykin (Lily Brown), Raphaël Coleman (Eric Brown), Samuel Honywood (Sebastian Brown), Holly Gibbs (Christianna Brown), Hebe and Zinnia Barnes (Agatha (Aggie) Brown), Kelly Macdonald (Evangeline), Angela Lansbury (Great Aunt Adelaide), Celia Imrie (Mrs. Selma Quickly), Imelda Staunton (Mrs. Blatherwick), Derek Jacobi (Mr. Wheen), Patrick Barlow (Mr. Jowls), Elizabeth Berrington

(Letitia), Adam Godley (Vicar), Claire Downes (Nanny Whetstone), Phyllida Law (Mrs. Partridge – voice). Widowed undertaker Cedric Brown has seven children who manage to drive off all the nannies he hires. The arrival of the mysterious Nanny McPhee eventually puts a stop to their antics. However, Great Aunt Agatha wishes Cedric to remarry for financial reasons and the awful Selma Quickly is in the frame. Can the children and nanny prevent this matrimonial disaster? Adapted from Christianna Brand's *Nurse Matilda* books. *Dir*. Kirk Jones.

Nanny McPhee and the Big Bang (2010) Emma Thompson (Nanny McPhee), Rhys Ifans (Phil Green), Maggie Gyllenhaal (Isabel Green), Asa Butterfield (Norman Green), Lil Woods (Megsie Green), Oscar Steer (Vincent Green), Ewan McGregor (Mr Rory Green), Eros Vlahos (Cyril Gray), Rosie Taylor-Ritson (Celia Gray), Ralph Fiennes (Lord Gray), Maggie Smith (Mrs Agatha "Aggie" Docherty), Sam Kelly (Mr Docherty), Sinead Matthews (Miss Topsey), Katy Brand (Miss Turvey), Bill Bailey (Farmer MacReadie), Nonso Anozie (Sgt Ralph Jeffreys), Daniel Mays (Blenkinsop), Ed Stoppard (Lt Addis), Toby Sedgwick (Enemy plane pilot). With her husband away fighting in WWI, Isabel is struggling to cope with the farm, a job and her three children. When the two Gray children are sent to the farm the situation worsens. Then one dark night Nanny McPhee arrives on the doorstep. *Dir*. Susanna White.

Nanny, The (1965) Bette Davis (Nanny), William Dix (Joey Fane), Wendy Craig (Virginia "Virgie" Fane), Jill Bennett (Aunt Pen), James Villiers (Bill Fane), Pamela Franklin (Bobby Medman), Jack Watling (Dr. Medman), Maurice Denham (Dr. Beamaster), Alfred Burke (Dr. Wills), Angharad Aubrey (Susy Fane). When young Joey Fane returns from boarding school he has attended since the death of his younger sister he seems to be illogically scared of the family Nanny. Based on the novel of the same name by Evelyn Piper. *Dir*. Seth Holt.

National Health, The (1973) Lynn Redgrave (Nurse Sweet/Nurse Betty Martin), Colin Blakely (Edward Loach), Eleanor Bron (Sister McFee/Sister Mary MacArthur), Donald Sinden (Mr. Carr/Senior Surgeon Boyd), Jim Dale (Barnet/Dr. Neil Boyd), Sheila Scott-Wilkenson (Nurse Powell/Cleo Norton), Neville Aurelius (Leyland/Monk), Gillian Barge (Dr. Bird), George Browne (The Chaplain), Patience Collier (The Lady Visitor), Jumoke Debayo (Nurse Lake), Robert Gillespie (Tyler), John Hamill (Kenny), Don Hawkins (Les), James Hazeldine (Student Doctor), Bob Hoskins (Foster), David Hutcheson (Mackie), Mervyn Johns (Rees), Bert Palmer (Flegg), Maureen Pryor (The Matron), Richie Stewart (Mortuary Attendant), Clive Swift (Ash), Graham Weston (Michael). Daily life in an underfunded NHS hospital is interwoven and contrasted with that of a "soap opera" hospital where everything seems wonderful. Based on the play by Peter Nichols. *Dir*. Jack Gold.

Navigators, The (2001) Dean Andrews (John), Thomas Craig (Mick), Joe Duttine (Paul), Steve Huison (Jim), Venn Tracey (Gerry), Andy Swallow (Len), Sean Glenn (Harpic), Charlie Brown (Jack), Juliet Bates (Fiona), John Aston (Bill Walters), Graham Heptinstall (Owen), Angela Saville (Tracy), Clare McSwain (Lisa), Megan Topham (Chloe), Abigail Pearson (Eve), Charlotte Hukin (Rose), Jamie Widowson (Michael), Nigel Harrison (Will Hemmings), Charles Armstrong (John Wilson). The effect the 1995 privatisation of British Rail has on five Sheffield railway workers. *Dir*. Ken Loach.

Nearly a Nasty Accident (1961)
Jimmy Edwards (Group Capt Kingsley), Kenneth Connor (AC 2 Alexander Wood), Shirley Eaton (Cpl Jean Briggs), Eric Barker (Air Minister), Jon Pertwee (General Birkinshaw), Ronnie Stevens (Flight Lt Pocock), Richard Wattis (Wagstaffe), Joyce Carey (Lady Trowborough), Peter Jones (Flight Lt Winters), Terry Scott (Sam Stokes), Charlotte Mitchell (Miss Chamberlain), Jack Watling (Flight Lt Grogan), Joe Baker (Watkins), Jack Douglas (Balmer). An RAF engineer can't help messing around with anything and everything mechanical, including, of course, the aircraft. *Dir*. Don Chaffey.

Nell Gwyn (1934) Anna Neagle (Nell Gwyn), Cedric Hardwicke (Charles II), Jeanne De Casalis (Duchess of Portsmouth), Muriel George (Meg), Helena Pickard (Mrs. Pepys), Dorothy Robinson (Mrs. Knipp), Esme Percy (Samuel Pepys), Miles Malleson (Chiffinch), Moore Marriott (Robin), Craighall Sherry (Ben), Lawrence Anderson (Duke Of York). Historical drama based around the romance between Charles II and the actress Nell Gwyn. *Dir*. Herbert Wilcox.

Neon Bible, The (1995) Jacob Tierney (David, aged 15), Drake Bell (David, aged 10), Gena Rowlands (Mae Morgan), Diana Scarwid (Sarah), Denis Leary (Frank), Bob Hannah (George), Aaron Frisch (Bruce), Leo Burmester (Bobbie Lee Taylor), Ian Shearer (Billy Sunday Thompson), Joan Glover (Flora), Tom Turbiville (Clyde), Peter McRobbie (Reverend Watkins), Dana Seltzer (Jo Lynne), Virgil Graham Hopkins (Mr. Williams), Duncan Stewart (Head Boy), Frances Conroy (Miss Scover). David is growing up in Georgia in the 1940s when his abusive father enlists in the army during World War II leaving him in the care of his mother and aunt. Based on the novel by John Kennedy Toole. *Dir*. Terence Davies.

Net, The (1953) Phyllis Calvert (Lydia Heathley), James Donald (Prof. Michael Heathley), Robert Beatty (Maj. Sam Seagram), Herbert Lom (Dr. Alex Leon), Muriel Pavlow (Caroline Cartier), Noel Willman (Dr. Dennis Bord), Walter Fitzgerald (Sir Charles Craddock), Patric Doonan (Brian Jackson), Maurice Denham (Prof. Carrington), Marjorie Fielding (Mother Heathley), Caven Watson (Dr. Ferguson), Herbert Lomas (George Jackson), Hal Osmond (Agent Lawson), Geoffrey Denton (Fisher), Cyril Chamberlain (Insp. Carter), Marianne Stone (Maisie), Tucker McGuire (Myrna). A spy in a group of scientists working on the prototype of a revolutionary new super-speed aircraft, known as the M7, murders one of them. Based on the novel by John Pudney. *Dir*. Anthony Asquith.

Neutral Port (1940) Will Fyffe (Capt Ferguson), Leslie Banks (George Carter), Yvonne Arnaud (Rosa Pirenti), Phyllis Calvert (Helen Carter), Hugh McDermott (Jim Grey), John Salew (Wilson), Cameron Hall (Charlie Baxter), Frederick Valk (Capt Traumer), Anthony Holles (Chief of Police), Sigurd Lohde (German Consul), Wally Patch (Fred), Dennis Wyndham (Terry), Jack Raine (Alf), Albert Lieven (Capt Grosskraft), Mignon O'Doherty (Miss Fleming). A British merchant ship attacked by a German U-Boat during WWII takes shelter in a neutral port. *Dir*. Marcel Varnel.

Never Let Go (1960) Richard Todd (John Cummings), Peter Sellers (Lionel Meadows), Elizabeth Sellars (Anne Cummings), Adam Faith (Tommy Towers), Carol White (Jackie), Mervyn Johns (Alfie Barnes), Noel Willman (Inspector Thomas), David Lodge (Cliff), Peter Jones (Alec Berger), John Bailey (Mackinnon), Nigel Stock (Regan), John Le Mesurier (Pennington), John Dunbar (Station Sergeant), Charles Houston (Cyril Spink), Cyril Shaps (Cypriot), Marianne Stone (Madge), David Gregory (Freddie), León García (Nick), Alex Murray (Pete), Larry Martin (Len), Jan Holden (Mrs. Hurst), Joe Wadham (Police Driver), Peter Pike (Martin Cummings), Roberta Tovey (Sandra Cummings), Gerald Paris (Plain Clothes Man). Peter Sellers, in a straight role, plays a London villain involved in a major car theft operation. One of his victims doggedly investigates him in an attempt to expose him and recover his own car. *Dir*. John Guillermin.

Never Say Never Again (1983) Sean Connery (James Bond), Kim Basinger (Domino Petachi), Klaus Maria Brandauer (Maximillian Largo), Barbara Carrera (Fatima Blush), Bernie Casey (Felix Leiter), Max von Sydow (Ernst Stavro Blofeld), Edward Fox (M), Rowan Atkinson (Nigel Small-Fawcett), Gavan O'Herlihy (Jack Petachi), Alec McCowen (Q), Pamela Salem (Miss Moneypenny), Saskia Cohen Tanugi (Nicole), Prunella Gee (Patricia Fearing), Valerie Leon (Lady in Bahamas), Milow Kirek (Kovacs), Pat Roach (Lippe), Anthony Sharp (Lord Ambrose). Largely a remake of *Thunderball*, the title referring to Connery saying in 1972 that he would "never again" play James Bond. Nuclear warheads are stolen and James has to track them down. Bond drives a black Bentley. The theme song is performed by Lani Hall. Based on the novel *Thurnderball* by Ian Fleming. *Dir*. Irvin Kershner

Never Take Sweets from a Stranger (1960) Patrick Allen (Peter Carter), Gwen Watford (Sally Carter), Janina Faye (Jean Carter), Felix Aylmer (Clarence Olderberry Sr.), Niall MacGinnis (Defense Counsel), Michael Gwynn (Prosecutor), Alison Leggatt (Martha), Bill Nagy (Clarence Olderberry Jr.), MacDonald Parke (Judge), Estelle Brody (Eunice Kalliduke), Robert Arden (Tom Demarest), Frances Green (Lucille), James Dyrenforth (Dr. Stevens), Robert Arden (Tom Demarest), Vera Cook (Mrs. Demarest), Budd Knapp (Hammond), Hazel Jennings (Mrs. Olderberry), Cal McCord (Charles Kalliduke), Gaylord Cavallaro (Neal Phillips), Sheila Robins (Miss Jackson), Larry O'Connor (Sam Kingsley), Helen Horton (Sylvia Kingsley), Shirley Butler (Mrs. Nash), Michael Hammond (Sammy Nash). A powerful and, for the time, hardnosed account of paedophilia and the wielding of localised power to pursue it. Young Jean Carter accuses the local landowner of making her dance naked for sweets. Her parents decide, against advice and warnings, to take him to court. *Dir.* Cyril Frankel.

New Lot, The (1943) Eric Ambler (Bren Gun Instructor), Ivor Barnard (Photographer), Robert Donat (Actor), Ian Fleming (Medical Officer), Philip Godfrey (Art Wallace), Kathleen Harrison (Keith's Mother), Bryan Herbert (Soldier), Raymond Huntley (Barrington), Mike Johnson (Railway Porter), Geoffrey Keen (Corporal), John Laurie (Harry Fyfe), Bernard Lee (Interviewing Officer), Albert Lieven (Czech Soldier), Bernard Miles (Ted Loman), Stewart Rome (Officer), Johnnie Schofield (Homeguard Sgt), John Slater (Soldier in Truck), Austin Trevor (Soldier Talking to Corporal), Peter Ustinov (Keith). A dramatised army training film showing the development of new recruits. It was later expanded for a commercial audience as *The Way Ahead* (1944). *Dir.* Carol Reed.

Next of Kin, The (1942) Mervyn Johns (No 23: Mr Davis), John Chandos (No 16), Nova Pilbeam (Beppie Leemans), Reginald Tate (Maj. Richards), Stephen Murray (Mr Barratt), Geoffrey Hibbert (Pvt. John), Philip Friend (Lt. Cummins), Phyllis Stanley (Miss Clare), Mary Clare (Mrs. Webster), Basil Sydney (Naval captain), Joss Ambler (Mr Vemon), Brefni O'Rorke (Brigadier), Alexander Field (Pvt. Durnford), David Hutcheson (Intelligence officer), Jack Hawkins (Major), Frederick Leister (Colonel), Torin Thatcher (German general), Charles Victor (Joe), Richard Norris (Pvt. Jimmy), Guy Maas (Frenchman), Thora Hird (ATS driver with puncture), Basil Radford (Careless talker on train), Naunton Wayne (Careless talker on train), J. Edgar Hoover (Narrator - prologue and epilogue), Johnnie Schofield (Lance Corporal), Frank Allenby (Wing Cmdr. Keaton). A WWII "training" film which was expanded for commercial release which, designed to show that "careless talk costs lives". A German spy network is shown piecing together information from various sources, including overheard conversations, and almost foiling an Allied raid. *Dir.* Thorold Dickinson.

Nicholas and Alexandra (1971) Michael Jayston (Tzar Nicholas II), Janet Suzman (Empress Alexandra), Roderic Noble (Tsarevich Alexei), Ania Marson (Grand Duchess Olga), Lynne Frederick (Grand Duchess Tatiana), Candace Glendenning (Grand Duchess Maria), Fiona Fullerton (Grand Duchess Anastasia), Laurence Olivier (Count Witte), Harry Andrews (Grand Duke Nicholas), Irene Worth (Dowager Empress Maria Feodorovna), Tom Baker (Grigori Rasputin), Jack Hawkins (Count Fredericks), Timothy West (Dr. Botkin), Jean-Claude Drouot (Mr. Gilliard), John Hallam (Nagorny), Guy Rolfe (Dr. Fedorov), John Wood (Colonel Kobylinsky), Eric Porter (Pyotr Stolypin), Michael Redgrave (Sergei Sazanov), Maurice Denham (Vladimir Kokovtsov), Ralph Truman (Rodzianko), Gordon Gostelow (Guchkov), John McEnery (Alexander Kerensky), Michael Bryant (Lenin), Brian Cox (Trotsky), James Hazeldine (Stalin), Steven Berkoff (Pankratov), Ian Holm (Commissar Yakovlev), Alan Webb (Yurovsky), Roy Dotrice (General Alexeiev), Richard Warwick (Grand Duke Dmitri Pavlovich), Curd Jürgens (German Consul), Alexander Knox (US Ambassador), Julian Glover (Georgy Gapon). Biopic of the last Russian royal family during the final years of the Russian Empire. Adapted from the book by Robert K. Massie. *Dir.* Franklin J. Schaffner.

Night and the City (1950) Richard Widmark (Harry Fabian), Gene Tierney (Mary Bristol), Googie Withers (Helen Nosseross), Hugh Marlowe (Adam Dunn), Francis L. Sullivan (Philip Nosseross), Herbert Lom (Kristo), Stanislaus Zbyszko (Gregorius), Mike Mazurki (The Strangler), Charles Farrell (Mickey Beer), Ada Reeve (Molly the Flower Lady), Ken Richmond (Nikolas of Athens), Peter Butterworth (Thug), Edward Chapman (Hoskins), James Hayter (Figler), Kay Kendall (One of Helen's Girls). Hustler Harry Fabian believes he has finally come up with a money-making scheme that can't fail. It involves crime boss Kristo and his father Gregorius. Based on the novel by Gerald Kersh. *Dir.* Jules Dassin.

Night Beat (1947) Anne Crawford (Julie Kendall), Maxwell Reed (Felix Fenton), Ronald Howard (Andy Kendall), Christine Norden (Jackie), Hector Ross (Don Brady), Fed Groves (PC Kendall), Sid James (Nixon), Nicholas Stuart (Rocky), Frederick Leister (Magistrate), Michael Medwin (Rocky), Cecil Bevan (Clerk of Court), Robert Cawdron (Police Recruit), Cyril Chamberlain (PC Rix). Two demobbed soldiers join the police force but one soon leaves and becomes involved in criminal activity. *Dir.* Harold Huth.

Night Boat to Dublin (1946) Robert Newton (Capt. David Grant), Raymond Lovell (Paul Faber), Guy Middleton (Capt. Tony Hunter), Muriel Pavlow (Marion Decker), Herbert Lom (Keitel), John Ruddock (Bowman), Martin Miller (Prof. Hansen), Brenda Bruce (Lily Leggett), Gerald Case (Inspector Emerson), Scott Forbes (Lieutenant Allen), Leslie Dwyer (George Leggett), Valentine Dyall (Sir George Bell), Derek Elphinstone (Naval Surgeon), Bruce Gordon (Hood), Marius Goring (Frederick Jannings), George Hirste (Station Official), Hubert Leslie (Ticket Collector), Olga Lindo (Mrs. Coleman), Stuart Lindsell (Inspector Martin), Gordon McLeod (Insp Longhurst), Joan Maude (Sidney Vane), Lawrence O'Madden (Capt Robert Wilson), Hay Petrie (Station Master), Wilfrid Hyde-White (Taxi Driver), Carroll Gibbons and Edmundo Ros (themselves). A missing Swedish scientist may be unwittingly passing secrets to the Germans via Ireland and British secret service agents are sent to Dublin in an attempt to forestall the Nazi plans. *Dir.* Lawrence Huntington.

Night Caller, The (1965) John Saxon (Dr Jack Costain), Maurice Denham (Dr Morley), Patricia Haines (Ann Barlow), Alfred Burke (Det Supt Hartley), Warren Mitchell (Reg Lilburn), Stanley Meadows (Det Tom Grant), Aubrey Morris (Thorburn), Ballard Berkeley (Cmdr Savage), Marianne Stone (Madge Lilburn), Geoffrey Lumsden (Col Davy), Barbara Stevens (Joyce Malone), Tony Wager (Pte Higgins), David Gregory (Pte Jones), Romo Gorrara (Lt), Robert Crewdson (Medra), John Carson (Major), Jack Watson (Sgt Hawkins). Aliens land in England looking for women to breed with. *Dir.* John Gilling.

Night Has Eyes, The (1942) James Mason (Stephen Deremid), Wilfrid Lawson (Jim Sturrock), Mary Clare (Mrs. Ranger), Joyce Howard (Marian Ives), Tucker McGuire (Doris), John Fernald (Dr. Barry Randall), Dorothy Black (Miss Fenwick), Amy Dalby (Miss Miggs), Jack Vyvian (Local Policeman). When teachers Marian and Doris holiday on the Yorkshire Moors a year after their friend Evelyn disappeared there they take refuge from a storm in a house occupied by shell-shocked pianist and composer Stephen Deremid. *Dir.* Leslie Arliss.

Night Invader, The (1943) Anne Crawford (Karen Lindley), David Farrar (Dick Marlow), Carl Jaffe (Count von Biebrich), Sybille Binder (Baroness von Klaveren), Marius Goring (Oberleutenant), Jenny Lovelace (Liesje von Klaveren). During WWII a British agent parachutes into the occupied Netherlands in an attempt to retrieve some important papers. *Dir.* Herbert Mason.

Night My Number Came Up, The (1955) Michael Redgrave (Air Marshal Hardie), Sheila Sim (Mary Campbell), Alexander Knox (Owen Robertson), Denholm Elliott (Fl. Lt. McKenzie), Ursula Jeans (Mrs Robertson), Ralph Truman (Lord Wainwright), Michael Hordern (Commander Lindsay), Nigel Stock (Pilot), Bill Kerr (Soldier), Alfie Bass (Soldier), George Rose (Bennett), Victor Maddern (Engineer), David Orr (The Co-pilot), David Yates (The Navigator), Doreen Aris (Miss Robertson), Richard Davies (Wireless Operator), Charles Perry (Kent), Geoffrey Tyrrell (Bennett's Secretary), Hugh Moxey (The Wing Commander), Nicholas Stuart (The Commandant), John Fabian (Traffic Controller), Percy Herbert (R.E.M.E. Sergeant), Robert Bruce (RAF Sergeant), Philip Vickers (American Radio Operator), Stratford Johns (Sergeant). At a dinner party a pilot relates a dream in which a plane with one of the fellow guests on board crashes. The other guest, an Air Vice Marshall thinks nothing of it until the next day when the events related in the dream begin to unfold in reality. Based on a real incident which happened to Sir Victor Goddard. *Dir*. Leslie Norman

Night of the Big Heat (1967) Christopher Lee (Godfrey Hanson), Patrick Allen (Jeff Callum), Peter Cushing (Dr. Vernon Stone), Jane Merrow (Angela Roberts), Sarah Lawson (Frankie Callum), William Lucas (Ken Stanley), Kenneth Cope (Tinker Mason), Percy Herbert (Gerald Foster), Thomas Heathcote (Bob Hayward), Anna Turner (Stella Hayward), Jack Bligh (Ben Siddle), Sydney Bromley (Old Tramp). In November a heat wave hits the remote Scottish island of Fara. Mysterious scientist Godfrey Hanson arrives to investigate, with a theory that the heat is being generated by alien visitors. Based on a novel by John Lymington. *Dir*. Terence Fisher.

Night of the Demon (1957) Dana Andrews (Dr John Holden), Peggy Cummins (Joanna Harrington), Niall MacGinnis (Dr Julian Karswell), Maurice Denham (Prof Henry Harrington), Athene Seyler (Mrs Karswell), Liam Redmond (Prof Mark O'Brien), Reginald Beckwith (Mr Meek), Ewan Roberts (Lloyd Williamson), Peter Elliott (Prof K.T. Kumar), Rosamund Greenwood (Mrs Meek), Brian Wilde (Rand Hobart), Richard Leech (Insp Mottrarn), Lloyd Lamble (Det Simmons), Peter Hobbes (Supt), Charles Lloyd Pack (Chemist), John Salew (Librarian), Janet Barrow (Mrs Hobart), Ballard Berkeley (1st Reporter). After a colleague Professor Harrington dies in mysterious circumstances, sceptical Dr Holden arrives in England and visits Karswell, the leader of a satanic cult which Harrington had warned him about. The remainder of the plot centres on the unwanted possession of a cursed parchment. Adapted from the M. R. James short story *Casting the Runes*. A cut version was released in the US as *Curse of the Demon*. *Dir*. Jacques Tourneur.

Night of the Eagle (1962) Peter Wyngarde (Norman Taylor), Janet Blair (Tansy Taylor), Margaret Johnston (Flora Carr), Anthony Nicholls (Harvey Sawtelle), Colin Gordon (Lindsay Carr), Kathleen Byron (Evelyn Sawtelle), Reginald Beckwith (Harold Gunnison), Jessica Dunning (Hilda Gunnison), Norman Bird (Doctor), Judith Stott (Margaret Abbott), Bill Mitchell (Fred Jennings). The wife of a psychology professor reveals she is a witch but insists that she is helping him with his career and protecting him from a rival. Also known as the rather less prosaic title *Burn, Witch, Burn!*. Based upon the Fritz Leiber novel *Conjure Wife*. *Dir*. Sidney Hayers.

Night to Remember, A (1958) Kenneth More (Second Officer Charles Herbert Lightoller), Ronald Allen (Mr. Clarke), Robert Ayres (Maj. Arthur Peuchen), Honor Blackman (Mrs. Liz Lucas), Anthony Bushell (Capt. Arthur Rostron – Carpathia), John Cairney (Mr. Murphy), Jill Dixon (Mrs. Clarke), Jane Downs (Mrs. Sylvia Lightoller), James Dyrenforth (Col. Archibald Gracie), Michael Goodliffe (Thomas Andrews), Kenneth Griffith (Wireless Operator John 'Jack' Phillips), Harriette Johns (Lady Richard), Frank Lawton (Chairman J. Bruce Ismay), Richard Leech (First Officer William Murdoch), David McCallum (Assistant Wireless Operator Harold Bride), Alec McCowen (Wireless Operator Harold Thomas Cottam – Carpathia), Tucker McGuire (Mrs. Margaret 'Molly' Brown), John Merivale (Robbie Lucas), Ralph Michael (Mr. Yates), Laurence Naismith (Capt. Edward John Smith), Russell Napier (Capt. Stanley Lord – Californian), Redmond Phillips (Mr. Hoyle), George Rose (Chief Baker Charles Joughin), Joseph Tomelty (Dr. William O'Loughlin), Patrick Waddington (Sir Richard), Jack Watling (Fourth Officer Joseph Boxhall), Geoffrey Bayldon (Wireless Operator Cyril Evans – Californian), Michael Bryant (Sixth Officer James Moody), Cyril Chamberlain (Quartermaster George Thomas Rowe), Bee Duffell (Mrs. Farrell), Harold Goldblatt (Benjamin Guggenheim), Gerald Harper (3rd Officer – Carpathia), Richard Hayward (Victualling Officer), Thomas Heathcote (Steward), Danuta Karell (Polish Mother), Andrew Keir (Chief Engineer Joseph Bell – Titanic), Christina Lubicz (Polish Girl), Barry MacGregor (Apprentice James Gibson - Californian), Edward Malin (Dining Saloon Steward), Patrick McAlinney (Mr. James Farrell), Helen Misener (Mrs. Ida Straus),

Mary Monahan (Kate), Howard Pays (Fifth Officer Harold Lowe), Philip Ray (Reverend Anderson), Harold Siddons (Second Officer Herbert Stone – Californian), Julian Somers (Mr. Bull - Man on Train), Tim Turner (Third Officer Charles Groves – Californian), Meier Tzelniker (Mr. Isador Straus), Jean Anderson (Stuffy Lady in Lifeboat), Roger Avon (Lookout Reginald Lee), Charles Belchier (Wallace Hartley - Orchestra Leader), Joan Benham (Lottie), Olwen Brookes (Miss Evans), Donald Churchill (Passenger), Sean Connery (Titanic Deck Hand), Glyn Houston (Stoker), Stratford Johns (Crewman on Upturned Lifeboat), Desmond Llewelyn (Seaman at Steerage Gate), Derren Nesbitt (Stoker Holding Oar on Upturned Lifeboat), Hal Osmond (Steward), Norman Rossington (James Kieran), Marianne Stone (Stewardess). A straightforward and very well told recounting of the final hours of RMS *Titanic* without any romanticised sub-plots to distract from the already dramatic enough story-telling. The film also benefits from a massive cast featuring some British acting stalwarts. Adapted from Walter Lord's book of the same name. *Dir*. Roy Ward Baker.

Night Train to Munich (1940) Margaret Lockwood (Anna Bomasch), Rex Harrison (Gus Bennett), Paul Henreid (Karl Marsen), Basil Radford (Charters), Naunton Wayne (Caldicott), James Harcourt (Axel Bomasch), Felix Aylmer (Dr Fredericks), Wyndham Goldie (Dryton), Roland Culver (Roberts), Eliot Makeham (Schwab), Raymond Huntley (Kampenfeldt), Austin Trevor (Capt Prada), Kenneth Kent (Controller), C.V. France (Adm Hassinger), Frederick Valk (Gestapo Officer), Morland Graham (Teleferic Attendant), Ian Fleming (Official at Home Office, MI5), Irene Handl (Station Master), Wally Patch (Fisherman), Billy Russell (Adolf Hitler). A Czech scientist who has developed a new form of armour plating escapes to England as the Germans march into Czechoslovakia. His daughter is arrested but later escapes with the aid of an undercover Nazi agent who hopes she will lead him to her father. The film also features the "comedy" Englishmen Charters and Caldicott, who first appeared in *The Lady Vanishes* (1938). *Dir*. Carol Reed.

Night Watch (1973) Elizabeth Taylor (Ellen Wheeler), Laurence Harvey (John Wheeler), Billie Whitelaw (Sarah Cooke), Robert Lang (Appleby), Tony Britton (Tony), Bill Dean (Walker), Michael Danvers-Walker (Sgt Norris), Rosario Serrano (Dolores), Pauline Jameson (Secretary), Linda Hayden (Girl in car), Kevin Colson (Carl), Laon Maybanke (Florist). A woman claims to have seen a murder from her window but there is no proof that a crime has taken place. *Dir*. Brian G Hutton.

Night We Dropped a Clanger, The (1959) Brian Rix (Aircraftman Arthur Atwood/Wing Cmdr. Blenkinsop), Cecil Parker (Air Vice-Marshal Sir Bertram Bukpasser), William Hartnell (Sgt. Bright), Leslie Phillips (Squadron Leader Thomas), Leo Franklyn (B.R. Belling), John Welsh (Squadron Leader Grant), Toby Perkins (Flight Lt. Spendal), Liz Fraser (Lulu), Vera Pearce (Madame Grilby), Sarah Branch (WAAF Hawkins), Charles Cameron (Gen. Gimble), Julian D'Albie (Air Marshal Carruthers), Arthur Brough (Adm. Bewdly), Ray Cooney (Corporal), Hattie Jacques (Ada), John Langham (Ricky), Roland Bartrop (Smythe), Denis Shaw (Hammerstein), Patrick Cargill (Fritz), Keith Banks (Cpl. Parker), Arnold Bell (Wing Cmdr. Jones), David Williams (Wing Cmdr. Priestly), Andrew Sachs (A.C.2 Briggs), Peter Allenby (Albert), Irene Handl (Mrs. Billingsgate). A comedy set during WWII where the double of a British agent is sent to Egypt to replace him whilst the real agent tries to deal with the V1 and V2 menace. *Dir*. Darcy Conyers.

Nil By Mouth (1997) Ray Winstone (Ray), Kathy Burke (Valerie), Charlie Creed-Miles (Billy), Laila Morse (Janet), Edna Doré (Kath), Chrissie Cotterill (Paula), Jon Morrison (Angus), Jamie Foreman (Mark), Steve Sweeney (Danny), Terry Rowley (M.C. in Club). It's grim down South. Ray rules the roost and kicks his brother-in-law Billy out of the house because of his drug addiction. The film is loosely based upon director Gary Oldman's own life growing up in South East London.

Nine Men (1943) Jack Lambert (Sgt Jack Watson), Gordon Jackson (Young 'un), Frederick Piper ('Badger' Hill), Grant Sutherland (Jock Scott), Bill Blewitt (Bill Parker), Eric

Micklewood ('Bookie' Lee), John Varley ('Dusty' Johnstone), Jack Horsman (Joe Harvey), Richard Wilkinson (Lieutenant Crawford), Giulio Finzi (Italian mechanic), Fred Griffiths (Base sergeant). During the North African campaign of WWII, a small British force of nine men finds itself stranded in the Libyan desert and has to fight off an attack by a much larger force of Italians. *Dir.* Harry Watt.

Nineteen Eighty-Four (1956) Edmond O'Brien (Winston Smith), Michael Redgrave (General O'Connor), Jan Sterling (Julia), David Kossoff (Mr Charrington), Mervyn Johns (Jones), Donald Pleasence (R. Parsons), Carol Wolveridge (Selina Parsons), Ernest Clark (Outer Party Announcer), Patrick Allen (Inner Party Official), Ronan O'Casey (Rutherford), Michael Ripper (Outer Party Orator), Ewen Solon (Outer Party Orator), Kenneth Griffith (Prisoner). In a dystopian future where everyone is watched by Big Brother, Winston Smith begins an affair with Julia. Based on the novel of the same name by George Orwell. *Dir.* Michael Anderson

Nineteen Eighty-Four (1984) John Hurt (Winston Smith), Richard Burton (O'Brien), Suzanna Hamilton (Julia), Cyril Cusack (Mr. Charrington), Gregor Fisher (Parsons), James Walker (Syme), Andrew Wilde (Tillotson), Corina Seddon (Mrs. Smith), Rupert Baderman (Young Winston Smith), Bob Flag (Big Brother), John Boswall (Emmanuel Goldstein), Phyllis Logan (The Telescreen Announcer - voice), David Trevena (Tillotson's Friend), David Cann (Martin), Anthony Benson (Jones), Peter Frye (Rutherford), Roger Lloyd-Pack (Waiter), Rupert Baderman (Winston Smith as a Boy), Corinna Seddon (Winston's Mother), Martha Parsey (Winston's Sister), Merelina Kendall (Mrs. Parsons), P.J. Nicholas (William Parsons), Lynne Gould (Susan Parsons), Pip Donaghy (Inner Party Speaker), Shirley Stelfox (Whore). See 1956 film for plot. Richard Burton's final film role. *Dir.* Michael Radford.

No Highway in the Sky (1951) James Stewart (Theodore Honey), Marlene Dietrich (Monica Teasdale), Glynis Johns (Marjorie Corder), Jack Hawkins (Dennis Scott), Janette Scott (Elspeth Honey), Elizabeth Allan (Shirley Scott), Ronald Squire (Sir John, Director), Jill Clifford (Peggy, Stewardess), Felix Aylmer (Sir Philip), Dora Bryan (Rosie, Barmaid), Maurice Denham (Maj Pearl), Wilfrid Hyde-White (Fisher, Inspector of Accidents), Niall MacGinnis (Capt Samuelson, Pilot), Kenneth More (Dobson, Co-Pilot), Pete Murray (Peter, the Radio Operator), Philip Ray (Burroughs), Roy Russell (Sir John's Butler), John Salew (Symes, Gander Inspector). Theodore Honey theorises that "Reindeer" aircraft will fail due to metal fatigue after 1440 hours flying and is sent to Labrador to investigate a recent crash. Unfortunately he finds himself flying to Labrador on another "Reindeer" which is close to its time limit and decides to inform both crew and passengers of the possibility of a crash. Based on the novel *No Highway* by Nevil Shute. *Dir.* Henry Koster.

No Limit (1935) George Formby (George Shuttleworth), Florence Desmond (Florrie Dibney), Edward Rigby (Grandfather Shuttleworth), Florence Gleason (Mrs Shuttleworth), Beatrix Fielden-Kaye (Mrs Horrocks), Howard Douglas (Turner), Jack Hobbs (Bert Tyldesley), Alf Goddard (Norton), Peter Gawthorne (Mr Higgins), Eva Lister (Rita), Evelyn Roberts (BBC Commentator), Ernest Sefton (Mr Hardacre), Arthur Young (Doctor). George builds his own motorbike and races in the Isle of Man TT. *Dir.* Monty Banks.

No Love for Johnnie (1961) Peter Finch (Johnnie Byrne), Stanley Holloway (Fred Andrews), Mary Peach (Pauline), Donald Pleasence (Roger Renfrew), Billie Whitelaw (Mary), Hugh Burden (Tim Maxwell), Rosalie Crutchley (Alice), Michael Goodliffe (Dr West), Mervyn Johns (Charlie Young), Geoffrey Keen (Prime Minister), Paul Rogers (Sydney Johnson), Dennis Price (Flagg), Peter Barkworth (Henderson), Fenella Fielding (Sheila), Derek Francis (Frank), Peter Sallis (MP). A British MP finds that he must eventually make a choice between being content with his career or being happy in his love life. Based on Wilfred Fienburgh's book. *Dir.* Ralph Thomas.

No Room at the Inn (1948) Freda Jackson (Mrs. Voray), Joy Shelton (Judith Drave), Hermione Baddeley (Mrs. Waters), Joan Dowling (Norma Bates), Ann Stephens (Mary O'Rane), Harcourt Williams (Reverend Allworth), Niall MacGinnis (O'Rane),

Sydney Tafler (Spiv), Frank Pettingell (Burrells), Betty Blackler (Lily), Jill Gibbs (Irene), Robin Netscher (Ronnie), Wylie Watson (Councilor Green), James Hayter (Councilor Trouncer), Eliot Makeham (News Editor), Dora Bryan (Spiv's Girlfriend), Pamela Deacon (Shirley Greenwood), Veronica Haley (Schoolgirl Friend), Billy Howard (Councillor Parkin), Vi Kaley (Pub Customer), Harry Locke (Tobacconist), Joyce Martyn (Schoolgirl Friend), Cyril Smith (Store Detective), Beatrice Varley (Mrs. Jarvis). Uncompromising film which highlights child abuse and neglect and the rather dismissive attitude to it at this time. During WWII orphan Mary is billeted on the outwardly good natured Mrs Voray who in fact treats all the children under her care with violence, cruelty and neglect. When Mary's teacher begins to have concerns, she goes to the council and the church but is rebuffed, with tragic consequences. Based on a play by Joan Temple and a screenplay written in part by poet Dylan Thomas. *Dir.* Daniel Birt.

No Sex Please, We're British (1973) Ronnie Corbett (Brian Runnicles), Ian Ogilvy (David Hunter), Susan Penhaligon (Penny Hunter), Beryl Reid (Bertha Hunter), Arthur Lowe (Mr Bromley), Michael Bates (Mr Needham), Cheryl Hall (Daphne), David Swift (Insp Paul), Deryck Guyler (Park keeper), Valerie Leon (Susan), Margaret Nolan (Barbara), Gerald Sim (Rev Mower), John Bindon (Pete), Stephen Greif (Niko), Michael Robbins (Car driver), Frank Thornton (Glass Shop Manager), Sydney Bromley (Rag & Bone Man), Michael Ripper (Traffic warden), Lloyd Lamble and Mavis Villiers (Americans), Brian Wilde (PC in park), Eric Longworth (Man with Lighter), Edward Sinclair (Postman), Robin Askwith (Baker's delivery man). Farce involving a bank clerk trying to dispose of pornography which has been sent to him by mistake. Based on Alistair Foot and Anthony Marriott's play. *Dir.* Cliff Owen.

No Surrender (1985) Michael Angelis (Mike), Avis Bunnage (Martha Gorman), James Ellis (Paddy Burke), Tom Georgeson (Mr. Ross), Bernard Hill (Bernard), Ray McAnally (Billy McCracken), Joanne Whalley (Cheryl), Mark Mulholland (Norman), J.G. Devlin (George Gorman), Vince Earl (Frank), Ken Jones (Ronny), Michael Ripper (Tony Bonaparte), Marjorie Sudell (Barbara), Joan Turner (Superwoman), Elvis Costello (Rosco de Ville). Set in Liverpool. A newly appointed ballroom manager discovers that his predecessor has hired it out on New Year's Eve to various different groups including hardline Irish Catholic Nationalists and hardline Protestant Unionists. *Dir.* Peter Smith.

No Trees in the Street (1959) Sylvia Syms (Hetty), Herbert Lom (Wilkie), Melvyn Hayes (Tommy), Ronald Howard (Frank), Stanley Holloway (Kipper), Joan Miller (Jess), Liam Redmond (Bill), Victor Brooks (Bookie's Clerk), Yvonne Buckingham (Girl), Fred Griffiths (Street Orator), David Hemmings (Kenny), Lily Kann (Mrs. Jacobson), Lloyd Lamble (Superintendent), Carole Lesley (Lova), Lana Morris (Marje), Edwin Richfield (Jackie), Richard Shaw (Reg), Campbell Singer (Inspector), Marianne Stone (Mrs. Jokel), Rita Webb (Mrs. Brown). Mainly in flashback, a young hoodlum is told a cautionary tale by a policeman. *Dir.* J. Lee Thompson.

Noose (1948) Carole Landis (Linda Medbury), Joseph Calleia (Sugiani), Derek Farr (Capt Jumbo Hyde), Stanley Holloway (Insp Kendall), Nigel Patrick (Bar Gorman), Ruth Nixon (Annie Foss), Carol van Derman (Mercia Lane), John Slater (Pudd'n Bason), Leslie Bradley (Basher), Reginald Tate (Editor), Edward Rigby (Slush), John Salew (Greasy Anderson), Robert Adair (Sgt Brooks), Hay Petrie (Barber), Uriel Porter (Coaly), Ella Retford (Nelly), Brenda Hogan (Maffy), Michael Golden (Moggie), Michael Ripper (Nelson). A US investigative journalist is out to put an end to the activities of black-market racketeer Sugiani. *Dir.* Edmond T. Gréville.

North West Frontier (1959) Kenneth More (Captain Scott), Lauren Bacall (Catherine Wyatt), Herbert Lom (Van Leyden), Wilfrid Hyde-White (Bridie), I.S. Johar (Gupta), Ursula Jeans (Lady Windham), Eugene Deckers (Peters), Ian Hunter (Sir John Windham), Jack Gwillim (Brigadier Ames), Govind Raja Ross (Prince Kishan), Basil Hoskins (A.D.C.), S.M. Asgaralli (Havildar), S.S. Chowdhary (Indian Soldier), Moultrie Kelsall (British Correspondent), Lionel Murton (American Correspondent), Jaron Yaltan (Indian Correspondent), Homi Bode

(Indian Correspondent), Frank Olegario (Rajah), Ronald Cardew (Staff Colonel at Halapur Station), Allan Cuthbertson (Monocled Officer). Muslim rebels attack a fortress in order to kill a young Hindu maharajah. Captain Scott puts the child and his American governess aboard a train and break out of the besieged palace on a journey which takes them across the sub-continent. *Dir*. J. Lee Thompson.

Notes on a Scandal (2006) Judi Dench (Barbara Covett), Cate Blanchett (Bathsheba "Sheba" Hart), Bill Nighy (Richard Hart), Andrew Simpson (Steven Connolly), Tom Georgeson (Ted Mawson), Michael Maloney (Sandy Pabblem), Joanna Scanlan (Sue Hodge), Shaun Parkes (Bill Rumer), Emma Williams (Linda), Phil Davis (Brian Bangs), Juno Temple (Polly Hart), Max Lewis (Ben Hart), Anne-Marie Duff (Annabel). Teacher Sheba Hart, who is having an affair with a student at her school, is befriended by colleague Barbara Covett and a relationship develops in which the older Barbara becomes a dominant and manipulative partner. Adapted from the novel of the same name by Zoë Heller. *Dir*. Richard Eyre.

Notting Hill (1999) Julia Roberts (Anna Scott), Hugh Grant (William "Will" Thacker), Emma Chambers (Honey Thacker), Hugh Bonneville (Bernie), Rhys Ifans (Spike), Tim McInnerny (Max), Gina McKee (Bella), James Dreyfus (Martin), Richard McCabe (Tony), Dylan Moran (Rufus), Alec Baldwin (Jeff King), Julian Rhind-Tutt ('Time Out' Journalist), Mischa Barton (12-Year-Old Actress), Emma Bernard (Keziah), Emily Mortimer (Perfect Girl), Samuel West (Anna's Co-Star), Patrick Barlow (Savoy Concierge). A Hollywood star and a Notting Hill book shop owner fall for each other. *Dir*. Roger Michell.

Nowhere Boy (2009) Aaron Johnson (John), Alex Ambrose (Young John), Kristin Scott Thomas (Aunt Mimi), David Threlfall (Uncle George), Anne-Marie Duff (Julia Lennon), Angelica Jopling (Julia - aged 8), Josh Bolt (Pete Shotton), Ophelia Lovibond (Marie Kennedy), James Johnson (Stan), David Morrissey (Bobby), Andrew Buchan (Fishwick), James Jack Bentham (Rod), Jack McElhone (Eric), Thomas Brodie-Sangster (Paul McCartney), Sam Bell (George Harrison), Colin Tierney (Alf). A biopic about the adolescence of John Lennon in particular his relationships with his guardian aunt and his birth mother and his growing interest in music and the forming of the Quarrymen. Based on a biography written by Lennon's half-sister Julia Baird. *Dir*. Sam Taylor-Wood.

Nuns on the Run (1990) Eric Idle (Brian Hope/Sister Euphemia), Robbie Coltrane (Charlie McManus/Sister Inviolata), Janet Suzman (Sister Liz), Camille Coduri (Faith Thomas), Robert Patterson ("Case" Casey), Doris Hare (Sister Mary), Lila Kaye (Sister Mary), Robert Morgan (Abbott), Winston Dennis (Morley), Tom Hickey (Father Seamus), Colin Campbell (Norm), Richard Simpson (Mr Norris), Nicholas Hewetson (Louis), Gary Tang (Ronnie Chang), David Forman (Henry Ho), Nigel Fan (Dwayne Lee), Ozzie Yue (Ernie Wong), Tatiana Strauss (Michelle), Wabei Siyolwe (Julie), Helen FitzGerald (Tracey), Stewart Harwood (Faith's Father), Peter Geeves (Faith's Brother). Crooks Brian and Charlie have to disguise themselves as nuns in order to escape their boss, the Triads and the police. *Dir*. Jonathan Lynn.

Nurse on Wheels (1963) Juliet Mills (Joanna Jones), Ronald Lewis (Henry Edwards), Joan Sims (Deborah Walcott), Noel Purcell (Abel Worthy), Esma Cannon (Mrs. Jones), Raymond Huntley (Vicar), Athene Seyler (Miss Farthingale), Norman Rossington (George Judd), Ronald Howard (Dr. Harold Golfrey), Joan Hickson (Mrs. Wood), Renée Houston (Mrs. Beacon), Jim Dale (Tim Taylor), George Woodbridge (Mr. Beacon), David Horne (Dr. Golfrey Senior), Deryck Guyler (Driving Examiner), Barbara Everest (Nurse Merrick), Brian Rawlinson (Policeman). Exploits of Joanna, the new district nurse. Made by the Carry On crew. *Dir*. Gerald Thomas.

O Lucky Man! (1973)
Malcolm McDowell (Michael Arnold "Mick" Travis / Plantation thief), Ralph Richardson (Monty / Sir James Burgess), Rachel Roberts as Gloria Rowe / Madame Paillard / Mrs Richards), Arthur Lowe (Mr Duff / Charlie Johnson / Dr Munda), Helen

Mirren (Patricia / casting call receptionist), Graham Crowden (Dr Millar /Prof Stewart / Meth drinker), Peter Jeffrey (Factory chairman / Prison governor), Dandy Nichols (Tea lady), Mona Washbourne (Neighbour / Usher / Sister Hallett), Philip Stone (Jenkins / Interrogator / Salvation Army maj), Mary MacLeod (Mrs Ball / Salvationist / Vicar's Wife), Michael Bangerter (William / Interrogator / Assistant / Released prisoner), Wallas Eaton (John Stone / Col Steiger / Prison Warder / Meths Drinker / Film Exec), Warren Clarke (MC / Warner / Male nurse), Bill Owen (Supt Barlow / Inspector Carding), Michael Medwin (Army capt / Power station technician / Duke of Belminster), Vivian Pickles (Good lady), Geoffrey Palmer (Examination doc / Basil Keyes), Christine Noonan (assembly line worker / Mavis), Geoffrey Chater (Bishop / Vicar), Anthony Nicholls (Gen /Judge), Brian Glover (Plantation Foreman/Bassett), Edward Judd (Oswald), Alan Price (Himself). The film follows the journey of Mick Travis who starts out as a coffee salesman, then works for an evil industrialist and ends up in jail. The second film in which Malcolm McDowell played a character named Mick Travis. *Dir*. Lindsay Anderson.

Oblong Box, The (1969) Vincent Price (Julian Markham), Christopher Lee (Dr. Neuhartt), Alister Williamson (Sir Edward Markham), Rupert Davies (Kemp), Uta Levka (Heidi), Sally Geeson (Sally), Alister Williamson (Edward), Peter Arne (Trench), Hilary Heath (Elizabeth), Maxwell Shaw (Hackett), Carl Rigg (Norton), Harry Baird (N'Galo), Godfrey James (Weller), James Mellor (Holt), John Barrie (Franklin), Ivor Dean (Hawthorne), Danny Daniels (Witchdoctor), Michael Balfour (Ruddock), Hira Talfrey (Martha), John Wentworth (Parson), Betty Woolfe (Mrs. Hopkins), Martin Terry (Sailor), Anne Clune (Prostitute), Jackie Noble (Prostitute), Colin Jeavons (Doctor), Hedgar Wallace (Major). When an escape plan goes awry, hideously disfigured Sir Edward Markham, who has been locked in a tower by his brother Julian, is buried alive. However, once dug up by grave robbers and resurrected by Doctor Neuhartt, he goes on a killing spree. *Dir*. Gordon Hessler.

Obsession (1949) Robert Newton (Dr Clive Riordan), Phil Brown (Bill Kronin), Sally Gray (Storm Riordan), Naunton Wayne (Supt Finsbury), James Harcourt (Aitkin), Betty Cooper (Miss Stevens), Michael Balfour (US sailor), Ronald Adam (Clubman), Roddy Hughes (Clubman), Allan Jeayes (Clubman), Olga Lindo (Mrs Humphries), Russell Waters (Flying Squad Det), Lyonel Watts (Clubman), Sam Kydd (Club steward), Stanley Baker (Policeman), Monty the dog. Clive plots the perfect murder to dispose of his wife's lover Bill but the whole plan might go awry thanks to her dog. Based on *A Man About A Dog* by Alec Coppel. *Dir*. Edward Dymtryk.

Octopussy (1983) Roger Moore (James Bond), Maud Adams (Octopussy), Louis Jourdan (Kamal Khan), Kabir Bedi (Gobinda), Steven Berkoff (General Orlov), Kristina Wayborn (Magda), Vijay Amritraj (Vijay), David Meyer & Anthony Meyer (Mischka & Grischka), Desmond Llewelyn (Q), Robert Brown (M), Geoffrey Keen (Fredrick Gray), Walter Gotell (General Gogol), Douglas Wilmer (Jim Fanning), Lois Maxwell (Miss Moneypenny), Michaela Clavell (Penelope Smallbone). Whilst tracking the stealing of Russian treasures (including a Faberge egg), which leads him to Kamal Khan and Octopussy in India, Bond also uncovers a plot to detonate a nuclear warhead on mainland Europe. Indian tennis player Vijay Amritraj had a career high world ranking of 16 in 1980. Bond drives a Mercedes 250SE. The opening theme, *All Time High* is sung by Rita Coolidge. The film's title is taken from a short story in Ian Fleming's short story collection *Octopussy and The Living Daylights* although the plot is different. *Dir*. John Glen

Odd Man Out (1947) James Mason (Johnny McQueen), Kathleen Ryan (Kathleen Sullivan), Robert Newton (Lukey), Cyril Cusack (Pat), F.J. McCormick (Shell), William Hartnell (Fencie), Fay Compton (Rosie), Denis O'Dea (Inspector), W.G. Fay (Father Tom), Maureen Delaney (Theresa O'Brien), Elwyn Brook-Jones (Tober), Robert Beatty (Dennis), Dan O'Herlihy (Nolan), Kitty Kirwan (Grannie), Wilfrid Brambell (Tram Passenger), Dora Bryan (Girl in Phone Kiosk). Johnny, the head of an illegal Irish organisation is wounded during a bank robbery and the film follows his attempts to elude the police search. Based on a novel by F. L. Green. *Dir.* Carol Reed.

Odessa File, The (1974) Jon Voight (Peter Miller), Maximilian Schell (Eduard Roschmann), Maria Schell (Frau Miller), Mary Tamm (Sigi), Derek Jacobi (Klaus Wenzer), Peter Jeffrey (David Porath), Klaus Löwitsch (Gustav Mackensen), Kurt Meisel (Alfred Oster), Hannes Messemer (General Richard Glücks), Garfield Morgan (Israeli General), Shmuel Rodensky (Simon Wiesenthal), Ernst Schröder (Werner Deilman), Günter Strack (Kunik), Noel Willman (Franz Bayer), Martin Brandt (Marx). In November 1963 journalist Peter Miller reads the diary of a holocaust survivor who has recently committed suicide. It sets him on the trail of a concentration camp commander, Eduard Roschmann and an organisation known by the acronym ODESSA which assists former members of the SS to obtain new identities. An adaptation of Freddie Forsyth's novel. *Dir.* Ronald Neame.

Odette (1950) Anna Neagle (Odette Sansom/Marie/Lise), Trevor Howard (Captain Peter Churchill/Raoul), Marius Goring (Colonel Henri), Bernard Lee (Jack), Peter Ustinov (Lt. Alex Rabinovich/Arnauld), Maurice Buckmaster (Himself), Alfred Schieske (Camp Commandant), Gilles Quéant (Jacques), Marianne Walla (S.S. Wardress), Fritz Wendhausen (Colonel), Marie Burke (Mme. Gliere), Wolf Frees (Major), Liselotte Goettinger (German POW camp officer), Campbell Gray (Paul), John Hunter (American Officer), Catherine Paul (Mother Superior), Derrick Penley (Jules), Guyri Wagner (Interrogator). The true story of Odette Sansom, a French woman who volunteered to join SOE (Special Operations Executive) during WWII. She was flown into occupied France where she fought with the French resistance until she was captured. *Dir.* Herbert Wilcox.

Of Human Bondage (1964) Kim Novak (Mildred), Laurence Harvey (Philip), Robert Morley (Dr Jacobs), Siobhan McKenna (Nora Nesbitt), Roger Livesey (Thorpe Athelny), Jack Hedley (Griffiths), Nanette Newman (Sally Athelny), Ronald Lacey (Matty Mathews), David Morris (Young Phillip), Anthony Booth (Martin). The tortuous love story of club-footed medical student Philip Carey and flighty Mildred Rogers. Adaptation of W. Somerset Maugham's novel of the same name. *Dir.* Ken Hughes.

Of Time and the City (2008) Documentary film where director Terence Davies recalls his early life in Liverpool using archive footage, contemporary and classical music and his own voiceover.

Offence, The (1972) Sean Connery (Det Sgt Johnson), Trevor Howard (Lt Cartwright), Vivien Merchant (Maureen Johnson), Ian Bannen (Kenneth Baxter), Peter Bowles (Det Insp Cameron), Derek Newark (Frank Jessard), Ronald Radd (Lawson), John Hallam (Panton), Richard Moore (Garrett), Anthony Sagar (Hill), Maxine Gordon (Janie Edmonds). The film follows the search for a child rapist and the arrest of a suspect and his interrogation. It also examines the cumulative effect of such horrors on Johnson, which leads to him attacking the suspect. Based upon the play *This Story of Yours* by John Hopkins. *Dir.* Sidney Lumet.

Oh Mr Porter! (1937) Will Hay (William Porter), Moore Marriott (Jeremiah Harbottle), Graham Moffatt (Albert Brown), Percy Walsh (Superintendent), Dave O'Toole (Postman), Sebastian Smith (Mr Trimbletow), Agnes Laughlan (Mrs Trimbletow), Dennis Wyndham (Grogan/One-Eyed Joe), Frederick Piper (Ledbetter), Frederick Lloyd (Minister), Frank Atkinson (Irishman in bar). A classic Hay, Marriott and Moffatt comedy which is loosely based on Arnold Ridley's play *The Ghost Train*. William Porter is made stationmaster of the isolated Irish station of Buggleskelly, with a staff of Old Harbottle and Young Albert. *Dir.* Marcel Varnel.

Oh! What a Lovely War (1969) Wendy Allnutt (Flo Smith), Colin Farrell (Harry Smith), Malcolm McFee (Freddie Smith), John Rae (Grandpa Smith), Corin Redgrave (Bertie Smith), Maurice Roëves (George Smith), Paul Shelley (Jack Smith), Kim Smith (Dickie Smith), Angela Thorne (Betty Smith), Mary Wimbush (Mary Smith), Paul Daneman (Czar Nicholas II), Ian Holm (President Poincaré), David Lodge (Recruiting Sergeant), Joe Melia (The Photographer), Guy Middleton (Sir William Robertson), Juliet Mills (Nurse), Nanette Newman (Nurse), Cecil Parker (Sir John), Gerald Sim (Chaplain), Thorley Walters (Staff Officer), Anthony Ainley (Third Aide), Michael Bates (Drunk

Lance Cpl), Edward Fox (Aide), Peter Gilmore (Pte Burgess), Norman Shelley (Staff Officer), Marianne Stone (Mill Girl), Dirk Bogarde (Stephen), Phyllis Calvert (Lady Haig), John Gielgud (Count Leopold Berchtold), Jack Hawkins (Emperor Franz Josef I), Kenneth More (Kaiser Wilhelm II), Laurence Olivier (Field Marshal Sir John French), Michael Redgrave (Gen Sir Henry Wilson), Vanessa Redgrave (Sylvia Pankhurst), Ralph Richardson (Sir Edward Grey), Maggie Smith (Music Hall Star), Susannah York (Eleanor), John Mills (Field Marshal Sir Douglas Haig). Musical about WWI, focusing on the four sons of the Smith family (Harry, Freddie, George and Jack). Using a series of symbolic settings the film moves through important moments in the war such as the assassination of Archduke Franz Ferdinand and the Christmas truce before moving into a darker mood. The film is based on the stage musical *Oh, What a Lovely War* which originated as a radio play, *The Long Long Trail* which was itself inspired by *The Donkeys* by Alan Clark. *Dir.* Richard Attenborough.

Oh... Rosalinda!! (1955) Anton Walbrook (Dr. Falke), Dennis Price (Maj. Frank), Ludmilla Tchérina (Rosalinda), Michael Redgrave (Col. Eisenstein), Mel Ferrer (Capt. Alfred Westerman), Anthony Quayle (Gen. Orlovsky), Anneliese Rothenberger (Adele), Oskar Sima (Frosch), Richard Marner (Col. Lebotov), Nicholas Bruce (Hotel receptionist), Arthur Mullard (Russian guard), Sari Barabas (Rosalinda - singing voice), Alexander Young (Capt. Westerman - singing voice), Dennis Dowling (Maj. Frank - singing voice), Walter Berry (Dr. Falke - singing voice). Based on the operetta *Die Fledermaus* by Johann Strauss but updated to Allied Powers occupied Vienna in the immediate post-WWII period. *Dirs.* Michael Powell and Emeric Pressburger.

Old Bill and Son (1941) Morland Graham (Old Bill), John Mills (Young Bill), Mary Clare (Maggie), Renee Houston (Stella Malloy), René Ray (Sally), Gus McNaughton (Alf), Ronald Shiner (Bert), Manning Whiley (Chimp), Janine Darcey (Françoise), Roland Culver (Colonel), Donald Stuart (Canuck), Nicholas Phipps (BBC Reporter), Allan Jeayes (Willoughby), Ian Fleming (Club Member). During WWII, Old Bill Busby, a veteran of the Great War, joins up to fight Nazis alongside his son. *Dir.* Ian Dalrymple.

Old Bones of the River (1938) Will Hay (Prof. Benjamin Tibbetts), Moore Marriott (Jerry Harbottle), Graham Moffatt (Albert Brown), Robert Adams (Bosambo), Jack London (M'Bapi), Wyndham Goldie (Commissioner Sanders), Jack Livesey (Capt. Hamilton), Western Brothers (The Voice of Reproach), Napoleon Florent (Chief Tahiti). Professor Tibbetts is a representative of the Teaching and Welfare Institute for the Reform of Pagans and sees it as his mission to educate the natives of Africa. Along the way he bumps into Harbottle and Brown, saves a baby from being sacrificed and sets off a native uprising. *Dir.* Marcel Varnel.

Old Mother Riley (1937) Arthur Lucan (Mrs. Riley), Kitty McShane (Kitty Riley), Barbara Everest (Mrs. Briggs), Patrick Ludlow (Edwin Briggs), Hubert Leslie (Captain Lawson), Edith Sharpe (Matilda Lawson), Syd Crossley (Butler), Edgar Driver (Bill Jones), Dorothy Vernon (Aggie Sparks), Zoe Wynn (Kay Stewart), G.H. Mulcaster (Prosecution), Charles Carson (Defense). Old Mother Riley and her daughter Kitty dispute the terms of a will. There were many Old Mother Riley films including *Old Mother Riley MP* (1938), *Old Mother Riley in Paris* (1938), *Old Mother Riley Joins Up* (1939), *Old Mother Riley in Society* (1940), *Old Mother Riley in Business* (1940), *Old Mother Riley's Circus* (1941), *Old Mother Riley's Ghosts* (1941) and *Old Mother Riley Overseas* (1943). *Dir.* Oswald Mitchell.

Oliver Twist (1948) John Howard Davies (Oliver), Alec Guinness (Fagin), Robert Newton (Bill Sikes), Kay Walsh (Nancy), Francis L. Sullivan (Mr Bumble), Henry Stephenson (Mr Brownlow), Mary Clare (Mrs Corney), Anthony Newley (Artful Dodger), Josephine Stuart (Oliver's Mother), Ralph Truman (Monks), Kathleen Harrison (Mrs Sowerberry), Gibb McLaughlin (Mr Sowerberry), Maurice Denham (Chief of Police), Michael Ripper (Barney), Michael Dear (Noah Claypole), Diana Dors (Charlotte), Frederick Lloyd (Mr Grimwig), Hattie Jacques (Singer at 'Three Cripples'). Orphan Oliver Twist runs away from a workhouse and becomes embroiled in the seedy underworld of

Victorian London. Based on Charles Dickens' novel. *Dir*. David Lean.

Oliver! (1968) Mark Lester (Oliver Twist), Ron Moody (Fagin), Oliver Reed (Bill Sikes), Shani Wallis (Nancy), Harry Secombe (Mr Bumble), Jack Wild (Artful Dodger), Hugh Griffith (Magistrate), Joseph O'Conor (Mr Brownlow), Leonard Rossiter (Mr Sowerberry), Hylda Baker (Mrs Sowerberry), Peggy Mount (Mrs Bumble), Joseph O'Conor (Mr. Brownlow), Sheila White (Bet), Megs Jenkins (Mrs Bedwin), Peter Butterworth (Shopkeeper). Kenneth Cranham (Noah Claypole), James Hayter (Mr Jessop), Elizabeth Knight (Charlotte), Fred Emney (Workhouse Chairman), A film version of the stage musical by Lionel Bart, based on *Oliver Twist* by Charles Dickens. The film won five Academy Awards: Best Picture, Best Director, Best Music, Best Art Direction-Set Decoration and Best Sound. *Dir*. Carol Reed.

On Approval (1944) Clive Brook (George, 10th Duke of Bristol), Beatrice Lillie (Maria Wislack), Googie Withers (Helen Hale), Roland Culver (Richard Halton), O.B. Clarence (Dr. Graham), Laurence Hanray (Parkes), Elliott Mason (Mrs. McCosh), Hay Petrie (Landlord), Marjorie Rhodes (Cook), Mollie Munks (Jeannie), E V H Emmett (Narrator). Comedy in which a couple attempt a "trial marriage" but another couple derails the plans. One of Beatrice Lillie's few films in her long career. Based on the play of the same name by Frederick Lonsdale. *Dir*. Clive Brook.

On Her Majesty's Secret Service (1969) George Lazenby (James Bond), Diana Rigg (Countess Tracy di Vicenzo), Telly Savalas (Ernst Stavro Blofeld/Comte Balthazar de Bleuchamp), Gabriele Ferzetti (Marc-Ange Draco), Ilse Steppat (Irma Bunt), Bernard Lee (M), Lois Maxwell (Miss Moneypenny), George Baker (Sir Hilary Bray), Bernard Horsfall (Shaun Campbell), Virginia North (Olympe), Angela Scoular (Ruby Bartlett), Catherine Schell (Nancy), Desmond Llewelyn (Q), Yuri Borionko (Grunther), Geoffrey Cheshire (Toussaint), Irvin Allen (Che Che), Julie Ege (The Scandinavian Girl), Mona Chong (The Chinese Girl), Sylvana Henriques (The Jamaican Girl), Sally Sheridan (The American Girl), Joanna Lumley (The English Girl), Zaheera (The Indian Girl), Anouska Hempel (The Australian Girl), Ingrid Back (The German Girl), Helena Ronee (The Israeli Girl), Jenny Hanley (The Irish Girl). After saving Tracy from committing suicide and refusing her father's offer a dowry of $1 million to marry her, James Bond begins to track down arch enemy Blofeld, who has a deadly plan involving bacteriological warfare agents. James eventually has a short-lived (literally) marriage to Tracy. George Lazenby's only outing as 007. Bond drives an Aston Martin DBS. The opening theme is instrumental but the secondary theme, *We Have All the Time in the World*, is sung by Louis Armstrong. Based on Ian Fleming's novel. *Dir*. Peter R. Hunt.

On the Beat (1962) Norman Wisdom (Norman Pitkin/Giulio Napolitani), Jennifer Jayne (Rosanna), Raymond Huntley (Sir Ronald Ackroyd), David Lodge (Insp Hobson), Esma Cannon (Mrs Stammers), Eric Barker (Doctor), Eleanor Summerfield (Sgt Wilkins), Ronnie Stevens (Oberon), Terence Alexander (Chief Supt Belcher), Maurice Kaufmann (Vince), Dilys Laye (American Lady), George Pastell (Manzini), Jack Watson (Police Sgt), Campbell Singer (Bollington), Lionel Murton (Man in Underground Train), Robert Rietty (Italian Lawyer), Marjie Lawrence (Crying Lady), Peggy Ann Clifford (Guilio's Mother), Jean Aubrey (Lady Hinchingford), Monte Landis (Mr Bassett), Mario Fabrizi (Newspaper Seller), Alfred Burke (Trigger O'Flynn), John Blythe (Chauffeur), Cyril Chamberlain (Cafe Proprietor), Tutte Lemkow (Billposter in Underground), Larry Martyn (Yob in Café), Julian Orchard (Wedding Photographer), Anita Sharp-Bolster (Hair-Salon Customer). Norman dreams of being a copper like his late father but has to content himself with washing police cars, having failed the height test. He is then recruited to do undercover work because of his resemblance to a jewel thief who masquerades as a hairdresser. *Dir*. Robert Asher.

On the Buses (1971) Reg Varney (Stan Butler), Doris Hare (Mum), Michael Robbins (Arthur Rudge), Anna Karen (Olive Rudge), Stephen Lewis (Inspector 'Blakey' Blake), Bob Grant (Jack Harper), Brian Oulton (Manager), Andrea Lawrence (Betty),

Pat Ashton (Sally), Pamela Cundell (Ruby), Pat Coombs (Vera), Wendy Richard (Housewife), Peter Madden (Mr. Brooks), David Lodge (Busman), Brenda Grogan (Bridget), Caroline Dowdeswell (Sandra), Nosher Powell (Betty's Husband). Stan and Bob decide to sabotage the new women bus drivers. The first spin-off film from the TV sitcom of the same name. *Dir*. Harry Booth.

On the Fiddle (1961) Alfred Lynch (Horace), Sean Connery (Pedlar), Cecil Parker (Group Capt Bascombe), Stanley Holloway (Cooksley), Alan King (Sgt Buzzer), Eric Barker (Doctor), Wilfrid Hyde-White (Trowbridge), Kathleen Harrison (Mrs Cooksley), Eleanor Summerfield (Flora McNaughton), Terence Longdon (Air Gunner), Victor Maddern (First Airman), Harry Locke (Huxtable), John Le Mesurier (Hixton), Peter Sinclair (Mr Pope), Edna Morris (Lil), Graham Stark (Sergeant Ellis), Jack Smethurst (Dai Tovey), Patsy Rowlands (Evie), Bill Owen (Corporal Gittens), Harold Goodwin (Corporal Reeves), Barbara Windsor (Mavis). Petty criminal Horace Pope is forced to enlist by a judge and spends his time in the army along with his mate Pedlar Pascoe trying to avoid fighting at all costs. Based on the novel *Stop at a Winner* by R.F. Delderfield. *Dir*. Cyril Frankel.

Once a Jolly Swagman (1949) Dirk Bogarde (Bill Fox), Bonar Colleano (Tommy Possey), Bill Owen (Lag Gibbon), Renée Asherson (Pat Gibbon), Thora Hird (Ma Fox), James Hayter (Pa Fox), Patric Doonan (Dick), Moira Lister (Dotty Liz), Sid James (Rowton), Dudley Jones (Taffy), Cyril Cusack (Duggie Lewis), Anthony Oliver (Derek Blake), Pauline Jameson (Mrs. Lewis), Russell Waters (Mr. Pusey), Sandra Dorne (Kay Fox), Stuart Lindsell (Christopher Yates), Frederick Knight (Chick), Michael Kent (Solicitor), Cyril Chamberlain (Reporter), June Bardsley (WAAF Flight Sergeant), Graham Doody (Dr. A.E. MacKenzie), Sam Kydd (Johnny Briggs). Bill Fox becomes a star of speedway but success goes to his head until his best friend is seriously injured. Based on the novel by Montagu Slater. *Dir*. Jack Lee.

Once More, with Feeling! (1960) Yul Brynner (Victor Fabian), Kay Kendall (Dolly Fabian), Gregory Ratoff (Maxwell Archer), Geoffrey Toone (Dr Richard Hilliard), Maxwell Shaw (Jascha Gendel /Grisha Gendel), Mervyn Johns (Mr Wilbur Jr), Martin Benson (Luigi Bardini), Harry Lockart (Chester), Shirley Anne Field (Angela Hopper). Musical genius Victor's career begins to slide when his wife walks out on him. Based on a play by Harry Kurnitz. Kay Kendall died before the film was released. *Dir*. Stanley Donen.

Once Upon a Dream (1949) Googie Withers (Carol Gilbert), Griffith Jones (Jackson), Guy Middleton (Maj Gilbert), Betty Lynne (Mlle. Louise), David Horne (Registrar), Geoffrey Morris (Registrar's Clerk), Raymond Lovell (Mr Trout), Noel Howlett (Solicitor), Agnes Lauchlan (Aunt Agnes), Mirren Wood (Conductress), Hubert Gregg (Capt Williams), Maurice Denham (Vicar), Mona Washbourne (Vicar's Wife), Dora Bryan (Barmaid). A wife dreams she has committed adultery with her officer husband's servant. But was it only a dream? *Dir*. Ralph Thomas.

Once Upon a Time in the Midlands (2002) Robert Carlyle (Jimmy), Rhys Ifans (Dek), Shirley Henderson (Shirley), Ricky Tomlinson (Charlie), Kathy Burke (Carol), Andrew Shim (Donut), Ryan Bruce (Emerson), Eliot Otis Brown Walters (Lake), Anthony Strachan (Jumbo), David McKay (Dougy), James Cosmo (Billy), Finn Atkins (Marlene), Kelly Thresher (Donna), Vanessa Feltz (Herself), Vicki Patterson (Audience Guest). After seeing his ex-girl and mother of his daughter being proposed to on television, small time crook Jimmy returns home to the Midlands to try and win her back. *Dir*. Shane Meadows.

One Day (2011) Anne Hathaway (Emma Morley), Jim Sturgess (Dexter Mayhew), Romola Garai (Sylvie), Rafe Spall (Ian), Ken Stott (Steven), Patricia Clarkson (Alison), Jodie Whittaker (Tilly), Jamie Sives (Mr. Jamie Hazeel), Georgia King (Suki Meadows), Matt Berry (Aaron), Joséphine de La Baume (Marie), Heida Reed (Ingrid), Amanda Fairbank-Hynes (Tara), Georgia King (Suki), Lorna Gayle (Mrs Major), Diana Kent (Mrs Cope), James Laurenson (Mr Cope, Matthew Beard (Murray Cope), Toby Regbo (Samuel Cope), Thomas Arnold (Colin), Sébastien Dupuis (Jean-Pierre), Eden Mengelgrein, Kayla Mengelgrein (Jasmine in

2001), Maisie Fishbourne (Jasmine in 2005), Emilia Jones (Jasmine in 2007 and 2011). The film follows Emma and Jim on a particular day of each year (15 July) from 1988 – the night they spend together on graduation – through to the present. Based on the book by David Nicholls. *Dir*. Lone Scherfig

One Good Turn (1954) Norman Wisdom (Norman), Joan Rice (Iris), Shirley Abicair (Mary), Thora Hird (Cook), William Russell (Alec Bigley), Joan Ingram (Matron Sparrow), Richard Caldicot (Mr. Bigley), Marjorie Fender (Tuppeny), Keith Gilman (Jimmy), Noel Howlett (Jeweller), David Hurst (Professor Dofee), Harold Kasket (Ivor Petrovitch), Ricky McCullough (Gunner Mac), Anthony Green (Martin), Michael Balfour (Boxing Booth Spectator), Lucy Griffiths (Nancy), Arthur Mullard (Boxer), Graham Stark (Boxing Competitor). Norman tries to raise money for the orphanage where he was brought up. *Dir*. John Paddy Carstairs.

127 Hours (2010) James Franco (Aron Ralston), Kate Mara (Kristi Moore), Amber Tamblyn (Megan McBride), Clémence Poésy (Rana, Aron), Lizzy Caplan (Sonja Ralston), Kate Burton (Donna Ralston), Treat Williams (Larry Ralston). The film is based on Ralston's autobiography *Between a Rock and a Hard Place* which describes how mountain climber Aron Ralston became trapped by a boulder in Robbers Roost, Utah in April 2003 and was eventually forced to amputate his own right arm in order to free himself. *Dir*. Danny Boyle.

One Million Years B.C. (1966) Raquel Welch (Loana), John Richardson (Tumak), Percy Herbert (Sakana), Robert Brown (Akhoba), Martine Beswick (Nupondi), Jean Wladon (Ahot), Lisa Thomas (Sura), Malya Nappi (Tohana), Richard James (Young Rock Man), William Lyon Brown (Payto), Frank Hayden (1st Rock Man), Terence Maidment (1st Shell Man), Micky De Rauch (1st Shell Girl), Yvonne Horner (Ullah). Tumak is expelled from the Rock tribe, meets Loana of the Shell tribe and her very fetching fur bikini. Remake of the equally fact free 1940 Hollywood film *One Million B.C.*. *Dir*. Don Chaffey.

One of Our Aircraft is Missing (1942) Godfrey Tearle (George Corbett), Eric Portman (Tom Earnshaw), Hugh Williams (Frank Shelley), Bernard Miles (Geoff Hickman), Hugh Burden (John Glyn Haggard), Emrys Jones (Bob Ashley), Pamela Brown (Else Meertens), Joyce Redman (Jet van Dieren), Googie Withers (Jo de Vries), Hay Petrie (Burgomeister), Selma Vaz Dias (Burgomeister's wife), Arnold Marlé (Pieter Sluys), Robert Helpmann (De Jong), Peter Ustinov (Priest), Alec Clunes (Organist), Hector Abbas (Driver), James B. Carson (Louis), Willem Akkerman (Willem), Joan Akkerman (Maartje), Peter Schenke (Hendrik), Valerie Moon (Jannie), John Salew (German Sentry), William D'Arcy (German Officer), David Ward (First German Airman), Robert Duncan (Second German Airman), Roland Culver (Naval Officer), Robert Beatty (Sgt. Hopkins), Michael Powell (Despatching Officer), Stewart Rome (Cmdr. Reynold). The crew of Wellington bomber "B for Bertie" is helped by the Dutch to get back to England after bailing out of the stricken aircraft over occupied Holland. A film made by The Archers production company under the authority of the Ministry of Information and aimed at raising morale during wartime. *Dirs*. Michael Powell and Emeric Pressburger.

One of Our Dinosaurs Is Missing (1975) Derek Nimmo (Lord Southmere), Peter Ustinov (Hnup Wan), Helen Hayes (Hettie), Joan Sims (Emily), Deryck Guyler (Harris), Clive Revill (Quon), Molly Weir (Scots nanny), Andrew Dove (Lord Castleberry), Max Harris (Truscott), Max Wall (Juggler), Natasha Pyne (Susan), Joss Ackland (B.J. Spence), Arthur Howard (Thumley), Hugh Burden (Haines), Bernard Bresslaw (Fan Choy), Roy Kinnear (Supt Grubbs), Leonard Trolley (Insp Eppers), Joe Ritchie (Cabbie), Percy Herbert (Mr Gibbons), Joan Hickson (Mrs Gibbons), John Laurie (Jock), Angus Lennie (Hamish), Jon Pertwee (Colonel), Kathleen Byron (Colonel's wife), Lucy Griffiths (Amelia), Aimée Delamain (Millicent), John Bardon (Bookie), Jane Lapotaire (Miss Prescott), Richard Pearson (Sir Geoffrey), Wensley Pithey (Bromley), Michael Elwyn (Haycock), Anthony Sharp (Home Sec), Frank Williams (Dr Freemo), Peter Madden (Sanders), Erik Chitty (Museum guard), Amanda Barrie (Mrs B.J. Spence). Queen's Messenger Lord Southmere has secreted a special microfilmed formula on a dinosaur skeleton in the Natural History Museum but shortly after passing this information on to his old nanny he is kidnapped by a Chinese gang led by Hnup Wan. Can Hettie, who enlists more nannies for the search, find the missing microfilm before the Chinese? Based on the 1970 novel *The Great Dinosaur Robbery* by David Forrest. *Dir*. Robert Stevenson.

One That Got Away, The (1957) Hardy Krüger (Franz Von Werra), Colin Gordon (Army Interrogator), Michael Goodliffe (RAF Interrogator), Terence Alexander (RAF Intelligence Officer), Jack Gwillim (Commandant, Grizedale), Andrew Faulds (Lieutenant – Grizedale), Julian Somers (Booking Clerk), Alec McCowen (Duty Officer, Hucknall), Richard Marner (German Prisoner), Cyril Chamberlain (Sergeant 'Later'), Peggy Ann Clifford (Train Conductor), Glyn Houston (Harry 'Hurricane'), Stratford Johns (Second Detective), Michael Ripper (Corporal), Norman Rossington (Sergeant – Swanick). The film recounts the true story of Franz von Werra, a Luftwaffe pilot shot down over England in 1940. After unsuccessful attempts to escape whilst in England he is sent by ship to Canada. *Dir*. Roy Ward Baker.

One Wild Oat (1951) Robertson Hare (Humphrey Proudfoot), Stanley Holloway (Alfred Gilbey), Sam Costa (Mr. Pepys), Andrew Crawford (Fred Gilbey), Vera Pearce (Mrs. Gilbey), June Sylvaine (Cherrie Proudfoot), Robert Moreton (Throstle), Constance Lorne (Mrs. Proudfoot), Gwen Cherrell (Audrey Cuttle), Irene Handl (Emily Pepys), Ingeborg von Kusserow (Gloria Samson), Charles Groves (Charles), Joan Rice (Annie), Audrey Hepburn (Hotel receptionist), Fred Berger (Samson), James Fox (Porter). When the neighbouring daughter and son of a barrister and greyhound owner fall in love, their respective fathers decide to delve into each other's backgrounds, with uncomfortable results for both men. *Dir*. Charles Saunders.

Onegin (1999) Ralph Fiennes (Yevgeni "Eugene" Onegin), Liv Tyler (Tatyana), Irene Worth (Princess Alina), Toby Stephens (Lensky), Martin Donovan (Prince Nikitin), Lena Headey (Olga), Alun Armstrong (Zaretsky), Simon McBurney (Triquet), Harriet Walter (Madame Larina), Elizabeth Berrington (Mlle Volkonsky). Bored St. Petersburg dandy inherits a landed estate from his uncle and attracts the attention of both his neighbour's fiancée and her sister. Based on Alexander Pushkin's verse novel *Eugene Onegin*. *Dir*. Martha Fiennes.

Only Two Can Play (1962) Peter Sellers (John Lewis), Mai Zetterling (Liz), Virginia Maskell (Jean Lewis), Kenneth Griffith (Ieuan Jenkins), Raymond Huntley (Vernon), David Davies (Benyon), Maudie Edwards (Mrs Edna Davies), Meredith Edwards (Clergyman on the Committee), John Le Mesurier (Salter), Frederick Piper (Mr Davies), Graham Stark (Hyman), Eynon Evans (Town Hall Clerk), John Arnatt (Bill), Sheila Manahan (Mrs Jenkins), Richard Attenborough (Gareth L. Probert), Desmond Llewelyn (Clergyman on Bus), Charles Lloyd Pack (Committee Member), Meg Wynn Owen (Dilys), Gerald Sim (Cigarette Thief at Party). The life of married librarian John Lewis is complicated when local councillor's wife Liz sets her sights on him. Based *That Uncertain Feeling* by Kingsley Amis. *Dir*. Sidney Gilliat.

Only When I Larf (1968) Richard Attenborough (Silas Lowther), David Hemmings (Bob), Alexandra Stewart (Liz Mason), Nicholas Pennell (Spencer), Melissa Stribling (Diana), Terence Alexander (Gee Gee Gray), Edric Connor (Awana), Clifton Jones (General Sakut), Calvin Lockhart (Ali Lin), Brian Grellis (Spider), David Healy (Jones), Alan Gifford (Poster). The activities of three confidence tricksters. Based on the book of the same name by Len Deighton. *Dir*. Basil Dearden.

Ooh... You Are Awful (1972) Dick Emery (Charlie Tully), Derren Nesbitt (Sid Sabbath), Ronald Fraser (Reggie Campbell Peek), Pat Coombs (Libby Niven), William Franklyn (Arnold Van Cleef), Cheryl Kennedy (Jo Mason), Norman Bird (Warder Burke), Roland Curram (Vivian), Liza Goddard (Liza Missenden Green), Ambrosine Phillpotts (Lady Missenden Green), Brian Oulton (Funeral Director), David Healy (Tourist), Steve Plytas (Signor Vittorio Ferruchi), Louis Negin (Emilio Ferruchi), Neil Wilson (Attendant Price), Henry Gilbert (Don Luigi), Anthony Stamboulieh (Dino), Guido Adorni (Carlo), Stefan Gryff (Capo Mafioso), Sheila Keith (Lady Magistrate), Larry Taylor (Hood), Jacki Harding (Police Trainee), Michael Sharvell-Martin (Jackson). Conmen Charlie and Reggie make £500,000 but before he can get his share Charlie is arrested. On his release Charlie meets Reggie but the latter is murdered. Charlie discovers that

265

Reggie had deposited the money in a Swiss bank account, the number to which is tattooed in separate parts on the posteriors of four young ladies. Charlie must find a way of getting to the bottom of the problem. All the while he is being shadowed by members of a criminal gang trying to kill him. *Dir*. Cliff Owen.

Operation Bullshine (1959) Donald Sinden (Lt Gordon Brown), Barbara Murray (Pte Betty Brown), Carole Lesley (Pte Marge White), Ronald Shiner (Gunner Slocum), Naunton Wayne (Maj Pym), Dora Bryan (Pte Cox), John Cairney (Gunner Willie Ross), Fabia Drake (Junior Commander Maddox A.T.S.), Joan Rice (Pte Finch), Daniel Massey (Bombardier Peter Palmer), Peter Jones (Gunner Perkins), Barbara Hicks (Sgt Merrifield), John Welsh (Brigadier), Cyril Chamberlain (Orderly Sergeant), Ambrosine Phillpotts (Reporter), Naomi Chance (Subaltern Godfrey A.T.S.), Marianne Stone (Sgt Cook), Harry Landis (Gunner Wilkinson), Brian Weske (Gunner Pooley), George Mikell (German Airman), Dorinda Stevens, Amanda Barrie, Marigold Russell, Julie Hopkins, Beverly Prowse, Margaret Simons, Pamela Searle, Eve Eden, Julie Alexander, Pat Gibson (A.T.S. Girls). An artillery officer is posted to an anti-aircraft battery staffed by ATS girls. Then his wife is posted to the same battery. Olympic swimming champion Judy Grinham features as a physical training instructor. *Dir*. Gilbert Gunn.

Operation Crossbow (1965) Sophia Loren (Nora), George Peppard (Lt John Curtis), Trevor Howard (Prof Lindemann), John Mills (Gen Boyd), Richard Johnson (Duncan Sandys), Tom Courtenay (Robert Henshaw), Jeremy Kemp (Phil Bradley), Anthony Quayle (Bamford), Lilli Palmer (Frieda), Paul Henreid (Gen Ziemann), Helmut Dantine (Gen Linz), Barbara Rütting (Hannah Reitsch), Richard Todd (Wing Cmdr Kendall), Sylvia Syms (Constance Babington Smith), John Fraser (Ft Lt. Kenny), Maurice Denham (RAF Officer), Patrick Wymark (Prime Minister Winston Churchill), Wolf Frees (German Police Insp), Moray Watson (Col Kenneth Post), Richard Wattis (Sir Charles Sims), Allan Cuthbertson (German Technical Examiner), Karel Stepanek (Prof Hoffer), Ferdy Mayne (German Officer at rocket plant), Robert Brown (Air Commodore), John Abineri (German Policeman), John Alderton (RAF 'Dakota' Navigator), Anton Diffring (German Soldier), Charles Lloyd Pack (Technical Examiner), Philip Madoc (German Police Officer). Fictionalised account of Crossbow, a real-life campaign of allied operations against the development and deployment of German long-range weapons during WWII (in particular the V1 and V2 weapons). The film tells the story from both the allied and German points of view. *Dir*. Michael Anderson.

Operation Snatch (1962) Terry-Thomas (Lt 'Piggy' Wigg), George Sanders (Maj Hobson), Lionel Jeffries (Evans), Jocelyn Lane (Bianca Tabori), Mark Eden (Mosquito Pilot), Mario Fabrizi (Tall Man), John Gabriel (Maj Frink), Gerard Heinz (Col Waldock), Bernard Hunter (Capt Baker), Dinsdale Landen (Capt Wellington), Howard H. Lang (P.T. Sgt), Angus Lennie (Vic), Jeremy Lloyd (Capt James), John Meillon (Medical Officer), Warren Mitchell (Contact Man), Lee Montague (Miklos Tabori), Nyree Dawn Porter (W.R.A.C. Officer), John Scott (Lt Gen Hepworth), Mark Singleton (P M's Secretary), Graham Stark (Soldier), Michael Trubshawe (Col Marston), James Villiers (Lt Keen), Ian Whittaker (Dyson), Ronnie Corbett (Soldier). The officer in charge of the Barbary Apes on Gibraltar during WWII decides to go behind enemy lines and capture a new ape. The film plays on the legend that if the apes leave the Rock then the British will also leave. *Dir*. Robert Day.

Orders to Kill (1958) Eddie Albert (Maj MacMahon), Paul Massie (Gene Summers), Lillian Gish (Mrs Summers), James Robertson Justice (Naval Commander), Irene Worth (Leonie), Leslie French (Marcel Lafitte), John Crawford (Maj Kimball), Lionel Jeffries (Interrogator), Anne Blake (Mme. Lafitte), Miki Iveria (Louise), Lillie Bea Gifford (Mauricette), Launce Maraschal (Gen Nolan), Robert Henderson (Col Snyder), William E. Greene (Mitchell), Ralph Nossek (Psychiatrist), Jacques B. Brunius (Commandant Morand). An American bomber pilot is chosen to go on a mission to Nazi-occupied Paris and kill a suspected double agent working in the French Resistance. *Dir*. Anthony Asquith.

Orlando (1992) Tilda Swinton (Orlando), Quentin Crisp (Elizabeth I), Jimmy Somerville (Falsetto/Angel), John Wood (Archduke Harry), John Bott (Orlando's father), Elaine Banham (Orlando's mother), Anna Farnworth (Clorinda), Sara Mair-Thomas (Favilla), Anna Healy (Euphrosyne), Dudley Sutton (James I), Simon Russell Beale (Earl of Moray), Matthew Sim (Lord Francis Vere), Charlotte Valandrey (Princess Sasha), Toby Stephens (Othello), Oleg Pogodin (Desdemona), Heathcote Williams (Nick Greene/Publisher), Thom Hoffman (William III), Sarah Crowden (Mary II), Billy Zane (Shelmerdine), Lol Coxhill (The Butler). A young man promises a dying Queen Elizabeth I that he will not grow old and then lives out the next 390 years, changing into a woman along the way. Based on Virginia Woolf's novel *Orlando: A Biography*. *Dir*. Sally Potter.

Oscar Wilde (1960) Robert Morley (Oscar Wilde), Ralph Richardson (Sir Edward Carson), Phyllis Calvert (Constance Wilde), John Neville (Lord Alfred Douglas), Dennis Price (Robert Ross), Alexander Knox (Sir Edgar Clarke), Edward Chapman (Marquis of Queensberry), Martin Benson (George Alexander), Robert Harris (Justice Henn Collins), Henry Oscar (Justice Wills), William Devlin (Solicitor-General), Stephen Dartnell (Cobble), Ronald Leigh-Hunt (Lionel Johnson), Martin Boddey (Insp. Richards), Leonard Sachs (Richard Legallienne), Tom Chatto (Clerk of Arraigns), Tony Doonan (Wood), Jack Gwillim (Barrister), Wilton Morley (Wilde's son). A biopic of the celebrated wit and playwright. *Dir*. Gregory Ratoff

Othello (1965) Laurence Olivier (Othello), Maggie Smith (Desdemona), Joyce Redman (Emilia), Frank Finlay (Iago), Derek Jacobi (Michael Cassio), Robert Lang (Roderigo), Kenneth MacKintosh (Lodovico), Anthony Nicholls (Brabantio), Sheila Reid (Bianca), Malcolm Terris (Senate Officer), Harry Lomax (Duke of Venice), Michael Turner (Gratiano), Terence Knapp (Duke's Officer), Keith Marsh (Senator), Tom Kempinski (Sailor), Nick Edmett (Messenger), David Hargreaves (Senate Officer), Edward Hardwicke (Montano), Christopher Timothy (Cypriot Officer), Roy Holder (Clown). A film of a stage production (National Theatre) of Shakespeare's play which famously features a controversial performance by a black-faced Olivier complete with unusual walk and voice. *Dir*. Stuart Burge.

Otley (1968) Tom Courtenay (Gerald Arthur Otley), Romy Schneider (Imogen), Alan Badel (Sir Alex Hadrian), James Villiers (Hendrickson), Leonard Rossiter (Johnson), Freddie Jones (Philip Proudfoot), Fiona Lewis (Lin), James Bolam (Albert), James Cossins (Geffcock), James Maxwell (Rollo), Edward Hardwicke (Lambert), Ronald Lacey (Curtis), Phyllida Laws (Jean), Geoffrey Bayldon (Inspector Hewett), Frank Middlemass (Bruce). A comedy thriller. Petty thief Otley finds his life turned into a series of chases when he is pursued by the police who wrongly want him for murder and by agents who think he is a spy. *Dir*. Dick Clement.

Our Girl Friday (1954) Joan Collins (Sadie Patch), George Cole (Jimmy Carrol), Kenneth More (Pat Plunkett), Robertson Hare (Professor Gibble), Hermione Gingold (Spinster), Walter Fitzgerald (Captain), Hattie Jacques (Mrs. Patch), Felix Felton (Mr. Patch), Lionel Murton (Barman), Anthony Tancred (Smithers), Michael Meacham (Schooner Officer), Peter Sellers (Parrot - voice). An heiress, a journalist, an economics professor and a stoker are marooned on a desert island following a collision at sea. Released in the US as *The Adventures of Sadie*. Based on Norman Lindsay's novel *The Cautious Amorist*. *Dir*. Noel Langley

Our Man in Havana (1959) Alec Guinness (Jim Wormold), Burl Ives (Dr. Hasselbacher), Maureen O'Hara (Beatrice Severn), Ernie Kovacs (Capt. Segura), Noel Coward (Hawthorne), Ralph Richardson ('C'), Jo Morrow (Milly Wormold), Grégoire Aslan (Cifuentes), Paul Rogers (Hubert Carter), Raymond Huntley (General), Ferdy Mayne (Prof. Sanchez), Maurice Denham (Admiral), Joseph P. Mawra (Lopez), Duncan Macrae (MacDougal), Gerik Schjelderup (Svenson), Hugh Manning (Officer), Karel Stepanek (Dr. Braun), Maxine Audley (Teresa),

John Le Mesurier (Louis), Rachel Roberts (Prostitute). A vacuum cleaner salesman in Cuba is engaged by British Intelligence to be its agent in Havana. Adapted from the novel of the same name by Graham Greene. *Dir.* Carol Reed.

Our Mother's House (1967) Dirk Bogarde (Charlie Hook), Margaret Brooks (Elsa), Pamela Franklin (Diana), Louis Sheldon Williams (Hubert), John Gugolka (Dunstan), Mark Lester (Jiminee), Phoebe Nicholls (Gerty), Gustav Henry (Willy), Parnum Wallace (Louis), Yootha Joyce (Mrs Quayle), Claire Davidson (Miss Bailey), Anthony Nicholls (Mr Halbert), Annette Carell (Mother), Gerald Sim (Bank Clerk), Edina Ronay (Doreen), Diana Ashley (Girl Friend), Garfield Morgan (Mr. Moley). When their abandoned mother dies, her seven children bury her in the back garden and continue to live as if she were still alive, fooling both neighbours and schoolteachers. Then their long gone father arrives and disrupts the household. *Dir.* Jack Clayton.

Out of True (1951) Jane Hylton (Molly Slade), Muriel Pavlow (Betty), David Evans (Arthur Slade), Mary Merrall (Granny), Beatrice Varley (Mrs Green), Robert Brown (Dr Dale), Sonia Williams (Nurse), Jean Anderson (Dr Bell). Dramatised documentary about the treatment of mental illness in Britain in the early 1950s. *Dir.* Philip Leacock.

Outcast of the Islands (1952) Ralph Richardson (Captain Tom Lingard), Trevor Howard (Peter Willems), Robert Morley (Elmer Almayer), Wendy Hiller (Mrs. Almayer), Kerima (Aissa), George Coulouris (Babalatchi), Wilfrid Hyde-White (Vinck), Frederick Valk (Hudig), Betty Ann Davies (Mrs. Williams), Dharma Emmanuel (Ali), Peter Illing (Alagappan), A.V. Bramble (Badavi), Annabel Morley (Nina Almayer), James Kenney (Ramsey), Marne Maitland (Mate). Set in Malaya, the bored, restless, and immoral Peter Willems cannot tame his passion for the chief's beautiful daughter and also clashes with the priggish trader Almayer. An adaptation of Joseph Conrad's novel, *An Outcast of the Islands. Dir.* Carol Reed.

Overlord (1975) Brian Stirner (Tom), Davyd Harries (Jack), Nicholas Ball (Arthur), Julie Neesam (The Girl), Sam Sewell (The Trained Soldier), John Franklyn-Robbins (Dad), Stella Tanner (Mum), Harry Shacklock (Stationmaster), David Scheuer (Medical Officer), Ian Liston (Barrack Guard), Lorna Lewis (Prostitute), Stephen Riddle (Dead German Soldier), Jack Le White (Barman), Mark Penfold (Photographer), Micaela Minelli (Little Girl), Elsa Minelli (Little Girl's Mother). A young soldier experiences premonitions of his death on the run up to the D-Day landings (Operation Overlord). *Dir.* Stuart Cooper.

Pair of Briefs, A (1962) Michael Craig (Tony Stevens), Mary Peach (Frances Pilbright), Brenda De Banzie (Gladys Worthing), James Robertson Justice (Mr. Justice Haddon), Roland Culver (Sir John Pilbright), Liz Fraser (Gloria Hoskins), Ron Moody (Sidney Pudney), Jameson Clark (George Lockwood), Charles Heslop (Peebles), Bill Kerr (Victor), Nicholas Phipps (Sutcliffe), Joan Sims (Gale Tornado), John Standing (Hubert Shannon), Amanda Barrie (Exotic dancer), Judy Carne (Exotic dancer), Barbara Ferris (Gloria Lockwood), Myrtle Reed (Barmaid), Terry Scott (Policeman), Graham Stark (Police witness), Ronnie Stevens (Hotel under-manager), Cyril Chamberlain (Policeman). Legal comedy. Two new barristers (Tony and Frances) find themselves on opposite sides in a case of restitution of conjugal rights and find themselves attracted to one another. *Dir.* Ralph Thomas.

Pandora and the Flying Dutchman (1951) James Mason (Hendrik), Ava Gardner (Pandora), Nigel Patrick (Stephen Cameron), Sheila Sim (Janet), Harold Warrender (Geoffrey Fielding), Mario Cabré (Juan Montalvo), Marius Goring (Reggie Demarest), John Laurie (Angus), Pamela Mason (Jenny), Patricia Raine (Peggy), Margarita D'Alvarez (Senora Montalvo), La Pillina (Spanish dancer), Abraham Sofaer (Judge), Francisco Igual (Vicente), Guillermo Beltrán (Barman), Lilli Molnar (Geoffrey's housekeeper), Phoebe Hodgson (Dressmaker), John Carew (Priest). Told in flashback. In Spain in 1930 American Pandora Reynolds seems unable to love any of her many admirers until the arrival of Hendrick van der Zee, a Dutchman with a secret. *Dir.* Albert Lewin.

Paper Tiger (1975) David Niven ('Walter Bradbury), Toshirô Mifune (Ambassador Kagoyama), Hardy Krüger (Müller), Ando (Koichi Kagoyama), Irene Tsu (Talah), Ivan Desny (Foreign Minister), Miiko Taka (Mme. Kagoyama), Jeff Corey (Mr King), Patricia Donahue (Mrs King), Ronald Fraser (Sgt Forster). Bradbury is taken on as a tutor to the son of the Japanese ambassador. He impresses Ando with his stories of derring-do during the war but when he and his young charge are kidnapped the "major" has to demonstrate that these heroics weren't just stories. *Dir.* Ken Annakin.

Parole Officer, The (2001) Steve Coogan (Simon Garden), Om Puri (George), Steven Waddington (Jeff), Ben Miller (Colin), Emma Williams (Kirsty), Stephen Dillane (Inspector Burton), Lena Headey (Emma), Justin Burrows (Mills), John Henshaw (Cochran), Omar Sharif (Victor), Jenny Agutter (Sarah), Richard Sinnott (Bank Manager), Simon Pegg (Deflated Husband). When parole officer Simon is falsely accused of murder his ex-clients help him try and prove his innocence. *Dir.* John Duigan.

Passage to India, A (1984) Judy Davis (Adela Quested), Peggy Ashcroft (Mrs Moore), Victor Banerjee (Dr Aziz Ahmed), James Fox (Richard Fielding), Alec Guinness (Prof Godbole), Nigel Havers (Ronny Heaslop), Michael Culver (Maj McBryde), Clive Swift (Maj Callendar), Art Malik (Ali), Saeed Jaffrey (Advocate Hamidullah), Roshan Seth (Advocate Amrit Rao), Richard Wilson (Turton), Antonia Pemberton (Mrs Turton), Ann Firbank (Mrs Callendar), Roshan Seth (Amritrao), Sandra Hotz (Stella Fielding), Rashid Karapiet (Das), H.S. Krishnamurthy (Hassan), Ishaq Bux (Selim), Moti Makan (Guide), Mohammed Ashiq (Haq), Phyllis Bose (Mrs Leslie), Sally Kinghorn (Ingenue), Z.H. Khan (Dr. Panna Lal), Ashok Mandanna (Anthony), Dina Pathak (Begum Hamidullah), Adam Blackwood (Mr Hadley), Duncan Preston (Club Member). Portrayal of the tensions existing between the British and Indian (and Anglo-Indian) communities in India during the 1920s, which come to a peak when Dr Aziz is accused of attempting to rape Adela. The film won two Oscars: Best Supporting Actress (Peggy Ashcroft), Best Music, Original Score (Maurice Jarre). Based on E. M. Forster's novel. *Dir.* David Lean.

Passing of the Third Floor Back, The (1935) Conrad Veidt (The Stranger), Anna Lee (Vivian), René Ray (Stasia), Frank Cellier (Wright), John Turnbull (Major Tomkin), Cathleen Nesbitt (Mrs. Tomkin), Ronald Ward (Chris Penny), Beatrix Lehmann (Miss Kite), Jack Livesey (Mr. Larkcom), Sara Allgood (Mrs. de Hooley), Mary Clare (Mrs. Sharpe), Barbara Everest (Cook), Alexander Sarner (The gramophone man), James Knight (The police inspector). A new lodger takes the room on the "third floor back" of a run-down boarding house. He begins to change the attitudes of the residents towards each other and the staff but comes into conflict with one of them. Based on the book of the same name by Jerome K Jerome. *Dir.* Berthold Viertel.

Passionate Friends, The (1949) Ann Todd (Mary Justin), Claude Rains (Howard Justin), Trevor Howard (Professor Steven Stratton), Betty Ann Davies (Miss Joan Layton), Isabel Dean (Pat Stratton), Arthur Howard (Smith - the Butler), Guido Lorraine (Hotel Manager), Marcel Poncin (Hall Porter), Natasha Sokolova (Chambermaid), Hélène Burls (Flowerwoman), Jean Serret (Emigration Official), Frances Waring (Charwoman), Wenda Rogerson (Bridge Guest), Wilfrid Hyde-White (Lawyer). When she meets Steven again after many years Mary rekindles her love for him even though she has now married a rich banker. *Dir.* David Lean.

Passionate Stranger, The (1957) Ralph Richardson (Roger Wynter/Sir Clement), Margaret Leighton (Judith Wynter/Leonie Hathaway), Patricia Dainton (Emily/Betty), Carlo Giustini (Carlo/Mario), Ada Reeve (Old Woman), Andree Melly (Marla), Frederick Piper (Mr. Poldy), Michael Shepley (Miles Easter), Thorley Walters (Jimmy), George Woodbridge (1st Landlord), Allan Cuthbertson (Dr. Stevenson), John Arnatt (Maurice Lamport/Martin), Barbara Archer (Doris - the barmaid), Marjorie Rhodes (Mrs. Poldy), Megs Jenkins (Millie), Michael Trubshawe (2nd Landlord), Alexander Gauge (MC at Dance), Barbara Graley (Secretary), Christopher Witty (Peter), Fred Tooze (Amos), Pat Ryan (Guard). A happily married novelist pens her latest romance about a woman who falls in love with her chauffeur. Her chauffeur finds the manuscript and believes it represents her real desires and tries to emulate the situations in the novel, much to the amusement of the novelist's husband. *Dir.* Muriel Box.

Passport to China (1961) Richard Basehart (Don Benton), Lisa Gastoni (Lola Sanchez), Athene Seyler (Mao Tai Tai), Eric Pohlmann (Ivono Kong), Alan Gifford (Charles Orme), Bernard Cribbins (Pereira), Burt Kwouk (Jimmy), Hedgar Wallace (Inspector Taylor), Marne Maitland (Han Po). When a pilot attempts to rescue a girl from Communist China, she wants him to take refugees back with him. Also known as *Visa to Canton*. *Dir*. Michael Carreras

Passport to Pimlico (1949) Stanley Holloway (Arthur Pemberton), Betty Warren (Connie Pemberton), Barbara Murray (Shirley Pemberton), Paul Dupuis (Sébastien de Charolais, Duke of Burgundy), John Slater (Frank Huggins), Jane Hylton (Molly Reed), Raymond Huntley (Mr. W.P.J. Wix), Philip Stainton (PC Spiller), Roy Carr (Benny Spiller), Sydney Tafler (Fred Cowan), Nancy Gabrielle (Mrs Cowan), Michael Knight (Monty Cowan), Hermione Baddeley (Edie Randall), Margaret Rutherford (Prof Hatton-Jones), Frederick Piper (Jim Garland), Roy Gladdish (Charlie Randall), Charles Hawtrey (Bert Fitch), Stuart Lindsell (Coroner), Naunton Wayne (Straker), Basil Radford (Gregg), Gilbert Davis (Bagshawe), Michael Hordern (Insp Bashford), Arthur Howard (Bassett), Bill Shine (Captain), Sam Kydd (Sapper), James Hayter (Commissionaire). A Royal Charter signed by Edward IV is revealed when a bomb explodes on a post-war bomb site at Pimlico in London. It states that the area is actually part of Burgundy and therefore outside British law and, more importantly in post-war Britain, rationing. *Dir*. Henry Cornelius.

Passport to Shame (1958) Odile Versois (Marie Louise 'Malou' Beaucaire), Diana Dors (Vicki), Herbert Lom (Nick Biaggi), Eddie Constantine (Johnny McVey), Brenda De Banzie (Aggie), Robert Brown (Mike), Elwyn Brook-Jones (Solicitor Heath), Yvonne Buckingham (Tart), Percy Cartwright (Registrar), Jackie Collins (English girl), Lana Morris (Girl), Pat Pleasence (Sally), Cyril Shaps (Willie), Denis Shaw (Mac), Pauline Stroud (Maria), Margaret Tyzack (June), Michael Caine (Man getting married), Anne Reid (Woman getting married), Joan Sims (Miriam). A French girl is persuaded to come to London ostensibly as a woman's companion but actually to be dragged into a prostitution ring. *Dir*. Alvin Rakoff.

Password Is Courage, The (1962) Dirk Bogarde (Sgt Maj Charles Coward), Maria Perschy (Irena), Alfred Lynch (Bill Pope), Nigel Stock (Cole), Reginald Beckwith (Unterofficer), Richard Marner (Schmidt), Ed Devereaux (Aussie), Lewis Fiander (Pringle), George Mikell (Necke), Richard Carpenter (Robinson), Bernard Archard (1st Prisoner of war), Ferdy Mayne (1st German officer at French farm), George Pravda (2nd German officer at French farm), Olaf Pooley (German doctor), Michael Mellinger (Feldwebel), Colin Blakely (German), Douglas Livingstone (Bennett). A POW escape story with a comedic touch based on a true story. *Dir*. Andrew L Stone.

Pastor Hall (1940) Wilfrid Lawson (Pastor Frederick Hall), Nova Pilbeam (Christine Hall), Seymour Hicks (General von Grotjahn), Marius Goring (Fritz Gerte), Brian Worth (Werner von Grotjahn), Percy Walsh (Herr Veit), Lina Barrie (Lina Veit), Eliot Makeham (Pippermann), Peter Cotes (Erwin Kohn), Edmund Willard (Freundlich), Hay Petrie (Nazi Pastor), Bernard Miles (Heinrich Degan), Manning Whiley (Vogel), J. Fisher White (Johann Herder), Barbara Gott (Frau Kemp). Based on the play of the same name by Ernst Toller which was itself based on the true story of Protestant minister Martin Niemuller, who was interned at Dachau concentration camp for criticising the Nazi party. A controversial film for the neutral USA to screen in 1940, it was released after the screening rights were acquired by the President's son James Roosevelt. Its US release also had a prologue tacked on which was delivered by First Lady Eleanor Roosevelt. Dir. Roy Boulting.

Paul (2011) Simon Pegg (Graeme Willy), Nick Frost (Clive Gollings), Seth Rogen (Paul - voice), Jason Bateman (Special Agent Lorenzo Zoil), Kristen Wiig (Ruth Buggs), Bill Hader (Agent Haggard), Blythe Danner (Tara Walton), Joe Lo Truglio (Agent O'Reilly), John Carroll Lynch (Moses Buggs), Jane Lynch (Pat Stevenson), David Koechner (Gus), Jesse Plemons (Jake),

Sigourney Weaver (Big Guy), Jeffrey Tambor (Adam Shadowchild), Steven Spielberg (Himself - voice), Brett Michael Jones (Keith Nash). Two British sci-fi enthusiasts travelling in the US in a Recreational Vehicle (RV) are asked for help by Paul, an alien. He has escaped from a top-secret military base and needs to rendezvous with a spacecraft from his home planet but Special Agent Zoil is on his trail. *Dir*. Greg Mottola.

Payroll (1961) Michael Craig (Johnny Mellors), Françoise Prévost (Katie Pearson), Billie Whitelaw (Jackie Parker), William Lucas (Dennis Pearson), Kenneth Griffith (Monty), Tom Bell (Blackie), Barry Keegan (Bert Langridge), Edward Cast (Det Sgt Bradden), Andrew Faulds (Det Insp Carberry), William Peacock (Harry Parker), Glyn Houston (Frank Moore), Joan Rice (Madge Moore), Vanda Godsell (Doll), Stanley Meadows (Bowen), Brian McDermott (Brent), Hugh Morton (Mr. John), Keith Faulkner (Alf), Bruce Beeby (Worth), Murray Evans (Billy), Kevin Bennett (Archie Murdock), Michael Barrington (Hay), Anthony Bate (Detective). The widow of a security van driver killed in a robbery plans to avenge her husband's death. Based on Derek Bickerton's novel. *Dir*. Sidney Hayers.

Peeping Tom (1960) Karlheinz Böhm (Mark Lewis), Moira Shearer (Vivian), Anna Massey (Helen Stephens), Maxine Audley (Mrs Stephens), Brenda Bruce (Dora), Miles Malleson (Elderly Gentleman customer), Esmond Knight (Arthur Baden), Martin Miller (Dr Rosan), Michael Goodliffe (Don Jarvis), Jack Watson (Chief Insp Gregg), Pamela Green (Milly), Miles Malleson (Elderly man), Esmond Knight (Arthur Baden), Shirley Anne Field (Diane Ashley). Now considered to be a fine film of its genre, on its release this was a controversial film which damaged director Powell's career. It is the story of a serial killer who murders women while using a portable film camera to record their dying expressions of terror. *Dir*. Michael Powell.

Penn of Pennsylvania (1941) Clifford Evans (William Penn), Deborah Kerr (Gulielma Maria Springett), Dennis Arundell (Charles II), Aubrey Mallalieu (Chaplain), D.J. Williams (Lord Arlington), O.B. Clarence (Lord Cecil), James Harcourt (George Fox), Charles Carson (Adm. Penn), Henry Oscar (Samuel Pepys), Max Adrian (Elton), John Stuart (Bindle), Maire O'Neill (Cook), Edward Rigby (Bushell), Joss Ambler (Lord Mayor), J.H. Roberts (Ford), Edmund Willard (Captain), Percy Marmont (Holme), Gibb McLaughlin (Indian Chief), Herbert Lomas (Captain Cockle), Gus McNaughton (Mate). A historical drama recounting the life of William Penn, the Quaker founder of Pennsylvania. *Dir*. Lance Comfort.

Penny Points to Paradise (1951) Harry Secombe (Harry Flakers), Alfred Marks (Edward Haynes), Peter Sellers (The Major/Arnold Fringe), Paddie O'Neil (Christine Russell), Spike Milligan (Spike Donnelly), Bill Kerr (Digger Graves), Freddie Frinton (Drunk), Vicki Page (Sheila Gilroy), Joe Linnane (Policeman), Sam Kydd (Porter/Taxi Driver). The Goons have a big screen outing in which Harry wins the football pools and is the target for forgers and money-hungry girls. *Dir*. Tony Young.

People That Time Forgot, The (1977) Patrick Wayne (Ben McBride), Doug McClure (Bowen Tyler), Sarah Douglas (Lady Charlotte 'Charly' Cunningham), Dana Gillespie (Ajor), Thorley Walters (Norfolk), Shane Rimmer (Hogan), Tony Britton (Captain Lawton), John Hallam (Chung-Sha), David Prowse (Executioner), Milton Reid (Sabbala), Kiran Shah (Bolum), Richard LeParmentier (Lt. Whitby), Jimmy Ray (Lt. Graham), Tony McHale (Telegraphist). A direct sequel to *The Land That Time Forgot* (1975) where the story follows a rescue expedition in the same country as before. Based on the novel by Edgar Rice Burroughs. *Dir*. Kevin Connor.

Percy (1971) Hywel Bennett (Edwin Anthony), Denholm Elliott (Emmanuel Whitbread), Elke Sommer (Helga), Britt Ekland (Dorothy Chiltern-Barlow), Cyd Hayman (Moira Warrington), Janet Key (Hazel Anthony), Tracey Crisp (Miss Elder), Antonia Ellis (Rita La Rousse), Tracy Reed (Mrs. Penney), Patrick Mower (James Vaile), Pauline Delaney (Sister Flanagan), Adrienne Posta (Maggie Hyde), Julia Foster (Marilyn), Sheila Steafel (Mrs. Gold), Arthur English (Pub Comic), Angus MacKay (TV producer), Rita Webb (Mrs. Hedges), Charles Hodgson (TV interviewer), Sue Lloyd (Bernice), Denise Coffey (Operator No 1), Edward Malin (Elderly patient), Margaretta Scott (Rita's Mother), Graham Crowden (Alfred Spaulton), T. P. McKenna (Meet the People Compere), Tony Haygarth (Purdey), Ronnie Brody (Reporter), Penny Brahms (Football Spectator), George Best (Himself). Shy Edwin is the recipient of the world's first penis transplant. His new member is that of the philanderer who was killed in the accident which emasculated him. He decides to investigate the dead man's past. *Dir*. Ralph Thomas.

Percy's Progress (1974) Leigh Lawson (Percy Edward Anthony), Elke Sommer (Clarissa), Denholm Elliott (Sir Emmanuel Whitbread), Judy Geeson (Dr. Fairweather), Harry H. Corbett (Prime Minister), Vincent Price (Stavos Mammonian), Adrienne Posta (Iris), Julie Ege (Miss Hanson), Barry Humphries (Dr. Anderson), James Booth (Jeffcot), Milo O'Shea (Dr. Klein), Ronald Fraser (Bleeker), Anthony Andrews (Catchpole), Bernard Lee (Barraclough), Madeline Smith (Miss UK), Alan Tilvern (General Dodds), Minah Bird (Miss America), Marianne Stone (Reporter), Alan Lake (Derry Hogan), George Coulouris (Prof. Godowski), Jenny Hanley (Miss Teenage Lust), Diane Langton (Maureen Sugden), Carol Hawkins (Maggie), Marika Rivera (Madame Lopez), Penny Irving (Chiquita), Michael Barratt (Himself), T.P. McKenna (London News Editor). A sequel to *Percy* (1971) – with a new actor playing the lead. Percy, the recipient of the world's first penis transplant, investigates an outbreak of impotency. *Dir*. Ralph Thomas.

Perfect Sense (2011) Ewan McGregor (Michael), Eva Green (Susan), Connie Nielsen (Jenny), Stephen Dillane (Samuel), Ewen Bremner (James), Kathryn Engels (Narrator), Denis Lawson (Boss), Liz Strange (Pretty Girl), Richard Mack (Apprentice Chef), James Watson (Bus Driver). During a global pandemic where the five human senses stop working one by one – starting with smell – a chef and an epidemiologist fall in love. *Dir*. David Mackenzie.

Perfect Strangers (1945) Robert Donat (Robert Wilson), Deborah Kerr (Catherine Wilson), Glynis Johns (Dizzy Clayton), Ann Todd (Elena), Roland Culver (Richard), Ivor Barnard (Chemist), Muriel George (Minnie), Allan Jeayes (Commander), Eliot Makeham (Mr Staines), Elliott Mason (Mrs Hemmings), Brefni O'Rorke (Mr Hargrove), Edward Rigby (Charlie), Jeanine Carre (Jeannie), Leslie Dwyer (Strupey), Peter Lawford (Introduction - USA Version), Henry B Longhurst (Petty Officer), Roger Moore (Soldier), Mollie Munks (Meg), Harry Ross (Bill), Bill Shine (Webster), Jack Vyvian (Barber). A couple in a humdrum marriage find their outlook transformed when WWII breaks out and he joins the Royal Navy and she becomes a Wren. Their confidence boosted they meet possible alternative partners and then meet up again for the first time after being separated for three years. The film won an Oscar for Best Writing, Original Story (Clemence Dane). *Dir*. Alexander Korda.

Performance (1970) James Fox (Chas/Johnny Dean), Mick Jagger (Mr Turner), Anita Pallenberg (Pherber), Michele Breton (Lucy), Ann Sidney (Dana), John Bindon (Moody), Stanley Meadows (Rosebloom), Allan Cuthertson (The Lawyer), Anthony Morton (Dennis), Johnny Shannon (Harry Flowers), Anthony Valentine (Joey Maddocks), Kenneth Colley (Tony Farrell), John Sterland (The Chauffeur), Laraine Wickens (Lorraine). When psychotic gangster Chas kills a bookmaker his boss has specifically told him not to approach, he hides out in the house of Mr Turner, a burnt out rock star. The film was made in 1968 but not released until 1970. *Dirs*. Donald Cammell and Nicolas Roeg.

Personal Services (1987) Julie Walters (Christine Painter), Shirley Stelfox (Shirley), Alec McCowen (Wing Commander Morten), Danny Schiller (Dolly), Tim Woodward (Timms), Victoria Hardcastle (Rose), Dave Atkins (Sydney), Ewan Hooper (Edward), Alan Bowyer (David Painter), Antony Carrick (Edgar), Beverley Foster (Elizabeth), Leon Lissek (Mr. Popozogolou), Peter Cellier (Mr. Marples), Benjamin Whitrow (Mr. Marsden), Stephen Lewis (Mr. Dunkley), Michelle Collins (June), Toni Palmer (Aunt Winnie), Nigel Le Vaillant (The Man). The story is inspired by Madam Cyn (Cynthia Payne) who ran a brothel in suburban London catering for the special wishes of older clients. *Dir*. Terry Jones.

Peter's Friends (1992) Stephen Fry (Peter Morton), Kenneth Branagh (Andrew Benson), Hugh Laurie (Roger Charleston),

Imelda Staunton (Mary Charleston), Emma Thompson (Maggie Chester), Alphonsia Emmanuel (Sarah Johnson), Rita Rudner (Carol), Ann Davies (Brenda), Tony Slattery (Brian), Nicola Wright (Brian's Wife), Phyllida Law (Vera), Richard Briers (Lord Morton), Alex Scott (Paul - age 7), Alex Lowe (Paul - age 17). Peter's friends from his university comedy group gather at his house for New Year celebrations. *Dir*. Kenneth Branagh.

Petulia (1968) Julie Christie (Petulia Danner), George C. Scott (Dr. Archie Bollen), Richard Chamberlain (David Danner), Arthur Hill (Barney), Shirley Knight (Polo), Pippa Scott (May), Kathleen Widdoes (Wilma), Roger Bowen (Warren), Richard Dysart (Motel Receptionist), Lou Gilbert (Mr. Howard), Nate Esformes (Mr. Mendoza), Maria Val (Mrs. Mendoza), Vincent Arias (Oliver), Eric Weiss (Michael), Kevin Cooper (Stevie), Joseph Cotten (Mr. Danner). Married to an abusive husband, socialite Petulia falls for a doctor in the midst of a divorce. Based on the novel *Me and the Arch Kook Petulia* by John Haase. *Dir*. Richard Lester.

Phantom of the Opera, The (1962) Herbert Lom (The Phantom/Professor Petrie), Heather Sears (Christine Charles), Edward de Souza (Harry Hunter), Michael Gough (Ambrose D'Arcy), Thorley Walters (Lattimer), Harold Goodwin (Bill), Marne Maitland (Xavier), Miriam Karlin (Charwoman), Patrick Troughton (The Rat Catcher), Renee Houston (Mrs. Tucker), Keith Pyott (Weaver). A retelling of the story by Gaston Leroux with the action moved from Paris to London. *Dir*. Terence Fisher.

Piccadilly (1929) Gilda Gray (Mabel Greenfield), Anna May Wong (Shosho), Jameson Thomas (Valentine Wilmot), Charles Laughton (Nightclub Diner), Cyril Ritchard (Victor Smiles), King Hou Chang (Jim), Hannah Jones (Bessie), Gordon Begg (Coroner), John Longden (Man from China), Ray Milland (Extra in Nightclub), Charles Paton (Doorman), Ellen Pollock (Vamp). A story of dancing, romantic entanglements and jealousy which leads to tragedy all set in a restaurant in Piccadilly. *Dir*. Ewald André Dupont.

Piccadilly Incident (1946) Anna Neagle (Diana Fraser), Michael Wilding (Capt Alan Pearson), Frances Mercer (Joan Draper), Coral Browne (Virginia Pearson), A.E. Matthews (Sir Charles Pearson), Edward Rigby (Judd), Brenda Bruce (Sally Benton), Leslie Dwyer (Sam), Maire O'Neill (Mrs Milligan), Michael Laurence (Bill Weston), Reginald Owen (Judge), Michael Medwin (Radio operator), Roger Moore (Guest). Wren Diana marries Alan after a whirlwind wartime romance. Posted to Singapore, her ship is torpedoed and all hands are reported lost. Alan remarries and has a child but is then stunned by Diana's return, she having been washed up on a desert island with a group of sailors for company. *Dir*. Herbert Wilcox.

Pickwick Papers, The (1952) James Hayter (Samuel Pickwick), James Donald (Nathaniel Winkle), Nigel Patrick (Mr. Jingle), Joyce Grenfell (Mrs. Leo Hunter), Hermione Gingold (Miss Tompkins), Hermione Baddeley (Mrs. Bardell), Donald Wolfit (Sergeant Buzfuz), Harry Fowler (Sam Weller), Kathleen Harrison (Rachel Wardle), Alexander Gauge (Tracy Tupman), Lionel Murton (Augustus Snodgrass), Diane Hart (Emily Wardle), Joan Heal (Isabella Wardle), William Hartnell (Irate Cabman), Athene Seyler (Miss Witherfield), Sam Costa (Job Trotter), George Robey (Tony Weller), Gerald Campion (Joe), Walter Fitzgerald (Mr. Wardle), Mary Merrall (Grandma Wardle), Raymond Lovell (Aide), Cecil Trouncer (Mr. Justice Stareleigh), D.A. Clarke-Smith (Dodson), Noel Willman (Mr. Perker), Max Adrian (Aide), Noel Purcell (Roker), Felix Felton (Dr. Slammer), Alan Wheatley (Fogg), Hattie Jacques (Mrs. Nupkins), Jack McNaughton (Mr. Nupkins), June Thorburn (Arabella Allen), Barry MacKay (Mr. Snubbins), Gibb McLaughlin (Foreman), Arthur Mullard (Onlooker), Dandy Nichols (Lady at Ball). Based on the novel of the same name by Charles Dickens. *Dir*. Noel Langley.

Pierrepoint (2006) Timothy Spall (Albert Pierrepoint), Juliet Stevenson (Annie Pierrepoint), Eddie Marsan (James 'Tish' Corbitt), Ben McKay (Timothy Evans), Michael Norton (Josef Kramer), Lizzie Hopley (Dorothea Waddingham), Cavan Clerkin (George Cooper), Christopher Fulford (Charlie Sykes), Ian Shaw (Percy), Maggie Ollerenshaw (Mary Pierrepoint), Claire Keelan (Jessie Kelly), Clive Francis (Field Marshall Montgomery), Sheyla Shehovich (Irma Grese), Keiran Flynn (Neville), Tobias

Menzies (Lieutenant Llewellyn), Mary Stockley (Ruth Ellis), Joyia Fitch (Elisabeth Volkenrath), James Corden (Kirky), Bernard Kay (Uncle Tom), Ann Bell (Violet Van Der Elst), Dominic Kemp (Medical Officer), Frances Shergold (Alice), Jack Lord (Jack Ellis), Jo Gould (Goss), Mary Jo Randle (Mrs. Corbitt), Neil Fitzmaurice (Cliff), Paul Ready (Anthony David Farrow), Peter Jonfield (Mr. Andrews), Robin Soans (Governor Paton-Walsh), Rodney Litchfield (Sellers), Scott Davidson (Josef Kramer), Suzie Sackie (Juana Bormanns), Warren Bertram (Fritz Klein). A biopic of Albert Pierrepoint, Britain's principal hangman from the time of his apprenticeship in the 1920s through WWII, after which he hanged 47 Nazi war criminals, and on to his resignation in 1956. *Dir.* Adrian Shergold.

Pillow Book, The (1996) Ewan McGregor (Jerome), Vivian Wu (Nagiko), Yoshi Oida (The Publisher), Ken Ogata (The Father), Hideko Yoshida (The Aunt/The Maid), Judy Ongg (The Mother), Ken Mitsuishi (The Husband), Yutaka Honda (Hoki), Barbara Lott (Jerome's Mother), Miwako Kawai (Young Nagiko), Lynne Langdon (Jerome's sister), Chizuru Ohnishi (Young Nagiko), Shiho Takamatsu (Young Nagiko), Aki Ishimaru (Young Nagiko). As a child Nagiko's father would write characters of good fortune on her face and on her birthdays he writes on her flesh in beautiful calligraphy, while her aunt reads a list of "beautiful things" from Sei Shōnagon's the book of observations (the "Pillow Book"). In her twenties she now seeks a lover who can match both her sexual desires and her admiration for poetry and calligraphy. *Dir.* Peter Greenaway.

Pimpernel Smith (1941) Leslie Howard (Prof Smith), Allan Jeayes (Dr Benckendorf), Peter Gawthorne (Sidimir Koslowski), Ernest Butcher (Weber), Ben Williams (Graubitz), Arthur Hambling (Jordan), Joan Kemp-Welch (Schoolteacher), Hugh McDermott (David Maxwell), Manning Whiley (Bertie Gregson), Philip Friend (Spencer), Laurence Kitchin (Clarence Elstead), Basil Appleby (Jock MacIntyre), David Tomlinson (Steve), Mary Brown (Student), Aubrey Mallalieu (Dean), W. Phillips (Innkeeper), Ilse Bard (Gretchen), Ernest Verne (German Officer), George Street (Schmidt), Raymond Huntley (Marx), Dennis Arundell (Hoffman), Francis L. Sullivan (Gen von Graum), Hector Abbas (Karl Meyer), Neal Arden (2nd Prisoner), Richard George (Prison Guard), Roddy Hughes (Zigor), Hugh Pryse (Wagner), Roland Pertwee (Embassy Official-Sir George Smith), Oriel Ross (Lady Willoughby), Mary Morris (Ludmilla Koslowski), A.E. Matthews (Earl of Meadowbrook), Percy Walsh (Dvorak), Bryan Herbert (Jaromir), Suzanne Clair (Salesgirl), Charles Paton (Steinhof). Archaeology professor Horatio Smith is supposedly investigating the origins of the Aryan race in Nazi Germany prior to the outbreak of WWII. In fact he, eventually with the help of his students, is releasing prisoners from concentration camps. Released in the US as *Mister V. Dir.* Leslie Howard.

Pink Floyd – The Wall (1982) Bob Geldof (Pink), Kevin McKeon (Young Pink), David Bingham (Little Pink), Christine Hargreaves (Pink's mother), Eleanor David (Pink's wife), Alex McAvoy (Teacher), Bob Hoskins (Rock-and-roll manager), Michael Ensign (Hotel manager), James Laurenson (J.A. Pinkerton - Pink's father), Margery Mason (Teacher's wife), Ellis Dale (Doctor), James Hazeldine (Lover), Jenny Wright, Joanne Whalley, Nell Campbell, Emma Longfellow, Lorna Barton (Groupies). A live-action/animated musical film based on the 1979 Pink Floyd album. It contains animations by Gerald Scarfe. *Dir.* Alan Parker.

Pit of Darkness (1961) William Franklyn (Richard Logan), Moira Redmond (Julie Logan), Bruno Barnabe (Maxie), Leonard Sachs (Clifton Conrad), Nigel Green (Jonathan), Bruce Beeby (Peter Mayhew), Humphrey Lestocq (Bill Underwood), Anthony Booth (Ted Mellis), Nanette Newman (Mary), Michael Balfour (Fisher), Jacqueline Jones (Mavis). A safe designer wakes up on waste ground with complete memory loss and finds out that he has been missing for three weeks, during which time a supposedly foolproof safe of his design has been opened. *Dir.* Lance Comfort.

Place of One's Own, A (1945) Margaret Lockwood (Annette), James Mason (Smedhurst), Barbara Mullen (Mrs Smedhurst),

Dennis Price (Dr Selbie), Helen Haye (Mrs Manning Tutthorn), Michael Shepley (Maj Manning Tutthorn), Dulcie Gray (Sarah), Moore Marriott (George), O.B. Clarence (Perkins), Helen Goss (Barmaid), Edie Martin (Cook), Gus McNaughton (PC Hargreaves), Muriel George (Nurse), John Turnbull (Sir Roland Jervis), Ernest Thesiger (Dr Marsham), Henry B. Longhurst (Inspector), Clarence Wright (Brighouse), Aubrey Mallalieu (Canon Mowbray). Ghost story in which a middle-aged couple buy an old house in the country which has been standing empty for 40 years. The wife's young companion soon begins to hear strange voices. *Dir.* Bernard Knowles.

Plague of the Zombies, The (1964) André Morell (Sir James Forbes), Diane Clare (Sylvia Forbes), Brook Williams (Dr Peter Tompson), Jacqueline Pearce (Alice Mary Tompson), John Carson (Squire Clive Hamilton), Alexander Davion (Denver), Michael Ripper (Sgt Jack Swift), Marcus Hammond (Tom Martinus), Dennis Chinnery (PC Christian), Roy Royston (Vicar), Louis Mahoney (Coloured Servant), Ben Aris (John Martinus). In 19th century Cornwall, a squire, who has lived most of his life in Haiti, is practicing voodoo on the locals and creating zombies. He now has his eye on Sylvia, the daughter of a man investigating the deaths of the villagers. *Dir.* John Gilling.

Plank, The (1967) Eric Sykes, Tommy Cooper, Jimmy Edwards, Roy Castle, Jimmy Tarbuck, Anna Carteret, John Junkin, Bill Oddie, Stratford Johns, Graham Stark, Jim Dale, Hattie Jacques, Rex Garner, Libby Morris, Joan Young, Barney Gilbraith, Clovissa Newcombe, Ronnie Brody, Johnny Speight, Kenny Lynch. A virtually silent short film except for sound effects and grunts as two builders try to get a plank back to the house they are working on. The plank used was sold at auction in 2011 for £1050. *Dir.* Eric Sykes.

Planter's Wife, The (1952) Claudette Colbert (Liz Frazer), Jack Hawkins (Jim Frazer), Anthony Steel (Hugh Dobson), Ram Gopal (Nair), Jeremy Spenser (Mat), Tom Macaulay (Jack Bushell), Helen Goss (Eleanor Bushell), Sonya Hana (Ah Mov), Andy Ho (Wan Li), Peter Asher (Mike Frazer), Yah Ming (Ah Siong), Shaym Bahadur (Putra), Ng Cheuk Kwong (Ho Tang), Bryan Coleman (Capt Dell), Don Sharp (Lt Summers), Maria Baillie (Arminah), Bill Travers (Planter), John Stamp (Len Carter), John Martin (Harry), Myrette Morven (Mildred Saunders), Alfie Bass (Soldier), Victor Maddern (Radio operator). Set during the Malayan Emergency, a rubber planter and his wife defend their homestead against terrorists. *Dir.* Ken Annakin.

Please Sir! (1971) John Alderton (Bernard Hedges), Deryck Guyler (Norman Potter), Noel Howlett (Maurice Cromwell), Joan Sanderson (Doris Ewell), Richard Davies (Mr Price), Erik Chitty (Mr Smith), Patsy Rowlands (Angela Cutforth), Peter Cleall (Eric Duffy), Carol Hawkins (Sharon Eversleigh), Liz Gebhardt (Maureen Bullock), David Barry (Frankie Abbott), Peter Denyer (Dennis Dunstable), Malcolm McFee (Peter Craven), Aziz Resham (Feisal), Brinsley Forde (Wesley), Jill Kerman (Penny Wheeler), Norman Bird (Reynolds), Barbara Mitchell (Mrs Abbott), Peter Bayliss (Mr Dunstable), Eve Pearce (Mrs Dunstable), Jack Smethurst (Bus Driver), Brenda Cowling (Mrs Duffy), Nicholas Locise (Nobbler), Richard Everett (Malcolm), Hayden Evans (Parsons), Fred Beauman (Joe), Daphne Heard (Old gypsy). Fenn Street School's Class 5c is taken on a two-week trip to an activity centre in the country. Spin-off from the ITV sitcom. *Dir.* Mark Stuart.

Please Turn Over (1959) Ted Ray (Edward Halliday), Jean Kent (Janet Halliday), Leslie Phillips (Dr. Henry Manners), Joan Sims (Beryl), Julia Lockwood (Jo Halliday), Tim Seely (Robert Hughes), Charles Hawtrey (Jeweler), Dilys Laye (Millicent Jones), Lionel Jeffries (Ian Howard), June Jago (Gladys Worth), Colin Gordon (Maurice), Joan Hickson (Saleswoman), Victor Maddern (Manager), Ronald Adam (Mr. Appleton), Cyril Chamberlain (Mr. Jones), Myrtle Reed (Mrs. Moore), Marianne Stone (Mrs. Waring), Leigh Madison (Cashier), Anthony Sagar (Barman), George Street (Removal Man), Noel Dyson (Mrs. Brent), Paul Cole (Newspaper Boy), Celia Hewitt (Young Woman), George Howell (Butcher's Boy). A comedy in which the apparently respectable residents of suburbia are surprised when Jo

Halliday publishes a novel called *The Naked Revolt* which she claims is based on the people in her community and in particular, her family. Based on the play *Book of the Month* by Basil Thomas. *Dir*. Gerald Thomas

Pleasure Girls, The (1965) Francesca Annis (Sally), Anneke Wills (Angela), Tony Tanner (Paddy), Rosemary Nicols (Marion), Suzanna Leigh (Dee), Colleen Fitzpatrick (Cobber), Hal Hamilton (Peter 'E'-Type), Ian McShane (Keith Dexter), Mark Eden (Prinny), Klaus Kinski (Nikko Stalmar), Jonathan Hansen (Ivor), Carol Cleveland (Ella), Yvonne Antrobus (Waitress), Julian Holloway (Hanger-on), Hugh Futcher (Pablo), Kate Binchy (Nurse), Tony Doonan (Reilly), Peter Diamond (Rat-Face), Brian Cant (Man in pub). A girl looking for a career in modelling moves to London during the Swinging Sixties. *Dir*. Gerry O'Hara.

Plunkett & Macleane (1999) Jonny Lee Miller (Capt James Macleane), Robert Carlyle (Will Plunkett), Liv Tyler (Lady Rebecca Gibson), Ken Stott (Thief Taker Chance), Alan Cumming (Lord Rochester), Michael Gambon (Lord Gibson), Tommy Flanagan (Eddie), David Walliams (Viscount Bilston), Matt Lucas (Sir Oswald), Alexander Armstrong (Winterburn), Ben Miller (Dixon), Noel Fielding (Brothel Gent), Nicholas Farrell (M.P.s Secretary), Iain Robertson (Highwayman Rob), Stephen Walters (Dennis), James Thornton (Catchpole), Terence Rigby (Harrison), Christian Camargo (Lord Pelham), Karel Polisenský (Newgate Priest), Neve McIntosh (Liz), David Foxxe (Lord Ketch), Claire Rushbrook (Lady Estelle), Tim McMullan (Bridegroom), Jeff Nuttall (Lord Morris), Dana Jurzova (Duchess of Stoke), Martin Serene (Josh), Victoria Harrison (Maria), Susan Porrett (Lady Newbold), Nichola McAuliffe (Lady Crombie), Anna Keaveney (Lady Marchant), Michael Culkin (Judge Beresteade). After the death of his partner in crime, highwayman Will Plunkett teams up with Captain Macleane but General Chance is on their trail. *Dir*. Jake Scott.

Pool of London (1951) Bonar Colleano (Dan MacDonald), Earl Cameron (Johnny Lambert), Susan Shaw (Pat), Renée Asherson (Sally), Moira Lister (Maisie), Max Adrian (Charlie Vernon/George), Joan Dowling (Pamela, Maisie's sister), James Robertson Justice (Engine Room Officer Trotter), Michael Golden (Customs Officer Andrews), Alfie Bass (Alf, a henchman), Christopher Hewett (Mike), Leslie Phillips (Harry, a sailor), John Longden (Det Insp Williams), Beckett Bould (The Murdered Watchman), Victor Maddern (First Tram Conductor), Laurence Naismith (Commissionaire), Sam Kydd (2nd Engineer), George Merritt (Captain of Dunbar), Arthur Mullard (Seaman on the Dunbar), Campbell Singer (Station Sgt). The merchant ship *Dunbar* docks in London and its crew goes ashore for the weekend, becoming involved in smuggling and petty crime. *Dir*. Basil Dearden.

Poor Cow (1967) Carol White (Joy), John Bindon (Tom), Queenie Watts (Aunt Emm), Kate Williams (Beryl), James Beckett (Tom's mate), Ellis Dale (Solicitor), Gladys Dawson (Bet), Anna Karen (Neighbour), Billy Murray (Tom's mate), Ron Pember (Petal), Phillip Ross (Shelley), Geraldine Sherman (Trixie), Gerald Young (Judge), Terence Stamp (Dave Fuller), Tony Selby and Wally Patch (Customers in Pub). The ironically named Joy runs-off with the criminal and abusive Tom when only eighteen, has a son, Johnny, and eventually has to resort to prostitution to make ends meet. *Dir*. Ken Loach.

Pope Must Die, The (1991) Robbie Coltrane (The Pope), Alex Rocco (Cardinal Rocco), Adrian Edmondson (Father Rookie), Paul Bartel (Monsignor Fitchie), Peter Richardson (Bish), Annette Crosbie (Mother Superior), Herbert Lom (Vittorio Corelli), Balthazar Getty (Joe Don Dante), Damir Mejovsek (Drunk Cardinal), Bozidar Smiljanic (Cardinal Spott), William Hootkins (Cardinal Verucci), Robert Stephens (Carmelengo), Janez Vajevec (Father Albini), Jeff Beck (Postman), John Sessions (Dino), Beverly D'Angelo (Veronica Dante). When the papal conclave mistakenly fails to elect the Mafia's candidate as Pope, the Mob decide that the new Pope must die. *Dir*. Peter Richardson.

Porridge (1979) Ronnie Barker (Norman Stanley Fletcher), Richard Beckinsale (Lennie Godber), Fulton Mackay (Mackay), Brian Wilde (Barrowclough), Peter Vaughan (Grouty), Geoffrey Bayldon (Treadaway – Governor), Christopher Godwin (Beal), Barrie Rutter (Oakes), Daniel Peacock (Rudge), Sam Kelly (Warren), Julian Holloway (Bainbridge), Ken Jones (Ives), Philip Locke (Banyard), Gorden Kaye (Dines), Karl Howman (Urquhart), Derek Deadman (Cooper), Tony Osoba (McClaren), Oliver Smith (McMillan), Zoot Money (Lotterby). After reluctantly breaking out of prison Fletch and Godber must break back in. Spin-off from the BBC sitcom. *Dir*. Dick Clement.

Portrait of Alison (1955) Terry Moore (Alison Ford), Robert Beatty (Tim Forrester), William Sylvester (Dave Forrester), Josephine Griffin (Jill Stewart), Geoffrey Keen (Insp Colby), William Lucas (Reg Dorking), Allan Cuthbertson (Henry Carmichael), Henry Oscar (John Smith), Terence Alexander (Fenby). Diamond smuggling gang murder a man who was about to expose them. The man's brother and an apparently dead actress investigate. Based on a TV programme of the same name. *Dir*. Guy Green.

Press for Time (1966) Norman Wisdom (Norman Shields/Emily Shields/Wilfred), Frances White (Liz Corcoran), Derek Bond (Maj. R.E. Bartlett), Angela Browne (Eleanor Lampton), Tracey Crisp (Ruby Fairchild), Allan Cuthbertson (Mr. Ballard), Noel Dyson (Mrs. Corcoran), Derek Francis (Ernest Corcoran), Peter Jones (Robin Willobey), David Lodge (Mr. Ross), Stanley Unwin (Mr. Nottage), Michael Balfour (Sewerman), Tony Selby (Harry Marshall), Hazel Coppen (Granny Fork), Totti Truman Taylor (Mrs. Doe Connor), Toni Gilpin (P.M.'s secretary), Gordon Rollings (Bus conductor), Imogen Hassall (Suffragette), Helen Mirren (Penelope Squires). Newspaper seller Norman is the grandson of the Prime Minister. His grandfather gets him a job as a cub reporter on the local paper in the seaside town of Tinmouth, with, as you might expect in a Norman Wisdom film, hilarious results. Helen Mirren makes an early appearance as a beauty contest entrant. Based on the book *Yea, Yea, Yea* by Angus McGill. *Dir*. Robert Asher.

Pride & Prejudice (2005) Keira Knightley (Elizabeth Bennet), Matthew Macfadyen (Mr. Darcy), Donald Sutherland (Mr. Bennet), Brenda Blethyn (Mrs. Bennet), Rosamund Pike (Jane Bennet), Talulah Riley (Mary Bennet), Carey Mulligan (Catherine "Kitty" Bennet), Jena Malone (Lydia Bennet), Simon Woods (Mr. Charles Bingley), Kelly Reilly (Caroline Bingley), Rupert Friend (Mr. George Wickham), Tom Hollander (Mr. William Collins), Claudie Blakley (Charlotte Lucas), Judi Dench (Lady Catherine de Bourgh), Rosamund Stephen (Anne de Bourgh), Cornelius Booth (Colonel Fitzwilliam), Penelope Wilton (Mrs. Gardiner), Peter Wight (Mr. Gardiner), Meg Wynn Owen (Mrs. Reynolds), Tamzin Merchant (Georgiana Darcy), Sinead Matthews (Betsy). An adaptation of the novel by Jane Austen centring on the proud Mr Darcy and the prejudiced Elizabeth Bennet. *Dir*. Joe Wright.

Priest (1994) Linus Roache (Father Greg Pilkington), Tom Wilkinson (Father Matthew Thomas), Robert Carlyle (Graham), Cathy Tyson (Maria Kerrigan), Christine Tremarco (Lisa Unsworth), Robert Pugh (Mr Unsworth), Lesley Sharp (Mrs Unsworth), James Ellis (Father Ellerton), Paul Barber (Charlie), Rio Fanning (Bishop), Jim R. Coleman (Funeral director), Gilly Coman (Ellie Molloy), Fred Pearson (Patrick), Jimmy Gallagher (Mick Molloy), Anthony Booth (Tommy), Kim Johnson (Mrs Gobshite), Keith Cole (Mr Gobshite), Valerie Lilley (Sister Kevin), John Bennett (Father Redstone). A priest struggles with a colleagues' breaking of the celibacy vows as well as his own homosexuality. *Dir*. Antonia Bird.

Prime Minister, The (1941) John Gielgud (Benjamin Disraeli), Diana Wynyard (Mary Disraeli), Will Fyffe (The Agitator), Owen Nares (Lord Derby), Fay Compton (Queen Victoria), Pamela Standish (Princess Victoria), Stephen Murray (Mr. W.E. Gladstone), Frederick Leister (Lord Melbourne), Nicholas Hannen (Sir Robert Peel), Anthony Ireland (Count D'Orsay), Irene Browne (Lady Londonderry), Joss Ambler (Earl of Carnarvon), Vera Bogetti (Lady Blessington), Barbara Everest (Baroness Lehzen), Lyn Harding (Bismarck), Gordon McLeod (John Brown), Leslie Perrins (Earl of Salisbury), Kynaston Reeves (Lord Stanley). A biopic of 19th Century British Prime Minister Benjamin Disraeli. *Dir*. Thorold Dickinson.

Prime of Miss Jean Brodie, The (1969) Maggie Smith(Jean Brodie), Robert Stephens (Teddy Lloyd), Pamela Franklin (Sandy), Gordon Jackson (Gordon Lowther), Celia Johnson (Miss Mackay), Diane Grayson (Jenny), Jane Carr (Mary McGregor), Shirley Steedman (Monica), Lavinia Lang (Emily Carstairs), Antoinette Biggerstaff (Helen McPhee), Margo Cunningham

(Miss Campbell), Isla Cameron (Miss McKenzie), Rona Anderson (Miss Lockhart), Ann Way (Miss Gaunt), Molly Weir (Miss Allison Kerr), Helena Gloag (Miss Kerr), Heather Seymour (Clara). Set in Edinburgh in the 1930s, Jean Brodie is a teacher at the Marcia Blaine School for Girls who uses unorthodox practices. She pays particular attention to the four girls in the "Brodie Set": Sandy, Monica, Jenny and Mary. However, her methods and her love life do not meet with the approval of everyone at the school. Based on Muriel Spark's novel. Maggie Smith won a Best Actress Oscar for her titular role. *Dir.* Ronald Neame.

Prince and the Pauper, The (1977) Oliver Reed (Miles Hendon), Raquel Welch (Lady Edith), Mark Lester (Edward/Tom), Charlton Heston (Henry VIII), Ernest Borgnine (John Canty), George C. Scott (Ruffler), Rex Harrison (The Duke of Norfolk), David Hemmings (Hugh Hendon), Harry Andrews (Hertford), Julian Orchard (St.John), Murray Melvin (Prince's Dresser), Lalla Ward (Princess Elizabeth), Felicity Dean (Lady Jane), Sybil Danning (Mother Canty), Graham Stark (Jester), Preston Lockwood (Father Andrew), Arthur Hewlett (Fat Man), Tommy Wright (Constable), Harry Fowler (Nipper), Richard Hurndall (Archbishop Cranmer), Don Henderson (Burly Ruffian), Sydney Bromley (Peasant), Ruth Madoc (Moll), Dudley Sutton (Hodge), Roy Evans (Night Owl), William Lawford (Mandrake), Peter O'Farrell (Linklight), Anthony Sharp (Dr. Buttes), Peter Cellier (Mean Man), Andrew Lodge (Captain of the Guard), Igor De Savitch (Master of Music), Dervis Ward (Forester), Michael Ripper (Edith's Servant), Jacques Le Carpentier (The Mute). Based on Mark Twain's story in which a pauper swaps places with the future King Edward VI. Released as *Crossed Swords* in the US. *Dir.* Richard Fleischer.

Prisoner, The (1955) Alec Guinness (The Cardinal), Jack Hawkins (The Interrogator), Wilfrid Lawson (The Jailer), Kenneth Griffith (The Secretary), Jeanette Sterke (The Girl), Ronald Lewis (The Guard), Raymond Huntley (The General), Mark Dignam (The Governor), Gerard Heinz (The Doctor). In a totalitarian state a popular cardinal is arrested for treason against the state. What follows is a battle of wills between the cardinal and his interrogator. *Dir.* Peter Glenville.

Private Angelo (1949) Peter Ustinov (Private Angelo), Godfrey Tearle (Count Piccologrando), Maria Denis (Lucrezia), Marjorie Rhodes (Countess), James Robertson Justice (Feste), Moyna MacGill (Marchesa Dolce), Robin Bailey (Simon Telfer), Harry Locke (Cpl Trivet), Bill Shine (Col Michael), John Harvey (Cpl McCunn), Diana Graves (Lucia). The misadventures of an Italian soldier during WWII. Adapted from the novel by Eric Linklater *Dirs.* Michael Anderson and Peter Ustinov.

Private Function, A (1984) Michael Palin (Gilbert Chilvers), Maggie Smith (Joyce Chilvers), Denholm Elliott (Dr Charles Swaby), Richard Griffiths (Henry Allardyce), Tony Haygarth (Leonard Sutcliff), John Normington (Frank Lockwood), Bill Paterson (Morris Wormold), Liz Smith (Joyce's Mother), Alison Steadman (Mrs Allardyce), Pete Postlethwaite (Douglas J. Nuttol), Jim Carter (Insp Noble), Rachel Davies (Mrs Forbes), Eileen O'Brien (Mrs Sutcliff), Reece Dinsdale (PC Penny), Philip Whileman (Preston Sutcliff), Charles McKeown (Medcalf), Susan Porrett (Mrs Dorcus Medcalf), Donald Eccles (Dorcus' Father), Denys Hawthorne (Grand Hotel Manager), Don Estelle (Barraclough), Eli Woods (Ernest), Amanda Gregan (Veronica Allardyce). As rationing continues in England after WWII, locals illegally raise a pig to kill to celebrate a royal wedding. Then somebody steals the pig. *Dir.* Malcolm Mowbray.

Private Life of Don Juan, The (1934) Douglas Fairbanks (Don Juan), Merle Oberon (Antonita), Bruce Winston (Cafe manager), Gina Malo (Pepita), Benita Hume (Dona Dolores), Binnie Barnes (Rosita), Melville Cooper (Leporello), Owen Nares (Antonio Martinez), Heather Thatcher (Anna Dora), Diana Napier (Lady of Sentiment), Joan Gardner (Carmen), Gibson Gowland (Don Alfredo), Barry MacKay (Rodrigo, the Impostor), Claud Allister (The Duke), Athene Seyler (Theresa), Hindle Edgar (Don Alfredo), Natalie Paley (Jealous Husband's Wife), Patricia Hilliard (Girl at the Castle), Lawrence Grossmith (Pedo), Morland Graham (Hector), Edmund Breon (Cardona). Ageing Don Juan returns to Seville but is threatened with jail by his wife. When an imposter is killed he attends his own funeral and decides that playing dead might be the solution to his problems. *Dir.* Alexander Korda.

Private Life of Henry VIII, The (1933) Charles Laughton (Henry VIII), Merle Oberon (Anne Boleyn), Wendy Barrie (Jane Seymour), Elsa Lanchester (Anne of Cleves), Binnie Barnes (Catherine Howard), Robert Donat (Thomas Culpeper), Franklin Dyall (Thomas Cromwell), Miles Mander (Wriothesley), Laurence Hanray (Archbishop Thomas Cranmer), William Austin (The Duke of Cleves), John Loder (Thomas Peynell), Everley Gregg (Catherine Parr). Charles Laughton *is* Henry VIII – well he certainly defined what Henry was apparently like in people's minds for many years after this film, especially the throwing of chicken bones over the shoulder during meals. The film is actually a rapid gallop through his many nuptials, omitting his divorced first wife, Catherine of Aragon, and starting with the execution of Anne Boleyn (wife number 2 – beheaded), and carrying on through Jane Seymour (died), Anne of Cleves (divorced), Catherine Howard (beheaded) and ending in old age with his marriage to Catherine Parr (survived). The film won one Academy Award: Best Actor in a Leading Role (Charles Laughton) and was the first British production to be nominated for the Academy Award for Best Picture. *Dir.* Alexander Korda.

Private Life of Sherlock Holmes, The (1970) Robert Stephens (Sherlock Holmes), Colin Blakely (Dr. John H. Watson), Geneviève Page (Gabrielle Valladon), Christopher Lee (Mycroft Holmes), Irene Handl (Mrs. Hudson), Clive Revill (Rogozhin), Tamara Toumanova (Madame Petrova), Stanley Holloway (1st Gravedigger), Mollie Maureen (Queen Victoria), Catherine Lacey (Old Woman), James Copeland (the guide), Jenny Hanley (a prostitute). A beautiful woman is fished half-drowned out of the Thames and begs Holmes to help her find her missing husband, an engineer. The trail leads Holmes and Watson to Scotland and in the process they cross paths with monks, midgets and the Loch Ness monster. Sherlock's smarter elder brother (by 7 years) Mycroft appears to hold the clue to the mystery. *Dir.* Billy Wilder.

Private's Progress (1956) Ian Carmichael (Pte Stanley Windrush), Ronald Adam (Doctor at Medical), Henry B. Longhurst (Mr Spottiswood), Peter Jones (Arthur Egan), Dennis Price (Brig Bertram Tracepurcel), Miles Malleson (Mr Windrush), Sally Miles (Catherine), David King-Wood (Gerald), Derrick De Marney (Pat), William Hartnell (Sgt Sutton), Brian Oulton (M.O. at Gravestone Camp), Michael Trubshawe (Col Fanshawe), John Le Mesurier (Psychiatrist), Jill Adams (Prudence Greenslade), Terry-Thomas (Maj Hitchcock), Thorley Walters (Capt Henry Bootle), John Warren (Sgt Maj Gradwick), Richard Attenborough (Pte Percy Cox), Ian Bannen (Pte Horrocks), Victor Maddern (Pte George Blake), Kenneth Griffith (Pte Dai Jones), George Coulouris (Padre), Basil Dignam (Col Martin), Glyn Houston (Cpl on Sick Call), Gerald Fox (Faceache), Christopher Lee (Maj Schultz), David Lodge (Lance Cpl Parsons), Wally Patch (Barman), Marianne Stone (Miss Sugden). Stanley Windrush is called up towards the end of the war and proves not to be office calibre. However, with the army staffed with men on the make such as Private Cox and Brigadier Tracepurcel, incompetence is no barrier to progress. Based on Alan Hackney's novel. *Dir.* John Boulting.

Prize of Arms, A (1962) Stanley Baker (Turpin), Helmut Schmid (Swavek), Tom Bell (Fenner), John Phillips (Colonel Fowler), Patrick Magee (Regimental Sergeant Major Hicks), John Westbrook (Captain Stafford), Jack May (Medical Officer), Frank Gatliff (Major Palmer), Michael Ripper (Corporal Freeman), John Rees (Sergeant Jones), Tom Adams (Corporal Glenn), Anthony Bate (Sergeant Reeves), Rodney Bewes (Private Maynard), Douglas Blackwell (Day), Glynn Edwards (Breakdown truck crewman), Stephen Lewis (Military Police Corporal), Fulton Mackay (Corporal Henderson), Stanley Meadows (Sergeant White), Garfield Morgan and Geoffrey Palmer (Military Policemen), Michael Robbins (Orford). A gang plan to steal an army payroll during the 1956 Suez Crisis. *Dir.* Cliff Owen.

Prospero's Books (1991) John Gielgud (Prospero), Michael Clark (Caliban), Michel Blanc (Alonso), Erland Josephson (Gonzalo), Isabelle Pasco (Miranda), Tom Bell (Antonio), Kenneth Cranham (Sebastian), Mark Rylance (Ferdinand), Gerard Thoolen (Adrian), Pierre Bokma (Francisco), Jim van der Woude (Trinculo), Michiel Romeyn (Stephano), Paul Russell (Ariel), James Thiérrée (Ariel), Orpheo (Ariel), Emil Wolk (Ariel), Marie Angel (Iris), Ute Lemper (Ceres), Deborah Conway (Juno). An interpretation of Shakespeare's *The Tempest. Dir.* Peter Greenaway.

Prudence and the Pill (1968) Deborah Kerr (Prudence Hardcastle), David Niven (Gerald Hardcastle), Robert Coote (Henry Hardcastle), Irina Demick (Elizabeth Brett), Joyce Redman (Grace Hardcastle), Judy Geeson (Geraldine Hardcastle), Keith Michell (Dr. Alan Hewitt), Edith Evans (Lady Roberta Bates), David Dundas (Tony Bates), Vickery Turner (Rose), Hugh Armstrong (Ted), Peter Butterworth (Chemist), Annette Kerr (Gerald's Secretary), Harry Towb (Racetrack Official). A film set firmly in the late 1960s. Women who think they are taking the contraceptive pill are in fact taking aspirin because various people for various reasons are making the switch. Based on a novel by Hugh Mills. *Dirs.* Fielder Cook and Ronald Neame.

Psychomania (1972) Nicky Henson (Tom Latham), Beryl Reid (Mrs Latham), George Sanders (Shadwell), Robert Hardy (Chief Inspr Heseltine), Mary Larkin (Abby Holman), Ann Michelle (Jane Pettibone), Roy Holder (Bertram), Denis Gilmore (Hatchet), Miles Greenwood (Chopped Meat), Peter Whitting (Gash), Rocky Taylor (Hinky), Patrick Holt (Sgt), Alan Bennion (PC), John Levene (PC), Jacki Webb (Mother), David Millett (Father), Roy Evans (Motorist), Bill Pertwee (Publican), Lane Meddick (Mr Pettibone), June Brown (Mrs Pettibone). Tom is the leader of a violent teen motorcycle gang, calling itself "The Living Dead", whilst his mother holds séances. Tom makes a pact with the devil to return from the dead (as you do) and members of the gang commit suicide, coming back as the undead. Also known as *The Death Wheelers*. George Sanders final film. *Dir.* Don Sharp.

Pumpkin Eater, The (1964) Anne Bancroft (Jo Armitage), Peter Finch (Jake Armitage), James Mason (Bob Conway), Janine Gray (Beth Conway), Cedric Hardwicke (Mr. James), Rosalind Atkinson (Mrs. James), Alan Webb (Mr. Armitage), Richard Johnson (Giles), Maggie Smith (Philpott), Eric Porter (Psychiatrist), Cyril Luckham (Doctor), Anthony Nicholls (Surgeon), John Franklyn-Robbins (Parson), John Junkin (Undertaker), Yootha Joyce (Woman at hairdresser's). Married three times and with a plethora of children, Jo is certain that her latest husband is being unfaithful and both partners feel the need to examine their marriage in more detail. Adapted by Harold Pinter from the novel by Penelope Mortimer. *Dir.* Jack Clayton.

Punch and Judy Man, The (1963) Tony Hancock (Wally), Sylvia Syms (Delia Pinner), Ronald Fraser (Mayor), Barbara Murray (Lady Caterham), John Le Mesurier (The Sandman), Norman Bird (Committee Man), Kevin Brennan (Landlord), Eddie Byrne (Ice Cream Assistant), Norman Chappell (Footman), Mario Fabrizi (Nevile Shanks), Carole Ann Ford (Girl in Kiosk), Gerald Harper (First Drunk), Hattie Jacques (Dolly Zarathusa), Hugh Lloyd (Edward Cox), Michael Ripper (Waiter), Peter Vaughan (Committee Man). Punch and Judy Man Wally Pinner is beset with a social climbing wife and the fact that he and his fellow beach front entertainers are no longer considered acceptable by the local council. An unexpected invitation to an official reception does not end well. *Dir.* Jeremy Summers.

Pure Hell of St Trinian's, The (1960) Cecil Parker (Prof Canford), George Cole ('Flash' Harry Cuthbert Edwards), Joyce Grenfell (Sgt Ruby Gates), Eric Barker (Culpepper-Brown), Thorley Walters (Butters), Irene Handl (Miss Harker-Parker), Dennis Price (Gore Blackwood), Sid James (Alphonse O'Reilly), Julie Alexander (Rosalie Dawn), Lloyd Lamble (Supt Samuel Kemp-Bird), Raymond Huntley (Judge), Nicholas Phipps (Major), Lisa Lee (Miss Brenner), John Le Mesurier (Minister of Education), George Benson (Defence Counsel), Elwyn Brook-Jones (Emir), Cyril Chamberlain (Army Captain), Michael Ripper (Liftman), Mark Dignam (Prosecuting Counsel), Monte Landis (Octavius), Warren Mitchell (Tailor), Clive Morton (V.I.P.), Wensley Pithey (Chief Constable), Bill Shine (Usher), Harold Berens (British Consul), Liz Fraser (WPC Susan Partridge), Sally Douglas (Harem Girl), Jill Gascoine (St Trinians Girl), Erica Rogers (Bobbie), Edina Ronay (Lavinia), Ann Wain (Lolita Chatterly). The girls are found innocent of burning down the school but are put in the custody of a dodgy professor. In no time the sixth form is on its way to the Middle East to be a sheik's harem, pursued by the Ministry of Education, the police and, of course, the formidable fourth form girls. *Dir* Frank Launder

Purely Belter (2000) Chris Beattie (Gerry McCarten), Greg McLane (Sewell), Charlie Hardwick (Mrs. McCarten), Roy Hudd (Mr. Sewell), Tim Healy (Mr. McCarten), Kevin Whately (Mr. Caird), Jody Baldwin (Gemma), Kerry Ann Christiansen (Bridget), Tracy Whitwell (Clare), Kate Garbutt (Baby Sheara), Laura Garbutt (Baby Sheara), Su Elliot (Mrs. Brabbin), Daniel James Lake (Matthew Brabin), Tracey Wilkinson (Mrs. Caird), Libby Davison (Miss Warren), Val McLane (Maureen), Willie Ross (Ginga), Adam Fogerty (Zak), Jo-Anne Horan (Waterstone's assistant), Anne Orwin (Auntie Maud), Rebekah Joy Gilgan (Cashier), Lynne Wilmot (Cashier), Michael Hodgson (Business man), Bill Gerard (Policeman), Phil Swinburne (Policeman), Joyce Gibbs (Magistrate), Christopher Connel (Vicar), Veronica Twidle (Old dear), Alan Shearer (Himself), Charlie Richmond (Mally), Chris Wiper (Jimmy), Richard Dawson (Bright boy), Helen Parker (Bright girl), Adam Moran (Darren), Anna-Marie Gascoigne (Dinner lady), Joanne Hickson (Janine), Madeleine Moffat (Mrs. Harvey). A comedy drama in which two likeable Geordie youngsters try to get money, by any means necessary, in order to get season tickets for Newcastle United FC. *Dir.* Mark Herman.

Purple Plain (1954) Gregory Peck (Squadron Leader Bill Forrester), Win Min Than (Anna), Brenda De Banzie (Miss McNab), Bernard Lee (Dr. Harris), Maurice Denham (Blore), Lyndon Brook (Carrington), Anthony Bushell (Col Aldridge), Josephine Griffin (Mrs. Bill Forrester), Ram Gopal (Mr. Phang), Peter Arne (Flight Lieutenant), Jack McNaughton (Sgt. Ralph Brown), Harold Siddons (Navigator Williams), Mya Mya Spencer (Dorothy). During operations flying a Mosquito in Burma during WWII, Squadron Leader Forrester is struggling to come to terms with the death of his wife in the London Blitz. On a routine flight his plane with two other crewmen on board is forced to ditch in Burma's central plain. *Dir.* Robert Parrish.

Pygmalion (1938) Leslie Howard (Professor Henry Higgins), Wendy Hiller (Eliza Doolittle), Wilfrid Lawson (Alfred Doolittle), Marie Lohr (Mrs. Higgins), Scott Sunderland (Colonel George Pickering), Jean Cadell (Mrs. Pearce), David Tree (Freddy Eynsford-Hill), Everley Gregg (Mrs. Eynsford-Hill), Leueen MacGrath (Clara Eynsford Hill), Esme Percy (Count Aristid Karpathy), Violet Vanbrugh (Ambassadress), Iris Hoey (Ysabel), Viola Tree (Perfide), Irene Browne (Duchess), Wally Patch (First Bystander), Leo Genn (Prince), Patrick Macnee (Extra), Anthony Quayle (Eliza's Hairdresser). In a satire on the rigid British class system of the day, Professor of phonetics Henry Higgins makes a bet that he can pass off cockney flower girl Eliza Doolittle as a duchess at an ambassador's garden party. The film won an Academy Award for Best Writing, Screenplay. It is based on the George Bernard Shaw play of the same name and adapted by him for the screen. It was later turned into the musical *My Fair Lady*. *Dirs.* Anthony Asquith and Leslie Howard.

Q Planes (1939) Laurence Olivier (Tony McVane), Ralph Richardson (Maj. Charles Hammond), Valerie Hobson (Kay Lawrence), George Curzon (Jenkins), George Merritt (Mr. Barrett), Gus McNaughton (Blenkinsop), David Tree (R. Mackenzie), Sandra Storme (Daphne), Hay Petrie (Stage Door Keeper), Frank Fox (Karl), George Butler (Air Marshal Gosport), Gordon McLeod (The Baron), John Longden (John Peters), Ronald Adam (Pollack), Patrick Aherne (Officer), Mark Daly (John), Roy Emerton (Viking First Mate), David Farrar (Viking Bo'sun), Ian Fleming (Air Ministry Officer), John Laurie (Newspaper Editor), Herbert Lomas (Mattie), Lewis Stringer (Foreign Agent), Jack Vyvian (Police Sergeant). British experimental bombers are disappearing on test flights and espionage is suspected. Hammond of the Yard is brought in to investigate. Released in the US as *Clouds Over Europe. Dirs.* Tim Whelan and Arthur B. Woods.

Quadrophenia (1979) Phil Daniels (Jimmy Cooper), Leslie Ash (Steph), Philip Davis (Chalky), Mark Wingett (Dave), Sting (Ace

Face), Ray Winstone (Kevin Herriot), Gary Shail (Spider), Garry Cooper (Peter Fenton), Toyah Willcox (Monkey), Trevor Laird (Ferdy), Andy Sayce (Kenny), Kate Williams (Mrs Cooper), Michael Elphick (Mr George Cooper), Timothy Spall (Harry), John Bindon (Harry North), Hugh Lloyd (Mr Cale). Set in 1965 at the height of the Mods v Rockers clashes, Jimmy joins his mates on a trip to Brighton for a Bank Holiday weekend and expected clash with the bikers. After the fight and arrests Jimmy struggles to recapture the excitement. Loosely based on The Who's rock opera. *Dir*. Franc Roddam.

Quantum of Solace (2008) Daniel Craig (James Bond), Olga Kurylenko (Camille Montes), Mathieu Amalric (Greene), Gemma Arterton (Strawberry Fields), Giancarlo Giannini (René Mathis), Jeffrey Wright (Felix Leiter), Judi Dench (M), Anatole Taubman (Elvis), David Harbour (Gregg Beam), Joaquín Cosío (General Medrano), Fernando Guillen Cuervo (Carlos), Jesper Christensen (Mr White), Rory Kinnear (Bill Tanner), Tim Pigott-Smith (Foreign Sec), Neil Jackson (Edmund Slate), Simon Kassianides (Yusef), Stana Katic (Corrine Veneau), Glenn Foster (Craig Mitchell), Oona Castilla Chaplin (Receptionist), Jesús Ochoa (Lt Orso), Lucrezia Lante della Rovere (Gemma), Glenn Foster (Mitchell), Paul Ritter (Guy Haines). The plot is carried over from *Casino Royale* as Bond seeks revenge for the death of Vesper Lynd. He investigates wealthy businessman Dominic Greene, a member of Quantum, who, although posing as an environmentalist, in fact intends to stage a coup d'état in Bolivia. Bond drives a Volvo S40T5. The theme song is *Another Way to Die* performed by Jack White and Alicia Keys. Based on a short story by Ian Fleming, the title comes from an explanation that in a relationship, once the "Quantum of Solace" drops to zero, humanity and consideration of one human for another is gone and the relationship is finished. *Dir*. Marc Forster.

Quartet (1948) W. Somerset Maugham (Himself – Host). Segment *The Facts of Life*: Basil Radford (Henry Garnet), Naunton Wayne (Leslie), Ian Fleming (Ralph), Jack Raine (Thomas), Angela Baddeley (Mrs Garnet), James Robertson Justice (Branksome), Jack Watling (Nicky), Nigel Buchanan (John), Mai Zetterling (Jeanne), Jean Cavall (Singer). Segment *The Alien Corn*: Dirk Bogarde (George Bland), Raymond Lovell (Sir Frederick Bland), Irene Browne (Lady Bland), Honor Blackman (Paula), George Thorpe (Uncle John), Mary Hinton (Aunt Maud), Françoise Rosay (Lea Makart). Segment *The Kite*: Bernard Lee (Prison Visitor), Frederick Leister (Governor), George Merritt (Prison Officer), George Cole (Herbert Sunbury), David Cole (Herbert as a Boy), Hermione Baddeley (Beatrice Sunbury), Mervyn Johns (Samuel Sunbury), Susan Shaw (Betty), Cyril Chamberlain (Reporter), Johnny Briggs (Boy on Common), Arthur Denton (Man on Common). Segment *The Colonel's Lady*: Cecil Parker (Col Peregrine), Nora Swinburne (Mrs Peregrine), J.H. Roberts (West), Claud Allister (Clubman), Wilfrid Hyde-White (Clubman), Ernest Thesiger (Henry Dashwood), Henry Edwards (Duke of Heverel), Linden Travers (Daphne), Felix Aylmer (Martin), John Salew (John Coleman), Lyn Evans (Bannock), Cyril Raymond (Railway Passenger), Clive Morton (Henry Blane), Margaret Withers (Gushing Woman), Ernest Butcher (Blanes Angestellter). Anthology, each based on a story by Somerset Maugham and introduced by him. *Dirs*. Ken Annakin (*The Colonel's Lady*), Arthur Crabtree (*The Kite*), Harold French (*The Alien Corn*), Ralph Smart (*The Facts of Life*).

Quatermass 2 (1958) Brian Donlevy (Prof Bernard Quatermass), John Longden (Lomax), Sid James (Jimmy Hall), Bryan Forbes (Marsh), William Franklyn (Brand), Vera Day (Sheila), Charles Lloyd Pack (Dawson), Tom Chatto (Vincent Broadhead), John Van Eyssen (The P.R.O.), Percy Herbert (Paddy Gorman), Michael Ripper (Ernie), John Rae (EJ 'Mac' McLeod), Marianne Stone (Secretary), Ronald Wilson (Young Man), Jane Aird (Mrs McLeod), Betty Impey (Kelly), Lloyd Lamble (Inspector), John Stuart (Commissioner), Gilbert Davis (Banker), Joyce Adams (Woman M.P.), Edwin Richfield (Peterson), Howard Williams (Michaels), Phillip Baird (Lab. Asst), Robert Raikes (Lab. Asst), John Fabian (Intern), George Merritt (Super), Arthur Blake (Constable), Michael Balfour (Harry). Aliens infiltrate the higher echelons of the British Government (doesn't seem unlikely) and set up an industrial plant to help the invasion force acclimatise to the Earth's atmosphere. Professor Quatermass investigates despite being hindered at every turn. Sequel to *The Quatermass Xperiment* (1956), based on the television serial *Quatermass II*. Released as *Enemy from Space* in the United States. *Dir*. Val Guest.

Quatermass and the Pit (1967) James Donald (Dr. Mathew Roney), Andrew Keir (Prof. Bernard Quatermass), Barbara Shelley (Barbara Judd), Julian Glover (Colonel Breen), Duncan Lamont (Sladden), Bryan Marshall (Captain Potter), Peter Copley (Howell), Edwin Richfield (Minister), Grant Taylor (Police Sergeant Ellis), Maurice Good (Sergeant Cleghorn), Robert Morris (Jerry Watson), Sheila Steafel (Journalist), Hugh Futcher (Sapper West), Hugh Morton (Elderly Journalist), Thomas Heathcote (Vicar), Noel Howlett (Abbey Librarian), Hugh Manning (Pub Customer), June Ellis (Blonde), Keith Marsh (Johnson), James Culliford (Corporal Gibson), Bee Duffell (Miss Dobson), Roger Avon (Electrician), Brian Peck (Technical Officer), John Graham (Inspector), Charles Lamb (Newsvendor). Workers digging on the London Underground call in a paleontologist when they discover skeletons and a metal object. He suspects that the bones are from a previously unknown apeman but Quatermass believes the bodies and artifacts are of Martian origin. The opening of the metal cylinder reveals the professor to be correct and the object seems to emanate an evil influence. *Dir*. Roy Ward Baker.

Quatermass Xperiment, The (1956) Brian Donlevy (Prof. Bernard Quatermass), Jack Warner (Insp. Lomax), Margia Dean (Mrs. Judith Carroon), Thora Hird (Rosemary 'Rosie' Wrigley), Gordon Jackson (BBC TV producer), David King-Wood (Dr. Gordon Briscoe), Harold Lang (Christie), Lionel Jeffries (Blake), Sam Kydd (Police Sergeant), Richard Wordsworth (Victor Carroon), Jane Aird (Mrs. Lomax), Margaret Anderson (Maggie), Jane Asher (Little Girl), Harry Brunning (Night Porter), Eric Corrie (Maggie's Boyfriend), Edward Dane (Station Policeman), Gron Davies (Charles Green), Basil Dignam (Sir Lionel Dean), Maurice Kaufmann (Marsh), Henry B. Longhurst (George), Arthur Lovegrove (Sgt. Bromley), Barry Lowe (Tucker), Marianne Stone (Central Clinic Nurse), Toke Townley (The Chemist), Stanley Van Beers (Dr. Ludwig Reichenheim), John Wynn (Det. Sgt. Best). When a rocket designed by Quatermass returns to Earth only one of the three astronauts on board is still present but he has been infected by an alien disease and is transmutating in a manner which will threaten all humanity. Based on the BBC Television serial *The Quatermass Experiment*. *Dir*. Val Guest.

Queen Kong (1976) Robin Askwith (Ray Fay), Rula Lenska (Luce Habit), Valerie Leon (Queen of the Nabongas), Roger Hammond (Woolf), John Clive (Comedian), Carol Drinkwater (Ima Goodbody), Brian Godfrey (Second Actor), Anthony Morton (Antique Dealer), Fiona Curzon (Police Secretary), Stanley Platts (Chief Constable), Linda Hayden (The Singing Nun), Barbara Allen, Suzy Arthur, Lela Babbick, Melita Clarke, Jeannie Collings, Kathryn Hayes, Annette Lynton, Vicki Michelle, Geraldine Gardner (Crew Girls). A giant female ape falls for a member of a film crew. *Dir*. Frank Agrama.

Queen of Hearts (1936) Gracie Fields (Grace), John Loder (Derek Cooper), Enid Stamp-Taylor (Yvonne), Fred Duprez (Zulenberg), Edward Rigby (Perkins), Julie Suedo (Rita Dow), Jean Lester (Mrs. Perkins), Hal Gordon (Stage Manager), Syd Crossley (Constable), Madeline Seymour (Mrs. Vandeleur), H.F. Maltby (Solicitor), Margaret Yarde (Mrs. Porter), Monty Banks (Montague Banking), Edith Fields (Violet), Tom Gill (Albert Perkins), Vera Hilliard (Emma), Mike Johnson (Walter), Patricia Russell (Sonia). After being mistaken for a patron of the arts seamstress Grace Perkins decides that if she pretends to back a new show, she might get the break in show business she wants. *Dir*. Monty Banks.

Queen of Spades (1949) Anton Walbrook (Capt. Herman Suvorin), Edith Evans (The Old Countess Ranevskaya), Yvonne Mitchell (Lizaveta Ivanova), Ronald Howard (Andrei), Mary

Jerrold (Old Varvarushka), Anthony Dawson (Fyodor), Miles Malleson (Tchybukin), Michael Medwin (Hovaisky), Athene Seyler (Princess Ivashin), Ivor Barnard (Bookseller), Maroussia Dimitrevitch (Gypsy singer), Violetta Elvin (Gypsy dancer), Pauline Tennant (Young countess), Jacqueline Clarke (Milliner's assistant), Josef Ramart (Countess' lover), Valentine Dyall (St. Germain's messenger), Gordon Begg (Gen. Volcholnikov), Gibb McLaughlin (Bird seller), Drusilla Wills (Countess' old servant), Aubrey Mallalieu (Fedya), George Woodbridge (Vassili), Pauline Jameson (Anyutka), Hay Petrie (Herman's servant), Brown Derby (The Countess' footman), Geoffrey Dunn (Hairdresser). An army officer tries to discover the secret of how a countess is unbeatable at cards. Based on a short story by Alexander Pushkin. *Dir.* Thorold Dickinson.

Queen, The (2006) Helen Mirren (HM The Queen), Michael Sheen (Prime Minister Tony Blair), James Cromwell (Prince Philip, Duke of Edinburgh), Helen McCrory (Cherie Blair), Alex Jennings (Charles, Prince of Wales), Roger Allam (Robin Janvrin), Sylvia Syms (HM Queen Elizabeth, The Queen Mother), Tim McMullan (Stephen Lamport), Mark Bazeley (Alastair Campbell), Douglas Reith (Lord Airlie), Robin Soans (Equerry), Lola Peploe (Janvrin's Secretary), Anthony Debaeck (Catholic Priest), Trevor McDonald (Newsreader), Jake Taylor Shantos (Prince William), Dash Barber (Prince Harry), Amanda Hadingue (Queen's Dresser), Gray O'Brien (Charles' Valet), Laurence Burg (Princess Diana), Michel Gay (Dodi Fayed). Mainly set in 1997 during the aftermath of the death of Princess Diana and the debate as to what should be the "correct" reaction to it by the Royal Family. Helen Mirren won a Best Actress Oscar for her role. *Dir.* Stephen Frears.

Quiet Wedding (1941) Margaret Lockwood (Janet Royd), Derek Farr (Dallas Chaytor), Marjorie Fielding (Mildred Royd), A.E. Matthews (Arthur Royd), Athene Seyler (Aunt Mary), Jean Cadell (Aunt Florence), Margaretta Scott (Marcia), David Tomlinson (John Royd), Sidney King (Denys), Peggy Ashcroft (Flower Lisle), Frank Cellier (Mr. Clayton), Roland Culver (Boofy Ponsonby), Michael Shepley (Marcia's Husband), Muriel Pavlow (Miranda), Margaret Halstan (Lady Yeldham), Roddy Hughes (Vicar), O.B. Clarence (First Magistrate), Wally Patch (Magistrate), Margaret Rutherford (Magistrate), Martita Hunt (Mme. Mirelle), Charles Carson (Mr. Johnson), Bernard Miles (PC). Based on the play of the same name by Esther McCracken which was also used for the 1958 film *Happy is the Bride. Dir.* Anthony Asquith.

Quiller Memorandum, The (1966) George Segal (Quiller), Alec Guinness (Pol), Max von Sydow (Oktober), Senta Berger (Inge Lindt), George Sanders (Gibbs), Robert Helpmann (Weng), Robert Flemyng (Rushington), Peter Carsten (Hengel), Ernst Walder (Grauber), Edith Schneider (Headmistress), Philip Madoc (Oktober's Man), Günter Meisner (Hassler), John Rees (Oktober's Man), John Moulder-Brown (Pupil). Quiller is sent to Berlin to investigate the death of two British agents and the rise of a neo-Nazi organisation led by an aristocrat named Oktober. An adaptation of the novel The Berlin Memorandum by Adam Hall. *Dir.* Michael Anderson.

Quills (2000) Geoffrey Rush (Marquis de Sade), Kate Winslet (Madeleine "Maddy" LeClerc), Joaquin Phoenix (Abbé du Coulmier), Michael Caine (Doctor Royer-Collard), Billie Whitelaw (Madame LeClerc), Stephen Marcus (Bouchon), Amelia Warner (Simone), Stephen Moyer (Prioux), Jane Menelaus (Renee Pelagie), Ron Cook (Napoleon Bonaparte), Patrick Malahide (Delbené), Elizabeth Berrington (Charlotte), Tony Pritchard (Valcour), Michael Jenn (Cleante), Danny Babington (Pitou), George Antoni (Dauphin), Edward Tudor-Pole (Franval), Harry Jones (Orvolle), Bridget McConnell (Madame Bougival), Pauline McLynn (Mademoiselle Clairwill), Rebecca Palmer (Michette), Toby Sawyer (Louison), Daniel Ainsleigh (Guerin), Alex Avery (Abbe du Maupas), Terry O'Neill (Gaillon), Diana Morrison (Mademoiselle Renard), Tom Ward (The Horseman). A re-imagining of the final years of the life of the Marquis de Sade. Incarcerated in the lunatic asylum at Charenton he is passing manuscripts to a publisher using laundry girl Maddy as an intermediary. Napoleon decides it is time to silence the scurrilous author. Adapted from the play of the same name by Doug Wright. *Dir.* Philip Kaufman.

Radio On (1980) David Beames (Robert), Lisa Kreuzer (Ingrid), Sandy Ratcliff (Kathy), Andrew Byatt (Deserter), Sue Jones-Davies (Girl), Sting (Just Like Eddie), Sabina Michael (Aunt), Katja Kersten (German Woman), Paul Hollywood (Kid). When DJ Robert's brother commits suicide he drives from London to Bristol, encountering various characters on the road. Shot in black and white with a New Wave soundtrack. *Dir.* Christopher Petit.

Raging Moon, The (1971) Malcolm McDowell (Bruce Pritchard), Nanette Newman (Jill Matthews), Georgia Brown (Sarah Charles), Bernard Lee (Uncle Bob), Gerald Sim (Reverend Corbett), Michael Flanders (Clarence Marlow), Margery Mason (Matron), Barry Jackson (Bill Charles), Geoffrey Whitehead (Harold Pritchard), Chris Chittell (Terry), Jack Woolgar (Bruce's Father), Norman Bird (Dr. Matthews), Constance Chapman (Mrs. Matthews), Michael Lees (Geoffrey), Geoffrey Bayldon (Mr. Latbury), Patsy Smart (Bruce's Mother), Theresa Watson (Gladys Pritchard), Sylvia Coleridge (Celia), Brook Williams (Hugh Collins), Richard Moore (Arnold Foster), George Hilsdon (George), Nelly Hanham (Margaret), Aimée Delamain (Alice), Jenny Logan (Night Nurse), Petra Markham (Mary), John Savident (Fete Guest), Michael Nightingale (Mr. Thomas), Paul Darrow (Doctor), Marianne Stone (1st Nurse). Bruce is paralysed in an accident whilst playing football and confined to a wheelchair. Then he meets Jill. *Dir.* Bryan Forbes.

Railway Children, The (1970) Dinah Sheridan (Mrs. Waterbury), Jenny Agutter (Bobbie Waterbury), Sally Thomsett (Phyllis Waterbury), Gary F. Warren (Peter Waterbury), Bernard Cribbins (Albert Perks), William Mervyn (Old Gentleman), Iain Cuthbertson (Charles Waterbury), Peter Bromilow (Doctor Forrest), Ann Lancaster (Ruth), Gordon Whiting (Shapanski/Szczepansky), Beatrix Mackey (Aunt Emma), Deddie Davies (Mrs. Nell Perks), David Lodge (Band Leader), Christopher Witty (Jim), Brenda Cowling (Mrs. Hilda Viney), Paddy Ward (Cart Man), Erik Chitty (Photographer), Sally James (Maid). The life of the Waterbury family is thrown into turmoil when father is sent to prison on charges of espionage. Mother and the three children (Bobbie, Phyllis and Peter) eventually have to move to a cottage in the countryside with a nearby railway line and station. Based on E. Nesbit's novel. *Dir.* Lionel Jeffries.

Rainbow, The (1989) Sammi Davis (Ursula), Paul McGann (Anton Skrebensky), Amanda Donohoe (Winifred Inger), Christopher Gable (Will Brangwen), David Hemmings (Uncle Henry), Glenda Jackson (Anna Brangwen), Dudley Sutton (MacAllister), Jim Carter (Mr Harby), Judith Paris (Miss Harby), Kenneth Colley (Mr Brunt), Glenda McKay (Gudrun Brangwen), Mark Owen (Jim Richards), Ralph Nossek (Vicar), Nicola Stephenson (Ethel), Molly Russell (Molly Brangwen), Alan Edmondson (Billy Brangwen), Rupert Russell (Rupert Brangwen), Richard Platt (Chauffeur), Bernard Latham (Uncle Alfred), John Tams (Uncle Frank). Coming of age story of Ursula Brangwen. Adapted from the D. H. Lawrence novel of the same name and a prequel to Lawrence's *Women in Love* which was also directed by Ken Russell.

Raining Stones (1993) Bruce Jones (Bob), Julie Brown (Anne), Gemma Phoenix (Coleen), Ricky Tomlinson (Tommy), Tom Hickey (Father Barry), Mike Fallon (Jimmy), Ronnie Ravey (Butcher), Lee Brennan (Irishman), Karen Henthorn (Young Mother), Christine Abbott (May), Geraldine Ward (Tracey), William Ash (Joe), Matthew Clucas (Sean), Anna Jaskolka (Shop Assistant), Jonathan James (Tansey). Bob tries to raise the money to buy his daughter a communion dress. *Dir.* Ken Loach.

Raising a Riot (1955) Kenneth More (Tony Kent), Shelagh Fraser (Mary Kent), Mandy Miller (Anne Kent), Gary Billings (Peter Kent), Fusty Bentine (Fusty Kent), Ronald Squire (Grampy), Olga Lindo (Aunt Maud), Lionel Murton (Harry), Mary Laura Wood (Jacqueline), Jan Miller (Sue), Nora Nicholson (Miss Pettigrew), Anita Sharp-Bolster (Mrs. Buttons), Michael Bentine (The Professor), Dorothy Dewhurst (Mary's Mother), Robin Brown (Junior), Cyril Chamberlain (Policeman), Erik Chitty (Mr. Buttons), Sam Kydd (Messenger), Victor Maddern (Guardsman), Bill Shine (Dotty). When his wife takes a trip to Canada, Tony is left in charge of their three precocious children. *Dir.* Wendy Toye.

Raising the Wind (1961) James Robertson Justice (Sir Benjamin Boyd), Leslie Phillips (Mervyn Hughes), Paul Massie (Malcolm

Stewart), Kenneth Williams (Harold Chesney), Liz Fraser (Miranda Kennaway), Eric Barker (Dr. Morgan Rutherford), Jennifer Jayne (Jill Clemons), Jimmy Thompson (Alex Spendlove), Sid James (Sid), Esma Cannon (Mrs. Deevens), Geoffrey Keen (Sir John), Jill Ireland (Janet), Victor Maddern (Removal Man), Lance Percival (Harry), Joan Hickson (Mrs. Bostwick), David Lodge (Taxi Driver), Ambrosine Phillpotts (Mrs. Featherstone), Brian Oulton (Concert Agent), Peter Howell (Prof. Lumb), George Woodbridge (Yorkshire Orchestra Leader), Cyril Chamberlain (L.A.M.A. Porter), Erik Chitty (Elderly Man at Concert), Jim Dale (Bass Trombone), John Antrobus (Street Musician), Tom Clegg (Street Musician), Frank Forsyth (Prof. Gerald Abrahams), Oliver Johnston (Prof. Parkin), Dorinda Stevens (Doris), Michael Nightingale (Invigilator), Bob Todd (Street Musician). From the team which brought you the *Carry On* series, the adventures of a group of flat-sharing musicians. *Dir.* Gerald Thomas.

Rake's Progress, The (1945) Rex Harrison (Vivian Kenway), Lilli Palmer (Rikki Krausner), Godfrey Tearle (Colonel Robert Kenway), Griffith Jones (Sandy Duncan), Margaret Johnston (Jennifer Calthorp), Guy Middleton (Fogroy), Jean Kent (Jill Duncan), Marie Lohr (Lady Angela Parks), Garry Marsh (Sir Hubert Parks), David Horne (Sir John Brockley), Alan Wheatley (Edwards), Brefni O'Rorke (Bromhead), John Salew (Burgess), Charles Victor (Old Sweat), Jan Van Loewen (Soldier), Joan Hickson (Miss Parker), Sidney Gilliat (Narrator - voice), Patricia Laffan (Miss Fernandez), Joan Maude (Alice), Kynaston Reeves (Oxford Dean), Jack Vyvian (Fred).
Vivian Kenway is a bounder, cad, womaniser and drunk. Perhaps the outbreak of war will be a turning point? *Dir.* Sidney Gilliat.

Rancid Aluminium (2000) Rhys Ifans (Pete Thompson), Joseph Fiennes (Sean Deeny), Tara Fitzgerald (Masha), Sadie Frost (Sarah Thompson), Steven Berkoff (Mr Kant), Keith Allen (Dr Jones), Dani Behr (Charlie), Andrew Howard (Trevor), Nick Moran (Harry), Olegar Fedoro (Naz), Barry Foster (Doctor), Brian Hibbard (Giovanni). After his father's death, Pete finds that the family firm is bust. Based on a novel of the same name by James Hawes. *Dir.* Edward Thomas.

Rasputin, the Mad Monk (1966) Christopher Lee (Rasputin), Barbara Shelley (Sonia), Richard Pasco (Dr. Zargo), Francis Matthews (Ivan), Suzan Farmer (Vanessa), Dinsdale Landen (Peter), Renée Asherson (Tsarina), Derek Francis (Innkeeper), Joss Ackland (The Bishop), Robert Duncan (Tsarvitch), Michael Cadman (Michael), Fiona Hartford (Tania), Bryan Marshall (Vasily), Brian Wilde (Vassily`s Father). Biopic of Grigori Rasputin and his influence within the Russian royal family. *Dir.* Don Sharp.

Rat, The (1937) Anton Walbrook (Jean Boucheron), Ruth Chatterton (Zelia de Chaumont), René Ray (Odile Verdier), Beatrix Lehmann (Marguerite), Mary Clare (Mere Colline), Felix Aylmer (Prosecuting Counsel), Hugh Miller (Luis Stets), Gordon McLeod (Caillard), Frederick Culley (Judge), Nadine March (Rose), George Merritt (Pierre Verdier), Leo Genn (Defending Counsel), Fanny Wright (Therese), Bob Gregory (Albert), Ivan Wilmot (Peter), J.H. Roberts (The Butler), Betty Marsden (Zelia's Maid), Stanley Lathbury (The Priest), Aubrey Mallalieu (The Jeweller). Zelia sets out to reform jewel thief Boucheron, who is known as "The Rat" but then his ward Odile confesses to a murder. Based on a play of the same name by Ivor Novello, who also starred in the 1925 film version. *Dir.* Thomas Bentley.

Ratcatcher (1999) William Eadie (James), Tommy Flanagan (George Gillespie), Mandy Matthews (Anne Gillespie), Michelle Stewart (Ellen Gillespie), Lynne Ramsay Jr. (Anne Marie Gillespie), Leanne Mullen (Margaret Anne), Thomas McTaggart (Ryan Quinn), John Miller (Kenny), Jackie Quinn (Mrs. Quinn), James Ramsay (Mr. Quinn), Anne McLean (Mrs. Fowler), Craig Bonar (Matt Monroe), Andrew McKenna (Billy), Mick Maharg (Stef), James Montgomery (Hammy), Stuart Gordon (Tommy), Stephen Sloan (Mackie), Molly Innes (Miss McDonald), Stephen King (Mr. Mohan), Ann Marie Lafferty (Rita), Marion Connell (Jesse), Donnie McMillan (Artie). In 1970s Glasgow, young

James Gillespie lives in a run-down flat with his dysfunctional family. *Dir.* Lynne Ramsay.

Rattle of a Simple Man (1964) Diane Cilento (Cyrenne), Harry H. Corbett (Percy Winthram), Michael Medwin (Ginger), Thora Hird (Mrs. Winthram), Charles Dyer (Chalky), Hugh Futcher (Ozzie), Carole Gray (District Nurse), Barbara Archer (Iris), David Saire (Mario), Alexander Davion (Ricardo), John Ronane (Willie), Michael Robbins (George), George Roderick (Papa), Marie Burke (Mama), Bryan Mosley (Mr Stratton), Marianne Stone (Barmaid), Brian Wilde (Fred). A naïve football fan from oop t'North finds life in London confusing when he comes down for the FA Cup Final and falls in love with a prostitute. *Dir.* Muriel Box.

Reach for Glory (1962) Harry Andrews (Capt. Curlew), Kay Walsh (Mrs. Curlew), Michael Anderson Jr. (Lewis Craig), Oliver Grimm (Mark Stein), Martin Tomlinson (John Curlew), Freddy Eldrett (Willy Aldrich), James Luck (Michael Freen), John Coker (Peter Joy), Michael Trubshawe (Maj. Burton), Arthur Hewlett (Vicar), Cameron Hall (Headmaster), Allan Jeayes (Crabtree), Richard Vernon (Dr. Aldrich), Russell Waters (Mr. Freeman), Patricia Hayes (Mrs. Freeman), George Pravda (Mr. Stein), John Rae (Lance Freeman), Alexis Kanner (Steven), Peter Furnell (Arthur Chettle), John Pike (Felix), Melvin Baker (Chettle's lieutenant), Olivia Breeze (Diana Aldrich). Evacuated teenagers play war games during WWII with tragic results. An adaptation of John Rae's novel *The Custard Boys*. *Dir.* Philip Leacock.

Reach for the Sky (1956) Kenneth More (Douglas Bader), Muriel Pavlow (Thelma Bader), Lyndon Brook (Johnny Sanderson), Lee Patterson (Turner), Alexander Knox (Mr. Joyce), Dorothy Alison (Nurse Brace), Michael Warre (Harry Day), Sydney Tafler (Robert Desoutter), Howard Marion-Crawford ("Woody" Woodhall), Jack Watling (Peel), Nigel Green (Streatfield), Anne Leon (Sister Thornhill), Charles Carson (Sir Hugh Dowding), Ronald Adam (Leigh-Mallory), Walter Hudd (Halahan), Basil Appleby (Crowley-Milling), Eddie Byrne (Mills), Beverley Brooks (Sally), Michael Ripper (West), Avice Landone (Douglas Bader's Mother), Eric Pohlmann (Adjutant at Prison Camp), Michael Gough (Flying Instructor Pearson). The biopic of Douglas Bader who overcame the loss of both legs in a flying accident in 1931 to become a fighter pilot in WWII. *Dir.* Lewis Gilbert.

Rebel, The (1961) Tony Hancock (Anthony Hancock), George Sanders (Sir Charles Broward), Paul Massie (Paul), Margit Saad (Margot), Grégoire Aslan (Carreras), Dennis Price (Jim Smith), Irene Handl (Mrs. Crevatte), John Le Mesurier (Office manager), Liz Fraser (Waitress), Nanette Newman (Josey), Mervyn Johns (Manager of Art Gallery), Peter Bull (Manager of Art Gallery), Oliver Reed (Artist in Café), Mario Fabrizi (Coffee Bar attendant). Anthony Aloysius St. John Hancock gives up his office job and pursues a career as an abstract artist. He moves to Paris where he expects to find more appreciation of his genius. *Dir.* Robert Day.

Red Beret, The (1953) Alan Ladd (Steve 'Canada' McKendrick), Leo Genn (Major J. Snow), Susan Stephen (Penny Gardner), Harry Andrews (R.S.M. Cameron), Donald Houston (Taffy Evans), Anthony Bushell (Major General A.B.C. Whiting), Patric Doonan (Flash), Stanley Baker (Sergeant Breton), Lana Morris (Pinky), Tim Turner (Rupert), Michael Kelly (Corporal Dawes), Anton Diffring (The Pole), Thomas Heathcote (Alf), Carl Duering (Rossi), John Boxer (Flight Sgt. Box), Harry Locke (Medical Orderly), Michael Balfour (American Sergeant), Guido Lorraine (German Officer), Dermot Palmer (Dakota Pilot), George Margo (American Crewman), Richard Ford (Wellington Pilot), Walter Gotell (German Sentry). A young man claiming to be a Canadian joins the British Army paratroop corps (the Red Berets) in 1941 but his commanding officer and newly acquired girlfriend believe there is more to him than he is letting on. *Dir.* Terence Young.

Red Shoes, The (1948) Moira Shearer (Victoria Page), Anton Walbrook (Boris Lermontov), Marius Goring (Julian Craster), Robert Helpmann (Ivan Boleslawsky), Léonide Massine (Grischa Ljubov), Albert Bassermann (Sergei Ratov), Ludmilla Tchérina (Irina Boronskaja), Esmond Knight (Livingstone 'Livy'

Montagne), Jean Short (Terry Tyler), Gordon Littmann (Ike Tanner), Julia Lang (A Balletomane), Austin Trevor (Professor Palmer), Eric Berry (Dimitri), Irene Browne (Lady Neston), Jerry Verno (Stage-Door Keeper), Derek Elphinstone (Lord Oldham), Marie Rambert (Madame Rambert), Joy Rawlins (Gwladys), Marcel Poncin (M. Boudin), Michel Bazalgette (M. Rideaut), Yvonne Andre (Vicky's Dresser). Talented young ballerina Victoria Page falls in love with composer Julian Craster, whose latest work is "The Red Shoes" based on the folk tale by Hans Christian Andersen. Impresario Lermontov is not impressed. Famous for the ballet sequences and its luxurious colour. The Red Shoes won two Academy Awards: Best Art Direction-Set Decoration and Best Music. *Dirs.* Michael Powell and Emeric Pressburger.

Regeneration (1997) Jonathan Pryce (Capt. William Rivers), James Wilby (2nd Lt. Siegfried Sassoon), Jonny Lee Miller (2nd Lt. Billy Prior), Stuart Bunce (2nd Lt. Wilfred Owen), Tanya Allen (Sarah), David Hayman (Maj. Bryce), Dougray Scott (Capt. Robert Graves), John Neville (Dr. Yealland), Paul Young (Dr. Brock), Alastair Galbraith (Capt. Campbell), Eileen Nicholas (Miss Crowe), Julian Fellowes (Timmons), David Robb (Dr. McIntyre), James McAvoy (Anthony Balfour). During WWI, after sending a letter to *The Times* protesting about the conduct of the war, poet Siegfried Sassoon is sent to Craiglockhart War Hospital, a psychiatric facility in Scotland. An adaptation of the novel by Pat Barker. *Dir.* Gillies MacKinnon.

Remains of the Day, The (1993) Anthony Hopkins (James Stevens), Emma Thompson (Sarah Kenton), James Fox (Lord Darlington), Christopher Reeve (Trent Lewis), Peter Vaughan (William Stevens), Paula Jacobs (Mrs. Mortimer), Ben Chaplin (Charlie), Steve Dibben (George), John Haycraft (Auctioneer), Caroline Hunt (Landlady), Hugh Grant (Cardinal), Tim Pigott-Smith (Benn), Lena Headey (Lizzie). Stevens is a very correct and emotionally repressed English butler at a country house once owned by Lord Darlington and newly in the possession of Congressman Lewis. Framed by a visit from Sarah, the film shows in flashback the house in the inter-war period when Sarah was housekeeper and found her love for Stevens apparently unreciprocated. Lord Darlington is also seen to be a Nazi sympathizer. Adapted by Ruth Prawer Jhabvala from the novel by Kazuo Ishiguro. *Dir.* James Ivory.

Rembrandt (1936) Charles Laughton (Rembrandt van Rijn), Gertrude Lawrence (Geertje Dirx), Elsa Lanchester (Hendrickje Stoffels), Edward Chapman (Fabrizius), Walter Hudd (Capt. Banning Cocq), Roger Livesey (Beggar Saul), John Bryning (Titus van Rijn), Sam Livesey (Auctioneer), Herbert Lomas (Harmenzs van Rijn), Allan Jeayes (Dr. Tulp), John Clements (Govaert Flinck), Raymond Huntley (Ludwick), Abraham Sofaer (Dr. Menasseh), Laurence Hanray (Heertsabeek), Austin Trevor (Marquis de Grand-Coeur), Henry Hewitt (Jan Six), Gertrude Musgrove (Elsa), Richard Gofe (Titus – Child), Basil Gill (Adrien van Rijn), John Turnbull (Minister), Marius Goring (Baron Leivens), Wilfrid Hyde-White (Civil Guardsman). A romanticised biopic of the great Flemish artist. *Dir.* Alexander Korda.

Reptile, The (1964) Noel Willman (Dr. Franklyn), Ray Barrett (Harry Spalding), Jennifer Daniel (Valerie Spalding), Jacqueline Pearce (Anna Franklyn), Michael Ripper (Tom Bailey), John Laurie (Mad Peter), Marne Maitland (The Malay), David Baron (Charles Spalding), Charles Lloyd Pack (The Vicar), Harold Goldblatt (The Solicitor), George Woodbridge (Old Garnsey). When Harry's brother Charles dies mysteriously, he and his wife Valerie move into Charles' cottage in a remote Cornish village. The locals (who are also dropping like flies) are not friendly and a neighbour urges them to leave. *Dir.* John Gilling.

Repulsion (1965) Catherine Deneuve (Carole Ledoux), Yvonne Furneaux (Helen Ledoux), Ian Hendry (Michael), John Fraser (Colin), Patrick Wymark (Landlord), Renee Houston (Miss Balch), Valerie Taylor (Madame Denise), James Villiers (John), Helen Fraser (Bridget), Hugh Futcher (Reggie), Monica Merlin (Mrs Rendlesham), Imogen Graham (Manicurist), Mike Pratt (Workman). When Carole is left alone in a flat in London after her sister goes on holiday, she suffers fits and nightmares, which spell tragedy for any man who calls to visit. *Dir.* Roman Polanski.

Restless Natives (1985) Vincent Friell (Will), Joe Mullaney (Ronnie), Teri Lally (Margot), Ned Beatty (Bender), Robert Urquhart (Baird), Bernard Hill (Will's father), Mel Smith (Pyle), Bryan Forbes (Driver), Nanette Newman (Passenger), Ann Scott-Jones (Will's mother), Rachel Boyd (Ilsa), Iain McColl (Nigel), Dave Anderson (Illingworth), Eiji Kusuhara (Presenter), Ed Bishop (Reporter), Laura Smith (Mary Harrison), Robin Brown (Angus Paterson), Sally Kinghorn (Courier). Will and Ronnie become tourist attractions as they begin to hold up tourist coaches wearing comedy masks. *Dir.* Michael Hoffman.

Return from the Ashes (1965) Maximilian Schell (Stanislaus Pilgrin), Samantha Eggar (Fabienne 'Fabi' Wolf), Ingrid Thulin (Dr. Michele 'Mischa' Wolf), Herbert Lom (Dr. Charles Bovard), Talitha Pol (Claudine), Mischa De La Motte (Mr. Friedheim), Rica Fox (Mrs. Friedheim), Vivienne Ventura (Receptionist). When Stan's Jewish wife survives the concentration camps she returns home to find he is sleeping with his stepdaughter. Stan then executes a plan which he believes will rid him of both women. *Dir.* J Lee Thompson.

Return of the Musketeers, The (1989) Michael York (D'Artagnan), Oliver Reed (Athos), Frank Finlay (Porthos), Richard Chamberlain (Aramis), Roy Kinnear (Planchet), Philippe Noiret (Cardinal Mazarin), Geraldine Chaplin (Queen Anne), Kim Cattrall (Justine de Winter), Christopher Lee (Rochefort), Eusebio Lázaro (Duke of Beaufort), Alan Howard (Oliver Cromwell), David Birkin (Louis XIV), Bill Paterson (Charles I), C. Thomas Howell (Raoul), Jean-Pierre Cassel (Cyrano de Bergerac), Billy Connolly (Caddie), Servane Ducorps (Olympe), William J. Fletcher (De Guiche), Laure Sabardin (Chevreuse), Marcelline Collard (Lamballe), Pat Roach (French Executioner), Jesús Ruyman (Headsman), Fernando De Juan (Ireton), Barry Burgues (Young Clerk), Leon Greene (Captain Groslow), Agata Lys (Duchesse de Longueville), Bob Todd (High Bailiff). Twenty years on from the events of the previous films an impoverished D'Artagnan is recruited for a mission by Cardinal Mazarin. Roy Kinnear was killed during the making of the film following a fall from a horse. Sequel to *The Three Musketeers* (1973) and *The Four Musketeers* (1974). Loosely based on the novel *Twenty Years After* by Alexandre Dumas, père. *Dir.* Richard Lester,

Revenge of Frankenstein, The (1958) Peter Cushing (Doctor Victor Stein), Francis Matthews (Doctor Hans Kleve), Eunice Gayson (Margaret Conrad), Michael Gwynn (Karl Immelmann), John Welsh (Dr. Bergman), Lionel Jeffries (Fritz), Oscar Quitak (Dwarf), Richard Wordsworth (Up Patient), Charles Lloyd Pack (President of the Medical Council), John Stuart (Inspector), Arnold Diamond (Dr. Malke), Marjorie Gresley (Countess Barscynska), Anna Walmsley (Vera Barscynska), George Woodbridge (Janitor), Michael Ripper (Kurt), Avril Leslie (Gerda), Ian Whittaker (Boy with Gerda), Julia Nelson (Inga), Robert Brooks Turner (Joseph the Groom). Baron Frankenstein is masquerading as Dr Stein and using his position at a hospital for the poor to harvest body parts for a new monster. The transplanting of his hunchback assistant Karl's brain into the monsters body goes well, at first. A sequel to *The Curse of Frankenstein* (1957). *Dir.* Terence Fisher.

Revenge of the Pink Panther (1978) Peter Sellers (Chief Insp Jacques Clouseau), Herbert Lom (Chief Insp Charles Dreyfus), Burt Kwouk (Cato Fong), Dyan Cannon (Simone Legree), Robert Webber (Philippe Douvier), Tony Beckley (Guy Algo), Robert Loggia (Al Marchione), Paul Stewart (Julio Scallini), André Maranne (Sgt François Chevalier), Graham Stark (Dr Auguste Balls), Alfie Bass (Fernet), Sue Lloyd (Claude Russo), Danny Schiller (Cunny), Douglas Wilmer (Police Commissioner), Ferdy Mayne (Dr Paul Laprone), Charles Augins (Vic Vancouver), John Wyman (Telly Toledo), Elisabeth Welch (Mrs Wu), Valerie Leon (Tanya), Adrienne Corri (Therese Douvier), Paul Antrim (Lookout), John Newbury (President), John Clive (President's Aide), Henry McGee (Officer Bardot), Andrew Sachs (Hercule Poirot), Christine Shaw (Nurse), Julian Orchard (Hospital Clerk), Michael Ward (Estate Agent), Maria Charles (Lady Client), Frank Williams (Gentleman Client), Rita Webb (Lady at Window), John Bluthal (Guard at Cemetery). The reports of Clouseau's death are greatly exaggerated so he decides to go undercover in order to discover who has been trying to kill him. *Dir.* Blake Edwards.

Revengers Tragedy (2002) Christopher Eccleston (Vindici), Derek Jacobi (The Duke), Diana Quick (The Duchess), Eddie Izzard (Lussurioso), Andrew Schofield (Carlo), Carla Henry

(Castiza), Justin Salinger (Ambitioso), Marc Warren (Supervacuo), Sophie Dahl (Imogen), Anthony Booth (Lord Antonio), Bianca Beyga (Young Castiza), Margi Clarke (Hannah), Carl Chase (Judge), Nichola Dixon (Imogen's Companion), Tony Maudsley (Executioner), Michael Starke (Nessio), Charles De'Ath (Sordido), Tom Williamson (Banisher), Kevin Knapman (Firework), Michael Ryan (Bomber), Jean Butler (Gloriana), Paul Reynolds (Junior), Fraser Ayres (Spurio), James McMartin (Boy), Ged McCormack (Referee), Sammy Duplay (Lad), Shaun Mason (Hippolito), Alex Cox (Duke's Driver). An adaptation of *The Revenger's Tragedy,* a Jacobean play which is attributed to Thomas Middleton. The film moves the action from a Renaissance Italian court to a futuristic dystopian Liverpool in the aftermath of a natural disaster. *Dir.* Alex Cox.

Revolver (2005) Jason Statham (Jake), Ray Liotta (Dorothy Macha), Francesca Annis (Lily Walker), André Benjamin (Avi), Vincent Pastore (Zach), Terence Maynard (French Paul), Andrew Howard (Billy), Stephen Walters (Joe), Ian Puleston-Davies (Eddie A), Jimmy Flint (Eddie B), Brian Hibbard (Eddie C), Mark Strong (Sorter), Anjela Lauren Smith (Doreen), Elana Binysh (Rachel), Mem Ferda (Macha's Goon), Shend (Teddy), Faruk Pruti (Ivan), Bill Moody (Al), Vincent Riotta (Benny). Con man Jake Green fresh out from seven years solitary confinement, is gunning for casino boss Dorothy (Mr D). Guy Ritchie issued a reedited version in 2007 in order to clarify some plot points after criticism that the film was too hard to follow. *Dir.* Guy Ritchie.

Rhubarb (1969) Kenneth Connor (Mr Rhubarb), Jimmy Edwards (Police Constable Rhubarb), Hattie Jacques (Nurse Rhubarb), Ann Lancaster (Mrs Rhubarb), Anastasia Penington (Baby Rhubarb), Gordon Rollings (Artist Rhubarb), Harry Secombe (Vicar Rhubarb), Johnny Speight (Gents Rhubarb), Graham Stark (Golfer Rhubarb), Eric Sykes (Insp Rhubarb), Sheree Winton (Girl Rhubarb). Short film in which the dialogue consists solely of the word "rhubarb". *Dir.* Eric Sykes.

Richard III (1955) Laurence Olivier (Richard III), Cedric Hardwicke (Edward IV), John Gielgud (George, Duke of Clarence), Ralph Richardson (Duke of Buckingham), Claire Bloom (The Lady Anne), Mary Kerridge (Queen Elizabeth), Pamela Brown (Jane Shore), Paul Huson (Edward, Prince of Wales), Alec Clunes (The Lord Hastings), Dan Cunningham (The Lord Grey), Douglas Wilmer (The Lord Dorset), Laurence Naismith (The Lord Stanley), Andrew Cruickshank (Brackenbury), Clive Morton (The Lord Rivers), Terence Greenidge (Scrivener), Norman Wooland (Catesby), Esmond Knight (Ratcliffe), John Laurie (Lovel), Stanley Baker (Henry, Earl of Richmond), Nicholas Hannen (Archbishop), Stewart Allen (Page to Richard), Russell Thorndike (First Priest), Michael Gough (Dighton, 1st murderer), Michael Ripper (Forrest, 2nd murderer), Helen Haye (Duchess of York), Andy Shine (Young Duke of York), Roy Russell (Abbot), George Woodbridge (Lord Mayor of London), Willoughby Gray (2nd Priest), Patrick Troughton (Tyrell). Adaptation of Shakespeare's history play with Olivier playing Richard III as very much an evil, deformed, manipulative creature who gets his just desserts. *Dir.* Laurence Olivier.

Richard III (1995) Ian McKellen (Richard III), John Wood (Edward IV), Nigel Hawthorne (George, Duke of Clarence), Jim Broadbent (Duke of Buckingham), Kristin Scott Thomas (Lady Anne), Annette Bening (Queen Elizabeth), Marco Williamson (Prince of Wales), Jim Carter (Lord Hastings), Christopher Bowen (Prince Edward), Matthew Groom (Richard of York), Kate Steavenson-Payne (Princess Elizabeth), Robert Downey Jr. (Lord Rivers), Maggie Smith (Duchess of York), Edward Hardwicke (Lord Stanley), Edward Jewesbury (King Henry VI), Dominic West (Earl of Richmond), Adrian Dunbar (James Tyrell), Roger Hammond (Archbishop Thomas), Tim McInnerny (Sir William Catesby), Bill Paterson (Sir Richard Ratcliffe), Denis Lill (Lord Mayor), Ryan Gilmore (George Stanley), Donald Sumpter (Brackenbury), Tres Hanley (Rivers' Mistress), Andy Rashleigh (Jailer in Tower), Stacey Kent (Ballroom Singer). Adaptation of Shakespeare's play brought into 1930s Britain with fascist overtones. *Dir.* Richard Loncraine.

Riff-Raff (1991) Robert Carlyle (Stevie), Emer McCourt (Susan), Jim R. Coleman (Shem), George Moss (Mo), Ricky Tomlinson (Larry), David Finch (Kevin), Richard Belgrave (Kojo), Ade Sapara (Fiaman), Derek Young (Desmonde), Bill Moores (Smurph), Luke Kelly (Ken Jones), Garrie J. Lammin (Mick), Willie Ross (Gus Siddon), Dean Perry (Wilf), Peter Mullan (Jake), John Kazek (Robert), Anne Marie Timoney (Fiona), Maureen Carr (Ellen). Just out of prison, Stevie moves from Glasgow to London and gets a job on a building site. *Dir.* Ken Loach.

Ring of Bright Water (1969) Bill Travers (Graham Merrill), Virginia McKenna (Mary MacKenzie), Peter Jeffrey (Colin Wilcox), Jameson Clark (Storekeeper), Helena Gloag (Mrs. Flora Elrich), Willie Joss (Lighthouse keeper), Roddy McMillan (Bus driver), Jean Taylor Smith (Mrs. Sarah Chambers), Phil McCall (Frank). After buying a young otter (Mij) in a London petshop, Graham moves to a cottage in Scotland and makes the acquaintance of Mary. Based upon Gavin Maxwell's novel. Husband and wife Travers and McKenna also made *Born Free* (1966) together. *Dir.* Jack Couffer.

Rita, Sue and Bob Too! (1987) Siobhan Finneran (Rita), Michelle Holmes (Sue), George Costigan (Bob), Lesley Sharp (Michelle), Kulvinder Ghir (Aslam), Willie Ross (Sue's Father), Patti Nichols (Sue's Mother), Danny O'Dea (Paddy), Maureen Long (Rita's Mother). Married man gets involved with two local girls who babysit for him. Adapted by Andrea Dunbar from her plays: *Rita Sue and Bob Too* and *The Arbor*. *Dir.* Alan Clarke.

Rob Roy, the Highland Rogue (1953) Richard Todd (Rob Roy MacGregor), Glynis Johns (Helen Mary MacPherson MacGregor), James Robertson Justice (Duke Campbell, of Argyll), Michael Gough (Duke of Montrose), Finlay Currie (Hamish MacPherson), Jean Taylor Smith (Lady Margaret Campbell MacGregor, of Glengyll), Jock MacKay (Neil MacCallum), Geoffrey Keen (Killearn), Archie Duncan (Dugal MacGregor), Russell Waters (Hugh MacGregor), Marjorie Fielding (Maggie MacPherson), Eric Pohlmann (King George I), Ina De La Haye (Countess von Pahlen), Michael Goodliffe (Robert Walpole), Martin Boddey (General Cadogan), Ewen Solon (Maj Gen Wightman), James Sutherland (Torcal), Abe Barker (Duncan MacIntosh), Howard Douglas (Donald Urquhart), Hamilton Keene (Fort Commandant), Henry Hewitt (Lord Parker), Malcolm Keen (Duke of Marlborough), Andrew Laurence (Lord Chamberlain), Paget Hunter (Earl of Berkeley), Derek Prentice (Viscount Townshend), Middleton Woods (Lord Carleton), Frank Webster (Lord Carteret), Robert Brooks Turner (Viscount Torrington), Rolph Hutcheson (John Treby), Max Gardner (Lord Evelyn) and the MacGregor clan: John McEnvoy (Nabby), Ian MacNaughton (Callum), Stevenson Lang (Keith), Charles Hubbard (Alasdair), Campbell Godley (James), Ted Follows (Douglas), Lionel Thomson (Donald), James Stuart (Ian), Lewis Schwarz (Wallace), Hugh Evans (Gordon). Disney version of Sir Walter Scott's hero. In post-1715 Jacobite Rebellion Scotland, supporters of the Stuarts are outlawed. *Dir.* Harold French.

Robbery (1967) Stanley Baker (Paul Clifton), Joanna Pettet (Kate Clifton), James Booth (Insp George Langdon), Frank Finlay (Robinson), Barry Foster (Frank), William Marlowe (Dave Aitken), Clinton Greyn (Jack), George Sewell (Ben), Glynn Edwards (Squad Chief), Michael McStay (Don), Martin Wyldeck (Chief constable), Rachel Herbert (School teacher), Patrick Jordon (Freddy), Barry Stanton (Car Lot owner), Kenneth Farrington (7th Robber), Robert Powell (Deltic Train Guard), Mike Pratt (Informant at Railway Station), John Savident (PC with Dog). Fictionalised re-telling of the 1963 Great Train Robbery. *Dir.* Peter Yates.

Robin and Marion (1976) Sean Connery (Robin Hood), Audrey Hepburn (Lady Marian), Robert Shaw (Sheriff of Nottingham), Nicol Williamson (Little John), Richard Harris (Richard I), Denholm Elliott (Will Scarlet), Ronnie Barker (Friar Tuck), Kenneth Haigh (Sir Ranulf), Ian Holm (King John), Bill Maynard (Mercadier), Esmond Knight (Old Defender), Veronica Quilligan (Sister Mary), Peter Butterworth (Surgeon), John Barrett (Jack),

Kenneth Cranham (Jack's Apprentice), Victoria Abril (Queen Isabella). On the death of Richard I, an ageing Robin Hood returns to Nottingham to find that Marian is now an Abbess at the local priory. *Dir.* Richard Lester.

Robin Hood (1991) Patrick Bergin (Sir Robert Hode/Robin Hood), Uma Thurman (Maid Marian), Jürgen Prochnow (Sir Miles Folcanet), Edward Fox (Prince John), Jeroen Krabbé (Baron Roger Daguerre), Owen Teale (Will Scarlett), David Morrissey (Little John), Jeff Nuttall (Friar Tuck), Danny Webb (Much the Miller), Carolyn Backhouse (Nicole), Barry Stanton (Miter), Conrad Asquith (Lodwick), Phelim McDermott (Jester), Caspar De La Mare (Sam Timmons), Cecily Hobbs (Mabel), Gabrielle Reidy (Lily). Stephen Pallister as Jack Runnel. Another, more traditional, retelling of the Robin Hood legend, this time concentrating on the oppression of the Saxons by the Normans. *Dir.* John Irvin.

Robin Hood (2010) Russell Crowe (Robin Longstride/Robin Hood), Cate Blanchett (Lady Marian), Mark Strong (Sir Godfrey), Oscar Isaac (King John), Mark Lewis Jones (Thomas Longstride), Kevin Durand (Little John), Mark Addy (Friar Tuck), Scott Grimes (Will Scarlet), Alan Doyle (Allan A'Dayle), William Hurt (William Marshal), Danny Huston (King Richard), Eileen Atkins (Eleanor of Aquitaine), Max von Sydow (Sir Walter Loxley), Jonathan Zaccaï (Philip II of France), Matthew Macfadyen (Sheriff of Nottingham), Léa Seydoux (Isabella of Angoulême). A version of the Robin Hood legend where Robin Longstride is an archer in the army of Richard I who deserts with some comrades after being imprisoned for speaking his mind. Whilst attempting to get home to England they disrupt an ambush of the Royal Guard which was returning to England to report the death of King Richard. Robin decides to impersonate one of the dead knights, Robert Loxley after promising to return his sword to his father Walter in Nottingham. *Dir.* Ridley Scott.

Rockets Galore! (1957) Jeannie Carson (Janet Macleod), Donald Sinden (Hugh Mander), Roland Culver (Captain Waggett), Catherine Lacey (Mrs. Waggett), Noel Purcell (Father James), Ian Hunter (Air Commodore Watchorn), Duncan Macrae (Duncan Ban), Jean Cadell (Mrs. Campbell), Gordon Jackson (George Campbell), Alex Mackenzie (Joseph Macleod), Carl Jaffe (Dr. Hamburger), Nicholas Phipps (Andrew Wishart), Jameson Clark (Constable Macrae), Ronnie Corbett (Drooby), James Copeland (Kenny McLeod), John Stevenson Lang (Reverend Angus), Reginald Beckwith (Mumford), Gabrielle Blunt (Catriona), Arthur Howard (Meeching), John Laurie (Capt. MacKechnie), Jack Short (Roderick). When a missile base is slated to be sited on the Hebridean island of Todday the locals try to discourage it by fair means or foul. Sequel to *Whisky Galore!*, based on Compton MacKenzie's novel. *Dir.* Michael Relph.

RocknRolla (2007) Mark Strong (Archy), Tom Wilkinson (Lenny Cole), Toby Kebbell (Johnny Quid), Gerard Butler (One-Two), Tom Hardy (Handsome Bob), Idris Elba (Mumbles), Karel Roden (Uri Omovich), Thandie Newton (Stella), Dragan Mićanović (Victor), Matt King (Cookie), Geoff Bell (Fred), Ludacris (Mickey), Gemma Arterton (June), Jeremy Piven (Roman), Jimi Mistry (The Councillor), Robert Stone (The Nightclub Bouncer), Jamie Campbell Bower (Rocker). A crime caper centred on real estate deals and a stolen painting. *Dir.* Guy Ritchie.

Rocky Horror Picture Show, The (1975) Tim Curry (Dr. Frank-N-Furter), Susan Sarandon (Janet Weiss), Barry Bostwick (Brad Majors), Richard O'Brien (Riff Raff), Patricia Quinn (Magenta), Nell Campbell (Columbia), Jonathan Adams (Dr. Everett V. Scott), Peter Hinwood (Rocky Horror), Charles Gray (The Criminologist), Meat Loaf (Eddie), Jeremy Newson (Ralph Hapschatt), Hilary Labow (Betty Munroe Hapschatt), Christopher Biggins (A Transylvanian). In a musical spoof of the usual Frankenstein/Dracula story, the car of young couple Bard and Janet gets a flat tyre and they try the nearby castle for help, wherein they discover a group of bizarre people who are holding an Annual Transylvanian Convention. Their host is the transvestite Dr. Frank-N-Furter. An adaptation of the rock musical stageplay, *The Rocky Horror Show*, written by Richard O'Brien. *Dir.* Jim Sharman.

Rogue Trader (1999) Ewan McGregor (Nick Leeson), Anna Friel (Lisa Leeson), Yves Beneyton (Pierre Beaumarchais), Betsy Brantley (Brenda Granger), Caroline Langrishe (Ash Lewis), Nigel Lindsay (Ron Baker), Tim McInnerny (Tony Hawes), Irene Ng (Bonnie Lee), Lee Ross (Danny Argyropoulos), Simon Shepherd (Peter Norris), John Standing (Peter Baring), Pip Torrens (Simon Jones), Tom Wu (George Seow), Daniel York (Henry Tan), Joanna David (Mrs. Peter Baring), Alexis Denisof (Fernando Gueller), Sharon Duce (Patsy Sims), Michael Garner (Alec Sims), Gaurav Kripalani (Aloysius), Michelle Lee (Susi), Danny Argyropoulos (Trader 1), Peter Sakon Lee (Trader 2), Rob Lemming (Trader 3), Guy Boardman (Trader 4), Jennifer Lim (Kim Wong), Karen Lim (Singapore Letting Agent), Kay Siu Lim (Policeman), Peter Quince (Nick's Father), Cristian Solimeno (Steve), Douglas Stark (Vicar). Fictionalised account of how future options trader Nick Leeson managed to bankrupt Barings Bank in 1995. Based on Leeson's book *Rogue Trader: How I Brought Down Barings Bank and Shook the Financial World*. *Dir.* James Dearden.

Roman Spring of Mrs. Stone, The (1961) Vivien Leigh (Karen), Warren Beatty (Paolo), Lotte Lenya (Contessa), Coral Browne (Meg), Jill St. John (Barbara), Jeremy Spenser (Young man), Stella Bonheur (Mrs. Jamison-Walker), Peter Dyneley (Lloyd Greener), Carl Jaffe (Baron Waldheim), Harold Kasket (Tailor), Viola Keats (Julia McIlheny), Cleo Laine (Singer), Bessie Love (Bunny), Elspeth March (Mrs. Barrow), Henry McCarty (Campbell Kennedy), Warren Mitchell (Giorgio), John Phillips (Tom Stone), Paul Stassino (Stefano - The Barber), Ernest Thesiger (Stefano), Mavis Villiers (Mrs. Coogan). After her husband dies on their flight to Rome, actress Karen Stone continues her stay in Italy and is introduced to young Paolo di Leo. Based on the novel by Tennessee Williams. *Dir.* José Quintero.

Romantic Age, The (1949) Mai Zetterling (Arlette), Hugh Williams (Arnold Dickson), Margot Grahame (Helen Dickson), Petula Clark (Julie Dickson), Carol Marsh (Patricia), Raymond Lovell (Hedges), Paul Dupuis (Henri Sinclair), Margaret Barton (Bessie), Marie Ney (Miss Hallam), Mark Daly (Withers), Judith Furse (Miss Adams), Betty Impey (Jill), Adrienne Corri (Norah), Jean Anderson (Miss Sankey). Comedy in which French exchange student Arlette decides to seduce the married art teacher at a girl's school which his daughter also attends. Released as *Naughty Arlette* in the United States. Based on the novel *Lycee des Jeunes Filles* by Serge Véber. *Dir.* Edmond T. Gréville.

Rome Express (1932) Esther Ralston (Asta Marvelle), Conrad Veidt (Zurta), Frank Vosper (Monsieur Jolif), Joan Barry (Mrs. Maxted), Donald Calthrop (Poole), Finlay Currie (Sam), Cedric Hardwicke (Alistair McBane), Gordon Harker (Tom Bishop), Harold Huth (George Grant), Eliot Makeham (Mills), Hugh Williams (Tony), Muriel Aked (Spinster). French detective Jolif investigates the theft of a Van Dyke painting which is believed to be on a train to Rome. Meanwhile there is a falling out amongst the thieves. *Dir.* Walter Forde.

Romeo and Juliet (1954) Laurence Harvey (Romeo), Susan Shentall (Juliet), Flora Robson (Nurse), Norman Wooland (Paris), Mervyn Johns (Friar Laurence), John Gielgud (Chorus), Bill Travers (Benvolio), Sebastian Cabot (Capulet), Lydia Sherwood (Lady Capulet), Ubaldo Zollo (Mercutio), Enzo Fiermonte (Tybalt), Giovanni Rota (Prince of Verona), Giulio Garbinetto (Montague), Nietta Zocchi (Lady Montague), Thomas Nicholls (Friar John), Mario Meniconi (Baldassare), Pietro Capanna (Sansone), Luciano Bodi (Abraham), Dagmar Josipovitch (Rosaline), Elio Vittorini (Bartolomeo). Adaptation of William Shakespeare's play. *Dir.* Renato Castellani.

Romeo and Juliet (1968) Leonard Whiting (Romeo), Olivia Hussey (Juliet), John McEnery (Mercutio), Milo O'Shea (Friar Laurence), Pat Heywood (The Nurse), Robert Stephens (The Prince of Verona), Michael York (Tybalt), Bruce Robinson (Benvolio), Paul Hardwick (Lord Capulet), Natasha Parry (Lady Capulet), Antonio Pierfederici (Lord Montague), Esmeralda Ruspoli (Lady Montague), Roberto Bisacco (Lord Paris), Roy Holder (Peter), Keith Skinner (Balthazar), Dyson Lovell (Sampson), Richard Warwick (Gregory), Roberto Antonelli (Abraham). Adaptation of William Shakespeare's play. *Dir.* Franco Zeffirelli.

Room at the Top (1959) Laurence Harvey (Joe Lampton), Simone Signoret (Alice Aisgill), Heather Sears (Susan Brown),

Donald Wolfit (Mr. Brown), Donald Houston (Charles Soames), Hermoine Baddeley (Elspeth), Allam Cuthbertson (George Aisgill), Raymond Huntley (Mr. Hoylake), John Westbrook (Jack Wales), Ambrosine Phillpotts (Mrs. Brown), Richard Pasco (Teddy), Beatrice Varley (Aunt), Delena Kidd (Eva), Ian Hendry (Cyril), Derren Nesbitt (Thug), Richard Caldicot (Taxi driver), Wendy Craig (Joan), Basil Dignam (Priest), Jack Hedley (Architect), Miriam Karlin (Gertrude), Prunella Scales (Council Office Worker). Ambitious Joe Lampton arrives in a new town and is attracted to Susan, the daughter of a local industrialist. Thwarted by her father sending her abroad, he transfers his affections to Alice, only for Susan to then come back into the picture. A sequel, *Life at the Top,* was made in 1965. The film won two Academy Awards: Best Actress in a Leading Role (Simone Signoret) and Best Writing, Screenplay Based on Material from Another Medium. *Dir.* Jack Clayton.

Room for Romeo Brass, A (1999) Andrew Shim (Romeo Brass), Ben Marshall (Gavin "Knocks" Woolley), Paddy Considine (Morell), Vicky McClure (Ladine Brass), Ladene Hall (Carol Brass), Frank Harper (Joe Brass), Julia Ford (Sandra Woolley), James Higgins (Bill Woolley), Bob Hoskins (Steven Laws), Martin Arrowsmith (Dennis Wardrobe), Darren O. Campbell (Darren), Johann Myers (Clifford). The friendship between Romeo and Gavin is disrupted by the arrival in their lives of Morell, who takes an interest in Romeo's sister Ladine. *Dir.* Shane Meadows.

Room with a View, A (1985) Maggie Smith (Charlotte Bartlett), Helena Bonham Carter (Lucy Honeychurch), Denholm Elliott (Mr. Emerson), Julian Sands (George Emerson), Simon Callow (The Reverend Mr. Beebe), Patrick Godfrey (The Reverend Mr. Eager), Judi Dench (Eleanor Lavish), Fabia Drake (Miss Catharine Alan), Joan Henley (Miss Teresa Alan), Amanda Walker (The Cockney Signora), Daniel Day-Lewis (Cecil Vyse), Maria Britneva (Mrs Vyse), Rosemary Leach (Mrs Honeychurch), Rupert Graves (Freddy Honeychurch), Peter Cellier (Sir Harry Otway), Mia Fothergill (Minnie Beebe). Whilst holidaying in Florence, Lucy meets and becomes attracted to George Emerson. When she returns home to England she accepts a marriage proposal from Cecil only to discover that George is moving to a cottage in her village. The film won three Academy Awards: Best Writing, Screenplay Based on Material from Another Medium, Best Art Direction-Set Decoration and Best Costume Design. An adaptation of E. M. Forster's novel. *Dir.* James Ivory.

Root of All Evil, The (1947) Phyllis Calvert (Jeckie Farnish), Michael Rennie (Charles Mortimer), John McCallum (Joe Bartle), Brefni O'Rorke (Farnish), Moore Marriott (Scholes), Hazel Court (Rushie Farnish), Arthur Young (George Grice), Reginald Purdell (Perkins), Hubert Gregg (Albert Grice), Stewart Rome (Sir George), George Carney (Bowser), Pat Hicks (Lucy), George Merritt (Landlord), Rory MacDermot (Overthwaite), Maureen Moore (Mrs. Scholes), Bryan Herbert (Stubley), Ellis Irving (Auctioneer), Diana Decker (Pam). A Gainsborough melodrama. Ambitious Jeckie Farnish sues grocer Albert Grice for breach of promise and uses the money she wins to drive him out of business. *Dir.* Brock Williams.

Rosencrantz & Guildenstern Are Dead (1990) Gary Oldman (Rosencrantz), Tim Roth (Guildenstern), Richard Dreyfuss (The Player), Livio Badurina (Tragedian), Tomislav Maretic (Tragedian), Mare Mlacnik (Tragedian), Serge Soric (Tragedian), Mladen Vasary (Tragedian), Zeljko Vukmirica (Tragedian), Branko Zavrsan (Tragedian), Joanna Roth (Ophelia), Iain Glen (Hamlet), Donald Sumpter (Claudius), Joanna Miles (Gertrude), Ljubo Zecevic (Osric), Ian Richardson (Polonius), Sven Medvesek (Laertes), Vili Matula (Horatio), John Burgess (Ambassador from England). Depiction of what happens to two minor characters from Shakespeare's *Hamlet* whilst they are not actually in the action of the play. Based on Tom Stoppard's play. *Dir.* Tom Stoppard.

Rosie Dixon – Night Nurse (1978) Debbie Ash (Rosie Dixon), Carolyne Argyle (Penny Green), Beryl Reid (Matron), John Le Mesurier (Sir Archibald MacGregor), Arthur Askey (Mr Arkwright), Liz Fraser (Mrs Dixon), John Junkin (Mr Dixon),

Lance Percival (Jake Fletcher), Bob Todd (Mr Buchanan), Christopher Ellison (Dr Adam Quint), Peter Mantle (Dr Tom Richmond), Ian Sharp (Dr Seamus MacSweeney), Jeremy Sinden (Dr Robert Fishlock), David Timson (Geoffrey Ramsbottom), Leslie Ash (Natalie Dixon), Joan Benham (Sister Tutor), Peter Bull (August Visitor), John Clive (Grieves), Glenna Forster-Jones (Staff Nurse Smythe), Patricia Hodge (Sister Belter), Harry Towb (Mr Phillips), Sara Pugsley (Night Sister), Claire Davenport (Mrs Buchanan), Jean Campbell-Dallas (Old Lady). Sex comedy about the adventures of a student nurse. Based on Christopher Wood's novel. *Dir.* Justin Cartwright.

Rotten to the Core (1965) Anton Rodgers (The Duke), Charlotte Rampling (Sara Capell), Eric Sykes (William Hunt), Ian Bannen (Lt. Percy Vine), Thorley Walters (Chief Constable Preston), Peter Vaughan (Sir Henry Capell), Dudley Sutton (Jelly), Kenneth Griffith (Lenny the Dip), James Beckett (Scapa Flood), Victor Maddern (Anxious O'Toole), Avis Bunnage (Countess de Wett), Frank Jarvis (Moby). Comedy crime caper. The Duke is the leader of a group of criminals who are planning a major robbery using a clinic as a front. *Dir.* John Boulting.

Royal Flash (1975) Malcolm McDowell (Captain Harry Flashman), Alan Bates (Rudi Von Sternberg), Florinda Bolkan (Lola Montez), Oliver Reed (Otto von Bismarck), Tom Bell (De Gautet), Joss Ackland (Sapten), Christopher Cazenove (Eric Hansen), Henry Cooper (John Gully), Lionel Jeffries (Kraftstein), Alastair Sim (Mr. Greig), Michael Hordern (Headmaster), Britt Ekland (Duchess Irma), Bob Hoskins (Police Constable), Arthur Brough (King Ludwig of Bavaria), Stuart Rayner (Speedicut), Leon Greene (Grundwig), David Jason (The Mayor), Rula Lenska (Helga), Bob Peck (Police Inspector). Flashman finds himself embroiled in a plot by Bismarck to make him impersonate a Danish prince and marry a German princess. Based on George MacDonald Fraser's second Flashman novel. *Dir.* Richard Lester.

Ruling Class, The (1972) Peter O'Toole (Jack Arnold Alexander Tancred Gurney - 14th Earl of Gurney), Alastair Sim (Bishop Bertie Lampton), Arthur Lowe (Daniel Tucker), Harry Andrews (Ralph Gurney - 13th Earl of Gurney), Coral Browne (Lady Claire Gurney), Michael Bryant (Dr. Herder), Nigel Green (McKyle), William Mervyn (Sir Charles Gurney), Carolyn Seymour (Grace Shelley), James Villiers (Dinsdale Gurney), Hugh Burden (Matthew Peake), Graham Crowden (Truscott), Kay Walsh (Mrs. Piggot-Jones), Patsy Byrne (Mrs. Treadwell), Joan Cooper (Nurse Brice), James Grout (Inspector Brockett), James Hazeldine (Fraser), Hugh Owens (Toastmaster), Griffith Davies (Inmate), Oliver MacGreevy (Inmate), Henry Woolf (Inmate), Neil Kennedy (Dr. Herder's Assistant), Ronald Adam (Lord), Cyril Appleton (McKyle's Assistant), Kenneth Benda (Lord Chancellor), Julian D'Albie (Lord), Declan Mulholland (Poacher). When a member of the aristocracy dies his insane heir ascends to his title. An adaptation of Peter Barnes' satirical stage play. *Dir.* Peter Medak.

Run Fat Boy Run (2007) Simon Pegg (Dennis Doyle), Thandie Newton (Libby Odell), Hank Azaria (Whit), Dylan Moran (Gordon), Harish Patel (Mr Goshdashtidar), India de Beaufort (Maya Goshdashtidar), Matthew Fenton (Jake), Simon Day (Vincent), Ruth Sheen (Claudine), Tyrone Huggins (Grover), Nevan Finegan (Mickey), Iddo Goldberg (News reporter), Floella Benjamin (Libby's mother), Chris Hollins (Sports reporter), Peter Serafinowicz (Sports commentator), Denise Lewis (Herself), Stephen Merchant (Man in suit), David Walliams (Customer), Michael Johnson (Marathon runner), Bill Bailey (Man dressed as Gandalf). Five years after leaving pregnant Libby whilst they were preparing to get married, Dennis discovers that she is seeing an American named Whit. When he finds out that Whit is running in a London marathon he decides he will do the same. *Dir.* David Schwimmer.

Run for Your Money, A (1949) Donald Houston (David 'Dai Number 9' Jones), Meredith Edwards (Thomas 'Twm' Jones), Moira Lister (Jo), Alec Guinness (Whimple), Hugh Griffith (Huw Price), Clive Morton (Editor), Julie Milton (Bronwen), Peter Edwards (Davies Manager), Joyce Grenfell (Mrs Pargiter), Leslie Perrins (Barney), Dorothy Bramhall (Jane Benson), Andrew

Leigh (The Pawnbroker), Edward Rigby (Beefeater), Desmond Walter-Ellis (Station Announcer), Mackenzie Ward (Stebbins), Meadows White (Guv'nor), Gabrielle Brune (Crooner), Ronnie Harries (Dan), Diana Hope (A Customer), Dudley Jones (Bleddyn), David Davies (The Burly Stranger), Tom Jones (Elderly Miner), Richard Littledale (Cinema Manager), Marianne Stone (Miss Carpenter). An Ealing comedy. Two Welsh miners win a competition for coal production and take a trip to London to watch the Wales v England rugby match at Twickenham. They miss the contact from the competition organisers and are led astray by various dodgy Londoners. *Dir.* Charles Frend.

Runaway Bus, The (1954) Frankie Howerd (Percy Lamb), Margaret Rutherford (Miss Cynthia Beeston), Petula Clark (Stewardess 'Nikki' Nicholls), George Coulouris (Ernest Schroeder), Toke Townley (Henry Waterman), Terence Alexander (Pilot Peter Jones), Belinda Lee (Janie Grey), John Horsley (Inspector Henley), Anthony Oliver (Uniformed Senior Airport Official), Stringer Davis (Transport officer), Michael Gwynn (Transport Dispatcher), Reginald Beckwith (Telephone man), Marianne Stone (Uniformed Airport Hostess), Lionel Murton (One of the American Travellers), Lisa Gastoni (The Airline Clerk), Richard Beynon (Transport officer), Sam Kydd (Chief of Security), Alastair Hunter (Detective Spencer). Comedy in which Percy, a bus driver for BOAC, has to transport passengers from a fog bound airport to the nearest clear one. However, one of the passengers is a criminal mastermind behind a gold bullion robbery at the airport they have just left and the loot is stashed on the bus. *Dir.* Val Guest.

Running Jumping & Standing Still Film, The (1960) Richard Lester, Peter Sellers, Spike Milligan, Mario Fabrizi, David Lodge, Leo McKern, Graham Stark, Bruce Lacey, Norman Rossington. A plotless eleven minute long film. Could involve people running, jumping and/or standing still. *Dirs.* Richard Lester and Peter Sellers.

Ryan's Daughter (1970) Robert Mitchum (Charles Shaughnessy), Trevor Howard (Father Collins), Christopher Jones (Randolph Doryan), John Mills (Michael), Leo McKern (Thomas Ryan), Sarah Miles (Rosy Ryan), Barry Foster (Tim O'Leary), Marie Kean (Mrs. McCardle), Arthur O'Sullivan (Mr. McCardle), Evin Crowley (Maureen), Douglas Sheldon (Driver), Gerald Sim (Captain), Barry Jackson (Corporal), Des Keogh (Lanky private), Niall Toibin (O'Keefe), Philip O'Flynn (Paddy), Donal Neligan (Maureen's boyfriend), Brian O'Higgins (Const. O'Connor), Niall O'Brien (Bernard), Owen Sullivan (Joseph). The married daughter of the bar owner in a remote Irish village falls for the commander of the nearby British army base, much to the annoyance of the locals, who are Nationalists to a man. The film won two Academy Awards: Best Actor in a Supporting Role (John Mills playing Michael – a deaf mute) and Best Cinematography (Freddie Young). *Dir.* David Lean.

Sabotage (1936) Sylvia Sidney (Mrs. Sylvia Verloc), Oskar Homolka (Karl Verloc), Desmond Tester (Stevie), John Loder (Detective Sergeant Ted Spencer), Joyce Barbour (Renee), Matthew Boulton (Superintendent Talbot), S.J. Warmington (Hollingshead), William Dewhurst (Professor A.F. Chatman), Pamela Bevan (Miss Chatham's Daughter), Peter Bull (Michaelis), Albert Chevalier (Cinema Commissioner), Clare Greet (Mrs. Jones), Charles Hawtrey (Youth at the Aquarium), Martita Hunt (Miss Chatham), Aubrey Mather (Greengrocer), Torin Thatcher (Yunct), Austin Trevor (Vladimir), Jack Vyvian (Detective). Terrorist Verloc runs a cinema but is under surveillance by the police. Realising he is under suspicion, Verloc gives his wife's young brother a bag containing a bomb to take onto the London Underground. Released as *The Woman Alone* in the United States. Based on the Joseph Conrad novel *The Secret Agent*. *Dir.* Alfred Hitchcock.

Sailor Beware! (1956) Peggy Mount (Emma Hornett), Shirley Eaton (Shirley Hornett), Ronald Lewis (Albert), Cyril Smith (Henry Hornett), Esma Cannon (Edie Hornett), Gordon Jackson (Carnoustie Bligh), Geoffrey Keen (Rev. Mr. Purefoy), Joy Webster (Daphne Pink), Thora Hird (Mrs. Lack), Eliot Makeham (Uncle Brummell), Fred Griffiths (Taxi Driver), George Rose (Waiter at Banfield's), Alfie Bass (Organist), Richard Beynon (Bearded Sailor), Michael Caine (Sailor), Paul Eddington (Bearded Sailor). Sailor Albert Tufnell begins to get cold feet

about his wedding to Shirley when he spends an evening in the presence of his future mother-in-law. Based on a play by Philip King and Falkland Cary. *Dir.* Gordon Parry.

Sailors Three (1940) Tommy Trinder (Tommy Taylor), Claude Hulbert (Llewellyn Davies), Michael Wilding (Johnny Wilding), Carla Lehmann (Jane Davies), James Hayter (Hans Muller), Jeanne De Casalis (Mrs Pilkington), Henry Hewitt (Professor Pilkington), Brian Fitzpatrick (Digby Pilkington), John Laurie (McNab), Harold Warrender (Pilot's Mate), Eric Clavering (Bartender), John Glyn-Jones (Best Man), John Wengraf (German Captain), Manning Whiley (German Commander), Victor Fairley (German Petty Officer), Robert Rendel (British Captain), Allan Jeayes (British Commander), Alec Clunes (British pilot), Derek Elphinstone (British Observer). A comedy with a few song and dance numbers. At the outset of WWII, three British sailors get drunk in a neutral port in South America and on returning to their ship discover they have actually boarded a German pocket battleship by mistake. *Dir.* Walter Forde.

Saint Joan (1957) Jean Seberg (St.Joan of Arc), Richard Widmark (The Dauphin, Charles VII), Richard Todd (Dunois, Bastard of Orleans), Anton Walbrook (Cauchon - Bishop of Beauvais), John Gielgud (Earl of Warwick), Felix Aylmer (Inquisitor), Archie Duncan (Robert de Baudricourt), Harry Andrews (John de Stogumber), Margot Grahame (Duchesse de la Tremouille), Barry Jones (De Courcelles), Francis De Wolff (La Tremouille), Finlay Currie (Archbishop of Rheims), Victor Maddern (English Soldier), Bernard Miles (Master Executioner), David Oxley ("Bluebeard',- Gilles de Rais), Patrick Barr (Captain La Hire), Sydney Bromley (Baudricourt's Steward), Kenneth Haigh (Brother Martin Ladvenu), David Langton (Captain of Warwick's Guard), Thomas Gallagher (Foul-Mouthed Frank), Norman Rossington (2nd Soldier at Burning). Screenplay by Graham Greene adapted from the George Bernard Shaw play of the same title. *Dir.* Otto Preminger.

Saint Meets the Tiger, The (1943) Hugh Sinclair (Simon Templar - The Saint), Jean Gillie (Pat Holm), Gordon McLeod (Insp. Claud Teal/Prof. Karn), Clifford Evans (Tidemarsh/The Tiger), Wylie Watson (Horace), Dennis Arundell (Lionel Bentley), Charles Victor (Bittle), Louise Hampton (Aunt Agatha Gurten), John Salew (Merridon), Arthur Hambling (Police constable), Amy Veness (Mrs. Donald Jones), Claude Bailey (Donald Jones), Noel Dainton (Burton), Eric Clavering (Frankie), Ben Williams (Joe Gallo), John Slater (Eddie), Tony Quinn (Paddy), Alf Goddard (Tailor), Joan Hickson (Aunt Agatha's Maid). The Saint investigates a gang of gold smugglers run by a villain known only as The Tiger. Based on the Leslie Charteris novel *Meet - The Tiger! Dir.* Paul L Stein.

Saint's Return, The (1953) Louis Hayward (Simon Templar), Naomi Chance (Carol Denby), Sydney Tafler (Max Lennar), Charles Victor (Chief Insp. Claud Teal), Jane Carr (Kate Finch), Harold Lang (Jarvis), William Russell (Keith Merton), Diana Dors (The Blonde), Fred Johnson (Irish Cassidy), Thomas Gallagher (Hoppy), Russell Napier (Col. Stafford), Sam Kydd (Barkley). Arriving in England in response to a telegram from a friend asking for help, The Saint finds that she has died in a suspicious accident. The trail leads him to a gambling gang. *Dir.* Seymour Friedman.

Saint's Vacation, The (1941) Hugh Sinclair (Simon Templar - The Saint), Sally Gray (Mary Langdon), Cecil Parker (Rudolph Hauser), Arthur Macrae (Monty Hayward), Leueen MacGrath (Valerie), Gordon McLeod (Inspector Teal), John Warwick (Gregory), Manning Whiley (Marko), Felix Aylmer (Charles Leighton), Ivor Barnard (Emil), Roddy Hughes (Valet). Whilst on holiday in Switzerland, The Saint tackles a German spy network. Based upon Leslie Charteris' novel *Getaway. Dir.* Leslie Fenton.

Sally in Our Alley (1931) Gracie Fields (Sally Winch), Ian Hunter (George Miles), Florence Desmond (Florrie Small), Ivor Barnard (Tod Small), Fred Groves (Alf Cope), Gibb McLaughlin (Jim Sears), Ben Field (Sam Bilson), Barbara Gott (Mrs. Pool), Renée Macready (Lady Daphne), Helen Ferrers (Duchess of Wexford), Leslie Mitchell (Party Guest). A British soldier is crippled during WWI and lets his girlfriend believe that he has been killed. However, years later, after he has been cured, he tries to contact her. *Dir.* Maurice Elvey.

Salome's Last Dance (1988) Glenda Jackson (Herodias/Lady Alice), Stratford Johns (Herod/Alfred Taylor), Nickolas Grace (Oscar Wilde), Douglas Hodge (John the Baptist/Lord Alfred 'Bosey' Douglas), Imogen Millais-Scott (Salome/Rose), Denis Lill (Tigellenus/Chilvers), Russell Lee Nash (Pageboy), Ken Russell (Cappadocian/Kenneth), David Doyle (A. Nubin), Warren Saire (Young Syrian), Kenny Ireland (1st Soldier), Michael Van Wijk (2nd Soldier), Paul Clayton (1st Nazarean), Imogen Claire (2nd Nazarean), Tim Potter (Pharisee), Matthew Taylor (Sadducean), Linzi Drew (1st Slave). The film is essentially a performance of Oscar Wilde's controversial play *Salome* within a framing device of Wilde putting on the play in a brothel in 1893. *Dir.* Ken Russell.

Saloon Bar (1940) Gordon Harker (Joe Harris), Elizabeth Allan (Queenie), Mervyn Johns (Wickers), Joyce Barbour (Sally), Anna Konstam (Ivy), Cyril Raymond (Harry Small), Judy Campbell (Doris), Al Millen (Fred), Norman Pierce (Bill Hoskins), Alec Clunes (Eddie Graves), Mavis Villiers (Joan), Felix Aylmer (Mayor), O.B. Clarence (Sir Archibald), Aubrey Dexter (Major), Helena Pickard (Mrs Small), Manning Whiley (Evangelist), Laurence Kitchin (Peter), Roddy Hughes (Doctor), Gordon James (Jim), Annie Esmond (Mrs. Truscott), Eliot Makeham (Meek Man), Roddy McDowall (Boy), Torin Thatcher (Mr. Garrod). Set largely in a pub where the regulars decide to prove that a fellow drinker is innocent of the murder for which he is soon to be hanged. A whodunit based on a play by Frank Harvey Jr. *Dir.* Walter Forde.

Salt and Pepper (1968) Sammy Davis Jr. (Charles Salt), Peter Lawford (Christopher Pepper), Michael Bates (Inspector Crabbe), Ilona Rodgers (Marianne Renaud), John Le Mesurier (Colonel Woodstock), Graham Stark (Sergeant Walters), Ernest Clark (Colonel Balsom), Jeanne Roland (Mai Ling), Robert Dorning (Club Secretary), Robertson Hare (Dove), Geoffrey Lumsden (Foreign Secretary), William Mervyn (Prime Minister), Llewellyn Rees ('Fake' Prime Minister), Mark Singleton ('Fake' Home Secretary), Michael Trubshawe ('Fake' First Lord), Francesca Tu (Tsai Chan), Oliver MacGreevy (Rack), Peter Hutchins (Straw), Jeremy Lloyd (Lord Ponsonby). Swinging London nightclub owners Salt and Pepper stumble across a plot to overthrow the British government. *Dir.* Richard Donner.

Salute the Toff (1952) John Bentley (The Honourable Richard Rollison), Carol Marsh (Fay), Valentine Dyall (Inspector Grice), Shelagh Fraser (Myra Lorne), June Elvin (Lady Anthea), Arthur Hill (Ted Harrison), Michael Golden (Benny Kless), Jill Allen (Cabaret singer), Roddy Hughes (Jolly), Wally Patch (Bert Ebbutt), Vi Stevens (Emily Ebbutt), Tony Britton (Draycott), John Forbes-Robertson (Gerald Harvey), Peter Bull (Lorne), Cyril Conway (The Wop), Deidre Doyle (Ma Kless). Det. Rollison ("The Toff") helps secretary Fay Gretton investigate the disappearance of her boss. *Dir.* Maclean Rogers.

Sammy and Rosie Get Laid (1987) Shashi Kapoor (Rafi Rahman), Frances Barber (Rosie Hobbs), Claire Bloom (Alice), Ayub Khan-Din (Sammy), Roland Gift (Danny/Victoria), Wendy Gazelle (Anna), Suzette Llewellyn (Vivia), Meera Syal (Rani), Badi Uzzaman (Ghost), Tessa Wojtczak (Bridget), Emer Gillespie (Eva), Lesley Manville (Margy), Mark Sproston (Young Policeman), Buster Bloodvessel (Ringerman), Nicholas Pritchard (Tory M.P), Valerie Buchanan (Danny's Girlfriend), Ade Sapara (Michael). Despite its title this isn't a throwback to the 1970's British sex comedies. A free living and free loving couple reassess their lifestyle during a visit by Sammy's father from India. *Dir.* Stephen Frears.

Sammy Going South (1963) Edward G. Robinson (Cocky Wainwright), Fergus McClelland (Sammy Hartland), Constance Cummings (Gloria van Imhoff), Harry H. Corbett (Lem), Paul Stassino (Spyros Dracandopolous), Zia Mohyeddin (The Syrian), Orlando Martins (Abu Lubaba), John Turner (Heneker), Zena Walker (Aunt Jane), Jack Gwillim (District Commissioner), Patricia Donahue (Kathy), Jared Allen (Bob), Guy Deghy (Doctor), Marne Maitland (Hassan). Sammy is orphaned in an air raid on Port Said during the 1956 Suez Crisis. He decides to travel the length of Africa in order to find his Aunt Jane who lives in Durban, South Africa. Along the way he encounters various characters including Cocky Wainwright, a diamond smuggler. *Dir.* Alexander MacKendrick.

San Demetrio, London (1943) Arthur Young (Captain George Waite), Walter Fitzgerald (Chief Engineer Charles Pollard), Ralph Michael (2nd. Officer Hawkins), Neville Mapp (3rd. Engineer Willey), Barry Letts (Apprentice John Jones), Michael Allen (Cadet Roy Housden), Frederick Piper (Boatswain W.E. Fletcher), Herbert Cameron (Pumpman Davies), John Owers (Steward), Gordon Jackson (Messboy John Jamieson), Robert Beatty ('Yank' Preston), Charles Victor (Deckhand), James McKechnie (Deckhand), John Coyle (Deckhand), Duncan McIntyre (Deckhand), Rex Holt (Deckhand), Mervyn Johns (Greaser John Boyle), Lawrence O'Madden (Capt. E.S.F. Fegen V.C.), James Donald (Gunnery Control Officer), James Sadler (Officer of the Watch), Peter Miller Street (Midshipman), David Horne (Mr. Justice Langton), Nigel Clarke (R.J.E. Dodds), James Knight (Capt. Smith), Diana Decker (Shopgirl). In 1942 the MV *San Demetrio* is damaged by enemy action in mid-Atlantic and abandoned by her crew but that is not the end of this true story. *Dirs.* Charles Frend and Robert Hamer.

Sanders of the River (1935) Paul Robeson (Bosambo), Leslie Banks (Commissioner R.G. Sanders), Nina Mae McKinney (Lilongo), Robert Cochran (Lieutenant Tibbets), Martin Walker (J. Ferguson), Richard Grey (Captain Hamilton), Tony Wane (King Mofolaba), Marqués De Portago (Farini), Eric Maturin (Smith), Allan Jeayes (Father O'Leary), Charles Carson (Governor of the Territory). Set in Nigeria, where the District Commissioner has to deal with gun runners and slave traders with the help of the local tribes. Based on the stories of Edgar Wallace. *Dir.* Zoltán Korda.

Sands of the Kalahari (1965) Stuart Whitman (Brian O'Brien), Stanley Baker (Mike Bain), Susannah York (Grace Munkton), Harry Andrews (Grimmelman), Theodore Bikel (Dr. Bondrachai), Nigel Davenport (Sturdevan), Barry Lowe (Detjens). The survivors of the crash of a private jet struggle to face the Kalahari desert, a pack of baboons and the internal strife within the group. *Dir.* Cy Endfield.

Sandwich Man, The (1966) Michael Bentine (Horace Quilby), Dora Bryan (Mrs. DeVere), David Buck (Steven Mansfield), Suzy Kendall (Sue), Harry H. Corbett (Mack), Bernard Cribbins (Harold), Diana Dors (First Billingsgate Lady), Anna Quayle (Second Billingsgate Lady), Ian Hendry (Policeman On Motorcycle), Stanley Holloway (Park Gardener), Wilfrid Hyde-White (Lord Uffingham), Michael Medwin (Sewer Man), Ron Moody (Rowing Coach), Terry-Thomas (Scoutmaster), Norman Wisdom (Boxing Vicar), Donald Wolfit (Car Salesman), Tracey Crisp (Girl in the Black Plastic Mac), Alfie Bass (Model Yachtsman), Leon Thau (Ram), Earl Cameron (Bernard), Hugh Futcher (Gogi), Peter Jones (Escapologist's Assistant), John Le Mesurier (Abadiah). A sandwich board advertiser roams the streets of London meeting friends, neighbours and eccentrics. *Dir.* Robert Hartford-Davis.

Sapphire (1959) Nigel Patrick (Supt Robert Hazard), Michael Craig (Insp Phil Learoyd), Yvonne Mitchell (Mildred), Paul Massie (David Harris), Bernard Miles (Ted Harris), Olga Lindo (Mrs Harris), Earl Cameron (Dr Robbins), Gordon Heath (Paul Slade), Jocelyn Britton (Patsy), Harry Baird (Johnnie Fiddle), Orlando Martins (Barman), Rupert Davies (Jack Ferris), Yvonne Buckingham (Sapphire), Robert Adams (Horace Big Cigar), Freda Bamford (Sgt Cook), Philip Lowrie (Student), Basil Dignam (Dr Burgess), Fenella Fielding (Lingerie Shop Manageress), Desmond Llewelyn (PC), Susan Stranks (Student), Peter Vaughan (Det Whitehead). The murder of pregnant Sapphire Robbins raises a number of questions, not least being why this black girl was passing herself off as white. *Dir.* Basil Dearden.

Saraband for Dead Lovers (1948) Stewart Granger (Count Philip Konigsmark), Joan Greenwood (Sophie Dorothea), Flora Robson (Countess Clara Platen), Françoise Rosay (The Electress Sophia), Frederick Valk (The Elector Ernest Augustus), Peter Bull (Prince George Louis), Anthony Quayle (Durer), Michael Gough (Prince Charles), Megs Jenkins (Frau Busche), Jill Balcon

(Knesbeck), David Horne (Duke George William), Mercia Swinburne (Countess Eleanore), Miles Malleson (Lord of Misrule). The affair between Count Philip and Sophie Dorothea, the wife of Prince George Louis, is ultimately doomed. Based on the novel by Helen Simpson. *Dir*. Basil Dearden.

Satanic Rites of Dracula, The (1973) Christopher Lee (Count Dracula), Peter Cushing (Lorrimer Van Helsing), Michael Coles (Inspector Murray), William Franklyn (Peter Torrence), Richard Vernon (Colonel Mathews), Maurice O'Connell (Agent Hanson), Joanna Lumley (Jessica Van Helsing), Richard Mathews (John Porter, MP), Patrick Barr (Lord Carradine), Lockwood West (General Sir Arthur Freeborne), Freddie Jones (Dr. Julian Keeley), Barbara Yu Ling (Chin Yang), Peter Adair (Doctor), Valerie Van Ost (Jane), John Harvey (Commissionaire), Maggie Fitzgerald (Vampire girl). Van Helsing is brought in by Scotland Yard to investigate vampirism and occult practices taking place in an English country house. *Dir*. Alan Gibson.

Saturday Night and Sunday Morning (1960) Albert Finney (Arthur Seaton), Shirley Anne Field (Doreen), Rachel Roberts (Brenda), Hylda Baker (Aunt Ada), Norman Rossington (Bert), Bryan Pringle (Jack), Robert Cawdron (Robbie), Edna Morris (Mrs. Bull), Elsie Wagstaff (Mrs. Seaton), Frank Pettitt (Mr. Seaton), Avis Bunnage (Mousy Woman), Colin Blakely (Loudmouth), Irene Richmond (Doreen's Mother), Louise Dunn (Betty), Anne Blake (Civil Defence Officer), Peter Madden (Drunken Man), Peter Sallis (Man in Suit). Arthur works in a Nottinghamshire textile factory and his only outlet is spending his wages on drink at the weekends. He starts an affair with Brenda, the wife of a co-worker, and also becomes attracted to Doreen. Then Brenda announces she is pregnant. An excellent example of the "kitchen sink" genre of the early 1960s which dealt with British working class life in a more realistic and gritty manner. An adaptation of Alan Sillitoe's novel. *Dir*. Karel Reisz.

Savage Messiah (1972) Dorothy Tutin (Sophie Brzeska), Scott Antony (Henri Gaudier), Helen Mirren (Gosh Boyle), Lindsay Kemp (Angus Corky), Michael Gough (M. Gaudier), John Justin (Lionel Shaw), Aubrey Richards (Mayor), Peter Vaughan (Museum Attendant), Ben Aris (Thomas Buff), Eleanor Fazan (Mdme. Gaudier), Otto Diamant (Mr. Saltzman), Imogen Claire (Mavis Coldstream), Maggy Maxwell (Tart), Susanna East (Pippa), Judith Paris (Kate), Robert Lang (Major Boyle). A biopic of French sculptor Henri Gaudier-Brzeska. *Dir*. Ken Russell.

Saving Grace (2000) Brenda Blethyn (Grace Trevethyn), Craig Ferguson (Matthew Stewart), Martin Clunes (Dr. Martin Bamford), Tchéky Karyo (Jacques Chevalier), Jamie Foreman (China MacFarlane), Bill Bailey (Vince), Valerie Edmond (Nicky), Tristan Sturrock (Harvey), Clive Merrison (Quentin Rhodes), Leslie Phillips (Rev. Gerald Percy), Diana Quick (Honey Chambers), Phyllida Law (Margaret Sutton), Linda Kerr Scott (Diana Skinner), Denise Coffey (Mrs. Hopkins), Paul Brooke (Charlie), Ken Campbell (Sgt. Alfred Mabely), John Fortune (Melvyn), Philip Wright (Nigel Plimpton), Darren Southworth (Terry), Magnus Lindgren (Tony), Dean Lennox Kelly (Bob), Johnny Bamford (Removal Boss), Bill Hallet (Postman), Alison Dillon (Secretary), Bill Weston (John Trevethyn). After her husband commits suicide Grace is pursued by debt collectors and decides to solve her financial crisis by growing and selling marijuana. *Dir*. Nigel Cole.

Scandal (1989) John Hurt (Stephen Ward), Joanne Whalley (Christine Keeler), Bridget Fonda (Mandy Rice-Davies), Ian McKellen (John Profumo), Leslie Phillips (Lord Astor), Britt Ekland (Mariella Novotny), Daniel Massey (Mervyn Griffith-Jones), Roland Gift (Johnnie Edgecombe), Jean Alexander (Mrs Keeler), Alex Norton (Det Insp), Ronald Fraser (Justice Marshall), Paul Brooke (John), Jeroen Krabbé (Eugene Ivanov), Keith Allen (Kevin), Ralph Brown (Paul Mann), Iain Cuthbertson (Lord Hailsham), Johnny Shannon (Peter Rachman), Susannah Doyle (Jackie), Joanna Dunham (Lady Bronwen Astor), Trevor Eve (Matinee Idol), Oliver Ford Davies (Mr. Woods), Deborah Grant (Valerie Profumo), Terence Rigby (James Burge), James Villiers (Conservative M.P.). A fictionalised account of the Profumo Affair of 1963 based on Anthony Summers' book *Honeytrap*. *Dir*. Michael Caton-Jones.

Scarlet Blade, The (1963) Lionel Jeffries (Col Judd), Oliver Reed (Capt Tom Sylvester), Jack Hedley (Edward Beverley/Scarlet Blade), June Thorburn (Claire Judd), Michael Ripper (Pablo), Harold Goldblatt (Jacob), Duncan Lamont (Maj Bell), Clifford Elkin (Philip Beverley), Suzan Farmer (Constance Beverley), John Harvey (Sgt Grey), Charles Houston (Drury), Douglas Blackwell (Blake), Michael Byrne (Lt. Hawke), Eric Corrie (Duncannon), Leslie Glazer (Gonzales), Denis Holmes (Chaplain), Robert Rietty (King Charles I), John Stuart (Beverley), Harry Towb (Cobb), John H. Watson (Fitzroy), George Woodbridge (Town Crier), John Woodnutt (Lt Wyatt). An English Civil war drama. The daughter of a Parliamentarian Colonel helps the Royalists, in particular the man known as The Scarlet Blade. *Dir*. John Gilling.

Scarlet Pimpernel, The (1934) Leslie Howard (Sir Percy Blakeney/The Scarlet Pimpernel), Merle Oberon (Lady Blakeney), Raymond Massey (Chauvelin), Nigel Bruce (The Prince of Wales), Bramwell Fletcher (The Priest), Anthony Bushell (Sir Andrew Ffoulkes), Joan Gardner (Suzanne de Tournay), Walter Rilla (Armand St. Just), Mabel Terry-Lewis (Countess de Tournay), O.B. Clarence (Count de Tournay), Ernest Milton (Robespierre), Edmund Breon (Col. Winterbottom), Melville Cooper (Romney), Gibb McLaughlin (The Barber), Morland Graham (Treadle), John Turnbull (Jellyband), Gertrude Musgrove (Sally), Allan Jeayes (Lord Grenville), A. Bromley Davenport (Brogard), William Freshman (Lord Hastings), Hindle Edgar (Lord Wilmot). An adaptation of the Baroness Orczy novel. *Dir*. Harold Young.

Scarlet Thread (1951) Kathleen Byron (Josephine), Laurence Harvey (Freddie), Sydney Tafler (Marcon), Arthur Hill (Shaw), Dora Bryan (Maggie), Eliot Makeham (Jason), Harry Fowler (Sam), Cyril Chamberlain (Mason), Renee Kelly (Eleanor), Hylton Allen (The Dean), Joyce Boorman (Daisy), Vi Kaley (Shooting Gallery Patron), Bill Shine (Basil). After a bystander is killed during a jewel heist, the criminals responsible hide out in a Cambridge college. *Dir*. Lewis Gilbert.

Scars of Dracula (1970) Christopher Lee (Count Dracula), Dennis Waterman (Simon Carlson), Jenny Hanley (Sarah Framsen), Christopher Matthews (Paul Carlson), Michael Gwynn (The Priest), Michael Ripper (Landlord), Patrick Troughton (Klove), Anouska Hempel (Tania), Wendy Hamilton (Julie), Bob Todd (Burgomaster), Delia Lindsay (Alice), Toke Townley (Elderly Waggoner), David Leland (First Policeman), Richard Durden (Second Policeman). Paul's brother Simon and his (Paul's) fiancé Sarah go to Dracula's castle in order to find out what has happened to him. Crucifixes, bats and neck biting are much in evidence. *Dir*. Roy Ward Baker.

Schizo (1976) Lynne Frederick (Samantha Gray), John Leyton (Alan Falconer), Stephanie Beacham (Beth), John Fraser (Leonard Hawthorne), Jack Watson (William Haskin), Queenie Watts (Mrs. Wallace), Trisha Mortimer (Joy), Paul Alexander (Peter McAllister), Robert Mill (Maitre), Colin Jeavons (Commissioner), Victor Winding (Sergeant), Raymond Bowers (Manager), Terry Duggan (Editor), Lindsay Campbell (Falconer), Diana King (Mrs. Falconer), Wendy Gilmore (Samantha's Mother), Victoria Allum (Samantha as a Child). Samantha is being stalked but nobody believes her. *Dir*. Pete Walker.

School for Scoundrels (1960) Ian Carmichael (Henry Palfrey), Terry-Thomas (Raymond Delauney), Alastair Sim (Mr. S. Potter), Janette Scott (April Smith), Dennis Price (Dunstan), Peter Jones (Dudley), Edward Chapman (Gloatbridge), John Le Mesurier (Head Waiter), Irene Handl (Mrs. Stringer), Kynaston Reeves (General), Hattie Jacques (1st Instructress), Hugh Paddick (Instructor), Barbara Roscoe (2nd Instructress), Gerald Campion (Proudfoot), Monte Landis (Fleetsnod), Jeremy Lloyd (Dingle), Charles Lamb (Carpenter), Anita Sharp-Bolster (Maid). Hapless Henry Palfrey attends courses run by Potter which promise to teach the student how to get the upper hand in any situation. The subtitle of the film is *How to Win Without Actually Cheating*. Inspired by the "Gamesmanship" series of books by Stephen Potter. *Dir*. Robert Hamer.

School for Secrets (1946) Ralph Richardson (Prof. Heatherville), Raymond Huntley (Prof. Laxton-Jones), John Laurie (Dr. McVitie), Ernest Jay (Dr. Dainty), David Tomlinson (Mr. Watlington), Finlay Currie (Sir Duncan Wills), Norman Webb (Dr. Wainwright), Michael Hordern (Lt. Cmdr. Lowther), Pamela Matthews (Mrs. Watlington), Joan Haythorne (Mrs. Laxton-

Jones), Joan Young (Mrs. McVitie), Ann Wilton (Mrs. Dainty), Richard Attenborough (Jack Arnold), David Hutcheson (Squadron Leader Sowerby), Patrick Waddington (Group Capt. Aspinall), Cyril Smith (Flight Sgt. Cox), James Hayter (Warrant Officer), D. Bradley Smith (Air Marshal Cotter), Robin Bailey (Wives' escort officer), Hugh Dempster (Sdr. Ldr. Slatter), Kenneth Buckley (Sdr. Ldr. Buckley), Paul Carpenter (Flt. Lt. Argylle), Anthony Dawson (Flt. Lt. Norton), Robert Long (Flying Officer Davies), Richard Mantell (Air Vice-Marshal), Murray Matheson (Wing Cdr. Allen), Anthony Wyckham (Flg. Off. Ogden), Peggy Evans (Daphne Adams), Ingrid Forrest (Penelope Birkenshaw), Geraldine Keyes (Phyllis Hammond), Bill Owen (Paratroop Sergeant), Joseph Almas (Dr. Klemmerhahn), Arthur Rieck (Lt. Hense), Marjorie Rhodes (Mrs. Arnold), Edward Lexy (Sir Desmond Prosser), Hugh Pryse (Sir Nicholas Hathaway), Aubrey Mallalieu (1st Club Member), Desmond Roberts (2nd Club Member), Guy Belmore (3rd Club Member), Alvar Liddell (BBC Announcer - voice), Kenneth More (Bomb Aimer). A fictionalised version of the improvement of the radar system that helped win the Battle of Britain. *Dir.* Peter Ustinov.

Scott of the Antarctic (1948) John Mills (Captain R.F. Scott R.N.), Diana Churchill (Kathleen Scott), Harold Warrender (Dr. E.A. Wilson), Anne Firth (Oriana Wilson), Derek Bond (Captain L.E.G. Oates), Reginald Beckwith (Lt. H.R. Bowers R.I.M.), James Robertson Justice (P.O.'Taff' Evans R.N.), Kenneth More (Lt. E.G.R. 'Teddy' Evans R.N.), Norman Williams (Chief Stoker W. Lashly R.N.), John Gregson (P.O. T. Crean R.N.), James McKechnie (Surgeon Lt. E.L. Atkinson R.N.), Barry Letts (Apsley Cherry-Gerrard), Dennis Vance (Charles S. Wright), Larry Burns (P.O. P. Keohane R.N.), Edward Lisak (Dimitri), Melville Crawford (Cecil Meares), Christopher Lee (Bernard Day), John Owers (F.J. Hooper), Bruce Seton (Lt. H. Pennell R.N.), Clive Morton (Herbert Ponting F.R.P.S.), Sam Kydd (Leading Stoker E. McKenzie R.N.), Mary Merrett (Helen Field), Percy Walsh (Chairman of Meeting), Noel Howlett (First Questioner), Philip Stainton (Second Questioner), Desmond Roberts (Admiralty Official), Dandy Nichols (Caroline), David Lines (Telegraph Boy). A recounting of Robert Falcon Scott's ill-fated expedition to the South Pole in 1910-12. *Dir.* Charles Frend.

Scream and Scream Again (1969) Vincent Price (Dr. Browning), Christopher Lee (Fremont), Peter Cushing (Major Heinrich Benedek), Alfred Marks (Detective Supt. Bellaver), Michael Gothard (Keith), Christopher Matthews (Dr. David Sorel), Judy Huxtable (Sylvia), Anthony Newlands (Ludwig), Kenneth Benda (Prof. Kingsmill), Marshall Jones (Konratz), Uta Levka (Jane), Yutte Stensgaard (Erika), Julian Holloway (Detective Constable Griffin), Judy Bloom (Helen Bradford), Peter Sallis (Schweitz), Clifford Earl (Detective Sgt. Jimmy Joyce), Nigel Lambert (Ken Sparten), David Lodge (Detective Inspector Phil Strickland), Amen Corner (Themselves). The unholy trinity of Cushing, Lee and Price together in this tale of a blood-draining serial killer running amok in 1960s London. The police investigation leads them to a scientist doing research, he says, into cancer. Based on the novel *The Disorientated Man* by Peter Saxon. *Dir.* Gordon Hessler.

Scrooge (1935) Seymour Hicks (Ebenezer Scrooge), Donald Calthrop (Bob Cratchit), Robert Cochran (Fred), Mary Glynne (Belle), Garry Marsh (Belle's husband), Oscar Asche (Spirit of Christmas Present), Marie Ney (Spirit of Christmas Past), C.V. France (Spirit of Christmas Future), Athene Seyler (Scrooge's charwoman), Maurice Evans (Poor man), Mary Lawson (Poor man's wife), Barbara Everest (Mrs. Cratchit), Eve Gray (Fred's wife), Morris Harvey (Poulterer with Prize Turkey), Philip Frost (Tiny Tim), D.J. Williams (Undertaker), Margaret Yarde (Scrooge's laundress), Hugh E. Wright (Old Joe), Charles Carson (Middlemark), Hubert Harben (Worthington). An adaptation of Charles Dicken's *A Christmas Carol*. *Dir.* Henry Edwards.

Scrooge (1951) Alastair Sim (Ebenezer Scrooge), Michael Hordern (Jacob Marley/Marley's Ghost), Michael J. Dolan (The Ghost of Christmas Past), Francis de Wolff (The Ghost of Christmas Present), C. Konarski (The Ghost of Christmas Future), Mervyn Johns (Bob Cratchit), Hermione Baddeley (Mrs.

Cratchit), John Charlesworth (Peter Cratchit), Glyn Dearman (Tiny Tim), George Cole (Young Ebenezer Scrooge), Carol Marsh (Fan), Roddy Hughes (Fezziwig), Hattie Jacques (Mrs. Fezziwig), Patrick Macnee (Young Jacob Marley), Jack Warner (Mr. Jorkin), Rona Anderson (Alice (Belle)), Brian Worth (Fred), Kathleen Harrison (Mrs. Dilber), Miles Malleson (Old Joe), Kathleen Harrison (Mrs. Dilber), Ernest Thesiger (Undertaker), Louise Hampton (Laundress), Eliot Makeham (Mr. Snedrig), Hugh Dempster (Mr. Groper), Richard Pearson (Mr Tupper), Douglas Muir (Businessman). Scrooge is visited by the ghost of his business partner and three spirits who try to show him how he got to be so miserable and miserly and how he might be capable of changing his ways. Possibly the definitive film version of Charles Dicken's *A Christmas Carol*. *Dir.* Brian Desmond Hurst.

Scrooge (1970) Albert Finney (Ebenezer Scrooge), Alec Guinness (Marley's ghost), Edith Evans (Ghost of Christmas Past), Kenneth More (Ghost of Christmas Present), Paddy Stone (Ghost of Christmas Yet to Come), David Collings (Bob Cratchit), Frances Cuka (Mrs. Cratchit), Richard Beaumont (Tiny Tim), Michael Medwin (Scrooge's nephew, Fred), Mary Peach (Fred's wife), Gordon Jackson (Fred's friend), Anton Rodgers (Tom Jenkins), Laurence Naismith (Fezziwig), Kay Walsh (Mrs. Fezziwig), Suzanne Neve (Isabel), Derek Francis (Portly gentleman), Roy Kinnear (Portly gentleman), Geoffrey Bayldon (Toyshop owner), Molly Weir (Woman debtor), Marianne Stone (Party guest). A musical film adaptation of Charles Dickens' short story, *A Christmas Carol*. The film's musical score was composed by Leslie Bricusse. *Dir.* Ronald Neame.

Scum (1979) Ray Winstone (Carlin), Mick Ford (Archer), Julian Firth (Davis), John Blundell (Banks), Phil Daniels (Richards), John Judd (Sands), Philip Jackson (Greaves), Peter Howell (Governor), John Grillo (Goodyear), Ray Burdis (Eckersley), Alan Igbon (Meakin), John Fowler (Woods), Bill Dean (Duke), P.H. Moriarty (Hunt), Nigel Humphreys (Taylor), Jo Kendall (Matron), Patrick Murray (Dougan). Deeply disturbing violent film which tells the story of a young offender named Carlin as he survives life in a borstal by a systematic campaign of violence which means he becomes the "Daddy" and can run the lives of the inmates in his own way. The story was originally made as a BBC play but it was withdrawn from being screened. It was subsequently remade as this film. *Dir.* Alan Clarke.

Sea of Sand (1958) Richard Attenborough (Brody), John Gregson (Capt. Bill Williams), Michael Craig (Capt. Tim Cotton), Vincent Ball (Sgt. Nesbitt), Percy Herbert ('Blanco' White), Barry Foster (Cpl. Matheson), Andrew Faulds (Sgt. Parker), George Murcell (Cpl. Simms), Ray McAnally (Sgt. Hardy), Harold Goodwin (Road Watch), Tony Thawnton (Capt. Tom), Wolf Frees (German Sergeant), George Mikell (German Officer), Martin Benson (German Half-track Officer), Dermot Walsh (Commanding Officer). The British Long Range Desert Group is tasked with blowing up a fuel dump behind enemy lines on the eve of El Alamein. *Dir.* Guy Green.

Sea Shall Not Have Them, The (1954) Michael Redgrave (Air Commodore Waltby), Dirk Bogarde (Flight Sgt. MacKay), Anthony Steel (Flying Officer Treherne), Nigel Patrick (Flight Sgt. Singsby), Bonar Colleano (Sgt. Kirby), James Kenney (Cpl. Skinner), Sydney Tafler (Cpl. Robb), Griffith Jones (Group Capt. Todd), Jack Watling (Flying Officer Harding), Guy Middleton (Squadron Leader Scott), Ian Whittaker (A.C.2 Milliken), Paul Carpenter (Lt Patrick Boyle, Sea Otter Pilot), George Rose (Tebbitt), Victor Maddern (Gus Westover), Eddie Byrne (Petty Officer Porter), Anton Diffring (German Pilot), Gudrun Ure (Kirby's Fiancee), Rachel Kempson (Mrs. Waltby), Joan Sims (Hilda Tebbitt), Michael Balfour (Dray), Glyn Houston (Knox), Michael Ripper (Botterhill), Graham Stark (Corporal). During WWII a bomber ditches in the sea and the survivors wait to be rescued. *Dir.* Lewis Gilbert.

Sea Wolves, The (1980) Gregory Peck (Colonel Lewis Gordon Pugh), Roger Moore (Captain Gavin Stewart), David Niven (Colonel W.H. Grice), Trevor Howard (Jack Cartwright), Barbara Kellerman (Mrs. Cromwell), Patrick Macnee (Major 'Yogi' Crossley), Kenneth Griffith (Wilton), Patrick Allen (Colin

Mackenzie), Wolf Kahler (Trompeta), Bernard Archard (Underhill), Martin Benson (Mr. Montero), Faith Brook (Mrs. Doris Grice), Allan Cuthbertson (Dickie Melborne), Edward Dentith (Lumsdaine), Clifford Earl (Sloane), Rusi Ghandhi (The Governor), Percy Herbert (Dennison), Patrick Holt (Barker), Donald Houston (Hilliard), Glyn Houston (Peters), Victor Langley (Williamson), Terence Longdon (Malverne), Michael Medwin (Radcliffe), W. Morgan Sheppard ("Patch" Lovecroft), John Standing (Finley), Graham Stark (Don Manners), Jack Watson (Maclean). A group made up of ex-pats and the Calcutta Light Horse, a reserve regiment, attack a German ship (in neutral Goa) which is suspected of passing on details of British merchant shipping movements to U-Boats. Based on an actual incident recounted in the book *Boarding Party* by James Leasor. *Dir.* Andrew V. McLaglen.

Séance on a Wet Afternoon (1964) Richard Attenborough (Billy Savage), Kim Stanley (Myra Savage), Mark Eden (Charles Clayton), Nanette Newman (Mrs. Clayton), Judith Donner (Amanda Clayton), Patrick Magee (Superintendent Walsh), Gerald Sim (Detective Sergeant Beedle), Diana Lambert (Sheila), Godfrey James (Mrs. Clayton's Chauffeur), Hajni Biro (Maid at Clayton's), Marian Spencer (Mrs. Wintry), Ronald Hines (Policeman Outside Clayton's), Michael Lees (Plain Clothes Policeman), Margaret Lacey (Woman at First Séance), Marie Burke (Woman at First Séance), Maria Kazan (Woman at First Séance), Lionel Gamlin (Man at Seances), Maggie Rennie (Woman at Second Séance). A medium persuades her husband to kidnap a child so that she can help the police find her and at the same time keep the ransom. *Dir.* Bryan Forbes.

Sebastiane (1976) Barney James (Severus), Neil Kennedy (Maximus), Leonardo Treviglio (Sebastian), Richard Warwick (Justin), Donald Dunham (Claudius), Daevid Finbar (Julian), Ken Hicks (Adrian), Lindsay Kemp (Dancer), Steffano Massari (Marius), Janusz Romanov (Anthony), Gerald Incandela (Leopard Boy), Robert Medley (Emperor Diocletian), Eric Roberts (Executioner). The later life and martyrdom of St Sebastian with homoeroticism to the fore. The dialogue is in (vulgar) Latin, with English subtitles provided for those not classically educated. *Dirs.* Derek Jarman and Paul Humfress.

Secret Agent (1936) John Gielgud (Richard Ashenden/Brodie), Peter Lorre (The General), Madeleine Carroll (Elsa Carrington), Robert Young (Robert Marvin), Percy Marmont (Caypor), Florence Kahn (Mrs. Caypor), Charles Carson ('R'), Lilli Palmer (Lilli). Sent on a mission to kill a spy, Ashenden kills an innocent tourist by mistake. He and his two partners, Elsa and The General try to make amends by eliminating the enemy agent. *Dir.* Alfred Hitchcock.

Secret Ceremony (1968) Elizabeth Taylor (Leonora), Mia Farrow (Cenci), Robert Mitchum (Albert), Peggy Ashcroft (Hannah), Pamela Brown (Hilda), Robert Douglas (Sir Alex Gordon), George Howell (First Cleaner), Penelope Keith (Hotel Assistant), Roger Lloyd-Pack (Cleaner), Angus MacKay (Vicar), Michael Strong (Dr. Walter Stevens). Prostitute Leonora's daughter has drowned and then she meets the physically and mentally fragile Cenci, who looks like the dead girl. In turn, Cenci thinks that Leonora resembles her own dead mother. The pair "adopt" one another but the situation is complicated by the arrival on the scene of Cenci's stepfather Albert. *Dir.* Joseph Losey.

Secret of Blood Island, The (1964) Jack Hedley (Sergeant Crewe), Barbara Shelley (Elaine), Patrick Wymark (Major Jocomo), Charles Tingwell (Major Dryden), Bill Owen (Bludgin), Peter Welch (Richardson), Michael Ripper (Tojoko). A female agent is helped to escape from a Japanese POW camp during WWII. A sequel to *The Camp on Blood Island* (1958). *Dir.* Quentin Lawrence.

Secret People (1952) Valentina Cortese (Maria Brentano/Brent/Lena Collins), Serge Reggiani (Louis Balan), Charles Goldner (Anselmo), Audrey Hepburn (Nora Brentano), Angela Fouldes (Nora Brentano as a child), Megs Jenkins (Penny), Irene Worth (Miss Jackson), Reginald Tate (Insp Eliot), Norman Williams (Police Sgt. Newcombe), Michael Shepley (Manager of the British Pavilion), Athene Seyler (Mrs Reginald Kellick), Sydney Tafler (Syd Burnett), Geoffrey Hibbert (Steenie), John Ruddock (Daly), Michael Allan (Rodd), John Field (Fedor Luki), Charlie Cairoli (Specialty act), Lionel Harris

(Frack), Rollo Gamble (Bentley), John Penrose (Bill), John Chandos (John), Michael Ripper (Charlie), Sam Kydd (Irish Police Sergeant), William Franklyn (Surgeon). Years after fleeing from a dictator, the Beltano family becomes involved in a plot to assassinate him. *Dir.* Thorold Dickinson.

Secrets & Lies (1996) Timothy Spall (Maurice Purley), Phyllis Logan (Monica Purley), Brenda Blethyn (Cynthia Purley), Claire Rushbrook (Roxanne Purley), Marianna Jean-Baptiste (Hortense), Elizabeth Berrington (Jane), Michelle Austin (Dionne), Lee Ross (Paul), Lesley Manville (Social Worker), Ron Cook (Stuart), Emma Amos (Girl with Scar), Brian Bovell (Hortense's Brother), Trevor Laird (Hortense's Brother), Claire Perkins (Hortense's Sister-in-Law), Elias Perkins McCook (Vardan Petrosian). Despite warnings, young black Hortense Cumberbatch, who was adopted, decides to trace her birth mother. Her research leads her to meet Cynthia, a white woman living with her daughter Roxanne, a street sweeper. Most of the performances were improvised after Leigh told each of the actors about their roles, and let them create their own lines. *Dir.* Mike Leigh.

Senna (2011) A documentary charting the career of Formula 1 world champion Ayrton Senna from his arrival in Britain in 1981 until his death in a crash at Imola in 1994, with particular emphasis on his time at McLaren and his rivalry with Alain Prost. *Dir.* Asif Kapadia

Sense and Sensibility (1995) Kate Winslet (Marianne Dashwood), Emma Thompson (Elinor Dashwood), James Fleet (John Dashwood), Harriet Walter (Fanny Dashwood), Gemma Jones (Mrs. Dashwood), Hugh Grant (Edward Ferrars), Alan Rickman (Col. Christopher Brandon), Emilie François (Margaret Dashwood), Elizabeth Spriggs (Mrs. Jennings), Robert Hardy (Sir John Middleton), Greg Wise (John Willoughby), Robert Hardy (Sir John Middleton), Imelda Staunton (Charlotte Jennings Palmer), Imogen Stubbs (Lucy Steele), Hugh Laurie (Mr. Palmer), Richard Lumsden (Robert Ferrars), Tom Wilkinson (Mr. Dashwood). The death of Mr Dashwood means that his estate passes to his son John by his first marriage and eventually leaves his widow and three daughters (Elinor, Marianne, and Margaret) with no choice but to move from their home and take up the offer of a small cottage in Devon. The plot then revolves around the loves of the two elder daughters, steady and dependable Elinor and hopelessly romantic Marianne. The screenplay by Emma Thompson is based on the novel of the same name by Jane Austen. The film won Thompson the Academy Award for Best Writing, Screenplay Based on Material Previously Produced or Published. *Dir.* Ang Lee.

Servant, The (1963) Dirk Bogarde (Hugo Barrett), James Fox (Tony), Sarah Miles (Vera), Wendy Craig (Susan), Catherine Lacey (Lady Mounset), Richard Vernon (Lord Mounset), Anne Firbank (Society Woman), Doris Knox (Older Woman), Patrick Magee (Bishop), Jill Melford (Younger Woman), Alun Owen (Curate), Harold Pinter (Society Man), Dorothy Bromiley (Girl Outside Phone Box), Johnny Dankworth (Jazz Bandleader). A commentary on the English class system. Aristocratic Tony moves to London and hires Barrett as his butler. Tony's girlfriend is suspicious of Barrett and once he introduces his "sister" Vera into the household, roles begin to become reversed. Adaptation by Harold Pinter from a novel by Robin Maugham (the nephew of Somerset Maugham). *Dir.* Joseph Losey.

Seven Days to Noon (1950) Barry Jones (Professor Willingdon), Olive Sloane (Goldie), André Morell (Superintendent Folland), Sheila Manahan (Ann Willingdon), Hugh Cross (Stephen Lane), Joan Hickson (Mrs. Peckett), Ronald Adam (The Prime Minister), Marie Ney (Mrs. Willingdon), Wyndham Goldie (Rev. Burgess), Russell Waters (Det. Davis), Martin Boddey (Gen. Willoughby), Victor Maddern (Private Jackson), Geoffrey Keen (Alf), Joss Ackland (Station Policeman), John Kevan (Major Fanshawe), James Knight (Mr. Cooper), Sam Kydd (Soldier in House Search), Henry McGee (Soldier), John Snagge (BBC Announcer), Marianne Stone (Woman in Phone Box). A nuclear scientist steals a nuclear weapon and gives the British government seven days until noon the following Sunday to stop nuclear research and stockpiling weapons. The film won an Academy Award for Best Writing, Motion Picture Story (Paul Dehn and James Bernard). *Dirs.* John Boulting and Roy Boulting.

Seven-Per-Cent Solution, The (1976) Nicol Williamson (Sherlock Holmes), Robert Duvall (Dr John Watson), Alan Arkin (Dr. Sigmund Freud), Vanessa Redgrave (Lola Deveraux), Laurence Olivier (Prof James Moriarty), Joel Grey (Lowenstein), Samantha Eggar (Mary Morstan Watson), Jeremy Kemp (Baron Karl von Leinsdorf), Charles Gray (Mycroft Holmes), Régine (Madame), Georgia Brown (Mrs Freud), Anna Quayle (Freda), Jill Townsend (Mrs Holmes), John Bird (Berger), Alison Leggatt (Mrs Hudson), Frederick Jaeger (Marker), Erik Chitty (The Butler), Jack May (Dr Schultz), Gertan Klauber (The Pasha), Leon Greene (Squire Holmes). Holmes visits Freud in Vienna in the hope of being cured of his heroin addiction but gets involved in a kidnapping case. Based on Nicholas Meyer's novel. *Dir.* Herbert Ross.

Seventh Survivor, The (1941) Felix Aylmer (Sir Elmer Norton), Jane Carr (Diane Winters), Martita Hunt (Mrs. Lindley), Wally Patch (Bob Sutton), Frank Pettingell (Thomas Pettifer), Ronald Shiner (Ernie), John Stuart (Robert Cooper), Linden Travers (Gillian Chase), Austin Trevor (Captain Hartzmann), Ralph Truman (Captain). The survivors in the lifeboat of a torpedoed ship during WWII include a German spy who is on the run carrying details of a U-Boat campaign. *Dir.* Leslie S. Hiscott.

Seventh Veil, The (1945) James Mason (Nicholas), Ann Todd (Francesca), Herbert Lom (Dr. Larsen), Hugh McDermott (Peter Gay), Albert Lieven (Maxwell Leyden), Yvonne Owen (Susan Brook), David Horne (Dr. Kendall), Manning Whiley (Dr. Irving), Grace Allardyce (Nurse), Ernest Davies (Parker), John Slater (James). A melodrama where in a series of flashbacks concert pianist Francesca, under hypnosis by Dr Larsen, talks about her life, removing successive "veils" to uncover memories of Nicholas, her controlling guardian, and the loves of her life. *Dir.* Compton Bennett.

Sex and Drugs and Rock and Roll (2010) Andy Serkis (Ian Dury), Naomie Harris (Denise), Ray Winstone (Bill Dury), Olivia Williams (Betty Dury), Noel Clarke (Desmond), Toby Jones (Hargreaves), Ralph Ineson (The Sulphate Strangler), Mackenzie Crook (Russell Hardy), Bill Milner (Baxter Dury), Michael Maloney (Graham), Arthur Darvill (Mick Gallagher), Luke Evans (Clive Richards), James Jagger (John Turnbull), Tom Hughes (Chaz Jankel), Clifford Samuel (Charlie Charles), Jennifer Carswell (Ruby), Stephanie Carswell (Mia), Joseph Kennedy (Davey Payne), Naomie Harris (Denise Roudette), Charlotte Beaumont (Jemima Dury), Wesley Nelson (Young Ian Dury). Shakraj Soornack (Norman Watt-Roy). A biopic of singer Ian Dury, in particular the impact on his career and relationships caused by his contraction of polio as a child. The title of the film is derived from a Dury song title. *Dir.* Mat Whitecross.

Sex Lives of the Potato Men (2004) Johnny Vegas (Dave), Mackenzie Crook (Ferris), Mark Gatiss (Jeremy), Lucy Davis (Ruth), Dominic Coleman (Tolly), Julia Davis (Shelley), Huss Garbiya (Beans), Evie Garratt (Joan's Mum), Natasha Anne Hamilton (Ruth's Mum), Robert Harrison (Kevin), Nick Holder (Gordon), Alfie Hunter (Matthew), Jenny Jay (Helen), Craig May (Ruth's Boyfriend), Ed Newbrook (Ruth's Dad), Kay Purcell (Gloria), Nicola Reynolds (Poppy), Kate Robbins (Joan), Angela Simpson (Vicky), Nicholas Tennant (Phil), Betty Trew (Katie), Adrian Chiles (Poppy's Brother). This is a film about the sex lives of a pair of chip shop potato delivery men. With that pitch it is a wonder and, according to media critics, a pity that it was ever made, especially as almost £1 million of public money from the National Lottery via the UK Film Council was used to fund the project. *Dir.* Andy Humphries.

Sexy Beast (2000) Ray Winstone (Gary 'Gal' Dove), Ben Kingsley (Don Logan), Ian McShane (Teddy Bass), Amanda Redman (Deedee Dove), James Fox (Harry), Cavan Kendall (Aitch), Julianne White (Jackie), Álvaro Monje (Enrique), Robert Atiko (Andy), Desirée Erasmus (Jean), Andy Lucas (Jimmy), Dionisio Mesa (Felipe), Eddie O'Connell (Bruno), Terence Plummer (Mike), Frank Scinto (Pete), Darkie Smith (Stan), Rocky Taylor (Raymond), Chris Webb (Nicky). Expert safe-cracker Gary Dove has happily retired to Spain with his wife and friends but then Don Logan arrives to get Gal to come back to London

and do one last job. And he won't take no for an answer. *Dir.* Jonathan Glazer.

Shadowlands (1993) Anthony Hopkins (CS "Jack" Lewis), Debra Winger (Joy Gresham), Edward Hardwicke (Warner "Warnie" Lewis), Joseph Mazzello (Douglas Gresham), James Frain (Peter Whistler), Julian Fellowes (Desmond Arding), Roddy Maude-Roxby (Arnold Dopliss), Michael Denison (Harry Harrington), Andrew Seear (Bob Chafer), Tim McMullan (Nick Farrell), John Wood (Christopher Riley), Andrew Hawkins (Rupert Parrish), Peter Howell (College President), Robert Flemyng (Claude Bird), Toby Whithouse (Frith), Daniel Goode (Lieven), Peter Firth (Dr. Craig), Scott Handy (Standish), Charles Simon (Barker), Giles Oldershaw (Marcus), Simon Cowell-Parker (John Egan). The story of the relationship which develops between reserved C S Lewis, Oxford academic and the author of the Narnia books who lives quietly with his brother Warnie, and divorced, combative, single mother Joy Gresham, an American poet. *Dir.* Richard Attenborough.

Shakespeare in Love (1998) Joseph Fiennes (William Shakespeare), Gwyneth Paltrow (Viola de Lesseps), Colin Firth (Lord Wessex), Ben Affleck (Ned Alleyn), Geoffrey Rush (Philip Henslowe), Judi Dench (Queen Elizabeth I), Tom Wilkinson (Hugh Fennyman), Rupert Everett (Christopher 'Kit' Marlowe), Imelda Staunton (Nurse), Antony Sher (Dr. Moth), Martin Clunes (Richard Burbage), Simon Callow (Edmund Tilney), Jim Carter (Ralph Bashford), Jill Baker (Lady de Lesseps), Patrick Barlow as Will Kempe, Sandra Reinton (Rosaline), Mark Williams (Wabash), Simon Day (First Boatsman), Joe Roberts (John Webster), Steven Beard (Makepeace). Young William Shakespeare is writing his latest play *Romeo and Ethel the Pirate's Daughter* whilst Viola, about to be married to compassionless Lord Wessex is dreaming of becoming an actress (which was impossible in Elizabethan theatre). The result is star-crossed lovers. The film won seven Academy Awards: Best Picture, Best Actress in a Leading Role (Gwyneth Paltrow), Best Actress in a Supporting Role (Judi Dench), Best Writing, Screenplay Written Directly for the Screen, Best Art Direction-Set Decoration, Best Costume Design (Sandy Powell), and Best Music, Original Musical or Comedy Score. *Dir.* John Madden.

Shallow Grave (1994) Ewan McGregor (Alex Law), Kerry Fox (Juliet Miller), Christopher Eccleston (David Stephens), Keith Allen (Hugo), Ken Stott (Detective Inspector McCall), Peter Mullan (Andy), Leonard O'Malley (Tim), Colin McCredie (Cameron), Jean Marie Coffey (Goth), Victoria Nairn (Visitor), Gary Lewis (Visitor), Robert David MacDonald (Lumsden), Kenneth Bryans (Police Officer), John Hodge (Detective Constable Mitchell), David Scoular (Cash Machine Victim), Grant Glendinning (Bath Victim). Three friends - David, a chartered accountant, Juliet, a doctor, and Alex, a journalist – share a flat in Edinburgh and decide they need another sharer. Then the new tenant, Hugo, expires leaving a suitcase behind. *Dir.* Danny Boyle.

Shame (2011) Michael Fassbender (Brandon Sullivan), Carey Mulligan (Sissy Sullivan), Nicole Beharie (Marianne), James Badge Dale (David), Hannah Ware (Samantha), Mari-Ange Ramirez (Alexa), Alex Manette (Steven), Elizabeth Masucci (Elizabeth), Rachel Farrar (Rachel), Loren Omer (Loren), Amy Hargreaves (Hotel Lover), Anna Rose Hopkins (Carly), Carl Low (Bouncer), Stanley Mathis (Conductor), Wenne Alton Davis (WPC). Brandon feels he is just about in control of his sex addiction but then his troubled sister Sissy arrives for a stay. *Dir.* Steve McQueen.

Shaun of the Dead (2004) Simon Pegg (Shaun Riley), Nick Frost (Ed), Kate Ashfield (Liz), Lucy Davis (Dianne), Dylan Moran (David), Penelope Wilton (Barbara), Bill Nighy (Phillip), Jessica Stevenson (Yvonne), Peter Serafinowicz (Pete), Rafe Spall (Noel), Jeremy Thompson (Himself), Martin Freeman (Declan), Reece Shearsmith (Mark), Tamsin Greig (Maggie), Julia Deakin (Yvonne's mum), Matt Lucas (Cousin Tom), Trisha Goddard (Herself), Mark Donovan (Hulking Zombie), Jack Fairbairn (Hulking Zombie 2), Patricia Franklin (Spinster), Chris Martin (Himself), Aaron (Himself), Keith Chegwin (Himself), Krishnan

Guru-Murthy (Himself), Carol Barnes (Herself), Rob Butler (Himself), Vernon Kay (Himself), Robert Popper (Newsreader), Rob Brydon (Newsreader Voiceover). Shaun's mundane existence is brought into sharp focus during a zombie apocalypse. *Dir.* Edgar Wright.

She (1965) Ursula Andress (Ayesha), Peter Cushing (Holly), Bernard Cribbins (Job), John Richardson (Leo), Rosenda Monteros (Ustane), Christopher Lee (Billali), André Morell (Haumeid), Princess Soraya (Soraya), Nosher Powell (British Soldier). Recently discharged from the army, Holly and Leo find the lost city of Kuma which is ruled over by the seemingly immortal Ayesha, also known as "she who must be obeyed". Leo's resemblance to one of Ayesha's past loves leads to inevitable tribulations. Based on the novel by H. Rider Haggard. *Dir.* Robert Day.

Sheriff of Fractured Jaw, The (1958) Kenneth More (Jonathan Tibbs), Jayne Mansfield (Kate), Henry Hull (Major Masters), Bruce Cabot (Jack), Robert Morley (Uncle Lucius), David Horne (James), Ronald Squire (Toynbee), William Campbell (Keeno), Sid James (The Drunk), Reed De Rouen (Clayborne), Charles Irwin (Luke), Donald Stewart (The Drummer), Clancy Cooper (A Barber), Gordon Tanner (Bud Wilkins), Eynon Evans (Manager), Tucker McGuire (Luke's Wife), Brandon Brady (Slim), Larry Taylor (The Gun Guard), Jack Lester (The Coach Driver), Nicholas Stuart (Feeney), Sheldon Lawrence (Johnny), Susan Denny (Cora), Charles Farrell (Bar Tender), Jonas Applegarth (Running Deer), Joe Buffalo (Red Wolf). Comedy in which a very British gun seller is mistaken for a gun-slinger in the Old West. He becomes the sheriff, brokers peace between feuding ranchers, wins the respect of the Native Americans and gains the love of a good woman. *Dir.* Raoul Walsh.

Sherlock Holmes (2009) Robert Downey Jr. (Sherlock Holmes), Jude Law (Dr John Watson), Rachel McAdams (Irene Adler), Mark Strong (Lord Blackwood), Eddie Marsan (Insp Lestrade), Geraldine James (Mrs Hudson), Robert Maillet (Dredger), Kelly Reilly (Mary Morstan), Hans Matheson (Lord Coward), James Fox (Sir Thomas Rotheram), William Hope (Ambassador Standish), William Houston (Constable Clark), Clive Russell (Capt Tanner), Oran Gurel (Reordan), David Garrick (McMurdo), James A. Stephens (Capt Philips), Amanda Grace Johnson (Young Woman Sacrifice), James Greene (Governor). After being hanged, serial killer Lord Blackwood apparently returns from the dead. As his power increases it is up to Holmes and Watson to foil his plans for world domination. *Dir.* Guy Ritchie.

Sherlock Holmes: A Game of Shadows (2011) Robert Downey Jr. (Sherlock Holmes), Jude Law (Dr. John Watson), Noomi Rapace (Madame Simza Heron), Jared Harris (Professor James Moriarty), Stephen Fry (Mycroft Holmes), Eddie Marsan (Inspector Lestrade), Geraldine James (Mrs. Hudson), Kelly Reilly (Mary Watson), Paul Anderson (Sebastian Moran), Fatima Adoum (Gypsy), Affif Ben Badra (Tamas), Daniel Naprous (Marko), Lancelot Weaver (Stefan), William Houston (Constable Clark), Wolf Kahler (Doctor Hoffmanstahl), Jack Laskey (Carruthers), Vladimir 'Furdo' Furdik (Andrzej), Stanley Kaye (Stanley), Thierry Neuvic (Claude Ravache), Laurence Possa (Rene Heron), Clive Russell (Captain Tanner), David Bailey (Robert Cecil). Holmes and the newly married Watson cross swords with the arch criminal Moriarty who is seemingly hell bent on starting a global war. *Dir.* Guy Ritchie.

Ship that Died of Shame, The (1955) Richard Attenborough (George Hoskins), George Baker (Bill Randall), Bill Owen (Birdie), Virginia McKenna (Helen Randall), Roland Culver (Maj. Fordyce), Bernard Lee (The Customs Officer), Ralph Truman (Sir Richard), John Chandos (Raines), Harold Goodwin (Second Customs Officer), John Longden (The Detective), Alfie Bass (Sailor), Stratford Johns (Garage Worker). At the end of WWII the crew of motor gun boat 1087 decide to buy the boat and use it for criminal activities. *Dir.* Basil Dearden.

Ships with Wings (1941) John Clements (Lt. Dick Stacey), Leslie Banks (Vice Adm. David Wetherby), Jane Baxter (Celia Wetherby), Ann Todd (Kay Gordon), Basil Sydney (Capt. Bill Fairfax), Edward Chapman ('Papa' Papadopoulos), Hugh Williams (Wagner), Frank Pettingell (Fields), Michael Wilding (Lt. David Grant), Michael Rennie (Lt Maxwell), Cecil Parker (German Air Marshal), John Stuart (Cmdr. Hood), Morland

Graham (CPO Marsden), Charles Victor (MacDermott), Hugh Burden (Sub Lt. Mickey Wetherby), Frank Cellier (Gen. Baradino Scarappa), Betty Marsden (Jean), John Laurie (Lt. Comdr. Reid), George Merritt (Surgeon), Charles Sturat (Von Rittau), Ian Fleming (Colonel). After Dick Stacey is dismissed from the Fleet Air Arm during WWII he sees a chance to redeem himself aboard an aircraft carrier. Ian Fleming (1888-1969) is an Australian actor famous for playing Dr Watson in a series of Sherlock Holmes movies. *Dir.* Sergei Nolbandov.

Shipyard Sally (1939) Gracie Fields (Sally Fitzgerald), Sydney Howard (Major Fitzgerald), Morton Selten (Lord Alfred Randall), Norma Varden (Lady Patricia Randall), Oliver Wakefield (Forsyth), Tucker McGuire (Linda Marsh), MacDonald Parke (Diggs), Richard Cooper (Sir John Treacher). Singer Sally and her father take over a pub near the Clydebank shipyards. She leads a campaign to keep the yard open when it is threatened with closure. *Dir.* Monty Banks.

Shiralee, The (1957) Peter Finch (Jim Macauley), Dana Wilson (Buster Macauley), Elizabeth Sellars (Marge Macauley), George Rose (Donny), Rosemary Harris (Lily Parker), Russell Napier (Mr. W.G. Parker), Niall MacGinnis (Beauty Kelly), Tessie O'Shea (Bella Sweeney), Sid James (Luke Sweeney), Charles 'Bud' Tingwell (Jim Muldoon), Reg Lye (Desmond), Barbara Archer (Shopgirl), Alec Mango (Papadoulos), John Phillips (Doctor), Bruce Beeby (Macauley's Solicitor), Lloyd Berrell (Slipery), John Cazabon (Charlie the Butcher), Mark Daly (Sam), Ed Devereaux (Christy), Bettina Dickson (Nurse), Guy Doleman (Son O'Neill), Gordon Glenwright (Pete). Itinerant worker Jim takes charge of his young daughter after he finds his wife having an affair. The new burdens of parenthood mean he has to change his ways. Based on the novel by D'Arcy Niland. *Dir.* Leslie Norman.

Shirley Valentine (1989) Pauline Collins (Shirley Valentine-Bradshaw), Tom Conti (Costas Dimitriades), Alison Steadman (Jane), Julia McKenzie (Gillian), Joanna Lumley (Marjorie Majors), Anna Keaveney (Jeanette), George Costigan (Dougie), Bernard Hill (Joe Bradshaw), Sylvia Syms (Headmistress), Gillian Kearney (Young Shirley Valentine), Catharine Duncan (Young Marjorie Majors), Cardew Robinson (Londoner), Tracie Bennett (Millandra), Ken Sharrock (Sydney), Karen Craig (Thelma), Gareth Jefferson (Brian). A Liverpool housewife, unhappy with the way her family ignore her, accepts an invitation to join her friend Jane who has won a holiday in Mykonos. The screenplay is by Willy Russell based on his one-character play of the same title. *Dir.* Lewis Gilbert.

Shooting Fish (1997) Dan Futterman (Dylan), Kate Beckinsale (Georgie), Stuart Townsend (Jez), Myles Anderson (Jez - Age 8), Jacob Macoby (Dylan - Age 8), Scott Charles (Samuel), Antonia Corrigan (Antonia), Rowena Cooper (Jez's Teacher), Jane Lapotaire (Dylan's Headmistress), Tom Chadbon (Mr. Greenaway), Phyllis Logan (Mrs. Ross), Peter McNamara (Geoff), Ralph Ineson (Mr. Ray), Nicola Duffett (Mrs. Ray), Claire Cox (Floss), Dominic Mafham (Roger), Arabella Weir (Mrs. Stratton-Luce), Nickolas Grace (Mr. Stratton-Luce), Annette Crosbie (Mrs. Cummins), Peter Capaldi (Mr. Gilzean), Peter O'Sullevan (Race Commentator - voice), Geoffrey Whitehead (Horse Owner). Dylan and Jez are con men ("shooting fish in a barrel") who during one scam hire Georgie to work for them as a secretary. However, her situation becomes a catalyst for them to think about changing their ways. *Dir.* Stefan Schwartz.

Shooting Party, The (1985) James Mason (Sir Randolph Nettleby), Edward Fox (Lord Gilbert Hartlip), Dorothy Tutin (Lady Minnie Nettleby), John Gielgud (Cornelius Cardew), Gordon Jackson (Tom Harker), Cheryl Campbell (Lady Aline Hartlip), Robert Hardy (Lord Bob Lilburn), Aharon Ipalé (Sir Reuben Hergesheimer), Joris Stuyck (Count Tibor Rakassyi), Rebecca Saire (Cicely Nettleby), Sarah Badel (Ida Nettleby), Rupert Frazer (Lionel Stephens), Judi Bowker (Lady Olivia Lilburn), John J. Carney (Jarvis), Ann Castle (Lady Mildred Stamp), Daniel Chatto (John), Mia Fothergill (Violet), Thomas Heathcote (Ogden), Barry Jackson (Weir), Jonathan Lacey (Dan Glass), Richard Leech (Dr. West), Jack May (Sir Harry Stamp), Deborah Miles (Ellen), Daniel Moynihan (Maidment), Patrick O'Connell (Charlie Lyne), Frank Windsor (Glass). Set in 1913, a year before the outbreak of the First World War, European aristocrats gather on an English country estate to take part in a shooting weekend. The differences between old school attitudes and manners and the new aristocracy begin to show. Based on the book of the same name by Isabel Colegate. *Dir.* Alan Bridges.

Shopping (1994) Sadie Frost (Jo), Jude Law (Billy), Sean Pertwee (Tommy), Fraser James (Be Bop), Sean Bean (Venning), Marianne Faithfull (Bev), Jonathan Pryce (Conway), Daniel Newman (Monkey), Lee Whitlock (Pony), Ralph Ineson (Dix), Eamonn Walker (Peters), Jason Isaacs (Market Trader), Chris Constantinou (Yuppie), Tilly Vosburgh (Mrs. Taylor), Melanie Hill (Sarah). Billy and Tommy lead rival gangs. Billy's girlfriend Jo wants him to change his ways but he wants to ram-raid the new shopping mall first. *Dir.* Paul W. S. Anderson.

Shore, The (2011) Ciarán Hinds (Joe), Conleth Hill (Paddy), Kerry Condon (Patricia), Maggie Cronin (Mary). Friends are reunited twenty-five years after The Troubles in Northern Ireland. The film won the Oscar for Best Live Action Short Film. *Dir.* Terry George

Shout at the Devil (1976) Lee Marvin (Colonel Flynn O'Flynn), Roger Moore (Sebastian Oldsmith), Barbara Parkins (Rosa O'Flynn/Oldsmith), Ian Holm (Mohammed), Reinhard Kolldehoff (Herman Fleischer), Horst Janson (Kyller), Karl Michael Vogler (Von Kleine), Gernot Endemann (Braun), Maurice Denham (Mr. Smythe), Jean Kent (Mrs. Smythe), Heather Wright (Cynthia Smythe), George Coulouris (El Keb), Murray Melvin (Lt. Phipps), Bernard Horsfall (Captain Joyce), Renu Setna (Mr. Raji), Gerard Paquis (Capt. da Silva), Robert Lang (Captain Henry), Peter Copley (Admiral Howe), Geoff Davidson (Mackintosh), Shalimar Undi (Nanny), Joe Mafela (Sergeant Dumu), Solomon Dungane (Luti), Ray Msengana (Ahmed). Set in German East Africa immediately before and during WWI. American O'Flynn and his son-in-law Oldsmith are in constant conflict with the German governor Fleischer, which boils over after the murder of Oldsmith's daughter and the outbreak of the war. Based on Wilbur Smith's novel. *Dir.* Peter R Hunt.

Show Goes On, The (1937) Gracie Fields (Sally Scowcroft), Owen Nares (Martin Fraser), John Stuart (Mack McDonald), Horace Hodges (Sam Bishop), Edward Rigby (Mr. Scowcroft), Amy Veness (Mrs. Scowcroft), Arthur Sinclair (Mike OHara), Cyril Ritchard (Jimmy), Jack Hobbs (Nicholson), Dennis Arundell (Felix Flack), Billy Merson (Manager), Frederick Leister (O.B. Dalton). A mill worker becomes a star. *Dir.* Basil Dean.

Sid and Nancy (1986) Gary Oldman (Sid Vicious), Chloe Webb (Nancy Spungen), David Hayman (Malcolm McLaren), Debby Bishop (Phoebe), Andrew Schofield (Johnny Rotten), Xander Berkeley (Bowery Snax), Courtney Love (Gretchen), Perry Benson (Paul Cook), Tony London (Steve Jones), Sy Richardson (Methadone Caseworker), Edward Tudor-Pole (Hotelier - UK), Biff Yeager (Detective), Rusty Blitz (Reporter), Anne Lambton (Linda), Kathy Burke (Brenda Windzor), Sara Sugarman (Abby National), Mark Monero (Jah Clive), Michele Winstanley (Olive McBollocks), Gloria LeRoy (Granma), Milton Selzer (Granpa). A film telling the ultimately tragic "love story" of Sid Vicious and Nancy Spungen. *Dir.* Alex Cox.

Silent Enemy, The (1958) Laurence Harvey (Lieutenant Crabb, R.N.V.R.), Dawn Addams (Third Officer Jill Masters, W.R.N.S.), Michael Craig (Leading Seaman Sid Knowles), John Clements (The Admiral), Sid James (Chief Petty Officer Thorpe), Alec McCowen (Able Seaman Morgan), Nigel Stock (Able Seaman Fraser), Ian Whittaker (Ordinary Seaman Thomas), Arnoldo Foà (Tomolino), Gianna Maria Canale (Conchita), Massimo Serato (Forzellini), Giacomo Rossi-Stuart (Rosati), Carlo Giustini (Fellini), Raymond Young (Celloni), David Lodge (Sergeant), Brian Oulton (Holford), Cyril Shaps (Miguel), Lee Montague (Miguel's Mate), John Lee (Flag Lieutenant), Terence Longdon (Lieutenant Bailey), Alan Webb (British Consul). A fictionalised account of the operation led by Lionel "Buster" Crabb against Italian divers attacking British warships in WWII. Based on Marshall Pugh's book *Commander Crabb*. *Dir.* William Fairchild.

Silver Dream Racer (1980) David Essex (Nick Freeman), Beau Bridges (Bruce McBride), Cristina Raines (Julie Prince), Clarke Peters (Cider Jones), Harry H. Corbett (Wiggins), Diane Keen

(Tina Freeman), Lee Montague (Jack Freeman), Sheila White (Carol), Patrick Ryecart (Benson), Ed Bishop (Al Peterson), T.P. McKenna (Bank Manager), David Baxt (Ben Mendoza), Barrie Rutter (Privateer), Doyle Richmond (Cider's Brother), Nick Brimble (Jack Davis), Malya Woolf (Mrs. Buonaguidi), Stephen Hoye (Clarke Nichols), Richard LeParmentier (Journalist), Murray Kash (TV Reporter), Bruce Boa (TV Reporter), Christopher Driscoll (Photographer), Leslie Schofield (Reporter), Robert Russell (Garage Mechanic), Morris Perry (Financier), Elisabeth Sladen (Bank Secretary), Jim McManus (Bike Salesman). When Nick Freeman's brother dies in a motorbike accident, he inherits a prototype bike that his brother has built and decides to race it. *Dir.* David Wickes

Silver Fleet, The (1943) Ralph Richardson (Jaap van Leyden), Googie Withers (Hélène van Leyden), Esmond Knight (Von Schiffer), Beresford Egan (Krampf), Frederick Burtwell (Captain Müller), Kathleen Byron (Schoolmistress), Willem Akkerman (Willem van Leyden), Dorothy Gordon (Janni Peters), Charles Victor (Bastiaan Peters), John Longden (Jost Meertens), Joss Ambler (Cornelis Smit), Margaret Emden (Bertha), George Schelderup (Dirk), Neville Mapp (Joop), Ivor Barnard (Admiral), John Carol (Johann), Philip Leaver (Chief of Police), Lawrence O'Madden (Captain Schneider), Anthony Eustrel (Lieutenant Wernicke), Charles Minor (Bohme), Valentine Dyall (Markgraf), Lieutenant Schouwenaar (Captain of the U-boat), Lieutenant Van Dapperen (Lieutenant of the U-boat). When the Nazis force the Dutch to start building submarines, some workers turn to sabotage. *Dirs.* Vernon Sewell and Gordon Wellesley.

Simba (1955) Dirk Bogarde (Alan Howard), Donald Sinden (Inspector Drummond), Virginia McKenna (Mary Crawford), Basil Sydney (Mr. Crawford), Marie Ney (Mrs. Crawford), Joseph Tomelty (Dr. Hughes), Earl Cameron (Karanja), Orlando Martins (Headman), Ben Johnson (Kimani), Frank Singuineau (Waweru), Huntley Campbell (Joshua), Slim Harris (Chege), Glyn Lawson (Mundati), Harry Quashie (Thakla), John Chandos (Settler at Meeting), Desmond Roberts (Colonel Bridgeman), Errol John (African Inspector), Willy Sholanke (Witch Doctor). Alan Howard's brother is murdered by the Mau Mau in Kenya and Alan decides to defend his brother's farm. *Dir.* Brian Desmond Hurst.

Simon and Laura (1955) Peter Finch (Simon Foster), Kay Kendall (Laura Foster), Muriel Pavlow (Janet Honeyman), Hubert Gregg (Bertie Burton), Maurice Denham (Wilson), Ian Carmichael (David Prentice), Richard Wattis (Controller of Television Drama), Thora Hird (Jessie), Terence Longdon (Barney), Clive Parritt (Timothy), Alan Wheatley (Adrian Lee), Beverley Brooks (Mabel), Hal Osmond (Effects Man), Tom Gill, David Morrell, Nicholas Parsons (T.V. Producers), Joan Hickson (Barmaid), Charles Hawtrey (Railway Porter), Cyril Chamberlain (Bert), Marianne Stone (Elsie), Muriel George (Grandma), Brian Wilde (Peter Harbottle), Barry Steele (Bert Harbottle), Esma Cannon (Laura from Newcastle), Philip Gilbert (Joe), Jill Ireland (Burton's Receptionist). A television producer decides to use a real-life acting couple in his new programme, unaware that the marriage is on the rocks. *Dir.* Muriel Box.

Sinbad and the Eye of the Tiger (1977) Patrick Wayne (Sinbad), Jane Seymour (Princess Farah), Damien Thomas (Prince Kassim), Taryn Power (Dione), Margaret Whiting (Zenobia), Patrick Troughton (Melanthius), Kurt Christian (Rafi), Nadim Sawalha (Hassan), Bruno Barnabe (Balsora), Bernard Kay (Zabid), Salami Coker (Maroof), David Sterne (Aboo-Seer). Sinbad and Princess Farah seek out the alchemist Melantius after Farah's brother Kassim is turned into a baboon by a curse. *Dir.* Sam Wanamaker.

Sing As We Go (1934) Gracie Fields (Gracie Platt), John Loder (Hugh Phillips), Dorothy Hyson (Phyllis Logan), Stanley Holloway (Policeman), Frank Pettingell (Uncle Murgatroyd Platt), Lawrence Grossmith (Sir William Upton), Morris Harvey (The Cowboy), Arthur Sinclair (The Great Maestro), Maire O'Neill (Madame Osiris), Ben Field (Nobby), Olive Sloane (Violet), Margaret Yarde (Mrs. Clotty), Evelyn Roberts (Parkinson), Norman Walker (Hezekiah Crabtree), Florence Gregson (Aunt Alice). A musical comedy drama. When Gracie is laid off from her job in a clothing mill during the Depression she decides to go to Blackpool. *Dir.* Basil Dean.

Sink the Bismark! (1960) Kenneth More (Capt Jonathan Shepard), Carl Möhner (Capt Lindemann), Dana Wynter (2nd Officer *Anne Davis*), Laurence Naismith (First Sea Lord), Karel Štěpánek (Admiral Günther Lütjens), Maurice Denham (Cmdr Richards), Mark Dignam (Capt, HMS *Ark Royal*), Michael Goodliffe (Capt Banister), Jack Gwillim (Capt, HMS *King George V*), Esmond Knight (Capt, HMS *Prince of Wales*), Michael Hordern (Adm Tovey, Commander-in-Chief, HMS *King George V*), Geoffrey Keen (Asst Chief of Naval Staff), Jack Watling (Signals Officer), Ernest Clark (Capt, HMS *Suffolk*), John Horsley (Capt, HMS *Sheffield*), Peter Burton (Capt - First Destroyer), Sydney Tafler (1st Workman), John Stuart (Capt, HMS *Hood*), Walter Hudd (Adm, HMS *Hood*), Edward R. Murrow (Himself). May 1941 and the film is largely played out on the bridges of warships and in the Admiralty War Room in London where the newly appointed Director of Operations Captain Shepard organises the hunt for the German battleship Bismark which is at large in the North Atlantic. Esmond Knight actually served as a gunnery officer on board HMS *Prince of Wales* and was almost blinded during the real battle. Based on the C S Forester book *Hunting the Bismark*. *Dir.* Lewis Gilbert.

633 Squadron (1964) Cliff Robertson (Wing Cmdr. Roy Grant), George Chakiris (Lt. Erik Bergman), Maria Perschy (Hilde Bergman), Harry Andrews (Air Vice Marshal Davis), Donald Houston (Group Capt. Don Barrett), Michael Goodliffe (Squadron Leader Frank Adams), John Meillon (Flight Lt. Gillibrand), John Bonney (Flight Lt. Scott), Angus Lennie (Flying Officer Hoppy Hopkinson), Scott Finch (Flying Officer Bissell), John Church (Flying Officer Evans), Barbara Archer (Rosie), Sean Kelly (Lt. Nigel), Julian Sherrier (Flight Lt. Singh), Geoffrey Frederick (Flight Lt. Frank), Suzan Farmer (WAAF Sgt. Mary Blake/Bissell0, Johnny Briggs (Lt Jones). The exploits of a fictional RAF squadron during WWII, its mission to destroy a German V-2 rocket fuel plant by bringing down the mountain under which it is located. The film also follows the travails of the Norwegian resistance which is attempting to aid the squadron. The popular stirring theme music was written by Ron Goodwin. It is believed that the scenes showing the attack through a fjord against anti-aircraft guns inspired the trench run sequence at the end of Star Wars IV. Based on the novel of the same name by Frederick E. Smith. *Dir.* Walter Graumon.

Sixty Glorious Years (1938) Anna Neagle (Queen Victoria), Anton Walbrook (Prince Albert), C. Aubrey Smith (Duke of Wellington), Walter Rilla (Prince Ernst), Charles Carson (Sir Robert Peel), Felix Aylmer (Lord Palmerston), Lewis Casson (Lord John Russell), Pamela Standish (Princess Royal), Gordon McLeod (John Brown), Henry Hallett (Joseph Chamberlain), Wyndham Goldie (Arthur J. Balfour), Malcolm Keen (William E. Gladstone), Frederick Leister (Herbert H. Asquith), Derrick De Marney (Benjamin Disraeli), Joyce Bland (Florence Nightingale), Frank Cellier (Lord Derby), Harvey Braban (Lord Salisbury), Aubrey Dexter (Prince of Wales), Stuart Robertson (Mr. Anson), Olaf Olsen (Prince Fredrick), Marie Wright (Maggie), Laidman Browne (Gen. Gordon), Greta Schröder (Baronin Lehzen), Robert Eddison (Lanternist Professor), Miles Malleson (Wounded Soldier). A biopic of Queen Victoria. A sequel to *Victoria the Great* (1937). *Dir.* Herbert Wilcox.

Skull, The (1965) Peter Cushing (Dr. Christopher Maitland), Patrick Wymark (Anthony Marco), Christopher Lee (Sir Matthew Phillips), Jill Bennett (Jane Maitland), Nigel Green (Inspector Wilson), Patrick Magee (Police Surgeon), Peter Woodthorpe (Bert Travers), Michael Gough (Auctioneer), George Coulouris (Dr. Londe), April Olrich (French Girl), Maurice Good (Pierre). The skull of the Marquis de Sade is offered to Dr Maitland but he is warned about its evil influence. *Dir.* Freddie Francis.

Sky West and Crooked (1966) Hayley Mills (Brydie White), Ian McShane (Roibin Krisenki), Annette Crosbie (Mrs. White), Laurence Naismith (Edwin Dacres), Geoffrey Bayldon (Rev. Phillip Moss), Pauline Jameson (Mrs. Moss), Norman Bird (Mr. Cheeseman), June Ellis (Mrs. Cheeseman), Hamilton Dyce (Bill Slim), Judith Furse (Mrs. Rigby), Anne Blake (Mrs. Potts), Jack Bligh (Fred Strong), Cyril Chamberlain (Hubberd), Margaret Lacey (Village Woman), Rachel Thomas (Grandmam), Gerald Lawson (Jabal Jones), Jacqueline Pearce (Cammellia), Alan Lake (Camlo), Irene Bradshaw (Rachel), Talfryn Thomas (Brand). Brydie is a young woman with the mentality of a teenager brought about by a shooting accident. Her latest "hobby" of burying dead animals in the local churchyard begins to upset the villagers, who already consider her to be a menace. *Dir.* John Mills.

Sleeping Car to Trieste (1948) Jean Kent (Valya), Albert Lieven (Zurta), Derrick De Marney (George Grant), Paul Dupuis (Detective Inspector Jolif), Rona Anderson (Joan Maxted), David Tomlinson (Tom Bishop), Bonar Colleano (Sergeant West), Finlay Currie (Alastair MacBain), Grégoire Aslan (Poirier), Alan Wheatley (Karl/Charles Poole), Hugh Burden (Mills), David Hutcheson (Denning), Claude Larue (Andrée), Zena Marshall (Suzanne), Leslie Weston (Randall), Michael Ward (Elvin), Eugene Deckers (Jules), Dino Galvani (Pierre), George De Warfaz (Chef du Train), Gerard Heinz (Ambassador), Michael Balfour (Spiegel), Yves Chanteau (French Station Official), Tony De Lungo (Beppo), Tony Etienne (Benoit), Christiana Forbes (Ilse), Armand Guinle (Lucien), Henrik Jacobsen (Embassy Butler), Andreas Malandrinos (Italian Police Inspector), Sheila Martin (Françoise), Primrose Milligan (Nursemaid), Oscar Nation (Luigi), David Paltenghi (Vincente), Marcel Poncin (Charles), Gaston Richer (Henri). A remake of the 1932 film *Rome Express* with the destination of the train changed and a stolen painting becoming a stolen diary. *Dir.* John Paddy Carstairs.

Sleuth (1972) Laurence Olivier (Andrew Wyke), Michael Caine (Milo Tindle), Alec Cawthorne (Inspector Doppler), John Matthews (Detective Sergeant Tarrant), Eve Channing (Marguerite Wyke), Teddy Martin (Police Constable Higgs). A game of cut and thrust using mindgames between crime detective fiction writer Wyke and hairdresser Tindle, who is the lover of Wyke's wife. The screenplay was adapted by Anthony Shaffer from his own play. *Dir.* Joseph L. Mankiewicz.

Sleuth (2007) Michael Caine (Andrew Wyke), Jude Law (Milo Tindle), Harold Pinter (Man on TV), Carmel O'Sullivan (Maggie), Kenneth Branagh (Man being questioned by Pinter on TV). Not so much of a remake of the 1972 film although the screenplay by Harold Pinter is an adaption of Anthony Shaffer's Tony Award-winning play. Michael Caine now takes on the role of the older man and Jude Law plays Caine's original role who is now an unemployed actor. *Dir.* Kenneth Branagh

Sliding Doors (1998) Gwyneth Paltrow (Helen), John Hannah (James), John Lynch (Gerry), Jeanne Tripplehorn (Lydia), Zara Turner (Anna), Douglas McFerran (Russell), Paul Brightwell (Clive), Nina Young (Claudia), Virginia McKenna (James's Mother), Kevin McNally (Paul), Terry English (Kind Cabbie), Paul Stacey (Man on Tube), Peter Howitt (Cheeky Bloke), Joanna Roth (Suspicious Girl), Neil Stuke (Defensive Bloke). Having just been fired from her PR job, Helen goes to get on a tube train (the sliding doors) and then in parallel we see her life in two strands – if she boards the train and if she misses it. *Dir.* Peter Howitt.

Slipper and the Rose, The (1976) Gemma Craven (Cinderella), Richard Chamberlain (Prince Edward), Margaret Lockwood (The Stepmother), Michael Hordern (The King), Lally Bowers (The Queen), Edith Evans (The Dowager Queen), Annette Crosbie (The Fairy Godmother), Kenneth More (The Lord High Chamberlain), Christopher Gable (John), Julian Orchard (Duke of Montague), Rosalind Ayres (Isobella, Stepsister), Sherrie Hewson (Palatine, Stepsister). A retelling of the classic fairy tale of Cinderella. *Dir.* Bryan Forbes.

Slumdog Millionaire (2008) Dev Patel (Jamal Malik), Ayush Mahesh Khedekar (Youngest Jamal), Tanay Chheda (Teenage Jamal), Freida Pinto (Latika), Rubina Ali (Youngest Latika), Tanvi Ganesh Lonkar (Teenage Latika), Madhur Mittal (Salim Malik), Azharuddin Mohammed Ismail (Youngest Salim), Ashutosh Lobo Gajiwala (Teenage Salim), Anil Kapoor (Prem Kumar), Irrfan Khan (Police Inspector), Saurabh Shukla (Head Constable Srinivas), Mahesh Manjrekar (Javed), Ankur Vikal (Maman), Rajendranath Zutshi (Millionaire show producer), Sanchita Choudhary (Jamal's mother), Mia Drake Inderbitzin (Adele), Shanjei Ramanathan (beggar boy). Crime, love and adventure as a young man from an impoverished background (a *slumdog*) who gets on the Indian version of *Who Wants to be a Millionaire*. As he progresses through the questions on the show suspicion arises that he may be cheating but when he is questioned by the police he explains in flashback how he comes to know the answers and the story of his life, his brother Salim and the love of his life, Latika. The film won eight Academy Awards: Best Motion Picture of the Year, Best Achievement in Directing (Danny Boyle), Best Achievement in Cinematography, Best Achievement in Film Editing, Best Achievement in Music Written for Motion Pictures, Original Score, Best Achievement in Music Written for Motion Pictures, Original Song (*Jai Ho*), Best Achievement in Sound Mixing, and Best Writing, Adapted Screenplay. *Dirs*. Danny Boyle and Loveleen Tandan.

Small Back Room, The (1949) David Farrar (Sammy Rice), Kathleen Byron (Susan), Jack Hawkins (R.B. Waring), Leslie Banks (Colonel A.K. Holland), Michael Gough (Captain Dick Stuart), Cyril Cusack (Corporal Taylor), Milton Rosmer (Professor Mair), Walter Fitzgerald (Brine), Emrys Jones (Joe), Michael Goodliffe (Till), Renée Asherson (A.T.S. corporal), Anthony Bushell (Colonel Strang), Henry Caine (Sergeant Major Rose), Elwyn Brook-Jones (Gladwin), James Dale (Brigadier), Sam Kydd (Crowhurst), June Elvin (Gillian), David Hutcheson (Norval), Sid James ('Knucksie' Moran), Roderick Lovell (Captain Pearson), James Carney (Sergeant Groves), Roddy Hughes (Welsh doctor), Geoffrey Keen (Pinker), Bryan Forbes (Peterson), Patrick Macnee (Man at Committee Meeting), Robert Morley (The Minister), Michael Powell (Gunnery Officer). Disabled bomb disposal expert Rice is pained by his artificial foot and turns to drink as a solution. This leads to a break-up with his girlfriend. However, the appearance of booby trap devices dropped by the Germans lead him to rediscover his expertise. Based on Nigel Balchin's novel of the same name. *Dirs*. Michael Powell and Emeric Pressburger.

Small Faces (1996) Joe McFadden (Alan), Steven Duffy (Bobby), Iain Robertson (Lex), Laura Fraser (Joanne Macgowan), Garry Sweeney (Charlie Sloan), Clare Higgins (Lorna Maclean), Kevin McKidd (Malky Johnson), Mark McConnochie (Gorbals), Steven Singleton (Welch), David Walker (Fabio), Ian McElhinney (Uncle Andrew), Paul Doonan (Jake), Colin Semple (Dowd), Colin McCredie (Doug), Debbie Welsh (Rebecca), Eilidh McCormick (Alice), Monica Brady (Aunt), Elizabeth McGregor (Mrs McGowan), Andy Gray (Tactless Man), Louise O'Kane (Polly), Lisa Mcintosh (Patty). Set in Glasgow in 1968 the three very different McLean brothers Alan, Bobby and Lex become involved in the local street gangs. *Dir*. Gillies MacKinnon.

Small Town Story (1953) Donald Houston (Tony Warren), Susan Shaw (Patricia Lane), Alan Wheatley (Nick Hammond), Kent Walton (Bob Regan), George Merritt (Michael Collins), Margaret Harrison (Jackie Collins), Norman Williams (Elton), Arthur Rigby (Alf Benson), Michael Balfour (Turner), Denis Compton (Himself), Raymond Glendenning (Commentator), Billy Milne (Trainer), Richard Wattis (Marsh), Molly Weir (Maid). A tussle over an inheritance leads to the kidnap of Oldchester United's star player during a vital promotion match. *Dir*. Montgomery Tully.

Small World of Sammy Lee, The (1961) Anthony Newley (Sammy 'Lee' Leeman), Julia Foster (Patsy), Robert Stephens (Gerry Sullivan), Wilfrid Brambell (Harry), Warren Mitchell (Lou Leeman), Miriam Karlin (Milly), Kenneth J. Warren (Fred), Clive Colin Bowler (Johnny), Toni Palmer (Joan), Harry Locke (Stage Manager), Roy Kinnear (Lucky Dave), Alfred Burke (Big Eddie), Al Mulock (Dealer), Cyril Shaps (Maurice 'Morrie' Bellman), Derek Nimmo (Rembrandt), Harry Baird (Buddy Shine), June Cunningham (Rita), Lynda Baron (Yvette). A comedian is pursued by debt collectors. *Dir*. Ken Hughes.

Smallest Show on Earth, The (1957) Virginia McKenna (Jean), Bill Travers (Matt), Peter Sellers (Percy Quill), Margaret Rutherford (Mrs Fazackalee), Bernard Miles (Old Tom), Francis De Wolff (Albert Hardcastle), Leslie Phillips (Robin Carter), June Cunningham (Marlene Hogg), Sid James (Mr. Hogg), George Cross (Commissionaire), George Cormack (Bell), Stringer Davis (Emmett), Michael Corcoran (Taxi Driver). Matt and Jean Spenser inherit a flea-pit cinema in Sloughborough which is staffed by three very long-term employees, played by Sellers, Rutherford and Miles. In addition they are being pressured to sell by rival cinema owner Hardcastle who wants to knock it down to make way for a car park. *Dir*. Basil Dearden.

Smashing Bird I Used to Know, The (1969) Madeleine Hinde (Nicki Johnson), Renée Asherson (Anne Johnson), Dennis Waterman (Peter), Patrick Mower (Harry Spenton), Faith Brook (Dr Sands), Janina Faye (Susan), David Lodge (Richard Johnson), Maureen Lipman (Sarah), Derek Fowlds (Geoffrey), Colette O'Neil (Miss Waldron), Megs Jenkins (Matron), Cleo Sylvestre (Carlien), Valerie Wallace (Muriel), Lesley-Anne Down (Diana), Cynthia Lund (Nicki, age 9), Sheila Steafel (Young Woman), Valerie Van Ost (Amanda), Joanna David (Schoolgirl). After her father is killed in a fair-ground accident Nicki has strained relationships with her mother and her mother's string of boyfriends, a violent clash with the latest of which ends with her being sent to a remand home – or "a perfumed zoo for teenage she-cats" as it is described on the film's promo poster. *Dir*. Robert Hartford-Davis.

Smashing Time (1967) Rita Tushingham (Brenda), Lynn Redgrave (Yvonne), Michael York (Tom Wabe), Anna Quayle (Charlotte Brillig), Irene Handl (Mrs. Gimble), Ian Carmichael (Bobby Mome-Rath), Jeremy Lloyd (Jeremy Tove), Toni Palmer (Toni), George A. Cooper (Irishman), Peter Jones (Dominic), Arthur Mullard (Cafe Boss), Ronnie Stevens (1st Waiter), John Clive (Sweeney Todd manager), David Lodge (The Caretaker), Murray Melvin (1st Exquisite), Bruce Lacey (Clive Sword), Cardew Robinson (Custard-Pie Vicar). Two young women from the North of England head for Swinging London with big plans to make their fortune. *Dir*. Desmond Davis.

Snapper, The (1993) Colm Meaney (Dessie Curley), Tina Kellegher (Sharon), Ruth McCabe (Kay Curley), Eanna MacLiam (Craig Curley), Peter Rowen (Sonny Curley), Joanne Gerrard (Lisa Curley), Colm O'Byrne (Darren Curley), Ciara Duffy (Kimberley Curley), Fionnuala Murphy (Jackie O'Keefe), Dierdre O'Brien (Mary), Karen Woodley (Yvonne Burgess), Pat Laffan (George Burgess), Virginia Cole (Doris Burgess), Denis Menton (Pat Burgess), Brendan Gleeson (Lester), Jack Lynch (Policeman), Stephen Kennedy (Supermarket Trainee Manager). Sharon Curley is pregnant but refuses to name the father of her baby (snapper) much to the consternation of all around her. Part of the *Barrytown Trilogy* (with *The Commitments* and *The Van*) written by Roddy Doyle. *Dir*. Stephen Frears.

Snatch (2000) Jason Statham (Turkish), Stephen Graham (Tommy), Alan Ford (Brick Top), Dennis Farina (Abraham "Cousin Avi" Denovitz), Brad Pitt (Mickey O'Neil), Vinnie Jones (Bullet Tooth Tony), Robbie Gee (Vinnie), Lennie James (Sol), Ade (Tyrone), Rade Šerbedžija (Boris The Blade), Benicio del Toro (Frankie "Four-Fingers"), Adam Fogerty (Gorgeous George), Mike Reid (Doug "The Head" Denovitz), Goldie ("Bad Boy" Lincoln), William Beck (Neil), Sam Douglas (Rosebud), Jason Flemyng (Darren), Andy Beckwith (Errol), Dave Legeno (John), Ewen Bremner (Mullet), Nicola Collins (Alex), Teena Collins (Susi), Jason Buckham (Gary), Mickey Cantwell (Liam), Sorcha Cusack (Mickey O'Neil's mother). Plots involving a stolen diamond, an unlicensed boxing promoter, match-fixing and gypsies. *Dir*. Guy Ritchie.

So Evil My Love (1948) Ray Milland (Mark), Ann Todd (Olivia), Geraldine Fitzgerald (Susan Courtney), Leo G. Carroll (Jarvis), Raymond Huntley (Henry Courtney), Raymond Lovell (Edgar Bellamy), Martita Hunt (Mrs. Courtney), Moira Lister (Kitty Feathers), Roderick Lovell (Sir John Curle), Muriel Aked (Miss Shoebridge), Finlay Currie (Dr. Krylie), Maureen Delaney (Curtis), Ivor Barnard (Mr. Watson), Ernest Jay (Smathers), Hugh Griffith (Coroner), Zena Marshall (Lisette), Eliot Makeham (Joe Helliwell), Guy Le Feuvre (Dr. Pound), Vincent Holman (Rogers), Chris Halward (Alice), John Wilder (Footman), Leonie Lamartine (Cafe proprietress), Clarence Rigge (Dr. Cunningham). Missionary's widow Olivia Harwood meets suave but amoral Mark Bellis, who becomes her lodger and then her lover. Completely under his spell she agrees to his blackmail scheme involving her old school friend Susan. Based on the novel of the same name by Marjorie Bowen (under the pseudonym Joseph Shearing). *Dir*. Lewis Allen.

So Little Time (1953) Maria Schell (Nicole de Malvines), Marius Goring (Oberst/Colonel Hohensee), Lucie Mannheim (Lotte Schönberg), Gabrielle Dorziat (Madame de Malvines), Barbara Mullen (Anna), John Bailey (Philipe de Malvines), David Hurst (Blumel/Baumann), Stanley Van Beers (Professor Perronet), Oscar Quitak (Gerard), Andree Melly (Paulette). A German officer and a Belgian woman who has lost family members in the war fall in love but surely their love cannot survive the pressures of the conflict? A rare post-war film where the Nazi protagonist is shown in a rather sympathetic light. Based on the novel *Je ne suis pas une Heroine* by Noelle Henry. *Dir.* Compton Bennett.

So Long at the Fair (1950) Jean Simmons (Vicky), Dirk Bogarde (George Hathaway), David Tomlinson (Johnny Barton), Marcel Poncin (Narcisse), Cathleen Nesbitt (Madame Hervé), Honor Blackman (Rhoda O'Donovan), Betty Warren (Mrs. O'Donovan), Zena Marshall (Nina), Eugene Deckers (Day Porter), Felix Aylmer (British Consul), André Morell (Doctor Hart), Austin Trevor (Police Commissaire), Natasha Sokolova (Charlotte), Nelly Arno (Madame Verni). Set in Paris in 1896 during the Paris *Exposition Universelle*. When Vicky Barton returns to the hotel where she and her brother Johnny are staying she finds both he and their room have disappeared. Everyone at the hotel disavows any knowledge of him. Adapted from Anthony Thorne's novel. *Dirs.* Terence Fisher and Anthony Darnborough.

Some Girls Do (1969) Richard Johnson (Hugh Drummond), Daliah Lavi (Baroness Helga Hagen), Beba Loncar (Pandora), James Villiers (Carl Petersen), Vanessa Howard (Robot Number Seven), Maurice Denham (Mr. Dudley Mortimer), Robert Morley (Miss Mary), Sydne Rome (Flicky), Adrienne Posta (Angela), Florence Desmond (Lady Manderville), Ronnie Stevens (Peregrine Carruthers), Virginia North (Robot Number Nine), Nicholas Phipps (Lord Dunnberry), George Belbin (Maj. Newman), Yutte Stensgaard (Robot Number One), Richard Hurndall (President of Aircraft Company), Marga Roche (Birgit), Douglas Sheldon (Kruger), Joanna Lumley (Robot on Suicide Mission). Hugh "Bulldog" Drummond is sent to investigate when people connected with the development of the SST1 supersonic airliner start dying. He is confronted by deadly robots masquerading as beautiful women. The second and final film in a projected Bulldog Drummond series, the other being *Deadlier than the Male* (1966). *Dir.* Ralph Thomas.

Something to Hide (1972) Peter Finch (Harry), Shelley Winters (Gabriella), Linda Hayden (Lorelei), Colin Blakely (Blagdon), John Stride (Sergeant Tom Winnington), Harold Goldblatt (Dibbick), Rosemarie Dunham (Elsie), Helen Fraser (Miss Bunyan), Jack Shepherd (Joe Pepper), Graham Crowden (Lay Preacher). When hen-pecked Harry Field picks up a pregnant teenaged hitchhiker his life dissolves into chaos and murder. Released in the US in 1976 as *Shattered*. Based on a novel by Nicholas Monsarrat. *Dir.* Alastair Reid.

Son of Rambow (2008) Bill Milner (Will Proudfoot), Will Poulter (Lee Carter), Neil Dudgeon (Brother Joshua), Adam Godley (Brethren Leader), Jessica Hynes (Mary Proudfoot), Anna Wing (Grandma), Eric Sykes (Frank), Charlie Thrift (Duncan Miller), Zofia Brooks (Tina), Tallulah Evans (Jess Proudfoot), Jules Sitruk (Didier Revol), Ed Westwick (Lawrence Carter), Asa Butterfield (Brethren Bo), Imogen Aboud (Young Mary), Adam Buxton (Chemistry Teacher), Paul Ritter (Geography Teacher), Edgar Wright (Metalwork Teacher), Emilie Chesnais (French Teacher), Finola McMahon (Gail Graham), Rachel Mureatroyd (Marie Plante), Taylor Richardson (David Smart), Peter Robinson (Lucas Dupont), Sam Kubrick-Finney (Danny), James Clarke (Shaun). A young boy, whose parents are members of the Plymouth Brethren strict religious sect and don't watch films or television, joins the school bad boy in making a home-made remake of the film *First Blood* (the first film to feature John Rambo). *Dir.* Garth Jennings.

Sorcerers, The (1967) Boris Karloff (Prof. Marcus Monserrat), Catherine Lacey (Estelle Monserrat), Ian Ogilvy (Mike Roscoe), Susan George (Audrey Woods), Elizabeth Ercy (Nicole), Victor Henry (Alan), Sally Sheridan (Laura Ladd), Alf Joint (Ron, the mechanic), Meier Tzelniker (The Jewish Baker), Gerald Campion (Customer in China Shop), Ivor Dean (Insp. Matalon), Peter Fraser (Detective George), Martin Terry (Tobacconist), Bill Barnsley (Constable in Fur Store), Maureen Booth (Dancer). A

couple develops a technique of experiencing someone's sensations through hypnosis. *Dir.* Michael Leaves.

Sound Barrier, The (1952) Ralph Richardson (John Ridgefield), Ann Todd (Susan Garthwaite), Nigel Patrick (Tony Garthwaite), John Justin (Philip Peel), Dinah Sheridan (Jess Peel), Joseph Tomelty (Will Sparks), Denholm Elliott (Christopher Ridgefield), Jack Allen (Windy Williams), Ralph Michael (Fletcher), Leslie Phillips (Controller). A drama centring on the problems facing pioneers in jet aircraft design and especially the hazards encountered by test pilots. The film won an Academy Award for Best Sound, Recording. *Dir.* David Lean

South American George (1941) George Formby (George Butters/Gilli Vanetti), Linden Travers (Carole Dean), Enid Stamp-Taylor (Frances Martinique), Jacques Brown (Enrico Richardo), Felix Aylmer (Mr Appleby), Ronald Shiner (Swifty), Alf Goddard (Slappy), Beatrice Varley (Mrs Butters), Herbert Lomas (Mr Butters), Gus McNaughton (George White), Mavis Villiers (Mrs Durrant), Eric Clavering (Mr Durrant). A dual role for George as both a successful and unsuccessful singer. *Dir.* Marcel Varnel.

South of Algiers (1953) Van Heflin (Nicholas Chapman), Wanda Hendrix (Anne Burnet), Eric Portman (Dr Burnet), Charles Goldner (Petris), Jacques François (Jacques Farnod), Jacques B. Brunius (Kress), Aubrey Mather (Prof Young), Alec Finter (Workman), Noelle Middleton (Stewardess), Rene Leplat (Dr Farnod), Simone Silva (Zara), Pierre Chaminade (Concierge), George Pastell (Hassan), Arnold Diamond (Spahi Officer), Marie-France (Yasmin), Michael Mellinger (Spahi N.C.O.), Alec Mango (Mahmoud). Released in the United States with the more descriptive title of *The Golden Mask*, this film follows archaeologist Burnet and his obsessive search for the Golden Mask of Moloch. He is accompanied in his quest by his daughter, her boyfriend and a journalist but his footsteps are dogged by Kress and Petris, two crooks who would also like to get their hands on the mask. *Dir.* Jack Lee.

South Riding (1938) Edna Best (Sarah Barton), Ralph Richardson (Robert Carne), Edmund Gwenn (Alfred Huggins), Ann Todd (Madge Carne), Marie Lohr (Mrs Beddows), Milton Rosmer (Alderman Snaith), John Clements (Joe Astell), Edward Lexy (Mr Holly), Joan Ellum (Lydia Holly), Glynis Johns (Midge Carne), Josephine Wilson (Mrs Holly), Gus McNaughton (Tadman), Herbert Lomas (Castle), Peggy Novak (Bessie Warbuckle), Lewis Casson (Lord Sedgmire), Felix Aylmer (Chairman of Council), Jean Cadell (Miss Dry), Skelton Knaggs (Reg Aythorne), Laura Smithson (Mrs Brimsley), Florence Gregson (Mrs Molton). School headmistress and local land owner take on the local council over a building scheme and fall in love in the process. Based on Winifred Holtby's novel. *Dir.* Victor Saville.

Spanish Gardener, The (1956) Dirk Bogarde (Jose), Jon Whiteley (Nicholas Brande), Michael Hordern (Harrington Brande), Cyril Cusack (Garcia), Maureen Swanson (Maria), Lyndon Brook (Robert Burton), Josephine Griffin (Carol Burton), Bernard Lee (Leighton Bailey), Rosalie Crutchley (Magdalena), Ina De La Haye (Jose's Mother), Geoffrey Keen (Dr. Harvey), Harold Scott (Pedro), Jack Stewart (Police Escort), Richard Molinas (Police Escort), Susan Lyall Grant (Maid), John Adderley (Taxi Driver), David Lander (Policeman). After being posted to Spain a father in the diplomatic service whose marriage has failed becomes jealous when his young son is taken under the wing of the Spanish gardener and takes the opportunity to blacken the man's character. Based on A. J. Cronin's novel. *Dir.* Philip Leacock.

Spare a Copper (1940) George Formby (George Carter), Dorothy Hyson (Jane Gray), Bernard Lee (Jake), John Warwick (Shaw), Warburton Gamble (Sir Robert Dyer), John Turnbull (Inspector Richards), George Merritt (Edward Brewster), Eliot Makeham (Fuller), Ellen Pollock (Lady Hardstaff), Edward Lexy (Night watchman), Jack Melford (Dame), Hal Gordon (Sergeant), Jimmy Godden (Manager), Grace Arnold (Music shop customer), Charles Carson (Admiral), Cyril Chamberlain (Policeman), Aubrey Mallalieu (Music Store Manager), Johnnie Schofield (Policeman), Ronald Shiner (Piano Mover), Jack Vyvian (Police Sergeant). A reservist policeman in Liverpool foils the plans of saboteurs to blow up a new British battleship. *Dir.* John Paddy Carstairs.

Spare the Rod (1961) Max Bygraves (John Saunders), Geoffrey Keen (Arthur Gregory), Donald Pleasence (Mr. Jenkins), Betty McDowall (Ann Collins), Peter Reynolds (Alec Murray), Jean Anderson (Mrs. Pond), Eleanor Summerfield (Mrs. Harkness), Mary Merrall (Miss Fogg), Aubrey Woods (Mr. Bickerstaff), Rory MacDermot (Mr. Richards), Richard O'Sullivan (Fred Harkness), Claire Marshall (Margaret), Jeremy Bulloch (Angell), Annette Robertson (Doris), June Archer (Gladys Weekes), Bryan Pringle (Drunken father). A rare big-screen outing for Max Bygraves, who plays a teacher whose reluctance to use corporal punishment is fully tested when he is assigned a class of unruly teenagers in their last year of school in the East End of London. *Dir.* Les Norman.

Sparrers Can't Sing (1963) James Booth (Charlie Gooding), Barbara Windsor (Maggie Gooding), Roy Kinnear (Fred Gooding), Avis Bunnage (Bridgie Gooding), Brian Murphy (Jack), George Sewell (Bert), Barbara Ferris (Nellie Gooding), Griffith Davies (Chunky), Murray Melvin (Georgie), Arthur Mullard (Ted), Peggy Ann Clifford (Ted's Wife), Wally Patch (Watchman), Bob Grant (Perce), Stephen Lewis (Caretaker), Victor Spinetti (Arnold), Jenny Sontag (Momma), May Scagnelli (Gran), Fanny Carby (Lil), Yootha Joyce (Barmaid), Janet Howse (Janet), Queenie Watts (Queenie), Harry H. Corbett (Greengrocer), Marjie Lawrence (Girl), Glynn Edwards (Charlie's Friend). Sailor-boy Charlie comes home to find his trouble and strife is shacked up with someone else and, to put the tin lid on it, has a baby an'all. Would you Adam and Eve it was released as *Sparrows Can't Sing* in the US and was in need of subtitles before the natives could understand it. *Dir.* Joan Littlewood.

Spiceworld (1997) Victoria Beckham (Victoria/Posh Spice), Melanie Brown (Mel B/Scary Spice), Emma Bunton (Emma/Baby Spice), Melanie Chisholm (Mel C/Sporty Spice), Geri Halliwell (Geri/Ginger Spice), Richard E. Grant (Clifford), Claire Rushbrook (Deborah), Roger Moore (The Chief), Naoko Mori (Nicola), Barry Humphries (Kevin McMaxford), Richard O'Brien (Damien Paparazzo), Alan Cumming (Piers Cuthbertson-Smyth), George Wendt (Martin Barnfield), Mark McKinney (Graydon), Michael Barrymore (Mr. Step), Jools Holland (Musical Director), Kevin McNally (Policeman), Kevin Allen (Gainer), Peter Sissons (Newsreader), Stephen Fry (Judge), Richard Briers (Bishop), Dominic West (Photographer), Bill Paterson (Brian), Jonathan Ross (Himself), Elvis Costello (Bartender), Elton John (Himself), Bob Geldof (Himself), Bob Hoskins (Geri's disguise), Jennifer Saunders (Fashionable woman), Meat Loaf (Dennis), Hugh Laurie (Poirot). A big screen outing for the Spice Girls much of the action involving them travelling around London on their own bus. *Dir.* Bob Spiers.

Spider and the Fly, The (1949) Eric Portman (Fernand Maubert), Guy Rolfe (Philippe Lodocq), Nadia Gray (Madeleine Saincaize), George Cole (Marc), John Carol (Jean Louis/Alfred Louis), Harold Lang (Belfort), Edward Chapman (Minister for War), Maurice Denham (Colonel de la Roche), John Salew (Minister's Secretary), May Hallatt (Monique), James Hayter (Mayor), Arthur Lowe (Town Clerk), Patrick Young (Captain le Maitre), Sebastian Cabot (Prefect at Amiens), Jeremy Spenser (Jacques), Madge Brindley (Jacques' Grandmother), Keith Pyott (Father Pletsier), Natasha Sokolova (Nicole Porte), Philip Stainton (Café Manager), Hal Osmond (Swiss Taxi Driver), Alastair Hunter (Watchman at Legation), Hattie Jacques (Café Michel Barmaid), Campbell Singer (Belfort's Escort). During WWI an ex-policeman, now a major in French intelligence, suggests a thief he knows should be hired to steal a list of German spies. *Dir.* Robert Hamer.

Split Second (1992) Rutger Hauer (Harley Stone), Kim Cattrall (Michelle), Alastair Duncan (Dick Durkin), Michael J. Pollard (The Rat Catcher), Alun Armstrong (Thrasher), Pete Postlethwaite (Paulsen), Ian Dury (Jay Jay), Roberta Eaton (Robin), Tony Steedman (O'Donnell), Steven Hartley (Foster), Sara Stockbridge (Tiffany), Ken Bones (Forensic Expert), Daimon Richardson (Police Officer), Dave Duffy (Nick 'The Barman'), Colin Skeaping (Drunk), Stewart Harvey-Wilson (Killer). Sci-fi set in a partly-flooded future London. Detective Harley Stone is on the trail of the serial killer who murdered his partner. *Dirs.* Tony Maylam and Ian Sharp.

Splitting Heirs (1993) Eric Idle (Tommy Patel/Thomas Henry Butterfly Rainbow Peace, Rick Moranis (Henry Bullock), Duke of Bournemouth), Barbara Hershey (Duchess Lucinda), Catherine Zeta-Jones (Kitty Farrant), John Cleese (Raoul P. Shadgrind), Sadie Frost (Angela), Stratford Johns (Butler), Brenda Bruce (Mrs. Bullock), William Franklyn (Andrews), Richard Huw (Brittle), Charu Bala Chokshi (Mrs Patel), Jeremy Clyde (14th Duke of Bournemouth), Eric Sykes (Jobson the Doorman). The "lost" heir to the Duke of Bournemouth becomes friends with the current heir. *Dir.* Robert Young.

Spring and Port Wine (1970) James Mason (Rafe Crompton), Diana Coupland (Daisy Crompton), Susan George (Hilda Crompton), Rodney Bewes (Harold Crompton), Hannah Gordon (Florence Crompton), Len Jones (Wilfred Crompton), Adrienne Posta (Betty Duckworth), Keith Buckley (Arthur Gasket), Avril Elgar (Betsy-Jane Duckworth), Frank Windsor (Ned Duckworth), Ken Parry (Pawnbroker), Bernard Bresslaw (Lorry Driver), Arthur Lowe (Mr. Aspinall), Marjorie Rhodes (Mrs. Gasket), Joseph Greig (Allan), Christopher Timothy (Joe), Bernard Smidowicz (Van Driver), Maria Mantella (Weaver). Set in Bolton. A strict father struggles to maintain authority over his family. Based on a stage play by Bill Naughton. *Dir.* Peter Hammond.

Spring in Park Lane (1948) Anna Neagle (Judy Howard), Michael Wilding (Lord Richard), Tom Walls (Uncle Joshua Howard), Peter Graves (Basil Maitland), Marjorie Fielding (Mildred Howard), Nigel Patrick (Mr. Bacon), G.H. Mulcaster (Perkins), Josephine Fitzgerald (Kate O'Malley), Lana Morris (Rosie), Nicholas Phipps (Marquis of Borechester), Catherine Paul (Lady Borechester), Cyril Conway (Antique Dealer), H.R. Hignett (Higgins), Tom Walls Jr. (Bates). Romantic comedy in which Lord Richard pretends to be a footman in the Howard household in order to raise money. *Dir.* Herbert Wilcox.

Spy in Black, The (1939) Conrad Veidt (Captain Hardt), Sebastian Shaw (Lt. Ashington/Cmdr. David Blacklock), Valerie Hobson (Frau Tiel/Jill Blacklock), Marius Goring (Lt. Felix Schuster), June Duprez (Anne Burnett), Athole Stewart (The Rev. Hector Matthews), Agnes Lauchlan (Mrs. Matthews), Helen Haye (Mrs. Sedley), Cyril Raymond (The Rev. John Harris), George Summers (Captain Walter Ratter), Hay Petrie (Engineer), Grant Sutherland (Bob Bratt), Robert Rendel (Admiral), Mary Morris (Chauffeuse), Margaret Moffatt (Kate), Kenneth Warrington (Commander Denis), Torin Thatcher (Submarine Officer), Esma Cannon (Maggie), Bernard Miles (Hans), Graham Stark (Bell Boy). During WWI a German submarine arrives off the Orkneys and the captain contacts the local schoolmistress, who is ostensibly a German agent. *Dir.* Michael Powell.

Spy Who Came in from the Cold, The (1965) Richard Burton (Alec Leamas), Claire Bloom (Nan Perry), Oskar Werner (Fiedler), Sam Wanamaker (Peters), George Voskovec (East German Defense Attorney), Rupert Davies (George Smiley), Cyril Cusack (Control), Peter van Eyck (Hans-Dieter Mundt), Michael Hordern (Ashe), Robert Hardy (Dick Carlton), Bernard Lee (Patmore), Beatrix Lehmann (Tribunal President), Esmond Knight (Old Judge), Anne Blake (Miss Crail), George Mikell (German Checkpoint Guard), Richard Marner (Vopo Captain), Warren Mitchell (Mr. Zanfrello), Richard Caldicot (Mr. Pitt), Walter Gotell (Holten), Philip Madoc (Young German Officer), Michael Ripper (Lofthouse). British agent Leamas is involved in a complex plot to undermine the reputation of an East German agent. An adaptation of the novel of the same name by John le Carré. *Dir.* Martin Ritt.

Spy Who Loved Me, The (1977) Roger Moore (James Bond), Barbara Bach (Anya Amasova), Curt Jürgens (Karl Stromberg), Richard Kiel (Jaws), Caroline Munro (Naomi), Walter Gotell (General Gogol), Bernard Lee (M), Desmond Llewelyn (Q), Lois Maxwell (Miss Moneypenny), Geoffrey Keen (Fredrick Gray), George Baker (Captain Benson), Edward de Souza (Sheikh Hosein). Bond teams up with Agent Triple X (Anya) in order to thwart the evil plans of megalomaniac Stromberg. Bond drives a white Lotus Esprit. The opening theme is *Nobody Does It Better* performed by Carly Simon. It was the first Bond theme song to be titled differently from the name of the film, although the phrase "the spy who loved me" is included in the lyrics. The film takes its title from Ian Fleming's novel but does not contain any elements of the novel's plot. *Dir.* Lewis Gilbert.

Spy with a Cold Nose, The (1966) Laurence Harvey (Dr. Francis Trevelyan), Daliah Lavi (Princess Natasha Romanova), Lionel Jeffries (Stanley Farquhar), June Whitfield (Elsie Farquhar), Eric Sykes (Wrigley), Eric Portman (British Ambassador), Denholm Elliott (Pond-Jones), Colin Blakely (Russian Premier), Robert Flemyng (Chief M.I.5), Bernard Archard (Russian Intelligence Officer), Robin Bailey (Man with Aston Martin), Genevieve (Nightclub Hostess), Nai Bonet (Belly Dancer), Paul Ford (American General), Michael Trubshawe (Braithwaite), Bruce Carstairs (Butler), Glen Mason ('Ark' Assistant), Norma Foster ('Ark' Nurse), Gillian Lewis (Lady Warburton), Wanda Ventham (Mrs. Winters), Amy Dalby (Miss Marchbanks), Julian Orchard (Policeman), John Forbes-Robertson (M.I.5 Workshop Director), Arnold Diamond (Agent in Water Wagon), R.S.M. Brittain (Commissionaire), Renee Houston (Lady Blanchflower), Marianne Stone (Mrs. Whitby). Spy spoof in which a British agent living in a semi-detached in Wimbledon with a nagging wife and three kids, devises a plan to spy on the Kremlin by giving the Soviet Premier a bulldog with a listening bug grafted inside its stomach. *Dir.* Daniel Petrie.

Squadron Leader X (1943) Eric Portman (Erich Kohler), Ann Dvorak (Barbara Lucas), Walter Fitzgerald (Inspector Milne), Martin Miller (Mr. Krohn), Beatrice Varley (Mrs. Krohn), Henry Oscar (Dr. Schultz), Barry Jones (Bruce Fenwick), Charles Victor (Marks), Mary Merrall (Miss Thorndike), Carl Jaffe (Luftwaffe Colonel), Marjorie Rhodes (Mrs. Agnew), Friedrich Richter (Inspector Siegel), David Peel (Michael Bertholt), Aubrey Mallalieu (Pierre), John Salew (Sentry). Disguised as an RAF pilot, Kohler fails in a mission to besmirch the British in the eyes of the Belgians and is helped to Britain in error by the Belgian Resistance who think he really is an RAF pilot. *Dir.* Lance Comfort.

Square Peg, The (1958) Norman Wisdom (Norman Pitkin/General Schreiber), Honor Blackman (Lesley Cartland), Edward Chapman (Mr. Grimsdale), Campbell Singer (Sergeant Loder), Hattie Jacques (Gretchen), Brian Worth (Henri Le Blanc), Terence Alexander (Captain Wharton), John Warwick (Colonel Layton), Arnold Bell (General Hunt), André Maranne (Jean-Claude), Victor Beaumont (Jogenkraut), Frank Williams (Captain Ford), Eddie Leslie (Medical officer), Victor Maddern (Cpl Motor Pool). A comedy set during WWII where road workers Norman Pitkin and Mr Grimsdale are drafted and sent to France to help prepare the Allied advance. Captured by the Germans, Norman uses his resemblance to a German officer to his and Mr Grimsdale's advantage. *Dir.* John Paddy Carstairs.

St Martin's Lane (1938) Charles Laughton (Charles), Vivien Leigh (Liberty "Libby"), Rex Harrison (Harley Prentiss), Larry Adler (Constantine Dan), Tyrone Guthrie (Gentry), Maire O'Neill (Mrs. Such), Gus McNaughton (Arthur Smith), Polly Ward (Frankie), Basil Gill (Magistrate), Helen Haye (Selina), David Burns (Hackett), Phyllis Stanley (Della), Edward Lexy (Mr. Such), Clare Greet (Old Maud), Alf Goddard (Doggie), Cyril Smith (Black Face), Romilly Lunge (Jan Duchesi), Ronald Ward (Jack Temperley), Bartlett Cormack (Strang), Edie Martin (Libby's Dresser), Ronald Shiner (Barman). Comedy drama set in London's theatreland. Busker Charles Staggers recruits Libby and forms a music troupe of street performers called The Co-operators. Then Libby is spotted by an impresario. Also known as *Sidewalks of London.* *Dir.* Tim Whelan.

St Trinian's (2007) Rupert Everett (Miss Camilla Dagey Fritton/Carnaby Fritton), Colin Firth (Geoffrey Thwaites), Russell Brand (Flash Harry), Talulah Riley (Annabelle Lealla Fritton), Gemma Arterton (Kelly Opposum Jones), Tamsin Egerton (Chelsea Parker), Antonia Bernath (Chloe), Amara Karan (Peaches), Paloma Faith (Andrea), Juno Temple (Celia), Kathryn Drysdale (Taylor), Lily Cole (Polly), Holly Mackie & Cloe Mackie (Tara & Tania), Lena Headey (Miss Dickinson), Fenella Woolgar (Miss Cleaver), Caterina Murino (Miss Maupassant), Jodie Whittaker (Beverly), Toby Jones (Bursar), Celia Imrie (Matron), Stephen Fry (Himself), Anna Chancellor (Miss Bagstock), Lucy Punch (Verity Thwaites), Mischa Barton (JJ French), Steve Furst (Bank Manager), Zoe Salmon (Emo Girl), Nathaniel Parker (Chairman of the National Gallery), Girls Aloud (School Band). St Trinian's school faces closure because of enormous debts. A national TV quiz and a painting in the National Gallery might prove the solutions to the problem. With a plot which has more than a passing resemblance to that of the 1937 Will Hay comedy *Good Morning Boys,* this was a reboot of the franchise more than 25 years after the previous film. *Dirs.* Oliver Parker and Barnaby Thompson.

St Trinian's 2: The Legend of Fritton's Gold (2009) Rupert Everett (Miss Camilla Dagey Fritton/Archibald Fritton/Reverend Fortnum Fritton), David Tennant (Sir Piers Pomfrey/Lord Pomfrey), Colin Firth (Geoffrey Thwaites), Talulah Riley (Annabelle Lealla Fritton), Sarah Harding (Roxy), Tamsin Egerton (Chelsea Parker), Clara Paget (Bella), Gabriella Wilde (Saffy), Juno Temple (Celia), Ella Smith (Lucy), Montserrat Lombard (Zoe), Zawe Ashton (Bianca), Jessica Agombar (Jessica), Cloe Mackie & Holly Mackie (Tania & Tara), Gemma Arterton (Kelly Opposum Jones), Celia Imrie (Matron), Toby Jones (Bursar), Jodie Whittaker (Beverly), Christian Brassington (Peters). A pair of rings are the secret to finding the legendary treasure stolen by Archibald Fritton from Lord Pomfrey. *Dir.* Oliver Parker and Barnaby Thompson.

Stage Fright (1950) Jane Wyman (Eve), Marlene Dietrich (Charlotte Inwood), Michael Wilding (Ordinary Smith), Richard Todd (Jonathan Cooper), Alastair Sim (Commodore Gill), Sybil Thorndike (Mrs. Gill), Kay Walsh (Nellie Goode), Miles Malleson (Mr. Fortesque), Hector MacGregor (Freddie Williams), Joyce Grenfell ('Lovely Ducks'), André Morell (Inspector Byard), Patricia Hitchcock (Chubby Bannister), Ballard Berkeley (Sergeant Mellish), Alfie Bass (Stage Hand), Cyril Chamberlain (Detective Sgt. Loomis), Basil Cunard (Mr. Tippett), Josephine Douglas (Valerie), Helen Goss (Miss Tippett), Irene Handl (Mrs. Mason), Lionel Jeffries (RADA Student). Actress Eve Gill helps Jonathan, on the run from the police, who suspect him of murdering Charlotte's husband. She goes undercover to try to prove his innocence. Hitchcock's cameo in this film is as a man staring at Eve in the street because she is talking to herself. Based on the novel *Man Running* by Selwyn Jepson. *Dir.* Alfred Hitchcock.

Staggered (1994) Martin Clunes (Neil Price), Michael Praed (Gary), Michele Winstanley (Tina), Kate Byers (Jackie), Sarah Winman (Hilary), David Kossoff (Elderly Man), Helena McCarthy (Elderly Woman), Sylvia Syms (Margaret), Sion Tudor Owen (Morris), Virginia McKenna (Flora), Jake D'Arcy (Pilot), John Forgeham (Inspector Lubbock), Dan Travers (Policeman), Steve Sweeney (Nutter), Dermot Crowley (Dr. Barnet), Anna Chancellor (Carmen Svennipeg), Bill Gavin (Old Man), Griff Rhys Jones (Graham), Julia Deakin (Brenda), Annette Ekblom (Caroline), Desmond McNamara (Traffic Policeman), Paul Brightwell (Longcoat), Ian Michie (Milkman), Michael Medwin (Sarah's Father), Neil Morrissey (Video Biographer), Richard Syms (Vicar). When Neil is abandoned naked on a Scottish island he must try and make it back to London for his wedding. *Dir.* Martin Clunes.

Stand Up, Virgin Soldiers (1977) Robin Askwith (Pvt. Brigg), Nigel Davenport (Sgt. Driscoll), George Layton (Pvt. Jacobs), John Le Mesurier (Col. Bromley-Pickering), Warren Mitchell (Morris Morris), Robin Nedwell (Lt. Grainger), Edward Woodward (Sgt. Wellbeloved), Irene Handl (Mrs. Phillimore), Pamela Stephenson (Bernice), Lynda Bellingham (Valerie), David Auker (Lantry), Robert Booth (Field), Peter Bourke (Villiers), Leo Dolan (Tasker), Brian Godfrey (Foster), Paul Rattee (Browning), Fiesta Mei Ling (Juicy Lucy), Miriam Margolyes (Elephant Ethel), Patrick Newell (M.O. Billings), John Clive (Man in wheelchair), Rosamund Greenwood (Miss Plant), Pearl Hackney (Miss Burns), Monica Grey (Mrs. Billings), Dino Shafeek (Indian watchman), Michael Halsey (MP), Ken Nazarin (Mujib). Set in 1950 during the Malayan Emergency, the lads on National Service are informed they must serve for another six months. They drown their sorrows and seek solace with the local lovelies and some nurses. A sequel to *Virgin Soldiers* (1969).

Based on the book of the same name by Leslie Thomas. *Dir*. Norman Cohen.

Stardust (1974) David Essex (Jim MacLaine), Adam Faith (Mike Menary), Larry Hagman (Porter Lee Austin), Ines Des Longchamps (Danielle), Rosalind Ayres (Jeanette), Marty Wilde (Colin Day), Edd Byrnes (TV Interviewer), Keith Moon (J. D. Clover), Dave Edmunds (Alex), Paul Nicholas (Johnny), Karl Howman (Stevie), Richard LeParmentier (Felix Hoffman), Peter Duncan (Kevin), John Normington (Harrap), David Daker (Ralph Woods), James Hazeldine (Brian), Charlotte Cornwell (Sally Porter), David Jacobs (Himself). Jim becomes a rock star but his relationships with those around him are destroyed by the trappings of fame – sex and drugs and rock and roll. A sequel to *That'll be the Day* (1973). *Dir*. Michael Apted.

Stardust (2007) Charlie Cox (Tristan Thorn), Claire Danes (Yvaine), Michelle Pfeiffer (Lamia), Joanna Scanlan (Mormo), Sarah Alexander (Empusa), Melanie Hill (Ditchwater Sal), Robert De Niro (Captain Shakespeare), Sienna Miller (Victoria Forester), Ben Barnes (Young Dunstan Thorn), Ricky Gervais (Ferdy the Fence), Peter O'Toole (King of Stormhold), Jason Flemyng (Primus), Rupert Everett (Prince Secundus), Mark Heap (Prince Tertius), Julian Rhind-Tutt (Prince Quartus), Adam Buxton (Prince Quintus), David Walliams (Prince Sextus), Mark Strong (Prince Septimus), Nathaniel Parker (Dunstan Thorn), Kate Magowan (Princess Una), David Kelly (Wall guard), Mark Williams (Billy, a goat), Henry Cavill (Humphrey), Jake Curran (Bernard), Olivia Grant (Bernard as a woman), Ian McKellen (The Narrator). A stone wall near the English village of Wall divides the real world from the magical kingdom of Stormhold. When the dying King of Stormhold throws a ruby into the sky it collides with a star causing them both to fall to earth. When Tristan from Wall is guided to the star he discovers it has taken the form of a young woman named Yvaine. He intends to take her home as a gift for Victoria, the girl he wants to marry but he doesn't realise that the star is also being hunted by the two surviving princes of Stormhold (Primus and Septimus) and the witch Lamia. This fantasy film is based on Neil Gaiman's novel of the same name. *Dir*. Matthew Vaughn.

Stars Look Down, The (1940) Michael Redgrave (Davey Fenwick), Margaret Lockwood (Jenny Sunley), Emlyn Williams (Joe Gowlan), Nancy Price (Martha Fenwick), Allan Jeayes (Richard Barras), Edward Rigby (Robert Fenwick), Linden Travers (Mrs. Laura Millington), Cecil Parker (Stanley Millington), Milton Rosmer (Harry Nugent, MP), George Carney (Slogger Gowlan), Ivor Barnard (Wept), Olga Lindo (Mrs. Sunley), Desmond Tester (Hughie Fenwick), David Markham (Arthur Barras), Aubrey Mallalieu (Hudspeth), Kynaston Reeves (Strother), Clive Baxter (Pat Reedy), James Harcourt (Will), Frederick Burtwell (Union Official), Dorothy Hamilton (Mrs. Reedy), Frank Atkinson (Miner), David Horne (Mr. Wilkins), Edmund Willard (Mr. Ramage), Ben Williams (Harry Brace), Scott Harold (Headmaster Strother), Lionel Barrymore (Narrator - U.S. release - voice), Vi Kaley (Old Woman). Davey leaves his mining village and goes to university. On graduating he marries Jenny and lives with her in her home town but back in the mining village danger looms. An adaption of the novel of the same name by A J Cronin. *Dir*. Carol Reed.

Starter for 10 (2006) James McAvoy (Brian Jackson), Dominic Cooper (Spencer), Simon Woods (Josh), Catherine Tate (Julie Jackson), Elaine Tan (Lucy Chang), Alice Eve (Alice Harbinson), Rebecca Hall (Rebecca Epstein), Charles Dance (Michael Harbinson), Lindsay Duncan (Rose Harbinson), Benedict Cumberbatch (Patrick Watts), Mark Gatiss (Bamber Gascoigne), John Henshaw (Des), Joseph Friend (Young Brian), James Gaddas (Martin Jackson), James Corden (Tone), Guy Henry (Dr. Morrison), Sule Rimi (Marcus), Ian Bonar (Colin), Reuben-Henry Biggs (Anthony Salmon), Bethan Bevan (Cordelia Sykes), Raj Ghatak (Nigel De Havilland), Tom Allen (Tristram Neville), Kenneth Hadley (Television Director). When Brian goes to Bristol University he jumps at the chance of being on the University Challenge team. He also starts to fall for his team mate

Alice. Screenplay by David Nicholls, adapted from his own novel. *Dir*. Tom Vaughan.

State Secret (1950) Douglas Fairbanks Jr. (Dr. John Marlowe), Jack Hawkins (Colonel Galcon), Glynis Johns (Lisa Robinson), Walter Rilla (General Niva), Karel Stepanek (Dr. Revo), Herbert Lom (Karl Theodor), Hans Olaf Moser (Sigrist), Guido Lorraine (Lieutenant Prachi), Robert Ayres (Arthur J. Buckman), Carl Jaffe (Janovic Prada), Gerard Heinz (Tomasi Bendel), Leonard Sachs (Dr. Poldoi), Leslie Linder (Andre), Anton Diffring (State Police Officer), Olga Lowe (Baba 'Robinson'), Therese Van Kye (Teresa 'Robinson'), Peter Illing (Macco), Arthur Reynolds (Compere), Richard Molinas (Red Nose), Eric Pohlmann (Cable Car conductor), Louis Wiechert (Christian), Gerik Schjelderup (Bartorek), Henrik Jacobsen (Mountain Soldier). After a surgeon is tricked into operating (unsuccessfully) on an Eastern European dictator, he is forced to flee the country's secret police who do not want the news of the dictator's loss to become known. Released as *The Great Manhunt* in the US. *Dir*. Sidney Gilliat.

Stealing Beauty (1996) Liv Tyler (Lucy Harmon), Sinéad Cusack (Diana Grayson), Donal McCann (Ian Grayson), Rebecca Valpy (Daisy Grayson), Jeremy Irons (Alex Parrish), Jean Marais (M. Guillaume), Rachel Weisz (Miranda Fox), Joseph Fiennes (Christopher Fox), D. W. Moffett (Richard Reed). After the suicide of her mother Lucy visits Italy where she will have her portrait painted. *Dir*. Bernardo Bertolucci.

Steptoe and Son (1972) Wilfrid Brambell (Albert Steptoe), Harry H. Corbett (Harold Steptoe), Carolyn Seymour (Zita), Arthur Howard (Vicar), Victor Maddern (Chauffeur), Fred Griffiths (Barman), Joan Heath (Zita's mother), Fred McNaughton (Zita's father), Lon Satton (Pianist), Patrick Fyffe (Arthur), Patsy Smart (Mrs. Hobbs), Mike Reid (Compere), Alec Mango (Hotel Doctor), Michael Da Costa (Hotel Manager). A big-screen spin-off from the BBC television comedy series about a pair of rag and bone men. After a whirlwind romance, Harold marries a stripper but the wedding, the honeymoon, and the marriage do not go well. *Dir*. Cliff Owen.

Steptoe and Son Ride Again (1973) Wilfrid Brambell (Albert Steptoe), Harry H. Corbett (Harold Steptoe), Milo O'Shea (Dr. Popplewell), Neil McCarthy (Lennie), Bill Maynard (George), Yootha Joyce (Lennie's Wife), George Tovey (Percy), Sam Kydd (Claude), Henry Woolf (Frankie Barrow), Geoffrey Bayldon (Vicar), Frank Thornton (Mr. Russell), Olga Lowe (Percy's wife), Richard Davies (Butcher), Diana Dors (Woman in Flat). The scrap metal dealers need a new horse to pull the cart but Harold buys a greyhound instead and gets into debt with a local loan shark. They try an insurance scam to get out of trouble. The second spin-off film from the television series Steptoe and Son. *Dir*. Peter Sykes.

Stiff Upper Lips (1997) Peter Ustinov (Horace), Prunella Scales (Aunt Agnes), Georgina Cates (Emily), Samuel West (Edward), Robert Portal (Cedric), Sean Pertwee (George), Frank Finlay (Hudson Junior), Brian Glover (Eric), David Artus (Hurdler), Kevin Furlong (Hurdler), Charles Simon (Hudson Senior), Anna Livia Ryan (Rosie), David Ashton (Dr. Henry), Richard Braine (Mr. Tweeb). Edward plans to pair off his sister Emily with his friend Cedric but Emily has other ideas. Aunt Agnes packs them all off to Italy and India. Parody of period dramas. *Dir*. Gary Sinyor.

Stitch in Time, A (1963) Norman Wisdom (Norman Pitkin), Edward Chapman (Mr. Grimsdale), Jeanette Sterke (Nurse Haskell), Jerry Desmonde (Sir Hector), Jill Melford (Lady Brinkley), Glyn Houston (Cpl. Welsh), Hazel Hughes (Matron), Patsy Rowlands (Amy), Peter Jones (Capt. Russell), Ernest Clark (Prof. Crankshaw), Lucy Appleby (Lindy), Vera Day (Betty), Frank Williams (Driver Nutall), Penny Morrell (Nurse Rudkin), Patrick Cargill (Dr. Meadows), Francis Matthews (Benson), John Blythe (Dale), Pamela Conway (Patient), Danny Green (Ticehurst), Johnny Briggs (Armed Robber), Michael Balfour (Workman with Mallet), Jill Carson (Nurse with Bouquet), Pat Coombs (Nurse), Michael Goodliffe (Doctor on Children's Ward), Julian Orchard (Man with Headache), Cardew Robinson (Pinching Patient), Marianne Stone (Mrs. Cutforth), Totti Truman

Taylor (Rich Woman Throwing Bracelet), Wanda Ventham (Nurse). When Mr Grimsdale ends up in hospital Norman, as usual, causes chaos on the wards but meets little Lindy, who hasn't spoken since her parents died in an accident. *Dir*. Robert Asher.

Stolen Face (1952) Paul Henreid (Dr. Philip Ritter), Lizabeth Scott (Alice Brent/Lily Conover), André Morell (David), Mary Mackenzie (Lily Conover), John Wood (Dr. John 'Jack' Wilson), Arnold Ridley (Dr. Russell), Susan Stephen (Betty), Diana Beaumont (May), Terence O'Regan (Pete Snipe), Dorothy Bramhall (Miss Simpson), John Bull (Charles Emmett), Janet Burnell (Maggie Bixby), Alexis France (Mrs. Emmett), Everley Gregg (Lady Millicent Harringay), Ambrosine Phillpotts (Miss Patten), Cyril Smith (Alf Bixby), Richard Wattis (Mr. Wentworth). A plastic surgeon remodels the face of a psychopathic patient to resemble that of a lost love and marries her. When the ex-love returns to him he is faced with a dilemma, especially as his wife has become uncontrollable. *Dir*. Terence Fisher.

Stolen Hours (1963) Susan Hayward (Laura Pember), Michael Craig (Dr. John Carmody), Diane Baker (Ellen), Edward Judd (Mike Bannerman), Paul Rogers (Dr. Eric McKenzie), Robert Bacon (Peter), Paul Stassino (Dalporto), Jerry Desmonde (Colonel), Ellen McIntosh (Miss Kendall), Gwen Nelson (Hospital Sister), Peter Madden (Reynolds). A socialite falls terminally ill. *Dir*. Daniel Petrie.

Storm Over the Nile (1955) Anthony Steel (Harry Faversham), Laurence Harvey (John Durrance), James Robertson Justice (General Burroughs), Mary Ure (Mary Burroughs), Ronald Lewis (Peter Burroughs), Ian Carmichael (Willoughby), Jack Lambert (Colonel), Raymond Francis (Colonel's Aide), Geoffrey Keen (Dr. Sutton), Michael Hordern (General Faversham), Ferdy Mayne (Dr. Harraz), Christopher Lee (Karaga Pasha), John Wynn (Sergeant), Avis Scott (Sergeant's Wife), Roger Delgado (Native Spy), Frank Singuineau (Native Servant), Ben Williams (Faversham's Butler), Vincent Holman (Burroughs' Butler), Paul Streather (Young Harry Faversham), Sam Kydd (Joe). Remake of *The Four Feathers* (1939) which was also directed by Zoltan Korda. *Dirs*. Zoltan Korda and Terence Young.

Stormy Monday (1988) Sean Bean (Brendan), Melanie Griffith (Kate), Tommy Lee Jones (Cosmo), Sting (Finney), James Cosmo (Tony), Mark Long (Patrick), Brian Lewis (Jim), Mick Hamer (Pianist), Andrzej Borkowski (Andrej), Caroline Hutchison (Jean), Scott Hoxby (Bob), Heathcote Williams (Peter Reed), Dulice Liecier (Carol), Prunella Gee (Mrs. Finney), Alison Steadman (Mayor). Brendan works for Newcastle night club owner Finney who is being pressured to sell up by corrupt American businessman Cosmo. Brendan becomes attracted to Kate, who has worked for Cosmo in the past. *Dir*. Mike Figgis.

Story of Gilbert and Sullivan, The (1953) Robert Morley (William S. Gilbert), Maurice Evans (Arthur Sullivan), Eileen Herlie (Helen D'Oyly Carte), Martyn Green (George Grossmith), Peter Finch (Richard D'Oyly Carte), Dinah Sheridan (Grace Marston), Isabel Dean (Mrs. Gilbert), Wilfrid Hyde-White (Mr. Marston), Muriel Aked (Queen Victoria), Michael Ripper (Louis), Bernadette O'Farrell (Jessie Bond), Ann Hanslip (Bride), Eric Berry (Rutland Barrington), Yvonne Marsh (Second bride), Lloyd Lamble (Joseph Bennett), Ian Wallace (Captain), Owen Brannigan (Principal bass baritone), Richard Warner (Cellier), Perlita Neilson (Lettie), Charlotte Mitchell (Charlotte), Stella Riley (Millicent), Leonard Sachs (Smythe), John Rae (Ferguson), Muir Mathieson (Conductor). A biopic of the composer Arthur Sullivan and librettist W S Gilbert and their relationship with each other and the impresario Richard D'Oyly Carte. *Dir*. Sidney Gilliat.

Strange Boarders (1938) Tom Walls (Tommy), Renée Saint-Cyr (Louise Blythe), Googie Withers (Elsie), Ronald Adam (Barstow), C.V. France (Col. Lionel Anstruther), Nina Boucicault (Mrs. Anstruther), Leon M. Lion (Luke), C. Denier Warren (Fry), Irene Handl (Mrs. Dewar), Marda Vanne (Mrs. Greatorex), Arthur Goullet (Senor Torres), George Curzon (Sir Charles), Bryan Powley (George Gateshead), Tyrell Davis (Hayes), Martita Hunt (Miss Pitter), Bernard Miles (Chemist). Comedy thriller. After an old lady carrying secret documents is hit by a bus and killed, honeymooning secret agent Tommy Blythe is sent to the boarding house where she lived to investigate. Meanwhile, his new wife has her own suspicions. *Dir*. Herbert Mason.

Stranger Came Home, A (1954) Paulette Goddard (Angie), William Sylvester (Philip Vickers), Patrick Holt (Job Crandall), Paul Carpenter (Bill Saul), Alvys Maben (Joan Merrill), Russell Napier (Insp. Treherne), Kay Callard (Jennie), David King-Wood (Sessions), Jeremy Hawk (Sgt. Johnson), Patricia Owens (Blonde), Jack Taylor (Brownie), Kim Mills (Roddy), Owen Evans (Redhead), Philip Lennard (Medical Examiner). Four years after he disappeared whilst on a fishing trip to Portugal with three friends, Philip Vickers returns home determined to revenge himself on the person or persons who tried to kill him. Released as *The Unholy Four* in the US. Based on a novel by George Sanders. *Dir*. Terence Fisher.

Straw Dogs (1971) Dustin Hoffman (David), Susan George (Amy), Peter Vaughan (Tom Hedden), T. P. McKenna (Major John Scott), Del Henney (Charlie Venner), Jim Norton (Chris Cawsey), Donald Webster (Riddaway), Ken Hutchison (Norman Scutt), Len Jones (Bobby Hedden), Sally Thomsett (Janice Hedden), Robert Keegan (Harry Ware), Peter Arne (John Niles), Cherina Schaer (Louise Hood), Colin Welland (Reverend Barney Hood), David Warner (Henry Niles). American David Sumner and his wife Amy move to her home village in Cornwall in order to avoid the protests in the US over the Vietnam War. However, the locals seem determined to take advantage of the quiet American. The situation soon escalates into rape and violence. A very controversial film on its release. Based upon the novel *The Siege of Trencher's Farm* by Gordon Williams. *Dir*. Sam Peckinpah.

Strawberry Roan (1944) William Hartnell (Chris Lowe), Carol Raye (Molly Lowe), Walter Fitzgerald (Walter Morley), Sophie Stewart (Mrs Morley), John Ruddock (John Dibben), Petula Clark (Kate Dibben), Wylie Watson (Bill Gurd), Joan Maude (Gladys Moon), Joan Young (Mrs. Dibben), Ellis Irving (Auctioneer), Kynaston Reeves (Horse Dealer), Norman Shelley (Dr Lambert), Patric Curwen (Vicar), Charles Doe (Silas), Percy Coyte (Fred), Pat Geary (Emily Dibben). City-girl marries a farmer but fails to adapt to life in the country. Based on A. G. Street's novel. *Dir*. Maurice Elvey.

Street Corner (1953) Peggy Cummins (Bridget Foster), Terence Morgan (Ray), Anne Crawford (Susan), Rosamund John (Sgt. Pauline Ramsey), Barbara Murray (WPC Lucy), Sarah Lawson (Joyce), Ronald Howard (David Evans), Eleanor Summerfield (Edna Hurran), Michael Medwin (Chick Farrar), Charles Victor (Muller), Dora Bryan (Prostitute), Eunice Gayson (Janet), Yvonne Marsh (Elsa), Isabel George (Helen), Archie Duncan (Chief Inspector), Michael Hordern (Det. Insp. Heron), Lloyd Lamble (Det. Sgt. Weston), Russell Waters (Det. Constable Brown), John Warwick (Insp. Gray), James Gilbert (PC Angus Ross), Joyce Carey (Miss Hopkins), Maurice Denham (Mr. Dawson), Thora Hird (Mrs. Perkins), Marjorie Rhodes (Mrs. Foster), Jean Anderson (Miss Haversham), Lily Kann (Mrs. Muller), Harold Lang (Len), Myrtle Reed (Ruby Masters), Leo Bieber (Herman J. Schultz), Brian Kent (Mr. Potter), Basil Lord (Ernie Hurran), Kathleen Michael (Mrs Dawson), Anthony Oliver (Stanley Foster), Fanny Rowe (C.O.), Pat Nye (C.S.M.), Dandy Nichols (Mrs. Furness), Campbell Singer (Desk Sgt. Bates), Brian Wilde (Pinky), Martin Wyldeck (Desk Sgt. Forbes). A documentary style dramatisation of the work of women PCs. *Dir*. Muriel Box.

StreetDance (3D) (2010) Flawless (The Surge), Diversity (Themselves), Nichola Burley (Carly), George Sampson (Eddie), Richard Winsor (Tomas), Ukweli Roach (Jay), Charlotte Rampling (Helena), Eleanor Bron (Madame Fleurie), Jeremy Sheffield (Michael), Chris Wilson (Cafe Parent), Rachel McDowall (Isabella), Patrick Baladi (Mr Harding), Jocelyn Jee Esien (Delilah), Tameka Empson (Sharonda), Jennifer Leung (Bex), Rhiann Keys (Ballet Dancer), Sianad Gregory (Chloe), Sascha Chang (Aimee), Daniella Masterson (Ballet Dancer), Teneisha Bonner (Shawna Melawani), Kofi Aggyman (Mack), Lex Milczarek (Boogie), Lil Steph (Steph), Richie Riz (Bouncer), Frank Harper (Fred). Street dance crews battle it out to win a competition and one of them has recruited ballet dancers! George Sampson, Diversity and Flawless all appeared on ITV's Britain's Got Talent, with George Sampson and Diversity being winners in 2008 and 2009 respectively. *Dirs*. Max Giwa and Dania Pasquini.

Stud, The (1978) Joan Collins (Fontaine Khaled), Oliver Tobias (Tony Blake), Sue Lloyd (Vanessa Grant), Walter Gotell (Benjamin Khaled), Mark Burns (Leonard Grant), Doug Fisher (Sammy), Emma Jacobs (Alex Khaled), Peter Lukas (Ian Thane), Natalie Ogle (Maddy), Merlyn Ward (Peter), Sarah Lawson (Anne Khaled), Peter Dennis (Marc), Minah Bird (Molly), Hilda Fenemore (Mrs. Blake), Bernard Stone (Mr. Blake), Jeremy Child (Lawyer), John Conteh (Himself). The bored wife of a businessman starts an affair with the manager of the disco she owns. Based on the novel of the same name by Jackie Collins. *Dir.* Quentin Masters.

Study in Terror, A (1965) John Neville (Sherlock Holmes), Donald Houston (Dr Watson), John Fraser (Lord Carfax), Anthony Quayle (Dr Murray), Barbara Windsor (Annie Chapman), Adrienne Corri (Angela), Frank Finlay (Insp Lestrade), Judi Dench (Sally Young), Charles Regnier (Joseph Beck), Cecil Parker (Prime Minister), Georgia Brown (Singer), Barry Jones (Duke of Shires), Robert Morley (Mycroft Holmes), Dudley Foster (Home Secretary), Peter Carsten (Max Steiner), Christiane Maybach (Polly Nichols), Kay Walsh (Cathy Eddowes), John Cairney (Michael Osborne), Edina Ronay (Mary Kelly), Avis Bunnage (Landlady), Barbara Leake (Mrs Hudson), Patrick Newell (PC Benson), Norma Foster (Liz Stride), Terry Downes (Chunky), Sally Douglas (Whore in Pub), Jeremy Lloyd (Rupert), Corin Redgrave (Rupert's Friend). Holmes and Watson on the trail of Jack the Ripper (again). It makes you wonder why Conan Doyle didn't think of it as a plot device. *Dir.* James Hill.

Submarine (2010) Craig Roberts (Oliver), Yasmin Paige (Jordana Bevan), Sally Hawkins (Jill Tate), Noah Taylor (Lloyd Tate), Paddy Considine (Graham), Gemma Chan (Kim-Lin), Steffan Rhodri (Mr. Davey), Melanie Walters (Judie Bevan), Sion Tudor Owen (Brynn Bevan), Darren Evans (Chips), Osian Cai Dulais (Mark Pritchard), Lily McCann (Zoe Preece), Otis Lloyd (Keiron), Elinor Crawley (Abby Smuts), Adrienne O'Sullivan (Jackie), Jonny Wier (Malcolm), Lydia Fox (Miss Dutton), Lynne Hunter (Gene), Claire Cage (News Reporter), Edwin Ashcroft (Dafydd), Andrew Phillips (Rhydian Bird). Oliver Tate is a 15 year-old who is concerned about his parent's sexlife, especially when an old flame of his mother's moves in next door. Oliver finally gets a girlfriend, at least until his social incompetence ruins the relationship. A coming-of-age comedy-drama adapted from the novel of the same name by Joe Dunthorne. *Dir.* Richard Ayoade.

Summer Holiday (1963) Cliff Richard (Don), Lauri Peters (Bobbie/Barbara), The Shadows (themselves), Melvyn Hayes (Cyril), Una Stubbs (Sandy), Teddy Green (Steve), Pamela Hart (Angie), Jeremy Bulloch (Edwin), Jacqueline Daryl (Mimsie), Madge Ryan (Stella), Lionel Murton (Jerry), Christine Lawson (Annie), Ron Moody (Orlando), David Kossoff (Magistrate), Wendy Barrie (Shepherdess), Nicholas Phipps (Wrightmore). Bus mechanic Don persuades London Transport to lend him and his friends a double-decker bus which they convert into a holiday caravan and drive across continental Europe as a publicity stunt. On the way to Athens they are joined by a girl trio and a young boy who is not all that he seems. The soundtrack includes the UK number 1 hits *Summer Holiday*, *Bachelor Boy*, *Foot Tapper* and *The Next Time*. *Dir.* Peter Yates.

Sunday Bloody Sunday (1971) Peter Finch (Daniel), Glenda Jackson (Alex), Murray Head (Bob), Peggy Ashcroft (Mrs. Grenville), Tony Britton (George Harding), Maurice Denham (Mr. Grenville), Bessie Love (Operator), Vivian Pickles (Alva Hodson), Frank Windsor (Bill Hodson), Thomas Baptiste (Professor Johns), Richard Pearson (Patient), June Brown (Woman Patient), Hannah Norbert (Daniel's Mother), Harold Goldblatt (Daniel's Father), Marie Burke (Aunt Astrid), Caroline Blakiston (Rowing Wife), Peter Halliday (Rowing Husband), Douglas Lambert (Man at Party), Jon Finch (Scotsman), Edward Evans (Husband at Hospital), Gabrielle Daye (Wife at Hospital), Daniel Day-Lewis (Teenage vandal). Dr Daniel Hirsh and Alex Greville are involved in a love triangle with artist Bob Elkin. *Dir.* John Schlesinger.

Sundowners, The (1960) Deborah Kerr (Ida), Robert Mitchum (Paddy), Peter Ustinov (Rupert Venneker), Glynis Johns (Mrs Firth), Dina Merrill (Jean Halstead), Michael Anderson Jr (Sean), Chips Rafferty (Quinlan), Lola Brooks (Liz Brown), Wylie Watson (Herb Johnson), John Meillon (Bluey Brown), Ronald Fraser (Ocker), Mervyn Johns (Jack Patchogue), Dick Bentley (Shearer), Molly Urquhart (Mrs. Bateman), Ewen Solon (Halstead), Bryan Pringle (PC Thomas). Paddy Carmody is a "sundowner", an itinerant sheep shearer always moving on to the next sheep station. However, his wife and son would like to settle down. *Dir.* Fred Zinnemann.

Sunshine (2007) Cillian Murphy (Robert Capa), Chris Evans (Mace), Michelle Yeoh (Corazon), Rose Byrne (Cassie), Troy Garity (Harvey), Hiroyuki Sanada (Kaneda), Benedict Wong (Trey), Mark Strong (Pinbacker), Cliff Curtis (Searle), Paloma Baeza (Capa's Sister), Archie Macdonald (Child), Sylvie Macdonald (Child), Chipo Chung (Icarus – voice). Seven years after Icarus I failed to kick-start the dying Sun, Icarus II is sent to complete the mission. On the way to the Sun they pick-up Icarus I's distress signal and decide to retrieve its payload. *Dir.* Danny Boyle.

Supergrass, The (1985) Adrian Edmondson (Dennis), Jennifer Saunders (Lesley Reynolds), Peter Richardson (Harvey Duncan), Robbie Coltrane (Det. Sgt. Troy), Nigel Planer (Gunter), Keith Allen (Wong), Dawn French (Andrea), Daniel Peacock (Jim Jarvis), Ronald Allen (Commander Robertson), Alexei Sayle (Motorbike Cop), Michael Elphick (Constable Collins), Patrick Durkin (Constable Franks), Marika Rivera (Bed and Breakfast Landlady), Rita Treisman (Mrs. Carter), Al Pillay (Mary). A comedy from *The Comic Strip Presents* team in which compulsive liar Dennis Carter boasts of being a drug smuggler in order to impress a girl and then gets recruited by the police to grass up his connections. *Dir.* Peter Richardson.

Sweeney 2 (1978) John Thaw (Detective Inspector Jack Regan), Dennis Waterman (Detective Sergeant George Carter), Denholm Elliot (ex-Detective Chief Superintendent Jupp), Ken Hutchison (Hill), Frederick Treves (McKyle), Nigel Hawthorne (Detective Chief Inspector Dilke), Anna Gaël (Mrs. Hill), Barry Stanton (Big John), John Flanagan (Willard), David Casey (Goodyear), Derrick O'Connor (Llewellyn), John Alkin (Det. Sgt. Tom Daniels), James Warrior (Det. Con. Jellyneck), Brian Gwaspari (White), Johnny Shannon (Harry), Toby Salaman (Doctor), Lewis Fiander (Gorran), Anna Nygh (Shirley Hicks), Michael J. Jackson (Soames), Lynn Dearth (Mrs. White), Fiona Mollison (Mrs. Haughton), Sarah Atkinson (Mrs. Mead), John Lyons (Mead), Brian Hall (Haughton), Matthew Scurfield (Jefferson), George Innes (Pete Beale), Roddy McMillan (Collie), Michael O'Hagan (Doyle), Arthur Cox (Detective), Georgina Hale (Switchboard Girl), Patrick Malahide (Major Conway), Yvon Doval (Mr. Mahmoun), Jim McManus (Barman), Marc Zuber (Andy), Leon Lissek (Cardona Alexandros), Stefan Gryff (Nino), Rosario Serrano (Mrs. Konstantikis). Regan is on the case of gold-plated Purdey shotgun wielding bank robbers. The second big screen spin-off from the television show *The Sweeney*. *Dir.* Tom Clegg.

Sweeney Todd: The Demon Barber of Fleet Street (1936) Tod Slaughter (Sweeney Todd), Stella Rho (Mrs. Lovatt), John Singer (Tobias Rag), Eve Lister (Johanna Oakley), Bruce Seton (Mark Ingerstreet), D.J. Williams (Stephen Oakley), Davina Craig (Nan), Jerry Verno (Stanley Pearley), Graham Soutten (The Beadle), Billy Holland (Parsons), Norman Pierce (Mr. Findlay), Aubrey Mallalieu (Trader Paterson), Ben Williams (Captain Stephenson). Tod Slaughter recreates his classic stage role in this typically melodramatic rendering of the famous tale of a barber, a trick barber's chair, a sharp blade and some piping hot meat pies. *Dir.* George King.

Sweeney! (1977) John Thaw (Detective Inspector Jack Regan), Dennis Waterman (Detective Sergeant George Carter), Barry Foster (Elliot McQueen), Ian Bannen (Charles Baker MP), Colin Welland (Frank Chadwick), Diane Keen (Bianca Hamilton), Michael Coles (Johnson), Joe Melia (Ronnie Brent), Brian Glover (Mac), Lynda Bellingham (Janice Wyatt), Morris Perry (Flying Squad Commander), Paul Angelis (Secret Serviceman), Nick

Brimble (Burtonshaw), John Alkin (Daniels), Bernard Kay (Matthews), Antony Scott (Johnson's Henchman), Sally Osborne (Sally), Susan Skipper (Chadwick's Secretary), Nadim Sawalha (Chairman of the Oil Producers' Conference). Whilst investigating the death of a prostitute Regan becomes embroiled in a web of political intrigue. Big screen spin-off from the television show *The Sweeney*. *Dir*. David Wickes.

Sword of Honour (1939) Geoffrey Toone (Bill Brown), Sally Gray (Lady Moira Talmadge), Dorothy Dickson (Mrs. Stanhope), Donald Gray (Stukely), Wally Patch (Pomeroy Brown), Peter Gawthorne (Lord Carhampton), Frederick Culley (Duke of Honiton), Maire O'Neill (Biddy), Gordon Begg (Grandpa Brown), Cyril Smith (Bright), Patrick Susands (Adjutant), Tommy Woodrooffe (Commentator). A recruit at Sandhurst makes a poor start but after riding in the Grand National goes on to win the Sword of Honour. *Dir*. Maurice Elvey.

Sword of Sherwood Forest (1960) Richard Greene (Robin Hood), Sarah Branch (Maid Marian), Peter Cushing (Sheriff of Nottingham), Richard Pasco (Edward, Earl of Newark), Nigel Green (Little John), Niall MacGinnis (Friar Tuck), Jack Gwillim (Archbishop Hubert Walter), Edwin Richfield (The Sheriff's Lieutenant), Oliver Reed (Lord Melton), Patrick Crean (Lord Ollerton), Vanda Godsell (The Prioress), Dennis Lotis (Alan A'Dale), Derren Nesbitt (Martin of Eastwood), James Neylin (Roger), John Franklin (Archbishop's Adjutant), Desmond Llewelyn (Wounded Fugitive), Anew McMaster (Judge), Adam Keane (Retford), John Hoey (Old Jack), Maureen Halligan (Portress). Robin meets Marian Fitzwalter, crosses swords with the Sheriff of Nottingham and gets involved in a plot to assassinate Hubert Walter, Chancellor of England and Archbishop of Canterbury. *Dir*. Terence Fisher.

Sylvia (2003) Daniel Craig (Ted Hughes), Gwyneth Paltrow (Sylvia Plath), Blythe Danner (Aurelia Plath), Michael Gambon (Professor Thomas), Sarah Guyler (Ted's Cambridge Girlfriend), Julian Firth (James Michie), David Birkin (Morecambe), Alison Bruce (Elizabeth), Lucy Davenport (Doreen), Andrew Havill (David Wevill), Amira Casar (Assia Wevill), Eliza Wade (Infant Frieda), Jeremy Fowlds (Mr. Robinson), Jared Harris (Al Alvarez), Liddy Holloway (Martha Bergstrom), John Mears (Charles Langridge), Derek Payne (Vicar), Sonia Ritter (Midwife), Anthony Strachan (Michael Boddy), Katherine Tozer (Myra Norris), Sam Troughton (Tom Hadley-Clarke). Beginning with their meeting at Cambridge in 1956 and ending with Sylvia's suicide in 1963, the film tells the true story of the romance between poets Sylvia Plath and Ted Hughes. *Dir*. Christine Jeffs.

Take a Girl Like You (1970) Hayley Mills (Jenny Bunn), Oliver Reed (Patrick Standish), Noel Harrison (Julian Ormerod), John Bird (Dick Thompson), Sheila Hancock (Martha Thompson), Aimi MacDonald (Wendy), Geraldine Sherman (Anna Le Page), Ronald Lacey (Graham McClintoch), John Fortune (Sir Gerald), Imogen Hassall (Samantha), Pippa Steel (Ted), Penelope Keith (Tory Lady), Nicholas Courtney (Panel Chairman), George Woodbridge (Publican), Jimmy Gardner (Voter), Nerys Hughes (Teacher), Jean Marlow (Mother), Howard Goorney (Labour Agent). Jenny is favoured with the attentions of several suitors including an older school-teacher colleague. Based on a Kingsley Amis novel. *Dir*. Jonathan Miller.

Take It Or Leave It (1981) Suggs (Suggs), Mark Bedford (Bedders), Lee Thompson (Lee), Carl Smyth (Carl), Dan Woodgate (Woody), Chris Foreman (Chris), Mike Barson (Barso), John Hasler (Hasler), Simon Birdsall (Simon), Andrew Chalk (Chalky), Ian Tokins (Toks). A biopic of the group Madness. *Dir*. Dave Robinson.

Take Me High (1974) Cliff Richard (Tim Matthews), Deborah Watling (Sarah Jones), Hugh Griffith (Sir Harry Cunningham), George Cole (Bert Jackson), Anthony Andrews (Hugo Flaxman), Richard Wattis (Sir Charles Furness), Madeline Smith (Vicki), Moyra Fraser (Molly Jones), Ronald Hines (Sam Jones), Jimmy Gardner (Hulbert), Noel Trevarthen (Paul), Graham Armitage (Boardman), John Franklyn-Robbins (Alderman), Peter Marshall (Grandson), Elizabeth Scott (Waitress), Polly Williams (Receptionist). Merchant banker Tim gets moved to Birmingham rather than hoped-for New York but finds love in a burger restaurant. *Dir*. David Askey.

Tale of Two Cities, A (1958) Dirk Bogarde (Sydney Carton), Dorothy Tutin (Lucie Manette), Cecil Parker (Jarvis Lorry), Stephen Murray (Dr. Manette), Athene Seyler (Miss Pross), Paul Guers (Charles Darnay), Marie Versini (Marie Gabelle), Ian Bannen (Gabelle), Alfie Bass (Jerry Cruncher), Ernest Clark (Stryver), Rosalie Crutchley (Madame Defarge), Freda Jackson (The Vengeance), Duncan Lamont (Ernest Defarge), Christopher Lee (Marquis St. Evremonde), Leo McKern (Attorney General-Old Bailey), Donald Pleasence (Barsad), Eric Pohlmann (Sawyer), Sam Kydd (Joe). Based on the Charles Dickens novel. *Dir*. Ralph Thomas.

Tales of Beatrix Potter, The (1971) Frederick Ashton (Mrs. Tiggy-Winkle), Alexander Grant (Pigling Bland / Peter Rabbit), Julie Wood (Mrs. Tittlemouse), Ann Howard (Jemima Puddleduck), Bob Mead (Fox), Garry Grant (Alexander), Sally Ashby (Mrs. Pettitoes/Tabitha), Brenda Last (Black Berkshire Pig), Michael Coleman (Jeremy Fisher), Wayne Sleep (Squirrel Nutkin/Tom Thumb), Lesley Collier (Hunca Munca), Leslie Edwards (Mr. Brown), Erin Geraghty (Beatrix Potter), Joan Benham (Nurse), Wilfred Babbage (Butler). Members of the Royal Ballet perform the tales of Beatrix Potter. *Dir*. Reginald Mills.

Tales of Hoffman, The (1951) Moira Shearer (Stella/Olympia - sung by Dorothy Bond), Ann Ayars (Antonia), Ludmilla Tchérina (Giulietta - sung by Margherita Grandi), Robert Rounseville (Hoffmann), Robert Helpmann (Lindorf/Coppélius/Dapertutto/Dr Miracle - sung by Bruce Dargavel), Pamela Brown (Nicklaus – sung by Monica Sinclair), Léonide Massine (Spalanzani/Schlemil/Franz), Frederick Ashton (Kleinsach/Cochenille), Mogens Wieth (Crespel), Lionel Harris (Pitichinaccio - sung by Rene Soames), Meinhart Maur - Luther, sung by Fisher Morgan), Edmond Audran (Stella's partner in Dragonfly ballet), Philip Leaver (Andreas), John Ford (Nathaniel), Richard Golding (Hermann). Hoffman tells of the three great loves of his life. An adaptation of Jacques Offenbach's opera *Les contes d'Hoffmann*. *Dirs*. Michael Powell and Emeric Pressburger.

Tall Guy, The (1989) Jeff Goldblum (Dexter King), Rowan Atkinson (Ron Anderson), Emma Thompson (Kate Lemmon), Geraldine James (Carmen), Anna Massey (Mary), Kim Thomson (Cheryl), Hugh Thomas (Dr. Karabekian), Emil Wolk (Cyprus Charlie), Harold Innocent (Timothy), Joanna Kanska (Tamara), Peter Kelly (Gavin), Tim Barlow (Mr. Morrow), Hugh Thomas (Dr. Karabekian), Charles Augins (Choreographer), Peter Brewis (Freddy), Angus Deayton (Actor in Agent's Office), Susan Field (Dr. Freud), Jason Isaacs (Doctor 2), Kate Lonergan (Stage Manager), Declan Mulholland (Doorman), Melvyn Bragg (Himself), John Inman (Himself), Suggs (Himself), Jonathan Ross (Himself). The straight man to comedian Ron Anderson suffers from chronic hay fever and falls for his nurse Kate. However, the course of true love...... *Dir*. Mel Smith.

Tamara Drewe (2010) Gemma Arterton (Tamara Drewe), Roger Allam (Nicholas Hardiment), Bill Camp (Glen McCreavy), Dominic Cooper (Ben Sergeant), Luke Evans (Andy Cobb), Tamsin Greig (Beth Hardiment), Jessica Barden (Jody Long), Charlotte Christie (Casey Shaw), John Bett (Diggory), Josie Taylor (Zoe), Pippa Haywood (Tess), Susan Wooldridge (Penny Upminster), Alex Kelly (Jody's mother), Lola Frears (Poppy Hardiment), Bronagh Gallagher (Eustacia), Amanda Lawrence (Mary), Zahra Ahmadi (Nadia Patel), Cheryl Campbell (Lucetta), Emily Bruni (Caitlin), Tom Allen (Vintner), Joel Fry (Steve Culley), Lois Winstone (Fran Redmond), James Naughtie (Interviewer). When Tamara returns to the village of Ewedown to sell her deceased mother's house she becomes the centre of attention. Based on the newspaper (*Guardian*) comic strip written by Posy Simmonds, itself based on Thomas Hardy's novel *Far from the Madding Crowd*. *Dir*. Stephen Frears.

Tamarind Seed, The (1974) Julie Andrews (Judith Farrow), Omar Sharif (Feodor Sverdlov), Anthony Quayle (Jack Loder), Dan O'Herlihy (Fergus Stephens), Sylvia Syms (Margaret Stephenson), Oskar Homolka (Gen. Golitsyn), Bryan Marshall (George MacLeod), David Baron (Richard Paterson), Celia Bannerman (Rachel Paterson), Roger Dann (Col. Moreau), Sharon Duce (Sandy Mitchell), George Mikell (Maj. Stukalov), Kate O'Mara (Anna Skriabina), Constantine Gregory (Dimitri Memenov). Judith, who works for the Home Office, and Feodor, assigned to the Soviet air attaché in Paris, begin an affair during the Cold War. Based on *The Tamarind Seed: A Novel* by Evelyn Anthony. *Dir.* Blake Edwards.

Target for Tonight (1941) A documentary which tells the story of the crew of "F for Freddie", a Wellington bomber, on a routine air raid over Germany. The film won an Honorary Academy Award for its vivid and dramatic presentation of the heroism of the RAF in a documentary film. *Dir.* Harry Watt.

Taste of Honey, A (1961) Dora Bryan (Helen), Robert Stephens (Peter), Rita Tushingham (Jo), Murray Melvin (Geoffrey), Paul Danquah (Jimmy), Michael Bilton (Landlord), Eunice Black (Schoolteacher), David Boliver (Bert), Margo Cunningham (Landlady), A. Goodman (Rag and Bone Man), Hazel Blears (Street Urchin). Teenager Jo has a one-night stand with a black sailor and, having been turfed out of her home by her remarried mother, moves in with a gay friend and soon discovers she is pregnant. Adaptation by Shelagh Delaney of her own play. *Dir.* Tony Richardson.

Taste the Blood of Dracula (1970) Christopher Lee (Dracula), Geoffrey Keen (William Hargood), Gwen Watford (Martha Hargood), Linda Hayden (Alice Hargood), Peter Sallis (Samuel Paxton), Anthony Higgins (Paul Paxton), Isla Blair (Lucy Paxton), John Carson (Jonathon Secker), Martin Jarvis (Jeremy Secker), Ralph Bates (Lord Courtley), Roy Kinnear (Weller), Michael Ripper (Inspector Cobb), Russell Hunter (Felix), Shirley Jaffe (Betty), Keith Marsh (Father), Peter May (Son), Reginald Barratt (Vicar), Madeline Smith (Dolly). Three men restore Dracula to life but he decides to take revenge on them for the death of his servant. *Dir.* Peter Sasdy.

Tea with Mussolini (1999) Cher (Elsa Morganthal Strauss-Almerson), Maggie Smith (Lady Hester Random), Judi Dench (Arabella), Lily Tomlin (Georgie Rockwell), Joan Plowright (Mary Wallace), Baird Wallace (Teenage Luca), Charlie Lucas (Young Luca), Michael Williams (British Consul), Jackie Basehart (Count Bernardini). A group of ex-patriot English women living in Italy are interned at the outbreak of WWII. An American woman who has been an irregular visitor is also interned when the Americans join the war. *Dir.* Franco Zeffirelli.

Telstar (2009) Con O'Neill (Joe Meek), Carl Barât (Gene Vincent), Kevin Spacey (Major Banks), Pam Ferris (Violet Shenton), JJ Feild (Heinz Burt), James Corden (Clem Cattini), Tom Burke (Geoff Goddard), Ralf Little (Chas Hodges), Mathew Baynton (Ritchie Blackmore), Jon Lee (Billy Fury), Callum Dixon (John Leyton), Nick Moran (Alex Meek), Jess Conrad (Larry Parnes), Justin Hawkins (Screaming Lord Sutch), Nigel Harman (Jess Conrad), Nick Thomas-Webster (Lord Justice Wignall), Alan Scally (George Bellamy), Jimmy Carr (Gentleman), Craig Vye (Mitch Mitchell), Chas Hodges (Mr. Brolin), John Leyton (Sir Edward), Robbie Duke (Stagehand), Mike Sarne (Backstage Manager), David Hayler (John Peel), Joan Hodges (Biddy Meek), Jim Field Smith (Ken Howard), Marcus Brigstocke (Alan Blaikley), Stephanie Dickens (Brenda), Louis Hennessey Hicks (Joe aged 13), Che Deedigan (Joe aged 9). A biopic of 1960s record producer Joe Meek who was responsible for hits such as "Telstar", "Have I the Right?", "Just Like Eddie" and "Johnny Remember Me" but was tortured by financial problems and his homosexuality. *Dir.* Nick Moran

Tempest, The (1979) Heathcote Williams (Prospero, the Right Duke of Milan), Toyah Willcox (Miranda, his daughter), Richard Warwick (Antonio, his brother), Peter Bull (Alonso, the King of Naples), David Meyer (Ferdinand, his son), Neil Cunningham (Sebastian, his brother), Karl Johnson (Ariel, an airy spirit), Jack Birkett (Caliban, a savage and deformed slave), Christopher Biggins (Stephano, a drunken mariner), Peter Turner (Trinculo, his friend), Ken Campbell (Gonzalo, an honest councillor), Elisabeth Welch (A Goddess), Claire Davenport (Sycorax), Kate Temple (Young Miranda). Based on Shakespeare's play. *Dir.* Derek Jarman

Ten Little Indians (1965) Hugh O'Brian (Hugh Lombard), Shirley Eaton (Ann Clyde), Fabian (Mike Raven), Leo Genn (General Sir John Mandrake V.C.), Stanley Holloway (Det. William Henry Blore), Wilfrid Hyde-White (Judge Arthur

Cannon), Daliah Lavi (Ilona Bergen), Dennis Price (Dr. Edward Armstrong), Marianne Hoppe (Elsa Grohmann), Mario Adorf (Joseph Grohmann), Christopher Lee (Mr. Owen - voice). Ten people are invited to a house high on a mountain top by a mysterious stranger. A film version of Agatha Christie's detective novel *And Then There Were None*. *Dir.* George Pollock.

10 Rillington Place (1971) Richard Attenborough (John Reginald Christie), Judy Geeson (Beryl Evans), John Hurt (Timothy John Evans), Pat Heywood (Mrs. Ethel Christie), Isobel Black (Alice), Phyllis MacMahon (Muriel Eady), Ray Barron (Workman Willis), Douglas Blackwell (Workman Jones), Gabrielle Daye (Mrs. Lynch), Jimmy Gardner (Mr. Lynch), Edward Evans (Detective Inspector), Tenniel Evans (Detective Sergeant), David Jackson, George Lee, Richard Coleman (Police Constables), André Morell (Judge Lewis), Robert Hardy (Malcolm Morris), Geoffrey Chater (Christmas Humphreys), Basil Dignam (Medical Board member), Sam Kydd (Furniture Dealer), Rudolph Walker (West Indian). Timothy Evans and his wife and daughter move into 10 Rillington Place, the home of their landlord John Christie. Evans does not know of the bodies buried in the garden or that he is about to entrust the lives of his family into the hands of a serial killer. Based on the book of the same name by Ludovic Kennedy. *Dir.* Richard Fleischer.

Term of Trial (1962) Laurence Olivier (Graham Weir), Simone Signoret (Anna), Sarah Miles (Shirley Taylor), Terence Stamp (Mitchell), Hugh Griffith (O'Hara), Roland Culver (Trowman), Dudley Foster (Detective Sergeant Keirnan), Frank Pettingell (Ferguson), Thora Hird (Mrs. Taylor), Norman Bird (Mr. Taylor), Allan Cuthbertson (Sylvan-Jones), Barbara Ferris (Joan), Ray Holder (Thompson), Derren Nesbitt (Lodger), Julia Foster (Virginia). A relationship develops between an alcoholic teacher who is disliked by his colleagues and one of his pupils. Based on the novel of the same name by James Barlow. *Dir.* Peter Glenville.

Tess (1979) Nastassja Kinski (Tess Durbeyfield), Peter Firth (Angel Clare), Leigh Lawson (Alec Stokes-d'Urberville), John Collin (John Durbeyfield), Rosemary Martin (Mrs. Durbeyfield), Carolyn Pickles (Miriam), Richard Pearson (Vicar of Marlott), David Markham (Reverend Clare), Pascale de Boysson (Mrs. Clare), Suzanna Hamilton (Izz Huett), Caroline Embling (Retty), Tony Church (Parson Tringham), Lesley Dunlop (Girl in henhouse), Sylvia Coleridge (Mrs. d'Urberville), Fred Bryant (Dairyman Crick), John Bett (Felix Clare), Tom Chadbon (Cuthbert Clare), Richard Pearson (Vicar of Marlott), Josine Comellas (Mrs. Crick), Arielle Dombasle (Mercy Chant), Gordon Richardson (Parson at wedding), Patsy Smart (Housekeeper), Dicken Ashworth (Farmer Groby), Patsy Rowlands (Landlady), Graham Weston (Constable). An adaptation of Thomas Hardy's novel *Tess of the d'Urbervilles*. *Dir.* Roman Polanski.

That Hamilton Woman (1941) Vivien Leigh (Emma Lady Hamilton), Laurence Olivier (Lord Horatio Nelson), Alan Mowbray (Sir William Hamilton), Sara Allgood (Mrs. Cadogan-Lyon), Gladys Cooper (Lady Frances Nelson), Henry Wilcoxon (Captain Hardy), Heather Angel (Streetgirl), Halliwell Hobbes (Rev. Nelson), Gilbert Emery (Lord Spencer), Miles Mander (Lord Keith), Ronald Sinclair (Josiah), Luis Alberni (King of Naples), Norma Drury Boleslavsky (Queen of Naples), Olaf Hytten (Gavin), Juliette Compton (Lady Spencer), Guy Kingsford (Captain Troubridge). An historical drama told largely in flashback about the life of Emma Lady Hamilton, including her dalliance with Charles Greville, her marriage to Sir William Hamilton and mainly about her affair with Horatio Nelson. The film won an Academy Award for Best Sound, Recording (Jack Whitney). *Dir.* Alexander Korda.

That Lady (1955) Olivia de Havilland (Ana de Mendoza), Gilbert Roland (Antonio Perez), Paul Scofield (King Philip II of Spain), Françoise Rosay (Bernardine), Dennis Price (Mateo Vasquez), Anthony Dawson (Don Inigo), Robert Harris (Cardinal), Peter Illing (Diego), José Nieto (Don Juan de Escobedo), Christopher Lee (Captain), Ángel Peralta (Rejoneador), Fernando Sancho (Diego). Set in the Spanish Court during the reign of Philip II.

Ana is a close friend of the king but after a scandal she is arrested. *Dir.* Terence Young.

That Riviera Touch (1966) Eric Morecambe (Eric Simpson), Ernie Wise (Ernest Clark), Suzanne Lloyd (Claudette), Paul Stassino (Le Pirate), Armand Mestral (Inspector Duval), Gerald Lawson (Coco), George Eugeniou (Marcel), George Pastell (Ali), Alexandra Bastedo (Girl at Roulette Table), Nicole Shelby (Woman in Casino), Peter Jeffrey (Mauron), Francis Matthews (Hotel Manager), Michael Forrest (Pierre), Clive Cazes (Renard), Paul Danquah (Hassim), Sally Douglas (Lady at Casino), Bettine Le Beau (French Lady at Casino), Steven Scott (Gaston). Eric and Ernie take a holiday in the South of France and get themselves unwittingly involved in a plan to smuggle jewels. *Dir.* Cliff Owen.

That'll Be The Day (1973) David Essex (Jim MacLaine), Ringo Starr (Mike), Rosemary Leach (Mrs. MacLaine), James Booth (Mr. MacLaine), Billy Fury (Stormy Tempest), Keith Moon (J.D. Clover), Rosalind Ayres (Jeanette), Brenda Bruce (Doreen), Robert Lindsay (Terry), Verna Harvey (Wendy), James Ottaway (Granddad), Deborah Watling (Sandra), Beth Morris (Jean), Daphne Oxenford (Mrs. Sutcliffe), Kim Braden (Charlotte), Ron Hackett (Policeman), Johnny Shannon (Jack), Karl Howman (Johnny), Patti Love (Sandra's Friend), Sue Holderness (Shirley), Alan Foss (Teacher), Natalie Kent (Mrs. Rimmer), Bernard Severn (Sutcliffe), Eugene Wallace (Stuart), Erin Geraghty (Joan), Sacha Puttnam (Young Jim). Restless Jim MacLaine wants to be a rock star but instead finds himself working in a number of different jobs including at a fun fair. *Dir.* Claude Whatham.

Theatre of Blood (1973) Vincent Price (Edward Lionheart), Diana Rigg (Edwina Lionheart), Charles Sinnickson (Vicar), Madeline Smith (Rosemary), Eric Sykes (Sgt. Dogge), Peter Thornton (Policeman), Ian Hendry (Peregrine Devlin), Harry Andrews (Trevor Dickman), Coral Browne (Miss Chloe Moon), Robert Coote (Oliver Larding), Jack Hawkins (Solomon Psaltery), Charles Gray (Solomon Psaltery – voice), Michael Hordern (George William Maxwell), Arthur Lowe (Horace Sprout), Robert Morley (Meredith Merridew), Dennis Price (Hector Snipe), Milo O'Shea (Insp Boot), Diana Dors (Maisie Psaltery), Joan Hickson (Mrs Sprout), Renée Asherson (Mrs Maxwell), Bunny Reed (Policeman). A Shakespearean actor fails to win a critic's award so he takes his revenge by submitting the critics to various types of death inspired by the Shakespeare plays in his final season. *Dir.* Douglas Hickox

There Was a Crooked Man (1960) Norman Wisdom (Davy Cooper), Alfred Marks (Adolf Carter), Andrew Cruickshank (McKillup), Reginald Beckwith (Station Master), Susannah York (Ellen), Jean Clarke (Freda), Timothy Bateson (Flash Dan), Paul Whitsun-Jones (Restaurant Gentleman), Fred Griffiths (Taxi Driver), Ann Hefferman (Hospital Sister), Rosalind Knight (Nurse), Reed De Rouen (Dutchman), Brian Oulton (Ashton), Glyn Houston (Smoking Machinist), Percy Herbert (Prison Warden), Edna Petrie (Woman at Assembly Hall), Jack May (Police Sergeant), Ronald Fraser (Gen. Cummins), Ed Devereaux (American Colonel), Sam Kydd (Foreman), Redmond Phillips (Padre). Davy Cooper is an explosives expert who falls foul of a criminal gang. He is caught and jailed, vowing to make amends when he gets released. An obscure Norman Wisdom film. *Dir.* Stuart Burge.

There's a Girl in My Soup (1970) Peter Sellers (Robert Danvers), Goldie Hawn (Marion), Tony Britton (Andrew Hunter), Nicky Henson (Jimmy), John Comer (John), Diana Dors (John's wife), Judy Campbell (Lady Heather), Gabrielle Drake (Julia), Nicola Pagett (Clare), Geraldine Sherman (Caroline), Thorley Walters (Manager of the Carlton Hotel), Ruth Trouncer (Gilly Hunter), Françoise Pascal (Paola), Christopher Cazenove (Nigel), Tom Marshall (Bryan), Raf De La Torre (Monsieur Le Guestier), Constantine Gregory (Michel Le Guestier), Avril Angers (English Tourist), George Lambert (Floor Waiter), Marianne Stone (Woman Reporter), Margaret Lacey (Autograph Hunter), Eric Barker (Wedding Guest), Mark Dignam (Wedding Guest), Lance Percival (Willie the Bridegroom), Caroline Seymour (Nigel's Girl Friend). A womanising television cookery show host falls for a teenage American girl. Based on the successful stage comedy. *Dir.* Roy Boulting.

There's Only One Jimmy Grimble (2000) Lewis McKenzie (Jimmy Grimble), Jane Lapotaire (Alice Brewer), Gina McKee (Donna), Ben Miller (Johnny Two Dogs), Wayne Galtrey (Walkway Kid), Ciaran Griffiths (Psycho), Bobby Power ('Gorgeous' Gordon Burley), Robert Carlyle (Eric Wirral), Samia Smith (Sara), Antony Marsh (Crane), Sean Delaney (Brick), Charles Denton (The Cat), Azmier Ahmed (Elvis), John McArdle (Headmaster), Ann Aris (Governor 1), Ray Winstone (Harry). He may be only a shy, much bullied schoolboy but Jimmy's abilities as a footballer seem to grow exponentially after an old woman presents him a pair of magical football boots. *Dir.* John Hay.

They Drive by Night (1938) Emlyn Williams (Shorty Matthews), Ernest Thesiger (Walter Hoover), Anna Konstam (Molly O'Neill), Allan Jeayes (Wally Mason), Anthony Holles (Murray), Ronald Shiner (Charlie), Yolande Terrell (Marge), Julie Barrie (Pauline), Kitty de Legh (Mrs. Mason), William Hartnell (Bus Conductor), Bernard Miles (Detective), Jack Vyvian (Jock McKenzie). Fresh out of prison Shorty discovers his girlfriend murdered and is afraid of being accused so tries to hide amongst a community of long-distance lorry drivers. Based on a James Curtis novel. *Dir.* Arthur B Woods.

They Flew Alone (1942) Anna Neagle (Amy Johnson), Robert Newton (Jim Mollison), Edward Chapman (Mr Johnson), Nora Swinburne (ATA Commandant), Joan Kemp-Welch (Mrs Johnson), Brefni O'Rorke (Mac), Charles Carson (Lord Wakefield), Martita Hunt (Miss Bland), Anthony Shaw (Official), Eliot Makeham (Mayor of Croydon), David Horne (Solicitor), Miles Malleson (Vacuum Salesman), Aubrey Mallalieu (Bill), Charles Victor (Postmaster), Hay Petrie (Old General), John Slater (Officer on Interview Panel), Cyril Smith (Radio Operator), George Merritt (Reporter), Muriel George (Kitty), Ian Fleming (Secretary), William Hartnell (Scotty), Arthur Hambling (Policeman), Peter Gawthorne (RAF Officer), Ronald Shiner (Mechanic). A biopic honouring Amy Johnson, who joined the Air Transport Auxilliary in 1940 and died in 1941 during a ferry flight. *Dir.* Herbert Wilcox.

They Made Me a Fugitive (1947) Trevor Howard (George Clement 'Clem' Morgan), Sally Gray (Sally Connor), Griffith Jones (Narcy), René Ray (Cora), Mary Merrall (Aggie), Charles Farrell (Curley), Michael Brennan (Jim), Jack McNaughton (Soapy), Cyril Smith (Bert), John Penrose (Shawney), Eve Ashley (Ellen), Phyllis Robins (Olga), Bill O'Connor (Bill), Maurice Denham (Mr. Fenshaw), Vida Hope (Mrs. Fenshaw), Ballard Berkeley (Det. Insp. Rockliffe), Derek Birch (Police Constable Murray), Sam Kydd (Eddie). Ex-RAF pilot is set-up by his boss and jailed for murder. He escapes to vow revenge. *Dir.* Alberto Cavalcanti.

They Met in the Dark (1943) James Mason (Richard Francis Heritage), Joyce Howard (Laura Verity), Tom Walls (Christopher Child), Phyllis Stanley (Lily Bernard), Edward Rigby (Mansel), Ronald Ward (Carter), David Farrar (Commander Lippinscott), Karel Stepanek (Riccardo), Betty Warren (Fay), Walter Crisham (Charlie), George Robey (Pawnbroker), Ronald Chesney (Max), Peggy Dexter (Bobby), Finlay Currie (Merchant Captain), Brefni O'Rorke (Detective Inspector Burrows), Patricia Medina (Mary), Eric Mason (Benson), Kynaston Reeves (Naval Officer), Herbert Lomas (Van Driver), Percy Walsh (Police Sergeant), Terence de Marney (Code Expert), Robert Sansom (Petty Officer Bill Grant), Alvar Liddell (Boothby, Radio Announcer), David Keir (Henry). Heritage is tricked by a female spy and cashiered from the navy. He tracks down the spy but finds her dead and teams up with Laura to solve the murder. Based on the novel *The Vanished Corpse* by Anthony Gilbert (a pseudonym used by Lucy Malleson). *Dir.* Karel Lamac.

They Were Not Divided (1950) Edward Underdown (Philip), Ralph Clanton (David), Helen Cherry (Wilhelmina), Stella Andrew (Jane), Michael Brennan (Smoke O'Connor), Michael Trubshawe (Major Bushey Noble), Rupert Gerard (Earl of Bentham), John Wynn ('45 Jones), Desmond Llewelyn ('77 Jones), Anthony Dawson (Michael), Estelle Brody (War Correspondent), Rufus Cruikshank (Sergeant Dean), R.S.M. Brittain (Regimental Sergeant Major), Christopher Lee (Chris Lewis), Alvin Floyd (Butch), Iain Murray (Commanding Officer), Robert Ayres (American Brigadier), David Rose (The General), Jacqueline Robert (Belgian Girl), Gene Price (Tex). The story of the Guards Armoured Division during WWII seen through the eyes of three recruits. The actions include Operation Market Garden, the Battle of the Bulge and the Ardennes Offensive. *Dir.* Terence Young.

They Were Sisters (1945) Phyllis Calvert (Lucy Moore), James Mason (Geoffrey Lee), Hugh Sinclair (Terry Crawford), Anne Crawford (Vera Sargeant), Peter Murray-Hill (William Moore), Dulcie Gray (Charlotte Lee), Barry Livesey (Brian Sargeant), Pamela Mason (Margaret Lee), Ann Stephens (Judith Lee), Helen Stephens (Sarah Sargeant), John Gilpin (Stephen Lee), Brian Nissen (John Watson), David Horne (Mr. Field), Brefni O'Rorke (Coroner), Roland Pertwee (Sir Hamish Nair), Amy Veness (Mrs. Purley), Thorley Walters (Channing), Joss Ambler (Blakemore), Roy Russell (Lethbridge), Edie Martin (Cook), Dora Sevening (Janet), Helen Goss (Webster). A Gainsborough melodrama about three sisters (Lucy, Vera and Charlotte) and their very different marriages. *Dir.* Arthur Crabtree.

Thief of Bagdad, The (1940) Conrad Veidt (Jaffar), Sabu (Abu), June Duprez (Princess), John Justin (Ahmad), Rex Ingram (Djinn), Miles Malleson (Sultan), Morton Selten (The Old King), Mary Morris (Halima), Bruce Winston (The Merchant), Hay Petrie (Astrologer), Adelaide Hall (Singer), Roy Emerton (Jailer), Allan Jeayes (The Story Teller). A sumptuous Arabian Nights adventure with all the trimmings, including a genie in a bottle, a beautiful princess, a mechanical flying horse, a deadly automaton and a flying carpet. Ahmad is the rightful king of Bagdad but is tricked by the evil Vizier Jaffar and thrown into prison where he meets young Abu, the best thief in the city. The production was switched from London to California owing to the outbreak of war and the influence of the Hays Office (censor) can be seen in the less revealing costumes of the harem girls where the scenes were filmed in the US. The film won three Academy Awards for Art Direction, Cinematography and Special Effects. *Dirs.* Michael Powell, Ludwig Berger, Tim Whelan, Alexander Korda, Zoltan Korda and William Cameron Menzies (last three uncredited).

Things to Come (1936) Raymond Massey (John Cabal/Oswald Cabal), Edward Chapman (Pippa Passworthy/Raymond Passworthy), Ralph Richardson (Rudolf a.k.a. The Boss), Margaretta Scott (Roxana Black/Rowena Cabal), Cedric Hardwicke (Theotocopulos), Maurice Braddell (Dr Edward Harding), Sophie Stewart (Mrs Cabal), Derrick De Marney (Richard Gordon), Ann Todd (Mary Gordon), Pearl Argyle (Catherine Cabal), Kenneth Villiers (Maurice Passworthy), Ivan Brandt (Morden Mitani), Anne McLaren (Child in 2036), Patricia Hilliard (Janet Gordon), Charles Carson (Great-Grandfather in 2036), Patrick Barr (World Transport official), John Clements (Enemy pilot), Antony Holles (Simon Burton), Allan Jeayes (Mr. Cabal in 1940), Pickles Livingston (Horrie Passworthy), Abraham Sofaer (Wadsky). Centring on a place called Everytown, this is a prediction of the future, beginning with a global war in 1940 which continues for decades and includes biological and gas warfare. The narrative moves on in stages until 2036. The screenplay is by H. G. Wells and adapts his novel *The Shape of Things to Come* and his non-fiction work *The Work, Wealth and Happiness of Mankind*. *Dir.* William Cameron Menzies

Third Man, The (1949) Joseph Cotton (Holly Martins), Orson Welles (Harry Lime), Trevor Howard (Major Calloway), Alida Valli (Anna Schmidt), Orson Welles (Harry Lime), Bernard Lee (Sergeant Paine), Wilfrid Hyde-White (Crabbin), Ernst Deutsch ('Baron' Kurtz), Siegfried Breuer (Popescu), Erich Ponto (Dr. Winkel), Paul Hoerbiger (Porter), Wilfrid Hyde-White (Crabbin), Hedwig Bleibtreu (Anna's Old Landlady), Eric Pohlmann (Waiter), Carol Reed (Opening Narrator). Set in a post-war Vienna which is still under the control of the allies. Writer Holly Martins is invited to the city by ex-schoolfriend Harry Lime but when he arrives he is told that Lime has died in a road accident. When various accounts of Lime's death do not tally, Martins decides all may not be as it appears. The film includes Harry Lime's much quoted assessment of the Swiss: 'In Italy for thirty years under the Borgias they had warfare, terror, murder, bloodshed - but they produced Michelangelo, Leonardo da Vinci, and the Renaissance. In Switzerland they had brotherly love, 500

years of democracy and peace, and what did that produce? The cuckoo clock". The haunting 'Harry Lime Theme' by Anton Karas is performed on a zither. The film won one Academy Award: Best Cinematography, Black-and-White. The screenplay was written by Graham Greene. *Dir.* Carol Reed.

39 Steps, The (1935) Robert Donat (Richard Hannay), Madeleine Carroll (Pamela), Lucie Mannheim (Miss Annabella), Godfrey Tearle (Professor Jordan), Peggy Ashcroft (Margaret), John Laurie (John), Helen Haye (Mrs. Louisa Jordan), Frank Cellier (Sheriff Watson), Wylie Watson (Mr. Memory), Gus McNaughton (Commercial traveller on Flying Scotsman). The film is very loosely based on John Buchan's novel *The Thirty-nine Steps* published in 1915. Richard Hannay is at a music hall when he meets Annabella Smith, who, as it transpires, is on the run from foreign agents. He agrees to hide her in his flat but during the night she is murdered. Suspecting he will be accused of the crime he goes on the run in an attempt to break the spy ring and in the process prove his innocence. Along the way he becomes involved with Pamela and they spend a good amount of the film handcuffed to each other. Hitchcock's cameo in this film is of a man tossing some litter as Richard and Annabella run from the music hall. *Dir.* Alfred Hitchcock

39 Steps, The (1958) Kenneth More (Richard Hannay), Taina Elg (Fisher), Brenda De Banzie (Nellie Lumsden), Barry Jones (Professor Logan), Reginald Beckwith (Lumsden),Faith Brook (Nannie), Michael Goodliffe (Brown), James Hayter (Mr. Memory), Andrew Cruickshank (Sheriff), Leslie Dwyer (Milkman), Joan Hickson (Miss Dobson), Sid James (Percy Baker). An updated version of Hitchcock's 1935 film. *Dir.* Ralph Thomas

39 Steps, The (1978) Robert Powell (Richard Hannay), David Warner (Sir Edmund Appleton), Eric Porter (Chief Superintendent Lomas), Karen Dotrice (Alex Mackenzie), John Mills (Scudder), George Baker (Sir Walter Bullivant), Ronald Pickup (Bayliss), Donald Pickering (Marshall), Timothy West (Porton), Miles Anderson (David Hamilton), Andrew Keir (Lord R). More closely based on Buchan's book than the 1935 and 1958 versions in being set in 1915 and the thirty-nine steps actually referring to a staircase, although it still deviates from it in having a love interest for Hannay. *Dir.* Don Sharp

This Happy Breed (1944) Robert Newton (Frank Gibbons), Celia Johnson (Ethel Gibbons), Amy Veness (Mrs. Flint), Alison Leggatt (Aunt Sylvia), Stanley Holloway (Bob Mitchell), John Mills (Billy Mitchell), Kay Walsh (Queenie Gibbons), Eileen Erskine (Vi), John Blythe (Reg Gibbons), Guy Verney (Sam Leadbitter), Betty Fleetwood (Phyllis Blake), Merle Tottenham (Edie), Laurence Olivier (Narrator). An episodic film which follows the story of one family who live at 17 Sycamore Road, Clapham Common from 1919 to 1939, with a background of the major events in England during that period. Based on a Noël Coward play. *Dir.* David Lean.

This Is England (2006) Thomas Turgoose (Shaun Field), Stephen Graham (Andrew "Combo" Gascoigne), Joe Gilgun (Richard "Woody" Woodford), Andrew Shim (Michael "Milky"), Vicky McClure (Lorraine "Lol" Jenkins), Rosamund Hanson (Michelle "Smell"), Andrew Ellis (Gary "Gadget"), Jack O'Connell ("Pukey" Nicholls), Danielle Watson (Trev), Chanel Cresswell (Kelly Jenkins), Kieran Hardcastle (Kes), Sophie Ellerby (Pob), Perry Benson (Meggy), George Newton (Banjo), Kriss Dosanjh (Mr. Sandhu), Jo Hartley (Cynthia), Michael Socha (Harvey). A 12 year-old schoolboy is befriended by a group of skinheads. Set in 1983, a spin-off series set three years later *This Is England '86*, was shown on Channel 4 in 2010 and another, *This Is England '88* in 2011. *Dir.* Shane Meadows

This is Spinal Tap (1984) Michael McKean (David St. Hubbins), Christopher Guest (Nigel Tufnel), Harry Shearer (Derek Smalls), Rob Reiner (Marty DiBergi), Tony Hendra (Ian Faith), David Kaff (Viv Savage), R.J. Parnell (Mick Shrimpton), June Chadwick (Jeanine Pettibone), Bruno Kirby (Tommy Pischedda), Ed Begley, Jr. (John "Stumpy" Pepys), Danny Kortchmar (Ronnie Pudding), Fran Drescher (Bobbi Flekman), Patrick Macnee (Sir Denis Eton-Hogg), Julie Payne (Mime waitress), Dana Carvey (Mime waiter),

Sandy Helberg (Angelo DiMentibelio), Zane Buzby (Rolling Stone reporter), Billy Crystal (Morty the Mime), Paul Benedict (Tucker "Smitty" Brown), Howard Hesseman (Terry Ladd), Paul Shortino (Duke Fame), Russ Kunkel (Eric "Stumpy Joe" Childs), Anjelica Huston (Polly Deutsch). The classic mockumentary covering the 1982 comeback American tour of the fictional heavy metal group Spinal Tap, the loudest band in the world (turning the dial up to 11) in order to promote their new album *Smell the Glove*. *Dir.* Rob Reiner.

This Man Is Dangerous (1941) James Mason (Mick Cardby), Mary Clare (Matron), Margaret Vyner (Mollie Bennett), Gordon McLeod (Inspector Cardby), Frederick Valk (Dr. Moger), Barbara Everest (Mrs. Cardby), Barbara James (Lena Morne), G.H. Mulcaster (Lord Morne), Eric Clavering (Al Meason), Terry Conlin (Detective Sergeant Trotter), W.G. Fay (Mr. Eslick), Brefni O'Rorke (Dr. Crosbie), Viola Lyel (Nurse), Anthony Shaw (Sir Wallace Benson), Michael Rennie (Inspector). Private detective Mick Cardby crosses swords with a gang which has kidnapped the daughter of Lord Morne. Based on the novel *They Called Him Death* by David Hume. *Dir.* Lawrence Huntington.

This Sporting Life (1957) Richard Harris (Frank Machin), Rachel Roberts (Mrs. Margaret Hammond), Alan Badel (Gerald Weaver), William Hartnell ('Dad' Johnson), Colin Blakely (Maurice Braithwaite), Vanda Godsell (Mrs. Anne Weaver), Anne Cunningham (Judith), Jack Watson (Len Miller), Arthur Lowe (Charles Slomer), Harry Markham (Wade), George Sewell (Jeff), Leonard Rossiter (Phillips), Peter Duguid (Doctor), Wallas Eaton (Waiter), Anthony Woodruff (Tom), Tom Clegg (Gower), Ken Traill (Trainer), Frank Windsor (Dentist). Former miner Frank Machin becomes the star of the local rugby league team but off the field his life is not so simple. Based on a novel of the same name by David Storey. *Dir.* Lindsay Anderson.

This Week of Grace (1933) Gracie Fields (Grace Milroy), Henry Kendall (Lord Clive Swinford), John Stuart (Henry Baring), Frank Pettingell (Mr. Milroy), Minnie Rayner (Mrs. Milroy), Douglas Wakefield (Joe Milroy), Vivian Foster (Vicar), Marjorie Brooks (Pearl Forrester), Helen Haye (Lady Warmington), Nina Boucicault (Duchess of Swinford). After Grace loses her job working at a factory she is taken on as housekeeper by the Duchess of Swinford and falls in love with the Duchess' nephew. *Dir.* Maurice Elvey.

This Year's Love (1999) Dougray Scott (Cameron), Jennifer Ehle (Sophie), Ian Hart (Liam), Sophie Okonedo (Denise), Douglas Henshall (Danny), Emily Woof (Alice), Catherine McCormack (Hannah), Kathy Burke (Marey), Jamie Foreman (Billy), Bronagh Gallagher (Carol), Eddie Marsan (Eddie), Alastair Galbraith (Willie), Reece Shearsmith (Tourist), Richard Armitage (Smug Man at Party), David Gray (Pub Singer). The inter-related love lives of a group of thirty-somethings in Camden. *Dir.* David Kane.

Those Magnificent Men in Their Flying Machines (1965) Stuart Whitman (Orvil Newton), Sarah Miles (Patricia Rawnsley), James Fox (Richard Mays), Alberto Sordi (Count Emilio Ponticelli), Robert Morley (Lord Rawnsley), Gert Fröbe (Colonel Manfred von Holstein), Jean-Pierre Cassel (Pierre Dubois), Irina Demick (Brigitte/Ingrid/Marlene/Françoise/Yvette/Betty), Eric Sykes (Courtney), Red Skelton (Neanderthal Man), Terry-Thomas (Sir Percy Ware-Armitage), Benny Hill (Fire Chief Perkins), Yûjirô Ishihara (Yamamoto), Flora Robson (Mother Superior), Karl Michael Vogler (Captain Rumpelstoss), Sam Wanamaker (George Gruber), Eric Barker (French Postman), Maurice Denham (Trawler Skipper), Fred Emney (Colonel), Gordon Jackson (MacDougal), Davy Kaye (Jean), John Le Mesurier (French Painter), Jeremy Lloyd (Lieutenant Parsons), Zena Marshall (Countess Sophia Ponticelli), Millicent Martin (Airline Hostess), Eric Pohlmann (Italian Mayor), Marjorie Rhodes (Maid), Norman Rossington (Assistant Fire Chief), William Rushton (Tremayne Gascoyne), Graham Stark (Fireman), Jimmy Thompson (Photographer), Michael Trubshawe (Niven), Tony Hancock (Harry Popperwell), James Robertson Justice (Narrator - voice), Gerald Campion (Fireman), Graham Chapman (Blonde man), Cicely Courtneidge (Muriel), Judy Huxtable (Girl on Beach), Ferdy Mayne (French Official), Ronnie Stevens (R.A.C. Officer). In 1910 Lord Rawnsley offers £10,000 to the winner of the *Daily Post* air race from London to Paris. American, British,

Italian, French, Japanese and German pilots take up the challenge. Subtitled: *Or How I Flew from London to Paris in 25 Hours 11 Minutes*. *Dir.* Ken Annakin.

Those Were the Days (1934) Will Hay (Magistrate Brutus Poskett), John Mills (Bobby Poskett), Iris Hoey (Agatha Poskett), Angela Baddeley (Charlotte Verrinder), Claud Allister (Captain Horace Vale), George Graves (Colonel Alexander Lukyn), Jane Carr (Minnie Taylor), Marguerite Allan (Eve Douglas), H.F. Maltby (Mr. Bullamy), Laurence Hanray (Wormington), Syd Crossley (Wyke), Wally Patch (Insp. Briggs), Jimmy Godden (Pat Maloney), Jimmy Hanley (Boy with bicycle), Ian Wilson (Tom Richardson). Will Hay, in his first film role, plays a beak trying to establish his wife's real age. The film's main action takes place at a music hall. Based on the farce *The Magistrate* by playwright Sir Arthur Wing Pinero. *Dir.* Thomas Bentley.

Three Cases of Murder (1955) Eamonn Andrews (Himself – introductions). *Lord Mountdrago* segment: Orson Welles (Lord Mountdrago), Alan Badel (Owen), André Morell (Dr. Audlin), Helen Cherry (Lady Mountdrago), Peter Burton (Under Secretary for Foreign Affairs), Evelyn Hall (Lady Connemara), David Horne (Sir James), John Humphry (Private Secretary), Zena Marshall (Beautiful Blonde). *You Killed Elizabeth* segment: John Gregson (Edgar Curtain), Elizabeth Sellars (Elizabeth), Emrys Jones (George Wheeler), Alan Badel (Harry), Emrys Jones (George Wheeler), Philip Dale (Sgt. Mallot), Christina Forrest (Susan), Maurice Kaufmann (Pemberton), Jack Lambert (Inspector Acheson). *The Picture* segment: Alan Badel (Mr. X), Hugh Pryse (Jarvis), Leueen MacGrath (Woman in the House), Eddie Byrne (Snyder), Ann Hanslip (The Girl), John Salew (Rooke). Three cases of murder – two of them with a supernatural element. *Dirs.* David Eady (*You Killed Elizabeth*), George More O'Ferrall (*Lord Mountdrago*), Wendy Toye (*The Picture*).

Three Hats for Lisa (1965) Joe Brown (Johnny Howjego), Sophie Hardy (Lisa Milan), Una Stubbs (Flora), Sid James (Sid Marks), Dave Nelson (Sammy), Peter Bowles (Pepper), Seymour Green (Signor Molfino), Josephine Blake (Miss Penny), Jeremy Lloyd (Guards Officer), Michael Brennan (Police Sergeant), Eric Barker (Station Sergeant), Howard Douglas (Cinema caretaker), Dickie Owen (Policeman), Norman Mitchell (Truck driver), Arnold Bell (Hilton Doorman), Barrie Gosney (Reporter). Musical comedy from the Swinging London era. A foreign film starlet and some cockneys tear around London in a game which involves stealing hats. *Dir.* Sidney Hayers.

Three Into Two Won't Go (1969) Rod Steiger (Steve Howard), Claire Bloom (Frances Howard), Judy Geeson (Ella Patterson), Peggy Ashcroft (Belle), Paul Rogers (Jack Roberts), Lynn Farleigh (Janet), Elizabeth Spriggs (Marcia), Sheila Allen (Beth). Steve starts an affair with Ella and then she moves into the family home. *Dir.* Peter Hall.

Three Lives of Thomasina, The (1964) Patrick McGoohan (Andrew McDhui), Karen Dotrice (Mary McDhui), Susan Hampshire (Lori MacGregor), Laurence Naismith (Reverend Angus Peddie), Jean Anderson (Mrs. MacKenzie), Wilfrid Brambell (Willie Bannock), Finlay Currie (Grandpa Stirling), Vincent Winter (Hughie Stirling), Denis Gilmore (Jamie McNab), Charles Carson (Doctor), Ewan Roberts (Constable McQuarrie), Oliver Johnston (Mr. Dobbie), Francis De Wolff (Targu), Nora Nicholson (Old Lady), Jack Stewart (Birnie), Matthew Garber (Geordie McNab), Elspeth March (Thomasina - voice), Rita Webb (Gypsy Granny). The story of a young girl, her cat, her widowed father (who is a vetinary surgeon) and a local woman healer. The life, and apparent death and rebirth of the cat has an effect on all the lives of the people involved with the pet. Based upon Paul Gallico's novel *Thomasina, the Cat Who Thought She Was God*. *Dir.* Don Chaffey.

Three Men in a Boat (1956) Laurence Harvey (George), Jimmy Edwards (Harris), David Tomlinson (J), Shirley Eaton (Sophie Clutterbuck), Lisa Gastoni (Primrose Porterhouse), Jill Ireland (Bluebell Porterhouse), Martita Hunt (Mrs. Willis), Joan Haythorne (Mrs. Porterhouse), Campbell Cotts (Ambrose Porterhouse), Adrienne Corri (Clara Willis), Noelle Middleton (Ethelbertha), Charles Lloyd Pack (Mr. Quilp), Robertson Hare (Photographer), A.E. Matthews (Crabtree), Miles Malleson (Baskcomb), Ernest Thesiger (3rd Old Gentleman), Shane Cordell (Girl Lover), Norman Rossington (Boy Lover), Alice Bowes

(Auntie), Kenneth Williams (Hampton Court Maze Attendant), Esma Cannon (Meek Woman), Toke Townley (Meek Man), Peggy Ann Taylor (Gertrude), Michael Barber (Harold). Three friends, George, Harris and J decide to escape from their respective woman troubles in London by embarking on a relaxing boat trip down the Thames taking with them their dog Montmorency. Based on the Jerome K. Jerome novel. *Dir.* Ken Annakin.

Three Musketeers, The (1973) Michael York (D'Artagnan), Oliver Reed (Athos), Frank Finlay (Porthos/O'Reilly), Richard Chamberlain (Aramis), Jean-Pierre Cassel (King Louis XIII), Geraldine Chaplin (Queen Anne of Austria), Charlton Heston (Cardinal Richelieu), Faye Dunaway (Milady de Winter), Christopher Lee (Count De Rochefort), Simon Ward (Duke of Buckingham), Raquel Welch (Constance Bonacieux), Spike Milligan (M. Bonacieux), Roy Kinnear (Planchet), George Wilson (Treville), Joss Ackland (D'Artagnan's Father), Gretchen Franklin (D'Artagnan's Mother), Nicole Calfan (Kitty), Michael Gothard (Felton), Sybil Danning (Eugenie), Gitty Djamal (Beatrice), Ángel del Pozo (Jussac), Rodney Bewes (Spy), Ben Aris (1st Musketeer), William Hobbs (Assassin), Francis De Wolff (Sea Captain). A reasonably humorous re-telling of the tale made famous by Alexandre Dumas, pere. Young Gascon D'Artagnan arrives in Paris determined to join the King's Musketeeers. Soon he finds himself joining Athos, Aramis and Porthos on a quest to save the Queen's reputation, in the process falling in love with Constance, the Queen's lady-in-waiting, crossing swords with Rochefort, and dealing with the dastardly whiles of Milady and Cardinal Richelieu. *Dir.* Richard Lester.

Three Weird Sisters, The (1948) Nancy Price (Gertrude Morgan-Vaughan), Mary Clare (Maude Morgan-Vaughan), Mary Merrall (Isobel Morgan-Vaughan), Nova Pilbeam (Claire Prentiss), Anthony Hulme (David Davies), Raymond Lovell (Owen Morgan-Vaughan), Elwyn Brook-Jones (Thomas), Edward Rigby (Waldo), Hugh Griffith (Mabli Hughes), Marie Ault (Beattie), David Davies (Police Sergeant), Hugh Pryse (Minister), Lloyd Pearson (Solicitor), Doreen Richards (Mrs. Probart), Bartlett Mullins (Dispenser), Wilfred Boyle (Solicitor's Clerk), Frank Dunlop (Ben), Belinda Marshall (Mrs. Bevan), Elizabeth Maude (Olwen Harries). Three sisters ask their rich younger brother to help them finance the repair of miners' cottages belonging to the failing mine which they own. However, he puts money before obligation, much to the sisters' dismay. Adapted from the novel *The Case of the Weird Sisters* by Charlotte Armstrong. *Dir.* Daniel Birt.

Thunder Rock (1942) Michael Redgrave (David Charleston), Barbara Mullen (Ellen Kirby), James Mason (Streeter), Lilli Palmer (Melanie Kurtz), Finlay Currie (Captain Joshua Stuart), Frederick Valk (Dr. Stefan Kurtz), Sybille Binder (Anne-Marie Kurtz), Frederick Cooper (Edward 'Ted' Briggs), Jean Shepherd (Mrs. Millie Briggs), Barry Morse (Robert), George Carney (Harry), Miles Malleson (Chairman of Directors), Bryan Herbert (Flanning), James Pirrie (Jim Sales), A.E. Matthews (Mr. Kirby), Olive Sloane (Woman Director), Tommy Duggan (Office Clerk), Tony Quinn (Office Clerk), Harold Anstruther (British Consul), Alfred Sangster (Director), Victor Beaumont (Hans), Vi Kaley (Old Woman In Cell), Milo Sperber (Mr. Hirohiti). Journalist David Charleston quits first his job and then Britain as he fails to convince people of the danger of the rise of fascism during the 1930s. He becomes a lighthouse keeper on Lake Michigan in Canada where he is visited by the spirits of the drowned from a shipwreck on the lake. They convince him he must not run away but return to Europe to fight. Based on the play of the same name by Robert Ardrey. *Dir.* Roy Boulting.

Thunderball (1965) Sean Connery (James Bond), Adolfo Celi (Emilio Largo), Claudine Auger (Dominique "Domino" Derval), Luciana Paluzzi (Fiona Volpe), Rik van Nutter (Felix Leiter), Bernard Lee (M), Guy Doleman (Count Lippe), Martine Beswick (Paula Caplan), Molly Peters (Patricia Fearing), Earl Cameron (Pinder), Paul Stassino (François Derval and Angelo Palazzi), Desmond Llewelyn (Q), Roland Culver (Home Secretary), Lois Maxwell (Miss Moneypenny), Philip Locke (Vargas), George Pravda (Ladislav Kutze), Michael Brennan (Janni), Bill Cummings (Quist). Bond is assigned to track down two stolen nuclear warheads. The film was remade as *Never Say Never Again*. Bond drives an Aston Martin DB5. The theme song is sung by Tom Jones. An adaptation of the novel of the same name by Ian Fleming. *Dir.* Terence Young.

Thunderbirds are Go (1966) Voice cast: Peter Dyneley (Jeff Tracy), Shane Rimmer (Scott Tracy), Sylvia Anderson (Lady Penelope Creighton-Ward), Jeremy Wilkin (Virgil Tracy/Space Colonel Harris), Matt Zimmerman (Alan Tracy/Messenger), David Graham (Gordon Tracy/Brains/Aloysius "Nosey" Parker), Ray Barrett (John Tracy/The Hood/Commander Casey), Christine Finn (Tin-Tin Kyrano), Paul Maxwell (Captain Paul Travers), Alexander Davion (Space Captain Greg Martin), Bob Monkhouse (Space Navigator Brad Newman/Swinging Star Announcer), Neil McCallum (Dr Ray Pierce), Charles Tingwell (Dr Tony Grant/PR Officer/SEC Board Member/Woomera Tracking Station), Cliff Richard (Cliff Richard Jr), The Shadows (Themselves). Two years after the Zero-X Mars mission is sabotaged by The Hood, another attempt is made, with International Rescue on standby. A big screen spin-off from the *Thunderbirds* television series. *Dir.* David Lane.

Thursday's Child (1943) Sally Ann Howes (Fennis Wilson), Wilfrid Lawson (Frank Wilson), Kathleen O'Regan (Ellen Wilson), Stewart Granger (David Penley), Eileen Bennett (Phoebe Wilson), Marianne Davis (Gloria Dewey), Gerhard Kempinski (Rudi Kauffmann), Felix Aylmer (Mr. Keith), Margaret Yarde (Mrs. Chard), Vera Bogetti (Madame Felicia), Percy Walsh (Charles Lennox), Michael Allen (Jim Wilson), Margaret Drummond (Wendy Keith), Ronald Shiner (Joe), Anthony Holles (Roy Todd), Patrick Aherne (Lance Sheridan). When Fennis is cast in a film, her sister is jealous and family tensions begin to rise to the surface. *Dir.* Rodney Ackland.

Tiara Tahiti (1962) James Mason (Capt. Brett Aimsley), John Mills (Lt. Col. Clifford Southey), Claude Dauphin (Henri Farengue), Herbert Lom (Chong Sing), Rosenda Monteros (Belle Annie), Jacques Marin (Desmoulins), Libby Morris (Adele Franklin), Madge Ryan (Millie Brooks), Gary Cockrell (Joey), Peter Barkworth (Lt. David Harper), Roy Kinnear (Capt. Enderby). The easy life of Brett Aimsley on Tahiti is spoilt by the arrival of his ex army commanding officer who is looking to open a hotel on the island. *Dir.* Ted Kotcheff.

Tiger Bay (1959) John Mills (Supt Graham), Horst Buchholz (Korchinsky), Hayley Mills (Gillie), Yvonne Mitchell (Anya), Megs Jenkins (Mrs Phillips), Anthony Dawson (Barclay), George Selway (Det Sgt Harvey), Shari (Christine), George Pastell ('POLOMA' Captain), Paul Stassino ('POLOMA' 1st. Officer), Marne Maitland (Dr Das), Meredith Edwards (PC Williams), Marianne Stone (Mrs Williams), Rachel Thomas (Mrs Parry), Brian Hammond (Dai Parry), Kenneth Griffith (Choirmaster), Eynon Evans (Mr Morgan), Christopher Rhodes (Insp Bridges), Edward Cast (Det Con Thomas), David Davies (Desk Sgt), Glyn Houston (Detective at Police Station). A young orphan girl witnesses the murder of a neighbour by a sailor but makes friends with him and he promises to take her with him when he next sails. However, the police are closing in. *Dir.* J. Lee Thompson.

Tiger in the Smoke (1956) Donald Sinden (Geoffrey Leavitt), Muriel Pavlow (Meg Elgin), Tony Wright (Jack Havoc), Bernard Miles (Tiddy Doll), Alec Clunes (Asst. Commissioner Oates), Laurence Naismith (Canon Avril), Christopher Rhodes (Chief Inspector Luke), Charles Victor (Will), Thomas Heathcote (Rolly Gripper), Sam Kydd (Tom Gripper), Kenneth Griffith (Crutches), Gerald Harper (Duds Morrison), Wensley Pithey (Detective Sergeant Pickett), Stanley Rose (Uncle), Stratford Johns (Police Constable), Brian Wilde (Trumps), Hilda Barry (Mrs. Talisman), Beatrice Varley (Lucy Cash), Percy Herbert (Copper), Dandy Nichols (Stall Attendant). A group of British ex-commandos trail the widow of their commanding officer who they believe hid treasure somewhere in Brittany. Very loosely based, in that it omits the main character, on the novel of the same name by Margery Allingham. *Dir.* Roy Ward Baker.

Till Death Us Do Part (1968) Warren Mitchell (Alf Garnett), Dandy Nichols (Else Garnett), Una Stubbs (Rita Garnett/Rawlins), Antony Booth (Mike Rawlins), Liam Redmond (Mike's Father), Shelagh Fraser (Mike's Mother), Geoffrey Hughes (Mike's brother), Bill Maynard (Bert), Brian Blessed (Sergeant), Sam Kydd (Fred), Frank Thornton (Valuation Officer), Ann Lancaster (Woman at Block of Flats), Michael Robbins (Pub Landlord), Pat Coombs (Neighbour), Kate Williams (Sergeant's Girlfriend), John D. Collins (RAF officer at Tube Station), Bob Grant (Man in Pub), Edward Evans (Jim). After a section set in early WWII London with the newly married Garnetts and a newly pregnant Else, the film switches to 1966 with a wedding and a World Cup Final. A spin-off from the television series. *Dir.* Norman Cohen.

Time Lock (1957) Robert Beatty (Pete Dawson), Lee Patterson (Colin Walker), Betty McDowall (Lucille Walker), Vincent Winter (The Boy), Robert Ayres (Insp. Andrews), Alan Gifford (George Foster), Larry Cross (Reporter), Sandra Francis (Evelyn Webb), Gordon Tanner (Dr. Hewitson), Jack Cunningham (Max Jarvis), Victor Wood (Howard Zeeder), Peter Mannering (Dr. Foy), Roland Brand (Police officer), Sean Connery (Welder No. 1). A little boy is trapped in a bank vault with only enough oxygen for ten hours. The race is on to release him. *Dir.* Gerald Thomas.

Time Without Pity (1957) Michael Redgrave (David Graham), Ann Todd (Honor Stanford), Leo McKern (Robert Stanford), Paul Daneman (Brian Stanford), Peter Cushing (Jeremy Clayton), Alec McCowen (Alec Graham), Renee Houston (Mrs. Harker), Lois Maxwell (Vickie Harker), Richard Wordsworth (Maxwell), George Devine (Barnes), Joan Plowright (Agnes Cole), Ernest Clark (Under-Secretary), Peter Copley (Prison Chaplain), Hugh Moxey (Prison Governor), Dickie Henderson (Comedian), Christina Lubicz (Jennie Cole). The father of convicted murderer Alec Graham has just 24 hours in order to save him from being hanged, during which time he comes across several possible suspects. *Dir.* Joseph Losey.

Tinker, Tailor, Soldier, Spy (2011) Gary Oldman (George Smiley), Colin Firth (Bill Haydon), Tom Hardy (Ricki Tarr), Mark Strong (Jim Prideaux), Ciarán Hinds (Roy Bland), Benedict Cumberbatch (Peter Guillam), David Dencik (Toby Esterhase), Stephen Graham (Jerry Westerby), Simon McBurney (Oliver Lacon), Toby Jones (Percy Alleline), John Hurt (Control), Svetlana Khodchenkova (Irina), Kathy Burke (Connie Sachs), Roger Lloyd-Pack (Mendel), Christian McKay (Mackelvore), Konstantin Khabensky (Polyakov), Tomasz Kowalski (Boris), Zoltán Mucsi (Hungarian agent). After a mission in Hungary goes wrong, British agent George Smiley is forced into retirement. However, after allegations are made that there is a "mole" in the Circus (British Intelligence) he is brought out of retirement to investigate. Anglo-French film based on the John le Carré novel. *Dir.* Tomas Alfredson.

Titfield Thunderbolt, The (1953) Stanley Holloway (Valentine), George Relph (Weech), Naunton Wayne (Blakeworth), John Gregson (Gordon), Godfrey Tearle (The Bishop), Hugh Griffith (Dan), Gabrielle Brune (Joan), Sid James (Hawkins), Reginald Beckwith (Coggett), Edie Martin (Emily), Michael Trubshawe (Ruddock), Jack MacGowran (Vernon Crump), Ewan Roberts (Alec Pearce), Herbert C. Walton (Seth), John Rudling (Clegg), Nancy O'Neil (Mrs. Blakeworth), Campbell Singer (Police Sergeant), Frank Atkinson (Station Sergeant), Wensley Pithey (A Policeman), Harold Alford (Guard), Ted Burbidge (Engine Driver), Frank Green (Fireman), George King (Fireman), Sam Kydd (Policeman). Comedy in which locals battle to save a railway branch line from being closed against competition from the local bus company. *Dir.* Charles Crichton.

To Catch a Spy (1971) Kirk Douglas (Andrej), Marlène Jobert (Fabienne), Trevor Howard (Sir Trevor Dawson), Tom Courtenay (Baxter Clarke), Patrick Mower (James Fenton), Bernadette Lafont (Simone), Bernard Blier (Webb), Sacha Pitoëff (Stefan), Richard Pearson (Haldane), Garfield Morgan (The Husband), Angharad Rees (Victoria), Isabel Dean (Celia), Jean Gilpin (Ground Stewardess), Robert Raglan (Ambassador), Sheila Steafel (Woman in Elevator). A comedy spy caper where a schoolteacher – a French woman married to a Brit - discovers her husband has been detained as a spy in the Soviet Union. Also released as *Keep Your Fingers Crossed*. *Dir.* Dick Clement.

To Die For (1995) Nicole Kidman (Suzanne Stone-Maretto), Matt Dillon (Larry Maretto), Joaquin Phoenix (Jimmy Emmett), Casey Affleck (Russell Hines), Illeana Douglas (Janice Maretto), Alison Folland (Lydia Mertz), Dan Hedaya (Joe Maretto), Wayne Knight (Ed Grant), Kurtwood Smith (Earl Stone), Holland Taylor (Carol Stone), Susan Traylor (Fay Stone), Maria Tucci (Angela Maretto), Tim Hopper (Mike Warden), Michael Rispoli (Ben DeLuca), Buck Henry (Mr. H. Finlaysson), Gerry Quigley (George), David Cronenberg (Man at lake), Joyce Maynard (Lawyer), George Segal (Conference speaker), Rain Phoenix (Tambourine player). Tagline: She'll do anything to get what she wants ...ANYTHING. Which just about sums up the relentless desire of Suzanne to graduate from local TV weathergirl to national news anchor. *Dir.* Gus Van Sant.

To Sir, with Love (1967) Sidney Poitier (Mark Thackeray), Christian Roberts (Denham), Judy Geeson (Pamela Dare), Suzy Kendall (Gillian Blanchard), Ann Bell (Mrs. Dare), Geoffrey Bayldon (Theo Weston), Faith Brook (Grace Evans), Patricia Routledge (Clinty Clintridge), Chris Chittell (Potter), Adrienne Posta (Moira Joseph), Lulu (Barbara 'Babs' Pegg), Edward Burnham (Florian), Rita Webb (Mrs. Joseph), Fiona Duncan (Euphemia Phillips), Fred Griffiths (Mr. Clark), Mona Bruce (Josie Dawes), Marianne Stone (Gert), Dervis Ward (Mr. Bell), Peter Atard (Ingham), Grahame Charles (Fernman), Michael Des Barres (Williams), Anthony Villaroel (Seales), Richard Willson (Curly), Lynne Sue Moon (Miss Wong), Jayne Peach (Jeanie Clarke), Gareth Robinson (Tich Jackson), Roger Shepherd ('Fats' Buckley), Ric Rothwell, Bob Lang, Eric Stewart (the band - 'The Mindbenders'). A black American teacher is confronted by a class of disruptive East London school children. The film deals with social and racial issues in an inner city school during the 1960s. Lulu's rendition of the title song reached the top of the US charts. Based on E. R. Braithwaite's semi-autobiographical novel. *Dir.* James Clavell.

To the Devil, a Daughter (1975) Richard Widmark (John Verney), Christopher Lee (Father Michael Rayner), Nastassja Kinski (Catherine Beddows), Honor Blackman (Anna Fountain), Denholm Elliott (Henry Beddows), Michael Goodliffe (George De Grass), Eva Maria Meineke (Eveline de Grass), Anthony Valentine (David), Derek Francis (The Bishop), Constantine Gregory (Kollde), Brian Wilde (Black Room Attendant), Howard Goorney (Critic), Frances de la Tour (Salvation Army Major), Izabella Telezynska (Margaret), Anna Bentinck (Isabel), Irene Prador (German Matron), Petra Peters (Sister Helle), William Ridoutt (Airport Porter), Ed Devereaux (Reporter). Catherine Beddows, a nun with The Children of the Lord run by Father Rayner, is on her annual birthday visit to her father. He asks the occult writer John Verney to try and protect her from the ordeal to come when she turns eighteen. Based on a Dennis Wheatley novel. *Dir.* Peter Sykes.

Tom & Viv (1994) Willem Dafoe (T. S Tom Eliot), Miranda Richardson (Vivienne Haigh-Wood), Rosemary Harris (Rose Haigh-Wood), Tim Dutton (Maurice Haigh-Wood), Nickolas Grace (Bertrand Russel), Geoffrey Bayldon (Harwent), Clare Holman (Louise Purdon), Philip Locke (Charles Haigh-Wood), Joanna McCallum (Virginia Woolf), Joseph O'Conor (Bishop of Oxford), John Savident (Sir Frederick Lamb), Michael Attwell (W.I. Janes), Sharon Bower (Secretary), Linda Spurrier (Edith Sitwell), Roberta Taylor (Ottoline Morrell), Christopher Baines (Verger), Anna Chancellor (Woman), James Greene (Dr. Cyriax), Lou Hirsch (Captain Todd), Edward Holmes (Telegraph Boy), Simon McBurney (Dr. Reginald Miller). A film depicting the relationship between T.S. Eliot and Vivienne Haigh-Wood based on the play *Tom & Viv* by Michael Hastings. *Dir.* Brian Gilbert

Tom Brown's Schooldays (1951) John Howard Davies (Tom Brown), Robert Newton (Dr. Thomas Arnold), John Charlesworth (East), James Hayter (Old Thomas), John Forrest (Flashman), Michael Hordern (Wilkes), Max Bygraves (Coach Guard), Francis De Wolff (Squire Brown), Diana Wynyard (Mrs. Thomas Arnold), Hermione Baddeley (Sally Harrowell), Kathleen Byron (Mrs. Brown), Amy Veness (Mrs. Wixie), Brian Worth (Judd), Rachel Gurney (Mrs. Arthur), Michael Brennan (Black Bart), Neil North (Diggs), Michael Ward (Master), Glyn Dearman (Arthur). Based on the novel of the same name by Thomas Hughes. *Dir.* Gordon Parry.

Tom Jones (1963) Albert Finney (Tom Jones), Susannah York (Sophie Western), Hugh Griffith (Squire Western), Edith Evans (Miss Western), Joan Greenwood (Lady Bellaston), Diane Cilento (Molly Seagrim), George Devine (Squire Allworthy), Joyce Redman (Mrs. Waters/Jenny Jones), David Tomlinson (Lord Fellamar), Rosalind Atkinson (Mrs. Miller), Angela Baddeley (Mrs. Wilkins), Wilfrid Lawson (Black George), Rosalind Knight (Mrs. Fitzpatrick), Jack MacGowran (Partridge), Freda Jackson (Mrs. Seagrim), David Warner (Blifil), James Cairncross (Parson Supple), Rachel Kempson (Bridget Allworthy), Peter Bull (Thwackum), George A. Cooper (Fitzpatrick), Jack Stewart (MacLachlan), Patsy Rowlands (Honour), John Moffatt (Square), Avis Bunnage (Innkeeper), Mark Dignam (Lieutenant), Michael Brennan (Jailer), Lynn Redgrave (Susan), Redmond Phillips (Lawyer Dowling), Julian Glover (Northerton). The adventures of a foundling of unknown parentage who through the machinations of Blifil and in consequence of his lowly status is sent out into the world, where he is beset with both mishaps and beautiful women. John Osborne's adaptation of Henry Fielding's novel *The History of Tom Jones, a Foundling*. The film won four Academy Awards: Best Picture, Best Director, Best Substantially Original Score (John Addison) and Best Writing, Screenplay Based on Material from Another Medium. *Dir*. Tony Richardson.

Tommy (1975) Roger Daltrey (Tommy Walker), Ann-Margret (Nora Walker), Oliver Reed (Uncle Frank), Elton John (The Pinball Wizard), Eric Clapton (The Preacher), John Entwistle (Himself), Keith Moon (Uncle Ernie/Himself), Paul Nicholas (Cousin Kevin), Jack Nicholson (The Specialist), Robert Powell (Group Captain Walker), Pete Townshend (Himself), Tina Turner (The Acid Queen), Arthur Brown (The Priest), Victoria Russell (Sally Simpson), Ben Aris (Rev. A. Simpson V. C.), Mary Holland (Mrs. Simpson), Gary Rich (Rock Musician), Dick Allan (President Black Angels), Barry Winch (Young Tommy), Eddie Stacey (Bovver Boy), Jennifer Baker (Nurse), Susan Baker (Nurse), Imogen Claire (Nurse). "That deaf, dumb and blind kid sure plays a mean pinball". Based upon The Who's rock opera album of the same name. *Dir*. Ken Russell.

Tommy Steele Story, The (1957) Tommy Steele (Himself), Patrick Westwood (Brushes), Tom Littlewood (Judo Instructor), Peter Lewiston (John Kennedy), John Boxer (Paul Lincoln), Cyril Chamberlain (Chief Steward), Brian Coleman (Hospital Doctor), Mark Daly (Junkshop Man), Lisa Daniely (Hospital Nurse), Hilda Fenemore (Mrs.Steele), Charles Lamb (Mr. Steele). A biopic of the then 21 year-old singer Tommy Steele, with Tommy playing himself. *Dir*. Gerard Bryant.

Tommy the Toreador (1959) Tommy Steele (Tommy Tomkins), Janet Munro (Amanda), Sid James (Cadena), Bernard Cribbins (Paco), Noel Purcell (Captain), Virgilio Teixeira (Parilla, the Bullfighter), José Nieto (Inspector Quintero), Ferdy Mayne (Lopez), Harold Kasket (Jose), Kenneth Williams (Vice-Consul), Eric Sykes (Martin), Manolo Blazquez (Matador), José Valero (Bullfighting enthusiast), Francis De Wolff (Hotel Proprietor), Tutte Lemkow (Bootblack), Warren Mitchell (Waiter), Edwin Richfield (Tommy's dresser), Andreas Malandrinos (Photographer), Charles Gray (Gomez), Sydney Tafler (Ramon). A Cockney sailor docks in Spain and tries his hand at bullfighting after being mistaken for a matador. *Dir*. John Paddy Carstairs.

Tomorrow at Ten (1964) John Gregson (Inspector Parnell), Robert Shaw (Marlowe), Alec Clunes (Anthony Chester), Alan Wheatley (Assistant Commissioner Bewley), Kenneth Cope (Sergeant Grey), Ernest Clark (Dr. Towers), Piers Bishop (Jonathan Chester), Helen Cherry (Robbie), William Hartnell (Freddy), Betty McDowall (Mrs. Parnell), Harry Fowler (Smiley), Renee Houston (Mrs. Maddox), Noel Howlett (Brain specialist), Trevor Reid (Q Detective). A little boy is kidnapped and the perpetrator tells the family that a bomb is set to go off the next day at ten o'clock in the house where he is being kept. Unfortunately, the kidnapper is killed before he can reveal the location! *Dir*. Lance Comfort.

Tomorrow Never Dies (1997) Pierce Brosnan (James Bond), Jonathan Pryce (Elliot Carver), Michelle Yeoh (Colonel Wai Lin), Teri Hatcher (Paris Carver), Götz Otto (Richard Stamper), Ricky Jay (Henry Gupta), Joe Don Baker (Jack Wade), Vincent Schiavelli (Dr. Kaufman), Judi Dench (M), Desmond Llewelyn (Q), Samantha Bond (Miss Moneypenny), Geoffrey Palmer (Admiral Roebuck), Colin Salmon (Charles Robinson), Julian Fellowes (Minister of Defence), Cecilie Thomsen (Professor Inga Bergstrom), Gerard Butler (Sailor), Julian Rhind-Tutt (Sailor). Media mogul Elliot Carver attempts to engineer a war between China and Britain. Bond drives a BMW 750iL and an Aston Martin DB5. The theme song is performed by Sheryl Crow. *Dir*. Roger Spottiswoode.

Tomorrow We Live (1943) John Clements (Jean Baptiste), Godfrey Tearle (Mayor Pierre Duchesne), Hugh Sinclair (Maj. von Kleist), Greta Gynt (Marie Duchesne), Judy Kelly (Germaine Bertan), Yvonne Arnaud (Mme. L. Labouche), Karel Stepanek (Seitz), Bransby Williams (Matthieu), Fritz Wendhausen (Cmndt. Frissette), Allan Jeayes (Pogo), Gabrielle Brune (Mrs. Frissette), Margaret Yarde (Fauntel), David Keir (Jacquier), Anthony Holles (Stationmaster), Olaf Olsen (Sergeant Major), D.J. Williams (Boileau), John Salew (Marcel LaBlanc), Walter Gotell (Hans), Victor Beaumont (Rabineau), Brefni O'Rorke (Moreau), Gibb McLaughlin (Dupont), Cot D'Ordan (Durand), Walter Hertner (Schultz), Herbert Lom (Kurtz), Townsend Whitling (Rougemont). A film made about the travails of the French Resistance and the brutal actions of the Nazis. The film was made with "the official co-operation of General de Gaulle and the French National Committee". *Dir*. George King.

Tony Draws a Horse (1950) Cecil Parker (Dr. Howard Fleming), Anne Crawford (Clare Fleming), Derek Bond (Tim Shields), Barbara Murray (Joan Parsons), Mervyn Johns (Alfred Parsons), Barbara Everest (Mrs. Parsons), Edward Rigby (Grandpa), Dandy Nichols (Mrs. Smith), Gabrielle Blunt (Grace), Marjorie Gresley (Mrs. Carey Brown), David Hurst (Ivan), Anthony Lang (Tony Fleming), Kynaston Reeves (Dr. Bletchley). An eminent doctor and his psychiatrist wife fall out over how to deal with their young son Tony after he draws a horse, complete with reproductive anatomy, on the wall of the surgery. Based on the Lesley Storm play. *Dir*. John Paddy Carstairs.

Too Hot To Handle (1960) Jayne Mansfield (Midnight Franklin), Leo Genn (Johnny Solo), Karlheinz Böhm (Robert Jouvel), Christopher Lee (Novak), Sheldon Lawrence (Diamonds Dielli), Danik Patisson (Lilliane Decker), Patrick Holt (Inspector West), Kai Fischer (Cynthia), Barbara Windsor (Ponytail). Penny Morrell (Terry), Katherine Keeton (Melody), Susan Denny (Marjorie), Judy Bruce (Maureen), Elizabeth Wilson (Jacki), Shari Kahn (Jungle), Martin Boddey (Mr. Arpels), John Salew (Moeller), Tom Bowman (Flash Gordon), Ian Fleming (Pawnbroker), Bill McGuffie (Piano player), Michael Balfour (Tourist guide), Larry Taylor (Mouth), June Elvin (Hostess), Morton Lowry (Dinelli's driver), Robin Chapman (Priest), Martin Sterndale (Editor), Harry Lane (Muscles). Nightclub owner Johnny Solo is receiving threats which he thinks originate from his rival Diamonds Dielli. Meanwhile his girlfriend, singer Midnight Franklin, is angling for him to get out of the business. *Dir*. Terence Young.

Too Late the Hero (1970) Michael Caine (Pvt. Tosh Hearne), Cliff Robertson (Lt. Sam Lawson), Ian Bannen (Pvt. Jock Thornton), Harry Andrews (Col. Thompson), Ronald Fraser (Pvt. Campbell), Denholm Elliott (Capt. Hornsby), Lance Percival (Cpl. McLean), Percy Herbert (Sgt. Johnstone), Patrick Jordan (Sergeant Major), Sam Kydd (Colour-Sergeant), William Beckley (Pvt. Currie), Martin Horsey (Pvt. Griffiths), Harvey Jason (Signalman Scott), Don Knight (Pvt. Connolly), Roger Newman (Pvt. Riddle), Michael Parsons (Pvt. Rafferty), Sean MacDuff (Pvt. Rogers), Frank Webb (Ensign), Henry Fonda (Capt. John G. Nolan), Ken Takakura (Maj. Yamaguchi). US Navy lieutenant is assigned a British unit to help send a signal from a Japanese communications station on New Hebrides. *Dir*. Robert Aldrich.

Too Many Crooks (1959) Terry-Thomas (Billy Gordon), George Cole (Fingers), Brenda De Banzie (Lucy), Bernard Bresslaw (Snowdrop), Sid James (Sid), Joe Melia (Whisper), Vera Day (Charmaine), Delphi Lawrence (Secretary), John Le Mesurier (Magistrate), Sydney Tafler (Solicitor), Rosalie Ashley (Angela), Nicholas Parsons (Tommy), Vilma Ann Leslie (Girl Journalist),

Edie Martin (Gordon's Mother), Tutte Lemkow (Swarthy Man), John Stuart (Inspector Jensen), Terry Scott (Fire Policeman), Cyril Chamberlain (Chief Fire Officer), Sam Kydd (Tramp), Wally Patch (Court Usher). When an incompetent gang of crooks kidnap a businessman's wife instead of his daughter he refuses to pay the ransom on the grounds that he doesn't want her back. His wife then takes over the gang and makes her husband's life a misery. *Dir*. Mario Zampi.

Topsy Turvy (1999) Jim Broadbent (W. S. Gilbert), Allan Corduner (Sir Arthur Sullivan), Ron Cook (Richard D'Oyly Carte), Lesley Manville (Lucy Gilbert), Dexter Fletcher (Louis), Timothy Spall (Richard Temple), Alison Steadman (Madame Leon), Andy Serkis (John D'Auban), Ashley Jensen (Miss Tringham), Sukie Smith (Clothilde), Martin Savage (George Grossmith), Eleanor David (Fanny Ronalds), Vincent Franklin (Rutland Barrington), Louise Gold (Rosina Brandram), Shirley Henderson (Leonora Braham), Kevin McKidd (Durward Lely), Dorothy Atkinson (Jessie Bond), Cathy Sara (Sybil Grey), Michael Simkins (Frederick Bovill), Naoko Mori (Miss 'Sixpence Please'), Eve Pearce (Gilbert's Mother), Charles Simon (Gilbert's Father), Theresa Watson (Maude Gilbert), Lavinia Bertram (Florence Gilbert), Roger Heathcott (Banton), Wendy Nottingham (Helen Lenoir), Stefan Bednarczyk (Frank Cellier), Geoffrey Hutchings (Armourer), Sam Kelly (Richard Barker), Nicholas Woodeson (Mr. Seymour), Richard Coyle (Mr. Hammond). As the popularity of their operettas might be beginning to wane, Sullivan and Gilbert cannot reach an agreement regarding Gilbert's latest story, which Sullivan feels is too similar to his previous efforts. However, inspiration strikes Gilbert after his wife takes him to an exhibition of Japanese arts and crafts. *Dir*. Mike Leigh.

Touch and Go (1955) Jack Hawkins (Jim Fletcher), Margaret Johnston (Helen Fletcher), June Thorburn (Peggy Fletcher), Roland Culver (Reg Fairbright), John Fraser (Richard Kenyon), James Hayter (Kimball), Alison Leggatt (Alice Fairbright), Margaret Halstan (Mrs Pritchett), Henry B. Longhurst (Mr Pritchett), Basil Dignam (Stevens), Bessie Love (Mrs Baxter), Alfred Burke (Man On Bridge), Liz Fraser (Girl On Bridge). After he quits his job Jim decides to emigrate to Australia despite the reluctance of his wife and daughter. *Dir*. Michael Truman.

Touch of Love, A (1969) Sandy Dennis (Rosamund Stacey), Ian McKellen (George Matthews), Eleanor Bron (Lydia Reynolds), John Standing (Roger Henderson), Michael Coles (Joe Hurt), Rachel Kempson (Sister Henry), Peggy Thorpe-Bates (Mrs. Stacey), Kenneth Benda (Mr. Stacey), Sarah Whalley (Octavia), Shelagh Fraser (Miss Gurnsey), Deborah Stanford (Beatrice), Margaret Tyzack (Sister Bennett), Roger Hammond (Mike), Maurice Denham (Doctor Prothero). Bookish Rosamund finds that she is pregnant after just one sexual encounter with TV announcer George. She eventually decides to keep the baby. *Dir*. Waris Hussein.

Touching the Void (2003) Brendan Mackey (Joe Simpson), Nicholas Aaron (Simon Yates), Ollie Ryall (Richard Hawking), Joe Simpson (Himself), Simon Yates (Himself), Richard Hawking (Himself). A documentary about Joe Simpson's and Simon Yates' disastrous attempt to climb the Siula Grande in the Peruvian Andes in 1985. Based on the book of the same name by Joe Simpson. *Dir*. Kevin Macdonald.

Town Like Alice, A (1956) Virginia McKenna (Jean Paget), Peter Finch (Joe Harman), Kenji Takaki (Japanese Sergeant), Tran Van Khe (Captain Sugaya), Jean Anderson (Miss Horsefall), Marie Lohr (Mrs. Dudley Frost), Maureen Swanson (Ellen), Renee Houston (Ebbey), Nora Nicholson (Mrs. Frith), Eileen Moore (Mrs. Holland), John Fabian (Mr. Holland), Vincent Ball (Ben), Tim Turner (British Sergeant), Vu Ngoc Tuan (Captain Yanata), Munesato Yamada (Captain Takata), Nakanishi (Captain Nishi), Ikeda (Kempetei Sergeant), Otokichi Ikeda (Kempetei Sergeant), Geoffrey Keen (Solicitor), June Shaw (Mrs. Graham), Armine Sandford (Mrs. Carstairs), Mary Allen (Mrs. Anderson), Virginia Clay (Mrs. Knowles), Bay White (Mrs. Davies), Philippa Morgan (Mrs. Lindsay), Dorothy Moss (Mrs. O'Brien), Gwenda Ewen (Mrs. Rhodes), Josephine Miller (Daphne Adams), Edwina Carroll (Fatima), Sanny Bin Hussan (Mat Amin), Charles Marshall (Well Digger), Jane White (Brenda), Cameron Moore (Freddie), Margaret Eaden (Jane), Dominic Lieven (Michael Rhodes), Peter John (Timothy), Meg Buckenham (Mary Graham), Geoffrey Hawkins (Robin), Sam Kydd (Australian Driver). Jean recalls (in flashback) how she survived being made prisoner in Malaya by the Japanese and became friendly with an Australian soldier who apparently sacrificed himself in order to save her and the women with her. Back in the present she discovers that the soldier did not die. Based on the novel by Nevil Shute. *Dir*. Jack Lee.

Trail of the Pink Panther (1982) Peter Sellers (Chief Insp. Jacques Clouseau (archive footage)), David Niven (Sir Charles Litton), Herbert Lom (Chief Insp. Charles Dreyfus), Richard Mulligan (Clouseau's Father), Joanna Lumley (Marie Jouvet), Capucine (Lady Simone Litton), Robert Loggia (Bruno Langois), Harvey Korman (Prof. Auguste Balls), Burt Kwouk (Cato Fong), Graham Stark (Hercule Lajoy), Peter Arne (Col. Bufoni), André Maranne (Sergeant Francois Duval), Ronald Fraser (Dr. Longet), Leonard Rossiter (Superintendant Quinlan (archive footage)), Marne Maitland (Deputy Commissioner Lasorde), Harold Kasket (President Sandover Haleesh), Denise Crosby (Denise), Daniel Peacock (Clouseau, age 18), Lucca Mezzofanti (Clouseau, age 8), Madlena Nedeva (Mme. Dreyfuss), Julie Andrews (Charwoman), Colin Blakely (Alec Drummond). Clouseau is once again on the trail of the jewel known as the Pink Panther when his plane crashes into the sea. This film contains no original material from Peter Sellers who had died in 1980. His performance only consists of flashbacks and outtakes from the previous films in the series. *Dir*. Blake Edwards.

Train of Events (1949) Segment *The Engine Driver*: Jack Warner (Jim Hardcastle), Gladys Henson (Mrs Hardcastle), Susan Shaw (Doris Hardcastle), Patric Doonan (Ron Stacey), Philip Dale (Hardcastle's fireman), Miles Malleson (Johnson), Leslie Phillips (Stacey's Fireman), Will Ambro (Lancashire Railwayman). Segment *The Prisoner-of-War*: Joan Dowling (Ella), Laurence Payne (Richard), Olga Lindo (Mrs. Bailey). Segment *The Composer*: Valerie Hobson (Stella), Irina Baronova (Irina Norozova), John Clements (Raymond Hillary), John Gregson (Malcolm Murray-Bruce), Gwen Cherrell (Charmian), Neal Arden (The Compere), Jacqueline Byrne (TV Announcer), Thelma Grigg (The Harpist). Segment *The Actor*: Peter Finch (Philip), Mary Morris (Louise), Laurence Naismith (Joe Hunt), Doris Yorke (Mrs Hunt), Michael Hordern (Plainclothesman), Charles Morgan (Plainclothesman), Guy Verney (Producer), Mark Dignam (Bolingbroke), Philip Ashley, Brian Coleman, Henry Hewitt, Lyndon Brook (Actors). A portmanteau film from Ealing Studios. In flashback as a train heads for a crash, three separate segments recall the events which lead to an actor, a composer and an ex prisoner-of-war taking the journey and a fourth segment centres on the train driver. *Dirs*. Sidney Cole (segment *The Engine Driver*), Charles Crichton (segment *The Composer*), Basil Dearden (segments *The Actor* and *The Prisoner-of-War*)

Trainspotting (1996) Ewan McGregor (Mark "Rent Boy" Renton), Ewen Bremner (Daniel "Spud" Murphy), Jonny Lee Miller (Simon "Sick Boy" Williamson), Kevin McKidd (Tommy MacKenzie), Robert Carlyle (Francis "Franco" Begbie), Kelly Macdonald (Diane Coulston), Peter Mullan (Swanney "Mother Superior"), James Cosmo (Mr. Renton), Eileen Nicholas (Mrs. Renton), Susan Vidler (Allison), Pauline Lynch (Lizzy), Shirley Henderson (Gail), Irvine Welsh (Mikey Forrester), Brianna Maja Harrington (The Baby), Dale Winton (Game Show Host). The life of a group of heroin addicts in 1980s Edinburgh focusing mainly on "Rent Boy" as he tries to get clean and the effect this has on his friends and family. Based on the novel of the same name by Irving Welsh. *Dir*. Danny Boyle.

Tread Softly Stranger (1958) Diana Dors (Calico), George Baker (Johnny Mansell), Terence Morgan (Dave Mansell), Patrick Allen (Paddy Ryan), Jane Griffiths (Sylvia), Joseph Tomelty (Joe Ryan), Thomas Heathcote (Sergeant Lamb), Russell Napier (Potter), Norman Macowan (Danny), Maureen Delaney (Mrs. Finnegan), Betty Warren (Flo), Chris Fay (Eric Downs), Timothy Bateson (Fletcher), John Salew (Pawnbroker), Andrew Keir (Inspector Harris), Sandra Francis (Linda). Brothers Dave and Johnny are encouraged by Dave's girlfriend Calico to steal Dave's firms' payroll. However, in the process the nightwatchman is killed. *Dir*. Gordon Parry.

Trench, The (1999) Paul Nicholls (Pte. Billy Macfarlane), Daniel Craig (Sgt. Telford Winter), Julian Rhind-Tutt (2Lt. Ellis Harte), Danny Dyer (LCpl. Victor Dell), James D'Arcy (Pte. Colin Daventry), Tam Williams (Pte. Eddie Macfarlane), Anthony Strachan (Pte. Horace Beckwith), Michael Moreland (Pte. George Hogg), Adrian Lukis (Lt. Col. Villiers), Ciarán McMenamin (Pte. Charlie Ambrose), Cillian Murphy (Pte. Rag Rookwood), John Higgins (Pte. Cornwallis), Ben Whishaw (Pte. James Deamis), Tim Murphy (Pte. Bone), Danny Nutt (Pte. Dieter Zimmermann), Charles Cartmell (Harold Faithfull), Tom Mullion (Nelson), Jenny Pickering (Maria Corrigan). Young British troopers wait in the trenches prior to going over the top on the disastrous first day of the Battle of the Somme on 1 July 1916. *Dir.* William Boyd.

Trent's Last Case (1952) Michael Wilding (Philip Trent), Margaret Lockwood (Margaret Manderson), Orson Welles (Sigsbee Manderson), John McCallum (John Marlowe), Miles Malleson (Burton Cupples), Hugh McDermott (Calvin C. Bunner), Jack McNaughton (Martin), Sam Kydd (Inspector Murch), Geoffrey Bayldon (Reporter in Court), John Chandos (Tim O'Reilly), Kenneth Williams (Horace Evans). When a major international financier is found dead the police decide that the death is suicide. However, journalist Philip Trent is convinced that it was in fact murder. Based on the novel of the same name by E. C. Bentley. *Dir.* Herbert Wilcox.

Trials of Oscar Wilde, The (1960) Peter Finch (Oscar Wilde), Yvonne Mitchell (Constance Wilde), James Mason (Sir Edward Carson), Nigel Patrick (Sir Edward Clarke), Lionel Jeffries (John Sholto Douglas, Marquis of Queensberry), John Fraser (Lord Alfred Douglas), Sonia Dresdel (Lady Wilde), Maxine Audley (Ada Leverson), James Booth (Alfred Wood), Emrys Jones (Robbie Ross), Lloyd Lamble (Charles Humphries), Paul Rogers (Frank Harris), Ian Fleming (Arthur), Naomi Chance (Lily Langtry), Laurence Naismith (Prince of Wales), Meredith Edwards (Auctioneer), Anthony Newlands (1st Clerk of Arraigns), Robert Percival (2nd Clerk of Arraigns), Michael Goodliffe (Charles Gill), Liam Gaffney (Willie Wilde), Derek Aylward (Lord Percy Douglas), William Kendall (Lord Ashford), Ronald Cardew (Lord Sonning), Cicely Paget-Bowman (Lady Queensberry), Campbell Singer (Inspector), Victor Brooks (PC), Alfred Burke (Reporter), A.J. Brown (Justice Collins), Charles Carson (Justice Charles), David Ensor (Justice Wills), Edward Evans (Sydney), Gladys Henson (Mrs Burgess, Landlady), John Welsh (Cafe Royal Manager), Richard Caldicot (Bookshop Owner). A fictionalised account of the libel action by Oscar Wilde against the Marquess of Queensberry and his subsequent trial for gross indecency. Aka *The Man with the Green Carnation*. *Dir.* Ken Hughes.

Triple Cross (1966) Christopher Plummer (Eddie Chapman), Romy Schneider (The Countess), Trevor Howard (Distinguished Civilian), Gert Fröbe (Colonel Steinhager), Claudine Auger (Paulette), Yul Brynner (Baron Von Grunen), Georges Lycan (Leo), Jess Hahn (Commander Braid), Harry Meyen (Lieutenant Keller), Gil Barber (Bergman), Jean-Claude Bercq (Major Von Leeb), Jean Claudio (Sergeant Thomas), Robert Favart (General Dalrymple), Gordon Jackson (British Sergeant). The film is loosely based on the true story of Eddie Chapman, believed by the Nazis to be their top spy in Great Britain whilst in fact he was an MI5 double agent known as "Zigzag". *Dir.* Terence Young.

Trollenberg Terror, The (1958) Forrest Tucker (Alan Brooks), Laurence Payne (Philip Truscott), Jennifer Jayne (Sarah Pilgrim), Janet Munro (Anne Pilgrim), Warren Mitchell (Professor Crevett), Frederick Schiller (Klein), Andrew Faulds (Brett), Stuart Saunders (Dewhurst), Colin Douglas (Hans), Derek Sydney (Wilde), Leslie Heritage (Carl). On a mountain in Norway, something is ripping the heads from climbers. Also known as *The Crawling Eye, Creature from Another World, The Creeping Eye,* and *The Flying Eye. Dir.* Quentin Lawrence.

Trottie True (1949) Jean Kent (Trottie True), James Donald (Lord Digby Landon), Hugh Sinclair (Maurice Beckenham), Lana Morris (Bouncie Barrington), Andrew Crawford (Sid Skinner), Bill Owen (Joe Jugg), Michael Medwin (Monty, Marquis of Maidenhead), Joan Young (Mrs. True), Harold Scott (Mr. True),

Tony Halfpenny (Perce True), Daphne Anderson (Bertha True), Carole Lesley (Clare as a child), Carol Leslie (Clara as a child), Dilys Laye (Trottie as a child), David Lines (Perce as a child), Campbell Cotts (Saintsbury), Heather Thatcher (Angela Platt-Brown), Mary Hinton (Duchess of Wellwater), Anthony Steel (The Bellaires' footman), Christopher Lee (Hon. Bongo Icklesham), Harcourt Williams (Duke Of Wellwater), Hattie Jacques (Daisy Delaware), Katharine Blake (Ruby Rubarto), Olwen Brookes (Lady Talman), Irene Browne (Duchess), Patrick Cargill (Party Guest), Ian Carmichael (Bill the Postman), Darcy Conyers (Claude), Francis De Wolff (George Edwardes), Gretchen Franklin (Martha), Helen Goss (Mrs. Bellaire), Elspet Gray (Honor Bellaire), Arthur Hambling (Mr. Jupp), Anne Holland (Countess of Burney), Mary Jones (Gladys True), Sam Kydd ('Bedford' Stage Manager), Roger Moore (Stage Door Johnny), James Neylin (Lord George Peasemarsh), Shaun Noble (Andy Galloway), Doris Rogers (Hon. Mrs. Seaton), Philip Stainton (Arthur Briggs), Philip Strange (Earl of Burney), Jack Vyvian (Uncle Sam) Set in the 1890s, Trottie is a music hall performer who has set her sights on stardom and thinks she needs the right romantic connections to reach that goal. *Dir.* Brian Desmond Hurst.

Trouble Brewing (1939) George Formby (George Gullip), Googie Withers (Mary Brown), Gus McNaughton (Bill Pike), Garry Marsh (A.G. Brady), C. Denier Warren (Major Hopkins), Beatrix Fielden-Kaye (Housekeeper), Joss Ambler (Lord Redhill), Ronald Shiner (Bridgewater), Martita Hunt (Mme Berdi), Esma Cannon (Maid), Basil Radford (Guest), Jack Vyvian (Policeman). After being paid out in counterfeit notes following a big win on the horses, George is determined to unmask the counterfeiting ring himself. *Dir.* Anthony Kimmins.

Trouble in Store (1953) Norman Wisdom (Norman), Lana Morris (Sally Wilson), Moira Lister (Peggy Drew), Megs Jenkins (Miss Gibson), Jerry Desmonde (Augustus Freeman), Margaret Rutherford (Miss Bacon), Eddie Leslie (Bill), Michael Brennan (Davis), Michael Ward (Wilbur), Joan Ingram (Miss Denby), Cyril Chamberlain (Alf), Ronan O'Casey (Eddie), Derek Bond (Gerald), Joan Sims (Edna), John Warren (Master of ceremonies), John Warwick (Robson), Hamlyn Benson (Mark), Esma Cannon (Lady Customer), Stringer Davis (Shop Assistant). Norman is up to his usual antics – this time in a department store – in the course of which he uncovers a robbery plot. *Dir.* John Paddy Carstairs.

Truth About Spring, The (1965) Hayley Mills (Spring Tyler), John Mills (Tommy Tyler), James MacArthur (William Ashton), Lionel Jeffries (Cark), Harry Andrews (Sellers), Niall MacGinnis (Cleary), David Tomlinson (Skelton), Lionel Murton (Simmons). A romantic comedy involving buried treasure and modern day (1960s) pirates of the Caribbean (with ne'er a Johnny Depp or Somalian in sight). *Dir.* Richard Thorpe.

Trygon Factor, The (1966) Stewart Granger (Supt. Cooper-Smith), Susan Hampshire (Trudy Emberday), Robert Morley (Hubert Hamlyn), Cathleen Nesbitt (Livia Embarday), Brigitte Horney (Sister General), Sophie Hardy (Sophie), James Robertson Justice (Sir John - voice: English version), Siegfried Schürenberg (Sir John - German Version), Eddi Arent (Emil Clossen), Diane Clare (Sister Claire), James Culliford (Luke Embarday), Allan Cuthbertson (Det. Thompson), Colin Gordon (Dice), Caroline Blakiston (White Nun), Richardina Jackson (Black Nun), Yuri Borionko (Nailer), Conrad Monk (Pasco), John Barrett (Guide), Jeremy Hawk (Bank Manager), Joseph Cuby (Receptionist), Inigo Jackson (Ballistics Expert), Russell Waters (Sgt. Chivers). A comedy crime film where a series of murders and burglaries leads Superintendent Cooper-Smith to investigate a mansion occupied by an odd family and a group of nuns. Based on the Edgar Wallace novel *Kate Plus Ten. Dir.* Cyril Frankel.

TT: Closer to the Edge (2011) A documentary about TT racing and riders, in particular covering the week of the Isle of Man TT races in 2010. *Dir.* Richard De Aragues.

Tudor Rose (1936) Nova Pilbeam (Lady Jane Grey), Cedric Hardwicke (Earl of Warwick), John Mills (Lord Guilford Dudley), Felix Aylmer (Edward Seymour), Leslie Perrins (Thomas Seymour), Frank Cellier (Henry VIII), Desmond Tester

(Edward VI), Gwen Ffrangcon Davies (Mary Tudor), Martita Hunt (Lady Grey), Miles Malleson (Duke Henry Grey), Sybil Thorndike (Ellen), Arthur Goullet (Sir John Gates), John Laurie (John Knox), John Turnbull (Arundel). The story of the life of the "Nine Days Queen". Throughout Lady Jane Grey's life she is used as a pawn by her family and then her husband's family in order to gain power. *Dir*. Robert Stevenson

Tunes of Glory (1962) Alec Guinness (Maj. Jock Sinclair), John Mills (Lt. Col. Basil Barrow), Dennis Price (Maj. Charles 'Charlie' Scott), Kay Walsh (Mary Titterington), John Fraser (Cpl. Piper Ian Fraser), Susannah York (Morag Sinclair), Gordon Jackson (Capt. Jimmy Cairns), Duncan Macrae (Pipe Maj. Duncan MacLean), Percy Herbert (RSM Riddick), Allan Cuthbertson (Capt. Eric Simpson), Paul Whitsun-Jones (Maj. 'Dusty' Miller), Gerald Harper (Maj. Hugo MacMillan), Richard Leech (Capt. Alec Rattray), Peter McEnery (2nd Lt. David MacKinnon), Keith Faulkner (Cpl. Piper Adam), Angus Lennie (Orderly Room Clerk), John Harvey (Sgt. Finney), Bryan Hulme (Cpl. Drummer), Andrew Keir (LCpl. Campbell), Eric Woodburn (Landlord), Andrew Downie (Cpl. Waiter), Jameson Clark (Sir Alan), Lockwood West (Provost), Gwen Nelson (Provost's Wife). When Jock Sinclair is overlooked in what he believes to be his rightful position as Commanding Officer he plots to undermine the authority of Basil Barrow who has been appointed in his stead. Based on the novel by James Kennaway *Dir*. Ronald Neame.

Tunnel, The (1935) Richard Dix (Richard 'Mack' McAllan), Leslie Banks (Frederick 'Robbie' Robbins), Madge Evans (Ruth McAllan), Helen Vinson (Varlia Lloyd), C. Aubrey Smith (Lloyd), Basil Sydney (Mostyn), Henry Oscar (Grellier), Hilda Trevelyan (Mary), Cyril Raymond (Harriman), Jimmy Hanley (Geoffrey McAllan), George Arliss (Prime Minister of Great Britain), Walter Huston (President of the United States), James Carew (Jim Barton), Pat Fitzpatrick (Geoffrey as a young child), Helen Haye (Oil Magnate). A science fiction film about two engineers who are building a tunnel from England to America. Based on the novel *Der Tunnel* by Bernhard Kellermann. *Dir*. Maurice Elvey.

Turn the Key Softly (1953) Yvonne Mitchell (Monica Marsden), Terence Morgan (David), Joan Collins (Stella Jarvis), Kathleen Harrison (Granny Quilliam), Thora Hird (Mrs. Rowan), Dorothy Alison (Joan), Glyn Houston (Bob), Geoffrey Keen (Mr. Gregory), Russell Waters (George Jenkins), Clive Morton (Walters), Toke Townley (Prison Guard). Three women from very different backgrounds (Monica, Stella and Mrs Quilliam) are all released from Holloway Prison on the same day having served their sentences. The film focuses on the events of their first day of freedom. *Dir*. Jack Lee.

Turned Out Nice Again (1941) George Formby (George Pearson), Peggy Bryan (Lydia), Elliott Mason (Mrs. Pearson), Edward Chapman (Uncle Arnold), O.B. Clarence (Mr. Dawson), Mackenzie Ward (Gerald Dawson), Ronald Ward (Nelson), John Salew (Largon), Wilfrid Hyde-White (Removal Man), Hay Petrie (Drunk), Michael Rennie (Diner), Jack Vyvian (Removal Man). George works for a traditional textile firm which makes underwear. When he develops a revolutionary new thread the company is not interested and gives him the sack, only to later regret the decision. *Dir*. Marcel Varnel.

28 Days Later... (2002) Cillian Murphy (Jim), Naomie Harris (Selena), Christopher Eccleston (Major Henry West), Megan Burns (Hannah), Brendan Gleeson (Frank), Ricci Harnett (Corporal Mitchell), Stuart McQuarrie (Sergeant Farrell), Noah Huntley (Mark), Leo Bill (Private Jones), Luke Mably (Private Clifton), Junior Laniyan (Private Bell), Ray Panthaki (Private Bedford), Sanjay Rambaruth (Private Davis), Marvin Campbell (Private Mailer), David Schneider (Scientist). The "rage" virus is released by animal activists and 28 days later coma victim Jim wakes up to find London deserted apart from psychotic people and a couple of survivors. *Dir*. Danny Boyle.

28 Weeks Later... (2007) Robert Carlyle (Don Harris), Rose Byrne (Major Scarlet Ross), Jeremy Renner (Sergeant Doyle), Harold Perrineau (Flynn), Idris Elba (General Stone), Imogen Poots (Tammy), Mackintosh Muggleton (Andy), Amanda Walker (Sally), Shahid Ahmed (Jacob), Garfield Morgan (Geoff), Emily Beecham (Karen), Catherine McCormack (Alice Harris), Beans El-Balawi (Boy in Cottage), Meghan Popiel (DLR Soldier), Stewart Alexander (Military Officer), Philip Bulcock (Senior Medical Officer), Chris Ryman (Rooftop Sniper), Tristan Tait (Soldier), William Meredith (Medical Officer), Matt Reeves (Bunker Soldier), Thomas Garvey (Bunker Major), Tom Bodell (Medical Centre Lobby Soldier). A British/Spanish sequel to 28 Days Later set six months after the events of the earlier film. A NATO force arrives in Britain to try to confirm that the infected have died of starvation and whether repopulation is possible. *Dir*. Juan Carlos Fresnadillo.

24 Hour Party People (2002) Steve Coogan (Tony Wilson), Conrad Murray (Bailey Brother), John Thomson (Charles), Shirley Henderson (Lindsay Wilson), Paddy Considine (Rob Gretton), Lennie James (Alan Erasmus), Andy Serkis (Martin Hannett), Sean Harris (Ian Curtis), John Simm (Bernard Sumner), Ralf Little (Peter Hook), Tim Horrocks (Stephen Morris), Danny Cunningham (Shaun Ryder), Chris Coghill (Bez), Paul Popplewell (Paul Ryder), Ron Cook (Derek Ryder), Kieran O'Brien (Nathan), Raymond Waring (Vini Reilly), Dave Gorman (John the Postman), Peter Kay (Don Tonay), Enzo Cilenti (Peter Saville), Rob Brydon (Ryan Letts). A film telling the story of the music scene in Manchester from the punk era through to the "Madchester" scene of the late 1980s and early 1990s. It follows the career of Tony Wilson, the head of Factory Records. *Dir*. Michael Winterbottom.

24 7: Twenty Four Seven (1997) Bob Hoskins (Alan Darcy), Danny Nussbaum (Tim), Justin Brady (Gadget), James Hooton (Wolfman Knighty), Darren O. Campbell (Darren Campbell), Karl Collins (Stuart), Johann Myers (Benny), Jimmy Hynd (Meggy), Mat Hand (Wesley Fagash), James Corden (Tonka). Alan Darcy opens a training gym to get kids off the street. *Dir*. Shane Meadows

Twice Round the Daffodils (1962)
Juliet Mills (Catty), Donald Sinden (Ian Richards), Donald Houston (John Rhodes), Kenneth Williams (Henry Halfpenny), Ronald Lewis (Bob White), Andrew Ray (Chris Walker), Joan Sims (Harriet Halfpenny), Jill Ireland (Janet), Lance Percival (George Logg), Sheila Hancock (Dora), Nanette Newman (Joyce), Renee Houston (Matron), Amanda Reiss (Dorothy), Mary Powell (Mrs. Rhodes), Barbara Roscoe (Mary), Olwen Brookes (Dorothy's mother), Frank Forsyth (Dorothy's father). Basically a rerun of Carry on Nurse. Both films were based on the play *Ring for Catty* and had a similar cast and crew. *Dir*. Gerald Thomas.

Twin Town (1997) Llyr Ifans (Julian Lewis), Rhys Ifans (Jeremy Lewis), Huw Ceredig (Fatty Lewis), Rachel Scorgie (Adie Lewis), Di Botcher (Jean Lewis), Dougray Scott (Terry Walsh), Dorien Thomas (Greyo), William Thomas (Bryn Cartwright), Jenny Evans (Bonny Cartwright), Sue Roderick (Lucy Cartwright), Brian Hibbard (Dai Rhys), Morgan Hopkins (Chip Roberts), Buddug Williams (Mrs Mort), Ronnie Williams (Mr Mort), Huw Ceredig (Fatty Lewis), Rachel Scorgie (Adie Lewis), Di Botcher (Jean Lewis), Mary Allen (Olive), David Hayman (Dodgy), Brian Hibbard (Dai Reese), Morgan Hopkins (Chip Roberts), Sion Tudor Owen (Dewi), William Thomas (Bryn Cartwright), Jenny Evans (Bonny Cartwright), Sue Roderick (Lucy Cartwright), Kevin Allen (TV Presenter), Paul Durden (Taxi Driver). When twins Julian and Jeremy fail to get compensation for their father's injury from his boss, small time gangster Bryn, the resulting feud quickly escalates into death and destruction. *Dir*. Kevin Allen.

Twins of Evil (1971) Peter Cushing (Gustav Weil), Kathleen Byron (Katy Weil), Mary Collinson (Maria Gellhorn), Madeleine Collinson (Frieda Gellhorn), David Warbeck (Anton Hoffer), Damien Thomas (Count Karnstein), Katya Wyeth (Countess Mircalla), Roy Stewart (Joachim), Isobel Black (Ingrid Hoffer), Harvey Hall (Franz), Alex Scott (Hermann), Dennis Price (Dietrich), Sheelah Wilcox (Lady in Coach), Inigo Jackson (Woodman), Judy Matheson (Woodman's Daughter), Kirsten Lindholm (Young Girl at Stake), Luan Peters (Gerta), Peter Thompson (Gaoler). Orphaned identical twins Maria and Frieda are sent to live with their stern "witchhunter" uncle Gustav. Frieda visits the castle of the mysterious Count Karnstein and is "vampirised". The third film in the so-called *The Karnstein Trilogy*, based on the book *Carmilla* by Sheridan Le Fanu. The other films in the trilogy are *The Vampire Lovers* (1970) and *Lust for a Vampire* (1971). *Dir*. John Hough.

Twisted Nerve (1968) Hayley Mills (Susan Harper), Hywel Bennett (Martin Durnley/Georgie), Billie Whitelaw (Joan Harper), Phyllis Calvert (Enid Durnley), Frank Finlay (Henry Durnley), Barry Foster (Gerry Henderson), Salmaan Peerzada (Shashie Kadir), Christian Roberts (Philip Harvey), Gretchen Franklin ('Clarkie'), Thorley Walters (Sir John Forrester), Timothy Bateson (Mr. Groom the Librarian), Clifford Cox (Insp. Goddard), Richard Davies ('Taffy' Evans), Basil Dignam (Doctor), Mollie Maureen (Lady Patient), Russell Napier (Prof. Fuller), Robin Parkinson (Shop Manager), Brian Peck (Det. Sgt. Rogers), Timothy West (Supt. Dakin), Marianne Stone (Store Detective). A young man pretends to be mentally challenged in order to stalk a girl and eliminate anyone who gets too close to her. *Dir*. Roy Boulting

Two for the Road (1967) Audrey Hepburn (Joanna Wallace), Albert Finney (Mark Wallace), Eleanor Bron (Cathy Manchester), William Daniels (Howard Manchester), Gabrielle Middleton (Ruth Manchester), Claude Dauphin (Maurice Dalbret), Nadia Gray (Francoise Dalbret), Georges Descrières (David), Jacqueline Bisset (Jackie), Judy Cornwell (Pat), Irène Hilda (Yvonne de Florac), Dominique Joos (Sylvia). Whilst driving to the South of France, Joanna and Mark revisit (through flashbacks) their early romance, marriage and married life through various road trips - in cars such as a white Mercedes-Benz 230SL roadster, an MG TD, a Triumph Herald, a VW Microbus and a Ford Country Squire. *Dir*. Stanley Donen.

2001: A Space Odyssey (1968) Keir Dullea (Dr. David Bowman), Gary Lockwood (Dr. Frank Poole), William Sylvester (Dr. Heywood R. Floyd), Douglas Rain (the voice of the HAL 9000), Daniel Richter (chief man-ape), Leonard Rossiter (Dr. Andrei Smyslov), Margaret Tyzack (Elena), Robert Beatty (Dr. Ralph Halvorsen), Frank Miller (mission controller), Edward Bishop (lunar shuttle captain). The film consists of four sections (The Dawn of Man, TMA-1, Jupiter Mission, and Jupiter and Beyond the Infinite) which in turn appear to deal with human evolution, technology, artificial intelligence, and extraterrestrial life. The film is partly based on Arthur C. Clarke's short story "The Sentinel" and focuses on a series of encounters between humans and mysterious black monoliths that are apparently affecting human destiny. The film includes a soundtrack of classical music (including The Blue Danube waltz by Johann Strauss II and the symphonic poem Also Sprach Zarathustra by Richard Strauss) which memorably accompanied visuals of spinning satellites and planetary bodies. *Dir*. Stanley Kubrick.

Two Way Stretch (1960) Peter Sellers (Dodger Lane), Lionel Jeffries (Prison Officer 'Sour' Crout), Wilfrid Hyde-White (Soapy Stevens), Bernard Cribbins (Lennie "The Dip" Price), David Lodge (Jelly Knight), Irene Handl (Mrs Price), Liz Fraser (Ethel), Maurice Denham (Horatio Bennett), Beryl Reid (Miss Pringle), George Woodbridge (Chief Prison Officer Jenkins), Cyril Chamberlain (Gate Warder – Day), Wallas Eaton (Gate Warder – Night), William Abney (Visiting Room Warder), Thorley Walters (Colonel Parkright), John Wood (Captain), Robert James (Police Superintendent), Walter Hudd (Reverend Patterson), Mario Fabrizi (Jones), Warren Mitchell (Tailor), John Glyn-Jones (Lawyer), Arthur Mullard (Fred). Dodger has devised the perfect crime. He'll escape from prison, do the robbery and then get back into jail before his escape is noticed. *Dir*. Robert Day.

Tyrannosaur (2011) Peter Mullan (Joseph), Olivia Colman (Hannah), Eddie Marsan (James), Samuel Bottomley (Samuel), Paul Popplewell (Bod), Ned Dennehy (Tommy), Sally Carman (Marie), Sian Breckin (Kelly), Paul Conway (Terry), Lee Rufford (Lee), Robin Butler (Jack), Robert Haythorne (Rob), Jag Sanghera (Gurav). Joseph's life is plagued by a seemingly uncontrollable temper and he turns to local charity shop worker Hannah to help him overcome his problems. *Dir*. Paddy Considine.

Ugly Duckling, The (1959) Bernard Bresslaw (Henry Jekyll/Teddy Hyde), Jon Pertwee (Victor Jekyll), Reginald Beckwith (Reginald), Maudie Edwards (Henrietta Jekyll), Jean Muir (Snout), Richard Wattis (Barclay), Elwyn Brook-Jones (Dandy), Michael Ripper (Benny), David Lodge (Peewee), Harold Goodwin (Norma Marla), Keith Smith (Figures), Michael Ward (Pasco), John Harvey (Sergeant Barnes), Jess Conrad (Bimbo), Mary Wilson (Lizzie), Geremy Phillips (Tiger), Ian Ainsley (Fraser), Jill Carson (Yum Yum), Cyril Chamberlain (Police Sergeant), Alan Coleshill (Willie), Robert Desmond (Dizzy), Shelagh Dey (Miss Angers), Jean Driant (M. Blum). A comic take on the Jekyll/Hyde story. Shy and awkward chemist's assistant Henry Jekyll takes a formula mixed by his uncle Victor and is transformed into suave but criminal Teddy Hyde. *Dir*. Lance Comfort.

Uncensored (1942) Eric Portman (Andre Delange), Phyllis Calvert (Julie Lanvin), Griffith Jones (Father de Gruyte), Raymond Lovell (von Koerner), Peter Glenville (Charles Neels), Frederick Culley (Victor Lanvin), Irene Handl (Frau von Koerner), Carl Jaffe (Kohlmeier), Felix Aylmer (Col. von Hohenstein), Eliot Makeham (Abbe De Moor), Walter Hudd (Van Heemskirk), Stuart Lindsell (Press Officer), J. H. Roberts (Father Corot), John Slater (Théophile), Peter Godfrey (Lou), Arthur Goullet (Jackson), Ben Williams (Arthur Backer), Aubrey Mallalieu (Louis Backer). A story about the organised resistance movement in occupied Belgium during WWII which centres on night club owner Delange, who publishes the anti-Nazi newspaper La Libre Belgique (Free Belgium). *Dir*. Anthony Asquith.

Uncle Silas (1947) Jean Simmons (Caroline Ruthyn), Katina Paxinou (Madame de la Rougierre), Derrick De Marney (Uncle Silas), Derek Bond (Lord Richard Ilbury), Sophie Stewart (Lady Monica Waring), Esmond Knight (Dr. Bryerly), Reginald Tate (Austin Ruthyn), Manning Whiley (Dudley Ruthyn), Marjorie Rhodes (Mrs. Rusk), John Laurie (Giles), Frederick Burtwell (Branston), George Curzon (Sleigh), O.B. Clarence (Vicar Clay), Frederick Ranalow (Rigg), Patricia Glyn (Mary Quince), Guy Rolfe (Sepulchre Hawkes), Robin Netscher (Tom Hawkes), John Salew (Grimstone). Set in the 19th Century. Teenager Caroline is heir to her father's fortune but on his death she is put under the guardianship of her impecunious Uncle Silas who is in league with his good for nothing son Dudley and her former governess Madame de la Rougierre. Together they conspire to get their hands on Caroline's estate before the time limit of the guardianship expires. An adaption of the novel of the same name by J. Sheridan Le Fanu. *Dir*. Charles Frank.

Under Capricorn (1949) Ingrid Bergman (Lady Henrietta Flusky), Joseph Cotten (Sam Flusky), Michael Wilding (Hon. Charles Adare), Margaret Leighton (Milly), Cecil Parker (The Governor), Denis O'Dea (Mr. Corrigan), Jack Watling (Winter), Harcourt Williams (The Coachman), John Ruddock (Mr. Potter), Bill Shine (Mr. Banks), Victor Lucas (The Rev. Smiley), Ronald Adam (Mr. Riggs), Francis De Wolff (Major Wilkins), G.H. Mulcaster (Dr. Macallister), Olive Sloane (Sal), Maureen Delaney (Flo), Julia Lang (Susan), Betty McDermott (Martha). Set in the 1830s. Charles Adare's uncle is the new Governor of New South Wales and Charles accompanies him to Australia in an attempt to reverse his poor fortunes. In Sydney he is befriended by Sam Flusky, a former convict who is now a successful businessman and married to the alcoholic Henrietta, who had been a friend of Charles' sister. Charles' attentiveness to Henrietta means that he is eventually caught between a jealous Sam and the Flusky's housekeeper Milly, who has her own agenda. Hitchcock makes two cameo appearances: he is seen first in the town square and later on the steps of Government House. Based on the novel of the same name by Helen Simpson. *Dir*. Alfred Hitchcock.

Under the Skin (1997) Samantha Morton (Iris Kelly), Claire Rushbrook (Rose Kelly), Rita Tushingham (Mum), Christine Tremarco (Vron), Stuart Townsend (Tom), Matthew Delamere (Gary), Mark Womack (Frank), Clare Francis (Elena), Joe Tucker (Sam), Daniel O'Meara (Max), Crissy Rock (Compere), Lisa Millett (Sylvia). Sisters Iris and Rose have to cope with the sudden death of their mother. *Dir*. Carine Adler.

Unearthly Stranger (1963) John Neville (Dr. Mark Davidson), Philip Stone (Prof. John Lancaster), Gabriella Licudi (Julie Davidson), Patrick Newell (Maj. Clarke), Jean Marsh (Miss Ballard), Warren Mitchell (Prof. Geoffrey D. Munro). The wife of a scientist on the brink of a breakthrough turns out to be an alien sent to Earth to prevent him completing his research. *Dir*. John Krish.

United 93 (2006) Khalid Abdalla (Ziad Jarrah), Sarmed al-Samarrai (Saeed al-Ghamdi), Omar Berdouni (Ahmed al-Haznawi), Jamie Harding (Ahmed al-Nami), Christian Clemenson (Tom Burnett), Trish Gates (Sandra Bradshaw), David Alan Basche (Todd Beamer), Cheyenne Jackson (Mark Bingham), Opal Alladin (CeeCee Lyles), Starla Benford (Wanda Anita Green), J.J. Johnson (Captain Jason Dahl), Nancy McDoniel (Lorraine G. Bay), Polly Adams (Deborah Welsh), Richard Bekins (William Joseph Cashman), Susan Blommaert (Jane Folger), Ray Charleson (Joseph DeLuca), Gary Commock (First Officer LeRoy Homer Jr.), Liza Colón-Zayas (Waleska Martinez), Lorna Dallas (Linda Gronlund), Denny Dillon (Colleen Fraser), Trieste Kelly Dunn (Deora Frances Bodley), Kate Jennings Grant (Lauren Grandcolas), Peter Hermann (Jeremy Glick), Tara Hugo (Kristin White Gould), Marceline Hugot (Georgine Rose Corrigan), Joe Jamrog (John Talignani), Corey Johnson (Louis J. Nacke), Masato Kamo (Toshiya Kuge), Tom O'Rourke (Donald Peterson), Simon Poland (Alan Anthony Beaven), Becky London (Jean Headley Peterson), Peter Marinker (Andrew Garcia), Jodie Lynne McClintock (Marion R. Britton), Libby Morris (Hilda Marcin), David Rasche (Donald Freeman Greene), Erich Redman (Christian Adams), Michael J. Reynolds (Patrick Joseph Driscoll), John Rothman (Edward P. Felt), Daniel Sauli (Richard Guadagno), Rebecca Schull (Patricia Cushing), Chloe Sirene (Honor Elizabeth Wainio), Olivia Thirlby (Nicole Carol Miller), Chip Zien (Mark Rothenberg), Leigh Zimmerman (Christine Snyder). A fact-based drama film chronicling the events aboard United Airlines Flight 93, which was hijacked during the 11 September 2001 attacks. *Dir.* Paul Greengrass.

Universal Soldier (1971) George Lazenby (Ryker), Ben Carruthers (Jesse), Robin Hunter (Bradshaw), Rudolph Walker (Mbote), Cy Endfield (Derek Bowden), Alan Barnes (Temple Smith), Guy Deghy (Timmerman), Edward Judd (Rawlings), Germaine Greer (Clara Bowden), Ronan O'Rahilly (Gered), Charles Owour (Mbote's Aide), Martin Wyldeck (Wilson), Ronald Leigh-Hunt (St. George), Anthony Newlands (Petrakis), Maggie Wright (Rawling's Secretary), Paul Dawkins (Chairman), Lynda Baron (Woman at Party). Ryker is a career mercenary who is commissioned to train an army for an exiled African leader. Lazenby financed and starred in this film rather than make a further appearance as James Bond. *Dir.* Cy Endfield.

Unpublished Story (1942) Richard Greene (Bob Randall), Valerie Hobson (Carol Bennett), Basil Radford (Lamb), Roland Culver (Stannard), Brefni O'Rorke (Denton), Miles Malleson (Farmfield), George Carney (Landlord), Muriel George (Landlady), André Morell (Marchand), Frederick Cooper (Trapes), George Thorpe (Major Edwards), Renee Gadd (Miss Hartley), Claude Bailey (George Roddington), Ronald Shiner (Agitator), Wally Patch (Taxi driver), John Longden (Metcalf), Aubrey Mallalieu (Warden), Edie Martin (Mrs. Duncan), Henry Morrell (Wigmore). Randall is an outspoken war correspondent with the Gazette who has had several stories censored and spiked. Together with fellow journalist Bennett he infiltrates an organisation known as People for Peace, ostensibly a pacifist movement but which is actually pro-Nazi. Will he manage to get his story told this time? *Dir.* Harold French.

Up in the World (1956) Norman Wisdom (Norman), Maureen Swanson (Jeannie Andrews), Jerry Desmonde (Maj. Willoughby), Michael Caridia (Sir Reginald), Colin Gordon (Fletcher Hethrington), Ambrosine Phillpotts (Lady Banderville), Michael Ward (Maurice), Jill Dixon (Sylvia), Edwin Styles (Conjuror), Hy Hazell (Yvonne), William Lucas (Mick Bellman), Lionel Jeffries (Wilson), Cyril Chamberlain (Harper), Michael Brennan (Prison Warder), Eddie Leslie (Max), Edward Lexy (Detective Superintendant), Bernard Bresslaw (Williams). Window cleaner Norman works at a wealthy woman's mansion and foils a kidnap attempt on the heir to the estate. However, as the heir has amnesia, thanks to a knock on the head, he cannot prevent Norman from being convicted of the attempted kidnap. *Dir.* John Paddy Carstairs.

Up Pompeii! (1971) Frankie Howerd (Lurcio), Michael Hordern (Ludicrus Sextus), Barbara Murray (Ammonia), Patrick Cargill (Nero), Lance Percival (Bilius), Julie Ege (Voluptua), Bill Fraser (Prosperus Maximus), Rita Webb (Cassandra), Bernard Bresslaw (Gorgo), Adrienne Posta (Scrubba), Russell Hunter (Jailor), Madeline Smith (Erotica), Royce Mills (Nausius), Ian Trigger (Odius), Aubrey Woods (Villanus), Hugh Paddick (Priest), Candace Glendenning (Stone Girl), Roy Hudd (M.C.), Laraine Humphrys (Flavia), Derek Griffiths (Steam Slave), Veronica Clifford (Boobia), Gaye Brown (Biggia), Kenneth Cranham (First Christian), Lally Bowers (Procuria), Billy Walker (Prodigious), Minah Bird (Girl Bather), Samantha Bond (Girl Bather), Sally Douglas (Titta), Carol Hawkins (Nero's Girl), Reuben Martin (Masseur), David Prowse (Muscular Man). The Prologue: Senator's slave Lurcio unwittingly comes into possession of a scroll listing the members of a plot to assassinate the Emperor Nero. Woe, woe and thrice woe! A big screen spin-off from the BBC comedy. First of the trilogy of 'Up' films. *Dir.* Bob Kellett.

Up the Chastity Belt (1971) Frankie Howerd (Lurkalot/Richard the Lionheart), Graham Crowden (Sir Coward de Custard), Bill Fraser (Sir Braggart de Bombast), Roy Hudd (Nick the Pick), Hugh Paddick (Robin Hood), Long John Baldry (Little John), Alan Rebbeck (Friar Tuck), Rita Webb (Maid Marian), Anna Quayle (Lady Ashfodel), Eartha Kitt (Scheherazade), Royce Mills (Knotweed), Anne Aston (Lobelia), Lance Percival (Reporter), Godfrey Winn (Archbishop of all England), Nora Swinburne (The Mistress of the Bed Chamber), David Kernan (Troubador), Lally Bowers (The Voice - voice), David Battley (Yokel), Veronica Clifford (Winnie the Pooh), Derek Griffiths (Saladin), Judy Huxtable (Gretel), Iain Cuthbertson (Teutonic Knight), Frank Thornton (Master of Ceremonies), Billy Walker (Chopper), Aubrey Woods (Vegetable Stall Owner), Sam Kydd (Locksmith), David Prowse (Sir Grumbell de Grunt), Ian Trigger (Lucky Charms Seller), Fred Emney (Mortimer), Dave King (Landlord). Serf Lurkalot is actually the identical twin brother of King Richard I. After being raised by pigs he finds employment with Sir Coward de Custard and eventually follows him to the crusades. Second of the 'Up' films. *Dir.* Bob Kellett.

Up the Creek (1958) David Tomlinson (Lt. Fairweather), Peter Sellers (Chief Petty Officer Doherty), Wilfrid Hyde-White (Admiral Foley), Vera Day (Lily), Liliane Sottane (Susanne), Tom Gill (Flag Lieutenant), Michael Goodliffe (Nelson), Reginald Beckwith (Publican), Lionel Murton (Perkins), John Warren (Cooky), Lionel Jeffries (Steady Barker), Howard Williams (Bunts), Peter Collingwood (Chippie), Barry Lowe (Webster), Edwin Richfield (Bennett), David Lodge (Scouse), Max Butterfield (Lofty), Malcolm Ranson (Small Boy), Sam Kydd (Bates), Frank Pettingell (Stationmaster), Donald Bisset (Farm Laborer), Leonard Fenton (Policeman), Basil Dignam (Coombes), Peter Coke (Commander Price), Jack McNaughton (Petty Officer), Larry Noble (Quartermaster), Patrick Cargill (Commander), Michael Ripper (Decorator). Comedy in which an incompetent and rocket-obsessed naval officer is passed on to command the oldest ship in the Royal Navy's moth-balled fleet in the hope that he can cause no more damage. This upsets the Chief Petty Officer, who has negotiated some very profitable business deals with the locals. Dir. Val Guest.

Up the Front (1972) Frankie Howerd (Lurk), Bill Fraser (Groping), William Mervyn (Lord Twithampton), Linda Gray (Lady Twithampton), Zsa Zsa Gabor (Mata Hari), Jonathan Cecil (Nigel), Madeline Smith (Fanny), Nicholas Bennett (Mallett), Mike Grady (Newsboy), Dora Bryan (Cora Crumpington), Stanley Holloway (Vincento), Veronica Clifford (Velma), Bob Hoskins (Recruiting Sgt.), Lance Percival (Von Gutz), Peter Bull (Von Kobler), Vernon Dobtcheff (Muller), Ingo Mogendorf (Captain Hamburger), Gertan Klauber (Donner), Stanley Lebor (Blitzen), Percy Herbert (Cpl. Lovechild), David Battley (Midgeley the Cook), Alan Rebbeck (Winking Soldier), Hermione Baddeley (Monique), Bozena (Frou Frou), Toni Palmer (Buttercup Girl), Delia Sainsbury (Buttercup Girl), Michael Brennan (M.P.), Harvey Hall (M.P.), Robert Coote (General Burke), Mischa De La Motte (Diplomat), Derek Griffiths (El Puncturo). Set during World War I, servant Lurk is hypnotized into bravery and finds himself on the Western Front. After he has the German master plan tattooed on his backside he becomes a target for German intelligence, including the spy Mata Hari. The third 'Up' film. *Dir.* Bob Kellett.

Up the Junction (1968) Suzy Kendall (Polly), Dennis Waterman (Pete), Maureen Lipman (Sylvie), Adrienne Posta (Rube), Liz Fraser (Mrs. McCarthy), Linda Cole (Pauline), Doreen Herrington

(Rita), Jessie Robins (Lil), Barbara Archer (May), Ruby Head (Edith), Susan George (Joyce), Sandra Williams (Sheilah), Michael Robbins (Figgins), Michael Gothard (Terry), Billy Murray (Ray), Michael Standing (John), Alfie Bass (Charlie), Aubrey Morris (Creely), Hylda Baker (Winnie), Shaun Curry (Ted), Olwen Griffiths (Fat Lil), Queenie Watts (Mrs. Hardy), Larry Martyn (Barrow Boy), Derek Ware (Ted's Friend). A Chelsea girl decides to break away from privilege by starting work in a sweet factory. She makes friends but now her problems really start. A big screen version of a BBC television drama. Based on the book of the same name by Nell Dunn. *Dir.* Neil Collinson.

Upstairs and Downstairs (1959) Michael Craig (Richard Barry), Anne Heywood (Kate Barry), Mylène Demongeot (Ingrid), James Robertson Justice (Mansfield), Claudia Cardinale (Maria), Sid James (P.C. Edwards), Joan Hickson (Rosemary), Joan Sims (Blodwen), Joseph Tomelty (Arthur Farringdon), Nora Nicholson (Edith Farringdon), Daniel Massey (Wesley Cotes), Austin Willis (McGuffey), Margalo Gillmore (Mrs. McGuffey), Reginald Beckwith (Parson), Cyril Chamberlain (Guard), Dilys Laye (Agency Girl), Irene Handl (Large Woman), William Mervyn (Kingsley), Eric Pohlmann (Mario), Jean Cadell (1st Old Lady), Barbara Everest (2nd Old Lady), Stephen Gregson (Paul), Nicholas Phipps (Harry), Jeremy Burnham (Frank), Nicholas Parsons (Brian), Madge Ryan (Policewoman), Betty Henderson (Bridget), Barbara Steele (Mary), Sam Kydd (Driver). Farce centring on a newly married couple's attempt to find suitable domestic staff. *Dir.* Ralph Thomas.

Upturned Glass, The (1947) James Mason (Michael Joyce), Rosamund John (Emma Wright), Pamela Mason (Kate Howard), Ann Stephens (Ann Wright), Morland Graham (Clay), Brefni O'Rorke (Dr. Farrell), Henry Oscar (Coroner), Jane Hylton (Miss Marsh), Sheila Huntington (1st Girl Student), Susan Shaw (2nd Girl Student), Peter Cotes (Male Student), Nuna Davey (Mrs. Deva), Judith Carol (Joan Scott-Trotter), Maurice Denham (Mobile Policeman), Janet Burnell (Sylvia), Lyn Evans (County Policeman), Cyril Chamberlain (Junior Doctor). A surgeon decides to take his own personal revenge against the woman he believes was responsible for the death of the woman he loved. *Dir.* Lawrence Huntingdon.

V for Vendetta (2005) Natalie Portman (Evey), Hugo Weaving (V), Stephen Rea (Finch), Stephen Fry (Deitrich), John Hurt (Adam Sutler), Tim Pigott-Smith (Creedy), Rupert Graves (Dominic), Roger Allam (Lewis Prothero), Ben Miles (Dascomb), Sinéad Cusack (Delia Surridge), Natasha Wightman (Valerie), John Standing (Lilliman), Eddie Marsan (Etheridge), Billie Cook (Little Glasses Girl), Guy Henry (Heyer), Cosima Shaw (Patricia), Tara Hacking (Vicky), Andy Rashleigh (Fred), Joseph Rye (Jones), Malcolm Sinclair (Major Wilson), Bradley Steve Ford (Evey's Brother), Madeleine Rakic-Platt (Young Evey), Selina Giles (Evey's Mother), Carsten Hayes (Evey's Father), Martin Savage (Denis), Imogen Poots (Young Valerie), Laura Greenwood (Sarah), Kyra Meyer (Christina), Paul Antony-Barber (Valerie's Father), Anna Farnworth (Valerie's Mother), Mary Stockley (Ruth). In the 2030s Britain is ruled by a totalitarian fascist government using concentration camps to remove opponents. Evey is rescued from being raped by a masked dissident calling himself V. On 5 November V destroys the Old Bailey and calls on the public to meet him in one year outside the Houses of Parliament, which he promises also to destroy. An adaptation of the *V for Vendetta* graphic novel by Alan Moore and David Lloyd. *Dir.* James McTeigue.

V.I.P.s, The (1963) Richard Burton (Paul Andros), Louis Jourdan (Marc Champselle), Elsa Martinelli (Gloria Gritti), Margaret Rutherford (Duchess of Brighton), Maggie Smith (Miss Mead), Rod Taylor (Les Mangrum), Orson Welles (Max Buda), Linda Christian (Miriam Marshall), Dennis Price (Commander Millbank), Richard Wattis (Sanders), Ronald Fraser (Joslin), David Frost (Reporter), Joan Benham (Miss Potter), Michael Hordern (Airport Director), Lance Percival (B.O.A.C. Officer), Martin Miller (Dr. Schwutzbacher), Peter Sallis (Doctor), Stringer Davis (Hotel Waiter), Clifton Jones (Jamaican Passenger), Moyra Fraser (Air Hostess), Duncan Lewis (Hotel Receptionist), Raymond Austin (Rolls Chauffeur), Cal McCord (Visitor), Jill Carson (Air Hostesses), Ann Castle (Lady Reporter), Betty Trapp (Waitress), Maggie McGrath (Waitress), Lewis Fiander (Third Reporter), John Blythe (Barman), Richard Briers (Meteorological Official), Richard Caldicot (Hotel Representative), Reginald Beckwith (Head Waiter), Terry Alexander (Captain), Frank Williams (Assistant to Airport Director), Clifford Mollison (Mr. River), Gordon Sterne (Official), Joyce Carey (Mrs. Damer), Robert Coote (John Coburn), Angus Lennie (Meteorological Man), Peter Illing (Mr. Damer). The film is set on a foggy day within the VIP lounge of Terminal 2, London Heathrow Airport. The delay to the flights caused by the fog has repercussions for all the waiting passengers on a financial level, a personal level or both. Margaret Rutherford won a Best Supporting Actress Oscar. *Dir.* Anthony Asquith.

Valiant (2005) Voice cast: Ewan McGregor (Valiant), Ricky Gervais (Bugsy), Pip Torrens (Lofty Thaddeus Worthington), Dan Roberts (Tailfeather), Brian Lonsdale (Toughwood), John Cleese (Mercury), Olivia Williams (Victoria), John Hurt (Felix), Annette Badland (Elsa), Jim Broadbent (Sergeant), Hugh Laurie (Wing Cmdr Gutsy), Tim Curry (Gen. Von Talon), Rik Mayall (Cufflingk), Mike Schlingmann (Underlingk), Sharon Horgan (Charles De Girl), Buckley Collum (Rollo), Sean Samuels (Jacques). An animated film set in 1944. Young woodpigeon Valiant signs up and joins the RHPS (Royal Homing Pigeon Service). *Dir.* Gary Chapman.

Vampira (1974) David Niven (Count Dracula), Teresa Graves (Countess Vampira), Nicky Henson (Marc), Jennie Linden (Angela), Linda Hayden (Helga), Bernard Bresslaw (Pottinger), Andrea Allan (Eve), Veronica Carlson (Ritva), Minah Bird (Rose), Freddie Jones (Gilmore), Frank Thornton (Mr. King), Peter Bayliss (Maltravers), Cathie Shirriff (Nancy), Aimi MacDonald (Woman in hotel), Patrick Newell (Man in hotel), Kenneth Cranham (Paddy), Carol Cleveland (Jane), Luan Peters (Pottinger's Secretary), Nadim Sawalha (Airline Representative), Marcia Fox (Air Hostess), Penny Irving (Playboy Bunny), David Rowlands (Drunk), Ben Aris (Policeman). Non-PC horror spoof centring on an aged Count Dracula hosting Playboy Bunnies at his castle in order to harvest their blood to resurrect his old lover, Vampira. *Dir.* Clive Donner.

Vampire Circus (1972) Laurence Payne (Professor Albert Müller), Domini Blythe (Anna Müller), Lynne Frederick (Dora Müller), Thorley Walters (Mayor), Adrienne Corri (Gypsy), Mary Wimbush (Elvira), Christina Paul (Rosa), Robin Sachs (Heinrich), Lalla Ward (Helga), Richard Owens (Dr. Kersch), John Moulder-Brown (Anton Kersch), Robin Hunter (Mr Hauser), Elizabeth Seal (Gerta Hauser), Barnaby Shaw (Gustav Hauser), John Bown (Mr Schilt), Jane Darby (Jenny Schilt), Robert Tayman (Count Mitterhaus), Skip Martin (Michael), Anthony Higgins (Emil), David Prowse (Strongman), Serena (Tiger-woman dancer). A village is cursed by a vampire and 15 years later his cousin arrives there with a circus of vampiric artistes, known as the Circus of Night. As prophesied in the curse the villagers and their children of the village begin to die. *Dir.* Robert Young.

Vampire Lovers, The (1970) Ingrid Pitt (Marcilla/Carmilla/Mircalla Karnstein), Madeline Smith (Emma Morton), Kate O'Mara (Mlle. Perrodot), Peter Cushing (General von Spielsdorf), George Cole (Roger Morton), Ferdy Mayne (Doctor), Douglas Wilmer (Baron Joachim von Hartog), Dawn Addams (The Countess), Jon Finch (Carl Ebhardt), Pippa Steel (Laura), Kirsten Lindholm (1st Vampire), Janet Key (Gretchin), Harvey Hall (Renton), Lindsay Kemp (Jester), John Forbes-Robertson (Man in Black), Charles Farrell (Landlord), Shelagh Wilcocks (Housekeeper), Joanna Shelley (Woodman's Daughter), Olga James (Village Girl), Jill Easter (Woodmans Wife), Sion Probert (Young Man In Tavern), Vicki Woolf (Landlords Daughter). Vampire Carmilla Karnstein is on the prowl for young women on whom she can feed. Part of the lesbian vampire themed Karnstein Trilogy of films - along with *Lust for a Vampire* (1971) and *Twins of Evil* (1972). *Dir.* Roy Ward Baker.

Van, The (1996) Colm Meaney (Larry), Donal O'Kelly (Brendan "Bimbo" Reeves), Ger Ryan (Maggie), Caroline Rothwell (Mary), Neilí Conroy (Diane), Rúaidhrí Conroy (Kevin), Brendan O'Carroll (Weslie), Stuart Dunne (Sam), Jack Lynch (Cancer), Laurie Morton (Maggie's Mum), Marie Mullen (Vera), Jon Kenny (Gerry McCarthy), Moses Rowen (Glenn), Linda McGovern (Jessica), Eoin Chaney (Wayne), Frank O'Sullivan (Wally), Jill Doyle (Mona), Barbara Bergin (Dawn), Charlotte Bradley (Anne Marie). When Brendan "Bimbo" Reeves gets laid off from his job as a baker he decides to sell fish and chips from a van with the help of his best friend Larry. The final part of the *Barrytown Trilogy* (with *The Commitments* and *The Snapper*) written by Roddy Doyle. *Dir.* Stephen Frears.

Velvet Goldmine (1998) Jonathan Rhys Meyers (Brian Slade), Christian Bale (Arthur Stuart), Ewan McGregor (Curt Wild), Toni Collette (Mandy Slade), Eddie Izzard (Jerry Devine), Emily Woof (Shannon), Joseph Beattie (Cooper), Michael Feast (Cecil), Lindsay Kemp (Pantomime Dame), Janet McTeer (Narrator – narrator). In 1984 journalist Arthur Stuart is assigned to write an article on the disappearance of his one-time hero and glam-rock star of the 1970s, Brian Slade. *Dir.* Todd Haynes.

Venetian Bird (1952) Richard Todd (Edward Mercer), Eva Bartok (Adriana Medova), John Gregson (Renzo Uccello), George Coulouris (Chief of Police Spadoni), Margot Grahame (Rosa Melitus), Walter Rilla (Count Boria), John Bailey (Lt. Longo), Sid James (Bernardo), Martin Boddey (Gufo), Michael Balfour (Moretto), Sydney Tafler (Boldesca), Miles Malleson (Grespi), Eric Pohlmann (Gostini), David Hurst (Minelli), Raymond Young (Luigi), Ferdy Mayne (Tio), Jill Clifford (Renata), Eileen Way (Woman Detective), Toni Lucarda (Nerva), Janice Kane (Ninetta), Meier Tzelniker (Mayor of Mirave). Mercer travels to Italy to reward someone who helped the Allies during WWII. However, he arrives to find that the man is in fact a criminal who may have faked his own death. *Dir.* Ralph Thomas.

Venus (2006) Peter O'Toole (Maurice), Leslie Phillips (Ian), Jodie Whittaker (Jessie), Vanessa Redgrave (Valerie), Richard Griffiths (Donald), Bronson Webb (Jessie's Boyfriend), Tim Faraday (Policeman), Beatrice Savoretti (Waitress), Philip Fox (Doctor), Cathryn Bradshaw (Jillian). Ian, an ageing actor, feels he needs someone to look after him so he turns to his niece Jessie. He finds her a real nuisance but his friend Maurice sees some potential and encourages her to take an interest in art, including doing some life modelling. *Dir.* Roger Michell.

Vera Drake (2004) Imelda Staunton (Vera Drake), Richard Graham (George), Eddie Marsan (Reg), Anna Keaveney (Nellie), Sally Hawkins (Susan), Alex Kelly (Ethel Drake), Daniel Mays (Sid Drake), Phil Davis (Stanley Drake), Sam Troughton (David), Ruth Sheen (Lily), Adrian Scarborough (Frank), Lesley Manville (Mrs. Wells), Marion Bailey (Mrs. Fowler), Lesley Sharp (Jessie Barnes), Peter Wight (Det. Inspector Webster), Martin Savage (Det. Sergeant Vickers), Leo Bill (Ronny), Sinéad Matthews (Young Woman), Chris O'Dowd (Sid's Customer), Allan Corduner (Psychiatrist), Jim Broadbent (Judge). In 1950s England, Vera is a devoted wife and mother and a pillar of the community. She is also a backstreet abortionist, performing her work as acts of charity for the women concerned. *Dir.* Mike Leigh.

Very Important Person (1961) James Robertson Justice (Sir Ernest Pease/Lt. Farrow RN), Leslie Phillips (Jimmy Cooper), Stanley Baxter ('Jock' Everett/Kommondant Stamfel), Eric Sykes (Willoughby), Richard Wattis (Woodcock), Godfrey Winn (Himself), Colin Gordon (Briggs), John Le Mesurier (Piggott), Norman Bird (Travers), Jeremy Lloyd ('Bonzo' Baines), John Forrest (Grassy Green), Jean Cadell (Lady Telling Story on TV show), Peter Myers (Shaw), Ronnie Stevens (Hankley), Ronald Leigh-Hunt (Clynes), Steve Plytas (Luftwaffe Officer), John Ringham (Plum Pouding), Joseph Fürst (Luftwaffe Interrogator), Norman Shelley (Fred Whittaker), Brian Oulton (1st Scientist), Frederick Piper (2nd Scientist), Joan Haythorne (Miss Rogers), Heidi Erich (German Frau), Derek Aylward (Stagehand), Ed Devereaux (Webber), Richard Marner (German Guard), Vincent Ball (Higgins). A comedy set in a POW camp during WWII. A brilliant scientist disguised as a Royal Navy officer is shot down over Europe, captured and taken to a POW camp. Once his identity is known to his fellow prisoners they begin to plan an escape. *Dir.* Ken Annakin.

Vessel of Wrath (1938) Charles Laughton (Ginger Ted' Wilson), Elsa Lanchester (Martha Jones), Robert Newton (The Controleur), Tyrone Guthrie (Dr. Owen Jones), Eliot Makeham (The Native Head Clerk), Dolly Mollinger (Lia), D.A. Ward (Albert), J. Solomon (Sgt. Henrik). A comedy drama in which a drunken beachcomber in Papua New Guinea meets his match in a woman missionary. *Dir.* Erich Pommer.

Vice Versa (1948) Roger Livesey (Paul Bultitude), Kay Walsh (Florence 'Fanny' Verlane), Petula Clark (Dulcie Grimstone), David Hutcheson (Marmaduke Paradine), Anthony Newley (Dick Bultitude), James Robertson Justice (Dr. Grimstone), Patricia Raine (Alice), Joan Young (Mrs. Grimstone), Vida Hope (1st Nanny), Vi Kaley (2nd Nanny), Ernest Jay (Bowler), Kynaston Reeves (Dr. Chawner), Harcourt Williams (Judge), Bill Shine (Lord Gosport), Andrew Blackett (Duke of Margate), John Willoughby (Lord Sevenoaks), Stanley Van Beers (Earl of Broadstairs), Robert Eddison (Mr. Blinkhorn), James Hayter (Bandmaster), Alfie Bass (Urchin), Hugh Dempster (Col. Ambrose), Peter Jones (Chawner), James Kenney (Coggs), Michael McKeag (Jolland), Timothy Bateson (Coker), John Glyn-Jones (Bindabun Doss), Frank Tickle (Clegg), Anton Rodgers (Pupil). Take one father who wishes he could return to his happy youth, add one son who wishes he could be more like his father and stir in a magical Indian idol. Result: classic body-swap comedy. Adaptation of the novel of the same name by F. Anstey. *Dir.* Peter Ustinov.

Vicious Circle, The (1957) John Mills (Dr. Howard Latimer), Derek Farr (Kenneth Palmer), Noelle Middleton (Laura James), Wilfrid Hyde-White (Maj. Harrington aka Robert Brady), Roland Culver (Detective Inspector Dane), Mervyn Johns (Dr. George Kimber), René Ray (Mrs. Ambler), Lionel Jeffries (Geoffrey Windsor), Lisa Daniely (Frieda Veldon), David Williams (The Detective Sergeant), Diana Lambert (Latimer's Office Nurse). Harley Street specialist Dr Latimer is drawn into a mystery when he finds in his flat the dead body of a woman he had briefly met a few days earlier and is then accused of her murder by the police. Based on a television series called *The Brass Candlestick* by Francis Durbridge. *Dir.* Gerald Thomas.

Victim (1961) Dirk Bogarde (Melville Farr), Sylvia Syms (Laura Farr), Dennis Price (Calloway), Nigel Stock (Phip), Peter McEnery (Barrett), Donald Churchill (Eddy), Anthony Nicholls (Lord Fullbrook), Hilton Edwards (P.H.), Norman Bird (Harold Doe), Derren Nesbitt (Sandy Youth), Alan MacNaughtan (Scott Hankin), Noel Howlett (Patterson), Charles Lloyd Pack (Henry), John Barrie (Detective Inspector Harris), John Cairney (Bridie), David Evans (Mickey), Peter Copley (Paul Mandrake), Frank Thornton (George). Successful barrister Melville Farr decides to take on a blackmail ring targeting homosexuals despite the fact that he is himself gay and it will ruin his career. Homosexual acts between consenting male adults were illegal until 1967. *Dir.* by Basil Dearden.

Victoria the Great (1937) Anna Neagle (Queen Victoria), Anton Walbrook (Prince Albert), Walter Rilla (Prince Ernest), H.B. Warner (Lord Melbourne), Mary Morris (Duchess of Kent), James Dale (Duke of Wellington), Felix Aylmer (Lord Palmerston), Charles Carson (Sir Robert Peel), Gordon McLeod (John Brown), C.V. France (Archbishop of Canterbury), Arthur Young (Rt. Hon. William Gladstone), Greta Schröder (Baroness Lehzen), Paul Leyssac (Baron Stockmar), Derrick De Marney (Younger Disraeli), Hugh Miller (Older Disraeli), Percy Parsons (President Lincoln), Hubert Harben (Lord Conyngham), Henry Hallett (Joseph Chamberlain), William Dewhurst (John Bright), Frank Birch (Sir Charles Dilke), Miles Malleson (Sir James), Robert Atkins (Garter King-at-Arms), Edgar Driver (Pearly King), Tom Heslewood (Sir Francis Grant), Moore Marriott (Train Driver), Lewis Casson (Archbishop of Canterbury), Charles Lefeaux (Earl of Albermarle), Ivor Barnard (Assassin), O.B. Clarence (Coachman-in-Chief), Clarence Blakiston (Duke of Sussex), Marie Wright (Old Kitty), Joyce Bland (Florence Nightingale), Wyndham Goldie (Cecil Rhodes), Joan Young (Miss Pitt), Aubrey Mallalieu (Bishop at the Palace). A biopic of Queen Victoria. *Dir.* Herbert Wilcox.

Victory (1996) Willem Dafoe (Axel Heyst), Sam Neill (Mr. Jones), Irène Jacob (Alma), Rufus Sewell (Martin Ricardo), Jean Yanne (Mr. Schomberg), Ho Yi (Wang), Bill Paterson (Capt. Davidson), Irm Hermann (Mrs. Schomberg), Graziano Marcelli (Pedro), Hansi Jochmann (Mrs. Zangiacomo), Simon Callow (Zangiacomo), Michael Lee (Chinese Gentleman), Leonard Maguire (McNab). Axel Heyst saves Alma from being sold to Schomberg. Based on the novel by Joseph Conrad. *Dir*. Mark Peploe.

View to a Kill, A (1985) Roger Moore (James Bond), Christopher Walken (Max Zorin), Tanya Roberts (Stacey Sutton), Grace Jones (May Day), Patrick Macnee (Sir Godfrey Tibbett), Patrick Bauchau (Scarpine), David Yip (Chuck Lee), Willoughby Gray (Dr. Carl Mortner), Fiona Fullerton (Pola Ivanova), Manning Redwood (Bob Conley), Alison Doody (Jenny Flex), Robert Brown (M), Desmond Llewelyn (Q), Lois Maxwell (Miss Moneypenny), Geoffrey Keen (Fredrick Gray), Walter Gotell (General Gogol), Papillon Soo Soo (Pan Ho), Daniel Benzali (W. G. Howe), Dolph Lundgren (Venz). Zorin has a cunning plan to flood Silicon Valley and corner the market in microchips. Bond has to stop him. This was Roger Moore's last outing as James Bond. Bond drives a Renault 11 and a Ford LTD. The theme song is performed by Duran Duran. *Dir*. John Glen.

Village of the Damned (1960) George Sanders (Gordon Zellaby), Barbara Shelley (Anthea Zellaby), Martin Stephens (David Zellaby), Michael Gwynn (Alan Bernard), Laurence Naismith (Doctor Willers), Richard Warner (Harrington), Jenny Laird (Mrs. Harrington), Sarah Long (Evelyn Harrington), Thomas Heathcote (James Pawle), Charlotte Mitchell (Janet Pawle), Pamela Buck (Milly Hughes), Rosamund Greenwood (Miss Ogle), Susan Richards (Mrs. Plumpton), Bernard Archard (Vicar), Peter Vaughan (PC Gobby), John Phillips (General Leighton), Richard Vernon (Sir Edgar Hargraves), John Stuart (Professor Smith), Keith Pyott (Dr. Carlisle). One day all the inhabitants of the English village of Midwich fall unconscious, as does anyone who goes into the village, or indeed flies over it. They wake up and are apparently unaffected until it is discovered two months later that all the women in the village of child-bearing age are pregnant. Then they all give birth on the same day and the resultant children begin to display odd behaviour. Based on the book *The Midwich Cuckoos* by John Wyndham. *Dir*. Wolf Rilla.

Villain (1971) Richard Burton (Vic Dakin), Ian McShane (Wolfe Lissner), T. P. McKenna (Frank Fletcher), Donald Sinden (Gerald Draycott), Fiona Lewis (Venetia), Joss Ackland (Edgar Lowis), Colin Welland (Tom Binney), Tony Selby (Duncan), Cathleen Nesbitt (Mrs Dakin), John Hallam (Terry), James Cossins (Brown), Anthony Sagar (Danny), Clive Francis (Vivian), Elizabeth Knight (Patti), Shirley Cain (Mrs Matthews), Burton plays a gay East London gangster with a sadistic streak, possibly "inspired" by Ronnie Kray. He is planning a wages snatch whilst also blackmailing an MP but the police seem to be closing in. *Dir*. Michael Tuchner.

Virgin and the Gypsy, The Joanna Shimkus (Yvette), Franco Nero (The Gypsy), Honor Blackman (Mrs. Fawcett), Mark Burns (Major Eastwood), Fay Compton (Grandma), Maurice Denham (The Rector), Kay Walsh (Aunt Cissie), Imogen Hassall (The Gypsy's Wife), Harriet Harper (Lucille), Norman Bird (Uncle Fred), Jeremy Bulloch (Leo), Ray Holder (Bob), Margo Andrew (Ella), Jan Chappell (Mary), Helen Booth (Cook), Laurie Dale (Thomas), Lulu Davies (Gypsy Grandmother). Does what it says on the tin – the virginal Yvette encounters a gypsy and is sexually attracted to him. Based on the D H Lawrence short story. *Dir*. Christopher Miles.

Virgin Soldiers, The (1969) Lynn Redgrave (Phillipa Raskin), Hywel Bennett (Pvt. Brigg), Nigel Davenport (Sgt. Driscoll), Nigel Patrick (R.S.M. Raskin), Rachel Kempson (Mrs. Raskin), Jack Shepherd (Sgt. Wellbeloved), Michael Gwynn (Bromley-Pickering), Tsai Chin (Juicy Lucy), Christopher Timothy (Cpl. Brook), Don Hawkins (Tasker), Geoffrey Hughes (Lantry), Roy Holder (Fenwick), Riggs O'Hara (Sinclair), Gregory Phillips (Foster), Wayne Sleep (Villiers), Peter Kelly (Sandy Jacobs), Marc Nicholls (Cutler), Alan Shatsman (Longley), Jonty Miller (Forsyth), Jolyon Jackley (LCpl. Browning), Robert Bridges (Sgt. Fred Organ), James Cosmo (Waller), Graham Crowden (Medical Officer), Dudley Jones (Doctor), Matthew Guinness (Maj. Cusper), Niranjan Singh (Sikh), Fuk Yew (Hallelujah), Brenda Bruce (Nursing Sister), Barbara Keogh (W.R.A.C.), David Bowie (Soldier), Warren Clarke (Soldier). A young British soldier in Singapore during the 1950's Malayan Emergency sets his sights on the daughter of the Regimental Sergeant Major but also gets involved with a local prostitute. Based on the book of the same name by Leslie Thomas. *Dir*. John Dexter.

Virgin Witch (1972) Ann Michelle (Christine), Vicki Michelle (Betty), Keith Buckley (Johnny), Patricia Haines (Sybil Waite), Neil Hallett (Gerald Amberly), James Chase (Peter), Paula Wright (Mrs. Wendell), Christopher Strain (Milkman), Esme Smythe (Horsewoman), Garth Watkins (Colonel), Helen Downing (Abby Darke), Peter Halliday (Club Manager), Prudence Drage, Maria Coyne (Coven members). Sisters Christine and Betty are lured to a Tudor mansion with the promise of a fashion shoot. Little do they know that the house is owned by the high priest of a secret coven. The film was due for release in 1971 but because of censorship problems was not finally released, with cuts, until 1972. *Dir*. Ray Austin.

Voice of Merrill, The (1952) Valerie Hobson (Alycia Roche), Edward Underdown (Hugh Allen), James Robertson Justice (Jonathan Roche), Henry Kendall (Ronald Parker), Garry Marsh (Inspector Thornton), Daniel Wherry (Pierce), Sam Kydd (Sergeant Baker), Ian Fleming (Doctor Forrest), Daphne Newton (Miss Quinn), Johnnie Schofield (Night Porter). Three people are implicated in the murder of a young female blackmailer. *Dir*. John Gilling.

Vote for Huggett (1949) Jack Warner (Joe Huggett), Kathleen Harrison (Ethel Huggett), Susan Shaw (Susan Huggett), Petula Clark (Pet Huggett), David Tomlinson (Harold Hinchley), Diana Dors (Diana Gowan), Peter Hammond (Peter Hawtrey), Amy Veness (Grandma Huggett), Hubert Gregg (Maurice Lever), John Blythe (Gowan), Anthony Newley (Dudley), Charles Victor (Mr Hall), Adrianne Allen (Mrs Hall), Frederick Piper (Mr Bentley), Empsie Bowman (Old Lady), Isa Bowman (Old Lady), Eliot Makeham (Mr Christie), Clive Morton (Mr Campbell), Norman Shelley (Mr Wilson), Lyn Evans (Sergeant Pike), Hal Osmond (Fishmonger), Elizabeth Hunt (Mrs Lever), Ferdy Mayne (Waiter). Third film featuring the Huggetts. Joe crosses swords with a corrupt local councillor when he calls for the building of a pleasure gardens as a war memorial. *Dir*. Ken Annakin. See also *Holiday Camp* (1947), *Here Come the Huggetts* (1948) and *The Huggetts Abroad* (1949).

Waking Ned (1999) Ian Bannen (Jackie O'Shea), David Kelly (Michael O'Sullivan), Fionnula Flanagan (Annie O'Shea), Susan Lynch (Maggie O'Toole), James Nesbitt (Pig Finn), Paul Vaughan (Narrator - voice), Adrian Robinson (Lotto Observer), Maura O'Malley (Mrs. Kennedy), Robert Hickey (Maurice O'Toole), Paddy Ward (Brendy O'Toole), James Ryland (Dennis Fitzgerald), Fintan McKeown (Pat Mulligan), Eileen Dromey (Lizzy Quinn), Kitty Fitzgerald (Kitty), Dermot Kerrigan (Father Patrick), Jimmy Keogh (Ned Devine), Brendan Dempsey (Jim Kelly), Matthew Devitt (Tom Toomey), Rennie Campbell (Rennie), Eamonn Doyle (Dicey Riley), Raymond MacCormac (The Whistler), Larry Randall (Father Mulligan). When Ned Devine dies on the night he wins the Irish Lottery, the rest of his village decide to try and claim the winnings. *Dir*. Kirk Jones.

Walkabout (1971) Jenny Agutter (Girl), Luc Roeg (White Boy), David Gulpilil (Black Boy), John Meillon (Man), Robert McDarra (Man), Peter Carver (No Hoper), John Illingsworth (Young Man), Hilary Bamberger (Woman), Barry Donnelly (Australian Scientist), Noeline Brown (German Scientist), Carlo Manchini (Italian Scientist). A young brother and sister are stranded in the Australian Outback after their father goes berserk and kills himself. They are befriended by an Aborigine boy who is on his "walkabout" from his tribe. Atmospheric classic, loosely based on the novel of the same name by James Vance Marshall. *Dir*. Nicolas Roeg.

312

Wallace and Gromit - Curse of The Were-Rabbit (2005) Voice cast: Peter Sallis (Wallace/Hutch), Ralph Fiennes (Victor Quartermaine), Helena Bonham Carter (Lady Campanula Tottington), Peter Kay (PC Mackintosh), Nicholas Smith (Reverend Clement Hedges), Liz Smith (Mrs. Mulch), John Thomson (Mr. Windfall), Mark Gatiss (Miss Blight), Vincent Ebrahim (Mr. Caliche), Geraldine McEwan (Miss Thripp), Edward Kelsey (Mr. Growbag), Dicken Ashworth (Mr. Mulch), Robert Horvath (Mr. Dibber), Pete Atkin (Mr. Crock), Noni Lewis (Mrs. Girdling), Ben Whitehead (Mr. Leaching). An Aardman Animations full-length clay-mation. Wallace and Gromit are running "Anti-Pesto", a firm dedicated to the protection of the local vegetables from rabbits – which is especially important with the annual Giant Vegetable Competition coming up. However, an industrial accident affects both Wallace and a captured rabbit and suddenly a giant beast is eating all the vegetables. The film won the Academy Award for the Best Animated Feature Film of the Year. *Dir.* Nick Park.

Waltzes from Vienna (1933) Esmond Knight (Johann "Schani" Strauss, the Younger), Jessie Matthews (Rasi), Edmund Gwenn (Johann Strauss, the Elder), Fay Compton (Countess Helga von Stahl), Frank Vosper (Prince Gustav), Robert Hale (Ebezeder), Marcus Barron (Drexter), Charles Heslop (Valet), Betty Huntley-Wright (Lady's Maid), Hindle Edgar (Leopold), Sybil Grove (Mme. Fouchett), Billy Shine Jr. (Carl), Bertram Dench (Engine driver), B. M. Lewis (Domeyer), Cyril Smith (Secretary). A definite oddity – a Hitchcock musical telling the story of the origin of the Strauss waltzes. There is no cameo appearance in this film. *Dir.* Alfred Hitchcock.

Wanted for Murder (1946) Eric Portman (Victor James Colebrooke, alias Tom Maren), Dulcie Gray (Anne Fielding), Derek Farr (Jack Williams), Roland Culver (Chief Insp. Conway), Stanley Holloway (Sgt. Sullivan), Barbara Everest (Mrs. Colebrooke), Bonar Colleano (Cpl. Nick Mappolo), Jenny Laird (Jeannie McLaren), Kathleen Harrison (Florrie), Bill Shine (Det. Ellis), Viola Lyel (Mabel Cooper), John Salew (Det. Walters), John Ruddock (Glover), Edna Wood (Miss Kemp), George Carney (Boat Rental Agent), Mary Mackenzie (Girl at Fair), Wilfrid Hyde-White (Guide in Madame Tussaud's), Moira Lister (Miss Willis), Gerhard Kempinski (Head Waiter), Caven Watson (Underground Attendant), Wally Patch (Merry-Go-Round Barker), Tony Quinn (Mugsy Knight). Chief Inspector Conway investigates a series of murders. The perpetrator is Victor, the son of a hangman who cannot control his urge to strangle women but has now fallen in love. Will his love be able to prevent him making Anne his next victim? Also known as *A Voice in the Night*. *Dir.* Lawrence Huntington.

War Horse (2011) Jeremy Irvine (Albert Narracott), Emily Watson (Rose Narracott), Peter Mullan (Ted Narracott), Niels Arestrup (Grandfather), David Thewlis (Lyons), Tom Hiddleston (Captain Nicholls), Benedict Cumberbatch (Major Jamie Stewart), Celine Buckens (Emilie), Toby Kebbell (Colin), Patrick Kennedy (Lieutenant Charlie Waverly), Leonard Carow (Private Michael Schröder), David Kross (Private Gunther Schröder), Matt Milne (Andrew Easton), Robert Emms (David Lyons), Eddie Marsan (Sergeant Fry), Nicolas Bro (Friedrich), Rainer Bock (Brandt), Hinnerk Schönemann (Peter), Geoff Bell (Sergeant Sam Perkins), Liam Cunningham (Army Doctor), Gerard McSorley (Market Auctioneer), Tony Pitts (Sergeant Martin), Pip Torrens (Major Tompkins), Philippe Nahon (French Auctioneer). The story of Joey, a thoroughbred horse who passes through numerous hands and hardships during WWI. Based on the children's novel of the same name by Michael Morpurgo and the subsequent stage adaptation. *Dir.* Steven Spielberg.

War Lover, The (1962) Steve McQueen (Capt. Buzz Rickson), Robert Wagner ('Bo'/Ed Bolland), Shirley Anne Field (Daphne), Gary Cockrell (2nd Lt. Marty Lynch), Michael Crawford (Sgt. Junior Sailen), Bill Edwards (Brindt), Chuck Julian (Lamb), Robert Easton (Handown), Al Waxman (Prien), Tom Busby (Farr), George Sperdakos (Bragliani), Bob Kanter (Haverstraw), Jerry Stovin (Emmet), Ed Bishop (Vogt), Richard Leech (Murika), Bernard Braden (Randall), Sean Kelly (Woodman), Charles De Temple (Braddock), Neil McCallum (Sully), Viera (Singer), Justine Lord (Street Girl), Louise Dunn (Hazel), Arthur Hewlett (Vicar), Frederick Jaeger (Air Crewman), Burt Kwouk (Air Crewman). During WWII, a gung-ho American bomber pilot has the trust of his crew despite his indiscipline. Both he and his co-pilot are attracted to the same English girl. Loosely based on the novel of the same name by John Hersey. *Dir.* Philip Leacock.

War Requiem (1989) Laurence Olivier (Old Soldier), Nathaniel Parker (Wilfred Owen), Tilda Swinton (Nurse), Sean Bean (German Soldier), Nigel Terry (Abraham), Patricia Hayes (Mother), Rohan McCullough (Enemy Mother), Owen Teale (Unknown Soldier), Jodie Graber (Young boy soldier), Antony Gabriel (Lieutenant Harper), Thomas Kett (Recruit). An adaptation, with no dialogue, of Benjamin Britten's musical piece of the same name. *Dir.* Derek Jarman.

Warlords of Atlantis (1978) Doug McClure (Greg Collinson), Peter Gilmore (Charles Aitken), Shane Rimmer (Captain Daniels), Lea Brodie (Delphine), Hal Galili (Grogan), John Ratzenberger (Fenn), Derry Power (Jacko), Michael Gothard (Atmir), Daniel Massey (Atraxon), Cyd Charisse (Atsil), Robert Brown (Captain Briggs), Donald Bisset (Professor Aitken). Charles Aitken and Greg Collinson find the lost underwater city of Atlantis but are captured and held prisoner along with the treacherous crew of the ship they were using for the expedition. Amongst fellow prisoners they find the captain of the *Mary Celeste* (why not?) and his daughter. *Dir.* Kevin Connor.

Warn That Man (1942) Gordon Harker (George Hawkins), Raymond Lovell (Hausemann/Lord Buckley), Finlay Currie (Captain Andrew Fletcher), Philip Friend (John Cooper), Jean Kent (Frances Lane), Frederick Cooper (Charles/Frampton), Carl Jaffe (Schultz), John Salew (Wilson), Veronica Rose (Miss Conway), Anthony Hawtrey (Brent), Anthony Holles (Waiter), Patrick Aherne (Mellows), Frank Bagnall (Lehmann), Friedrich Richter (Wolheim), Leonard Sharp (Miles). A comedy thriller in which a Nazi plot to kidnap Winston Churchill doesn't take into account the resourcefulness of three British sailors. *Dir.* Lawrence Huntington.

Watcher in the Woods, The (1980) Bette Davis (Mrs. Aylwood), Lynn-Holly Johnson (Jan Curtis), Kyle Richards (Ellie Curtis), Carroll Baker (Helen Curtis), David McCallum (Paul Curtis), Benedict Taylor (Mike Fleming), Frances Cuka (Mary Fleming), Richard Pasco (Tom Colley), Ian Bannen (John Keller), Katharine Levy (Karen Aylwood), Eleanor Summerfield (Mrs. Thayer), Georgina Hale (Young Mrs. Aylwood), Dominic Guard (Young John Keller). An Anglo-American family moves to a house in England and the children begin to experience various paranormal activities which seem to centre on a girl who had disappeared from the house years before. The film was re-edited and re-released in 1981 with a new ending. Based on the novel of the same name by Florence Engel Randall. *Dir.* John Hough.

Water (1985) Michael Caine (Governor Baxter Thwaites), Valerie Perrine (Pamela Weintraub), Brenda Vaccaro (Dolores Thwaites), Leonard Rossiter (Sir Malcolm Leveridge), Billy Connolly (Delgado Fitzhugh), Dennis Dugan (Rob Waring), Fulton Mackay (Reverend Eric), Jimmie Walker (Jay Jay), Dick Shawn (Deke Halliday), Fred Gwynne (Franklin Spender), Trevor Laird (Pepito), Alan Igbon (Cuban). Chris Tummings (Garfield Cooper), Kelvin Omard (Nado), Oscar James (Miguel), Charles Thomas Murphy (Ken), Felicity Dean (Sarah), William Hootkins (Ben Branch), Alan Shearman (Charlesworth), Bill Bailey (Hollister), Richard Pearson (Foreign Secretary), Maureen Lipman (Prime Minister), Jacqueline De Peza (Lucille), Lucita Lijertwood (Delgado's Mother), Alfred Molina (Pierre), Ruby Wax (Spenco Executive), Eric Clapton, Ray Cooper, Jon Lord, Mike Moran, Chris Stainton, Ringo Starr, Jenny Bogle, Anastasia Rodriguez (The Singing Rebels' Band), Paul Heiney (Kessler). The tranquility of the Caribbean island of Cascara is disturbed when an abandoned oil rig begins spouting very pure water. This was Leonard Rossiter's last film. BBC television presenter Paul Heiney had a part in the film as part of the tv series *In at the Deep End*, where he and fellow presenter Chris Serle were challenged to master a variety of professions. *Dir.* Dick Clement.

Waterloo Road (1945) John Mills (Jim Colter), Stewart Granger (Ted Purvis), Alastair Sim (Dr. Montgomery), Joy Shelton (Tillie Colter), Alison Leggatt (Ruby), Beatrice Varley (Mrs. Colter), George Carney (Tom Mason), Leslie Bradley (Mike Duggan), Jean Kent (Toni), Ben Williams (Cpl Lewis), Anna Konstam

313

(May), Vera Frances (Vera Colter), Wylie Watson (Tattooist), George Merritt (Air Raid Warden), Frank Atkinson (George), Nellie Bowman (Tillie's Mother), Amy Dalby (Tillie's Aunt), Wallace Lupino (Tillie's Uncle), Arthur Denton (Fred), Ian Fleming (Officer at Station), Peter Hammond (Arthur). During WWII a soldier receives news that his wife is having an affair and goes AWOL to sort it out. In the process a draft dodging spiv gets his richly deserved come-uppance. *Dir.* Sidney Gilliat.

Watership Down (1978) Voice cast: John Hurt (Hazel), Richard Briers (Fiver), Michael Graham Cox (Bigwig), John Bennett (Capt. Holly), Ralph Richardson (Chief Rabbit), Simon Cadell (Blackberry), Terence Rigby (Silver), Roy Kinnear (Pipkin), Richard O'Callaghan (Dandelion), Denholm Elliott (Cowslip), Lynn Farleigh (Cat), Mary Maddox (Clover), Zero Mostel (Kehaar), Harry Andrews (Gen. Woundwort), Hannah Gordon (Hyzenthlay), Nigel Hawthorne (Capt. Campion), Clifton Jones (Blackavar), Derek Griffiths (Vervain), Michael Hordern (Frith), Joss Ackland (Black Rabbit), Michelle Price (Lucy). When Fiver has a vision that the warren where he and his brother Hazel live will soon be destroyed he sets out with Hazel and some friends to set up a new one. After many adventures they reach Watership Down. Will they be safe now? Art Garfunkel's song from the film, *Bright Eyes*, reached the top of the UK charts. An animated film based on the book of the same name by Richard Adams. *Dir.* Martin Rosen.

Way Ahead, The (1944) David Niven (Lieutenant Jim Perry), Stanley Holloway (Pvt. Ted Brewer), James Donald (Pvt. Evan Lloyd), John Laurie (Pvt. Luke), Leslie Dwyer (Pvt. Sid Beck), Hugh Burden (Pvt. Bill Parsons), Jimmy Hanley (Pvt. Geoffrey Stainer), William Hartnell (Sgt. Ned Fletcher), Reginald Tate (The Training Company Commanding Officer), Leo Genn (Captain Edwards), John Ruddock (Chelsea Pensioner), A. Bromley Davenport (Chelsea Pensioner), Renée Asherson (Marjorie Gillingham), Mary Jerrold (Mrs. Gillingham), Raymond Lovell (Mr. Jackson), A.E. Matthews (Colonel Walmsley), Jack Watling (Buster), Peter Ustinov (Rispoli), Lloyd Pearson (Thyrtle), Raymond Huntley (Pvt. Herbert Davenport), Penelope Dudley-Ward (Mrs. Perry), Esma Cannon (Mrs. Brewer), Eileen Erskine (Mrs. Hilda Parsons), Grace Arnold (Mrs. Fletcher), Trevor Howard (Officer on Ship), John Salew (Sam), Tessie O'Shea (Herself). During WWII a young officer tries his best to turn recruits into soldiers, initially earning their enmity but eventually their respect. The benefit of the training is put to the test as the battalion defends its position during the North Africa campaign. An expanded and rewritten version of *The New Lot* (1943) and released in the US as *The Immortal Battalion*. *Dir.* Carol Reed.

Way to the Stars, The (1945) Michael Redgrave (Flt Lt. David Archdale), John Mills (Pt Officer Peter Penrose), Rosamund John ('Toddy' Todd), Douglass Montgomery (Johnny Hollis), Renée Asherson (Iris Winterton), Stanley Holloway (Mr. Palmer), Basil Radford (Tiny Williams), Felix Aylmer (Rev. Charles Moss), Bonar Colleano (Joe Friselli), Joyce Carey (Miss Winterton), Trevor Howard (Squadron Leader Carter), Nicholas Stuart (Col. Rogers), Bill Owen (Sgt. 'Nobby' Clarke), Grant Miller (Wally Becker), Jean Simmons (A Singer), Johnnie Schofield (Jones), Charles Victor (Corporal Fitter), David Tomlinson ('Prune' Parsons), Hartley Power (Col. Page), Vida Hope (Elsie), Hugh Dempster ('Tinker' Bell), Charles Farrell (American Orderly), Anthony Dawson (Bertie Steen), Bill Logan (Radio Operator), John Howard (Shelter Officer), Murray Matheson (Joe Lawson), John McLaren ('Cheerio' Chester), Jacqueline Clarke (Waitress), Alf Goddard (P.T. Instructor), Caven Watson (RAF Corporal), Sydney Benson (Fred), Peter Cotes (Aircraftman), Ian Warner McGilvray (Little Peter), Ann Wilton (Schoolmistress). The lives, loves and deaths of the British and American airmen at an English airfield during the early years of WWII. Also known as *Johnny in the Clouds*. *Dir.* Anthony Asquith.

We Dive at Dawn (1943) John Mills (Lt. Taylor), Louis Bradfield (Lt. Brace), Ronald Millar (Lt. Johnson), Jack Watling (Lt. Gordon), Reginald Purdell (C/P.O. Dabbs), Caven Watson (C/P.O. Duncan), Niall MacGinnis (C/P.O. Mike Corrigan), Eric

Portman (L/S. Hobson), Leslie Weston (L/S Tug Wilson), Norman Williams ('Canada'), Lionel Grose ('Spud'), David Peel ('Oxford'), Philip Godfrey ('Flunkey'), Robb Wilton ('Pincher'), Marie Ault (Mrs. Metcalfe), Frederick Burtwell (Sidney Briggs), Ian Fleming (Captain), Philip Friend (Humphries), Walter Gotell (Luftwaffe Captain), Vincent Holman (Danish Captain), Joan Hopkins (Ethel Dabbs), Vi Kaley (Old Lady), John Salew (Drake), Johnnie Schofield (Policeman), John Slater (Charlie), David Trickett (Peter Hobson), Beatrice Varley (Mrs. Dabbs), Josephine Wilson (Alice Hobson), After being recalled early from shore leave the crew of submarine *Sea Tiger* is sent on a mission to seek out and sink the German battleship *Brandenburg*. *Dir.* Anthony Asquith.

We Need to Talk about Kevin (2011) Tilda Swinton (Eva Khatchadourian), John C. Reilly (Franklin), Ezra Miller (Kevin Khatchadourian), Jasper Newell (Kevin aged 6 to 8), Rocky Duer (infant Kevin), Ashley Gerasimovich (Celia), Siobhan Fallon (Wanda), Alex Manette (Colin), Kenneth Franklin (Soweto), James Chen (Dr. Foulkes). Told in flashback, Eva looks at the events which led to her son Kevin to commit multiple murders. Based on Lionel Shriver's novel of the same name. *Dir.* Lynne Ramsay.

Weak and the Wicked, The (1954) Glynis Johns (Jean Raymond), Diana Dors (Betty Brown), John Gregson (Dr. Michael Hale), Olive Sloane (Nellie Baden), Rachel Roberts (Pat), Jane Hylton (Babs Peters), Athene Seyler (Millie Williams), Jean Taylor Smith (Grange Prison Governor), Cecil Trouncer (Judge), Ursula Howells (Pam Vickers), Edwin Styles (Seymour), Sid James (Syd Baden), Eliot Makeham (Grandad Baden), Joan Haythorne (Blackdown Prison Governor), Joyce Heron (Prison Matron Arnold), Anthony Nicholls (Prison Chaplain), Josephine Stuart (Andy), Paul Carpenter (Joe), Sybil Thorndike (Mabel Wicks), A.E. Matthews (Harry Wicks), Barbara Couper (Prison Doctor), Mary Merrall (Mrs. Skinner), Marjorie Rhodes (Suzie), Josephine Griffin (Miriam), Simone Silva (Tina), Thea Gregory (Nancy), Irene Handl (Waitress), Sandra Dorne (Stella), Ballard Berkeley (Police Detective). The film follows Jean through her time in prison and, in flashback, tells the story of how she ended up there, together with the stories of other inmates in two women's prisons. *Dir.* J Lee Thompson.

Went the Day Well? (1942) Leslie Banks (Oliver Wilsford), C.V. France (The Vicar), Valerie Taylor (Nora), Marie Lohr (Mrs. Fraser), Harry Fowler (Young George), Elizabeth Allan (Peggy), Frank Lawton (Tom Sturry), Thora Hird (Ivy), Muriel George (Mrs. Collins), Patricia Hayes (Daisy), Mervyn Johns (Charlie Sims), Norman Pierce (Jim Sturry), Hilda Bayley (Cousin Maud), Edward Rigby (Bill Purvis), Johnnie Schofield (Joe Garbett), Ellis Irving (Harry Drew), Grace Arnold (Mrs. Owen), Philippa Hiatt (Mrs. Bates), Basil Sydney (Major Ortler), David Farrar (Lieut. Jung), John Slater (Sergeant), Eric Micklewood (Soldier), Irene Arnold (Mrs. Drew), Kathleen Boutall (Mrs. Sturry), Lillian Ellias (Bridget), Gerard Heinz (Schmidt), Robert McDermott (BBC Announcer), Josephine Middleton (Mrs. Carter), Gerald Moore (Johnnie Wade), Charles Paton (Harry Brown), Anthony Pilbeam (Ted Garbett), Arthur Ridley (Father Owen), Janette Scott (Child), Norman Shelley (Bob Owen), Mavis Villiers (Violet), Jack Vyvian (Postman), Josie Welford (June). Told in flashback, the film recounts the events in a typically sleepy English village which is taken over by a group of German paratroopers disguised as British soldiers who are the vanguard of an invasion force. After being betrayed by the Nazi-loving local squire, the villagers eventually alert the local British forces to the deception and the German's end up with only just enough English soil to bury them all in. The squire also gets what he deserves. Classic unofficial propaganda of the type the British film industry produced during WWII wrapped up in a well-told, well-acted and at times very dark story, which was originally written by Graham Greene. *Dir.* Alberto Cavalcanti.

We're Going to Be Rich (1938) Gracie Fields (Kit Dobson), Victor McLaglen (Dobbie), Brian Donlevy (Yankee Gordon), Coral Browne (Pearl), Ted Smith (Tim), Gus McNaughton (Broderick), Charles Carson (Keeler), Syd Crossley (Jake), Hal

Gordon (Charlie), Robert Nainby (Judge), Charles Harrison (Rat Face), Tom Payne (Kinch), Don McCorkindale (Killer), Joe Mott (Manager), Alex Davies (Kimberley Kid). Set in the 1880s, a drifter and his wife leave Australia and head for the gold fields of South Africa. *Dir*. Monty Banks.

West is West (2010) Om Puri (George Khan), Aqib Khan (Sajid Khan), Linda Bassett (Ella Khan), Jimi Mistry (Tariq), Emil Marwa (Maneer), Vijay Raaz (Tanvir), Vanessa Hehir (Esther), Robert Pugh (Mr. Jordan), Ila Arun (Basheera Khan), Zita Sattar (Neelam Haqq), Thomas Russell (Hughsy), Raj Bhansali (Zaid), Dhanalaxmi Padmakumar (Raushana Khan), Sheeba Chaddha (Rehana Khan), Nadim Sawalha (Pir Naseem), Kamal Arora (Master Eyaz), Sunil Soni (Field Worker), Kalra Chander (Abdullah), Sujata Kumar (Mrs. Haqq), Enid Dunn (Eunice), John Branwell (Store Detective), Yograj Singh (Customs Official), Karamjit Anmol (Cousin 1), Sanjeev Attari (Cousin 2). George Khan is worried that his son Sajid, is turning his back on his Pakistani heritage, so he decides to take him for a visit to Pakistan. The sequel to *East is East* (1999). *Dir*. Andy De Emmony.

Western Approaches (1944) A dramatised documentary using active naval servicemen rather than actors which tells the story of seamen adrift in the Atlantic in a lifeboat after a U-Boat has torpedoed their ship. *Dir*. Pat Jackson.

Wetherby (1985) Vanessa Redgrave (Jean), Ian Holm (Stanley Pilborough), Judi Dench (Marcia Pilborough), Tim McInnerny (John Morgan), Stuart Wilson (Mike Langdon), Suzanna Hamilton (Karen Creasy), Tom Wilkinson (Roger Braithwaite), Marjorie Yates (Verity Braithwaite), Joely Richardson (Young Jean), Katy Behean (Young Marcia), Robert Hines (Jim Mortimer), Ian Bleasdale (Teacher), Howard Crossley (Policeman), Penny Downie (Chrissie), David Foreman (Young Malay), Christopher Fulford (Arthur), Matthew Guinness (Randall), Bert King (Mr. Mortimer), Richard Marris (Sir Thomas), Guy Nicholls (Mr. Varley). A stranger commits suicide in Wetherby and it seems his death will have an effect on Jean Travers, in whose house he died, and on her friends. *Dir*. David Hare.

What a Carve Up! (1961) Sid James (Sid Butler), Kenneth Connor (Ernie Broughton), Shirley Eaton (Linda Dickson), Donald Pleasence (Everett Sloane), Dennis Price (Guy Broughton), Michael Gough (Fisk - the Butler), Valerie Taylor (Janet Broughton), Esma Cannon (Aunt Emily), George Woodbridge (Dr. Edward Broughton), Michael Gwynn (Malcolm Broughton), Philip O'Flynn (Arkwright/Gabriel Broughton), Timothy Bateson (Porter), Frederick Piper (Hearse Driver), Adam Faith (Himself).
A group of relatives are summoned to the reading of a will at a remote mansion. During the night they begin to be murdered one by one. A comedy horror film loosely based on the novel *The Ghoul* by Frank King. *Dir*. Pat Jackson.

Whatever Happened to Harold Smith? (1999) Tom Courtenay (Harold Smith), Michael Legge (Vincent Smith), Lulu (Irene Smith), Laura Fraser (Joanna Robinson), Stephen Fry (Dr. Peter Robinson), Charlotte Roberts (Lucy Robinson), Amanda Root (Margaret Robinson), David Thewlis (Nesbit), Charlie Hunnam (Daz), James Corden (Walter). As Harold Smith becomes a minor celebrity due to his psychic powers, his son is desperately trying to date office colleague Joanna. *Dir*. Peter Hewitt.

What's Good for the Goose (1969) Norman Wisdom (Timothy), Sally Geeson (Nikki), Sarah Atkinson (Meg), Sally Bazely (Margaret Bartlett), Stuart Nichol (Bank Manager), Derek Francis (Harrington), Terence Alexander (Frisby), Paul Whitsun-Jones (Clark), David Lodge (Porter), Karl Lanchbury (Pete), Hilary Pritchard (Cashier in Disco), H.H. Goldsmith (Policeman), Thelma Falls-Hand (Bank Clerk), George Meaton (Third Speaker), Duncan Taylor (Other Banker), Jonathon Cox (First Son), Patrick Goggin (Second Son), Sally Begley (Daughter), John Alder, Phil May, John Povey, Dick Taylor, Wally Waller (The Pretty Things). A Norman Wisdom sex comedy! Married Timothy Bartlett goes on a business trip and has an affair with a young woman. *Dir*. Menahem Golan.

When Brendan Met Trudy (2000) Peter McDonald (Brendan), Flora Montgomery (Trudy), Maynard Eziashi (Edgar), Marie Mullen (Mother), Pauline McLynn (Nuala), Don Wycherley

(Niall), Eileen Walsh (Siobhán), Barry Cassin (Headmaster), Robert O'Neill (Dylan). Shy teacher and film buff Brendan meets Trudy, a free-spirited girl who begins to lead him into wicked ways. Written by Roddy Doyle. *Dir*. Kieron J. Walsh.

When Saturday Comes (1996) Sean Bean (Jimmy Muir), Emily Lloyd (Annie Doherty), Craig Kelly (Russel Muir), Melanie Hill (Mary Muir), John McEnery (Joe Muir), Ann Bell (Sarah Muir), Ian Taylor (Young Jimmy Muir), Tony Currie (Himself), Mel Sterland (Captain), Pete Postlethwaite (Ken Jackson), Rebecca Nichols (Stripper), Chris Walker (Mac), John Higgins (Rob), Tim Gallagher (Steve), Peter Gunn (Tommy), Nick Waring (Gerry), James McKenna (George McCabe), Alex Norton (Factory Boss). Factory worker Jimmy Muir is scouted by local football team Hallam FC with prospects of even greater footballing heights at Sheffield United. *Dir*. Maria Giese.

Where Angels Fear to Tread (1991) Rupert Graves (Philip Herriton), Helena Bonham Carter (Caroline Abbott), Judy Davis (Harriet Herriton), Giovanni Guidelli (Gino Carella), Helen Mirren (Lilia), Barbara Jefford (Mrs. Herriton). Sophie Kullmann (Irma), Thomas Wheatley (Mr. Kingcroft), Vass Anderson (Mr. Abbott), Sylvia Barter (Mrs. Theobald), Eileen Davies (Ethel), Siria Betti (Hotel-Keeper), Giovanni Guidelli (Gino Carella), Anna Lelio (Perfetta), Luca Lazzareschi (Spiridione). Period drama. When recently widowed Lilia Herriton visits Tuscany and marries a local dentist, her family is not pleased. When she dies in childbirth her friend Caroline, and in-laws Philip and Harriet go to Italy to take custody of the baby. Based on the novel of the same title by E. M. Forster. *Dir*. Charles Sturridge.

Where Eagles Dare (1968) Richard Burton (Maj. Smith), Clint Eastwood (Schaffer), Mary Ure (Mary Ellison), Patrick Wymark (Col. Turner), Michael Hordern (Adm. Rolland), Donald Houston (Christiansen), Peter Barkworth (Berkeley), William Squire (Thomas), Robert Beatty (Gen. George Carnaby), Brook Williams (Sgt. Harrod), Neil McCarthy (Sgt. Jock MacPherson), Vincent Ball (Carpenter), Anton Diffring (Col. Kramer), Ferdy Mayne (Rosemeyer), Derren Nesbitt (Von Happen), Victor Beaumont (Col. Weissner), Ingrid Pitt (Heidi), John G. Heller (German Major), Guy Deghy (Maj. Wilhelm Wilner), Olga Lowe (Lt. Anne-Marie Kernitser), Max Faulkner (Sgt. Hartmann). During WWII, a group of crack commandos are dropped into Germany ostensibly on a mission to rescue a captured American general who knows the plans for D-Day. The screenplay was written by Alistair MacLean who also wrote the novel. *Dir*. Brian G. Hutton.

Where Is Parsifal? (1983) Tony Curtis (Parsifal Katzenellenbogen), Berta Domínguez (D.Elba), Erik Estrada (Henry Board II), Peter Lawford (Montague Chippendale), Ron Moody (Beersbohm), Donald Pleasence (Mackintosh), Orson Welles (Klingsor), Christopher Chaplin (Ivan), Nancy Roberts (Ruth), Ava Lazar (Sheila). Peter Lawford's final screen appearance. A bit of a curiosity in that, although it was shown at the Cannes Film Festival and released in France, it had no UK or US distribution and no original English language versions exist. *Dir*. Henri Helman

Where the Spies Are (1965) David Niven (Dr. Jason Love), Françoise Dorléac (Vikki), John Le Mesurier (MacGillivray), Cyril Cusack (Rosser), Eric Pohlmann (Farouk), Richard Marner (Josef), Paul Stassino (Simmias), George Pravda (1st Agent), Noel Harrison (Jackson), Ronald Radd (Stanilaus), Alan Gifford (Security), Bill Nagy (Aeradio), George Mikell (Assassin), Nigel Davenport (Parkington), Gábor Baraker (2nd Agent), Geoffrey Bayldon (Lecturer), Derek Partridge (Duty Officer), Robert Raglan (Sir Robert), Riyad Gholmieh (1st Taxi Driver), Muhsen Samrani (2nd Taxi Driver), Basil Dignam (Major Harding), Gordon Tanner (Inspector). James Bond-ish spy spoof. The projected series of films were canned after the first effort. Based on the James Leasor book *Passport to Oblivion*. *Dir*. Val Guest.

Where There's a Will (1936) Will Hay (Benjamin Stubbins), Graham Moffatt (Willie), Norma Varden (Lady Margaret Wimpleton), Hartley Power (Duke Wilson), Gina Malo (Goldie Kelly), H.F. Maltby (Sir Roger Wimpleton), Peggy Simpson (Barbara Stubbins), Gibb McLaughlin (Martin, The Butler), Eddie Houghton (Slug Riley), Hal Walters (Nick Harris), John Turnbull (Detective Collins), Sybil Brooke (Mrs Peabody, Landlady), Davina Craig (Lucie, The Maid). Stubbins is fooled into vacating his solicitor's office so that crooks can use it in a bank robbery. *Dir.* William Beaudine.

Where's Jack? (1969) Tommy Steele (Jack Sheppard), Stanley Baker (Jonathan Wild), Alan Badel (The Lord Chancellor), Dudley Foster (Blueskin), Fiona Lewis (Edgworth Bess Lyon), Sue Lloyd (Lady Darlington), Noel Purcell (Leatherchest), Eddie Byrne (Rev. Wagstaff), Ivan Dixon (Naval Officer), Michael Douglas (Constable), Michael Elphick (Hogarth), Roy Evans (Mr. Hind), Howard Goorney (Surgeon), John Hallam (The Captain), Dafydd Havard (Clerk), Fred Johnson (Merchant), Harold Kasket (The King), John Kelly (Proprietor), Esmond Knight (Ballad Singer), Leon Lissek (Deeley), Yole Marinelli (Lady Clarissa), William Marlowe (Tom Sheppard), Skip Martin (Dwarf), John Morley (Judge), Caroline Munro (Madame Vendonne), Cardew Robinson (Lord Mayor), Liam Sweeney (Austin), George Woodbridge (Hangman), Jack Woolgar (Mr. Woods), Carla Challoner (Emma), Loretta Clarke (Lady Mayoress). A version of the rivalry between notorious 18th Century highwayman and gaol-escapee Jack Shepherd and infamous "thief-taker" Jonathan Wild. *Dir.* James Clavell.

Where's That Fire? (1940) Will Hay (Captain Benjamin Viking), Moore Marriott (Jeremiah Harbottle), Graham Moffatt (Albert Brown), Peter Gawthorne (Fire Chief), Eric Clavering (Hank Sullivan), Hugh McDermott (Jim Baker), Charles Hawtrey (Woodley), Dave O'Toole (Postman), Frank Atkinson (Town Clerk), Clifford Buckton (1st Driver), George Carney (Councillor), Wilson Coleman (Doctor), David Keir (Councillor), Philip Leaver (Chief Crook). As might be expected Viking, Harbottle and Brown are probably the worst firemen in history and even manage to have their engine stolen. What's worse is that the engine is going to be used in a heist at the Tower of London. *Dir.* Marcel Varnel.

While I Live (1947) Sonia Dresdel (Julia Trevelyan), Carol Raye (Sally Grant), Tom Walls (Nehemiah), Patricia Burke (Christine Sloan), Clifford Evans (Peter Sloan), John Warwick (George Grant), Audrey Fildes (Olwen), Ernest Butcher (Ambrose), Enid Hewitt (Ruth), Sally Rogers (Hannah), Charles Victor (Sergeant Pearne), Edward Lexy (Selby), Johnnie Schofield (Alfie), John Martyn (Onlooker), Brenda Cameron (Mary), Diana Lake (Lucy), Doreen Fischer (Ethel). Pianist Olwen Trevelyan falls to her death after being disturbed by her sister whilst sleepwalking. Exactly 25 years later a young woman with no memory of who she is turns up at the sister's door and starts playing Olwen's last unfinished composition. The musical theme "The Dream of Olwen" composed by Charles Williams which ran throughout the film became a popular piano piece. *Dir.* John Harlow.

Whisky Galore! (1949) Basil Radford (Captain Paul Waggett), Catherine Lacey (Mrs Waggett), Bruce Seton (Sergeant Odd), Joan Greenwood (Peggy Macroon), Wylie Watson (Joseph Macroon), Gabrielle Blunt (Catriona Macroon), Gordon Jackson (George Campbell), Jean Cadell (Mrs Campbell), James Robertson Justice (Dr Maclaren), Morland Graham (The Biffer), John Gregson (Sammy MacCodrun), James Woodburn (Roderick MacRurie), James Anderson (Old Hector), Jameson Clark (Constable Macrae), Duncan Macrae (Angus McCormac), Mary MacNeil (Mrs. McCormac), Norman Macowan (Captain MacPhee), Alastair Hunter (Captain MacKechnie), Compton MacKenzie (Captain Buncher), Finlay Currie (Narrator), A.E. Matthews (Colonel Linsey-Woolsey). In 1943, as the inhabitants of Todday in the Outer Hebrides contemplate the end of the whisky supply on the island, their prayers are answered when the freighter S.S. *Cabinet Minister*, with cargo consisting of 50,000 cases of the spirit, runs aground in heavy fog late one night. Adapted from the novel of the same name by Compton MacKenzie which itself was based on the real-life 1941 shipwreck of the S.S. *Politician* with its cargo of whisky near the island of Eriskay. *Dir.* Alexander Mackendrick.

Whisperers, The (1967) Edith Evans (Mrs. Ross), Nanette Newman (The Girl Upstairs), Harry Baird (The Man Upstairs), Jack Austin (Police Sergeant), Gerald Sim (Mr. Conrad), Lionel Gamlin (Mr. Conrad's Colleague), Ronald Fraser (Charlie Ross), Kenneth Griffith (Mr. Weaver), Avis Bunnage (Mrs. Noonan), John Orchard (Grogan), Peter Thompson (Publican), Sarah Forbes (Mrs. Ross When Young), Penny Spencer (Mavis Noonan), Kaplan Kaye (Jimmie Noonan), Michael Robbins (Mr. Noonan), Frank Singuineau (Negro Doctor), Michael Francis (Plain-Clothes Policeman), Robin Bailey (Psychiatrist), Eric Portman (Archie Ross), George Spence (Caretaker), Leonard Rossiter (Assistance Board Officer), Margaret Tyzack (Hospital Almoner), Clare Kelly (Prostitute), Charlie Bird (Man in N.A.B. Office), Max Bacon (Mr. Fish), Robert Russell (Andy), Alan O'Keefe (1st Attacker), Francis Flynn (2nd Attacker), Glen Farmer (1st Redeemer), Oliver MacGreevy (2nd Redeemer). An old lady, who hears voices whispering to her, finds some money hidden by her thief son and believes her fantasies of being an heiress are becoming reality. Based on the novel by Robert Nicolson. *Dir.* Bryan Forbes.

Whistle Down the Wind (1961) Hayley Mills (Kathy Bostock), Bernard Lee (Mr. Bostock), Alan Bates (The Man), Norman Bird (Eddie), Diane Clare (Sunday School Teacher), Patricia Heneghan (Salvation Army Girl), John Arnatt (Superintendent Teesdale), Elsie Wagstaff (Auntie Dorothy), Hamilton Dyce (The Vicar), Howard Douglas (The Vet), Ronald Hines (PC Thurstow), Gerald Sim (Detective), Roy Holder (Jackie). A film where a group of schoolchildren believe that a murderer hiding out in a barn is in fact Jesus Christ. Based on the novel of the same name by Mary Hayley Bell (Hayley Mills' mother). *Dir.* Bryan Forbes.

White Corridors (1951) Googie Withers (Dr. Sophie Dean), James Donald (Neil Marriner), Godfrey Tearle (Mr. Groom Sr.), Petula Clark (Joan Shepherd), Jean Anderson (Sister Gater), Timothy Bateson (Dr. Cook), Fabia Drake (Miss Farmer), Henry Edwards (Phillip Brewster), Lyn Evans (Pedlar), Grace Gavin (Sister Abbott), Helen Harvey (Nurse Miller), Gerard Heinz (Dr. Macuzek), H.S. Hills (Tranter), Mary Hinton (Matron), Humphrey Howarth (Chandler), Brand Inglis (Tommy Briggs), Megs Jenkins (Mrs. Briggs), Barry Jones (Dr. Shoesmith), Avice Landone (Sister Jenkins), Bernard Lee (Burgess), Moira Lister (Dolly Clark), Jean Lodge (Night Nurse), Dandy Nichols (Char), Mary Pratt (Rose Dawson), Basil Radford (Retired Civil Servant), Johnnie Schofield (Night Porter), Philip Stainton (Sawyer), Patrick Troughton (Sailor), Jack Watling (Dick Groom), Dana Wynter (Marjorie Brewster). A hospital drama in the early days of the National Health Service with the emphasis on the personal lives of the doctors and nurses and some dramatic medical action surrounding a young boy with blood poisoning. *Dir.* Pat Jackson.

White Mischief (1987) Greta Scacchi (Diana Lady Broughton), Charles Dance (Josslyn Hay), Joss Ackland ('Jock' Delves Broughton), Sarah Miles (Alice de Janzé), Geraldine Chaplin (Nina Soames), Ray McAnally (Morris), Murray Head (Lizzie), John Hurt (Gilbert Colvile), Trevor Howard (Jack Soames), Susan Fleetwood (Gladys, Lady Delamer), Catherine Neilson (Lady June Carberry), Hugh Grant (Hugh), Alan Dobie (Harragin), Gregor Fisher (McPherson), Jacqueline Pearce (Idina), Tristram Jellinek (Land Agent), Tim Myers (Raymond de Trafford), Sean Mathias (Gerald Portman), Douglas Chege (Kiptobe), Wensley Pithey (Sheridan), Stephan Chase (Carberry), Louis Mahoney (Abdullah), David Quilter (Chief Superintendent Poppy), John Rees (Baines), Olivier Pierre (Kaplan), Anthony Benson (Fox), Nigel Le Vaillant (Reporter), Susannah Harker (Young Girl). A dramatization of the events known as the "Happy Valley murder case" in Kenya in 1941, when Sir Henry "Jock" Delves Broughton was tried for the murder of Josslyn Hay, Earl of Erroll. Based on a book by James Fox. *Dir.* Michael Radford.

Who Dares Wins (1982) Lewis Collins (Capt. Peter Skellen), Judy Davis (Frankie Leith), Richard Widmark (Secretary of State Arthur Currie), Edward Woodward (Commander Powell), Robert Webber (General Ira Potter), Tony Doyle (Colonel Hadley), John Duttine (Rod Walker), Kenneth Griffith (Bishop Crick), Rosalind Lloyd (Jenny Skellen), Ingrid Pitt (Helga), Norman Rodway (Ryan), Maurice Roëves (Maj. Steele), Bob Sherman (Hagen), Mark Ryan (Mac), Patrick Allen (Police Commissioner), Zig Byfield (SAS trooper Baker), Nick Brimble (SAS trooper Williamson), Anna Ford (Newsreader), Aharon Ipalé (Malek), Paul Freeman (Sir Richard), Briony Elliott (Baby Samantha), Alan Mitchell (Harkness), Richard Coleman (Mr. Martin), Nigel

Humphreys (Sgt. Pope), Stephen Bent (Neil), Jon Morrison (Dennis), Trevor Byfield (Baker), John Woodnutt (Harold Staunton). An SAS officer infiltrates a terrorist group. The title is the motto of the Special Air Service. *Dir*. Ian Sharp.

Who Done It? (1956) Benny Hill (Hugo Dill), Belinda Lee (Frankie Mayne), David Kossoff (Zacco), Garry Marsh (Det. Insp. Hancock), George Margo (Barakov), Ernest Thesiger (Sir Walter), Denis Shaw (Otto Stumpf), Frederick Schiller (Gruber), Thorley Walters (Raymond Courtney), Philip Stainton (Jimmy Maddox), Warwick Ashton (PC. Roberts), Stratford Johns (PC Coleman), Charles Hawtrey (Disc Jockey), Irene Handl (Customer), Glyn Houston (Arresting Policeman). Hugo Dill is a would-be detective who uncovers a spy ring. *Dir*. Basil Dearden.

Whoops Apocalypse (1986) Stuart Saunders (Governor of Santa Maya), Marc Smith (Dan Hickey), Loretta Swit (President Barbara Adams), John Benfield (Secret Service agent), Ben Robertson (Secret Service agent), Peter Cook (Sir Mortimer Chris), Alexander Davion (Maguadoran general), Herbert Lom (Gen. Mosquera), Daniel Benzali (William Kubert), Richard Pearson (Michael Sumpter), Ian Richardson (Bendish), Christopher Coll (Flag Lt. Gerald Beaverstone), Christopher Malcolm (Gallagher), Ian McNeice (Thrush), Joanne Pearce (Princess Wendy), Ed Bishop (Wink Persiman), Rik Mayall (Specialist Catering Commander), Graeme Garden (Man who walks to the phone). Spin-off from the television series of the same name, which did not go on general release until 1988. *Dir*. Tom Bussmann.

Wicked Lady, The (1945) Margaret Lockwood (Barbara Worth), James Mason (Captain Jerry Jackson), Patricia Roc (Caroline), Griffith Jones (Sir Ralph Skelton), Michael Rennie (Kit Locksby), Felix Aylmer (Hogarth), Enid Stamp Taylor (Lady Henrietta Kingsclere), Francis Lister (Lord Kingsclere), Beatrice Varley (Aunt Moll), Amy Dalby (Aunt Doll), Martita Hunt (Cousin Agatha), David Horne (Martin Worth), Emrys Jones (Ned Cotterill), Helen Goss (Mistress Betsy), Muriel Aked (Mrs. Munce). A Gainsborough Pictures melodrama set in the 17th century. Barbara Worth seduces her best friend's bridegroom the day before the wedding, marries him and then embarks on a career as a highwayman. Based on the novel *The Life and Death of the Wicked Lady Skelton* by Magdalen King-Hall. *Dir*. Leslie Arliss

Wicked Lady, The (1983) Faye Dunaway (Lady Barbara Skelton), Alan Bates (Jerry Jackson), John Gielgud (Hogarth), Denholm Elliott (Sir Ralph Skelton), Prunella Scales (Lady Kingsclere), Oliver Tobias (Kit Locksby), Glynis Barber (Caroline), Joan Hickson (Aunt Agatha), Helena McCarthy (Moll Skelton), Mollie Maureen (Doll Skelton), Derek Francis (Lord Kingsclere), Marina Sirtis (Jackson's Girl), Nicholas Gecks (Ned Cotterell), Hugh Millais (Uncle Martin), John Savident (Squire Thornton), Dermot Walsh (Lord Marwood), Marc Sinden (Lord Dolman), Glynis Brooks (Ned's Wife), Mark Burns (King Charles II), Teresa Codling (Nell Gwynne), Celia Imrie (Servant at Inn), Marianne Stone (Customer in Shop), Louise English (Servant). A remake of the 1945 film melodrama. *Dir*. Michael Winner.

Wicker Man, The (1973) Edward Woodward (Sergeant Howie), Christopher Lee (Lord Summerisle), Diane Cilento (Miss Rose), Britt Ekland (Willow), Ingrid Pitt (Librarian), Lindsay Kemp (Alder MacGregor), Russell Waters (Harbour Master), Aubrey Morris (Old Gardener/Gravedigger), Irene Sunters (May Morrison), Walter Carr (School Master), Roy Boyd (Broome), Peter Brewis (Musician), Gerry Cowper (Rowan Morrison), John Hallam (PC McTaggart). A cult horror classic. Devout Christian and celibate Sgt.Howie travels to Summerisle to investigate the disappearance of a young girl and discovers that the locals worship the pagan gods of the Celts. *Dir*. Robin Hardy.

Wild Bill (2011) Charlie Creed-Miles (Bill), Will Poulter (Dean), Liz White (Roxy), Sammy Williams (Jimmy), Leo Gregory (Terry), Neil Maskell (Dicky), Iwan Rheon (Pill), Jaime Winstone (Helen), Charlotte Spencer (Steph), Amanda Henderson (Steph's Friend), Dixie Arnold (Police Officer), Peter-Hugo Daly (Keith), Elly Fairman (Miss Treedley), Jason Flemyng (John), Graham Fletcher-Cook (Police Driver), Billy Holland (Mini Hoodie), Aaron Ishmael (Boz), Radoslaw Kaim (Jonas), Peter McCabe (Roland), Mark Monero (Freddy), Andy Serkis (Glen), Hardeep Singh Kohli (Raj), Morgan Watkins (Viktoras), Lee Whitlock (Boss), Olivia Williams (Kelly). Hardman Bill comes out of

prison after eight years to find that his two sons are fending for themselves as his wife has gone off with her new boyfriend. He suddenly has to adapt to being a proper father. *Dir*. Dexter Fletcher.

Wild Geese II (1985) Scott Glenn (John Haddad), Barbara Carrera (Kathy Lukas), Edward Fox (Alex Faulkner), Laurence Olivier (Rudolf Hess), Robert Webber (Robert McCann), Robert Freitag (Stroebling), Kenneth Haigh (Col. Reed-Henry), Stratford Johns (Mustapha El Ali), Derek Thompson (Hourigan), Paul Antrim (Murphy), John Terry (Michael), Ingrid Pitt (Hooker), Patrick Stewart (Russian General), Michael Harbour (KGB Man), David Lumsden (Joseph), Frederick Warder (Jamil), Malcolm Jamieson (Pierre), Billy Boyle (Devenish). A group of mercenaries are hired to extract Hess from Spandau Prison in Berlin. Based on the novel *The Square Circle* by Daniel Carney. Sequel to *The Wild Geese*. Dir. Peter R Hunt.

Wild Geese, The (1978) Richard Burton (Col. Allen Faulkner), Roger Moore (Lt. Shawn Fynn), Richard Harris (Capt. Rafer Janders), Hardy Krüger (Lt. Pieter Coetze), Stewart Granger (Sir Edward Matherson), Winston Ntshona (Julius Limbani), John Kani (Sgt. Jesse Blake), Jack Watson (RSM Sandy Young), Frank Finlay (Fr. Geoghagen), Kenneth Griffith (Arthur Witty), Barry Foster (Thomas Balfour), Ronald Fraser (Sgt. Jock McTaggart), Ian Yule (Sgt. Tosh Donaldson), Patrick Allen (Rushton), Rosalind Lloyd (Heather), David Ladd (Sonny), Paul Spurrier (Emile Janders), Jeff Corey (Mr. Martin), Brook Williams (Samuels), Percy Herbert (Keith), Glyn Baker (Esposito), Sydney Chama (Clark), Ken Gampu (Alexander), Jane Hylton (Mrs. Young), Joe Cole (Derek), John Alderson (Randy), Terence Longdon (Anonymous Man), Patrick Holt (Skyjacker), John Dennison (Matherson's butler), Thomas Baptiste (Col. Mboya), Jules Walters (Mboya's ADC), Valerie Leon (Croupier), Suzanne Danielle (Girl at Party). A team of mercenaries are recruited to rescue the imprisoned leader of an African country. *Dir*. Andrew V. McLaglen.

Wildcats of St Trinian's, The (1980) Sheila Hancock (Olga Vandemeer), Michael Hordern (Sir Charles Hackforth), Joe Melia (Flash Harry), Thorley Walters (Hugo Culpepper Brown), Rodney Bewes (Peregrine Butters), Deborah Norton (Miss Brenner), Maureen Lipman (Miss Katy Higgs), Julia McKenzie (Miss Dolly Dormancott), Ambrosine Phillpotts (Mrs Mowbray), Rose Hill (Miss Martingale), Diana King (Miss Mactavish), Luan Peters (Poppy Adams), Barbara Hicks (Miss Coke), Rosalind Knight (Miss Walsh), Patsy Smart (Miss Warmold), Bernadette O'Farrell (Miss Carfax), Sandra Payne (Miss Taylor), Frances Ruffelle (Angela Hall/Princess Roxanne), Hilda Braid (Miss Summers), Lisa Vanderpump (Ursula), Ballard Berkeley (Humphry Wills), Alex Kingston (Schoolgirl). The girls of St Trinian's decide to go on strike (as befitting it's year of release perhaps). Not the best of the franchise. *Dir:* Frank Launder.

Wimbledon (2004) Paul Bettany (Peter), Kirsten Dunst (Lizzie), James McAvoy (Carl Colt), Bernard Hill (Edward Colt), Eleanor Bron (Augusta Colt), Celia Imrie (Mrs Kenwood), Nikolaj Coster-Waldau (Dieter Prohl), Sam Neill (Dennis Bradbury), Austin Nichols (Jake Hammond), Kirsten Taylor Montjoy Hunter (Elizabeth Hammond), Jon Favreau (Ron Roth), Jonathan Timmins (The Ballboy), Robert Lindsay (Ian Frazier), Vikas Punna (Ajay Bhatt), Murphy Jensen (Ivan Dragomir), Alun Jones (Tom Cavendish), Rebecca Dandeniya (Arliyia Rupesindhe) and as themselves, John McEnroe, Chris Evert, Mary Carillo and John Barrett. British tennis pro Peter Colt has decided to call it a day and retire after he competes at Wimbledon. He finds that there is a mutual attraction between himself and US tennis ace Lizzie Bradbury, much to the disapproval of her father. *Dir*. Richard Loncraine.

Wind in the Willows, The (1996) Voice cast: Terry Jones (Mr. Toad), Steve Coogan (Mr. Mole), Eric Idle (Mr. Rat), Nicol Williamson (Mr. Badger), Antony Sher (The Chief Weasel), Stephen Fry (The Judge), John Cleese (Mr. Toad's Lawyer), Michael Palin (The Sun), Bernard Hill (The Engine Driver), Nigel Planer (The Car Salesman), Julia Sawalha (The Jailer's Daughter), Victoria Wood (The Tea Lady), Don Henderson (The Sentry). An animated version of Kenneth Grahame's children's book. *Dir*. Terry Jones.

Wind of Change, The (1961) Donald Pleasence ('Pop' Marley), Johnny Briggs (Frank Marley), Ann Lynn (Josie Marley), Hilda Fenemore (Gladys), Glyn Houston (Sgt. Parker), Norman Gunn (Ron), Bunny May (Smithy), David Hemmings (Ginger), Patricia Garwood (Lina), Ken McGregor (Man from Café), Angela Douglas (Denise), Topsy Jane (Peggy), Antonita Dias (Sylvia), Rosemary Frankau (Woman in Mews), Bertie Green (Bus Conductor). Frank is a young unemployed white man in Notting Hill who is drawn into a fight where a black boy is killed and his own sister is stabbed. He begins to questions his racist attitudes. The title is taken from British Prime Minister Harold Macmillan's Wind of Change speech given in Cape Town in February 1960. *Dir.* Vernon Sewell.

Wind that Shakes the Barley, The (2006) Cillian Murphy (Damien O'Donovan), Pádraic Delaney (Teddy O'Donovan), Liam Cunningham (Dan), Orla Fitzgerald (Sinéad Ní Shúilleabháin), Laurence Barry (Micheál Ó Súilleabháin), Mary Murphy (Bernadette), Mary O'Riordan (Peggy), Myles Horgan (Rory), Martin Lucey (Congo), Roger Allam (Sir John Hamilton), John Crean (Chris Reilly), Damien Kearney (Finbar), Frank Bourke (Leo), Shane Casey (Kevin), Máirtín de Cógáin (Sean), William Ruane (Johnny Gogan), Fiona Lawton (Lily), Sean McGinley (Father Denis), Kevin O'Brien (Tim). Set during the Irish War of Independence and the Irish Civil War, the O'Donovan brothers join the Irish Republican Army to fight for Irish independence but history decrees they will eventually end up on different sides. *Dir.* Ken Loach.

Windbag the Sailor (1936) Will Hay (Captain Ben Cutlet), Moore Marriott (Jerry Harbottle), Graham Moffatt (Albert), Norma Varden (Olivia Potter-Porter), Kenneth Warrington (Yates), Dennis Wyndham (Jim Maryatt), Amy Veness (Emma Harbottle), Leonard Sharp (Crew member), Percy Walsh (Captain, 'Rob Roy'). Although he has only ever sailed a coal barge, Captain Cutlet is a definite windbag when it comes to telling of his adventures on the high seas. However, this gets him into trouble when he is persuaded to command the leaky *Rob Roy*. The first film to feature Hay, Marriott and Moffatt together. *Dir.* William Beaudine.

Windom's Way (1957) Peter Finch (Alec Windom), Mary Ure (Lee Windom), Natasha Parry (Anna Vidal), Robert Flemyng (Col. George Hasbrook), Michael Hordern (Patterson), Grégoire Aslan (Mayor Lollivar), John Cairney (Jan Vidal), Marne Maitland (Commissioner Belhedron), George Margo (Police Officer Lansang), Kurt Siegenberg (Kosti), Martin Benson (Samcar, Rebel Commander), Sanny Bin Hussan (Father Amyan), Burt Kwouk (Father Amyan's Aide). Set during the Malayan Emergency, a doctor tries to mediate between planters and villagers and at the same time deal with his socialite wife. *Dir.* Ronald Neame

Window in London, A (1939) Michael Redgrave (Peter), Sally Gray (Vivienne), Paul Lukas (Zoltini), Hartley Power (Max Preston), Patricia Roc (Pat), Glen Alyn (Andrea), Gertrude Musgrove (Telephonist), George Carney (Night Watchman), Bryan Coleman (Constable), Alf Goddard (Tiny), Wilfred Walter (Foreman), George Merritt (Manager), John Salew (Reporter). A man on a train believes he has witnessed a murder in a block of flats by the railway line. *Dir.* Herbert Mason.

Wings of the Dove, The (1997) Helena Bonham Carter (Kate Croy), Linus Roache (Merton Densher), Alison Elliott (Millie Theale), Elizabeth McGovern (Susan Stringham), Charlotte Rampling (Aunt Maude), Michael Gambon (Lionel Croy), Alex Jennings (Lord Mark), Alexander John (Butler), Diana Kent (Merton's Party Companion), Georgio Serafini (Eugenio). Period drama. Kate's aunt wants her to marry well but Kate has her eye on poor journalist Merton. The arrival of the vivacious but ailing Millie on the scene may offer a way out. Based on the novel of the same name by Henry James. *Dir.* Iain Softley.

Wings of the Morning (1937) Henry Fonda (Kerry Gilfallen), Annabella (Maria, Duchess of Leyva), Leslie Banks (Lord Clontarf), Stewart Rome (Sir Valentine), Irene Vanbrugh (Old Marie), Harry Tate (Paddy), Helen Haye (Aunt Jenepher), Edward Underdown (Don Diego), Mark Daly ('Jimmy' Brannigan), Sam

Livesey (Angelo). A gypsy woman who left Ireland for Spain returns nearly fifty years later with her granddaughter, who falls for a horse trainer. *Dir.* Harold D. Schuster.

Winslow Boy, The (1948) Robert Donat (Sir Robert Morton), Cedric Hardwicke (Arthur Winslow), Neil North (Ronnie Winslow), Margaret Leighton (Catherine Winslow), Kathleen Harrison (Violet), Francis L. Sullivan (Attorney General), Marie Lohr (Grace Winslow), Jack Watling (Dickie Winslow), Basil Radford (Desmond Curry), Walter Fitzgerald (First Lord), Frank Lawton (John Watherstone), Nicholas Hannen (Colonel Watherstone), Hugh Dempster (Agricultural Member), Evelyn Roberts (Hamilton MP), W.A. Kelley (Brian O'Rourke), Marie Michelle (Mrs. Curry), Mona Washbourne (Miss Barnes), Ivan Samson (Captain Flower), Kynaston Reeves (Lord Chief Justice), Ernest Thesiger (Mr. Ridgeley Pierce), Stanley Holloway (Comedian), Noel Howlett (Mr. Williams), Wilfrid Hyde-White (Wilkins). When Ronnie Winslow is expelled from the naval academy at Osborne for stealing a postal order his family go to great lengths in order to prove him innocent. An adaptation of Terence Rattigan's play of the same name. *Dir.* Anthony Asquith.

Winslow Boy, The (1999) Jeremy Northam (Sir Robert Morton), Nigel Hawthorne (Arthur Winslow), Rebecca Pidgeon (Catherine Winslow), Guy Edwards (Ronnie Winslow), Gemma Jones (Grace Winslow), Matthew Pidgeon (Dickie Winslow), Aden Gillet (John Watherstone), Colin Stinton (Desmond Curry), Sarah Flind (Violet), Neil North (First Lord), Lana Bilzerian (Undermaid), Eve Bland (Suffragette), Sara Stewart (Miss Barnes), Perry Fenwick (Fred), Alan Polonsky (Mr. Michaels), Chris Porter (MP), Jim Dunk (Colleague), Duncan Gould (Commons Reporter), Ian Soundy (Local Reporter). An adaptation of Terence Rattigan's play of the same name. *Dir.* David Mahmet.

Wisdom of Crocodiles, The (1999) Jude Law (Steven Grlscz), Elina Löwensohn (Anne Levels), Timothy Spall (Inspector Healey), Jack Davenport (Sergeant Roche), Colin Salmon (Martin), Hitler Wong (Noodles Chan), Kerry Fox (Maria Vaughan), Anastasia Hille (Karen), Joseph O'Conor (Mr. Nancarrow), Rupert Farley (Priest), Diane Howse (Mrs. Healey), Cliff Parisi (Labourer). Steven drinks blood to keep himself alive. Based on the book of the same name by Paul Hoffman. *Dir.* Po-Chih Leong.

Wish You Were Here (1987) Emily Lloyd (Lynda Mansell), Tom Bell (Eric), Jesse Birdsall (Dave), Clare Clifford (Mrs. Parfitt), Barbara Durkin (Valerie), Geoffrey Hutchings (Hubert Mansell), Charlotte Barker (Gillian), Chloë Leland (Margaret), Charlotte Ball (Lynda - aged 11), Pat Heywood (Aunt Millie), Abigail Leland (Margaret - aged 7), Geoffrey Durham (Harry Figgis), Neville Smith (Cinema manager), Heathcote Williams (Dr. Holroyd), Val McLane (Maisie Mathews), Susan Skipper (Lynda's Mother), Lee Whitlock (Brian), Sheila Kelley (Joan Figgis), William Lawford (Uncle Brian), Pamela Duncan (Mrs. Hartley), Bob Flag (Mental Patient), Val McLane (Maisie Mathews), Kim McDermott (Vickie), Ben Daniels (Policeman). Cheeky but naïve teenager Lynda's life changes completely when she becomes pregnant by one of her father's friends. *Dir.* David Leland.

Witches, The (1966) Joan Fontaine (Gwen Mayfield), Kay Walsh (Stephanie Bax), Alec McCowen (Alan Bax), Ann Bell (Sally Benson), Ingrid Boulting (Linda Rigg), John Collin (Dowsett), Michele Dotrice (Valerie Creek), Gwen Ffrangcon Davies (Granny Rigg), Duncan Lamont (Bob Curd), Leonard Rossiter (Dr. Wallis), Martin Stephens (Ronnie Dowsett), Carmel McSharry (Mrs. Dowsett), Viola Keats (Mrs. Curd), Shelagh Fraser (Mrs. Creek), Bryan Marshall (Tom), Yemi Ajibade (Mark), Kitty Atwood (Mrs. McDowall), John Barrett (Mr. Glass), Rudolph Walker (Mark). A school teacher has a breakdown after a run-in with a witch doctor in Africa and returns to England. As bad luck would have it she ends up teaching in a village which is the home to a coven of witches looking to sacrifice one of her pupils. *Dir.* Cyril Frankel.

Witches, The (1990) Anjelica Huston (Miss Eva Ernst/Grand High Witch), Mai Zetterling (Helga Eveshim), Jasen Fisher (Luke

Eveshim), Rowan Atkinson (Mr. Stringer), Bill Paterson (Mr. Jenkins), Brenda Blethyn (Mrs. Jenkins), Charlie Potter (Bruno Jenkins), Jane Horrocks (Miss Irvine), Anne Lambton (Woman in Black), Sukie Smith (Marlene), Rose English (Dora), Jenny Runacre (Elsie), Annabel Brooks (Nicola), Emma Relph (Millie), Nora Connolly (Beatrice), Rosamund Greenwood (Janice), Angelique Rockas (Henrietta), Jim Carter (Head Chef), Roberta Taylor (Witch Chef), Brian Hawksley (Elderly Waiter), Debra Gillett (Waitress), Darcy Flynn (Luke's Mother), Vincent Marzello (Luke's Father), Serena Harragin (Doctor), Grete Nordrå (Norwegian Witch), Elsie Eide (Erica), Kristin Steinsland (Child Helga), Merete Armand (Erica's Mother), Ola Otnes (Erica's Father). After Luke is orphaned his grandmother takes him on holiday. The hotel they are staying in is host to a convention of witches who wish to rid the world of all children. Adaptation of Roald Dahl's book of the same name. *Dir.* Nicolas Roeg.

Witchfinder General (1968) Vincent Price (Matthew Hopkins), Ian Ogilvy (Richard Marshall), Rupert Davies (John Lowes), Patrick Wymark (Oliver Cromwell), Wilfrid Brambell (Master Loach), Hilary Heath (Sara Lowes), Robert Russell (John Stearne), Nicky Henson (Trooper Robert Swallow), Tony Selby (Tom Salter), Michael Beint (Captain Gordon), Bernard Kay (Fisherman), Beaufoy Milton (Priest), Sally Douglas (Girl at Hoxne Inn), Peter Haigh (Lavenham Magistrate), Godfrey James (Webb), Margaret Nolan (Girl at Inn). During the English Civil War Matthew Hopkins begins a reign of terror in East Anglia as he moves from village to village accusing people of being witches and extracting confessions under torture. *Dir.* Michael Reeves.

Withnail and I (1987) Richard E Grant (Withnail), Paul McGann (Peter Marwood, "I"), Richard Griffiths (Uncle Monty), Ralph Brown (Danny), Michael Elphick (Jake), Daragh O'Malley (Irishman), Michael Wardle (Isaac Parkin), Una Brandon-Jones (Mrs. Parkin), Noel Johnson (General), Irene Sutcliffe (Waitress), Eddie Tagoe (Presuming Ed), Llewellyn Rees (Tea Shop Proprietor), Robert Oates (Policeman One), Anthony Wise (Policeman Two). Set in 1969, two unemployed young actors leave their filthy flat in Camden and journey to a cottage in the Lake District belonging to Withnail's gay uncle Monty. Unfortunately the holiday does not turn out to be as restful as they had hoped. *Dir.* Bruce Robinson.

Without a Clue (1988) Michael Caine (Sherlock Holmes/Reginald Kincaid), Ben Kingsley (Dr. John Watson), Jeffrey Jones (Inspector George Lestrade), Lysette Anthony (Lesley Giles), Paul Freeman (Professor James Moriarty), Pat Keen (Mrs. Hudson), Matthew Savage (Wiggins), Nigel Davenport (Lord Smithwick), Tim Killick (Sebastian Moran), Peter Cook (Norman Greenhough), John Warner (Peter Giles), Matthew Sim (Lesley Giles), Fredrick Fox (Priest), Harold Innocent (Lord Mayor), Gerald Fitzwalter (Johnson), George Sweeney (John Clay), Murray Ewan (Archie), Jennifer Guy (Lord Mayor's daughter). A film built around the premise that Dr Watson is in fact the genius and hires an actor to play the part of the fictional Sherlock Holmes. *Dir.* Thom Eberhardt.

Witness For the Prosecution (1957) Tyrone Power (Leonard Vole), Marlene Dietrich (Christine Vole/Helm), Charles Laughton (Sir Wilfred Robarts), Elsa Lanchester (Miss Plimsoll), John Williams (Brogan-Moore), Henry Daniell (Mayhew), Ian Wolfe (Carter), Torin Thatcher (Mr. Myers), Norma Varden (Mrs Emily Jane French), Una O'Connor (Janet McKenzie), Francis Compton (Judge), Philip Tonge (Inspector Hearne), Ruta Lee (Diana). When Leonard Vole stands trial for murder his barrister is surprised to find that his wife is a prosecution witness. *Dir.* Billy Wilder.

Wittgenstein (1993) Karl Johnson (Ludwig Wittgenstein), Clancy Chassay (Young Ludwig Wittgenstein), Michael Gough (Bertrand Russell), Tilda Swinton (Lady Ottoline Morrell), John Quentin (Maynard Keynes), Kevin Collins (Johnny), Lynn Seymour (Lydia Lopokova), Jill Balcon (Leopoldine Wittgenstein), Sally Dexter (Hermine Wittgenstein), Gina Marsh (Gretyl Wittgenstein), Vanya Del Borgo (Helene Wittgenstein), Ben Scantlebury (Hans Wittgenstein), Howard Sooley (Kurt Wittgenstein), David Radzinowicz (Rudolf Wittgenstein), Jan Latham-Koenig (Paul Wittgenstein), Nabil Shaban (Martian). A biopic of the Austrian philosopher Ludwig Wittgenstein. *Dir.* Derek Jarman.

Woman in a Dressing Gown (1957) Yvonne Mitchell (Amy Preston), Anthony Quayle (Jim Preston), Sylvia Syms (Georgie Harlow), Andrew Ray (Brian Preston), Carole Lesley (Hilda), Michael Ripper (Pawnbroker), Nora Gordon (Mrs. Williams), Marianne Stone (Hairdresser), Olga Lindo (Manageress), Harry Locke (Wine merchant), Max Butterfield (Harold), Roberta Woolley (Christine), Melvyn Hayes (Newsboy). Amy is a disorganised woman who spends much of her time wearing a dressing gown rather than getting dressed. She is shocked when her husband asks for a divorce so that he can marry a co-worker. *Dir.* J. Lee Thompson

Woman in Black, The (2012) Daniel Radcliffe (Arthur Kipps), Ciarán Hinds (Sam Daily), Janet McTeer (Mrs. Daily), Sophie Stuckey (Stella Kipps), Misha Handley (Joseph Kipps), Liz White (Jennet Humfrye), Alisa Khazanova (Alice Drablow), Daniel Cerqueira (Keckwick), Tim McMullan (Mr Jerome), Aoife Doherty (Lucy Jerome), Roger Allam (Mr Bentley), Alexia Osborne (Victoria Hardy), Victor McGuire (Gerald Hardy), David Burke (PC Collins), Ashley Foster (Nathaniel). A young solicitor is sent to Eel Marsh House, a dilapidated mansion with a terrible history. Based on Susan Hill's novel of the same name. *Dir.* James Watkins.

Woman in Question, The (1950) Jean Kent (Agnes/Madame Astra), Dirk Bogarde (R.W. (Bob) Baker), John McCallum (Michael Murray), Susan Shaw (Catherine Taylor), Hermione Baddeley (Mrs. Finch), Charles Victor (Albert Pollard), Duncan Macrae (Supt. Lodge), Lana Morris (Lana Clark), Joe Linnane (Inspector Butler), Vida Hope (Shirley Jones), John Boxer (Detective Lucas), Albert Chevalier (W.T. Gunter), Julian D'Albie (Police Surgeon), Anthony Dawson (Inspector Wilson), Richard Dunn (Police Sergeant), Ian Fleming (Doctor). Investigations reveal that a murdered woman was viewed very differently by the various people interviewed concerning her death. *Dir.* Anthony Asquith.

Woman of Straw (1964) Gina Lollobrigida (Maria Marcello), Sean Connery (Anthony 'Tony' Richmond), Ralph Richardson (Charles Richmond), Alexander Knox (Detective Inspector Lomer), Johnny Sekka (Thomas), Laurence Hardy (Baynes, the butler), Peter Madden (Yacht Captain), Danny Daniels (Fenton), Noel Howlett (Assistant Solicitor), Michael Goodliffe (Solicitor), Peggy Marshall (Wardress), André Morell (Judge). A rich old man's nurse is persuaded by his scheming nephew to marry the sick man and thus inherit the man's fortune and share it with him. *Dir.* Basil Dearden.

Women in Love (1969) Alan Bates (Rupert Birkin), Oliver Reed (Gerald Crich), Glenda Jackson (Gudrun Brangwen), Jennie Linden (Ursula Brangwen), Eleanor Bron (Hermione Roddice), Alan Webb (Thomas Crich), Vladek Sheybal (Loerke), Catherine Willmer (Mrs. Crich), Phoebe Nicholls (Winifred Crich), Sharon Gurney (Laura Crich), Christopher Gable (Tibby Lupton), Michael Gough (Tom Brangwen), Norma Shebbeare (Mrs. Brangwen), Nike Arrighi (Contessa), James Laurenson (Minister), Michael Graham Cox (Palmer). The story of two sisters (Gudrun and Ursula) and the men in their lives, friends Gerald and Rupert with different attitudes to the meaning of love. The film won one Academy Award: Best Actress in a Leading Role (Glenda Jackson). Adapted from the novel of the same name by D. H. Lawrence. *Dir.* Ken Russell.

Wonderful Life (1964) Cliff Richard (Johnnie), Walter Slezak (Lloyd Davis), Susan Hampshire (Jenny Taylor), Melvyn Hayes (Jerry), Una Stubbs (Barbara Tate), Derek Bond (Douglas Leslie), Joseph Cuby (Miguel), Richard O'Sullivan (Edward), Gerald Harper (Sheik/Scotsman/Harold), Bruce Welch, John Rostill, Brian Bennett, Hank B. Marvin (The Shadows). Some young people decide that the film they are making could be improved by adding a few song and dance numbers. *Dir.* Sidney J Furie.

Wonderland (1999) Shirley Henderson (Debbie), Gina McKee (Nadia), Molly Parker (Molly), Ian Hart (Dan), John Simm (Eddie), Stuart Townsend (Tim), Kika Markham (Eileen), Jack Shepherd (Bill), Enzo Cilenti (Darren), Sarah-Jane Potts (Melanie), David Fahm (Franklyn), Ellen Thomas (Donna), Peter Marfleet (Jack), Nathan Constance (Alex), Anton Saunders (Danny), Abby Ford (Nurse), Michelle Jolly (Midwife), Rebecca Lenkiewicz (Policewoman), Vanessa Pratt (Kelly), Mark Sproston (Rupert). The story of Bill and Eileen and their three daughters

Debbie, Nadia and Molly over the course of a long November weekend. *Dir*. Michael Winterbottom.

Wonderwall (1968) Jack MacGowran (Prof. Oscar Collins), Jane Birkin (Penny), Irene Handl (Mrs. Peurofoy), Richard Wattis (Perkins), Iain Quarrier (Young Man), Beatrix Lehmann (Mother), Brian Walsh (Photographer), Sean Lynch (Riley), Bee Duffell (Mrs. Charmer), Noel Trevarthen (Policeman), Suki Potier (Girl at party), Anita Pallenberg (Girl at Party). A reclusive professor becomes obsessed with his model neighbour Penny Lane after he sees her through a hole in the wall dividing their apartments. *Dir*. Joe Massot.

Wooden Horse, The (1950) Leo Genn (Peter Howard), David Tomlinson (Phil), Anthony Steel (John Clinton), David Greene (Bennett), Peter Burton (Nigel), Patrick Waddington (Senior British Officer), Michael Goodliffe (Robbie), Anthony Dawson (Pomfret), Bryan Forbes (Paul), Dan Cunningham (David), Peter Finch (Australian in Hospital), Philip Dale (Bill White), Russell Waters ('Wings' Cameron), Ralph Ward (Adjutant), Franz Schafheitlin (Camp Commandant), Herbert Eilitz (Camp guard), Lis Løwert (Kamma), Jacques B. Brunius (André), Helge Erickssen (Sigmund), Meinhart Maur (Hotel proprietor), Walter Gotell (The follower), Walter Hertner (German policeman), Hans Meyer (Charles aka Charlie - Head ferret), Paul Stockman (Hunky), Bill Travers (Prisoner). A fictionalised version of the true story of the escape from a German POW camp by using a wooden horse used for gymnastics to conceal the entrance to an escape tunnel. Based on the book of the same name by Eric Williams. *Dir*. Jack Lee.

World Is Not Enough, The (1999) Pierce Brosnan (James Bond), Denise Richards (Dr. Christmas Jones), Robert Carlyle (Renard), Sophie Marceau (Elektra King), Robbie Coltrane (Valentin Zukovsky), Judi Dench (M), Colin Salmon (Charles Robinson), Desmond Llewelyn (Q), John Cleese (R), Samantha Bond (Miss Moneypenny), Serena Scott Thomas (Dr. Molly Warmflash), John Seru (Gabor), Ulrich Thomsen (Sasha Davidov), Goldie (Bullion), Maria Grazia Cucinotta (Giulietta da Vinci). Sir Robert is assassinated and Bond is assigned to protect his daughter from the evil Renard, a KGB agent-turned-terrorist. This was Desmond Llewelyn's last appearance as Q before his death in a car accident. Bond drives a silver coloured BMW Z8. The theme song is performed by Garbage. *Dir*. Michael Apted.

World Owes Me a Living, The (1945) David Farrar (Paul Collyer), Judy Campbell (Moira Barrett), Sonia Dresdel (Eve Heatherley), Jack Livesey (Jack Graves), Eric Barker (Chuck Rockley), John Laurie (Matthews), Anthony Hawtrey (Jerry), Wylie Watson (Conductor), Joss Ambler (Man in bar), Stewart Rome (Air Vice-Marshal), Amy Veness (Mrs. Waterman), Mackenzie Ward (Tommy Tindsley). Paul suffers amnesia after crashing his plane during WWII but his memory is gradually restored as we see (in flashback) his recollections of his earlier life. Based on a novel by John Llewellyn-Rhys. *Dir*. Vernon Sewell.

Wrong Arm of the Law, The (1962) Peter Sellers (Pearly Gates), Lionel Jeffries (Inspector Fred 'Nosey' Parker), Bernard Cribbins (Nervous O'Toole), Davy Kaye (Trainer King), Nanette Newman (Valerie), Bill Kerr (Jack Coombes), Ed Devereaux (Bluey May), Reg Lye (Reg Denton), John Le Mesurier (Assistant Commissioner), Graham Stark (Sid Cooper), Martin Boddey (Superintendent J.S. Forest), Irene Browne (Dowager), Arthur Mullard (Brassknuckles), Dermot Kelly (Misery Martin), Vanda Godsell (Annette), Tutte Lemkow (Siggy Schmoltz), Barry Keegan (Alf), Michael Caine (Police Station PC), Dick Emery (Man in Flat 307), John Junkin (Maurice), Dennis Price (Educated Ernest), Cardew Robinson (Mailman), Gerald Sim (Airfield Official), Marianne Stone (Woman at Meeting). Two rival London criminal gangs join with police in trying to catch an Australian gang who have moved in on their patch by committing robberies dressed as coppers. *Dir*. Cliff Owen.

Wrong Box, The (1966) John Mills (Masterman Finsbury), Ralph Richardson (Joseph Finsbury), Michael Caine (Michael Finsbury), Peter Cook (Morris Finsbury), Dudley Moore (John Finsbury), Nanette Newman (Julia Finsbury), Peter Sellers (Dr. Pratt), Tony Hancock (Detective), Wilfrid Lawson (Peacock), Thorley Walters (Lawyer Patience), Cicely Courtneidge (Major Martha), Diane Clare (Mercy), Gerald Sim (First Undertaker), Irene Handl (Mrs. Hackett), John Le Mesurier (Dr. Slattery), Jeremy Lloyd (Brian Harvey), James Villiers (Sydney Sykes), Graham Stark (Ian Fife), Nicholas Parsons (Alan Scrope), Willoughby Goddard (James Wragg), Valentine Dyall (Oliver Harmsworth), Leonard Rossiter (Vyvyan Montague), Hamilton Dyce (Derek Digby), Hilton Edwards (Lawyer), Timothy Bateson (Clerk), Donald Oliver (Gunner Sergeant), Totti Truman Taylor (Lady at Launching), Jeremy Roughton (Bugler), Frank Singuineau (Native Bearer), Michael Lees (Young Digby), Avis Bunnage (Queen Victoria), Gwendolyn Watts (Maidservant), Vanda Godsell (Mrs. Goodge), Peter Graves (Military Officer), Tutte Lemkow (Strangler), Marianne Stone (Spinster), John Junkin (First Engine Driver), Roy Murray (Fred the Stoker), Donald Tandy (Ticket Collector), Lionel Gamlin (Second Engine Driver), Martin Terry (Stoker), Michael Bird (Countryman), George Selway (Railway Vanman), Josef Behrmann (Railway Vanman), Norman Rossington (First Rough), Thomas Gallagher (Second Rough), Charlie Bird (Benn's Vanman), Tony Thawnton (Second Undertaker), Temperance Seven (Themselves), Reg Lye (Third Undertaker), George Spence (Workman in Road), Norman Bird (Clergyman), Penny Brahms (Female on Moors), David Lodge (Corpse Remover), Juliet Mills (Mannish Woman on Train), André Morell (Club Butler). A black comedy in which two elderly brothers are the last surviving members of a tontine. Their direct descendants want to make sure that they get their hands on the fortune. *Dir*. Bryan Forbes.

Wrong Trousers, The (1993) Peter Sallis (Wallace – voice). Animated film featuring Wallace, Gromit, a pair of mechanical trousers and a sinister penguin named Feathers. It won the 1993 Academy Award for Animated Short Film. *Dir*. Nick Park.

Wuthering Heights (1970) Anna Calder-Marshall (Catherine Earnshaw Linton), Timothy Dalton (Heathcliff), Harry Andrews (Mr. Earnshaw), Pamela Brown (Mrs. Linton), Judy Cornwell (Nelly Dean), James Cossins (Mr. Linton), Rosalie Crutchley (Mrs. Earnshaw), Hilary Dwyer (Isabella Linton), Julian Glover (Hindley Earnshaw), Hugh Griffith (Dr. Kenneth), Morag Hood (Frances Earnshaw), Ian Ogilvy (Edgar Linton), Peter Sallis (Mr. Shielders), Aubrey Woods (Joseph). The lives of the Earnshaw children, Hindley and Catherine, are disrupted when their father adopts a gypsy boy and brings him back to Wuthering Heights, their house on the moors. Hindley is upset by the perceived dilution of his father's affections whilst Catherine is attracted to wild Heathcliff. Their passion is destined to destroy so many lives. Based on the early chapters of the classic Emily Bronte novel of the same name. *Dir*. Robert Fuest.

Wuthering Heights (1992) Ralph Fiennes (Heathcliff), Juliette Binoche (Cathy Earnshaw/Cathy Linton), Jeremy Northam (Hindley Earnshaw), Simon Shepherd (Edgar Linton), Sophie Ward (Isabella Linton), Janet McTeer (Nelly Dean), Jason Riddington (Hareton Earnshaw), Jonathan Firth (Linton Heathcliff), Sinéad O'Connor (Emily Bronte), Simon Ward (Mr. Linton), Dick Sullivan (Parson), Robert Demeger (Joseph), Paul Geoffrey (Mr. Lockwood), John Woodvine (Mr. Earnshaw), Jennifer Daniel (Mrs. Linton), Janine Wood (Frances Earnshaw), Jonathan Firth (Linton Heathcliff), Jon Howard (Young Heathcliff), Jessica Hennell (Young Cathy), Trevor Cooper (Dr. Kenneth), Steven Slarke (Hindley Earnshaw age 16), Rupert Holliday-Evans (Vicar), Sean Bowden (Young Hareton). An adaptation of the novel of the same name by Emily Bronte, which unlike most film versions also includes the story of the children of Cathy, Hindley and Heathcliff. *Dir*. Peter Kosminsky.

X the Unknown (1956) Dean Jagger (Dr. Adam Royston), Edward Chapman (John Elliott), Leo McKern (Insp. McGill), Anthony Newley (LCpl. 'Spider' Webb), Jameson Clark (Jack Harding), William Lucas (Peter Elliott), Peter Hammond (Lt. Bannerman), Marianne Brauns (Zena), Ian MacNaughton (Haggis), Michael Ripper (Sgt. Harry Grimsdyke), John Harvey (Major Cartwright), Jane Aird (Vi Harding), Norman Macowan (Old Tom), Neil Hallett (Unwin), Kenneth Cope (Sapper Lansing), Michael Brooke (Willie Harding), Frazer Hines (Ian

Osborn), Robert Bruce (Dr. Kelly), Edward Judd (2nd Soldier), Shaw Taylor (Police Radio Operator). Mysterious radiation is leaking from a bottomless crack near Glasgow. After the deaths of soldiers and locals, Dr Royston investigates. *Dir*. Leslie Norman.

Xtro (1983) Philip Sayer (Sam Phillips), Bernice Stegers (Rachel Phillips), Danny Brainin (Joe Daniels), Maryam d'Abo (Analise Mercier), Simon Nash (Tony Phillips), Peter Mandell (Clown), David Cardy (Michael), Anna Wing (Mrs. Goodman), Robert Fyfe (Doctor), Katherine Best (Jane), Robert Pereno (Ben), Sean Crawford (Commando), Tim Dry (Monster), Arthur Whybrow (Mr. Knight), Anna Mottram (Teacher), Susie Silvey (Woman in Cottage), Robert Austin (Van Driver), Vanya Seager (Paula Phillips). Sam is abducted by aliens and reappears three years later with an extra-terrestrial core. *Dir*. Harry Bromley Davenport.

Yangtse Incident: The Story of HMS Amethyst (1957) Richard Todd (Lt. Cmdr. Kerans, RN), William Hartnell (Leading Seaman Frank), Akim Tamiroff (Col. Peng), Donald Houston (Lt Weston RN), Keye Luke (Capt. Kuo Tai), Sophie Stewart (Miss Charlotte Dunlap), Robert Urquhart (Flt Lt Fearnley RAF), James Kenney (Lt Hett RN), Richard Leech (Lt Strain RN), Michael Brill (Lt Berger RN), Barry Foster (PO McCarthy RN), Thomas Heathcote (Mr. Monaghan RN), Sam Kydd (AB Walker RN), Ewen Solon (ERA Williams RN), John Charlesworth (Roberts), Kenneth Cope (Mr. McNamara), Alfred Burke (Petty Officer), John A. Tinn (Chinese pilot), Keith Rawlings (Crocker), Richard Coleman (Lt. Cmdr. Skinner), Murray Leask (Petty Officer), Ian Bannen (AB Bannister RN), Ray Jackson (Telegraphist French, RN), Gordon Whiting (Surgeon Lt. Alderton), Bernard Cribbins (Sonar Operator), Gene Anderson (Ruth Worth), Cyril Luckham (Commander-in-Chief Far Eastern Station), Allan Cuthbertson (Captain Donaldson RN), Ballard Berkeley (Lt. Col. Dewar-Curie). A fictionalised account of the true story of HMS *Amethyst*, which was trapped on the Yangtse during the Chinese Civil War. *Dir*. Michael Anderson.

Yank at Oxford, A (1938) Robert Taylor (Lee Sheridan), Lionel Barrymore (Dan Sheridan), Maureen O'Sullivan (Molly Beaumont), Vivien Leigh (Elsa Craddock), Edmund Gwenn (Dean of Cardinal), Griffith Jones (Paul Beaumont), C.V. France (Dean Snodgrass), Edward Rigby (Scatters), Morton Selten (Cecil Davidson, Esq.), Claude Gillingwater (Ben Dalton), Tully Marshall (Cephas), Walter Kingsford (Dean Williams), Robert Coote (Wavertree), Peter Croft (Ramsey), Noel Howlett (Tom Craddock), Ronald Shiner (Bicycle repairman), Jon Pertwee (Extra). An American receives a scholarship to attend Oxford University and, after a shaky start, settles in and makes friends. However, just before his father arrives for a visit, he is expelled from the college. *Dir*. Jack Conway. The film was parodied in the 1940 Laurel and Hardy film *A Chump at Oxford* and remade in 1984 as *Oxford Blues*. A 1942 sequel *A Yank at Eton* was less successful.

Yanks (1979) Richard Gere (Matt Dyson), Lisa Eichhorn (Jean Moreton), Vanessa Redgrave (Helen), William Devane (John), Chick Vennera (Danny Ruffelo), Wendy Morgan (Mollie), Rachel Roberts (Mrs. Clarrie Moreton), Tony Melody (Mr. Jim Moreton), Martin Smith (Geoff), Philip Whileman (Billy), Derek Thompson (Ken), Simon Harrison (Tim), Joan Hickson (Mrs. Moody), Arlen Dean Snyder (Henry), Annie Ross (Red Cross lady), Tom Nolan (Tom G.I. drummer), John Ratzenberger (Corporal Cook), Antony Sher (G.I. at cinema). American G.I.s and English women begin relationships while the Yanks are billeted in a Lancashire town during the preparations for D-Day. *Dir*. John Schlesinger.

Years Between, The (1946) Michael Redgrave (Michael Wentworth), Valerie Hobson (Diana Wentworth), Flora Robson (Nanny), James McKechnie (Richard Llewellyn), Felix Aylmer (Sir Ernest Foster), Dulcie Gray (Judy), John Gilpin (Robin Wentworth), Yvonne Owen (Alice), Wylie Watson (Venning), Esma Cannon (Effie), Lyn Evans (Ames), Joss Ambler (Atherton), Ernest Butcher (Old Man), Katie Johnson (Old Man's Wife), Muriel Aked (Mrs. May), Michael Hordern (MP). Three years after his presumed death in a plane crash Michael Wentworth returns to his wife and reveals that he was organising resistance in Occupied Europe. An adaptation of the play of the same name by Daphne du Maurier. *Dir*. Compton Bennett.

Yellow Canary (1943) Anna Neagle (Sally), Richard Greene (Lieutenant Commander Jim Garrick), Nova Pilbeam (Betty

Maitland), Albert Lieven (Jan Orlock), Lucie Mannheim (Madame Orlock), George Thorpe (Colonel Charles Hargraves), Marjorie Fielding (Lady Maitland), Franklin Dyall (Captain Foster), Margaret Rutherford (Mrs. Towcester), Claude Bailey (Major Fothergill), Sybille Binder (Madame Orlock's Attendant), Valentine Dyall (German Commander), Cyril Fletcher (Entertainer), Grace Allardyce (Maitland's Maid), Madge Brindley (Newspaper Seller at Railway Station), Paul Dupuis (Paul), Leslie Dwyer (Ship's Steward), Aubrey Mallalieu (Reynolds). Upper class Sally Maitland is such a well-known Nazi sympathiser that she has to leave Britain for Canada when WWII breaks out. But is she all she appears? *Dir*. Herbert Wilcox.

Yellow Rolls-Royce, The (1964) Ingrid Bergman (Gerda Millett), Rex Harrison (Lord Charles Frinton), Shirley MacLaine (Mae Jenkins), Jeanne Moreau (Lady Eloise Frinton), George C. Scott (Paolo Maltese), Omar Sharif (Davich), Alain Delon (Stefano), Art Carney (Joey Friedlander), Joyce Grenfell (Hortense Astor), Edmund Purdom (Fane), Michael Hordern (Harnsworth), Lance Percival (Assistant Car Salesman), Roland Culver (Norwood), Moira Lister (Lady Angela St. Simeon), Harold Scott (Taylor), Richard Pearson (Osborn), Isa Miranda (Duchesse d'Angouleme), Grégoire Aslan (Albanian Ambassador), Riccardo Garrone (Bomba), Wally Cox (Ferguson), Carlo Croccolo (Michele), Guy Deghy (Mayor), Martin Miller (Head Waiter). The stories of three owners of a distinctive yellow 1930 Rolls-Royce Phantom II during the 1930s and early 1940s. From the same team which produced *The V.I.P.s* (1963) with an equally international all-star cast. *Dir*. Anthony Asquith.

Yellow Submarine (1968) Voice cast: The Beatles (Sgt. Pepper's Lonely Hearts Club Band), Paul Angelis (Chief Blue Meanie/Ringo), John Clive (John), Dick Emery (Jeremy Hilary Boob, Ph.D - Nowhere Man/Lord Mayor/Max), Geoffrey Hughes (Paul), Lance Percival (Young/Old Fred), Peter Batten (George). An animated film using music by The Beatles. The band must save Pepperland from the terrible Blue Meanies. *Dir*. George Dunning.

Yesterday's Enemy (1959) Stanley Baker (Captain Langford), Guy Rolfe (Padre), Leo McKern (Max), Gordon Jackson (Sgt. MacKenzie), David Oxley (Doctor), Richard Pasco (2nd Lt. Hastings), Philip Ahn (Yamazuki), Bryan Forbes (Dawson), Wolfe Morris (Informer), David Lodge (Perkins), Percy Herbert (Wilson), Russell Waters (Brigadier), Barry Lowe (Turner), Burt Kwouk (Japanese Soldier), Donald Churchill (Elliott). During WWII a small group of British soldiers reach a Burmese village and manage to kill the Japanese soldiers who controlled it. They find a dead Japanese officer carrying a map with markings which they do not understand. The British captain threatens to execute villagers unless the meaning of the markings is revealed. *Dir*. Val Guest.

Yield to the Night (1956) Diana Dors (Mary Price Hilton), Yvonne Mitchell (Matron Hilda MacFarlane), Michael Craig (Jim Lancaster), Marie Ney (Prison Governess), Olga Lindo (Senior Matron Hill), Joan Miller (Matron Barker), Marjorie Rhodes (Matron Brandon), Geoffrey Keen (Prison Chaplain), Liam Redmond (Prison Doctor), Dandy Nichols (Mrs. Price), John Charlesworth (Alan Price), Mona Washbourne (Mrs. Thomas), Alec Finter (Mr. Thomas), Athene Seyler (Miss Bligh), Joyce Blair (Doris), Charles Clay (Bob), Michael Ripper (Roy), Harry Locke (Fred Hilton), Molly Urquhart (Mason), Mercia Shaw (Lucy Carpenter), Peggy Livesey (Prison Nurse), Charles Lloyd Pack (Mary's Lawyer), Frank Hawkins (Detective Sergeant), Marianne Stone (New Matron Richardson). Told using flashbacks, Mary Hilton, who is in the condemned cell waiting to be hanged for the murder of her lover Jim's mistress, reflects on the events which led her there. The film was also known as *Blonde Sinner,* which rather downplays Miss Dors effective performance in a role for which she wouldn't normally have been seen. Based on the novel of the same title by Joan Henry. *Dir*. J. Lee Thompson.

You Only Live Twice (1967) Sean Connery (James Bond), Akiko Wakabayashi (Aki), Mie Hama (Kissy), Tetsurô Tanba (Tiger Tanaka), Teru Shimada (Mr. Osato), Karin Dor (Helga Brandt), Donald Pleasence (Blofeld), Bernard Lee ('M'), Lois Maxwell (Miss Moneypenny), Desmond Llewelyn ('Q'), Charles Gray (Henderson), Tsai Chin (Ling), Peter Fanene Maivia (Car

Driver), Burt Kwouk (Spectre 3), Michael Chow (Spectre 4), Ronald Rich (Hans), Jeanne Roland (Bond's Masseuse), David Toguri (Assassin in Bedroom), John Stone (Submarine Captain), Norman Jones (Astronaut), Paul Carson (Astronaut), Laurence Herder (Astronaut), Richard Graydon (Astronaut), Bill Mitchell (Astronaut), George Roubicek (Astronaut), Anthony Ainley (Hong Kong Policeman), Vic Armstrong (Ninja), Robin Bailey (Foreign Secretary), George Baker (NASA Engineer), Ed Bishop (Hawaii CapCom), Richard Marner (Russian Spacecraft Communicator), Shane Rimmer (Hawaii Radar Operator), Brian Wilde (1st Policeman). After a US space craft is "captured" Bond is sent to Japan to discover which organization could have been behind the highjacking. His investigations eventually lead him to an extinct Japanese volcano. The only car really featured in this film is a Toyota 2000GT convertible but Bond flies an autogyro known as "Little Nellie". The title song was sung by Nancy Sinatra and the screenplay completed by Roald Dahl from material using the original Ian Fleming story of the same name and additional ideas from Harold Bloom. *Dir.* Lewis Gilbert.

Young Adam (2003) Ewan McGregor (Joe), Tilda Swinton (Ella Gault), Peter Mullan (Les Gault), Emily Mortimer (Cathie Dimly), Jack McElhone (Jim Gault), Therese Bradley (Gwen), Ewan Stewart (Daniel Gordon), Stuart McQuarrie (Bill), Pauline Turner (Connie), Alan Cooke (Bob M'bussi), Rory McCann (Sam), Michael Carter (Prosecutor), Struan Rodger (Judge), Mathew Zajac (Forensics Expert), Mhairi Morrison (Cathie's Flatmate), John Comerford (Jury Foreman), Anne Marie Timoney (Mrs Gordon), John Yule (Clerk of the Court), Sandy Neilson (Defence Counsel), Des Hamilton (Witness), Eddie Dahlstrom (Blind Man). Set in Scotland in the early 1950s, young drifter Joe Taylor is working on a barge on the River Clyde when he pulls the body of a half naked woman out of the water. From flashbacks it is clear that Joe and the dead woman once had a relationship. Based on the novel of the same name by Alexander Trocchi. *Dir.* David Mackenzie.

Young and Innocent (1937) Nova Pilbeam (Erica Burgoyne), Derrick De Marney (Robert Tisdall), Percy Marmont (Colonel Burgoyne), Edward Rigby (Old Will), John Longden (Inspector Kent), Mary Clare (Erica's Aunt), George Curzon (Guy), Basil Radford (Erica's Uncle), Pamela Carme (Christine Clay), George Merritt (DS Miller), J. H. Roberts (Solicitor), Jerry Verno (Lorry driver), H. F. Maltby (Police sergeant), John Miller (Police Constable), Jack Vyvian (Police Constable), Syd Crossley (Policeman), Bill Shine (Cafe manager), Torin Thatcher (Lodging House Caretaker). When Robert Tisdall is wrongly accused of Christine's murder he goes on the run with the aid of Erica, the daughter of a Chief Constable. Hitchcock's cameo in this film is as a clumsy press photographer. Loosely based on Josephine Tey's novel *A Shilling for Candles*. *Dir.* Alfred Hitchcock.

Young Cassidy (1965) Rod Taylor (John Cassidy), Maggie Smith (Nora), Julie Christie (Daisy Battles), Michael Redgrave (W.B. Yeats), Edith Evans (Augusta, Lady Gregory), T. P. McKenna (Tom), Jack MacGowran (Archie), Siân Phillips (Ella), Flora Robson (Mrs. Cassidy), Julie Ross (Sara), Robin Sumner (Michael), Philip O'Flynn (Mick Mullen), Pauline Delaney (Bessie Ballynoy), Harry Brogan (Murphy), Eddie Golden (Captain White), James Fitzgerald (Charlie Ballynoy), Eamon Kelly (Feeney), Harold Goldblatt (Abbey Theatre Manager), Daniel Skidd (Shelly), Henry B. Longhurst (Doctor), David Kelly (O'Brien). A dramatisation of the life of playwright Sean O'Casey based on O'Casey's autobiography *Mirror in my House*. *Dirs.* John Ford and Jack Cardiff.

Young Lovers, The (1954) Odile Versois (Anna Szobek), David Knight (Ted Hutchens), Joseph Tomelty (Moffatt), Theodore Bikel (Joseph), Paul Carpenter (Gregg Pearson), Peter Illing (Dr. Weissbrod), John McLaren (Col. Margetson), David Kossoff (Geza Szobek), Bernard Rebel (Stefan), Jill Adams (Judy), Robin Bailey (Thomas Cook cashier), Dora Bryan (Switchboard Operator), Peter Dyneley (Regan), Percy Herbert (Richards), Sam Kydd (Driver), Victor Maddern (Sailor), Betty Marsden (Mrs. Forrester), Aubrey Mather (Waiter), Joan Sims (Telephone Operator), Anna and Ted meet and fall in love. The only problem

is that she is Russian, he is American and it is the 1950s. *Dir.* Anthony Asquith.

Young Mr Pitt, The (1942) Robert Donat (William Pitt), Robert Morley (Charles James Fox), Phyllis Calvert (Eleanor Eden), John Mills (William Wilberforce), Geoffrey Atkins (William Pitt, as a boy), Jean Cadell (Mrs. Sparry), Raymond Lovell (George the Third), Agnes Lauchlan (Queen Charlotte), Felix Aylmer (Lord North), Ian McLean (Dundas), Max Adrian (Richard Sheridan), A. Bromley Davenport (Sir Evan Nepean), John Salew (Smith), Herbert Lom (Napoleon), Albert Lieven (Tallerand), Stephen Haggard (Lord Nelson), Stuart Lindsell (Earl Spencer), Henry Hewitt (Addington), Frederick Culley (Sir William. Farquhar), Leslie Bradley (Gentleman Jackson), Roy Emerton (Dan Mendoza), Hugh McDermott (Mr. Melvill), Alfred Sangster (Lord Grenville), Kathleen Byron (Millicent Grey), Esma Cannon (Servant at Lord Auckland's), Leslie Dwyer (Servant at Lord Auckland's), Leo Genn (Danton), Frederick Leister (Lord Auckland), Aubrey Mallalieu (Somerset), Ronald Shiner (Man in Stocks), Jack Watling (Atkinson). A biopic of British Prime Minister William Pitt the Younger paralleling his struggles against Revolutionary France and Napoleon with the (then) current conflict with Hitler. *Dir.* Carol Reed.

Young Ones, The (1961) Cliff Richard (Nicky), Robert Morley (Hamilton Black), Carole Gray (Toni), Jet Harris, Hank B. Marvin, Tony Meehan, Bruce Welch (The Shadows), Teddy Green (Chris), Richard O'Sullivan (Ernest), Melvyn Hayes (Jimmy), Annette Robertson (Barbara), Robertson Hare (Chauffeur), Sonya Cordeau (Dorinda), Sean Sullivan (Eddie), Harold Scott (Dench), Gerald Harper (Watts), Rita Webb (Woman in Market). When faced with the demolition of their youth club by developer Hamilton Black, the gang decide to "put on a show right here", but Nicky has a secret. *Dir.* Sidney J. Furie.

Young Poisoner's Handbook, The (1995) Hugh O'Conor (Graham Young), Tobias Arnold (Young Graham Young), Ruth Sheen (Molly), Roger Lloyd-Pack (Fred), Norman Caro (Mr. Goez), Dorothea Alexander (Mrs. Goez), Charlotte Coleman (Winnie), Paul Stacey (Dennis), Samantha Edmonds (Sue), Robert Demeger (Mr. Dexter), Jack Deam (Mick), Peter Pacey (Dickie Boone), Joost Siedhoff (Dr. Scott), Vilma Hollingbery (Aunty Panty), Frank Mills (Uncle Jack), Rupert Farley (Nurse Trent), Dirk Robertson (Nurse Hopwood), Chris Lawson (Prison Officer), Malcolm Sinclair (Dr. Triefus), Charlie Creed-Miles (Berridge), Antony Sher (Dr. Ernest Zeigler), Cate Fowler (Social Services Woman), John Abbott (Chairman), Hazel Douglas (Edna), Arthur Cox (Ray), John Thomson (Nathan), Jean Warren (Debra), Simon Kunz (John), Frank Coda (Billy), Tim Potter (Simon), Roger Frost (Factory Manager), David Savile (Chief Medical Inspector), Mark Kempner (Mark). Loosely based biopic of Graham Young, known as "The Teacup Murderer". After being incarcerated as a teenager for killing his step-mother by putting thallium in her food and drink, Graham is released and finds work at a factory which uses thallium in its production process. Soon his workmates begin to feel ill. *Dir.* Benjamin Ross.

Young Victoria, The (2010) Emily Blunt (Queen Victoria), Rupert Friend (Prince Albert of Saxe-Coburg and Gotha), Miranda Richardson (Duchess of Kent), Mark Strong (Sir John Conroy), Jim Broadbent (King William IV), Harriet Walter (Queen Adelaide), Paul Bettany (Lord Melbourne), Thomas Kretschmann (King Leopold I of Belgium), Jesper Christensen (Baron Stockma), Jeanette Hain (Baroness Louise Lehzen), Julian Glover (Duke of Wellington), Michael Maloney (Sir Robert Peel), Michiel Huisman (Prince Ernest of Saxe-Coburg and Gotha), Johnnie Lyne-Pirkis (Prince Ernest Augustus, Duke of Cumberland), Liam Scott (Prince Augustus Frederick, Duke of Sussex), Dave A. Hewitt (Duke of Norfolk), Danny Dalton (Prince of Prussia), Sophie Roberts (Lady Emma Portman), Rachael Stirling (Duchess of Sutherland), Genevieve O'Reilly (Lady Flora Hastings), Roddy Weaver (William IV's Chief Footman), David Robb (Lord John Russell), Emily Eby (Lady Eliza), Alice Glover (Duchess of Montrose), David Horovitch (Sir James Clark), Bernard Lloyd (Archbishop of Canterbury), Morven Christie (Watson), Josef Altin (Edward Oxford),

322

Michaela Brooks (Young Victoria Age 11), Grace Smith (Young Victoria Age 5), Robert Cambrinus (Kammerherr Turner), Tom Fisher (Lord Chamberlain), Johnnie Lyne-Pirkis (Earl of Derby), Iain Mitchell (Speaker), Malcolm Sinclair (Charles Kemble), Julia St. John (Marchioness of Hastings), Princess Beatrice of York (Lady-in-waiting). A biopic depicting the early life and reign of Queen Victoria and her marriage to Prince Albert of Saxe-Coburg and Gotha. The film won one Academy Award: Best Costume Design. *Dir* Jean-Marc Vallée.

Young Winston (1972) Robert Shaw (Lord Randolph Churchill), Anne Bancroft (Lady Randolph Churchill), Simon Ward (Winston Churchill), Jack Hawkins (Mr. Welldon), Ian Holm (George E. Buckle), Anthony Hopkins (David Lloyd George), Patrick Magee (General Bindon Blood), Edward Woodward (Captain Aylmer Haldane), John Mills (General Kitchener), Peter Cellier (Captain 35th Sikhs), Ronald Hines (Adjutant 35th Sikhs), Pat Heywood (Mrs. Everest), Laurence Naismith (Lord Salisbury), Basil Dignam (Joseph Chamberlain), Robert Hardy (Headmaster), Russell Lewis (Winston Churchill - age 7), Pat Heywood (Mrs. Everest), William Dexter (Arthur Balfour), Basil Dignam (Joseph Chamberlain), Richard Leech (Mr. Moore), Clive Morton (Dr. Robson Roose), Robert Flemyng (Dr. Buzzard), Reginald Marsh (Prince of Wales), Jane Seymour (Pamela Plowden), Dinsdale Landen (Capt. Weaver), Julian Holloway (Capt. Baker), Thorley Walters (Major Finn), Patrick Holt (Col. Martin), Gerald Sim (Engineer), Andrew Faulds (Mounted Boer), Maurice Roëves (Sergeant Major Brockie), James Cossins (Barnsby), John Woodvine (John Howard), Norman Rossington (Daniel Dewsnap), Pippa Steel (Clementine Hozier), Dino Shafeek (Sikh Soldier), Michael Audreson (Winston Churchill - age 13), Edward Burnham (Henry Labouchere), Colin Blakely (Butcher), Norman Bird (Party Chairman), A biopic of the early life of Winston Churchill covering his school days, his army service in India and the Sudan, his experiences as a war correspondent in the Boer War, and his election to Parliament at the age of 26. Based on the book *My Early Life: A Roving Commission by Winston Churchill*. *Dir*. Richard Attenborough.

Young Wives' Tale (1951) Joan Greenwood (Sabina Pennant), Nigel Patrick (Rodney Pennant), Derek Farr (Bruce Banning), Guy Middleton (Victor Manifold), Athene Seyler (Nanny Gallop), Helen Cherry (Mary Banning), Audrey Hepburn (Eve Lester), Fabia Drake (Nanny Blott), Selma Vaz Dias (Ayah), Irene Handl (Nanny), Carole James (Elizabeth), Jack McNaughton (Cab driver), Joan Sanderson (Nurse). A shy woman shares a house with two couples. Comedy ensues, apparently. *Dir*. Henry Cass.

Your Witness (1950) Robert Montgomery (Adam Heyward), Michael Ripper (Samuel 'Sam' Baxter), Leslie Banks (Col. Roger Summerfield), Felix Aylmer (The British Judge), Andrew Cruickshank (Sir Adrian Horth), Patricia Cutts (Alex Summerfield), Harcourt Williams (Richard Beamish), Stanley Baker (Police Sergeant), Jenny Laird (Mary Baxter), Ann Stephens ('Sandy' Summerfield), Wylie Watson (Mr. Widgery), Noel Howlett (Martin Foxglove), James Hayter (Prouty), John Sharp (PC Hawkins), Shelagh Fraser (Ellen Foster), Meadows White (Warder), Dandy Nichols (Waitress), Erik Chitty (Judge's Clerk), Amy Dalby (Mrs. Widgely), Philip Dale (Jim Foster), Wensley Pithey (Alfred), Hal Osmond (Taxi Driver), Lyonel Watts (Vicar), Derrick Penley (Clerk of Assize), Ruth Lee (Miss Hubert). American lawyer Adam Heyward travels to England to defend wartime friend Sam Baxter who is facing trial for the murder of his business partner. *Dir*. Robert Montgomery.

Zarak (1956) Victor Mature (Zarak Khan), Michael Wilding (Major Michael Ingram), Anita Ekberg (Salma), Bonar Colleano (Biri), Eunice Gayson (Cathy Ingram), Finlay Currie (The Mullah), Peter Illing (Ahmad), Bernard Miles (Hassu the one-eyed), Eddie Byrne (Kasim), Patrick McGoohan (Moor Larkin), Frederick Valk (Haji Khan), André Morell (Maj. Atherton), Harold Goodwin (Sgt. Higgins), Alec Mango (Akbar), Oscar Quitak (Youssuff), George Margo (Chief jailer), Arnold Marlé (Flower seller), Conrad Phillips (Johnson), Tom Clegg (Mahmud), Andy Ho (Lee Feng), Geoffrey Keen (Carruthers), Tutte Lemkow (Sword Dancer), Eric Pohlmann (Tobacco seller). Set in the 19th Century, Zarak is caught kissing his father's youngest wife Salma and narrowly escapes with his life before becoming a bandit and thorn in the side of the British, in particular Major Ingram. Tagline: Pillage! Plunder! Passion! The film was noted, even in the House of Lords, for the skimpiness of Miss Ekberg's costume. Loosely based on the book *The Story of Zarak Khan* by A.J. Bevan. *Dir*. Terence Young.

Zed & Two Noughts, A (1985) Andréa Ferréol (Alba Bewick), Brian Deacon (Oswald Deuce), Eric Deacon (Oliver Deuce), Frances Barber (Venus de Milo), Joss Ackland (Van Hoyten), Jim Davidson (Joshua Plate), Agnès Brulet (Beta Bewick), Guusje van Tilborgh (Caterina Bolnes), Gerard Thoolen (Van Meegeren), Ken Campbell (Stephen Pipe), Wolf Kahler (Felipe Arc-en-Ciel), Geoffrey Palmer (Fallast). The wives of two zoologist twins are killed in a car crash. The brothers then begin to examine the nature of the human condition. *Dir*. Peter Greenaway.

Zeta One (1969) James Robertson Justice (Maj. Bourdon), Charles Hawtrey (Swyne), Robin Hawdon (James Word), Anna Gaël (Clotho), Brigitte Skay (Lachesis), Dawn Addams (Zeta), Valerie Leon (Atropos), Lionel Murton (W), Yutte Stensgaard (Ann Olsen), Angela Grant (Angvisa Girl), Wendy Lingham (Edwina 'Ted' Strain), Rita Webb (Clippie), Carol Hawkins (Zara), Steve Kirby (Sleuth), Paul Baker (Bourdon's Assistant), Walter Sparrow (Stage Manager), Alan Haywood (Pilot), Anna Turnard (Miss Johnson), Yolande Del Mar (Striptease Artist), Rose Howlett (Fat Lady). Alien women (mainly topless) from the planet (anagram experts might want to look away now) Angvia arrive on Earth and begin to abduct women. The presence of British film comedy greats such as Robertson-Justice and Hawtrey does nothing to rescue the film. *Dir*. Michael Cort.

Zulu (1964) Stanley Baker (Lt. John Chard), Michael Caine (Lt. Gonville Bromhead), Jack Hawkins (Rev. Otto Witt), Ulla Jacobsson (Margareta Witt), James Booth (Pvt. Henry Hook), Nigel Green (Colour Sgt. Frank Bourne), Ivor Emmanuel (Pvt. Owen), Paul Daneman (Sgt. Robert Maxfield), Glynn Edwards (Cpl. William Allen), Neil McCarthy (Pvt. John Thomas), David Kernan (Private Hitch), Gary Bond (Private Cole), Peter Gill (Private 612 John Williams), Patrick Magee (Surgeon-Major James Henry Reynolds), Richard Davies (Private 593 William Jones), Denys Graham (Private 716 Robert Jones), Dickie Owen (Corporal Schiess), Gert Van den Bergh (Lieutenant Josef Adendorff), Dennis Folbigge (Commissary James Langley Dalton), Larry Taylor (Hughes), Kerry Jordan (Company Cook), Ronald Hill (Bugler), Chief Mangosuthu Buthelezi (Cetewayo), Daniel Tshabalala (Jacob), Ephraim Mbhele (Red Garters), Simon Sabela (Dance Leader), Richard Burton (Narrator). After a force of Zulus destroys a British Army at Isandhlwana on 22 January 1879, 4000 warriors advance on Rorke's Drift, where a hospital and supply dump is guarded by just 139 Welsh infantrymen. Lieutenants Chard and Bromhead muster the force and construct defences in what appears to be a hopeless task. With some poetic licence, the film is in fact relatively accurate (for a piece of entertainment). After the actual Rorke's Drift battle, 11 Victoria Crosses were awarded, the highest number ever given in a single conflict. *Dir* Cy Endfield.

Famous British (and Irish) Comedy Entertainers

Abbot, Russ Born Russell Allan Roberts, 16 September 1947, Chester, Cheshire. Russ served a 15-year apprenticeship as drummer with *The Black Abbots*, a musical comedy group in the style of *The Barron Knights* and *The Grumbleweeds*. After appearances on ITV's *The Comedians* and *Who Do You Do?*, Russ became a regular on *Freddie Starr's Variety Madhouse* in 1979, before taking over the star role the following year, the show title being changed to *Russ Abbot's Madhouse*. For the next ten years Russ and his team including, at various times, Michael Barrymore, Susie Blake, Les Dennis, Bella Emberg, Dustin Gee, Sherrie Hewson and Jeffrey Holland, won plaudits for their comedy sketches within the framework of various Russ Abbot shows before being adjudged too corny by the BBC. His greatest comedy characters include, Basildon Bond (a secret agent based on James Bond), Cooperman (an impression of Tommy Cooper as Superman), Fritz Crackers (a deranged German), Fatman (an overweight opera singer), Barratt Holmes (a detective based on Sherlock Holmes), Jimmy McJimmy (an orange-haired Scotsman whose only audible words were 'see you Jimmy'), and Vince Prince (a Teddy boy). Russ also has a fine easy-listening singing voice and reached number seven in the UK Charts with his 1984 song "Atmosphere". After a period in the doldrums Russ went on to show considerable acting talent in the ITV drama series *September Song* (1991-93) and has become a competent stage actor, notably playing Fagin in *Oliver*, Bottom in *A Midsummer Night's Dream*, Alfred P Doolittle in *My Fair Lady*, Grandpa Potts in *Chitty Chitty Bang Bang*, Roger De Bris in *The Producers* and the Tin Man in the *Wizard of Oz*. In 2008 he joined the cast of *Last of the Summer Wine* for the show's 30th series and more recently has appeared in *Casualty* and *The Sarah Jane Adventures*. In 2012 he is set for a cameo role in *Run For Your Wife*, the film version of Ray Cooney's farce. Russ married Patricia Simpson in 1967, and has four children: Erika, Richard, Gary and Christopher, and two grandchildren, Laine (b. 1995) and Charlotte (b. 2004).

Aherne, Caroline Born 24 December 1963, Ealing, London, but raised from the age of two in Wythenshawe, Manchester. Caroline gathered a huge fan-base in the 1980s with her irreverent portrayal of the Irish nun, Sister Mary Immaculate, with which she won the inaugural *City Life Comedian of the Year* in 1990. Mitzi Goldberg, lead singer of the comedy country and western act The Mitzi Goldberg Experience was another early comic avatar of Caroline's on the Manchester circuit. *The Fast Show* (1994) was undoubtedly Caroline's springboard towards national recognition and her inspired comedy caricatures included the tactless checkout girl and the impressionable teenager. In 1995 her spoof *The Mrs Merton Show*, projected Caroline to superstardom and her success and popularity steadily grew although her television appearances became increasingly sporadic. *The Royle Family* in which she starred and co-wrote (with Craig Cash) won numerous awards but unfortunately Caroline's private life was not blessed with the same degree of good fortune. Her marriage to Joy Division/New Order bassist Peter Hook broke down in 1997 and her subsequent partner, BBC technician Matt Bowers, died of stomach cancer. In 2001 Caroline announced her retirement from television and emigrated to Australia. Within a year she had written and produced *Dossa and Joe* - a sitcom about an Aussie couple who don't do very much. She returned to Britain in 2002. By now Caroline worked even more sparingly than before and in recent years has confined her output to a few *Royle Family* specials and the co-writing of the ITV1 comedy-drama *The Fattest Man in Britain*, which aired in December 2009.Caroline has fought ongoing battles with alcohol and depression although has maintained a positive attitude and remains the mistress of her own destiny as an unrivalled comedy talent who stands alongside any of the great female performers.

Allen, Chesney See *Crazy Gang*.

Allen, Dave Born David Tynan O'Mahony, 6 July 1936, Tallaght, County Dublin. The great Irish comic began his working life as a newspaper journalist on the *Drogheda Argus* before coming to England in 1955 and working as a Redcoat at Butlins in Skegness. His first television appearance was as host of the BBC talent show *New Faces* (1959) but his big break came while touring Australia in 1963 when he was offered his own chat show on Channel 9, *Tonight with Dave Allen*. Returning to Britain the following year he initially had a regular spot on *The Val Doonican Show* before reprising his Australian series on ITV in 1967. After joining the BBC in 1968 his various shows mixing stand-up and sketches ran for the next 25 years. Stand-up is probably not the most descriptive of terms as Dave was always perched on a stool with glass of whiskey (sic) in one hand and cigarette in the other, pontificating on the absurdities of the human condition and in particular sex and religion. Impressionists had a field-day with the Allen trademark mannerisms and would often over-emphasise the fact that Dave had the tip of one of his fingers missing, as a result of a car accident in his youth, by constantly placing the missing digit in prominent view of the camera. As time went on he chose religion as the recurrent theme of both his gags and his sketches and was often in trouble with Catholic groups and watchdog societies for his irreverence. Allen proved he was an accomplished actor in 1972 when he made his stage debut at the Royal Court in Edna O'Brien's *A Pagan Place* and furthered this opinion on his television debut in the ITV production of Alan Bennett's *One Fine Day* in 1979. He died 10 March 2005.

Andrews, Archie See Television and Radio section: *Educating Archie*.

Ant and Dec Anthony McPartlin born 18 November 1975, and Declan Donnelly born 25 September 1975, both in Newcastle-Upon-Tyne, England, are not perhaps the most obvious act to include in an all-time list of the top comedy entertainers as neither is a natural comedian but such is their degree of comfort in working together they have wide appeal, each taking it in turns to play the stooge to the other's taunts and thus portraying an ever-changing comic pathos. They began their professional life in 1989 as child-actors in the successful Newcastle-based soap opera *Byker Grove* (although the young Ant had built some television experience with a brief stint on the children's classic, *Why Don't You?*). They subsequently went on to have a successful pop career as 'PJ and Duncan' (their character names in the soap) on leaving *Byker Grove* in 1993, having a No 9 hit with *Let's Get Ready To Rhumble* in July 1994 before clocking up a further dozen top-20 hits. In 1995 the duo moved into television presenting, initially having their own sketch show on Children's BBC and, in 1997, an early evening show on Channel 4. After presenting various other BBC programmes they signed to the ITV network in the early 2000s. They enjoyed success fronting ITV's Saturday morning children's programmes *SMTV Live* and *CD:UK* alongside Cat Deeley. They subsequently moved to Saturday evening to present fare aimed at adults such as *Friends Like These* (for the BBC), *Pop Idol*, *Ant & Dec's Saturday Night Takeaway* and *Ant & Dec's Push the Button*. Their highest audience figures to date were obtained whilst presenting *I'm a Celebrity, Get Me Out of Here!* in February 2004. It is a running joke that many people do not know which of them is Ant, and which Dec. In fact, a 2004 Daily Mirror poll found that 70% of viewers could not tell them apart. As a result, photographs of the duo are now almost always taken with Ant on the left and Dec on the right. In 2005, as part of the ITV Network's 50th birthday celebrations, they were back on television fronting *Ant & Dec's Gameshow Marathon*, a celebration of some of ITV's most enduring gameshows from the past 50 years. They have also, albeit infrequently, returned to acting. They played themselves in the film *Love Actually* (in which Bill Nighy's character referred to Dec as "Ant or Dec"). They have returned to their Geordie roots in a one-off tribute to *The Likely Lads* (in which they remade one of the classic episodes) and by returning to *Byker Grove* for Geoff's funeral. Their recent projects include the film *Alien Autopsy*, the TV show *Soccer Aid,* the game show *PokerFace* and the variety show

Britain's Got Talent. In September 2008 the lads braved Taliban shells at Kandahar Airport while waiting to catch a military flight to Camp Bastion in Helmand province to present a Pride of Britain Award to the Medical Emergency Response Team (MERT), who rescue injured colleagues from the front line in Afghanistan. Ant married Lisa Marie Armstrong (born 25 October 1976, Oxford), a former member of pop band Deuce and now make-up expert for ITV's *This Morning* programme, in 2006 whilst Dec was in a relationship with actress Clare Buckfield between 1993 and 2003 and Sky Sports presenter Georgie Thompson between January 2009 and April 2011.

Armstrong and Miller Alexander Armstrong (born 14 August 1970, Rothbury, Northumberland) and Ben Miller (born 24 February 1966, London) are products of the Cambridge Footlights. They first performed their comedy sketch show at the Edinburgh Fringe in 1994 and returned in 1996, when they were nominated for the Perrier Comedy Award. The following year they began the first of four series of *Armstrong and Miller* (1997-2001) for Channel 4, and reprised their act for a short series in 2007 for the BBC. The characters they play invariably poke fun at class distinction and pomposity, Armstrong specializing in the arrogant upper-class twit. Individually they are both talented actors, Miller starring on film as 'Bough', sidekick to Rowan Atkinson's titular character in the film *Johnny English* (2003) and on television as Lester in ITV's sci-fi drama *Primeval* (2007). Armstrong, the cousin of television chef Clarissa Dickson-Wright, has concentrated more on television broadcasting in recent years and has become a regular presenter of the BBC's satirical panel game *Have I Got News For You* and in October 2008 he was offered the job as replacement for Des O'Connor as the host of the Channel 4 game show *Countdown* but turned it down as he did not want to be typecast as a gameshow host although rather ironically is currently hosting the BBC gameshow *Pointless.*

Askey, Arthur Born 6 June 1900, Liverpool, Merseyside. Arthur honed his comedic skills on the concert party circuit before receiving his big break on the BBC radio show *Band Waggon* in 1938 as 'Big-Hearted Arthur'. At 5ft 2ins and nine stone wet, the bespectacled Arthur's brand of mischievous, hyperactive humour and silly songs endeared him to generations of fans. His film credits include *Charley's Big-Hearted Aunt* (1940), *The Ghost Train* (1941) and the box-office flop *Bees in Paradise* (1943). His catchphrases include 'before your very eyes' (a reference to his television series of the same name which was performed live), 'I thang you' (sic), 'hello playmates' and 'doesn't it make you want to spit?' Towards the end of his career Arthur appeared on numerous panel game shows and played pantomime dame as 'Martha' for many years. Bad circulation caused him to have both his legs amputated in later life and he died 16 November 1982.

Atkinson, Rowan Born Rowan Sebastian Atkinson, 6 January 1955, Newcastle-upon-Tyne, Tyne and Wear. Rowan attended Durham Cathedral Choristers' School; St Bees School; Newcastle University; and Queen's College, Oxford (BSc, MSc), before launching his career as a professional comedian, actor and writer after gaining experience in university revues. He established his reputation in the irreverent sketch show *Not the Nine O'Clock News* (1979-82) co-starring with Griff Rhys Jones, Mel Smith and Pamela Stephenson, before being elevated to super-stardom via four series of the sitcom *Blackadder* (1983-89). The silent, but magnificently irritating, *Mr Bean* (1990-95) made Rowan a global star. *The Thin Blue Line* (1995-96) was a less successful but well-received sitcom set around a dysfunctional police station. A prodigious talent, in 1981 Rowan became the youngest person to have a one-man show in London's West End. He married Sunetra Sastry in 1990 and has two children. He also owns his own production company, Tiger Television. His film credits include *Never Say Never Again* (1983), *The Tall Guy* (1989), *The Appointment of Dennis Jennings* (1989), *The Witches* (1990), *Hot Shots! Part Deux* (1993), *The Lion King*, (1994 - voice of Zazu the Hornbill), *Four Weddings and a Funeral* (1994), *Johnny English* (2003*), Keeping Mum* (2005 – a rare straight role), *Mr Bean's Holiday* (2007) and *Johnny English Reborn* (2011). A shy man off-camera, possibly because of a congenital speech impediment, (which was used to great comic effect throughout the *Blackadder* series with his slow deliberate pronunciation of key words), but there is no doubting the quality of his work in

television and film. Rowan is also a celebrated stage actor and his West End live shows include *The Nerd* (1984) and *The Sneeze* (1988). In 2009 he returned to the stage as Fagin in Lionel Bart's musical *Oliver!,* produced by Andrew Lloyd Webber and Cameron Mackintosh. Rowan's great passion is his love of cars and he is one of the few members of Equity who holds a Large Goods Vehicle (LGV) licence. His collection of cars is dominated by Aston Martins, including the DB7 Vantage used in *Johnny English* – he is not a lover of the Porsche.

Bailey, Bill Born Mark Bailey, 13 January 1964, Bath. Stand-up comedian, musician and actor. The son of a GP and ward sister, Bill is a classically-trained musician and it was his propensity to play the song "Won't You Come Home Bill Bailey" on the guitar, whilst at school, which eventually led to his stage name. His early professional gigs were as part of various double-acts but his first notable success came in 1995 with his touring one man show *Bill Bailey's Cosmic Jam* which was shown on Channel 4 under the name *Bill Bailey Live*. Bill's distinctive looks (goatee beard and long hair), and the eerie sound of the theremin he played in his early days, help to create an atmosphere of surrealism as the basis for his humour. In actuality Bill is a true sci-fi fan and named his son Dax after the *Star Trek: Deep Space 9* character. In 1998 the BBC gave him his own television show, *Is It Bill Bailey?* and after winning the Best Live Stand-Up award at the British Comedy Awards in 1999, Bill's television career really took off. He co-starred in the Channel 4 sitcom, *Black Books*, between 2000 and 2004 and in 2005 furthered his burgeoning acting career by voicing the sperm whale in the film version of *The Hitchhiker's Guide to the Galaxy*. His other films include: *Hot Fuzz* (2007), *Nanny McPhee and the Big Bang* (2010), *Burke and Hare* (2010) and *Chalet Girl* (2011). More recently, Bill has become a regular team captain on *Never Mind the Buzzcocks* (series 11-21) had cameo roles in television drama series *Skins* and *Hustle* and presented a Channel 4 series *Wild Thing I Love You*, which perhaps surprisingly had nothing to do with rock-and-roll but was in fact a series focusing on the protection of Britain's wild animals.

Baker, Hylda Born 4 February 1905, Farnworth, Lancashire. Hylda was a child performer who wrote, produced, directed and starred in her own shows during the music hall days. Her monologues were full of malapropisms and double-entendres delivered with a confident authority which added to the comic effect. This stage persona was all but reprised in two popular sitcoms, *Nearest and Dearest* (1968-73) and *Not On Your Nellie* (1974-75). Hylda also had minor roles in a number of films including *Saturday Night and Sunday Morning* (1960), *Up the Junction* (1968) and *Oliver!* (1968). In 1978, aged 73, she became an unlikely pop star when a spoof version of "You're The One That I Want" from the musical *Grease*, reached No 22 in the UK Charts and earned her and co-"singer" Arthur Mullard a slot on *Top of the Pops*. Unfortunately the performance has gone down in pop history as the most comically inept ever and the song disappeared from the charts overnight. Hylda suffered from Alzheimer's disease in the last few years of her life and died at a retirement home in Epsom, Surrey, 1 May 1986.

Barker, Ronnie Born Ronald William George Barker, 25 September 1929, Bedford, Bedfordshire. Ronnie worked as a character actor at Aylesbury Repertory Company from 1948 but after working on several radio shows found fame as Able Seaman Johnson in *The Navy Lark*. His first television break came on *The Frost Report* as resident comedy actor alongside John Cleese and Ronnie Corbett. *The Ronnie Barker Playhouse* followed introducing the character Lord Rustless who became the lead character in his 1969 series *Hark at Barker*. It was in 1971 that the first series of *The Two Ronnies* hit our screens and for the next 16 years the teaming of Messrs Barker and Corbett remained one of the best-loved double acts on television, many of their classic sketches being written by Ronnie B under his pen-name of Gerald Wiley. Ronnie was equally successful in his own right throughout this period, initially reprising his Lord Rustless character in *His Lordship Entertains* before introducing the character Norman Stanley Fletcher in the classic series *Porridge* (1974-77), reprised in *Going Straight* in 1978. The other classic Barker series, *Open All Hours*, began as a modest pilot on BBC2 in 1973 and it wasn't until 1976 that the first series proper began. Series Two and Three aired on BBC1 in 1982 and 1983 and have remained popular through several repeat runs. *The Magnificent Evans* (1984) and *Clarence* (1988) were less well-received but highly watchable. Following the recording of *Clarence*, incidentally written by Ronnie under the pseudonym Bob Ferris, the great man announced his retirement to run an antique shop in Chipping Norton, Oxfordshire. He died 3 October 2005, Adderbury, Oxfordshire, after a long period of heart disease. See also entries in the radio and television section for *Bold As Brass, Clarence, The Frost Report, Hark at Barker, It's A Square World, The Magnificent Evans, The Navy Lark, Open All Hours, Porridge, Seven Faces Of Jim, Seven of One, Six Dates With Barker*, and *The Two Ronnies*.

Baron Cohen, Sacha Born Sacha Noam Baron Cohen, 13 October 1971, Hammersmith, London. Educated at Haberdashers' Aske's school (as was Matt Lucas) Baron Cohen is a comic actor mainly known for his comic creations, Ali G (a hip hop gangsta and leader of the West Staines Massiv), Borat (a Kazakhstani reporter), and Brüno (a flamboyantly camp Austrian fashion reporter). Ali G made his television debut in 1998 on *The Eleven O'Clock Show* on Channel 4, which incidentally also introduced Ricky Gervais to the viewing public. *Da Ali G Show* began in 2000, and won the BAFTA for Best Comedy in the following year. Although Ali G (Alistair Leslie Graham) was the main character of the series Baron Cohen's two other comic personas were frequently depicted. Ali would often interview guests such as politician Tony Benn, who would be blissfully unaware of the spoof, and the garishly track-suited "voice of da yoof" would embark on a cross-examination of his guest in the sort of irreverent cruel style previously observed by Paul Kaye in his Dennis Pennis persona. Baron Cohen's creation of Borat Sagdiyev was depicted in the highly successful film *Borat: Cultural Learnings of America for Make Benefit Glorious Nation of Kazakhstan* (2006). The joke here was again the character's believability as a real foreign person struggling with language and culture barriers to create comic effect. Unfortunately because of the necessity for obscurity to make the gag work, Sacha announced the retirement of his two most famous characters in December 2007 and did likewise to his third creation Brüno after the 2009 premier of the film of the same name. His other films include: *The Jolly Boys' Last Stand* (2000), *Ali G Indahouse* (2002), *Madagascar* (2005 - voice of Julien), *Talladega Nights: The Ballad of Ricky Bobby* (2006) and *Sweeney Todd: The Demon Barber of Fleet Street* (2007). He wed long time partner, Australian actress Isla Fisher, in 2010 and the pair have two daughters, Olive (b. 2007) and Elula (b. 2010). Sacha is due to star as Freddie Mercury in *Mercury*, an upcoming film about the period in *Queen*'s history from 1971 leading up to the Live Aid concert in 1985. Other forthcoming projects include a role as the dictator of a fictional Arab country in the 2012 film, *The Dictator*.

Barrymore, Michael Born Michael Kieran Parker, 4 May 1952, Bermondsey, London. Michael began as a Butlins Redcoat before turning professional and working mainly in pubs and clubs. His marriage to dancer Cheryl Cocklin (stage name: Cheryl St Claire) in 1976 (died 2005) caused a turnabout in his fortunes and through her devoted guidance, and much support from the *Daily Mirror*, he became a much-loved comedian, his catchphrase "awight at the back" becoming the nation's favourite. He began as a support in *Russ Abbot's Madhouse* (1981-83) and by the mid-1990s he was the most successful comedian in Britain (his *My Kind of People* attracting 13m viewers at its peak), but the excesses of his private life began to take their toll. In 1995 he announced his homosexuality after reporters spotted him in the White Swan in East London (a traditional gay pub). His marriage was dissolved and in 1999 he 'married' his then boyfriend Shaun Davis in Honolulu, Hawaii. His popular sitcom *Bob Martin* (2000-01) proved he was not just a madcap comedian and it appeared a new career in acting beckoned, but by now he was beginning to be reviled in newspapers for his wayward tendencies. In March 2001, Stuart Lubbock, a guest at his house in Harlow, Essex, was found dead in his swimming pool and three months later Barrymore was arrested on suspicion of being in possession

of, and supplying a Class B drug. After checking into a psychiatric unit, the Marchwood Priory in Hampshire, and later a similar institution in Arizona, Barrymore came home to find his career in tatters, the general public no longer able to laugh at his onstage antics as his private indiscretions blurred their vision. An attempt to carve out a career in New Zealand faltered and he returned home to the UK in January 2006 to take part in *Celebrity Big Brother* but, although his runners-up spot seemed to suggest the nation had again warmed to him, the Stuart Lubbock Affair was never far from the surface and his career in showbusiness appears to be almost over. In 2011 he was a contestant in the Channel 4 reality television show *Celebrity Coach Trip* but he was hospitalized during the trip suffering seemingly from anxiety attacks. He was later convicted of cocaine possession. See entries in the television section for *Animals Do the Funniest Things, Big Brother, The Friday Night Project, Kids Say the Funniest Things, My Kind of Music, The Salon, Saturday Live, Strike It Lucky, Who Do You Do?*.

Baxter, Stanley Born 24 May 1926, Glasgow, Scotland. Sir Harry Lauder and Mae West were early successful impersonations for the great Scottish mimic in a 20-minute vaudeville routine put together with the help of his mother while still in his teens. During World War II he worked in Forces Radio in Malaya and formed a friendship with Kenneth Williams. After the war he worked as a stage actor until making his television debut in the 1952 BBC series *Shop Window*. Stanley's first feature film appearance was a minor part in *Geordie* (1955) but more prominent roles followed in *Very Important Person* (1961), *Crooks Anonymous* (1962) and *The Fast Lady* (1963). *The Stanley Baxter Show* aired on BBC in 1963 and ran for eight years before the more lavish ITV series of *The Stanley Baxter Picture Show* began in 1972 with characters such as Alan Wicked, Malcolm Gibberidge, Glandy Jackson, Hicky Denderson, Benny Pill, John Bitumen, and an assortment of dames which he also played in his annual pantos in Glasgow and Edinburgh. These shows were big budget productions and were consequently sporadic but eagerly-awaited and always well-received. Stanley retired in 1998, a year after his wife (Moira) of 46 years died although he does occasional voice-over work.

Bentine, Michael Born Michael Bentin, 26 January 1922, Watford, Hertfordshire. The son of a Peruvian immigrant, Michael had a tragic youth being unable to speak for 13 years but recovered to receive a public school education at Eton. An RAF Intelligence officer during World War II, it was then he decided to become a comedian, initially teaming up with boyhood friend Tony Sherwood and then meeting Harry Secombe who introduced him to Spike Milligan and Peter Sellers at the Grafton Arms pub in London. It was at this meeting that the idea for the BBC radio classic *The Goon Show* was born, the first show airing 28 May 1951 (under the name *Crazy People*). Michael was involved in the first 43 episodes before going solo, his act being based upon a mad professor character created by 'Monsewer' Eddie Gray, of Crazy Gang fame. *The Bumblies* (1954) was a BBC children's puppet series presented by 'professor' Michael Bentine but his major breakthrough came with his BBC sketch show *It's A Square World* (1960-64) with its state-of-the-art special effects including an imaginary flea-circus with Bentine giving a running commentary on the order of events. *Michael Bentine's Potty Time* ran from 1974-80 and consisted of 78 episodes of children's sketches based around puppet characters the Pottys. In later life Michael developed an interest in the paranormal, being convinced he had previously walked the earth in a variety of guises. He also starred in two feature films, *Down Among the Z Men* (1952) and *The Sandwich Man* (1966). He died 26 November 1996.

Bhaskar, Sanjeev Born 31 October 1963, Ealing, London. Sanjeev gained a degree in marketing from The Hatfield Polytechnic (now the University of Hertfordshire) before landing a job as a marketing executive at IBM. He entered showbusiness as part of a double act with musician Nitin Sawhney under the name The Secret Asians. The pair were given a show on BBC Radio, which eventually grew into the award-winning BBC TV sketch show *Goodness Gracious Me*. On film, Sanjeev made his debut in *Notting Hill* (1999). Other films include: *The Mystic*

Masseur (2001), *The Guru* (2002), *Anita and Me* (2002 - as Mr Kumar), *L'entente cordiale* (2006), *Jhoom Barabar Jhoom* (2007), *It's a Wonderful Afterlife* (2010), *Jackboots on Whitehall* (2010 - voice of Rupee) and *London Boulevard* (2010 - as Dr Raju). In 2007, Sanjeev presented a four part documentary for the BBC, *India with Sanjeev Bhaskar*, in which he travelled to India with director Deep Sehgal and among many entertaining pieces, visited his father's ancestral home which is now in Pakistan. On stage, he made his musical theatre debut as King Arthur in *Spamalot* at London's Palace Theatre in 2008. He was awarded an OBE in 2005 and in a memorable year he also married Meera Syal (see separate entry) and their first child, a son, Shaan, was born at the Portland Hospital on 2 December 2005. Sanjeev was appointed as the University of Sussex's new Chancellor in February 2009. For all his success as a comedian, writer and actor (he has gained huge critical acclaim for his portrayal of *The Indian Doctor*) Sanjeev will always be remembered for creating one of television's greatest comic characters, Sanjeev Kumar, in the spoof chat show (*Kumars at No 42*) that had star guests falling over themselves to appear. See also entry for Tommy Tiernan and entries in the radio and television section for *Captain Butler*, *Goodness Gracious Me*, *The Indian Doctor*, *The Kumars at No. 42*, *Love Soup*, and *Mumbai Calling*.

Bonn, Issy Born Benjamin Levine, 21 April 1893, London. Music Hall comedian and singer who became famous for his BBC radio shows before and after the Second World War. Issy also starred in two films, the Carroll Levis musical *Discoveries* (1939) and the Arthur Askey comedy *I Thank You* (1941). His image is one of many that appear on the cover for The Beatles "Sergeant Pepper's Lonely Hearts Club Band" album and quiz aficionados will know that it is his head above Paul McCartney's head. He gave up comedy to become a well-known theatrical agent and died on his birthday 21 April 1977.

Boyce, Max Born 27 September 1945, Glynneath, Neath Port Talbot, South Wales. Max's father died in a mining accident soon after his birth and for ten years Max himself worked down the pits. He became an all-round entertainer; singer, story-teller, poet and comedian. His comedy LPs include *Live at Treorchy* (1973), *We All Had Doctor's Papers* (1975) (the first comedy album to reach number one), *The Incredible Plan* (1976) and *I Know Cos I Was There* (1978) ('I Was There' the title of a 1979 book by Boyce becoming a slogan forever associated with Max). The transition from comedy folk singer to fully-fledged comedian was made in 1976 when Max was given his first BBC television show and began a stand-up routine based around his Welsh background and in particular his beloved rugby. Max had regular series for the next decade before diversifying into other forms of entertainment although remaining a stand-up comic of the highest order. He was awarded the MBE in the millennium new year's honours list.

Boyle, Frankie Born Francis Martin Patrick Boyle, 16 August 1972, Glasgow, Scotland. Frankie began his professional life as a stand-up comedian in 1995 and is known for his irreverent humour and acerbic wit both as a performer and a writer (regular columnist in the Scottish Daily Record and occasional guest columnist in The Sun as well as writing for other comedians such as Jimmy Carr and Sean Lock). Boyle was a panellist for the first seven series of *Mock the Week* (the topical celebrity panel game, hosted by Dara Ó Briain) between 2005 and 2009 and was often involved in controversy standing accused of disparaging and hurtful remarks towards swimmer Rebecca Adlington and Her Majesty the Queen. In October 2009 Boyle's autobiography, *My Shit Life So Far*, was published. In Oct 2009 he piloted a sketch and stand-up show for Channel 4, entitled *Deal With This, Retards*, which was eventually made into a six-episode series the following year under the title *Frankie Boyle's Tramadol Nights*. Frankie lives in Glasgow with his partner, Shereen Taylor, and has two children, a daughter (b. 2004) and a son (b. 2007).

Brand, Jo Born Josephine Grace Brand, 23 July 1957, Wandsworth, London. Jo worked as a psychiatric nurse before taking up a career in stand-up comedy in the mid-1980s, acquiring the stage name, "The Sea Monster". Jo was advised at this time by her then lover, Malcolm Hardee, one of the most well-known agent/comedians in the country. Her first television gig was on the Channel 4 variety show *Saturday Night Live* (1985-87). With her Doc Marten boots, and her large size and short hair, the public often thought Jo was a lesbian, particularly as her style of emasculating humour often highlighted the inadequacies of the male species. In actual fact Jo has been happily married (to Bernie Bourke) since 1997 and has two children. Originally regarded as an alternative comedienne Jo's transition into the mainstream was confirmed when she obtained her own series on Channel 4, *Jo Brand Through the Cakehole* (1993). In recent years Jo has taken part in several reality television shows and has become an ever-present panellist on television shows such as *Have I Got News For You*, *Never Mind The Buzzcocks*, *QI* and *Countdown*. Jo also co-hosts (with Mark Lamarr) a popular Saturday morning Radio 2 music show when Jonathan Ross is otherwise engaged. In 2011 Jo won a BAFTA for Best Female Performance in a Comedy Role for her portrayal of nurse Kim Wilde in *Getting On*, the BBC4 sitcom based in an NHS hospital.

Brand, Russell Born 4 June 1975, Grays, Essex. Russell made his screen debut in an episode of *The Bill* in 1994 but first came to public attention in 2004 as the irreverent host of the sister show to Big Brother 5, *Big Brother's Eforum*, on E4. Brand also hosted the show during Big Brother 6 and 7 (its name now changed to *Big Brother's Big Mouth*) before leaving to rediscover his roots as a stand-up comic. Russell hosted a popular Saturday evening music show on BBC Radio 2 from November 2006 until October 2008. In an episode of the show broadcast on 18 October 2008, Russell and fellow Radio 2 presenter Jonathan Ross made a series of phone calls to actor Andrew Sachs that crudely discussed Sachs' granddaughter. The *Mail on Sunday* published the story with a very negative spin and both presenters were later suspended by the BBC and Russell resigned from his show. Russell is a former heroin addict, sex addict and alcoholic and has had numerous run-ins with the police, having been arrested on several occasions for public indecency. His camp dress sense and manner has made him an unlikely target for female predators and tabloid discussion of his sexual preferences is on par with that of Robbie Williams' and David Walliams'. Although Russell's 2007 autobiography, *My Booky Wook*, became a best-seller his first major film role as Flash Harry in *St Trinian's*, released soon after the book launch, was given a lukewarm reception by film critics. His performance in the title role of the remake of *Arthur* (2011) came in for similar criticism. Other films include: *Penelope* (2008 - as Sam), *Forgetting Sarah Marshall* (2008 - as Aldous Snow) and its sequel *Get Him to the Greek* (2010), *Despicable Me* (2010 - voice of Dr Nefario), *The Tempest* (2010 - as Trinculo), *Hop* (2011 - as "Hoff Knows Talent") and *Rock of Ages* (2012 - as Lonny Barnett). Russell married American singer and actress Katy Perry (born Katheryn Elizabeth Hudson, 25 October 1984) on 23 October 2010 in a traditional Hindu ceremony, near the Ranthambhore tiger sanctuary in Rajasthan, India. Russell filed for divorce in Los Angeles, California in December 2011.

Bresslaw, Bernard See entry in cinema section.

Brough, Peter See Television and Radio section: *Educating Archie*.

Brown, Roy Chubby Born Royston Vasey, 5 February 1945, Grangetown, North Yorkshire. Stand-up comedian, who despite placing second in one of the *New Faces* talent showcases in the 1970s almost exclusively plays to live, rather than television, audiences due to the adult nature of his act. Chubby performs wearing a multi-coloured patchwork jacket and trousers, white shirt, red bow tie and moccasins. His head is adorned with flying helmet and goggles. His act typically begins with him jigging around while his audience shouts "You fat bastard!" repeatedly, to which he eventually responds "Fuck off!". This formatted style is similar to that employed by Al Murray in his pub landlord guise albeit a shade or two bluer. In 1995 Chubby had an unlikely No. 3 UK Chart Hit with the band Smokie, *Living Next Door to Alice (Who the Fuck is Alice)*. Chubby's real name, Royston Vasey, was famously used for the fictional village in the comedy television series *The League of Gentlemen*. He also made several cameo appearances as the foul-mouthed mayor of the village.

Brydon, Rob Born Robert Brydon Jones, 3 May 1965, Swansea, Wales. It will be no surprise to know that Rob began his career as a radio presenter with Radio Wales, his versatility making him popular as DJ, impressionist, comedian and pundit. Initially known as a voice-over artist (Rob voiced the main character, Lewton, in the *Discworld* computer game *Discworld Noir* as well as numerous television adverts), he eventually found small roles in several successful films (for example as a traffic warden in *Lock, Stock and Two Smoking Barrels*). *Marion and Geoff* was Rob's breakthrough role and he quickly became a popular game show panellist and interviewee (invariably being asked to perform the Tom Jones' clearing of the throat effect). Rob is an excellent stand-up comedian but excels in comedic acting roles, his portrayal of Bryn West in *Gavin and Stacey*, winning him many honours. He also has a fine singing voice and in 2009 had a No 1 UK Chart single with *Islands in the Stream* on behalf of Comic Relief. His recent autobiography is entitled, *Small Man in a Book*. Rob has collaborated with Steve Coogan on several projects, notably the 2006 film, *A Cock and Bull Story*. See also entries in the radio and television section for *Gavin and Stacey, I'm Sorry I Haven't A Clue, Just A Minute, Little Britain, Live at the Apollo, Marion and Geoff, The Rob Brydon Show, The Trip*, and *Would I Lie To You?*

Carr, Alan See entry in television section.

Carr, Jimmy Born James Anthony Patrick Carr, 15 September 1972, Hounslow, London. After graduating from Cambridge University with a 2:1 degree in Political Sciences, Jimmy became a marketing executive for Shell before taking the plunge into stand-up comedy. His screen debut came in *Meet Ricky Gervais* (2000) a show he also wrote for. Jimmy's stand-up routines are notable for their deadpan staccato delivery and short gags. His quick-wittedness has made him a regular panellist on radio and television game shows. During an episode of the BBC game show *Would I Lie To You?* he divulged that he had been a Catholic until his mid-twenties, and remained a virgin until the age of 26 due to his faith, but then became aware of the writings of Richard Dawkins and renounced his religion, becoming an atheist. He currently lives in North London with his girlfriend, Karoline Copping, a commissioning editor for *Five*. See also entries in the television section for *8 Out of 10 Cats, The 11 O'Clock Show, Live at the Apollo*, and *The Friday Night Project*.

Carrott, Jasper Born Robert Norman Davis, 14 March 1945, Acocks Green, Birmingham. In his teens Jasper worked as a trainee buyer at a city centre department store, The Beehive, with schoolfriend Bev Bevan who later became the drummer with *The Move* and *ELO*. After university, in 1969, he started his own folk club, "The Boggery", in nearby Solihull and initially performed folk songs. Rather as with Russ Abbott and Billy Connolly, eventually the banter between songs became the focal point of his act and a wonderful incisive stand-up was born. In August 1975 he had a No. 5 UK Chart hit with *Funky Moped*. However it was the non-broadcastable B-side, *Magic Roundabout*, a risqué parody of the children's TV programme, which contributed to the record's huge sales. By now Jasper had developed an act based around all things Brummie, including the accent, culture, and especially his beloved Birmingham City FC. In 1978 Jasper was given his own series, *An Audience with Jasper Carrott*, which aired on ITV and then moved to the BBC to star in the Saturday night live comedy show, *Carrott's Lib*. Jasper was then given various vehicles for his humour by the BBC, including *Carrott's Commercial Breakdown*, which broadcast weird and wacky adverts from around the world, and the sketch and stand-up shows *Carrott Confidential, 24 Carrott Gold, The Jasper Carrott Trial* and *Canned Carrott*, which featured a regular police drama spoof called *The Detectives*, co-starring Robert Powell, which was spun off into its own series. He has written three humorous autobiographical books, *A Little Zit on the Side* (1979), *Sweet and Sour Labrador* (1982) and *Carrott Roots...and Other Myths* (1986), and also wrote a novel, *'Shop! or A Store is Born'*. Jasper was part owner of the production company *Celador*, makers of the internationally successful *Who Wants To Be A Millionaire?*. In 2006, he and wife Hazel sold their shares in the company for over £10m as part of a management buyout deal. His daughter, Lucy Davis (b. 1973), is an actress best known for playing Dawn in *The Office*. See also entries in the television section for *All About Me, The Detectives*, and *Golden Balls*.

Castle, Roy See entry in cinema section

Champion, Harry Born William Crump, in 1866, Shoreditch, London. Affectionately known as 'Cockney Bill of London Town'. He first appeared in the Music Hall, aged 15, under the name Will Conray but after appearing at the Queen's Poplar, London, in 1888, he changed his stage name to Harry Champion. His songs, usually rendered at lightning-speed, include *Any Old Iron, I'm Henery the Eighth, Boiled Beef and Carrots, You Don't Want to Keep on Showing it, Don't do it Again Matilda, Ginger You're Barmy, Never Let Your Braces Dangle, Cover it Over Quick Jemima, Let's Have a Basin of Soup, My Old Iron Cross, Standard Bread, You Ought to See the Missus in a Harem Skirt, I'm Getting Ready For My Mother-in-Law, The Old Dun Cow Caught Fire, I'm Proud of My Old Bald Head, Home Made Sausages, Ragtime Ragshop, I'm William the Conqueror, What a Mouth*, and *You Can't Help Laughing Can Yer?* Harry was one of music hall's most successful artists and continued working into his seventies. He died in London in January 1942.

Chaplin, Charlie See entry in cinema section.

Chester, Charlie Born 26 April 1914, Eastbourne, East Sussex. Chester was a boy singer who turned to comedy in his early teens and rose to prominence with his BBC Radio comedy sketch show *Stand Easy* in the 1940s. The show was adapted for television as *The Charlie Chester Show* (1949-60) and was responsible for making a star of the great Arthur Haynes. Charlie returned to radio broadcasting on the Light Programme (later Radio 2) and could be heard regularly virtually up to his death on 26 June 1997.

Chevalier, Albert Born Albert Onesime Britannicus Gwathveoyd Louis Chevalier, 21 March 1861, Notting Hill, London. The son of a French father and Welsh mother, Albert showed acting promise at a young age and until reaching the age of 30 he played straight roles on the stage. In 1891, he began a successful music hall career as a singer dressed in pearly costermonger uniform, often carrying his wares in a basket. His brother, Charles Ingle (born Auguste Chevalier), wrote the music for many of his songs and also managed him. Albert became an instant success on both sides of the Atlantic, his most popular song being *My Old Dutch* (1892), lyrics by Albert and music by Charles. The famous chorus of the song is almost as well known today as it was then: *We've been together now for forty years, An' it don't seem a day too much, There ain't a lady livin' in the land, As I'd "swop" for my dear old Dutch*. The song was a tribute to his wife, Florrie, the daughter of George 'Champagne Charlie' Leybourne. Albert died, 10 July 1923. He is buried with his son and father in law George Leybourne at Abney Park Cemetery, Stoke Newington, London.

Clary, Julian Born Julian Peter McDonald Clary, 25 May 1959, Teddington, London. The ultra-camp master of innuendo and double entendre began his career as a fake keyboardist for pop band *Thinkman*, before entering the alternative comedy scene in the early 1980s, first as Gillian Pieface, and later as The Joan Collins Fanclub, complete with heavy glam make up and outrageous attire, sometimes involving leather and hinting at bondage. During his early television performances as The Joan Collins Fan Club (which he was eventually forced to abandon by the actress issuing a cease and desist order to prevent him using her name in his comedy stage act) he was accompanied by his pet dog "Fanny the Wonder Dog". Julian became much sought after by the mid to late 1980s and co-hosted the short-lived ITV game show *Trick Or Treat* (1989) with Mike Smith, before achieving greater success later that year with his own high-camp Channel 4 gameshow, *Sticky Moments with Julian Clary*. He later starred in the 1992 audience participation sitcom *Terry and Julian* with Lee Simpson, again for Channel 4. His next series was the BBC's studio-based *All Rise for Julian Clary* in 1996, in which he played a judge in a mock courtroom setting. His comedy tours have included: The Mincing Machine Tour (1989), My Glittering Passage (1993) and Lord of the Mince (2009). Julian made his film debut as Don Juan Diego in *Carry on Columbus* (1992). In 1993 he appeared at the British Comedy Awards where he made a controversial joke, comparing the set to Hampstead Heath and stating that he had just been fisting the then Chancellor of the Exchequer Norman Lamont. In 2004, he took part in the BBC series *Strictly Come Dancing*, finishing third with his partner Erin

Boag. Julian has published comedy books: *My Life With Fanny The Wonder Dog* (1989) and *How To Be A Man* (1992) and an autobiography, *A Young Man's Passage*, which covers his life and career up to the 1993 Norman Lamont incident. He has also published two novels, *Murder Most Fab* (2007) and *Devil in Disguise* (2009). Julian lives in Ashford in Kent and is a close friend and neighbour of fellow comedians Paul Merton and Paul O'Grady. See also entries in the television section for *The All Star Talent Show, It's Only TV... But I Like It, Monte Carlo Or Bust, Mr and Mrs, National Lottery, Saturday Live,* and *Who Do You Think You Are?*

Cleese, John Born John Marwood Cleese, 27 October 1939, Weston-super-Mare. John is the only child of Muriel Cross, an acrobat, and Reginald Francis Cheese an insurance salesman. His family's surname was changed to "Cleese" in 1915, upon his joining the Army. John studied law at Downing College, Cambridge, and joined the Cambridge Footlights where he met his future writing partner Graham Chapman. His first television credit was as a writer on *That Was The Week That Was* (1963), but he became nationally known as a contributor of *The Frost Report* and in particular the recurring sketches where he was one of three people in a line-up representing the British class system (the other two being Ronnie Barker and Ronnie Corbett). Each sketch would start something along the lines "I look down on him as I have a fabulously good job" and would invariably end with Ronnie Corbett uttering "I know my place". John will always be identified as a member of the *Monty Python* team but in *Fawlty Towers* he wrote and starred in one of the most successful sitcoms of all time. His film debut came in *Interlude* (1968). Other films include: *The Magic Christian* (1969), *The Rise and Rise of Michael Rimmer* (1970), *And Now for Something Completely Different* (1971), *Anyone for Sex?* (1973), *Monty Python and the Holy Grail* (1975), *The Strange Case of the End of Civilization as We Know It* (1977), *Life of Brian* (1979), *The Great Muppet Caper* (1981), *Time Bandits* (1981 - as Robin Hood), *Privates on Parade* (1983), *The Meaning of Life* (1983), *Yellowbeard* (1983), *Silverado* (1985 - as Sheriff Langston), *Clockwise* (1986 - as Brian Stimpson), *A Fish Called Wanda* (1988 - as Archie Leach), *Erik the Viking* (1989), *Splitting Heirs* (1993), *Frankenstein* (1994), *The Jungle Book* (1994), *The Wind in the Willows* (1996), *Fierce Creatures* (1997 - as Rollo Lee), *Parting Shots* (1999), *The World Is Not Enough* (1999 - as 'R'), *Isn't She Great* (2000), *Rat Race* (2001), *Harry Potter and the Philosopher's Stone* (2001 - as Nearly Headless Nick), *Pluto Nash* (2002), *Harry Potter and the Chamber of Secrets* (2002), *Die Another Day* (2002 - as 'Q'), *Charlie's Angels: Full Throttle* (2003), *Shrek 2* (2004 - voice of the king), *Around the World in 80 Days* (2004), *Valiant* (2005 - voice of Mercury), *Charlotte's Web* (2006 - voice of Samuel the Sheep), *Shrek the Third* (2007), *The Day the Earth Stood Still* (2008), *The Pink Panther 2* (2009 - as Dreyfus), *Shrek Forever After* (2010), *Spud* (2010) and *Winnie the Pooh* (2011 - as narrator). John also produced and acted in a number of successful business training films, including *Meetings, Bloody Meetings* and *More Bloody Meetings*. These were produced by his company Video Arts. To add to the Cleese fortunes, he wrote two books on relationships: *Families and How to Survive Them*, and *Life and How to Survive It*. The books are presented as a dialogue between John and Robin Skynner, the group analyst and family therapist. John has been married three times, to actresses Connie Booth (1968–78) and Barbara Trentham (1981–1990) and American psychotherapist Alyce Eichelberger (1992–2008), his last marriage seriously depleting the aforementioned Cleese fortunes to the tune of £12m. In April 2010, John revealed on *The Graham Norton Show* that he had begun a new relationship with a woman 31 years his junior, Jennifer Wade. See also entries in the radio and television section for *At Last The 1948 Show, Broaden Your Mind, Desert Island Discs, The Dick Emery Show, Doctor in the House, Fawlty Towers, The Frost Report, I'm Sorry I'll Read That Again, It's A Knockout, Marty, Monty Python's Flying Circus, Ripping Yarns, Rutland Weekend Television, That Was The Week That Was, What the Ancients Did For Us,* and *Whoops! Apocalypse*.

Clitheroe, Jimmy Born James Robinson Clitheroe, 24 December 1921, Clitheroe, Lancashire. As well as his radio and television career, which is described elsewhere, Jimmy made his film debut

in *Old Mother Riley in Society* (1940). Other films include: *Much Too Shy* (1942), *Rhythm Serenade* (1943), *Somewhere in Politics* (1949), *School for Randle* (1949), *Stars in Your Eyes* (1957), *Rocket to the Moon* (1967 - as General Tom Thumb), and his last film, *The Magic Christian* (1969). Jimmy never married, and lived with his mother in Blackpool. He died from an overdose of sleeping pills on the day of her funeral on 6 June 1973. The title of the 1970s BBC TV sitcom, *Some Mothers Do 'Ave 'Em*, was based on Jimmy's catchphrase. See also entries in the radio and television section for *The Clitheroe Kid*, and *That's My Boy*.

Collins, Justin Lee See entry in television section under *Heads or Tails*.

Coltrane, Robbie See entry in cinema section.

Conley, Brian Born Brian Paul Conley, 7 August 1961, Paddington, London. After studying Performing Arts at The Barbara Speake Stage School he worked as a Pontins' Bluecoat at the age of sixteen before becoming a warm-up man on various BBC television shows. After making appearances on the Jimmy Cricket vehicle, *And There's More* (1985-88), Brian was given his own ITV show *Brian Conley: This Way Up* (1989-90), a mixture of sketches and stand-up. A popular Conley creation was Nick Frisbee and his sidekick Larry The Loafer (operated by Ray Tizzard), which coined Brian's most famous catchphrase "It's a Puppet". Nick and Larry were to be seen again on Brian's next ITV series, *The Brian Conley Show* (1992-95) which also introduced Brian's alter-ego, "Dangerous Brian". The dare-devil stuntman would appear in a silver boilersuit complete with blue lycra balaclava. When Brian referred to himself as "dangerous", a close-up shot would see him pulling random faces quickly with his ears wiggling extremely fast. *Gladiators* commentator John Sachs invariably reported the stunts taking place. Another recurring character was "Septic Peg", a parody of Mystic Meg who featured in the original National Lottery show. After a gap of five years Brian had another ITV series of *The Brian Conley Show* (2000-02) but this was more focused on chat with several Hollywood A-listers rather than comedy, although the series was littered with sketches, usually topically-based. Brian has a fine singing voice and he was nominated for a Laurence Olivier Award for his performance as Al Jolson in the stage musical *Jolson* (1995). His other stage portrayals include Caractacus Potts in *Chitty Chitty Bang Bang* and he is currently playing Brother Love in *Brother Love's Travelling Salvation Show*, a tribute to the music of Neil Diamond. Brian married his wife, Anne-Marie, in 1996 and they have two daughters. See also entries in the television section for *The Grimleys, Let Me Entertain You, The Life and Times of Vivienne Vyle, National Lottery* and *Time After Time*.

Connolly, Billy Born 24 November 1942, Glasgow, Scotland. Began his working life as an apprentice welder in the Upper Clyde shipyards before joining Tam Harvey and Gerry Rafferty in the folk-group *The Humblebums* as a banjo player. Developing a stand-up act based around observations of the absurdities of life he became a household name in Scotland after his debut at the Edinburgh Festival in the *Great Northern Welly Boot Show* (1972) before a performance on the BBC *Parkinson* chat-show, coupled with a top-ten comedy album *Cop Yer Whack of This* (1975), brought him recognition all over Britain. Billy's cheerful vulgarity both in language and looks struck a chord with the public and whether he was talking of incontinence knickers, footwarmers, religion or politics, the irreverence of his routines mattered not, he was simply hilariously funny. He married his second wife comedienne Pamela Stephenson in 1989. The Big Yin, as he is called by his fans, has had success as a singer, D.I.V.O.R.C.E. making No 1 in the UK chart in 1975; television comedy actor, in the American series *Head of the Class* (later renamed *Billy*); straight television actor in *Down Among the Big Boys* (1993); and film actor in *Mrs Brown* (1997). His other films include: *The Return of the Musketeers* (1989), *The Big Man* (1990), *Indecent Proposal* (1993), *Pocahontas* (1995 - voice of Ben), *Muppet Treasure Island* (1996 - as Billy Bones), *Beverly Hills Ninja* (1997), *Middleton's Changeling* (1998), *Still Crazy* (1998), *The Debt Collector* (1999), *The Boondock Saints* (1999), *Gabriel & Me* (2001), *The Man Who Sued God* (2001 - as Steve Myers), *White Oleander* (2002), *Timeline* (2003), *The Last Samurai* (2003 - as Zebulon Gant), *Lemony Snicket's A Series of Unfortunate*

Events (2004 - as Uncle Monty), *The X Files: I Want to Believe* (2008), *The Boondock Saints II: All Saints Day* (2009), *Good Sharma* (2010), *Gulliver's Travels* (2010) and *The Ballad of Nessie* (2011). An ill-advised remark concerning the soon-to-be murdered hostage victim Ken Bigley during a stand-up gig in October 2004 severely affected his popularity for a time although Billy himself has always claimed he was misquoted.

Coogan, Steve See entry in cinema section.

Cook, Peter Born 17 November 1937, Torquay, Devon. A product of the famous Cambridge Footlights, Peter came to prominence via *Beyond the Fringe* (1960-63) a stage-comedy revue also starring former fellow Oxbridge students Jonathan Miller, Alan Bennett and Dudley Moore which was televised in 1964 and gave birth to the trend in satirical comedy already begun in *That Was The Week That Was* (1962-63). His cameos on *On the Braden Beat* (1964) as E.L. Wisty, a working man's philosopher seated on a park bench pontificating on all and sundry, became an eagerly awaited part of the show. Peter again worked with Dudley Moore on *Not Only........But Also* (1965-70) the classic BBC sketch show which was originally to be a vehicle for the talents of Moore but soon became known as not only Peter Cook but also Dudley Moore. Classic sketches from this period included Peter as Sir Arthur Streeb-Greebling attempting to teach ravens to fly underwater, the ballad of Spotty Muldoon, and the 'Dagenham Dialogues' where Pete and Dud would engage in improbable but highly-entertaining conversations. This period proved to be the happiest of Cook's life although a mix of heavy drinking and boredom created rifts with Dudley and his creative juices appeared to dry up. Pete and Dud struggled on through the 1970s joining up for the three controversial 'Derek and Clive' recordings (1976-78) and the Sherlock Holmes spoof *Hound of the Baskervilles* (1978) before Dudley left for America and beckoning superstardom. Peter carried on alone by hosting *Revolver* (1978) a short-lived pop show before a disastrous venture in an American sitcom *The Two of Us* (1981-82) as butler Robert Brentwood. His low-point arrived in 1986 when he took the role of sidekick in the BBC chat-show *Joan Rivers: Can We Talk*. As in the first *Not Only...But Also...* programme Peter was not happy playing second fiddle to anyone and made no attempt at humour throughout the six programme run, a particularly ironic moment came when guest comedian Bernard Manning, not known for his sharp wit, turned to him and mocked his lack of humour and the great man, known to have the sharpest most innovative comic brain bar none, merely stared back in uncomfortable silence. There were still traces of the comic genius which inspired a generation and a performance on the *Clive Anderson Talks Back* chat-show in December 1993 where Peter was interviewed in the guise of four separate characters was particularly revealing of his immense talent when he could be bothered. Peter's varied life had included films such as *Bedazzled* (1967), satirical magazine ownership (he became the proprietor of *Private Eye* in 1962), and he opened the first satirical nightclub in the UK in 1961, *The Establishment*. Peter was married three times, to Wendy Snowden (1963-1971), actress Judy Huxtable (1973-89) and Lin Chong, from 1989 until his death, of gastrointestinal haemorrhage, on 9 January 1995, Hampstead, London. In 2004 he was the runaway winner of a poll by professional comedians as the Comedian's Comedian.

Cooper, Tommy Born 19 March 1921, Caerphilly, South Wales. The 6ft 4ins magician/comedian with the over-sized feet would top many people's list as the all-time greatest funny man. Tommy only had to walk on stage to have an audience in hysterics, his trademark fez atop his dishevelled head of hair, a bewildered expression fixed firmly on his sad and lonely face. More often than not he would start with a nervous frantic laugh while attempting to wipe away a stream of perspiration with a white handkerchief, all the time reassuring us that he was in full control. The pretext of his act was of a bungling magician who could rarely manage to perform even the simplest of tricks effectively although occasionally he would surprise the audience by pulling off a seemingly difficult illusion to their (and his) obvious delight. After service in the Horse Guards during World War II Tommy had a successful stint at the Windmill Theatre before an appearance at the London Palladium in 1952 led to his first television series, *It's Magic* (1952). For the next 32 years Tommy was never off our television screens whether it be starring in his own series or guesting on someone else's, his appeal was universal, being loved by the general public and fellow professionals alike. He died on stage at Her Majesty's Theatre, London, during a live television performance on 15 April 1984. Many tributes have been paid to Tommy's work over the years, the most recent being a West End portrayal of his genius by actor Jerome Flynn in *Jus' Like That* (his catchphrase of many years).

Corbett, Ronnie Born 4 December 1930, Edinburgh, Scotland. The other half of the Two Ronnies double-act began his professional life after his obligatory national service gaining a small part in the 1952 film *You're Only Young Twice*. He worked the night club circuit for the next six years until gaining another tiny part in *Rockets Galore* (1958) and then became a regular on the hugely popular BBC children's show *Crackerjack*. Ronnie was spotted by David Frost while doing his adult act at Winstons night club and *The Frost Report* followed, where he first teamed up with Ronnie Barker. Various television series followed before he reprised his partnership with Ronnie B in the first *Two Ronnies* series in 1971. Ronnie's expertise at stand-up became an integral part of the show and his five-minute monologue while seated in an easy chair consisted of a myriad of side jokes while finally arriving at the punchline of the main story. Ronnie has worked on a variety of television projects since the retirement, and subsequent death of Ronnie B. Already awarded an OBE, he was appointed Commander of the Order of the British Empire (CBE) in the 2012 New Year Honours for services to entertainment and charity. See also entries in the television section for *Ant & Dec's Push the Button, Crackerjack, the Frost Report, Hark at Barker, Love Soup, No - That's Me Over Here!, Now Look Here, Prince of Denmark, Sorry !,* and The Two Ronnies.

Crazy Gang See entry in cinema section.

Cricket, Jimmy Born James Mulgrew, 17 October 1945, Cookstown, Co. Tyrone, Northern Ireland. After leaving school at sixteen and working in a betting shop for two years Jimmy worked on the holiday camp circuit for many years. His big break came in 1980 when he appeared on the ITV series *Search for a Star*, hosted by Steve Jones. After several appearances on another ITV variety show, *Starburst*, in 1982 and 1983, Jimmy appeared on the 1984 Royal Variety Performance which led to him gaining his own ITV series, *And There's More* (1985-88), which featured the first television performances of both Brian Conley and Rory Bremner. Jimmy invariably appeared in his trademark outfit of cut-off trousers, dinner jacket, black felt hat worn sideways in the style of a German army helmet, and wellies marked "L" and "R" but worn on the wrong feet. The hat was an addition to his act given to him by the BBC when he made an earlier appearance on *The Good Old Days*. A popular theme of Jimmy's comedy is stereotypical Irish logic, and the ubiquitous letter from his "Mammy" which would have endings such as "PS I was going to send you a £5 postal order but had already sealed the envelope". Sadly, Jimmy's style of good clean wholesome humour has gone out of fashion for television audiences but at his height he was one of the highest paid comedians on the circuit.

Crowther, Leslie Born Leslie Douglas Sargent Crowther, 6 February 1933, West Bridgford, Nottingham. Leslie's introduction to showbusiness was as one of the so-called 'Ovaltineys' who appeared on Radio Luxembourg to advertise the popular beverage. A talented pianist and stage actor before building a reputation as a radio comic on *Variety Playhouse* (1960) and then on television in the BBC children's show *Crackerjack* (1960-68), where his zany antics made him very much the star of the show. After hosting the BBC's variety series *The Black and White Minstrel Show* he turned his hand to situation comedy starring in the BBC series *The Reluctant Romeo* (1967), and the ITV series' *My Good Woman* (1972-74), and *Big Boy Now!* (1976-77). Before the days of Noel Edmonds visiting hospital wards at Christmas it was Leslie's domain and for many years these visits were a staple of Christmas morning on the BBC. In 1984 he hosted the ITV game show *The Price is Right* and in 1990 *Stars in Their Eyes*.

Leslie married Jean Stone in March 1954. They had five children, Caroline, Charlotte, Nicholas and twins Lindsey & Elizabeth, an actress (b. 9 December 1954). Caroline was married to the late rock musician Phil Lynott, and his youngest child Nick works as a radio presenter. In 1992 Leslie had a serious car accident necessitating brain surgery and he never fully recovered. His autobiography, written after his accident was entitled, *The Bonus of Laughter* (1994). He died on 29 September 1996, Royal United Hospital, Bath. See also entries in the radio and television section for *The Black and White Minstrel Show, Children's Favourites, Crackerjack, My Good Woman, The Price is Right, Runaround, Stars In Their Eyes,* and *Whodunnit?*

Davidson, Jim Born James Cameron Davidson, 13 December 1953, Blackheath, London. Jim got the bug for showbusiness when he was chosen to appear in *Ralph Reader's Gang Show* at the Golders Green Hippodrome aged 12 and he subsequently appeared on television in the *Billy Cotton Band Show*. On leaving school he played drums in a local band whilst having a variety of jobs before auditioning for *Opportunity Knocks* in 1975. Hughie Green summarily dismissed him but a year later he won an edition of the television talent show *New Faces* and was runner-up in the final. He then became a regular stand-up act on variety shows featuring his very non-politically correct character of Chalkie White, a West Indian stereotype. Although Jim is often vilified for this portrayal, in truth it was never offensive and when you consider TV sitcoms such as *Curry and Chips* and *Love Thy Neighbour* were fresh in the memory, Jim's act was deemed perfectly acceptable and in fact audiences loved it. He received his own series between 1979 and 1986 and developed his police-mocking catchphrase of 'nick-nick', in reality having several run-ins with the police, usually on driving charges. During the height of his fame Jim won the *TV Times* award as "Funniest Man On Television". He remains a popular stand-up performer and still performs in his adult pantomime work, including productions with titles such as: *Boobs in the Wood* and *SINderella*. Jim's has written two autobiographies *The Full Monty* (1993) and *Close to the Edge* (2001). He received the OBE in 2001 for services to entertainment and has always been identified with his work entertaining the British Armed Forces overseas. He is currently the Chairman of The British Forces Foundation charity which aims to promote the well-being and esprit de corps of service personnel. Jim has been married five times, to Sue Walpole (1971–72; 1 child), Julie Gullick (1981–86; 1 child), Alison Holloway (1987–88), Tracy Hilton (1990–2000; 3 children) and Michelle Cotton (2010-present). In 2006 he was declared bankrupt, a result of maintenance payments from his marriages and diminishing income. A controversial man, standing accused of being a racist, homophobe and wife-beater but in essence a very talented all-round entertainer touched by the demons that so many of his ilk are plagued with. See also entries in the television section for *Big Break, The Dark Side of Fame, The Generation Game, Hell's Kitchen, Home James, New Faces,* and *Up the Elephant and Round the Castle.*

Dawson, Les Born 2 February 1931, Collyhurst, Manchester. Les was a jobbing stand-up act until success on the talent show *Opportunity Knocks* in 1967 propelled him to stardom. His first television series was the ITV production *Sez Les* (1969-76) where Les introduced several regular characters for sketches, notably Cosmo Smallpiece. From series 4 onwards he developed a great double-act with Roy Barraclough as two old biddies, Cissie Braithwaite and Ada Shufflebotham, who would put the world to rights in across-the-garden-wall conversations, an act which was inspired by the Rochdale-born comedian Norman Evans (1901-62) who had earlier had the same act but used an unseen neighbour. Les moved to BBC in 1978 and over the next 10 years 33 editions of *The Les Dawson Show* showcased his talents for mother-in-law jokes and wordy descriptive preambles to jokes. Of portly build himself, Les introduced a dancing group of overweight ladies called the Roly Polys to his BBC shows. Les loved the English language and wrote several novels and actually began his professional life as a writer and pianist in Paris - the piano-playing was developed as part of his comedy act where he would play off-key for comedic effect. His two autobiographies were: *A Clown Too Many* (1986) and *No Tears for the Clown* (1992). Les was married twice, to Margaret (1960 until her death

in 1986 from cancer. They had three children: Julie, Pamela and Stuart) and Tracy, from 6 May 1989 until his death on 10 June 1993, Whalley Range, Manchester, while filming the ITV drama series *Demob*. They had a daughter, Charlotte (b. 3 October 1992). See also entries in the television section for *Blankety Blank, It's A Knockout, Joker's Wild,* and *Opportunity Knocks.*

Dee, Jack Born James Andrew Innes Dee, 24 September 1961, Petts Wood, near Bromley, London. Jack worked as a waiter at The Ritz, Piccadilly, before briefly courting the idea of becoming a priest. He decided to become a full-time comedian after appearing at an open-mike evening at Soho's Comedy Store in 1986. The doleful stand-up comedian came to prominence after winning the Best Stage Newcomer at the 1991 Comedy Awards. Channel 4 gave him his own series (1992-94) and his deadpan delivery remained popular throughout the 1990s and into the millennium. Despite a serious drinking problem in his youth Jack starred in advertisements for John Smith's Bitter in the 1990s and was sometimes referred to as "the midget with the widget" due to his 5' 6½" (1.69 m) height. *Jack Dee's Happy Hour* (2000-01) a successful BBC series where Dee would be interrupted by Jed Cake (voice of Hugh Dennis), a latter day Max Headroom. Jack has also been a winner on *Celebrity Big Brother* and has now turned to straight acting to supplement his comedic career. His film debut came in *The Steal* (1995). Other films include: *Four Play* (2001), *Spivs* (2004), *Short Order* (2005) and *The Last Drop* (2006). In 2004 he played the role of Steven Sharples MP the self-styled 'Deputy Home Secretary' alongside Warren Clarke and Dervla Kirwan in the television film *The Deputy*. Jack married Susan Jane Hetherington in 1989. They have four children, Hattie Jane Innes (b. 1992, Wandsworth), Phoebe Jane Innes (b. 1995, Westminster) and twins, Miles Lionel Innes and Charles Lionel Innes (b. 1998, Westminster). He published *Thanks For Nothing: The Jack Dee Memoirs*, in 2009. His television credits include guest appearances in series such as *Silent Witness, Dalziel and Pascoe* and *Jonathan Creek*. See also entries in the radio and television section for *Big Brother, The Grimleys, I'm Sorry I Haven't A Clue, It's Only TV... But I Like It, Just A Minute, Lead Balloon, Live at the Apollo, The Mary Whitehouse Experience, Monte Carlo Or Bust,* and *Shooting Stars.*

Dodd, Ken Born Kenneth Arthur Dodd, 8 November 1927, Knotty Ash, Liverpool. Ken started his professional life as a ventriloquist (he still incorporates this skill into his stage act on occasion) but developed a comedy routine as Professor Chuckabutty, operatic tenor and sausage knotter. Ken had a great voice as is witnessed by four top-ten hits including his signature tune of *Love is Like a Violin* (No. 8 in 1960), *The River* (No. 3 in 1965), *Promises* (No. 6 in 1966) and the best-selling record of 1965, *Tears* (No. 1). Another popular song, *Happiness*, only reached No. 31 in the UK Charts in 1964 but has become a favourite for his live performances. Despite his great singing voice, with his buck teeth (the result of a cycling accident), eccentric hairstyle and crooked fingers, his true genius was as a stand-up comedian. He turned pro in 1954 and worked with Jimmy Clitheroe in Blackpool before summer seasons in 1955 and 1956 supporting Morecambe and Wise led him to the top of the bill there himself in 1958. Appearances at the Palladium and the Royal Command Performance led to his first BBC television series *The Ken Dodd Show* (1959-69). Ken introduced a fictitious world called Diddyland complete with a diminutive group of Diddymen, including Dicky Mint and Mick the Marmalizer who worked in a jam-butty mine, and the Hon Nigel Ponsonby-Smallpiece, who was so rich he owned a pond full of 18-carat goldfish. The success of the Diddymen in Ken's act led to a puppet series of Ken Dodd and the Diddymen (1969-72) where Diddyland, in the centre of Knotty Ash, now boasted the highest sunshine rate in the world and had snuff quarries, a broken-biscuit repair works and the Knotty Ash gravy wells. Ken's fame was such that he even had his own comic strip in the popular children's *TV Comic*. Ken remains the best-loved stand-up comedian on the circuit with his Doddyism catchprases of 'plumpshious' and 'tattifilarious' and his trademark 'tickling stick' which was often the precursor of his famous one-liners beginning "have you been tickled today missus" of "how tickled I am". He is legendary for over-running his scheduled time when working although the audience is usually so entranced they never mind missing last trains home. Although he works mainly in the music hall tradition, he has occasionally appeared in drama, including as Malvolio in Shakespeare's *Twelfth Night* on stage in Liverpool in 1971; on television in the cameo role of 'The Tollmaster' in the 1987 *Doctor Who* story *Delta and the Bannermen*; and as Yorick (in silent flashback) in Kenneth Branagh's film version of Shakespeare's *Hamlet* in 1996. Ken was famously cleared of tax evasion charges in the 1980s but typically took it all in good heart and is as popular as ever. His autobiography, *Look At It My Way*, was published in November 2009. See also entries in the radio and television section for *Face to Face, the Good Old Days*, and *Worker's Playtime*.

Drake, Charlie Born Charles Edward Springall, 19 June 1925, Southwark, London. With his diminutive (5ft 1in) stature, blond curly hair, childlike manner and natural flair for knockabout slapstick (he was a ju-jitsu instructor at Butlins), Charlie was, particularly in the early years of his career, a popular comedian with children but by the 1960s had developed a universal and international appeal. Charlie made his television debut in an episode of *The Centre Show* (BBC) on 7 July 1953, in the period when he was an aspiring stand-up comic. In 1954 he teamed up with lanky 6ft 4in comedian Jack Edwardes, who he had first met during war service, to form a double-act. Following their 1954 appearance in the talent show *Showcase* (BBC), the distinctive-looking pair refashioned their act to appeal more to children, adopting the stage names 'Mick and Montmorency' (Charlie was the latter). As such they made appearances in the children's magazine series *Jigsaw* (BBC, 1954-55), followed by *Mick and Montmorency* (ITV, 1955-58), occasionally billed under the title *Jobstoppers*. By 1956 Charlie began to gain huge popularity as a solo artist on various variety shows and this led to the BBC offering him a one-off showcase *Laughter in Store* (BBC, broadcast 3 January 1957), followed by such BBC series as *Drake's Progress* (1957-58), *Charlie Drake In...* (1958-60), and *The Charlie Drake Show* (1960-63). His television fame led to four disappointing attempts at film stardom between 1960 and 1967: *Sands of the Desert* (d. John Paddy Carstairs, 1960), *Petticoat Pirates* (d. David MacDonald, 1961), *The Cracksman* (d. Peter Graham Scott, 1963) and *Mr. Ten Per Cent* (d. Peter Graham Scott, 1967), *The Cracksman* being by far the most successful of the four. In 1963, he returned to ITV, where he was to remain for the rest of his comedy career, apart from the one BBC series, *The Charlie Drake Show* (1967-68), from which a compilation of sketches won him the Charlie Chaplin Award for Best Comedy at the 1968 Montreux Television Festival. The hilarious 1812 Overture sketch, with Charlie conducting and playing all the instruments of the orchestra, winning another Golden Rose and being widely acclaimed as the funniest sketch of all time (although sadly missing from various recent polls!). Charlie's ITV series included *The Charlie Drake Show* (1963), *Who Is Sylvia?* (1967) and *Slapstick and Old Lace* (1971), but it was *The Worker* (1965-70), with Drake as the proverbial little man who is unable to hold down a job, which was his crowning achievement. By the 1980s Charlie mainly concentrated on straight dramas, notably as the unscrupulous moneylender Smallweed in *Bleak House* (BBC, 1985), one of a party of Welshmen on a wife-hunting mission in the TV film *Filipina Dreamgirls* (BBC, broadcast 15 September 1991) and, stretching credibility to its limits, as a crime boss in an episode of the thriller series *99-1* (ITV, 1994-95). He also starred in several stage plays by Shakespeare and Pinter. Charlie suffered a serious stroke in 1995 and did not work after this, classing himself as 'semi-retired' although he did appear in a documentary series reflecting on his life *Drake's Progress* (BBC2, 25 December 2001). Charlie captured the heart of the nation from the time he made his radio debut in 1951 as a budding amateur vocalist (Charlie had four Top 30 hits between 1958 and 1961 with novelty records *Splish Splash* (No 7, Aug 1958), *Volare* (No 28, Oct 1958), *Mr Custer* (No 12, Oct 1960) and *My Boomerang Won't Come Back* (No 14, Oct 1961), through his early years as straightman to the likes of Jimmy Wheeler (it was during a Wheeler sketch, playing opposite the 5ft 10ins dancer Janet Ball that Charlie coined his famous catchphrase "Hello, my darlings") and ultimately being honoured with numerous series of his own. Charlie was famous for doing his own stunts during his slapstick era and on one occasion it led to the cancellation of a whole television series when a stunt went wrong. The third series of *The Charlie Drake Show* entitled *Bingo Madness* began at 8pm on Tuesday 24 October 1961 and was broadcast live. During a well-rehearsed stunt routine Charlie was pulled through a bookcase and thrown through a window but it was soon clear something was wrong. Charlie lay unconscious for three days suffering from a fractured skull which caused the five remaining programmes in the series to be cancelled. Charlie fractured his skull again the following year in a car accident and this possibly led to the depression that was to haunt him for the rest of his life. Charlie married two dancers (Heather 1953-71 and Elaine 1976-84), he had three children with his first wife and it was his love of young glamorous dancers that contributed to his falling foul of Equity when he tried to employ attractive non-union members to perform in his shows and was subsequently banned from performing outside London. Charlie died on 23 December 2006, Brinsworth House, Twickenham. See also entries in the television section for *Bleak House, Who Is Sylvia?*, and *The Worker*.

Éclair, Jenny Born Jenny Clare Hargreaves, 16 March 1960, Kuala Lumpur, Malaysia. Jenny's family returned to England when she was two years old and she went to school in Lytham St Annes. She studied at Manchester Polytechnic School of Theatre and joined a cabaret group, variously referred to as Kathy Lacreme and the Rum Babas and Cathy La Crème and the Rum Babies. Jenny's first job was at Camberwell Arts College as a life model. She then saw an advert in 'The Stage' looking for novelty acts, and she found work performing punk poems. Her television acting debut came as a waitress in an episode of *Auf Wiedersehen, Pet* in 1983. In 1995 she became the first female solo winner of the Edinburgh Festival's Perrier Comedy Award. In 1997 she played 'Josie' in the stage play *Steaming*. More recently she has appeared in episodes of *The Bill* (2007) and *Skins* (2010). Jenny appeared in the 2010 series of *I'm a Celebrity... Get Me Out Of Here!* And ultimately finished in third place behind Stacey Solomon and Shaun Ryder. In 2011, she has returned to being a panellist on *Loose Women*, a show she was a panellist on in 2003. Her long-time partner is Geof Powell, and they have a daughter, Phoebe (b. 1989). See also entries in the television section for *Al Murray's Multiple Personality Disorder, The Comedy Network, Grumpy Old Men/Women* and *Packet of Three*.

Edmondson, Ade Born Adrian Charles Edmondson, 24 January 1957, Bradford, West Yorkshire. Best-known for his collaborations with Rik Mayall and for his marriage to Jennifer Saunders (see separate entries). Ade's university nickname of "Eddie Monsoon," a play on his surname, inspired the name of Jennifer's character, Edina Monsoon in *Absolutely Fabulous*. Ade's solo projects include playing Brad Majors in the 1990 West End run of *The Rocky Horror Show*, alongside Tim McInnerny as Frank-N-Furter and Ed Tudor-Pole as Riff-Raff. He has also had straight acting roles in series such as *Jonathan Creek* and *Holby City*. In March 2011, Ade gave a winning performance of The Dying Swan on BBC1's *Lets Dance for Comic Relief* (and was promptly smacked on the head at the end of the act by his old sparring partner Rik Mayall) and later that month he hosted the ITV1 six-part series *The Dales*, in which he followed a number of families who live and work in the Yorkshire Dales. A talented musician, in 2008, he founded the band *The Bad Shepherds*, performing punk and new wave classics on traditional instruments. He has also directed pop videos for *The Pogues, 10,000 Maniacs, Sandie Shaw* and *Squeeze* amongst others. Ade has made it known that for future projects he will now use his birth name of Adrian rather than his nickname Ade. See also entries in the television section for *Absolutely Fabulous, Bottom, The Comic Strip Presents, Filthy Rich and Catflap, Happy Families, Hell's Kitchen, Holby City, Jonathan Creek, Monte Carlo Or Bust, Press Gang, Saturday Live, Teenage Kicks*, and *The Young Ones*.

Edwards, Jimmy Born James Keith O'Neill Edwards, 23 March 1920, Barnes, London. Jimmy served as a Flight Lieutenant in the Royal Air Force during the Second World War, winning the Distinguished Flying Cross. His Dakota was shot down at Arnhem in 1944 and as a result he had plastic surgery (he was a member of the Guinea Pig Club) which he disguised with a huge handlebar moustache which became his most distinguishing feature and trademark throughout his career. Jimmy's radio career took off in 1948 in *Take It From Here* (1948-60) where his character of Pa Glum elevated him to instant stardom. His television career reached similar heights via his madcap headmaster role in the children's series *Whack-O!* (1956-60; 1971-72). Jimmy came out as a homosexual in the 1970s following his six-part comedy series *The Six Faces of Jim* and this seriously affected his television work as his image was one of being the chauvinistic Jack-the-lad. Jim maintained an active stage career, notably alongside Eric Sykes in their theatrical farce *Big Bad Mouse*. He also appeared in several films, notably *Three Men in a Boat* (1956). Jim published his autobiography, *Six of the Best*, in 1984, as a follow-up to his earlier memoir *Take it From Me*. He was an accomplished player of both the tuba and euphonium and a keen amateur polo player, being a member at Ham Polo Club. He died 7 July 1988, in London. See also entries in the radio and television section for *Bold As Brass, Seven Faces Of Jim, Take It From Here, Variety Bandbox*, and *Whack-O!*

Elen, Gus Born 22 July 1862, Pimlico, London. A contemporary of Albert Chevalier, Gus was a coster comedian and singer in the music halls from 1891, after his comedy partner, a man named Daniels, died in a boating accident. His most famous song was probably, *If it Wasn't for the Houses in Between*, with the immortal lyrics: *Wiv a ladder and some glasses, You could see to 'Ackney marshes, If it wasn't for the 'ouses in between*. One of the most popular performers of his day, Gus died 17 February 1940, Balham, London, and is buried in Streatham Park Cemetery.

Emery, Dick Born Richard Gilbert Emery, 19 February 1915, St Pancras, London. Dick had show business in his blood, his parents being a successful double-act, Callan and Emery. During World War II, he deserted from the RAF to work in a London show and was caught and imprisoned. On his release he joined *Ralph Reader's Gang Show* before gaining a regular spot at the Windmill Theatre, London, alongside a developing Tony Hancock. The BBC radio show *Educating Archie* (1956-58) established him as a brilliant mimic and when the series transferred to television in 1958, Dick became a television regular. He next appeared in the classic situation comedy *The Army Game*, playing Private 'Chubby' Catchpole in series five (1960-61) before being given his own BBC series *The Dick Emery Show* (1963-81), a young John Cleese being one of his early writers. Characters included Hettie (the sexually-repressed spinster), the buck-toothed Church of England vicar, Clarence (the camp socialite with the catchphrase of 'Hello Honky Tonk'), James Maynard Kitchener Lampwick (the short-breathed First World War veteran) and Mandy (the pretty sweet blonde with the catchphrase 'Ooh, you are awful.....but i like you' when replying to the interviewer's double entendre. This stock phrase was usually followed with a manly shove of the interviewer and Mandy tripping in her high heels on departing and finally destroying the illusion of femininity by walking away bandy-legged. His other popular recurring character was Gaylord the gormless denim-clad bovver boy (in a double act with his long suffering father, played by Roy Kinnear) where, each week, he would mess up and utter the catchphrase "Dad, I think I got it wrong again". Dick also appeared in several films, notably, *The Fast Lady* (1963), *The Wrong Arm of the Law* (1963), *Ooh... You Are Awful* (1974 as Charlie Tully) and *Find the Lady* (1976). He also had a wonderful singing voice and often included a musical interlude midway through his shows. Despite his various camp creations Dick was very much heterosexual. He married five times and had numerous affairs, usually with long-legged blondes. He died 2 January 1983 while filming the second series of his latest project *Dick Emery Presents*. He is survived by his four children, Gilbert, Nicholas, Michael and Eliza. See also entries in the radio and television section for *The Army Game, Educating Archie* and *It's A Square World*.

Emney, Fred Born Frederick Arthur Round Emney, 12 February 1900, Prescot, Lancashire. Fred grew up in London and made his first stage appearance at the age of 15, becoming both a regular in the West End and in the USA during the succeeding years. The gruff, witty, monocle-wearing, cigar-smoking Churchill-lookalike appeared several times on pre-war television in sketches with Richard Hearne (later to become famous as Mr Pastry), but when the television service resumed after hostilities had ceased, commitments prevented him from returning to the medium until *Emney Enterprises* (1954-57), the BBC show in which Fred was aided in his sketches by Deryck Guyler, Rita Webb and Kenneth Connor. *The Fred Emney Show* (1957) followed and Fred was hardly off our screens for the next 20 years. His film performances included his debut *Brewster's Millions* (1935), *She Couldn't Say No* (1940), *Just William* (1940), *The Fast Lady* (1962), *Those Magnificent Men in their Flying Machines* (1965), *The Sandwich Man* (1966), *The Assassination Bureau* (1969), *Lock Up Your Daughters!* (1969), *The Italian Job* (1969), *The Magic Christian* (1969), *Doctor in Trouble* (1970), *Up the Chastity Belt* (1971), and his last film, *Adventures of a Private Eye* (1977). Fred's act was that of a lovable rogue, his upper-class pomposity contrasting with his desire to buck the system ensured his audience warmed to him as someone who had worked out life's absurdities and used them to his advantage. His mannerisms were much mimicked by impressionists of the day which is testament to his unfailing popularity. He died on Christmas Day 1980, Bognor Regis, West Sussex. See also entries in the television section for *Hugh and I*, and *Pinky and Perky*.

Enfield, Harry Born Henry Richard Enfield, 30 May 1961, Horsham, West Sussex. Educated at the independent Worth School in West Sussex, and later the University of York, Harry's first television gig came supplying voices for *Spitting Image* in 1984. Harry gained national fame on Channel 4's *Saturday Live* in 1985 portraying several characters that captured the public's imagination and he was immediately thrust to stardom. He next took on the title role in the 1989 Channel 4 TV film, *Norbert Smith – a Life*, a mockumentary charting the life and career of the fictitious British actor. The film was presented as if it were an edition of the ITV arts programme *The South Bank Show*, and featured Melvyn Bragg, playing himself as the interviewer visiting Sir Norbert at his home, and encouraging him to reminisce about his past career. In 1993 he presented the Channel 4 arts series *Harry Enfield's Guide To Opera* (1993). In 2000 Harry starred in the feature film *Kevin & Perry Go Large* and in 2004 he appeared as King George VI in *Churchill: The Hollywood Years*, a satire on Hollywood's tendency to change history. In January 2012 he starred with Simon Callow in the film *Acts of Godfrey*. Harry also played Jim Stonem in the E4 series, *Skins* (2007-09). He married Lucy Lyster in 1997 and they have one son, Archie Edward (b. 1997) and two daughters, Poppy Sophia (b. 1999) and Nell Florence (b. 2003). Harry was previously in a relationship with Alison Owen, the mother of Alfie and Lily Allen. They lived together for three years but separated 1995. He is best known for his collaborations with Paul Whitehouse and numerous television series. See also entries in the television section for *Celeb, Harry Enfield's Television Programme, Men Behaving Badly, Ruddy Hell! It's Harry and Paul, Saturday Live*, and *Spitting Image*.

Evans, Lee Born 25 February 1964, Avonmouth, Bristol. Brought up in Billericay, Essex (where he still resides), Lee followed his father into showbusiness after unsuccessful spells as a boxer and a pop musician (he played drums in a punk rock band called *The Forgotten Five*). After a failed audition for *Opportunity Knocks* in 1986, Lee began to gain guest spots on television shows following an appearance on the ITV chatshow *After Ten with Tarbuck* in 1988. By 1995, Lee was offered his own sitcom, *The World of Lee Evans*, in which he played the character of Lee in four separate stories, rather like the earlier Tony Hancock series, although far more manic. Lee's comedy style can be described as a cross between Norman Wisdom and Tommy Cooper, although at 5' 9" (1.75 m) Lee is much taller than Norman and sweats even more than Tommy. Lee's stand-up routines appear to be uncontrolled slap-stick mayhem, the perpetual sweat dripping from every pore lending itself to a certain audience sympathy, but in actual fact Lee is a very accomplished all-round entertainer, singing, dancing and playing several instruments. His film debut came in *Funny Bones* (1995 - as Jack Parker). Other films include: *The Fifth*

Element (1997 - as Fog), MouseHunt (1997 - as Lars Smuntz), There's Something About Mary (1998 - as Tucker), The Ladies Man (2000 - as Barney), The Martins (2001 - as Robert Martin), Plots with a View (2002 - as Delbert Butterfield), Vacuums (2003 - as Toady), The Medallion (2003 - as Arthur Watson) and Freeze Frame (2004 - as Sean Veil). Lee also provided the voice for Zippo in the 2002 TV miniseries Dinotopia and Train in the 2005 film The Magic Roundabout. He is also a very fine stage actor, having played Leo Bloom in the London production of The Producers along with Nathan Lane, with whom he also starred in MouseHunt. On television he has played Alfred Polly in the 2007 TV drama The History of Mr Polly and in 2009 he played Dr Malcolm Taylor in Doctor Who – Planet of the Dead. Lee married Heather Nudds in 1984. They have a daughter, Mollie (b. 1994).

Feldman, Marty See entry in cinema section.

Ferguson, Craig Born 17 May 1962, Glasgow, Scotland. The Cumbernauld-raised Scottish comedian and actor is not perhaps an obvious choice for inclusion among such comic luminaries that dwell on these pages but his earning power as the current host of CBS's The Late Late Show demands enormous respect. Ferguson, from an entertainment-based family (His sister Lynn, and brother Scott are also in showbusiness), went largely unheralded in Britain, his appearances on the alternative comedy circuit under the stage-name Bing Hitler were received with mixed reviews. After enjoying success at the Edinburgh Festival, Craig moved to Los Angeles in 1994. He was best known in the U.S. for his role on The Drew Carey Show, where he played Nigel Wick, Drew Carey's boss, complete with an over-the-top English accent. In December 2004, it was announced that Ferguson would be the successor to Craig Kilborn on CBS's The Late Late Show. Ferguson's first show aired on January 4, 2005, and his 15-minute opening monologue is usually based around a leading news item of the day. Craig also demonstrates his mimic skills, characterising people such as Michael Caine (in space), Sean Connery, Larry King, Mick Jagger, Dr. Phil, and Prince Charles, in a variety of amusing wigs. Craig is reported to earn $8 million a year on American television. His feature film debut came in The Big Tease (1999). Other films include: Saving Grace (2000), The Soul Keeper (2002), Lemony Snicket's A Series of Unfortunate Events (2004), Lenny the Wonder Dog (2005) and Winnie the Pooh (2011 - voice of Owl). He released a novel Between the Bridge and the River on 10 April 2006 and an autobiography American on Purpose: The Improbable Adventures of an Unlikely Patriot in 2009. Craig is a life-long fan of Scottish football team Partick Thistle F.C. He sports three tattoos: the Join, or Die political cartoon on his right forearm; a Ferguson family crest with the Latin motto Dulcius ex asperis ("Sweetness out of difficulty") on his upper right arm in honour of his father; and the Ingram family crest on his upper left arm in honour of his mother. He is also a keen aviator. He has been married three times, to Anne Hogarth (1983-86), Sascha Corwin (1998-2004) and Megan Wallace-Cunningham (2008–present).

Field, Sid See entry in cinema section.

Fielding, Noel Born 21 May 1973, Westminster, London. Noel was educated at Croydon Art College and Buckinghamshire Chilterns University College (now Buckinghamshire New University). He is best known for his collaborations with Julian Barratt (b. Julian Barratt Pettifer, 4 May 1968, Leeds). Their Edinburgh Festival debut in 1998 won them the much coveted Perrier Award for Best Newcomer, the humour based around surreal, sometimes non sequitur, but hilariously funny dialogue. Later that year they made their television debut in the six-episode comedy sketch series, Unnatural Acts, on the Paramount Comedy Channel, now known as Comedy Central. This series was the inspiration for a later Radio 4 series, The Mighty Boosh, and a subsequent television series. On film, Noel debuted in Plunkett & Macleane (1999). Other films include: Bunny and the Bull (2009), Come on Eileen (2010) and Horrid Henry: The Movie (2011 - as Ed Banger). He also appeared in the television movie, Surrealissimo: The Trial of Salvador Dali (2002), Dali being a significant influence on Noel's colourful dress sense and indeed artistic flair. He held his first exhibition, Psychedelic Dreams of the Jelly Fox, at Maison Bertaux, a patisserie in Greek Street, Soho in early 2008. A second exhibition, Bryan Ferry Vs The Jelly Fox, took place at Maison Bertaux, from 5 July 2010 through to 5 January 2011. More recently, Noel performed a dance to "Wuthering Heights" (in true Kate Bush style) for the 2011 edition of Let's Dance for Comic Relief. Despite his camp appearance, Noel was in a long-term relationship with Delia Gaitskell (stage name: Dee Plume) a member of the electropunk band Robots in Disguise. Following their split in 2009, after nine years together, Noel began dating XFM London radio DJ Lliana Bird. Julian has been in a long-term relationship with comedy actress Julia Davis for some years. See also entries in the radio and television section for The Comedy Network, Gas, The It Crowd, Michael McIntyre's Comedy Roadshow, The Mighty Boosh, Nathan Barley, and Never Mind the Buzzcocks.

Fields, Gracie See entry in cinema section.

Flanagan, Bud See Crazy Gang.

Formby, George See entry in cinema section.

Forsyth, Bruce Born Bruce Joseph Forsyth-Johnson, 22 February 1928, Edmonton, Greater London. As a young boy, Bruce attended The Latymer School, and at the age of eight he was captivated by Fred Astaire films. He trained to dance in Tottenham and Brixton. Bruce's stage career began when he was just fourteen, in a song, dance and accordion act called "Boy Bruce, the Mighty Atom". After the war, he spent some years learning his craft on stage, travelling the UK, doing summer seasons, pantomimes and circuses, where he became well known for his comedy strong-man act. It wasn't until 1958 that Bruce became a household name after being asked to compère Val Parnell's weekly TV variety show, Sunday Night at the London Palladium. He continued this role for three series over the following four years. His popularity increased and Bruce was able to turn his hand to new ventures such as his ever-popular one-man shows in which he would dance, sing, play the piano and of course fool around. Bruce vies with Bob Monkhouse as the 'king of the game show hosts' and from 1971 to 1977 drew in huge audiences as host of the BBC's The Generation Game. In 1978 he left the BBC to present the less successful Bruce Forsyth's Big Night, for ITV. Unfortunately this Saturday night extravaganza went on for three hours and although it had high spots such as the return of The Glums, it had no real direction or variety. Despite this rare turkey he remained with ITV and hosted many popular game shows. Since 2004 he has been lead presenter alongside his co-host Tess Daly on BBC television's Strictly Come Dancing. During his presenting career Bruce has become especially well-known for his catch phrases, "Nice to see you, to see you nice", "Good game, good game" and "Didn't they do well?" (from The Generation Game) and "It's gonna be a good night tonight if you play your cards right" and "You get nothing for a pair - not in this game" (from Play Your Cards Right). In 1998 Bruce celebrated his 70th birthday and to commemorate his career was asked to appear at the London Palladium in a week-long revival of his one-man show which culminated in a 90-minute edition of Sunday Night at the London Palladium. A seasoned entertainer who has spent more than sixty years in front of the camera, telling gags, engaging audiences, singing, dancing, playing piano, and acting. His feature films include Star! (1968 - as Arthur Lawrence), Can Heironymus Merkin Ever Forget Mercy Humppe and Find True Happiness? (1969 - as Uncle Limelight), Bedknobs and Broomsticks (1971 - as Swinburne), The Magnificent Seven Deadly Sins (1971 - as Clayton) and Pavlova: A Woman for All Time (1983 - Alfred Batt). Bruce's talents and popularity have been recognised and in May 2005 Bruce unveiled a bronze bust of himself in the Cinderella Bar at the London Palladium. He was appointed a Commander of the Order of the British Empire in the 2006 New Year Honours list and in 2008, was awarded a BAFTA Academy Fellowship Award. In December 2007, his catchphrase 'Nice to see you, to see you nice' was voted the most popular UK catchphrase by the British public. It was originally said to Bruce in a TV advert for the TV Times in 1970 but he immediately made it his own. Bruce has always been associated with beautiful women and his extra-marital relationships in the 1960s included the 1964 Miss World Ann Sidney and singing star Kathy Kirby. He has been married three times, to his early dance partner Penny Calvert (1953-73) with whom he had three daughters: Debbie, Julie and Laura; his co-host from *The Generation Game* Anthea Redfern (1973–79) with whom he had two daughters: Charlotte and Louisa; and the 1975 Miss World Wilnelia Merced (1983–present) with whom he has a son, Jonathan Joseph Forsyth Johnson. His daughter Julie was a member of the Pop Group *Guys 'n' Dolls* and, after marrying band member Dominic Grant, formed the duo *Grant & Forsyth*. In 1988, Julie wrote the UK's Eurovision Song Contest entry "Go" performed by Scott Fitzgerald, which was pipped by Celine Dion by a single point. Bruce's great-great-great-great grandfather William Forsyth (1737–1804) was a founder of the Royal Horticultural Society and gave his name to the plant genus Forsythia. Following years of media lobbying, Bruce was finally made a Knight Bachelor in the 2011 Birthday Honours for services to entertainment and charity. See also entries in the radio and television section for *Didn't They Do Well!*, *Educating Archie*, *The Generation Game*, *Hollywood or Bust*, *Play Your Cards Right*, *The Price is Right*, *Strictly Come Dancing*, *Sunday Night at the London Palladium*, *Take It From Here*, *Takeover Bid*, *Tripper's Day*, *Who Do You Think You Are?*, *The Worker*, and *You Bet!*

French, Dawn Born Dawn Roma French, 11 October 1957, Holyhead, Anglesey, Dawn was born of English parents, her father being a member of the Royal Air Force, being stationed at RAF Valley, Anglesey. He later committed suicide, aged 45, when Dawn was nineteen. In 1977, Dawn studied at the Central School of Speech and Drama, where she met her future comedy partner, Jennifer Saunders. Both came from RAF backgrounds and had grown up on the same base. Although initially disliking one another they eventually shared a flat whilst at college and became friends and formed a double-act called *The Menopause Sisters*. Dawn progressed from this to make her screen debut in the 1981 BBC2 film short, *The Comic Strip*, a tongue-in-cheek "behind the scenes" look at the Comic Strip comedy club. On 9 March 1987, Dawn and Jennifer launched their sketch show *French and Saunders*, which ran for seven series over a period of twenty years. The early series' were known for the small-scale low-budget humour featuring a set of geriatric dancers and a bongos/keyboard music duo called *Raw Sex*, played by Simon Brint and Rowland Rivron. The true vocal talent spot was taken by Kirsty MacColl. Gradually the shows became known for their spoofs on Hollywood films and pop icons. The final series in 2007 was retitled *A Bucket o' French and Saunders*, and was shown as a retrospective, showing 20 years of the *French and Saunders* sketch show. The series also included new pre-recorded sketches, which were interspersed between the classic sketches. Dawn's solo projects include films and adverts. She played The Fat Lady in the film adaptation of *Harry Potter and the Prisoner of Azkaban*, replacing the late Elizabeth Spriggs, who played the character in the first film of the series. Dawn also provided the voice for the character Mrs Beaver in *The Chronicles of Narnia: The Lion, the Witch and the Wardrobe* (2005) and the voice of Miss Miriam Forcible in the 2009 stop-motion 3D fantasy, *Coraline*. For many years she became popular for her appearances in the Terry's Chocolate Orange adverts saying the famous line "It's not Terry's, it's mine!" and she is currently the voice of W H Smith and Tesco adverts. Dawn also has her own line of clothes, Sixteen47, taking its name from the statistic that 47% of the British female population are at least a size 16. Her best-selling epistolary autobiography, *Dear Fatty* (2008), was named from her pet name for Jennifer. Dawn married fellow comedian Lenny Henry in 1984 but they announced their split in 2010. They have an adopted daughter, Billie. Despite her championing of the fuller-bodied woman, Dawn has lost eight stone recently and has dieted down to 11 stone! See also entries in the television section for *Absolutely Fabulous*, *The Comic Strip Presents*, *Girls on Top*, *Happy Families*, *Jam and Jerusalem*, *Lark Rise To Candleford*, *Let Them Eat Cake*, *Murder Most Horrid*, *Psychoville*, *Roger and Val Have Just Got In*, *Saturday Live*, *The Vicar Of Dibley*, *Wild West*, and *The Young Ones*.

Frinton, Freddie Born Frederick Bittiner Coo, 17 January 1909, Grimsby, Lincolnshire. Brought up by foster parents, Freddie moved into music hall after being fired from his job in a Grimsby fish processing plant, for continually playing the fool. He became a household name as a comedian during World War II and after the war began a film career, his debut being *Trouble in the Air* (1948). His other films include: *Penny Points to Paradise* (1951) playing a drunk – a part he perfected in his stage act although he himself was tee-total, *Forces' Sweetheart* (1953), *Stars in Your Eyes* (1957), *Make Mine Mink* (1960) and *What a Whopper* (1961). In 1945, Freddie first performed the sketch *Dinner for One* in Blackpool. As he had to pay a royalty every time he performed the sketch, he bought the rights in the 1950s, which turned out to be a very insightful decision. In 1963, Frinton's *Dinner for One* was recorded by the Norddeutscher Rundfunk (NDR) German television station, and bizarrely, the non-subtitled English language sketch became a German New Year's Eve tradition in the same way as the Marx Brothers films had done so in the UK. In the sixteen-minute short Freddie plays James, butler to Miss Sophie (played by May Warden). Miss Sophie entertains her friends every year but as they are all dead it is left to James to take their place. As each course is served with the accompanying sherry, port, brandy and champagne, James becomes increasingly drunk. The sketch is also a permanent New Year's Eve fixture throughout Scandinavia and Belgium. In Britain Freddie is best known for his elastic facial expressions and the sitcom, *Meet the Wife*. He died 16 October 1968, London, and is buried in Hanwell Cemetery. See also entries in the television section for *Meet the Wife*, and *Thicker Than Water*.

Fry, Stephen See entry in cinema section.

Fyffe, Will Born 16 February 1885, Dundee, Scotland. Will's film career began as long ago as 1914 with his role of Welshman Lewis Bach in the silent movie *The Maid of Cefn Ydfa* (1914) but it was in the 1930s and 1940s that the future music hall star would make his best known films as a character actor in British and Hollywood films. His best known films include: *Rolling Home* (1935), *Owd Bob* (1938 - as Adam McAdam), *The Mind of Mr. Reeder* (1939 - as J. G. Reeder), *Annie Laurie* (1939 - as Will Laurie), *They Came by Night* (1940) and his last film, *The Brothers* (1947). Will's act in the music halls was varied, incorporating many different comedy guises, but it was his epic song routines that he will be remembered. His approach would be to start his song, pause in the middle to give a comic monologue with further detail of the song's storyline, and then resume the song where he left off. He topped the bill at the 1937 Royal Command Performance at the London Palladium. His best-known song was *I belong to Glasgow*, written in 1927, the memorable chorus being *I belong to Glasgow, Dear old Glasgow town; But what's the matter wi' Glasgow, For it's goin' roun' and roun'! I'm only a common old working chap, As anyone here can see, But when I get a couple o' drinks on a Saturday, Glasgow belongs to me!* Ironically, one of the lines in the song reads 'We went in a hotel, where we did very well'. It was by falling from a hotel room window that Will met his death on 14 December 1947, St Andrews. He was buried at Lambhill Cemetery in his adopted home city of Glasgow, three days later.

Gervais, Ricky Born Ricky Dene Gervais, 25 June 1961, Whitley, Reading. Ricky's father was a Franco-Ontarian who emigrated from Canada while on foreign duty during the Second World War. He met his future wife, Eva House, during a blackout and they settled in Whitley. Ricky originally studied biology at University College London in 1979 but changed to philosophy after two weeks, eventually obtaining an upper second-class honours degree. During his time at UCL, he met producer and novelist, Jane Fallon (b. 9 December 1960), with whom he has been in a relationship since 1982. In 1983, during his final year at UCL, Ricky formed a pop duo, *Seona Dancing*, with his friend Bill Macrae. They were signed by *London Records*, but their first two records *More to Lose* (117) and *Bitter Heart* (70) failed to break into the UK singles charts and they split up the following year. Ricky later had a heavy metal band called *The Sacred Hearts* which also failed to set the world alight. By 1997 Ricky was 'head of speech' at the radio station Xfm London and hired his future collaborator Stephen Merchant as his assistant, although Stephen was unknown to him at the time. Ricky first came to prominence by replacing Ali G in the topical slot of the satirical Channel 4 comedy programme *The 11 O'Clock Show* in early 1999, in which his character used as many expletives as was allowable. He next went on to present his own comedy chat series for Channel 4 called *Meet Ricky Gervais* (2000), written by Ricky, Stephen Merchant, Jimmy Carr and another close friend, Robin Ince. Unfortunately the tongue-in-cheek style of the show did not go down well with the viewing public who did not get the joke, which was perhaps a little more subtle than Steve Coogan's Alan Partridge effort. The show regularly featured darts assistant, Tony Green, as his stooge, but perhaps because Ricky used his own name on the show it was perceived as a straight talk show and cancelled after one series. Ricky also wrote for Channel 5's *The Jim Tavare Show*. His big television break came in 2001 with *The Office*, which has since become a hit all over the world. His next venture, *Extras*, was also a huge hit on both sides of the Atlantic. The *Ricky Gervais Show* is a comedy audio show starring Ricky, Stephen Merchant, and their mutual friend Karl Pilkington, which was later adapted into an animated televised version debuting for HBO and Channel 4 in 2010. The show started in November 2001 on *Xfm*, London and aired in weekly periods. In November 2005, Guardian Unlimited offered the show as a podcast series of 12 shows. Throughout January and February 2006, the podcast was consistently ranked the number one podcast in the world and appeared in the *2007 Guinness World Record* for the world's most downloaded podcast, having gained an average of 261,670 downloads per episode during its first month. The three friends have subsequently made a travel documentary television series broadcast on Sky1 and Science Channel entitled, *An Idiot Abroad* (2010). In 2002, Ricky beat entrepreneur Grant Bovey on a split decision in a three-round charity boxing contest shown by the BBC as part of its Comic Relief programming. Ricky has also completed a trilogy of stand-up tours, Animals (2003), Politics (2004) and Fame (2007). He released a children's book in 2004, *Flanimals* (illustrated by his friend Rob Steen), which depicted nonsense animals. Its sequels include *More Flanimals* (2005), *Flanimals of the Deep* (2006) and *Day of the Bletching* (2007). His film debut was *Dog Eat Dog* (2001). Other films include: *Valiant* (2005 - voice of Bugsy the pigeon), *For Your Consideration* (2006 - as Martin Gibb), *Night at the Museum* (2006 - as Dr McPhee), *Stardust* (2007 - as Ferdy the Fence), *Ghost Town* (2008 - as Pincus), *Night at the Museum 2* (2009), *The Invention of Lying* (2009 - as Mark Bellison), *Cemetery Junction* (2010 - as Mr Taylor) and *Spy Kids: All the Time in the World* (2011 - voice of Argonaut). He also voices Mole in the forthcoming film *The Wind in the Willows*. Ricky is a huge fan of *The Simpsons*. He wrote the episode *Homer Simpson, This Is Your Wife* (2006), becoming the first celebrity to both write and guest star (as Charles Heathbar) in an episode. Ricky has hosted the Golden Globes for the past three years. His latest television creation is *Derek*, a sitcom about Derek Noakes, a 49-year-old retirement home worker, who "loves animals, Rolf Harris, Jesus, *Deal or No Deal, Million Pound Drop* and *Britain's Got Talent* - but his main hobby is autograph hunting". The pilot is to air in April 2012. See also entries in the television section for *Bruiser, Comedy Lab, The 11 O'Clock Show, Extras, The Office,* and *The Sketch Show*.

Gold, Jimmy See *Crazy Gang*.

Goodies A trio of British comedians. Tim Brooke-Taylor (b. 17 July 1940, Buxton, Derbyshire), (David) Graeme Garden (b. 18 February 1943, Aberdeen, Scotland) and Bill Oddie (b. 7 July 1941, Rochdale, Lancashire) who created, wrote, and starred in the surreal comedy series *The Goodies*. The three actors met as students at the University of Cambridge, where Tim was studying law, Graeme, medicine and Bill, English. They all became members of the Cambridge University Footlights Club, with Tim becoming president in 1963, and Graeme succeeding him in 1964 (he himself being succeeded by none other than Eric Idle). The three comedy actors have had lengthy careers both as a team and in solo projects. See entries in the radio and television section for *At Last The 1948 Show, Broaden Your Mind, Crossroads, The Frost Report, The Goodies, I'm Sorry I Haven't A Clue, I'm Sorry I'll Read That Again, Jamie's Fowl Dinners, Just A Minute, Marty, Mastermind, Me and My Girl, No - That's Me Over Here!,* *On the Braden Beat, One Foot in the Grave, Twice a Fortnight,* and *Who Do You Think You Are?*

Gray, Eddie See *Crazy Gang*.

Grenfell, Joyce See entry in cinema section.

Hancock, Tony Born 12 May 1924, Hall Green, Birmingham. Anthony John Hancock was brought up in his father's pub, the Railway Hotel, in Bournemouth. John Hancock was also the resident comedian and all-round entertainer in his pub and the love of show business formulated in the young Hancock from these roots. During World War II, Tony joined the RAF and, following a failed audition for ENSA, he subsequently joined *Ralph Reader's Gang Show*. Once de-mobbed Tony became resident comedian at the Windmill Theatre and had his first big break on the radio shows *Workers' Playtime, Variety Bandbox* and *Educating Archie*. His first venture into television was in four episodes of *Kaleidoscope* in 1951. In 1954, Tony was given his own BBC radio show, *Hancock's Half Hour*, which ran until 1959. This title was used by Tony for his popular television show from 1956. In 1960, Tony made a memorable appearance on the BBC's *Face to Face*, and this is often considered to be a seminal moment in his career as he subsequently became very analytical about himself and his comedy, eventually ditching his co-stars and then his scriptwriters. Tony appeared in five feature films *Orders Are Orders* (1954 - as Lieutenant Wilfred Cartroad), *The Rebel* (1961 - as Anthony Hancock), *The Punch and Judy Man* (1962 - as Wally Pinner), *Those Magnificent Men in Their Flying Machines* (1965 - as Harry Popperwell) and *The Wrong Box* (1966 - as a detective). Tony was married twice, to fashion model Cicely Romanis (1950-65) and his publicist Freddie Ross, from 1965 until just before his death in 1968. Tony had an affair with John Le Mesurier's second wife, Joan, during his marriage to Freddie. Alcoholism and increasing paranoia blighted Tony's later career and he committed suicide in Sydney, Australia, on 24 June 1968. The master of comic timing and observation was found dead in his Latimer Road, Bellevue Hill apartment with an empty vodka bottle by his right hand and amphetamines by his left. In a suicide note he wrote "Things just seemed to go too wrong too many times". His ashes were brought back to the UK by satirist Willie Rushton. See also entries in the radio and television section for *Citizen James, Educating Archie, Face to Face, Hancock's Half Hour, Here's Harry, Kaleidoscope, Not So Much A Programme, Steptoe and Son, Variety Bandbox,* and *Worker's Playtime*.

Handley, Tommy See entry in cinema section.

Hart, Miranda Born Miranda Katharine Hart-Dyke, 14 December 1972, Torquay, Devon. Miranda comes from good stock. She is the daughter of Captain David Hart Dyke, who was in command of HMS *Coventry* during the 1982 Falklands War when it was sunk by the Argentinian Air Force and later went on to be Aide-de-Camp to HM The Queen. Miranda is also first cousin to celebrated plant hunter Tom Hart Dyke. Despite graduating with a 2:1 in politics from, the then, Bristol Polytechnic, Miranda always intended to be a comedienne and took to it quite naturally, touring one-woman shows as the basis for her early style of self-deprecating humour. The sketch show *Smack the Pony* (2001) was Miranda's first television break as a writer and performer, and she showed her versatility as an actress by playing straight roles in the 2004 drama series *William and Mary* and the 2005 television film *My Family and Other Animals*. Miranda has also made appearances in *Absolutely Fabulous, The Vicar of Dibley,* and *Lead Balloon*. Her sitcom, *Miranda*, has won several television awards. Miranda has broken into the US market by playing Crabman in the US comedy *My Name is Earl*, although the extreme make-up prevents her from being immediately recognisable. In 2012, Miranda began to appear in the BBC One drama series, *Call the Midwife*, playing the character of Camilla 'Chummy' Fortescue-Cholmeley-Browne. See also entries in the radio and television section for *Hyperdrive, Miranda, The 99p Challenge, Not Going Out* and *Smack the Pony*.

Hay, Will See entry in cinema section.

Haynes, Arthur Born 19 May 1914, Hammersmith, London. After teaming up with Charlie Chester to entertain the troops during World War II, Arthur became a member of Chester's team on the radio series *Stand Easy* (1946-49) but his break came when he appeared on the 1956 ITV show *Strike A New Note* and the following year he was given his own ITV series. His most popular character between 1957 and 1960 was Oscar Pennyfeather, an entirely silent characterisation whose 'conscience' would be expressed by his comedy foil, more often than not Nicholas Parsons. Arthur's best-loved character was undoubtedly the all-knowing argumentative tramp who proudly adorned a row of medals on his chest. Johnny Speight was responsible for many of the sketches involving Arthur and the similarity to Alf Garnett is more than superficial. The on-screen relationship with Dermot Kelly as Arthur's Irish tramp sidekick was always popular and the 15 series of *The Arthur Haynes Show* between 1957 and 1966 were invariably prime time Saturday evening viewing. Arthur appeared in two feature films, *Strange Bedfellows* (1965) and *Doctor in Clover* (1966) and appeared on The Ed Sullivan Show in the autumn of 1966 and was due to start a 16th series for ITV but died of a heart attack on 19 November 1966.

Hearne, Richard Born 30 January 1908, Norwich, Norfolk, England. From a circus background, Richard became well-versed in all aspects of musical variety and became an accomplished acrobat, specialising in stunt falling. This expertise led to the creation of his greatest character, Mr Pastry, a bumbling old doddery fool who was forever falling over. Mr Pastry made his television debut on 19 August 1946 in a short BBC film, *The Village Store*, alongside his wife Yvonne Hearne. He was 37-years-old but doffed 'granny' glasses and bowler hat to give the impression of being very old and to make the illusion even more convincing he sprinkled flour on his hair and moustache and walked in staccato fashion. Between 1946 and 1962 Mr Pastry was never off our television screens either starring in his own series or making cameo appearances in others. His popularity during this period cannot be underestimated, children of all ages would be spellbound by his antics whether it be making pastry or acting as Britain's favourite odd-job man. His fame was not confined to these shores and his films such as *Mr Pastry at the Circus* (1960) gave him fame throughout Europe and America, where he made numerous appearances on the Ed Sullivan Show. In France he was known as Papa Gâteau, in Germany Mr Sugar Tart. Richard Hearne, in the guise of Mr Pastry remained popular throughout the 1960s but without his own series he gradually semi-retired in the 1970s through ill-health and disillusionment at the increasing trend of smutty television. He died of a heart attack on 25 August 1979.

Henderson, Dickie Born 30 October 1922, London, England. The son of a Yorkshire comedian of the same name, best known for making the original British recording of the popular song "Tiptoe Through the Tulips". Dickie Jr was steeped in show business making his first appearance in the 1933 Noel Coward film, *Cavalcade*. Initially he was part of a family act (The Henderson Twins and Dickie) with his two sisters, but once they married the act broke up. Having cut his teeth in Hollywood Dickie developed an American-style delivery in the mould of Bob Hope but he was more than just a stand-up comedian he was also a fine actor, juggler, song and dance man, and gymnast. After making his British television debut on Arthur Askey's *Before your Very Eyes* (1956) he was given his own ITV series *The Dickie Henderson Show* (1957-59) with former light-heavyweight boxing champion Freddie Mills appearing with him in various sketches. This series was renamed the *Dickie Henderson Half-Hour* (1958-59) before resorting back to its former name and becoming a sitcom co-starring June Laverick and Lionel Murton (1960-68). Dickie was also a regular compere on Val Parnell's *Sunday Night at the London Palladium* in 1958 and appeared in three specials with Bob Monkhouse in 1977 and 1978 (*I'm Bob, He's Dickie*), their friendship dating back to when Dickie stood in for Bob on his popular quiz show, *For Love or Money* (1960). In 1948 he married Dixie Jewel Ross (b. 9 August 1929, Loraine, Texas; d. 10 July 1963 – on the day of their 15th wedding anniversary), a member of the Ross Sisters song and dance trio. They had a son Matthew and a daughter Linda. His second marriage, to Gwynneth lasted until his death, from cancer, on 22nd September 1985.

Henry, Lenny Born Lenworth George Henry, 29 August 1958, Dudley, England. Lenny came to prominence in 1975 winning an edition of the popular talent-show *New Faces*, aged 16, his act consisting of impersonating famous people of the day such as Muhammad Ali and Tommy Cooper. Five years touring as compere of the *Black and White Minstrels* (ironically the only black member of the cast) gave Lenny all-round experience and regular appearances as Sonny Foster in the ground-breaking black sitcom *The Fosters* (1976-77) turned him into a formidable entertainer. He enjoyed further success on the Saturday morning children's programme *Tiswas* (and lesser success on the adult version *OTT*) in the late 1970s and early 1980s resorting back to mimicking stars such as naturalist David Bellamy and newsreader Trevor McDonald (in the guise of Trevor McDoughnut). Lenny also developed new fictional characters such as Algernon Spencer Churchill Gladstone Disraeli Palmerston Pitt-the-Younger Razzamatazz, a Rastafarian with a penchant for condensed-milk sandwiches, and Theophilus P Wildebeeste, a soul singer and 'sex machine' (inspired by singers Barry White, Tom Jones and Teddy Pendergrass). The comedy sketch show *Three of a Kind* (1981-83) gave Lenny yet another chance to re-invent himself and he was rewarded with his own series of *The Lenny Henry Show* (1984-88; 1994-95; 2004-05), the 1987/88 series being a sitcom with Lenny playing Delbert Wilkins the 'wickedly crucial' London DJ. Lenny returned to the sitcom format for three series of *Chef* (1993-96) playing super-cook Gareth Blackstock before starring in the highly-acclaimed mini-series *Hope and Glory* (1999-2000) playing headmaster Ian George, his first straight dramatic role. Lenny has managed to remain at the top of the British comedy tree with fresh routines and characters and his likeable personality has continued to endear him to audiences everywhere. On film he made his debut in *The Suicide Club* (1988) and he has also appeared in *True Identity* (1991), *Harry Potter and the Prisoner of Azkaban* (2004 – voice of Shrunken Head), *MirrorMask* (2005) and *Penelope* (2006). On stage, Lenny has appeared in the title role of *Othello* in the Northern Broadsides production, at the West Yorkshire Playhouse in Leeds. In 2009, Lenny became the face of budget hotel operator Premier Inn and continues to star in adverts for them. In 1984, he married comedienne Dawn French and it was a union that blessed both their careers, although they did eventually divorce in October 2010. They have an adopted daughter, Billie (b. 1991). See also entries in the television section for *Big & Small, The Black and White Minstrel Show, Chef, The Fosters, Hope and Glory, The Jack Docherty Show, Live at the Apollo, New Faces, OTT , Saturday Live, Three Of A Kind, TISWAS,* and *The Young Ones*.

Hill, Benny Born Alfred Hawthorne Hill, 21 January 1924, Southampton, England. Benny took his stage name from the great American comedian Jack Benny, although after being demobbed after World War II, his career was anything but on par with his namesake. He struggled to work consistently on radio and for a while in the late 1940s played straight-man to Reg Varney in a moderately successful double-act. He made his television debut on the BBC show *Music-Hall* (1949) and developed a reputation as a fine satirical impressionist when hosting the BBC talent series *Showcase* (1954). He was named 'Personality of the Year' in the *Daily Mail National Television Awards* in 1955 and this elevated him to stardom, the first comedy star to make his name in television rather than first having a radio or stage career. *The Benny Hill Show* (1955-89) ran in various guises for 34 years, initially on the BBC and then ITV until the powers to be at Thames decided his particular brand of bawdy seaside postcard humour was not politically correct. There is no doubt Benny revelled in his stylised parade of scantily-dressed buxom assistants in various sketches and his use of the double-entendre was in *Carry On* film proportions, but this format kept his shows at the top for four decades. His musical sketches contain some classic comedy moments and even spawned a UK No 1 hit in *Ernie - the fastest milkman in the west* - (1971). The lisping numskull Fred Scuttle, complete with beret and greeting of 'yeth thir' while saluting humbly, was a popular character creation and a mischievous roll of the eyes was enough to let us know that he wasn't quite as stupid as the interviewer thought. Despite the accusations of repetitiveness in his shows Benny was a great comic innovator and classic moments popped up on a regular basis. On one occasion while playing the beleaguered potential son-in law asked to tea, he would persistently shrug his shoulders and wave his hands while uttering "no, no, no" as his girlfriend's mother asked him to say 'when' as she slid the knife along to an ever-diminishing slice of battenberg cake. He would finally relent and mum would cut off the most miniscule slice only for Benny to slyly look to the camera and surprise us all by picking up the whole cake and leaving the thin slice on the plate. During another sketch Benny could be seen sitting outside an inn playfully dangling a piece of rope in front of a sobbing companion. When asked by another companion why the man was crying the fourth member of the group proclaims "he's okay, it's just that his father was hung this morning"..........sheer genius. On film he made his debut as Hugo Dill in *Who Done It?*. Other films include: *Light Up the Sky!* (1960), *Chitty Chitty Bang Bang* (1968 - as the toymaker) and his last feature film, *The Italian Job* (1969).Benny suffered with ill health after his series was cancelled and was advised to have a heart bypass in early 1992. His body was found propped up in front of the television in his Teddington flat on 20 April 1992, he had died of a heart-attack up to two days earlier.

Hill, Harry Born Matthew Keith Hall, 1 October 1964, Woking, Surrey. Harry qualified as a doctor and initially worked as a semi-pro comedian before winning the Perrier Award as best newcomer on the Edinburgh Festival Fringe. His larger-than-life appearance - bald head, extra-large horn-rimmed glasses, extra-extra-large shirt collars, suede shoes and drainpipe pin-striped suit with a proliferation of pens in his breast-pocket - coupled with a staccato delivery style, make him a unique act. *Harry Hill's Fruit Corner* (BBC Radio 4, 1993-97) led to various television series beginning with *Harry Hill's Fruit Fancies* (1994) which gave the viewing public its first glimpse of the off-the-wall brand of good clean humour that characterises his act. *Harry Hill's Television Burp* has won him fresh acclaim as an innovative and clever presenter and *An Audience with Harry Hill* (2004) confirmed his status as a true comic genius. See also entries in the television section for *Harry Hill's TV Burp, The Jack Jackson Show*, and *You've Been Framed*.

Hinge and Bracket George Logan (b. 7 July 1944, Glasgow) and Patrick Fyffe (b. 23 January 1942, Stafford; died 11 May 2002, from spinal cancer). George and Patrick made their first appearance as Hinge and Bracket in 1974 at the Edinburgh Festival. Dr Evadne Hinge (Logan) was a pianist, arranger and foil for Dame Hilda Bracket (Fyffe). Together they played two elderly spinster musicians who shared a house (The Old Manse or Utopia Ltd.) in the fictional village of Stackton Tressel in Suffolk. They amused themselves with recitals of Gilbert & Sullivan, Noel Coward and Ivor Novello. They employed an eccentric housekeeper, Maud, played in various radio series by character actress Daphne Heard. Hinge and Bracket gained a wider audience when they transferred their act to television via three series of *Dear Ladies* on BBC 2, between 1983 and 1985, scripts written by Gyles Brandreth. After the death of his stage partner, George retired from the stage and opened a bed-and-breakfast in France.

Hope and Keen See entry in television section.

Hope, Bob Born Leslie Townes Hope, 29 May 1903, Eltham, London. His English father, William Henry Hope, was a stonemason from Weston-super-Mare and his Welsh mother, Avis Townes, was a light opera singer. His family moved to America when he was four-years-old, and he grew up in Cleveland Ohio. Bob began his career in 1914 when he entered and won a Charlie Chaplin imitator contest. He was a professional boxer for a time, under the name Packy East, before eventually entering show business by doing vaudeville in the 1920s. His first wife was his vaudeville partner Grace Louise Troxell, whom he married on 25 January 1933. The marriage proved to be short-lived and following a quickie divorce he married Dolores DeFina, on 19 February 1934. A devoutly Roman Catholic (Hope was to convert to Roman Catholicism at a later date) Bronx-born nightclub singer of Irish and Italian extraction, she was known professionally as Dolores Reade and had met Hope two months earlier at The Vogue, a Manhattan nightclub where she was performing. Dolores

and Bob remained together until Hope's death sixty-nine years later – the longest marriage in Hollywood history to date. They adopted four children, all from the same orphanage in Evanston, Illinois. Bob's growing reputation in the 1930s led him to move on to radio, movies, television, and just about everything else. His fame began with several Broadway musicals including *Roberta, Say When*, the 1936 *Ziegfeld Follies* and, with Ethel Merman, *Red, Hot and Blue*. Then, in his film debut *The Big Broadcast of 1938*, Bob introduced (in duet with Shirley Ross) the song that became his trademark, *Thanks for the Memory*. The sentimental nature of the music allowed Bob and his writers to come up with endless variations of the song to fit specific circumstances, such as saying farewell to troops whilst on tour. As a movie star he was best known for *The Cat and the Canary* (1939), *My Favorite Brunette* (1947), *The Paleface* (1948), *Fancy Pants* (1950), *Casanova's Big Night* (1954), *Call Me Bwana* (1963) and the "Road To" movies where he starred alongside Bing Crosby and Dorothy Lamour in *Road to Singapore* (1940 - as Ace Lannigan), *Road to Zanzibar* (1941 - as Hubert 'Fearless' Frazier), *Road to Morocco* (1942 - as Orville 'Turkey' Jackson / Aunt Lucy), *Road to Utopia* (1946 - as Chester Hooton), *Road to Rio* (1947 - as Hot Lips Barton), *Road to Bali* (1952 as Harold Gridley) and *The Road to Hong Kong* (1962 - as Chester Babcock). His last feature film was a cameo in *Spies Like Us* (1985). He never won any Oscars for his films, though the Academy of Motion Picture Arts and Sciences, otherwise honoured him five times, with two honorary Oscars, two Special Awards and the Jean Hersholt Humanitarian Award. As host of the Academy Awards ceremony – a role he filled 18 times between 1939 and 1977 – he once quipped "Well, it's Oscar time, or as it's known at my house, Passover." On 6 May 1941, at March Field, California, Bob performed his first United Service Organizations (USO) show. He continued to travel and entertain troops for the rest of World War II, the Korean War, the Vietnam War and didn't retire until after the 1990-91 Persian Gulf War. By the time Bob made his radio debut in 1937, NBC was mainly just a radio network. His first regular series for NBC Radio was the "Woodbury Soap Hour". One year later, he had the first of many shows to bear his name, and in the decades that followed he became one of the world's most-loved entertainers, a friend of several American Presidents and the host of Pro-Am golf tournaments and, from 1953, Christmas television specials. A signature portion of his yuletide specials was his performance of "Silver Bells" (from his 1951 film *The Lemon Drop Kid*), usually done as a duet with a featured female guest star (through the years done with such stars as Olivia Newton-John and Brooke Shields). His final television special was in 1996, with guest Tony Danza helping him to salute all the Presidents of the United States he had known over the years. Although a huge star by then, Bob made his television debut on Easter Sunday 1950 on *The Colgate Comedy Hour*. By 1951 he also appeared on another budget variety show, *Chesterfield Sound Off Time* and also made numerous guest appearances on various comedy shows such as *I Love Lucy, The Danny Thomas Show*, and *The Jack Benny Show*, where the two great comics began to manufacture an on-going 'rivalry' based on great friendship and mutual respect. *The Bob Hope Show* ran from 1953-75, although Bob did not stop doing TV specials until 1996, when he pretty much retired from show business, except for a K-Mart commercial that aired in 1997. Bob was an excellent golfer, playing to a four handicap at his best. The Bob Hope Classic (now known as the Humana Challenge and changed to 4 rounds in 2012) was founded in 1960, and for many years was the only FedEx Cup tournament that took place over five rounds. The tournament made history in 1995, when Bob teed up for the opening round in a foursome that included Presidents Gerald R. Ford, George H.W. Bush and Bill Clinton – the only time ever that three presidents participated in a golf foursome. Despite two rumours of Bob's premature death in 1998 he did eventually die of pneumonia on Sunday, 27 July 2003, at Toluca Lake, California, and is interred in San Fernando Mission Cemetery in Los Angeles, California.

Howard, Russell Born Russell Joseph Howard, 23 March 1980, Bristol. Russell began his professional career in 2004 when he was commissioned by BBC Radio 1 to write and perform on the comedy series, *The Milk Run.* He was one of several comedians picked as the best comedy talent from the 2005 Edinburgh Festival Fringe that recorded spots for the 'Edinburgh and Beyond show' which aired on Paramount Comedy 1 in 2006. From 2009 he took over as compère of this show from Al Murray. His routine is based on political satire, surrealism and observational humour. In 2006 he had his own show on BBC 6 Music, assisted by fellow comedian Jon Richardson, in a Sunday morning slot previously hosted by Russell Brand. In 2009 he began a BBC3 comedy series, *Russell Howard's Good News,* which is currently in its fourth series. A regular on panel shows, see also entries in the television section for *Live at the Apollo,* and *Mock The Week.*

Howerd, Frankie Born Francis Alick Howard, 6 March 1917, York. Francis appeared on stage at a young age but his early hopes of becoming a serious actor were thwarted after he failed an audition for RADA. He began his off-the-cuff comedy routines during World War II whilst serving in the Army. Despite suffering from terrible stage fright, he continued to work after the war, beginning his professional career in the summer of 1946 in a touring show called *For the Fun of It.* He then began working in radio, making his debut at the start of December 1946 in the BBC's *Variety Bandbox.* Frankie's reputation grew thanks to excellent material written by the likes of Eric Sykes, Galton and Simpson and Johnny Speight. In 1954, he made his feature film debut opposite Petula Clark in *The Runaway Bus* (as Percy Lamb), a film specifically written for Frankie. Other films include: *The Ladykillers* (1955), *Further Up the Creek* (1958), *The Cool Mikado* (1963), *The Fast Lady* (1963), *The Great St. Trinian's Train Robbery* (1966), *Carry on Doctor* (1967 - as Francis Bigger), *Carry on Up the Jungle* (1970 - as Professor Inigo Tinkle), *Up the Chastity Belt* (1971 - as Lurkalot / Richard the Lionheart), *Up Pompeii* (1971 - as Lurcio), *The House in Nightmare Park* (1977) and his last feature film, *Sgt. Pepper's Lonely Hearts Club Band* (1978 - as Mr Mustard). Despite his initial success in films Frankie was very much a television performer. His routine consisted of engaging the audience directly as a whole as if he was making them privy to some confidential information, usually to the detriment of his employers, the BBC or ITV. Occasionally he would feign innocence about his obvious and risqué double entendres while mockingly censuring the audience for finding them funny. Frankie would rarely tell jokes but he was a master at weaving a story where the journey was laced with improbable situations. He had numerous catchphrases while relating his stories, "Oooh, no missus" and "Titter ye not" were mainstays and another old favourite was "I was flabbergasted, in fact my flabber has never been so gasted". Frankie's fame was at its height in the 1970s when his iconic television series *Up Pompeii* showed his talents to the full. Several spin-offs, on stage, film and television followed and he was at the top of his profession by the end of the decade. After a lull of several years without a regular television show Frankie returned to television screens in the Channel 4 show *Superfrank!* (1987), scripted by Miles Tredinnick and Vince Powell. In the last years of his career, he developed a cult following with student audiences and performed a one-man show at universities small theatrical venues all over the country. Throughout his career, Frankie concealed his homosexuality from both his audience and his mother. Sexual acts between consenting males were illegal in England and Wales until 1967 and illegal in Scotland until 1981 and it would have been professional suicide for him to 'come out'. Frankie was in a relationship with his manager, Dennis Haymer for more than 30 years, although several showbusiness friends have detailed Frankie's propensity for bold advances to both gay and straight men. Frankie had a close friendship with singer / presenter Cilla Black. He died, of heart failure, on 19 April 1992, Fulham, London. See also entries in the radio and television section for *Children's Favourites, Up Pompeii!, Variety Bandbox, Whoops Baghdad!* and *Worker's Playtime.*

Hudd, Roy Born 16 May 1936, Croydon, London. Roy began his professional life as a Butlins Redcoat at Clacton in Essex. He was a great fan of the music hall and had the opportunity to appear on the same bill as Max Miller at the Finsbury Park Empire in 1959 (Roy is now President of the Max Miller Appreciation Society). He made his television debut in an episode of the ITV series, *Our House* (1960) and progressed to a larger role in *Not So Much A Programme, More A Way Of Life* (1964-65), a satirical show in the mould of *That Was The Week That Was,* and the following year he landed his own TV show, *The Illustrated Weekly Hudd,* which demonstrated his skills as a comedy entertainer and sketch-writer. Various television series followed but it was his topical BBC Radio 2 show *The News Hudd Lines* (1975-2001) which won him critical acclaim, the mix of sharp writing and excellent performances by his team, including June Whitfield and Chris Emmett, giving the show a cutting contemporary edge while managing to afford nostalgic indulgences which pleased young and old listeners alike. Roy's love of the music hall has never diminished and he became president of the British Music Hall Society. In 1983 he won a Laurence Olivier Theatre Award for *Underneath the Arches,* a musical pastiche of Flanagan and Allen. As a character actor Roy has excelled and after his acclaimed performance in Dennis Potter's dark 1993 drama *Lipstick On Your Collar,* Potter wrote another role for him in the chilling *Karaoke* (1996), his Spoonerism-afflicted Ben Baglin lightening Potter's posthumous tale. Roy has played undertaker Archie Shuttleworth in *Coronation Street,* off-and-on since 2002, and as in all his character portrayals gives him his unique stamp, in this case it was Archie's professional ability to gauge a person's exact height on first sighting! He was awarded the OBE in 2003. Roy made his film debut in *The Blood Beast Terror* (1968). Other films include: *Up the Chastity Belt* (1971), *Up Pompeii* (1971), *The Magnificent Seven Deadly Sins* (1971), *The Alf Garnett Saga* (1972), *A Kind of Hush* (1999) and *Purely Belter* (2000). See also entries in the television section for *Common as Muck, Coronation Street, The Good Old Days, Lipstick on your Collar,* and *Not So Much A Programme.*

Idle, Eric Born 29 March 1943, South Shields, Tyne and Wear. In 1962 Eric won a place at Pembroke College, Cambridge, to read English. He joined the Cambridge Footlights after being auditioned by Bill Oddie and Tim Brooke-Taylor. He quickly rose in the Footlight ranks, working with David Gooderson, Richard Eyre and Humphrey Barclay, who would later help in the formation of the Python team. Despite having the difficult task of following Chapman and Cleese's phenomenally successful revue show *A Clump of Plinths,* Eric led a triumphant production at the 1964 Edinburgh Festival (where he first met Michael Palin and Terry Jones), and the next year was elected chairman of the Footlights where he was responsible for throwing the doors open to women for the first time, including celebrated feminist author Germaine Greer. He began his professional life writing for *The Frost Report* and the popular radio series *I'm Sorry I'll Read That Again* before making the occasional appearance at *At Last the 1948 Show* (the title suggested by John Cleese relating to the length of time it took programme controllers to green-light a show), a forerunner of the Python series. He then teamed up with Terry Jones and Michael Palin to write, and star in a similarly surreal children's series *Do Not Adjust Your Set. Monty Python's Flying Circus* turned Eric into a superstar and inspired a future generation of comedians. When the Python television series ended in the mid-1970s Eric's next project was *Rutland Weekend Television,* a comedy sketch show based around 'Britain's smallest television network'. Eric befriended ex-Beatle George Harrison at this time and George not only made a guest appearance in the Christmas special but also inspired one of Eric's most successful projects, *The Rutles* (1978). A spoof documentary modelled on the real-life career of *The Beatles,* the full-length television film tracked the deeds of the "Pre-Fab Four" (containing tracks penned by Neil Innes that closely parodied *Beatles* tracks); it also managed to pull in a wide range of stars, including Dan Aykroyd, Bill Murray, Michael Palin, Mick Jagger and George Harrison (who played an interviewer of the band). During the late 1970s and early 1980s, Eric's career in the U.S. took off and he became a regular host of *Saturday Night Live* (along with Michael Palin), as well as earning a guest spot in the film *National Lampoon's European Vacation* (1985). His starring film roles include *The Adventures of Baron Munchausen* (1988) and *Nuns on the Run* (1990). Other films include: *And Now for Something Completely Different* (1971 – his debut), *The Meaning of Life* (1983),

Yellowbeard (1983), Missing Pieces (1992), Mom and Dad Save the World (1992), Splitting Heirs (1993), Casper (1995), The Wind in the Willows (1996 - as Rat), An Alan Smithee Film: Burn Hollywood Burn (1997), Journey Into Your Imagination (1999), Dudley Do-Right (1999), 102 Dalmatians (2000 - voice of Waddlesworth), Shrek the Third (2007 - voice of Merlin), Delgo (2008 - voice of Spig) and Wolf Sheep (2010). Eric also has had hit records with the (self-penned) theme tune to the hit BBC sitcom One Foot in the Grave and Always Look on the Bright Side of Life (from the 1979 film The Life of Brian), which reached No 3 in the UK Charts in 1991 after being adopted as a football chant. More recently, his musical Spamalot (a musical based on the 1975 film Monty Python and The Holy Grail) has been playing to packed houses on Broadway. This post-Python success with Python-esque material has led to Eric being criticised for demeaning (and milking) the glorious memory of Python. Eric has been married twice, to Australian actress Lyn Ashley (1969-75 - they have a son, Carey b. 1973) and American Tania Kosevich since 1981. They have a daughter, Lily (b. 1990). See also entries in the radio and television section for At Last The 1948 Show, Broaden Your Mind, Do Not Adjust Your Set, The Frost Report, Hark at Barker, I'm Sorry I'll Read That Again, Monty Python's Flying Circus, No - That's Me Over Here!, One Foot in the Grave, and Rutland Weekend Television.

Izzard, Eddie See entry in cinema section.

Jacques, Hattie See entry in cinema section.

James, Jimmy Born James Casey, 20 May 1892, Portrack, Stockton-on-Tees. Jimmy began his stage career, aged 12, joining the vocal act 'Willy Netta's Singing Jockeys' as 'Terry the blue-eyed Irish boy'. During the Great War, he was a sergeant in the Northumberland Fusiliers but was invalided out. Jimmy initially worked as a double act, The Two Jimmies, with his great uncle Jimmy Howells. His big break came when he replaced the young Max Miller who had walked out of a show. By 1930 he was appearing at the London Palladium, earning £100 a week. His act was very much ahead of its time with surreal observational humour and few gags. Jimmy often played a chain-smoking drunk and like Freddie Frinton, who performed a similar routine, he too was teetotal. In the 1940s Jimmy developed one of the funniest stage routines in variety history with his two stooges, Bretton Woods (later known as Eli Woods, more familiarly known as 'Our Eli') and Hutton Conyers (played by various members of the Casey family and, from 1956 to 1959 by a young Roy Castle). Their most famous routine was probably the 'elephant-in-the-box' where the dim-witted Hutton Conyers (Jimmy named the character after a village near Ripon) would walk on stage with a shoe-box purporting to have all manner of huge animals inside it. Jimmy's nephew, Jack Casey, who worked under the name Eli Woods, would often receive the sympathetic laughter. 'Our Eli' was tall and gormless, had a stammer and wore ill-fitting clothes. After Jimmy's death, his son, James Casey (1922-2011), producer of The Clitheroe Kid and discoverer of Les Dawson, often replaced his father to keep the act alive. Jimmy also appeared in several films, notably opposite Norman Evans (who played his wife) in Over The Garden Wall (1950) and Those People Next Door (1953) where he and Eli perform a cameo reprising Jimmy's drunk routine. Jimmy appeared at the Royal Variety Performance in 1953 and stole the show with his routine The Chipster—a lecture on the occupational hazards of preparing chips. Towards the end of his career Jimmy made guest appearances on popular variety shows of the day and also had his own series' Home James (1956) and Meet the Champ (1960) where he played a boxing promoter. In 1921 he married music hall dancer Isabelle Darby and they had one son, the aforementioned James Casey. Jimmy died 4 August 1965, Blackpool, Lancashire.

James, Sid See entry in cinema section.

Jewel, Jimmy Born James Arthur Thomas Marsh, 4 December 1909, Sheffield, South Yorkshire. Jimmy, the son of a Yorkshire comedian, initially worked under the name Maurice Marsh before adopting his father's stage name. He had a long career as a solo comedian before teaming up with his cousin Ben Warriss (b. 29 May 1909, apparently in the same bed as Jimmy; d. 14 January

1993, Twickenham, London) in 1934 and taking over the mantle of Britain's best-loved double-act from Flanagan and Allen. Jimmy appeared in several films, including Rhythm Serenade (1943 - his debut), The Man Who Had Power Over Women (1970), Nearest and Dearest (1972), Rocinante (1987), The Krays (1990 - as Cannonball Lee) and his last film, American Friends (1991). He also appeared with his partner Ben Warriss in What a Carry On! (1949) and Let's Have a Murder (1950). Jimmy and Ben starred in the popular post-war radio series Up the Pole, in which the premise was that they maintained a residence at the North Pole. Morecambe and Wise, and to a lesser extent, Mike and Bernie Winters, became the nation's favourite double acts in the 1960s and Jewel and Warriss split up in 1966. Ironically, Ben, who was the straight-man, now toured as a solo comedian while Jimmy, the comedian, then turned to television to carve out a successful career as an actor both in straight and comic roles. See also entries in the television section for Hideaway, Nearest and Dearest, Spring and Autumn, and Thicker Than Water.

Jones, Terry Born Terence Graham Parry Jones, 1 February 1942, Colwyn Bay, North Wales. Terry was educated at the Royal Grammar School in Guildford and had the distinction of being head boy in his final year before reading English and History at St Edmund Hall, Oxford, where he first met Michael Palin, whilst performing with The Oxford Revue. Throughout the 1960s Terry worked closely with Michael both as writer and performer, his best known work undoubtedly being as a member of the Monty Python team. Terry was equally at home playing a middle-aged woman or the bowler-hatted "man in the street". A talented director, Terry had a lot of input into the Python style and also directed several of the Python films. His genius was not so much as a comedian but as someone who had an eye for comic situations, for example his marvellous depiction of the grotesquely obese Mr Creosote during the climax of Monty Python's The Meaning of Life. Terry once commented that to the best of his knowledge Ireland had only ever banned four movies, three of which he had directed: The Meaning of Life (1983), Monty Python's Life of Brian (1979) and Personal Services (1987). Other film acting credits include: Jabberwocky (1977), Erik the Viking (1989) and The Wind in the Willows (1996 - as Toad). Terry was the creator and co-producer of the Canadian/French animated television series Blazing Dragons (1996-98). Based on Arthurian Legends, a coinciding graphic adventure video game was released for the original PlayStation and Sega Saturn in 1996 by Crystal Dynamics. He has written books and presented television documentaries on medieval and ancient history and has also written numerous works for children, including Fantastic Stories, The Beast with a Thousand Teeth, and a collection of Comic Verse called The Curse of the Vampire's Socks. Since January 2009, he has provided narration for The Legend of Dick and Dom, a CBBC fantasy series set in the Middle Ages. Terry married Alison Telfer in 1970, and they have two children together, Sally (b. 1974) and Bill (b. 1976). Although remaining married to Alison, Terry formed a liaison with student Anna Söderström and in September 2009 Anna gave birth to his third child, a daughter, Siri. See also entries in the television section for At Last The 1948 Show, Broaden Your Mind, The Complete and Utter History of Britain, Do Not Adjust Your Set, The Frost Report, Marty, Monty Python's Flying Circus, Ripping Yarns, Twice a Fortnight, and The Young Ones.

Kay, Peter Born 2 July 1973, Bolton, England. Peter's breakthrough came in 1997 when he won the Channel 4 comedy talent competition So You Think You're Funny?, and the following year, his show at the Edinburgh Festival was nominated for the Perrier Award. He next wrote and played five characters in The Services (1998), a spoof documentary set in a motorway service station. Peter then developed the fake-documentary style into a series, That Peter Kay Thing (2000), in which, as well as writing the series, he played fifteen characters. The multi-award-winning Phoenix Nights turned Peter into a superstar of comedy and his man-next-door persona and stereotypical no-nonsense northern delivery has won him a huge following. His commercials for John Smith's bitter have also won awards and have featured him as a

Sunday League footballer, an Olympic diver, a curry eating Dad and a disc jockey. In Spring 2005 Peter collaborated with Tony Christie to have a huge UK and Ireland No 1 hit with *Is This The Way To Amarillo?*, in 2007 he recorded *I'm Gonna Be 500 Miles* with The Proclaimers featuring Brian Potter (Peter) & Andy Pipkin (Matt Lucas) for Comic Relief, which also made UK No 1 and in 2009 he had a third UK chart-topper with his Animated All Star Band and *The Official BBC Children In Need Medley*. His other top-ten hits are *Sleep* with Texas in 2006 (6) and the two recordings he brought out in 2008 as Geraldine McQueen, *The Winner's Song* (2) and *Once Upon A Christmas Song* (5). He also had a UK No 11 hit with *I Know Him So Well*, recorded in his Geraldine guise with Susan Boyle for Comic Relief 2011. On film, Peter has appeared as George in the TV film short, *Two Minutes* (1996) and as Ronnie in the full-length TV film, *Butterfly Collectors* (1999) before making his feature debut as Flipper in *Going Off Big Time* (2000). His other films include: *Blow Dry* (2001), *24 Hour Party People* (2002), *The League of Gentlemen's Apocalypse* (2005 - as Simon Pig) and *Wallace & Gromit in The Curse of the Were-Rabbit* (2005 - voice of PC Mackintosh). Peter has written two autobiographies, *The Sound of Laughter* (2006) and *Saturday Night Peter* (2009). See also entries in the television section for *Comedy Lab, Coronation Street, Gas, Peter Kay's Britain's Got the Pop Factor*, and *Peter Kay's Phoenix Nights*.

Kaye, Paul See *Anyone For Pennis* in the television section.

King, Dave Born David Kingshott, 23 June 1929, Twickenham, London. Began his career as a member of Morton Fraser's Harmonica Gang, a music-hall variety act fronted by a midget. After his National Service he took over from Benny Hill as compere of the BBC TV series *Showcase*, before receiving his own BBC sketch series (1955-57) written by Sid Green and Dick Hills, later famous as writers for Morecambe and Wise. Following a brief hospitalisation with appendicitis Dave transferred *The Dave King Show* to ITV (1958-63) and he became one of the brightest stars on television with a catalogue of classic characters from simple-minded labourers to angry young bonneted babies. Although Dave reprised his sketch format in a one-off series in 1980 he turned his hand to sitcoms and stand-up between 1964 and 1980 before becoming a straight actor with parts in television series such as *The Sweeney, Pennies from Heaven, Minder, Heartbeat*, and *Rumpole of the Bailey*, as well as playing Jack Duckworth's brother in *Coronation Street*. Dave appeared in many films, notably *Pirates of Tortuga* (1961 - his debut), *Go to Blazes* (1962), *Up the Chastity Belt* (1971), *Cuba* (1979), *The Long Good Friday* (1980) *Reds* (1981), *Revolution* (1985) and his last film, *Rude Awakening* (1989). He also had three top-twenty hits, *Memories are Made of This* (1956) reaching No. 5. Dave married dancer, Jean Hart (who pre-deceased him) and they had two daughters, Cheyenne and Kiowa. He died on 15 April 2002. See also entries in the television section for *Coronation Street, Little Big Time, Pennies From Heaven*, and *That's Your Funeral*.

King, Hettie Born Winifred Emms, 21 April 1893, Barrow-in-Furness. Hettie initially appeared with her comedian father Will King (William Emms 1856-1954) from the age of six, singing and dancing to his accompaniment and generally fooling about. When aged 12 she first appeared in Shoreditch, London, working as a male impersonator and soon topped the bills all over the world as a debonair man about town, and in costume as the soldiers and sailors of both world wars. She amused her public with comic songs and in particular her two greatest songs, *All the Nice Girls Love a Sailor* and *Piccadilly*, She appeared on the stage for over seventy years, and continued working in variety and Summer shows with remarkable verve and vitality until shortly before her death at the age of 79 on 28th September 1972.

King, Nosmo Born H. Vernon Watson in 1886, Thorney, nr Peterborough. He turned pro, aged 25, performing an act mimicking the comedians of the day. Then, when Frank Tinney, the American black-faced comedian, came to the UK, Watson added a successful impression of him to his repertoire and this prompted him to change his act to a black-faced routine. From then on he would appear in white bowler hat, braided uniform, white glasses and blackface make-up, calling himself Nosmo King, Watson taking his stage name from a partly-opened backstage door at a Leeds theatre he was working in. The stage act of Nosmo King & Hubert developed when his son Jack Watson joined him as straight man after leaving school in the 1930s. During WWII Nosmo again worked alone when Hubert joined up. He died in 1952 and is buried in Thorney, Cambridgeshire.

Kitson, Daniel Born 2 July 1977, Denby Dale, West Yorkshire. Daniel began performing comedy routines, aged 16, before studying drama at Roehampton Institute (now Roehampton University). He was nominated for the 2001 Perrier Comedy Award at the Edinburgh Festival Fringe for his show *Love, Innocence and the Word Cock* before winning it the following year for the show *Something*. Daniel is known for his surreal 'story shows' and in particular *Stories For the Wobbly-Hearted* and *C-90*. His stand-up routines are based on observational humour and self-deprecation, his easy style and big bushy beard make him memorable. He has by and large shunned television work after having an unhappy experience working with Peter Kay on *That Peter Kay Thing* and *Peter Kay's Phoenix Nights*, although in his teens, he appeared as a contestant on the ITV quiz show *Blockbusters*, hosted by Bob Holness. In 2007 he was voted 27th in the one-off Channel 4 show *100 Greatest Stand-Ups* and in an updated version in 2010, placed 23rd.

Knox, Ted See *Crazy Gang*.

Krankies Scottish comedy duo Janette Tough (b. 16 May 1947, Stirlingshire) and Ian Tough (b. 26 March 1947, Glasgow). Although in reality the Krankies have been married since 1969, in the act they portray schoolboy Wee Jimmy Krankie (Janette), and Jimmy's father (Ian), Jennifer's act was influenced by Wee Georgie Wood, (b. 17 December 1894, Jarrow; d. 19 February 1979) who, when fully grown, was 4 ft 9 in (1.45 m) tall and became one of the greatest music hall acts ever playing a child. Janette herself was a mere 4' 5½" (1.36 m) and with her hair hidden under her school cap and decked out in short trousers and blazer, was very believable in her role. After appearing as presenters on *Crackerjack* in the late 1970s they were given their own series in the 1980s *The Krankies Klub* (1982-84) and *The Krankies Elektronik Komik* (1985-87). Although semi-retired in the 1990s they still perform in the occasional pantomime.

Lauder, Sir Harry Born Henry Lauder, 4 August 1870, Portobello, Edinburgh. Harry began his adult working life as a coalminer in Hamilton supplementing his income by singing in local clubs. In 1891, Harry married Ann Vallance, the daughter of a colliery manager. His first professional engagement, in Larkhall, was for five shilling for the night and over the course of the next twenty years he established himself as Scotland's greatest entertainer, commanding $1,000 a night during his US tours. In 1912 he was top of the bill at Britain's first ever Royal Command Variety performance, in front of King George V. At the peak of his fame he was the highest-paid performer in the world and the first British artiste to sell a million records. Harry's appeal was universal. He performed in full Highland regalia, singing songs with a Scottish theme and honing his line of patter to great comic effect. His popular songs, some romantic, some comedic, include: *Just a wee deoch and doris, My Bonnie, Bonnie Jean, Stop yer ticklin', Jock, That's the reason noo I wear a kilt, When I get back again tae bonnie Scotland*, and his two most famous, *I love a lassie*, and *Roamin' in the gloamin'*, During the Great War, Harry's only son, John (1891–1916), a captain in the 8th Argyll and Sutherland Highlanders, was killed in action on 28 December 1916 at Poiziers. Harry wrote the song *Keep Right on to the End of the Road* in memory of John. On film, Harry starred in *Huntingtower* (1927), *Auld Lang Syne* (1929) and *The End of the Road* (1936). He also wrote a number of books, notably, *A Minstrel in France* (1918), *Between You and Me* (1919), *Roamin' in the Gloamin'* (1928), *My Best Scotch Stories* (1929) and *Wee Drappies* (1931). He was knighted in 1919 and after his wife's death in 1927 he went into semi-retirement, although he entertained the troops during WWII. Sir Harry died 26 February 1950, Strathaven, Lanarkshire. Sir Winston Churchill described him as "Scotland's greatest ever ambassador!"

Laurel, Stan Born Arthur Stanley Jefferson, 16 June 1890, Ulverston, Cumbria. Arthur's family moved to Glasgow when he was a child and he began working at Glasgow's Metropole Theatre where his father was manager. At age 16, Arthur gave his first professional comedy performance on stage at The Panopticon in Glasgow. Four years later he joined Fred Karno's troupe of actors, and for some time was Charlie Chaplin's understudy working under the name of Stan Jefferson. The Karno troupe toured America in 1916 and Stan made his film debut in the comedy short *Nuts in May* (1917) opposite Australian actress Mae Dahlberg (1888-1969) whom he later worked with in music hall and lived with between 1919 and 1925. Mae maintained that it was she who suggested Stan change his name from Jefferson to Laurel. Stan first met his future comedy partner, Oliver Hardy (1892–1957), while working on a silent film short *The Lucky Dog* (1921). After Mae went back to Australia Stan joined the Hal Roach studio, and began directing films, including a 1926 production called *Yes, Yes, Nanette*, starring Oliver Hardy (cast as Babe Hardy). Stan and Ollie next appeared in *45 Minutes from Hollywood* (1926), albeit in minor roles. *Duck Soup*, *Slipping Wives*, and *With Love and Hisses*, saw the pair teamed up again in 1927 and later that year Hal Roach marketed them as a double-act of Laurel and Hardy and their films took a subtle change of tack with them invariably appearing in almost every scene together. Early films together include: *Putting Pants on Philip* (1927), *The Battle of the Century* (1927) and *Should Tall Men Marry?* (1928), before making the first film where they played 'Stan and Ollie' *Leave 'Em Laughing* (1928). Most of their films in the next seven years are timeless comedy shorts and include, in 1928: *Flying Elephants, The Finishing Touch, You're Darn Tootin', Should Married Men Go Home?, Early to Bed, Two Tars, Habeas Corpus,* and *We Slip Up*; in 1929: *Liberty, Wrong Again, That's My Wife, Big Business, Unaccustomed As We Are* (their first talkie), *Double Whoopee, Berth Marks, Men O'War, Perfect Day,* and *Angora Love*; in 1930: *Radiomania, Night Owls, Blotto, Brats, Below Zero, Hog Wild,* and *Another Fine Mess*, which was a talkie re-make of their silent movie *Duck Soup*; in 1931: *Chickens Come Home, Laughing Gravy, Pardon Us* (their first feature length film), *Come Clean, One Good Turn, Beau Chumps* (aka *Beau Hunks*); in 1932: *Helpmates, Any Old Port!, The Music Box* (won an Academy Award for Best Short Subject. You'll know it as the one with the piano and the stairs), *The Chimp, County Hospital, Scram, Pack Up Your Troubles* (2nd feature film), and *Towed in a Hole*; in 1933: *Twice Two, Me and My Pal, The Midnight Patrol, Busy Bodies, Dirty Work,* and *Sons of the Desert* (feature length); in 1934: *Going Bye-Bye!, Them Thar Hills, The Live Ghost,* and *Babes in Toyland* (feature film); in 1935: *Tit for Tat, The Fixer Uppers, Thicker Than Water,* and *Bonnie Scotland* (feature film). From 1936 Laurel and Hardy concentrated mainly on feature-length films, including: *The Bohemian Girl* (1936), *Our Relations* (1936), *Way Out West* (1937 - the one that gave them a posthumous hit with the *Trail of the Lonesome Pine*), *Swiss Miss* (1938), *Block-Heads* (1938), *The Flying Deuces* (1939), *A Chump at Oxford* (1940), *Saps at Sea* (1940 - their last Hal Roach film), *Great Guns* (1941), *A-Haunting We Will Go* (1942), *Air Raid Wardens* (1943), *The Dancing Masters* (1943), *The Big Noise* (1944), *Nothing But Trouble* (1944), *The Bullfighters* (1945), and their last film, *Robinson Crusoeland* (1951 - aka *Utopia* and *Atoll K*) by which time both men were quite ill. After Hardy's death, Stan retired and lived at a modest apartment at the Oceana Hotel in Santa Monica, California. He was always available to talk to fans and his phone number was in the telephone directory. Both Dick Van Dyke and Jerry Lewis rang Stan at the beginning of their careers and subsequently visited him. Stan was married five times to four different women, Lois Neilson (1926–35), Virginia Ruth Rogers (1935–1937; 1941–1946), Vera Ivanova Shuvalova (1938–1940) and Ida Kitaeva Raphael, from 1946 until his death, from a heart-attack on 23 February 1965. At his funeral, Buster Keaton was overheard to say "Chaplin wasn't the funniest, I wasn't the funniest, this man was the funniest." Dick Van Dyke gave the eulogy, reading *A Prayer for Clowns*.

Laurie, Hugh See entry in film section.

Leno, Dan Born George Wild Galvin, 20 December, 1860, Somers Town, Camden, London. Dan made his debut at the Cosmotheca Music Hall in Paddington when he was billed as Little George, the Infant Wonder, Contortionist and Posturer. In the 1880s he became the most popular music hall act in England, performing in up to 20 shows a night, specialising in clog dancing, a pursuit in which he became world champion in 1880. Dan blossomed into playing various characters including a policeman, Spanish bandit, fireman, shopwalker, doctor, beefeater, waiter, recruiting sergeant, bathing attendant, and hairdresser. It was his portrayal of pantomime dames, particularly his *You know Mrs. Kelly?...* routine, which increased his stardom. He proved to be so popular that he even entertained Edward VII at Sandringham in the early part of his reign, later earning the nickname the King's Jester. In 1902 Dan suffered a mental breakdown and died 31 October 1904. His funeral was a huge public occasion, the biggest funeral for an actor or comedian since the death of David Garrick.

Leybourne, George Born Joe Sanders, in 1842, Newcastle. George was a popular British music hall performer, often nicknamed "Champagne Charlie" after the popular song of the day. He would enter in immaculate evening dress, with top hat, tails, gloves, cane, and scarf, waving a bottle of vintage Moet & Chandon. George also wrote the lyrics for "The Flying Trapeze" in 1867 (music by Gaston Lyle), the lyrics based on the exploits of trapeze artist Jules Léotard, and the tune based on Jacques Offenbach's "Le Papillon", Act 2, Scene 1. The phenomenal success of the song popularised Champagne sales and Moet & Chandon employed George as a celebrity promoter contracting him to drink nothing but Champagne in public. George's daughter Florrie married Albert Chevalier and was the inspiration for Chevalier's hit "My Old Dutch." George Leybourne died 15 September 1884, Islington, and is buried at Abney Park Cemetery, Stoke Newington.

Little and Large Comedy double act comprising straight man Syd Little (born Cyril Mead, 19 December 1942, Manchester) and comic Eddie Large (born Edward Hugh McGinnis, 25 June 1941, Glasgow). Beginning their act as pub singers in 1962 they won the 1971 series of the talent show *Opportunity Knocks* and for twenty years appeared on television with Eddie being the comic impressionist while Syd, the butt of Eddie's jokes, always aspiring to be given a chance to sing a serious song. Their two BBC shows *The Little and Large Telly Show* (1976-77) and *The Little and Large Show* (1978-91) ran for fifteen years before the new wave of comedians condemned them to panto and the cabaret circuit as solo artists. Eddie had a heart transplant in 2003 but is now fully recovered although he jokes "with the 20 pills I take each day I don't need a pair of maracas". See also entries in the television section for *Opportunity Knocks*, and *Who Do You Do?*

Little Tich Born Harry Relph, 21 July 1867, Cudham, nr Bromley, Greater London. Harry was one of 15 children of the landlord of the village pub, the Blacksmith's Arms. I can vouch that the pub still stands and is full of memorabilia of its most famous son. At 4' 6" (1.37 m) in height fully grown, it is probably no surprise that Harry performed his comic routines under the name Little Tich. He took his name from Arthur Orton, who was known as the Tichborne claimant in a celebrated 19th-century legal case in which Orton claimed to be Sir Roger Tichborne, the missing heir to the lucrative Tichborne Baronetcy. Harry had several strings to his bow as a comedian. He dressed up as a woman to play The Spanish Señora, and was also a very convincing pantomime dame, appearing with the likes of Marie Lloyd and Dan Leno. His male characters included The Gendarme, and The Tax Collector, but his most popular routine was his Big Boot dance, which involved him wearing a pair of 28-inch slapshoes. Little Tich would appear on stage, top hat tilted and hands in pocket, and perform a very clever routine involving slapping the boots together and getting his fingers caught, walking on tiptoe, balancing his top hat on his nose and even bending over in the shoes to pick the hat up directly onto his head (having dropped it on the floor on purpose earlier in the act). Harry was unusual in having five fingers and a thumb on each hand, and six toes on each foot. In 1909, he was made an officer of the French Academy, for his performances at the Folies Bergère. His final appearance was in 1927 at the Alhambra Theatre in London, with Jack Hylton's Band, and he died at Hendon after a long illness in 1928.

Lloyd, Marie Born Matilda Alice Victoria Wood, 12 February 1870, Hoxton, London. She made her debut at the Royal Eagle Music Hall (later became The Grecian) under the name of Bella Delamare in 1885 but changed her name to Marie Lloyd soon after. Her first success was with a song entitled *The Boy I Love Is Up in the Gallery* and she became a star turn, becoming known as the 'Queen of the Music Hall', making appearances in America, South Africa and Australia. Between 1891 and 1893 she appeared in pantomime with Dan Leno and excelled in this but always preferred the halls. Marie was married three times, to Percy Courtenay from 1887-1905 (although they were estranged from 1894), Alec Hurley, a noted music hall artist of the day, from 1905 until his death in 1913 (although they were estranged from 1910) and Irish jockey Bernard Dillon (who won the Epsom Derby in 1910 on Lemberg) from 1914, although once again the marriage deteriorated. Marie began to copy the drinking habits of her husband and her act suffered accordingly. Her final performance was in Edmonton on 4 October 1922, and her last song was *It's A Bit of a Ruin that Cromwell Knocked About a Bit.* Her most famous songs included *Oh Mr Porter* and *My Old Man Said Follow the Van.* She died on 7th October 1922.

Lowe, Arthur See entry in cinema section.

Lucan, Arthur Born Arthur Towle, 16 September 1885, Sibsey, near Boston, Lincolnshire. Arthur was a jobbing music hall artist from the turn of the century but while touring Ireland he met and married Kitty McShane (1898-1964) and they developed a double-act, Lucan and McShane (Harry adopted the name Lucan in Dublin as he needed an Irish surname to find work, legend has it that he gleaned the name from Lucan's Dairy). Their most famous sketch was 'Bridget's Night Out' in which Arthur played Mrs O'Flynn, an old woman dressed in black. An appearance in the 1934 Royal Command Performance led to a film series and the character's name was changed to 'Old Mother Riley' and Kitty played her daughter also named Kitty. The first film in 1937 was called *Old Mother Riley* and the 15th and last *Mother Riley Meets the Vampire* (1952). Arthur died on the 17th May 1954 in the wings of the Tivoli Theatre in Hull.

Lucas, Matt Born Matthew Richard Lucas, 5 March 1974, Paddington, London. Matt grew up in Stanmore, Middlesex and attended Haberdashers' Aske's school (as did Sacha Baron Cohen). He met his long-time collaborator David Walliams at the National Youth Theatre, and they caught up with each other again at Bristol University. Together they worked out a routine around a character Sir Bernard Chumley and brought this to the Edinburgh Festival (1994-96). His major television solo work includes *The Smell Of Reeves and Mortimer, Bang Bang It's Reeves and Mortimer,* and *Randall and Hopkirk.* He became a household name after teaming up with Bob Mortimer and Vic Reeves on *Shooting Stars,* where he played George Dawes, who, dressed as a baby (Matt has had alopecia since the age of six), played the drums exuberantly whilst giving the scores and punctuated affairs with some hilariously surreal one-liners. Not just a performer, Matt also wrote for *Da Ali G Show.* Superstardom came when teaming up again with Walliams to make the multi award-winning series *Little Britain.* Matt is openly gay, and based the character Daffyd Thomas on himself, recalling how he felt he was "the only gay in the village" when growing up. In 2005 he took his first role in a television drama, a supporting part as a Venetian Duke in the BBC historical serial *Casanova,* written by Russell T. Davies. He made his film debut, as an air steward, in *Jilting Joe* (1998). His other films include: *Plunkett & Macleane* (1999), *Shaun of the Dead* (2004), *Cold and Dark* (2005), *Astro Boy* (2009 - voice of Sparx), *Alice in Wonderland* (2010 - as Tweedledee / Tweedledum), *The Infidel* (2010), *Gnomeo & Juliet* (2011 - voice of Benny), *Bridesmaids* (2011) and the upcoming *Small Apartments* (2012). He also starred as the irrepressible Mr Toad in *The Wind in the Willows,* a 2006 television film adaptation of the Kenneth Grahame novel. On stage, Matt played the part of infamous performance artist Leigh Bowery, in Boy George's musical Taboo, at The Venue, London, in 2002. He also played the role of Thénardier in a special one-off performance celebrating the 25th anniversary of *Les Misérables,* held at the O2 Arena in London, which he reprised at The Queen's Theatre, in 2011. Matt has also had a UK No. 1 hit in 2007 in his guise of Andy Pipkin, opposite Peter Kay as Brian Potter, with the

Proclaimers' song *I'm Gonna Be 500 Miles,* in aid of Comic Relief. In December 2006, Matt entered into a civil partnership with Kevin McGee, but this was subsequently dissolved in October 2008. Kevin hanged himself in October 2009 causing Matt to pull out of a London production of *Prick Up Your Ears,* being replaced by Con O'Neill. See also entries in the radio and television section for *Come Fly With Me, Down the Line, Krōd Mändoon and the Flaming Sword of Fire, Little Britain, Rock Profile* and *Shooting Stars.*

McIntyre, Michael Born Michael Hazen James McIntyre, 21 February 1976, Merton, London. Michael attended Merchant Taylors' School, local state school Woodhouse College, and Edinburgh University, dropping out after a year to pursue a career as a scriptwriter. Michael's Canadian father, Ray Cameron, was one of the writers of *The Kenny Everett Television Show* and his Hungarian mother, Kati, was a dancer. His parents divorced when he was seven, after which Ray remarried and moved to Los Angeles; and subsequently died of a heart attack when Michael was 17. Michael's thoughts soon turned to comedy when he realised he could write his own material and he became an ever-present on the comedy club circuit. His television debut was as a pundit on Channel 5's *That's So Last Week* (2005), a panel game, on the subject of celebrity news, gossip and comment. His big break came with his appearance in the 2006 Royal Variety Performance. Michael's first DVD, *Live & Laughing,* is the fastest-selling debut stand-up DVD and his second DVD, *Hello Wembley,* has also sold well. In 2009 he won Best Live Stand-up at the British Comedy Awards. In 2010, Michael released his autobiography, *Life and Laughing: My Story,* and also became the youngest-ever host of the Royal Variety Performance. In 2011, he appeared as a judge on the fifth series of *Britain's Got Talent.* Michael, a keen Spurs supporter, lives in Muswell Hill, North London with his aromatherapist wife Kitty, and their two sons, Lucas (b. 2005) and Oscar (b. 2008). Kitty is the youngest of actor Simon Ward's three daughters. See also entries in the television section for *Live at the Apollo, Michael McIntyre's Comedy Roadshow* and *Walk on the Wild Side*

Mack, Lee Born Lee Gordon McKillop, 4 August 1968, Southport, Lancashire. Like many comedians Lee was the school clown and amused his friends with impressions of Bobby Ball. He worked as a bingo caller and a stableboy before entering showbusiness. The story goes that the first horse he ever rode out was the legendary Red Rum, three-time winner of the Grand National, but by then retired. Lee eventually became a Bluecoat at Pontins, first at Yarmouth, then at Morecambe. He became a stand-up comedian in 1994 and after very few open mike sessions won the prestigious *So You Think You're Funny* at the 1995 Edinburgh Festival Fringe. He made his television debut as host of *Gas,* the Channel 4 comedy showcase. On radio, Lee has played the part of Graham, the security guard in the original radio version of *The Mighty Boosh,* and currently presents his own Radio 2 show. On television, Lee has been a panelist on almost every celebrity game show possible but since 2006 has starred in the sitcom *Not Going Out.* See also entries in the radio and television section for *Gas, Just A Minute, Live at the Apollo, Not Going Out, The Sketch Show, They Think It's All Over,* and *Would I Lie To You?*

Manford, Jason Born Jason John Manford, 26 May 1981, Salford, Greater Manchester. As a teenager, Jason was a finalist in the 2000 Channel 4 *So You Think You're Funny* competition at the Edinburgh Fringe Festival. In 2005 he was nominated for the Perrier Award at the festival for his debut one-man show *Urban Legend.* This gave his career a springboard into television work and he has become a regular panelist on many of the current celebrity game shows. In a rare straight acting role, Jason appeared in Channel 4's *Shameless* in 2007 as a security guard that is seduced by Karen Maguire. In March 2010, Jason hosted a pilot for a new ITV comedy show called *Comedy Rocks,* featuring stand up comedians as well as musical interludes. The pilot was subsequently followed by a six-part series in January 2011. In July 2010, he became the new presenter of BBC One's *The One Show* but resigned in November 2010 to "concentrate on his family" following tabloid newspaper revelations that he exchanged sexually-oriented Twitter messages with fans. See also entries in the television section for *As Seen On TV, 8 Out of 10*

Cats, Live at the Apollo, Michael McIntyre's Comedy Roadshow, Odd One In, The One Show and *Walk on the Wild Side*

Manning, Bernard Born Bernard John Manning, 13 August 1930, Ancoats, Manchester. Bernard was of Russian Jewish and Irish descent, a fact that he later felt gave him entitlement to make jokes with impunity. He began his career entertaining his fellow soldiers during his National Service in the late 1940s. In those days Bernard was a ballad singer who fronted many big bands of the day. He turned to comedy as a natural progression from his other job as a club compere and in 1959 he and his father bought The Embassy, a converted billiard hall on the Rochdale Road, Harpurhey, three miles north of Manchester. The Embassy Club gave Bernard an outlet to develop his stand-up act and also play host to many aspiring comics and variety acts. Bernard made his television debut in the ITV comedy showcase *The Comedians* (1971) and was a familiar face on television for the next 20 years. His style was a quickfire stream of gags, often poking fun at ethnic minorities, religion and public figures, although in the last few years of his career he created an act around clean jokes, repeatedly pleading "nothing blue about that". Unfortunately, much as he tried, he could never shake off the tag of being a racist. He even named his house in Alkrington, Greater Manchester "Shalom", the Hebrew word for "peace". The truth be known his jokes could be offensive but no more than the current crop who seem to take great delight in 'roasting' fellow artistes and public figures within the bounds of a perceived political correctness. So in a way Bernard was merely a victim of a changing society, his type of joke heard in pubs all over the country but no longer fit for television consumption. Fiercely proud of his career (often citing the amount of money he had made when interviewed), Bernard was a simple working class man with values to match. His defiant nature would never allow him to apologise for his act but he did once say "I dragged myself up by my bootlaces. I don't drink or smoke, I don't take drugs. I have never been a womaniser. I was brought up right with good parents and I have never been in trouble or harmed no-one. And I love my family". Bernard died in North Manchester General Hospital, 18 June 2007. Weeks after his death he made his final screen 'appearance' in Channel 4's *Bernard Manning from Beyond the Grave*, an eerie retrospective of his life where he presented his own obituary. See also entries in the television section for *The Comedians, Coronation Street, OTT (Over The Top),* and *Wheeltappers' and Shunters Social Club.*

Mayall, Rik Born Richard Michael Mayall, 7 March 1958, Harlow, Essex. Although born in the appropriately comic-sounding hamlet of Matching Tye, in the Epping Forest area of Essex, Rik was raised in Droitwich, Worcestershire. After attending The King's School, Worcester he studied drama at the University of Manchester in 1976, where he befriended Ade Edmondson. He performed sketches and stand-up in The Comedy Store and The Comic Strip Club in London as part of a double act with Ade called *Twentieth Century Coyote*. Rik came to prominence playing his alter-ego of Brummie investigative journalist Kevin Turvey in *A Kick Up The Eighties* (1981) and *The Man Behind the Green Door* (1982) before rising to stardom playing Rik in the anarchic BBC comedy series *The Young Ones* (1982-84). He and the other three cast members had a number-one hit single in April 1986 with *Living Doll*. Rik to-date has starred in 17 of the one-off comedy classics *The Comic Strip Presents* (1982-present). His only minor flop was *Filthy, Rich and Catflap* (1987) but this was followed by the more successful *The New Statesman* (1987-92) in which his character of Alan Beresford B'Stard, Conservative MP for Haltemprice, struck a chord with the public as a parody of the existing political sleaze, at its height during this period. *Bottom* (1991-95) was a sitcom teaming Rik with his old sparring partner Ade Edmondson and was really an extension of their earlier successful partnership as the Dangerous Brothers. A film version, *Guest House Paradiso*, was released in 1999 with the character names changed to "Richard Twat" and "Edward Elizabeth Ndingombaba". *Rik Mayall Presents* (1993; 1995) reminded his fans of his great versatility, honed from touring in various Shakespearean productions. In 1995 he

provided the voice of a malevolent baby in the BBC mini-sitcom *How To Be A Little Sod*. In the spring of 1998, Rik had a serious quad bicycle accident near his home in Devon, which put him on the critical list. He has since made a full recovery and in 2002 he starred in the ITV sitcom *Believe Nothing* as an egotistical Nobel prize-winning Oxford professor named Adonis Cnut, a member of the Council for International Progress, an underground organisation that aspires to control the world. In 2005 he starred in another ITV series, *All About George*. Shy and reticent off screen, Rik remains one of the outstanding comedy talents of recent years. On film he made his debut as a policeman in *The Orchard End Murder* (1980). Other films include: *Eye of the Needle* (1981), *An American Werewolf in London* (1981), *Shock Treatment* (1981), *Whoops Apocalypse* (1988), *Eat the Rich* (1988), *Drop Dead Fred* (1991), *The Princess and the Goblin* (1991 - voice of Prince Froglip), *Little Noises* (1992), *Carry on Columbus* (1992 - as The Sultan), *The Snow Queen* (1995 - voice of the Robber King), *Bring Me the Head of Mavis Davis* (1997), *A Monkey's Tale* (1999 - as Gerard the Gormless), *Merlin: The Return* (2000 - as Merlin), *Kevin of the North* (2001), *Day of the Sirens* (2002), *Oh Marbella!* (2003), *Cold Dark* (2003), *Chaos and Cadavers* (2003), *Churchill: The Hollywood Years* (2004), *Valiant* (2005 - voice of Cufflingk), *Snow White: The Sequel* (2007), *Just for the Record* (2010), *Errors of the Human Body* (2011), *Eldorado* (2011 - as Chef Mario) and *Johnny English Reborn* (2011 – as Dirty Finger). On stage, Rik co-starred, with Stephen Fry, in Simon Gray's production of the play *Cell Mates*, at the Albery Theatre. The play opened on 17 February 1995, but Fry left the London production after three days and although Simon Ward replaced him, the production closed the following month. Rik married former Scottish make-up artist Barbara Robbin in 1985. They have three children, Rosie (b. 1986), Sidney (b. 1988) and Bonnie (b. 18 September 1995). See also entries in the television section for *The Bill, Blackadder Goes Forth, Blackadder II, Bottom, The Comic Strip Presents, Filthy Rich and Catflap, A Kick Up the Eighties, The New Statesman, Saturday Live, Shoebox Zoo, Wood and Walters,* and *The Young Ones.*

Merton, Paul Born Paul James Martin, 9 July 1957, Parsons Green, London. Paul changed his name to Merton in deference to an existing Equity member, Merton being the area of London where he grew up. After leaving school with no formal qualifications, Paul worked at the Tooting Employment Office for several years. It was not until April 1982 while performing at the Comedy Store in Soho that he developed the laconic style which was to become his trademark. Despite severe health problems in the mid-1980s Paul gradually carved out a living as a comedian, making his screen debut in an episode of the anarchic *The Young Ones* and later gaining stardom in the improvisation series *Whose Line Is It Anyway*. Despite a brief period of mental incapacitation Paul recovered to receive further plaudits as a team captain on the topical news quiz *Have I Got News For You* (1990-present), taking time out to star in two series of sketch shows and the popular ITV series *Paul Merton in Galton & Simpson's...*(1996-97) where he recreated some classic sketches, notably six in the *Hancock's Half-Hour* series which suited his style perfectly. Between 1999 and 2007 Paul hosted *Room 101*, a chat show in which guests are offered the chance to discuss their pet hates and consign them to the oblivion of Room 101. After seven nominations for a BAFTA award for Best Entertainment Performance, he finally won the award in April 2003, ironically defeating fellow HIGNFY star Angus Deayton who had just recently been fired from the show. He has been a member of the London improvisation group The Comedy Store Players since 1985 (current members include Josie Lawrence, Neil Mullarkey, Lee Simpson, Andy Smart, Jim Sweeney and Richard Vranch; former members include Sandi Toksvig and Mike Myers). Paul has also presented three travel documentary series for Channel Five, *Paul Merton in China* (2007), *Paul Merton in India* (2008) and *Paul Merton in Europe* (2010). His most recent television projects have been a three part documentary series, *Paul Merton's Birth of Hollywood*, on BBC2 in 2011 and a special 10-episode television special of *Just A Minute* (2012). Paul has been married three times, to actress Caroline Quentin (1990-98), actress and producer Sarah Parkinson (married unofficially in the Maldives in 2000 but officially three months before her death on 23 September 2003, of breast cancer) and comedienne Suki Webster since 2009. See also entries in the radio and television section for *Hancock's Half Hour, Have I Got News for You, Just A Minute, Rex the Runt, Room 101, Saturday Live, Whose Line Is It Anyway?* and *The Young Ones*.

Miller, Max Born Thomas Henry Sargent, 21 November 1894, Brighton, Sussex. Harry, as he was then known, left school aged 12 and drifted from job to job before serving in the army in WWI and gaining a reputation as an entertainer. He formed a concert party and met Kathleen Marsh (1896-1972), a contralto. They married in 1921 and although touring together for a short time, Kathleen eventually became his manager and suggested his change of name. Max wrote his own songs and developed a unique line of patter. He dressed in a flower-patterned suit, plus-fours, matching shoes, white trilby on the tilt, and kipper tie. He would come on stage to the sound of the orchestra playing his signature tune *Mary from the Dairy*, then tempt the audience to choose from one of two gag-books - the 'Blue Book' or the 'White Book'. Inevitably they would pick the blue one and the act would begin. His legendary timing and delivery, full of sly looks over his shoulders giving the impression he was telling you something he oughtn't, have never been surpassed and he always had complete control of his audience. In May 1931 he appeared in his first Royal Variety Performance (he also appeared in 1937 and 1950). The following year he made *Confessions of a Cheeky Chappie*, the first of numerous recordings, initially on the Broadcast Twelve Records label, before transferring to HMV, Philips and Pye, for whom he made his last recording (with Lonnie Donegan) in 1963. On film, he made his debut in *The Good Companions* (1933). Other films include: *Friday the Thirteenth* (1933), *Channel Crossing* (1933), *Princess Charming* (1934), *Things Are Looking Up* (1934), *Get Off My Foot* (1935), *Educated Evans* (1936), *Take It from Me* (1937), *Don't Get Me Wrong* (1937), *Thank Evans* (1938), *Everything Happens to Me* (1938), *The Good Old Days* (1939), *Hoots Mon!* (1940) and his last feature film, *Asking for Trouble* (1942). His last screen appearance was opposite Terry-Thomas in a 1959 BBC special, *Around the Town*. Max can undoubtedly lay claim to being the greatest British stand-up comedian. He was never overtly rude, and would be considered very tame by today's standards, but he was occasionally banned from BBC radio, his double-entendres being deemed too much, and it was such a ban that ultimately ended his career. For all his fame, Max rarely left his home town of Brighton. In his book *Roy Hudd's Cavalcade of Variety Acts*, Roy tells of a conversation he had with the great comic at the end of his career. Max, known as The Cheeky Chappie, had been packing out theatres since the 1930s, but on this particular evening in 1959, as he stood in the wings watching another act perform to an audience of around thirty people, he turned to Roy and made an announcement. "It's all over," he said, referring to the age of variety. "When I'm dead and gone the game's finished." Prophetic words indeed! His most famous catchphrases include: "Now, there's a funny thing", "It's people like you who give me a bad name" and "They don't make 'em anymore, duck!" The Max Miller Appreciation Society was founded in 1999. Max died of a heart-attack, 7 May 1963, Brighton.

Milligan, Spike Born Terence Alan Patrick Sean Milligan, 16 April 1918, Ahmednagar, India. Spike was born the son of an Irish Captain in the British Raj in India. His mother was English and Spike began his education in India and completed it in Lewisham. He joined the British Army in 1940 serving as a gunner in the Royal Artillery and this period later inspired a great collection of work, including his best-selling memoirs *Adolf Hitler: My Part In His Downfall* (1971) which was made into a film in 1972, Spike playing the part of his father. Other books inspired by this period in Spike's life include: *Monty: His Part in My Victory* (1976) and *Mussolini: His Part in My Downfall* (1978). A singer and trumpeter who made his radio debut in *Opportunity Knocks* (1949), Spike met Harry Secombe during the war and it was Harry that introduced Spike to Jimmy Grafton at the aptly-named Grafton Arms, and Milligan and Grafton wrote scripts for several radio shows before they pitched the idea for the

Goon Show to the BBC. The show aired on the Home Service (now Radio 4) from 28 May 1951, although the BBC decided to use the name *Crazy People* for the first year. Spike played several characters notably, Count Jim Moriarty, Minnie Bannister and the intellectually-challenged Eccles, as well as writing much of the script at his small office above a grocer's shop at 130 Uxbridge Road, Shepherd's Bush, collaborating alongside Eric Sykes on the later scripts. The Goons had two UK Top-Ten hits with *I'm Walking Backwards for Christmas/Bluebottle Blues* (No 4 – June 1956) and *Bloodnok's Rock 'N' Roll Call/Ying Tong Song* (No 3 - September 1956). Spike's former army friend, musician Harry Edgington, was nicknamed Edge-ying-Tong which gave birth to Spike's most memorable musical creation. While Peter Sellers became a star of the big screen, Spike enjoyed similar success on television although he was no stranger to film. Spike made his film debut in *Penny Points to Paradise* (1951 - as Spike Donnelly). Other films include: *Down Among the Z Men* (1952 - as Pte Eccles), *Suspect* (1960), *Watch Your Stern* (1961), *Invasion Quartet* (1961), *What a Whopper* (1961), *Postman's Knock* (1962), *The Bed Sitting Room* (1969 – based on a play of the same title co-written by Spike and John Antrobus), *The Magic Christian* (1969), *The Magnificent Seven Deadly Sins* (1971), *Rentadick* (1972), *The Adventures of Barry McKenzie* (1972), *Alice's Adventures in Wonderland* (1972 - as Gryphon), *Ghost in the Noonday Sun* (1973), *The Three Musketeers* (1973), *Digby, the Biggest Dog in the World* (1973), *The Great McGonagall* (1974), *The Cherry Picker* (1974), *Barney* (1976), *The Last Remake of Beau Geste* (1977), *The Hound of the Baskervilles* (1978), *Life of Brian* (1979), *History of the World: Part I* (1981) and his last feature film, *Yellowbeard* (1983). His last film appearance was in the film short, *The Big Freeze* (1993). On television, Spike played the pipe-smoking, dressing-gowned Dr Strabismus in *The World of Beachcomber* (1968-69) and this was followed by the even more surreal *Q* series (1969-82). Spike also ventured into the world of sitcoms with the controversial Johnny Speight-written *Curry and Chips* (1969) where he played a blacked-up Kevin 'Paki-Paddy' O'Grady. From the days of the first Goon Shows which inspired a generation of comics to listen to and draw inspiration from Goon classics such as *Tales of Old Dartmoor* and *The Tale of Men's Shirts* which were immortalised on vinyl; through several books such as *Puckoon* (1963) *Where Have All the Bullets Gone?* (1985) and *Peacework* (1991), the latter two being autobiographies, Spike showed an unequalled comedy genius despite having to overcome manic depression which caused him to be hospitalised on several occasions. The Prince of Wales was a huge fan, and Spike caused a stir by jokingly calling his friend a "little grovelling bastard" on live television in 1994. A naturalised Irishman, Spike was given an honorary knighthood in 2001. He was married three times, to June Marlow (1952–60), Patricia 'Paddy' Ridgeway (1962–78) and Shelagh Sinclair, from 1983 until his death on 27 February 2002, Rye, Sussex. Spike had three children with his first wife: Laura, Seán and Síle; and a daughter, actress Jane Milligan (b. 1966) by his second. He also fathered a son, James (b. 1976), in an affair with Margaret Maughan. Spike's gravestone in the grounds of St Thomas, Winchelsea, East Sussex has an epitaph which reads "Duirt mé leat go raibh mé breoite", Irish for "I told you I was ill." It is impossible to quantify Spike's influence on the realm of entertainment. His partnership with Peter Sellers can only be compared to that of Lennon and McCartney in the music world. Two very different geniuses brought together to obliterate everything that went before or since. See also entries in the radio and television section for *The Adventure Game, Curry and Chips, Eamonn Andrews Show, The Goon Show, Gormenghast, The Idiot Weekly, Price 2d, Marty, Oh in Colour, Q, A Show Called Fred, Six Dates With Barker, The Six-Five Special, Sykes and A..., Telegoons, The Two Ronnies,* and *The World of Beachcomber*.

Mitchell, David Born David James Stuart Mitchell, 14 July 1974, Salisbury, Wiltshire. Comedy actor and writer best known for his collaborations with Robert Webb, whom he met at Cambridge University; both performing in the Cambridge Footlights, of which David became President. Apart from his numerous appearances on panel game shows David has also gone solo on several acting projects, notably as technical expert Owen in the Radio 4 sitcom *Think the Unthinkable* (2001) and surgeon Dr

Toby Stephens in the BBC2 sitcom *Doctors and Nurses* (2004). In 2007 David and Robert starred in the feature film, *Magicians*, in which David played traditional magician Harry. Also in 2007, David played writer Harry Kane in the American romantic comedy film, *I Could Never Be Your Woman*. David excels in the sketch show format but is equally at home ad-libbing as a panel show guest or performing stand-up routines. See also entries in the radio and television section for *Best of the Worst, Bruiser, The Bubble, Dead Ringers, The Jack Docherty Show, Jam and Jerusalem, Just A Minute, Peep Show, 10 O'Clock Live, That Mitchell and Webb Look,* and *Would I Lie To You?*

Monkhouse, Bob Born Robert Alan Monkhouse, 1 June 1928, Beckenham, Kent. Bob's grandfather was a prosperous Methodist businessman who owned Monk and Glass, the famous custard powder company. Bob was educated at Dulwich College where he showed a great aptitude for drawing and by the age of twelve was drawing strip-cartoons for children's comics *Hotspur* and *Wizard* as well as supplying stories for the *Beano* and *Dandy*. On leaving school he became a cartoon film animator with a side line in selling jokes to top comedians, notably Max Miller. In 1947, while fulfilling his National Service obligation, he made his radio debut with *Ralph Reader's Gang Show* and the following year made his television debut in the BBC young talent show *New To You*. In 1949 he became the first comedian to be put under exclusive contract to the BBC and this gave him the platform to appear on many of the network's variety shows as a stand-up comedian although by now he had also developed a successful writing partnership with Denis Goodwin. Bob's first television series was *Fast And Loose* (1954-55) in which he and Denis wrote and performed all the sketches, a proliferation of stand-up shows and sitcoms followed. In 1956, he was the host of *Do You Trust Your Wife?*, the British version of an American gameshow. He went on to host more than 30 different quiz shows on British television. In the 1960s he interrupted his busy schedule as a night-club entertainer to host *Candid Camera* and *Sunday Night at the London Palladium* before taking over from Jackie Rae as the host of *The Golden Shot*. Bob became the master of the gameshow but did return to his stand-up roots in the 1990s. He was a man of many talents, starring in films such as *The Secret People* (1952 – his debut), *Carry On Sergeant* (1958), *Dentist in the Chair* (1960), *Dentist on the Job* (1961) and *She'll Have to Go* (1962 - his last feature). Bob also possessed an encyclopedic memory of trivia, particularly of silent movie comedy of which he had a huge collection. He also wrote gags for Bob Hope and Frank Sinatra. In July 1995, Bob had one of his joke books stolen and he offered a £15,000 reward for its return. The book was eventually returned 18 months later. Bob was married twice, to Elizabeth Thompson (1949-72) and Jacqueline Harding, from 1973 until his death. He had three children from his first marriage, but only his daughter Abigail survived him. His son Gary Alan, suffered from cerebral palsy and died in 1992, aged 40; his other son Simon died of a heroin overdose in a hotel in Northern Thailand in 2001. Bob died on 29 December 2003, Eggington, Bedfordshire after a two-year battle against prostrate cancer. On 12 June 2007, he posthumously appeared on a British TV advertisement promoting awareness of prostate cancer. The ad, recorded before Bob's death included the poignant quip "What killed me kills one man per hour in Britain. That's even more than my wife's cooking." See also entries in the radio and television section for *The Big Noise, Candid Camera, Celebrity Squares, The Clitheroe Kid, Face to Face, Family Fortunes, For Love or Money, The Golden Shot, Just A Minute, Opportunity Knocks, Rex the Runt, The $64,000 Dollar Question, Sunday Night at the London Palladium, Wipeout, Worker's Playtime,* and *You Rang M'Lord.*

Moran, Dylan Born 3 November 1971, Navan, County Meath, Ireland. Dylan attended St. Patrick's Classical School in Navan at the same time as fellow comic Tommy Tiernan and Irish television presenter Hector Ó hEochagáin. He left school, aged 16, with no qualifications but encouraged by the school to pursue a career in the arts he eventually developed a stand-up act that he first performed at Dublin's Comedy Cellar in 1992. His persona of a tousle-haired, world-weary Irishman with ever-present cigarette and glass of wine may draw comparisons with Dave Allen but in actuality Dylan's act is far more surreal, although he does feed threads of observational humour into his routine. In 1993, he won the *So You Think You're Funny* award at the Edinburgh Festival and three years later he became the youngest person to win the Perrier Comedy Award at the festival, for his *Gurgling for Money* routine, which he toured around the UK with the following year. Interestingly, the only other comedian to win the two big Edinburgh Festival awards is Tommy Tiernan. In 1998 he made an impact in the BBC2 sitcom *How Do you Want Me?* and in 2000 he rose to stardom in the Channel 4 sitcom *Black Books*. His subsequent tours have included Ready, Steady, Cough (2002), Monster (2004) and Monster II (2004). He made his film debut as Rufus the thief in *Notting Hill* (1999). Other films include: *The Actors* (2003), *Shaun of the Dead* (2004), *A Cock and Bull Story* (2005), *Run Fatboy Run* (2007), *A Film with Me in It* (2008) and *The Decoy Bride* (2011). Dylan married his wife Elaine on 6 September 1997 in London. They live in Edinburgh and have two children, Siobhan and Simon. See also entries in the television section for *Black Books,* and *How Do you Want Me?*

Morecambe, Eric Born John Eric Bartholomew, 14 May 1926, Morecambe, Lancashire. Eric first met Ernie Wise (b. Ernest Wiseman, 27 November 1925, Leeds) at a talent contest in Hoylake in 1939 and worked with him on an occasional basis from 1941. During World War II, Ernie served in the Merchant Navy while Eric became a Bevin Boy, conscripted to work in a coal mine in Accrington from May 1944 until invalided out 11 months later because of a heart defect. After the war, on the advice of Eric's mother Sadie, they became an official double-act, making their television debut on 28 September 1951 on the BBC's young talent show *Parade of Youth*, having already been heard on radio on *Workers' Playtime* and *Variety Fanfare* (BBC North's equivalent of *Variety Bandbox*). Their first television series together was *Running Wild* (1954) for the BBC and was a disastrous flop but the lads persevered and started to gather a populist following while becoming the resident comedy act on *The Winifred Atwell Show* (1956) with Johnny Speight writing for them. They had more success in their 1957 series *Double Six,* before switching to ITV for their next series, *Two of a Kind* (1961-68). Sid Green and Dick Hills were the writers of this series and also took part in many of the sketches as 'Sid and Dick' and this chemistry proved inspired. It was during this period that many of Eric's catchphrases were developed, he would often refer to Ernie as having 'short fat hairy legs' or greet him with 'you can't see the join' (implying he was wearing a wig........he wasn't), at other times he would stick his open hand under Ernie's chin and say 'get out of that' or slap him on each cheek with his open palm. The shows would always end with a recurring joke - in one series it was the telling of a joke which began 'There were two old men sitting in deckchairs' (of course some natural disaster would inevitably occur to prevent the punchline being told) in another there was a door they had to walk through but never managed to do so for a variety of bizarre reasons. *The Morecambe and Wise Show* (1968-77) moved to the BBC but Eric suffered his first heart attack after the first series and Sid and Dick decided to stop writing for them for a more certain future with ITV. Eddie Braben was called in and Eric and Ernie continued to thrive albeit within a subtle change of act, Eric's attacks on Ernie now being replaced largely by his verbal abuse of their guests. New catchphrases such as "I'll Smash Your Face In" and "More Tea Ern?" were added to the old and Ernie's plays 'wot he wrote' attracted the cream of theatrical greats, John Mills, Eric Porter, Glenda Jackson, Diana Rigg and Peter Cushing to name but a few. During performances Eric would often be heard to say "what do you think of it so far?" with the inevitable answer from an inanimate object of "rubbish". The shows kept to their successful formula of having a recurring ending and this would invariably be the rather overweight Janet Webb walking to the front of the stage with the end credits rolling and thanking the audience for attending 'her' show. Harmonica player Arthur Tolcher was used in later series playing a speedy rift on the mouth organ but always being interrupted by Eric's plea of "not now Arthur". Eric also developed a propensity to throw up imaginary objects into the air while catching them in a brown paper bag, a trick which became popular in every household. In 1976, they were both awarded the OBE. ITV lured the lads back in 1978 with a lucrative contract for Christmas specials and four series. Morecambe and Wise were undoubtedly the greatest British double-act of all time, they made three films together, The Intelligence Men (1964), That Riviera Touch (1966) and The Magnificent Two (1967). Eric also wrote several books. In 1981 he published Mr Lonely, a tragicomic novel about a stand-up comedian. He focused more on writing during what were to be the final years of his life. Morecambe and Wise duly made a series for showing during the autumns of 1980 to 1983. They also appeared together recalling their music hall days in a one-hour special on ITV on 2 March 1983, called Eric & Ernie's Variety Days. During this time Eric published two more novels: The Reluctant Vampire (1982) and its sequel, The Vampire's Revenge (1983). Morecambe and Wise's final show together was the 1983 Christmas special for ITV. Five months after the Christmas special, Morecambe took part in a show hosted by close friend and comedian Stan Stennett (born 30 July 1925, Cardiff) at the Roses Theatre in Tewkesbury, Gloucestershire. After his performance, Eric suffered a massive heart attack and died at Cheltenham General Hospital later that evening, 28 May 1984. Eric married Joan Bartlett on 11 December 1952. They had two children: Gail (b. 14 September 1953) and Gary (b. 21 April 1956) and an adopted son, Steven (b. 1969 and adopted in 1973). In his leisure time, Eric was a keen birdwatcher, and the statue of him at Morecambe shows him wearing his binoculars. He was also an enthusiastic football fan and a director of Luton Town. A West End Show, The Play What I Wrote, appeared in 2001 as a tribute to the duo. Directed by Kenneth Branagh, each performance featured a different guest celebrity, including Kylie Minogue, Roger Moore, Nigel Havers and most notably Prince Charles, who was a huge fan of the duo. In 1999 Eric was voted the funniest person of the 20th century in a British internet poll; Eric pulled in 26% of the votes, beating his contemporary performer Tommy Cooper into second. Ernie continued to work after Eric's death, as he was a solo performer before teaming up with Eric, but his heart wasn't really in it. He married the dancer Doreen Blythe in 1953 and had no children. He died, also from a heart-attack, on 21 March 1999, Gerrards Cross, Buckinghamshire See also entries in the television section for Hope and Keen, Variety Bandbox, and Worker's Playtime.

Morris, Chris Born 15 June 1962, Bristol. Brought up in Cambridgeshire, Chris, the offspring of two doctors, read zoology at Bristol University before deciding to begin his brand of anarchic comedy at BBC Radio Cambridgeshire. He developed a style similar to the one now used by comedian Harry Hill whereby clever editing gave rise to some innovative spoofs and parodies. Chris progressed to BBC Radio Bristol and Greater London Radio but was sacked from both for on-air pranks. His first appearance on national radio was on Christmas Day 1990 when he informed the BBC Radio 1 listeners that the Pet Shop Boys were to record a song with Myra Hindley, the 'Moors Murderer', and was promptly sacked. His next radio show was Radio 4's On the Hour (1991) a spoof news show that became a BBC television show in 1994 under the title The Day Today. Chris played the frontman for the show which saw the introduction of Steve Coogan's character of Alan Partridge as the sports correspondent. Later in the year he was invited back to Radio 1 where he teamed up with Peter Cook in the guise of Sir Arthur Streeb-Greebling. Chris next wrote and starred in Channel 4's Brass Eye (1997) which developed the extreme satirical theme of The Day Today and had a recurrent theme of asking famous people to comment on news items unaware that they were ludicrous and fictional. The subject matter, including references to paedophilia, rape, incest and buggery, led to record numbers of viewer complaints. The Channel 4 late-night show Jam (2000), a re-working of his radio show Blue Jam, and it's even later-night adult version Jaaaaam (2000) continued Chris's irreverent comedy output. In 2003 he was listed in The Observer as one of the 50 funniest people in British comedy and in December 2004 was listed at No.11 in the Channel 4 show The Comedian's Comedian, in which foremost writers and performers ranked their 50 favourite acts. Perhaps this elevated ranking, above the likes of Spike Milligan, reflects the short memories of the judges but there is no doubt that the reclusive Morris has earned his place in this list as a true innovator of British comedy. In 2002, Chris directed the film short, My Wrongs, about a man led astray by a sinister talking dog. It was the first film project of Warp Films, and won a BAFTA for best short film. Chris has recently directed his first feature-length film Four Lions (2010) about a group of inept British terrorists. He currently lives in Brixton, with literary agent Jo Unwin, and has two sons Charles Peter (b. 1996, Lambeth) and Frederick Rudolf (b. 1999, Lambeth). See also entries in the television section for Brass Eye, The Day Today, The It Crowd, and Nathan Barley.

Mortimer, Bob See entry for Vic Reeves

Murray, Al Born Alastair James Hay Murray, 10 May 1968, Stewkley, Buckinghamshire. Al was bitten by the performing bug whilst performing with the Oxford Revue in between studying modern history at the university. At this time Al shared a passion with other great comedians such as Peter Sellers, Russ Abbot, Jim Davidson, Lee Evans and Matt Lucas – he was a drummer. Although he began his professional life as a sound-effect impressionist he is best known for his Pub Landlord act which first saw the light of day in 1994 as the tour support act for Harry Hill. The character 'Guv' from Sky One's sitcom Time Gentlemen Please (2000-02) was played by Al, based on his pub landlord persona. Al made his television debut in The Word (1991) before co-starring in the Harry Hill comedy vehicle, Fruit Fancies (1994). He was nominated for the Perrier Award at the Edinburgh Festival Fringe in 1996, 1997 and 1998 before finally winning the award in 1999. In 2007 he was voted number sixteen on Channel 4's hundred greatest stand-up lists. In 2008 and 2009 Al appeared on Jools Holland's annual Hootenanny and every time Jools attempted an interview with the comedian the only response forthcoming was "Hootenanny". Interestingly, Al is a great-great-great-grandson of William Makepeace Thackeray. See also entries in the radio and television section for Al Murray's Happy Hour, Al Murray's Multiple Personality Disorder, Fact Hunt, Fist of Fun, Hell's Kitchen, Live at the Apollo, Michael McIntyre's Comedy Roadshow and Walk on the Wild Side

Murray, Chic Born Charles Thomas McKinnon Murray, 6 November 1919, Greenock, Inverclyde. Chic began his career as a musician in amateur groups such as "The Whinhillbillies" and "Chic and His Chicks" while an apprentice at the Kincaid shipyard, Inverclyde, in 1934. He began his professional life as part of a double act with his wife, Maidie Dickson, often billed as "The Tall Droll with the Small Doll" as he was 6'3" while she was 4'11". By the mid-1950s Chic had gone solo and developed more of a surreal line in patter, although his dead-pan delivery revealed a master class in comedy timing whether telling a long elaborate tall tale or a pithy one-liner. Chic was known as the comedian's comedian, ever changing his act and maintaining a compelling standard. When delivering a particularly subtle line he would often pause and pull an exasperated expression to give the audience time to digest what he had said. Chic didn't need props but was invariably dressed in smart blazer and tie (or bow) with the omnipresent bunnet atop his head. He made rare excursions into film, making his debut in Casino Royale (1966). Other films include: Secrets of a Door-to-Door Salesman (1974), I'm Not Feeling Myself Tonight (1976), The Ups and Downs of a Handyman (1976), What's Up Superdoc! (1978), What's Up Nurse! (1978) and his last film, Gregory's Girl (1981). On television, he made his debut in David Nixon's BBC comedy series Showtime in 1961 and was a regular guest on all the leading variety shows during the next two decades. One of Chic's last television appearances was as a balaclava-clad itinerant poacher, causing problems on the Glendarroch Estate, in Take The High Road. Chic was still performing stand-up as well as ever right up to his death on 29 January 1985, Edinburgh. He was survived by his wife Maidie (d. May 2010). See also entries in the television section for Comedy Bandbox, Joker's Wild, and The White Heather Club.

Naughton, Charlie See Crazy Gang.

Nervo, Jimmy See Crazy Gang.

Noble, Ross Born Ross Markham Noble, 5 June 1976, Cramlington, Northumberland. At the age of eleven Ross realised he was dyslexic and settled for a non-academic career. Before deciding on comedy he dabbled in street juggling, stilt-walking and singing (backing vocals for the Kane Gang). He also joined the youth theatre section of the People's Theatre, Newcastle upon Tyne. By the age of fifteen he performed his first comedy routine at his local comedy club. His act is largely based on absurd humour, although his quick-witted interaction with his audience often gives him room for banter and clever comic responses, particularly to heckling. He first appeared on Australian television in 1999 and lived there for a time until burned out by a forest fire in 2009. In Britain he gained a Perrier Award nomination in 1999 for his Edinburgh Festival show Laser Boy, and the following year won a Time Out award in Edinburgh for his Chickenmaster show. Other tours have included: Slackers' Playtime (2001–2002), Sonic Waffle (2002–2003), Unrealtime (2003–2004), Noodlemeister (2004), Randomist (2005), Fizzy Logic (2006), Nobleism (2007), Things (2009), Nonsensory Overload (2010-12) and Mindblender (2012). On British television he has appeared on numerous panel shows including, Room 101, QI, and Have I Got News for You. He has also appeared on the Irish chat show Tubridy Tonight, and several radio shows such as Just A Minute and I'm Sorry I Haven't a Clue. Ross and his Australian-born wife Fran, have a daughter, Elfie. He also has a famous uncle, Mickey Hutton, who was a popular Geordie television presenter and stand-up. Ross is a keen motorcyclist and after crashing and dislocating his collarbone outside a hospital in April 2006, he treated the staff to his Stephen Hawking impression. His latest of numerous DVDs is The Headspace Cowboy, highlights of an Australian tour.

O'Briain, Dara Born 4 February 1972, Bray, County Wicklow. Dara attended University College, Dublin, where he studied mathematics and theoretical physics and was the co-founder and co-editor of The University Observer college newspaper. In 1994, he won the Irish Times National Debating Championship and The Irish Times/Gael Linn National Irish language debating championship. Dara began working at RTÉ as a children's TV presenter and at the same time began performing stand-up gigs on the Irish comedy circuit. He was a regular at the Kilkenny Cat Laughs and the Edinburgh Festival. Already a well-known face on Irish television by the end of the 1990s, Dara presented the weekend mainstream game show It's a Family Affair for RTÉ. It was the first time he worked with former Channel 4 commissioning editor Séamus Cassidy. They later set up the production company Happy Endings Productions, and together they produced (and Dara presented) the chat show Buried Alive (2003) and most famously, in Ireland, the weekly topical comedy-style chat show, The Panel (2003–06). In Britain, Dara has become a household name for his appearances on shows such as Never Mind the Buzzcocks, Have I Got News for You, and QI. See also entries in the radio and television section for The Apprentice, Don't Feed The Gondolas, Echo Island, Mock the Week, and Three Men In A Boat.

O'Carroll, Brendan Popular Irish comedian and actor now famous in Britain as Agnes Brown, the loud, foul-mouthed Irish matriarch in the popular BBC1 sitcom, Mrs Brown's Boys (2012). See Brendan O'Carrolls Hot Milk and Pepper in the television section for fuller biography.

O'Connor, Des Born Desmond Bernard O'Connor, 12 January 1932, Stepney, London. Des was evacuated to Northampton during World War II and was briefly a professional footballer on the books of Northampton Town. He began his professional life as a Butlins Redcoat and after National Service became a polished stand-up comedian and compere. Des made his television debut on the ITV show, Spot the Tune, in 1957. When Buddy Holly toured the UK in March 1958, Des was his warm-up act and compere. After several appearances on shows such as Six-Five Special and Thank Your Lucky Stars, Des made several appearances as guest and host on Val Parnell's Sunday Night At The London Palladium. The Des O'Connor Show (1963-73) propelled him to superstardom and his stooge, Jack Douglas in the character of Alf Ippititimus, also enjoyed great popularity throughout this period. His subsequent television shows, Des O'Connor Entertains (1974–76), Des O'Connor Tonight (1977–

2002) and Today with Des and Mel (2002–06), a live afternoon chat and light entertainment show co-hosted by Melanie Sykes, has meant that Des has never been off our screens. He remains a class act as shown in a one-off special of An Audience With Des O'Connor (2001). He also has a fine singing voice and, despite the tongue-in-cheek disparaging remarks from Eric Morecambe which became a recurrent theme in the Morecambe and Wise Show, has sold millions of records including the 1968 No 1 I Pretend and several Top 20 hits such as Careless Hands (No. 6 in 1967), 1-2-3 O'Leary (No. 4 in 1968), the classic Dick-A-Dum-Dum (No. 14 in 1969) and The Skye Boat Song (No. 10 in 1986 – with Roger Whittaker). He was awarded a CBE in the 2008 Birthday Honours. Des has been married four times, to Butlins performer Phyllis Gill (1953-59), with whom he has a daughter, Karen; dancer Gillian Vaughan (1960-82), with whom he has two daughters, TJ and Samantha; model Jay Rufer (1985-90), with whom he has a daughter, Kristina; and singer Jodie Brooke Wilson (2007-present), with whom he has a son Adam. His autobiography, published in 2001, is entitled Bananas Can't Fly! See also entries in the television section for Countdown, For Love or Money, National Lottery, Sunday Night at the London Palladium, and Take Your Pick.

O'Doherty, David Born David Nicholas O'Doherty, 18 December 1975, Dublin, Ireland. Among numerous other jobs, David worked in telemarketing before making his stand-up debut at Dublin's Comedy Cellar in 1998. In actual fact David's act should be described as sit-down as he is invariably sat with an electronic keyboard on his lap delivering his comic songs with a dry sarcasm that he describes as "Very low energy musical whimsy" in his song "FAQ for the DOD". In 1999, he won the Channel 4 So You Think You're Funny comedy competition at the Edinburgh Fringe and he has been winning awards ever since despite making very few appearances on British television. His first full show, The Story of the Boy Who Saved Comedy, received a nomination for Perrier Best Newcomer when it was performed at the Edinburgh Fringe and in August 2008, he won the If.comedy award at the fringe for his show Let's Comedy, which included advice on how to dislodge a badger if stuck to your leg. David is also an author and playwright. His first written work, published in 2001, is a children's book entitled Ronan Long Gets It Wrong. His first play, written with Bryan Quinn, is entitled Saddled and claims to be "the world's first theatrical production to feature live repair of audience members' bicycles". The bicycle theme was recurrent in David's first television series, The Modest Adventures of David O'Doherty, which began airing on RTÉ Two in May 2007. In the first of the six episodes David attempts to cycle from Dublin to Galway, for a show later that night but quits 100 kilometres from his destination. The second episode showed David's attempt at having a minor hit with the CD, Orange, which indeed did peak at No. 30 in the Irish charts. The following year David made his film debut in the comedy thriller A Film with Me in It (2008). In Britain, David has appeared on 8 Out of 10 Cats and Never Mind the Buzzcocks, presenting shows in 2010 and 2011. He has also appeared on the Australian equivalent to Buzzcocks, Spicks and Specks.

O'Grady, Paul See entry in television section

Oliver, Vic See entries in the television section for Desert Island Discs and Life With the Lyons.

O'Shea, Tessie Born Teresa Mary O'Shea, 13 March 1913, Cardiff, Wales. Tessie appeared on stage as a singer and dancer from the age of six, billed as "The Wonder of Wales". By her teens she was an international star known for her comedy songs, larger-than-life personality and her banjolele playing. As Tessie began to put on weight in the 1930s she adopted the theme song "Two Ton Tessie from Tennessee". She was undoubtedly one of Britain's most loved music hall entertainers with her combination of over-the-top outfits (usually oversized hats, striped stockings and elastic boots) and great booming voice as she belted out such bawdy favourites as "Don't Have Any More, Missus Moore" and "Hold Your Hand Out, Naughty Boy." By the late 1930s Tessie had become a major star on radio and stage and won the hearts and respect of soldiers everywhere touring with ENSA during

World War II. She later went out on the road with bandleader Bill Cotton in a highly successful musical revue called "Tess and Bill." Tessie had huge success on Broadway with her scene-stealing part of a fish-and-chips seller singing "London" in *The Girl Who Came to Supper*, a 1963 musical adaptation of Terrance Rattigan's play *The Sleeping Prince*, and was rewarded with a Tony for her efforts. She was one of Ed Sullivan's guests on the famous 9 February 1964 show that featured the US debut of *The Beatles*. This raised public awareness of Tessie and she returned to Broadway in 1966 with the musical *A Time for Singing*, which was based on Richard Llewellyn's *How Green Was My Valley*. Tessie won an Emmy nomination in 1968 for her feisty, atmospheric musical turn in Jack Palance's version of *Dr. Jekyll and Mr. Hyde*. On film, she made her debut in *Holidays with Pay* (1948). Other films include: *Somewhere in Politics* (1949), *The Shiralee* (1957), *The Russians Are Coming! The Russians Are Coming!* (1966), *The Best House in London* (1969) and her last film, *Bedknobs and Broomsticks* (1971). Back in Britain in the 1970s she appeared to great advantage on television shows such as *The Good Old Days*. Tessie died of congestive heart failure on 21 April 1995, East Lake Weir, Florida.

Palin, Michael Born Michael Edward Palin, 5 May 1943, Broomhill, Sheffield. Michael attended Shrewsbury School and read modern history at Brasenose College, Oxford, where he met Terry Jones and performed with him in the Oxford Revue. On leaving university the pair re-united and wrote for various BBC shows including *The Ken Dodd Show*, *The Billy Cotton Bandshow*, and *The Illustrated Weekly Hudd*. As a performer Michael will inevitably always be identified with *Monty Python* but much the same as John Cleese, Michael too followed up with a classic comedy series, *Ripping Yarns*. Michael made his film debut in the *Monty Python* film spin-off *And Now for Something Completely Different* (1971). Other films include: *Monty Python and the Holy Grail* (1975), *Jabberwocky* (1977), *Life of Brian* (1979), *Time Bandits* (1981), *The Missionary* (1982), *The Meaning of Life* (1983), *A Private Function* (1984), *Brazil* (1985), *American Friends* (1991), *The Wind in the Willows* (1996) and *Fierce Creatures* (1997 - as Adrian 'Bugsy' Malone) – many of these films he also contributed to as writer. He won a BAFTA as Best Supporting Actor for his role of Ken Pile in *A Fish Called Wanda* (1988). After *Ripping Yarns*, Michael began a new career as a travel writer and travel documentarian, his journeys having taken him around the world. In 2000 he received a CBE for his services to television. Michael married Helen Gibbins in 1966. They have three children and a grandchild. His youngest child, Rachel (b.1975) is a BBC TV director, whose work includes *Masterchef: The Professionals*. See also entries in the radio and television section for *Around the World in 80 Days, At Last The 1948 Show, Broaden Your Mind, The Complete and Utter History of Britain, Do Not Adjust Your Set, The Frost Report, Full Circle, GBH, Great Railway Journeys, Hark at Barker, Hemingway Adventure, Himalaya, It's A Knockout, Just A Minute, Marty, Monty Python's Flying Circus, Pole to Pole, Ripping Yarns, Rutland Weekend Television, Sahara, Timewatch,* and *Twice a Fortnight*.

Platt, Ken Born 17 February 1921, Leigh, Lancashire. As with so many entertainers of the day, Ken joined the Army in 1942 and was posted to North Africa where he appeared in a concert party, *The Forest Mummers*. Ken played the ukelele and was billed as 'the Pocket George Formby', in homage to his idol. He subsequently joined the Combined Services Entertainment unit and after being demobbed Ken initially worked in his own grocery store in Leigh while doing stand-up at night. In 1950 he became resident comedian on the BBC's popular radio show *Variety Fanfare*. The series, broadcast on the northern Home Service, ran for two years and made Ken a household name. It was on radio that Ken was in his true element with his immaculate timing and brilliant ad-libbing. The classic radio series *Worker's Playtime* enhanced Ken's career and gave him national recognition. With his flat cap and droll delivery, he was best remembered by the catchphrase with which he began every performance: "Allo, I won't take me coat off - I'm not stoppin'!". When his brand of music hall act became a thing of the past Ken became a character actor and after minor roles in *Crossroads* and *The Liver Birds* he starred in his own Yorkshire Television sitcom, *Our Kid*, playing

Ben Buslingthorpe. He died 2 October 1998, Blackpool. See also entries in the radio and television section for *Comedy Bandbox, Crossroads, Spot the Tune, Wild Wild Women,* and *Worker's Playtime*.

Powell, Sandy Born Albert Arthur Powell, 30 January 1900, Bridgegate, Rotherham. Show business was in Sandy's (his preferred name derives from the colour of his hair) blood from an early age becoming a boy vocalist aged seven and then assisting his mother in a puppet show. His career took-off when he became a 'Scottish' comedian, wearing a kilt that was given to him by his mother. He starred in the pantomime *Cinderella* in 1915 and he subsequently hardly missed a year thereafter. His film debut was as Ginger Dick in *The Third String* (1932). Other films include: *Can You Hear Me, Mother?* (1935), *Leave it to Me* (1936). *It's a Grand Old World* (1937), *I've Got a Horse* (1938) and his last film, *Cup Tie Honeymoon* (1948). He also had a very successful recording career and made more than 80 records (notably, *The Lost Policeman* and *Gracie and Sandy at the Coronation*, which he made with Gracie Fields). Sandy's career went from strength to strength and throughout the 1940s and 1950s he was a household name. On television he was a regular on variety shows of the day, and appeared in three Royal Variety Performances. He also toured abroad with his comic songs and a very successful ventriloquist act where his dummy would literally fall apart. His catchphrase 'can you hear me mother?' would always be heard at the start of his radio series and became the title for his 1976 autobiography. He did a lot of charity work, particularly for his local hospital in Rotherham, and also gave free concerts for the unemployed. He was awarded the MBE in the 1975 Queen's Honours List. He performed with his Starlight company in the Eastbourne Pier theatre for over fifteen seasons in the 1950s and 1960s, earning himself the sobriquet 'Mr Eastbourne' and he was still performing occasionally up to his death on 26 June 1982.

Ray, Ted Born Charles Olden, 21 November 1905, Wigan, Lancashire. His family moved to Liverpool when he was but a few days old and he has always been considered a Liverpudlian. He began his professional life as a comic under the name Hugh Neek and then became a violinist performing as Nedlo the Gypsy Violinist (Nedlo being his name backwards). He changed his name to Ted Ray in 1930, in honour of the famous British golfer. Initially describing his act as 'fiddling and fooling' he abandoned the violin after World War II and only sporadically used it as a comedy prop in the vein of Jack Benny (the American comedian who perfected a similar act years earlier). In 1949 Ted was given his own BBC radio show *Ray's A Laugh* which ran until 1961 and co-starred Australian actress Kitty Bluett as his wife, Fred Yule as his brother-in-law and Kenneth Connor as Sidney Mincing. Patricia Hayes was also a regular as was a young Peter Sellers. Another radio series, *Does the Team Think?*, that ran throughout the 1960s, showed Ted's extraordinary skill at ad-libbing. This series also starred Jimmy Edwards, Arthur Askey and Cyril Fletcher and numerous guest panelists such as Tommy Trinder, Jimmy Wheeler and David Tomlinson, but it was Ted's contribution of quick-fire gags that always gained the loudest applause. On television, Ted enhanced his popularity by starring in *The Ted Ray Show* (1955-59), *Hip Hip Who Ray* (1956) and *It's Saturday Night* (1959), alongside his actor son Robin (1934-98). Robin became famous as a classical music expert on the television series *Face The Music*. Ted's other son, Andrew (1939-2003) was a child star of several films in the 1950s. Ted's film debut was in *Meet Me Tonight* (1952). Other films include: *Escape by Night* (1953), *My Wife's Family* (1956), *The Crowning Touch* (1959), *Carry On Teacher* (1959) and his last film, *Please Turn Over* (1960). A particular party-piece Ted acquired, and later copied by Bob Monkhouse and others, was to ask an audience to give him a word or phrase as a theme and he would tell a joke about it. He died of a heart attack on 8 November 1977, London. See also entries in the television section for *Joker's Wild*, and *Spot the Tune*.

Read, Al Born 3 March 1909, Broughton, Salford. Al worked as a sausage maker in his father's business for years while working part-time as an after-dinner speaker and comedian in the clubs. *The Al Read Show* was one of the most popular radio comedy shows in the UK in the 1950s and 1960s. His catchphrases "Right Monkey", "You've met 'em!" and "You'll be lucky, I say you'll be lucky!" were well known throughout the land. His first Royal Variety Performance at the London Palladium was in 1954 and he made numerous guest appearances on variety shows as well as having several television series of his own. Al was the master of the comedy monologue, a sort of northern version of Bob Newhart. He died 9 September, 1987.

Reeves, Vic Born James Roderick Moir, 24 January 1959, Leeds, West Yorkshire. Brought up in Darlington, Jim began his showbusiness career as a punk rocker but soon turned to comedy. He joined the alternative comedy circuit under many different guises, including a loudmouth American called Jim Bell, Tappy Lappy, a tap dancer wearing a Bryan Ferry mask with planks on his feet, a beat poet called Mister Mystery and, eventually, "The North-East's Top Light Entertainer" Vic Reeves – and the name stuck. He put together comedy nights at Goldsmith's Tavern in New Cross, London, where he was often heckled by a young Legal Aid solicitor named Robert Renwick 'Bob' Mortimer (b. 23 May 1959, Acklam, Middlesbrough). The comic chemistry was apparent and they initially formed a band called *The Potter's Wheel* before teaming up for a stage-show *Vic Reeves Big Night Out*. Reeves and Mortimer made their television debut on the short-lived chat show *One Hour with Jonathan Ross* (1989), in the game show segment known as knock down ginger. *Vic Reeves Big Night Out* became a television show in 1990 after Jonathan Ross persuaded Channel 4 chief executives to see the show, now at the Albany Empire, Deptford. Switching to BBC and giving Bob a more prominent role as a fully-fledged equal partner, *The Smell of Reeves and Mortimer* (1993-95) followed by *Shooting Stars* and *Bang Bang It's Reeves and Mortimer* (1999) engaged the lads in the same surreal off-the-wall humour that became their trademark. In recent years, despite suffering from rheumatoid arthritis, which flares up in stressful situations, Bob has been seen defeating Les Dennis in the first-ever celebrity boxing match (in aid of Sport Relief, 2002) and Vic accompanying his wife Nancy Sorrell into the Australian jungle to compete in *I'm a Celebrity, Get Me Out of Here* (2004). Vic's part in the Churchill car insurance adverts was hastily re-voiced by another actor after he was involved in a drink-driving accident in March 2005 and banned from driving for 32 months. Vic is also a promising artist and his drawings and paintings have been used in his television shows and formed a major part of his 1999 book, *Sun Boiled Onions*. He recently played Eric Morecambe's father, George, in the BBC2 television film, *Eric and Ernie* (2011). Vic has been married twice, to Sarah Vincent (1990-99) and Nancy Sorrell (2003-present). He has two children Alice Vincent (b. 1993) and Louis Vincent (b. 1997) from his first marriage and twin girls Elizabeth and Nell (b. 2006) from his second. Bob is married to Lisa Matthews and has two children, Harry (b. 1997) and Tom (b. 1998). See also entries in the television section for *I'm a Celebrity Get Me Out Of Here, Randall and Hopkirk (Deceased), Shooting Stars, The Tube,* and *Who Do You Think You Are?*

Reid, Beryl See entry in cinema section.

Robey, George Born George Edward Wade, 20 September 1869, Herne Hill, London. George had a middle-class upbringing and used his 'plummy' voice and looks as tools to instigate laughter. He took his stage name from a firm of Birmingham builders, but changed his original stage name from Roby to Robey on a whim and then made it permanent by deed-poll. At first he worked as an assistant to a stage hypnotist, 'professor' Kennedy, before debuting in the Oxford Music Hall in June 1891. George could work an audience better than any of his contemporaries and the more he asked the screaming hordes to 'desist' the more raucous the laughter became. George was equally at home playing a pantomime dame, collarless cleric with full comic red nose and darkened eyebrows, or singing in various styles, as he was working comedy routines - a true all-round entertainer. On film, he debuted in *Doing His Bit* (1917). Other films include: *The Rest Cure* (1923), *Don Quixote* (1923 - as Sancho Panza), *Henry V* (1944 - as Sir John Falstaff), and his last film, *The Pickwick Papers* (1952 - as Tony Weller). Although he initially turned down a knighthood for the lesser honour of CBE as he felt unworthy of the higher accolade, he relented in the final year of his life and he was consequently dubbed 'the prime minister of mirth'. He died on 29 November 1954, Saltdean, Brighton.

Ross, Jonathan See entry in the television section under *Friday Night With Jonathan Ross*.

Sadowitz, Jerry Born 4 November 1961, New Jersey, USA. Following the break-up of his parent's marriage, his mother returned to her native Scotland and Jerry was brought up in Glasgow. He took a keen interest in magic as a child and began his comedy magic act at his local pub, the Weavers Inn, then run by comedienne Janey Godley. In his early days he was managed by the legendary showbiz agent and comedian Malcolm Hardee (1950-2005), who billed him as "too shocking to appear on TV". This was indeed true to a certain extent as Jerry is certainly in the Chubby Brown/Bernard Manning school of stand-up, his irreverent humour causing controversy wherever he goes. After parting from Hardee he was part of a short-lived double act with Logan Murray in the early 1990s and their propensity for poking fun in bad taste ensured they would never be booked for TV work. Jerry has made rare excursions into television land, notably with the BBC 2 series *The Pall Bearer's Revue* (1992) and the Channel 5 series *The People vs. Jerry Sadowitz* (1998-99) in which he challenged members of the public to talk to him interestingly with the hope of winning £10,000. The prize was never paid and the punters were mercilessly abused by Jerry. Despite the lack of mainstream success Jerry's shows are invariably sold-out. He has always been popular at the Edinburgh Fringe whether performing magic or stand-up, his "Rabbi Burns" character (a cross between a Jew and the famous Scottish poet) being particularly popular. Jerry does an excellent impersonation of Jimmy Savile and the clean version was seen on *Stewart Lee's Comedy Vehicle* (BBC2, 2009). Jerry is widely acclaimed as one of the best close-up magicians in the business and in 2007 he was voted the 15th greatest stand-up comic on Channel 4's *100 Greatest Stand-Ups*.

Saunders, Jennifer Born Jennifer Jane Saunders, 6 July 1958, Sleaford, Lincolnshire. Her mother was a biology teacher, and her father an Air Marshal in the RAF. Jennifer is known for her long-time collaboration with Dawn French (see separate entry). Her solo projects include guest starring in the American sitcoms *Roseanne* and *Friends*, and winning the American People's Choice Award for voicing the wicked Fairy Godmother in the DreamWorks' animation *Shrek 2* (2004) performing the song "Holding Out for a Hero". She also voiced Miss Spink in the animated film *Coraline* (2009). Other films include: *In the Bleak Midwinter* (1995), *Muppet Treasure Island* (1996), *Spice World* (1997), *Fanny & Elvis* (1999) and *Absolument fabuleux* (2001), a French film based on *Absolutely Fabulous*. Jennifer married fellow comedian Adrian Edmondson in 1985. They have three daughters, Eleanor Rose (b. 22 January 1986, Hammersmith), Beatrice Louise (b. 19 June 1987, Kensington and Chelsea) and Freya Domenica (b. 16 October 1990, Wandsworth). Beatrice followed in her father's footsteps and studied drama at the University of Manchester where she became a member of all-female comedy troupe Lady Garden. All three of Jennifer's daughters have appeared in *Jam and Jerusalem*. Jennifer has recently battled against breast cancer but is currently in remission. Along with Dawn French, she declined an OBE in 2001. See also entries in the television section for *Absolutely Fabulous, The Comic Strip Presents, French and Saunders, Girls on Top, Happy Families, Jam and Jerusalem, Let Them Eat Cake, The Life and Times of Vivienne Vyle, Saturday Live,* and *The Young Ones*.

Saveen See *Ventriloquists*.

Sayle, Alexei Born Alexei David Sayle, 7 August 1952, Anfield, Liverpool. Alexei's mother was of Lithuanian Jewish descent and his father was English. His parents were members of the Communist Party of Great Britain and in the aftermath of the May 1968 French uprising, Alexei joined the party. He attended the Chelsea College of Art and Design. When The Comedy Store opened in London in 1979, he responded to an advert for would-be comedians and became its first master of ceremonies. After honing his act at the Edinburgh Festival Fringe he began to make television appearances in 1980. His political roots form a firm foundation for his cutting-edge style of stand-up although he has a lighter surreal side too. His trademark appearance is a shaved head, five o'clock shadow, and a suit that is two sizes too small; his delivery is often loud and sometimes manic. At the height of his fame he had several BBC2 serials, including *Alexei Sayle's Stuff* (1988–91), *The All New Alexei Sayle Show* (1994–95) and *Alexei Sayle's Merry-Go-Round* (1998). He made his film debut as Golodkin in *Gorky Park* (1983). Other films include: *The Supergrass* (1985), *The Bride* (1985), *Whoops Apocalypse* (1986), *Solarbabies* (1986), *Siesta* (1987), *The Love Child* (1987), *Indiana Jones and the Last Crusade* (1989), *Carry On Columbus* (1992), *Reckless Kelly* (1993), *Rhinoceros Hunting in Budapest* (1997), *Swing* (1999), *Arabian Nights* (2000), *Don't Walk* (2001), *The Tale of Tarquin Slant* (2004), *Upstaged* (2005) and *The Thief Lord* (2006). Alexei also had a No 15 UK Chart hit in 1984 with *'Ulllo John Got A New Motor?* See also entries in the television section for *The Comic Strip Presents, Common as Muck, Great Railway Journeys, Horrible Histories, OTT (Over The Top), Tipping the Velvet, Whoops! Apocalypse,* and *The Young Ones.*

Secombe, (Sir) Harry Born 8 September 1921, Swansea, South Wales. Harry served his country in the Royal Artillery during World War II and appeared in Forces shows where he displayed a great comic talent. *The Goon Show* (1951-60) propelled him to radio stardom and his 1955 BBC series *Secombe Here!*, written by his great friend Jimmy Grafton, made him a television star. *The Harry Secombe Show* (1955-57), written by Eric Sykes, became the first weekly variety show on the newly-formed ITV and his regular character of Fred Nerk lent itself to any stupid person becoming know as a 'nerk'. By 1959 Harry had developed his singing voice enough for it to become an integral part of his act and he began to make guest appearances on other people's variety shows as a singer. In 1967 his rendition of *This Is My Song* reached No 2 in the UK Charts. Harry made several series during the 1960s and 70s notably, *Secombe and Friends* (1959-66), *Secombe at Large* (1959), *Who Is Secombe* (1963), and *The Harry Secombe Show* (1968-1973). He presented the religious programme *Highway* in the 1980s but still turned up in comedic roles, blowing his famed raspberries and showing his great wit. By now he was only half the man he used to be having lost several stone through doctor's orders. Ill-health plagued him throughout the 1990s and after suffering a stroke he filmed a touching reflective programme portraying his life after becoming semi-paralysed. Knighted in 1981, Harry was simply a good guy, probably the best-loved man in showbusiness. He starred in the stage-show *Pickwick* and the film *Oliver!* in the 1960s and was known as the Welsh Goon. Although he played only the one main character, Neddie Seagoon, throughout the 241 editions, his character was often the lead role around which all the story lines revolved. Harry met Myra Atherton at the Mumbles dance hall. They were married from 1948 until his death on 11 April 2001. They had four children: Jennifer, Andy, David and Katy. See also entries in the radio and television section for *Educating Archie, The Goon Show, Highway, The Idiot Weekly, Price 2d, Songs of Praise, Stars On Sunday, Telegoons,* and *Variety Bandbox.*

Sellers, Peter Born Richard Henry Sellers, 8 September 1925, Southsea, Hampshire. Although christened Richard Henry, his parents always called him Peter, after his elder stillborn brother. His father, Yorkshire-born entertainer Bill Sellers was a protestant while his mother, Agnes (always known as Peggy) also an entertainer, was Jewish. Peter's great-great-grandfather on his mother's side was Daniel Mendoza, the 18th century British prizefighter who, although a middleweight, won world heavyweight boxing titles. Peter began his career in revue at the age of five. He later developed a double act "Altman and Sellers" with his friend Derek Altman before working as drummer in a dance band. During WWII he was an airman in the Royal Air Force, rising to corporal, though his poor eyesight restricted him to ground staff. His tour of duty included India and Burma and, like his father before him, he joined the Entertainments National Service Association and developed his drumming. By the end of the war in 1945, more than four out of five British entertainers had worked for ENSA. In 1946, Peter became entertainment director of a holiday camp and two years later he worked as a vaudeville comedian at the Windmill Theatre, London. He made his film debut in *Penny Points to Paradise* (1951) and in May of that year the long-running BBC radio show *Crazy People* (became

the *Goon Show* in June 1952) began. Peter, played a variety of characters including Hercules Grytpype Thynne, Major Denis Bloodnok, Henry Crun and the downtrodden falsetto-voiced Bluebottle, whose interaction with Spike Milligan's character of Eccles became a much-loved, and imitated, part of the show. Although the original series ended on 28 January 1960, after 241 editions, it was revived from time-to-time as one-off nostalgic specials and a very successful television puppet version using the voices of Sellers, Secombe and Milligan, entitled *The Telegoons* (1963-64). At this time Peter became the first man on the cover of Playboy—he appeared on the April 1964 cover dressed as a Sheik with Karen Lynn, re-creating Valentino's famous silent film role. Peter had by now become the top British comedy actor of his generation through classic films such as *The Lady Killers* (1955), *The Mouse That Roared* (1959), *I'm All Right, Jack* (1959), for which he won a BAFTA, *Two-Way Stretch* (1960), *Heavens Above* (1963) and *The Wrong Arm of the Law* (1963). His international profile was raised after playing opposite Sophia Loren in *The Millionairess* (1961) but it was *The Pink Panther* (1963), and its sequels *A Shot in the Dark* (1964), *The Return of the Pink Panther* (1975), *The Pink Panther Strikes Again* (1976), *Revenge of the Pink Panther* (1978) and *Trail of the Pink Panther* (1982), playing the hapless incompetent Inspector Jacques Clouseau, that elevated him to international superstar status. Other films include: *Carlton-Browne of the F.O.* (1959), *The Battle of the Sexes* (1959), *Mr. Topaze* (1961), a film he also directed, *Only Two Can Play* (1962), *The Road to Hong Kong* (1962), *Lolita* (1962), *Dr. Strangelove or: How I Learned to Stop Worrying and Love the Bomb* (1964), playing the roles of Group Captain Lionel Mandrake / President Merkin Muffley / Dr. Strangelove, *The World of Henry Orient* (1964), *What's New Pussycat* (1965), *The Wrong Box* (1966), *After the Fox* (1966), *Casino Royale* (1967), *I Love You, Alice B. Toklas!* (1968), *The Magic Christian* (1969), a film he also wrote, *There's a Girl in My Soup* (1970), *Alice's Adventures in Wonderland* (1972 - as The March Hare), *Soft Beds, Hard Battles* (1974), in which he played six roles: Général Latour / Major Robinson / Herr Schroeder/ Adolf Hitler / The President / Prince Kyoto, *The Great McGonagall* (1974 - as Queen Victoria), *Murder by Death* (1976), *The Prisoner of Zenda* (1979), playing three roles: Rudolf IV / Rudolf V / Syd Frewin, *Being There* (1979 - as Chance), winning a Golden Globe, and his last film *The Fiendish Plot of Dr. Fu Manchu* (1980), playing two roles: Dennis Nayland Smith / Dr. Fu 'Fred' Manchu. Peter also released several comedy singles, many of them produced by George Martin and released on the Parlophone record label. These include: *Any Old Iron* (1957 - UK No 17), *Goodness Gracious Me* (1960 -UK No 4, with Sophia Loren), *Bangers and Mash* (1961 - UK No 22, with Sophia Loren) and *A Hard Day's Night* (1965 - UK No 14), consisting of Peter speaking the lyrics using the stereotypical voice of an actor playing Shakespeare's Richard III. Peter was undoubtedly one of the greatest all-time comedy actors, as happy playing a cockney, Frenchman, American, Egyptian, Welshman or American, but struggled with the day-to-day rigours of having to be Peter Sellers, resorting to advice from TV astrologer Maurice Woodruff towards the end of his career. Peter was married four times, to Anne Howe (1951-61), Swedish actress Britt Ekland (1964-68), Australian model Miranda Quarry (1970-74) and English actress Lynne Frederick (1977-80). He had two children, Michael and Sarah by his first wife and a daughter, Victoria (b. 20 January 1965, London) by his second. Peter died on 24 July 1980, London and his last joke was to have *In the Mood* played at his funeral. It was a song he despised. See also entries in the radio and television section for *BBC, The Goon Show, The Idiot Weekly, Price 2d, A Show Called Fred, Sykes, Telegoons, Variety Bandbox,* and *Worker's Playtime.*

Skinner, Frank Born Christopher Graham Collins, 28 January 1957, West Bromwich, West Midlands. Although not fully committing himself to study while at school, he graduated from Birmingham Polytechnic (now Birmingham City University) in 1981 with a degree in English and in 1982 gained a Masters degree in English Literature at the University of Warwick. After several years on the dole, he eventually worked as a lecturer in English at Halesowen College before taking the plunge into full-time comedy in 1989, taking his stage name from a member of his father's dominoes team. In 1991 he won the Perrier Award at the

Edinburgh Fringe, beating Jack Dee and Eddie Izzard in a vintage year. Frank's style is a laid-back chat-to-his-audience with keen observations and often topical slant. Although not averse to telling jokes, Frank is at his best when using his natural quick wit to bounce off an audience or his frequent collaborator David Baddiel (b. 28 May 1964, New York). He has worked with his best friend and ex-flatmate on the popular late night ITV entertainment show *Fantasy Football League* (1994-96; 1998; 2004) and on the ITV improvisation show *Baddiel and Skinner Unplanned* (2000-05). The duo also co-wrote and performed the football song *Three Lions* with the Lightning Seeds and the England national football team for Euro 96, and re-released it for the 1998 World Cup. The song reached No.1 in the UK charts both times. *The Frank Skinner Show* was a hugely popular chat show which began on BBC 1 in 1995 and moved to ITV for its final series' in 2000-01. In recent years Frank has returned to touring as a stand-up comedian interspersed with a regular Saturday morning slot on the London-based independent Absolute Radio. He is currently hosting *Frank Skinner's Opinionated*, on BBC 2 on Friday evenings and the revamped version of *Room 101*. Frank became an alcoholic in his youth but has abstained throughout his most successful years. See also entries in the television section for *Blue Heaven, The Culture Show, Packet of Three,* and *Shane.*

Starr, Freddie Born Frederick Leslie Fowell, 9 January 1943, Huyton, Liverpool. Freddie had a small part in the 1958 film *Violent Playground* before fronting Liverpool rock band *The Midnighters*. He then joined musical impressionist group the *Delmonts* and won the talent show *Opportunity Knocks* three times. He appeared on the 1970 Royal Variety Performance. On turning solo Freddie became the star of the London Weekend Television series *Who Do You Do* (1972-76) impersonating Elvis Presley, Mick Jagger, Norman Wisdom, Max Wall, Adolf Hitler and Tarzan. In February 1974 he had a UK No 9 hit with the ballad, *It's You*. His star was still on the ascendance when he starred in *Freddie Starr's Variety Madhouse* (1979) but his fortunes soon changed when his turbulent private life began to encroach on his performances. To boost Freddie's failing career well-known fabricator of media stories, Max Clifford, concocted a story, FREDDIE STARR ATE MY HAMSTER, which headlined in *The Sun* on 13 March 1986. This story duly placed Freddie back in the public eye and he had something of a renaissance for the next few years, being given his own TV show and recording two 'Audience Withs', the second of which was panned by the critics. A keen sports fan, Freddie supports Everton FC and he was the owner of Miinnehoma, the winning horse in the 1994 Grand National at Aintree. His autobiography, *Unwrapped,* was published in 2001. A comic genius at his very best but a run-of-the-mill performer at his worst, Freddie suffered a major heart attack in April 2010 and underwent triple heart bypass surgery. In November 2011 he entered the Queensland jungle as a contestant on *I'm A Celebrity...Get Me Out of Here!* and although proving that he was definitely incapable of eating a hamster during the first eating trial, Freddie sustained an allergic attack and had to leave the jungle soon after. See also entries in the television section for *Joker's Wild, Opportunity Knocks,* and *Who Do You Do?*

Syal, Meera Born Feeroza Syal, 27 June 1961, Wolverhampton. A comedienne, writer, playwright, singer, journalist and actress, whose Punjabi-born parents came to Britain from New Delhi. She began her professional life as a writer, notably as part of the team of the Channel 4 series *Tandoori Nights* and individually writing the screenplay for the Gurinder Chadha film *Bhaji on the Beach* (1993). Meera is perhaps most famous for playing Granny Kumar in the comedy chat show *The Kumars at No. 42*. In 2005 she married Sanjeev Bhaskar who played her grandson in the series and also collaborated with her on the hit radio and television sketch show *Goodness Gracious Me*. She achieved a number one record in March 2003 with Gareth Gates and her co-stars from *The Kumars*, with *Spirit in the Sky*, the Comic Relief single. Her debut novel, *Anita and Me* (1996), is a semi-autobiographical work about a young Punjabi girl, and her relationship with the white Anita as they grow up in the fictional Midlands village of Tollington in the 1970s. It was a GCSE English literature set text

for the examination years 2004 and 2005. She was awarded the MBE in the New Year's Honours List of 1997. On film, she made her debut as Rehana in *Majdhar* (1983). Other films include: *Sammy and Rosie Get Laid* (1987), *Beautiful Thing* (1996), *Sixth Happiness* (1997), *Girls' Night* (1998), *Anita and Me* (2002 - as Auntie Shaila), *The King of Bollywood* (2004), *Scoop* (2006), *Jhoom Barabar Jhoom* (2007), *Mad Sad & Bad* (2009), *Desert Flower* (2009) and *You Will Meet a Tall Dark Stranger* (2010). Meera has been married twice, to journalist Shekhar Bhatia (1989–2002) and actor Sanjeev Bhaskar (see separate entry). Meera has a son, Shaan (b. 2005) by Sanjeev and a daughter, Chameli, from her first marriage. See also entries in the radio and television section for *All About Me, The Amazing Mrs Pritchard, Beautiful People, Bedtime, Goodness Gracious Me, Holby City, In Deep, The Kumars at No. 42, MIT: Murder Investigation Team, The Real McCoy, Tandoori Nights,* and *Who Do You Think You Are?*

Sykes, Eric Born 4 May 1923, Oldham. Eric has reached the top of his profession as both a performer and writer. He has provided material for many of the major comedy stars including Bill Fraser, Frankie Howerd, Peter Sellers, Harry Secombe and Spike Milligan, as well as writing for top radio series *Variety Bandbox* and *Educating Archie* - It said a lot for Eric's scripts that a ventriloquist became a successful radio act. As a performer Eric will always be associated with the long-running BBC series *Sykes And A.........*(1960-65) alongside Hattie Jacques, Richard Wattis and later, Deryck Guyler. The 60 episodes included classics such as *Sykes And A Bath* and *Sykes And A Plank* (later made into an all-star special). Eric and Hattie were so closely associated with their characters that much of the general public believed they were brother and sister in real life. Another 68 episodes of Sykes were recorded from 1972 until 1979 and Eric is still performing as energetically as ever. His trademark spectacles have no lenses and merely act as a bone-conducting hearing aid as he has bean deaf for over 50 years. His film credits include: his debut *Orders Are Orders* (1954), *Kill or Cure* (1962), *Village of Daughters* (1962), *Heavens Above!* (1963), *The Bargee* (1964), *One Way Pendulum* (1964), *Those Magnificent Men in Their Flying Machines* (1965), *Rotten to the Core* (1965), *The Spy with a Cold Nose* (1966), *Shalako* (1968), *Monte Carlo or Bust* (1969), *Theatre of Blood* (1973), *The Others* (2001), *Harry Potter and the Goblet of Fire* (2005 – as Frank Bryce) and the TV film *Agatha Christie's Poirot: Hallowe'en Party* (2010). Eric married Edith Eleanore Milbrandt on 14 February 1952 and they have three daughters, Catherine, Julie, Susan, and a son, David. See also entries in the radio and television section for *Curry and Chips, The Goon Show, The Idiot Weekly, Price 2d, Juke Box Jury, Sykes, Sykes and A, Telegoons, Teletubbies,* and *Variety Bandbox.*

Tarbuck, Jimmy Born 6 February 1940, Liverpool. Jimmy was a Butlins Redcoat before enjoying a meteoric rise as a stand-up comedian after making his television debut in *Comedy Bandbox* (19 October 1963) and eight days later appearing on *Val Parnell's Sunday Night at the London Palladium,* a show he later compered. Jimmy's cheeky personality, gap-tooth a la Terry-Thomas and lively wit made him one of the most popular stand-up comics of the 1960s; his trendy appearance gave him the tag of being 'the fifth Beatle'. An ever-present on our screens, Tarby has hosted chat-shows, game-shows - *Full Swing* (BBC 1996), *Tarby's Frame Game* (ITV 1987-89) - and variety shows (he was compere of *Live From Her Majesty's* when Tommy Cooper died on stage), and his love of a round of golf is well-known. On film, he made his one and only appearance, as Norman Vaughan, in the Charles Bronson film *Twinky* (1970) a film in which Norman Vaughan also appeared - as Jimmy Tarbuck! Jimmy is the father of actress and television presenter Liza Tarbuck (b. 21 November 1964, Liverpool). See also entries in the television section for *Comedy Bandbox, Sunday Night at the London Palladium,* and *Winner Takes All.*

Tarri, Suzette See entry for Catherine Tate

Tate, Catherine Born Catherine Ford, 12 May 1968, Bloomsbury, London. Catherine was brought up in the then new grade II listed residential and shopping area, the Brunswick

Centre, in Bloomsbury. After attending various Catholic schools in the area she eventually joined a drama group at the Salesian College in Battersea and then trained at the Central School of Speech and Drama. She made her television debut in the ITV sitcom *Surgical Spirit* in 1991 and spent most of the 1990s playing minor roles in television series such as *The Bill*, *Men Behaving Badly* and *London's Burning*. Catherine gravitated towards stand-up comedy in 1996 and made her breakthrough in the BBC2 sketch show, *Big Train* in 1998. She subsequently appeared in comedy series such as *The Harry Hill Show*, *Barking* and *That Peter Kay Thing*. In 2004 she was given her own series and elevated to super-stardom thanks to characters such as Lauren Cooper and Joannie 'Nan' Taylor which combined her acting skills and her sharp comic observations. The foul-mouthed Nan in particular became a sensation. In a throwback to the type of character once portrayed by the music hall star Suzette Tarri (1900-55), Nan told it as it was albeit with rather more floral language than Suzette used to use. On film Catherine made her feature debut as Tallulah Riggs-Wentworth in *Love and Other Disasters* (2006). Other films include: *Starter for 10* (2006), *Sixty Six* (2006), *Scenes of a Sexual Nature* (2006), *Mrs. Ratcliffe's Revolution* (2007), *Gulliver's Travels* (2010 - as Queen Isabelle) and *Monte Carlo* (2011 - as Alicia Winthrop Scott). Catherine's long-time partner was stage manager Twig Clark until the summer of 2011. They have a daughter, Erin Johanna (b. 2003, London). Since October 2011 Catherine has been dating *Take That* star Jason Orange. See also entries in the radio and television section for *Attention Scum!*, *Big Train*, *The Catherine Tate Show*, *Down the Line*, *Dr Who*, and *Wild West*.

Tate, Harry Born Ronald Macdonald Hutchinson, 4 July 1872. The Scottish music hall star took his stage name from Henry Tate & Sons, Sugar Refiners, for whom he worked briefly before turning pro. Like many music hall performers he began as an impressionist, imitating well-known performers such as Dan Leno, George Robey and Eugene Stratton. His first big success came with his 'Motoring' sketch, in which he, a chauffeur and his idiotic son completely failed to get the car started to take the son to college. The son sat in the back of the car making inane comments such as "It's amazing, pa-pa", and "Goodbye-eee" (which became Tate's best-known catchphrase and was the inspiration for the popular World War I song). Later sketches included 'Fishing', 'Running an Office', 'Golfing', 'Fortifying The Home' (Tate: 'I say the house is fortified'. Son: 'No, pa-pa.. it's forty-six!') and 'Selling a Car' (which he performed at the 1919 Royal Command performance). Harry made his film debut as Major Gore in *Her First Affaire* (1932) opposite Ida Lupino. Other films include: *My Lucky Star* (1933), *I Spy* (1934), *Look Up and Laugh* (1935), *Hyde Park Corner* (1935), *Midshipman Easy* (1935), *Variety Parade* (1936), *Keep Your Seats, Please* (1936), *Wings of the Morning* (1937), *Take a Chance* (1937) and his last film, *Sam Small Leaves Town* (1937). Several of Harry's catchphrases went into the English language for a time - 'Goodbye-ee', and 'How's your father?' (said as a get-out for not being able to answer something) - and the expression 'I don't think', used ironically by Harry as in 'He's a nice chap - I don't think', often with the addition of a subtle touch of his bristling moustache. Harry's real son Ronnie, acted with the company from after the First World War, playing parts such as the chauffeur in 'Motoring'. When his father died on 14 February 1940, as a result of a stroke, Ronnie kept the act going for some years as 'Harry Tate Junior'. Interestingly, the earliest known celebrity personalised number plate was owned by Harry. It was simply T 8, a precursor of text-speak!

Tavaré, Jim Born in Essex in 1963, Jim trained at RADA but then became a stand-up comedian, specializing in a unique double bass act. Jim would dress up in classical musician garb and walk on with his large instrument in tow. Although he is an accomplished musician, he would concentrate more on comedy patter interspersed with musical interludes. By the end of the 1990s his act had been seen on numerous television shows so he branched out into other comedy avenues, notably *The Sketch Show* (see entry in the television section), *The Jim Tavaré Show* (C5 -1999, co-written with Ricky Gervais) and *Jim Tavaré Pictures Presents...* (BBC2 – 2005, co-written with Al Murray). To Harry Potter fans he is Tom, the owner of the Leaky Cauldron, in *Harry Potter and the Prisoner of Azkaban* (2004). Other films include: *Rabbit Fever* (2006), *Dirty South* (2010), *Subprime* (2010), *The Black Box* (2010) and *Exit 13* (2011).

Three Monarchs Comedy harmonica act, founded in 1946, consisting of Eric York, Jimmy Prescott and the undoubted star of the trio, Les Henry, better known as Cedric Monarch. Les was actually born Henry Leslie on 20 October 1920 but reversed his name when he became a professional musician. After WWII he was asked by Harry Secombe and Spike Milligan to join them in a new venture with the working title of *The Goons* but by then he had already promised to perform with the Monarchs and he quickly established himself as a star turn. All three were very accomplished harmonica players but it was Les's ability to play the downtrodden poor-relation to the other two which endeared him to audiences. With his distinctive goatee beard, falsetto voice and silly walk, Les was an act guaranteed to make an audience laugh out loud. The Monarchs appeared on all the variety shows of the day and made their first appearance on the Royal Variety Performance in 1952. In 1965 Jimmy Prescott went solo and was replaced by David Conway, who had first played with the Monarchs whilst on tour in South Africa with a thirteen-year-old Helen Shapiro. After the trio disbanded in 1981 'Cedric' became a successful solo cabaret act. He died on 12 January 2007.

Tiernan, Tommy Born 16 June 1969, Carndonagh, Inishowen, County Donegal, Ireland. Tommy attended the same school as Dylan Moran, St. Patrick's Classical School, Navan, and emulated Dylan by winning the *So You Think You're Funny* award at the Edinburgh Festival (1996) and two years later winning the Perrier Comedy Award at the festival. Tommy's best friend, television presenter Hector Ó hEochagáin also attended St Patrick's. Tommy started doing stand up comedy at the G.P.O club in Galway City before making his television debut on the BBC's *The Stand-up Show* (1995-2000) in 1996, then hosted by Ardal O'Hanlon who had just replaced original host Barry Cryer. Tommy took over as host for the final two series in 1999. Also in 1999 Tommy starred alongside Sanjeev Bhaskar (Rick Roy) and Omid Djalili (Hoss) in the Channel 4 sitcom, *Small Potatoes*, in which he played Ed Hewitt, a man who works in a video store. He made his film debut in *Angela Mooney Dies Again* (1996). Other films include: *The MatchMaker* (1997), *Hold Back the Night* (1999) and *About Adam* (2000). Tommy made the first of several controversial appearances on Ireland's *The Late Late Show* in 1998. He caused such outrage with his irreverent sketch on the Crucifixion that angry protesters arrived at R.T.E Studios to protest, before the live show had ended. His act has always been controversial and Tommy has poked fun at drug addicts, homosexuals, disabled people, religion and the Holocaust and on several occasions complaints have been upheld by the Broadcasting Complaints Commission. On 12 April 2009, Tommy set the Guinness World Record for the longest stand-up comedy show by an individual, 36 hours and 15 minutes at Nuns Island in Galway. This record has subsequently been superseded. Tommy married his manager, Yvonne, on 9 August 2009 at Castle Leslie, famous for previously hosting the wedding of Paul McCartney and Heather Mills. See also entries in the television section for *The Comedy Network*, and *Michael McIntyre's Comedy Roadshow*.

Tilley, Vesta Born Matilda Alice Powles 13 May 1864, Worcester, Worcestershire. She made her first stage appearance at the age of three at St George's Theatre in Nottingham, a music hall managed by her father Harry Powles. Originally billed as the Great Little Tilley this was soon changed to Vesta Tilley, the Vesta being a popular brand of matches of the day whose name derived from the Roman goddess of the hearth. Vesta was consequently dubbed 'The goddess of fire'. Her first appearance as a male impersonator was at Day's Concert Hall, Birmingham in 1872 and she went down a storm and had a great repertoire of male impersonations by the time she was nine. In 1890 she married Walter de Frece, the son of a theatre proprietor. Walter later became a Conservative MP. Vesta's comedy routine was well-rehearsed and she revealed all the stereotypical male foibles and eccentricities in her act which particularly appealed to the women in her audience. Her clothes were always immaculate and she became a fashion icon for men particularly when impersonating dandies and fops. During World War I Walter wrote recruiting songs for Vesta and she became known as

England's greatest recruiting sergeant with songs such as *The Army of Today's All Right*, *Six Days' Leave* and *Jolly Good Luck to the Girl Who Loves a Soldier*. On a successful tour of America Vesta appeared in Fred Karno's famous sketch 'The Mumming Birds' with Charlie Chaplin and Stan Laurel. Her greatest songs include *Burlington Bertie* and *Following in Father's Footsteps*. She retired in 1920 and died on 16 September 1952, in London.

Trinder, Tommy See entry in cinema section.

Ullman, Tracey Born Trace Ullman, 30 December 1959, Slough. Tracey had a rather tragic early life, her Polish father dying of a heart attack while reading a book to her when she was six-years-old. A natural mimic, Tracey trained at the Italia Conti Academy stage school and initially worked as a dancer, joining the "Second Generation" dance troupe. Her first screen appearance was as Lisa MacKenzie in the short-lived BBC drama series *MacKenzie* (1980). Her feature film debut came in *Give My Regards to Broad Street* (1984). Other films include: *Plenty* (1985 - as Alice Park), *Jumpin' Jack Flash* (1986 - as Fiona), *I Love You to Death* (1990 - as Rosalie Boca), *Household Saints* (1993 - as Catherine Falconetti), *Robin Hood: Men in Tights* (1993 - as Latrine), *I'll Do Anything* (1994 - as Beth Hobbs), *Bullets Over Broadway* (1994 - as Eden Brent), *Prêt-à-Porter* (1994 - as Nina Scant), *Panic* (2000 - as Martha), *Small Time Crooks* (2000 - as Frenchy), *A Dirty Shame* (2004 - as Sylvia Stickles), *Corpse Bride* (2005 - voice of Nell Van Dort / Hildegarde), *Kronk's New Groove* (2005 - voice of Ms Birdwell), *I Could Never Be Your Woman* (2007- as Mother Nature) and *The Tale of Despereaux* (2008 - voice of Mig). After considerable British success as actress and mimic in the 1980s Tracey emigrated to the USA (becoming an American citizen in December 2006) and had further success with *The Tracey Ullman Show* (1987-90), more famous nowadays for introducing *The Simpsons* to the world. Tracey later voiced the character of Emily Winthrop in a 1991 episode, *Bart's Dog Gets an F*. She has also appeared in *Ally McBeal* (1998-99 - as psychotherapist Dr Tracey Clark), voiced the 'Telephone Voice' in *Mumbai Calling* (2008) and gone back to her sketch roots in the Showtime series *State of the Union* (2008-10). As a pop singer she has had three Top-Ten UK singles in 1983, *Breakaway* (No 4 - famous for her performance with a hairbrush as a microphone), *They Don't Know* (No 2) and *Move Over Darling* (No 8). Her fourth single, *My Guy*, only reached No 23 in 1984 but was famous for its video featuring Neil Kinnock, the then leader of the Labour Party. Tracey married producer Allan McKeown on 27 December 1983; they have two children, Mabel Ellen McKeown (b. 1986) and John Albert Victor McKeown (b. 1991). Mabel, who now works for Harriet Harman in a Labour Party funded job, unsuccessfully ran as the Labour Party candidate in the by-election in Cremorne in Kensington and Chelsea Council in 2010. See also entries in the television section for, *Girls on Top*, *A Kick Up the Eighties*, *MacKenzie*, *Saturday Live*, and *Three Of A Kind*.

Varney, Reg Born Reginald Alfred Varney, 11 July 1916, Canning Town, London. On leaving school at 14, Reg worked as a messenger boy and a page boy before beginning his career as an all-round entertainer, singing, dancing, and playing piano and accordion. His first professional gig was at the Plumstead Radical Club in Woolwich, for which he was paid the princely sum of eight shillings and sixpence (42½p). After World War II he concentrated on comedy and between 1948 and 1951 formed an occasional double-act with Benny Hill, who was the straight man. Reg won superstar status playing the foreman Reg in the BBC sitcom *The Rag Trade* (1961-63) and followed this with another classic series *The Valiant Varneys* (1964-65) where the premise was to look back at the exploits of Reg's fictional ancestors. *Beggar My Neighbour* (1966-68) cemented his reputation as one of the best-loved British television actors but his greatest success was undoubtedly *On the Buses* (1969-73), the 1971 spin-off film becoming the highest-grossing British box-office film of the year. His other films included: *Miss Robin Hood* (1952 – his debut), *Joey Boy* (1965), *The Great St. Trinian's Train Robbery* (1966), *Mutiny on the Buses* (1972), *Go for a Take* (1972), *Holiday on the Buses* (1973) and his last film, *The Best Pair of Legs in the Business* (1974). Reg left *On The Buses* mid-way through its

seventh and final series to star in his own ITV variety show where he reprised his earlier music hall act. In 1975, Reg felt that it was time for him to return to sitcom. He came up with an idea for a show about Billingsgate Market fish porters – *Down the Gate* (1975-76) which was not well received by fans or critics. Reg only made occasional television appearances after this series, mainly due to ill health (he suffered a heart-attack in 1965 and another in 1981). His last screen appearances were in the TV film *Red Peppers* (1991) and as a bingo caller in *Paul Merton's Life of Comedy* (1995). At 5' 2½" (1.59 m), Reg's autobiography was appropriately called *The Little Clown*. A little-known fact is that Reg was the first person in the United Kingdom to use a cashpoint machine when he withdrew £10 in £1 notes at the Barclays hole-in-the-wall in Enfield, North London on 27th June 1967. Reg's wife, Lilian Emma Varney, died in East Devon in 2002, aged 92, and Reg died peacefully in his sleep on 16 November 2008, in a nursing home in Budleigh Salterton, Devon. He was survived by his daughter Jeanne Marley. See also entries in the television section for *Beggar My Neighbour*, *On the Buses*, and *The Rag Trade*.

Vegas, Johnny Born Michael Joseph Pennington, 11 September 1971, St Helens, Merseyside. After studying art and ceramic design at Middlesex University, he initially tried to carve out a career as a potter but eventually worked as a barman and began to drink heavily. He made his screen debut as a contestant on the ITV show *Win, Lose or Draw*. His mentor at this time was the famous (some would say infamous) comedian, prankster and agent, Malcolm Hardee (5 January 1950 – 31 January 2005). His career took off when he won the Festival Critics' Award at the 1997 Edinburgh Festival, and was the first newcomer to be nominated for the Perrier Award. His style was similar to Alexei Sayle, with angry rants at the establishment but delivered in an almost unintelligible high-pitched but husky voice which made him a very real character to his public. Johnny's appearance is also that of a bloke down the pub; slightly overweight, lived-in face and laconic expression. His early shows even contained elements of his private life, with onstage pottery, verbal abuse of the audience, and drunkenness. A second career breakthrough occurred in 2001 when he appeared as "Al" in a series of adverts for ITV Digital with a knitted monkey (voiced by Ben Miller). He made his film debut as Jackie Symes in *The Virgin of Liverpool* (2003). Other films include: *Blackball* (2003), *Cheeky* (2003), *Sex Lives of the Potato Men* (2004), *Terkel in Trouble* (2004), *The Libertine* (2004) and *Gridiron UK* (2011). Johnny has the distinction of being the only person to complete a lap of the *Top Gear* track at Dunsfold without holding a driving licence. He has been married twice, to Catherine Donnelly (2002-08) and Irish TV producer Maia Dunphy (April 2011 - present). He has a son, Michael Laurence Pennington (b. 2003) with his first wife. See also entries in the television section for *Attention Scum!*, *Benidorm*, *Bleak House*, *Happiness*, *Tipping the Velvet* and *Win, Lose or Draw*

Ventriloquists Perhaps the best-known ventriloquist act in British history was **Archie Andrews** (see entry for Educating Archie in the radio and television section). Other popular acts of music hall, radio and television include the following: **Saveen and Daisy May** - Albert Saveen (1915-94) had fourteen puppet characters including Daisy May - a tiny schoolgirl dummy, Andy the Spiv - a cockney boy, a sad little boy adopted by Daisy May called Sonny, and a dog who used to say "Drop Dead!" in a very droll posh voice whenever Mr. Saveen or Daisy spoke to him. The dolls were always packed away in a suitcase when Saveen had finished with them and they could be heard arguing together inside the suitcase and making rude remarks about Saveen. During part of the show, the dummy dog would bark incessantly. Saveen would tell it to be quiet, whereupon it would reply in a posh voice "No I won't! ". Later in the act, Saveen would point to a real dog sitting very still on a chair. The dummy dog would sniff him, ask if he could talk and suggest that he was stupid. At the end of the act, the dog on the chair (called Mickey) would open a false lower jaw (operated by Saveen) and say "Why don't you shut that ruddy dog up!" and then jump down and walk away, being a very well trained real dog. Saveen, who always appeared immaculately dressed in Top Hat and Tails, was the first ventriloquist to have his own radio show, beating Peter Brough and Archie Andrews to it by just a matter of weeks. **Ray Alan and Lord Charles** – Although Ray (b. Raymond Alan Whyberd, 18 September 1930, Greenwich, London; d. 24 May 2010, Reigate, Surrey) was known for voicing the small boy, Tich, and his pet duck Quackers in the popular children's TV series, *Tich and Quackers* in the 1960s and 1970s, he will always be remembered for his long association with the upper crust Lord Charles, who made his television debut (complete with his catchphrase "you silly arse") in *The Good Old Days* in the early 1960s. **Arthur Wilkinson Worsley** (b. 16 October 1920, Failsworth, Manchester; d. 14 July 2001, Blackpool, Lancashire) was the best known television ventriloquist from the 1950s until the 1970s. He was known for his deadpan look and impeccable technique; letting his dummy, Charlie Brown, do all the talking. At his peak Arthur was probably the world's finest vent. **Terry Hall** (b. 20 November 1926, Chadderton, Lancashire; d. 3 April 2007, Coventry, West Midlands) was one of the first ventriloquists to use a non-human puppet. Terry initially worked a boy dummy, Mickey Finn, and won a talent show aged 15. In 1954 he created Lenny the Lion and became one of the most popular variety acts in Britain. Lenny's catchphrase was "Aw, don't embawass me!". Lenny advertised Trebor Mints in the early 1960s and also had his own television show (see entry in the television section for *The Lenny the Lion Show*). Interestingly, David Bowie's father, Hayward Jones, worked on the show, and launched the Lenny the Lion Fan Club. **Roger De Courcey** (b. 10 December 1944, London) found fame as winner of the 1976 *New Faces* televised talent competition, operating his dummy, Nookie Bear. Although Roger's act for television was family-orientated, his stage act was surprisingly blue. **Dennis Spicer** (1936-64) was a very talented ventriloquist with a variety of dummies, including James Green and Maxwell Monkey, Sexy Rexy The Wolf, Puppy Doll The Poodle, Rikki Tikki The Tiger, The Ugly Duckling and Russian bear. He died in a car crash on the A1, near RAF Wittering, near Stamford, Lincolnshire on 15 November 1964, aged 28. **Keith Harris** (b. 21 September 1947, Lyndhurst, Hampshire) had two famous creations, Orville the Duck and Cuddles the Monkey. Orville is a green duckling who wears nothing but a nappy with a large safety pin on the front. He speaks in a much-mimicked falsetto voice. Orville appeared on BBC television from 1982 to 1990 on *The Keith Harris Show*, which also featured Cuddles. Keith and Orville released the single *Orville's Song*, reaching number 4 in the UK Singles Chart in January 1983. Cuddles was orange in colour, with a blue face. He wore a white shirt collar and blue tie, and his catchphrase was "I hate that duck." *Orville and Cuddles* was a BBC series that ran from 1991-92.

Vine, Tim Born Timothy Mark Vine, 4 March 1967, Cheam, Surrey. Tim was educated at Epsom College in Surrey (as was his elder brother, journalist and television presenter Jeremy Guy Vine, b. 17 May 1965, Epsom). Tim is made in the Ken Dodd mould of bombarding his audience with jokes, specialising in quick-fire one-liners and puns. He is a regular at the Edinburgh Festival Fringe and his *Tim Vine Fiasco* show won him the Perrier newcomer award in 1995. His tours include Current Puns (2006), Punslinger (2008) and The Joke-amotive (2010). For his Punslinger tour he dressed in full cowboy outfit, complete with Stetson and six guns. In July 2008, he recorded a performance at the Bloomsbury Theatre in London, which was released as a DVD entitled *So I Said To This Bloke*. On 7 October 2004, Tim told 499 jokes in an hour to break the Guinness World Record, beating the previous record of 362. Each joke had to get a laugh from the paying audience to count towards the record. He held the record until May 2005, when Australian comedian, Anthony "Lehmo" Lehmann told 549 jokes. The late Bob Monkhouse said of Tim, "he has taken the trick of word play and extended it to lengths no one has ever dared before. A very funny man indeed." On television, Tim has presented the game show *Fluke* on Channel 4, *Housemates* on BBC One and *Fort Boyard Takes on the World* on Challenge. A regular on reality shows, Tim appeared as a contestant on *Comic Relief does Fame Academy* in 2007, and later that year appeared with his brother Jeremy on the celebrity version of ITV's *Who Wants to be a Millionaire* where they raised £1000 for the Fire Services National Benevolent Fund. In January 2009, Tim won an edition of *Celebrity Mastermind*, choosing Elvis Presley as his specialist subject, he scored 28 points, donating his prize money to the Cure Parkinson's Trust. He also appeared on a celebrity edition of *Total Wipeout* in December 2009. In August 2010, Tim won the prize for the funniest joke of that year's Edinburgh Fringe, following a public vote from a judged shortlist. His winning joke was "I've just been on a once-in-a-lifetime holiday. I'll tell you what, never again". As well as being a talented singer, Tim is also a fine musician and plays guitar, keyboards and drums, sometimes at his local church. See also entries in the television section for *Channel Five, Not Going Out, The Sketch Show*, and *Whittle*.

Wall, Max Born Maxwell George Lorimer, 12 March 1908, Brixton, London. Max began his professional life in 1922 billed as 'the boy with the educated feet'. He gradually included comedy into his dance act and his best-known characterisation became Professor Wallofski, world-famous concert pianist. The act would begin with the professor being unable to play his piano as his arms were of different lengths and the comic adjustments always caused hilarity. When his arms were fully outstretched he would squat and drag his knuckles along the floor and become a human monkey before ending the act by isolating his hip joints in a series of comic struts across the stage. Comedians such as Dickie Henderson and Billy Dainty later copied this part of Max's act, always performed to dramatic drum beats. John Cleese also based his famous Ministry of Silly Walks sketch on Max's act. With the demise of the music hall Max became a very able straight actor and an early role was as Wally Soper in *Crossroads*. He appeared in several films, making his debut in *On the Air* (1934). Other films include: *Save a Little Sunshine* (1938), *Come Dance with Me* (1950), *Chitty Chitty Bang Bang* (1968), *The Nine Ages of Nakedness* (1970), *One of Our Dinosaurs Is Missing* (1975), *Jabberwocky* (1977), *The Hound of the Baskervilles* (1978), *Hanover Street* (1979), *Little Dorrit* (1988) and his last film, *Strike It Rich* (1990). Max died after a fall at Simpson's restaurant in the Strand, London on 21 May 1990. He was survived by four sons, Michael, Melvin, Martin and Meredith, and a daughter, Maxine. See also entries in the radio and television section for *Born and Bred, Coronation Street, Variety Bandbox*, and *Who Do You Do?*

Walliams, David Born David Edward Williams, 20 August 1971, Borough of Reigate and Banstead, Surrey. David began his professional career in the Bob Mills' presented *Gamesworld* (Sky One, 1993) where he appeared in various roles each week, his first being "Lesley Luncheonmeat". For the next few years he presented children's programmes, took bit-parts in television and film dramas, and even resorted to writing scripts for Ant and Dec before discovering his comic boots on teaming up with Matt Lucas to make the multi award-winning series *Little Britain*. David made his film debut in the short *Clancy's Kitchen* (1997) and his feature debut in *Plunkett & Macleane* (1999). Other films include: *Shaun of the Dead* (2004 - as the uncredited voice of a News Reporter), *A Cock and Bull Story* (2005), *Stoned* (2005), *Marie Antoinette* (2006), *Stardust* (2007), Run Fatboy Run (2007), *Virgin Territory* (2007), *The Chronicles of Narnia: Prince Caspian* (2008 - voice of Bulgy Bear), *Marmaduke* (2010) and *Dinner for Schmucks* (2010). He also took the title role in the TV film *Frankie Howerd: Rather You Than Me* (2008). On 4 July 2006 he swam the English Channel for the charity Sport Relief. In 2008 his debut novel, *The Boy In The Dress*, was published and the following year, *Mr Stink* was published. Both children's books are illustrated by Quentin Blake. After much speculation as to his sexuality David married Dutch model Lara Stone in May 2010, his comedy partner Matt Lucas acting as best man. Later in the year he released his third book *Billionaire Boy* in October 2011 his fourth, *Gangsta Granny*; both illustrated by Tony Ross. See also entries in the television section for *Come Fly With Me, Little Britain*, and *Rock Profile*.

Walters, Elsie & Doris Florence Elsie Waters (1893–1990) and Doris Waters (1904–78), who were sisters of Jack Warner (see entry in cinema section) became legends of stage, screen and radio via their Cockney characterisations, Gert & Daisy. The sisters appeared in three films together *Gert and Daisy's Weekend* (1942), *Gert and Daisy Clean Up* (1942) and *It's in the Bag*

(1944) and were regulars on *Workers' Playtime* (see entry in radio section) where they would usually pontificate on all and sundry, but in particular their husbands, Bert and Wally. In 1959 they appeared in an ITV television series *Gert and Daisy*.

Walters, Julie See entry in cinema section.

Western Brothers Kenneth 'Ken' Alfred Western (b. 10 September 1899, London; d. 24 January 1963) was a civil servant who turned to the world of entertainment and, in 1925, met and formed his partnership with (Ernest) George Western (b. 23 July 1895, died 16 August 1969), actually his second cousin although, "the two cads" or "the perfectly polite pair" as they were formerly called, were most successful as "the Western Brothers". By 1926 the monocled pair of 'upper-class toffs' (they were not in the least upper-class in reality) became famous for their vaudeville act lampooning the establishments of the times, *Vaudeville Vanities*, and performed their act at a Sunday concert at the Palladium. Their fame grew and they boasted their own "coat of arms" their motto being "Adsum Ard Labor". Their songs were composed and performed by George on the piano and Ken, who provided the lyrics, leaning against it. They would burlesque anything from the government of the day to world events, and even the old school tie. In 1935, playing before King George V and Queen Mary, they made the first of their two appearances at Royal Command variety performances. Ken and George took their act on the road throughout the late 1940s, and although their popularity was in decline, they continued to appear as late as 1950. They shared the billing with Julie Andrews and Enso Toppano in Harold Fielding's *Music For The Millions* in August 1950 at the Winter Gardens in Bournemouth and a young Tony Hancock toured with them at this time. Their songs included *We're Frightfully BBC* and *Keeping Up the Old Traditions*.

Wheeler, Jimmy Born Ernest Remnant, 16 September 1910, Battersea, London. The fiddle-playing stand-up comedian chose his stage name by a combination of fate and history. The 'Jim' part he picked up from entertainer George Formby Sr, who - when summoning him for a curtain-call - nicknamed the comedian 'lucky Jim'; the 'Wheeler' came from his father's old double-act 'Wheeler and Wilson' (Eventually, the youngster played his part in the team, playing Wheeler to his father's Wilson). The mustachioed Wheeler was a regular performer on stage, films and radio but the comic was first and foremost a music-hall performer; his act usually ending with his catchphrase "Aye, aye, that's your lot". Jimmy made a successful transition to television towards the end of his career with *The Jimmy Wheeler Show* (BBC, 1956-57) and *Tess And Jim* (BBC, 1956) starring alongside Tessie O'Shea. He died 8 October 1970.

Whitehouse, Paul Born 17 May 1958, Stanleytown, Rhondda Valley. Although Paul's parents are both Welsh and he lived in Wales until he was four-years-old, Paul's humour stems from his North London roots. He came to prominence in 1990, after appearing in *Harry Enfield's Television Programme*, developing his most famous character Mike 'Smashie' Smash opposite Enfield's Dave 'Nicey' Nice (two disc jockeys unmistakably based on Tony Blackburn and Alan Freeman). It was teaming up with his old university pal Charlie Higson to write and star in the comedy sketch series *The Fast Show* which propelled him to stardom. Characters including, Ron Manager (a football pundit), 'unlucky' Alf (who delighted in screaming 'bugger' on his latest misfortune), Rowley Birkin QC (the unintelligible but very posh sounding barrister) and Chris Jackson aka 'The Crafty Cockney' (a 'geezer' who was a little bit wooor and a little bit waayyy and as such would 'nick anything', made Paul a household name and his teaming up with Mark Williams as the irritating, sex-obsessed menswear assistants with their ingratiating catchphrase 'ooh! suit you sir' was irritatingly popular throughout the series run. Perhaps Paul's most comically poignant creation was Ted (an Irish estate worker) who had to contend with the affections of Lord Ralph Mayhew (a repressed homosexual), played by Higson. *Ted and Ralph* (1998) later became a TV Movie, Ralph eventually declaring his love for Ted via the Elvis Presley hit *Burning Love* during a karaoke session and they were last seen romping gaily through a field, hand in hand. Paul showed his comic versatility in

Help (2005) playing a different character in the therapist's chair in each of six episodes (the therapist, Peter, played by Chris Langham). In 2007 Paul teamed up again with Harry Enfield in the very popular *Harry and Paul* BBC1 sketch show. On the big screen Paul has appeared in *Kevin & Perry Go Large* (2000), *Harry Potter and the Prisoner of Azkaban* (2004 - as Sir Cadogan), *Finding Neverland* (2004), *Corpse Bride* (2005), *Alice in Wonderland* (2010 - voice of the March Hare) and *Burke and Hare* (2010). See also entries in the radio and television section for *Bellamy's People, Down the Line, The Fast Show, Happiness, Harry Enfield's Television Programme, Help, Randall and Hopkirk (Deceased), Ruddy Hell! It's Harry and Paul,* and *Saturday Live.*

Williams, Kenneth Born Kenneth Charles Williams, 22 February 1926, Islington, London. With his flaring nostrils, exaggerated preciseness of speech, often mimicked cry of "Matron" and mastery of the double entendre immortalised in so many Carry On films, Kenneth entertained the public for 40 years. Beginning his working life as a map-maker at Stanfords (a job he reprised during his army service), he joined the Newquay Players in 1948 making his stage debut in *The First Mrs Fraser* (1948). Ken acted in repertory companies in Swansea, Guildford, Bromley and Worthing. His screen debut was in *Trent's Last Case* (1952). Other early films include: *The Beggar's Opera* (1952), and *The Seekers* (1954). His big break came in 1954 when he joined Sid James and Bill Kerr as regular cast members of the radio show *Hancock's Half Hour* (transferred to television in 1956). It was during this series Kenneth created his most famous catchphrase "Stop Messing About". *Carry On Sergeant* (1958) was the first of the successful comedy film series that made both him, and the genre, a national institution. In 1959 he left Hancock and joined the cast of a new topical radio sketch show *Beyond Our Ken* (which spawned an even more successful sequel *Round the Horne*). Ken's characters included Peasmold Gruntfuttock and Sandy (opposite the equally camp Julian, played by Hugh Paddick, and notable for their double entendres and use of the underground gay slang, Polari), Rambling Syd Rumpo, the eccentric folk singer, and Dr Chou N Ginsberg MA (failed), the evil mastermind whose plans were continually thwarted by Secret Agent Kenneth Horne (the sudden death of the genial host prematurely ended the series). Returning to films, Ken appeared in *Raising the Winds* (1961) and *Twice Round the Daffodils* (1962) but will always be most associated with the Carry On films in which he appeared in 25 finishing with *Carry On Emmanuelle* (1978); his only later film being *The Princess and the Cobbler* (1993 – voice of goblet / Tickle). He played such characters as Citizen Camembert - The Big Cheese in *Carry On Don't Lose Your Head* (1966) and the Khazi of Kalabar in *Carry On Up the Khyber* (1968). Rather than list all the Carry Ons Kenneth starred in it is perhaps easier to mention the five in which he did not appear: *Carry On Cabby* (1963), *Carry On Up the Jungle* (1970), *Carry On Girls* (1973), *Carry On England* (1976) and *Carry On Columbus* (1992). An accomplished stage actor - his Dauphin in G B Shaw's St Joan was particularly well received in the mid 1950s. In 1957 he was a star of the first West End production of *Share My Lettuce*, a musical written by Bamber Gascoigne whilst still an undergraduate and he also starred in *The Private Ear and the Public Eye* (1962) opposite Maggie Smith. In 1980 he directed *Loot* by his late friend Joe Orton at The Lyric, Hammersmith. Hosting *International Cabaret* (1966-68; 1974) was a surprise success for Ken, whose immaculate dress and superbly comic and well-informed links gave the television series a gravitas it perhaps did not deserve. In the latter part of his career Ken became one of the most popular guests on the chat-show circuit, his natural wit, obsession with his health, particularly his dysfunctional bottom (it is rumoured that Ken never allowed anyone to use his toilet for fear of his secret being outed), and his sculpture of the English language, endeared him to millions. He wrote *Acid Drops* (1980) and *Back Drops* (1983) in collaboration with Gyles Brandreth and *Just Williams: An Autobiography* (1985). His diaries were published in 1993. He died from an overdose of barbiturates taken while suffering pain from a severe stomach ulcer and chronic back pain, on 15 April 1988, Euston, London. In 2006, Michael Sheen played Kenneth in the highly acclaimed BBC Four drama *Kenneth Williams: Fantabulosa!* See also entries in the radio and television section for *Beyond Our Ken, Hancock's Half Hour, International Cabaret, Jackanory, Just A Minute, Round the Horne*, and *Willo the Wisp*.

Wilton, Rob Born Robert Wilton Smith, 28 August 1881, Everton, Liverpool. Hugely popular star of music hall, films and radio, often as a befuddled policeman, fireman, member of the Home Guard, and most memorably as Mr Muddlecombe, JP. Rob made his film debut in *Love, Life and Laughter* (1934). Other films include: *The Secret of the Loch* (1934), *A Fire Has Been Arranged* (1935), *Two's Company* (1936), *We Dive at Dawn* (1943) and his last film, *The Love Match* (1955). His catchphrase of "The day war broke out", said in a confused northern tone with hand nervously covering his face, began many of his famous monologues. He married actress Florence Palmer and she accompanied him in his act. The often-mimicked star died 1 May 1957, London.

Winters, Bernie Born Bernard Weinstein, 6 September 1932, Islington, London. Younger brother of Mike (b. 15 November 1930), together forming a double-act often dubbed the poor man's Morecambe and Wise, but in fact at their height rivalled the great men in the nation's affection, albeit on ITV throughout their careers. Mike played the straight-man with ideas while Bernie played the amiable buffoon in a slightly over-sized bowler hat with no idea at all, and when feeling threatened by Mike's sharpness would merely either use his catchphrase of 'I'll Smash Yer Face In' or hunch his shoulders, show his teeth and mutter 'Eeeeeeeeeeeee', occasionally squeezing Mike's cheek and calling him 'choochie face'. The brothers first appeared on television together in the BBC's *Variety Parade* (1955) and were regulars on British TV's first pop show *Six-Five Special* (1957-58). Bernie made his film debut in *Idol on Parade* (1959) and although a film career was planned he decided to stick with his brother and they began to appear regularly on all the main variety shows on television eventually gaining their own series in 1966. Mike and Bernie had an acrimonious split in 1978 and Mike left for North America to become a businessman and writer. Bernie continued to work on his own and had great success with his new partner, Schnorbitz a St Bernard dog, always by his side although doing little. Bernie died of stomach cancer on 4 May 1991 having made his peace with his brother. See also entries in the television section for *The Six-Five Special, The Strange World of Gurney Slade, Whose Baby?*, and *Hope and Keen*.

Wisdom, Norman Born Norman Joseph Wisdom, 4 February 1915, Marylebone, London. After leaving school aged 11, Norman had a variety of jobs including errand boy, cabin boy in the merchant navy, miner, waiter and page boy, before joining the army as a bandsman in 1931 and being posted to Lucknow, India, becoming the flyweight boxing champion of his regiment. On leaving the army in 1946 he worked for a short time as a chauffeur before choosing a life in showbusiness as a visual comedian, using skills he developed while entertaining his regiment. He turned professional later that year under his own name after using the stage name Dizzy Wizzy, having already developed his famous persona of the downtrodden put-upon working class little man - he was 5' 2" (1.57 m) – wearing cloth cap askew, with peak turned up (much in vogue nowadays of course) and a suit at least two sizes too small, crumpled shirt collar and a mangled tie. Norman initially gained a reputation as the straight man for the magician David Nixon but his comedic genius was soon apparent. His first television series came in the form of 2 x 45 minute BBC sketch shows *Wit and Wisdom* (1948) with Beryl Reid assisting him and Dorothy Squires performing the musical interlude. He made his film debut with a small cameo as a shadow boxer in *A Date with a Dream* (1948) but the success of his second BBC television outing, *The Norman Wisdom Show* (1952-57) launched him to superstar status and he took the lead role in his second film appearance, *Trouble in Store* (1953). Other films include: *One Good Turn* (1955), *Man of the Moment* (1955), *Up in the World* (1956), *Just My Luck* (1957), *The Square Peg* (1958), *Follow a Star* (1959), *There Was a Crooked Man* (1960), *The Bulldog Breed* (1960 – in which Michael Caine and Oliver Reed appeared in a cinema fight scene), *On the Beat* (1962), *A*

Stitch in Time (1963), *The Early Bird* (1965), *Press for Time* (1966), *The Night They Raided Minsky's* (1968) and his last feature film, *Five Children and It* (2004 - as Nesbitt). In 2007, he came out of retirement to take a role in a film short, *Expresso*. Norman's film persona struck a chord in communist countries and he was revered in parts of Russia and became a national icon in Albania. He was the top box-office comedian in Britain throughout the 1950s and 1960s but also made the occasional television series, and two of his six appearances on Val Parnell's Sunday Night at the London Palladium are regarded as Comedy masterpieces. Both were while working opposite then host Bruce Forsyth and although the first is lost the reprise has been shown regularly as a showcase for his talents. Norman showed a great propensity for straight acting as a cancer sufferer in *Going Gently* (1981) and made cameo appearances in *Casualty* (1998) and *Coronation Street* (2004). His catchphrase immortalised by many impressionists was 'Mr Grimsdale' and his uncontrollable fits of laughter were also much impersonated. Norman was married twice, to Doreen Brett (1941–46) with whom he had a son, Michael (b. 1945) and Freda Simpson (1947–68) with whom he had two children, Nicholas (b. 1953, who played first-class cricket for Sussex) and Jacqueline (b. 1954). His signature tune was *Don't Laugh At Me (Cause I'm a Fool)*. Norman was knighted in 2000 and during the ceremony, once he had received his knighthood, he walked away and performed his trademark trip over his feet which the Queen smiled and laughed at. He died on 4 October 2010 at Abbotswood nursing home, Ballasalla, Isle of Man. See also entries in the television section for *Coronation Street, Going Gently, Last of the Summer Wine, Sunday Night at the London Palladium, Who Do You Do?"*

Wood, Victoria Born 19 May 1953, Prestwich, Lancashire. Began her professional life by winning the ITV talent show *New Faces* with a mix of music and comedy. By 1976 Victoria had gained a regular spot on the BBC consumer programme *That's Life* singing a topical song each week at the piano. Her big break came after writing a play entitled *Talent* (1979) for Granada television and teaming up with Julie Walters to play the two lead roles. Victoria reunited with Julie for the ITV sketch show *Wood and Walters* (1981-82) and in *Victoria Wood - As Seen On TV* (1985-87) in which Julie again joined her old friend in a superb parody of bad soap operas *Acorn Antiques*. The two were seen at their finest in the 1994 television film *Pat and Margaret*, in which Julie and Victoria (who also wrote the script) played sisters whose lives had taken very different paths. Victoria has rarely been off our screens in the past 30 years whether it be starring in her own shows or guesting on other shows with her comic musical masterpieces such as the classic *Let's Do It*. Her writing talents were to the fore again with the BBC sitcom *dinnerladies* (1998-2000) which became cult viewing. Her marriage to magician Geoffrey Durham (The Great Soprendo), whom she married in March 1980, ended in October 2002. They have two children, Grace (b. 1988) and Henry (b. 1992). Her most recent successes have included winning two BAFTA awards for her one-off ITV drama, *Housewife, 49* (2006) and creating the award-winning TV film *Eric and Ernie* (2011) in which she also played the part of Sadie Bartholomew, Eric's mother. Victoria was awarded the OBE in 1997 and the CBE in 2008. See also entries in the radio and television section for *dinnerladies, Great Railway Journeys, Just A Minute, New Faces, That's Life, Victoria Wood As Seen On TV*, and *Wood and Walters*.

Worth, Harry Born Harry Bourlon Illingworth, 20 November 1917, Hoyland Common, nr Barnsley. Harry's father died in a mining accident the year after his birth but, as was the custom, Harry followed him down the pit, aged 14, and worked at the colliery for eight years before joining the RAF at the outbreak of WWII. Harry made his debut as a ventriloquist in 1946 with dummies named Fotheringay and Clarence, but was persuaded to pursue a career as a stand-up comedian by Stan Laurel and Oliver Hardy, who he supported between 1952 and 1954. Harry's natural nervousness created a comedy genius in the persona of a bespectacled bumbling incompetent and between 1960 and 1980 he was rarely off our screens, his fictional address of 52 Acacia Avenue, Woodbridge, becoming as famous as Tony Hancock's. Harry was also famous for beginning the national trend of standing astride the corner of glass shop windows while raising an arm and leg laterally to give the impression of floating in mid-air (this was the opening sequence of his television series *Here's Harry*. His much mimicked catchphrase was "My Name Is Harry Worth. I don't know why - but, it is!" He died on 20 July 1989. See also entries in the radio and television section for *Here's Harry*, *Oh Happy Band!*, and *Variety Bandbox*

A1 A1 are an Anglo-Norwegian boyband who were formed in 1998 and signed to Columbia Records. The four members were Ben Adams (born Benjamin Anthony Edward Stephens, Ascot, Berkshire, 22 November 1981), Paul Marazzi (born Paul Thomas Leo Marazzi, Wanstead, London, 24 January 1975), Mark Read (born Mark Daniel Read, Worcester Park, London, 7 November 1978) and Christian Ingebrigtsen (born in Oslo, Norway, 25 January 1977). The band's first record, *Be The First to Believe*, reached number six in the UK singles chart in July 1999 and later in the year their next two singles, *Summertime Of Our Lives* (No 5, Aug 1999) and the double A-sided *Ready or Not / Everytime* (No 3, Nov 1999) fared even better. In December, their first studio album, 'Here We Come' (No 20, Dec 1999 – No 4 in Norway) was released and featured all three of their hits to date. The following year was even more successful for the lads. In March, *Like A Rose* (No 6) became the fourth track from their debut album to make the UK Top 10, but in September, *Take On Me*, became their first Number 1 single and in November, *Same Old Brand New You*, also topped the UK charts. Both singles simultaneously topped the Norwegian chart. In October, their second album, 'The A List' (No 14), was released and contained all three of their hits that year as well as their only hit of 2001, *No More* (No 6, Feb 2001). In February 2002, *Caught in the Middle* (No 2) ensured that the band's first eight singles all made the Top 10. In May 2002, *Make It Good* (11) became their final single and the first one not to make the Top 10. In June 2002, their third and final studio album, 'Make It Good' (No 15) was released and included their two hits of earlier in the year as well as *Nos Differences*, a French version of *Caught In The Middle* which was released as a single in Norway, featuring Eve Angeli on vocals. Despite winning a BRIT Award for British Breakthrough Act in 2001, Paul Marazzi left A1 to form a band called Snagsby and the group disbanded. Christian immediately embarked on a solo career back in his native Norway. On June 15, 2009, Mark released a solo album 'Peace at Last'. After a couple of years writing, Ben made a comeback with a new solo recording contract and his first solo single, *Sorry*, reached No 18 on the UK Singles Chart in June 2005. Following his appearance on *Celebrity Big Brother* in 2009 (he came fifth), the remaining members reformed and have had some success in the Norwegian charts.

Russ Abbot see Comedy section

ABC New Wave band formed in 1977 as Vice Versa before changing their name to ABC in 1980 and becoming known as a New Romantic band when Martin Fry (b. Stockport, Greater Manchester, 9 March 1958) joined them. The original line-up was Mark Lickley (bassist 1980-82), Dave Robinson (drummer 1980-82), Steve Singleton (b. 17 April 1959; saxophonist 1980-84), Mark Andrew White (b. Sheffield, Yorkshire, 1 April 1961; guitarist/keyboards player 1980-92) and Fry, who had previously interviewed the group for his fanzine *Modern Drugs* and was asked to join them to play synthesiser – later vocals. The group's first single, *Tears Are Not Enough*, reached number 19 in the UK charts in October 1981 but their next three singles *Poison Arrow* (No 6, Feb 1982), *The Look Of Love* (No 4, May 1982) and *All Of My Heart* (No 5, Aug 1982 – No 3 in Ireland), all peaked in the Top 10. Their two Top 20 hit singles were *That Was Then but This Is Now* (No 18, Oct 1983) and *When Smokey Sings* (No 11, May 1987). The band's six studio albums: 'The Lexicon of Love' (No 1, Jun 1982 – No 24 in US), 'Beauty Stab' (No 12, Nov 1983), 'How to be a... Zillionaire!' (No 28, Oct 1985), 'Alphabet City' (No 7, Oct 1987), 'Up' (No 58, Oct 1989), and 'Abracadabra' (No 50, Aug 1991) were all highly acclaimed. Style icons Fiona Russell-Powell (b. 2 April 1963 and using the name Eden) and David Yarritu worked with the band for the video recordings from 'How to be a... Zillionaire!' and ABC used a technique known as video scratching (where video follows the rhythm of the music) to good effect for the single *Be Near Me*, from the album and although only reaching Number 26 in the UK, this single reached number nine in the US charts (*When Smokey Sings* at number five being their only other US Top Ten hit). The group split in 1992 but Martin resurrected ABC in 1997 to produce the album 'Skyscraping' (97) in collaboration with Glenn Gregory of Heaven 17 and Keith Lowndes - working as Honeyroot. David Palmer, the band's drummer between 1982 and 1986, rejoined Fry for VH1's Bands Reunited in 2004 and, following a US tour in 2006, Fry and Palmer, together with keyboardist Chuck Kentis, put together a new ABC album, 'Traffic' in 2008. Mark White released solo albums, 'Life' in 1994 and 'Tunch' four years later. He refused to take part in the reunion project. Martin Fry, complete with his trademark gold lamé suit, is still performing and touring.

Adam Ant/Adam & The Ants
Adam Ant (born Stuart Leslie Goddard, Marylebone, London, 3 November 1954) began his professional life as bass player for Bazooka Joe and the Lillets, the band best known as the headline act when the Sex Pistols played their first concert on 6 November 1975 at Central Saint Martins College of Art and Design in London. The comedienne Arabella Weir (born in San Francisco, California, 6 December 1957) was one of the Lillets' backing singers. Goddard left Bazooka Joe and formed a group called the B-Sides (which rehearsed but never played a concert). He became anorexic after his 1975 marriage to Carol Mills: "I just didn't eat. I wasn't attempting to slim, I was attempting to kill myself," he later recalled. A drugs overdose left him in Colney Hatch mental hospital. He was discharged into his wife's care when he was 21. He changed his name to Adam Ant and formed The Ants in 1977 with the original line-up being Lester Square (born Thomas Woodburne Bruce Hardy, in Canada, 17 April 1954; lead guitarist), Andy Warren (b. 1961; bassist) and Paul Flanagan only lasting a few months as, at various times Matthew Ashman (born in Mill Hill, London, 3 November 1960, d. London, 21 November 1995 of diabetes; guitarist), Dave Barbarossa (b. 1961; drummer), Johnny Bivouac, Leigh Gorman (born in London, 1961; bassist), Merrick (born Christopher Merrick Hughes, London, 3 March 1954 ; drummer), Terry Lee Miall, Kevin Mooney (born in Greenwich, London, 5 May 1962; bassist), Marco Francesco Andrea Pirroni (born in Camden, London, 27 April 1959; guitarist), Gary Brian Tibbs (born in Northwood, Middlesex, 25 January 1958; bassist), Terry Lee Miall and Mark Ryan (born in London 1959; guitarist) all became Ants. The band's manager and erstwhile vocalist was the model and actress Jordan (b. Seaford, East Sussex 23 June 1955 as Pamela Rooke). She worked for (Dame) Vivienne Westwood and the SEX boutique in Kings Road, London and is credited with creating the punk look, although much of the styling of The Ants, which placed them at the forefront of the New Romantic bands, was achieved by Adam himself. The band's first two singles, *Young Parisian* (1978) and *Zerox* (1979), failed to chart, although the former did reach number nine in the charts when re-released in December 1980. That year brought success with the release of their second studio album, 'Kings of the Wild Frontier' (N0 1, Nov 1980) which topped the album charts, went platinum in the UK and gold in the USA. It also spawned three successful singles: *Kings of the Wild Frontier* which reached number 48 but hit the two spot on its re-release in February 1981, *Dog Eat Dog* (No 4, Oct 1980) and *Antmusic* (No 2, Dec 1980) which stopped one short of the top spot. Their first album effort, 'Dirk Wears White Sox' (released in 1979) now began to sell and peaked at number 16 in January 1981. Adam & The Ants consolidated their success with their third studio album 'Prince Charming' which reached number two in November 1981. The album contained the group's two chart-toppers: *Stand and Deliver* (No 1, May 1981 - the video featuring Adam's then little-known actress girlfriend Amanda Donohoe) and *Prince Charming* (No 1, Sep 1981 – the video featuring Diana Dors) plus *Ant Rap* (No 3, Dec 1981). Their last single release was *Deutscher Girls* (No 13, Feb 1982) from the 1977 Derek Jarman film *Jubilee* (which featured Adam as Kid). The Ants disbanded. Gorman, Ashman and Barbarossa joined Bow Wow Wow and Adam went solo hitting the top spot in May 1982 with *Goody Two Shoes* from the album 'Friend or Foe' (No 5, Oct 1982). Unfortunately Adam's musical career seemed to peak at this point as apart from the single *Puss 'n Boots* reaching number five in October 1983, he has failed to appear in the Top 10 ever

since. His second studio album, 'Strip', reached number 20 in November 1983 but subsequent releases 'Vive Le Rock' (1985), 'Manners & Physique' (1990) and 'Wonderful' (1995) peaked at numbers 42, 19 and 24 respectively. He turned to acting and began carving out a successful career on both side of the Atlantic (including an appearance as a menacing villain in *The Equalizer*) until a recurrence of his mental health problems enforced a premature retirement. A second marriage (to Lorraine Gibson in 1997) was no more successful than the first. In September 2003, he was sectioned under the Mental Health Act. Three years later, in September 2006, he published his autobiography entitled *Stand & Deliver*. Adam has recently tried to resurrect his career and his sixth studio album 'Adam Ant Is the Blueblack Hussar in Marrying the Gunner's Daughter' is due to be released in 2012.

Adele Rhythm'n'blues and soul singer-songwriter Adele (b. Tottenham, London, 5 May 1988 as Adele Laurie Blue Adkins) was offered a record contract by XL Recordings after being discovered via her MySpace webpage launched on 31 December 2004. She attended the BRIT School of Performing Arts in Croydon along with contemporaries such as Amy Winehouse, Katie Melua and Kate Nash. She was a classmate of Jessie J and Leona Lewis. Adele graduated in May 2006. Her first record, *Hometown Glory*, reached number 19 in the charts and is a eulogy to her London roots. Adele's debut album, '19', was released on 28 January 2008, a week after the lead single, *Chasing Pavements*. The single remained in the Top 40 for 14 weeks, peaking at number two, while the album topped the charts in its first week. Two other singles from the album reached the Top 20 in 2008, *Cold Shoulder* (18) and *Make You Feel My Love* (4). Her career in the US took off following a *Saturday Night Live* appearance later that year and a subsequent appearance in the TV comedy drama *Ugly Betty*. At the 2009 Grammy Awards, Adele received the awards for Best New Artist and Best Female Pop Vocal Performance. British Prime Minister Gordon Brown sent a thank-you letter to Adele that stated "with the troubles that the country's in financially, you're a light at the end of the tunnel." Her second album, '21', was released on 19 January 2011 and *Rolling in the Deep*, the first single from the album, topped the US charts and peaked at number two in the UK. The album topped the charts in the UK, US and Ireland as did the second single from the album, *Someone Like You*, after a staggering performance of the song at the 2011 BRIT Awards. Adele's first album '19' re-entered the UK album chart alongside '21' whilst first and second singles *Rolling in the Deep* and *Someone Like You* were in the top 5 of the UK singles chart, making Adele the first living artist to achieve the feat of two top-five hits in both the Official Singles Chart and the Official Albums Chart simultaneously since the Beatles in 1964. Although the third single from the album narrowly failed to make the UK Top 10, *Set Fire to the Rain* (11) did top the US Billboard Hot 100. More records started to tumble and the success of '21' earned Adele the accolade of becoming the first artist to sell more than 3 million copies of an album in a year in the UK. Among other record-breaking feats, Adele is the first female artist to have three singles in the Top 10 of the Billboard Hot 100 at the same time, and the first female artist to have two singles in the top five of the Billboard Hot 100 simultaneously. Just for good measure '21' is also the longest running number one album by a female solo artist on the UK and US Albums Chart. By the end of 2011, '21' sold over 3.4 million copies in the UK, and became the biggest-selling album of the 21st century, overtaking Amy Winehouse's 'Back to Black'. In November 2011 Adele underwent laser microsurgery at Massachusetts General Hospital after suffering a throat haemorrhage. She made her live comeback at the Grammy Awards in February 2012 and became the second female artist after Beyoncé Knowles in Grammy Awards history to win six categories in a single night. At the 2012 BRIT Awards she received two awards: Best British Female Solo Artist and British Album of the Year although the second was slightly tarnished when James Corden interrupted (at the behest of ITV bosses) her victory speech in order to accommodate Blur's closing set.

All Saints Girlband formed by Londoners Melanie Ruth Blatt (b. Camden, 25 March 1975), Shaznay Lewis (b. Islington, 14 October 1975 as Tricia Marie Lewis) and Simone Rainford (b. Camden, December 1975) in 1993. Although the girls considered calling themselves Spice they settled on All Saints 1.9.7.5., derived from All Saints Road (close to their label ZTT's London recording studio) and the fact that all three were born in the same year. Their first performance was at the Notting Hill Carnival in 1994. The group's two singles failed to chart and, after creative differences with Melanie, Simone left and ZTT dropped the other two. The Anglo-Canadian Appleton sisters Nicole (b. Hamilton, Ontario, 7 December 1974) and Natalie (b. Mississauga, Ontario, 14 May 1973) joined and the 1.9.7.5. suffix was dropped. They signed to London Records and their eponymously titled debut album was released on 24 November 1997 and reached second place in the charts. It went quintuple platinum in the UK, triple platinum in Canada, double platinum in Australia, platinum in Switzerland and America and gold in Holland. The group released seven singles from the album. *I Know Where It's At* peaked at number four and went gold in Australia. Oddly, their second single was released with two different titles – *Let's Get Started* and *If You Wanna Party (I Found Lovin')* – but it failed to chart anywhere. The third single, *Never Ever*, established All Saints internationally. It hit the top spot in the UK (for one week), Australia (for seven weeks) and New Zealand, number two in Ireland and Top 10 in most of Europe except Germany where it stalled at 18. *Never Ever* sold more than a million copies in Britain going double platinum and won two BRIT Awards in 1998 for Best Single and Best Video. The fourth single was the double A-side *Under the Bridge/Lady Marmalade*, which went to Number 1 in May 1998. *Bootie Call* was the fifth single off the album and their third UK number one. The last single, *War Of Nerves*, peaked at number seven. In November 1998, All Saints won the Breakthrough Artist gong at the MTV Europe Music Awards in Milan. On 14 October 2000, All Saints released their second album, 'Saints And Sinners', and it went one better than 'All Saints' spending a week in the top spot although it only went double platinum. Of the three single releases two went to Number 1 (*Pure Shores*, which was their only Irish Number 1, and *Black Coffee*) and one reached number seven (*All Hooked Up*). Disharmony in the group led to a split in 2001 and they all worked on solo projects with varying degrees of success. Blatt had one Top 10 (*TwentyFourSeven* with Artful Dodger in 2001) and one Top 20 hit (*Do Me Wrong* in 2003) before her label dropped her. Appleton (the sisters' offshoot) hit number two with *Fantasy* (written with Andy Hayman and Gareth Young) in the autumn of 2002 and number five with *Don't Worry* in spring 2003. Their album, 'Everything's Eventual', reached number nine and a third single *Everything Eventually* reached 38 after which they were dropped by their label. They published an autobiography *Together* in October 2002. Lewis released two singles, *Never Felt Like This Before* (eight) and *You* (56) and an album 'Open' (22) and collaborated with Wideboys on *Daddy O*, which stalled at 32 on the Singles Chart. In 2006, the four girls reunited and signed with Parlophone. Their third and final studio album, 'Studio 1', reached number 40 in the charts in 2006 and a single from the album, *Rock Steady*, peaked at three. Another single, *Chick Fit*, was due for release in early 2007 but was eventually only made available as a download and failed to chart. Parlophone subsequently dropped the band and a planned tour was cancelled. Lewis continues to write songs. The other three who first acted together at the Sylvia Young Theatre School (and professionally in the 2000 black comedy, *Honest*, playing the Chase sisters), have appeared on various television programmes. Natalie married Liam Howlett of The Prodigy on 6 June 2002 (her brief first marriage was to stripper Carl Robinson) and appeared on *I'm a Celebrity... Get Me Out of Here!* where she appeared to be afraid of everything in the jungle. She left the programme after the public voted for her to do five bush tucker trials. Nicole was engaged to Robbie Williams before she married his musical rival Liam Gallagher on St Valentine's Day 2008, seven years after she gave birth to their son, Gene. She is co-host of ITV2 and ITV Mobile music show *The Hot Desk* with Melanie Blatt, Dave Berry and Emma Willis. Blatt has appeared as a guest on *I'm a Celebrity... Get Me Out of Here Now!* In a recent nationwide poll to determine the sexiest female group of all time, more than 12,000 television viewers voted for the girl band or singer they thought had the most sex appeal and All Saints beat the Spice Girls into second spot.

allSTARS* Pop group that consisted of Sandi Lee Hughes, Thaila Zucchi (b. at Swindon, Wiltshire 19 January 1981); Ashley Taylor Dawson (b. at Manchester 11 January 1982); Rebecca Hunter (b. at Northampton 12 July 1981) and Sam Bloom – the initial letter of their Christian names gave the group its name. They appeared on the CITV show, *STARStreet**, between 2001 and 2002. They had four Top 20 singles with their cover of Bucks Fizz's *Land Of Make Believe* reaching number nine. They split in June 2002. Thaila Zucchi appeared as fake housemate Pauline in *Big Brother 8*. Ashley Taylor Dawson played Darren Osborne in *Hollyoaks* and was nominated for three British Soap Awards in 2010. Rebecca Hunter played Melanie in the soap *Family Affairs* for two years before emigrating to America.

Lily Allen Lily Rose Beatrice Allen (b. Hammersmith, London, 2 May 1985) is the singer-songwriting daughter of the actor Keith Allen and film producer Alison Owen. Her parents split up when she was four-years-old and her mother began to date comedian Harry Enfield. Despite her early singing style being distinctly Cockney-oriented, Lily in fact attended some of the top public schools in the country including Prince Charles's junior alma mater, Hill House in Knightsbridge, London. Unfortunately her personality was more suited to St Trinian's and Lily was expelled from several schools for drinking and smoking. Despite having the same rebellious nature as her father Lily showed considerable promise as a musician from a young age although it was as an actress that we first saw her on screen - as a lady-in-waiting in the 1998 film *Elizabeth*, which was co-produced by her mother. When her family went on holiday to Ibiza, Lily decided to remain there, initially earning money by working at a Plastic Fantastic record store and dealing ecstasy. It was in Ibiza she met her first manager, George Lamb (b. West London, 20 December 1979), the television presenter son of actor Larry Lamb. She signed for London Records in 2002, changed her management, but left without releasing any material. After studying to become a florist for a while, in early 2005 Lily signed to Regal Recordings who gave her a £25,000 advance to make an album. In November 2005, she began posting song demos on her MySpace page and soon had tens of thousands of "friends". Lily's debut album, 'Alright, Still', was released in July 2006 and reached number two in the charts (No 6 in Ireland and No 20 in US), but her debut single from the album, *Smile*, also released in July, went one better and topped the charts. Three other singles from the album were *LDN* (No 6, Sep 2006), *Littlest Things* (No 21, Dec 2006) and the double A-side *Alfie / Shame for You* (No 15, Mar 2007), inspired by her younger brother. The B-side of *Smile*, *Cheryl Tweedy*, was not on the album. The subject of the song originally thought that it was a tribute until she heard it. It was anything but. Lily's career began to develop in the same controversial manner as her father's. The press knew she was always good for a choice comment or three regarding fellow artistes and began to hound her for stories. On 28 June 2007, Lily was arrested for allegedly assaulting photographer Kevin Rush while she was leaving a nightclub in London's West End. Photos of her drunk and topless (Lily has posed topless for *GQ*) at the Cannes Film Festival in 2008 were also widely covered in the press. Her appearance at the 2008 Glamour Awards also generated criticism, as she showed up intoxicated wearing a dress covered in decapitated Bambi figures, and had an on-stage, expletive-laced exchange with Sir Elton John. In May 2009, French football magazine *So Foot* published a fake interview in which Lily was quoted as making derogatory remarks about David and Victoria Beckham and Ashley and Cheryl Cole. Some of the material was reprinted in the British tabloid *The Sun*. Both publications later apologised and paid damages to Lily. Her private life did not impinge on her music career and Lily's second album, 'It's Not Me It's You', topped the

charts in the UK, Canada and Australia in February 2009 and produced Lily's second Number 1 single, *The Fear* (No 1, Jan 2009). Other singles from this album were *Not Fair* (No 5, Mar 2009 – No 3 in Ireland), *Fuck You* -aka *Guess Who Batman* (No 104, Jul 2009 but No 1 in Belgium), *22* (No 14, Aug 2009 – No 12 in Ireland), *Who'd Have Known* (No 39, Nov 2009) and her final solo single before she announced her 'retirement' *Back To The Start*, which was only released in Australia. Lily has also had three UK top ten singles collaborating firstly with Mark Ronson, *Oh My God* (No 8, Jul 2007) and then Professor Green, *Just Be Good to Green* (No 5, Jun 2010) and finally with American R&B artist T-Pain, *5 O'Clock* (No 6, Sep 2011). Lily sang backing vocals on the Kaiser Chief's *Never Miss a Beat* (No 5, Oct 2008) and has also recorded tracks with Basement Jaxx, Robbie Williams, Dizzee Rascal and Mick Jones as well as performing on the 2009 charity single, *Beds Are Burning*. In 2008 Lily hosted her own chatshow on BBC3, *Lily Allen and Friends*. In 2009, Karl Lagerfeld, the head designer for Chanel, personally hired and photographed Lily for a campaign to promote a luxury line of handbags he was launching. In 2010 she opened a fashion rental shop "Lucy in Disguise" with her older sister Sarah. In 2011 Lily launched her own record label, In the Name Of, financially backed by Sony Music, and plans to resume her recording career in the near future. Lily married Sam Cooper, the owner of a building company, on 11 June 2011 at St. James church in Cranham, Gloucestershire and she subsequently gave birth to a daughter, Ethel Mary, on 25 November 2011.

Amen Corner Cardiff-based band formed in late 1966 by Dennis Ronald Bryon (born in Cardiff, 14 April 1949; drummer); Blue Weaver (born Derek John Weaver, Cardiff, 11 March 1947; organist); Clive Taylor (born in Cardiff, 27 April 1948; bassist); Neil Jones (born in Llanbradach, 25 March 1949; guitarist); Allan Jones (born in Swansea, 6 February 1947; saxophonist); Mike Joseph Smith (born in Swansea, 4 November 1947; tenor saxophonist) and front-man Andy Fairweather Low (born in Ystrad Mynach, Hengoed, 2 August 1948; vocalist). The band's first single, *Gin House Blues*, reached the number 12 spot in the charts in July 1967 and the following year they had Top 10 successes with *Bend Me, Shape Me* (No 3, Jan 1968) and *High in the Sky* (No 6, Jul 1968). In January 1969, they topped the charts with *If Paradise Is Half As Nice* and followed this with *Hello Susie* (No 4, Jun 1969). Their last single was a cover of *Get Back* by The Beatles but it failed to chart and the saxophone players left the band which was renamed Fair Weather in 1970. They had just the one charting single, *Natural Sinner* (No 6, Jul 1970) and split in 1971. Blue Weaver (who is actually listed under that name on official documents) left to join The Strawbs (when Rick Wakeman departed for Yes) but left them in 1973 to tour with Mott the Hoople. Andy Fairweather Low enjoyed solo success that included two Top 10 singles *Reggae Tune* (No 10, Sep 1974) and *Wide-Eyed And Legless* (No 6, Dec 1975). He has since collaborated with The Who, Roger Waters, Joe Satriani, Eric Clapton and has toured with Bill Wyman's Rhythm Kings and the Big Chris Barber Band, often playing guitar.

Peter Andre Peter James Andre was born in Harrow on 27 February 1973 to Greek-Cypriot parents but raised in Australia. He was discovered on the Australian television talent show *New Faces* in 1990 and although his early singles, *Drive Me Crazy*, *Gimme Little Sign*, *Funky Junky* and *Let's Get it On/Do You Wanna Dance?*, made little impact in the UK charts, the last three all made the Australian Top 20. His eponymously titled debut album reached number 27 in the Australian charts in 1993 but failed to dent the UK charts. However, his second album, 'Natural', released on the Mushroom label, reached number 11 in Australia but topped the UK charts in 1996 and spawned the hit single *Mysterious Girl* (No 2, Jun 1996). Peter was as well known for his toned body as his singing voice. He moved to England where he had six consecutive Top 10 hits: *Flava* (No 1, Sep 1996), *I Feel You* (No 1, Dec 1996), *Natural* (No 6, Mar 1997), *All about Us* (No 3, Aug 1997) and *Lonely* (No 6, Nov 1997). Andre's third studio album, 'Time', reached number 28 in the UK album charts in November 1997 and in 1998 his last major chart successes were *All Night, All Right* (No 16, Jan 1998) featuring

Warren G, and *Kiss The Girl* (No 9, Jul 1998) before being dropped by his record company. It was six years before he troubled the chart compilers again after he appeared on the third series of the reality show *I'm A Celebrity... Get Me Out Of Here!* He finished in third place but more importantly he met and ended up marrying the model Jordan (see entry in the miscellaneous section). He re-released *Mysterious Girl* and it made the top spot for one week in March 2004. *Insania*, a song he often performed in the jungle, reached number three that same year. In 2009, he returned to the Top 10 with *Behind Closed Doors*, which made number four and was taken from the album 'Revelation' which peaked at number three. In 2006 he and then-wife Jordan released an album entitled 'A Whole New World' and it made it to number 20 while the title track made number 12 on the singles chart. Another album, 'Accelerate', released in November 2010, reached number 10 in the UK charts. Away from the music industry Peter has released a fragrance for women called Unconditional and a counterpart for men named Conditional. In 2010, he released a book, *My World: In Pictures and Words,* which became a best-seller. See also entries in the television section for *The Five O'Clock Show, I'm a Celebrity Get Me Out Of Here, Odd One In,* and *Star Stories.*

The Animals Newcastle-based group formed in 1962 by vocalist Eric Burdon (born in Walker, Newcastle-upon-Tyne, 11 May 1941), bassist Chas Chandler (born Bryan James Chandler, Heaton, Tyne & Wear, 18 December 1938; d. Newcastle General Hospital, Heaton, 17 July 1996 of an aortic aneurysm), keyboard player Alan Price (born in Fatfield, Tyne & Wear, 19 April 1942), drummer John Steel (born in Gateshead, 4 February 1941) and guitarist Hilton Stewart Paterson Valentine (born in North Shields, 21 May 1943). *Baby Let Me Take You Home* (No 21, Apr 1064) was the first Animals hit but it was their second single, *House Of The Rising Sun* (No 1, Jun 1964), produced by Mickie Most (born in Aldershot, 20 June 1938; died in London, 30 May 2003) with its haunting melody and Valentine's memorable guitar riff, that ensured the group's place in pop history by topping the charts on both sides of the Atlantic. Other Top 10 singles followed: *I'm Crying* (No 8, Sep 1964), *Don't Let Me Be Misunderstood* (No 3, Feb 1965), *Bring It on Home to Me* (No 7, Apr 1965), *We Gotta Get out Of This Place* (No 2, Jul 1965), *It's My Life* (No 7, Oct 1965) and *Don't Bring Me Down* (No 6, Jun 1966). In May 1965, Alan left to reform another Alan Price Combo, which, with Chandler and Steel had been the forerunner of The Animals. The touring combo became the Alan Price Set before their first single *I Put a Spell on You* was released in March 1966 and reached number nine. Further hits in this guise included *Hi Lili Hi Lo* (No 11, Jul 1966), *Simon Smith And His Amazing Dancing Bear* (No 4, Mar 1967), *The House That Jack Built* (No 4, Aug 1967) and *Don't Stop the Carnival* (No 13, Jan 1968) before Price began to collaborate with Georgie Fame: *Rosetta* (No 11, Apr 1971) being a commercial success for them. Eventually, Alan went solo and had a Top 10 hit with *Jarrow Song* (No 6, May 1974) and a minor hit with *Just For You* (No 43, Apr 1978). His last single release, *Changes*, reached number 54 in 1988. In 1973, he wrote the music for the Lindsay Anderson film *O Lucky Man!*, and in 1981 he wrote the songs for the stage musical, *Andy Capp*. Alan also acted in the 1975 film *Alfie Darling*, a sequel to the film *Alfie*, during the course of which he became romantically involved with his co-star, Jill Townsend (famous as Dulcey in the western series *Cimarron Strip*). In The Animals, Mick William Gallagher (born in Newcastle-upon-Tyne, 29 October 1945) initially replaced Price before Dave Rowberry (born in Mapperley, Nottinghamshire, 4 July 1940; d. London, 6 June 2003 of a perforated ulcer) became keyboard player a few months later. John Steel left the band in February 1966 and was replaced by Barry Jenkins (born Colin Ernest Jenkins, in Leicester, 22 December 1944), but the group disbanded soon after. In December 1966, Eric Burdon recruited Jenkins, John Weider (born in London, 21 April 1947; guitarist/violinist), Vic Briggs (born in Twickenham, 14 February 1945; guitarist/pianist), and Danny McCulloch (born in London, 18 July 1945; bassist) and the group became known as Eric Burdon & the Animals. In that incarnation, they had just one Top 10 hit *San Franciscan Nights*, which made number seven in October 1967. In April 1968, Briggs and McCulloch were replaced by Zoot Money (born George Bruno Money, Bournemouth, 17 July 1942; keyboards player) and Andy Summers (see entry for The Police). The band split in February 1969 and did not reform until 1975. They have since toured in various guises. Burdon played with the Californian band, War, for some time but now tours with his own band, Eric Burdon And The New Animals, having lost a legal battle with John Steel over who is entitled to use the name The Animals. Chandler managed The Jimi Hendrix Experience and Slade. His second wife was Madeleine Stringer, the 1977 Miss United Kingdom.

Another Level Boyband formed in 1997 and signed to BMG-Northwestside. The four members were Mark Baron (born 17 August 1974), Bobak Kianoush (born 1 November 1978), Wayne Williams (born 19 January 1978) and Dane Bowers (born in Sutton, Surrey, 29 November 1979). Jo Charrington auditioned the group – Bowers and Williams from the BRIT School and Baron and Kianoush from modelling agencies. The band's first single release, *Be Alone No More* (No 6, Feb 1998) entered the Top 10 but their second single, *Freak Me* (No 1, Jul 1998) topped the charts and gained them a MOBO Award for Best Single. Other Top 10 singles were: *I Guess I Was A Fool* (No 5, Nov 1998), *I Want You For Myself* (No 2, Jan 1999 – with Ghostface Killah), *From the Heart* (No 6, Jun 1999), *Summertime* (No 7, Sep 1999) and *Bomb Diggy* (No 6, Nov 1999). They had one Top 10 album 'Nexus' (No 7, Sep 1999). The band then split up to concentrate on solo projects, Bowers having UK Top 10 hits with *Buggin' Me* (No 6, Apr 2000), a collaboration with the garage production duo, True Steppers, *Out Of Your Mind* (No 2, Aug 2000) a collaboration with True Steppers and Victoria Beckham, *Shut Up And Forget About It* (No 9, Mar 2001) and *Another Lover* (No 9, Jul 2001), the latter two hits released under his Christian name and the first of which is thought to have been written about his two-year relationship with the model Jordan (aka Katie Price). Dane has appeared on several reality shows including *Come Dine With Me* and Channel 4's *Celebrity Big Brother* in January 2010 where he was runner-up to transvestite cage fighter Alex Reid, who subsequently became Jordan's second husband.

Applejacks The Applejacks were notable for being the first so-called 'Brumbeat' group to reach the Top 10 of the UK Singles Chart. Formed in 1961 as The Crestas, the band comprised Martin Baggott (b. 20 October 1947; lead guitar), Phil Cash (b. 9 October 1947; rhythm guitar), Megan Davies (b. 25 March 1944; bass) and Gerry Freeman (b. 5 May 1943; drums). When Don Gould (b. 23 March 1947; organ) joined the group in early 1962 their name was changed to The Jaguars. Originally an instrumental group in the vein of The Shadows, when Al Jackson (b. 21 April 1945; vocalist) joined in July 1962 they became a rock'n'roll band and changed their name yet again to The Applejacks. On signing with Decca in 1963 they were given an early song by the soon to be prolific songwriters Les Reed and Geoff Stephens. *Tell Me When* rose to number seven in the singles chart in March 1964 and the power of this song coupled with the novelty of having a female bass guitarist seemed to ensure a bright future. Their second single was a Lennon-McCartney number, *Like Dreamers Do*, which reached number 20 in June 1964 and their third single, *Three Little Words*, managed to get to number 23 in October 1964. The band then fell out with their label over their next record. Decca insisted they record *Chim Chim Chiree* (from the recently released musical film *Mary Poppins*) but The Applejacks refused and although Decca released several more singles throughout 1965 none of them charted and their final single, *You've Been Cheating*, released in 1967, went unnoticed. The band resorted to playing local gigs and cruise ships. Megan and Gerry were married in 1965 and Megan eventually gave up gigging to become a nurse and then a hospital administrator. Interestingly, Megan was also the only member of the band not born in either Birmingham or Solihull – and despite several pop music reference books claiming that she is the sister of Ray and Dave Davies of The Kinks, the Sheffield-born bassist is no relation whatsoever. See also The Honeycombs.

Arctic Monkeys Indie Rock band founded in 2002 and who came to public prominence via the internet. The group, all born in Sheffield, consists of lead vocalist/guitarist Alex Turner (born Alexander David Turner, 6 January 1986), guitarist Jamie Cook (born Jamie Robert Cook, 8 July 1985) - currently dating glamour model and Page Three girl Katie Downes (b. 16 May 1984), bassist Nick O'Malley (born 5 July 1985) and drummer Matt Helders (born 7 May 1986). Andy Nicholson left the group in May 2006 before their American tour unable to cope with the pressures of fame and joined Reverend and the Makers and was replaced by O'Malley. Singer Glyn Jones was only briefly with the band in its early days. The Arctic Monkeys played their first gig on 13 June 2003 at The Grapes in Sheffield. The band's recording debut was a limited edition EP released on their own Bang Bang label, *Five Minutes With Arctic Monkeys*, in May 2005. It featured two songs, *Fake Tales Of San Francisco* and *From The Ritz To The Rubble*. Having now signed to the Domino label, their first single, *I Bet You Look Good On The Dancefloor*, was released on 17 October 2005 and went straight in at Number 1 in the UK Singles Chart. Their second single, *When the Sun Goes Down*, was released the following month and also topped the charts. Both singles were from their first album, 'Whatever People Say I Am, That's What I'm Not', which was released on 23 January 2006 and not only topped the UK and Irish Album Charts but also became the fastest-selling debut album in UK chart history outselling the rest of the Top 20 album chart combined in its first week. A second EP, *Who the Fuck Are Arctic Monkeys?*, was released on 24 April 2006, but was disqualified from charting as it contained five tracks. The first post-Nicholson single was *Leave before the Lights Come On* (No 4, Aug 2006). Their second album, 'Favourite Worst Nightmare', released on 23 April 2007, also made it to Number 1 in the charts in the UK and Ireland and created yet another record when all 12 of the album tracks, plus six other songs, made it into the UK Top 200, *Brianstorm* (No 2, Apr 2007), *Fluorescent Adolescent* (No 5, Jul 2007) and *Teddy Picker* (No 20, Dec 2007) being the highest entries. In August 2009 the band's third studio album, 'Humbug', was released and followed a familiar pattern by attaining top spot in the charts in the UK and Ireland although the single releases, *Crying Lightning* (No 12, Jul 2009), *Cornerstone* (No 94, Nov 2008) and *My Propeller* (No 90, Mar 2010) not having the same measure of success. Their fourth studio album 'Suck it and See' (No 1, Jun 2011) emulated their first three by topping the UK Albums Chart but only peaked at No 3 in Ireland. In doing so, Arctic Monkeys became only the second band in history to debut four albums in a row at the top of the charts; a certain Liverpudlian combo achieving the record of seven. Alex Turner is also front man of The Last Shadow Puppets who had a chart-topping album with 'The Age of the Understatement' (No 1, Apr 2008 and No 2 in Ireland). He was dating the television presenter Alexa Chung from October 2007 until July 2011. In August 2011 Alex began dating American model and actress Arielle Vandenberg. In May 2006, Gordon Brown, the then Chancellor of the Exchequer, claimed that he had Arctic Monkeys, Beethoven, Bach, The Beatles, Coldplay, U2 and James Blunt on his iPod. He told an interviewer, "The Arctic Monkeys really wake you up in the morning."

Rick Astley Singer-songwriter Richard Paul Astley (born in Newton-le-Willows, Merseyside, 6 February 1966) began his music career gigging as a drummer in various local bands, the last of which was the soul band FBI. When the lead singer quit in 1985, Rick was elevated to that position and was quickly discovered by record producer Pete Waterman who employed him at his PWL recording studio in London. If his first single, *When You Gonna*, is discounted (a non-charting collaboration with Lisa Carter) Astley has the distinction of being the only male solo artist to have his first eight singles all chart in the UK Top 10. His debut solo single release, *Never Gonna Give You Up*, released in August 1987, topped the charts in 25 countries including the UK and

USA, although only reaching number two in Ireland. It became the best-selling record of 1987 in the UK. The follow-up single, *Whenever You Need Somebody* (No 3, Oct 1987) was also the title track of his debut UK album, released in November 1987 and immediately topping the charts. This album also spawned the double A-sided *When I Fall in Love* / *My Arms Keep Missing You* (No 2, Dec 1987) and *Together Forever* (No 2, Feb 1988) which topped the charts Stateside. Another track from the album, *It Would Take a Strong Strong Man*, was aimed at the American market only and duly peaked at number 10 on the Billboard Hot 100. *She Wants to Dance With Me* (No 6, Sep 1988) and *Take Me to Your Heart* (No 8, Nov 1988) were both from his second studio album 'Hold Me In Your Arms', which peaked at number eight in the charts in January 1989, the title track reaching number 10 in the singles chart the following month. Rick received a mainly negative press for the perception that he was merely a product of the SAW hits factory and on returning from a world tour he decided to leave them although he maintained RCA as his label. After a fallow year in the recording studio, he released the single, *Cry for Help*, in January 1991 and this was to be his eighth, and final, UK Top 10 entry, reaching number seven. His third studio album, 'Free', was released in March 1991 and reached number nine in the UK album charts. His next album, 'Body and Soul', was released in 1993 but failed to chart and Astley took time out to enjoy his family although he featured on the Elton John single, *Can You Feel the Love Tonight* (No 14, Jul 1994). In December 2001 his fifth studio album, 'Keep It Turned On', was released by Polydor, but only in continental Europe, although a greatest hits album charted in the UK in 2002. Rick's sixth studio album, 'Portrait', reached number 26 in the UK album charts in 2005. Two years later, he became the focus of an internet prank whereby web browsers were tricked into watching Rick Astley's video of *Never Gonna Give You Up* by following a link that claimed to be something else. The phenomenon became known as Rickrolling and raised his profile to the extent that he was voted Best Act Ever by internet users at the MTV Europe Music Awards in 2008! In December 2008, *Never Gonna Give You Up* made a brief return to the charts spending a solitary week at number 73.

Atomic Kitten Liverpool-based girl band founded in 1997 by Andy McCluskey (born George Andrew McCluskey, Heswall, Wirral, 24 June 1959) who had previously co-founded Orchestral Manoeuvres in the Dark (with Paul Humphreys) in 1978. The original line-up of Atomic Kitten consisted of Kerry Jayne Elizabeth Katona (born at Warrington General Hospital, Cheshire, 6 September 1980), Elizabeth Margaret "Liz" McClarnon (born in Liverpool, 10 April 1981) and Heidi India Range (born in Liverpool, 23 May 1983) was short-lived as Range left the band in 1999 (see Sugababes entry) and was replaced by Natasha Maria Hamilton (born in Liverpool, 17 July 1982). The group's debut album, 'Right Now', was released by Virgin Records on 23 October 2000 and reached number 39. Subsequently the title track was released as their debut single and rose to number 10 in the UK Singles Chart in December 1999. Three further tracks, *See Ya* (No 6, Apr 2000), *I Want Your Love* (No 10, Jul 2000) and *Follow Me* (No 20, Oct 2000) did quite well but chiefly due to Virgin's huge promotion. The label was about to drop the band but was persuaded to release one more single from the album, *Whole Again*, which topped the UK charts in February 2001. A month prior to this, Kerry left the band and had an abortive attempt at a solo career. She married former Westlife star Brian McFadden on 5 January 2002 (with Natasha as bridesmaid) but the couple divorced in 2006 after having two children, Molly Marie McFadden (b. 31 August 2001) and Lilly-Sue (b. 3 February 2003). On 14 February 2007, Kerry married taxi driver Mark Croft and six days later, on 20 February 2007, the couple's daughter Heidi Elizabeth Croft was born. Their second child Maxwell Mark (b. 11 April 2008) was given his Christian name after her publicist Max Clifford. The couple separated in 2010. Kerry has been the centre of drug scandals, financial meltdowns, assault charges and mental health problems and Max ensures she is always in the news. Despite being criticised for smoking and drinking alcohol during her pregnancies Kerry has twice been named Celebrity Mum of the Year (see separate section). Kerry was replaced in Atomic Kitten by Jenny Frost (born in Wallasey,

Merseyside, 22 February 1978), formerly a member of Precious, the group which represented the United Kingdom at the 1999 Eurovision Song Contest (finished twelfth) with their debut song, *Say It Again*, which reached number six in the charts. In August 2001, a sixth track from Atomic Kitten's 'Right Now' album was released, *Eternal Flame*, a cover of The Bangles hit, and this became their second Number 1 UK single. 'Right Now' was then re-released with Frost featuring on the tracks and all the promotional videos. It soared to the top of the UK album charts. It went double platinum in the UK. In June 2002, the single *It's OK!* (No 3) was released and in September *The Tide Is High (Get The Feeling)* became their third, and final, chart-topper. Their second album, 'Feels So Good', featuring both successful singles, was released on 9 September 2002, and also topped the charts. It went double platinum in the UK and platinum in Australia and New Zealand. Two other tracks from the album, the double A-sided *The Last Goodbye/Be With You* (No 2, Dec 2002) and *Love Doesn't Have to Hurt* (No 4, Apr 2003) also reached the Top 10 before their third studio album, 'Ladies Night', was released on 10 November 2003, reaching number five in the album charts. It, too, went platinum. The single *If You Come To Me* (No 3, Nov 2003) and the album title track *Ladies Night* (No 8, Dec 2003), featuring Kool And The Gang, both made the Top 10. Atomic Kitten released the third track from the album, the double A-sided single, *Someone Like Me/Right Now 2004* (No 8, Mar 2004) as a supposed farewell to their fans, as they intended to split in 2004, but subsequently decided to reunite for a one-off single in aid of the charity World Vision and released, *Cradle*, in the UK where it peaked at number 10 in 2005. Two subsequent singles, *All Together Now (Strong Together)*, in 2006, and *Anyone Who Had a Heart*, in 2008, failed to make an impact on the UK charts and the band last worked together in January 2008. Natasha played the role of Mrs Johnston in *Blood Brothers* at the Phoenix Theatre in London's West End since January 2011 while Liz had a Top 10 UK single with the double A-sided *Woman In Love/I Get The Sweetest Feeling* (No 5, Feb 2006) and originated the role of Paulette in the first UK tour of Legally Blonde the musical. Jenny appeared on the 2005 edition of *I'm a Celebrity... Get Me Out of Here!* and was the fourth to be voted out of the jungle. From 2008-2011 she presented the BBC3 show *Snog Marry Avoid?* Frost also showed her sporting prowess in the live Channel 4 show *Famous and Fearless* in January 2011. On 4 March 2012, Natasha confirmed that the group were reuniting for a summer tour, including a performance at the Queen's Diamond Jubilee.

Average White Band Anglo-Scottish soul-funk band formed in 1971, the original line-up being Roger Ball (born in Broughty Ferry, Dundee, 4 June 1944; alto sax/keyboards), Malcolm "Molly" Duncan (born in Montrose, 24 August 1945; tenor sax), Alan Gorrie (born in Perth, 19 July 1946; bass/guitar/keyboards/vocals), Robbie McIntosh (born in Dundee, 6 May 1950, d. at Hollywood, California 23 September 1974; drums) and Onnie McIntyre (born in Lennoxtown, 25 September 1945; rhythm guitar/vocals). The following year they were joined by Hamish Stuart (born in Glasgow, 8 October 1949; bass, guitar and vocals). Despite the band's poor sales of their debut album, 'Show Your Hand' (1973, re-issued in 1975 as 'Put It Where You Want It'), their second album, 'AWB', released in August 1974, fared much better, reaching number six in the UK album charts and topping the US charts. In the meantime Robbie McIntosh died of an accidental heroin overdose at a party following a concert at the Troubadour in Los Angeles. According to the report in *Time*, McIntosh and Gorrie took what they thought was cocaine, but was actually heroin. The mistake cost McIntosh his life, while Gorrie was saved by the intervention of fellow partygoer Cher, who kept him conscious long enough to recover. The party host was subsequently indicted for murder by a grand jury. Steve Ferrone (born in Brighton, East Sussex, 25 April 1950) took over from McIntosh and the English drummer became the only non-Scot and only black member of the band. The group's first single from the 'AWB' album, *Pick Up The Pieces* (No 6, Feb 1975) oddly enough replicated the performance of the LP on both sides of the

Atlantic by reaching number six in the UK and topping the US charts. Average White Band's third studio album, 'Cut The Cake', released in June 1975, again fared better in the States (reaching number 10) than it did in Britain (where it stalled at 28). 'I Feel No Fret' (15) in 1979 and 'Shine' (14) in 1980 were their only other UK Top 20 albums and *Let's Go Round Again* (12) in 1980, their only other Top 20 single. Average White Band disbanded in 1982, Ferrone going on to work with Duran Duran, Stuart joining Paul McCartney's touring group and the others concentrating on solo projects. In 1989, Gorrie, McIntyre and Ball reunited to record the LP, 'Aftershock', with guitarist and drummer Alex Ligertwood (born in Glasgow, 18 December 1946), best known as the lead singer of Santana, and Eliot Lewis, who replaced Hamish Stuart as lead singer and also co-wrote the album with Gorrie. Roger Ball left the band shortly after the release of 'Aftershock', and was replaced by Fred Vigdor (aka Freddy V). Brian Dunne subsequently became the band's drummer until 2006 when Rocky Bryant replaced him for the 2006 tour. In 2002, Eliot Lewis left the Average White Band and was replaced by Klyde Jones. AWB still gig regularly although Gorrie and McIntyre are the only two original members of the band.

Babyshambles see entry for Pete Doherty

Badfinger Anglo-Welsh rock band originally called The Iveys who signed to The Beatles' Apple label in 1968 and changed their name the following year to Badfinger. Although the band had several changes of line-up both before and after their chart successful years, the classic line-up during those years was Pete Ham (born in Swansea, 27 April 1947; d. in Woking, Surrey, 24 April 1975; guitar, piano and vocals), Tom Evans (born in Liverpool, 5 June 1947; d. in London, 19 November 1983; bass and vocals), Joey Molland (born Joseph Charles Molland, in Liverpool, 21 June 1947; guitar and vocals) and Mike Gibbins (born in Swansea, 12 March 1949 d. 4 October 2005; drummer). Between 1970 and 1972 they put three records in the Top 10 – *Come and Get It* (No 4, Jan 1970; written and produced by Paul McCartney as the soundtrack of the film, The Magic Christian, with Tom Evans providing lead vocals), *No Matter What* (No 5, Jan 1971; written by Pete Ham who also provided lead vocals) and *Day After Day* (No 10, Jan 1972; produced by George Harrison with Paul McCartney on piano and Pete Ham providing lead vocals). In 1970 Ham and Evans wrote the song *Without You*, which topped the charts for Harry Nilsson in 1971 and reached number three for Mariah Carey in 1994. It also featured in the film *Bridget Jones's Diary* (2001). Badfinger were hampered by the legal problems following the break-up of The Beatles and hired Stan Polley to sort out the mess. However, problems continued and in 1974, their new record label Warners was forced to withdraw the album, 'Wish You Were Here' (seven weeks after release). It left the band members financially embarrassed. After a night out at a pub together, where Pete had drunk ten whiskies, Tom drove him home at three o'clock in the morning and some time during the night Pete hanged himself in his garage studio, three days before his 28th birthday, criticising Polley in the suicide note: "P.S. Stan Polley is a soulless bastard. I will take him with me." For months leading up to that fateful night Pete had shown self-harming tendencies by stubbing out cigarettes on his arms. The group disbanded immediately and the remaining members joined other groups. In 1982 both Joey Molland and Tom Evans toured with bands calling themselves Badfinger, which created a lot of personal and professional conflict. On 19 November 1983, Tom and Joey had an altercation on the telephone regarding past Badfinger income still in escrow from the Apple era, and in particular the "Without You" songwriting royalties that Tom was now receiving but Joey felt should be shared by the group and their former manager. Following this argument, Tom hanged himself in the garden at his home in Richmond, England. There is no doubt that Badfinger became embroiled in the machinations of big business and lost out summarily. For the short time they were productive they were a quality act and their power pop songs stand the test of time. All three of their UK Top 10 singles also featured in the Top 10 in America and a fourth single, *Baby Blue* peaked at No 14 on the US Hot 100 in 1972.

Badly Drawn Boy Badly Drawn Boy is the nom de chanson of Damon Gough (born in Dunstable, Bedfordshire, 2 October 1969), an alternative singer/songwriter who took his name in 1995 from the television show *Sam and His Magic Ball*. BDB's debut album, 'The Hour of Bewilderbeast' (No 13, Jun 2000) won the 2000 Mercury Prize and £20,000. His second album 'About a Boy' (No 6, Apr 2002) was the score for the film of the same name. His next two albums also made the Top 10 'Have You Fed the Fish'? (No 10, Nov 2002) and 'One Plus One Is One' (No 9, Jun 2004), although the latter was not critically well received and led to the eventual set-up of his own label, BDB Records. It took until the spring of 2002 for BDB to score a Top 20 hit when he reached No 16 with *Silent Sigh*. Other Top 20 hits are *You Were Right* (No 9, Oct 2002) and *Born Again* (No 16, Jan 2003).

Bad Manners Bad Manners are a 2 Tone ska band best known for its bald, heavyweight lead singer Buster Bloodvessel (born Douglas Trendle, Hackney, London, 6 September 1958). Founded in 1976 by pupils from Woodberry Down Comprehensive School, north London other members of the band have included: Louis 'Alphonso' Cook (guitar), Winston Bazoomies (born Alan Sayag; harmonica), Brian 'Chew-It' Tuit (drums), David Farren (bass), Paul Hyman (trumpet), Gus 'Hot Lips' Herman (trumpet), Chris Kane (sax), Andrew 'Marcus-Absent' Marson (sax) and Martin Stewart (keyboards). They signed to Magnet Records in 1980 and their first chart hit came in March of that year when *Ne-Ne Na-Na Na-Na Nu-Nu* reached number 28 spending 14 weeks on the hit parade. *Lip Up Fatty* also spent 14 weeks on the chart but penetrated the Top 20 reaching number 15 in June. In the autumn of 1980 *Special Brew* became their joint most successful single when reached it reached No 3. In the summer of 1981 *Can Can* also reached the No 3 position. An LP, 'Gosh It's... Bad Manners', was their only album to reach the Top 20, stalling at No 18. *Walking In The Sunshine* (No 10, Sep 1981) and *My Girl Lollipop (My Boy Lollipop)* (No 9, Jul 1982) were their last Top 10 hits and the group left Magnet in 1983. They split in 1986 but Buster quickly reformed the group with original personnel Cook, Stewart (left 1991), Bazoomies and Kane (left in 1990 to become a music teacher). Between 1995 and 1998, Buster ran a hotel called Fatty Towers in Margate, Kent. Using various musicians, he still tours under the name Bad Manners.

Long John Baldry The man who gave half his name to Elton John was born John William Baldry on 12 January 1941. His nickname came about because he was 6ft 7in tall. In 1962 he sang with Alexis Korner's Blues Incorporated. In 1964 he was front-man of the Cyril Davies R&B All Stars who became Long John Baldry and His Hoochie Coochie Men following Davies's death. This band evolved into Steampacket with Rod Stewart sharing vocal duties with Baldry. Steampacket split in 1966 and Long John joined Bluesology (see entry for Elton John). Long John's debut single as a solo artist, *Let The Heartaches Begin* (No 1, Nov 1967) topped the charts and he had a further Top 20 hit with *Mexico* (No 15, Oct 1968) which was inevitably played frequently during the Olympic Games of that year. In 1978, John released the album 'Baldry's Out' to announce his homosexuality to the world. He suffered from mental health problems and was institutionalised at one stage. John emigrated to Canada where he became a voice actor and died on 21 July 2005 at Vancouver General Hospital, of a lung infection.

Bananarama The most successful British girl group (until the Spice Girls) was founded in 1979 by Siobhan Fahey (born Siobhan Máire Deirdre Fahey, Dublin, Ireland, 10 September 1958), Keren Jane Woodward (born in Bristol, 2 April 1961) and Sarah Elizabeth Dallin (born in Bristol, 17 December 1961). In 1981 they recorded their first song *Aie A Mwana* but it was early 1982 before they entered the Top 75 for the first time when they worked with the Fun Boy Three on *It Ain't What You Do (It's the Way That You Do It)*, which peaked at number four. The Fun Boy Three returned the favour by guesting on *Really Saying Something*, which reached number five. On 2 March 1983, they

released their debut album, 'Deep Sea Skiving' and it made it to No 7 in the UK and 63 on the Billboard Hot 100, spawning the Top 10 singles, *Shy Boy* (No 4, Jul 1982), *Na Na Hey Hey Kiss Him Goodbye* (No 5, Feb 1983) and the aforementioned *It Ain't What You Do*. Their eponymously titled second album was released on 21 April 1984 and peaked at No 16 in Britain and No 30 in America. It contained *Cruel Summer* (No 8, Jul 1983), the song that gave them their first Top 10 hit Stateside. *Robert De Niro's Waiting* from the same album reached number three in March 1984, their (joint) highest placing in the UK. On 30 May 1986, they released the Stock Aitken Waterman produced *Venus*, a remake of the Shocking Blue hit. By coincidence both versions reached number eight in the UK and topped the charts in America. In October 1987, *Love In The First Degree* equalled their top placing in the UK. *I Want You Back* (No 5, Apr 1988) became their last solo Top 10 hit. In February 1989 they released a charity version of *Help!* with French & Saunders and Kathy Burke under the name Lananeeneenoonoo. Siobham, who had married Dave Stewart of Eurythmics left and was replaced in March 1988 by Jacquie O'Sullivan (born in London, 7 August 1960) and *I Want You Back* was re-recorded with her vocals instead of Fahey's. O'Sullivan left after the release of *Tripping On Your Love*, the fourth single from the album 'Pop Life' (released 18 May 1991). 'Please Yourself' (released: 3 April 1993), an album featuring just Dallin and Woodward peaked at 46 and was their last Top 50 chart entry. After a gap of 12 years, Bananarama returned to the charts in 2005 with *Move In My Direction*, which reached number 14. It is, to date, their last Top 20 single.

Dame Shirley Bassey Born at Tiger Bay, a suburb of Cardiff, Wales on 8 January 1937 Shirley Veronica Bassey has had a chart career that spans 50 years. Her first single, *Burn My Candle (At Both Ends)*, was released in February 1956 but it was not until early 1957 that she entered the charts with the *Banana Boat Song* (No 8, Feb 1957). Her fourth chart entry *As I Love You* (No 1, Dec 1958) topped the UK Singles Chart and was swiftly follwed by *Kiss Me Honey Honey Kiss Me* (No 3, Dec 1958). After *As Long As He Needs Me* (No 2, Aug 1960) from Lionel Bart's *Oliver!* Shirley was back at the top of the charts with the double-A side *Reach For The Stars/Climb Ev'ry Mountain* (No 1, Jul 1961). Further Top 10 success followed with *I'll Get By* (No 10, Nov 1961) before she recorded *Tonight* (No 21, Feb 1962) from *West Side Story* and *What Now My Love* (No 5, Aug 1962). Arguably Shirley's most critically-acclaimed hit was the Lieber and Stoller penned, George Martin produced *I (Who Have Nothing)* (No 6, Sep 1963) although in America it was Tom Jones who had the bigger hit with this song, reaching No 14 in 1970. Shirley's version of the theme to *Goldfinger* (No 21, Oct 1964) gave her only Top 40 hit in America reaching No 8. Surprisingly, Shirley's other best-known song *Big Spender* (No 21, Oct 1967) from the musical *Sweet Charity*, also narrowly missed out on the Top 20 but this is no reflection on the public affection for the song but rather tells the tale of the Beatles' effect, flower power and the general dominance of groups in a golden era of music. The following year Shirley left Britain to become a tax exile. In 1970, she returned to the charts for the first time in three years with the George Harrison-penned *Something* (No 4, Jun 1970), equalling the chart position of the original Beatles recording. The album of the same name reached number five, Shirley's highest charting studio album. In August 1971, she reached No 6 with *For All We Know* and in March 1973, No 8 with *Never Never Never*, her last chart Top 20 hit to date although Shirley was sampled on the Kanye West hit single *Diamonds from Sierra Leone* (no 8, Jul 2005). It was a different story with LPs. Between 1970 and 1979, Shirley put 18 albums onto the UK Albums Chart. In 1971, she recorded the theme song for the Bond film *Diamonds Are Forever* (No 38, Jan 1972) and her record third Bond theme outing came eight years later with *Moonraker*. The stats alone barely do the legendary diva justice. Shirley lays claim, with artists such as Elton John, Tom Jones, Cliff Richard and Rod Stewart, to being one of the greatest international solo artists Britain has produced. Her 1984 album 'I Am What I Am' included a little known song entitled *This is My Life* which became the definitive show-stopper and the song her fans insisted she closed her shows with, Shirley sometimes teasing her audience with several encores before giving her impassioned performance of the song. Shirley is still knocking out Top 20 albums, her most recent being the compilation 'Get the Party Started' (No 6, Jun 2007) and 'The Performance' (No 20, Nov 2009) her first studio album of original compositions in three decades. Shirley famously appeared on the *Morecambe and Wise Christmas Show* in 1971 (Eric often referring to her as Burly Chassis) where, in a memorable scene Shirley lost a shoe during a performance and Eric as a props man replaces it with a large boot! Shirley also had several series of her own from 1976. On 29 September 2011, the BBC broadcast a 70 minute drama, entitled *Shirley*, depicting Bassey's early life and career. Ruth Negga played the title role. Unusually the drama did not need to use any hyperbole to tell the story of Shirley's colourful and sometimes tragic life. Her first husband, Kenneth Hume was gay and their two daughters Sharon (b. 1954) and Samantha (b. 1963) are of doubtful parentage, Hume suggesting that Peter Finch may have been Samantha's father. After Kenneth died in 1967 Shirley married Sergio Novak, the assistant manager of the Excelsior Hotel in Rome. They divorced in 1979. Novak served as Shirley's manager throughout their marriage. With Novak she adopted her grand-nephew, Mark. In 1985, Shirley's daughter Samantha, age 21, was found dead in the River Avon in Bristol, suicide was suspected. Shirley was created a Dame Commander of the Order of the British Empire (DBE) on 31 December 1999 "For services to entertainment". See also entries in the television section for *The Life and Times of Vivienne Vyle*, and *Stars in Their Eyes*.

Bay City Rollers The Bay City Rollers were Tartan teenyboppers, all from Edinburgh, Scotland, who became one of the most successful pop groups of the 1970s, "Rollermania" sweeping the world for a brief period. Although personnel changed, the mainstays were Les McKeown (born 12 November 1955; vocalist), Alan Longmuir (born 20 June 1948; bassist), Stuart Wood (born 25 February 1957; guitarist), Eric Faulkner (born 21 October 1953; guitarist) and Derek Longmuir (born 19 March 1951; drummer). The Longmuirs and Gordon Clark founded a group called The Saxons in 1966 and later changed the name supposedly by throwing a dart at a map of America. It landed at Bay City, Michigan, the birthplace of Madonna. David Paton (1969-1970) and Billy Lyall (1969-1971) were briefly members before forming Pilot. In 1971, the Bay City Rollers recorded *Keep On Dancing* after impresario Jonathan King suggested it. The song reached number nine in September 1971 but it would not be until 1974 that they really made their mark. The year before McKeown had replaced Clark as lead singer. McKeown rerecorded the vocals for *Remember (Sha La La La)* and it reached number six. They followed up with *Shang-A-Lang* (No 2, Apr 1974), *Summerlove Sensation* (No 3, Jul 1974) and *All Of Me Loves All Of You*" (No 4, Oct 1974). In early 1975 they had their own television series entitled *Shang-A-Lang* and in the spring their version of the Four Seasons' *Bye, Bye, Baby* stayed at Number 1 for six weeks. *Give A Little Love* (No 1, Jul 1975) became their second chart-topper of 1975 and that year they also hit the top spot on the Billboard Hot 100 with *Saturday Night*, a song that failed to chart at all in the UK two years previously. After scoring two more Top 10 hits, *Money Honey* (No 3, Nov 1975) and *Love Me Like I Love You* (No 4, Apr 1976), Alan Longmuir left the group and Ian Mitchell took his place temporarily before himself being replaced by Pat McGlynn. *I Only Wanna Be with you* (No 4, Sep 1976) and *It's a Game* (No 16, May 1977) were their last Top 20 hits in the UK. Alan Longmuir rejoined in 1978 for an American television show and a new album but both flopped. At the end of that year McKeown left to go solo and the group fired their long-time manager Tam Paton. They changed their name to The Rollers and recruited Duncan Faure as the new lead singer. Three albums flopped and they split in 1981. Various line-ups tried to tour in the 1980s and 1990s but without great success. In 2000, Derek Longmuir was convicted of possessing child pornography and sentenced to 300 hours community service.

Beady Eye see entry for Oasis

The Beatles The 'Fab Four' dominated the 1960's music scene and became the first British pop group to be successful in America, leading the British Invasion in 1964. The band was originally formed in 1957 and known as The Quarrymen (after Quarry Bank High School which John Lennon and some of the other original group members attended), then Johnny and The Moondogs (temporarily in October 1958 for a television talent show), the Silver Beatles (from 1960) and finally from early 1961 The Beatles (in tribute to Buddy Holly's backing band the Crickets). John Lennon (born at Oxford Street Maternity Hospital, Liverpool, 9 October 1940; vocals, guitar and harmonica; killed in New York, 8 December 1980, aged 40) met (Sir James) Paul McCartney (born at Walton Hospital, Liverpool, 18 June 1942; bass and vocals) at a church fete on 6 July 1957. Paul remembers John as being drunk that day. Nonetheless, Lennon invited him to join the group. Two songs recorded that day by The Quarrymen were sold in 1994 for £78,500. On 7 August 1957, The Quarrymen played The Cavern, a Mathew Street club, for the first time although Paul was absent (he was away with the Scouts). George Harrison (born at Wavertree, Liverpool, 24 February 1943 – not 25th as George believed for many years; guitar and vocals) joined the Quarrymen in February 1958. In early 1960, Stuart Sutcliffe (b. 23 June 1940), a friend of John's from art school, joined the band as a bass player. Drummer Tommy Moore (b. Liverpool, 1924; d. 1981) joined them that same year but left on 13 June to return to his job as a forklift truck driver. Drummer (Randolph) Peter Best (b. Madras, India, 24 November 1941) joined the group on 12 August 1960, a day before they were to go to Hamburg to play a season of club dates. In June 1961, The Beatles (without Sutcliffe) backed Tony Sheridan in West Germany on four songs. The first release *My Bonnie* credited to Tony Sheridan and the Beat Brothers failed to make the West German charts. In July 1961, Sutcliffe elected to leave The Beatles and lived in Hamburg with his girlfriend Astrid Kirchherr. On 9 November 1961, Jewish businessman Brian Epstein (1934-1967) visited The Cavern for the first time after hearing about the group and on 10 December became their manager. On 1 January 1962, they auditioned for Decca (see entry for The Shadows) but did not impress. On 5 January 1962, *My Bonnie* was released in the UK and eventually staggered to No 48 in June 1963. On 10 April 1962, Stu Sutcliffe died of a brain aneurysm in Hamburg. He was 22. In the summer, The Beatles signed with Parlophone (part of EMI) and recorded at Abbey Road on 6 June. In August, the group sacked Pete Best. He was replaced by Ringo Starr (b. Richard Starkey, Dingle, Liverpool, 7 July 1940), the drummer with Rory Storm and the Hurricanes. John was once asked if Ringo was the best drummer in the world and replied jokingly, "He's not even the best drummer in The Beatles." Released on Parlophone, *Love Me Do* was the first Beatles song to enter the charts, doing so in October 1962 and reaching number 17 and spending 18 weeks in the Hit Parade. Parlophone's A&R man (Sir) George (Henry) Martin (b. London, 3 January 1926) produced all The Beatles' singles. Three months after *Love Me Do*, *Please, Please Me* became their first Top 10 hit, missing the top spot by one place. *From Me to You* went one better and spent seven weeks at Number 1. It would be the first of 17 UK chart-toppers for the Fab Four between 1963 and 1969. *She Loves You* had two stints at Number 1 in late 1963 and was replaced at the top by *I Want to Hold Your Hand*, the first instance of a group replacing themselves at Number 1. In 1964 in America, *I Want to Hold Your Hand* was replaced at the top spot by *She Loves You*, which was in turn succeeded by *Can't Buy Me Love*, the first instance of a group replacing themselves at Number 1 twice. In America, The Beatles had 20 chart-toppers. Most of the group's songs were credited to Lennon-McCartney although the majority were written by one or other of them. As with Elvis Presley, The Beatles began appearing in films including *A Hard Day's Night* (1964) and *Help!* (1965) but unlike Presley's the Beatles' films became the template for future highly-regarded films of the genre. The most critically acclaimed being the cartoon *Yellow Submarine*

(1968) which while based on the band's music did not feature the group - instead actors provided the voices of The Beatles. In March 1966, John gave an interview to the *Evening Standard* in which he said that the Beatles were "more popular than Jesus". The remarks caused barely a ripple in the UK but uproar in the USA where outraged Christians arranged burnings of Beatles records and memorabilia. It almost caused the cancellation of an American tour. Two months earlier, the group had angered Americans with the cover for the compilation album 'Yesterday and Today', which featured the foursome in butcher's garb surrounded by raw meat and mutilated dolls. The Beatles' last tour ended on 29 August 1966 at Candlestick Park, San Francisco. On 9 November 1966, John met the *avant garde* Japanese artist Yoko Ono at the Indica Gallery in London. On 6 December 1966 the group began recording their eighth studio album 'Sgt. Pepper's Lonely Hearts Club Band', an experimental LP which would be the first major pop album to include its complete lyrics - which were printed on the back cover. The album topped the charts in the UK and USA and sold more than 32million copies. The front cover (created by Jann Haworth and Peter Blake) contained a montage of wax figures of the Beatles surrounded by photos and models of personalities from the arts, architecture, politics, sport and literature. They included Aleister Crowley (occultist), Mae West (actress), Lenny Bruce (comedian), Edgar Allan Poe (writer), Bob Dylan (singer/songwriter), two images of Shirley Temple (actress), Sir Robert Peel (Prime Minister), Laurel & Hardy (actors), Marilyn Monroe (actress), Fred Astaire (dancer and actor), Dylan Thomas (poet), Tony Curtis (actor), Sonny Liston (boxer), Sigmund Freud (psychoanalyst), Stu Sutcliffe (former band member), Marlon Brando (actor), Tom Mix (cowboy actor), Oscar Wilde (writer), Tyrone Power (actor), Issy Bonn (comedian), GB Shaw (playwright), Lewis Carroll (writer), T. E. Lawrence (of Arabia), Diana Dors (actress), Albert Einstein (physicist), Marlene Dietrich (actress) and little-known Liverpool footballer Albert Stubbins! In 1967, The Beatles became involved with the Maharishi Mahesh Yogi, an Indian mystic, who influenced their thinking. On 25 June, the band performed their newest single *All You Need Is Love* on *Our World*, the first live global television link. In August 1967, they went to Bangor, North Wales for a retreat with the Maharishi. While they were away, Brian Epstein died of a drugs overdose. In December 1967, *Magical Mystery Tour* was released and made Number 1 in America. The film of the same name, premiered on Boxing Day, and was described as "blatant rubbish" by the *Daily Express* and "a colossal conceit" by the *Daily Mail*. One of the problems was that the film was shot in colour but shown on BBC1 in black and white – another problem was that the surreal nature of the content was probably a little ahead of its time. The film certainly contained excellent songs and some beautifully eccentric comic interludes, notably, Ringo's Aunt Jessie's lascivious daydreams about the tour bus conductor Buster Bloodvessel (played by the beautifully eccentric Ivor Cutler), Bonzo Dog Doo-Dah Band's performance of *Death Cab For Cutie*, sung by the even more eccentric Vivian Stanshall (see separate entry), Victor Spinetti's depiction of a stereotypical howling British Sgt Major, and the scene in which John plays a waiter who shovels spaghetti on a fat woman's plate -die-hard fans loved it. With Epstein dead the group turned to an unlikely saviour, the Maharishi and travelled to his ashram in Rishikesh, India. However, they became disillusioned by him when they heard rumours that he had made sexual advances to the actress Mia Farrow, although George remained a devotee of eastern religions to the end of his life. John wrote the song *Sexy Sadie* about him and later said, "We believe in meditation, but not the Maharishi and his scene." The band began to split in 1968 and indeed Ringo walked out for a while and Paul took over drumming duties. John enamoured of Yoko Ono, lost interest in writing with McCartney. On 22 November 1968 'The Beatles' (a double LP that came to be known as the "White Album") was released, the first on Apple Records. From March 1968 until June 1969 the group had four consecutive Number 1s: *Lady Madonna*, *Hey Jude* (about Julian Lennon, John's eldest son), *Get Back* and the last Beatles Number 1 *The Ballad Of John And Yoko* about the couple's often fraught relationship with the press. The final live performance by The Beatles, accompanied by Billy Preston, was filmed on the rooftop of the Apple Corps building at 3 Savile Row, London, on 30 January 1969. The group began squabbling about who managed their financial affairs. John, George and Ringo favoured Allen Klein, who had negotiated contracts for The Rolling Stones. Paul wanted John Eastman who had become his brother-in-law on 12 March 1969. Five months later, on 20 August, all four Beatles appeared in a studio for the last time as they finished the Abbey Road track *I Want You (She's So Heavy)*. Exactly, one month later, John left The Beatles. The 'Abbey Road' album spent more than 80 weeks on the chart, topping it for 11 and sold four million copies within two months. The second release from the album *Something* was the only song by George to appear as a Beatles' A-side. On 3 January 1970, the last new song, Harrison's *I Me Mine,* was recorded. John did not take part. Paul then announced his departure on 10 April 1970. *Let It Be* (the single) peaked at number two while 'Let It Be' (the album) got to Number 1 in 1970. John, Paul, George and Ringo all released solo albums in 1970. Two double greatest hits albums '1962-1966' and '1967-1970', were released in 1973 and are known as the Red and Blue albums (due to the colour of their cover). The hope that one day The Beatles would reform ended on 8 December 1980 when John was shot dead outside his Manhattan home by a deranged man named Mark Chapman. The Beatles were inducted into the Rock and Roll Hall of Fame in 1988. George and Ringo attended the ceremony along with John's widow, Yoko Ono, and his two sons, Julian and Sean. In 1994, *Live at the BBC* was the first official release of previously unissued Beatles' performances in 17 years. That year George, Paul and Ringo reunited for the *Anthology* project, the culmination of work begun in the late 1960s by Neil Aspinall, the group's former road manager. A five-part television series (watched by 400million people), an eight-volume video set and three two-CD box sets were released as part of the project. On 13 November 2000, '1', a compilation featuring every Beatles British chart-topper, was released. It became the fastest-selling album of all time, with 3.6million sold in the first week and more than 12 million in three weeks worldwide. It was a Number 1 chart hit in at least 28 countries, including the UK and America. George died from lung cancer on 29 November 2001. The Beatles' twelve original UK albums were 'Please Please Me' (1963), 'With The Beatles' (1963), 'A Hard Day's Night' (1964), 'Beatles for Sale' (1964), 'Help!' (1965), 'Rubber Soul' (1965), 'Revolver' (1966), 'Sgt. Pepper's Lonely Hearts Club Band' (1967), 'The Beatles' (1968 - aka The White Album), 'Yellow Submarine' (1969), 'Abbey Road' (1969) and 'Let It Be' (1970) – all topped the charts bar 'Yellow Submarine' which stalled at No 3 in February 1969. They also had four compilation chart-toppers 'The Beatles at the Hollywood Bowl' (1977), 'Live at the BBC' (1994), 'Anthology 2' (1996) and '1' (2000). Their 17 UK single No 1s were: *From Me To You* (Apr 1963), *She Loves You* (Aug 1963), *I Want To Hold Your Hand* (Dec 1963), *Can't Buy Me Love* (Mar 1964), *A Hard Day's Night* (Jul 1964), *I Feel Fine* (Dec 1964), *Ticket to Ride* (Apr 1965), *Help* (Jul 1965), *Day Tripper/We Can Work It Out* (Dec 1965), *Paperback Writer* (Jun 1966), *Yellow Submarine/Eleanor Rigby* (Aug 1966), *All You Need Is Love* (Jul 1967), *Hello Goodbye* (Nov 1967), *Lady Madonna* (Mar 1968), *Hey Jude* (Sep 1968), *Get Back* (Apr 1969) and *The Ballad of John and Yoko* (Jun 1969). The only other records not to top the UK singles chart when the band were active were the double-A side *Penny Lane/Strawberry Fields Forever* (No 2, Feb 1967), the *Magical Mystery Tour* (Double EP) (No 2, Dec 1967), the double-A side *Something/Come Together* (No 4, Nov 1969) and *Let it Be* (No 2, Mar 1970). Of all their numerous re-releases only *Love Me Do* (No 4, Oct 1982) fared better than the original release. Several other, previously unreleased, records charted in the years following their break-up including: *Yesterday* (No 8, Mar 1976), *Baby It's You* (No 7, Apr 1995), *Free as a Bird* (No 2, Dec 1995) and *Real Love* (No 4, Mar 1996). As individuals their UK chart output includes **George** Harrison singles: *My Sweet Lord* (No 1, Jan 1971 and No 1, Jan 2002), *Bangla Desh* (No 10, Aug 1971), *Give Me Love (Give Me Peace On Earth)* (No 8, Jun 1973), *All Those Years Ago* (No 13, May 1981 – tribute to John with Paul, Ringo and Linda McCartney), *Got My Mind Set On You* (No 2, Oct 1987) and *When We Was Fab* (No 25, Feb 1988). Albums: 'All Things Must Pass' (No 4, Dec 1970), 'Living in the Material World' (No 2, Jul 1973), 'Somewhere in England' (No 13, Jun

1981) and 'Cloud Nine' (No 10, Nov 1987). George married model Pattie Boyd in January 1966, with Paul as best man. They split up in 1974 and Pattie moved in with Eric Clapton and they subsequently married. George subsequently married Olivia Trinidad Arias in 1978. They had one son, Dhani Harrison (born 1 August 1978). **John** Lennon singles: *Give Peace A Chance* (No 2, Jul 1969), *Cold Turkey* (No 14, Nov 1969), *Instant Karma* (No 5, Feb 1970), *Power to the People* (N0 7, Mar 1971), *Happy Xmas (War is Over)* (No 4, Dec 1972) all crediting the Plastic Ono Band, then on his own *Imagine* (No 6, Nov 1975) and then the four posthumous hits *(Just Like) Starting Over* (No 1, Nov 1980), the re-released *Happy Xmas (War Is Over)* (No 2, 20 Dec 1980) and *Imagine* (No 1 , 27 Dec 1980) and finally *Woman* (No 1, Jan 1981). John also had a No 6 hit with *Nobody Told Me* in January 1984. The song was recorded (but uncompleted) shortly before his death in 1980 and completed by his widow Yoko Ono in 1983. Albums: 'Imagine' (No 1, Oct 1971), 'Sometime in New York City' (No 11, Oct 1971), 'Mind Games' (No 13, Dec 1973), 'Walls and Bridges' (No 6, Oct 1974), 'Rock 'N' Roll' (No 6, Mar 1975), 'Shaved Fish' (No 8, Mar 1975 - compilation), 'Double Fantasy' (No 1, Nov 1980) and the compilations 'The John Lennon Collection' (No 1, Nov 1982), 'Milk and Honey' (No 3, Feb 1984) and 'Working Class Hero: The Definitive Lennon' (No 11, Oct 2005). John married Cynthia Powell in August 1962 and was divorced in 1968. They had one son, (John Charles) Julian Lennon (born in Liverpool, 8 April 1963). He married Yoko Ono in March 1969. They had one son, Sean Taro Ono Lennon (born in New York, 9 October 1975). **Sir Paul** McCartney (he was knighted in 1997) singles: *Another Day* (No 2, Feb 1971) and then a proliferation of singles with his band, Wings, *Give Ireland Back To The Irish* (No 16, Feb 1972), *Mary Had A Little Lamb* (No 9, May 1972), *Hi Hi Hi/C Moon* (No 5, Dec 1972), *My Love* (No 9, Apr 1973), *Live and Let Die* (No 9, Jun 1973), *Helen Wheels* (No 12, Nov 1973), *Jet* (No 7, Mar 1974), *Band On The Run* (No 3, Jul 1974), *Junior's Farm* (No 16, Nov 1974), *Listen To What The Man Said* (No 6, May 1975), *Silly Love Songs* (No 2, May 1976), *Let 'Em In* (No 2, Aug 1976), *Mull of Kintyre/Girls' School* (No 1, Nov 1977), *With A Little Luck* (No 5, Apr 1978), *Goodnight Tonight* (No 5, Apr 1979) and post-Wings singles, *Wonderful Christmas Time* (No 6, Dec 1979), *Coming Up* (No 2, Apr 1980), *Waterfalls* (No 9, Jun 1980), *Ebony and Ivory* (No 1, Apr 1982 with Stevie Wonder), *The Girl Is Mine* (No 8, Nov 1982 with Michael Jackson), *Say Say Say* (No 2, Oct 1983 with Michael Jackson), *Pipes of Peace* (No 1, Dec 1983), *No More Lonely Nights* (No 2, Oct 1984), *We All Stand Together* (No 3, Nov 1984 with the Frog Chorus), *Once Upon A Long Ago* (No 10, Nov 1987), *Ferry 'Cross the Mersey* (No 1, May 1989 with Christians, Holly Johnson, Gerry Marsden and Stock Aitken Waterman in aid of the Hillsborough football disaster), *My Brave Face* (No 18, May 1989), *This One* (No 18, Jul 1989), *Put it There* (No 32, Feb 1990), *All My Trials* (No 35, Dec 1990), *Hope of Deliverance* (No 18, Jan 1993) and *Dance Tonight* (No 26, Jun 2007). Albums: 'McCartney' (No 2, May 1970), 'Ram' (No 1, Jun 1971 with Linda McCartney), 'Wings Wildlife' (No 11, Dec 1971), 'Red Rose Speedway' (No 5, May 1973), 'Band on the Run' (No 1, Dec 1973), 'Venus and Mars ' (No 1, Jun 1975), 'Wings at the Speed of Sound' (No2, Apr 1976), 'Wings Over America' (No 8, Jan 1977), 'London Town' (No 4, Apr 1978), 'Back to The Egg' (No6, Jun 1979) and the post-Wings period 'McCartney II' (No 1, May 1980), 'Tug of War' (No 1, May 1982), 'Pipes of Peace' (No 4, Nov 1983), 'Give My Regards to Broad Street' (No 1, Nov 1984), 'Press to Play' (No 8, Sep 1986), 'Flowers in the Dirt' (No 1, Jun 1989), 'Off the Ground' (No 5, Feb 1993), 'Flaming Pie' (No 2, May 1997), 'Chaos and Creation in the Backyard' (No 10, Sep 2005), 'Memory Almost Full' (No 5, Jun 2007) and 'Kisses on the Bottom' (No 3, Feb 2012). Paul has thrice collaborated with producer Youth (of Killing Joke and Orb fame) under the alias the Fireman, and released the electronica albums: 'Strawberries Oceans Ships Forest' (1993), 'Rushes' (1998) and 'Electric Arguments' (2008). He also recorded the soundtracks for the films *The Family Way* (1966) and *The Honorary Consul* (1983) as well as recording several highly regarded classical pieces, notably *The Liverpool Oratorio,* Paul's first official foray into classical music; released in 1991 and composed in collaboration with Carl Davis to commemorate The Royal Liverpool Philharmonic Orchestra's 150th anniversary. Other classical pieces include: *Standing Stone* (1997), *Ecce Cor Meum* (2006) and *Ocean's Kingdom* (2011). Paul married American photographer Linda Eastman (Born in New York, 24 September 1941; d. 17 April 1998) in 1969. The McCartneys had three children together: Mary Anna (born in London, 28 August 1969), Stella Nina (born in London, 13 September 1971) and James Louis (born in London, 12 September 1977). His second marriage to Heather Mills (born in Aldershot, Hampshire, 12 January 1968) in 2002 ended in an acrimonious divorce in 2008). They have a daughter, Beatrice Milly (born 28 October 2003). Paul married New Yorker Nancy Shevell in a civil ceremony at Old Marylebone Town Hall, London on 9 October 2011. **Ringo** Starr singles: *It Don't Come Easy* (No 4, Apr 1971), *Back Off Boogaloo* (No 2, Apr 1972), *Photograph* (No 8, Oct 1973) and *You're Sixteen* (No 4, Feb 1874), the latter two both topping the US chart. Although Ringo had several more American hits the only other in the UK was in his Thomas the Tank engine guise on the chart-topping *The Official BBC Children in Need Medley* in 2009. Albums: 'Sentimental Journey' (No 7, Apr 1970), 'Ringo' (No 7, Dec 1973) and 'Goodnight Vienna' (No 30, Dec 1974). Ringo decided to concentrate on a movie career and notable films include: *Candy* (1968), *The Magic Christian* (1969), *That'll Be the Day* (1973), *Son of Dracula* (1974 alongside Harry Nilsson), *Lisztomania* (1975 as The Pope), *Sextette* (1978), *Caveman* (1981), *Give My Regards to Broad Street* (1984), *Alice in Wonderland* (1985 as The Mock Turtle) and *The Return of Bruno* (1988). Ringo married Maureen Cox on 11 February 1965 but divorced in 1975. They had three children Zak (born 13 September 1965), Jason (born 19 August 1967) and Lee (born 11 November 1970). Maureen died in 1994. His second marriage, on 27 April 1981, was to actress Barbara Bach (born Barbara Goldbach, New York, 27 August 1947).

Beautiful South Formed from the ashes of The Housemartins by Paul Heaton (born Bromborough, Cheshire, 9 May 1962) and Dave Hemingway (born in Hull 20 September 1960), The Beautiful South had a dozen UK Top 20 hits. Heaton and Hemingway were joined by Sean Welch (born in Enfield, London, 12 April 1965; bassist and former roadie for The Housemartins), Dave Stead (born in Huddersfield, Yorkshire, 15 October 1966; drummer), Dave Rotheray (born in Hull, 9 February 1963; guitarist) and Briana Corrigan (born in Belfast, 30 May 1965; vocalist) who was replaced in 1994 by Jacqui Abbott (born in St Helens, Merseyside, 10 November 1973; vocalist), who left in 2000 and was succeeded by Alison Wheeler (born 4 March 1972; vocalist) who was with the band from 2003 until it disbanded on 30 January 2007 citing "musical similarities". 'Welcome to the Beautiful South' (No 2, Nov 1989) the debut album by the group spawned three hit singles, *Song For Whoever* (No 2, Jun 1989), *You Keep It All In* (No 8, Sep 1989) and *I'll Sail This Ship Alone* (No 31, Dec 1989). *A Little Time* (No 1, Oct 1990) from their second album 'Choke' (No 2, Nov 1990) gave the band its only No 1 spending a solitary week atop the charts. Two further albums, '0898: Beautiful South' (No 4, Apr 1992) and 'Miaow' (No 6, Apr 1994) made the Top 10 before their compilation 'Carry on Up the Charts: the Best of the Beautiful South' (No 1, Nov 1994) gave them the Christmas No 1 album, their first chart-topping LP. The singles *Rotterdam* (No 6, Oct 1996) followed by *Don't Marry Her* (No 8, Dec 1996) both came from the million-selling album 'Blue Is The Colour' (No 1, Nov 1996). In the meantime, Corrigan left the band in 1992 after disagreements with Heaton but was not officially replaced for two years (by St Helens supermarket shelf-stacker Jacqui Abbott). The album 'Quench' (No 1, Oct 1998) gave the band their third consecutive chart-topper and spawned the singles *Perfect 10* (No 2, Oct 1998) and *How Long's a Tear Take to Dry* (No 12, Mar 1999). Their final two Top 10 albums were 'Painting it Red' (No 2, Oct 2000) and 'Superbi' (No 6, May 2006). The band split in January 2007 but

Dave Hemingway, Dave Stead and Alison Wheeler and six new members formed The New Beautiful South in 2008 (renamed The South in 2010).

Bee Gees One of the most successful pop groups of all time, the Bee Gees have charted in the UK in the Sixties, Seventies, Eighties, Nineties and Noughties. The trio of Gibb brothers, born in Douglas, Isle of Man, consisted of Barry Alan Crompton, CBE (born 1 September 1946), Maurice Ernest, CBE (born 22 December 1949; d. Miami Beach, Florida, 12 January 2003) and Robin Hugh, CBE (born 22 December 1949; d. London, 20 May 2012). They began their musical careers at Redcliffe, Queensland, Australia where their parents had emigrated with older sister Lesley and baby brother Andy (born Andrew Roy Gibb, in Manchester, 5 March 1958 – d. in Oxford, 10 March 1988) in 1958. It was their twelfth single, *Spicks And Specks* (named Best Single of the Year by *Go-Set*, Australia's most influential music paper), that gained them their first chart entry down under. In January 1967, they returned to the UK and under the patronage of Robert Stigwood they made their chart debut three months later with *New York Mining Disaster 1941* (No 12, Apr 1967). A second release, *To Love Somebody*, reached only 41 in the summer of 1967 but has subsequently been covered by numerous artistes including The Animals, Janis Joplin, Gram Parsons, Rod Stewart, Bonnie Tyler, Jimi Somerville, Nina Simone, and Michael Bolton. The Bee Gees' first charting album, appropriately named 'Bee Gees' 1st' (No 8, Aug 1967) reached No 7 in America. Their next LP, 'Horizontal' (No 16, Feb 1968), contained the group's first UK Number 1 *Massachusetts* (No 1, Sep 1967 and No 11 in USA). Their next two songs *World* (No 9, Nov 1967) and *Words* (No 8, Jan 1968 and No 15 in USA) continued their chart success before *Jumbo/The Singer Sang His Song* (No 25, Mar 1968 and No 57 in USA) was a comparative flop. Their second UK chart-topper *I've Gotta Get a Message to You* (No 1, Aug 1968) peaked at No 8 Stateside. After the reflective single *First of May* (No 3, Feb 1969) Robin became irritated that Stigwood favoured Barry. Robin left the band in the middle of 1969 and made his point by having a huge hit with *Saved by the Bell* (No 2, Jul 1969) before he returned to the fold. Sister Lesley temporarily replaced Robin in the Bee Gees. In his absence *Don't Forget to Remember* reached number two in Britain in August 1969 but a lowly 73 in America. Barry and Maurice actually split before the three brothers reunited in 1970. On 28 January 1971, they recorded *How Can You Mend a Broken Heart*, which became their first American No 1. *Run to Me* reached number nine in 1972 and then the group vanished from the charts until 1975 when they began their disco phase with *Jive Talkin'* (No 5, Jun 1975 and No 1 in USA). *Nights on Broadway*, which reached number seven in America but did not chart in Britain, firmly established Barry's new falsetto range. The soundtrack for the hit film *Saturday Night Fever*, which revolutionised not only the Bee Gees' career but also made white suits and chest hair temporarily fashionable, followed. The brothers wrote the songs "virtually in a single weekend" working from only a rough script. Three singles, *How Deep Is Your Love* (No 3, Oct 1977), *Stayin' Alive* (No 4, Feb 1978) and *Night Fever* (No 1, Apr 1978) topped the charts in the United States. *Too Much Heaven*, the Bee Gees contribution to the "Music for UNICEF" fund, charted at No 3 in the UK. The following year, *Tragedy* (No 1, Feb 1979) became their fourth UK chart-topper. The soundtrack to *Saturday Night Fever* sold more than 40million copies worldwide. In 1978, Barry wrote the title track to the hit film *Grease*. The Billboard Hot 100 chart of 25 March 1978 contained a remarkable five Gibb-composed songs in the Top 10. It was the first time this had happened since April 1964 when The Beatles held the first five slots. Barry Gibb became the only songwriter to have four consecutive Number 1s in America besting the Lennon-McCartney 1964 achievement. The Bee Gees also co-starred with Peter Frampton in the flop film *Sgt. Pepper's Lonely Hearts Club Band* (1978). The group did not chart in the UK between 1980 and 1987 when they returned to the top with *You Win Again* (No 1, Sep 1987). They worked with other artistes, composing and singing backing vocals on the Barbra Streisand transatlantic No 1 *Woman In Love*. In 1982, Dionne Warwick took their *Heartbreaker* to number three in the UK and

Dolly Parton and Kenny Rogers reached No 1 in America and Top 10 in Britain with *Islands in the Stream*. In 1985, Diana Ross topped the charts with *Chain Reaction*. Andy Gibb, who was a huge solo star with three chart-topping US singles to his name, died aged barely 30 on 10 March 1988 after a life of alcohol and drugs. In the next decade Maurice joined Alcoholics Anonymous. In the nineties they had UK Top 10 success with *Secret Love* (No 5, Mar 1991), *For Whom the Bell tolls* (No 4, Nov 1993), *Alone* (No 5, Mar 1997) and *Immortality* (No 5, Jul 1998 - a duet with Celine Dion). In 2001, the Bee Gees released their last album of new material as a group, *This Is Where I Came In*. Maurice died unexpectedly on 12 January 2003 at 53 from a heart attack after suffering complications from a twisted intestine. The remaining brothers retired the group name. In 2009, Barry and Robin sang on dancing reality shows in Britain and America. On Sunday 20 May, 2012 at 10:46pm, Robin Gibb died of colo-rectal cancer. In a tribute upon his death, longtime friend and former Prime Minister Tony Blair said: "Robin was not only an exceptional and extraordinary musician and songwriter, he was a highly intelligent, interested and committed human being. He was a great friend with a wonderful open and fertile mind and a student of history and politics." Barry told the world that Robin's wish was for *How Deep Is Your Love* to be played at his funeral.

Beverley Sisters The Bethnal Green-born trio consisting of Joy (born Joycelyn Chinery, 5 May 1929), Babs (born Babette Chinery, 5 May 1932) and Teddy (born Hazel Chinery, 5 May 1932) – had six Top 40 hits in the Fifties: *I Saw Mommy Kissing Santa Claus* (No 6, Nov 1953), *Willie Can* (No 23, Apr 1956), *I Dreamed* (No 24, Feb 1957), *Little Drummer Boy* (No 6, Feb 1959), *Little Donkey* (No 14, Nov 1959) and *Green Fields* (No 29, Jun 1960). Based on the American Andrews Sisters, the Beverly Sisters had a resurgence in the Eighties when they became very popular among the gay community. They appear in *Guinness World Records* as the world's longest surviving vocal group without a line-up change. Joy married England football captain Billy Wright on 28 July 1958. The daughters of Joy (Vicky and Babette) and Babs (Sasha) formed a group called The Little Foxes. The Beverleys were ever-presents on television variety shows throughout the 1960s and 1970s and are still going strong today. They were awarded the M.B.E. in the 2006 Queen's New Years Honours List for their services to music. Interestingly, Joy, who is three years older than the twins was also born on 5 May, which makes birthdays interesting.

B*Witched Irish girl group made up of twin sisters Edele and Keavy Lynch (born in Dublin, Ireland, 15 December 1978 - the sisters of Boyzone's Shane Lynch), Sinéad Maria O'Carroll (born in Dublin, Ireland, 14 May 1973) and Lindsay Gael Christian Elaine Armaou (born in Athens, Greece, 18 December 1978). Originally called D'Zire, they became Sister before adopting the B*Witched moniker. The group released their debut single *C'Est La Vie* (No 1, Jun 1998 and No 1 in Ireland and No 9 in US) on the Glowworm label and it topped the charts at the end of its first week of sales. Their next three singles releases: *Rollercoaster* (No 1, Oct 1998), *To You I Belong* (No 1, Dec 1998) and *Blame it on the Weatherman* (No 1, Mar 1999) performed similarly to give the girls the distinction of being the first group to have their first four singles enter the chart at number one, although only the first topped the charts in their native Ireland. Their eponymous debut album (which contained all four chart-toppers) was released on 12 October 1998 and reached number three in the UK and 12 in the US but topped the Irish Albums Chart. B*Witched's second album, 'Awake and Breathe' (released 18 October 1999) also topped the charts in Ireland and made five in Britain but stalled at No 91 in America. Their subsequent UK singles were: *Jessie Hold On* (No 4, Oct 1999 – No 6 in Ireland), *I Shall Be There* (No 13, Dec 1999 – featuring Ladysmith Black Mambazo) and *Jump Down* (No 16, Apr 2000 – No 26 in Ireland). The band also took part in the BRITS Trust *Thank Abba For The Music* (No 4, Mar 1999 – No 5 in Ireland) project, its release coinciding with the debut of the ABBA musical Mamma Mia!. During a tour of America, B*Witched appeared on the American soap opera *General Hospital* on 4 July 2001. The group split in September 2002 after their label dropped them and Sinéad decided to leave.

369

Lindsay Armaou married Lee Brennan of 911 in September 2006. The Lynches continued to work, initially under the name Ms Lynch, but changed this to Barbarellas in October 2010. They released a single, *Body Rock*, on 31 January 2011 and an album 'Night Mode' three months later. Sinéad managed a girl group, Minx, until 2004, and then set up a youth musical workshop, Star Academy. In November 2007 she appeared in an episode of the Irish soap opera *Fair City* as a hotel receptionist. More recently she has presented *Inside & Out*, a makeover show for TV3 Ireland.

Blind Faith see entry for Cream

James Blunt Singer-songwriter, James Hillier Blount, was born in Tidworth, Wiltshire, 22 February 1974, the son of Charles Blount, a Colonel in the British Army Air Corps and Jane Blount. James attended Elstree School in Woolhampton and Harrow School before gaining an army sponsored place at the University of Bristol from which he graduated with a BSc in sociology in 1996. The army sponsorship meant that he was required to complete a minimum of four years in the armed forces and consequently trained at the Royal Military Academy Sandhurst. James gained a commission as a second lieutenant in the Life Guards, a unit of the Household Cavalry, and rose to the rank of captain. Whilst serving with the Life Guards he was assigned the job of guarding the Queen Mother's coffin in April 2002. He left the army on 1 October 2002, after serving for six years. Although in 2002 James began using the surname Blunt, his legal name still remains Blount and is pronounced in the same way, he just feels that Blunt is easier for people to spell. In 2003 his debut album 'Back to Bedlam' was recorded in Los Angeles. In October 2004 the album was released in the UK and several tracks were released over the course of the next year. James released *High* in *October* 2004 and *Wisemen* in March 2005 but neither made a huge impact until the third single from the album, *You're Beautiful*, was released in May 2005 and after entering the UK chart at number 12 climbed to the number one spot after six weeks (also topping the Irish and US chart). The previously released album, *Back to Bedlam* subsequently climbed to number one on the UK Albums Chart in the UK and Ireland and peaked at No 2 in USA. In November 2005 the fourth single from the album was released and *Goodbye My Lover* peaked at No 9 on the UK chart. In September of 2007 following huge success in America James released a second album 'All The Lost Souls' which went Gold after only four days selling 65,000 copies and by January 2008 had sold 600,000 copies in the UK, again topping the albums chart in Britain and Ireland. The cover depicts a thousand photos of James displayed as a chronologic photomosaic. The first single released from the album was *1973*, which peaked at No 4 in the UK. James' third studio album 'Some Kind of Trouble' was released in November 2010 and reached No 4 in the UK although to-date he has had no further Top 10 singles. James has received numerous awards, including; *MTV Europe Music Awards, Best New Act* (2005), *Q Awards, Best New Act* (2005), *BRIT Awards, Best Pop Act and Best Male Vocalist* (2006), *Ivor Novello Awards, International Hit Of The Year* (2006) *and World Music Awards, Best New Artist in the World and Biggest Selling British Artist in the World* (2006). Although guarded of his own personal life, James was instrumental in introducing his sister to her eventual husband Guy Harrison after offering her for "sale" on eBay (it's a long story!). In February 2012, it was announced that James was one of six alleged victims who had filed for damages in new civil cases against *News International* in the phone hacking affair.

Blur Four-man band: Damon Albarn (born Whitechapel, London, 23 March 1968; lead vocals) Graham Leslie Coxon (born Rinteln, West Germany, 12 March 1969; guitar), (Steven) Alexander James (born Boscombe, Bournemouth, 21 November 1968; bass) and David Alexander De Horne Rowntree (born Colchester, 8 May 1964; drums). In 1988 Damon and Graham met Alex whilst studying at Goldsmith's College in London. Following the departure and arrival of new members to the group, at the time named Seymour, an A&R man from Food Records attended a gig. He decided from the outset that he wanted to sign the band, but that their name didn't quite fit. They were renamed Blur and signed a contract in March 1990 and for the next six months toured the UK and created a fan base. It was a slow-burner initially. In October 1990 Blur released *She's So High*, which struggled to No 48 in the UK Singles Chart. Their next single, *There's No Other Way*, which was produced by Stephen Street, managed to get to number eight in the Charts in April 1991 but it would be a further two years until their next Top 10 single. *Bang!* Blur's third single failed to top its predecessor only managing to get to 24 in the Charts. In 1991 Blur released their first album 'Leisure' which peaked at No 7 in the albums chart in September. 1992 started out in a bad way for the band, they were £60,000 in debt so decided to tour the United States to try and recoup some of their money. They failed, and were miserable and homesick. On returning to the UK they recorded 'Modern Life is Rubbish' in December 1992 but the record company were not happy with the album and sent the band back in to the studio to compile new songs. *For Tomorrow*, is what the band came up with, first released as a single this peaked at 28 on the UK Singles Chart. In May 1993 the album was released but climbed only to number 15 on the UK Albums Chart. 'Parklife' was released on 25 April 1994 which included songs such as *End of a Century, To The End, Girls & Boys* (No 5, Mar 1994) and the title track, *Parklife* (No 10, Sep 1994) and became the first of five chart-topping albums, in May 1994. In 1995 Blur won four BRIT Awards. In September 1995 'The Great Escape' was released and a particular single from this album, *Country House*, raised the rivalry between Blur and Oasis. Blur's label Food Records moved the original release date to the same day as Oasis's *Roll with It* and the British media dubbed this battle for the number one spot the 'Battle of Britpop'. In the event, *Country House* (No 1, Aug 1995) won the 'battle', Blur managing to outsell the Manchester band 274,000 to 216,000, however to redress the balance the sales for Blur's album 'The Great Escape' (No 1, Sep 1995) were lower than those for Oasis's album '(What's the Story) Morning Glory'. Other Top 10 single tracks from the album were: *The Universal* (No 5, Nov 1995), *Stereotypes* (No 7, Feb 1996) and *Charmless Man* (No 5, May 1996). Through 1996 Blur struggled to stay together, there were fights amongst the band members, sometimes physical, although they put their problems aside long enough to record and release their fifth album 'Blur' (No 1, Feb 1997). The album shot straight to number one in the UK Albums chart and the first single released from the album, *Beetlebum* went straight in at number one in the UK singles chart the same month. The album also produced two further Top 10 tracks, *Song 2* (No 2, Apr 1997) and *On Your Own* (No 5, Jun 1997). Following the success of the album, Blur decided to go on a nine month world tour. In February 1998 they approached William Orbit to help produce their next album; recording was to start in June of this year. In August, Graham released a solo album 'The Sky is Too High' (No 31). In March 1999 Blur released their sixth album '13' which debuted at number one in the UK Albums chart and produced the single track *Tender* (No 2, Mar 1999). A fallow period then occurred when the band only had one Top 10 single, *Music is My Radar* (No 10, Oct 2000) until Graham left in 2002, standing accused of being disruptive. He had worked on one of the songs in the bands new album, which at the time had yet to be released. 'Think Tank' was released in May 2003. For the tour that followed the albums release, Blur hired Simon Tong (The Verve). The album went straight to number one on the UK Albums Chart to become their fifth consecutive No 1 studio album. It also won Best Album at the 2004 BRIT Awards and spawned the single *Out of Time* (No 5, Apr 2003). The band members concentrated on their solo projects until, in December 2008, it was revealed that Blur would be playing at Hyde Park on 3 July 2009, and that the line up would include Graham Coxon. Tickets sold out within two minutes of release. On 21 February 2012, Blur were awarded the Outstanding Contribution to Music award at the 2012 BRIT Awards. They went on to perform five songs: *Girls & Boys, Song 2, Parklife* (with Phil Daniels), *Tender* and *This is a Low* (James Corden controversially cutting short Adele's victory speech for Best British Album to accommodate the band). Interestingly, Dave Rowntree, who has previously stood as a Labour Party candidate, is training to become a solicitor and graduates from law school in September 2012, just weeks after Blur play at the Olympics closing ceremony in Hyde Park for which they are reforming. See also entry for Gorillaz.

David Bowie David Robert Jones was born in Brixton, London, 8 January 1947. The singer, musician, songwriter and actor is perhaps only surpassed by The Beatles as having the greatest influence on British popular music. The son of Haywood Stenton Jones and Margaret Mary Burns relocated with his family to nearby Bromley in 1953. For Christmas 1959 David received a plastic saxophone from his mother and this soon developed into a love of the recorder, guitar and piano. David attended Bromley Tech High School until he was 15 when an incident with his friend, George Underwood forced him to miss several months of his final year so that doctors could attempt to keep him from losing his vision after George punched him in the eye over a row over a girl. It was this incident that left David having one of his blue eyes looking a permanent watery green. Despite the altercation the two men remained good friends and George even did the artwork for some of David's early albums. In late 1962, now fully recovered and working as an electrician's mate, David formed his first band, Konrads, with George and various other friends. David's penchant for reinventing himself was developed very early in his career; his first three records: *Liza Jane* (1964 - as Davie Jones with the King Bees), *I Pity the Fool* (1965 - as The Manish Boys) and *You've Got a Habit of Leaving* (1965 - as Davy Jones & the Lower Third) all being recorded with different groups and indeed his fourth record *Can't Help Thinking About Me* (1966 - as David Bowie with The Lower Third), although keeping the same personnel, was recorded under his now familiar name taken from the American frontiersman Jim Bowie who gave his name to the Bowie knife. At this time David was influenced by blues and folk music and his half brother, Terry Burns, had also introduced him to modern jazz. Terry had a great impact on David's formative years; a manic depressive, with whom I socialised a lot with during his long stays at Cane Hill mental hospital, Terry loved the likes of Anthony Newley, and in particular Neil Diamond, and David's voice had more than a passing similarity to the former in early records such as *The Laughing Gnome* (failing to chart in 1967 but reaching No 6 in 1973). His very affable older brother (who ultimately took his own life) was a constant reminder to David that he might too have this self-destructive gene and the fear of mental illness haunted him throughout his formative years. After several more changes of group (including Turquoise, Feathers, The Buzz and a brief flirtation with The Riot Squad - as replacement for Graham Bonney), David finally had chart success with his single *Space Oddity* which was released around the time of the first moon landing and reached No 5 in the UK chart in September 1969. Although he had already appeared in a 1967 film short, *The Image*, and on television briefly as a pundit and in a Lyons Maid ice cream advert, David's performance on *Top of the Pops* singing the haunting lyrics on acoustic guitar, made him an overnight sensation. The space folk theme was gradually developed in collaboration with Mick Ronson from February 1970 and eventually became the space rock phenomena, Ziggy Stardust and The Spiders from Mars. Originally gigging as The Hype, the band included Tony Visconti for a very short period and also the likes of Rick Wakeman during his pre-Yes era (while with the Strawbs) and Marc Bolan as a session guitarist just before he went huge later in 1970. A pioneer of glam rock, Bowie, according to music historians Schinder and Schwartz, has joint responsibility with Bolan for creating the genre. Ziggy Stardust and The Spiders from Mars debuted at the Toby Jug pub in Tolworth on 10 February 1972 and made an immediate impact leading to an American tour beginning at Cleveland, Ohio. A subsequent concept LP, 'The Rise and Fall of Ziggy Stardust and the Spiders from Mars', became David's first charting album (No 5, Jul 1972) and a single from the album, *Starman* peaked at No 10 in the UK chart in June 1972. The interest in David's new persona of Ziggy brought a

rush of sales for David's earlier albums and 'Hunky Dory', which was released the previous year, peaked at No 3 in the UK album chart in September 1972, the most noteworthy tracks being *Oh! You Pretty Things*, which was a No 12 hit for Peter Noone in May 1971, and *Life On Mars*, which was later released as a single and reached No 3 in June 1973. David also had a No 12 hit with the non-album single *John, I'm Only Dancing* in September 1972 as well as writing *All the Young Dudes* (No 3, Aug 1972) specifically for Mott the Hoople. David produced several other acts around this time, including Lou Reed, Iggy Pop and Lulu (see separate entry). 1973 was a big year for Bowie, having two No 1 albums with 'Aladdin Sane' and 'Pin-Ups', the first mentioned producing the Top 10 singles *The Jean Genie* (No 2, Dec 1972) and *Drive-In Saturday* (No 3, Apr 1973) as well as the song *Cracked Actor* which became the title for the 1975 *Omnibus* documentary on David's drug-taking days during the Ziggy era. After totally immersing himself in the Ziggy character for almost 18 months, David made a surprise on-stage "retirement" at London's Hammersmith Odeon on 3 July 1973. In October of that year, David had a No 3 hit with a cover version of *Sorrow*, from the 'Pin-Ups' album. In June 1974 'Diamond Dogs' became David's third-successive No 1 album, having earlier had single success with the album track *Rebel Rebel* (No 5, Feb 1974). David next entered his so-called Plastic Soul era with the release of the 'Young Americans' LP (No 2, Feb 1975) and became one of the world's greatest pop icons after cementing his reputation in America with the Billboard No 1 single, *Fame* (on which John Lennon provided backing vocals) in September 1975. Although this record only peaked at No 17 in the UK, the following month he had his first UK No 1 single with the re-issue of *Space Oddity*. The Thin White Duke period followed with the release of the album 'Station to Station' (No 5, Feb 1976) and David has never been out of the public consciousness ever since. His list of UK Top 10 singles continued with: *Knock On Wood* (No 10, Sept 1974), *Golden Years* (No 8, Nov 1975), *Sound and Vision* (No 3, Feb 1977 –the epitome of David's so-called Berlin period), *Boys Keep Swingin'* (No 7, May 1979), *Ashes to Ashes* (No 1, Aug 1980), *Fashion* (No 5, Nov 1980), *Under Pressure* (No 1, Nov 1981 – a collaboration with Queen), *Peace On Earth / Little Drummer Boy* (No 3, Nov 1982 – a duet with Bing Crosby recorded in 1977), *Let's Dance* (No 1, Mar 1983), *China Girl* (No 2, Jun 1983), *Modern Love* (No 2, Sep 1983), *Blue Jean* (No 6, Sep 1984), *Dancing In the Street* (No 1, Sep 1985 – with Mick Jagger), *Absolute Beginners* (No 2, Mar 1986) and *Jump They Say* (No 9, Mar 1993). His list of UK Top 10 studio albums continued with: 'David Live' (No 2, Nov 1974), 'Changesonebowie' (No 2, Jun 1976), 'Low' (No 2, Jan 1977), 'Heroes' (No 3, Oct 1977), 'Stage' (No 5, Oct 1978), 'Lodger' (No 4, Jun 1979), 'Scary Monsters and Super Creeps' (No 1, Sep 1980), 'Let's Dance' (No 1, Apr 1983), 'Tonight'; (No 1, Oct 1984 – recorded after his Serious Moonlight tour; the title track duetted with Tina Turner), 'Never Let Me Down' (No 6, May 1987), 'Tin Machine' (No 3, Jun 1989 – as part of his brief interlude as a member of band of the same name), 'Changesbowie' (No 1, Mar 1990), Black Tie White Noise (No 1, Apr 1993), 'Outside' (No 8, Oct 1995), 'Earthling' (No 6, Feb 1997), 'Hours' (No 5, Oct 1999), 'Bowie at the Beeb' (No 7, Oct 2000), 'Heathen' (No 5, Jun 2002) and 'Reality' (No 3, Sep 2003). Never predictable, David played two anonymous gigs (one in Dublin and one in Stratford-upon-Avon) under the name The Tao Jones Index. David has also had a sporadic but for the most part critically acclaimed acting career. He studied mime with Lindsay Kemp in 1968 and formed his own mime troupe *Feathers* before making his big screen debut in *The Virgin Soldiers* (1969). His first major film role was as alien visiting earth, Thomas Jerome Newton, in *The Man Who Fell to Earth* (1976). David played opposite Marlene Dietrich in her last film performance in *Just a Gigolo* (1978) and the following year began a lengthy Broadway run as John (aka Joseph) Merrick, *The Elephant Man*. His other major films include: *The Hunger* (1983), *Merry Christmas, Mr Lawrence* (1983), *Absolute Beginners* (1986), *Labyrinth* (1986), *The Last Temptation of Christ* (1988 - as Pontius Pilate) and *The Prestige* (2006 – as Nikola Tesla). He also voiced the role of Emperor Maltazard in the English version of the part-animated, part-live action feature film *Arthur and the Invisibles* (2007). David turned down the opportunity to play Max

Zorin in the Bond film *A View to a Kill* (1985). At one time thought to be bisexual, if not fully homosexual, in recent years David has taken the Cliff Richard stance of refusing to talk publicly about his sexual preferences. David has been married twice, to (Mary) Angela Barnett (1970-80, Bromley Registry Office) and Somali-born Supermodel Iman (1992-present, Lausanne, Switzerland). He has a child from each marriage, film director Duncan Zowie Haywood Jones (b. Beckenham, 30 May 1971) and a daughter Alexandria Zahra Jones (b. New York City, 15 August 2000). He also has a step-daughter, Zulekha, from Iman's first marriage to basketball player Spencer Haywood. See also entries in the television section for *The Buddha of Suburbia*, *Extras*, *Old Grey Whistle Test*, *Omnibus*, *Only Fools and Horses*, and *Stella Street*

Boy George see entry for Culture Club

Boyzone In 1993, an advertisement was placed in several Irish newspapers by theatrical manager Louis Walsh (born Michael Louis Vincent Walsh, Kiltimagh, Co. Mayo, Ireland, 5 August 1952) for budding young pop stars to become 'the Irish Take That'. Following the auditions six people were selected including Richard Rock, the son of Dickie Rock (born Richard Rock, in Dublin, 10 October 1936) a famous Irish singer who led the equally famous Miami Showband to thirteen top ten hits, including seven number ones on the Irish Singles Chart. Although only known in the UK because of the murder of three of the band on 31 July 1975 during The Troubles, In Ireland their success attracted the kind of mass hysteria normally reserved for the Beatles. Richard Jr eventually dropped out of the band at an early stage and after Mark Walton was replaced by Mikey Graham (born Michael Christopher Charles Graham, 15 August 1972), the quintet was completed by Ronan Keating (born Ronan Patrick John Keating, 3 March 1977), Stephen Gately (born Stephen Patrick David Gately, 17 March 1976; d. in Majorca, 10 October 2009), Keith Duffy (born Keith Peter Thomas Francis John Duffy, 1 October 1974) and Shane Lynch (born Shane Eamon Mark Stephen Lynch, 3 July 1976), all five being born in Dublin. Before even entering a recording studio and dressed in very unflattering attire, the lads made an appearance on RTÉ's *The Late Late Show* with host Gay Byrne at his professional best as he watched the lad's amateurish gyrations to backing tapes.

They were signed to Polygram in 1994 and by now were a finely-honed professional band. They initially released *Working My Way Back to You* in Ireland only and it peaked at No 3 in the Irish Singles Chart. They then took Britain by storm with a proliferation of hits. Their first four albums 'Said and Done' (No 1, Sep 1995). 'A Different Beat' (No 1, Nov 1996), 'Where We Belong' (No 1, Jun 1998) and the compilation album 'By Request' (No 1, Jun 1999) topped the charts in both the UK and Ireland. Their UK chart singles began with a cover of the Osmonds hit, *Love Me for a Reason* (No 2, Dec 1994 – No 1 in Ireland) and all of their subsequent UK singles until the time of their split placed No 4 or higher. The complete list includes: *Key to my Life* (No 3, Apr 1995 – No 1 in Ireland), *So Good* (No 3, Aug 1985– No 1 in Ireland), *Father and Son* (No 2, Nov 1985– No 1 in Ireland), *Coming Home Now* (No 4, Mar 1996– No 1 in Ireland), *Words* (No 1, Oct 1996– No 1 in Ireland), *A Different Beat* (No 1, Dec 1996– No 2 in Ireland), *Isn't it a Wonder* (No 2, Mar 1997– No 3 in Ireland), *Picture of You* (No 2, Aug 1997– No 2 in Ireland), *Baby Can I Hold You/Shooting Star* (No 2, Dec 1997– No 2 in Ireland), *All that I Need* (No 1, May 1998– No 1 in Ireland), *No Matter What* (No 1, Aug 1998– No 1 in Ireland), *I Love the Way You Love Me* (No 2, Dec 1988– No 2 in Ireland), *When the Going Gets Tough* (No 1, Mar 1999– No 2 in Ireland), *You Needed Me* (No 1, May 1999– No 2 in Ireland) and *Every Day I Love You* (No 3, Dec 1999– No 1 in Ireland). *No Matter What* was Boyzone's best selling single during their career and the only hit they had in America. In June 1999, Stephen Gately revealed that he was gay and was in love with the ex-Caught in the Act member Eloy de Jong. Later in the year Ronan Keating released his first solo single, *When You Say Nothing at All* (No 1,

Aug 1999 – No 1 in Ireland), an Alison Krauss song which he had recorded for the movie Notting Hill. In January 2000 Boyzone decided to split temporarily to pursue solo projects. Ronan continued his solo career with a string of hits including: *Life is a Rollercoaster* (No 1, Jul 2000 - No 1 in Ireland), *The Way You Make Me Feel* (No 6, Dec 2000 - No 8 in Ireland), *Lovin' Each Day* (No 2, Apr 2001- No 4 in Ireland), *If Tomorrow Never Comes* (No 1, May 2002 - No 3 in Ireland), *I Love It When We Do* (No 5, Sep 2002 - No 12 in Ireland), *We've Got Tonight* (No 4, Dec 2002 - featuring Lulu; No 10 in Ireland), *The Long Goodbye* (No 3, May 2003 - No 10 in Ireland), *Lost for Words* (No 9, Nov 2003 – No 23 in Ireland), *She Believes (In Me)* (No 2, Feb 2004 - No 17 in Ireland), *Last Thing on My Mind* (featuring LeAnn Rimes) (No 5, Jun 2004 - No 10 in Ireland), *I Hope You Dance* (No 2, Sep 2004 - No 4 in Ireland), *Father and Son* (featuring Yusuf Islam) (No 2, Dec 2004 - No 16 in Ireland) and *All Over Again* (featuring Kate Rusby) (No 6, May 2006 - No 11 in Ireland). His Top 10 albums include: 'Ronan' (No 1, Aug 2000 – No 2 in Ireland), 'Destination' (No 1, Jun 2002 – No 3 in Ireland), 'Bring You Home' (No 3, Jun 2006 – No 16 in Ireland) and 'Songs for My Mother', released on 16 March 2009 and topping the UK and Irish charts on 22 March, Mother's Day. **Ronan** won the All Ireland under-13 200m title and his parents wanted him to go on and win an Olympic medal. During the Boyzone era and his very successful solo career Ronan has been a talented television presenter, hosting the Eurovision Song Contest and Miss World among many other shows. Ronan sang at the World Cup opening party in June 2006 in front of no less than 250,000 people and later that year posed naked for Cosmopolitan magazine. He even co-managed Westlife in their early days but had a bitter falling out with Louis Walsh, his manager and Westlife co-manager, which took several years to heal. Since 2010 Ronan has served as a judge on the Australian version of *The X Factor*. He married model Yvonne Connolly in April 1998 and together, the couple have three children: Jack (b. 15 March 1999), Marie (b. 18 February 2001) and Ali (b. 7 September 2005). In April 2012 the couple announced they had split in late 2011. **Keith** Duffy became an acclaimed actor and presenter; with notable roles in the soap operas *Coronation Street* and *Fair City* (see television section). After the band split **Mikey** Graham suffered from depression but recovered to train as an actor in America, and then studied Music Technology and Sound Production after his solo career as a singer failed. Mikey was a contestant on *Dancing on Ice* in 2010. **Shane** Lynch married Easther Bennett, lead singer of Eternal, on 8 March 1998, but they separated in July 2000. Shane's sisters, twins Keavy and Edele Lynch, found fame as members of the girl group B*Witched, which became the first group to replace members of their own family at number one in the charts. Thus the Lynch family offshoots have enjoyed eleven No 1 UK singles (six for Boyzone, four for B*Witched and one for Eternal). Shane was in the second series of the Channel 4 reality television show, *The Games*, in 2004 and received a gold medal, showing good form as an athlete. A keen motor racing enthusiast, Shane raced a Marcos, TVR and then Mosler from 2002 to 2006 for the Eclipse Motorsport team in the British GT Championship, and came within a few laps of winning the 2003 British GT Championship at the last race of the season at Brands Hatch when he crashed into a spinning backmarker he was lapping. In recent years he has become an actor and played Eli Knox the chairman of Harchester United in the Sky One football drama, Dream Team. Shane became a Christian in 2003. He married singer Sheena White on 22 August 2007, and on 25 October 2008, Sheena gave birth to their daughter Billie Rae. **Stephen** Gately had initial success as a solo singer making his debut with the UK Top 10 double-A side *New Beginning/Bright Eyes* (No 3, Jun 2000) but Polydor eventually dropped him from their label. In December 2002, Stephen took the lead role in Bill Kenwright's new production of Tim Rice and Andrew Lloyd Webber's *Joseph and the Amazing Technicolor Dreamcoat*, which previewed in Oxford before moving to Liverpool over Christmas and finally to London's West End and the New London Theatre in Drury Lane in February 2003. From September 2004 until March

2005 he played the Child Catcher in *Chitty Chitty Bang Bang* at the London Palladium. Stephen was also in the second series of ITV's *Dancing on Ice* with his dancing partner Kristina Lenko. They went out in eighth place on 10 February 2007. He entered into a civil relationship in March 2006 with internet businessman Andrew Cowles. On 16 November 2007, Boyzone made a comeback appearance as part of *Children In Need* on BBC1 in the UK. They subsequently embarked on a tour tour beginning on 25 May 2008 at Belfast's Odyssey arena and finishing at Carlisle Bitts Park on 23 August 2008. *Love You Anyway* (No 5, Sep 2008 - No 3 in Ireland) continued their long run of Top 5 hit singles. In late summer 2009, Boyzone completed their Better Tour and on 10 October 2009, Stephen died while on holiday in Majorca, with his partner Andrew Cowles. The official verdict was death by natural causes, owing to an acute pulmonary oedema. In March 2010 the remaining quartet released the album 'Brother' in memory of Stephen. The album topped the UK and Irish charts and spawned the single *Gave It All Away* (No 9, Mar 2010) which topped the Irish Singles Chart. Boyzone are currently planning a 2013 tour to celebrate the 20th anniversary of the band forming.

Joe Brown see entry for The Shadows

Sam Brown see entry for The Shadows

Kate Bush Catherine "Kate" Bush (born Bexleyheath, Greater London, 30 July 1958) came to prominence, aged 19, with her chart-topping debut single *Wuthering Heights* (No 1, Feb 1978) her much-imitated high-pitched quirky voice and ethereal dance movements bringing something different to the pop scene. Interestingly, Kate's birthday is the same as Emily Jane Brontë (30 July 1818 – 19 December 1848), on whose novel of the same name the song was based. Kate's other Top 10 singles include: *Man with the Child in his Eyes* (No 6, Jun 1978), *Babooshka* (No 5, Jul 1980), *Running up that Hill* (No 3, Aug 1985), *Don't Give Up* (No 9, Nov 1986 - with Peter Gabriel) and King of the Mountain (No 4, Oct 2005). Kate has also had several successful albums: 'The Kick Inside' (No 3, Mar 1978), 'Lionheart' (No 6, Nov 1978), 'Never for Ever' (No 1, Sep 1980), 'The Dreaming' (No 3, Sep 1982), 'Hounds of Love' (No 1, Sep 1985), 'The Whole Story' (No 1, Nov 1986 - compilation), 'The Sensual World' (No 2, Jan 1989), The Red Shoes' (No 2, Nov 1993), 'Aerial' (No 3, Nov 2005), 'Director's Cut' (No 3, Nov 2005) and '50 Words for Snow' (No 5, Nov 2011).

Busted The pop/punk rock band began life under the name The Termites at the turn of the new Millennium, becoming Buster (after the name of a friend of the band's dog) and ultimately Busted after the original line-up disbanded leaving just James Bourne (born James Elliot Bourne, Rochford, Essex, 13 September 1983; guitar and vocals) and Matt Willis (born Matthew James Willis, Tooting, South London, 8 May 1983; drums and vocals). The duo initially recruited Tom Fletcher (see entry for McFly) as lead guitarist and vocalist, but he was later replaced by Charlie Simpson (born Charles Robert Simpson, Woodbridge, Suffolk, 7 June 1985). In early 2002 the trio signed to Universal and by August they had featured on the front cover of *Smash Hits* before releasing their debut single, *What I Go to School For* (No 3, Sep 2002) the following month. The lads then had a string of hits that either equalled or bettered this initial success: *Year 3000* (No 2, Jan 2003), *You Said No* (No 1, May 2003), *Sleeping with the Light On* (No 3, Aug 2003), *Crashed the Wedding* (No 1, Nov 2003), *Who's David* (No 1, Feb 2004), *Air Hostess* (No 2, Jun 2004) and *3AM / Thunderbirds Are Go!* (No 1, Jul 2004). Busted also featured on the chart-topping UK and Irish charity single *Do They Know It's Christmas?* (No 1, Nov 2004) as part of Band Aid 20. Both their studio albums 'Busted' (Sep 2002) and 'A Present for Everyone' (Nov 2003) peaked at No 2 on the UK Albums Chart although, as with their single releases, fared less well in Ireland. Their live album 'A Ticket for Everyone' (No 11, Nov 2004) contained twelve tracks recorded during the Manchester leg of their 'A Present for Everyone' tour, in March 2004. On Christmas Eve 2004, Charlie announced his departure from the band to concentrate more on Fightstar, an English alternative rock band from London, comprising guitarist and vocalist Alex Westaway, bassist Dan Haigh and drummer Omar Abidi, whose debut EP 'They Liked You Better When You Were Dead' released on February 28, 2005 through Sandwich Leg Records, proved a critical success. Charlie also released a solo acoustic album 'Young Pilgrim' which peaked at Nor 6 on the UK Albums Chart in 2011. The other two members of Busted decided to move on to other projects when Charlie left and James initially formed Son of Dork that had two single releases, *Ticket Outta Loserville* (No 3, Nov 2005) and *Eddie's Song* (No 10, Jan 2006). James, a big fan of the film *Back to the Future* like his friend Tom Fletcher, is now pursuing a solo career under the name of Future Boy, inspired by the film. After a brief stint in rehab (Matt has had both drug and alcohol problems) after the Busted split, Matt began a solo career and had three Top 20 UK hits on the Mercury label: *Up All Night* (No 7, May 2006), *Hey Kid* (No 11, Aug 2006) and *Don't Let It Go to Waste* (No 19, Dec 2006) featuring Imogen Heap on vocals. The last named single was the title track of his debut album and was released just days before Matt won the reality show *I'm a Celebrity... Get Me out of Here!* Since his jungle success Matt has begun a presenting career (see entries in the television section for *Britannia High*, and *I'm a Celebrity Get Me Out Of Here*). Matt married model and television presenter Emma Griffiths (born in Birmingham, 20 March 1976) in July 2008 and the pair have since frequently worked together. The couple have two children, a daughter Isabelle Catherine (b. 20 June 2009) and a son Ace Billy (b. 25 November 2011).

Captain Sensible see entry for The Damned

Carrott, Jasper see entry in the comedy section

Catatonia Welsh rock band formed in 1992 by vocalist Cerys Matthews (born Cerys Elizabeth Matthews, Cardiff, Wales, 11 April 1969) and guitarist Mark Roberts (born Llanrwst, Wales, 3 November 1969). In the embryonic stages the band had an ever-changing line-up but by the time of their chart success in the mid-1990s the remaining members were bassist Paul Jones (born Colwyn Bay, 5 February 1967), guitarist Owen Powell (born Cambridge, England, 9 July, 1969) and drummer Aled Richards (born Carmarthen, Wales, 5 July 1969). Dafydd Ieuan (born Bangor, Gwynedd, Wales, 1 March 1969) was a member of Catatonia from 1993-96 before joining Super Furry Animals (see separate entry). The band's first charting single, *Sweet Catatonia* (No 61, Feb 1996) was also the original name of the group but the oxymoronic adjective was dropped once they realised that Catatonia was in fact a very disturbing mental state of rigidity sometimes suffered by schizophrenics. Catatonia had three UK Top 10 singles: *Mulder and Scully* (No 3, Jan 1998) and *Road Rage* (No 5, May 1998) from their chart-topping album 'International Velvet' (No 1, Feb 1998) and *Dead from the Waist Down* (No 7, Apr 1999) from their follow-up album 'Equally Cursed and Blessed' (No 1, Apr 1999) which also topped the charts. After their third album 'Paper Scissors Stone' (No 6, Aug 2001) Cerys began to suffer from anxiety and nervous exhaustion due to the pressures of fronting a much-in-demand band. On 21 September 2001, the group officially disbanded. Mark, who had previously been in a long-term relationship with Cerys, teamed up again with Paul Jones in 2004, to form another Welsh band Sherbet Antlers, together with John Griffiths and Kevs Ford from the Welsh dance band Llwybr Llaethog. The duo later went on to form a new band - Y Ffyrc (meaning The Forks), this name interestingly being an anagram of Y Cyrff, the band they were in together prior to joining Catatonia. Owen became a judge on the S4C show *Wawffactor* (Wow Factor) throughout its run from 2003-06, the Welsh equivalent of *X Factor* famously seeing Duffy finishing runner-up, behind Lisa Pedrick, in the first series. Aled now drums for Cardiff-based Bristolian songstress Amy Wadge. Cerys had already been involved in projects outside the band before the split. In 1998 she collaborated with the Liverpudlian group Space on *The Ballad of Tom Jones* (No 4, Mar 1998) and the following year recorded with the man himself on *Baby, It's Cold Outside* (No 17, Dec 1999). After Catatonia broke up she moved to Nashville, Tennessee and began to work more anonymously in an environment that suited. She eventually married and had a child but subsequently divorced and moved back to her home in Pembrokeshire permanently. In 2007 Cerys appeared on ITV's *I'm a Celebrity... Get Me out of Here!*, coming fourth behind eventual winner, Christopher Biggins, but becoming involved with fellow contestant, former *Eastenders* actor Marc Bannerman. The relationship was short-lived. Cerys still records regularly but more recently she has presented various programmes for BBC radio. Her latest gig has been as guest mentor for the Tom Jones' team on the UK version of *The Voice*.

The Chemical Brothers Acid House and hip hop electronic music duo famous for sampling (taking a portion of an existing recording and reworking it into a different piece). Comprising Tom Rowlands (b. Kingston upon Thames, London, 11 January 1971) and Ed Simons (b. Herne Hill, South London, 9 June 1970), the two public school friends both attended the University of Manchester (basically because of their love for the Manchester music scene) and in 1992 began working as DJs under the name "The 237 Turbo Nutters" - after the number of their house on Dickenson Road, Manchester and a reference to their Blackburn raving days. By October 1994 they had moved to London and began producing their own instrumental hip hop tracks under the name The Dust Brothers. The following year they changed their name after the US production duo of the same name, famous for their work with the Beastie Boys, threatened legal action. The now familiar name was a corruption of one of their early tracks *Chemical Beats*. The change of name had immediate success as their fourth single (and first under their new identity) *Leave Home*, released on the Junior Boy's Own label, became the band's first UK chart hit, peaking at No 17. Oddly, it stayed at number 17 for 8 weeks, the most weeks a record has stayed at the same place, apart from chart-toppers. Their next single, *Life is Sweet*, featured the uncredited vocals of Tim Burgess of The Charlatans, and reached No 25 in September 1995. In the meantime they brought out their first album 'Exit Planet Dust' (No 9, Jul 1995) which featured both their Top 30 hits as well as *Chemical Beats*. 1996 was a big year for the duo. In January their *Loops of Fury* EP reached number 13 and this proved not to be unlucky for them as they signed to Virgin and their next single, *Setting Sun*, featuring the uncredited lead vocals of Noel Gallagher, entered the UK chart at No 1 in October 1996. Six months later their next single, *Block Rockin' Beats* (No 1, Apr 1997) containing a sample of Schoolly D's *Gucci Again* and re-working of the bassline from 23 Skidoo's single *Coup*, topped the UK chart and also won a 1997 Grammy Award for Best Rock Instrumental Performance. The Chemical Brother's next five studio albums all topped the UK chart, 'Dig Your Own Hole' (No 1, Apr 1997), 'Surrender' (No 1, Jul 1999), 'Come With Us' (No 1, Feb 2002), 'Push the Button' (No 1, Feb 2005) and 'We Are the Night' (No 1, Jul 2007). Their seventh album 'Further' was released in June 2010 but was deemed ineligible to chart in the UK due to all copies giving buyers the chance to win an iPad (UK chart regulations forbid merchandise or prizes being used as enticements to buy releases). Other Top 10 singles include: *Hey Boy Hey Girl* (No 3, Jun 1999), *Let Forever Be* (No 9, Aug 1999, featuring Noel Gallagher), *It Began in Afrika* (No 8, Sep 2001), *Star Guitar* (No 8, Jan 2002) and *Galvanize* (No 3, Jan 2005, featuring Q-Tip). Recently the duo has composed music for films such as *Black Swan* (2010) and *Hanna* (2011).

Chicory Tip Maidstone-based band consisting of vocalist Peter Hewson (born Gillingham, Kent, 1 September, 1945), guitarist Rick Foster (born Maidstone, Kent, 7 July 1946), bassist Barry Magyer (born Maidstone, Kent, 1 June 1946) and drummer Brian Shearer (born in Lewisham, 4 May 1951). Their debut charting single, *Son of My Father* (No 1, Jan 1972), written by Giorgio Moroder and Pete Bellotte, not only topped the UK Singles Chart but was also the first UK No 1 to feature a synthesiser. Foster left the band in October 1972 and was replaced by Rod Cloutt (born Gillingham, Kent, 26 January 1949). The group had two further Top 20 singles, *What's Your Name* (No 13, May 1972) and *Good Grief Cristina* (No 17, Mar 1973). Chicory Tip disbanded in 1975,

but later reformed to play gigs on the 1970s revival nostalgia circuit.

Chipmunk (born Jahmaal Noel Fyffe, Tottenham, London, 26 November 1990) is a hip hop rapper and songwriter, who shortened his stage name to Chips in January 2012. In 2008 he released his debut single, *Beast* (featuring Loick Essien) which despite no backing from his record label managed to register on the charts albeit a lowly No 181. After being rewarded with a MOBO Award later in the year he signed to the British arm of Columbia Records. His debut album 'I am Chipmunk' (No 2, Oct 2009) spawned the singles, *Chip Diddy Chip* (No 21, Mar 2009) notable for having introduced Chipmunk's trademark "che" vocalisation, and *Diamond Rings* (No 6, Jul 2009) featuring Scottish singer Emeli Sandé. The song samples *Miss Ska-Culation* by Roland Al and the Soul Brothers. The third official single from the album (*Beast* was only a promotional single), *Oopsy Daisy* (No 1, Oct 2009 and No 7 in Ireland) featuring vocals by R&B singer Dayo Olatunji, topped the UK Singles Chart beating The Saturdays who charted at Number 2 with *Forever Is Over*. Ironically the song contains the line "And now I feel like The Saturdays all week, cos me and my heart got crazy issues". The fourth official single from the album, *Look for Me* (No 5, Dec 2009) features vocals by Talay Riley. The album garnered platinum sales of over 300,000 copies and in-line with its sound sales, a new platinum edition of the album was released on May 3, 2010 featuring four new songs, including new single *Until You Were Gone* (No 3, Apr 2010) featuring Dutch singer-songwriter Esmee Denters. Chipmunk's second album 'Transition' (No 10, Apr 2011) spawned the Top 10 single *Champion* (No 2, Nov 2010) featuring American singer Chris Brown. He has also featured on *Tiny Dancer (Hold Me Closer)* (No 3, Apr 2009) a collaboration with British musician, DJ and rapper Ironik (see separate entry). Another Top 10 Chipmunk accreditation was as part of the Young Soul Rebels on the charity single, *I Got Soul* (No 10, Oct 2009) in aid of War Child. Chipmunk announced his signing to American rapper T.I's Grand Hustle Records in March 2012 following the conclusion of his two-album record deal with Columbia Records. In May 2012 Chips featured in the video for Tulisa's chart-topping debut solo single *Young*.

Chumbawamba Alternative music group formed in 1982 but not coming to national and international prominence until 1997 with the success of their album 'Tubthumper' (No 19, Sep 1997) which spawned the two Top 10 singles, *Tubthumping* (No 2, Aug 1997 and No 6 in USA) and *Amnesia* (No 10, Jan 1998). The personnel at the time of their greatest commercial success included Jude Abbott (trumpet and vocals), Dunston Bruce (percussion and vocals), Paul Greco (bass), Harry Hamer (drums), Danbert Nobacon (vocals), Alice Nutter (vocals), Allen 'Boff' Whalley (guitar) and Louise "Lou" Watts (keyboards). Chumbawamba was at the forefront of the 1980s anarcho-punk movement, frequently playing benefit gigs in squats and small halls for causes such as animal rights, the anti-war movement, and community groups. The group had a loyal fanbase while they were signed to the small One Little Indian label but once they signed to EMI just prior to their mainstream chart success many considered their capitalist decision-making was flying in the face of everything the band purported to stand for. Back on track, Chumbawamba are still performing to their simpatico fans. Incidentally, for those who don't know, Tubthumping is that song with the repetitive lyric "I Get Knocked Down but I Get Up Again, You're Never Gonna Keep Me Down"

Petula Clark see entry in the film section

Coldplay British alternative rock band formed in 1996 by lead vocalist Chris Martin (born Christopher Anthony John Martin, Exeter, Devon, 2 March 1977) and lead guitarist Jonny Buckland (born Jonathan Mark Buckland, Islington, London, 11 September 1977) at University College London (Chris graduated with First Class honours in Greek and Latin). Originally calling themselves

Pectoralz, the lads were joined by their classmate Guy Berryman (born Guy Rupert Berryman, Kirkcaldy, Scotland, 12 April 1978) on bass and Will Champion (born in Southampton, 31 July 1978) on drums; Will actually joining the band on his nineteenth birthday, by which time the band had changed its name to Starfish. Chris also recruited his longtime school friend Phil Harvey, who was studying classics at the University of Oxford, to be the band's manager and unofficial fifth member. After changing their name to Coldplay in 1998 they eventually signed to Parlophone in early 1999. Chris sacked Will in a fit of pique at this time but relented soon after and then assured the security of band members by announcing a future democracy on all decisions and an equal profit-sharing scheme on royalties. Their debut album 'Parachutes' (No 1, Jul 2000) topped the UK Albums Chart and won the 2001 BRIT Award for Best Album. It spawned their first charting single *Shiver* (No 35, Mar 2000) plus the Top 10 singles *Yellow* (No 4, Jul 2000) and *Trouble* (No 10, Nov 2000). Their second album 'A Rush of Blood to the Head' (No 1, Sep 2002) emulated the first by topping the chart and winning the 2003 BRIT Award for Best Album, but went one better by spawning three Top 10 singles: *In My Place* (No 2, Aug 2002), *The Scientist* (No 10, Nov 2002) and *Clocks* (No 9, Apr 2003). Coldplay's third album 'X&Y' (No 1, Jun 2005) became the best-selling album worldwide in 2005 and also gave them their first No 1 Stateside. The album spawned the singles *Speed of Sound* (No 2, May 2005), *Fix You* (No 4, Sep 2005) and *Talk* (No 10, Dec 2005) and won the 2006 BRIT Award for Best Album. The band's perfect record was maintained with their fourth studio album 'Viva la Vida or Death and All His Friends' (No 1, Jun 2008), produced by former Roxy Music keyboard and synthesiser player Brian Eno (born Brian Peter George St. John le Baptiste de la Salle Eno, Woodbridge, Suffolk, 15 May 1948), which debuted at number one in 36 countries, including the USA, and spawned the singles *Violet Hill* (No 8, May 2008) and their first chart-topping single *Viva la Vida* (No 1, May 2008 and No 1 in USA). The album won the Grammy for Best Rock Album at the 2009 Grammy Awards. The band's fifth studio album 'Mylo Xyloto' (No 1, Oct 2011) continued the production partnership with Eno and topped the charts of 30 countries including the USA. The album spawned the single *Every Teardrop Is a Waterfall* (No 6, Jun 2011) and their second chart-topper *Paradise* (No 1, Sep 2011). On 21 February 2012, Coldplay were awarded the BRIT Award for Best British group for the third time. Chris met American actress Gwyneth Paltrow in 2002 backstage at a Coldplay gig after the death of the actress's father, Bruce Paltrow. The couple married on 5 December 2003. They have two children, a daughter, Apple Blythe Alison Martin (born in London, 14 May 2004) and a son, Moses Bruce Anthony Martin (born in New York City, 8 April 2006). Actor Simon Pegg and Martin's bandmate Jonny Buckland are Apple's godfathers.

Billy Connolly see entry in the comedy section

The Cranberries Although never having a UK Top 10 hit single the Limerick-based alternative rock band are worthy of passing mention if only for the unequalled stage presence and much-copied lilting vocals of their lead vocalist Dolores O'Riordan (born Dolores Mary Eileen O'Riordan, Limerick, 6 September 1971) never shown to better effect than on the single *Zombie* (No 14, Oct 1994 and No 3 in Ireland). Interestingly, although the album from which *Zombie* was taken 'No Need to Argue' (No 2, Oct 1994) is often considered their finest album it was their debut album 'Everybody Else Is Doing It, So Why Can't We?' (No 1, Mar 1993) which topped the UK Albums Chart.

Cream Often referred to as the world's first successful supergroup, as all three members had a modicum of success with previous bands (Clapton with the Yardbirds and John Mayall & the Bluesbreakers, Bruce with Manfred Mann and Baker with Alexis Korner and Graham Bond), in actuality the term describes the member's subsequent attachments and the high regard in which they are held in the hierarchy of popular music. Jack Bruce, the Scottish lead vocalist and bass player was born John Symon Asher Bruce, in Bishopbriggs, East Dunbartonshire, on 14 May 1943; lead guitarist and backing vocalist Eric Clapton, was born

Eric Patrick Clapton, in Ripley Surrey, on 30 March 1945; and drummer Ginger Baker, was born Peter Edward Baker, in Lewisham, South London, on 19 August 1939. The idea for the group came about in July 1966 when Ginger invited Eric to join his new, yet unnamed, band. Eric agreed with the proviso that he also invited Jack Bruce. This was initially a sticking-point as all three had collaborated on various ventures previously and Ginger and Jack didn't get on, in fact when Jack was with the Graham Bond Organisation Ginger fired him from the band. Despite their previous problems the three united as Cream – the name unpretentiously indicating that they were already considered the "cream of the crop" amongst blues and jazz musicians. Cream made its unofficial debut at the Twisted Wheel on 29 July 1966 and two nights later made its official debut at the Sixth Annual Windsor Jazz & Blues Festival. Although the trio never had a Top 10 UK single during their two short years recording together their music influenced future generations of rockers and they popularised the use of the wah-wah pedal even before Jimi Hendrix. Their best known singles include: *Wrapping Paper* (No 34, Oct 1966, their debut single), *I Feel Free* (No 11, Dec 1966), *Strange Brew* (No 17, Jun 1967), *Anyone For Tennis* (No 40, Jun 1968), *Sunshine of Your Love* (No 25, Oct 1968 and their biggest US hit at No 5), *White Room* (No 28, Jan 1969) and *Badge* (No 18, Apr 1969), the last named being co-written by Eric Clapton and George Harrison (who also played rhythm guitar as 'L'Angelo Misterioso') with Ringo Starr supplying the line "I told you 'bout the swans, that they live in the park". Incidentally, the previously unnamed track from the 'Goodbye' album was so named after Eric misread George Harrison's writing of the word Bridge, which was merely a reference to the bridge section of the song! Cream were a very successful album group, their four studio LPs all making the UK Top 10; 'Fresh Cream' (No 6, Dec 1966) and 'Disraeli Gears' (No 5, Nov 1967), on the Reaction label; 'Wheels of Fire' (No 3, Aug 1968 but No 1 in USA and the world's first platinum-selling double album featuring the iconic Clapton guitar riff on the track *Crossroads*) and 'Goodbye' (No 1, Mar 1969) with Polydor. Their appropriately named final album topped the charts several months after they played their final gig in London on 26 November 1968. The frailty of the relationship between Bruce and Baker ultimately caused the break-up of the band and almost immediately Eric and Ginger recruited ex Spencer Davis Group and Traffic frontman Steve Winwood (born Stephen Lawrence Winwood, Handsworth, Birmingham, 12 May 1948) and ex Family bassist Rick Grech (born Richard Roman Grech, Bordeaux, France, 1 November 1946; died of kidney failure due to alcoholism 17 March 1990) to form Blind Faith – sometimes attributed to be the first so-called "super-group". In fact Eric had already played with Winwood in his 1966 band Eric Clapton and the Powerhouse, perhaps a precursor of the super-group genre, with Paul Jones playing harmonica with the group. The short-lived Blind Faith collaboration produced one album 'Blind Faith' which topped the charts in September 1969. Eric then went on to play with The Plastic Ono Band, Delaney & Bonnie, and Derek and the Dominos with which he had a Top 10 hit with *Layla* (No 7, Aug 1972). His subsequent Top 10s include: *I Shot the Sheriff* (No 9, Jul 1974), a reissue of *Layla* (No 4, Mar 1982), *Tears in Heaven* (No 5, Feb 1992, inspired by the death of his four-year-old son Conor, who fell from the 53rd floor of the East 57th Street NYC apartment where he lived with his mother) and *Love Can Build a Bridge* (No 1, Mar 1995) a collaboration with Cher, Chrissie Hynde and Ninah Cherry released in aid of Comic Relief. Eric also had success with the albums '461 Ocean Boulevard' (No 3, Aug 1974 but No 1 in USA), 'No Reason to Cry' (No 8, Sep 1976), 'Slowhand' (No 23, Nov 1977 but No 2 in USA), 'Behind the Sun' (No 8, Mar 1985), 'August' (No 3, Dec 1986), 'Journeyman' (No 2, Nov 1989) , 'Unplugged' (No 2, Sep 1992), 'From the Cradle' (No 1, Sep 1994), 'Pilgrim' (No 6, Mar 1998), 'Reptile' (No 7, Mar 2001), 'Me and Mr Johnson' (No 10, Apr 2004) and 'Clapton' (No 7, Oct 2010). Ginger, Steve and Rick then formed Ginger Baker's Air Force, a jazz-rock fusion band which also included ex Moody Blues guitarist Denny Laine (born Brian Frederick Arthur Hines, Birmingham, 29 October 1944) and musical innovator Graham Bond (born Graham John Clifton Bond, Romford, Essex, 28 October 1937; died under the wheels of a train at Finsbury Park station, London, 8 May 1974 in a probable suicide induced by depression and chronic drug addiction).

Culture Club Band formed in London in 1981 amid the burgeoning New Romantic movement, based around flamboyant, eccentric fashion and 'New Wave' music, the group's founder, Boy George (born George Alan O'Dowd, Bexley, Kent, 14 June 1961 – to Irish parents) epitomising all the elements of the movement. Prior to the formation of Culture Club, George had been supplying guest vocals (under the name Lieutenant Lush) for the Malcolm McLaren-managed Bow Wow Wow, a group of good looking former Adam and the Ants' musicians who were fronted by Annabella Lwin (born Myint Myint Aye – translates as High High Cool - in Yangon, Myanmar, 31 October 1966) and were set up to promote the fashion lines of McLaren's business partner Vivienne Westwood. Annabella began to resent George's dominance within the group and the friction prompted him to enlist bassist Mikey Craig (born Michael Emile Craig, Hammersmith, London, 15 February 1960), drummer Jon Moss (born Jonathan Aubrey Moss, Wandsworth, London, 11 September 1957) and guitarist Roy Hay (born Roy Ernest Hay, Southend, Essex, 12 August 1961) to form Culture Club, the name deriving from the diverse backgrounds and ethnicities of its members. Signed to the Virgin label, the group's first two singles, *White Boy* and *I'm Afraid of Me*, both failed to chart but their third single, the reggae-influenced *Do You Really Want to Hurt Me* (No 1, Sep 1982) topped the charts in the UK, Ireland, several European countries and Canada, eventually peaking at No 2 in the USA in early 1983. Helen Terry (born 25 May 1956) supplied backing vocals on this and several other Culture Club tracks. The group's first album 'Kissing to Be Clever' (No 5, Oct 1982) contained all three previously released singles. Their next single, *Time (Clock of the Heart)* (No 3, Nov 1982 and No 4 in Ireland) again performed well all over the world, having its highest peak, No 2, on the American Billboard Hot 100. A string of hits followed, including: *Church of the Poison Mind* (No 2, April 1983), *Karma Chameleon* (No 1, Sep 1983 – also No 1 in Ireland and USA), *Victims* (No 3, Dec 1983) and *It's a Miracle* (No 4, Mar 1984) all tracks from their chart-topping second album 'Colour By Numbers' (No 1, Oct 1983) which also peaked at No 2 in the USA. *The War Song* (No 2, Oct 1984) from the album 'Waking Up with the House on Fire' (No 2, Nov 1984) topped the Irish Singles Chart and *Move Away* (No 7, Mar 1986) from the album 'From Luxury to Heartache' (No 10, Apr 1986) became their last Top 10 single before splitting due to friction between George and Jon but also because of George's cocaine and heroin addiction. In 1998, George and Jon put their differences aside and the band reunited for a short tour, subsequently scoring a UK Top 10 single with *I Just Wanna Be Loved* (No 4, Oct 1998). The group's manager, Tony Gordon, has stated on several occasions that Culture Club may reunite in the future. As a solo artist George has had typical severe highs and lows, his melodic style, often classified as blue-eyed soul, heard at its best on his chart-topping first solo release, *Everything I Own* (No 1, Mar 1987 and No 1 in Ireland). Although he has had no further Top 10 success to-date he formed Jesus Loves You, a band that produced a mixture of electronic dance music, Indian classical music and western pop music between 1989 and 1992, their best known single being, *Bow Down Mister* (No 27, Feb 1991) released on the More Protein label. George has also been involved in numerous charity releases, including *Do They Know It's Christmas* (1984) for Bandaid, *Let It Be* (1987) for Ferry Aid, *Wishing Well* (1987) for G.O.S.H, *What's Going On* (1989) for Life Aid Armenia and *Grief Never Grows Old* (2006) for One World Project. In 1995, Kirk Brandon sued George for libel claiming that George mentioned a non-existent love affair between them in George's autobiography, *Take It Like a Man* (1995). George won the court case and Brandon was ordered to pay £200,000 in costs. Brandon subsequently declared himself bankrupt, which resulted in George paying over £60,000 in legal fees. In 2002, George was portrayed as one of the leading protagonists in the West End musical *Taboo*. His character was originally played by Euan Morton whilst George himself played Leigh Bowery for a time both in the London show and on Broadway. In December 2008, George was convicted in Snaresbrook Crown Court, London, of the assault and false imprisonment of Audun Carlsen. The following month he was sentenced to 15 months' imprisonment for these offences. Initially sent to HMP Pentonville in London, George was later transferred to the Category C HMP Edmunds Hill in Newmarket, Suffolk. In May 2009, George was released after serving four months of his sentence and was required to wear an ankle monitor for 90 days. In December 2009, George had his request to appear on the final series of Channel 4's *Celebrity Big Brother* turned down by the Probation Service. George was portrayed on film by Douglas Booth in the BBC2 drama documentary *Worried About the Boy* (2010). Apart from the much-publicised fling with Kirk Brandon, George also had a relationship with band member Jon Moss but is probably even more famous for his friendship with pop singer Peter Robinson (born Kingston, Jamaica, 3 November 1962), better known as Marilyn, who had a No 4 UK single in November 1983 with *Calling Your Name*.

Curved Air Five-piece progressive rock band formed in 1970 from previous members of Sisyphus: Darryl Way (b. Taunton, Somerset, 17 December 1948; electronic violin), Francis Monkman (b. Hampstead, North London, 9 June 1949; keyboards and guitar), Florian Pilkington-Miksa (b. Roehampton, South West London, 3 June 1950; drums) and Rob Martin - replaced as bassist by Ian Eyre (b. Knaresborough, Harrogate, North Yorkshire, 11 September 1949) before recording - who were joined by former Strawb vocalist Sonja Kristina (b. Brentwood, Essex, 14 April 1949) who became the mainstay of the band. The band was named after the album 'A Rainbow in Curved Air' by American composer Terry Riley. In December 1970 their debut album 'Air Conditioning' reached No 8 in the UK chart, on the Warner Brothers label, and in August 1971 *Back Street Luv* peaked at No 4 in the UK singles chart. Although regarded as a one-hit-wonder, as indeed the band never had another chart entry, this song, written by Ian, Sonja and Darryl, with its driving beat and haunting melody, was one of the most memorable of the decade. Incidentally, Darryl Way, though the chief writer of the song, did not play on the original recording. Original band members had gone their separate ways by the mid-1970s although with ever-changing line-ups the group staggered on through most of the decade, Sonja by now being the only original member. Stewart Copeland became the band's drummer in 1974 and remained with them for two years prior to forming The Police. He married Sonja in 1982 but they divorced in 1991. Francis became a founding member of Sky in 1978 and composed the soundtrack for the film *The Long Good Friday*. Curved Air reunited briefly in 1990 and again in 2008 although by now Sonja had toned down her sexy on-stage act somewhat.

Jim Dale see entry in the film section

The Damned Punk rock band formed in London in 1976 and notable for being the first of the genre from the UK to release a single, *New Rose* (No 81, Oct 1976) and an album 'Damned Damned Damned' (No 36, Feb 1977). The Damned's only Top 10 success was with *Eloise* (No 3, Feb 1986) a cover of the earlier Paul and Barry Ryan hit. At various times the band have included bassist Captain Sensible (born Raymond Ian Burns, Balham, London, 24 April 1954; famous for his red beret and chart-topping solo hit, *Happy Talk*, in June 1982), drummer Rat Scabies (born Christopher Millar, Kingston upon Thames, 30 July 1957; famous for being the central character of the book *Rat Scabies And The Holy Grail*, written by former music journalist Christopher Dawes), lead vocalist Dave Vanian (born David Lett, Hemel Hempstead, Hertfordshire, 12 October 1956; famous for being one of the early influences for British Goth fashion and also for being an erstwhile grave digger), guitarist Brian James (born Brian Robertson, Hammersmith, west London, 18 February 1955; famous for being a member of the Crawley-based garage band Bastard and punk band London SS, who included musicians who later found fame in The Clash and Generation X), keyboard player Monty Oxy Moron (born Montgomery Gillan, Brighton, East Sussex, 27 September 1961; famous for being a former member of Punk Floyd), American bass guitarist Patricia Morrison (born in Los Angeles, California, 14 January 14; famous for being a member of Sisters of Mercy and for marrying Dave Vanian in 1996), bassist Stu West (born in Lincolnshire, 24 December 1964; famous for replacing Morrison when she retired after giving birth in 2004) and drummer Pinch (born Andrew Pinching, Grantham, Lincolnshire, 5 September 1965; famous for being a current member alongside Dave, Monty, Stu and the Captain).

Def Leppard Heavy-metal rock band formed at Tapton School in Sheffield in 1977, initially known as Atomic Mass. After several personnel changes the group settled on the Sheffield-born trio Rick 'Sav' Savage (born 2 December 1960; bass), Pete Willis (born 16 February 1960; guitar) and Joe Elliott (born 1 August 1959; lead vocals), and after changing their name, firstly to Deaf Leopard and ultimately Def Leppard, they recruited drummer Rick Allen (born in Dronfield, Derbyshire, 1 November 1963) and guitarist Steve Clark (born in Sheffield, 23 April 1960; d. 8 January 1991). In July 1982 Pete Willis was fired for drinking on the job and was replaced by Phil Collen (born in Hackney, London, 8 December 1957) former guitarist with the glam band Girl. On 31 December 1984, Rick Allen lost his left arm in a car crash on the A57 in Sheffield, when his Corvette swerved off the road on a sharp bend and went through a drystone wall. Despite the severity of the accident, Rick was committed to continuing his role as Def Leppard's drummer, and worked with Simmons to design a customised electronic drum kit which enabled him to use his feet as well as his remaining arm. Although the band never sought a replacement drummer, in August 1986 Jeff Rich was brought in to play alongside Rick but after missing a gig accidentally the band realised that Rick was able to play a full function within the band and Jeff left to join Status Quo. The next tragedy the band had to overcome was the death of Steve Clark in January 1991. Steve had been in and out of rehab for some time as his drinking escalated out of control and he had been given leave of absence to sort himself out six months before his death, from a mixture of excessive alcohol with anti-depressants and painkillers. To this point Def Leppard had released the successful albums 'On Through the Night (No 15, Mar 1980), 'Pyromania' (No 18, Mar 1983) and the chart-topping 'Hysteria' (No 1, Aug 1987) and they decided to release 'Adrenalize' (No 1, Apr 1992) as a quartet after the death of Clark, and as with 'Hysteria' it topped the charts on both sides of the Atlantic. In the month the album topped the charts Def Leppard recruited Irish rock guitarist Viv Campbell (born in Belfast, 25 August 1962) who had been a member of Whitesnake since 1987. The present line-up has now been established for twenty years. Despite being a typical rock band, Def Leppard have charted in the Top 10 three times: *Animal* (No 6, Aug 1987), *Let's Get Rocked* (No 2, Mar 1992) and *When Love & Hate Collide* (No 2, Oct 1995). On 23 October 1995, the band entered the *Guinness Book of World Records* by performing three concerts in three continents in one day (Tangiers, Morocco; London, England; and Vancouver, Canada).

Cathy Dennis The singer-songwriter, record producer and actress, is one of the unsung heroines of the pop world. Catherine Roseanne Dennis was born in Norwich on 25 March 1969. At the age of 17 she was signed to Simon Fuller's 19 Management Company after being spotted recording Stevie Wonder-influenced demos at The Kitchen in Norwich. At the time she was working for Norwich Union but had gained a lot of musical experience playing gigs with her father's Alan Dennis Band at British holiday camps. Cathy's initial chart success was in collaboration with British house music producer Daniel Kojo Poku (aka Dancin' Danny D) under the name D Mob. Her debut single *C'Mon And Get My Love* (No 15, Oct 1989 and No 10 in USA) and follow-up *That's The Way of the World* (No 48, Apr 1990) established her as a relevant artist and she then produced a solo album on the Polydor label 'Move to This' (No 3, Aug 1991) which spawned four singles, *Touch Me (All Night Long)* (No 5, May 1991 and No 2 in USA), *Just Another Dream* (No 13, Jul 1991 and No 9 in USA), *Too Many Walls* (No 17, Oct 1991 and No 8 in USA) and

Everybody Move (No 25, Dec 1991). Her second album 'Into the Skyline' (No 8, Jan 1993) was released in December 1992 and featured the singles *You Lied to Me* (No 34, Aug 1992), *Irresistible* (No 24, Nov 1992), *Falling* (No 32, Feb 1993) and *Why* (No 23, Feb 1994) - the latter being credited to D Mob with Cathy Dennis. Her third album 'Am I the Kinda Girl?' was released in 1996. It was a diversion from the dance-pop sound of her previous releases and was more in line with the Britpop trend and featured collaborations with Guy Chambers of The Lemon Trees and Andy Partridge of XTC. Although failing to chart in the Top 75 it did spawn the singles *West End Pad* (No 25, Aug 1996), *Waterloo Sunset* (No 11, Mar 1997) and *When Dreams Turn to Dust* (No43, Jun 1997). In 1999, Cathy turned her hand to acting, appearing alongside S Club 7 in episode 8 of their TV series *Miami 7* in which she played an actress starring as the lead role in a fictional show called "Alien Hunter". Cathy then turned her attention to writing songs for other artists, mainly those on the books of Simon Fuller. She had already written one of the songs (*Find the Key to Your Life* featuring David Morales) for the 1991 film *Teenage Mutant Ninja Turtles II the Secret of the Ooze* and also co-wrote (with D Mob and Paul Taylor) an album track *Love's on Every Corner* for Dannii Minogue's second album 'Get into You' (1993). To-date she has written, or co-written, eight UK No 1 singles: *Never Had a Dream Come True* (S Club 7 2000), *Have You Ever* (S Club 7 2001), *Can't Get You Out of My Head* (Kylie Minogue 2001), *Anything Is Possible* (Will Young 2002), *Toxic* (Britney Spears 2004), *About You Now* (Sugababes 2007), *I Kissed a Girl* (Katy Perry 2008 - also No 1 in USA) and *Once* (Diana Vickers 2010). Cathy has won five Ivor Novello Awards, written several other Top 10 songs on both sides of the Atlantic and just for good measure wrote the theme song to the television series *American Idol*.

Dire Straits Rock band, formed in 1977 by former journalist and teacher Mark Knopfler (born Mark Freuder Knopfler, in Glasgow, 12 August 1949) which had an ever-changing personnel until they disbanded in 1995; John Illsley (born in Leicester, 24 June 1949) being the only other constant member. Dire Straits had four chart-topping albums 'Love Over Gold' (Oct 1982), 'Brothers in Arms' (May 1985), 'Money for Nothing' (Oct 1988) and 'On Every Street' (Sep 1991). Other Top 10 albums included: 'Communique' (No 5, Jun 1979), 'Making Movies' (No 4, Oct 1980), 'Alchemy – Dire Straits Live' (No 3, Mar 1984) and 'On the Night' (No 4, May 1993). Their single successes include: *Sultans of Swing* (No 8, Mar 1979), *Romeo and Juliet* (No 8, Jan 1981), *Private Investigations* (No 2, Sep 1982), *Money for Nothing* (No 4, Jul 1985) and *Walk of Life* (No 2, Jan 1986). Released in May 1985, *Brothers in Arms* entered the UK Albums Chart at No 1 and spent a total of 228 weeks in the charts. It went on to become the best-selling album of 1985 in the UK and was similarly successful in the US, peaking at No 1 on Billboard 200 for nine weeks, going multi-platinum and selling nine million copies. Mark's family settled in his mother's home town of Blyth, Northumberland when he was seven-years-old and many of his songs reflect his North Eastern upbringing.

Ken Dodd see entry in the comedy section

Pete Doherty Pete Doherty (born in Hexham, Northumberland, 12 March 1979) is a talented musician, writer, actor, poet and artist but unfortunately is probably best known for his troubled personal life. Pete's father was of Irish Catholic descent. He was an officer in the British army which meant Pete grew up flitting between garrisons at home and overseas. He did well at school and at sixteen won a poetry competition and was rewarded with a tour of Russia organised by the British Council (Pete's mother is of Jewish Russian descent). He initially got a job as a grave-filler at Willesden Cemetery. After dropping out of university he moved into a London flat (they nicknamed the Camden Road flat "The Delaney Mansions") with friend and fellow musician Carl Barât (born Carl Ashley Raphael Barât, Basingstoke, Hampshire, 6 June 1978) with whom he founded The Libertines (named after the Marquis de Sade's novel *Lusts of the Libertines*) in 1997. The two guitarist/vocalists shared front-man duties and recruited bassist John Hassall (born John Cory Hassall, in London, 17 February

1981) and drummer Gary Powell (born Gary Armstrong Powell, New York, 11 November 1969). The band's second album 'The Libertines' (No 1, Aug 2004) topped the UK Albums Chart and spawned the Top 10 single *Can't Stand Me Now* (No 2, Aug 2004). The group disbanded in 2004 but reunited in 2010 to play a series of shows, including slots at the 2010 Reading and Leeds Festivals. Before the break-up of The Libertines, Pete had already formed indie band, Babyshambles. The band's line-up underwent several changes before eventually stabilizing in late summer of 2004 with Pete on vocals and guitar, Patrick Walden on guitar, Gemma Clarke on drums and Drew McConnell on bass. On the night Babyshambles were due to play their first gig, Pete was arrested for burglary; his victim none other than his Libertine co-founder Carl Barât. After serving two months of a six-month sentence Pete was met at the gate by Carl and initially began playing again with the Libertines but the rivalry between the two front-men inevitably caused friction. Eventually concentrating solely on Babyshambles, the band was constantly overshadowed by Pete's drug addiction and criminal behaviour. On one occasion, the band walked off the stage when it became obvious that Doherty was too drunk to perform. A riot ensued at the London Astoria when Pete failed to turn up at all. The band's debut album, 'Down In Albion' (No 10, Nov 2005) spawned the singles *Killamangiro* (No 8, Nov 2004), *Fuck Forever* (No 4, Aug 2005) and *Albion* (No 8, Nov 2005). In August 2006, Babyshambles signed to Parlophone and three months later released *Janie Jones*, a cover of the Clash song. It reached No 17 and profits went to Joe Strummer's charity. Two more singles *Beg, Steal Or Borrow* and *The Blinding* were limited editions available only to attendees at a festival and buyers of *The Big Issue*. On 1 October 2007 Babyshambles released the album 'Shotter's Nation' (No 5, Oct 2007) which spawned the singles *Delivery* (No 6, Sep 2007) and *You Talk* (No 54, Dec 2007). A third album track, *Side of the Road*, released in 2010, failed to chart at all. The present line-up includes: lead guitarist Mick Whitnall, bass guitarist Drew McConnell and former Supergrass drummer Danny Goffey. In June 2007 Orion published *The Books of Albion: The Collected Writings of Peter Doherty*, a collection of journals in which Pete records poetry, drawings, and photos over the course of his career. He has also had art exhibitions in London and Paris, which caused controversy due to artworks made with Pete's own blood. More recently Pete has completed his role as Octave in the French film *La confession d'un enfant du siècle* (Confession of a Child of the Century) starring alongside Charlotte Gainsbourg and Lily Cole. Pete met model Kate Moss (see entry in miscellaneous section) in January 2005 at Kate's 31st birthday party and the couple had an on-off relationship for two years before briefly becoming engaged in October 2007. Pete has a son, Astile Louis Doherty (born Camden, London, 12 July 2003) with singer Lisa Moorish (born 1972, Walworth, London) who also has a daughter, Molly (b. March 1998) fathered by Liam Gallagher.

Lonnie Donegan Anthony James Donegan was born in Glasgow, Scotland on 29 April 1931. He took his stage name from US blues singer Lonnie Johnson. He joined Ken Colyer's jazzmen on guitar and banjo in 1952, leaving to join Chris Barber's Jazz Band in 1954. Lonnie then formed his own band (the Lonnie Donegan Skiffle Group) and shot to fame when *Rock Island Line* (No 8, Jan 1956) made the Top 10 on both sides of the Atlantic. Over the next six years he managed 17 Top 10 hits including three No 1s: *Cumberland Gap* (Apr 1957), *Gamblin' Man/Putting on the Style* (Jun 1957) and *My Old Man's a Dustman* (Mar 1960). *The Lonnie Donegan Show* was always high in the television ratings and the 'King of Skiffle' (Lonnie's version of American Folk Music dubbed 'Skiffle' because of its jazz content) was the most influential and successful British act of the pre-Beatles era. Whether it was singing doleful melodies such as *Tom Dooley* (No 3, Nov 1958) and *I Wanna Go Home* (No 5, May 1960) or rousing songs such as *Does Your Chewing Gum Lose It's Flavour (On the Bedpost Overnight)* (No 3, Feb 1959) and *The Battle of New Orleans* (No 2, Jun 1959), he established a unique style of

performance and also popularised the sale of his trademark 'Martin' guitars all over the world. His other well-known singles included: *Lost John* (No 2, Apr 1956), *Bring A Little Water Sylvie/Dead or Alive* (No 7, Sep 1956), *Don't You Rock Me Daddy-O* (No 4, Jan 1957), *My Dixie Darling* (No 10, Oct 1957), *Grand Coolie Dam* (No 6, Apr 1958), *Lorelei* (No 10, Aug 1960), *Have A Drink On Me* (No 8, May 1961), *Michael Row the Boat/Lumbered* (No 6, Aug 1961), *The Comancheros* (No 14, Jan 1962) and *Pick A Bale Of Cotton* (No 11, Aug 1962). Lonnie suffered from heart problems for many years but made a very successful tour of Britain and America in the late 1990s, often fronting the concerts of life-long fan Van Morrison. He was awarded the MBE in 2000 and died 3 November 2002, midway through a successful British tour.

Charlie Drake see entry in the comedy section

Duran Duran New Romantic band formed in 1978 by John Taylor (born Nigel John Taylor, 20 June 1960; bass), Nick Rhodes (born Nicholas James Bates, 8 June 1962; keyboards) and Stephen Duffy (born Stephen Anthony James Duffy, 30 May 1960) who were joined the following year by Roger Andrew Taylor (born 26 April 1960; drums) and Andy Arthur Taylor (born 16 February 1961, Cullercoats, Tyne and Wear; guitar), the first non Birmingham-born member of the band. The lads became the resident band at the famous Birmingham Rum Runner nightclub. There were several other nightclubs in close proximity, and one was called Barbarella's. They would go on to name the band after the villain from *Barbarella* (1968), Roger Vadim's cult science-fiction film starring Jane Fonda in the title role. The villain, played by Milo O'Shea, is named "Dr. Durand Durand". Stephen left Duran Duran in 1979 for a solo career and after forming the band Tin Tin in 1982 he became known as Stephen 'Tin Tin' Duffy. He later collaborated with Alex James of Blur, Justin Welch of Elastica (drums), and Alex's friend Charlie Bloor to form the short-lived group Me Me Me; the band's first, and only single, *Hanging Around* was released on August 5, 1996 and reached No 19 on the UK Singles Chart. In 1980 Simon Le Bon (born Simon John Charles Le Bon, Bushey, Hertfordshire, 27 October 1958) signed up to Duran Duran as lead vocalist. Simon first appeared on our television screens in a Persil ad when he was six-years-old. Incidentally, none of the Taylors are related, and Roger Taylor is not to be confused with the Queen drummer of the same name. After signing to EMI, *Planet Earth*, their first charting single, rose to No 12 in Feb 1981. Other successful singles include: *Girls on Film* (No 5, Jul 1981), *Hungry Like the Wolf* (No 5, May 1982), *Save a Prayer* (No 2, Aug 1982), *Rio* (No 9, Nov 1982), *Is There Something I Should Know* (No 1, Mar 1983), *Union of the Snake* (No 3, Oct 1983), *New Moon on Monday* (No 9, Feb 1984), *The Reflex* (No 1, Apr 1984 and No 1 in Ireland and USA), *Wild Boys* (No 2, Nov 1984), *A View to a Kill* (No 2, May 1985 but No 1 in USA), *Notorious* (No 7, Nov 1986), *All She Wants Is* (No 9, Jan 1989), *Ordinary World* (No 6, Jan 1993), *Electric Barbarella* (No 23, Jan 1999) and *What Happens Tomorrow* (No 11, Jan 2005). They also had one chart-topping album, *Seven and the Ragged Tiger* (No 1, Dec 1983 and No 8 in USA). The band still play together although Andy Taylor left in 2006, and was replaced by London guitarist Dom Brown as a session player and touring member. Arcadia was the offshoot group formed in 1985 by Simon Le Bon, Nick Rhodes and Roger Taylor, during a break in Duran Duran's schedule. They had a Top 10 hit with *Election Day* (No 7, Oct 1985). Meanwhile, the other two members of Duran Duran (John Taylor and Andy Taylor) joined Power Station, fronted by Robert Palmer (born Robert Allen Palmer, Batley, West Yorkshire, 19 January 1949; d. 26 September 2003) although Roger Taylor also provided percussion on more than one occasion. Soon after the successful single *Some Like It Hot* (No 14, Mar 1985) the group disbanded and Robert went on to have a very successful solo career with hits such as *Addicted to Love* (No 5, May 1986), *I Didn't Mean to Turn You On* (No 9, Jul 1986), *She Makes My Day* (No 6, Oct 1988), *I'll Be Your Baby Tonight* (No 6, Nov 1990) and *Mercy*

Mercy Me – I Want You (No 9, Jan 1991). Simon famously married model Yasmin Parvaneh (born in Oxford, 29 October 1964) on 27 December 1985. They have three daughters: Amber Rose Tamara (b. August 25, 1989 – now a model), Saffron Sahara (b. 25 September 1991) and Tallulah Pine (b. 10 September 1994). Simon is also famous for being the original 'Rock Star Sailor' drawing international media attention after his maxi yacht, Drum, lost her keel and capsized during the Fastnet race, just off Falmouth, Cornwall. Before being rescued, he and other crew members were trapped underwater, inside the hull, for forty minutes. Despite the accident, Simon participated in the 1985-1986 Whitbread Round the World Race, coming in third overall in elapsed time, Drum being skippered by Skip Novak.

Sophie Ellis-Bextor Sophie Michelle Ellis-Bextor was born in London on 10 April 1979, the daughter of film director Robin Bextor and actress and presenter, Janet Ellis. Sophie's parents divorced when she was four-years-old. The singer, song-writer and model first appeared on television aged six, in an episode of the children's magazine programme *Blue Peter*, hosted by her mother. At the age of thirteen Sophie appeared with the W11 Children's Opera. Her musical career began in 1997 with a band called theaudience (*sic*). Their one and only album 'theaudience' (No 22, Aug 1998) was preceded by the tracks, *I Got the Wherewithal* (No 170, Oct 1997), *If You Can't Do It When You're Young; When Can You Do It?* (No 48, Feb 1998), *A Pessimist Is Never Disappointed* (No 27, May 1998) and *I Know Enough (I Don't Get Enough)* (No 25, Jul 1998). Sophie also sang on *Black Holes for the Young* the B-side of the Manic Street Preachers' 1998 single *The Everlasting*. After theaudience split up in December 1998 Sophie took a year out from singing and auditioned for the role of Satine in the film *Moulin Rouge!*, a part which eventually went to Nicole Kidman. She next collaborated with Italian DJ Cristiano Spiller by adding vocals to his then-instrumental club track *Groovejet* (No 1, Aug 2000). This chart-topping success attracted record labels and in October 2000 Sophie signed with Polydor as a solo artist, her debut album 'Read My Lips' (No 2, Sep 2001) showing off her deliciously quirky voice to good effect by spawning four successful singles, *Take Me Home* (No 2, Aug 2001), *Murder on the Dancefloor* (No 2, Dec 2001 and No 1 in Russia), *Get Over You/Move This Mountain* (No 3, Jun 2002) and *Music Gets the Best of Me* (No 14, Nov 2002). Her second album 'Shoot from the Hip' (No 19, Oct 2003) produced two Top 10 singles, *Mixed Up World* (No 7, Oct 2003) and *I Won't Change You* (No 9, Dec 2003). August 2006 saw Sophie announced as the new face of high street fashion chain, Monsoon. In 2007, her third album 'Trip the Light Fantastic' (No 7, May 2007) produced three singles, *Catch You* (No 8, Feb 2007), *Me and My Imagination* (No 23, May 2007) and *Today the Sun's on Us* (No 64, Aug 2007). In May 2008 Sophie was hired by cosmetics brand Rimmel as one of their new faces and later that year (Aug 24) Sophie performed a live cover version of Carly Simon's *Nobody Does It Better* outside Buckingham Palace as part of the Visa London 2012 Handover Party in the Mall. Her fourth studio album 'Make a Scene' (No 33, Apr 2011) was less successful than her others despite the lead single, *Heartbreak (Make Me a Dancer)*, a collaboration with production team the Freemasons, peaking at number 13 on the UK singles chart in July 2009 and another track, *Bittersweet* (No 25, May 2010) also performing well in the charts. Sophie and her husband, bass guitarist (with The Feeling) Richard Jones, married on 25 June 2005 in Italy. Their first two children, Sonny (b. 23 April 2004) and Kit (b. 5 November 2008) were both born prematurely and their third child, Ray Holiday was born on 25 April 2012.

Jennifer Ellison see entry in the miscellaneous section

Emerson, Lake and Palmer Progressive rock supergroup founded in 1970, consisting of Keith Emerson (born Keith Noel Emerson, Todmorden, West Yorkshire, 2 November 1944; keyboards), Greg Lake (born Gregory Stuart Lake, Poole, Dorset, 10 November 1947; bass guitar, vocals, guitar) and Carl Palmer (born Carl Frederick Kendall Palmer, Handsworth, Birmingham, 20 March 1950; drums, percussion). The ELP sound is dominated by the Hammond organ and Moog synthesiser of the flamboyant Emerson. The band's compositions are influenced across its genres of hard rock, jazz and classical music as epitomised by their only Top 10 UK single *Fanfare for the Common Man* (No 2, Jun 1977), Adapted by Keith Emerson from Aaron Copland's 1942 piece of the same name. ELP's successful albums include: 'Tarkus' (No 1, Jun 1971), 'Pictures at an Exhibition' (No 3, Dec 1971), 'Trilogy' (No 2, Jul 1972) and 'Brain Salad Surgery' (No 2, Dec 1973). The band split in 1979 but Keith and Greg reunited in 1986 with Cozy Powell taking over drumming duties from Carl Palmer. Carl returned the following year and former Rainbow drummer Cozy Powell (see entry for Whitesnake) joined Black Sabbath in 1988 before dying in a car crash while driving his Saab 9000 at 104 mph (167 km/h) in bad weather on the M4 motorway near Bristol on 5 April 1998. ELP are still gigging sporadically. Keith Emerson began his career with Nice, Greg Lake with King Crimson alongside Robert Fripp (born Wimborne Minster, Dorset, 16 May 1946), Peter John Sinfield (born Fulham, London, 27 December 1943), Ian McDonald (born Osterley, Middlesex, 25 June 1946) and Michael Giles (born Waterlooville, Hampshire, 1 March 1942) who together made the iconic album 'In the Court of the Crimson King' (No 5, Nov 1969), the track *21st Century Schizoid Man* known for its heavily distorted vocals sung by Greg Lake, a driving mechanical rhythm and piercingly loud saxophone and guitar, along with its instrumental middle section, called "Mirrors". Carl Palmer previously played with Crazy World of Arthur Brown, Atomic Rooster and Chris Farlowe.

Estelle Estelle Fanta Swaray was born in Hammersmith on 18 January 1980, to a Senegalese mother and a Grenadian father. Estelle grew up among a large family in the west London suburb and before she fell in love with Hip Hop (mainly her uncle's influence) gospel music was her staple diet (mainly her mother's influence) with a little bit of reggae. At the age of 17, Estelle began working in a Hip Hop record shop, Deal Real, in Soho and developed her passion for both rap and R&B by gigging in the evenings and building up a reputation as the 'Queen of the M.I.C.'. After signing record deals with V2 and Atlantic Records, Estelle, formerly known as Est'elle in her street rapping days, broke into the UK chart with her debut single, *1980* (No 14, Jul 2004), named after the year of her birth. The follow-up single, *Free* (No 14, Oct 2004) was released at the same time as the album both tracks appeared on, 'The 18th Day' (No 35, Oct 2004). This album was named after the day of her birth, the number 18 being significant in Estelle's life. It was on this day in January 1980 that her mother almost died in giving birth to her. It was also on her 18th birthday that Estelle decided to embark on a musical career. This album also contained two tracks produced by John Legend, *Hey Girl* and *Freedom*, on both of which he also added vocals. Estelle subsequently won a MOBO Award for Best Newcomer. A third single from the album, *Go Gone* (No 32, Mar 2005) did not perform as well as the first two tracks. Estelle's second album 'Shine' (No 6, Mar 2008) was preceded by the lead single, *Wait a Minute (Just a Touch)* which was produced by, and featured, The Black Eyed Peas member will.i.am, but failed to have any impact on the charts. However, the second single, *American Boy* (No 1, Mar 2008 - No 2 in Ireland, No 9 in USA) featuring Kanye West reached number one in the UK Singles Chart on downloads alone. Estelle's third album 'All of Me' was released in February 2012 in the United States and in March in the UK.

Eurythmics Pop rock duo, Annie Lennox (born in Aberdeen, 25 December 1954) and Dave Stewart (born David Allan Stewart in Sunderland, 9 September 1952) first played together in 1977 as part of a larger group known as Catch - the other two members being Peet Coombes (b. 1952, d. 1997; guitar and vocals) and Eddie Chin (b. 1948; bass guitar). In 1979 Catch recruited drummer Jim Toomey and changed their name to The Tourists. Under this name they managed two Top 10 singles, *I Only Want To Be With You* (No 4, Nov 1979) and *So Good to Be Back Home Again* (No 8, Feb 1980) on the Logo label. By the end of 1980 The Tourists had split up and Dave and Annie signed to RCA under the new theatrical name Eurythmics - named after the 'Rhythm Gymnastics' style of dance mime devised by Emile

Jacques-Dalcroze. Their first charting album 'Sweet Dreams (Are Made of This)' (No 3, Feb 1983) spawned two Top 10 singles, the title track which peaked at No 2 in February 2003 (but became their only US No 1) and *Love Is A Stranger* (No 6, Apr 1983) which was released in 1982 but did little until the album started to sell. The follow-up chart-topping album 'Touch' (No 1, Nov 1983) produced three further Top 10 singles, *Who's that Girl?* (No 3, Jul 1983), *Right By Your Side* (No 10, Nov 1983) and *Here Comes The Rain Again* (No 8, Jan 1984). Their next single, *Sexcrime (Nineteen Eighty-Four)* (No 4, 1984) was written as part of the soundtrack to the film *Nineteen Eighty-Four* (1984). The Eurythmics' next album 'Be yourself Tonight' (No 3, May 1985) included the tracks *Would I Lie To You* (No 17, Apr 1985) and the UK and Ireland chart-topping single, *There Must Be an Angel (Playing with My Heart)* (No 1, Jul 1985). It also produced *It's Alright (Baby's Coming Back* (No 12, Jan 1986) and *Sisters Are Doing It For Themselves* (No 9, Nov 1985) a collaboration with Aretha Franklin. Subsequent successful albums include: 'Revenge' (No 3, Jul 1986) which spawned their last Top 10 single *Thorn In My Side* (No 5, Sep 1986), 'Savage' (No 7, Nov 1987) and 'We Too Are One' (No 1, Sep 1989) which they were, in the UK and Sweden. They also scored a third UK No 1 album with a 'Greatest Hits' compilation in March 1991 by which time they had split to concentrate on solo projects. They reformed in the late 1990s to produce the album 'Peace' (No 4, Oct 1999) and again in 2005 to release the single *I've Got A Life* (No 14, Oct 2005). During the hiatus Dave began writing film soundtracks and had a big international hit in 1990 with the instrumental track *Lily Was Here* (featuring saxophonist Candy Dulfer) which reached No 6 in the UK Singles Chart. He also formed a band called The Spiritual Cowboys, releasing two albums with this group in the early 1990s. The versatile guitarist, producer and songwriter also co-created the comic books *Walk-In* (2006) and *Zombie Broadway* (2008), both published by *Virgin Comics*. He has collaborated with many of the world's leading pop artists and his latest project is as part of Mick Jagger's new band, SuperHeavy, a supergroup formed in May 2011, consisting of Mick, Dave, Joss Stone, A. R. Rahman, and Damian Marley. Their debut album 'SuperHeavy' peaked at No 13 in the UK and No 26 in the USA. Having previously been married from 1973 to 1977, Dave wed former Bananarama member Siobhan Fahey (who later formed Shakespears Sister) in 1987. The couple have two children (Sam and Django) but divorced in 1996. On 4 August 2001, he married Dutch photographer Anoushka Fisz with whom he has two daughters, Kaya and Indya. After taking time out to have a baby, Annie released her first solo album 'Diva' (No 1, Apr 1992). She had previously collaborated with Al Green on *Put a Little Love in Your Heart* (No 28, Dec 1988 – No 9 in USA) which was released as the ending theme song to the 1988 film *Scrooged*. The album 'Diva' won Best British Album at the 1993 Brit Awards to add to Annie's ever-growing hoard of BRITS. It also spawned several successful tracks including her debut solo single, *Why* (No 5, Mar 1992) plus *Walking on Broken Glass* (No 8, Aug 1992) and *Little Bird* (No 3, Feb 1993), the B-side of which (*Love Song For A Vampire*) featured in the 1992 film *Bram Stoker's Dracula*. Her next album 'Medusa' (No 1, Mar 1995) also topped the charts and included Annie's version of *No More I Love You's* (No 2, Feb 1995), written by Joseph Hughes and David Freeman and originally released by their band, The Lover Speaks, in 1986. Annie's last three albums 'Bare' (No 3, Jun 2003 – No 4 in USA), 'Songs Of Mass Destruction' (No 7, Oct 2007 – No 9 in USA) and 'A Christmas Cornucopia' (No 16, Nov 2010 – No 35 in USA) were all commercial successes on both sides of the Atlantic. As at the beginning of 2012 Annie has won eight BRIT awards, four Grammy Awards and an MTV Video Music Award. In 2004, she won both the Golden Globe and the Academy Award for Best Original Song for *Into the West*, written for the soundtrack to the feature film *The Lord of the Rings: The Return of the King*. A tireless worker for human rights (as is Dave Stewart), she received an OBE in 2009. As a performer she has been erstwhile dubbed "The Greatest White Soul Singer Alive".

Example The singer and rapper (born Elliot John Gleave, Hammersmith, London, 20 June 1982) rather ingeniously took his stage name from his initials E.G. - an abbreviation of the Latin phrase "exempli gratia", which means "for example". In 2000, he attended Royal Holloway, University of London to study film directing but started garage MCing to make some money. After graduation, Elliot worked in Australia for a year in the props departments of films such as *Star Wars Episode III: Revenge of the Sith*. On returning to the UK he became a voiceover artist and editor for the Paramount Comedy Channel (now Comedy Central) and also worked as an editor at MTV Networks. He released his first studio album 'What We Made' on 17 September 2007 through The Beats, a subsidiary of 679 Recordings owned by Mike Skinner. It made little impact as did any of the three singles released, *I Don't Want To, So Many Roads*, and *Me & Mandy*. Things changed in 2009 with the release of his single, *Watch the Sun Come Up* (No 19, Sep 2009) on the data label, the first single from Example's second album 'Won't Go Quietly' (No 4, Jun 2010). The Top 10 album was preceded by the title track, *Won't Go Quietly* (No 6, Jan 2010). Other tracks released as singles, *Kickstarts* (No 3, Jun 2010 – No 8 in Ireland), *Last Ones Standing* (No 27, Sep 2010) and Two Lives (No 84, Nov 2010) had mixed success. Example's third studio album 'Playing in the Shadows' (No 1, Sep 2011) released on the Ministry of Sound label, topped the UK Albums Chart and placed No 6 in Ireland. It was preceded by the lead single, *Changed the Way You Kiss Me* (No 1, Jun 2011) which was eagerly awaited after it had premiered on BBC Radio 1 as Zane Lowe's "Hottest Record in the World" on 24 March 2011. The track went straight to No 1 on release. The follow-up single, *Stay Awake* (No 1, Aug 2011 – No 16 in Ireland) was given the same glowing reference by Zane Lowe in July 2011 and the result was the same. A third single from the album, *Natural Disaster* (No 37, Oct 2011) featuring Dutch DJ Laidback Luke was less successful as was the fourth, *Midnight Run* (No 30, Dec 2011). He has worked with many contemporary artists including, Professor Green and Ed Sheeran, his most successful collaboration being with Tottenham-born rapper Wretch 32 (see separate entry) on his single *Unorthodox* (No 2, Apr 2011). In February 2008 he attempted a stand-up comedy routine as part of BBC2's *The Culture Show*. Mentored by Richard Herring, Example spent six weeks writing and practicing his set which culminated in his first ever stand-up show in front of 60 paying customers in a Covent Garden pub. A week later Example appeared on the bill with Richard Herring, Phill Jupitus and Harry Hill at the Lyric Hammersmith.

The Faces see entry for Rod Stewart

Adam Faith Although Adam was one of Britain's finest natural character actors (see entry in cinema section) he began his professional life in 1957 working as an assistant film editor for Rank Screen Service and whilst there formed a skiffle group, The Worried Men, made up of his fellow workmates. The group played in Soho coffee bars after work, and became the resident band at The 2i's Coffee Bar, where they appeared on the BBC Television live music programme *Six-Five Special*. The producer, Jack Good, was impressed by Adam and arranged a solo recording contract with HMV that failed to produce any chart success. Adam returned to his job at National Studios at Elstree until March 1959, when he then auditioned for a BBC TV rock and roll show, *Drumbeat*. The producer, Stewart Morris (later of *Top of the Pops* fame), gave him a contract for three shows, extended to the full 22-week run. At this time Adam's recordings were arranged by John Barry (1933-2011) who after their first film collaboration *Beat Girl* (Adam's first film and John's first film for which he wrote the soundtrack) led to both being in great demand. Adam had already signed to Parlophone and his first single on that label, *What Do You Want* (No 1, Nov 1959) not only topped the UK chart and became Parlophone's first UK chart-topper in the process, but Adam's unique staccato voice modelled on Buddy Holly's rendition of *It Doesn't Matter Anymore* gave the public (and numerous impressionists) a popular catchphrase in the pronunciation of the lyric 'baby' as 'bay-beh'. Adam's next six singles, *Poor Me* (No 1, Jan 1960), *Someone Else's Baby* (No 2, Apr 1960), *When Johnny Comes Marching Home/Made You* (No 5, Jun 1960), *How About That* (No 4, Sep 1960), *Lonely Pup (In A Christmas Shop)* (No 4, Nov 1960) and *Who Am I/This Is It!* (No 5, Feb 1961) gave him the distinction of being the first British act to have his first seven chart entries all in the Top 5. His other well known hits include: *The Time Has Come* (No 4, Oct 1961), *As You Like It* (No 5, May 1962), *Don't That Beat All* (No 8, Aug 1962), *The First Time* (No 5, Sep 1963) and *Message To Martha (Kentucky Bluebird)* (No 12, Nov 1964). His only Top 10 album was his debut release 'Adam' (No 6, Nov 1960). In December 1960, Adam became the first pop artist to appear on the hard-hitting TV interview series *Face to Face* with John Freeman. This 'honour' raised the profile of pop music and gave it an importance it had never before experienced. Adam married Jackie Irving in 1967 and they had one daughter Katya Faith who became a television producer. After his own pop career ended, Adam went on to produce Roger Daltrey's first solo album and to manage Leo Sayer before becoming a highly successful actor and businessman.

Paloma Faith Singer-songwriter and actress (born Paloma Faith Blomfield, Hackney, London, 21 July 1985; to a Spanish father and an English mother) who was trained in ballet and contemporary dance as a youngster. Whilst studying for an MA in theatre directing (Scenography) at Central Saint Martins College of Art and Design, Paloma funded her course by a string of exotic jobs including: sales assistant at Agent Provocateur, singer in a burlesque cabaret, life model and magician's assistant. Signed to the epic label, Paloma's only impression on the UK Top 10 has been with her debut album 'Do You Want the Truth or Something Beautiful?' (No 9, Sep 2009). The lead single from the album (her debut single), *Stone Cold Sober* (No 17, Jun 2009) was followed by *New York* (No 15, Sep 2009) which features a rousing gospel chorus by the London-based Souls of Prophecy Gospel Choir. Although Paloma has had no further Top 20s to-date she remains a burgeoning star in great demand by other artists as a collaborator. As an actress Paloma made her feature film debut in *St Trinian's* (2007 – as Andrea) and followed this up with *The Imaginarium of Doctor Parnassus* (2009 - as Sally the girlfriend of the Devil) and the horror film *Dread* (2009 – as Clara Thornhill). On television she made her debut in the comedy detective drama series *Mayo* (2006) starring Alistair McGowan and Jessica Oyelowo. She later appeared in an episode of the BBC police drama HolbyBlue.

Fatboy Slim Norman Quentin Cook (born Quentin Leo Cook, Bromley, Greater London, 31 July 1963) is a DJ, electronic dance music musician, and record producer better known by his stage name Fatboy Slim. Raised in Reigate in Surrey, he met Paul Heaton (see entry for The Beautiful South) at Reigate College and formed a band called the Stomping Pondfrogs. Whilst studying at Brighton Polytechnic he began to develop his DJing skills on the ebullient local club scene. In 1985 Norman replaced vocalist Ted Key in Paul Heaton's group the Housemartins, which was formed a year earlier, in Hull. The Housemartins had a Top 10 UK single with *Happy Hour* (No 3, Jun 1986) followed by the chart-topping *Caravan of Love* (No 1, Dec 1986). They also had three Top 10 albums 'London 0 Hull 4' (No 3, Jul 1986), 'The People Who Grinned Themselves to Death' (No 9, Oct 1987) and 'Now That's What I Call Quite Good' (No 8, May 1988). After dissolving in 1989 Paul went on to form Beautiful South (see separate entry) whilst Norman initially became a record remixer, fronting the Urban All Stars and then briefly a solo artist before forming Beats International with keyboard player Andy Boucher, drummer Luke Cresswell and vocalists, Lester Noel, D.J. Baptiste, MC Wildski and ex *Grange Hill* actress Lindy Layton (born Belinda Kimberley Layton, Chiswick, London, 7 December 1970). Their first release *Dub Be Good to Me* (No 1, Feb 1990) topped the UK singles chart and was followed by *Won't Talk about It* (No 9, May 1990). Their one and only album 'Let Them Eat Bingo' peaked at No 17 in April 1990. Norman disbanded them in 1993 and went on to launch another group called Freak Power (with horn player Ashley Slater and singer Jesse Graham) which had one successful

album 'Drive-Thru Booty' (No 11, Apr 1995) and one Top 10 single *Turn On, Tune In, Cop Out* (No 3, Mar 1995). Norman also recorded under the name Pizzaman to have two Top 20 singles, *Happiness* (No 19, Nov 1995) and *Trippin' on Sunshine* (No 18, Jun 1996) and also under the name The Mighty Dub Katz (with Gareth Hansome - aka GMoney) scoring three minor hits, the most successful being *Magic Carpet Ride* (No 24, Aug 1997). It was however as Fatboy Slim that he achieved the greatest success. His first Top 10 single was *The Rockafeller Skank* (No 6, Jun 1998) which featured the repeated line "Right about now, the funk soul brother. Check it out now, the funk soul brother", which is a vocal sample of rapper Lord Finesse on the track *Vinyl Dog Vibe* by Vinyl Dogs. The single also included samples of the songs *Sliced Tomatoes* by the band Just Brothers, *I Fought the Law (And the Law Won)* by Bobby Fuller, *Beat Girl* by John Barry and his Orchestra and *Peter Gunn* by Art of Noise featuring Duane Eddy. Despite being a global hit Norman had to award all his royalties to the featured artists he sampled in order to have the song released. This unfortunately is an occupational hazard of creative samplers. In October 1998 the album 'You've Come A Long Way Baby' was released and topped the UK chart and is often considered a benchmark album in big beat music. The album's title was taken from a marketing slogan for the cigarette brand Virginia Slims and the cover depicts an obese young lad, dressed in a T-shirt with the slogan "I'm #1 so why try harder". As well as *The Rockafeller Skank*, the album contained three more Top 10 tracks, *Gangster Trippin* (No 3, Oct 1998), *Praise You* (No 1, Jan 1999) and *Right Here, Right Now* (No 2, May 1999). The multi-award-winning music video for *Praise You*, Norman's first solo No 1 single, was directed by Spike Jonze, who also starred in the film under the pseudonym Richard Koufey alongside the fictional Torrance Community Dance Group. Norman's next album 'Halfway Between the Gutter and the Stars' (No 8, Nov 2000) was preceded by its lead single *Sunset (Bird of Prey)* (No 9, Oct 2000) and succeeded by the double-A side track *Star 69/Weapon of Choice* (No 10, May 2001). The music video for *Weapon of Choice* featured actor Christopher Walken dancing. It won multiple awards at the 2001 MTV Video Music Awards and won the 2002 Grammy Award for Best Short Form Video. Although Norman has not produced any further Top 10 studio output to-date, his album 'Palookaville' (No 14, Oct 2004) was highly-acclaimed and a return to traditional music with traditional instruments, Norman himself supplying bass and his long-time collaborator Simon Thornton also playing guitar. The album title became a temporary name of Brighton and Hove Albion F.C.'s Withdean Stadium, due to their sponsorship deal with Skint Records, the label that produced all of Norman's output as Fatboy Slim. Norman's compilation album 'The Greatest Hits – Why Try Harder' peaked at No 2 in the UK albums chart in June 2006 and also gave him his one and only Irish No 1. Norman has also been responsible for successful remixes for Lateef the Truthspeaker, Cornershop, Beastie Boys, A Tribe Called Quest, and Wildchild. Norman formed The Brighton Port Authority in 2008 and it was thought that his Fatboy Slim days were over, however in early 2012 he performed a live DJ set on the main stage at Ultra Music Festival in Miami, Florida under his most illustrious name. Norman married TV personality Zoë Ball in 1999 at Babington House in Somerset. They hit a rocky spell at the beginning of 2003 and split up for a while but were reconciled three months later. They have a son, Woody Fred Cook (b. 15 December 2000) and a daughter, Nelly May Lois (b. 14 January 2010). Although he received treatment for alcohol dependency in 2009, Norman managed to complete the Brighton marathon in a time of 4:53:10 in April 2010. He is also a 12% shareholder in Brighton & Hove Albion, the football club he has supported since moving to Brighton in the late 1980s. See also entry for Rizzle Kicks.

Bryan Ferry Born in Washington, Tyne and Wear, 26 September 1945, Bryan studied fine art at the University of Newcastle upon Tyne under Richard Hamilton (see entry in the miscellaneous section) and this was later to influence his pop career. Whilst working as a ceramics teacher in London he formed The Banshees, and later, together with Graham Simpson, The Gas Board. Although these bands had moderate success his real breakthrough came in November 1970 when he and Graham formed Roxy Music. The band members have included Phil Manzanera, Andy MacKay, Paul Thompson, Eddie Jobson, David O'List, Dexter Lloyd, Rik Kenton, John Gustafson, John Wetton, Gary Tibbs, Neil Hubbard, Andy Newmark, Alan Spenner and Brian Eno. Their debut single *Virginia Plain*, reached No. 4 in the British charts and their only No 1 came in February 1981 with *Jealous Guy*, a tribute to John Lennon, and ironically the only Roxy record not written by Bryan. Roxy's other hits include: *Pyjamarama* (No 10, Mar 1973), *Street Life* (No 9, Nov 1973), *Love is the Drug* (No 2, Oct 1975), *Dance Away* (No 2, Apr 1979), *Angel Eyes* (No 4, Aug 1979), *Over You* (No 5, May 1980), *Oh Yeah (On the Radio)* (No 5, Aug 1980), *The Same Old Scene* (No 12, Nov 1980), *More than This* (No 6, Apr 1982) and *Avalon* (No 13, Jun 1982). They had three chart-topping studio albums: 'Stranded' (No 1, Nov 1973) the cover featuring Bryan's then girlfriend and 1973 Playmate of the Year, Marilyn Cole, 'Flesh and Blood' (No 1, Jun 1980) and 'Avalon' (No 1, May 1982). Although Bryan has performed on and off with Roxy throughout the band's different incarnations, his solo career has always run parallel and often with greater success. His first solo album *These Foolish Things* (No 5, Nov 1973) contained a typically quirky rendition of the title track, a standard number often attributed as one of a group of 'Mayfair Songs' like *A Nightingale Sang in Berkeley Square*. The album also spawned Bryan's debut single, a stirring cover of Bob Dylan's *A Hard Rain's Gonna Fall*, which reached No 10 in September 1973. Other hits include *Let's Stick Together* (No 4, Jun 1976 - his highest placed solo recording), *This is Tomorrow* (No 9, Feb 1977) and *Slave To Love* (No 10, May 1985). He has also had two solo No 1 albums with the studio album 'Boys and Girls' (No 1, Jun 1985) and the compilation album 'Street Life – 20 Greatest Hits' (No 1, Apr 1986). Bryan is a style icon and often collaborates with fashion designer Antony Price for clothing and image consultations. Known for his relationships with several high-profile models such as Jerry Hall (Bryan first met Jerry when she posed for the Roxy Music album cover for 'Siren' –No 4 - in Wales during the summer 1975) and Amanda Lear (who was photographed with a black jaguar for the cover of the 'For Your Pleasure' album, which also reached No 4). Bryan eventually married model Lucy Helmore (the model on the front cover of the album 'Avalon') in 1982 and the couple have four sons: Otis, Isaac, Tara and Merlin. In 2004, Otis, joint master of the south Shropshire hunt, stormed the House of Commons in protest at anti-hunting legislation. After 21 years of marriage, Bryan and Lucy divorced in 2003. In recent years Bryan has made cameo roles in several films including *The Porter* (2004) and *Breakfast On Pluto* (2005). In June 2011 Bryan was made a CBE in the Queen's Birthday Honours for his contribution to the British music industry. In early January 2012, Bryan married Amanda Sheppard, one of his son's ex-girlfriends, in a private ceremony on the Turks and Caicos Islands.

Fightstar see entry for Busted

Fleetwood Mac see entry for Rod Stewart

Florence and the Machine Stylised as Florence + the Machine, the indie pop band, consists of lead singer Florence Welch (born Florence Leontine Mary Welch, Camberwell, London, 28 August 1986) and a collaboration of other artists who provide backing music. Florence is the niece of *Private Eye* satirist and *Daily Mail* columnist Craig Brown (born 23 May 1957, Hayes, Middlesex). She attended the independent Alleyn's School in Dulwich and later, the Camberwell College of Arts. Despite being diagnosed with dyslexia and dyspraxia she managed to perform adequately at school but was always destined for a musical career. In 2006 she began gigging with her friend, keyboard player Isabella Summers, the girls calling themselves Florence Robot/Isa Machine. By the following year this was shortened to Florence and the Machine. Other musicians were recruited and after Isabella left the group temporarily the 'Machine' had become the

generic name of the band on her return. The current band members include: Robert Ackroyd (guitar and backing vocals), Chris Hayden (drums, percussion and backing vocals), Isabella Summers (keyboards and backing vocals), Mark Saunders (bass guitar and backing vocals) and Tom Monger (harp). The band's debut single, *Kiss with a Fist*, was released through Moshi Moshi Records on 9 June 2008 in the UK and stalled at No 51. Two further singles, *Dog Days Are Over* (No 23, Dec 2008) and *Rabbit Heart (Raise It Up)* (No 12, Jun 2009) faring progressively better, the first named reaching No 21 in America and No 6 in Ireland. All three singles were tracks from their debut album 'Lungs' which was released on 6 July 2009 by Island Records and by January 2010 had topped the UK Albums Chart as well as placing No 14 on the US Billboard 200 and No 2 on the Irish Albums Chart. Another track from 'Lungs', *You've Got the Love* (No 5, Nov 2009) a cover version of the song *You Got the Love* by The Source featuring Candi Staton albeit with a slightly different title, was originally released as the B-side of *Dog Days Are Over* but on re-release has become their most successful single to-date. The album, produced by Paul Epworth, James Ford, Charlie Hugall and Stephen Mackey (former member of Pulp) contains several songs about violence and death, a subject that has preoccupied (and sometimes caused depression) Florence since her youth when she experienced the deaths of two of her grandparents. The band's second album 'Ceremonials' (No 1, Oct 2011) also topped the Irish Albums chart and peaked at No 6 in the USA, the lead single *Shake it Out* (No 12, Sep 2011) rising to No 2 in the Irish Singles Chart. On 26 April 2012, the band released *Breath of Life*, a song which was recorded as the official theme song for the 2012 film *Snow White and the Huntsman*. The stage appearance of Florence is distinctive; often wearing short skirts or hotpants (although sometimes long elaborate gypsy-style dresses) the natural brunette is distinguished by her long flowing dyed red hair. Her quirky style is reminiscent of Kate Bush, Cyndi Lauper and performers of that ilk although she herself cites American singer Grace Slick as her chief influence.

Samantha Fox see entry in the miscellaneous section

Billy Fury Ronald Wycherley was born in Liverpool on 17 April 1940. After buying his first guitar at the age of 14, he was fronting his own group within a year although simultaneously working full-time on a tugboat and later as a stevedore. He won a talent competition and started composing his own songs. In 1958 he attended a concert in Birkenhead, run by impresario Larry Parnes, in the hope of interesting the already famous young singer Marty Wilde in some of his songs he had written. Instead, in an episode that has become pop music legend, Parnes (he of the epithet *Parnes, Shillings and Pence*) pushed young Ron up on stage and he was such an immediate success that Parnes signed him, added him to the tour, and renamed him 'Billy Fury'. After signing with Decca his debut single *Maybe Tomorrow* (No 18, Feb 1959) was followed by the less impressive *Margo* (No 28, Jun 1959) but his profile was raised by appearing in a televised play *Strictly for Sparrows*, and subsequently as a regular on the pioneering TV pop show *Oh Boy!* Billy's first album 'The Sound of Fury' (No 18, Jun 1960) featured a young Joe Brown on lead guitar. Another famous story surrounding Billy revolved around Parnes' sacking Billy's backing band, The Blue Flames (later famous when their pianist Georgie Fame came to the fore). Larry held auditions in Liverpool and one of the acts seen were The Beatles (who for the first time called themselves The Silver Beetles). They were offered the job for £20 a week on condition that they sacked their bassist Stuart Sutcliffe. John Lennon refused and the band left after Lennon had secured Billy's autograph! The Tornados (see separate entry) were eventually recruited as his backing band and toured and recorded with Billy from January 1962 to August 1963. It might seem ironic that John had asked for Billy's autograph when he himself was destined to become just about the biggest name in pop history, but the truth is Billy actually had more Top 40 charting singles in the 1960s than even the Fab Four could muster, a total of 24 to The Beatles 23, and Billy managed it all in a six-year period! Despite, famously again, never scoring a No 1 hit, Billy's Top 10 singles included, *Colette* (No 9, Mar 1960), *Halfway To Paradise* (No 3, May 1961), *Jealousy* (No 2, Sep 1961), *I'd Never Find Another You* (No 5, Dec 1961), *Last Night Was Made For Love* (No 4, May 1962), *When Will You Say I Love You* (No 3, May 1963), *In Summer* (No 5, Jul 1963), *It's Only Make Believe* (No 10, Jul 1964) and *In Thoughts of You* (No 9, Jul 1965). He also had further album success with 'Halfway to Paradise' (No 5, Sep 1961) the title track becoming his most iconic song, 'Billy' (No 6, May 1963) and the live album 'We Want Billy!' (No 14, Oct 1963) which featured his previous hits plus cover versions of several R&B classics such as *Unchain My Heart*. In 1962 he appeared in his first feature film, *Play It Cool*, modelled on the Elvis movies. It also featured Helen Shapiro, Danny Williams, Shane Fenton (later to become Alvin Stardust) and Bobby Vee. In 1965 he appeared in his most famous film, the musical comedy *I've Gotta Horse*, which was based around Billy's famous (again) love for animals. The film also co-starred Amanda Barrie, The Bachelors, Michael Medwin and Jon Pertwee. Two heart operations put his career on hold for a while but in 1973, he starred as Stormy Tempest (modelled on Rory Storm) alongside David Essex and Ringo Starr in the film *That'll Be the Day*. Billy had rheumatic fever as a child, leaving him with a weakened heart. His version of *Unchain My Heart*, made famous by Ray Charles, seems somewhat poignant given Billy's medical history and is as touching as when Ray himself sings the line "and let me see" in his other classic, *Take These Chains From My Heart*. Billy's career was undoubtedly blighted by ill health. His moody good looks and impeccable hair was seen as a danger to women. He was more of a sex symbol than either Marty Wilde or Cliff Richard and was perceived as the 'King of Cool' and the true 'British Elvis'. Billy's last public appearance was at the Sunnyside, Northampton, in December 1982. He died of heart failure on 28 January 1983. In 2003 a bronze statue of Billy was unveiled at the National Museum of Liverpool Life.

Michelle Gayle Beautiful black former *Grange Hill* actress (born Michelle Patricia Gayle, in London 2 February 1971) who in 1987, as Fiona Wilson, began singing in the programme as part of a rap duo named Fresh'n'Fly. In 1990, she joined the cast of *EastEnders* as Hattie Tavernier, leaving in 1993. In August of that year, she charted with *Looking Up*, which reached number 11. Thirteen months later, she entered the charts with *Sweetness* – her first Top 10 hit, peaking at number four. Her eponymously titled debut album reached number 30 that year. Eight days before Christmas 1994, she charted with *I'll Find You*, which made number 26. Michelle's other singles include: *Happy Just to Be with You* (No 11, Aug 1995), *Do You Know* (No 6, Feb 1997) and *Sensational* (No 14, Apr 1997). In 2008, she co-wrote and recorded *Woo (U Make Me)* as an entry for *Song For Europe*. It came second in the competition on 1 March but it didn't chart. She received three BRIT Award nominations: two in 1995 for Best Single and Best Female, and one three years later for Best Female. She was married to ex-footballer Mark Bright for 10 years but divorced in April 2008. Her first novel, *Pride And Premiership*, was published in May 2011.

Genesis Prog rock band formed in 1967 at Charterhouse School and comprising Peter Gabriel (born in Chobham, Surrey, 13 February 1950; vocals and flute); Tony Banks (born in East Hoathly, Sussex, 27 March 1950; keyboards); Mike Rutherford (born Michael John Cleote Crawford Rutherford, in Guildford, Surrey, 2 October 1950; bass); Anthony Phillips (born in Chiswick, London, 23 December 1951; guitar) and Chris Stewart (born in 1950; drums). Old Carthusian Jonathan King signed them in 1968 after seeing them in a concert at the school and named them (Gabriel's Angels was discarded). Their first single, *The Silent Sun*, was released in February 1968. In summer that year, John Silver (born in 1950) replaced Stewart. In March 1969, they released 'From Genesis To Revelation' on Decca Records. In August 1969, Silver left and John Mayhew (born in Ipswich, Suffolk, 27 March 1947; d. in Scotland, 26 March 2009, of a heart-related condition) took over the drums. A year later, he was replaced by Phil Collins (born in Chiswick, London, 30 January 1951). Phillips left in 1972, suffering from stage fright. In October 1972, 'Foxtrot' was Genesis' first album to chart, reaching No 12. Their next two charted albums, 'Genesis Live' and 'Selling England by the Pound' (both 1973) reached nine and three respectively. In April 1974, their single *I Know What I Like (In Your Wardrobe)* became their first entry on the charts peaking at 21. A double disc concept album *The Lamb Lies down on Broadway* was released on 18 November 1974 and reached No 10. Gabriel left in 1975 and was replaced as lead singer by Collins. Steve Hackett left in 1977 to pursue a solo career. In March 1978, Genesis charted with *Follow You Follow Me*, which was their first Top 10 single, reaching No 7. From 1978 until 1996 Genesis consisted of the trio of Collins, Banks and Rutherford with other musicians being added as necessary. Their Top 10 singles include: *Turn It on Again* (No 8, Mar 1980), *Abacab* (No 9, Aug 1981), The EP *3X3* (No 10, May 1982), *Mama* (No 4. Sep 1983), *No Son Of Mine* (No 6, Nov 1991), *I Can't Dance* (No 7, Jan 1992) and *Invisible Touch* (No 7, Nov 1992). Their Top 10 albums include: 'A Trick of the Trail' (No 3, Feb 1976), 'Wind and Wuthering' (No 7, Jan 1977), 'Seconds Out' (No 4, Oct 1977), '…And Then There Were Three' (No 3, Apr 1978), 'Duke' (No 1, Apr 1980), 'Abacab' (No 1, Sep 1981), 'Three Sides Live' (No 2, Jun 1982), 'Genesis' (No 1, Oct 1983), 'Invisible Touch' (No 1, Jun 1986), 'We Can't Dance' (No 1, Nov 1991), 'Live – The Way We Walk Volume 1: The Shorts' (No 3, Nov 1992) and 'Live – The Way We Walk Volume 2: The Longs' (No 1, Jan 1993). Phil Collins left in 1996 but rejoined 10 years later for a tour. He was replaced from 1996-98 by Ray Wilson (born in Dumfries, Scotland, 8 September 1968). During the Wilson era they charted with the album 'Calling All Stations' (No 2, Sep 1997). On 15 March 2010, Genesis was inducted into the Rock and Roll Hall of Fame. Gabriel has had four solo Top 10 hits: *Games without Frontiers* (No 4, Feb 1980), *Sledgehammer* (No 4, Apr 1986), *Don't Give Up* (No 9, Nov 1986 – with Kate Bush) and *Steam* (No 10, Jan 1993). Bizarrely, he also called his first four solo albums 'Peter Gabriel' (the third in 1980 reaching No 1) and the fifth 'Peter Gabriel Plays Live' (No 8, Jun 1983). His sixth album, 'So', also topped the charts, in May 1986. Collins, a child actor, has had the greatest solo success of his band mates. He has charted with more than 30 singles including *In The Air Tonight* (No 2, Jan 1981), *You Can't Hurry Love* (No 1, Dec 1982), *Against All Odds* (No 2, Apr 1984), *Sussudio* (No 12, Jan 1985), *Easy Lover* (No 1, Mar 1985; a duet with Philip Bailey), *One More Night* (No 4, Apr 1985), *Separate Lives* (No 4, Nov 1985 – with Marilyn Martin), *A Groovy Kind Of Love* (No 1, Sep 1988), *Two Hearts* (No 6, Nov 1988), *Another Day In Paradise* (No 2, Nov 1989), I Wish it Would Rain Down (No 7, Jan 1990), Both Sides of the Story (No 7, Oct 1993) and Dance into the Light (No 9, Oct 1996) plus six chart-topping albums 'Face Value' (Feb 1981, which spent 274 weeks on the chart), 'No Jacket Required' (Mar 1985, which spent 176 weeks on the chart), '…But Seriously' (Dec 1989), 'Both Sides of the Story' (Nov 1993), '…Hits' (Oct 1998) and 'Going Back' (Sep 2010). Under the guise of Mike and The Mechanics, Rutherford reached No 2 with *The Living Years* in 1989. An album of the same name also got to No 2.

Gerry and the Pacemakers Part of the Mersey invasion, Gerry and the Pacemakers was the first band to reach Number 1 with their first three releases (a record broken by the Spice Girls in 1997). Gerry was Gerry Marsden (born at 8 Menzies Street, Toxteth, Liverpool, 24 September 1942; lead guitar/vocals) and The Pacemakers were Gerry's brother Fred (born at 8 Menzies Street, Toxteth, Liverpool 23 November 1940; d. in Southport, 9 December 2006; drums), Les Chadwick (born John Leslie Chadwick, Aigburth, Liverpool, 11 May 1943; bass) and Arthur McMahon (piano). They were founded in 1959 as the Mars Bars (hoping to get sponsored by the confectionery giant who instead insisted the name was changed). McMahon left in May 1961 and was replaced by Les Maguire (born in Wallasey, 27 December 1941). In June 1962, Gerry and the Pacemakers were Brian Epstein's second signing and they began their chart career with *How Do You Do It?* (a song written by Mitch Murray that Adam Faith had rejected) in March 1963. Two months later, *I Like It* (another Murray composition) gave them a second chart-topper. *You'll Never Walk Alone* from Rodgers and Hammerstein's

Carousel was their third and final Number 1. The Marsden-penned *I'm the One* stalled at number two in January 1964 and *Don't Let the Sun Catch You Crying* reached number six in April of that year. Their last Top 10 hit was *Ferry Cross the Mersey*, which reached number eight in December 1964. They disbanded in October 1966. Gerry has also been part of two chart-topping charity records. In 1985 the multinational charity group 'The Crowd' assembled by Graham Gouldman of 10cc, to raise funds for the victims of the Bradford City football fire, recorded *You'll Never Walk Alone* (No 1, Jun 1985) the anthem for Liverpool football club. In 1989 The Christians, Holly Johnson, Paul McCartney, Stock Aitken Waterman and Gerry topped the chart with *Ferry Cross the Mersey* (No 1, May 1989) a charity record in aid of the Hillsborough disaster.

Girl Thing A girlband comprising Jodi Albert (born Chingford, Essex, 22 July 1983), Anika Bostelaar, Linzi Martin, Michelle Barber and Nikki Stuart. They had one Top 10 hit in 2000 with *Last One Standing*, which reached number eight. A second release, *Girls on Top*, stalled at 25 and a planned album release was cancelled. Jodi later appeared in *Hollyoaks* and married Irish boybander Kian Egan. See also entry for Hear'Say.

Girls Aloud Girl band formed from contestants on the reality show *Popstars The Rivals* on 30 November 2002. The girls were managed by Louis Walsh until 2005 when he was replaced by Hilary Shaw. The group comprises Cheryl Cole (born Cheryl Ann Tweedy, Newcastle upon Tyne, 30 June 1983), Nadine Elizabeth Louise Coyle (born Londonderry, Northern Ireland, 15 June 1985), Sarah Harding (born Sarah Nicole Hardman, Ascot, Berkshire, 17 November 1981), Nicola Maria Roberts (born Stamford, Lincolnshire, 5 October 1985) and Kimberley Jane Walsh (born Bradford, West Yorkshire, 20 November 1981). Kimberley and Nicola were not in the original selection of 10 potential members, however, Hazel Kaneswaren was deemed too old and Nicola Ward refused to sign a contract believing that she was being exploited. Javine Hylton (see separate entry) was one of the unlucky five not ultimately chosen and the other four rejects formed the group Clea (taken from their initials.) Signed to Polydor, Girls Aloud's debut single *Sound Of The Underground* (No 1, Dec 2002) spent four weeks at Number 1 in the UK and also became their only No 1 single in Ireland. It was later revealed that this catchy tune with the iconic guitar riff was originally recorded by another girl group, Orchid, the Girls Aloud vocals merely added over the top. Before their second release, *No Good Advice* (No 2, May 2003) five months later, Cole was charged with racially aggravated assault after an altercation with a black lavatory attendant Sophie Amogbokpa at Harper's nightclub in Guildford. It was alleged that Cheryl had called the attendant a 'jigaboo'. A jury found her guilty of assault occasioning actual bodily harm, but cleared her of racially aggravated assault. The judge sentenced Cole to 120 hours community service and ordered her to pay her victim £500 in compensation, as well as £3,000 towards prosecution costs. In June 2003, their debut album 'Sound Of The Underground' reached number two. Described as a mix of "Blondie and Bananarama, with a smattering of the Spice Girls at their best thrown in," the album included the tracks, *Girls Allowed*, written for the group by ex-Westlife star Bryan McFadden, and *Some Kind of Miracle*, co-written by former B*Witched member Edele Lynch. Girls Aloud's next 18 single releases all reached the Top 10: *Life Got Cold* (No 3, Aug 2003), *Jump* (No 2, Nov 2003), *The Show* (No 2, Jun 2004), *Love Machine* (No 2, Sep 2004), the Children In Need charity single *I'll Stand by You* (No 1, Nov 2004), *Wake Me Up* (No 4, Feb 2005), *Long Hot Summer* (No 7, Aug 2005), *Biology* (No 4, Nov 2005), *See the Day* (No 9, Dec 2005), *Whole Lotta History* (No 6, Mar 2006), *Something Kinda Ooooh* (No 3, Oct 2006), *I Think We're Alone Now* (No 4, Dec 2006), *Walk This Way* (Sugababes vs. Girls Aloud) (No 1, Mar 2007), *Sexy! No No No..* (No 5, Aug 2007), *Call the Shots* (No 3, Nov 2007), *Can't Speak French* (No 9, Mar 2008), *The Promise* (No 1, Oct 2008) and *The Loving Kind* (No 10, Jan 2009). Only Oasis before them has had more

consecutive Top 10 singles. Their 21st and final single to-date, *Untouchable*, was written by Girls Aloud's usual team of Miranda Cooper, Brian Higgins and his production team Xenomania but unfortunately stalled at No 11 in May 2009, thus ending their long streak of twenty-consecutive Top 10s. Their four subsequent studio albums are: 'What Will the Neighbours Say?' (No 6, Nov 2004), 'Chemistry' (No 11, Dec 2005), 'Tangled Up' (No 4, Nov 2007) and 'Out of Control' (No 1, Nov 2008). In October 2006, Girls Aloud released their first greatest hits collection, 'The Sound Of Girls Aloud' which went straight in at Number 1 and sold more than a million copies. *The Promise* won a BRIT Award for Best Single in 2009. In July that year the group announced its intention to take a year off. Although it has now been the best part of three years the band has not officially split. In August 2010, **Nicola**, who in 2008 had launched Dainty Doll, a make-up range for girls with pale skin like hers (she used fake tan for much of Girls Aloud's early history), said that she did not expect a reunion before 2012. In December 2006, she revealed that she had split with long time boyfriend Carl Egerton. She then dated Carl Davies for a year and there were rumours that they had planned to marry, however, in November 2008, she attended Sarah Harding's birthday party with Charlie Fennell. Nicola's debut solo album 'Cinderella's Eyes' (No 17, Sep 2011) spawned the singles *Beat of My Drum* (No 27, Jun 2011) and *Lucky Day* (No 40, Sep 2011). **Sarah** has turned to acting, appearing in the two recent *St Trinians* films as well as the forthcoming film of Ray Cooney's farce, *Run for Your Wife*. She has also launched a new nightclub called Kanaloa, signed a £100,000 deal to model Ultimo lingerie and can be seen as the face of Coca-Cola Zero in Ireland. Sarah has been linked to Kian Egan of Westlife, Calum Best, Alex Zane and Tom Crane amongst others. **Nadine** entered Ireland's version of the talent show *Popstars* in 2001, whilst attending Thornhill College. Although she managed to get to the end and into the group, Six, she was asked to leave as she had lied about her age on the application form for the show. She was 16, two years too young. In November 2010, Nadine released a solo album 'Insatiable' which reached No 20 in the Irish Albums Chart, as did the title track, *Insatiable*, in the Irish Singles Chart. In January 2008, Nadine dated former American football player Jason Bell, and the two were engaged until their split in May 2011. **Kimberley** starred as Young Cosette in a regional production of Les Misérables as a child and later appeared in ITV's *The Book Tower*. An accomplished actress, she applied for the role of Maria Sutherland in *Coronation Street* and made the final three along with Suzanne Shaw, losing out to Samia Smith. Since the band's hiatus she has fronted the 2009 Autumn/Winter collection for the fashion chain New Look and in July 2010, she became a presenter on music talk-show, *Suck My Pop*, on the Viva channel. In January 2011 Kimberley's vocals featured on the Aggro Santos song *Like U Like* which placed number eight and thirteen on the UK Singles Chart and Irish Singles Chart respectively. On 5 October 2011, Kimberley took over from Amanda Holden as Princess Fiona in the West End production of *Shrek the Musical*. **Cheryl** grew up in Heaton, Newcastle. As a youngster she won Boot's Bonniest baby competition, Mothercare Happy Faces Portrait competition, Best Looking girl in Newcastle and also appeared in two British Gas advertisements. She joined the Royal Ballet's summer school when she was nine years old. She became Mrs Cheryl Cole Tweedy when she married footballer Ashley Cole in Barnet, North West London in July 2006. In June 2008, she was named as the replacement for Sharon Osbourne as a judge for the fifth series of *The X Factor* alongside Dannii Minogue, Simon Cowell and Louis Walsh and subsequently ended up as the victorious judge, mentoring Alexandra Burke. Cheryl returned for the sixth series in 2009 and again emerged as the winning judge, mentoring Joe McElderry. Unfortunately the seventh series was not a happy one for Cheryl as her category failed to win for the first time, her marriage hit the rocks and she contracted malaria! With her health restored Cheryl became a judge on the American version of *The X Factor* alongside Simon Cowell, L.A. Reid, and Paula Abdul but was replaced after three weeks by Nicole Scherzinger. Outside Girls Aloud Cheryl has had the most successful recording career of the five girls. Her first two studio albums '3 Words' (No 1, Oct 2009) and 'Messy Little Raindrops' (No 1, Oct 2010) both topped the UK Albums Chart and placed second in Ireland. The lead singles of these albums, *Fight for This Love* (No 1, Oct 2009) and *Promise This* (No 1, Oct 2010) topped both the UK Singles Chart and Irish Singles Chart. Her other Top 20 singles include: *Parachute* (No 5, Mar 2010 – No 4 in Ireland) and *The Flood* (No 18, Jan 2011). Cheryl sang some of the vocals for will.i.am's single, *Heartbreaker* (No 4, May 2008, - No 7 in Ireland) and collaborated again with the rapper on the title track of her debut album, *3 Words* (No 4, Dec 2009 – No 7 in Ireland). Cheryl also supplied vocals for the Helping Haiti UK and Irish chart-topper, *Everybody Hurts* (No 1, Apr 1993).

The Goons see entry in the comedy section

Gorillaz Virtual band created in 1998 by Damon Albarn and comic book artist and designer Jamie Hewlett (the co-creator of the comic *Tank Girl*). The band has four animated members: 2D (lead vocals, keyboard and melodica), Murdoc Niccals (bass guitar and drum machine), Noodle (guitar, keyboard and occasional vocals) and Russel Hobbs (drums and percussion). The music in actuality is provided by a wide assortment of artists, Damon being the only permanent contributor. To-date the band has released four studio albums 'Gorillaz' (No 3, Apr 2001), 'Demon Days' (No 1, May 2005), 'Plastic Beach' (No 2, Mar 2010) and 'The Fall' (No 12, Dec 2010). Their debut single *Clint Eastwood* peaked at No 4 in March 2001. The pinnacle of their career came in September 2005 with their collaboration with Shaun Ryder (of Happy Mondays, Black Grape and Australian jungle fame) on *Dare (song)* reaching No 1 in the UK singles chart. The music video for *Dare* consists of a giant disembodied head (Shaun Ryder) being kept alive by machinery in a wardrobe belonging to Noodle (who performs most of the vocals in the video). Other Top 10 singles include: *19/2000* (No 6, Jul 2001), *Feel Good Inc* featuring vocals from De La Soul (No 2, May 2005) and *Dirty Harry* featuring Bootie Brown (No 2, Nov 2005). The multi-award-winning band is currently 'resting' due to disagreements between Damon and Jamie. See also entry for Blur.

Calvin Harris The Scottish DJ, singer, songwriter, and record producer, was born Adam Richard Wiles in Dumfries on 17 January 1984. A life-long lover of electronic music, Calvin was discovered on MySpace by American record producer Tommie Sunshine in 2006 and signed to EMI (publishing) and Sony BMG (recording). His debut album 'I Created Disco' (No 8, Jun 2007) was released by Fly Eye Records and Columbia Records, preceded by the singles *Acceptable in the 80s* (No 10, Mar 2007) and *The Girls* (No 3, Jun 2007). As a producer Calvin worked with pop singer Kylie Minogue, co-writing and producing two songs on her 2007 album 'X' - *Heart Beat Rock* and *In My Arms*, the latter a top ten hit in the UK. Calvin returned to work with Minogue on her album 'Aphrodite' (2010), co-producing the track *Too Much*. In June 2008 Calvin collaborated with rapper Dizzee Rascal and singer Chrome on the single *Dance wiv Me* which went straight to number one and stayed there for four weeks. The record mixed the grime roots of Rascal with the dance music of Harris and R&B of Chrome. In August 2009, Calvin produced Dizzee Rascal's next single, *Holiday*, which also reached number one and also featured vocals by Chrome although unlike *Dance wiv Me*, Harris doesn't sing any lines. Calvin's second album 'Ready for the Weekend' (No 1, Aug 2009) topped the UK chart and was preceded by the lead single *I'm Not Alone* (No 1, Apr 2009 and No 4 in Ireland) which knocked Lady Gaga's *Poker Face* off the top spot in it's first week of release. The title track *Ready for the Weekend* (No 3, Aug 2009) and *Flashback* (No 18, Nov 2009 featuring the vocals of Ayah Marar) were other successful singles from the album. Calvin's other Top 10 singles include: *Bounce* (featuring Kelis) (No 2, Jun 2011) and *Feel So Close* (No 2, Aug 2011 and also No 2 in Ireland). His latest single, *Let's Go*, the third track from his forthcoming third studio album was released in April 2012. The song features vocals from American pop and R&B singer-songwriter, record producer, dancer and actor Ne-Yo. On 14 November 2010, Calvin invaded the stage of *The X Factor* during a performance by Jedward,

holding a pineapple on his head and bending over to point at his buttocks. He was subsequently evicted from the studio by the security team and told not to return to fulfil his booking as a "Celebrity Guest" on the ITV2 programme *The Xtra Factor*. In 2011, he toured with Rihanna in Australia, Poland and the UK as a support act on her Loud Tour and subsequently produced and performed on her single *We Found Love* (No 1, Sep 2011) although did not provide any vocals. In November 2011, Calvin teamed up with another Scottish DJ Matt Burns (credited as 'BURNS') to produce and perform on Ghanaian musician Tinchy Stryder's single *Off The Record* which stalled at No 24 in the UK chart but peaked at No 23 in the Scottish chart.

Hear'Say British pop group created in February 2001 from the winners of *Popstars* (see entry in television section). The five chosen singers: Danny Foster (born Hackney, London, 3 May 1979), Myleene Klass (born Myleene Angela Quinn, Gorleston, Norfolk, 6 April 1978), Kym Marsh (born Kimberley Gail Marsh, Whiston, Merseyside, 13 June 1976), Suzanne Shaw (born Suzanne Crowshaw, Bury, Greater Manchester, 29 September 1981) and Noel Sullivan (born Cardiff, 28 July 1980) had immediate chart success when their debut single *Pure and Simple* (No 1, Mar 2001) went straight to number one in the UK Singles Chart on 24 March 2001. The song was a cover version of a song originally released a year earlier by Girl Thing (see separate entry) who were dropped from Polydor Records to make way for Hear'Say. The single was followed by an equally successful debut album 'Popstars' (No 1, Apr 2001). The album featured cover versions of *Monday Monday* by The Mamas & the Papas and *Bridge over Troubled Water* by Simon & Garfunkel, alongside original tracks. After another number one single, *The Way to Your Love* (No 1, Jun 2001 – No 10 in Ireland) the group were given their own ITV show, *Hear'Say It's Saturday*. By the end of the year the group's popularity began to wane. Their third single, *Everybody* (No 4, Nov 2011 and No 23 in Ireland) was the title track of their second album which stuttered to No 24 in the UK Albums Chart. In February 2002, Kym announced that she was leaving and following auditions mirroring the procedure through which the original members of Hear'Say were chosen, one of the group's former dancers, Johnny Shentall (born 3 September 1978) joined the band. Johnny was a member of short-lived group BOOM! but is probably more famous as the husband of Steps singer Lisa Scott-Lee (born Rhyl, St Asaph, Denbighshire, Wales, 5 November 1975). After several disappointing gigs, in August 2002, Hear'Say released their only single post-Marsh, *Lovin' Is Easy*. The track entered the charts at No 6 but dropped outside of the UK Top 20 the following week. Hear'Say disbanded on 1 October 2002, citing negative public reaction as the main reason. Following the breakup, **Myleene** went on to record a classical album for Polydor before becoming a presenter on CD:UK. She has since become a mainstream presenter and serial reality contestant and host (see entries in the television section for *The All Star Talent Show, Escape From Scorpion Island, Gok's Fashion Fix, I'm a Celebrity Get Me Out Of Here, Last Choir Standing, The One Show, The People's Quiz*, and *Popstar to Operastar*. **Kym** initially became a solo artist, having two UK Top 10 singles, *Cry* (No 2, Apr 2003) and *Come on Over* (No 10, Jul 2003) and a Top 10 album 'Standing Tall' (No 9, Aug 2003) on the Island label, before she was dropped due to low sales. After making her television acting debut in a 2005 episode of BBC soap opera *Doctors*, and subsequently appearing in an episode of Channel 4 late night soap *Hollyoaks: In The City*, playing a character called Ruth Parry, Kym joined the cast of *Coronation Street* as Michelle Connor on 3 April 2006. She was married to actor Jack Ryder (born Jack Seigfried Ryder, Woolwich, London, 21 September 1981) between 2002 and 2009 but has been dating *Hollyoaks* actor Jamie Lomas (he plays Warren Fox) since July 2008. Kym has two children, David Ryan (b. 1995) and Emily May (b. 1997) from a previous relationship with Dave Cunliffe and, despite tragically losing her son, Archie Jay Lomas, who had been born 18 weeks premature on 11 February 2009 and had died moments after birth, Kym gave birth to a baby girl, Polly, on 23 March 2011. See also section for Celebrity Mums of the Year. **Suzanne** had gained a lot of showbusiness experience before she auditioned for Hear'Say. She appeared in musicals, an Esso advert, a BBC children's series *Elidor* (1995 as Helen), *Holby City* (2000 as Tanya Cunningham) and just for good measure Suzanne was part of an ABBA tribute band, The Right Stuff. She also tried out for the part of Maria Sutherland in *Coronation Street*, and made it to the final three along with Girls Aloud member Kimberley Walsh, but lost out to Samia Smith. Since the demise of the band Suzanne has established herself as an actress in musical theatre and television. In April 2010 she started a seventeen month stint in *Emmerdale* playing Eve Birch / Jenson. Suzanne is a dab hand at winning reality shows also being successful in series 3 of the popular ITV1 ice skating program *Dancing on Ice*. After a lengthy romance with record producer Terry Adams she got engaged to him during her Hear'Say days but broke it off after meeting actor Darren Day whilst touring with him in the musical Summer Holiday. The couple had a son, Corey Mackenzie Day (born in Kent, Dec 2004) but by the following spring their relationship was over. Suzanne married Jason King (born Jason Griffiths, Tenbury Wells, Worcestershire, 6 January 1975) of duo JK and Joel (born Joel Hogg in Scarborough, North Yorkshire, 31 May 1977) fame (presenters of *Hider in the House* and *Escape from Scorpion Island*) on 14 June 2009 but separated from him by February 2012. See also section for Celebrity Mums of the Year. **Danny** first displayed his vocal talent on the Michael Barrymore music quiz show *My Kind of Music*. Post-Hear'Say he took part in the third series of Channel 4 sports-based reality show *The Games*, as replacement for injured actor Jonathon Morris but nowadays gigs with his own soul band, Danny Foster & The Big Soul Corporation. **Noel** came from the traditional Welsh choir background although was working as a waiter before being chosen for Hear'Say. He initially went into musical theatre when the band broke up and after a brief return to reality television in *Five's Trust Me – I'm a Holiday Rep*, he worked in America hosting *Simply Ballroom* and then moving to Reno and Branson as part of the Twelve Irish Tenors. Noel returned to musical theatre in Britain, playing the lead role of Galileo Figaro in the 2011 UK tour of *We Will Rock You*.

Hi-Gate see entry for Yomanda

The Hollies Manchester-based band formed in 1961 as the Fourtones by vocalist Allan Clarke (born Harold Allan Clarke, Salford, 5 April 1942), guitarist and vocalist Graham Nash (born Graham William Nash, Blackpool, 2 February 1942), bassist Eric Haydock (born Stockport, 3 February 1942) and drummer Donald Rathbone (born Wilmslow, Cheshire, October 1942). Guitarist Vic Steele (born Victor Winston Farrell, Manchester, 8 May 1945) joined the band later in the year and their name was changed to the Deltas. In 1962 they changed their name once again to The Hollies, by way of homage to Buddy Holly. After Steele left in 1963 they were signed to Parlophone and almost immediately Don Rathbone also left; their replacements were guitarist Tony Hicks (born Anthony Christopher Hicks, Nelson, Lancashire, 16 December 1945) and drummer Bobby Elliott (born Robert Hartley Elliott, Burnley Lancashire, 8 December 1941. The band gained a reputation for close vocal harmonies and although their debut single, *(Ain't That) Just Like Me* (No 25, May 1963) failed to make the Top 20, their next 21 singles certainly did beginning with: *Searchin'* (No 12, Aug 1963), *Stay* (No 8, Nov 1963), *Just One Look* (No 2, Feb 1964), *Here I Go Again* (No 4, May 1964), *We're Through* (No 7, Sep 1964), *Yes I Will* (No 9, Jan 1965) and their first UK number one, *I'm Alive* (No 1, May 1965). By now The Hollies had become part of the British Invasion of America and their next single *Look Through Any Window* (No 4, Sep 1965 – No 32 in USA) written by future 10cc member Graham Gouldman, who had earlier in the year written the Yardbirds' hit *For Your Love*, became their first US Top 40 hit. The B-side of this single, *So Lonely*, written by Clarke, Hicks and Nash (like so many of their hits under the name L. Ransford as the management felt there wasn't enough space on the record for all three names) was recorded by the Everly Brothers. The band's next single, *If I Needed Someone* (No 20, Dec 1965) was written by George Harrison and *I Can't Let Go* (No 2, Feb 1966)

was written by Chip Taylor (actor Jon Voight's brother), who also wrote *Wild Thing*. Eric Haydock left the band at this point and was replaced by Bernie Calvert (born Bernard Bamford Calvert, Brierfield, Lancashire, 16 September 1942) who had previously played with Tony Hicks and Bobby Elliott in the Dolphins. *Bus Stop* (No 5, Jun 1966 – No 5 in USA) also written by Gouldman, became the band's first Top 10 US single. *Stop Stop Stop* (No 2, Oct 1966 – No 7 in USA) became the first single in which Clarke, Hicks and Nash were credited under their own names. *On A Carousel* (No 4, Feb 1967 – No 11 in USA) was the first single in which Graham took over lead vocals as opposed to his usual three-part harmonies shared with Alan and Tony. *Carrie-Anne* (No 3, Jun 1967 – No 9 in USA) was followed by *King Midas in Reverse* (No 18, Sep 1967) a song written solely by Graham in an effort to get away from what he called the typical commercial "Moon, June, Spoon" lyrics which were their bread and butter. Although the record was critically acclaimed it failed to break the Top 50 in the States and this failure hit Graham very hard and he began to become disillusioned. After *Jennifer Eccles* (No 7, Mar 1968) and *Listen to Me* (No 11, Oct 1968) the band were gigging one night, coincidentally on Bobby's birthday, 8 December 1968, after which Graham announced he was quitting the band to relocate to Los Angeles to join forces with former Buffalo Springfield guitarist Stephen Stills and ex-Byrds singer David Crosby to form the supergroup, Crosby, Stills & Nash. Graham was replaced by Terry Sylvester (born Allerton, Liverpool, 8 January 1947) to take over guitar and vocal duties, the first post-Nash single being *Sorry Suzanne* (No 3, Mar 1969). Their next single, *He Ain't Heavy, He's My Brother* (No 3, Oct 1969 – No 7 in USA) featuring Elton John on piano, featured Allan as the frontman; a role he acquired after Graham's departure. The record was re-released in September 1988 following its use in a television advertisement for Miller Lite beer, and subsequently became their second chart-topping single. The band had two further Top 20 singles, *I Can't Tell the Bottom from the Top* (No 7, Apr 1970) and *Gasoline Alley Bred* (No 14, Oct 1970) before their record of 21 consecutive Top 20s ended with *Hey Willy* (No 22, May 1971). The apparent demise of the band's fortunes prompted Allan to leave the band temporarily to pursue a solo career and he was replaced by Swedish singer Mikael Rickfors. Ironically, Allan's solo projects were not commercial successes but the last single he recorded with The Hollies, *Long Cool Woman in a Black Dress* (No 32, Sep 1972) which he had co-written with Roger Cook and Roger Greenaway, reached No. 2 in the USA to become their most successful single ever there. Rickfors left the band in July 1973 to make way for the return of Allan Clarke. Their last Top 10 single was *The Air That I Breathe* (No 2, Feb 1974 – No 6 in USA). The Hollies were never really considered an album band for whatever reason although they did make plenty of LPs and had quite a lot of success. Their debut album 'Stay With The Hollies' (No 2, Feb 1964) was their most successful studio album despite only featuring cover songs for which they were famous in their early career. 'Hollies Sings Dylan' (No 3, May 1969) was another successful album and 'Distant Light' released in the USA in October 1971 peaked at No 21. They did have a UK chart-topping compilation album 'The Hollies Greatest' (No 1, Aug 1968). The group have never officially disbanded and continue to gig with ever-changing line-ups. Allan retired in 2000 and was replaced by Carl Wayne (born Colin David Tooley, Winson Green, Birmingham, 18 August 1943; died, of cancer, 31 August 2004), former lead singer of The Move. Present members of the band include: bassist Ray Stiles, formerly a member of 1970s chart-topping glam rock group Mud, keyboard player Ian Parker, former member of the Tom Robinson Band and Clannad, vocalist Peter Howarth plus Tony and Bobby. The Hollies were inducted to the Rock and Roll Hall of Fame in 2010.

The Honeycombs The Honeycombs were a London-based pop group often confused with The Applejacks (see separate entry) by dint of both bands having female instrumentalists which was almost unique at the time. Formed, as The Sheratons, in 1963 by hairdresser Martin Murray (born in London, 7 October 1939; rhythm guitar), his salon assistant Honey Lantree (born Ann Margot Lantree, Hayes, Middlesex, 28 August 1943; drums and vocals), her brother John Lantree (born John David Lantree, Newbury, Berkshire, 20 August 1940; Bass) and friends Denis D'Ell (born Denis James Dalziel, Whitechapel, London, 10 October 1943 - died of cancer 6 July 2005; lead vocals and harmonica) and Alan Ward (born in Nottingham, 12 December 1945; lead guitar). Martin left in November 1964 and was replaced by Peter Pye (born Walthamstow, London, 12 July 1946). The songwriting team of Ken Howard and Alan Blaikley spotted the group in the Mildmay Tavern in the Balls Pond Road in Islington. They gave them some songs for an audition with Joe Meek and one of them, *Have I the Right* (No 1, Jul 1964) impressed Joe so much he recorded it there and then, provided the B-side, *Please Don't Pretend Again*, and eventually released it with Pye Records in June 1964. Louis Benjamin (1922–1994), Pye's later chairman changed the name of the group to The Honeycombs as a pun on Ann's nickname and former profession. As well as topping the UK Singles Chart, the song made No 5 in the States and No 3 in Ireland. It was the third No 1 single Joe Meek produced at his Holloway Road studio (the other two being *Johnny Remember Me* by John Leyton and *Telstar* by The Tornados). Unfortunately The Honeycombs could never equal the success of their debut single and although they did have a subsequent hit with *That's the Way* (No 12, Aug 1965) by the following year most of the band had left and they officially disbanded in 1967. In the 1990s the band reformed to go on the very popular nostalgia circuit. There are presently two bands calling themselves the Honeycombs, one led by founder member Martin Murray and the other by later member Tony Harte. There is also yet another Hybrid calling itself The New Honeycombs.

The Housemartins see entries for Fatboy Slim and The Beautiful South

Hudson Ford see entry for The Strawbs

Engelbert Humperdinck Arnold George Dorsey was born in Madras, British India, 2 May 1936, to a British Army office father and Indian mother. His family relocated to England when he was ten-years-old and he was brought up in Leicester. A professional saxophone player in his early teens, he took up singing when he was 17 and began working under the name Gerry Dorsey (the idea for the name coming from his impression of Jerry Lewis). After National Service he began a recording career with Decca although with very little success; his first single, *I'll Never Fall in Love Again*, not charting. After suffering from TB in 1961 he resumed his career working the clubs until an old friend, Gordon Mills, who had newly begun to manage the career of Tom Jones, suggested the name change (borrowed from the 19th-century German composer of the popular opera Hansel and Gretel) that would soon spark a popularity previously unconsidered. His first single under his new name, *Release Me*, was previously a hit in America for Little Esther Phillips in 1962, but Engelbert's version not only gave Decca a No 1 on the UK Chart in January 1967, but also remained in the charts for more than a year in a single run (only Acker Bilk has ever emulated this feat). Engelbert went on to have a second No 1 with *The Last Waltz* in August 1967 and also six further Top 10 singles: *There Goes My Everything* (No 2, May 1967), *Am I That Easy To Forget* (No 3, Jan 1968), *A Man Without Love* (No 2, Apr 1968), *Les Bicyclettes De Belsize* (No 5, Sep 1968), *The Way It Used To Be* (No 3, Feb 1969) and *Winter World Of Love* (No 7, Nov 1969). During this period Engelbert also had several hit albums: 'Release Me' (No 6, May 1967), 'The Last Waltz' (No 3, Nov 1967), 'A Man Without Love' (No 3, Aug 1968), 'Engelbert' (No 3, Mar 1969) and 'Engelbert Humperdinck' (No 5, Dec 1969). He also had a No 1 greatest hits album in December 1974 and two further Top 10 compilation albums; 'At His Very Best' (No 5, Apr 2000) and 'His Greatest Love Songs' (No 4, Mar 2004). Engelbert married showjumper Patricia Healey in 1964. They have four children and nine grandchildren. He was chosen as the UK entrant (singing *Love Will Set You Free*) for the 2012 Eurovision Song Contest in Baku, Azerbaijan (the oldest competitor ever) and placed second-to-last.

Javine Hylton The artist usually referred to by her Christian name, Javine, was born Javine Dionne Hylton, to a white mother and black father, in Kensington, London, 27 December 1981. Her first professional gig was playing Nala in a production of *The Lion King* in London's West End, a role she held for two years. Javine's destiny as a solo singer was decided for her when she narrowly missed out on making the final cut for Girls Aloud (see separate entry) after taking part in ITV's *Popstars: The Rivals*. After signing to Virgin's pop-oriented Innocent label, her debut single, *Real Things* (No 4, Jul 2003) which featured a sample of M.O.P.'s (Mashed Out Posse) *Ante Up*, became her most successful to-date. Javine's four other singles: *Surrender (Your Love)* (No 15, Nov 2003), *Best of My Love* (No 18, Jun 2004), the double-A side *Don't Walk Away / You've Got a Friend* (No 16, Aug 2004) and *Touch My Fire* (No 18, May 2005) all made the Top 20; the last named being the UK's entry for the Eurovision Song Contest for 2005 (see entry in television section) and her first for Island Records. Javine's debut album 'Surrender' was released in June 2004 but flopped and she was dropped by Innocent later in the year. In an up and down 2006, Javine was convicted of driving with excess alcohol in her body in March and was subsequently banned from driving for 18 months. She then began to concentrate on reality television and went on to win Series 4 of the Channel 4 programme *The Games*. She began an affair with fellow *Games* competitor MC Harvey (born Michael Harvey Jr, Plymouth, Devon, 1 May 1979) who had married Alesha Dixon only the year before, and by November 2006, after much acrimony, the marriage was over and her relationship with the former So Solid Crew star was cemented. Whilst appearing on *Never Mind the Buzzcocks*, Alesha's friend Jamelia (born Jamelia Niela Davis, Hockley, Birmingham, 11 January 1981) referred to Javine as "a slag". Javine gave birth to MC Harvey's daughter, Angel Hylton Harvey, in February 2008. In September 2009, Javine split with MC Harvey after discovering that he had been unfaithful to her. In recent years Javine has appeared in BBC Three's *Celebrity Scissorhands*, BBC Two's *The Underdog Show* and Channel Four's *Celebrity Come Dine With Me*.

Billy Idol Born at Stanmore, Middlesex as William Michael Albert Broad on 30 November 1955, Billy was one of the most visible punks thanks in no small measure to his peroxide hair. Formerly lead singer of Generation X, he enjoyed more success Stateside than in his home country and received three Grammy nominations. He charted between 1984 and 1994 in Britain but only scored three Top 10 hits: *White Wedding* (No 6, Jul 1985), *Rebel Yell* (No 6, Sep 1985) and *Mony Mony* (No 7, Oct 1987) although still touring with Steve Stevens, the guitarist who played for Michael Jackson.

Frank Ifield Coventry-born singer, born 30 November 1937, who topped the charts four times in the early Sixties. When he was eight, Frank's parents moved to Australia where he learned to yodel and became very popular Down Under. He returned to the UK in November 1959 and the following year made his chart debut with *Lucky Devil*, which got to number 22. The follow-up *Gotta Get A Date* stalled at 49 in September 1960. In July 1962, he entered the charts with *I Remember You*, which stayed at Number 1 for seven weeks. The double A-side, *Lovesick Blues / She Taught Me to Yodel*, in October of the same year gave Frank his second Number 1 and he completed the hat-trick with *The Wayward Wind* (No 1, Jan 1963), making him the first Briton to have three successive chart-toppers. His debut album, 'I'll Remember You' (No 3, Feb 1963) was followed by the single, *Nobody's Darling But Mine* (No 4, Apr 1963). Frank returned to the top of the charts with his next release *Confessin' (That I Love You)* in June 1963. He then toured the UK for the remainder of the year. While Vee-Jay Records temporarily had the US rights to a number of The Beatles' recordings, they released an album called 'Jolly What!', consisting of four studio Beatles songs (all previously released), plus eight Frank Ifield recordings. This LP has subsequently become one of the rarest Beatles' albums. Frank's LPs 'Born Free' (No 3, Sep 1963), 'Blue Skies' (No 10, Mar 1964) and the compilation album 'Greatest Hits' (No 9, Dec 1964), ensured that all four of his charted albums made the Top

10. In 1962 and 1976, Frank entered A Song for Europe finishing second the first time and last (of 12) the second time. His last chart appearance for 25 years came in December 1966 but in December 1991, he made a surprise return with *The Yodelling Song* (aka *She Taught Me to Yodel*) featuring the Backroom Boys, which reached number 40. Frank is still performing and has written the first volume of his autobiography, *I Remember Me*.

Ironik DJ and Rapper Ironik (born James Christian Charters, Camden, London, 18 January 1988) has thus far had UK Top 10 hits with: *Stay With Me (Everybody's Free)* (No 5, Jun 2008) which samples lyrics of the songs *Everybody's Free (To Feel Good)* by Quindon Tarver, which itself is a cover of the Rozalla hit *Everybody's Free,* and *Written In The Stars* by Westlife; and *Tiny Dancer* (No 3, three, 2009) a collaboration with Chipmunk and Sir Elton John (see separate entries). Both singles were from his debut album 'No Point in Wasting Tears' (No 21, Sep 2008). Another Top 10 Ironik accreditation was as part of the Young Soul Rebels on the charity single, *I Got Soul* (No 10, Oct 2009) in aid of War Child. He was nominated as Best Newcomer at the 2008 MOBO Awards and Best UK Act at the 2009 MOBOs. The handsome young musician often uses lyrics reflecting street violence but ironically (no pun intended) he was robbed and stabbed in his right buttock on 6 November 2010 whilst returning home to his north London home from a gig in Essex in the middle of the night. Thankfully Ironik is fully fit again and soon to release his, eponymously titled, second album.

The Jam Three-piece punk-influenced mod band from Woking, Surrey who scored four No 1 singles and a No 1 album in the early Eighties. Formed in 1972, their early line-up was changeable before it settled on Paul Weller (born John William Weller, Sheerwater, near Woking, Surrey, 25 May 1958; vocalist/lead guitarist), Rick Buckler (born Paul Richard Buckler, Woking, Surrey, 6 December 1955; drummer) and Bruce Foxton (born in Woking, Surrey, 1 September 1955; bass guitarist). On 29 April 1977, Polydor released The Jam's debut single, *In The City*, a song about police brutality, which reached No 40. An album of the same name was released the following month and reached No 20. In March 1978, The Jam released *News of the World* (No 27) written and sung by Foxton. The song is used as the theme to the comedy show *Mock the Week*. After the album 'This is the Modern World' (No 22, Nov 1977) their third LP 'All Mod Cons' (No 6, Nov 1978) became their first Top 10 album and spawned the single *David Watts* (No 25, Aug 1978) a cover of a Kink's song written by Ray Davies about his love for a fellow shoolboy. Three more singles charted before they finally breached the Top 10 with *The Eton Rifles* (No 3, Nov 1979) from the album, 'Setting Sons' (No 4, Nov 1979). In 1980, they released two singles, the double A-sided *Going Underground/Dreams Of Children* (10 March 1980) and *Start* (11 August 1980), and both reached No 1, the latter appearing on the album 'Sound Affects' (No 2, Dec 1980). In 1981, another track from the album, *That's Entertainment* reached No 21 while the non-album singles *Funeral Pyre* (No 4, Jun 1981) and *Absolute Beginners* (No 4, Oct 1981) both reached the same spot in the charts. In early 1982, *Town Called Malice/Precious* (No 1, Feb 1982) from the album 'The Gift' (No 1, Mar 1982) – the band's final studio album – became their third No 1 single, the album also topping the chart. In the summer, another track from the album, *Just Who is the Five O'Clock Hero* (No 8, Jul 1982) was followed by the non-album soul ballad *The Bitterest Pill (I Ever Had To Swallow)* (No 2, Sep 1982). In December 1982, *Beat Surrender* (released 26 November 1982) became their last No 1 hit. That month the group embarked on a farewell tour, finishing at the Brighton Centre on 11 December 1982. In early 1983, Paul Weller formed The Style Council with Mick Talbot of The Merton Parkas. The duo was later joined by drummer Steve White and Weller's then-wife, vocalist Dee C. Lee. They had three Top 10 albums: 'Café Bleu' (US title: My Ever Changing Moods) (No 2, Mar 1984), 'Our Favourite Shop' (US title: Internationalists) (No 1, May 1985) and 'The Cost of Loving' (No 2, Feb 1987) and seven top 10 singles:

Speak Like A Child (No 4, Mar 1983), *Long Hot Summer/Paris Match* (No 3, Aug 1983), My *Ever Changing Moods* (No 5, Feb 1984), *Groovin' (You're the Best Thing)/Big Boss Groove* (No 5, May 1984), *Shout to the Top* (No 7, Oct 1984), *Walls Come Tumbling Down!* (No 6, May 1985) and *It Didn't Matter* (No 9, Jan 1987). After they split in 1989, Paul pursued a solo career and made 11 studio albums all of which were in the Top 10: 'Paul Weller' (No 8, Sep 1992), 'Wild Wood' (No 2, Sep 1993), 'Stanley Road' (No 1, May 1995), 'Heavy Soul' (No 2, Jul 1997), 'Heliocentric' (No 2, Apr 2000), 'Illumination' (No 1, Sep 2002), 'Studio 150' (No 2, Sep 2004), 'As Is Now' (No 4, Oct 2005), '22 Dreams' (No 1, Jun 2008), 'Wake Up the Nation' (No 2, Apr 2010) and 'Sonik Kicks' (No 1, Mar 2012). He has also had five top 10 singles: *The Changingman* (No 7, May 1995), *You Do Something to Me* (No 9, Jul 1995), *Peacock Suit* (No 5, Aug 1996), *It's Written in the Stars* (No 7, Sep 2002) and *From the Floorboards Up* (No 6, Jul 2005). Bruce Foxton had three minor hits before joining Stiff Little Fingers in 1990, where he remained until January 2006. Rick Buckler formed Time UK with Tom Robinson Band guitarist Danny Kustow. They released three singles. A 1986 collaboration between Foxton and Buckler under the name Sharp did not trouble the chart compilers. In 2006, Weller stated that The Jam would never reform. He said, "Me and my children would have to be destitute and starving in the gutter before I'd even consider that." Buckler and Foxton have toured as From The Jam.

Jessie J Singer / songwriter Jessica Ellen Cornish (born Chadwell Heath, Essex, 27 March 1988) showed an aptitude for showbusiness from a young age. She attended Colin's Performing Arts School and as an 11-year old-was cast in Andrew Lloyd Webber's West End production of *Whistle Down the Wind*. Unlike her two older sisters, Jessica was not academically-inclined and at the age of 16 she enrolled at the BRIT School and, aged 17, joined a girl group, Soul Deep. Jessie graduated in May 2006 along with singers Adele and Leona Lewis. Later that year she suffered a minor stroke which made her realise the uncertainty of life and gave her the impetus to risk a pop career. After Jessie left Soul Deep she toured as the support act for Cyndi Lauper and created her own fan base under her stage name of Jessie J. In November 2010 Jessie released her debut single, *Do It Like a Dude*, which peaked at number two on the UK Singles Chart. Her follow-up single, *Price Tag*, featuring American rapper Bobby Ray Simmons Jr. (aka B.o.B), was released in January 2011 and the following month topped the chart in the UK, Ireland, France and New Zealand. The single also reached number twenty-three on the Billboard Hot 100 in the United States, giving her global fame. Her debut album 'Who You Are' was released in February 2011 and reached number two on the UK Chart. The album contained her first two singles plus her subsequent next four, *Nobody's Perfect* (No 9, Jun 2011), *Who's Laughing Now* (No 16, Aug 2011), *Domino* (released in Sep 2011 but No 1, Jan 2012 and also No 1 in Ireland and No 6 in USA) and the title track *Who You Are* (No 8, Nov 2011). In November, Jessie also recorded *Up*, a duet with James Morrison from his album 'The Awakening'. The single reached No 30 in the UK chart by the end of 2011. Jessie is openly bi-sexual displaying no preference for either gender. Midway through 2011 Jessie had an accident whilst rehearsing and ruptured tendons in her foot causing her to have to perform sitting on a throne for several months. The accident has prompted her not to wear extreme high heels. Jessie is currently working as a coach and mentor alongside artistes will.i.am (of The Black Eyed Peas), Tom Jones and Danny O'Donoghue (of The Script) on the BBC talent show, *The Voice*.

JLS The four London-based vocalists first came to public attention during the fifth series of ITV reality talent show *The X Factor* in 2008, ultimately finishing runners-up. Oritsé Williams (born in London, 27 November 1986) was inspired to put the band together when he was nineteen-years-old in order to raise some money to help his mother who suffers from Multiple sclerosis. He first recruited singer and actor Marvin Humes (born in London, 18

March 1985) who had already experienced Top 10 chart success with *Love You Like Mad* (No 7, Feb 2004) as a member of the Simon Webbe-managed band VS and also appeared regularly in BBC One's *Holby City*. Next to join was Aston Merrygold (born in Peterborough, Cambridgeshire, 13 February 1988) who also had showbusiness experience as Cookie in the pre-school children's show *Fun Song Factory* on CITV. The final member of the quartet to sign up was Jonathan "JB" Gill (born in London, 7 December 1986). Originally working under the name UFO (Unique Famous Outrageous) the lads had to change their name when auditioning for *X Factor* as that name was already registered as a professional act. They agreed to go with the name JLS (Jack the Lad Swing), from their style created with their production/songwriting team Tracklacers, combining the phrase "Jack the lad" and the urban music of New Jack Swing. Following their success on the show, Simon Cowell's record company, Syco, announced that they were to sign JLS but by the following month Simon had decided to concentrate his efforts on series winner Alexandra Burke and revoked the offer. JLS were immediately signed to Epic Records in January 2009 and six months later their debut single, *Beat Again* (No 1, Jul 2009) topped the UK Singles Chart and placed No 3 in Ireland. The song won Best British Single at the MOBO Awards 2009 and 2010 BRIT Awards making them the first act from *X Factor* to win a Brit Award. Their follow-up single, *Everybody in Love* (No 1, Nov 2009) also topped the UK Singles Chart and went one better than *Beat Again* in Ireland by peaking at No 2. In the same month, the band's debut album 'JLS' (No 1, Nov 2009) went straight to No 1 in the UK and Ireland. A third track from the album, *One Shot* (No 6, Feb 2010) peaked at No 6 in the UK and No 11 in Ireland. *The Club Is Alive* (No 1, Jul 2010 – No 4 in Ireland) was released as the lead single for their second album 'Outta This World' (No 2, Nov 2010 - No 4 in Ireland) and became their third chart-topping single. The second track from the album, *Love You More* (No 1, Nov 2010 – No 12 in Ireland), also topped the UK Singles Chart and served as the official Children in Need charity single for 2010. A third track, *Eyes Wide Shut* (No 8, Feb 2011 - No 14 in Ireland) was remixed to feature Tinie Tempah for its single release. *She Makes Me Wanna* (No 1, Jul 2011 – No 2 in Ireland) featuring American singer-songwriter Dev, was the lead single for their third studio album and became their fifth UK No 1 single. The album itself 'Jukebox' (No 2, Nov 2011 – No 5 in Ireland) spawned two further hit singles: *Take a Chance on Me* (No 2, Nov 2011 - No 13 in Ireland) and *Do You Feel What I Feel?* (No 16, Dec 2011 and No 29 in Ireland). Their latest single, *Proud* (No 6, Mar 2012 – No 28 in Ireland) was the official Sport Relief charity single. JLS have also featured on three further UK chart-topping singles: *Hero* (Oct 2008) as part of The X Factor Finalists, *Everybody Hurts* (Feb 2010) as part of Helping Haiti, and *Wishing on a Star* (Nov 2011) by *The X Factor* Finalists 2011 featuring JLS and One Direction. The group have also released their own documentary film titled *JLS: Eyes Wide Open 3D*, making them the first British music act ever to release a 3D film. JLS have become patrons of several charities but have also released branded condoms with Durex under the campaign line "Just Love Safe", as part of a charitable initiative they have established called the JLS Foundation, where they are working together with sexual health charities to promote safe sex and family planning. The four socially aware young lads have won numerous awards including four MOBOs and two BRITs. See also entry for The Saturdays.

Sir Elton John Flamboyant knighted singer-songwriter whose private life has guaranteed him acres of newsprint. Sir Elton Hercules John was born as Reginald Kenneth Dwight in Pinner, Middlesex on 25 March 1947. He began taking piano lessons when he was just four and after studying at the Royal Academy of Music joined his first band Corvettes (later to become Bluesology) in the early Sixties. In July 1965, he wrote Bluesology's first release *Come Back Baby* and they turned professional that year. In December 1966, Long John Baldry became lead singer and later the band evolved into a nine-piece outfit including Elton Dean on sax. The group became known as the John Baldry Show and began touring. Six months later, disillusioned by the way the band had developed, Reg Dwight auditioned for Liberty Records and although he failed the audition

he was given some lyrics written by Bernie Taupin (born in Sleaford, Lincolnshire, 22 May 1950). They discovered that they had identical musical tastes and began composing by post. They only met when 20 songs had been written. Their first composition (credited to John/Taupin) was called *Scarecrow*. Dwight had recently dispensed with his birth name and borrowed the names of his former bandmates Baldry and Dean. On 7 November 1967, the duo were signed to Dick James Music as staff writers at a salary of £10 per week. On 22 November 1967, *Let the Heartaches Begin* by Long John Baldry became the 240th UK No 1. The B-side, *Lord You Made the Night Too Long*, was the first record to bear the names of John/Taupin. On 1 March 1968, the first solo Elton John single was released and the same month Roger Cook recorded their song *Skyline Pigeon*. In January 1969, Elton auditioned unsuccessfully to be lead singer of Robert Fripp's band King Crimson. On 3 June that year, his debut album, 'Empty Sky', was released. While waiting for his big break, he played piano as a session musician including on The Hollies' *He Ain't Heavy, He's My Brother* and worked as a backing singer for The Scaffold. The following year, on 10 April, his eponymously titled album entered the charts and spawned his first chart single *Your Song* (No 7, Jan 1971). 'Elton John' reached number five in the UK and went one better in the USA. In 1971, John Reid became Elton's manager and sometime lover. The two men would fall out spectacularly 27 years later. In 1972, *Rocket Man (I Think It's Going To Be A Long, Long Time)* (No 2, Apr 1972) became Elton's second consecutive Top 10 hit whilst *Crocodile Rock* (No 5, Nov 1972) topped the US chart. The last named single was from the album 'Don't Shoot Me I'm Only the Piano Player', which was released in February 1973 and topped the charts on both sides of the Atlantic, spawning a second single, *Daniel* (No 4, Jan 1973). In the summer of that year, *Saturday Night's Alright for Fighting* (No 7, Jul 1973) and *Goodbye Yellow Brick Road* (No 6, Sep 1973) were lead singles for the album of the same name which topped the charts on both sides of the Atlantic in November 1973. In March 1974, the iconic track *Candle in the Wind* entered the charts where it stalled at number 11. The fourth single from the 'Goodbye Yellow Brick Road' album was *Benny and the Jets* (No 37, Feb 1974) which topped the US Singles Chart. In the summer of 1974 the album 'Caribou' reached Number 1 in the UK and US Album Charts and spawned the singles, *Don't Let the Sun Go Down on Me* (No 16, Jun 1974) and *The Bitch is Back* (No 15, Sep 1974). That autumn, the first greatest hits LP was released and also went to No 1, spending 84 weeks on the chart in the UK. It also went to Number 1 in America. On the same day the greatest hits album entered the British charts, Elton also entered the singles chart with a cover of The Beatles' *Lucy in the Sky with Diamonds* (No 10, Nov 1974). In America, it went to the top of the chart, as did the follow-up *Philadelphia Freedom*, which reached 12 in Britain. In 1975 Elton released the albums 'Captain Fantastic and the Dirt Brown Cowboy' (No 2, Jun 1975) and 'Rock of the Westies' (No 5, Nov 1975) both LPs topping the US Albums Chart. Later that year Elton appeared as the Local Lad in The Who's rock opera *Tommy* and the following spring he released *Pinball Wizard* (No 7, Mar 1976) from the film soundtrack. That summer, he had his first Number 1 single in the United Kingdom, a duet with Kiki Dee, *Don't Go Breaking My Heart* (released 21 June 1976). It sold more than a million copies in America where it also topped the charts. In an interview with *Rolling Stone* in November 1976, Elton admitted that he was bisexual. In October 1977, his second greatest hits LP charted and reached number six. On 3 November 1977, during a concert at Empire Pool, Wembley, Elton announced that he was retiring from performing. After the success of *Don't Go Breaking My Heart* in 1976, Elton did not put another song in the UK Top 10 until January 1979 when *Song For Guy* (released 28 November 1978) reached number four. The song was about Guy Burchett, a motorcycle messenger for Elton's record label. He had died in an accident aged seventeen. On 21 May 1979, Elton began an eight-concert run in Leningrad, the first Western pop star to play in the Soviet Union. That month, he also played Israel. Later in the year Elton and Bernie Taupin began working together again after a brief hiatus. A third greatest hits album was released in 1980. Despite releasing singles and albums, Elton did not return to the Top 10 until *Blue Eyes* in the spring of

1982 reached number eight. Just over a year later he released the album 'Too Low for Zero' (No 7, Jun 1983) which spawned the singles, *I Guess That's Why They Call It the Blues* (No 5, Apr 1983 - featuring Stevie Wonder on harmonica) and *I'm Still Standing* (No 4, Jul 1983). In the autumn of that year, he reached number 20 with a third track *Kiss the Bride*. It may have been an omen for surprising many who believed him homosexual rather than bisexual as he then married sound engineer Renate Blauel on St Valentine's Day 1984 at Darling Point, Sydney, Australia. The marriage lasted three years. His next album 'Breaking Hearts' (No 2, Jun 1984) spawned the singles *Sad Songs Say So Much* (No 7, May 1984) and *Passengers* (No 5, Aug 1984). The following year the album 'Ice on Fire' (No 2, Nov 1985) spawned the single *Nikita* (No 3, Oct 1985) which was aided by a video produced by Ken Russell. On 13 July 1985, he appeared at Wembley for the charity concert Live Aid. In the winter of 1985, he sang on *That's What Friends Are For* (No 16, Nov 1985), a joint effort with Dionne Warwick, Gladys Knight and Stevie Wonder, which reached No 1 in America with the profits going to Aids research. In January 1987, he underwent surgery on his throat. Several non-cancerous polyps were removed from his vocal cords. He did not perform live again until April but the month before issued a writ for libel against *The Sun*, which alleged he had indulged in drug-fuelled romps with rent boys. In early 1988, an orchestral rendition of *Candle in the Wind* peaked at number six in America and went one better in the UK, six places higher than its original chart placing. On 17 November 1988, he and his wife were divorced and the following month on 12 December *The Sun* settled its libel case agreeing to pay substantial damages and print a front page apology. Elton's next album 'Sleeping with the enemy' (No 1, Sep 1989) spawned the single *Sacrifice* which charted in November 1989, but stalled at No 55. Seven months later, and reissued as a double-A single with *Healing Hands*, it gave him his first solo British No 1. It topped the charts for six weeks. A fourth greatest hits album went to Number 1, charting in November 1990. His next single, *Don't Let the Sun go Down on Me* (No 1, Dec 1991), a duet with George Michael of his earlier hit, topped the charts in both the US and UK. In November 1993, he released the album 'Duets' (No 5, Dec 1993) which included the George Michael duet and spawned the Top 10 singles *True Love* (with Kiki Dee) (No 2, Nov 1993) and *Don't Go Breaking My Heart* (with RuPaul) (No 7, Feb 1994). Elton then collaborated with Tim Rice to write the songs for the 1994 Disney film *The Lion King*. At the 67th Oscars on 27 March 1995, three of the five nominees for Best Song were from *The Lion King*. Elton won with *Can You Feel the Love Tonight* (No 14 Jul 1994). The song also won him the Best Male Pop Vocal Performance gong at the 37th Grammy Awards on 1 March 1995. A second compilation entitled 'Love Songs' was issued in 1995, 13 years after the first one. On 31 August 1997, Diana, Princess of Wales died in a Paris car crash and, a week later at her funeral, he sang Bernie Taupin's revised lyrics to *Candle In The Wind* to commemorate the princess. *Candle In The Wind 1997* topped the charts on both side of the Atlantic as well as Australia, Austria, Belgium, Canada, Finland, France, Germany, Holland, Ireland, Italy, Japan, New Zealand, Norway, Sweden and Switzerland. Eleven times Platinum, it eventually sold more than 33 million copies. It is the best-selling single in UK Chart history; Elton's fourth British and ninth US Number 1 (topping the charts for 14 weeks) and the only single ever certified Diamond in America where it sold more than 11 million copies. It also won Elton the Best Male Pop Vocal Performance gong at the 40th Grammy Awards ceremony in 1998. Later that year, *The Lion King* was adapted for Broadway and in 1999 Elton composed music for a Disney production of *Aida* (with lyrics by Tim Rice), for which they received the Tony Award for Best Original Score at the 54th Tony Awards, and the Grammy Award for Best Musical Show Album at the 43rd Grammy Awards. In 2000, John and Rice collaborated again to write songs for DreamWorks' animated film *The Road to El Dorado*. Elton then collaborated with Blue on the single sorry *Seems to be the Hardest Word* (No 1, Dec 2002) which featured on their album 'One Love'. In August 2003, Elton

scored another No 1 single with *Are You Ready for Love* and eighteen months later another with *Ghetto Gospel* (No 1, Feb 2005) collaborating with Tupac Shakur. In 2005, he also composed the score for *Billy Elliot The Musical* with playwright Lee Hall. An album, 'The Union' was released on 19 October 2010, a collaboration with American singer-songwriter Leon Russell. In 1976 Elton became chairman and director of Watford Football Club, appointing Graham Taylor as manager. He sold the club to Jack Petchey in 1987 but remained his life-long president. In 1997 he re-purchased the club from Petchey and once again became chairman, eventually stepping down in 2002 although continuing as president of the club. Having been named a Commander of the Order of the British Empire in 1996, Elton received a knighthood from Queen Elizabeth II for "services to music and charitable services" in 1998. Elton met David Furnish (born in Scarborough, Ontario, Canada, 25 October 1962) on 30 October 1993 and they held a civil partnership ceremony on 21 December 2005 at Windsor Guildhall. After failing to adopt a Ukrainian child, they had a son (to a surrogate mother) Zachary Jackson Levon Furnish-John, born in California on Christmas Day 2010. On the boy's birth certificate, Elton was registered as the father while David was named under the mother category in computer documents.

Sir Tom Jones Welsh vocalist (born Thomas John Woodward, Treforest, Pontypridd, 7 June 1940) whose love of music was formed in childhood when at the age of twelve he contracted tuberculosis and spent two years bed-ridden, passing the time by listening to music and drawing. In March 1957, Tom married his childhood sweetheart Melinda Trenchard when he discovered she was pregnant. Both Tom and 'Linda' were aged just sixteen. Their son, Mark, was born a month after the wedding. To support his young family Tom initially took a job working in a glove factory but was later employed as a vacuum cleaner salesman and later still, a bricklayer's mate. He supplemented his income by gigging as the frontman for Welsh beat group, Tommy Scott and the Senators. Although recording several tracks with the legendary producer Joe Meek, Tom had little success outside South Wales until one evening in the summer of 1964 while playing the Top Hat in Cwmtillery, Blaenau Gwent, Tom was spotted by Madras-born Welsh songwriter Gordon Mills (15 May 1935 - 29 July 1986). Gordon was a much-respected musician who had won competitions for his harmonica playing and as a member of The Viscounts, had chart success with *Short'nin' Bread* (No 16, Oct 1960) and *Who Put the Bomp* (No 21, Sep 1961). He also wrote the Top 10 hits, *I'll Never Get Over You* (No 4, Jul 1963) for Johnny Kidd and the Pirates, and *I'm the Lonely One* (No 8, Feb 1964) for Cliff Richard and the Shadows. Gordon took Tom to London, changed his name from Woodward to Jones and arranged a recording contract with Decca. Tom's first single, *Chills and Fever*, was released in November 1964 but made no impact on the charts. However his second single, *It's Not Unusual* (No 1, Feb 1965) topped the charts after being heavily promoted on Radio Caroline, and also peaked at No 10 on the American chart. Tom spent much of the next year gigging around the UK with his backing band, The Squires, but took time out to record the successful film themes, *What's New Pussycat* (No 11, Aug 1965 – No 3 in USA and No 1 in Canada) and *Thunderball* (No 35, Jan 1966). Tom won the Grammy Award for Best New Artist for 1965. By the mid-1960s The Beatles had killed off many established male recording artists but Gordon was shrewd enough to continually reinvent Tom and his next phase from rock singer to balladeer probably ensured his longevity. In November 1966 Tom had his second UK No 1 single with *Green Green Grass of Home,* which became Decca's first single by a UK artist to sell over a million copies. A proliferation of hit singles followed over the course of the next five years, including: *Detroit City* (No 8, Feb 1967), *Funny Familiar Forgotten Feeling* (No 7, Apr 1967), *I'll Never Fall in Love Again* (No 2, Jul 1967), *I'm Coming Home* (No 2, Nov 1967), *Delilah* (No 2, Feb 1968), *Love Me Tonight* (No 9, May 1969), *Without Love* (No 10, Dec 1969), *Daughter of Darkness* (No 5, Apr 1970), *I (Who Have Nothing)* (No 16, Aug

1970), *She's A Lady* (No 13, Jan 1971), *Till* (No 2, Oct 1971) and *The Young New Mexican Puppeteer* (No 6, Apr 1972). During this period Tom also had several successful albums, including the chart-topping 'Delilah' in 1968, plus the internationally successful ITV television variety show, *This Is Tom Jones*, which ran from 1969 until 1971. Tom first performed in Las Vegas (at the Flamingo) in 1967 and became friends with Elvis Presley, who he had first met two years earlier in Hawaii whilst Elvis was filming *Paradise, Hawaiian Style*. Tom has played Vegas for at least one week every year for the past 40 years and it was at Caesar's Palace in the early 1970s that young women in the audience first started to throw their knickers (and sometimes bras and hotel keys) at Tom during his performances. Between 1969 and 1974 Tom's resident guitarist was the legendary Big Jim Sullivan (born James George Tomkins, Uxbridge, Middlesex, 14 February 1941) who subsequently also became a friend of Presley's. Tom moved to the United States in 1974 on the advice of his accountant to avoid Britain's newly introduced 83% top rate of tax, buying Dean Martin's former mansion in the East Gate Old Bel Air in Los Angeles. In March 1975 Tom released a '20 Greatest Hits' album which topped the UK chart. Before Sullivan left, Tom was already in a bit of a slump recording-wise although still hugely popular in Vegas. Gordon decided to reinvent him yet again, as a country singer and although his first charting song in this genre, *Say you'll Stay until Tomorrow* (No 40, Apr 1977) topped the US Billboard Hot Country Singles and also placed No 15 in the US Billboard Hot 100, it was only a minor UK hit, and indeed his last for exactly a decade. After Gordon died of cancer in 1986, Tom's son Mark became his manager and free from all the frustrations that inevitably accompanies long-term management, Tom's career once again took off. Tom re-entered the singles chart with *A Boy from Nowhere* (No 2, Apr 1987) and the following year collaborated with The Art of Noise to have a further Top 10 single with *Kiss* (No 5, Oct 1988). In the 1990s Tom had a brief recording hiatus although still active. In June 1992 he made his first appearance at the Glastonbury Festival (situated near Pilton, Somerset and organised by Michael Eavis) and in 1993 he appeared as himself in episodes of *The Fresh Prince of Bel-Air* and *The Simpsons*. On the back of this he released the singles *All You Need Is Love* (No 19, Feb 1993), *Gimme Shelter* (New Model Army with Tom Jones) (No 23, Jul 1993) and *If I Only Knew* (No 11, Nov 1994). In 1997 Tom did the soundtrack for the comedy film *The Full Monty*, recording *You Can Leave Your Hat On*. The popularity of the film raised Tom's profile once again and in October 1999 he had his third No 1 album with 'Reload' a collection of cover duets which spawned the singles: *Burning Down the House* (No 7, Sep 1999 – with The Cardigans), *Baby, It's Cold Outside* (No 17, Dec 1999 – with Cerys Matthews), *Mama Told Me Not to Come* (No 4, Mar 2000 – with Stereophonics), *Sex Bomb* (No 3, May 2000 – with Mousse T) and *You Need Love Like I Do* (No 24, Nov 2000). Other tracks included: *Are You Gonna Go My Way* (with Robbie Williams), *Sunny Afternoon* (with Space), *Sometimes We Cry* (with Van Morrison), *Lust for Life* (with The Pretenders), *Ain't That a Lot of Love* (with Simply Red), *Never Tear Us Apart* (with Natalie Imbruglia) and *Motherless Child* (with Portishead). Tom has remained as popular as ever into the new Millennium. In 2004 he teamed up with pianist Jools Holland and released 'Tom Jones & Jools Holland' a roots rock 'n' roll album, which peaked at No. 5 in the UK Albums Chart. On 28 May 2005, in celebration of his approaching 65th birthday, Tom returned to his homeland to perform a concert in Ynysangharad Park, Pontypridd before a crowd of about 20,000. This was his first performance in Pontypridd since 1964. In April 2006 Tom was the featured vocalist on Chicane's (Nick Bracegirdle) version of *Stoned in Love* (No 7, Apr 2006) and in March 2009 he featured on the No 1 Comic Relief single, *(Barry) Islands in the Stream*, a collaboration with actors Ruth Jones and Rob Brydon, in character as Vanessa Jenkins and Bryn West from the hit BBC show *Gavin & Stacey*. Robin Gibb also provided backing vocals which meant the Gibb Brothers had achieved No. 1 songs in five successive decades, the first songwriters to do this. In July 2010, Tom's 39th studio album 'Praise & Blame' his first release with Island Records, containing the much-acclaimed tracks, *Burning Hell* and *Nobody's Fault but Mine*, reached No 2 in the UK Albums Chart.

In May 2011 Tom appeared as guest vocalist on Hugh Laurie's debut album 'Let Them Talk'. Having been awarded an OBE in 1999, Tom received a knighthood from Queen Elizabeth II for "services to music" in 2006. He has of course been linked to many women over the course of his career although remaining married to Linda. Apart from Mark, Tom has another son, Jonathan Berkery (b. 1988) after a brief fling with model Katherine Berkery. Tom has never met Jonathan and denied paternity for 20 years, despite DNA evidence, although finally admitting it in 2008. Tom is currently a coach and mentor on the BBC television show *The Voice UK*.

Kaiser Chiefs Indie rock quintet who formed in 1996 and are named after the South African football team Kaizer Chiefs. Leeds-born trio, Nick Hodgson (born 20 October 1977; drummer), Nick "Peanut" Baines (born 21 March 1978; keyboardist) and (James) Simon Rix (born 18 October 1977; bassist) were all in the same class at St Mary's School, Menston, Bradford. When Rix and Baines left for university in 1996 Hodgson met Andrew White (born in Leeds, West Yorkshire, 28 August 1974; guitarist) and Ricky Wilson (born Charles Richard Wilson, Keighley, West Yorkshire, 17 January 1978; lead vocalist/percussion). The latter three formed the band Runston Parva and they signed to Beggars Banquet, releasing three singles and an album. The band was dropped and on the return of Baines and Rix adopted the name Parva before eventually becoming Kaiser Chiefs. They debuted on the singles chart in May 2004 with *Oh My God* but it only reached No 66. Ten months later, their debut album 'Employment' was released and reached No 2, going quintuple platinum. It was shortlisted for the Mercury Prize but lost to Antony And The Johnsons. *Oh My God* was re-released in February 2005 and peaked at No 6. *I Predict A Riot* hit the number 22 spot in winter of 2004 but on its re-release (now as a double-A side with *Sink that Ship*) in August 2005, made it to No 9. Other tracks from the album included *Everyday I Love You Less And Less* (No 10, May 2005) and *Modern Way* (No 11, Nov2005). Their second album, 'Yours Truly, Angry Mob' (No 1, Feb 2007), topped the chart in the UK (45 in the USA) and featured the No 1 hit single *Ruby* (No 1, Feb 2007). A second release off the LP, *Everything Is Average Nowadays*, peaked at No 19 and a third single, *The Angry Mob*, stalled at No 22. The fourth single, *Love's Not A Competition (But I'm Winning)*, was available from 12 November on the band's website only. Their third album, 'Off With Their Heads' (No 2, Oct 2008) spawned the Top 10 single *Never Miss a Beat* (No 5, Oct 2008). After a three-year gap, their fourth studio album 'The Future Is Medieval' (No 10, Jun 2011) was released on their website. Fans could pick 10 from 20 available songs and pay £7.50 for their "own" album. Later fans could buy the chosen albums and if they did, the "compiler" was given £1. The album was later re-issued in North America, under the new title 'Start the Revolution Without Me'.

Katy B The singer-songwriter, born Kathleen Anne Brien, Peckham, South London, 8 May 1989, is a graduate of the BRIT School. Katy had been working with British underground grime, garage and house record producers from the age of fifteen and was a very experienced performer before being signed by the Rinse label. Her debut single was *Katy on a Mission* (No 5, Sep 2010), co-written by Katy, Rinse FM founder Geeneus and Croydon-based dubstep music producer, Benga (born Adegbenga Adejumo, London, 28 November 1986), who also produced the record. Dubstep is a genre of electronic dance music that originated in South London, and consists of tightly coiled productions with overwhelming bass lines and reverberant drum patterns, clipped samples, and occasional vocals. Katy's follow-up single, *Lights On* (No 4, Dec 2010) featured Ms. Dynamite (see separate entry). Her third UK Top 10 single, *Broken Record* (No 8, Mar 2011) was followed by the release of her debut album, 'On a Mission' (No 2, Apr 2011). The album has had five tracks released as singles thus far, the aforementioned three Top 10 hits plus *Easy Please Me* (No 25, Jun 2011) and *Witches' Brew* (No 128, Aug 2011) which were both disappointing commercially. Another track on the album, *Perfect Stranger* (No 16, Oct 2010) was released as a single under the name Magnetic Man (a trio of dubstep producers and DJs, Benga, Skream and Artwork aka

Having A Lovely Time) featuring Katy B. The track is also on the trio's debut album 'Magnetic Man' (No 5, Oct 2010).

Johnny Kidd and the Pirates see entry for The Tornados

The Kinks see entry for Rod Stewart

Labrinth The English singer-songwriter and record producer was born Timothy McKenzie in Hackney, London on 1 April 1989. After attending Stoke Newington School, where he first became interested in a musical career, Timothy began working as a producer under the name Labrinth. In February 2010, he appeared as an uncredited guest artist on British rapper Tinie Tempah's debut single, *Pass Out* (No 1, Feb 2010 – No 6 in Ireland) having also produced and co-written the track. Four months later he featured on Tinie's follow-up single, *Frisky* (No 2, Jun 2010 – No 3 in Ireland) although this time was given a credit. Later in the month Labrinth signed to Simon Cowell's record label, Syco, the signing being the first for six years not to have arisen from one of Simon's reality shows. Labrinth's debut single, *Let the Sun Shine* (No 3, Sep 2010) was produced and written by Labrinth and his manager Marc Williams (aka Da Diggler) and established his credentials as a solo artist. Throughout 2010 and 2011, Labrinth either wrote material for or produced tracks for many up-and-coming artists, notably Etta Bond, who became the first signing to his own label within Syco, which he named Odd Child Recordings. For his second single release, *Earthquake* (No 2, Oct 2011 – No 12 in Ireland) he reversed roles with Tinie Tempah, who now became the featured artist on one of his records. In November 2011, Labrinth appeared on and produced the Children in Need 2011 charity single, a cover of the Massive Attack song *Teardrop*. Under the name The Collective, the group were assembled by Take That member Gary Barlow, and included Chipmunk, Wretch 32, Mz. Bratt, Dot Rotten, Rizzle Kicks, Ed Sheeran, Ms. Dynamite and Tulisa Contostavlos. The single reached a disappointing No 24 on the UK Singles Chart, the lowest-charting Children in Need single in sixteen years. Labrinth's third single, *Last Time* (No 4, Mar 2012 – No 14 in Ireland) was also co-written with his manager Marc Williams. Labrinth's debut album 'Electronic Earth' was released in April 2012 and has currently peaked at No 2 on the UK Albums Chart. The fourth single from the album, *Express Yourself*, was featured on a semi-final edition of *Britain's Got Talent* on 9 May 2012.

The Last Shadow Puppets see entry for Arctic Monkeys

Led Zeppelin Rock group formed in 1968 as the New Yardbirds by guitarist Jimmy Page (born James Patrick Page, Heston, Middlesex, 9 January 1944), vocalist Robert Plant (born Robert Anthony Plant, West Bromwich, West Midlands, 20 August 1948), bassist John Paul Jones (born John Baldwin, Sidcup, Kent, 3 January 1946) and drummer John 'Bonzo' Bonham (born John Henry Bonham, Redditch, Worcestershire, 31 May 1948). Jimmy Page joined The Yardbirds in 1966 to play bass guitar. Shortly after, he switched from bass to lead guitar, creating a dual-lead guitar line up with Jeff Beck (who had replaced Eric Clapton in 1965). Following the departure of Beck in October 1966, The Yardbirds lost impetus and played their final gig in July 1968. Jimmy Page formed the New Yardbirds in October 1968. He had originally intended to form a supergroup with Beck and Who members Keith Moon and John Entwistle but this didn't happen. The New Yardbirds had become Led Zeppelin by the end of 1968. Apparently Keith had commented that a supergroup containing John, Jimmy, Jeff and himself would go down like the proverbial "lead balloon". Their manager, Peter Grant, later dropped the 'a' in lead so that those unfamiliar with the phrase would not pronounce it "leed" and at the same time he changed "balloon" into "zeppelin". From the start the band had a policy of not releasing singles preferring their albums not to be perceived as composite formations of disparate tracks but carefully crafted entities. Consequently Zeppelin have never had a UK Top 20 single although after their debut album 'Led Zeppelin' reached No 6 in

April 1969 their next eight albums all topped the UK chart: 'Led Zeppelin II' (1969), 'Led Zeppelin III' (1970), 'Led Zeppelin IV' (1971), 'Houses of the Holy' (1973), 'Physical Graffiti' (1975), 'Presence' (1976), the live album 'The Song Remains the Same (1976) and 'In Through the Out Door' (1979). All bar the last mentioned and Led Zeppelin IV (which both stalled at No 2) topped the US Albums chart. On 24 September 1980 after a rehearsal was cut short, the band retired to Jimmy Page's house, The Old Mill House in Clewer, Windsor. John Bonham had been drinking heavily all day, eventually falling to sleep and taken to bed, where he was placed on his side. The following day, he was found dead, his death recorded as asphyxiation from vomit. The group immediately disbanded. In 1982, the surviving members of the group released an album of out-takes from various sessions during Zeppelin's career, entitled 'Coda' (No 4, Dec 1982). On 13 July 1985, Page, Plant and Jones reunited for the Live Aid concert at JFK Stadium, Philadelphia. The three members again reunited in May 1988, for their label's (Atlantic Records) 40th Anniversary concert. In October 1990 the compilation album 'Remasters' was released and peaked at No 10 in the UK. In 1994, Page and Plant reunited in the form of a 90 minute "UnLedded" MTV project. They later released an album called 'No Quarter' (No 7, Nov 1994) which featured some reworked Led Zeppelin songs. The duo made another album 'Walking into Clarksdale' (No 3, Apr 1998) and the track *Most High* was awarded a Grammy Award for Best Hard Rock Performance in 1999. In 2003 a triple-disc live album of a 1972 tour of California 'How the West Was Won' reached No 5 in the UK but topped the charts in the USA. Their only other UK Top 10 album was the compilation 'Mothership' (No 4, Nov 2007). One of Zeppelin's best-known tracks is *Whole Lotta Love* from the album Led Zeppelin II. The song has been widely covered by many artists. It was famous in the UK for having been the theme music for the long-running television programme *Top of the Pops* during the 1970s and 1980s although that instrumental version was a collaboration by Alexis Korner's CCS (Collective Consciousness Society) and the TOTP orchestra. Another iconic Zeppelin track is the 8.02 minute long classic *Stairway to Heaven* from the band's untitled fourth album – variously referred to as Led Zeppelin IV, Four Symbols, Untitled, The Runes, The Hermit, and ZoSo, the latter of which is derived from the symbol used by Jimmy Page for the album sleeve. Amongst the many awards received by the band are a Grammy Lifetime Achievement Award (2005) and Polar Music Prize (2006). Jimmy Page received an OBE in 2005 and Robert Plant a CBE in July 2009. On 12 January 1995, Led Zeppelin was inducted into the United States Rock and Roll Hall of Fame and the UK Music Hall of Fame in November 2006. After his father's death Jason John Bonham (born Dudley, West Midlands, 15 July 1966) played drums with Led Zeppelin on several occasions, including the Ahmet Ertegün Tribute Concert at The O2 Arena in London in 2007. Robert Plant had a successful solo career, his highest charting UK single being *Big Log* (No 11, Jul 1983) from the album 'The Principle of Moments' (No 7, Jul 1983). He also had a successful album with American bluegrass-country singer Alison Krauss (born Illinois, July 23, 1971), 'Raising Sand' peaking at No 2 in the UK and USA in November 2007. John Paul Jones has collaborated with numerous acts since the demise of Zeppelin and is currently part of Them Crooked Vultures, a supergroup with Dave Grohl of Foo Fighters fame and Queens of the Stone Age frontman Josh Homme.

John Leyton Actor and singer (born John Dudley Leyton, Frinton-on-Sea, Essex, 17 February 1939) who rose to fame in 1960 with his portrayal of Ginger in a 1960 Granada TV adaptation of *Biggles*. He was managed by Australian impresario and entertainment entrepreneur Robert Stigwood (b. 1934) who later went on to manage Cream and The Bee Gees as well as produce theatrical productions like Hair and Jesus Christ Superstar and film productions including *Saturday Night Fever*. John's first charting single, *Johnny Remember Me* (No 1, Aug 1961) coincided with his role of singer Johnny Saint Cyr in the popular ATV television series *Harpers West One* (see entry in the television section) and topped the UK Singles Chart. It was produced by Joe Meek at his Holloway Road studio (see entry for The Honeycombs). John's follow-up single *Wild Wind* (No 2, Oct 1961) was his only other Top 10 single but he carved out an acting career in film and television, again starting at the very top with his role of tunnel king RAF Flight Lieutenant William 'Willie' Dickes in *The Great Escape* (1963).

The Libertines see entry for Pete Doherty

Little Mix Girl group formed in 2011 specifically for the eighth series of *The X Factor*, where they became the first group to win in the programme's eight-year history. The four members: Perrie Edwards (b. South Shields, Tyne and Wear 28 April 1993), Jesy Nelson (b. Romford, London 30 September 1991), Leigh-Anne Pinnock (b. High Wycombe, Buckinghamshire 3 January 1992) and Jade Thirlwall (b. South Shields, Tyne and Wear 3 July 1993) initially auditioned as solo entrants but Perrie and Jesy were eventually placed into four-member group Faux Pas while Jade and Leigh-Anne joined three-member group Orion. However, both groups failed to make it through to the judges' houses. A subsequent decision to select two members from each group to form the four-piece group Rhythmix proved successful and the girls were mentored by N-Dubz member Tulisa Contostavlos. In October 2011, midway through the series, Rhythmix announced their change of name following a request from a Brighton-based children's music charity of the same name. The girl's struck up an immediate rapport with fans and Jesy in particular garnered a lot of sympathy due to the struggles with her weight. Their winner's single was a cover of Damien Rice's song *Cannonball*, and topped the UK Singles Chart on 18 December 2011 while also taking the Christmas number one spot on the Irish Singles Chart. Little Mix had already been part of The X Factor Finalists 2011 UK and Irish chart-topper, *Wishing on a Star*, the month before their solo group effort. This record also featured JLS and One Direction.

Pixie Lott Singer-songwriter, dancer and actress (born Victoria Louise Lott, Bromley, London, 12 January 1991), her nickname being given to her by her mother at birth because she was "such a tiny, cute baby who looked like a fairy". Pixie studied at the Italia Conti Academy of Theatre Arts. A precocious talent, at the age of thirteen she appeared in the West End production of *Chitty Chitty Bang Bang* at the London Palladium and the following year appeared in BBC1's *Celebrate the Sound of Music* as Louisa von Trapp. After signing to Mercury records she released her debut album 'Turn it Up' (No 6, Sep 2009). The album's first two singles, *Mama Do (Uh Oh, Uh Oh)* (No 1, Jun 2009) and *Boys and Girls* (No 1, Sep 2009) both peaked at number one on the UK Singles Chart, while subsequent tracks *Cry Me Out* (No 12, Nov 2009), *Gravity* (No 20, Mar 2010), *Turn It Up* (No 11, Jun 2010) and *Broken Arrow* (No 12, Oct 2010) all reached the Top 20, the latter only appearing on the US version of the album. *All About Tonight* (No 1, Sep 2011), the lead single from her second album 'Young Foolish Happy' (No 18, Nov 2011) gave her a third UK number one hit. The album has thus far spawned two further Top 10 singles, *What Do You Take Me For?* (No 10, Nov 2011 - featuring Pusha T) and *Kiss the Stars* (No 8, Jan 2012). Pixie has also had two Top 10 hits: as part of the Young Soul Rebels on the charity single, *I Got Soul* (No 10, Oct 2009) in aid of War Child, and with Tinchy Stryder on *Bright Lights* (No 7, Mar 2012). As a songwriter Pixie has written for several artists, most notably perhaps the track, *You Broke My Heart*, for Alexandra Burke's debut album 'Overcome'. Pixie made her film debut as Judy, Fred Figglehorn's crush, in *Fred: The Movie* (2010) starring alongside Lucas Cruikshank. The long-haired, long-legged blonde was voted No 45 in 2010 and No 31 in 2011 in FHM's 100 Sexiest Women list.

Lulu The petite (5ft 1ins) Glasgow-bred singer (born Marie McDonald McLaughlin Lawrie, Lennoxtown, Stirlingshire, 3 November 1948) began her professional career as part of a local group The Gleneagles (later changing their name to The Luvvers), discovered by Tony Gordon, owner of the Phonograph disco. Tony's sister Marion Massey became Lulu's manager and signed her to Decca. Lulu first heard the Isley Brothers' song *Shout* in a local Glasgow club, sung by Alex Harvey (born in Glasgow, 5 February 1935; died, from a heart-attack, in Zeebrugge, Belgium, 4 February 1982) later front-man of The Sensational Alex Harvey Band who had a Top 10 hit with *Delilah* (No 7, Jul 1975), when she was 12-years-old and made this her debut single, now aged 15 and backed by The Luvvers. *Shout* (No 7, May 1964) elevated Lulu to stardom and John Lennon went on record as saying it was the record of the year. It was however a hard song to follow and although now a solo singer and enjoying huge television success Lulu only had one further Top 10 hit, *Leave a Little Love* (No 8, Jun 1965) in the following three years. In 1966 she toured Poland with The Hollies, the first British female singer to appear live behind the Iron Curtain. On her return she was dropped by Decca and signed to Columbia to be produced by Mickie Most (see entry for The Animals). This prompted an upturn in her fortunes. Her debut single for her new label, *The Boat that I Row* (No 6, Apr 1967) written by Neil Diamond, gave her a great boost but better was to come when, in June, the film *To Sir, with Love* was released. Lulu not only appeared (as Barbara "Babs" Pegg) in the film but also sang the haunting title song which reached No 1 in the US Singles Chart and became Billboard magazine's No 1 pop single for 1967 although rather bizarrely only appeared on the B-side of *Let's Pretend* (No 11, June 1967) in Britain. After showing her comedic acting ability in a 1967 BBC TV series, Lulu was given her own TV series in 1968, which ran annually until 1975 under various titles including *Lulu's Back in Town, Happening For Lulu, Lulu* and *It's Lulu*, which featured her *To Sir, with Love* co-star Adrienne Posta. Her BBC series' featured music and comedy sketches and on one occasion Jimi Hendrix appeared and after playing about two minutes of *Hey Joe*, Jimi stopped and announced "We'd like to stop playing this rubbish and dedicate a song to The Cream, regardless of what kind of group they may be in, dedicate to Eric Clapton, Ginger Baker and Jack Bruce". He then broke into *Sunshine of Your Love*. Hendrix was told he would never work at the BBC again. Lulu's subsequent hits included: *Love Loves to Love Love* (No 32, Nov 1967), *Me the Peaceful Heart* (No 9, Feb 1968) and *I'm a Tiger* (No 9, Nov 1968). She married Maurice Gibb (of the Bee Gees) at Gerrards Cross in 1969 but their honeymoon had to be postponed due to Lulu representing the UK in the Eurovision Song Contest in Madrid with *Boom Bang-A-Bang* (No 2, Mar 1969). The UK ended joint-winners with Spain, (*Vivo Cantando* by Salomé), Netherlands, (*De Troubadour* by Lenny Kuhr) and France, (*Un Jour, un Enfant* by Frida Boccara) all on 18 votes each. Lulu's marriage had its ups and downs and eventually ended in divorce in 1973 chiefly due to Maurice's drinking problem. Lulu remained on good terms with Maurice (22 December 1949 – 12 January 2003) right up until his death. After another brief hiatus in her career Lulu performed the title song for the James Bond film *The Man with the Golden Gun* (1974) and then had her first Top 10 hit in five years with *The Man Who Sold the World* (No 3, Jan 1974) written and produced by David Bowie, who also sang backing vocals and played the saxophone riff. In 1977 Lulu married hairdresser John Frieda. They divorced in 1991. They had one son, Jordan Frieda (b. 17 June 1977) who is now an actor and took the title role in the controversial TV movie, *Prince William* (2002), about Prince William of Wales, with whom Jordan attended Eton College. Work dried up for Lulu gradually throughout the 1980s. She remained in the public eye early in the decade with her frequent appearances in the Freemans fashion catalogue. She then appeared in the Adam and the Ants video for *Ant Rap* in 1981. She won the Rear of the Year award in 1983, had a Top 10 hit with a re-recording of *Shout* (No 8, Jul 1986) and then replaced Julie Walters as Adrian Mole's mother on television. By the third time of playing Peter Pan in consecutive years up to 1989 she parted from her manager, Marion Massey, after more than 25 years, for most of which they were not only business partners but also good friends. After an inauspicious start to the 1990s Lulu had a Top 20 hit with *Independence* (No 11, Jan 1993) and then collaborated with Take That on their chart-topping single *Relight My Fire* (No 1, Oct 1993) and subsequently supported the band on their 1994 tour. Lulu has worked on television in some capacity ever since, occasionally returning to the studios to record albums and less occasionally the film studio, notably starring alongside Tom Courtenay and Stephen Fry in the British movie,

Whatever Happened to Harold Smith? (1999). In 2000 Lulu was made an OBE. Her last Top 10 hit was *We've Got Tonight* (No 4, Nov 2002) a collaboration with Ronan Keating. Her autobiography, published later in the year was titled *I Don't Want to Fight* after the Top 10 song she co-wrote for Tina Turner in 1993. Around this time Lulu started to use her late mother's birth name before she was adopted by the McDonald family and called herself Lulu Kennedy-Cairns. Almost 50 years after beginning her show business career Lulu is as popular as ever. One of her most recent television appearances was as a contestant on *Strictly Come Dancing* in November 2011, partnering Brendan Cole. In May 2012, she appeared in an episode of ITV series Piers Morgan's Life Stories where she admitted relationships with Davy Jones, David Bowie, George Best and Scottish actor Angus McFadden. She also made a tearful apology to Marion for their split. See also entries in the television section for *Absolutely Fabulous, Eurovision Song Contest, Juke Box Jury, Just The Two Of Us, National Lottery, Secret Diary of Adrian Mole, Aged 13 3/4, Three Of A Kind,* and *Titch and Quackers*.

McFly Surf/pop/punk rock band formed in 2003 by Tom Fletcher (born Thomas Michael Fletcher, Harrow, London, 17 July 1985; lead vocals, guitar and piano) after narrowly missing out on a place with Busted, for whom he subsequently wrote the chart-topping double-A sided single *3AM / Thunderbirds Are Go!*, and co-wrote (with James Bourne) two other Busted No 1 singles, *Crashed the Wedding* and *Who's David?*. Whilst helping to write Busted's second album 'A Present for Everyone' Tom met Danny Jones (born Daniel Alan David Jones, Bolton, Greater Manchester, 12 March 1986; lead vocals and guitar) and struck up a songwriting partnership with a view to starting their own band. A classified ad for a bass player and drummer was placed in the NME magazine and Dougie Poynter (born Dougie Lee Poynter, Corringham, Essex, 30 November 1987; bass and vocals) and Harry Judd (born Harry Mark Christopher Judd, Chelmsford, Essex, 23 December 1985; drums) were recruited. Tom suggested the name McFly, as he was a huge *Back to the Future* fan and particularly a fan of Michael J Fox's character, Marty McFly. The story goes that Danny didn't like the name at first but after watching the film he changed his mind on noticing that the name on the side of the manure truck was "D. Jones". Their debut single, *5 Colours in Her Hair* (No 1, Mar 2004), co-written by Tom, Danny and Busted's James Bourne, topped the UK Singles Chart and placed No 7 in Ireland. Their subsequent UK singles are; from the album 'Room on the 3rd Floor' (No 1, Jul 2004), *Obviously* (No 1, Jun 2004), *That Girl* (No 3, Sep 2004) and the title track, *Room on the 3rd Floor* (No 5, Nov 2004); from the album 'Wonderland' (No 1, Aug 2005), *All About You / You've Got a Friend* (No 1, Mar 2005), *I'll Be OK* (No 1, Aug 2005), *I Wanna Hold You* (No 3, Oct 2005) and *Ultraviolet / The Ballad of Paul K* (No 9, Dec 2005); from the album 'Motion in the Ocean' (No 6, Nov 2006), *Don't Stop Me Now / Please, Please* (No 1, Jul 2006 - the official Sport Relief 2006 release), *Star Girl* (No 1, Oct 2006), *Sorry's Not Good Enough / Friday Night* (No 3, Dec 2006) and *Baby's Coming Back / Transylvania* (No 1, May 2007); from their 'Greatest Hits' (No 4, Nov 2007) album, *The Heart Never Lies* (No 3, Oct 2007); from the album 'Radio:Active' (No 8, Sep 2008), *One for the Radio* (No 2, Jul 2008), *Lies* (No 4, Sep 2008) and *Do Ya / Stay with Me* (No 18, Nov 2008 - the official Children in Need Single for 2008) and from the album 'Above the Noise' (No 20, Nov 2010), *Party Girl* (No 6, Sep 2010), *Shine a Light* (No 4, Nov 2010 - featuring Taio Cruz) and *That's the Truth* (No 35, Mar 2011). The double-A side *All About You / You've Got a Friend*, was the official Comic Relief charity single for 2005 and the band's only Irish chart-topper. The band are ever-presents on television and in March 2007 guest starred in the *Top Gear* comic relief show *Top Gear of the Pops*, where they were given a challenge to come up with a song without using the words 'love', 'baby', or 'heart'. In addition, they had to include the words 'sofa', 'administration', and 'Hyundai'. It was later renamed 'Sofa, Hyundai Administration' and placed as a B Side on *The Heart Never Lies* Single. Later in 2007 McFly made a cameo appearance

in an episode of the science fiction series *Doctor Who*. The lads are no strangers to reality television either, Danny participated in 2010's *Popstar to Operastar* and, during a brief hiatus, Dougie won the eleventh series of *I'm a Celebrity...Get Me Out of Here!* on 4 December 2011 and, not to be outdone, Harry then won the ninth series of *Strictly Come Dancing* later in the month. Tom also took on *The Cube* in a celebrity special and walked away with £100,000 for his charity. On the relationship front, since late 2009, Danny has been dating and living with Miss England 2007 Georgia Horsley (having previously dated Miss England 2008 Laura Coleman). Dougie dated Frankie Sandford of The Saturdays, until the pair briefly split up in March 2010, reunited in April, but finally split up for good in November 2010. After spending some time in rehab following the split, due to his depression, he cleared his mind in the Australian jungle and is currently dating artist Lara Carew-Jones.

Malcolm McLaren see entry for The Sex Pistols

Manic Street Preachers Welsh alternative rock band formed in 1986 by Oakdale Comprehensive School friends James Dean Bradfield (born Pontypool, Monmouthshire, 21 February 1969; lead guitar and vocals), Nicky Wire (born Nicholas Allen Jones, Blackwood, Caerphilly, 20 January 1969; bass) and Sean Moore (born Sean Anthony Moore, Pontypool, Monmouthshire, 30 July 1968; drums). Another school-friend Richey Edwards (born Richard James Edwards, Blackwood, Caerphilly, 22 December 1967; rhythm guitar) began as their roadie but, after starting a song-writing partnership with Nicky in 1988 whilst they were both studying at Swansea University, he became their rhythm guitarist although miming his playing on early gigs. Both lads graduated with degrees in Political history, Richey gaining a 2:1 degree and Nicky a 2:2. Nicky had intended to be a footballer, having already captained the Welsh under-15 national schoolboys' team; however injuries put paid to this ambition. Despite his lack of musical ability Richey's thought-provoking lyrics and intensity gave the band a cutting edge. On 15 May 1991, he gained notoriety following an argument with NME journalist, and later BBC Radio disc jockey, Steve Lamacq (born Basingstoke, 16 October 1965), who questioned the band's authentic punk roots after a gig at the Norwich Arts Centre. An exasperated Richey responded by carving the words "4 Real" into his forearm with a razor blade he was carrying. The injury required eighteen stitches. Unfortunately this statement was a natural reply from an increasingly disturbed young man who had a history of self-harming, depression and alcohol abuse. The Manics had a UK Top 10 single with *Theme from M.A.S.H. (Suicide is Painless)* (No 7, Sep 1992) and two Top 10 Albums 'Gold Against the Soul' (No 8, Jul 1993) and 'The Holy Bible' (No 6, Sep 1994), the latter often considered to be one of the greatest albums of all time and a true work of genius. Richey wrote most of the lyrics for the album but it took a hefty toll on his health and he was hospitalised at the Priory Hospital in Roehampton the month before its release. On checking out Richey appeared to have his drinking under control but by then he was also suffering from anorexia nervosa and was hardly eating at all. On 1 February 1995, Richey disappeared from the Embassy Hotel at Bayswater Road in London after checking out at 7:00 am. His car was found abandoned on 17 February 1995 at the Severn View service station near the Severn Bridge, which has since acquired notoriety for being a suicide spot. His passport and credit cards were found in his car. On 23 November 2008 Richey was officially presumed dead by his family on the coroner's advice although no body has ever been found. The Manic's first album after Richey's disappearance 'Everything Must Go' (No 2, Jun 1996) garnered the 1997 BRIT Award for Best Album and included several songs written by Richey. The album spawned the Top 10 singles, *A Design for Life* (No 2, Apr 1996), *Everything Must Go* (No 5, Aug 1996), *Kevin Carter* (No 9, Oct 1996) and *Australia* (No 7, Dec 1996) and also ensured the Manics won the 1997 BRIT Award for Best Band. Perversely the suicide theme recurred regularly in Richey's life. Apart from the references already made, the

Manic's debut single in August 1988 was *Suicide Alley*, and Richey's lyrics for the single, *Kevin Carter* were a tribute to the South African Pulitzer Prize winning photographer, Kevin Carter, who tragically took his own life in 1994. The remaining trio had considerable success with their next album 'This is My Truth Tell Me Yours' (No 1, Sep 1998) - a quotation taken from a speech given by Welsh British Labour Party politician Aneurin Bevan - which not only topped the charts and duplicated their 1997 BRIT performance by winning the awards for Best Album and Best Band but also spawned their first chart-topping UK single, *If You Tolerate This Your Children Will Be Next* (No 1, Sep 1998 - The song is in the Guinness World Records as the number one single with the longest title without brackets) as well as the Top 10 hit, *You Stole the Sun from My Heart* (No 5, Mar 1999). In January 2000 the Manics released their limited-edition single *The Masses Against the Classes* (No 1, Jan 2000) which was a non-album track and, despite no promotion by the band and no promotional video by their label, Epic, topped the UK Singles Chart and gave them their first Top 10 Irish hit single when it placed 7th on the Irish Singles Chart. The band's next album 'Know Your Enemy' (No 2, Mar 2001) spawned the Top 10 singles, *So Why So Sad* (No 8, Mar 2001) and *Found That Soul* (No 9, Mar 2001) which surprisingly, after a year's hiatus, were released on the same day. Their remaining Top 10 studio albums were 'Send Away the Tigers' (No 2, May 2007), 'Journal for Plague Lovers' (No 3, May 2009) and 'Postcards from a Young Man' (No 3, Sep 2010). The band's other Top 10 singles to-date include: *There by the Grace of God* (No 6, Oct 2002), *The Love of Richard Nixon* (No 2, Oct 2004), *Empty Souls* (No 2, Jan 2005), the last two mentioned from the album 'Lifeblood' (No 13, Nov 2004), *Your Love Alone Is Not Enough* (No 2 Apr 2007 - featuring Nina Persson of The Cardigans) and *Autumnsong* (No 10, Jul 2007) from the aforementioned album 'Send Away the Tigers'.

Manuel and His Music of the Mountains This was a name under which the well-known television orchestra leader Geoff Love (born Todmorden, West Yorkshire, 4 September 1917; d. 8 July 1991) recorded from time to time, notably having a huge hit with *Rodrigo's Guitar Concerto De Aranjuez (Theme from 2nd Movement)* (No 3, Jan 1976) an interpretation of the iconic *Concierto de Aranjuez* written in 1939 by the Spanish composer Joaquín Rodrigo. Apart from being a beautiful piece of music, it is worthy of mention for topping the charts for three hours before it was noticed a computer breakdown had occurred and the chart was recalculated. Geoff later became resident band leader on shows with Max Bygraves, Frankie Vaughan and Des O'Connor to name but three. He also composed the theme music for the ITV sitcom *Bless This House*. One of Geoff's sons, Adrian Love (born in York, 3 August 1944) was a popular radio disc jockey and television presenter. The mixed-race blood of his father didn't seem to filter through to Adrian who was very light-skinned and his great height too made them a strikingly contrasting father and son. Adrian was seriously injured in a car crash in December 1997 and suffered a collapsed lung a year later and died on 10 March 1999, eight years after his father.

Marilyn see entry for Culture Club

Joe Meek see entry for The Tornados

Gary Miller Gary was born Neville Williams, Blackpool, Lancashire, 1924. Following a promising football career he signed to Columbia in 1953, after being spotted by talent scout Norman Newell, his first record being *Yellow Rose of Texas* (No 13, October 1955). Gary's only UK Top 10 single was *Robin Hood*, the theme from the popular Saturday afternoon series sung by Dick James, which reached No 10 in January 1956. Despite having several other minor hits (all on the Pye label) Gary is best remembered for providing the singing voice for Troy Tempest in the Gerry Anderson series *Stingray* and in particular the end titles theme for the series, *Aqua Marina*, composed by Barry Gray. After gaining minor acting roles in series such as *The Saint* and *Gideon's Way*, Gary died, of a heart attack, on 15 June 1968.

Ms. Dynamite Born Niomi Arleen McLean-Daley, Archway, North London, 26 April 1981, to a Jamaican father and Scottish mother, the garage, hip hop, R&B singer MC and rapper is the eldest of eleven siblings, one of whom is a grime artist known as Akala. Originally working under the name Lady Dynamite, Niomi, while working at the radio station RAW FM, was discovered by Richard Forbes (Aka DJ Sticky) at a West End club. She provided vocals for Sticky's garage hit *Booo!* (No 12, Jun 2001) and was subsequently signed by Polydor. Her debut album 'A Little Deeper' (No 10, Jun 2002) spawned the Top 20 singles *It Takes More* (No 7, Jun 2002), *Dy-na-mi-tee* (No 5, Sep 2002) and *Put Him Out* (No 19, Dec 2002). Her first public performance was at the closing ceremony of the 2002 Commonwealth Games at the City of Manchester Stadium. Ms. Dynamite won the 2002 MOBO Awards for Best British Act, Best Newcomer and Best Single for *It Takes More* plus the Mercury Music Prize for her debut album. She also won two BRIT Awards at the 2003 ceremony: Best British Female Solo Artist and Best British Urban Act. However meteoric Ms. Dynamite's rise to fame had become, unfortunately her demise was equally as spectacular. Initially taking time off to have her son, Shavaar, her second album 'Judgement Days' (No 43, Oct 2005) only received tepid reviews, although the success of the title track *Judgement Day/Father* (No 25, Sep 2005) showed she still had a fan base. On the 6 January 2006, Ms Dynamite was arrested outside a London nightclub, after a brawl in which she punched a male police officer in the face whilst in custody. She was convicted and sentenced to sixty hours of community service and disappeared from the public spotlight until resurfacing as a reality show contestant on the ITV cookery-based show *Hell's Kitchen* (2009). Her fourth place raised her profile once more and the following year she was featured on Katy B's second single, *Lights On*. See separate entry.

Mis-Teeq R&B girl group originally formed as a quartet in 1999, Zena McNally (born Birmingham, West Midlands, 8 March 1979) leaving to pursue a solo career after the release of their first single, *Why* (No 8, Jan 2001). The remaining trio of Alesha Anjanette Dixon (born Welwyn Garden City, Hertfordshire, 7 October 1978), Su-Elise Michelle Nash (born Dulwich, London, 22 May 1981) and Sabrina Fredrica Washington (born Gravesend, Kent, 27 October 1978) had two Top 10 albums 'Lickin' on Both Sides' (No 3, Oct 2001) and 'Eye Candy' (No 6, Apr 2003) and several more Top 10 singles: *All I Want* (No 2, Jun 2001), *One Night Stand* (No 5, Oct 2001), *B With Me* (No 5, Mar 2002), *Roll On / This Is How We Do It* (No 7, Jun 2002), *Scandalous* (No 2, Mar 2003) and *Can't Get It Back* (No 8, Jul 2003). *Scandalous* was released in the US in May 2004 and reached No 35 on the Billboard Hot 100 chart, making it their only US hit. The song was featured as the theme of the film *Catwoman* (2004) starring Halle Berry. Their final single was *Style* (No 13, Nov 2003) before their label, Telstar Records went bankrupt eventually leading to the group splitting up in 2005. **Sabrina,** the lead singer with Mis-Teeq, has subsequently carved out a career as a reality television star, winning *Celebrity Scissorhands* in 2008 and appearing as a contestant on *I'm a Celebrity...Get Me out of Here!* in 2009, however attempts to resurrect her pop career have thus far stalled, her debut solo single *OMG (Oh My Gosh)*, released on 5 April 2010, failing to make much impact. **Su-Elise,** who had begun a business degree before the success of Mis-Teeq, decided to continue with her studies and after gaining teaching qualifications opened her own performing arts school, the "Su-Elise Stage School" based in Gravesend, Kent. Su-Elise makes the occasional television appearance, mainly on panel shows, but remains hopeful of returning to singing professionally in the future. **Alesha,** the MC of Mis-Teeq, initially pursued a solo career with Polydor but after disappointing sales of her first two singles, *Lipstick* (No 14, Aug 2006) and *Knockdown* (No 27, Nov 2006) her debut album 'Fired Up' was postponed indefinitely (although released in Japan) and she was dropped by her label. Alesha then decided on the reality television route and signed up for *Strictly Come Dancing* in 2007, and eventually won. This television exposure led to a successful comeback, which included her signing to Asylum Records, an offshoot of Warner Music Group. Her second solo album 'The Alesha Show' (No 11, Nov

2008) spawned the successful singles, *The Boy Does Nothing* (No 5, Nov 2008), *Breathe Slow* (No 3, Feb 2009) and *Let's Get Excited* (No 13, May 2009). Alesha's third album 'The Entertainer' (No 84, Nov 2010) was less successful and she subsequently parted from Asylum. In September 2009 Alesha became a judge on the seventh series of *Strictly Come Dancing*, controversially replacing fellow judge Arlene Phillips. In January 2012, shortly after completing the ninth series of *Strictly*, Alesha quit to become a judge on *Britain's Got Talent*. In June 2005, after a five-year relationship, Alesha married MC Harvey, of So Solid Crew, in a private ceremony at Brocket Hall, Hertfordshire. See also entry for Javine Hylton.

Mumford & Sons Folk rock band named after multi-instrumentalist and vocalist Marcus Mumford (born Marcus Oliver Johnston Mumford in Anaheim, California, 31 January 1987). Marcus's family moved back to their native England when he was six months old. He attended King's College School in Wimbledon where he first met future band member Ben Lovett. In December 2007 Marcus and Ben were joined by Country Winston Marshall and Ted Dwane to form Mumford & Sons, the suffix '& Sons' referring to the traditional names of many family firms. All four members of Mumford & Sons play numerous stringed and percussion instruments as well as complimenting each other with tight vocal harmonies. After becoming identified as part of the so-called "West London folk scene" the band toured Ireland and their debut album 'Sigh No More' was released (on the Island label) in October 2009 and topped the Irish Albums chart. The album's title was taken from a song performed in Shakespeare's *Much Ado About Nothing* and several lines from the play appear in the title track's lyrics. The album was a slow-burner in the UK Albums Chart, entering at No 11 on 11 October 2009 but eventually peaking at No 2 on 20 February 2011, in its 72nd week on the chart and following its Album of the Year win at the 2011 BRIT Awards. It also reached No 2 on the US Billboard 200. Five tracks have so far been released as singles, *Little Lion Man* (Aug 2009), *Winter Winds* (Dec 2009), *The Cave* (Feb 2010), *Roll Away Your Stone* (Jun 2010) and *White Blank Page* (Nov 2010). Although yet to have a Top 20 UK single, *The Cave* reached No 10 on the Irish Singles Chart in March 2010 and became one of the most-played songs of the year. The official music video for *The Cave* features the four band members driving on scooters through the roads of Goa while singing the song in tandem with four Indian men in marching band uniforms to whom they gave their instruments at the start of the video. The band was so unknown before the record became a hit that many viewers thought that the four Indian men were Mumford & Sons! Marcus married actress Carey Mulligan (see entry in cinema section) in Somerset on 21 April 2012. He was previously in a relationship with folk musician Laura Marling (born Laura Beatrice Marling in Eversley, Hampshire, 1 February 1990) who won Best Female Solo Artist at the 2011 Brit Awards and whom he often supported as drummer. See also entry for Noah and the Whale.

N-Dubz The British hip hop group comprising the Camden Town-born trio, Fazer (born Richard Rawson, February 5, 1987) and cousins Dappy (born Costadinos Contostavlos, 11 June 1987) and Tulisa Contostavlos (born Tula Paulinea Contostavlos, 13 July 1988) were formed in 2000 in their pre-teen schooldays. Under the management of Dappy's father, Byron Contostavlos (formerly of Mungo Jerry), they performed initially as the Lickle Rinsers Crew and then NW1, after the area they hail from. They changed their name to N-Dubz and, released their first single, *You Better Not Waste My Time*, as a digital download in August 2006 but made little impact on the charts. After winning a MOBO Award for Best Newcomer in 2007, they signed to Polydor and re-released, *You Better Not Waste My Time*, which peaked at No 26 in October 2007. In the meantime Byron died on 12 April 2007 and in August 2008 the group left Polydor and signed with All Around the World records. Their debut album 'Uncle B' (No 11, Nov 2008) was dedicated to Byron and spawned the successful singles, *Ouch* (No 22, Sep 2008), *Papa Can You Hear Me?* (No

19, Nov 2008) and *Strong Again* (No 24, Feb 2009). N-Dubz' second album 'Against All Odds' (No 6, Nov 2009) produced their highest-charting single, *I Need You* (No 5, Nov 2009) and the collaboration with Mr Hudson, *Playing with Fire* (No 14, Jan 2010). Their third and final studio album 'Love.Live.Life' (No 7, Nov 2010) spawned the singles, *We Dance On* (featuring Bodyrox) (No 6, May 2010 – No 9 in Ireland), *Best Behaviour* (No 10, Oct 2010) and *Girls* (No 18, Dec 2010). N-Dubz were also credited on Tinchy Stryder's mega-hit *Number 1* (No 1, Apr 2009) which was exactly that, in both the UK and Ireland. Although this song only featured vocals by Dappy, a new version was recorded for the N-Dubz album 'Against All Odds' featuring lines by all three members of the band. Another Top 10 N-Dubz accreditation was as part of the Young Soul Rebels on the charity single, *I Got Soul* (No 10, Oct 2009) in aid of War Child. US label Def Jam signed the group in early 2011 but by August they had parted company due to artistic differences. Whilst on a short holiday Dappy announced to Tulisa and Fazer his desire to go solo and the group disbanded officially on 15th March 2012. The group have never been far away from controversy either in their professional or private life. Critics have blamed their videos for inciting violence and prejudice with their "them and us" attitude towards the ruling classes. In December 2008, Dappy pleaded guilty to two counts of assault at Chelmsford Magistrates Court, after reportedly spitting in a girl's face while drunk on a night out. He received four weeks' imprisonment, suspended for 12 months. The following January he was arrested and bailed after being accused of making death threats with a gun. Later that month Dappy and Fazer were escorted from a BA flight from Edinburgh to London by police after it touched down, after allegedly threatening other passengers. In November 2009, Fazer was caught without car insurance in St Albans, Hertfordshire, while driving his BMW and was banned for 6 months. This has since meant that he has been refused an American visa. On 12 January 2010, N-Dubz appeared on The Chris Moyles Show on BBC Radio 1. The show received a text message from a caller complaining that Dappy was "vile" and "a little boy with a silly hat" and that N-Dubz were "losers". Dappy secretly copied the girl's phone number from the studio console and, the following day, tried calling her and sent threatening messages including: "Your [sic] gonna die. U sent a very bad msg towards Ndubz on The Chris Moyels [sic] show yesterday Morning and for that reason u will never be left alone!!! u say sorry I will leave u alone u ****." The girl claimed that she continued to receive messages after declining to apologise but N-Dubz management later apologised on his behalf and offered free tickets to one of his concerts, although Dappy has not apologised to her personally. Dappy lives with his girlfriend, Kaye Vassell and their two sons, Gino (b. Jan 2009) and Milo (b. Dec 2010). His debut solo release, *No Regrets* (No 1, Sep 2011) topped the UK Singles Chart and peaked at No 8 in Ireland. Fazer, born to a Jamaican mother and an English father, is a competent pianist. Along with his N-Dubz colleagues, he appeared in the interactive television series *Dubplate Drama*, as the character Flames, although his part wasn't as big as Dappy's part as Sleazy, or Tulisa's part as cocaine-addict Laurissa. Tulisa was born to an Irish mother, Anne Byrne (who, with her three sisters, was a member of the 1980's band Jeep) and a Greek Cypriot father, Steve Contostavlos, who, like Dappy's father, was also a member of Mungo Jerry). She had a difficult childhood and twice tried to kill herself as a teenager and was also an habitual self-harmer. On 30 May 2011, Tulisa was confirmed as a judge for the eighth series of *The X Factor*, alongside Louis Walsh, Kelly Rowland and Gary Barlow, and ultimately mentored the winning act, Little Mix. All through the series Tulisa was afraid of being exposed in public "as a slapper" by engaging in a video showing an intimate moment with a former boyfriend. In early 2012 this video, taken by London-based DJ/rapper, Justin Edwards, appeared on the internet. Tulisa sought an injunction but was unable to legally block the tape worldwide and later recorded a video response in which she clarified the relationship on her YouTube account "Tulisaconto", stating that she was both heartbroken and devastated by its release by her ex-boyfriend. Despite this controversy her public appeal remains solid and in May 2012 her debut solo single, *Young*, entered the UK chart at number one on the day she was named *FHM* magazine's Sexiest Woman in the World. Tulisa has previously been in a relationship with band-mate Fazer but is currently dating actor Jack O'Connell.

Anthony Newley see entry in the film section

Noah and the Whale Indie folk band formed in 2006 and presently consisting of frontman Charlie Fink (born in Twickenham, 16 May 1986), violinist and keyboard player Tom Hobden, bassist Matt Owens, drummer Michael Petulla and guitarist / keyboard player Fred Abbott. During the band's early years Charlie had a relationship with Laura Marling, who appears on their debut album 'Peaceful, the World Lays Me Down' (No 5, Aug 2008 and No 32 in Ireland). Laura later had a relationship with Marcus Mumford the leader of another "West London folk scene" band. The first single from the album, *5 Years Time* (No 7, Aug 2008 – No 10 in Ireland) was originally released in 2007, but was re-released on 4 August 2008, and became their first top-ten hit. The music video features the band performing in a football stadium, and playing in the park. During the video, Laura Marling who provides backing vocals for the group is seen playing a tin whistle and also giving the camera a two-finger sign. Although the popular band have had no further Top 10 hits they have recorded two further successful albums 'The First Days of Spring' (No 16, Aug 2009) and 'Last Night on Earth' (No 8, Mar 2011). The first official single from the album, *L.I.F.E.G.O.E.S.O.N*, was released in January 2011 and peaked at number 14 in the UK Singles Chart.

Noel Gallagher's High Flying Birds see entry for Oasis

Now That's What I Call Music! This entry differs from all the others in this section inasmuch as Now! (As it is often abbreviated to) is neither a band nor solo artist but rather a very successful brand. The first album from the series was released in the UK and Ireland on 28 November 1983 and went straight to No 1 the following week. It included eleven chart-topping singles of that year, *You Can't Hurry Love* (Phil Collins), *Is There Something I Should Know?* (Duran Duran), *Red Red Wine* (UB40), *Give It Up* (KC and the Sunshine Band), *Total Eclipse of the Heart* (Bonnie Tyler), *Karma Chameleon* (Culture Club), *Too Shy* (Kajagoogoo), *Down Under* (Men at Work), *Baby Jane* (Rod Stewart), *Wherever I Lay My Hat (That's My Home)* (Paul Young) and *Candy Girl* (New Edition) plus nineteen other popular songs of the year. What made Now! so different from other "various artists" compilations was that not only were the songs by original artists but also the fact that the LPs were double albums distributed by an amalgam of all the leading record labels which ensured many of the leading artists were included. The brand took its name from a 1920s advertising poster hanging in an office for Danish meat products which showed a pig listening to a whistling cockerel. In recent years three Now! compilations are released per annum and the latest one 'Now 81' was released in April 2012. The most popular Now! album to-date is 'Now 44' (released in 1999). The album contains ten songs that reached number one on the UK Singles Chart: *Baby One More Time* (Britney Spears), *Mambo No. 5 (A Little Bit Of...)* (Lou Bega), *Blue (Da Ba Dee)* (Eiffel 65), *Tragedy* (Steps), *Mi Chico Latino* (Geri Halliwell), *She's the One* (Robbie Williams), *When You Say Nothing At All* (Ronan Keating), *Lift Me Up* (Geri Halliwell), *We're Going to Ibiza!* (Vengaboys) and *King of My Castle* (Wamdue Project) and remains in the Top 50 all-time selling British albums. 'Now 62' in 2005 was the first Now! album to be released as a digital download across online music stores.

Oasis The Manchester-based rock group grew out of an earlier band called Rain, named after the B side of The Beatles' hit *Paperback Writer*. Rain were formed in early 1991 and consisted of Paul ' Guigsy' McGuigan (born Barton-upon-Irwell, Lancashire, 9 May 1971; bass guitar), Paul 'Bonehead' Arthurs (born Burnage, Manchester, 23 June 1965; guitar), Tony McCarroll (born Levenshulme, Manchester, 27 June 1971; drums)

and Chris Hutton (vocals). Liam Gallagher (born William John Paul Gallagher, Burnage, Manchester, 21 September 1972; vocals and tambourine) replaced Hutton almost immediately and promptly suggested the change of name to Oasis (inspired by an Inspiral Carpets tour poster that hung in the Gallagher brothers' bedroom and listed the Oasis Leisure Centre in Swindon, Wiltshire). Oasis played their first live gig on 18 August 1991 at the Boardwalk club in Manchester. Liam's elder brother Noel Gallagher (born Noel Thomas David Gallagher, Longsight, Manchester, 29 May 1967; guitar and vocals) was in the audience and although not overly impressed with the musicality of the band expressed a desire to join them under the condition he would be the leader and sole song writer and that the group would focus on becoming a commercial success. Noel in fact brought a lot to the table. He had worked as a roadie for the aforementioned Inspiral Carpets and had witnessed first hand the vagaries of being professional musicians. He also had a vast backlist of unrecorded songs and thought the raw Manchester band a perfect vehicle for them. After a period of rehearsing some of Noel's songs the band went on the road and it was at a gig in May 1993, at King Tut's Wah Wah Hut club in Glasgow, they were spotted by Creation Records co-owner Alan McGee and signed almost immediately. The band's debut single, *Supersonic*, was released in April 1994, reaching number 31 in the charts. Their second single, *Shakermaker* (No 11, Jul 1994) became the subject of a plagiarism suit, with Oasis paying $500,000 in damages to The New Seekers for the unlicensed use of a line from *I'd Like to Teach the World to Sing* (the song made famous from its use in Coca-Cola adverts in the 1970s). The band continued with a proliferation of hits, all written by Noel unless stated, including: *Live Forever* (No 10, Aug 1994), *Cigarettes and Alcohol* (No 7, Oct 1994), *Whatever* (No 3, Dec 1994 co-written with Neil Innes), *Some Might Say* (No 1, May 1995), *Roll with It* (No 2, Aug 1995), *Wonderwall* (No 2, Nov 1995), *Don't Look Back In Anger* (No 1, Mar 1996), *D'You Know What I Mean* (No 1, Jul 1997), *Stand By Me* (No 2, Oct 1997), *All Around The World* (No 1, Jan 1998), *Go Let It Out* (No 1, Feb 2000), *Who Feels Love?* (No 4, Apr 2000), *Sunday Morning Call* (No 4, Jul 2000), *The Hindu Times* (No 1, Apr 2002), *Stop Crying Your Heart Out* (No 2, Jun 2002), *Little By Little/She Is Love* (No 2, Oct 2002), *Songbird* (No 3, Feb 2003 first written by Liam), *Lyla* (No 1, May 2005), *The Importance of Being Idle* (No 1, Aug 2005), *Let There Be Love* (No 2, Nov 2005), *Lord Don't Slow Me Down* (No 10, Oct 2007), *The Shock of the Lightning* (No 3, Sep 2008), *I'm Outta Time* (No 12, Dec 2008 the second song by Liam) and *Falling Down* (No 10, Mar 2009). Oasis beat the record of Madness (whose first 20 singles all made the Top 20) for consecutive UK Top 20s but the Manchester band managed it in style by having 22 consecutive Top 10s! On the album front their debut release 'Definitely Maybe' topped the UK chart in September 1994 and their six subsequent studio albums did likewise: '(What's the Story) Morning Glory?' (No 1, Oct 1995), 'Be Here Now' (No 1, Aug 1887), 'Standing on the Shoulder of Giants' (No 1, Mar 2000), 'Heathen Chemistry' (No 1, Jul 2002), 'Don't Believe the Truth' (No 1, May 2005) and 'Dig Out Your Soul' (No 1, Oct 2008). In addition the band had success with the compilation albums 'The Masterplan' (No 2, Nov 1998), 'Stop the Clocks' (No 2, Nov 2006) and 'Time Flies... 1994–2009' (No 1, Jun 2010) as well as the live album 'Familiar to Millions' (No 5, Nov 2000). In May 1995 after the band's first UK No 1, Tony McCarroll was replaced as drummer by Alan White (born in south London, 26 May 1972) who was himself replaced by Ringo Starr's son Zak Starkey (born Hammersmith, London, 13 September 1965) in 2004, although Zak continued to perform with The Who, a collaboration going back to 1996. The rigours of touring, excesses of youth and inter-personnel tensions caused Noel, Liam and Guigsy at various times to take breaks from the band (Guigsy actually being replaced temporarily by Scott McLeod in September 1995) but it was Bonehead who left permanently, in August 1999, and was replaced by Gem Archer (born Colin Murray Archer, Durham, 7 December 1966). Two weeks later Guigsy followed suit and was replaced by Andy Bell (born Andrew Piran Bell, Cardiff, Wales, 11 August 1970). At the turn of the new Millennium, Creation Records folded and Oasis consequently formed their own label, Big Brother, which released all of Oasis' subsequent records in the UK and Ireland from the beginning of 2000. In May 2008, Zak left the band after recording 'Dig Out Your Soul' and was replaced by former Icicle Works drummer Chris Sharrock (born Bebington, Merseyside, 30 May 1964) on their tour although like Zak, Chris did not have official member status and Oasis remained as a four-piece. On 7 September 2008 while performing at the Virgin Festival in Toronto, a member of the audience ran on stage and physically assaulted Noel breaking three of his ribs. On 28 August 2009, following yet another fight between the Gallagher brothers, the group's manager announced the cancellation of their concert at the Rock en Seine festival near Paris just minutes before it was about to begin, and issued a statement that the group "does not exist anymore". Noel confirmed that he had resigned via their website the same night. The following week Liam announced he was planning to continue with Oasis despite Noel's departure. In November 2009 Liam announced that he, Gem Archer and Andy Bell (all former members of Oasis) would be joined by Chris Sharrock (an unofficial member of Oasis) to form Beady Eye. The band released *Bring the Light* as a promotional single on 15 November 2010, as a free download. A limited physical release followed, and charted at number sixty-one on the UK Singles Chart. A second promotional single, *Four Letter Word*, was released on 26 December 2010. Beady Eye's first official single, *The Roller*, was released in January 2011 and peaked at No 31. Their debut album 'Different Gear, Still Speeding' was released in February 2011 and peaked at No 3 in the UK. Two subsequent singles, *Millionaire* (No 71, May 2011) and *The Beat Goes On* (No 64, Jul 2011) have fared moderately in the charts. Keyboard player Jay Darlington and guitarist Jeff Wootton have been slated to become full members in 2012. Liam, a staunch Manchester City F.C. supporter and life-long fan of John Lennon, married Patsy Kensit on 7 April 1997. However, in January 1998, Lisa Moorish bore a daughter, Molly, who was conceived during an affair in Los Angeles only a week after he and Patsy were married. Liam and Patsy's only child together, son Lennon Francis Gallagher, was born in September 1999. The couple divorced a year later. Liam's second son, Gene Gallagher, was born to Nicole Appleton on 2 July 2001. In 2004, Gallagher made headlines when it was revealed that he regularly paid £2000 in child support for his son Lennon Francis and daughter Molly. Furthermore, he criticised musician Pete Doherty, the father of Lisa Moorish's other child, for his alleged lack of child support. Liam married Nicole Appleton on 14 February 2008 at Westminster Register Office, the same venue where he married his first wife, actress Patsy Kensit. Noel initially gigged solo throughout 2010 but perhaps prompted by Beady Eye he decided to start a project called Noel Gallagher's High Flying Birds, explaining that the inspiration for the band's name was from dual sources. The idea to prefix the name with "Noel Gallagher's" was formed whilst washing up dishes listening to the album Peter Green's Fleetwood Mac, while the latter part of the name was taken from the song *High Flying Bird* by Jefferson Airplane. The band originates from Manchester and includes former Oasis session pianist Mike Rowe, drummer Jeremy Stacey of The Lemon Trees, The Zutons bassist Russell Pritchard and guitarist Tim Smith. Their debut album 'Noel Gallagher's High Flying Birds' was released in October 2011 and entered the UK chart at No 1, selling more than 600,000 copies by the end of February 2012. The track *The Death of You and Me* was released as the lead single on 19 August 2011 and peaked at No 15 in the UK single chart. A second track from the album, *AKA... What a Life!*, was released in September 2011 and peaked at No 20 in the UK chart. Other tracks due for release in 2012 include *If I Had a Gun..* and *Dream On*. In June 1997, Noel married Meg Mathews, who gave birth to their daughter, Anaïs Gallagher, on 27 January 2000. Since their divorce in 2001, Noel has been in a relationship with Scottish publicist Sara MacDonald. He wrote *Waiting for the Rapture* about their meeting at club Space on Ibiza in June 2000. They have two sons, Donovan Rory MacDonald Gallagher (b. 22 September 2007) and Sonny Patrick MacDonald Gallagher (b. 1 October 2010). Noel and Sara were married on 18 June 2011 in a private ceremony at the Lime Wood Hotel in the New Forest

National Park. Noel's best friend Russell Brand was best man at the wedding. See also entry for Blur to explain the so-called Battle of Britpop.

Sinead O'Connor Sinéad Marie Bernadette O'Connor was born at Glenageary, County Dublin on 8 December 1966 and after a brief stint in a local band, Ton Ton Macoute, rose to fame with her debut solo album, 'The Lion and the Cobra' (released November 1987) which reached No 27 in the UK Albums chart in January 1988. Her debut single, *Mandinka*, was taken from the album and reached No 17 in the UK single chart (No 6 in Ireland), also in January 1988. Sinead's follow-up album, 'I Do Not Want What I Haven't Got' topped the UK chart in March 1990 and her second single, *Nothing Compares 2 U* (a cover of a Prince song), taken from the album, also topped the charts, in January 1990 (topping the Irish charts in July and remaining there for 11 weeks). Although her next album, 'Am I Not Your Girl?' reached No 6 in September 1992, Sinead had no further top-ten singles or albums. She has however maintained a high profile through her statements and gestures such as her ordination as a priest, Mother Bernadette Mary, despite being female with a Roman Catholic background. On 3 October 1992, Sinead appeared on the live American late-night television sketch comedy and variety show, *Saturday Night Live*, and after singing an a cappella version of Bob Marley's "War", she presented a photo of Pope John Paul II to the camera while singing the word "evil", and proceeded to tear the photo into pieces whilst shouting "Fight the real enemy". This protest was aimed at child-abuse, rife in the Roman Catholic Church. Sinead has been married four times, to music producer John Reynolds (they have a son, Jake), journalist Nicholas Sommerlad, musical collaborator Steve Cooney, and Irish therapist Barry Herridge, whom she met online. Her last wedding, on 9 December 2011 in Las Vegas, lasted a little over a fortnight. Apparently her husband was upset that Sinead spent her wedding day attempting to track down some cannabis!

One Direction Boyband who came to prominence after placing third in the seventh series of the ITV reality singing show, *The X Factor*, in 2010. As with the 2011 series winners Little Mix; Louis Tomlinson (born Doncaster, South Yorkshire, 24 December 1991), Harry Styles (born Evesham, Worcestershire, 1 February 1994), Liam Payne (born Wolverhampton, West Midlands, 29 August 1993), Zayn Malik (born Bradford, West Yorkshire, 12 January 1993) and Niall Horan (born Mullingar, County Westmeath, Ireland, 13 September 1993) originally applied as solo singers but were eventually put together on the suggestion of guest judge Nicole Scherzinger. After finishing runners up behind Matt Cardle and Rebecca Ferguson, the band signed a £2 million record contract with Simon Cowell's company Syco Records. One Direction's debut single, *What Makes You Beautiful* (No 1, Sep 2011) topped the charts in the UK and Ireland and peaked at No 4 on the Billboard Hot 100. It also won the Best British Single award at the 2012 BRIT Awards. Their second single, *Gotta Be You* (No 3, Nov 2011 and No 3 in Ireland) was released a week before their debut album 'Up All Night' (No 2, Nov 2011 and No 2 in Ireland) which featured collaborations with Savan Kotecha, Rami Yacoub, RedOne, Ed Sheeran, Steve Mac, Toby Gad and Carl Falk. In the USA, 'Up All Night' was released by Columbia and went straight to number one on the Billboard 200, thus making One Direction the first UK group to debut at number one with their first album. The third release from the album, *One Thing* (No 9, Feb 2012 and No 6 in Ireland) gave the band their third successive Top 10 single. One Direction have also featured on the chart-topping UK hits *Heroes* (as part of The X Factor Finalists 2010) and *Wishing on a Star* (The X Factor Finalists 2011 featuring JLS and One Direction). In America the band are perceived as a new wave of "British Invasion" and have been marketed accordingly; Niall is considered the "cute little Irish one", Zayn the "quiet and mysterious one", Liam "the sensible one", Harry "the charming one" and Louis "the funny one." The band is currently being sued for trademark infringement by a low profile Californian music group who go by the same name. It was

Harry that actually came up with the name One Direction as he thought it would sound good when *The X Factor* announcer Peter Dickson read their name out loud on the live shows. Harry briefly dated English television presenter Caroline Flack (see entry in the miscellaneous section), which caused widespread media controversy over their fifteen-year age gap, but has recently rekindled a friendship with childhood sweetheart Felicity Skinner. He currently lives in North London with best friend and bandmate Louis Tomlinson, the two sometimes referred to by the portmanteau "Larry Stylinson" by their fans. Louis is currently in a relationship with Hollister model and Manchester University student Eleanor Calder. Liam, who is known for having a dysfunctional kidney, is currently in a relationship with dancer, Danielle Peazer. Zayn dated X Factor runner up, Rebecca Ferguson, for four months in 2011, which caused controversy because of their six year age difference but he has also had an on-off relationship with Little Mix singer Perrie Edwards which is currently on apparently. Niall, who is happily single, has a fear of birds since he was attacked by a pigeon while on the toilet as a child. At least two of the band might well now have a fear of koalas after Harry and Liam were peed on by one during a trip down under in April 2012. Up to 80 per cent of Australian koalas are infected with the STD Chlamydia!

Plan B Rapper, singer-songwriter, actor and film director (born Benjamin Paul Ballance-Drew, Forest Gate, London, 22 October 1983) who first came to public attention as a hip hop artist releasing his critically acclaimed debut album 'Who Needs Actions When You Got Words' (No 30, Jun 2006). Although the lead single for the album, the double A-sided *Sick 2 Def / No Good* made no impression on the charts the follow-up *Mama (Loves a Crackhead)* (No 41, Jul 2006) produced by Ben and sampling *I Can't Go for That (No Can Do)* by Hall & Oates, narrowly missed out on the Top 40 boosted by his first television appearance on *Later... with Jools Holland* performing an acoustic version of the song. In 2009 Ben collaborated with Chase & Status - an Electronic music production duo consisting of Saul Milton (Chase) and Will Kennard (Status) on the Top 10 single *End Credits* (No 9, Oct 2009). The song was used in the video game F1 2010 and also featured in the Michael Caine film *Harry Brown*, in which Ben co-starred. He has also contributed songs to the soundtracks of British films such as *Adulthood* (2008), in which he also played the role of Dabs, and *Shifty* (2009). Ben's second album 'The Defamation of Strickland Banks' (No 1, Apr 2010 and No 7 in Ireland) was a chart-topping concept album telling the fictitious story of sharp-suited Strickland Banks, who finds fame as a soul singer only to have it all taken away when sent to prison for a crime he didn't commit. The album spawned the single *She Said* (No 3, Feb 2010 and No 2 in Ireland) the video for which (set in a courtroom) starred Ben as Strickland Banks alongside Vicky McClure as his girlfriend plus Kaya Scodelario as the female lead. The song became one of the most-played singles of 2010. Other singles from the album include: *Stay Too Long* (No 9, Jan 2010), *Prayin* (No 16, Jul 2010) and *The Recluse* (No 35, Oct 2010). As a film actor Ben has also appeared in British crime thriller *4.3.2.1* (2010 - as Terry) and *Turnout* (2011 - as John). In 2012, he is due to release his first film as a director *Ill Manors*. Other projects Ben is working on include a third album 'The Ballad of Belmarsh', a film of *The Defamation of Strickland Banks* and an updated film version of *The Sweeney* (as George Carter) opposite Ray Winstone as Regan. Incidentally, the reasoning behind's Ben's working name of Plan B is that although he has a beautiful soul voice his 'Plan B' is his cutting-edge rapping – although Ben himself puts it rather more modestly!

The Police Founded by American drummer Stewart Copeland (b. Alexandria, Virginia, USA, 16 July 1952) in early 1977 after the demise of his progressive rock band Curved Air. Stewart was brought up in Egypt which is why many sources assume his birthplace of Alexandria is the African city. He was joined by vocalist and bass player Sting and guitarist Henry Padovani to cut their first single, *Fall Out*, on the Illegal Records label, part of the Faulty Products group of companies owned by Copeland's brother Miles, who would later become the band's manager. The record unsurprisingly failed to chart on its original May 1977 release date as the band had only begun to gig two months earlier, but it did manage a No 47 UK chart position on re-release in November 1979. In March and April 1977, the threesome toured as a support act for Cherry Vanilla and for Wayne County & the Electric Chairs. In May, ex-Gong musician Mike Howlett invited Sting and former Eric Burdon and the Animals guitarist Andy Summers (born Poulton-le-Fylde, Lancashire, 31 December 1942), to form a project band with him for a Gong reunion, which they named Strontium 90. The drummer Howlett had in mind, Chris Cutler, was unavailable to play, so Sting brought along Stewart Copeland. Strontium 90 recorded several demo tracks, and performed at a Gong reunion concert in Paris on 28 May 1977. An album with some of these live and studio tracks (along with the first recorded version of *Every Little Thing She Does Is Magic*) was released 20 years later in 1997 under the name Strontium 90: Police Academy. The foursome also performed at a London club as The Elevators in July 1977. Later that month, Copeland, Sting, Padovani, and Summers began performing as a four-piece version of the Police but Henry left in August 1977 and the band remained a trio for the remainder of its duration. Their debut album, 'Outlandos D'Amour' was released in 1978 and peaked at No 6 on the UK Albums chart in April 1979, two singles from the LP, *Roxanne* (No 12, Apr 1979) and *Can't Stand Losing You* (No 2, Jul 1979), both raising the profile of the now popular band. In October 1979, the group released their second album, 'Reggatta de Blanc', and this immediately went to the top of the charts and spawned the UK chart-topping singles *Message in a Bottle* (No 1, Sep 1979) and *Walking on the Moon* (No 1, Dec 1979). The instrumental title track *Reggatta de Blanc* won the Grammy Award for Best Rock Instrumental Performance. After the single *So Lonely* (No 6, Feb 1980), the band's next studio album, 'Zenyatta Mondatta', became their second chart-topper in October 1980 and spawned the singles *Don't Stand So Close to Me* (No 1, Sep 1980) and *De Do Do Do, De Da Da Da* (No 5, Dec 1980). In October 1981 'Ghost in the Machine' became their third UK chart-topper and singles from this album included: *Invisible Sun* (No 2, Sep 1981), *Every Little Thing She Does Is Magic* (No 1, Oct 1981) and *Spirits in the Material World* (No 12, Dec 1981). In June 1983 'Synchronicity' became their fourth successive chart-topping album and *Every Breath You Take* (No 1, May 1983) and *Wrapped Around Your Finger* (NO 7, July 1983) their final Top 10 singles; the last mentioned topping the Irish charts and thereby giving the group five UK No 1 singles but six Irish chart-toppers. During the group's 1983 Shea Stadium concert, Sting felt that performing at the venue was their "Everest" and decided to pursue solo projects, and although 'Every Breath You Take – The Singles' (No 1, Nov 1986) became their fifth successive chart-topping album, by the end of the year they had effectively disbanded. A decade on another chart-topping album was released 'The Very Best of Sting and The Police' (No 1, Nov 1997) and yet another decade on the band reunited for a world tour commencing at the 49th Annual Grammy Awards on 11 February 2007 in Los Angeles and ending at Madison Square Garden, New York City on August 7, 2008. See also solo entry for Sting.

Queen English rock band originally formed in 1970 consisting of frontman Freddie Mercury (born Farrokh Bulsara, Stone Town, Zanzibar, 5 September 1946), lead guitarist Brian May (born Brian Harold May, Hampton, London, 19 July 1947), bassist John Deacon (born John Richard Deacon, Oadby, Leicestershire, 19 August 1951) and drummer Roger Taylor (born Roger Meddows Taylor, Dersingham, Norfolk, 26 July 1949). In 1968, Brian May; then a student at London's Imperial College, formed the band, Smile, with bassist Tim Staffell and they were eventually joined by drummer Roger Taylor. Tim was attending Ealing Art College and by the time he left the band in 1970 to join Humpy Bong (with Irish musician Jonathan Kelly and Australian child actor Colin Petersen, a former drummer with the Bee Gees) his college friend, Farrokh Bulsara had become well established as Smile's frontman. The first change of name was Farrokh's own name to Freddie and then, at Freddie's request, Smile became Queen. In February 1971 Queen recruited John Deacon and began to play their first gigs, mainly in the London area, and initially specialising in the sort of prog rock made famous by bands such as King Crimson and Pink Floyd. In 1972 the band signed to EMI and was subsequently managed by John Reid (Elton John's manager). Whilst writing songs for Queen's eponymously titled debut album, Freddie created the fantasy world of Rhye which featured heavily in several tracks but it was one in particular, *My Fairy King*, with its lyric "Mother Mercury, look what they've done to me" that prompted Freddie to change his surname to Mercury. The album was released in July 1973 (eventually peaking at No 24 a year later) and included two non-charting singles, *Keep Yourself Alive* and *Liar* plus an instrumental version of *Seven Seas of Rhye*. Their second album 'Queen 2' (No 5, Mar 1974) spawned their first charting single, the revamped *Seven Seas of Rhye* (No 10, Mar 1974). Queen's subsequent hit singles up until the death of Freddie Mercury include: from the album 'Sheer Heart Attack' (No 2, Nov 1974 – No 12 in US), *Killer Queen* (No 2, Oct 1974) and *Now I'm Here* (No 11, Jan 1975); from the album 'A Night at the Opera' (No 1, Nov 1975 – No 4 in US), *Bohemian Rhapsody* (No 1, Nov 1975 – No 1 in Ireland and No 9 in US) and *You're My Best Friend* (No 7, Jul 1976); from the album 'A Day at the Races' (No 1, Dec 1976 – No 5 in US), *Somebody to Love* (No 2, Nov 1976); from the album 'News of the World' (No 4, Oct 1977 – No 3 in US), *We Are the Champions / We Will Rock You* (No 2, Oct 1977); from the album 'Jazz' (No 2, Nov 1978 – No 6 in US), *Bicycle Race / Fat Bottomed Girls* (No 11, Oct 1978) and *Don't Stop Me Now* (No 9, Feb 1979); from the album 'The Game' (No 1, Jun 1980 – No 1 in US), *Crazy Little Thing Called Love* (No 2, Oct 1979 – No 1 in US) and *Another One Bites the Dust* (No 7, Sep 1980); from the album 'Flash Gordon' (No 10, Dec 1980 – soundtrack for the film, *Flash* (No 10, Dec 1980); from the album 'Hot Space' (No 4, May 1982), *Under Pressure* (with David Bowie) (No 1, Nov 1981); from the album 'The Works' (No 2, Feb 1984), *Radio Ga Ga* (No 2, Feb 1984), *I Want to Break Free* (No 3, Apr 1984) and *It's a Hard Life* (No 6, Jul 1984); from the album 'A Kind of Magic' (No 1, Jun 1986), *One Vision* (No 7, Nov 1985), *A Kind of Magic* (No 3, Mar 1986) and *Who Wants to Live Forever* (No 24, Sep 1986); from the album 'The Miracle' (No 1, May 1989), *I Want it All* (No 3, May 1989) and *Breakthru'* (No 7, Jul 1989) and from the album 'Innuendo' (No 1, Feb 1991), *Innuendo* (No 1, Jan 1991), *I'm Going Slightly Mad* (No 22, Mar 1991) and *The Show Must Go On* (No 16, Oct 1991). After Freddie died of an AIDS-related illness on 24 November 1991 the double-A sided single *Bohemian Rhapsody / These Are the Days of Our Lives* (No 1, Dec 1991 – No 2 in US) was released and not only topped the charts once again but was also awarded a second BRIT for Best Single after first winning one fifteen years earlier. In his final months Freddie recorded as much material as he could in order that the band might have enough for one final album. Queen's 15th studio album 'Made in Heaven' (No 1, Nov 1995) which was "Dedicated to the immortal spirit of Freddie Mercury", debuted at No. 1 in the UK and sold more than 20 million copies worldwide. The album spawned the singles *Heaven for Everyone* (No 2, Nov 1995), *A Winter's Tale* (No 6, Dec 1995), *Too Much Love Will Kill You* (No 15, Mar 1996), *Let Me Live* (No 9, Jun 1996) and *You Don't Fool Me* (No 17, Nov 1996). In addition to their studio albums and various live albums, Queen also had two chart-topping 'Greatest Hits' albums in 1981 and 1991 plus the chart-topping *FIVE Live EP* (No 1, May 1993 – with George Michael and Lisa Stansfield). As featured artists the band also had a Top 10 hit with *Another One Bites the Dust* (No 5, Nov 1998 – with Wyclef Jean featuring Pras Michel and Free) and another chart-topper with *We Will Rock You* (No 1, Jul 2000 – with Five). Queen was one of the best live bands in the world and their flamboyant frontman gave the performance of his life at Wembley during the Live Aid gig for famine relief on 13 July 1985. Freddie totally stole the show with his mix of hard rock and soulful ballads and at times led the entire crowd of 72,000 in thundering unified refrains. The band opened with Freddie's iconic chorusless *Bohemian Rhapsody*, a song that originally remained at number one in the UK Singles Chart for nine weeks and gave the band their first top ten hit on the US Billboard Hot 100. Twenty

minutes later they closed with their rock anthem *We Are the Champions*. After Freddie's death Queen never officially disbanded. John Deacon retired in 1997 and Paul Rodgers (ex frontman with Free and Bad Company) often guested with the band although never actually joining Queen. Brian studied physics and mathematics at Imperial College, graduating with a BSc (Hons) degree and ARCS in physics with Upper Second-Class Honours. He has had success as a solo artist with the album 'Back to the Light' (No 6, Oct 1992) and the singles *Driven by You* (No 6, Dec 1991) and *Too Much Love Will Kill You* (No 5, Sep 1992). More recently he featured on Dappy's single, *Rockstar* (No 2, Feb 2012). He married actress Anita Dobson in 2000. Freddie too had solo success with the album 'Mr Bad Guy' (No 6, May 1985) and the singles, *Love Kills* (No 10, Sep 1984), *The Great Pretender* (No 4, Mar 1987), *In My Defence* (No 8, Dec 1992) and his posthumous chart-topper *Living On My Own* (No 1, Jul 1993). His duet with Montserrat Caballe, *Barcelona*, originally peaked at No 8 in November 1987 but was re-released after his death and reached No 2 in August 1992.

Damien Rice The Irish singer-songwriter, multi-instrumentalist and record producer, born in Celbridge, County Kildare, 7 December 1973, formed the Irish rock band Juniper in 1991 along with old schoolfriends Paul Noonan, Dominic Philips, David Geraghty and Brian Crosby. Damien (calling himself Dodima Rice whilst with the band) became disillusioned with the artistic compromises forced upon him by Polygram and he left the group in 1998 and became a farmer in Tuscany. The remaining members of Juniper reformed as Bell-X1. Returning to Ireland, Damien released his first solo album 'O' in February 2002 and this made No 2 in the Irish Albums Chart and No 8 in the UK. Although the first single from the album, *The Blower's Daughter*, only rose to No 38 in the Irish Singles Chart, the record was highly-acclaimed and the second release from the album, *Cannonball* was released in the UK in May 2002 and made No 32 on its first re-release in May 2003. Several re-releases later Damien's song peaked at No 9 in the UK in October 2011 and No 13 in Ireland. The song was picked as the winner's song for the British *The X Factor* in its eighth series and was released by the series winners Little Mix on 11 December 2011, topping the British and Irish Singles Charts in the first week of release. After having an Irish chart-topping compilation EP in 2004, Damien's second studio album '9' was released in November 2006 and topped the Irish Albums Chart, made No 4 in the UK and stalled at a creditable No 22 in the USA. In 2007 Damien appeared at the Glastonbury Festival and also played at the T in the Park music event in Scotland in the second week of July (the T standing for the sponsors Tennents), the Latitude Festival in Suffolk and the V Festival - an annual music festival held during the penultimate weekend of August. The event is held at two parks simultaneously which share the same bill; artists perform at one location on Saturday and then swap on Sunday. The sites are located at Hylands Park in Chelmsford and Weston Park in South Staffordshire. In recent years Damien has made musical contributions to charitable projects such as the Songs for Tibet, Freedom Campaign and the Enough Project. His songs can also regularly be heard on film and television on both sides of the Atlantic.

Sir Cliff Richard Harry Rodger Peavoy Webb was born at Lucknow, India on 14 October 1940 to an English father and Anglo-Indian mother. Cliff's family returned to England in 1948 and lived in Cheshunt. He was heavily influenced by Elvis Presley and after forming the Quintones vocal group in 1957 and then singing with the Dick Teague Skiffle Group, he eventually formed, The Drifters in 1958, and as Cliff Richard and the Drifters reached No.2 in the charts with *Move It* in September of that year and swiftly followed this up with *High Class Baby* (No 7, Nov 1958). His film debut was as Curley Thompson in Terence Young's *Serious Charge* (1959), in which Anthony Quayle played a vicar accused of improper behaviour towards a young girl who has a crush on him. Concentrating more on his music, Cliff gained a No 10 UK chart hit with *Mean Streak* in May 1959 and his first

No.1 followed in July with *Living Doll*, backed by *The Drifters*, who by now had changed their name to *The Shadows* (see separate entry) to distinguish themselves from the American soul group of the same name. *Travellin' Light* (Oct 1959) became Cliff's second No 1 and this was followed by *Voice in the Wilderness* (No 2, Jan 1960). By now Cliff was well established as the best-selling British pop artist and he had regular Top-10 hits throughout the 1960s with: *Fall in Love With You* (No 2, Mar 1960), *Please Don't Tease* (No 1, Jun 1960), *Nine Times Out of Ten* (No 3, Sep 1960), *I Love You* (No 1, Dec 1960), *Theme for a Dream* (No 3, Mar 1961), *Gee Whiz It's You* (No 3, Mar 1961), *A Girl Like You* (No 3, Jun 1961), *When the Girl in Your Arms is the Girl in Your Heart* (N0 3, Oct 1961), *The Young Ones* (No 1, Jan 1962), *I'm Looking Out the Window / Do You Want to Dance?* (No 2, May 1962), *It'll Be Me* (No 2, Sep 1962), *The Next Time / Bachelor Boy* (No 1, Dec 1962), *Summer Holiday* (No 1, Feb 1963), *Lucky Lips* (No 4, May 1963), *It's All in the Game* (No 2, Aug 1963), *Don't Talk To Him* (No 2, Nov 1963), *I'm the Lonely One* (No 8, Feb 1964), *Constantly* (No 4, Apr 1964), *On the Beach* (No 7, Jul 1964), *The Twelfth of Never* (No 8, Oct 1964), *I Could Easily Fall* (No 9, Dec 1964), *The Minute You're Gone* (No 1, Mar 1965), *Wind Me Up (Let Me Go)* (No 2, Nov 1965), *Visions* (No 7, Jul 1966), *Time Drags By* (No 10, Oct 1966), *In the Country* (No 6, Dec 1966), *It's All Over* (No 9, Mar 1967), *The Day I Met Marie* (No 10, Aug 1967), *All My Love* (No 6, Nov 1967), *Congratulations* (No 1, Mar 1968), *Big Ship* (No 8, May 1969) and *Throw Down a Line* (No7, Sep 1969 - with Hank Marvin). All of Cliff's UK chart-toppers bar *Summer Holiday, I Love You* and *The Minute You're Gone*, also reached No 1 in Ireland although to make up for the shortfall he also topped the Irish charts with *A Voice In The Wilderness, Lucky Lips* and *Don't Talk To Him*. On film Cliff followed *Serious Charge* with the role of Bert Rudge (aka Bongo Herbert) in *Expresso Bongo* (1960) but made his big screen breakthrough as Nicky in *The Young Ones* (1961). Cliff followed this up with films in a similar vein; bright musical comedies with a young cast including *The Shadows*, Melvin Hayes and Una Stubbs. The most popular is the perennial favourite *Summer Holiday* (1963) in which Cliff's character, Don, drives a London Transport double-decker bus through Europe. Cliff's other two films in this vein are *Wonderful Life* (1964 – as Johnnie) and the rarely shown *Finders Keepers* (1966 – as Cliff). He was billed as Cliff Richard Jr. and reduced to a marionette in *Thunderbirds are GO* (1966). His only other films are the Billy Graham-inspired *Two a Penny* (1967 – as Jamie Hopkins) and the Birmingham-based musical comedy *Take me High* (1973 – as Tim Matthews). Cliff had his own television show *It's Cliff Richard* (1970-71) and finished 2nd in the 1968 Eurovision Song Contest with *Congratulations*, losing out by a single vote to the Spanish entry *La, La, La*. It was later alleged that the Spanish dictator Francisco Franco rigged the vote to ensure Spain hosted the competition the following year. Cliff also came 3rd in 1973 with *Power to All Our Friends*, later to become his first single on the EMI label following his release from Columbia. After *Goodbye Sam Hello Samantha* (No 6, Jun 1970 but No 1 in Ireland), Cliff had a dip in his pop career in the 1970s and his only subsequent UK Top 10s were: *Power to All Our Friends* (No 4, Mar 1973), *Devil Woman* (No 9, May 1976) and *We Don't Talk Anymore* (No 1, Jul 1979 and also No 1 in Ireland). The 1980s brought a resurgence and his UK Top 10s were: *Carrie* (No 4, Feb 1980), *Dreamin'* (No 8, Aug 1980), *Wired For Sound* (No 4, Aug 1981), *Daddy's Home* (No 2, Nov 1981), *The Only Way Out* (No 10, Jul 1982), *She Means Nothing To Me* (No 9, Feb 1983 - with Phil Everly), *True Love Ways* (No 8, Apr 1983), *Please Don't Fall In Love* (No 7, Nov 1983), *Living Doll* (No 1, Mar 1986 - with The Young Ones and Hank), *All I Ask of You* (No 3, Oct 1986 – with Sarah Brightman), *My Pretty One* (No 6, Jun 1987), *Some People* (No 3, Aug 1987), *Mistletoe & WIne* (No 1 Christmas 1988), *The Best of Me* (No 2, Jun 1989) and *I Just Don't Have the Heart* (No 3, Aug 1989). Again Cliff fared a little better in Ireland for chart-toppers in the 1980s with the Sarah Brightman duet reaching No 1. In the 1990s Cliff again began to have a relatively quiet chart period with *Saviour's Day* (No 1, Christmas 1990 but only No 5 in Ireland), *We Should Be Together* (No 10, Dec 1991), *I Still Believe In You* (No 7, Dec 1992), *Peace In Our Time* (No 8, Mar 1993), *Can't Keep This Feeling In* (No 10, Oct 1998) and his last

chart topper *The Millenium Prayer* (Christmas 1999 but only No 3 in Ireland) bringing his total of chart-toppers to 14 both in the UK and Ireland. In the new Millennium he has had UK Top 10s with *Santa's List* (No 5, Dec 2003), *Somethin' Is Goin' On* (No 9, 2004), *21st Century Christmas / Move It* (No 2, Dec 2006 - with Brian May & Brian Bennett) and *Thank You for a Lifetime* (No 3, 2008). He has released more than 130 singles in the UK and has also had seven UK album chart-toppers and despite rather controversially not receiving any airplay on Radio 1 since the 1990s continues to sell records. Cliff made his "legitimate" stage debut in *Five Finger Exercise* (1970) and his acting career includes *The Potting Shed* (1971), *Time* (1986) and *Heathcliff* (1996). Cliff was awarded the OBE in 1980 for his services to music and was knighted in 1995 for his work with charities, becoming the first UK pop star to be so honoured. In 1996 he famously led the Wimbledon Centre Court crowd in singing during a rain delay when asked by Wimbledon officials to entertain the crowd. In 1964, Cliff announced his Christianity to the world and began to perform gospel concerts to huge audiences. In 1967 he starred in the film *Two a Penny*, released by Billy Graham's World Wide Pictures, in which he played a young man who gets involved in drug dealing. In 1975 he released the single *Honky Tonk Angel* produced by Hank Marvin and John Farrar, but as soon as he was notified that a honky-tonk angel was Southern US slang for a prostitute, he ordered EMI to withdraw it. Cliff's first serious girlfriend was Australian dancer Delia Wicks and he has also dated dancer Jackie Irving and former tennis player Sue Barker. Cliff currently lives with a former Roman Catholic priest, John McElynn, whom he met in 2001 while doing charity work in the United States. Cliff has called on the Church of England to affirm people's commitment to same-sex marriage. Apart from his London home he also owns a home in Portugal from where he produces quality wine. See also entries in the television section for *Coronation Street, Drumbeat, Eurovision Song Contest, It's A Knockout, Oh Boy!, Trainer,* and *The Young Ones*.

Rizzle Kicks North London-born mixed-race hip hop duo based in Brighton, consisting of Jordan "Rizzle" Stephens (born 25 January 1992) and Harley "Sylvester" Alexander-Sule (born 23 November 1991). The two childhood friends both attended the BRIT School where Jordan studied Media and Harley studied Theatre. They formed Rizzle Kicks in 2008, the group's name a corruption of 'Green Rizla', an early nickname given to Jordan by a football team-mate after a crew of the same name from the school that he attended at the time. The nickname evolved into 'Rizzle' and the duo decided on the suffix 'kicks' due to their shared love of football. Whilst gigging and making promotional videos, the lads finished college and Harley went on to work as an assistant drama teacher, whilst Jordan was employed selling burgers at the Corals Greyhound Stadium in Hove. In November 2010, they signed to Island Records, after their YouTube videos caught the attention of label executives. In June 2011, the duo released a promotional single, *Prophet (Better Watch It)* accompanied by a stop motion style video made up of 960 photographic stills. The track was initially offered as a free download, before being released on iTunes. Their first official single, *Down with the Trumpets* (No 8, Sep 2011) spent a total of 13 weeks in the UK Top 40. They next featured on *Heart Skips a Beat* by Olly Murs, which topped the UK chart in its first week on 28 August 2011. On 23 October, they released their second official single *When I Was a Youngster* (No 8, Oct 2011) which includes a ska sample from *Revolution Rock* by The Clash. The video features a cameo from Ed Sheeran throwing shoes at Rizzle Kicks. Their debut album 'Stereo Typical' was released on 31 October 2011 and has thus far peaked at No 5 on the UK Albums Chart. Their third single *Mama Do the Hump* (produced by Fatboy Slim) was released on 16 December, eventually peaking at No 2 in January 2012. The lo-fi video features a cameo from James Corden. Their fourth single, *Traveller's Chant*, was released in April, 2012.

Rolling Stones The evergreen icons that are the Stones had their heyday in the 1960s when they were rivals of The Beatles, and certainly outrocked the Fab Four in the eyes of the media as regards raw rock lifestyle and the usual popstar indulgences. The settled group members throughout most of the decade were: Brian Jones (Lewis Brian Hopkin Jones, born Cheltenham, Gloucestershire, 28 February 1942, guitar, harmonica), Mick Jagger (Michael Philip Jagger, born Dartford, Kent, 26 July 1943, vocals and harmonica), Keith Richards (born Dartford, Kent, 18 December 1943, guitar and vocals), Bill Wyman (William George Perks, born Lewisham, London, 24 October 1936, bassist) and Charlie Watts (Charles Robert Watts, born Camden, London, 2 June 1941, drums). However, the first person to respond to Brian Jones's advertisement in *Jazz News* of 2 May 1962 for musicians to form a rhythm & blues group was Scottish keyboard player Ian Stewart (Ian Andrew Robert Stewart, born Pittenweem, Fife, 18 July 1938). The following month both Mick and Keith joined the group and, with Dick Taylor on bass and Tony Chapman on drums, played their first gig under the name The Rollin' Stones at the Marquee Club on 12 July 1962. By January 1963, Bill and then Charlie had joined, replacing a series of bassists and drummers and in April they recruited teenaged publicist Andrew Loog Oldham (born Paddington, London, 29 January 1944) as their manager. Andrew had been the Beatles' PR man and he had a vision for the Stones' image to be that of an "anti-Beatles" – rough, raunchy and bad. His first decision was to dispense with Andrew's on-stage presence because his clean-cut, square-jawed look did not fit the required image. Andrew in fact became the band's road manager and session player and until the day he died, of a heart-attack on 12 December 1985 whilst waiting to see a doctor for breathing problems, he remained an integral part of the set-up. Mainly due to Decca regretting not signing The Beatles when they had the chance, Andrew managed to negotiate an advantageous recording contract. A cover of Chuck Berry's *Come On* was the Rolling Stones' first single, released on 7 June 1963 and peaking at No 21 on the UK singles chart in July 1963. The success of their first record initiated a UK tour in the latter-half of the year and while on tour they recorded the Lennon–McCartney song *I Wanna Be Your Man*, which reached No.12 in the UK charts in November 1963. Their third single, Buddy Holly's *Not Fade Away*, was released in February 1964 and reached No 3. By this time the group had attracted a huge fan base and their first two albums and next five singles all topped the UK charts. Although Brian, by dint of forming the band, was initially the leader and media darling, the songwriting collaboration of Jagger/Richards, which produced the majority of the group's catalogue of hits, brought them to the fore. Andrew Oldham, who had produced their records and managed the band sold out to Allen Klein and by early 1967 had no input to the band's music. In March 1967, Anita Pallenberg, Brian's girlfriend of two years, left him for Richards (subsequently having three children together), thus creating an even bigger rift between himself and the two former classmates at Wentworth Primary School in Dartford. In 1969 Brian's diminishing contributions to the band and his inability to tour, due to his asthma, drug addiction, alcohol abuse and various legal implications, prompted him to leave the group three weeks before drowning in his swimming pool at Cotchford Farm in East Sussex on 3 July 1969. The following year the group's contracts with both Allen Klein and Decca Records ended, and they formed their own record company, Rolling Stones Records; 'Sticky Fingers', featuring an elaborate cover design by Andy Warhol, becoming the band's first album on their own label. Brian's replacement Mick Taylor (Michael Kevin Taylor, born Welwyn Garden City, Hertfordshire, 17 January 1949), a former member of John Mayall's Bluesbreakers (1966–69), remained with the band until leaving voluntarily in 1974 and being replaced by former Faces guitarist Ronnie Wood (Ronald David Wood, born Hillingdon, Middlesex, 1 June 1947). Bill Wyman retired from the band in 1993 and his replacement, American bassist Darryl Jones, has never been made a full member. Their full list of Top 10 studio albums include: 'The Rolling Stones' (No 1, Apr 1964), 'The Rolling Stones No. 2' (No 1, Jan 1965), 'Out of Our Heads' (No 2, Oct 1965), 'Aftermath' (No 1, Apr 1966), 'Between the Buttons' (No 3, Jan 1967), 'Their Satanic Majesties Request' (No 3, Dec 1967), 'Beggars Banquet'

(No 3, Dec 1968), 'Let It Bleed' (No 1, Dec 1969), 'Sticky Fingers' (No 1, May 1971), 'Exile on Main Street' (No 1, Jun 1972), 'Goats Head Soup' (No 1, Sep 1973), 'It's Only Rock 'n Roll' (No 1, Nov 1974), 'Black and Blue' (No 2, May 1976), 'Some Girls' (No 2, Jun 1978), 'Emotional Rescue' (No 1, Jul 1980), 'Tattoo You' (No 2, Sep 1981), 'Undercover' (No 3, Nov 1983), 'Dirty Work' (No 4, Apr 1986), 'Steel Wheels' (No 2, Sep 1989), 'Voodoo Lounge' (No 1, Jul 1994), 'Bridges to Babylon' (No 6, Oct 1997) and 'A Bigger Bang' (No 2, Sep 2005). The group's live album 'Get Yer Ya-Yas Out! The Rolling Stones in Concert' also topped the charts in September 1970. Their Top 10 single releases after *Not Fade Away* include: *It's All Over Now* (No 1, Jul 1964), *Little Red Rooster* (No 1, Nov 1964), *The Last Time* (No 1, Mar 1965), *(I Can't Get No) Satisfaction* (No 1, Aug 1965), *Get Off of My Cloud* (No 1, Oct 1965), *19th Nervous Breakdown* (No 2, Feb 1966), *Paint It, Black* (No 1, May 1966), *Have You Seen Your Mother, Baby, Standing in the Shadow?* (No 5, Sep 1966), *Let's Spend the Night Together/Ruby Tuesday* (No 3, Jan 1967), *We Love You/Dandelion* (No 8, Aug 1967), *Jumpin' Jack Flash* (No 1, May 1968), *Honky Tonk Women* (No 1, Jul 1969), *Brown Sugar/Bitch/Let it Rock* (No 2, Apr 1971), *Tumbling Dice* (No 5, Apr 1972), *Angie* (No 5, Sep 1973), *It's Only Rock 'n Roll (But I Like It)* (No 10, Aug 1974), *Fool to Cry* (No 6, May 1976), *Miss You/Far Away Eyes* (No 3, Jun 1978), *Emotional Rescue* (No 9, Jul 1980) and *Start Me Up* (No 7, Aug 1981). More recently their video accompanying the single *Undercover of the Night* (No 11, Nov 1983) was banned by the BBC for being too violent and their version of Bob and Earl's *Harlem Shuffle* with Bobby Womack on backing vocal went to No 5 on the US Billboard Hot 100 chart, and No13 in the UK. Mick Jagger is undoubtedly one of the greatest front men ever to grace a stage. Away from the Stones he has had a film career beginning with the title role in *Ned Kelly* (1970). Other films include: *Performance* (1970 – as Turner), *Running Out of Luck* (1987 - as Mick), *Freejack* (1992 - as Vacendak), *Bent* (1997 - as Greta), *Enigma* (2001), *The Man from Elysian Fields* (2001 - as Luther) and *The Bank Job* (2008). He has also had a number one record with David Bowie, *Dancing in the Street* (Sep 1985). Mick has been married twice, to Nicaraguan-born Bianca De Macias (1971-78) and American model Jerry Hall (1990-99). He has seven children by four women; a daughter Karis Jagger Hunt (b. 4 November 1970) with American singer Marsha Hunt; a daughter Jade Sheena Jezebel Jagger (b. 21 October 1971) with Bianca; four children with Jerry Hall i.e. daughters Elizabeth Scarlett Jagger (b. 2 March 1984) and Georgia May Ayeesha Jagger (b. 12 January 1992) and sons James Leroy Augustin Jagger (b. 28 August 1985) and Gabriel Luke Beauregard Jagger (b. 9 December 1997); and a son Lucas Maurice Morad Jagger (b. 18 May 1999) with Brazilian fashion model Luciana Gimenez. Mick was knighted in 2003.

Mark Ronson see entry in the miscellaneous section

Mike Sarne Singer, director and actor (born Michael Scheuer, Paddington, London, 6 August 1940) who specialised in novelty records, his first single being the Joe Meek-produced chart-topper *Come Outside* (No 1, May 1962) which included comic interjections by actress Wendy Richard (born Wendy Emerton, in Middlesbrough, 20 July 1943; died in London, 26 February 2009). His follow-up single, *Will I What* (No 18, Aug 1962) observed a similar theme of Cockney interjections albeit this time by singer Billie Davis (born Carol Hedges, Woking, Surrey, 22 December 1945) who later suffered a broken jaw in a car crash (see entry for The Shadows). Mike began his professional life as an extra in films such as *Sink the Bismarck!* (1960) and *The Guns of Navarone* (1961); his first credited acting role being in the British comedy film *No Kidding* (1961 – as Henri). He also had television roles in series such as *The Avengers* (1961), *Scales of Justice* (1962), *No Hiding Place* (1965) and *Man in a Suitcase* (1968). In 1970 he directed *Myron Breckinridge*, starring Mae West and Raquel Welch in the title role. Mike has continued to have small roles in many popular television series. See also entry in television section for *Criss Cross Quiz*.

Saturdays Girlband formed in 2007 by Polydor Records and signed to Fascination Records, a sub-label of Polydor. The five-girl group comprises Una Healy (born Una Theresa Healy, Thurles, County Tipperary, 10 October 1981), Mollie King (born Mollie Elizabeth King, Wandsworth, London, 4 June 1987), Frankie Sandford (born Francesca Sandford, Havering, London, 14 January 1989), Vanessa White (born Vanessa Karen White, Burnley, Lancashire, 30 October 1989) and Rochelle Wiseman (born Rochelle Eulah Eileen Wiseman, Barking, Greater London, 21 March 1989). Rochelle and Frankie were both former members of S Club 8 (originally known as S Club Juniors) and Rochelle also presented children's television programme *Smile* from 2004 to 2006. The Saturdays' debut single *If This is Love* (No 8, Jul 2008) sampled a heavily-synthesised backing rhythm from Yazoo's 1982 song *Situation*. The follow-up single *Up* (No 5, Oct 2008) was released at the same time as their debut album 'Chasing Lights' (No 9, Oct 2008). Three further tracks from the album, *Issues* (No 4, Jan 2009), *Just Can't Get Enough* (No 2, Mar 2009 - the official 2009 Comic Relief single) and *Work* (No 22, Jun 2009) cemented their position as a tour de force. Their second album, 'Wordshaker' (No 9, Oct 2009) produced the lead single *Forever is Over* (No 2, Oct 2009) and *Ego* (No 9, Jan 2010). They then produced a mini-album 'Headlines!' (No 3, Aug 2010) which spawned the singles *Missing You* (No 3, Aug 2010) and *Higher* (No 10, Oct 2010) featuring American rapper Flo Rida. Their third album 'On Your Radar' (No 23, Nov 2011) was preceded by the lead single *Notorious* (No 8, May 2011) and the tracks *All Fired Up* (No 3, Sep 2011) and *My Heart Takes Over* (No 15, Nov 2011). Although yet to have either a chart-topping single or album, the band are firmly established as one of the country's leading live bands and have already had their own reality show on ITV2, *The Saturdays: 24/7* (2010). They also became the face of hair removal product, Veet in 2009 and the face of women's deodorant, Impulse in 2010. Several members of the band have high-profile relationships. Una is engaged to England national rugby union player Ben Foden and on 13 March 2012, gave birth to the couple's first child, a daughter, Aoife Belle Foden. Rochelle, the niece of football manager and former England international footballer Paul Ince, has been in a relationship with JLS member Marvin Humes since March 2010. She announced their engagement via Twitter on 31 December 2011. Frankie dated McFly bassist Dougie Poynter for two years but finally split with him in November 2010. She has been dating Manchester City footballer, Wayne Bridge since December 2010. Mollie is friends with Prince Harry of Wales but she has denied any romantic inclinations. See also entry for The Wanted.

Screaming Lord Sutch The erstwhile 'rock singer' and 'politician' was born David Edward Sutch in Hampstead, London on 10 November 1940. Although he never had a charting single (his best-known record, *Jack the Ripper*, being banned by the BBC) David warrants a passing mention by dint of his profile. His name, inspired by Black American singer Screamin' Jay Hawkins, was given an aristocratic theme although David had no ties whatsoever to the peerage. In the early 1960s he was produced by Joe Meek and became a popular television personality with his outrageous stage act that was a precursor of the shock-rock purveyed by American rock legend Alice Cooper. David was of course the founder of the Official Monster Raving Loony Party and served as its leader from 1983-99, during which time he stood in numerous parliamentary elections, invariably losing his deposit. David suffered from manic depression and committed suicide by hanging on 16 June 1999.

The Script Irish rock band consisting of frontman Danny O'Donoghue (born Dublin, 3 October 1980), guitarist Mark Sheehan (born Dublin, 29 October 1976) and drummer Glen Power. Danny and Mark had previously been members of boyband Mytown between 1996 and 2001. Mytown won the 1999 *Smash Hits* Newcomers Award and had a minor UK hit with *Party All Night* (No 22, Mar 1999). The Script released their debut single, *We Cry*, in April 2008 and it peaked at No 9 on the Irish Singles chart and No 15 on the UK Singles Chart. The follow-up single, *The Man Who Can't Be Moved*, fared even

better, making No 2 in both the UK and Ireland in July 2008 and breaking into the Billboard Hot 100 at No 86. Their debut album 'The Script' was then released in August 2008 and topped the charts in the UK and Ireland and made No 64 in the USA. In July 2009, The Script opened for Paul McCartney in New York and for U2 at Dublin's Croke Park. Their second album 'Science & Faith' topped the charts in the UK and Ireland in September 2010 but made a significant breakthrough in the States, peaking at No 3. The lead single from the album, *For the First Time*, topped the Irish Singles Chart in August 2010 and peaked at No 4 in the UK and No 23 in the USA. Danny is currently a coach on *The Voice UK*, a BBC reality show seeking to find a star recording artist irrespective of looks or profile. Danny's fellow judges are Jessie J, Sir Tom Jones and will.i.am with Reggie Yates and Holly Willoughby as presenters.

Peter Sellers see entry in the comedy section

The Sex Pistols Anarchic punk band formed in 1975 by vocalist Johnny Rotten (born John Joseph Lydon, 31 January 1956), guitarist Steve Jones (born Stephen Philip Jones, 3 September 1955), bassist Glen Matlock (born 27 August 1956) and drummer Paul Cook (born Paul Thomas Cook, 20 July 1956). All four members were London born. The Sex Pistols' origins lay with a band formed in 1972 by Jones and Cook along with their friend, guitarist Wally Nightingale (born Warwick Alan Nightingale, in West Kensington, London; d. from complications of substance abuse, 6 May 1996). The band was variously known as The Strand, and on occasion The Swankers, before Malcolm McLaren (born Malcolm Robert Andrew McLaren, Stoke Newington, London, 22 January 1946; d. Bellinzona, Ticino, Switzerland, 8 April 2010) became their manager in 1975 and renamed them after his boutique 'Sex' and the Shakespearean character 'Pistol'. Malcolm's second change was to get rid of Wally and recruit Glen and John (who was given the moniker Johnny Rotten by Steve Jones, apparently because of his bad dental hygiene). After EMI released the band's first single, *Anarchy in the UK* (No 38, Dec 1976) on 26th November 1976 the label set about lining up promotional work for the Pistols. The band announced itself to the British public on 1 December 1976 on a live early evening broadcast of Thames Television's *Today* programme. Appearing as last-minute replacements for fellow EMI artists Queen, the band duly over-imbibed on the production company's hospitality and the result was a drunken exchange with host Bill Grundy. The interview began with Grundy admonishing various members of the band for swearing and ended in a tirade of abuse from Steve Jones after Grundy made a throw-away remark to Siouxsie Sioux (born Susan Janet Ballion, in London, 27 May 1957) the lead singer of rock band Siouxsie and the Banshees, who was also making her debut on the show. Grundy asked Siouxsie if she was enjoying herself to which she replied "Yes, I always wanted to meet you" to which Grundy responded, "Did you really? We'll meet afterwards, shall we?" This prompted Steve Jones to interject "You dirty sod. You dirty old man". The dialogue continued thus Grundy: *Well keep going chief, keep going. Go on. You've got another five seconds. Say something outrageous.* Jones: *You dirty bastard.* Grundy: *Go on, again.* Jones: *You dirty fucker.* Grundy: *What a clever boy.* Jones: *What a fucking rotter.* This anti-establishment derring-do laid the foundations for a generation of downtrodden working class youth who identified with the band's ethos. Although the programme was broadcast only in the Greater London region, it made the national news and the tabloid newspapers had a field day with the story; the *Daily Mirror* famously running the headline "The Filth and the Fury!" Thames Television suspended Grundy for his part in the debacle and in January 1977 EMI dropped the band from their label. Worse was to come when the band's chief songwriter Glen Matlock was replaced by Johnny Rotten's friend Sid Vicious (born John Simon Ritchie, later known as John Beverley, Lewisham, London, 10 May 1957; d. 2 February 1979) who had previously played drums with Siouxsie and the Banshees, in February 1977. In March, the band were signed to A&M Records but immediately dropped after protests from several of their existing artists, notably Rick Wakeman. From this inauspicious start the band actually got signed by Virgin Records in May and their gigs were spectacularly popular with Sid's pioneering pogo dance starting a craze amongst their fans. In May 1977 the band's second single, *God Save the Queen* (no 2, Jun 1977) peaked at number 2 (behind Rod Stewart's double A-side *I Don't Want to Talk About it /The First Cut is the Deepest*) on the official UK Singles Chart although reaching No 1 on the NME charts amid controversy that the record had been deliberately downgraded not to cause offence around the time of the Queen's Silver Jubilee. Considering the BBC and the Independent Broadcasting Authority banned the record it was a monumental effort to become one of the best-selling records of the year despite no media exposure whatsoever. Incidentally, before the group signed to Virgin, a small amount of copies of *God Save the Queen*, had been pressed on the A&M label and are now amongst the most valuable records ever pressed in the UK, with a resale value in excess of £10,000 a copy, depending on the condition of the disc. The irreverent record cover, depicting a picture of Queen Elizabeth II with the words 'GOD Save THE QUEEN' covering her eyes and the words 'SeX PISTOLS' covering her mouth, was designed by Jamie Reid and in 2001 was named No 1 in a list of 100 greatest record covers of all time by *Q* Magazine. In October 1977 the band released their debut album (which was destined to become their only studio album) 'Never Mind the Bollocks, Here's the Sex Pistols' (No 1, Nov 1977), Older versions of most of the album's songs also appearing on a bootleg album called *Spunk*, which was made prior to Matlock leaving the band. In fact, because of Sid's inadequacies on his newly-learnt bass guitar Glen was an integral part of the recording of this album giving input as songwriter and musician to many of the songs. Despite the album being banned by Boots, W. H. Smith and Woolworth's, the album topped the UK Albums Chart amid much controversy, the manager of the Nottingham Virgin record shop and label owner, a certain Richard Branson (see entry in miscellaneous section), was prosecuted (unsuccessfully) for having it displayed in his shop window! Apart from *Anarchy in the UK*, the album also spawned the singles, *Pretty Vacant* (No 6, Jul 1977) and *Holidays in the Sun* (No 8, Oct 1977). In January 1978, the Sex Pistols embarked on a disastrous US tour. By now Sid's heroin addiction had become a major problem and although he attempted to gig clean his severe withdrawal symptoms led to on-stage violent outbursts against US fans only too ready to accommodate him. On 17 January 1978 the band split up. On 30 June, a double-A side single credited to the Sex Pistols was released: on one side, Great Train Robber Ronnie Biggs sang *No One Is Innocent* and on the other, Sid 'sang' the classic *My Way*, both songs accompanied by Jones and Cook. The single reached No 7 on the charts, eventually outselling all the singles with which Rotten was involved. After leaving the Pistols, Johnny Rotten reverted to his birth name of Lydon, and formed Public Image Ltd. (PiL) with former Clash member Keith Levene and school friend Jah Wobble. PiL had two Top 10 singles: *Public Image* (No 9, Oct 1978) and *This is Not a Love Song* (No 5, Sep 1983). Ironically, Malcolm McLaren, who was one of the prime reasons for Johnny leaving The Sex Pistols, went on to have greater solo success than Lydon, scoring Top 10 single success with *Buffalo Gals* (No 9, 1982) and *Double Dutch* (No 3, 1983). Steve Jones, well known during his Pistols days for his "hanky on the head", and his perm, continued to play with various bands, as did Paul Cook. Sid relocated to New York and began performing as a solo artist, with his American girlfriend Nancy Spungen (born Nancy Laura Spungen, Philadelphia, Pennsylvania, 27 February 1958) acting as his manager. On 12 October 1978, Nancy was found dead in the Hotel Chelsea room she was sharing with Vicious, with stab wounds to her stomach and dressed only in her underwear. Police recovered drug equipment from the scene and Sid was arrested and charged with her murder. While free on bail, he smashed a beer mug in the face of Todd Smith, Patti Smith's brother, and was arrested again on an assault charge. On 9 December 1978 he was sent to Rikers Island jail, where he spent 55 days and underwent cold-turkey detox. He was released on 1 February 1979; sometime during the early hours of the following morning, Sid died of a heroin overdose, not having the opportunity to defend the accusation that many people close to him felt was untrue. 'The Great Rock 'n' Roll Swindle', the soundtrack album of the film of the same name, was released by Virgin Records on 24 February 1979. Four Top Ten singles were spawned from the Swindle recordings, one more than had appeared on Never Mind the Bollocks. The aforementioned *No One Is Innocent/My Way* was followed by Sid's cover of *Something Else* (No 3, Mar 1979), a double-A side with *Friggin' in the riggin'* and the biggest-selling single ever under the Sex Pistols name, Jones singing an original, Silly Thing (No 6, Apr 1979) and Sid's second Cochran cover, C'mon Everybody (No 3, Jun 1979). The original four Sex Pistols reunited in 1996 for the six-month Filthy Lucre Tour and have had several reunions since. See also entries in the miscellaneous section for Vivienne Westwood; the television section for *Captain Butler, I'm a Celebrity Get Me Out Of Here*, and *Never Mind the Buzzcocks*; and the cinema section for *The Great Rock'n'Roll Swindle* (1980) and *The Filth and the Fury* (2000).

The Shadows Young pop fans could be forgiven for dismissing The Shadows as merely being Cliff Richard's backing band in the early stages of his career but the reality is the Shadows are the third most successful UK charted hit-singles act, behind Elvis Presley and Cliff himself, and more than half their hits were produced without their famous front-man. The Shads were UK pioneers of the now traditional four-man group (lead, rhythm and bass guitarists and drummer) and inspired a generation of musicians to pick up the guitar and have a go. In the five-year period before Beatlemania swept the country Cliff and The Shads dominated the British music scene in a way that could never be imagined these days. Together on live performances Cliff and The Shads became the ultimate band having great variety in their output, but the public accepted them as artists in their own right too and their fan bases were often quite different. Perhaps because The Shads were almost exclusively an instrumental group this arrangement worked well. The origins of The Shads were indeed as a backing band for Cliff. Formed in 1958 under the name The Drifters the band consisted of guitarists Ken Pavey (b. 1932) and Norman Mitham (b. 1941) plus drummer Terry Smart (b. 1942) and front-man/guitarist Harry Webb (before he became Cliff Richard). Ian Samwell (born Ian Ralph Samwell, Lambeth, London, 19 January 1937; d. 13 March 2003) saw the band perform at the 2i's Coffee Bar in Soho and subsequently joined them as rhythm guitarist. Ian wrote their first smash hit, *Move it* (No 2, Sep 1958). Oddly, none of the four founding members of The Shadows were founding members of The Drifters. This came about in September 1958 when The Drifters were signed for Jack Good's *Oh Boy!* (see entry in television section). Norrie Paramor, the Artiste and Repertoire Manager (A&R Man) for EMI's Columbia Records, had already signed Cliff but had concerns about his backing group. He asked Cliff's manager, Johnny Foster, to go to the 2i's coffee bar and seek out guitarist Tony Sheridan but Johnny's attention was drawn to another guitarist wearing Buddy Holly glasses - Hank Marvin (born Brian Robson Rankin, Newcastle upon Tyne, 28 October 1941). Hank agreed to join under the condition his friend Bruce Welch (born Bruce Cripps, Bognor Regis, West Sussex, 2 November 1941) who he was currently playing with in The Five Chesternuts (named from their drummer Pete Chester -born 1942 - son of comedian Charlie Chester) was also offered a place. Marvin and Welch replaced Pavey and Mitham and shortly after, Jet Harris (born Terence Harris, Kingsbury, London, 6 July 1939; d. 18 March 2011) was recruited to replace Samwell, who was by now the group's bass player. When Terry Smart left soon after, Harris recommended his friend Tony 'The Baron' Meehan (born Daniel Joseph Anthony Meehan, Hampstead, North London, 2 March 1943; d. 28 November 2005) whom he had played with previously as a member of Wally Whyton's (born Wallace Victor Whyton, in London, 23 September 1929; d. 22 January 1997) band the Vipers Skiffle Group. Wally of course went on to become a huge star of children's television in the mid-1960s presenting the ITV tea-time shows *Small Time, Lucky Dip, Tuesday Rendezvous* (on which The Beatles made their second television appearance, performing

Love Me Do), *Five O'Clock Club, Ollie and Fred's Five O'Clock Club* and *Five O'Clock Funfair.* So by the time of Cliff's first No 1 single, *Living Doll* (No 1, Jul 1959) The Drifters had become Hank on lead guitar, Bruce on rhythm guitar, Jet (named from his sprinting prowess as a child) on bass and Tony on drums. By now, known as Cliff Richard and The Drifters, the band released their first solo (separate from Cliff) single, *Feeling Fine* (a rare vocal excursion and notable for Jet's trademark scream). This record was withdrawn from the US market after an injunction was raised by the American band of the same name. Their second single, *Jet Black*, was subsequently released in the States under the name the Four Jets. Their third single, *Saturday Dance* (another vocal), was released in Britain under the name The Drifters but prompted a name change to The Shadows by the time they recorded *Travellin' Light* (No 1, Oct 1959) with Cliff in the autumn of 1959. Jet was perceived as the leader of the band, at least by the public, and it was he that gave them the new name while he and Hank were relaxing at the lads' local, the Six Bells in Ruislip in July 1959. The first of a proliferation of solo instrumental hits followed. *Apache* (No 1, Jul 1960), written by Jerry Lordan, topped the charts throughout most of Europe. Bert Weedon (see separate entry) recorded *Apache* a few months earlier and his version peaked at No 24 in July on the back of The Shadow's success. Interestingly, the Shad's recorded *Apache* at the EMI Abbey Road Studio in London and although often considered to be their first solo effort, Cliff actually played a Chinese drum at the beginning and end to provide an atmosphere of stereotypical Native American music. The distinctive sound of Hank's guitar was developed using the tremolo arm of his famous red Fender Stratocaster and also an Italian-built echo chamber given to him by singer-guitarist Joe Brown (born Joseph Roger Brown, Swarby, Lincolnshire, 13 May 1941). Joe Brown and the Bruvvers went on to have hits with *A Picture of You* (No 2, May 1962), *It Only Took a Minute* (No 6, Nov 1962) and *That's What Your Will Do* (No 3, Feb 1963) and Joe's sense of humour ensured he remained a television personality long after the hits dried up. His daughter, Sam (born Stratford, London, 7 October 1964) also had a successful pop career, her biggest hit being *Stop* (No 4, Feb 1989). Following *Apache*, the Shad's had Top 10 hits with *Man of Mystery/The Stranger* (No 5, Nov 1960), *F.B.I.* (No 6, Feb 1961), *The Frightened City* (No 3, May 1961) and *Kontiki* (No 1, Sep 1961). In October 1961 Tony Meehan left the group to work as an arranger/producer and session drummer for Joe Meek. Fans of the Shad's found this a strange move to make for such a successful drummer within an iconic group but the truth is there were tensions among the Shad's. Although Tony was long gone by the time of the Shad's chart-toping *Wonderful Land* (No 1, Mar 1962) the single was recorded while he was still with the group. In fact *Wonderful Land* remained at the top of the UK Singles Chart for eight weeks. Brian Bennett (born Brian Laurence Bennett, Palmers Green, 9 February 1940) replaced Tony as drummer but in April 1962 another bombshell was to hit the band when Jet Harris suddenly quit. The story given out at the time was that Jet was suffering from nervous exhaustion and stage-fright (which was partly true) but the full truth was a little more sinister. Jet had been suffering from depression and alcohol dependency from almost the beginning of his marriage to Carol Costa in 1959. Costa, the first of Jet's four wives, had been having an affair with Cliff Richard, and remains the only woman Cliff has ever admitted to sleeping with. After Bruce Welch made an off-hand remark about Jet's wife's ongoing affair with Cliff things became impossible. After signing to Decca, Jet had a couple of solo hits before teaming up with his old friend Tony Meehan to have three huge hits during 1963, *Diamonds* (No 1, Jan 1963), *Scarlett O'Hara* (No 2, Apr 1963) and *Applejack* (No 4, Sep 1963). Jimmy Page was the session guitarist who worked on *Diamonds* and John Paul Jones toured with the duo in the summer of 1963. Unfortunately a spate of drunken incidents began to take their toll but in September 1963 the Jet Harris and Tony Meehan partnership was ultimately ended by a serious car crash. Jet was returning home from a concert in Worcester with his girlfriend Billie Davis (see entry for Mike Sarne) when their chauffeur-driven limousine crashed in the West Midlands. Jet received head injuries that seriously affected his already troubled career and it was not until 1966 he recovered sufficiently to play again, briefly

becoming a member of the Jeff Beck Group. In recent years Jet enjoyed playing with Hank and Bruce at Shad reunions but died of cancer on 18 March 2011. Interestingly, before Tony linked up with Jet he auditioned The Beatles (Paul McCartney, John Lennon, George Harrison and Pete Best) on 1 January 1962, for Decca. Eventually the band was rejected in favour of The Tremeloes, who had auditioned the same day. After a brief spell touring with the Tony Meehan Combo and a few reunions with the Shads, Tony became a psychologist in the 1990s and retired from the music industry. He died on 28 November 2005. Jet was replaced in the Shads by Brian "Licorice" Locking (born in Bedworth, Warwickshire, 22 December 1938), his nickname stemming from his ability to play the clarinet (nicknamed the licorice stick). Both Brians had previously played together in Marty Wilde's backing group The Wildcats, who also recorded instrumentals as The Krew Kats. The Top 10 hits continued to flow and included: *Guitar Tango* (No 4, Aug 1962), *Dance On!* (No 1, Dec 1962), *Foot Tapper* (No 1, Mar 1963), *Atlantis* (No 2, Jun 1963) and *Shindig* (No 6, Sep 1963) before, in October 1963 Licorice Locking left to spend more time as a Jehovah's Witness and was replaced by John Rostill (born John Henry Rostill in Birmingham, 16 June 1942; d. Radlett, Hertfordshire, 26 November 1973) who popularised the Burns guitar. After *Geronimo* (No 11, Dec 1963) which Licorice Locking had already recorded, the new line-up was first heard on *The Rise and Fall of Flingel Bunt* (No 5, May 1964). The character Flingel Bunt was an imaginary character invented by the actor Richard O'Sullivan (see entry in cinema section), a friend of The Shadows. The full title was given to the tune after the group had been to see the film *The Rise and Fall of Legs Diamond* (1960). Although the hits continued, notably *Genie with the Light Brown Lamp* (No 17, Dec 1964) and *Stingray* (No 19, Jun 1965) the Shads were no longer making the Top 10 as the Mersey Sound, and in particular The Beatles, began to monopolise the charts. In December 1968 the group decided to split, after Bruce left, although hybrid formations continued, the most famous being Marvin, Welch & Farrar. John Farrar (born in Melbourne Australia, 8 November 1946) was a guitarist and vocalist who gave the band a new dimension and the trio specialised in close harmonies as well as instrumental music, often playing with the cream of session musicians such as drummer Clem Cattini (see entry for The Tornados). None of the different versions of the Shads caught the public imagination so in 1973 Hank, Bruce and Brian Bennett decided to reform the group with John Farrar replacing John Rostill. After the 1968 break-up John Rostill toured with Tom Jones and intended to rejoin the Shads but he was electrocuted in his home recording studio whilst playing the guitar and died on 26 November 1973, Bruce Welch finding his body. The biggest success of the reformed band was *Let Me Be the One* (No 12, Mar 1975) which was the UK entry for the Eurovision Song Contest. The Shadows recorded six options, seen each week on a weekly television show *It's Lulu*, televised on BBC1 and hosted by Lulu, a former Eurovision winner herself. *Let Me Be the One*, composed by Paul Curtis, placed second to the Dutch entry, Teach-In's *Ding-A-Dong* in the Eurovision final in Stockholm. Other hit singles included: *Don't Cry for Me Argentina* (No 5, Dec 1978) and *Theme from the Deer Hunter (Cavatina)* (No 9, Apr 1979). The band has continued to play with various line-ups, Licorice Locking occasionally guesting. In December 2004 The Shads were each awarded the Order of the British Empire although Hank politely declined his. The Shadows were innovators in several fields. Their three-move strut in harmony to the music they were playing gave the group a dynamic feel which has been much-imitated ever since. Hank's use of echo machines and tremolo lever also popularised these effects in the UK. Another lesser known innovation was not to have the group's name on the drums in the traditional way but instead to have the name of the drummer!

Ed Sheeran Ginger-haired singer-songwriter Edward Christopher Sheeran was born in Halifax, West Yorkshire, on 17 February 1991, to Irish and English parents, before moving to Framlingham, Suffolk as a child. He is a cousin of Belfast-born TV journalist and presenter Gordon Burns who also admits to have been ginger when a young man. A self-taught guitarist and

405

songwriter, Ed began gigging at a young age. After reading an interview with James Morrison that stated that James had done 200 gigs in a year, Ed decided to beat that figure and in 2009, played 312 gigs. In April 2010, after leaving his old management company, he bought a ticket to Los Angeles, and played open mic nights all over LA, before being spotted by actor and musician Jamie Foxx who invited him to stay at his house and record for the rest of his stay. Throughout 2010, Ed's fan-base grew as a result of media attention via YouTube and *The Independent* newspaper, plus celebrity praise from the likes of England football captain Rio Ferdinand and pop star Elton John. In January 2011, Ed released his final independent EP, *No.5 Collaborations Project* featuring appearances by grime artists such as Wiley, JME, Devlin, Sway and Ghetts. In April 2011 Ed was signed to Asylum / Atlantic Records and released his debut single, *The A Team* (No 3, Jun 2011 and No 3 in Ireland), which sold more than 50,000 copies in it's first week. His second single, *You Need Me, I Don't Need You* (No 4, Aug 2011 - No 19 in Ireland), third, *Lego House* (No 5, Nov 2011 - No 5 in Ireland) and fourth, *Drunk* (No 9, Feb 2012 - No 7 in Ireland)   cemented his position as a mainstream popular artist. All four singles were from his debut chart-topping album '+' (No 1, Sep 2011 – No 2 in Ireland). In addition to his solo efforts Ed's voice has also featured on several less successful singles such as *If I Could* (Wiley featuring Ed Sheeran), *Young Guns* (Lewi White featuring Ed Sheeran, Yasmin, Griminal & Devlin), *Teardrop* (as part of The Collective) and *Hush Little Baby* (Wretch 32 featuring Ed Sheeran). The fifth track from '+', *Small Bump*, is due to be released in May 2012. At the 2012 BRIT awards, Ed won the British Breakthrough Act and British Solo Male Artist categories.

Sky Instrumental classical / rock fusion band formed in 1978 by classical guitarist John Williams (born Melbourne, Australia, 24 April 1941), former Blue Mink and T. Rex bassist Herbie Flowers (born Brian Keith Flowers, Isleworth, Middlesex, 19 May 1938) and former Curved Air keyboards player Francis Monkman. By 1979 the trio were joined by guitarist Kevin Peek and drummer Tristan Fry. The group's only Top 10 UK single was *Toccata* (No 5, Apr 1980) although their first four albums, 'Sky' (No 9, Jun 1979), 'Sky 2' (No 1, Apr 1980), 'Sky 3' (No 3, Mar 1981) and 'Sky 4 – Forthcoming' (No 7, Apr 1982) all reached the UK Top 10. Francis left in 1980 and was replaced by Steve Gray and John left the group in 1983. Although the group has never officially disbanded it has not toured since 1995 and there are no future plans. John continues to be one of the world's greatest classical guitarists. He was once married to broadcaster Sue Cook (born Susan Lorraine Thomas, Ruislip, Middlesex, 30 March 1949). Herbie currently works as a bass guitar teacher at Ardingly College and has impressive credentials for the job. In his day he was one of the most sought-after session musicians in Britain, probably only bettered by Clem Cattini (see entry for The Tornados). He has collaborated with many of the world's top musicians and famously played the iconic twin interlocking bass lines (on double bass and overdubbed fretless bass guitar) on Lou Reed's *Walk on the Wild Side*. He also composed Clive Dunn's novelty chart-topper *Grandad* (No 1, Jan 1971).

The Small Faces see entry for Rod Stewart

Son of Dork see entry for Busted

The Spice Girls In February 1994, Heart Management – which comprised father-and-son management team Bob and Chris Herbert plus financier Chic Murphy – placed an advertisement in *The Stage* asking for young streetwise females, aged 18-23, who could sing and dance, to audition with a view to gaining a recording deal. The original chosen line-up was Michelle Stephenson (born Abingdon, Oxfordshire, 3 January 1977,) Victoria Caroline Adams (born Harlow, Essex, 17 April 1974), Melanie Janine Brown (born Harehills, Leeds, West Yorkshire, 29 May 1975, Lianne Morgan - later replaced by Melanie Jayne Chisholm (born Whiston, Merseyside, 12 January 1974) and

Suzanne Tinker - later replaced by Geraldine Estelle Halliwell (born Watford, Hertfordshire, 6 August 1972). By July Michelle had left the band (then named Touch) and was replaced by Emma Lee Bunton (born Finchley, London, 21 January 1976). Frustrating months ensued in which little happened except demos being cut, on which one track called *Sugar and Spice*, written by Tim Hawes, inspired a name change to Spice and before the year was out, The Spice Girls. In March 1995 the girls parted from Heart Management and signed with Simon Fuller of 19 Entertainment and by September had signed a deal with Virgin Records. The next few months were spent touring the west coast of America and writing album tracks. On 7th of June 1996, they released their debut single *Wannabe* and aided by an accompanying video played endlessly on The Box music channel plus their first live TV slot on ITV's *Surprise Surprise*, the record made No 1 in the UK, Ireland and USA (among many other countries) and won the BRIT award for Best Single. In October 1996 their second single, *Say You'll Be There*, also topped the UK chart (No 2 in Ireland and 3 in the States) and won them a second BRIT (Best Video) at the 1997 awards. In November 1996, the Spice Girls released their debut album 'Spice' and this topped the UK chart as well as the Irish and American. To round off a fantastic year their third single, *2 Become 1* (USA No 4) became the first of three consecutive Christmas No 1s for the girls. At the aforementioned BRIT awards the group opened proceedings with *Who Do You Think You Are*, with Geri Halliwell wearing a Union Jack mini-dress, which became one of pop history's most famed outfits. In March 1997, the double A-side of *Mama/Who Do You Think You Are* became their fourth successive No 1, thus making The Spice Girls the most successful debut act of all time, beating Gerry and the Pacemakers, Frankie Goes to Hollywood and Robson and Jerome, all of whom topped the charts with their first three releases. *Girl Power!*, The Spice Girls' first book and manifesto was launched later that month at the Virgin Megastore and became an immediate best-seller. The group also performed a live show for members of the Royal Family and playfully breached royal protocol when Mel B and then Geri Halliwell planted kisses on Prince Charles' cheeks and pinched his bottom. In October 1997, *Spice Up Your Life* (No 2 in Ireland, 18 in the States), became the group's fifth-consecutive No 1 single and in December, *Too Much* (No 4 in Ireland, 9 in the States), their sixth; both from their second album 'Spiceworld' (No 1, Nov 1997). This album also topped the Irish chart and placed third on the US. On Boxing Day 1997 the film, *Spiceworld,* premiered (see entry in film section) but by then they had already fired Simon Fuller and had taken over the running of the band themselves. Their seventh single, *Stop* (No 2, Mar 1998 and No 3 and 16 respectively in Ireland and US) and eighth, *Viva Forever* (No 1, Aug 1998 and No 2 in Ireland), both from the 'Spiceworld' album became the last chart hits of the five girls as Geri had announced her departure very publicly on 31 May 1998. The original lineup also had a No 9 UK hit as part of England United in June 1998 with *How Does It Feel To Be (On Top of the World)*, the official England World Cup song. Geri's departure was the subject of a lawsuit by Aprilia World Service BV, a manufacturer of motorcycles and scooters. On 9 March 1998, Halliwell informed the other members of the group of her intention to withdraw from the group, yet the girls signed an agreement with AWS on 24 March and participated in a commercial photo shoot on 4 May in Milan, eventually concluding a contract with AWS on 6 May 1998. The Court of Appeal held that their conduct constituted a misrepresentation, allowing AWS to rescind their contract with the Spice Girls. This is now the leading case in English law on misrepresentation by conduct. *Goodbye* (No 1, Dec 1998 and No 11 in USA) became The Spice Girls third Christmas No 1 and, after an eight-month recording-break, the post-Halliwell band began to start work on their third album 'Forever' (No 2, Nov 2000); the lead single, the double A-side *Holler/Let Love Lead the Way* (No 1, Nov 2000 and No 3 in Ireland) giving them their ninth UK chart-topper. This album only peaked at No 15 in Ireland and 39 in the States. In December 2000, the group announced that they would be concentrating on their solo careers for the foreseeable future, although pointing out that they might get back together at some point. In June 2007 all five members of the band reunited to work on a 'Greatest Hits' album (No 2, Nov 2007) which was released with two new tracks; the single, *Headlines (Friendship Never Ends)* and *Voodoo*. The album peaked at number two in the UK, and became their first number-one album in Australia. It also reached No 9 in Ireland but stalled at No 93 in the Billboard Hot 100. The group's comeback single, *Headlines (Friendship Never Ends)*, was announced as the official Children in Need charity single for 2007 and although reaching No 11 in the UK in November 2007 only peaked at 29 in Ireland and No 90 in the States. The first come-back appearance on stage by the Spice Girls was made at the Kodak Theatre in Hollywood, where the group performed at the Victoria's Secret Fashion Show in November before kicking off a world tour in Vancouver on 2 December 2007. In February 2008, it was announced that due to personal and family commitments their tour would come to a premature end in Toronto on 26 February 2008, resulting in tour dates in Beijing, Hong Kong, Shanghai, Sydney, Cape Town and Buenos Aires being cancelled. A list of their solo Top 10 output follows: **Victoria Beckham** (Posh Spice) albums - Victoria Beckham (No 10, Oct 2001) singles - *Out of Your Mind* (featuring True Steppers & Dane Bowers) (No 2, Aug 2000), *Not Such an Innocent Girl* (No 6, Sep 2001), *A Mind of Its Own* (No 6, Feb 2002), *Let Your Head Go* (No 3, Dec 2003) and *This Groove* (No 3, Dec 2003). Her autobiography *Learning to Fly* (2001) became an instant best-seller. Her second book, a fashion advice guide, entitled *That Extra Half an Inch: Hair, Heels and Everything In Between*, was published on 27 October 2006. Victoria has taken part in several documentaries about her life with the Spice Girls but made a bigger impact in the world of fashion after becoming a British ambassador for Dolce and Gabbana although making her name in that field through her collaboration with Italian designer Roberto Cavalli. In November 2011, she was awarded the "Designer of the Year" gong at the annual British Fashion Awards. See also entry for David Beckham in the miscellaneous section. **Mel B** (Scary Spice) singles - *I Want You Back* featuring Missy Elliott (No 1, Sep 1998), *Tell Me* (No 4, Aug 2000) and *Feels So Good* (No 5, Feb 2001) all from her debut album 'Hot' which stalled at No 28 on the UK chart. In 2002, Mel released her autobiography, *Catch A Fire*. She has had a varied television career, the highlight being her runner-up spot in the fifth season of the U.S. television show *Dancing with the Stars* in 2007. She married Dutch dancer Jimmy Gulzar in Little Marlow, Buckinghamshire, on 13 September 1998 and changed her stage name to Melanie G for a while. They have a daughter, Phoenix Chi Gulzar (b. Westminster, London, 19 February 1999). After divorcing Gulzar in 2000, Mel had an affair with actor Eddie Murphy and gave birth to daughter Angel Iris Murphy Brown on Eddie Murphy's 46th birthday, 3 April 2007. Murphy initially disputed the parentage but DNA evidence proved he was the father. In June 2007 she married film producer Stephen Belafonte and subsequently gave birth to her third child, a daughter Madison Brown Belafonte (b. 1 September 2011). **Emma Bunton** (Baby Spice) albums – 'A Girl Like Me' (No 4, Apr 2001) and 'Free Me' (No 7, Feb 2004) singles - *What I Am* (featuring Tin Tin Out) (No 2, Nov 1999), *What Took You So Long?* (No 1, Apr 2001), *Take My Breath Away* (No 5, Aug 2001), *Free Me* (No 5, May 2003), *Maybe* (No 6, Nov 2003), *I'll Be There* (No 7, Jan 2004) and *Downtown* (No 3, Nov 2006). Emma trained at the Sylvia Young Theatre School in Marylebone and appeared briefly in the BBC series *EastEnders* in 1992 as a mugger and also made a brief appearance as a prostitute in the BBC drama series *To Play the King*. See also entries in the television section for *Absolutely Fabulous, Dancing On Ice*, and *Strictly Come Dancing*. Emma's long-term partner since 2000 is former Damage and CherryBlackStone lead singer Jade Jones. She announced her engagement to Jade during an episode of *Dancing on Ice* on 23 January 2011. The couple have two sons: Beau Lee Jones (b. London, 10 August 2007) and Tate Lee Jones (b. 6 May 2011). **Melanie Chisholm** (Sporty Spice) albums - 'Northern Star' (No 4, Oct 1999) and 'Reason' (No 5, Mar 2003) singles - *Goin' Down* (No 4, Sep 1999), *Northern Star* (No 4, Nov 1999), *Never Be the Same Again* (featuring Lisa Lopes) (No 1, Mar 2000), *I Turn to You* (No 1, Aug 2000), *Here It Comes Again* (No 7, Feb 2003),

Next Best Superstar (No 10, Apr 2005) and as featured artist *When You're Gone* (Bryan Adams featuring Melanie C) (No 3, Nov 1998). In November 2009, Melanie played the role of Mrs Johnstone for six months in the musical *Blood Brothers* by Willy Russell in London's West End. She has been in a relationship with property developer Thomas Starr since 2002 and Melanie gave birth to their first child, a daughter, Scarlet Starr, on 22 February 2009. Mel has 11 tattoos on her body the most visible a crucifix on her upper left bicep. **Geri Halliwell** (Ginger Spice) albums – 'Schizophonic' (No 4, Jun 1999) and 'Scream If You Wanna Go Faster' (No 5, May 2001) singles - *Look at Me* (No 2, May 1999), *Mi Chico Latino* (No 1, Aug 1999), *Lift Me Up* (No 1, Nov 1999), *Bag It Up* (No 1, Mar 2000), *It's Raining Men* (No 1, Apr 2001), *Scream If You Wanna Go Faster* (No 8, Jul 2001), *Calling* (No 7, Nov 2001) and *Ride It* (No 4, Nov 2004). In 1999 she wrote an autobiography *If Only*, and in 2008 a book series named *Ugenia Lavender*. On 14 May 2006, Geri gave birth to her daughter, Bluebell Madonna Halliwell, by caesarean section at London's Portland Hospital. The father has never been named but is thought to be Sacha Gervasi.

The Stargazers Vocal group formed in 1949 by Cliff Adams and Ronnie Milne. Of the other original members: Marie Benson, Fred Datchler and Dick James, it is the last named that is the most interesting. Dick James (12 December 1920 – 1 February 1986) was born Reginald Leon Isaac Vapnick. Under the name Lee Sheridan he was a member of the Henry Hall band before signing up for war duty in 1942. After the war he changed his name and sung with Geraldo's band for a time until beginning a four-year stint with The Stargazers. He left the group at the beginning of 1953 (replaced by Bob Brown), missing out on their recording career, but enjoying a measure of solo success with UK Top 20 hits *Robin Hood* (No 14, Jan 1956) and *Garden of Eden* (No 18, Jan 1957); the first mentioned charting soon after being heard as the theme tune for the popular ITV adventure series starring Richard Greene. Dick later sang the theme tune to another ITV series, *The Buccaneers*, but as his singing career declined he entered the music-publishing business and formed the DJM (Dick James Music) record label. After Brian Epstein played him The Beatles' second single *Please Please Me*, Dick decided to promote the record and organised the groups big television break on *Thank Your Lucky Stars*. This was the beginning of a long association with the Fab Four which included forming Northern Songs Ltd with them. Ultimately the relationship broke down when Dick sold the company which led to The Beatles losing the rights to their own songs. Dick also signed Elton John and all his hits up until his first No 1, *Don't Go Breaking My Heart* (which was on Elton's own Rocket label), were on the DJM label. Again this association ended acrimoniously, in 1985, with Elton suing Dick over the rights to his earlier material. Dick died of a heart attack soon after. As for The Stargazers, their first single, *Broken Wings* reached the top of the UK chart in February 1953 but later in the year Ronnie Milne left to emigrate to Canada and was replaced by Dave Cary. At this time the group was backing Petula Clark in her early recordings. In February 1954 their second single, *I See the Moon*, also topped the charts and they had a third No 1 in December 1954 with *Finger of Suspicion* (with Dickie Valentine). Two further Top 10 singles followed: *Close the Door* (No 6, Sep 1955) and *Twenty Tiny Fingers* (No 4, Nov 1955) before they disbanded; Fred Datchler going on to form The Polkadots. Fred's son, Clark, found fame in the 1980s as lead singer and multi-instrumentalist with Johnny Hates Jazz.

Status Quo The Quo were founded in 1962, as The Spectres, by two Catford schoolmates Francis Rossi (born Francis Dominic Nicholas Michael Rossi, Forest Hill, London, 29 May 1949; guitar and vocals) and Alan Lancaster (born Alan Charles Lancaster, Peckham, London, 7 February 1949; bassist). They were later joined by drummer John Coghlan (born John Robert Coghlan, Dulwich, London, 19 September 1946) and keyboardist Roy Lynes (born Roy Alan Lynes, Redhill, Surrey, 25 October 1943) who replaced their original organist Jess Jaworski but left in 1971. In 1967 guitarist and vocalist Rick Parfitt (born Richard John Parfitt, Woking, Surrey, 12 October 1948) joined, after befriending Rossi two years earlier at Butlin's Minehead whilst

Rick was playing as Ricky Harrison in a musical trio called The Highlights. This quintet became Traffic, Traffic Jam, The Status Quo, finally settling on the name Status Quo in 1969. The Quo's first single, *Pictures of Matchstick Men* (No 7, Jan 1968) recorded before Rick joined them, was written by Rossi whilst sitting on the toilet. The so-called bubblegum psychedelia feel of the song was perfectly attuned to the 'Flower Power' era and the simple four note riff intro epitomised Quo's early music. Although their second single, *Black Veils Of Melancholy*, failed to make much impression on the charts the band have subsequently had a string of hit singles, including: *Ice In the Sun* (No 8, Aug 1968 – written by Marty Wilde and Ronnie Scott), *Paper Plane* (No 8, Jan 1973), *Caroline* (No 5, Sep 1973), *Break the Rules* (No 8, May 1974), *Down Down* (No 1, Dec 1974), *Roll Over Lay Down* (No 9, May 1975), *Rain* (No 7, Feb 1976), *Wild Side of Life* (No 9, Dec 1976), *Rockin' All Over the World* (No 3, Oct 1977), *Whatever You Want* (No 4, Sep 1979), *What You're Proposing* (No 2, Oct 1980), *Something 'Bout You Baby I Like* (No 9, Feb 1981), *Rock 'N' Roll* (No 8, Nov 1981), *Dear John* (No 10, Mar 1982), *Marguerita Time* (No 3, Dec 1983), *The Wanderer* (No 7, Oct 1984), *Rollin' Home* (No 9, May 1986), *In the Army Now* (No 2, Oct 1986), *Dreamin'* (No 15, Dec 1986), *Running All Over the World* (No 17, Aug 1988), *Burning Bridges (On and Off and On Again)* (No 5, Dec 1988), *Anniversary Waltz – Part 1* (No 2, Sep 1990), *Anniversary Waltz – Part 2* (No 16, Dec 1990), *Come on You Reds* (No 1, Apr 1994 - released as Manchester United F.C. with Status Quo), *Jam Side Down* (No 17, Aug 2002) and *The Party Ain't Over Yet* (No 11, Sep 2005). Their successful albums include: 'Piledriver' (No 5, Dec 1972), 'Hello!' (No 1, Sep 1973), 'Quo' (No 2, May 1974), 'On the Level' (No 1, Feb 1975), 'Blue for You' (No 1, Mar 1976), 'Rockin' All Over the World' (No 5, Nov 1977), ' If You Can't Stand the Heat..' (No 3, Oct 1978), 'Whatever You Want' (No 3, Oct 1979), 'Just Supposin'' (No 4, Oct 1980), 'Never Too Late' (No 2, Mar 1981), '1+9+8+2' (aka 1982) (No 1, Apr 1982), 'Back To Back' (No 9, Nov 1983), 'In the Army Now' (No 7, Aug 1986), 'Rock 'til You Drop' (No 10, Sep 1991), 'Don't Stop' (No 2, Feb 1996), 'In Search of the Fourth Chord' (No 15, Sep 2007) and 'Quid Pro Quo' (No 10, May 2011). Quo became one of the world's great rock bands by the mid-1970s signing a pioneering sponsorship deal with Levi's in 1976 as they were identified with the cool Levi-clad look more than any other rock band. At this time Andy Bown (born Andrew Steven Bown, in London, 27 March 1946) joined the Quo as bassist and keyboardist. Andy, who found fame alongside Peter Frampton as a member of Herd, which had hit singles with *From the Underworld* (No 6, Sep 1967), *Paradise Lost* (No 15, Dec 1967) and *I Don't Want Our Loving to Die* (No 5, Apr 1968) had previously played with Quo as a session musician. John Coghlan left the group in late 1981, to be replaced by Pete Kircher (born Peter Derek Kircher, Folkestone, Kent, 21 January 1945), formerly of the 1960s band Honeybus. Alan Lancaster left the band in 1985 amid bitter acrimony after Francis and Rick began recording a new album under the name of "Status Quo" unbeknown to Alan, who was by now living in Australia. Alan's final performance with Quo was at Wembley Stadium on 13 July 1985 for the opening of Live Aid. He was replaced by John 'Rhino' Edwards (born John Victor Edwards, Chiswick, London, 9 May 1953). Pete Kircher left Quo soon after and was replaced by Jeff Rich (born in Hackney, London, 8 June 1953). Rick underwent quadruple by-pass surgery in 1997 but returned with a performance at the Norwich City Football Club ground three months later. Drummer Matt Letley (born 29 March 1961) joined the band in 2000 as replacement for Jeff Rich. In December 2008, they released their 75th single and first Christmas single, *It's Christmas Time*, which peaked at No 40 in the UK Singles Chart. Quo are far from the three-chord instrumentalists they sometimes modestly portray themselves as but in actuality are great innovators, for instance, *Whatever You Want*, written by by Rick Parfitt and Andy Bown, and arguably their greatest recording, is played with the low 'E' string of the guitars tuned to a D to give the unique contrast to the driving beat. Francis and Rick were awarded the OBE in the New Year Honours 2010 for their services to music.

Tommy Steele Thomas William Hicks was born at Bermondsey, London on 17 December 1936. Amongst many jobs he spent over four years in the Merchant Navy (1951-55) before forming a skiffle group called *The Cavemen* with future actor Mike Pratt and future composer Lionel Bart. Tommy was signed up by Decca after a session at the 2i's coffee bar and Larry Parnes (aka "Parnes, shillings and pence") guided his early career. Backed by the Steelmen he reached No.13 with *Rock with the Caveman* (Oct 1956) and gained his only No.1 with his second release, *Singin' the Blues* (Dec 1956). Tommy went on to make 30 singles, six more of which made the UK top 10: *Butterfingers* (No 8, May 1957), *Water Water / Handful of Songs* (No 5, Aug 1957), *Nairobi* (No 3, Mar 1958), *Come On, Let's Go* (No 10, Nov 1958), *Little White Bull* (No 6, Dec 1959) and *What a Mouth* (No 5, Jun 1960). He co-wrote songs after 1958 under the name Jimmy Bennett. He was Britain's first rock and roll idol. There followed an amazingly quick-off-the-mark film bio *The Tommy Steele Story* (1957) and his full feature screen debut *The Duke Wore Jeans* (1958). He followed up with *Tommy the Toreador* (1959), from which the popular children's song *Little White Bull* was taken. By that point his career had begun to move from a pop performer to being an all-round entertainer. He began his stage career in pantomime but progressed to the legitimate theatre by appearing at the Old Vic in *She Stoops to Conquer* (1960-61). His films include *Half a Sixpence* (1967), in which he had appeared on stage in London and Broadway, *The Happiest Millionaire* (1967) and *Finian's Rainbow* (1968). He then played Feste in a TV production of *Twelfth Night* (1969). His other films include *Where's Jack* (1969 - as highwayman Jack Sheppard) and *Quincy's Quest* (1979 – based on Tommy's children's novel *Quincy*). He has also starred in the stage musicals *Hans Christian Anderson, Singin' in the Rain, Some Like it Hot* and *Scrooge*. He entered the Guinness Book of Records when his *An Evening with Tommy Steele* (1979-80) became the longest running one-man show in West End history. Tommy has also made more than 1,700 appearances at the London Palladium, wrote the novels *Final Run* (1983) and *Four Faces of Ada* (1993), an autobiography *Bermondsey Boy: Memories of a Forgotten World* (2006) and is an accomplished painter and sculptor. Tommy married Ann Donoghue in 1960. They have one daughter, Emma. He received the OBE in 1980. Tommy is a talented artist and his Eleanor Rigby sculpture was given to the City of Liverpool as a tribute to the Beatles and stands in Stanley Street, not far from the Cavern Club. He has another sculpture featuring two rugby players on display at Twickenham Stadium. He has also exhibited paintings at the Royal Academy. On 21 April 2008, during a BBC Radio 2 interview, theatre impresario Bill Kenwright claimed that in 1958, Elvis Presley, then 23, "flew in for a day and Tommy showed him round London. He showed him the Houses of Parliament and spent the day with him". Tommy's statement on the controversy was that "It was two young men sharing the same love of their music. I swore never to divulge publicly what took place and I regret that it has found some way of getting into the light. I only hope he can forgive me." Press officers employed by Stagecoach, the company that owns Prestwick Airport, the previously considered only place Elvis ever trod on British soil, rapidly issued a statement requesting proof of these claims. The plot thickened when Lamar Fike, a former member of the Memphis Mafia, who lived with Presley at the time, posted a claim that it was he, not Elvis, who visited London and Tommy Steele for a day in 1958.

Rod Stewart The husky-voiced rocker was born Roderick David Stewart in Highgate, North London on 10 January 1945, to an English mother and Scottish father. As a youngster Rod was a typical working-class lad, his interests were trains, particularly model railways, and football, captaining his school team and playing centre-half for Middlesex Schools. An early musical influence was Al Jolson. Rod's father bought him a guitar in

January 1959 and within a year he was playing in a band. Although leaving school, aged 15, and becoming a silk screen printer Rod's ambition was to pursue a career as a professional footballer. He started an apprenticeship with third division Brentford FC in 1961 but the daily rigour of travelling coupled with the discipline of cleaning the boots of the first team players ate away at Rod's enthusiasm and he left after a couple of months. As many a quiz buff will know, Rod then became a grave-digger at Highgate cemetery for a while before fronting a band called The Raiders and auditioning for Joe Meek (see entry for The Tornados). Ironically, Joe loved the band but hated the front-man. Rod left and Joe took The Raiders on, changed their name to The Moontrekkers, and after a UK No 50 single, *Night of the Vampire*, disappeared without trace. Rod spent his late teens living in a beatnik houseboat at Shoreham-by-Sea and involving himself in left-wing politics, being arrested on three occasions for taking part in sit-ins on behalf of organisations such as CND. All this time Rod was learning his craft by playing harmonica and busking at Leicester Square, usually alongside folk-singer Wizz Jones. Eventually Rod and Wizz took their act to Paris and then Barcelona, where Rod was promptly arrested for vagrancy and deported back to England. In early 1962 he joined the Ray Davies Quartet for a short time. Ray (born Raymond Douglas Davies, Fortis Green, London, 21 June 1944) later co-founded The Kinks with his brother Dave (born David Russell Gordon Davies, Fortis Green, London, 3 February 1947). The Kinks had numerous hits including: *You Really Got Me* (No 1, Aug 1964), *All Day and All of the Night* (No 2, Oct 1964), *Tired of Waiting for You* (No 1, Jan 1965), *Till the End of the Day* (No 8, Dec 1965), *Dedicated Follower of Fashion* (No 4, Mar 1966), *Sunny Afternoon* (No 1, Jun 1966), *Waterloo Sunset* (No 2, May 1967), *Autumn Almanac* (No 3, Oct 1967), *Days* (No 12, Jul 1968), *Lola* (No 2, Jul 1970), *Apeman* (No 5, Dec 1970) and *Death of a Clown* (No 3, Jul 1967) which was released as a solo effort by Dave. It was around this time that Rod adopted the Mod look and made feather-cut hair fashionable for men. In January 1964 Rod was amusing himself playing his harmonica at Twickenham railway station whilst waiting for a train home when Long John Baldry approached him and invited him to join his group, which became the Hoochie Coochie Men. The two singers had a mutual friend in the bisexual Dave Davies, with whom Long John had a brief relationship. Although John and Rod went their own ways in October 1964 they joined up again the following year to form Steampacket, which also included Julie Driscoll (born in London, 8 Jun 1947) who later had a huge hit with Bob Dylan's *This Wheels on Fire* (No 5, Apr 1968). Rod also made an abortive attempt at a solo career, recording the Sam Cooke song *Shake*. Cooke had become a major influence on Rod's style of singing. After leaving Steampacket in March 1966 Rod joined Shotgun Express, a band that included drummer Mick Fleetwood (born Michael John Kells Fleetwood, Redruth, Cornwall, 24 June 1947) and guitarist Peter Green (born Peter Allen Greenbaum, Bethnal Green, London, 29 October 1946) who would go on to form Fleetwood Mac together and have a chart-topping single with *Albatross* (No 1, Dec 1968) composed by Green. In the post-green era (Lindsey Buckingham, Mick Fleetwood, Christine McVie, John McVie, Stevie Nicks) Fleetwood Mac released one of the best-selling albums of all-time 'Rumours' (No 1, Feb 1977) which was No 1 on both sides of the Atlantic and spawned the iconic track, *The Chain*, a sample of which has been used by the BBC to introduce their F1 Grand Prix coverage. Other chart-topping albums include: 'Tusk' (No 1, Oct 1979), 'Tango in the Night' (No 1, Apr 1987) and 'Behind the Mask' (No 1, Apr 1990). In February 1967 Rod joined the Jeff Beck Group and first played with Ronnie Wood (see entry for The Rolling Stones). The two friends left in July 1969 to join The Small Faces after the departure of Steve Marriott (born Stephen Peter Marriott, East Ham, London, 30 January 1947; d. 20 April 1991) to form the supergroup Humble Pie with Greg Ridley, Jerry Shirley and former Herd vocalist/guitarist Pete Frampton (born Peter Kenneth Frampton, Bromley, London, 22 April 1950) and having a huge hit with their debut single, *Natural Born Bugie* (No 4, Aug 1969). Rod and Ronnie joined existing members of The Small Faces - Ronnie Lane, (born Ronald Frederick Lane, Plaistow, London, 1 April 1946; d. from multiple slerosis, in Colorado, USA, 4 June 1997), Ian McLagan (born Ian William Patrick McLagan, Isleworth, London, 12 May 1945), and Kenney Jones (see entry for The Who) and soon decided to call the new line-up The Faces. The Small Faces had considerable success with singles such as *Sha La La La Lee* (No 3, Feb 1966), *All or Nothing* (No 1, Aug 1966), *My Mind's Eye* (No 4, Nov 1966), *Here Comes the Nice* (No 12, Jun 1967), *Itchycoo Park* (No 3, Aug 1967) and *Lazy Sunday* (No 2, Apr 1968) and the hits continued under their new name The Faces; *Stay With Me* (No 6, Dec 1971), *Cindy Incidentally* (No 2, Feb 1973) and the double-A side *Pool Hall Richard/I Wish it Would Rain* (No 8, Dec 1973) all reaching the Top 10 as did the album 'A Nod Is as Good as a Wink... to a Blind Horse' (No 2, Mar 1971 and No 6 in the USA). Rod also had a solid solo career which continued after The Faces broke up at the end of 1975. Rod's numerous solo hit singles include: *Maggie May / Reason to Believe* (No 1, Sep 1971 and No 1 in USA), *You Wear It Well* (No 1, Aug 1972), *In a Broken Dream* (No 3, Sep 1972 - with Aussie band Python Lee Jackson), *Angel/ What's Made Milwaukee Famous (Has Made a Loser Out of Me)* (No 4, Nov 1972), *Oh No Not My Baby* (No 6, Sep 1973), *Sailing* (No 1, Aug 1975), *This Old Heart of Mine* (No 4, Nov 1975), *Tonight's the Night* (Gonna Be Alright) (No 5, Jun 1976), *The Killing of Georgie (Part I and II)* (No 2, Aug 1976), *I Don't Want to Talk About It/The First Cut Is the Deepest* (No 1, Apr 1977), *You're in My Heart* (The Final Acclaim) (No 3, Oct 1977), *Hot Legs/I Was Only Joking* (No 5, Jan 1978), *Ole Ola (Mulher Brasileira)* (No 4, May 1978 - featuring The Scottish World Cup Football Squad '78), *Da Ya Think I'm Sexy?* (No 1, Nov 1978 and No 1 in USA), *Tonight I'm Yours (Don't Hurt Me)* (No 8, Oct 1981), *Young Turks* (No 11, Dec 1981 and No 5 in USA), *Baby Jane* (No 1, Jun 1983), *What Am I Gonna Do* (No 3, Aug 1983), *Some Guys Have All the Luck* (No 15, Jul 1984), *Every Beat of My Heart* (No 2, Jul 1986), *Downtown Train* (No 10, Jan 1990 and No 3 in USA), *It Takes Two* (No 5, Nov 1990 – with Tina Turner), *Rhythm of My Heart* (No 3, Mar 1991), *Tom Traubert's Blues* (Waltzing Matilda) (No 6, Dec 1992), *Have I Told You Lately* (No 5, Jun 1993) and *All for Love* (No 2, Jan 1994 - with Bryan Adams and Sting). Rod's hit albums include: 'Every Picture Tells A Story' (No 1, Jul 1971 and No 1 in USA), 'Never A Dull Moment' (No 1, Aug 1972), 'Sing it Again Rod' (No 1, Aug 1973), Smiler' (No 1, Oct 1974), 'Atlantic Crossing' (No 1, Aug 1975), 'A Night on the Town' (No 1, July 1976), 'Foot Loose and Fancy Free' (No 3, Nov 1977), 'Blondes Have More Fun' (No 3, Dec 1978 and No 1 in USA), 'Greatest Hits, Vol. 1' (No 1, Oct 1979), 'Foolish Behaviour' (No 4, Nov 1980), 'Body Wishes' (No 5, Jun 1983), 'Camouflage' (No 8, Jun 1984), 'Vagabond Heart' (No 2, Apr 1991), the live album 'Unplugged...and Seated' (No 2, Jun 1993), 'A Spanner in the Works' (No 4, Jun 1995), 'It Had to Be You: The Great American Songbook' (No 8, Nov 2002), 'As Time Goes By: The Great American Songbook 2' (No 4, Oct 2003), 'Stardust: The Great American Songbook 3' (No 3, Oct 2004 and No 1 in USA), 'Thanks for the Memory: The Great American Songbook, Volume IV' (No 3, Oct 2005 and No 2 in USA), 'Still the Same... Great Rock Classics of Our Time' (No 4, Oct 2006 and No 1 in USA) 'Soulbook' (No 9, Oct 2009 and No 4 in USA) and 'Fly Me to the Moon...The Great American Songbook Volume V' (No 5, Oct 2010 and No 4 in USA). Rod was awarded the CBE in 2007 but despite an international career which rivals most of Britain's musical knights has yet to be given the ultimate accolade. His girlfriends have included model Dee Harrington (1971-75), actress Britt Ekland (1975-77) and model Kelly Emberg (1983-90) with whom he had a daughter, Ruby Stewart (b. 17 June 1987). Rod has been married three times, to actress and model Alana Hamilton (1979-84) with whom he has a daughter, Kimberly Stewart (see entry in the miscellaneous section) and a son, Sean Stewart (b. 1 September 1980); model Rachel Hunter (1990-2006) with whom he has two children, Renée Stewart (b. 1 June 1992) and Liam McAlister Stewart (b. 5 September 1994); and since 2007 model Penny Lancaster, with whom he has two sons, Alastair Wallace Stewart (b. 27 November 2005) and Aiden Stewart (b. 16 February 2011). Rod also had a daughter, Sarah Streeter (b. 1963) in his teens, with his Art student girlfriend, Susannah Boffey.

Sting Born Gordon Matthew Thomas Sumner, 2 October 1951, Wallsend, Newcastle-upon-Tyne, Tyne & Wear. The singer, composer and actor studied at Warwick University and initially worked as a ditch digger and English teacher before playing in music groups of various genres including Dixieland Jazz. He got his nickname because of a yellow and black striped shirt he wore. Sting was a founding member of the group The Police in 1977 and together they scored five No 1 UK hit singles and six chart-topping albums (four studio plus two compilations). He has also had a very successful solo career, his first solo single, *Spread a Little Happiness*, from the 1982 film *Brimstone and Treacle*, peaking at No 16 in August 1982. Other memorable singles include: *Russians* (No 12, Dec 1985), the Quentin Crisp tribute *Englishman in New York* (No 15, Aug 1990), *It's Probably Me* (No 30, Aug 1992) a collaboration with Eric Clapton which featured in the film *Lethal Weapon 3* (1992), *If I Ever Lose My Faith In You* (No 14, Feb 1993) for which he won a Grammy for Best Male Pop Vocal Performance, *Fields of Gold* (No 16, Jun 1993), *Demolition Man* (No 21, Nov 1993) which featured in the film of the same name, *All For Love* (No 2, Jan 1994 but No 1 in Ireland) a collaboration with Bryan Adams and Rod Stewart which featured in the film *The Three Musketeers* (1993), *When We Dance* (No 9, Oct 1994), *This Cowboy Song* (No 15, Feb 1995) a collaboration with Pato Banton which featured in the film *Terminal Velocity* (1995), *Desert Song* (No 15, Jan 2000) featuring Cheb Mami, and *Rise and Fall* (No 2, May 2003) a collaboration with Craig David. In addition his first solo UK album 'The Dream of the Blue Turtles' reached No 3 in June 1985 and he has had a steady stream of subsequent hit albums including: 'Nothing Like The Sun' (No 1, Oct 1987), 'The Soul Cages' (No 1, Feb 1991), 'The Summoner's Tales' (No 2, Mar 1993), 'Mercury Falling' (No 4, Mar 1996), 'Brand New Day' (No 5, Oct 1999), 'All This Time' (No 3, Nov 2001) and 'Sacred Love' (No 3, Oct 2003). Sting has also guested on records by Tina Turner (*On Silent Wings* in 1996), Dire Straits (*Money For Nothing* in 1985) and of course Band Aid (*Do They Know It's Christmas* in 1984) to name but three of many. He made his screen debut as Ace in *Quadrophenia* (1979). Other films include *Radio On* (1980), *Brimstone & Treacle* (1982), *Dune* (1984), *Plenty* (1985), *The Bride* (1985 – as Baron Frankenstein), *Giulia e Giulia* (1987), *The Adventures of Baron Munchausen* (1988), *Stormy Monday* (1988), *The Grotesque* (1995), notable for featuring Sting in nude scenes, *Lock Stock and Two Smoking Barrels* (1998), *Bee Movie* (2007 – as himself) and *Brüno* (2009 – as himself). He has gained Academy Award nominations for Best Original Song for *The Emperor's New Groove* (2000), *Until... in Kate & Leopold* (2001) and *You Will Be My Ain True Love* in *Cold Mountain* (2003). Sting's first marriage was to actress Francis Tomelty (1976-84). The couple had two children: Joseph (b. 23 November 1976), a member of the band Fiction Plane, and Fuchsia Catherine (b. 17 April 1982). His second marriage is to film producer Trudie Styler (1992-present) with whom he has four children: Bridget Michael (b. 19 January 1984), Jake (b. 24 May 1985), Eliot Pauline (b. 30 July 1990), and Giacomo Luke (b. 17 December 1995). Sting and Trudie started the Rainforest Foundation in 1989 and their names are synonymous with worthy charitable projects. He was appointed CBE in 2004. See also entry for The Police.

The Strawbs Folk rock/ prog rock band formed in 1967 by guitarist and vocalist Dave Cousins (born David Joseph Cousins, Hounslow, Middlesex, 7 January 1945) and guitarist Tony Hooper (born Eastry, Kent, 14 September 1943) as the Strawberry Hill Boys. In the late 1960s they became the first UK act to be signed to A&M Records (formed in 1962 by Herb Alpert and Jerry Moss). The early ever-changing line-up included Sandy Denny (see Fairport Convention) who was replaced by Sonja Kristina (See Curved Air). Rick Wakeman was also a member from March 1970 until joining Yes in July 1971 (see separate entries). The other early members included drummer Richard Hudson (born Tottenham, London, 9 May 1948) and his Elmer Gantry's Velvet Opera band-mate and fellow drummer John Ford (born Fulham,

London, 1 July 1948). After the 'From the Witchwood' album (No 39, July 1971), Wakeman departed to join Yes, being replaced by Blue Weaver who had previously been with Amen Corner and Fairweather. This lineup produced what many feel to be the archetypal Strawbs album 'Grave New World' (No 11, Feb 1972) before yet another change saw the departure of Hooper, who was replaced by Dave Lambert, formerly of rock group Fire and the King Earl Boogie Band. The next album 'Bursting at the Seams' (No 2, Feb 1973) included the band's two most successful singles *Lay Down* (No 12, Oct 1972) and the iconic *Part of the Union* (No 2, Jan 1973) written by Hudson and Ford, themed on the Woody Guthrie/Almanac Singers' song *Union Maid* albeit with different music. Musical differences cut swathes through the band and Hudson and Ford now left to form the unimaginatively named band Hudson-Ford, complete with backing group Micky Keene (guitar), Chris Parren (keyboards) and Gerry Conway (later replaced by Ken Law) on drums. In August 1973 Hudson-Ford had a UK No 8 single with the ever-popular *Pick Up the Pieces*. After *Burn Baby Burn* (No 15, Feb 1974) their popularity waned and after splitting up in 1977 the two lads reformed again two years later as The Monks and had a one-hit-wonder with *Nice Legs Shame About Her Face* (No 19, Apr 1979). The Strawbs themselves are still going strong in both acoustic and electronic versions. A recent addition to the band has been Rick Wakeman's son Oliver, a keyboardist like his father.

Sugababes Girlband formed in 1998 by All Saints manager Ron Tom as The Sugababies. The three London-born girls Siobhán Donaghy (born Siobhán Emma Donaghy, 14 June 1984), Mutya Buena (Born Rosa Isabel Mutya Buena, 21 May 1985) and Keisha Buchanan (born Keisha Kerreece Fayeanne Buchanan, 30 September 1984) were signed as individual performers but Tom decided to place them in a group that, by the time they signed to London Records, became Sugababes. The band's debut single, *Overload*, peaked at number 6 on the UK Singles Chart in September 2000. Their debut album 'One Touch' (No 26, Dec 2000) spawned three further singles, *New Year* (No 12, Dec 2000), *Run for Cover* (No 13, Apr 2001) and *Soul Sound* (No 30, Jul 2001). Despite this respectable performance their label dropped them and they eventually signed to Island Records. During a Japanese promotional tour in August 2001, Siobhán left the group and was replaced by Heidi Range (see Atomic Kitten entry). Their first post-Donaghy single, *Freak Like Me* (No 1, May 2002), containing a sample from Gary Numan's *Are Friends Electric*, topped the UK chart and placed second on the Irish chart. The follow-up single, *Round Round* (No 1, Aug 2002) also debuted on top of the UK Singles Chart and peaked at number 2 in Ireland. The following month their second album 'Angels With Dirty Faces' (No 2, Sep 2002) was released and to-date has become their highest-selling album, selling in excess of a million copies. The third single from the album, the double-A side *Angels with Dirty Faces /Stronger* (No 7, Nov 2002 - No 13 in Ireland) gained the girls their third consecutive UK Top 10 hit. The track *Angels with Dirty Faces* was chosen as the theme tune to *The Powerpuff Girls Movie*, the 2002 American animated film based on the Cartoon Network animated television series of the same name. A fourth single from the album, *Shape* (No 11, Mar 2003 - No 9 in Ireland) contained a sample of Sting's *Shape of my Heart*. The group's third album 'Three' (No 3, Nov 2003) was preceded by lead single *Hole in the Head* (No 1, Oct 2003 – No 2 in Ireland), which became the group's third UK number 1 single and only single to-date to chart in the United States, reaching number 96 on the Billboard Hot 100. The follow-up single *Too Lost in You* (No 10, Dec 2003 – No 13 in Ireland) appeared on the soundtrack to the film *Love Actually*. Two other tracks from the album made the UK Top 10, *In the Middle* (No 8, Mar 2004 – No 13 in Ireland) and *Caught in a Moment* (No 8, Aug 2004 – No 28 in Ireland). The group's fourth album 'Taller in More Ways' (No 1, Oct 2005 – No 7 in Ireland) was preceded by the lead single *Push the Button* (No 1, Sep 2005 – No 1 in Ireland). In October 2005 the group was number 1 on the singles, album, airplay and download charts simultaneously, making them the first girl group to achieve such a feat. Their next single, *Ugly* (No 3, Dec 2005 – No 7 in Ireland) became their last before the announcement just before Christmas that Mutya had left the group due to personal reasons and was replaced by Amelle Berrabah (born Aldershot, Hampshire, 22 April, 1984). In March 2006 the next track from the album, *Red Dress* (No 4, Mar 2006 – No 12 in Ireland) was released after Amelle re-recorded Mutya's vocals heard on 'Taller in More Ways'. After a brief hiatus the group's first original post-Buena single, *Easy* (No 8, Nov 2006 – No 18 in Ireland) was followed by *Walk this Way* (No 1, Mar 2007 – No 14 in Ireland) the official Comic Relief charity single recorded with Girls Aloud. The Sugababes fifth studio album 'Change' (No 1, Oct 2007), was preceded by lead single, *About You Now* (No 1, Sep 2007), written by Cathy Dennis (see separate entry) and American producer Dr. Luke, signalling the second occasion in which the band were simultaneously number one on the UK album, single, download and airplay charts. In the 2009 edition of *Guinness Book of World Records*, *About You Now* was listed as the "first track by a British pop act to top the singles chart solely on downloads". The groups' sixth studio album, 'Catfights and Spotlights' (No 8, Oct 2008 – No 32 in Ireland) produced the single, *Girls* (No 3, Sep 2008). In August 2009 Amelle featured on Tinchy Stryder's number one hit *Never Leave You*, co-written with Taio Cruz. This gave her the distinction of being the only member of the Sugababes, past and present, to achieve a number one single outside the group. In September 2009 Keisha Buchanan, the sole original member of the group, left the Sugababes and was replaced by Jade Ewen (born Jade Almarie Louise Ewen, Plaistow, London, 24 January 1988), the UK's 2009 Eurovision Song Contest entrant. The band's seventh studio album 'Sweet 7' (No 14, Mar 2010 – No 35 in Ireland) was preceded by the lead single *Get Sexy* (No 2, Sep 2009), it was the last single to feature Keisha. The second single from the album, *About a Girl* (No 8, Nov 2009 – no 14 in Ireland) was followed by *Wear My Kiss* (No 7, Feb 2010 – No 9 in Ireland). In January 2012 it was announced that the group were taking a break to work on solo projects although singer-songwriter Emeli Sande confirmed to MTV News that she was writing songs for the original line-up consisting of Keisha, Mutya and Siobhan. Heidi has recently appeared in the seventh series of ITV entertainment show, *Dancing on Ice*. See also line-up of Band Aid 20 at the end of the UK chart section.

Super Furry Animals Welsh rock band formed in Cardiff in 1993, and fairly unusual inasmuch as they have had the same line-up throughout their history: Gruff Rhys (born Gruffydd Maredudd Bowen Rhys, Haverfordwest, Pembrokeshire, 18 July 1970; lead vocals, guitar), Huw Bunford (born Huw Cennydd Bunford, Cardiff, 15 September 1967; lead guitar, vocals), Guto Pryce (born Guto Dafydd Pryce, Cardiff, 4 September 1972; bass guitar) and brothers Cian Ciaran (born Bangor, Gwynedd, 16 June 1976; keyboards, synthesisers, guitar, vocals) and Dafydd Ieuan (born Bangor, Gwynedd, 1 March 1969; drums, vocals). The name of the band came from T-shirts being printed by Rhys' sister for the fashion and music collective Acid Casuals. After gigging at the Camden Monarch club in London in late 1995, they were noticed by Creation Records boss Alan McGee and signed to his label. Having their roots in techno rock, the band has never had a Top 10 UK single, although faring better in the UK Albums Chart with four Top 10 LPs, 'Radiator' (No 8, Aug 1997), 'Guerrilla' (No 10, Jun 1999), 'Rings Around the World' (No 3, Jul 2001) and 'Phantom Power' (No 4, Jul 2003). There most notorious single is *The Man Don't Give a Fuck* (No 22, Dec 1996) which contains samples from Steely Dan's *Showbiz Kids*, and is a tribute to ex-Reading and Cardiff footballer Robin Friday. The single's packaging features a photograph of the footballer Robin Friday showing a V sign to Luton Town goalkeeper Milija Aleksic whilst playing for Cardiff City. The artwork also features a dedication to the memory of Friday "and his stand against the 'Man'" alongside the Welsh proverb "Stwffiwch y dolig ddim y twrci" which roughly translates into English as "Stuff Christmas not a turkey". This track cemented the band as cool cult heroes, as the song contained the word "fuck" over 50 times and therefore received practically no airplay whatsoever. Another seminal single release was the EP *Ice Hockey Hair* (No 12, Jun 1998). The four-track EP's power-ballad title song refers to an alternative name for the

mullet haircut. Another track, *Smokin*, was commissioned by Channel 4 for a programme about sloth presented by Howard Marks as part of a series on the Seven Deadly Sins. SFA's highest-charting single to-date is *Northern Lites* (No 11, May 1999). After the demise of Creation in 1999, SFA signed with one of Sony's subsidiaries, Epic. Their first single release for the label, *Juxtaposed With U* (No 14, Jul 2001) has echoes of the so-called plastic soul of David Bowie's album 'Young Americans' and was inspired by the Paul McCartney and Stevie Wonder track *Ebony and Ivory*. The track was from the album 'Rings Around the World' which was the first album by any artist to be simultaneously released on both audio CD and DVD. The album also contained the track, *Receptacle For the Respectable*, featuring Paul McCartney on "carrot and celery rhythm track". The album was nominated for the Mercury Music Prize in 2001. The ceremony took place on the day after the terror attacks on the World Trade Center and the Pentagon, and SFA's performance of the album track *It's Not the End of the World?* had a macabre irony to it. See also entries for Catatonia, and Rhys Ifans in the cinema section.

Take That Vocal quintet put together in 1990 by Manchester-based pop impresario Nigel Martin-Smith who had chart success the previous year with the artist Damian (born Damian Davey, in Manchester, 30 September 1964) who had a UK top 10 hit with a cover of *The Time Warp* (No 7, Aug 1989). Take That comprises Gary Barlow (born Frodsham, Cheshire, 20 January 1971), Howard Paul Donald (born Droysden, Manchester, 28 April 1968), Jason Thomas Orange (born Crumpsall, Manchester, 10 July 1970), Mark Anthony Patrick Owen (born Oldham, Lancashire, 27 January 1972) and Robbie Williams (born Robert Peter Williams, Stoke-on-Trent, Staffordshire, 13 February 1974). Their first television performance was on *The Hitman & Her* (1990), the exposure leading to bookings up and down the country in clubs, schools and corporate events. After signing to RCA Records, the band's breakthrough single was *It Only Takes a Minute* (No 7, Jun 1992), which was quickly followed by *I Found Heaven* (No 15, Aug 1992 - featuring lead vocals by Robbie), *A Million Love Songs* (No 7, Oct 1992) and *Could It Be Magic* (No 3, Dec 1992 – featuring lead vocals by Robbie) - all four of which were tracks on their debut album 'Take That and Party' No 2, Sep 1992). Their second album 'Everything Changes' (No 1, Oct 1993) not only topped the UK Albums Chart but also spawned six Top 10 singles, including four No 1s, i.e. *Why Can't I Wake Up with You* (No 2, Feb 1993), *Pray* (No 1, Jul 1993), *Relight My Fire* (No 1, Oct 1993 – with Lulu), *Babe* (No 1, Dec 1993 and No 1 in Ireland – featuring lead vocals by Mark), *Everything Changes* (No 1, Apr 1994 -featuring lead vocals by Robbie) and *Love Ain't Here Anymore* (No 3, Jul 1994). Take That's third studio album 'Nobody Else' (No 1, May 1995) spawned three chart-topping singles, *Sure* (No 1, Oct 1994 and No 3 in Ireland), *Back For Good* (No 1, Apr 1995 and No 7 in USA) and *Never Forget* (No 1, Aug 1995 – featuring lead vocals by Howard), the last two also topping the Irish Singles Chart. Whilst undertaking their first World Tour in 1995 cracks began to appear in the band's close-knit unity and the other four members became concerned about Robbie's burgeoning drug problem and erratic behaviour. On 13 February 1996 (Robbie's 22nd birthday) Take That formally announced that they were disbanding. No reasons were given although they had made it clear to Robbie they did not want him to complete the 'Nobody Else' tour with them. In April, a 'Greatest Hits' compilation topped the charts and spawned a cover of The Bee Gees' *How Deep Is Your Love* (No 1, Mar 1996), the first single released by Take That without Robbie, and their last single until they reformed in 2005. As solo performers the lads had varying fortunes. Gary had initial success, both his first two singles *Forever Love* (No 1, Jul 1996 - used as the soundtrack to the film The Leading Man) and *Love Won't Wait* (No 1, May 1997 – co-written by Madonna and Shep Pettibone) topping the UK Singles Chart as did his debut solo album 'Open Road' (No 1, May 1997). However, the title track from this album was destined to be his last UK Top 10 solo single when it peaked at No 7 in November 1997. Gary was of course the leading songwriter of the band and the main vocalist but he was not the most popular member of the group with the fans and he suffered a backlash from them once Robbie was established as a superstar. Howard became almost suicidal when the band split and things didn't improve for him when his solo career failed to take off, his one recording, *Speak without Words*, remaining unreleased. He eventually returned to DJing and became popular throughout the European circuit. Howard was one of the founders of the DJ band Sonic Fly along with King Brain and Bart Van Der Zwaan. Jason was the only group member who did not consider a solo career in music, instead he travelled through Europe for a year before trying his hand at an acting career, which eventually led to him playing DJ Brent Moyer in the Lynda La Plante thriller *Killer Net*, shown on Channel 4 in 1998. When the harsh reality of constant auditions and long-term breaks ensued Jason decided to attend South Trafford College in Greater Manchester in 2001, studying A-level English, and an access course including psychology, biology, and history. Mark had two Top 10 singles, *Child* (No 3, Nov 1996) and *Clementine* (No 3, Feb 1997) under the Bertelsmann Music Group, (BMG) label before being dropped after another single, *I Am What I Am*, stalled at number 29 in August 1997. After five barren years Mark won the second series of *Celebrity Big Brother* in November 2002 and subsequently signed a deal with Universal Records and having a further Top 10 single with *Four Minute Warning* (No 4, Aug 2003) before once again being dropped. Robbie, ironically perhaps in light of all that had gone before, not only had the most successful solo career of the quintet but went on to become one of the most successful British acts in pop history. Robbie's solo career was initially delayed by legal wrangles but he was eventually allowed to sign to Chrysalis in June 1996 and his first single release was a cover of George Michael's *Freedom* (No 2, Aug 1996). His subsequent chart success was relentless and includes seven consecutive chart-topping studio LPs, his full album listing being as follows: 'Life Thru a Lens' (No 1, Oct 1997) which spawned the singles *Old Before I Die* (No 2, Apr 1997), *Lazy Days* (No 8, Jul 1997), *Angels* (No 4, Dec 1997) and *Let Me Entertain You* (No 3, Sep 1998); 'I've Been Expecting You' (No 1, Nov 1998) which spawned the singles *Millennium* (No 1, Sep 1998), *No Regrets* (No 4, Dec 1998), *Strong* (No 4, Mar 1999) and *She's the One / It's Only Us* (No 1, Nov 1999); 'Sing When You're Winning (No 1, Dec 2001) which spawned the singles *Rock DJ* (No 1, Aug 2000), *Kids* (No 2, Oct 2000 – featuring Kylie Minogue), *Supreme* (No 4, Dec 2000), *Let Love Be Your Energy* (No 10, Apr 2001) and *Eternity / The Road to Mandalay* (No 1, Jul 2001); 'Swing When You're Winning' (No 1, Dec 2001) which spawned the single *Somethin' Stupid* (No 1, Dec 2001 – with Nicole Kidman); 'Escapology' (No 1, Nov 2002) which spawned the singles *Feel* (No 4, Dec 2002), *Come Undone* (No 4, Apr 2003), *Something Beautiful* (No 3, Aug 2003) and *Sexed Up* (No 10, Nov 2003); 'Greatest Hits' (No 1, Oct 2004) which spawned the singles *Radio* (No 1, Oct 2004) and *Misunderstood* (No 8, Dec 2004); 'Intensive Care' (No 1, Oct 2005) which spawned the singles *Tripping* (No 2, Oct 2005) and *Advertising Space* (No 8, Dec 2005); 'Rudebox' (No 1, Oct 2006) which spawned the singles *Rudebox* (No 4, Sep 2006), *Lovelight* (No 8, Nov 2006) and *She's Madonna* (No 16, Mar 2007 – with Pet Shop Boys); 'Reality Killed the Video Star' (No 2, Nov 2009) which spawned the singles *Bodies* (No 2, Oct 2009) and *You Know Me* (No 6, Dec 2009) and 'In and Out of Consciousness: Greatest Hits 1990–2010' (No 1, Oct 2010) which spawned the single *Shame* (No 2, Oct 2010), a duet with Gary Barlow, the first time that both Gary and Robbie had performed together on a song since the latter left Take That in 1995. Robbie also recorded the album 'Live at Knebworth' (aka Live Summer 2003) (No 2, Sep 2003) and had a Top 10 single, *My Culture* (No 9, Apr 2002) collaborating with British trip-hop duo 1 Giant Leap and Maxi Jazz, as well as supplying vocals for the Helping Haiti UK and Irish chart-topper, *Everybody Hurts* (No 1, Apr 1993). He has accrued seventeen BRIT Awards—more than any other artist. Robbie also provided songs for soundtracks of several films, notably *Have You Met Miss Jones?* for the film *Bridget Jones' Diary* (2001) and *Beyond the Sea*, which was featured over the credits of the film *Finding Nemo* (2003) – both tracks from the 'Swing When You're

Winning' album. Meanwhile, after filming a 2005 documentary about the group and officially re-uniting, a four-piece Take That, without Robbie, announced their 2006 "Ultimate Tour". Since their reunion Take That have had UK chart-topping albums with 'Beautiful World' (No 1, Nov 2006) which spawned the singles *Patience* (No 1, Nov 2006), *Shine* (No 1, Feb 2007) and *Rule the World* (No 2, Oct 2007 – written for the film *Stardust*) and 'The Circus' (No 1, Dec 2008) which spawned the singles *Greatest Day* (No 1, Nov 2008) and *Said It All* (No 9, Jun 2009). Robbie, a lifelong supporter of Port Vale, based in his home town of Stoke-on-Trent, had been battling a lethargy caused by a type of hormone imbalance for some years and although he was at this time at the very top of his profession the Take That reunion coincided with a grave sense of dissatisfaction within him. In 2008 he stopped gigging, almost as if he was content to see the success of the second-coming of Take That but did not want to rain on their parade. On 11 October 2009 Robbie published a 12-track compilation album, titled Songbook, as a free CD for the newspaper *The Mail on Sunday*. That same evening he returned from his brief hiatus by performing on *The X Factor* results show, singing his new single *Bodies* for the first time live. On 15 July 2010, Robbie announced he was returning to Take That. He subsequently departed from EMI (although signing with Universal in October 2011 for his parallel solo career). On 7 August 2010, Robbie married the Turkish American actress Ayda Field at his home in Los Angeles. Now, as a quintet again, Take That released the album 'Progress' (No 1, Nov 2010), which became the fastest selling album since 2000 and the second fastest selling album in UK history. The album spawned the chart-topping single *The Flood* (No 1, Oct 2010), the first single to feature Robbie since his return to the band. On 19 May 2011, Take That announced a new EP entitled *Progressed*, which contained eight tracks written by the band since they had reunited as a five piece. It was packaged alongside the record breaking album 'Progress' and returned the band to No 1 in the UK Albums Chart the week after it was released on 13 June 2011. On 4 October 2011, it was announced that the five piece Take That were currently on a break after the completion of their European leg of the Progress tour, with Gary judging on *The X Factor*, whilst Robbie is recording new solo material. On 30 March 2012 Robbie announced that he and his wife would become parents for the first time.

Tinie Tempah British rapper (born Patrick Chukwuemeka Okogwu, Plumstead, London, 7 November 1988) of Nigerian descent, who first came to the fore in 2006 when he was featured heavily on the British digital music television station Channel AKA (formerly Channel U). Tinie gained experience gigging and collaborating with numerous artists and his manager, Dumi, had bold plans for him when scout and music consultant Jade Richardson saw him performing at the 2009 Wireless Festival and called Parlophone Records who signed him up immediately. Tinie released his debut single, *Pass Out*, on 28 February 2010, and it entered the UK Singles Chart at No 1. Producer and writer Labrinth (born Timothy McKenzie, Hackney, London, 4 March 1989) provides uncredited vocals on the song. After performing *Pass Out* with American rapper Snoop Dogg on 25 June 2010 at Glastonbury (on the Pyramid stage) it was remixed and released in the States in November 2010. The song won Best British Single at the 2011 BRIT Awards and Best Contemporary Song at the 2011 Ivor Novello Awards. Tinie's second single, *Frisky* (No 2, Jun 2010) also featured Labrinth and although stalling at No 2 in the UK improved on his debut No 6 in Ireland by placing No 3 in the Irish Singles Chart. Tinie's third single, *Written in the Stars* (No 1, Sep 2010) featuring the vocals of US singer Eric Turner, became a global hit and not only topped the UK and Irish charts but made No 12 on the Billboard Hot 100. All three singles were on Tinie's debut album 'Disc-Overy' (No 1, Oct 2010) which topped the UK Albums Chart, placed No 2 in Ireland and a creditable No 21 in USA. The next track from the album which was released as a single was *Miami 2 Ibiza* (No 4, Oct 2010 - No 5 in Ireland) a collaboration with the Swedish House Mafia which also features on their album 'Until One'. Other successful tracks include: *Invincible* (No 11, Dec 2010 – No 13 in Ireland) featuring guest vocals from American recording artist, Kelly Rowland, and *Wonderman* (No 12, Mar 2011 – No 16 in Ireland) featuring guest vocals by Ellie Goulding. Tinie has had two further Top 10 UK hits as a featured artist, with JLS, *Eyes Wide Shut* (No 8, Feb 2011 – No 14 in Ireland) and Labrinth, *Earthquake* (No 2, Oct 2011 – No 12 in Ireland). At the Brit Awards in 2012, Tinie announced the name of his second album is to be called 'Demonstration'.

The Tornados Instrumental group formed by Joe Meek (born Robert George Meek, Newent, Gloucestershire, 5 April 1929) with members including lead guitarist Alan Caddy (born in Chelsea, 2 February 1940; d. 16 August 2000), rhythm guitarist George Bellamy (born in Sunderland, 8 October 1941 – he is the father of Matthew Bellamy, frontman of British rock band, Muse), keyboard player Roger LaVern (born Roger Jackson, Kidderminster, Worcestershire, 11 November 1938), bassist Heinz Burt (born Heinz Henry Georg Schwartze, Detmold, Germany, 24 July 1942; d. 7 April 2000, Weston, Hampshire) and drummer Clem Cattini (born in Stoke Newington, 28 August 1938). Their debut hit single, *Telstar* (No 1, Aug 1962 and No 1 in Ireland) is famous for being the first single by a British band to reach number one on the US Billboard Hot 100, and also the only instrumental single to top the charts on both sides of the Atlantic. The record was named after the AT&T communications satellite Telstar, which was the first such satellite to relay television signals. Telstar 1 went into orbit in July 1962 and Joe Meek wrote, produced and released the single just five weeks later. The record is also famous for its distinct electronic sound, produced on a keyboard instrument called a clavioline, and its space age effects which were largely produced in Joe's recording studio – a small flat above a shop at 304 Holloway Road, Islington. Unfortunately the record which is estimated to have sold over five million copies worldwide was the subject of a plagiarism suit and Joe received no royalties during his lifetime. Joe, a closet homosexual, was convicted of "importuning for immoral purposes" in 1963 and fined £15. He later suffered from depression and had an unhealthy obsession with the late Buddy Holly. On 3 February 1967, the eighth anniversary of Holly's death, Meek killed his landlady Violet Shenton with a single barrelled shotgun at his home/studio and then he turned the gun (belonging to Heinz) on himself. Ironically, the plagiarism lawsuit against Meek was ruled in his favour three weeks after his death. The Tornados never scaled the same heights after *Telstar* although having hits with *Globetrotter* (No 5, Jan 1963), *Robot* (No 17, Mar 1963) and *The Ice Cream Man* (No 18, Oct 1963). They also played the theme music for *The Scales of Justice* (see television section). Of the band members, Heinz went solo (literally by also dropping his surname) in 1963 under Joe's guidance and had a hit with *Just Like Eddie* (No 5, Aug 1963) a tribute to Eddie Cochran. He died from motor neurone disease in 2004. Both Alan Caddy and Clem Cattini had previously played with Johnny Kidd and the Pirates from 1959-61 and featured on their chart-topping single *Shakin' All Over* (No 1, Jun 1960) but had left the Pirates by the time of their other Top 10 single, *I'll Never Get Over You* (No 4, Jul 1963). Johnny Kidd (born Frederick Heath, Willesden, North London, 23 December 1935) formed the band as Freddie Heath and The Nutters and after the name change would invariably wear a black eye patch over his right eye. He died, tragically, aged 30, on 7 October 1966, when the car in which he was travelling as a passenger had a head-on collision with another car on the A58, Bury New Road, Breightmet, near Radcliffe, Lancashire. Pirates' bassist Nick Simper, who later became an original member of Deep Purple, was also in the car with Kidd but suffered only cuts and a broken arm. Johnny was cremated at Golders Green Crematorium, London. After Clem left the Tornados in 1965 he became a successful session musician, featuring on 44 different UK number one singles. The Tornados eventually disbanded in 1968. The B-side of their final single, in 1966, *Do You Come Here Often?*, was the first openly "gay" pop record release by a UK major label. It started off as a standard organ-inspired instrumental, but Joe interjected a casual conversation between what sounds like two stereotypical camp men (Dave Watts playing keyboards and Rob Gale playing guitar). The song was featured, along with other gay-flavoured releases, on a 2006 compilation CD, Queer Noises. See also entry for Billy Fury and for *Telstar* in the film section.

UB40 The reggae band named after the card issued to the jobless (Unemployment Benefit Form 40) was formed in 1978 by brothers Ali Campbell (born Alistair Ian Campbell, 15 February 1959; vocalist) and Robin Campbell (born 25 December 1954; lead guitarist) along with a mix of school friends. The band numbered Earl Falconer (born 23 January 1957; bassist), Mickey Virtue (born 19 January 1957; keyboards player), Brian Travers (born 7 February 1959; saxophonist), Jimmy Brown (born 20 November 1957; drummer) and Norman Hassan (born 26 January 1958; percussionist). They were all born in Birmingham. UB40 played their first gig at The Hare & Hounds Pub in Kings Heath, Birmingham for a friend's birthday party on 9 February 1979. They were soon joined by toaster (a sort of chanting rapper) Astro (born Terence Wilson, Birmingham, 24 June 1957). Their first single, *King/Food for Thought* was released on a local independent label and reached number four. *King* was about the Reverend Dr Martin Luther King and *Food For Thought* about African famine. A follow-up, *My Way of Thinking/I Think It's Gonna Rain* entered the charts in June 1980 and made it to number six. Their debut album, 'Signing Off' (so-called because that's what they were doing), was released on 29 August 1980 entering the charts the following week, hitting second place and spending 71 weeks on the chart. It caused controversy when it was released with cover artwork featuring an actual UB40. The album gave the band a fan base among disaffected youth and admirers of Two-Tone and ska music. In November 1980, *The Earth Dies Screaming/Dream A Lie* reached number 10. In early 1981, they formed their own label, DEP International, and their first release was the album 'Present Arms' (No 2, Jun 1981). In August of that year, released their anthem *One In Ten* (No 7, Aug 1981). The song is not about the number of people then officially without a job and claiming state benefits as generally supposed but about government statistics and how they are used to manipulate people. Their LP 'Labour Of Love' (No 1, Sep 1983 – No 8 in USA) returned them to their reggae roots and topped the charts in Britain and went top 20 in America. It also spawned UB40's first Number 1 single – a reggae version of Neil Diamond's *Red Red Wine* (released 20 August 1983), which topped the charts in America, New Zealand, Holland and Ireland. *Please Don't Make me Cry* made it to number 10 in October of that year. Their only top 10 single in 1984 was *If It Happens Again* (No 9, Sep 1984). In August 1985 they topped the charts with *I Got You Babe*, the group duetting with Chrissie Hynde. Eight years later, in May 1993, they completed their hat-trick of Number 1s with *(I Can't Help) Falling in Love With You*, which topped the charts on both sides of the Atlantic. The song was used as the main theme to the flop film *Sliver* (1993), which starred Sharon Stone. Other Top 10 singles included: *Don't Break My Heart* (No 3, Oct 1985), *Sing Our Own Song* (No 5, Jul 1986), *Breakfast in Bed* (No 6, Jun 1988 – featuring Chrissie Hynde), *Homely Girl* (No 6, Nov 1989), *Kingston Town* (No 4, Mar 1990), *I'll Be Your Baby Tonight* (No 6, Nov 1990 – featuring Robert Palmer), *Higher Ground* (No 8, Aug 1993) and *Come Back Darling* (No 10, Oct 1998). Top 10 albums include: 'UB44' (No 4, Sep 1982), 'Geffery Morgan' (No 3, Oct 1984), 'Rat in the Kitchen' (No 8, Jul 1986), 'Promises and Lies' (No 1, Jul 1993) and 'Guns in the Ghetto' (No 7, Jul 1997). In February 2008, Ali left the band acrimoniously but was later replaced by another Campbell brother, Duncan, the twin of Robin. Their last album, 'TwentyFourSeven', with the original line-up was released on 4 May 2008 by way of a giveaway in *The Mail On Sunday*. On 21 June 2008, a full 17-track version of the album was released and became their first to fail to reach the Top 50. Mickey Virtue also departed that year. In February of the following year, UB40, with new lead singer Duncan Campbell released 'Labour Of Love 4'. It peaked at number 24.

Ultravox New Wave rock band founded as Tiger Lily in 1973 by vocalist John Foxx (born Dennis Leigh, Chorley, Lancashire, 26 September 1948). He was aided by Bass player Chris St John (born Christopher Thomas Allen, Tottenham, London, 14 July 1952), guitarist Stevie Shears (born in Dagenham, Essex, *ca* 1954) and in early 1974 by drummer Warren Cann (born in Victoria,

British Columbia, Canada, 20 May 1950). They played their first official gig at the Marquee club in August 1974 after which violinist Billy Currie (born William Lee Currie, Huddersfield, West Yorkshire, 1 April 1950), then known as Billy Curry, joined. A single, a cover of Fats Waller's *Ain't Misbehavin'* was released on 14 March 1975. The band's name was changed several times from The Zips, Fire of London, London Soundtrack, and The Damned before settling on Ultravox! (Latin for Beyond the Voice) by 1976; the name change coinciding with Chris St John deciding to start calling himself Chris Cross. They signed to Island Records in August 1976 and in early 1977 their first single *Dangerous Rhythm* and eponymous debut album co-produced by Steve Lillywhite and Brian Eno was released. Ultravox! was heavily influenced by Roxy Music, The New York Dolls, David Bowie and Kraftwerk. In early March 1978, Stevie Shears was sacked and replaced by Robin Simon (born Robert Simon, Halifax, West Yorkshire, 12 July 1956). During that year, the exclamation mark was dropped. In January 1979, Island Records dropped the band after they failed to excite America and two months later Foxx left. Just as it seemed the band would disappear, James "Midge" Ure (born in Gambuslang, Lanarkshire, Scotland, 10 October 1953) joined as lead singer, guitarist and keyboardist in April 1979. Midge had been part of Slik (No 1 single with *Forever and Ever* in Jan 1976), The Rich Kids, Visage, and for a brief period, Thin Lizzy. With Ure revitalising the band they were signed to Chrysalis and their next album 'Vienna' (No 3, Jul 1980) was the first to chart and the single of that name was stopped from being No 1 only by the humorous *Shaddap You Face* by Joe Dolce in January 1981, although it did manage to top the chart in Ireland. The follow-up single, *All Stood Still* (No 8, Jun 1981) also made the Top 10. Other UK Top 10 albums included 'Rage in Eden' (No 4, Sep 1981), 'Quartet' (No 6, Oct 1982), 'Lament' (No 8, Apr 1984) and 'U-Vox' (No 9, Oct 1986). In June 1982, Midge reached No 7 with a cover of *No Regrets*. In May 1984, the band reached number three with *Dancing With Tears In My Eyes* and in November of that year a greatest hits album 'The Collection' was released and reached number two, going triple platinum. Midge was then asked by Bob Geldof to co-write and produce the Band Aid single, *Do They Know It's Christmas?*, with him. In September 1985, a solo hit reached Number 1 with *If I Was* and the following month an album 'The Gift' made it to number two. Cann left the band in 1986, going to America to try to become an actor. Mark Brzezicki (born Slough, Berkshire, 21 June 1957), previously with Big Country, took his place. Ultravox officially split up in 1988. Currie reformed the band in 1992 but with all new personnel. It was not successful and the band remained dormant until the spring of 2009 when Warren Cann, Chris Cross, Billy Currie and Midge Ure reformed for a UK tour. In 2011, the band announced that a new album 'Brilliant' will be released in May 2012.

U2 Irish band who have become the most successful band of the last 30 years putting more than 50 singles on the charts since their first, *Fire* (No 35) on 8 August 1981. Formed at Mount Temple Comprehensive School, Dublin, on 25 September 1976, by drummer Larry Mullen, Jr (born in Dublin, Ireland, 31 October 1961) - the other members of the band consisted of vocalist Bono (born Paul Hewson, Dublin, Ireland, 10 May 1960), guitarist The Edge (born David Evans, Barking, Essex, 8 August 1961 to Welsh parents), bassist Adam Clayton (born in Chinnor, Oxfordshire, 13 March 1960), The Edge's elder brother, guitarist Dik Evans, Ivan McCormick and Peter Martin. They called themselves Feedback. Martin did not stay after the first rehearsal and McCormick left a little while later. In March 1977, Feedback became The Hype. A year later, Dik Evans walked out mid-gig at the Presbyterian Church Hall in Howth as quintet The Hype metamorphosed into quartet U2. That month, U2 won £500 and studio time in a talent competition resulting in their first demo tape at Keystone Studios in Dublin in May 1978. Paul McGuinness became their manager at that time. U2's first release (in September 1979), an EP called *Three*, was only available in Ireland. In December 1979, they played their first gigs in England but were all but ignored. In February 1980, their second single *Another Day* was released but again was only available in Ireland. In March, 1980 U2 signed to Island Records and released their first single available outside Ireland, *11 O'Clock Tick Tock* two months later. Towards the end of the year, they released their debut album 'Boy'. It peaked at number 52 in August 1981. Their second album 'October' (No 11, Oct 1981) was released amid a religious crisis which threatened to split the band. On 12 March 1983 their third album 'War' entered the charts at Number 1. The lead single from the album, *New Year's Day* (No 10, Jan 1983) gave U2 their first UK Top 10 and peaked at No 2 in Ireland. The album also included the controversial *Sunday Bloody Sunday*, which reached seven on the Billboard Hot 100. During the 'War' tour, U2 recorded the 'Under A Blood Red Sky' (No 2, Nov 1983) live album. In October 1984, 'The Unforgettable Fire', produced by Brian Eno, went into the charts at Number 1. The lead single, *Pride (In The Name Of Love)* (No 3, Sep 1984), about the Reverend Dr Martin Luther King Jr, peaked at No 2 in Ireland and was their first US Top 40 hit (reaching No 33). The follow-up single, *The Unforgettable Fire* (No 6, May 1985) topped the Irish Singles Chart. In July 1985, U2 appeared at Wembley for Live Aid. Their fifth album, 'The Joshua Tree', entered the UK and Irish charts at No 1 in March 1987. It became the fastest-selling album in British chart history, and was No 1 for nine weeks in America. The first two singles, *With or without You* (No 4, Mar 1987) and *I Still Haven't Found What I'm Looking For* (No 6, Jun 1987) became U2's first No 1s Stateside as well as topping the Irish chart. 'The Joshua Tree' won U2 their first two Grammy Awards and also spawned a third UK Top 10 single, *Where the Streets Have No Name* (No 4, Sep 1987), which stalled at No 11 in America but topped the Irish chart. An album recorded during 'The Joshua Tree' Tour entitled *Rattle and Hum* (No 1, Oct 1988) topped the UK, Irish and US charts. The album spawned the singles, *Desire* (No 1, Oct 1988 and No 1 in Ireland), *Angel of Harlem* (No 9, Dec 1988 and No 3 in Ireland), *When Love Comes to Town* (No 6, Apr 1989 and No 1 in Ireland – featuring BB King) and *All I Want is You* (No 4, Jun 1989 and No 1 in Ireland). In October 1990, U2 began work on their seventh studio album, 'Achtung Baby', which was released in November 1991. It peaked at number two in Britain but topped both the US and Irish charts. Successful singles from the album included: *The Fly* (No 1, Nov 1991 and No 1 in Ireland), *Mysterious Ways* (No 13, Dec 1991 but No 1 in Ireland and No 9 in US), *One* (No 7, Mar 1992 but No 1 in Ireland) and *Even Better Than the Real Thing (Remix)* (No 8, Jul 1992). 'Zooropa', released in the summer of 1993, also reached the Number 1 slot in the UK, Ireland and USA. The only UK Top 10 single from the album was *Stay (Faraway, So Close)* (No 4, Dec 1993 but No 1 in Ireland). U2's next single was *Hold Me, Thrill Me, Kiss Me, Kill Me* (No 2, Jun 1995 but No 1 in Ireland) which featured in the film *Batman Forever*. In November 1995, they released the critically panned album 'Original Soundtracks 1' under the name Passengers. It reached number 12 but spawned the single, *Miss Sarajevo* (No 6, Dec 1995). Bono cites *Miss Sarajevo* as his favourite U2 song. In March 1997 their album 'Pop' topped the charts of 35 countries including the UK, Ireland and USA, and spawned the singles, *Discothèque* (No 1, Feb 1997 and No 1 in Ireland), *Staring at the Sun* (No 3, Apr 1997 and No 4 in Ireland), *Last Night on Earth* (No 10, Aug 1997 and No 11 in Ireland) and *Please* (No 7, Oct 1997 and No 6 in Ireland). The following year a greatest hits album reached No 1 in the UK and Ireland and No 2 in America and spawned the single, *Sweetest Thing* (No 3, Oct 1998 and No 1 in Ireland), originally released in 1987 as a B-side on the *Where the Streets Have No Name* single. Their next album 'All That You Can't Leave Behind' (No 1, Nov 2000 and No 1 in Ireland) spawned the singles *Beautiful Day* (No 1, Dec 2000 and No 1 in Ireland), *Stuck in a Moment You Can't Get Out Of* (No 2, Feb 2001 and No 1 in Ireland), *Elevation* (No 3, Jul 2001 and No 1 in Ireland) and *Walk On* (No 5, Dec 2001 and No 1 in Ireland). U2's compilation album 'The Best of 1990–2000' topped the charts in the UK, Ireland and USA and spawned the single *Electrical Storm* (No 5, Oct 2002 and No 2 in Ireland). In January 2004 U2 collaborated with English Dance Pop group LMC on the single *Take Me to the Clouds Above* which topped the UK chart and reached No 3 in Ireland. Their next album, 'How to Dismantle an Atomic Bomb' was released in November 2004 and topped the charts in the UK, Ireland and USA; spawning the singles *Vertigo* (No 1, Nov 2004 and No 1 in Ireland), *All Because of You* (No 4, Feb 2005 and No 4 in Ireland), *Sometimes You Can't Make It on Your Own* (No 1, Feb 2005 and No 3 in Ireland) and *City of Blinding Lights* (No 2, Jun 2005 and No 8 in Ireland). The album and its singles won Grammy Awards in all eight categories in which they were nominated and U2 were subsequently inducted into the Rock'n'Roll Hall Of Fame. The following year, the band was criticised in the Dail when it was revealed that they had moved their publishing business to Holland after the Irish government capped tax exemption for artists to €250,000. After the singles, *One* (No 2, Jun 2006 and No 2 in Ireland - with Mary J Blige), *The Saints Are Coming* (No 3, Oct 2006 and No 1 in Ireland - with Green Day) and *Windows in the Sky* (No 4 Jan 2007 and No 5 in Ireland) they collaborated with The Dubliners, Kíla, and "A Band of Bowsies" – which included artists such as Ronan Keating, Sinead O'Connor, Chris De Burgh, Bob Geldof, Shane McGowan and Andrea Corr – for the charity single *The Ballad of Ronnie Drew*, in aid of the Irish Cancer Society. The record topped the Irish Singles Chart. U2's 12th album, 'No Line on the Horizon', was released in February 2009 and went straight in at Number 1 in more than 30 countries including the UK, Ireland and USA, but produced no hit singles from it. In April 2011, U2's 360° Tour became the highest-grossing tour in music history, earning more than $558million and breaking the previous record, which was held by the Rolling Stones. U2 have been nominated for 34 Grammys and won 22, the most by any band. They are also the recipients of seven BRIT Awards. In Ireland, U2 have won 14 Meteor Awards since their inception in 2001. Bono's investment group Elevation put money into the social networking site Facebook in 2009, taking 2.3% of the company. After Facebook was floated on the stock exchange in May 2012 Bono and his team of directors shared in excess of £1 billion. Bono's post-flotation comment was "Contrary to reports, I'm not a billionaire or going to be richer than any Beatle - and not just in the sense of money, by the way, the Beatles are untouchable - those billionaire reports are a joke."

The Verve The Wigan-based rock group were formed in 1989 by vocalist Richard Ashcroft (born Richard Paul Steven Ashcroft, Wigan, 11 September 1971), guitarist Nick McCabe (born Nicholas John McCabe, St Helens, Lancashire14 July 1971), bassist Simon Jones (born Simon Robin David Jones, Liverpool, 29 May 1972) and drummer Peter Salisbury (born Peter Anthony Salisbury, Bath, 24 September 1971). From the outset Ashcroft and McCabe, who met at Winstanley Sixth Form College in Wigan, had a love-hate relationship and would often clash, Richard having the showmanship required of a good front-man whilst Nick was more introverted and detached from the group's machinations. The band's first gig was at a friend's birthday party at the Honeysuckle Pub, in Wigan, on 15 August 1990. After being signed to Hut Records in 1991 they began to release singles that hovered around the nether regions of the charts, their first real impact coming with the album 'A Storm in Heaven' (No 27, Jun 1993). On 12 July 1994 the band were due to play at the travelling North American alternative rock festival, Lollapalooza, but on the day before Richard was hospitalised for dehydration after a heavy drinking session and Peter was arrested for destroying a hotel room in Kansas in a drug-fuelled rage. In good old showbusiness tradition they both managed to play at Lollapalooza the very next day. Back in Britain the band gigged regularly with Oasis in their early days. The Verve's second charting album 'A Northern Soul' (No 13, July 1995), whose title was a reference to the popular soul movement in Britain during the 1960s and at its height in the 1970s, fared well but still did not spawn a Top 20 single. Richard dedicated track five of the album to Oasis guitarist Noel Gallagher after Noel had dedicated the song *Cast No Shadow* to him. By October 1995 tensions between Richard and Nick split the band up and when they decided to reunite a few weeks after the breakup, Nick did not rejoin them. The new band originally hired former Suede guitarist Bernard Butler, but he spent only a couple of days with the band. The group then chose guitarist and keyboardist Simon Tong (born in Wigan, 9 July 1972) an old school friend credited with originally teaching Richard and Simon to play guitar. Apart from a solo performance by Richard supporting Oasis in New York the band made no live appearances in 1996. In early 1997, Richard asked Nick to return to the band and after he accepted they remained a quintet thereafter. Their next album 'Urban Hymns' (No 1, Oct 1997) not only topped the UK Albums Chart, but ironically deposed their great friends and rivals Oasis ('Be Here Now') in the process. The album spawned three Top 10 singles, the first of which, *Bitter Sweet Symphony* (No 2, Jun 1997) peaked at No 3 in Ireland and No 12 in USA. The record is based on music from an Andrew Loog Oldham adaptation of a Rolling Stones song, *The Last Time*, and involved some legal controversy surrounding plagiarism charges as, even though the group had secured permission to use a sample of four bars of an orchestral rendition of the song, it was successfully argued that the group had relied too heavily on the song's original vocal melody as well, and they were forced to surrender copyright and royalties to Mick Jagger and Keith Richards. The second single from the album, *The Drugs Don't Work* (No 1, Sep 1997) gave them their first, and only, UK chart-topper and peaked at No 3 in Ireland. The third single from the album, *Lucky Man* (No 7, Dec 1997) was not as successful commercially as the other two but U2 front-man Bono cites it as one of six songs that he wished he had written from the last 20 years of music. The Verve gained the BRIT Award for Best British Group and Best Album in 1998. On 7 June 1998 a post-performance fight at Düsseldorf-Philipshalle left Nick McCabe with a broken hand and Richard Ashcroft with a sore jaw which seemed to confirm the bubbling hostility had returned. The Verve played their last gig at Slane Castle in Ireland on 29 August 1998 and, after a long period of inactivity, finally announced a permanent split in April 1999. Since the split Richard has had three Top 10 solo albums with 'Alone with Everybody' (No 1, Jun 2000), 'Human Conditions' (No 3, Oct 2002) and 'Keys to the World' (No 2, Jan 2006) plus two Top 10 singles: *A Song for the Lovers* (No 3, Apr 2000) and *Break the Night with Colour* (No 3, Jan 2006). Richard had been adamant that The Verve would never reform, once remarking: "You're more likely to get all four Beatles on stage", however on 26 June 2007, the band's reunion (minus Simon Tong) was announced by Jo Whiley on BBC Radio 1. After extensive touring they released the album 'Forth' (No 1, Aug 2008) which topped the UK Albums Chart and spawned the single *Love is Noise* (No 4, Aug 2008). The same old internal discontent reared its ugly head yet again and the band split for a third time with Richard once again stating, on 7 July 2010, the band "is over for good" – we shall see!

Diana Vickers The blonde wispy singer-songwriter was born in Blackburn, Lancashire on 30 July 1991. Diana first came to public attention on the fifth series of British talent show *The X Factor* in 2008 when she became the bookie's favourite from the outset although ultimately being eliminated in the semi-finals. A bout of laryngitis midway through the competition did not help her cause and in week five she was allowed to miss the live show, the first time the producers have ever offered this concession to any act. After the series end it was initially announced that Diana would be signed by Sony Music under the Syco label along with JLS and Eoghan Quigg but this plan was later dropped and she eventually signed to Sony Music's RCA Records. Her debut single, *Once*, written by Cathy Dennis and Eg White for Diana's debut album 'Songs from the Tainted Cherry Tree' (No 1, May 2010 and No 7 in Ireland), topped the UK Singles Chart. Diana also topped the UK and Irish charts previously with *Hero* (Oct 2008) as part of The X Factor Finalists. Her second single from her debut album, *The Boy Who Murdered Love*, stalled at No 36 in the UK. The album was originally slated to be released in November 2009 but was postponed due to Diana's title role in the West End show *The Rise and Fall of Little Voice*. Diana appeared at many festivals throughout Summer 2010, including T4 on the Beach (one day music event held annually on the beach at Weston-super-Mare since July 2005 and televised for Channel 4), Oxygen Festival (an annual four-day rock music festival held since 2004 on Punchestown racecourse, Co Kildare) and iTunes Festival (an annual music festival and concert series held at The Roundhouse art centre in London since 2007 and sponsored by Apple Inc). Diana's third single, *My Wicked Heart* (No 13, Oct 2010) was originally going to be the lead single for her debut album but ultimately became the lead single for her forthcoming second album 'Music to Make Boys Cry'. In May 2011 Diana unveiled her debut fashion line for Very.co.uk titled "Dee V" reinforcing her signature quirky fashion sense. On 30 June 2011 Diana announced that she had parted company with her label by mutual consent and for purely creative reasons. She has subsequently signed with Virgin Records. Diana has recently been dating One Night Only frontman, George Craig.

Rick Wakeman Richard Christopher Wakeman was born in Perivale, London, 18 May 1949. In 1968, he secured a place at the Royal College of Music, where he studied piano, clarinet, orchestration and modern music. He left a year later in favour of session music work (see entry for David Bowie). Between 1970 and 1971 he was a member of The Strawbs and between 1971-74 and 1976-80 a member of Yes. As a solo artist he made a series of concept albums 'Journey to the Centre of the Earth', a collaboration with the London Symphony Orchestra, topping the UK chart in May 1974. His other Top 10 albums included: 'The Six Wives of Henry VIII' (No 7, Feb 1973), 'The Myths and Legends of King Arthur and the Knights of the Round Table' (No 2, Apr 1975) and 'No Earthly Connection' (No 9, Apr 1976). Rick also produced the soundtracks for the films *Lisztomania* (1975) and *Crimes of Passion* (1984). In 1989, he joined with three fellow ex-Yes members to form Anderson Bruford Wakeman Howe (ABWH) and after collaborating with Yes on the studio album 'Union' (No 7, May 1991) formed a supergroup version of Yes that toured for the remainder of the year. Rick again joined Yes in 1996 for the two 'Keys to Ascension' albums and again in 2002, remaining with the band until 2008. Although Rick is an accomplished keyboard player in all their many guises, he is probably best known as an exponent of the Mellotron – an analogue electronic musical instrument that uses a bank of pre-recorded magnetic tape strips, each of which is activated by a separate key on its keyboard and lasts approximately 8 seconds. In recent years Rick has carved out a new career as a raconteur, wit and panel show regular. He has also been a regular contributor to the BBC 2 show *Grumpy Old Men*. Rick has been married three times, to Rosaline Woolford (1970-77) with whom he had two sons, Oliver (b. 26 February 1972) and Adam (b. 11 March 1974); Danielle Corminboeuf (1980) with whom he had a son Benjamin (b. 1978); and to former Page 3 model Nina Carter (1984-2007) with whom he had a daughter Jemma Kiera (b. 12 February 1983) and a son Oscar (b. May 1986). Rick also has a daughter, Manda (b. 9 May 1986) with his long time friend, designer and seamstress Denise Gandrup. In his twenties, Rick suffered three heart attacks.

The Wanted British-Irish boy band made up of Max George (born Max Albert George, Manchester, 6 September 1988), Siva Kaneswaran (born Blanchardstown, Dublin, 16 November 1988), Jay McGuiness (born Newark, Nottinghamshire, 24 July 1990), Tom Parker (born Bolton, 4 August 1988) and Nathan Sykes (born Abbeydale, Gloucester, 18 April 1993). The Wanted were formed in 2009 through a mass audition by Jayne Collins, who also put together The Saturdays (see separate entry). After signing to Geffen Records, their debut release, *All Time Low* (No 1, Jul 2010) topped the UK Singles Chart and peaked at No 19 in Ireland and was the lead single for their first album 'The Wanted' (No 4, Oct 2010 – No 11 in Ireland). Two subsequent tracks from the album, *Heart Vacancy* (No 2, Oct 2010) and *Lose My Mind* (No 19, Dec 2010) also made the Top 20. Their second studio album 'Battleground' (No 5, Nov 2011 – No 4 in Ireland) spawned the singles, *Gold Forever* (No 3, Mar 2011 - released in aid of Comic Relief), *Glad You Came* (No 1, Jul 2011 - No 1 in Ireland and No 3 in US), *Lightning* (No 2, Oct 2011 – No 5 in Ireland) and *Warzone* (No 21, Dec 2011). The band has recently completed a UK arena tour, supported by another Jayne Collins' creation, Parade (Emily Biggs, Lauren Deegan, Bianca Claxton,

Jessica Agombar and Sian Charlesworth) whose debut single, *Louder,* reached number 10 in the UK Singles Chart in March 2011. Max is engaged to actress Michelle Keegan (born Stockport, Greater Manchester, 3 June 1987) who plays Tina McIntyre in the soap opera *Coronation Street*.

Bert Weedon Although almost unknown to the public today, Herbert Maurice William Weedon was one of the most influential figures in music in the 1950s and 1960s. Born in East Ham on 10 May 1920, his how-to play guitar books, *Play in a Day*, were devoured by George Harrison, Jeff Beck, Eric Clapton, Brian May, Mike Oldfield, The Shadows and almost every budding guitarist. He was the first British guitarist to hit the charts with *Guitar Boogie Shuffle* (No 10, May 1959). Mr Guitar Man, as he was known, put eight singles and two albums onto the charts and reached the Number 1 slot in 1976 with his album '22 Golden Guitar Greats'. He was often associated with The Shadows and played many of their hits, reproducing the tremolo and echo sound made famous by Hank Marvin. Much of his earnings came from supporting bigger names like Frank Sinatra and Rosemary Clooney when they toured and English acts like Dickie Valentine and Alma Cogan in the studio. Bert became something of a television personality with or without the guitar and followed Wally Whyton as foil for many a children's television puppet star. He was awarded an OBE in 2001 and died on 20 April, 2012.

Westlife Irish boyband formerly co-managed by Boyzone's Ronan Keating formed on 3 July 1998 and made up of Nicholas Bernard James Adam "Nicky" Byrne (born in Dublin, 9 October 1978; vocalist – his father-in-law is former taoiseach Bertie Aherne), Kian John Francis Egan (born in Sligo, 29 April 1980; vocalist), Markus Michael Patrick Feehily (born in Sligo, 28 May 1980; vocalist), Shane Steven Filan (born in Sligo, 5 July 1979; vocalist) and Brian Nicholas McFadden (born in Dublin, 12 April 1980; vocalist – he left in 2004. In the band his Christian name was spelled Bryan to facilitate autograph signing. He was married to former Atomic Kitten singer Kerry Katona from 5 January 2002 to their separation in September 2004). Westlife are the only act to have their first seven singles go straight to Number 1 in the UK whereas in America they have only managed to chart once with *Swear It Again*, which made it to number 20 on the Hot 100 in 2000. In Britain, only Elvis Presley and The Beatles have had more chart toppers. Egan, Feehily and Filan were originally part of a group called Six As One along with Derrick Lacey, Graham Keighron and Michael Garrett. They later changed their name to IOYOU. Filian's mother contacted boyband manager Louis Walsh who in turn asked Simon Cowell to look at them but he was not impressed with Lacey, Keighron and Garrett. They were sacked and Byrne and McFadden were recruited after auditions in Dublin. The new band was named Westside but since another group already was using that name, it was changed to Westlife. The group's first single, *Swear It Again* (No 1, May 1999), topped the charts in Britain and Ireland. As did their second, third and fourth releases *If I Let You Go* (No 1, Aug 1999), *Flying Without Wings* (No 1, Oct 1999) and the double-A side *I Have A Dream/Seasons In The Sun* (No 1, Dec 1999 - surprising everyone by knocking Cliff Richards' *The Millennium Prayer*, off the top spot for Christmas). Their eponymously titled debut album topped the charts in their homeland but stalled in second spot in the UK. It was also the biggest dropper in album history falling from three to 37 in one week. *Fool Again* (No 1, Apr 2000), the last single to be released from 'Westlife' reached the top spot in England but only number two in Ireland. A duet with Mariah Carey released on 18 September 2000, *Against All Odds* (the Phil Collins song credited as Mariah Carey featuring Westlife), gave them their sixth UK and fifth Irish Number 1. On 6 November 2000, 'Coast to Coast', the group's second album was released and topped the charts in Britain and Ireland. *My Love* (No 1, Nov 2000) also topped the charts on both sides of the Irish Sea but *What Makes A Man* (No 2, Dec 2000) failed to become their eighth consecutive UK Number 1, peaking at No 2 in the UK and Ireland. Bob The Builder's *Can We Fix It?* (voiced by actor Neil Morrisey) stopped

Westlife claiming the Christmas No 1 that year. They quickly resumed their winning ways when their cover of Billy Joel's *Uptown Girl* (No 1, Mar 2001) hit the top slot in both their home country and Britain. The group then launched their Where Dreams Come True Tour. *Queen Of My Heart* (No 1, Nov 2001) gave them their ninth Number 1 and their third album 'World of Our Own' (released 12 November 2001) also reached Number 1 as did the title single (released 18 February 2002) from it. *Bop Bop Baby* (released 20 May 2002) became their least successful single to date peaking at number five in the UK and went one better in Ireland. *Unbreakable* (released 4 November 2002), became their 11th chart-topper. Westlife completed their second world tour (World of Our Own Tour) in the autumn of 2002. Their next two singles *Tonight /Miss You Nights* (No 3, Apr 2003) and *Hey Whatever* (No 4, Sep 2003) both failed to top the charts but *Mandy* (No 1, Nov 2003) a cover of the Barry Manilow classic (although written by Scott English and Richard Kerr), was No 1 in the UK and Ireland. 'Turnaround' (released 24 November 2003), the group's fourth studio album, also hit the top slot. *Obvious* (released 23 February 2004) made it to No 3 in Britain and Ireland. Two weeks later, McFadden left the group and Westlife continued as a quartet. His first solo effort, *Real To Me* (released 6 September 2004), entered the charts at No 1 but Brian has met with mixed fortune in the rest of his career. A Rat Pack-inspired album '…Allow Us To Be Frank' (released 6 November 2004) reached number three in the UK. In August 2005, Feehily publicly revealed he was gay during an interview with the British tabloid *The Sun*. A year passed before Westlife's next release. *You Raise Me Up* (No 1, Oct 2005 and No 1 in Ireland) became the 13th occasion on which they hit the top slot. Following their successful collaboration with Mariah Carey, Westlife teamed up with another diva, Diana Ross, to record *When You Tell Me That You Love Me*, which reached number two in the UK and Ireland in December 2005. Their sixth studio album 'Face to Face' (No 1, Dec 2005) topped the charts in the UK and Ireland. *Amazing* (No 4, Feb 2006 and No 2 in Ireland) was the group's lowest selling single to date. Their seventh studio album, 'The Love Album' (released 20 November 2006), went to Number 1 in Britain, Ireland and Norway. A cover version of Bette Midler's *The Rose* (No 1, Nov 2006 and No 1 in Ireland) became their 14th UK No 1. Almost a year later, 'Back Home', their eighth studio album, was released on 5 November 2007 and although it was a chart-topper in Britain and Ireland it fared less well in the rest of Europe. A single from it, a cover of Michael Bublé's *Home*, reached number three (No 2 in Ireland) at the end of 2007. *I'm Already There* (2007) was not released as a single but made it to number 62 on the strength of downloads after an appearance on *The X Factor*. In March 2008, *Us against the World* entered the UK charts where it peaked at number eight (No 6 in Ireland). Nine months later, *I'm Already There* re-entered the charts as a download but fared worse than it did the first time round and stalled at 63. In November 2009, the group made a comeback with a new album 'Where We Are', which reached number two in Britain and Ireland and a new single *What About Now*, which coincidentally also reached number two in Britain and Ireland. *Safe* (released 14 November 2010) reached number 10 (No 4 in Ireland), their 25th Top 10 single in the United Kingdom. An album, 'Gravity' (released 22 November 2010) reached number three in Britain but topped the charts in the group's homeland. Westlife also had two compilation albums reach the top of the charts in Ireland, 'Unbreakable: The Greatest Hits Volume' (Nov 2002) and 'Greatest Hits' (Nov 2011) but although the first named also topped the UK Albums Chart, the second stalled at No 4. On 19 October 2011, Westlife announced they were splitting after a farewell tour in 2012.

Wet Wet Wet Scottish pop band formed at Clydebank High School in 1982 and consisting of Marti Pellow (born Mark McLachlan, in Clydebank, 23 March 1966; vocalist), Graeme Clark (born in Glasgow, 15 April 1965; bassist), Neil Mitchell (born in Helensburgh, Dunbartonshire, 8 June 1965; keyboards player) and Tommy Cunningham (born in Drumchapel, Glasgow, 22 June 1964; drummer). Of the group, Cunningham said, "It was either crime, the dole, football, or music – and we chose music." They began rehearsing in Graeme Clark's mum's kitchen and took their name from a Scritti Politti song *Getting Having And*

Holding. In 1983, unofficial member Graeme Duffin joined them and two years later they signed a record deal. Their debut single *Wishing I Was Lucky* reached number six in the singles chart in 1987. Their first album 'Popped In Souled Out' hit the Number 1 slot, spent 72 weeks on the chart and was home to three more hit singles *Sweet Little Mystery* (1987, five), *Angel Eyes (Home And Away)* (1987, five) and *Temptation* (1988, 12). Their next release, a cover of The Beatles' *With A Little Help From My Friends*, recorded for the charity ChildLine, gave them their first No 1. A second album, 'The Memphis Sessions', reached number three and was bested by one place by their third album 'Holding Back The River' (1989). *Sweet Surrender* from the album made it to number four. Their next five singles did not live up to their previous success with only, *Break Away* (1989), breaking into the Top 20 (at 19). 1992 started off brilliantly for Wet Wet Wet with *Goodnight Girl* topping the singles chart (their only self-penned No 1) and 'High On The Happy Side' topping the album charts. Then came another period of comparative chart failure although 'End Of Part One (Their Greatest Hits)' topped the album charts in 1993. In 1994, the group had their biggest hit when their version of The Troggs's *Love Is All Around* (released on 9 May 1994) spent an incredible 15 weeks on top of the UK charts helped by its appearance in the smash Hugh Grant film *Four Weddings And A Funeral* (1994). It also went to No 1 in Australia, Austria, Holland, New Zealand, Norway and Sweden. It reached number two in France, Germany, Ireland and Switzerland. It failed to equal the run by Bryan Adams's *(Everything I Do) I Do It for You* because their record company wanted to promote their next single *Julia Says* which reached number three. The 1995 album 'Picture This' became their second consecutive chart-topper. The 1997 effort, '10', failed to complete a hat-trick stalling at number two. Then Tommy Cunningham left in fury after discovering that the other three wanted to revise his royalty share downwards. In 1999, Pellow followed him out of the band although his departure was due to his heroin habit. Two years later, he returned to the music industry with his debut solo single and album, *Close To You* (nine) and 'Smile' (seven). In 2004, their differences behind them, Wet Wet Wet reformed releasing the single *All I Want* and another greatest hits album. Three years later, on 5 November 2007, they released a new single *Too Many People*, which made it only to No 46. An album, 'Timeless', followed a week later. A second single from the album, *Weightless*, was released on 4 February and charted at number 10 before dropping in its second week to number 96, the largest ever fall for a Top 10 single in the UK, besting the previous record held by *The Wedding Present*. The group continue to record and play gigs.

Wham! The most commercially successful boyband of the 1980s hailed from Bushey, Hertfordshire, and consisted of school friends George Michael (born Georgios Kyriacos Panayiotou, Finchley, London, 25 June 1963) and Andrew Ridgeley (born in Windlesham, Surrey, 26 January 1963). The duo met at Bushey Meads Comprehensive School and joined a ska band named The Executive, alongside two of their former school friends David Mortimer (b. 14 July 1962, who as David Austin would have some minor chart success) and Andrew Leaver. Wham! signed to Innervision Records and, along with backing singers Amanda Washbourn and Shirlie Holliman, made appearances in local clubs before their debut single *Wham Rap!* was released in June 1981 and promptly disappeared. In October 1982, *Young Guns (Go For It!)* entered the charts and reached the number three slot thanks in no small part to their performance on *Top Of The Pops* when George wore espadrilles, an open suede jacket, and rolled-up denim jeans. Dee C. Lee had replaced Washbourn as a backing singer and was herself succeeded by Helen "Pepsi" Demacque the following year. A reworked *Wham Rap!* made it to number eight in early 1983. Four months later, *Bad Boys* entered the charts and peaked at number two. In July 1983, their first LP, 'Fantastic', began what was to be 116 weeks on the hit parade. Realising that they needed to change their "bad boy" image, the duo hired new managers in Jazz Summers and Simon Napier-Bell. Wham! released *Club Tropicana* which reached number four that same summer. Wham! then fell out with Innervision Records and sued to be released from their contract. During the dispute Innervision released *Club Fantastic Megamix*, a medley of non-single album songs from 'Fantastic', which George and Andrew urged fans to boycott. The result was the bankruptcy and disappearance of Innervision and no new releases for three years until Wham! signed with Epic. Their first Epic release *Wake Me Up Before You Go-Go* was also their first No 1. It became notable also for Pepsi and Shirlie wearing Katharine Hamnett T-shirts bearing various legends. It was followed by Michael's first solo single (although co-credited on the writing to Ridgeley) *Careless Whisper*, also a chart-topper. *Freedom* (No 1, Oct 1984) gave Wham! their second consecutive No 1 single while 'Make It Big' gave them their second consecutive No 1 album. George took part in the Band Aid charity single *Do They Know It's Christmas?* which meant that in 1984 he topped the charts as a solo artist, and part of a duo and an ensemble/group. *Do They Know It's Christmas?* prevented Wham! from enjoying a hat-trick of chart-toppers as it kept their now classic festive song *Last Christmas* off the top spot. In 1985, Wham! became the first Western pop group to perform in communist China. In September, *I'm Your Man* charted and became Wham!'s third No 1 and the re-issued *Last Christmas* reached number six. In the spring of 1986, Michael and Ridgeley announced that Wham! would end that summer. The Edge Of Heaven was their fourth and last No 1 and the duo played a farewell gig before 73,000 fans at Wembley Stadium on 28 June 1986. In 1990, Ridgeley had a brief sojourn into the lower reaches of the charts with *Shake* hitting number 58 but, for the most part, he has lived a quiet life of domestic bliss in Cornwall with his girlfriend, Keren Woodward, the singer from Bananarama. His former partner has rarely been out of the press though and not always for musical reasons. It all started well: *A Different Corner* (released in 1986 while Wham! were still active) reached No 1, as did his post-Wham! duet with Aretha Franklin *I Knew You Were Waiting (For Me)*, and also topped the Billboard Hot 100. The song was co-written by Simon Climie, later to achieve success as one-half of Climie Fisher and won a Grammy for Michael and Franklin for Best R'n'B Performance. Also in 1987, Michael reached number three with the raunchy *I Want Your Sex* and No 2 with *Faith* from the album of the same name (which was released in October 1987 and reached No 1). In America, many radio stations banned *I Want Your Sex* and when it made the charts DJ Casey Kasem (who provided the voice of Shaggy in the cartoon series *Scooby Doo (Where Are You!)*) refused to say the song's title, calling it merely "the new single by George Michael". *Father Figure*, Michael's premier release in 1988, was his first single in five years not to make the Top 10, reaching its zenith position 11 in January. In the spring, *One More Try* returned Michael to the Top 10 finishing at eight but *Monkey* finished at a disappointing 13th position. In America, things were different and all four songs topped the Billboard Hot 100. *Kissing A Fool*, the last release of 1988, reached number 18 in the UK and five in America. Michael was absent from the charts until August 1990 when he released *Praying For Time*, which although it reached only number six in Britain was Michael's sixth Number 1 in the USA. On 3 September, his second album, 'Listen Without Prejudice Volume 1' was released and became his second No 1 going quadruple Platinum. Michael's next four releases, *Waiting for That Day*, *Freedom 90*, *Heal The Pain* and *Cowboys and Angels* did comparatively badly reaching 23, 28, 31 and 45 respectively before a duet with Elton John on *Don't Let The Sun Go Down On Me* returned him to the No 1 spot on both sides of the Atlantic in 1991. Six months later, *Too Funky* charted and reached fourth position. At this time, 'Listen Without Prejudice Volume 2' was abandoned although it might have been related to Michael's growing discomfort with his record label, Sony. As with Wham!, he began a legal battle to extricate himself from his contract with his record label and it would be four years before he began releasing new solo material. Michael was absent from the public stage until November 1994 when he performed his new song *Jesus To A Child*, a tribute to his dress designer boyfriend Anselmo Feleppa (b. in Brazil 21 August 1956) who had died of Aids on 26 March 1993. When the song was finally released (on Virgin) in January 1996, it went straight in at No 1, and the follow-up *Fastlove* also topped the charts. *Fastlove* is about his affair with banker Brett Charles and it is Michael's last No 1 to date. In May 1996, George released his third studio album, 'Older', and it, too, went to No 1 to give him a hat-trick of solo No 1 albums followed by a fourth chart-topper, albeit a compilation, *Ladies & Gentlemen: The Best Of George Michael*. The album was released as part of his settlement to leave Sony. *Spinning the Wheel* reached number two in the UK and was followed by *Older/I Can't Make You Love Me* (1997, three), *Star People 97* (1997, two) and another double A-side *You Have Been Loved/The Strangest Thing 97* (1997, two) then it started to go wrong for George. On 7 April 1998, his homosexuality an open secret in showbusiness circles but unknown to the public at large, became widely known when he was arrested for cottaging in a Beverly Hills public lavatory. He was fined $810 and sentenced to 80 hours' community service. He mocked the incident in his next song, *Outside* (released on 25 October 1998), which made it to number two in the UK but in America where they saw little to laugh about in his actions it did not chart at all and, indeed, George has not has a record on the Billboard Hot 100 since *Fastlove*. Given No choice, George admitted that he was gay and had been in a relationship with American businessman Kenny Goss since June 1996. Since his arrest, George's chart positions have been poor by his very high standards. He has released the following records, on various different labels: *As* (with Mary J. Blige, 1999, four), *Freeek!* (2002, seven), *Shoot The Dog* (2002, seven; a song criticising Britain's close relationship with the United States), *Amazing* (2004, eight), *Flawless (Go To The City)* (2004, eight), *Round Here* (2004, 32), *John and Elvis Are Dead* (2005), *An Easier Affair* (2006, 13), *This Is Not Real Love* (with Mutya Buena, 2006, 15) and *December Song (I Dreamed of Christmas)* (2008, 14). In December 1999, he released the album 'Songs from the Last Century', a compilation of old favourites and reworked new songs. It reached No 2 making it the only solo album not to get to No 1. His album, 'Patience', his first original work since 1996, went straight in at No 1 on the charts in March 2004. On 26 February 2006, George was arrested for Class C drugs and received a police caution. On 23 July 2006, the *News Of the World* revealed that he had been seen cruising on Hampstead Heath. After first saying that he intended to sue for libel, Michael then admitted that he often seeks anonymous sex and that boyfriend Goss does not mind. In November 2006, his second greatest hits album, 'Twenty Five', was released and went straight in at No 1. On 8 May 2007, George pleaded guilty to driving while unfit through drugs after he was arrested at Cricklewood when his car blocked others at a set of traffic lights. He was banned from driving for two years, and given community service. On 9 June 2007, he became the first singer to perform at the new Wembley Stadium but was later fined £130,000 for going 13 minutes over the allowed time. On 19 September 2008, he was arrested in a public convenience near Hampstead Heath for possession of Class A and C drugs and received another police caution. On 4 July 2010, he drove into the shop window of a Snappy Snaps store in Hampstead and was again arrested. On 12 August, George was "charged with possession of cannabis and with driving while unfit through drink or drugs". Twelve days later, at Highbury Corner Magistrates' Court he pleaded guilty to driving while under the influence of drugs. On 14 September, he was sentenced to eight weeks in prison, a fine and a five-year driving ban. On 11 October, he was released from Highpoint Prison, Suffolk on after serving half his sentence. George subsequently contracted pneumonia in November 2011 and spent a period of time in intensive care in a Vienna hospital.

Whitesnake Heavy metal band that like many of their ilk have had greater success with albums than with singles. Although they have charted 21 times only two singles, *Is This Love* (No 9, Jun 1987) and *Here I Go Again* (No 9, Oct 1987) have made the Top 10. In 1976, David Coverdale (born in Saltburn-by-the-Sea, North Yorkshire, 22 September 1951) left Deep Purple who he had been with since 1973 and the following year founded Whitesnake. Originally called The White Snake Band, the members played on both his solo albums, 'White Snake' (1977) and 'Northwinds' (1978), and consisted of Bernie Marsden (born in Buckingham, Buckinghamshire, 7 May 1951; guitarist), Micky Moody (born in Middlesbrough, 30 August 1950; guitarist), Neil Murray (born in Edinburgh, 27 August 1950; bassist), David "Duck" Dowle (born in London, 20 October 1953; drummer), and Brian Johnston (keyboards player) who was quickly replaced by Pete Solley, formerly of Procol Harum. In June 1978, Whitesnake made their first appearance on the singles chart with the EP *Snakebite*, which made it to number 61. Five months later, they made their album chart debut with 'Trouble', which peaked at number 50, followed 11 months later by 'Lovehunter', controversial because of its cover (by Chris Achilleos), which was a drawing of a naked woman straddling a coiled snake. The album reached number 29 in October 1979. *Long Way From Home* did slightly better on the singles chart reaching No 55 but their third chart entry was to that time their most successful, *Fool For Your Loving* making it to No 13 in the spring of 1980. In June 1980, they charted with the album 'Ready and Willing' (No 6, Jun 1980) and in November of that year, 'Live... In The Heart of the City' entered the charts and went one better. In spring 1981, Whitesnake released 'Come an' Get It' which missed the top spot by just one place. Coverdale's daughter, Jessica, fell ill and he took time off to look after her. When Whitesnake went back into the studio, David introduced a new line-up replacing Marsden, Ian Paice (born in Nottingham, 29 June 1948; drummer, he joined in 1979) and Murray with Mel Galley (b. March 8, 1948; d. at Heath Hayes, Cannock, Staffordshire July 1, 2008; bassist), Colin Hodgkinson (born in Peterborough, 14 October 1945; bassist) and bringing in Cozy Powell (born Colin Flooks, in Cirencester, Gloucestershire, 29 December 1947; d. at M4, Bristol 5 April 1998) as the new drummer. The new album, 'Saints & Sinners' (1982), made it to No 9 and included the single *Here I Go Again*, which peaked at No 34 as a double A-side with *Bloody Luxury*. In the summer of 1983, *Guilty Of Love* made it to No 31. In 1984, Whitesnake had another change of personnel – former Thin Lizzy guitarist John Sykes (born in Reading, Berkshire, 29 July 1959) replaced Moody, and Neil Murray returned replacing Hodgkinson. Galley was sacked after discussing reforming his old band, Trapeze. In 1985, Cozy Powell left to join Emerson, Lake & Powell and was replaced by Aynsley Dunbar (born in Liverpool 10 January 1946). The following year, Coverdale fell ill with a sinus infection that threatened his voice. The eponymously titled album that had been delayed because of his illness was finally released on 7 April 1987 and went octuple platinum in America reaching No 2 on the Billboard 200 chart and No 8 in the UK. The popularity was aided by its raunchy videos on MTV that featured sexy actress Tawny Kitaen (born Julie Kitaen, San Diego, California 5 August 1961), whom Coverdale married on 17 February 1989. In the summer and autumn of 1987, Whitesnake enjoyed their two Top 10 singles. In June, *Is This Love* reached number nine and in October, a remixed version of *Here I Go Again* entered the charts and also reached number nine. The band charted with *Give Me All Your Love* (1988, 18), *Fool for Your Loving* (1989, 43), *The Deeper The Love* (1990, 35) and *Now You're Gone* (1990, 31) before Coverdale broke them up. He worked on various projects with Jimmy Page before reforming Whitesnake in 1994 for a greatest hits tour. Coverdale hired Warren DeMartini (born in Chicago, Illinois, 10 April 1963; guitarist), Adrian Vandenberg (born in The Hague, Holland, 31 January 1964; guitarist), Rudy Sarzo (born Rodolfo Maximiliano Sarzo Lavieille Grande Ruiz Payret y Chaumont, in Havana, Cuba, 18 November 1950; bassist), Denny Carmassi (drummer) and Paul Mirkovich (born in Los Angeles, California 20 March 1963; keyboards player). The band then split up for a further three years until, in 1997, Coverdale and Vandenberg reformed for a new Whitesnake album 'Restless Heart', which made No 34 in the UK. A single from it, *Too Many Tears*, made it to number 46. At the end of 1997, Coverdale again split up Whitesnake. In December 2003, Coverdale reformed Whitesnake for the group's 25th year anniversary. The group released two albums 'Good to Be Bad' (2008) and 'Forevermore' (2011) and continues to perform around the world.

David Whitfield David Whitfield was a hugely popular ballad singer who topped the charts for 10 weeks in 1954 with *Cara Mia*.

David was born on 2 February 1926 at Hull, East Yorkshire the third of eight children. He began singing with the local church choir and then when he was 17 joined the Royal Navy. His singing career began in earnest in the Far East and on demob in 1949 David entered a talent show in the Southampton area. He was disqualified because the audience clapped so much he was unable to finish his song, as the rules stated. After winning the Hughie Green talent show *Opportunity Knocks* on Radio Luxembourg in 1950, he was offered an eight-month touring contract with the show. When the tour ended, he returned to Hull and got a job as a coalman's mate while singing in clubs in the evenings and weekends. An offer from Hughie Green led to David singing in London hotels and he was subsequently signed to Decca Records. In January 1953, he recorded *Marta* (with Nat Temple and his orchestra) which sold more than 20,000 copies. Three months later he released his second single, *I Believe*, which sold 75,000 copies and narrowly failed to make the charts (which in those days consisted only of a Top 12). In October, he entered the charts for the first time with *Bridge of Sighs*, which reached number nine in its solitary week on the chart. His second single, *Answer Me* (recorded with Stanley Black and His Orchestra) was released two weeks later and spent 14 weeks on the Hit Parade including two separate runs of a week at Number 1 with sales of 700,000 copies. This massive hit single was all the more remarkable for the fact that the BBC placed a partial ban on it under its original title of *Answer Me, Oh Lord*, as it was mistakenly construed as anti-Christian in its questioning of God. *Rags to Riches* made it to number three after it entered the charts in December 1953. *The Book* (No 5, Feb 1954) continued David's run in the Top 10. In the summer, aided by Mantovani and his orchestra, David spent 10 weeks at Number 1 with *Cara Mia*, selling more than three and a half million copies worldwide and being a hit in America, then a rare feat for an English singer. The song earned Whitfield a Gold Disc in 1956, the first British male singer to achieve that honour (Vera Lynn being the first British singer to be awarded a Gold Disc, for *Auf Wiederseh'n Sweetheart*). *Santo Natale* (No 2, Nov 1954) and *Beyond the Stars* (No 8, Feb 1955) continued his stay in the Top 10 before *Mama* (No 12, May 1955) ruined the run of seven consecutive Top 10 hits. The status quo soon returned with *Ev'rywhere* (No 3, Jul 1955), *When You Lose The One You Love* (No 7, Nov 1955) and *My September Love* (No 3, Mar 1956). The dawn of the rock 'n' roll era then began to impinge on David's recording career and his remaining hits had mixed fortunes as follows: *My Son John* (No 22, Aug 1956), *My Unfinished Symphony* (No 25, Aug 1956), *The Adoration Waltz* (No 9, Jan 1957 – with the Roland Shaw Orchestra), *I'll Find You* (No 27, Apr 1957 – featured in the 1957 film *Sea Wife*), *Cry My Heart* (No 22, Feb 1958), *On The Street Where You Live* (No 16, May 1958), *The Right To Love* (No 30, Aug 1958) and his last chart entry, the re-released *I Believe* (No 49, Nov 1960). David then returned to theatres, both for operatic concerts and musicals, and also appeared in pantomimes to earn his living. In 1954 he had begun his first world tour and appeared in America, Canada, Australia, New Zealand, South Africa and the Far East. It was while on tour that he suffered a brain haemorrhage and died in a Sydney hospital on 15 January 1980. He left only a paltry amount of money. In 1987, the David Whitfield International Appreciation Society was formed and serves to keep alive David's music and memory. The society has thus far succeeded in naming a rose and a star after David; published a biography entitled *Cara Mia: The David Whitfield Story;* and are presently in the throes of erecting a bronze statue of the great tenor in his home town of Hull. The aforementioned Dame Vera Lynn is the patron of the society.

The Who Influential "mod" group formed at Shepherd's Bush, London in 1964 that evolved out of the Detours, a local youth club band formed in 1961. Their original personnel were Roger Daltrey, CBE (born Roger Harry Daltrey, at Hammersmith Hospital, London, 1 March 1944; vocalist), Pete Townshend (born Peter Dennis Blandford Townshend, at Chiswick Hospital, London, 19 May 1945; guitarist), John Entwistle (born John Alec Entwistle, at Hammersmith Hospital, London, 9 October 1944; d. in room 658, Hard Rock Hotel and Casino, Las Vegas, Nevada, 27 June 2002, of a cocaine-induced heart attack while in bed with a stripper-groupie; bassist), Colin Dawson (vocalist) and bricklayer Doug Sandom (b. 1936; drummer). The latter two were sacked and the band recruited Keith Moon (born Keith John Moon, at Central Middlesex County Hospital, London, 23 August 1946; d. at Flat 12, 9 Curzon Place, Mayfair, London 7 September 1978, of a drug overdose; drummer). The Detours changed their name to The Who in February 1964 but when Peter Alexander Edwin Meaden (born in Edmonton, London, 11 November 1941; d. 29 July 1978, of a drugs overdose), an advertising executive, became their manager that summer they became The High Numbers and released *Zoot Suit/I'm the Face* on 3 July 1964. When the release flopped they reverted to The Who and hired Kit Lambert (born in Knightsbridge, London, 11 May 1935; d. in London, 7 April 1981, of a cerebral haemorrhage after falling down the stairs of his mother's house) and Chris Stamp (born in London, 6 July 1942, the younger brother of Terence Stamp). Lambert and Stamp positioned The Who as a mod band. In September 1964, during a gig at the Railway Tavern in Harrow and Wealdstone, Townshend, broke the head of his guitar by accident and after seeing the crowd reaction a gimmick was born. Despite their popularity no major labels seemed interested in signing The Who even after a successful run at the Marquee Club at 90 Wardour Street, Soho, that began in November 1964. Finally, Shel Talmy, an independent producer, spotted them and signed the group to Decca who sublet them to Brunswick. They scored a Top 10 hit with their first release, the Kinks-influenced *I Can't Explain* (No 8, Feb 1965) which peaked at No 93 on the American Billboard Hot 100. The group followed that with *Anyway, Anyhow, Anywhere* (No 10, May 1965), written by Daltrey and Townshend, which did not chart in the USA. Their next single *My Generation* (No 2, Nov 1965) one of the first songs with a bass guitar solo, stalled at number 74 in America. The Who decided it wanted to sever its ties with Shel Talmy because they saw the deal as punitive. When he refused to renegotiate they went ahead and recorded *Substitute* (No 5, Mar 1966) on the Reaction label. Shel sued but the matter was settled out of court with Talmy retaining rights to all of The Who's royalties until the end of the decade. The Who followed up with *A Legal Matter* (No 32, Mar 1966), the first song not to get into the Top 10. The lads were back on track with *I'm a Boy* (No 2, Sep 1966) about transvestism, *Happy Jack* (No 3, Dec 1966), about mental illness, and *Pictures Of Lily* (No 4, Apr 1967), about masturbation. On 18 June 1967, The Who played the Monterey Pop Festival and shocked the crowd when at the end of their set Pete began smashing his guitar. Roadies ran onstage to rescue expensive microphones. That autumn The Who released *I Can See for Miles* (No 10, Oct 1967) which became their biggest hit in America, being the only one to breach the Top 10 of the Billboard Hot 100 making it No 9. *Dogs* (No 25, Jun 1968) and *Magic Bus* (No 26, Oct 1968) were comparative disappointments in terms of chart performance although the latter became a concert staple. It was The Who's next project that was a landmark in modern music. 'Tommy', the first rock opera, was recorded in London between 19 September 1968 and 7 March 1969 and released as a double LP on 23 May 1969. Pete Townshend wrote the vast majority of the story about the "deaf, dumb and blind boy" who led a messianic cult. 'Tommy' reached number two in Britain and four in America and five of the songs were released as singles: *Pinball Wizard* (No 4, Mar 1969), *Go To The Mirror!* (Jul 1969), *I'm Free* (Jul 1969), *Christmas* (Nov 1969) and *See Me, Feel Me* (Oct 1970), the last four not charting in the UK although the last named peaked at No 12 in the USA. The band performed much of Tommy at Woodstock that year and demanded that they be paid ($11,200) for their performance. During the set, a drugged up Yippie leader Abbie Hoffman, determined to further publicise the case of poet John Sinclair who had been sentenced to 10 years in prison for giving two marijuana cigarettes to an undercover policeman, grabbed a microphone and shouted, "I think this is a pile of shit, while John Sinclair rots in prison!" Townshend pulled the microphone from him and yelled, "Fuck off! Fuck off my fucking stage!" before hitting Hoffman with his guitar. The Who's first live album, 'Live at Leeds' (No 3, May 1970) is often cited as the best live rock album of all time. On 4 January 1970, while trying to escape a fracas at the Red Lion pub in Hatfield, Hertfordshire, a car containing Keith Moon ran over and killed Keith's friend and minder Neil Boland. Keith was absolved of all blame but felt a personal guilt for the rest of his life. Pete Townshend began working on his next major project, a sci-fi rock opera to be called *Lighthouse* but it was abandoned and several of its songs were incorporated into the album 'Who's Next', which reached Number 1 in September 1971, the band's only chart-topper. Seven years later in September 1978, The Who released 'Who Are You', which revisited the *Lighthouse* idea by including new science fiction related songs by John Entwistle with a slightly changed plot. The album reached number six in Britain. In 1970, The Who became the first rock act to play the Metropolitan Opera House in New York. In the summer of 1971, the group reached number nine with *Won't Get Fooled Again*. While Townshend worked on 'Quadrophenia' (No 2, Nov 1973), The Who produced *Let's See Action* (No 16, Oct 1971), *Join Together* (No 9, Jun1972) and *Relay* (No 21, Jan 1973) and released the album 'Meaty Beefy Big and Bouncy' (No 9, Dec 1971). On 19 October 1973, 'Quadrophenia' was released – another rock opera but this time about a mentally ill youth called Jimmy who took part in the Mods and Rockers clashes at Brighton in the early 1960s. It spent 13 weeks on the UK chart reaching number two on both sides of the Atlantic. In October 1974, The Who released the outtakes album 'Odds & Sods' which peaked at number 10. On 26 March 1975 the film version of 'Tommy' was released with an all-star cast (see entry in the cinema section). Directed by Ken Russell, the film was nominated for two Oscars – Best Actress for Ann-Margret and Best Music, Scoring Original Song Score and/or Adaptation for Pete Townshend. On 3 October 1975, The band released their seventh studio album 'The Who by Numbers'. The LP reached number seven on the UK album chart and number eight on the Billboard 200 in America. On 6 December 6, 1975, The Who created a world record for the most attendees at an indoor concert when 75,962 fans saw them at the Pontiac Silverdome. *Squeeze Box* reached number 10 in Britain in January 1976. Almost six months later, on May 31, 1976 they played The Valley, the home of Charlton Athletic, in what was listed in *The Guinness Book Of Records* for more than 10 years as the noisiest concert in the world measuring more than 120 decibels. There was a chart hiatus of two years while Townshend assessed what effect punk would have on The Who. In July 1978 *Who Are You* entered the charts and peaked at 18 (No 14 in the USA) while on 18 August 1978 'Who Are You' (No 6, Dec 1978) the album was released. In America, it became their fastest selling album but its success was overshadowed by the death of Keith Moon. On 6 September 1978, Moon went to a film preview of *The Buddy Holly Story* and then to dinner with Paul and Linda McCartney. He returned, with girlfriend Annette Walter-Lax, to the Mayfair flat that he was renting from Harry Nilsson. Mamas And Papas singer Mama Cass Elliot had died in the flat in July 1974. There Moon took 32 tablets of Clomethiazole (Heminevrin), a drug to help alleviate his alcohol withdrawal symptoms as he tried to give up drink. Six were enough to cause death. Keith was cremated at Golders Green Crematorium. In 1979, rumours of a split were dismissed when Small Faces drummer Kenney Jones (born in Stepney, London, 16 September 1948) replaced Moon with the sticks. A documentary retrospective *The Kids Are Alright* and *Quadrophenia* were released. Just as it seemed that things were picking up after the tragedy of Keith's death, another disaster struck. On 3 December 1979, 11 fans were killed and 26 injured during a pre-gig stampede at the Riverfront Coliseum in Cincinnati, Ohio. In March 1981, the album 'Face Dances' (No 2) spawned the single *You Better You Bet* (No 9, Mar 1981). Following the album 'It's Hard' (No 11, Sep 1982), the band undertook a farewell tour although they reunited for Live Aid in 1984. In 1981, Townshend's marriage had collapsed due to his heavy drinking and he became a heroin addict. When, two years later, he was unable to write new music he announced that he was leaving in December. He worked on solo projects. In 1988, Jones left the band after the group won the British Phonographic

Industry's Lifetime Achievement Award and the following year The Who began a 25th anniversary reunion tour. Simon Phillips (born in London, 6 February 1957) played drums and Steve "Boltz" Bolton took over on lead guitar. Two new releases, *Athena* (No 40, Oct 1982) and the EP *Ready Steady Who* (No 58, Nov 1983), were the last singles chart entries for The Who apart from two re-issues of *My Generation* in 1988 and 1996. They went on tour in 1996 and 1997 and three years later, the three surviving members contemplated a new album but their plans were halted by Entwistle's death in 2002. Townshend and Daltrey continue to perform as The Who, and in 2006 they released the studio album 'Endless Wire' (No 9, Oct 2006 and No 7 in USA) which reached the Top 10 on both sides of the Atlantic. Roger Daltrey was the only member of The Who to have a solo Top 10 hit when he reached number five in April 1973 with *Giving It All Away*. In 2003, police cautioned Townshend after he accessed child pornography sites on the internet.

Kim Wilde Blonde bombshell singer who later found success as a gardener. Kim Wilde was born Kim Smith at Chiswick on 18 November 1960, the eldest daughter of 1950s singer Marty Wilde (see below) and Joyce Baker (b. May 1941) of The Vernons Girls (named after the pools company for which they all worked). In late 1980, Wilde was signed to RAK Records by producer Mickie Most who was also one of the Mr Nastys on TV talent show *New Faces*. In January 1981, her debut single *Kids In America* shot to number two in the UK although it stuttered to 25 in America in the summer of 1982. A second single, *Chequered Love*, reached number four in summer 1981. It would be her last Top 10 success for more than five years. Her eponymously titled debut album made it to No 3 in the UK. She continued to release singles, which fared less well in Britain with each one: *Water On Glass* (1981, 11), *Cambodia* (1981, 12), *View From A Bridge* (1982, 16), *Child Come Away* (1982, 43), *Love Blonde* (1983, 23) and *Dancing In The Dark* (1983, 67) which resulted in her leaving RAK and signing with MCA. A second album with RAK, 'Select' (1982) had made it to number 19 but a third, 'Catch As Catch Can' (1983), flopped only scraping to 90. Wilde's first chart hit with MCA, *The Second Time*, spent six weeks on the Hit Parade and reached No 29. An album, 'Teases & Dares', only made it to number 66. A second single, *The Touch*, was not a success, stalling at 56 but the third, the rockabilly *Rage to Love* (produced by Dave Edmonds), made it to No 19. A greatest hits album released by RAK peaked at 78. Just as her career seemed over, a cover of The Supremes' *You Keep Me Hangin' On* reached No 2 in the UK (in winter 1986) and topped the charts in the USA (in June 1987) – the fifth female Brit to earn that position after Petula Clark, Lulu, Sheena Easton, and Bonnie Tyler. In April 1987, she charted in the UK with *Another Step (Closer to You)* (recorded with Junior Giscombe and reaching six) and at Christmas as (the other Mel & Kim) with Mel Smith on *Rockin' Around The Christmas Tree* (for the charity Comic Relief and peaking at three). In June 1988, she charted with her album 'Close' and spent 38 weeks on the chart reaching a very respectable number eight. The following month, *You Came* entered the charts and reached number three. *Never Trust A Stranger* (1988, seven) and *Four Letter Word* (1988, six) ended her run of Top 10 hits and the highest subsequent placings have been 12 for *If I Can't Have You* in 1993 and 16 for *Love Is Holy* in 1992. Her last, to date, chart entry has been *This I Swear* which made it to number 46 in 1996. Wilde's career has been more successful in Europe, scoring a Top 10 hit in Belgium, Austria, Germany, Holland and Switzerland in 2003 with *Anyplace, Anywhere, Anytime*, a duet with German pop star Nena. In 2006, Kim signed a record deal with EMI Germany and four years later joined Starwatch who released her eleventh studio album, 'Come Out and Play' on 17 August 2010. Kim has presented television programmes about gardening and written two books on the subject.

Marty Wilde Fifties heartthrob who more recently has became more famous as Kim Wilde's dad. Marty Wilde was born with the decidedly unglamorous name of Reginald Leonard Smith at Blackheath, south London on 15 April 1939. He was for a short time in a skiffle group before landing a residency as Reg Patterson at the Condor Club, London, in 1957 where he came to the attention of songwriter Lionel Bart who told impresario Larry Parnes who in turn persuaded Jack Good to hire Marty for his ITV show *Oh Boy!* They fell out when Good refused to let Wilde sing *Misery's Child* and then effectively replaced him with (Sir) Cliff Richard who became the country's leading teen idol. In July 1958, Wilde entered the charts for the first time with *Endless Sleep*, his first Top 10 hit which spent 16 weeks and made it to No 4. He went one better with *Donna* (1959) and one better still with *A Teenager In Love* (1959) even though he wasn't actually a teenager at the time. *Sea Of Love* peaked at No 3 and the self-penned *Bad Boy* (1959) reached No 7. His marriage on 2 December 1959 to Joyce Baker (b. May 1941) of The Vernons Girls (named after the pools company for which they all worked) further dented his teen appeal. He started appearing on stage in shows such as *Bye Bye Birdie,* and Parnes attempted to promote Wilde as an actor but Marty was less than keen. His last Top 10 hit was a cover of Bobby Vee's *Rubber Ball*, which made nine in early 1961. Marty turned to writing songs and with Ronnie Scott, he wrote the 1968 number two hit *Jesamine* for The Casuals (under the pseudonyms Frere Manston and Jack Gellar), *Ice in the Sun* for Status Quo (1968, eight) and *I'm A Tiger* for Lulu (1968, nine). In the 1970s, he tried to promote his son Ricky (b. 1961 as Richard James Reginald Steven Smith) as England's answer to Little Jimmy Osmond. Ricky later wrote many of the songs for his big sister, Kim (see above). Marty Wilde's younger daughter Roxanne (b. 1979) is also a singer.

Amy Winehouse Amy was a powerful contralto who was equally at home singing jazz, rhythm and blues or soul but ultimately became more famous for her turbulent personal life than her prodigious singing talent. Born at Southgate, London on 14 September 1983, Amy Jade Winehouse signed to Simon Fuller's 19 Management in 2002. In 2003, her debut album 'Frank' (released on 20 October 2003) originally peaked at No 13 on the UK Albums chart in January 2004 and was nominated for the Mercury Prize (following her death it was reissued and rose to No 3 in August 2011). However her first four singles all failed to dent the Top 50. Nevertheless, her debut chart single *Stronger Than Me*, which peaked at 71, won the Ivor Novello Award for Best Contemporary Song Musically & Lyrically in 2004. Two years later, she finally cracked the Top 10 with her song about addictions *Rehab*, which made it to number seven and won her a second Ivor Novello Award. She performed the song at the 27th BRIT Awards, held at Earls Court on 15 February 2007 and won the gong for Best British Female. Her second album, 'Back To Black' (released on 30 October 2006), was nominated but lost out to Arctic Monkeys with 'Whatever People Say I Am, That's What I'm Not'. It topped the UK Album Charts in January 2007 and has to date sold more than 10million copies worldwide. It went octuple platinum in Britain, double platinum in America where it reached number two on the Billboard Hot 200, and number one in Argentina, Austria, Belgium, Denmark, France, Germany, Holland, Ireland, New Zealand, Norway, Poland, Portugal, Spain and Switzerland. It has returned to the top of the UK charts on two occasions the last being in July 2011 following her death. The title track originally stalled at No 25 in the UK Singles chart but again, rose to No 8 in July 2011 following her death. Despite her album success, the only real one made the Top 10 Singles Chart during her lifetime although *Valerie* by Mark Ronson featuring Winehouse reached number two. Amy's version of the track peaked at 37. In 2007, despite being white and Jewish, Amy won the MOBO (Music of Black Origin) for Best UK Female. In 2008, she won her third Ivor Novello Award for *Love Is A Losing Game*. The song first entered the UK Singles Chart at 46 in 2007. However, following her death the song re-entered the chart at a new peak of 33. At the 50th Annual Grammy Awards ceremony, she won five gongs equalling the record (with Lauryn Hill, Alicia Keys, Beyoncé Knowles, Norah Jones, and Alison Krauss) for the second-most awards won by a female artist in a single ceremony. 'Back To Black' won Best Pop Vocal Album, while *Rehab* won Best Female Pop Vocal Performance, Song of the Year and Record of the Year while Amy won Best New Artist. Reports of a third album continued to circulate until Amy was found dead at her north London home on 23 July 2011. An inquest showed that she had drunk bottles of vodka and was more than five times over the drink drive limit. She was 27 and joined "The Stupid Club" – musicians who had died at that age and who include Janis Joplin, Jimi Hendrix, Brian Jones, Kurt Cobain, Jim Morrison and many more. In the aftermath of her death 'Back To Black' returned to the Number 1 slot and went on to become the best-selling album of the 21st Century, overtaking James Blunt's 2005 debut album, 'Back to Bedlam'. In December 2011, the aforementioned third album, 'Lioness: Hidden Treasures' was released posthumously and sold almost 200,000 copies in its first week to top the UK album chart. The album contains her final recording, *Body and Soul*, a duet with American singer Tony Bennett for his latest album, 'Duets II'. The song received the Grammy for Best Pop Duo/Group Performance at the 54th Grammy Awards on February 12th, 2012. Amy's father Mitch Winehouse, picked up the award with his wife Janis, saying, "We shouldn't be here. Our darling daughter should be here. These are the cards that we're dealt."

Wizzard Pop group founded by Roy Wood (born in Birmingham, 8 November 1946 - not as Ulysses Wood as he once flippantly claimed but as Roy Adrian Wood) after he had tired of The Move and Electric Light Orchestra. Wizzard was formed in July 1972 with Bill Hunt (keyboards player; his nephew played with The Wonder Stuff), Rick Price (vocalist/bassist), Hugh McDowell (cello), Nick Pentelow (saxophonist), Keith Smart (drummer) and Charlie Grima (drummer). Wizzard's first appearance was at the Wembley Rock'n'Roll Festival that year and made their chart debut reaching No 6 with *Ball Park Incident* in December 1972. Wizzard improved on that by reaching No 1 with their next two hits *See My Baby Jive* (Apr 1973 - it also topped the charts in Ireland) and *Angel Fingers* (Sep 1973). The same year, they reached No 4 with *I Wish It Could Be Christmas Every Day*, which has become a perennial festive favourite. For their stage performances Wood coloured his hair and beard, wore make-up and stuck stars to his face. In spring 1974, *Rock'N'Roll Winter* reached No 6 and at Christmas 1976, *Are You Ready To Rock* made it to No 8, but apart from re-releases of *I Wish It Could Be Christmas Every Day* that marked the end for Wizzard. Attempts to break America in 1975 ended in failure because of a lack of money. In 1977, Wood, Rick Price and Mike Burney formed the Wizzo band but it ended in March 1978 whereupon Roy has performed solo or supported other bands with the Roy Wood Rock & Roll Band. In 1986, he reached No 45 with a cover version of *Waterloo* with Doctor And The Medics. Fourteen years later, he teamed up with furry environmentalists The Wombles to get to 22 with *I Wish It Could Be A Wombling Merry Christmas Every Day*. He continued to record solo material alongside the first incarnation of Wizzard and reached number eight in the winter of 1973-1974 with *Forever*.

Wretch 32 Rapper (born Jermaine Scott, Tottenham, London, 9 March 1985) who was a member of the grime collective "Combination Chain Gang", before forming The Movement with fellow rappers Scorcher (real name Tayo Jarrett) and Ghetts (real name Justin Reginald Clarke Samuel). Wretch 32 got his first big break when he performed at the first annual MP3 Music Awards in 2007 but he didn't make it into mainstream music consciousness until he appeared at Radio 1's Big Weekend, as part of the new 'BBC Introducing' music brand in 2009. By then he had already released his debut studio album 'Wretchrospective' which failed to make any impact in 2008, prior to Wretch's signing with record label Ministry of Sound. On 6 December 2010, he was named as one of the nominees for BBC's Sound of 2011, an annual poll which predicts artists that will progress during the upcoming year. His debut single, *Traktor* (No 5, Jan 2011) featuring the uncredited vocals of L, showed the poll to be correct. Wretch 32's second album 'Black and White' (No 4, Aug 2011) spawned three other singles to-date: *Unorthodox* (No 2, Apr 2011 – see entry for Example), *Don't Go* (No 1, Aug 2011) featuring vocals from Josh Kumra, and the less successful, *Forgiveness* (No 49, Dec 2011) featuring vocals from Etta Bond. The fifth track from the album, *Hush Little Baby*, featuring the vocals of Ed Sheeran is due for release in May 2012.

Yazoo Pop duo formed in 1981 at Basildon, Essex by former Depeche Mode songwriter Vince Clarke (synthesiser) and Alison Moyet (vocals). The name originates from Yazoo Records, a blues label. A little know rock band in America called Yazoo sued the Essex duo and forced them to be known as Yaz in the States. Their first single, *Only You*, was released on 15 March 1982 and reached No 2 but a cover version by the Flying Pickets went one better the following year. Yazoo's follow-up *Don't Go* (released on 3 July 1982) peaked at No 3 and their first album 'Upstairs at Eric's' (1983) made it to No 2 and achieved a platinum disc. *The Other Side of Love*, their third single reached 13. A second album *You and Me Both* (1983) reached No 1. *Nobody's Diary* from that LP was their final Top 10 hit peaking at three. They went their separate ways Moyet going solo and Clarke forming The Assembly then Erasure. *Situation*, a remixed version of the B-side of *Only You*, was released in 1990 and reached 14. Nine years later, a remixed version of *Only You* was released. In 2008 they reformed for a brief tour, and a live album, 'Reconnected Live', of the tour was released on 27 September 2010. Alison's solo singles include: *Love Resurrection* (no 10, Jun 1984), *All Cried Out* (No 8, Oct 1984), *That Old Devil Called Love* (No 2, Mar 1985), *Is This Love?* (No 3, Nov 1986), *Weak in the Presence of Beauty* (No 6, Mar 1987) and *Love Letters* (No 4, Nov 1987). She also had a chart-topping debut solo album 'Alf' in November 1984 and a chart-topping compilation album 'Singles' in June 1995.

Yazz Tall bleached blonde singer (born in Shepherd's Bush, London 19 May 1960 as Yasmin Evans, the daughter of a Jamaican father and English mother) who played keyboards in a band called Pastiche while she was still at school. She worked as a catwalk model to earn money to finance a music career. In 1988 she worked with production duo Coldcut on their Top 10 single *Doctorin' the House* (credited to Coldcut featuring Yazz and the Plastic Population). Five months later, Yazz and the Plastic Population with production by Coldcut entered the charts with *The Only Way Is Up*, which reached No 1 and stayed there for five weeks. *Stand Up For Your Love Rights* credited just to Yazz reached No 3 and her debut album 'Wanted' charted in November 1988 and also reached No 3. *Fine Time* (No 9, Feb 1989) was her last Top 10 and after taking time out to recover from the hectic lifestyle she found her fan base had moved on by the time she started gigging again. Yasmin released several more records including *How Long* with Aswad in 1993 and a cover of The Jackson 5's 1971 hit *Never Can Say Goodbye* in 1997 but they all stalled in the lower reaches of the charts. In 1996, she became Christian and later moved to Spain where she sings in the local Calahonda Baptist Church. Her other albums have been: 'The Wanted Remixes' (1989), 'One On One' (1994), 'Natural Life' (1997), 'At Her Very Best' (2001), 'Tribute To Burt Bacharach And Hal David' (2002) and 'Running Back To You' (2007).

Yes Prog rock band formed in London in 1968 who have sold more than 30million albums. Like AC/DC and Led Zeppelin, they are best known for album rather than single releases, reaching the Top 10 on just one occasion with *Wonderous Stories* (No 7, Sep 1977). In the USA they fared rather better reaching Number 1 with *Owner Of A Lonely Heart* in 1983, the song stalling at 28 in the UK. Chris Squire (b. Kingsbury, London, 4 March 1948; bassist) has been the only constant in the group, which has seen many personnel changes in its existence. Squire and Jon Anderson (b. Accrington, Lancashire, 25 October 1944; vocalist) founded the group having met in a Soho nightclub, La Chasse, where Anderson was working. Yes played their first gig at East Mersea Youth Camp on 4 August 1968. Their eponymously titled first album was released on 25 July 1969 but did not chart. The following year, the second album, 'Time And A Word', released in the summer of 1970 hit the number 45 slot. 'The Yes Album', released in early 1971, made it to number four. Between 1970 and 2003, Yes had 22 albums on the chart with 'Tales From Topographic Oceans' (No 1, Dec 1973) and 'Going For The One' (No 1, Jul 1977) both topping the UK chart. Over the years, many musical greats have plied their trade with yes including Peter Banks, Steve Howe, Trevor Rabin, Billy Sherwood (guitarists), Geoff Downes, Tony Kaye, Igor Khoroshev, Patrick Moraz, Oliver Wakeman and Rick Wakeman (keyboards players), Bill Bruford and Alan White (drummers) as well as Trevor Horn before he became a successful producer. See separate entry for Rick Wakeman.

Yomanda Yomanda was one of many pseudonyms used by Northern Irish DJ Paul Masterson (b. at Belfast) with which he charted four times getting to number eight with *Synth And Strings* in July 1999. Paul also recorded under the name Hi-Gate as a collaboration with Judge Jules – real name Julius O'Riordan) and had three hits under this name, *Pitchin' (In Every Direction)* peaking at No 6 in January 2000. His other noms de chansons include: Amen! UK, Candy Girls (with Rachel Auburn), Celine Diablo, The Clergy, Dorothy, Erotixs, Sleazesisters, Subway, Succargo, Sushi, VPL, Wand and Working Class Hero.

Jimmy Young Known to a generation as a Radio 2 DJ, Sir Jimmy Young (b. Cinderford, Gloucestershire, 21 September 1921 as Leslie Ronald Young) was a very successful singer in the 1950s and had two Number 1s and six other Top 20 hits. Polygon Records signed him in 1950 and his first record was cut the following year – the aptly titled *Too Young*. In 1952, he joined Decca and in January 1953 charted with *Faith Can Move Mountains*, making the number 11 slot. *Eternally* made it to number eight in August 1953 and he then made it to the Number 1 slot twice with *Unchained Melody* (No 1, May 1955) and *The Man From Laramie* (No 1, Sep 1955). His other hits were *Someone On Your Mind* (No 13, Dec 1955), *Chain Gang* (No 9, Mar 1956), *Wayward Wind* (No 27, Mar 1956), *Rich Man Poor Man* (No 25, Jun 1956), *More* (No 4, Sep 1956), *Round And Round* (No 30, May 1957), *Miss You* (No 15, Oct 1963) and a remake of *Unchained Melody* which only got to number 43 in March 1964. He worked on Radio 1 from 1967 until 1973 when he then transferred to Radio 2 and hosted their flagship programme along the way interviewing every British Prime Minister and most of the Royal Family. The 'JY Prog' as it was affectionately known, ran for the best part of 30 years. His distinctive theme music was "Town Talk" by Ken Woodman & His Piccadilly Brass. His familiar closing catchphrase was "This is Jimmy Young saying BFN – Bye For Now" and not the often attributed TTFN (Ta Ta For Now) which in fact was a catchphrase of Tommy Handley in *ITMA*. Jimmy was knighted in 2002, a short time before he retired. However in recent months his dulcet tones have again been gracing the airwaves on Radio 2.

Karen Young One-hit wonder, Karen Young (b. Sheffield, 1 January 1946) had her solitary hit in the autumn of 1969 when she made number six with *Nobody's Child*. She retired from the music industry in 1974.

Paul Young Born in Luton on 17 January 1956, white soul boy Paul Antony Young began taking piano lessons when he was 14 but on leaving school at 16 he began work at the local Vauxhall car plant. In evenings and in his spare time, he played with various bands, the first being Kat Kool & The Kool Kats. In the mid-1970s, he joined Streetband as lead singer. They reached number 18 with the double A-side *Toast/Hold On* in late 1978 before splitting in December 1979. Paul founded The Q-Tips but they had no chart success and they split in 1982. Backed by The Royal Family and backing singers Maz Roberts and Kim Leslie aka The Fabulous Wealthy Tarts, Paul embarked on a solo career. His first two singles, *Iron Out the Rough Spots* and *Love Of The Common People* flopped but his cover of the little known Marvin Gaye song *Wherever I Lay My Hat (That's My Home)* hit the top spot in the summer of 1983 (although it stalled at 70 in America). His debut album 'No Parlez' made it to Number 1 and spent 119 weeks on the chart. His second charting single *Come Back And Stay* reached number four in the UK and 22 in the USA. Young re-released *Love Of The Common People* and saw it rise to number two in Britain in September 1983. The following year he had two more Top 10 hits in the UK, *I'm Gonna Tear Your Playhouse Down* (No 9, Oct 1984) and *Everything Must Change*

(No 9, Dec 1984) and in 1985 *Everytime You Go Away* (N0 4, Mar 1985), gave him his only USA Number 1. He was also one of the featured artists on the Band Aid single *Do They Know It's Christmas?* A tour of America that year put pressure on his vocal chords. His second album 'The Secret Of Association', released in 1985, also made Number 1 and spent 49 weeks on the charts. His subsequent albums include 'Between Two Fires' (No 4, Nov 1986), 'Other Voices' (No 4, Jun 1990) and a chart-topping compilation 'From Time to Time' (No 1, Sep 1991). In March 1991 he made it to number four duetting with Italian blues singer Zucchero on *Senza Una Donna (Without A Woman)*. In 1995 Paul formed Los Pacaminos, a stetson-wearing Tex-Mex inspired combo known for performing songs such as *La Bamba* and *Speedy Gonzales*. In 2006, he appeared on BBC1's *Celebrity MasterChef* and in 2007 on ITV's *Hell's Kitchen* (he came fourth of 10 celebrities). Paul has been married to former model Stacey Smith since 1987. Stacey was the hostess on the disastrous revival of *Mr & Mrs* hosted by Julian Clary in 1999. Together they have three children: daughters Levi (b. March 1987), Layla (b. August 1994), and son Grady Cole (b. January 1996).

Will Young Winner (in February 2002) of the first series of *Pop Idol*, Will Robert Young (b. Wokingham, Berkshire, 20 January 1979) has subsequently sold more than eight million albums worldwide. Young hit the top spot in the UK Singles Chart with four of his first five charted singles. The first, the double A-side *Evergreen/Anything Is Possible* (released 25 February 2002) became the fastest-selling debut in British chart history, selling 403,027 copies on its day of release (1,108,659 copies in its first week) and more than 1.7million in total. On 31 December 2009, Radio 1 revealed that it was the biggest selling single of the decade in the UK. *Evergreen* was nominated for a BRIT Award as Best Single. *Light My Fire* (released 27 May 2002) was his second Number 1 followed by *The Long And Winding Road* (a duet with Gareth Gates who he had beaten to win Pop Idol, released as a double A-side with Gates's song *Suspicious Minds*). His fourth Number 1 (charting in November 2002) was another double A-side *Don't Let Me Down/You And I* (released in aid of the charity Children in Need). Young was away from the charts for more than a year. He returned in December 2003, the year he won a British Breakthrough Act BRIT Award, and reached Number 1 with *Leave Right Now* (released 24 November 2003). *Your Game* (March 2004) made it to number three and won the Best British Single BRIT Award; *Friday's Child* (released 5 July 2004) hit fourth slot; *Switch It On* (released 14 November 2005) peaked at number five; *All Time Love* (released 16 January 2006) made it to number three; *Who Am I* (released 24 April 2006) made it to number 11; *Changes* (released 15 September 2008) reached number 10; despite publicity on *The X Factor* and *Children In Need*, *Grace* (released 22 December 2008) tanked at 33. His next two singles *Let It Go* (released 2 March 2009) and *Hopes & Fears* (released 8 November 2009) fared even worse reaching 58 and 65 respectively. His first album, 'From Now On', was released on 7 October 2002, went double platinum and reached Number 1 as did his second album, 'Friday's Child' (released 1 December 2003) – which went quadruple platinum. Album number three arrived on 21 November 2005 and was entitled 'Keep On'. It reached number two and went triple platinum. Will's fourth album 'Let It Go' was released on 29 September 2008 and reached number two. It too went platinum. His fifth album 'Echoes' was released on 22 August 2011 and topped the charts and of course also went platinum. The first single from the album, *Jealousy*, peaked at No 5 in August 2011. In 2005 Will appeared in the British comedy film, *Mrs Henderson Presents*, alongside Bob Hoskins and Dame Judi Dench and in 2007 trod the boards in the Royal Exchange Theatre's production of *The Vortex* by Noël Coward. In 2010 he appeared in the Marple TV film *The Mirror Crack'd from Side to Side* and later in the year guest starred in an episode of *Skins*. Will has also authored two books *Anything is Possible* (2002) and *On Camera, Off Duty* (2004). Openly gay, Will remains tight-lipped as to his personal life despite constant media speculation.

Lena Zavaroni Petite and Scottish Lena Zavaroni came to public attention in 1974, aged 10, on the Hughie Green talent show

Opportunity Knocks with the song *Ma! (He's Making Eyes At Me)*. Lena Hilda Zavaroni was born at Greenock on 4 November 1963 and won *Opportunity Knocks* for five consecutive weeks. This led to work on both sides of the Atlantic. Her album, 'Ma' reached number eight in the UK and she sang for US President Gerald Ford at the White House. In 1977, she fell victim to anorexia nervosa but blamed her plummeting weight on career pressure. In 1979, she began her own show on BBC *Lena Zavaroni And Music*, which ran until 1982. Her 1989 marriage to computer consultant Peter Wiltshire broke up after just 18 months. She fell further and lived on £48.80 a week benefits and in 1999 the diminutive (Lena was 4' 10" in her stocking feet) singer was accused of stealing a packet of jelly worth 50p, although the charges were later dropped. She suffered from depression and had drug treatments and electroconvulsive therapy to try and beat her anorexia. She died of pneumonia on 1 October 1999, three weeks after she underwent a psychosurgical operation at the University Hospital of Wales in Cardiff. She was just 35-years-old.

Zig & Zag Irish puppets created by Mick O'Hara and Ciaran Morrison best known in the UK for their appearances from 1992 with Chris Evans on *The Big Breakfast*. Zig (b. at Zog, 29 February 1971 as Zigmund Ambrose Zogly) and Zag (b. at Zog, 29 February 1971 as Zagnatius Hillary Zogly) had two Top 30 hits – *Them Girl Them Girls* entered the charts on Christmas Eve 1994 and reached number five and *Hands Up! Hands Up!* reached number 21 the following summer, the duo having been signed by Simon Cowell.

The Zutons Indie rock band who hail from Liverpool, formed in 2001 but who did not chart until 2004. In September 2002, they put out *Devil's Deal*, a three-track release. In the spring of 2003 they released *Creepin' And A Crawlin'* followed that November by *Haunts Me*, a download only single. The Zutons are made up of Dave McCabe, Russell Pritchard, Sean Payne and Abi Harding. Their first single to chart was *Pressure Point* in January 2004 and it reached number 19. (In America, the song was featured in an advertisement for Levi's.) A second single charting in April 2004, *You Will Won't You*, fared slightly worse stalling at 22. Their debut album, 'Who Killed….. The Zutons?', entered the charts in May 2004, reached number nine and was nominated for the 2004 Mercury Music Prize. In 2005, the Zutons were nominated for the British Breakthrough Act Award at the BRITs. A second album, 'Tired Of Hanging Around' (released on 17 April 2006) contained their two Top 10 singles *Why Won't You Give Me Your Love?* and *Valerie*, both of which peaked at number nine. *Always Right Behind You* finished a disappointing 26 and spent just four weeks on the chart. It came from their third album, 'You Can Do Anything', which was released on 2 June 2008. In December 2008, their record label, Sony/BMG, dropped The Zutons. In September 2010, Dave McCabe was found guilty of assault at Liverpool Crown Court, after headbutting Peter Appleby, a man he believed assaulted his girlfriend. McCabe was sentenced to 150 hours of community service and ordered to pay Appleby £1,500 in compensation. Russell is currently playing bass with Noel Gallagher's High Flying Birds although The Zutons are still gigging.

UK Top Ten Singles (listed alphabetically by song title) Between 1952 and 2011

A And E (10) Goldfrapp (2008)
A Team, The (3) Ed Sheeran (2011)
Abacab (9) Genesis (1981)
Abba-Esque EP (1) Erasure (1992)
ABC (8) Jackson 5 (1970)
About A Girl (8) Sugababes (2009)
About You Now (1) Sugababes (2007)
Abracadabra (2) Steve Miller Band (1982)
Abraham Martin And John (9) Marvin Gaye (1970)
Absolute Beginners (2) David Bowie (1986)
Absolute Beginners (4) Jam (1981)
Absolutely Everybody (7) Vanessa Amorosi (2000)
Absolutely Fabulous (6) Pet Shop Boys (1994)
Acapella (5) Kelis (2010)
Acceptable In The 80s (10) Calvin Harris (2007)
Achilles Heel (re-issue) (8) Toploader (2000)
Achy Breaky Heart (3) Billy Ray Cyrus (1992)
Activ 8 (Come With Me) (3) Altern 8 (1991)
Addam's Groove (4) MC Hammer (1991)
Addicted To Bass (2) Puretone (2002)
Addicted To Love (5) Robert Palmer (1986)
Addictive (3) Truth Hurts featuring Rakim (2002)
Adelante (2) Sash (2000)
Adoration Waltz (9) David Whitfield (1957)
Advertising Space (8) Robbie Williams (2005)
Affirmation (8) Savage Garden (2000)
Africa (3) Toto (1983)
African Waltz (9) Johnny Dankworth (1961)
Afrika Shox (7) Leftfield / Bambaataa (1999)
After The Love Has Gone (4) Earth Wind & Fire (1979)
After The Love Has Gone (5) Steps (1999)
After You're Gone / Sacred Trust (2) One True Voice (2002)
Agadoo (2) Black Lace (1984)
Again (6) Janet Jackson (1993)
Against All Odds (1) Mariah Carey & Westlife (2000)
Against All Odds (1) Steve Brookstein (2005)
Against All Odds (Take A Look At Me Now) (2) Phil Collins (1984)

Age Of The Understatement, The (9) Last Shadow Puppets (2008)
Ain't Gonna Bump No More (2) Joe Tex (1977)
Ain't Got No – I Got Life / Do What You Gotta Do (2) Nina Simone (1968)
Ain't It Fun (9) Guns 'N' Roses (1993)
Ain't It Funny (3) Jennifer Lopez (2001)
Ain't It Funny (remix) (4) Jennifer Lopez (2002)
Ain't Misbehavin' (3) Tommy Bruce & The Bruisers (1960)
Ain't No Doubt (1) Jimmy Nail (1992)
Ain't No Love (Ain't No Use) (3) Sub Sub and Melanie Williams (1993)
Ain't No Mountain High Enough (6) Diana Ross (1970)
Ain't No Other Man (2) Christina Aguilera (2006)
Ain't No Pleasing You (2) Chas & Dave (1982)
Ain't No Stoppin' Us (8) DJ Luck & MC Neat featuring JJ (2000)
Ain't No Stoppin' Us Now (5) McFadden & Whitehead (1979)
Ain't No Sunshine (8) Michael Jackson (1972)
Ain't Nobody (1) LL Cool J (1997)
Ain't Nobody (8) Course (1997)
Ain't Nobody (8) Rufus & Chaka Khan (1984)
Ain't Nobody (remix) (6) Rufus & Chaka Khan (1989)
Ain't Nobody Better (10) Inner City (1989)
Ain't Nothing Goin' On But The Rent (5) Gwen Guthrie (1986)
Ain't Talkin' 'Bout Dub (7) Apollo Four Forty (1997)
Ain't That A Shame (7) Pat Boone (1955)
Ain't That Funny (8) Jimmy Justice (1962)
Ain't That Just The Way (6) Lutricia McNeal (1997)
Air Hostess (2) Busted (2004)
Air That I Breathe, The (2) Hollies (1974)
Air That I Breathe, The (6) Simply Red (1998)
Airplanes (1) BoB featuring Hayley Williams (2010)
Airport (4) Motors (1978)
Airwave (10) Rank 1 (2000)
Aisha (9) Death In Vegas (2000)
Albatross (1) Fleetwood Mac (1968)
Albatross (re-issue) (2) Fleetwood Mac (1973)
Albion (8) Babyshambles (2005)
Alcoholic (10) Starsailor (2001)
Alejandro (7) Lady Gaga (2010)

Alfie (9) Cilla Black (1966)
Alice I Want You Just For Me (9) Full Force (1985)
Alive (5) S Club (2002)
Alive And Kicking (7) Simple Minds (1985)
Alive And Kicking / Love Song (re-issue) (6) Simple Minds (1992)
All About Lovin'You (9) Bon Jovi (2003)
All About Tonight (1) Pixie Lott (2011)
All About Us (3) Peter Andre (1997)
All About Us (8) Tatu (2005)
All About You / You've Got A Friend (1) McFly (2005)
All Alone Am I (7) Brenda Lee (1963)
All Along The Watchtower (5) Jimi Hendrix Experience (1968)
All Around My Hat (5) Steeleye Span (1975)
All Around The World (1) Lisa Stansfield (1989)
All Around The World (1) Oasis (1998)
All Because Of You (6) Geordie (1973)
All Because Of You (4) U2 (2005)
All By Myself (6) Celine Dion (1996)
All Cried Out (8) Alison Moyet (1984)
All Day And All Of The Night (2) Kinks (1964)
All Day And All Of The Night (7) Stranglers (1988)
All Falls Down (10) Kanye West] featuring Syleena Johnson (2004)
All Fired Up (3) The Saturdays (2011)
All 4 Love (5) Color Me Badd (1991)
All For Love (2) Bryan Adams, Rod Stewart & Sting (1994)
All For You (3) Janet Jackson (2001)
All Good Things (Come To An End) (4) Nelly Furtado (2006)
All Hooked Up (7) All Saints (2001)
All I Ask Of You (3) Cliff Richard & Sarah Brightman (1986)
All I Ever Need Is You (8) Sonny & Cher (1972)
All I Ever Wanted (2) Basshunter (2008)
All I Have (2) Jennifer Lopez featuring LL Cool J (2003)
All I Have To Do Is Dream / Claudette (1) Everly Brothers (1958)
All I Have To Do Is Dream (3) Bobbie Gentry & Glen Campbell (1969)
All I Have To Give (2) Backstreet Boys (1998)
All I Really Want To Do (4) Byrds (1965)
All I Really Want To Do (9) Cher (1965)
All I See Is You (9) Dusty Springfield (1966)
All I Wanna Do (4) Sheryl Crow (1994)
All I Wanna Do (4) Dannii Minogue (1997)
All I Wanna Do Is Make Love To You (8) Heart (1990)
All I Want (2) Mis-Teeq (2001)
All I Want For Christmas Is You (2) Mariah Carey (1994)
All I Want For Christmas Is You (re-emergence) (4) Mariah Carey (2007)
All I Want Is You (4) U2 (1989)
All I Want Is You (4) 911 (1998)
All In My Head (7) Kosheen (2003)
All Kinds Of Everything (1) Dana (1970)
All Mine (8) Portishead (1997)
All My Life (5) Foo Fighters (2002)
All My Life (8) K-Ci & JoJo (1998)
All My Love (6) Cliff Richard (1967)
All Night Long (4) Alexandra Burke featuring Pitbull (2010)
All Night Long (5) Rainbow (1980)
All Night Long (All Night) (2) Lionel Richie (1983)
(All Of A Sudden) My Heart Sings (10) Paul Anka (1959)
All Of Me Loves All Of You (4) Bay City Rollers (1974)
All Of My Heart (5) ABC (1982)
All Of My Life (9) Diana Ross (1974)
All Or Nothing (1) Small Faces (1966)
All Or Nothing (4) O-Town (2001)
All Out Of Love / Beauty And The Beast (10) H & Claire (2002)
All Over (2) Lisa Maffia (2003)
All Over Again (6) Ronan Keating & Kate Rusby (2006)
All Right Now (2) Free (1970)
All Right Now (remix) (8) Free (1991)
All Rise (4) Blue (2001)
All She Wants Is (9) Duran Duran (1989)
All Shook Up (re-entry) (1) Elvis Presley with The Jordanaires (1957)

All Star Hit Parade (2) Various Artists (1956)
All Stood Still (8) Ultravox (1981)
All Summer Long (1) Kid Rock (2008)
All That I Need (1) Boyzone (1998)
All That She Wants (1) Ace Of Base (1993)
All The Love In The World (10) Dionne Warwick (1982)
All The Lovers (3) Kylie Minogue (2010)
All The Small Things (2) Blink 182 (2000)
All The Things She Said (9) Simple Minds (1986)
All The Things She Said (1) Tatu (2003)
All The Time And Everywhere (9) Dickie Valentine (1953)
All The Way (3) Craig David (2005)
All The Way (re-entry) (3) Frank Sinatra (1957)
All The Way From Memphis (10) Mott The Hoople (1973)
All The Young Dudes (3) Mott The Hoople (1972)
All This Time (1) Michelle (2004)
All Time Love (3) Will Young (2006)
All Time Low (1) The Wanted (2010)
All Together Now (4) Farm (1990)
All Together Now 2004 (5) Farm featuring SFX Boys Choir (2004)
All You Good Good People EP (8) Embrace (1997)
All You Need Is Love (1) Beatles (1967)
Ally's Tartan Army (6) Andy Cameron (1978)
Almaz (4) Randy Crawford (1986)
Almost Here (3) Brian McFadden & Delta Goodrem (2005)
Almost There (2) Andy Williams (1965)
Almost Unreal (7) Roxette (1993)
Alone (8) Petula Clark (1957)
Alone (3) Heart (1987)
Alone (5) Bee Gees (1997)
Alone (7) Lasgo (2002)
Alone Again (Naturally) (3) Gilbert O'Sullivan (1972)
Alone Without You (8) King (1985)
Alphabet Street (9) Prince (1988)
Alright (6) Jamiroquai (1997)
Alright / Time (2) Supergrass (1995)
Alright Alright Alright (3) Mungo Jerry (1973)
Also Sprach Zarathustra 2001 (7) Deodato (1973)
Alternate Title (2) Monkees (1967)
Always (3) Atlantic Starr (1987)
Always (2) Bon Jovi (1994)
Always (4) Erasure (1994)
Always And Forever / Mind Blowing Decisions (remix) (9) Heatwave (1978)
Always Be My Baby (3) Mariah Carey (1996)
Always Breaking My Heart (8) Belinda Carlisle (1996)
Always Come Back To Your Love (3) Samantha Mumba (2001)
Always Look On The Bright Side Of Life (3) Monty Python (1991)
Always On My Mind (9) Elvis Presley (1972)
Always On My Mind (1) Pet Shop Boys (1987)
Always On Time (6) Ja Rule featuring Ashanti (2002)
Always There (6) Incognito featuring Jocelyn Brown (1991)
Always Where I Need To Be (3) Kooks (2008)
Always Yours (1) Gary Glitter (1974)
Am I That Easy To Forget (3) Engelbert Humperdinck (1968)
AM To PM (3) Christina Milian (2002)
Amateur Hour (7) Sparks (1974)
Amazing (4) George Michael (2004)
Amazing (4) Westlife (2006)
Amazing Grace (5) Judy Collins (1970)
Amazing Grace (1) Pipes & Drums & Military Band Of The Royal Scots Dragoon Guards (1972)
Ambitions (6) Joe McElderry (2010)
America (2) Razorlight (2006)
America: What Time Is Love (4) KLF (1992)
American Boy (1) Estelle featuring Kanye West (2008)
American Dream (3) Jakatta (2001)
American Idiot (3) Green Day (2004)
American Life (2) Madonna (2003)
American Pie (2) Don McLean (1972)
American Pie (1) Madonna (2000)
Americanos (4) Holly Johnson (1989)
Amigo (9) Black Slate (1980)

Amnesia (10) Chumbawamba (1998)
An American Trilogy (8) Elvis Presley (1972)
An Everlasting Love (10) Andy Gibb (1978)
An Honest Mistake (7) Bravery (2005)
An Innocent Man (8) Billy Joel (1984)
Analogue (All I Want) (10) A-Ha (2006)
And I Love You So (3) Perry Como (1973)
And The Beat Goes On (2) Whispers (1980)
And The Heavens Cried (6) Anthony Newley (1961)
Anfield Rap (Red Machine In Full Effect) (3) In Liverpool FC (1988)
Angel / What Made Milwaukee Famous (Has Made A Loser Out Of Me) (4) Rod Stewart (1972)
Angel (5) Madonna (1985)
Angel (4) Simply Red (1996)
Angel (1) Shaggy featuring Rayvon (2001)
Angel Eyes / Voulez Vous (3) Abba (1979)
Angel Eyes (4) Roxy Music (1979)
Angel Eyes (Home And Away) (5) Wet Wet Wet (1987)
Angel Eyes (7) Raghav (2005)
Angel Face (4) Glitter Band (1974)
Angel Fingers (1) Wizzard (1973)
Angel Of Harlem (9) U2 (1988)
Angel Of Mine (4) Eternal (1997)
Angel Street (8) M People (1998)
Angela Jones (7) Michael Cox (1960)
Angelo (1) Brotherhood Of Man (1977)
Angels (4) Robbie Williams (1997)
Angels With Dirty Faces / Stronger (7) Sugababes (2002)
Angie (5) Rolling Stones (1973)
Angie Baby (5) Helen Reddy (1975)
Animal (6) Def Leppard (1987)
Animal Nitrate (7) Suede (1993)
Anitina (The First Time) / Pump Up The Volume (1) Marrs (1987)
Annie I'm Not Your Daddy (2) Kid Creole & The Coconuts (1982)
Annie's Song (1) John Denver (1974)
Annie's Song (3) James Galway (1978)
Anniversary Waltz, The – Part 1 (2) Status Quo (1990)
Another Brick In The Wall Part II (1) Pink Floyd (1979)
Another Chance (1) Roger Sanchez (2001)
Another Day (2) Paul McCartney (1971)
Another Day (7) Whigfield (1994)
Another Day (9) Lemar (2004)
Another Day In Paradise (2) Phil Collins (1989)
Another Day In Paradise (5) Brandy & Ray J (2001)
Another Lover (9) Dane (2001)
Another Night (2) MC Sar & The Real McCoy (1994)
Another One Bites The Dust (7) Queen (1980)
Another One Bites The Dust (5) Queen featuring Wyclef Jean, Pras Michel and Free (1998)
Another Rock And Roll Christmas (7) Gary Glitter (1984)
Another Step (Closer To You) (6) Kim Wilde & Junior (1987)
Another Suitcase In Another Hall (7) Madonna (1997)
Another Way To Die (9) Jack White & Alicia Keys (2008)
Answer Me (1) David Whitfield (1953)
Answer Me (1) Frankie Laine (1953)
Answer Me (9) Barbara Dickson (1976)
Ant Rap (3) Adam & The Ants (1981)
Ante Up (7) MOP featuring Busta Rhymes (2001)
Anthem, The (10) Good Charlotte (2003)
Antmusic (EP) (2) Adam & The Ants (1980)
Antmusic / No Regrets (4) Robbie Williams (1998)
Any Dream Will Do (1) Jason Donovan (1991)
Any Dream Will Do (2) Lee Mead (2007)
Any Way That You Want Me (8) Troggs (1966)
Anyone Can Fall In Love (4) Anita Dobson (1986)
Anyone Of Us (Stupid Mistake) (1) Gareth Gates (2002)
Anyone Who Had A Heart (1) Cilla Black (1964)
Anything (5) Culture Beat (1994)
Anything (2) 3T (1996)

Anything For You (10) Gloria Estefan and The Miami Sound Machine (1988)
Anything Is Possible / Evergreen (1) Will Young (2002)
Anytime You Need A Friend (8) Mariah Carey (1994)
Anyway Anyhow Anywhere (10) Who (1965)
Anywhere For You (4) Backstreet Boys (1997)
Anywhere Is (7) Enya (1995)
Apache (1) Shadows (1960)
Apeman (5) Kinks (1970)
Apologize (3) Timbaland featuring One Republic (2007)
Applejack (4) Jet Harris & Tony Meehan (1963)
April Love (7) Pat Boone (1957)
April Skies (8) Jesus & Mary Chain (1987)
Are Friends Electric (1) Tubeway Army (1979)
Are You Gonna Go My Way (4) Lenny Kravitz (1993)
Are You Lonesome Tonight (1) Elvis Presley with The Jordanaires (1961)
Are You Lonesome Tonight? (re-issue) (2) Elvis Presley (2005)
Are You Ready For Love (1) Elton John (2003)
Are You Ready To Rock (8) Wizzard (1974)
Are You Sure (2) Allisons (1961)
Aria (5) Mr Acker Bilk, his Clarinet & Strings (1976)
Arms Around The World (4) Louise (1997)
Arms Of Mary (5) Sutherland Brothers & Quiver (1976)
Army Of Lovers (3) Lee Ryan (2005)
Army Of Me (10) Björk (1995)
Around The World (4) Ronnie Hilton (1957)
Around The World (5) Bing Crosby (1957)
Around The World (8) Gracie Fields (1957)
Around The World (7) East 17 (1994)
Around The World (5) Daft Punk (1997)
Art For Art's Sake (5) 10CC (1975)
Arthur's Theme (Best That You Can Do) (7) Christopher Cross (1982)
As (4) George Michael & Mary J Blige (1999)
As I Love You (re-entry) (1) Shirley Bassey (1959)
As Long As He Needs Me (2) Shirley Bassey (1960)
As Long As You Love Me (3) Backstreet Boys (1997)
As Tears Go By (9) Marianne Faithfull (1964)
As Time Goes By (5) Dooley Wilson (1977)
As Usual (5) Brenda Lee (1964)
As You Like It (5) Adam Faith (1962)
Ashes To Ashes (1) David Bowie (1980)
Ass Like That (4) Eminem (2005)
At My Most Beautiful (10) REM (1999)
At Night (6) Shakedown (2002)
At The Club / Saturday Night At The Movies (re-entry) (3) Drifters (1972)
At The Hop (3) Danny & The Juniors (1958)
Atlantis (2) Shadows (1963)
Atmosphere (7) Russ Abbot (1984)
Atomic (1) Blondie (1980)
Attention To Me (9) Nolans (1981)
Auf Weidersehen (10) Vera Lynn (1952)
Australia (7) Manic Street Preachers (1996)
Autobahn (11) Kraftwerk (1975)
Automatic (2) Pointer Sisters (1984)
Automatic High (2) S Club Juniors (2002)
Automatic Lover (4) Dee D Jackson (1978)
Automatically Sunshine (10) Supremes (1972)
Autumn Almanac (3) Kinks (1967)
Autumnsong (10) Manic Street Preachers (2007)
Avenging Angels (6) Space (1998)
Away From Here (8) Enemy (2007)
Axel F (2) Harold Faltermeyer (1985)
Axel F / Keep Pushin' (7) Clock (1995)
Axel F (1) Crazy Frog (2005)
Ay Ay Ay Ay Moosey (10) Modern Romance (1981)
Ayo Technology (2) 50 Cent featuring Justin Timberlake & Timbaland (2007)
Babe (1) Take That (1993)
Babe (6) Styx (1980)

Babooshka (5) Kate Bush (1980)
Baby (3) Justin Bieber featuring Ludacris (2010)
Baby Baby (4) Frankie Lymon & Teenagers (1957)
Baby Baby (2) Amy Grant (1991)
Baby Baby (5) Corona (1995)
Baby Boy (2) Beyonce featuring Sean Paul (2003)
Baby Boy (4) Big Brovaz (2003)
Baby Can I Hold You / Shooting Star (2) Boyzone / Stephen Gately (1997)
Baby Come Back (1) Equals (1968)
Baby Come Back (1) Pato Banton (1994)
Baby Come On Over (5) Samantha Mumba (2001)
Baby Don't Change Your Mind (4) Gladys Knight & The Pips (1977)
Baby Face (2) Little Richard (1959)
Baby Goodbye (5) Friday Hill (2005)
Baby I Don't Care (3) Transvision Vamp (1989)
Baby I Don't Care (6) Jennifer Ellison (2003)
Baby I Know (10) Rubettes (1977)
Baby I Love You (8) Dave Edmunds (1973)
Baby I Love You (8) Ramones (1980)
Baby I Love You (3) Jennifer Lopez (2004)
Baby I Love Your Way – Freebird (6) Will To Power (1989)
Baby I Love Your Way (2) Big Mountain (1994)
Baby It's You (7) Beatles (1995)
Baby It's You (8) JoJo featuring Bow Wow (2004)
Baby Jane (1) Rod Stewart (1983)
Baby Jump (re-entry) (1) Mungo Jerry (1971)
Baby Love (1) Supremes (1964)
Baby Make It Soon (9) Marmalade (1969)
Baby Now That I've Found You (1) Foundations (1967)
Baby One More Time (1) Britney Spears (1999)
Baby Please Don't Go (10) Them (1965)
Baby Roo / Where The Boys Are (5) Connie Francis (1961)
Babycakes (1) 3 Of A Kind (2004)
Babylon (5) David Gray (2000)
Babylon's Burning (7) Ruts (1979)
Baby's Coming Back / Transylvania (1) McFly (2007)
Baby's Got A Temper (5) Prodigy (2002)
Bachelor Boy / Next Time, The (1) Cliff Richard and The Shadows (1962)
Back For Good (1) Take That (1995)
Back Here (re-issue) (5) BBMak (2001)
Back Home (1) England World Cup Squad (1970)
Back In My Life (4) Alice Deejay (1999)
Back Off Boogaloo (2) Ringo Starr (1972)
Back Street Luv (4) Curved Air (1971)
Back To Basics (10) Shapeshifters (2005)
Back to Black (8) Amy Winehouse (2011)
Back to Life (However Do You Want Me) (1) Soul II Soul featuring Caron Wheeler (1989)
Back to The Sixties (4) Tight Fit (1981)
Back Together Again (3) Roberta Flack & Donny Hathaway (1980)
Backstage (4) Gene Pitney (1966)
Bad (3) Michael Jackson (1987)
Bad Actress (10) Terrorvision (1996)
Bad Bad Boy (10) Nazareth (1973)
Bad Boy (7) Marty Wilde (1959)
Bad Boys (1) Alexandra Burke featuring Flo Rida (2009)
Bad Boys (2) Wham! (1983)
Bad Day (2) Daniel Powter (2005)
Bad Day (8) REM (2003)
Bad Girl (10) Madonna (1993)
Bad Intentions (4) Dr Dre featuring Knoc-Turn'al (2002)
Bad Moon Rising (1) Creedence Clearwater Revival (1969)
Bad Romance (1) Lady Gaga (2009)
Bad To Me (1) Billy J Kramer And The Dakotas (1963)
Bad Touch, The (4) Bloodhound Gang (2000)
Badman Riddim (Jump) (7) Vato Gonzalez featuring Foreign Beggars (2011)
Bag It Up (1) Geri Halliwell (2000)
Baggy Trousers (3) Madness (1980)
Bailamos (4) Enrique Iglesias (1999)
Baker Street (2) Undercover (1992)

Baker Street (3) Gerry Rafferty (1978)
Ball Of Confusion (7) Temptations (1970)
Ball Park Incident (6) Wizzard (1972)
Ballad Of Bonnie And Clyde (1) Georgie Fame (1967)
Ballad Of Davy Crockett (2) Bill Hayes (1956)
Ballad Of Davy Crockett, The (3) Tennessee Ernie Ford (1956)
Ballad Of John And Yoko (1) Beatles (1969)
Ballad Of Paladin (10) Duane Eddy (1962)
Ballad Of Paul K, The / Ultraviolet (9) McFly (2005)
Ballad Of Tom Jones, The (4) Space with Cerys of Catatonia (1998)
Ballroom Blitz, The (2) Sweet (1973)
Bamboogie (2) Bamboo (1998)
Banana Boat Song (8) Shirley Bassey (1957)
Banana Boat Song (Day-O) (2) Harry Belafonte (1957)
Banana Republic (3) Boomtown Rats (1980)
Banana Rock (9) Wombles (1974)
Banana Splits (7) Dickies (1979)
Band Of Gold (1) Freda Payne (1970)
Band Of Gold (6) Don Cherry (1956)
Band On The Run (3) Paul McCartney & Wings (1974)
Bang Bang (2) B A Robertson (1979)
Bang Bang (My Baby Shot Me Down) (3) Cher (1966)
Bang Bang Bang (6) Mark Ronson & The Business Int (2010)
Bang Bang You're Dead (5) Dirty Pretty Things (2006)
Bangin' Man (3) Slade (1974)
Bangla-Desh (10) George Harrison (1971)
Banks Of The Ohio (6) Olivia Newton-John (1971)
Banner Man (3) Blue Mink (1971)
Barbados (1) Typically Tropical (1975)
Barbara Ann (3) Beach Boys (1966)
Barber's Adagio For Strings (4) William Orbit (1999)
Barbie Girl (1) first hit Aqua (1997)
Barcelona (2) Freddy Mercury & Montserrat Caballë (1987)
Barcelona (re-issue) (2) Freddy Mercury & Montserrat Caballë (1992)
Barrel Of A Gun (4) Depeche Mode (1997)
(Barry) Islands In The Stream (1) Vanesa Jenkins & Bryn West featuring Sir Tom Jones & Robin Gibb (2009)
Bartender And The Thief, The (3) Stereophonics (1998)
Basket Case (7) Green Day (1995)
Bass Down Low (10) Dev featuring The Cataracs (2011)
Bat Out Of Hell (re-issue) (8) Meat Loaf (1993)
Batdance (2) Prince (1989)
Battle (10) Wookie featuring Lain (2000)
Battle Of New Orleans (2) Lonnie Donegan & His Skiffle Group (1959)
Be Aggressive / I'm Easy (3) Faith No More (1993)
Be Alone No More (6) Another Level (1998)
Be Careful (7) Sparkle featuring R Kelly (1998)
Be Cool (7) Paffendorf (2002)
Be Faithful (1) Fatman Scoop featuring The Crooklyn Clan (2003)
Be Mine (10) Robyn (2008)
Be Mine (4) Lance Fortune (1960)
Be My Baby (4) Ronettes (1963)
Be My Baby (6) Vanessa Paradis (1992)
Be My Girl (2) Jim Dale (1957)
Be Quick Or Be Dead (2) Iron Maiden (1992)
Be The First To Believe (6) A1 (1999)
Be There (8) UNKLE featuring Ian Brown (1999)
Be With You / Last Goodbye (2) Atomic Kitten (2002)
Beat Again (1) JLS (2009)
Beat Dis (2) Bomb The Bass (1988)
Beat It (3) Michael Jackson (1983)
Beat Mama (9) Cast (1999)
Beat Surrender (1) Jam (1982)
Beat The Clock (10) Sparks (1979)
Beatles Movie Medley (10) Beatles (1982)
Beatnik Fly (8) Johnny & The Hurricanes (1960)
Beautiful (1) Christina Aguilera (2003)
Beautiful (10) Matt Darey with Marcella Woods (2002)
Beautiful (8) Akon featuring Kardinal Offishall & Colby O'Donis (2009)
Beautiful Day (1) U2 (2000)

Beautiful Girl (1) Sean Kingston (2007)
Beautiful Liar (1) Beyonce & Shakira (2007)
Beautiful Monster (1) Ne-Yo (2010)
Beautiful Ones (8) Suede (1996)
Beautiful People (4) Chris Brown featuring Benny Benassi (2011)
Beautiful Stranger (2) Madonna (1999)
Beauty And The Beast (9) Celine Dion & Peabo Bryson (1992)
Beauty And The Beast / All Out of Love (10) H & Claire (2002)
Because I Got High (1) Afroman (2001)
Because I Love You (The Postman Song) (6) Stevie B (1991)
Because Of You (3) Scanty Sandwich (2000)
Because Of You (4) Ne-Yo (2007)
Because Of You (7) Kelly Clarkson (2005)
Because The Night (5) Patti Smith Group (1978)
Because They're Young (2) Duane Eddy (1960)
Because We Want To (1) Billie (1998)
Because You Loved Me (5) Celine Dion (1996)
Because You're Mine (3) Mario Lanza (1952)
Because You're Mine (6) Nat 'King' Cole (1952)
Because You're Mine (re-entry) (10) Nat 'King' Cole (1953)
Bed Sitter (4) Soft Cell (1981)
Bedrock (9) Young Money featuring Lloyd (2010)
Beds Are Burning (re-issue) (6) Midnight Oil (1989)
Bedshaped (10) Keane (2004)
Bedtime Story (4) Madonna (1995)
Beep (2) Pussycat Dolls featuring Will I Am (2006)
Beetlebum (1) Blur (1997)
Before (7) Pet Shop Boys (1996)
Beg Steal Or Borrow (2) New Seekers (1972)
Beggin' (5) Madcon (2008)
Begin The Beguine (1) Julio Iglesias (1981)
Behind A Painted Smile (5) Isley Brothers (1969)
Behind Closed Doors (4) Peter Andre (2009)
Behind The Groove (6) Teena Marie (1980)
Behind These Hazel Eyes (9) Kelly Clarkson (2005)
Being Boiled (6) Human League (1982)
Being Brave (10) Menswear (1996)
Being Nobody (3) Richard X vs Liberty X (2003)
Being With You (1) Smokey Robinson (1981)
Belfast (8) Boney M (1977)
Belfast Child (1) Simple Minds (1989)
Believe (1) Cher (1998)
Believe In Me (8) Utah Saints (1993)
Belissima (4) DJ Quicksilver (1997)
Bell Bottom Blues (4) Alma Cogan (1954)
Belly Dancer (Bananza) (5) Akon (2005)
Ben (5) Marti Webb (1985)
Ben (7) Michael Jackson (1972)
Bend It (2) Dave Dee, Dozy, Beaky, Mick & Tich (1966)
Bend Me Shape Me (3) Amen Corner (1968)
Bernadette (8) Four Tops (1967)
Best Behaviour (10) N-Dubz (2010)
Best Disco In Town, The (10) Ritchie Family (1976)
Best In Me (8) Let Loose (1995)
Best Of Me, The (2) Cliff Richard (1989)
Best Of My Love (4) Emotions (1977)
Best Of You (4) Foo Fighters (2005)
Best Thing I Never Had (3) Beyoncé (2011)
Best Thing That Ever Happened To Me (7) Gladys Knight & The Pips (1975)
Best Things in Life Are Free (4) Luther Vandross & Janet Jackson (1992)
Best Things In Life Are Free, The (remix) (7) Luther Vandross & Janet Jackson (1995)
Best Years Of Our Lives (4) Modern Romance (1982)
Best, The (5) Tina Turner (1989)
Best, The (re-emergence) (9) Tina Turner (2010)
Bette Davis Eyes first and biggest hit (10) Kim Carnes (1981)
Better Best Forgotten (2) Steps (1999)
Better Day (9) Ocean Colour Scene (1997)
Better In Time / Footprints In The Sand (2) Leona Lewis (2008)
Better Love Next Time (8) Dr Hook (1980)

Better Off Alone (2) DJ Jurgen presents Alice DeeJay (1999)
Better The Devil You Know (2) Kylie Minogue (1990)
Better The Devil You Know / Say You'll Be Mine (4) Steps (1999)
Better Watch Out (10) Ant & Dec (1996)
Beverly Hills (9) Weezer (2005)
Beware Of The Dog (10) Jamelia (2006)
Beyond The Reef / It's Only Love (3) Elvis Presley (1980)
Beyond The Stars (8) David Whitfield (1955)
Big Apple (8) Kajagoogoo (1983)
Big Bad John (2) Jimmy Dean (1961)
Big Big World (5) Emilia (1998)
Big Boss Groove / Groovin' (You're The Best Thing) (5) Style Council (1984)
Big Boys Don't Cry / Rockin' Robin (10) Lolly (1999)
Big Brother UK TV Theme (4) Element Four (2000)
Big Fun (4) Gap Band (1986)
Big Fun (8) Inner City (1988)
Big Girl (You Are Beautiful) (9) Mika (2007)
Big Girls Don't Cry (2) Fergie (2007)
Big Hunk O' Love, A (4) Elvis Presley with The Jordanaires (1959)
Big In Japan (8) Alphaville (1984)
Big Love (9) Fleetwood Mac (1987)
Big Man (2) Four Preps (1958)
Big Mistake (2) Natalie Imbruglia (1998)
Big Seven (8) Judge Dread (1972)
Big Ship (8) Cliff Richard (1969)
Billie Jean (1) Michael Jackson (1983)
Billie Jean (re-emergence) (10) Michael Jackson (2009)
Billionaire (3) Travie Mccoy featuring Bruno Mars (2010)
Bills Bills Bills (6) Destiny's Child (1999)
Billy Don't Be A Hero (1) Paper Lace (1974)
Bimbo (7) Ruby Wright (1954)
Bing Bang (Time To Dance) (4) Lazy Town (2006)
Biology (4) Girls Aloud (2005)
Bionic Santa (10) Chris Hill (1976)
Bird Dog (2) Everly Brothers (1958)
Bird Of Paradise (6) Snowy White (1983)
Birdhouse In Your Soul (6) They Might Be Giants (1990)
Birdie Song (The Birdie Dance) (2) Tweets (1981)
Bitch (6) Meredith Brooks(1997)
Bitch / Brown Sugar / Let It Rock (2) Rolling Stones (1971)
Bits And Pieces (2) Dave Clark Five (1964)
Bitter Sweet Symphony (2) Verve (1997)
Bitterest Pill (I Ever Had To Swallow) (2) Jam (1982)
Black And Gold (2) Sam Sparro (2008)
Black And White (6) Greyhound (1971)
Black And White Town (6) Doves (2005)
Black and Yellow (5) Wiz Khalifa (2011)
Black Betty (7) Ram Jam (1977)
Black Coffee (1) All Saints (2000)
Black Hills Of Dakota (7) Doris Day (1954)
Black Is Black (2) La Belle Epoque (1977)
Black Is Black (2) Los Bravos (1966)
Black Night (2) Deep Purple (1970)
Black Or White (1) Michael Jackson (1991)
Black Skin Blue-Eyed Boys (9) Equals (1970)
Black Suits Comin' (Nod Ya Head) (3) Will Smith featuring Tra-Knox (2002)
Black Superman (Muhammad Ali) (7) Johnny Wakelin & Kinshasa Band (1975)
Black Velvet (2) Alannah Myles (1990)
Blackberry Way (1) Move (1968)
Black-Eyed Boy (5) Texas (1997)
Blame It On The Boogie (4) Big Fun (1989)
Blame It On The Boogie (8) Jacksons (1978)
(Blame It) On The Pony Express (7) Johnny Johnson and the Bandwagon (1970)
Blame It On The Weatherman (1) B*Witched (1999)
Blanket On The Ground (6) Billie Jo Spears (1975)
Bleeding Love (1) Leona Lewis (2007)

Bless You (5) Tony Orlando (1961)
Blind Faith (5) Chase & Status featuring Liam Bailey (2011)
Blind Vision (10) Blancmange (1983)
Blinded By The Light (6) Manfred Mann's Earth Band (1976)
Blinded By The Lights (10) Streets (2004)
Blinded By The Sun (7) Seahorses (1997)
Block Rockin' Beats (1) Chemical Brothers (1997)
Blockbuster (1) Sweet (1973)
Blood On The Dancefloor (1) Michael Jackson (1997)
Blood Sweat And Tears (6) V (2004)
Bloodnok's Rock 'N' Roll Call / Ying Tong Song (3) Goons (1956)
Blossom Fell, A (10) Ronnie Hilton (1955)
Blossom Fell, A (3) Nat 'King' Cole (1955)
Blossom Fell, A (9) Dickie Valentine (1955)
Blow The House Down (10) Living In A Box (1989)
Blow Ya Mind (6) Lock 'N' Load (2000)
Blowing Wild (2) Frankie Laine (1954)
Blue (Da Ba Dee) (1) Eiffel 65 (1999)
Blue Angels (6) Pras (1998)
Blue Bayou / Mean Woman Blues (3) Roy Orbison (1963)
Blue Eyes (3) Don Partridge (1968)
Blue Eyes (8) Elton John (1982)
Blue Guitar (8) Justin Hayward & John Lodge (1975)
Blue Is The Colour (5) Chelsea FC (1972)
Blue Jean (6) David Bowie (1984)
Blue Monday (re-entry) (9) New Order (1983)
Blue Monday (remix) (3) New Order (1988)
Blue Moon (1) Marcels (1961)
Blue Moon (9) Elvis Presley (1956)
Blue Moon / Only You (9) John Alford (1996)
Blue Orchid (9) White Stripes (2005)
Blue Room (8) Orb (1992)
Blue Savannah (3) Erasure (1990)
Blue Star (The Medic Theme) (2) Cyril Stapleton Orchestra (1955)
Blue Suede Shoes (10) Carl Perkins (1956)
Blue Suede Shoes (9) Elvis Presley (1956)
Blue Tango (8) Ray Martin Orchestra (1952)
Blue Tango (re-entry) (10) Ray Martin Orchestra (1952)
Blue Velvet (2) Bobby Vinton (1990)
Blueberry Hill (re-entry) (6) Fats Domino (1956)
Bluebottle Blues / I'm Walking Backwards For Christmas (4) Goons (1956)
Blurred (6) Pianoman (1996)
Blurry (8) Puddle Of Mudd (2002)
Bo Diddley (4) Buddy Holly (1963)
Boat That I Row, The (6) Lulu (1967)
Bobby's Girl (3) Susan Maughan (1962)
Bodies (2) Robbie Williams (2009)
Body And Soul (9) Mai Tai (1985)
Body Groove (3) Architechs featuring Nana (2000)
Body II Body (5) Samantha Mumba (2000)
Body Talk (4) Imagination (1981)
Bodyshakin' (3) 911 (1997)
Bohemian Like You (re-issue) (5) Dandy Warhols (2001)
Bohemian Rhapsody (1) Queen (1975)
Bohemian Rhapsody (9) G4 (2005)
Bohemian Rhapsody (re-issue) / These Are The Days Of Our Lives (1) Queen (1991)
Bomb Diggy (6) Another Level (1999)
Bomb! (These Sounds Fall Into My Mind) (5) Bucketheads (1995)
Boney M Megamix (7) Boney M (1992)
Bonkers (1) Dizzee Rascal & Armand Van Helden (2009)
Boogie 2nite (2) Booty Luv (2006)
Boogie Nights (2) Heatwave (1977)
Boogie Oogie Oogie (3) A Taste Of Honey (1978)
Boogie Wonderland (4) Earth Wind & Fire with The Emotions (1979)
Book Of Days (10) Enya (1992)
Book Of Love (8) Mudlarks (1958)
Book, The (5) David Whitfield (1954)
Book, The (re-entry) (10) David Whitfield (1954)
Boom Bang-A-Bang (2) Lulu (1969)

Boom Boom Boom (1) Outhere Brothers (1995)
Boom Boom Boom Boom (1) Vengaboys (1999)
Boom Boom Pow (1) Black Eyed Peas (2009)
Boom! Shake The Room (1) Jazzy Jeff & The Fresh Prince (1993)
Boombastic (1) Shaggy (1995)
Bootie Call (1) All Saints (1998)
Bootylicious (2) Destiny's Child (2001)
Bop Bop Baby (5) Westlife (2002)
Borderline (2) Madonna (1986)
Born Free (6) Vic Reeves & The Roman Numerals (1994)
Born in England (9) Twisted X (2004)
Born In The USA / I'm On Fire (5) Bruce Springsteen (1985)
Born Slippy (2) Underworld (1996)
Born This Way (3) Lady Gaga (2011)
Born To Be Alive (10) Patrick Hernandez (1979)
Born To Be With You (5) Dave Edmunds (1973)
Born To Be With You (8) Chordettes (1956)
Born To Make You Happy (1) Britney Spears (2000)
Born To Try (3) Delta Goodrem (2003)
Born Too Late (5) Poni-Tails (1958)
Born With A Smile On My Face (2) Stephanie De Sykes with Rain (1974)
Boss Drum (4) Shamen (1992)
Both Sides Now (14) Judy Collins (1970)
Both Sides Of The Story (7) Phil Collins (1993)
Boulevard Of Broken Dreams (5) Green Day (2004)
Bounce (2) Calvin Harris featuring Kelis (2011)
Bouncer, The (7) Kicks Like A Mule (1992)
Bound 4 Da Reload (Casualty) (1) Oxide & Neutrina (2000)
Bow Wow (That's My Name) (6) Lil Bow Wow (2001)
Boxer Beat (3) Jo Boxers (1983)
Boxer, The (6) Simon & Garfunkel (1969)
Boy Does Nothing, The (5) Alesha Dixon (2008)
Boy From New York City (2) Darts (1978)
Boy From Nowhere, A (2) Tom Jones (1987)
Boy Is Mine, The (2) Brandy & Monica (1998)
Boy Named Sue, A (4) Johnny Cash (1969)
Boy You Knock Me Out (3) Tatyana Ali featuring Will Smith (1999)
Boys (7) Britney Spears featuring P Williams (2002)
Boys (Summertime Love) (3) Sabrina (1988)
Boys And Girls (1) Pixie Lott (2009)
Boys Are Back In Town, The (8) Thin Lizzy (1976)
Boys Cry (8) Eden Kane (1964)
Boys Keep Swinging (7) David Bowie (1979)
Boys Of Summer, The (2) DJ Sammy (2003)
Boys Will Be Boys (re-entry) (3) Ordinary Boys (2006)
Brand New Key (4) Melanie (1972)
Brass In Pocket (1) Pretenders (1979)
Break Away (6) Beach Boys (1969)
Break My Stride (4) Matthew Wilder (1984)
Break The Night With Colour (3) Richard Ashcroft (2006)
Break The Rules (8) Status Quo (1974)
Break Your Heart (1) Taio Cruz (2009)
Breakaway (4) Tracey Ullman (1983)
Breakdance Party (9) Break Machine (1984)
Breakfast At Tiffany's (1) Deep Blue Something (1996)
Breakfast In America (9) Supertramp (1979)
Breakfast In Bed (6) UB40 featuring Chrissie Hynde (1988)
Breakin' ... There's No Stopping Us Now (5) Ollie & Jerry (1984)
Breakin' Down The Walls Of Heartache (4) Johnny Johnson & The Bandwagon (1968)
Breaking Free (9) Cast Of High School Musical (2006)
Breaking Up Is Hard To Do (3) Partridge Family (1972)
Breaking Up Is Hard To Do (7) Neil Sedaka (1962)
Breakout (4) Swing Out Sister (1986)
Breakthru (7) Queen (1989)
Breath Of Life (8) Erasure (1992)
Breathe (1) Blu Cantrell featuring Sean Paul (2003)
Breathe (1) Prodigy (1996)
Breathe (4) Erasure (2005)
Breathe Again (2) Toni Braxton (1994)
Breathe Easy (4) Blue (2004)
Breathe In (6) Lucie Silvas (2005)
Breathe Slow (3) Alesha Dixon (2009)

Breathless (1) Corrs (2000)
Breathless (6) Shayne Ward (2007)
Breathless (8) Jerry Lee Lewis (1958)
Breeze And I, The (5) Caterina Valente (1955)
Breeze On By (8) Donny Osmond (2004)
Brianstorm (2) Arctic Monkeys (2007)
Bridge Of Sighs, The (9) David Whitfield (1953)
Bridge Over Troubled Water (1) Simon & Garfunkel (1970)
Bridget The Midget (Queen of the Blues) (2) Ray Stevens (1971)
Bright Eyes (1) Art Garfunkel (1979)
Bright Eyes / New Beginning (3) Stephen Gately (2000)
Brimful Of Asha (remix) (1) Cornershop (1998)
Bring A Little Water Sylvie / Dead Or Alive (7) Lonnie Donegan & His Skiffle Group (1956)
Bring It All Back (1) S Club 7 (1999)
Bring It On / My Lover's Prayer (5) Alistair Griffin featuring Robin Gibb (2004)
Bring It On Home To Me (7) Animals (1965)
Bring Me Edelweiss (5) Edelweiss (1989)
Bring Me To Life (1) Evanescence (2003)
Bring Your Daughter ... To The Slaughter (1) Iron Maiden (1991)
Bringing On Back The Good Times (9) Love Affair (1969)
Britannia Rag (re-entry) (5) Winifred Atwell (1953)
British Hustle / Peace On Earth (8) Hi Tension (1978)
Brits 1990, The (2) Various Artists (1990)
Broken Bones (8) Love Inc (2003)
Broken Down Angel (9) Nazareth (1973)
Broken Hearted Melody (7) Sarah Vaughan (1959)
Broken Heels (8) Alexandra Burke (2009)
Broken Record (8) Katy B (2011)
Broken Silence (9) So Solid Crew (2003)
Broken Strings (2) James Morrison featuring Nelly Furtado (2008)
Broken Wings (4) Mr Mister (1985)
Broken Wings (6) Art & Dotty Todd (1953)
Broken Wings (re-entry) (1) Stargazers (1953)
Brontosaurus (7) Move (1970)
Brother Louie (4) Modern Talking (1986)
Brother Louie (7) Hot Chocolate (1973)
Brown Girl In The Ring / Rivers Of Babylon (1) Boney M (1978)
Brown Sugar / Bitch / Let It Rock (2) Rolling Stones (1971)
Brown-eyed Handsome Man (3) Buddy Holly (1963)
Bubblin' (9) Blue (2004)
Buck Rogers (5) Feeder (2001)
Buddy / The Magic Number (7) De La Soul (1989)
Buffalo Gals (9) Malcolm McLaren and The World Famous Supreme Team (1982)
Buffalo Soldier (4) Bob Marley & The Wailers (1983)
Buffalo Stance (3) Neneh Cherry (1988)
Bug A Boo (9) Destiny's Child (1999)
Buggin' Me (6) True Steppers with Dane Bowers (2000)
Build Me Up Buttercup (2) Foundations (1968)
Bullet In The Gun (2000 remix) (7) Planet Perfecto (2000)
Bulletproof (1) La Roux (2009)
Bulls On Parade (8) Rage Against The Machine (1996)
Bump N' Grind (8) R Kelly (1995)
Bump, The (3) Kenny (1974)
Bunsen Burner (9) John Otway (2002)
Buona Sera (7) Acker Bilk & His Paramount Jazz Band (1960)
Burn (1) Usher (2004)
Burning Bridges (On And Off And On Again) (5) Status Quo (1988)
Burning Down The House (7) Tom Jones & The Cardigans (1999)
Burning Heart (5) Survivor (1986)
Burning Love (7) Elvis Presley (1972)
Bus Stop (5) Hollies (1966)
Business (6) Eminem (2003)
But I Do (3) Clarence 'Frogman' Henry (1961)
Butterfingers (re-entry) (8) Tommy Steele (1957)
Butterfly (1) Andy Williams (1957)
Butterfly (3) Crazy Town (2001)
Buttons (3) Pussycat Dolls featuring Snoop Dogg (2006)

Buzzin' (6) Mann featuring 50 Cent (2011)
B With Me (5) Mis-Teeq (2003)
By The Way (2) Red Hot Chili Peppers (2002)
Bye Bye Baby (1) Bay City Rollers (1975)
Bye Bye Baby (7) TQ (1999)
Bye Bye Bye (3) N Sync (2000)
Bye Bye Love (6) first hit Everly Brothers (1957)
C Moon / Hi Hi Hi (5) Wings (1972)
Ca Plane Pour Moi (8) Plastic Bertrand (1978)
Cabaret / What A Wonderful World (1) Louis Armstrong and his All-Stars (1968)
Calendar Girl (8) Neil Sedaka (1961)
California (9) Phantom Planet (2005)
California Dreamin' (re-entry) (9) Mamas & The Papas (1997)
California Gurls (1) Katy Perry featuring Snoop Dogg (2010)
California King Bed (8) Rihanna (2011)
California Love (6) 2Pac featuring Dr Dre (1996)
California Man (7) Move (1972)
Call Me (1) Blondie (1980)
Call Me (2) Spagna (1987)
(Call Me) Number One (2) Tremeloes (1969)
Call Me When You're Sober (4) Evanescence (2006)
Call My Name (10) Charlotte Church (2005)
Call On Me (1) Eric Prydz (2004)
Call The Shots (3) Girls Aloud (2007)
Call Up The Groups (3) Barron Knights with Duke D'Mond (1964)
Call, The (8) Backstreet Boys (2001)
Calling (7) Geri Halliwell (2001)
Calling All The Heroes (6) It Bites (1986)
Calling Occupants Of Interplanetary Craft (9) Carpenters (1977)
Calling Your Name (4) Marilyn (1983)
Calm Down Dearest (9) Jamie T (2007)
Camels (9) Santos (2001)
Camouflage (4) Stan Ridgway (1986)
Can Can (3) Bad Manners (1981)
Can Can You Party (8) Jive Bunny & The Mastermixers (1990)
Can I Have It Like That (5) Pharrell featuring Gwen Stefani (2005)
Can I Play With Madness (3) Iron Maiden (1988)
Can I Take You Home Little Girl (10) Drifters (1975)
Can I Touch You ... There (6) Michael Bolton (1995)
Can The Can (1) Suzi Quatro (1973)
Can We Fix It? (1) Bob The Builder (2000)
Can You Feel It (6) Jacksons (1981)
Can You Feel It / Hip to Hip (5) V (2004)
Can You Feel The Force (5) Real Thing (1979)
Can You Forgive Her (7) Pet Shop Boys (1993)
Candida (9) Dawn (1971)
Candle In The Wind (re-issue) (5) Elton John (1988)
Candle In The Wind 97 / Something About The Way You Look Tonight (1) Elton John (1997)
Candy (5) Aggro Santos featuring Kimberly Wyatt (2010)
Candy (6) Mandy Moore (2000)
Candy Girl (1) New Edition (1983)
Candy Man (6) Brian Poole & TheTremeloes (1964)
Candy Shop (4) 50 Cent (2005)
Canned Heat (4) Jamiroquai (1999)
Cannonball (1) Little Mix (2011)
Cannonball (9) Damien Rice (2011)
Can't Be With You Tonight (2) Judy Boucher (1987)
Can't Buy Me Love (1) Beatles (1964)
Can't Fight The Moonlight (1) LeAnn Rimes (2000)
Can't Get By Without You (2) Real Thing (1976)
Can't Get By Without You (The Second Decade Remix) (6) Real Thing (1986)
Can't Get Enough (10) Raghav (2004)
Can't Get Enough (8) Soulsearcher (1999)
Can't Get Enough Of Your Love Babe (8) Barry White (1974)
Can't Get It Back (8) Mis-Teeq (2003)
Can't Get Used To Losing You (2) Andy Williams (1963)
Can't Get Used To Losing You (3) Beat (1983)

430

Can't Get You Out Of My Head (1) Kylie Minogue (2001)
Can't Give You Anything (But My Love) (1) Stylistics (1975)
Can't Help Falling In Love (3) Andy Williams (1970)
Can't Help Falling In Love (4) Stylistics (1976)
Can't Help Falling in Love / Rock A Hula Baby (1) Elvis Presley with The Jordanaires (1962)
Can't Help Falling In Love / Rock A Hula Baby (re-issue) (3) Elvis Presley (2005)
Can't Hold Us Down (6) Christina Aguilera featuring Lil' Kim (2003)
Can't I (9) Nat 'King' Cole (1953)
Can't I (re-entry) (10) Nat 'King' Cole (1953)
Can't I (re-entry) (6) Nat 'King' Cole (1953)
Can't Keep This Feeling In (10) Cliff Richard (1998)
Can't Nobody (5) Kelly Rowland (2003)
Can't Shake The Feeling (8) Big Fun (1989)
Can't Speak French (9) Girls Aloud (2008)
Can't Stand Losing You (re-release) (2) Police (1979)
Can't Stand Me Now (2) Libertines (2004)
Can't Stay Away From You (7) Gloria Estefan & Miami Sound Machine (1989)
Can't Take My Eyes Off You (4) Boystown Gang (1982)
Can't Take My Eyes Off You (5) Andy Williams (1968)
Can't Take My Eyes Off You / Where The Streets Have No Name / How Can you Expect To Be Taken Seriously (4) Pet Shop Boys (1991)
Can't Wait Another Minute (7) Five Star (1986)
Can't You See That She's Mine (10) The Dave Clark Five (1964)
Cantina Band / Star Wars Theme (7) Meco (1977)
Capstick Comes Home / The Sheffield Grinder(3) Tony Capstick (1981)
Captain Beaky / Wilfred the Weasel (5) Keith Michell (1980)
Captain Of Her Heart, The (8) Double (1986)
Car 67 (7) Driver 67 (1978)
Car Wash (4) Christina Aguilera featuring Missy Elliott (2004)
Car Wash (9) Rose Royce (1976)
Cara Mia (1) David Whitfield with Mantovani (1954)
Caramel (9) City High featuring Eve (2002)
Caravan Of Love (1) Housemartins (1986)
Careless Hands (6) Des O'Connor (1967)
Careless Whisper (1) George Michael (1984)
Caribbean Disco Show, The (8) Lobo (1981)
Caribbean Queen (No More Love On the Run) (6) Billy Ocean (1984)
Carnation / Going Underground (6) Liam Gallagher and Steve Craddock (1999)
Carnaval De Paris (5) Dario G (1998)
Carnival (72) first hit Cardigans (1995)
Carnival Girl (9) Texas featuring Kardinal Offishall (2003)
Carnival Is Over, The (1) Seekers (1965)
Carolina Moon / Stupid Cupid (1) Connie Francis (1958)
Caroline (5) Status Quo (1973)
Carrie (4) Cliff Richard (1980)
Carrie-Anne (3) Hollies (1967)
Carry Me Home (9) Gloworm (1994)
Carry Out (6) Timbaland featuring Justin Timberlake (2010)
Cars (1) Gary Numan (1979)
Cartoon Heroes (7) Aqua (2000)
Casanova (9) Levert (1987)
Case Of The Ex (3) Mya (2001)
Cassius (7) Cassius 1999 (1999)
Cast Your Fate To The Wind (5) Sounds Orchestral (1964)
Castle Rock / Cut Some Rug (7) Bluetones (1996)
Castles In The Sky (3) Ian Van Dahl (2001)
Cat Amongst The Pigeons / Silent Night (2) Bros (1988)
Cat Crept In, The (2) Mud (1974)
Catch A Falling Star (9) Perry Como (1958)
Catch The Wind (4) Donovan (1965)
Catch Us If You Can (5) Dave Clark Five (1965)
Catch You (8) Sophie Ellis-Bextor (2007)
Cathy's Clown (1) Everly Brothers (1960)
Cats In The Cradle (7) Ugly Kid Joe (1993)
Caught In A Moment (8) Sugababes (2004)
Caught In The Middle (2) A1 (2002)
Caught Out There (4) Kelis (2000)

Caught Up (9) Usher (2005)
Causing A Commotion (4) Madonna (1987)
Cecilia (4) Suggs and Louchie Lou & Michie One (1996)
Celebration (3) Madonna (2009)
Celebration (7) Kool & The Gang (1980)
Centerfold (3) J Geils Band (1982)
Certain Smile, A (4) Johnny Mathis (1958)
C'est La Vie (1) B*Witched (1998)
C'est La Vie (3) Robbie Nevil (1986)
Cha Cha Slide (1) DJ Casper (2004)
Chain Gang (9) Jimmy Young (1956)
Chain Gang (9) Sam Cooke (1960)
Chain Reaction (1) Diana Ross (1986)
Chain Reaction / One For Sorrow (2) Steps (2001)
Chains (6) Tina Arena (1994)
Champion (2) Chipmunk featuring Chris Brown (2011)
Chance (9) Big Country (1983)
Change (10) Lisa Stansfield (1991)
Change (4) Tears For Fears (1983)
Change (8) Daniel Merriweather featuring Wale (2009)
Change Would Do You Good, A (8) Sheryl Crow (1997)
Changed the Way You Kiss Me (1) Example (2011)
Changes (1) Ozzy & Kelly Osbourne (2003)
Changes (10) Will Young (2008)
Changes (3) 2Pac (1999)
Changing Partners (10) Bing Crosby (1954)
Changing Partners (4) Kay Starr (1954)
Changing Partners (re-entry) (9) Bing Crosby (1954)
Changingman, The (7) Paul Weller (1995)
Chanson D'Amour (1) Manhattan Transfer (1977)
Chant No. 1 (I Don't Need This Pressure On) (3) Spandau Ballet (1981)
Charlie Brown (6) Coasters (1959)
Charly (3) Prodigy (1991)
Charmaine (6) Bachelors (1963)
Charmless Man (5) Blur (1996)
Chase The Sun (5) Planet Funk (2001)
Chasing Cars (6) Snow Patrol (2006)
Chasing Cars (re-entry) (9) Snow Patrol (2007)
Chasing Pavements (2) Adele (2008)
Ch-Check It Out (8) Beastie Boys (2004)
Check On It (3) Beyonce featuring Slim Thug (2006)
Check Out The Groove (10) Bobby Thurston (1980)
Check This Out (6) LA Mix (1988)
Checkin' It Out (3) Lil' Chris (2006)
Cheeky Song (Touch My Bum) (2) Cheeky Girls (2002)
Chelsea Dagger (5) Fratellis (2006)
Chequered Love (4) Kim Wilde (1981)
Cherish (3) Madonna (1989)
Cherish (4) Kool & The Gang (1985)
Cherish / Could It Be Forever (2) David Cassidy (1972)
Cherry Pink And Apple Blossom White (1) Perez 'Prez' Prado (King of the Mambo) (1955)
Cherry Pink And Apple Blossom White (1) Eddie Calvert (1955)
Chi Mai (The Theme From The Life And Times Of Lloyd George) (2) Ennio Morricone (1981)
Chicka Boom (5) Guy Mitchell (1953)
Chicka Boom (re-entry) (4) Guy Mitchell (1954)
Chicken Song, The (1) Spitting Image (1986)
Child (3) Mark Owen (1996)
Child's Prayer, A (7) Hot Chocolate (1975)
Children (2) Robert Miles (1996)
Children Of The Revolution (2) T Rex (1972)
China Girl (2) David Bowie (1983)
China In Your Hand (1) T'Pau (1987)
China Tea (5) Russ Conway (1959)
Chiquitita (2) Abba (1979)
Chirpy Chirpy Cheep Cheep (1) Middle Of The Road (1971)
Chocolate (6) Kylie Minogue (2004)
Chocolate Box (9) Bros (1989)
Chocolate Salty Balls (1) Chef (1998)
Choose Life (6) PF Project featuring Ewan McGregor (1997)
Chorus (3) Erasure (1991)
Chosen Few, The (7) Dooleys (1979)
Christmas Alphabet (1) Dickie Valentine (1955)

Christmas Island (8) Dickie Valentine (1956)
Christmas Time (Don't Let The Bells End) (2) Darkness (2003)
Church Of The Poison Mind (2) Culture Club (1983)
Cigarettes And Alcohol (7) Oasis (1994)
Cinderella Rockefella (1) Esther & Abi Ofarim (1968)
Cindy Incidentally (2) Faces (1973)
Cindy Oh Cindy (5) Eddie Fisher (1956)
Circle In The Sand (4) Belinda Carlisle (1988)
Circle, The (6) Ocean Colour Scene (1996)
Circles (4) New Seekers (1972)
Circus, The (6) Erasure (1987)
City Of Blinding Lights (2) U2 (2005)
Clair (1) Gilbert O'Sullivan (1972)
Clairvoyant, The (6) Iron Maiden (1988)
Clap Back / Reigns (9) Ja Rule (2003)
Clapping Song, The (6) Shirley Ellis (1965)
Classic (8) Adrian Gurvitz (1982)
Classical Gas (9) Mason Williams (1968)
Claudette / All I Have To Do Is Dream (1) Everly Brothers (1958)
Cleanin' Out My Closet (4) Eminem (2002)
Clementine (3) Mark Owen (1997)
Clementine (8) Bobby Darin (1960)
Cleopatra's Theme (3) Cleopatra (1998)
Climb Ev'ry Mountain / Reach For The Stars (1) Shirley Bassey (1961)
Climb, The (1) Joe McElderry (2009)
Clint Eastwood (4) Gorillaz (2001)
Clocks (9) Coldplay (2003)
Close (To The Edit) (8) Art Of Noise (1984)
Close The Door (6) Stargazers (1955)
Close To You (6) Carpenters (1970)
Close To You (7) Maxi Priest (1990)
Close To You (9) Marti Pellow (2001)
Closer (1) Ne-Yo (2008)
Closer (10) Travis (2007)
Closer Than Close (4) Rosie Gaines (1997)
Closer to Me (4) Five (2001)
Closest Thing To Crazy, The (10) Katie Melua (2003)
Clothes Off!!! (5) Gym Class Heroes (2007)
Cloud Lucky Seven (2) Guy Mitchell (1953)
Cloud Number 9 (6) Bryan Adams (1999)
Clouds Across The Moon (6) Rah Band (1985)
Club Can't Handle Me (1) Flo Rida featuring David Guetta (2010)
Club Is Alive, The (1) JLS (2010)
Club Tropicana (4) Wham! (1983)
C'Mon Everybody (3) Sex Pistols (1979)
C'Mon Everybody (6) Eddie Cochran (1959)
Co-Co (2) Sweet (1971)
Coco Jamboo (8) Mr President (1997)
Cognoscenti Vs Intelligentsia (4) Cuban Boys (1999)
Cold As Ice (4) MOP (2001)
Colette (9) Billy Fury (1960)
Collide (4) Leona Lewis & Avicii (2011)
Colourblind (1) Darius (2002)
Colours (4) Donovan (1965)
Combine Harvester (Brand New Key) (1) Wurzels (1976)
Come and Get It (4) Badfinger (1970)
Come And Stay With Me (4) Marianne Faithfull (1965)
Come As You Are (9) Beverley Knight (2004)
Come As You Are (9) Nirvana (1992)
Come Baby Come (3) K7 (1993)
Come Back And Shake Me (3) Clodagh Rodgers (1969)
Come Back And Stay (4) Paul Young (1983)
Come Back Brighter (8) Reef (1997)
Come Back Darling (10) UB40 (1998)
Come Back My Love (2) Darts (1978)
Come Back To What You Know (6) Embrace (1998)
Come Get Some (7) Rooster (2004)
Come In Out Of The Rain (8) Wendy Moten (1994)
Come Into My Life (7) Joyce Sims (1988)
Come Into My World (8) Kylie Minogue (2002)

Come Live With Me (5) Heaven 17 (1983)
Come On Eileen (1) Dexy's Midnight Runners (1982)
Come On England (2) England's Barmy Army (2004)
Come On Girl (5) Taio Cruz (2008)
Come On Let's Go (10) Tommy Steele (1958)
Come On Over (10) Kym Marsh (2003)
Come On Over Baby (All I Want Is You) (8) Christina Aguilera (2000)
Come On Over To My Place (re-issue) (9) Drifters (1972)
Come On You Reds (1) Manchester United Football Club (1994)
Come Outside (1) Mike Sarne with Wendy Richard (1962)
Come Play With Me (10) Wedding Present (1992)
Come Prima (2) Marino Marini & His Quartet (1958)
Come Softly To Me (6) Fleetwoods (1959)
Come Softly To Me (9) Frankie Vaughan & The Kaye Sisters (1959)
Come To Me (4) P Diddy featuring Nicole Scherzinger (2006)
Come Together / Something (4) Beatles (1969)
Come Together / Remember The Time (3) Michael Jackson (1992)
Come Tomorrow (4) Manfred Mann (1965)
Come Undone (4) Robbie Williams (2003)
Come What May (2) Vicky Leandros (1972)
Come With Me (2) Puff Daddy featuring Jimmy Page (1998)
Come With Me (6) Special D (2004)
Comes A-Long A-Love (1) Kay Starr (1952)
Comfortably Numb (10) Scissor Sisters (2004)
Coming Around (5) Travis (2000)
Coming Around Again (10) Carly Simon (1987)
Coming Home (4) Diddy-Dirty Money featuring Skylar Grey (2011)
Coming Home Now (4) Boyzone (1996)
Coming Up (2) Paul McCartney (1980)
Commander (9) Kelly Rowland featuring David Guetta (2010)
Common People (2) Pulp (1995)
Communication (Somebody Answer The) (5) Mario Piu (1999)
Complete (4) Jaimeson (2003)
Complex (6) Gary Numan (1979)
Complicated (3) Avril Lavigne (2002)
Compliments On Your Kiss (2) Red Dragon with Brian & Tony Gold (1994)
Computer Love / The Model (re-entry) (1) Kraftwerk (1981)
Concrete And Clay (1) Unit Four Plus Two (1965)
Condemnation (9) Depeche Mode (1993)
Confessin' (1) Frank Ifield (1963)
Confessions Part II / My Boo (5) Usher (2004)
Confide In Me (2) Kylie Minogue (1994)
Confusion / Last Train To Electric Light London (8) Orchestra (1979)
Congratulations (1) Cliff Richard (1968)
Constantly (4) Cliff Richard (1964)
Contact (6) Edwin Starr (1979)
Control Myself (2) LL Cool J featuring Jennifer Lopez (2006)
Controversy (5) Prince (1993)
Conversations (7) Cilla Black (1969)
Convoy (2) C W McCall (1976)
Convoy G.B. (4) Laurie Lingo & The Dipsticks (1976)
Cookie Jar (6) Gym Class Heroes featuring The Dream (2008)
Cool For Cats (2) Squeeze (1979)
Cool Water (2) Frankie Laine (1955)
Cooler Than Me (5) Mike Posner (2010)
Cornflake Girl (4) Tori Amos (1994)
Coronation Rag (re-entry) (5) Winifred Atwell (1953)
Cosmic Girl (6) Jamiroquai (1996)
Cotton Eye Joe (1) Rednex (1994)
Cottonfields (5) Beach Boys (1970)
Could Have Told You So (6) Halo James (1989)
Could I Have This Kiss Forever (7) Whitney Houston & Enrique Iglesias (2000)
Could It Be Forever / Cherish (2) David Cassidy (1972)
Could It Be I'm Falling In Love (5) David Grant & Jaki Graham (1985)

Could It Be Magic (3) Take That (1992)
Could You Be Loved (5) Bob Marley & The Wailers (1980)
Couldn't Get It Right (10) Climax Blues Band (1976)
Could've Been (4) Tiffany (1988)
Counting Teardrops (4) Emile Ford & The Checkmates (1960)
Country Girl (5) Primal Scream (2006)
Country House (1) Blur (1995)
Country Roads (7) Hermes House Band (2001)
County Grammar (see Hot S**t county Grammar)
Cover Girl (4) New Kids On The Block (1990)
Coward Of The County (1) Kenny Rogers (1980)
Cowpuncher's Cantata (re-entry) (6) Max Bygraves (1953)
Coz I Luv You (1) Slade (1971)
Crack A Bottle (4) Eminem featuring Dr Dre & 50 Cent (2009)
Crackers International EP (2) Erasure (1988)
Cracklin' Rosie (3) Neil Diamond (1970)
Cradle (10) Atomic Kitten (2005)
Cradle Of Love (2) Johnny Preston (1960)
Crank That (Soulja Boy) (2) Soulja Boy Tellem (2007)
Crash (5) Primitives (1988)
Crashed The Wedding (1) Busted (2003)
Crazy (1) Gnarls Barkley (2006)
Crazy (2) Seal (1990)
Crazy (remix) (6) Mark Morrison (1996)
Crazy Chick (2) Charlotte Church (2005)
Crazy Crazy Nights (4) Kiss (1987)
Crazy For You (2) Madonna (1985)
Crazy For You (remix) (2) Madonna (1991)
Crazy For You (2) Let Loose (1994)
Crazy Horses (2) Osmonds (1972)
Crazy In Love (1) Beyonce (Knowles) (2003)
Crazy Little Party Girl (7) Aaron Carter (1998)
Crazy Little Thing Called Love (2) Queen (1979)
Crazy Love (10) M J Cole (2000)
Crazy Rap (10) Afroman (2002)
Creep (re-entry), The (10) Ken Mackintosh Orchestra (1954)
Creep (7) Radiohead (1993)
Creep (re-issue) (6) TLC (1996)
Creeps, The (7) Camille Jones vs Fedde Le Grande (2007)
Creeps, The (Get On The Dancefloor) (9) Freaks (2007)
Creeque Alley (9) Mamas & The Papas (1967)
Criticize (4) Alexander O'Neal (1987)
Crockett's Theme (2) Jan Hammer (1987)
Crocodile Rock (5) Elton John (1972)
Crocodile Shoes (4) Jimmy Nail (1994)
Cross My Broken Heart (6) Sinitta (1988)
Crossfire (8) Brandon Flowers (2010)
Crossroads (1) Blazin' Squad (2002)
Crown, The (6) Gary Byrd & The GB Experience (1983)
Cruel Summer (8) Ace Of Base (1998)
Cruel Summer (8) Bananarama (1983)
Cruise Into Christmas (10) Jane McDonald (1998)
Cruising / So Macho (2) Sinitta (1986)
Crunch, The (6) Rah Band (1977)
Crush (4) Jennifer Paige (1998)
Crush On You (5) Jets (1987)
Crush On You (9) Aaron Carter (1997)
Cry (2) Kym Marsh (2003)
Cry For Help (7) Rick Astley (1991)
Cry For You (5) September (2008)
Cry Just A Little Bit (3) Shakin' Stevens (1983)
Cry Me A River (2) Justin Timberlake (2003)
Cry Wolf (5) A-Ha (1986)
Cryin' In The Rain (6) Everly Brothers (1962)
Crying (1) Don McLean (1980)
Crying Game, The (5) Dave Berry (1964)
Crying In The Chapel (re-entry) (7) Lee Lawrence (1953)
Crying In The Chapel (1) Elvis Presley with The Jordanaires (1965)
Crying In The Chapel (re-issue) (2) Elvis Presley (2005)
Crystal (8) New Order (2001)
Cubik / Olympic (10) 808 State (1990)
Cuddly Toy (re-issue) (4) Roachford (1989)
Cuff Of My Shirt (9) Guy Mitchell (1954)
Cult Of Snap (8) Snap (1990)

Cum On Feel The Noize (1) Slade (1973)
Cumberland Gap (1) Lonnie Donegan & His Skiffle Group (1957)
Cumberland Gap (10) Vipers Skiffle Group (1957)
Cupid (6) Johnny Nash (1969)
Cupid (7) Sam Cooke (1961)
Cupid's Chokehold (3) Gym Class Heroes (2007)
Cupid – I've Loved You For A Long Time (4) Detroit Spinners (1980)
Curtain Falls (4) Blue (2004)
Cut Some Rug / Castle Rock (7) Bluetones (1996)
Cutt Off (8) Kasabian (2005)
Cutter, The (8) Echo And The Bunnymen (1983)
C U When You Get There (3) Coolio featuring 40 Thevz (1997)
D.I.S.C.O. (2) Ottowan (1980)
D.I.V.O.R.C.E. (1) Billy Connolly (1975)
Da Da Da (2) Trio (1982)
Da Doo Ron Ron (5) Crystals (1963)
Da Funk / Musique (7) Daft Punk (1997)
Da Ya Think I'm Sexy? (1) Rod Stewart (1978)
Da Ya Think I'm Sexy? (7) N-Trance featuring Rod Stewart (1997)
Da Ya Think I'm Sexy? (10) Girls Of FHM (2004)
Daddy Cool (6) Boney M (1976)
Daddy Cool / The Girl Can't Help It (6) Darts (1977)
Daddy's Home (2) Cliff Richard (1981)
Dakota (1) Stereophonics (2005)
Damned On 45 / Glad It's All Over (6) Captain Sensible (1984)
Dance Away (2) Roxy Music (1979)
Dance Dance (8) Fall Out Boy (2006)
Dance Dance Dance (Yowsah Yowsah Yowsah) (6) Chic (1977)
Dance For Me (6) Sisqo (2001)
Dance Into The Light (9) Phil Collins (1996)
Dance Little Lady Dance (6) Tina Charles (1976)
Dance On (1) Shadows (1962)
Dance The Night Away (4) Mavericks (1998)
Dance To The Music (7) Sly & The Family Stone (1968)
Dance With Guitar Man (4) Duane Eddy & The Rebelettes (1962)
Dance With Me (10) Debelah Morgan (2001)
Dance With The Devil (3) Cozy Powell (1973)
Dance (With U) (2) Lemar (2003)
Dance Wiv Me (1) Dizzee Rascal featuring Calvin Harris & Chrome (2008)
Dance Yourself Dizzy (2) Liquid Gold (1980)
Dancin' Party (4) Showaddywaddy (1977)
Dancing In The City (3) Marshall Hain (1978)
Dancing In The Dark (re-entry) (4) Bruce Springsteen (1985)
Dancing In The Dark (10) Micky Modelle vs Jessy (2006)
Dancing In The Moonlight (remix) (7) Toploader (2000)
Dancing In The Street (1) David Bowie & Mick Jagger (1985)
Dancing In The Street (re-issue) (4) Martha Reeves & The Vandellas (1969)
(Dancing) On A Saturday Night (2) Barry Blue (1973)
Dancing On My Own (8) Robyn (2010)
Dancing On The Ceiling (7) Lionel Richie (1986)
Dancing On The Floor (Hooked On Love) (10) Third World (1981)
Dancing Queen (1) Abba (1976)
Dancing Tight (4) Galaxy featuring Phil Fearon (1983)
Dance with Me Tonight (1) Olly Murs (2011)
Dancing With Tears In My Eyes (3) Ultravox (1984)
Dancing With The Captain (8) Paul Nicholas (1976)
Dandelion / We Love You (8) Rolling Stones (1967)
Danger Games (8) Pinkees (1982)
Danger High Voltage (2) Electric Six (2003)
Dangerous / Listen To Your Heart (6) Roxette (1990)
Dani California (2) Red Hot Chili Peppers (2006)
Daniel (4) Elton John (1973)
Dare (1) Gorillaz (2005)
Darlin' (6) Frankie Miller (1978)
Dat (6) Pluto Shervington (1976)
Daughter Of Darkness (5) Tom Jones (1970)
Davy's On The Road Again (6) Manfred Mann's Earth Band (1978)
Day After Day (10) Badfinger (1972)
Day And Night (1) Billie Piper (2000)

Day I Met Marie, The (10) Cliff Richard (1967)
Day n Nite (2) Kid Cudi vs Crookers (2009)
Day The Rains Came, The (1) Jane Morgan (1958)
Day Trip To Bangor (Didn't We Have A Lovely Time) (3) Fiddler's Dram (1979)
Day Tripper / We Can Work It Out (1) Beatles (1965)
Day We Caught The Train, The (4) Ocean Colour Scene (1996)
Day We Find Love, The (4) 911 (1997)
Day Without Love, A (6) Love Affair (1968)
Daydream (2) Lovin' Spoonful (1966)
Daydream Believer (5) Monkees (1967)
Daydreamer / The Puppy Song (1) David Cassidy (1973)
Daydreamin' (6) Tatyana Ali (1998)
Days Of Pearly Spencer, The (4) Marc Almond (1992)
Daysleeper (6) REM (1998)
D-Days (10) Hazel O'Connor (1981)
De Do Do Do De Da Da Da (5) Police (1980)
Dead And Gone (4) TI featuring Justin Timberlake (2009)
Dead End Street (5) Kinks (1966)
Dead From The Waist Down (7) Catatonia (1999)
Dead Giveaway (8) Shalamar (1983)
Dead Or Alive / Bring A Little Water Sylvie (7) Lonnie Donegan & His Skiffle Group (1956)
Dead Ringer For Love (5) Meat Loaf (1981)
Dean And I, The (10) 10CC (1973)
Dear Jessie (5) Madonna (1989)
Dear John (10) Status Quo (1982)
Dear Lonely Hearts (4) Nat 'King' Cole (1962)
Dear Prudence (3) Siouxsie & The Banshees (1983)
Death Of A Clown (3) Dave Davies (1967)
Debora / One Inch Rock (re-issue) (7) Tyrannosaurus Rex (1972)
December 1963 (Oh What A Night) (1) Four Seasons (1976)
Deck Of Cards (re-entry) (5) Wink Martindale (1963)
Dedicated Follower Of Fashion (4) Kinks (1966)
Dedicated To The One I Love (2) Mamas & The Papas (1967)
Dedicated To The One I Love (6) Bitty McLean (1994)
Dedication to My Ex (Miss That) (3) Lloyd featuring André 3000 & Lil Wayne (2011)
Deep (5) East 17 (1993)
Deep Deep Trouble (7) Simpsons featuring Bart & Homer (1991)
Deeper And Deeper (6) Madonna (1992)
Deeper Love, A (5) Aretha Franklin(1994)
Deeper Shade Of Blue (4) Steps (2000)
Deeper Underground (1) Jamiroquai (1998)
Deepest Blue (7) Deepest Blue (2003)
Deeply Dippy (1) Right Said Fred (1992)
Deja Vu (1) Beyonce featuring Jay-Z (2006)
Delaware (3) Perry Como (1960)
Delilah (2) Tom Jones (1968)
Delilah (7) Sensational Alex Harvey Band (1975)
Delivery (6) Babyshambles (2007)
Delta Lady (4) Joe Cocker (1969)
Dem Girlz (I Don't Know Why) (10) Oxide & Neutrino featuring Kowdean (2002)
Denial Twist, The (10) White Stripes (2005)
Denis (2) first hit Blondie (1978)
Desiderata (7) Les Crane (1972)
Design For Life, A (2) Manic Street Preachers (1996)
Desire (1) U2 (1988)
Destination Calabria (4) Alex Gaudino featuring Crystal Waters (2007)
Detroit City (8) Tom Jones (1967)
Devil Gate Drive (1) Suzi Quatro (1974)
Devil In Disguise Elvis Presley see You're The) Devil In Disguise
Devil Woman (5) Marty Robbins (1962)
Devil Woman (9) Cliff Richard (1976)
Devil You Know, The (10) Jesus Jones (1993)
Devil's Answer, The (4) Atomic Rooster (1971)
Diamond Rings (6) Chipmunk featuring Emeli Sande (2009)
Diamonds (1) Jet Harris & Tony Meehan (1963)
Diamonds From Sierra Leone (8) Kanye West (2005)
Diana (1) Paul Anka (1957)

Diane (1) Bachelors (1964)
Diary Of Horace Wimp, The (8) Electric Light Orchestra (1979)
Did You Ever (2) Nancy Sinatra & Lee Hazlewood (1971)
Didn't I Blow Your Mind / Let's Try Again (8) New Kids On The Block (1990)
Die Another Day (3) Madonna (2002)
Different Beat, A (1) Boyzone (1996)
Different Corner, A (1) George Michael (1986)
Different World (3) Iron Maiden (2007)
Dilemma (1) Nelly featuring Kelly Rowland (2002)
Dime And A Dollar (8) Guy Mitchell (1954)
Dip It Low (2) Christina Milian (2004)
Dirtee Cash (10) Dizzee Rascal (2009)
Dirtee Disco (1) Dizzee Rascal (2010)
Dirty (1) Christina Aguilera featuring Redman (2002)
Dirty Cash (2) Adventures Of Stevie V (1990)
Dirty Diana (4) Michael Jackson (1988)
Dirty Harry (6) Gorillaz (2005)
Dirty Picture (6) Taio Cruz featuring Kesha Dirty (2010)
Disappointed (6) Electronic (1992)
Disco Connection (10) Isaac Hayes (1976)
Disco Duck (Part One) (6) Rick Dees & His Cast Of ldiots (1976)
Disco Stomp (6) Hamilton Bohannon (1975)
Disco's Revenge (9) Gusto (1996)
Discotheque (1) U2 (1997)
Disco 2000 (7) Pulp (1995)
Distant Drums (1) Jim Reeves (1966)
Disturbia (3) Rihanna (2008)
Divine Emotions (8) Narada (1988)
Dizzy (1) Tommy Roe (1969)
Dizzy (1) Vic Reeves & The Wonder Stuff (1991)
DJ (3) H & Claire (2002)
DJ / Stop (9) Jamelia (2004)
DJ Got Us Falling In Love (10) Usher featuring Pitbull (2010)
DJ Got Us Falling In Love (7) Usher featuring Pitbull (2010)
Do Anything You Wanna Do (9) Eddie & The Hotrods (1977)
Do I Do (10) Stevie Wonder (1982)
Do It Again (1) Beach Boys (1968)
Do It Like a Dude (2) Jessie J (2011)
Do It Do It Again (9) Raffaella Carra (1978)
Do Nothing / Maggie's Farm (4) Specials (1980)
Do Somethin' (6) Britney Spears (2005)
Do That To Me One More Time (7) Captain & Tennille (1980)
Do The Bartman (1) Simpsons (1991)
Do The Conga (10) Black Lace (1984)
(Do) The Hucklebuck (5) Coast To Coast (1981)
(Do The) Spanish Hustle (10) Fatback Band (1976)
Do They Know It's Christmas (1) Band Aid (1984)
Do They Know It's Christmas Band Aid (re-entry) (3) (1985)
Do They Know It's Christmas (1) Band Aid II (1989)
Do They Know It's Christmas? (1) Band Aid 20 (2004)
Do This Do That (8) Freefaller (2005)
Do U Still (7) East 17 (1996)
Do Wah Diddy (9) DJ Otzi (2001)
Do Wah Diddy Diddy (1) Manfred Mann (1964)
Do What You Do (6) Jermaine Jackson (1985)
Do What You Gotta Do / Ain't Got No - I Got Life (2) Nina Simone (1968)
Do Ya Do Ya (Wanna Please Me) (10) Samantha Fox (1986)
Do you Believe in Love / Power of Love, The (9) Huey Lewis & The News (1986)
Do You Feel My Love (8) Eddy Grant (1980)
Do You Know (6) Michelle Gayle (1997)
Do You Know (I Go Crazy) (8) Angel City (2004)
Do You Know The Way To San Jose (8) Dionne Warwick (1968)
Do You Know? (The Ping Pong Song) (3) Enrique Iglesias (2007)
Do You Love Me (1) Brian Poole & The Tremeloes (1963)
Do You Mind (1) Anthony Newley (1960)
Do You Really Like It (1) DJ Pied Piper & Master of Ceremonies (2001)
Do You Really Want To Hurt Me (1) Culture Club (1982)

434

Do You See The Light (Looking For) (10) Snap featuring Niki Harris (1993)
Do You Wanna Dance (7) Barry Blue (1973)
Do You Wanna Touch Me? (Oh Yeah) (2) Gary Glitter (1973)
Do You Want Me (5) Salt-N-Pepa (1991)
Do You Want To (4) Franz Ferdinand (2005)
Do You Want to Dance / I'm Looking Out The Window (2) Norrie Paramor / Cliff Richard & The Shadows (1962)
Do You Want To Know A Secret (2) Billy J Kramer And The Dakotas (1963)
Dock Of The Bay, The (Sittin' On) (3) Otis Redding (1968)
Doctor Doctor (3) Thompson Twins (1984)
Doctor Jones (1) Aqua (1998)
Doctor My Eyes (9) Jackson 5 (1973)
Doctor Pressure (3) Mylo vs Miami Sound Machine (2005)
Doctorin' The House (6) Coldcut with Yazz & Plastic Population (1988)
Doctorin' The Tardis (1) Timelords (1988)
Doctor's Orders (7) Sunny (1974)
Does Your Chewing Gum Lose Its Flavour (3) Lonnie Donegan (1959)
Does Your Mother Know (4) Abba (1979)
Doesn't Really Matter (5) Janet Jackson (2000)
Doesn't Mean Anything (8) Alicia Keys (2009)
Dog Eat Dog (4) Adam & The Ants (1980)
Doin' The Do (7) Betty Boo (1990)
Doing Alright With The Boys (6) Gary Glitter (1975)
Dolce Vita (5) Ryan Paris (1983)
Dollar In The Teeth / Return Of Django (5) Upsetters (1969)
Dolly My Love (10) Moments (1975)
Dolphins Were Monkeys (3) Ian Brown (2000)
Dominick the Donkey (3) Lou Monte (2011)
Dominique (7) Singing Nun (Soeur Sourire) (1963)
Domino Dancing (7) Pet Shop Boys (1988)
Don Quixote (10) Nik Kershaw (1985)
Donald Where's Your Troosers (re-issue) (4) Andy Stewart (1989)
Donna (2) 10CC (1972)
Donna (3) Marty Wilde (1959)
Don't (2) Elvis Presley with The Jordanaires (1958)
Don't Answer Me (6) Cilla Black (1966)
Don't Be A Stranger (3) Dina Carroll (1993)
Don't Be Stupid (You Know I Love You) (5) Shania Twain (2000)
Don't Blame Me (8) Frank Ifield (1964)
Don't Bother (9) Shakira (2006)
Don't Break My Heart (3) UB40 (1985)
Don't Bring Me Down (10) Pretty Things (1964)
Don't Bring Me Down (6) Animals (1966)
Don't Bring Me Down (3) Electric Light Orchestra (1979)
Don't Call Me Baby (re-issue) (1) Madison Avenue (2000)
Don't Call This Love (3) Leon Jackson (2008)
Don't Cha (1) Pussycat Dolls featuring Busta Rhymes (2005)
Don't Cry (8) Guns 'N' Roses (1991)
Don't Cry Daddy (8) Elvis Presley (1970)
Don't Cry For Me Argentina (1) Julie Covington (1976)
Don't Cry For Me Argentina (5) Shadows (1978)
Don't Cry For Me Argentina (3) Madonna (1996)
Don't Do It Baby (9) Mac & Katie Kissoon (1975)
Don't Ever Change (5) Crickets (1962)
Don't Forbid Me (2) Pat Boone (1957)
Don't Forget To Remember (2) Bee Gees featuring Colin Peterson (1969)
Don't Get Me Wrong (10) Pretenders (1986)
Don't Give Me Your Life (2) Alex Party (1995)
Don't Give Up (9) Peter Gabriel & Kate Bush (1986)
Don't Give Up (1) Chicane featuring Bryan Adams (2000)
Don't Give Up On Us (1) David Soul (1976)
Don't Go (3) Yazoo (1982)
Don't Go (1) Wretch 32 featuring Josh Kumra (2011)
Don't Go Breaking My Heart (1) Elton John & Kiki Dee (1976)
Don't Go Breaking My Heart (7) Elton John & RuPaul (1994)
Don't Hold Your Breath (1) Nicole Scherzinger (2011)
Don't It Make My Brown Eyes Blue (5) Crystal Gayle (1977)
Don't Knock The Rock (7) Bill Haley & His Comets (1957)

Don't Know Much (2) Linda Ronstadt with Aaron Neville (1989)
Don't Laugh At Me (3) Norman Wisdom (1954)
Don't Leave Me (6) Blackstreet (1997)
Don't Leave Me This Way (5) Harold Melvin & The Bluenotes (1977)
Don't Leave Me This Way (1) Communards (1986)
Don't Let Go (3) David Sneddon (2003)
Don't Let Go (Love) (5) En Vogue (1997)
Don't Let It Die (2) Hurricane Smith (1971)
Don't Let Me Be Misunderstood (3) Animals (1965)
Don't Let Me Down / You And I (2) Will Young (2002)
Don't Let Me Get Me (6) Pink (2002)
Don't Let The Stars Get In Your Eyes (1) Perry Como (1953)
Don't Let The Sun Catch You Crying (6) Gerry & The Pacemakers
Don't Let The Sun Go Down On Me (1) George Michael with Elton John (1991)
Don't Lie (6) Black Eyed Peas (2005)
Don't Look Any Further (9) M People (1993)
Don't Look Back In Anger (1) Oasis (1996)
Don't Love You No More (4) Craig David (2005)
Don't Make Me Wait (10) 911 (1996)
Don't Make Me Wait / Megablast (6) BombThe Bass featuring Merlin & Antonia / Lorraine & Lose (1988)
Don't Make My Baby Blue (10) Shadows (1965)
Don't Marry Her (8) Beautiful South (1996)
Don't Miss The Partyline (7) Bizz Nizz (1990)
Don't Need The Sun To Shine (To Make Me Smile) (9) Gabrielle (2001)
Don't Phunk With My Heart (3) Black Eyed Peas (2005)
Don't Play Your Rock 'N' Roll To Me (8) Smokie (1975)
Don't Speak (1) No Doubt (1997)
Don't Stand So Close To Me (1) Police (1980)
Don't Stay Away Too Long (3) Peters & Lee (1974)
Don't Stop (3) ATB (1999)
Don't Stop (Wiggle Wiggle) (1) Outhere Brothers (1995)
Don't Stop Me Now (9) Queen (1979)
Don't Stop Me Now / Please Please (1) McFly (2006)
Don't Stop Movin' (5) Livin' Joy (1996)
Don't Stop Movin' (1) S Club 7 (2001)
Don't Stop The Music (7) Yarbrough & Peoples (1980)
Don't Stop Till You Get Enough (3) Michael Jackson(1979)
Don't Take Away The Music (4) Tavares (1976)
Don't Talk Just Kiss (3) Right Said Fred with Jocelyn Brown (1991)
Don't Talk To Him (2) Cliff Richard & The Shadows (1963)
Don't Talk To Me About Love (7) Altered Images (1983)
Don't Tell Me (8) Blancmange (1984)
Don't Tell Me (4) Madonna (2000)
Don't Tell Me (5) Avril Lavigne (2004)
Don't That Beat All (8) Adam Faith (1962)
Don't Think I'm Not (9) Kandi (2000)
Don't Think You're The First (10) Coral (2003)
Don't Throw Your Love Away (1) Searchers (1964)
Don't Treat Me Like A Child (3) Helen Shapiro (1961)
Don't Turn Around (1) Aswad (1988)
Don't Turn Around (5) Ace Of Base (1994)
Don't Walk Away (7) Jade (1993)
Don't Wanna Go Home (1) Jason Derülo (2011)
Don't Wanna Let You Go (9) Five (2000)
Don't Wanna Lose This Feeling (5) Dannii Minogue (2003)
Don't Wanna Lose You (6) Gloria Estefan (1989)
Don't Want To Forgive Me Now (7) Wet Wet Wet (1995)
Don't Waste My Time (8) Paul Hardcastle featuring Carol Kenyon (1986)
Don't Worry (2) Kim Appleby (1990)
Don't Worry (5) Appleton (2003)
Don't Worry Be Happy (2) Bobby McFerrin (1988)
Don't You (Forget About Me) (7) Simple Minds (1985)
Don't You Love Me (3) Eternal (1997)
Don't You Rock Me Daddy-O (10) Vipers Skiffle Group (1957)
Don't You Rock Me Daddy-O (4) Lonnie Donegan & His Skiffle Group (1957)
Don't You Think It's Time (6) Mike Berry & The Outlaws (1963)
Don't You Want Me (1) Human League (1981)

435

Don't You Want Me (6) Felix (1992)
Don't You Want Me (remix) (10) Felix (1995)
Doo Wap (That Thing) (3) Lauryn Hill (1998)
Doodah! (7) Cartoons (1999)
Dooms Night (8) Azzido Da Bass (2000)
Doop (1) Doop (1994)
Double Barrel (1) Dave & Ansil Collins (1971)
Double Dutch (3) Malcolm McLaren (1983)
Dove (I'll Be Loving You) (9) Moony (2002)
Down Boy (2) Holly Valance (2002)
Down Deep Inside (Theme From The Deep) (5) Donna Summer (1977)
Down Down (1) Status Quo (1974)
Down for Whatever (6) Kelly Rowland featuring The WAV.s (2011)
Down 4 U (4) Irv Gotti Presents (2002)
Down On The Beach Tonight (7) Drifters (1974)
Down On The Street (9) Shakatak (1984)
Down To Earth (3) Curiosity Killed The Cat (1986)
Down Under (1) Men At Work (1983)
Down with the Trumpets (8) Rizzle Kicks (2011)
Down Yonder (8) Johnny & The Hurricanes (1960)
Downhearted (3) Eddie Fisher (1953)
Downtown (2) Petula Clark (1964)
Downtown (remix) (10) Petula Clark (1988)
Downtown (3) Emma Bunton (2006)
Downtown Train (10) Rod Stewart (1990)
Dr Beat (6) Miami Sound Machine (1984)
Dr Kiss Kiss (8) 5000 Volts (1976)
Dr Love (4) Tina Charles (1976)
Dragnet (7) Ray Anthony (1953)
Dragnet (re-entry) (9) Ted Heath Orchestra (1953)
Dragostea Din Tei (3) O-Zone (2004)
Drama! (4) Erasure (1989)
Dreadlock Holiday (1) 10CC (1978)
Dream A Lie / The Earth Dies Screaming (10) UB40 (1980)
Dream Baby (2) Roy Orbison (1962)
Dream Catch Me (7) Newton Faulkner (2007)
Dream Lover (1) Bobby Darin (1959)
Dream On (6) Depeche Mode (2001)
Dream To Me (9) Dario G (2001)
Dreamboat (1) Alma Cogan (1955)
Dreamer (remix) (1) Livin' Joy (1995)
Dreamin' (5) Johnny Burnette (1960)
Dreaming (2) Blondie (1979)
Dreamin' (8) Cliff Richard (1980)
Dreaming (9) Glen Goldsmith (1988)
Dreaming (10) Ruff Driverz presents Arrola (1998)
Dreamlover (9) Mariah Carey (1993)
Dreams (1) Gabrielle (1993)
Dreams (6) Corrs (1998)
Dreams (8) Game (2005)
Dream's A Dream, A (6) Soul II Soul (1990)
Dreams Can Tell A Lie (10) Nat 'King' Cole (1956)
Dreams Of Children / Going Underground (1) Jam (1980)
Dress You Up (5) Madonna (1985)
Drifting Away (9) Lange featuring Skye (2002)
Drinking In L.A. (re-issue) (3) Bran Van 3000 (1999)
Drive (5) Cars (1984)
Drive (re-entry) (4) Cars (1985)
Drive-In Saturday (3) David Bowie (1973)
Driven By You (6) Brian May (1991)
Driving In My Car (4) Madness (1982)
Drop Dead Gorgeous (7) Republica (1997)
Drop It Like It's Hot (10) Snoop Dogg featuring Pharrell (2004)
Drop The Boy (2) Bros (1988)
Drops Of Jupiter (Tell Me) (10) Train (2001)
Drowned World (Substitute For Love) (10) Madonna (1998)
Drowning (9) Backstreet Boys (2002)
Drowning In Berlin (9) Mobiles (1982)
Drugs Don't Work, The (1) Verve (1997)
Dry County (9) Bon Jovi (1994)

Dry Your Eyes (1) Streets (2004)
Dub Be Good To Me (1) Beats International with Lindy Layton (1990)
Duck Sauce (3) Barbra Streisand (2010)
Dude (7) Beenie Man (2004)
Duke Of Earl (6) Darts (1979)
Dumb (3) 411 (2004)
Dyna-Mite (4) Mud (1973)
Dy-Na-Mi-Tee (5) Ms Dynamite (2002)
Dynamite (1) Taio Cruz (2010)
D'You Know What I Mean? (1) Oasis (1997)
E.T. (3) Katy Perry featuring Kanye West (2011)
Each Time (2) E-17 (1998)
Each Time You Break My Heart (5) Nick Kamen (1986)
Early In The Morning (8) Vanity Fare (1969)
Earth Angel (4) Crew Cuts (1955)
Earth Dies Screaming, The / Dream A Lie (10) UB40 (1980)
Earthquake (2) Labrinth featuring Tinie Tempah (2011)
Earth Song (1) Michael Jackson (1995)
Easy (9) Commodores (1977)
Easy (8) Sugababes (2006)
Easy Lover (1) Philip Bailey duet with Phil Collins (1985)
Eat You Alive (10) Limp Bizkit (2003)
Ebb Tide (9) Frank Chacksfield (1954)
Ebeneezer Goode (1) Shamen (1992)
Ebony And Ivory (1) Paul McCartney with Stevie Wonder (1982)
Ebony Eyes / Walk Right Back (1) Everly Brothers (1961)
E-Bow The Letter (4) REM (1996)
Echo Beach (10) Martha & The Muffins (1980)
Ecuador (2) Sash featuring Rodriguez (1997)
Eddie's Song (10) Son Of Dork (2006)
Edelweiss (2) Vince Hill (1967)
Edge of Glory, The (6) Lady Gaga (2011)
Edge Of Heaven, The / Where Did Your Heart Go (1) Wham! (1986)
Eenie Meenie (9) Sean Kingston & Justin Biebe (2010)
Ego (9) Saturdays (2009)
Egyptian Reggae (5) Jonathan Richman & Modern Lovers (1977)
Eighteen Strings (9) Tinman (1994)
Eighteen With A Bullet (7) Pete Wingfield (1975)
Eighth Day (5) Hazel O'Connor (1980)
Einstein A Go-Go (5) Landscape (1981)
Either Way (8) Twang (2007)
Eleanor Rigby / Yellow Submarine (1) Beatles (1966)
Elected (4) Alice Cooper (1972)
Election Day (7) Arcadia (1985)
Electric Avenue (2) Eddy Grant (1983)
Electric Avenue (remix) (5) Eddy Grant (2001)
Electrical Storm (5) U2 (2002)
Electricity (5) Suede (1999)
Electricity (4) Elton John (2005)
Elenore (7) Turtles (1968)
Elephant Stone (8) Stone Roses (1990)
Elevation (3) U2 (2001)
Eloise (2) Barry Ryan (1968)
Eloise (3) Damned (1986)
Elusive Butterfly (5) Bob Lind (1966)
Elusive Butterfly (5) Val Doonican (1966)
Elvis Ain't Dead (8) Scouting For Girls (2007)
Embarrassment (4) Madness (1980)
Emma (3) Hot Chocolate (1974)
Emotion (3) Destiny's Child (2001)
Emotional Rescue (9) Rolling Stones (1980)
Empire (9) Kasabian (2006)
Empire State Of Mind (2) Jay-Z featuring Alicia Keys (2009)
Empire State Of Mind (Part 2) (4) Alicia Keys (2010)
Empty Souls (2) Manic Street Preachers (2005)
Encore Une Fois (2) Sash (1997)
End Credits (9) Chase & Status featuring Plan B (2009)
End Is The Beginning Is The End, The (10) Smashing Pumpkins (1997)
End Of The Line (5) Honeyz (1998)

End Of The Road (1) Boyz II Men (1992)
Endless Love (7) Diana Ross & Lionel Richie (1981)
Endless Love (3) Luther Vandross & Mariah Carey (1994)
Endless Sleep (4) Marty Wilde (1958)
England We'll Fly the Flag / This Time (We'll Get It Right) (2)
England World Cup Squad (1982)
England's Irie (6) Black Grape, Joe Strummer & Keith Allen (1996)
English Country Garden (5) Jimmie Rodgers (1962)
Enjoy The Silence (6) Depeche Mode (1990)
Enjoy The Silence 04 (7) Depeche Mode (2004)
Enjoy Yourself (5) A+ (1999)
Enola Gay (8) Orchestral Manoeuvres In The Dark (1980)
Enter Sandman (5) Metallica (1991)
Erase / Rewind (7) Cardigans (1999)
Ernie (The Fastest Milkman In The West) (1) Benny Hill (1971)
Erotica (3) Madonna (1992)
Escape (2) Enrique Iglesias (2002)
Escaping (3) Dina Carroll (1996)
Especially For You (1) Kylie Minogue & Jason Donovan (1988)
Especially For You (3) Denise & Johnny (1998)
Et Les Oiseaux Chantaient (And The Birds Were Singing) (4)
Sweet People (1980)
Eternal Flame (1) Bangles (1989)
Eternal Flame (1) Atomic Kitten (2001)
Eternally (8) Jimmy Young (1953)
Eternity / The Road To Mandalay (1) Robbie Williams (2001)
Eton Rifles, The (3) Jam (1979)
European Female (9) Stranglers (1983)
Evacuate The Dancefloor (1) Cascada (2009)
Evapor 8 (6) Altern 8 (1992)
Eve Of Destruction (3) Barry McGuire (1965)
Eve Of War, The (remix) (3) Jeff Wayne's War Of The Worlds (1989)
Even After All (10) Finley Quaye (1997)
Even Better Than The Real Thing (remix) (8) U2 (1992)
Even The Bad Times Are Good (4) Tremeloes (1967)
Ever Fallen In Love (9) Fine Young Cannibals (1987)
Evergreen / Anything Is Possible (1) Will Young (2002)
Everlasting Love (1) Love Affair (1968)
Everlasting Love (5) Cast From Casualty (1998)
Evermore (3) Ruby Murray (1955)
Every Beat Of My Heart (2) Rod Stewart (1986)
Every Breath You Take (1) Police (1983)
Every Day Hurts (3) Sad Cafe (1979)
Every Day (I Love You More) (2) Jason Donovan (1989)
Every Day Of My Life (5) Malcolm Vaughan (1955)
Every Little Step (6) Bobby Brown (1989)
Every Little Thing She Does Is Magic (1) Police (1981)
Every Loser Wins (1) Nick Berry (1986)
Every Morning (10) Sugar Ray (1999)
Every Teardrop Is a Waterfall (6) Coldplay (2011)
Every Time You Go Away (4) Paul Young (1985)
Everybody (9) Tommy Roe (1963)
Everybody (6) Clock (1995)
Everybody (7) Progress presents The Boy Wunda (1999)
Everybody (4) Hear'Say (2001)
Everybody (Backstreet's Back) (3) Backstreet Boys (1997)
Everybody Dance (9) Chic (1978)
Everybody Get Together (8) Dave Clark Five (1970)
Everybody Get Up (2) Five (1998)
Everybody Gonfi-Gon (7) Two Cowboys (1994)
Everybody Hurts (7) REM (1993)
Everybody Hurts (1) Helping Haiti (2010)
Everybody In Love (1) JLS (2009)
Everybody In The Place (EP) (2) Prodigy (1992)
Everybody Knows (2) Dave Clark Five (1967)
Everybody Wants To Rule The Tears For Fears World (2) (1985)
Everybody Wants To Run The Tears For Fears World (5) (1986)
Everybody's Changing (4) Keane (2004)
Everybody's Free (To Feel Good) (6) Rozalla (1991)
Everybody's Free (To Wear Sunscreen) (1) Baz Luhrmann (1999)
Everybody's Got To Learn Sometime (5) Korgis (1980)
(Everybody's Got To Learn Sometime) I Need Your Loving (3)
Baby D (1995)

Everybody's Laughing (10) Phil Fearon & Galaxy (1984)
Everybody's Somebody's Fool (5) Connie Francis (1960)
Everyday (3) Slade (1974)
Everyday (5) Bon Jovi (2002)
Everyday I Love You (3) Boyzone (1999)
Everyday I Love You Less And Less (10) Kaiser Chiefs (2005)
Everyday Is Like Sunday (9) Morrissey (1988)
Everyone's Gone To The Moon (4) Jonathan King (1965)
Everything (6) Mary J Blige (1997)
Everything About You (3) Ugly Kid Joe (1992)
Everything Changes (1) Take That (1994)
Everything Counts (6) Depeche Mode (1983)
Everything I Am (6) Plastic Penny (1968)
(Everything I Do) I Do It For You (1) Bryan Adams (1991)
(Everything I Do) I Do It For You (7) Fatima Mansions (1992)
Everything I Have Is Yours (re-entry) (8) Eddie Fisher (1953)
Everything I Own (1) Ken Boothe (1974)
Everything I Own (1) Boy George (1987)
Everything Is Alright (Uptight) (10) C J Lewis (1994)
Everything Is Beautiful (6) Ray Stevens (1970)
Everything Must Change (9) Paul Young (1984)
Everything Must Go (5) Manic Street Preachers (1996)
Everything She Wants / Last Christmas (2) Wham! (1984)
Everything's Alright (9) Mojos (1964)
Everything's Gonna Be Alright (5) Sweetbox (1998)
Everytime / Ready Or Not (3) A1 (1999)
Everytime (1) Britney Spears (2004)
Everytime We Touch (2) Cascada (2006)
Everytime You Need Me (3) Fragma featuring Maria Rubia (2001)
Everywhere (4) Fleetwood Mac (1988)
Evil Hearted You / Still I'm Sad (3) Yardbirds (1965)
Evil That Men Do, The (5) Iron Maiden (1988)
Evil Woman (10) Electric Light Orchestra (1976)
Ev'rywhere (3) David Whitfield (1955)
Exceeder (3) Mason (2007)
Excerpt From A Teenage Opera (2) Keith West (1967)
Ex-Factor (4) Lauryn Hill (1999)
Exodus (Theme From 'Exodus') (6) Ferrante & Teicher (1961)
Experiments With Mice (7) Johnny Dankworth (1956)
Express Yourself (5) Madonna (1989)
Extended Play EP (7) Bryan Ferry (1976)
Exterminate (2) Snap featuring Niki Harris (1993)
Eye Level (re-entry) (1) Simon Park Orchestra (1973)
Eye Of The Tiger (1) Survivor (1982)
Eyes On You (6) Jay Sean featuring Rishi Rich Project (2004)
Eyes Wide Shut (8) JLS featuring Tinie Tempah (2011)
F**k Forever (4) Babyshambles (2005)
F**k It (I Don't Want You Back) (1) Eamon (2004)
F**kin' Perfect (aka Perfect) (10) Pink (2011)
F.L.M. (7) Mel & Kim (1987)
F.U.R.B. (F U Right Back) (1) Frankee (2004)
Fable (7) Robert Miles (1996)
Fabulous (8) Charlie Gracie (1957)
Faces (8) 2 Unlimited (1993)
Fade To Grey (8) Visage (1980)
Fairground (1) Simply Red (1995)
Fairytale (10) Alexander Rybak (2009)
Fairytale Of New York (2) Pogues featuring Kirsty MacColl (1987)
Fairytale Of New York Pogues featuring (re-issue) (3) Kirsty MacColl (2005)
Fairytale Of New York Pogues featuring (re-entry) (6) Kirsty MacColl (2006)
Fairytale Of New York (re-emergence) (4) Pogues featuring Kirsty MacColl (2007)
Faith (2) George Michael (1987)
Faith Can Move Mountains (7) Johnnie Ray & The Four Lads (1952)
Faith Can Move Mountains (10) Nat 'King' Cole (1953)
Faith Can Move Mountains (11) Jimmy Young (1953)
Fall In Love With You (2) Cliff Richard & The Shadows (1960)
Fallin' (3) Alicia Keys (2001)
Falling (9) Roy Orbison (1963)
Falling (7) Julie Cruise (1990)

Falling Apart At The Seams (9) Marmalade (1976)
Falling Down (10) Oasis (2009)
Falling In Love Again (8) Eagle-Eye Cherry (1998)
Falling Into You (10) Celine Dion (1996)
Falling Stars (3) Sunset Strippers (2005)
Fame (1) Irene Cara (1982)
Familiar Feeling (10) Moloko (2003)
Family Affair (8) Mary J Blige (2001)
Famous Last Words (8) My Chemical Romance (2007)
Fancy Pants (4) Kenny (1975)
Fanfare For The Common Man (2) Emerson Lake & Palmer (1977)
Fantastic Day (9) Haircut 100 (1982)
Fantasy (5) Black Box (1990)
Fantasy (4) Mariah Carey (1995)
Fantasy (2) Appleton (2002)
Fantasy Island (2) Tight Fit (1982)
Far Away Eyes / Miss You (3) Rolling Stones (1978)
Far Far Away (2) Slade (1974)
Farewell – Bring It On Home To Me / You Send Me (7) Rod Stewart (1974)
Farewell Is A Lonely Sound (8) Jimmy Ruffin (1970)
Farewell My Summer Love (7) Michael Jackson (1984)
Fascinating Rhythm (9) Bass-O-Matic (1990)
Fascination (6) Alphabeat (2008)
Fascination (see Keep Feeling Fascination)
Fashion (5) David Bowie (1980)
Fast Car (5) Tracy Chapman (1988)
Fast Car (4) Tracy Chapman (2011)
Fast Food Song (2) Fast Food Rockers (2003)
Fast Love (1) George Michael (1996)
Faster Kill Pussycat (7) Paul Oakenfold (2006)
Fat Lip (8) Sum 41 (2001)
Fat Neck (10) Black Grape (1996)
Father (10) LL Cool J (1998)
Father And Son (2) Boyzone (1995)
Father And Son (2) Ronan Keating & Yusuf Islam (2004)
Father Christmas Do Not Touch Me / The In Betweenies (7) Goodies (1974)
Fattie Bum Bum (8) Carl Malcolm (1975)
Favourite Shirts (Boy Meets Girl) (4) Haircut 100 (1981)
Favourite Things (2) Big Brovaz (2003)
FBI (6) Shadows (1961)
Fear Of The Dark (live) (8) Iron Maiden (1993)
Fear, The (1) Lily Allen (2009)
Feel (4) Robbie Williams (2002)
Feel Good (7) Phats & Small (1999)
Feel Good Inc (2) Gorillaz (2005)
Feel Good Time (3) Pink featuring William Orbit (2003)
Feel It (1) Tamperer featuring Maya (1998)
Feel It Boy (9) Beenie Man featuring Janet (2002)
(Feel Like) Heaven (6) Fiction Factory (1984)
Feel So Close (2) Calvin Harris (2011)
Feel So Good (10) Mase (1997)
Feel So Real (5) Steve Arrington (1985)
Feel The Beat (5) Darude (2000)
Feel The Need In Me (4) Detroit Emeralds (1973)
Feelings (4) Morris Albert (1975)
Feels Just Like It Should (8) Jamiroquai (2005)
Feels Like Heaven (5) Urban Cookie Collective (1993)
Feels Like I'm In Love (1) Kelly Marie (1980)
Feels So Good (5) Melanie B (2001)
Feet Up (2) Guy Mitchell (1952)
Fernando (1) Abba (1976)
Ferry Cross The Mersey (8) Gerry & The Pacemakers (1964)
Ferry Cross The Mersey (1) Christians, Johnson, McCartney, Marsden & Stock Aitken Waterman (1989)
Fever (5) Peggy Lee with Jack Marshall's Music (1958)
Fever (6) Madonna (1993)
Fields Of Fire (400 Miles) (10) Big Country (1983)
50:50 / Lullaby (5) Lemar (2003)
Figaro (1) Brotherhood Of Man (1978)

Fight For This Love (1) Cheryl Cole (2009)
Fighter (3) Christina Aguilera (2003)
Fill Me In (1) Craig David (2000)
Fill My Little World (10) Feeling (2006)
Filmstar (9) Suede (1997)
Filthy / Gorgeous (5) Scissor Sisters (2005)
Final Countdown, The (1) Europe (1986)
Finally (re-issue) (2) Ce Ce Peniston (1992)
Finally Found (4) Honeyz (1998)
Find My Love (7) Fairground Attraction (1988)
Find The Time (7) Five Star (1986)
Fine Time (9) Yazz (1989)
Finest Dreams (8) Richard X featuring Kelis (2003)
Finger Of Suspicion (1) Dickie Valentine with The Stargazers (1954)
Fings Ain't Wot They Used To Be (5) Max Bygraves (1960)
Fire (1) Crazy World Of Arthur Brown (1968)
Fire (3) Kasabian (2009)
Fire Brigade (3) Move (1968)
Fire It Up / Turn It Up (2) Busta Rhymes (1998)
Fireflies (1) Owl City (2010)
Firestarter (1) Prodigy (1996)
Firewire (9) Cosmic Gate (2001)
Firework (3) Kate Perry (2010)
First Cut Is The Deepest / I Don't Want To Talk About It (1) Rod Stewart (1977)
First Night, The (6) Monica (1998)
First Of May (6) Bee Gees (1969)
First Of The Gang To Die (6) Morrissey (2004)
First Time (9) Sunblock (2006)
First Time, The (5) Adam Faith with The Roulettes (1963)
First Time, The (1) Robin Beck (1988)
Fit But You Know It (4) Streets (2004)
Five Colours In Her Hair (1) McFly (2004)
5-4-3-2-1 (5) Manfred Mann (1964)
Five Live EP (1) George Michael, Queen, Lisa Stansfield (1993)
5 O'clock (6) T-Pain featuring Lily Allen & Wiz Khalifa (2011)
5-7-0-5 (8) City Boy (1978)
5 Years Time (7) Noah & The Whale (2008)
Fix (7) Blackstreet (1997)
Fix You (4) Coldplay (2005)
Flap Your Wings / My Place (1) Nelly (2004)
Flash (10) Queen (1980)
Flash (5) BBE (1997)
Flashdance ... What A Feeling (2) Irene Cara (1983)
Flashdance (3) Deep Dish (2004)
Flat Beat (1) Mr Oizo (1999)
Flava (1) Peter Andre (1996)
Flawless (7) Ones (2001)
Flawless (Go To The City) (8) George Michael (2004)
Flip Reverse (2) Blazin' Squad (2003)
Flirtation Waltz (re-entry) (10) Winifred Atwell (1953)
Float On (1) Floaters (1977)
Flood, The (2) Take That (2010)
Floral Dance, The (2) Brighouse & Rastrick Brass Band (1977)
Flowers (2) Sweet Female Attitude (2000)
Flowers In The Rain (2) Move (1967)
Floy Joy (9) Supremes (1972)
Fluorescent Adolescent (5) Arctic Monkeys (2007)
Flux (8) Bloc Party (2007)
Fly Away (1) Lenny Kravitz (1999)
Fly By II (6) Blue (2002)
Fly On The Wings Of Love (8) XTM & DJ Chucky presents Annia (2003)
Fly, The (1) U2 (1991)
Flying (4) Cast (1996)
Flying The Flag (For You) (5) Scooch (2007)
Flying Without Wings (1) Westlife (1999)
Focus (7) Emma's Imagination (2010)
Fog On The Tyne (Revisited) (2) Gazza & Lindisfarne (1990)
Folk Singer, The (4) Tommy Roe (1963)
Follow Da Leader (5) Nigel & Marvin (2002)

Follow Me (3) Uncle Kracker (2001)
Follow The Rules (9) Livin' Joy (1996)
Follow You Follow Me (7) Genesis (1978)
Food For Thought / King (4) UB40 (1980)
Fool Again (1) Westlife (2000)
Fool No More (4) S Club 8 (2003)
Fool Such As I, A / I Need Your Love Tonight (1) Elvis Presley with The Jordanaires (1959)
Fool Such As I, A / I Need Your Love Tonight (re-issue) (2) Elvis Presley (2005)
Fool To Cry (6) Rolling Stones (1976)
Foolish (4) Ashanti (2002)
Foolish Beat (9) Debbie Gibson(1988)
Fool's Gold / What The World Is Waiting For (8) Stone Roses (1989)
Foot Tapper (1) Shadows (1963)
Footloose (6) Kenny Loggins (1984)
Footprints In The Sand / Better In Time(2) Leona Lewis (2008)
Footsee (9) Wigan's Chosen Few (1975)
Footsteps (4) Steve Lawrence (1960)
For All We Know (6) Shirley Bassey (1971)
For America (10) Red Box (1986)
For Lovers (7) Wolfman featuring Pete Doherty (2004)
For Once In My Life (3) Stevie Wonder (1968)
For The First Time (4) Script (2010)
For The Good Times (7) Perry Como (1973)
For Whom The Bell Tolls (4) Bee Gees (1993)
(For You) I'll Do Anything You Want Me To (5) Barry White (1975)
For Your Babies (9) Simply Red (1992)
For Your Eyes Only (8) Sheena Easton (1981)
For Your Love (3) Yardbirds (1965)
Forever (4) Chris Brown (2008)
Forever (8) Roy Wood (1973)
Forever (6) Damage (1996)
Forever (6) N-Trance (2002)
Forever And Ever (1) Slik (1976)
Forever And For Always (6) Shania Twain (2003)
Forever Autumn (5) Jeff Wayne's War Of The Worlds featuring Justin Hayward (1978)
Forever Is Over (2) Saturdays (2009)
Forever Love (1) Gary Barlow (1996)
Forever Yours (4) Alex Day (2011)
Forget Me Not (7) Vera Lynn (1952)
Forget Me Not (re-entry) (5) Vera Lynn (1952)
Forget Me Not (3) Eden Kane (1962)
Forget Me Nots (8) Patrice Rushen (1982)
Forget You (aka Fuck You) (1) Cee Lo Green (2010)
Forgive Me (5) Leona Lewis (2008)
Forgive Me Girl / Working My Way Back To You (1) Detroit Spinners (1980)
Forgot About Dre (7) Dr Dre featuring Eminem (2000)
48 Crash (3) Suzi Quatro (1973)
Found A Cure (6) Ultra Naté (1998)
Found That Soul (9) Manic Street Preachers (2001)
Foundations (2) Kate Nash (2007)
Four Bacharach And David Songs EP (2) Deacon Blue (1990)
Four From Toyah EP (4) Toyah (1981)
Four Letter Word (6) Kim Wilde (1988)
Four Minute Warning (4) Mark Owen (2003)
4 Minutes (1) Madonna featuring Justin Timberlake & Timbaland (2008)
4 My People (5) Missy Elliott (2002)
4 Seasons Of Loneliness (10) Boyz II Men (1997)
Fox On The Run (5) Manfred Mann (1968)
Fox On The Run (2) Sweet (1975)
Frankie (1) Sister Sledge (1985)
Freak Like Me (1) Sugababes (2002)
Freak Me (1) Another Level (1998)
Free (1) Deniece Williams (1977)
Free (4) Ultra Naté (1997)
Free (7) DJ Quicksilver (1997)
Free As A Bird (2) Beatles (1995)
Free Me (7) Cast (1997)
Free Me (5) Emma (2003)

Freed From Desire (3) Gala (1997)
Freedom (1) Wham! (1984)
Freedom (2) Robbie Williams (1996)
Freedom Come Freedom Go (6) Fortunes (1971)
Freeek! (7) George Michael (2002)
Freestyler (2) Bomfunk MCs (2000)
Freight Train (5) Charles McDevitt Skiffle Group and Nancy Whiskey (1957)
French Kiss (2) Lil' Louis (1989)
French Kissin' In The USA (8) Deborah Harry (1986)
Fresh! (6) Gina G (1997)
Friday I'm In Love (6) Cure (1992)
Friday On My Mind (6) Easybeats (1966)
Friday's Child (4) Will Young (2004)
Friend Or Foe (9) Adam Ant (1982)
Friendly Persuasion (3) Pat Boone (1956)
Friends (8) Arrival (1970)
Friends And Neighbours (re-entry) (3) Billy Cotton & His Band (1954)
Friends Forever (5) Thunderbugs (1999)
Friggin' In The Riggin' / Something Else (3) Sex Pistols (1979)
Frightened City (3) Shadows (1961)
Frisky (2) Tinie Tempah featuring Labrinth (2010)
From A Distance (6) Bette Midler (1991)
From A Jack To A King (2) Ned Miller (1963)
From A Window (10) Billy J Kramer And The Dakotas (1964)
From Me To You (1) Beatles (1963)
From New York To L.A. (6) Patsy Gallant (1977)
From Paris To Berlin (2) Infernal (2006)
From The Floorboards Up (6) Paul Weller (2005)
From The Heart (6) Another Level (1999)
From The Underworld (6) Herd (1967)
From This Moment On (9) Shania Twain (1998)
Frontin' (6) Pharrell Williams featuring Jay-Z (2003)
Frozen (1) Madonna (1998)
Frozen Orange Juice (10) Peter Sarstedt (1969)
Full Metal Jacket (I Wanna Be Your Drill Instructor) (2) Abigail Mead & Nigel Goulding (1987)
Funeral Pyre (4) Jam (1981)
Funkin' For Jamaica (N.Y.) (10) Tom Browne (1980)
Funky Gibbon / Sick Man Blues (4) Goodies (1975)
Funky Jam / Rocks (7) Primal Scream (1994)
Funky Moped / Magic Roundabout (5) Jasper Carrott (1975)
Funky Weekend (10) Stylistics (1976)
Funkytown (2) Lipps Inc (1980)
Funny Familiar Forgotten Feeling (7) Tom Jones (1967)
Funny How Love Can Be (8) Ivy League (1965)
G.H.E.T.T.O.U.T. (10) Changing Faces (1997)
G.L.A.D. (10) Kim Appleby (1991)
Galvanize (3) Chemical Brothers (2005)
Gambler (4) Madonna (1985)
Gamblin' Man / Putting On The Style (1) Lonnie Donegan & His Skiffle Group (1957)
Game Boy / Please Don't Go (1) KWS (1992)
Game Of Love (2) Wayne Fontana & The Mindbenders (1965)
Games People Play (6) Joe South (1969)
Games Without Frontiers (4) Peter Gabriel (1980)
Gangsta Lovin' (6) Eve featuring Alicia Keys (2002)
Gangsta's Paradise (1) Coolio featuring LV (1995)
Gangster Trippin' (3) Fatboy Slim (1998)
Gangsters (6) Special AKA (1979)
Garden Of Eden (1) Frankie Vaughan (1957)
Gasolina (5) Daddy Yankee (2005)
Gave It All Away (9) Boyzone (2010)
Gay Bar (5) Electric Six (2003)
Gaye (8) Clifford T Ward (1973)
Gee Baby (4) Peter Shelley (1974)
Gee Whiz It's You (4) Cliff Richard & The Shadows (1961)
Genie In A Bottle (1) Christina Aguilera (1999)
Genie In A Bottle / Save Yourself (10) Speedway (2003)
Geno (1) Dexy's Midnight Runners (1980)
Gentle On My Mind (2) Dean Martin (1969)
George Best – A Tribute (4) Brian Kennedy (2005)
Georgy Girl (3) Seekers (1967)
Get A Life (3) Soul II Soul (1989)

Get Away (1) Georgie Fame & The Blue Flames (1966)
Get Back (1) Beatles with Billy Preston (1969)
Get Busy (4) Sean Paul (2003)
Get Dancing (8) Disco Tex & Sex-OLettes (1974)
Get Down (1) Gilbert O'Sullivan (1973)
Get Down (9) Groove Armada featuring Stush (2007)
Get Down On It (3) Kool & The Gang (1981)
Get Get Down (5) Paul Johnson (1999)
Get Here (4) Oleta Adams (1991)
Get It (10) Darts (1979)
Get It On (1) T Rex (1971)
Get Lost (10) Eden Kane (1961)
Get Low / Lovers And Friends (10) Lil Jon & The East Side Boyz (2005)
Get Off Of My Cloud (1) Rolling Stones (1965)
Get Outta My Dreams Get Into My Car (3) Billy Ocean (1988)
Get Over You / Move This Mountain (3) Sophie Ellis-Bextor (2002)
Get Ready (10) Temptations (1969)
Get Ready For This (2) 2 Unlimited (1991)
Get Right (1) Jennifer Lopez (2005)
Get Sexy (2) Sugababes (2009)
Get Shaky (9) Ian Carey Project (2009)
Get The Girl! Kill The Baddies! (9) Pop Will Eat Itself (1993)
Get The Message (8) Electronic (1991)
Get The Party Started (2) Pink (2002)
Get Together (7) Madonna (2006)
Get Up (Before The Night Is Over) (2) Technotronic featuring Ya Kid K (1990)
Get Up And Boogie (7) Silver Convention (1976)
Get UR Freak On (4) Missy Elliott (2001)
Get Your Number / Shake It Off (9) Mariah Carey (2005)
Getaway (6) Texas (2005)
Gett Off (4) Prince & The New Power Generation (1991)
Gettin' Over You (1) David Guetta featuring Chris Willis, Fergie & LMFAO (2010)
Gettin' Jiggy Wit It (3) Will Smith (1998)
Ghetto Child (7) Detroit Spinners (1973)
Ghetto Gospel (1) 2Pac featuring Elton John (2005)
Ghetto Heaven (10) Family Stand (1990)
Ghetto Romance (7) Damage (2000)
Ghetto Superstar (2) Pras Michel, Ol' Dirty Bastard and Mya (1998)
Ghost Town (1) Specials (1981)
Ghostbusters (2) Ray Parker Jr (1984)
Ghosts (5) Japan (1982)
Ghosts / History (5) Michael Jackson (1997)
Giddy-Up-A-Ding-Dong (4) Freddie Bell & The Bellboys (1956)
Gift Of Christmas (9) Childliners (1995)
Gigi (8) Billy Eckstine (1959)
Gilly Gilly Ossenfeffer Katzenellen Bogen By The Sea (7) Max Bygraves (1954)
Gimme All Your Lovin' (10) ZZ Top (1984)
Gimme Dat Ding (6) Pipkins (1970)
Gimme Gimme Gimme (A Man After Midnight) (3) Abba (1979)
Gimme Hope Jo'Anna (7) Eddy Grant (1988)
Gimme Little Sign (8) Brenton Wood (1967)
Gimme More (3) Britney Spears (2007)
Gimme Some Loving (2) Spencer Davis Group (1966)
Gimme Some More (5) Busta Rhymes (1999)
Gimme The Light (remix) (5) Sean Paul (2003)
Ginny Come Lately (5) Brian Hyland (1962)
Girl (6) Destiny's Child (2005)
Girl All The Bad Guys Want (8) Bowling For Soup (2002)
Girl Can't Help It, The (9) Little Richard (1957)
Girl Can't Help It, The / Daddy Cool (6) Darts (1977)
Girl Crazy (7) Hot Chocolate (1982)
Girl Don't Come (3) Sandie Shaw (1964)
Girl I'm Gonna Miss You (2) Milli Vanilli (1989)
Girl Is Mine, The (8) Michael Jackson & Paul McCartney (1982)
Girl Like You, A (3) Cliff Richard & The Shadows (1961)
Girl Like You, A (4) Edwyn Collins (1995)

Girl Of My Best Friend, The (9) Elvis Presley with The Jordanaires (1976)
Girl On TV (6) Lyte Funkie Ones (2000)
Girl You Know It's True (3) Milli Vanilli (1988)
Girlfriend (8) Pebbles (1988)
Girlfriend (1) Billie (1998)
Girlfriend (2) N Sync (2002)
Girlfriend (10) B2K (2003)
Girlfriend (2) Avril Lavigne (2007)
Girlie Girlie (7) Sophia George (1985)
Girls (3) Moments & Whatnauts (1975)
Girls (3) Sugababes (2008)
Girls And Boys (5) Blur (1994)
Girls And Boys (6) Good Charlotte (2003)
Girls Girls Girls (7) Sailor (1976)
Girls Just Want To Have Fun (2) Cyndi Lauper (1984)
Girls Like Us (7) B15 Project with Chrissy D & Lady G (2000)
Girls On Film (5) Duran Duran (1981)
Girls' School / Mull Of Kintyre (1) Wings (1977)
Girls Talk (4) Dave Edmunds (1979)
Girls, The (3) Calvin Harris (2007)
Give A Little Love (1) Bay City Rollers (1975)
Give A Little Love (7) Daniel O'Donnell (1998)
Give In To Me (2) Michael Jackson (1993)
Give It Away (9) Red Hot Chili Peppers (1994)
Give It Away (9) Deepest Blue (2004)
Give It To Me (1) Timbaland featuring Nelly Furtado & Justin Timberlake (2007)
Give It 2 Me (7) Madonna (2008)
Give It To You (5) Jordan Knight (1999)
Give It Up (1) KC & The Sunshine Band (1983)
Give It Up (re-entry) (5) Goodmen (1993)
Give Me A Little More Time (5) Gabrielle (1996)
Give Me A Reason (9) Triple Eight (2003)
Give Me Back My Heart (4) Dollar (1982)
Give Me Everything (1) Pitbull featuring Ne-Yo, Afrojack & Nayer (2011)
Give Me Just A Little More Time (3) Chairmen Of The Board (1970)
Give Me Just A Little More Time (2) Kylie Minogue (1992)
Give Me Love (Give Me Peace On Earth) (8) George Harrison (1973)
Give Me The Night (7) George Benson (1980)
Give Me Your Word (1) Tennessee Ernie Ford (1955)
Give Peace A Chance (2) John Lennon & The Plastic Ono Band (1969)
Giving It All Away (5) Roger Daltrey (1973)
Giving You Up (6) Kylie Minogue (2005)
Glad All Over (1) Dave Clark Five (1963)
Glad It's All Over / Damned On 45 (6) Captain Sensible (1984)
Glad You Came (1) The Wanted (2011)
Glamorous (6) Fergie featuring Ludacris (2007)
Glass Of Champagne, A (2) Sailor (1975)
Globetrotter (5) Tornados (1963)
Gloria (6) Laura Branigan (1982)
Glorious (4) Andreas Johnson (2000)
Glory Of Love (3) Peter Cetera (1986)
Glow / Musclebound (10) Spandau Ballet (1981)
Glow Worm (10) Mills Brothers (1953)
Go (10) Moby (1991)
Go (Before You Break My Heart) Gigliola Cinquetti (8) (1974)
Go Away Little Girl (6) Mark Wynter (1962)
Go Buddy Go / Peaches (8) Stranglers (1977)
Go Let It Out (1) Oasis (2000)
Go Now (1) Moody Blues (1964)
Go On Move (7) Reel 2 Real with The Mad Stuntman (1994)
Go West (2) Pet Shop Boys (1993)
Go Wild In The Country (7) Bow Wow Wow (1982)
God Gave Rock And Roll To You (4) Kiss (1992)
God Is A DJ (6) Faithless (1998)
God Only Knows (2) Beach Boys (1966)
God Save The Queen (2) Sex Pistols (1977)

Goin' Down (4) Melanie C (1999)
Goin' Home (4) Osmonds (1973)
Going Back (10) Dusty Springfield (1966)
Going Back To My Roots (4) Odyssey (1981)
Going Back To My Roots / Rich In Paradise (9) FPI Project present Paolo Dini (1989)
Going For Gold (8) Shed Seven (1996)
Going In With My Eyes Open (2) David Soul (1977)
Going Nowhere (9) Gabrielle (1993)
Going Out (5) Supergrass (1996)
Going Under (8) Evanescence (2003)
Going Underground / Carnation (6) Liam Gallagher & Steve Cradock (1999)
Going Underground / Dreams Of Children (1) Jam (1980)
Gold (2) Spandau Ballet (1983)
Gold (10) Artist Formerly Known As Prince (1995)
Gold Digger (2) Kanye West featuring Jamie Foxx (2005)
Gold Forever (3) The Wanted (2011)
Golden Brown (2) Stranglers (1982)
Golden Skans (7) Klaxons (2007)
Golden Touch (9) Razorlight (2004)
Golden Years (8) David Bowie (1975)
Golden Years EP, The (8) Motorhead (1980)
Goldeneye (10) Tina Turner (1995)
Goldfinger (5) Ash (1996)
Gone Till November (3) Wyclef Jean (1998)
Gonna Get Along Without You Now (8) Viola Wills (1979)
Gonna Make You A Star (1) David Essex (1974)
Gonna Make You An Offer You Can't Refuse (8) Jimmy Helms (1973)
Gonna Make You Sweat (Everybody Dance Now) (3) C & C Music Factory (1990)
Good Enough (4) Dodgy (1996)
Good Feeling? (1) Flo Rida (2011)
Good Girl (6) Alexis Jordan (2011)
Good Golly Miss Molly (8) Little Richard (1958)
Good Heart, A (1) Feargal Sharkey (1985)
Good Life (4) Inner City (1988)
Good Life (Buena Vida) (remix) (10) Inner City (1999)
Good Luck Charm (1) Elvis Presley with The Jordanaires (1962)
Good Luck Charm (re-issue) (2) Elvis Presley (2005)
Good Morning Freedom (10) Blue Mink (1970)
Good Morning Judge (5) 10CC (1977)
Good Morning Starshine (6) Oliver (1969)
Good Old Arsenal (16) Arsenal FC First Team Squad (1971)
Good Old Rock 'N' Roll (7) Dave Clark Five (1969)
Good The Bad And The Ugly, The (1) Hugo Montenegro (1968)
Good Thing (7) Fine Young Cannibals (1989)
Good Thing (8) Eternal (1996)
Good Thing Going (We've Got A Good Thing Going) (4) Sugar Minott (1981)
Good Times (5) Chic (1979)
Good Times (1) Roll Deep (2010)
Good Timin' (1) Jimmy Jones (1960)
Good Tradition (10) Tanita Tikaram (1988)
Good Vibrations (1) Beach Boys (1966)
Good Year For The Roses, A (6) Elvis Costello (1981)
Goodbye (2) Mary Hopkin (1969)
Goodbye (1) Spice Girls (1998)
Goodbye Jimmy Goodbye (10) Ruby Murray (1959)
Goodbye Mr A (4) Hoosiers (2007)
Goodbye My Love (4) Searchers (1965)
Goodbye My Love (2) Glitter Band (1975)
Goodbye My Lover (9) James Blunt (2005)
Goodbye Sam Hello Samantha (6) Cliff Richard (1970)
Goodbye Stranger (9) Pepsi & Shirlie (1987)
Goodbye To Love / I Won't Last A Day Without You (9) Carpenters (1972)
Goodbye Yellow Brick Road (6) Elton John (1973)
Goodies (1) Ciara featuring Petey Pablo (2005)
Goodness Gracious Me (4) Peter Sellers and Sophia Loren (1960)
Goodnight Girl (1) Wet Wet Wet (1992)
Goodnight Midnight (4) Clodagh Rodgers (1969)
Goodnight Tonight (5) Wings (1979)
Goody Two Shoes (1) Adam Ant (1982)

Google Eye (10) Nashville Teens (1964)
Gorgeous / Filthy (5) Scissor Sisters (2005)
Gossip Folks (9) Missy Elliott featuring Ludacris (2003)
Got My Mind Set On You (2) George Harrison (1987)
Got Some Teeth (8) Obie Trice (2003)
Got The Feelin' (3) Five (1998)
Got 'Til It's Gone (6) Janet Jackson (1997)
Got To Be Certain (2) Kylie Minogue (1988)
Got To Be There (5) Michael Jackson (1972)
Got To Get It (4) Culture Beat (1993)
Got To Get You Into My Life (6) Cliff Bennett & The Rebel Rousers (1966)
Got To Give It Up (7) Marvin Gaye (1977)
Got To Have Your Love (4) Mantronix featuring Wondress (1990)
Got To Have Your Love (2) Liberty X (2002)
Gotham City (9) R Kelly (1997)
Gotta Be You (10) 3T (1997)
Gotta Be You (3) One Direction (2011)
Gotta Get Thru This (1) Daniel Bedingfield (2001)
Gotta Have Something In The Bank Frank (8) Kaye Sisters (1957)
Gotta Have Something In The Bank Frank (8) Frankie Vaughan & The Kaye Sisters (1957)
Gotta Pull Myself Together (9) Nolans (1980)
Gotta Tell You (2) Samantha Mumba (2000)
Govinda (7) Kula Shaker (1996)
Grace Kelly (1) Mika (2007)
Granada (10) Frankie Laine (1954)
Granada (re-entry) (9) Frankie Laine (1954)
Grand Coolie Dam (6) Lonnie Donegan & His Skiffle Group (1958)
Grand Piano (9) Mixmaster (1989)
Grandad (1) Clive Dunn (1970)
Grandma's Party (9) Paul Nicholas (1976)
Gravel Pit (6) Wu-Tang Clan (2000)
Gravity (7) Embrace (2004)
Grease (3) Frankie Valli (1978)
Grease Megamix (3) John Travolta & Olivia Newton-John (1990)
Great Balls Of Fire (1) Jerry Lee Lewis (1957)
Great Beyond, The (3) REM (2000)
Great Pretender, The / Only You (5) Platters (1956)
Great Pretender, The (9) Jimmy Parkinson (1956)
Great Pretender, The (4) Freddie Mercury (1987)
Greatest Day (1) Take That (2008)
Greatest Love Of All (8) Whitney Houston (1986)
Green Door (2) Frankie Vaughan (1956)
Green Door (8) Jim Lowe (1956)
Green Door (1) Shakin' Stevens (1981)
Green Green Grass Of Home (1) Tom Jones (1966)
Green Leaves Of Summer, The (7) Kenny Ball & His Jazzmen (1962)
Green Light (1) Roll Deep (2010)
Green Manalishi (With The Two Pronged Crown), The (10) Fleetwood Mac (1970)
Green Onions (7) Booker T & The MG's (1979)
Green Tambourine (7) Lemon Pipers (1968)
Grenade (1) Bruno Mars (2011)
Grey Day (4) Madness (1981)
Grief Never Grows Old (4) One World Project (2005)
Groove Is In The Heart / What Is Love (2) Deee-Lite (1990)
Groove, The (7) Rodney Franklin (1980)
Groovejet (If This Ain't Love) (1) Spiller (2000)
Groover, The (4) T Rex (1973)
Groovin' (8) Young Rascals (1967)
Groovin' With Mr Bloe (2) Mr Bloe (1970)
Groovin' (You're The Best Thing) / Big Boss Groove (5) Style Council (1984)
Groovy Kind Of Love, A (2) Mindbenders (1966)
Groovy Kind Of Love, A (1) Phil Collins (1988)
Groovy Train (6) Farm (1990)
Guaglione (2) Perez 'Prez' Prado & His Orchestra (1995)
Guantanamera (7) Sandpipers (1966)
Gudbuy T'Jane (2) Slade (1972)
Guess I Was A Fool (5) Another Level (1998)
Guiding Star (9) Cast (1997)

Guilt (8) Nero (2011)
Guilty (10) Pearls (1974)
Guilty (2) Blue (2003)
Guilty Conscience (5) Eminem featuring Dr Dre (1999)
Guitar Boogie Shuffle (10) Bert Weedon (1959)
Guitar Tango (4) Shadows (1962)
Guns Don't Kill People Rappers Do (3) Goldie Lookin Chain (2004)
Gym And Tonic (1) Spacedust (1998)
Gypsies Tramps And Thieves (4) Cher (1971)
Gypsy Woman (La Da Dee) (2) Crystal Waters (1991)
H.A.P.P.Y. Radio (9) Edwin Starr (1979)
Ha Ha Said The Clown (4) Manfred Mann (1967)
Had Enough (4) Enemy (2007)
Half A Heart (8) H & Claire (2002)
Half As Much (3) Rosemary Clooney (1952)
Halfway Down The Stairs (7) Muppets (1977)
Halfway To Paradise (3) Billy Fury (1961)
Hallelujah (5) Milk & Honey featuring Gali Atari (1979)
Hallelujah (1) Alexandra Burke (2008)
Hallelujah (2) Jeff Buckley (2008)
Hallelujah Freedom (10) Junior Campbell (1972)
Hallowed Be Thy Name (live) (9) Iron Maiden (1993)
Halo - Walking On Sunshine (9) Glee Cast (2010)
Halo (10) Texas (1997)
Halo (4) Beyonce (2009)
Hammer To the Heart (6) Tamperer featuring Maya (2000)
Hand On Your Heart (1) Kylie Minogue (1989)
Hand That Feeds, The (7) Nine Inch Nails (2005)
Handbags And Gladrags (4) Stereophonics (2001)
Handful Of Songs / Water Water (5) Tommy Steele (1957)
Hands Off – She's Mine (9) Beat (1980)
Hands To Heaven (4) Breathe (1988)
Hands Up (Give Me Your Heart) (3) Ottowan (1981)
Handy Man (3) Jimmy Jones (1960)
Hang On In There Baby (3) Johnny Bristol (1974)
Hang On In There Baby (3) Curiosity (1992)
Hang On Sloopy (5) McCoys (1965)
Hang On To Your Love (8) Jason Donovan (1990)
Hangin' Tough (1) New Kids On The Block (1990)
Hanging On The Telephone (5) Blondie (1978)
Hanky Panky (2) Madonna (1990)
Happenin' All Over Again (4) Lonnie Gordon (1990)
Happening, The (6) Supremes (1967)
Happiness (3) Alexis Jordan (2010)
Happy (8) MN8 (1995)
Happy (2) Leona Lewis (2009)
Happy Birthday (2) Altered Images (1981)
Happy Birthday (2) Stevie Wonder (1981)
Happy Birthday Sweet Sixteen (3) Neil Sedaka (1961)
Happy Days And Lonely Nights (6) Ruby Murray (1955)
Happy Ending (7) Mika (2007)
Happy Hour (3) Housemartins (1986)
Happy Jack (3) Who (1966)
Happy People / U Saved Me (6) R Kelly (2004)
Happy Talk (1) Captain Sensible (1982)
Happy To Be On An Island Demis Roussos In The Sun (5) (1975)
Happy Together (10) Jason Donovan (1991)
Happy Wanderer Obernkirchen (Der Fröhliche Wanderer) (2) Children's Choir (1954)
Happy Whistler, The (8) Don Robertson (1956)
Happy Xmas (War Is Over) (4) John & Yoko with The Plastic Ono Band (1972)
Happy Xmas (War Is Over) (2) John & Yoko with The Plastic Ono Band (re-entry) (1980)
Happy Xmas (War Is Over) (5) Idols (2003)
Hard Day's Night, A (1) Beatles (1964)
Hard Day's Night, A (14) Peter Sellers (1965)
Hard Habit To Break (8) Chicago (1984)
Hard Headed Woman (2) Elvis Presley with The Jordanaires (1958)
Hard Knock Life (Ghetto Anthem) (2) Jay-Z (1998)

Hard Rain's Gonna Fall, (10) Bryan Ferry (1973)
Hard To Beat (9) Hard-Fi (2005)
Hard To Say I'm Sorry (4) Chicago (1982)
Hard To Say I'm Sorry (7) Az Yet featuring Peter Cetera (1997)
Harder I Try, The (2) Brother Beyond (1988)
Harlem Shuffle (7) Bob & Earl (1969)
Harvest For The World (10) Isley Brothers (1976)
Harvest For The World (8) Christians (1988)
Hate It Or Love It (4) Game featuring 50 Cent (2005)
Haters (8) So Solid Crew presents Mr Shabz (2002)
Hats Off To Larry (6) Del Shannon (1961)
Have A Cheeky Christmas (10) Cheeky Girls (2003)
Have A Drink On Me (8) Lonnie Donegan & His Group (1961)
Have A Nice Day (5) Stereophonics (2001)
Have A Nice Day (6) Bon Jovi (2005)
Have I The Right (1) Honeycombs (1964)
Have I The Right (6) Dead End Kids (1977)
Have I Told You Lately (5) Rod Stewart (1993)
Have You Ever (1) S Club 7 (2001)
Have You Ever Been In Love (10) Leo Sayer (1982)
Have You Ever Really Loved A Woman (4) Bryan Adams (1995)
Have You Seen Her (3) Chi-Lites (1972)
Have You Seen Her / Oh Girl (re-issue) (5) Chi-Lites (1975)
Have You Seen Her (8) MC Hammer (1990)
Have You Seen Your Mother Baby Standing In The Shadow (5) Rolling Stones (1966)
Haven't Met You Yet (5) Michael Buble (2009)
Hawkeye (7) Frankie Laine (1955)
Hazard (3) Richard Marx (1992)
He Ain't Heavy He's My Brother (3) Hollies (1969)
He Ain't Heavy He's My Brother (re-issue) (1) Hollies (1988)
He Ain't No Competition (6) Brother Beyond (1988)
He Wasn't Man Enough (5) Toni Braxton (2000)
Head Over Feet (7) Alanis Morissette (1996)
Heal The World (2) Michael Jackson (1992)
Healing Hands / Sacrifice (re-issue) (1) Elton John (1990)
Hear The Drummer (Get Wicked) (3) Chad Jackson (1990)
Heard It All Before (9) Sunshine Anderson (2001)
Heart (1) Pet Shop Boys (1988)
Heart And Soul (4) T'Pau (1987)
Heart Full Of Soul (2) Yardbirds (1965)
Heart Never Lies, The (3) McFly (2007)
Heart Of A Man, The (5) Frankie Vaughan (1959)
Heart Of A Teenage Girl, The (10) Craig Douglas (1960)
Heart Of Asia (3) Watergate (2000)
Heart Of Glass (1) Blondie (1979)
Heart Of Gold (10) Neil Young (1972)
Heart Of My Heart (7) Max Bygraves (1954)
Heart On My Sleeve (6) Gallagher & Lyle (1976)
Heart Skips a Beat (1) Olly Murs featuring Rizzle Kicks (2011)
Heart Vacancy (2) Wanted (2010)
Heartache (2) Pepsi & Shirlie (1987)
Heartache Avenue (7) Maisonettes (1982)
Heartaches By The Number (re-entry) (5) Guy Mitchell (1959)
Heartbeat (3) Ruby Murray (1954)
Heartbeat (7) Showaddywaddy (1975)
Heartbeat (2) Nick Berry (1992)
Heartbeat / Tragedy (1) Steps (1998)
Heartbeat (10) Scouting For Girls (2008)
Heartbeat (8) Enrique Iglesias featuring Nicole Scherzinger (2010)
Heartbeats (9) Jose Gonzalez (2006)
Heartbreak Hotel (2) Elvis Presley (1956)
Heartbreak Hotel / Hound Dog (re-issue) (10) Elvis Presley (1971)
Heartbreaker (2) Dionne Warwick (1982)
Heartbreaker (5) Mariah Carey featuring Jay-Z (1999)
Heartbreaker (4) Will I Am featuring Cheryl Cole (2008)
Heartbroken (2) T2 featuring Jodie Aysha (2007)
Heartless (10) Kanye West (2009)
Heart-Shaped Box (5) Nirvana (1993)
Heaven (1) DJ Sammy & Yanou featuring Do (2002)

Heaven (2) Emeli Sandé (2011)
Heaven For Everyone (2) Queen (1995)
Heaven Is A Halfpipe (4) OPM (2001)
Heaven Is A Place On Earth (1) Belinda Carlisle (1987)
Heaven Knows I'm Miserable Now (10) Smiths (1984)
Heaven Must Be Missing An Angel (4) Tavares (1976)
Heaven Must Have Sent You (3) Elgins (1971)
Heaven's What I Feel (4) Gloria Estefan (1998)
Heavyweight Champion Of The World (8) Reverend & The Makers (2007)
Hell Raiser (2) Sweet (1973)
Hello (1) Lionel Richie (1984)
Hello Goodbye (1) Beatles (1967)
Hello Hello I'm Back Again (2) Gary Glitter (1973)
Hello Hurray (6) Alice Cooper (1973)
Hello Little Girl (9) Fourmost (1963)
Hello Mary Lou / Travellin' Man (2) Ricky Nelson (1961)
Hello Suzie (4) Amen Corner (1969)
Hello This Is Joanie (The Telephone Answering Machine Song) (6) Paul Evans (1978)
Hello, Dolly! (4) Louis Armstrong and the All Stars (1964)
Help! (1) Beatles (1965)
Help / La Na Nee Nee Noo Noo (3) Bananarama (1989)
Help Me Make It Through The Night (6) John Holt (1974)
Help The Aged (8) Pulp (1997)
Help Yourself (5) Tom Jones (1968)
Here (In Your Arms) (4) Hellogoodbye (2007)
Here And Now / You'll Be Sorry (4) Steps (2001)
Here Comes My Baby (4) Tremeloes (1967)
Here Comes Summer (1) Jerry Keller (1959)
Here Comes That Feeling (5) Brenda Lee (1962)
Here Comes The Hotstepper (4) Ini Kamoze (1995)
Here Comes The Night (2) Them (1965)
Here Comes The Rain Again (8) Eurythmics (1984)
Here Comes The Sun (10) Steve Harley (1976)
Here 4 One (6) Blazin' Squad (2004)
Here I Am (5) Bryan Adams (2002)
Here I Go Again (4) Hollies (1964)
Here I Go Again (remix) (9) Whitesnake (1987)
Here I Stand (10) Bitty McLean (1994)
Here In My Heart (1) Al Martino (1952)
Here It Comes Again (4) Fortunes (1965)
Here It Comes Again (7) Melanie C (2003)
Here We Go Round The Mulberry Bush (8) Traffic (1967)
Here With Me (4) Dido (2001)
Here's Where The Story Ends (7) Tin Tin Out featuring Shelley Nelson (1998)
Hernando's Hideaway (1) Johnston Brothers (1955)
Hero (7) Mariah Carey (1993)
Hero (1) Enrique Iglesias (2002)
Hero (4) Chad Kroeger featuring Josey Scott (2002)
Hero (1) X Factor Finalists (2008)
Heroes (1) X Factor Finalists (2010)
Heroes And Villains (8) Beach Boys (1967)
Hersham Boys (6) Sham 69 (1979)
He's Gonna Step On You Again (4)John Kongos (1971)
He's In Town (3) Rockin' Berries (1964)
He's Misstra Know It All (10) Stevie Wonder (1974)
He's The Greatest Dancer (6) Sister Sledge (1979)
Hey Baby (Uuh, Aah) (1) DJ Otzi (2001)
Hey Baby (2) No Doubt (2002)
Hey Baby (Unofficial World Cup Remix) (10) DJ Otzi (2002)
Hey Boy Hey Girl (3) Chemical Brothers (1999)
Hey Child (3) East 17 (1997)
Hey DJ I Can't Dance To That Music You're Playing (7) Beatmasters featuring Betty Boo (1989)
Hey Dude (2) Kula Shaker (1996)
Hey Girl (10) Small Faces (1966)
Hey Girl Don't Bother Me (1) Tams (1971)
Hey Joe (1) Frankie Laine (1953)
Hey Joe (6) Jimi Hendrix Experience (1967)
Hey Jude (1) Beatles (1968)
Hey Little Girl (2) Del Shannon (1962)
Hey Ma (8) Cam'ron featuring Juelz Santana (2003)
Hey Mamma (6) Black Eyed Peas (2004)

Hey Matthew (9) Karel Fialka (1987)
Hey Music Lover (6) S Express (1989)
Hey Now (Girls Just Want To Have Fun) (4) Cyndi Lauper (1994)
Hey Now (Mean Muggin) (9) Xzibit (2005)
Hey Paula (8) Paul & Paula (1963)
Hey Rock And Roll (2) Showaddywaddy (1974)
Hey Sexy Lady (10) Shaggy (2002)
Hey There (4) Rosemary Clooney (1955)
Hey There (5) Johnnie Ray (1955)
Hey There Delilah (2) Plain White T's (2007)
(Hey There) Lonely Girl (4) Eddie Holman (1974)
Hey Whatever (4) Westlife (2003)
Hey Ya! (3) Outkast (2003)
(Hey You) The Rocksteady Crew (6) Rocksteady Crew (1983)
Hey! Baby (2) Bruce Channel (1962)
Hi Hi Hi / C Moon (5) Wings (1972)
Hi Ho Silver (5) Jim Diamond (1986)
Hidden Agenda (10) Craig David (2003)
Hide U (6) Kosheen (2001)
Hideaway (10) Dave Dee, Dozy, Beaky, Mick & Tich (1966)
Hideaway (9) De'Lacy (1995)
Hi-Fidelity (5) Kids From Fame (1982)
High (8) Cure (1992)
High (4) Lighthouse Family (1998)
High Class Baby (7) Cliff Richard with The Drifters (1958)
High Energy (5) Evelyn Thomas (1984)
High Hopes (re-entry) (6) Frank Sinatra (1959)
High In The Sky (6) Amen Corner (1968)
High Life (8) Modern Romance (1983)
High Noon (Do Not Forsake Me) (7) Frankie Laine (1952)
High Time (4) Paul Jones (1966)
High Voltage / Points Of Authority (9) Linkin Park (2002)
Higher (10) Saturdays featuring Flo Rida (2010)
Higher (8) Taio Cruz featuring Kylie Minogue & Travie McCoy (2011)
Higher Ground (8) UB40 (1993)
Higher State Of Consciousness (8) Josh Wink (1995)
Higher State Of Consciousness (remix) (7) Josh Wink (1996)
Hillbilly Rock Hillbilly Roll (7) Woolpackers (1996)
Hindu Times, The (1) Oasis (2002)
Hip To Hip / Can You Feel It (5) V (2004)
Hippy Chick (re-entry) (8) Soho (1991)
Hippy Hippy Shake (2) Swinging Blue Jeans (1963)
Hips Don't Lie (1) Shakira featuring Wyclef Jean (2006)
His Latest Flame (see Marie's The Name)
History (8) Mai Tai (1985)
History / Ghosts (5) Michael Jackson (1997)
History Maker (4) Delirious? (2010)
Hit 'Em High (The Monstars' Anthem) (8) B Real BustaRhymes / Coolio / LL Cool J / Method Man (1997)
Hit And Miss (10) John Barry Seven (1960)
Hit Me With Your Rhythm Stick (1) Ian Dury & The Blockheads (1978)
Hit That Perfect Beat (3) Bronski Beat (1985)
Hit The Road Jack (6) Ray Charles (1961)
Hold Back The Night (5) Trammps (1975)
Hold It Against Me (6) Britney Spears (2011)
Hold Me (3) P J Proby (1964)
Hold Me Close (1) David Essex (1975)
Hold Me In Your Arms (10) Rick Astley (1989)
Hold Me Now (4) Thompson Twins (1983)
Hold Me Now (2) Johnny Logan (1987)
Hold Me Thrill Me Kiss Me (3) Muriel Smith (1953)
Hold Me Thrill Me Kiss Me Kill Me (2) U2 (1995)
Hold Me Tight (5) Johnny Nash (1968)
Hold My Hand (1) Don Cornell (1954)
Hold My Hand (10) Michael Jackson featuring Akon (2010)
Hold On (5) En Vogue (1990)
Hold On (6) Wilson Phillips (1990)
Hold On Me (10) Phixx (2003)
Hold On Tight (4) Electric Light Orchestra (1981)
Hold On To My Love (7) Jimmy Ruffin (1980)
Hold Tight (4) Dave Dee, Dozy, Beaky, Mick & Tich (1966)
Hold You Down (6) Jennifer Lopez featuring Fat Joe (2005)
Hold Your Head Up (5) Argent (1972)

Holding Back The Years (2) Simply Red (1986)
Holding On For You (5) Liberty X (2002)
Holding Out For A Hero (2) Bonnie Tyler (1985)
Hole In My Shoe (2) Traffic (1967)
Hole In My Shoe (2) Neil (1984)
Hole In The Ground (9) Bernard Cribbins (1962)
Hole In The Head (1) Sugababes (2003)
Holiday (6) Madonna (1984)
Holiday (re-entry) (2) Madonna (1985)
Holiday (re-issue) (5) Madonna (1991)
Holiday (1) Dizzee Rascal (2009)
Holiday Rap (6) MC Miker G & Deejay Sven (1986)
Holidays In The Sun (8) Sex Pistols (1977)
Hollaback Girl (8) Gwen Stefani (2005)
Holler / Let Love Lead The Way (1) Spice Girls (2000)
Hollywood (2) Madonna (2003)
Holy Cow (6) Lee Dorsey (1966)
Holy Smoke (3) Iron Maiden (1990)
Homburg (6) Procol Harum (1967)
Home (3) Westlife (2007)
Home Lovin' Man (7) Andy Williams (1970)
Homecoming (9) Kanye West (2008)
Homely Girl (5) Chi-Lites (1974)
Homely Girl (6) UB40 (1989)
Homeward Bound (9) Simon & Garfunkel (1966)
Homing Waltz (9) Vera Lynn (1952)
Honey (2) Bobby Goldsboro (1968)
Honey (re-issue) (2) Bobby Goldsboro (1975)
Honey (3) Mariah Carey (1997)
Honey Come Back (4) Glen Campbell (1970)
Honey Honey (10) Sweet Dreams (1974)
Honey To The Bee (3) Billie (1999)
Hong Kong Garden (7) Siouxsie & The Banshees (1978)
Honky Tonk Women (1) Rolling Stones (1969)
Hooked On Classics (2) Royal Philharmonic Orchestra (1981)
Hooray Hooray (It's A Cheeky Holiday) (3) Cheeky Girls (2003)
Hooray Hooray It's A Holi-Holiday (3) Boney M (1979)
Hoots Mon (1) Lord Rockingham's XI (1958)
Hopelessly Devoted To You (2) Olivia Newton-John (1978)
Horny (5) Mark Morrison (1996)
Horny (2) Mousse T vs Hot 'N' Juicy (1998)
Horse With No Name (re-entry) (3) America (1972)
Hot (6) Inna (2010)
Hot Diggity (Dog Ziggity Boom) (4) Perry Como (1956)
Hot In Herre (4) Nelly (2002)
Hot Love (1) T Rex (1971)
Hot 'n' Cold (4) Katy Perry (2008)
(Hot S**t) Country Grammar (7) Nelly (2000)
Hot Stuff (9) Arsenal FC (1998)
Hot Stuff (Let's Dance) (7) Craig David (2007)
Hot Toddy (6) Ted Heath Orchestra (1953)
Hotel (3) Cassidy featuring R Kelly (2004)
Hotel California (8) Eagles (1977)
Hotel Room Service (9) Pitbull (2009)
Hotlegs / I Was Only Joking (5) Rod Stewart (1978)
Hound Dog (2) Elvis Presley (1956)
Hound Dog / Heartbreak Hotel (re-issue) (10) Elvis Presley (1971)
Hounds Of Love (8) Futureheads (2005)
House Arrest (3) Krush (1987)
House Nation (re-entry) (8) Housemaster Boyz and The Rude Boy Of The House (1987)
House Of Fun (1) Madness (1982)
House Of Love (10) East 17 (1992)
House Of The Rising Sun (1) Animals (1964)
House Of The Rising Sun (4) Frijid Pink (1970)
House That Jack Built, The (4) Alan Price Set (1967)
House That Jack Built, The (9) Tracie (1983)
Housecall (remix) (8) Shabba Ranks featuring Maxi Priest (1993)
How 'Bout Us (5) Champaign (1981)
How About That! (4) Adam Faith (1960)

How Am I Supposed To Live Without You (3) Michael Bolton (1990)
How Bizarre (5) OMC (1996)
How Can I Be Sure (1) David Cassidy (1972)
How Can I Love You More (remix) (8) M People (1996)
How Can We Be Lovers (10) Michael Bolton (1990)
How Can you Expect To Be Taken Seriously / Can't Take My Eyes Off You / Where The Streets Have No Name (4) Pet Shop Boys (1991)
How Come (4) D12 (2004)
How Come, How Long (10) Babyface featuring Stevie Wonder (1997)
How Deep Is Your Love (3) Bee Gees (1977)
How Deep Is Your Love (1) Take That (1996)
How Deep Is Your Love (9) Dru Hill (1998)
How Do I Live (7) LeAnn Rimes (1998)
How Do You Do It (1) Gerry & The Pacemakers (1963)
How Do You Want Me To Love You? (10) 911 (1998)
(How Does It Feel To Be) On Top Of The World (9) England United (1998)
How High (6) Charlatans (1997)
How Many Tears (10) Bobby Vee (1961)
(How Much Is) That Doggie In The Window (1) Lita Roza (1953)
(How Much Is) That Doggie In The Window (9) Patti Page (1953)
How Much Love (10) Leo Sayer (1977)
How Soon (10) Henry Mancini Orchestra (1964)
How To Save A Life (4) Fray (2007)
How We Do (5) Game featuring 50 Cent (2005)
How We Roll (2) Loick Essien featuring Tanya Lacey (2011)
How Will I Know (5) Whitney Houston (1986)
How Wonderful You Are (2) Gordon Haskell (2001)
How You Remind Me (4) Nickelback (2002)
Howzat (4) Sherbet (1976)
Human (8) Human League (1986)
Human (3) Killers (2008)
Human Nature (10) Gary Clail On USound System (1994)
Human Nature (8) Madonna (1995)
Humpin' Around (remix) (8) Bobby Brown (1995)
Hundred Mile High City (4) Ocean Colour Scene (1997)
Hundred Pounds Of Clay, A (9) Craig Douglas (1961)
Hung Up (1) Madonna (2005)
Hungry Like The Wolf (5) Duran Duran (1982)
Hunting High And Low (5) A-Ha (1986)
Hurdy Gurdy Man (4) Donovan (1968)
Hurry Up England – The People's Anthem (10) Sham 69 & The Special Assembly (2006)
Hurry Up Harry (10) Sham 69 (1978)
Hurt (4) Manhattans (1976)
Hurt (8) Leona Lewis (2011)
Hurt So Good (4) Susan Cadogan (1975)
Husan (7) Bhangra Knights vs Husan (2003)
Hush (2) Kula Shaker (1997)
Hush (3) LL Cool J featuring 7 Aurelius (2005)
Hustle, The (3) Van McCoy & Soul City Symphony (1975)
Hymn To Her (8) Pretenders (1986)
Hyperballad (8) Björk (1996)
Hypnotize (10) Notorious BIG (1997)
I (Who Have Nothing) (6) Shirley Bassey (1963)
I Ain't Gonna Stand For It (10) Stevie Wonder (1980)
I Am ... I Said (4) Neil Diamond (1971)
I Am A Cider Drinker (Paloma Blanca) (3) Wurzels (1976)
I Am Blessed (7) Eternal (1995)
I Am The Beat (6) Look (1980)
I Beg Your Pardon (5) Kon Kan (1989)
I Begin To Wonder (2) Dannii Minogue (2003)
I Believe (1) Frankie Laine (1953)
I Believe (2) Bachelors (1964)
I Believe (6) EMF (1991)
I Believe (11) Marcella Detroit (1994)
I Believe (re-issue) (7) Happy Clappers (1995)
I Believe / Up On The Roof (1) Robson & Jerome (1995)
I Believe (In Love) (8) Hot Chocolate (1971)

I Believe I Can Fly (1) R Kelly (1997)
I Believe In A Thing Called Love (2) Darkness (2003)
I Believe In Christmas (9) Tweenies (2001)
I Believe In Father Christmas (2) Greg Lake (1975)
I Believe In You (2) Kylie Minogue (2004)
I Believe My Heart (2) Duncan James & Keedie (2004)
I Belong To You (6) Gina G (1996)
I Bet You Look Good On The Dancefloor (1) Arctic Monkeys (2005)
I Breathe Again (5) Adam Rickett (1999)
I Can Do It (7) Rubettes (1975)
I Can Hear Music (10) Beach Boys (1969)
I Can Hear The Grass Grow (5) Move (1967)
I Can Help (6) Billy Swan (1974)
I Can Make You Feel Good (7) Shalamar (1982)
I Can Make You Feel Good (8) Kavana (1997)
I Can Make You Love Me / Older (3) George Michael (1997)
I Can Only Disappoint U (8) Mansun (2000)
I Can Prove It (8) Phil Fearon (1986)
I Can See Clearly Now (5) Johnny Nash (1972)
I Can See For Miles (10) Who (1967)
I Can't Break Down (2) Sinead Quinn (2003)
I Can't Control Myself (2) Troggs (1966)
I Can't Dance (7) Genesis (1992)
I Can't Explain (8) Who (1965)
(I Can't Get No) Satisfaction (1) Rolling Stones (1965)
I Can't Go For That (No Can Do) (8) Daryl Hall & John Oates (1982)
I Can't Help Myself (re-issue) (10) Four Tops (1970)
I Can't Help Myself (7) Lucid (1998)
(I Can't Help) Falling In Love With You (1) UB40 (1993)
I Can't Leave You Alone (9) George McCrae (1974)
I Can't Let Go (2) Hollies (1966)
I Can't Let Maggie Go (8) Honeybus (1968)
I Can't Read You (6) Daniel Bedingfield (2003)
I Can't Stand It (7) Captain Hollywood Project (1990)
I Can't Stand The Rain (5) Eruption (1978)
I Can't Stand Up For Falling Down (4) Elvis Costello (1980)
I Can't Stop Loving You (1) Ray Charles (1962)
I Can't Stop Lovin'You (Though I Try) (6) Leo Sayer (1978)
I Can't Take The Power (7) Off-Shore (1990)
I Can't Tell A Waltz From A Tango (4) Alma Cogan (1954)
I Can't Tell The Bottom From The Top (7) Hollies (1970)
I Can't Wait (2) Nu Shooz (1986)
I Close My Eyes And Count To Ten (4) Dusty Springfield (1968)
I Could Be Happy (7) Altered Images (1981)
I Could Be So Good For You (3) Dennis Waterman with The Dennis Waterman Band (1980)
I Could Easily Fall (In Love With You) (9) Cliff Richard & The Shadows (1964)
I Couldn't Live Without Your Love (6) Petula Clark (1966)
I Did What I Did For Maria (2) Tony Christie (1971)
I Didn't Know I Loved You (Til I Saw You Rock 'N' Roll) (4) Gary Glitter (1972)
I Didn't Mean To Turn You On (9) Robert Palmer (1986)
I Die:You Die (6) Gary Numan (1980)
I Don't Believe In If Anymore (8) Roger Whittaker (1970)
I Don't Care (7) Shakespears Sister (1992)
I Don't Feel Like Dancin' (1) Scissor Sisters (2006)
I Don't Know Anybody Else (4) Black Box (1990)
I Don't Know Why (7) Eden Kane (1962)
I Don't Like Mondays (1) Boomtown Rats (1979)
I Don't Need A Man (7) Pussycat Dolls (2006)
I Don't Wanna Dance (1) Eddy Grant (1982)
I Don't Wanna Fight (7) Tina Turner (1993)
I Don't Wanna Get Hurt (7) Donna Summer (1989)
I Don't Wanna Know (1) Mario Winans featuring Enya & P Diddy (2004)
I Don't Wanna Lose You (8) Tina Turner (1989)
I Don't Want A Lover (8) Texas (1989)
I Don't Want Our Loving To Die (5) Herd (1968)
I Don't Want To (9) Toni Braxton (1997)
I Don't Want To Miss A Thing (4) Aerosmith (1998)
I Don't Want To Put A Hold On You (3) Berni Flint (1977)

I Don't Want To Talk About It / First Cut Is The Deepest (1) Rod Stewart (1977)
I Don't Want To Talk About It (3) Everything But The Girl (1988)
I Drove All Night (7) Cyndi Lauper (1989)
I Drove All Night (7) Roy Orbison (1992)
I Eat Cannibals Part 1 (8) Toto Coelo (1982)
I Feel Fine (1) Beatles (1964)
I Feel For You (1) Chaka Khan (1984)
I Feel For You (9) Bob Sinclair (2000)
I Feel Like Buddy Holly (7) Alvin Stardust (1984)
I Feel Love (1) Donna Summer (1977)
I Feel Love (medley) (3) Bronski Beat with Marc Almond (1985)
I Feel Love (re-issue) (8) Donna Summer (1995)
I Feel So Bad / Wild In The Country (4) Elvis Presley with The Jordanaires
I Feel The Earth Move (7) Martika (1989)
I Feel You (8) Depeche Mode (1993)
I Feel You (1) Peter Andre (1996)
I Finally Found Someone (10) Barbra Streisand & Bryan Adams (1997)
I Found Lovin' (7) Fatback Band (1987)
I Found Lovin' (9) Steve Walsh (1987)
I Found Someone (5) Cher (1987)
I Found U (6) Axwell featuring Max C (2007)
I Get A Kick Out Of You (7) Gary Shearston (1974)
I Get A Little Sentimental Over You (5) New Seekers (1974)
I Get Around (7) Beach Boys (1964)
I Get Lonely (5) Janet Jackson (1998)
I Get So Lonely (5) Nat 'King' Cole & The Four Knights (1954)
I Get So Lonely (re-entry) (10) Nat 'King' Cole & The Four Knights (1954)
I Get The Sweetest Feeling (9) Jackie Wilson (1972)
I Get The Sweetest Feeling (re-issue) (3) Jackie Wilson (1987)
I Get The Sweetest Feeling / Woman In Love (5) Liz McClarnon (2006)
I Get Weak (10) Belinda Carlisle (1988)
I Go Ape (9) Neil Sedaka (1959)
I Go To Sleep (7) Pretenders (1981)
I Got 5 On It (3) Luniz (1996)
I Got Soul (10) Young Soul Rebels (2009)
I Got Stung / OneNight (1) Elvis Presley (1959)
I Got Stung / One Night (re-issue) (1) Elvis Presley (2005)
I Got You Babe (1) Sonny & Cher (1965)
I Got You Babe (1) UB40 featuring Chrissie Hynde (1985)
I Got You Babe / Soda Pop (5) Avid Merrion, Davina McCall & Patsy Kensit (2004)
I Gotta Feeling (1) Black Eyed Peas (2009)
I Guess That's Why They Call It The Blues (5) Elton John (1983)
I Have A Dream (2) Abba (1979)
I Have A Dream / Seasons In The Sun (1) Westlife (1999)
I Have Forgiven Jesus (10) Morrissey (2004)
I Have Nothing (3) Whitney Houston (1993)
I Haven't Stopped Dancing Yet (9) Pat & Mick (1989)
I Hear You Knocking (1) Dave Edmunds (1970)
I Hear You Now (8) Jon & Vangelis (1980)
I Heard It Through The Grapevine (1) Marvin Gaye (1969)
I Heard It Through The Grapevine (re-issue) (8) Marvin Gaye (1986)
I Hope You Dance (2) Ronan Keating (2004)
I Just Called To Say I Love You (1) Stevie Wonder (1984)
I Just Can't Help Believing (6) Elvis Presley (1971)
I Just Can't Stop Loving You (1) Michael Jackson (1987)
(I Just) Died In Your Arms Tonight (4) Cutting Crew (1986)
I Just Don't Have The Heart (3) Cliff Richard (1989)
I Just Don't Know What To Do With Myself (3) Dusty Springfield (1964)
I Just Wanna Be Loved (4) Culture Club (1998)
I Just Wanna Live (9) Good Charlotte (2005)
I Just Want To Make Love To You (5) Etta James (1996)
I Kissed A Girl (1) Katy Perry (2008)
I Knew I Loved You (10) Savage Garden (1999)
I Knew You Were Waiting (For Me) (1) Aretha Franklin & George Michael (1987)
I Know Him So Well (1) Elaine Paige & Barbara Dickson (1985)

I Know Him So Well / Words Are Not Enough /(5) Steps (2001)
I Know What You Want (3) Busta Rhymes & Mariah Carey featuring The Flipmode Squad (2003)
I Know Where It's At (4) All Saints (1997)
I Know You Want Me (Calle Ocho) (4) Pitbull (2009)
I Like It (1) Gerry & The Pacemakers (1963)
I Like It (9) Narcotic Thrust (2004)
I Like It (4) Enrique Iglesias featuring Pitbull (2010)
I Like The Way (3) Bodyrockers (2005)
I Like To Move It (5) Reel 2 Real With The Mad Stuntman (1994)
I Lost My Heart To A Starship Trooper (6) Sarah Brightman & Hot Gossip (1978)
I Love It When We Do (5) Ronan Keating (2002)
I Love My Chick (8) Busta Rhymes (2006)
I Love My Radio (My Deejay's Taffy Radio) (6) (1987)
I Love Rock 'N' Roll (4) Joan Jett & The Blackhearts (1982)
I Love The Sound Of Breaking Glass (7) Nick Lowe (1978)
I Love The Way You Love Me (2) Boyzone (1998)
I Love To Love (1) Tina Charles (1976)
I Love You (1) Cliff Richard & The Shadows (1960)
I Love You (10) Donna Summer (1977)
I Love You Always Forever (5) Donna Lewis (1996)
I Love You Anyway (5) Boyzone (2008)
I Love You Baby (3) Paul Anka (1957)
I Love You Because (5) Jim Reeves (1964)
I Love You Love Me Love (1) Gary Glitter (1973)
I Love You Smile (2) Shanice (1992)
I Luv U (7) Ordinary Boys (2007)
I Luv U Baby (remix) (2) Original (1995)
I Miss You (9) Haddaway (1993)
I Miss You (8) Blink 182 (2004)
I Must Be Seeing Things (6) Gene Pitney (1965)
I Need a Doctor (8) Dr. Dre featuring Eminem & Skylar Grey (2011)
I Need a Dollar (2) Aloe Blacc (2011)
I Need A Girl (Part One) (4) P Diddy featuring Usher & Loon (2002)
I Need A Lover Tonight (7) Ken Doh (1996)
I Need A Miracle (8) Cascada (2007)
I Need Air (10) Magnetic Man featuring Angela Hunte (2010)
I Need Love (8) LL Cool J (1987)
I Need You (3) BVSMP (1988)
I Need You (10) Deuce (1995)
I Need You (5) N-Dubz (2009)
I Need You Tonight (3) Professor Green featuring Ed Drewett (2010)
I Need Your Love Tonight / Fool Such As I, A (1) Elvis Presley with The Jordanaires (1959)
I Need Your Love Tonight / Fool Such as I, A (re-issue) (2) Elvis Presley (2005)
I Need Your Lovin' (8) Alyson Williams (1989)
I Only Have Eyes For You (1) Art Garfunkel (1975)
I Only Want To Be With You (4) Dusty Springfield (1963)
I Only Wanna Be With You (4) Bay City Rollers (1976)
I Only Want To Be With You (4) Tourists (1979)
I Owe You Nothing (1) Bros (1988)
I Predict A Riot / Sink That Ship (re-issue) (9) Kaiser Chiefs (2005)
I Pretend (1) Des O'Connor (1968)
I Put A Spell On You (9) Alan Price Set (1966)
I Put A Spell On You (re-issue) (8) Sonique (2000)
I Quit (4) Bros (1988)
I Quit (8) Hepburn (1999)
I Remember Elvis Presley (The King Is Dead) (4) Danny Mirror (1977)
I Remember You (1) Frank Ifield (1962)
I Saw Him Standing There (8) Tiffany (1988)
I Saw Mommy Kissing Santa Claus (3) Jimmy Boyd (1953)
I Saw Mommy Kissing Santa Claus (re-entry) (6) Beverley Sisters (1953)
I Say A Little Prayer (4) Aretha Franklin (1968)

I Second That Emotion (9) Japan (1982)
I See A Star (8) Mouth & Macneal (1974)
I See The Moon (1) Stargazers (1954)
I Shot The Sheriff (9) Eric Clapton (1974)
I Shot The Sheriff (2) Warren G (1997)
I Should Be So Lucky (1) Kylie Minogue (1988)
I Should Have Known Better (1) Jim Diamond (1984)
I Shoulda Loved Ya (8) Narada Michael Walden (1980)
I Still Believe (3) Ronnie Hilton (1954)
I Still Believe In You (7) Cliff Richard (1992)
I Still Haven't Found What I'm Looking For (6) U2 (1987)
I Still Haven't Found What I'm Looking For (6) Chimes (1990)
I Surrender (3) Rainbow (1981)
I Swear (2) All-4-One (1994)
I Think I Love You (10) Kaci (2002)
I Think I'm Paranoid (9) Garbage (1998)
I Think It's Going To Rain / My Way Of Thinking (6) UB40 (1980)
I Think Of You (5) Merseybeats (1964)
I Think We're Alone Now (1) Tiffany (1988)
I Think We're Alone Now (4) Girls Aloud (2006)
I Thought It Was Over (9) Feeling (2008)
I Touch Myself (10) Divinyls (1991)
I Try (7) Macy Gray (1999)
I Turn To You (1) Melanie C (2000)
I Understand (5) Freddie & The Dreamers (1964)
I Wanna Be A Hippy (6) Technohead (1996)
I Wanna Be The Only One (1) Eternal featuring BeBe Winans (1997)
I Wanna Be U (6) Chocolate Puma (2001)
I Wanna Dance Wit Choo (6) Disco Tex & Sex-OLettes (1975)
I Wanna Dance With Somebody (Who Loves Me) (1) Whitney Houston (1987)
I Wanna Do It With You (8) Barry Manilow (1982)
(I Wanna Give You) Devotion (2) Nomad (1991)
I Wanna Go Home (The Wreck Of The John 'B') (5) Lonnie Donegan & Wally Stott Orchestra (1960)
I Wanna Have Your Babies (7) Natasha Bedingfield (2007)
I Wanna Hold You (3) McFly (2005)
I Wanna Hold Your Hand (9) Dollar (1979)
I Wanna Love You (3) Akon featuring Snoop Doggy Dogg (2007)
I Wanna Love You Forever (7) Jessica Simpson (2000)
I Wanna Sex You Up (1) first hit Color Me Badd (1991)
I Wanna Stay With You (6) Gallagher & Lyle (1976)
I Want Candy (9) Bow Wow Wow (1982)
I Want It All (3) Queen (1989)
I Want It That Way (1) Backstreet Boys (1999)
I Want Love (9) Elton John (2001)
(I Want To Be) Elected (9) Mr Bean and The Smear Campaign with Bruce Dickinson (1992)
I Want To Be Free (8) Toyah (1981)
I Want To Break Free (3) Queen (1984)
I Want To Hold Your Hand (1) Beatles (1963)
I Want To Know What Love Is (1) Foreigner (1984)
I Want To Stay Here (3) Steve & Eydie (1963)
I Want To Wake Up With You (1) Boris Gardiner (1986)
I Want You Back (2) Jackson 5 (1970)
I Want You Back (5) Bananarama (1988)
I Want You Back (remix) (8) Michael Jackson & The Jackson 5 (1988)
I Want You Back (1) Melanie B featuring Missy Misdemeanor' Elliott (1998)
I Want You Back (4) Cleopatra (1998)
I Want You Back (5) N Sync (1999)
I Want You For Myself (2) Another Level / Ghostface Killah (1999)
I Want Your Love (4) Chic (1979)
I Want Your Love (5) Transvision Vamp (1988)
I Want Your Love (10) Atomic Kitten (2000)
I Want Your Sex (3) George Michael (1987)
I Was Kaiser Bill's Batman (5) Whistling Jack Smith (1967)
I Was Made For Dancin' (4) Leif Garrett (1979)

I Was Made To Love Her (5) Stevie Wonder (1967)
I Was Only Joking / Hotlegs (5) Rod Stewart (1978)
I (Who Have Nothing) (6) Shirley Bassey (1963)
I Will (4) Ruby Winters (1977)
I Will Always Love You (1) Whitney Houston (1992)
I Will Always Love You (6) Rik Waller (2002)
I Will Come To You (5) Hanson (1997)
I Will Return (5) Springwater (1971)
I Will Survive (16) Arrival (1970)
I Will Survive (1) Gloria Gaynor (1979)
I Will Survive (remix) (5) Gloria Gaynor (1993)
I Wish (5) Stevie Wonder (1976)
(I Wish I Knew How It Would Feel To Be) Free / One (6) Lighthouse Family (2001)
I Wish I Was A Punk Rocker (With Flowers in My Hair) (1) Sandi Thom (2006)
I Wish It Could Be Christmas Everyday (4) Wizzard (1973)
I Wish It Would Rain Down (7) Phil Collins (1990)
I Wish It Would Rain / Pool Hall Richard (8) Faces (1973)
I Wonder (4) Dickie Valentine (1955)
I Wonder Why (2) Showaddywaddy (1978)
I Wonder Why (5) Curtis Stigers (1992)
I Won't Change You (9) Sophie Ellis-Bextor (2004)
I Won't Forget You (3) Jim Reeves (1964)
I Won't Last A Day Without You / Goodbye To Love (9) Carpenters (1972)
I Won't Let The Sun Go Down On Me (re-issue) (2) Nik Kershaw (1984)
I Won't Let You Down (3) PhD (1982)
I Won't Let You Go (5) James Morrison (2011)
I Won't Run Away (7) Alvin Stardust (1984)
I Wouldn't Trade You For The World (4) Bachelors (1964)
I.O.U. (2) Freeez (1983)
Ice Ice Baby (1) Vanilla Ice (1990)
Ice In The Sun (8) Status Quo (1968)
I'd Do Anything For Love (But I Won't Do That) (1) Meat Loaf (1993)
I'd Lie For You (And That's The Truth) (2) Meat Loaf (1995)
I'd Like To Teach The World To Sing (1) New Seekers (1971)
I'd Love You To Want Me (5) Lobo (1974)
I'd Never Find Another You (5) Billy Fury (1961)
I'd Rather Jack (8) Reynolds Girls (1989)
Icky Thump (2) White Stripes (2007)
Idle Gossip (3) Perry Como (1954)
If (1) Telly Savalas (1975)
If Anyone Finds This I Love You (4) Ruby Murray with Anne Warren (1955)
If I Can't / Them Thangs (10) 50 Cent / G-Unit (2004)
If I Can't Have You (4) Yvonne Elliman (1978)
If I Could Turn Back The Hands Of Time (3) R Kelly (1999)
If I Could Turn Back Time (6) Cher (1989)
If I Didn't Care (9) David Cassidy (1974)
If I Give My Heart To You (4) Doris Day (1954)
If I Give My Heart To You (re-entry) (3) Joan Regan (1954)
If I Had A Hammer (4) Trini Lopez (1963)
If I Had Words (3) Scott Fitzgerald and Yvonne Keely with The St Thomas More School Choir (1978)
If I Let You Go (1) Westlife (1999)
If I Never See You Again (3) Wet Wet Wet (1997)
If I Only Had Time (3) John Rowles (1968)
If I Said You Have A Beautiful Body Would You Hold It Against Me (3) Bellamy Brothers (1979)
If I Told You That (9) Whitney Houston & George Michael (2000)
If I Was (1) Midge Ure (1985)
If I Were A Boy (1) Beyonce (2008)
If I Were A Carpenter (9) Bobby Darin (1966)
If I Were A Carpenter (7) Four Tops (1968)
If I Were A Rich Man (9) Topol (1967)
If It Happens Again (9) UB40 (1984)
If It Makes You Happy (9) Sheryl Crow (1996)
If Not For You (7) Olivia Newton-John (1971)
If Not You (5) Dr Hook (1976)
If Only I Could (3) Sydney Youngblood (1989)
(If Paradise Is) Half As Nice (1) Amen Corner (1969)

If She Should Come To You (4) Anthony Newley (1960)
If That's OK With You / No U Hang Up (2) Shayne Ward (2007)
If The Kids Are United (9) Sham 69 (1978)
If The Whole World Stopped Loving (3) Val Doonican (1967)
If There's Any Justice (3) Lemar (2004)
If This Is Love (8) Saturdays (2008)
If Tomorrow Never Comes (1) Ronan Keating (2002)
If We Ever Meet Again (3) Timbaland featuring Katy Perry (2010)
If Ya Gettin' Down (2) Five (1999)
If You Believe (re-entry) (7) Johnnie Ray (1955)
If You Buy This Record Your Life Will Be Better (3) Tamperer featuring Maya (1998)
If You Can't Give Me Love (4) Suzi Quatro (1978)
If You Can't Stand The Heat (10) Bucks Fizz (1982)
If You Come Back (1) Blue (2001)
If You Come To Me (3) Atomic Kitten (2003)
If You Don't Know Me By Now (9) Harold Melvin & The Bluenotes (1973)
If You Don't Know Me By Now (2) Simply Red (1989)
If You Ever (2) East 17 featuring Gabrielle (1996)
If You Go Away (8) Terry Jacks (1974)
If You Go Away (9) New Kids On The Block (1991)
If You Gotta Go Go Now (2) Manfred Mann (1965)
If You Gotta Make A Fool Of Somebody (3) Freddie & The Dreamers (1963)
If You Had My Love (4) Jennifer Lopez (1999)
If You Leave Me Now (1) Chicago (1976)
If You Let Me Stay (7) Terence Trent D'Arby (1987)
If You Love Me (8) Brownstone (1995)
If You Only Let Me In (6) MN8 (1995)
If You Think You Know How To Love Me (3) Smokie (1975)
If You Tolerate This Your Children Will Be Next (1) Manic Street Preachers (1998)
If You Wanna Party (9) Molella with The Outhere Brothers (1995)
If You Were With Me Now (4) Kylie Minogue & Keith Washington (1991)
If You're Looking For A Way Out (6) Odyssey (1980)
If You're Not The One (1) Daniel Bedingfield (2002)
Ignition (remix) (1) R Kelly (2003)
Iko Iko (10) Natasha (1982)
Il Silenzio (8) Nini Rosso (1965)
III / Jack Mix II (4) Mirage (1985)
I'll Be (9) Foxy Brown featuring Jay-Z (1997)
I'll Be Back (5) Arnee & The Terminators (1991)
I'll Be Home (1) Pat Boone (1956)
I'll Be Loving You (Forever) (5) New Kids On The Block (1990)
I'll Be Missing You (1) Puff Daddy & Faith Evans with 112 (1997)
I'll Be OK (1) McFly (2005)
I'll Be Ready (4) Sunblock (2006)
I'll Be Satisfied (10) Shakin' Stevens (1982)
I'll Be There (4) Jackson 5 (1970)
I'll Be There (2) Mariah Carey (1992)
I'll Be There (7) Emma (2004)
I'll Be There For You (Theme From Friends) (3) Rembrandts (1995)
I'll Be There For You / You're All I Need To Get By (10) Method Man featuring Mary J Blige (1995)
I'll Be There For You (re-entry) (5) Rembrandts (1997)
I'll Be Your Angel (9) Kira (2003)
I'll Be Your Baby Tonight (6) Robert Palmer & UB40 (1990)
I'll Come When You Call (6) Ruby Murray (1955)
I'll Do Anything You Want Me To (see For You I'll Do Anything You Want Me To)
I'll Find My Way Home (6) Jon & Vangelis (1981)
I'll Fly For You (9) Spandau Ballet (1984)
I'll Get By (10) Shirley Bassey (1961)
I'll Keep You Satisfied (4) Billy J Kramer And The Dakotas (1963)
I'll Make Love To You (5) Boyz II Men (1994)
I'll Never Break Your Heart (8) Backstreet Boys (1996)
I'll Never Fall In Love Again (2) Tom Jones (1967)
I'll Never Fall In Love Again (1) Bobbie Gentry (1969)

I'll Never Find Another You (1) Seekers (1965)
I'll Never Get Over You (4) Johnny Kidd & The Pirates (1963)
I'll Pick A Rose For My Rose (10) Marv Johnson (1969)
I'll Remember (Theme From With Honours) (7) Madonna (1994)
I'll Say Forever My Love (7) Jimmy Ruffin (1970)
I'll Stand By You (10) Pretenders (1994)
I'll Stand By You (1) Girls Aloud (2004)
I'll Stop At Nothing (4) Sandie Shaw (1965)
I'll Take You Home Again Kathleen (7) Slim Whitman (1957))
I'm A Believer (1) Monkees (1967)
I'm A Believer (3) EMF & Reeves & Mortimer (1995)
I'm A Boy (2) Who (1966)
I'm A Clown / Some Kind Of Summer (3) David Cassidy (1973)
I'm A Man (9) Spencer Davis Group (1967)
I'm A Man (8) Chicago (1970)
I'm A Man Not A Boy (7) North & South (1997)
I'm A Slave For You (4) Britney Spears (2001)
I'm A Tiger (9) Lulu (1968)
I'm a Wonderful Thing Baby (4) Kid Creole & The Coconuts (1982)
I'm Alive (1) Hollies (1965)
I'm Alive / Kiss From A Rose (4) Seal (1995)
I'm Alive (6) Stretch 'N'Vern present Maddogg (1996)
(I'm Always Hearing) Wedding Bells (5) Eddie Fisher (1955)
I'm Always Touched (By Your Presence Dear) (10) Blondie (1978)
I'm Coming Home (2) Tom Jones (1967)
I'm Crying (8) Animals (1964)
I'm Doing Fine Now (4) Pasadenas (1992)
I'm Easy / Be Aggressive (3) Faith No More (1993)
I'm Every Woman (remix) (8) Chaka Khan (1989)
I'm Every Woman (4) Whitney Houston (1993)
I'm Free (5) Soup Dragons (1990)
I'm Gonna Be Alright (3) Jennifer Lopez (2002)
I'm Gonna Be 500 Miles (1) Proclaimers featuring Brian Potter & Andy Pipkin (2007)
I'm Gonna Be Strong (2) Gene Pitney (1964)
I'm Gonna Get Me A Gun (6) Cat Stevens (1967)
I'm Gonna Get You (3) Bizarre Inc featuring Angie Brown (1992)
I'm Gonna Getcha Good (4) Shania Twain (2002)
I'm Gonna Make Me Love Me (3) Diana Ross & The Supremes and The Temptations (1969)
I'm Gonna Make You Mine (2) Lou Christie (1969)
I'm Gonna Run Away From You (4) Tami Lynn (1971)
I'm Gonna Tear Your Playhouse Down (9) Paul Young (1984)
I'm In Heaven (9) Jason Nevins / UKNY featuring Holly James (2003)
I'm In Love (I Wanna Do It) (10) Alex Gaudino (2010)
I'm In The Mood For Dancing (3) Nolans (1979)
I'm Into Something Good (1) Herman's Hermits (1964)
I'm Into You (9) Jennifer Lopez featuring Lil Wayne (2011)
I'm Leaving It (All) Up To You (2) Donny & Marie Osmond (1974)
I'm Like A Bird (5) Nelly Furtado (2001)
I'm Looking Out The Window / Do You Want to Dance (2) Norrie Paramor / Cliff Richard & The Shadows (1962)
I'm Mandy Fly Me (6) 10CC (1976)
I'm Not A Girl Not Yet A Woman (2) Britney Spears (2002)
I'm Not Alone (1) Calvin Harris (2009)
I'm Not In Love (1) 10CC (1975)
I'm Not Scared (7) Eighth Wonder (1988)
I'm On Fire (4) 5000 Volts (1975)
I'm On Fire / Born In The USA (5) Bruce Springsteen (1985)
I'm Only Sleeping / Off On Holiday (7) Suggs (1995)
I'm Outta Love (6) Anastacia (2000)
I'm Over You (2) Martine McCutcheon (2000)
I'm Real (4) Jennifer Lopez (2001)
I'm Right Here (5) Samantha Mumba (2002)
I'm Still In Love With You (6) Sean Paul featuring Sasha (2004)
I'm Still Standing (4) Elton John (1983)
I'm Still Waiting (1) Diana Ross (1971)
I'm Stone In Love With You (9) Stylistics (1972)

I'm Stone In Love With You (10) Johnny Mathis (1975)
I'm Telling You Now (2) Freddie & The Dreamers (1963)
I'm The Leader Of The Gang (I Am) (1) Gary Glitter (1973)
I'm The Lonely One (8) Cliff Richard & The Shadows (1964)
I'm The One (2) Gerry & The Pacemakers (1964)
I'm The Urban Spaceman (5) Bonzo Dog Doo-Dah Band (1968)
I'm Too Sexy (2) Right Said Fred (1991)
I'm Walking Backwards For Christmas / Bluebottle Blues (4) Goons (1956)
I'm Walking Behind You (1) Eddie Fisher with Hugo Winterhalter's Orchestra and Sally Sweetland (1953)
I'm With Stupid (8) Pet Shop Boys (2006)
I'm With You (7) Avril Lavigne (2003)
I'm Your Angel (3) Celine Dion & R Kelly (1998)
I'm Your Baby Tonight (5) Whitney Houston (1990)
I'm Your Man (1) Wham! (1985)
I'm Your Man (2) Shane Richie (2003)
Imagine (6) John Lennon (1975)
Imagine (re-entry) (1) John Lennon (1980)
Imagine (re-issue) (3) John Lennon (1999)
Imitation Of Life (6) REM (2001)
Immortality (5) Celine Dion with The Bee Gees (1998)
Importance Of Being Idle, The (1) Oasis (2005)
Impossible (9) Shontelle (2010)
In A Broken Dream (3) Python Lee Jackson (1972)
In A Golden Coach (3) Billy Cotton & His Band (1953)
In A Golden Coach (7) Dickie Valentine (1953)
In All The Right Places (8) Lisa Stansfield (1993)
In Betweenies, The / Father Christmas Do Not Touch Me (7) Goodies (1974)
In Da Club (3) 50 Cent (2003)
In Demand (6) Texas (2000)
In Dreams (6) Roy Orbison (1963)
In Dulce Jubilo / On Horseback (4) Mike Oldfield (1975)
In For The Kill (2) La Roux (2009)
In My Arms (10) Kylie Minogue (2008)
In My Defence (8) Freddie Mercury (1992)
In My Eyes (9) Milk Inc (2002)
In My Head (1) Jason Derulo (2010)
In My Own Time (4) Family (1971)
In My Place (2) Coldplay (2002)
In My System (10) Tinchy Stryder (2010)
In Our Lifetime (4) Texas (1999)
In Summer (5) Billy Fury (1963)
In The Air Tonight (2) Phil Collins (1981)
In The Air Tonight (remix) (4) Phil Collins (1988)
In The Army Now (2) Status Quo (1986)
In The Bad Bad Old Days (8) Foundations (1969)
In The Closet (8) Michael Jackson (1992)
In The Country (6) Cliff Richard & The Shadows (1966)
In The End (8) Linkin Park (2001)
In The Ghetto (2) Elvis Presley (1969)
In The Middle (8) Sugababes (2004)
In The Middle Of Nowhere (8) Dusty Springfield (1965)
In The Morning (6) Coral (2005)
In The Morning (3) Razorlight (2006)
In The Name Of The Father (8) Black Grape (1995)
In The Navy (2) Village People (1979)
In The Shadows (3) Rasmus (2004)
In The Summertime (1) Mungo Jerry (1970)
In The Summertime (5) Shaggy featuring Rayvon (1995)
In The Year 2525 (Exordium And Terminus) (1) Zager & Evans (1969)
In These Arms (9) Bon Jovi (1993)
In Thoughts Of You (9) Billy Fury (1965)
In Too Deep (6) Belinda Carlisle (1996)
In Yer Face (9) 808 State (1991)
In Your Arms (Rescue Me) (8) Nu Generation (2000)
In Your Eyes (7) George Benson (1983)
In Your Eyes (3) Kylie Minogue (2002)
In Your Room (8) Depeche Mode (1994)
In Zaire (4) Johnny Wakelin (1976)

Incommunicado (6) Marillion (1987)
Incomplete (8) Backstreet Boys (2005)
Incredible (remix) (8) M-Beat featuring General Levy (1994)
Incredible (What I Meant To Say) (9) Darius (2003)
Independent Women Part 1 (1) Destiny's Child (2000)
Indian Love Call (7) Slim Whitman (1955)
Indian Reservation (3) Don Fardon (1970)
Indiana Wants Me (2) R Dean Taylor (1971)
Infinite Dreams (6) Iron Maiden (1989)
Infinity (5) Guru Josh (1990)
Infinity (3) Guru Josh Project (2008)
Informer (2) Snow (1993)
Inner Smile (6) Texas (2001)
Innocent Eyes (9) Delta Goodrem (2003)
Innuendo (1) Queen (1991)
Insane / Say What You Want (re-recording) (4) Texas featuring The Wu-Tang Clan (1998)
Insania (3) Peter Andre (2004)
Insanity (3) Oceanic (1991)
Insatiable (8) Darren Hayes (2002)
Inside (1) Stiltskin (1994)
Inside Out (3) Odyssey (1982)
Insomnia (3) Faithless (1996)
Instant Karma (5) John Lennon & The Plastic Ono Band (1970)
Instant Replay (8) Dan Hartman (1978)
Instant Replay (10) Yell! (1990)
Instinction (10) Spandau Ballet (1982)
Interesting Drug (9) Morrissey (1989)
Intergalactic (5) Beastie Boys (1998)
International Bright Young Thing (7) Jesus Jones (1991)
Into The Groove (1) Madonna (1985)
Into The Valley (10) Skids (1979)
Intuition (7) Linx (1981)
Invisible (7) D-Side (2003)
Invisible Sun (2) Police (1981)
Invisible Touch (live) (7) Genesis (1992)
Ire Feelings (Skanga) (9) Rupie Edwards (1974)
Iris (3) Goo Goo Dolls (2011)
Irish Blood English Heart (3) Morrissey (2004)
Irish Rover, The (8) Pogues & The Dubliners (1987)
Irish Son (6) Brian McFadden (2004)
Iron Lion Zion (5) Bob Marley & The Wailers (1992)
Irreplaceable (4) Beyonce (2006)
Is It Any Wonder (3) Keane (2006)
Is It Cos I'm Cool (9) Mousse T featuring Emma Lanford (2004)
Is It Just Me (8) Darkness (2006)
Is There Anybody Out There (5) Bassheads (1991)
Is There Something I Should Know (1) Duran Duran (1983)
Is This Love (9) Bob Marley & The Wailers (1978)
Is This Love? (3) Alison Moyet (1986)
Is This Love (9) Whitesnake (1987)
Is This The Way To Amarillo (1) Tony Christie featuring Peter Kay (2005)
Is This The Way To The World Cup? (8) Tony Christie (2006)
Island In The Sun (3) Harry Belafonte (1957)
Island Of Dreams (5) Springfields (1962)
Islands In The Stream (7) Kenny Rogers & Dolly Parton (1983)
Islands In The Stream (See Barry Islands in the Stream)
Isle Of Innisfree (3) Bing Crosby (1952)
Isn't It A Wonder (2) Boyzone (1997)
Isn't She Lovely (4) David Parton (1977)
Israelites (1) Desmond Dekker & Aces (1969)
Israelites (re-issue) (10) Desmond Dekker (1975)
Issues (4) Saturdays (2009)
It Ain't What You Do It's The Way That You Do It (4) Fun Boy Three & Bananarama (1982)
It Began In Afrika (8) Chemical Brothers (2001)
It Can't Be Right (8) 2play featuring Raghav & Naila Boss (2004)
It Didn't Matter (9) Style Council (1987)
It Doesn't Have To Be This Way (5) Blow Monkeys (1987)
It Doesn't Matter (3) Wyclef Jean (2000)
It Doesn't Matter Anymore (1) Buddy Holly (1959)
It Don't Come Easy (4) Ringo Starr (1971)
It Feels So Good (remix) (1) Sonique (2000)
It Girl (4) Jason Derülo (2011)

It Hurts So Much (8) Jim Reeves (1965)
It Is Time To Get Funky (9) D Mob (1989)
It Keep Rainin' (Tears From Eyes) (2) Bitty McLean (1993)
It Miek (7) Desmond Dekker & Aces (1969)
It Might As Well Rain Until September (3) Carole King (1962)
It Must Be Him (2) Vikki Carr (1967)
It Must Be Love (4) Madness (1981)
It Must Be Love (re-issue) (6) Madness (1992)
It Must Have Been Love (3) Roxette (1990)
It Must Have Been Love (re-issue) (10) Roxette (1993)
It Only Takes A Minute (9) One Hundred Ton And A Feather (1976)
It Only Takes A Minute (7) Take That (1992)
It Only Took A Minute (6) Joe Brown & The Bruvvers (1962)
It Should Have Been Me (5) Yvonne Fair (1976)
It Started With A Kiss (5) Hot Chocolate (1982)
It Takes More (7) Ms Dynamite (2002)
It Takes Scoop (9) Fatman Scoop featuring The Crooklyn Clan (2004)
It Takes Two (5) Rod Stewart & Tina Turner (1990)
It Wasn't Me (1) Shaggy featuring Rikrok (2001)
Itchycoo Park (3) Small Faces (1967)
Itchycoo Park (re-issue) (9) Small Faces (1975)
It'll Be Me (2) Cliff Richard & The Shadows (1962)
It's A Fine Day (5) Opus III (1992)
It's A Hard Life (6) Queen (1984)
It's A Heartache (4) Bonnie Tyler (1977)
It's A Love Thing (9) Whispers (1981)
It's A Miracle (4) Culture Club (1984)
It's A Sin (1) Pet Shop Boys (1987)
It's All Coming Back To Me Now (3) Celine Dion (1996)
It's All Coming Back To Me Now (6) Meat Loaf featuring Marion Raven (2006)
It's All Gravy (9) Romeo featuring Christina Milian (2002)
It's All In The Game (1) Tommy Edwards (1958)
It's All In The Game (2) Cliff Richard & The Shadows (1963)
It's All In The Game (5) Four Tops (1970)
It's All Over (9) Cliff Richard (1967)
It's All Over Now (1) Rolling Stones (1964)
It's Almost Tomorrow (1) Dreamweavers (1956)
It's Alright (5) Pet Shop Boys (1989)
It's Alright (3) East 17 (1993)
It's Been So Long (4) George McCrae (1975)
It's Chico Time (1) Chico (2006)
It's Different For Girls (5) Joe Jackson (1980)
It's For You (7) Cilla Black (1964)
It's Four In The Morning (3) Faron Young (1972)
It's Getting Better (8) Mama Cass (1969)
It's Goin' Down (7) X-Ecutioners (2002)
It's Gonna Be A Cold Cold Christmas (4) Dana (1975)
It's Gonna Be Me (9) N Sync (2000)
It's Good News Week (5) Hedgehoppers Anonymous (1965)
It's Grim Up North (10) Justified Ancients Of Mu Mu (1991)
It's Impossible (4) Perry Como (1971)
It's In His Kiss (6) Linda Lewis (1975)
It's Late (3) Ricky Nelson (1959)
It's Like That (1) Run DMC vs Jason Nevins (1998)
It's Like That (5) Mariah Carey (2005)
It's Love (Trippin') (6) Goldtrix presents Andrea Brown (2002)
It's My Life (7) Animals (1965)
It's My Life (2) Dr Alban (1992)
It's My Life (3) Bon Jovi (2000)
It's My Party (9) Lesley Gore (1963)
It's My Party (1) Dave Stewart with Barbara Gaskin (1981)
It's No Good (5) Depeche Mode (1997)
It's Not Right But It's OK (3) Whitney Houston (1999)
It's Not That Easy (7) Lemar (2006)
It's Not Unusual (1) Tom Jones (1965)
It's Now Or Never (1) Elvis Presley with The Jordanaires (1960)
It's Now Or Never (re-issue) (9) Elvis Presley (2005)
It's Oh So Quiet (4) Björk (1995)
It's OK (3) Atomic Kitten (2002)
It's Only Love / Beyond The Reef (3) Elvis Presley (1980)
It's Only Make Believe (1) Conway Twitty (1958)
It's Only Make Believe (10) Billy Fury (1964)

It's Only Make Believe (4) Glen Campbell (1970)
It's Only Make Believe (10) Child (1978)
It's Only Rock And Roll (10) Rolling Stones (1974)
It's Only Us / She's The One (1) Robbie Williams (1999)
It's Over (1) Roy Orbison (1964)
It's Over (8) Funk Masters (1983)
It's Over (10) Level 42 (1987)
It's Over (10) Clock (1997)
It's Raining (2) Darts (1978)
It's Raining (10) Shakin' Stevens (1981)
It's Raining Men (3) Weather Girls (1984)
It's Raining Men (1) Geri Halliwell (2001)
It's The Way You Make Me Feel / Too Busy Thinking 'Bout My Baby (2) Steps (2001)
It's Time For Love (5) Chi-Lites (1975)
It's Too Late (6) Carole King (1971)
It's Too Late (8) Quartz introducing Dina Carroll (1991)
It's Too Soon To Know (7) Pat Boone (1958)
It's Wonderful (To Be Loved By You) (6) Jimmy Ruffin (1970)
It's Written In The Stars (7) Paul Weller (2002)
It's You (9) Freddie Starr (1974)
It's Your Life (5) Smokie (1977)
Itsy Bitsy Teeny Weeny Yellow Polka Dot Bikini (8) Brian Hyland (1960)
Itsy Bitsy Teeny Weeny Yellow Polka Dot Bikini (1) Bombalurina (1990)
I've Been A Bad Bad Boy (5) Paul Jones (1967)
I've Been Losing You (8) A-Ha (1986)
I've Been Thinking About You (2) Londonbeat (1990)
I've Got A Little Puppy (4) Smurfs (1996)
I've Got A Little Something For You (2) MN8 (1995)
I've Got You (6) Martine McCutcheon (1999)
I've Got You Under My Skin (4) Frank Sinatra with Bono (1993)
I've Gotta Get A Message To You (1) Bee Gees (1968)
(I've Had) The Time Of My Life (6) Bill Medley & Jennifer Warnes (1987)
(I've Had) The Time Of My Life (8) Bill Medley & Jennifer Warnes re-entry (1990)
I've Lost You (9) Elvis Presley (1970)
I've Never Been To Me (1) Charlene (1982)
I've Told Every Little Star (7) Linda Scott (1961)
I've Waited So Long (3) Anthony Newley (1959)
Jack In The Box (4) Clodagh Rodgers (1971)
Jack In The Box (7) Moments (1977)
Jack Mix II / III (4) Mirage (1985)
Jack Mix IV (8) Mirage (1987)
Jack That House Built, The (6) Jack 'N' Chill (1988)
Jack Your Body (1) Steve 'Silk' Hurley (1987)
Jackie Wilson Said (I'm In Heaven When You Smile) (5) Dexy's Midnight Runners (1982)
Jacques Your Body (Make Me Sweat) (9) Les Rythmes Digitales (2005)
Jai Ho (You Are My Destiny) (3) A R Rahman featuring The Pussycat Dolls (2009)
Jailhouse Rock (1) Elvis Presley (1958)
Jailhouse Rock (re-issue) (1) Elvis Presley (2005)
James Bond Theme (Moby's Re-Version) (8) Moby (1997)
James Dean (I Wanna Know) (4) Daniel Bedingfield (2002)
Jamming / Punky Reggae Party (9) Bob Marley & The Wailers (1977)
January (1) Pilot (1975)
Japanese Boy (1) Aneka (1981)
Jar of Hearts (4) Christina Perri (2011)
Jarrow Song (6) Alan Price (1974)
Jazz It Up (7) Reel 2 Real (1996)
JCB Song (1) Nizlopi (2005)
Je Ne Sais Pas Pourquoi (2) Kylie Minogue (1988)
Je T'Aime ... Moi Non Plus (2) Jane Birkin & Serge Gainsbourg (1969)
Je T'Aime ... Moi Non Plus Jane Birkin & Serge (re-issue) (1) Gainsbourg (1969)
Je T'Aime (Moi Non Plus) (9) Judge Dread (1975)

Jealous Guy (1) Roxy Music (1981)
Jealous Mind (1) Alvin Stardust (1974)
Jealousy (2) Billy Fury (1961)
Jealousy (5) Will Young (2011)
Jean Genie, The (2) David Bowie (1972)
Jeans On (3) David Dundas (1976)
Jeepster (2) T Rex (1971)
Jennifer Eccles (7) Hollies (1968)
Jennifer Juniper (5) Donovan (1968)
Jenny From The Block (3) Jennifer Lopez (2002)
Jerk It Out (re-issue) (8) Caesars (2005)
Jerusalem (10) Fat Les 2000 (2000)
Jesamine (2) Casuals (1968)
Jesse Hold On (4) B*Witched (1999)
Jesus To A Child (1) George Michael (1996)
Jet (7) Paul McCartney & Wings (1974)
Jet Set / Stereotype (6) International Specials (1980)
Jig A Jig (7) East Of Eden (1971)
Jilted John (4) Jilted John (1978)
Jingle Bell Rock (7) Max Bygraves (1959)
Jingle Bells / U Can't Touch this (5) Crazy Frog (2005)
Jive Talkin' (5) Bee Gees (1975)
Jive Talkin' (7) Boogie Box High (1987)
Joan Of Arc (5) Orchestral Manoeuvres in the Dark (1981)
Joanna (7) Scott Walker (1968)
Joanna / Tonight (2) Kool & The Gang (1984)
Joe Le Taxi (3) Vanessa Paradis (1988)
John And Julie (6) Eddie Calvert (1955)
Johnny Come Home (8) Fine Young Cannibals (1985)
Johnny Reggae (3) Piglets (1971)
Johnny Remember Me (1) John Leyton (1961)
Johnny Will (4) Pat Boone (1961)
Join In And Sing Again (9) Johnston Brothers (1955)
Join Together (9) Who (1972)
Joker, The (1) Steve Miller Band (1990)
Jolene (7) Dolly Parton (1976)
Journey, The (3) 911 (1997)
Joy (4) Soul II Soul (1992)
Joy And Pain (10) Donna Allen (1989)
Joybringer (9) Manfred Mann's Earth Band (1973)
Joyride (4) Roxette (1991)
Judas (8) Lady Gaga (2011)
Judy In Disguise (With Glasses) (3) John Fred & The Playboy Band (1968)
Judy Teen (5) Cockney Rebel (1974)
Juicebox (5) Strokes (2005)
Juke Box Jive (3) Rubettes (1974)
Julia Says (3) Wet Wet Wet (1995)
Julie Ann (1) Kenny (1975)
Julie Do Ya Love Me (8) White Plains (1970)
Juliet / Tell Me Girl (What Are You Gonna Do) (1) Four Pennies (1964)
Jump (7) Van Halen (1984)
Jump (2) Kris Kross (1992)
Jump (2) Girls Aloud (2003)
Jump (9) Madonna (2006)
Jump Around (re-issue) / Top O' The Morning (8) House Of Pain (1993)
Jump (For My Love) (6) Pointer Sisters (1984)
Jump In My Car (3) David Hasselhoff (2006)
Jump They Say (9) David Bowie (1993)
Jump To The Beat (3) Stacy Lattisaw (1980)
Jump To The Beat (8) Dannii Minogue (1991)
Jumpin' (6) Liberty X (2003)
Jumpin' Jumpin' (5) Destiny's Child (2000)
Jumping Jack Flash (1) Rolling Stones (1968)
Jungle Rock (3) Hank Mizell (1976)
Just A Dream (8) Nelly (2010)
Just A Girl (re-issue) (3) No Doubt (1997)
Just A Lil Bit (10) 50 Cent (2005)
Just A Little (1) Liberty X (2002)
Just A Step From Heaven (8) Eternal (1994)

Just An Illusion (2) Imagination (1982)
Just Another Day (5) Jon Secada (1992)
Just Around The Hill (8) Sash (2000)
Just Be Good To Green (5) Professor Green featuring Lily Allen (2010)
Just Can't Get Enough (8) Depeche Mode (1981)
Just Can't Get Enough (2) Saturdays (2009)
Just Can't Get Enough (3) The Black Eyed Peas (2011)
Just Dance (1) Lady Gaga featuring Colby O'Donis (2009)
Just Don't Want To Be Lonely (9) Freddie McGregor (1987)
Just For Tonight (9) One Night Only (2008)
Just For You (10) Glitter Band (1974)
Just For You (8) M People (1997)
Just Got Lucky (7) Jo Boxers (1983)
Just Like A Pill (1) Pink (2002)
Just Like A Woman (10) Manfred Mann (1966)
Just Like Eddie (5) Heinz (1963)
(Just Like) Starting Over (1) John Lennon (1980)
Just Looking (4) Stereophonics (1999)
Just Lose It (1) Eminem (2004)
Just Loving You (6) Anita Harris (1967)
Just My Imagination (Running Away With Me) (8) Temptations (1971)
Just One Look (2) Hollies (1964)
Just One More Night (8) Yellow Dog (1978)
Just One Smile (8) Gene Pitney (1966)
Just Say No (5) Grange Hill Cast (1986)
Just The Two Of Us (2) Will Smith (1998)
Just The Way I'm Feeling (10) Feeder (2003)
Just The Way You Are (8) Milky (2002)
Just The Way You Are (Amazing) (1) Bruno Mars (2010)
Just Walkin' In The Rain (1) Johnnie Ray (1956)
Just Want You To Know (8) Backstreet Boys (2005)
Just What I Always Wanted (8) Mari Wilson (1982)
Just When I Needed You Most (8) Randy Vanwarmer (1979)
Just Who Is The Five O'Clock Hero (8) Jam (1982)
Justified And Ancient (2) KLF with Tammy Wynette (1991)
Justify My Love (2) Madonna (1990)
Ka-Ching (8) Shania Twain (2003)
Karma Chameleon (1) Culture Club (1983)
Karma Police (8) Radiohead (1997)
Kate Bush On Stage EP (10) Kate Bush (1979)
Katy On A Mission (5) Katy B (2010)
Kayleigh (2) Marillion (1985)
(Keep Feeling) Fascination (2) Human League (1983)
Keep Me A Secret (5) Ainslie Henderson (2003)
Keep On Dancing (9) Bay City Rollers (1971)
Keep On Dancin' (8) Gary's Gang (1979)
Keep On Jumpin' (7) Lisa Marie Experience (1996)
Keep On Jumpin' (8) Todd Terry with Martha Wash and Jocelyn Brown (1996)
Keep On Loving You (7) REO Speedwagon (1981)
Keep On Moving (5) Soul II Soul featuring Caron Wheeler (1989)
Keep On Movin' (1) Five (1999)
Keep On Running (1) Spencer Davis Group (1965)
Keep On Walkin' (10) Ce Ce Peniston (1992)
Keep Pushin' / Axel F (7) Clock (1995)
Keep Searchin' (We'll Follow The Sun) (3) Del Shannon (1965)
Keep The Faith (5) Bon Jovi (1992)
Kernkraft 400 (2) Zombie Nation (2000)
Ketchup Song (Asereje), The (1) Las Ketchup (2002)
Kevin Carter (9) Manic Street Preachers (1996)
Kewpie Doll (9) Perry Como (1958)
Kewpie Doll (10) Frankie Vaughan (1958)
Key The Secret, The (2) Urban Cookie Collective (1993)
Key To My Life (3) Boyzone (1995)
Kickstart (3) Example (2010)
Kid's Last Fight, The (3) Frankie Laine (1954)
Kids (2) Robbie Williams & Kylie Minogue (2000)
Kids In America (2) first hit Kim Wilde (1981)
Killamangiro (8) Babyshambles (2004)
Killer (1) Adamski (1990)
Killer (EP) (8) Seal (1991)
Killer (4) ATB (2000)
Killer On The Loose (10) Thin Lizzy (1980)

Killer Queen (2) Queen (1974)
Killing In The Name (re-emergence) (1) Rage Against The Machine (2009)
Killing Me Softly With His Song (6) Roberta Flack (1973)
Killing Me Softly (1) Fugees (1996)
Killing Moon (9) Echo And The Bunnymen (1984)
Killing Of Georgie (Parts 1 And 2), The (2) Rod Stewart (1976)
Kind Of Magic, A (3) Queen (1986)
Kinda Love (8) Darius (2004)
King / Food For Thought (4) UB40 (1980)
King Creole (2) Elvis Presley with The Jordanaires (1958)
King Of My Castle (1) Wamdue Project (1999)
King Of Rock 'N' Roll, The (7) Prefab Sprout (1988)
King Of The Cops (6) Billy Howard (1975)
King Of The Mountain (4) Kate Bush (2005)
King Of The Road (1) Roger Miller (1965)
King Of The Road (EP) (9) Proclaimers (1990)
Kings Of The Wild Frontier (2) Adam & The Ants (1981)
Kingston Town (4) UB40 (1990)
Kinky Afro (5) Happy Mondays (1990)
Kinky Boots (5) Patrick MacNee & Honor Blackman (1990)
Kiss (9) Dean Martin (1953)
Kiss (re-entry) (5) Dean Martin (1953)
Kiss (6) Prince & The Revolution (1986)
Kiss (5) Art Of Noise featuring Tom Jones (1988)
Kiss (When The Sun Don't Shine (3) Vengaboys (1999)
Kiss And Say Goodbye (4) Manhattans (1976)
Kiss From A Rose / I'm Alive (4) Seal (1995)
Kiss Kiss (1) Holly Valance (2002)
Kiss Me (4) Stephen 'Tin Tin' Duffy (1985)
Kiss Me (4) Sixpence None The Richer (1999)
Kiss Me Honey Honey Kiss me (3) Shirley Bassey (1958)
Kiss Me Thru The Phone (6) Soulja Boy Tellem featuring Sammie (2009)
Kiss The Girl (9) Peter Andre (1998)
Kiss The Rain (4) Billie Myers (1998)
Kiss You All Over (6) Exile (1978)
Kisses Sweeter Than Wine (7) Jimmie Rodgers (1957)
Kisses Sweeter Than Wine (8) Frankie Vaughan (1957)
Kissin' Cousins (10) Elvis Presley with The Jordanaires (1964)
Kissin In The Back Row Of The Movies (2) Drifters (1974)
Kites (9) Simon Dupree & The Big Sound (1967)
Klubbhopping (10) Klubbheads (1996)
Knee Deep In The Blues (3) Guy Mitchell (1957)
Knights Of Cydonia (10) Muse (2006)
Knock Knock Who's There (2) Mary Hopkin (1970)
Knock On Wood (10) David Bowie (1974)
Knock On Wood (6) Amii Stewart (1979)
Knock On Wood / Light My Fire (remix) (7) Amii Stewart (1985)
Knock Out (8) Triple Eight (2003)
Knock Three Times (1) Dawn (1971)
Knock You Down (5) Keri Hilson Featuring Kanye West & Ne-Yo (2009)
Knocked It Off (8) B A Robertson (1979)
Knockin' On Heaven's Door (2) Guns 'N' Roses (1992)
Knockin' On Heaven's Door / Throw These Guns Away (1) Dunblane (1996)
Knowing Me Knowing You (1) Abba (1977)
Kon-Tiki (1) Shadows (1961)
Koochy (4) Armand Van Helden (2000)
Kowalski (8) Primal Scream (1997)
Krafty (8) New Order (2005)
Kung-Fu (9) 187 Lockdown (1998)
Kung Fu Fighting (1) Carl Douglas (1974)
Kung Fu Fighting (8) Bus Stop featuring Carl Douglas (1998)
La Bamba (1) Los Lobos (1987)
La Dee Dah (4) Jackie Dennis (1958)
La Isla Bonita (1) Madonna (1987)
La La La Hey Hey (7) Outhere Brothers (1995)
La Mer (Beyond The Sea) (8) Bobby Darin (1960)
La Na Nee Nee Noo Noo / Help (3) Bananarama (1989)
La Primavera (3) Sash (1998)
Labelled With Love (4) Squeeze (1981)
Labour Of Love (6) Hue & Cry (1987)
Ladies Knight (9) Kool & The Gang (1979)

Ladies Night (8) Atomic Kitten featuring Kool & The Gang (2003)
Lady (Hear Me Tonight) (1) Modjo (2000)
Lady D'Arbanville (8) Cat Stevens (1970)
Lady Eleanor (3) Lindisfarne (1972)
Lady In Red, The (1) Chris De Burgh (1986)
Lady Lynda (6) Beach Boys (1979)
Lady Madonna (1) Beatles (1968)
Lady Marmalade / Under The Bridge (1) All Saints (1998)
Lady Marmalade (1) Christina Aguilera, Lil' Kim, Mya & Pink (2001)
Lady Rose (5) Mungo Jerry (1971)
Lady Willpower (5) Union Gap featuring Gary Puckett (1968)
Ladyboy Is Mine, The (10) Stuntmasters (2001)
Lambada (4) Kaoma (1989)
Lamplight (7) David Essex (1973)
Land Of Make Believe, The (1) Bucks Fizz (1981)
Land Of Make Believe, The (9) Allstars (2002)
Larger Than Life (5) Backstreet Boys (1999)
Last Christmas / Everything She Wants (2) Wham! (1984)
Last Christmas (re-issue) (6) Wham! (1985)
Last Farewell, The (2) Roger Whittaker(1975)
Last Friday Night (T.G.I.F.) (9) Katy Perry (2011)
Last Goodbye / Be With You (2) Atomic Kitten (2002)
Last Kiss, The (6) David Cassidy (1985)
Last Night In Soho (8) Dave Dee, Dozy, Beaky, Mick & Tich (1968)
Last Night On Earth (10) U2 (1997)
Last Night Was Made For Love (4) Billy Fury (1962)
Last Of The Famous International Playboys (6) Morrissey (1989)
Last One Standing (8) Girl Thing (2000)
Last Request (5) Paolo Nutini (2006)
Last Resort (3) Papa Roach (2001)
Last Thing On My Mind (6) Steps (1998)
Last Thing On My Mind (5) Ronan Keating & Leann Rimes (2004)
Last Time, The (1) Rolling Stones (1965)
Last Train Home (8) Lostprophets (2004)
Last Train to London / Confusion (8) Electric Light Orchestra (1979)
Last Train To San Fernando (2) Johnny Duncan & Blue Grass Boys (1957)
Last Train To Trancentral (2) KLF (1991)
Last Waltz, The (1) Engelbert Humperdinck (1967)
Lately (3) Stevie Wonder (1981)
Lately (6) Samantha Mumba (2001)
Lately (6) Lisa Scott-Lee (2003)
Laugh At Me (9) Sonny (1965)
Laughing Gnome, The (6) David Bowie (1973)
Launch, The (2) DJ Jean (1999)
Lavender (5) Marillion (1985)
Lay All Your Love On Me (3) Racey (1978)
Lay All Your Love On Me (7) Abba (1981)
Lay Down Your Arms (1) Anne Shelton (1956)
Lay Lady Lay (5) Bob Dylan (1969)
Lay Your Hands (4) Simon Webbe (2005)
Layla (7) Derek & The Dominoes (1972)
Layla (re-issue) (4) Derek & The Dominoes (1982)
Lazy (9) Suede (1997)
Lazy (2) X-Press 2 featuring David Byrne (2002)
Lazy Days (8) Robbie Williams (1997)
Lazy River (2) Bobby Darin (1961)
Lazy Song, The (1) Bruno Mars (2011)
Lazy Sunday (2) Small Faces (1968)
LDN (6) Lily Allen (2006)
Le Freak (7) Chic (1978)
Leader Of The Pack (re-issue) (3) Shangri-Las (1972)
Leader Of The Pack (re-issue) (7) Shangri-Las (1976)
Lean On Me (7) Mud (1976)
Lean On Me (Ah-Li-Ayo) (3) Red Box (1985)
Lean On Me (3) Club Nouveau (1987)
Learnin' The Blues (2) Frank Sinatra with Nelson Riddle (1955)

Leave (Get Out) (2) JoJo (2004)
Leave A Light On (4) Belinda Carlisle (1989)
Leave A Little Love (8) Lulu (1965)
Leave Before The Lights Come On (4) Arctic Monkeys (2006)
Leave Home (17) Chemical Brothers(1995)
Leave Me Alone (2) Michael Jackson (1989)
Leave Right Now (1) Will Young (2003)
Leave Them All Behind (9) Ride (1992)
Leavin' On A Jet Plane (2) Peter Paul & Mary (1970)
Leaving New York (5) REM (2004)
Leeds Leeds Leeds (Marching On Together) (10) Leeds United Team & Supporters (2010)
Leeds United (10) Leeds United FC (1972)
Left My Heart In Tokyo (7) Mini Viva (2009)
Left Outside Alone (3) Anastacia (2004)
Left To My Own Devices (4) Pet Shop Boys (1988)
Legacy EP (7) Mansun (1998)
Legend Of Xanadu (1) Dave Dee, Dozy, Beaky, Mick & Tich (1968)
Lego House (5) Ed Sheeran (2011)
Lenny (10) Supergrass (1995)
Les Bicyclettes De Belsize (5) Engelbert Humperdinck (1968)
Lessons In Love (3) Level 42 (1986)
Let 'Em In (2) Wings (1976)
Let Forever Be (9) Chemical Brothers (1999)
Let It Be (2) Beatles (1970)
Let It Be (1) Ferry Aid (1987)
Let It Rain (10) East 17 (1995)
Let It Rock / Memphis Tennessee (6) Chuck Berry (1963)
Let It Rock / Bitch/ Brown Sugar (2) Rolling Stones (1971)
Let It Rock (5) Kevin Rudolf featuring Lil' Wayne (2009)
Let Love Be Your Energy (10) Robbie Williams (2001)
Let Love Lead The Way / Holler (1) Spice Girls (2000)
Let Me Be Your Fantasy (1) Baby D (1994)
(Let Me Be Your) Teddy Bear (3) Elvis Presley with The Jordanaires (1957)
Let Me Blow Ya Mind (4) Eve featuring Gwen Stefani (2001)
Let Me Clear My Throat (8) DJ Kool (1997)
Let Me Entertain You (3) Robbie Williams (1998)
Let Me Go Lover (3) Dean Martin (1955)
Let Me Go Lover (5) Ruby Murray (1955)
Let Me Go Lover (9) Teresa Brewer with The Lancers (1955)
Let Me Go Lover (10) Kathy Kirby (1964)
Let Me In (2) Osmonds (1973)
Let Me Kiss You (8) Morrissey (2004)
Let Me Live (9) Queen (1996)
Let Me Love You (2) Mario (2005)
Let Me Show You (5) Camisra (1998)
Let Me Think About It (2) Ida Corr vs Fedde Le Grand (2007)
Let Me Try Again (5) Tammy Jones (1975)
Let The Bass Kick In Miami Girl (9) Chuckie & LMFAO (2009)
Let The Beat Control Your Body (2) 2 Unlimited (1994)
Let The Heartaches Begin (1) Long John Baldry (1967)
Let The Music Play (9) Barry White (1975)
Let The Sunshine (3) Labrinth (2010)
Let There Be Drums (3) Sandy Nelson (1961)
Let There Be Love (6) Simple Minds (1991)
Let There Be Love (2) Oasis (2005)
Let Your Head Go / This Groove (3) Victoria Beckham (2004)
Let Your Love Flow (7) Bellamy Brothers (1976)
Let Your Yeah Be Yeah (5) Pioneers (1971)
Let's All Chant (8) Michael Zager Band (1978)
Let's Dance (2) Chris Montez (1962)
Let's Dance (re-entry) (9) Chris Montez (1972)
Let's Dance (1) David Bowie (1983)
Let's Dance (1) Five (2001)
Let's Get Ready To Rhumble (9) PJ & Duncan (1994)
Let's Get Rocked (2) Def Leppard (1992)
Let's Get Serious (8) Jermaine Jackson (1980)
Let's Get Together Again (8) Glitter Band (1974)
Let's Get Together No. 1 (6) Big Ben Banjo Band (1954)
Let's Go All The Way (3) Sly Fox (1986)

Let's Go Crazy / Take Me With You (7) Prince & The Revolution (1985)
Let's Go Round Again (10) Louise (1997)
Let's Go To San Francisco (4) Flowerpot Men (1967)
Let's Groove (3) Earth Wind & Fire (1981)
Let's Hang On! (4) Four Seasons featuring The Sound Of Frankie Valli (1965)
Let's Have A Ball (4) Winifred Atwell (1957)
Let's Have A Ding Dong (3) Winifred Atwell (1955)
Let's Have A Party (2) Winifred Atwell (1953)
Let's Have A Quiet Night In (8) David Soul (1977)
Let's Have Another Party (1) Winifred Atwell (1954)
Let's Hear It For The Boy (2) Deniece Williams (1984)
Let's Make A Night To Remember (10) Bryan Adams (1996)
Let's Party (1) Jive Bunny & The Mastermixers (1989)
Let's Put It All Together (9) Stylistics (1974)
Let's Spend The Night Together Ruby Tuesday (3) / Rolling Stones (1967)
Let's Stay Together (7) Al Green (1972)
Let's Stay Together (6) Tina Turner (1983)
Let's Stick Together (Let's Work Together) (4) Bryan Ferry (1976)
Let's Talk About Sex (2) Salt-N-Pepa Featuring Psychotropic (1991)
Let's Think About Living (6) Bob Luman (1960)
Let's Try Again / Didn't I Blow Your Mind (8) New Kids On The Block (1990)
Let's Twist Again (remix) (2) Chubby Checker (1961)
Let's Twist Again / The Twist (re-issue) (5) Chubby Checker (1975)
Let's Wait Awhile (3) Janet Jackson (1987)
Let's Walk Thata-Way (4) Doris Day & Johnnie Ray (1953)
Let's Work Together (2) Canned Heat (1970)
Letter From America (3) Proclaimers (1987)
Letter To You, A (10) Shakin' Stevens (1984)
Letter, The (5) Box Tops (1967)
Levels (4) Avicii (2011)
Licence To Kill (6) Gladys Knight (1989)
Lick Ya Down (9) Cover Drive (2011)
Lie To Me (10) Bon Jovi (1995)
Lies (4) McFly (2008)
Life (6) Haddaway (1993)
Life (8) Des'ree (1998)
Life Ain't Easy (4) Cleopatra (1998)
Life For Rent (8) Dido (2003)
Life Got Cold (3) Girls Aloud (2003)
Life Is A Flower (5) Ace Of Base (1998)
Life Is A Minestrone (7) 10CC (1975)
Life is A Rollercoaster (1) Ronan Keating (2000)
Life Is Too Short Girl (9) Sheer Elegance (1976)
Life Less Ordinary, A (10) Ash (1997)
Life On Mars (3) David Bowie (1973)
Lifeline (7) Spandau Ballet (1982)
Lifestyles Of The Rich And Famous (8) Good Charlotte (2003)
Lift Me Up (1) Geri Halliwell (1999)
Lifted (4) Lighthouse Family (1996)
Light My Fire (6) Jose Feliciano (1968)
Light My Fire / 137 Disco Heaven (medley) (5) Amii Stewart (1979)
Light My Fire / Knock On Wood (remix) (7) Amii Stewart (1985)
Light My Fire (re-issue) (7) Doors (1991)
Light My Fire (7) Clubhouse featuring Carl (1994)
Light My Fire (1) Will Young (2002)
(Light Of Experience) De Jale (4) Doina Georghe Zamfir (1976)
Light Of My Life (8) Louise (1995)
Lighters (10) Bad Meets Evil featuring Bruno Mars (2011)
Lightning (2) The Wanted (2011)
Lights On (4) Katy B featuring Ms. Dynamite (2010)
Like A Baby (1) Len Barry (1966)
Like A G6 (5) Far East Movement / Cataracs / Dev (2010)
Like A Prayer (1) Madonna (1989)
Like A Prayer (3) Madhouse (2002)
Like A Rolling Stone (4) Bob Dylan (1965)
Like A Rose (6) A1 (2000)
Like A Virgin (3) Madonna (1984)

Like Clockwork (6) Boomtown Rats (1978)
Like Glue (3) Sean Paul (2003)
Like I Do (3) Maureen Evans (1962)
Like I Love You (2) Justin Timberlake (2002)
Like I've Never Been Gone (3) Billy Fury (1963)
Like Sister And Brother (7) Drifters (1973)
Like This (4) Kelly Rowland featuring Eve (2007)
Like To Get To Know You Well (4) Howard Jones (1984)
Like Toy Soldiers (1) Eminem (2005)
Like U Like (8) Aggro Santos featuring Kimberley Walsh (2011)
Lil Star (3) Kelis featuring Cee Lo (2007)
Lily The Pink (1) Scaffold (1968)
Lily Was Here (6) Dave A Stewart with Candy Dulfer (1990)
Lion Sleeps Tonight, The (1) Tight Fit (1982)
Lipstick On Your Collar (3) Connie Francis (1959)
Liquid Dreams (3) O-Town (2001)
Liquidator (9) Harry J Allstars (1969)
Listen (re-emergence) (8) Beyonce (2008)
Listen To What The Man Said (6) Wings (1975)
Listen To Your Heart (10) Sonia (1989)
Listen To Your Heart (7) DHT featuring Edmee (2005)
Listen To Your Heart / Dangerous (6) Roxette (1990)
Little Arrows (2) Leapy Lee (1968)
Little Bad Girl (4) David Guetta featuring Taio Cruz & Ludacris (2011)
Little Bird / Love Song For A Vampire (3) Annie Lennox (1993)
Little Bit Me A Little Bit You, A (3) Monkees (1967)
Little Bit More, A (2) Dr Hook (1976)
Little Bit More, A (1) 911 (1999)
Little Bit Of Lovin' (8) Kele Le Roc (1998)
Little Bit Of Luck, A (9) DJ Luck & MC Neat (1999)
Little Bit Of Soap, A (5) Showaddywaddy (1978)
Little Bitty Tear, A (9) Burl Ives (1962)
Little By Little / She Is Love (2) Oasis (2002)
Little Children (1) Billy J Kramer And the Dakotas (1964)
Little Darlin' (3) Diamonds (1957)
Little Devil (9) Neil Sedaka (1961)
Little Donkey (3) Nina & Frederick (1960)
Little Drummer Boy - Peace On Earth (3) David Bowie and Bing Crosby (1982)
Little Drummer Boy - Peace On Earth (3) Bandaged (2008)
Little Drummer Boy (6) Beverley Sisters (1959)
Little Fluffy Clouds (10) Orb (1993)
Little L (5) Jamiroquai (2001)
Little Less Conversation, A (1) Elvis vs JXL (2002)
Little Less Conversation, A (re-issue) (3) Elvis vs JXL (2005)
Little Lies (5) Fleetwood Mac (1987)
Little Love And Understanding, A (10) Gilbert Becaud (1975)
Little Loving, A (6) Fourmost (1964)
Little Man (4) Sonny & Cher (1966)
Little Miss Lonely (8) Helen Shapiro (1962)
Little More Love, A (4) Olivia Newton-John (1978)
Little Peace, A (1) Nicole (1982)
Little Red Corvette / 1999 (re-issue) (2) Prince (1985)
Little Red Monkey (10) Frank Chacksfield (1953)
Little Red Rooster (1) Rolling Stones (1964)
Little Respect, A (4) Erasure (1988)
Little Respect, A (3) Wheatus (2001)
Little Shoemaker, The (7) Petula Clark (1954)
Little Sister / (Marie's The Name) His Latest Flame (re-issue) (3) Elvis Presley (2005)
Little Star, The / Power of Good-Bye (6) Madonna (1998)
Little Things (5) Dave Berry (1965)
Little Things Mean A Lot (1) Kitty Kallen (1954)
Little Time, A (1) Beautiful South (1990)
Little Town Flirt (4) Del Shannon (1963)
Little White Bull (6) Tommy Steele (1959)
Little Willy (4) Sweet (1972)
Live And Let Die (9) Paul McCartney & Wings (1973)
Live And Let Die (5) Guns 'N' Roses (1991)
Live Forever (10) Oasis (1994)
Live In Trouble (7) Barron Knights (1977)
Live Is Life (6) Opus (1985)
Live It Up (3) Mental As Anything (1987)
Live Like Horses (9) Elton John & Luciano Pavarotti (1996)

Live The Dream (7) Cast (1997)
Live To Tell (2) Madonna (1986)
Live Together (10) Lisa Stansfield (1990)
Live Twice (7) Darius (2005)
Live Your Life (2) TI featuring Rihanna (2008)
Liverpool Lou (7) Scaffold (1974)
Livin' It Up (re-issue) (5) Ja Rule featuring Case (2002)
Livin' La Vida Loca (1) Ricky Martin (1999)
Livin' On A Prayer (4) Bon Jovi (1986)
Livin' Thing (4) Electric Light Orchestra (1976)
Living Daylights, The (5) A-Ha (1987)
Living Doll (1) Cliff Richard & The Drifters (1959)
Living Doll (1) Cliff Richard & The Young Ones with Hank
Marvin (1986)
Living In A Box (5) Living In A Box (1987)
Living In America (5) James Brown (1986)
Living In The Past (3) Jethro Tull (1969)
Living Next Door To Alice (5) Smokie (1976)
Living Next Door To Alice (Who The F**K Is Alice) (3) Smokie
featuring Roy 'Chubby' Brown (1995)
Living On My Own (1) Freddie Mercury (1993)
Living On The Ceiling (7) Blancmange (1982)
Living On Video (9) Trans X (1985)
Living Years, The (2) Mike & The Mechanics (1989)
L-L-Lucy (10) Mud (1975)
Loadsamoney (4) Harry Enfield (1988)
Loca People (1) Sak Noel (2011)
Loch Lomond (9) Runrig featuring The Tartan Army (2007)
Locked Up (5) Akon (2005)
Loco (5) Fun Lovin' Criminals (2001)
Loco In Acapulco (7) Four Tops (1988)
Locomotion (5) Orchestral Manoeuvres In The Dark (1984)
Loco-Motion, The (2) Little Eva (1962)
Loco-Motion, The (2) Kylie Minogue (1988)
Logical Song, The (7) Supertramp (1979)
Logical Song, The (2) Scooter (2002)
Lola (2) Kinks (1970)
Lola's Theme (1) Shapeshifters (2004)
Lollipop (2) Mudlarks (1958)
Lollipop (6) Chordettes (1958)
London Bridge (3) Fergie (2006)
London Nights (2) London Boys (1989)
Lone Ranger, The (5) Quantum Jump (1979)
Loneliness (1) Tomcraft (2003)
Lonely (6) Peter Andre (1997)
Lonely (1) Akon (2005)
Lonely At The Top (10) Ordinary Boys (2006)
Lonely Boy (3) Paul Anka (1959)
Lonely Bull, The (3) Herb Alpert & The Tijuana Brass (1963)
Lonely Girl (see Hey There Lonely Girl)
Lonely Pup (In A Christmas Shop) (4) Adam Faith with The
Children (1960)
Lonely This Christmas (1) Mud (1974)
Long And Winding Road, The / Suspicious Minds (1) Will Young
& Gareth Gates (2002)
Long Goodbye, The (3) Ronan Keating (2003)
Long-Haired Lover From Liverpool (1) Little Jimmy Osmond
(1972)
Long Hot Summer / Paris Match (3) Style Council (1983)
Long Hot Summer (7) Girls Aloud (2005)
Long Live Love (1) Sandie Shaw (1965)
Long Tall Glasses (4) Leo Sayer (1974)
Long Tall Sally (3) Little Richard (1957)
Long Train Runnin (7) Doobie Brothers (1993)
Look, The (7) Roxette (1989)
Look At Me (2) Geri Halliwell (1999)
Look At That Girl (1) Guy Mitchell (1953)
Look Away (7) Big Country (1986)
Look For A Star (7) Garry Mills (1960)
Look For Me (7) Chipmunk featuring Talay Riley (2009)
Look Homeward Angel (7) Johnnie Ray (1957)
Look Mama (10) Howard Jones (1985)

Look Of Love, The (4) ABC (1982)
Look Of Love, The (9) Madonna (1987)
Look Through Any Window (4) Hollies (1965)
Look Wot You Dun (4) Slade (1972)
Lookin' Through The Windows (9) Jackson 5 (1972)
Looking For Love (8) Karen Ramirez (1998)
Looking Through The Eyes Of Love (9) Partridge Family starring
David Cassidy (1973)
Looking Through The Eyes Of Love (3) Gene Pitney (1965)
Loop Di Love (4) Shag (1972)
Loop-De-Loop (5) Frankie Vaughan (1963)
Lord Don't Slow Me Down (10) Oasis (2007)
Lorelei (10) Lonnie Donegan (1960)
Lose Control (7) Missy Elliott (2005)
Lose My Breath (2) Destiny's Child (2004)
Lose Yourself (1) Eminem (2002)
Losing My Mind (6) Liza Minnelli (1989)
Losing You (10) Brenda Lee (1963)
Losing You (9) Dusty Springfield (1964)
Lost For Words (9) Ronan Keating (2003)
Lost In France (9) Bonnie Tyler (1976)
Lost In Music (remix) (4) Sister Sledge (1984)
Lost In Space (4) Apollo Four Forty (1998)
Lost In Space (6) Lighthouse Family (1998)
Lost John / Stewball (2) Lonnie Donegan Skiffle Group (1956)
Lost Without You (4) Delta Goodrem (2003)
Louder (1) DJ Fresh featuring Sian Evans (2011)
Louder (10) Parade (2011)
Loungin' (7) LL Cool J (1996)
Love ... Thy Will Be Done (9) Martika (1991)
Love Action (I Believe In Love) (3) Human League (1981)
Love Ain't Gonna Wait For You / Say Goodbye (2) S Club
(2003)
Love Ain't Here Anymore (3) Take That (1994)
Love Aint Gonna Wait For You / Say Goodbye (2) S Club (2003)
Love And Affection (10) Joan Armatrading (1976)
Love And Kisses (8) Dannii Minogue (1991)
Love And Marriage (3) Frank Sinatra (1956)
Love And Pride (2) King (1985)
Love And Understanding (10) Cher (1991)
Love At First Sight (2) Kylie Minogue (2002)
Love Can Build A Bridge (1) Cher, Chrissie Hynde, Neneh
Cherry and Eric Clapton (1995)
Love Can't Turn Around (10) Farley 'Jackmaster' Funk and
Jessie Saunders (1986)
Love Cats, The (7) Cure (1983)
Love Changes Everything (2) Climie Fisher (1988)
Love Changes Everything (2) Michael Ball (1989)
Love City Groove (7) Love City Groove (1995)
Love Come Down (7) Evelyn 'Champagne' King (1982)
Love Doesn't Have To Hurt (4) Atomic Kitten (2003)
Love Don't Cost A Thing (4) Jennifer Lopez (2001)
Love Don't Let Me Go (Walking Away) (3) David Guetta vs The
Egg (2006)
Love Don't Live Here Anymore (2) Rose Royce (1978)
Love Don't Live Here Anymore (3) Jimmy Nail (1985)
Lovefool (2) Cardigans (1997)
Love Grows (Where My Rosemary Goes) (1) Edison Lighthouse
(1970)
Love Guaranteed (7) Damage (1997)
Love Hangover (10) Diana Ross (1976)
Love Hurts (4) Jim Capaldi (1975)
Love I Lost, The (3) West End featuring Sybil (1993)
Love In The First Degree (3) Bananarama (1987)
Love In This Club (4) Usher featuring Young Jeezy (2008)
Love Is A Many-Splendoured Thing (2) Four Aces featuring Al
Alberts (1955)
Love Is A Stranger (6) Eurythmics (1983)
Love Is All Around (5) Troggs (1967)
Love Is All Around (1) Wet Wet Wet (1994)
Love Is Contagious (7) Taja Seville (1988)
Love Is Gone (9) David Guetta (2007)

Love Is In The Air (5) John Paul Young (1978)
Love Is Life (6) Hot Chocolate (1970)
Love Is Like A Violin (8) Ken Dodd (1960)
Love Is Like Oxygen (9) Sweet (1978)
Love Is Noise (4) Verve (2008)
Love Is Only A Feeling (5) Darkness (2004)
Love Is The Drug (2) Roxy Music (1975)
Love Is The Law (3) Seahorses (1997)
(Love Is) The Tender Trap (2) Frank Sinatra (1956)
Love Kills (10) Freddie Mercury (1984)
Love Letters (4) Ketty Lester (1962)
Love Letters (6) Elvis Presley (1966)
Love Letters (4) Alison Moyet (1987)
Love Letters In The Sand (2) Pat Boone (1957)
Lovelight (8) Robbie Williams (2006)
Love Like A Man (10) Ten Years After (1970)
Love Like You And Me (10) Gary Glitter (1975)
Love Lockdown (8) Kanye West (2008)
Love Machine (3) Miracles (1976)
Love Machine (2) Girls Aloud (2004)
Love Makes The World Go Round (6) Perry Como (1958)
Love Me (6) Yvonne Elliman (1976)
Love Me / Talking In Your Sleep (6) Martine McCutcheon (1999)
Love Me Do (re-entry) (4) Beatles (1982)
Love Me For A Reason (1) Osmonds (1974)
Love Me For A Reason (2) Boyzone (1994)
Love Me Forever (5) Marion Ryan (1958)
Love Me Like I Love You (4) Bay City Rollers (1976)
Love Me Love My Dog (3) Peter Shelley (1975)
Love Me Or Leave Me (8) Sammy Davis Jr (1955)
Love Me Tonight (9) Tom Jones (1969)
Love Missile F1-11 (3) Sigue Sigue Sputnik (1986)
Love Of A Lifetime (9) Honeyz (1999)
Love Of My Life (9) Dooleys (1977)
Love Of Richard Nixon, The (2) Manic Street Preachers (2004)
Love Of The Common People (9) Nicky Thomas (1970)
Love Of The Common People (2) Paul Young (1983)
Love On A Mountain Top (10) Robert Knight (1973)
Love On The Line (6) Blazin' Squad (2002)
Love On Your Side (9) Thompson Twins (1983)
Love Plus One (3) Haircut 100 (1982)
Love Really Hurts Without You (2) Billy Ocean (1976)
Love Resurrection (10) Alison Moyet (1984)
Love Rollercoaster (7) Red Hot Chili Peppers (1997)
Love Sex Magic (5) Ciara featuring Justin Timberlake (2009)
Love Shack (2) B-52's (1990)
Love Shine A Light (3) Katrina & The Waves (1997)
Love Song (4) Sara Bareilles (2008)
Love Song / Alive And Kicking (re-issue) (6) Simple Minds (1992)
Love Song For A Vampire / Little Bird (3) Annie Lennox (1993)
Love Spreads (2) Stone Roses (1994)
Love Story (Vs Finally) (8) Layo & Bushwacka (2003)
Love Story (2) Taylor Swift (2009)
Love The Way You Lie (2) Eminem featuring Rihanna (2010)
Love Theme From A Star is Born (Evergreen) (3) Barbra Streisand (1977)
Love Theme From Thornbirds, The (10) Juan Martin (1984)
Love To Hate You (4) Erasure (1991)
Love To Love You Baby (4) Donna Summer (1976)
Love Today (6) Mika (2007)
Love Town (6) Booker Newbury III (1983)
Love Train (9) O'Jays (1973)
Love Train (4) Holly Johnson (1989)
Love Will Save The Day (10) Whitney Houston (1988)
Love Won't Wait (1) Gary Barlow (1997)
Love Worth Waiting For, A (2) Shakin' Stevens (1984)
Love X Love (10) George Benson (1980)
Love You Like Mad (7) VS (2004)
Love You More (1) JLS (2010)
Love You Save, The (7) Jackson 5 (1970)
Lovely Day (7) Bill Withers (1978)
Lovely Day (remix) (4) Bill Withers (1988)
Lover's Concerto, A (5) Toys (1965)

Lovers And Friends / Get Low (10) Lil Jon & The East Side Boyz (2005)
Lovers Of The World Unite (7) David & Jonathan (1966)
Love's Been Good To Me (8) Frank Sinatra (1969)
Love's Got A Hold On My Heart (2) Steps (1999)
Love's Gotta Hold On Me (4) Dollar (1979)
Love's Just A Broken Heart (5) Cilla Black (1966)
Love's Theme (10) Love Unlimited Orchestra (1974)
Love's Unkind (3) Donna Summer (1977)
Lovesick Blues (1) Frank Ifield (1962)
Lovestruck (10) Madness (1999)
Lovin' Each Day (2) Ronan Keating (2001)
Lovin' Is Easy (6) Hear'Say (2002)
Lovin' Things (6) Marmalade (1968)
Loving Kind, The (re-emergence) (10) Girls Aloud (2009)
Loving You (2) Minnie Riperton (1975)
Low (2) Flo Rida featuring T-Pain (2008)
LSF (10) Kasabian (2004)
LSI (6) Shamen (1992)
Lucille (10) Little Richard (1957)
Lucille / So Sad (To Watch Good Love Go Bad) (4) Everly Brothers (1960)
Lucille (1) Kenny Rogers (1977)
Lucky (5) Britney Spears (2000)
Lucky Lips (4) Cliff Richard & The Shadows (1963)
Lucky Man (7) Verve (1997)
Lucky Number (3) Lene Lovich (1979)
Lucky Stars (3) Dean Friedman (1978)
Lucy In The Sky With Diamonds (10) Elton John (1974)
Lullaby (5) Cure (1989)
Lullaby (9) Shawn Mullins (1999)
Lullaby / 50:50 (5) Lemar (2003)
Lumbered / Michael Row The Boat (6) Lonnie Donegan & His Group (1961)
Luv Me Luv Me (5) Shaggy (2001)
Luv Shine (10) Booty (2007)
Luv U Better (7) LL Cool J (2002)
Luvstruck (9) Southside Spinners (2000)
Lyla (1) Oasis (2005)
Ma Baker (2) Boney M (1977)
Ma (He's Making Eyes At Me) (2) Johnny Otis Show (1957)
Ma (He's Making Eyes At Me) (10) Lena Zavaroni (1974)
Macarena (2) Los Del Rio (1996)
Macarthur Park (4) Richard Harris (1968)
Macarthur Park (5) Donna Summer (1978)
Mack The Knife (1) Bobby Darin (1959)
Mad About You (9) Bruce Ruffin (1972)
Mad Passionate Love (6) Bernard Bresslaw (1958)
Mad World (3) first hit Tears For Fears (1982)
Mad World (1) Michael Andrews featuring Gary Jules (2003)
Madame Helga (4) Stereophonics (2003)
Made You / When Johnny Comes Marching Home (5) Adam Faith with John Barry Orchestra (1960)
Madness (Is All In My Mind) / Tomorrow's (Just Another Day) (8) Madness (1983)
Maggie May / Reason To Believe (1) Rod Stewart (1971)
Maggie's Farm / Do Nothing (4) Specials (1980)
Magic Fly (2) Space (1977)
Magic Moments (1) Perry Como (1958)
Magic Number, The / Buddy (7) De La Soul (1989)
Magic Roundabout / Funky Moped (5) Jasper Carrott (1975)
Magical Mystery Tour EP (2) Beatles (1967)
Mah Na Mah Na (8) Piero Umiliani (1977)
Maid Of Orleans (The Waltz Joan of Arc) (4) Orchestral Manoeuvres in the Dark (1982)
Main Title Theme From Man With The Golden Arm (9) Billy May Orchestra (1956)
Make It A Party (7) Winifred Atwell (1956)
Make It Easy On Yourself (1) Walker Brothers (1965)
Make It Soon (9) Tony Brent (1953)
Make It With You (5) Bread (1970)
Make It With You (7) Let Loose (1996)
Make Love To Me (8) Jo Stafford (1954)
Make Luv (1) Room 5 featuring Oliver Cheatham (2003)
Make Me An Island (3) Joe Dolan (1969)

Make Me Smile (Come Up And See Me) (1) Steve Harley & Cockney Rebel (1975)
Make You Feel My Love (4) Adele (2010)
Makes Me Wonder May (2) Maroon 5 (2007)
MakeThe World Go Away (8) Eddy Arnold (1966)
Makin' Love (9) Floyd Robinson (1959)
Making Up Again (7) Goldie (1978)
Making Your Mind Up (1) Bucks Fizz (1981)
Male Stripper (4) Man 2 Man meet Man Parrish (1987)
Malt And Barley Blues (5) McGuinness Flint (1971)
Mama / Robot Man (2) Connie Francis (1960)
Mama (5) Dave Berry (1966)
Mama (4) Genesis (1983)
Mama / Who Do You Think You Are (1) Spice Girls (1997)
Mama – Who Da Man? (3) Richard Blackwood (2000)
Mama Do (Uh Oh Uh Oh) (1) Pixie Lott (2009)
Mama Told Me Not To Come (3) Three Dog Night (1970)
Mama Told Me Not To Come (4) Tom Jones & The Stereophonics (2000)
Mama Used To Say (7) Junior (1982)
Mama Weer All Crazee Now (1) Slade (1972)
Mambo Italiano (1) Rosemary Clooney & The Mellomen (1954)
Mambo No 5 (A Little Bit Of ...) (1) Lou Bega (1999)
Mambo No 5 (1) Bob The Builder (2001)
Mamma Mia (1) Abba (1975)
Man (Uh-Huh) (7) Rosemary Clooney (1954)
Man From Laramie, The (1) Jimmy Young (1955)
Man In The Mirror (re-emergence) (2) Michael Jackson (2009)
Man Of Mystery / The Stranger (5) Shadows (1960)
Man Of The World (2) Fleetwood Mac (1969)
Man On Fire / Wanderin' Eyes (6) Frankie Vaughan (1957)
Man On The Edge (10) Iron Maiden (1995)
Man Who Can't Be Moved, The (2) Script (2008)
Man Who Sold The World, The (3) Lulu (1974)
Man With The Child In His Eyes (6) Kate Bush (1978)
Man Without Love, A (2) Engelbert Humperdinck (1968)
Man! I Feel Like A Woman (3) Shania Twain (1999)
Manchild (5) Neneh Cherry (1989)
Mandy (9) Eddie Calvert (1958)
Mandy (1) Westlife (2003)
Maneater (6) Daryl Hall & John Oates (1982)
Maneater (1) Nelly Furtado (2006)
Manic Monday (2) Bangles (1986)
Many Of Horror (When We Collide) (8) Biffy Clyro (2010)
Marblehead Johnson (7) Bluetones (1996)
March Of The Siamese Kenny Ball & His
Marcheta (8) Karl Denver (1961)
Marguerita Time (3) Status Quo (1983)
Maria (8) P J Proby (1965)
Maria (1) Blondie (1999)
Maria Elena (5) Los Indios Tabajaras (1963)
Maria Maria (6) Santana featuring The Product G&B (2000)
Marie (9) Bachelors (1965)
(Marie's The Name) His Latest Flame / Little Sister (1) Elvis Presley (1961)
(Marie's The Name) His Latest Flame / Little Sister (re-issue) (3) Elvis Presley (2005)
Martha's Harbour (10) All About Eve (1988)
Mary Had A Little Boy (8) Snap (1990)
Mary Had A Little Lamb (9) Wings (1972)
Mary's Boy Child (1) Harry Belafonte (1957)
Mary's Boy Child (re-entry) (10) Harry Belafonte (1958)
Mary's Boy Child / Oh My Lord (1) Boney M (1978)
Mary's Prayer (3) Danny Wilson (1988)
Mas Que Nada (10) Echobeatz (1998)
Mas Que Nada (6) Sergio Mendes / Black Eyed Peas (2006)
Mass Destruction (7) Faithless (2004)
Massachusetts (1) Bee Gees (1967)
Masses Against The Classes, The (1) Manic Street Preachers (2000)
Master And Servant (9) Depeche Mode (1984)
Masterblaster (Jammin') (2) Stevie Wonder (1980)

Masterblaster 2000 (5) DJ Luck & MC Neat featuring JJ (2000)
Matchstalk Men And Matchstalk Cats And Dogs (1) Brian & Michael (1978)
Material Girl (3) Madonna (1985)
Matinee (8) Franz Ferdinand (2004)
Matthew And Son (2) Cat Stevens (1967)
May I Have The Next Dream With You (8) Malcolm Roberts (1968)
May You Always (9) Joan Regan (1959)
Maybe (6) Emma (2003)
Maybe Baby (4) Crickets (1958)
Maybe That's What It Takes (3) Alex Parks (2003)
Maybe Tomorrow (3) Stereophonics (2003)
Me Against The Music (2) Britney Spears featuring Madonna (2003)
Me And My Life (4) Tremeloes (1970)
Me And U (6) Cassie (2006)
Me And You And A Dog Named Boo (4) Lobo (1971)
Me And You Versus The World (9) Space (1996)
Me Julie (2) Shaggy & Ali G (2002)
Me The Peaceful Heart (9) Lulu (1968)
Mean Streak (10) Cliff Richard & The Drifters (1959)
Mean Woman Blues / Blue Bayou (3) Roy Orbison (1963)
Measure Of A Man / With A Little Help From My Friends (1) Sam & Mark (2004)
Meet Me Halfway (1) Black Eyed Peas (2009)
Meet Me On The Corner (2) Max Bygraves (1955)
Meet Me On The Corner (5) Lindisfarne (1972)
(Meet) The Flintstones (3) BC-52s (1994)
Megablast / Don't Make Me Wait (6) BombThe Bass featuring Merlin & Antonia / Lorraine & Lose (1988)
Megamix (6) Technotronic (1990)
Mellow Yellow (8) Donovan (1967)
Melody Of Love (10) Ink Spots (1955)
Melting Pot (3) Blue Mink (1969)
Memories Are Made Of This (1) Dean Martin (1956)
Memories Are Made Of This (5) Dave King featuring The Keynotes (1956)
Memory (6) Elaine Paige (1981)
Memphis Tennessee / Let It Rock (6) Chuck Berry (1963)
Men In Black (1) Will Smith (1997)
Mercy (1) Duffy (2008)
Mercy Mercy Me – I Want You (9) Robert Palmer (1991)
Merry Christmas Everyone (1) Shakin' Stevens (1985)
Merry Gentle Pops (9) Barron Knights with Duke D'Mond (1965)
Merry Xmas Everybody (1) Slade (1973)
Mess Of Blues, A (2) Elvis Presley with The Jordanaires (1960)
Message In A Bottle (1) Police (1979)
Message To You Rudy, A / Nite Club (10) Specials featuring Rico (1979)
Message Understood (6) Sandie Shaw (1965)
Message, The (8) Grandmaster Flash & The Furious Five (1982)
Metal Guru (1) T Rex (1972)
Mexicali Rose (8) Karl Denver (1961)
Mexico (15) Long John Baldry (1968)
MFEO (8) Kavana (1997)
Mi Chico Latino (1) Geri Halliwell (1999)
Miami (3) Will Smith (1998)
Miami 2 Ibiza (4) Swedish House Mafia vs Tinie (2010)
Miami Hit Mix / Xmas Through Your Eyes (8) Gloria Estefan (1992)
Miami Vice Theme (5) Jan Hammer (1985)
Michael (1) Highwaymen (1961)
Michael Row The Boat / Lumbered (6) Lonnie Donegan & His Group (1961)
Michelle (1) Overlanders (1966)
Mickey (2) Toni Basil (1982)
Mickey (4) Lolly (1999)
Midas Touch (8) Midnight Star (1986)
Midlife Crisis (10) Faith No More (1992)
Midnight In Chelsea (4) Jon Bon Jovi (1997)
Midnight In Moscow (2) Kenny Ball & His Jazzmen (1961)

Midnight Rider (10) Paul Davidson (1975)
Midnight Train To Georgia (10) Gladys Knight & The Pips (1976)
Mighty Quinn (1) Manfred Mann (1968)
Milk (10) Garbage featuring Tricky (1996)
Milk And Alcohol (9) Dr Feelgood (1979)
Milkshake (2) Kelis (2004)
Millennium (1) Robbie Williams (1998)
Millennium Prayer, The (1) Cliff Richard (1999)
Million Dollar Bill (5) Whitney Houston (2009)
Million Love Songs, A (7) Take That (1992)
Millionaire (3) Kelis featuring Andre 3000 (2004)
Mind Blowing Decisions / Always And Forever (remix) (9) Heatwave (1978)
Mind Of Its Own, A (6) Victoria Beckham (2002)
Minute You're Gone, The (1) Cliff Richard (1965)
Miracles (10) Pet Shop Boys (2003)
Mirror In The Bathroom (4) Beat (1980)
Mirror Man (2) Human League (1982)
Mirror Mirror (9) Pinkerton's Assorted Colours (1966)
Mirror Mirror (4) Dollar (1981)
Misfit (7) Curiosity Killed The Cat (1987)
Misfit (6) Amy Studt (2003)
Miss Independent (6) Kelly Clarkson (2003)
Miss Independent (6) Ne-Yo (2008)
Miss Perfect (5) Abs featuring Nodesha (2003)
Miss Sarajevo (6) Passengers (1995)
Miss You / Far Away Eyes (3) Rolling Stones (1978)
Miss You Like Crazy (2) Natalie Cole (1989)
Miss You Nights / Tonight (3) Westlife (2003)
Mis-Shapes / Sorted For E's And Wizz (2) Pulp (1995)
Missing (remix) (3) Everything But The Girl (1994)
Missing You (9) John Waite (1984)
Missing You (3) Chris De Burgh (1988)
Missing You (3) Saturdays (2010)
Mississippi (1) Pussycat (1976)
Mistletoe And Wine (1) Cliff Richard (1988)
Misty (2) Ray Stevens (1975)
Misty Blue (5) Dorothy Moore (1976)
Misunderstood (8) Robbie Williams (2004)
Mixed Up World (7) Sophie Ellis-Bextor (2003)
Mmm Mmm Mmm Mmm (2) Crash Test Dummies (1994)
Mmmbop (1) Hanson (1997)
Mo Money Mo Problems (6) Notorious BIG featuring 112 (1997)
Moan And Groan (7) Mark Morrison (1997)
Mobile (4) Ray Burns with Eric Jupp and Orchestra (1955)
Mockingbird (4) Eminem (2005)
Mockingbird Hill (10) Migil Five (1964)
Model, The / Computer Love (re-entry) (1) Kraftwerk (1981)
Modern Girl (8) Sheena Easton (1980)
Modern Love (2) David Bowie (1983)
Moi ... Lolita (9) Alizee (2002)
Moment Like This, A (1) Leona Lewis (2006)
Moments In Soul (7) JT & The Big Family (1990)
Mona (2) Craig McLachlan & Check 1-2 (1990)
Mona Lisa (5) Conway Twitty (1959)
Monday Monday (3) Mamas & The Papas (1966)
Money (5) Flying Lizards (1979)
Money (5) Jamelia featuring Beenie Man (2000)
Money For Nothing (4) Dire Straits (1985)
Money Honey (3) Bay City Rollers (1975)
Money Money Money (3) Abba (1976)
Monkey Spanner (7) Dave & Ansil Collins (1971)
Monsieur Dupont (6) Sandie Shaw (1969)
Monster (4) Automatic (2006)
Monster Mash (3) Bobby 'Boris' Pickett & the Crypt- Kickers (1973)
Montego Bay (3) Bobby Bloom (1970)
Mony Mony (1) Tommy James & The Shondells (1968)
Mony Mony (7) Billy Idol (1987)
Moody Blue (6) Elvis Presley (1977)
Moon River (1) Danny Williams (1961)
Moonglow / Theme From Picnic (7) Morris Stoloff (1956)
Moonlight Shadow (4) Mike Oldfield featuring Maggie Reilly (1983)

Moonlighting (2) Leo Sayer (1975)
Moonlighting Theme (8) Al Jarreau (1987)
Moonshine Sally (10) Mud (1975)
More (4) Jimmy Young (1956)
More (10) Perry Como (1956)
More And More Party Pops (5) Russ Conway (1959)
More I See You, The (3) Chris Montez (1966)
More More More (5) Andrea True Connection (1976)
More More More (3) Rachel Stevens (2004)
More Party Pops (10) Russ Conway (1958)
More Than A Woman (7) Tavares (1978)
More Than A Woman (2) 911 (1998)
More Than A Woman (1) Aaliyah (2002)
More Than Ever (Coma Prima) (5) Malcolm Vaughan with The Mike Sammes Singers (1958)
More Than I Can Say / Staying In (4) Bobby Vee (1961)
More Than I Can Say (2) Leo Sayer (1980)
More Than I Needed To Know (5) Scooch (2000)
More Than In Love (2) Kate Robbins & Beyond (1981)
More Than This (6) Roxy Music (1982)
More Than This (5) Emmie (1999)
More Than Words (2) Extreme (1991)
More To This World (8) Bad Boys Inc (1994)
More You Ignore Me The Closer I Get, The (8) Morrissey (1994)
Morning After Dark (6) Timbaland featuring Nelly Furtado & Soshy (2009)
Morning Has Broken (9) Cat Stevens (1972)
Morning Side Of The Mountain (5) Donny & Marie Osmond (1974)
Morningtown Ride (2) Seekers (1966)
Most Beautiful Girl, The (2) Charlie Rich (1974)
Most Beautiful Girl In The World, The (1) Artist Formerly Known As Prince (1994)
Most Girls (5) Pink (2000)
Mother And Child Reunion (5) Paul Simon (1972)
Mother Nature And Father Time (7) Nat 'King' Cole (1953)
Mother Of Mine (2) Neil Reid (1972)
Motorhead Live (6) Motorhead (1981)
Motown Song, The (10) Rod Stewart with The Temptations (1991)
Mouldy Old Dough (1) Lieutenant Pigeon (1972)
Moulin Rouge (1) Mantovani & His Orchestra (1953)
Moulin Rouge (re-entry) (10) Mantovani & His Orchestra (1953)
Mountain Greenery (re-entry) (4) Mel Tormé (1956)
Mountains (5) Biffy Clyro (2008)
Move Any Mountain (remix) (4) Shamen (1991)
Move Away (7) Culture Club (1986)
Move Closer (1) Phyllis Nelson (1985)
Move It (2) Cliff Richard and The Drifters (1958)
Move It / 21st Century Christmas (2) Cliff Richard (2006)
Move Mania (8) Sash featuring Shannon (1998)
Move Move Move (The Red Tribe) (6) 1996 Manchester Utd FA Cup Squad (1996)
Move On Baby (7) Cappella (1994)
Move Over Darling (8) Doris Day (1964)
Move Over Darling (8) Tracey Ullman (1983)
Move This Mountain / Get Over You (3) Sophie Ellis-Bextor (2002)
Move Ya Body (6) Nina Sky (2004)
Move Your Body (Elevation) (7) Xpansions (1991)
Move Your Body (3) Eiffel 65 (2000)
Move Your Feet (3) Junior Senior (2003)
Moves Like Jagger (2) Maroon 5 featuring Christina Aguilera (2011)
Movies (5) Alien Ant Farm (2002)
Moviestar (5) Stereophonics (2004)
Movin' Too Fast (2) Artful Dodger & Romina Johnson (2000)
Moving (9) Supergrass (1999)
Moving On Up (2) M People (1993)
Mozart Symphony No. 40 in G Minor (5) Waldo De Los Rios (1971)
Mr Blobby (1) Mr Blobby (1993)
Mr Blue Sky (6) Electric Light Orchestra (1978)
Mr Brightside (10) Killers (2004)
Mr Hankey The Christmas Poo (4) Mr Hankey (1999)

Mr Know It All (4) Kelly Clarkson (2011)
Mr Loverman (re-issue) (3) Shabba Ranks (1993)
Mr Sandman (5) Dickie Valentine (1954)
Mr Sandman (9) Four Aces featuring Al Alberts (1955)
Mr Saxobeat (3) Alexandra Stan (2011)
Mr Sleaze (3) Stock Aitken Waterman (1987)
Mr Soft (8) Cockney Rebel (1974)
Mr Tambourine Man (1) Byrds (1965)
Mr Vain (1) Culture Beat (1993)
Mr Wendal / Revolution (4) Arrested Development (1993)
Mr Wonderful (5) Peggy Lee (1957)
Mr Writer (5) Stereophonics (2001)
Mrs Robinson (4) Simon & Garfunkel (1968)
Mrs Robinson (EP) (9) Simon & Garfunkel (1969)
Ms Grace (1) Tymes (1974)
Ms Jackson (2) Outkast (2001)
(Mucho Mambo) Sway (2) Shaft (1999)
Mulder And Scully (3) Catatonia (1998)
Mull Of Kintyre / Girls' School (1) Wings (1977)
Multiplication (5) Bobby Darin (1961)
Mundian To Bach Ke (5) Panjabi MC (2003)
Munich (10) Editors (2006)
Murder On The Dancefloor (2) Sophie Ellis-Bextor (2001)
Musclebound / Glow (10) Spandau Ballet (1981)
Music (3) John Miles (1976)
Music (1) Madonna (2000)
Music And Lights (5) Imagination (1982)
Music Gets The Best Of Me (14) Sophie Ellis Bextor (2002)
Music Is My Radar (10) Blur (2000)
Music Of The Night, The (7) Michael Crawford (1987)
Music Of Torvill And Dean EP, (9) Richard Hartley & The Mike Reed Orchestra (1984)
Music Sounds Better With You (2) Stardust (1998)
Music To Watch Girls By (9) Andy Williams (1999)
Music's No Good Without Me, The (8) Cher (2001)
Musique / Da Funk (7) Daft Punk (1997)
Must Be The Music (8) Joey Negro featuring Taka Boom (2000)
Must To Avoid, A (6) Herman's Hermits (1965)
My All (4) Mariah Carey (1998)
My Arms Keep Missing You / When I Fall In Love (2) Rick Astley (1987)
My Baby Just Cares For Me (5) Nina Simone (1987)
My Baby Loves Lovin' (9) White Plains (1970)
My Band (2) D12 (2004)
My Best Friend's Girl (3) Cars (1978)
My Boo / Confessions Part II (5) Usher (2004)
My Boy (5) Elvis Presley (1974)
My Boy Lollipop (2) Millie (1964)
My Brother Jake (4) Free (1971)
My Camera Never Lies (1) Bucks Fizz (1982)
My Cherie Amour (4) Stevie Wonder (1969)
My Coo-Ca-Choo (2) Alvin Stardust (1973)
My Culture (9) 1 Giant Leap featuring Maxi Jazz and Robbie Williams (2002)
My Destiny (7) Lionel Richie (1992)
My Ding-A-Ling (1) Chuck Berry (1972)
My Dixie Darling (10) Lonnie Donegan & His Skiffle Group (1957)
My Doorbell (10) White Stripes (2005
My Ever Changing Moods (5) Style Council (1984)
My Eyes Adored You (5) Frankie Valli (1975)
My Favourite Mistake (9) Sheryl Crow (1998)
My Favourite Waste Of Time (3) Owen Paul (1986)
My First Kiss (7) 3OH!3 featuring Kesha (2010)
My Friend (1) Frankie Laine (1954)
My Friend Stan (2) Slade (1973)
My Friend The Sea (7) Petula Clark (1961)
My Generation (2) Who (1965)
My Girl (3) Madness (1980)
My Girl (re-issue) (2) Temptations (1992)
My Girl Lollipop (My Boy Lollipop) (9) Bad Manners (1982)
My Guy (5) Mary Wells (1964)

My Happiness (4) Connie Francis, David Rose Orchestra (1959)
My Happy Ending (5) Avril Lavigne (2004)
My Heart Has A Mind of Its Own (3) Connie Francis (1960)
My Heart Sings (see All of a Sudden - Paul Anka)
My Heart Will Go On (1) Celine Dion (1998)
My Hometown / Santa Claus Is Comin' To Town (9) Bruce Springsteen (1985)
My Humps (3) Black Eyed Peas (2005)
My Immortal (7) Evanescence (2003)
My Kind Of Girl (5) Matt Monro (1961)
My Life Would Suck Without You (1) Kelly Clarkson (2009)
My Little Lady (6) Tremeloes (1968)
My Little One (6) Marmalade (1971)
My Love (4) Petula Clark (1966)
My Love (9) Paul McCartney & Wings (1973)
My Love (5) Julio Iglesias featuring Stevie Wonder (1988)
My Love (8) Kele Le Roc (1999)
My Love (1) Westlife (2000)
My Love (2) Justin Timberlake featuring TI (2006)
My Love And Devotion (10) Doris Day (1952)
My Love For You (9) Johnny Mathis (1960)
My Love Is Your Love (2) Whitney Houston (1999)
My Lover's Prayer / Bring It On (5) Alistair Griffin featuring Robin Gibb (2004)
My Lovin' (4) En Vogue (1992)
My Mind's Eye (4) Small Faces (1966)
My Name (10) McLean (2010)
My Name Is (2) Eminem (1999)
My Name Is Jack (8) Manfred Mann (1968)
My Name Is Prince (7) Prince & The New Power Generation (1992)
My Neck My Back (Lick It) (4) Khia (2004)
My Oh My (2) Slade (1983)
My Oh My (6) Aqua (1998)
My Old Man's A Dustman (Ballad Of A Refuse Disposal Officer) (1) Lonnie Donegan & His Group (1960)
My Old Piano (5) Diana Ross (1980)
My One Temptation (7) Mica Paris (1988)
My Perfect Cousin (9) Undertones (1980)
My Place / Flap Your Wings (1) Nelly (2004)
My Prayer (4) Platters (1956)
My Prayer (9) Gerry Monroe (1970)
My Prerogative (6) Bobby Brown (1988)
My Prerogative (3) Britney Spears (2004)
My Pretty One (6) Cliff Richard (1987)
My Resistance Is Low (3) Robin Sarstedt (1976)
My Sentimental Friend (2) Herman's Hermits (1969)
My September Love (re-entry) (3) David Whitfield (1956)
My Sharona (6) Knack (1979)
My Ship Is Coming In (3) Walker Brothers (1965)
My Simple Heart (9) Three Degrees (1979)
My Son My Son (1) Vera Lynn with The Frank Weir Orchestra (1954)
My Special Angel (3) Malcolm Vaughan (1957)
My Star (5) Ian Brown (1998)
My Sweet Lord (1) George Harrison (1971)
My Sweet Lord (re-issue) (1) George Harrison (2002)
My Toot Toot (6) Denise La Salle (1985)
My True Love (9) Jack Scott (1958)
My Vision (6) Jakatta featuring Seal (2002)
My Way (5) Frank Sinatra (1969)
My Way (10) Dorothy Squires (1970)
My Way (9) Elvis Presley (1977)
My Way / No One Is Innocent (7) Sex Pistols (1978)
My Way (6) Limp Bizkit (2001)
My Way Of Thinking / I Think It's Going To Rain (6) UB40 (1980)
My Weakness Is None Of Your Business (9) Embrace (1998)
Mysterious Girl (2) Peter Andre featuring Bubbler Ranx (1996)
Mysterious Girl (re-issue) (1) Peter Andre (2004)
Mysterious Times (2) Sash featuring Tina Cousins (1998)
N Dey Say (6) Nelly (2005)

Na Na Hey Hey Kiss Him Goodbye (9) Steam (1970)
Na Na Hey Hey Kiss Him Goodbye (5) Bananarama (1983)
Na Na Is The Saddest Word (5) Stylistics (1975)
Na Na Na (10) Cozy Powell (1974)
Nairobi (3) Tommy Steele (1958)
Naïve (5) Kooks (2006)
Naked (5) Louise (1996)
Naked In The Rain (4) Blue Pearl (1990)
Name Of The Game, The (1) Abba (1977)
Nancy Boy (4) Placebo (1997)
Nasty Girl (9) Inaya Day (2005)
Nasty Girl (1) Notorious BIG featuring Diddy, Nelly, Jagged Edge & Avery Storm (2006)
Nathan Jones (5) Supremes (1971)
National Express (8) Divine Comedy (1999)
Native New Yorker (5) Odyssey (1977)
Natural (6) Peter Andre (1997)
Natural (3) S Club 7 (2000)
Natural Born Bugie (4) Humble Pie (1969)
Natural Sinner (6) Fair Weather (1970)
Naturally (7) Selena Gomez & The Scene (2010)
Nature's Law (2) Embrace (2006)
Naughty Girl (10) Beyonce (2004)
Naughty Lady Of Shady Lane (5) Dean Martin (1955)
Naughty Lady Of Shady Lane (6) Ames Brothers (1955)
Neanderthal Man (2) Hotlegs (1970)
Need You Tonight (2) INXS (1988)
Needin' U (8) David Morales presents The Face (1998)
Needles And Pins (1) Searchers (1964)
Needles And Pins (10) Smokie (1977)
Negotiate With Love (10) Rachel Stevens (2005)
Nellie The Elephant (4) Toy Dolls (1984)
Nelson Mandela (9) Special AKA (1984)
Nessaja (4) Scooter (2002)
Nessun Dorma (2) Luciano Pavarotti (1990)
Never / These Dreams (re-issue) (8) Heart (1988)
Never Again (9) Kelly Clarkson (2007)
Never Be Lonely (9) Feeling (2006)
Never Be The Same Again (1) Melanie C with Lisa Left Eye Lopes (2000)
Never Be Your Woman (8) Naughty Boy presents Wiley featuring Emeli (2010)
Never Can Say Goodbye (2) Gloria Gaynor (1974)
Never Can Say Goodbye (4) Communards (1987)
Never Do A Tango With An Eskimo (6) Alma Cogan (1955)
Never Ending Song Of Love (2) New Seekers (1971)
Never Ending Story (4) Limahl (1984)
Never Ever (1) All Saints (1997)
Never Felt Like This Before (8) Shaznay Lewis (2004)
Never Forget (1) Take That (1995)
Never Gonna Give You Up (6) Musical Youth (1983)
Never Gonna Give You Up (1) Rick Astley (1987)
Never Gonna Leave Your Side (1) Daniel Bedingfield (2003)
Never Gonna Let You Go (7) Tina Moore (1997)
Never Had A Dream Come True (6) Stevie Wonder (1970)
Never Had A Dream Come True (1) S Club 7 (2000)
Never Knew Love Like This Before (4) Stephanie Mills (1980)
Never Leave You (1) Tinchy Stryder featuring Amelle (2009)
Never Leave You (Uh Oooh Uh Oooh) (2) Lumidee (2003)
Never Let Her Slip Away (5) Andrew Gold (1978)
Never Let Her Slip Away (5) Undercover (1992)
Never Let You Down (7) Honeyz (1999)
Never Miss A Beat (5) Kaiser Chiefs (2008)
Never Never (4) Assembly (1983)
Never Never Never (8) Shirley Bassey (1973)
Never Say Goodbye (9) Karl Denver (1962)
Never Too Late (4) Kylie Minogue (1989)
Never Trust A Stranger (7) Kim Wilde (1988)
New Beginning (Mamba Seyra) (8) Bucks Fizz (1986)
New Beginning / Bright Eyes (3) Stephen Gately (2000)
New Day Has Come, A (7) Celine Dion (2002)
New Direction (2) S Club Juniors (2002)
New England, A (7) Kirsty MacColl (1985)
New Moon On Monday (9) Duran Duran (1984)
New Song (3) Howard Jones (1983)

New Years Day (10) U2 (1983)
New York Groove (9) Hello (1975)
Next Best Superstar (10) Melanie C (2005)
Next Episode, The (3) Dr Dre featuring Snoop Dogg (2001)
Next Time, The / Bachelor Boy (1) Cliff Richard and The Shadows (1962)
Nice Guy Eddie (10) Sleeper (1996)
Night Birds (9) Shakatak (1982)
Night Chicago Died, The (3) Paper Lace (1974)
Night Fever (1) Bee Gees (1978)
Night Games (6) Graham Bonnet (1981)
Night Has A Thousand Eyes, The (3) Bobby Vee (1963)
Night Of Fear (2) Move (1967)
Night Owl (5) Gerry Rafferty (1979)
Night They Drove Old Dixie Down, The (6) Joan Baez (1971)
Night To Remember, A (5) Shalamar (1982)
Night To Remember, A (6) Liberty X (2005)
Night, The (7) Frankie Valli & The Four Seasons (1975)
Nights In White Satin (re-entry) (9) Moody Blues (1972)
Nights On Broadway (6) Candi Staton (1977)
Nightshift (3) Commodores (1985)
Nikita (3) Elton John (1985)
Nine Million Bicycles (5) Katie Melua (2005)
911 (9) Wyclef Jean featuring Mary J Blige (2000)
9pm (Till I Come) (1) ATB (1999)
Nine Times Out Of Ten (3) Cliff Richard & The Shadows (1960)
9 To 5 (3) Sheena Easton (1980)
Nine2Five (6) Ordinary Boys featuring Lady Sovereign (2006)
Nineteen (1) Paul Hardcastle (1985)
1999 (re-entry) (10) Prince (1999)
1999 / Little Red Corvette (re-issue) (2) Prince (1985)
1973 (4) James Blunt (2007)
19 / 2000 (6) Gorillaz (2001)
Nineteenth Nervous Breakdown (2) Rolling Stones Breakdown (1966)
99 Red Balloons (1) Nena (1984)
99 Ways (5) Tab Hunter (1957)
Nite Club / A Message To You Rudy (10) Specials featuring Rico (1979)
No Air (3) Jordin Sparks featuring Chris Brown (2008)
No Arms Can Ever Hold You (7) Bachelors (1964)
No Charge (1) J J Barrie (1976)
No Diggity (9) Blackstreet (1996)
No Doubt About It (2) Hot Chocolate (1980)
No Fronts (9) Dog Eat Dog (1996)
No Good (Start The Dance) (4) Prodigy (1994)
No Good 4 Me (6) Oxide & Neutrino featuring Megaman (2000)
No Good Advice (2) Girls Aloud (2003)
No Honestly (7) Lynsey De Paul (1974)
No Letting Go (3) Wayne Wonder (2003)
No Limit (1) 2 Unlimited (1993)
No Matter How I Try (5) Gilbert O'Sullivan (1971)
No Matter What (5) Badfinger (1971)
No Matter What (1) Boyzone (1998)
No Milk Today (7) Herman's Hermits (1966)
No More (6) A1 (2001)
No More (I Can't Stand It) (8) Maxx (1994)
No More (Baby I'Ma Do Right) (6) 3LW (2001)
No More Drama (9) Mary J Blige (2002)
No More Heroes (8) Stranglers (1977)
No More I Love Yous (2) Annie Lennox (1995)
No More Lonely Nights (2) Paul McCartney (1984)
No More Mr Nice Guy (10) Alice Cooper (1973)
No More Tears (Enough Is Enough) (3) Donna Summer & Barbra Streisand (1979)
No More The Fool (5) Elkie Brooks (1986)
No No No (5) Destiny's Child (1998)
No One (6) Alicia Keys (2007)
No One But You (3) Billy Eckstine (1954)
No One Is Innocent / My Way (7) Sex Pistols (1978)
No One Quite Like Grandma (1) St Winifred's School Choir (1980)
No Other Love (1) Ronnie Hilton (1956)
No Particular Place To Go (3) Chuck Berry (1964)
No Promises (2) Shayne Ward (2006)

No Regrets (7) Walker Brothers (1976)
No Regrets (9) Midge Ure (1982)
No Regrets / Antmusic (4) Robbie Williams (1998)
No Regrets (1) Dappy (2011)
No Scrubs (3) TLC (1999)
No Son Of Mine (6) Genesis (1991)
No Surprises (4) Radiohead (1998)
No Tomorrow (1) Orson (2006)
No U Hang Up / If That's OK With You (2) Shayne Ward (2007)
No Woman No Cry (2) Fugees (1996)
No Woman No Cry (re-entry) (8) Bob Marley & The Wailers (1981)
No Worries (4) Simon Webbe (2005)
Nobody Does It Better (7) Carly Simon (1977)
Nobody I Know (10) Peter & Gordon (1964)
Nobody Knows (4) Tony Rich Project (1996)
Nobody Needs Your Love (2) Gene Pitney (1966)
Nobody Told Me (6) John Lennon (1984)
Nobody Wants To Be Lonely (4) Ricky Martin & Christina Aguilera (2001)
Nobody's Child (6) Karen Young (1969)
Nobody's Darlin' But Mine (4) Frank Ifield (1963)
Nobody's Diary (3) Yazoo (1983)
Nobody's Fool (9) Haircut 100 (1982)
Nobody's Perfect (9) Jessie J (2011)
North Country Boy (4) Charlatans (1997)
Northern Lights (10) Renaissance (1978)
Northern Star (4) Melanie C (1999)
Not A Dry Eye In The House (7) Meat Loaf (1996)
Not Afraid (5) Eminem (2010)
Not Fade Away (3) Rolling Stones (1964)
Not Fair (5) Lily Allen (2009)
Not Gonna Get Us (7) Tatu (2003)
Not In Love (5) Enrique featuring Kelis (2004)
Not Over Yet (6) Grace (1995)
Not Over Yet (9) Diana Ross (1999)
Not Such An Innocent Girl (6) Victoria Beckham (2001)
Nothin' On You (1) BoB featuring Bruno Mars (2010)
Nothing (9) A (2002)
Nothing Can Divide Us (5) Jason Donovan (1988)
Nothing Compares 2 U (1) Sinead O'Connor (1990)
Nothing Else Matters (6) Metallica (1992)
Nothing Hurts Like Love (3) Daniel Bedingfield (2004)
Nothing Lasts Forever (8) Echo And The Bunnymen (1997)
Nothing Really Matters (7) Madonna (1999)
Nothing Rhymed (8) Gilbert O'Sullivan (1970)
(Nothin' Serious) Just Buggin' (7) Whistle (1986)
Nothing's Gonna Change My Love For You (1) Glenn Madeiros (1988)
Nothing's Gonna Stop Me Now (8) Samantha Fox (1987)
Nothing's Gonna Stop Us Now (1) Starship (1987)
Nothing's Real But Love (10) Rebecca Ferguson (2011)
Notorious (7) Duran Duran (1986)
Notorious (8) The Saturdays (2011)
November Rain (4) Guns 'N' Roses (1992)
Novocaine For The Soul (10) Eels (1997)
Now (3) Al Martino (1953)
Now Is The Time (5) Jimmy James & The Vagabonds (1976)
Now That We Found Love (2) Heavy D & The Boyz (1991)
Now That We've Found Love (10) Third World (1978)
Now Those Days Are Gone (8) Bucks Fizz (1982)
Now You're Gone (1) Basshunter featuring DJ Mental Theo's Bazzheadz (2008)
N-R-G (12) Adamski (1990)
Nu Flow (3) Big Brovaz (2002)
Nuff Vibes EP (5) Apache Indian (1993)
Number Of The Beast, The (re-issue) (3) Iron Maiden (2005)
Number 1 (6) Tweenies (2000)
Number 1 (9) Goldfrapp (2005)
Number 1 (1) Tinchy Stryder featuring N-Dubz (2009)
Number One (see Call Me Number One)
Numero Uno (9) Starlight (1989)

Nut Rocker (1) B Bumble and the Stingers (1962)
Nutbush City Limits (4) Ike & Tina Turner (1973)
03 Bonnie & Clyde (2) Jay-Z featuring Beyonce Knowles (2003)
O L'Amour (7) Dollar (1987)
O Superman (2) Laurie Anderson (1981)
O.T.B (On The Beach) / Reachers of Civilisation (4) York (2000)
Object Of My Desire (7) Dana Rayne (2005)
Ob-La-Di Ob-La-Da (1) Marmalade (1968)
Obsession (5) Animotion (1985)
Obvious (3) Westlife (2004)
Obviously (1) McFly (2004)
Off On Holiday / I'm Only Sleeping (7) Suggs (1995)
Off The Wall (7) Michael Jackson (1979)
Oh (4) Ciara featuring Ludacris (2005)
Oh Babe What Would You Say? (4) Hurricane Smith (1972)
Oh Baby I... (4) Eternal (1994)
Oh Boy (3) Crickets (1957)
Oh Boy (1) Mud (1975)
Oh Boy (The Mood I'm In) (8) Brotherhood Of Man (1977)
Oh Carol (3) Neil Sedaka (1959)
Oh Carol (5) Smokie (1978)
Oh Carolina (1) Shaggy (1993)
Oh Diane (9) Fleetwood Mac (1982)
Oh Girl / Have You Seen Her (re-issue) (5) Chi-Lites (1975)
Oh Happy Day (4) Johnston Brothers (1953)
Oh Happy Day (2) Edwin Hawkins Singers (1969)
Oh Julie (1) Shakin' Stevens (1982)
Oh Lori (8) Alessi (1977)
Oh Mein Papa (1) Eddie Calvert (1953)
Oh My God (6) Kaiser Chiefs (2005)
Oh My God (8) Mark Ronson featuring Lily Allen (2007)
Oh My Gosh (8) Basement Jaxx (2005)
Oh My Lord / Mary's Boy Child (1) Boney M (1978)
Oh My Papa (9) Eddie Fisher (1954)
Oh My Papa (re-entry) (10) Eddie Fisher (1954)
Oh No Not My Baby (6) Rod Stewart (1973)
Oh Pretty Woman (1) Roy Orbison (1964)
Oh Well (2) Fleetwood Mac (1969)
Oh What A Circus (3) David Essex (1978)
Oh Yeah (6) Ash (1996)
Oh Yeah (On The Radio) (5) Roxy Music (1980)
Oh Yes! You're Beautiful (2) Gary Glitter (1974)
Ohh! What A Life (10) Gibson Brothers (1979)
Oi (8) Platinum 45 featuring More Fire Crew (2002)
OK? (10) Julie Covington, Rula Lenska, Charlotte Cornwell and Sue Jones-Davies (1977)
OK (7) Big Brovaz (2003)
Okay! (4) Dave Dee, Dozy, Beaky, Mick & Tich (1967)
Ol' Rag Blues (9) Status Quo (1983)
Old Before I Die (2) Robbie Williams (1997)
Older / I Can Make You Love Me (3) George Michael (1997)
Oldest Swinger In Town (6) Fred Wedlock (1981)
Ole Ola (Mulher Brasilieira) (4) Rod Stewart and Scottish World Cup Football Squad '78 (1978)
Oliver's Army (2) Elvis Costello & The Attractions (1979)
Olympic / Cubik (10) 808 State (1990)
Omen (4) Prodigy (2009)
OMG (1) Usher featuring Will I Am (2010)
On A Carousel (4) Hollies (1967)
On A Mission (9) Gabriella Cilmi (2010)
On A Night Like This (2) Kylie Minogue (2000)
On A Ragga Tip (2) SL2 (1992)
On A Saturday Night (see Dancing On A Saturday Night)
On A Slow Boat To China (3) Emile Ford & The Checkmates (1960)
On Her Majesty's Secret Service (7) Propellerheads / David Arnold (1997)
On Horseback / In Dulce Jubilo (4) Mike Oldfield (1975)
On My Knees (4) 411 featuring Ghostface Killah (2004)
On My Own (2) Patti LaBelle & Michael McDonald (1986)
On My Radio (8) Selecter (1979)

On Our Own (Theme from Ghostbusters II) (4) Bobby Brown (1989)
On The Beach (7) Cliff Richard & The Shadows (1964)
On the Floor (1) Jennifer Lopez featuring Pitbull (2011)
On The Inside (3) Lynne Hamilton (1989)
On The Radio (7) Martine McCutcheon (2001)
On The Rebound (1) Floyd Cramer (1961)
On The Road Again (8) Canned Heat (1968)
On The Ropes (EP) (10) Wonder Stuff (1993)
On The Street Where You Live (1) Vic Damone (1958)
On Your Own (5) Blur (1997)
Once (1) Diana Vickers (2010)
Once Upon A Christmas Song (5) Geraldine (2008)
Once Upon A Dream (7) Billy Fury (1962)
Once Upon A Long Ago (10) Paul McCartney (1987)
One (7) U2 (1992)
One (2) Mary J Blige & U2 (2006)
One / (I Wish I Knew How It Would Feel To Be) Free (6) Lighthouse Family (2001)
One (Your Name) (7) Swedish House Mafia / Pharrell (2010)
One, The (10) Elton John (1992)
One, The (8) Backstreet Boys (2000)
One And One (3) Robert Miles featuring Maria Nayler (1996)
One And One Is One (3) Medicine Head (1973)
One And Only, The (1) Chesney Hawkes (1991)
One By One (7) Cher (1996)
One Day At A Time (1) Lena Martell (1979)
One Day I'll Fly Away (2) Randy Crawford (1980)
One Day In Your Life (1) Michael Jackson (1981)
One For Sorrow (2) Steps (1998)
One For Sorrow / Chain Reaction (2) Steps (2001)
One For The Radio (2) McFly (2008)
One I Love, The (8) David Gray (2005)
One In Ten (7) UB40 (1981)
One Inch Rock / Debora (re-issue) (7) Tyrannosaurus Rex (1972)
One Kiss From Heaven (9) Louise (1996)
One Love / People Get Ready (5) Bob Marley & The Wailers (1984)
One Love (4) Stone Roses (1990)
One Love (8) Prodigy (1993)
One Love (3) Blue (2002)
One Man Band (6) Leo Sayer (1974)
One Minute Man (10) Missy Elliott featuring Ludacris (2001)
One Moment In Time (1) Whitney Houston (1988)
One More Chance (5) Michael Jackson (2003)
One More Night (4) Phil Collins (1985)
One More Time (2) Daft Punk (2000)
One More Try (8) George Michael (1988)
One Nation Under A Groove (9) Funkadelic (1978)
One Night / I Got Stung (1) Elvis Presley (1959)
One Night / I Got Stung (re-issue) (1) Elvis Presley (2005)
One Night In Heaven (6) M People (1993)
One Night Stand (5) Mis-Teeq (2001)
10538 Overture (9) Electric Light Orchestra (1972)
One Of Us (3) Abba (1981)
One Of Us (6) Joan Osborne (1996)
One Shining Moment (10) Diana Ross (1992)
One Shot (6) JLS (2010)
One Step Beyond (7) Madness (1979)
One Step Closer (2) S Club Juniors (2002)
One Step Further (2) Bardo (1982)
One Step Too Far (6) Faithless featuring Dido (2002)
One Sweet Day (6) Mariah Carey & Boyz II Men (1995)
1 Thing (4) Amerie (2005)
137 Disco Heaven / Light My Fire (medley) (5) Amii Stewart (1979)
One To Another (3) Charlatans (1996)
1, 2 Step (3) Ciara featuring Missy Elliott (2005)
1-2-3 (3) Len Barry (1965)
1-2-3 (9) Gloria Estefan & Miami Sound Machine (1988)
1234 (8) Feist (2007)
1-2-3-4 Get With The Wicked (10) Richard Blackwood (2000)
1-2-3 O'Leary (4) Des O'Connor (1968)
One Vision (7) Queen (1985)
One Way Love (9) Cliff Bennett & The Rebel Rousers (1964)

One Way Ticket (9) Eruption (1979)
One Way Ticket (8) Darkness (2005)
One Week (5) Barenaked Ladies (1999)
One Wild Night (10) Bon Jovi (2001)
One Word (9) Kelly Osbourne (2005)
Onion Song (9) Marvin Gaye & Tammi Terrell (1969)
Only Fools (Never Fall In Love) (10) Sonia (1991)
Only Girl In The World (1) Rihanna (2010)
Only Living Boy In New Cross, The (7) Carter The Unstoppable Sex Machine (1992)
Only Love (2) Nana Mouskouri (1986)
Only One I Know, The (9) Charlatans (1990)
Only One Road (8) Celine Dion (1995)
Only One Woman (5) Marbles (1968)
Only Rhyme That Bites, The (10) MC Tunes vs 808 State (1990)
Only Sixteen (1) Craig Douglas (1959)
Only The Lonely (re-entry) (1) Roy Orbison (1960)
Only Thing That Looks Good On Me is You, The (6) Bryan Adams (1996)
Only Way Is Up, The (1) Yazz & The Plastic Population (1988)
Only Way Out, The (10) Cliff Richard (1982)
Only When You Leave (3) Spandau Ballet (1984)
Only Yesterday (2) Carpenters (1975)
Only You (3) Hilltoppers (1956)
Only You / The Great Pretender (5) (1956)
Only You (2) Yazoo (1982)
Only You (1) Flying Pickets (1983)
Only You (4) Praise (1991)
Only You / Blue Moon (9) John Alford (1996)
Only You (2) Ashanti (2005)
Only You Can (3) Fox (1975)
Ooh Aah ... Just A Little Bit (1) Gina G (1996)
Ooh La La (2) Wiseguys (1999)
Ooh La La (4) Goldfrapp (2005)
Ooh La La La (Let's Go Dancin') (6) Kool & The Gang (1982)
Ooh Stick You! (8) Daphne & Celeste (2000)
Ooh To Be Ah (7) Kajagoogoo (1983)
Ooh-Wakka-Doo-Wakka-Day (8) Gilbert O'Sullivan (1972)
Oops (Oh My) (5) Tweet (2002)
Oops Up (5) Snap (1990)
Oops Up Side Your Head (6) Gap Band (1980)
Oops! ... I Did It Again (1) Britney Spears (2000)
Oopsy Daisy (1) Chipmunk (2009)
Open Arms (4) Mariah Carey (1996)
Open Road (7) Gary Barlow (1997)
Open You Mind (7) Usura (1993)
Open Your Heart (6) Human League (1981)
Open Your Heart (4) Madonna (1986)
Open Your Heart (9) M People (1995)
Opera Song, The (Brave New World) (3) Jurgen Vries featuring CMC (2003)
Operation Blade (Bass In The Place) (5) Public Domain (2000)
Opposites Attract (2) Paula Abdul with The Wild Pair (1990)
Ordinary World (6) Duran Duran (1993)
Ordinary World (5) Aurora featuring Naimee Coleman (2000)
Original Prankster (6) Offspring (2000)
Orinoco Flow (1) Enya (1988)
Orville's Song (4) Keith Harris & Orville (1982)
Ossie's Dream (Spurs Are On Their Way to Wembley) (5) Tottenham Hotspur FA Cup Final Squad (1981)
Our Favourite Melodies (9) Craig Douglas (1962)
Our House (5) Madness (1982)
Our Lips Are Sealed (7) Fun Boy Three (1983)
Our Velocity (9) Maximo Park (2007)
Out In The Fields (5) Gary Moore & Phil Lynott (1985)
Out Of Reach (4) Gabrielle (2001)
Out Of Space / Ruff In The Jungle (5) Prodigy (1992)
Out Of The Blue (9) Delta Goodrem (2004)
Out Of Time (1) Chris Farlowe (1966)
Out Of Time (5) Blur (2003)
Out Of Touch (7) Uniting Nations (2004)
Out Of Your Mind (2) True Steppers, with Dane Bowers and Victoria Beckham (2000)
Outside (2) George Michael (1998)
Outside Of Heaven (1) Eddie Fisher (1953)

Outta Control (7) 50 Cent featuring Mobb Deep (2005)
Outta Here (7) Esmee Denters (2009)
Over And Over (1) Nelly featuring Tim McGraw (2005)
Over Under Sideways Down (10) Yardbirds (1966)
Over You (5) Roxy Music (1980)
Overload (6) Sugababes (2000)
Overprotected (4) Britney Spears (2002)
Owner Of A Lonely Heart (9) Max Graham vs Yes (2005)
Oxygene Part IV (4) Jean-Michel Jarre (1977)
P.I.M.P. (5) 50 Cent (2003)
Pacific (10) 808 State (1989)
Pack Up (4) Eliza Doolittle (2010)
Pain Killer (5) Turin Brakes (2003)
Paint It Black (1) Rolling Stones (1966)
Paint Your Target (9) Fightstar (2005)
Painter Man (10) Boney M (1979)
Pale Shelter (5) Tears For Fears (1983)
Paloma Blanca (10) George Baker Selection (1975)
Pandora's Box (7) Orchestral Manoeuvres In the Dark (1991)
Pandora's Kiss (5) Louise (2003)
Papa Don't Preach (1) Madonna (1986)
Papa Don't Preach (3) Kelly Osbourne (2002)
Papa's Got A Brand New Pigbag (3) Pigbag (1982)
Paparazzi (4) Lady Gaga (2009)
Paper Plane (8) Status Quo (1973)
Paper Roses (7) Kaye Sisters (1960)
Paper Roses (2) Marie Osmond (1973)
Paper Sun (5) Traffic (1967)
Paperback Writer (1) Beatles (1966)
Parachute (5) Cheryl Cole (2010)
Paradise? (1) Coldplay (2011)
Paradise City (6) Guns 'N' Roses (1989)
Paralysed (8) Elvis Presley (1957)
Paranoid (4) Black Sabbath (1970)
Paranoid Android (3) Radiohead (1997)
Parisienne Walkways (8) Gary Moore (1979)
Paris Match / Long Hot Summer (3) Style Council (1983)
Parklife (10) Blur (1994)
Part Of The Union (2) Strawbs (1973)
Part-Time Lover (3) Stevie Wonder (1985)
Party (2) Elvis Presley with The Jordanaires (1957)
Party All Night (Sleep All Day) (9) Sean Kingston (2011)
Party Fears Two (9) Associates (1982)
Party For Two (10) Shania Twain featuring Mark McGrath (2004)
Party Girl (6) McFly (2010)
Party People … Friday Night (5) 911 (1997)
Party Pops (24) Russ Conway (1957)
Party Rock Anthem (1) LMFAO featuring Lauren Bennet & GoonRock (2011)
Party's Over, The (9) Lonnie Donegan (1962)
Pasadena (4) Temperance Seven (1961)
Pass And Move (It's The Liverpool FC & The Liverpool Groove) (4) Boot Room Boyz (1996)
Pass It On (5) Coral (2003)
Pass Out (1) Tinie Tempah (2010)
Pass That Dutch (10) Missy Elliott (2003)
Pass The Dutchie (1) Musical Youth (1982)
Passengers (5) Elton John (1984)
Passion (remix) (6) Gat Decor (1996)
Patches (2) Clarence Carter (1970)
Patience (10) Guns 'N' Roses (1989)
Patience (1) Take That (2006)
Patricia (8) Perez Prado & His Orchestra (1958)
PATT (Party All The Time) (8) Sharam (2006)
Peace (8) Sabrina Johnston (1991)
Peace In Our Time (8) Cliff Richard (1993)
Peace On Earth / British Hustle (8) Hi Tension (1978)
Peace On Earth - Little Drummer Boy (3) David Bowie & Bing Crosby (1982)
Peaches (8) Presidents of the United States of America (1996)
Peaches / Go Buddy Go (8) Stranglers (1977)
Peacock Suit (5) Paul Weller (1996)

Pearl In The Shell (7) Howard Jones (1984)
Pearl's A Singer (8) Elkie Brooks (1977)
Peek-A-Boo (7) New Vaudeville Band (1967)
Peggy Sue (6) Buddy Holly (1957)
Penny And Me (10) Hanson (2005)
Penny Lane / Strawberry Fields Forever (2) Beatles (1967)
People Are People (4) Depeche Mode (1984)
People Everyday (2) Arrested Development (1992)
People Get Ready / One Love (5) Bob Marley & The Wailers (1984)
People Hold On (4) Lisa Stansfield vs Dirty Rotten Scoundrels (1997)
People Like You People Like Me (5) Glitter Band (1976)
Pepe (2) Duane Eddy (1961)
Pepper Box (6) Peppers (1974)
Perfect (1) Fairground Attraction (1988)
Perfect 10 (2) Beautiful South (1998)
Perfect Day (1) Various Artists (1997)
Perfect Gentleman (4) Wyclef Jean (2001)
Perfect Moment (1) Martine McCutcheon (1999)
Perfect Year, The (5) Dina Carroll (1993)
Perfidia (4) Ventures (1960)
Perseverance (5) Terrorvision (1996)
Personality (6) Anthony Newley (1959)
Personality (9) Lloyd Price (1959)
Peter Gunn (8) Art Of Noise featuring Duane Eddy (1986)
Peter Gunn Theme (6) Duane Eddy (1959)
Petite Fleur (9) Chris Barber's Jazz Band (1959)
Phantom Of The Opera, The (7) Sarah Brightman & Steve Harley (1986)
Phatt Bass (9) Warp Brothers vs Aquagen (2000)
Phenomenon (9) LL Cool J (1997)
Phorever People (5) Shamen (1992)
Photograph (8) Ringo Starr (1973)
Physical (7) Olivia Newton-John (1981)
Piano Party (10) Winifred Atwell (1959)
Pick A Part That's New (4) Stereophonics (1999)
Pick Up The Pieces (8) Hudson-Ford (1973)
Pick Up The Pieces (6) Average White Band (1975)
Pickin' A Chicken (9) Eve Boswell with Glen Somer Orchestra (1955)
Picture Of You, A (2) Joe Brown & The Bruvvers (1962)
Picture Of You (2) Boyzone (1997)
Picture This (12) Blondie (1978)
Pictures Of Lily (4) Who (1967)
Pictures Of Matchstick Men (7) Status Quo (1968)
Pie Jesu (3) Sarah Brightman & Paul Miles-Kingston (1985)
Piece Of Me (2) Britney Spears (2008)
Piece Of My Heart (7) Shaggy featuring Marsha (1997)
Pieces Of Me (4) Ashlee Simpson (2004)
Pied Piper (5) Crispian St Peters (1966)
Pinball Wizard (4) Who (1969)
Pinball Wizard (7) Elton John (1976)
Pink Cadillac (5) Natalie Cole (1988)
Pipes Of Peace (1) Paul McCartney (1983)
Pitchin' (In Every Direction) (6) Hi-Gate (2000)
Pjanoo (2) Eric Prydz (2008)
Place Your Hands (6) Reef (1996)
Play (3) Jennifer Lopez (2001)
Play Me Like You Play Your Duane Eddy & The Guitar (9) Rebelettes (1975)
Play That Funky Music (7) Wild Cherry (1976)
Play That Funky Music (10) Vanilla Ice (1991)
Played A Live (The Bongo Song) (6) Safri Duo (2001)
Playing With Knives (4) Bizarre Inc (1991)
Please (7) U2 (1997)
Please Come Home For Christmas (7) Bon Jovi (1994)
Please Don't Fall In Love (7) Cliff Richard (1983)
Please Don't Go (3) Donald Peers (1968)
Please Don't Go (3) KC & The Sunshine Band (1979)
Please Don't Go / Game Boy (1) KWS (1992)
Please Don't Go (4) No Mercy (1997)

Please Don't Make Me Cry (10) UB40 (1983)
Please Don't Tease (1) Cliff Richard & The Shadows (1960)
Please Don't Turn Me On (4) Artful Dodger featuring Lifford (2000)
Please Don't Let Me Go (1) Olly Murs (2010)
Please Forgive Me (2) Bryan Adams (1993)
Please Help Me I'm Falling (9) Hank Locklin (1960)
Please Mr Postman (2) Carpenters (1975)
Please Please / Don't Stop Me Now (1) McFly (2006)
Please Please Me (2) Beatles (1963)
Please Stay (10) Kylie Minogue (2000)
Please Tell Him That I Said Hello (8) Dana (1975)
Poetry In Motion (1) Johnny Tillotson (1960)
Point Of View (3) DB Boulevard (2002)
Points of Authority / High Voltage (9) Linkin Park (2002)
Poison (2) Alice Cooper (1989)
Poison (3) Nicole Scherzinger (2010)
Poison Arrow (6) ABC (1982)
Poison Ivy (7) Lambrettas (1980)
Poker Face (1) Lady Gaga (2009)
Pon De Replay (2) Rihanna (2005)
Pool Hall Richard / I Wish it Would Rain (8) Faces (1973)
Poor Little Fool (4) Ricky Nelson (1958)
Poor Man's Son (5) Rockin' Berries (1965)
Poor Me (1) Adam Faith (1960)
Poor People Of Paris (1) Winifred Atwell (1956)
Pop (9) N Sync (2001)
Pop Go The Workers (5) Barron Knights with Duke D'Mond (1965)
Pop Muzik (2) M (1979)
Pop Ya Colla (2) Usher (2001)
Popcorn (5) Hot Butter (1972)
Poppa Piccolino (2) Diana Decker (1953)
Poppa Piccolino (re-entry) (5) Diana Decker (1954)
Poppiholla (7) Chicane (2009)
Porcelain (5) Moby (2000)
Portrait Of My Love (3) Matt Monro (1960)
Portsmouth (3) Mike Oldfield (1976)
Positive Tension / So Here We Are (5) Bloc Party (2005)
Positively Fourth Street (8) Bob Dylan (1965)
Power Of A Woman (5) Eternal (1995)
Power Of Good-Bye / Little Star, The (6) Madonna (1998)
Power Of Love, The (1) Frankie Goes To Hollywood (1984)
Power Of Love, The (1) Jennifer Rush (1985)
Power Of Love, The / Do you Believe in Love (9) Huey Lewis & The News (1986)
Power Of Love, The (re-issue) (10) Frankie Goes To Hollywood (1993)
Power Of Love, The (4) Celine Dion (1994)
Power Of Love, The (re-issue) (6) Frankie Goes To Hollywood (2000)
Power Rangers (3) Mighty Morphin Power Rangers (1994)
Power To All Our Friends (4) Cliff Richard (1973)
Power To The People (7) John Lennon & The Plastic Ono Band (1971)
Power, The (1) Snap (1990)
Praise You (1) Fatboy Slim (1999)
Pray (8) MC Hammer (1990)
Pray (1) Take That (1993)
Prayer, The (4) Bloc Party (2007)
Praying For Time (6) George Michael (1990)
Precious / Town Called Malice (1) Jam (1982)
Precious (4) Depeche Mode (2005)
Pretend (2) Nat 'King' Cole (1953)
Pretend (4) Alvin Stardust (1981)
Pretender, The (8) Foo Fighters (2007)
Pretty Blue Eyes (4) Craig Douglas (1960)
Pretty Flamingo (1) Manfred Mann (1966)
Pretty Fly (For A White Guy) (1) Offspring (1999)
Pretty Good Year (7) Tori Amos (1994)
Pretty Green Eyes (2) Ultrabeat (2003)
Pretty Little Angel Eyes (5) Showaddywaddy (1978)
Pretty Little Black-Eyed Susie (2) Guy Mitchell (1953)
Pretty Paper (6) Roy Orbison (1964)
Pretty Vacant (6) Sex Pistols (1977)

Price Of Love, The (2) Everly Brothers (1965)
Price Tag (1) Jessie J featuring B.o.B (2011)
Pride (In The Name Of Love (3) U2 (1984)
Prince Charming (1) Adam & The Ants (1981)
Princess In Rags (9) Gene Pitney (1965)
Private Emotion (9) Ricky Martin featuring Meja (2000)
Private Investigations (2) Dire Straits (1982)
Private Number (8) Judy Clay & WilliamBell (1968)
Private Number (3) 911 (1999)
Prize Of Gold (6) Joan Regan (1955)
Problems (6) Everly Brothers (1959)
Professional Widow (remix) (1) Tori Amos (1997)
Promiscuous (3) Nelly Furtado featuring Timbaland (2006)
Promise Me (3) Beverley Craven (1991)
Promise, The (1) Girls Aloud (2008)
Promise This (1) Cheryl Cole (2010)
Promised Land (9) Elvis Presley (1975)
Promises (6) Ken Dodd (1966)
Promises (1) Nero (2011)
Propane Nightmares (9) Pendulum (2008)
Proper Crimbo (4) Bo Selecta (2003)
Proper Education (2) Eric Prydz vs Floyd (2007)
Protect Your Mind (For The Love Of A Princess) (4) DJ Sakin & Friends (1999)
Proud Mary (8) Creedence Clearwater Revival (1969)
Proud One, The (5) Osmonds (1975)
Prove Your Love (8) Taylor Dayne (1988)
Pub With No Beer, A (3) Slim Dusty (1959)
Public Image (9) Public Image Ltd (1978)
Pump It (3) Black Eyed Peas (2006)
Pump Up The Jam (2) Technotronic featuring Felly (1989)
Pump Up The Volume / Anitina (The First Time) (1) Marrs (1987)
Punky Reggae Party / Jamming (9) Bob Marley & The Wailers (1977)
Puppet On A String (1) Sandie Shaw (1967)
Puppy Love (1) Donny Osmond (1972)
Puppy Love / Sleigh Ride (6) S Club Juniors (2002)
Puppy Song, The / Daydreamer (1) David Cassidy (1973)
Pure And Simple (1) Hear'Say (2001)
Pure Morning (4) Placebo (1998)
Pure Shores (1) All Saints (2000)
Purple Haze (3) Jimi Hendrix Experience (1967)
Purple Hills / Purple Pills (2) D12 (2001)
Purple Pills / Purple Hills (2) D12 (2001)
Purple Rain (8) Prince & The Revolution (1984)
Push It (9) Garbage (1998)
Push It / Tramp (2) Salt-N-Pepa (1988)
Push The Button (1) Sugababes (2005)
Push The Feeling On (remix) (3) Nightcrawlers featuring John Reid (1995)
Pushbike Song, The (2) Mixtures (1971)
Puss 'N' Boots (5) Adam Ant (1983)
Put Em High (6) Stonebridge featuring Therese (2004)
Put The Needle On It (7) Dannii Minogue (2002)
Put Your Arms Around Me (10) Texas (1997)
Put Your Hands Together (7) D Mob (1990)
Put Your Hands Up For Detroit (1) Fedde Le Grande (2006)
Put Your Head On My Shoulder (7) Paul Anka (1959)
Put Your Love In Me (10) Hot Chocolate (1977)
Put Your Records On (2) Corinne Bailey Rae (2006)
Putting On The Style / Gambling Man (1) Lonnie Donegan & His Skiffle Group (1957)
Pyjamarama (10) Roxy Music (1973)
Pyramid Song (5) Radiohead (2001)
Quarter To Three (7) Gary US Bonds (1961)
Que Sera Mi Vida (5) Gibson Brothers (1979)
Queen Of Clubs (7) KC & The Sunshine Band (1974)
Queen Of My Heart (1) Westlife (2001)
Queen Of New Orleans (10) Jon Bon Jovi (1997)
Question (2) Moody Blues (1970)
Quiereme Mucho (Yours) (3) Julio Iglesias (1982)
Quit Playing Games (With My Heart) (2) Backstreet Boys (1997)
Rabbit (8) Chas & Dave (1980)
Race, The (7) Yello (1988)

Race With The Devil (8) Gun (1968)
Rachel (10) Al Martino (1953)
Rachmaninoff's Variation On A Theme (9) Winifred Atwell (1954)
Radancer (6) Marmalade (1972)
Radar Love (7) Golden Earring (1973)
Radio (1) Robbie Williams (2004)
Radio Gaga (2) Queen (1984)
Radioactive (7) Kings Of Leon (2010)
Rag Doll (2) Four Seasons featuring Frankie Valli (1964)
Ragamuffin Man (8) Manfred Mann (1969)
Rage Hard (4) Frankie Goes To Hollywood (1986)
Rags To Riches (re-entry) (3) David Whitfield (1954)
Rags To Riches (9) Elvis Presley (1971)
Rain (7) Status Quo (1976)
Rain (7) Madonna (1993)
Rain (Supa Dupa Fly), The Missy 'Misdemeanor' (first hit) Elliott (1997)
Rain Or Shine (2) Five Star (1986)
Rain Rain Rain (8) Frankie Laine, The Four Lads and The Buddy Cole Quartet (1954)
Rain, The (4) Oran 'Juice' Jones (1986)
Rainbow (3) Marmalade (1970)
Rainbow Valley (5) Love Affair (1968)
Raincloud (6) Lighthouse Family (1997)
Raindrops (Encore Une Fois) (9) Sash featuring Stunt (2008)
Raindrops Keep Falling On My Head (10) Sacha Distel (1970)
Rainy Day Women Nos 12 And 35 (7) Bob Dylan (1966)
Ramblin' Rose (5) Nat 'King' Cole (1962)
Ramona (4) Bachelors (1964)
Randy (9) Blue Mink (1973)
Ranking Full Stop / Tears Of A Clown (6) Beat (1979)
Rapper's Delight (3) Sugarhill Gang (1979)
Rapture (5) Blondie (1981)
Rapture (2) IIO (2001)
Rasputin (2) Boney M (1978)
Rat Race / Rude Boys Outa Jail (5) Specials (1980)
Rat Trap (1) Boomtown Rats (1978)
Rave On (5) Buddy Holly (1958)
Raving I'm Raving (2) Shut Up & Dance (1992)
Rawhide (6) Frankie Laine (1959)
Ray Of Light (2) Madonna (1998)
Reach (2) S Club 7 (2000)
Reach For The Stars / Climb Ev'ry Mountain (1) Shirley Bassey (1961)
Reach Out I'll Be There (1) Four Tops (1966)
Reach Up (Papa's Got A New Pig Bag (6) Brand Perfecto Allstarz (1995)
(Reach Up For The) Sunrise (5) Duran Duran (2004)
Reachers of Civilisation / O.T.B (On The Beach) (4) York (2000)
Read All About It (1) Professor Green featuring Emeli Sandé (2011)
Ready For The Floor (6) Hot Chip (2008)
Ready For The Weekend (3) Calvin Harris (2009)
Ready Or Not (1) Fugees (1996)
Ready Or Not (5) Course (1997)
Ready Or Not / Everytime (3) A1 (1999)
Ready Willing And Able (7) Doris Day (1955)
Real Girl (2) Mutya Buena (2007)
Real Gone Kid (8) Deacon Blue (1988)
Real Good Time (7) Alda (1998)
Real Love (8) Time Frequency (1993)
Real Love (4) Beatles (1996)
Real Slim Shady, The (1) Eminem (2000)
Real Thing, The (1) Tony Di Bart (1994)
Real Thing, The (6) 2 Unlimited (1994)
Real Thing, The (9) Lisa Stansfield (1997)
Real Things (4) Javine (2003)
Real To Me (1) Brian McFadden (2004)
Real Wild Child (Wild One) (10) Iggy Pop (1986)
Real World (9) D-Side (2003)

Really Saying Something (5) Bananarama with Fun Boy Three (1982)
Reason (8) Ian Van Dahl (2002)
Reason To Believe / Maggie May (1) Rod Stewart (1971)
Reasons To Be Cheerful (Part 3) (3) Ian Dury & The Blockheads (1979)
Rebel Rebel (5) David Bowie (1974)
Rebel Yell (6) Billy Idol (1985)
Red (5) Daniel Merriweather (2009)
Red Alert (5) Basement Jaxx (1999)
Red Balloon (7) Dave Clark Five (1968)
Red Blooded Woman (5) Kylie Minogue (2004)
Red Dress (7) Alvin Stardust (1974)
Red Dress (4) Sugababes (2006)
Red Letter Day, A (9) Pet Shop Boys (1997)
Red Light Spells Danger (2) Billy Ocean (1977)
Red Red Wine (1) UB40 (1983)
Red River Rock (3) Johnny & The Hurricanes (1959)
Reet Petite (The Sweetest Girl in Town) (6) Jackie Wilson (1957)
Reet Petite (The Sweetest Girl in Town) (re-issue) (1) Jackie Wilson (1986)
Reflections (5) Diana Ross & The Supremes (1967)
Reflections Of My Life (3) Marmalade (1969)
Reflex, The (1) Duran Duran (1984)
Refugees (9) Tears (2005)
Reggae Tune (10) Andy Fairweather- Low (1974)
Regret (4) New Order (1993)
Regulate (5) Warren G & Nate Dogg (1994)
Rehab (7) Amy Winehouse (2006)
Reigns / Clap Back (9) Ja Rule (2003)
Relax (1) Frankie Goes To Hollywood (1983)
Relax (re-issue) (5) Frankie Goes To Hollywood (1993)
Release Me (1) Engelbert Humperdinck (1967)
Release Me (3) Agnes (2009)
Relight My Fire (1) Take That featuring Lulu (1993)
Remedy (6) Little Boots (2009)
Remember (Sha-La-La) (6) Bay City Rollers (1974)
Remember Me (7) Diana Ross (1971)
Remember Me (8) Blue Boy (1997)
Remember Me This Way (3) Gary Glitter (1974)
Remember The Time / Come Together (3) Michael Jackson (1992)
Remember You're A Womble (3) Wombles (1974)
Remember You're Mine / There's a Goldmine in The Sky (5) Pat Boone (1957)
Reminisce / Where The Story Ends (8) Blazin' Squad (2003)
Renaissance (5) M People (1994)
Rendezvous (8) Craig David (2001)
Rendez-Vu (4) Basement Jaxx (1999)
Renegade Master '98 (remix) (3) Wildchild (1998)
Rent (8) Pet Shop Boys (1987)
Renta Santa (10) Chris Hill (1975)
Re-Offender (7) Travis (2003)
Replay (1) Iyaz (2010)
Requiem (4) London Boys (1989)
Re-Rewind The Crowd Say Bo Selecta (2) Artful Dodger featuring Craig David (1999)
Rescue Me (3) Madonna (1991)
Rescue Me (8) Ultra (1999)
Respect (10) Aretha Franklin (1967)
Respect Yourself (7) Bruce Willis (1987)
Respectable (1) Mel & Kim (1987)
Resurrection (3) PPK (2001)
Resurrection Shuffle, The (3) Ashton Gardner & Dyke (1971)
Return Of Django / Dollar in the Teeth (5) Upsetters (1969)
Return Of The Los Palmas Seven, The (7) Madness (1981)
Return Of The Mack (1) Mark Morrison (1996)
Return To Innocence (3) Enigma (1994)
Return To Me (2) Dean Martin (1958)
Return To Sender (1) Elvis Presley with The Jordanaires (1962)
Return To Sender (re-issue) (5) Elvis Presley (2005)
Reunited (4) Peaches & Herb (1979)

Reverence (10) Jesus & Mary Chain (1992)
Reverence (10) Faithless (1997)
Reverend Black Grape (9) Black Grape (1995)
Revolution / Mr Wendal (4) Arrested Development (1993)
Reward (6) Teardrop Explodes (1981)
Rewind / Erase (7) Cardigans (1999)
Rhinestone Cowboy (4) Glen Campbell (1975)
Rhythm Is A Dancer (1) Snap (1992)
Rhythm Is A Mystery (3) K-Klass (1991)
Rhythm Of My Heart (3) Rod Stewart (1991)
Rhythm Of The Night (4) DeBarge (1985)
Rhythm Of The Night, The (2) Corona (1994)
Rhythm Of The Rain (5) Cascades (1963)
Rhythm Of The Rain (9) Jason Donovan (1990)
Rich Girl (4) Gwen Stefani featuring Eve (2005)
Rich In Paradise / Going Back To My Roots (9) FPI Project present Paolo Dini (1989)
Richard III (2) Supergrass (1997)
Ricochet (8) Joan Regan & The Squadronaires (1953)
Ricochet (re-entry) (9) Joan Regan & The Squadronaires (1954)
Riddle, The (3) Nik Kershaw (1984)
Ride A White Swan (2) T Rex (1970)
Ride It (4) Geri (2004)
Ride Like The Wind (3) East Side Beat (1991)
Ridin' (2) Chamillionaire featuring Krayzie Bone (2006)
Ride On Time (1) Black Box (1989)
Ride Wit Me (3) Nelly featuring City Spud (2001)
Riders In The Sky (8) Ramrods (1961)
Ridin' Solo (2) Jason Derulo (2010)
Right Back Where We Started From (8) Maxine Nightingale (1975)
Right Back Where We Started From (4) Sinitta (1989)
Right By Your Side (10) Eurythmics (1983)
Right Here (3) SWV (1993)
Right Here Right Now (2) Fatboy Slim (1999)
Right Here Waiting (2) Richard Marx (1989)
Right In The Night (Fall In Love With Music) (re-issue) (10) Jam & Spoon featuring Plavka (1995)
Right Now (10) Atomic Kitten (1999)
Right Now (Na Na Na) (6) Akon (2008)
Right Now / Someone Like Me (8) Atomic Kitten (2004)
Right Round (2) Flo Rida featuring Kesha Right (2009)
Right Said Fred (10) Bernard Cribbins (1962)
Right There (3) Nicole Scherzinger featuring 50 Cent (2011)
Ring My Bell (1) Anita Ward (1979)
Ring Ring (Ha Ha Hey) (10) De La Soul (1991)
Rio (9) Duran Duran (1982)
Rip It Up (4) Bill Haley & His Comets (1956)
Rip It Up (8) Orange Juice (1983)
Rise (1) Gabrielle (2000)
Rise & Fall (2) Craig David featuring Sting (2003)
Rise And Fall Of Flingel Bunt, The (5) Shadows (1964)
Rise To The Occasion (10) Climie Fisher (1987)
River Deep Mountain High (3) Ike & Tina Turner (1966)
River Of Dreams, The (3) Billy Joel (1993)
River, The (3) Ken Dodd (1965)
Riverdance (9) Bill Whelan and Anuna and RTE Concert Orchestra (1994)
Rivers Of Babylon / Brown Girl In The Ring (1) Boney M (1978)
Riverside (Let's Go) (2) Sidney Samson featuring Wizard Sleeve (2010)
Road Rage (5) Catatonia (1998)
Road To Hell (Part 2), The (10) Chris Rea (1989)
Road To Mandalay, The / Eternity (1) Robbie Williams (2001)
Road To Nowhere (6) Talking Heads (1985)
Robert De Niro's Waiting (3) Bananarama (1984)
Robin Hood (10) Gary Miller (1956)
Robot Man / Mama (2) Connie Francis (1960)
Roc Ya Body (Mic Check 1 2) (5) MVP (2005)
Rock 'N' Roll (8) Status Quo (1981)
Rock 'N' Roll Winter (6) Wizzard (1974)
Rock A Hula Baby / Can't Help Falling in Love (1) Elvis Presley with The Jordanaires (1962)
Rock A Hula Baby / Can't Help Falling In Love (re-issue) (3) Elvis Presley (2005)

Rock And Roll (Parts 1 And 2) (2) Gary Glitter (1972)
Rock And Roll Waltz (1) Kay Starr (1956)
Rock Around The Clock Bill Haley & His (re-entry) (1) Comets (1955)
Rock Around The Clock Bill Haley & His (re-entry) (5) Comets (1956)
Rock DJ (1) Robbie Williams (2000)
Rock Island Line (8) Lonnie Donegan Skiffle Group (1956)
Rock Me Amadeus (1) Falco (1986)
Rock Me Gently (2) Andy Kim (1974)
Rock My Heart (9) Haddaway (1994)
Rock On (3) David Essex (1973)
Rock Steady (3) All Saints (2006)
Rock The Boat (6) Hues Corporation (1974)
Rock The Boat (4) Forrest (1983)
Rock This Party (Everybody Dance Now) (3) Bob Sinclar & Cutee B (2006)
Rock This Town (9) Stray Cats (1981)
Rock Wit U (Awww Baby) (7) Ashanti (2003)
Rock With You (7) Michael Jackson (1980)
Rock Your Baby (1) George McCrae (1974)
Rock Your Baby (8) KWS (1992)
Rock Your Body (2) Justin Timberlake (2003)
Rock-A-Beatin' Boogie (4) Bill Haley & His Comets (1955)
Rock-A-Billy (1) Guy Mitchell (1957)
Rockafeller Shank, The (6) Fatboy Slim (1998)
Rockaria! (9) Electric Light Orchestra (1977)
Rocket (6) Mud (1974)
Rocket Man (2) Elton John (1972)
Rockin' All Over The World (3) Status Quo (1977)
Rockin' Around The Christmas Tree (6) Brenda Lee (1962)
Rockin' Around The Christmas Tree (3) Mel & Kim (1987)
Rockin' Good Way, A (5) Shakin' Stevens & Bonnie Tyler (1984)
Rockin' Over The Beat (9) Technotronic featuring Ya Kid K (1990)
Rockin' Robin (3) Michael Jackson (1972)
Rockin' Robin / Big Boys Don't Cry (10) Lolly (1999)
Rockin' Roll Baby (6) Stylistics (1974)
Rockin' Through The Rye (3) Bill Haley & His Comets (1956)
Rocking Goose (3) Johnny & The Hurricanes (1960)
Rockit (8) Herbie Hancock (1983)
Rocks / Funky Jam (7) Primal Scream (1994)
Rockstar (2) Nickelback (2007)
Rocksteady Crew (see Hey You The Rocksteady Crew)
Rodrigo's Guitar Concerto De Aranjuez (3) Manuel & The Music Of The Mountains (1976)
Rok Da House (5) Beatmasters with The Cookie Crew (1988)
Roll Away The Stone (8) Mott The Hoople (1973)
Roll On / This Is How We Do It (7) Mis-Teeq (2002)
Roll Over Beethoven (6) Electric Light Orchestra (1973)
Roll Over Lay Down (9) Status Quo (1975)
Roll With It (2) Oasis (1995)
Rollercoaster (1) B*Witched (1998)
Rollin' (1) Limp Bizkit (2001)
Rollin' Home (9) Status Quo (1986)
Rolling in the Deep (2) Adele (2011)
Rolling Stone (5) David Essex (1975)
Romeo (3) Petula Clark (1961)
Romeo (4) Mr Big (1977)
Romeo (6) Basement Jaxx (2001)
Romeo (3) Romeo Dunn (2002)
Romeo And Juliet (8) Dire Straits (1981)
Roobarb And Custard (7) Shaft (1991)
Rooftops (A Liberation Broadcast) (8) Lostprophets (2006)
Room In Your Heart (5) Living In A Box (1989)
Room On The 3rd Floor (5) McFly (2004)
Rose Garden (3) Lynn Anderson (1971)
Rose Marie (1) first hit Slim Whitman (1955)
Rose, The (1) Westlife (2006)
Rosemary Goes) (1) (1970)
Roses (4) Outkast (2004)
Roses Are Red (3) Ronnie Carroll (1962)
Roses Are Red (8) Mac Band with McCampbell Brothers (1988)
Rosie (4) Don Partridge (1968)

Rotterdam (5) Beautiful South (1996)
Roulette (1) Russ Conway (1959)
Round And Round (9) Jaki Graham (1985)
Round Round (1) Sugababes (2002)
Roundabout (5) Funky Town (8) Pseudo Echo (1987)
Roussos Phenomenon EP, The (1) Demis Roussos (1976)
Rubber Ball (4) Bobby Vee (1961)
Rubber Ball (9) Marty Wilde (1961)
Rubber Bullets (1) 10CC (1973)
Rubberneckin' (remix) (5) Elvis Presley (2003)
Ruby (1) Kaiser Chiefs (2007)
Ruby Don't Take Your Love To Town (2) Kenny Rogers & The
First Edition (1969)
Ruby Tuesday (9) Melanie (1970)
Ruby Tuesday / Let's Spend The Night Together (3) Rolling
Stones (1967)
Rude Boy (2) Rihanna (2010)
Rude Boys Outa Jail / Rat Race (5) Specials (1980)
Rudebox (4) Robbie Williams (2006)
Ruff In The Jungle Bizness / Out Of Space (5) Prodigy (1992)
Rule The World (2) Take That (2007)
Rumble In The Jungle (3) Fugees featuring A Tribe Called Quest,
Busta Rhymes and Forte (1997)
Run (5) Snow Patrol (2004)
Run (1) Leona Lewis (2008)
Run Away (6) MC Sar & The Real McCoy (1995)
Run Baby Run (10) Newbeats (1971)
Run For Home (10) Lindisfarne (1978)
Run For Your Life (6) Matt Cardle (2011)
Run It (2) Chris Brown featuring Juelz Santana (2006)
Run Run Away (7) Slade (1984)
Run Run Run (6) Jo Jo Gunne (1972)
Run This Town (1) Jay-Z featuring Rihanna & Kanye West
(2009)
Run To Him (6) Bobby Vee (1961)
Run To Me (9) Bee Gees (1972)
Run To The Hills (7) Iron Maiden (1982)
Run To The Hills (re-issue) (9) Iron Maiden (2002)
Run To The Sun (6) Erasure (1994)
Run To You (3) Rage (1992)
Runaway (1) Del Shannon (1961)
Runaway (6) Janet Jackson (1995)
Runaway (2) Corrs (1999)
Runaway Boys (9) Stray Cats (1980)
Runaway Train (re-entry) (7) Soul Asylum (1993)
Runner, The (10) Three Degrees (1979)
Running Bear (1) Johnny Preston (1960)
Running In The Family (6) Level 42 (1987)
Running Scared (9) Roy Orbison (1961)
Running Up That Hill (3) Kate Bush (1985)
Running With The Night (9) Lionel Richie (1983)
Rush Rush (6) Paula Abdul (1991)
Rushes (5) Darius (2002)
Russian Roulette (2) Rihanna (2009)
S&M (Come On) (3) Rihanna (2011)
S Club Party (2) S Club 7 (1999)
S**t On You (10) D12 (2001)
S.O.S. (6) Abba (1975)
Sabre Dance (5) Love Sculpture (1968)
Sacred Trust / After You're Gone (2) One True Voice (2002)
Sacrifice / Healing Hands (re-issue) (1) Elton John (1990)
Sad Songs (Say So Much) (7) Elton John (1984)
Sad Sweet Dreamer (1) Sweet Sensation (1974)
Saddle Up (9) David Christie (1982)
Sadness Part 1 (1) Enigma (1990)
Safe (10) Westlife (2010)
Safety Dance, The (6) Men Without Hats (1983)
Said It All (9) Take That (2009)
Sail On (8) Commodores (1979)
Sailing (1) Rod Stewart (1975)
Sailing (re-entry) (3) Rod Stewart (1976)

Sailing On The Seven Seas (3) Orchestral Manoeuvres In The
Dark (1991)
Sailor (1) Petula Clark (1961)
Sailor (10) Anne Shelton (1961)
Saint, The (3) Orbital (1997)
Saints Are Coming, The (2) U2 & Green Day (2006)
Saints Rock 'N' Roll, The (5) Bill Haley & His Comets (1956)
Sale Of The Century (10) Sleeper (1996)
Sally (4) Gerry Monroe (1970)
Salsoul Nugget (If U Wanna) (6) M & S presents The Girl Next
Door (2001)
Saltwater (6) Julian Lennon (1991)
Saltwater (6) Chicane with Maire Brennan of Clannad (1999)
Salva Mea (remix) (9) Faithless (1996)
Sam (6) Olivia Newton-John (1977)
Samba De Janeiro (8) Bellini (1997)
Same Jeans (3) View (2007)
Same Old Brand New You (1) A1 (2000)
San Bernadino (7) Christie (1970)
San Franciscan Nights (7) Eric Burdon & The Animals (1967)
San Francisco (Be Sure To Wear Some Flowers In Your Hair) (1)
Scott McKenzie (1967)
Sanctify Yourself (10) Simple Minds (1986)
Sandstorm (8) Cast (1996)
Sandstorm (3) Darude (2000)
Sandy (2) John Travolta (1978)
Santa Bring My Baby Back (To Me) (7) Elvis Presley (1957)
Santa Claus Is Comin' To Town / My Hometown (9) Bruce
Springsteen (1985)
Santa's List (5) Cliff Richard (2003)
Santo Natale (2) David Whitfield (1954)
Satan (3) Orbital (1997)
Satellite Of Love 04 (10) Lou Reed (2004)
Satisfaction (2) Benny Benassi presents The Biz (2003)
Satisfy You (8) Puff Daddy featuring R Kelly (2000)
Saturday Love (6) Cherelle with Alexander O'Neal (1985)
Saturday Night (3) Drifters (1972)
Saturday Night (1) Whigfield (1994)
Saturday Night (6) Suede (1997)
Saturday Night At The Movies / At the Club (re-entry) (3)
Drifters (1972)
Saturday Night At the Movies / What Becomes Of The Broken
Hearted / You'll Never Walk Alone (1) Robson & Jerome (1996)
Saturday Night's Alright For Fighting (7) Elton John (1973)
Savage, The (10) Shadows (1961)
Save A Prayer (2) Duran Duran (1982)
Save Me (4) Dave Dee, Dozy, Beaky, Mick & Tich (1966)
Save Our Love (8) Eternal (1994)
Save The Best For Last (3) Vanessa Williams (1992)
Save The Last Dance For Me (2) Drifters (1960)
Save the World (10) Swedish House Mafia (2011)
Save Tonight (6) Eagle-Eye Cherry (1998)
Save Your Kisses For Me (1) Brotherhood Of Man (1976)
Save Your Love (1) Renee & Renato (1982)
Save Yourself / Genie In A Bottle (10) Speedway (2003)
Saved By The Bell (2) Robin Gibb (1969)
Saving All My Love For You (1) Whitney Houston (1985)
Saviour's Day (1) Cliff Richard (1990)
Say A Little Prayer (10) Bomb The Bass featuring Maureen
(1988)
Say Cheese (10) Fast Food Rockers (2003)
Say Goodbye / Love Ain't Gonna Wait For You (2) S Club
(2003)
Say Hello Wave Goodbye (3) Soft Cell (1982)
Say I (4) Christina Milian featuring Young Jeezy (2006)
Say I Won't Be There (5) Springfields (1963)
Say I'm Your No.1 (7) Princess (1985)
Say It Again (7) Jermaine Stewart (1988)
Say It Again (6) Precious (1999)
Say It Isn't So (10) Bon Jovi (2000)
Say It Isn't So (4) Gareth Gates (2003)
Say It Right (10) Nellie Furtado (2007)

Say My Name (3) Destiny's Child (2000)
Say Say Say (2) Paul McCartney & Michael Jackson (1983)
Say Say Say (Waiting 4 U) (4) Hi-Tack (2006)
Say What You Want (3) Texas (1997)
Say What You Want / Insane (re-recording) (4) Texas featuring The Wu-Tang Clan (1998)
Say Wonderful Things (6) Ronnie Carroll (1963)
Say You Love Me (7) Simply Red (1998)
Say You Say Me (8) Lionel Richie (1985)
Say You'll Be Mine (1) Spice Girls (1996)
Say You'll Be Mine / Better The Devil You Know (4) Steps (1999)
Say You're Mine Again (6) June Hutton with Axel Stordahl (1953)
Scandalous (2) Mis-Teeq (2003)
Scarlett O'Hara (2) Jet Harris & Tony Meehan (1963)
Scatman (3) Scatman John (1995)
Scatman's World (10) Scatman John (1995)
School's Out (1) Alice Cooper (1972)
Scientist, The (10) Coldplay (2002)
Scotch On The Rocks (8) Band Of The Black Watch (1975)
Scream (3) Michael Jackson & Janet Jackson (1995)
Scream If You Wanna Go Faster (8) Geri Halliwell (2001)
Se A Vide (That's The Way Life Is) (8) Pet Shop Boys (1996)
Sea Of Love (3) Marty Wilde (1959)
Sealed With A Kiss (3) Brian Hyland (1962)
Sealed With A Kiss (re-issue) (7) Brian Hyland (1975)
Sealed With A Kiss (1) Jason Donovan (1989)
Search For The Hero (9) M People (1995)
Searchin' (I Gotta Find A Man) (6) Hazell Dean (1984)
Searchin' My Soul (1) Vonda Shepard (1998)
Searching (4) China Black (1994)
Seaside Shuffle (2) Terry Dactyl & The Dinosaurs (1972)
Seasons In The Sun (1) Terry Jacks (1974)
Seasons In The Sun / I Have A Dream (1) Westlife (1999)
Secret (5) Madonna (1994)
Secret Love (1) Doris Day (1954)
Secret Love (4) Kathy Kirby (1963)
Secret Love (5) Bee Gees (1991)
Secret Lovers (10) Atlantic Starr (1986)
Secrets (9) Eternal (1996)
Secrets That You Keep, The (3) Mud (1975)
See Emily Play (6) Pink Floyd (1967)
See It In A Boy's Eyes (5) Jamelia (2004)
See My Baby Jive (1) Wizzard (1973)
See My Friend (10) Kinks (1965)
See The Day (3) Dee C Lee (1985)
See The Day (9) Girls Aloud (2005)
See Ya (6) Atomic Kitten (2000)
See You (6) Depeche Mode (1982)
See You Later Alligator (7) Bill Haley & His Comets (1956)
Self Control (5) Laura Branigan (1984)
Semi-Detached Suburban Mr James (2) Manfred Mann (1966)
Send In The Clowns (6) Judy Collins (1975)
Senses Working Overtime (10) XTC (1982)
Sentinel (10) Mike Oldfield (1992)
Senza Una Donna (Without A Woman) (4) Zucchero & Paul Young (1991)
Separate Lives (4) Phil Collins & Marilyn Martin (1985)
September (3) Earth Wind & Fire (1978)
Serenade (re-entry) (8) Slim Whitman (1956)
Serious (8) Donna Allen (1987)
Sesame's Treet (2) Smart Es (1992)
Set Adrift On Memory Bliss (3) PM Dawn (1991)
Set Me Free (9) Kinks (1965)
Set Me Free (7) Jaki Graham (1986)
Set You Free (remix) (2) N-Trance (1995)
Set You Free (2nd remix) (4) N-Trance (2001)
Setting Sun (1) Chemical Brothers (1996)
7 Days (1) Craig David (2000)
Seven Days And One Week (3) BBE (1996)
Seven Drunken Nights (7) Dubliners (1967)
Seven Little Girls Sitting In The Back Seat (3) Avons (1959)
Seven Lonely Days (re-entry) (6) Gisele McKenzie (1953)
7 Nation Army (7) White Stripes (2003)

Seven Seas Of Rye (10) Queen (1974)
7 Seconds (3) Youssou N'Dour featuring Neneh Cherry (1994)
Seven Tears (1) Goombay Dance Band (1982)
7 Ways To Love (8) Cola Boy (1991)
Sewn (7) Feeling (2006)
Sex On Fire (1) Kings Of Leon (2008)
Sex On Fire (re-emergence) (6) Kings Of Leon (2009)
Sex On The Beach (2) T-Spoon (1998)
Sexbomb (3) Tom Jones & Mousse T (2000)
Sexcrime (Nineteen Eighty-Four) (4) Eurythmics (1984)
Sexed Up (10) Robbie Williams (2003)
(Sexual) Healing (4) Marvin Gaye (1982)
Sexy and I Know It (5) LMFAO (2011)
Sexy Chick (1) David Guetta featuring Akon (2009)
Sexy Eyes (4) Dr Hook (1980)
Sexy Love (5) Ne-Yo (2006)
Sexy MF / Strollin' (4) Prince & The New Power Generation (1992)
Sexy No No No (5) Girls Aloud (2007)
Sexyback (1) Justin Timberlake (2006)
Sha La La (3) Manfred Mann (1964)
Sha La La La Lee (3) Small Faces (1966)
Shackles (Praise You) (5) Mary Mary (2000)
Shaddup You Face (1) Joe Dolce Music Theatre (1981)
Shake It (6) Metro Station (2009)
Shake It Off (9) Get-A-Way (4) Maxx (1994)
Shake It Off / Get Your Number (9) Mariah Carey (2005)
Shake Rattle And Roll (4) Bill Haley & His Comets (1954)
Shake Ur Body (7) Shy FX & T Power featuring Di (2002)
Shake Ya Tailfeather (10) Nelly / P Diddy / Murphy Lee (2003)
Shake You Down (6) Gregory Abbott (1986)
Shake Your Body (Down To The Ground) (4) Jacksons (1979)
Shake Your Head (4) Was (Not Was) (1992)
Shake Your Love (7) Debbie Gibson (1988)
Shakespeare's Way With Words (10) One True Voice (2003)
Shakin' All Over (1) Johnny Kidd & The Pirates (1960)
Shakin' Stevens EP, The (2) Shakin' Stevens (1982)
Shalala Lala (5) Vengaboys (2000)
Shame (2) Robbie Williams & Gary Barlow (2010)
Shame Shame Shame (6) Shirley & Company (1975)
Shang-A-Lang (2) Bay City Rollers (1974)
Shape Of My Heart (4) Backstreet Boys (2000)
Shapes Of Things (3) Yardbirds (1966)
Sharing You (10) Bobby Vee (1962)
Shattered Dreams (5) Johnny Hates Jazz (1987)
Shazam! (4) Duane Eddy (1960)
She (1) Charles Aznavour (1974)
She Bangs (3) Ricky Martin (2000)
She Believes (In Me) (2) Ronan Keating (2004)
She Don't Let Nobody (4) Chaka Demus & Pliers (1993)
She Drives Me Crazy (5) Fine Young Cannibals (1989)
She Is Love / Little By Little (2) Oasis (2002)
She Loves You (1) Beatles (1963)
She Makes Me Wanna (1) JLS featuring Dev (2011)
She Makes My Day (6) Robert Palmer (1988)
She Makes My Nose Bleed (9) Mansun (1997)
She Means Nothing To Me (9) Phil Everly / Cliff Richard (1983)
She Moves In Her Own Way (7) Kooks (2006)
She Said (3) Plan B (2010)
She Wants To Dance With Me (6) Rick Astley (1988)
She Wants To Move (5) NERD (2004)
She Wants You (3) Billie (1998)
She Wears My Ring (3) Solomon King (1968)
She Wears Red Feathers (1) Guy Mitchell (1953)
She Will Be Loved (4) Maroon 5 (2004)
She Wolf (4) Shakira (2009)
She'd Rather Be With Me (4) Turtles (1967)
Sheffield Grinder, The / Capstick Comes Home (3) Tony Capstick (1981)
Sheila (3) Tommy Roe (1962)
Sheila Take A Bow (10) Smiths (1987)
Sherry (8) Four Seasons (1962)
Sherry (10) Adrian Baker (1975)
She's A River (9) Simple Minds (1995)
She's A Star (9) James (1997)

She's Always A Woman (7) Fyfe Dangerfield (2010)
She's Got Claws (6) Gary Numan (1981)
She's Got That Vibe (3) R Kelly (1994)
She's Leaving Home (1) Billy Bragg with Cara Tivey (1988)
She's Not You (1) Elvis Presley with The Jordanaires (1962)
She's Not You (re-issue) (3) Elvis Presley (2005)
She's On It (10) Beastie Boys (1987)
She's Out Of My Life (3) Michael Jackson (1980)
She's So Lovely (7) Scouting For Girls (2007)
She's The One / It's Only Us (1) Robbie Williams (1999)
Shindig (6) Shadows (1963)
Shine (5) Aswad (1994)
Shine (1) Take That (2007)
Shine (6) Lovefreekz (2005)
Shine A Light (4) McFly featuring Taio Cruz (2010)
Shine A Little Love (6) Electric Light Orchestra (1979)
Shine On (8) Degrees Of Motion featuring Biti (1994)
Shining Light (8) Ash (2001)
Shiny Happy People (6) REM (1991)
Ship Of Fools (6) Erasure (1988)
Shirley (6) Shakin' Stevens (1982)
Shiver (8) Natalie Imbruglia (2005)
Shock Of The Lightning, The (3) Oasis (2008)
Shocked (6) Kylie Minogue (1991)
Shoop Shoop Song (It's In His Kiss), The (1) Cher (1991)
Shoot Me With Your Love (7) D:Ream (1995)
Shooting Star (3) Flip & Fill (2002)
Shooting Star / Baby Can I Hold You (2) Boyzone / Stephen Gately (1997)
Shortsharpshock EP (9) Therapy? (1993)
Shot You Down (3) Audio Bullys featuring Nancy Sinatra (2005)
Shotgun Wedding (6) Roy C (1966)
Shotgun Wedding (re-issue) (8) Roy C (1972)
Should I Stay Or Should I Go Clash (re-issue) (1) (1991)
Shoulda Woulda Coulda (10) Beverley Knight (2002)
Shout (7) Lulu & The Luvvers (1964)
Shout (4) Tears For Fears (1984)
Shout (8) Lulu (1986)
Shout (7) Louchie Lou & Michie One (1993)
Shout (10) Ant & Dec (1997)
Shout (1) Shout For England featuring Dizzee Rascal & James Corden (2010)
Shout To The Top (7) Style Council (1984)
Show, The (7) Doug E Fresh & The Get Fresh Crew (1985)
Show, The (2) Girls Aloud (2004)
Show Me Heaven (1) Maria McKee (1990)
Show Me Love (6) Robin S (1993)
Show Me Love (remix) (9) Robin S (1997)
Show Me Love (8) Robyn (1998)
Show Me The Meaning Of Being Lonely (3) Backstreet Boys (2000)
Show Me The Way (10) Peter Frampton (1976)
Show Me You're A Woman (8) Mud (1975)
Show Must Go On, The (2) Leo Sayer (1973)
Show You The Way To Go (1) Jacksons (1977)
Showing Out (Get Fresh At The Weekend) (3) Mel & Kim (1986)
Shuffle, The (4) Van McCoy (1977)
Shut Up (7) Madness (1981)
Shut Up (2) Black Eyed Peas (2003)
Shut Up And Drive (8) Rihanna (2007)
Shut Up And Forget About It (9) Dane (2001)
Shut Up And Let Me Go (re-entry) (6) Ting Tings(2008)
Shy Boy (4) Bananarama (1982)
Shy Guy (2) Diana King (1995)
Sick And Tired (4) Anastacia (2004)
Sick Man Blues / Funky Gibbon (4) Goodies (1975)
Side By Side (7) Kay Starr (1953)
Side Saddle (1) Russ Conway (1959)
Sideshow (3) Barry Biggs (1976)
Sight For Sore Eyes (6) M People (1994)
Sign, The (2) Ace Of Base (1994)
Sign O' The Times (10) Prince (1987)

Sign Of The Times (3) Belle Stars (1983)
Sign Your Name (2) Terence Trent D'Arby (1988)
Signal Fire (4) Snow Patrol (2007)
Signature Tune Of 'The Army Game' (5) Michael Medwin, Bernard Bresslaw, Alfie Bass and Leslie Fyson (1958)
Signs (2) Snoop Dogg featuring Charlie Wilson & Justin Timberlake (2005)
Silence (remixes) (3) Delirium featuring Sarah McLachlan (2000)
Silence Is Easy (9) Starsailor (2003)
Silence Is Golden (1) Tremeloes (1967)
Silent Night (8) Bing Crosby (1952)
Silent Night / Cat Amongst The Pigeons (2) Bros (1988)
Silhouettes (10) Cliff Richard (1990)
Silhouettes (3) Herman's Hermits (1965)
Silly Games (2) Janet Kay (1979)
Silly Love Songs (2) Wings (1976)
Silly Thing (6) Sex Pistols (1979)
Silver Dream Machine (4) David Essex (1980)
Silver Lady (1) David Soul (1977)
Silver Machine (3) Hawkwind (1972)
Silver Star (3) Four Seasons (1976)
Simon Says (2) 1910 Fruitgum Co (1968)
Simon Smith and his Amazing Dancing Bear (4) Alan Price Set (1967)
Simon Templar / Two Pints Of Lager And A Packet Of Crisps Please (7) Splodgeness-abounds (1980)
Simple Game (3) Four Tops (1971)
Since I Don't Have You (10) Guns 'N' Roses (1994)
Since U Been Gone (5) Kelly Clarkson (2005)
Since Yesterday (5) Strawberry Switchblade (1984)
Since You've Been Gone (6) Rainbow (1979)
Sing (3) Travis (2001)
Sing Baby Sing (3) Stylistics (1975)
Sing For The Moment (6) Eminem (2003)
Sing It Back (4) Moloko (1999)
Sing Me (8) Brothers (1977)
Sing Our Own Song (5) UB40 (1986)
Singin' In The Rain (re-issue) (1) Mint Royale (2008)
Singing The Blues (1) Guy Mitchell (1956)
Singing The Blues (1) Tommy Steele (1956)
Single (3) Natasha Bedingfield (2004)
Single Ladies (Put A Ring On It) (7) Beyonce (2008)
Sink That Ship / I Predict A Riot (re-issue) (9) Kaiser Chiefs (2005)
Sir Duke (2) Stevie Wonder (1977)
Sister (10) Bros (1989)
Sister Jane (9) New World (1972)
Sisters Are Doin' It For Themselves (9) Eurythmics & Aretha Franklin (1985)
Sit Down (2) James (1991)
Sit Down (remix) (7) James (1998)
(Sittin' On) The Dock Of The Bay (3) Otis Redding (1968)
Sitting Down Here (5) Lene Marlin (2000)
Six Teens, The (9) Sweet (1974)
6 Underground (remix) (9) Sneaker Pimps (1997)
16 Bars (7) Stylistics (1976)
Sixteen Reasons (9) Connie Stevens (1960)
Sixteen Tons (1) Tennessee Ernie Ford (1956)
Sixteen Tons (10) Frankie Laine (1956)
Size Of A Cow, The (5) Wonder Stuff (1991)
Sk8er Boi (8) Avril Lavigne (2003)
Skin Deep (7) Duke Ellington (1954)
Skin Deep (9) Ted Heath Orchestra (1954)
Skweeze Me Pleeze Me (1) Slade (1973)
Sky (2) Sonique (2000)
Sky High (9) Jigsaw (1975)
Skye Boat Song, The (10) Roger Whittaker & Des O'Connor (1986)
Slam Dunk (Da Funk) (10) Five (1997)
Slam Jam (4) WWF Superstars (1992)
Slave To Love (10) Bryan Ferry (1985)
Sledgehammer (4) Peter Gabriel (1986)

Sleep (6) Texas (2006)
Sleeping Satellite (1) Tasmin Archer (1992)
Sleeping With The Light On (3) Busted (2003)
Sleepy Shores (8) Johnny Pearson Orchestra (1971)
Sleigh Ride / Puppy Love (6) S Club Juniors (2002)
Slight Return (2) Bluetones (1996)
Slightest Touch, The (4) Five Star (1987)
Sloop John B (2) Beach Boys (1966)
Slow (1) Kylie Minogue (2003)
Slow Down (10) John Miles (1977)
Slow Down (4) Bobby Valentino (2005)
Slow Jamz (3) Twista (2004)
Slowhand (10) Pointer Sisters (1981)
Smack My Bitch Up (8) Prodigy (1997)
Smack That (1) Akon featuring Eminem (2006)
Smalltown Boy (3) Bronski Beat (1984)
Smarty Pants (9) First Choice (1973)
Smells Like Teen Spirit (7) Nirvana (1991)
Smile (2) Nat 'King' Cole (1954)
Smile (1) Lily Allen (2006)
Smiley Faces (10) Gnarls Barkley (2006)
Smoke (5) Natalie Imbruglia (1998)
Smoke Gets In Your Eyes (1) Platters (1959)
Smokers Outside The Hospital Doors (7) Editors (2007)
Smooth (3) Santana featuring Rob Thomas (2000)
Smooth Criminal (8) Michael Jackson (1988)
Smooth Criminal (3) Alien Ant Farm (2001)
Smurf Song, The (2) Father Abraham & Smurfs (1978)
Snake (10) R Kelly featuring Big Trigger (2003)
Snap Megamix (10) Snap (1991)
Snooker Loopy (6) Matchroom Mob with Chas & Dave (1986)
Snoopy Vs The Red Baron (8) Royal Guardsmen (1967)
Snoopy Vs The Red Baron (4) Hotshots (1973)
Snot Rap (9) Kenny Everett (1983)
Snow Coach (7) Russ Conway (1959)
So Cold The Night (8) Communards (1986)
So Confused (6) 2play featuring Raghav & Jucxi (2004)
So Emotional (5) Whitney Houston (1987)
So Good (3) Boyzone (1995)
So Good (10) Rachel Stevens (2005)
So Good To Be Back Home Again (8) Tourists (1980)
So Hard (4) Pet Shop Boys (1990)
So Here We Are / Positive Tension (5) Bloc Party (2005)
So Lonely (6) Police (1980)
So Lonely (8) Jakatta (2002)
So Long Baby (10) Del Shannon (1961)
So Macho / Cruising (2) Sinitta (1986)
So Much Love To Give (9) Freeloaders featuring The Real Thing (2005)
So Pure (3) Baby D (1996)
So Sad (To Watch Good Love Go Bad) / Lucille (4) Everly Brothers (1960)
So Sick (1) Ne-Yo (2006)
So What (1) Pink (2008)
So Why So Sad (8) Manic Street Preachers (2001)
So Yesterday (9) Hilary Duff (2003)
So You Win Again (1) Hot Chocolate (1977)
So Young (6) Corrs (1998)
Sober (9) Pink (2009)
Soda Pop / I Got You Babe (5) Avid Merrion, Davina McCall & Patsy Kensit (2004)
Softly As I Leave You (10) Matt Monro (1962)
Softly Softly (1) Ruby Murray (1955)
Softly Whispering I Love You (4) Congregation (1971)
Soldier (4) Destiny's Child featuring TI & Lil' Wayne (2005)
Soldier Blue (7) Buffy St Marie (1971)
Soley Soley (5) Middle Of The Road (1971)
Solid (3) Ashford & Simpson (1985)
Solid Gold Easy Action (2) T Rex (1972)
Solitaire (4) Andy Williams (1973)
Solitary Man (9) Him (2004)
Solo (3) Iyaz (2010)
Solomon Bites The Worm (10) Bluetones (1998)
Solsbury Hill (10) Erasure (2003)
Some Girls (2) Racey (1979)

Some Girls (9) Ultimate Kaos (1994)
Some Girls (2) Rachel Stevens (2004)
Some Kind of Summer / I'm a Clown (3) David Cassidy (1973)
Some Kinda Fun (10) Chris Montez (1963)
Some Might Say (1) Oasis (1995)
Some Of Your Lovin' (8) Dusty Springfield (1965)
Some People (3) Cliff Richard (1987)
Somebody Help Me (1) Spencer Davis Group (1966)
Somebody Stole My Gal (6) Johnnie Ray (1953)
Somebody To Love (2) Queen (1976)
Somebody To Love (3) Boogie Pimps (2004)
Somebody Told Me (re-issue) (3) Killers (2005)
Somebody's Watching Me (6) Rockwell (1984)
Somebody's Watching Me (3) Beatfreakz (2006)
Someday (9) Ricky Nelson (1958)
Someday (I'll Come Back) (10) Lisa Stansfield (1992)
Someday (4) Eternal (1996)
Someday (6) Nickelback (2003)
Someday I'll Be Saturday Night (7) Bon Jovi (1995)
Someone (6) Johnny Mathis (1959)
Someone Else's Baby (2) Adam Faith (1960)
Someone Else's Roses (5) Joan Regan (1954)
Someone Like Me / Right Now (8) Atomic Kitten (2004)
Someone Like You (10) Russell Watson & Faye Tozer (2002)
Someone Like You (1) Adele (2011)
Someone Loves You Honey (9) Lutricia McNeal (1998)
Someone Someone (2) Brian Poole & The Tremeloes (1964)
Someone's Looking At You (4) Boomtown Rats (1980)
Something / Come Together (4) Beatles (1969)
Something (4) Shirley Bassey (1970)
Something (4) Lasgo (2002)
Somethin' Is Goin' On (9) Cliff Richard (2004)
Somethin' Stupid (1) Nancy Sinatra & Frank Sinatra (1967)
Somethin' Stupid (1) Robbie Williams & Nicole Kidman (2001)
Something About The Way You Look Tonight / Candle In The Wind 97 (1) Elton John (1997)
Something About You (6) Level 42 (1985)
Something About You (9) Jamelia (2006)
Something Beautiful (3) Robbie Williams (2003)
Something Better Change / Straighten Out (9) Stranglers (1977)
Something 'Bout You Baby I Like (9) Status Quo (1981)
Something Changed (10) Pulp (1996)
Something Deep Inside (4) Billie Piper (2000)
Something Else / Friggin' In The Riggin' (3) Sex Pistols (1979)
Something For The Pain (8) Bon Jovi (1995)
Something Goin' On (5) Todd Terry (1997)
Something Good (4) Utah Saints (1992)
Something Good 08 (8) Utah Saints (2008)
Something In The Air (1) Thunderclap Newman (1969)
Something Inside) So Strong (4) Labi Siffre (1987)
Something Kinda Ooooh (3) Girls Aloud (2006)
Something Old Something New (9) Fantastics (1971)
Something Tells Me (Something Is Gonna Happen Tonight) (3) Cilla Black (1971)
Something's Burning (8) Kenny Rogers & The First Edition (1970)
Something's Gotten Hold Of My Heart (5) Gene Pitney (1967)
Something's Gotten Hold Of My Heart (1) Marc Almond featuring Gene Pitney (1989)
Something's Happening (6) Herman's Hermits (1968)
Sometimes (2) Erasure (1986)
Sometimes (3) Britney Spears (1999)
Sometimes You Can't Make It On Your Own (1) U2 (2005)
Somewhere (6) P J Proby (1964)
Somewhere (9) Pet Shop Boys (1997)
Somewhere Along The Way (3) Nat 'King' Cole (1952)
Somewhere Else (2) Razorlight (2005)
Somewhere I Belong (10) Linkin Park (2003)
Somewhere In My Heart (3) Aztec Camera (1988)
Somewhere Only We Know (3) Keane (2004)
Somewhere Out There (8) Linda Ronstadt & James Ingram (1987)
Somewhere Somehow (7) Wet Wet Wet (1995)
Son Of A Gun (remix) (6) JX (1995)
Son Of A Preacher Man (9) Dusty Springfield (1968)
Son Of Hickory Holler's Tramp (2) O C Smith (1968)

Son Of My Father (1) Chicory Tip (1972)
Song 4 Lovers (5) Liberty X (2005)
Song 4 Mutya (Out Of Control) (8) Groove Armada (2007)
Song For Guy (4) Elton John (1978)
Song For The Lovers, A (3) Richard Ashcroft (2000)
Song For Whoever (2) Beautiful South (1989)
Song Of The Dreamer (10) Johnnie Ray (1955)
Songbird (3) Oasis (2003)
Song 2 (2) Blur (1997)
Sorrow (4) Merseys (1966)
Sorrow (3) David Bowie (1973)
Sorry (1) Madonna (2006)
Sorry I'm A Lady (8) Baccara (1978)
Sorry Seems To Be The Hardest Word (1) Blue featuring Elton John (2002)
Sorry Suzanne (3) Hollies (1969)
Sorry's Not Good Enough (3) McFly (2006)
Sorted For E's And Wizz / Mis-Shapes (2) Pump (1995)
SOS (2) Rihanna (2006)
Soulmate (7) Natasha Bedingfield (2007)
Sound (9) James (1991)
Sound And Vision (3) David Bowie (1977)
Sound Of Drums (3) Kula Shaker (1998)
Sound Of Silence, The (3) Bachelors (1966)
Sound Of The Underground (1) Girls Aloud (2002)
Southern Freeez (8) Freeez (1981)
Souvenir (3) Orchestral Manoeuvres In The Dark (1981)
Sowing The Seeds Of Love (5) Tears For Fears (1989)
Space Jungle, The (7) Adamski (1990)
Space Oddity (5) David Bowie (1969)
Space Oddity (re-issue) (1) David Bowie (1975)
Spaceman (1) Babylon Zoo (1996)
Spaceship (5) Tinchy Stryder featuring Dappy (2011)
Spanish (8) Craig David (2003)
Spanish Eyes (re-issue) (5) Al Martino (1973)
Spanish Flea (3) Herb Alpert & The Tijuana Brass (1965)
Spanish Harlem (14) Aretha Franklin (1971)
Spanish Hustle (see Do The Spanish Hustle)
Speak Like A Child (4) Style Council (1983)
Speak To Me Pretty (3) Brenda Lee (1962)
Special AKA Live EP, The (1) Special AKA (1980)
Special Brew (3) Bad Manners (1980)
Special Years, The (7) Val Doonican (1965)
Speechless (9) D-Side (2003)
Speed Of Sound (2) Coldplay (2005)
Speedy Gonzales (2) Pat Boone (1962)
Spice Up Your Life (1) Spice Girls (1997)
Spin The Black Circle (10) Pearl Jam (1994)
Spinning Around (1) Kylie Minogue (2000)
Spinning The Wheel (2) George Michael (1996)
Spirit In The Sky (1) Norman Greenbaum (1970)
Spirit In The Sky (1) Dr & The Medics (1986)
Spirit In The Sky (1) Gareth Gates featuring The Kumars (2003)
Splish Splash (7) Charlie Drake (1958)
Squeeze Box (10) Who (1976)
S-S-Single Bed (4) Fox (1976)
St Anger (9) Metallica (2003)
St Elmo's Fire (Man In Motion) (6) John Parr (1985)
St Therese Of The Roses (re-entry) (3) Malcolm Vaughan (1956)
St Valentine's Day Massacre Motorhead & EP (5) Girlschool (1981)
Staccato's Theme (4) Elmer Bernstein (1959)
Stagger Lee (7) Lloyd Price (1959)
Stairway Of Love (3) Michael Holliday (1958)
Stairway To Heaven (8) Neil Sedaka (1960)
Stairway To Heaven (8) Far Corporation (1985)
Stairway To Heaven (7) Rolf Harris (1993)
Stan (1) Eminem (2000)
Stand And Deliver (1) Adam & The Ants (1981)
Stand By Me (re-issue) (1) Ben E King (1987)
Stand By Me (2) Oasis (1997)
Stand By Your Man (1) Tammy Wynette (1975)

Stand Tough (7) Point Break (2000)
Stand Up For Your Love Rights (2) Yazz (1988)
Stand Up Tall (10) Dizzee Rascal (2004)
Standing In The Road (4) Blackfoot Sue (1972)
Standing In The Shadows Of Love (6) Four Tops (1967)
Standing In The Way Of Control (7) Gossip (2007)
Standing On The Corner (4) King Brothers (1960)
Star 69 (10) Fatboy Slim (2001)
Star Girl (1) McFly (2006)
Star Guitar (8) Chemical Brothers (2002)
Star People '97 (2) George Michael (1997)
Star To Fall (4) Cabin Crew (2005)
Star Trekkin' (1) Firm (1987)
Star Wars Theme / Cantina Band (7) Meco (1977)
Stardust (7) David Essex (1974)
Staring At The Sun (3) U2 (1997)
Staring At The Sun (5) Rooster (2005)
Starlight (2) Supermen Lovers with Mani Hoffman (2001)
Starmaker (3) Kids From Fame (1982)
Starman (10) David Bowie (1972)
Starry Eyed (1) Michael Holliday (1960)
Starry Eyed (4) Ellie Goulding (2010)
Starry-Eyed Surprise (6) Oakenfold (2002)
Stars (8) Simply Red (1991)
Stars Are Blind (5) Paris (2006)
Stars On 45 (2) Starsound (1981)
Stars On 45 Vol.2 (2) Starsound (1981)
Starstrukk (3) 3OH!3 featuring Katy Perry (2009)
Start (1) Jam (1980)
Start Me Up (7) Rolling Stones (1981)
Start Without You (1) Alexandra Burke featuring Laza Morgan (2010)
Starting Over (see Just Like Starting Over)
Starting Together (2) Su Pollard (1986)
Starz In Their Eyes (2) Just Jack (2007)
State Of Mind (8) Holly Valance (2003)
Stay (1) Shakespears Sister (1992)
Stay (2) Sash featuring La Trec (1997)
Stay (8) Hollies (1963)
Stay (4) Eternal (1993)
Stay (Faraway So Close) (4) U2 (1993)
Stay Another Day (1) East 17 (1994)
Stay Awake (1) Example (2011)
Stay (I Missed You) (6) Lisa Loeb & Nine Stories (1994)
Stay On These Roads (5) A-Ha (1988)
Stay Out Of My Life (9) Five Star (1987)
Stay Together (3) Suede (1994)
Stay Too Long (9) Plan B (2010)
Stay With Me (6) Faces (1971)
Stay With Me (Baby) (10) Rebecca Wheatley (2000)
Stay With Me (5) Ironik (2008)
Stayin' Alive (4) Bee Gees (1978)
Stayin' Alive (2) N-Trance featuring Ricardo Da Force (1995)
Staying In / More Than I Can Say (4) Bobby Vee (1961)
Steady As She Goes (4) Raconteurs (2006)
Steal My Sunshine (8) Len (1999)
Steam (10) Peter Gabriel (1993)
Steam (7) East 17 (1994)
Step Back In Time (4) Kylie Minogue (1990)
Step By Step (2) New Kids On The Block (1990)
Step Inside Love (8) Cilla Black (1968)
Step Off (Part 1) (8) Grandmaster Melle Mel & Furious Five (1984)
Step On (5) Happy Mondays (1990)
Steppin' Out (6) Joe Jackson (1983)
Stereo Hearts (3) Gym Class Heroes featuring Adam Levine (2011)
Stereo Love (4) Edward Maya featuring Vika Jigulina (2010)
Stereotype / Jet Set (6) International Specials (1980)
Stereotypes (7) Blur (1996)
Stewball / Lost John (2) Lonnie Donegan Skiffle Group (1956)
Stick It Out (4) Right Said Fred & Friends (1993)

Stickwitu (1) Pussycat Dolls (2005)
Still (4) Commodores (1979)
Still D.R.E. (6) Dr Dre featuring Snoop Doggy Dogg (2000)
Still I'm Sad / Evil Hearted You (3) Yardbirds (1965)
Still On Your Side (8) BBMak (2001)
Still Water (Love) (10) Four Tops (1970)
Stillness In Time (9) Jamiroquai (1995)
Stole (2) Kelly Rowland (2003)
Stolen (4) Jay Sean (2004)
Stomp (6) Brothers Johnson (1980)
Stomp (1) Steps (2000)
Stoned In Love (7) Chicane featuring Tom Jones (2006)
Stoned Love (3) Supremes (1971)
Stonk, The (1) Hale & Pace & The Stonkers (1991)
Stool Pigeon (7) Kid Creole & The Coconuts (1982)
Stop (4) Sam Brown (1989)
Stop (2) Spice Girls (1998)
Stop / DJ (9) Jamelia (2004)
Stop And Stare (4) OneRepublic (2008)
Stop Crying Your Heart Out (2) Oasis (2002)
Stop In The Name Of Love (7) Supremes (1965)
Stop Living The Lie (1) David Sneddon (2003)
Stop Me (2) Mark Ronson featuring Daniel Merriweather (2007)
Stop Sign (10) Abs (2003)
Stop Stop Stop (2) Hollies (1966)
Stop The Cavalry (3) Jona Lewie (1980)
Stop The Rock (10) Apollo Four Forty (1999)
Storm In A Teacup (7) Fortunes (1972)
Story Of My Life, The (1) Michael Holliday (1958)
Story Of My Life (9) Kristian Leontiou (2004)
Story Of The Blues, The (3) Wah (1982)
Story Of Tina, The (10) Al Martino (1954)
Straight From The Heart (9) Doolally (1999)
Straight Up (3) Paula Abdul (1989)
Straighten Out / Something Better Change (9) Stranglers (1977)
Stranded (3) Lutricia McNeal (1998)
Strange And Beautiful (7) Aqualung (2002)
Strange Currencies (9) REM (1995)
Strange Kind Of Woman (8) Deep Purple (1971)
Strange Lady In Town (6) Frankie Laine (1955)
Strange Little Girl (7) Stranglers (1982)
Stranger, The / Man Of Mystery (5) Shadows (1960)
Stranger In Moscow (4) Michael Jackson (1996)
Stranger In Paradise (1) Tony Bennett (1955)
Stranger In Paradise (6) Four Aces featuring Al Alberts (1955)
Stranger In Paradise (6) Tony Martin (1955)
Stranger On The Shore (2) Acker Bilk with Leon Young Strings (1961)
Strangers In The Night (1) Frank Sinatra (1966)
Strangest Thing '97, The / You Have Been Loved (2) George Michael (1997)
Strawberry Fair (3) Anthony Newley (1960)
Strawberry Fields Forever / Penny Lane (2) Beatles (1967)
Strawberry Fields Forever (3) Candy Flip (1990)
Streak, The (1) Ray Stevens (1974)
Street Dance (3) Break Machine (1984)
Street Life (9) Roxy Music (1973)
Street Life (5) Crusaders (1979)
Street Spirit (Fade Out) (5) Radiohead (1996)
Street Tuff (3) Rebel MC & Double (1989)
Streets Of London (2) Ralph McTell (1974)
Streets Of Philadelphia (2) Bruce Springsteen (1994)
Strings Of Life (Stronger On My Own) (6) Soul Central featuring Kathy Brown (2005)
Strollin / Sexy MF (4) Prince & The New Power Generation (1992)
Strong (4) Robbie Williams (1999)
Strong Enough (5) Cher (1999)
Stronger (7) Britney Spears (2000)
Stronger / Angels With Dirty Faces (7) Sugababes (2002)
Stronger (1) Kanye West (2007)
Strut Your Funky Stuff (10) Frantique (1979)
Stuck (9) Stacie Orrico (2003)
Stuck In A Moment You Can't Get Out Of (2) U2 (2001)
Stuck In The Middle (4) Louise (2001)

Stuck In The Middle With You (8) Stealer's Wheel (1973)
Stuck On You (3) Elvis Presley with The Jordanaires (1960)
Stuck On You (9) Trevor Walters (1984)
Stupid Cupid / Carolina Moon (1) Connie Francis (1958)
Stupid Girl (4) Garbage (1996)
Stupid Girls (4) Pink (2006)
Stutter (7) Joe (2001)
Stutter Rap (No Sleep 'Til Bedtime) (4) Morris Minor & The Majors (1987)
Substitute (5) Who (1966)
Substitute (re-issue) (7) Who (1976)
Substitute (2) Clout (1978)
Substitute (8) Liquid Gold (1980)
Subterranean Homesick Blues (9) Bob Dylan (1965)
Suburban Knights (7) Hard-Fi (2007)
Suburbia (8) Pet Shop Boys (1986)
Such A Night (1) Johnnie Ray (1954)
Sucu Sucu (9) Laurie Johnson (1961)
Suddenly (4) Billy Ocean (1985)
Suddenly (3) Angry Anderson (1988)
Suddenly There's A Valley (7) Petula Clark (1955)
Suddenly You Love Me (6) Tremeloes (1968)
Suedehead (5) Morrissey (1988)
Sugar And Spice (2) Searchers (1963)
Sugar Baby Love (1) Rubettes (1974)
Sugar Candy Kisses (3) Mac & Katie Kissoon (1975)
Sugar Me (5) Lynsey De Paul (1972)
Sugar Moon (6) Pat Boone (1958)
Sugar Sugar (1) Archies (1969)
Sugar Town (6) Nancy Sinatra (1967)
Sugar We're Goin Down (re-issue) (8) Fall Out Boy (2006)
Sugarbush (8) Doris Day & Frankie Laine (1952)
Sukiyaki (6) Kyu Sakamoto (1963)
Sukiyaki (10) Kenny Ball & His Jazzmen (1963)
Sultana (5) Titanic (1971)
Sultans Of Swing (8) Dire Straits (1979)
Summer (The First Time) (9) Bobby Goldsboro (1973)
Summer Holiday (1) Cliff Richard and The Shadows (1963)
Summer In The City (8) Lovin' Spoonful (1966)
Summer Night City (5) Abba (1978)
Summer Nights (10) Marianne Faithfull (1965)
Summer Nights (1) John Travolta & Olivia Newton- John (1978)
Summer of Love / When I Said Goodbye (5) Steps (2000)
Summer Of Love (8) Lonyo (2000)
Summer Of My Life (7) Simon May (1976)
Summer Set (5) Acker Bilk and his Paramount Jazz Band (1960)
Summer Son (5) Texas (1999)
Summer Sunshine (6) Corrs (2004)
Summerlove Sensation (3) Bay City Rollers (1974)
Summertime (8) Jazzy Jeff & The Fresh Prince (1991)
Summertime (7) Another Level featuring TQ (1999)
Summertime Blues (18) first hit Eddie Cochran (1958)
Summertime City (4) Mike Batt (1975)
Summertime Of Our Lives (5) A1 (1999)
Sun Ain't Gonna Shine Anymore, The (1) Walker Brothers (1966)
Sun Always Shines On TV, The (1) A-Ha (1985)
Sun And The Rain, The (5) Madness (1983)
Sun Arise (3) Rolf Harris (1962)
Sun Goes Down (4) David Jordan (2008)
Sun Goes Down (Living It Up), The (10) Level 42 (1983)
Sun Hits The Sky (10) Supergrass (1997)
Sun Is Shining (3) Bob Marley vs Funkstar De Luxe (1999)
Sunchyme (2) Dario G (1997)
Sunday Girl (1) Blondie (1979)
Sunday Morning Call (4) Oasis (2000)
Sundown (4) S Club 8 (2003)
Sunlight (8) DJ Sammy (2003)
Sunny (3) Boney M (1977)
Sunny (10) Boogie Pimps (2004)
Sunny Afternoon (1) Kinks (1966)
Sunrise (7) Simply Red (2003)
Sunrise (9) Angel City (2005)
Sunset (Bird Of Prey) (9) Fatboy Slim (2000)
Sunshine (9) Gabrielle (1999)
Sunshine (3) Gareth Gates (2003)

Sunshine (3) Twista (2004)
Sunshine After The Rain (10) Elkie Brooks (1977)
Sunshine After The Rain, The (4) Berri (1995)
Sunshine Girl (8) Herman's Hermits (1968)
Sunshine Of Your Smile, The (9) Mike Berry (1980)
Sunshine On A Rainy Day (re-mix) (4) Zoe (1991)
Sunshine Superman (2) Donovan (1966)
Super Bass (8) Nicki Minaj (2011)
Super Trouper (1) Abba (1980)
Superfly Guy (5) S Express (1988)
Superfreak (7) Beatfreakz (2006)
Superman (Gioca Jouer) (9) Black Lace (1983)
Supermarioland (8) Ambassadors Of Funk with MC Mario (1992)
Supermassive Black Hole (4) Muse (2006)
Supernature (8) Cerrone (1978)
Supernova (2) Mr Hudson featuring Kanye West (2009)
Superstar (3) Jamelia (2003)
Superstar (4) Lupe Fiasco featuring Matthew Santos (2008)
Supreme (4) Robbie Williams (2000)
Sure (1) Take That (1994)
Surfin' Bird (3) The Trashmen (2010)
Surrender (Torna Surriento) (1) Elvis Presley with The Jordanaires (1961)
Surrender (10) Diana Ross (1971)
Surrender (7) Swing Out Sister (1987)
Surrender (Torna Surriento) (re-issue) (2) Elvis Presley (2005)
Surrender Your Love (7) Nightcrawlers featuring John Reid (1995)
Surround Yourself With Sorrow (3) Cilla Black (1969)
Survivor (1) Destiny's Child (2001)
Susan's House (9) Eels (1997)
Suspicion (9) Elvis Presley (1976)
Suspicious Minds (2) Elvis Presley (1969)
Suspicious Minds (8) Fine Young Cannibals (1986)
Suspicious Minds / The Long and Winding Road (1) Will Young and Gareth Gates (2002)
Sven Sven Sven (7) Bell & Spurling (2001)
Swagger Jagger (1) Cher Lloyd (2011)
Swallowed (7) Bush (1997)
Swamp Thing (3) Grid (1994)
Sway (6) Dean Martin (1954)
Sway (Mucho Mambo) (2) Shaft (1999)
Swear It Again (1) Westlife (1999)
Sweat (4) Snoop Dogg vs. David Guetta (2011)
Sweat (A La La La La Long) (re-entry) (3) Inner Circle (1993)
Swedish Rhapsody (2) Mantovani & His Orchestra (1953)
Swedish Rhapsody (re-entry) (4) Ray Martin Orchestra (1953)
Sweet About Me (re-entry) (6) Gabriella Cilmi (2008)
Sweet Caroline (8) Neil Diamond (1971)
Sweet Child O' Mine (remix) (6) Guns 'N' Roses (1989)
Sweet Disposition (6) Temper Trap (2009)
Sweet Dream (7) Jethro Tull (1969)
Sweet Dreams (Are Made Of This) (2) Eurythmics (1983)
Sweet Dreams (5) Beyonce (2009)
Sweet Dreams My LA Ex (2) Rachel Stevens (2003)
Sweet Escape, The (2) Gwen Stefani featuring Akon (2007)
Sweet Harmony (8) Beloved (1993)
Sweet Inspiration (10) Johnny Johnson & The Bandwagon (1970)
Sweet Like Chocolate (1) Shanks & Bigfoot (1999)
Sweet Little Mystery (5) Wet Wet Wet (1987)
Sweet Love 2K (3) Fierce (2000)
Sweet Lullaby (10) Deep Forest (1994)
Sweet Nothin's (4) Brenda Lee (1960)
Sweet Old-Fashioned Girl (3) Teresa Brewer (1956)
Sweet Soul Music (7) Arthur Conley (1967)
Sweet Surrender (6) Wet Wet Wet (1989)
Sweet Talkin' Guy (re-issue) (4) Chiffons (1972)
Sweet Talkin'Woman (6) Electric Light Orchestra (1978)
Sweetest Smile (8) Black (1987)
Sweetest Thing (3) U2 (1998)
Sweetness (4) Michelle Gayle (1994)
Sweets For My Sweet (1) Searchers (1963)

Sweets For My Sweet (3) C J Lewis (1994)
Swing The Mood (1) Jive Bunny & The Mastermixers (1989)
Swing Your Daddy (4) Jim Gilstrap (1975)
Swingin' Shepherd Blues (3) Ted Heath Orchestra (1958)
Swinging On A Star (7) Big Dee Irwin (1963)
Swiss Maid (2) Del Shannon (1962)
Switch (4) Will Smith (2005)
Switch It On (5) Will Young (2005)
Swords Of A Thousand Men (6) Ten Pole Tudor (1981)
Sylvia (4) Focus (1973)
Sylvia's Mother (2) Dr Hook (1972)
Sympathy For The Devil (9) Guns 'N' Roses (1995)
Synth And Strings (8) Yomanda (1999)
System Addict (3) Five Star (1986)
Taboo (10) Glamma Kid featuring Shola Ama (1999)
Tahiti (8) David Essex (1983)
Tainted Love (1) Soft Cell (1981)
Tainted Love (5) Soft Cell / Marc Almond (1991)
Tainted Love (5) Marilyn Manson (2002)
Take A Bow (1) Rihanna (2008)
Take A Chance On Me (1) Abba (1978)
Take a Chance On Me (2) JLS (2011)
(Take A Little) Piece Of My Heart (9) Erma Franklin (1992)
Take A Look Around (Theme from MI 2) (3) Limp Bizkit (2000)
Take Back The City (6) Snow Patrol (2008)
Take Care (9) Drake featuring Rihanna (2011)
Take Control (10) Amerie (2007)
Take Five (6) Dave Brubeck Quartet (1961)
Take Good Care Of My Baby (3) Bobby Vee (1961)
Take Good Care Of Yourself (9) Three Degrees (1975)
Take Me Away (9) Stonebridge featuring Therese (2005)
Take Me Back (3) Tinchy Stryder featuring Taio Cruz (2009)
Take Me Bak 'Ome (1) Slade (1972)
Take Me Home (2) Sophie Ellis-Bextor (2001)
Take Me Out (3) Franz Ferdinand (2004)
Take Me There (7) Blackstreet & Mya featuring Mase and Blinky Blink (1998)
Take Me To The Clouds Above (1) LMC vs U2 (2004)
Take Me To The Mardi Gras (7) Paul Simon (1973)
Take Me To Your Heart (8) Rick Astley (1988)
Take Me With You / Let's Go Crazy (7) Prince & The Revolution (1985)
Take My Breath Away (1) Berlin (1986)
Take My Breath Away (re-entry) (3) Berlin (1990)
Take My Breath Away (5) Emma Bunton (2001)
Take My Heart (9) Al Martino (1952)
Take On Me (2) A-Ha (1985)
Take On Me (1) A1 (2000)
Take That Look Off Your Face (3) Marti Webb (1980)
Take These Chains From My Heart (5) Ray Charles (1963)
Take Your Shoes Off (3) Cheeky Girls (2003)
Take Your Time (10) Mantronix featuring Wondress (1990)
Taken For Granted (10) Sia (2000)
Takes Two To Tango (6) Louis Armstrong (1952)
Talk (10) Coldplay (2005)
Talk About Our Love (6) Brandy featuring Kanye West (2004)
Talk Of The Town (8) Pretenders (1980)
Talking In Your Sleep / Love Me (6) Martine McCutcheon (1999)
Tammy (2) Debbie Reynolds (1957)
Tap Turns On The Water (5) CCS (1971)
Tarzan Boy (3) Baltimora (1985)
Taste Of Aggro, A (3) Barron Knights (1978)
Tattva (4) Kula Shaker (1996)
Tea For Two Cha Cha (3) Tommy Dorsey Orchestra and Warren Covington (1958)
Teacher / The Witches Promise (4) Jethro Tull (1970)
Tear Fell, A (2) Teresa Brewer (1956)
Teardrop (10) Massive Attack (1998)
Teardrops (5) Shakin' Stevens (1984)
Teardrops (3) Womack & Womack (1988)
Tearin' Up My Heart (9) N Sync (1999)
Tears (1) Ken Dodd (1965)

Tears I Cried, The (8) Glitter Band (1975)
Tears In Heaven (5) Eric Clapton (1992)
Tears Of A Clown / Ranking Full Stop (6) Beat (1979)
Tears Of A Clown, The (1) Smokey Robinson & The Miracles (1970)
Tears On My Pillow (1) Johnny Nash (1975)
Tears On My Pillow (1) Kylie Minogue (1990)
Tease Me (3) Chaka Demus & Pliers (1993)
Teddy Bear (4) Red Sovine (1981)
Teddy Bear (see Let Me Be Your Teddy Bear)
Teen Beat (9) Sandy Nelson (1959)
Teenage Dirtbag (2) Wheatus (2001)
Teenage Dream (2) Katy Perry (2010)
Teenage Life (8) Daz Sampson (2006)
Teenage Rampage (2) Sweet (1974)
Teenager On Love, A (2) Marty Wilde (1959)
Teenagers (9) My Chemical Romance (2007)
Telegram Sam (1) T Rex (1972)
Telephone (re-emergence) (1) Lady Gaga featuring Beyonce (2010)
Telephone Line (8) Electric Light Orchestra (1977)
Telephone Man (6) Meri Wilson (1977)
Teletubbies Say Eh-Oh! (1) Teletubbies (1997)
Tell Her About It (4) Billy Joel (1983)
Tell Him (10) Billie Davis (1963)
Tell Him (6) Hello (1974)
Tell Him (3) Barbra Streisand & Celine Dion (1997)
Tell It To My Heart (3) Taylor Dayne (1988)
Tell It To My Heart (9) Kelly Llorenna (2002)
Tell Laura I Love Her (1) Ricky Valance (1960)
Tell Me (4) Melanie B (2000)
Tell Me (8) P Diddy featuring Christina Aguilera (2006)
Tell Me A Story (5) Jimmy Boyd & Frankie Laine (1953)
Tell Me A Story (5) Jimmy Boyd (1953)
Tell Me Girl (What Are You Gonna Do) / Juliet (1) Four Pennies (1964)
Tell Me What He Said (2) Helen Shapiro (1962)
Tell Me When (7) Applejacks (1964)
Tell Me When (6) Human League (1995)
Tell Me Why (The Riddle) (7) Paul Van Dyk featuring Saint Etienne (2000)
Telstar (1) Tornados (1962)
Temma Harbour (6) Mary Hopkin (1970)
Temple Of Love (3) Sisters Of Mercy (1992)
Temptation (1) Everly Brothers (1961)
Temptation (2) Heaven 17 (1983)
Temptation (remix) (4) Heaven 17 (1992)
Tender (2) Blur (1999)
Tenderly (10) Nat 'King' Cole (1954)
Tennessee Wig Walk (4) Bonnie Lou (1954)
Tequila (5) Champs (1958)
Tequila (2) Terrorvision (1999)
Terry (4) Twinkle (1964)
Terry's Theme From Limelight (2) Frank Chacksfield (1953)
Terrys Theme From Limelight (3) Ron Goodwin Orchestra (1953)
Tetris (6) Doctor Spin (1992)
Tha Crossroads (8) Bone Thugs-NHarmony (1996)
Thank Abba For The Music (4) Steps, Tina Cousins, Cleopatra, B*Witched and Billie (1999)
Thank God I Found You (10) Mariah Carey (2000)
Thank U (5) Alanis Morissette (1998)
Thank U Very Much (4) Scaffold (1967)
Thank You (3) Dido (2001)
Thank You (2) Jamelia (2004)
Thank You For A Lifetime (3) Cliff Richard (2008)
Thanks For The Memory (Wham Bam Thank You Mam) (7) Slade (1975)
That Don't Impress Me Much (3) Shania Twain (1999)
That Girl (3) McFly (2004)
That Girl Belongs To Yesterday (7) Gene Pitney (1964)
That Golden Rule (10) Biffy Clyro (2009)
That Look In Your Eye (5) Ali Campbell (1995)
That Ole Devil Called Love (2) Alison Moyet (1985)
That Same Old Feeling (5) Pickettywitch (1970)

That Sounds Good To Me (4) Jive Bunny & The Mastermixers (1990)
That'll Be The Day (1) Crickets (1957)
That's All Right (re-issue) (3) Elvis Presley (2004)
That's Amore (2) Dean Martin and Dick Stabile Orchestra (1954)
That's Livin' Alright (3) Joe Fagin (1984)
That's My Goal (1) Shayne Ward (2005)
That's My Home (7) Mr Acker Bilk & his Paramount Jazz Band (1961)
That's The Way (I Like It) (4) KC & The Sunshine Band (1975)
That's The Way It Is (10) Mel & Kim (1988)
That's The Way Love Goes (2) Janet Jackson (1993)
That's The Way Love Is (8) Ten City (1989)
That's What Friends Are For (8) Deniece Williams (1977)
That's What I Like (1) Jive Bunny & The Mastermixers (1989)
That's What Love Will Do (3) Joe Brown & The Bruvvers (1963)
That's You (10) Nat 'King' Cole (1960)
That's Not My Name (1) Ting Tings (2008)
The Official BBC Children In Need Medley (1) Peter Kay's Animated All Star Band (2009)
The Way I Are (1) Timbaland featuring Keri Hilson & DOE (2007)
Them Girls Them Girls (5) Zig & Zag (1994)
Them Thangs / If I Can't (10) 50 Cent / G-Unit (2004)
Theme For a Dream (3) Cliff Richard & The Shadows (1961)
Theme From A Summer Place (2) Percy Faith & his Orchestra (1960)
Theme From A Threepenny Opera (Mack The Knife) (8) Louis Armstrong and his All-Stars (1956)
Theme From Dixie (7) Duane Eddy (1961)
Theme From Harry's Game (5) Clannad (1982)
Theme From M.A.S.H. (Suicide Is Painless) (1) MASH (1980)
Theme From M.A.S.H. Manic Street (Suicide Is Painless) (7) Preachers (1992)
Theme From Mahogany (Do You Know Where You're Going To) (5) Diana Ross (1976)
Theme From Mission Adam Clayton and Impossible (7) Larry Mullen (1996)
Theme From New York New York (re-issue) (4) Frank Sinatra (1986)
Theme From Picnic / Moonglow (7) Morris Stoloff (1956)
Theme From S-Express (1) S-Express (1988)
Theme From Shaft (4) Isaac Hayes (1971)
Theme From The Deerhunter (Cavatina) (9) Shadows (1979)
Theme From The Legion's Last Patrol (4) Ken Thorne Orchestra (1963)
Theme From The Threepenny Opera (9) Dick Hyman Trio (1956)
Theme From Z Cars (8) Johnny Keating Orchestra (1962)
Then He Kissed Me (2) Crystals (1963)
Then I Kissed Her (4) Beach Boys (1967)
There Are More Questions Than Answers (9) Johnny Nash (1972)
There But For Fortune (8) Joan Baez (1965)
There By The Grace Of God (6) Manic Street Preachers (2002)
There Goes My Everything (2) Engelbert Humperdinck (1967)
There Goes My Everything (6) Elvis Presley (1971)
There Goes My First Love (3) Drifters (1975)
There Goes The Fear (3) Doves (2002)
There Is A Mountain (8) Donovan (1967)
There It Is (5) Shalamar (1982)
There Must Be A Reason (9) Frankie Laine (1954)
There Must Be A Way (7) Frankie Vaughan (1967)
There Must Be An Angel (Playing With My Heart) (1) Eurythmics (1985)
There There (4) Radiohead (2003)
There There My Dear (7) Dexy's Midnight Runners (1980)
There You Go (6) Pink (2000)
There You'll Be (3) Faith Hill (2001)
There You'll Be (re-emergence) (10) Faith Hill (2008)
(There'll Be Bluebirds Over) The White Cliffs Of Dover / Unchained Melody (1) Robson & Jerome (1995)
There's A Ghost In My House (3) R Dean Taylor (1974)
There's a Goldmine in The Sky / Remember You're Mine (5) Pat Boone (1957)
There's A Heartache Following Me (6) Jim Reeves (1964)
There's A Kind Of Hush (7) Herman's Hermits (1967)

There's A Whole Lot Of Loving (2) Guys & Dolls (1975)
There's No Other Way (8) Blur (1991)
There's Nothing I Won't Do (4) JX (1996)
(There's) Always Something There To Remind Me (1) Sandie Shaw (1964)
These Are The Days Of Our Lives / Bohemian Rhapsody (re-issue) (1) Queen (1991)
These Are The Times (4) Dru Hill (1999)
These Boots Are Made Walking (1) For Nancy Sinatra (1966)
These Boots Are Made For Walkin' (4) Jessica Simpson (2005)
These Days (7) Bon Jovi (1996)
These Dreams / Never (re-issue) (8) Heart (1988)
These Words (1) Natasha Bedingfield (2004)
They (4) Jem (2005)
They Don't Care About Us (4) Michael Jackson (1996)
They Don't Know (2) Tracey Ullman (1983)
They Don't Know (3) So Solid Crew (2001)
(They Long To Be) Close To You (6) Carpenters (1970)
They're Coming To Take Me Away Ha-Haaa! (4) Napoleon XIV (1966)
Thieves In The Temple (7) Prince (1990)
Thing Called Love, A (4) Johnny Cash (1972)
Things (2) Bobby Darin (1962)
Things Can Only Get Better (6) Howard Jones (1985)
Things Can Only Get Better (remix) (1) D:Ream (1994)
Things I've Seen (6) Spooks (2001)
Things That Make You Go Hmmm ... (4) C & C Music Factory (1991)
Things We Do For Love, The (6) 10CC (1976)
Think Of You (7) Whigfield (1995)
Think Twice (1) Celine Dion (1994)
Thinking About Your Love (4) Kenny Thomas (1991)
Thinking It Over (5) Liberty (2001)
Thinking Of Me (4) Olly Murs (2010)
This Ain't A Love Song (6) Bon Jovi (1995)
This Ain't A Love Song (1) Scouting For Girls (2010)
This Ain't A Scene It's An Arms Race (2) Fall Out Boy (2007)
This Charming Man (re-issue) (8) Smiths (1992)
This Corrosion (7) Sisters Of Mercy (1987)
This Day (10) Emma's Imagination (2010)
This Groove / Let Your Head Go (3) Victoria Beckham (2004)
This Guy's In Love With You (3) Herb Alpert (1968)
This Is A Call (5) Foo Fighters (1995)
This Is How We Do It / Roll On (7) Mis-Teeq (2002)
This Is It! / Who Am I (5) Adam Faith (1961)
This Is It (9) Melba Moore (1976)
This Is It (10) Dannii Minogue (1993)
This Is My Song (1) Petula Clark (1967)
This Is My Song (2) Harry Secombe (1967)
This Is Not A Love Song (5) Public Image Ltd (1983)
This Is Tomorrow (9) Bryan Ferry (1977)
This Little Bird (6) Marianne Faithfull (1965)
This Love (3) Maroon 5 (2004)
This Old Heart Of Mine (Is Weak For You) (3) Isley Brothers (1968)
This Old Heart Of Mine (4) Rod Stewart (1975)
This Ole House (1) Rosemary Clooney (1954)
This Ole House (4) Billie Anthony with Eric Jupp Orchestra (1954)
This Ole House (1) Shakin' Stevens (1981)
This One's For The Children (9) New Kids On The Block (1990)
This Time (We'll Get It Right) / England We'll Fly the Flag (2) England World Cup Squad (1982)
This Time I Know It's For Real (3) Donna Summer (1989)
This Town Ain't Big Enough For Both Of Us (2) Sparks (1974)
This Town Ain't Big Enough For Both Of Us (6) British Whale (2005)
This Used To Be My Playground (3) Madonna (1992)
This Wheel's On Fire (5) Julie Driscoll, Brian Auger & The Trinity (1968)
Thong Song (3) Sisqo (2000)
Thorn In My Side (5) Eurythmics (1986)

Those Were The Days (1) Mary Hopkin (1968)
Thought I'd Died And Gone To Heaven (8) Bryan Adams (1992)
Thousand Miles, A (6) Vanessa Carlton (2002)
3 (7) Britney Spears (2009)
3AM / Thunderbirds (1) Busted (2004)
3AM Eternal (1) KLF featuring Children of The Revolution (1991)
Three Bells, The (6) Browns (1959)
Three Coins In The Fountain (1) Frank Sinatra (1954)
Three Coins In The Fountain (5) Four Aces featuring Al Alberts (1954)
3 Is Family (9) Dana Dawson (1995)
3 Lions (1) Baddiel & Skinner and Lightning Seeds (1996)
3 Lions '98 (1) Baddiel & Skinner and Lightning Seeds (1998)
3 Lions (re-issue) (9) Baddiel & Skinner and Lightning Seeds (2006)
3 Lions (re-emergence) (10) Baddiel & Skinner and The Lightning Seeds (2010)
Three Little Pigs (5) Green Jelly (1993)
Three Steps To Heaven (1) Eddie Cochran (1960)
Three Steps To Heaven (2) Showaddywaddy (1975)
Three Times A Lady (1) Commodores (1978)
3 x 3 EP (10) Genesis (1982)
3 Words (re-emergence) (4) Cheryl Cole featuring Will I Am (2009)
Thriller (10) Michael Jackson (1983)
Through The Barricades (6) Spandau Ballet (1986)
Through The Rain (8) Mariah Carey (2002)
Through The Wire (9) Kanye West (2004)
Throw Down The Line (7) Cliff Richard & Hank Marvin (1969)
Throw These Guns Away / Knockin' On Heaven's Door (1) Dunblane (1996)
Thunder (4) East 17 (1995)
Thunder In My Heart Again (1) Meck featuring Leo Sayer (2006)
Thunder In The Mountains (4) Toyah (1981)
Thunderbirds / 3AM (1) Busted (2004)
Thunderbirds Are Go (5) FAB featuring MC Parker (1990)
Ticket Outta Loserville (3) Son Of Dork (2005)
Ticket To Ride (1) Beatles (1965)
Tide Is High, The (1) Blondie (1980)
Tide Is High (Get The Feeling), The (1) Atomic Kitten (2002)
Tie a Yellow Ribbon Round the Old Oak Tree (1) Dawn featuring Tony Orlando (1973)
Tie Me Kangaroo Down Sport (9) Rolf Harris (1960)
Tiger Feet (1) Mud (1974)
Tik Tok (4) Kesha (2009)
(Til) I Kissed You (2) Everly Brothers (1959)
Till (2) Tom Jones (1971)
Till The End Of The Day (8) Kinks (1965)
Tilt Ya Head Back (5) Nelly & Christina Aguilera (2004)
Time (9) Craig Douglas (1961)
Time, The (1) Black Eyed Peas (2010)
Time (Clock Of The Heart) (3) Culture Club (1982)
Time / Alright (2) Supergrass (1995)
Time After Time (3) Cyndi Lauper (1984)
Time Drags By (10) Cliff Richard & The Shadows (1966)
Time Has Come, The (4) Adam Faith (1961)
Time Is Now, The (2) Moloko (2000)
Time Is Running Out (8) Muse (2003)
Time Is Tight (4) Booker T & The MG's (1969)
Time To Burn (3) Storm (2000)
Time To Grow (9) Lemar (2005)
Time To Say Goodbye (Con Te Partiro) (2) Sarah Brightman & Andrea Bocelli (1997)
Time Warp (remix), The (7) Damian (1989)
Times They Are A-Changin' (9) Bob Dylan (1965)
Tin Soldier (9) Small Faces (1967)
Tiny Dancer (Hold Me Closer) (3) Ironik featuring Chipmunk & Elton John (2009)
Tipsy (4) J-Kwon (2004)
Tired Of Being Alone (4) Al Green (1971)
Tired Of Waiting For You (1) Kinks (1965)

To Be Or Not To Be (9) B A Robertson (1980)
To Be With You (3) Mr Big (1992)
To Be With You Again (10) Level 42 (1987)
To Cut A Long Story Short (5) Spandau Ballet (1980)
To Earth With Love (10) Gay Dad (1999)
To Know Him Is To Love Him (2) Teddy Bears (1958)
To Know You Is To Love You (5) Peter & Gordon (1965)
To Live And Die In L.A. (10) Makaveli (1997)
To Love Somebody (5) Nina Simone (1969)
To Love Somebody (8) Jimmy Somerville (1990)
To The Moon And Back (3) Savage Garden (1998)
To You I Belong (1) B*Witched (1998)
Tobacco Road (6) Nashville Teens (1964)
Toca's Miracle (1) Fragma (2000)
Toccata (5) Sky (1980)
Together (6) Connie Francis (1961)
Together (8) P J Proby (1964)
Together Again (4) Janet Jackson (1997)
Together Forever (2) Rick Astley (1988)
Together In Electric Dreams (3) Giorgio Moroder & Phil Oakey (1984)
Together We Are Beautiful (1) Fern Kinney (1980)
Tokoloshe Man (4) John Kongos (1971)
Tokyo Melody (9) Helmut Zacharias (1964)
Tom Dooley (3) Lonnie Donegan & His Skiffle Group (1958)
Tom Dooley (5) Kingston Trio (1958)
Tom Hark (2) Elias & His Zigzag Jive Flutes (1958)
Tom Hark (6) Piranhas (1980)
Tom Tom Turnaround (6) New World (1971)
Tom Traubert's Blues (Waltzing Matilda) (6) Rod Stewart (1992)
Tom's Diner (2) DNA featuring Suzanne Vega (1990)
Tomboy (10) Perry Como (1959)
Tomorrow (8) Johnny Brandon, The Phantoms, and Norman Warren (1955)
Tomorrow (9) Sandie Shaw (1966)
Tomorrow's (Just Another Day) / Madness (Is All In My Mind) (8) Madness (1983)
Tonight / Joanna (2) Kool & The Gang (1984)
Tonight (3) New Kids On The Block (1990)
Tonight / Miss You Nights (3) Westlife (2003)
Tonight I Celebrate My Love (2) Peabo Bryson & Roberta Flack (1983)
Tonight (I'm Lovin' You) (5) Enrique Iglesias featuring Ludacris & DJ Frank E (2011)
Tonight I'm Yours (Don't Hurt Me) (8) Rod Stewart (1981)
Tonight Tonight (7) Smashing Pumpkins (1996)
Tonight's The Night (Gonna Be Alright) (5) Rod Stewart (1976)
Too Bad (9) Nickelback (2002)
Too Blind To See It (5) Kym Sims (1991)
Too Busy Thinking 'Bout My Baby (5) Marvin Gaye (1969)
Too Busy Thinking 'Bout My Baby / The Way You Make Me Feel (2) Steps (2001)
Too Close (1) Blue (2001)
Too Funky (4) George Michael (1992)
Too Good To Be Forgotten (10) Chi-Lites (1974)
Too Good To Be Forgotten (5) Amazulu (1986)
Too Hot (9) Coolio (1996)
Too Late For Goodbyes (6) Julian Lennon (1984)
Too Little Too Late (4) JoJo (2007)
Too Lost In You (10) Sugababes (2003)
Too Many Broken Hearts (1) Jason Donovan (1989)
Too Much (6) Elvis Presley with The Jordanaires (1957)
Too Much (2) Bros (1989)
Too Much (1) Spice Girls (1997)
Too Much Heaven (3) Bee Gees (1978)
Too Much Love Will Kill You (5) Brian May (1992)
Too Much Too Little Too Late (3) Johnny Mathis & Deniece Williams (1978)
Too Nice To Talk To (7) Beat (1980)
Too Shy (1) Kajagoogoo (1983)
Too Soon To Know (3) Roy Orbison (1966)
Too Young (5) Donny Osmond (1972)
Too Young To Die (10) Jamiroquai (1993)
Too Young To Go Steady (8) Nat 'King' Cole (1956)

Top O' The Morning / Jump Around (re-issue) (8) House Of Pain (1993)
Top Of The World (5) Carpenters (1973)
Top Of The World (2) Brandy featuring Mase (1998)
Torch (2) Soft Cell (1982)
Torn (2) Natalie Imbruglia (1997)
Torn Between Two Lovers (4) Mary MacGregor (1977)
Torn On The Platform (7) Jack Penate (2007)
Tossing And Turning (3) Ivy League (1965)
Total Eclipse Of The Heart (1) Bonnie Tyler (1983)
Total Eclipse Of The Heart (5) Nicki French (1995)
Total Eclipse Of The Heart (9) Glee Cast (2010)
Touch It (6) Busta Rhymes (2006)
Touch Me (I Want Your Body) (3) Samantha Fox (1986)
Touch Me (3) 49ers (1989)
Touch Me (All Night Long) (5) Cathy Dennis (1991)
Touch Me (1) Rui Da Silva featuring Cassandra (2001)
Touch Me In The Morning (9) Diana Ross (1973)
Touch My Body (5) Mariah Carey (2008)
Touch The Sky (6) Kanye West featuring Lupe Fiasco (2006)
Touch Too Much, A (8) Arrows (1974)
Tower Of Strength (1) Frankie Vaughan (1961)
Town Called Malice / Precious (1) Jam (1982)
Toxic (1) Britney Spears (2004)
Toxygene (4) Orb (1997)
Toy Balloons (7) Russ Conway (1961)
Toy Boy (4) Sinitta (1987)
Toy Soldiers (5) Martika (1989)
Tracks Of My Tears, The (9) Smokey Robinson & The Miracles (1969)
Tracy (4) Cufflinks (1969)
Tragedy (1) Bee Gees (1979)
Tragedy / Heartbeat (1) Steps (1998)
Trail Of The Lonesome Pine, Laurel & Hardy with
Train Of Thought (8) A-Ha (1986)
Trains and Boats and Planes (4) Burt Bacharach (1965)
Traktor (5) Wretch 32 featuring L (2011)
Tramp / Push It (2) Salt-N-Pepa (1988)
Transylvania / Baby's Coming Back (1) McFly (2007)
Trapped (3) Colonel Abrams (1985)
Trash (3) Suede (1996)
Travellers Tune (5) Ocean Colour Scene (1997)
Travellin' Band (8) Creedence Clearwater Revival (1970)
Travellin' Light (1) Cliff Richard & The Shadows (1959)
Travellin' Man / Hello Mary Lou (2) Ricky Nelson (1961)
Tribal Dance (4) 2 Unlimited (1993)
Tribute (Right On) (5) Pasadenas (1988)
Trick Me (2) Kelis (2004)
Trip To Trumpton, A (6) Urban Hype (1992)
Trippin' (8) Mark Morrison (1996)
Tripping (2) Robbie Williams (2005)
Trooper, The (re-issue) (5) Iron Maiden (2005)
Trouble (10) Coldplay (2000)
Trouble (7) Pink (2003)
True (1) Spandau Ballet (1983)
True (4) Jaimeson featuring Angel Blu (2003)
True Blue (1) Madonna (1986)
True Faith (4) New Order (1987)
True Faith (remix) (9) New Order (1994)
True Love (4) Bing Crosby & Grace Kelly (1956)
True Love (2) Elton John – duet with Kiki Dee (1993)
True Love Never Dies Flip & Fill featuring (re-issue) (7) Kelly Llorenna (2002)
True Love Ways (2) Peter & Gordon (1965)
True Love Ways (8) Cliff Richard (1983)
Truly (6) Lionel Richie (1982)
Truly Madly Deeply (4) Savage Garden (1998)
Truly Madly Deeply (4) Cascada (2006)
Try Again (5) Aaliyah (2000)
Try Me Out (6) Corona (1995)
Try Sleeping With A Broken Heart (7) Alicia Keys (2010)
Try To Remember / Way We Were, The (4) Gladys Knight & The Pips (1975)
T-Shirt (6) Shontelle (2009)
Tu M'Aimes Encore (To Love Me Again) (7) Celine Dion (1995)

Tubthumping (2) Chumbawamba (1997)
Tulips From Amsterdam / You Need Hands (3) Max Bygraves with The Clark Brothers (1958)
Tumble And Fall (5) Feeder (2005)
Tumbling Dice (5) Rolling Stones (1972)
Tunnel Of Love (10) Fun Boy Three (1983)
Turn (8) Travis (1999)
Turn Around (3) Phats & Small (1999)
Turn Back Time (1) Aqua (1998)
Turn It On Again (8) Genesis (1980)
Turn It Up / Fire It Up (2) Busta Rhymes (1998)
Turn Me On (2) Kevin Lyttle (2003)
Turn Off The Light (4) Nelly Furtado (2001)
Turn On Tune In Cop Out (re-issue) (3) Freak Power (1995)
Turn The Music Up (8) Players Association (1979)
Turning Japanese (3) Vapors (1980)
Turtle Power (1) Partners In Kryme (1990)
Tusk (6) Fleetwood Mac (1979)
Tweedle Dee (4) Little Jimmy Osmond (1973)
Tweedle Dee Tweedle Dum (2) Middle Of The Road (1971)
Twelfth Of Never, The (8) Cliff Richard (1964)
Twelfth Of Never, The (1) Donny Osmond (1973)
12:51 (7) Strokes (2003)
20th Century Boy (3) T Rex (1973)
21st Century Christmas / Move It (2) Cliff Richard (2006)
25 Or 6 To 4 (7) Chicago (1970)
Twenty Four Hours From Tulsa (2) Gene Pitney (1963)
Twenty Four Seven (6) Artful Dodger featuring Melanie Blatt (2001)
21 Questions (6) 50 Cent (2003)
21 Seconds (1) So Solid Crew (2001)
Twenty Tiny Fingers (4) Stargazers (1955)
Twilight Time (3) Platters (1958)
2012 It Ain't The End (9) Jay Sean featuring Nicki Minaj (2010)
Twilight Zone (2) 2 Unlimited (1992)
Twist, The / Let's Twist Again (re-issue) (5) Chubby Checker (1975)
Twist (Yo Twist), The (2) Fat Boys & Chubby Checker (1988)
Twist And Shout (4) Brian Poole & The Tremeloes (1963)
Twist And Shout (4) Salt-N-Pepa (1988)
Twist And Shout (10) Deacon Blue (1991)
Twist And Shout (1) Chaka Demus & Pliers (1993)
Twistin' The Night Away (6) Sam Cooke (1962)
2 Become 1 (1) Spice Girls (1996)
Two Can Play That Game (re-entry) (3) Bobby Brown (1995)
2 Faced (3) Louise (2000)
2-4-6-8 Motorway (5) Tom Robinson Band (1977)
Two Hearts (6) Phil Collins (1988)
2 Hearts (4) Kylie Minogue (2007)
Two In A Million / You're My Number One (2) S Club 7 (1999)
Two Kinds Of Teardrops (5) Del Shannon (1963)
Two Little Boys (1) Rolf Harris (1969)
Two More Years (7) Bloc Party (2005)
Two Pints Of Lager And A Packet Of Crisps Please / Simon Templar (7) Splodgeness-abounds (1980)
Two Princes (3) Spin Doctors (1993)
2 Times (2) Ann Lee (1999)
Two Tribes (1) Frankie Goes To Hollywood (1984)
U And Me (10) Cappella (1994)
U And Ur Hand (10) Pink (2006)
U Can't Touch This (3) MC Hammer (1990)
U Got It Bad (5) Usher (2001)
U Got 2 Know (6) Cappella (1993)
U Got 2 Let The Music (2) Cappella (1993)
U Know What's Up (2) Donell Jones (2000)
U Make Me Wanna (4) Blue (2003)
U R The Best Thing (remix) (4) D:Ream (1994)
U Remind Me (3) Usher (2001)
U Saved Me / Happy People (6) R Kelly (2004)
U Sure Do (re-entry) (4) Strike (1995)
Ugly (3) Sugababes (2005)
Ugly (7) Bubba Sparxxx (2001)

Ugly Duckling, The (10) Mike Reid (1975)
Uh La La La (10) Alexia (1998)
Ultraviolet / The Ballad Of Paul K (9) McFly (2005)
Um Um Um Um Um Um (5) Wayne Fontana & The Mindbenders (1964)
Umbrella (1) Rihanna featuring Jay-Z (2007)
Un Banc Un Arbre Une Rue (9) Severine (1971)
(Un Dos Tres) Maria (6) Ricky Martin (1997)
Una Paloma Blanca (5) Jonathan King (1975)
Unbelievable (3) EMF (1990)
Un-Break My Heart (2) Toni Braxton (1996)
Unbreakable (1) Westlife (2002)
Unchained Melody (1) Jimmy Young (1955)
Unchained Melody (2) Al Hibbler (1955)
Unchained Melody (10) Les Baxter His Chorus and Orchestra (1955)
Unchained Melody (re-issue) (1) Righteous Brothers (1990)
Unchained Melody / (There'll Be Bluebirds Over) The White Cliffs Of Dover (1) Robson & Jerome (1995)
Unchained Melody (1) Gareth Gates (2002)
Uncle John From Jamaica (6) Vengaboys (2000)
Under Pressure (1) Queen & David Bowie (1981)
Under Pressure (ice Ice Baby) (2) Jedward featuring Vanilla Ice (2010)
Under The Boardwalk (2) Bruce Willis (1987)
Under The Bridge / Lady Marmalade (1) All Saints (1998)
Under The Bridges Of Paris (6) Dean Martin (1955)
Under The Bridges Of Paris (7) Eartha Kitt (1955)
Under The Moon Of Love (1) Showaddywaddy (1976)
Under The Thumb (10) Amy Studt (2003)
Under Your Thumb (3) Godley & Crème (1981)
Underneath Your Clothes (3) Shakira (2002)
Underwater Love (4) Smoke City (1997)
Undivided Love (5) Louise (1996)
Unfaithful (2) Rihanna (2006)
Unforgettable Fire, The (6) U2 (1985)
Uninvited (8) Freemasons featuring Bailey Tzuke (2007)
Union Of The Snake (3) Duran Duran (1983)
United States Of Whatever (10) Liam Lynch (2002)
United We Stand (10) Brotherhood Of Man (1970)
Universal, The (5) Blur (1995)
Unleash The Dragon (6) Sisqo (2000)
Unorthodox (2) Wretch 32 featuring Example (2011)
Unpretty (6) TLC (1999)
Until It Sleeps (5) Metallica (1996)
Until It's Time For You To Go (5) Elvis Presley (1972)
Until The End Of Time (4) 2Pac (2001)
Until The Time Is Through (2) Five (1998)
Until You Were Gone (3) Chipmunk featuring Esmee Denters (2010)
Untouched (8) Veronicas (2009)
Unwritten (6) Natasha Bedingfield (2004)
Up (5) Saturdays (2008)
Up All Night (7) Matt Willis (2006)
Up And Down (4) Vengaboys (1998)
Up Around The Bend (3) Creedence Clearwater Revival (1970)
Up Middle Finger (7) Oxide & Neutrino (2001)
Up On The Roof (10) Kenny Lynch (1962)
Up On The Roof / I Believe (1) Robson & Jerome (1995)
Up The Junction (2) Squeeze (1979)
Up The Ladder To The Roof (6) Supremes (1970)
Up To The Wildstyle (10) Porn Kings vs DJ Supreme (1999)
Up Town Top Ranking (1) Althia & Donna first and only hit (1977)
Up Up And Away (6) Johnny Mann Singers (1967)
Up Where We Belong (7) Joe Cocker & Jennifer Warnes (1983)
Uprising (9) Muse (2009)
Upside Down (2) Diana Ross (1980)
Upside Down (10) A Teens (2001)
Uptown Girl (1) Billy Joel (1983)
Uptown Girl (1) Westlife (2001)
Us Against The World (8) Westlife (2008)

Use It Up And Wear It Out (1) Odyssey (1980)
Use Somebody (re-emergence) (2) Kings Of Leon (2008)
Vacation (10) Connie Francis (1962)
Valentine (9) T'Pau (1988)
Valerie (9) Zutons (2006)
Valerie (2) Mark Ronson featuring Amy Winehouse (2007)
Vaya Con Dios (7) Les Paul & Mary Ford (1953)
Venus (8) Shocking Blue (1970)
Venus (8) Bananarama (1986)
Venus (4) Don Pablo's Animals (1990)
Venus In Blue Jeans (4) Mark Wynter (1962)
Vertigo (1) U2 (2004)
Victim Of Love (7) Erasure (1987)
Victims (3) Culture Club (1983)
Video Games (9) Lana Del Rey (2011)
Video Killed The Radio Star (1) Buggles (1979)
Vienna (2) Ultravox (1981)
Vienna Calling (10) Falco (1986)
View To A Kill, A (2) Duran Duran (1985)
Vincent (1) Don McLean (1972)
Vindaloo (2) Fat Les (1998)
Violet Hill (8) Coldplay (2008)
Virginia Plain (4) Roxy Music (1972)
Virtual Insanity (3) Jamiroquai (1996)
Vision Of Love (9) Mariah Carey (1990)
Visions (7) Cliff Richard (1966)
Viva Bobby Joe (6) Equals (1969)
Viva Forever (1) Spice Girls (1998)
Viva La Radio (6) Lolly (1999)
Viva La Vida (1) Coldplay (2008)
Viva Las Vegas (10) ZZ Top (1992)
Vogue (1) Madonna (1990)
Voice In The Wilderness (2) Cliff Richard & The Shadows (1960)
Voice Within, The (9) Christina Aguilera (2003)
Volare (2) Dean Martin (1958)
Volare (10) Domenico Modugno (1958)
Voodoo Child (3) Rogue Traders (2006)
Voodoo Chile (1) Jimi Hendrix Experience (1970)
Voulez Vous / Angel Eyes (3) Abba (1979)
Voyage Voyage (5) Desireless (1988)
Wait (7) Robert Howard & Kym Mazelle (1989)
Waiting For A Girl Like You (8) Foreigner (1981)
Waiting For A Star To Fall (9) Boy Meets Girl (1988)
Waiting For An Alibi (9) Thin Lizzy (1979)
Waiting For The Train (7) Flash & The Pan (1983)
Waiting For Tonight (5) Jennifer Lopez (1999)
Wake Me Up (4) Girls Aloud (2005)
Wake Me Up Before You Go Go (1) Wham! (1984)
Wake Me Up When September Ends (8) Green Day (2005)
Wake Up (7) Hilary Duff (2005)
Wake Up Boo! (9) Boo Radleys (1995)
Wake Up Little Susie (2) Everly Brothers (1957)
Walk Away (4) Matt Monro (1964)
Walk Away From Love (10) David Ruffin (1976)
Walk Away Renee (3) Four Tops (1967)
Walk Don't Run (8) Ventures (1960)
Walk Hand In Hand (2) Tony Martin (1956)
Walk In The Black Forest, A (3) Horst Jankowski (1965)
Walk Like A Panther '98 (10) The All Seeing I, with Tony Christie (1999)
Walk Like An Egyptian (3) Bangles (1986)
Walk Of Life (2) Dire Straits (1986)
Walk On (5) U2 (2001)
Walk On By (5) Leroy Van Dyke (1962)
Walk On By (9) Dionne Warwick (1964)
Walk On By (6) Sybil (1990)
Walk On By (7) Gabrielle (1997)
Walk On The Wild Side (10) Lou Reed (1973)
Walk On Water (10) Milk Inc (2002)
Walk Right Back / Ebony Eyes (1) Everly Brothers (1961)
Walk Right In (10) Rooftop Singers (1963)
Walk Right Now (7) Jacksons (1981)
Walk Tall (3) Val Doonican (1964)
Walk The Dinosaur (10) Was (Not Was) (1987)
Walk This Way (1) Sugababes vs Girls Aloud (2007)

Walk This Way (8) Run DMC (1986)
Walk With Me (10) Seekers (1966)
Walkaway (9) Cast (1996)
Walkin' (7) CCS (1971)
Walkin' Back To Happiness (1) Helen Shapiro (1961)
Walkin' Miracle, A (6) Limmie & The Family Cookin (1974)
Walkin' To Missouri (9) Tony Brent (1952)
Walkin' To Missouri (re-entry) (7) Tony Brent (1953)
Walking Away (3) Craig David (2000)
Walking In The Air (5) Aled Jones (1985)
Walking In The Rain (10) Partridge Family starring David Cassidy (1973)
Walking In The Rain (7) Modern Romance (1983)
Walking On Broken Glass (8) Annie Lennox (1992)
Walking On Sunshine (10) Bad Manners (1981)
Walking On Sunshine (4) Rocker's Revenge (1982)
Walking On Sunshine (8) Katrina & The Waves (1985)
Walking On The Moon (1) Police (1979)
Walking Wounded (6) Everything But The Girl (1996)
Wall Street Shuffle, The (10) 10CC (1974)
Walls Come Tumbling Down (6) Style Council (1985)
Waltz Away Dreaming (10) Toby Bourke with George Michael (1997)
Wand'rin' Star (1) Lee Marvin (1970)
Wanderer, The (10) Dion (1962)
Wanderer, The (7) Status Quo (1984)
Wanderin' Eyes (6) Charlie Gracie (1957)
Wanderin' Eyes / Man On Fire (6) Frankie Vaughan (1957)
Wanna Be Startin' Something (8) Michael Jackson (1983)
Wannabe (1) first hit Spice Girls (1996)
Wanted (4) Perry Como (1954)
Wanted (re-entry) (4) Al Martino (1954)
Wanted (3) Dooleys (1979)
War (3) Edwin Starr (1970)
War Baby (6) Tom Robinson (1983)
War Of Nerves (7) All Saints (1998)
War Song, The (2) Culture Club (1984)
Warpaint (5) Brook Brothers (1961)
Warrior's Dance (9) Prodigy (2009)
Warwick Avenue (3) Duffy (2008)
Watching Me Watching You (10) David Grant (1983)
Watching The Detectives (15) Elvis Costello (1977)
Water Water / Handful Of Songs (5) Tommy Steele (1957)
Watercolour (4) Pendulum (2010)
Waterfalls (9) Paul McCartney (1980)
Waterfalls (4) TLC (1995)
Waterloo (1) Abba (1974)
Waterloo Sunset (2) Kinks (1967)
Wavin' Flag (2) K'Naan (2010)
Way Down (1) Elvis Presley (1977)
Way Down (re-issue) (2) Elvis Presley (2005)
Way Down Yonder In New Orleans (3) Freddy Cannon (1960)
Way I Am, The (8) Eminem (2000)
Way It Used To Be, The (3) Engelbert Humperdinck (1969)
Way Love Goes, The (8) Lemar (2010)
Way Of Life (6) Family Dogg (1969)
Way To Your Love, The (1) Hear'Say (2001)
Way We Were, The / Try To Remember (4) Gladys Knight & The Pips (1975)
Way You Make Me Feel, The (3) Michael Jackson (1987)
Way You Make Me Feel, The (6) Ronan Keating (2000)
Way You Move, The (7) Outkast featuring Sleepy Brown (2004)
Way, The (Put Your Hand In My Hand) (5) Divine Inspiration (2003)
Wayward Wind (8) Tex Ritter (1956)
Wayward Wind (9) Gogi Grant (1956)
Wayward Wind (1) Frank Ifield (1963)
We All Follow Man United (10) Manchester United Football Club (1985)
We All Stand Together (3) Paul McCartney & The Frog Chorus (1984)
We Are (8) Ana Johnsson (2004)
We Are Detective (7) Thompson Twins (1983)
We Are Family (8) Sister Sledge (1979)
We Are Family (remix) (5) Sister Sledge (1993)

We Are Glass (5) Gary Numan (1980)
We Are Golden (4) Mika (2009)
We Are The Champions (2) Queen (1977)
We Are The World (1) USA For Africa (1985)
We R Who We R (1) Kesha (2011)
We Be Burnin' (2) Sean Paul (2005)
We Belong Together (2) Mariah Carey (2005)
We Call It Acieed (3) D Mob (1988)
We Can Work It Out / Day Tripper (1) The Beatles (1965)
We Close Our Eyes (5) Go West (1985)
We Come 1 (3) Faithless (2001)
We Dance On (6) N-dubz featuring Bodyrox (2010)
We Didn't Start The Fire (7) Billy Joel (1989)
We Do It (5) R & J Stone (1976)
We Don't Have To ... (2) Jermaine Stewart (1986)
We Don't Need Another Hero (Thunderdome) (3) Tina Turner (1985)
We Don't Talk Anymore (1) Cliff Richard (1979)
We Found Love (1) Rihanna featuring Calvin Harris (2011)
We Got A Love Thang (6) Ce Ce Peniston (1992)
We Gotta Get Out Of This Place (2) Animals (1965)
We Have A Dream (5) Scotland World Cup Squad (1982)
We Have All The Time In The World (3) Louis Armstrong (1994)
We Just Be Dreamin' (3) Blazin' Squad (2003)
We Like To Party! (Vengabus) (3) Vengaboys (1999)
We Love You / Dandelion (8) Rolling Stones (1967)
We Made It (10) Busta Rhymes featuring Linkin Park (2008)
We Made You (4) Eminem (2009)
We No Speak Americano (1) Yolanda Be Cool vs D Cup (2010)
We Should Be Together (10) Cliff Richard (1991)
We Take Mystery (To Bed) (9) Gary Numan (1982)
(We Want) The Same Thing (6) Belinda Carlisle (1990)
We Will Make Love (2) Russ Hamilton (1957)
We Will Rock You (1) Five & Queen (2000)
We'll Bring The House Down (10) Slade (1981)
We're All Alone (6) Rita Coolidge (1977)
We're Going To Ibiza! (1) Vengaboys (1999)
We're Gonna Do It Again (6) Manchester Utd Football Squad & Stryker (1995)
We're On The Ball (3) Ant & Dec (2002)
We're Through (7) Hollies (1964)
We've Got It Goin' On (3) Backstreet Boys (1996)
We've Got Tonight (4) Ronan Keating featuring Lulu (2002)
Weak In The Presence Of Beauty (6) Alison Moyet (1987)
Wear My Kiss (7) Sugababes (2010)
Wear My Ring Around Your Neck (3) Elvis Presley with The Jordanaires (1958)
Wearing My Rolex (2) Wiley (2008)
Weather With You (7) Crowded House (1992)
Wedding Bells (7) Godley & Crème (1981)
Wedding Bells (see I'm Always Hearing Wedding Bells)
Wedding, The (3) Julie Rogers (1964)
Wee Rule (6) Wee Papa Girl Rappers (1988)
Weekend, The (7) Michael Gray (2004)
Weightless (10) Wet Wet Wet (2008)
Welcome Home (1) Peters & Lee (1973)
Welcome To My World (6) Jim Reeves (1963)
Welcome To The Black Parade (1) My Chemical Romance (2006)
Welcome To The Cheap Seats (EP) (8) Wonder Stuff (1992)
(Welcome) To The Dance (5) Des Mitchell (2000)
Welcome To The Pleasure Frankie Goes To Dome (2) Hollywood (1985)
Welcome To Tomorrow (6) Snap featuring Summer (1994)
Well I Ask You (1) Eden Kane (1961)
West End Girls (1) Pet Shop Boys (1985)
Westside (4) TQ (1999)
Wet Dream (10) Max Romeo (1969)
Wham Rap (8) Wham! (1983)
What (3) Soft Cell (1982)
What A Difference A Day Made (6) Esther Phillips (1975)
What a Feeling (6) Alex Gaudino featuring Kelly Rowland (2011)
What A Girl Wants (3) Christina Aguilera (2000)

What A Waste (9) Ian Dury & The Blockheads (1978)
What A Wonderful World / Cabaret (1) Louis Armstrong and his All-Stars (1968)
What A Wonderful World (1) Eva Cassidy & Katie Melua (2007)
What About Now (2) Westlife (2009)
What About Us (4) Brandy (2002)
What Am I Gonna Do (3) Rod Stewart (1983)
What Am I Gonna Do With You (5) Barry White (1975)
What Are You Doing Sunday (3) Dawn featuring Tony Orlando (1971)
What Became Of The Likely Lads (9) Libertines (2004)
What Becomes Of The Broken Hearted (10) Jimmy Ruffin (1966)
What Becomes Of The Broken Hearted (re-issue) (4) Jimmy Ruffin (1974)
What Becomes Of The Broken Hearted / Saturday Night At the Movies / You'll Never Walk Alone (1) Robson & Jerome (1996)
What Can I Do (3) Corrs (1998)
What Can I Say (10) Boz Scaggs (1977)
What Can You Do For Me (10) Utah Saints (1991)
What Do I Do (5) Phil Fearon & Galaxy (1984)
What Do I Have To Do (6) Kylie Minogue (1991)
What Do You Take Me For? (10) Pixie Lott featuring Pusha T (2011)
What Do You Want (1) Adam Faith (1959)
What Do You Want To Make Those Eyes At Me For (1) Emile Ford & The Checkmates (1959)
What Do You Want To Make Those Eyes At Me For (5) Shakin' Stevens (1987)
What Goes Around Comes Around (4) Justin Timberlake featuring Tanya Stephens (2007)
What Have I Done To Deserve This (2) Pet Shop Boys & Dusty Springfield (1987)
What Have You Done For Me Lately (3) Janet Jackson (1986)
What Hurts The Most (10) Cascada (2007)
What I Am (2) Tin Tin Out featuring Emma Bunton (1999)
What I Go To School For (3) Busted (2002)
What If (6) Kate Winslet (2001)
What Is Love (2) Howard Jones (1983)
What Is Love / Groove Is In The Heart (2) Deee-Lite (1990)
What Is Love (2) Haddaway (1993)
What It Feels Like For A Girl (7) Madonna (2001)
What I've Done (6) Linkin Park (2007)
What I've Got In Mind (4) Billie Jo Spears (1976)
What Kinda Boy You Looking For Girl (10) Hot Chocolate (1983)
What Made Milwaukee Famous (Has Made A Loser Out Of Me) / Angel (4) Rod Stewart (1972)
What Makes A Man (2) Westlife (2000)
What Makes You Beautiful (1) One Direction (2011)
What My Heart Wants To Say (5) Gareth Gates (2002)
What Now My Love (5) Shirley Bassey (1962)
What The World Is Waiting For / Fool's Gold (8) Stone Roses (1989)
What Time Is Love (5) KLF with Children of The Revolution (1990)
What Took You So Long (1) Emma Bunton (2001)
What Would I Be (2) Val Doonican (1966)
What Would You Do (3) City High (2001)
What You Got (4) Abs (2002)
What You Waiting For (4) Gwen Stefani (2004)
What You're Made Of (7) Lucie Silvas (2004)
What You're Proposing (2) Status Quo (1980)
What'd I Say (10) Jerry Lee Lewis (1961)
What'll I Do / Whoops Now (9) Janet Jackson (1995)
What's Another Year (1) Johnny Logan (1980)
What's Going On (6) Artists Against Aids Worldwide (2001)
What's It Gonna Be (2) H Two O featuring Platnum (2008)
What's It Gonna Be?! (6) Busta Rhymes featuring Janet (1999)
What's Love Got To Do With It (3) Tina Turner (1984)
What's Love Got To Do With It (2) Warren G featuring Adina Howard (1996)
What's Luv (4) Fat Joe featuring Ashanti (2002)

*What's My Name? (2) Rihanna featuring Drake (2010)
What's So Different (10) Ginuwine (1999)
What's The Colour Of Money (7) Hollywood Beyond (1986)
What's The Frequency Kenneth (9) REM (1994)
What's Up (2) 4 Non Blondes (1993)
What's Up (6) DJ Miko (1994)
What's Your Flava (8) Craig David (2002)
Whatcha Say (3) Jason Derulo (2009)
Whatcha Think About That (9) Pussycat Dolls (2009)
Whatever (3) Oasis (1994)
Whatever I Do (Wherever I Go) (4) Hazell Dean (1984)
Whatever U Want (9) Christina Milian featuring Joe Budden (2004)
Whatever Will Be Will Be (1) Doris Day (1956)
Whatever You Want (4) Status Quo (1979)
Whatta Man (7) Salt-N-Pepa with En Vogue (1994)
Wheels (8) String-A-Longs (1961)
When (1) Kalin Twins (1958)
When (3) Showaddywaddy (1977)
When A Child Is Born (1) Johnny Mathis (1976)
When A Man Loves A Woman (4) Percy Sledge (1966)
When A Man Loves A Woman (re-issue) (2) Percy Sledge (1987)
When A Man Loves A Woman (8) Michael Bolton (1991)
When A Woman (6) Gabrielle (2000)
When Doves Cry (4) Prince (1984)
When Doves Cry (10) Ginuwine (1997)
When Forever Has Gone (2) Demis Roussos (1976)
When I Fall In Love (2) Nat 'King' Cole (1957)
When I Fall In Love (4) Donny Osmond (1973)
When I Fall In Love / My Arms Keep Missing You (2) Rick Astley (1987)
When I Fall In Love (re-issue) (4) Nat 'King' Cole (1987)
When I Grow Up (9) Garbage (1999)
When I Grow Up (3) Pussycat Dolls (2008)
When I Lost You (6) Sarah Whatmore (2002)
When I Need You (1) Leo Sayer (1977)
When I Need You (5) Will Mellor (1998)
When I Said Goodbye / Summer of Love (5) Steps (2000)
When I Think Of You (10) Janet Jackson (1986)
When I Was a Youngster (8) Rizzle Kicks (2011)
When I'm Dead And Gone (2) McGuinness Flint (1970)
When I'm Gone (4) Eminem (2005)
When I'm Good And Ready (5) Sybil (1993)
When Johnny Comes Marching Home / Made You (5) Adam Faith with John Barry Orchestra (1960)
When Julie Comes Around (10) Cufflinks (1970)
When Love And Hate Collide (2) Def Leppard (1995)
When Love Comes To Town (6) U2 with B B King (1989)
When Love Takes Over (1) David Guetta featuring Kelly Rowland (2009)
When Mexico Gave Up The Rumba (6) Mitchell Torok (1956)
When My Little Girl Is Smiling (9) Craig Douglas (1962)
When My Little Girl Is Smiling (9) Jimmy Justice (1962)
When She Was My Girl (3) Four Tops (1981)
When The Girl In Your Arms Is The Girl In Your Heart (3) Cliff Richard (1961)
When The Going Gets Tough (1) Boyzone (1999)
When The Going Gets Tough The Tough Get Going (1) Billy Ocean (1986)
When The Heartache Is Over (10) Tina Turner (1999)
When The Lights Go Out (4) Five (1998)
When The Sun Goes Down (1) Arctic Monkeys (2006)
When We Collide (1) Matt Cardle (2010)
When We Dance (9) Sting (1994)
When We Were Young (10) Bucks Fizz (1983)
When Will I Be Famous (2) Bros (1988)
When Will I Be Loved (4) Everly Brothers (1960)
When Will I See You Again (1) Three Degrees (1974)
When Will You Say I Love You (3) Billy Fury (1963)
When You Ask About Love (4) Matchbox (1980)
When You Believe (4) Mariah Carey & Whitney Houston (1998)
When You Believe (1) Leon Jackson (2007)
When You Come Back To Me (2) Jason Donovan (1989)
When You Look At Me (3) Christina Milian (2002)

When You Lose The One You Love (7) David Whitfield with Mantovani (1955)
When You Say Nothing At All (1) Ronan Keating (1999)
(When You Say You Love Somebody) In the Heart (7) Kool & The Gang (1984)
When You Tell Me That You Love Me (2) Diana Ross (1991)
When You Tell Me That You Love Me (2) Westlife featuring Diana Ross (2005)
When You Walk In The Room (3) Searchers (1964)
When You Wasn't Famous (8) Streets (2006)
When You Were Young (2) Killers (2006)
When You're Gone (3) Bryan Adams featuring Melanie C (1998)
When You're In Love With A Beautiful Woman (1) Dr Hook (1979)
(When You're) Young And In Love (7) Flying Pickets (1984)
When You're Gone (3) Avril Lavigne (2007)
Whenever Wherever (2) Shakira (2002)
Whenever You Need Somebody (3) Rick Astley (1987)
Where Are You Baby (3) Betty Boo (1990)
Where Are You Now (My Love) (1) Jackie Trent (1965)
Where Did Our Love Go (3) Supremes (1964)
Where Did Our Love Go (8) Donnie Elbert (1972)
Where Did Your Heart Go / Edge Of Heaven, The (1) Wham! (1986)
(Where Do I Begin) Love Story (4) Andy Williams (1971)
Where Do You Go (2) No Mercy (1997)
Where Do You Go To My Lovely (1) Peter Sarstedt (1969)
Where Is The Love (1) Black Eyed Peas (2003)
Where Love Lives (remix) (9) Alison Limerick (1996)
Where The Boys Are / Baby Roo (5) Connie Francis (1961)
Where The Story Ends / Reminisce (8) Blazin' Squad (2003)
Where The Streets Have No Name (4) U2 (1987)
Where The Streets Have No Name / How Can you Expect To Be Taken Seriously / Can't Take My Eyes Off You (4) Pet Shop Boys (1991)
Where The Wind Blows (2) Frankie Laine (1953)
Where Them Girls At (3) David Guetta featuring Flo Rida & Nicki Minaj (2011)
Where Will The Baby's Dimple Be (6) Rosemary Clooney and Mellomen, with the Buddy Cole Quartet (1955)
Where's The Love (4) Hanson (1997)
Where's Your Head At? (9) Basement Jaxx (2001)
Wherever I Lay My Hat (That's My Home) (1) Paul Young (1983)
Wherever You Are (1) The Military Wives Choir featuring Gareth Malone (2011)
Wherever You Will Go (3) Calling (2002)
Wherever You Will Go (3) Charlene Soraia (2011)
Which Way You Goin' Billy (7) Poppy Family (1970)
Whip My Hair (2) Willow (2010)
Whiskey In The Jar (6) Thin Lizzy (1973)
Whispering Grass (1) Windsor Davies & Don Estelle (1975)
Whistle For The Choir (9) Fratellis (2006)
Whistle Song (Blow My Whistle B***h) (5) DJ Aligator Project (2002)
White Christmas (6) Mantovani & His Orchestra (1952)
White Christmas (5) Bing Crosby (1977)
White Flag (2) Dido (2003)
White Horses (10) Jacky (1968)
White Lines (Don't Do It) (7) Grandmaster & Melle Mel (1984)
White Sport Coat, A (6) King Brothers (1957)
White Wedding (6) Billy Idol (1985)
Whiter Shade Of Pale, A (1) Procol Harum (1967)
Who Am I (10) Beenie Man (1998)
Who Am I / This Is It! (5) Adam Faith (1961)
Who Are We (6) Ronnie Hilton (1956)
Who Do You Love Now (Stringer) (3) Riva featuring Dannii Minogue (2001)
Who Do You Think You Are / Mama (1) Spice Girls (1997)
Who Feels Love? (4) Oasis (2000)
Who Found Who (10) Jellybean featuring Elisa Fiorillo (1987)
Who Is It (10) Michael Jackson (1992)
Who Killed Bambi (6) Ten Pole Tudor (1979)
Who Knew (5) Pink (2006)
Who Let The Dogs Out (2) Baha Men (2000)

Who Loves You (6) Four Seasons (1975)
Who Needs Love Like That (10) Erasure (1992)
Who Says You Can't Go Home (5) Bon Jovi (2006)
Who The Hell Are You (10) Madison Avenue (2000)
Who You Are (8) Jessie J (2011)
Who's David? (1) Busted (2004)
Who's In The House (8) Beatmasters featuring Merlin (1989)
Who's Leaving Who (4) Hazell Dean (1988)
Who's Sorry Now (1) Connie Francis (1958)
Who's That Chick (6) David Guetta featuring Rihanna (2011)
Who's That Girl (3) Eurythmics (1983)
Who's That Girl (1) Madonna (1987)
Who's That Girl (6) Eve (2001)
Whodunit (5) Tavares (1977)
Whole Again (1) Atomic Kitten (2001)
Whole Lotta History (6) Girls Aloud (2006)
Whole Lotta Love (3) Goldbug (1996)
Whole Lotta Shakin' Goin' On (8) Jerry Lee Lewis (1957)
Whole Lotta Woman (1) Marvin Rainwater (1958)
Whole Of The Moon (re-issue), The (3) Waterboys (1991)
Whoomph! (There It Is) (4) Clock (1995)
Whoops Now / What'll I Do (9) Janet Jackson (1995)
Why (1) Anthony Newley (1960)
Why (3) Donny Osmond (1972)
Why (10) Carly Simon (1982)
Why? (6) Bronski Beat (1984)
Why (5) Annie Lennox (1992)
Why (2) 3T featuring Michael Jackson (1996)
Why (10) Glamma Kid (1999)
Why (8) Mis-Teeq (2001)
Why (7) DJ Sammy (2005)
Why Can't I Wake Up With You (2) Take That (1993)
Why Can't This Be Love (8) Van Halen (1986)
Why Do Fools Fall In Love (1) Frankie Lymon & Teenagers (1956)
Why Do Fools Fall In Love (4) Diana Ross (1981)
Why Do You Love Me (7) Garbage (2005)
Why Does It Always Rain On Me? (10) Travis (1999)
Why Don't You Get A Job? (2) Offspring (1999)
Why Oh Why Oh Why (6) Gilbert O'Sullivan (1973)
Why Won't You Give Me Your Love (9) Zutons (2006)
Wichita Lineman (7) Glen Campbell (1969)
Wicked Game (10) Chris Isaak (1990)
Wicker Man, The (9) Iron Maiden (2000)
Wide Boy (9) Nik Kershaw (1985)
Wide-Eyed And Legless (6) Andy Fairweather- Low (1975)
Wiggle It (3) 2 In A Room (1991)
Wig-Wam Bam (4) Sweet (1972)
Wild Boys (2) Duran Duran (1984)
Wild Horses (9) Susan Boyle (2009)
Wild In The Country / I Feel So Bad (4) Elvis Presley with The Jordanaires
Wild One (7) Bobby Rydell (1960)
Wild One, The (7) Suzi Quatro (1974)
Wild Side Of Life (9) Status Quo (1976)
Wild Thing (2) Troggs (1966)
Wild West Hero (6) Electric Light Orchestra (1978)
Wild Wild West (2) Will Smith featuring Dru Hill (1999)
Wild Wind (2) John Leyton (1961)
Wild World (5) Maxi Priest (1988)
Wild World (8) Jimmy Cliff (1970)
Wildest Dreams (6) Iron Maiden (2003)
Wilfred the Weasel / Captain Beaky (5) Keith Michell (1980)
Will I? (5) Ian Van Dahl (2001)
Will I Ever (7) Alice Deejay (2000)
Will 2K (2) Will Smith (1999)
Will You (8) Hazel O'Connor (1981)
Will You Be There (9) Michael Jackson (1993)
Will You Love Me Tomorrow (4) Shirelles (1961)
Wimoweh (4) Karl Denver (1962)
Winchester Cathedral (4) New Vaudeville Band (1966)
Wind Beneath My Wings (5) Bette Midler (1989)

Wind Beneath My Wings (3) Steven Houghton (1997)
Wind Cries Mary (6) The Jimi Hendrix Experience (1967)
Wind It Up (3) Gwen Stefani (2006)
Wind Me Up (Let Me Go) (2) Cliff Richard & The Shadows (1965)
Wind Of Change (2) Scorpions (1991)
Windmills Of Your Mind (8) Noel Harrison (1969)
Window In The Skies (4) U2 (2007)
Wings Of A Butterfly (10) Him (2005)
Wings Of A Dove (2) Madness (1983)
Winner Takes It All, The (1) Abba (1980)
Winner's Song, The (2) Geraldine (2008)
Winter In July (7) Bomb The Bass (1991)
Winter World Of Love (7) Engelbert Humperdinck (1969)
Winter's Tale, A (2) David Essex (1982)
Winter's Tale, A (6) Queen (1995)
Wipe Out (5) Surfaris (1963)
Wipeout (2) Fat Boys & The Beach Boys (1987)
Wire To Wire (5) Razorlight (2008)
Wired For Sound (4) Cliff Richard (1981)
Wires (4) Athlete (2005)
Wish You Were Here (8) Eddie Fisher (1953)
Wishful Thinking (9) China Crisis (1984)
Wishing (10) Buddy Holly (1963)
Wishing (If I Had A Photograph Of You) (10) A Flock Of Seagulls (1982)
Wishing I Was Lucky (6) Wet Wet Wet (1987)
Wishing On A Star (3) Rose Royce (1978)
Wishing On A Star (10) Fresh 4 featuring Lizz E (1989)
Wishing on a Star (1) The X Factor Finalists 2011 featuring JLS & One Direction (2011
Wishing Well (7) Free (1973)
Wishing Well (4) Terence Trent D'Arby (1987)
Wishing You Were Somehow Here Again (7) Sarah Brightman (1987)
Witch Doctor (5) Don Lang & His Frantic Five (1958)
Witch Doctor (2) Cartoons (1999)
Witch, The (8) Rattles (1970)
Witch Queen Of New Orleans, The (2) Redbone (1971)
Witches Promise, The / Teacher (4) Jethro Tull (1970)
With A Girl Like You (1) Troggs (1966)
With A Little Help From Friends (10) Young Idea (1967)
With A Little Help From My Friends (1) Joe Cocker (1968)
With A Little Help From My Friends (1) Wet Wet Wet (1988)
With A Little Help From My Friends / Measure of a Man (1) Sam & Mark (2004)
With A Little Luck (5) Wings (1978)
With All My Heart (4) Petula Clark (1957)
With Every Heartbeat (1) Robyn with Kleerup (2007)
With My Own Eyes (10) Sash (2000)
With Or Without You (4) U2 (1987)
With Ur Love (3) Cher Lloyd featuring Mike Posner (2011)
With You (7) Jessica Simpson (2004)
With You (8) Chris Brown (2008)
With You I'm Born Again (2) Billy Preston & Syreeta (1979)
Without Love (10) Tom Jones (1969)
Without Me (1) Eminem (2002)
Without You (1) Nilsson (1972)
Without You (1) Mariah Carey (1994)
Without You (6) David Guetta featuring Usher (2011)
Woman (1) John Lennon (1981)
Woman (9) Neneh Cherry (1996)
Woman (Uh-Huh) (7) Jose Ferrer (1954)
Woman In Love, A (1) Frankie Laine (1956)
Woman In Love (3) Three Degrees (1979)
Woman In Love (1) Barbra Streisand (1980)
Woman In Love / I Get The Sweetest Feeling (5) Liz McClarnon (2006)
Woman Trouble (6) Artful Dodger & Robbie Craig with Craig David (2000)
Womanizer (3) Britney Spears (2008)
Wombling Merry Christmas (2) Wombles (1974)

Wombling Song, The (4) Wombles (1974)
Wonder Of You, The (1) Elvis Presley (1970)
Wonder Of You, The (re-issue) (4) Elvis Presley (2005)
Wonderful (1) Ja Rule featuring R Kelly & Ashanti (2004)
Wonderful Christmastime (6) Paul McCartney (1979)
Wonderful Copenhagen (5) Danny Kaye (1953)
Wonderful Land (1) Shadows (1962)
Wonderful Life (8) Black (1987)
Wonderful Time Up There, A (2) Pat Boone (1958)
Wonderful Tonight (3) Damage (1997)
Wonderful World (7) Herman's Hermits (1965)
Wonderful World (re-issue) (2) Sam Cooke (1986)
Wonderful World (8) James Morrison (2006)
Wonderful World Beautiful People (6) Jimmy Cliff (1969)
Wonderful World Of The Young (8) Danny Williams (1962)
Wonderland (8) Big Country (1984)
Wonderwall (2) Mike Flowers Pops (1995)
Wonderwall (2) Oasis (1995)
Wondrous Stories (7) Yes (1977)
Won't Get Fooled Again (9) Who (1971)
Won't Go Quietly (6) Example (2010)
Won't Take It Lying Down (7) Honeyz (2000)
Won't Talk About It (9) Beats International (1990)
Wood Beez (Pray Like Aretha Franklin) (10) Scritti Politti (1984)
Wooden Heart (1) Elvis Presley (1961)
Wooden Heart (re-issue) (2) Elvis Presley (2005)
Woodstock (1) Matthews Southern Comfort (1970)
Woo-Hah!! Got You All In Check (8) Busta Rhymes (1996)
Word Girl, The (6) Scritti Politti featuring Ranking Ann (1985)
Word Up (3) Cameo (1986)
Word Up (8) Gun (1994)
Words (8) Bee Gees (1968)
Words (2) F R David (1983)
Words (1) Boyzone (1996)
Words Are Not Enough / I Know Him So Well (5) Steps (2001)
Wordy Rappinghood (7) Tom Tom Club (1981)
Work (4) Kelly Rowland (2008)
Work It (6) Missy Elliott (2002)
Work It (7) Nelly featuring Justin Timberlake (2003)
Work It Out (7) Beyonce (2002)
Work Rest And Play EP (6) Madness (1980)
Work That Body (7) Diana Ross (1982)
Workaholic (4) 2 Unlimited (1992)
Working In A Coalmine (8) Lee Dorsey (1966)
Working My Way Back To You / Forgive Me Girl (1) Detroit Spinners (1980)
World (9) Bee Gees (1967)
World At Your Feet (3) Embrace (2006)
World Hold On (Children Of The Sky) (9) Bob Sinclar featuring Steve Edwards (2006)
World In Motion (1) Englandneworder (1990)
World Of Our Own, A (3) Seekers (1965)
World Of Our Own (1) Westlife (2002)
World Without Love, A (1) Peter & Gordon (1964)
World's Greatest, The (4) R Kelly (2002)
Worried About Ray (5) Hoosiers (2007)
Would I Lie To You (1) Charles & Eddie (1992)
Would You? (3) Touch & Go (1998)
Wouldn't Change A Thing (2) Kylie Minogue (1989)
Wouldn't It Be Good (4) Nik Kershaw (1984)
Wow (re-entry) (5) Kylie Minogue (2008)
Wrapped Around Your Finger (7) Police (1983)
Written In The Stars (10) Elton John & LeAnn Rimes (1999)
Written In The Stars (1) Tinie Tempah featuring Eric Turner (2010)
Wrong (8) Everything But The Girl (1996)
Wrong Impression (10) Natalie Imbruglia (2002)
Wuthering Heights (1) Kate Bush (1978)
X Gon' Give It To Ya (6) DMX (2003)
Xanadu (1) Olivia Newton-John and ELO (1980)
X-Files, The (2) Mark Snow (1996)
X-Files (8) DJ Dado (1996)
Xmas Through Your Eyes / Miami Hit Mix (8) Gloria Estefan (1992)
Y Viva Espana (4) Sylvia (1974)

Y.M.C.A. (1) Village People (1978)
Yeah (1) Usher featuring Lil' Jon & Ludacris (2004)
Yeah 3x (6) Chris Brown (2011)
Yeah Yeah (2) Bodyrox featuring Luciana (2006)
Year 3000 (2) Busted (2003)
Years May Come Years May Go (7) Herman's Hermits (1970)
Yeh Yeh (1) Georgie Fame & The Blue Flames (1964)
Yellow (4) Coldplay (2000)
Yellow River (1) Christie (1970)
Yellow Rose Of Texas (2) Mitch Miller (1955)
Yellow Submarine / Eleanor Rigby (1) Beatles (1966)
Yes (8) McAlmont & Butler (1995)
Yes I Will (9) Hollies (1965)
Yes My Darling Daughter (10) Eydie Gorme (1962)
Yes Sir I Can Boogie (1) Baccara (1977)
Yes Tonight Josephine (1) Johnnie Ray (1957)
Yesterday (8) Matt Monro (1965)
Yesterday (8) Beatles (1976)
Yesterday (4) Wet Wet Wet (1997)
Yesterday Has Gone (4) Cupid's Inspiration (1968)
Yesterday Man (3) Chris Andrews (1965)
Yesterday Once More (2) Carpenters (1973)
Yesterdays / November Rain (8) Guns 'N' Roses (1992)
Yester-Me Yester-You Yesterday (2) Stevie Wonder (1969)
Ying Tong Song / Bloodnok's Rock 'N' Roll Call (3) Goons (1956)
Ying Tong Song (re-issue) (9) Goons (1973)
You (10) Ten Sharp (1992)
You (2) S Club 7 (2002)
You Ain't Seen Nothing Yet (2) Bachman-Turner Overdrive (1974)
You Always Hurt The One You Love (6) Clarence 'Frogman' Henry (1961)
You And I / Don't Let Me Down (2) Will Young (2002)
You Are Alive (4) Fragma (2001)
You Are Everything (5) Diana Ross & Marvin Gaye (1974)
You Are My Destiny (6) Paul Anka (1958)
You Are My World (30) Communards (1985)
You Are Not Alone (1) Michael Jackson (1995)
You Are Not Alone (1) X Factor Finalists 2009 (2009)
You Are The Sunshine Of My Life (7) Stevie Wonder (1973)
You Belong To Me (1) Jo Stafford (1952)
You Better You Bet (9) Who (1981)
You Came (3) Kim Wilde (1988)
You Can Call Me Al (4) Paul Simon (1986)
You Can Do It (2) Ice Cube featuring Mack 10 & MS Toi (2004)
You Can Do Magic (3) Limmie & The Family Cookin (1973)
You Can Get It If You Really Want (2) Desmond Dekker (1970)
You Can Never Stop Me Loving You (10) Kenny Lynch (1963)
You Can't Hurry Love (3) Supremes (1966)
You Can't Hurry Love (1) Phil Collins (1982)
You Could Be Mine (3) Guns 'N' Roses (1991)
You Do Something To Me (9) Paul Weller (1995)
You Don't Bring Me Flowers (5) Barbra & Neil (1978)
You Don't Care About Us (5) Placebo (1998)
You Don't Have To Be A Baby To Cry (6) Caravelles (1963)
You Don't Have To Be A Star (To Be in My Show) (7) Marilyn McCoo & Billy Davis Jr (1977)
You Don't Have To Go (3) Chi-Lites (1976)
You Don't Have To Say You Love Me (1) Dusty Springfield (1966)
You Don't Have To Say You Love Me (9) Elvis Presley (1971)
You Don't Have To Say You Love Me (5) Guys & Dolls (1976)
You Don't Know (1) Helen Shapiro (1961)
You Don't Know Me (9) Ray Charles (1962)
You Don't Know Me (1) Armand Van Helden (1999)
You Don't Love Me (No No No) (3) Dawn Penn (1994)
You Drive Me Crazy (2) Shakin' Stevens (1981)
(You Drive Me) Crazy (5) Britney Spears (1999)
You Gave Me Love (10) Crown Heights Affair (1980)
You Get What You Give (5) New Radicals (1999)
You Give Me Something (5) James Morrison (2006)
You Got It (3) Roy Orbison (1989)
You Got It (The Right Stuff) (1) New Kids On The Block (1989)
You Got Soul (6) Johnny Nash (1969)

You Got The Dirtee Love (Live At The BRIT Awards 2010) (2) Florence & The Machine & Dizzee Rascal (2010)
You Got The Love (3) (re-entry) Source featuring Candi Staton (1997)
You Got The Love (4) Source featuring Candi Staton (1991)
You Got The Love (7) Source featuring (2nd remix) Candi Staton (2006)
You Got The Love (5) Florence & The Machine (2009)
You Got What It Takes (7) Marv Johnson (1960)
You Got What It Takes (2) Showaddywaddy (1977)
You Gotta Be (re-issue) (10) Des'ree (1999)
You Gotta) Fight For Your Right (To Party) (11) Beastie Boys (1987)
You Had Me (9) Joss Stone (2004)
You Have Been Loved / The Strangest Thing '97 (2) George Michael (1997)
You Have Killed Me (3) Morrissey (2006)
You Held The World In Your Arms (9) Idlewild (2002)
You Just Might See Me Cry (2) Our Kid (1976)
You Keep It All In (8) Beautiful South (1989)
You Keep Me Hangin' On (8) Supremes (1966)
You Keep Me Hangin' On (2) Kim Wilde (1986)
You Know Me (6) Robbie Williams (2009)
You Know My Name (7) Chris Cornell (2006)
You Little Thief (5) Feargal Sharkey (1986)
You Make It Real (7) James Morrison (2008)
You Make Me Feel Brand New (2) Stylistics (1974)
You Make Me Feel Brand New (7) Simply Red (2003)
You Make Me Feel Like Dancing (2) Leo Sayer (1976)
You Make Me Feel (Mighty Real) (8) Sylvester (1978)
You Make Me Feel (Mighty Real) (5) Jimmy Somerville (1990)
You Make Me Sick (9) Pink (2001)
You Make Me Wanna (1) Usher (1998)
You Might Need Somebody (4) Shola Ama (1997)
You Must Have Been A Beautiful Baby (10) Bobby Darin (1961)
You Must Love Me (10) Madonna (1996)
You Need Hands / Tulips From Amsterdam (3) Max Bygraves with The Clark Brothers (1958)
You Need Me, I Don't Need You (4) Ed Sheeran (2011)
You Needed Me (1) Boyzone (1999)
You Only Tell Me You Love Me When You're Drunk (8) Pet Shop Boys (2000)
You Raise Me Up (1) Westlife (2005)
You Really Got Me (1) Kinks (1964)
You Rock My World (2) Michael Jackson (2001)
You Said No (1) Busted (2003)
You See The Trouble With Me (2) Barry White (1976)
You See The Trouble With Me (1) Black Legend (2000)
You Send Me / Farewell – Bring It On Home To Me (7) Rod Stewart (1974)
You Sexy Thing (2) Hot Chocolate (1975)
You Sexy Thing (remix) (10) Hot Chocolate (1987)
You Sexy Thing (re-issue) (6) Hot Chocolate (1997)
You Should Be ... (3) Blockster (1999)
You Should Be Dancing (5) Bee Gees (1976)
You Should Really Know (8) The Pirates featuring Enya, Shola Ama, Naila Boss & Ishani (2004)
You Showed Me (8) Lightning Seeds (1997)
You Spin Me Round (Like A Record) (1) Dead Or Alive (1985)
You Spin Me Round (re-issue) (5) Dead Or Alive (2006)
You Stole The Sun From My Heart (5) Manic Street Preachers (1999)
You Take Me Up (2) Thompson Twins (1984)
You To Me Are Everything (1) Real Thing (1976)
You To Me Are Everything (The Decade Re-mix 76-86) (5) Real Thing (1986)
You Took My Heart (7) Pepper & Piano (2010)
You Wear It Well (1) Rod Stewart (1972)
You Were Made For Me (3) Freddie & The Dreamers (1963)
You Were On My Mind (2) Crispian St Peters (1966)
You Were Right (9) Badly Drawn Boy (2002)
You Win Again (1) Bee Gees (1987)

You Won't Find Another Fool Like Me (1) New Seekers (1973)
You Won't Forget About Me (7) Dannii Minogue vs Flower Power (2004)
You You You (6) Alvin Stardust (1974)
You'll Answer To Me (5) Cleo Laine (1961)
You'll Be Sorry / Here And Now (4) Steps (2001)
You'll Never Find Another Love Like Mine (10) Lou Rawls (1976)
You'll Never Know (6) Shirley Bassey (1961)
You'll Never Stop Me From Loving You (1) Sonia (1989)
You'll Never Walk Alone (1) Gerry & The Pacemakers (1963)
You'll Never Walk Alone (1) Crowd (1985)
You'll Never Walk Alone / What Becomes Of The Broken Hearted / Saturday Night At the Movies (1) Robson & Jerome (1996)
You'll See (5) Madonna (1995)
You're A Lady (3) Peter Skellern (1972)
You're A Superstar (7) Love Inc (2002)
You're All I Have (7) Snow Patrol (2006)
You're All I Need To Get By / I'll Be There For You (10) Method Man featuring Mary J Blige (1995)
You're All That Matters To Me (6) Curtis Stigers (1992)
You're Beautiful (1) James Blunt (2005)
You're Driving Me Crazy (1) Temperance Seven (1961)
You're Gone (7) Marillion (2004)
You're Gorgeous (3) Babybird (1996)
(You're) Having My Baby (6) Paul Anka featuring Odia Coates (1974)
You're History (7) Shakespears Sister (1989)
You're In My Heart (3) Rod Stewart (1977)
You're Makin' Me High (7) Toni Braxton (1996)
You're More Than A Number In My Little Red Book (5) Drifters (1976)
You're Moving Out Today (6) Carole Bayer Sager (1977)
You're My Best Friend (7) Queen (1976)
You're My Number One / Two In A Million (2) S Club 7 (1999)
You're My World (1) Cilla Black (1964)
You're No Good (3) Swinging Blue Jeans (1964)
You're Not Alone (1) Olive (1997)
You're Sixteen (3) Johnny Burnette (1961)
You're Sixteen (4) Ringo Starr (1974)
You're So Vain (3) Carly Simon (1972)
You're Still The One (10) Shania Twain (1998)
(You're The) Devil In Disguise (1) Elvis Presley with the Jordanaires (1963)
(You're The) Devil In Disguise (re-issue) (2) Elvis Presley (2005)
You're The First The Last My Everything (1) Barry White (1974)
You're The One I Love (3) Shola Ama (1997)
You're The One That I Want (1) John Travolta & Olivia Newton-John (1978)
You're The One That I Want John Travolta & (re-issue) (4) Olivia Newton- John (1998)
You're The Voice (6) John Farnham (1987)
You've Got A Friend (4) James Taylor (1971)
You've Got A Friend (9) Brand New Heavies (1997)
You've Got A Friend / All About You (1) McFly (2005)
You've Got It Bad (7) Ocean Colour Scene (1996)
You've Got Me Dangling On A String (5) Chairmen of the Board (1970)
You've Got Your Troubles (2) Fortunes (1965)
You've Lost That Lovin' Feelin' (1) Righteous Brothers (1965)
You've Lost That Lovin' Feelin' (2) Cilla Black (1965)
You've Lost That Lovin' Feelin' (re-issue) (10) Righteous Brothers (1969)
You've Lost That Lovin' Feelin' (re-issue) (3) Righteous Brothers (1990)
Young And Foolish (10) Edmund Hockridge (1956)
Young At Heart (8) Bluebells (1984)
Young At Heart (re-issue) (1) Bluebells (1993)
Young Forever (re-emergence) (10) Jay-Z featuring Mr Hudson (2010)
Young Gifted And Black (5) Bob & Marcia (1970)

Young Girl (1) Union Gap featuring Gary Puckett (1968)
Young Girl (re-issue) (6) Gary Puckett & The Union Gap (1974)
Young Guns (Go For It) (3) Wham! (1982)
Young Hearts Run Free (2) Candi Staton (1976)
Young Love (1) Tab Hunter (1957)
Young Love (1) Donny Osmond (1973)
Young Lovers (9) Paul & Paula (1963)
Young New Mexican Puppeteer, The (6) Tom Jones (1972)
Young Ones, The (1) Cliff Richard & The Shadows (1962)
Young Parisians (9) Adam & The Ants (1980)
Your Body (10) Tom Novy featuring Michael Marshall (2005)
Your Christmas Wish (8) Smurfs (1996)
Your Game (3) Will Young (2004)
Your Love Alone Is Not Enough (2) Manic Street Preachers (2007)

Your Love Is King (6) Sade (1984)
Your Loving Arms (remix) (6) Billie Ray Martin (1995)
Your Song (7) Elton John (1971)
Your Song (4) Elton John & Alessandro Safina (2002)
Your Song (2) Ellie Goulding (2010)
Your Woman (1) White Town (1997)
Yummy Yummy Yummy (5) Ohio Express (1968)
Zabadak! (3) Dave Dee, Dozy, Beaky, Mick & Tich (1967)
Zambesi (2) Lou Busch and his Orchestra (1956)
Zephyr Song, The (11) Red Hot Chili Peppers (2002)
Zing A Little Zong (10) Bing Crosby & Jane Wyman (1952)
Zoom (2) Fat Larry's Band (1982)
Zorba's Dance (6) Marcello Minerbi (1965)

Notes: The artists on Perfect Day were the BBC Symphony Orchestra with Andrew Davis, Thomas Allen, Brett Anderson (Suede), Laurie Anderson, Joan Armatrading, Bono (U2), David Bowie, Boyzone, Brodsky Quartet, Ian Broudie (Lightning Seeds), Burning Spear, Robert Cray, Evan Dando (Lemonheads), Dr John, Gabrielle, Lesley Garrett, Emmylou Harris, Huey Morgan (Fun Lovin' Criminals), Elton John, Tom Jones, Shane McGowan, Courtney Pine, Lou Reed, Skye (Morcheeba), Heather Small (M People), Suzanne Vega, Visual Ministry Orchestra, Sheona White, Tammy Wynette.

The artists on the various recordings of Do They Know It's Christmas were: **Band Aid** - Keren Woodward, Sarah Dallin, Siobhan Fahey (Bananarama); Bob Geldof, Johnny Fingers, Simon Crowe, Pete Briquette (Boomtown Rats); David Bowie; Phil Collins; Boy George, Jon Moss (Culture Club); Simon Le Bon, Nick Rhodes, Andy Taylor, John Taylor, Roger Taylor (Duran Duran); Holly Johnson (Frankie Goes to Hollywood); Martin Ware, Glenn Gregory (Heaven 17); Robert 'Kool' Bell, James Taylor, Dennis Thomas (Kool and the Gang); Marilyn; Paul McCartney; George Michael; Jody Watley (Shalimar); Tony Hadley, John Keeble, Gary Kemp, Martin Kemp, Steve Norman (Spandau Ballet); Francis Rossi, Rick Parfitt (Status Quo); Sting; Adam Clayton, Bono (U2); Midge Ure, Chris Cross, (Ultravox); Paul Weller; Paul Young. **Band Aid II** - Bananarama, Big Fun, Bros, Cathy Dennis, D Mob, Jason Donovan, Kevin Godley, Glen Goldsmith, Kylie Minogue, The Pasadenas, Chris Rea, Cliff Richard, Jimmy Somerville, Sonia, Lisa Stansfield, Technotronic, Wet Wet Wet. **Band Aid 20** - Damon Albarn (made the tea); Tim Wheeler (Ash); Daniel Bedingfield; Natasha Bedingfield; James Bourne, Mattie Jay, Charlie Simpson (Busted); Chris Martin (Coldplay); Ed Graham, Dan Hawkins, Justin Hawkins, Frankie Poullain (The Darkness); Dido; Ms Dynamite; Grant Nichols (Feeder); Bob Geldof; Neil Hannon (The Divine Comedy); Jamelia; Tom Chaplin, Richard Hughes, Tim Rice-Oxley (Keane); Beverley Knight; Lemar; Shaznay Lewis; Paul McCartney; Madonna; Katie Melua; Roisin Murphy (Moloko); Skye (Morcheeba); Jonny Greenwood, Thom Yorke (Radiohead); Dizzee Rascal; Richard Colburn, Gary Lightbody, Mark McClell, John Quinn (Snow Patrol); Rachel Stevens; Joss Stone; Keisha Buchanan, Mutya Buena, Heidi Range (The Sugababes); Danny Goffey (Supergrass); Ben Carrigan, Connor Deasy, Kevin Horan, Padraic MacMahon, Daniel Ryan (The Thrills); Andy Dunlop, Fran Healy, Dougie Payne, Neil Primrose (Travis); Olly Knights, Gail Paradjanian (Turin Brakes); Bono, The Edge (U2); Midge Ure; Robbie Williams; Will Young. The featured artists in the original recording with their lyrics are as follows: (**Paul Young**) It's Christmas time, There's no need to be afraid. At Christmas time, We let in light and we banish shade (**Boy George**) And in our world of plenty We can spread a smile of joy, Throw your arms around the world at Christmas time (**George Michael**) But say a prayer, Pray for the other ones, At Christmas time it's hard (**Simon Le Bon**) But when you're having fun, There's a world outside your window (**Sting**) And it's a world of dread and fear, Where the only water flowing is (**Bono joins in**) The bitter sting of fears, And the Christmas bells that are ringing, Are clanging chimes of doom (**Bono only**) Well, tonight thank God it's them instead of you (**All**) And there won't be snow in Africa this Christmas time, The greatest gift they'll get this year is life, Where nothing ever grows, No rain or river flows, Do they know it's Christmas time at all? Feed the world, Let them know it's Christmas time, Feed the world, Do they know it's Christmas time at all? (**Paul Young**) Here's to you raise a glass for everyone, Here's to them underneath the burning sun, Do they know it's Christmas time at all? (**All**) chorus repeat.

The official BBC Children in Need Medley performed by Peter Kay's Animated All Star Band consisted of the following songs, in order: 'Can You Feel It' (The Jacksons), 'Don't Stop' (Fleetwood Mac/Status Quo), 'Jai Ho' (A R Rahman & The Pussycat Dolls), 'Tubthumping' (Chumbawamba), 'Never Forget' (Take That), 'Hey Jude' (The Beatles), 'One Day Like This' (Elbow).

The artists performing Everybody Hurts as Helping Haiti in order of appearance: Leona Lewis, Rod Stewart, Mariah Carey, Cheryl Cole, Mika, Michael Bublé, Joe McElderry, Miley Cyrus, James Blunt, Gary Barlow, Mark Owen, Jon Bon Jovi, James Morrison, Alexandra Burke, Jason Orange, Susan Boyle, JLS, Shane Filan, Mark Feehily, Kylie Minogue, Robbie Williams, Kian Egan, Nicky Byrne.

UK Chart Christmas Number Ones

1952 Here in My Heart – Al Martino
1953 Answer Me – Frankie Laine
1954 Let's Have Another Party – Winifred Atwell
1955 The Christmas Alphabet – Dickie Valentine.
1956 Just Walkin' in the Rain – Johnnie Ray
1957 Mary's Boy Child – Harry Belafonte
1958 It's Only Make Believe – Conway Twitty
1959 What Do You Want to Make Those Eyes at Me For - Emile Ford
1960 I Love You – Cliff Richard and the Shadows
1961 Moon River – Danny Williams
1962 Return to Sender – Elvis Presley
1963 I Want to Hold Your Hand – Beatles
1964 I Feel Fine – Beatles
1965 Day Tripper/We Can Work It Out – Beatles
1966 Green Green Grass of Home – Tom Jones

1967 Hello Goodbye – Beatles
1968 Lily the Pink – Scaffold
1969 Two Little Boys – Rolf Harris
1970 I Hear You Knockin' – Dave Edmunds
1971 Ernie (The Fastest Milkman in the West) – Benny Hill
1972 Long Haired Lover from Liverpool – Little Jimmy Osmond
1973 Merry Xmas Everybody – Slade
1974 Lonely This Christmas – Mud
1975 Bohemian Rhapsody – Queen
1976 When a Child Is Born – Johnny Mathis
1977 Mull of Kintyre/Girls' School – Wings
1978 Mary's Boy Child – Boney M
1979 Another Brick in the Wall – Pink Floyd
1980 There's No One Quite Like Grandma – St Winifred's School Choir
1981 Don't You Want Me – Human League

1982 Save Your Love – Renee and Renato
1983 Only You – Flying Pickets
1984 Do They Know It's Christmas – Band Aid
1985 Merry Christmas Everyone – Shakin' Stevens
1986 Reet Petite – Jackie Wilson
1987 Always on My Mind – Pet Shop Boys
1988 Mistletoe and Wine – Cliff Richard
1989 Do They Know It's Christmas? – Band Aid II
1990 Saviour's Day – Cliff Richard
1991 Bohemian Rhapsody / These Are the Days of Our Lives – Queen
1992 I Will Always Love You – Whitney Houston
1993 Mr. Blobby – Mr. Blobby
1994 Stay Another Day – East 17
1995 Earth Song – Michael Jackson
1996 2 Become 1 – Spice Girls
1997 Too Much – Spice Girls
1998 Goodbye – Spice Girls
1999 I Have a Dream/Seasons in the Sun – Westlife
2000 Can We Fix It – Bob The Builder
2001 Somethin' Stupid – Robbie Williams and Nicole Kidman
2002 Sound Of The Underground – Girls Aloud
2003 Mad World – Michael Andrews featuring Gary Jules
2004 Do They Know It's Christmas? – Band Aid 20
2005 That's My Goal – Shayne Ward
2006 A Moment Like This – Leona Lewis
2007 When You Believe – Leon Jackson
2008 Hallelujah – Alexandra Burke
2009 Killing In the Name – Rage Against the Machine
2010 When We Collide - Matt Cardle
2011 Wherever You Are - Military Wives

A for Andromeda Julie Christie (Christine / A for Andromeda), Peter Halliday (John Fleming), Esmond Knight (Professor Reinhart), Mary Morris (Professor Madeleine Dawnay), Patricia Kneale (Judy Adamson), Donald Stewart (General Vandenberg), John Hollis (Kaufman). Science fiction series set nine years in the future. A message from an alien civilisation 200 light years away in Andromeda (M31) is detected by the newly built radio telescope at Bouldershaw Fell, in the Yorkshire Dales. Scientist John Fleming soon recognises it as a plan for a complex computer - which is duly built at a rocket research establishment at Thorness, a remote Scottish island. Christine, a lab assistant, is operating the computer alone one evening when she falls under its influence, grasps the terminals and the high voltage kills her. This is written off as an accident, but the computer subsequently generates instructions for a new and complex DNA synthesis which leads to the rapid growth of an embryo and, within a few months, a fully grown woman with a striking resemblance to Christine (only her hair colour had changed from brunette to blonde). Andromeda, as the new creation comes to be known, communicates directly with the computer through the terminals and is in many ways just an extension of the machine, brilliant but without emotion. Fleming becomes convinced that the computer is intent on world domination and that it must be destroyed. However it becomes increasingly valuable to the British Government, designing a new anti-satellite missile and a new enzyme for healing damaged tissue, and also working on economic problems. A battle develops between the various government agencies and the Swiss business cartel, Intel, headed by the evil Kaufman. The first series ends with Andromeda presumed drowned, but she re-appeared in a 1962 sequel, *The Andromeda Breakthrough*, with Susan Hampshire replacing Christie, who was contracted for the film *Crooks Anonymous*. Both series were created by BBC producer John Elliot from a storyline by Cambridge astronomer and novelist Fred Hoyle. This truly thought-provoking and often terrifying series undoubtedly created an upsurge of interest in sci-fi on television and like the earlier *Quatermass* series paved the way for the approach of *Dr Who*. BBC 1961.

A.J.Wentworth, BA Arthur Lowe (A.J. Wentworth), Marion Mathie (Matron), Harry Andrews (Reverend R. Gregory Saunders). Sit-com set in Burgrove, a boys' preparatory school in Wilminister. Arthur James Wentworth is an absent minded maths teacher in a 1940s prep school and 'Squid' Saunders his aloof headmaster. The stories were based on stories by H. F. Ellis and adapted by Basil Boothroyd. Only six episodes were made before Arthur Lowe died. ITV 1982.

A. P. Herbert's Misleading Cases Alastair Sim (Mr Justice Swallow), Roy Dotrice (Albert Haddock), Avice Landon (Mrs Haddock), Thorley Walters (Sir Joshua Hoot QC). Much-loved comedy series notable for a rare television excursion by Sim, the magnificent portrayal of Haddock by Dotrice and the excellent writing of Herbert aided by such as Alan Melville, Christopher Bond, Michael Gilbert and Henry Cecil. It has become a matter of principle for Albert Haddock to not let archaic laws and bye-laws dictate the way he lives his life. Whenever he takes on the injustices of life he normally ends up having to defend his stance in a court of law. A court that is frequently presided over by the increasingly amused Mr Justice Swallow and Mr Haddock's long-suffering adversary Sir Joshua Hoot QC. Based on A.P. Herbert's many judicial 'summings up' of "Misleading Cases" for Punch magazine, the stories exposed the legal absurdities we are forced to live with. The second series was entitled *Misleading Cases* before reverting back to the original title for the final outing which saw the absurdities played out in colour for the first time. BBC1 1967-71

Absolute Power Stephen Fry (Charles Prentiss), John Bird (Martin McCabe), James Lance (Jamie Front), Zoe Telford (Alison Jackman), Nicholas Burns (Nick Mayer), Sally Bretton (Cat Durnford), Henry Hereford (Will Cookson). TV adaption of a BBC radio comedy series, created by Mark Tavener. It started in 2000 on BBC Radio 4, with the fourth and last radio series broadcast in 2004. The television series was written by Guy Andrews, Mark Lawson and Andrew Rattenbury, and had the tag "spin is dead, long live PR". Unlike most radio to TV sitcom transfers, none of the TV episodes were based on a radio episode. The series revolves around the machinations of Prentiss McCabe, a PR agency whose offices play host to a succession of minor celebrities, politicians and high-flying businessmen who all need photo-shoots arranging and soundbites composing. Ethics are not a priority; the firm's staff will lie, cheat and possibly steal as long as it makes their clients look good. Two television series, each of six episodes were shown. The title is taken from a quotation by the historian Lord Acton that "power tends to corrupt, and absolute power corrupts absolutely". BBC2 2003; 2005.

Absolutely Comedy sketch show, the cast and crew being mainly Scottish. The principal writers and performers were Moray Hunter, Jack Docherty, Peter Baikie, Gordon Kennedy (all of whom had performed together as The Bodgers for many years), Morwenna Banks and John Sparkes (a Welsh comedian). Recurring characters included Mr Muzak a smug pianist (played by Baikie), club host Frank Hovis (played by Sparkes), McGlashan (played by Docherty) an extreme Scottish patriot, who supported anglophobia, McGlashan's camp agent McMinn (Kennedy), Calum Gilhooley (played by Hunter) the most boring man in the world, Denzil and Gwynedd (played by Sparkes and Banks) who made ethnic jokes and mocked the Welsh language, The Little Girl (played by Banks) who would always sit on a very large table and describe a topic in an overexcited bluster, the sketches often ending with her exclaiming, "It is, it's true!" and George and Donald McDiarmid (played by Docherty and Hunter), George would dress in a black pinstripe suit and tie, while Don McDiarmid (no relation) would dress in tweed, a bow tie, and an unusual pair of glasses with one lens at a right angle. George would often find Don annoying in some manner. C4 1989-93. The characters Don and George went on to get their own sit-com on Channel 4 in 1993, *Mr Don & Mr George*.

Absolutely Fabulous Jennifer Saunders (Edina Monsoon), Joanna Lumley (Patsy Stone), Julia Sawalha (Saffron Monsoon), Jane Horrocks (Bubble / Katy Grin), June Whitfield (June, Edina's mother), Miranda Richardson (Bettina), Kathy Burke (Magda), Eleanor Bron (Patsy's mother). Created by Dawn French and Jennifer Saunders (who also wrote the series). Edina is a twice divorced international PR guru sharing her three-storey house (in swanky W11) with her mother and daughter Saffy (sired by Edina's bisexual second husband Justin). She also has a son, Serge (sired by Edina's first husband Marshall, a television evangelist), who turns up in Series 5. Her Bolly-swilling, label-shopping lifestyle is funded by income from her two businesses, Monsoon PR and, by Series 4, Radical TV. Her supremely outrageous behaviour is only rivalled by that of her lifelong friend Patsy Stone (Christened Eurydice Collette Klytemnestra Dido Bathsheba Patricia Rabelais Stone by her mother). As Harvey Nichols happens to be on the way to the office the girls tend to spend a disproportionate amount of time and money in the store. Bubble is Edina's long-suffering secretary and Katy Grin is Bubble's ex *Blue Peter*- presenting cousin who turns up in Series 4 as Edina's business partner at Radical TV. Guest stars (playing themselves) have included: Twiggy, Lady Victoria Hervey, Michael Greco, Stephen Gately, Richard Madeley, Judy Finnigan, Lulu, Emma Bunton, Kirsty Wark, Mark Kermode, La Roux, Zandra Rhodes, Naomi Campbell, Christopher Biggins, Nicky Clarke, Bruce Oldfield, Sacha Distel, Christian Lacroix, Annegret Tree, Erin O'Connor, Whoopi Goldberg, Deborah Harry, Graham Norton, Rufus Wainwright, Minnie Driver, Elton John, Jean-Paul Gaultier, Richard Curtis and Perou. The theme tune *Wheels On Fire* (written by Bob Dylan and Rick Danko) is sung by Julie Driscoll and Ade Edmondson. The character of Edina Monsoon is allegedly modelled on the equally famous PR guru Lynn Franks. First shown on BBC2 in 1992 but then on BBC1 (1993-96, 2001-04). A series of specials ran from Christmas 2011 and are scheduled to continue into 2012.

According to Bex Jessica Hynes nee Stevenson (Bex Atwell), Greg Wise (Charles Mathers), Raquel Cassidy (Chris), Clive Russell (Jack Atwell), Zita Sattar (Jan), Oliver Chris (Ryan), Rhea Seehorn (Christine Firth). Sitcom created by Fred Barron. Bex is a twenty-something single woman who works as a secretary and who lives in London. She is looking for the perfect man and the perfect job, but in both she ends with second best. Unfortunately the only thing memorable able this comedy was the title of the eight episodes: "Stuck in the Middle With You", "Papa's Got a Brand New Bag", "The Time Warp", "Breaking Up Is Hard To Do", "Gimme Shelter", "Private Dancer", "Hanging on the Telephone" and "Nothing But Flowers". The story goes that Jessica Hynes thought the series so bad that she sacked her agent for putting her up for it. BBC1 2005.

Ace of Wands Michael Mackenzie (Tarot), Judy Loe (Lillian 'Lulli' Palmer), Tony Selby (Sam Maxsted), Donald Layne-Smith (Mr Sweet), Petra Markham (Mikki Diamond), Roy Holder (Chas Diamond), Willoughby Goddard (Tun-Ju). Children's adventure series created by Trevor Preston and Pamela Lonsdale. The Ace of Wands of the title is Tarot, a performing magician and escapologist with some real psychic powers. He is assisted in his adventures by Mr Sweet and, in the first two seasons, by Lulli (who has a telepathic relationship with Tarot) and Sam. For the third and final series in 1972, Tarot is accompanied by Mikki and her brother Chas. Completing the team is Ozymandias, played by Fred, a Malayan fishing owl. Ozzie's main purpose is to sit on his open perch in Tarot's flat looking inscrutable. Tarot is billed as 'a 20th century Robin Hood, with a pinch of Merlin and a dash of Houdini'. The super-villains he encounters include Madame Midnight, Ceribraun, Mama Doc (who turns people into dolls which bleed when broken) and Mr Stabs (played by Russell Hunter). ITV 1970-72.

Adam Adamant Lives! Gerald Harper (Adam Llewellyn De Vere Adamant), Juliet Harmer (Georgina Jones), Jack May (William E. Simms), Peter Ducrow (The Face). The Edwardian adventurer of the title is entombed by his arch-enemy, the leather-masked The Face, in 1902 but in 1966 a gang of London workmen discover his body and thaw it out with his 99-year-old body still in its 36-year-old immaculate and somewhat enhanced condition due to a preservative drug. The contrast between Adam's strict morals and the permissive society of the Sixties is the main source of humour in the series. Ably assisted by trendy local DJ Georgina (who happened to be well-versed in the legend of the great man) Adam reprised his former Robin Hood role in the surrounds of an increasingly psychedelic-looking London and in the second series encountered his old nemesis The Face. Adam's athleticism and mental faculties are key features as was the very popular mini he chose as his preferred mode of transport. The series, created by Donald Cotton and Richard Harris, was produced by Verity Lambert. Kathy Kirby sang the Bond-style theme. The lyrics were "Bold as a knight in white armour, Cold as a shot from a gun, if you should look for a man who loves danger, to whom love is a stranger, this man is one" followed by a chorus of Adam Adamant repeated several times and then faded. BBC 1966-67.

Adam and Joe Show, The London-born comedians Adam Offord Buxton (born 7 June 1969) and Joseph Murray "Joe" Cornish (born 20 December 1968) began working on comedy material during their time at Westminster School together, where they created numerous amateur films along with their friend Louis Theroux. Some of these films were submitted to Channel 4's home video showcase *Takeover TV* in 1994; Adam making his television debut on this show as a man called "Louise" dressed as a Klingon, complaining about *Star Trek: The Next Generation* being taken off the air. The following year Adam became presenter of this series and Joe joined him later in the run. Following this they created *The Adam and Joe Show*, a series of short sketches interspersed with links filmed in what was purportedly Adam and Joe's bedsit. Each week, Adam and Joe would re-create a popular current feature film using stuffed toys and elaborate cardboard sets. Other memorable segments included *Vinyl Justice*, where Adam and Joe would dress as policemen to raid rock stars' homes, then examine their record collections for embarrassing items to which the star would then be forced to dance to; and a parody of British television shows using *Star Wars* action figures, Obi-Wan Kenobi being portrayed as a drunk vagrant. C4 1996-2001

Adam Smith Andrew Keir (Adam Smith), Kara Wilson (Helen Smith), Freddie Earlle (Alasdair McCaig), Tom Conti (Dr Calvi), Brigit Forsyth (Annie Smith), Michael Elphick (Ben Davies), Janet Munro (Elizabeth Crichton). Religious drama series in which a Scots minister, following his wife's death, questions the purpose of his local ministry but finds it in his spiritual work for the community. ITV 1972-73

Adrian Mole: The Cappuccino Years See *The Secret Diary of Adrian Mole*

Adventure Game, The Charmian Gradwell (Gnoard), Christopher Leaver (Gandor the butler), Moira Stuart (Darong), Ian Messiter (Argond), Kenny Baker (His Highness The Rangdo), Bill Homewood (Dagnor the backwards-talking Australian), Sarah Lam (Dorgan the benevolent one). Game Show originally broadcast on BBC1 in 1980 as a children's programme but transferred to BBC2 in 1981 in an evening slot to cater for its growing adult popularity. The premise of the show was for three contestants with varying degrees of celebrity status to suspend their belief for the duration and enter the world of Arg. Charmian Gradwell replaced Moira Stuart as the seemingly all-knowing but secretive host of the show for the first of the BBC2 series, the format involving the rescue of former Blue Peter presenter Lesley Judd (who turned out to be a double-agent throughout the series). By series three the format was changed again to give the contestants a series of mental and physical tests culminating in the last survivor having to play the traditional Arg game of Drogna which necessitated a hazardous journey through a vortex grid of assorted colours and shapes and possible annihilation by the Red Salamander of Arg. If successful the victor claimed the Great Crystal of Arg. The programme grew to cult status by the fourth series largely due to a combination of the school ma'am charm and drive of Charmian Gradwell, the intensity of some of the contestants, the complexity of plot, the cameos by such as Bill Homewood's clever and convincing backwards talk, the Spike Milligan look-a-like old butler and the shy Rangdo (often taking the form of an aspidistra or a teapot). From the moment the show began with the gentle guitar pluckings and the narrator's opening parable of: "Many light years away on the far side of the galaxy in a region often visited by time travellers... lies Arg, a small planet of little consequence. Naturally the inhabitants of Arg get a bit fed up with trippers and tend to discourage them, often they will even nick the essential crystal off their time machines and hide it" you were transported to a fantasy world for an hour. The series was created by Patrick Dowling. BBC1 1980, BBC2 1981-86.

Adventure Weekly Brent Oldfield (Peter Perkins), Ian Ellis ('Tubby' Taylor), Frank Barry ('Swot' English), Len Jones (Andy Rogers), Elizabeth Dear (Frederica 'Fred' Somers), Bartlett Mullins (Mr Filling). Children's drama series. Five budding junior journalists run their own newspaper, the *Adventure Weekly*, in the fictitious town of Cliffsea on the south coast. Twelve-year-old Peter Perkins is the editor (mainly because his father owns the local rag, *The Cliffsea Recorder*), ardent Cliffsea United fan Tubby Taylor is the sports editor, Swot English is the roving reporter and Andy Rogers the newspaper's photographer. The pig-tailed Fred Somers is the last to join the team but soon becomes the ace reporter clearly outshining the lads in all departments. BBC1 1968-69.

Adventurer, The Gene Barry (Gene Bradley), Barry Morse (Mr Parminter), Catherine Schell (Diane Marsh), Garrick Hagon (Gavin Jones), Stuart Damon (Vince), Oliver Tobias (Jack Vincent). Adventure series created by Monty Berman and Dennis Spooner. Although the star of the show was an American working for US Intelligence the production was very much a British concern. Gene Bradley, a jet-setting movie star, moonlights as a detective via commissions from his manager Mr Parminter and employs his acting skills along the way. ITV 1972-73.

African Patrol John Bentley (Chief Inspector Paul Derek). The premise of this drama series was for British Patrol officer Paul Derek to solve various mysteries, often involving murder and corruption. John Bentley went on to greater fame as Hugh Mortimer, the second husband of Meg Richardson in *Crossroads*. African Patrol was produced and directed by George Breakston and is memorable for being filmed entirely on location in Kenya. ITV 1958-59

After Dark Late night live discussion programme which ran on Channel 4 between 1987 and 1997, and revived on the BBC in 2003. *After Dark* had a cult following, courted controversy and was famous for its arguments between its guests.

After Henry Prunella Scales (Sarah France), Joan Sanderson (Eleanor Prescott), Janine Wood (Clare France), Jonathan Newth (Russell Bryant), Peggy Ann Wood (Vera Poling), Edward de Souza (Sam Greenland), Anne Priestley (Mary). Sarah France is 42 and a widow of two years, her GP husband, Henry, having been killed in a car crash. Dr France has left Sarah well provided for, with a large Edwardian detached house in the leafy suburb of Stipton, about 70 miles out of London, which she shares with their 18-year-old daughter Clare and her seventy-something mother Eleanor. Much of the humour derives from the vain attempts of Sarah to reconcile the generations amicably in order to cope...... After Henry. Written by Simon Brett, *After Henry* was originally a BBC Radio Series (Radio 4) and was transferred to television with the same two stars although the roles of Clare and Russell were originally played by Gerry Cowper and Benjamin Whitrow. ITV 1988-92

After You've Gone Nicholas Lyndhurst (Jimmy Venables), Celia Imrie (Diana Neal), Dani Harmer (Molly Venables), Ryan Sampson (Alex Venables), Amanda Abbington (Siobhan Casey), Vincent Ebrahim (Bobby), Lee Oakes (Kev), Jocelyn Jee Esien (Lucy), Samantha Spiro (Ann), Nicky Henson (David Casey). Sitcom created by Fred Barron of *My Family* fame. Handyman Jimmy Venables moves back into the marital home to look after his children Alex and Molly after his former wife Ann goes to Africa to help victims of a flood. Unfortunately for Jimmy, his former mother-in-law Diana Neal, a teacher, decides to move in to help him out. Other characters include Jimmy's girlfriend, Siobhan, a hairdresser who becomes a barmaid at The Leek and Shepherd in Series 2; Jimmy's assistant, Kev; and Bobby, the landlord of the aforementioned pub. The theme song is performed by Jamie Cullum. BBC1 2007-08

Agatha Christie's Poirot David Suchet (Hercule Poirot), Hugh Fraser (Captain Arthur Hastings), Philip Jackson (Inspector/Chief Inspector Japp), Pauline Moran (Miss Felicity Lemon), Zoë Wanamaker (Ariadne Oliver). The cases of the fastidious Belgian sleuth who by exercising his 'little grey cells' helps the police unravel mysteries in 1930s Britain. The series created a glossy, generic atmosphere and indulged in the expensive and beautifully crafted period trappings of the era, including cars, aircraft, fashions and architecture. The décor was also crucial, with the layout of Poirot's Whitehaven Mansions flat (actually Florin Court in Charterhouse Square, near Holborn) central to the episode The Third Floor Flat (broadcast on 5 February 1989). This style is brilliantly evoked in Pat Gavin's animated title sequence and by Christopher Gunning's memorable theme tune. The Suchet portrayal has never really been off our screens since its first broadcast on ITV 8 January 1989, with feature-length episodes shown in 1996 and 1997 followed by a two-part dramatisation of *The Murder of Roger Ackroyd* (2002) and further single adventures. ITV 1989-

Agony Maureen Lipman (Jane Lucas), Simon Williams (Laurence Lucas), Maria Charles (Bea), Jeremy Bulloch (Rob), Peter Denyer (Michael), Diana Weston (Val), Jan Holden (Diana), Peter Blake (Andy Evol), Bill Nighy (Vincent Fish), Robert Gillespie (Mr Mince), Doon Mackichan (Debra), David Harewood (Daniel). Real-life press and radio 'agony aunt' Anna Raeburn advised and (for the first series) co-wrote this sometimes daring and always entertaining sitcom about her own work, casting Maureen Lipman as a cosmopolitan Jewish wife and mother, Jane Lucas - radio broadcaster and author of the problem page in *Person* magazine. The premise of the sitcom is that Jane spends so much time sorting out other people's problems that she is unable to handle her own, and numerous they are, She has an ex-public schoolboy husband, Laurence, who works as a psychiatrist, but has philandering tendencies at odds with his Christian nature; a needy and manipulative archetypal Jewish widowed mother, Bea; a magazine boss, Diana, who is impossible to work for; a gung-ho office secretary, Val; and, at Happening Radio 242, a DJ colleague, Andy, who is shallow and narcissistic. The only people

to offer Jane real comfort and support are the well-adjusted Rob and Michael, her gay neighbours. The series was first broadcast on ITV 11 March 1979, and ran for 20 episodes over three seasons. It was revived by the BBC under the title *Agony Again* in 1995 with Jane now the host of the TV talk show *Lucas Live*. The problems of the past remain however revolving around her now ex-husband and new man, Daniel, and her gay son, Michael. ITV 1979-81; BBC1 1995.

Ain't Misbehavin' Robson Green (Eric Trapp), Jerome Flynn (Eddie Wallis), Julia Sawalha (Dolly Nightingale), Warren Mitchell (Ray Smiles), Jane Lapotaire (Clara Van Trapp), Jim Carter (Maxie Morrell), James Cosmo ('Big' Malky Fraser), June Brown (Mrs Jilks), George Melly (Bing Williams), Graham Stark (Spadger), Heidi Monsen (Dolores Deville). Following the success of *Soldier, Soldier*, Jerome Flynn again teamed up with Robson Green for this musical comedy drama set in the 1940 Blitz of wartime London. The story revolves around the exploits of Eddie Wallis and Eric Trapp - an unlikely pair. Wallis is a man of principle who was discharged from the RAF on medical grounds after suffering blackouts following his heroic crash-landing in a Blenheim Bomber. He was devastated at rejection by the RAF. He takes a train to London on which he meets the gorgeous Dolly Nightingale and the story's romantic interest is set up. The lads join the Ray Smiles Orchestra and find themselves embroiled amidst inter-gang rivalries. The three-part comedy drama was directed by Norman Stone, written by Bob Larbey, and produced by Robson & Jerome's own company *Clapp Trapp*. ITV 1997

Ain't Misbehavin' Peter Davison (Clive Quigley), Nicola Pagett (Sonia Drysdale), Lesley Manville and Karen Drury (Melissa Quigley), John Duttine (Dave Drysdale), Polly Hemingway (Mrs Ramona Whales), Ian McNeice and Paul Brooke (Chuck Purvis), Barry Stanton (Lester Whales). Clive thinks he is happily married but Sonia informs him that her husband Dave is engaged in an affair with his wife Melissa. At first Clive refuses to believe Sonia but he is convinced when they follow the errant couple to a secret rendezvous. Clive is devastated, and after contemplating suicide, joins Sonia in a campaign to split up the affair. Other characters in this unyielding plot are Chuck Purvis, the private detective Clive and Sonia hire, and Lester and Ramona Whales - Ramona is Clive's secretary, and her jealous husband Lester, an exterminator, is convinced that his wife is having an affair with Clive, and takes to following him around. Paul Jones sang the title song (a version of the Fats Waller classic), Roy Clarke wrote the series and Tony Dow was the producer. BBC1 1994-95.

Airline Roy Marsden (Jack Ruskin), Richard Heffer (Peter Witney), Sean Scanlan (Jock McEvoy), Polly Hemingway (Jennie Shaw), Terence Rigby (Ernie Cade). Eight-part drama series. On being demobbed after World War Two, former RAF pilot Jack Ruskin starts his own airline business in partnership with Peter Witney. Jack's girlfriend Jennie Shaw was played by Polly Hemingway, the then real-life wife of Roy Marsden. Tony Hatch supplied the theme music. ITV 1982.

Airline The 1998 ITV documentary was made following the success of the BBC's *Airport*. The series concentrated on the staff of Britannia Airways, and later Easyjet, and in particular Luton Airport check-in girl Katrina Leeder.

Airport The 1996 BBC1 documentary about various aspects of working life at Heathrow Airport made a star of Aeroflot supervisor Jeremy Spake. In 2001 a spin-off series focused on the staff at Miami Airport.

Al Murray's Happy Hour Murray's pub landlord comedy act thinly disguised in a chatshow format. His catchphrases include "All hail to the ale!", "...beautiful British name!", "Say filthy", "Pint for the fella... Glass of white wine/ fruit-based drink for the lady!" and "I was never confused". The finely formatted show begins with an audience participation routine with Al shouting "Where would we be without rules?" and as the stock reply comes back "France!" his next question is "and where would we be with too many rules?" to which the standard reply is "Germany!" and thus the stand- up routine goes on to the first commercial break with Al introducing his "Pub of the Week" and "Big Bob", an oversized member of the studio audience. His guests are then interviewed with Al always in character as the caricature of a stereotypical pub landlord. ITV 2007-8. See also *Al Murray's*

Multiple Personality Disorder, Fact Hunt and Al Murray's entry in the British and Irish comedy section.

Al Murray's Multiple Personality Disorder Sketch series showcasing new characters for the first time since creating The Pub Landlord in 1994. Written by Al Murray, Simon Brodkin, Mark Augustyn, John Camm, Chris England, Paul Hawksbee, Will McLean, Tony MacMurray and Daniel Maier. Co-starring Jenny Eclair, Simon Brodkin, Laura Solon, Katy Wix, Kim Wall, Sadie Hasler, Colin Holt and Hassani Shapi. Guest appearances by John Barrowman, Duncan Bannatyne and Peter Davison. Creations include: **Peter Taylor** - the embarrassing West Country dad, who "luuuuuuurrrves seeeeex!"; **Barrington Blowtorch** - a silver-tongued Victorian gentleman thief; **Horst Schwull** - Hitler's most trusted aide, who's just a little on the 'kamp' side; The **Radio Ad Couple** - a husband-and-wife team who voice radio commercials and never turn off the adspeak; **Gary Parsley** - the outrageous, over-demanding piano-playing '70s rock star who has let fame go to his head; **Intolerant Vicar** - a Scottish clergyman who likes to keep things traditional. ..apart from his temper; **Roger Dennis** - the airline pilot who always gives his passengers a little too much information over the tannoy; The **Celeb News Tramps** - a pair of homeless chaps who chat about what they glean from the newspapers they sleep under; **Gay Best Friend** - not your typical Gay Best Friend, Gaz likes beer, heavy metal, and er, women; **Mobile Phone Shop Assistants** - a parody of all that is bad about customer service; **Jason Bent** - the Premiership footballer who's always ready with a memorable soundbite after the match; **Lee Nelson** – philosophy according to a misguided cheeky chav from Bermondsey; **Duncan's Den** - entrepreneur Duncan Bannatyne is looking to invest one million pounds in a new business venture. Unfortunately, desperate divorcee Carole Price is pitching most of the ideas. ITV 2009.

Alan Carr: Chatty Man Alan Carr, born in Weymouth, Dorset, 14 June 1976 is a stand-up comedian and television presenter. *Chatty Man* is a comedy chat show with probing interviews and irreverent humour. C4 2009- See also *Alan Carr's Celebrity Ding Dong* and *The Friday Night Project*.

Alan Carr's Celebrity Ding Dong Celebrity game show hosted by stand-up comedian Alan Carr. C4 2008

Alan Titchmarsh Show, The Alan Fred Titchmarsh, born in Ilkley, West Yorkshire, 2 May 1949 is a gardener, novelist and broadcaster. Alan was a natural choice as a television gardening pundit, being heavily influenced from a young age by the original celebrity gardener Percy Thrower (who he affectionately refers to as Percy Chucker). Alan began his broadcasting career as a horticultural expert on the BBC news magazine show, *Nationwide*. His natural communication skills and professional expertise led to his long association with the BBC coverage of the Chelsea Flower Show (1983-2008) and he was soon in demand as a mainstream presenter of non-gardening programmes. *The Alan Titchmarsh Show* is a daytime magazine show discussing topical subjects with celebrity guests, The third series in 2008 ran a competition to find a soprano to sing alongside Jonathan Ansell in the *A Night At The Opera* tour. The judging panel comprised David Grant, Ruthie Henshall and Jonathan Shalit and the eventual winner was Olivia Safe. In 2009 a similar exercise was undertaken to find 'the people's crooner', the judges comprising Pete Waterman, Carrie Grant and Tom Lewis. The winner was Jason Isaacs. The 2010 singing competition was open to pensioners and the prize was for the winner to sing on the Christmas record of the Chelsea Pensioners. Brenda Sokell was the winner and the judges included Elaine Paige, Jodie Prenger and Heather Small amongst others. ITV 2007- See also *Ask the Family, British Isles - A Natural History, Gardener's World, The Great British Village Show, Ground Force, Pebble Mill At One, Points of View, Songs of Praise*.

Alas Smith and Jones Following their success in *Not the Nine O'Clock News*, Mel Smith (born London, 3 December 1952) and Griff Rhys Jones (born Cardiff, 16 November 1953) teamed up again and formed their own production company (TalkBack) and after a brief try-out in 1982 their comedy sketch show began two years later. BBC1 1984-87. A 40-minute special *Alas Sage and Onion* aired in 1988 and in 2006 the lads teamed up again in *The Smith and Jones Sketchbook* which showed the best of their previous series blended with some brand new 'head-to-heads', the famed sketches depicting the duo deliberating on all and sundry while peering into each other's eyes.

Alcock and Gander Beryl Reid (Mrs Marigold Alcock), Richard O'Sullivan (Richard Gander), John Cater (Ernest). Six-part sitcom written by Johnnie Mortimer and Brian Cooke. Marigold Alcock inherits her husband's business upon his death. The companies, whose headquarters are above a strip club in Soho, include Sotheby's Racing Service Ltd and Hugh Blanding's Detective Agency. The elderly Ernest is her office assistant, while her partner is Richard Gander, who was given partnership in the company after an Alcock Economy Coach Tour went wrong. ITV 1972.

Alfred Hitchcock Presents The benign countenance of portly film director Alfred Hitchcock welcomed viewers to stories of terror, horror, suspense, and twisted endings for an entire decade beginning in 1957. The great man himself only directed about 20 of the 300-plus episodes but the likes of Robert Altman, William Friedkin and Sydney Pollack ensured the stories of authors such as Ray Bradbury, Roald Dahl and HG Wells were given a Hitchcock air of suspense. While the staccato sound of Gounod's *Funeral March of a Marionette* played its haunting melody the silhouette of Hitchcock in profile would appear on the screen and the master of suspense would commence each 30 minute episode either laying the foundation of plot or very often making totally unrelated comments (This worked very nicely when the series was revived in the 1980s as his vignettes could be tagged on to new episodes). By 1962 a series of one-hour episodes were shown under the title of *The Alfred Hitchcock Hour* with the opening sequence changed to a line drawing of Hitchcock's profile drawn by Hitchcock himself. ITV 1957-66.

Alfresco Early comedy sketch vehicle for Robbie Coltrane, Ben Elton, Stephen Fry, Hugh Laurie, Siobhan Redmond and Emma Thompson. The title was a reference to the fact that many outdoor sketches were shot with hand-held cameras. Two series were broadcast on ITV 1983-84.

All About Me Jasper Carrott (Colin Craddock), Meera Syal (Rupinder Craddock - series 1), Nina Wadia (Rupinder Craddock - series 2 and 3), Jamil Dhillon (Raj), Ryan Cartwright (Peter Craddock), Natalia Kills (Sima), Robert Cartin (Leo Craddock), Alina Iqbal (Kavita), Jonty Stephens (Billy), Richard Lumsden (Charles), Amanda Root (Miranda), Luke Allder (Voice of Raj). Sitcom created by Steve Knight about life in a mixed-race Birmingham family as seen through the eyes of Raj, a teenager with cerebral palsy. BBC1 2002-04

All At No. 20 Maureen Lipman (Sheila Haddon), Lisa Jacobs (Monica Haddon), Gary Waldhorn (Richard Beamish), Gabrielle Glaister (Carol), Gregory Doran (Chris), David Bannerman (Hamish), Martin Clunes (Henry), Carol Hawkins (Candy). Sitcom created by Richard Ommanney. A recently widowed housewife is forced to take in a variety of lodgers in order to make ends meet. ITV 1986-87.

All Creatures Great and Small Christopher Timothy (James Herriot), Robert Hardy (Siegfried Farnon), Peter Davison (Tristan Farnon), Carol Drinkwater and Lynda Bellingham (Helen Alderson / Herriot), Mary Hignett (Mrs Hall the housekeeper). Based on the autobiographical novels of James Herriot the drama series was inspired by the success of the earlier feature films. The veterinary practice was situated at Skeldale House in the North Riding town of Darrowby (the real-life Askrigg). The oft-featured pekingese owned by Mrs Pumphrey (Margaretta Scott) was named 'Tricki Woo'. Three series were shown between 1978 and 1980 and a further four between 1988 and 1990 with two Christmas Specials in 1983 and 1985. BBC1 1978-90. Over Christmas 2011, the BBC screened a three-episode prequel, *Young James Herriot*, about Herriot's time at University, with Iain de Caestecker in the title role.

All Gas and Gaiters Derek Nimmo (Rev Mervyn Noote), William Mervyn (Bishop), Robertson Hare (Archdeacon), John Barron and Ernest Clark (The Dean). Sitcom based around St

Ogg's Cathedral. The series began life as a Comedy Playhouse presentation of 1966. All five series were written by the husband and wife team of Edwin Apps and Pauline Devaney. BBC1 1966-71.

All in Good Faith Richard Briers (Rev Philip Lambe), Barbara Ferris and Susan Jameson (Emma Lambe), James Campbell (Peter Lambe), Lydia Smith (Miranda Lambe), James Cossins (Major Andrews), T.P. McKenna and John Woodvine (Oscar Randolph), Frank Middlemiss (Desmond). Sitcom, written by John Kane, involving a middle-aged vicar who leaves his safe country parish to take up a more challenging position in the Midlands town of Edendale. ITV 1985-88.

All Ireland Talent Show, The Presented by Gráinne Seoige, the show replaced *You're A Star* as an Irish version of *Britain's Got Talent*. Twenty five finalists made the television stages and the first winners were the Mulkerrin Brothers. The winner of the second series was Chloe Coyle and the third series, Daniel Furlong. The judges were John Creedon, Bláthnaid Ní Chofaigh, Shane Lynch (replaced by Amanda Brunker for series 3), Dana and Dáithí Ó Sé. RTÉ 1 2009-11. *The All Ireland Talent Show Backstage* was a companion show that aired on RTÉ 2 from season two, hosted by Aidan Power and Dustin the Turkey. The series was axed in July 2011 and replaced by *The Voice of Ireland* based on the hit US TV series *The Voice*.

All Night Long Keith Barron (Bill Chivers), Maureen Beattie (Vanda), Dinah Sheridan (Clare), Angus Lennie (Tom), Jacqueline Reddin (Terry), Jan Winters (WPC Jackson), John Phythian (PC Digby), Paul Grunert (Wally), Robert McKewley (Courtney). Sitcom set in a London bakery, the action taking place through the night as the employees prepare the daily bread for local hotels and cafés amid frequent interruptions from a motley crew of visitors. The owner of the business, Bill Chivers, is an ex burglar who learned baking while doing a spell in prison and is trying his utmost to turn over a new leaf, despite the temptations of London's night urchins. Helping Chivers at the bakery are, Vanda, an illegally employed Romanian who is a better baker than her boss; Tom, a confused Scot prone to boasting that he 'was once the shortest man ever to work for British Rail'; and young Courtney, given the chance to prove himself by Chivers after he is caught breaking into the bakery in the first episode. Others visitors include Clare a wheelchair-bound crime writer who uses the night-bakery life to inspire her; Wally, a shady mini-cab driver; Terry, a striptease and stripagram act; and the comic coppers Digby & Jackson. Digby is prone to want to arrest Chivers for anything and everything while Jackson leans the other way, not least because she fancies the ex-con. Written by Dick Fiddy and Mark Wallington, the six-episode series never caught the public's imagination in the same way as the later *dinnerladies*, but had some great under-stated comedy performances from an excellent cast. BBC1 1994.

All Our Yesterdays Presenters: James Cameron (1960), Brian Inglis (1961-73), Bernard Braden (1987-89). Nostalgic documentary series looking back 25 years in time using old cinema newsreels. The Brian Inglis years were the most memorable as they portrayed graphic and sometimes horrifying footage of World War Two. First broadcast on ITV 1960-73 and resurrected 1987-89.

All Quiet On The Preston Front See *Preston Front*.

All Square See *It's A Square World*.

All Star Talent Show, The For five weeks, six celebrities displayed a variety of hidden talents with the winner at the end of each episode returning for the final at the end of the series. In addition, the runner-up with the most votes at the end of the series also got to perform again in the final. Presented by Andi Peters and Myleene Klass, with Julian Clary making up the judging panel alongside two guest judges. The overall winner was Zimbabwean cricketer Henry Olonga showing off a fine operatic voice. *Five* 2006.

All the Small Things Sarah Lancashire (Esther Caddick), Neil Pearson (Michael Caddick), Sarah Alexander (Layla), Richard Fleeshman (Kyle Caddick), Bryan Dick (Jake Barton), Clive Rowe (Clifford 'Shrek' Beale), Jo Woodcock (Georgia Caddick), Jamie Birtwhistle (Fred Caddick), Annette Badland (Ethel Tonks) and David Fleeshman (Gilbert 'Jabba' Tonks). Drama series created and developed by Debbie Horsfield, following the lives

and ambitions of a church choir and its members. The programme's title is taken from a song on American band Blink-182's 1999 album, *Enema of the State*. BBC1 2009

'Allo 'Allo Gorden Kaye (René Artois), Carmen Silvera (Edith Artois), Vicki Michelle (Yvette), Guy Siner (Lt Gruber), Francesca Gonshaw (Maria), Kirsten Cooke (Michelle Dubois), Richard Marner (Colonel Kurt Von Strohm), Sam Kelly (Captain Hans Geering), Richard Gibson and David Janson (Herr Otto Flick), Kim Hartman (Helga Geerhart), John Louis Mansi (Englebert Von Smallhausen), Hilary Minster (General Von Klinkerhoffen), Arthur Bostrom (Officer Crabtree), Sue Hodge (Mimi La Bonque), Jack Haig, Derek Royle, Robin Parkinson (Monsieur Leclerc), Kenneth Connor (Monsieur Alphonse), Rose Hill (Fanny), John D. Collins (Flying Officer Fairfax), Nicholas Frankau (Flying Officer Carstairs), Gavin Richards and Roger Kitter (Captain Alberto Bertorelli). Veiled spoof of the earlier BBC drama *Secret Army*. In *Secret Army*, Bernard Hepton had starred as Albert, a café owner involved in the resistance. In 'Allo 'Allo Kaye plays René Artois, a café owner in the town of Nouvion who becomes unwittingly involved with the resistance when they use his establishment as a base from which to hatch plans to smuggle two British airmen back to Blighty. Introducing each episode of the serial farce by talking to camera in order to update viewers with the plot, René's love-life is often the main sub-plot. He is married to Edith, a formidable woman who entertains in the café by singing, but he is also enjoying a passionate affair with the beautiful Yvette, a leggy waitress at the café, and their constant attempts to steal a few precious moments alone are often thwarted. René himself is the target of the unwanted attentions of Lieutenant Gruber, aide-de-camp to the Gestapo's Herr Flick. The patronage of Flick and other Germans causes René further problems when resistance agent Michelle embroils him in her half-baked secret plans. Throughout the 85 episodes there were recurrent themes, including Herr Flick's pursuit of a valuable painting (The Fallen Madonna With The Big Boobies, by Van Clomp). Early on in the series, to escape the wrath of the SS, René fakes his own death and continues through the remainder of the episodes as his own fictitious twin brother. This deception prompts aged lothario Monsieur Alfonse into pursuing René's 'widow', with a view to marriage. This prospect had its attractions because it would allow René to plight his troth with Yvette, but the drawbacks - losing the café and his savings - prove overwhelming and so he thwarts the courtship. Other characters in the show include the fat, mentally-challenged German Von Strohm and his colleague Hans Geering; ice queen Helga, Herr Flick's right-hand-woman; diminutive waitress Mimi La Bonque; and Edith's mother Fanny 'Fifi' Lafanne, who eventually marries Leclerc. The original Leclerc was played by Jack Haig but following the actor's death the writers invented Leclerc's twin brother who was played initially by Derek Royle and later by Robin Parkinson. David Janson appeared as Hitler in an episode of series eight and he returned to the cast for series nine, this time taking over the role of Herr Flick. The show had a cunning method of dealing with language problems. French characters spoke their native tongue with pantomime-style exaggerated French accents, but when they spoke English they adopted equally exaggerated posh Oxford accents. The English characters spoke English normally, but when they spoke French it was with a poor, almost incomprehensible cod French accent. This was especially true of the Englishman named Crabtree, who survived in Nouvion disguised as a gendarme and who's strangulated English-French gave the show its most memorable catchphrase with his customary greeting 'Good Moaning'. The show's other principal catchphrase was resistance leader Michelle's, 'Leesen verrry carefully, I weel zay zis only once...' The series, written by Jeremy Lloyd and David Croft, won numerous awards. BBC1 1984-92.

Always and Everyone Martin Shaw (Robert Kingsford), Niamh Cusack (Dr Christine Fletcher), David Harewood (Mike Gregson), Esther Hall (Louise Macken), Paul Warriner (Stuart Phelan), David Partridge (Dr David Scobie), Jane Slavin (Cathy Jordan), Kim Vithana (Yvonne), Connor McIntyre (Terry Harker), Cathy Tyson (Stella), Tamzin Malleson (Kate Brady), Bill Rodgers (Freddie), Dean Williamson (Alan), Jane Danson (Sam Docherty), Michael Kitchen (Jack Turner), Michele Austin (Poppy Jonston),

Parminder Nagra (Sunita Verma), Bhasker Patel (Raj Verma), Judy Holt (Jean Kenning), Don Gallagher (Jeffrey Drummond), Ben Taylor (James Da Costa), Silas Carson (Raz Amin), David Fleeshman (Gareth), Jaye Griffiths (Ruth Cole), James Murray (Danny Barton), Dominic Mafham (Andrew Argyle), Catherine Russell (Issy), Katie McEwen (Judy Enshaw), Ellie Haddington (Carla), Beatrice Kelley (Annie). The everyday lives of the doctors and nurses running the A & E department of the busy city hospital, St. Victor's. The title is the motto of the hospital, but is also a pun on the initial letters "A & E", hospital shorthand for "Accident and Emergency." ITV 1999-2002, by the third series in 2001 the title became *A & E*.

Amazing Mrs Pritchard, The Jane Horrocks (Prime Minister Rosamund 'Ros' Jane Pritchard), Steven Mackintosh (Ian Pritchard), Carey Mulligan (Emily Pritchard), Jemma McKenzie-Brown (Georgina Pritchard), Jodhi May (Miranda Lennox), Janet McTeer (Catherine Walker), Frances Tomelty (Kitty Porter), Geraldine James (Hilary Rees-Benson), Selina Cadell (Dorothy Crowther), Meera Syal (Liz Shannon), Siobhan Finneran (Beverley Clarke), Jonathan Aris (Richard Leavis), Sally Phillips (Meg Bayliss), Tom Mison (Ben Sixsmith), Robert Portal (Paul Critchley), Dilys Laye (Queen Elizabeth II). Six-part drama series written by Sally Wainwright, revolving around Ros Pritchard, a woman with no previous political experience who becomes Prime Minister of the United Kingdom. BBC1 2006.

Amazon with Bruce Parry The intrepid traveller made an epic journey across South America from the source of the Amazon in the Peruvian Andes to its vast mouth 4,000 miles away on Brazil's Atlantic coast. On the way Bruce explored the devastation wreaked by oil companies along the river banks and had many adventures, from trying to be accepted by the Peruvian Achuar tribe to brushing with cocaine dealers. BBC2 2008. See also *Tribe*.

Ambassador Pauline Collins (Harriet Smith), Denis Lawson (John Stone), William Chubb (Stephen Tyler), Owen Roe (Kevin Flaherty), Dominic Mafham (Julian Wadham), Alison McKenna (Jennifer), Sarah Markland (Becky), Tim Matthews (Nate Smith), Tom Connolly (Sam Smith), Eve Matheson (Catherine Grieve), Peter Egan (Michael Cochrane), Gina Moxley (Eileen), Sinead Clarkin (Susan). Harriet Smith, the new British ambassador to Ireland, desperately wants to make her mark in this historically difficult posting and try to put the tragic murder of her husband behind her (he was killed by a bomb intended for her). Harriet wants to be just and fair in her dealings with the Irish government and to try to make the relationship between the two governments less adversarial in nature. However, the situation is made considerably worse for her and her trusted assistant, John Stone (later Catherine Grieve), by her son Nate who refuses to accept the consequences of her new ambassadorial role and still blames her for his father's death. BBC1 1998-99.

America Alistair Cooke's *America* was a 13-part television series about the United States and its history, first broadcast in both Britain and the US in 1972, and followed by a book of the same title. It was a great success in both countries, and resulted in Cooke being invited to address the joint Houses of the United States Congress as part of Congress's bicentennial celebrations. Alistair Cooke said that, of all his work, America was what he was most proud of; it is the result and expression of his long love of his naturalised country. Cooke was once asked how long it took him to make the series. "I do not want to be coy," he replied, "but it took 40 years." BBC2 1972.

An Actor's Life for Me John Gordon-Sinclair (Robert Neilson), Gina McKee (Sue Bishop), Victor Spinetti (Desmond Shaw). Robert Neilson, a struggling actor convinced that he is on the verge of the big time although to-date he has only secured one important job, as the face of Doberman aftershave. His agent Desmond and his girlfriend Sue do their best to keep his feet on the ground but Robert maintains his head in the clouds always fantasising about starring with such names as Kim Basinger. Paul Mayhew-Archer's comedy started out on BBC Radio 2 with John Gordon-Sinclair in the role of Robert Wilson (changed to Neilson for television), Caroline Quentin as Sue and Gary Waldhorn as

Desmond. Following the 1991 run on BBC1, it returned to radio once more, this time with Gina McKee reprising her television role as replacement for Quentin.

And Mother Makes Three Wendy Craig (Sally Harrison / Redway), Robin Davies (Simon Harrison), David Parfitt (Peter Harrison), Valerie Lush (Auntie Flo), George Selway (Mr Campbell), Richard Coleman (David Redway), Miriam Mann and Maxine Gordon (Jane Redway), Tony Britton (Joss Spencer), Charlotte Mitchell (Monica Spencer). Sally Harrison is a widow faced with the everyday tribulations of raising two well-meaning but nonetheless troublesome children (Simon and Peter), plus a cat and a goldfish, is 'helped' by her aunt, all the while enjoying some occasional male interest and holding down a job as assistant to a vet (Mr Campbell). Sally married father-of-one widower and antiquarian bookseller David Redway in the final series, leading to the sequel called *And Mother Makes Five* (ITV 1974-76) where Sally works at David's antiquarian bookshop. David's daughter Jane was played by Miriam Mann in *And Mother Makes Three* (ITV 1971-73) but Maxine Gordon took over the role in *And Mother Makes Five* (Tony Britton and Charlotte Mitchell also joined the cast as neighbours).

Andy Pandy The puppet series was first shown on 11 July 1950. Andy Pandy is a chubby faced toddler who wears a blue-and-white striped tunic with matching hat and lives in a picnic basket. He first appears alone but was then joined by his inseparable pal Teddy and later a rag doll called Looby Loo. Maria Bird brought Andy out to play, opera singers Gladys Whitred and Julia Williams sang the songs and Audrey Atterbury (mother of Paul Atterbury of *Antiques Roadshow* fame, on whom it is rumoured Andy was modelled!) and Molly Gibson pulled the strings. The excitement for children was when Andy and Teddy had their backs to the rag doll who would then come alive to the sound of 'here we go Looby Loo, here we go Looby light, here we go Looby Loo, all on a Saturday night'. The 15-minute episodes, shown on Tuesdays as part of the original *Watch with Mother* series, would end with the song 'Time to go home, Time to go home, Andy and Teddy it's time to go home' and the two heroes would jump into the basket. Only 26 original episodes were made, they were seen time and time again, and in 1970, 13 new episodes were made in colour with Vera McKechnie as narrator and Valerie Cardnell providing the songs (the puppeteers were Cecil and Madge Stavordale and Christopher Leith). An all-new *Andy Pandy* was made in 2002, with no strings attached! Produced by Cosgrove Hall, the new stop-frame animated toddler now lived in a house, as did Teddy and Looby. New characters included Hissy Missy (a snake / draught excluder), Bilbo the sailor, Tiffo the dog, and Orbie the bouncing ball. Tom Conti performed the narrative. The original series was created by Freda Lingstrom and Maria Bird. BBC 1950-57, BBC1 1970, BBC2 2002-05

Angels Fiona Fullerton (Patricia Rutherford), Julie Dawn Cole (Jo Longhurst), Karan David (Sita Patel), Lesley Dunlop (Ruth Fullman), Clare Gifford (Shirley Brent), Erin Geraghty (Maureen Morahan), Faith Brooks (Heather Windrup), Jeremy Wilkin (Stewart Farrar), Debbie Ash (Sarah Regan), Shirley Cheriton (Katy Betts/Smart), Pauline Quirke (Vicky Smith), Kathryn Apanowicz (Rose Butchins), Judith Jacob (Beverley Slater), Bill Owen (Harry Jamieson), Geoffrey Palmer (Lawrence Rutherford), Kate Saunders (Brenda Cotteral), Christopher Strauli (Brian Hollis), Bill Treacher (Mr Carter), David Troughton (John Overton), Richard Caldicot (Dr Collins), Rita Webb (Mrs White), Irene Handl (Annie). Created by writer Paula Milne, Angels originally chronicled the personal and professional lives of six student nurses (Pat, Jo, Sita, Ruth, Shirley and Maureen) based at the fictitious St Angela's Hospital in London's Battersea district (The setting eventually changed to Heath Green Hospital in Birmingham and the cast grew considerably). Dubbed the Z-Cars of nursing by some critics due to its authentic semi-documentary approach, the series began as a 50-minute weekly drama, but changed to two half-hour episodes a week in 1979 and exterior scenes were shot in the grounds of St. James's Hospital, Balham. BBC1 1975-83

Animal Hospital Presenters: Rolf Harris, Shauna Lowry, Lynda Bryans, Steve Knight, Mairi McHaffie, Rhodri Williams, Christa Hart, Edwina Silver, Jamie Darling. Began on BBC 1 as Animal Hospital Live in August 1994, a twice-daily report (over five days) on the events at Harmsworth Memorial Hospital in Holloway, London. A Christmas Day special followed and then another series in January 1995 entitled *Animal Hospital Week*, the chief veterinary surgeon David Grant being the human star and snowy the poodle and Dolly the bull, the animal stars. Rolf Harris recorded a special *Animal Hospital Down Under* from the Currumbin Wildlife Sanctuary in Queensland at Christmas 1995 (the series becoming known as *Animal Hospital* earlier that year). From 1996 until the show's demise in 2004, *Animal Hospital* ran with two series a year with the autumn series remaining at Harmsworth and the spring series visiting new locations under the title 'On the Hoof', the first location was Bedford's Whipsnade Wild Animal Park, and since then Hamden Veterinary Hospital in Aylesbury (1997), Harmsworths' RSPCA Hospital, Putney in London (1998 this became the year-round venue at this time although in 2000 visits to Salford and Stapeley Grange, near Nantwich, were made). Lorraine Heggessey, the former controller of BBC1, was one of the executive producers. BBC1 1994-2004

Animal Magic The popularity of this natural history series which ran for over 20 years was undoubtedly due to its presenter Johnny Morris, who not only travelled the world's zoos and nature reserves (although Bristol Zoo was featured heavily) to showcase some of the world's most interesting animals, but also dubbed the 'voices' in order to tell a story that left the young viewer spellbound. Chimpanzees and camels were always fair game for a few anecdotes as their natural jaw movements gave spectacular effect to the dubbing technique. Terry Nutkins joined Johnny towards the end of the series run in the 1980s. BBC1 1962-83

Animal Rescue Squad Wildlife series anchored by Michaela Strachan and Matt Baker. Animal Rescue Squad followed the efforts of dedicated zoologists, vets and volunteers to help animals around the world. The programmes focused on the unsung heroes of animal conservation and protection, who work tirelessly to improve the lives of creatures in zoos, safari parks, wildlife reserves and public areas. The series also examined the life-and-death dramas that unfold in vets' surgeries up and down the country on a daily basis. *Five* 2008

Animal, Vegetable, Mineral? A popular early fortnightly television panel game created by Paul Johnstone and hosted by Cambridge University Fellow Glyn Daniel (although the pilot show was presided over by Lionel Hale and the poet John Betjeman stood in for Daniel during one series). The concept of the show was for a panel of celebrated archaeologists, art historians, natural history experts and scientists to identify unusual and interesting museum items. Guests included such luminaries as Sir Mortimer Wheeler, Julian Huxley, Adrian Digby, Norman Cook, W. E. Swanton, Jacquetta Hawkes and Professor Thomas Bodkin. The man responsible for selecting the items to be shown to the panel was none other than the young David Attenborough, who also acted as camera director on the show. There was a brief but unsuccessful revival of the show in 1971 hosted by Professor Barry Cunliffe. The title was taken from the long-running radio show *Twenty Questions*. BBC 1952-59; BBC2 1971. See *Life in Cold Blood*

Animals Do the Funniest Things Home-video show where the animals are the stars. Hosts have included Michael Barrymore (1999), Tony Blackburn (2003), Tara Palmer-Tomkinson (2003) and Stephen Mulhern (2004-06). ITV 1999-2006

Animals of Farthing Wood, The Rupert Farley (Fox), Stacy Jefferson (Adder), Ron Moody (Toad, Mole and Badger), Jeremy Barrett (Mr Rabbit), Sally Grace (Weasel and Owl), Pamela Keevil Kral (Mrs Squirrel), Jon Glover (Scarface). Telemagination animation series of 39 episodes. A group of animals have to leave their home, the Farthing Wood which was destroyed by the people. They travel to the famous White Deer Park and want to make a new home there. Fox is their leader and Toad their guide. Also with them are Badger, a very old resident of the Farthing Wood, Owl, which is very wise and often helps them, and Mole, the little friend of Badger. ITV 1993-95.

Another Bouquet See *Bouquet of Barbed Wire*.

Ant & Dec's Push the Button Game show hosted by Anthony McPartlin and Declan Donnelly. Contesting families compete over four games to win a jackpot of up to £100,000. The final game consists of remembering a sequence of flashing lights generated by DAVE (Dynamic Audio Visual End Game). The series was sponsored by Maltesers and narrated by Ronnie Corbett. ITV 2010- See entry for Ant and Dec in the comedy section.

Ant & Dec's Saturday Night Takeaway Variety show hosted by Anthony McPartlin and Declan Donnelly. Games during the seven year run included Mr and Mesmerised, Court in the Act, Where's your Shed At?, STOP! That's Mine, Stars in their Lives, Shame That Tune, This Is Your Diary, Prankety Prank, Wedding Daze, How The Other Half Lives, Trouble & Strife, Grab the Ads, Ant v Dec (hosted by Kirsty Gallacher), Imitation Street and I'm a Believer. Each show ended with a contestant from the audience attempting to win 20 items advertised during a randomly-chosen programme from the preceding week. ITV 2002-9. See entry for Ant and Dec in the comedy section.

Antiques Roadshow When *Going For A Song* ended its original run in 1977 it was sadly missed, and by 1979 Bruce Parker and Arthur Negus (and occasionally Angela Rippon) began co-hosting the still-popular travelling antiques show on Sunday afternoons. Members of the public bring their prized antiques to the roadshow venues and there is invariably a surprise in store for a lucky punter. Experts have included David Battie and Hugh Morley-Fletcher (porcelain), Simon Bull (timepieces), Roy Butler (militaria), Fergus Gambon and Eric Knowles (ceramics and glass), David Collins and Philip Hook (paintings), John Bly (furniture) and the 'potaholic' Henry Sandon and his son John Sandon. Hugh Scully joined the team of presenters in 1981 and when Arthur Negus retired in 1983 he became the mainstay of the programme until his departure in 2000 when Michael Aspel then took over the reins. Michael retired in January 2008 and was replaced by Fiona Bruce. BBC1 1979-

Any Answers? See *Any Questions?*

Any Dream Will Do? In 2006, the BBC1 audience and Andrew Lloyd Webber solved a problem like Maria and catapulted telesales girl Connie Fisher to stardom in *The Sound Of Music*. The following year, the BBC launched a nationwide talent search to find a male lead for *Joseph And The Amazing Technicolor Dreamcoat*. Joining musical composer and producer Andrew Lloyd Webber and presenter Graham Norton was the *Any Dream Will Do* panel - Broadway and West End leading lady Denise Van Outen, *Torchwood* star John Barrowman, acclaimed theatre producer Bill Kenwright, and outspoken and opinionated voice coach Zoe Tyler. Lee Mead won the series and again was a great success in the West End. BBC1 2007 See also *I'd Do Anything*.

Any Questions? Topical debate radio programme broadcast by BBC Radio 4 on Friday evenings and repeated on Saturday afternoons, when it is followed by a phone-in response programme, *Any Answers?*. It typically features a panel of four politicians from the three major UK political parties and other public figures who answer questions put to them by the audience, with a neutral chairman. First broadcast on 12 October 1948 as a programme on the Home Service in the West of England. It has been broadcast nationally since 1950, initially on the BBC Light Programme and repeated on the Home Service and later Radio 4. The programme has gone out exclusively on Radio 4 since 10 April 1970. It has had four chairmen in its history: Freddie Grisewood from 1948 to December 1967, David Jacobs from December 1967 to July 1983, John Timpson from July 1983 to July 1987 and Jonathan Dimbleby from July 1987; Nick Clarke has been Jonathan's occasional substitute in recent years.

Anyone For Pennis Paul Kaye (born 1965 in Clapham, south London to Jewish parents) is an English comedian and actor who made his name as shock interviewer Dennis Pennis, a fictional geeky American who first appeared on screen in *The Sunday Show* in the spring of 1995. Later in the year celebrity interviewer Dennis Pennis, written by Kaye and his friend Anthony Hines, was given his own series. The technique of conducting comic interviews in disguise was pioneered in 1974-75 on Australian TV by actor Garry McDonald, in the guise of his fictional TV host character Norman Gunston. The series changed its title to Very Important Pennis from 1996 but continued in the same vein of cruel jibes at unsuspecting celebrities. There was some controversy when Pennis asked of Steve Martin: "Hey Steve - how come you're not funny anymore?" Martin subsequently cancelled all scheduled press interviews. Kaye later stated it was the sole interview he regretted making whilst playing the Pennis character. In 1997 Paul 'killed off' the character although has maintained an eagerness to resurrect him in the future. BBC2 1995-97.

Apparitions Martin Shaw (Father Jacob), Elyes Gabel (Vimal), John Shrapnel (Cardinal Bukovak), Luigi Diberti (Monsignor Vincenzo), Rick Warden (Astaruth), Romy Irving (Donna), Michelle Joseph (Sister Anne), Sarah-Jayne Steed (Sarah). Supernatural drama series written and directed by Joe Ahearne. Father Jacob, a priest working to promote candidates for sainthood, becomes drawn in to exorcism as he discovers a dark battle between good and evil – a battle that threatens the future of the human race itself. BBC1 2008

Appleyards, The Frederick Piper and Douglas Muir (Mr Appleyard), Constance Fraser (Mrs Appleyard), David Edwards (John Appleyard), Maureen Davis, Tessa Clarke and Sylvia Bidmead (Janet Appleyard), Derek Rowe (Tommy Appleyard), Patricia Wilson, Patricia Fryer and Carol Olver (Margaret Appleyard), Robert Dickens (Ronnie Grant), John Garley (Joe), Douglas Hurn (Mr Wheeler). Broadcast once a fortnight in the BBC's Children's Television slot, The Appleyards is generally regarded as Britain's first television soap opera. Telling the ups and downs of a suburban Home Counties family, the show, which picked up a number of awards during its five year run, was transmitted live on Thursdays around 4.30 to 5.00pm with a repeat performance the following Sunday. Each episode was approximately 20 minutes in length. The theme music for the series, 'Looking Around' by Colin Smith (alias Lloyd Thomas), was played into the studio live off a 78rpm record. The family consisted of Mr and Mrs Appleyard and their four children, teenagers Janet and John, and their younger siblings Margaret and Tommy. A Christmas reunion, *Christmas With The Appleyards*, was shown in 1960. BBC 1952-57 and 1960.

Apprentice, The Reality show in which 14 potential apprentices vie for a position worth an annual salary of £100,000 in Sir Alan Sugar's business empire, overlooked by his very able assistants Nick Hewer and Margaret Mountford (replaced by Karen Brady in 2010). The first series winner in 2005 was Tim Campbell; the second in 2006 was Michelle Dewberry, the third in 2007 was Simon Ambrose, the fourth in 2008, Lee McQueen, the fifth in 2009, Yasmina Siadatan and the sixth in 2010, Stella English. The seventh series in 2011 was fought for a partnership deal with Lord Sugar whereby the electronics magnate invested £250,000 into the business plan of the winner. Tom Pellereau, a 32-year-old inventor, was the ultimate winner. For the 2006 series onwards a sister programme, *The Apprentice: You're Fired!* follows the regular show and consists of an after-show interview of the rejected candidate. This show was presented by Adrian Chiles until Dara O'Briain took over the mantle for Series 6 in 2010. *The Apprentice* format is based on an earlier American series of the same name in which the winner was hired by Donald Trump. A junior version of the show began in 2010, the winner - 17 year old Arjun Rajyagor - receiving £25,000 in funding for his future prospects and further education. The 2011 winner was Zara Brownless BBC2 2005-

Aquarius Presenters: Humphrey Burton, Russell Harty, Peter Hall. Late-night arts magazine programme which was designed as a rival to the BBC's *Omnibus*. It was succeeded by *The South Bank Show* in 1978. ITV 1970-77.

Archers, The Radio soap opera broadcast on BBC Radio 4. It is the world's longest running radio soap and was originally billed as an "everyday story of country folk". The Archers is set in the fictional Midlands village of Ambridge close to Borchester, in the county of Borsetshire, an imaginary county situated between the real counties of Worcestershire and Warwickshire, south of Birmingham in the West Midlands (where the show is recorded). Ambridge itself is sometimes said to be based upon the village of Inkberrow in Worcestershire, where the village pub, The Old Bull,

was the model for the pub The Bull in Ambridge. Other local villages include Penny Hassett, Loxley Barratt, Darrington, Hollerton, Edgeley, Waterley Cross and Lakey Green. The county town of Borsetshire is the cathedral city of Felpersham. Anywhere further away from Ambridge may be referred to humorously with comments such as 'but that's on the other side of Felpersham!'. Many of the storylines concern the title characters, the middle-class Archer family, who own and manage Brookfield Farm. The farm has been passed down the generations from original owner Dan (now deceased) to his son Phil (also deceased) and is now co-owned by three of Phil's children: David (who manages it with his wife Ruth), Elizabeth and Kenton. There are six episodes a week running from Sunday to Friday. All except the Friday evening episode are re-broadcast the following day, and all episodes are edited into a Sunday morning omnibus. Over Easter 1950, a pilot series was broadcast to the English Midlands; it was decided to commission the series for a longer national run. (In the pilot series the Archers' farm was not called Brookfield but 'Wimberton Farm'.) Since 1 January 1951, a fifteen-minute episode (since 1998, twelve minutes) has been transmitted across the UK each weekday, at first on the BBC Light Programme and subsequently on the BBC Home Service (now Radio 4). Originally produced with collaborative input from the Ministry of Agriculture, it was conceived as a means of disseminating information to farmers and smallholders to help increase productivity in the post-war years of rationing and food shortages. Some long-term listeners still refer to "the Min. of Ag. bit" although the programme's educational remit, and the involvement of the government, ended in 1972. The actor Norman Painting played the character of Phil Archer continuously from the first trial series in 1950 until his death on 29 October 2009. As a script writer, his first episode was the one in which Phil's first wife, Grace (Ysanne Churchman), was killed in a fire on the launch day of ITV. Painting had reviewed the initial script of the episode, and substantially rewrote it, gaining his first writing credit as "Bruno Milna". He wrote around 1,200 episodes, culminating in the 10,000th episode. Other characters include **Jill Archer** (Patricia Greene) the second wife of Phil Archer and matriarch of the family. Together they have four children - twins Shula and Kenton, and David and Elizabeth. **Shula Hebden Lloyd,** (Judy Bennett) is the elder daughter of Phil and Jill and twin sister of Kenton. Her first husband, Mark Hebden, a solicitor, was killed in a road accident in 1994. **Kenton Archer** (Richard Attlee, formerly played by Graeme Kirk) is portrayed as the wayward member of the Archer family. **David Archer** (Timothy Bentinck, formerly played by Nigel Carrivick) is the second son of Phil and Jill and has assumed responsibility for Brookfield Farm. **Ruth Archer,** née Pritchard (Felicity Finch) is the wife of David Archer. **Christine Barford** (Lesley Seaward, formerly played by Pamela Mant) is the younger sister of Phil Archer. **Lilian Bellamy,** née Archer (Sunny Ormonde, formerly played by Elizabeth Marlowe) is the twice-widowed, gin-soaked, chain-smoking second daughter of Jack and Peggy Archer. **Tony Archer** (Colin Skipp) is the youngest child and only son of Jack and Peggy Archer. **Helen Archer** (Louiza Patikas, formerly played by Frances Graham and Bonnie Engstrom), Tony and Pat Archer's daughter, makes a cheese called "Borchester Blue" in the farm dairy and runs the organic farm shop, Ambridge Organics, in Borchester. **Tom Archer** (Tom Graham) is the younger son of Tony and Pat. **Joe Grundy** (Edward Kelsey, formerly played by Reg Johnstone and Haydn Jones) is the oldest of the well-established local family, and often provides comic relief. **Eddie Grundy** (Trevor Harrison) is Joe's son. **Clarrie Grundy** née Larkin (Rosalind Adams, formerly played by Heather Bell and Fiona Mathieson) is Eddie Grundy's long-suffering wife. **William Grundy** (Philip Molloy) is the elder son of Eddie and Clarrie. He is gamekeeper for Borchester Land – his boss is Brian Aldridge. **Emma Grundy,** née Carter (Felicity Jones) is the daughter of Susan and Neil Carter, who were horrified when their daughter announced she was marrying into the Grundy family. **Ed Grundy** (Barry Farrimond) is the younger son of Eddie and Clarrie. **Jack Woolley** (Arnold Peters, formerly played by Philip Garston-Jones) is a self-made man originally from Stirchley in

Birmingham who owns the village shop. Until recently he also owned local country-house hotel Grey Gables (now owned by Caroline Sterling and her husband Oliver), the cafe (managed by Kenton Archer) and the Borchester Echo (the local newspaper). **Peggy Woolley**, née Perkins, formerly Archer (June Spencer, briefly played by Thelma Rogers) is the widow of Jack Archer, Phil's elder brother. **Brian Aldridge** (Charles Collingwood) is considered by some the resident 'baddie' of the piece and by others as one of the most interesting and subtle characters in the programme. Married to Jack and Peggy Archer's daughter Jennifer, he is primarily a farmer, but has interests in a string of businesses and is a partner in Tom Archer's sausage business. Brian has had numerous extra-marital affairs during his marriage to Jennifer, including one with the Irish-born translator Siobhan Hathaway, which produced a child, Ruairí. He has an uncomfortable relationship with his gay step-son, Adam, and this has been the source of some friction with his wife. He is exceptionally close to his stepdaughter, Debbie. **Jennifer Aldridge**, née Archer (Angela Piper) is the elder daughter of Peggy Woolley. **Adam Macy** (Andrew Wincott) is the first son of Jennifer Aldridge (his presumed father was former Brookfield farmhand Paddy Redmond). **Debbie Aldridge** (Tamsin Greig) is the daughter of Jennifer and Roger Travers-Macy, but chooses to use the surname of her stepfather Brian. **Nigel Pargetter** (Graham Seed, formerly by Nigel Caliburn) is the eccentric aristocratic owner of Lower Loxley Hall, a mansion on the outskirts of Ambridge. **Elizabeth Pargetter**, née Archer (Alison Dowling) is Phil and Jill's youngest daughter and, along with Kenton, at first rejected village life, attempting a career in publicity in London. **Mike Tucker** (Terry Molloy) lost an eye in a farming accident, for which Brian Aldridge was responsible. **Roy Tucker** (Ian Pepperell) was formerly part of a teenage gang which perpetrated a series of racist attacks on Usha Gupta. **Hayley Tucker**, née Jordan (Lorraine Coady, formerly played by Lucy Davis) comes from Birmingham and first appeared as John Archer's girlfriend. **Brenda Tucker** (Amy Shindler) has had some controversial short-term relationships, with Debbie's husband, with Lilian's then (much younger) lover and with Lilian's son. **Neil Carter** (Brian Hewlett), is another business failure. Susan wanted him to be a white collar worker but he decided that he is a pigman. He used to be Tom's partner in piggery. The family lived in a caravan until he finished building a house on his own land. He dislikes all Grundys but especially Ed, who, until his disappearance, lived in the caravan with Emma and George. **Susan Carter**, née Horrobin (Charlotte Martin) briefly became the most notorious Archers character ever when her imprisonment at Christmas 1993 for assisting her armed-robber brother Clive Horrobin led to the launch of the "Free the Ambridge One" campaign. Questions were asked in the House of Commons of then Home Secretary Michael Howard. **Usha Gupta** (Souad Faress, formerly played by Sudha Bhuchar) works as a solicitor in Felpersham and is one of very few minority ethnic characters in the series. **Rev Alan Franks** (John Telfer) was appointed vicar of Ambridge and neighbouring parishes in 2003, moving from Nottingham where he had previously worked as an accountant and a non-stipendiary minister. **Caroline Sterling**, neé Bone, for a while Pemberton (Sara Coward) moved to the village in the 1977, aged 22, when she was hired by Sid as barmaid in the Bull. **Sid Perks** (Alan Devereux) is landlord of the village pub, The Bull. **Kathy Perks** (Hedli Niklaus), formerly married to Sid now lives at April Cottage with her son Jamie. **Lynda Snell** (Carole Boyd) is the inhabitant of Ambridge Hall, wife of computer expert Robert Snell. **Dan Archer** (Harry Oakes, Monte Crick, Edgar Harrison and Frank Middlemass) was the first owner of Brookfield and the patriarch of the Archer family. The character survived the deaths of the first three actors before finally being killed off in 1986. **Doris Archer** (Gwen Berryman), Dan's wife and mother of Phil Archer and his siblings. Her death was discovered by Shula in 1980. **Grace Archer** (Monica Gray and Ysanne Churchman) was Phil Archer's first wife and the first major character to be killed off. The episode featuring her death was first broadcast on 22 September 1955. The previous night, which happened to be the night that ITV (now ITV1), the UK's first commercial television channel was launched, she received fatal injuries, trying to rescue her horse, Midnight, from a fire. This was seen as a ploy to keep loyal viewers and listeners away from the new station. **Tom Forrest** (George Hart and Bob Arnold) was Doris Archer's brother and a gamekeeper. **Walter Gabriel** (Robert Mawdesley and Chris Gittins), originally a smallholder, was a friend of the Archers' and provided comic relief in the years before the Grundy family were introduced. Walter continually tried to romance Mrs. Perkins, Peggy's mother, who he referred to as Mrs P. Walter Gabriel's phrase "My old pal, my old beauty" remains one of the most enduringly-remembered phrases associated with The Archers, even among non-listeners. **Nelson Gabriel** (Jack May), Walter's son, was for many years the most disreputable character in the village. He had a mysterious criminal past, but latterly ran a bar in Borchester before suddenly disappearing. He died in strange circumstances in South America. On 7th May 2004 listeners to *The Archers* heard a door open with a slow creak, and then a muffled cry. Brian Aldridge had just discovered his gamekeeper, Greg Turner, lying on the floor of a hut with a bullet in his brain. It was the first suicide in the radio drama's 53-year history. *The Archers'* widely recognised theme tune is called *Barwick Green*. It is a "maypole dance" from the suite My Native Heath, written in 1924 by the Yorkshire composer Arthur Wood. The series made national headlines in early 2011 when Vanessa Whitburn, editor since 1992, accidentally revealed on BBC Radio 4's *Today* programme that Nigel Pargetter had died after falling from the roof of his stately home. In April 2011 a youth-oriented spin-off show, *Ambridge Extra*, complete with re-vamped music by British folk group Bellowhead, aired on the digital station Radio 4 Extra, focusing on the younger characters such as Pip Archer, Alice Carter and sulky teenager Jamie Perks. The new show is broadcast twice-weekly in 15 minute slots, with an omnibus edition on Sundays.

Are You Being Served John Inman (Mr Wilberforce Humphries), Mollie Sugden (Mrs Betty Slocombe), Arthur Brough (Mr Ernest Grainger), Frank Thornton (Capt Stephen Peacock), Nicholas Smith (Mr Cuthbert Rumbold), Arthur English (Mr Harman), Wendy Richard (Miss Shirley Brahms), Mike Berry (Mr Spooner), Trevor Bannister (Mr Dick Lucas), Kenneth Waller ('Old' Mr Grace), Alfie Bass (Mr Harry Goldberg), James Hayter (Mr Percival Tebbs), Larry Martyn (Mr Mash). Sitcom written by Jeremy Lloyd and David Croft. Set in the clothes department on the first floor of Grace Brothers, the programme made a star of the camp Inman with his character's catchphrase of "I'm Free" finding its way into many an impersonator's act. BBC1 1973-85. A short-lived spin-off *Grace and Favour* ran for two series in 1992-93 with the cast transferring to the run-down Millstone Manor.

Arena Arts documentary series running sporadically on BBC2 since 1975 and having editors such as Alan Yentob, Nigel Finch and Anthony Wall. One of the most memorable programmes was a profile of David Bowie, *Cracked Actor*, in which Yentob captured the essence of the tortured soul of a pop icon. This 1975 documentary (shown here in 1978) was originally shown as part of the Omnibus series in 1975.

Armchair Theatre When it began on ITV in 1956 with the play *The Outsider*, starring David Kossoff and Adrienne Corri, the series captured a respectable audience rating but it wasn't until 1958, and the arrival of Canadian producer Sydney Newman, that it gained a reputation for the ruthless, down-to-earth, gritty, 'kitchen sink' stories that had the cream of British actors rushing to showcase their talents. Newman's approach was to abandon established dramas and go for a gritty realism with a series of specially commissioned plays by young playwrights such as Harold Pinter, Robert Miller, Ray Rigby and Alun Owen. Pinter's first TV play during that period was *A Night Out*, and was followed that same year by Owen's *Lena, O My Lena*, which starred Billie Whitelaw and Peter McEnery in a terse story of a Liverpool student who falls in love with a factory worker. The earlier productions went out live but this practise was stopped after a tragic night in 1958 when actor Gareth Jones collapsed and died during a performance in *Underground*. There were two major spin-offs from *Armchair Theatre*, John Wyndham's 1962 play *Dumb Martian*, which became the pilot for *Out Of This World*, and James Mitchell's *Magnum for Schneider* (1967), which eventually became the pilot for *Callan*. By this time though Sidney Newman had been headhunted by the BBC, where he became Head of Drama and devised possibly the most famous

BBC series of all time, *Doctor Who*. During the summer months from 1960 onwards the series was alternatively called *Armchair Summer Theatre* and *Armchair Mystery Theatre*. However, when ABC lost its franchise to Thames Television in the late 1960s the series was dropped before being resurrected in 1974 as *Armchair Cinema*, a short-lived series of filmed works, which had the distinction of producing Ian Kennedy Martin's *Regan* (4 June 1974), which the following year became the classic British cop series *The Sweeney*. Between 1978 and 1980 *Armchair Theatre* was resurrected for the last time as *Armchair Thriller*.

Armstrong and Miller Show, The Comedy sketch show that followed on from the duo's four series of Armstrong and Miller which aired on the Paramount Comedy Channel between 1997 and 2001 (the last two series in 1999 and 2001 being shown on Channel 4). Popular recurring characters are the Two World War II airmen who speak with stereotypically cut-glass accents but use the language of the equally stereotypical chav, peppering their sentences with words such as "innit", "blad" and "like". BBC1 2007-. See entry in the comedy section.

Army Game, The William Hartnell (CSM Percy Bullimore), Bill Fraser (Sgt Claude Snudge), Michael Medwin (Corporal Springer), Harry Fowler (Corporal 'Flogger' Hoskins), Charles Hawtrey and Keith Smith (Pte 'Prof' Hatchett), Bernard Bresslaw (Pte 'Popeye' Popplewell), Alfie Bass (Pte 'Excused Boots' Bisley), Norman Rossington and Keith Banks (Pte 'Cupcake' Cook), Frank Williams (Capt Pocket), Mario Fabrizi (Lance Corporal Ernest 'Moosh' Merryweather), Dick Emery (Pte 'Chubby' Catchpole), Geoffrey Sumner and Jack Allen (Major Upshot-Bagley), Bernard Hunter (Capt Pilsworthy), C. B. Poultney (Major Geoffrey Gervaise Duckworth), Ted Lune (Pte Bone), Robert Desmond (Pte Billy Baker), Arthur Mullard (Basher Briggs). This was the most popular comedy show of its day. Set in Hut 29 of the Surplus Ordnance Depot at Nether Hopping, near Itchwick, Staffordshire, the series followed the exploits of a motley bunch of army conscripts. A young Marty Feldman was one of the writers. The series was at its peak between 1958 and 1960 when the characters of Bootsie, Popeye, Cupcake and Prof (Charles Hawtrey), under the guidance of Corporal Springer, invariably managed to get one over on their immediate superior officer Snudge. Bill Fraser and Alfie Bass reprised their popular roles in *Bootsie and Snudge*. ITV 1957-61

Around the World in 80 Days Michael Palin's reconstruction of Phileas Fogg's journey aired on BBC1 in 1989.

Art Attack The red-sweatered Neil Buchanan hosted the CITV show throughout its run and also comes up with many of the ideas to encourage children to get involved with painting. Neil's favourite Art Attack was Lolly Lettering, consisting of a lolly stick, snapped in two and dipped into ink, which enables some very posh calligraphy. His favourite big Art Attack was creating a portrait of the Queen with £250,000 in ten pound notes (loaned from the Bank of England). ITV 1989-2007

Arthur C. Clarke's Mysterious World The celebrated science fiction writer hosted this documentary series from his home in Sri Lanka. Aired on ITV in 1980 and narrated by Gordon Honeycombe, the series concentrated on some of the world's real-life natural phenomena.

Arthur of the Britons Oliver Tobias (Arthur), Rupert Davies (Cerdig), Jack Watson (Llud), Brian Blessed (Mark of Cornwall), Michael Gothard (Kai), George Marishka (Yorath, chief of the Jutes). This series strips away the elaborate medieval view of Camelot, and presents Arthur as a 6th century Welsh chief of a small Celt tribe in Britain constantly under attack from raiders from the East led by Cerdig and from the South led by Mark of Cornwall. Arthur's two confederates Llud and Kai were popular characters and the young Saxon Kai in particular became the hero of the series in the way that Lancelot had done in the traditional story. The fight scenes were authentically shot and the series made a star of the young moody-looking Oliver Tobias. ITV 1972-73

As Seen On TV Television-based celebrity panel game show presented by Steve Jones with team captains Fern Britton and Jason Manford. BBC1 2009

As Time Goes By Judi Dench (Jean Pargetter/Hardcastle), Geoffrey Palmer (Lionel Hardcastle), Moira Brooker (Judith Pargetter/Hanson/Deacon), Philip Bretherton (Alistair Deacon), Jenny Funnell (Sandy), Frank Middlemas (Rocky Hardcastle), Joan Sims (Madge Hardcastle), Moyra Fraser (Penny), Paul Chapman (Stephen), Janet Henfrey (Mrs Bale), David Michaels (Harry), Vivienne Martin (Gwen Flack), Tim Wylton (Lol Ferris). Sitcom created by Colin Bostock-Smith and written by Bob Larbey. Lionel, an ex-army officer and Kenyan coffee planter who returns to England to write his memoirs, entitled *My Life In Kenya*, seeks the help of a temporary secretary to take care of the typing, an agency offers him the services of Judith Pargetter. Lionel invites her out to dinner but chances to meet too with her mother Jean who owns the agency 'Type For You'. During the Korean War she and Lionel had been very close, intent on marriage, but one vital letter went astray and each thought the other had given up. The point now was, could the old fires be stoked after a 38-year parting? And what about the twice-married Judith, who was rather keen on Lionel herself? Such was the situation and the dilemmas at the start of the first series. By the 1995 series Jean and Lionel were married but things were never that simple for the sometimes irascible couple who were both too independent to settle easily into married life. The theme tune was sung by Joe Fagin. BBC1 1992-2005

Ascent of Man Born in Poland in 1908, Californian-based Jacob Bronowski was a mathematician, biologist, philosopher and historian. With several literary critical works to his name, he was a clear choice to provide David Attenborough's BBC2 with the follow-up to the international success of Kenneth Clarke's *Civilisation*. Begun in 1969 and taking four years to complete, the 13-part series arrived on our screens on 5 May 1973. Intended as a digest of the history of science for general viewers, and to match the claims of the Clarke series, it actually ranged further afield than the eurocentric *Civilisation*, although Bronowski retained a rather odd dismissal of pre-Colombian science and technology in the New World. The series faced, however, perhaps a greater challenge than its predecessor, in that the conceptual apparatus of science is less obviously telegenic than the achievements of culture. Nonetheless, the device of the "personal view" which underpinned the series of televisual essays gave the ostensibly dry materials a human warmth that allied them successfully with the presenter-led documentaries already familiar on British screens. *The Ascent of Man* covers, not in strict chronological order but according to the strongly evolutionary model suggested in the title, the emergence of humanity, the agricultural revolution, architecture and engineering, metallurgy and chemistry, mathematics, astronomy, Newtonian and relativistic mechanics, the industrial revolution, Darwinism, atomic physics, quantum physics, DNA and, in the final program, what we would now call neurobiology and cognitive science and artificial intelligence. Sadly, Bronowski died a year after the completion of his masterpiece, possibly from nervous exhaustion at the work load he undertook to bring this series to fruition. BBC2 1973.

Ashes To Ashes A 24-episode sequel (shown over three series of eight episodes) to the critically-acclaimed and multi award-winning *Life On Mars*. Philip Glenister reprised his role as DCI Gene Hunt (swapping the Ford Cortina for an Audi Quattro), flanked by his faithful sidekicks, Ray Carling (played by Dean Andrews) and Chris Skelton (played by Marshall Lancaster). In this series Gene is thrown together with sexy, intelligent, DCI Alex Drake (played by Keeley Hawes). Single mother to daughter Molly, Alex has rapidly risen through the ranks of the Met and, in the modern world of 2008, skilfully uses psychological profiling to capture suspects. When Alex and her daughter are kidnapped she makes a daring attempt at escape, resulting in an horrific accident. Alex suddenly finds herself in 1981 interacting with familiar characters, not just from her own life-time, but also from the detailed reports logged by none other than Sam Tyler, which Alex has previously spent months pouring over. Daniel Mays joined the cast for Series Three, as DCI Jim Keats. The final episode revealed that all the *Life on Mars / Ashes to Ashes* characters were actually dead and existing in some sort of purgatory for police officers, DCI Keats representing the dark side. All except Gene disappear into the Railway Arms for a pint; and the series ends with a newly dead officer arriving, demanding his iPhone and asking where his office has gone. BBC1 2008-10

Ask Aspel BBC1 Children's request show hosted by Michael Aspel sporadically between 1970 and 1981 taking over from *Junior Points of View* as the young viewer's feedback programme.

Ask the Family Popular panel game hosted by Robert Robinson, BBC1 1967-84, consisting of two family teams, usually mum, dad, and kids, taking part in a series of mind-boggling rounds culminating in a series champion. Alan Titchmarsh faithfully revived the show in 1999 on UK Gold (later shown on BBC1) but a somewhat less faithful version was aired on BBC2 in 2005 hosted by children's television presenters Dick and Dom.

At Home with the Braithwaites Amanda Redman (Alison Braithwaite), Peter Davison (David Braithwaite), Lynda Bellingham (Pauline Farnell), Sylvia Syms (Marion Riley), Judy Holt (Elaine Fishwick), Julie Graham (Megan Hartnoll), Sarah Smart (Virginia Braithwaite), Kevin Doyle (Mike Hartnoll), Ishia Bennison (Denise Skidmore), Garry Cooper (Colin Skidmore). Alison Braithwaite is married to David. Together they live with their three daughters. Alison's life is turned upside down when she discovers that the Eurolottery ticket her youngest daughter got her for her birthday has landed her a mega £38,000,000. In a bid to be responsible she decides to use the money for charitable purposes and decides to keep the win a secret from her family. The Yorkshire TV Production was written by Sally Wainwright. ITV 2000-03

At Last The 1948 Show Undoubtedly an inspiration for Monty Python, the sketch show was written by, and starred John Cleese, Tim Brooke-Taylor, Graham Chapman and Marty Feldman; with (the lovely) Aimi Macdonald linking sketches wearing skimpy costumes and talking in her whiny over-the-top manner. Eric Idle and Bill Oddie made occasional appearances and David Frost was the Executive Producer of the show that was a stepping-stone for all its stars. The famous Four Yorkshiremen sketch (a development of the Four Sidney Lotterbies sketch) first saw light of day in this show and not Monty Python as is commonly thought. The full sketch follows: Michael Palin (First Yorkshireman), Graham Chapman (Second Yorkshireman), Terry Jones (Third Yorkshireman), Eric Idle (Fourth Yorkshireman). The Scene: Four well-dressed men are sitting together at a vacation resort with 'Farewell to Thee' playing in the background on Hawaiian guitar. FIRST YORKSHIREMAN: Aye, very passable, that, very passable bit of risotto. SECOND YORKSHIREMAN: Nothing like a good glass of Château de Chasselas, eh, Josiah? THIRD YORKSHIREMAN: You're right there, Obadiah. FOURTH YORKSHIREMAN: Who'd have thought thirty year ago we'd all be sittin' here drinking Château de Chasselas, eh? FIRST YORKSHIREMAN: In them days we was glad to have the price of a cup o' tea. SECOND YORKSHIREMAN: A cup o' cold tea. FOURTH YORKSHIREMAN: Without milk or sugar. THIRD YORKSHIREMAN: Or tea. FIRST YORKSHIREMAN: In a cracked cup, an' all. FOURTH YORKSHIREMAN: Oh, we never had a cup. We used to have to drink out of a rolled up newspaper. SECOND YORKSHIREMAN: The best we could manage was to suck on a piece of damp cloth. THIRD YORKSHIREMAN: But you know, we were happy in those days, though we were poor. FIRST YORKSHIREMAN: Because we were poor. My old Dad used to say to me, "Money doesn't buy you happiness, son". FOURTH YORKSHIREMAN: Aye, 'e was right. FIRST YORKSHIREMAN: Aye, 'e was. FOURTH YORKSHIREMAN: I was happier then and I had nothin'. We used to live in this tiny old house with great big holes in the roof. SECOND YORKSHIREMAN: House! You were lucky to live in a house! We used to live in one room, all twenty-six of us, no furniture, 'alf the floor was missing, and we were all 'uddled together in one corner for fear of falling. THIRD YORKSHIREMAN: Eh, you were lucky to have a room! We used to have to live in t' corridor! FIRST YORKSHIREMAN: Oh, we used to dream of livin' in a corridor! Would ha' been a palace to us. We used to live in an old water tank on a rubbish tip. We got woke up every morning by having a load of rotting fish dumped all over us! House? Huh. FOURTH YORKSHIREMAN: Well, when I say 'house' it was

only a hole in the ground covered by a sheet of tarpaulin, but it was a house to us. SECOND YORKSHIREMAN: We were evicted from our 'ole in the ground; we 'ad to go and live in a lake. THIRD YORKSHIREMAN: You were lucky to have a lake! There were a hundred and fifty of us living in t' shoebox in t' middle o' road. FIRST YORKSHIREMAN: Cardboard box? THIRD YORKSHIREMAN: Aye. FIRST YORKSHIREMAN: You were lucky. We lived for three months in a paper bag in a septic tank. We used to have to get up at six in the morning, clean the paper bag, eat a crust of stale bread, go to work down t' mill, fourteen hours a day, week-in week-out, for sixpence a week, and when we got home our Dad would thrash us to sleep wi' his belt. SECOND YORKSHIREMAN: Luxury. We used to have to get out of the lake at six o'clock in the morning, clean the lake, eat a handful of 'ot gravel, work twenty hour day at mill for tuppence a month, come home, and Dad would thrash us to sleep with a broken bottle, if we were lucky! THIRD YORKSHIREMAN: Well, of course, we had it tough. We used to 'ave to get up out of shoebox at twelve o'clock at night and lick road clean wit' tongue. We had two bits of cold gravel, worked twenty-four hours a day at mill for sixpence every four years, and when we got home our Dad would slice us in two wit' bread knife. FOURTH YORKSHIREMAN: Right. I had to get up in the morning at ten o'clock at night half an hour before I went to bed, drink a cup of sulphuric acid, work twenty-nine hours a day down mill, and pay mill owner for permission to come to work, and when we got home, our Dad and our mother would kill us and dance about on our graves singing Hallelujah. FIRST YORKSHIREMAN: And you try and tell the young people of today that ..... they won't believe you. ALL: They won't! ITV 1967.

Atletico Partick Gordon Kennedy (Jack Roan), Tom McGovern (Ally), Ronnie Letham (Gazza), Iain McColl (Pettigrew), Steven McNicoll (Lachie), Aline Mowatt (Karen Roan), Clive Russell (Bonner), Anne Marie Timoney (Marie). The problems with portraying authentic action has resulted in few sitcoms with a sporting theme but Atletico Partick overcame this problem by having its protagonists play in an amateur Sunday league team which enabled overweight, lumbering actors with few football skills to accurately portray their real-life counterparts. The central character was Jack Roan, a midfield player with a passion for the game, a low sex-drive and a sensual but maritally unfulfilled wife, Karen who is having an affair with Ally, an Atletico Partick player renowned for his sexual philandering. Jack's closest friend is Pettigrew who has his own marital problems (his wife has taken up witchcraft), and most of the other major team members have similar problems. Typical of writer Ian Pattison (the creator of *Rab C Nesbitt*), there were dark undertones beneath the slapstick surface and some serious issues were tackled. BBC1 1996.

Attention Scum! Six-episode anarchic comedy series created by Stewart Lee and Simon Munnery (also known by his stagename of Alan Parker: Urban Warrior), who also starred in the series as his other persona of the League Against Tedium. The series contained surreal stand-up routines atop a transit van and sketches including regulars such as "24 Hour News", performed by Johnny Vegas, operatic intermissions by Kombat opera (Richard Thomas and Lori Lixenberg) and additional routines by the likes of Catherine Tate and Kevin Eldon. The format was based on a 1994 cabaret act, Club Zarathustra, co-founded by Munnery and Lee, and performed at the Edinburgh Festival. BBC2 2001

Auf Wiedersehen Pet Tim Healy (Dennis Patterson), Jimmy Nail ('Oz' Osbourne), Kevin Whately (Neville Hope), Gary Holton (Wayne), Pat Roach (Brian 'Bomber' Busridge), Timothy Spall (Barry Taylor), Christopher Fairbank (Albert Moxey), Julia Tobin (Brenda Hope), Michael Elphick (Magowan). Three Geordie labourers (Oz, Neville and Dennis), a cockney carpenter (Wayne), a Bristolian jack-of-all-trades (Bomber), a Scouse scallywag (Moxey) and a Brummie electrician (Barry) soon become friends after they meet up on a Dusseldorf building site and engage in a series of adventures. Written by Dick Clement and Ian La Frenais and first aired on ITV in 1983, the series became a must-view watch for millions of fans. The second series began in 1986 with the Magnificent Seven reunited to renovate the Derbyshire mansion of gangland boss Ally Fraser (Bill Paterson) and ended up in Spain with them building a swimming pool for the Newcastle-based gangster. Sadly, Gary Holton died during

495

filming of the follow up series in Spain. The show's closing theme song *That's Living Alright* was a top-three hit for Joe Fagin in 1984. In 2002 the gang reunited again (on BBC1) and now Dennis is driving a taxi; Barry's driving a Bentley and has a beautiful Russian wife; Neville's still married to Brenda and is selling prefabricated houses over the Internet; Moxey's working for a local gangster; while Bomber's just been doing 'this and that'. But the series begins with Oz announced as having died. All is soon revealed as Oz arrives at his own wake as the reformed Leonard Jeffrey Osborne (after a spell in prison). Wayne's death is however announced at Oz's 'funeral' but his son Wyman Norris (Noel Clarke) joins the gang. While Oz was behind bars, he met disgraced MP Jeffrey Grainger (Bill Nighy), and the pair have a proposal that should make the whole gang a fortune. Land on either side of the Middlesbrough Transporter Bridge is ripe for development. But the bridge has to go, and the lads' job is to organise its removal. They need to raise £75,000 for the hire of foreign labour to pull the bridge down. But they stand to make £250,000 by selling the bridge. And thus the scene is set for the Magnificent Seven to ride again into the Arizona Desert to sell the bridge to the Chocanaw Americans. A new theme song accompanied this series *Why Aye Man* by Mark Knopfler. The follow up series had the lads flying off to Cuba as representatives of the Overseas Estates Development (OED) department which arranges for British workmen to travel round the world fixing up British Government property, and Neville is recruited by MI6 and is forced to work undercover. Pat Roach died during the filming of this series and the final Christmas special in 2004 (set in Laos) referred to Bomber as having settled down in Arizona. ITV 1983-86; BBC1 2002-04.

Auntie's Bloomers BBC's answer to *It'll Be Alright On The night* began in 1991 and ran sporadically throughout the 90s. Hosted by Terry Wogan the programme followed the tried and tested format of showing embarrassing out-takes of BBC recordings. *Auntie's Sporting Bloomers* (1995-97), also hosted by Terry, was a spin-off series and there have been several other hybrid series.

Avengers, The Patrick MacNee (John Steed), Honor Blackman (Cathy Gale), Diana Rigg (Emma Peel), Linda Thorson (Tara King), Patrick Newell (Mother), Ian Hendry (Dr David Keel), Ingrid Hafner (Carol Wilson), Julie Stevens (Venus Smith), Jon Rollason (Dr Martin King), Douglas Muir (One-Ten), Arthur Hewlett (One-Twelve), Rhonda Parker (Rhonda). Produced by ABC and first broadcast on ITV in January 1961, The Avengers began as a spin-off from the less popular 1960 drama *Police Surgeon* in which Ian Hendry played Dr Geoffrey Brent and Ingrid Hafner his secretary Amanda Gibbs. The producer Leonard White made these two characters the basis for his new series of *The Avengers*, albeit with a change of names, and Steed was initially a minor role. The first episode saw Dr Keel's wife murdered by a drugs gang and his plea for help to British Intelligence agent John Steed, hence the title of the series. Steed's bosses at this time were One-Ten and One-Twelve. By the time the 161st and last episode had aired in September 1969 The Avengers had become one of the most popular television series of all time, eventually reaching audiences in 120 countries, a record that still stands today. John Steed was the common thread of the series, during the course of which he had six different partners. After physician Dr. David Keel came two seasons of anthropologist and judo expert Catherine Gale, who was not always Steed's partner during the show's second season; occasionally he was accompanied by physician Dr. Martin King or jazz singer Venus Smith. Much of the show's international popularity was due however to the eventual pairing of Steed and Emma Peel. The series which started as a serious secret agent drama now became a stylish blend of espionage, fantasy, fashion, humour, manners and quasi-science fiction that had international appeal. Each episode began with a typical arty shot of two champagne glasses, one upturned, with Steed appearing in the background dressed in a Pierre Cardin suit, bowler hat, umbrella on his arm, about to pop open the champers when a gun-in-hand Mrs Peel appears to nonchalantly shoot off the cork before they eventually raise a toast to each other. Steed then draws a sword from his umbrella in order to cut and deliver a red carnation to his partner who promptly places it in his lapel, all the time Laurie Johnson's dramatic music resounding majestically in the background (Johnny Dankworth's original theme was replaced with the introduction of colour and the selling to the American market). Produced by Albert Fennell and Brian Clemens these magnificent stylised episodes invariably began with a top agent being bumped off in outlandish fashion by some megalomaniac intent on world domination although quite often the surreal and sometimes absurd situations were shown to be perfectly reasonable at the denouement although the tongue-in-cheek splendour of it all was apparent right up until the closing shots of the two action heroes departure in an evermore bizarre mode of transport. For the record Steed lived at 3 Duchess Mews, London, drove a vintage Bentley and insisted his coffee be stirred anticlockwise (remind you of anyone?), his trademark bowlers were often steel reinforced and often demobilised attackers. Mrs Peel was a karate expert who drove a Lotus Elan and was thought to be the widow of test pilot Peter Peel, although he eventually turned up alive which caused Mrs Peel to retire from the service. Unknown actress Linda Thorson replaced Diana Rigg as the ever-grinning relatively unathletic Tara King who brought a dash of flirtation to the part and the rarely seen wheelchair-bound controller 'Mother' was given a more prominent and regular role. Among the most memorable, and scary, episodes was *The House That Never Was* whereby Steed and Mrs Peel are involved in an automobile accident on their way to attending a party at a soon-to-close air base, but they arrive to find the place completely deserted. After a series of strange experiences, Steed is knocked out and reawakens at the scene of the auto accident, this time without Emma, and returns to the air base to find the party in full swing. The key to the mystery may be the milk float that is heard making its rounds the whole time. The three episodes including the killing machines, known as cybernauts, were also interesting diversions of an always surprising and inspiring series. Fennell and Clemens managed to persuade Patrick Macnee to reprise his role in the 1976-77 series of *The New Avengers* with Joanna Lumley playing former ballerina Purdey and Gareth Hunt playing weapons expert and martial artist Mike Gambit. ITV 1961-69.

Babes in the Wood Karl Howman (Charlie), Samantha Janus (Ruth), Denise Van Outen (Leigh), Natalie Walter (Caralyn), Mark Hayford (Benito), Madeleine Curtis (Frankie). Sitcom written by Geoff Deane (former vocalist with pop group Modern Romance). The raunchy adventures of three independent twenty-something blondes who share a flat in St John's Wood, London (hence the title). Ruth, is the neurotic and overbearing one, Leigh the streetwise ladette, and Caralyn the vague and rather stupid one. Across the hall is their neighbour Charlie Lovall, one-time owner of a successful chain of video shops, now divorced and having to contend with diminished wealth because his ex-wife has cleaned him out. The only remnant of his past success is his Porsche, a vehicle which he refers to as 'the lovewagon'. Charlie has a love-hate relationship with the girls, and Ruth in particular, whom he insists on calling Ruthie, much to her chagrin. Beyond the flat is Bar Coda, where Leigh works as a stroppy waitress for Benito, an ex public-schoolboy who looks down his nose at her and her 'common' friends. Frankie replaced Ruth as a babe in Series 2. ITV 1998-99.

Baby Ballroom Reality television series presented by Kate Thornton. Twelve pairs of juvenile ballroom dancers, aged between six and eleven, competed for the title of Baby Ballroom Champion. The three celebrity judges were singer Ray Quinn, actress Bonnie Langford and dance tutor Pierre Dulaine. The public decided the eventual winners, Kim and Josh. ITV 2007

Bachelor Father Ian Carmichael (Peter Lamb), Gerald Flood (Harry), Joan Hickson (Mrs Pugsley), Colin Gordon (Mr Gibson), Pauline Yates (Mrs Moore), Rona Anderson (Mary), Briony McRoberts (Anna), Ian Johnson (Ben), Roland Pickering and Andrew Bowen (Donald), Beverley Simons (Jane), Michael Douglas (Freddie), Kevin Moran (Christopher), Geraldine Cowper (Jo), Jacqueline Cowper (Ginny), Diana King (Nora). Delightful comedy based on the true-life circumstances of Peter Lloyd

Jeffcock, bachelor foster parent of 12 children. Ian Carmichael chose to play the big-hearted wealthy bachelor as his next television excursion following his hugely successful portrayal of Bertie Wooster in *The World of Wooster* and although it never reached the same level of popularity with the viewers it was a heart-warming experience. BBC1 1970-71.

Bachelors Walk Keith McErlean (Barry), Don Wycherley (Raymond), Simon Delaney (Michael). Radio Telefís Éireann comedy drama series created by Tom Hall, Kieran Carney and John Carney and based around three single men living in a house in Dublin's Bachelors Walk. RTE 1 2001-03. After three series a one-off Christmas special which aired on Boxing Day (St Stephen's Day) 2006 on RTÉ Two, brought the story to a conclusion.

Bad Boys Freddie Boardley (Fraser Hood), Karl Howman (Wayne Todd), Alex Norton (Malky Mulherron), Simon Donald (Inspector McKenna), Masami Kikuchi (James), Malcolm Shields (Rumey), Ashley Jensen (Morag), Aline Mowat (Betty Hood), Sally Howitt (Maureen). Wayne Todd is fresh out of Wandsworth prison and decides to run a pub in Glasgow with his old cell mate Fraser Hood. However, investigations are already under way, as Fraser's nightclub has been destroyed by an explosion, and he soon finds himself caught up in the violent gangland of Glasgow. BBC1 1995-96.

Bad Girls ITV drama set in G Wing of the fictional Larkhall women's prison. In the first series the liberal Wing Governor Helen Stewart (Simone Lahbib) struggles to impose her authority over inmates and officers alike. Inmate Rachel Hicks (Joanne Froggatt) makes a mortal enemy of G-Wing's psychotic-bisexual-lifer, Michelle 'Shell' Dockley (Debra Stephenson) and Dockley's henchwoman Denny Blood (Alicia Eyo) with calamitous results; difficult prisoner Nikki Wade (Mandana Jones) falls in love with Helen; unscrupulous warder Jim Fenner (Jack Ellis) forms an alliance with Dockley, and the Wing Governor ultimately falls for the charms of the intellectual Nikki. Over the course of the following eight series the over-the-top storylines were criticised for their violence and tawdriness but the viewing figures always reflected a tolerance by the viewing public. Series 8 experienced the arrival of new Deputy Governor Lou Stoke as assistant to Governor Joy Masterson. Other cast members include Victoria Alcock (Julie Saunders), Anthonia Lanre Ajose (Femi Bada), Isabelle Amyes (Barbara Hunt), Denise Black (Jessie Devlin), Luisa Bradshaw-White (Lorna Rose), Kellie Bright (Cassie Tyler), Victoria Bush (Tina Purvis/O'Kane), Pauline Campbell (Al Mackenzie), Lara Cazalet (Zandra Plackett), Nathan Constance (Josh Mitchell), Sharon Duncan-Brewster, Nicole Faraday (Snowball Merriman), Lindsey Fawcett (Shaz Wiley), Oliver Fox (Sean Parr), Helen Fraser (Sylvia Hollamby), James Gaddas (Neil Grayling), Linda Henry (Yvonne Atkins), Michael Higgs (Dr Thomas Waugh), Claire King (Karen Betts), Jane Lowe (Monica Lindsay), Siobhan McCarthy (Roisin Connor), Philip McGough (Dr Nicholson), Ashley Miller (Carol Byatt), Kika Mirylees (Julie Johnston), Kerry Norton (Maxi Purvis), Kim Oliver (Buki Lester), Kate O'Mara (Virginia O'Kane), Paul Opacic (Mark Waddle), Helen Schlesinger ('Mad' Tessa Spall), Joe Shaw (Dominic McAllister), Kate Steavenson-Payne (Charlotte Myddleton), Kim Taylforth (Marilyn Fenner), Gideon Turner (Robin Dunstan), Lisa Turner (Gina Rossi), Eugene Walker (Officer Blakeson), Tracey Wilkinson (Di Barker), Jade Williams (Rhiannon Dawson), Amanda Barrie (Bev Tull), Amanda Donohoe (Lou Stoke), Stephanie Beacham (Phyl Oswyn), Sid Owen (Donny Kimber), Nicola Stapleton (Janine Nebeski), Angela Bruce (Mandy Goodhue), Helen Fraser (Sylvia Hollamby), Dannielle Brent (Natalie Buxton), Colin Salmon (Dr Rowan Dunlop), Kika Mirylees (Julie Johnston), Antonia Okonma (Darlene Cake), Liz May Brice (Pat Kerrigan), Ellie Haddington (Joy Masterton). ITV 1999-2006

Bagpuss Each episode opens with the staccato chimed music by Sandra Kerr and John Faulkner before Oliver Postgate (who also wrote and co-created the series) begins "Once upon a time, Not so long ago, There was a little girl and her name was Emily, And she had a shop. There it is. It was rather an unusual shop because it didn't sell anything. You see, everything in that shop window was a thing that somebody had once lost, and Emily had found, and brought home to Bagpuss, Emily's cat Bagpuss, the most

Important, the most beautiful, the most magical, saggy old cloth cat in the whole wide world" The girl seen as Emily in the sepia sequences at the start of the programme was Emily Firmin, daughter of co-creator Peter Firmin. Emily (who doesn't appear in the stories) owns a Victorian lost-and-found shop (Bagpuss & Co) and when she recites her magical spell, Emily awakens her pink-and-white striped cloth cat (who can make his thoughts visible in bubbles above his head) and when he wakes up, all his friends come to life and begin to repair whatever item Emily has found. The friends include Professor Yaffle, full name Augustus Barclay Yaffle, the carved wooden book-end. He is the brains of the outfit, or so he'd like to think. He is very knowledgeable, but a bit proud, and the mice love to play tricks on him to bring him down a peg or two. Gabriel Croaker (voiced by John Faulkner), of the "Tea-Time Toads" is a banjo-playing toad, who lives on top of the round tin on the shelf. Madeleine Remnant (voiced by Sandra Kerr) is a rag doll, who sits in a wicker chair. She never moves anywhere, and is happy to be a mother to the mice, tell stories and sing songs with Gabriel. The mice are really the major characters, and tend to get involved in everything that goes on. Their pride and joy is the Marvellous Mechanical Mouse Organ, which plays rolls of music, and projects a picture onto the screen, like a television. The six mice are Charliemouse, who wears a grey checked suit, and appears to be their leader, Eddiemouse, who wears a blue suit with a green jacket, Janiemouse, who wears a pink dress with a red waistcoat, Jenniemouse, who wears a blue dress, Lizziemouse, who wears a blue flowery dress with a blue waistcoat, and Williemouse, who wears a flowery top and red trousers. Only 13 episodes were made and first broadcast on BBC1 in 1974, although they have been repeated on numerous occasions.

Baking Made Easy Former Oxford model Lorraine Pascale (b. 17 November 1972) tried a number of career paths including modelling, interior design, hypnotherapy and working as a mechanic. She first came to attention as the first black British model to appear on the cover of American *Elle*. She took a Prue Leith diploma cookery course in 2005 and after gaining her diploma established herself as a specialist cakemaker, with an exclusive contract with Selfridges (at the suggestion of Marco Pierre White). Lorraine opened her own shop, Ella's Bakehouse, in Covent Garden and has recently studied at Thames Valley University in Culinary Arts. This BBC2 series, first shown in January 2011, was followed by *Home Cooking Made Easy,* which aired later in the year.

Balamory Action series for pre-school children created by Brian Jameson and based around the small island community of Balamory in Scotland (real-life Tobermory on the Isle of Mull) where the action often takes place in one of the many coloured houses. 'What's the story in Balamory today?' Characters include, Archie the kilted inventor (who lives in the pink castle, which is in fact at Fenton Tower in North Berwick. Archie is played by Miles Jupp.), Miss Hoolie the local school teacher and main character (who always wears a green cardigan with stripes and a green skirt. Miss Hoolie is played by Julie Wilson Nimmo.), PC Plum (played by Andrew Agnew) the local bobby who loves riding around the town on his bicycle, Josie Jump the fitness guru (who lives in the yellow house and was originally played by Buki Akib but replaced by Kasia Haddad in 2005), Spencer the painter (who lives in the orange house. Played by Rodd Christensen.), Penny Pocket (played by Kim Tserkezie) who helps Suzi Sweet (Played by Mary Riggans) in the shop, and Edie McCredie (Played by Juliet Kadzow) and her bus "Daisy" which is often parked outside the Post Office. BBC and Cbeebies 2002-05.

Baldy Man, The A series of dialogue-free, visual narratives - with two distinct stories per half-hour - that was strongly reminiscent of *Mr Bean*. The Baldy Man (Gregor Fisher) is an intensely vain, irritating chap who, inside or outside his stone-clad bungalow, cannot stop admiring himself in anything that gives off a reflection. What the Baldy Man somehow doesn't notice is what the rest of us see: he's a rotund, sweaty, deeply unattractive man with but a few strands of hair greased across his pate, someone unable to fathom human relationships and who endures a succession of mishaps with inanimate objects. The character of the Baldy Man was created by Fisher and Colin Gilbert for *Naked Video* but really caught the eye in a 1989 series of photo-booth

TV commercials for Hamlet cigars, in which, vainly, he tried to obscure his shiny head before the flash popped. ITV 1995-98.

Balls of Steel Comedy series hosted by Mark Dolan, where his special guests perform stunts or hidden camera set-ups in the presence of celebrities or the British public. Regular contributors include Alex Zane who presents a fake game show; Thaila Lucia Zucchi (best known for her appearance on Big Brother 8 as a fake Australian housemate) who plays a bunny boiler who flirts with a man whilst in the company of his girlfriend to provoke a reaction from her; Jason Attar (replaced by Barrie Hall for Series 2) as the 'Annoying Devil'; and Michael Locke and Matthew Pritchard who go by the names Pancho and Pritchard and deliberately inflict extreme pain on themselves. This is the only segment to take place within the Balls of Steel studio, rather than being shown on the video screen. C4 2005- *Massive Balls of Steel* is a highlights show on E4.

Ballykissangel Stephen Tompkinson (Father Clifford), Dervla Kirwan (Assumpta Fitzgerald), Tony Doyle (Brian Quigley), Niall Tobin (Father MacAnally), Gary Whelan (Brendan Kearney), Peter Caffrey (Padraig O'Kelly), Peter Hanly (Ambrose Egan), Tina Kellegher (Niamh Quigley/Egan/Dillon), Lorcan Cranitch (Sean Dillon), Frankie McCafferty (Donal), Deirdre Donnelly (Siobhan Mehigan/Kearney), Birdy Sweeney (Eamon Byrne), Victoria Smurfit (Orla O'Connell), Don Wycherley (Father Aidan O'Connell), Aine Ni Mhuiri (Kathleen), Joe Savino (Liam), Bosco Hogan (Dr Michael Ryan), Doreen Keogh (Imelda Egan), John Cleere (Kevin), Kate McEnery (Emma Dillon), Robert Taylor (Father Vincent Sheahan), Catherine Cusack (Frankie Sullivan), Katie Cullen (Grainne Dooley), Ciaran Owens (Dermot Dooley), Marion O'Dwyer (Oonagh Dooley), James Ellis (Uncle Minto), Jimmy Nesbitt (Leo McGarvey), Colin Farrell (Danny Byrne), Alan Barry (Supt/Insp. Foley), Owen Teale (Conor Devlin). First broadcast on BBC 1 in 1996. Father Clifford, an English priest, is transferred to a small Irish village and attempts to come to terms with the natural prejudices of some of the locals. At the end of Series Three in 1998 Stephen Tompkinson and Dervla Kirwan left the series, their poignant closing scene depicting Father Clifford embracing the dying Assumpta. Father Aidan O'Connell became the new priest on the block but the series developed into something of a soap opera and began to focus more on the interesting group of characters rather than any one individual. Sadly, Birdy Sweeney died during filming of the fourth series and Tony Doyle during filming of the final series, shown in 2001. *Ballykissangel* was filmed in Avoca, Co Wicklow, and such was the enormous popularity of the series, Avoca became a major tourist attraction. Ex *That's Life* presenter Kieran Prendiville created the series. BBC1 1996-2001.

Band of Gold Cathy Tyson (Carol Johnson), Geraldine James (Rose Garrity), Barbara Dickson (Anita Braithwaite), Samantha Morton (Tracy Richards), Tony Doyle (George Ferguson), Lena Headey (Colette), Ruth Gemmell (Gina Dickson), Richard Moore (Curly), Anthony Milner (Bob), David Schofield (Insp/DCI Newall). Drama series created by Kay Mellor. The series begins with Gina Dickson, a young mother in Yorkshire, throwing out her abusive husband and borrowing from a loan shark to pay off her debts. She meets Carol, a prostitute who teaches Gina how to "work the lane" (a reference to "Lumb Lane" which is a real street in Manningham, Bradford), and introduces her to the world of ponces, punters, and police. Gina also meets Carol's friends: Rose, an older hooker who rules the lane, Anita, a selfish middle-class schemer, and Tracey, a young runaway who's hooked on drugs and her pimp. Despite Carol's warnings, Gina discovers the worst that can happen to a woman who works the lane (she is murdered). By the end of the six-part series Carol and her friends decide to pack it in, go legit, and form a business (a cleaning co-operative named Scrubbit) that will get back at the loan shark. The theme song *Love Hurts* was performed by Barbara Dickson. By Series Three only Cathy and Rose remained of the original four girls and the series name became *Gold*. ITV 1995-97.

Band Waggon Comedy radio show broadcast by the BBC from 1938 to 1939 and starring Arthur Askey and Richard Murdoch. Many of their sketches had Arthur and Richard sharing a top floor flat in Broadcasting House along with Lewis the goat, and pigeons named Basil, Lucy, Ronald and Sarah. Other regular characters included Mrs Bagwash the char and her daughter Nausea, both of whom were often referred to but never heard. Arthur was courting Nausea but he never seemed to be getting anywhere. The lad's adventures often ended violently with Arthur typically falling off a ladder or such-like, but always ended with the famous Bandwaggon crash. A corner of the stage was roped off like a boxing ring, and a large pile of assorted metal objects were piled up inside. At the appropriate moment it was pushed over by a sound effects man. One of Bandwaggon's most popular features was 'Mr Walker wants to know', in which actor Syd Walker played an old Cockney junkman. He would enter to the sound of his signature tune - *Any rags bottles or bones*. Then he would relate some recent events in his life and ask listeners to write in and advise him what to do, with his phrase 'What would you do chums?'. Bandwaggon only ran for a total of 55 shows, but it had an enormous impact. It established a new formula - a regular weekly comedy and music show at the same time each week. It was also the first comedy show to be designed specifically for the radio, as opposed to one made up of variety acts.

Bargain Hunt Follow-on programme from *The Great Antiques Hunt*. Two teams of two are given a budget to spend at an antiques fair to buy several items which they would later sell. An expert is assigned to each team to help them decide what to buy. The teams each have one hour to buy whatever they wanted with the money. One week later the items purchased are sold in a real auction and the team which makes the most profit (or the least loss) is the winner. If the team makes a profit then they keep it. Originally airing as a daytime BBC1 show hosted by David Dickinson in 2000, it was promoted into a prime-time slot in 2002, whereupon Tim Wonnacott took over a daytime version. The primetime version was axed in April 2005 but the daytime version continues.

Barlow at Large Stratford Johns (Det Chief Supt Charles Barlow), Norman Comer (Det. Sgt Rees), Derek Newark (Det. Insp. Tucker). Created by Elwyn Jones, this spin-off from *Softly Softly* saw Barlow assigned, rather uncomfortably, to the Home Office. In 1974 the title changed to *Barlow*. BBC1 1971-75. See also *Z Cars* and *Second Verdict*.

Baron, The Steve Forrest (John Mannering 'The Baron'), Sue Lloyd (Cordelia Winfield), Colin Gordon (John Alexander Templeton-Green), Paul Ferris (David Marlowe). Stories of an American millionaire antique dealer who drives a Jensen (registration BAR 1) and is really an undercover agent. Mannering's nickname is taken from his family's ranch in Texas. The series was produced by Monty Berman with music by Edwin Astley, and the stories were loosely based on the character created by John Creasey. ITV 1966-67.

Baron, The Reality show aired over three weekly episodes in which Suzanna Shaw, Malcolm McLaren and Mike Reid (the latter two now both deceased) competed for a vacant Baronial title in the small Scottish town of Gardenstown, near Banff, Aberdeenshire. The show saw Mike elected into the aristocracy, winning the esteemed title Baron of Troup, beating off competition from the legendary Sex Pistols manager and the former pop singer. Mike Reid died in between shooting and airing and Mike's wife Shirley holds the title 'Baroness of Troup' and the title of The Baron can be passed down to the Reid family descendants. ITV 2008

Battle of the Brains General knowledge quiz show hosted by Paddy O'Connell. Two teams of six plus a non-playing captain went head-to-head in a game where the captains decided who answered the questions. The show's tagline was "It's not what they know, but who they know". Nicky Campbell replaced Paddy for Series Two. BBC2 2008-09

BBC The British Broadcasting Corporation was founded on 18 October 1922 and its first radio transmission was on 14 November of that year, from station 2LO, located at Marconi House, London. The organization is often referred to as "the Beeb", a nickname originally dubbed by Peter Sellers in The Goon Show in the 1950s, when he referred to the "Beeb Beeb Ceeb". It was then borrowed, shortened and popularised by Kenny Everett. Another nickname, now less commonly used, is "Auntie", possibly a reference to the 'aunties' and 'uncles' who were presenters of children's programmes in early days. On 1 October 1936 the first television broadcasts took place, from a converted wing of Alexandra Palace in London. It was very much a rich man's luxury in the early days and by the time it was taken off the air, two days before Britain declared war on Germany, there were less than 20,000 television sets in Britain. The last pre-war programme aired on 1 September 1939; it was a Mickey Mouse cartoon, *Mickey's Gala Premiere*. BBC television returned on 7 June 1946 at 3 p.m. Jasmine Bligh, one of the original announcers, uttered the first words saying, 'Good afternoon everybody. How are you? Do you remember me, Jasmine Bligh?' The Mickey Mouse cartoon of 1939 was repeated twenty minutes later. Alexandra Palace was the home of the channel until the early 1950s when the majority of production moved to the Lime Grove Studios, and then in 1960 the headquarters moved to its present site, the purpose-built BBC Television Centre at White City, also in London. BBC2 was launched in April 1964 and the original station then became BBC 1. Prior to its launch, BBC2 was promoted on the BBC channel by animated adverts featuring the campaign mascots "Hullabaloo" (a mother kangaroo) and "Custard" (her joey). The intended launch date of 20 April 1964 was put back a day due to a power failure, *Play School* eventually becoming the first programme to be shown officially on the new channel. BBC2 was broadcast only on the 625 line UHF system, so was not available to viewers with 405-line VHF sets. BBC1 and ITV later joined BBC2 on 625-line UHF but continued to simulcast on 405-line VHF until 1985. In July 1967, BBC2 became the first channel in Europe to begin regular broadcasts in colour, the thirteen part series *Civilisation* was created to showpiece the new colour technology. During the evenings, alternative programmes are broadcast on BBC Two Northern Ireland, BBC Two Scotland and BBC Two Wales. In addition, BBC Wales broadcasts a special, digital-only channel, BBC 2W, which contains more opt-outs than BBC Two Wales, an analogue-only service. BBC Two Northern Ireland's offering includes local news and weather updates, whilst BBC Scotland broadcasts variations from the main network on BBC Two Scotland, such as Newsnight Scotland, and often Gaelic-language programmes under the banner "BBC Two Alba". BBC Choice was launched on 23 September 1998. It was the first British TV channel to broadcast exclusively in digital format. BBC 3 replaced BBC Choice and was launched on 9 February 2003, eleven months after the originally planned launch date (and the launch of BBC Four which was launched on 2 March 2002). BBC 3 and BBC 4 programmes are beyond the scope of this book. The BBC runs ten national domestic radio stations, the main five being Radios 1, 2, 3, 4 and 5 Live. Radio 1 (FM: 97.7 MHz - 99.7 MHz) was launched at 7.00am on 30 September 1967 with disc jockey Tony Blackburn playing "Flowers in the Rain" by The Move. Radio 2 (FM: 88.1 MHz - 89.7 MHz), launched at the same time as Radio 1, and evolved from the Light Programme which had been broadcasting since 1945. Radio 3 (FM: 90 MHz - 93 MHz) was launched as The BBC Third Programme on 29 September 1946 but changed its name in line with Radio 1 and 2. Similarly, Radio 4 evolved from the Home Service, launched in 1939. Radio 5 Live (MW: 693 kHz, 909 kHz) was launched as Radio 5 at 9am on 27 August 1990 and became Radio 5 Live on 28 March 1994. BBC radio headquarters is at Broadcasting House, Portland Place, London; the building itself is designed in the shape of a ship. The BBC is primarily funded by levying television licence fees. Its motto is "Nation Shall Speak Peace Unto Nation". Director-Generals of the BBC have included Sir John Reith (1927–1938), Sir Frederick Ogilvie (1938–1942), Sir Cecil Graves and Robert W. Foot (joint Directors-General, 1942–1943), Robert W. Foot (1942–1944), Sir William Haley (1944–1952), Sir Ian Jacob (1952–1959), Sir Hugh Greene (1960–1969), Sir Charles Curran (1969–1977), Sir Ian Trethowan (1977–1982), Alasdair Milne (1982–1987), Sir Michael Checkland (1987–1992), John Birt (1992–2000), Greg Dyke (2000–2004) and Mark Thompson (June 22, 2004 -present).

BBC Young Musician of the Year Televised biennial music competition designed for British musicians, all of whom must be eighteen years of age or under. The competition was founded in 1978 by Humphrey Burton and Walter Todds, both of whom are former members of the BBC Television Music Department. In 1994, the use of percussion instruments was permitted, alongside the existing keyboard, string, brass and woodwind categories. The full list of winners: 1978 Michael Hext (trombone); 1980 Nicholas Daniel (Oboe); 1982 Anna Markland (Piano); 1984 Emma Johnson (Clarinet); 1986 Alan Brind (Violin); 1988 David Pyatt (Horn); 1990 Nicola Loud (Violin); 1992 Freddy Kempf (Piano) ; 1994 Natalie Clein (Cello); 1996 Rafal Zambrzycki Payne (Violin); 1998 Adrian Spillett (Percussion); 2000 Guy Johnston (Cello); 2002 Jennifer Pike (Violin); 2004 Nicola Benedetti (Violin); 2006 Mark Simpson (Clarinet); 2008 Peter Moore (Trombone), 2010 Lara Omeroglu (Piano). Peter Moore, aged 12, was the youngest winner of the award. Natalie Clein became the first British winner of the Eurovision Competition for Young Musicians. BBC2 1978-

Beadle's About Jeremy James Anthony Gibson Beadle (born in Hackney, 12 April 1948 and died North London 30 January 2008) was an iconic wit, raconteur, charity fundraiser and television presenter. This hidden camera show based on the earlier *Candid Camera*, where members of the public became victims of elaborate practical jokes, at its peak attracted approximately 15 million viewers, making it one of ITV's most popular Saturday night programmes during that period. Jeremy would often deliver the 'reveal' dressed as a policeman and in 1993, a man was arrested for trying to pull the beard off a policeman, thinking it was Jeremy Beadle in disguise! ITV 1986-96. See also *Game For A Laugh*.

Bear Grylls Born Edward Michael Grylls, Bembridge, Isle of Wight, 7 June 1974, the son of the late Conservative party politician Sir Michael Grylls and grandson of Patricia Ford, an Ulster Unionist Party MP. Bear is a television presenter and adventurer who lives on a barge on the River Thames and an island in North Wales. His Channel 4 series *Bear Grylls: Born Survivor* (first shown on the Discovery Channel in 2006 and known as *Man vs. Wild* in America), in which he is parachuted into remote locations all around the world to display survival techniques, has come in for constant media criticism for stage-management of scenes and Bear's comfortable 'base camp'. In July 2009, Grylls was appointed the youngest ever Chief Scout at the age of 35.

Bear's Tale, A See *Bo' Selecta!*

Beat the Boss CBBC game show presented by Saira Khan. Two teams, "The Bright Sparks" and "The Big Shots", children and adults respectively, have to create a product that will appeal to the children's market. The team with the most votes wins and then the winners get a limousine ride while the losers take the bus. Cameron Johnson replaced Khan as presenter in 2009. BBC1 2006- In September 2008, an Irish version of the show in Irish language started on BBC Northern Ireland. Hosted by Céara Ní Choinn, it is titled Gaisce Gnó (Be the Business).

Beat the Star Game show, hosted by Vernon Kay, in which a member of the public goes head-to-head with a celebrity in a series of physical and mental challenges in a bid to win a £50,000 cash prize. If the celebrity reigned supreme then the kitty was rolled over to the following week for the first series but for the second series a rolled over amount was defended by the host in an end-of-series finale hosted by Phillip Schofield. Undefeated super-middleweight boxer Joe Calzaghe comfortably won this challenge and the lion's share of the £150,000 rollover for his two designated charities. ITV 2008-09

Beautiful People Luke Ward-Wilkinson (Simon Doonan), Aidan McArdle (Andy Doonan), Layton Williams (Kylie Parkinson), Olivia Colman (Debbie Doonan), Sophie Ash (Ashlene Doonan), Meera Syal (Aunty Hayley), Sarah Niles (Reba), Tameka Empson (Johoyo), Gary Amers (Sacha), Brenda Fricker (Narg), Samuel Barnett (Narrator as Simon in present day scenes). 12-part drama series written by Jonathan Harvey. Set in Reading during the late 1990s, 14-year-old Simon Doonan and his best friend Kyle, better known as Kylie, dream of living in London with the "beautiful people". Simon lives with his dysfunctional family: the gin drinking mother (Debbie), blind ex-druggie hippie aunt (Hayley), slutty sister (Ashlene), Irish wine-experimental father (Andy) and briefly, his angel-turned-devil grandmother (Narg). BBC2 2008-09

Bed-Sit Girl, The Sheila Hancock (Sheila Ross), Dilys Laye (Dilys), Derek Nimmo (David), Hy Hazell (Liz). Sitcom written by Ronald Wolfe and Ronald Chesney. Sheila, a typist living in a bed-sit, has aspirations for a better life. BBC 1965-66.

Bedtime Sheila Hancock (Alice Oldfield), Timothy West (Andrew Oldfield), Alun Armstrong (Neil Henshaw), Emma Pierson (Sapphire), Doon Mackichan (Faith), Kevin McNally (Simon), Claire Skinner (Sarah Newcombe), Stephen Tompkinson (Paul Newcombe), Meera Syal (Ruby), Adam Paul Harvey (Ralph), Sienna Miller (Stacey – Ralph's girlfriend), James Bolam (Ronnie). Comedy drama series written by Andy Hamilton, revolving around the bedtime conversations of couples – or in one case a father and son – living in adjoining houses on a suburban London street. BBC1 2001-03.

Beggar My Neighbour Reg Varney (Harry Butt), Pat Coombs (Lana Butt), Peter Jones (Series 1) and Desmond Walter-Ellis (Gerald Garvey), June Whitfield (Rose Garvey). Sitcom written by Ken Hoare and Mike Sharland, its premise being the attempts of the Garveys to match the lifestyle of the more affluent Butts. BBC1 1967-68.

Beiderbecke Affair, The James Bolam (Trevor Chaplin), Barbara Flynn (Jill Swinburne), Dudley Sutton (Mr Carter), Keith Smith (Mr Wheeler), Dominic Jephcott (DS/DI Hobson), Terence Rigby (Big Al), Danny Schiller (Little Norm), Colin Blakely (Chief Supt. Forrest), Beryl Reid (Sylvia). Drama series written by Alan Plater. Trevor teaches woodwork at Leeds Comprehensive and likes to listen to jazz. His girlfriend Jill teaches English and wants to help save the planet. Trevor is looking for a set of Bix Beiderbecke records and this leads to meeting a beautiful platinum blonde, a suspicious detective sergeant and a strange pair of men running a junior football team. Big Al and Little Norm agree to help Trevor and Jill with their school supplies problems. Jill decides to stand as a local councillor. A tale of black economies, council corruption and many strange characters all set to a background of Bix Beiderbecke (performed by Frank Ricotti with Kenny Baker recreating Beiderbecke's cornet solos). The opening theme was "Crying All Day" by Bix Beiderbecke and Frankie Trumbauer. First aired on ITV in 1985, the six-part series was so successful it spawned a two-part sequel, *The Beiderbecke Tapes* (1987) concerning the dumping of nuclear waste; and a further four-part sequel, *The Beiderbecke Connection* (1988).

Belfry Witches Laura Sadler (Skirty Marm), Lucy Davis (Old Noshie). Based on the children's book series by author and journalist Kate Saunders, the CBBC drama followed the fortunes of two witches, banished to Earth from Witchland, as they caused mayhem in a quiet English village. BBC1 1999-2000.

Bellamy's People Spin off from the BBC Radio 4 show *Down the Line*. The show stars Rhys Thomas as Gary Bellamy the former radio host who has now transferred to television, travelling around Britain in his Triumph Stag 'personality vehicle' meeting the people of Britain and trying to find out what makes them tick. Charlie Higson and Paul Whitehouse direct, produce and also co-star in the series. Other contributors include Simon Day, Felix Dexter, Amelia Bullmore, Lucy Montgomery, Adil Ray & Robert Popper as a variety of characters. BBC2 2010.

Benidorm Steve Pemberton (Mick Garvey), Johnny Vegas (Geoff Maltby a.k.a. The Oracle), Elsie Kelly (Noreen, Geoff's Mum), Siobhan Finneran (Janice Garvey), Hannah Hobley (Chantelle Garvey), Oliver Stokes (Michael Garvey), Geoffrey Hutchings (Mel Harvey), Sheila Reid (Madge), Crissy Rock (Janey York), Margi Clarke (Dorothy), Niky Wardley (Kelly), Nicholas Burns (Martin Weedon), Janine Duvitski (Jacqueline Stewart), Hugh Sachs (Gavin Ramsbottom), Kenny Ireland (Donald Stewart), Abigail Cruttenden (Kate Weedon), Paul Bazely (Troy), Tim Healy (Leslie), Denise Welch (Scary Mary), Una Stubbs (Diana), Robin Askwith (Gary), Adam Gillen (Liam Marshall), Kathryn Drysdale (Natalie Jones), Shelley Longworth (Sam Wood), Tony Maudsley (Kenneth), Louie Spence (Marvin), Selina Griffiths (Pauline Mamood née Maltby) and the late Wendy Richards (Sylvia). Sitcom written by Derren Litten exploiting the working-class stereotype of the popular Spanish tourist destination. Cilla Black and Su Pollard had cameo roles as themselves. ITV 2007-

Benny Hill Show, The See entry in comedy section. Incidentally, the popular theme tune that accompanied the manic chase routines was *Yakety Sax*, composed by Boots Randolph (1927-2007).

Bergerac John Nettles (Det Sgt Jim Bergerac), Terence Alexander (Charlie Hungerford), Liza Goddard (Philippa Vale), Louise Jameson (Susan Young), Celia Imrie (Marianne Bellshade), Sean Arnold (Chief Insp. Barney Crozier). Drama series created by Robert Banks Stewart. An alcoholic policeman works for the Bureau des Etrangers (which deals with crimes involving non-island residents) on the island of Jersey. He drives around in a burgundy-coloured 1947 Triumph sports car and often gets physical in his quest for justice and sometimes in his quest for love. The theme tune was composed by George Fenton. BBC1 1981-91.

Beryl's Lot Carmel McSharry (Beryl Humphries), Mark Kingston and George Selway (Tom Humphries), Brian Capron (Jack Humphries), Verna Harvey (Rosie Humphreys), Anita Carey (Babs Humphries), Robin Askwith (Fred Pickering), Queenie Watts (Freda). Comedy drama. As her fortieth birthday approaches, Beryl Humphries realises that there must be more to life than running the family home, being a mother of three, milkman's wife, and a 'char' for others, and she decides to improve her 'lot', enrolling for philosophy evening classes and otherwise breaking her conventions. The series was inspired by the life of Margaret Powell - who, in her sixties, was transformed, seemingly overnight, from household servant to best-selling author and explosively giggly celebrity - and she served as script consultant during the first series. The main writer, Kevin Laffan, created the rural soap Emmerdale Farm in 1972. ITV 1973-77.

Best of the Worst Panel game created by Giles Pilbrow and Colin Swash which featured two teams of two players, one captained by David Mitchell and the other by Johnny Vaughan (the other two panellists being television personalities). The show looked at the worst things ever to happen in the world, such as the person with the worst luck, the worst diet, or the worst inventions. The four rounds were Pick the Worst, Bottom Five, Which ends the Worst? and Wall of Worst. C4 2006

Between the Lines Neil Pearson (Det. Supt. Tony Clark), Tom Georgeson (DI Harry Naylor), Siobhan Redmond (DS Maureen Connell), Tony Doyle (Chief Supt. John Deakin), Francesca Annis (Angela Berridge), Bernard Hill (Chief Constable Harmsworth). Police drama set in the Complaints Investigation Bureau (CIB) - the department responsible for investigating other police officers - of London's Metropolitan Police. The first two series had stories based around various different aspects of the darker side of the police, ranging from such topics as petty corruption, racism and sexual harassment through to grand conspiracy, with some plot threads running through the series over several episodes. The series also dealt with the personal lives of its less-than-clean-cut characters, particularly the womanising lead character Tony Clark, and is also notable for its inclusion of a lesbian character in a major role (Mo Connell). In the third and final series, the focus changed significantly, moving away from the police force to other areas of security and espionage. BBC1 1992-94.

Beyond Our Ken Radio comedy programme written by Eric Merriman and Barry Took (Series 1 and 2). All seven series of weekly Tuesday evening shows were hosted by comedian Kenneth Horne (27 February 1907, St Pancras, London – 14 February 1969, Dorchester Hotel, London). Characters included: Fanny Haddock (Betty Marsden's parody of Fanny Cradock), Hankie Flowered (Bill Pertwee's impersonation of Frankie Howerd), Ricky Livid (Hugh Paddick's working-class pop singer whose name was a mickey-take of contemporary pop singers' names such as Marty Wilde and Billy Fury) and Arthur Fallowfield (Kenneth Williams' country yokel who was based on Dorset farmer Ralph Wightman, a regular contributor to the BBC radio programme *Any Questions?*) Fallowfield's reply to any question was invariably "Well, I think the answer lies in the soil!" Williams and Paddick also played a couple of camp men-about-town, Rodney and Charles, a precursor of Julian and Sandy (see Round The Horne). BBC Light Programme (became Radio 2) 1958-64.

Big & Small Live action comedy for pre-schoolers, following the lives of the purple puppet with pink spots on his back, Big, and the smaller orange one aptly named, Small, both played by Lenny Henry. Other characters such as Ruby, a pink mouse with red hair; Twiba, a green worm that lives in an apple in the apple tree (Twiba is an acronym which stands for "The Worm In Big's Apple"); two green frogs that live in the backyard pond and T-Rex, Big's stuffed animal, and favourite possession (disliked by Small).are played by Imelda Staunton. Part of the CBeebies menu. BBC 2008-

Big Big Talent Show, The Jonathan Ross hosted the star-spotting talent show. Ventriloquist Paul Zurdin won the first series and comedian Ed Byrne the second. Garry Bushell cast his critical eye over the acts before the result was announced. The show helped to launch the career of Charlotte Church who appeared towards the end of the run in 1997 to introduce her aunt and was asked to sing by Jonathan (although she had previously sung on *Talking Telephone Numbers* the previous month). ITV 1996-97.

Big Boy Now! Leslie Crowther (Tony Marchant), Fabia Drake (Heather Marchant), Derek Farr (Captain Edgar Bingham). Sitcom written by Ronnie Taylor. A middle-aged estate agent is still living at home with his mother, the domineering Heather, who thinks he is still her 'little boy'. To break her hold on him, he tries to forge a relationship between her and Captain Bingham in the hope he will marry her. ITV 1976-77.

Big Breadwinner Hog Peter Egan (Hog), Alan Browning (Izzard), Godfrey Quigley (Ryan), Donald Burton (Ackerman), Timothy West (Lennox). Eight-episode gangland drama series written by Robin Chapman and directed by Mike Newell (six episodes) and Michael Apted (two episodes) as a follow up to *Spindoe*. The series portrays the rise of vicious young extortioner and thief, Hogarth (commonly known as Hog), to the top of the London criminal fraternity. Hog exploits the resources of a declining gangster, Ryan, to take over the dominant crime syndicate Scot-Yanks, controlled by the equally ruthless and manipulative Lennox. ITV 1969.

Big Break Snooker-based quiz show hosted by Jim Davidson and professional snooker player John Virgo (who threw in a trick shot for good measure). Three contestants answer questions in order to win their professional snooker player partners time to pot balls and thus win them prizes. The three sections of the show were entitled "red hot", "pocket money" and "make or break". The show's theme song is The Snooker Song, from the musical The Hunting of the Snark composed by Mike Batt and performed by Captain Sensible. BBC1 1991-2002.

Big Breakfast, The The early morning entertainment show originally had Bob Geldof (a director of the production company Planet 24) conducting a series of pre-recorded interviews but the show soon developed a personality of weird and wackiness and made stars of several of its presenters, who included: Chris Evans, Gaby Roslin, Paula Yates, Keith Chegwin, Mark Lamarr, Mark Little, Paul Ross, Richard Orford, Lily Savage, Zoe Ball, Danni Minogue, Sharron Davies, Rick Adams, Vanessa Feltz, Denise Van Outen, Johnny Vaughan, Melanie Sykes, Kelly Brook, Sara Cox, Lisa Tarbuck, Gail Porter, Richard Bacon, Paul Tonkinson, Donna Air and Amanda Byram. C4 1992-2002.

Big Brother Game-show based on an original format by John de Mol, the Dutch supremo of Endemol Productions. The first series aired in Holland in 1999 and was a huge success and was quickly established globally. *Big Brother* first aired in the British Isles on Channel 4, 18 July 2000 when ten housemates, Anna, Andrew, Caroline, Craig, Darren, Melanie, Nick, Nichola, Sada and Thomas, entered the Big Brother house (initially a bungalow in Bow, London, but now a mock-up house at Boreham Wood Studio, Hertfordshire). Nick Bateman was evicted for cheating and replaced by Claire Strutton. The first winner was Craig Philips who donated his £70,000 first prize to charity and began a career as a television DIY presenter. Other housemates fared less well although Nick Bateman hosted a game-show based on duplicity, Sada Walkington (the first-ever British evictee) wrote a book, and Nichola Holt became a porn star. Marjorie was the pet chicken and Juanita the toy baby. Series 2 was won by Irishman

Brian Dowling, who became a children's television presenter, and housemates Helen and Paul began a romance that continued outside the house. Series 3 was won by Kate Lawler, a very successful presenter, and was famous for having its first walkout, Sunita leaving after less than a week. Other highlights included the doughty Scot Sandy Cummings climbing the walls and escaping over the roof of the house; the ongoing romance of Lee Davey and Sophie Pritchard; the cult following of model Alex Sibley; the beginning of the promising television career of Alison Hammond and the Jade Goody phenomenon. Jade became famous for her lack of general knowledge, believing that East Anglia was a foreign country and that Einstein lived with Sherlock Holmes! Series 4 was won by Cameron Stout, who was the first housemate to leave the house (he was flown in to the Big Brother Africa house midway through the series before returning to triumph). This series appeared to be the end for BB as viewing figures were drastically down on previous series but they did pick up towards the end when the evicted Jon Tickle re-entered the house as an agitator working for Big Brother. Series 5 was won by Nadia Almada, a 27-year-old Portuguese transsexual, who beat Jason Cowan, a 30-year-old Scottish air steward for the title. This series recaptured the attention of the viewing public with its infamous night of violence when the police had to be called to calm things down in the house and Emma Greenwood was evicted from the house following several warnings. There was also the first in-house "romance" (apparently underneath the dining table) between Stuart Wilson and Michelle Bass. Another BB5 housemate had a brief career as a nude model. A companion show: *Big Brother's Big Mouth*, formerly named Big Brother's Eforum, was introduced along with Big Brother 5. It was hosted by Russell Brand until BB8 when a series of guest presenters were used, including main show presenter Davina McCall. Series 6 was won by Anthony Hutton, a 23-year-old trainee hairdresser, who narrowly beat Eugene Sully for the title. The star of this series was the production company (in the guise of Big Brother) who constantly surprised both viewers and housemates with secret gardens, secret missions, twists on nominations and inspired contestant choices including the aristocratic Tory speech-writer Derek Laud, the equally articulate but more street-wise rapper Science (real name Kieron Harvey), the refreshingly honest Kinga Karolczak, and geeky (in the mould of Jon Tickle) Eugene. The strong favourite for the BB6 title was Eugene until Big Brother offered him half of the winner's prize money (£50,000) two days before the final and the acceptance of this tipped the balance towards Anthony. The series also had an intense friendship between two of the male contestants and a duplicitous Zimbabwean contestant who was given the loudest and longest boos of any inmate in BB history although bizarrely ending up in third position. Series 7 was won by 24-year-old Tourette's sufferer Pete Bennett, the overwhelming favourite from the outset. BB7 threw up the usual batch of characters including the temperamental Nikki Grahame, excitable Shahbaz, 'ghetto-girl' Aisleyne, all-things Welsh-loving Glyn, DJ Sp(o)iral and burping Jayne, to name but a few. BB8 provoked another controversy by evicting a housemate for using the word nigger to describe a fellow inmate only for the victim herself to imply another housemate was a paedophile by suggesting he slept with 15-year-old boys, to which no action was taken. Brian Belo was the winner of this series and the runners-up were the universally popular twins Amanda and Sam. BB9 was won by 24-year-old trainee teacher Rachel Rice, BB10 by 24-year-old busty blonde Sophie Reade and BB11 by another busty blonde, Josie Gibson, who immediately re-entered the house to take part in the show's swansong effort *Ultimate Big Brother*, but alas the 25-year-old farm girl from Bristol walked after four days to be reunited with her Australian house mate John James Parton. The eventual winner of this final series was Brian Dowling. Another companion show: *Big Brother On the Couch*, aired during BB8. Davina McCall has been the presenter on eviction nights throughout the run and Dermot O'Leary hosted *Big Brother's Little Brother*, a daily update on all the news in the house and a showcase for evictees, until January 2008 when George Lamb replaced him. *Celebrity Big Brother* began in 2001 the first winner being comedian Jack Dee. Former Take That star Mark Owen won the second series and the third series was won by former Happy

Mondays star, Bez. The fourth series in January 2006 was the most controversial and popular series to-date. Housemates included transvestite pop star Pete Burns, controversial MP George Galloway, NBA basketball superstar Dennis Rodman, and disgraced entertainer Michael Barrymore. The twist in the plot was to include a non-celebrity, Chantelle Houghton, among the residents, and the blonde Paris Hilton look-a-like pipped Michael to the title. The 2007 series was won by Bollywood actress Shilpa Shetty who remained stoic throughout despite the bullying tactics of three of the female contestants. After respite of a year the show returned in 2009 and was won by Ulrika Jonsson. The 2010 series was won by cage fighter Alex Reid, who promptly married Katie Price (aka Jordan) on leaving the house. The series was transferred to Channel 5 (now *Five*) in 2011. Hosted by Brian Dowling, the celebrity version was won by Irish traveller and reality star Paddy Doherty whilst the regular winner was Aaron Allard-Morgana, a 30-year-old contract manager from Weston-super-Mare. The regular spin-off show for this series, *Big Brother's Bit on the Side*, was hosted by Emma Willis with help from Alice Levine and Jamie East.C4 2000-10; C5 2011-. In January 2012, Denise Welch was the surprise winner of the celebrity version of the show.

Big Deal Ray Brooks (Robby Box), Sharon Duce (Jan Oliver), Lisa Geoghan (Debby Oliver). A middle-age gambler is set on changing his ways and settle down to a life of bliss with his girlfriend and her teenage daughter. As so often Ray Brooks played a most-convincing loveable rogue with a heart of gold and this series was enormously popular throughout its run. BBC1 1984-86.

Big Fat Gypsy Weddings See *My Big Fat Gypsy Wedding*

Big Jim and the Figaro Club Bob Hoskins (Narrator), Norman Rossington (Big Jim), David Beckett (Chick), Sylvester McCoy (Turps), Gordon Rollings (Old Ned), Roland Curram (Harold Perkins). "Big Jim" started life as a one-off television play in 1979, written by Ted Walker. Set during the early days of the welfare state in Britain, the working-class narrator has been to university. Home on vacation he looks up his old mates from the gang of council builders he worked with. 'Big Jim' is the foreman, Harold Perkins is their snooping, petty-minded manager. It turns out Perkins has started an affair with Big Jim's wife and the narrator gets caught up in two revenge plots. It is a tradition in the work gang that when one member "calls on Figaro", "every bugger calls on Figaro" - a sort of all-for-one-and-one-for-all (and not to be done lightly). Even after 25 years or so the narrator is still so committed to the club's code of silence that he says he can never tell us who Figaro is (or was). BBC1 1979; 1981. Norman Rossington also played Big Jim in the BBC Radio 4 version of *Big Jim and the Figaro Club* in 1987.

Big Noise, The Bob Monkhouse (Bob Mason), Norman Rossington (Kim Hunter). Six-part sitcom created by Bob Monkhouse and Denis Goodwin, with additional material by Frank Muir. Episodes in the uneasy lift of a top pop Disc Jockey. BBC 1964.

Big Time, The Esther Rantzen produced and presented this series which gave ordinary people a chance to achieve lifelong ambitions. Esther discovered international singing star Sheena Easton during the second series in 1980. BBC1 1976-80.

Big Train Surreal British television comedy sketch show created by Arthur Mathews and Graham Linehan. The first series, broadcast in 1998, was a writing collaboration while the second, in 2002, was penned solely by Mathews. Contributors included: Simon Pegg, Mark Heap, Kevin Eldon, Amelia Bullmore, Julia Davis, Rebecca Front, Tracy-Ann Oberman, Catherine Tate. A recurring sketch from the first series was a stare-out competition accompanied by commentary from BBC football commentator Barry Davies and Phil Cornwell. The title of the show is derived from the song run during the credits. The song "Big Train" was recorded by Max Greger and his Orchestra. BBC2 1998; 2002

Bigger Picture with Graham Norton, The Graham Norton informally and satirically discusses the week's news with an eclectic panel of celebrity guests. The show begins with the celebrities being shown in mocked-up photographs of themselves in scenes involving other celebrities, and ends with the guests introducing other mocked up photographs that humourously explain the recent behaviour of other celebrities. The third series was retitled *Graham Norton's Bigger Picture*. BBC1 2005-06

Biggest Loser, The Weight-losing reality show that started life on LIVINGtv in 2005, presented by motoring journalist Vicki Butler-Henderson (b. 16 February 1972). When the programme transferred to terrestrial television for its third series, ITV Breakfast presenter Kate Garroway (b. 4 May 1967) took over as host. The fourth series was presented by Davina McCall. The winners to-date are Aaron Howlett (2005), Jodie Prenger (2006 – who two years later became the winner of BBC talent show *I'd Do Anything*), Kevin Sage (2009) and Wil Graham (2011). In the first two series, the person who won the competition received £25,000 in cash, the third series winning prize was reduced to £10,000 but was reverted to the £25,000 cash prize in the fourth series. ITV 2009; 2011-

Biggles Neville Whiting (Inspector James 'Biggles' Bigglesworth), John Leyton (Ginger), David Drummond (Bertie), Carl Duering (Von Stalheim). In this production, Capt. W. E. Johns' flying ace had left the Air Force with his chums ginger and Bertie and was attached to Scotland Yard as a Detective Air Inspector. John Leyton had a successful pop career following this series. ITV 1960.

Bill, The Although not quite the longest-lasting - Taggart began a few months earlier, *The Bill*, at 2,400 episodes, stands as the most voluminous police drama in British television history. It began as *Woodentop*, a one-hour segment by Geoff McQueen for Thames' Storyboard anthology (1983) chronicling the arrival of probationary PC Jim Carver (Mark Wingett) and WPC June Ackland (Trudie Goodwin) of London's Metropolitan Police, both attached to the fictional Sun Hill police station in the equally fictional Canley district of London's East End. Although only intended as a one-off drama a full series was commissioned and first broadcast on 16 October 1984, its title now changed to *The Bill*. In a bold decision, the series, already shot on video rather than film, had a unique writing format whereby a police officer was filmed in every scene. Among many popular characters to have come and gone over the years are slightly bent copper Frank Burnside, eternally patient desk sergeant Bob Cryer, scruffy-but-kind 'Tosh' (the late Kevin Lloyd) and Viv Martella (Nula Conwell), dramatically killed-off after nine years service. Among its most potent storylines was the relationship of homosexual Sergeant Craig Gilmore and the closeted PC Luke Ashton; the famous siege and fire of Sun Hill in 2002; and the several bent copper threads of D.S. Don Beech, D.S. Phil Hunter and P.C. Gabriel Kent. *The Bill* began as a series of one-hour episodes, switched to a soap-style twice-weekly half-hour format in 1987, increased to three episodes, each of thirty minutes, per week in 1988 and ten years later, in 1998, returned to hour-long episodes, which later became twice-weekly, heralding its most popular period. The show became a proving ground for rising young actors, including Robert Carlyle (Tom Ward in 1990), Kathy Burke (Sherry Brooks in 1989 and Wendy the negotiator in 1991) and Sean Bean (Horace Clark in 1984). More recently it attracted strong guest stars, including Denise Van Outen (Melanie Lehmann in 1998), Hugh Laurie (Harrap in 1998) and Rik Mayall (Patrick Massie in 1997). The early introduction of a Black PC, Lyttleton (Ronny Cush), created a stir, as did the first openly gay characters, PC Craig Gilmore (Hywel Simons) and WPC Gemma Osborne (Jane Danson). The Bill celebrated its 20th anniversary with a live episode in October 2003 but by now the storylines were becoming fantastic bordering on totally unbelievable. Following several changes in format, including a move to a post-watershed time slot, the series wasn't quite able to out-pace Taggart, and eventually came to the end of its run after 26 years, the final episode broadcast on 31 August 2010. Ironically, the final two-parter was among the strongest storylines since its inception, Jack Meadows giving a quite moving valedictory speech to his men which quite cleverly doubled as Simon Rouse thanking his fellow actors and indeed the viewing public for its support throughout the years. *The Bill*'s iconic theme music for

25 years was known as "Overkill". The following is an alphabetical list of regular cast members: Nicola Alexis (P.C. Ruby Buxton), Colin Alldridge (P.C. Phil Young), Lysette Anthony (Rachel Heath), Pal Aron (D.C. Brandon Kane), Ray Ashcroft (D.S. Geoff Daly), Michele Austin (P.C. Yvonne Hemmingway), Alex Avery (S.C. Terence 'Terry' Stanley Knowels), Micah Balfour (P.C. Benjamin Gayle), Stephen Beckett (P.C. Mike Jarvis), Rae Baker (D.C. Juliet Becker), Colin Blumenau (P.C. Francis 'Taffy' Edwards), Russell Boulter (D.S. John Boulton), John Bowler (P.C. Roger Valentine), Carl Brincat (P.C. Adam Bostock), Moya Brady (Front Desk Officer Roberta Cryer), Joy Brook (D.C. Kerry Holmes), Ralph Brown (P.C. Pete Muswell), Mike Burnside (DAC Trevor Hicks), Tom Butcher (P.C. Steve Loxton), Bruce Byron (D.C. Terry Perkins), Todd Carty (P.C. Gabriel Kent), Caroline Catz (P.C./D.S. Rosie 'Rosebud' Fox), Lolita Chakrabarti (P.C. Jamilla Blake), Graham Cole (P.C. Stamp 1984-2009), Karl Collins (D.C. Danny Glaze), Nula Conwell (W.P.C./W.D.C. Viv Martella), Beth Cordingly (P.C. Kerry Young), Tom Cotcher (D.C. Alan Woods), Matthew Crompton (P.C. Sam Harker), Liz Crowther (Sgt. Jane Kendall), Ronnie Cush (P.C. Abe Lyttleton), Larry Dann (Sgt. Alec Peters), Jane Danson (P.C. Gemma Osbourne), Holly Davidson (P.C Roz Clarke), Libby Davison (D.C./D.S./Acting D.I. Liz Rawton), Anita Dhiri (D.C. Grace Dasari), Gregory Donaldson (D.C. Tom Proctor), Jonathan Dow (P.C. Barry Stringer), Peter Ellis (Ch. Supt. Charles Brownlow), Christopher Ellison (D.S. Frank Burnside), Tania Emery (D.C. Kate Spears), Iain Fletcher (D.C. Rod Skase), Russell Floyd (D.C. Ken Drummond), Victor Gallucci (D.C. Tom 'Vic' Baker), Vickie Gates (Marilyn Chambers), Vicki Gee-Dare (P.C. Suzanne Ford), Lisa Geoghan (P.C./CAD Officer Polly Page), Trudie Goodwin (W.P.C./Sgt. June Ackland 1983-2007), Gary Grant (D.C. Paul Riley), Jaye Griffiths (D.I. Sally Johnson), Ciaran Griffiths (P.C. Gary Best), Ashley Gunstock (P.C. Frank), Mark Haddigan (P.C. Timothy Able), Luke Hamill (CAD Officer Dean McVerry), Louise Harrison (P.C. Donna Harris), Steven Hartley (Supt. Tom Chandler), Huw Higginson (P.C. George Garfield), Michael Higgs (P.C. Eddie Santini), Robert Hudson (P.C. Smith), Chris Humphreys (P.C. Richard Turnham), Connie Hyde (P.C. Cathy Bradford), Jon Iles (D.C. Mike Dashwood), Seeta Indrani (W.P.C. Norika Datta), Raji James (D.S. Vik Singh), Thusita Jayasundera (D.C./D.S. Ramani De Costa), Larry Lamb (C.P.S. Lawyer Jonathan Fox), Andrew Lancel (D.I. Neil Manson), Kelly Lawrence (W.P.C. Claire Brind), Roger Leach (Sgt. Tom Penny), Mark Letheren (Simon Kitson), Kevin Lloyd (D.C. Alfred 'Tosh' Lines 1988-98), James Lloyd (P.C. Ryan Hunter), Andrew Mackintosh (D.S. Alistair Greig), Daniel Macpherson (P.C. Cameron Tait), Suzanne Maddock (P.C. Cass Rickman), Martin Marquez (D.S. Danny Pearce), Scott Maslen (D.S. Phil Hunter), Andrea Mason (W.P.C. Debbie Keane), Lisa Maxwell (D.S./Acting D.I. Samantha Nixon), Lesley Mcguire (Jenny Delaney / Quinnan), Nick Miles (CH/Commander/Borough Commander Guy Mannion), Sam Miller (Sgt. John Maitland), Lynne Miller (W.P.C. Cathy Marshall), Steve Morley (Sgt. Stuart Lamont), Billy Murray (D.S. Don Beech), Scott Neal (P.C. Luke Ashton), Bernie Nolan (Sgt. Sheelagh Murphy), Cyril Nri (Supt. Adam Okaro), Hywel Simons (Sgt. Craig Gilmore), Peter O'Brien (D.I./D.C. Peter Cavanuagh), Tony O'Callaghan (Sgt. Matthew Boyden 1991-2003), Roland Oliver (Sgt. Joseph Corrie0, Gary Olsen (P.C. Dave Litten), Diane Parish (D.C. Eva Sharpe), Andrew Paul (P.C. Dave Quinnan), Kerry Peers (W.D.C. Suzi Croft), Robert Perkins (Sgt. Ray Steele), Ben Peyton (P.C. Ben Hayward), John Phythian (D.C. Scott Henderson), Carolyn Pickles (D.C.I. Kim Reid), Mark Powley (P.C. Melvin), Mary Jo Randle (W.D.C./W.D.S Jo Morgan), Nick Reding (P.C. Pete Ramsey), Eric Richard (Sgt. Bob Cryer 1984-2001), Natalie J. Robb (P.C. Andrea Dunbar), Ben Roberts (Ch. Insp. Conway), Samantha Robson (P.C. Vicky Hagen), Sally Rogers (Sgt. Jo Masters), Natalie Roles (D.S. Debbie McAllister), George Rossi (D.C. Duncan Lennox), Simon Rouse (D.C.I/Supt Jack Meadows 1989-2010), Clara Salaman (D.S. Claire Stanton), John Salthouse (D.I. Roy Galloway), Tony Scannell (D.S. Roach), Shaun Scott (D.I. Chris Deakin), Ged Simmons (D.I. Alex Cullen), Chris Simmons (D.C. Mickey Webb 2000-10), Sonesh Sira (P.C. Danesh Patel), Simon Slater (Insp. Brian Kite), Mark Spalding (Ch. Insp. Paul Stritch), Lucy Speed (D.S. Stevie Moss), Jeff Stewart (P.C. Reg Hollis 1984-2008), Nick Stringer (P.C. Ron Smollett), Colin Tarrant (Insp. Andrew Monroe), Roberta Taylor (Insp. Gina Gold), Barbara Thorn (Insp. Frazer), Kim Tiddy (P.C. Honey Harman), Ofo Uhiara (P.C. Lance Powell), Paul Usher (P.C. Des Taviner), Chris Walker (P.C. Nick Shaw), Eamonn Walker (P.C. Malcolm Haynes), Alex Walkinshaw (P.C./Sgt. Dale Smith), Jane Wall (P.C. Di Worrell), Clive Wedderburn (P.C. Gary McCann), Alan Westaway (P.C. Nick Slater), Gary Whelan (D.I. Harry Haines), Philip Whitchurch (Ch. Insp. Philip Cato), Natasha Williams (P.C. Delia French), Mark Wingett (P.C./D.C. Jim Carver 1983-2005), Clive Wood (D.C.I. Gordon Wray), Rene Zagger (P.C. Nick Klein). ITV 1984-2010. Spin-offs from The Bill included: *Burnside* (2000), *Beech is Back* (2001) and *MIT: Murder Investigation Team* (2003-05) – see separate entry.

Bill and Ben Revival of the earlier *The Flowerpot Men* with John Thomson providing the voice of Bill and Jimmy Hibbert speaking for Ben. See In the new version, instead of the all-too-obvious strings and wobbly wooden frames, Bill and Ben had malleable metal skeletons beneath brightly-coloured rubber faces and resin bodies; and Little Weed had undergone an image change from the squeaky little sunflower of the earlier series into an "earth-mother". Other characters included Whoops the Worm, Ketchup the Tomato and Pry the Magpie. BBC1 2000.

Bill Brand Jack Shepherd (Bill Brand), Cherie Lunghi (Alex Ferguson), Arthur Lowe (Watson), Jonathan Pryce (Jamie Finn), Geoffrey Palmer (Malcolm Freer), Sharon Duce (Sian), Lynn Farleigh (Miriam "Mim" Brand), Jean Boht (Edna Copple), Lynne Carol (Elsie Wright), Peter Davison (Renshaw), Robert Hardy (Mr Marples), Carol Drinkwater (Pat), Nigel Hawthorne (Browning). Created and written by Trevor Griffiths and directed by Roland Joffé, this 11-part drama concerns a young lecturer who becomes a Labour Party MP representing Leighley. ITV 1976.

Billy Bunter of Greyfriars School Gerald Campion (William George Bunter). Billy Bunter, known to one and all as the 'Fat Owl Of The Remove', was the invention of the writer Charles Hamilton, who worked under the pseudonym Frank Richards. The stories of Bunter's cowardly, greedy adventures first appeared in print in 1908, and he found especial fame through the pages of the popular children's paper *The Magnet* and in dozens of books. The character translated superbly to television in this popular sitcom, in which Gerald Campion (who was 31 when he first played the part) was cast as the chubby, cake-loving, 'cripes' and 'yaroo'-uttering, work-shy, bespectacled boy in check-trousers. Mr Quelch and the beastly schoolboy posse of Harry Wharton, Bob Cherry, Frank Nugent, Hurree Jamset Ram Singh and Johnny Bull were played by a variety of actors. (A young and then unknown Michael Crawford appeared as Frank Nugent in the 1959 series, and Anthony Valentine and David Hemmings also found work in the programme at this time.) Although well into his eighties, the inexhaustible Frank Richards wrote all of the TV episodes, scripting the last series shortly before his death in 1961. BBC 1952-61.

Billy Cotton Band Show Popular Sunday lunchtime radio programme on the Light Programme (later became BBC Radio2) from 1949 to 1968, hosted by cockney band leader, Billy Cotton (6 May 1899 – 25 March 1969), who began each show with the cry "Wakey-Wake-aaaay!", followed by his band's signature tune "Somebody Stole My Gal". The show transferred to BBC Television in 1956, the variety series airing on Saturday or Sunday evenings, under various names, until 1965. As well as being a gifted musician, mainly drums, Billy was also an accomplished footballer and racing car driver. His son, Bill Cotton, later became BBC's head of variety and presenter Fearne Cotton is his nephew's granddaughter.

Billy Liar Jeff Rawle (Billy Fisher), Barbara (Sally Watts), Colin Jeavons (Mr Shadrack). Keith Waterhouse and Willis Hall adapted Waterhouse's novel for this 26-episode sitcom. Billy is apprenticed as an undertaker's assistant but spends his life daydreaming. ITV 1973-74.

Birds of a Feather Pauline Quirke (Sharon Theodopolopoudos), Linda Robson (Tracey Stubbs), Lesley Joseph (Dorien Green), Peter Polycarpou and David Cardy (Chris Theodopolopoudos).

Sitcom created by Laurence Marks and Maurice Gran. Two sisters are experiencing starkly different lifestyles: Sharon lives in a dilapidated tower block and is locked into a loveless marriage to the shiftless waster Chris; Tracey, on the other hand, is happily wed to the successful Darryl and they have a son, Garth, whom they are putting through public school. The couple live in a huge neo-Georgian house ('Dalentrace') in Bryan Close, Chigwell, a real-life Essex millionaire's row populated by footballers, TV stars, pools winners, wide-boys made good and other worthies. Both sisters' lives are turned upside down, however, when their husbands are caught red-handed on a heist and sent to jail, convicted of armed robbery. Well conversant with Chris's shortcomings, Sharon is hardly surprised, but Tracey, innocent of Darryl's criminal activities, is 'totally gobsmacked'. Despite their differences, the sisters find themselves compatriots in adversity and for reasons of companionship and convenience Sharon moves in with the well-to-do Tracey. Tracey's next door neighbour is the gossipy, sex-obsessed Dorien, a snobbish Jewess, ostensibly happily married to accountant Marcus but actually indulging in a flurry of flings with muscular toy boys. She breezes in and out of the Stubbs' household and, despite her perennial rudeness and obvious disdain for the womens' social standing, gradually becomes good friends with them. Most early episodes centred around the difficulties of the prisoners' wives coming to terms with the separation and trying to get on with their own lives, but, inevitably, as the series progressed, it gathered a different momentum, latter episodes concentrating on the relationships and adventures of the three women, never exactly forgetting the original concept but occasionally ignoring it when the need arose. BBC1 1989-98.

Bit of a Do, A David Jason (Ted Simcock), Gwen Taylor (Rita Simcock), Wayne Foskett (Elvis Simcock), David Thewlis (Paul Simcock), Paul Chapman (Laurence Rodenhurst), Nicola Pagett (Liz Rodenhurst/Simcock), Michael Jayston (Neville Badger), Sarah-Jane Holm (Jenny Rodenhurst/Simcock), Tim Wylton (Rodney Sillitoe), Stephanie Cole (Betty Sillitoe), David Yelland (Gerry Lansdown), Karen Drury (Carol Fordinbridge), Diana Weston (Corinna Price-Rodgerson), Malcolm Tierney (Geoffrey Ellsworth-Smythe), Amanda Wenban (Lucinda Snellmarsh), Tracy Brabin (Sandra), Malcolm Hebden (Eric). Sitcom written by David Nobbs. Ted Simcock is a blunt no-nonsense Yorkshire businessman who owns Jupiter Foundry, makers of toasting forks, coal scuttles, fire-irons, boot scrapers and door knockers. In the opening episode Ted's youngest son Paul marries Jenny Rodenhurst, the already-pregnant daughter of upper-crust dentist Laurence Rodenhurst. The union brings together two ill-fitting families, both obsessed with class, albeit from different ends of the spectrum. Each of the 13 episodes was set at a party, highlighting a new development in the status quo between the two families, which covered every aspect of life's rich tapestry. ITV 1989.

Bit of Fry and Laurie, A Comedy sketch series, starring Stephen Fry and Hugh Laurie, broadcast over four series alternating between BBC1 and BBC2, the pilot show being broadcast on BBC2 in 1987. The 26 episodes can best be described as a cross between *The Two Ronnies* and *Not Only But Also*, with a dash of *Monty Python* thrown in. Clever wordplay and innuendo were staple diets and the series frequently broke the fourth wall whereby characters would revert into their real-life actors mid-sketch, or the camera would pan off set into the studio. In addition, the show was punctuated with non-sequitur vox pops in a similar style to those of *Monty Python's Flying Circus*. Hugh would also frequently play piano with the non-musical Stephen sometimes helping out on comical numbers. BBC 1987; 1989-95

Black and White Minstrel Show, The Variety show created by George Inns from a 1957 show, *Television Minstrels* (BBC TV 2 September 1957) as part of the National Radio Show in London. A series of one-off shows soon developed into a regular series with a forty-five minute non-stop format of Mississippi tunes and Country and Western songs. The music, conducted by George Mitchell, was interpreted by the Mitchell Minstrels and the Television Toppers Dance Troupe. The soloists included Tony Mercer, John Boulter and Dai Francis. During the early years, various comedians such as Leslie Crowther, Stan Stennett and George Chisholm acted as link-men between the slick song and dance routines. The Show won the 1961 *Golden Rose Of Montreux* at the height of it's fame but became under increasing scrutiny from pressure groups which felt black people were being caricatured (all the minstrels were white men who blacked up). Despite the changing tide of what was considered respectful viewing, the show trundled along until 1 July 1978, and ironically by then, the occasional host had become none other than Lenny Henry, a black comedian who had toured with them for years! BBC1 1958-78

Black Beauty, The Adventures of Judi Bowker (Victoria Gordon), William Lucas (Dr James Gordon), Roderick Shaw (Kevin Gordon), Stacy Dorning (Jenny Gordon), Charlotte Mitchell (Amy Winthrop), Tom Maiden (Albert), Michael Culver (Squire Armstrong), Black Jet (Black Beauty). Drama series based on Anna Sewell's classic novel set on a spacious country estate in 1877. In the first episode, The Fugitive, (broadcast on ITV 17 September 1972), a widower Dr James Gordon moves from Victorian London to the village of Five Oaks to set up a country practice. After saving the life of the invalid owner of a magnificent black stallion, the Gordons are presented with him as a thank-you. His daughter, Vicky, names him Black Beauty. Thus ensued many exciting adventures for Vicky and brother Kevin, aided and abetted by Beauty. For the second series, previously unseen Gordon sibling Jenny arrived from schooling in London to replace Vicky. 16 years after the final episode, *The New Adventures of Black Beauty* saw Dr Gordon and the grown-up Jenny emigrate to New Zealand in 1902 (William Lucas and Stacy Dorning resuming their roles), with stepdaughter Vicky (Amber McWilliams) charged with looking after a new black steed. ITV 1972-74; 1990.

Black Books Bill Bailey (Manny Bianco), Dylan Moran (Bernard Black), Tamsin Greig (Fran Katzenjammer). Sitcom written by Dylan Moran, Graham Linehan, Arthur Mathews, Kevin Cecil and Andy Riley. Black Books is a second-hand bookshop in London run by an Irishman named Bernard, who is totally unsuited to running such an establishment, making no effort to sell, closing at strange hours on a whim, and appearing to be in a constant alcoholic stupor. He also hates his customers (sometimes physically abusing them) and is often comatose at his desk. Help comes in the shape of Manny Bianco, a hairy, bumbling individual, who he does manage to sell a book to (The Little Book Of Calm). Manny becomes Bernard's assistant although he is not a natural salesman himself. Next door is Fran, an anxious, frustrated woman who (in the first series) runs a sort of new-age shop selling the most unlikely bits of arty junk. (In the second, her shop was neither seen nor mentioned.) Fran is friends with Bernard and, through him, with Manny; together the trio become embroiled in escapades that are fantastically ludicrous, but very funny. C4 2000-04.

Blackadder Goes Forth Rowan Atkinson (Captain Edmund Blackadder), Tony Robinson (Private S. Baldrick), Hugh Laurie (Lt. The Honourable George Colthurst St Barleigh), Stephen Fry (General Sir Anthony Cecil Hogmanay Melchett), Tim McInnerny (Captain Kevin Darling), Miranda Richardson (Nurse Mary), Rik Mayall (Lord Flashheart). The fourth series of Blackadder was set in the trenches of World War I and the 'hero' plays his usual cowardly self, attempting to flee the inevitable carnage by any manner or means possible. Written by Richard Curtis and Ben Elton, the series comes to a most heart-wrenching conclusion when all the 'ordinary men' are ordered to go 'over the top' to their certain deaths. The slow motion action fades silently into a field of swaying poppies. BBC1 1989

Blackadder II Rowan Atkinson (Lord Edmund Blackadder), Tony Robinson (Baldrick), Miranda Richardson (Queen Elizabeth I), Stephen Fry (Lord Melchett), Tim McInnerny (Lord Percy), Patsy Byrne (Nursie), Rik Mayall (Lord Flashheart), Hugh Laurie (Prince Ludwig/Simon Partridge), Tom Baker (Captain Rum), Simon Jones (Sir Walter Raleigh), Miriam Margolyes (Lady Whiteadder). The second series of Blackadder was set in

Elizabethan England towards the end of the 16th century, the 'hero' being the great-grandson of the Black Adder of the first series. Ben Elton replaced Rowan Atkinson as the co-writer with Richard Curtis. BBC1 1986.

Blackadder the Third Rowan Atkinson (Edmund Blackadder), Tony Robinson (Baldrick), Hugh Laurie (George, Prince of Wales), Helen Atkinson-Wood (Mrs Miggins), Robbie Coltrane (Dr Samuel Johnson), Miranda Richardson (Amy Hardwood), Stephen Fry (The Duke of Wellington). The third series of Blackadder was set in Georgian England around the turn of the 19th century and the 'hero' was now the butler of the idiotic Prince Regent. Written by Richard Curtis and Ben Elton. BBC1 1987.

Blackadder, The Rowan Atkinson (Edmund, Duke of Edinburgh aka The Black Adder), Tony Robinson (Baldrick), Tim McInnerny (Percy), Brian Blessed (Richard IV), Elspet Gray (Queen), Robert East (Harry, Prince of Wales), Miriam Margolyes (Princess Maria). Written by Richard Curtis and Rowan Atkinson. The first of the four series of historical comedies, although good, is generally considered inferior to the others. Set in the 15th century, during the Wars of the Roses, the 'hero' is allegedly the son of Richard IV, one of the Princes in the Tower. The series was filmed at Alnwick Castle, Northumberland. BBC1 1983.

Blackeyes Michael Gough (Maurice James Kingsley), Carol Royle (Jessica), Nigel Planer (Jeff), Gina Bellman (Blackeyes), John Shrapnel (Detective Blake), Colin Jeavons (Jamieson), Dennis Potter (Narrator). Four-part drama by Dennis Potter with music by Max Harris. Maurice, a novelist, writes a book about a beautiful young model named 'Blackeyes' which is actually based on events in the life of his niece Jessica (Blackeyes being her working name as a model), with whom he has a tortured relationship. BBC2 1989.

Blackhearts in Battersea Celia Imrie (Duchess Of Battersea), Philip Jackson (Eustace Buckle), Ronald Pickup (Duke Of Battersea), John Altman (Midwink), Annette Badland (Dolly Buckle), Barry Ewart (John Daggett), Stephen Moore (Abednigo Twite). Children's drama serial written by Joan Aiken and James Andrew Hall. In early nineteenth century London the rightful Duke of Battersea finds himself cheated out of his inheritance. BBC1 1995-96.

Blackpool David Morrissey (Ripley Holden), David Tennant (DI Peter Carlisle), Sarah Parish (Natalie Holden), Georgia Taylor (Shyanne Holden), Thomas Morrison (Danny Holden), Steve Pemberton (Adrian Marr). Six-part musical comedy drama serial, created by Peter Bowker, revolving around the murder of a young man in a Blackpool arcade. The series had surreal comic moments and was notable for its sound track which sung along with and accompanied by quirky dance routines acted out by the characters, reminiscent of the style Dennis Potter employed in *Pennies From Heaven* and *The Singing Detective*. BBC1 2004. A one-off sequel, *Viva Blackpool*, starring David Morrissey and Georgia Taylor reprising their roles as Ripley Holden, and his daughter Shyanne, was shown on the BBC on Saturday June 10, 2006.

Blake's 7 Gareth Thomas (Roj Blake), Paul Darrow (Kerr Avon), Sally Knyvette (Jenna Stannis), Michael Keating (Vila Restal), Jan Chappell (Cally from Auron), Josette Simon (Dayna Mellanby), David Jackson (Gan Olag), Steven Pacey (Capt Del Tarrant), Peter Tuddenham (voice of Zen, Orac and Slave – the first voice of Orac was Derek Farr), Glynis Barber (Soolin), Jacqueline Pearce (Servalan). In the third century of the second calendar, seven incongruous prisoners escape whilst on the way to a penal colony on Cygnus Alpha and form a team to combat the evil Terran Federation. Cult science fiction series created by Terry Nation which was often criticised for its shaky sets but always maintained a faithful core of fans. The title character was gone by the end of Series 2 and computer expert Avon became the chief freedom fighter in the war against the daemonic Servalan. The rebel's spacecrafts were The Liberator (computers: Zen and Orac) and then Scorpio (computer: Slave). Gan Olag was implanted with a 'Brain Limiter' to stop him killing. BBC1 1978-81.

Blandings Castle Ralph Richardson (Clarence, 9th Earl of Emsworth), Stanley Holloway (Beach), Meriel Forbes (Lady Constance), Derek Nimmo (The Hon. Freddie Threepwood). Six-part adaptation of the PG Wodehouse stories. BBC1 1967.

Blankety Blank Game show presented by Terry Wogan (1979-83), Les Dawson (1984-90 and Lily Savage (1998-2002). A celebrity panel of six were asked to complete a potentially risqué statement read out by the host in the hope it would marry with that of a member of the public. The show had a semi-final with two contestants vying to gain six matching answers in order to play the Supermatch game and the chance to play again in the final head-to-head at the end of the show. The Supermatch consisted of an audience poll of top answers to end a well-known word or phrase and the contestant had to attempt to choose the most popular answer worth 50, 100 or 150 Blanks. Prizes were modest but the losers all received a Blankety Blank Chequebook And Pen. BBC1 1979-90, 1998-2000; ITV 2001-02.

Bleak House Denis Lawson (John Jarndyce), Anna Maxwell Martin (Esther Summerson), Patrick Kennedy (Richard Carstone), Carey Mulligan (Ada Clare), Nathaniel Parker (Harold Skimpole), Gillian Anderson (Lady Dedlock), Pauline Collins (Miss Flite), Timothy West (Sir Leicester Dedlock), Charles Dance (Mr Tulkinghorn), Alun Armstrong (Bucket), Burn Gorman (Guppy), Alistair McGowan (Mr Kenge), Ian Richardson (The Chancellor), Johnny Vegas (Krook), Matthew Kelly (Old Mr Turveydrop), Warren Clarke (Boythorn), Richard Griffiths (Mr Bayham Badger), Charlie Brooks (Jenny), Natalie Press (Caddy Turveydrop / Caddy Jellyby), Lisa Tarbuck (Mrs Jellyby), John Lynch (Nemo), Phil Davis (Smallweed). 15-part adaptation of the Dickens' classic by Andrew Davies, first broadcast on BBC1 in 2005. A popular BBC2 series of 1985 starred Diana Rigg as Lady Dedlock, Denholm Elliott as John Jarndyce, Peter Vaughan as Tulkinghorn, Charlie Drake as Smallweed, Bernard Hepton as Krook and Philip Franks as Richard Carstone.

Bless Me Father Arthur Lowe (Father Charles Duddleswell). Sitcom based at St Jude's in the London suburb of Fairwater with Lowe playing an Irish priest having to overcome a series of disasters. The series was written by Peter de Rosa, a former Catholic priest who wrote books under the pseudonym Neil Boyd. ITV 1978-81.

Bless this House Sid James (Sid Abbott), Diana Coupland (Jean Abbott), Robin Stewart (Mike Abbott), Sally Geeson (Sally Abbott), Anthony Jackson (Trevor), Patsy Rowlands (Betty). Domestic sitcom created by Vince Powell and Harry Driver. Produced by future *Fifteen-to-One* host William G Stewart. ITV 1971-76.

Blind Date Game show presented by Cilla Black. The show consisted of two halves, the first involved a man or woman asking three questions to three unseen members of the opposite sex in order to gauge their suitability for a blind date and later the gender would be reversed so that four men and four women would be showcased in total. The second half of the programme would consist of a film of how last week's contestants 'got on' on their date and a studio appearance with a summing-up by the 'protagonists'. The first couple to marry as a result of meeting on *Blind Date* were Sue Middleton and Alex Tatham in 1991. Actress Amanda Holden (1990) and presenter Jenni Falconer (1994) were once contestants on the show. The catchy theme tune was composed by Laurie Holloway and the announcer was Graham Skidmore for all but the final series when he was replaced by Tommy Sandhu. ITV 1985-2003.

Blockbusters Quiz show for contestants aged 16-18, hosted by Bob Holness (1998-2012). The avuncular Holness asked a series of questions the answers of which began with a letter of the alphabet chosen by either an individual or the opposing team of two. The winner of each round would be put on the 'hot spot' and attempt to go on a gold run to win prizes. "Can I have a P please Bob" became a popular catchphrase. ITV 1983-94. The series was revived on BBC2 in 1997 with Michael Aspel as presenter, and again on Sky One in 2000 with Lisa Tarbuck as presenter.

Blooming Marvellous Sarah Lancashire (Liz Deakin), Clive Mantle (Jack Deakin). Sitcom based around the mid-life crisis of a Yorkshire couple who decide to start a family. BBC1 1997-98.

Blott on the Landscape David Suchet (Blott), George Cole (Sir Giles Lynchwood MP), Simon Cadell (Dundridge), Geraldine James (Lady Maud Lynchwood), Julia McKenzie (Mrs Forthby), Geoffrey Bayldon (Ganglion). Adaption by Malcolm Bradbury of Tom Sharpe's black comic novel. Filmed at Stanage Park, near Ludlow. BBC2 1985.

Blue Heaven Frank Skinner (Frank Sandford), Conleth Hill (Roache), Paula Wilcox (Ivy Sandford), John Forgeham (Jim Sandford). Six-part sitcom written by Frank Skinner. Frank, a Brummie musician forms a duo with his mate Roache and aims to get a break into the bigtime. C4 1994.

Blue Murder Caroline Quentin (DCI Janine Lewis), Ian Kelsey (DI Richard Mayne), Saskia Wickham (DCS Louise Hogg), Nicolas Murchie (DS Tony Shap), Paul Loughran (DS Ian Butchers), Rhea Bailey (DC Lisa Goodall), Belinda Everett (DC Kat Skerton), Tina O'Brien (Amy Kirkland). Police drama series created by Cath Staincliffe. ITV 2003-09.

Blue Peter Children's magazine programme first broadcast over 50 years ago with more than 4,000 live editions having been produced. Presenters: Christopher Trace (1958-67) (former army-oficer who was Charlton Heston's stand-in on *Ben Hur*), Leila Williams (1958-62) (the previous year's Miss Great Britain), Anita West (1962), Valerie Singleton (1962-72), John Noakes (1965-78), Peter Purves (1967-78), Lesley Judd (1972-79), Simon Groom (1978-86), Christopher Wenner (1978-80),Tina Heath (1979-80), Sarah Greene (1980-83), Peter Duncan (1980-84), and (1985-86), Janet Ellis (1983-87), Michael Sundin (1984-85), Mark Curry (1986-89), Caron Keating (1986-90), Yvette Fielding (1987-92), John Leslie (1989-94), Diane-Louise Jordan (1990-96), Anthea Turner (1992-94), Tim Vincent (1993-97), Romana D'Annunzio (1996-98), Richard Bacon (1997-98), Stuart Miles (1994-99), Katy Hill (1995-2000), Simon Thomas (1999-2005), Konnie Huq (1997-2008), Matt Baker (1999-2006), Liz Barker (2000-06), Zoe Salmon (2004-08), Gethin Jones (2005-08), Andy Akinwolere (2006-), Helen Skelton (2008-), Joel Defries (2008-). The theme tune is Barnacle Bill and the famous ship logo was designed by Tony Hart. Pets have included the dogs Petra, Shep, Patch, Goldie, Bonnie, Mabel, Lucy and Meg; the cats Jason, Jack, Jill, Willow, Kari, Oke and Smudge; and the tortoises Fred/Freda, Maggie, Jim, George and Shelley. BBC1 1958- See also *Echo Island.*

Blue Planet, The Natural history series presented by David Attenborough and first broadcast on BBC 1 in 2001. See *Life in Cold Blood*

Bo' Selecta! Sketch show written and performed by Leigh Francis in his guise of Avid Merrion, a perpetual neck-brace wearer and stalker from the fictitious country Aracnipuss, who conducts celebrity interviews whilst wearing an array of grotesque latex masks, each one vaguely resembling a celebrity such as Elton John, David Blaine, Kelly Osbourne, Michael Jackson, Mel B and Craig David. Caroline Flack made several appearances as Bubbles throughout the run. Another recurring character on the show is 'the Bear', a perverted, foul-mouthed teddy who spews a constant barrage of filth at his guests, often before exposing himself. The series title is based on a line from the Craig David song "Re-Rewind". The show also introduced the fictional character Keith Lemon who now has his own quiz show, *Celebrity Juice*. After the third series of Bo' Selecta!, the Bear was given his own short-lived spin-off show in 2005 called *A Bear's Tail*, Patsy Kensit featuring in several episodes. C4 2002-04

Bob Martin Sitcom written by Bob Mills and Jeff Pope with Michael Barrymore playing the title character, a troubled daytime game show host. His extremely camp producer, Greg, was played by Denis Lawson and his assistants Vinnie and Beverley by Keith Allen and Tracey Ann Oberman. ITV 2000-01

Bob Says Opportunity Knocks See *Opportunity Knocks.*

Bob the Builder Neil Morrisey (voice of Bob), Kate Harbour (voice of Wendy, Dizzy and Mrs Potts), Rob Rackstraw (voice of Scoop, Muck, Roley, Spud and Travis), Rupert Degas (voice of Skip). Children's animation series created by Keith Chapman and inspired by the Kafka short story, 'A Departure'. Set in Bob's yard in the town of Bobsville; Bob and his crew of talking machines - Scoop the yellow digger, Muck the red bulldozer, Lofty the blue crane, Roley the green steamroller and Dizzy the orange cement mixer (who seems to have a crush on Scoop) teach the value of teamwork, problem solving and achieving something by working together. Other characters include Spud the scarecrow, Wendy (Bob's business partner), Farmer Pickles, Bernard Bentley (the building inspector and later Mayor of Bobsville), Mr Sabatini (runs the local pizza shop), Mrs Potts (owner of Tommy the Tortoise, or is it a turtle?), Mr Dixon (postman and brother to a famous football goalkeeper), Pilchard (Bob's pet cat), Bird (Roley's best friend), Travis (Farmer Pickles' cyan tractor), Sumsy (a maroon and yellow striped forklift, owned by Farmer Pickles), Mrs Percival (school headmistress), JJ (the parts supplier), Molly(JJ's daughter) and Skip (a yellow skip-carrier owned by JJ). The series, first broadcast on BBC1 in 1999, is now shown as part of the children's Cbeebies slot. The lyrics to the theme song are as follows: *Bob the Builder! Can we fix it? Bob the Builder! Yes we can! Scoop, Muck and Dizzy, and Roley too; Lofty and Wendy, join the crew. Bob and the gang have so much fun; working together, they get the job done. Bob the Builder! Can we fix it? Bob the Builder! Yes we can! (I think so!). Pilchard and Bird, Travis and Spud; playing together, like good friends should. Bob the Builder! Can we fix it? Bob the Builder! Yes we can! (Yes!).Can We fix It* was the best-selling single of 2000 with sales of 853,000 copies and it went on to top the million by the following year. Bob's follow-up single *Mambo No 5* also topped the UK Charts in 2001. In the second series the title became *Bob the Builder: Project: Build-It*. Bob hears of a contest to build a new community in a remote area called Sunflower Valley, outside of Bobsville. He moves from Bobsville with Wendy and the team and builds a new yard there. Bob convinces his father, Robert, to come out of retirement and take over the Bobsville building business. It is not known whether Bob will return to Bobsville or not.

Bod Children's animated cartoon series based on four original *Bod* books (*Bod's Apple, Bod's Present, Bod's Dream* and *Bod and the Cherry Tree*) by Joanna and Michael Cole. Thirteen five-minute episodes were created for transmission on the BBC as part of the *Watch with Mother* series and originally shown in 1975. Narrated by John Le Mesurier and Maggie Henderson, Bod is a boy who lives in a town with Aunt Flo, PC Copper, Frank the Postman and Farmer Barleymow. Each of the characters have their own theme music (performed by Derek Griffiths) which is heard when they appear. There is also another set of characters who appear in each episode called *Alberto Frog and his Amazing Animal Band*. This segment featured short extracts from famous pieces of classical music as part of the story, and always ended with Alberto choosing a different flavour of milkshake as his reward for solving a problem.

Bognor David Horovitch (Bognor), Joanna McCallum (Monica), Ewan Roberts (Parkinson), Tim Meats (Lingard), Peter Jeffrey (Milburn Port). Light-hearted twice-weekly drama series created by Tim Heald. Simon Bognor was an agent of a special investigations department of the Board Of Trade. If a newspaper editor was murdered or some bounders tried to kill a champion poodle or steal the formula for a new type of honey, Bognor was, despite being a bit dim, the man to sort it out. The poor man's 007, you might say. He was happily married to the lovely Monica, though occasionally pretty women threw themselves his way. His boss was the gruff Parkinson. ITV 1981-82.

Bold As Brass Jimmy Edwards (Ernie Briggs), Beryl Reid (Bessie Briggs), Jill Hyem (Peggy Briggs), Ronnie Barker (Mr. Oakroyd). Sitcom written by Ron Watson and David Climie concerning the exploits of brass band-mad Ernie Briggs and his long-suffering wife, Bessie. BBC 1963-64.

Bonekickers Julie Graham (Dr. Gillian Magwilde), Adrian Lester (Dr. Ben Ergha), Hugh Bonneville (Professor Gregory 'Dolly' Parton), Gugu Mbatha-Raw (Viv Davis), Burn Gorman (Major Banks), Joe Grossi (Monk), Duane Henry (Anthony), William Hope (Preston Lester), Shauna Macdonald (Boudica), Michael Maloney (Professor Daniel Mastiff), Tamzin Merchant (Helena), Patrick Monckeberg (Gruber), David Oakes (Alfred Tennyson), Sam Spiegel (Henri), Trevor White (Bobby), Anthony Green (Marcus Quintanus). Six-part drama series about a dynamic team of archaeologists. Created by Matthew Graham and Ashley Pharoah. BBC1 2008.

Boon Michael Elphick (Ken Boon), Neil Morrissey (Rocky Cassidy), Lesley-Anne Sharp (Debbie Yates). A big-hearted ex-fireman begins a courier service, The Texas Rangers, and becomes an urban cowboy-cum-detective, cruising the Midland streets on his 650cc BSA Norton which he calls White Lightning. ITV 1986-92.

Bootsie and Snudge Alfie Bass (Bootsie), Bill Fraser (Snudge), Clive Dunn (Henry Beerbohm 'Old' Johnson), Robert Dorning (Hesketh Pendleton). Created by Marty Feldman and Barry Took. Spin-off from the *Army Game* with the two popular characters now situated as major-domo (Snudge) and boot-boy (Bootsie) in a gentleman's club. ITV 1960-63. A short ITV series of 1964, *Foreign Affairs*, saw Fraser and Bass reprise their roles and another in 1974, albeit with a reversal of fortune after Bootsie won the football pools. Another vehicle for the two stars was the short-lived ITV series *Vacant Lot* (1967) with Bill Fraser playing William Bendlove and Alfie Bass playing Alf Grimble.

Borderers, The Michael Gambon (Gavin Ker), Edith McArthur (Margaret Ker), Iain Cuthbertson (Sir Walter Ker of Cessford), Nell Brennan (Agnes Ker - Series 1), Eileen Nicholas (Agnes Ker - Series 2), Margaret Greig (Grizel Ker), Joseph Brady (Rab - Series 1), James Garbutt (Rab - Series 2), Ross Campbell (Jamie Ker), Russell Waters (Pringle). Historical drama series set in the 16th century, chronicling the lives of the Ker family, particularly the dashing young head of the family, Gavin Ker, who live in the Scottish Middle March as part of the border reiver community. Created by Bill Craig. BBC1 1968-70

Borgias, The Adolfo Celi (Rodrigo Borgia), Anne-Louise Lambert (Lucrezia Borgia), Oliver Cotton (Cesare Borgia), Louis Selwyn (Jofre Borgia), George Camiller (Juan Borgia), Maurice O'Connell (Michelotto), Alfred Burke (Giuliano della Rovere). Historical drama series, created by Mark Shivas, and set in Italy during the 15th century, telling the story of Rodrigo Borgia - the future Pope Alexander VI - and his family, including his son Cesare and daughter Lucrezia. The 10 episodes follow events from 1492 when Rodrigo is elected pope and concludes in 1507 with Cesare's violent death. BBC2 1981.

Born and Bred Kate Williams (Marge Benge), Constance Chapman (Rose Tonsley), James Grout (Frank Benge), Gorden Kaye (Ray Benge), Richard O'Callaghan (Stephen Benge), Gillian Raine (Daphne Benge), Susie Blake (Pam Redstone), Trevor Peacock (Dennis Tonsley), Max Wall (Tommy Tonsley), Joan Sims (Molly Peglar). Comedy drama series created by Douglas Livingstone, inspired by the Adam Faith vehicle, *Budgie*. Two warring London families, the working-class Tonsleys, headed by the grumpy Tommy, and the middle-class Benges, led by the ultra-snobbish Frank, attempt to get along. Two series of six episodes were broadcast. ITV 1978; 1980.

Born Survivor: Bear Grylls See *Bear Grylls*

Bottom Rik Mayall (Richard "Ritchie" Richard), Ade Edmondson (Edward Elizabeth "Eddie" Hitler). Two friends, who live above a Hampstead shop, spend their lives attacking one another. Sitcom created by the show's stars, reprising their stage act and spawning a series of stage shows. The character names come from Mayall's and Edmondson's own nicknames for each other. Incidentally, the "Eddie" is taken from "Eddie Monsoon", Edmondson's nickname since University. The theme tune is performed by The Bum Notes, a jazz ensemble featuring Edmondson. The series was produced by Ed Bye. BBC2 1991-92; 1995. The series was made into a film adaptation in 1999 entitled *Guest House Paradiso* (albeit with different character names: Richard Twat and Eddie Elizabeth Ndingobamba).

Bounder, The Peter Bowles (Howard Booth), George Cole (Trevor Mountjoy), Rosalind Ayres (Mary Mountjoy), Isla Blair (Laura Miles). Sitcom written by Eric Chappell. Howard Booth is a Raffles-like cultured cad, newly released from prison after serving two years for fraud. Sadly, jail has not altered his disposition, a fact that does not go unnoticed by his much put-upon estate agent brother-in-law Trevor Mountjoy. Howard moves in as the Mountjoys' lodger, thanks to his sister Mary's propensity to be wrapped around his finger. As the title suggests, Howard is a bounder through and through, pathologically compelled to lie, cheat and deceive, suckering men and women alike, all of whom fall for his suave manner and Savile Row suits. One person not so easily conquered, however, is Laura, an attractive widow who lives next door to the Mountjoys and whom Howard pursues because she's wealthy. ITV 1982-83.

Bouquet of Barbed Wire Frank Finlay (Peter Manson), Sheila Allen (Cassie Manson), Susan Penhaligon (Prue Manson/Sorenson), James Aubrey (Gavin Sorenson), Deborah Grant (Sarah Francis). Written by Andrea Newman and based on her 1969 novel about the intertwined relationships, both sexual and emotional, of the Manson family. ITV 1976. A sequel *Another Bouquet* was broadcast in 1977 with Sarah Francis becoming the new femme fatale after Prue died in childbirth in the first series. A critically-acclaimed remake of the original series, adapted by Guy Andrews, was broadcast on ITV in 2010 starring Trevor Eve as Peter, Hermione Norris as Cassie, Imogen Poots as Prue, Tom Riley as Gavin and Jemima Rooper as Sarah.

Bowler George Baker (Stanley Bowler), Renny Lister (Doreen Bowler), Fred Baumann (Reg), Gretchen Franklin (Mum). Spin off series from *The Fenn Street Gang* written by John Esmonde and Bob Larbey (who only wrote two episodes of Fenn Street), focusing on the wealthy villain with fingers in a whole range of extremely shady pies but whose main aim in life is to become 'accepted' among the 'upper crust' of society. ITV 1973.

Boyd QC Michael Denison (Richard Boyd QC), Charles Leno (Jack – his clerk). Courtroom drama series written by Jack Roffey, a real-life court official. Britain's answer to Perry Mason was usually hired as counsel for the defence although he could equally well find himself appearing for the prosecution. His credibility as a defence lawyer was unsurpassed but, unlike his American counterpart he didn't always win his cases. The theme tune was called 'Royalty' and was composed by Robert Farnon. ITV 1956-64.

Boys From the Blackstuff Bernard Hill (Yosser Hughes), Michael Angelis (Chrissie Todd), Julie Walters (Angie Todd), Gary Bleasdale (Kevin Dean), Jean Boht (Miss Sutcliffe), James Ellis (a drunkard), Malloy (Pete Postlethwaite), Alan Igbon (Loggo Logmond), Peter Kerrigan (George Malone), Tom Georgeson (Dixie Dean). A gang of tarmac layers are laid off with tragic results. The most memorable episode of Alan Bleasdale's five-part drama was *Yosser's Story*, the fourth of the five parts. It concerned the desperate would-be brickie Yosser Hughes with his catchphrase 'gissa job' and 'I can do dat'. Although some of the scenes were disturbing, the black humour gave the viewer a rollercoaster of emotions. While receiving the sacrament of Confession, Yosser relays his plight to the priest thus: "I'm desperate father" to which the priest replies "Call me Dan my son" and Yosser then gives a tearful "I'm desperate Dan"......pathos at its best! Yosser was actually first seen on screen in a 1980 TV film, *The Black Stuff*, where he was also played by Hill. BBC2 1982. The series was so successful upon its original broadcast that only nine weeks after it had finished transmission, it was re-shown on the higher-profile BBC1.

Boys From the Bush Tim Healy (Reg Toomer), Chris Haywood (Dennis Tontine), Pat Thomson (Doris Toomer), Mark Haddigan (Leslie), Nadine Garner (Arlene Toomer), Kirsty Child (Corrie), Kris McQuade (Delilah). Light-hearted drama series written by Douglas Livingstone. Two detectives, one British, one Australian, operate a detective agency Melbourne Confidential, from above a brothel. Reg is an avid QPR fan and hates Australia although living there for the past 20 years. BBC1 1991-92.

Bracken Gabriel Byrne (Pat Barry), Niall Tóibín (Mr Daly), Mick Lally (Miley Byrne), Joe Lynch (Dinny Byrne), Dana Wynter (Jill Daly). Irish soap opera set in and around County Wicklow in the Republic of Ireland. Gabriel Byrne's character first appeared in *The Riordans*, and the characters of Dinny and Miley Byrne were later to become the central stars of *Glenroe*. RTÉ One 1978-82.

Braden's Week When Canadian presenter Bernard Braden joined the BBC following the end of his popular series *On the Braden Beat*, this next offering was almost a reprise of the format, albeit now including a team of reporters/researchers, notably Esther Rantzen. The series ended in controversial fashion when Braden was sacked for advertising Stork margarine on ITV, the BBC feeling it was inappropriate for the host of a consumer programme to be seen endorsing commercial goods. BBC1 1968-72.

Brain of Britain The annual competition for the *Brain of Britain* title began on the Light Programme in 1953 as a knock-out quiz slot within a programme called *What Do You Know?* (Created by John P. Wynn and chaired by Franklin Engelmann). The slot was transferred to the BBC Home Service (became Radio 4 on 30

September 1967) in the 1960s and renamed *Brain of Britain*. On the death of Engelmann, in 1972, Robert Robinson became chairman and, apart from illnesses causing Russell Davies to replace him for the 2004 series and Peter Snow for the 2007 series, hosted the show until announcing his retirement in 2010 (Russell Davies now taking over the reins permanently). The quiz consists of eight general knowledge rounds and a section in the middle where members of the public get the opportunity to set a question for the contestants. Ian Gillies, who served many years as 'Mycroft' (a reference to Sherlock Holmes' smarter brother), the final arbiter of contestants' answers, died in April 2002 after a long illness. He gave up his job as an advertising account manager to lend his amazing general knowledge to the BBC full-time for over 30 years providing the questions that intrigued, delighted and challenged the Radio 4 audience. Kevin Ashman, who emulated Ian by being crowned 'Brain of Britain', 'Brain of Brains' and 'Top Brain' (a series of competitions concerning previous winners), replaced Ian under the guise of 'Jorkins' (the largely unseen, but often confided in, member of the partnership of Spenlow & Jorkins in Dickens' David Copperfield). Kevin stood down in 2007. The series was produced by Richard Edis for most of its run. The full list of winners is as follows: Martin Dakin (1954), Arthur Maddock (1955), Anthony Carr (1956), Rosemary Watson (1957), David Keys (1958), Dr Reginald Webster (1959), Patrick Bowing (1960), Irene Thomas (1961), Henry Button (1962), Ian Barton (1963), Ian Gillies (1964), Robert Crampsey (1965), Richard Best (1966), Lt Cmdr Loring (1967), Ralph Raby (1968), T.D.Thomson (1969), Ian Matheson (1970), Fred Morgan (1971), A. Lawrence (1972), Glyn Court (1973), Roger Pritchard (1974), Winifred Lawson (1975), Thomas Dyer (1976), Martin Gostelow (1977), James Nesbitt (1978), Arthur Gerard (1979), Tim Paxton (1980) Peter Barlow (1981), John Pusey (1982), Sue Marshall (1983), Peter Bates (1984), Richard Fife (1985), Stephen Gore (1986), Ian Sutton (1987), Paul Monaghan (1988), Barbara Thompson (1989), Jim Eccleson (1990), Chris Wright (1991), Mike Billson (1992), Geoffrey Colton (1993), Ian Wynn-Mackenzie (1994), Ian Kinloch (1995), Kevin Ashman (1996), Daphne Fowler (1997), Guy Herbert (1998), Leslie Duncalf (aka Booth, 1999), Mike Smith-Rawnsley (2000), Tom Corfe (2001), Dr David Jones (2002), David Steadman (2003), Alan Bennett (2004), Christopher Hughes (2005), Pat Gibson (2006), Mark Bytheway (2007) , Geoff Thomas (2008), Ian Bayley (2009), Dr Iwan Thomas (2010) and Ray Ward (2011). The programme is no longer completed in a calendar year so Ian Bayley's victory for instance was begun in 2009 but completed in 2010. The theme music to the programme is Mozart's *Eine Kleine Nachtmusik* (A Little Night Music). Every three years, the annual winners traditionally returned for a *Brain of Brains* competition; every third winner of those contests competed in the *Top Brain* contest, possibly eight years after their original triumph. *Brain of Brain* winners: 1962 Irene Thomas, 1965 Ian Gillies, 1974 Roger Pritchard, 1977 Tom Dyer, 1980 James Nesbitt, 1983 Peter Barlow, 1986 Richard Fife, 1989 Glen Binnie (finished runner-up to Barbara Thompson in the 1989 series but took her place in Brain of Brain when she was unavailable to appear), 1992 Mike Billson, 1995 Geoffrey Colton, 1998 Kevin Ashman, 2001 Leslie Duncalf, 2004 Alan Bennett., 2007 Mark Bytheway. *Top Brain* winners: 1971 Ian Gillies, 1980 Roger Pritchard, 1989 Peter Barlow, 1998 Kevin Ashman, 2007 Mark Bytheway. Both *Brain of Brains* and *Top Brain* have now been discontinued.

Brainbox Challenge Clive Anderson hosted this challenging quiz in which contestants battled it out to win money from the 'Brain Bank' by proving themselves in a sequence of brain games which tested their memory, language, visual, numerical and spatial skills. BBC2 2008.

Brains Trust, The Discussion programme began on BBC Radio in 1941 and transferred to BBC television between 1955 and 1961 and revived for a short run on BBC2 in 1996. Chairmen: Hugh Ross Willliams, Michael Flanders, Norman Fisher, Alan Melville, Hubert Gregg, Malcolm Muggeridge, Bernard Braden, Robert Kee, Mary Ann Sieghart (1996 revival). Guest panellists included Dr Jacob Bronowski, Bertrand Russell, Egon Ronay and Dr Jonathan Miller (1996 revival).

Brainstorm Science-based quiz hosted by Kenny Everett with help from Cleo Rocos. Four contestants competed for "watts" of brainpower in order to win the final Brain Drain game to prevent being "evaporated". BBC1 1988

Brass Timothy West (Bradley Hardacre), Caroline Blakiston (Patience Hardacre), Geoffrey Hinsliff and Geoffrey Hutchings (George Fairchild). Comedy drama series written by Julian Roach and John Stevenson. The first two series were broadcast on ITV and the third on Channel 4. Set in the fictional northern town of Utterley during the 1930s. The Hardacres are a well-to-do family with interests in mining, munitions and cotton milling. The Fairchilds are a less well-off family with various members showing open hostility towards their 'betters'. ITV 1983-84; C4 1990.

Brass Eye Controversial spoof of current-affairs television and the role of celebrity in the UK. Chris Morris was the inspiration behind, and the lead contributor of, this irreverent but ground-breaking programme which became known for tricking celebrities and politicians into throwing support behind public awareness campaigns for made-up issues that were often absurd or surreal (such as a drug called cake). Other contributors included Doon Mackichan, Mark Heap, Barbara Durkin, David Cann and Kevin Eldon. First broadcast on C4 in 1997, the six-episode series was followed by a one-off 2000 programme on the subject of paedophilia.

Brat Camp Reality television show about a group of unruly teenagers, who are sent away to a special camp for misbehaving teens. The first series was based at Red Cliff Ascent and followed the fortunes of six children; the second series at Turn About Ranch; and the third series at the Aspen Achievement Academy; all in the Utah desert. Series 2 increased the induction to seven children and Series 3 to seven girls. Series 4 was set in a Wilderness Therapy Unit in Idaho and included the parents of four children to make them take responsibility for their kids' behaviour. Series 5 followed a similar format but was set in an Arizona unit. C4 2005-07

Bread Peter Howitt and Graham Bickley (Joey Boswell), Jean Boht (Nellie), Ronald Forfar (Freddie), Victor McGuire (Jack), Gilly Coman and Melanie Hill (Aveline), Jonathan Morris (Adrian), Nick Conway (Billy), Peter Byrne (Derek), Rita Tushingham (Celia Higgins). Sitcom created by Carla Lane and set in Liverpool, and quite often the DHSS, featuring the Boswell's attempts to buck the system with pride. BBC1 1986-91.

Breakfast Time Britain's first national breakfast magazine programme. Presenters included, Frank Bough, Selina Scott, Nick Ross, Mike Smith, Debbie Greenwood, Sue Cook, Sally Magnusson, Kirsty Wark and Jeremy Paxman. Other contributors included the fitness guru Diana Moran (aka The Green Goddess), Russell Grant (Horoscopes), Francis Wilson (Weather) and Glynn Christian (Cookery). First broadcast BBC1, 17 January 1983. In 1989 the name changed to *Breakfast News* with newsreaders such as Nicholas Witchell and Jill Dando now at the helm. In 2000 the programme became *Breakfast* and the current presenters include Bill Turnbull, Sian Williams, Susanna Reid and Charlie Stayt.

Bremner, Bird and Fortune Satirical show uniting the long-standing team of John Bird and John Fortune (the Two Johns) with the satirical impressionist Rory Bremner. The show is almost entirely political, but in recent series different genres of sketches have been introduced. The programme ranges from small sketches and a regular stand-up impressionism section by Bremner to heavily researched, bitingly satirical three-handed historical narratives, as well as ending with a, usually political, musical number. Actresses Pauline McLynn (Mrs Doyle in Father Ted) and Frances Barber add a further dimension to some of the sketches. C4 1999-

Brendan O'Carrolls Hot Milk and Pepper The youngest of eleven children, Brendan O'Carroll was born in Dublin in 1955. His mother, Maureen was a Labour TD (MP) and a huge influence on his life. He left school at 12 and worked as a waiter, trying many other occupations in his spare time - disco manager, milkman, pirate radio disc-jockey, and painter-decorator. For a time he ran his own bar and cabaret lounge before being persuaded to try the comedy circuit with an act built around his fascination for carrots. The gigs were small at first and included his own version of *Blind Date*, but word soon got round about this original and outrageous funnyman. The real turning point in Brendan's career was his first appearance on *The Late Late Show*, Ireland's longest-running chat show, also shown weekly on C4 in the UK. The studio audience and the viewers loved him. His first video *Live at the Tivoli* went straight to No 1, knocking U2 off the top slot and pushing Garth Brooks to No 3. In 1994 he was voted Ireland's No 1 Variety Entertainer at the National Entertainment Awards. *Hot Milk and Pepper,* named after a cure for constipation, was commissioned by RTÉ 1 in 1996 as a replacement for the Sunday night slot previously occupied by the quiz *Where in the World*. Brendan's sidekick on the show was Gerry Browne, who became high profile during the show for alleging he was beaten up by three xenophobic British policemen. Brendan's success on the show led to film parts in The Van (1996) and Angela's Ashes (1999) as well as tv roles in *The Royal Family* (2000) and *The Fattest Man in Britain* (2009). Brendan has also published several novels. In 2005, Brendan married actress Jennifer Gibney.

Brideshead Revisited Anthony Andrews (Lord Sebastian Flyte), Jeremy Irons (Charles Ryder), Diana Quick (Lady Julia Flyte), Laurence Olivier (Lord Alex Marchmain), John Gielgud (Edward Ryder), Clair Bloom (Lady Marchmain), Jane Asher (Celia Mulcaster/Ryder). Eleven-part drama series written by John Mortimer, based on Evelyn Waugh's novel. Sebastian Flyte and Charles Ryder meet at Oxford and become friends after Sebastian breaks his foot and needs a companion. Charles becomes involved with Sebastian's family which is landed gentry and Catholic in a Protestant England. The story is told in flashback as Charles, now an officer in the British Army, is moved with his company to an English country home that he discovers to be Brideshead, the Flyte family home where he has a series of memories of his youth and young manhood, his loves, life, and a journey of faith and anguish. ITV 1981.

Brief, The Alan Davies (Henry Farmer), Cherie Lunghi (Cleo Steyn), Christopher Fulford (Ray Scanlon), Zara Turner (Polly Graham), Steven Alvey (Paul Bracewell), Linda Bassett (Maureen Tyler). Courtroom drama series written by Dusty Hughes. Newly single and temporarily homeless, criminal barrister Henry Farmer's finances are still suffering as a result of his gambling addiction and alimony payments to his ex-wife and son in Australia. Despite his shambolic life, Henry is a formidable courtroom operator with a tremendous gift of cross-examination and a silver tongue for the vital closing speech. Alan decided to discontinue the role after two series and it was widely reported that this was because of filming interfering with his Arsenal addiction; a rumour that Alan has always strongly denied. ITV 2004-05

Britain's Best Dish Daytime cookery show hosted by Mark Nicholas. The three judges, Ed Baines, John Burton Race and Jilly Goolden, sought the best starter, main course and pudding. The first series winners were: Starter - Tiddy Oggy; Main Course - Slow roast belly of pork winner; Pudding - Sticky toffee pudding. The overall winner, as decided by a national vote was the Slow roasted belly of pork. The second series was followed by *Britain's Best Celebrity Dish*. ITV 2007-

Britain's Got Talent For nine days in June 2007 an eclectic array of amateur talent performed in front of judges Simon Cowell, Piers Morgan, and Amanda Holden with the winner receiving £100,000 and an automatic slot at the Royal Variety Performance in front of the Queen and members of the Royal Family at the Empire Theatre in Liverpool. Hosted by Ant and Dec the series, based on the tried and tested X Factor format, had an ITV2 counterpart called *Britain's Got More Talent*, presented by magician and former CITV presenter, Stephen Mulhern. The first ever winner of *Britain's Got Talent* was 36-year-old mobile phone salesman Paul Potts who captivated the audience with his rich operatic voice. The second series in 2008 was rich in talent and the bookies' favourites Faryl Smith (a 12-year-old opera singer) and Escala (a female quartet of electric violin and cello players) failed to reach the final three, the winner being George Sampson,

a 14-year-old dancer. The third series in 2009 followed the same format as the previous two years with the same prize up for grabs. Susan Boyle, a 48-year-old singer whose performance at the auditions had already made her a star before the live final, was surprisingly beaten into second place by the 11-member dance troupe, Diversity. The fourth series in 2010 was unusual inasmuch as the bookies' favourites Spelbound - made up of 13 acrobats, aged from 12 to 24 – duly won despite strong competition from the likes of Janey Cutler, an 81-year-old Scottish songstress and body-popping duoTwist and Pulse. The fifth series in 2011 was won by Scottish vocalist Jai McDowall who beat hot-favourite Ronan Parke, a twelve-year-old singing sensation. ITV 2007-

Britannia High Georgina Hagen (Lauren), Sapphire Elia (Claudine), Rana Roy (Lola), Mitch Hewer (Danny), Matthew James Thomas (Jez), Marquelle Ward (BB), Sophie Powles (Ronnie), Mark Benton (Mr Frank Nugent), Adam Garcia (Stefan – the dance teacher). Musical drama series focusing on the lives of a group of young adults and their mentors at the fictional London theatre school Britannia High. Based on an idea by choreographer Arlene Phillips and theatre impresario David Ian, the eight-part first series features an original soundtrack and incidental music by Take That member Gary Barlow. Guy Chambers, Steve Mac, Andy Hill, Mark Owen and Elliot Kennedy also contributed to the musical component of the show while the writing team consisted of Jonathan Harvey, Damon Rochefort, Julie Jones, Kirstie Falkous and John Reiger. In addition to the main cast, the series featured cameo performances from Girls Aloud, Boyzone, Matt Willis and Gemma Bissix. ITV 2008.

British Isles - A Natural History Eight-part documentary taking viewers on a journey from the formation of what is now the British Isles some 3 billion years ago to the present day, revealing how natural and human forces have shaped the landscape. Presented by Alan Titchmarsh each of the 50-minute episodes was followed by a 10-minute short specific to each region of the country. BBC1 2004.

Brittas Empire, The Chris Barrie (Gordon), Pippa Heywood (Helen Brittas), Julia St John (Laura Lancing), Harriet Thorpe (Carole Parkinson), Michael Burns (Colin Wetherby), Russell Porter (Tim Whistler), Tim Marriott (Gavin Featherly), Jill Greenacre (Linda Perkin), Judy Flynn (Julie Porter). Sitcom, created by Richard Fegen and Andrew Norriss, based around the inept staff of the Whitbury Newtown Leisure Centre, particularly the overbearing and manic manager Gordon Brittas. BBC1 1991-97.

Broaden Your Mind Comedy series starring Tim Brooke-Taylor and Graeme Garden, who were joined by Bill Oddie for the second series - the first time all three of them had performed together on television. Subtitled 'an encyclopaedia of the air' the series' consisted mainly of short sketches with the odd monologue thrown in. Writers included Tim Brooke-Taylor, Graeme Garden, Bill Oddie, Michael Palin, Terry Jones, John Cleese, Graham Chapman, Eric Idle, Terry Gilliam, Roland MacLeod, Marty Feldman, Barry Cryer, Barry Took, Jim Franklin, Simon Brett and Chris Stuart-Clark. BBC2 1968-69.

Broker's Man, The Kevin Whately (Jimmy Griffin), Annette Ekblom (Sally Griffin), Danny Worters (Dominic Griffin), Holly Davidson (Jodie Griffin), Al Ashton (Vinnie Stanley), Jill Baker (Claudette Monro-Foster), Sarah-Jane Potts (Harriet Potter - first series), Charlotte Bellamy (Harriet Potter - second series), Peter Firth (Alex 'Godzilla' Turnbull - first series), John McEnery (Alex 'Godzilla' Turnbull - second series). Drama series about an ex-policeman, Jimmy Griffin, who now uses his detective skills while working for insurance companies. Two series, each of six episodes, were made, the most notable episode being 'Kith and Kin' as it was the last screen appearance of former matinee idol Anthony Steel. BBC1 1997-98

Brookside Channel 4 soap opera created by Phil Redmond and set in Liverpool. First aired on the opening night of Channel 4 (2 November 1982) the final episode going out on 4 November 2003. It is especially well-known for broadcasting the first pre-watershed lesbian kiss (between Beth Jordache and Margaret Clemence) on British television in 1994, as well as a storyline featuring consensual incestuous sexual relations between two sibling characters. In the final episode, drug dealer Jack Michaelson, played by Paul Duckworth, was hanged from his own bedroom window. The lynch mob, who had all been wronged by Michaelson in recent weeks, included Jimmy Corkhill, Steve and Marty Murray, Tim O'Leary and Sean Smith. Full cast listed alphabetically: Betty Alberge (Edna Cross), Gladys Ambrose (Julia Brogan), Tony Armatrading (Charles Weekes), Marcia Ashton (Jean Crosbie), Dicken Ashworth (Alan Partridge), David Banks (Graeme Curtis), Paul Barber (Greg Salter), Judith Barker (Audrey Manners), Jonathan Barlow (Don Summerhill), John Basham (Adrian Roache), Debra Beaumont (Deborah Lawson), Jenny Beaver (Alison Matthews), Kate Beckett (Jenny Swift), Robert Beck (Peter Harrison), Paula Belle, Victoria Bennett (Emily Farnham), Mark Birch (Ducksie Brown), Joanne Black (Kirsty Brown), Christopher Blake (Tim Derby), Kamilla Blanche (Avril), Freddie Boardley (Alasdair Finnegan), Eamon Boland (Ken Dinsdale), Gerard Bostock (Tony Dixon), Tommy Boyle (Kenny Maguire), Nigel Bradshaw (Victor), Hilda Braid (Molly Partridge), Gil Brailey (Heather's boss), Jill Brassington (Gina Brookes Philips), Matthew Brenher (Marcus Seddon), Paul Broughton (Eddie Banks), Duggie Brown (Ray Piper), Eithne Browne (Chrissy Rogers), Faith Brown (Anne Bradley), John Burgess (David 'Bing' Crosbie), Mark Burgess (Gordon Collins), Diane Burke (Katie Rogers), Malandra Burrows (Lisa Morrisey), Amanda Burton (Heather Haversham/Huntingdon/Black), John Burton (Alan Gordon), Andrew Butler (Daniel 'Danny' Simpson), Michelle Byatt (Nikki White), Paul Byatt (Michael 'Mike' Dixon), Richard Calkin (Fredrico 'Fred' Gonzalez), Jennifer Calvert (Cheryl Boyanowsky), Ken Campbell (Oscar Dean), Marji Campi (Jessie Shadwick/Hilton), Jonathan Caplan (Brian Kennedy) Neil Caple (Martin 'Marty' Murray), Kevin Carson (Geoff 'Growler' Rogers), Katrin Cartlidge (Lucy Collins), Simon Chadwick (Dave Burns), Stephanie Chambers (Gabby Parr (2002 - 2003), Tiffany Chapman (Rachel Jordache/Wright/Dixon), Carl Chase (Joey Godden), Peter Christian (Frank Rogers), George Christopher ('Little' Jimmy Corkhill Jr.), Angela Clarke (Elsa), Edward Clayton (Arthur Parkinson), Rosy Clayton (Diane McAllister), Billie Clements (Imelda Clough), Margaret Clifton (Mona Harvey/Fallon), Steven Cole (Leo Johnson), Suzanne Collins (Nikki Shadwick), Carol Connor (Carmel O'Leary), Bill Cookson (Dick Ronson), Kenneth Cope (Ray Hilton), Peter Corey (Freddie Spence), Hilary Crane (Irene Harrison), Matthew Crompton (Darren Murphy and Dan Morrissey), Paul Crosby (Mark Potter), Nigel Crowley (Gordon Collins), Robert T. Cullen (Gizzmo Hawkins), Jane Cunliffe (Laura Wright/Gordon-Davies), Lucinda Curtis (Carolyn Roebuck), Robert Dallas (Richard de Saville), Pauline Daniels (Maria Benson), Chris Darwin (Joey Woods), Anne-Marie Davies (Katrina Evans), Neil Davies (Robbie Moffat), Raine Davison (Mary Bowers), Bill Dean (Harry Cross), Letitia Dean (Dawn - 1984), Timothy Deenihan (Dr. Darren Roebuck), Les Dennis (Jeff Evans), Stephen Donald (Carl Banks), Hannah Dowd (Kylie Stanlow/Corkhill), Philip Dowd (Christian Wright), Jackie Downey (Fee Phelan), Jodie Draper (Paula Heneghan), Barbara Drennan (Niamh Musgrove), Karen Drury (Susannah Morrisey/Farnham), Ray Dunbobbin (Ralph Hardwicke), Stephen Dwyer (Garry Salter), Christian Ealey (Matt Musgrove), Natalie Earl (Kelly Musgrove), Vince Earl (Ronald 'Ron' Dixon), David Easter (Pat Hancock), Annette Ekblom (Debbie Gordon), Brenda Elder (Barbara Black), Jennifer Ellison (Emily Shadwick/O'Leary), Louis Emerick (Mick Johnson), Norman Eshley (Alun Jones), Tina Fairclough (Bagga), Chelsea Farrell (Paige Kelly/Howard), Lisa Faulkner (Louise Hope), Andrew Fillis (Gary Stanlow), Kate Fitzgerald (Doreen Corkhill), Neil Fitzmaurice as Neil Anthony (Sinnott), Pauline Fleming (Val Walker), Alexandra Fletcher (Jacqueline 'Jacqui' Dixon/Farnham), Steven Fletcher (Steven 'Steve' Murray), Gene Foad (James Fleming), Bernadette Foley (Margi Shadwick), Paula Frances (Diana Spence/Corkhill), Marie Francis (Chris Myers), Anna Friel (Beth Jordache), Callum Gablin (Luke Smith), Vickie Gates (Leanne Powell), Sylvia Gatril (Lesley Donnelly), Gabrielle Glaister (Patricia Farnham), Philip Glancy (Scott Black), Helen Grace (Georgia Simpson), Ebony Gray (Cassie Charlton), Norman Gregory (Derek Hobbs), Sheila Grier (Sandra Maghie), Geraldine Griffiths (Carol Thompson), Andrew Hall (Martin Howes),Gillian Hanna (Brenna Jordache), Jodie Hanson (Marianne Dwyer), John Harding (Sam Martin), Sean Harrison (Andrew Taylor), Lee Hartney (Simon Howe), Barbara Hatwell (Anthea Russell/Brindley/Dixon), Ann Haydn-Edwards (Teresa Nolan), Mary Healey (Ruth Sweeney), Andy Henderson (Andy Carlton), Ian Hendry (Davy Jones), Reanne Henesy (Louise Daniels), Jenny Hesketh (Louise Mitchell), Jean Heywood (Kitty Hilton), Derek Hicks (Sean Roach), Polly Highton (Barbara Newton), Beverly Hills (Elaine Davies Johnson), Ruth Holden (Grace Hardwicke), Jason Hope (PC Rod Corkhill), Cliff Howells (George Jackson), Samuel J. Hudson (Ryan Musgrove), Ben Hull (Dr. Gary Parr), Amanda Humphrey (Karen Dalton), Marcus Hutton (Nathan Cuddington), Michael J. Jackson (Ollie Simpson), Carla Jarrett (Gemma Johnson), Tracey Jay (Michelle Jones), Sue Jenkins (Jackie Corkhill), Saul Jephcott (Mike Stevens), Francis Johnson (Ellis Johnson), Meg Johnson (Brigid McKenna), Sue Johnston (Sheila Grant/Corkhill), Gareth Ryan Jones (Matthew Farnham), Naomi Kamanga (Gemma Johnson), Sam Kane (Peter Phelan), Jason Kavanagh (Luke Musgrove), Gillian Kearney (Debbie McGrath), Anna Keaveney (Marie Jackson), Diane Keen (Molly Marchbank), Arthur Kelly (Geoff Wright), Gerard Kelly (Callum Finnegan), Justine Kerrigan (Tracy Corkhill), Roberta Kerr (Sally Haynes), Ian Kershaw (Bennet), Noreen Kershaw (Kathy Roach), Tony King (Adam Black), Al T. Kossy (Alec O'Brien), Adam Kotz (Roy Williams), Renny Krupinski (Sizzler), Sarah Lam (Caroline Choi), Katy Lamont (Adele Murray), Ronnie Leek (Mr. Binenan), Geoffrey Leesley (John Harrison), Cheryl Leigh (Vicki Cleary), Mark Lennock (Tony Dixon), Kwong Chee Leong (Stephen Choi), Matthew Lewney (Lee Banks), Rachael Lindsay (Sammy Rogers/Daniels/Deveraux), John Line (John Swift), Stacey Liu (Michelle Tan), Suzette Llewellyn (Yvonne 'Vonnie' Johnson), Dugald Bruce Lockhart (Mark Wilcox), Leon Lopez (Jerome Johnson), Elizabeth Lovelady (Melanie O'Leary), Linda Lusardi (Frankie), David Lyon (Stuart Gordon), Kenneth MacDonald (George Webb), Cheryl Mackie (Megan Brindley),Vincent Maguire (Brian Lawrence), Cheryl Maiker (Marcia Barrett), Sandra Maitland (Amanda 'Mandy' Jordache/Dutton), Tina Malone (Moe McGee), Tom Mannion (James Markham), Irene Marot (Deborah 'D-D' Dixon), Andrea Marshall (Sarah Banks), Bryan Matheson (Gerald Fallon), James Mawdsley (Brian 'Bumper' Humphries), William Maxwell (Jack Sullivan), Dinah May (Samantha Partridge), John McArdle (Billy Corkhill), Lynsey McCaffrey (Ruth Gordon Smith), Danny McCall (Owen Daniels), Adam McCoy (Josh McLoughlin), Philip McGough (Charlie Dawson), Ashley McKechnie (Kevin Taylor), Sean McKee (Jamie Henderson), Nicholas McKenna (Carl Crawford), Jack McMullen (Josh McLoughlin Dixon), Terry Melia (Kevin), Will Mellor (Paul Howard), Ian Michie (Guy Willis), Greg Milburn (Terry Gibson), Annie Miles (Sue Harper/Sullivan), Kris Mocherri (Ali Gordon), Clive Moore (Derek O'Farrell), Mark Moraghan (Karl Trevor/Colin Lambert/Greg Shadwick), Angela Morant (Barbara Harrison), Jane Morant (Andrea Parkin), Jacqueline Morgan (Dorothy Wright), Ian Morris (Mark Gossage), Dan Mullane (Joey Musgrove), Lawrence Mullin (Steve Matthews), Megan Munro (Leah Musgrove), Brian Murphy (George Manners), Bryan Murray (Trevor Jordache), Jack Mythen (William "Wills" Corkhill), Julie Neubert (Joan Hope), Katy Newell (Cathy Walker), Lesley Nicol (Shelley Rimmer), Lesley Nightingale (Beryl 'Bel' Simpson), Amanda Noar (Rose Finnegan), Amanda Nolan (Lisa Morrisey), Bernie Nolan (Diane Murray), Jessica Noon (Kirsty Gordon), Anna Norbury (Alice Farnham), Richard Norton (Shane Cochrane), Doc O'Brien (George Williams), Eileen O'Brien (Gladys Charlton), Simon O'Brien (Damon Grant), John O'Gorman (Neil 'Tommo' Thompson), Shelagh O'Hara (Karen Grant), Philip Olivier (Timothy 'Tinhead' O'Leary), Stuart Organ (Kevin Cross), Suzanne Packer (Josie Johnson/Brooks), Stifyn Parri (Christopher Duncan), Guy Parry (Dr. Neil Kelly), Sherril Parsons (Cheryl Smith), Greg Pateras (Clint Moffat), Allan Patterson (Gary Jackson), Steven Patterson (Little George Jackson), Simon Paul (Ben O'Leary), Julie Peasgood (Fran Pearson), Kerry Peers (Helen Carey), Kazia Pelka (Anna Wolska),

510

Tricia Penrose (WPC Emma Reid), Joanna Phillips-Lane (Karyn Clark), Alexandra Pigg (Petra Taylor) Steven Pinder (Max Farnham), Steven Pinner (Jonathan Gordon-Davies), Mickey Poppins (Lance Powell), Patricia Potter (Victoria Seagram/Wilcox/Shadwick), Eric Potts (Mr. Moore), Sharon Power (Lyn Matthews/Rogers), Vincent Price (Jason Shadwick), Glynn Pritchard (Christy Murray), Robert Pugh (John Clarke), Raymond Quinn (Anthony 'Tony' Murray), Georgia Reece (Eleanor Kitson), Brian Regan (Terry Sullivan), Debbie Reynolds (Katie Rogers), Diana Ricardo (Lana Costello), Kate Riding (Sally Dinsdale), Louisa Rix (Alison Dicks), Claire Robinson (Ronnie Williams), Crissy Rock (Amber), Christian Rodska (Joe O'Rourke), Lynda Rooke (Penny Riozzi), Dave Rooney (Roy Heneghan), Sharon Rosita (Kate Moses), Alan Rothwell (Nicholas Black), John Sandford (Nat Simpson), Sunetra Sarker (Nisha Batra), Maggie Saunders (Lucy Collins), Leeon Sawyer (Leo Johnson), Tony Scoggo (Matty Nolan), Graham Seed (Mr. Thornton), Ken Sharrock (J C Bradley), Helen Sheals (Jan Murray), Peggy Shields (Mrs. McArdle), Joanne Sidwell (Ruth Black), Barry Sloane (Sean Smith), Doreen Sloane (Annabelle Collins), Kirk Smith (Keith Rooney), Robert Smith (Gizzmo Hawkins), Hayley Smitton (Sharon Bridges), Rob Spendlove (Roger Huntingdon), Alyson Spiro (Alison Gregory), Michael Starke (Thomas 'Sinbad' Sweeney), Shirley Stelfox (Madge Richmond), Brian Stephens (Tom Curzon), Nicola Stephenson (Margaret Clemence), Colette Stevenson (Helen Massey) Dean Sullivan (Jimmy Corkhill), Adam Sunderland (Liam Riley), Anna Sung (Jessica Choi), Allan Surtees (Cyril Dixon), Claire Sweeney (Lindsey Corkhill/Stanlow/Phelan), Paul Swinnerton (Rob Dexter), Mary Tamm (Penny Crosbie), Kim Taylforth (Pauline Robson), Kerrie Thomas (Viv), Malcolm Tierney (Tommy McArdle), Heather Tomlinson (Tanya Davies), Ricky Tomlinson (Bobby Grant), Richard Trinder (Shaun Brookes), Susan Twist (Rosie Banks), Paul Usher (Barry Grant), Matthew Walker (Matthew), Angela Walsh (Carol Salter), Stephen Walters (Geoff 'Growler' Rogers), Gordon Warnecke (Dil Palmar), Susie Ann Watkins (Joe Halsall), Danny Webb (Gavin Taylor), Hilary Welles (Angela Lambert), Martin Wenner (Dr. Tony Hurrell), Alexandra Westcourt (Shelly Bower), John Whitehall (Milkman), Julianne White (Sarah Townes), Sarah White (Beverly 'Bev' McLoughlin/Gonzales/Dixon), Jonathan Whiteley (Craig Charleston), Jim Wiggins (Paul Collins), Edward Wiseman (Harvey), Sarah Withe (Jules Bradley/Simpson), Christopher Wright (Geoffrey Fletcher), David Yip (Michael Choi). C4 1982-2003

Brothers, The Jean Anderson (Mary Hammond), Glyn Owen and Patrick O'Connell (Edward Hammond), Gabrielle Drake (Jill Hammond), Colin Baker (Paul Merroney), Mark McManus (Harry Carter), Liza Goddard (April Winter/Merroney), Kate O' Mara (Jane Maxwell). Drama series created and produced by Gerard Glaister. Three brothers fight for control of the family haulage firm. Mike Pratt (Randall and Hopkirk (Deceased) played the character Don Stacey in his final role before his untimely death. BBC1 1972-76.

Bruce's Price Is Right See *The Price Is Right*

Bruiser Comedy sketch show written by David Mitchell and Robert Webb with additional material by Richard Ayoade, Ricky Gervais, Bash Doran, Richard Parker, James Bachman, Jason Doll-Steinberg, Daniel Lander, David Tomlinson and Russell Young. Cast members were Olivia Colman, David Mitchell, Robert Webb, Martin Freeman, Matthew Holness and Charlotte Hudson. Recurring characters included the vulgar IT technician which was the precursor of Simon in the sitcom *The Office*, also played by Holness, who calls everything a wank. BBC2 2000

Brush Strokes Karl Howman (Jacko), Mike Walling (Eric), Nicky Croydon (Jean), Howard Lew Lewis (Elmo Putney), Gary Waldhorn (Lionel Bainbridge). Sitcom written by John Esmonde and Bob Larbey. A chirpy cockney painter and decorator has an eye for the ladies. The theme song *Because Of You* was performed by Dexy's Midnight Runners. BBC1 1986-91.

Bubble, The News-based celebrity panel game show. Three celebrities were locked away in a media-free zone for four days. When they were released and took part on the show they had to decide which stories that had been in the media were true or had been made up. Presented by comedian David Mitchell. BBC2 2010.

Buccaneer Bryan Marshall (Tony Blair), Clifford Rose (Charles Burton), Pamela Salem (Monica Burton), Carolyn Courage (Kim Hayward), Mark Jones (Ray Mason), Cecil Humphreys (Paul Blair), Shirley Anne Field (Janet Blair). 13-episode drama series written by N.J. Crisp and Eric Paice, revolving around a developing air freight business. BBC2 1980.

Buccaneers, The Robert Shaw (Capt Dan Tempest), Peter Hammond (Lt Beamish), Wilfrid Downing (Dickon), Edwin Richfield (Armando), Roger Delgado (Estaban), Terence Cooper (Blackbeard). Set in the British Caribbean territory of New Providence in the early 18th century, the adventures on the high seas of Dan Tempest and his ex-pirate crew aboard 'The Sultana' now fighting for the British against the Spanish. There were 39 episodes broadcast and Shaw did not appear until the third episode, the first two episodes setting the scene. The series was shot at Nettlefold Studios, Walton-on-Thames, with the sea scenes filmed off the coast of Falmouth in Cornwall. The theme song began "Let's go A-Roving, A-Roving, A-Roving" and was sung by Dick James. ITV 1956-57.

Buddha of Suburbia, The Naveen Andrews (Karim Amir), Roshan Seth (Haroon Amir), Brenda Blethyn (Margaret Amir), John McEnery (Uncle Ted). Drama series written by Hanif Kureishi and Roger Michell with theme song by David Bowie. Set in Bromley, south London, in the 1970s. Karim's mother is English and his father is Indian which gives Karim some problems with life in British society which can be racist and intolerant He particularly experiences this when he attempts to become an actor. BBC2 1993.

Budgie Adam Faith (Ronald 'Budgie' Bird), Iain Cuthbertson (Charlie Endell), Lynn Dalby (Hazel), Georgina Hale (Jean Bird), John Rhys-Davies (Laughing Spam Fritter), Rio Fanning (Grogan). Written by Keith Waterhouse and Willis Hall, this enormously popular series starred former pop idol Faith, in his first television acting role, as a cockney wide-boy working on the fringes of propriety via his malevolent boss Charlie Endell. A serious car crash forced Adam to announce his retirement from acting in 1973 thus preventing a third series being made. ITV 1971-72. The series spawned a spin-off *Charles Endell Esquire* in 1979 but due to an ITV technicians' strike which took the network (Scottish Television) off the air for three months, the series was postponed and only six episodes were made.

Bullseye Darts-based game show hosted by Jim Bowen. The series spawned catchphrases such as "Let's have a look at what you would 'ave won" and "Let's have a bit of bully". The announcer was Tony Green and all the top professional dart players took part in the charity section after the mid-show commercial break. ITV 1981-95. The format was revived on Challenge in 2006 with Phoenix Nights star, Dave Spikey, as host alongside Tony Green.

Bulman Don Henderson (George Bulman), Siobhan Redmond (Lucy McGinty), Thorley Waters (William Dugdale). Having left the police force in disgust, the eccentric and bad-tempered detective George Kitchener Bulman sets himself up as a private investigator in this third appearance of the character (see also *The XYY Man* and *Strangers*). Bulman is quirkier than in his earlier manifestations, he is taken to wearing fingerless grey gloves, using an asthma inhaler, carrying a plastic bag and driving a 2CV car. ITV 1985-87.

Busman's Holiday Quiz Show between two teams representing a particular trade, industry or profession, the winners having the opportunity to see how their jobs are performed elsewhere in the world. Presenters: Julian Pettifer, Sarah Kennedy, Elton Welsby. ITV 1985-93.

Butterflies Wendy Craig (Ria Parkinson), Geoffrey Palmer (Ben Parkinson) Andrew Hall (Russell Parkinson), Nicholas Lyndhurst (Adam Parkinson), Bruce Montague (Leonard Dunn). Sitcom based on the midlife crises of an attractive middle-class woman and her dentist husband. The title is a reference to Ben's hobby but also an allusion to how the Parkinsons were pinned down like those in Ben's collection. Series created by Carla Lane and broadcast BBC2 1978-80 and 1983.

Button Moon The adventures of Mr Spoon, who in each episode would travel to Button Moon with his wife Mrs Spoon and his daughter Tina in his homemade rocket-ship. Once on Button Moon (which hung in "blanket sky") they would have an adventure before heading home. They would often use their telescope to watch creatures on Junk Planet and other distant worlds. Mr Spoon and the Spoon Family live at Cardboard Box House, Treacle Street. Narrated by Robin Parkinson, the puppet series was written by Ian Allen and the theme song was performed by husband and wife Peter Davison and Sandra Dickinson. ITV 1980-88.

By Any Means See *Charley Boorman: Ireland to Sydney*

By the Sword Divided Sharon Maughan (Anne Lacey/Fletcher), Julian Glover (Sir Martin Lacey), Tim Bentinck (Sir Thomas Lacey), Rob Edwards (John Fletcher), Jeremy Clyde (King Charles I), Peter Jeffrey (Oliver Cromwell), Simon Treves (King Charles II), Simon Butteriss (Hugh Brandon) and Christopher Baines (Prince Rupert). Historical drama series created by John Hawkesworth. A family is torn apart by the English Civil War. BBC1 1983-85.

Byker Grove Soap opera set around the Newcastle-based Byker Grove Youth Centre. Created by Adele Rose and most memorable for giving the world the comedy double-act of 'Ant 'n Dec' via their successful but short-lived pop career as PJ and Duncan. Cast in alphabetical order includes: Grant Adams (Ed), Donna Air (Charlie Charlton), Jody Baldwin (Cher), Lyndyann Barrass (Spuggie), Chris Beattie (Joe Dakin), Alex Beebe (Adam Brett), Dominic Beebe (Luke Brett), Nicola Bell (Debbie Dobson), Caspar Berry (Martin 'Gill' Gillespie), Stephen Bradley (Speedy), Daymon Britton (Dom Meredith), Stephen Carr (Barney Hardy), Michelle Charles (Marilyn 'Charley' Charlton), Kerry Ann Christiansen (Flora), Gary James Crawford (Greg Watson), Colin Cuthbert (Carter), Luke Dale (Frew), Declan Donnelly (Duncan between 1989-93), Kimberly Dunbar (Karen), Matthew Edgar (Jamie), Nicola Ewart (Jemma Dobson), Billy Fane (Geoff Keegan), Bill Fellows (Mr. Rivers), Jonathan Ferguson (Binnie), Nick Figgis (Jake), Duncan Ford (Alan), Alexia Gibb (Nat), Rory Gibson (Lee Ratcliffe), Tracy Gillman (Jeanette Wilson), Claire Graham (Anna Turnbull), Gemma Graham (Amanda Bewick), Thomas Graham (Robert), Craig Grieveson (Ian Webster), Jill Halfpenny (Nicola Dobson between 1989-92), Siobhan Hanratty (Nikki Watson), Charlie Hardwick (Sian), Christopher Hardy (Robert), Vicky Hawkins (Claire Rivers), Louise Henderson (Laura), Pete Hepple (Liam), Jayni Hoy (Leah Carmichael), Adam Ironside (Bill Dakin), Leah Jones (Harry), Gregory A. Kyprianou (Simon Rivers), Rory Lewis (Eve Johnson), Emma Littlewood (Stella Reece), Gavin Makel (Rob), Phil Matthews (Dean Sinton), Joanne Mcintosh (Brigid O'Hagan), Ant McPartlin (Peter 'PJ' Jenkins between 1990-93), Sally McQuillan (Donna Bell), Paul Meynell (Stumpy), Nicholas Nancarrow (Bradley Clayton), David Oliver (Marcus Bewick), Anne Orwin (Lou Gallagher), Ronan Paterson (Sgt. Tom), Danny Ponton (Hugo), Craig Reilly (Winston), Oz Reth (Jesus), Neil Shearer (Andrew 'Cas' Pearson), Andrew Hayden Smith (Ben Carter), Andrew Smith (Alfie Turnbull), Leanne Adele Taylor (Terraise O'Hagan), Victoria Taylor (Angel O'Hagan), Lyndsey Todd (Chrissie Van Den Berg), Jade Turnbull (Regina O'Hagan), Gauri Vedhara (Sita), Lucy Walsh (Julie Warner), Michelle Warden (Joanne), Daniel Waterston (Mickey), Louis Watson (Ollie Guinane), Amanda Webster (Hayley), Holly Wilkinson (Emma Miller), Lynne Wilmot (Tina), Chris Woodger (Terry). In March 2008 Gallowgate Productions, the TV production company owned by Ant McPartlin and Declan Donnelly, purchased the rights to Byker Grove. BBC1 1989-2006

C.A.T.S. Eyes Jill Gascoine (Maggie Forbes), Rosalyn Landor (Pru Standfast) Leslie Ash (Frederica 'Fred' Smith), Don Warrington (Nigel Beaumont), Tracy-Louise Ward (Tessa Robinson). Created by Terence Feely as a British version of Charlie's Angels with a female detective agency (Eyes Enquiry Agency) acting as a front for a Home Office security team known as C.A.T.S. (Covert Activities Thames Section). ITV 1985-87.

Cadfael Derek Jacobi (Brother Cadfael), Michael Culver (Prior Robert), Julian Firth (Brother Jerome), Terrence Hardiman (Abbot Radulfus), Sean Pertwee (Sheriff Hugh Beringar – Series 1), Eoin McCarthy (Beringar - Series 2 & 3), Anthony Green (Beringar – Series 4), Michael Grandage (King Stephen), Sarah Badel (Sister Magdalen , Avice of Thornbury), Anna Friel (Sioned), Maggie O'Neill (Aline Siward). Based on the novels of the late Edith Pargeter writing under the name "Ellis Peters", the 13 feature-length episodes, adapted by Simon Burke and Russell Lewis, remained largely true to the books. Cadfael ap Meilyr ap Dafydd, was born in May 1080 during the early Norman occupation of Britain. He fought as a Crusader at the turn of the century and became a Benedictine monk in middle-age. The stories are set during the civil war between the forces of King Stephen and the would-be Queen Matilda. The crusader-turned-monk uses his botanical knowledge to solve mysteries in and around Shrewsbury Abbey in Shropshire. The films were shot in Hungary (mainly Budapest) and used local actors both as extras and in speaking roles. ITV 1994-98.

Caesars, The Roland Culver (Augustus), Eric Flynn (Germanicus), Andre Morell (Tiberius), Barrie Ingham (Sejanus), Ralph Bates (Caligula), Freddie Jones (Claudius), Sonia Dresdel (Livia). Historical drama first shown on ITV in 1968.

Call Me Mister Steve Bisley (Jack Bartholomew), Dermot Crowley (Det Sgt McBride), David Bamber (Fred Hurley), Dulice Liecier (Julie Columbus), Haydn Gwynne (Bridget Bartholomew), Rupert Frazer (Philip Bartholomew), Michael Medwin (Sir Basil Kinthly). Anglo-Australian drama series written by Robert Banks Stewart, Glenn Chandler and Terry Hodgkinson. Former Aussie policeman Jack Bartholomew moves to Britain when he discovers he is heir to a family title. Not really getting on with his newly-discovered family he starts working as a private Detective. BBC1 1986.

Call My Bluff Presenters: Robert Robinson, Bob Holness, Robin Ray, Joe Melia, Peter Wheeler, Fiona Bruce. Popular panel show where two celebrity teams of three gave unlikely definitions of obscure words. Although Robin Ray was the original presenter the name of Robert Robinson is synonymous with the show, taking over in 1967 and presiding over matters until 1988. Robert Morley and Frank Muir were the first team captains and Patrick Campbell took over from Morley in the show's most popular period throughout the 1970s and Arthur Marshall subsequently replacing him in the 1980s. The show was revived in 1996 with Bob Holness as chairman and Alan Coren and Sandy Toksvig the team captains. Fiona Bruce took over the chair in 2003 and Rod Liddle replaced Toksvig. BBC2 1965-88 and 1996-2005.

Call Oxbridge 2000 See *Emergency Ward 10*

Callan Edward Woodward (David Callan), Russell Hunter (Lonely), Ronald Radd, Michael Goodliffe, Derek Bond, William Squire (Hunter), Anthony Valentine (Toby Meres), Patrick Mower (Cross). The classic spy series started as an Armchair Theatre production *A Magnum For Schneider* with Peter Bowles playing Toby Meres. ITV 1967-72. Edward Woodward reprised his most famous role in a one-off 90-minute episode in 1981 entitled *Wet Job*.

Camberwick Green Created by Gordon Murray and narrated by Brian Cant, the children's puppet series took over the Monday *Watch with Mother* slot from *Picture Box*. Animated by Bob Bura and John Hardwick. Characters included Capt Snort, Sgt Major Grout, Windy Miller of Colley's Mill, Mickey Murphy the Baker, Dr Mopp, Thomas Tripp the Milkman, Mrs Dingle the Postmistress, Mrs Honeyman the chemist's wife, Jonathan Bell the farmer, Mr Crockett the garage owner, Mr Dagenham the salesman, Peter Hazel the postman, Packet the post office puppy, Roger Varley the chimney sweep, Mr Carraway the fishmonger, PC McGarry (No 452). Each episode opens and ends with a shot of a musical box from which one of the villagers slowly emerges to allow viewers to follow them as they go about their day whereupon some minor tragedy would inevitably occur and the gallant lads at Pippin Fort are called upon to restore order. First broadcast on BBC1 in 1966 the 13 episodes were frequently repeated and the series spawned two spin-offs *Trumpton* and *Chigley*.

Camelot Joseph Fiennes (Merlin), Jamie Campbell Bower (King Arthur), Tamsin Egerton (Guinevere), Peter Mooney (Kay), Philip

Winchester (Leontes), Eva Green (Morgan), Claire Forlani (Queen Igraine), Clive Standen (Gawain), Diarmaid Murtagh (Brastias), Chipo Chung (Vivian), Jamie Downey (Ulfius), Sinéad Cusack (Sybil), Lara Jean Chorostecki (Bridget), James Purefoy (King Lot), Sebastian Koch (King Uther), Daragh O'Malley (Leodegrance), Sean Pertwee (Sir Ector), Lauren Coe (Lady of the Lake). Irish/Canadian historical-fantasy-drama created by Chris Chibnall and Michael Hirst, loosely based on the Arthurian legend as told by Geoffrey of Monmouth and Thomas Malory. The series was shown after the watershed due to its graphic nudity and language. C4 2011

Camomile Lawn, The Felicity Kendal (Helena Cuthbertson), Paul Eddington (Richard Cuthbertson), Jennifer Ehle (Calypso), Rosemary Harris (Calypso when older), Tara Fitzgerald (Polly), Virginia McKenna (Polly when older), Toby Stephen (Oliver), Richard Johnson (Oliver when older), Rebecca Hall (Sophy), Claire Bloom (Sophy when older), Ben Walden (Walter), Joss Brook (David Floyer), Jeremy Brook (Paul Floyer), Oliver Cotton (Max Erstweiler), Trudy Weiss (Monika), Nicholas Le Prevost (Hector/Hamish). Four-part dramatisation of Mary Wesley's novel adapted by Ken Taylor, highlighting the lives and loves of a family of cousins from 1939 to the present. The story begins with a funeral and uses the reminiscences of those gathered to fill in details in the lives of Richard and Helena and their nieces and nephews. Calypso was notably played by mother and daughter actresses Rosemary Harris and Jennifer Ehle. C4 1992.

Campbells, The Malcolm Stoddard (Dr James Campbell), Amber Lea Weston (Emma Campbell), John Wildman (Neil Campbell), Eric Richards (John Campbell), Cedric Smith (Captain Thomas Sims), Wendy Lyon (Rebecca Sims), Brigit Wilson (Harriet Sims), Julien Poulin (Gabriel Leger), Rosemary Dunsmore (Mary MacTavish). Set during the Highland Clearances of Scotland in the 19th century, the story concerns the Campbell family's attempt to start a new life in Canada. ITV 1986-90.

Campion Peter Davison (Albert Campion), Brian Glover (Magersfontein Lugg his Manservant), Andrew Burt (Chief Inspector Stanislaus Oates). Margery Allingham's aristocratic sleuth solves crimes in the East Anglian countryside of the 1930s driving around in a vintage Lagonda. BBC1 1989-90.

Candid Camera Presenters: Bob Monkhouse, Jonathan Routh, Peter Dulay. "Smile, you're on Candid Camera" became one of the most popular catchphrases in the 1960s when the bowler-hatted Jonathan Routh delivered the punchline to some outrageous hidden-camera stunts that were spoken of in pubs and clubs with more affection than the latest plot of Corrie or the Saturday football results. The most famous wind-up concerned Routh 'driving' (actually being pushed) to a garage and enquiring of mechanics as to why his car wouldn't start only for the non-plussed staff to lift the bonnet to find the distinct lack of an engine. Eventually Routh became too well-known as an actor and replaced Bob Monkhouse as the show's presenter, his partner in crime Arthur Atkins taking a more prominent role as he had more nondescript looks. The show originally aired on ITV 1960-67 and was revived in 1974 by Peter Dulay.

Canterbury Tales, The A series of six single dramas adapted from one of Geoffrey Chaucer's 14th century Canterbury Tales which are transferred to a modern, 21st century setting, but still set along the traditional Pilgrims' route to Canterbury. The anthology series was conceived by Laura Mackie and Franc Roddam and starred James Nesbitt, Dennis Waterman, Billie Piper, Kenny Doughty (*The Miller's Tale*); Julie Walters, Paul Nicholls, Bill Nighy (*The Wife of Bath*); John Simm, Chiwetel Ejiofor, Keeley Hawes (*The Knight's Tale*); Om Puri, Nitin Ganatra, Indira Varma (*The Sea Captain's Tale*); Jonny Lee Miller, William Beck (*The Pardoner's Tale*); and Andrew Lincoln, Nikki Amuka-Bird (*The Man of Law's Tale*). Julie Walters won a Best Actress Award at the British Academy Television Awards, for her role as Beth. BBC1 2003.

Cape Wrath David Morrissey (David Brogan), Lucy Cohu (Evelyn Brogan), Felicity Jones (Zoe Brogan), Harry Treadaway (Mark Brogan), Scot Williams (Tom Tyrell), Nina Sosanya (Samantha), Kate Steavenson-Payne (Alison Tyrell), Melanie Hill (Brenda Ogilvie), Tom Hardy (Jack Donnelly), Ralph Brown (Bernard Wintersgill), Ella Smith (Jezebel Ogilvie), David Smallbone (Green Suit), Tony Lee (Meadowlands Guard). Eerie,

tense drama series. The Brogans move to a seemingly idyllic suburb, Meadowlands, to escape something sinister in their past. They meet Brenda, their hyperactive and highly strung neighbour who speaks of almost nothing but the beauty of her daughter Jezebel; Jack Donnelly, the local handyman who feeds off people's fear of him; Wintersgill, a police detective who ensures the residents remain lawful and dispenses justice as he sees fit, and keeping an eye on them all is the seemingly impenetrable 'handler' Samantha. All have something to hide. C4 2007.

Capital City Douglas Hodge (Declan McConnachie), Trevyn McDowell (Michelle Hauptmann), William Armstrong (Max Lubin), Jason Isaacs (Chas Ewell), Joanna Kanska (Sirkka Nieminen), John Bowe (Leonard Ansen), Rolf Saxon (Hudson Talbot III), Saira Todd (Hillary Rollinger). Drama series created by Andrew MacLear, focusing on the lives of investment bankers in London living and working on the corporate trading floor for the fictional international bank Shane-Longman. ITV 1989-90.

Captain Butler Craig Charles (Captain Butler), Roger Griffiths (Cliff), Sanjeev Bhaskar (Adeel), Shaun Curry (Bosun), Lewis Rae (Roger). Six-episode sitcom written by John Smith and Rob Sprackling. Set in the late 18th century during the golden age of piracy, Butler is the captain of a motley crew of wannabe pirates. The stories are light-hearted and full of intended historical inaccuracies (such as the crew reading girlie magazines). The series' theme tune was The Sex Pistols version of "Friggin' In The Riggin'" C4 1997.

Captain Pugwash BBC1 animated pirate series created by John Ryan that ran from 1957-66. Characters included Capt Horatio Pugwash (Skipper of the Black Pig), Barnabas and Willy, Master Mate, Tom, and Cut Throat Jake. "Dollopping doubloons! Coddling catfish! Lolloping landlubbers! Staggering stalactites! Nautical Nitwits! Kipper me capstans! Tottering turtles! Plundering porpoises! Jumping jellyfish! Harrowing hurricanes!" were among the favourite exclamations of the rotund pirate Captain Pugwash to the work-shy crew of his ship *The Black Pig* as they sailed the Seven Seas and encountered adventures. The overtly brave but ultimately reticent captain was a simple man and no match for his various shiver-me-timbers foes but fortunately he was regularly rescued from the clutches of black-bearded arch villain Cut-Throat Jake (of *The Flying Dustman*) by the cunning and courage of the Black Pig's cabin boy Tom. Originally, a very basic animated programme, in which speech was simulated by moving a piece of card behind the character's open mouths, the BBC screened a colour version in 1974 and ITV gave a state-of-the-art reworking of 26 new episodes in 1998. Theme Music The Trumpet Hornpipe performed on the accordion by Tommy Edmondson. Narrator: Peter Hawkins. It is an urban myth that there were characters with names such as Master Bates, Seaman Staines, and Roger the Cabin Boy and also that the theme tune was entitled The Hornblower.

Captain Scarlet and the Mysterons Supermarionation series created and produced by Gerry and Sylvia Anderson. Set in 2068, the series follows the continuing battle of Spectrum (the world's security command) against the Mysterons, who have launched war against Earth after their Martian city has been mistakenly destroyed by a group of Earthling explorers, led by Spectrum's Captain Black. The Mysterons possess incredible abilities, not least of which is their power of retro-metabolism (recreation of destroyed matter). They can take an object, or a person, which has been destroyed, and recreate it to an exact copy and use it to exact their revenge on Earth. It's by the powers of the Mysterons that Captain Scarlet is killed, in the first episode, along with Captain Black, they are both recreated to try to assassinate the World President but although Captain Black becomes a Mysteron agent it is discovered that Captain Scarlet remains free of their influence but his body now heals at an incredible rate, and he can even recuperate from a fatal wound and is in effect indestructible and ready to take on the aliens who had tried to make him their slave. Voices: Francis Matthews (Paul Metcalfe/Captain Scarlet), Donald Gray (Charles Gray/Colonel White), Ed Bishop (Adam Svenson/Captain Blue), Paul Maxwell (Bradley Holden/Captain Grey), Sylvia Anderson (Magnolia Jones/Melody Angel), Liz Morgan (Juliette Pointon/Destiny Angel), Janna Hill (Karen Wainwright/Symphony Angel), Liz Morgan (Diane Sims/Rhapsody Angel), Lian-Shin (Chan Kwan/Harmony Angel),

Donald Gray (Conrad Turner/Captain Black), Charles Tingwell (Edward Wilkie/Dr Fawn), Gary Files (Patrick Donaghue/Captain Magenta), Jeremy Wilkin (Richard Frazier/Captain Ochre), Cy Grant (Seymour Griffiths/Lt Green), Paul Maxwell (World President), Donald Gray (The Voice of the Mysterons). Colonel White's Spectrum base is called Cloudbase. The five female pilots include two Americans, one Japanese, one French and a British girl born in Chelsea (Rhapsody). Lt Green was Trinidadian. The Angel Interceptor Aircraft Codeword was SIG (Spectrum is Green). ITV 1967-68.

Cardiac Arrest Helen Baxendale (Dr Claire Maitland), Andrew Lancel (Dr Andrew Collin), Pooky Quesnel (Dr Monica Broome), Ahsen Bhatti (Dr Rajesh Rajah), Jo Dow (Dr James Mortimer), Nicholas Palliser (Mr Paul Tennant), Jayne Mackenzie (Staff Nurse Caroline Richards), Peter O'Brien (Dr Cyril "Scissors" Smedley). Written by Dr Ged Mercurio (under the name John MacUre) the medical drama described a world of lazy nurses, rule-bending consultants and constantly stressed junior doctors, who often had to cope with situations beyond their experience. A second season episode, featuring a haemophiliac spectacularly bleeding to death through his nose, prompted the BBC to preface the following week's episode with a reassurance that nose bleeds are rarely fatal. BBC1 1994-96.

Carry On Laughing Jack Douglas (Lord Peter Flimsy / Ethelred / Colonel Yackoff / Sir Jethro / Sir Gay / Clodson / Dick Darcy / Master of the Rolls / Lord Essex), Kenneth Connor (King Philip / King Arthur / Nickoff / Athelstan / Punter / Sir William / Sir Harry Bulgen-Plunger / Stanley), Joan Sims (Lady Guinevere / Madame Olga / Lady Isobel / Lady Kate / Amelia Forbush / Else / Mrs Breeches), Barbara Windsor (Lady Miranda / Lady Mary Airy-Fairy / Marie / Lottie / Vera Basket / Sarah), Peter Butterworth (Oliver Cromwell / Merlin / Count Yerackers / Friar Roger / Lord Gropefinger), David Lodge (Sir Simon de Montfort / William the Conqueror / Inspector Bungler / Duke Boris), Norman Chappell (Sir William), Bernard Bresslaw (Dr Pavingstone / Sir Pureheart / Sir Lancelot / Starkers / Klanger), Sid James (Sir Francis Drake / Arnold Basket / Prince Rupert / Baron Hubert / Lovelace), Sherrie Hewson (Virginia Bulgen-Plunger / Nurse Millie Teazel), Victor Maddern (Charlie / Todd), Hattie Jacques (Queen Elizabeth I), Andrew Ray (Willie Bulgen-Plunger), Carol Hawkins (Lilly), Brian Capron (Trumpeter). 13-part sitcom very much akin to the humour of the film series. Dave Freeman and Lew Schwarz wrote six episodes a piece while Barry Cryer and Dick Vosburgh penned the other. ITV 1975.

Casanova Frank Finlay (Giovanni Casanova), Norman Rossington (Lorenzo), Zienia Merton (Cristina), Christine Noonan (Barberina), Patrick Newell (Schalon). Six-part drama by Dennis Potter based on the life of the great Venetian Lothario. The drama portrays Casanova reflecting on his life from a prison cell. BBC2 1971. A 2005 mini-series of the same title was shown on BBC3 and starred Peter O'Toole as the older Casanova looking back on his life, David Tennant as his young self and Dervla Kirwan as his mother.

Casanova '73 Leslie Phillips (Henry Newhouse), Jan Holden (Carole Newhouse), Madeline Smith (Tessa). Six-part sitcom written by Ray Galton and Alan Simpson. Henry Newhouse (a literal translation of the Italian "casa nova") has a way with the ladies, much to the annoyance of his wife, Carole, and niece, Tessa. The risqué humour caused a slot transfer after three episodes, with *Mastermind,* which was originally shown as a late-night quiz. BBC1 1973.

Case Histories of Scotland Yard Drama series, with a varying cast, hosted by Edgar Lustgarten and based on actual Scotland Yard case files. ITV 1955.

Cash in the Attic Reality show where the object is for a featured family to make enough money for them to achieve their goals by means of selling hidden treasures. Presenters have included Lorne Spicer, Ben Fogle, Alistair Appleton, Angus Purden, Jennie Bond, Angela Rippon, Chris Hollins, Aled Jones and Gloria Hunniford. Resident experts have included Paul Hayes, Jonty Hearnden, James Rylands and John Cameron. BBC1 2002-11

Castaway 2000 and 2007 Castaway 2000 was a series of BBC 1 programs covering the adventures of 36 specially selected people who had agreed to give up on the hullabaloo of modern living and turn their attentions to a simpler way of life for a year on the beautiful Outer Hebridean island of Taransay in the Western Isles of Scotland. Some of the 'contestants' failed to stay the course but one notable exception was Ben Fogle (and his black labrador, Inca), a Picture Editor at society magazine Tatler who became something of a pin-up for the ladies and subsequently carved out a successful media career. Castaway returned seven years on with a new shape and new twists. Presented by Danny Wallace, the show differed from the previous series inasmuch as there was originally just one set of castaways; this time the group evolved throughout the three months of the project, and one viewer was to join the experiment on Great Barrier Island, New Zealand during the run. Each week, live on BBC One, the castaways had to make a group decision that had a crucial effect on their island lives. BBC 3 screened a spin-off show on weekday evenings called *Castaway: The Last 24 Hours,* hosted by Richard Bacon. The winner of the 2007 version was Jonathan Shearer, 41, from the island of Benbecula in Scotland.

Casualty Medical drama series set in the casualty department of Holby (a thinly disguised Bristol) City Hospital. Created by Jeremy Brock and Paul Unwin. Recent cast list (in alphabetical order) with dates joining: Matt Bardock (Jeff Collier – 2007), William Beck (Dylan Keogh - 2011), Charles Dale (Mackenzie "Big Mac" Chalker – 2007), Michael French (Nick Jordan – 1998), Jane Hazlegrove (Kathleen "Dixie" Dixon – 2006), Madeleine Mantock (Scarlett Conway – 2011), Tony Marshall (Noel Garcia – 2008), Steven Miller (Lenny Lyons – 2009), Michael Obiora (Lloyd Asike - 2011), Suzanne Packer (Tess Bateman - 2003), Charlotte Salt (Sam Nicholls - 2011), Sunetra Sarker (Zoe Hanna – 2007), Derek Thompson (Charlie Fairhead - 1986), Christine Tremarco (Linda Andrews - 2010). Other cast members have included, in historical order of appearance: Brenda Fricker (Megan Roach - 1986-90; 1998; 2007; 2010), Bernard Gallagher (Ewart Plimmer - 1986-88), Julia Watson (Barbara 'Baz' Samuels /Hayes / Fairhead - 1986, 1995-98), George Harris (Clive King -1986), Catherine Shipton (Lisa 'Duffy' Duffin - 1986-93, 1998-2003), Robson Green (Jimmy Powell - 1989-92), Ian Bleasdale (Josh Griffiths – 1989-2007), Nigel Le Vaillant (Julian Chapman - 1990-92), Mamta Kaash (Beth Ramanee - 1990-92), Patrick Robinson (Martin 'Ash' Ashford - 1990-96), Eamon Boland (Tony Walker - 1990), Caroline Webster (Jane Scott - 1990-94), Robert Daws (Simon Eastman - 1992-93), Clive Mantle (Mike Barratt - 1992-96), Jason Merrells (Matt Hawley - 1994-97), Lisa Coleman (Jude Korcanik - 1994-97), Sue Devaney (Liz Harker - 1994-97), Claire Goose (Tina Seabrook - 1997-2000), Gerald Kyd (Sean Maddox - 1998-2006), Kwame Kwei-Armah (Finlay Newton - 1999-2004), Philip Bretherton (Andrew Bower - 2000-01), Will Mellor (Jack Vincent - 2001-03), Kieron Forsyth (Tom Harvey - 2000-01), Judy Loe (Jan Goddard - 2001-03), Lee Warburton (Tony Vincent - 2001-03), Martina Laird (Comfort Jones – 2001-06), Simon MacCorkindale (Harry Harper – 2002-08), Sarah Manners (Bex Reynolds - 2003-05), Maxwell Caulfield - Jim Brodie (2003-04), Leanne Wilson (Claire Guildford - 2003-05), Liz Carling (Selena Manning - 2003-07), James Redmond (John 'Abs' Denham – 2003-08), Will Thorp (Paul 'Woody' Joyner - 2004-05), Georgina Bouzova (Ellen Zitek - 2004-06), Rebekah Gibbs (Nina Farr - 2004), Luke Bailey (Sam Bateman – 2004-07), Elyes Gabel (Guppy Sandhu – 2004-07), Ben Price (Nathan Spencer -2005-07), Susan Cookson (Maggie Coldwell – 2005-09), Janine Mellor (Kelsey Phillips – 2005-09), Joanne King (Cynthia "Cyd" Pyke - 2006-07), Kip Gamblin (Greg Fallon – 2006-08), Sam Grey (Alice Chantrey – 2006-10), Peter O'Brien (Theo "Stitch" Lambert - 2007), Matthew Needham (Toby De Silva - 2007-09), Tristan Gemmill (Adam Trueman – 2007-11), Georgia Taylor (Ruth Winters – 2007-11), Lysette Anthony (Rachel Houston 2007; Amanda 2009), Ivana Bašić (Snezana Lalovic - 2008-09), Abdul Salis (Curtis Cooper - 2008-09), Gillian Kearney (Jessica Harrison - 2008-10), Ben Turner (Jay Faldren – 2008-11), Laura Aikman (May Phelps – 2009-

10),Sophia Di Martino (Pauline "Polly" Emmerson - 2009-11), Will Sharpe (Yuki Reid – 2009-11), Lucy Gaskell (Kirsty Clements - 2010-11), Hasina Haque (Madiha "Mads" Durrani - 2010-11). BBC1 1986- See also *Holby City*.

Catchphrase Game show wherein two contestants compete to solve computer-generated 'dingbats' in order to win prizes (many of the 'catchphrases' involved an animated robot named Mr Chips). The series spawned its own catchphrase of "say what you see". Presenters: Roy Walker (1986-1999), Nick Weir (2000-01), Mark Curry (2002). ITV 1986-2002.

Catchword Game show presented by Paul Coia. The main part of the game involved a computer (named Bryan) generating three letters, the contestant having to come up with the longest word they can think of which contains those letters within a few seconds. This was the show that gave us such regulars as "Antidisestablishmentarianism", "Floccinaucinihilipilification" and the longest word in any English-language dictionary, "Pneumonoultramicroscopicsilicovolcanokoniosis" (45 letters; a lung disease caused by breathing in certain particles. It is also spelt - coniosis). Other word game rounds included looking for a hidden word in a sentence, anagrams and synonyms. BBC2 1989-97.

Catherine Tate Show, The Comedy sketch show written by Catherine Tate, Aschlin Ditta and Derren Litten. Performers include Catherine Tate, Jonathan McGuinness, Ella Kenion, Sue Elliot Nicholls, Aschlin Ditta, Michael Brandon, Matthew Horne, Derren Litten, Angela McHale, Bruce MacKinnon, Lee Ross and Niky Wardley. Characters include: Lauren, the modern-day schoolgirl constantly troubled by current parlance (infecting the country with the catchphrases 'Am I bovvered?', 'Are you disrespecting my family?' and 'Are you calling me a pikey?'); the cockney Nan Taylor who, while appearing to be pleasant, is actually a foul-mouthed racist, her catch phrase being 'What a fucking liberty'; Bernie the incompetent nurse - An Irish nurse who teeters on being sacked in every episode. She frequently makes inappropriate remarks to her patients, takes critically ill members of the public on wild nights out, has illicit relationships with any interested staff members and mixes up the records of patients both living and dead; Margaret - the frightened woman - A woman who screams with terror at everyday noises like a pop-up toaster (Catherine based this character on her mother); Bunty Carmichael the over-aged majorette - A woman who insists on being allowed to perform in a children's baton twirling team, as there is no age limit. Her obsession with the club results in the owner contacting the police and obtaining a restraining order; Elaine Figgis the bride of a killer - A woman who appears in a documentary, following her engagement and eventual marriage to a convicted killer on Death Row in the US; The austere woman - who disapproves of the behaviour of everybody around her, before passing wind loudly and unashamedly; and The unhappy Northern couple - who express their disgust at meals they have had in restaurants. After complaining about the food and prices, they use their catchphrase: "The dirty bastards!". Subsequent editions introduced Derek, an overtly effeminate man constantly outraged at the widespread assumption he is gay. His catchphrase is "How very dare you!", as well as the overuse of the word "dear". He is sometimes seen with a male companion, Leslie; and Moo Shepherd, a hugely competitive dog trainer from Birmingham whose dog Lady Penelope ends up coming last at an important contest. The show's theme tune for the first series was *In These Shoes?* by Kirsty MacColl. BBC2 2004-07

Cathy Come Home Carol White (Cathy Ward), Ray Brooks (Reg Ward). Written by Jeremy Sandford and directed by Ken Loach. This kitchen-sink drama, shown under *The Wednesday Play* banner, about a despairing mother without a roof over her head brought the homeless charity 'Shelter' to the awareness of many. BBC1 1966.

Catweazle Geoffrey Bayldon (Catweazle), Robin Davies (Carrot Bennett), Peter Butterworth (Groome), Gary Warren (Cedric Collingford). Story of an 11th Century wizard stranded in the 20th Century and befriend by young Carrot Bennett. For the second series of 13 episodes, Cedric Collingford became the wizard's young confidante. ITV 1970-71.

CBBC Sister channel to Cbeebies primarily aimed at older children. Programmes include *Ace Lightning, Animadness, The Basil Brush Show, Beat the Boss, Best of Friends, Blue Peter, Bring It On, Chucklevision, Crush, Dick and Dom in Da Bungalow, Eureka TV, Hider in the House, Incredible Games, The Makeshift, Maya and Miguel, Nelly Nut Live, Newsround, One Minute Wonders, Oscar Charlie, Pablo the Little Red Fox, Roar, Scooby-Doo and Scrappy-Doo, Scoop, Shoebox Zoo, SMart, So Little Time, Space Hoppers, Stake Out, Super Rupert, The Story of Tracy Beaker, UGetMe, Watch My Chops, Xchange, X-PeriMENTAL, Zig Zag, Zombie Hotel*. Otis the Aardvark was a puppet presenter on Children's BBC (Dave Chapman was the puppeteer). Otis mainly presented the afternoon links alongside the main CBBC presenters. He left in 1999 and was replaced by another puppet called Emlin the Gremlin, who proved to be short-lived. Other presenter characters have included: Monsieur Pamplemousse, Jam Lady, Oucho T. Cactus, and Ted Metrie. The current continuity presenter is Saffron Coomber (since January 2011).

Cbeebies Digital BBC channel aimed at children under six-years-old. Launched on 11 February 2002 it broadcasts from 06.00 to 19.00 on Freeview (where it shares bandwidth with BBC Four, broadcast after 19.00), cable and digital satellite. The CBBC Channel is its sister channel for older children. Programmes include Andy Pandy, Barnaby Bear, Bill & Ben, Bits and Bobs, Bob the Builder, Boo!, Boogie Beebies, Brum, Clifford the Big Red Dog, Come Outside, Ethelbert the Tiger, Fimbles, Fireman Sam, In the Night Garden, Jackanory Junior, Numberjacks, Pingu, Playdays, Postman Pat with Jess the Cat, Roly Mo Show, Rubbadubbers, SMarteenies, Something Special, Teletubbies, Tikkabilla, Tweenies, The Story Makers, Smarteenies, The Shiny Show, Tikkabilla. Some of the shows are also included in the CBBC schedules.

Celeb Harry Enfield (Gary Bloke), Amanda Holden (Debs Bloke), Rupert Vansittart (Johnson), Frances Barber (Suzi), Leo Bill (Troy Bloke), Alison King (Zoe), Alison Steadman (Grandma). Sitcom about an ageing millionaire rock star. ITV 2002.

Celebrity Five Go To…… Five celebrities embark on a holiday and have to vote each other off until down to the final two when the best holidaymaker is then judged by the people responsible for looking after them during their stay. To-date two series of this reality show has been broadcast. The first series in January 2011 included Emma Ridley (3rd, the winner), Antony Costa (the winner), Russell Grant (2nd), Jan Leeming (5th) and Derek Conway (4th). The destination was Turkey. The second series in May 2011 included Stuart Baggs (5th), Ed Giddins (the winner), Sheila Ferguson (3rd), Paula Hamilton (4th) and Christopher Biggins (2nd). The destination was South Africa and the narrator of the series was Jane McDonald. C4 2011

Celebrity Juice Comedy panel show hosted by Leigh Francis in his alter ego of Keith Lemon. Two teams captained by Holly Willoughby and Fearne Cotton are tested on their knowledge of topical celebrity news over a series of eclectic rounds. Rufus Hound, who was originally one of the four guests during the first series which aired on ITV2 in 2008, became a permanent member of Fearne's team from the second series onwards. Although remaining an ITV2 show throughout its first three series the third series was repeated on ITV1 and the 30-minute episodes were lengthened to 45 minutes for this series. Since the third series, the show has also featured Jedward, David Hasselhoff and Verne Troyer as the regular challengers in the VT challenges.

Celebrity Love Island Reality television programme that follows twelve single people as they go to a Fiji island with the stated aim of finding love. Each week a male and a female contestant are eliminated until just one pair is left, making the 'ultimate couple'. The first series was presented by Patrick Kielty and Kelly Brook. The series was won by Jayne Middlemiss and Fran Cosgrave. The second series was entitled *Love Island*, dropping Celebrity from the show name as the contestants included non-celebrities. The added twist was that there were six women and five men and the men initially had to pick a partner; Sophie Anderton being the unfortunate woman left behind initially. The eventual winners were Bianca Gascoigne and Calum Best, a contestant from the previous season who was whisked in midway through the series to triumph. Fearne Cotton replaced Kelly Brook as Patrick Kielty's co-presenter. ITV 2005-06

Celebrity Scissorhands Reality show (originally screened on BBC3) that was part of the BBC's Children in Need charity campaign, in which celebrities cut people's hair while trained and watched by professional hairdresser Lee Stafford. *Visage* frontman Steve Strange, who was a contestant on the first series, returned as assistant manager for series two and three. The presenters were Alex Zane (series one) and George Lamb (series two and three) and the voice-over artist was Sarah Cawood. Produced by Endemol, the format was similar to their previous production *The Salon*. BBC1 2006-08.

Celebrity Squares Bob Monkhouse asked nine celebrities, each one housed in a noughts and crosses grid-box, a true or false question whereupon two contestants took alternate turns to either agree or disagree in order to win the round. The voice-overs were provided by Kenny Everett and one of the main question contributors in the early series was none other than master prankster Jeremy Beadle. ITV 1975-79, 1993-95.

Chain Reactions A six-part series chronicling Ireland's modern history focusing each week on a different strand of Irish society and the radical changes it has undergone over the last 25 years. Presented by Simon Delaney. RTÉ1 2005

Champions, The Stuart Damon (Craig Stirling), William Gaunt (Richard Barrett), Alexandra Bastedo (Sharon McCready). Endowed with the qualities of superhumans by a lost Tibetan tribe after a plane crash in the Himalayas, the three intrepid Champions of Law, Order and Justice use their powers to their best advantage while working for the Geneva-based International Agency, 'Nemesis'. ITV 1968-69.

Chance in a Million Simon Callow (Tom Chance), Brenda Blethyn (Alison Little). Sitcom based around the hapless Tom Chance's propensity for disaster somewhat aided by his peculiar staccato speech which often led to confusion. C4 1984-86.

Chancer Clive Owen (Stephen Crane/Derek 'Dex' Love, Leslie Phillips (James Xavier Blake), Susannah Harker (Jo Franklyn), Sean Pertwee (Jamie Douglas), Peter Vaughan (Thomas Franklyn), Tom Bell (John Love). Stephen Crane works for Kleber's Bank and develops an ambitious plan to acquire new investors, but a shady past under a different name catches up with him. He is called in to rescue Douglas Motors, a collapsing sports car company owned by the stylish Douglas family. The second season of the drama opens with the Chancer finishing a prison sentence for insider trading. ITV 1990-91.

Changing Rooms Hosted by Carol Smillie (Series 1-13). Home Modernisation and Interior Decorating show where two sets of neighbours swapped keys to transform a room in each other's home, with only two days and a set budget and the considerable help of celebrity designers. Presenters included Graham Wynne, Nick Knowles, John Craven, Nicki Chapman, Dominic Littlewood, Laurence Llewelyn Bowen, Anna Ryder-Richardson, Oliver Heath and Linda Barker. DIY experts: Andy Kane and Craig Phillips. BBC 2 1996-97, BBC1 1998-2003.

Channel Four The United Kingdom's fourth terrestrial channel was launched on 2 November 1982, although much of Wales began receiving its own version S4C (Welsh: Sianel Pedwar Cymru, meaning Channel 4 Wales) the day before. In fact, S4C was a distinct brand and consisted of largely Welsh-speaking programmes as made by HTV, the BBC, or from independent companies. Originally, limited frequency space meant that Channel 4 could not be broadcast alongside S4C, though some C4 programmes were aired at less popular times on the Welsh variant, a practice that carried on up until the closure of S4C's analogue transmissions in 2010. The first voice ever heard on Channel 4 was that of continuity announcer Paul Coia (b. 19 June 1960, Glasgow), his introduction to the new channel being "Good afternoon. It's a pleasure to be able to say to you: Welcome to Channel Four", before heading into a montage of clips from its programmes set to the station's signature tune, "Fourscore", written by Lord David Dundas, which would form the basis of the station's jingles for its first decade. The first programme to air on the channel was the teatime game show *Countdown*. Since 1994, the headquarters of the channel has occupied a distinctive, purpose-built building with curved front and dramatic concave glazed wall, designed by Richard Rogers, at 124 Horseferry Road, Westminster. Chairmen of C4 have included Edmund Dell (1982–1987), Richard Attenborough (1987–1992), Michael Bishop (1993–1997), Vanni Treves (1998–2003), Luke Johnson (2004–2010) and Terry Burns (2010–Present). Chief Executives have included Jeremy Isaacs (1981–1987), Michael Grade (1988–1997), Michael Jackson (1997–2002), Mark Thompson (Mar 2002 – Jun 2004), Andy Duncan (Jul 2004 - Nov 2009), Anne Bulford (Interim) (Nov 2009 - Jan 2010) and David Abraham (Jan 2010 – present).

Channel Five The United Kingdom's fifth terrestrial channel was launched by the Spice Girls (with an adaptation of Manfred Mann's *5-4-3-2-1*) on Sunday 30 March 1997 at 6:00 pm. Tim Vine and Julia Bradbury were the channel's first presenters, introducing previews of forthcoming shows under the banner "Give me 5!". On Monday 21 August 2002, Channel 5 changed its name to *Five*. The channel currently experiences an audience share of approximately 5 per cent.

Charles Endell Esquire See *Budgie*

Charley Boorman: Ireland to Sydney Charley Boorman was born in Wimbledon, 23 August 1966. He is the son of costume designer Christel Kruse and film director John Boorman. A sometime actor, Charley befriended Ewan McGregor whilst they were shooting *The Serpent's Kiss* (1997) and in 2004 they set off on their first journey across several continents. On 12 April 2008, Charley started another adventure, accompanied by director Russ Malkin and Mungo, the cameraman. This time the aim was to travel from his home in County Wicklow, Ireland to Sydney, Australia, "By Any Means" (the alternative title of the series). Although motorbikes were the preferred form of transport, all manner of other vehicles were used commensurate with the country they were visiting. Lucy Trujillo, Russ Malkin and Liz Mercer produced the six-part series that resulted from this adventure. The title music was performed by Jamiroquai and the opening graphics by Alex Dinnin and Matt Knott. BBC2 2008. See also *Long Way Round*.

Charmer, The Nigel Havers (Ralph Ernest Gorse), Bernard Hepton (Donald), Rosemary Leach (Joan), Fiona Fullerton (Clarice), Judy Parfitt (Alison Warren), Abigail McKern (Pamela Bennett). Based on the books by Patrick Hamilton concerning the caddish Ralph and his propensity to seduce a variety of women before relieving them of the family silver. After he cons Joan Plumleigh-Bruce out of £1,000 he has to contend with her estate agent friend Donald Stimpson who is hell-bent on revenge, all the time Ralph himself is truly enamoured by the beautiful Clarice Mannors. ITV 1987.

Chase, The Weekday quiz show hosted by Bradley Walsh. Four contestants endeavour to answer more questions correctly than a general knowledge expert in order to win cash prizes; the show finale being a race against the clock. The four resident quiz players in the guise of The Chaser are Anne Hegerty, Shaun Wallace, Mark Labbatt and the most recent addition, Paul Sinha. ITV 2009-

Cheaters, The John Ireland (John Hunter), Robert Ayres (Walter Allen). Popular series depicting the investigations of insurance inspector John Hunter on behalf of the Eastern Insurance company. ITV 1960-62.

Chef Lenny Henry (Gareth Blackstock), Caroline Lee Johnson (Janice), Roger Griffiths (Everton). Sitcom based around a French restaurant Le Château Anglais in the Oxfordshire Cotswolds. BBC1 1993-96.

Chefs A list of celebrity chefs in alphabetical order: Jane Asher, Ed Baines, Cheryl Baker, Mary Berry, Galton Blackiston, Heston Blumenthal, Ross Burden, Michael Caines, Richard Corrigan, Fanny and Johnny Craddock, Clarissa Dickson Wright, Hugh Fearnley-Whittingstall, Keith Floyd, Silvana Franco, Daniel Galmiche, Rose Gray, Sophie Grigson, Phillip Harben, Ainsley Harriott, Angela Hartnett, Mary Henry, Annabel Karmel, Lawrence Keogh, Graham Kerr, Nigella Lawson, Jeremy Lee, Tom Lewis, Alastair Little, James Martin, Paul Merrett, Michael Moore, Nick Nairn, Jean-Christophe Novelli, Jamie Oliver, Lorraine Pascale, Jennifer Paterson, Arthur Potts Dawson, John

Burton Race, Gordon Ramsay, Paul Rankin, Gary Rhodes, Simon Rimmer, Ruth Rogers, Roux Brothers (Albert and Michel), Oliver Rowe, Nigel Slater, Delia Smith, Rick Stein, James Tanner, Tony Tobin, Brian Turner, Phil Vickery, Lesley Waters, Marco Pierre White, Kevin Woodford, Antony Worrall Thompson, Mario Wyn-Jones, Aldo Zilli.

Chelmsford 123 Jimmy Mulville (Aulus Paulinus), Rory McGrath (Badvoc), Neil Pearson (Mungo). Sitcom set in Roman Britain of 123 AD. C4 1988-90.

Chewin' the Fat
Comedy sketch show that poked fun at Scottish, US and English stereotypes, merging farce, outrageous humour and social commentary. Contributors included Ford Kiernan, Greg Hemphill, Karen Dunbar, Paul Riley, Gordon McCorkell, Julie Wilson Nimmo, Tom Urie and Mark Cox. Starting as a radio series on BBC Radio Scotland, the television show was first broadcast on BBC1 Scotland but series three and four, as well as highlights from the first two series, were later broadcast to the rest of the UK. Although the last series ended in February 2002, every year there is a 'Hogmanay Special' shown on New Year's Eve on BBC1 Scotland, and regular 'greatest hits' series are shown. Popular characterisations included Ronald Villiers, the hopeless actor; the lighthouse keepers ('Gonnay nae dee that...jist, gonnay naw!' became a phrase on everyone's lips in Scotland); The Glasgae Banter Boys; The Old Slapper; know-all Harry with his wife Linda and their pal George; The Two Neds ("ya couple of fannies".); Betty, an OAP with X-rated memories of the Second World War; The Big Man; Eco-terrorist, The Lonely Shopkeeper, and The Boy That's Just Started Masturbating - which was dropped after the stars grew tired of people in the street shouting "wank!" at them). BBC1 1999-2002. *Chewin' the Fat* also gave birth to two spin-off shows, *Still Game*, which focused on the two old men in the show, Jack and Victor, and *The Karen Dunbar Show*, which is a sketch show featuring Karen Dunbar.

Chief, The Tim Pigott-Smith (Chief Constable John Stafford), Karen Archer (Asst. Chief Constable Anne Stewart), Judy Loe (Dr. Elizabeth Stafford), Eamon Boland (Jim Gray), TP McKenna (Colin Fowler), Martin Shaw (Chief Constable Alan Cade). Police Drama ITV 1990-95. Martin Shaw's character took over as the title character in 1993.

Chigley Described as a hamlet near Camberwick Green, Trumptonshire. Characters included Mr Clutterbuck the builder, Chippy Minton the carpenter (and his son Nibbs), Lord Belborough of Wingstead Hall, Mr Cresswell the owner of the biscuit factory, Mr Clamp the greengrocer, Harry Farthing the potter, Mr Swallow the Treadles Wharf docks supervisor, Mr Brackett the butler and various characters from both Camberwick Green and Trumpton. Lord Belborough ran a steam train known as Bessie for the benefit of the locals. A six o'clock whistle sounded the end of each episode. Songs were by Freddie Phillips and all 13 episodes were narrated by Brian Cant. First broadcast on BBC1 in 1969.

Child Of Our Time It all began when the BBC followed the birth of 25 babies born in the new millennium. The idea behind the series is to follow the families as their children grow up. It uses a fascinating mix of observational filming, interviews and experiments to help us learn more about child development. Parys Lapper is one of the babies featured in this 20-year project. His mother Alison, an artist who was born with no arms and shortened legs, participates in the series on an equal basis to the other families featured. Professor Robert Winston returns to the children born in the year 2000 to discover how they're developing in the regular series updates. BBC1 2001-

Children in Need Although the format originally aired on radio on Christmas Day 1927 it was in 1980 that the BBC decided to give over its whole evening viewing schedule in order to raise money for various charities. Held on the third Friday in November, and hosted throughout by Sir Terry Wogan, the 1980 appeal raised £1.2m but in recent years this has grown to more than £30m. Pudsey Bear, with his bandaged right eye and forlorn countenance, is the mascot for the appeal.

Children's Favourites Much-loved Saturday morning music request programme for children first broadcast on the Light Programme in 1954 and presented by Derek "Uncle Mac" McCulloch. By way of homage to his parting catchphrase on *Children's Hour*, Derek would begin proceedings with the immortal line "Hello children, everywhere!". The iconic theme tune known in every household in the land was *Puffin' Billy* by Edward White played by Melodi Light Orchestra. When Derek retired in 1965 various guest presenters took over before Leslie Crowther became its permanent host. After Radio 1 and Radio 2 were launched in 1967, the show was re-named *Junior Choice* and was broadcast simultaneously on both stations. Leslie's busy work schedule meant he had to stand down in 1968 and he was replaced by Ed "Stewpot" Stewart (born 23 April 1941 in Exmouth, Devon) who turned out to be an inspired choice with ratings topping 17 million at times. *Puffin' Billy* was now replaced by an instrumental version of The Seekers hit *Morningtown Ride*, played by Stan Butcher's Birds 'n Brass. In 1980 Stewpot was replaced by Tony Blackburn and by 1982 the name *Junior Choice* was dropped in favour of *Tony Blackburn's Saturday Show* and continued until 23 September 1984, after which Blackburn left Radio 1. Although Peter Powell took over the weekend breakfast show, the link with the "Uncle Mac" era was finally broken. Among the most frequently requested songs were: *The Laughing Policeman* (Charles Penrose), *The Runaway Train* (Michael Holliday), *Nellie the Elephant* (Mandy Miller), *Poppa Piccolino* (Petula Clark), *The Bee Song* (Arthur Askey), *There's A Hole In My Bucket* (Nina and Frederick), *The Ugly Duckling* (Danny Kaye), *The Three Little Fishes* (Frankie Howerd), *The Hippopotamus Song* (Flanders and Swann), *Little White Bull* (Tommy Steele), *Tubby the Tuba* (Danny Kaye), *Sparky's Magic Piano* (Henry Blair - this one used to scare children and adults alike!), *My Old Man's a Dustman* (Lonnie Donegan), *Thumbelina* (Danny Kaye), *Beep Beep* - The Bubble Car Song (The Playmates – this too was a little scarey) and *There Was an Old Lady Who Swallowed a Fly* (Burl Ives).

Children's Hour Broadcast from 1922 to 1964, originally from the BBC's Birmingham station, before transferring to the BBC Home Service, at the outbreak of World War II. Parts of the programme were also rebroadcast by the BBC World Service. For the last three years of its life (from 17 April 1961 until 27 March 1964), the title *Children's Hour* was no longer used, the programmes in its time slot, going out under the umbrella heading of *For the Young*. *Children's Hour* was broadcast from 5pm to 6pm on weekdays and was aimed at an audience aged about 5 to 15 years. Popular series on *Children's Hour* included: *Jennings at School, Just So Stories, Toytown* (Derek was famous for playing Larry the Lamb*), Inishban, Mary Plain, Norman and Henry Bones, Nature Parliament, Out with Romany, Sherlock Holmes, Worzel Gummidge* and *Winnie the Pooh*. Plymouth-born Derek Ivor Breashur McCulloch (18 November 1897 - 1 June 1967) will forever be associated with the programme. under the guise of "Uncle Mac". Derek joined the BBC in 1926 as an announcer and was immediately involved in Children's Hour although also having the distinction of commentating on the first radio broadcast of the FA Cup Final in 1927. Derek took control of *Children's Hour* in 1933 and stated his policy as: "Nothing but the best is good enough for children... our wish is to stimulate their imaginations, direct their reading, encourage their various interests, widen their outlook and inculcate the Christian virtues of love of God and their neighbours". His sign-off line "Goodnight children, everywhere", became more poignant after the evacuation of many children from their homes at the start of the Second World War. Already having lost an eye in the Great War, Derek also lost his left leg in a road traffic accident in 1938 but his general ill health never transcended over the air waves. Violet Carson (later to become Ena Sharples in *Coronation Street*) was an ever-present on *Children's Hour* as "Aunty Vi". Another interesting regular was Arthur Burrows. "Uncle Arthur" was the first Director of Programmes on the BBC and is famous for two records. At 6pm on 14 November 1922, he read the BBC's first-ever, on-air news bulletin and at 5pm on 24 December 1922, he played Father Christmas in the play *The Truth About Father Christmas* - considered to be the first official broadcast of a radio drama. See also entry for *Children's Favourites*.

Children's Ward Carol Harvey (DR Charlotte Woods), Andrew Hall (Dave Spencer), Ian McCulloch (Dr McKeown), Tim Stanley (Nurse Gary Miller), Nina Baden-Semper (Jan Stevens), Tim Vincent (Billy Ryan), Chris Bisson (JJ), Chloe Newsome (Thea

Bartlett), Michael Friel (Danny Phillips), Emma Belton and Jane Danson (Paula James), Tina O'Brien (Claire), Brigit Forsyth (Sylvia Dickinson), Ralf Little (Robbie), Vicky Binns (Tash Naylor), Tim Robbins (Ewan), Nicola Stephenson (Amanda), Kieran O'Brien (Lee Jones), Rebecca Callard (as Rebecca Sowden (Fiona Brett), Rita May (Mags), Alan Rothwell (Dr Davies). Children's medical drama set on Ward B1 of South Park General Hospital. Between 1995 and 1999 the series was retitled *The Ward*. ITV 1989-2000.

Child's Play Celebrity panel game hosted by Michael Aspel in which word definitions were given by toddlers with the panel having to guess what the children were describing. ITV 1984-88.

Chinese Detective, The David Yip (Det Sgt Johnny Ho). Created by Ian Kennedy Martin this police drama concerned a Chinese detective working in the Limehouse area of London. BBC1 1981-82.

Chocky Andrew Ellams (Matthew Gore), Glynis Brooks (voice of Chocky), Carol Drinkwater (Mary Gore), James Hazeldine (David Gore), Ed Bishop (Dr Deacon). The story of young Matthew Gore, an intelligent boy from the Home Counties of England who is chosen by a mysterious extra-terrestrial visitor (Chocky) who is never seen except by Matthew (on rare occasions), as a source of information about life on earth. The drama follows the story as his parents witness a strange change in Matthew's behaviour as he becomes more attentive and inquisitive about life around him. His schoolwork improves dramatically, as does his artistic talent and manual dexterity on computer games. In the final episode when Chocky leaves Matthew for good, she is able to explain to his father David who she is, why she has been here, and why she is leaving. At this point the original book by John Wyndham ends, although Thames produced two further series, *Chocky's Children* and *Chocky's Challenge*. ITV 1984-86.

Choir, The Three-part documentary following the highs and lows of London Symphony Orchestra Choir Master Gareth Malone, as he attempted to take 30 R&B-obsessed comprehensive school kids, who have never sung before, to compete in the World Choir Games in China. BBC2 2006. A sequel *The Choir – Boys Don't Sing* was shown on BBC2 in 2008, now set in Lancaster School – a large boys'-only state school in Leicester, rather than the Middlesex comprehensive of the original series. Yet another sequel *The Choir Revisited* was broadcast in 2009. The most recent series, *The Choir: Military Wives* was aired in November 2011 and was set in two British Army bases in Devon (Chivenor Barracks and Royal Citadel, Plymouth). In this three-part series, Gareth enlisted voices for an all-women choir from the wives and girlfriends of military personnel deployed to Afghanistan. The culmination of the programme was a performance by the Military Wives Choir in The Royal British Legion's Remembrance parade at the Royal Albert Hall on 12 November 2011. As a spin-off of the series, the Military Wives Choir recorded a CD single of the song *Wherever You Are* especially composed for the programme by Paul Mealor. The song became the Christmas number-one single, after outselling the release by *The X Factor* winners *Little Mix*

Chorlton and the Wheelies Fenella the Wicked Kettle Witch (who lives in Spout Hall) hates to see people having fun, so she uses an evil sadness spell to turn Wheelie World into a gloomy place. But one day, a mysterious egg appears, and out pops a Happiness Dragon named Chorlton. Fenella's spell is broken, and Wheelie World will never be the same again! Three series (39 episodes) were made and shown originally on ITV 1976-79.

Christmas Lights See *Northern Lights*.

Chronicle Long-running series tracing new developments in historical research. Regular presenters included Magnus Magnusson (1966-80), John Julius Norwich (1967-80), Andrew Faulds (1978-84) and David Drew (1984-90). BBC 1966-90.

Chucklevision Barry Elliot (b. 24 December, 1944) and Paul Elliot (b. 18 October, 1947), better known as The Chuckle Brothers, are Rotherham-born comedians from a dynasty of funny men (their father was a well-known Gang Show performer whose stage name was Gene Patton and their older brothers, Jimmy and Brian, who are known professionally as The Patton Brothers, are a double act who they often work with both in the series and on stage). The Chuckle Brothers won the television talent shows *Opportunity Knocks* in 1967 and *New Faces* in 1974 but their lasting legacy is *Chucklevision*, the long-running BBC children's show that sees the pair in some unlikely but hilarious situations. Jimmy Patton plays their boss, No Slacking, in the series. The other claim to fame for Paul and Barry is that they won the first series of *Celebrity Coach Trip*. BBC 1987-

Churchill's People Richard Johnson (Claudius), Tom Conti (Tom Mackenzie), Jeremy Irons (Samuel Ross), Ray Barrett (Leo Hennessey), Edward Fox (Aaron Graham), Charles Gray (Duke of Portland), Alan Lake (Valentine Joyce), George Sewell (Colonel Michelburn), Alan Howard (King Alfred), Patrick Stewart (Wulfric), Anna Massey (Queen Ealswith), Brian Blessed (Guthrum), Sam Kydd (George Campsie), Nigel Stock (Earl Howe), Robert Hardy (King Oswy), Leo McKern (King Pender), Dinsdale Landen (William the Ewerer), Dennis Waterman (Harold Godwinsson), John Justin (Vice-Admiral Buckner), Brian Cox (William Wallace), Elisabeth Sellars (Albrida), Philip Madoc (Williams), Alfred Lynch (King James I), Ian Hendry (William Davenant), Bernard Hepton (Oliver Cromwell), Paul Darrow (Marcellus), John Turner (Sir Walter Raleigh), John Nettleton (Sir Francis Bacon), Hugh Dickson (Sir Robert Cecil), Gemma Jones (Margaret Paston), Geoffrey Matthews (Archbishop of York), Daniel Brian (King Charles I), Patrick Allen (Donald MacAmnay), Arthur Lowe (Epillicus, the Barber), Ian Charleson (John Ross), Rodney Bewes (Bob Pott), Rita Webb (Mrs Trundle), Arthur Mullard (Jack Plaster). Series of 26 historical dramas based on Winston Churchill's *A History of the English-Speaking Peoples*. Each episode dealt with a particular period in British history and despite the major stars involved the production quality was best described as variable. BBC1 1974-75.

Cinema Film review programme. Presenters included Bamber Gascoigne (the first), Derek Granger, Mike Scott, Mark Shivas, Michael Parkinson, Clive James and Brian Trueman. ITV 1964-75.

Citizen James Sid James (Sidney Balmoral James) Bill Kerr (William 'Bill' Kerr) Liz Fraser (Liz Fraser), Sydney Tafler (Charlie). Written by Ray Galton, Alan Simpson, Sid Green and Dick Hills, this sitcom was Sid James' first effort after his somewhat acrimonious split with Tony Hancock. BBC 1960-62.

Citizen Smith Robert Lindsay (Walter Henry 'Wolfie' Smith), Mike Grady (Ken Mills), Tony Millan (Tucker), Cheryl Hall (Shirley Johnson), Peter Vaughan and Tony Steedman (Charlie Johnson). Wolfie is leader of the 'Tooting Popular Front' with his catchphrase 'Power to the People'. Lindsay's girlfriend in the series was played by Cheryl Hall, his real-life wife at the time. The series was written by John Sullivan. BBC1 1977-80.

CITV The brand name used for the majority of children's television output on ITV's television stations, including the ITV Network, breakfast broadcaster GMTV and the ITV plc-owned CITV Channel as well as non ITV plc owned regions. CITV (Children's Independent Television) currently airs on weekend mornings on ITV. CITV also has its own channel, which was launched by ITV plc on 11 March 2006. Produced by Central Independent Television, Children's ITV first aired in January 1983, and consisted of programmes with recorded links in between, initially featuring a different presenter each month. Recorded links continued until 1987, when it started to be broadcast live, echoing Children's BBC which had started two years earlier. Before being known as Children's ITV the timeslot was briefly branded as "Watch IT!" and was presented locally rather than having national coverage. The flagship Saturday morning programmes have included No. 73, The Saturday Show , The Saturday Starship, Get Fresh, Motormouth, Ghost Train, Gimme 5, What's Up Doc?, Scratchy & Co, Telegantic Megavision, SM:TV Live and Ministry of Mayhem.

City Central Paul Nicholls (PC Terry Sydenham), Dave Hill (PC Pete Redfern), Ian Aspinall (PC Colin Jitlada), Sean McKenzie (PC Nick Green), Ian Burfield (DS Ray Pickering), Stephen Lord (PC Steve Jackson), Lorraine Ashbourne (Sgt Yvonne Mackey), Terence Harvey (Chief Insp George Barnard), Ashley Jensen (PC

Sue Chappell). The everyday public and private lives of the detectives, policemen and policewomen who work at the inner-city Christmas Street police station in Manchester. BBC1 1998-2000.

City Hospital Medical documentary series broadcast live from Guy's Hospital and St Thomas' Hospital in London, and The Princess Anne Maternity Hospital in Southampton. The show followed real patients and staff and featured daily live-to-air footage of actual surgical operations, as they were being performed. Presenters included Nadia Sawalha, Matt Baker, Ainsley Harriott, Andi Peters, Nick Knowles, Sian Williams, Roger Black and Matthew Kelly. BBC1 2002-07.

City Lights Gerard Kelly (Willie Melvin), Andy Gray (Chancer), Jan Wilson (Mum), Jonathan Watson (Brian), Dave Anderson (Mr McLelland), Iain McColl (Tam),
Elaine C Smith (Irene), Louise Beattie (Vicki - series 1), Elaine Collins (Janice McLachlan - series 2 & 3), Ann Bryson (Fiona - series 4 & 5). Scottish sitcom written by Bob Black. Bank-teller Willie Melvin's lofty ideas of becoming a successful novelist run riot after he wins a short-story competition, causing him no end of problems. His acquaintances also suffer, with friend Brian, boss Mr McLelland, and Chancer, a dodgy sort who spends some time in jail (between series one and two). Willie also has a couple of romances during the series, most notably with Janice, whom he almost marries. By the end of the run, however, he is courting Fiona. Ashley Jensen made her screen debut in a 1990 episode, *The Front*. BBC2 1987-91 See also *Northern Lights* for entry on the 2007 drama series *City Lights*

Civilisation The premise for the series, which was fully *titled Civilisation: a personal view by Kenneth Clark* , was explained by Clark with a quote from John Ruskin: "Great nations write their autobiographies in three manuscripts - the book of their deeds, the book of their words and the book of their art. Not one of these books can be understood unless we read the two others, but of the three the only trustworthy one is the last." And for 13 weeks he attempted to show how two thousand years of the creative urge had moulded western civilisation. The eminent art historian and former chairman of the Independent Television Authority (ITA) became an unlikely television star via this seminal work. BBC2 1969.

Clangers, The Clangers were the pink and woolly, mouse-like creatures which live on a blue planet and took their names from the sound made when they battened down their dustbin-lid hatches and retreated underground. Other inhabitants of the planet were the Froglets, Soup Dragon and Iron Chicken. Created by Oliver Postgate and Peter Firmin. BBC1 1969-74.

Clarence Ronnie Barker (Clarence Sale), Josephine Tewson (Jane Travers). Sitcom written by Ronnie Barker under the pseudonym Bob Ferris. Clarence is a real-life Mr Magoo who retires to the countryside, and goes from one mishap to another due to his short-sightedness. The series was inspired by *The Removals Person* by Hugh Leonard, an earlier programme in the 1971 LWT comedy series, *Six Dates With Barker*. BBC1 1988.

Classical Star Reality television series whereby young talented classical musicians auditioned for the chance to enter the Classical Star Music Academy with the chance of a recording contract at the end of it. The first episode showed the audition process resulting in the naming of the nine successful candidates to enter the academy. Renowned cellist Matthew Barley was the academy principal and the judges were conductors Charles Hazlewood and Jason Lai plus celebrated double bass player Chi-chi Nwanoku and producer and manager Steve Abbott. Pianist Sophie Cashell ultimately won the contract with Universal Classics and Jazz. BBC2 2007.

Clayhanger Peter McEnery (Edwin Clayhanger), Janet Suzman (Hilda Lessways), Louise Purnell (Janet Orgreave), Thelma Whiteley (Maggie Clayhanger), Joyce Redman (Auntie Hamps), Harry Andrews (Darius Clayhanger), Bruce Purchase (Big James), Anne Carroll (Clara Benbow), Clive Swift (Albert Benbow), Denis Quilley (George Cannon), Denholm Elliott (Tertius Inkpen). Twenty-six-part adaptation of Arnold Bennett's novel. ITV 1976.

Cleopatras, The Actresses who played the Cleopatras: Michelle Newell, Elizabeth Shepherd, Caroline Mortimer, Sue Holderness, Amanda Boxer, Prue Clarke, Pauline Moran. Referred to as

'horror-comic' in style, partly because of the casual horror of life under the Cleopatras, but more prophetically perhaps because critics dubbed it a comic-horror of a series. The director of all eight episodes was John Frankau who strived for authenticity (this consisted mainly of having bare-chested handmaids and bare-headed nobles, including Amanda Boxer's shaven-headed portrayal of Cleopatra Tryphaena) but asked for over-the-top performances from his actors which almost parodied the pre-Christian era. The use of modern vernacular did not help. Typically miscast actors included Robert Hardy as Julius Caesar and Richard Griffiths as Pot Belly. BBC2 1983.

Clitheroe Kid, The The Clitheroe Kid was James Robertson Clitheroe (1921-73), Jimmy Clitheroe to most, who by some strange coincidence did come from the town of that name without having to change his family name! At his full height he was 4ft 3in, and played the naughty schoolboy on the Light Programme (Radio 2) between 1957 and 1972. Although plausible from a distance, he was not really able to pass himself off as a youngster close up, so a TV career did not really take off too well, but at the peak of his fame the radio show was raking in about 10 million listeners, although by the end this had dropped to a tenth of that figure. The scripts were generally written by James Casey and Frank Roscoe, with the shows production by James Casey. The series sprang from a single show broadcast on 24 April 1956 as part of a Variety Playhouse series. The regular but ever-changing cast consisted of Jimmy Clitheroe, Eddie Leslie, Peter Sinclair, Judith Chalmers, Rosalie Williams, Fred Fairclough, Brian Truman, John Broadbent, Bob Monkhouse, Jack Watson, Herbert Smith, Jack Howarth, Fred Ferris, Shirley King, Violet Carson, Tom Harrison, and Patrick Wells. A television version of the show retitled, *Just Jimmy*, was broadcast on ITV between 1964 and 1968 with Mollie Sugden playing Jimmy's mother in the series.

Clocking Off Sarah Lancashire (Yvonne Kolakowski), Philip Glenister (James 'Mack' Mackintosh), Lesley Sharp (Trudy Graham), Siobhan Finneran (Julie O'Neill), Diane Parish (Sylvia Robinson), Christine Tremarco (Katherine Mackintosh), Jason Merrells (Martin Leach), Lindsey Coulson (Bev Ratcliffe/Aindow), Ricky Tomlinson (Ronnie Anderson), Nicola Stephenson (Suzie Davidson), Pam Ferris (Pat Fletcher), Claire Sweeney (Katrina Wilkes), Christopher Eccleston (Jim Calvert), Ashley Jensen (Babs Leach), Tina O'Brien (Adele Kolakowski). Interconnected dramas about the lives of a group of workers at a Manchester textile factory, with each episode focusing on the home life of a different character. BBC1 2000-03.

Clothes Show, The Selina Scott, the Queen of Breakfast TV, and style guru Jeff Banks were recruited by BBC Pebble Mill to demystify the world of fashion. The idea was to mix reports from the catwalk with items on how to delude yourself you could achieve model looks and still have change from a twenty pound note. The show was an instant hit. The Clothes Show format stood the test of time, and various changes of line-up - other presenters during the show's run included Caryn Franklin, Jane Lomas, Jasmine Fadhli, Siobhan Maher, Lucy Pilkington, Raj Dhanda, Sheryl Simms, Vanessa Scott, Ann-Marie Gwatkin, Ged Gray, Margerita Taylor, Tim Vincent and Brenda Emmanus. BBC1 1986-98.

Cluedo Series 1 - Stephanie Beacham (Mrs Peacock), Robin Nedwell (Rev. Green), Tracy-Louise Ward (Miss Scarlett), Robin Ellis (Col. Mustard), Kristoffer Tabori (Prof. Plum), June Whitfield (Mrs White). Christmas Special - Kate O'Mara (Mrs Peacock), David Robb (Col. Mustard), Derek Nimmo (Rev. Green), Ian Lavender (Prof. Plum), Toyah Willcox (Miss Scarlett), Joan Sims (Mrs White). Series 2 - Rula Lenska (Mrs Peacock), Michael Jayston (Col. Mustard), Richard Wilson (Rev. Green), David McCallum (Prof. Plum), Koo Stark (Miss Scarlett), Mollie Sugden (Mrs White). Series 3 - Susan George (Mrs Peacock), Lewis Collins (Col. Mustard), Christopher Biggins (Rev. Green), Tom Baker (Prof. Plum), Lysette Anthony (Miss Scarlett), Pam Ferris (Mrs White). Series 4 - Joanna Lumley (Mrs Peacock), Leslie Grantham (Col. Mustard), Nicholas Parsons (Rev. Green), John Bird (Prof. Plum), Jerry Hall (Miss Scarlett), Liz Smith (Mrs White). Whodunnit? Game show based on the board game and set in the fictional Arlington Grange. The first series, and the following Christmas special, were hosted by James

Bellini and had two teams of one celebrity and one viewer competing against each other in order to solve the dastardly crime. In series 2-4, hosted by Richard Madeley, there were just two pairs of celebrities competing against each other. After 25 minutes of suspicion, deception and deduction, the murderer was finally unveiled to give a pre - prepared monologue of a confession, under a spotlight, direct to camera. Oddly, no one ever solved the murder prematurely but although the formatting led to fix allegations the series was always about the journey and not the destination. ITV 1990-93

Cluff Leslie Sands (Sergeant Caleb Cluff), Eric Barker and Michael Bates (Inspector Mole), John Rolfe (DC Barker). Cluff first appeared in an episode of the anthology series 'Detective' (an episode entitled 'The Drawing' broadcast on 6th April, 1964). He was a plodding sort of detective, much more at home taking a good walk with his pipe in his mouth, his chestnut walking stick in his hand and his faithful dog, Clive (a half-breed black and tan) by his side. But any no-gooder underestimating the tweed-suited detective would do so at their own cost because Cluff's slow methodology belied a skilfully perceptive insight into human nature and behaviour, particularly in the criminal mind. Set in the fictional Yorkshire moorland town of Gunnershaw. The series was created and written by Gil North. BBC 1964-65.

Clunk Click See *Jim'll Fix It*.

Coach Trip Reality television show whereby seven teams of two travel around Europe on a coach for 30 days and are voted off by their fellow contestants and replaced by another couple. By the fourth series the journey had been extended to 50 days. The tour guide is Brendan Sheerin. The driver for series one was Chris Groombridge and for subsequent series, Paul Donald. The narrator for the first two series was Andy Love; for the third and fourth series, David Quantick, and for the fifth series onwards, Dave Vitty. There has also been several series of *Celebrity Coach Trip*; the first winners being Paul and Barry Elliott (better known as *The Chuckle Brothers*). C4 2005-

Coast Geographer and writer Nicholas Crane presented this ambitious expedition around the entire coast of the UK. His expert team consisted of archaeologist Neil Oliver, zoologist Miranda Krestovnikoff, Anatomist Dr Alice Roberts and anthropologist Mark Horton. All but one of the episodes in the first series ended with Nicholas Crane stating that in the British Isles, "Remember, you are never more than 72 miles from the sea!" BBC2 2005-

Cold Feet James Nesbitt (Adam Williams), Helen Baxendale (Rachel Bradley), John Thomson (Pete Gifford), Robert Bathurst (David Marsden), Fay Ripley (Jenny Gifford), Hermione Norris (Karen Marsden), Jacey Salles (Ramona Ramirez), Kimberley Joseph (Jo Ellison). Comedy drama about three couples: Adam and Rachel; Pete Gifford and his wife Jenny (Fay Ripley); and David Marsden and his wife Karen. Adam and Rachel meet and, after many ups and downs, seem to be building a happy, lasting relationship. Fate, however, intervenes to spoil Adam's happiness. David and Karen are both tempted into extra-marital relationships. Eventually, they decide to go their separate ways. Pete and Jenny also separate and are eventually divorced. Pete later remarries, but his second marriage is very short-lived. ITV 1998-2003.

Colditz Jack Hedley (Lt Col John Preston), Robert Wagner (Flt Lt / Major Phil Carrington), David McCallum (Flt Lt Simon Carter), Bernard Hepton (Kommandant), Anthony Valentine (Major Horst Mohn), Edward Hardwicke (Capt Pat Grant), Christopher Neame (LT Dick Player), Dan O'Herlihy (Lt. Col. Max Dodd), Jeremy Kemp (Squadron Leader Tony Shaw). Based on the book by Pat Reid, a real-life survivor of Colditz, a POW camp thought to be escape-proof. Castle Colditz's official designation is Oflag IV C. BBC1 1972-74.

Colin's Sandwich Mel Smith (Colin), Louisa Rix (Jenny Anderson), Mike Grady (Des), Andrew Robertson (Mr Travers), Tony Haase (Trevor Blacklock), Lee Cornes (Graham), Jane Booker (Sarah), Michael Medwin (John Langley), Nicholas Ball (Alan Hunter). Sitcom written by Paul Smith and Terry Kyan. Colin Watkins, a British Rail office worker with ambitions to become a professional writer dreams of becoming the next Stephen King. His smart and together girlfriend, Jenny tries to humour him in his quest, as does his sympathetic friend Des, but bad luck seems to conspire to ensure that Colin never quite grabs his slice of fame. BBC2 1988-90.

Colonel March of Scotland Yard Boris Karloff (Colonel Perceval March), Ewan Roberts (Inspector Ames). Based on stories by Carter Dickson (John Dickson Carr), the one-eyed Colonel March (he wore a black patch over his left eye) works for D-3 (The Department of Queer Complaints) and solves improbable mysteries. ITV 1956-57.

Colour of Money, The Prime-time Saturday evening game show billed as the most stressful show on television. Co-hosted by Chris Tarrant and Millie Clode, the show was effectively a variation of *Deal Or No Deal* with a contestant having to open boxes to reveal sums of money varying from one to £20,000 in order to attain a predetermined figure that, if achieved, is kept. The stress part comes in not as one might think at the player having to put up with Chris's banal comments but at having to stop the clock, which counts up to the value of the box, before the total is achieved, for instance, if the box contains the maximum £20k the contestant will have a 20 second count-up and can say stop at any point, banking any monies accrued along the way. If they are timed out they lose all the money and have to reach their target with fewer boxes remaining. ITV 2009

Come Dancing The first-ever episode of Come Dancing was shown on 29 September 1949. An erroneous entry in the Guinness Book of Records citing 1950 as its debut year has cost many a quiz player dearly in years before, and after, the truth was out in 1992. Some sources have also mentioned 1948 as its debut year but the mistake is probably an over compensation of the correct year or a reference to its companion show of *Television Dancing Club*, which did indeed start in 1948. The ballroom dancing showcase was created by Eric Morley and ran on BBC for almost 50 years although until 1953 it followed a dance master class format and was non-competitive. Its presenters included Leslie Mitchell, McDonald Hobley, Sylvia Peters, Brian Johnston, Pete Murray, Don Moss, Peter Marshall, Angela Rippon, David Jacobs, Terry Wogan, Peter West, Peter Dimmock, Rosemarie Ford, Noel Edmonds, Judith Chalmers, Keith Fordyce and Michael Aspel. The last episode of the show proper was shown on 11 September 1995 although there were several *International Come Dancing* specials shown in 1996 and 1998. Although the theme is dance, the show is often cited as being the longest-running music show on television, although *Friday Night Is Music Night*, on the radio, has far greater longevity. BBC 1949-98

Come Dine With Me Five amateur chefs take it in turn to host a dinner party for the other four contestants each competitor then rating the host's performance with the winner winning a £1,000 cash prize. Occasionally the format has been tinkered with by having only four chefs and there have also been several celebrity specials. Dave Lamb adds the comic voice-overs. C4 2005-

Come Fly With Me Mockumentary comedy series created by and starring Matt Lucas and David Walliams. The series is a spoof of documentaries such as Airport and Airline and follows the activity at a fictional airport and three fictional airlines: FlyLo (a budget airline), Our Lady Air (an Irish budget airline) and Great British Air (a major international British airline). Characters include: Omar Baba (Walliams) - The owner of FlyLo; Precious Little (Lucas) – The aptly named skiving manager of the airport's coffee kiosk; Moses Beacon (Walliams) – The executive passenger liaison officer for Great British Air, who also runs a charity called WishWings; Tommy Reid (Lucas) – A young Scottish man working at the airport's Happy Burger, hoping to work his way up to becoming a pilot; Ian Foot (Walliams) - The airport's chief immigration officer; Fearghal O'Farrell (Lucas) – The gay air steward of Our Lady Air; Penny Carter (Walliams) - A first-class stewardess for Great British Air's long haul flights, with scathing views of passengers in the economy-class cabin; Melody Baines (Walliams) and Keeley St Clair (Lucas) – Liverpudlian check-in staff for FlyLo; Simon (Lucas) and Jackie Trent (Walliams) - A husband-and-wife pilot team with marital problems, flying for Great British Air; Ben Roberts (Walliams) and James Stewart (Lucas) – Airport customs officers, with rather unconventional methods of cataloguing the illegal substances they find; Peter (Lucas) and Judith Surname (Walliams) – Holiday makers who have suffered several horrific and surreal trips abroad with FlyLo; and Terry (Walliams) and John (Lucas) – The much put-upon Father-and-son baggage handlers. Many scenes were filmed at Robin Hood Airport Doncaster and London Stansted Airport. The series is narrated by Lindsay Duncan. BBC1 2010-

Comedians, The In 1971 Johnnie Hamp, who was formerly responsible for the early television appearances of artistes such as *The Beatles*, created a stand-up comedy show introducing innumerable new faces to the British public. The series featured mainly Northern stand-up comedians drawn from the club circuit. These included Mike Reid, Charlie Williams, Frank Carson, Colin Crompton, Ken Goodwin, Mick Miller, George Roper, Stan Boardman, Bernard Manning, Russ Abbot, Lennie Bennett, Jim Bowen, Duggie Brown, Bobby Knutt, Paul Melba, Tom O'Connor and Roy Walker. All these artistes recorded a 20-minute routine in front of a live Manchester audience and the result was edited into seven 30-minute shows. The format was a ratings winner and eleven series were made in total, although Johnnie gave way as producer to Ian Hamilton for the final series in 1992. ITV 1971-74; 1979, 1984-85; 1992.

Comedy Bandbox Saturday evening comedy showcase series that kickstarted the careers of Les Dawson, Dick Emery, Mike Yarwood, Dave Allen and Jimmy Tarbuck as well as showcasing existing stars such as Ken Platt and Chic Murray. Originally hosted by comedy double-act Hope and Keen, and entitled *Saturday Bandbox* for its first series, other hosts included Don Arroll and David Nixon. Interestingly, despite the huge success of the series it was never shown in the London area as it was aimed primarily at working-class audiences farther north. ITV 1962-66

Comedy Lab Generic name of a television series which has aired irregularly since 1998 and showcases pilots of experimental comedy shows. Shows that have gone on to spawn full series include *Trigger Happy TV, Fonejacker, School of Comedy, That Peter Kay Thing, Meet the Magoons* and *FM.* A 1999 show, *Golden Years*, was notable for an early writing collaboration between Ricky Gervais and Stephen Merchant. In the show Ricky played Clive Meadows, a David Bowie fanatic determined to play his idol on *Stars in their Eyes*. C4 1998-

Comedy Network, The Stand-up comedy showcase hosted by Boothby Graffoe. Among the performers were Jim Tavaré, Stewart Lee, Jenny Eclair, Sean Lock, Ed Byrne, Julian Barratt, Jason Freeman, Adam Bloom, Junior Simpson, Dave Gorman, Neil Bromley, Chris Addison, Kevin Eldon, Tommy Tiernan and Alan Parker Urban Warrior (alias Simon Munnery). C4 1997-99. See also *Gas*.

Comic Strip Presents, The Financed by theatrical impresario Michael White, the Comic Strip club opened in October 1980 at the Boulevard Theatre in London. The eight-strong core team at the venue comprised Alexei Sayle, Arnold Brown and three double-acts: Rik Mayall and Ade Edmondson, Nigel Planer and Peter Richardson; and Dawn French and Jennifer Saunders. Peter Richardson took a list of comedy film ideas to Jeremy Isaacs, head of Britain's fourth TV channel, due to open in November 1982, whereupon six films were commissioned. With the exceptions of Arnold Brown (whom Comic Strip TV viewers never saw) and Alexei Sayle (who showed up in only six of the 38 films), the six other protagonists appeared in most of the productions. Added, to round off the eight were Pete Richens (who co-scripted a good many of them and had tiny roles in two latter productions) and Robbie Coltrane, who had not played the Comic Strip club but was brought in as a friend by Rik Mayall. These eight formed their own production company, Comic Strip Productions, with Peter Richardson the linchpin and driving force of the collective. All 38 films are distinct productions, self-contained from the others, the first film, an Enid Blyton parody *Five Go Mad In Dorset*, went out on the opening night of C4, and four of the other films were screened soon after. The films kept coming, at reasonably regular intervals, and switched in 1990 to BBC2 (*South Atlantic Raiders*). All the while, the various players were enjoying glorious success with other TV productions (*The Young Ones* and *French And Saunders* to name but two) and the 'alternative' comedians rapidly became primary stars of the medium. After a five year break, the team returned to the screen (and to C4) in 1998 (*Four Men In A Car*). The 38th production *Four Men In A Plane* was broadcast on 4 January 2000 and the 39th, *Sex Actually* was broadcast on 28 December 2005. The latest offering, *The Hunt for Tony Blair*, aired on 14 October 2011 and starred Stephen Mangan in the title role and Jennifer Saunders as Margaret Thatcher. C4 1982-88, BBC2 1990-93, C 4 1998-2000; 2005; 2011

Common as Muck Edward Woodward (Nev), Tim Healy (Foxy), Neil Dudgeon (Ken), Roy Hudd (John Parry), Shirley Stelfox (Jean), Richard Ridings (Bernard), Stephen Lord (Jonno), Kathy Burke (Sharon), Frank Finlay (Derek), Alexei Sayle (Reg Vickers). A team of dustmen fight to prevent their jobs being privatised. In the second series Nev has retired after 45 years in the job. BBC1 1994 and 1997.

Compact Ronald Allen (Ian Harmon), Carmen Silvera (Camilla Hope), Vincent Ball (David Rome), Jean Harvey (Joanne Minster), Donald Morley (Mr Arnold Babbage). Popular BBC soap set in Enterprise House, the high-rise Victoria offices of *Compact*, a glossy women's magazine. Created by Hazel Adair and Peter Ling. BBC1 1962-65.

Complete and Utter History of Britain, The Written and performed by Terry Jones and Michael Palin, the premise was to replay history as if television had been around at the time, for instance, interviewing the vital characters in the dressing-room after the Battle of Hastings; having Samuel Pepys present a TV chat-show; showing an estate agent trying to sell Stonehenge to a young couple looking for their first home ('It's got character, charm and a slab in the middle'); and replaying Caesar's home-movie footage of his British invasion. The scope of the series was 'The Dawn Of History' to Oliver Cromwell and each episode took the form of short (three- to four-minute) sketches within the given historical theme, combining film inserts shot on location with video-tape shot in the LWT studio. The surreal humour was easily identifiable with the style of their earlier *Do Not Adjust Your Set* and other pre-Python series such as *At Last The 1948 Show*. Other actors performing in sketches included Colin Gordon, Roddy Maude-Roxby, Wallas Eaton, Melinda May, Diana Quick, Ted Carson, Johnny Vyvyan, John Hughman and Colin Cunningham. ITV 1969.

Comrade Dad George Cole (Reg Dudgeon), Barbara Ewing (Treen Dudgeon), David Garlick (Bob Dudgeon), Doris Hare (Gran). This futuristic seven-part sitcom was set in 1999, London now being known as Londongrad (part of USSR/GB) since the bloodless Soviet coup of 27 June 1989. BBC2 1986.

Connections Game show originally hosted by Sue Robbie who was succeeded by Richard Madeley (with Marian Chantar) from series three. Although it was primarily a teenager's show, an adult version hosted by Simon Potter aired in 1989-90. Contestants answered questions and were given a depiction of a person or object and had to work out the connection between them for bonus points. During the Simon Potter era, the end game involved being given the first and last of eight pictures and then, with the help of up to three clues, having to identify the next picture in the sequence, which would have a connection of some sort (such as a shared surname) with the pictures before and after it. One example was: The Walker Cup; Doris Speed (who played Annie Walker in Coronation Street) etc. Initially the jackpot was £1,000 but this was reduced to £400 when the series became daytime viewing. ITV 1985-90.

Connie Stephanie Beacham (Connie). A leading light in the rag trade is cheated out of her business but her steely grit and determination leads her to take a job at the Midlands-based House of Bea as a springboard for past glories. The theme song of this popular series was written by Willy Russell. ITV 1985.

Coogan's Run Six-episode comedy drama written by Steve Coogan, Patrick Marber, David Tyler, Graham Linehan, Arthur Mathews, Geoffrey Perkins and Henry Normal. Characters portrayed by Coogan include Paul, Pauline and Peter Calf, Gareth Cheeseman, Ernest Moss, Mike Crystal (aka Clint Stallone), Guy Crump and Tim Fleck. The title of each of the six episodes were *Get Calf, Dearth of a Salesman, A Handyman For All Seasons, Thursday Night Fever, Natural born Quizzers, The Curator*. Other character actors appearing included Alison Steadman, John Thomson, Felicity Montagu and Graham Fellows. BBC2 1995

Cool For Cats Britain's first television pop music show, playing a selection of latest releases. Originally hosted by Ker Robertson but after two months he was succeeded by Kent Walton for the remainder of its five-year run. ITV 1956-61.

Copycats Two families battle it out in a range of hilarious games based on the idea of Chinese Whispers and involving anything from remote control football boots to motorized toilets. A typical game will have the first member of the family miming an action and this must be copied along the line of the remaining members of the family and then guessed. Presented by Sam Nixon and Mark Rhodes as part of the CBBC menu in 2010. See *Sam and Mark's Guide to Dodging Disaster*

Coronation Street Britain's longest-running television soap opera was created by Tony Warren and first broadcast on Friday 9 December 1960 on ITV, where it continues to be scheduled. The programme is produced by Granada Television, the ITV1 franchise for the northwest England, and was initially shown only in that area; it was networked in May 1961. The working title of the show was Florizel Street, but a tea lady at Granada named Agnes remarked that 'Florizel' sounded too much like a disinfectant! Coronation Street is set in the fictitious industrial town of Weatherfield (loosely based on Salford). The show's iconic theme music, a solo brass piece reminiscent of northern band music, was written by Eric Spear and has been only slightly modified since the show's beginning. In Britain, Coronation Street was broadcast on Mondays and Wednesdays at 7:30pm for many years but in recent years the scheduling has been less rigid. Repeat episodes (and specials) can be seen on ITV2, with the omnibus usually shown on Saturday and Sunday. TV3 Ireland (part-owned by Granada), simulcasts 'Corrie' with ITV. Famous cameo appearances have included Noddy Holder in a live broadcast celebrating 40 years of Corrie; Sir Trevor McDonald, as himself, in 2000; The Duke of Bedford also as himself in 1973; Honor Blackman who played Rula Romanoff, an ageing wife-swapper who wanted to swap with Norris and Rita, in 2004; music star Cliff Richard who appeared in a scene, but had his back to the camera. The main characteristics of him in the scene, which was shot in the Rovers, were black hair, and a jumper which had the words 'Rock and Roll' across it; Graham Fellows, the comedian-pop star who created the fictional personas Jilted John and John Shuttleworth, had a cameo role in one episode and later returned as truck driver Les Charlton, a regular at Gail's café; Davy Jones of The Monkees made an appearance before he became famous in 1961 (and again in 1972) as Ena Sharples's grandson Colin Lomax; Bolton comedian Peter Kay played a shopfitter in 1997 and made a cameo appearance over two episodes in January 2004 as Eric Garside, a man who went on a date with Shelley Unwin; Joanna Lumley of *Absolutely Fabulous* and *The New Avengers* fame played Elaine Perkins, a girlfriend of Ken Barlow, in 1973; Sir Ian McKellen starred in 10 episodes in 2005 as con-merchant 'novelist' Melvin Hutchwright; Peter Noone of Herman's Hermits played Len Fairclough's son, Stanley, in 1961; Status Quo, the legendary rock band, appeared as themselves on Friday 23rd September 2005, when they assaulted Les for an incident which involved him 20 years previously. They appeared again on 31 October 2005 to play at Les and Cilla's wedding; The Prince of Wales, who played himself in a walk-on part); comedy legend Norman Wisdom, played fitness fanatic Ernie Crabbe in one episode in 2004; Sue Johnston, best known for her roles as Sheila Grant in *Brookside* and Barb Royle in *The Royle Family*, played Mrs. Chadwick in 1982; Patricia Routledge, better known as Hyacinth Bucket in the BBC sitcom *Keeping Up Appearances*, appeared in 1961 as Sylvia Snape; Zöe Lucker, who played Tanya Turner in *Footballers' Wives*, played Sonia Leach in 1996; Prunella Scales, best known as Sybil Fawlty in *Fawlty Towers*, played bus conductress Eileen Hughes in 1961; Martin Shaw, who played Doyle in the ITV action series *The Professionals*, played hippy Robert Croft in 1968; Joanne Whalley, who starred in the acclaimed BBC dramas *Edge of Darkness* and *The Singing Detective* before a Hollywood career beckoned, played Pamela Graham in 1974; Robin Askwith, star of several 'confessions' films made a brief appearance as a saucy tour guide in 2007; also

in 2007, Keith Barron, star of numerous comedy dramas, joined the cast as a former husband of Angela (Norris's ex). The following is the present cast list in alphabetical order as at the end of December 2011 with their character name and date started in brackets: Kate Anthony (Pam Compton / Hobsworth 2008), Peter Armitage (Maurice Allen 1977 and Bill Webster 1984-85; 1995-97, 2006–), Sam Aston (Chesney Brown / Battersby-Brown - 2003), Alex Bain (Simon Barlow – 2003), Elliott and Ollie Barnett (Baby Liam Connor - 2009), Jaxon and Maddox Beswick (Jack Dobbs - 2010), Katie Cavanagh (Julie Carp – 2008), Craig Charles (Lloyd Mullaney – 2005 absent at present while Craig films new episodes of Red Dwarf but scheduled to return in 2012), Pattie Clare (Mary Taylor - 2008), Sue Cleaver (Eileen Grimshaw - 2000), Stephanie Cole (Sylvia Goodwin - 2011), Michelle Collins (Stella Price - 2011), Charlie Condou (Marcus Dent - 2007–08; 2011), Antony Cotton (Sean Tully - 2003), Jane Danson (Leanne Battersby/Tilsley - 1997), Eileen Derbyshire (Emily Nugent / Bishop / Swain - 1961), Zennon Ditchett (Aadi Alahan - 2006), Sally Dynevor nee Whittaker (Sally Seddon / Webster - 1986), Helen Flanagan (Rosie Webster - 2000), Georgia May Foote (Katy Armstrong – 2010), Kate Ford (Tracy Preston / Barlow – 2002), Chris Fountain (Tommy Duckworth – 2011), Chris Gascoyne (Peter Barlow - 2000), Lisa George (Beth - 2011), Samia Ghadie (Maria Sutherland / Connor - 2000), Tanisha Gorey (Asha Alahan - 2006), Simon Gregson (Steve McDonald - 1989), Shobna Gulati (Sunita Parekh/Alahan - 2001), Natalie Gumede (Kirsty Soames - 2011), Peter Gunn (Brian Packham – 2010), Alan Halsall (Tyrone Dobbs - 1998), Jimmi Harkishin (Dev Alahan - 1999), Malcolm Hebden (Carlos 1974 and Norris Cole - 1994), Julie Hesmondhalgh (Hayley Patterson/Cropper - 1998), Tony Hirst (Paul Kershaw – 2010), Judy Holt (Mrs Grice 1991 and Lesley Kershaw - 2011), Cherylee Houston (Izzy Armstrong - 2010), Michelle Keegan (Tina McIntyre - 2008), Katherine Kelly (Becky Granger / McDonald - 2006), Alison King (Carla Connor - 2006), Anne Kirkbride (Deirdre Hunt / Langton / Barlow / Rachid - 1972), Barbara Knox (Rita Littlewood / Fairclough / Sullivan - 1964), Andrew Lancel (Frank Foster – 2011), Paula Lane (Kylie Turner / Platt – 2010), Ellie Leach (Faye Butler - 2011), Michael Le Vell (Neil Grimshaw 1981 and Kevin Webster - 1983), Philip Lowrie (Dennis Tanner - 1960-68; 2011), Kym Marsh nee Ryder (Michelle Connor - 2006), Jennie McAlpine (Fiz Brown / Stape - 2001), Oliver Mellor (Matt Carter - 2010), John Michie (Karl Munro - 2011), Elle Mulvaney (Amy Barlow – 2004), David Neilson (Roy Cropper - 1995), Sue Nicholls (Audrey Potter / Roberts - 1979), Mikey North (Gary Windass - 2008), Nikki Patel (Amber Kalirai 2005-09; 2011), Sadie Pilbury and Harriet Atkins (Hope Stape - 2010), Ben Price (Nick Tilsley – 2009), Ian Pulestan-Davies (Owen Armstrong – 2010), William Roache (Ken Barlow - 1960) , Debbie Rush (Anna Windass - 2008), Jeremy Sheffield (Danny Stratton - 2011), Jack P. Shepherd (David Platt - 2000), Gwen Taylor (Anne Foster – 2011), Ryan Thomas (Jason Grimshaw - 2000), Catherine Tyldesley (unnamed midwife 2006; Eva Price 2011), Brooke Vincent (Sophie Webster - 2004), Andrew Whyment (Wayne 1999 and Kirk Sutherland - 2000), Helen Worth (Gail Potter / Tilsley / Platt / Hillman / McIntyre - 1974).

This is a comprehensive list of all former named Corrie stars sorted in the same manner as above: Owen Aaronovitch (Jon Lindsay 1997-98), Lewis Ablett (Billy Mallett 1998-2000), William Abney (Rev Copley 1977 and Jim Lorimer 1980), Andy Abrahams (unnamed shop assistant 2000 and Brian Hudson 2001), Zaraah Abrahams (Joanne Jackson 2005-07), Dawn Acton (Tracy Barlow / Preston 1988-99), Justine Adams (Nurse Cooper 1999 and 2002, WPC Hall 2001 and WPC Jessop 2002), Sally Adams (extra in 1977 and Registrar 1999), Peter Adamson (Len Fairclough 1961-83), Roger Adamson (David Graham 1964), Guido Adorni (Waiter 1974), Mark Adshead (Mark Hillkirk 1973), Sara Aimson (Dr Sarah Morris 1981), Betty Alberge (Florrie Lindley 1960-65), Richard Albrecht (Derek Heavey 1999 and 2002), Gordon Alcock (Arthur Billyard 1996), Victoria Alcock (Mary Docherty 1998), Jill Alex (Mrs Simms 1977 and 1979), Jean Alexander (Hilda Ogden 1964-87), Johnny Allan

(Barney Moss 1976 and Barney Holt 1980), Eric Allen (Les Fox 1977), Fiona Allen (Julia Stone 1999), Jack Allen (Arthur Walker 1969), Genevieve Allenbury (Irene Muir 1996), David Allister (Peter Bromley 1984), Michael Altha (Walter Crombie 1975), Rachel Ambler (Gill Collins 1982), Gladys Ambrose (Mre Hindle 1979), Georgina Anderson (Eunice Watts 1988 and 1995), Simeon Andrews (Father Donnelly 1995), Michael Angelis (Franny Slater 1972), Robert Angell (Alan Rush 2001), Callen Angelo (Gary Strauss 1967-68 and 1970), Avril Angers (Norah Dawson 1961), Tony Anholt (David Law 1975), Holly Quin-Ankrah (Cheryl Gray 2010-11), Lysette Anthony (Lydia Radcliffe 2010), Nigel Anthony (Mr Melia 1984), Philip Anthony (Maurice Rowe 1968), Josephine Antosz (Mrs Holt 1978), Mina Anwar (Ravinder Kalirai 2005-06), Kathryn Apanowicz (Carol Starkey 1995), Cyril Appleton (Jim Conran 1978), Annabelle Apsion (Patricia Hillman 2002), Ann Aris (Mrs Mottershead 1978 and various unnamed roles 1995-98), Debbie Arnold (Sylvie Hicks 1981-82), Dickie Arnold (George Benton 1976, Tiny Stubbs 1977 and Ossie Oswald 1980), Dominic Arnold (Brett Grundy 2000), Steven Arnold (Ashley Peacock 1995-2010), Pal Aron (Sonny Dhillon 2006-07), Rod Arthur (unnamed site foreman 1989, blood donor 1991 and Tim Hedges 1996), William Ash (Johnny James 2002), Jayne Ashbourne (Amy Goskirke 2000), Bridget Ashburn (Christine Glover 1984), Barbara Ashcroft (Mrs Ferguson 1976), Ray Ashcroft (Tim Gibbs 1978 and Steve Holt 1986-87), Dean Ashton (Aidan Critchley 2002-03), Dicken Ashworth (Geoff Horton 1992-2000), Ian Aspinall (Darren Whateley 1989), Mark Aspinall (David Denton 1983), Emily Aston (Becky Palmer 1996-97), Joseph Aston (Tommy Duckworth 2000), Michael Atha (Walter Crombie 1975), Frank Atkinson (Sam Leach 1962), Michael Atkinson (Delivery Man 1982, Mr Ryan 1997 and Colin Fielding 2001), Rebecca Atkinson (Stephanie Mills 2002), Rosalind Ayres (Alison Wright 1974), Martin Bacon (Wayne Fletcher 1980), Wendy Bacon (Sharon Fletcher 1980), John Baddeley (Douglas Preston 1967), Nicholas R. Bailey (Lee Middleton 1996-97), Amanda Bairstow (Susan Denton 1983), George Baker (Cecil Newton 2003), Victoria Baker (Christopher Hewitt 1962-85), Peter Baldwin (Derek Wilton 1976-97), Michael Ball (Malcolm Nuttall 1985), Geoffrey Banks (Herbert Townsend 1996 and Wally 2001), Thomas Baptiste (Johnny Alexander 1963), Jonathan Barclay (John Spencer 1981), Anthony Barclay (Karl Harper 2001-02), Jessica Barden (Kayleigh Morton 2007-08), Ashley Barker (Terry 1981 and Mr Yorke 1998-99), Judith Barker (Janet Reid/Barlow 1969-77), Melanie Barker (Clare Machin 2000), Tim Barker (Mr Brown 1997), Ginni Barlow (Mrs Taylor 1978), Jonathan Barlow (Jeff Singleton 1987), Thelma Barlow (Mavis Riley/Wilton 1971-97), Lynda Baron (Renee Turnbull 1997), Roy Barraclough (I-Spy Dwyer 1968 and Alec Gilroy 1972-75, 1986-92, 1996-98), Steve Barratt (Terry Bates 1972), John Barrett (Monty Shawcross 1980), Amanda Barrie (Alma Sedgewick / Baldwin / Halliwell 1981-2001), John Barrie (Jimmy Frazer 1972), Keith Barron (George Trench 2007), Alice Barry (Elsie Birch 2002), June Barry (Joan Walker 1961-63), Jim Bartley (Michael Ryan 1974), Tony Barton (Pat Hegherty 1998-2001), John Basham (Nigel Ridley 1989-90), Romy Baskerville (unnamed secretary 1989 and Sue Jeffers 1990-97), Geoffrey Bateman (Philip Lightfoot 1976), Rupert Bates (Mr Hutton 1997), Lee Battle (Simon Green 2000-01), John Batty (Cliff Humphries 1976), Eileen Battye (Ms Deakin 2000), Lois Baxter (Marie Stanton 1976-77), Susie Baxter (Dotty Sutherland 2000 and 2008), Peter Bayliss (Charlie Bracewell 1989), Stephanie Beacham (Martha Fraser 2009), Oliver Beamish (Richard Willmore 1992-94; 2011), Tim Beasley (Roger Caulfield 2001), Andrew Beaumont (Robin Smethurst 1977), Ivan Beavis (Harry Hewitt 1960-67), Clare Beck (Jean Crabtree 1997), Robert Beck (Jimmy Dockerson 2008-09), David Beckett (Dave Barton 1990-91), Linda Beckett (Edith Foster 1983), Stephen Beckett (Dr. Matt Ramsden 2000-02 and 2005), Richard Beckinsale (PC Wilcox 1969), Samantha Beckinsale (Lorraine Mason 1996), Harry Beety (Alec Yardley 1984), Geoffrey Beevers (Mr Liston 1978), Michael Begley (PC Bentley 1996-97), Sasha Behar (Maya Sharma 2003-04), Joe Belcher (George Carter 1981), Neil Bell (Simon Farrah 2002), Stephen Bell (Luke Quinn 2010), Jane Bellamy (Margaret Frost 1997), Rebecca Bellamy (Jackie Mosley 2001), Derek Benfield (Walter Greenhalgh 1961-69), Lesley Bennett (Sister Baker 1980), Nigel Bennett (Colin Bailey 1977), Tracie Bennett (Sharon Gaskell / Bentley 1982-84 and 1999), Ishia Bennison (Mrs Mawdsley 2000), Stephen Bent (Dave Turner 2002), Benjamin Beresford (Joshua Peacock 2004-11), Luke Beresford (Freddie Peacock 2010-11), Niall Beresford (Freddie Peacock 2010-11), Carol Berlyne (Shirley Bennett 1981), Sheila Bernette (Sister Delaney 1973), Charise Berry (WPC / Stripper 2001), Suzanne Bertish (Viv Fay 1998), Nicola Bertram (Gillian Davies 2001), James Berwick (Ralph Curtis 1978), Anthony Beswick (Vernon Bradshaw 2000-01 and Mike Scott 2008-09), Robert Bettison (Tom Pickup 1977), George Betton (Wally Tanner 1966), Janette Beverley (Elaine Pollard 1984), Nigel Betts (Mr Weir 2000 and Eddie 2007), Ted Beyer (Arthur Jones 1980), Ace Bhatti (Jayesh Parekh 2005-06), Stephen Billington (Greg Kelly 1998-99), Michael Bilton (Norman Pearson 1983), Vicky Binns (Molly Compton / Dobbs 2005-10), Frank Birch (Milman Ross Jonas 1976-77), Norman Bird (Joe Hibbert 1978), Philip Bird (Gregory Stephens 2000-01), Chris Bisson (Vikram Desai 1999-2002), Denise Black (Denise Osbourne 1992-97 and 2007), Joe Black (Herbert Cook 1979), Michael Blackham (Brian Thomas 1966), Susie Blake (Bev Unwin 2003-06), Joy Blakeman (Marie Ramsden 1990 and Jayne Reid 2001), Margaret Blakemore (June Meadows 2000), Toby Blanchard (Mr Swift 1982), Nicholas Blane (Neville Green 1998-99), Andrea Blidgeon (Lucy Foyle 1974), Paul Blidgeon (Vernon Foyle 1974), Ian Blower (Mr Phelps 1996 and Mr Matthews 1999), Pat Blyton (Dorothy Millington 1977), Freddie Boardley (Ian McAllister 1980), Lee Boardman (Jez Quigley 1999-2000), Eamon Boland (Ronnie Stubbs 1988 and Frank O'Connor 2000-01), Clive Bonelle (Wilf 2000), Stella Bonheur (Emmeline Tanner 1967), Imogen Boorman (Vanessa Morgan 1992), Jane Booker (Mrs Hall 1996), Neil Boorman (Gerald Lickley 1999), Anthony Booth (Malcolm Wilkinson 1960-61), Lee Booth (Paul Clayton 2000-01), Matthew Booth (Matt Broughall 2002), Tracey Booth (Chloe Bebbington 2002), Bruce Bould (John Summers 1978), Emma Bowe (Jayne Morgan 2001), John Bowe (Duggie Ferguson 1999-2002), Holly Bower (Amy Barlow 2004), Sharon Bower (WPC Rogers 1978), Robin Bowerman (Mr Lucas 1998 and Ralph Merryweather 2000), Debbie Bowers (Trish Keegan 1982), Lally Bowers (Mrs. Arkinstall 1966), John Bowler (John Wilding 2002), Todd Boyce (Stephen Reid 1996, 1997 and 2007), Alexandra Boyd (Clarissa Mason 2008), Niven Boyd (Paul Fisher 1997-98), Roy Boyd (Mr Franklin 1978), Tommy Boyle (Frank Bradley 1970 and Phil Jennings 1990-91), Tracy Brabin (Tricia Armstrong 1994-97), Lisa Bracewell (Phillippa Robson 1978), David Bradley (Det Sgt Simms 1980), Elizabeth Bradley (Councillor Adams 1978 – credited as Margaret Bradley - and Maud Grimes 1993-99), Ken Bradshaw (Jason Riley 1998), Patricia Brake (Viv Baldwin 2005-06), Roy Brandon (Barry Pollard 1985), John Branwell (Ed Malone 1996), Christine Brennan (Dawn Watson 1997, Dr Neville 1998, PC Jones 2000 and Belinda Sawyer 2002), Philip Bretherton (Robert Weston 1991 and Ian Davenport 2004-05), Bridget Brice (Sonia Price 1981), David Brierley (Harold 1983), Roger Brierley (Lanky Potts 1976), Tommy Brierley (Old Man in Café 1981 and Tommy Shankley 1983), Stephen Brigden (Dr Maitland 1983), Ali Briggs (Freda Burgess 2005-10), Johnny Briggs (Mike Baldwin 1976-2006), Theresa Brindley (Cathy Power 1994), Kate Brisley (Sandra Rogers 1990), Judy Brooke (Paula Maxwell 1992-94), Philip Brook (Adrian Gosthorpe 1991), Ray Brooks (Norman Phillips 1963-64), Michael Brophy (Mr Daventry 1999), Margaret Brough (Mrs Pye 1982), June Broughton (Joan Lowther 1982 and Enid Crump 2010), Denton Brown (Waiter 1999 and Max Dale 2000), Duggie Brown (George Freeman 1997), Jemma Brown (Sandra Buckley 1996), Julie Brown (unnamed mother 1999 and Julie Reardon 2002), June Brown (Mrs. Parsons 1970), Martina Brown (Amanda Stephens 2000-01), Melanie Brown (Chantal Clarke 1998), Susan Brown (Connie Clayton 1985 and Maureen Tully 2006), Wenda Brown (Teresa Meakin 1976), Alan Browning (Alan Howard 1969-1974), Patricia Browning (Pauline Stringer 1980), Angela Bruce (Janice Stubbs 1978), Lorraine Brunning (Mrs Medlock 1997), Margot Bryant (Minnie Caldwell 1960-76), Christine Buckley (Florrie Banks 1977), Terence Budd (Neil Foxall 1975), Amelia Bullmore (Steph Barnes 1990-92 and 1995), Avis Bunnage (Alice Burgess 1961), Ken Burgess (Alec

Dewhurst 1980), Andy Burke (Trevor Stamp 2002), David Burke (John Benjamin 1966), Ian Burns (Ronnie Burgess 1981), Alison Burrows (WPC Latimer 1998 and WPC Milner 2000), Justin Burrows (unnamed paramedic 1999-2001 and DS Tony Trafford 2001-02), Maxine Burth (Nurse Sloane 2000), John Burton (DC Cody 1997), Margaret Burton (Poppy Watts 1980), Neville Buswell (Ray Langton 1966-78 and 2005), Richard Butler (Jim Schofield 1962), Paul Butterworth (PC Conway 1979 and PC Reed 1981), Michael Byrne (Ted Page 2008-10), Jim Bywater (Wilf Starkey 1985), Juliet Cadzow (Jacqui McIntyre 1997), Sean Caffrey (Frank Riley 1968), Clare Calbraith (Robyn 2005), David Calder (Ted Thomas 1978-79), Richard Caldicot (Rev Smedley 1977), Beverley Callard (Liz McDonald 1989–98; 2000–01; 2003; 2004–11), Gillian Cally (Maureen Shepherd 2001), Robert Calvert (DC Gough 2000), Nicholas Camm (DS Johnson 2000), Marji Campi (Dulcie Froggatt 1984-87), Joan Campion (Florrie Todd 1979), Chris Canavan (Dusty 1976), Toni Cannon (Sharon Dobbs 1978), Jonathan Caplan (Martin Cheveski 1980), Penny Capper (Cheryl Jones 1997), Brian Capron (Donald Worthington 1981-82 and Richard Hillman 2001-03), Tony Capstick (Harvey Nuttall 1995, 97 and 99), Fanny Carby (Amy Burton 1987-88), Anita Carey (Brenda Summers 1978 and Joyce Smedley 1996-97), Denis Carey (Ozzie 1978), Gary Cargill (DS Phil Campbell 2006, 2007 and 2008), Timothy Carlton (Richard Cresswell 1977-78), Katy Carmichael (Lucy Richards / Barlow 2002-03), Lynne Carol (Martha Longhurst 1960-64), Gary Carp (Richard Dickinson 1981), Jack Carr (Tony Cunliffe 1984), Kit Carradice (Alice 1996), Olivia Carruthers (Suzanne Holbrook 2011), Violet Carson (Ena Sharples 1960-80), Dominic Carter (DC Hooch 2008-09), Fabian Cartwright (Billy Wyatt 1988), Stephen Casey (Det Insp Grey 1998), Murray Cash (Mike Ritchie 1973), Jane Casson (Faye Marie Schofield 1973), Ralph Casson (Mr Bellis 2000), Ann Castle (Moira Maxwell 1965), Brenda Castle (Mrs Watson 1978 and 1979), Claire Cathcart (Yvonne Bannister 1996), Angela Catherall (Muriel Clough 1978), Amelia Cauldwell (Chloe 2006-07), Deborah Chad (Helen Cooper 2000-01), Amber Chadwick (Amy Barlow 2007-2010), Nicholas Chagrin (unnamed surgeon 1998 and Fabrice Sancier 2000), John Challis (Det Sgt Phillips 1977), Holly Chamarette (Tracy Barlow 1985-88), Bara Chambers (Mrs Tetlow 1980), Vicki Chambers (Michelle Fenton 1981 and Sally Waterman 1983-85), Belinda Chapman (WPC Mitchell 1995), Stephen Chapman (Roger Hinde 2002), Maria Charles (Lena Thislewood 2004-06), Carl Chase (Cyril McGregor 1982), Connor Chatburn (Morgan Middleton 1998), Mark Chatterton (Neville Hawthorne 1986, 2005 and 2007 and Gordon Blinkhorn 1992-93), Helen Cherry (Sybil Cudlipp 1973), Peter Childs (Cliff Mortam 1978 and Mr Emery 1980), Dennis Chinnery (Steve Bassett 1977), Ken Christiansen (Jerry Hopkins 1999-2000), Sushil Chudasama (Scooter Makuna 2005), Margi Clarke (Jackie Dobbs 1998-99 and 2009-10), Warren Clarke (Kenny Pickup 1966 and Gary Bailey 1968), Richard Clay-Jones (Mr Healey 1978), Edward Clayton (Tom Casey 1989-90), Rosy Clayton (Barbara Davies 1996 and Steph Hughes 2001), Caroline Clegg (unnamed estate agent 2000 and Dr Pearce 2002), Keith Clifford (Charlie West 1997-99 and Frank Nicholls 2007), Ina Clough (Mrs Laight 1997), Hazel Clyne (Glenda Fox 1981), Dario Coates (Alex Neeson 2007-08), Mary-Ann Coburn (Mrs Harris 2001), Martin Cochrane (Stuart Boswell 1996), Michael Cochrane (Bob Fay 1998), Nicholas Cochrane (Andy McDonald 1989-97, 2000, 2004 and 2009), Frank Coda (Mario Bonarti 1961), Christopher Coghill (Vole 1998), Adam Colclough (Colin Baxter 1995 and unnamed bodyguard 1999), Richard Cole (Mal Price 1996, Mr Downing 1999 and Insp Pearce 2001), Lesley Coleman (Dr Lamball 1998), Sylvia Coleridge (Sonia Forrester 1978), Ian Colin (Arthur Forsythe-Jones 1962), Christopher Coll (Victor Pendlebury 1982-92), Daniel Coll (Colin Applegate 2000), John Collin (Douglas Pickens 1969), Emma Collinge (Rosie Webster 1990-99), Jonathan Collins (Trevor Ogden 1964), Nigel Collins (Ernie Kershaw 2000 and Tommy 2001), Stephen Collins (Joshua Peacock 2003), Phil Collinson (Bob Wright 1997), Christopher Colquhoun (Matt Davis 2009-10), Gilly Coman (Judy 1978 and Sugar Le Mar 1981), Shane Connaughton (John Smith 1970), Vicky Connett (Kirsten Grant 2000), Stephen Connor (Mr Jewson 2000), Barry Conway (unnamed security guard 1996 and Carl Mason 2000), Jim Conway (Roy Stevenson 1979), Nick Conway (Mr Jameson 1997), Chris Cook (Mark Redman 1992-94), Joe Cook (PC Maskall 1977, 80, 82, 83), Linda Cook (Jill Morris 1967), Juliet Cooke (Muriel Fielding 1981), Ryan Cooke (Cameron McIntyre 2006), Trish Cooke (Registrar 2003), Barrie Cookson (Ted Brownlow 1977), Mia Louise Cookson (Bethany Platt 2000), Susan Cookson (Mrs Briscoe 1998), Collette Cooper (Carol Mills 2002), Garry Cooper (DC Richardson 1989), George A. Cooper (William Piggott 1964), Jack Cooper (Kenzie Judd 2008-09), Kenneth Cope (Jed Stone 1961-66 and 2008-09), Paul Copley (Ivor Priestley 2007), Susan Cormack (Wendy Rawnsley 2002), Delia Corrie (Dr Judith Hollins 1981), Chelsea Corrigan (Lauren Riding 2002), Deirdre Costello (Gina Fletcher 1971 and Connie Parker 1987-88), Orla Cottingham (Julie Howard 2002), Prim Cotton (Pam Mitchell 1983), Eric Coudrill (PC Bowman 1996), Simon Coury (Mr Hallam 2000), Alan Cowan (Simon 1996), Corrine Ray Coward (Janette Foster 2002), Gabrielle Cowburn (Judi Spencer 1984), Christine Cox (Renee Dodds 1990, Margaret Dunbar 1996 and Mrs Ferris 1998), Clifford Cox (Eric Turner 1974), Frances Cox (Mrs Bolton 1980 and Aunt Cissie 1991), Jane Cox (Mrs. Shaw 1991), Sue Cox (Jill Sykes 1973), Jonathan Coy (Stanley Fairclough 1977), David Craig (Dr Harris 1979), Pamela Craig (Jackie Marsh 1966), Thomas Craig (Tommy Nelson/Harris 2002-05), Kenneth Cranham (Ray Harrison 1968), Frank Crawshaw (Arnold Tanner 1961), David Crellin (Graham Baxter 1996, Jimmy Clayton 2005 and Colin Fishwick 2010), Nesba Crenshaw (Carrie Meyer 1996), Bernard Cribbins (Wally Bannister 2003), Bill Croasdale (Mr Fearnley 1978 and unnamed registrar 1980), Frank Crompton (Councillor Harold Chapman 1972, 76, 78 and 1980), Matthew Crompton (Dan Mason 2007-08), Anna Cropper (Joan Akers 1962), Hugh Cross (DCI Castle 1967 and 1970), Fred Crossley (George Mulliner 1970), Angela Crow (Doreen Lostock 1961-63), Daniel Crowder (Ray Connell 2000), Bob Cryer (Inspector Johnson 1998), Nailah Cumberbatch (Jessie Jackson 2005-06), Ronald Cunliffe (Stanley Fairclough 1967-77), Anne Cunningham (Linda Tanner / Cheveski 1960-68 and 1984), Danny Cunningham (Jimmy Sykes 2000-01), Glenn Cunningham (Gordon Fletcher 1998 and Bob Critchley 2002-03), Kieran Cunningham (Dave Bonsall 2010), Mary Cunningham (Sandra Hesketh 1999), Susan Cunningham (Tina Shapiro 2000), Shaun Curry (Harry Fox 1981), Catherine Cusack (Carmel Finnan 1992-93), Sorcha Cusack (Helen Connor 2008), Patricia Cutts (Blanche Hunt 1974), Lesley Daine (Josie Steele 1976), Lois Daine (Jean Mosley 1970), David Daker (Basil Griffin 1968, Gordon Lewis 1981 and 1984-85), Charles Dale (Dennis Stringer 2000-02), Niamh Daly (Carol Delaney 1997-2000), Gary Damer (Wayne Haynes 2000-01), Sarah Dangerfield (Linda Norton 1979), Tara Daniels (WPC Burrows 1996), Tim Dantay (Neil Flynn 1998), David Darbyshire (Lenny Larkin 2000), Maureen Darbyshire (Zilla 1974), Alison Darling (Lydia Summers 2000), Chris Darwin (Billy Nelson 1982), Sam Dastor (Jimmy 1981), Alan David (Glyn Thomas 1973), Joel David (various unnamed roles 1981-93, Eric Warburton 1996 and Mr Cooper 2004), David Davies (Lt. Comm. Prince 1971), Andrew Davidson (Wayne Summers 1978), Danny Davies (Charlie Palmer 1996), Diana Davies (Norma Ford 1972-73), Eirwynn Davies (Fred Bigginshaw 1975), Judith Davies (Mrs Hargreaves 1989), Rachel Davies (Donna Parker 1975), Richard Davies (Idris Hopkins 1974-75), Ron Davies (George Wardle 1985), Terence Davies (Dick Rawlins 1978), Judith Davis (Mrs Stevens 1983 and Mrs Groves 1997), Maureen Davis (Mavis Fox 1963), Noel Davis (Johnny Wade 1967), Elizabeth Dawn (Vera Duckworth 1974-2008), Marion Dawson (Matilda Grimshaw 1962), Yvonne Dawson (Margaret 1998), Vicky Day (Fatima 1976), Gabrielle Daye (Beattie Pearson 1975-83), Julia Deakin (Brenda Fearns 2003-04), Kate Deakin (Connie Reeves 2001), Stephanie Deakin (Stephanie 2004), Jack Deam (Phil Simmonds 2000-01), Peter Dean (Jeff Bateman 1980), Iain De Caestecker (Adam Barlow 2001-03), Constantine De Goguel (Vince Denton 1977), Olivier De

Grossouvre (Olivier Madar 2000), Alexander Delamere (Robert Hastings 2001), Alex De Marcus (Cliff Beresford 2002), Zulema Dene (Sarah Brookes 1992), Sue Devaney (Debbie Webster 1984-85), Myrtle Devenish (Mrs Ashbrook 1997), Andy Devine (Jason Ross 2000), Ayesha Dharker (Tara Mandel 2008-09), Leena Dhingra (Mina Parekh 2001 and 2004), Charlie Dickinson (unnamed locksmith 1996 and Gordon Holness 2002), Rob Dickson (Brian Roscoe 1988-89), Russell Dickson (Dave Barnes 1978-79), Peter Dineen (Father Bradley 1997), Reece Dinsdale (Joe McIntyre 2008-10), Jonathan Dixon (Darryl Morton 2007-09), Michael Dixon (Christopher Pitcher 2006), Russell Dixon (Dave Barnes 1979 and Councillor Harold Potts 1992-93), Shirley Dixon (Joyce Lomas 1982), Steve Dixon (Paul Sidall 1980 and unnamed taxi driver 1984), Eric Dodson (Reverend James 1968), Pip Donaghy (Eddie Baines 1996), Elaine Donnelly (Caroline Wilson/Clegg 1982), James Donnelly (Reuben Ward 1970), John Donnelly (Dobber Dobson 1998), Shaun Dooley (Richie Fitzgerald 1997-98), Veronica Doran (Marion Willis/Yeats 1982-83), Tupele Dorgu (Kelly Crabtree 2004-10), Christopher Dormer (Peter Barlow 1986), Robert Dorning (Edward Wormold 1965 and Alderman Rogers 1972), Kenny Doughty (Jake Harman 2009), Lyn Douglas (Alice Nelson 1979), Su Douglas (Mrs Bardsley 1996), Katherine Dow Blyton (Nicola Owens 1996, Dr Groves 1998 and Liz Morrisey 2001), Patricia Downing (Pauline Stringer 1980), Tony Doyle (Sean Regan 1972), Gabrielle Drake (Inga Olsen 1967), Keith Drinkel (Maurice Gregory 2001-02 and Bob 2005), Betty Driver (Betty Turpin/Williams 1969-2011), Lauren Drummond (Christie Wells 2001), Karen Drury (Angie 1978), Barbara Dryhurst (Maggie Knight 1978 and Miss Johnson 2001-02), Franck Dubosc (Patrice Podevin 1987), Sharon Duce (Paula Carp 2009), Peter Dudley (Donald Anderson 1978 and Bert Tilsley 1979-83), Carl Duering (Klaus Muller 1992), Keith Duffy (Ciaran McCarthy 2002-11), Michael Duggan (Gary Turner 1974), Paul Duncan (Andy Rowlands 1979-81), Peter Duncan (Christopher Cullen 1974), Rosemarie Dunham (Sylvia Mathews 1976), Enid Dunn (Joan Lawson 2002), Andrew Dunn (Roger Stiles 2007), Ian Dunn (Vinnie Powers 2009-10), Pat Dunn (Pat Barnes 1998), Nick Dunning (Mr Gillatt 1998), Matthew Dunster (Ryan Sykes 2000-01), Louise Duprey (Amy Nelson 1993), Patrick Durkin (Joe Williams 1978), Joe Duttine (D.S. Carr - 2010), John Duttine (Alec Baker 1977), Dave Dutton (Bert Latham 1990-91 and Harry Benson 1998-99), Leslie Dwyer (Jacko Dugdale 1978), Trevor Dwyer-Lynch (Patrick Tussel 2002-05), Kevin Dyer (PC Park 1996 and Graham Larkin 2001), Anne Dyson (Effie Spicer 1968-69), Noel Dyson (Ida Barlow 1960-61), Freddie Earlle (Sam Owens 1993), Mark Eden (Wally Randle 1981 and Alan Bradley 1986-89), David Edge (Tony Hill 1984), Emma Edmondson (Mel Morton 2007-08), Darryl Edwards (Tommy Duckworth 1992-97), Jenny Edwards (Terri Clayton 1977), Maudie Edwards (Elsie Lappin 1960), Meredith Edwards (Bert Gosling 1975), Tommy Edwards (Doug Clayton 1978), Colin Edwynn (PC Jimmy Conway 1967-72), Brenda Elder (Flo 1972, Mrs Hillkirk 1973, Eunice Wheeler 1975, Mrs Mossop 1983 and Elsie Seddon 1986-97), Steve Elder (DI Fox 1998), Rachael Elizabeth (Abi Sharpe 2008), John Elkington (Chris Melton 2002), Rosalind Elliot (Karen Lomax 1972), Su Elliot (Julie Dewhurst 1991-92), Catriona A. Elliott (Liz Turnbull 1986), Frank Elliott (Det Sgt Whiteley 1981), Jack Ellis (Harry Mason 2007-08), June Ellis (Winnie Dyson (1991), Peter Ellis (Reg Sudworth 1980), John Elmes (Leo Firman 1995), Michael Elphick (Douglas Wormold 1974), Paul Elsam (Dazz Isherwood 1984), Victoria Elton (Paul Cheveski 1961), Ian Embleton (Colin Barnes 1993, 1998-2000), Vicky Entwistle (Janice Battersby 1997-2011), Elizabeth Estensen (Pam Middleton 1996-98), Ashley Evans (Christine Hargreaves 2001), Edward Evans (Lionel Petty 1965-66), Howell Evans (Tegwin Thomas 2000), Jessie Evans (Mrs Cook 1967 and Granny Megan Hopkins 1974-75), Lucy Evans (Lauren Wilson 2007-08), Mandy Evans (Wanda 1991), Tenniel Evans (Insp Vaughan 1980), Chris Fairbank (Ginger 1981), Amanda Fairclough (Diane Goodhoe 2001 and Nurse Shaw 2002), Deborah Fairfax (Dr Summers 1991), Souad Faress (Urmila Alahan 2001), Suzan Farmer (Wendy Nightingale(1976 and Sally Robson 1978), Simon Farnaby (Greg Bamfield 1996), Colin Farrell (Frank Holmes 1976 and Colin Fanshawe 1998), Kenneth Farrington (Billy Walker 1961-84),

Kate Faulkner (Lisa Sugden 2001), Peter Faulkner (Professor Barker 1998), Andrew Faulkner (Richard Taylor 1998), Gaynor Faye (Judy Mallett 1995-99), Ray Fearon (Nathan Harding 2005-2006), Fred Feast (Fred Gee 1975-84), Benjamin Feitelson (Roger Floriet 1977), Graham Fellows (Les Charlton 1982), Jean Ferguson (Mrs Mallett 1999; Dorothy Hoyle 2010-11), Samantha Ferguson (Jason Lomax 1972), Barbara Ferris (Nona Willis 1961), Emma Louise Field (Lucy Moffatt 1982), Susan Field (Ethel Tyson 1963), John Lloyd Fillingham (Neil Mitchell 1992-93), Chris Finch (Karl Foster 2003-04), Christabel Finch (Tracy Langton/Barlow (1977-83), John Finn (DS Rearden 2001), Siobhan Finneran (Josie Phillips 1989-90), Daryl Fishwick (Mandy Turner 1988), Martin Fisk (PC White 1980), Annie Fitzmaurice (DS Groves 2001; Jane Kenworthy 2010), Caleb Flanagan (Brad Armstrong 1997), Sean Flannigan (Bernie Marsh 1975), David Fleeshman (unnamed Morris Dancer 1976, Paul Haines 1979 and Supt Jevons 2000), Richard Fleeshman (Craig Nelson/Harris 2002-06), James Fleet (Robbie Sloan 2010), Pauline Fleming (Penny King 2003-06), Barrie Fletcher (Insp Gorman 1980), Diane Fletcher (Angela Hawthorne 1994-95 and 2005), Freddie Fletcher (Bob Whitely 1982), Gerard Fletcher (Mr Sparrow 1998), Mark Fletcher (Vic 1980), Maggie Flint (Mrs Bannister 1980), Ian Flintoff (George Urquhart 1996 and 1998), Finton Flynn (Russ Gray 2010-11), Kieran Flynn (Aiden O'Donnell 1998-99), Maureen Flynn (Sarah Malone 1996), Adam Fogarty (Mr Horner 1998), Fine Time Fontayne (Henry Wakefield 1985), Miranda Forbes (Beryl Challis 1978), Patricia Ford (Joyce Banks 1978 and Pauline Walsh 1985), Brigit Forsyth (Babs Fanshawe (1998), Dudley Foster (Tom Hayes 1961), Joanna Foster (Susan Barlow 2001), Megan Foster (Becky Mallet 1998-2000), Maggie Fox (Ruth Audsley 2001), Paul Fox (Mark Redman 1999-2001 and 2006), William Fox (Douglas Cresswell 1969), Julie Foy (Gina Seddon 1988-89), Ben Frain (Paul Davies 1996 and Philip Hodson 1999), Andrew Frame (John Dalton 1998), Derek Francis (Charles Beaumont 1977), Joan Francis (Dot Greenhalgh 1961-69), Adrienne Frank (Lucy Goodwin 1979), Sabina Franklyn (Eve Wilson 2009-10), Helen Fraser (Magenta Savannah 1998), Alan French (Christian Locke 2001), Brenda Fricker (Staff Nurse Maloney 1977), Joanne Frogatt (Zoe Tattersall 1997-99), Nicholas Fry (Mr. Simpson 1990-91), Patricia Fuller (Sandra Butler 1969-70), Jason Furnival (DS Trotter 1999; Andrew Hoskins 2001; DS Woodhead 2002 and Mark Kenworthy 2010), Paul Gabriel (DC David Brett 2002), James Gaddas (Robert Prescott 1989 and/Vinny Sorrell 1999-2000), Ian Gain (PC Mick Hopwood 2002-03), Sean Gallagher (Paul Connor 2006-07), Tina Gambe (Sonia Marshall 2003-05), Mike Gant (Batesey 1978), James Garbutt (Wilf Gaskell 1996-97), Nicola Gardener (Dr Cunningham 1997), Jimmy Gardner (Tiny Hargreaves 1978), Chris Garner (Malcolm Fairhurst 1999), Steve Garti (Sean Swift 2000), Anna Gascoigne (Kath Barnes 1998), Fred Gaunt (DS Bell 1978 and 1982), Craig Gazey (Graeme Proctor 2008-11), Nicholas Gecks (Mr Marriott 2000), Peter Geddis (Larry Wolstenhulme 1995), Donald Gee (Roger Crompton 1994), Prunella Gee (Doreen Heavey 1999 and 2002-04), William Geldart (Kevin Haggerty 1976), Tristan Gemmill (Will Griffiths 2000), Colin George (Jimmy Graham 1974), Valerie Georgeson (Elaine Dennett 1977), Alan Gerrard (George Scully 1973), Sally Gibson (unnamed shop customer 1977, 79 and Mrs Rigby 1982), Derrick Gilbert (CPO Henderson 1978), Joseph Gilgun (Jamie Armstrong 1994-97), Jamie Gill (Mark Jackson 1992), Terry Gilligan (PC Johnstone 1978, Sgt Perryman 1999 and DS Taylor 2001), David Gilmore (Frank 1974), Lindsay Gilmour (Penny Shaw 1981), Gabrielle Glaister (Debs Brownlow 2000), Elizabeth Glennon (unnamed shop customer 1976 and Mrs Elton 1977), Brian Glover (Fred Henshaw 1972), Julie Glover (DC Yeats 2002), Jane Godber (Annie Woodford 2002), Paul Goddard (Stephen 1995-96), Charmayne Golaub (Lucy Armitage 1988), Michael Goldie (Bob Statham 1983), Stuart Golland (Ernie Wagstaff 2000), Frances Goodall (unnamed shop customer 1976 and Gladys Turnbull 1981), Tony Goodall (Asst Div Officer Scott 1979), Julia Goodman (Hilary Forrest 1996), Harold Goodwin (Joss Shackleton 1991), Julie Goodyear (Bet Lynch/Gilroy 1966, 1970-95 and 2002-03), Burn Gorman (Ben Andrews 1998), Sandra Gough (Irma Ogden/Barlow 1964-68 and 1970-71), Peter Gowen (Simon Beatty 1991-92), Penny Gowling (Mrs Harbottle

1978), Howard Grace (Steve Dunthorne 1982), Sally Grace (Doreen Lovell 1980), Mike Grady (Les Grimes 1975), Alexander Graham (Jamie Ramsden 1990), Denys Graham (Walter Jenkins 1976), Stephen Graham (Lee Sankey 1999), Olga Grahame (Ruby Green 1977), Glyn Grain (Fraser Henderson 1996-97), Barbara Grant (Mary Bedford 1973), Sheri Graubert (Dr Jones 1998), Diane Grayson (Liz Brocklebank 1977), Christina Greatrex (Cherie Watkins 1992), Nigel Greaves (Paul Cheveski 1972), Constantine Gregory (Vince Denton 1977), Lyndam Gregory (Sammy Patel 1982-83), Nigel Gregory (Frank Mills 1985-86), Norman Gregory (DS Thornton 1978), David Grellin (Graham Baxter 1996), Martin Gresham (unnamed vicar 2001 and John Carter later in 2001), Judy Gridley (Elaine Prior Webster 1984-85), Angela Griffin (Fiona Middleton 1992-98), John Griffin (DC Simon Cavanagh 2000), Robin Griffith (Mr Ellis 1979), Ciaran Griffiths (Dean Sykes 2000), Frank Grimes (Barry Connor 2009), Andrew Grose (Tim Munson 1999-2000), Stephen Guilfoyle (Matt Graham 1997), Peter Guinness (Ray Sykes 2000-02), Margo Gunn (Linda Lindsay 1997-98), Robert Gwilym (Sgt Johnny Johnstone 1996), Graham Haberfield (Jerry Booth 1962-68 and 1971-75), Pearl Hackney (Ethel Bostock 1973 and Daisy Hibbert 1978, 1980), Ellie Haddington (Josie Clarke 1994-97), George Hagan (Rev A. Challenor 1978), Will Haigh (Glen Middleham 2000-01), Martyn Hainstock (Granville Norbury 1996), Jill Halfpenny (Rebecca Hopkins 1999-2000), Andrew Hall (Marc Selby 2011), Brenda Hall (Mrs Dodwell 1981), Gordon Hall (Harold 1978 and unnamed van driver 1979), Suzanne Hall (Kimberly Taylor 1989-93), Mark Hallett (Nick Norbury 1990-92 and Boris Weaver 2000-05), Tom Halliday (Tom Schofield 1965), Steve Halliwell (Mr Toft 1984), Bella Hamblin (Nurse Wilson 2001), Michael Hamilton (Sol Pepper 2002), Paul Hamilton (unnamed rugby player 1977 and Fireman Hollis 1979), Norah Hammond (Nancy Leathers 1961-62), Madison Hampson (Amy Barlow (2005-06), Martin Hancock (Geoffrey 'Spider' Nugent (1997-2003), Stephen Hancock (Ernest Bishop (1967 and 1969-78), Trevor Hancock (Mr Dolan 1999), Richard Hannant (PC Woolfe 2000), Chris Hannon (Luigi 2007-08), Tim Hans (Sgt Graham 2002), Sophiya Haque (Poppy Morales 2008-09), Michelle Hardwick (Sheila Dickson 1997 and Naomi Russell 1998), Betty Hardy(Clara Midgeley 1965-66), Doris Hare (Alice Pickens 1968-69), Christine Hargreaves (Christine Hardman/Appleby 1960-63), Christopher Hargreaves (Carl Foster 1998), David Hargreaves (Bob Birchall 1977), Diana Harker (Mrs Pendlebury 1983), Lewis Harney (Daniel Osbourne 1996), Richard Harrington (Owen Williams 1999), Dean Harris (Alan Skidmore 1980), Louise Harrison (Dawn Prescott 1989), Barry Hart (unnamed piano player 1978 and Les Boden 1980), Emma Hartley-Miller (Dawn Coghill 2010), Lee Hartney (Shane Mallett 1999), James Harvey (Chris Wheelan 1978), Terence Harvey (John Harris QC 2000), Ian Hastings (John Lane 1976), Nigel Havers (Lewis Archer 2009-10), Julia Haworth (Claire Casey / Peacock 2003-11), Don Hawkins (Trevor Ogden 1973 and 1983-84), Thomas Hawkesford (Mark Redman 1983), Paul Hawkyard (Paul Beck 2000), Graeme Hawley (unnamed policeman 1998, Desmond Worthing 2001 and John Stape 2007-11), Mike Hayward (Vince Denton 1975 and Mr Williams 1999), Andrew Haywood (Nigel Johnson 1976), Philip Hazelby (Mr Robinson 1999), Jane Hazlegrove (Sue Clayton 1985), Brendan P. Healey (Gerry 1996), Mary Healey (Thelma James 1977 and Yvonne Pendlebury 1990), Matt Healy (DC Flannery 2001), Tim Healy (unnamed bingo checker 1976 and Brian Tully 2006), Katie Heannau (Susan Barlow 1965-70), Richard Heap (DI Tyler 2000 and Stephen Rawlings 2001), Daphne Heard (Lizzie Hinchcliffe 1978), Phil Hearne (Chris Shawcross 1983, PC Naylor 1990 and DS Mallory 1992), Joan Heath (May Hardman 1960), Jean Heller (Alice 1979), Kathryn Hellier (Kathy Miller 1978), Kathleen Helm (Agnes Greenwood 1968), Polly Hemingway (Nurse Phillips 1979), Patricia Heneghan (Marian Lund 1961), Jennifer Hennessey (Bernie Sayers 2009), Del Henney (Eddie Duncan 1971), Zoë Henry (Log Thwaite 1998 and Casey Cardwell 2007), John Henshaw (Mick Murphy 1996), Karen Henthorn (Teresa Bryant 2007-10), Martin Herdman (Ron Harris

1997), Randal Herley(Ernie Sadler 1981 and Sidney Templeton 1999), Ronald Herman (George Handforth 1977), Martyn Hesford (Harvey Stone 1979), Jason Hetherington (D.S. Wyatt 1998), Donald Hewlett (Bob Maxwell 1965), Verity Hewlett (WPC Meyers 1996), Sherrie Hewson (Maureen Naylor /Holdsworth / Elliott 1993-97 and 2006), Jean Heywood (Alice Kirby 1983), Brian Hibbard (Doug Murray 1992-93), Jimmy Hibbert (Andy Lewis 1998 – racing commentator), Derek Hicks (Malcolm Bradford 1998), Ian Hicks (Ronnie Burgess 1981), John Higgins (Sgt Stevens 1970), Lois Higgins (Dr Wilson 2000), Polly Highton (Sister Lynne Woods 1990-91), Mark Hignett (Frank Starkie 1967), Andy Hill (Darren Briscoe 1976-77), David Hill (Tony Parsons 1970), Peter Hill (Sgt Cottam 1976), Rupert Hill (Jamie Baldwin 2004-08; 2011), Steven Hillman (unnamed jury foreman 1996, unnamed repo man 1998 and Rich Raven 2000), Jane Hills (Melanie Power 1996), Terence Hillyer (Terry Goodwin 1983 and Sean Skinner 1995-97), Pippa Hinchley (Elaine Fenwick 1993-94), Gerry Hinks (Mr Bottomley 1997 and unnamed man in pub 1999), Madge Hindle (Renee Bradshaw / Roberts 1976-80), Becky Hindley (Charlotte Hoyle 2010), Frazer Hines (Roger Wain 1965), Geoffrey Hinsliff (Eric Bailey 1977 and Don Brennan 1987-97), Tina Hobley (Samantha Failsworth 1996-98), Alan Hockey (Jim Nelson 1979), Jane Hogarth (Judith Roberts 2000), Paul Holowaty (Neil Ferns 2000), Ruth Holden (Vera Lomax 1960-66), Noddy Holder (Stan Potter 2000), Roy Holder (Michael Butterworth 1963), Jane Hollowood (Janice Baker 1994), Denis Holmes (Brian Foley 1961), Dominic Holmes (Daniel Osbourne 1995-97 and 2007), Linda Jane Holmes (Grace Kershaw 2000), Michelle Holmes (Tina Fowler 1989-90), Paul Holowaty (Neil Fearns 2000), Morag Hood (Sally Frost 1967), Ewan Hooper (Mr Stowe 1997), Denice Hope (Peggy Jones 2002), Taryn Hopkins (Samantha Summers 1978), Tim Horand (Pedro 1974), Jeff Hordley (unnamed nightclub manager 1997 and Wayne 1998), Anne Hornby (WPC Phillips 1997), John Horsley (Rev Nuttall 1983), Paula J Horton (Carol Morgan 1997), Robert Horwell (Nick Neeson 2007-08), Jane Hott (Sylvia Monroe 2000), Steven Houghton (Jeff Cullen 2011), David Hounslow (unnamed prison officer 1998 and Derek 2007), Debbie Howard (Dr Marius 1998 and Shirley Stewart 2000-01), Lisa Howard (Miss Finch 2000), Rita Howard (Helen Ormerod 1977 and unnamed shop customer 1981), Jack Howarth (Albert Tatlock 1960-84), Jeni Howarth Williams (Sheila Hayes 2001), Cliff Howells (Terry Seymour 1991), William Hoyland (Geoffrey Hardcastle MP 1976), Stephen Hoyle (Gary 2003), Roy Hudd (Archie Shuttleworth 2002-03; 2006; 2010), Lucy-Jo Hudson (Katy Nelson/Harris 2002-05), Robert Hudson (Trevor 1998), Tom Hudson (Paul Clayton 2007-08), Geoffrey Hughes (Phil Ferguson 1967 and Eddie Yeats 1974-87), Sean Hughes (Pat 2007), Glenn Hugill (Alan McKenna 1996-97), Steve Huison (Michael Pearce 1997 and Eddie Windass 2008-11),), Annie Hulley (Lorna Ferguson 1980 and Gwen Davies 1999-2000), Eric Hulme (James Pilling 1996 and Mr Fearns 2000), Alan Hulse (Harry Brown 1977, Peter Cross 1980, Mr McKellar 1982, Dave Craig 1988, unnamed drivers 1991 and 1998), Andrew Hulse (Peter Bryant 1996), Chris Humphreys (Clive Parnell 1991), Nigel Humphreys (Dickie Fleming 1968-70), Kathryn Hunt (Angela Nelson/Harris 2002-05), Sandra Hunt (unnamed receptionist 1996, Mrs Jones 1999 and Sandy George 2002), Alan Hunter (DC Burton 1977 and Peter Shaw 1988), Cathy Hytner (Jilly West 1978), Alan Igbon (Tony Stewart 2003), Emily Iggulden (Lauren Hickson 1996), William Ilkley (Nick Horrocks 1997 and 2000), Ralph Ineson (Zack 2005), George Innes (Stuart Draper 1974), Nicholas Irons (James Kitching 1999), George Irving (Nick Cavanagh 1988), Michael Irving (Eric Broadhurst 1982), Boris Isarov (Mr Tchernikow 1983), Kate Isitt (Dr Vickers 1999), Peter Ivatis (Mr Nesbit 1977), Neil Iveson (Amjad Iqbal 2005), William Ivory (Eddie Ramsden 1990), George Jackos (Sergei Kasparov 1999), Barry Jackson (Sid Garfield 1978), Brandon Jackson (Joshua Peacock 2002), Philip Jackson (Smitty 1982 – credited as Peter Jackson), Sally Jane Jackson (Karen Oldfield 1980), Steve Jackson (Trevor Dean 2010-11), Warren Jackson (Nicky Tilsey/Platt 1981-96), Joseph Jacobs (Marcus Wrigley 1998-99),

Saeed Jaffrey (Ravi Desai 1999), Daniel James (DC Wright 2000), Godfrey James (Sam Briscoe 1997), Jennifer James (Geena Gregory 2000-02), Lawrence James (Colin Appleby 1962), Matthew James (Robbie 1997), Polly James (Audrey Hargreaves 1967), Sophie James (Justine Davenport 2004-05), Susan Jameson (Myra Booth 1963-64 and 1968), Rob James-Collier (Liam Connor 2006-08), Kathy Jamieson (Sandra Arden 1990-91), Kaleem Janjua (Mr Gupta 1989 and Soresh Parekh 2001, 2004), John Jardine (Mr Lewis 1977, Tony Watkins 1980, Barry Platt 1987 and Randolf Taylor 1990-92), Olivia Jardith (Mrs. Oaks 1992), Stan Jay (George Dickenson 1963), Paul Jaynes (Dennis Lawton 1983), Michael Jayston (unnamed judge 2000), Linda Jean-Barry (Lynn Watts 1981), Pauline Jefferson (unnamed women 1979, 1990 and Hermione Fairfax 2002), Sue Jenkins (Gloria Todd 1985-88), Gillian Jephcott (Carol Glover 2001), Poppy Jhakra (Minnie Chandra 2008-09), Milton Johns (Brendan Scott 1991-93), Darren Johnson (PC Malcolm 1995, PC McMahon 1998, PC Henshaw 1999, 2000 and PC Robinson 2002), Meg Johnson (unnamed drunk 1972, Brenda Holden 1976 and Eunice Nuttall/Gee 1981-82 and 1999), Noel Johnson (Peter Smith 1976), Vicky Johnson (unnamed shop manager 1995 and Paula Clegg 1998), Alex Johnston (Mr Bannister 1980), Hope Johnstone (Janet Bamford 1987-88), Sue Johnston (Mrs. Chadwick 1982), Casey-Lee Jolleys (Stacey "Orchid" Hilton 2004-06), Bruce Jones (Les Battersby / Battersby-Brown 1997-2007), Davy Jones (Colin Lomax 1961), Iain Jones (Dean Matthews 1983 and Mickey Edwards 2002), Jacqueline Jones (Philippa Scopes 1962), Judi Jones (Pam Hargreaves 2001), Kathy Jones (Tricia Hopkins 1973-76), Ken Jones (Harry Eastham 1967), Kenneth Jones (Arthur Burrows 1971), Maggie Jones (Blanche Hunt (1974-78, 1981, 1996, 1997, 1998-2010), Nicholas Jones (Mark Howard 1970), Norman Jones (Det Insp Brewster 1978-79), Suranne Jones (Mandy Phillips 1997, Karen Phillips / McDonald 2000-04), Indira Joshi (Maya Desai 2000 and Grishma Parekh 2010), Paddy Joyce (Tommy Deakin 1968-1974), Vernon Joyner (Stuart Hodges 1964), Edward Judd (Geoff Siddall 1982), John Judd (Dr Cannon 1977 and Sammy Chadwick 1982), John Junkin (Bill Fielding 1981), Gordon Kane (Henry Fraser 2001), Sam Kane (Gary Adams 2001), Shainey Karn (Rosalyn Greenwood 1986), Murray Kash (Mike Ritchie 1973), Helen Kay (Jo Simpson 2001), Julian Kay (Robert Preston 1996-99), Peter Kay (unnamed shopfitter 1997 and Eric Garside 2004), Richard Kay (Keith Sadler 1980), Carol Kaye (Maureen Slater 1983), Gorden Kaye (Bernard Butler 1969-70), Lila Kaye (Rose Bonnetti 1966), Barry Keegan (Jim Mount 1965), Robert Keegan (Jacko Ford 1972), Iain Keith (Sandy Lester 1980), Bob Keller (Bob Neale 1969), Beatrice Kelley (Carol Palmer 1996), Arthur Kelly (Monkey Gibbons 1975-77 and 1982), Clare Kelly (Edith Tatlock 1969), Craig Kelly (Luke Strong 2009), Elizabeth Kelly (Edie Burgess 1971), Sam Kelly (Bob Challis 1983), Joan Kempson (Edna Miller 1998, 2000-01 and Iris Merry 2001), Eileen Kennally (Brenda Riley 1966 and Maureen Webb 1980), Matt Kennard (Duncan Styles 2000), Ann Kennedy (Lynne Johnson 1975), Joyce Kennedy (Freda Todd 1976 and Alma Walsh 1978), Kevin Kennedy (Norman 'Curly' Watts 1983-2003), Laurence Kennedy (Dr Cole 1998), Neil Kennedy (Jud Johnston 1970), Sayan Kent (unnamed doctor 1997 and Gabrielle Smith 2001), Bill Kenwright (Gordon Clegg 1967-69, 1974, 1975, 1982, 1984, 1995), Barbara Keogh (Jessie Wilcox 1996), Doreen Keogh (Concepta Riley/Hewitt 1960-75), Mike Keogh (PC Basson 2002), Jill Kerman (Maggie Dunlop/Redman 1982-84, 1991-94), Roberta Kerr (Wendy Crozier 1989-90), Colin Kerrigan (Gary Grimshaw 1987), Ian Kershaw (Malcolm Bradford 1998, Duncan Stott 1999 and Mick Crompton), Rosie Kerslake (Linda Farrell 1988), Ayub Khan-Din (Hanif Ruparell 1992-93), Josie Kidd (Margaret Lacey 1971), Melanie Kilburn (Evelyn Sykes/Elliott 2000-02), Alison King (Milly Webster 1982), Dave King (Bernard Lane 1978 and Clifford Duckworth 1994-95), Leah King (Sarah Louise Tilsley 1987), Lyndsey King (Sarah Louise Tilsley/Platt 1987-99), Ben Kingsley (Ron Jenkins 1966-67), Jacqueline Kington (Molly Hardcastle 2000-02), Hellen Kirby (Lauren Green 2000 and unnamed nurse 2002), John Kirk (James Wright 1998), Ken Kitson (Jim Hinton 1977, Phil Moss 1982 and Marty Kelly 2001), Rosalind Knight (Mrs Ramsden 1981), Tom Knight (DS Neil 1997), Timothy Knightley (Royston Bell 1999-2000), Andrew Knott (Liam Shepherd 1997), Jo-Anne Knowles (Gilly Saunders (1996, Mrs Hardy 1999, DC Anne Short 2001), Bobby Knutt (Ron Sykes 1980-83), Sally Knyvette (Margi Quigley 2000), Anne Kristen (Olive Rowe 1971), Renny Krupinski (Harry Pringle 1999), Sam Kydd (Frankie Baldwin 1980-82), Susan Kyd (Samantha Benson 1984), John Labonowski (Frank Miller 1982), Nicky Ladanowski (Merle Jackson 2003), Keith Ladd (Mr Crosbie 1996, unnamed court clerk 2000 and Ron Rafferty 2002), Paul Lally (Dr Crawford 1980), Georgina Lamb (Pauline Boswell 2002), Rebecca Lamb (Fran Mooney 2000 and Sheila Cunningham 2002), Sarah Lancashire (Wendy Farmer 1987 and Raquel Wolstenhulme / Watts 1991-96 and 1999), Marshall Lancaster (Slug 2006-09), David Landberg (Don Ashton 1985), Eric Lander (Ron Cooke 1972-74), Nikki Landowski (Saskia Benson 2000), John F. Landry (Jim Stoker 1971 and Clifford Willis 1976), Gregory Lane (Ernest Brighouse 1999), Josie Lane (Dolly Fairbrother 1976), Maggy Lane (Mrs Slater 1982), Poppy Lane (Freda Loftus 1978), Julia Lang (Mrs Rankin and Ethel Platt 1977), Gordon Langford-Rowe (George Docherty 2000-01), John Langford (Mr Stott 1997), Bruno Langley (Darren Michaels 2000 and Todd Grimshaw 2001-04; 2007; 2011), Andrew Langtree (Leon 2009), Bernard Latham (Mr Pritchard 1977), Jody Latham (Liam Clarke 2000), Frank Lauder (Pete Hickman 1997), James Lauren (Jeff Prior 2000), Rachel Laurence (Mrs Houghton 1981 and unnamed Miss Weatherfield), Natalie Lawless (Jenny Lyons 2000-01), Marjie Lawrence (Marj Griffin 1968 and Dawn Sampson 1978), Brian Lawson (Syd Kippax 1983), Charles Lawson (Jim McDonald 1989-2000, 2003, 2004, 2005; 2009-11), Kate Layden (Shadow 1996 and Jean Walters 1999), Dilys Laye (Isabel Stephens 2000-01), Penny Leatherbarrow (Mrs Lester 1978, Cath Spinks 1997 and unnamed nurse 1999), Howard Lee (Howard Lee 2009-11), Jamie Lee (Pat Gordon 2008), Kate Lee (WPC Harris 1979 and Kath Simpson 1982), Ronnie Leek (DS Dave O'Grady 1997), Freddie Lees (Norman Leach 1973), Michael Lees (Sgt Oldfield 1980 and Ralph Dobson 1990-91), Geoffrey Leesley (Tommy Cox 1978 and Gordon Clegg 2002), Geoffrey Leeson (Gordon Clegg 2002), Johnny Leeze (Mr Slater 1982 and Harry Clayton 1985), Simon Lenagan (Alex 2002-03), Rula Lenska (Claudia Colby 2009-11), Rachel Leskovac (Natasha Blakeman 2008-10), Arthur Leslie (Jack Walker 1960-70), Rita Lester (Mrs Winters 1983), Jonathan Guy Lewis (Ian Bentley 1999), Lisa Lewis (Shirley Armitage 1983-89), Rhoda Lewis (Lilian Smith 1969), Tom Lewis (Jonathan Broughton 1993-94), Mark Lindley (Nick Wilding 1991-99), Sally Lindsay (Shelley Unwin/Barlow 2001-06), Maureen Lipman (Lillian Spencer 2002), Renny Lister (Jean Stark 1961), Ian Liston (Danny Burrows 1974), Rodney Litchfield (Wilf Morton 2007), Ralf Little (Mark Stranks 1999), Susan Littler (Sharon Duffy 1972), Harry Littlewood (Sam Littlewood 1977, 1980 and Arnold Swift 1988), Andrew Livingstone (Charlie Figgis 1996), Douglas Livingstone (Cliff Stone 1969), Sydney Livingstone (Roy Thornley 1976), Alison Lloyd (unnamed woman in hospital 1980 and Aunty Monica 1999), Bernard Lloyd (Judge Yeomans 1998), Kevin Lloyd (Don Watkins 1983-84), Howard Lloyd-Lewis (Mr Carter 1982), Tom Lloyd-Roberts (Mr Boyce 2000 and Councillor Naysmith 2002), Josephine Lloyd-Welcome (Dr Patel 2004; 2008; 2009; 2010), Kate Lock (Sue Jackson 1981), Clifford Lockwood (Benny Higgins 2000), Jamie Lomas (PC Stubbs 2002), Michael Loney (Ian Latimer 1986), Matthew Long (Roger Nightingale 1976), Terence Longdon (Wilf Stockwell 1981-82), Henry B. Longhurst (Harry Dunscombe 1968), Matthew Long (Roger Nightingale 1976), Jeffrey Longmore (Bernard Clough 1981-82 and Joe Dillon 1997), Eric Longworth (Nathaniel Lumley 1976), Ray Lonnen (Maurice Gordon 1975), Angela Lonsdale (WPC / Sgt. / Insp. Emma Taylor / Watts 2000-03), David Lonsdale (Peter Barlow 1986-88), Robert Lonsdale (Dan Staveley 2002), Peter Lorenzelli (Cassius 1976, Bob Scott 1978, unnamed barman 1980, Vinny Morris 1984 and George Owens 1997), Barbara Lott (Ethne Willoughby 1972), Arthur Lowe (Leonard Swindley 1960-65), Jane Lowe (Doreen Thornley 1976), Paul Lowther (Colin Jackson 1981), Gary Lucas (Mr Smedley 1990), William Lucas (Dennis Maxwell 1971), Zoe Lucker (Sonia Leach 1996), John Ludlow (James Buckley 1976), Joanna Lumley (Elaine Perkins 1973), Doel Luscombe (DI Seabright 1970), Alan Luxton (Doug West 1976), Joe Lynch (Ron

Mather 1978-79), Sean Lynch (Jack Barker 1976), Dave Lynn (Shirelle 1996), Joyce Lynn (Mrs Stone 1976), Carolyn Lyster (Jennifer Swann 1971), Donna Lythgoe (Brenda Fox 1996 and Nurse Dooley 2000), Ray MacAllan (Vinnie 2004), Terence Macarthy (Tony Bolton 1974), Dorian Macdonald (Paul Reece 2000), Oliver MacGreevy (Bert Tate 1967), Fulton MacKay (Dr Graham 1961), Stephen MacKenna (George Dixon 1997), Roland MacLeod (Rev Bernard Morten 1993-94), Edward MacLiam (Tim White 2005), Oliver Maguire (Joe Mooney 1976), Gina Maher (Debbie Nuttall 1981-82), James Mair (DS Downing 2002), John Malcolm (George Harrop 1972 and Frank Pritchard 1981), Stephen Mallatratt (Peter Hockley 1979 and Geoff Moffatt 1982), Calvin Malone (Gordon Davies 1961), Nick Maloney (Dave Hinchcliffe 1983 and PC Simons 1998), Layizha Malovich (Dr Sally Clarke 2002), George Malpas (Uncle Wilf 1983), Terence Mann (Andrew Turner 1996 and Mr Hardy 1999), Bernard Manning (himself 1971), Francesca Manning (Sandra Milligan 2002), Elizabeth Mansfield (Joan Wakefield 1999-2000), Doreen Mantle (Joy Fishwick 2010-11), Lesley Manville (Jill Mason 1982), Debbie Margolis (Janet Locke 2001), Ray Marioni (Marco 1983), Harry Markham (Handel Gartside 1970-71 and 1976), Dani Marks (Joyce Walters 1978), Matthew Marsden (Chris Collins 1997-98), Jim Marsh (Mr Firth 1978, Reg 1981 and unnamed vicar 1999), Keith Marsh (George Marsden 1980, Harry Ashton 1988 and Uncle Mervyn 1999), Reginald Marsh (Dave Smith 1962-76), Alex Marshall (Yvonne Chappell 1971), Wendy Marshall (Renee Delafonte 1973), Len Marten (Tom Hopwood 1987), Ian Martin (Gary Pearce 1976), Jay Martin (Billy Brown 2005), Peter Martin (Jack Livesey 1976), Rosemary Martin (Ginnie Spencer 1975), Trevor Martin (Arthur Whittaker 1984), Bob Mason (Terry Bradshaw 1976), Hilary Mason (Amy Wilton 1976), Ralph Mason (Major Blake 1975), Jamilla Massey (Upma Parekh 2010-11), James Masters (Ernie Ratcliffe 1985, Sgt Grant 1995, Insp Todd 1999 and Alasdair Troughton 2001), Geoffrey Matthews (Neil Crossley 1963), Sally Ann Matthews (Jenny Bradley 1986-91 and 1993), Andrew Mawdsley (Adam White 2002), Robert Maxfield (Horace Steel 2009), Paul Maxwell (Steve Tanner 1967-68), William Maxwell (Frank Skinner 1982), Bunny May (George Pickup 1963), Olwen May (Rev Jessica Lundy 1999-2000), Rita May (Marjorie Pitts 1978, Freda Woods 1981, Miss Wilberforce 2000, Brenda Kelly 2001 and Connie Rathbone 2009-10), Eileen Mayers (Sheila Birtles / Crossley 1961-63, 1966-74), Bill Maynard (Mickey Malone 1970), Patricia Maynard (Veronica Holdsworth 1991), Patrick McAlinney (Tickler Murphy 1964), Brian McAllistair (David Johnson 1989), Deborah McAndrew (Angie Freeman 1990-93 and 1996-98), Susan McArdle (Lyn Fullwood 2010), Fiona McArthur (Hazel Broughton 1993-94), Nichola McAuliffe (Anita Scott 2001-02), Bill McCabe (Eddie Goulden 1969), Gillian McCann (Audrey Bright / Fleming 1968-70), Rhys McConnochie (Toni 1977), Ron McCormick (Herbert Siddall 1976), Charles McCurdy (Dennis Norton 1996), Brian McDermott (Roger Mullholland 1981), Harry McDermott (Max Turner 2010-11), Terry McDonald (Mr Settle 1979), Dave McEale (Tommo Jackson 1978), Andrea McEwan (Lisa Ditchfield 2005-), Clare McGlinn (Charlie Ramsden 2000-02), John McGregor (Dr Brooks 1976), Lloyd McGuire (PCLyle 1980), Bill McGuirk (Frank Wilson 1979), Tony McHale (Dave Lester 1978), Vivian McKee (Miss Hirst 1976), Ian McKellen (Mel Hutchwright aka Lionel Hipkiss 2005), Joseph McKenna (Peter Barlow 1977), Janice McKenzie (Mrs Paton 2000), Lizzie McKenzie (Phyliss Jameson 1978), Donald McKillop (Jack Walsh 1979 and 1982), Mary McLeod (Mary Handforth 1977), Adrian McLoughlin (Mr Bycroft 1995), James McMartin (Darren Dobbs 1999), Roddy McMillan (Roy Johnson 1975), Una McNulty (Anna Leith 1997 and Mrs Gardner 2000), Michael McStay (Alan Hoyle 2011), Alan Meadows (Brian McDonald 1976 and unnamed registrar 1995), Stanley Meadows (Laurie Fraser 1963), Michael Melia (Sgt Cummins 1979), Tom Mennard (Sam Tindall 1985-89), Ian Mercer (Pete Jackson 1987 and Gary Mallett 1995-2000), Colin Meredith (Laurence Burford 2002), Connie Merigold (Gertie Robson 1974), Kathy Meryck (Mrs Lambert 1980), Cynthis Michaelis (Norah Seddon 1978),

David Michaels (Jon Welch 1994-96), Philip Middlemiss (Des Barnes 1990-98), Ashleigh Middleton (Sophie Webster 1994-97), John Middleton (John Hargreaves 1993), James Midgley (PC Harper 2000), Giles Milan (PC Graham 2001 and Guy Northam 2002), Jim Millea (Carl Armstrong 1994 and 1996), Brian Miller (Tom Elliot 1991), David Miller (Don Grady 1976 and unnamed salesman 1979), Frank Mills (Ivor Mortlake 1976 and Billy Williams 1995-97), Norman Mills (unnamed coastguard 1997 and Mr Horner 1999), Caroline Milmoe (Lisa Horton / Duckworth 1992-93), Ann Milton (Susan Schofield 1962), Charlotte Mitchell (Margaret Swain 1982), Susan Mitchell (Anna McIntyre 2008), Geraldine Moffatt (Arlene Jones (1980), Sarah Moffett (Kelly Thomson 1996-97), Dearbhla Molloy (2009), Simon Molloy (Jim Pitts 1976, Mr Pollard 1987, unnamed clerk of court 1996 and Evelyn Hunter-Roachford 1999), Steve Money (Ted 1997 and Eric Sutherland 2000-01, 2005 and 2008), Tony Monroe (Arnie Scanlon 2003), Helen Moon (Spud 2001), Gordon Mooney (Jim Simmonds 2001), Tony Mooney (Phil Rodgers 2002), Alan Moore (Maurice Jones 1989), Christine Moore (Nurse Purcell 1978 and Gloria Longhurst 1981), Damien Moore (Mr Boyle 2001), Heather Moore (Sandra Petty 1965), Richard Moore (Harry McLean 1976 and George Hepworth 1985), Vivienne Moore (Sister Hopkins 1983), William Moore (Cyril Turpin 1969-72), Rani Moorthy (Dr Kin 2002), Josh Moran (PC Marsh 1995), Kevin Moreton (Kevin Marsh 1975), Garfield Morgan (Vince Plummer 1961), Sharon Morgan (Mrs Ellis 1979), Paul Moriarty (Colin Harvey 1971), Carrie Morley (Mrs Fox 1979), Donald Morley (Walter Fletcher 1961 and Leo Slater 1969), Ken Morley (Reg Holdsworth 1989-95), Louisa Morris (Amy Barlow 2005), Ted Morris (Ted Loftus 1973), Campbell Morrison (Neville Rose 2000), Ray Mort (Harry Bailey 1960-62), Bryan Mosley (Alf Roberts 1961, 1963 and 1971-99), Jennifer Moss (Lucille Hewitt 1960-74), Carole Mowlam (Anne Woodley 1977), Alex Moxham (Graham Bellis 2000), Henry Moxon (Arthur Harvey 1974), Sharon Muircroft (Fiona Cavanagh 1988), Lawrence Mullin (Steve Fisher 1976-79), Cheryl Murray (Suzie Birchall 1977-79 and 1983), James Murray (Sandy Hunter 1998), Leonie Murray (Sandra Pringle 1978), Valerie Murray (Dr Patel 1979), Bill Nagy (Greg Flint 1967 and 1970), Jacqueline Naylor (Christine Naden 1996), Amanda Simms 1998 and unnamed registrar 2000), Amer Nazir (Mr Aziz 2001), Al Nedjari (Samir Rachid 1994-95), Catherine Neilson (Karen Barnes 1978-79), Conrad Nelson (Tim Woods 1999), Fiona Nelson (Cathy Savage 1976 and unnamed shop customer 1978), Michelle Newell (Gill Gregory 2001-02), Patrick Newell (Mr Mullins 1978), Holly Newman (Julie Hudson 1996 and Lorraine Brownlow 1997-2000), Chloe Newsome (Vicky Arden / McDonald 1991-96 and 1998), Andrew Newton-Lee (Liam Strong 2003), Madelaine Newton (Mary McKenna 1997), Dave Nicholls (Chris Jacobs 2000 and Buster 2002), Guy Nicholls (Harry 1983), Patti Nicholls (Mrs Stubbs 1980), Yvonne Nicholson (Sally Norton 1977 and 1979), James Nickerson (Mr Brumwell 1996, Peter Phelan 1998, Mr Roe 2000 and Keith Greenacre 2002), Lesley Nightingale (Josie Clark 1979), Carole Nimmons (Sarah Ridley 1983-85), Carol Noakes (DC Robinson 2000), Nora-Jane Noone (Louise 2005), Peter Noone (Stanley Fairclough 1961), Fenella Norman (Christine Glover 2000), John Normington (Mr Groves 1997), Andrew Norris (Philip Harper 2000), Maggie Norris (Claire Palmer 1996-97), Michael Norris (Dave 1999), Len Norton (Sid Clarke 1981), Tony Nyland (unnamed bookmaker 2000 and Gerry Imlach 2002), Christopher Oakswood (Mark Redman 1983-84), Ann O'Brien (Florrie Smethurst 1985), Eileen O'Brien (Marjorie Proctor 1983), Kieran O'Brien (Craig Lee 1993), Tina O'Brien (Sarah Louise Platt 1999-2007), Joe O'Byrne (DC Hammond 2001 and Jack Henshaw 2002), Angela O'Doherty (Beryl Freeman 1999), Micky O'Donoughue (Nipper Harris 1982), Maureen O'Farrell (Jacqui Henderson 1997), Vicky Ogden (Margo Richardson 1987), Yvonne O'Grady (Yvonne Casey 2006-07; 2010), Michael O'Hagan (Jim Sedgewick 1980), Martin Oldfield (Tom Hudson 1983 and Edward Welch 2002), Beverley Oldham (Janice 1982), Geoff Oldham (Arthur Watts 2002), Paul Oldham (Matt Stapleton 1981 and unnamed plumber 1999), Colette O'Neil (Ruth Winters

528

1966), Caroline O'Neill (Andrea Clayton 1985 and 2000-01), John O'Neill (Luke Ashton 2001-02), Lesley Clare O'Neill (Debi Scott 1993), Seamus O'Neill (Mr Pollard 1983 and Maurice Preston 1996), Wanda Opalinska (Wiki Dankowska 2007-09), Thomas Ormson (David Platt 1990-99), Tony Osoba (Wesley McGregor 1982 and Peter Ingram 1990), Bill Owen (Charlie Dickinson 1971), Clare Owen (Rosemary Fraser 1964), Glyn Owen (Norman Lindley 1965), Jonathan Owen (The Great Orlando 2001), John Owens (Mr Irwin 1977), Daphne Oxenford (Esther Hayes 1960-72), John Oxley (Harvey Shaw 1974), June Page (Lorraine Tindall 1981), Stanley Page (Donald Gorman 1976), Helene Palmer (Ida Clough 1978-89 and 1995-98), George Panther (Frank 1976 and Bill Mountford 1978), Dave Parke (Tommo Jackson 1978), Tony Parke (Dave Lester 1978), Emma Parker (Anna Wilson 2000), Kirsten Parker (Ruth Morgan 1998), Sacha Parkinson (Sian Powers 2009-11), Sue Parkinson (Dorothy Buxton 1996), Sarah Parks (unnamed midwife 1998 and DS Pullen 2001), Christine Parle (Sandra Walker 1997), Katherine Parr (Amy Preston 1967), Guy Parry (Jay Rodgers 2002), Ken Parry (Benny Stone 1977), Marc Parry (Mr Aspinall 2001), Alan Partington (Joe Stark 1976, unnamed coin dealer 1980, Sophie Partington (Angela Willis 1999), Harry Slater 1996 and Mr Irwin 1999), Harish Patel (Umed Alahan 2009), Suzie Patterson (Susan Barlow 1977-79 and 1981-83), Bobby Pattinson (unnamed barman 1978 and Frank Elliott 1979), Maxine Peake (Belinda Peach 1999), Eve Pearce (Betty Lawson 1967), Jennifer Pearcey (Eileen Wolstenhulme 1995), Fred Pearson (Curly Watkins 1982), Logan Blake Pearson (Liam Connor Jr - 2009), Lynne Pearson (Carol Baldwin 2005-06), Ted Peart (Ted Cooper 1999), Brian Peck (Tommy Ball 1979), Anthony Pedley (Herbert Cook 1979 and Harry Scott 1979), Tony Peers (Peter Mallett 1999), Caroline Pegg (Hilary Pugsley 2010-11), Barbara Peirson (Pat Marshall 1980), Kazia Pelka (Linda Jackson 1987 and Hazel Wilding 2002), Charles Pemberton (Johnny Mann 1973), Frank Pemberton (Frank Barlow 1960-71), Tara Pendergast (Kerry Irving 2000), Ann Penfold (Edith Firman 1995 and 1996), Arthur Pentelow (George Greenwood 1968-71), Rosy Perkins (Kath Harris 2002), Lynne Perrie (Ivy Tilsley/Brennan 1971-94), Lloyd Peters (Tony Lawson 2002), Lorraine Peters (Kitty Earnshaw 1983), Luan Peters (Lorna Shawcross 1971), Wendi Peters (Cilla Brown/Battersby-Brown 2003-07), Alita Petrof (Pam 1996), Rosaling Philips (WPC Berry 1997), Neil Phillips (Des Foster 1983), Patricia Phoenix (Elsie Tanner / Howard 1960-73 and 1976-84), Robert Pickervance (Dr Phillips 2000), Carolyn Pickles (Michelle Turnbull 1975 and Moira Kelly / Wood 1998), John Pickles (DI Conroy 1976, PC Handley 1978 and Arthur Watts 1995), Rebecca Pike (Amy Barlow 2004-05), Jacqueline Pilton (Mrs Payne 2000), Jacqueline Pirie / Chadwick (Linda Sykes / Baldwin 1998-01), Wensley Pithey (Wilfred Perkins 1972), Nigel Pivaro (Terry Duckworth 1983-87, 1992-93, 1996-97, 1999-2002 and 2008), Blair Plant (DS/DI Reynolds 1998-2000), Jenny Platt (Violet Wilson 2004-08; 2011), Angela Pleasence (Monica Sutton 1968), Steve Plytas (Leo Bonarti 1961), Ray Polhill (Wayne Farrell 1992-93), Robin Polley (Rob Allison 2002), Norah Pollitt (Fay 1977), Phillip Pollitt (unnamed shop customer 1978 and Wayne Gaskell 1982), Eva Pope (Tanya Pooley 1993-94), Peter Postlethwaite (DS Cross 1981), Eric Potts (Colin Dearing 1989, Mr Saxton 1996, Diggory Compton 2005-06), Graham Poutney (Kevin 1977), Gwyneth Powell (Diana Kenton 1976), Benedict Power (Tufty 1999), Samantha Power (Emma Baxter 1995), Mark Powley (Rob Lucas 2001), Daniel Poyser (PC Dawson 1998, PC Thomson 2000 and PC Watson 2001), Mark Prentice (PC Warner 2000 and 2001), Duncan Preston (Dennis Stokes 2004), Mark Price (Craig Whitely 1982), Sheila Price (Nurse Gray 1978), Tom Price (Alec Hobson 1982), Cheryl Prime (Kathy Barrett 1982), Glynn Pritchard (Malcolm Fox 1996), Nicholas Pritchard (Mr Massey 1996), Colin Prockter (Rodney Bostock 1995), Carl Proctor (DC Weston 2000), David Prosho (Josh Cunningham 2000), Julian Protheroe (Glynn Petrie 1997),Kay Purcell (Rhona Summers 1997), Parvez Qadir (Naveen Alahan 2002-03), John Quayle (Captain Platt 1964 and Anthony Stephens 2000-01), Christopher Quinn (Jim Douglas 1978), James Quinn (John Sinclair 2000), Mary Quinn (Phyllis Gregory 1962), Ramone Quinn (Finlay Bryant 2007-08), Chris Quinten (Brian Tilsley 1978-89), Diana Quiseekay (Sophie Edwards 1975), Sue Race

(Phyllis Lomax 1982), Naomi Radcliffe (unnamed secretary 1996 and Alison Wakefield / Webster (1998-2000), Malcolm Raeburn (Dr Williams 2000), Paul Raffield (Dr Stirling 1996), Anne Raitt (Doreen Horten 1992-2000), Craig Ralph (unnamed youth 1979 and Andy 1984), Bud Ralston (an extra 1960-76 and Wilf Bottomley 1977-78 and 1983), Helen Rappaport (Eileen Hicks 1983), Neil Ratcliffe (Damian Ogden 1983), Raad Rawi (Ranjiv Alahan 2001), Brian Rawlinson (Joe Makinson 1961, 1963 and 1970), Janet Rawson (Louise Clayton 1980), Carol Ray (Mary 1979), Freddie Rayner (Sam Turner 1977-78), Andrew Readman (DC Cannon 1995 and 1996), Ian Reddington (Vernon Tomlin 2005-08), Ian Redford (Les Carter 1980 and Keith Appleyard 2005-06), Richard Redpath (Nigel Chadwick 1990), Llewellyn Rees (Herbert James 1973), Martin Reeve (Ian Renwick 1996 and Lester Middleman 1999), Anne Reid (Valerie Tatlock/Barlow 1961-71), Nicola Reynolds (WPC Tate 1996 and unnamed shop customer 1998), Claire Rhodes (Rachel Graves 2000), Peter Richard (Gary Pendleton 1976), Charles Richards (Sgt Farnell 1999), Gavin Richards (Alex Christie 1994), Natalie Richards (Nicolette Seddon 2005), Stan Richards (Arthur Stokes 1977), Edwin Richfield (Jack Broadley 1977), Laura Richmond (Dr Andrea Cannon 1998), Dominic Rickhards (Michael Wall 1998 - 2000), Adam Rickitt (Nick Tilsley 1997-99 and 2002-04), Vincenzo Ricotta (Sgt Johnny Johnstone 1990), Derek Riddell (Adam Newbould 1997-98), Elizabeth Rider (Kathleen Gutteridge 1999), Graham Rigby (Sid Lambert 1965, Mr Fox 1979 and Archie Wardle 1995), David Riley (Micky Brooks 1976), Eamonn Riley (Mr Carter 1992-93, unnamed court usher 1998 and Peter Hartnell 2000-01), Eddie Riley (Melvin Lush 2002), Julie Riley (Margaret Reece 2000), Jean Rimmer (Avril Carter 1983), Shane Rimmer (Joe Donnelli 1968-70 and Malcolm Reid 1988), Michael Ripper (Wally Fisher 1976), Renny Rister (Jean Stark 1961), Elizabeth Ritson (Alison Dougherty 1986), Rebecca Ritters (Jules Robinson 2002), Louisa Rix (Carole Gordon 1978), James Roache (James Cunningham 2011), Linus Roache (Peter Barlow 1975; Lawrence Cunningham 2010), Sarah Roache (Judge Alderman 2007), Andy Robb (Darren Whateley 1998), Ted Robbins (DJ 2000), Jeffrey Robert (Jeff Longton 1991), Christine Roberts (Penny Bowes 2001), Ivor Roberts (Tommy Silcock 1972 and George Daly 1987), Michael Roberts (Francois de Jealis 2000), Sam Robertson (Adam Barlow 2004-07), Lynda Roddke (Ruth Horner 2000), Lynn Roden (Brenda Kingston 2000), Sue Roderick (Megan Morgan 1989), Bill Rodgers (Dave Woods 1996 and Mr Booth 2000), Irena Rodic (Kasia Barowicz 2007),Tania Rodrigues (Joanne Khan 1990), Christian Rodska (Mr Newton 1980), Mitzi Rogers (Jenny Sutton/Tanner 1968), Muriel Rogers (Eileen Tibson 1978), Iain Rogerson (Harry Flagg 2002-04), Mavis Rogerson,(Edna Gee 1971-75), Jon Rollason (David Robbins 1963-64, 1969 and 1971), Gordon Rollings (Charlie Moffit 1964-65), Marcus Romer (DS Wilson 2001), Angela Rooks (Eunice Watts 2002), David Roper (Bob Bradshaw 2000), Mark Roper (PC Binding 1997-98), David Ross (Lester Fontayne 1994), Vivienne Ross (Stella Rigby 1985-95), Alan Rothwell (David Barlow 1960-61 and 1963-1968), Lil Roughley (Lorraine Thomson 1996), Patricia Routledge (Sylvia Snape 1961), Joanna Rowden (Paula Shipley 2000), Patricia Rowe (Gladys 1979), Philip Rowson (D.C. Glynn 2010), Max Rubin (Paul Katowski 2002), Ruth Alexander Rubin (Lisa Dalton 2008-09), Thelma Ruby (Lily Dempsey 1996), Claire Rushbrook (Mrs Bennett 1999), Clive Russell (Scotch Tommy 1991 and Phil Nail 2005-06), Grant Russell (unnamed fireman 1998 and Paul Wheeler 1999), Naomi Russell (Bobbi Lewis 2002), Sue Russell (Mrs Shaw 1979), William Russell (Ted Sullivan 1992), Kate Rutter (Jo Marsh 1996), Conor Ryan (Len Windass 2008-09), Francesca Ryan (Miranda Peters 1998-99), Naomi Ryan (Bobbi Lewis 2000-02), Emma Rydal (Maz O'Loughlin 2003), Mark Ryder (Jason Pearce 1978), Penny Ryder (Geraldine Milne 1997), Ann Rye (Ruby Mottram 1991), Alec Sabin (Colin Lomax 1972), Andrew Sachs (Ramsay Clegg 2009), Leonard Sachs (Sir Julius Berlin 1974), Amber Sainsbury (Kerry Fletcher 2002), Johnny St George (Councillor Spooner 1978), John Saint Ryan (Charlie Whelan 1993-94), John Salthouse (Simon Lodge 1976), Rachel Sanders (DI Daley 1998), Nicola Sanderson (Claire Connell 2000), Nikki Sanderson (Candice Stowe 1999-2005), Chris Sanford (Walter Potts 1963-64), Rebecca Sarker (Nita Desai 1999-2000),

Christopher Saul (Mr Imison 1998), Maggie Saunders (Alison Dunkley 1995-96), Stuart Saunders (Harold Dewhurst 1971), Joan Savage (Celeste Pickersgill 2000), John Savident (Fred Elliott 1994-2006), Marcus Saville (Paul Cheveski 1966), Prunella Scales (Eileen Hughes 1961), Sean Scanlan (Les Pringle 1985), Andrew Scarborough (Harvey Reuben 2000-01), David Scase (Dr. Lowther 1987), Rory Scase (Bob Mackay 1977), Malcolm Scates (Dr Hutchinson 1999), Anthony Schaeffer (Dr Edwards 1980 and unnamed various 2000-01), Greta Schmidt (Carole 1981), Andrew Schofield (Norman Mannion 1979), Meriel Schofield (Miss Dalton 1999, Joanne Duggan 2000 and Toni Melton 2002), Peter Schofield (Joe Dawson 1978), Joan Scott (Winifred Willis 1983 and Olive Clarke 1993), Angela Scoular (Sue Silcock 1972), Samantha Seagar (Jodie Morton 2007), Joe Searby (Raymond Attwood 1982), Paul Seed (Father Harris 1979 and 1981), George Selway (Frank Bebbington 1979), Louis Selwyn (Martin Downes 1974), Anne Sessions (WPC Walters 1976), Dannie Seward (Robbie 1998), Anthony Shaeffer (Malcolm Teeson 1995), Shireen Shah (Dr Jaiswal 1995), Patricia Shakesby (Susan Cunningham 1960-61), Paul Shane (Dave the Rave 1977 and Frank Roper 1979), Madhav Sharma (Prem Mandal 2008), John Sharp (Les Clegg 1968), Bernie Shaw (Les Johnson 1979), Charlene Shaw (Imelda 2011), Martin Shaw (Robert Croft 1968), Richard Shaw (Dan Johnson 1980), Tracy Shaw (Maxine Heavey / Peacock 1995-2003), Michael Sheard (Arthur Dabner 1989), Norman Shelley (Henry Foster 1967), Susanna Shelling (Colette Graham 2000), Mark Shepherd (Jeff Walters 1981), Sally Sheridan (Lyn Hargreaves 1996 and unnamed registrar 2000), Sam Sherry (Lol Unsworth 1978), Maggie Shevlin (Jean Cooper 1973), Lisa Shingler (Rachel Forbes 1997-98), Jack Shinn (Harry 1977), Julie Shipley (Jill Marriott 1976 and Christine Millwood 1985), Marlene Sidaway (Mrs Briscoe 1976, Mrs Fletcher 1982 and Brenda Taylor 1990-92), Nicholas Sidi (Stuart Hamilton 1998), Sophie Sigston (Dr Plowman 1998), Gerald Sim (Ted Farrell 1982), David Simeon (Bobby Simpson 1981 and Dr Gareth Bird 1998), Mark Simkin (Craig Brennan 2000), Paula Simms (Mrs Stowe 2000-01), William Simons (Harry Bates 1972), Joe Simpson (unnamed reporter 1997, Sgt Roper 1999 and Alex Swinton 2000-01), Paul Simpson (Jason Stubbs 1988-89), Richard Sinnott (Peter Lloyd 1993, Roger 1997 and Paul Birch 2000), Irene Skillington (Carole Burns 1988, Barbara Day 1998 and Connie Clayton 2000), Elisabeth Sladen (Anita Reynolds 1970), Tony Slattery (Eric Talford 2005-06), Jane Slavin (Wendy Neeson 2007-08), Doreen Sloane (Hilary Dodds 1972-3), Anthony Smee (John Ridley 1981), Jack Smethurst (Percy Bridges 1967, Johnny Webb 1980-83 and Stan Wagstaff 2001), Derek Smith (Harry Bishop 1966), Loveday Smith (Jakki Nye 1996), Max Smith (Alec Young 1979 and Graham Bell 1981), Rachel Smith (Alison Rathbone 1993), Lucille Soong (Jasmine Choong 1969), Leslie Southwick (Eric Briggs 1967), Brian Southwood (Dr McLaren 1979 and unnamed judge 2001), John Southworth (Mr Conway 1997), Mark Spalding (DC Beewood 2003), Joe Speare (Clive Middleton 1996-97), Doris Speed (Annie Walker 1960-83), Kathy Staff (Vera Hopkins 1973-75), Richard Standing (Danny Hargreaves 1999-2001), Jiri Stanislav (Mr Karp 1983), Emma Stansfield (Ronnie Clayton 2005-06), Barry Stanton (Tony Ditchburn 1981), Lesley Staples (Mrs Hardcastle 1999 and Irene Rafferty 2002), Michael Starke (Jerry Morton 2007-08), Alan Starkey (Neville Radd 1976), Paul Stassino (Miklos Zadic 1968), Maggie Steed (Ellen Smith 1970), Tony Steedman (D.I. Patterson 1972), Bill Steel (Bernard McKenna 1997), Eve Steele (Anne Malone 1996-98), Richard Steele (DS Jones 1970), Shirley Stelfox (Shirley Henderson 1994), Stan Stennett (Norman Crabtree 1976-77), Debra Stephenson (Frankie Baldwin 2004-06), Shelagh Stephenson (Sandra Webb 1981), Elaine Stevens (Pip Mistral 1964), Vicki Stevens (Lorraine Ramsden 1995), Colette Stevenson (Lynette Campion 1991), Cyriack Stevenson (Tom Bowden 2001), Garry Stewart (Duncan Craig 1980), Joy Stewart (Freda Barry 1974), Patrick Stewart (unnamed fire officer 1967), Christine Stirling (Jessica Andrews 1984), Matt Stirling (Gary Ryan 1994), Richard Stone (Mr Hart 1996 and Bob Wakefield 2000), Hannah Stoner (Jess 2000), Amy Stratton (unnamed estate agent 2001 and Davina Dawes 2002), John Stratton (Archie Crabtree 1972), Nick Stringer (Frank Harvey 1984-85 and Jump Jackson 1997), Caroline Strong (Mrs Allen 2000), Marjorie Sudell (Edie Riley 1977), Caroline Sugden (unnamed receptionist 1999 and Gemma Richards 2000), Mollie Sugden (Nellie Harvey (1965, 1971-74 and 1976), Anna Summerfield (Beryl Thorn 1967), Jill Summers (Bessie Procter 1972 and Phyllis Pearce 1982-96), Marjorie Sundell (Edie Kenyon 1977), Allan Surtees (Ben Critchley 1981), Clare Sutcliffe (Vicki Bright 1972), Irene Sutcliffe (Maggie Clegg/Cooke 1968-74), Maureen Sutcliffe (Gaynor Burton 1974), Joanna Swain (Mrs Oldred 2000), Gabriel Swartland (Dr Hughes 2001), Bryan Sweeney (Chris Ashton 1975), Charles Swift (Iain Gibson 2010), Helen Swift (Alison Oakley 1989), Tim Swinton (Malcolm Green 2000 and Tom Price 2002), Leigh Symonds (Mr Mason 2000), Will Tacey (Peter Webster 1979, Mr Powell 1983, Dr Keane 1998 and unnamed registrar 2001), Maggie Tagney (Shirley Preston 1996 and Joan 2009), Stephanie Tague (Michelle Robinson 1985), Mary Tamm (Polly Ogden 1973 and Diana Black 2002), Elizabeth Tan (Xin Proctor 2011), Ash Tandon (PC Daullah 2002), Stella Tanner (Laura Howard 1972), William Tarmey (unnamed darts player 1977, Jack Rowe 1978 and Jack Duckworth 1979-2010), Annabelle Tarrant (Alice Watts 2000), Brian Tattersall (Lance Harrison 1995), Emma Taylor (Pip 2000, Mrs Brook 2001 and Trish Farrah 2002), Emma Taylor (Mrs Brook 2001 and Trish Farrah 2002), Georgia Taylor (Toyah Battersby 1997-2003), Kenneth Alan Taylor (Cecil Newton 1987-90), Neve Taylor (Jo Doyle 2001), Samuel Taylor (Jonathan Wright 1974), Shirin Taylor (Jackie Ingram / Baldwin 1990-92), Susan Tebbs (Wendy Nightingale 1976), Peter Temple (Rodney Whitworth 1990 and Josh Reynolds 1996-97), Catherine Terris (Marjorie Pearce 1978 and Mrs Bell 1981), Malcolm Terris (Eric Firman 1994 and 1998), Gareth Thomas (Mel Ryan 1971), Madoline Thomas (Bertha Lumley 1976), Michael Thomas (Richard Armstrong 1986), Talfryn Thomas (Dirty Dick 1971-72), William Thomas (Rev Whittaker 1999), Alan Thompson (Mr Smedley 1976), Ben Thompson (Ryan Connor 2006-10), Jemma Thompson (Claudette Munro 2002), John Thomson (Jesse Chadwick 2008-10), Caitlin Thorburn (Verity Gibson 2010), Lynda Thornton (Viv Radford 1998), Will Thorp (Chris Gray 2010-11), Mark Thrippleton (Simon Hanson 1997), Sarah Thurston (Caroline Clegg 1995 and 2002), Paula Tilbrook (Stella Rigby 1977, Olive Taylor-Brown 1980 and Vivian Barford 1991-93), Anny Tobin (Beryl Peacock 1999 and 2002-06), Frances Tomelty (Christine Peters 1972), Steve Tomlin (Rev Trippet 1997), James Tomlinson (Harry Wiggins 1971, Mr Wainwright 1982 and Paul Rigby 1989), Jacqueline Tong (Jackie Moffatt 1982), Ronald Top (Johan 1998), John Tordoff (Norman Hill 1978 and Keith Hesketh 1999), Susan Tordoff (Warder Maggie Veitch 1998), Michelle Totton (unnamed bike thief 1996 and Wendy Jones 2000), William Travis (Sgt Major Partridge 2010), Christine Tremarco (Lucy Johnson 1980), Tilly Tremayne (Dr Marian Taylor 1998), Richard Trinder (Paul Buckley 1997), Cindy Truman (Fifi La Touche 1976 and Sandra Pitt 1979), Kevin Tucker (unnamed journalist 2000 and Craig Rowe 2002), Jayne Tunnicliffe (Yana Lumb 2005-07), Andrew Turner (Christian Gatley 2007), Linsey Turner (Cheryl Smedley 1976), Michael Turner (Arthur Webster 1981), Stephanie Turner (Shirley Walton 1968), Teddy Turner (Chalky Whiteley 1982-83), Tony Turner (Paddy Thompson 1998), Johnny Tweed (Baz Wilson 1977), Susan Twist (Donna Stout 2002), Robert Vahey (Rev Hope 1974 and 1978), Anthony Valentine (George Wilson 2009-10), Lex van Delden (Dirk Van Der Stek 1981), Peter Vaughan (Arthur Johnson 1966), Harvey Virdi (Nina Mandal 2008), Kim Vithana (Frances Stillman 1997-98), Sandra Voe (Mrs Harrison 1978 and Brenda Palin 1980), Wendy Votel (Pauline Stokes 1982), Barbara Waddington (Myra 1981), Bill Waddington (Eric Summers 1978, George Turner 1980 and Percy Sugden 1983-97), Johnny Wade (Eddie 1998), Mark Wadsworth (Phil Jones 1999 and unnamed reporter 2000), Tammy Wakefield (unnamed paramedic 2000 and Vicky Jones 2001), Ernst Walder (Ivan Cheveski 1960-67), Chris Walker (Ray Thorpe 1997 and Ed Jackson 2005-06), Richard

Walker (Norris Stephens 1983), Wendy Jane Walker (Susan Barlow / Baldwin 1970-75 and 1985-87), Max Wall (Harry Payne 1978), Sue Wallace (Mrs Fletcher 1980), Larry Waller (Mickey 1997), Kenneth Waller (Arthur Watts 1985), Mike Walling (Clifford Ford 2006), Dominic Wallis (Chris Fox 1995), Peter Wallis (Tony Newall 1980 and Great Uncle Bert 1999), Bradley Walsh (Danny Baldwin 2004-06), Peter Walsh (Mr Parr 2000), Julian Walsh (Wayne Pickles 1988), Amy and Emily Walton (Bethany Platt 2000-07), Helen Warburton (Vicky Arden 1990), Lee Warburton (Tony Horrocks 1995-98), Joan Ward (Mrs Watson 1976), Lottie Ward (Diane 1981 and Mrs Dawson 1983), Bill Ward (Charlie Stubbs 2003-07), Michael Wardle (Bill Sutton 1981), George Waring (Councillor Tattersall 1977 and Arnold Swain 1980-81), Darren Warner (Mr Poulson 1997), Eddie Warren (George MacDonald 1976), Marcia Warren (Gladys Braithewaite 2000), Paul Warriner (Ben Williams 1990-92, John Arnley 2002-03, DC Redfern 2010-11), James Warrior (Tony Hayes 1980), Dilys Watling (Merle Baker 1966), Jack Watson (Petty Officer Bill Gregory 1961-62, 1970 and 1983-84), Kenneth Watson (Ralph Lancaster 1975-80), Tom Watson (Frank Turner 1965), Gwendolyn Watts (Candy Brown 1971), Peter Watts (Mr Seymour 1997 and 1998), Sally Watts (Sandra Stubbs 1988), Gillian Waugh (Mrs Easton 1998-99 and Sue Green 2000), Robert Weatherby (Kieran Hargreaves 1999-2001), David Webb (Keith Lucas 1970), Clarie Webzell (Ms Bairstow 1997), Denise Welch (Natalie Horrocks/Barnes 1997-2000), Vin Welch (Bob Barnes 1998), Jerold Wells (Ted Ashley 1964), Lori Wells (Kath Goodwin 1984-85), Kelly Wenham (Danielle Spencer 2002), Robin Wentworth (Arthur Dewhurst 1961), David Westbrook (Dr Hawkins 2001), Graham Weston (George Livesley 1978), Julie Westwood (Dr Minshull 1999), Joanne Whalley (Pamela Graham 1974), Kevin Whately (Kevin 1981), John Wheatley (Gary Hankin 1977 and Joe Broughton 1993-94), Nicola Wheeler (Melanie Tindel 1999), Robert Whelan (Mr Hollands 2002), Lucy Whipday (Shannon Tattersall 1997-98), Dylan and Hayden Whitbread (Freddie Peacock 2006-10), Dorothy White (Joan Walker / Davies 1978), John White (Bob Atkinson 1980), Ruth Whitehead (Lisa Woods 1987-88), Thelma Whiteley (Edith Wilton 1997), June Whitfield (May Penn 2010), Tony Whittle (unnamed taxi driver 1995 and Stuart Leigh 2000), Paula Wilcox (Janice Langton 1969), Jeannette Wild (Dawn Perks 1977), John Wild (Tommy Gregg 1982), Christopher Wilkinson (Dr Nicholls 1998 and unnamed police officer 2002), Geoffrey Wilkinson (Alec Keegan 1979 and Ralph Alwood 1998), Shelley Willetts (Alison Oakley 1998), Alan Williams (unnamed caretaker 1999 and Brian Haverstock 2001), David Williams (Barry Halstead 1995), Jeni Williams (unnamed check-in girl 1999 and Sheila Hayes 2001), Rosalie Williams (Mrs Lacey 1978), Rosemary Williams (WPC Kathy Lane 1980), Victoria Williams (Janice Berry 1975), Bob Williamson (Neil Collier 1978), Dean Williamson (Ronnie Clegg 1998), Sarah Wills (Janine Carr 1996), Dylan Wilson (Charlie Corry 2008 and Connor and Liam McCheyne 2011), Flo Wilson (Kerry Matthews 1998), Sean Wilson (Martin Platt 1985-2005), Martin Wimbush (Robert Manders 1978), Anthony Wingate (Mr Woodhouse 1979), Helen Wingrave (Nurse Chambers 1999), Tom Wisdom (Tom Ferguson 1999-2000), Margery Withers (Hetty Thorpe 1971), Rita Wolf (Flick Khan 1990), Paula Wolfenden (unnamed waitress and nurse 2000 and Andrea Dawson 2002), Stuart Wolfenden (Mark Casey 1989-91), Sally Womersley (Val Rayner 2001 and Margaret Goodbody 2002), Greg Wood (Rick Neelan 2009-10), Jane Wood (Mrs Spencer 1981), Terry Wood (Arnold Pettifer 1976), Keith Woodason (Gerry Turner 1997), Jennie Woodford (Karen Olsen 1967), Caroline Woodruff (unnamed receptionist 1998 and Miss Harper 2001), John Woodvine (Alan Hoyle 2010), Emma Woodward (Sophie Webster 1997-2004), James Wooldridge (unnamed police officer 2010), Jack Woolgar (Arthur Noblett 1970), Dean Worswick (Warren Shipley 2000), Vincent Worth (Walter Byford 1999), Kaye Wragg (Melanie 1997), Jonathan Wrather (Joe Carter 2002-03), Mary Wray (Wendy Williams 1978), Ann Wrigg (Flora Swain 1980-81), Jonathan Wright (Timothy Spencer 2002), Scott Wright (Sam Kingston 2000-02), Tommy Wright (Jack Clayton 1980), Bernard Wrigley (Mr Shaw 1991, Stan Waller 1996 and Marvin Winstanley 1999), William Wymar (Ted Bates 1965), Gilbert Wynne (Maurice

Dodds 1981), Stephen Yardley (Martin Barrett 1974), Bernard Youens (Stan Ogden 1964-84), Andrea Young (Melanie Hesketh 1995), Barbara Young (Betty Ridgeway 1961, Dot Stockwell 1982, Barbara Platt 1991 and Doreen Fenwick 2007) , Benny Young (Brian Dunkley 1995-96), Danny Young (Warren Baldwin 2004-06), Jeremy Young (Benny Lewis 1972), Paul Young (Jock MacCall 1999), Nicholas Zabel (Darren Michaels 2001), Matt Zarb (Goran Milanovich 2002), Joanne Zorian (Charlotte Morris 2002), Damian Zuk (Mickey Hegarty (1997).

Count Duckula Spin-off series from *Dangermouse* with David Jason voicing the green vegetarian vampire duck's voice. Other voices include Brian Trueman (Nanny), Jack May (Igor), Jimmy Hibbert (Von Goosewing), Barry Clayton (Narrator). Ruby Wax voices various characters. Count Duckula was a vegetarian vampire because of a mix-up during reincarnation in which Nanny and Igor used ketchup instead of blood. ITV 1988-93.

Countdown Words and numbers game, based on the French original, *Des Chiffres et Des Lettres*, devised by Armand Jammot. Produced by Yorkshire Television in Leeds, it was the first programme broadcast on Channel 4, on 2 November 1982. From November 1982 until July 2005, it was hosted by the very popular Richard Whiteley (d. 26 June 2005). After a period of mourning Des Lynam was chosen as the show's new presenter, recording his first shows in October 2005. Des O'Connor replaced Des Lynam in January 2007 and in January 2009 was himself replaced by Jeff Stelling. At the same time Rachel Riley, 22, replaced Carol Vorderman as the numbers guru. In the early days Beverley Isherwood and Cathy Hytner were the glamorous co-hosts dispensing the letters and numbers at the contestant's request but to save on budget these jobs were amalgamated and taken over by Carol Vorderman, one of two resident numbers expert (the other being Linda Barrett) who had previously merely shown her method of solving the numbers game. Each show consists of two contestants playing a series of words and numbers rounds, the winner carrying over to the next day for a maximum of eight-consecutive appearances before returning towards the end of the series to play in the knockout stage to decide the series champion. The letters round consists of nine letters being chosen, one point per letter being awarded for the longest word, this being doubled to a maximum 18 points for a nine-lettered word (only the longest word scoring). The numbers game consists of six numbers being chosen from a pool (the numbers 1-9, 10, 25, 50, 75 and 100 being available, two each of every single digit number and one each of every double digit number) in order to make a randomly generated three-digit number by using any combination of addition, subtraction, multiplication or division. eg if the six numbers happened to be 1, 5, 9, 25, 75, and 100 and the three-digit number generated by Cecil (Cecil was the random number generator and stood for Countdown Electronic Calculator In Leeds) happened to be 463 then one possible solution would be to subtract the 9 and the 1 from 100 to give 92 then multiply this by the 5 to give 460 and then divide the 75 by the 25 to give the remaining 3. After each letters round 'Dictionary Corner' is consulted to compare the contestant's offering to a pairing of lexicographer and celebrity. There have been many lexicographers (usually from the Oxford Union Press) used over the years such as Catherine Clark, Della Thompson, Richard Sampson and Susie Dent (who has become the resident) and innumerable (and often innumerate) celebrities! Champions of Countdown have included Harvey Freeman, Tim Morrissey, Wayne Summers, Don Reid, Chris Rogers, Alan Saldanha, Michael Wylie, Damian Eadie and Mark Nyman; the last three ultimately joining the production team. C4 1982- Nick Hewer (of *The Apprentice* fame) is scheduled to replace Jeff Stelling in January 2012.

Counterpoint The perennial music quiz, covering the full classical repertoire, with a generous smattering of show-tunes, jazz, rock and pop. Twenty-seven members of the public compete to prove themselves Radio 4's musical mastermind of the year. Originally hosted by Ned Sherrin until his death in 2006. In the chair for the 2007 series was Edward Seckerson with Paul Gambaccini taking over from 2008. Ian Gillies (*Brain of Britain*'s Mycroft) was the adjudicator until 2000 in the guise of 'young' Grove and David Kendrick and Stephen Holland took over the role of Grove in 2001. The Counterpoint theme is Bach's 'Partita in E major', arranged and performed by Jacques Loussier. Radio 4 1986-

Coupling Jack Davenport (Steve Taylor), Gina Bellman (Jane Christie), Sarah Alexander (Susan Walker), Kate Isitt (Sally Harper), Ben Miles (Patrick Maitland), Richard Coyle (Jeff Murdock). Steven Moffat sitcom based around the confused sex lives of six friends often resulting in a battle of the sexes. The catchy theme song *Perhaps, Perhaps, Perhaps*, was sung by Mari Wilson. BBC2 2000-04.

Cowboy Trap Daytime drama series in which Clive Holland and his team try to fix the bad jobs that builders have left behind in homes across the country. For the second series the title became *Cowboy Builders*. BBC1 2009-.

Cracker Robbie Coltrane (Eddie 'Fitz' Fitzgerald), Barbara Flynn (Judith Fitzgerald), Geraldine Somerville (DS Jane 'Panhandle' Penhaligon), Christopher Eccleston (DCI David Bilborough), Ricky Tomlinson (DCI Wise). Created by Jimmy McGovern this multi-award winning drama centred around a criminal psychologist working freelance for the Greater Manchester Police at the Anson Road station. Fitz is described most accurately by Penhaligon as "able to spot a guilty cough in a football crowd but not know if World War III was breaking out in his living room" as he bumbles from one disaster to the next in his private life. Hard-drinking, compulsively gambling, rude, arrogant, and ultimately philandering with the aforementioned Panhandle; Fitz, for all his faults, possesses a brilliantly incisive brain that could understand the criminal mind in an almost 'but for the grace of God go I' manner. ITV 1993-96.

Crackerjack Children's entertainment show with a mix of games, slapstick sketches, and musical interludes. The original host, Eamonn Andrews, devised a very popular game called 'Double or Drop' whereby a series of questions would be asked and for every correct answer a child would be loaded up with a prize but for every wrong answer they would have to tote a cabbage, all prizes dropped would be confiscated. All contestants would be given a coveted Crackerjack pencil. Subsequent hosts were Leslie Crowther (who previously had a double-act with Peter Glaze in the Eamonn Andrews era), Michael Aspel, Ed Stewart and Stu Francis. Regular performers included Jack Douglas, Joe Baker, Ronnie Corbett, Peter Glaze, Jillian Comber, Pip Hinton, Christine Holmes, Don Maclean, Jacqueline Clarke, Jan Hunt, Bernie Clifton, The Krankies, Leigh Miles, The Great Soprendo (Geoffrey Durham), and Basil Brush. First broadcast on BBC 1 on 14 September 1955 and ended on 21 December 1984.

Crane Patrick Allen (Richard Crane), Sam Kydd (Orlando O'Connor), Gerald Flood (Colonel Mahmoud), Laya Raki (Halima). Adventure series. Escaping the boredom of everyday life Crane decides against continuing in the rat race and emigrates to Casablanca in Morocco and buys a shabby bar by the beach. However, to make life more interesting he moonlights as an affable smuggler and really makes his living by running illicit cigarettes and drink, but will not touch arms or drugs. ITV 1963-65. *Orlando* was a spin-off series.

Crazy People See *The Goon Show*

Cranford Francesca Annis (Lady Ludlow, the Lady of Hanbury Court), Eileen Atkins (Deborah Jenkyns, the moral guardian of the town), Claudie Blakley (Martha, a maid to the Jenkyns sisters), Deborah Findlay (Augusta Tomkinson, a spinster), John Bowe (Dr Morgan, the appreciated surgeon of the town), Andrew Buchan (Jem Hearne, a carpenter and Martha's fiancé), Jim Carter (Captain Brown, retired officer on half-pay), Judi Dench (Matilda 'Matty' Jenkyns, Deborah's sister), Barbara Flynn (The Honourable Mrs Jamieson, a widow with aristocratic pretensions), Michael Gambon (Thomas Holbrook, a farmer and Miss Matty's admirer), Philip Glenister (Edmund Carter, Lady Ludlow's land agent), Lesley Manville (Mrs Rose, Dr Harrison's housekeeper), Joe McFadden (Dr Jack Marshland, Dr Harrison's friend), Julia McKenzie (Mrs Forrester, a widow), Julia Sawalha (Jessie Brown, Captain Brown's daughter), Martin Shaw (Peter Jenkyns, The Jenkyns sisters' long-lost brother), Imelda Staunton (Octavia Pole, a town gossip). Five-part mini-series based on works of Elizabeth Gaskell published between 1849 and 1858. Set in the early 1840s

in the fictional village of Cranford in the county of Cheshire, the story focuses primarily on the town's single and widowed middle class female inhabitants who are comfortable with their traditional way of life and place great store in propriety and maintaining an appearance of gentility. Eileen Atkins won a BAFTA for Best Actress. BBC1 2007. A two-part sequel, *Return to Cranford* was broadcast by BBC as a Christmas special in December 2009. Judi Dench, Imelda Staunton, Julia McKenzie, Deborah Findlay, and Barbara Flynn reprised their roles, with Jonathan Pryce, Celia Imrie, Lesley Sharp, Nicholas Le Prevost, Jodie Whittaker, Tom Hiddleston, Michelle Dockery, Matthew McNulty and Rory Kinnear joining the cast.

Cribb Alan Dobie (DS Cribb), William Simons (Constable Thackeray), David Waller (Chief Insp Jowett). Victorian police drama series Based on the novels of Peter Lovesey. ITV 1980-81.

Crime of Passion Anthony Newlands (President of the Court), Daniel Moynihan (Maitre Savel), John Phillips (Maitre Lacan), Bernard Archer (Maitre Dubois). Created by Ted Willis and using authentic French court cases concerning crimes of passion (a legitimate defence in French law). Lacan and Savel are the respective prosecution and defence lawyers in each episode. ITV 1970-73.

Crime Sheet Raymond Francis (Det Chief Supt. Tom Lockhart). Sequel to *Murder Bag* saw Lockhart promoted to Chief Super and widening his area of expertise to crimes other than murder. ITV 1959. The short-lived series, created by Glyn Davies, soon evolved into the hugely popular *No Hiding Place*.

Crime Traveller Michael French (Jeff), Chloe Annett (Holly), Sue Johnston (Chief Insp. Kate Grisham). Science fiction drama concerning policeman Jeff Slade travelling backwards and forwards in time in a machine built by the father of police science officer Holly Turner. Eight episodes, BBC1 1997.

Crimewatch UK Combining dramatic re-enactments of unsolved crimes with public pleas for help, the series was originally hosted by Nick Ross and Sue Cook (left in 1995). Jill Dando replaced Sue Cook until her tragic death in 1999. Fiona Bruce co-hosted the series with Nick Ross between January 2000 and 2 July 2007, when Nick presented his final episode after 23 years. Fiona left in January 2008, to take over Michael Aspel's role on *The Antiques Roadshow*, and was replaced by Kirsty Young and Matthew Amroliwala. One of the two original resident police officers, Helen Phelps, later left the force to join the production team of the show. Rav Wilding (born 16 October, 1977) is a former policeman, who specialized on the criminals 'Caught on Camera' segment of the show between 2004 and December 2011. Nick Ross invariably signed off the monthly show with the words "Don't have nightmares. Do sleep well". BBC1 1984-

Criminal Justice Five-part thriller written by Peter Moffat. Ben Whishaw (Ben Coulter), Pete Postlethwaite (Hooch), David Harewood (Freddie Graham), Maxine Peake (Juliet Miller), Bill Paterson (DCI Box), Con O'Neil (Stone), Sophie Okonedo (Jack Woolf), Lindsay Duncan (Alison Slaughter). Ben's ordeal begins when he wakes up to find a sexy young woman stabbed to death in her bed. And, what's worse, he can't remember what happened the night before. The series became a talking point for the moral ethics of advocates in court. Should a defence lawyer act for a person when their guilt is evident? BBC1 2008.

Criss Cross Quiz Quiz show based on the noughts and crosses board, hosted by Jeremy Hawk (Father of Actress Belinda Lang), between 1957 and 1962 and then Barbara Kelly. ITV 1957-67. A children's version Junior Criss Cross Quiz ran for the same time period and was also originally hosted by Jeremy Hawk. Other presenters included Chris Kelly, Mike Sarne, Chris Howland, Bob Holness, Gordon Luck, Peter Wheeler, Bill Grundy and Danny Blanchflower. The shows derived their format from the American *Tic Tac Dough*.

Crocodile Shoes Jimmy Nail (Jed Shepperd). Also created and written by Jimmy Nail this drama series concerned a Geordie lathe operator who makes a name for himself as a country singer. *Crocodile Shoes, Cowboy Dreams* and *Calling Out Your Name*, were all hit singles from the series. BBC1 1994-96.

Crossroads The hugely popular soap, created by Hazel Adair and Peter Ling, first aired on Monday 2 November 1964 as replacement for *Lunchbox* and was shown five days a week. To improve production quality the output was reduced to four a week in 1967 and three a week in 1980. Further revamps took place in the early 1980s, not least of which was the sacking of its main star Noele Gordon in 1981 (although she was subsequently recalled for cameo roles before she became too ill to act). Also in 1981, Roger Tonge, who played Meg's wheelchair-bound son Sandy Richardson died after a long fight with Hodgkin's Disease. Roger died at the age of just 35 and in a case of life imitating art, he was forced to use the wheelchair off set for the last few years of his life. In 1985 the title of the soap was changed to *Crossroads Motel* and the then motel owners Barbara and David Hunter were replaced by new owner, Nicola Freeman. In 1986, William Smethurst, the producer who had previously revived the flagging fortunes of *The Archers*, took over and yet more high-profile sackings occurred during his tenure, notably Sue Hanson and Paul Henry. This earned him the epithet 'Butcher Bill'. Smethurst also changed the title again to *Crossroads Kings Oak*, but none of these changes prevented the series being axed (final episode shown on 4 April 1988 with actress Jane Rossington rather aptly uttering the final words (as she had also spoken the first words 24 years earlier). Public demand ensured a reprise albeit 13 years later. *Crossroads* was revived in March 2001, the only characters returning from the original run being Doris Luke, Jill Harvey, Adam Chance and Jill's daughter Sarah-Jane Harvey. Kathy Staff soon left the show, citing the amount of sex as the reason. She told ITV Teletext she felt it was no longer the family-friendly show she had originally been part of. The decision to kill Jill Harvey at the hand of her ex-husband Adam Chance three months into the series' revival, was unpopular with fans as Chance's psychopathic tendencies seemed non sequitur with his previous character which at worst was that of a loveable rogue. It also meant of course there was hardly a character remaining from the original series. This was the beginning of the end but the final nail was when the decision was made to camp up the production and Jane Asher was brought in to play the new central character of glamorous, but bitchy Angel Samson and a series of 'celebrity' actors ensured the show had finally lost all credibility. The Thistle Hotel in Cheltenham, Gloucestershire, was used as the outside of the fictional motel featured in the show's original opening credits. The Paul McCartney version of Tony Hatch's original theme tune which was used to revamp the soap is the final track on Wings' *Venus and Mars* LP. Notable cast members: Tony Adams (Adam Chance 1978-88 and 2001-02), Freema Agyeman (Lola Wise 2003), Ronald Allen (David Hunter 1969-1985), Carl Andrews (Joe MacDonald 1978-86), Joy Andrews (Tish Hope 1965-80), Lysette Anthony (Roxanne Doyle-Wells 1964), Jane Asher (Angel Samson 2003), Vincent Ball (Kevin McArthur 1964-73), John Bentley (Hugh Mortimer 1965-76), Gillian Betts (Josefina Rafael 1965-66), Lionel Blair (Valentine Starwood 2003), Johnny Briggs (Clifford Leyton 1973-75), Peter Brookes (Vince Parker 1964-75), Tim Brooke-Taylor (Murray Simpson 2003), Max Brown (Mark Russell 2001-02), Edward Clayton (Stan Harvey 1966-78), Jess Conrad (Philip Bailey 1978), Sophie Cook (Sarah-Jane Harvey 1987), Peter Dalton (Minty Sutton 2001-02), David Davenport (Malcolm Ryder 1968-69), Les Dennis (Dr Harry Richmond 2003), Gabrielle Drake (Nicola Freeman 1985-88), Sorrel Dunger (Sarah-Jane Harvey 1975-83), Sandor Elès (Paul Ross 1982-86), Claire Faulconbridge (Miranda Pollard 1980-85), David Fennell (Brian Jarvis 1964-75), Fine Time Fontayne (Ken Dolman 2002), Freddy Foote (Chris Hunter 1972-73), John Forgeham (Jim Baines 1976-78), Sonia Fox (Sheila Harvey 1970-76), Ann George (Amy Turtle 1966-76), Zeph Gladstone (Vera Downend 1966-77), Joanne Good (Carole Sands 1982-84), Noelle Gordon (Meg Richardson / Mortimer 1964-81 and 1983), Jane Gurnett (Kate Russell 2001-03), Jimmy Hanley (Jimmy Gudgeon 1964-66), Susan Hanson (Diane Lawton / Parker / Hunter 1965-87), Janet Hargreaves (Rosemary Hunter 1973-80), Paul Henry (Benny Hawkins 1975-88), Dee Hepburn (Anne-Marie Wade 1985-88), Sherrie Hewson (Virginia Raven 2001-03), Peter Hill (Arthur Brownlow 1976-82), Stephen Hoye (Chris Hunter 1974-80), Carolyn Jones (Sharon Metcalfe 1977-83), Brian Kent (Dick Jarvis 1964-71), Sam Kydd (Mr Walton 1976-77), Angus Lennie (Shughie McFee 1974-80), Sue Lloyd (Barbara Brady / Hunter 1975-85), Neil McCaul (Patrick Russell 2001), Malcolm McDowell (Crispin Ryder 1964), Lynette McMorrough (Glenda Brownlow / Banks 1976-83), Reginald Marsh (Reg Lamont 1982-84), Terry Molloy (Stan Harvey 1987), David Moran (Kevin Banks 1980-85), Anthony Morton (Carlos Rafael 1964-67), Holly Newman (Sarah-Jane Harvey 2001-02), Sue Nicholls (Marilyn Gates 1964-68), Emma Noble (Suzie Samson 2003), Kate O'Mara (Lady Alice Fox 2003), Ken Platt (Arthur Loomis 1964), Stephen Rea (Pepe Costa 1964), John Rhys-Davies (Gareth 1964), Terence Rigby (Tommy "Bomber" Lancaster 1986-88), Kate Robbins (Kate Loring 1980), Linda Robson (Wanda Wise 2003), Jane Rossington (Jill Richardson / Harvey / Chance 1964-88 and 2001), Di Sherlock (Oona Stocks 2002-03), Kathy Staff (1978-85 and 2001-02), Anthony Steel (Philip Warner Bligh 1978), Stan Stennett (Sid Hooper 1982-87), Ramon Tikaram (Eddie Weaver 2002), Roger Tonge (Sandy Richardson 1964-81), Pamela Vezey (Kath Brownlow / Fellowes 1976-87), Max Wall (Wally Soper). ITV 1964-88 and 2001-03

Crosswits Game show with a crossword theme. Hosted by Barry Cryer (1985-87) and Tom O'Connor (1987-98). Two contestants would solve cryptic crosswords with the help of celebrities. The late John Junkin was an outstanding player. ITV 1986-98.

Crown Court Over three half-hour episodes, usually shown from Wednesday to Friday, a criminal case was introduced to the viewer in the form of black and white stills with narration by Peter Wheeler. The case was then presented before a judge and jury at the fictitious Fulchester Crown Court, London. The twist was that the jury was made up entirely of members of the public, and the verdict they reached on Friday afternoon was completely unscripted. The cream of British television and stage actors appeared at some point, the most frequent appearances being by Richard Wilson as barrister Jeremy Parsons QC and William Mervyn as Justice Campbell. ITV 1972-84. ITV reprised the format in a 1998 drama entitled *Verdict*, starring Peter Davison.

Crown Prosecutor Tom Chadbon (Lenny Monk), David Daker (Ben Campbell), Deborah Grant (Sheila Cody), Jessica Hynes nee Stevenson (Jackie South), Paris Jefferson (Nina Fisher-Holmes), Shaun Parkes (Eric Jackson), Michael Praed (Marty James). Legal drama featuring an ensemble cast who brought cases before local magistrates in the United Kingdom. Each one of ten episodes generally featured a primary plot centred on an unfolding court case, along with two subplots that advanced the development of the show's cast of characters. BBC1 1995.

Cruise, The Twice-weekly docu-soap set aboard the cruise-ship *Galaxy* as it toured the Caribbean. The ship's resident singer, Jane McDonald, became a national television star as a result of the series. BBC1 1998.

Crystal Maze, The Game show with contestants (aged under 40) partaking in a series of mental and physical challenges in order to gain crystals which were exchanged for time during the jackpot run at the end of the show (this involved collecting floating strips of gold foil). The four fantasy zones were Aztec, Futuristic, Medieval and Industrial. The two presenters were Richard O'Brien (1990-94) and Edward Tudor-Pole (1994-95). C4 1990-95.

Crystal Tipps and Alistair Children's animation series created by Hilary Hayton and produced by Q3 of London. Frizzy-haired Crystal and her grey grinning square-headed dog Alistair are the best of friends. Together they hatch spectacular peacocks, throw custard pies at one another, poke each other with extended tickling sticks and float high in the sky in giant bubbles. Crystal even has her own big-propellered biplane. In Crystal and Alistair's world life is big, bright, splashy fun with ne'er a grown-up in sight, and every day is a big-hair day. Fifty 5-minute episodes were made as well as an additional 20 minute special called Crystal's Christmas Special in which she and Alistair escape the snows of winter for sunnier climes, where they encounter Santa Claus off on his holidays too! BBC1 1972-74.

Cube, The Award-winning game show presented by Phillip Schofield offering contestants the opportunity to win up to £250,000 by completing a series of physical challenges within 'The Cube' (a 4x4x4 metre perspex cube). Each contestant is given nine lives and each time they fail a game, one life is lost, and the contestant must repeat the game. Any contestant who runs out of lives while trying to win a game loses all of the money they have accumulated. The seven tasks offer increasing values of £1,000, £2,000, £10,000, £20,000, £50,000, £100,000, and £250,000, the contestant can bail out at any time before commencing the next game and keep any money accrued. Additional help is offered by way of 'Simplify' whereby the player will have the task made easier in order to protect lives, and 'Trial Run' which gives the contestant the chance to have a dry run before deciding whether to undertake the challenge. A faceless female character, known as the 'body', demonstrates each game before its commencement. ITV 2009-

Cuckoo Waltz, The David Roper (Chris Hawthorne), Diane Keen (Felicity 'Fliss' Hawthorne), Lewis Collins (Gavin Rumsey), Ian Saynor (Adrian Lockett), Clare Kelly (Connie Wagstaffe), John McKelvey (Austen). Sitcom concerning hard-up newly-weds Chris and Fliss Hawthorne sharing their sparsely furnished Chorlton-cum-Hardy accommodation with a lodger, Gavin, who purports to be Chris's best friend while secretly harbouring carnal desires for his wife. Chris is a young northern newspaper reporter with a mortgage, and a wife who has newly delivered twins, Gavin is a wealthy young air-freight executive used to the luxury life and lavish spending sprees. Forced to leave his matrimonial home when he splits from his wife Carol, Gavin moves his fancy furniture, Scalextric, hi-fi, abundantly stocked wardrobe, drinks cabinet and fast cars into chez Hawthorne, at first only for a couple of days but then, it seems, indefinitely. Gavin flaunts his wealth while the disinterested Fliss wonders what has happened to her life: three A-levels to her name and she's up to her hands in nappy-rash cream. Also closely involved in Chris and Fliss's lives are their neighbour Austen Tweedale and Fliss's prudish, interfering and materially-obsessed mother Connie. When the series returned after a three-year gap, Lewis Collins had become a star of *The Professionals* and the new lodger was Adrian Lockett. ITV 1975-77, 1980.

Cuffy See *The Shillingbury Tales.*

Culture Show, The Weekly arts magazine programme focusing on the latest developments in the world of film, music, visual art, fashion and the performing arts. Presenters have included Verity Sharp, Kwame Kwei-Armah, Andrew Graham-Dixon (current), Mark Kermode, Tom Dyckhoff, Clemency Burton-Hill, Mark Radcliffe, Tim Samuels, Matthew Sweet, Danny Robbins. Stewart Lee, Frank Skinner, Grace Dent, Charlie Brooker, and Russell Brand. BBC2 2004-

Curry and Chips Spike Milligan (Kevin O'Grady aka Paki-Paddy), Eric Sykes (The Foreman), Norman Rossington (Norman). Written by Johnny Speight this controversial comedy was set in Lillicrap Ltd, a factory making cheap souvenirs. The humour was based around racial jibes towards a blacked-up Spike Milligan playing a Pakistani with an Irish father. ITV 1969.

Cutting Edge Umbrella title for a series of occasional documentaries that portray stories focusing mainly on political and social issues. An early story *Graham Taylor: The Impossible Job*, featured the England national football team's unsuccessful attempt to qualify for the 1994 World Cup. This programme gave rise to Taylor's catchphrase, "Do I not like that". Another early broadcast *Shops and Robbers* received one of Channel 4's highest ever audiences. The series took a sabbatical for a few years but returned in 2005 with a steady stream of 'cutting edge' stories including *The 9/11 Faker and The Virgin Daughters*. A 2010 story, *My Big Fat Gypsy Wedding*, spawned a spin-off series of its own. C4 1990-

Cutting It Amanda Holden (Mia Bevan), Sarah Parish (Allie Henshall), Jason Merrells (Gavin Ferraday), Ben Daniels (Finn Bevan), Angela Griffin (Darcey Henshall), Cherie Lunghi (Zinnia). Written by Debbie Horsfield this popular drama centred around rival Manchester hairstylists. BBC1 2002-05.

Dad's Army Arthur Lowe (Capt George Mainwaring - a bank manager), John Le Mesurier (Sgt Arthur Wilson), Clive Dunn (L/Corporal Jack Jones - a butcher), John Laurie (Pte James Frazier - an undertaker), James Beck (Pte Joe Walker - a spiv), Ian Lavender (Pte Frank Pike - a silly boy), Arnold Ridley (Pte Charles Godfrey), Bill Pertwee (ARP Warden William Hodges - a greengrocer), Frank Williams (Revd Timothy Farthing - the

vicar), Edward Sinclair (Maurice Yeatman - the verger), Colin Bean (Pte Sponge), Pamela Cundell (Mrs Marcia Fox), Janet Davies (Mrs Mavis Pike), Talfryn Thomas (Pte Cheeseman). Created by Jimmy Perry and David Croft and set in Walmington-on-sea (Supposedly Bexhill) during World War II, this nostalgic comedy about the exploits of members of the Home Guard is always near the top of any polls of the nation's favourite sitcom. The theme tune was composed by Derek Taverner and played by the Band Of The Coldstream Guards and featured Bud Flanagan singing Jimmy Perry's lyrics thus: *Who do you think you are kidding Mr. Hitler, if you think we're on the run? We are the boys who will stop your little game. We are the boys who will make you think again. 'Cus who do you think you are kidding Mr. Hitler, if you think old England's done? Mr. Brown goes off to town on the 8:21. But he comes home each evening and he's ready with his gun. So watch out Mr. Hitler: You have met your match in us. If you think you can push us we're afraid you've missed the bus. 'Cos who do you think you are kidding Mr. Hitler, if you think old England's done?* BBC1 1968-77.

Dalziel and Pascoe Warren Clarke (Det Supt Andrew Dalziel), Colin Buchanan (DS/DI Peter Pascoe). Written by Stephen Lowe, based on Reginald Hill's books about the two detectives who are total opposites, but whose different skills complement one another, making a crime-busting team second to none. Dalziel (pronounced 'de-yell') is a blunt-talking, politically incorrect, Yorkshireman. He's from the old school of policing, in complete contrast to his younger side-kick, the fast-track university educated Pascoe. The action takes place in the fictional Yorkshire town of Wetherton. BBC1 1996-2007

Damon and Debbie Three-part spin-off of *Brookside* that aired on Channel 4 in 1987.

Dance X Reality television show that aimed to find a mega-talented dancing group which could also sing a bit. Presented by Ben Shephard the two teams were 'managed' by Bruno Tonioli and Arlene Phillips with the help of a dance and vocal coach. Bruno's group consisting of Claire Mealor, Marie McGonigle, Marquelle Ward, Phoenix and Rana Roy were the winners and were subsequently given the name 'Pulse' by readers of *The Sun* newspaper. BBC1 2007. The main Saturday show was followed by Dance Xtra on BBC3.

Dancing On Ice Partnered by a professional and coached by the UK's most famous Ice Dance Olympic Champions, Jane Torvill and Christopher Dean, who also return to skate together for the first time since they retired in 1998, various celebrities compete against each other to gain marks from a distinguished panel of experts and votes from the viewing public. The series is hosted by Phillip Schofield and Holly Willoughby and the judging panel were Karen Barber, Nicky Slater, Jason Gardiner and head judge Robin Cousins for the first five series. The fifth judge has changed from series to series, Karen Kresge (Series 1), Natalia Bestemianova (Series 2), Ruthie Henshall (Series 3 and 4) and Emma Bunton (Series 5 and 6). For Series 6 there were only three judges, after Nicky Slater was dropped and Karen Barber demoted to mentor. The announcer is Marc Silk and the commentator Tony Gubba. The winners of the first series were actress Gaynor Faye and Daniel Whiston, the second series was won by England rugby star Kyran Bracken and Melanie Lambert, the third series by singer Suzanne Shaw and Matt Evers, the fourth series by singer Ray Quinn and Maria Filippov, the fifth series by actress Hayley Tamaddon and Daniel Whiston and the sixth series by actor Sam Attwater and Brianne Delcourt. ITV 2006-. The seventh series, scheduled to begin in January 2012, has Robin Cousins joined by two new judges, Louie Spence and Katarina Witt whilst Christine Bleakley replaces Holly Willoughby as co-presenter.

Danger! 50,000 Volts! Eight-episode spoof of the outdoors survival genre written and presented by Nick Frost, in which survival experts demonstrated how to improvise solutions to dangerous problems. A feature of the series was the clever and humorous use of 'danger' iconography in the graphic design of segment titles, identifying the show with the British tradition of stoic resolve in the face of (comically) overwhelming odds. Bruce Parry made several cameo appearances. Channel 5 (now Five)

2002. There were several spin-off ventures, including *Danger! Incoming Attack!* (2003) and a film short collaboration with Simon Pegg *Danger! 50,000 Zombies!* (2004), in which Simon played Zombie Hunter Dr. Russel Fell.

Danger Man Patrick McGoohan (John Drake), Peter Madden (Hobbs). Hugely popular action series created by Ralph Smart. John Drake worked for NATO initially and travelled the world as a secret agent to preserve world peace. From 1962 the series changed its format from 30 minutes to full hour-long episodes and Drake was now working as a Special Security Agent for M19, a branch of the British Secret Service. ITV 1960-68.

Danger UXB Anthony Andrews (Lt Brian Ash), Maurice Roeves (Sgt James), Judy Geeson (Susan Mount), Norman Chappell (Cpl Mould), Deborah Watling (Norma Baker), Kenneth Cranham (Sapper/L/Cpl Jack Salt), Iain Cuthbertson (Dr David Gillespie), Ken Farrington (Capt/Major Francis), Jeremy Sinden (Lt Ivor Rogers). Brian Ash is a young Lieutenant assigned to the 97 Tunnelling Company of the Royal Engineers in the early days of World War II and subsequently re-assigned to a UXB unit. UXB is the signal that an aerial bomb has not exploded (UneXploded Bomb). Ash's job is to deactivate bombs made by German technicians some of which have fuses specifically designed to kill him. The series takes the viewer from the Blitz through to D-Day, concentrating on the Lieutenant's harrowing job (where the average life-span of a sapper was a mere seven weeks), his love affair with Susan Mount, and the stresses and strains of wartime on the civilians and military in England. ITV 1979.

Dangerfield Nigel Le Vaillant (Dr Paul Dangerfield), Amanda Redman (Dr Joanna Stevens), George Irving (DI Ken Jackson), Sean Maguire and Tim Vincent (Marty Dangerfield), Nicola Cowper (DS Helen Diamond), Lisa Faulkner and Tamzin Malleson (Alison Dangerfield), Nadim Sawalha (Dr Shaaban Hamada), Kim Vithana (Kate Durrani), Michael Melia (DI Frank Dagley), Nigel Havers (Dr Jonathan Paige), Jane Gurnett (DI Gillian Cramer), Sam Loggin (Jojo). Set in Warwick and Leamington Spa, *Dangerfield* tells of the trials of London police surgeon Dr Paul Dangerfield who relocates to Warwickshire following the tragic death of his wife Celia in a car crash. A single parent to teenagers Alison and Marty, Dangerfield first works under the watchful eye of Birmingham-born DI Ken Jackson then in Series 3 and 4 is presented with other police bosses including DS Helen Diamond and DI Frank Dagley. After a suitable period of mourning Dangerfield finds time to briefly romance feisty barrister Kate Durrani and on a more long-term basis, his medical colleague Dr Joanna Stevens. Following his daughter's marriage during Series 4, Paul Dangerfield decides to leave Warwickshire and at the end of that series, is replaced by his GP friend Dr Jonathan Paige whose police boss is attractive DI Gillian Cramer. The series kept the name Dangerfield as Paige's base was The Dangerfield Health Centre. BBC1 1995-99.

Dangermouse Cartoon series created by Mike Harding and Brian Trueman and written by Brian Trueman and Angus Allen. Voices: David Jason (Dangermouse and Nero), Terry Scott (Penfold and Leatherneck), Brian Trueman (Stiletto Mafioso), Edward Kelsey (Baron Greenback and Colonel K). Dangermouse is the strongest, the quickest, the greatest super agent in the world. He's a suave, super-cool, black eyepatch-wearing white mouse based at a postbox outside 221b Baker Street, the home of Sherlock Holmes. 'DM' as he's known, has a spectacled hamster sidekick called Penfold who never hangs around long enough to even glimpse danger. Still, this dynamic duo are given death-defying missions from Colonel K (a walrus) of the Secret Service. These mostly lead down a well-trodden path to the door of that most fiendish of villains, Baron Silas Greenback (a toad). The Baron aims to take over the world by any means necessary. To assist him he has Stiletto, an incompetent mock-Italian crow (who could often be heard to mutter "Si Barone" despite giving the impression he never really understood at all), Leatherneck, an even more incompetent crow, and a big white furry caterpillar called Nero who chatters and grumbles disaffectedly on his master's arm. Other characters include Doctor Augustus P. Crumhorn III (a mad scientist), Professor Squarkencluck (a mole who Invented the Mark III, DM's flying car), Agent 57 (an ally of Dangermouse who is always undercover and later gained the ability to alter his own molecular structure to transform into any appearance he

wished), Flying Officer Buggles Pigeon (one of Colonel K's agents), Isambard Sinclair (the unseen narrator - voiced by David Jason), and The Singer (the unseen woman who sings the opening and closing theme song - voiced by Prunella Scales). Penfold's real name is revealed as Wilbraham Keith Benedict, the only son of Arthur Wigglesworth and Bronwen Merionedd Ysptty Ystwyth Penfold (nee O'Herlihy). DM was educated at Eton, Cambridge, Oxford, Harvard, the Sorbonne and Wurternberg, and holds a B.A., B.Sc., M.A., M.Sc., and P.H.D. Stiletto's real name is Nasaccio Mafiosa Cornetto. Nero is of the species Creepio Nastissimus. His full title is Instar Emperor Nero the Second of Chorlton-Cum-Hardy - Chorlton-Cum-Hardy being the real-life address of Cosgrove Hall's studios, the makers of the series. Count Duckula, a character from one of the episodes was given his own spin-off series. As well as creating the character of Baron Greenback, Mike Harding also provided the music. Each episode began with the words *He's the greatest, he's fantastic. Wherever there is danger he'll be there. He's the ace, he's amazing. He's the strongest, he's the quickest, he's the best. Danger Mouse. He's terrific, he's magnific. He's the greatest Secret Agent in the world. Danger Mouse, Powerhouse. He's the fastest, he's the greatest, he's the best. Danger Mouse, Danger Mouse, Danger Mouse.* 89 episodes were made and originally broadcast on ITV 1981-87, 1991-92.

Dani's House Dani Harmer (Dani), Klariza Clayton (Sam), Harry Culverhouse (Toby), Darragh Mortell (Jack), James Gandhi (Ben), Sebastian Applewhite (Max), Steff White (Ruby), Millie Innes (Maisy). Children's sitcom based around Dani, a 17-year-old actress and singer who has to look after her 10-year-old brother Max, and 6-month-old baby brother. Dani usually hangs out with her two best friends, Sam and Toby (and in later series a DJ named Jack). Other characters include Max's dim-witted friend Ben and Coordinator Zang and Zark - Two green aliens who are travelling together across the universe. They enjoy watching their favourite human show "Dani's House", learning something new every episode. Part of the CBBC menu; guest stars have included Professor Brian Cox, presenter Zöe Salmon, and actor Matt Di Angelo. BBC 2008-

Dark Season Victoria Lambert (Marcie), Ben Chandler (Tom), Kate Winslet (Reet), Brigit Forsyth (Miss Maitland), Grant Parsons (Mr Eldritch), Jacqueline Pearce (Miss Pendragon). Six-part children's science fiction series created by Russell T Davies (later of Dr Who fame). Three teenagers, Marcie, Tom and Reet battle to save their school from the devilish actions of Mr Eldritch and Miss Pendragon, he complete with dark shades and she with an even more sinister black bejewelled turban. The short-lived series is now famous for being the second screen role for the young Kate Winslet (a Sugar Puffs advert with the Honey Monster being her first). BBC1 1991.

Dark Side of Fame, The Piers Morgan interviewed various celebrities about the downside of being famous. The eclectic choice of subjects for each of the eight shows were Pamela Anderson, Jim Davidson, Jason Donovan, Tracey Emin, Mickey Rourke, Nancy Dell'Olio, Bruce Jones and Chantelle Houghton. BBC1 2008.

Darling Buds of May, The David Jason (Sidney Charles 'Pop' Larkin), Pam Ferris (Ma Larkin), Catherine Zeta-Jones (Mariette Larkin/Charlton), Philip Franks (Cedric 'Charley' Charlton), Michael Jayston (Ernest Bristow). Written by Bob Larbey, Richard Harris and Paul Wheeler and based on H. E. Bates' five Larkin books concerning the boisterous Pop Larkin and his family who run a 22-acre smallholding in the delightful Kent countryside. ITV 1991-93.

Dave King Show, The See Dave King's entry in the comedy section.

David Copperfield David Yelland (David Copperfield), Patience Collier (Betsey Trotwood), David Troughton (Ham Peggotty), Arthur Lowe (Wilkins Micawber), Martin Jarvis (Uriah Heep), Beth Morris (Dora Spenlow), Jonathan Kahn (Young David Copperfield), Anthony Andrews (James Steerforth). Highly acclaimed five-part mini-series based on the classic work of Charles Dickens. BBC1 1974. The BBC actually covered this timeless work several times, notably in 1999 when the cast included Ciarán McMenamin (David Copperfield), Daniel Radcliffe (Young David Copperfield), Emilia Fox (Clara

Copperfield), Pauline Quirke (Peggotty), Michael Elphick (Barkis), Bob Hoskins (Micawber), Ian McKellen (Creakle), and Nicholas Lyndhurst (Uriah Heep). A 1986 BBC ten-part mini-series starred Colin Hurley (David Copperfield), Simon Callow (Wilkins Micawber), Nyree Dawn Porter (Mrs Steerforth), David Dexter (Young David Copperfield).

David Dickinson Show, The David Dickinson was born David Gulessarian in Cheadle Heath, Stockport, 16 August 1941. At age 19 David served three years of a four-year prison sentence for fraud, most of which was spent at Strangeways in Manchester. Whilst working as agent for his wife (cabaret singer Lorne Lesley) he developed an interest in antiques and initially opened various shops before eventually deciding to concentrate on selling antiques at major fairs. He specialised in 18th and 19th century furniture and works of art. In 1998, a chance meeting with a TV producer at a barbecue led to Dickinson's first television appearance, a two-part documentary for the BBC following his preparation for a show at Olympia. David next became the resident antiques expert on *This Morning*, allegedly because of his resemblance to Ian McShane's portrayal of *Lovejoy* (see separate entry) and his four-year stint hosting the game show *Bargain Hunt* secured his fame. On leaving the show in 2004 he took part in *Strictly Come Dancing* and the following year entered the jungle as a contestant on *I'm a Celebrity... Get Me Out of Here!* Earlier in 2005 *Dealing with Dickinson* was a short-lived success but *Dickinson's Real Deal* (first aired in 2006) has been a more lasting success and remains popular on ITV. David's dark complexion (often implied to be a fake tan, although he claims that it's due to his Armenian ancestry) and numerous catchphrases have made him fair game for imitation. Catchphrases include: "Do you mind if I call you girls?", "it's real bobby-dazzler", "it's a load of tat," and "it's cheap as chips!". In 2010 David (nicknamed The Duke after his favourite actor John Wayne) was given his own daytime chat show, assisted by his 'butler' Ralph. One segment of the show is Seal The Deal, an antiques-based guessing game giving a member of the audience a chance to win some money. ITV 2010

Day of the Triffids, The Dougray Scott (Bill Masen), Joely Richardson (Jo Playton), Brian Cox (Dennis Masen), Vanessa Redgrave (Durrant), Eddie Izzard (Torrence), Jason Priestley (Coker), Jenn Murray (Susan), Ewen Bremner (Walter Strange), Lizzie Hopley (Hilda), Julia Joyce (Imogen). Two-part adaptation of John Wyndham's novel by Patrick Harbinson. The drama opens in the jungles of Zaire, where 30 years before Triffid expert Dr. Bill Masen's mother was attacked and killed by one of the plants. BBC1 2009.

Daybreak Weekday breakfast television programme originally presented by Adrian Chiles and Christine Bleakley until they were replaced by Dan Lobb and Kate Garraway in December 2011. The show was launched in September 2010 as replacement for *GMTV* (see separate entry). The magazine show which features news, entertainment stories, celebrity interviews, competitions, consumer and health items had a high-profile launch but ratings fell throughout 2011.

Day Today, The Satire spoofing current affairs TV programmes featuring a team who had all been involved in a BBC radio show, *On The Hour* (13 editions from 9 August 1991 to 28 December 1992; 12 on Radio 4, the last on Radio 1), which had taken a similarly juicy swipe at radio current affairs programming. Both the radio and TV shows were produced by Armando Iannucci and featured a number of recurring characters, most notably the sports correspondent Alan Partridge, later to be granted his own TV show, *Knowing Me...Knowing You* which, in turn, led to *I'm Alan Partridge*. Other regulars included political cartoonist Brant (played by David Schneider), 'enviromation' presenter Rosie May (Rebecca Front), business correspondent Collaterlie Sisters (Doon Mackichan), inept political reporter Peter O'Hanrahanrahan (Patrick Marber) and the show's smarmy front-man played by Chris Morris. BBC2 1994.

Dead Ringers Comedy impressions show devised by producer Bill Dare that began life on BBC Radio 4. Actors included Jon Culshaw, Jan Ravens, Phil Cornwell, Kevin Connelly, Kate

Robbins, Mark Perry, Simon Lipson and Alistair McGowan. The principal writers were Tom Jamieson and Nev Fountain with contributions from Simon Blackwell, Jon Culshaw, Jan Ravens, John Finnemore, David Mitchell, Richard Ward, Jonathan Morris, Colin Birch, Carl Carter and Tony Cooke. A televised version ran for five years. BBC Radio 4 2000-07 and BBC2 2002-2007.

Deadline Midnight Armine Sandford (Jane Smith), Glyn Houston (Mike Grieves), Jeremy Young (Neville Crane), Bruce Beeby (Matt Stewart), Jane Merrow (Dilys Jones). 39-episode drama series set in the offices of *The Globe* newspaper. Notable for the first screen appearance of Sarah Miles as Vi Vernon in a 1961 episode, *Manhunt*. ITV 1961.

Deadly Knowledge Show, The Daytime quiz show pitting two teams of two players against each other. Dave Berry, the host, engaged in lengthy preambles to questions which often went off on a tangent before settling. Four multiple-choice answers were supplied. An interesting later round was where players had to buzz in for their partners to answer the question. C4 2005-06

Deadly 60 Wildlife presenter Steve Backshall (born in Surrey, 21 April 1973) tracks down 60 of the world's deadliest animals. Part of the CBBC menu.

Deal or No Deal Game show hosted by Noel Edmonds in which 22 contestants stand over boxes containing varying amounts from 1p to £250,000, the tension mounting when each one is opened on the command of another contestant who has brought their box to the table with a view to either open it last and receive the contents or settle on an offer made by the dastardly, but unseen 'banker'. Each one of the 22 box-openers eventually gets a turn which means a new player is added every day. The banker makes a bid for the player's box after five choices and then again after every third box is opened. This is by no means set in stone and variations can occur at the banker's discretion. The object is to maintain the 'power five' (amounts from £35,000 to £250,000) as long as possible in order to gain a huge offer. To-date only four players (all young women) have won the top prize although on several occasions the player has been in possession of the £250,000 but has been happy to settle for a lower amount rather than risk oblivion. Laura Pearce had the choice of accepting £45,000 or chancing her luck on the final two boxes, one holding the jackpot and the other £3,000. She gambled successfully. The second winner was given an even better deal. Alice Munday, had dealt at £17,500 two rounds before the end and was left with the 1p and the £250,000 as her final two boxes. The banker then offered her the 'banker's gamble' allowing her back into live play in return for the money. Alice accepted the challenge and won. Suzanne Mulholland became the third jackpot winner on 13 May 2011. The Sligo-born Bristolian declined £165,000 after creating the dream £100,000/£250,000 finish. She then accepted the swap and box 21 came up trumps for her. Suzanne also won a Week for 2 in Florida along the way as it was the banker's birthday. The fourth winner was twenty-year-old Tegen Roberts in September 2011. Tegen, who is in remission from Hodgkins Disease, turned down her final offer of £77,000 as she had the safety valve of £20,000. As each show progresses the psychological pressure mounts on the contestant. It is a simple format which lends itself to the *Countdown* propensity for fast-forwarding through the links although the banality of the intercourse has a certain comic effect. C4 2005-`

Dealing With Dickinson See *The David Dickinson Show*

Dear Ladies See entry for Hinge and Bracket in the comedy section.

Dear Mother Love Albert Rodney Bewes (Albert Courtnay), Garfield Morgan (A C Strain), Sheila White (Vivian McKewan), Geraldine Newman (Mrs McKewan), Liz Gebhardt (Doreen Bissel - Series 3), Amelia Bayntun (Ada Bissel), Cheryl Hall (Doreen Bissel - Series 4). Whatever happened to the Likely Lads? Well Rodney Bewes went on to co-write this sitcom with Derrick Goodwin. As well as creating, writing, producing and starring in the series Rodney also managed to find time to sing the theme song he co-wrote with Mike Hugg. Albert Courtney is fresh down south from up north. He regularly writes home to his mother, grossly exaggerating the events that have happened to him in London. He finds work in a confectionary company, moves into a flat he shares with two young women and eventually gets engaged to Doreen Bissel. By the fourth and final series Albert has lost his job and Doreen subsequently dumps him. ITV 1969-72

Death of a Princess Suzanne Abou Taleb (Princess Misha'al), Paul Freeman (Ryder), Judy Parfitt (Elsa Gruber). A journalist investigates a newspaper story of the execution of an Arab princess. This two-hour simulated documentary drama by Antony Thomas sparked off a diplomatic incident between Britain and Saudi Arabia. The story concerned a 19-year-old Islamic princess who was publicly executed for adultery and although no country was cited as the perpetrator of this deed the Saudi government took exception to the open criticism of Islamic doctrine and normality was only restored once Foreign Secretary Lord Carrington had openly condemned the film. ITV 1980.

Dee Time See Simon Dee.

Demons Philip Glenister (Rupert Galvin), Christian Cooke (Luke Rutherford), Holliday Grainger (Ruby), Zoe Tapper (Mina Harker), Saskia Wickham (Jenny Rutherford), Mackenzie Crook (Gladiolus Thrip), Rick English (Gilgamel), Kevin McNally (Tobias Tibbs), Ciarán McMenamin (Quincey), Laura Aikman (Alice). Six-part supernatural drama series created by Johnny Capps and Julian Murphy and written by Peter Tabern, Howard Overman and Lucy Watkins. Luke Rutherford learns that he is the last descendant of the Van Helsing line by the sudden arrival of his American godfather Rupert Galvin. Luke is briefed to challenge the gathering dark forces (with a little help from his best friend Ruby) whilst trying to live an ordinary teenage life in London. Rupert Galvin helps train Luke with the assistance of Mina Harker, a blind concert pianist with vampire-like tendencies who is an authority on half-lives (i.e. vampires, demons, zombies, and werewolves). Demons that get the rough treatment from the team include vampires Gladiolus Thrip and Quincey, Gilgamesh – a grotesque 'travesty' with cloven hooves and taloned wings, Tobias – the arrogant part-man- part-rat, and Alice - a 3,000 year old harpy with a taste for young human flesh. ITV 2009.

Dempsey and Makepeace Michael Brandon (Lt James Dempsey), Glynis Barber (Det Sgt Harriet Makepeace), Ray Smith (Chief Supt Gordon Spikings), Tony Osoba (DS Charles Jarvis). A streetwise New York cop from Manhattan's Ninth Precinct, who was forced to kill his own partner after unearthing corruption, is transferred to Britain and forms an uneasy partnership with Lady Harriet Makepeace, a stunning blonde aristocrat with a distant claim to the throne. They work for S110, a covert division of Scotland Yard. The two stars later married in real-life. ITV 1985-86.

Department S Peter Wyngarde (Jason King), Joel Fabiani (Stewart Sullivan), Rosemary Nichols (Annabelle Hurst), Dennis Alaba Peters (Sir Curtis Seretse). Created by Monty Berman and Dennis Spooner. Three special agents solve impossible cases on behalf of B501 a secret government department controlled by Sir Curtis Seretse. ITV 1969-70. See also entry for *Jason King*.

Desert Island Discs Originally introduced by Roy Plomley and now the longest running music programme in the history of radio. Guests are invited to imagine themselves as "castaways" on a desert island, and asked to choose the eight pieces of music they would take with them; discussion of their choices permits a review of their life. They also choose one book (excluding the Bible and the works of Shakespeare which are already deemed present on the island) and one luxury item which must be inanimate and have no practical use. The signature tune is called *By the Sleepy Lagoon* by Eric Coates. The first castaway on 29 January 1942 was comedian (and son-in-law of Winston Churchill having been married to Sarah Churchill from 1936-1945) Vic Oliver (born Victor Oliver von Samek in Vienna, Austria, 8 July 1898 – d. 15 August 1964). Several Prime Ministers of the United Kingdom have been guests on the programme, although only John Major appeared while in office. Other guests have included Noël Coward, Dame Judi Dench, John Malkovich, Princess Margaret, George Clooney, Stephen Hawking, John Cleese and Rowan Williams. After Roy Plomley's death in 1985, *Desert Island Discs* was presented by Michael Parkinson (1985-88), Sue Lawley (1988-2006) and Kirsty Young (2006-). BBC Radio 4 1942-

Desmond's Norman Beaton (Desmond Ambrose), Carmen Munroe (Shirley Ambrose), Ram John Holder (Porkpie Grant). Sitcom based around a Peckham barber's shop; the hub of the local West Indian community. C4 1989-94.

Detectives, The Jasper Carrott (DC Bob Louis), Robert Powell (DC Dave Briggs), George Sewell (Supt Frank Cottam). Sitcom created by Steve Knight and Mike Whitehill, concerning two inept police detectives who bumble their way through various cases, often achieving results despite themselves. BBC1 1993-97.

Dial 999 Robert Beatty (DI Mike Maguire), Duncan Lamont (DI Winter), John Witty (DS West). Canadian Mountie Mike Maguire is seconded to London on work experience. The opening of each of the 39 episodes began with a night view of London across the Thames with the cigarette-smoking Maguire uttering "Dial 9-9-9. When in London, that's what you do to call the police. I know- I'm a policeman from Canada attached to Scotland Yard. My name's Mike Maguire." ITV 1958-59.

Dick and Dom in da Bungalow Saturday morning children's show hosted by Richard McCourt and Dominic Wood. Six children take part in games to win prizes. One of the most popular items of the show concerns the two hosts visiting various public places and shouting the word "BOGIES" louder than their invited guests! BBC and digital CBBC Channel 2002- 06

Dick and Dom's Ask the Family See *Ask the Family*

Dick Barton - Special Agent Noel Johnson (Dick Barton), Alex McCrindle (Jock Anderson), John Mann (Snowey White). Dick Barton appeared in 711 fifteen-minute episodes between 1946 and 1951 on the Light Programme beginning at 6.45 pm on Monday, 7 October 1946. With his two best mates by his side, Jock and Snowey, and a host of crime-busting gadgets, the former Captain Richard Barton of the Commandos became a national hero in post-war Britain. At his peak, over 15 million listeners tuned in to his adventures. Dick's Girlfriend (who made an early exit) was Jean Hunter, played by Lorna Dermott. The announcer who rapped out 'Dick Barton...Special Agent!' was Hamilton Humphries. Although Geoffrey Webb and Edward J. Mason wrote the radio scripts, Barton was actually created by BBC producer Norman Collins, who had visions of a "cloak and dagger soap opera" every evening. The producer was Neil Tuson. The first series ended on 30 May 1947, but Dick was back on 6 October in a new serial. The third series, beginning with 'The JB Case', started 20 September 1948. The serial beginning 26 September 1949 introduced a new Dick Barton, Duncan Carse, a real-life adventurer and oceanographer. The announcer was changed, too; John Fitchen replacing Humphries. Another Dick Barton, Gordon Davies, took over from 3 October 1950, with a new producer, Archie Campbell. The final episode was broadcast on 30 March 1951. There was a two-week, 10 part revival for the BBC's Jubilee, starting 6 November 1972. Noel Johnson and John Mann reprising their partnership. The signature tune was *The Devil's Gallop* composed by Charles Williams. A short-lived ITV television series of 1979 was broadcast with Tony Vogel as Dick, Anthony Heaton as Snowey, and James Cosmo as Jock.

Dick Emery Show, The See entry for Dick Emery in the comedy section.

Dick Turpin Richard O'Sullivan (Dick Turpin), Michael Deeks ('Swift' Nick Smith), Christopher Benjamin (Sir John Glutton), David Daker (Capt Nathan Spiker), Alfie Bass (Isaac Rag). Tales of the 18th-century highwayman. ITV 1979-82.

Dickinson's Real Deal See *The David Dickinson Show*.

Didn't They Do Well! Game show vehicle for Bruce Forsyth where studio contestants are pitted against actual questions from BBC quizzes shown in the past and asked by way of archive footage by the likes of Noel Edmonds, Anne Robinson, Jeremy Paxman, Kenny Everett and Mike Read. The jackpot was £32,000. BBC1 2004

Diggit Children's TV show which replaced *Saturday Disney,* and *Disney Club* on Sunday mornings and consisted of mainly Disney cartoons although *Sonic Underground* was a notable exception. Originally presented by Paul Ballard (known on screen as Des) and Fearne Cotton, other presenters included Liam Dolan, Victoria Hickson, Phil Gallagher (Voiceover), Laura Jaye, Danielle Nicholls, Abbie Pethullis, Gail Porter, Jack Stratton and Reggie Yates. The shows name changed to *Diggin' It* in 2003 and aptly included a giant puppet named "It". ITV 1998-2005. See also *Up on the Roof* and *Toonattik*.

Dinner Date Reality dating/cooking show in which a person chooses three dates from a pool of five suitors based on the menus they have prepared. In a format similar to *Come Dine With Me* the person then attends dinner with their three blind dates before deciding on which one to have another date with at the expense of the production company. ITV 2010-

Dinnerladies Victoria Wood (Brenda Furlong), Thelma Barlow (Dolly Bellfield), Celia Imrie (Philippa Moorcroft), Maxine Peake (Twinkle), Anne Reid (Jean), Duncan Preston (Stan Meadowcroft), Andrew Dunn (Tony Martin), Shobna Gulati (Anita), Julie Walters (Petula Gardeno), Christopher Greet (Mr Michael), Jane Hazlegrove (Lisa), Sue Devaney (Jane). Sitcom written by Victoria Wood. Bren works in the factory canteen at HWD Components based in Manchester. The canteen is managed by Tony, who has a "thing" for Bren (he is a chemotherapy survivor who later becomes her boyfriend). Julie Walters plays a marvellous cameo role as Bren's dotty mum, Petula (who lives in a caravan). The title is deliberately billed with a lower-case 'd'. BBC1 1998-2000.

District Nurse Nerys Hughes (Megan Roberts), John Ogwen (David Price), Margaret John (Gwen Harries), Philip Raymond (Hugh Morris), Rio Fanning (Dr O'Casey), Deborah Manship (Nesta Mogg), Ken Morgan (Teg), Gareth Potter (Bryn Morris), Ian Saynor (Dylan Roderick), Elen Roger Jones (Sarah Hopkin), Ifan Huw Dafydd (Revd Geraint Rhys), Freddie Jones (Dr Emlyn Isaacs). Created by Tony Holland and Julia Smith, this popular series concerned the new health visitor of the conservative South Wales mining village of Pencwm during the late 1920s. Megan Roberts is from North Wales and is viewed with some suspicion initially but manages to win over the locals. For the third series (now set in 1932), Megan has moved to the seaside town of Glanmor, where she resides in the busy household of Dr Isaacs. BBC1 1984-87.

Divided Daytime quiz show hosted by Andrew Castle. Three contestants pool their knowledge in order to get through several rounds of questions, the first round consisting of five, the second four, the third three and the fourth two. The questions are worth more money as the team progresses although their value diminishes the longer they take to answer. The team is allowed two wrong answers, the penalty being the halving of the accumulated fund, or else leave with nothing. They can choose to leave at the end of any round but the decision must be unanimous. There is a cruel twist at the end whereby the accumulated fund is divided into three unequal shares, the players having to decide which share they deserve, the time and money ebbing away the longer they pontificate. After 100 seconds the fund becomes zero. ITV 2009-10

Dixon of Dock Green Jack Warner (PC/Sgt George Dixon), Peter Byrne (PC/DC/DS/DI Andy Crawford), Billie Whitelaw, Jeanette Hutchinson and Anna Dawson (Mary Dixon/Crawford), Arthur Rigby (Sgt Flint). The popular series was the creation of writer Ted Willis, who not only wrote the series over its 20 years on British television but also had a controlling hand in the production. Altogether some 307 episodes were made, at first running 30 minutes and later clocking in at 45 minutes. And of course the early episodes were in black and white while the later ones were in colour. The figures of both Dixon and Warner were already well known to the British public from the cameo role in the 1949 Ealing film *The Blue Lamp*, where the warm, avuncular policeman was shot and killed at the hands of a young thug (played by Dirk Bogarde). In the television series Dixon was the stereotypical 'bobby-on-the-beat', with a heart of gold. A widower raising an only daughter Mary (later to marry Andy Crawford), Dixon was promoted in1964, replacing Sgt Flint as desk sergeant. BBC1 1955-76.

Do Not Adjust Your Set Written and performed by Eric Idle, Michael Palin and Terry Jones. Billed as 'The Fairly Pointless Show' this children's comedy sketch show was the direct forerunner of Monty Python and introduced the wonderful animations of Terry Gilliam to the surreal world that was to become Python. A highlight of the show was the Captain Fantastic slot (played by David Jason) who was constantly thwarting death at the hands of his nemesis Mrs Black (played by Denise Coffey). The Bonzo Dog Doo-Dah Band provided the musical interlude to this ground-breaking children's series which appealed to all ages. ITV 1967-69.

Doc Martin Martin Clunes (Dr Martin Ellingham), Stewart Wright (PC Mark Mylow), Stephanie Cole (Joan Norton), Joe Absolom (Al Large), Ian McNeice, Lucy Punch (Elaine Denham), Caroline Catz (Louisa Glasson), Katherine Parkinson (Pauline Lamb), Dame Eileen Atkins (Aunt Ruth), Jessica Ransom (Morwenna Newcross), Louise Jameson (Eleanor Glasson). Comedy drama series created by Dominic Minghella. Surgeon Martin Ellingham's glittering career comes crashing down around him when he develops a blood-phobia which prevents him conducting operations. He makes a life-changing decision to retrain as a GP, and applies for a vacant post in the sleepy Cornish hamlet of Portwenn, where he spent childhood holidays. If the patients were expecting tea and sympathy from their curmudgeonly GP they were soon disappointed. Despite his surgical brilliance, he has no personnel skills, and his understanding of humans is practically non-existent. ITV 2004-. Clunes starred in a television film of the same name in 2003 playing Dr Martin Bamford (first played by Clunes in the 2000 television film *Saving Grace* and reprised in *Doc Martin and the Legend of the Cloutie* later in 2003). Although this character visits a small Cornish fishing village (Port Isaac), that is where the similarity ends and the characters are totally different.

Doctor Finlay Tannochbrae 20 yrs on (real-life Auchtermuchty in Fife) with Dr Finlay played by David Rintoul and the character's Christian name changed to John. Dr Cameron was played by Ian Bannen and Janet by Annette Crosbie. ITV 1993-96. See *Dr Finlay's Casebook*

Doctor in the House Barry Evans (Michael Upton), Robin Nedwell (Duncan Waring), Geoffrey Davies (Dick Stuart-Clark), George Layton (Paul Collier), Martin Shaw (Huw Evans), Ernest Clark (Professor Geoffrey Loftus). Based on the books by Richard Gordon, the medical sitcom was set at St Swithins Teaching Hospital. John Cleese wrote several episodes of both this series and the spin-offs. ITV 1969-70. Spin-off series' included *Doctor at Large* (1971) and *Doctor in Charge* (1972-73), both starring Richard O'Sullivan as nerdy Laurence Bingham, *Doctor at Sea* (1974). *Doctor on the Go* (1975-77) and *Doctor Down Under* (1981).

Doctors Weekday medical soap set in the fictional Midland town of Letherbridge, somewhere close to Birmingham. Its storylines deal with the lives of staff and patients at the fictional Mill Health Centre and its offshoot, Letherbridge University's Campus Surgery, although earlier episodes were set at the Riverside Surgery and, later in the storyline, The Best Practice was also featured. Initially the soap focused on reformed alcoholic Mac Mcguire and his team. His Mill Health Centre managed by his wife Kate. Recent cast members in alphabetical order include: Sophie Abelson (Cherry Malone), Owen Brenman (Dr. Heston Carter), Matthew Chambers (Dr. Daniel Granger), Charlie Clemmow (Imogen Hollins), Lu Corfield (Dr. Freya Wilson), Elisabeth Dermot-Walsh (Dr. Zara Carmichael), Janet Dibley (Dr Elaine Cassidy), Diane Keen (Julia Parsons), Lorna Laidlaw (Mrs. Tembe), Marian McLoughlin (Marina Bonnaire), Adrian Lewis Morgan (Dr. Jimmi Clay), Jan Pearson (Karen Hollins), Simon Rivers (Dr. Kevin Tyler), Chris Walker (Sgt Rob Hollins), Nicolas Woodman (Jack Hollins). Former cast members include: Mark Adams (Phil Thompson), Lysette Anthony (Joanne Oaksey 2007; Marcelle D'Arby 2010), Nicole Arumugam (Dr Kali Hamada), Donnaleigh Bailey (Michelle Corrigan), Ariyon Bakare (Dr Benjamin Kwarme), Colin Baker (Charles Dillon), Lynda Baron (Barbara Cross), Amanda Barrie (Margo Phillips), Gary Beadle (PC Wilson), Jean Boht (Sylvia Wharton), Yvonne Brewster (Ruth Harding), Guy Burgess (Jerry Walsh), Tom Butcher (Dr Marc Eliot), Selina Chilton (Ruth Pearce), Maggie Cronin (Kate McGuire), Darren Day (David Wilde), Barbara Drennan (Leigh Ashworth), Sharon Duce (Rachel Wilson), Ray

Fearon (Malcolm Tumelo), Eva Fontaine (Faith Walker), Brigit Forsyth (Pauline Hasland), Mark Frost (Dr Steve Rawlings), Gareth Hale (Eddie Platt), Vicky Hall (Trudy Wilson), Seeta Indrani (Dr. Lily Hassan), Sue Jenkins (Brenda MacGyver), Jacqueline King (Wendy Sheffield), Akbar Kurtha (Dr Rana Mistry), Ian Lavender (Ian Bardwell), Charles Lawson (Bill McQueen), Jacqueline Leonard (Dr Caroline Powers), Neil McCaul (Howard Bond), Philip McGough (Dr. Charlie Bradfield), Sarah Manners (Joanna Helm), Sarah Matravers (Gabby French), Rita May (Eileen Neville), Carli Norris (Anoushka Flynn), Tom O'Connor (Father Tom), Tessa Peake-Jones (Sue Bond), Laurence Penry-Jones (Dr Oliver Berg), Colin Prockter (David Allen), Ian Reddington (Martin Brown), Natalie J. Robb (Dr Jude Carlyle), Ted Robbins (Kenny Rock), Alan Rothwell (Frank Conway), Paul Shane (Bill Joseph), Richard Standing (Father David), Sheila Steafel (Dorothy Maples), David Sturzaker (Dr. Simon Bond), Sylvia Syms (Dorothy Holland), Mary Tamm (Jemma Forrester), Roberta Taylor (Rachel Whiting), Christopher Timothy (Dr Brendan 'Mac' McGuire 2000-06), Tabitha Wady (Katrina Bullen), Corrinne Wicks (Dr Helen Thompson). BBC1 2000-

Dombey and Son Julian Glover (Paul Dombey), Lysette Anthony (Florence Dombey), Shirley Cain (Miss Tox), Emrys James (Captain Cuttle), Sharon Maughan (Edith Dombey), James Cossins (Major Bagstock), Max Gold (Walter Gay), Jenny McCracken (Polly Toodle), Barbara Hicks (Mrs Pipchin), Neal Swettenham (Mr Toots). Ten-part mini-series based on the classic Dickens' novel. BBC1 1983.

Don Quick, The Adventures of A short-lived attempt by LWT to bring adult concepts combined with satire and sci-fi that lasted just six episodes. The stories were loosely based on the adventures of Don Quixote and featured Ian Hendry as Captain Don Quick - a member of the Intergalactic Maintenance Squad. Along with his sidekick Sgt. Sam Czopanser (Ronald Lacey) he would land on a different planet each week to carry out some routine maintenance, and become embroiled in trying to right imaginary wrongs. His delusions of grandeur would result in him imagining himself to be an ambassador for Earth and he invariably upset local traditions and balances resulting in negative consequences for the population. ITV 1970.

Donovan Tom Conti (Joe Donovan), Samantha Bond (Kate Donovan), Ryan Cartwright (Seth Donovan), Amelia Bullmore (Evie Strauss). Drama written by Mike Cullen. A retired forensic expert is called back to work when his name is found written in blood on the wall at the scene of a murder. Pathologist (Joe) Donovan heads a team of FIU (Forensics Investigation Unit) operatives who solve crime using scientific means. ITV 2004-05

Don't Ask Me Popular science programme featuring David Bellamy, Magnus Pyke and Miriam Stoppard answering questions from a studio audience. Presenters and pundits included Derek Griffiths, Colin Welland, Marion Davies, Maggie Makepiece, Adrienne Posta, Austin Mitchell, Rob Buckman and Brian Glover. The flute-driven theme was House Of The King by Dutch rock band Focus (the B-side of chart hit Sylvia). The programme's title was changed to *Don't Just Sit There* in 1979. ITV 1974-79.

Don't Call Me Stupid Celebrity version of *Swapheads*, hosted by Alexander Armstrong. ITV 2007. The show featuring Michael Howard and Wayne Sleep, although part of the original series, was not broadcast until June 2009. The parliamentary register of members' interests listed Michael Howard's fee as between £5000 and £10,000 for appearing on this show, while George Galloway commanded a fee of between £10,000 and £15,000.

Don't Drink the Water See *On The Buses.*

Don't Feed The Gondolas Irish topical panel show similar in format to the BBC's *Have I Got News For You*. The host was Seán Moncrieff, and the regular panellists were Brendan O'Connor and Dara Ó Briain. A running gag throughout the series had the host making prank calls under the alias 'Monica Loolly', claiming to be from a small town in Galway named Ahascragh. The show's title derives from a remark made by a Wicklow County Councillor, during a meeting regarding Blessington Lake, a reservoir in Co Wicklow. When the meeting proposed putting a gondola on the lake, he remarked: "That's all very well, but who's going to feed it? RTÉ 1998-2000

Don't Forget Your Toothbrush Live Saturday night game show hosted by Chris Evans. The ultimate winning prize was a holiday. There would be two on offer but to qualify you needed to have a passport and you needed to have the next seven days off work and be prepared to leave immediately after the show (hence the title). Two series were made, the first co-hosted with Rachel Tatton-Brown and the second with Jadine Doran. C4 1994-95.

Don't Get Done, Get Dom Reality television series which helps consumers get good deals when purchasing goods. Presented by Dominic Littlewood. BBC1 2006-

Don't Just Sit There See *Don't Ask Me*

Don't Scare the Hare Game show hosted by the white-bespectacled Jason Bradbury and narrated by Sue Perkins. Contestants attempted a series of challenges to win prize money of £15,000 - failure to successfully complete the challenges risked "scaring" a giant robotic hare. The prime-time Saturday evening show was cancelled after six episodes due to poor ratings. BBC1 2011

Don't Try This At Home Saturday evening challenge game show presented by Davina McCall featuring members of the public performing daredevil challenges. Davina's co-presenters included Darren Day (series 1 only), Kate Thornton, and Paul Hendy. The show was narrated by Russ Williams. ITV 1998-2001

Don't Wait Up Nigel Havers (Dr Tom Latimer), Tony Britton (Dr Toby Latimer), Jane How (Helen Latimer), Dinah Sheridan (Angela Latimer). Written by George Layton. Sitcom concerning father and son doctors forced to share a flat. Tom is a hardworking National Health Service GP while his father a rather pompous Harley Street dermatologist. BBC1 1983-90.

Doomwatch John Paul (Dr Spencer Quist), Simon Oates (Dr John Ridge), Joby Blanshard (Colin Bradley), Robert Powell (Tobias 'Toby' Wren). Created by Kit Pedler and Gerry Davis (creators of the Cybermen for the *Dr Who* series) and billed as science-fact rather than science-fiction, Doomwatch was a drama series concentrating on the dangers and threats to world ecology, both natural and man-made. The Department of Observation and Measurement of Scientific Work (nicknamed Doomwatch)- is a section of the Ministry of National Security whose remit is to act as a watchdog group investigating current scientific work, and ensuring that the welfare of the general public and the environmental is not compromised. It is led by Doctor Spencer Quist, a gruff no-nonsense Nobel Prize-winning mathematician, who is driven to champion the cause for ecological awareness following his work on the Manhattan Project (creation of the first atom bomb) and the death of his wife Helena of radiation poisoning. He is assisted by Doctor John Ridge, a chemist in his late thirties who is not only a ladies' man, but who also has a shady past and connections to MI6 and Colin Bradley, the team's electronics engineer, who looks after the department's computer and undertakes any required scientific tests. Other members would come and go over the three seasons, but particularly well-known is Toby Wren, a physics postgraduate from Cambridge who meets a dramatic end in season one's finale *Survival Code*. BBC1 1970-72. A feature film based on the series was made in 1972.

Door, The Two-part game show hosted by Chris Tarrant and Amanda Holden. Six celebrities passed through a series of doors and took on a number of tough challenges, the last star standing claiming a cash prize for their chosen charity. The contestants were The Saturdays singer Frankie Sandford (Eliminated first); actresses Louisa Lytton and Jennie McAlpine (Eliminated 2nd and 3rd respectively); television present Michael Underwood (placed 3rd), actor Dean Gaffney (runner-up) and Boyzone member Keith Duffy (the winner). ITV 2010.

Dotto Game show hosted by Robert Gladwell, Jimmy Hanley and Shaw Taylor during its two year run. Two contestants answered questions in order to join dots to reveal a celebrity's face. The first contestant to guess the mystery person received a cash sum for every unjoined dot left on the board (there were 50 dots at start of play). The series was based on an American show which was taken off as part of the 'Quiz Show Scandal' whereby sponsors of the show were accused of favouring interesting contestants and feeding them answers so they could continue as reigning champions. ITV 1958-60.

Double Your Money Originally airing on Radio Luxembourg this popular quiz show was transferred to television in 1955 with its host, Hughie Green, reprising his role. London-born Hughie (1920–97) was a child star of stage and screen before serving as a pilot in the Royal Canadian Air Force. After his death from lung cancer the story broke that he was the father of television presenter Paula Yates. In this long-running series contestants answered questions on a selected subject and doubled their money from £1 to £32 and were then given a chance to play for up to £1,000 on the Treasure Trail Game. Bobby Charlton won the jackpot of £1,000 answering questions on pop music. Hughie's assistants included Valerie Drew, Jean Clarke, Julie De Marco, Nancy Roberts, Sabrina, Barbara Roscoe and Anita West. He also had two former contestants as hostesses, Alice Earrey (a 77-year-old former char lady) and the most famous of all, Monica Rose. Chirpy cockney Monica won £8 answering questions on famous women as a 15-year-old in 1963 and became an instant hit with her matter-of-fact irreverent behaviour. Hughie invited her back as hostess and she remained as such throughout the final four years of the show's run. The theme song went: *Double Your Money and try to get rich, Double Your Money, without any hitch, Double Your Money, it's your lucky day, Double Your Money and take it away!* ITV 1955-68. The show was revamped in 1971 and was renamed *The Sky's The Limit* and ran on ITV until 1974 with Hughie and Monica co-hosting (Monica tragically committed suicide in 1994, aged 45). See *Take Your Pick*

Down the Gate Reg Varney (Reg Furnell), Dilys Laye (Irene Furnell), Reg Lye (Old Wol), Tony Melody (Len Peacock), Percy Herbert (Mr Preston). Sitcom set in Billingsgate fish market and written by Maurice Sellar and Roy Tuvey. Reg Varney created the series, his character being a fish porter happily married to the social-climbing Irene, who was forever trying to impress important people such as the bank manager, and would lose her cool whenever her husband came home late and stinking of mackerel. Reg's best mate was 'Old Wol', and Mr Preston was his demanding boss. ITV 1975-76

Down the Line Spoof radio phone-in created by *The Fast Show* team of Paul Whitehouse and Charlie Higson. *Down The Line* is hosted by Gary Bellamy (played by Rhys Thomas). Regular 'callers' include: Christopher Nibbs from Pevensey Bay; who refers to himself as 'Nibbsy' or 'The Nibbster'; Khalid, who only repeats previous topics of the show followed by the stock phrase 'what is point?'; the 'pearly king', a cheery cockney who talks about the 'pearly way'; Humphrey Milner; an elderly gentleman who uses endless examples to illustrate his point; Graham Downs, a morbidly obese loser with a sinus problem who often says he would "really like to get married"; Chuck Perry, who laughs uncontrollably at his own jokes; and the military man, who responds to every topic stating that he is from a military background and that he would drive a van packed with explosives into the "issue" be it education or global warming. Contributors include: Paul Whitehouse, Charlie Higson, Simon Day, Lucy Montgomery, Amelia Bullmore, Matt Lucas, Felix Dexter, Mark Gatiss, Catherine Tate, Arabella Weir, Robert Popper, Louis Vause, Simon Godley, Phoebe Higson, Sam Ward, Dave Cummings, and Fiona Whitehouse. BBC Radio 4 2006-11

Downton Abbey Dame Maggie Smith (Violet, Dowager Countess of Grantham), Hugh Bonneville (Robert, Earl of Grantham), Elizabeth McGovern (Cora, Countess of Grantham), Penelope Wilton (Mrs Isobel Crawley), Dan Stevens (Matthew Crawley), Michelle Dockery (Lady Mary Crawley), Laura Carmichael (Lady Edith Crawley), Jessica Brown Findlay (Lady Sybil Crawley), Jim Carter (Charles Carson - the butler), Phyllis Logan (Mrs Elsie Hughes - the housekeeper), Lesley Nicol (Mrs Patmore -the cook), Brendan Coyle (John Bates – Lord Grantham's valet), Siobhan Finneran (Sarah O'Brien – Lady Grantham's maid), Rob James-Collier (Thomas - the first footman), Thomas Howes (William Mason - second footman), Joanne Froggatt (Anna Smith - head housemaid), Rose Leslie (Gwen Dawson - housemaid), Sophie McShera (Daisy – scullery maid), Christine Lohr (Mrs Bird - Matthew Crawley's Cook), Allen Leech (Tom Branson - chauffeur), Andrew Westfield (Lynch - groom), Kevin Doyle (Joseph Molesley - Matthew Crawley's butler and valet), Nicky Henson (Mr Charles Grigg), Allen Leech (Tom Branson), Brendan Patricks (The Hon. Evelyn Napier), Theo James (Mr Kemal Pamuk), Charlie Cox (Duke of Crowborough), Robert Bathurst (Sir Anthony Strallan), Samantha Bond (Lady Rosamund Painswick), Zoe Boyle (Miss Lavinia Swire), Cal Macaninch (Henry Lang), Clare Calbraith (Jane Moorsum), Iain Glen (Sir Richard Carlisle), Maria Doyle Kennedy (Vera Bates), Lachlan Nieboer (Lieutenant Edward Courtenay), Daniel Pirrie (Major Charles Bryant), Trevor White (Major Patrick Gordon), Paul Copley (Mr Mason), Kevin McNally (Mr Bryant), Christine Mackie (Mrs Bryant). Nigel Havers appeared as Lord Hepworth in the 2011 Christmas special. Drama series written by Julian Fellowes, Shelagh Stephenson and Tina Pepler. Set in 1912, in a stately home named Downton Abbey, it follows the lives of the aristocratic Crawley family and the servants who work for them. Lord and Lady Carnarvon gave permission for their Highclere Castle home in Berkshire to be used as Downton Abbey although the servant's living quarters were constructed at Ealing Studios and outdoor scenes were filmed at Bampton in Oxfordshire. ITV 2010-

Down Your Way BBC radio series which ran from 1946 to 1992, originally on the Home Service and then on BBC Radio 4, usually broadcast on Sundays. It visited towns around the United Kingdom, spoke to residents and played their choice of music. It vividly evoked the local and regional distinctiveness as it roved around the United Kingdom. The first edition on 29th December 1946 visited Lambeth and featured local man-about-town Montague 'Monty' Modlyn (1921-94) who later became a popular radio and television presenter known for his acquired cockney accent and direct interview technique. *Down Your Way* was hosted by Stewart MacPherson (from its inception until 1950), Richard Dimbleby (1950-55), Franklin Engelmann (1955 until his death in 1972) and Brian Johnston (1972-87). In 1975, despite then being the second most popular programme on radio, it was taken off the air as an 'economy measure'. It was subsequently reinstated, after a storm of popular protest. From 1987 until its demise in 1992 it had a different celebrity host every week, who would visit a place of significance in their own lives - effectively turning it into "Down My Way" and blending it into the then-emerging celebrity culture. Its gentle signature tune was called *Horseguards, Whitehall* by Haydn Wood (composer of the popular second world war song *Roses of Picardy*).

Dr Finlay's Casebook Bill Simpson (Dr Alan Finlay), Andrew Cruickshank (Dr Angus Cameron), Barbara Mullen (Janet). Hugely popular medical drama set in 1920's Tannochbrae (real-life Callander). The base for the practice was Arden House. The stories were based on *The Adventures of a Black Bag* by doctor-novelist AJ Cronin (dramatised on Radio 4 in 2001 with John Gordon-Sinclair as Dr Finlay). BBC2 1962-71.

Dr Who First Dr Who was William Hartnell (1963-66) followed by Patrick Troughton (1966-69), Jon Pertwee (1970-74), Tom Baker (1974-81), Peter Davison (1982-84), Colin Baker (1984-86), Sylvester McCoy (1987-89, 1996), Paul McGann (1996), Christopher Eccleston (2005), David Tennant (2006-10) and Matt Smith (2010-). Other television Doctors have included Richard Hurndall who took William Hartnell's part in The Five Doctors (1983), Trevor Martin who played the part in a stage play in 1974, Richard E Grant who played the Doctor in an internet-only audio drama, Joanna Lumley who played the Doctor in a Comic-Relief spoof, and Peter Cushing who appeared as the Doctor in two Feature Films. The original crew were William Russell (Ian Chesterton), Jacqueline Hill (Barbara Wright), and Carole Ann Ford (Susan Foreman, the Doctor's granddaughter). Other assistants include, in the Hartnell era:, Maureen O'Brien (Vicki), Peter Purves (Steven Taylor), Jackie Lane (Dorothea 'Dodo' Chaplet), Michael Craze (Ben Jackson), Anneke Wills (Polly); in the Troughton era: Michael Craze (Ben Jackson), Anneke Wills (Polly), Frazer Hines (Jamie McCrimmon), Deborah Watling (Victoria Waterfield), Wendy Padbury (Zoe Herriot); in the Pertwee era: Caroline John (Liz Shaw), Katy Manning (Jo Grant), Elizabeth Sladen (Sarah Jane Smith); in the Tom Baker era:

Elizabeth Sladen (Sarah Jane Smith), Ian Marter (Surgeon-Lt Harry Sullivan), Louise Jameson (Leela), Mary Tamm & Lalla Ward (Romanadvoratrelundar 'Romana'), Matthew Waterhouse (Adric), Sarah Sutton (Nyssa), Janet Fielding (Tegan Jovanka), voices of John Leeson and David Brierley (K9); in the Davison era: Matthew Waterhouse (Adric), Sarah Sutton (Nyssa), Janet Fielding (Tegan Jovanka), Mark Strickson (Vizlor Turlough), Nicola Bryant (Perpugillian 'Peri' Brown); in the Colin Baker era: Nicola Bryant (Perpugillian 'Peri' Brown), Bonnie Langford (Melanie Bush); in the McCoy era: Bonnie Langford (Melanie Bush), Sophie Aldred (Dorothy 'Ace'); in the McGann film: Daphne Ashbrook (Dr Grace Holloway), Yee Jee Tso (Chang Lee). The Doctor is from the Planet Gallifrey. The six actors who have played the Master are (1) Roger Delgado, (2) Peter Pratt, (3) Geoffrey Beevers, (4) Anthony Ainley, (5) Eric Roberts, (6) John Simm (who regenerated from the Professor Yana character played by Derek Jacobi during the David Tennant era. Tardis: Time And Relative Dimension In Space. The series was axed in 1989 but resurrected in March 2005, the Doctor being played by Christopher Eccleston, and his assistant Rose Tyler, by Billie Piper. Their first adversaries were the Autons and the series was mainly written by Russell T Davies, who also acted as an Executive Producer. Eccleston left after one series and was replaced by David Tennant. Noel Clarke joined Billie Piper briefly as assistant to the David Tennant regeneration and both Elizabeth Sladen and K9 reprised their earlier roles in an episode during this period. Billie Piper left the series in the autumn of 2006 and was replaced by Freema Agyeman as the Time-lord's assistant Martha Jones. Comedian Catherine Tate replaced Agyeman in 2008, reprising her role of Donna Noble from the Christmas special of 2007. Both Piper and Agyeman made guest appearances in subsequent episodes. In an episode in the 2008 series, The Doctor's Daughter, the Timelord gave birth to a daughter on the planet Messaline by cell reproduction. Donna dubbed this generated anomaly Jenny. Jenny (Georgia Moffett) was shot at the end of the episode but in true Timelord fashion was resurrected and began her own journey through space. At Easter 2010 the Matt Smith era began with Karen Gillan as his assistant Amy Pond, and Arthur Darvill accompanying them briefly as Rory, Amy's fiancé but becoming more of a regular feature in 2011. First broadcast on BBC 1, 23 November 1963, the classic sci-fi series was an instant hit. The opening episode, An Unearthly Child, saw schoolteachers Barbara Wright and Ian Chesterton become intrigued by one of their pupils, Susan Foreman, who shows uncommon ability in the sciences but lacks rudimentary knowledge of other subjects. They visit her home address - a junkyard at 76 Totters Lane - where they meet her grandfather, the Doctor. The Doctor and Susan are aliens who travel through time and space in their ship, the TARDIS, which looks like an ordinary police box but actually houses a huge gleaming control room. The TARDIS takes the four of them to a pre-historic Earth landscape where they encounter a tribe that has lost the secret of fire. The series really took off the following month when the intrepid travellers landed on the planet Skaro where they met two indigenous races - the Daleks, malicious mutant creatures of the Kaled race saved by a power-crazed scientist Davros and encased in armoured super-structures, and the Thals, beautiful humanoids with pacifist principles. The Daleks at this time, although very scary with their eerie silent movement, roving eye and deadly ray gun attachment, were limited to travel within their metallic city but this inevitable drawback to world domination was eventually addressed and they were later able to ascend stairs by the power of flight. Other popular super-villains include, the Cybermen (silver robots from Earth's twin planet, Mondas), the Martian Ice Warriors, the Zarbi (giant ants), the Yeti (furry robots based on the abominable snowman), the Sea Devils (underwater creatures who surface to reclaim the planet), the Silurians (reptilian relatives of the Sea Devils) and The Rani (a deadly fellow Time Lord of the Doctor's played by Kate O'Mara). A radio version starring Jon Pertwee, Elizabeth Sladen and Nicholas Courtney (who played UNIT-United Nations Intelligence Taskforce- commander Lethbridge Stewart during the eras of Troughton, Pertwee, Tom Baker, Davison and McCoy) aired on Radio 5 in 1993 with a second serial aired on Radio 2 in 1996. Another spin-off series, *K9 and*

Friends, was shown in December 1981 (see also *The Sarah Jane Adventures* and *Torchwood*). Music to Dr Who was composed by Ron Grainer, initially realised by Delia Derbyshire of the BBC Radiophonic Workshop, and later rearranged by Peter Howell (1980), Dominic Glynn (1986), Keff McCulloch (1987), John Debney (1996) and Murray Gold (2005). The Daleks were the creation of Terry Nation (see *Blake's Seven*) and the main voice of the Daleks was actor Roy Skinner (almost as famous for voicing glove puppets Zippy and George in Rainbow). The series has spawned over 200 original novels and 100 audio dramas sold on CD. 108 episodes from the 1960s are currently missing, wiped by the BBC although some of them are saved as audio tapes. BBC 1 1963-89, 1996 and 2005-

Dragon's Den Reality show where entrepreneurs pitch their ideas to secure investment finance from the 'Dragons'; elite business experts, the premise being the 'contestants' must extract the whole of their asked-for funding from the multi-millionaire panellists or miss out completely. The series is presented by Evan Davis and the five original panellists were Duncan Bannatyne, Rachel Elnaugh (replaced by Deborah Meaden from series three), Peter Jones, Doug Richard (replaced by Richard Farleigh from series three and himself replaced by James Caan from series five who in turn was replaced by Hilary Devey from series nine) and Simon Woodroffe (replaced by Theo Paphitis from series two). The dramatic theme tune and background music were composed by John Watt. BBC2 2005- . Spin-off series include *Where Are They Now*, a follow-up on some of the projects success or otherwise and *Dragon's Den: Outside the Den*, a profile of the 'Dragons'.

Draw In Your Chair The Hogmanay favourite of the 1950s, with Roddy McMillan, *Draw In Your Chair* was the predecessor to *The White Heather Club*. It featured impromptu chat and traditional Scottish music, features which have been the mainstay of subsequent BBC Scotland Hogmanay shows.

Driving School The 1997 BBC 1 documentary series about the ups and downs of seven driving school pupils. Maureen Rees, a 55-year-old police station cleaner, was the undoubted star of the show and went on to become a star of other reality shows and was also honoured with a *This Is Your Life* show. Maureen's driving was awful and her poor bus-driving husband Dave often bore the brunt of her tongue in stressful situations.

Drop the Dead Donkey Robert Duncan (Gus Hedges), Neil Pearson (Dave Charnley), Jeff Rawle (George Dent), Stephen Tompkinson (Damien Day), David Swift (Henry Davenport), Haydn Gwynne (Alex Pates), Victoria Wicks (Sally Smedley). Topical satirical sitcom written by Andy Hamilton and Guy Jenkin and recorded the night before transmission in order to include breaking news. Gus Hedges is the editor of *Globelink News*, owned by the unseen Sir Royston Merchant. Original working title for the show was 'Dead Belgians Don't Count', the eventual title alluding to a story bumped from the news agenda by a more important story or time constraints. C4 1990-98.

Drumbeat Short-lived pop music showcase for the rock stars of the day, initially hosted by Gus Goodwin but soon replaced by Trevor Peacock. The show was devised as BBC's antidote to ITV's *Oh Boy* series and followed the quick-moving format (instead of Cliff Richard as a regular guest, Adam Faith was booked). Many of the top budding British rock stars appeared during its four-month run, including Billy Fury, Marti Wilde and Cliff Richard. BBC 1959.

Duchess of Dukes Street, The Gemma Jones (Louisa Leyton/Trotter), Christopher Cazenove (Charles Tyrrell), Richard Vernon (Major Toby Smith-Barton), Donald Burton (Augustus 'Gus' Trotter), (Maureen O'Brien (Lizzie), Jan Francis (Irene Baker), June Brown (Mrs Violet Leyton), Lalla Ward (Lottie). Loosely based on the life story of Rosa Lewis, a kitchen maid, who became manageress of the Cavendish Hotel in Jermyn Street. Louisa Trotter works her way up from being a skivvy to assistant chef and ultimately the owner of the Bentink Hotel, 20 Duke Street, London. Her life and happenings among the guests and staff of the hotel make up the 31 episodes. BBC1 1976-77.

Duel Hosted by Nick Hancock. Quiz show testing general knowledge and skill. Players took each other on in head-to-head duels of knowledge, battling for the jackpot, which started at £100,000 if four successful duels were completed. ITV 2008

Dumped Originally entitled Eco-Challenge, this reality television show involved 11 contestants living for three weeks on a purpose-built landfill site near Croydon in south London. Presented by Rob Holdway. C4 2007.

Dustbinmen, The John Woodvine and Brian Wilde (Bloody Delilah), Bryan Pringle ('Cheese and Egg' Petty), Graham Haberfield (Winston Platt), Trevor Bannister (Heavy Breathing), John Barrett ('Smelly' Ibbotson). Created and Produced by Jack Rosenthal, the sitcom concentrated on a gang of northern refuse collectors going about their daily shirking routine aboard their dustcart, affectionately dubbed 'The Thunderbird Three'. It was this series that established the word 'pigging' as a euphemism for the stronger sort of language that binmen might use given some of the circumstances the lads found themselves in. ITV 1969-70.

Duty Free Keith Barron (David Pearce), Gwen Taylor (Amy Pearce), Neil Stacy (Robert Cochran), Joanna Van Gyseghem (Linda Cochran), Carlos Douglas (Carlos). Sitcom written by Eric Chappell and Jean Warr. Two couples meet in a Spanish hotel and a relationship instantly transpires between the husband of one marriage (David) and the wife of the other (Joanna). Episodes reflected their desire to get things together while the spouses Amy and Neil tried their all to keep them apart. ITV 1984-86.

Eamonn Andrews Show Eamonn Andrews was born in Synge Street, Dublin, 19 December 1922. He began his career as an amateur boxer (becoming an All-Ireland Juvenile Champion) and went on to be a sports commentator on Radio Éireann. In 1950, he began presenting programmes for the BBC, notably, *What's My Line?* (1951-63 and 1984-87), *This Is Your Life* (1955-64), and *Crackerjack*. When *This Is Your Life* was revived by ITV in 1969 Eamonn again played the genial host until his death on 5 November 1987. Eamonn also chaired the Radio Éireann Authority between 1960 and 1964, overseeing the introduction of television to Ireland and establishing the Irish State Broadcaster as an independent semi-state body. Eamonn was much loved and much impersonated. His notoriety for dubious off-the-cuff links which didn't work — such as 'speaking of cheese sandwiches, have you come far?' was parodied by Seamus Android in the BBC radio programme *Round the Horne* in the 1960s. Despite all these achievements Eamonn was also the nation's top chat-show host. *The Eamonn Andrews Show* began on the BBC in 1956 and ran for two series. Written by Sid Green and Dick Hills it consisted of comedy sketches aided each week by numerous guest stars, including Spike Milligan (who appeared in three of the shows) and Warren Mitchell (two). In 1964 until 1969 Eamonn had his own late-night show on ITV, again called *The Eamonn Andrews Show*, but now a very different format. He maintained the light-hearted laid-back approach but now showed he was a natural interviewer of everyone from The Beatles to Muhammad Ali. He also introduced several popular music acts on his show, notably Clodagh Rodgers.

Early Doors John Henshaw (Ken Dixon), Craig Cash (Joe), Phil Mealey (Duffy), Mark Benton (Eddie Bell), Christine Bottomley (Melanie Bell), Lorraine Cheshire (Joan Bell), Susan Cookson (Tanya), Rodney Litchfield (Tommy), James McAvoy (Liam - Mel's boyfriend - Series 1), Rita May (Jean Dixon), James Quinn (Phil), Peter Wight (Nige), Lee Ingleby (Dean - Mel's boyfriend - Series 2), Lisa Millett (Debbie), Sue McArdle (Nicola), Maxine Peake (Janice), Joan Kempson (Winnie). Sitcom written by Craig Cash and Phil Mealey who also appear in the series playing best mates Joe and Duffy. The action is set in the Grapes, a small public house in Manchester, where Ken the landlord, son of Jean, father of Melanie and potential partner for part-time barmaid Tanya, attempts to maintain order among his motley regulars. The theme music for the series is "Small World" by Roddy Frame from the 2002 album *Surf*. BBC2 2003-04

Eastenders Long-running soap opera created by producer Julia Smith and script editor Tony Holland set in the fictional London Borough of Walford E20. EastEnders is filmed at the BBC Elstree Centre in Borehamwood, Hertfordshire. First broadcast on 19 February 1985 (Reg Cox was murdered by Nick Cotton in this episode), the action in EastEnders is centred in and around Albert Square and in particular The Queen Victoria Public House, street market, night club, car lot, community centre, café, chip shop, Walford East tube station and various residencies. Albert Square is thought to be based on the real life Fassett Square in Dalston, east London, an area where Tony Holland lived. In true soap fashion many of the families in Albert Square are related to each other in some form or other. In the early days the Watts, Fowlers and Beales were the mainstays before the Mitchells began to dominate proceedings with the Beales, Wicks, Butchers, Slaters, Brannings, Jacksons, Masoods and Johnsons all having a large family presence. Adam Woodyatt is the longest-serving member of the cast having been an ever-present since the very first episode. For its 25th anniversary in February 2010, a live episode of EastEnders was broadcast concerning the revelation of Archie Mitchell's (Larry Lamb) murderer, which ultimately turned out to be Stacey Slater although only actress Lacey turner was informed, literally 30 minutes before the episode commenced. The EastEnders theme tune was composed by Simon May and Leslie Osborne and has spawned several remixes notably a vocal version "Anyone Can Fall in Love", lyrics by Don Black, and recorded in 1986 by EastEnders cast member Anita Dobson, which reached number four on the UK Singles Chart. This was not the most successful song by a cast member however, that accolade goes to "Every Loser Wins", a 1986 No 1 for Nick Berry. Notable figures who have made appearances in Walford over the years have included Boris Johnson and Robbie Williams. The following is the present cast list as at the end of December 2011: Adam Woodyatt (Ian Beale), Dot Branning June Brown (Dot Cotton / Branning), Sid Owen (Ricky Butcher), Charlie Brooks (Janine Butcher - previously played by Rebecca Michael and Alexia Demetriou), Steve McFadden (Phil Mitchell), Lindsey Coulson (Carol Jackson), Patsy Palmer (Bianca Jackson), Hetti Bywater (Lucy Beale - previously played by Eva Brittin-Snell, Casey Anne Rothery and Melissa Suffield), Jamie Foreman (Derek Branning – previously played by Terence Beesley), Perry Fenwick (Billy Mitchell), James Forde (Liam Butcher - previously played by Jack and Tom Godolphin, Gavin and Mitchell Vaughan, Nathaniel Gleed), Laila Morse (Mo Harris), Rudolph Walker (Patrick Trueman), Joshua Pascoe (Ben Mitchell – previously played by Matthew Silver, Morgan Whittle and Charlie Jones), Jessie Wallace (Kat Moon), Shane Richie (Alfie Moon), Laurie Brett (Jane Beale), Nicola Stapleton (Mandy Salter), Gillian Wright (Jean Slater), Diane Parish (Denise Johnson / Fox), Jake Wood (Max Branning), Jo Joyner (Tanya Branning / Jessop), Lorna Fitzgerald (Abi Branning), Jacqueline Jossa (Lauren Branning – previously played by Madeline Duggan), Linda Henry (Shirley Carter), Jamie Borthwick (Jay Brown), Cheryl Fergison (Heather Trott), Nina Wadia (Zainab Masood), Steve John Shepherd (Michael Moon), Rita Simons (Roxy Mitchell), Himesh Patel (Tamwar Masood), Tanya Franks (Rainie Cross), Nitin Ganatra (Masood Ahmed), Scott Maslen (Jack Branning), John Partridge (Christian Clarke), Shona McGarty (Whitney Dean), Maisie Smith (Tiffany Dean), Marc Elliott (Syed Masood), Meryl Fernandes (Afia Khan), Tameka Empson (Kim Fox), Ricky Norwood (Fatboy), Danielle Harold (Lola Pearce), George Layton (Norman Simmonds), Michael French (David Wicks), Tony Discipline (Tyler Moon), Preeya Kalidas (Amira Masood), Ann Mitchell (Cora Cross), Matt Lapinskas (Anthony Moon), Ricky Grover (Andrew Cotton), Polly Perkins (Rose Cotton), Chucky Venn (Ray Dixon) and long-time extras Jane Slaughter (Tracey) and Ulric Browne (Winston). A list of past actors in alphabetical order follows: Joe Absolom (Matthew Rose), Kacey Ainsworth (Little Mo Mitchell), James Alexandrou (Martin Fowler - previously played by Jon Peyton Price), John Altman (Nick Cotton), Devon Anderson (Billie Jackson - previously played by Bluey Robinson), Robin Askwith (Jason Le Fell), Sam Attwater (Leon Small), Kylie Babbington (Jodie Gold), Nick Bailey (Dr. Anthony Trueman), Nicholas Ball (Terry Bates), Marc Bannerman (Gianni di Marco), John Bardon (Jim Branning), Alexandra Bastedo (Cynthia Marshall), Gary Beadle (Paul Trueman), Tiana Benjamin (Chelsea Fox), Hywel Bennett (Jack Dalton), Liam Bergin (Danny Mitchell), Nick Berry (Simon Wicks – returning in January 2012), Ace Bhatti (Yusef Khan),

Gemma Bissix (Clare Bates), Stefan Booth (Greg Jessop), William Boyde (James Willmott-Brown), Rachel Bright (Poppy Meadow), Ray Brooks (Joe Macer), Brian Capron (Jerry McKenzie), Todd Carty (Mark Fowler - previously played by David Scarboro), Natalie Cassidy (Sonia Fowler), Tony Caunter (Roy Evans), Shirley Cheriton (Debbie Wilkins), Charlie Clements (Bradley Branning), Michelle Collins (Cindy Beale), Phil Daniels (Kevin Wicks), Linda Davidson (Mary Smith), Ross Davidson (Andy O'Brien), Bobby Davro (Vinnie Monks), Letitia Dean (Sharon Watts / Mitchell / Rickman), Peter Dean (Pete Beale), Matt Di Angelo (Deano Wicks), Anita Dobson (Angie Watts), Madeline Duggan (Lauren Branning), Christopher Ellison (Len Harker), Michael Elphick (Harry Slater), David Essex (Eddie Moon), Leonard Fenton (Dr. Harold Legg), Alex Ferns (Trevor Morgan), Fine Time Fontayne (Sid Holliday), Alex Francis (Bobby Beale - previously played by Kevin Curran), Gretchen Franklin (Ethel Skinner), Dean Gaffney (Robbie Jackson), Michelle Gayle (Hattie Tavernier), Susan George (Margaret Walker), Don Gilet (Lucas Johnson), Leslie Grantham (Den Watts), Michael Greco (Beppe di Marco), Ricky Groves (Garry Hobbs), Jill Halfpenny (Kate Mitchell), Nigel Harman (Dennis Rickman), Charlie G. Hawkins (Darren Miller), Nicky Henson (Jack Edwards), Oscar James (Tony Carpenter), Simone James (Becca Swanson), Louise Jameson (Rosa di Marco), Samantha Janus / Womack (Ronnie Mitchell), Ashley Jensen (Fiona Morris), Paul Kaye (Douglas Baker), Robert Kazinsky (Sean Slater), Martin Kemp (Steve Owen), Ross Kemp (Grant Mitchell), Emer Kenny (Zsa Zsa Carter), Larry Lamb (Archie Mitchell), Ian Lavender (Derek Harkinson), Thomas Law (Peter Beale - previously played by Francis Brittin-Snell, Alex Stevens, Joseph Shade and James Martin), Sophie Lawrence (Diane Butcher), Dilys Laye (Maxine Palmer), Zöe Lucker (Vanessa Gold), Sean Maguire (Aidan Brosnan), Derek Martin (Charlie Slater), Martine McCutcheon (Tiffany Mitchell), Neil McDermott (Ryan Malloy), Paul J. Medford (Kelvin Carpenter), Will Mellor (Warren Stamp), Jonny Lee Miller (Jonathan Hewitt), Jimi Mistry (Dr Fonseca), Bunmi Mojekwu (Mercy Olubunmi), Ron Moody (Edwin Caldecott), Cathy Murphy (Julie Perkins), Anthony Newley (Vince Watson), Tracy-Ann Oberman (Chrissie Watts), Tamzin Outhwaite (Melanie Owen), Belinda Owusu (Libby Fox), Brittany Papple (Louise Mitchell - previously played by Rachel Cox and Danni Bennatar), Cliff Parisi (Minty Peterson), Christopher Parker (Spencer Moon), David Proud (Adam Best), Sandy Ratcliff (Sue Osman), Ian Reddington (Richard Cole), Mike Reid (Frank Butcher), Wendy Richard (Pauline Fowler), Michelle Ryan (Zoe Slater), Jack Ryder (Jamie Mitchell), Pam St. Clement (Pat Butcher / Evans - Pat died on New Years Day 2012), Nejdet Salih (Ali Osman), Lucy Speed (Natalie Evans), David Spinx (Keith Miller), Michael-Joel David Stuart (Jordan Johnson), Una Stubbs (Caroline Bishop), Joe Swash (Mickey Miller), Ron Tarr (Big Ron), Gillian Taylforth (Kathy Beale / Mitchell), Roberta Taylor (Irene Raymond), Ellen Thomas (Grace Olubunmi), Kara Tointon (Dawn Swann), Bill Treacher (Arthur Fowler), Susan Tully (Michelle Fowler), Lacey Turner (Stacey Slater), Bill Ward (Mike Parker), Hannah Waterman (Laura Beale), Tom Watt (Lofty Holloway), Barbara Windsor (Peggy Mitchell - previously played by Jo Warne), Anna Wing (Lou Beale), Stephen Woodcock (Clyde Tavernier), Edward Woodward (Tommy Clifford), Angela Wynter (Yolande Trueman).

Echo Beach Short-lived television soap opera set in the fictional Cornish coastal town of Polnarren and created by Tony Jordan as a British version of American series *Beverly Hills 90210*. The plot centred around Susan Penwarden and her ex-lover Daniel Marrack, who after a long absence, and following the death of his wife, returns to Polnarren to run a beachfront cafe and surf shop with his daughter Abi and son Brae. Mixed reviews and falling ratings led to its axing after the first run of 12 weekly episodes. The problem with *Echo Beach* was that it was treated as something of a spoof as it was borne out of its sister show *Moving Wallpaper* and viewers had difficulty understanding its relevance. Martine McCutcheon (Susan Penwarden), Jason Donovan (Daniel Marrack), Hugo Speer (Mark Penwarden), Hannah Lederer-Alton (Abi Marrack), Christian Cooke (Brae Marrack), Ed Speleers (Jimmy Penwarden), Laura Greenwood (Grace Penwarden), Chandeep Uppal (Narinder Gurai), Jonathan Readwin (Charlie

Morgan), Naomi Ryan (Jackie Hughes), Marcus Patric (Ian Brenton), Susie Amy (Angela Cole), Gwyneth Powell (Ivy Trehearne), Johnny Briggs (Fin Morgan). The theme song was a cover of Martha and the Muffins' "Echo Beach" performed by Gabriella Cilmi. ITV 2008. See *Moving Wallpaper*.

Echo Four-Two Eric Lander (DI Harry Baxter). Spin-off police series from *No Hiding Place* found Harry Baxter promoted to Detective Inspector. ITV 1961.

Echo Island Irish television programme for children and young adults, shown as part of the daytime viewing under the banner of The Den. Echo Island began broadcasting in 1994 with two episodes a week, which was extended to four episodes the following year with two of these being Irish language editions. The series was similar in format to the BBC's Blue Peter but in later years proved a useful showcase for some of the best young rock bands in Ireland. A number of current Irish media presenters either began, or spent part of, their early careers on *Echo Island*, including Dara Ó Briain, Derek Mooney, Bláthnaid Ní Chofaigh, Tom Ó Brannagáin, Carrie Crowley, Mary Kingston, Peter O'Meara, Danann Breathnach, Sinéad Chaomhánach, Sharon Ní Fhinneadha and Christine Ní Chearraláin. RTÉ Network 2 1994-99 See also Jo Maxi

Ed and Oucho's Excellent Inventions A man and his pet cactus put together viewers' requests for inventions. Ed is played by actor Ed Petrie while Oucho T Cactus is performed by Warrick Brownlow-Pike. Part of the CBBC menu first aired in 2009.

Edgar Wallace Mysteries Low-budget film series made as second features and produced at Merton Park Studios for Anglo-Amalgamated between 1960 and 1965. They were generally loosely based adaptations of original stories by Wallace, updated to reflect contemporary settings. The memorable opening sequence was a slowly revolving bust of Edgar Wallace to the accompaniment of the Man of Mystery theme, written by Michael Carr. It was later recorded by *The Shadows* who had a No. 1 hit record in the UK. The films, usually about an hour in length, were later shown on ITV at various times.

Edge of Darkness Bob Peck (Ronald Craven), Joanne Whalley (Emma Craven), Joe Don Baker (Darius Jedburgh), Jack Watson (James Godbolt), Kenneth Nelson (Grogan), Tim McInnerny (Terry Shields), Zoe Wanamaker (Clemmy), Alan Cuthbertson (Chilwell). The mysterious death of his activist daughter (Emma), leads her straight-laced father (Ronald), a police inspector in Yorkshire, through a haunting revelation of the murkiness of the British Nuclear Policy of the eighties. Written by Troy Kennedy Martin with incidental music by Eric Clapton. First broadcast on BBC2 in 1985, the series was repeated almost immediately on BBC1.

Edna, The Inebriate Woman Patricia Hayes (Edna), Barbara Jefford (Josie), Pat Nye (Irene). Written by Cathy Come Home scribe Jeremy Sandford, this powerful drama, part of the *Play For Today* series, showcased the talents of one of the nation's leading character actresses and comedy stooges, playing the part of a down-and-out alcoholic, schizophrenic ex-con (Edna) who nobody wants to know. BBC1 1971.

Educating Archie Archie Andrews was a ventriloquist's dummy voiced by Peter Brough (1916-99). In 1950 he was given his own BBC radio show called *Educating Archie*. The programme was scheduled in the slot formerly filled by the highly successful *Take It From Here* and by the end of the initial twelve-week run, *Educating Archie* was holding a regular audience of twelve million listeners. The show then ran on for thirty weeks without a break, with Robert Moreton as Archie's tutor, Max Bygraves as an odd-job man and Hattie Jacques as Agatha Dinglebody and various supporting roles. Harry Secombe was a regular contributor. A young girl soprano, only thirteen, was the resident singer. Her name was Julie Andrews. Beryl Reid also made a breakthrough in this show, firstly as naughty schoolgirl Monica and later as the Brummie, Marlene. After its first break, the show returned in 1951with Tony Hancock as Archie's new tutor and his catchphrase of "Flippin' Kids" became common parlance. Max Bygraves (who also become a star with catch-phrases such as "That's a good idea - son!" and "I've arrived, and to prove it, I'm here!") then left, and Alfred Marks took over. By the end of the final series in 1959, Bruce Forsyth and Sid James had also taken their turns as Archie's tutor. The series transferred to television in

1958 (starring Dick Emery and Irene Handl), largely scripted by Marty Feldman, but, bizarrely perhaps, was never as popular as the radio series. Interestingly, Archie was not the first ventriloquism act to get its own BBC Radio show; Saveen and Daisy May had beaten them to it by just a few weeks (see comedy section). In November 2005, the original Archie Andrews doll was sold at auction in Taunton for £34,000 to Colin Burnett-Dick, a care-home director from Halland, East Sussex. Archie's new voice is Steve Hewlett, 31, from Basingstoke.

Edward and Mrs Simpson Edward Fox (Edward), Cynthia Harris (Mrs Wallis Warfield Simpson), Peggy Ashcroft (Queen Mary), David Waller (Stanley Baldwin), Andrew Ray (George, Duke of York), Marius Goring (King George V), Nigel Hawthorne (Walter Monckton), Jessie Matthews (Aunt Bessie). The story of Edward VIII's abdication. Based on the biography by Frances Donaldson, the seven-part drama series portrays Mrs Simpson as a calculating schemer. ITV 1978.

Edward the Seventh Timothy West (Edward as an Adult), Charles Sturridge (Edward as a Teenager), Annette Crosbie (Queen Victoria), Robert Hardy (Prince Albert), John Gielgud (Disraeli), Michael Hordern (Gladstone), Francesca Annis (Lillie Langtry), Harry Andrews (Col. Bruce / General Bruce), Christopher Neame (Kaiser Wilhelm II). 13-part biopic written by David Butler based on the biography by Philip Magnus. ITV 1975.

Edwardian Country House, The, Real-life upstairs and downstairs. 19 volunteers find that life in a grand house (Manderston, just south of Edinburgh) in the early 20th century is plagued by all-too familiar themes: money, power and class. For three months, the household functioned as it would have done in pre-first world war Britain. Every participant in the experiment agreed not just to live with Edwardian technology, but to abide by Edwardian standards of behaviour and to adapt to a complicated set of rules that governed everything in their daily lives. Upstairs were the Olliff-Cooper family from Hampshire, cast as Lords of the Manor, downstairs were butler Hugh Robert Edgar, housekeeper Jean Davies, chef Denis Dubiard, ladies' maid Eva Morrison, footman Charlie Gray, children's tutor Reji Raj-Singh, plus assorted parlour-maids among a staff of twelve. C4 2002. See *The 1900 House.*

Edwardians, The Robert Powell (Charles Stewart Rolls), Michael Jayston (Frederick Henry Royce), Nigel Davenport (Sir Arthur Conan Doyle), Judy Parfitt (E. Nesbit), Virginia McKenna (Daisy, mistress of Edward VII), Ron Moody (Robert Baden-Powell), Georgia Brown (Marie Lloyd), Timothy West (Horatio Bottomley), Anthony Hopkins (David Lloyd George). Series of eight dramatisations of early 20th century figures of note. BBC2 1972-73.

Eggheads BBC Panel game in which a team of five crack quizplayers take on an assortment of quiz teams in order to protect their Egghead reputation. The prizemoney increases £1,000 every day the Eggheads aren't beaten. Presided over by Dermot Murnaghan, the Egghead team consists of Kevin Ashman (*Brain of Britain* and *Mastermind* champion), CJ De Mooi (multiple quiz show winner), Daphne Fowler (*Brain of Britain* and *15-to-1* champion), Chris Hughes (*International Mastermind* and *Brain of Britain*) and Judith Keppel (first winner of £1m on *Who Wants To Be A Millionaire*). From 2008 Jeremy Vine alternated with Dermot as host and also presented a spin-off show *Are you An Egghead?*, devised in order to give a member of the public the chance to join the talented team. Barry Simmons won the series and became the sixth Egghead, although only five ever play at any one time. *Are you An Egghead?* Returned in 2009 and former World Quiz champion Pat Gibson won the series and ultimately joined the crack squad. BBC1 2003-04, BBC2 2005-

8 Out of 10 Cats Comedy panel game based on statistics and opinion polls, the show's title deriving from the well-known advertising tagline for Whiskas cat food "8 out of 10 cats prefer Whiskas". Interestingly, the first advert ever screened during the show's commercial break was for Whiskas. Hosted by Jimmy Carr, the show features two teams of two celebrities, captained by Sean Lock and Jon Richardson (replacing Jason Manford after the

tenth series in 2010 who himself replaced Dave Spikey after the fourth series). C4 2005-

Eldorado Patricia Brake (Gwen Lockhead), Campbell Morrison (Drew Lockhead), Josh Nathan (Blair Lockhead), Polly Perkins (Trish Valentine), William Lucas (Stanley Webb). Short-lived soap set in the Spanish fishing village of Los Barcos. Created by Julia Smith and Tony Holland, this euro soap was made by Cinema Verity (an independent production company) but was axed by new BBC 1 controller, Alan Yentob, 12 months after it had begun. BBC1 1992-93.

11 O'Clock Show, The Late-night satirical comedy series which featured topical sketches and commentary on news items. Hosted by Iain Lee and Daisy Donavan (for Series 2 to 4), the programme is notable for launching the careers of Ricky Gervais, Sacha Baron Cohen, Mackenzie Crook, Jimmy Carr and Charlie Brooker. Original hosts were Brendon Burns and Fred MacAulay, and the final hosts (Series 5) were Jon Holmes and Sarah Alexander. C4 1998-2000

Eleventh Hour Patrick Stewart (Professor Ian Hood), Ashley Jensen (Rachel Young). Four part thriller written by Stephen Gallagher, following the adventures of Professor Ian Hood, Special Advisor to the government's Joint Sciences Committee, who troubleshoots threats stemming from or targeting "scientific endeavour." He is joined by Rachel Young, a Special Branch operative who acts primarily as his bodyguard, as Hood has made powerful enemies through his work. ITV 2006.

Elizabeth R Glenda Jackson (Elizabeth), Robert Hardy (Robert Dudley), Ronald Hines (William Cecil), Daphne Slater (Mary Tudor), Vivian Pickles (Mary Queen of Scots), John Woodvine (Sir Francis Drake), Nicholas Selby (Sir Walter Raleigh), Bernard Hepton (Thomas Cranmer), Rachel Kempson (Kat Ashley), Jason Kemp (Edward VI), Rosalie Crutchley (Catherine Parr), Leonard Sachs (Count de Feria), Esmond Knight (Bishop de Quadra), Stephen Murray (Sir Francis Walsingham), Michael Williams (Duke of Alencon), Margareta Scott (Catherine De Medici), Robin Ellis (Earl of Essex), David Collings (Sir Anthony Babington), Peter Jeffrey (Philip II, King of Spain), John Nettleton (Francis Bacon), Angela Thorne (Lettice Knollys), Patrick O'Connell (O'Neill, Earl of Tyrone), Hugh Dickson (Sir Robert Cecil), Peter Egan (Earl of Southampton). Six-part drama detailing the life and reign of the Virgin Queen. BBC2 1971.

Emergency Ward 10 Rosemary Miller (Nurse Pat Roberts), Jill Browne (Staff Nurse/Sister Carole Young), Charles Tingwell (Dr Alan Dawson), Desmond Carrington (Dr Chris Anderson), John Carlisle (Mr Lester Large), Ray Barrett (Dr Don Nolan), Jane Rossington (Nurse Kate Ford), Paul Darrow (Mr Verity), John Alderton (Dr Richard Moone), Pik-Sen Lim (Nurse Kwe Kim-Yen/Kwai), Richard Thorp (Dr John Rennie), Glyn Owen (Dr Patrick 'Paddy' O'Meara), Frazer Hines (Tim Birch), Tom Adams (Mr Guy Marshall). Created by Tessa Diamond. Set in the Oxbridge General Hospital, Emergency Ward 10 was Britain's first twice-weekly, long-running drama series. ITV 1957-67. A short spin-off series, *Call Oxbridge 2000*, followed Dr Rennie into private practice and this spawned another entitled, *24-Hour Call.*

Emma Romola Garai (Emma), Michael Gambon (Mr Woodhouse), Jonny Lee Miller (Mr George Knightley), Robert Bathurst (Mr Weston), Poppy Miller (Isabella Knightley), Laura Pyper (Jane Fairfax), Rupert Evans (Frank Churchill), Jamie Glover (Henry Knightley). Four-part adaptation of the classic Jane Austen novel. BBC1 2009.

Emmerdale Soap opera known as *Emmerdale Farm* until 1989. Created by Kevin Laffan it is set in the fictional village of Emmerdale somewhere in West Yorkshire. The village was known as Beckindale until it changed its name in 1994 after a plane crash devastated the area The first episode witnessed the funeral of patriarch Jacob Sugden and the controversy surrounding his bequest of Emmerdale Farm to his absent son Jack. The Sugdens have remained at the forefront of plots although superseded by the Tates during the nineties and then the Dingles and the Kings into the new millennium. The Woolpack is the local pub, currently owned by Diane Sugden, and other local businesses include Home Farm Stables (recently owned by Natasha Wylde and Katie Sugden until taken over by the Maceys), The Grange B&B, the post office (run by Viv Hope who also owned the café until her death in the fire started by corrupt policeman Nick Henshall in 2011), Sharma and Sharma Sweet Factory, Dingle Automotives, Emmerdale Haulage (owned by Carl and Jimmy King), Butlers Farm Farmers (run by John Barton, Andy Sugden and Adam Barton) and Emmerdale Veterinary Clinic (run by Paddy Kirk and Rhona Goskirk). The current cast list as at the end of December 2011 in order of their first appearance follows: Richard Thorp (Alan Turner), Christopher Chittell (Eric Pollard), Isabel Hodgins (Victoria Sugden - previously played by Jessica Haywood and Hannah Midgley), Paula Tilbrook (Betty Eagleton), Steve Halliwell (Zak Dingle), James Hooton (Sam Dingle), Kelvin Fletcher (Andy Sugden), Jane Cox (Lisa Dingle), Mark Charnock (Marlon Dingle), John Middleton (Ashley Thomas), Dominic Brunt (Paddy Kirk), Eden Taylor-Draper (Belle Dingle - played as a baby by James and Emily Mather), Elizabeth Estensen (Diane Sugden née Lambert, previously Blackstock), Jeff Hordley (Cain Dingle), Emma Atkins (Charity Tate), Shirley Stelfox (Edna Birch), Tony Audenshaw (Bob Hope - the barman at the Woolpack), Patrick Mower (Rodney Blackstock), Nicola Wheeler (Nicola King), Sammy Winward (Katie Sugden), Zoe Henry (Rhona Goskirk), Annelise Manojlovic (Gabby Thomas - previously played by Jemma Giles), Lucy Pargeter (Chastity "Chas" Dingle), Charley Webb (Debbie Dingle), Charlotte Bellamy (Laurel Thomas), Meg Johnson (Pearl Ladderbanks), Danny Miller (Aaron Livesy - previously played by Danny Webb), Charlie Hardwick (Val Pollard), Tom Lister (Carl King), Nick Miles (Jimmy King), Freddie Jones (Sandy Thomas), Matthew Wolfenden (David Metcalfe), Sian Reese-Williams (Genesis Walker), Lesley Dunlop (Brenda Walker), Kitty McGeever (Lizzie Lakely), James Thornton (John Barton), Natalie J. Robb (Moira Barton), Adam Thomas (Adam Barton), Sophie Powles (Holly Barton), Grace Cassidy (Hannah Barton), Chris Bisson (Jai Sharma), Rik Makarem (Nikhil Sharma), Fiona Wade (Priya Sharma - previously played by Effie Woods), Jason Merrells (Declan Macey), Natalie Anderson (Alicia Gallagher), Pauline Quirke (Hazel Rhodes), Chelsea Halfpenny (Amy Wyatt), Dominic Power (Cameron Murray), Kurtis Stacey (Alex Moss), Gemma Oaten (Rachel Breckle), Luke Roskell (Sean Spencer), Kelli Hollis (Ali Spencer), Alicya Eyo (Ruby Haswell), Trudie Goodwin (Georgia Sharma), Bhasker Patel (Rishi Sharma). **A list of past actors in alphabetical order** follows: Peter Amory (Chris Tate), Peter Armitage (Wilf Butler), Katharine Barker (Dolly Skilbeck 1977-79), Vicky Binns (Ollie Reynolds), Norman Bowler (Frank Tate), Leah Bracknell (Zoe Tate), Malandra Burrows (Kathy Brookman), Andrew Burt (Jack Sugden 1972-76), Beverley Callard (Angie Richards), Lorraine Chase (Steph Forsythe), George Costigan (Charlie Haynes), Alice Coulthard (Maisie Wylde), Kelsey-Beth Crossley (Scarlett Nicholls), Drew Dawson (Jock MacDonald), Amanda Donohoe (Natasha Wylde), Jack Downham (Noah Tate - previously played by Alfie Mortimer), Ken Farrington (Tom King), Anna Friel (Poppy Bruce), Rokhsaneh Ghawam-Shahidi (Leyla Harding), Sandra Gough (Doreen Shuttleworth 1984, 1991 and Nellie Dingle 1994-96), Angela Griffin (Tina), Billy Hartman (Terry Woods), Sherrie Hewson (Lesley Meredith), (Frazer Hines (Joe Sugden), Michelle Holmes (Lindsay Carmichael and Britt Woods), Clive Hornby (Jack Sugden 1980-2008), Louise Jameson (Sharon Crossthwaite), Ross Kemp (Graham Lodsworth), Patsy Kensit (Sadie King 2004-06), Claire King (Kim Marchant / Tate), Bobby Knutt (Albert Dingle), Sally Knyvette (Kate Sugden), Oscar Lloyd (Will Wylde), Philip Madoc (Paul Pargrave), Ronald Magill (Amos Brearly), Lesley Manville (Rosemary Kendall 1974-76), Reginald Marsh (Bob Molesworth), Patricia Maynard (Jill Turner), Sheila Mercier (Annie Pearson / Sugden/ Kempinski / Brearly), Sheree Murphy (Tricia Dingle), Lyndon Ogbourne (Nathan Wylde), Lynn Paul (Freda Darby), Deena Payne (Viv Hope), Arthur Pentelow (Henry Wilks), Conrad Phillips (Christopher Meadows), Jacqueline Pirie (Tina Dingle), Duncan Preston (Doug Potts), Frederick Pyne (Matt Skilbeck), Stan Richards (Seth Armstrong 1978-2004), Lisa Riley (Mandy Dingle), Jean Rogers (Dolly Skilbeck - 1980-91), Suzanne Shaw (Eve Jenson - previously

played by Raine Davison), Marc Silcock (Jackson Walsh), Kathy Staff (Winnie Purvis), James Sutton (Ryan Lamb), Maggie Tagney (Nellie Dingle 2000), Kim Thomson (Faye Lamb), Angela Thorne (Charlotte Verney), Linda Thorson (Rosemary King), Toke Townley (Sam Pearson), Wanda Ventham (Heather Bannerman), Tanya Vital (Adele Allfrey), Joanne Whalley (Angela Read 1977), Jack Woolgar (Charlie Nelson), Oliver Young (Joseph Tate).

Empire Road Norman Beaton (Everton Bennett), Joe Marcell (Walter Isaacs), Corinne Skinner-Carter (Hortense Bennett), Wayne Laryea (Marcus Bennett), Nalini Moonasar (Ranjanaa Kapoor), Rudolph Walker (Sebastian Moses). Written by Guyanan Michael Abbensetts, Empire Road was the first drama to be written, performed and directed entirely by black artists. Filmed in the Handsworth area of Birmingham, the series focuses on the relationship between the West Indian and Asian inhabitants of a residential street. BBC2 1978-79.

Enemy at the Door Alfred Burke (Major Richter), Emily Richard (Clare Martel), Antonia Pemberton (Olive Martel), Bernard Horsfall (Dr Philip Martel), Simon Cadell (Hauptmann Reinicke). Drama depicting life in the Channel Islands during the German occupation. Written by Michael Chapman. ITV 1978-80.

Englishman Abroad, An Alan Bates (Guy Burgess), Coral Browne (Coral Browne). Single drama directed by John Schlesinger recounting the meeting between actress Coral Browne (playing herself) and the traitor Burgess who had defected to the Soviet Union with Donald Maclean in 1951. The two meet in 1958 while Browne is in a touring company of Hamlet in Moscow and they continue their correspondence when she returns home. BBC1 1983.

Eòrpa Eòrpa (Scottish Gaelic for Europe) is a highly-acclaimed 30-minute current affairs programme broadcast weekly, in Scottish Gaelic with English subtitles, on BBC Two Scotland. The series first aired in 1993, and covers social and political issues affecting Europe generally but also has a strong local content in and around the Western Isles. Presenters have included Susie Algie, Alasdair Fraser, Derek Mackay, Colin Mackinnon, Anna Macleod, John Morrison. The current presenters are Iain Macinnes, Darren Laing and Roddy Angus Munro.

Epic Win Short-lived Saturday evening game show in which a celebrity panel of three evaluated a price (from £1 to £1,000) that they believed the contestant deserved for undertaking a skill challenge. Presented by Alexander Armstrong, the resident panellist was comedian Micky Flanagan and the announcer was Joe Lycett. BBC1 2011.

Epitaph for a Spy Peter Cushing (Josef Vadassey), Vivienne Burgess (Odette Martin). Six-part mini-series. In 1937 France, an innocent photographer is arrested for espionage. BBC 1953.

Equalizer, The Edward Woodward (Robert McCall). 'Got a problem? Odds against you? Call the Equalizer. Tel:212 555 4200' Thus read the newspaper advertisement of the Manhattan-based former US Government espionage agent. Although the series was American (first shown on CBS) it is included by nature of its very British star. Stewart Copeland of the rock group Police composed the theme music. ITV 1986-90.

Errol the Hamster See *Roland Rat*

Escape From Scorpion Island Children's television adventure show in which contestants try to gain freedom from a mysterious island by performing various challenges to improve their chances of escaping. Presenters have included Caroline Flack and Reggie Yates (Series 1), JK and Joel (Series 2-3), Myleene Klass and Johnny Pitts (Series 4-5). Since Series 3 in 2009 the programme has aired as part of the CBBC menu. BBC1 2007; BBC2 2008-

Eureka! Short-lived children's programme about inventions. Produced by Clive Doig and hosted by Jeremy Beadle, contributors included, Sylvester McCoy, Simon Gipps-Kent, Bernard Holley, Madeline Smith, Pascal King, and Mike Savage. BBC 1981.

Eureka Street Dervla Kirwan (Aoirghe), Mark Benton (Chuckie Lurgan), Vincent Regan (Jake Jackson), Elisabeth Röhm (Max). Four-part adaptation of Robert McLiam Wilson's novel. A group of people from Northern Ireland try to make sense of their lives in the face of sectarian and political polarisation. Chucky is an overweight 30-year-old who comes up with a business idea, thus making things change for himself in an almost miraculous manner. His friend Jake is an unusually sensitive repossession man, and his life too begins to change when he meets Aoirghe, a woman from the other side of the sectarian divide. BBC2 1999.

Eurotrash Late-night comical review of weird and wacky news from around the world, and as the title suggests, usually focusing on trash reports on pop culture-related items, with a fair amount of pornography thrown in. Originally presented by Antoine de Caunes and Jean-Paul Gaultier, with narrative voiceover by British comic actress Maria McErlane, the 30-minute programmes were conceived in Paris for London-based Rapido Television, the English voice translations in series 1 being provided by Davina McCall and by Kate Robbins for later series. A recurring item was the ever-increasing bust of French porn star Lolo Ferrari (b. Eve Valois, 9 February 1963; d. 5 March 2000). Other regulars included, Pepe and Popo, two cardboard giraffes made from toilet paper tubes, and the Belgian singer Eddy Wally. Graham Norton was a roving reporter for the 1998 series and Victoria Silvstedt was a semi-regular during 2003, often appearing in the studio with de Caunes to present the Naked Germans of the Week feature. C4 1993-2007. See also *Rapido*

Eurovision Song Contest The annual song contest began in 1956 and although the BBC covered the event only seven countries took part, the six that formed the European Coal and Steel Community France, Italy, Germany, Belgium, Netherlands and Luxembourg, plus the host country Switzerland. The United Kingdom took part in all subsequent years apart from 1958. Only on one occasion (2003) has the UK entry received no points. The qualifying shows in the UK have been variously called *Festival of British Popular Songs, Eurovision Song Contest British Final, A Song for Europe, Great British Song Contest, Eurovision: Making Your Mind Up, Eurovision: Your Decision,* and since 2009, *Eurovision: Your Country Needs You.* The following is a list of UK entrants with their placing in brackets. 1957 Patricia Bredin "All" (6th), 1959 Pearl Carr & Teddy Johnson "Sing, Little Birdie" (2nd), 1960 Bryan Johnson "Looking High, High, High" (2nd), 1961 The Allisons "Are You Sure" (2nd), 1962 Ronnie Carroll "Ring-a-Ding Girl" (4th), 1963 Ronnie Carroll "Say Wonderful Things" (4th), 1964 Matt Monro "I Love the Little Things" (2nd), 1965 Kathy Kirby "I Belong" (2nd), 1966 Kenneth McKellar "A Man Without Love" (7th), 1967 Sandie Shaw "Puppet on a String" (1st), 1968 Cliff Richard "Congratulations" (2nd), 1969 Lulu "Boom Bang-a-Bang" (joint 1st), 1970 Mary Hopkin "Knock Knock, Who's There?" (2nd), 1971 Clodagh Rodgers "Jack in the Box" (4th), 1972 The New Seekers "Beg, Steal or Borrow" (2nd), 1973 Cliff Richard "Power to All Our Friends" (3rd), 1974 Olivia Newton-John "Long Live Love" (4th), 1975 The Shadows "Let Me Be the One" (2nd), 1976 Brotherhood of Man "Save Your Kisses for Me" (1st), 1977 Lynsey de Paul & Mike Moran "Rock Bottom" (2nd), 1978 Co-Co "The Bad Old Days" (11th), 1979 Black Lace "Mary Ann" (7th), 1980 Prima Donna "Love Enough for Two" (3rd), 1981 Bucks Fizz "Making Your Mind Up" (1st), 1982 Bardo "One Step Further" (7th), 1983 Sweet Dreams "I'm Never Giving Up" (6th), 1984 Belle and the Devotions "Love Games" (7th), 1985 Vikki Watson "Love Is" (4th), 1986 Ryder "Runner in the Night" (7th), 1987 Rikki "Only the Light" (13th), 1988 Scott Fitzgerald "Go" (2nd), 1989 Live Report "Why Do I Always Get it Wrong?" (2nd), 1990 Emma "Give a Little Love Back to the World" (6th), 1991 Samantha Janus "A Message to Your Heart" (10th), 1992 Michael Ball "One Step Out of Time" (2nd), 1993 Sonia "Better the Devil You Know" (2nd), 1994 Frances Ruffelle "Lonely Symphony (We Will Be Free)" (10th), 1995 Love City Groove "Love City Groove" (10th), 1996 Gina G "Ooh Aah... Just a Little Bit" (8th), 1997 Katrina and the Waves "Love Shine a Light" (1st), 1998 Imaani "Where Are You?" (2nd), 1999 Precious "Say It Again" (12th), 2000 Nicki French "Don't Play That Song Again" (16th), 2001 Lindsay "No Dream Impossible" (15th), 2002 Jessica Garlick "Come Back" (3rd), 2003 Jemini "Cry Baby" (26th), 2004 James Fox "Hold On to Our Love" (16th), 2005 Javine Hylton "Touch My Fire" (22nd), 2006 Daz Sampson "Teenage Life" (18th), 2007 Scooch "Flying the Flag (for You)" (23rd), 2008 Andy Abraham "Even If" (25th), 2009 Jade Ewen "It's My Time"

(5th), 2010 Josh Dubovie "That Sounds Good To Me" (25th), 2011 Blue "I Can" (11th). Ireland made its Eurovision debut in 1965 and has won the contest on a record seven occasions. Ireland missed the 1983 contest in Munich due to financial problems at RTÉ and the 2002 contest in Tallinn through relegation. Johnny Logan's first winning song was written by Shay Healy but Johnny wrote the 1984, 1987 and 1992 entries, the first two under the name Sean Sherrard. A full list of Irish entrants follow: 1965 Naples, Italy "Walking The Streets In The Rain" Butch Moore (6th), 1966 Luxembourg "Come Back To Stay" Dickie Rock (4th), 1967 Vienna "If I Could Choose" Sean Dunphy (2nd), 1968 London "Chance Of A Lifetime" Pat McGeegan (4th), 1969 Madrid "Wages Of Love" Muriel Day (7th), 1970 Amsterdam "All Kinds Of Everything" Dana (1st), 1971 Dublin "One Day Love" Angela Farrell (11th), 1972 Edinburgh "Ceol An Ghrá" ("Music Of Love") Sandie Jones (15th), 1973 Luxembourg "Do I Dream" Maxi (10th), 1974 Brighton "Cross Your Heart" Tina (Reynolds) (7th), 1975 Stockholm "That's What Friends Are For" The Swarbriggs (9th), 1976 The Hague "When" Red Hurley (10th), 1977 London "It's Nice To Be In Love Again" The Swarbriggs Plus Two (3rd), 1978 Paris "Born To Sing" Colm T. Wilkinson (5th), 1979 Jerusalem "Happy Man" Cathal Dunne (5th), 1980 The Hague "What's Another Year" Johnny Logan (1st), 1981 Dublin "Horoscopes" Sheeba (5th), 1982 Harrogate "Here Today, Gone Tomorrow" The Duskeys (11th), 1984 Luxembourg "Terminal 3" Linda Martin (2nd), 1985 Gothenburg "Wait Until The Weekend Comes" Maria Christian (6th), 1986 Bergen "You Can Count On Me" Luv Bug (4th), 1987 Brussels "Hold Me Now" Johnny Logan (1st), 1988 Dublin "Take Him Home" Jump The Gun (8th), 1989 Lausanne "The Real Me" Kiev Connolly & The Missing Passengers (18th), 1990 Zagreb "Somewhere In Europe" Liam Reilly (2nd), 1991 Rome "Could It Be That I'm In Love" Kim Jackson (10th), 1992 Gothenburg "Why Me?" Linda Martin (1st), 1993 Millstreet, Ireland "In Your Eyes" Niamh Kavanagh (1st), 1994 Dublin "Rock 'N' Roll Kids" Paul Harrington And Charlie McGettigan (1st), 1995 Dublin "Deamin'" Eddie Friel (14th), 1996 Oslo "The Voice" Eimear Quinn (1st), 1997 Dublin "Mysterious Woman" Marc Roberts (2nd), 1998 Birmingham "Is Always Over Now?" Dawn (Martin) (9th), 1999 Jerusalem "When Your Need" The Mullans (17th), 2000 Stockholm "Millennium Of Love" Eamonn Toal (6th), 2001 Copenhagen "Without Your Love" Gary O'Shaughnessy (21st), 2003 Riga "We've Got The World" Mickey Harte (11th), 2004 Istanbul "If My World Stopped Turning" Chris Doran (22nd), 2005 Kiev "Love?" Donna & Joe (failed to qualify for final), 2006 Athens "Every Song Is A Cry For Love" Brian Kennedy (10th), 2007 Helsinki "They Can't Stop The Spring" Dervish (24th and last), 2008 Belgrade, Serbia "Irelande Douze Points" Dustin the Turkey (failed to qualify for final), 2009 Moscow "Et Cetera" Sinead Mulvey & Black Daisy (failed to qualify for final), 2010 Oslo "It's For You" Niamh Kavanagh (23rd), 2011 Düsseldorf "Lipstick" Jedward (8th).
BBC1 1956-

Ever Decreasing Circles Richard Briers (Martin Bryce), Penelope Wilton (Ann Bryce), Peter Egan (Paul Ryman), Stanley Lebor (Howard Hughes), Geraldine Newman (Hilda Hughes). Domestic sitcom created by John Esmonde and Bob Larbey. Martin Bryce lives in a quiet suburban close with his wife Anne. He does his best to organise the leisure time of all of the other inhabitants of the close, running umpteen societies and doing good works. Martin is quite happy with his lot until Paul Ryman moves in next door. Paul is a successful businessman, running his own hairdressing salon. Without even trying, he brings out Martin's innate inferiority complex. BBC1 1984-89.

Everybody's Equal Game show hosted by Chris Tarrant. 200 contestants were asked a question with four options, those answering incorrectly being eliminated until less than ten players survived, at which point they faced four questions which were worth £50 each. The player who correctly answered the final question the fastest went on to play the final round. The winning contestant attempted to place four things into the correct order, to win £1000. If they got it wrong, the money was divided equally between all the other contestants. ITV 1989-91. See also *Whittle*.

Every Second Counts Quiz show hosted throughout its run by Paul Daniels. Three married couples took turns to answer rapid-fire multiple-choice questions in order to win vital seconds on the clock which would be carried forward by the winner to the jackpot run climaxing the show. BBC1 1986-89.

Executive Stress Penelope Keith (Caroline Fielding/Fairchild), Geoffrey Palmer and Peter Bowles (Donald Fairchild), Wanda Ventham (Sylvia), Prunella Gee (Valerie Davenport). Donald Fairchild is an executive with Oasis Publishing. When the company is taken over by a US conglomerate, the Frankland Organisation, Donald is made the Sales And Marketing Director. His wife Caroline comes to work for the company as the Editorial Director, using her maiden name, as there is an unwritten law that a married couple cannot work together. Later, their secret comes out and they are made joint managing directors. Geoffrey Palmer was unable to return to the programme for the second series because of other commitments, Peter Bowles taking over the role of Donald. ITV 1986-88.

Expert, The Marius Goring (Dr John Hardy), Ann Morrish (Dr Jo Hardy), Sally Nesbitt (Jane Carter), Victor Winding (DCI Fleming). The meticulously researched drama series was created by Gerard Glaister, whose uncle had been Professor of Forensic Science at Glasgow University. John Hardy is a Warwickshire pathologist working with his GP wife to aid the local police with their investigations. BBC2 1968-71, 1976.

Extras Ricky Gervais (Andy Millman), Ashley Jensen (Maggie Jacobs), Stephen Merchant (Darren Lamb), Shaun Williamson (as himself although Barry from Eastenders to everyone else). Ricky Gervais' eagerly-awaited follow-up to *The Office* saw him cast as Andy Millman, a man who gave up his day job to follow his dream to become an actor. So far the breaks haven't come and he's had to get by doing 'extra' work. Egged on by his best friend Maggie, also an extra, Andy perseveres and is desperate to start landing some serious speaking roles but unfortunately his agent, Darren, is probably the worst agent in the history of show business. Guests in the first series, playing caricatures of themselves include Ben Stiller, Les Dennis, Ross Kemp, Vinnie Jones, Kate Winslet, Patrick Stewart and Samuel L Jackson. In the second series Andy's new sitcom, *When The Whistle Blows*, raises his profile thanks to his heavily-accented catchphrase "Are you 'avin' a laugh?" Lisa Tarbuck plays Rita, the central character. Guests in the second series include David Bowie, Daniel Radcliffe, Orlando Bloom, Sir Ian McKellen, Chris Martin, Robert De Niro, Diana Rigg, Keith Chegwin, Jonathan Ross and Robert Lindsay. A 2007 Christmas Special saw Andy finally becoming an A-lister and no longer confiding in Maggie. Andy ultimately ends up on Celebrity Big Brother and realizes the error of his ways and gives a heartfelt speech to the viewing nation before driving off to Heathrow with Maggie. Ashley Jensen won two British Comedy Awards (Best Actress and Best Newcomer) for her performance as Maggie in 2005. First broadcast on BBC2 2005-07

Eyes Down Paul O'Grady (Ray Temple), Rosie Caveliero (Christine McMurray), Edna Doré (Mary Hardcastle), Neil Fitzmaurice (Bobby Rutt), Sheridan Smith (Sandy Beech), Michelle Butterly (Pamela Henderson) Hazel Douglas (Kathline), Margaret John (Kay), Beatrice Kelley (Kitty), Tony Maudsley (Martin), Eugene Salleh (Terry). Fourteen-part comedy series written by Angela Clarke and starring Paul O'Grady as the manager of The Rio, a Liverpool Bingo Hall. BBC1 2003-04

F Word, The Themed food magazine show based around Gordon Ramsay cooking a three course meal at the F Word restaurant for 50 assorted people. Ramsay chats to guests, offers tips and throws out challenges along the way. C4 2005-

Fabian of Scotland Yard Bruce Seton (DI Robert Fabian). One of television's first police heroes, pipe-smoking no-thrills Inspector Fabian of Scotland Yard would scream around the streets of London in his sturdy Humber Hawk squad car. Through 39 episodes he stalked the wrongdoers and unravelled mysteries with quiet competence. The series was based on the career of former Scotland Yard Detective Inspector Robert Fabian who usually appeared briefly before the final fade-out to wind up the story. The introduction to the programme was as follows: "In the

nation's war on crime, Scotland Yard is the brain of Great Britain's man-hunting machine. Routine, detailed science and tenacity; these are the weapons used by squads of highly trained men. Men like former Superintendent Robert Fabian, hailed by the press as one of England's greatest detectives!" This was followed by ringing of a police car bell and screech of tyres and the stirring theme music. BBC 1954-56.

Face the Music Light-hearted classical music-based quiz hosted by Joseph Cooper. Three celebrities would try and identify classical music pieces disguised in some way. Popular rounds included the 'dummy-keyboard' round where Joseph played on a silent piano and challenged the celebs to identify the piece of music from the beats of the host playing the piano. Bernard Levin, Michael Bentine, Joyce Grenfell, Richard Baker and Robin Ray were regulars. Ray was famous for giving chapter and verse on his favourite pieces and unerringly managed to quote the opus numbers! BBC 2 1967-79 and 1983-84.

Face to Face Chat-show hosted by John Freeman, former editor of *The New Statesman* and later to become British Ambassador to the USA. Freeman asked straight forward and often probing questions to intellectually heavyweight personalities of the day such as Dr Martin Luther King, Bertrand Russell, Carl Jung, Lord Reith and Dame Edith Sitwell, but the show found a new popular audience in its second season when the legendary comedian Tony Hancock was given the Freeman treatment and first showed the signs of insecurity that was to blight his subsequent career. Other popular guests included pop singer Adam Faith, racing driver Stirling Moss and gruff *What's My Line* panellist Gilbert Harding who was reduced to tears when questioned about his mother (who, unbeknown to Freeman, had recently died). BBC 1959-62. The show was revived on BBC2 between 1995 and 1997 with Jeremy Isaacs as host, guests including Bob Monkhouse, Lauren Bacall, Paul Eddington, Anthony Hopkins, Ken Dodd, Stephen Sondheim, Diana Rigg, Harold Pinter and Roddy Doyle.

Fact Hunt Late night comedy quiz show hosted by Al Murray in his pub landlord guise. Fact Hunt was originally a section of Al Murray's Edinburgh stage show, whereby large members of the audience were invited on stage to answer questions, and the audience would shout out "Fact Hunt" to large guffaws! ITV 2005.

Fáilte Towers Reality television show airing daily between August 2nd and 17th 2008 and featuring 13 celebrities who ran a hotel for sixteen days and nights in order to win money for their designated charities. The contestants were Don Baker Blues (musician),John Creedon (RTÉ radio personality), Evelyn Cusack (RTÉ weather presenter), Brian Dowling (Big Brother winner), Michelle Heaton (former Liberty X member), Jennifer Maguire (Apprentice UK contestant), Donna and Joseph McCaul (You're A Star winners), Patricia McKenna (Green Party MEP), Sean Ó Domhnaill (Former GAA Gaelic footballer), Liz O'Kane (RTÉ presenter), Luke Thomas (Pop singer) and Clare Tully (Page 3 Model). The name is a play on the BBC sitcom Fawlty Towers - Fáilte is the Irish language word for "welcome". The hotel used in the series was Bellingham Castle in Castlebellingham, County Louth. The show was presented by Aidan Power and Baz Ashmawy and the judges were Bibi Baskin, Dublin restaurateur Derry Clarke and Castle Leslie hotelier Sammy Leslie. Each night the three lowest scoring contestants were marched into the Oliver Plunkett Suite to face the judges and one of them had to 'check out'. The winner of the show was John Creedon. RTÉ One 2008

Fair City The longest running and most popular Irish soap opera. Created by Margaret Gleason and set in the fictional town of Carrigstown, a suburb of the fair city of Dublin. Four families: the O'Hanlons, the Kellys, the Clarkes and the Corcorans, originally dominated the plots but were gradually usurped throughout the nineties by the Phelan, Doyle, Molloy and Halpin families before concentrating more on individuals. Local businesses include McCoys pub, Phelan's corner shop (formerly Doyle's), The Hungry Pig diner (formerly The Bistro), Vino's Tapas Bar (formerly Rainbows Sandwich Bar), Acorn Cabs dispatch centre, the Northside Post newspaper and the Helping Hand charity shop. The present cast list as at the end of December 2011 includes, in alphabetical order: Jim Bartley (Bela Doyle), Maclean Burke (Damien Halpin), Victor Burke (Wayne Molloy), Catherine Byrne (Judith Dillon), Eileen Colgan (Esther Roche), Sam Peter Corry

(Robert Daly), Alan Devine (Louie Gleeson), Dave Duffy (Leo Dowling), Martha Fitzpatrick (Charlotte Lynch), Patrick Fitzpatrick (Zumo Bishop), Sarah Flood nee McDowall (Suzanne Doyle / Halpin), Sorcha Furlong (Orla Kirwan), Aoibhin Garrihy (Neasa Dillon), Tom Hopkins (Christy Phelan), Tom Jordan (Charlie Kelly), Kevin Joyce (Zak Dillon), Stephanie Kelly (Sash Bishop), Cal Kenealy (Mark Halpin), Aoibheann McCaul (Caoimhe Dillon), Lewis Magee (Denzo Bishop), Ryan Matthews (Sean Cassidy), Geoff Minogue (Tommy Dillon), Eamon Morrissey (Cass Cassidy), Clelia Murphy (Niamh Cassidy), Rachel Sarah Murphy (Jo Coughlan / Fahey), Bryan Murray (Bob Charles), Mick Nolan (Ray O'Connell), Helen Norton (Vivienne Lynch), Enda Oates (Pete Ferguson), Ciara O'Callaghan (Yvonne Doyle / Gleeson), Liana O'Cleirigh (Laura Halpin), James O'Donoghue (Benjamin Fahey), Sam O'Mahony (Finn McGrath), Aisling O'Neill (Carol Foley / Meehan), Alan O'Neill (Keith McGrath), Tommy O'Neill (John Deegan), David O'Sullivan (Decco Bishop), Kerrie O'Sullivan (Dearbhla Dillon), Seamus Power (Dermot Fahey), Niamh Quirke (Rachel Brennan), Michael Sheehan (Dean Dowling), Martina Stanley (Dolores Molloy), Margaret Toomey (Eileen Bishop), Tony Tormey (Paul Brennan). **Famous past actors include**: Mojisola Adebayo (Gina Udenze), Joan Brosnan Walsh (Mags Kelly), Jenny Kavanagh (Cleo Cullen / Collins), Cian & Cathal Byrne (Benjamin Fahey), Asaf B. Goldfrid (Avi Bar Lev), Nathan Gordon (Duncan Stonehouse), Lisa Harding (Connie Boylan), Pat Nolan (Barry O'Hanlon), Gerard Byrne (Malachy Costello), Yare Jegbefume (Felix Jones), Vicky Byrne (Kylie Kavanagh), Kate Thompson (Justine Molloy), Gemma Doorly (Sarah O'Leary), Wesley Doyle (Doug Ferguson), Marian Caparrós (Oxanna), Steve Cash (Colm Joyce), Doireann Ní Chorragáin (Ali O'Shea / Foley), Declan Conlon (Turlough Norris), Jean Costello (Rita Doyle), Una Crawford O'Brien (Renee Phelan), Amelia Crowley (Fiona Piggott), Sandra Curran (Una Norris), Aoife Doyle (Louise Doyle), Keith Duffy (Ringo Leyden), Lisa Dwan (Zoe Burke), Hilda Fay (Tracey McGuigan), Aoife Finnegan (Clare Gogan), Joe Gallagher (Dominic Kavanagh), Julie Hale (Terry Deegan), Aaron Harris (Detective Garda Sgt. Myles Bryne), Frances Healy (Clare Whelan), David Johnston (Ken Fahey) , Una Kavanagh (Heather Lyons / Daly), Anne Kent (Angela O'Connell), Deirdre Lawless (Gina Cassidy), Vinnie McCabe (Seamus McAleer), Alan McMahon (Adam Birmingham), Jose Mantero (Patrick Maloney), Philip Michael (Joshua Udenze), David Mitchell (Jimmy Doyle), Seamus Moran (Mike Gleeson), William Morgan (Morgan Dalton), Mireia Pomar Natal (Magda Reyes), Gareth O'Connor (Pierce Stanley), Tom O'Leary (Brendan Daly), Anne O'Neill (Sue Kenny), Tommy O'Neill (John Deegan), Ryan O'Shaughnessy (Mark Halpin), Aimee O'Sullivan (Beth Kenny), Tatiana Ouliankina (Lana Borodin / Dowling), Orlaith Rafter (Robin McKenna Doyle), Ciaran Reilly (Anthony Brady), Bairbre Scully (Deirdre Burke), Carmel Stephens (Geraldine Creagh / Fahey). RTÉ One 1989-

Fairly Secret Army Geoffrey Palmer (Major Harry Kitchener Wellington Truscott). Sitcom written by David Nobbs. A retired British Army major, once of the Queen's Own West Mercian Lowlanders, tries to fight the forces of anarchy by setting up a supposedly secret taskforce. C4 1984-86.

Faith in the Future See *Second Thoughts*

Faking It Reality television series. Each programme follows a volunteer from one walk of life who lives and trains with an expert from a completely different field. After a four-week crash course in their mentor's area of expertise, the volunteer is put to the test by competing against genuine practitioners. Judges (who in most cases aren't initially aware that there is a faker in the line-up) are asked to pick a winner, and then pick out the fake. There is no particular prize for success - the fakers do it just for the experience. Challenges have included dog trainer, polo player, wrestler, bouncer, pop-video director, garage MC, surfer, drag queen, stuntman, showjumper, conductor, conceptual artist, chef, football manager, rock musician, hairdresser, ballroom dancer, fashion photographer, racing driver, yachtswoman. The programme has won several prestigious awards including the Montreux Television Festival 2003 Golden Rose (awarded for the best TV programme overall - punk rocker Chris Sweeney becoming an orchestral conductor). C4 2000-05

Fall and Rise of Reginald Perrin, The Leonard Rossiter (Reginald Iolanthe Perrin / Martin Wellbourne), Pauline Yates (Elizabeth Perrin), John Barron (CJ), Sue Nicholls (Joan Greengross), Geoffrey Palmer (Jimmy), John Horsley (Doc Morrisey), Bruce Bould (David Harris-Jones), Trevor Adams (Tony Webster). David Nobbs adapted his 1975 comic novel *The Death Of Reginald Perrin* as the first series of this quintessentially British sitcom (it was retitled *The Fall And Rise Of Reginald Perrin* for paperback). Leonard Rossiter lent an outstanding empathetic quality to the role. The plot centred on Sunshine Desserts, a confectionary company where Perrin worked as a desk-bound sales executive. The business was run by C J, a tall, powerful figure wont to begin most of his statements with the all-purpose introduction 'I didn't get where I am today by...' followed by a baffling example of what he did or didn't do to arrive at his present status. CJ also had an interesting method of gaining domination over his employees at meetings by employing whoopee cushions to disarm them (or perhaps he was merely stark raving bonkers). Reggie's colleagues, Tony Webster and David Harris-Jones, were equally superficial and lacking in original thoughts, meeting any suggestion with a simple one-word platitude, 'Great!' (Tony) or 'Super!' (David). The dithering company doctor was of a similar ilk, knowing nothing about medicine and living in the hope that a sick female employee might 'feel chesty' so that he could have an opportunity to examine the problem area. Then there is Reggie's secretary Joan, a middle-aged bundle of simmering sexuality, fatally attracted to Reggie and liable at any moment to pounce on him. At home, Reggie's wife Elizabeth is pleasant and understanding, but it's her very tolerance and unchanging reliability that grates on Reggie and adds to his malaise. Then there was Reggie's exceedingly boring son-in-law Tom, who made appalling home-made wine, and his wildly off-centre brother-in-law Jimmy, whose military background seemed to have cast him adrift in civilian life where he appeared hopelessly out of his depth, using militaristic forms of speech to explain his predicament ('No food. Bit of a cock-up on the catering front'). From episode one, Reggie's life was brain-numbingly predictable and repetitive - the train ride into London from his Norbiton home was always 11 minutes late (Reggie began each working day relating to Joan the variety of reasons). The signs that he was going off the rails were also suggested by his bizarre habit of visualising a hippopotamus whenever thinking of his mother-in-law. Gradually madness became the order of the day. In a last-ditch attempt to preserve his sanity and escape the rat-race, he faked his own suicide by leaving a pile of clothes on a beach and walking off into the sunset. Wondering what it would be like to attend his own funeral, Reggie then wore a fake beard, called himself Martin Wellbourne and fell in love anew with Elizabeth, who recognised his true identity but, for a while, pretended otherwise. In the second series Reggie revealed that he was not dead and reacquainted himself with his relatives and old work colleagues. After a brief spell working at a piggery for a Mr Pelham, and warding off the advances of a dowdy spinster Miss Erith, Reggie launched a shop, Grot, dedicated to selling useless things, and was amazed when it became a massive global success. Reggie remarried Elizabeth, who had become a Grot business executive, and when Sunshine Desserts collapsed he relocated his former colleagues at the Grot HQ. But still Reggie was numbed by routine and eerily found himself taking on the traits and mannerisms of C J. The second series ended with Perrin, his wife and C J all faking their suicides. The third series saw Reggie gather the usual crew to launch Perrins, a self-contained commune for the middle-aged and middle-class, where its members could learn to live in harmony and then set out to spread the gospel. A fourth series *The Legacy of Reginald Perrin*, followed in 1996, without Leonard Rossiter who had died in 1984, the remaining cast members (plus Patricia Hodge as Geraldine Hackstraw) forming yet another company, Broscor (Bloodless Revolution Of Senior Citizens and the Occupationally Rejected). BBC1 1976-79, 1996. A remake entitled *Reggie Perrin* began on BBC1 in 2009 with Martin Clunes playing Reggie as a product executive in charge of disposable razors at 'Groomtech'. Other cast members included Neil Stuke as Reggie's overbearing boss, Chris Jackson, Fay Ripley as Nicola Perrin, Reggie's wife, Geoffrey Whitehead as William, Nicola's father and Reggie's father-in-law, Wendy Craig as Reggie's mother, Kerry Howard as Reggie's secretary and Lucy Liemann as Jasmine Strauss, one of Reggie's colleagues and his sexual fantasy figure. Simon Nye wrote the updated version (assisted by David Nobbs).

Fallen Hero Del Henney (Gareth Hopkins), Wanda Ventham (Dorothy Hopkins). A lad from the Welsh valleys, about to collect his first rugby union cap, decides to switch codes and become a star in the northern leagues. Now aged 35 his life is suddenly changed when he suffers a career-ending leg injury. ITV 1978-79.

Fame Academy Reality television show searching for future singing stars. Hosted by Patrick Kielty and Cat Deeley with guest judges, Series 1 - Richard Park, Kevin Adams and Carrie Grant; Series 2 - Richard Park, Robin Gibbs, Carrie and David Grant, Jeremy Milnes was the tutor. The first series winner was David Sneddon and the second, Alex Parks. The top five students from the inaugural Fame Academy - David Sneddon, Sinead Quinn, Lemar Obika, Malachi Cush and Ainslie Henderson - have all since signed record deals. BBC1 2002-03. Claudia Winkleman hosted regular updates within the Fame Academy House (Witanhurst, in Highgate Village, North London - the second largest stately home in London) on BBC3. Three celebrity editions of Fame Academy were shown as part of Comic Relief, Will Mellor winning in 2003, Edith Bowman 2005, and Tara Palmer-Tomkinson in 2007.

Family at War, A Colin Douglas (Edwin Ashton), Shelagh Fraser (Jean Ashton), Barbara Flynn (Freda Ashton), Coral Atkins (Sheila Ashton), John Nettles (Ian McKenzie). Ups and downs of the Yorkshire-born Ashton family residing in Liverpool between May 1938 and the end of World War II. The 52-episode series by John Finch was semi-autobiographical. The memorable opening title sequence showed a demolished sand-castle to symbolise the sign of the times. ITV 1970-72.

Family Fortunes Game show played by two teams made up of family members. 100 people were polled on a variety of questions and the teams have to decide how the public voted. Presenters: Bob Monkhouse (1980-83), Max Bygraves (1983-85), Les Dennis (1987-2002), Andy Collins (2002) and Vernon Kay (2006-). ITV 1980-2002; 2006-.

Family, The Fly on the Wall look at the Wilkins family from Reading, the original reality television family. Director Paul Watson and his camera crew spent three months, 18 hours a day, filming Margaret and Terry and their children Gary, Marian, Heather and Chris; the resulting series, broadcast over 12 weeks, gaining audiences of 10 million, made a star out of Margaret. It might seem pretty tame nowadays but at the time the liberated Wilkins allowing their daughter Marian to live at home with her boyfriend caused some controversy. BBC1 1974. In 2008 Channel 4 produced an eight-part series of the same name and type, this time concentrating on the Hughes family from Canterbury in Kent. Simon and Jane, and their four children, Jessica (who lives down the road with her fiancé and their year-old baby), Emily, 19 (the "wild child"), Charlotte, 17 (the "clever one") and Tom, 14. They were filmed for 100 days, using 21 tiny cameras dotted around their semi-detached house. The title narration was by John Simm and the director was Jonathan Smith.

Famous, Rich and Jobless Actor Larry Lamb, television gardener Diarmuid Gavin, interior designer Meg Matthews, and model-turned-mechanic Emma Parker Bowles swapped their fame and fortune for a world of joblessness, job-hunting and surviving on the poverty line and benefits. Kitted out in old clothes and having just under 10 pounds a day to live on, they were guided by Emma Harrison, founder of A4e (the largest employment agency in the world), and Craig Last, a former youth worker for the charity Centrepoint. At the beginning of their eight day experience they were sent to four unemployment blackspots across the country; Larry went to Hartlepool, Diarmuid to Hackney, Meg to Ebbw Valley, and Emma to Wolverhampton. BBC1 2010.

Far Pavilions, The Ben Cross (Ashton 'Ash' Pelham-Martyn), Amy Irving (Princess Anjuli), Christopher Lee (Kaka-Ji-Rao), Omar Sharif (Koda Dad), John Gielgud (Major Sir Louis Cavagnari), Rossano Brazzi (The Rana of Bhithor), Rupert Everett (George Garforth). The series was adapted by Julian Bond from the novel by M. M. Kaye and the music was provided by Carl Davis. Ash had been brought up to think of himself as Indian rather than officer class, and is torn between the British and Indian cultures and his forbidden love for the sultry Anjuli. C4 1984.

Farrell See *Prime Time*

Farrington of the F.O. Angela Thorne (Harriet Farrington), John Quayle (Major Willoughby-Gore), Joan Sims (Annie Begley), Tony Haygarth (Fidel Sanchez). Sitcom created by Dick Sharples. Harriet Farrington arrives to take charge at a small, unimportant British Consulate in "one of the armpits of Latin America". She is horrified to find out how indolent and scheming her staff are, and - with more than a hint of Margaret Thatcher about her mannerisms - sets out to turn the Consulate around. The second, and final, series was simply called Farrington. ITV 1986-87.

Fast Show, The Fast-paced comedy sketch show created by Charlie Higson and Paul Whitehouse and starring Whitehouse as Rowley Birkin QC (I was very drunk), Ted, The 13th Duke of Winburne, Ken (Suit You!), Archie (the pub bore), Chris Jackson (he's a little bit werrrr a little bit weyyyyy), Brilliant (the innocent teenager), Unlucky Alf (Oh Bugger!), Monster, Arthur Atkinson (How queer!), Lyndsay Mottram, Ron Manager (based on Alec Stock). Charlie Higson as Colin Hunt (the office wag), Ralph (Lord of the Manor), Swiss Toni (the bequiffed car salesman), Bob Fleming (genial host of Country Matters), Johnny the Painter, Simon Bush. Simon Day as Billy Bleach (pub know-it-all), Carl Hooper (That's Amazing!), Dave Angel (eco warrior), Monkfish (as played by Johnny Actor), Competitive Dad, Tommy Cockles. Mark Williams as Jesse (This week I shall mostly be eating...), Kenneth (Suit You Sir!), Patrick Nice, The Headmaster. Caroline Aherne as Checkout Girl, Our Janine, Renee. John Thomson as Louis Balfour (presenter of Jazz Club), Professor Denzil Dexter, Chip the Deaf Stuntman. Arabella Weir as No Offence (cosmetic salesperson), Insecure Woman (Does My Bum Look Big In This?). There were also characters portrayed by Rhys Thomas, Paul Shearer and Eryl Maynard. The show's theme music was *Release Me.* BBC2 1994-97. *The Last Fast Show Ever* was screened at Christmas 2000. A spin-off comedy, *Ted and Ralph*, was screened in December 1998 and Swiss Toni was given his own series on BBC3 in 2003. A new online edition of the show was screened in November 2011.

Fat Friends Drama series created by Kay Mellor. Gaynor Faye (Lauren Harris), Ruth Jones (Kelly Chadwick), James Corden (Jamie Rymer), Lisa Riley (Rebecca Petterson), Alison Steadman (Betty Simpson), Lynda Baron (Norma Patterson), Janet Dibley (Carol McGary), Gareth Miller (Tom), Paul Warriner (Paul Thompson), Jonathan Ryland (Kevin Chadwick), Kathryn Hunt (Val Lorrimer). The trials and tribulations of a gang of overweight people attending a slimming club in the Headingley district of Leeds run by Carol, an advocate of the 'Super Slimmers' diet. Gaynor Faye is the real-life daughter of Kay Mellor. This series brought together James Corden and Ruth Jones who went on to co-write *Gavin and Stacey*. ITV 2000-05

Father & Son Dougray Scott (Michael O'Connor), Sophie Okonedo (Connie Turner), Ian Hart (Tony Conroy), Stephen Rea (Augustine Flynn), Reece Noi (Sean O'Connor), Wunmi Mosaku (Stacey Cox), Simon Delaney (George), John Kavanagh (John O'Connor), Terence Maynard (Barrington), Imani McLaren (Imani Turner), Flora Montgomery (Anna), Darren Morfitt (Blanchflower). Four-part crime thriller written by Frank Deasy. Michael O'Connor is recently returned to his native Ireland, after spending several years imprisoned in the United Kingdom. A parallel storyline follows O'Connor's son and sister-in-law in Manchester. The intelligent script with several sub-plots and twists ensures the viewer needs to stay focused. First broadcast on RTÉ One in June 2009 and then on ITV in 2010.

Father Brown Kenneth More (Father Brown), Dennis Burgess (Flambeau). Based on the saintly sleuth created by G. K. Chesterton. ITV 1974.

Father Dear Father Patrick Cargill (Patrick Glover), Natasha Pyne (Anna Glover), Ann Holloway (Karen Glover), Noel Dyson (Matilda 'Nanny' Harris), Joyce Carey (Mrs Glover), Ursula Howells (Barbara Mossman), Dawn Addams (Georgie Thompson). Domestic sitcom concerning a divorced spy novelist attempting to find the right woman while having to contend with two demanding daughters, a dotty mother, a fussy nanny, ex-wife, and agent. ITV 1968-73. An Australian version starring Cargill and Noel Dyson aired in the UK in 1978.

Father Ted Dermot Morgan (Father Ted Crilly), Ardal O'Hanlon (Father Dougal McGuire), Frank Kelly (Father Jack Hackett), Pauline McLynn (Mrs Doyle), Graham Norton (Father Noel Furlong). Sitcom about three priests and their housekeeper who live on Craggy Island, off the coast of Galway, Ireland. The central character is Ted Crilly, exiled to Craggy Island for embezzling a charity fund (the sick child hoping for a visit to Lourdes was deprived and Ted went to Las Vegas on the proceeds). His assistants are the dimwitted novice priest, Father Dougal McGuire, similarly exiled for an incident involving nuns, and the hard-drinking all-swearing Father Jack Hackett (catchphrases "drink" and "feck off"), who was also exiled by the church for an unspecified wedding ceremony outrage. Mrs Doyle is their well-meaning tea-making housekeeper (catchphrase when asking if you would like more tea "go on go on go on go on go on go on"). The other stars of the show were writers Graham Linehan and Arthur Mathews, who managed to create a refreshingly novel style that combined witty, oddball dialogue with mindbogglingly extreme situations, encompassing anything from the priests entering the Eurovision Song Contest, to Father Ted and a gang of his fellow priests being lost for hours in the women's lingerie section of a department store. And the writers weren't above indulging themselves by introducing silly names: Ted Crilly himself, but also characters like Father Dick Byrnes, Father Todd Unctious, randy milkman Pat Mustard and Sampras, Dougal's pet rabbit. (The character of Father Ted, incidentally, first appeared in Mathews' standup routine.) It was the improbable storylines that made the series almost universally popular as the irreverent humour was so over the top it was difficult for Christians to take real offence as church rituals were never caricatured. Sadly, as the third series was about to air, principal star Dermot Morgan died suddenly, aged just 45. An annual 'TedFest' takes place on the Aran Islands every February to commemorate the series, the date coinciding with the anniversary of its stars' premature death. C4 1995-98. The 25 episodes were also shown on Monday nights on Ireland's Network 2.

Fattest Man in Britain, The Timothy Spall (Georgie Godwin), Bobby Ball (Morris Morrissey), Frances Barber (Janice), Aisling Loftus (Amy), David Williams (Mad Bob), Archie Lal (Raj), Richard Riddell (Joe), Brendan O'Carroll (Father O'Flaherty), Alice Barry (Joyce), Tim Woodward (Morley Raisin). Comedy-drama written by Caroline Aherne and Jeff Pope. Georgie Godwin, housebound for 23 years, is a tourist attraction in Rochdale, thanks to greedy agent, taxi-driver Morris who brings visitors to hear Georgie sing and touch the 'fattest man in Britain'. Devoted neighbour Janice is Georgie's only other regular outside contact until he meets Amy, a pregnant teenager fleeing a violent boyfriend, whom Georgie takes in as a lodger. Amy wants Georgie to lose weight for his own safety, while Morris encourages him to pile on the pounds as a money-spinner for them both, arranging for him to take part in a local television weigh-in, to see if he is fatter than rival claimant Big Brian. The story was inspired by the real-life case of Jack Taylor (1946 - 2006) from Bradford who took part in a TV weigh-in with Barry Austin (who played Big Brian in this film) in 2001 for the title of The Fattest Man in Britain. ITV 2009.

Fawlty Towers John Cleese (Basil Fawlty), Prunella Scales (Sybil Fawlty), Andrew Sachs (Manuel), Connie Booth (Polly Sherman), Ballard Berkeley (Major Gowen), Brian Hall (Terry), Gilly Flower (Miss Abitha Tibbs), Renee Roberts (Miss Ursula Gatsby). Sitcom set in a hotel at 16 Elwood Avenue, Torquay, run by a stressed and moronic lunatic who can't seem to please his guests, has a shaky marriage with a cruel and self-centered woman, and a Spanish porter (he's from Barcelona and knows 'nathing') who can barely speak English. Fortunately he has an intelligent and attractive maid to help him out of the various situations he gets into. The 12 episodes (six shown in 1975 and six in 1979) are: A Touch of Class (the one with Lord Melbury's

scam), The Builders, The Wedding Party, The Hotel Inspectors, Gourmet Night (the one where Basil vents his frustration on his car), The Germans, Communication Problems ("What did you expect to see out of a Torquay hotel bedroom window? Sydney Opera House perhaps? The Hanging Gardens of Babylon? Herds of wildebeest sweeping majestically...!"), The psychiatrist, Waldorf Salad, The Kipper and the Corpse, The Anniversary, Basil the Rat (Manuel believes it to be a Siberian hamster). BBC2 1975, 1979.

FBi Interactive See *Fully Booked*

Fee Fi Fo Yum Children's game show presented by Les Dennis as part of the CBBC menu. Broadcast on the fictional GTV (Giant Television) station where gameshows rule and *Fee Fi Fo Yum* is the most popular. Two teams of 'humunchies' (human children) compete in a series of challenges on the dinner table of Brian the Giant (played by Nigel Cooper), the losing team suffering the fate of being eaten by him. BBC1 2010.

Fellows, The See *The Man in Room 17*.

Fenn Street Gang Peter Cleall (Eric Duffy), David Barry (Frankie 'Hank' Abbott), Peter Denyer (Dennis Dunstable), Barbara Mitchell (Mrs Abbott), Liz Gebhardt (Maureen Bullock), George Baker (Bowler), Carol Hawkins (Sharon Eversleigh), Malcolm McFee and Leon Vitali (Peter Craven). Spin off series from *Please Sir* focusing on the relationships between the former schoolfriends. Sharon (now played by Carol Hawkins, who had also appeared in the role in the *Please, Sir!* movie) and Duffy continued the very bumpy relationship they had started in the third year at school, becoming engaged at the end of the second series and marrying in the third. Frankie Abbott - calling himself Hank Abbott - continued to live out his comic-book fantasies, fashioning himself as a clumsy, over-disguised amateur detective and having a relationship with Maureen, who trained as a nurse. And Craven became a wide-boy, working for a cockney crook named Bowler who had fingers in all manner of nefarious pies and was definitely the lord of the local manor. 'Privet' Hedges (John Alderton) appeared in two episodes. ITV 1971-73. George Baker was cast as Craven's boss and the role was so successful that it led to a spin-off, *Bowler*.

Fiddlers Three Peter Davison (Ralph West), Paula Wilcox (Ros), Charles Kay (J J Morley), Peter Blake (Harvey), Cindy Day (Norma), Tyler Butterworth (Osborne). Sitcom written by Eric Chappell. Ralph is happily married to Ros. He works in the Accounts Department of a large organisation. Along with the rest of the staff, Ralph seems to spend more time dabbling in office politics and angling for promotion than he does working. The three fiddlers of the title - Ralph, Harvey and Osborne , although workshy, were not prone to embezzlement. The plotline was a reworking of an earlier Chappell sitcom, *The Squirrels*. ITV 1991.

15 Storeys High Sean Lock (Vince Clarke), Benedict Wong (Errol Spears). Sitcom created by Sean Lock, Martin Trenaman and Mark Lamarr. Set in a London tower block, the series was originally entitled *Sean Lock's 15 Minutes of Misery* and aired in the late night comedy spot on BBC Radio 4. The second series introduced Sean's flatmate Errol Spears (played by Peter Serafinowicz) and as the show was extended to 30 minutes the name became *15 Storeys High*. Two series were subsequently televised and Sean Lock's character became Vince and Errol was now played by Benedict Wong. The series was initially broadcast on BBC Choice (the forerunner to BBC Three) in 2002 but then repeated on BBC2 the following year. BBC Radio 4 1998-2000; BBC2 2003-04

Fifteen to One General Knowledge Quiz Hosted by William G Stewart. In the first round 15 hopefuls, beginning with three lives, stood in an arc and were asked two questions in turn, a wrong answer would lose a life but two wrong answers was game over and an early bath. Round two was the nomination round where a contestant could nominate any of the remaining players to answer the next question until only three remained. The final round consisted of 40 questions, initially on the buzzer, the contestant then having the choice of answering the next question, and therefore jeopardising a life, or nominating an opponent. The top daily scorers were listed on a finals board and the top 15 were invited back to the end-of-series Grand Final. The Grand Final winners were: 1988 - Jon Goodwin, Mal Collier, 1989 - Kevin Ashman, Andrew Francis, 1990 - Anthony Martin , Mike Kirby, 1991 - Thomas Dyer, Anthony Martin, 1992 - Julien Allen, Barbara Thompson, 1993 - Anthony Martin, Glen Binnie, 1994 - Stanley Miller, Leslie Booth (aka Duncalf), 1995 - Leslie Booth (aka Duncalf), Ian Booth, 1996 - Arnold O' Hara, Martin Riley, 1997 - Trevor Montague, Bill Francis, Nick Terry, 1998 - Nick Terry, Bill McKaig, Paul Hillman, 1999 - Nick Terry (twice), 2000 - Les Arnott, Dag Griffiths, Matti Watton, 2001 - Daphne Fowler (twice), 2002 - Matti Watton, David Good, 2003 - Jack Welsby/Dave Steadman (tie), John Harrison. Mal Collier won the Champion of Champions event held at Christmas 1997. The voice-overs were by Anthony Hyde, Laura Calland, Philip Lowrie and Sarah Wynter at various times. C4 1988-2003.

Fifth Gear Channel Five motoring magazine show which was designed to replace the BBC's *Top Gear* after it was 'cancelled' in 2001, but now running parallel with it after Top Gear was relaunched after the first series. Presenters have included Tiff Needell, Quentin Willson, Vicki Butler-Henderson, Tom Ford, Jason Plato, Johnny Smith and Tim Lovejoy. One of the features of the programme is the 'infamous' shoot outs, between similarly priced, similarly powerful cars, or, recently, cars versus bikes. These shoot outs take place at the Ty Croes circuit on the Isle of Anglesey. Five 2002-

55 Degrees North Don Gilet (DS Nicky Cole), Dervla Kirwan (Claire Maxwell), Andrew Dunn (Sgt Rick Astel), George Harris (Errol Hill), Mark Stobbart (PC Martin Clark), Michael Hodgson (DS Frank Maguire), Darren Morfitt (DS Patrick Yates), Emma Cleasby (Sgt Katherine Brookes), Jaeden Burke (Matty Cole). Detective series written by Timothy Prager. A London detective sergeant moves to Newcastle after blowing the whistle on a corrupt colleague. BBC1 2004-05.

Film 72….. The film review programme actually started in 1971 for the South-East only, with Jacky Gillott as host. In 1972 the show was networked nationally with Joan Bakewell, Frederic Raphael and Barry Norman alternating as hosts before Norman took sole possession in 1973. Norman handed over the reins to Jonathan Ross for the 1999 series onwards and Claudia Winkleman replaced Ross in September 2010. BBC 1 1971-

Filthy Rich and Catflap Nigel Planer (Filthy Ralph aka Ralph Filthy), Rik Mayall (Richard Rich), Ade Edmondson (Eddie Catflap). All six episodes were written by Ben Elton. Richie Rich, a minor celebrity with a feckless nonentity of an agent, Filthy Ralph, and a dipsomaniac minder, Eddie Catflap, works on the fringes of stardom. BBC2 1987.

Filthy Rotten Scoundrels Documentary series featuring the work of environment officers across the UK, as they tackle astonishing and flagrant cases of fly-tipping. BBC1 2010-11

Final Cut, The See *House of Cards*

Fine Romance, A Judi Dench (Laura Dalton), Michael Williams (Mike Selway), Susan Penhaligon (Helen Barker), Richard Warwick (Phil Barker), Geoffrey Rose (Harry). Sitcom written by Bob Larbey. Laura is a translator by profession, a happy spinster. Reluctantly, (because she knows her younger sister Helen and her husband Phil are incurable matchmakers), she goes to one of their parties and sure enough, is introduced to bachelor Mike, also in his forties, a landscape gardener who drives around in a van. Laura feigns interest in Mike in order to fool Laura and Phil and escape the party as soon as possible. As the first series develops so the couple are drawn to one another, as much through boredom as anything else, but soon they begin an on-off relationship. ITV 1981-84.

Finger Tips Children's television series about creating things out of household items. Presenters have included Stephen Mulhern (Series 1-4), Fearne Cotton (Series 1-3), Naomi Wilkinson (Series 4-5) and Tim Dixon (Series 5). ITV 2001-04; 2008-

Fingerbobs Puppet creations of Joanne and Michael Cole. Presented by bearded Playschool refugee Rick Jones in the guise of Yoffy, a maker of finger puppets. Only 13 episodes were made and introduced Scampi, Flash the tortoise, Enoch the woodpecker, Louise the squirrel, Curly the sheep, Twit the owl, Gulliver the seagull and Fingermouse (who managed his own series in 1985), each having their own song. BBC1 1972.

Fingersmith Elaine Cassidy (Maud Lilly), Sally Hawkins (Sue Trinder), Imelda Staunton (Mrs Sucksby), Rupert Evans (Richard 'Gentleman' Rivers), Polly Hemingway (Mrs Stiles), Sarah Badel (Mrs Frobisher), Charles Dance (Mr Christopher Lilly), David Troughton (Mr Ibbs). Two–part adaptation of Sarah Waters' Man Booker Prize nominated novel. Sue Trinder is a fingersmith (slang for pickpocket) who lives in the slums of London with a baby farmer (person who looks after unwanted babies) Mrs Sucksby. When a once rich man, who gambled all his money away, presents them with a scam that has a payout of 40,000 pounds, Sue signs on to swindle rich heiress Maud Lilly. Sue will pose as Maud's maid so that Mr.Rivers (the gentleman) can get close to and eventually marry her. Their plan is to put Maud in the madhouse and take the money for themselves. All goes astray though when Sue falls in love with Maud. And the question is: Who can you trust? BBC1 2005.

Fire Crackers Joe Baker (Jumbo), Alfred Marks (Charlie). Sitcom based around inept local firemen working in the fictional Cropper's End (population 70). The local pub is the Cropper's Arms. ITV 1964-65.

Fireball XL5 Supermarionation series created by Gerry and Sylvia Anderson. Characters include Colonel Steve Zodiac, Professor Matthew Matic, Venus (voiced by Sylvia Anderson), Commander Zero, Lt 90, Zoonie, Robert the Robot (voiced by Gerry Anderson). The blond dare devil Steve Zodiac worked for World Space Patrol in the year 2063. Commander Zero was based in Space City. Thirty nine episodes were made. The closing theme song Fireball was performed by Don Spencer, the lyrics being: *I wish I was a spaceman, the fastest guy alive. I'd fly you 'round the universe, In fireball xl5. Way out in space together. Conquerors of the sky. My heart would be a fireball. A fireball. Every time I gaze into your starry eyes. We'd take a path to Jupiter and maybe very soon. We'd cruise along the Milky Way and land upon the Moon. To a wonderland of stardust. We'll zoom our way to mars. My heart would be a fireball. A fireball. And you would be my Venus of the stars.* ITV 1962-63

Fireman Sam Animation series created by Rob Lee and narrated by John Alderton. Brave, resourceful and calm in a crisis, Fireman Sam is a pillar of the community and the hero of the Pontypandy fire service. On the word of Station Officer Steele (a moustachioed Windsor Davies look-a-like), Sam, with colleagues Trevor Evans and Elvis Cridlington, hops aboard his engine, Jupiter (reg no. J999), to aid cats stuck up trees, children trapped in railings or shops engulfed in flames. Adventures in the Welsh valleys frequently centre on Bella Lasagne's cafe or Dilys Price's grocery store, with Dilys's son Norman often involved. The better behaved twins Sarah and James are also quite often involved. The series first aired in Welsh on S4C in 1986 under the title *Sam Tân*, Maldwyn Pope singing the theme song. The original series comprised 32x10 min episodes, with a 1x20 min Christmas Special. A new 26x10 min series of *Fireman Sam* was produced by Siriol Production in Cardiff, Wales in 2003. The series uses the latest techniques in puppet animation and introduces some great new characters to the show - including the bush pilot, Tom; the Flood family; and of course, Dusty the dog! *Fireman Sam* is used by Fire Brigades across the UK to deliver a safety message to children. S4C 1986; BBC 1987-88, 1990, 1994. *Fireman Sam* is now shown on the BBC as part of the Cbeebies menu.

First Born Charles Dance (Edward Forester), Julie Peasgood (Ann Forester), Philip Madoc (Lancing), Sharon Duce (Emily Jessop), Jamie Foster (Gor), Gabrielle Anwar (Nell Forester), Beth Pearce (young Nell). Ted Whitehead wrote this controversial series based on Maureen Duffy's novel *Gor Saga* about a scientist who successfully breeds a half ape/half human from female gorilla cells and his own sperm which he names Gordon, or Gor. Eventually Gor is beaten to death by his mother, a gorilla named Mary but the consequences do not end there. Forester's daughter Nell gives birth to Gor's daughter! BBC1 1988.

First Churchills, The Susan Hampshire (Sarah Churchill, Duchess of Marlborough), John Neville (John Churchill, Duke of Marlborough), John Standing (Sidney Godolphin), Robert Robinson (Louis XIV), Margaret Tyzack (Princess Anne), John Ringham (Laurence Hyde), Jill Balcon (Abigail Hill / Masham), Sheila Gish (Mary, duchess of York). 12-part mini-series depicting the early history of the Churchill family. BBC1 1969.

First Class Children's quiz show originally hosted by Louise Batchelor who was swiftly replaced by Debbie Greenwood. Two teams compete to answer the most questions correctly - and fastest on the buzzer. Some rounds were open to all, some specific to one player. The 'Spinning Gold Disc' was a particular highlight, where segments of a Compact Disc - a new concept in those days - were removed to reveal a pop star. Another game involved playing a Hangman game on a BBC micro where you had to guess a country by revealing certain letters. The computer used to keep score was named Eugene. The star prize for the whole series was a BBC micro for your school and the honour to play a special extra show against some of the cast of *Grange Hill*, and later *Eastenders*. BBC1 1984-87.

First Lady, The Sitcom created by Philip Levene. The series starred Thora Hird as crusading local councillor Sarah Danby and was set around the fictional borough of Furness in Lancashire (actually Barnsley in Yorkshire). BBC1 1968-69.

Fist of Fun Comedy sketch show that began life as a BBC Radio 1 series in 1993, before being given the first of two series on BBC2 in 1995. Written by and starring the comedy double act of (Stewart) Lee and (Richard) Herring, other contributors included Ronni Ancona, Peter Baynham, Kevin Eldon, Rebecca Front, Mel Giedroyc, Alistair McGowan, Ben Moor, Al Murray, Sue Perkins, Sally Phillips and John Thomson. BBC2 1995-96. See *This Morning With Richard Not Judy* and *Lionel Nimrod's Inexplicable World*

Five Daughters Adam Kotz (D), Juliet Aubrey (Maire Alderton), Natalie Press (Paula Clennell), Ian Hart (DCS Stewart Gull), Sarah Lancashire (Rosemary Nicholls), Vicky McClure (Stacy Nicholls), Jaime Winstone (Anneli Alderton), Chris McCalphy (Steve Wright). Three-part dramatised documentary about the killings of five young women by Steve Wright in the Ipswich area in 2006, concentrating on the last few days of the victims' lives, the effects of their deaths on their families, and the police investigation to find the murderer. Based on the personal testimonies of many of those most closely involved. BBC1 2010.

Five O'Clock Club Twice-weekly light entertainment children's show originally introduced by Muriel Young and Howard Williams. It was the new title for what had been previously known as *Small Time* (1955-62),and *Tuesday Rendezvous* (1962-63), as ATV attempted to repeat the BBC's consistent success with children's shows by coming up with a cross between *Blue Peter* and *Crackerjack*. The show featured regular items such as "Happy Cooking" with Fanny and Johnny Craddock (reprising a similar role in the Muriel Young-hosted *Lucky Dip*), Graham Dangerfield talking about pets, Jimmy Hanley (father of future *Magpie* presenter Jenny) making models and Bert Weedon giving guitar lessons. Wally Whyton replaced Howard Williams and for an entire generation of children the show entered its most fondly remembered era. But the undoubted stars of the show were a pair of glove puppets called Ollie Beak and Fred Barker, the first television glove puppets with attitude. The show's original glove puppet, Pussy Cat Willum, was cast aside and replaced by Ollie Beak when *Small Time* became *Tuesday Rendezvous* and now Ollie the Owl was joined by Fred the Dog, the pair becoming so popular that in 1965 the show was re-titled *Ollie and Fred's Five O'Clock Club*. ITV 1963-66.

Five O'Clock Show, The Weekday tea-time chat show hosted by a series of famous faces, Peter Andre presenting for the first two weeks. C4 2010. Another tea time show of the same name, although more often known as *Richard Hammond's Five O'Clock Show* (in which the Top Gear presenter co-hosted with Mel Giedroyc) aired on ITV in 2006.

Fixer, The Andrew Buchan (John Mercer), Peter Mullan (Lenny Douglas), Tamzin Outhwaite (Rose Chamberlain), Jody Latham (Calum McKenzie), Elisa Terren (Manuela), Liz White (Jess Mercer), Elliot Cowan (Matt Symmonds). Drama series created by Ben Richards. Ex-special forces operative and convicted murderer John Mercer is awarded an early release from prison on the condition that he becomes an assassin for the government, responsible for eliminating criminals and renegade police officers that are beyond the law. ITV 2008-09.

Flame Trees of Thika Hayley Mills (Tilly Grant), David Robb (Robin Grant), Ben Cross (Ian Crawfurd), Holly Aird (Elspeth Grant), John Nettleton (Major), Sharon Maughan (Lettice Palmer), Paul Onsongo (Juma), Tony Osoba (Ahmed), Mick Chege (Njombo), Steve Mwenesi Sammy). Flame Trees chronicles the efforts of the Grant family to establish a coffee farm in the unpromising Kenyan (known as The East African Protectorate at this time) bush in 1913. Based on the autobiographical novel of the same name by Elspeth Huxley. ITV 1981.

Flaxton Boys, The Peter Firth (Archie Weekes), David Smith (Jonathan Flaxton), James Hayter (Nathan), Peter Clay (Capt. Andrew Flaxton), David Bradley (Peter Weekes), Victor Winding (Barnaby Sweet), Gorden Kaye (P.C. Joseph), Jill Summers (Mary Porter). Four series (13 episodes in each) of this historical children's television series, set in the West Riding of Yorkshire, were made, each set in a different era, spanning the years 1854 to 1945, and including 1890 and 1928. The cast changed totally from series to series but is notable for the television debut of Peter Firth (see entry in cinema section) in the first series. The producer was Jess Yates and the series creator none other than darts commentator Sid Waddell. Filming for the series took place at Ripley Castle, four miles north of Harrogate. The memorable theme tune was an extract from Sergei Prokofiev's *Classical Symphony*. ITV 1969-73.

Flog It! Unwanted antiques are valued by experts, and then sold in a real-life auction. The show is most often presented by Cornwall dealer Paul Martin, though occasionally antiques expert Kate Alcock steps into the breach. Many of the resident antiques valuers will be familiar to anyone who has ever watched *Bargain Hunt*. The team includes Philip Serrell, David Barby, James Braxton, Kevin Jackson, James Lewis, Adam Partridge and Thomas Plant. BBC2 2002-

Flowerpot Men, The In 1952 The Flowerpot Men joined Andy Pandy as part of the pre-school-age children's light entertainment fare which became *Watch With Mother* the following year. The identical puppets, Bill and Ben were made out of flowerpots, their hands made out of large gardening gloves, and feet of hobnailed boots. Their 'flibadobs' and 'flobadobs' (their language was officially called Oddle Poddle) were the only way of telling them apart as Bill's voice was a light falsetto and Ben's a distinct bass. They lived in two giant flowerpots at the bottom of the garden, behind the potting shed. They would secretly pop their head over the flowerpot when the gardener went home for a bit of lunch, have a rascally adventure and return to their pots by the end of the programme as the gardener footstep's were heard. Keeping counsel was their neighbour Little Weed, who alerted them to any danger with a shrill "weeeeeeeeed" and a tortoise friend called Slowcoach made frequent visits. The burning issue of the day was always "Was it Bill or was it Ben?" sung in a beautiful soprano by the narrator. At this point every child would scream at their television set (some would act a little more reserved) "It was Bill" or "It was Ben". The perpetrator of the meddlesome prank would then be known by one of our heroes turning around to reveal their name. A recurrent theme was for the narrator to mention "and I think the little house knew something about it! Don't You?" The series was created by Freda Lingstrom and Maria Bird with Peter Hawkins providing the voices of both Bill and Ben, and Gladys Whitred and Julia Williams adding the songs. In 2000, The Flowerpot Men were revived by the BBC as a new 13-part series entitled *Bill and Ben*. BBC 1952-54.

Flumps, The The Flumps were created by Julie Holder. The much-repeated 13 episodes were produced by David Yates and narrated by Gay Soper. The Flumps were a family of sweet-natured furballs with distinct Yorkshire accents. There were six characters, Father Flump, Mother Flump, Grandfather and the three children, Posie (a girl) and the two boys Perkin and young Pootle. The stories focused on such gentle premises as getting vegetables to grow, fun with magnets, lending a hand, roller-skating, and keeping secrets. Grandfather was renowned for his ability to play his Flumpet, a cross between a trumpet and a horn which 'parped' like a tuba. When he wasn't flumpeting,

Grandfather would inevitably be found dozing with his moustache 'breezing' and his toes 'rippling' with contentment as he snoozed. Perkin, meanwhile, was renowned for his moods, and was regularly heard sounding-off about the other Flumps, or situations. Animation was by David Kellahar and music by Paul Reade. BBC1 1977.

Flying Doctor, The Richard Denning (Dr Greg Graham), Jill Adams (Mary Meredith the nurse), Peter Madden (Dr Jim Harrison the assistant), Alan White (Charley Wood the pilot), James Copeland (Alec Macleod the radio-operator). UK-Australian adventure series starring Richard Denning as the American doctor of the title. The series followed the cases of a flying doctor serving remote bush areas of Australia. The interior scenes were filmed at Elstree Studios and the Exterior scenes were filmed in Australia by Crawford Productions. ITV 1959-61.

Flying Swan, The Margaret Lockwood (Mollie Manning), Julia Lockwood (Carol Manning), Nerys Hughes (Maisie). Six-part drama series set in a hotel. BBC 1965.

Follyfoot Gillian Blake (Dora), Steve Hodson (Steve), Arthur English (Slugger), Desmond Llewelyn (The Colonel), Christian Rodska (Ron Stryker), Paul Guess (Lewis Hammond). Based on Monica Dickens (great granddaughter of Charles Dickens) 1963 novel Cobbler's Dream, *Follyfoot* is set in a retirement home for old or unwanted horses in Yorkshire (filmed in Harewood, near Leeds), invariably rescued from a cruel fate or cruel owners. The farm is run by The Colonel; his niece Dora; Steve, a former juvenile delinquent; and Ron, a ne'er-do-well motorcyclist with a heart of gold. The resident cook was Slugger, the Colonel's ex batman and a former boxer. In the middle of the farm stands a burnt out tree that had been struck by lightning during a storm one night and the Colonel believes that it will bloom again given enough care and attention, so everyone who passes it by is required to throw a bucket of water over its roots, making it a symbol of the work undertaken in the horse sanctuary, as well as something of a supposedly good luck charm. The theme tune The Lightning Tree was written by Steven Francis and performed by The Settlers. The lyrics were as follows: *Down in the meadow where the wind blows free, in the middle of a field stands a lightning tree. It's limbs all torn from the day it was born for the tree was born in a thunderstorm. Grow, grow, the lightning tree, it's never too late for you and me; Grow, grow, the lightning tree, never give in too easily. Down in the meadow where the wind blows light, the lightning struck in the middle of the night. Limbs stripped bare by the lightning flare the lightning flare was a wild affair. (Chorus) Down in the meadow where the wind blows cold, the lightning tree stands stiff and old. Branches bent when the lightning rent the lightning rent from the firmament. (Chorus). Down in the meadow with the wind in the west, the lightning tree faced up to the test. Its heart went snap when it took the rap, the terrible rap of the thunder clap. (Chorus). Down in the meadow when the wind blows free, a whispering breeze in the lightning tree. Dreams come true if you want them to if you want them to, then it's up to you. (Chorus x 3). Lightning Tree x 3.* ITV 1971-73.

Food and Drink Long-running food magazine. Presenters have included Simon Bates, Gillian Miles, Chris Kelly, Henry Kelly, Susan Grossman, Jilly Goolden, Michael Barry, Oz Clarke, Paul Heiney, Antony Worrall Thompson, and Emma Crowhurst. BBC2 1982- 2000.

Footballers' Wives Gary Lucy (Kyle Pascoe), Gillian Taylforth (Jackie Pascoe), Susie Amy (Chardonnay Lane Pascoe), Nathan Constance (Ian Walmsley), Katharine Monaghan (Donna Walmsley), Zöe Lucker (Tanya Turner/Laslett), Cristian Solimeno (Jason Turner), Jesse Birdsall (Roger Webb), Daniel Schutzmann (Salvatore Biagi), John Forgeham (Frank Laslett), Philip Bretherton (Stefan Hauser), Ben Richards (Bruno Milligan), Alison Newman (Hazel Bailey), Laila Rouass (Amber Gates), Ben Price (Conrad Gates), Jamie Davis (Harley Lawson), Sarah Barrand (Shannon Donnelly-Lawson), Peter Ash (Darius Fry), Joan Collins (Eva de Wolffe), Jessica Brooks (Freddie Hauser), Julie Le Grand (Nurse Jeanette Dunkley), Tom Swire (Sebastian Webb), Billie Wackrill (Holly Walmsley), Micaiah Dring (Marie Minshull), Sam Graham (Archie Malloch), Chad Shepherd (Ronald Bateman), Leanne Baker (Lara Bateman), Nick Lopez (Tel Harper), Paula Wilcox (Marguerite Laslett), Helen Latham (Lucy Milligan), Marcel McCalla (Noah Alexander), Graham Norton (Brendan Spunk). Drama series revolving around the private lives of a group of professional footballers. The show is based around the fictional Earls Park Football Club and one of the chief focuses throughout several series has been the vile Tanya Turner, at first the widow of footballer Jason Turner, before marrying Frank Laslett, the chairman of Earls Park, and then being briefly engaged to footballer Conrad Gates. Joan Collins joined the cast for Series Five, playing a glamorous magazine mogul. ITV 2002-06

For Love of Money Game show based on the hugely popular 1958 US show of the same name where contestants answered general knowledge questions and could either take the offered prize or gamble on winning a higher sum of money ranging from nine shillings to 9999 shillings. Bob Monkhouse hosted 46 episodes between 1959 and 1960 and Des O'Connor took over for the final 26 shows. Dickie Henderson and Keith Fordyce stood in for Bob for the occasional show. Ann Taylor, Julie Stevens, Joy Webster and Nicky Allen were the hostesses and Barry Faber the announcer. ITV 1959-61

For One Night Only Old-fashioned variety shows hosted by Vernon Kay and Joan Rivers. The shows followed the tried and tested format of singers, dancers and speciality acts interspersed with comedy patter from the two hosts. ITV 2008-09

For the Love of Ada Irene Handl (Ada Cresswell/Bingley), Wilfred Pickles (Walter Bingley), Jack Smethurst (Leslie Pollitt), Barbara Mitchell (Ruth Pollitt). Sitcom written by Vince Powell and Harry Driver. Ada is a widow in her 70s and Walter is the gravedigger who buried her husband. The couple become friendly and a relationship gradually develops. Ada's daughter, Ruth lives next door with her husband Leslie, and they don't really approve of the relationship but reluctantly accept it. By the end of the second series the pensioners wed. ITV 1970-71. A film spin-off was made in 1972 with the cast reprising their roles and introduced a young Patsy Kensit in her first screen role.

For the Rest of Your Life Rather over-complicated game show produced by Endemol in which coupled contestants try to earn a cash sum paid to them monthly for a term of years. The game begins with the players choosing one of three envelopes to decide the base prize. The first part of the main game sees them trying to multiply this up into a more substantial monthly amount by choosing light sticks from their pods; white lights increase the sum by the amount of the base while red lights correspondingly decrease the amount. Three red lights is game over so a certain amount of caution is necessary. Once the monthly amount has been established the second part of the game involves playing for time. The person who revealed the coloured lights now goes into an isolation booth where they are kept informed of how the game is going, but not of what their partner is saying. Eleven white lights and four reds now count for months for which the money won in the first half is paid, from one month up to The Rest of Your Life (40 years is the maximum). The player in the studio decides whether to stick or continue after each white light is uncovered, the one in the booth makes the same decision, of which the other player, and the viewers, are not informed. After the main player has finished, either by sticking or by uncovering all the reds and losing the money, the other is brought out of the booth, and the game is run through again to see if the boothed player saved or lost them thousands of pounds by sticking earlier than their partner and thus ending the game. Presented by Nicky Campbell, the unscreened pilot was presented by Bradley Walsh. ITV 2007-09

Forever Green John Alderton (Jack Boult), Pauline Collins (Harriet Boult), Daisy Bates (Freddy Boult), Paola Dionisotti (Lady Patricia Broughall), Ian Lindsay (Ted Hubbard (1989)), Wendy van der Plank (Hilly), Nimer Rashed (Tom Boult). Jack Boult, a former rally driver, and his second wife Harriet, a former nurse, move from the bustle of London, following a fortunate inheritance, and start a new life in a cottage at Meadows Green Farm in the west country, together with Jack's children Freddy and Tom. With the help of Lady Patricia Broughall, a local landowner, and her grand-daughter, Hilly, who lives in a railway carriage in the woods, they become involved in tackling various environmental issues such as badger-baiting and horse-stealing. ITV 1989, 1992.

Forsyte Saga, The Kenneth More (Jolyon 'Jo' Forsyte), Eric Porter (Soames Forsyte), Nyree Dawn Porter (Irene Heron/Forsyte), Terence Alexander (Montague Dartie), Joseph O'Connor (Jolyon 'Old Jolyon' Forsyte), John Welsh (James Forsyte), Margaret Tyzack (Winifred Forsyte/Dartie), Fay Compton (Ann Forsyte), Lana Morris (Helene Hilmer/Forsyte), Susan Hampshire (Fleur Forsyte), Michael York (Jolyon 'Jolly' Forsyte), Martin Jarvis (Jolyon 'Jon' Forsyte), Maggie Jones (Smither), Nicholas Pennell (Michael Mont), John Barcroft (George), Suzanne Neve (Holly). Based on the series of novels and stories by John Galsworthy concerning the tumultuous events in the lives of three generations of the insular and aristocratic Forsyte family from 1879 to 1926. BBC2 1967. The series was repeated on BBC1 in 1968 and managed audiences in excess of 18 million at its peak. A remake of the series was shown on ITV in 2002 with Rupert Graves in the Kenneth More role, Damian Lewis as Soames and Corin Redgrave as Jolyon Forsyte Sr. A second series *The Forsyte Saga: To Let* was shown in 2003.

Fort Boyard Gameshow presented by Melinda Messenger based on the French show *Les Clés de Fort Boyard,* created by Jacques Antoine. The format is similar to another Antoine creation, *The Crystal Maze,* although focusing more on physical challenges rather than mental ones. Set and filmed on the real Fort Boyard in France, the programme starred Leslie Grantham as the eponymous Boyard, the dastardly master of the fort who sets the challenges for the contestants. Geoffrey Bayldon played the eccentric professor who became mad after Boyard kept him prisoner in the watchtower. His job is to ask the contestants riddles in order for them to progress successfully. Other characters include Jacques and Jules (André Bouchet and Alain Prévost respectively), two dwarves who lead the team through the Fort in between challenges (Deni replaces Jules later in the show); the Tiger Master who turns a statue shaped as a tiger's head to release the gold or close the gate in the Treasure Room (replaced by Monique -played by Monique d'Angeon- after the first series; and La Boule (played by Yves Marchesseau), who bangs the gong to indicate the start and end of time and locks the contestants in the cages when they fail to get out of challenge rooms in time. Four series were broadcast. *Five* 1998-2001. The show transferred to Challenge TV in 2003 with Jodie Penfold presenting, Christopher Ellison performing the Boyard role and Tom Baker asking the riddles as the insane mariner Captain Baker.

Fortune: Million Pound Giveaway Richard Madeley introduced a conveyor-belt of members of the public who attempted to convince five millionaires that they deserved a slice of their money. The Fortune Five were Jeffrey Archer, Duncan Bannatyne, Jacqueline Gold, Simon Jordan and Kanya King. ITV 2007

Fortunes of War Kenneth Branagh (Guy Pringle), Emma Thompson (Harriet Pringle), Rupert Graves (Simon Boulderstone), Robert Stephens (Castlebar), Ronald Pickup (Prince Yakimov), Vernon Dobtcheff (Prince Hadjimoscos), Ronald Fraser (Cmdr. Sheppey), Greg Hicks (Aiden Pratt), Alan Bennett (Lord Pinkrose), Beryl Cooke (Gladys Twocurry), Philip Madoc (Freddie von Flugel), Jeremy Sinden (Lord Lisdoonvarna), Jack Watling (Sir Desmond Hooper), James Villiers (Inchcape). Mini-series written by Alan Plater. Guy Pringle and his new wife, Harriet, are members of the English community in Bucharest, Romania, on the eve of World War II. The series chronicles their adventures as war begins and focuses too on the many and varied characters that cross and re-cross their path as they flee before the advancing German armies to Athens and then to Cairo. BBC1 1987.

Forty Minutes Current affairs programme. BBC2 1982-94. See *Man Alive.*

Fortysomething Hugh Laurie (Paul Slippery), Anna Chancellor (Estelle Slippery), Sheila Hancock (Gwendolen Hartley), Lolita Chakrabarti (Surinder), Peter Capaldi (Dr Ronnie Pilfrey), Benedict Cumberbatch (Rory Slippery), Neil Henry (Daniel Slippery), Joe Van Moyland (Edwin Slippery). Six-part comedy drama series written by Nigel Williams, based on his 1999 novel of the same name. Paul Slippery is a doctor facing a mid-life

crisis. His wife Estelle is starting a new career as a headhunter. His three sons, Rory, a student at the fictitious University of Reigate, Daniel, and Edwin, are sex-obsessed. Meanwhile, Paul appears to hear the inner thoughts of others. Other characters include Paul's partner and nemesis, Dr. Ronnie Pilfrey, Estelle's new employer, Gwendolen Hartley, and Surinder, Paul's assistant. ITV 2003

Fosters, The Norman Beaton (Samuel Foster), Isabelle Lucas (Pearl Foster), Carmen Munro (Vilma), Lenny Henry (Sonny Foster). Sitcom that broke new ground as Britain's first series to feature an all-black cast. ITV 1976-77.

Four Feather Falls Voices: Nicholas Parsons (Tex Tucker), Kenneth Connor (Rocky, Dusty and Pedro), David Graham (Grandpa Twink and Fernando), Denise Bryer (Ma Jones and Little Jake). Tex Tucker was the sheriff of Four Feather Falls. Once, when Tex was crossing a desolate trail he came across a little Indian boy. Night was drawing in and, with it, the cold. At night the Indian boy woke from his sleep screaming 'Kalamakooya' and a great Indian chief appeared. He caused great magical things to happen. As a reward for finding and caring for his son, he gave Tex four magic feathers. One gave Dusty (his dog) the power of speech, another did the same for Rocky (his horse), and the remaining two made Tex's guns swivel and fire automatically whenever he was in danger. This was the first puppet show to use electronic lip-synch and eye movement so the voices really appeared to come from the puppets' mouths. The producer Gerry Anderson named this process "Supermarionation" although he did not use the title until his *Supercar* series was produced. Michael Holliday recorded the songs from the series, including 'Phantom Rider', 'Two Gun Tex' and the title song. ITV 1958.

Four In A Bed See *Three In A Bed*

Four Just Men, The Jack Hawkins (Ben Manfred MP), Dan Dailey (Tim Collier), Richard Conte (Jeff Ryder), Vittorio De Sica (Ricco Poccari), Andrew Keir (Jock - Hawkins episodes), Honor Blackman (Nicole- Dailey episodes), June Thorburn (Vicky - Conte episodes), Lisa Gastoni (Giulia - De Sica episodes). Based on the 1906 novel by Edgar Wallace, this popular series highlighted each one its stars working alone in their crusade against crime and corruption (38 episodes in which none of the four stars appear together apart from the opening sequence). As the opening credits rolled with the four signing their pact to tackle injustice around the world (at the request of their wartime leader, Colonel Bacon) this narration would be heard: *Throughout time there have been men to whom justice has been more important than life itself. From these ranks come four men prepared to fight valiantly on the side of justice, wherever the need may be. Joined together in this cause they are -* THE FOUR JUST MEN. ITV 1959-60.

Fox Peter Vaughan (Billy Fox), Elizabeth Spriggs (Connie Fox), Ray Winstone (Kenny Fox), Larry Lamb (Joey Fox), Bernard Hill (Vin Fox), Derrick O'Connor (Ray Fox), Eamon Boland (Phil Fox). Written by Trevor Preston. The story of the Fox family, dominated by their patriarch Billy Fox, a retired Covent Garden market porter who is regarded with awe by the residents of Clapham where most of the action takes place. He has five sons by two marriages, and although he is a family man, the sons struggle to form their own identity under his shadow. There is a particular tension between Billy and his intellectual son, Phil, a left-wing firebrand, which is exacerbated when Phil refuses to attend his youngest brother's (Kenny) vital boxing match, the ramifications of which rumble on throughout the series. When Billy dies, the family tries to hold itself together, but individual trials and tribulations create division, and Phil departs to the US in order to work through his feelings. The other brothers were Vin, a construction worker; Joey, a womanising taxi-driver and publican Ray, the eldest and often wisest of the bunch. 13 episodes ITV 1980.

Foyle's War Detective drama series created by Anthony Horowitz. Set in Hastings during the 1940s, Detective Chief Superintendent Christopher Foyle attempts to catch criminals profiteering from the war effort and the aftermath thereof. He is ably assisted by his driver Sam Stewart and Detective Sergeant Paul Milner. Michael Kitchen (Foyle), Anthony Howell (Paul Milner), Honeysuckle Weeks (Samantha "Sam" Stewart). The show was cancelled after six series but revived in 2010 for a further three feature-length episodes. ITV 2002-08; 2010.

Fraggle Rock Children's television series created by Jim Henson, primarily featuring a cast of Muppet creatures called Fraggles, with music by Philip Balsam and Dennis Lee. The vision of Fraggle Rock articulated by Jim Henson was to depict a fun world, but also a world with a relatively complex system of symbiotic relationships between different "races" of creatures, an allegory to the human world, where each group was somewhat unaware of how interconnected and important they were to one another. On Fraggle Rock, a rugged outcrop off the southern coast of England, stood a lighthouse. The lighthouse-keeper is an old sea-salt simply called The Captain, played by Fulton Mackay (The captain was later replaced by his nephew PK, played by John Gordon Sinclair and then by BJ, played by Simon O'Brien). The captain only has his faithful old hound Sprocket as company but underneath the weather-beaten building lurks a fantastic subterranean world. Fraggles are small humanoid creatures, about 22 inches tall, that come in a wide variety of colours and have tails that bear a tuft of fur on the end. They live in a system of natural caves called Fraggle Rock that are filled with all manner of creatures and features, and which seem to connect to at least two different worlds. Fraggles live a very carefree life, spending most of their time playing, exploring, and generally enjoying themselves. They live on a diet of radishes and "doozer sticks". The series focused on one group of Fraggles in particular; Gobo, Mokey, Red, Wembley, and Boober. They form a tight-knit group of friends, and each has a distinctive personality type. Gobo is the "leader", level-headed and practical, and considers himself chiefly an explorer. Mokey is highly spiritual and artistic, being quiet and contemplative. Red, on the other hand, is exuberant and athletic; she is one of the best swimmers among the Fraggles. Wembley is nervous and pathologically indecisive, though no coward when push comes to shove. Boober's cardinal trait is depression and anxiety, and his favourite activity is washing socks. Within Fraggle Rock lives a second species of small humanoid creatures, the pudgy green ant-like Doozers. Standing only 6 inches tall, Doozers are the antithesis of Fraggles; and as such are dedicated to work and industry although the Fraggles tend to eat their fabulous constructions. Gobo's Uncle Matt discovered the door to the human world, known by Fraggles as "Outer Space"; its inhabitants known as "Silly Creatures". In another exit from Fraggle Rock live a small family of Gorgs, giant furry humanoids standing 22 feet tall. The husband and wife of the family consider themselves the King and Queen of the Universe, with their son Junior as its prince and heir, but to all appearances they are really simple farmers with a rustic house and garden patch. Fraggles are considered a pest by the Gorgs, as they steal radishes. (In one episode it is revealed that the Gorgs use radishes to make "anti-vanishing cream" that prevents them from becoming invisible. Thus, the three main races of the Fraggle Rock universe - Fraggles, Doozers and Gorgs - are all dependent on the radishes for their own particular reason). Also in the Gorgs' world is a sapient compost heap called Marjory, and her two rat-like sidekicks Philo and Gunge. The Fraggles consider the Trash Heap to be all-wise and go to her for advice regularly. Only Philo and Gunge called her Marjory; the Fraggles called her Madame Trash Heap. She wasn't much of a principal character on the show but did appear in nearly every episode. Madame Trash Heap was played by Jerry Nelson. After Fraggle Rock ended, Philo went into retirement, but Gunge appeared on Dinosaurs and Mopatop's Shop. Philo was played by Dave Goelz and Gunge was played by Richard Hunt. Other creatures included The Blob, a giant rolling blob that has a generally amorphous shape but has some kind of mouth somewhere; Convincing John, a Fraggle who uses his fast talking musical numbers to convince Fraggles to do anything; The Poisonous Cackler, a large, fearsome, scorpion-like creature who enjoys eating smoke bombs; and The Spider Fly, a flying insect capable of turning into an avuncular Fraggle-like being and granting wishes. The first episode aired on 10 January 1983, and the last episode aired on 30 March 1987, for a total of five seasons, with a total of 96 episodes. ITV 1983-87

Francis Durbridge Presents Francis Durbridge (1912-98) was born in Hull Yorkshire. After studying English at Birmingham University he worked briefly as a stockbroker before becoming a full-time writer. His first book, *Send for Paul Temple* (1938), a collaboration with John Thewes, was a novelisation of his BBC radio serial that began in that year (See *Paul Temple*). Durbridge wrote various cliff-hanger thriller series for BBC Television between 1952 and 1980, beginning with *The Broken Horseshoe* (Britain's first television thriller series, a six-parter produced live from a tiny studio at Alexandra Palace). The first serial to be transmitted under the 'Francis Durbridge Presents' banner was *The World of Tim Frazer*, starring Jack Hedley as an undercover agent. This 18-part series first aired on 15 November 1960. All his subsequent series were prefixed by his name, including Paul Temple (although he did not write any of the stories for television). Durbridge also wrote Paul Temple novels in collaboration with Douglas Rutherford and Charles Hatten (those with Rutherford were even published under the name "Paul Temple" thus making the fictional writer a "real" one.) Durbridge also wrote four Paul Temple stories which were turned into films *Send for Paul Temple* (1946) with Anthony Hulme playing the hero, *Calling Paul Temple* (1948), *Paul Temple's Triumph* (1950) and *Paul Temple Returns* (1952), John Bentley taking over the role in the last three films.

Frank Stubbs Promotes Timothy Spall (Frank Stubbs), Lesley Sharp (Petra Dillon), Daniella Westbrook (Dawn Dillon), Roy Marsden (Blick), Nick Reding (Dave Giddings), Hazel Ellerby (Diane Stubbs). Created by Simon Nye. Frank Stubbs (Timothy Spall) is a down-at-heel ticket tout with grand ideas. He has an ambition to become a 'high class' promoter of famous and talented performers but in reality, his ambitions tend to outstrip his capabilities. ITV 1993-94.

Frankenstein's Cat CBBC animated series based on the picture book created by Curtis Jobling. Each 11-minute episode follows the exploits of hyperactive Franken-pet Nine (voiced by Joe Pasquale) and his best friend Lottie (voiced by Alex Kelly) as they continually outwit the citizens of Oddsburg. Other characters include Nine's three ugly sisters, Igora (a chicken), Heidi (a hamster) and Fifi (a dog); Clever Trevor, Pipsquawk, Sweeny, Bigtop, Mr Crumble – and of course – Dr Frankenstein. BBC1 2008.

Freezing Hugh Bonneville (Matt), Elizabeth McGovern (Elizabeth), Tom Hollander (Leon). Sitcom written by James Wood and directed by Simon Curtis. Leon, an agent, moves in with Elizabeth, an Oscar-nominated American actress, and her British publisher husband, Matt, themselves working together from home for the first time. Originally a one-off comedy as part of BBC Four's *Tight Spot* season in February 2007, which then became the first episode of the series when it aired on BBC2 in 2008.

French and Saunders BBC2 1987-88; 1990; 1993; 1996; 2004; 2007. Plus various specials. See entries for Dawn French and Jennifer Saunders in the comedy section.

Fresh Fields Julia McKenzie (Hester Fields), Anton Rodgers (William Fields), Ballard Berkeley (Guy Penrose), Ann Beach (Sonia Barratt), Fanny Rowe (Nancy Penrose). Sitcom created by John Chapman. Hester is a middle-aged woman with a grown-up daughter. Although happily married to William and well provided for, she can't help feeling that there's something missing in her life. She embarks on a seemingly endless quest for self-improvement which tends to frustrate and infuriate William. Three years after the end of the final series, a sequel entitled *French Fields* began taking the couple from the leafy lanes of Barnes to the grape yards of Northern France. ITV 1984-86, 1989-91.

Friday Night Armistice, The See *The Saturday Night Armistice*.

Friday Night Is Music Night Broadcast live between 8pm and 10pm on Fridays, originally from the Mermaid Theatre in London or the Watford Colosseum, although now the longest-running radio music show travels to many other theatres and concert halls throughout the UK. The resident orchestra is the BBC Concert Orchestra, which was formed at the beginning of proceedings in 1952, and has a wide and flexible repertoire, ranging from classical works and grand opera to light music and popular songs. Its Principal Conductors over the years have been Gilbert Vinter,

Sir Charles Mackerras, Vilem Tausky, Marcus Dods, Ashley Lawrence and, since 1989, Barry Wordsworth. Each programme begins with the orchestra playing the introduction of an adapted version of Charles Williams's *High Adventure*, followed by the presenter uttering the immortal title words. This happens again at the close of the programme, with the announcer ending on "I hope that once again we have proved that Friday Night IS Music Night". Presenters have included Richard Baker, Robin Boyle, Ken Bruce, Russell Davies, Paul Gambaccini, Aled Jones, Brian Kay, Jimmy Kingsbury and Clare Teal. BBC Light Programme (Radio 2 since 1967) 1952-

Friday Night Live See *Saturday Live.*

Friday Night Project, The Comedy chat and sketch show originally presented by comics Jimmy Carr, Rob Rouse, Sharon Horgan and roving reporter Lucy Montgomery with occasional appearances from Abi Titmuss. The presenters were joined each week by a guest presenter and guest band. Guest presenters have included Vinnie Jones, Kelly Osbourne and Kelly Brook whilst the bands Fightstar, The Bravery, Moby and The Futureheads have also featured. From the second series onwards the regular hosts were comedians Justin Lee Collins and Alan Carr with segments from Debra Stephenson and Chantelle Houghton. The guest hosts for the second series were: Billie Piper (Episode 1), Lorraine Kelly (Episode 2) (Editors as the Guest Band), Christian Slater (Episode 3) (The Kooks as the Guest Band), Denise van Outen (Episode 4) (Boy Kill Boy as the Guest Band), Michael Barrymore (Episode 5) (The Ordinary Boys as the Guest Band), Jamie Oliver (Episode 6) (Kubb as the Guest Band), Jessie Wallace (Episode 7) (Hard-Fi as the Guest Band), Trisha Goddard (Episode 8) (The Automatic as the Guest Band). Originally broadcast on Friday nights, the show moved to Sunday nights for its seventh series in 2008 and changed its name accordingly. C4 2005-09

Friday Night With Jonathan Ross Jonathan Stephen Ross, born in Camden, north London, 17 November 1960, is a radio and television presenter, and film critic who was awarded the OBE in 2005. Jonathan is the son of actress Martha Ross and he himself made his television debut as an actor, aged nine, in an oft-shown television advert for Rice Krispies. He has three other famous brothers, Simon (the founder of Cactus TV), Miles (a television producer, actor and writer) and Paul (a television presenter; b. April 1956, Leytonstone, London). After attending university in London and gaining an East European History degree, Jonathan worked as a researcher on Channel 4's late-night show *Loose Talk* before the station gave him his own show *The Last Resort* in 1987. He married author, journalist and broadcaster Jane Goldman in 1988 and together they established the television production company Hotsauce TV. The couple have two daughters, Betty and Honey, and a son, Harvey. An avid fan of comic books, Jonathan recently published, *Turf*, a five-issue comic book limited series, illustrated by Tommy Lee Edwards and published by Image Comics. Friday Night With Jonathan Ross was a late night chat show which displayed Jonathan's own brand of irreverent humour and light-hearted banter. As well as the closing musical act Jonathan had a resident house band, 4 Poofs and a Piano. BBC1 2001-10. After leaving the BBC in 2010 (see entry for Russell Brand in the comedy section) he transferred his show to ITV under the name *The Jonathan Ross Show*. See also entries for *The Big Big Talent Show, Extras, Film 72....., It's Only TV... But I Like It, Jonathan Creek, Rex the Runt, Shooting Stars,* and *They Think It's All Over.*

Frost Programme David Paradine Frost was born in Tenterden, Kent, 7 April 1939. Like so many of his peers he was part of the Cambridge Footlights in his University days. He first made his name on the BBC series *That Was the Week That Was* before appearing in a succession of programmes with Frost in the title of the show, including this highly acclaimed offering which showed the beginning of the transition from the comedian to the serious interviewer. Frost pioneered such TV techniques as directly involving the audience in the discussions and blending comedy sketches with current affairs. From this time on Frost's mixture of politics and entertainment would draw mixed responses from

critics. At this time his "ad-lib interviewing" style, as he calls it, was characterized by rather remorseless fire on well-chosen subjects, and led to his label as the "tough inquisitor". Frost interviewed most of the world's leaders at some point but his finest hour was a confrontation on live TV with the reviled insurance swindler Dr Emil Savundra on 3 February 1967. Savundra had asked to be interviewed by Frost, confident that his charm would sway public opinion in his favour. By the end it is clear which of them the studio audience was rooting for. This occasion led to Lord Justice Salmon's warning that trial by TV should not be tolerated in a civilised society. ITV 1966-68

Frost Report, The Topical satire show introduced by David Frost with the now legendary "Hello, good evening and welcome!". The shows were written by Graham Chapman, John Cleese, Eric Idle, Terry Jones, Michael Palin, Marty Feldman, Tim Brooke-Taylor and John Law. The sketches were performed by John Cleese, Ronnie Barker, Ronnie Corbett, Sheila Steafel, Nicky Henson and Tom Lehrer. Each programme featured a song by Julie Felix. A compilation of the best moments entitled *Frost Over England*, won the Golden Rose of Montreaux in 1967. BBC1 1966-67.

Full Circle Michael Palin's 1997 BBC travel dialogue began and ended at Little Diomede Island in the Bering Strait. Following the Pacific Rim the journey was completed within the deadline of one calendar year (1995) and covered 50,000 miles.

Full Stretch Kevin McNally (Baz Levick), Reece Dinsdale (Tarquin Woods), Sue Johnston (Grace Robbins), Rowena King (Tessa Knowles), David Howey (Norman Love). Six-part sitcom written by Dick Clement and Ian La Frenais. Baz Levick, an ex-footballer, is now the proprietor of the Ivory Towers Limousine Car Service. The fast-talking Baz has to use all his ingenuity and charm to fend off competitors and keep his business on the road, while his team of hard-working drivers find themselves chauffeuring everyone from rock stars to insufferable aristocrats. David Bowie makes a cameo appearance in the series and actress Helen McCrory makes her screen debut in an episode as Vicki Goodall. ITV 1993

Fully Booked Children's television magazine show produced by BBC Scotland and originally presented by Zoë Ball and Grant Stott. The show was set in a fictional Scottish hotel and its stars were said to be guests at the hotel. The puppet Morag the cow was the hotel's receptionist. Other characters included Wee Alistair McAlistair, Jan Van Da Vall and Les Vegas all played by Paul Brophy. The show originally aired on Saturday mornings but was moved to Sunday mornings from the summer of 1996 when the extended Saturday CBBC was renamed Saturday Aardvark, with Otis being a key feature. Also at this time Zoe Ball was replaced by Sarah Vandenbergh. In 1998 a new team arrived in the form of Chris Jarvis, Gail Porter and Tim Vincent. For the last series Gail was replaced by Kate Heavenor. BBC2 1995-99. In 2000 *Fully Booked* was replaced by *FBi* (Fully Booked Interactive), back on Saturday mornings. Heavenor was retained, whilst the other presenters were replaced by Vernon Kay and former Boyzone member Keith Duffy.

Funland Daniel Mays (Carter Krantz), Judy Parfitt (Mercy Woolf), Ian Puleston-Davies (Shirley Woolf), Frances Barber (Connie Woolf), Kenny Doughty (Liam Woolf), Emily Aston (Ruby Woolf), Kris Marshall (Dudley Sutton), Sarah Smart (Lola Sutton), Roy Barraclough (Rev Onan Van Kneck), Mark Gatiss (Ambrose Chapfel), Beth Cordingly (Vienna Keen), Burn Gorman (Tim Timothy), Philip Jackson (Leo Finch), Brian Hibbard (Willy Woolf), Kevin Eldon (Shadowman), Geoffrey Hutchings (Howdie Doodre), Cheryl Campbell (Lola's Mother), Shaun Williamson (Cliff). Comedy drama series written by Simon Ashdown and Jeremy Dyson. Set in Blackpool over one long weekend. Carter Krantz arrives in the seaside town to avenge the death of his mother. Without a penny to his name and carrying only a fragment of paper containing the words 'Ambrose Chapel', he is sucked into the most disturbing of mysteries. The dysfunctional Woolf family are at the heart of everything that happens: there's Shirley Woolf, a borderline psycho; his mother, the evil and manipulative Mercy; and his foolhardy wife Connie. Other characters include Dudley and Lola Sutton, hoping for a dirty weekend to spice up their marriage; Ambrose Chapfel, a Dutch repressed taxidermist; Rev Onan Van Kneck, the corrupt town Mayor; Vienna Keen, the enigmatic lap-dancer; Leo Finch who runs the Shangri-la guesthouse; and the mysterious Shadowman. First aired on BBC3 in 2005 and repeated on BBC2 2006.

Fuse, The Weekday game show hosted by former rugby player Austin Healey. Six contestants were challenged to take on 'The Fuse' and quickly answer questions to prevent a fortune going up in smoke, before competing against one another to take the prize money home. ITV 2009.

Gaffer, The Bill Maynard (Fred Moffat), Russell Hunter (Harry). Sitcom written by Graham White. Fred Moffat is the ducking-and-diving owner of Moffat Engineering Company, a firm perennially on the brink of disaster. ITV 1981-83.

Gambit Game show based on the card game pontoon. Originally hosted by Fred Dinenage (1978-81) assisted by Michelle Lambourne. Tom O'Connor took over in 1982. ITV 1978-83.

Game for A Laugh Based on the 1950s US game show, *People Are Funny*, the show mixed hidden-camera pranks with audience participation stunts and pre-recorded items. The four original presenters were Jeremy Beadle, Henry Kelly, Matthew Kelly and Sarah Kennedy, who would all career down the steps at the top of the show and plant themselves on stools in the centre of the stage. By the final series in 1985 only Jeremy Beadle remained of the originals (he was joined by Rustie Lee, Martin Daniels, Lee Peck and Debbie Rix. The show would invariably end with the words "Watching you watching us, watching us watching you". This show was undoubtedly the springboard for the more elaborate pranks Jeremy was to be involved in at a later date. ITV 1981-85. See also *Beadle's About*.

Game On Ben Chaplin and Neil Stuke (Matthew Malone), Matthew Cottle (Martin Henson), Samantha Janus (Mandy Wilkins), Tracy Keating (Clare Monohan), Mark Powley (Jason), Crispin Bonham-Carter (Archie Glenister). Sitcom written by Andrew Davies and Bernadette Davis, focusing on the sexual adventures and misadventures of three twenty-somethings living under the same roof. Ben Chaplin (in the first series) played Matthew, a wealthy, workshy landlord who, because of a strange phobia, never leaves the flat. Matthew Cottle was cast as the hapless, sexually innocent Martin, and Samantha Janus played the ambitious but confused and deeply insecure Mandy. BBC2 1995-98.

Games, The Ten celebrities spent six weeks training in six different sporting disciplines which were then put to the test live every night for a week. The men and women competed in a different sport every night and the live nightly show was when the final of an event was held (the qualifying heats, if any, were usually shown live in the afternoons on E4). Contestants score five points for winning an event, three for second, two for third, one for fourth and zero for coming last with a bonus point if they beat their personal best on the night. The money raised from ticket sales, viewer polls and telephone competitions went into a big pot and the celebrities took a cut for their charities in proportion to the amount of points scored during the week. A wide variety of events were on offer from swimming, judo, floor exercises and speed skating for the women to diving, weightlifting, vaulting horse and curling for the men. The final day featured the track and field events from the Don Valley stadium in Sheffield and the crowning of the champions. The show was co-presented by Jamie Theakston and Jayne Middlemiss (Kirsty Gallacher taking over for Series 4). The athletes spent the week living in the "athlete's village" at the Don Valley Stadium, and this being a reality show, a reasonable amount of time was given over to gossip from the night previous. Participants Series 1 - Boys: Harvey (winner), James Hewitt, Bobby Davro, Lee Latchford-Evans, Jean-Christophe Novelli. Girls: Azra Akin (Miss World) and Teri Dwyer (joint winners), Mel C, Gail Porter, Josie d'Arby. Series 2 - Boys: Shane Lynch and Jarrod Batchelor (Mr Gay UK) (joint winners), Pat Sharp, Romeo, Charles Ingram. Girls: Lady Isabella Hervey (winner), Jodie Marsh, Charlie Dimmock, Katy Hill, Linda Lusardi. Series 3 - Boys: Philip Olivier (winner), Craig Charles, Chesney Hawkes, Jonathon Morris (replaced by Danny Foster), Kevin Simm. Girls: Kirsty Gallacher (winner), Lisa Maffia, Mel Giedroyc, Her Royal Highness Princess Tamara Czartoryski-Borbon, Anna Walker. Series 4 - Boys: Jade Jones

(winner), Radio One DJ, JK (Jason King) Peter Duncan, MC Plat'num aka Marcel Somerville from the Blazin' Squad and Adam Rickitt. Girls: Javine (winner), Michelle Gayle, Amanda Lamb, Bernie Nolan and Liberal Democrat MP Julia Goldsworthy. C4 2003-06

Gardener's World Originally hosted by Ken Burras (1968-69), other presenters include Percy Thrower (1969-76) who also hosted its black-and-white forerunner *Gardening Club* on BBC1; Arthur Billitt (1976-79); Geoff Hamilton (1979-96); Alan Titchmarsh (1996-2002); Monty Don (2003-08), Toby Buckland (2008-10). Assistant presenters have included Peter Seabrook, Clay Jones, Stefan Buczacki, Geoffrey Smith, Diarmuid Gavin, Pippa Greenwood, Carol Klein, Bob Flowerdew, Rachel De Thame, Ali Ward and Jo Swift. BBC2 1968-

Gardening Club The forerunner of *Gardener's World* was originally screened from a rooftop garden at the BBC's Lime Grove studio, where Percy Thrower (1913-88) offered sound advice to gardeners nationwide. BBC1 1955-67.

Garnock Way Eileen McCallum (Jean Ross), Gerard Slevin (Alex Ross), Bill Henderson (Tod Baxter), Ginni Barlow (Effie Murdoch), Bill McCabe (Harry Murdoch), John Stahl (PC Scoular). Short-lived soap opera set in a Scottish mining village somewhere between Glasgow and Edinburgh. The lack of traditional Scottish settings did not sit well with programme planners and the soap eventually made way for *Take The High Road*. ITV 1976-79

Garrow's Law Andrew Buchan (William Garrow), Alun Armstrong (John Southouse), Lyndsey Marshal (Lady Sarah Hill), Rupert Graves (Sir Arthur Hill, Bt), Aidan McArdle (Silvester), Michael Culkin (Judge Buller). Period legal drama about the 18th-century lawyer William Garrow. BBC1 2009-

Gas Stand up comedy showcase modelled on the same lines as *The Comedy Network*. Hosted by Lee Mack clowning about both on stage and in the middle of the audience, presenting up to three other stand up acts every week, on an animated set designed to attract younger viewers. The performers tended to be a little on the unconventional side, which was one of the appealing features of the show - it was never straightforward stand up or boring observations. There was a certain amount of overlap between *Gas* and *The Comedy Network* in terms of performers. Comedians who featured include Noel Fielding, Julian Barratt, Will Smith, Peter Kay, Chris Addison, Steve Furst (as Lenny Beige), Mike Gunn, Martin Bigpig, Brendan Burns, Andy Robinson, Jason Byrne, Mitch Benn, Gina Yashere, Hovis Presley, David Hadingham and Simon Evans. At the end of the last episode, a title card came up announcing the death of host Lee Mack following the recording of the show and then the card continued to scroll through the names of the stand up clubs he had 'died' in. C4 1997-1998.

Gavin and Stacey Matthew Horne (Gavin Shipman), Joanna Page (Stacey Shipman née West), James Corden (Neil Smith), Ruth Jones (Nessa Jenkins), Alison Steadman (Pam Shipman), Larry Lamb (Mick Shipman), Rob Brydon (Bryn West), Melanie Walters (Gwenyth 'Gwen' West), Sheridan Smith (Ruth Smith), Pam Ferris (Catherina Smith), Robert Wilfort (Jason West), Steffan Rhodri (Dave Coaches), Julia Davis (Dawn Sutcliffe), Adrian Scarborough (Peter Sutcliffe), Margaret John (Doris). Sitcom written by Ruth Jones and James Corden. Two sets of best-friends, Gavin (A Spurs supporter) and Smithy (A West Ham supporter) from Billericay in Essex and Stacey and Nessa from Barry in the Vale of Glamorgan, develop romantic links and the first series ended with the marriage of the two eponymous characters and the pregnancy of Nessa by Smithy (Baby Neil is born in Series Two). Nessa is known for her fantastic stories and her catchphrase "what's occurring?". As with Jones' other award-winning comedy series, *Nighty Night*, this series originally aired on BBC3 and was later shown on BBC2 and BBC1. 2007-10 See *Fat Friends*

Gay Byrne Show, The Gabriel Mary Byrne, known as Gay Byrne (nicknamed Gaybo) was born in Dublin, 5 August 1934. After being educated at Synge Street CBS (Christian Brother School) he attended Trinity College, Dublin, (which Catholics could not attend without a bishop's dispensation, but Archbishop McQuaid granted one to Byrne, with the proviso that he did not join any of the University's clubs). He later entered the world of insurance before moving into broadcasting in 1958 when he became a presenter on Radio Éireann. He also worked with Granada Television and the BBC in England before finally working exclusively for the new Irish service. Gay also introduced many popular programmes such as *Jack Pot, Film Night* and *The Rose of Tralee*, and his name is synonymous with *The Late Late Show*, but he was also a successful radio broadcaster and is best remembered for this two hour morning show, *The Gay Byrne Show* (1972-1999). He is married to Kathleen Watkins, a well-known harpist and singer, and they have two daughters. Few would disagree that for many years he has been a legendary figure amongst the Irish people and he has been referred to as "the most famous man in Ireland". In 1989 he wrote his autobiography entitled *The Time of My Life*. In 1999 he was awarded the freedom of Dublin City.

GBH Robert Lindsay (Michael Murray), Stephen Hall (young Michael Murray), Michael Palin (Jim Nelson), Lindsay Duncan and Michelle Atkinson (Barbara Critchley / Douglas), Julie Walters (Lilian Murray), Jane Dawson aka Danson (Eileen Critchley), Anna Friel (Susan Nelson). Drama series written by Alan Bleasdale. Michael Murray is an ambitious and charismatic politician. Jim Nelson is a much loved headmaster of a local school for disturbed children. When the paths of these two men cross, things are destined never to be the same again. C4 1991.

Gems Cornelius Garrett (Alan Stone), Jonty Miller (George Rudd), Steven Mann (Stephen Stone), Margo Cunningham (Shirley Campbell), Anjela Belli (Christina Scott), Cindy O'Callaghan (Cally Johnson), Shelley Borkum (Jean Briggs), William Armstrong (Paul Currie), Janet McTeer (Stephanie Wilde). Daytime drama series created by Tessa Diamond. ITV 1985-88

General Hospital Medical soap opera set in a fictitious Midlands town. The series followed the romantic and professional adventures of its doctors and nurses. After 110 twice-weekly afternoon episodes, *General Hospital* was given a primetime slot on Friday evening. The move saw the episode lengths double from 30 to 60 minutes and story lines were given more depth. Cast list included: Tony Adams (Dr Neville Bywater), Lynda Bellingham (Nurse Hilda Price), Judy Buxton (Nurse Katy Shaw), David Garth (Dr Matthew Armstrong), Monica Grey (Sister Edwards), Lewis Jones (Dr William Parker-Brown), James Kerry (Dr Martin Baxter), Ronald Leigh-Hunt (Dr Robert Thorne), Carmen Munroe (Sister Washington), Peggy Sinclair (Sister Helen Chapman), Ian White (Dr Peter Ridge), Patricia Maynard (Dr Joanna Whitworth), Pippa Rowe (Sister Holland), Kate Lee (Dr Helen Sanders), Tom Adams (Dr Guy Wallman), Eric Lander (Dr Richard Kirby), Jill Balcon (Dr Catherine Eliot), Brian Capron (Ernie Penrose), Sally Knyvette (Nurse Rowland), Rosemary Nicols (Dr Sara Lacey). ITV 1972-79

Generation Game, The Game show involving four couples with the two members of each team a generation apart. The four couples split into two sets of two couples who faced off against each other. The winners faced each other in the final and the winners of the final played the conveyor belt game, in which a contestant had to attempt to recall 20 items that flashed past them (one of which was inevitably a cuddly toy). Original theme music sung by Bruce Forsyth: *Life is the name of the game, And I wanna play the game with you. Life can be terribly tame, If you don't play the game with two. Yeah life is a go-as-you-please. And I need some place to go with you. Life can be oh-such-a-tease, If you don't play the game with two.* Catchphrases that Bruce immortalised during his tenure as host included "Good game, good game!", "Give us a twirl, Anthea", "Let's meet the eight who are gonna generate", "What's on the board, Miss Ford!" and ultimately "Ohh! Didn't they do well?" Bruce's co-host throughout his first stint as host was Anthea Redfern (who he met at a Lovely Legs competition and married on Christmas Eve 1973). The format was devised by a Dutch housewife, its Dutch title being Een Van De Aacht (One From Eight). When Bruce joined ITV in 1978 he was replaced by Larry Grayson with co-host Isla St Clair and his catchphrase was "What are the Scores on the Doors" among others. The show was axed in 1982 but was revived in 1990 with Bruce back in control for a further four-year stint with

Rosemarie Ford as his co-host. Near the end of the Brucie run, for one reason or another Jim Davidson stood in for an episode and proved so popular that when Brucie left he did it full time. Rosemarie Ford left too and in came Sally Meen as Jim's co-host. The chemistry between Jim and Sally was not quite right and she was replaced by Melanie Stace (Lea Kristensen replaced Melanie for the final series). BBC1 1971-82; 1990-2002.

Gentle Touch Jill Gascoine (DI Maggie Forbes), Derek Thompson (Det Sgt Jimmy Fenton), William Marlowe (DCI Russell), Paul Moriarty (DS Jake Barratt). This series had the distinction of being the first police drama series on British television with a female protagonist. Premiering on ITV in April 1980, it beat the BBC's *Juliet Bravo* (1980-85) to the punch by four months. Forbes worked out of London's Seven Dials police station. ITV 1980-84.

George and Mildred Brian Murphy (George Roper), Yootha Joyce (Mildred Roper), Norman Eshley (Jeffrey Fourmile), Sheila Fearn (Ann Fourmile). Written by Johnnie Mortimer and Brian Cooke. Spin-off sitcom from *Man About the House*, featuring the former landlord and landlady from the series now moved upmarket into a new home at 46 Peacock Crescent, Hampton Wick, Suburbia. For Mildred it was her long-awaited climb up the class structure - she called it a 'town house'. For George - lazy, mostly unemployed (he did work for a short while as a traffic warden) and aggressively determined to preserve his working-classness - it was a terraced house. Their differences were exacerbated by the influence of their posh neighbours, the Fourmiles. ITV 1976-79.

George and the Dragon Sid James (George Russell), Peggy Mount (Gabrielle Dragon), John Le Mesurier (Colonel Maynard), Keith Marsh (Ralph). Sitcom written by Vince Powell and Harry Driver. Chauvinist chauffeur George meets his match when the retired Colonel hires the formidable Gabrielle Dragon as the new housekeeper. The odd couple lock horns in some memorable scenes. ITV 1966-68.

George Gently Martin Shaw (Inspector George Gently), Lee Ingleby (DS John Bacchus). Drama series written by Peter Flannery and Mick Ford. Set in the 1960s and based on the *Inspector Gently* novels by Alan Hunter, the stories are set in Northumberland rather than the Norfolk portrayed in the books. BBC1 2007-

Get A Grip Short-lived topical satire show hosted by Ben Elton and Alexa Chung. ITV 2007.

Get Fresh Children's television programme that replaced *The Saturday Starship* and starred Gareth "Gaz Top" Jones, Charlotte Hindle, and Gilbert the Alien (a puppet voiced by Phil Cornwell). The series was broadcast from a different location each week and featured the Millenium Dustbin, a fictional space ship in which the presenters would travel the country. Two ever-present cartoons were The Centurions and The Adventures of the Galaxy Rangers. ITV 1986-88. *Get Fresh Sunday* was a Sunday morning edition of the show airing at the same period and was presented by Michael J. Bassett. This spin-off featured The Adventures of Teddy Ruxpin and Gummi Bears.

Get Some In! Tony Selby (Corporal Percy Marsh), Robert Lindsay and Karl Howman (Jakey Smith), Madge Hindle (Min), David Janson (Ken Richardson). Sitcom written by John Esmonde and Bob Larbey. The title refers to getting some National Service in. Set in RAF Skelton in 1955 and focusing on 'C' Flight, nicknamed the 'erks' by the bullying Corporal Marsh. The third series saw the cast move to RAF Midham, and the final one (with Karl Howman replacing Lindsay, who had demobbed to star in Citizen Smith) was set in the hospital at RAF Druidswater. Tony Selby, as Corporal Marsh, had previously appeared in a similar role in an episode of Esmonde and Larbey's *The Fenn Street Gang*. ITV 1975-78

Getting On Jo Brand (Nurse Kim Wilde), Vicki Pepperdine (Dr Pippa Moore), Joanna Scanlan (Sister Den Flixter), Ricky Grover (Matron Hilary Loftus). Sitcom based around Ward B4, a geriatric backwater in an NHS trust hospital. This is the world of slips, trips and hips; healthcare at its least glamorous. Originally shown on BBC4 in 2009, the three-part series, written by its three female co-stars, was repeated on BBC2 in 2010.

Ghost Squad Michael Quinn (Nick Craig), Neil Hallett (Tony Miller), Donald Wolfit (Sir Andrew Wilson), Angela Browne (Helen Winters), Anthony Marlowe (Geoffrey Stock), Clare Nielson (Jean 'Porridge' Carter), Ray Barrett (Peter Clarke), Ray Austin (Billy Clay). Drama series created by John Gosling and Anthony Kearey. An elite division of Scotland Yard investigates cases that fall outside the scope of normal police work. Canadian actor Michael Quinn was replaced by Australian actor Ray Barrett for the third and final series which was also retitled *G.S.5*. ITV 1961-64

Ghost Squad, The Elaine Cassidy (Det Constable Amy Harris), Emma Fielding (Det Supt Carole McKay), Jonas Armstrong (Det Sgt Pete Maitland). Crime drama series created by Tom Grieves concerning an undercover police squad which investigates police when suspected of corruption. C4 2005

Ghost Train Children's Saturday morning show presented by Frances Dodge who had supposedly inherited a ghost train from her grandmother and with the help of fellow presenters Paul J Medford and Sabra Williams managed to escape the clutches of the evil Barry Mafia (played by Joe Hall). Inside the train were Gerard the aliens' favourite broadcaster (played by Angelo Abela) and Nobby the Sheep (played by Simon Buckley and later to star in the replacement show *Gimme 5*). The show followed the tried and tested format of live studio guests, cartoons and competitions. ITV 1989-91

Ghosts of Motley Hall, The Freddie Jones (Sir George Uproar), Nicholas Le Prevost (Sir Francis 'Fanny' Uproar), Arthur English (Bodkin), Sean Flanagan (Matt), Sheila Steafel (The White Lady), Peter Sallis (Mr Gudgin). Richard Carpenter, who had written *Catweazle*, conceived and wrote *The Ghosts Of Motley Hall*, lightly humorous stories that centred on a dilapidated empty mansion populated by five ghosts, the irascible Victorian general Sir George Uproar, who had led his soldiers so ignominiously to their deaths; the gambler Sir Francis, nicknamed Fanny, an 18th-century fop who had died of drinking and duelling; the vague but mysteriously moaning White Lady; Matt, a Regency-period stable boy who was not a part of Motley Hall's heritage but came to the ghosts' rescue in the first episode, stayed and became their nominal leader because he was the only spook who could roam beyond the house; and Bodkin, jester to the original Uproar, Sir Richard, back in the 16th-century. Mr Gudgin was the local estate agent, proud of his links with the last Uproar (Sir Humphrey, killed by an elephant in 1976) and determined to see that Motley Hall did not fall into the hands of motley purchasers. ITV 1976-78.

Gibberish Short-lived daytime game show hosted by Kenny Everett. Regular panellists, who answered questions in as entertaining way as possible, included Danny Baker, Barry Cryer, Jessica Martin, Steve Punt, Jan Ravens and Carol Vorderman. BBC1 1992.

Gideon's Way John Gregson (Commander George Gideon), Alexander Davion (Chief Inspector David Keen), Daphne Anderson (Kate Gideon). Police drama based on the books of John Creasey (aka J.J.Marric) followed a film version, *Gideon's Day* (1958) starring Jack Hawkins. ITV 1965-66.

Gimme 5 Children's Saturday morning magazine show presented by Jenny Powell, Lewis MacLeod (replaced by Paul Leyshon for Series 2), Matthew Davies and Nobby the Sheep (played by Simon Buckley). The two-hour show included live guests, cartoons, competitions and games. ITV 1992-94. See *Ghost Train*

Gimme Gimme Gimme Kathy Burke (Linda La Hughes), James Dreyfus (Tom Farrell), Beth Goddard (Suze), Brian Bovell (Jez), Rosalind Knight (Beryl Merit). Sitcom written by Jonathan Harvey. Linda La Hughes, the self-styled 'Auburn Jerry Hall', who lives her life trying to fend off romantic approaches from every man who sets eyes on her (I don't think, as music hall star Harry Tate might have said!), shares a flat with Tom, the undiscovered acting genius gagging for his big break on the route to stardom. He dreams of being rescued from his dull existence by Peak Practice's Simon Shepherd, his knight in shining armour. The script is so over the top that you just have to laugh, however un-PC it may be! Linda's foul mouth might be vulgar and offensive coming from anyone other than Kathy Burke, who

carries off the role with comfortable ease and leads the audience to sympathise with Linda rather than hate her. BBC2 1999-2000; BBC1 2001.

Girls on Top Tracey Ullman (Candice Valentine), Dawn French (Amanda Ripley), Jennifer Saunders (Jennifer Marsh), Ruby Wax (Shelley Dupont), Joan Greenwood (Lady Carlton). Written by Dawn French, Jennifer Saunders and Ruby Wax. Female version of *The Young Ones* concerning four zany girls. Amanda, a feminist writer for the women's magazine "Spare Cheeks" lucks into an apartment in Kensington. In order to pay the rent to Lady Carlton, the crazy romantic -novelist (with a stuffed pet dog named Josephine), who lives downstairs and owns the flat, she has to take in Shelley, a loud-mouthed American actress; Jennifer, a retarded friend from childhood and Candice (pronounced Candeece) a blonde hypochondriac who previously lived there and has nowhere else to go. Alan Rickman, a close friend of Ruby Wax, appeared in two episodes in 1985, as the voice of RADA and Dimitri. ITV 1985-86.

Give My Head Peace Satirical comedy series poking fun at northern Irish politicians and paramilitary groups. Starring Tim McGarry (Da), Damon Quinn (Cal), Martin Reid (Uncle Andy), Michael McDowell (Billy), Olivia Nash (Ma), Nuala McKeever (Emer), Alexandra Ford (Dympna) and BJ Hogg (Big Mervyn). The first four mentioned actors are known as the Hole in the Wall Gang. The series' title stems from a common Northern Irish phrase meaning 'leave me alone'. The theme song, "She Says" was performed by The Saw Doctors. BBC1 (NI) 1998-2008

Give Us A Break Robert Lindsay (Mickey Noades), Paul McGann (Mo Morris). Sitcom written by Geoff McQueen. Mickey, an East End ducker-and-diver takes a Liverpudlian snooker prodigy under his wing. BBC1 1983.

Give Us A Clue Boys versus girls celebrity charades hosted by Michael Aspel (1979-83) and Michael Parkinson (1984-91). The team captains were Lionel Blair and Una Stubbs (later replaced by Liza Goddard). The theme music was an arrangement of the *Grange Hill* theme "Chicken Man" by Alan Hawkshaw. ITV 1979-91. The game show was revived on BBC1 in 1997 with new host Tim Clark and team captains Julie Peasgood and Christopher Blake.

Gladiators Every week two male and two female contenders would battle it out against the Gladiators over a series of gruelling events, culminating in the Eliminator, the ultimate test of strength, stamina and willpower. The winners of the heats progressed into the later rounds, until only the series champions remained. Gladiators was filmed in front of 7,000 people at the National Indoor Arena in Birmingham. The Gladiators were Ace (Warren Furman), Amazon (Sharron Davies), Cobra (Michael Willson), Diesel (Darren Crawford), Falcon (Bernadette Hunt), Flame (Kimbra Standish), Fox (Tammy Baker), Gold (Lize van der Walt), Hawk (Alex Georgijev), Hunter (James Crossley), Jet (Diane Youdale), Khan (Radvik Nekic), Laser (Tina Andrew), Lightning (Kim Betts), Nightshade (Judy Simpson), Panther (Helen O'Reilly), Phoenix (Sandy Young), Raider (Carlton Headly), Rebel (Jennifer Stoute), Rhino (Mark Smith), Rio (Janie Omorogbe), Rocket (Pauline Richards), Saracen (Mike Lewis), Scorpio (Nikki Diamond), Shadow (Jefferson King), Siren (Alison Paton), Trojan (Mark Griffin), Vogue (Suzanne Cox), Vulcan (John Seru), Warrior (Mike Ahearne), Wolf (Mike van Wiljk), Zodiac (Kate Staples). The presenters were Ulrika Jonnson and John Fashanu (later replaced by Jeremy Guscott). The referee was John Anderson and the commentator was John Sachs. The timekeeper was Andrew Norgate and the cheerleaders were G-Force. The male and female series winners were 1992: Weininger Irwin and Vanda Fairchild; 1993: Phil Norman and Jean Klenk; 1994: Paul Field and Eunice Huthart; 1995: Mark Everitt and Janet Allen; 1996: Mark Mottram and Andreya Wharry; 1997: Piers Bryant and Audrey Garland; 1998: Dave Walter and Jane Smith. ITV 1992-98. A children's version of Gladiators - Gladiators Train to Win - ran for four series between 1994 and 1997, presented by Daley Thompson, Sharron Davies and Kyran Bracken amongst others.

Glenroe Long-running Sunday night soap created by Wesley Burrowes and set in the fictional rural village of Glenroe in County Wicklow (real-life village of Kilcoole). The series was a spin-off from *Bracken*. In 1991 *Glenroe* became the first show to be subtitled by RTÉ. Cast in alphabetical order: Paul Bennett (Sergeant Roche), Emmet Bergin (Dick Moran), Carmel Callan (Nuala Brennan / Maher), Liam Carney (Kevin Haughey), Robert Carrickford (Stephen Brennan), Cyril Cusack (Uncle Peter), Donall Farmer (Father Tim Devereux), Barbara Griffin (Bernadette Timlin), William Heffernan (Blackie Connors), Laura Howard (Eileen Synnot), David Kelly (Sylvie Dolan), Louise Kerr (Catherine Daly), Mick Lally (Miley Byrne), Joe Lynch (Dinny Byrne), Mary McEvoy (Biddy Byrne), John-Paul McGarry (Joseph Timlin), Joe McKinney (Dan Reilly), Eunice MacMenamin (Fidelma Kelly), Isobel Mahon (Michelle Haughey), Tim Murphy (Conor Sheehy), Enda Oates (Rev. George Black), Geraldine Plunkett (Mary McDermott-Moran), Mario Rosenstock (Dr. David Hanlon), Alan Stanford (George Manning), Kate Thompson (Terry Kileen), Maureen Toal (Teasy McDaid), Lucy Vigne-Welch (Fiona March Black). RTÉ One 1983-2001. See *Bracken* and *The Riordans*.

Glittering Prizes, The Tom Conti (Adam Morris), Barbara Kellerman (Barbara Morris), Angela Down (Joyce Hadleigh/Bradley), Malcolm Stoddard (Dan Bradley), Leonard Sachs (Lionel Morris), Anna Carteret (Barbara Ransome / Parks), Dinsdale Landen (Gavin Pope), Eric Porter (Stephen Taylor), Clive Merrison (Bill Bourne), John Gregg (Alan Parks), Mark Wing-Davey (Mike Clode). Written by Frederic Raphael and chronicling the lives of a group of friends who first meet as students at Cambridge in 1953. Adam Morris, who becomes a wealthy novelist, was the lead in three of the six 75-minute plays, which see him facing a series of events and relationships which are intended to impact upon his development as a person. BBC2 1976. The series was revived in 2005 on BBC Radio 4 with Jamie Glover taking the role of Adam and Jemma Redgrave as Barbara.

Glums, The See *Take It From Here*.

GMTV Good Morning Television began broadcasting in January 1993 and was the breakfast television franchise for the UK's ITV network until replaced by ITV Breakfast Limited on 3 September 2010, with the newly rebranded ITV Breakfast launching new weekday breakfast programmes *Daybreak* and *Lorraine* on 6 September 2010. The slot began with a news hour from 6.00am to 7.00am (originally called *The Reuters News Hour*) and other segments included: *Rise and Shine* (a Saturday morning children's series), *Toonattik* (a weekend children's slot featuring a selection of both British and imported cartoons presented by Jamie Rickers and Anna Williamson, with relief presenters such as Chloe Bale, Laura Hamilton and Nigel Clarke), *Wakey! Wakey!* (presented by Kerry Newell and later by Sue Monroe, the weekday slot was replaced by *The Fluffy Club* from 2006), *The Fluffy Club* (pre-school weekday slot presented by Mandisa Taylor and Tiny Little Fluff, a puppet duckling), *Sunday Best* (magazine slot presented by Eamonn Holmes and Anne Davies before being revamped and hosted by former TV-am presenter Mike Morris), *Entertainment Today* (the Friday slot presented by Ben Shephard and Jenni Falconer with Michael Underwood later introduced as a presenter),*The Richard Arnold Show* (replaced *Entertainment Today* in 2007), *Up on the Roof* (weekend slot presented by Jamie Rickers replaced by toonattik in 2005) and *Diggit/Diggin' It* (cartoon slot that replaced *Saturday Disney* and the Sunday morning *Disney Club* in 1998). The flagship fashion, food and celebrity gossip slot was *GMTV with Lorraine* (Kelly). See also *Daybreak*.

Gnomes of Dulwich, The Sitcom written by Jimmy Perry concerning the *Hugh and I* partnership of Terry Scott and Hugh Lloyd playing a big and small gnome respectively and pontificating on the human passers-by. John Clive played the third 'old' Gnome. BBC1 1969.

God's Gift Late-night (often in the middle of the night) game show presented from the studio floor by Davina McCall (series 1) and Claudia Winkleman (series 2). Stuart Hall provided the voiceover for both series although Jimmy Savile voiced on some later editions in series 2. Each week five male contestants competed for the votes of a female audience by participating in a series of bizarre games designed to test their sex appeal. The winner's prize would be to take an audience member of his choice

out on a date, which was then filmed for broadcast in the following week's show. The 1993 winner of Mr Gay UK Anthony Morley, who was later convicted of murder and cannibalism, appeared in a special edition in 1996 and one of the audience members was his future victim Damian Oldfield. ITV 1995-96. See also *Man O Man*

Going For A Song Max Robertson presided over the panel game between connoisseurs and customers whereby antiques would be passed along the panel and at first identified and then given an estimated auction value, points being awarded dependent on how near the estimate corresponded to the actual value. The show made a star of Arthur Negus, an antiques expert who specialised in Chippendale furniture, particularly in mahogany. The series ran on BBC1 between 1965 and 1977 and was revived in 1995 with Michael Parkinson taking over as chairman and Tony Slattery and Leslie Ash the team captains. This series ran until 2001 with Mariella Frostrup, Kit Hesketh-Harvey, Penny Smith and Lucinda Lambton, all having stints as team captains. Michael Aspel presided over the final series and the captains were Rachel de Thame and Mark Porter.

Going For Gold Euro quiz show hosted by Henry Kelly. The programme followed a repechage-style format where contestants representing various European countries stayed with the show for the whole week. Seven contestants would appear on Monday, and the first four to answer elimination questions correctly went into "the first round proper". The three rejects together with the three that would be knocked-out during Monday's contest, would come back on Tuesday, and so on. The winner of each daily show would return on Friday's finale and each weekly winner would return again for the series finals. The final round of the contest consisted of Henry Kelly reading out a long description of a famous person, place or object (always beginning with "What am I?" or "Who am I?"). Henry revealed more and more information as the time went on. However, the number of points available reduced from 4 down to just 1, so the quicker you could buzz in, the more points you got. The first series winner was Daphne Fowler (now more famous as an Egghead) representing England. BBC1 1987-96. The show was revived on Five from 13 October 2008 until 20 March 2009. The new version, featuring only contestants from the UK and Ireland, was broadcast live and hosted by newsreader John Suchet.

Going Gently Norman Wisdom (Bernard Flood), Fulton Mackay (Austin Miller), Judi Dench (Sister Scarli), Stephanie Cole (Gladys Hood). Highly acclaimed single drama adapted by Thomas Ellice from the novel by Robert C. S. Downsby. Directed by Stephen Frears and shown as one of the episodes in the BBC2 *Playhouse* series. Bernard, a retired salesman who is dying of cancer, and fellow sufferer Austin, live out their last days in a hospital ward. Norman Wisdom won rave reviews for his touching performance in a rare straight role. BBC2 1981.

Going Live! Saturday morning children's light entertainment show carrying the baton forward from *Multi-Coloured Swap Shop* and *Saturday Superstore*, hosted by Sarah Greene and Phillip Schofield (not forgetting his puppet pal Gordon the Gopher). The show was a mixture of cartoons, children's games and some more serious ecological issues. Warm-up man Peter Simon was given a stint in front of the camera hosting the popular 'Double Dare' action-quiz slot (later replaced by 'Run the Risk' with Peter Simon and Shane Richie). When Phillip left to join the West End production as Joseph (of the Amazing Dreamcoat) Sarah was joined by Kristian Schmid. BBC1 1987-93. The baton was passed on to *Live and Kicking* in 1993.

Going Straight See *Porridge*.

Gok's Fashion Fix Gok Wan, born Ko-Hen Wan, in Leicester on 9 September 1974, is a British fashion consultant and television presenter. Between 2006 and 2008 Gok presented four series of the Channel 4 show *How to Look Good Naked*, where he offered advice and encouragement to women who were insecure about the way they looked and ultimately built up their confidence enough for them to strip naked for the camera. To compliment the show he wrote a book to accompany the series, entitled *How to Look Good Naked: Shop for Your Shape and Look Amazing!* In 2009

Gok co-presented another Channel 4 series, *Miss Naked Beauty*, with Myleene Klass; the six-episodes portraying all aspects of beauty pageantry. The winner was Shona Collins. *Gok's Fashion Fix* began on Channel 4 in 2008 and is currently on its third series. Gok travels around the country visiting all sorts of diverse people but many having one thing in common, a lack of dress sense. He is famous for his over-use of the word "literally" and his nickname of "bangers" for women's breasts.

Gold See *Band Of Gold*

Golden Balls Daily weekday game show hosted by Jasper Carrott. Four players are initially dealt out four balls worth varying amounts of money up to a maximum of £75,000. Four of the 12 balls are "killer balls" which will come into effect in the end game by dividing the potential winnings by 10 if selected. Two of each player's balls are on show, the rest are known only to each player. A vote is taken after some banter aimed at ensuring entry into the second round and one player has to leave with their balls. Three more balls are added in round two, including one more killer, the three remaining contestants now holding five balls but only two known to their competitors. Another vote is taken and the two finalists enter the final round with 11 balls, yet another killer being added. Each person now picks a ball to get rid of (Bin) and then another to add to the jackpot (Win). Any killer balls chosen to 'win' only divides the amount already clocked up, so if you pick up a killer to win when £10,000 is stored then your total drops to £1000 but any cash balls chosen after this are worth the full amount. The best bit of the game now follows. After they make up their row of five winners, they are given two more balls each: Split and Steal. If both choose Split, they share the remaining cash. If one says Split and the other says Steal, the stealer gets all the cash. If they both say Steal, they both go home with nothing. Jasper gives the contestants 30 seconds to have a chat at what they might do and the television audience is left to ponder the outcome. Amanda Grant looks after the Golden Balls. ITV 2007-10

Golden Shot, The Game show featuring contestants directing a crossbow bolt at various targets in order to win prizes. Presenters included Jackie Rae (1967), Bob Monkhouse (1967-71 and 1974-75), Norman Vaughan (1972), Charlie Williams (1974). The original hostesses (known as the Golden Girls) were Anita Richardson, Andrea Lloyd and Carol Dilworth (the wife of Tremeloes guitarist Chip Hawkes, and mother of Chesney). Jackie Rae only hosted 14 shows and gave the command "Heinz the bolt" at the commencement of proceedings. When Bob Monkhouse took over this catchphrase became "Bernie the bolt" although the crossbow loader was actually named Derek Young (when the show was transferred from Boreham Wood to Birmingham in 1968, Alan Bailey replaced Derek and on occasion did Johnny Baker). Towards the end of Bob's first reign only Carol Dilworth remained of the Golden Girls and she was joined by Cheri Gilham and the ever-popular Anne Aston (she who couldn't count). Bob left under a cloud in 1971 after being sacked by Francis Essex ATV's Head of Light Entertainment for being implicated in a bribery scandal after he was spotted receiving a gift from Wilkinson's Sword representative Bob Brooksby. The following weekend a "his and hers" Wilkinson Sword grooming kit was featured as the bronze prize on The Shot and Essex smelt collusion. In reality the gift Monkhouse had received was only a collectable book, "The Shy Photographer" but perhaps surmising he was rooting out the old boy's network, Essex visited Monkhouse at home and told him he was going to dismiss him from the show. The public were to be told that the decision to leave had been Monkhouse's with ATV issuing a statement to the press that read: "Bob is being released to find opportunities for his abilities elsewhere". Indeed that was how things remained until Monkhouse himself revealed all in his 1993 autobiography "Crying With Laughter". Both Norman Vaughan and Charlie Williams were experienced stand-up comedians and Vaughan in particular was experienced at live television but ratings dropped during both tenures and Essex eventually asked Bob to return for the final series. Anne Aston was joined by Wei Wei Wong as hostesses. ITV 1967-75.

Goldplated David Schofield (John White), Barbara Marten (Beth White), Kelly Harrison (Cassidy Tallow), Darren Tighe (Darren White), Poppy Miller (Terese White), Gary Whelan (Leo Cascarino), Nicholas Shaw (Justin White), Jaime Winstone (Lauren White), Naomi Bentley (Naomi), Nichola Burley (Donna), Sandra Huggett (Bo Blonde), Jacqueline Leonard (Faye Blonde), Georgina Mellor (Anna Blonde), Angela Holmes (Charlotte), Keith Clifford (Ray Borrigard), Jason Furnival (Councillor Smeaton), Ace Bhatti (Haq), Lisa Millett (Jacqui Quail) Kenny Doughty (Coll), Isabelle and Niamh Earnshaw (Baby Johnnie). Eight-part drama written by Jimmy Gardner, set in the 'golden triangle' of Wilmslow, Prestbury and Alderley Edge. John White and his wife Beth work hard to drag themselves up from their working class roots via their own construction firm. They swap the British Legion for the Country Club and their Manchester terrace for an eight bedroom mansion in the Cheshire triangle. Their first born Darren is John's deputy in the family business and Darren's wife Terese is the social climbing daughter of a local golf pro. John and Beth's youngest, Justin and Lauren, now in their twenties, have never worked a day in their lives. Then along comes Cassidy to complicate John's life. *Goldplated* lifts the lid on a world of conspicuous consumption in which wealth, or at least the perception of it, is everything. C4 2006.

Good Guys, The Nigel Havers (Guy McFadyean), Keith Barron (Guy Lofthouse), David Langton (Ronald McFadyean), Leslie Grantham (Nick Toth), Imogen Boorman (Jenny Toth), Hilary Gish (Sarah), Isla Blair (Maggie), Jenny Agutter (Grizel), Jean Alexander (Maud Layton), Thora Hird (Edna Wood), Edward Fox (John Montgomerie), Richard Griffiths (Archie Phillips), Michael Kitchen (Graham Croxley), Arabella Weir (Annabel West), Derek Nimmo (Stephen Wolfe). Light-hearted drama series not to be confused with the current popular American action-comedy series. ITV 1992-93.

Good Life, The Richard Briers (Tom Good), Felicity Kendall (Barbara Good), Penelope Keith (Margo Leadbeatter), Paul Eddington (Jerry Leadbeatter). Sitcom written by John Esmonde and Bob Larbey. Middle-aged suburban couple, Tom and Barbara Good, decide to go back to the land and turn their Surbiton home into a self-sufficient farm-cum-allotment, growing their own food, keeping animals (they had a pet cockerel named Lenin and goat named Geraldine) and making their own tools and equipment. This creates friction with their neighbours, especially the rather snobbish Margo. BBC1 1975-78.

Good Morning Scotland Scottish breakfast radio news programme first aired on BBC Radio Scotland on 31 December 1973 with presenters David Findlay and John Milne. The longest-running radio show broadcast from Scotland, consists of news and sport items, business, travel and weather bulletins as well as interviews, in-depth reports and a daily religious slot Thought for the Day. Current presenters are Isabel Fraser, Gillian Marles and Gary Robertson. Previous hosts include John Milne, Douglas Kynoch, Mary Marquis, James Cox, Neville Garden, Eddie Mair, Anne MacKenzie, Derek Bateman, Mhairi Stuart, Abeer MacIntyre, Gillian Marles, and Aasmah Mir.

Good Old Days, The Transmitted from the Leeds City Varieties Theatre by Leonard Sachs (originally Don Gemmell), the variety acts worked in a music hall atmosphere with the audience dressed in Edwardian costume of the early 20th century. Regular guests included Tessie O'Shea, Danny La Rue, Roy Hudd, Roy Castle, Ray Alan and Ken Dodd. Every show was ended with a rendition of 'Down at the Old Bull and Bush'. BBC1 1953-83.

Goodies, The Popular comedy series starring Tim Brooke-Taylor, Graeme Garden and Bill Oddie as the arch-benefactors of society, The Goodies. Always ready to right wrongs on their tandem (three-seater bicycle), sometimes saving London from a giant cat, sometimes guarding the Crown Jewels. BBC2 1970-77; 1980; ITV 1981-82. A one-off *Return of the Goodies* was screened at Christmas 2005 on BBC2.

Goodness Gracious Me Asian sketch show which first appeared on the radio. When producer Anil Gupta took the idea to BBC television the executive producer Jon Plowman suggested the team first assemble a radio pilot, a cheap way of demonstrating the potential of an untried idea. This pilot led to a full radio series, which quickly won a prestigious Sony Award. Impressed by its aural successes, Plowman decided the time was right to switch the show to television. The show's four stars were Sanjeev Bhaskar, Meera Syal, Kulvinder Ghir and Nina Wadia. Regular characters included Smeeta Smitten, Showbiz Kitten (Syal), a Bollywood gossip columnist; the nouveau riche Kapoor family, who were desperate to be fully English and insisted their name was pronounced Cooper; Mr 'Everything Comes From India' ('The royal family? Indian! Have arranged marriages, live in the same house and all work for the family business. Indian!'); the Indian mother who could 'make it at home for nothing'; Bollywood superstar Chunky La Funga; the tactless suitor whose verbal gaffes always leave him asking for the 'cheque please'; Asian street kids the Bhangra Muffins; charlatan His Serene Calmness the Guru Maharishi Yogi; and the alcoholic marsupial 'Skipinder, The Punjabi Kangaroo'. Memorable sketches include the Delhitubbies and the much-repeated one about a group of young Indians visiting a restaurant for an "English", amusingly ordering 'something bland'. BBC Radio 4 1996-98; BBC2 1998-2000.

Goodnight Sweetheart Nicholas Lyndhurst (Gary Sparrow), Michelle Holmes and Emma Amos (Yvonne Sparrow), Dervla Kirwan and Elizabeth Carling (Phoebe Bamford/Sparrow), Victor McGuire (Ron Wheatcroft), Christopher Ettridge (PC Reg Deadman), David Benson (Noël Coward). Sitcom created by Laurence Marks and Maurice Gran. Gary Sparrow wanders down Ducketts Passage in the East End of London and finds himself back in 1940. He goes into a pub called the Royal Oak and meets the lovely Phoebe Bamford. When Gary finds that he can move between the 1990s and the 1940s at will, he quickly develops a double life. In the 1990s, he has his bossy wife Yvonne, his job as a TV repairman and his best friend Ron Wheatcroft. In the 1940s, he has a developing relationship with Phoebe. She's married when Gary first meets her but, after she becomes a widow, Gary marries her and becomes a time-travelling bigamist. He also fathers a son much older than he is himself. After the third series, Dervla Kirwan left and was replaced by Liz Carling. Michelle Holmes also left, to be replaced by Emma Amos. BBC1 1993-99.

Goon Show, The Outrageous and original radio comedy show written mainly by Spike Milligan (with contributions from John Antrobus, Larry Stephens, Maurice Wiltshire and Jimmy Grafton) and performed by Michael Bentine (for the first 43 episodes), Peter Sellers, Harry Secombe and Spike Milligan. The first series, broadcast on the BBC Home Service (later to become Radio 4) in 1951, was entitled *Crazy People*; whilst the remaining nine annual series (ending in 1960) were given the title *The Goon Show*. The surreal and ridiculous plots were the inspiration for the next generation of comedy icons including Peter Cook and Dudley Moore, and the Monty Python crew. All ten series were recorded at the BBC's Camden studios (now a nightclub named KOKO) and Series 4 was written by Eric Sykes after Spike had suffered one of his numerous breakdowns during Series 3. The central character was originally the madcap inventor Dr Osric Pureheart (a role Michael Bentine was later to play in several television series) and when Michael departed to pursue a solo career Neddy Seagoon (Harry Secombe) became the central stooge. The 30-minute shows were formatted to include a ridiculous storyline such as prisoners from Dartmoor Prison being allowed a holiday to France but with the proviso they are kept locked up thus necessitating an attempt to float the prison across the English Channel. Of course one of the lags tunnels his way out during the crossing and discovers....Water! The first interlude would usually be a jazz harmonica recital by Max Geldray and the second another jazz number (Spike was a huge jazz fan and very accomplished musician) by the Ray Ellington Quartet. The original producer of the show was Dennis Main Wilson but the longest incumbent was Peter Eton. Of the numerous catchphrases that became legend the most famous three were "He's fallen in the water!" (Little Jim), "You dirty, rotten swine, you! You deaded me!" (Bluebottle), and "You silly, twisted boy, you." (Grytpype-Thynne), all voiced by Peter Sellers. Various attempts were made to televisualise the Goons including *The Idiot Weekly, Price 2d* (1956), *A Show Called Fred* (1956), *Son of Fred* (1956) and *The Telegoons* (1963-64). In 1972 *The Last Goon Show of All*, was broadcast on BBC Radio 4 and BBC2 as part of the celebrations of the 50th anniversary of the BBC. See also the individual biographies of the four Goons in the comedy section.

Gordon Ramsay Gordon James Ramsay was born in Johnstone, Renfrewshire, Scotland, 8 November 1966. He is a television chef who trained under Marco Pierre White at Harveys in Wandsworth Common, London (now the site of Chez Bruce). Gordon appeared in several cookery-based shows before beginning his television career proper in 2004 with *Hell's Kitchen* (see separate entry). Later that year he began the first series of *Ramsay's Kitchen Nightmares* for Channel 4. The format saw Gordon visit an ailing restaurant and offer advice to help improve its fortunes in just one week. The series ran for five years. In 2005 *The F Word* (also called *Gordon Ramsay's F Word*) began on Channel 4 with each episode based around Ramsay preparing a three-course meal at the F Word restaurant for 50 guests, including celebrities, who participate in conversations, challenges, and cook-offs against the multi-award-winning chef. By November 2011 he had been awarded 13 Michelin stars. Controversy has surrounded Gordon as to his actual professional football career as a member of the Rangers development youth squad although he himself rarely talks about the situation. In 1996, he married schoolteacher Cayetana Elizabeth Hutcheson. The couple have four children, Megan Jane (b. 1998), twins Jack Scott and Holly Anna (b. 2000), and Matilda Elizabeth (b. 2002). Gordon's father-in-law, Chris Hutcheson, was until 2010 responsible for the business operations of Ramsay's restaurant empire. Known for his over-use of swear words and cosmetic surgical procedures, Gordon's autobiography is entitled, *Humble Pie*.

Gormenghast Jonathan Rhys Meyers (Steerpike), Celia Imrie (Lady Gertrude), Christopher Lee (Flay), Warren Mitchell (Barquentine), Neve McIntosh (Lady Fuchsia), John Sessions (Dr Prunesquallor), Fiona Shaw (Irma Prunesquallor), June Brown (Nannie Slagg), Lynsey Baxter (Cora Groan), Zoë Wanamaker (Clarice Groan), George Antoni (Bookman), Sean Hughes (Poet), Stephen Fry (Professor Bellgrove), Richard Griffiths (Swelter), Ian Richardson (Lord Groan), Windsor Davies (Rottcodd), Olga Sosnovska (Keda), Eric Sykes (Mollocks), Spike Milligan (De'Ath), Andrew N. Robertson (Titus - 17 years), Gregor Fisher (The Fly), Mark Williams (Professor Perch), Martin Clunes (Professor Flower), Steve Pemberton (Professor Mule), Phil Cornwell (Professor Shred), James Dreyfus (Professor Fluke). Four-episode mini-series based on the *Gormenghast* series by Mervyn Peake. BBC1 2000.

Governor, The Janet McTeer (Helen Hewitt), Derek Martin (Gary Marshall), Ron Donachie (Russell Morgan), Sophie Okonedo (Moira Levitt), David Nicholls ('Jumbo' Jackson), Christine Moore (Mavis O'Connell). Drama series written by Lynda La Plante. Helen Hewitt is the first woman put in charge of Barfield, a maximum security prison that had been nearly destroyed by a disastrous riot and subsequent fire. Despite being greeted with open hostility by inmates and little enthusiasm by prison staff, she is determined to clean up the place. ITV 1995-96.

Grace and Favour See *Are You Being Served?*

Graham Norton's Bigger Picture See *The Bigger Picture with Graham Norton*

Graham Norton Show, The Graham Norton was born in Clondalkin, Co Dublin, 4 April 1963. Graham is an all round entertainer who has acted on stage and screen as well as being adept at stand-up comedy and presenting on radio and television. This late-night chat show originally aired on BBC2 in February 2007 but was transferred to BBC1 in October 2009. See also *How Do You Solve A Problem Like Maria?*, *The Bigger Picture with Graham Norton, The One And Only, I'd Do Anything, Who Do You Think You Are?, Strictly Dance Fever*, and *Wogan*.

Grandad Clive Dunn (Charlie Quick). Sitcom created by Clive Dunn and written by Bob Block. Charlie Quick, known to all and sundry as Grandad, the elderly but sprightly caretaker of the Parkview Rehearsal Hall. The eager OAP tries to help but he mostly hinders the acting and dancing students who hired the venue. BBC1 1979-84. The hit record of the same name by Clive was recorded in 1970 and may have been the inspiration for the series but Clive specialised in playing the pensioner characters for more than 30 years.

Grandma's House Simon Amstell (Simon), Linda Bassett (Grandma), Geoffrey Hutchings (Grandpa), Rebecca Front (Tanya), James Smith (Clive), Samantha Spiro (Auntie Liz), Jamal Hadjkura (Adam). Comedy drama series written by Simon Amstell and Dan Swimer. TV presenter Simon Amstell plays a version of himself in this six-part comedy, each episode being set at Grandma's house, where Simon's family frequently meet to catch up. BBC2 2010-

Grandstand Long-running Saturday afternoon sports programme. Presenters have included Peter Dimmock, David Coleman, Frank Bough, Des Lynam and Steve Rider. Australian Len Martin, a voiceover artist heard on Movietone newsreels, was famous for reading the Grandstand football results from 1958 to 1995. BBC1 1958-2007. There have been several Grandstand Extras over the years, notably *Sunday Grandstand*.

Grange Hill Todd Carty (Peter "Tucker" Jenkins), Michelle Herbert (Trisha Yates), Susan Tully (Suzanne Ross), George Armstrong (Alan Humphries), Letitia Dean (Lucinda Oliver), Peter Moran (Douglas "Pogo" Patterson), Erkan Mustafa (Roland Browning), Gwyneth Powell (Bridget McCluskey), Mark Savage (Norman "Gripper" Stebson), Sean Maguire (Terence "Tegs" Ratcliffe), Michael Cronin (Mr Geoff "Bullet" Baxter – PE teacher and later deputy head), Lee MacDonald (Samuel "Zammo" Maguire), Chris Perry-Metcalf (Patrick "Togger" Johnson), Iain Robertson (Sean Pearce), Michael Sheard (Maurice Bronson), Reggie Yates (Carl Fenton), Laura Sadler (Judi Jeffreys), John Holmes - later credited as John McMahon (Luke "Gonch" Gardener), Bradley Sheppard (Paul "Hollo" Holloway). Children's soap opera created by Phil Redmond and set in Northam, a fictional area of north London, but more precisely the local comprehensive school, Grange Hill. Although Bridget McCluskey was the school's head throughout the show's heyday period of the 1980s there have been many others. The first head was Mr Starling (Denys Hawthorne) and the last was Miss Gayle (Cathy Tyson) although she did not appear in the final series. One of the most famous storylines was the descent into drug addiction by Zammo McGuire which spawned a UK No 5 single by the cast in 1986, *Just Say No*. Anthony Mingella was the script editor during this period. The theme music for the first 12 years, which returned for the final series, was "Chicken Man" by Alan Hawkshaw. In a tragic irony, Laura Sadler's character was killed off in 1989, after slipping and falling out of a burning building, paralleling her real life death four years later. BBC1 1978-2008. See also *Tucker's Luck*.

Grease Is the Word: Live Reality television show hosted by Zoe Ball, the aim being to find a couple to play Sandy Dumbrowski and Danny Zuko in Grease the musical in the West End in the summer of 2007. Putting his reputation on the line by judging the potential hopefuls (as well as producing the eventual winners) was renowned Theatre Producer David Ian who was joined on the judging panel by multi-millionaire, showbiz impresario (and *I'm A Celebrity* favourite) David Gest; choreographer to the stars and judge on hit TV show *So You Think You Can Dance* Brian Friedman and *The X Factor* mentor and 80s' pop icon Sinitta. The executive producer of the series was Simon Cowell. ITV 2007

Great Antiques Hunt, The Hosted by Jilly Goolden, this game show consisted of two pairs of contestants spending a fixed budget on antiques before selling those items at auction in order to beat their opponents. The winners would then choose an antique from a set of five in the hope they pick the most valuable item. BBC1 1994-99. See Bargain Hunt.

Great British Journeys Presenter Nicholas Crane travelled by foot, horse and bicycle, on eight epic endurance journeys, through Britain's wildest landscapes, following in the footsteps of the greatest indigenous explorers. The eight original journeys were: Thomas Pennant - A Tour in Scotland & Voyage to the Hebrides (1772), William Gilpin's Observations on the River Wye (1770), Celia Fiennes's Horse Ride from London to the Scottish Border (1698), William Cobbett's Rural Rides (1821-6), Gerald of Wales Journey through Wales (1188), Daniel Defoe's Tour Through the Whole Island of Great Britain (1724-26), John Leland's Journey Through the West Country (1533-42) and H V Morton's Search for Scotland (1928-1933). BBC2 2007

Great British Menu Top British and Northern Irish chefs compete for the chance to cook one course of a four course banquet for various luminaries. Presented by Jenny Bond, the first series banquet was for the Queen on her 80th birthday; the second to cook for the British Ambassador to France at the British Embassy in Paris; the third to prepare a banquet to be held at the Gherkin in London, hosted by Heston Blumenthal, the fourth series chefs competed to cook at a celebratory dinner for British troops returning from Afghanistan and the fifth series was to cook at a banquet hosted by the Prince of Wales for outstanding local food suppliers. The judges are Prue Leith, Matthew Fort and Oliver Peyton. The music to the series was written by Daniel Pemberton. BBC2 2006-

Great British Railway Journeys Travel documentary series presented by Michael Portillo. Victorian cartographer George Bradshaw's Railway Companion is used by Michael to draw a comparison with modern Britain with that of the early years of the reign of Queen Victoria when the railways were in their infancy. The four journeys undertaken are Liverpool to Scarborough; Preston to Kirkcaldy; Swindon to Penzance; and Buxton to London. Each journey warrants five half-hour episodes. BBC2 2010- See *Great Railway Journeys*.

Great British Village Show, The From growing the biggest and best vegetables to decorating elaborate cakes, presenters Alan Titchmarsh, James Martin and Angellica Bell visit six regional competitions in some of the most beautiful stately homes in Britain. Head judge was Medwyn Williams. BBC 1 2007.

Great Britons In 2002 the BBC organised a national poll to find the greatest Briton who has ever lived. A short list of 100 names was drafted and showcased in the initial programme in the series and then the top ten were given their own one hour specials with, the ten nominees being championed by various experts or celebrity fans. In November 2002, the British public voted Sir Winston Churchill the Greatest Briton of all time. The Top Ten Great Britons (and their champions) were: 1. Winston Churchill - 456,498 votes (28.1%) - Mo Mowlam; 2. Isambard Kingdom Brunel - 398,526 votes (24.6%) - Jeremy Clarkson; 3. Diana, Princess of Wales - 225,584 votes (13.9%) - Rosie Boycott; 4. Charles Darwin - 112,496 votes (6.9%) - Andrew Marr; 5. William Shakespeare - 109,919 votes (6.8%) - Fiona Shaw; 6. Isaac Newton - 84,628 votes (5.2%) - Tristram Hunt; 7. Queen Elizabeth I - 71,928 votes (4.4%) - Michael Portillo; 8. John Lennon - 68,445 votes (4.2%) - Alan Davies; 9. Horatio Nelson - 49,171 votes (3%) - Lucy Moore; 10. Oliver Cromwell - 45,053 (2.8%) votes - Richard Holmes. BBC 2002.

Great Egg Race, The Teams of university boffins would create weird and frequently Heath-Robinson-like gadgets out of shockingly scant apparatus in order to crack problems like building bridges to support someone's weight, burglar alarm detectors that people couldn't avoid triggering, or indeed the weekly challenge of transporting an egg over some great distance without breaking it! Originally hosted by Lesley Judd and Professor Heinz Wolff the format changed in the 1980s and Wolff became the sole host of the new 'challenge' format. BBC2 1978-86.

Great Expectations Gary Bond (Pip), Francesca Annis (Estella), Maxine Audley (Miss Havisham), Neil McCarthy (Joe Gargery), Richard O'Sullivan (Herbert Pocket), Peter Vaughan (Mr. Jaggers), Bernard Hepton (Wemmick), Norman Scace (Pumblechook), Hannah Gordon (Biddy), Shirley Cain (Mrs Gargery), Ronald Lacey (Orlick), John Tate (Magwitch). Eight-part adaptation of the classic Charles Dickens' novel. BBC 1967. The BBC also made a 12-part mini-series in 1981 with Gerry Sundquist as Pip, Joan Hickson as Miss Havisham, Stratford Johns as Abel Magwitch, and Patsy Kensit as Young Estella. The most recent BBC effort was a three-part mini-series shown over Christmas 2011 starring Ray Winstone as Abel Magwitch, Gillian Anderson as Miss Havisham and 19-year-old Douglas Booth as Philip "Pip" Pirrip.

Great Italian Escape, The Documentary series following the lives of Richard and Sarah Turnbull, who have emigrated from the UK to Tuscany. The couple use their experience of six years of living in Italy to advise some of the stream of new British arrivals on everything they'll need to know about their adopted homeland. C4 2008. Jamie Oliver also had an Italian escape the year before this six-episode series.

Great Pretender, The Daytime quiz show hosted by Chris Tarrant. Six contestants had to answer questions but faced the possibility of being voted off by their rivals in the early rounds if showing too much form. Once down to the last four players Chris told each player if they were leading or not and that player had to try and convince the others that it was one of the others in order to keep the accrued money. At the final voting stage if the leading contestant successfully bluffed their way through then they won all the money but if the remaining three all voted for the leader then they shared the pot amongst themselves. ITV 2007

Great Railway Journeys Travel documentary series where famous faces make an epic train journey through sometimes familiar areas of the world. The first series in 1980 was entitled *Great Railway Journeys of the World* and presenters included Ludovic Kennedy, Michael Palin, Michael Frayn and Eric Robson. The second series in 1994 saw Clive Anderson,, Mark Tully, Natalia Makarova and Michael Palin (again) make nostalgic journeys and by now the series was given its present title. The third series in 1996 had episodes presented by Victoria Wood, Ben Okri, Alexei Sayle and Chris Bonington. The final series in 1999 saw Ian Hislop, Rick Stein, Nick Hancock, Danny Glover and Stephen Tompkinson make meaningful journeys. This series also had an episode presented by Michael Portillo making a journey through his fatherland of Spain (Granada to Salamanca) and this eventually led to a further series entitled *Great British Railway Journeys*. BBC2 1980-99. In 1983 the BBC made a series on rail travel, presented by Brian Blessed and Michael Wood among others, entitled *Great Little Railways*, featuring narrow gauge railways.

Great War, The The story of World War 1 told in 26 episodes and narrated by Sir Michael Redgrave. Other voices included Emlyn Williams as David Lloyd George and Sir Ralph Richardson as Douglas Haig. BBC2 1964

Green Green Grass, The John Challis (Boycie), Sue Holderness (Marlene), Jack Doolan (Tyler), Roy Marsden (Danny Driscoll), Christopher Ryan (Tony Driscoll). Sitcom spin-off from *Only Fools and Horses*, also written by John Sullivan. Boycie is in trouble with the Driscoll Brothers - "the South London Mafia" - imminently due for release from a prison sentence they think he grassed them up for. He decides not to hang around to find out just how angry they are, quickly selling his house and successful car dealership and moving his family (wife Marlene and teenage son Tyler) from Peckham to a comparatively isolated country farm in Shropshire. BBC1 2005-

Grimleys, The Brian Conley (Doug Digby), James Bradshaw (Gordon Grimley), Amanda Holden (Geraldine Titley), Noddy Holder (Neville Holder), Craig Kelly (Dave Trebilock), Nigel Planer (Baz Grimley). Sitcom written by Jed Mercurio. Set on the Jericho Council Estate, Dudley in 1975. Doug Digby is a PE teacher with a sadistic streak. He divides his time between making his pupils as miserable as possible and chasing after English teacher Geraldine Titley. Young Gordon Grimley also fancies Miss Titley, but has little or no chance of success with her. He has to look on as the awful Mr Digby moves in on his beloved. By the third series Digby is dead and Dave Trebilock is the new love interest of Miss Titley. Former Slade frontman Noddy Holder plays a genial music teacher and performs the odd song. The pilot for the series was broadcast in 1997 as part of ITV's *Comedy Premieres* season, Jack Dee playing Doug Digby and Samantha Janus playing Geraldine Titley. ITV 1999-2001.

Groovy Fellers, The Short-lived sitcom written by and starring Jools Holland (as himself) and Rowland Rivron (as a Martian). The six-part series began with Jools nursing a pint in a Northumberland pub when in walked a Martian. Jools and the Martian then set off around Britain on a series of surreal adventures to try and find the meaning of life on Earth. C4 1989.

Ground Force Garden makeover show created by Peter Bazalgette. Unsuspecting householders were given the full treatment by Alan Titchmarsh, Charlie Dimmock and Tommy Walsh (assisted by Will Shanahan). Alan left in 2002 and was replaced by Kirsty King. BBC2 1997-98; BBC1 1998-2005

Growing Pains of Adrian Mole, The See *The Secret Diary of Adrian Mole*

Growing Pains of PC Penrose, The Paul Greenwood (PC Michael 'Rosie' Penrose), Bryan Pringle (Sgt Flagg), David Pinner (PC Buttress). Police sitcom written by Roy Clarke (a former policeman). Rosie is a probationary police constable stationed in the small Yorkshire town of Slagcaster. Sergeant Flagg has the job of turning the naive young Rosie into a competent policeman. BBC1 1975. The second series was entitled *Rosie*. See separate entry.

Grumpy Old Men/Women Conversational-style series in which various 40 plus television personalities pontificated on all manner of things that make them grumpy. Narrated by Geoffrey Palmer, contributors to the men's series have included Jeremy Clarkson, Bob Geldof, A. A. Gill, Nigel Havers, Tony Hawks, Simon Hoggart, John Humphrys, Des Lynam, Rory McGrath, Bill Nighy, John O'Farrell, Matthew Parris, John Peel, Tim Rice, Will Self, Lemn Sissay, Tony Slattery, Arthur Smith, Rick Stein, Rick Wakeman and Don Warrington. The women's series (narrated by Alison Steadman for the first two series and Judith Holder for the third) began a year later and contributors have included Lynn Barber, Stephanie Beacham, Jilly Cooper, Annette Crosbie, Jenny Eclair, Sheila Ferguson, Kathryn Flett, Lynne Franks, Muriel Gray, Bonnie Greer, Germaine Greer, Sheila Hancock, Michele Hanson, Charlie Hardwick, Indira Joshi, Dillie Keane, India Knight, Helen Lederer, Angie Le Mar, Maureen Lipman, Aggie MacKenzie, Jane Moore, Nina Myskow, Fiona Phillips, Eve Pollard, Esther Rantzen, Linda Robson, Pam St Clement, Janet Street-Porter, Jenni Trent Hughes, Arabella Weir, Ann Widdecombe and Kim Woodburn. BBC2 2003-06. An Irish version, hosted by Gay Byrne, *Gaybo's Grumpy Men* was produced by RTÉ in 2005 and contributors included Paraic Breathnach, Dave Fanning, Gary Kavanagh, Gerry Lundberg, David Norris, Brendan O'Carroll, Páidí Ó Sé, Cathal O'Shannon, John O'Shea, Alan Stanford, Steve Wall, and of course Gay himself.

Hadleigh Gerald Harper (James Hadleigh), Hilary Dwyer (Jennifer Caldwell/Hadleigh), Gerald James (Charles Caldwell), Jane Merrow (Anne Hepton). The life and times of James Hadleigh, the squire of Melford Park, in the West Riding of Yorkshire. ITV 1969-73; 1976. The series was a spin-off from a 1968 series *Gazette*, the story of a weekly newspaper owned by Hadleigh's father.

Hairy Bikers, The Dave Myers and Simon 'Si' King (from Barrow-in-Furness and Newcastle-upon-Tyne respectively), are collectively known as The Hairy Bikers. The two 50 something 'foodies' have presented four series of travel-cum-food-based shows *The Hairy Bikers' Cookbook* (renamed *The Hairy Bikers Ride Again* for series three, and *The Hairy Bakers* for series four). Dave, a former make-up artist, and Si, a film location manager, used all their accumulated production knowledge (and love of food) to entertain viewers in a humorous but interesting fashion. BBC2 2004-08. A further BBC2 daytime show, *The Hairy Bikers Food Tour of Britain*, aired in 2009, with the lads travelling the length and breadth of Britain and Northern Ireland. See *Two Fat Ladies*.

Hallelujah! Thora Hird (Captain Emily Ridley). Sitcom written by Dick Sharples. A Salvation Army worker has served faithfully for 42 years but her superiors feel she is now too old so she is sent to the 'sinful' Yorkshire town of Brigthorpe with the spec of turning things round in four weeks. By the second series Emily is installed at the Mill Street Citadel in Blackwick. The opening sequence portrayed the good captain in a marching band booming out 'When the Saints Go Marching In'. ITV 1983-84.

Hall's Pictorial Weekly When first broadcast on RTÉ, 29 September 1971, the show's full title was *Hall's Pictorial Weekly Incorporating the Provincial Vindicator*. Hosted by Frank Hall and set in the office of a mythical small newspaper, it combined a mixture of social and political satirical sketches with bizarre rural news items (the first show had Hall attempting to establish where exactly is the centre of Ireland). The fictional town where the series was set was called Ballymagash. In testament to the show's popularity the name Ballymagash entered every day usage as a term for any small Irish town in the 1970s. The show had its origins in the *Newsbeat* programme, in which its editor Frank Hall toured Ireland in search of colourful characters and off-beat situations. According to Hall, it occurred to him one day that he would be much more the master of the situation, if he simply sat at home and wrote the sketches, instead of looking for stories around the country. The series was at its strongest during the 1973-1977 term of the Fine Gael-Labour Party coalition government. So sharp and constant was its satirical send-up of the government ministers of the time, that it is generally accepted that the programme played an important part in bringing the coalition into disrepute and perhaps even contributed to bringing it down. Ireland at the time had a very volatile economic situation and the show spared no political expense in portraying the then Taoiseach, Liam Cosgrave, as the "Minister for Hardship," while the Minister for Finance, Richie Ryan, was portrayed as "Richie Ruin". The show also portrayed the former Taoiseach Jack Lynch (played by Frank Kelly) as a rather benign pipe-smoking figure. The political party he led, Fianna Fáil, was also lampooned as being called "Feel and Fall". *Hall's Pictorial Weekly* ended in 1982 after twelve years and over 250 episodes. Frank Hall (1921-95) began his professional life as a journalist with the Irish Independent and the Evening Herald. After that, he moved to RTÉ where he worked in the newsroom. From 1964 to 1971 he presented *Newsbeat*, a regional television news programme. He also presented *The Late Late Show* for the 1968/1969 season.

Hamish Macbeth Robert Carlyle (Hamish Macbeth), James Young (Tusker Gray), Ralph Riach (TV John McIver), Jimmy Yuill and Billy Riddoch (Lachlan), Stuart Davids (Lachie Jr), Duncan Duff (Doc Brown), Brian Pettifer (Rory Campbell), Shirley Henderson (Isobel Sutherland), Brian Alexander (Jubel), Iain McColl (Neil the Bus), Rab Christie (Jimmy Soutar), Anne Lacey (Esme), Valerie Gogan (Alex MacLaine), Stuart McGugan (Barney), Barbara Rafferty (Agnes), Morag Hood (Delores Balfour), David Ashton (Major Roddy Maclean). Hamish Macbeth is a laid-back pot-smoking police constable in the small Scottish town of Lochdubh (pronounced 'Lochdoo' - real-life Plockton), who occasionally bends the rules when it suits him or when it can help some of his fellow eccentric townsfolk. Hamish has two women in his life, the beautiful novelist Alex and the plain local newswoman Isobel, and a dog Wee Jock (a West Highland terrier). Based on characters created by Marion Chesney 'M.C.' Beaton, from her series of mystery novels. BBC1 1995-97.

Hammer House of Horror In 1980 Hammer Films created this series which ran for 13 episodes with 51 min per episode. In a break from their cinema format, these featured plot twists, which usually saw the protagonists fall into the hands of that episode's horror. These varied from sadistic shopkeepers with hidden pasts, to witches and satanic rites. The series was marked by a sense of dark irony, its haunting title music, and the intermingling of horror with the commonplace. Among many memorable episodes was *The Silent Scream*, in which Peter Cushing played an apparently personable pet shop owner working on the concept of "prisons without walls" whilst harbouring a dark secret. Brian Cox, later the first actor to play Hannibal Lecter in Michael Mann's *Manhunter*, was the guinea pig. ITV 1980.

Hancock's Half Hour Tony Hancock (Anthony Aloysius Hancock), Sidney James (Sidney James). Written by Ray Galton and Alan Simpson. Based on his famous 1954 radio show of the same name, the TV run consolidated 'the lad himself' as Britain's leading comic of the day. Hancock's character was invariably a loser, whose aspirations and plans were dashed by fate, circumstance, Sid James or, more often than not, his own pomposity or unfettered ambition. Hancock suffered the slings and arrows of outrageous fortune ruefully, occasionally lamenting his lot with the heartfelt phrase 'Stone me, what a life'. The character's position and profession changed from week to week, and the intentionally unreal feel of the production was compounded by the irregularly recurring support cast of actors appearing in different roles - affectionately named the East Cheam Repertory Company after the Surrey town in which the TV show, like the radio version, was ostensibly located (Hancock's abode, 23 Railway Cuttings, became the most famous address in British comedy). Sidney James, Hancock's friend and confidante, though also his nemesis, was the only constant player, but three of Hancock's radio regulars Hattie Jacques, Bill Kerr and Kenneth Williams appeared in the second TV series and stalwarts such as Johnny Vyvyan, Alec Bregonzi, John Vere, Mario Fabrizi, Irene Handl and Hugh Lloyd provided sterling support throughout. When Sid left in 1960 the last BBC series was broadcast under the title of Hancock, although the same opening sequence remained with Tony appearing in Homburg and heavy coat uttering in breathless tones the title of the series. It was this series that produced the classic episodes *The Blood Donor, The Lift*, and *The Radio Ham*. BBC 1956-61. Tony made a further six episodes without Galton & Simpson for ITV in 1963 but these were not as well-received. In 1996-97 Paul Merton reprised Hancock's role in several of his classic sketches in the ITV series Paul Merton in Galton & Simpson's..... See Tony Hancock's entry in comedy section.

Hanged Man ,The Colin Blakely (Lew Burnett), Michael Williams (Alan Crowe), Gary Watson (John Quentin), William Lucas (George Pilgrim), Julian Glover (Joe Denver), Jenny Hanley (Druscilla), Peter Halliday (Jean-Claud de Salle), William Russell (Peter Kroger), Gareth Hunt (Eddie Malone). Eight-part crime drama series created and written by Edmund Ward. After the third attempt on his life construction boss Lew Burnett decides to stay 'dead' - so that he can stay alive. With the help of his friend Alan Crowe, he goes undercover and can no longer fall back on his money or influence, just the wits and hands with which he built up his own small empire. He is in a state of transition - symbolised by the Hanged Man of the Tarot. ITV 1975.

Hannah Helen Ryan (Hannah Mole), Tim Pigott-Smith (Mr Samuel Blenkinsop), Kathleen Helme (Mrs Gibson), Judi Maynard (Mrs Riddings), Constantine Gregory (Captain Nicholas Foxe), Jenny Beamish (Nancy), Jane Freeman (Lilla Spencer-Smith), Alan MacNaughton (Mr Robert Corder), Oriane Grieve (Ethel Corder), Patsy Kensit (Ruth Corder). Four-part period drama written by Lee Langley and E.H. Young. Hannah, a middle aged housekeeper, arrives in Radstowe to make a fresh start. She finds employment, friendship and romance but two men who know her "sordid" past threaten her newly found happiness. BBC1 1980.

Happiness Paul Whitehouse (Danny), Fiona Allen (Rachel Roche), Mark Heap (Terry Roche), Clive Russell (Angus O'Connor), Pearce Quigley (Sid), Johnny Vegas (Charlie Doyle), Tim Plester (Toby C). Bittersweet comedy series written by Paul Whitehouse and Dave Cummings, following Danny Spencer, a voice-over actor with a mid-life crisis, and his friends in their pursuit, successful or otherwise, of happiness. BBC2 2001-03

Happy Ever After Terry Scott (Terry Fletcher), June Whitfield (June Fletcher), Beryl Cooke (Aunt Lucy), Pippa Page (Susan Fletcher), Caroline Whitaker (Debbie Fletcher). Terry and his wife June are a typical middle-class couple living in a typical middle-class suburban house. Their two daughters, Susan and Debbie have grown up and left home (although appearing on occasions) but the newly-found domestic tranquility is disturbed when June's 73-year-old Aunt Lucy decides to move in with them, complete with her pet mynah bird (Gunga Din). BBC1 1974-78. See *Terry and June*.

Happy Families Jennifer Saunders (Granny, Cassie, Madeleine, Joyce, Roxanne Fuddle), Ade Edmondson (Guy Fuddle), Dawn French (Cook), Stephen Fry (Dr De Quincy), Helen Lederer (Flossie), Jim Broadbent (Dalcroix), Hugh Laurie (Jim), Una Stubbs (Mother Superior). Six-episode sitcom written by Ben Elton, telling the story of the dysfunctional Fuddle family. The plot centred around Guy's attempts to find his four sisters - all played by Saunders - for a family reunion. BBC2 1985.

Happy Holidays Hattie Jacques (Mrs Mulberry), John Le Mesurier (Mr Mulberry), Clive Dunn (Mr Grimble), Carole Lorimer (Kate Holliday), Colin Campbell (Bill Holliday), Robert Scroggins (Cliff Holliday), Anthony Lang (Roger Holliday). Comedy serial written by Peter Ling made by the BBC Children's Television department and broadcast throughout the school holidays of 1954. In it, real life husband and wife John Le Mesurier and Hattie Jacques play Mr and Mrs Mulberry - a childless couple, who, for the summer, look after four children whose own parents are in Ceylon. When the Mulberry's London flat proves to be too small to accommodate all of them they take off for the seaside where the action takes place at the end of a disused pier. BBC 1954.

Hardware Martin Freeman (Mike), Peter Serafinowicz (Kenny), Ken Morley (Rex), Ryan Cartwright (Steve), Susan Earl (Anne), Ella Kenion (Julie). Sitcom created by Simon Nye. Mike, Steve and Kenny work for Rex in Hamway's Hardware Store, in London. The humour revolves around the sometimes over-enthusiastic DIY customers and the banter at the next-door-but-one "Nice Day Cafe", where Mike's girlfriend Anne works with Julie. The show's opening theme was *A Taste of Honey* by Herb Alpert's Tijuana Brass. ITV 2003-04.

Hark at Barker Ronnie Barker (Lord Rustless), Frank Gatliff (Badger), Josephine Tewson (Mildred Bates), David Jason (Dithers). Rustless is a rumbustious, cigar-smoking aristocrat with bushy white eyebrows and a moustache, and with sex keenly on the brain, a man who grows mustard and cress for a living. The character was first seen in the second edition of *The Ronnie Barker Playhouse*, screened on 10 April 1968, conceived by the playwright Alun Owen. Barker's interpretation of Rustless was based on a similarly larger-than-life character he had played, under various names, in repertory in his pre-TV years. The scripts for these 15 half-hours came from a team of writers, with Peter Caulfield (a pseudonym for Alan Ayckbourn, who was employed as a BBC radio drama producer at the time and was not supposed to work elsewhere), John Brendan, Bernard McKenna and Gerald Wiley (a pseudonym for Barker himself) involved in virtually all the editions to a greater or lesser extent. The shows had an unusual style, in that the situation, Rustless addressing the camera from Chrome Hall, recurred in every edition, but the comedy was 'broken' - ie, sketch - based loosely around a particular topic. As a consequence, Ronnie played an extraordinary number of roles in each show, as many as eight, and multi-tasking was required of the other actors too: David Jason was not only the heavily hirsute, doddering, gibberish-spouting, aged gardener Dithers but had other parts to contend with; Ronnie Corbett appeared in one edition in three different roles, there were also occasional parts for David Jason's real-life brother, Arthur White. Michael Palin also made a guest appearance, indeed the Monty Python connection was quite strong: Eric Idle contributed to the scripts and good use was made of caricatures drawn by Terry Gilliam. ITV 1969-70. Barker reprised the role in the 1972 BBC2 series *His Lordship Entertains* (written by Barker under the pseudonym Jonathan Cobbald).

Harley Street Paul Nicholls (Robert Fielding), Suranne Jones (Martha Eliot), Rosie Day (Tess Eliot), Lucy Brown (Maya), Oliver Dimsdale (Felix Quinn), Cush Jumbo (Hannah Fellows), James Fox (Dr Harvey Cost). Short-lived medical drama series created by Marston Bloom and notable as the first drama ITV aired in high definition. ITV 2008.

Harpers West One Norman Bowler (Roger Pike), Graham Crowden (Edward Cruickshank), Tristram Jellinek (Mike Gilmore), Jan Holden (Harriet Carr), Tenniel Evans (Charlie Pugh), Wendy Richard (Susan Sullivan), Vivian Pickles (Julie Wheeler), Arthur Hewlett (Aubrey Harper), John Leyton (Johnny St. Cyr), Philip Latham (Oliver Backhouse). Drama series co-created by John Whitney, the future Director-General of IBA. According to the publicity blurb, this series was "shopping with the lid off" and featured all the life and loves of a big London West End department store. The characters are real, the carpets are plush, the atmosphere is authentic - Yes madam, you'll enjoy buying at Harpers - that's our slogan". John Leyton played a pop singer and his rendition of *Johnny Remember Me* during the series became one of the best-selling records of 1961. ITV 1961-63.

Harry and Paul See *Ruddy Hell! It's Harry & Paul*

Harry Enfield's Television Programme Sketch show written by Harry Enfield, Paul Whitehouse, Charlie Higson and Geoffrey Perkins. The main contributors were Harry Enfield, Paul Whitehouse, Kathy Burke, Martin Clunes and Jon Glover. Originally airing on BBC2, the series was renamed *Harry Enfield and Chums* and given a BBC1 slot in 1994. The most popular characters were Smashie and Nicey (i.e. Fab FM DJs Dave Nice

and Mike Smash who seemed to share a love of "You Ain't Seen Nothing Yet" by Bachman-Turner Overdrive); Wayne and Waynetta Slob and the two chav's daughters Frogmella and Spudulika; Michael Paine the "nosey neighbour" (played by Whitehouse in the style of Michael Caine) and Mr You-Don't-Wanna-Do-It-Like-That (with his catchphrase of "Only Me!"). BBC2 1990-92, BBC1 1994-97.

Harry Hill's TV Burp Multi-award-winning show taking a comical look at the past week's television programmes, the humour often emanating from Harry's deftness at setting the scene for each clip and his surreal pieces to camera. Although Harry does most of the writing himself, Brenda Gilhooly, Paul Hawksbee, Dan Maier, Joe Burnside and David Quantick also help write the weekly show. Before the commercial break there is always a fight to decide which of two people or things from a scene are "best". ITV 2001-

Harry's Game Ray Lonnen (Capt Harry James Brown), Derek Thompson (Billy Downes), Benjamin Whitrow (Davidson), Linda Robson (Theresa McCorrigan), Gil Brailey (Josephine Laverty), Geoffrey Russell (Home Secretary), Nicholas Day (Bannen), Geoffrey Chater (Colonel George Frost), Charles Lawson (Seamus Duffryn), Rita Howard (Mrs. Duffreyn). Three-part thriller written by Gerald Seymour. The IRA has affected a ruthless and brutal slaughter of a Cabinet Minister in London, forcing the Prime Minister to take a personal interest in finding the murderer. A special kind of hunter is needed. Captain Harry Brown is sent alone onto the streets of Belfast to track down the killer. *Harry's Game* is a game of cat and mouse in which there can be no winner and one slip-up means death. The haunting theme song to the series reached the top five of the British charts for Clannad, a feat made even more impressive when one considers that the song is in Gaelic! ITV 1982.

Hart Beat See *Vision On*.

Have A Go Wilfred Pickles (b. Halifax, Yorks, 13 October 1904, d. 26 March 1978) began announcing in 1938 and was an occasional newsreader (the first with a regional accent) on National programme from 1941. Wilfred was also an accomplished comic actor and wit but it was the long-running BBC radio show *Have A Go* that he will always be remembered. Radio's most popular audience participation show, in which ordinary folk did party pieces and answered simple quiz questions, ran from 1946-67 and at its peak received 20 million listeners. Pickles' catch-phrases - among them 'How do, how are yer?', 'Are yer courting?' and 'Give him the money, Mabel' (a reference to wife Mabel Myerscough) - were much quoted; and the show's title remains an epithet for the extraordinary bravery of ordinary people. Wilfred and Mabel, took the programme to church halls throughout the length and breadth of the land 'bringing the people to the people'. The original producer was Barney Colehan (and the catchphrase was "Give 'em the money, Barney!"). The original prize money was £1 17/6, awarded in instalments of 2/6, 5/-, 10/- and 1 guinea. Violet Carson (Ena Sharples in Coronation Street) was resident pianist until 1953, when Harry Hudson took over, followed in 1966 by Eric James. The resounding opening theme, sung in gung-ho Gracie Fields style, was as follows *Have a go, Joe, come on and have a go, You can't lose owt, it costs you nowt, To make yourself some dough. So hurry up and join us, don't be shy and don't be slow. Come on Joe, have a go!*

Have I Got News for You Two celebrity duos play against each other in this topical current affairs satirical quiz hosted by Angus Deayton, until his high-profile sacking in 2002 following tabloid revelations about his private life. Since his demise the series has been hosted by various guest presenters, although the two team captains, Paul Merton and Ian Hislop have been ever-present (apart from one series when Paul was substituted by guest captains). In a famous edition when politician Roy Hattersley failed to turn up for the recording he was substituted by a tub of lard. BBC 2 1990-2000; BBC 1 2000- An extended version of the show *Have I Got a Bit More News for You* began on BBC2 in 2007. See also *Don't Feed The Gondolas*

Hazell Nicholas Ball (James Hazell), Roddy McMillan ('Choc' Minty), Desmond McNamara (Cousin Tel). Hazell first appeared in the 1974 novel *Hazell Plays Solomon*, introducing himself as "The biggest bastard who ever pushed your bell-button." He was the creation of novelist and sports writer Gordon Williams and footballer-turned-manager Terry Venables, using the joint pseudonym 'P.B. Yuill'. In transferring his adventures to the small screen, producers June Roberts and Tim Aspinall presented Hazell as a slightly tarnished East End version of Raymond Chandler's immortal detective Philip Marlowe. Following his retirement from the force due to a damaged ankle, Hazell turns to drink and destroys his marriage. Reformed and dried out, he now works as a private investigator, helped by his cousin Tel, with his main sparring partner a Scottish CID officer named 'Choc' Minty. ITV 1978-80.

HeadJam Game show hosted by Vernon Kay which featured two teams, each consisting of a member of the public and a celebrity. Contestants played a variety of rounds, answering questions about popular culture and the team with the most points at the end played a final round, named "HeadJam", in which the member of the public had to memorise and then deliver the answers to eight questions in order. Series originally aired during the summer of 2004 on BBC3, with a repeat soon afterwards on BBC2.

Heads or Tails Justin Lee Collins, sometimes known as JLC, was born in Bristol, 28 July 1974. He began his showbusiness career as a stand-up comic but soon ventured into radio and television presenting. He and wife Karen have two children (as at July 2010), Archie and Harvey. This daytime game show offered contestants large cash prizes if they could guess correctly whether it was heads or tails when Justin tossed a coin. *Five* 2009. See also *The Friday Night Project*

Heartbeat Nick Berry (PC/Sgt Nick Rowan 1992-98), Derek Fowlds (Oscar Blaketon), Bill Maynard (Claude Jeremiah Greengrass), Niamh Cusack (Doctor Kate Rowan), Jonathan Kerrigan (PC Rob Walker), Clare Calbraith (Dr.Tricia Summerbee), Jason Durr (PC Mike Bradley), Geoffrey Hughes (Vernon Scripps), Peter Benson (Bernie Scripps), Mark Jordon (PC Phil Bellamy), William Simons (PC Alf Ventress), Tricia Penrose (Gina Ward), Duncan Bell (Sgt Dennis Merton), David Michaels (Neil Bolton), Kazia Pelka (Maggie Bolton), Juliette Gruber (Jo Weston), Philip Franks (Sgt Raymond Craddock), David Lonsdale (David Stockwell), Steven Blakely (PC Geoff Younger), John Duttine (Sgt George Miller), Gwen Taylor (Peggy Armstrong), Lisa Kay (Nurse Carol Cassidy), Joe McFadden (PC Joe Mason), Rupert Ward-Lewis (PC Don Wetherby), Nikki Sanderson (Dawn Bellamy). Created by Johnny Byrne, Heartbeat's setting, some of the early storylines, and many of the characters, were taken from the *Constable* novels by Nicholas Rhea (pen-name of former Yorkshire policeman Peter Walker). The stories feature an English policeman in a rural village in North Yorkshire during the 1960s, although cast changes and story developments have resulted in a group of village characters sharing the attention with the local village bobby. The Heartbeat title refers to an English bobby 'on the beat', the medical stories that are woven into each episode, and the way each programme puts a finger on the pulse of the rural community of Aidensfield. Kate Rowan, PC Nick Rowan's wife, and the local GP, is diagnosed with cancer and dies at the end of series 5 and Nick departs during series 7 (to become a Canadian Mountie). Buddy Holly's *Heartbeat*, sung by Nick Berry, was the programme's theme song. The series was axed in 2010 although ITV has left it open to continue at a later date. ITV 1992-2010. A spin-off series *The Royal*, set in a cottage hospital, St Aidan's Royal Free, in neighbouring Elsinby, began on ITV in 2003, starring Julian Ovenden as Dr David Cheriton, Robert Daws as Dr Gordon Ormerod, Amy Robbins as Dr Jill Weatherill, Wendy Craig as Matron and Susan Hampshire as Elizabeth Middleditch. This series was also axed in 2010.

Hearts and Bones Damian Lewis (Mark Rose), Dervla Kirwan (Emma Rose), Hugo Speer (Richard Rose), Amanda Holden (Louise Slaney), Sarah Parish (Amanda Thomas), Rose Keegan (Sinead Creagh). Drama series created by Stewart Harcourt, about a group of friends who move from Coventry to London. Emma is in a seven-year relationship with Mark Rose, with whom she has a son named Sam. She marries him although she loves his brother

Rich - a butcher. Rich lives with his girlfriend Louise who is a hairdresser, but he finds the temptation of a dalliance with Emma hard to resist, especially when his relationship with Louise comes under strain when Louise's mother becomes ill. BBC1 2000-01

Hearts and Minds Current affairs programme presented by Noel Thompson for BBC Northern Ireland. Shown on both BBC1 and BBC2 the show features discussion among the chief Northern Irish politicians about the week's events. At the end of the show there is always a comedy monologue by Tim McGarry.

Hearts of Gold Esther Rantzen handed out gongs to deserving members of the public. Co-presenters included Michael Groth, Joy Aldridge, Mike Smith, Carol Smillie and Mickey Hutton. BBC1 1988-96.

Heaven and Earth Show Sunday morning religious magazine which looked at topical spiritual issues and religious beliefs. Presenters included Simon Biagi, Anita Anand, Max Flint, Diarmuid Gavin, Esther McVey, Juliet Morris, Amanda Redington, Rowland Rivron, Kate Sanderson, Kate Silverton, Kevin Woodford, Philippa Forrester, Yvette Fielding, Phil Hammond and Gloria Hunniford. Reporters included Paul Ross, John Walters, Toyah Willcox, Mike Harding, Edward Enfield, Allan Beswick and Alice Beer. BBC1 1998-2007.

Hector's House Television stick puppet series that began on BBC1 in 1965 and ran for more than 50 episodes repeated on numerous occasions well into the 1970s. Originally a French production (Its French title being La Maison de Toutou - The House of the Doggie), the five-minute segments were revoiced (in Noel Coward-style) for the British market and shown just before the late afternoon news. The main characters were Hector the Dog (voiced by Paul Bacon), Zsazsa the Cat (voiced by Lucie Dolène) and Kiki the Frog (voiced by Denise Bryer). Hector and ZsaZsa lived in a house with a beautiful garden and Kiki (invariably dressed in a pink smock) would visit, and together with ZsaZsa, begin to give Hector a hard time, each episode ending with Hector's catchphrase "I'm a Great Big Old Hector".

Heir Hunters Daytime television programme focusing on attempts to find missing or unknown heirs, entitled to deceased people's estates before the British Treasury lawfully collects the money. The show follows the work of Probate researchers to show how time-consuming research positively impacted people's lives. The first series was presented by Nadia Sawalha, while the second, third, fourth and fifth are narrated by Lisa Faulkner. BBC1 2007-

Helicopter Heroes Television documentary/reality series following a team of helicopter paramedics aboard an air ambulance across Yorkshire. Presenters have included Rav Wilding, Richard Hammond, Lee Davison and Darren Axe. BBC1 2007-09

Hell's Kitchen Cookery-based reality show first broadcast in the UK on ITV in 2004, featuring chef Gordon Ramsay and presented by Angus Deayton. The show, which ran nightly for two weeks, placed ten celebrities in a specially constructed London restaurant kitchen with the task of catering for a clientèle of famous people. The celebrities were Edwina Currie, Abi Titmuss, Matt Goss, Belinda Carlisle, Al Murray, Dwain Chambers, Tommy Vance (who replaced Roger Cook), Jennifer Ellison, James Dreyfus, and Amanda Barrie. Jennifer Ellison was declared the winner after a series of public elimination votes. The second series featured ten members of the public competing for a prize of £250,000 with which the winner could start their own restaurant. They were split into two teams of five, one red - tutored by Gary Rhodes, and the other blue - led by Jean-Christophe Novelli. A new and much larger restaurant was built to accommodate the fact that there were now two kitchens. The only things that remained the same in the second series were the music and the presenter, who was still Angus Deayton. Elimination was still down to voting. 46-year-old caterer Terry Miller won the series. The third series in 2007 reverted back to the celebrity format and saw Marco Pierre White become the kitchen's sole chef. The celebrities were Rosie Boycott, Abigail Clancy, Jim Davidson, Brian Dowling, Kelly LeBrock, Barry McGuigan, Anneka Rice, Lee Ryan, Adele Silva and Paul Young. The Maitre D' was Nick Munier. Former boxer Barry McGuigan exited victorious. The fourth series in 2009 was won by *Dynasty* actress Linda Evans who narrowly beat Ade

Edmondson in the public vote after hot favourite Bruce Grobbelaar walked out for personal reasons.

Help Comedy series written and performed by Paul Whitehouse and Chris Langham, concerning a psychotherapist, Peter Strong (Langham) and his therapy sessions with a variety of patients, invariably played by Whitehouse. Other contributors were Mark Williams and Olivia Colman in cameos as patients, Alison Senior as a patient's wife, Alison King as Strong's secretary, and Langham's real-life daughter Emily as a patient's prodigious daughter. Langham's trial and subsequent finding of guilt on charges of possessing child pornography prevented further series. BBC2 2005.

Hemingway Adventure One hundred years after the birth of Ernest Hemingway, Michael Palin set out to discover the man behind the legend: a hard-drinking, controversial figure who wrote like a dream. Michael's travels took him to seven countries and three continents. The book of the series is not to be confused with his earlier best-selling novel *Hemingway's Chair*. BBC1 1999.

Henry's Cat Animation series created by Stan Hayward and produced by Bob Godfrey (see *Roobarb*). Henry's Cat is a plump lazy feline who enjoys a host of surreal adventures (which turn out to be daydreams) much to the disapproval of the establishment figures of constable bulldog or Farmer Giles. Henry's Cat's gang were a laid back bunch, including Chris Rabbit, Pansy Pig, Mosey Mouse, Sammy Snail, Douglas Dog, Philippe Frog, Ted Tortoise and Denise Duck. Henry's Cat's arch enemy was the evil Rum Baa Baa. Henry himself was never seen. BBC1 1983-87.

Herbs, The Stop-frame animated series created by Michael Bond, concerning the adventures of the animals living in the walled English country garden of Sir Basil and Lady Rosemary. One of the characters, Parsley the Lion, went on to have his own series. Other characters were Dill the Dog, Sage the Owl, Bayleaf the Gardener, Constable Knapweed, Mr Onion the schoolteacher (and his pupils, the Chives), Aunt Mint , Tarragon the Dragon, Belladonna and Pashana Bedi the Snake-Charmer. Narrated by Gordon Rollings. The magic word that opened the gate to the garden was 'Herbidacious'. BBC1 1968.

Here Come the Double Deckers Peter Firth (Scooper), the leader , Michael Audreson (Brains) a geek, Gillian Bailey (Billie), a tomboy, Bruce Clark (Sticks), an American boy, Brinsley Forde (Spring), the only black member of the gang, Debbie Russ (Tiger), who also had a stuffed tiger called Tiger, and Douglas Simmonds (Doughnut), who is constantly hungry. Seventeen-part children's drama series revolving around the adventures of seven children whose HQ was an old red double-decker London bus in an unused works yard. Each weekly episode saw the gang having unlikely adventures in such exotic locations as hovercrafts, chocolate factories, camp sites, and haunted stately homes. Peter Firth went on to become a prominent adult actor, appearing in *Equus, The Hunt for Red October, Tess, Pearl Harbor* and *Spooks* (see entry in cinema section). Co-star Brinsley Forde later became the lead singer in *Aswad*. Adult guest stars included, Julian Orchard, Norman Vaughan, David Lodge, Bob Todd, Liz Fraser, Clive Dunn, Pat Coombs, Betty Marsden, Hugh Paddick, Jane Seymour, Frank Thornton, Michael Sharvell-Martin, Robin Askwith, Graham Stark, Sam Kydd and Melvyn Hayes (Albert) who also co-produced the series. BBC1 1971

Here's Harry Popular sitcom starring Harry Worth as a bumbling, trilby-hatted, well-meaning citizen, living with his cat, Tiddles, in the northern town of Woodbridge. Harry's character had elements of Frank Spencer, Tony Hancock and Victor Mildrew and he often confused himself and all around him. BBC 1960-65. See Harry Worth's entry in the comedy section.

Hetty Wainthropp Investigates Patricia Routledge (Henrietta 'Hetty' Wainthropp), Derek Benfield (Robert Wainthropp), Dominic Monaghan (Geoffrey Shawcross), John Graham Davies (DCI Adams), Suzanne Maddock (Janet Fraser), Wanda Ventham (Margaret Balshaw). Drama series created by John Bowen and David Cook, who created the character of Hetty in his novel *Missing Persons*. To make ends meet and to stop Geoffrey, a local, homeless teenager, from becoming a juvenile delinquent,

Hetty Wainthropp, a sprightly, intelligent pensioner looking for a new challenge, decides to become a private investigator much to the disgust and disbelief of her idle husband, Robert. Once she has made up her mind she becomes an unstoppable force and, led by Hetty, the three set forth to investigate crimes of less interest to the local police force in and around their little village in the beautiful Lancashire countryside. BBC1 1996-98.

Hideaway Ken Hutchison (Colin Wright), Clare Higgins (Ann Wright), Harold Innocent (Arnie), Tony Selby (Terry Staples), Gabrielle Anwar (Tracy Wright), Gary Whelan (Tommy), Ron Moody (Det Sgt Albert Adams), Jimmy Jewel (Robert Hammel). Six-part mini-series. A former criminal decides to go straight and moves to the country with his family to start his own life, but he is pursued by his former associates. BBC1 1986

Hi-De-Hi Paul Shane (Ted Bovis), Ruth Madoc (Gladys Pugh), Simon Cadell (Jeffrey Fairbrother), David Griffin (Squadron Leader Clive Dempster, DFC), Jeffrey Holland (Spike Dixon), Su Pollard (Peggy Ollerenshaw), Felix Bowness (Fred Quilley), Leslie Dwyer (Mr Partridge), Diane Holland (Yvonne Stewart-Hargreaves), Barry Howard (Barry Stewart-Hargreaves), Nikki Kelly (Sylvia), Rikki Howard (Betty), Penny Irving (Mary), The Webb Twins (The Twins Bruce and Stanley), Susan Beagley (Tracey), Linda Reagan (April), Laura Jackson (Dawn), Ben Aris (Julian Dalrymple-Sykes), Kenneth Connor (Uncle Sammy Morris). Sitcom written by Jimmy Perry and David Croft. In 1959, Jeffrey Fairbrother, a Cambridge archaeologist, leaves his university teaching post and takes a job as Entertainments Manager at (Joe) Maplins Holiday Camp, Crimpton-on-sea. He immediately begins to attract the amorous attentions of the Chief Yellowcoat, Gladys Pugh. Other characters include comic Ted Bovis, his assistant Spike Dixon, wannabe-Yellowcoat Peggy Ollerenshaw, childrens' entertainer Mr Partridge, ex-jockey Fred Quilly and dancing instructors Yvonne and Barry Stuart-Hargreaves. By the fifth series Simon Cadell had left and was replaced by David Griffin as the camp boss. Jimmy Perry, who was a former Butlins Red Coat, composed the theme song *Holiday Rock*. There were eight series and 58 episodes. BBC1 1981-88.

Hider in the House Presented by JK and Joel (Jason King and Joel Ross). CBBC programme whereby a celebrity had to be hidden in a house by the children without one of the parents (occasionally another relative) finding out. The children involved also underwent a series of tasks to win prizes which they received if the parent failed to find the celebrity. To prevent the parent being alerted to the cameramen a bogus show named *Our House* was set up as a cover for the 48-hour game of hide-and-seek. In Series 2 the cover programme's name was changed to *Big Kidz*. At this time the show also went through a reformatting, with JK and Joel being joined by presenter, Kate Edmonson of the cover show *Big Kidz* and them having to go undercover as too many people knew about *Hider in the House*. BBC2 2007-8

High Life, The Siobhan Redmond (Shona Spurtle), Alan Cumming (Sebastian Flight), Forbes Masson (Steve McCracken), Patrick Ryecart (Captain Hilary Duff). Sitcom written by Alan Cumming and Forbes Masson . Welcome aboard Air Scotia - flying out of Scotland's Prestwick Airport with the most useless cabin crew ever to push a drinks trolley! The pilot was broadcast in 1994, followed by a series proper the following year. BBC2 1994; 1995

High Living See *Take The High Road*

High Road See *Take The High Road*

High Stakes Game show, hosted by Jeremy Kyle (b. 7 July 1965, Reading, Berkshire) in which contestants climb a cash pyramid by avoiding danger numbers. Each contestant can use up to 10 clues which highlight the danger number. The only way to win more than £25,000 is to guess several numbers on the way. ITV 2011.

High Street Dreams Jo Malone and Nick Leslau help budding entrepreneurs develop products to sell in High Street shops and Supermarkets. The four-episode series delved into the fashion industry, food and drink market, home and garden equipment, and children's toys and games. BBC1 2010.

Highway A roving version of *Stars on Sunday* presented by Sir Harry Secombe. The religious theme would take the form of Sir Harry's guests reading scripture, singing hymns or merely talking of their faith. Harry would always offer a few songs of his own for good measure. ITV 1983-93.

Hilary Marti Caine (Hilary Myers), Caroline Moody (Lyn), Philip Fox (Wesley), Jack Smethurst (Kimberley), Philip Madoc (George), Sandra Carrier (Angela). Sitcom written by Peter Robinson and Peter Vincent for the comic impressionist Marti Caine. Hilary is a Putney-based chat-show researcher (Eagle Television's Searchlight show) with a 19-year-old son and a pet mynah bird named Arthur (voiced by Percy Edwards). She is prone to move from one disaster to the other but is always well-meaning. BBC2 1985-86.

Himalaya Michael Palin's 2004 travels on behalf of the BBC took him to the Earth's greatest mountain range, 1800 miles from the borders of Afghanistan to southwest China. As with so many of his previous journeys *Himalaya* spawned a best-selling book of the series.

Hippies Simon Pegg (Ray), Julian Rhind-Tutt (Alex), Sally Phillips (Jill), Darren Boyd (Hugo). Six-part television comedy series created by Arthur Mathews and Graham Linehan, the writing partnership of *Father Ted*, although the scripts of *Hippies* were written by Arthur alone. Set in 'Swinging London' during 1969, Ray Purbbs is the editor of a counterculture magazine called *Mouth*, which he produces in his flat in Notting Hill Gate. He is aided by Alex Picton-Dinch, Hugo Yemp, and Jill Sprint, who is also Ray's girlfriend, or he thinks she is his girlfriend. BBC2 1999.

His Lordship Entertains See *Hark at Barker*

History Man, The Anthony Sher (Dr Howard Kirk), Geraldine James (Barbara Kirk), Isla Blair (Flora Beniform), Laura Davenport (Annie Callendar), Paul Brooke (Henry Beamish), Maggie Steed (Myra Beamish), Chloe Salaman (Anne Petty), Michael Hordern (Professor Marvin), Miriam Margolyes (Melissa Tordoroff), Veronica Quilligan (Felicity Phee). Christopher Hampton's four-part adaptation of Malcolm Bradbury's novel of varsity vices. Set in October 1972, Howard Kirk is an unpleasant sociology lecturer at Watermouth University whose lifestyle is threatened by allegations of gross moral turpitude. BBC2 1981.

History of Britain by Simon Schama, A Schama, a professor of art history and art at New York's Columbia University, wrote and presented this 17-part history of his native country with the help of reconstructions and site visits. BBC2 2000-02.

Hitch-Hiker's Guide to the Galaxy, The Simon Jones (Arthur Dent), David Dixon (Ford Prefect), Sandra Dickinson (Trillian), David Learner (Marvin), Stephen Moore (Marvin's voice), Mark Wing-Davey (Zaphod Beeblebrox), Peter Jones (The book voice). Douglas Adams' fantasy was originally broadcast on BBC Radio 4 in March 1978, with the second series first being heard in January 1980. The series was brought to television the following year. Arthur Dent is having one of those days when you have trouble taking in all the information you get. He hardly has time to take in the fact that his friend Ford Prefect wasn't from Guildford as he had thought for the past 15 years but was in fact an alien, before he learns that the Earth is going to be destroyed to make way for an intergalactic highway. The pyjama-clad Dent then travels with Prefect aboard a demolition spacecraft manned by the vile sadistic Vogons, who terrorise all and sundry with their appalling poetry. They eventually flee and join the Heart of Gold, a hijacked spaceship manned by galactic celebrity Zaphod Beeblebrox, a two-headed part-time conman and full-time Galactic President, who is heading for the lost planet of Magrathea. His crew consists of Trillian (an earthling named Trisha McMillan) and Marvin a paranoid android, who has the brain the size of a planet. On their travels they encounter Startibartfast, the architect of the fjords, the Golgafrinchians, former telephone operatives and pan-dimensional beings disguised as white mice who are desperately seeking the meaning of life, the universe and everything (which is ultimately made known to be 42). A yellow ear-insert called a Babel Fish simultaneously translates from one spoken language to another enables the journey to be sufferable. Following many adventures the travellers arrive at Milliways, the Restaraunt at the End of the Universe, but all is not what it seems. BBC2 1981.

HolbyBlue Twenty-part spin-off series from *Holby City* created by Tony Jordan. The police drama is based at Holby South station set in the fictional city of Holby. Cast includes Cal Macaninch (DI John Keenan), Tim Pigott-Smith (DCI Harry Hutchinson), Richard Harrington (DS Luke French), Kacey Ainsworth (Jenny Black), Zöe Lucker (Kate Keenan), James Hillier (Christian Young), Chloe Howman (Kelly Cooper), Kieran O'Brien (Robert Clifton), Joe Jacobs (William "Billy" Jackson), Elaine Glover (Lucy Slater), David Sterne (Edward "Mac" McFadden), Oliver Milburn (DCI Scott Vaughan), James Thornton (PC Jake Loughton), Kevin Doyle (Sean Burrows). BBC1 2007-08.

Holby City Spin-off series from *Casualty* created by Tony McHale and Mal Young and set in the same hospital but concentrating on a surgical ward. Recent cast list as at the end of December 2011 includes: Tina Hobley (Chrissie Williams), Hugh Quarshie (Ric Griffin), Paul Bradley (Elliot Hope), Hari Dhillon (Michael Spence), Rosie Marcel (Jac Naylor), James Anderson (Oliver Valentine), Bob Barrett (Sacha Levy), Olga Fedori (Frieda Petrenko), Edward MacLiam (Greg Douglas), Guy Henry (Henrik Hanssen), Jimmy Akingbola (Antoine Malick), Laila Rouass (Sahira Shah), Adam Astill (Dan Hamilton), Lauren Drummond (Chantelle Lane), Sarah-Jane Potts (Eddie McKee), Joseph Millson (Luc Hemingway). **Previous cast members include:** Kelly Adams (Mickie Hendrie, Scott Adkins (Bradley Hume), Jane Asher (Lady Anne-Marie Byrne), Rakie Ayola (Kyla Tyson), Adam Best (Matt Parker), Emma Catherwood (Penny Valentine 2009-11), Tom Chambers (Sam Strachan 2006-08), Sharon D Clarke (Lola Griffin), Ade Edmondson (Percival 'Abra' Durant 2005-08), Jeremy Edwards (Danny Shaughnessy), Michael French (Nick Jordan 1999-2010), Angela Griffin (Jasmine Hopkins 1999-2001), Martin Hancock (Reg Lund), Paul Henshall (Dean West), Jaye Jacobs (Donna Jackson), La Charné Jolly (Elizabeth Tait), Verona Joseph (Jess Griffin), Patsy Kensit (Faye Byrne 2007-10), Denis Lawson (Tom Campbell-Gore 2002-04), Phyllis Logan (Muriel McKendrick), Art Malik (Zubin Khan), Clive Mantle (Mike Barrett 1999-2000), Sharon Maughan (Tricia Williams 2003-06), Amanda Mealing (Connie Beauchamp), Patricia Potter (Diane Lloyd), Duncan Pow (Linden Cullen), Robert Powell (Mark Williams 2005-11), Siobhan Redmond (Janice Taylor), Luke Roberts (Joseph Byrne), Meera Syal (Tara Sodi 2009), Susannah York (Helen Grant 2003). BBC1 1999-

Hold the Back Page David Warner (Ken Wordsworth), Eric Allan (Reg), Gil Brailey (Alison), Lee Whitlock (Charlie Wordsworth), Peter-Hugo Daly (Steve Stevens), David Horovitch (Russell de Vries). Ken Wordsworth is a sports journalist who after going through a divorce needs a pay rise. He leaves the quality newspaper he writes for and joins a very low market tabloid where he is soon dubbed 'The Poet Laureate of Sport. His salary duly increases as a result and this fuels some legendary drinking sessions in a pub called 'The Inkwell'. Amongst the people he now mixes with is a journalist from another tabloid called Steve Stevens. He proves nothing is too low for a tabloid journalist and will stop at nothing for a story. Each one of the ten episodes featured a different sport. BBC1 1985-86.

Holding Out For A Hero Game show hosted by Gethin Jones. Three contestants answered questions worth between £1,000 and £25,000 each on behalf of a hero of their choice. By using a combination of skill, luck and strategy, they could double and treble the worth of a particular question in order to beat the other two rivals. Although the losers were given the consolation prize of £3,000 for their charity, it was sometimes heartbreaking to witness the loss of tens of thousands of pounds for very worthy charitable causes. ITV 2011

Hole in the Wall Dale Winton originally hosted this Saturday evening game show where team captains Anton Du Beke and Darren Gough, plus two other celebrities, have to contort their bodies through holes in an approaching wall or else face a watery demise. The winning team wins £10,000 for their chosen charity. Anton replaced Dale as presenter in 2009 and new team captains were Austin Healey and Joe Swash. BBC1 2008-

Holiday Long-running holiday magazine. Presenters included Frank Bough, Des Lynam, Cliff Michelmore, Joan Bakewell, Jill Dando, Anne Gregg, John Carter, Craig Doyle, Anneka Rice, Eamonn Holmes and Laurence Llewellyn Bowen. BBC1 1969-2007

Holly & Fearne Go Dating Six-part reality series with Holly Willoughby and Fearne Cotton choosing a date each for a contestant looking for love, the show culminating with a dinner date at the Hell's Kitchen restaurant in London, where the lonely heart got to enjoy the company of both dates, one after the other. At the end of the night one date would be chosen as the winner with the prospect of a future relationship. ITV 2007

Holly & Stephen's Saturday Showdown See *Ministry of Mayhem*

Hollyoaks Soap opera devised by Phil Redmond. Set in the fictional suburb of Chester, Hollyoaks, and centred round Hollyoaks Community College, a local higher education academy. Hollyoaks is the only British soap to use incidental music as a transition between scenes. Present cast list as at end of December 2011, in alphabetical order: James Atherton (Will Savage), David Atkins (Rob Edwards), Nicole Barber-Lane (Myra McQueen), Hollie-Jay Bowes (Michaela McQueen), Scarlett Bowman (Maddie Morrison), PJ Brennan (Doug Carter), Jonny Clarke (Bart McQueen), Tosin Cole (Neil Cooper), Claire Cooper (Jacqui McQueen), Stephanie Davis (Sinead O'Connor), Ashley Taylor Dawson (Darren Osborne), Calvin Demba (Scott Sabeka), Lucy Dixon (Tilly Evans), Laurie Duncan (Callum Kane), Alexandra Fletcher (Diane O'Connor), Jessica Forrest (Leanne Holiday), Jessica Fox (Nancy Hayton), Jazmine Franks (Esther Bloom), Karen Hassan (Lynsey Nolan), Bianca Hendrickse-Spendlove (Texas Longford), Ellis Hollins (Tom Cunningham), David Kennedy (Dirk Savage), Dylan Llewellyn (Martin "Jono" Johnson), Danny Mac (Mark "Dodger" Savage), Montana Manning (Jodie Wilde), Ashley Margolis (Ricky Campbell), James McKenna (Jack Osborne), Gemma Merna (Carmel Valentine), Jennifer Metcalfe (Mercedes Fisher), Andrew Moss (Rhys Ashworth), Tamaryn Payne (Annalise Appleton), Helen Pearson (Frankie Osborne), Abi Phillips (Liberty Savage), Nick Pickard (Tony Hutchinson – longest surviving character), Jorgie Porter (Theresa McQueen), Kieron Richardson (Ste Hay), Steven Roberts (George Smith), Emmett J. Scanlan (Brendan Brady), Tom Scurr (Barney Harper-McBride), Anna Shaffer (Ruby Button), Rachel Shenton (Mitzeee), Ashley Slanina-Davies (Amy Barnes), Joe Tracini (Dennis Savage), Stephanie Waring (Cindy Hutchinson), Bronagh Waugh (Cheryl Brady), Holly Weston (Ash Kane), Connor Wilkinson (Finn O'Connor), **A list of past actors in alphabetical order follows:** Jodi Albert (Debbie Dean), Andonis Anthony (Phil Sharpe), Lysette Anthony (Yvonne Summers), Debbie Arnold (Janice Bolton), Dean Aspen (Duncan Smith), Gemma Atkinson (Lisa Hunter), Alice Barlow (Rae Wilson), Ali Bastian (Becca Dean), Stephen Beard (Archie Carpenter), Jennifer Biddall (Jessica Harris), Gemma Bissix (Clare Devine 2006-09), Shaun Blackstock (Taylor Sharpe), Brian Bovell (Leo Valentine), Sarah Jane Buckley (Kathy Barnes), Alison Burrows (Kathleen McQueen), Alex Carter (Lee Hunter), Tracey Childs (Patty Cornwell), Saira Choudhry (Anita Roy), Emily Corselli (Meriel Vaughn), Ross Davidson (Andy Morgan), Garnon Davies (Elliot Bevan), Kris Deedigan (Des Townsend), Elize Du Toit (Izzy Davies), Terri Dwyer (Ruth Osborne), Jeremy Edwards (Kurt Benson), Nathalie Emmanuel (Sasha Valentine), Lucy Evans (Rachel Osborne), Sonny Flood (Josh Ashworth), Chris Fountain (Justin Burton), Joel Goonan (Gaz Bennett), Kelly Greenwood (Zara Morgan), Jessica Hall (Sheila Buxton), Suzanne Hall (Suzanne Ashworth), Tony Hirst (Mike Barnes), Paul Holowaty (Stephen "Macki" Mackintosh), Dominique Jackson (Lauren Valentine), Darren Jeffries (Sam "OB" O'Brien), Claire King (Andrea Mason), Beth Kingston (India Longford), Darren John Langford (Spencer Gray), Elliot James Langridge (Dave Colburn), Sarah Lawrence (Darlene Taylor), Zoë Lister (Zoe Carpenter), Matt Littler (Max Cunningham 1997-2008), Lydia Lloyd-Henry (Amber Sharpe), Gary Lucy (Luke Morgan), Stuart Manning (Russ Owen), Grant Masters (Martin Campbell), Gerard McCarthy (Kris Fisher), Will Mellor (Jambo Bolton), Jim Millea (Neville Ashworth), Nico Mirallegro (Barry Newton), Tiffany Mulheron (Natalie Osborne), Sheree Murphy (Eva Strong), Helen Noble (Abby Davies), Phina Oruche (Gabby Sharpe), Lee Otway (David "Bombhead" Burke), Julie Peasgood (Jacqui Hudson), John Pickard (Dominic Reilly), Mark Powley (Johnno Dean 2002-03), Cassie Powney (Mel Burton), Connie Powney (Sophie Burton), Anthony Quinlan (Gilly Roach), Emma Rigby (Hannah Ashworth), Kent Riley (Zak Ramsey), Samantha Rowley (Clare Devine 2005-06), Helen Russell-Clark (Jem Costello), Kevin Sacre (Jake Dean), Ben Sherriff (Max Cunningham 1995-97), Alvin Stardust (Greg Anderson 1995-96), Carley Stenson (Steph Cunningham), Liz Stooke (Angela Cunningham), Davinia Taylor (Jude Cunningham), Kerrie Taylor (Lucy Benson), Neil Toon (Kyle Ryder), Stephen Uppal (Ravi Roy), Glen Wallace (Malachy Fisher), Melissa Walton (Loretta Jones), Lydia Waters (Holly Hutchinson), Colin Wells (Johnno Dean 2003-05), Ricky Whittle (Calvin Valentine), Amy Yamazaki (Charlotte Lau). C4 1995-

Hollywood or Bust Game show vehicle for Bruce Forsyth in which contestants re-enacted scenes from classic movies. Volunteers from the audience auditioned for the lead male and female roles of the show's themed film. These "auditions" involved reading from autocues that were written to make it look like you were reading wrong. This was a steal from Brucie's earlier show *The Generation Game*. ITV 1984.

Home Again Samantha Janus (Ingrid), Bruce Mackinnon (Mark), Sinead Cusack (Sheila), Peter Egan (Graham). Sitcom written by James Hendrie and Ian Brown. Continually failing to get onto the property ladder, newlyweds Ingrid and Mark are forced to move into her parents' spare room. BBC1 2006.

Home James Jim Davidson (Jim London), George Sewell (Robert Palmer), Harry Towb (Henry Compton), Sherrie Hewson (Paula). Jim Davidson reprises his character first seen in *Up the Elephant and Round the Castle*. After Jim's house is demolished he finds employment as a delivery driver with Palmer Electronics but is promptly dismissed for failing to do his duty. He is brought back onto the payroll when Jim is proved innocent but now is employed as the chauffeur by the company boss Robert Palmer. ITV 1987-90

Home to Roost John Thaw (Henry Willows), Reece Dinsdale (Matthew Willows), Elisabeth Bennett (Enid Thompson), Joan Blackham (Fiona Fennell). Sitcom written by Eric Chappell. Henry Willows is a middle aged, divorced man who lives happily alone. Then one day, there's a knock on the door and Henry finds his 17-year-old son Matthew standing outside. Matthew has decided to move in with his father after being thrown out by his mother. Henry isn't convinced that this is a good idea but decides to give it a go. ITV 1985-90.

Home Truths Radio 4 Saturday morning show presented by John Peel from its inception in 1998 until his death in 2004. The programme was born out of a previous Peel-fronted show, *Offspring*, and helped introduce the veteran DJ, best known for playing ground-breaking music on Radio 1, to a new audience concentrating on domestic issues. Among the diverse features he dealt with included a nine-year-old boy who acted as a carer for his severely epileptic mother, to a woman talking about her enthusiasm for sniffing her pets. Following John's death a series of guest presenters were employed including writer David Stafford, musician Tom Robinson and comedian Linda Smith but Radio 4 controller Mark Damazer announced the show would end in the spring of 2006.

Homes Under The Hammer Daytime television series following the fortunes of three properties bought at auction and often requiring some refurbishment. A presenter will view the property prior to going up for auction giving their opinion on it and its potential problems as well as attractive features. A local estate agent will also be invited to give their opinion on the property. The auction will then be shown and the final sale price revealed. The buyer is then interviewed and the property reviewed several months later when the renovations are complete. Presenters have included Lucy Alexander, Martin Roberts, Graham Barnfield and Alan Driscoll. BBC1 2003-

Honest Amanda Redman (Lindsay Carter), Danny Webb (Mack Caster), Matthew McNulty (Taylor Carter and Vin Carter), Laura Haddock (Kacie Carter), Eleanor Wyld (Lianna Carter), Sean Pertwee (Sgt Bain). Six-part comedy drama series written by Jack Williams. A family of tricksters, thieves and blackmailers have been a mini crime wave for years but things are about to change as mum Lindsay decides enough is enough when dad Mack is banged up for four years for robbery: it's time the family went straight. But some of her children have other ideas. The eldest, twin sons Taylor and Vin may look identical but the similarities end there. While mum's favourite Taylor toils away at law school, Vin's more interested in following in dad's footsteps. And then there's Kacie, who dreams of a career on the catwalk, but in the meantime has to get by on jobseeker's allowance. The youngest, 15-year-old Lianna, is the smartest of the lot. But even she's no angel, blackmailing her deputy headmistress so she can bunk off school! ITV 2008.

Hoobs, The Much-repeated children's television puppet show created and produced by The Jim Henson Company. The five Hoobs: HubbaHubba (Blue), Roma (Orange), Tula (Pink), Iver (Purple), and Groove (Green), are from Hoobland and the stories centre on their interaction with earthlings. In each episode they attempt to increase their knowledge by finding an answer to a question which is then placed in the great Hoobopaedia created by Hubba Hubba. Whilst Hubba Hubba remains in Hoobland; Iver, Groove, and Tula live in the Hoobmobile; and Roma travels to various parts of the world on his motorbike "Picki Picki". The hoobs are accompanied by musicians the Motorettes Tootle (Blue – blows) Twang (Red - strums) and Timp (Yellow - bangs), who also look after the engine room of the Hoobmobile. Hoobs have their own language and regular viewers will know that Tiddlypeeps are children, Wrinklypeeps are old people and Squigglytiddlypeeps are babies. The puppeteers are Donald Austen (Iver), Julie Westwood (Tula), John Eccleston, Mark Jefferis and Brian Herring (Groove), Gillie Robic (Roma), Mark Jefferis and Brian Herring (Hubba Hubba), Mark Jefferis, Rebecca Nagan and Wim Booth (Motorettes). C4 2000-02

Hope and Glory Lenny Henry (Ian George), Amanda Redman (Debbie Bryan), Clive Russell (Phil Jakes), Pippa Guard (Ian Woolley), William Gaminara (Colin Ward), Lee Warburton (Tony Elliot), Richard Griffiths (Leo Wheeldon), Sara Stephens (Sally Bell), Martin Trenaman (Mike Waters), Valerie Lilley (Elaine Rawlings), Phyllis Logan (Annie Gilbert), Gresby Nash (Matt Bennett). Adapted from the story written by Lucy Gannon, *Hope and Glory* is a drama set in a failing inner London grammar school, seen though the eyes of the new headmaster, Ian George. He is young and innovative and turns down a well-paid, influential government position to save Hope Park Comprehensive School. BBC1 1999-2000.

Hope and Keen Mike Hope and Albie Keen (both born in 1935) were cousins (The sons of comedians Syd and Max Harrison) who were stationed together in the RAF, where their love of physical training enabled them to become Olympic gymnastic coaches. After demobilisation they decided to remain together and tour an acrobatic act around provincial theatres, but when the premise wore thin they focused on comic routines and became a success, appearing on *Val Parnell's Sunday Night At The London Palladium* and in the 1965 *Royal Variety Show*. Their screen debut came as the short-lived hosts of *Comedy Bandbox* in 1962 and their first television series, a nine-episode sketch show written by Sid Green and Dick Hills (ITV 1965) located them in curious foreign climes (Gold Nugget Creek, Old Pekin, Casablanca, Tropicsville, Zieto Tierra, Greece, Moonaboola, on board the SS Bounty and in Ballyduro) for comic effect. The Scottish double-act never reached the dizzy heights of popularity enjoyed by Morecambe and Wise but at their height in the mid to late 1960s rivalled Mike and Bernie Winters in popularity. Their sharp routines and well-timed pratfalls during karate sketches added a new dimension to the usual comedy routines prevalent at the time.
In 1970 they switched to the BBC for *Hope and Keen's Crazy House* which encompassed zany goings-on in different rooms, one of which featured a performing musical guest. The regular cast featured Peter Goodwright as an ancient butler and Ruth Kettlewell as their larger-than-life cook. In the second series, the setting was changed to a bus (and the title was changed accordingly) and Hope and Keen set out on an adventure to find their Uncle Ebenezer's lost treasure - a quest that took them all over Britain. The lads are still working together professionally on Caribbean cruises and pantomime.

Horizon BBC Two's flagship 50-minute science documentary series exploring topical scientific issues and their effects for the future. The ongoing programme first aired on 2 May 1964 with *The World of Buckminster Fuller*, exploring the theories and structures of the American inventor of the Geodesic Dome. This first programme included the *Horizon* mission statement, *The aim of Horizon is to provide a platform from which some of the world's greatest scientists and philosophers can communicate their curiosity, observations and reflections, and infuse into our common knowledge their changing views of the universe.* To-date, more than a thousand episodes have been broadcast. BBC2 1964-

Hornblower Ioan Gruffudd (Horatio Hornblower), Robert Lindsay (Captain / Commodore / Admiral Sir Edward Pellew), Jamie Bamber (Lieutenant Archie Kennedy), Paul Copley (Matthews - the Bosun), Sean Gilder (Styles the Bosun's Mate), Jonathan Coy (Lieutenant / Captain Bracegirdle), Simon Sherlock (Oldroyd), Chris Barnes (Finch), Paul McGann (Lt William Bush), Lorcan Cranitch (Wolfe), Philip Glenister (Hobbs), Julia Sawalha (Maria Mason), David Warner (Captain James Sawyer). Umbrella title of a series of eight television drama films based on C. S. Forester's novels about the fictional character Horatio Hornblower, a Royal Naval officer during the French Revolutionary Wars and the Napoleonic Wars. Originally shown on ITV between 1998 and 2003, the series has recently been repeated on ITV3.

Horrible Histories CBBC sketch show based on the Terry Deary book series of the same name. The quirky, bloody, gruesome but entertaining stories are all based on historical fact although stretched to their comic limits. Subject matters include: Savage Stone Age, Groovy Greeks, Rotten Romans, Potty Pioneers, Putrid Pirates, Slimy Stuarts, Smashing Saxons, Cut-Throat Celts, Terrible Tudors, Measly Middle Ages, Frightful First World War, Woeful Second World War, Vile Victorians, Vicious Vikings, Ruthless Rulers, Awful Egyptians (Original book was titled "Awesome Egyptians"), Gorgeous Georgians and Wicked Witches. Mathew Baynton is the chief actor and writer for the television series. Special guests have included: Terry Deary, David Baddiel, Dave Lamb (voice only of course), Alexei Sayle, Meera Syal and Steve Punt. The show was repackaged for a prime-time BBC One slot in 2011 with Stephen Fry as host. The new six-part series featured a selection of the best clips from Series 1 and 2, and new segments featuring Fry, who replaced the puppet host Rattus Rattus. BBC1 2009; BBC2 2010; BBC1 2011-
A spin-off game show entitled *Gory Games* started airing in May 2011, starring Dave Lamb, Scott Brooker and John Eccleston (Puppeteer for Rattus Rattus).

Hospital, The This documentary series began in the accident and emergency wards of two Midlands hospitals (City Hospital, Birmingham and Heartlands Hospital, Birmingham) where doctors and nurses working on the frontline are left to pick up the pieces of a young generation who binge-drink to excess. The second episode of three concentrated on the cost of teenage mothers to an already stretched health service while the third episode in the series looked at the cost of Britain's increasingly obese teens. The second series began with an episode focusing on the West London Centre for Sexual Health examining young people's matter-of-fact attitude to sexually transmitted infections. C4 2009-10

Hot Milk and Pepper See *Brendan O'Carrolls Hot Milk and Pepper*

Hot Shoe Show, The Dance (and the occasional song) show, presented by Wayne Sleep with regular guest dancers Bonnie Langford, Cherry Gillespie and Finola Hughes. BBC1 1983-84.

Hotel Babylon Nigel Harman (Sam Franklin), Anna Wilson-Jones (Juliet Miller), Dexter Fletcher (Tony Casemore), Martin Marquez (Gino Primirola), Ray Coulthard (James Schofield), Alexandra Moen (Emily James), Michael Obiora (Ben Trueman), Amy Nuttall (Melanie Hughes), Danira Govic (Tanja Mihajlov), Tamzin Outhwaite (Rebecca Mitchell), Natalie Mendoza (Jackie Clunes), Lee Williams (Jack Harrison), Max Beesley (Charlie Edwards), Emma Pierson (Anna Thornton-Wilton), Paul Telfer (Luke Marwood). Drama series following the lives of workers at a glamorous five-star hotel. Based on the book by Imogen Edwards-Jones, the programme was ignominiously cancelled after four series and 32 episodes leaving many unanswered questions. BBC1 2006-09

Hotel Inspector, The In each episode a celebrated hotelier (Ruth Watson in series 1–3; Alex Polizzi in series 4–present) visits a struggling British hotel and tries to turn their fortunes by giving advice and suggestions to the owner. C5 2005- In January 2012 Alex Polizzi was scheduled to begin a new BBC series on similar lines, entitled *The Fixer*.

Hounded Rufus Hound (Rufus Hound), Colin McFarlane (Dr Muhahahaha), Nadine Marshall (Steve), Steven Wickham (Future Rufus), Eva Alexander (Gill), Colin Ryan (Barry). Children's comedy series starring Rufus Hound. The comedian is chased through space and time by the evil Dr Muhahahaha who is prone to dastardly deeds such as beaming powerful Grot Particles across the universe to Earth giving everyone there really bad breath. Rufus must thwart Dr Mu and find his way home. At the end of each adventure, if Rufus beats the evil doctor, he rewinds time and the day begins, finding himself back in his flat about to start the same fateful day again...and again, and again. Part of the CBBC menu. 2010.

Hour, The Ben Whishaw (Freddie Lyon), Dominic West (Hector Madden), Romola Garai (Bel Rowley), Anton Lesser (Clarence Fendley), Julian Rhind-Tutt (Angus McCain), Anna Chancellor (Liz Storm), Kelly-Jayne Adams (Alice the PA), Jamie Lawton (Don the don). Six-episode drama series created by Abi Morgan and set around a new BBC current affairs programme at the time of the Suez Crisis in 1956. BBC2 2011

Hour of Mystery Ten-episode anthology drama series depicting classic mystery stories. Introduced by Donald Wolfit, the stories were: *Duet for Two Hands* (15 June 1957), *The Man in Half Moon Street* (22 June 1957), *The Woman in White* (29 June 1957), *Confess, Killer* (13 July 1957), *The Man with Red Hair* (20 July 1957), *Night Must Fall* (27 July 1957), *Sound Alibi* (10 August 1957), *Spare Your Pity* (17 August 1957), *A Murder Has Been Arranged* (24 August 1957), *Portrait in Black* (7 September 1957). ITV 1957.

House of Cards Ian Richardson (Francis Urquhart), Sussanah Harker (Mattie Storin), Diane Fletcher (Elisabeth Urquhart), Colin Jeavons (Tim Stamper), James Villiers (Charles Collingridge), Michael Kitchen (The King), John Bird (Bryan Brynford-Jones), Kitty Aldridge (Sarah Harding), Isla Blair (Claire Carlsen). Dramatisation by Andrew Davies of Michael Dobbs' novel concerning the ruthless Government whip Francis Urquhart's determination to become Prime Minister at any cost. Mattie Storin, a young reporter, begins to have suspicions as to the integrity of the scheming politician and what follows made this series compelling viewing. Francis Urquhart's catchphrase "You might well think that; but I couldn't possibly comment" has become part of the English political language. In the follow-up series *To Play the King* Urquhart (aka 'FU') was by now firmly entrenched at No.10. The third series *The Final Cut* saw Urquhart's empire crumbling. Michael Dobbs was uncredited for this series, apparently due to not being happy with Andrew Davies' adaptation. BBC1 1990; 1993; 1995.

House of Eliott Stella Gonet (Beatrice Eliott), Louise Lombard (Evangeline Eliott), Barbara Jefford (Lady Lydia Eliott), Peter Birch (Arthur Eliott), Aden Gillett (Jack Maddox), Phyllida Law (Edith Duglass), Cathy Murphy (Tilly Watkins/Foss). A lavish 12-part Saturday night drama series, created by Eileen Atkins and Jean Marsh, set in the 1920s and revolving around the lives of two sisters and their battle to set up their own fashion house. Beatrice and Evangeline Eliott (12 years her junior) are left penniless when their father (a respected Highgate doctor) dies but fight tooth and nail to make a go of the House of Eliott. BBC1 1991-94.

Housewive's Choice Immensely popular radio record request programme broadcast every morning from 1946 to 1967 on the BBC Light Programme. The iconic theme music was *In A Party Mood* by Jack Strachey. Aberdeen-born musician George Elrick (29 December 1903 – 15 December 1999) was compere for most of the show's run and would invariably sign off each show by singing the words 'I'll be with you all again tomorrow morning'

over the theme tune, and noting 'This is Mrs Elrick's wee son George saying thanks for your company - and cheerio!'.

How Educational children's programme explaining how things happen. The original presenters were Fred Dinenage, Jack Hargreaves, Jon Miller and Bunty James. Jack tended to take the role of an avuncular know-it-all displaying all the practical 'Hows', Jon was the sensible science-based one and Fred played the naughty prankster who asked 'Hows' such as 'how do you get an egg into a milk bottle'. Bunty kept a motherly watch over Fred while displaying qualities of humour and practicality in her Hows. Each programme began and ended with the team raising their palms in the traditional Native American greeting while drums beat out the theme tune. Jill Graham replaced Bunty in the 1970s and was herself replaced by Marian Davies towards the end of the run. ITV 1966-81. The format was revived between 1990 and 2006 under the title *How 2* with original presenter Fred Dinenage being joined by Gareth Jones and Carol Vorderman (1990-96) (variously replaced by Sian Lloyd (1997), Gail Porter (1998) and Gail McKenna (2000-06). There has also been several spin-off *How* specials.

How Clean Is Your House? Unlikely hit show where expert cleaners Kim Woodburn (born Patricia Mary MacKenzie, 25 March 1942, Eastney, Hampshire) and Aggie MacKenzie (born 12 October 1955, Rothiemurchus, Aviemore) visit filthy homes and then clean them. C4 and S4C 2003-09. *Too Posh To Wash* was a spin-off of *How Clean Is Your House?* shown on C4 and S4C, in 2004.

How Do They Do It? Programme exploring how ordinary objects are made and utilised. Presenters include Robert Llewellyn, Dominic Frisby, Rupert Degas and Iain Lee. Originally shown on the Discovery Channel from 2006, a revamped version aired on *Five* in 2008.

How Do You Solve A Problem Like Maria? Ten would-be Maria von Trapps battled it out on Saturday nights during the summer of 2006, the ultimate prize being the leading role in the West End production of *The Sound of Music*. Graham Norton presented and three judges, John Barrowman, David Ian and Zoe Tyler passed comments but Andrew Lloyd Webber had the final say on who was voted off each week, although the viewer finally chose the winner. Connie Fisher, a 23-year-old call-centre worker, was the favourite from the beginning and ultimately won the prize, and indeed has been a resounding success in the West End. BBC1 2006.

How Do you Want Me? Dylan Moran (Ian Lyons), Charlotte Coleman (Lisa Lyons), Mark Heap (Derek Few), Emma Chambers (Helen Yardley), Frank Finlay (Astley Yardley), Peter Serafinowicz (Dean Yardley). Sitcom written by Simon Nye. Naïve urban man, Ian Lyons, is newly wed to country girl Lisa Yardley. After a year living in London they move to the village of Snowle, where her unpleasant father, Astley, breeds turkeys. He and most of Lisa's family, which includes her sister Helen and her boorish brother, Dean, take a dislike to Ian. Life is also complicated by Lisa's ex-boyfriend Derek, who still holds a candle for her. BBC2 1998-99.

How Green Was My Valley Stanley Baker (Gwilym Morgan), Siân Phillips (Beth Morgan), John Clive (Cyfartha), Keith Drinkel (Ianto Morgan), Mike Gwilym (Owen Morgan), Nerys Hughes (Bronwen Morgan), Sue Jones-Davies (Angharad Morgan), Ray Smith (Dai Bando), Jeremy Clyde (Iestyn Evans), Dominic Guard (Huw Morgan), Rhys Powys (Young Huw), Gareth Thomas (Rev. Mr Gruffyd). Elaine Morgan's highly acclaimed six-part adaptation of Richard Llewellyn's novel about life in a Welsh mining valley. BBC1 1975-76.

How to Look Good Naked See *Gok's Fashion Fix*

Howard's Way Maurice Colbourne (Tom Howard), Jan Harvey (Jan Howard), Glyn Owen (Jack Rolfe), Stephen Yardley (Ken Masters), Tony Anholt (Charles Frere), Nigel Davenport (Sir Edward Frere), Kate O'Mara (Laura Wilde), Susan Gilmore (Avril Rolfe), Tracey Childs (Lynne Howard/Dupont), Dulcie Gray (Kate Harvey), Michael Denison (Admiral Redfern). Drama series created by Gerard Glaister and Allan Prior. Tom Howard is made redundant from his job as a senior aircraft designer and decides to invest his skill, time and redundancy money in a run-down local boat building establishment named 'Mermaid Yard'. The decision puts a great strain on his marriage and causes problems with other members of his family. Howard's Way is set on the River Hamble in Tarrant (real-life Bursledon). Tom's yacht is *The Flying Fish*. The theme tune *Always There* performed by Marti Webb and the Simon May Orchestra reached No 13 in the charts in 1986. Tragically, Maurice Colbourne died of a heart-attack in 1989 and the series ended after one more series. BBC1 1985-90.

Hugh and I Terry Scott (Terry Scott), Hugh Lloyd (Hugh Lloyd), Patricia Hayes (Griselda Wormold), Vi Stevens (Mrs Scott), Fred Emney (Lord Popham). Sitcom written by John Chapman. Terry is a youngish bachelor who lives with his mother. He's a bit of a dreamer who wants to get rich as quickly and as easily as possible. He comes up with new "get rich quick" scheme after another, causing endless problems for himself and his friend, Hugh Lloyd. In the final series, Hugh wins some money on the Premium Bonds and the pair set off on a world cruise. BBC 1962-66. A short-lived sequel, *Hugh And I Spy* was transmitted in 1968. See also *The Gnomes of Dulwich*.

Human Jungle, The Herbert Lom (Dr Roger Corder), Sally Smith (Jennifer Corder), Mary Yeomans (Nancy Hamilton, Dr Corder's secretary), Michael Johnson (Dr Jimmy Davis), Mary Steel (Jane Harris, assistant to Dr. Corder). Drama series about a psychiatrist based in Harley Street, London. Widower Dr Roger Corder sometimes struggles with his relationship with his headstrong teenage daughter Jennifer but is more successful in getting to the root of the deep, and sometimes bizarre, emotional distress suffered by his featured patient in each of the 26 episodes. Margaret Lockwood as a washed-up actress, Joan Collins as a stripper, and Jess Conrad as a pop-star, appeared in memorable episodes and Janina Faye as an ice-skater (Verity Clarke) who had lost her nerve on the ice epitomised the ability of Herbert Lom's portayal to bring a sense of tension and gravitas to the series. *The Human Jungle* theme music was composed by Bernard Ebbinghouse and played by John Barry and his orchestra. ITV 1963-65.

Hunter's Walk Ewan Hooper (DS Smith), Davyd Harries (Sgt Ken Ridgeway), David Griffith (PC Parfitt, credited as Mark Griffith), Duncan Preston (PC Fred Pooley), David Simeon (DC 'Mickey' Finn), Ruth Madoc (Betty Smith), Charles Rea (P.C. Harry Coombs). Police drama series created by Ted Willis and set in the Midlands town of Broadstone (actually Rushden, Northants). ITV 1973-76.

Hustle Robert Vaughan (Albert Stroller), Adrian Lester (Mickey "Bricks" Stone), Marc Warren (Danny Blue), Robert Glenister (Ash Morgan), Jaime Murray (Stacie Monroe), Rob Jarvis (Eddie), Matt Di Angelo (Sean Kennedy), Kelly Adams (Emma Kennedy). Drama series created and written by Tony Jordan. Five con-artists join forces to enjoy the economies of scale and divisions of labour. Habitual gambler Albert's job in the team is to pick the right targets ('Put up the mark') for his colleagues. Danny is the joker in the pack, a 'grifter' who excels at card tricks and pick-pocketing. Ash is the technical and practical brains of the operation. Stacie uses her feminine wiles to ensnare unsuspecting marks. She causes 'distraction' while another gang member, usually Mickey or Danny targets the male victim. Mickey is the leader of the team, and master of the long con. An all-rounder, Mickey has the skills of all the male members of the group and belies his 'ordinary' appearance with extraordinary abilities. Eddie is the hapless licencee of the premises the team frequent. The popular series has a unique style with occasional freeze-frame scenes where our heroes are the only animate objects, asides to camera, flashback denouements and frequent contemporary music tracks. The 'stings' themselves become almost incidental but are always entertaining even if predictable at times. In series four Mickey leaves the group for a long term solo project and is replaced by short con artist Billy Bond played by former So Solid Crew rap star Ashley Walters and Danny becomes leader of the gang. Mickey returns in series five but Danny and Stacie remain in New York to work and are replaced by brother and sister team Sean and Emma Kennedy. BBC1 2004-

Hyperdrive Nick Frost (Space Commander Michael "Mike/Lucky Jack/Hendo" Henderson), Kevin Eldon (First Officer Eduardo Pauline York), Miranda Hart (Diplomatic Officer

Chloe Teal), Stephen Evans (Navigator Dave Vine), Dan Antopolski (Technical Officer Karl Jeffers), Petra Massey (Sandstrom), Maggie Service voices a variety of computers. Science fiction sitcom written by Kevin Cecil and Andy Riley. Set in the year 2152, *H.M.S. Camden Lock*'s mission is to protect Britain's interests in a changing galaxy. The design for the spaceship is based on the BT Tower and is a 'Wendover' class ship measuring 376m long by 90m wide. The ship's registration is XH558 - the same serial number as the RAF's last flying Avro Vulcan bomber. The shuttlebay doors on the Camden are shown with the Union Jack embossed on them, which is part of the patriotic theme of the series. *Camden Lock* is powered by P-Rods, with the P standing for Perfectly safe, although it is rumoured to stand for Plutonium. Her maximum speed is 170 Vs -- any higher and the Reactors overheat. Her maximum crush depth is 197 atmospheres. BBC2 2006-07

I Am Not an Animal Steve Coogan (Mark the Bird), Julia Davis (Claire the Rat), Kevin Eldon (Hugh the Monkey), Arthur Mathews (Niall the Rabbit), Simon Pegg (Kieron the Cat), Amelia Bullmore (Winona the Dog), John Shrapnel (Narrator). Animated comedy series, created by Peter Baynham, about the only six talking animals in the world, whose cosseted existence in a vivisection unit is turned upside down when they are liberated by animal rights activists. BBC2 2004

I Claudius Derek Jacobi (Claudius), Sian Phillips (Livia), Brian Blessed (Octavian / Augustus), George Baker (Tiberius), John Hurt (Caligula), Patrick Stewart (Sejanus), Christopher Biggins (Nero), Ian Ogilvy (Drusus), Christopher Guard (Marcellus), John Paul (Agrippa), Simon MacCorkindale (Lucius), David Robb (Germanicus), Patricia Quinn (Livilla), Fiona Walker (Agrippina), John Castle (Postumus), James Faulkner (Herod), John Rhys-Davies (Naevius Sutorius Macro), Stratford Johns (Piso), Sheila White (Messalina), Beth Morris (Drusilla), Kevin McNally (Castor), Bernard Hill (Gratus), Norman Eshley (Marcus), John Cater (Narcissus), Bernard Hepton (Pallas), Peter Bowles (Caractacus). Jack Pulman's 12-part adaptation of Robert Graves' two novels *I Claudius* and *Claudius the God*. The mini-series follows the history of the Roman Empire, from approximately the death of Marcellus (23 BC) to Claudius' own death in 54 AD. As Claudius narrates his life, we witness Augustus' attempts to find an heir, often foiled by his wife Livia who wants her son Tiberius to become emperor. We also see the conspiracy of Sejanus, the infamous reign of Caligula, and Claudius' own troubled period of rule. BBC2 1976.

I Didn't Know You Cared Stephen Rea (Carter Brandon), Keith Drinkel (Carter Brandon), Robin Bailey (Uncle Mort), John Comer (Mr Brandon), Liz Smith (Mrs Brandon), Deirdre Costello (Linda Preston), Liz Goulding (Pat), Bert Palmer (Uncle Staveley). Sitcom written by Peter Tinniswood, based upon his books *A Touch of Daniel*, *I Didn't Know You Cared* and *Except You're A Bird*. Set in a working class household, in South Yorkshire in the 1970s the family life plots revolve around the thoughts of Carter Brandon (played in the first two series by Irish film star Stephen Rea). Uncle Staveley (remembered for his catchphrase, "I heard that! Pardon?") always appears with the ashes of Corporal Parkinson - one of his comrades from World War I - in a box around his neck. BBC1 1975-79. In the various BBC Radio 4 spin-offs aired between 1987 and 1996, Stephen Thorne played Uncle Mort, with Peter Skellern as Carter Brandon.

I Own Britain's Best Home and Garden Laurence Llewelyn-Bowen and a panel of experts scrutinized 12 of the country's most extraordinary gardens. The judges were straight-talking garden designer Anne Wareham, esteemed RHS Chelsea judge Mark Gregory and horticultural author Laetitia Maklouf. In a Dragons' Den style conclusion to each show, the three contenders had to defend their gardens against the judges' criticisms before the victor was announced. The six-part series evolved from *I Own Britain's Best Home*, shown on Five earlier in the year, presented by Melissa Porter, Charlie Luxton and Russell Harris. *Five* 2008.

I Thought You'd Gone Peter Jones (Gerald), Pat Heywood (Alice), Ian Gelder (Tony), Rosalind Knight (Ruby Pugh), Rowena Roberts (Sue). Seven-part comedy series written by Kevin Laffen and Peter Jones, who also starred as the main protagonist. Just when they were beginning to enjoy life alone, a middle-aged couple find their grown-up children wanting to return home. ITV 1984.

I'd Do Anything The BBC's follow-up to *Any Dream Will Do*, this time searching for an unknown performer to play Nancy and three young performers to take it in turns to play Oliver in a West End revival of the British musical *Oliver!* The show, named after a song from *Oliver*, was hosted by Graham Norton with Andrew Lloyd Webber again overseeing the programme together with theatrical producer Cameron Mackintosh. Regulars John Barrowman and Denise Van Outen were joined by Barry Humphries as the judging panel of the show. Although Lord Lloyd Webber could save either one of the bottom two each week, as voted by viewers, the final three were totally at the mercy of the public. Jodie Prenger, a 28-year-old singer, ultimately won the vote for Nancy and Gwion Jones, Harry Stott and Laurence Jeffcoate were announced as the three winning Olivers. BBC1 2008.

Identity Aidan Gillen (DI John Bloom), Keeley Hawes (Det Supt Martha Lawson), Holly Aird (Tessa Stein), Elyes Gabel (DC Jose Rodriguez), Shaun Parkes (DS Anthony Wareing), Patrick Baladi (Asst Commissioner Hugh Wainwright). Six-part drama series, created by Ed Whitmore, which follows an elite police unit formed to combat the explosion of identity-related crime. The unit, formed and led by DSI Lawson, recruits John Bloom, an ex-undercover cop, who knows first hand what it's like to pretend to be someone you are not. He's also only too aware of how easy it is to lose your own identity when you're living a lie. ITV 2010.

Idiot Weekly, Price 2d, The Short-lived sitcom/sketch show starring Peter Sellers as the editor of a run-down Victorian newspaper, the headlines of which prompted sketch recreations. This six-episode series was the first attempt to televisualise the Goon humour (although Harry Secombe did not take part due to prior commitments). Spike Milligan was the chief writer and actors included Peter Sellers, Spike Milligan, Eric Sykes, Valentine Dyall, Kenneth Connor, Graham Stark and June Whitfield. Patti Lewis and Max Geldray provided the musical interludes. ITV 1956. See *The Goons*

I'm a Celebrity Get Me Out Of Here Reality television set in the North Queensland rainforest of Australia and introduced by Ant McPartlin and Declan Donnelly. First broadcast on ITV 1, 2002. The premise of the show is that celebrity campers take part in a series of 'Bush Tucker Trials' (usually involving some sort of creepy-crawlies) to earn food for the remaining tribe members while the general viewing public offer their judgement by way of a daily elimination vote resulting in a winner being crowned 'King (or Queen) of the Jungle'. The celebrities have included: Series 1 - Nigel Benn, Tony Blackburn (winner), Rhona Cameron, Darren Day, Uri Geller, Christine Hamilton, Nell McAndrew, Tara Palmer-Tomkinson. Series 2 - Linda Barker, Chris Bisson John Fashanu, Catalina Guirado, Siân Lloyd, Wayne Sleep, Phil Tufnell (winner), Danniella Westbrook, Toyah Willcox, Antony Worrall Thompson. Series 3 - Peter Andre, Alex Best, Jennie Bond, Lord Charles Brocket, Jordan, John Lydon, Kerry Katona (as Kerry McFadden - winner), Diane Modahl, Mike Read, Neil Ruddock, Sophie Anderton. Series 4 - Sophie Anderton, Natalie Appleton, Paul Burrell, Fran Cosgrave, Antonio Fargas, Sheila Ferguson, Brian Harvey, Joe Pasquale (winner), Vic Reeves. Series 5 - Antony Costa, Kimberley Davies, David Dickinson, Jenny Frost, Mike Goldman, Jilly Goolden, Elaine Lordan, Sheree Murphy, Jimmy Osmond, Sid Owen, Carol Thatcher (winner). Series 6 - Toby Anstis, Faith Brown, Malandra Burrows, Jason Donovan, Dean Gaffney, David Gest, Myleene Klass, Jan Leeming and Matt Willis (winner). Series 7 - Marc Bannerman, Christopher Biggins (winner),John Burton Race, Janice Dickinson, Lynne Franks, Malcolm McLaren, Rodney Marsh and Cerys Matthews. Series 8 - Dani Behr, Robert Kilroy-Silk, Timmy Mallett, Martina Navratilova, Brian Paddick, Esther Rantzen, Joe Swash (winner), George Takei, David Van Day and Simon Webbe. Series 9 - Gino D'Acampo (winner), Joe Bugner, Samantha Fox, George Hamilton, Colin McAllister, Katie Price (Jordan's second appearance), Justin Ryan, Jimmy White and Kim Woodburn. Series 10 - Linford Christie, Kayla Collins, Jenny

Eclair, Britt Ekland, Sheryl Gascoigne, Alison Hammond, Nigel Havers, Dom Joly, Gillian McKeith, Lembit Öpik, Shaun Ryder, Aggro Santos, Stacey Solomon (winner). Series 11 - Willie Carson, Lorraine Chase, Jessica-Jane Clement, Antony Cotton, Stefanie Powers, Dougie Poynter (winner), Crissy Rock, Emily Scott, Pat Sharp, Sinitta, Freddie Starr, Fatima Whitbread, Mark Wright. Presenters of the ITV 2 supporting programme *I'm a Celebrity Get Me Out Of Here- Now!* have included Louise Loughman, Mark Durden-Smith, Tara Palmer-Tomkinson, Matt Brown, Emma Willis, Brendon Burns, Kelly Osbourne, Jeff Brazier, Matt Willis, Caroline Flack, Joe Swash, Russell Kane and Laura Whitmore.

I'm Alan Partridge Steve Coogan (Alan Partridge), Felicity Montagu (Lynn). Sitcom written by Peter Baynham, Armando Iannucci and Steve Coogan. After the end of the first series of Alan's BBC chat show, *Knowing me Knowing You with Alan Partridge*, and the divorce from his wife Carol, Alan is now living in Linton Travel Tavern. He now works for Radio Norwich covering the early morning slot. In the second series Alan moved out of the hotel and into a mobile home while awaiting the completion of his new house. He now hosts the late night show on Radio Norwich as well as a cable TV game show called Skirmish. BBC2 1997; 2002.

I'm Sorry I Haven't A Clue The self-styled "antidote to panel games" was a spin-off from *I'm Sorry I'll Read That Again* and chaired from its inception on 11 April 1972 by the inimitable Humphrey Lyttelton (known affectionately as "Humph"), until his death in April 2008. The BBC Radio comedy show consists of a panel of four comedians, split into two teams and "given silly things to do" by its genial host. The original panellists were Bill Oddie, Graeme Garden, Tim Brooke-Taylor and Jo Kendall with Barry Cryer sometimes filling in for Humph as chairman but eventually replacing Kendall as a panellist. In 1974 Oddie was replaced by Willie Rushton (1937-96) and from then until Willie's death the establishment remained constant, the fourth seat then being taken by a variety of comedy stars. Dave Lee was the original pianist on the show but Colin Sell, the butt of many impromptu jokes, has been the pianist on much of the run, Neil Innes standing-in on several occasions. Since 18 May 1985, the show's routines have included a fictional and completely silent scorer, "whose job is eased by the fact no points are actually awarded". This role is usually filled by "the lovely Samantha" — who would like to sit on Humph's left hand! When Samantha has been unavailable her role has sometimes been filled by the Swedish stand-in scorer, Sven, or occasionally another substitute, Monica. Since 1978 *Mornington Crescent* has been a popular game featured on the show. The game, the rules of which are deliberately not explained, satirises complicated strategy games and consists of each player in turn announcing a landmark or street, most often a tube station on the London Underground system; the winner being the first to announce "Mornington Crescent", a station on the Northern Line. The humour of the game was that while its rules were invoked and argued on the show, they were never explained. Willie Rushton is honoured by a Comic Heritage blue plaque at Mornington Crescent. The theme music is called "The Schickel Shamble", by Ron Goodwin, and is from the film *Monte Carlo or Bust*. The show returned in the summer of 2009 with rotating chairmen, Stephen Fry, Rob Brydon and Jack Dee, who became the sole presenter in November 2009.

I'm Sorry I'll Read That Again Billed as 'a radio custard pie' this iconic series starred Graeme Garden, Tim Brooke-Taylor, Bill Oddie, John 'Otto' Cleese, Jo Kendall and David Hatch (who later went on to produce the show and eventually became Controller of Radio 2 and Radio 4). The show was a liberal smattering of silly impressions, awful puns, and mild smut but was also totally anarchic, with the audience controlling much of the show in later series. The show's title comes from a sentence commonly used by BBC newsreaders following a mispronunciation or grammatical faux pas. Bill Oddie and Graeme Garden wrote the scripts with contributions from the others, plus Eric Idle, Graham Chapman, Anthony Buffery, Alan Hutchkinson, Elizabeth Lord, Chris

Stuart-Clark and Humphrey Barclay, who also created the show. The musical links and songs were provided by Dave Lee and his band although the show always ended with a sign-off song from Bill Oddie performed as "Angus Prune" and referred to by the announcer as "The Angus Prune Tune". The pilot of the series was a recording of the West End show, *Cambridge Circus*, which aired on the 30th December 1963. *Cambridge Circus* originated at the Cambridge University Footlights Club, and sprang from the revue entitled "A Clump of Plinths". Recurring themes and catchphrases included the mention of rhubarb tart as a much-loved food that would act as a bribe to enhance performance; The Tillingbourne Folk and Madrigal Society performing their renditions of everything from football chants to current pop tunes including the never-ending folk song "There was a Ship that put to Sea all in the Month of May"; John Cleese's obsession with ferrets; and the inappropriate use of the opening bars of Beethoven's Fifth for comedic effect. ISIRTA, as it was affectionately known by fans, was also famous for its Christmas pantomime specials. These were always good value and John Cleese's character of 'King Rat' was often central to the lack of plot. BBC Home Service (became Radio 4 in 1967) 1963-73. See *I'm Sorry I Haven't A Clue*.

In All Directions BBC radio comedy that ran from 1952-55, featuring actors Peter Jones and Ustinov as themselves in a car in London perpetually searching for Copthorne Avenue. The comedy derived from the characters they met along the way, often also played by themselves. The show was unusual for the time in that it was largely improvised – with the tape subsequently edited for broadcast by Frank Muir and Denis Norden, who also sometimes took part. Two of the more popular characters were Morris and Dudley Grosvenor, two rather stupid East End spivs whose sketches always ended with the phrase "Run for it Dudley" (or Morry as appropriate). Jones reprised the character of Dudley in the 1960 film, *School for Scoundrels*, but was now known as Dudley Dorchester. The film was based on the Stephen Potter 'Gamesmanship' books and Peter later starred in the TV series *One-Upmanship,* also based on Potter's books.

In at the Deep End Chris Searle and Paul Heiney took it in turn to learn new skills in this series which was a precursor of *Faking It.* BBC1 1982-84; 1987.

In Deep Nick Berry (Liam Ketman), Stephen Tompkinson (Garth O'Hanlon), Lisa Maxwell (Pamela Ketman), Karianne Henderson (Nicola Ketman), Buster Reece (Max Ketman), Meera Syal (Marta Drusic), Fiona Allen (Sophie), Carli Norris (Kelly). Police drama written by Peter Jukes and Stephen Brady. Undercover detectives Liam Ketman and Garth O'Hanlon submerge themselves in various dangerous criminal worlds as they go deep undercover to investigate serious crime. Liam is married and is forced to lie to his wife to protect his cover. He pays regular visits to police psychiatrist Marta Drusic to keep himself sane in the duplicitous life he is forced to lead. Garth is single and much stronger mentally, seemingly having no problem with the dangers of the job. BBC1 2001-03

In Loving Memory Sitcom created by Dick Sharples. Set in the fictional Lancashire town of Oldshaw during the 1930s. In the opening episode Jeremiah Unsworth (Freddie Jones), the proprietor of an undertakers, dies. This leaves his widow Ivy (Thora Hird) and gormless nephew Billy (Christopher Beeny) to take over the business. As in other Thora Hird comedies the actual location was in Yorkshire (the village of Luddenden). The pilot episode aired in 1969 but it was ten years later before being commissioned. ITV 1979-86.

In Sickness And In Health See *Till Death Us Do Part*.

In The Grid Gameshow based on the game of 'battleships' where two contestants chose grid numbers such as A1, C3 etc in order to win cash prizes. Some grid squares were good and others offered penalties. The winner of the game played on a jackpot board at the end and was allowed to return the following day. Presented by Les Dennis with theme music by Marc Sylvan. *Five* 2006-07.

In The Night Garden... An interpretation of a nursery rhyme picture book featuring lots of characters based loosely on toys, living together within a happy and caring community. Narrated by Sir Derek Jacobi and filmed mostly in live action, featuring a mix of actors in costumes, puppetry and computer animation. Each character has their own unique song and dance, with Igglepiggle and Upsy Daisy playing important roles as their emotional and comic interaction is an essential part of the narratives of many of the episodes. The Tombliboos live inside a lovely round bush, which has many different levels inside where the Tombliboos enjoy playing with their special blocks as well as their drums and piano. Makka Pakka lives in a little cave with his favourite stones. He also has a little soap and sponge to make sure all of the Garden stones and all of the faces of the other characters are clean and tidy. He travels around the Garden pushing his Og-Pog, which carries his sponge, his uff-uff dryer and his special trumpet. The Pontipines are a large family that lives in a semi-detached house at the foot of a tree. Their next-door neighbours are the Wottingers. The Pontipines and the Wottingers are two families of ten, with eight children, four of which are boys and four are girls. The Haahoos are six enormous great billowy forms that make their way through the Garden like puffy pillows, calling to each other as they meet up to go to sleep in a big pillowy pile. The Ninky Nonk is a wonderful train of many differently sized and shaped carriages and the Pinky Ponk is an airship, speckled with many fins and large landing lights and providing wonderful aerial views of all of the Garden's splendour. Created by Anne Wood and Andy Davenport, the partnership responsible for co-creating *Teletubbies*. Part of the Cbeebies diet for children aged between 1 and 4. BBC 2007-

In Town Tonight BBC Radio topical chat show broadcast on the Home Service every Saturday evening from 1933 to 1960. Its opening sequence consisted of a voice crying "Stop" to interrupt the sound of busy central London, before an announcer said "Once more we stop the mighty roar of London's traffic and, from the great crowds, we bring you some of the interesting people who have come by land, sea and air to be In Town Tonight". At the end of the programme the voice would say "Carry on, London". The original presenter was Birmingham-born Eric Maschwitz (10 June 1901–27 October 1969). Eric was a talented screenwriter who wrote the screenplays of several successful films in the 1930s and 1940s, but he is perhaps best remembered today for his lyrics to 1940s popular songs such as *A Nightingale Sang in Berkeley Square* and *These Foolish Things*. Eric was married to actress Hermione Gingold from 1926-45. One of the regular contributors to the programme was Hertfordshire-born BBC cricket commentator Brian Johnston (24 June 1912 - 5 January 1994) who had his own segment, "Let's Go Somewhere" from 1948 to 1952. During this run Brian stayed in the Chamber of Horrors alone for a night, rode a circus horse, lay under a passing train, was hauled out of the sea by a helicopter and was attacked by a police dog. Towards the end of its run *In Town Tonight* was simultaneously broadcast on BBC Television, presented by John Ellison. The television version always started with a view of Piccadilly Circus. After its demise the programme was replaced by *In Town Today*, which was broadcast at lunchtime and ran until 1965. The theme music was the *Knightsbridge March* by the then little known composer Eric Coates, who subsequently went on to monopolise the radio theme tune market.

Inbetweeners, The Simon Bird (Will McKenzie), Joe Thomas (Simon Cooper), James Buckley (Jay Cartwright), Blake Harrison (Neil Sutherland), Emily Head (Carli D'Amato), Henry Lloyd-Hughes (Mark Donovan), Emily Atack (Charlotte "Big Jugs" Hinchcliffe). Sitcom Written by Damon Beesley and Iain Morris. Set in and around Rudge Park Comprehensive and following the struggles of four sixth formers who are neither part of the school's trendy "in-crowd" nor school "nerds", but somewhere inconsequentially "inbetween". Will moves from a "posh private school" to the sixth form at the local comprehensive school and eventually makes friends with Simon, Neil and Jay after they initially try to avoid him. Simon is the oldest of the four and the first to learn how to drive. Having passed his test his father buys him a small, yellow Fiat Cinquecento Hawaii. Jay is obsessed with sex, with almost all his comments being about the subject, although his actual practical experience of it is always hugely exaggerated. Neil is the slowest member of the group but can do the robot and has a crush on his biology teacher Miss Timms. Originally shown on E4 in 2008 but transferred to Channel 4 later in the year. The current series (3) reaches a natural conclusion with the lads completing their schooling. C4 2008-10. In 2011 a very successful film, *The Inbetweeners Movie*, was released with much of the cast reprising their roles.

Indian Doctor, The Sanjeev Bhaskar (Dr Prem Sharma), Ayesha Dharker (Kamini Sharma), Mark Williams (Richard Sharpe), Naomi Everson (Gina Nicolli), Ifan Huw Dafydd (Owen Griffiths), Beth Robert (Sylvia Sharpe), Alexander Vlahos (Tom Evans), Mali Harries (Megan Evans), Erica Eirian (Sian Davies), Jacob Oakley (Dan Griffiths). Drama series created by Deep Sehgal and Tom Ware and written by Bill Armstrong. Set in 1963; a backwater Welsh mining town's doctor dies and the only replacement the union representative can find arrives, straight from India. To everyone's surprise, he's better educated and more cultured then any of the local residents and he is friendly and eager to help. His wife, Kamini, however looks down on the 'peasants' and wants him to move to London. The first series came to a climax with the manipulative colliery manager Richard Sharpe, being exposed as deliberately ignoring safety warnings to develop productivity in his attempts to further his own career. BBC1 2010-

Indoor League, The Former cricket legend Freddie Trueman presided over events at the mock Yorkshire boozer which held all manner of indoor sports including, shove-ha'penny, bar billiards, arm-wrestling, darts, table-football, pool and table-skittles. The competition was serious, with many household names taking part, but the intimate atmosphere created a sense of keen amateurism popular with the viewing audience. Commentators included Sid Waddell, Dave Lanning, Keith Macklin, Kent Walton, Neil Hawke, Neil Cleminson, Bill Maynard, Fraser Davy and Hector O. Meades. The pipe-smoking Fred would end each lunchtime show with a hearty 'I'll see thee'. ITV 1973-78.

Informer, The Ian Hendry (Alex Lambert), Heather Sears (Janet Lambert), Jean Marsh (Sylvia Parrish), Neil Hallett (DS Piper), Tony Selby (Cass). Created by Geoffrey Bellman and John Whitney. Disgraced and disbarred lawyer uses his accumulated knowledge to earn a living from both sides of the law as a paid informer, passing on information to Detective Sergeant Piper. This series was a fore-runner of *In Deep* with Lambert masquerading undercover as a business consultant, not even his wife knowing his true identity. ITV 1966-67.

Inigo Pipkin George Woodbridge (Mr Inigo Pipkin), Wayne Laryea (Johnny), Charles McKeown (Charlie the Dustman), Jumoke Debayo (Bertha), Jonathan Kydd (Tom), Paddy O'Hagan (Peter Potter), Sue Nicholls (Mrs Muddle). Voices: Nigel Plaskitt (Narrator/Hartley Hare/Tortoise/Mooney), Heather Tobias (Pig/Topov/Octavia), Loraine Bertorelli (Pig/Topov/Octavia/Pigeon), Elizabeth Lindsay (Topov/Octavia), Diana Eden (Mrs P), Anne Rutter (Pig), Alex Knight (Pig). Fun exploits with the animal residents of 'Pipkins' Puppeteer's Workshop: Pig, Topov the monkey, Tortoise, Octavia the ostrich and Hartley Hare. Mr Pipkin actor George Woodbridge died five weeks into making the second series and an episode was given over to explaining Mr Pipkin's death. With the series retitled *Pipkins* (1974-81), assistant Johnny (played by former Crawley athlete Wayne Laryea) ran the shop as an agency, helping people in all kinds of strange ways. ITV 1973-81.

Innes Book of Records Former Bonzo Dog Doo Dah Band member Neil Innes performed musical parodies of established pop stars. BBC2 1979-81.

Innocence Project, The Stephen Graham (Andrew Lucas), Lloyd Owen (Professor Jon Ford), Christine Bottomley (Sarah Shawcross), Luke Treadaway (Adam Solomons), Oliver James (Nick Benitz), Ruth Bradley (Beth McNair), Shelley Conn (Dr Eve Walker), Ruta Gedmintas (Mary Jarvis), Thomas Turgoose (Dizzy). Drama series created by BBC Northern Ireland and written by Oliver Brown. Professor Jon Ford sets up *The Innocence Project*, in partnership with a select group of law students. They take on clients with little hope – who have possibly been wrongly convicted. The series is notable for an early screen performance by Thomas Turgoose (of *This is England* fame) in the role of delinquent Dizzy who is attempting to put his life back on track. The series was scrapped ignominiously after eight episodes due to poor ratings. BBC1 2006-07.

Inside George Webley Roy Kinnear played the depressive bank clerk George Webley, created by Keith Waterhouse and Willis Hall. ITV 1968-70.

Inside Sport Late-night sports-talk show presented by Gabby Logan. BBC1 2007-

Inspector Alleyn Mysteries, The Patrick Malahide (Chief Insp Roderick Alleyn), William Simons (Insp Brad Fox), Belinda Lang (Agatha Troy). Character created by Ngaio Marsh. In this popular series the 'toff' policeman's activities are confined to the period following World War II. BBC1 1993-94.

Inspector Lynley Mysteries, The Nathaniel Parker (Insp Thomas Lynley), Sharon Small (DS Barbara Havers), Lesley Vickerage and Catherine Russell (Helen Clyde / Lynley). The series, originally adapted from the novels of Elizabeth George, concerns the aristocratic crime-fighter Inspector Lynley, 8th Earl of Asherton, who owns a plush Chelsea home and drives a Bristol 410 (In the first episode he drove a Peugeot 607 and in subsequent early episodes, a Jensen Interceptor although in the books he drove a Bentley). He works with DS Havers, a young lady from the opposite side of the tracks, living at home in Acton with her sick parents. The unlikely pairing made a formidable crime-busting duo. BBC1 2001-08.

Inspector Morse John Thaw (Chief Insp Endeavour Morse), Kevin Whatley (Det Sgt Robbie Lewis), James Grout (Chief Supt Strange), Peter Woodthorpe (Max), Amanda Hillwood (Dr Grayling Russell), Norman Jones (Chief Supt Bell), Clare Holman (Dr Laura Hobson), Judy Loe (Adele Cecil). Colin Dexter's Morse is a multi-faceted officer of the Thames Valley Police Force. The curmudgeonly Oxford graduate has a fondness for booze, crosswords, and Wagnerian opera. He also has an unfortunate love life, and a propensity to leap to conclusions, but ultimately possesses a brilliant mind. Morse drives a 1960 Mark 2 maroon Jaguar (it was a Lancia in the books), accompanied by his genial Geordie sergeant, Lewis. The TV show's haunting theme tune was by Barrington Pheloung, and based on the Morse Code for the letters M-O-R-S-E. Dexter chose the name Morse after Sir Jeremy Morse, the former chairman of Lloyds Bank. The series proper ran on ITV between 1987 and 1993 but a series of specials continued until the last-ever episode aired in 2000. See also *Lewis*.

Instant Restaurant Two amateur cooks went head to head to see if they've got what it takes to create a restaurant in their own homes for one night only - and make a profit. Presented by Nadia Sawalha. BBC2 2010.

International Cabaret Variety show, presented by Kenneth Williams, in which three international acts, from around the world, would perform in each show. BBC2 1966-68; 1974

Interpol Calling Charles Korvin (Insp Paul Duval), Edwin Richfield (Insp Mornay). 39 episodes of this popular police drama were made and set around the Paris HQ of the International Police Organisation. Each episode began with a speeding car crashing through a checkpoint amid a hail of bullets and the opening announcement. 'Crime knows no frontiers. To combat the growing menace of the international criminal, the police forces of the world have opened up their national boundaries. At their headquarters in Paris, scientifically equipped to match the speed of the jet age, sixty-three nations have linked together to form the International Criminal Police Organisation, INTERPOL!' ITV 1959-60.

Into the Labyrinth Pamela Salem (Belor), Charlie Caine (Phil), Ron Moody (Rothgo), Lisa Turner (Helen), Simon Henderson (Terry). Children's drama series written by Gary Hopkins and produced by Harlech Television. Three children stumble upon the imprisoned sorcerer Rothgo and are drawn into a mysterious search through time for the magical Nidus which has been stolen by the evil witch Belor. ITV 1981-82.

Intrigue Edward Judd (Gavin Grant), Caroline Mortimer (Val Spencer). Drama series created by Tony Williamson. An industrial espionage agent and his assistant investigate the world of big business. ITV 1966.

Invisible Man, The Lisa Daniely (Diane Brady – The Invisible Man's widowed sister), Deborah Watling (Sally Brady – Diane's daughter), Ernest Clarke (Sir Charles Anderson). In the original series Dr Peter Brady's body was played by Johnny Scripps and the voice was that of Tim Turner although no actor was billed. Scientist Peter Brady becomes invisible following his experiments into light refraction. While working on an antidote he uses his power of invisibility to solve crimes. Ralph Smart produced this series based on the HG Well's character. The eerie incidental music, particularly when Brady moved around invisibly, added to the suspense of the plots. ITV 1958-59. A more faithful version of the HG Wells' novel was shown on BBC1 in 1984 with Pip Donaghy playing the title role of Griffin in a six-part series. David McCallum also played the character (now named Dr Daniel Westin) in a 1975 American series.

Invisibles, The Warren Clarke (Syd Woolsey), Anthony Head (Maurice Riley), Dean Lennox Kelly (Hedley Huthwaite), Jenny Agutter (Barbara Riley), Emily Head (Grace Riley), Paul Barber (Young Nick), Mina Anwar (Helen Huthwaite), Darren Tighe (Joe Woolsey). Comedy drama series written by William Ivory. Maurice and Syd are old friends who return from the good life on the Costa del Crime to a quiet Devon fishing village. They plan to eke out their retirement fishing and availing themselves of the NHS after one last job. However, crime has moved on and they've got new things to learn. BBC1 2008.

Ireland: A Television History Robert Kee's 13-part series followed the country's development from pre-Christian times, through various uprisings down the centuries, the famine of 1845 and up to the present, with a specific emphasis on the creation of the modern independent republic and the roots of the Troubles. More importantly, the series presented many British viewers with their first detailed insight into the history of Irish politics, especially the issues surrounding sovereignty and identity in Northern Ireland. RTE screened the last two episodes uncut, despite the fact that they contained statements from organisations banned in that country. RTE / BBC2 1980-81.

Irish RM, The Peter Bowles (Major Sinclair Yeates), Doran Godwin (Philippa Butler/Yeates), Bryan Murray (Florence Macarthy 'Flurry' Knox), Lise-Ann McLaughlin (Sally Knox), Beryl Reid (Mrs Knox). Series based on the 1899 book *Some Experiences of an Irish RM*, By Edith Somerville and Martin Ross (pen name of Violet Florence Martin), adapted for television by Rosemary Anne Sisson. When Major Sinclair Yeates leaves his home in England to work as the Irish Resident Magistrate, he finds that the justice system needs tempering somewhat to suit the local needs. Ulster / RTE /C4 1983-85.

It Ain't Half Hot Mum Windsor Davies (RSM B.L. Williams), Melvyn Hayes (Gunner / Bombardier 'Gloria' Beaumont), George Layton (Bombardier 'Solly' Solomons), Michael Bates (Rangi Ram), Don Estelle (Gunner 'Lofty' Sugden), Donald Hewlett (Colonel Reynolds), Michael Knowles (Captain Ashwood), Christopher Mitchell (Gunner Nigel Parkin), John Clegg (Gunner 'Paderewski' Graham), Stuart McGugan (Gunner Mackintosh), Kenneth MacDonald (Gunner 'Nobby' Clark), Mike Kinsey (Gunner 'Nosher' Evans), Dino Shafeek (Char Wallah Muhammed), Babar Bhatti (Punka Wallah Rumzan), Andy Ho (Ah Syn the cook). Sitcom created by Jimmy Perry and David Croft. The adventures of a Royal Artillery concert party towards the end of the Second World War. Initially based in Deolali, India, the company were later sent to entertain the troops in Burma. The motley crew were the responsibility of Sergeant Major Williams, a gruff Welsh RSM who referred to his charges as 'A bunch of pooftahs' and whose favourite command was "Shut Up!". The concert party included Bombardier "Solly" Solomons (written out after the early episodes), Bombardier Beaumont (who was very effeminate, dressed up in drag for the concerts, and was constantly referred to as 'Gloria'), an intellectual pianist referred to by Williams as 'Mr La-de-Da' Gunner Graham, chief vocalist "Lofty" Sugden (so called because he was extremely short) and Gunner Parkins (who the Sgt Major treated kindly and referred to as 'Lovely Boy' because he believed him to be his illegitimate son), Scotsman Gunner Mackintosh, and Gunners Clark and Evans. Each episode opened with the troops singing the theme song 'meet the gang...'cos the boys are here, the boys to entertain you!' BBC1 1974-81.

It Crowd, The Chris O'Dowd (Roy Tenneman), Richard Ayoade (Maurice Moss), Katherine Parkinson (Jen Barber), Chris Morris (Denholm Reynholm), Matt Berry (Douglas Reynholm), Noel Fielding (Richmond Avenal), Tom Binns (Nolan). Sitcom written by Graham Linehan and set in the Information Technology department of the London offices of Reynholm Industries. The humour emanates from the three-strong IT support team, i.e. geeky technicians Roy and Maurice plus their computer-illiterate boss, Jen, herself hired by the equally technophobic Denholm. C4 2006-

ITMA Tommy Handley and Ted Kavanagh wrote the scripts for this very popular wartime radio programme together with producer Francis Worsley. The name of the programme derived from a topical catchphrase. Whenever Hitler made some new territorial claim, the newspaper headlines would proclaim 'It's That Man Again'. The programme started on a trial basis in July 1939. The setting was a pirate commercial radio ship, from which Tommy Handley broadcast, assisted by Cecilia Eddy as his secretary Cilly, Eric Egan as a mad Russian inventor, Sam Heppner and Lionel Gamlin. These early editions were modelled on *Bandwaggon* (see separate entry). *ITMA* returned in September 1939 for a weekly series in which Tommy Handley was Minister of Aggravation and Mysteries at the Office of Twerps. With a new cast, Vera Lennox as his secretary Dotty, Maurice Denham as Mrs Tickle the office char and Vodkin the Russian inventor, Jack Train as Funf the elusive German spy, and Sam Costa. One of the regular features was Radio Fakenburg, a send up of Radio Luxembourg which had stopped broadcasting during the War. For the third series in June 1941, the show was renamed *It's That Sand Again*. It was set in a seedy seaside resort called Foaming-at-the-Mouth, with Tommy (as the town's Mayor), Sydney Keith, Horace Percival, Dorothy Summers and Fred Yule. New characters were invented: Lefty and Sam, the gangsters (Train and Keith); Deepend Dan the Diver (Percival), Claude and Cecil, the over-polite handymen (Train and Percival) and Ali Oop (Percival), a Middle Eastern vendor of saucy postcards and other dubious merchandise. In September 1941, the show reverted back to *ITMA*. This time they were joined by Dino Galvani as Tommy Handley's Italian secretary Signor So-So and Clarence Wright as a commercial traveller who never sold anything but didn't seem to care. Dorothy Summers played the office char, Mrs. Mopp, sent by the "Labour" to dust the Mayor's dado. By September 1942, Foaming-at-the-Mouth had a war factory but it was never mentioned what it was supposed to be producing - even the workers didn't seem to know. Colonel Humphrey Chinstrap (Jack Train) made his first appearance, and rapidly became one of the most popular characters. The colonel was a dipsomaniac army officer who turned almost any innocent remark into the offer of a drink with his catchphrase 'I don't mind if I do'. (Jack Train also appeared as Colonel Chinstrap in at least one edition of *The Goon Show*, as an old army pal of Denis Bloodnok.) The following series saw the war factory turned into a spa, a holiday camp and a hotel. In the next series Tommy was Squire of Much Fiddling and Jack Train introduced a new character called Mark Time, an elderly man who answered all questions with 'I'll 'ave to ask me Dad'. Newcomer Diana Morrison played Miss Hotchkiss. The first post-war series was joined by Carleton Hobbs, Hugh Morton, Mary O'Farrell, Michele de Lys and Lind Joyce. Tommy was now appointed Governor of a South Sea island called Tomtopia. During the journey to this new paradise, Tommy met Curly Kale (Carleton Hobbs), the chef who hated food but loved terrible puns; George Gorge (Fred Yule), a glutton who could eat any quantity of 'lovely grub' and Sam Fairfechan (Hugh Morton), the contradictory Welshman. Accompanying them on the journey was Colonel Chinstrap. The local population included Bigga Banga (Fred Yule), the native chief who spoke only Utopi language, his daughter and translator Banjeleo (Lind Joyce); Wamba M'Boojah (Hugh Morton), another Tomtopian native whose Oxbridge accent was the result of a spell as an announcer with the BBC's Overseas Service, and Major Munday (Carleton Hobbs), an ex-British army officer who had lived in isolation since the Boer war and now believed that England was exactly as it had been in the nineteenth century. A year later Tommy was appointed the Governments adviser on industrial and scientific affairs. The series investigated the radio industry, organisation of a fuel saving campaign and a PR programme for England. Hattie Jacques joined up as Sophie Tuckshop, the greedy schoolgirl, whose prandial excesses were invariably followed by a giggle and 'but I'm all right now'. The final series began in September 1948. Down on his luck, Tommy was now a permanent resident at Henry Hall (the tramps guesthouse), run by Miss Hotchkiss. For the milestone 300th episode on 28th October 1948, the setting was Madame Tussauds' Waxworks in London. Here passing through a door marked 'The Hall of ITMA's Past', Tommy was reunited with many favourite characters from Foaming-at-the-Mouth and Tomtopia, with Dino Galvani, Horace Percival, Clarence Wright, Lind Joyce and Dorothy Summers all making guest appearances. The very last ITMA went out on 6th January 1949. Tommy Handley died suddenly of a cerebral haemorrhage three days later. The Radio Times shows that there was an ITMA show scheduled for 13th January, but this was to be replaced by a special tribute programme.

It's A Knockout Iconic game show adapted from the French show *Intervilles*, in which teams representing a town or city, took part in absurd games, often water-based and often wearing giant foam costumes, for comic effect. The first series was a domestic competition between Yorkshire and Lancashire, the first show winners being Blackpool, although the Grand Final was won by Bridlington. Presenters were McDonald Hobley (1966), David Vine (1967-71) and Stuart Hall (1971-82) with Eddie Waring co-hosting throughout the run and Arthur Ellis also refereeing the domestic version throughout. Stuart's enthusiasm and uncontrollable fits of laughter became synonymous with the show. *It's A Knockout* became a feeder show for the European version *Jeux Sans Frontières*, also shown on the BBC and the British presenters also hosted these shows although the international referees were Gennaro Olivieri and Guido Pancaldi (Eddie was the British referee for JSF). Although *Jeux Sans Frontières* had been running in Europe since 1965, Great Britain did not participate until 1967, when they were pitted against Belgium (B), France (F), West Germany (D), Italy (I) and Switzerland (CH). Bridlington, representing GB, finishing last. In 1969 Britain had its first international success when Shrewsbury became the first British heat winner and then went on to win the Grand Final, albeit a tied effort with Germany. BBC1 1966-82. *The Grand Knockout Tournament* (known *as It's a Royal Knockout*) was a one-off charity event, organized by Prince Edward, which the BBC aired on 15 June 1987. The show featured Prince Edward, The Princess Royal, The Duke of York and The Duchess of York as non participating team captains, each of whom supported a different charity. Participating celebrities included Jenny Agutter, Anthony Andrews, Rowan Atkinson, Michael Brandon, John Cleese, Ian Charleson, Ben Cross, Margot Kidder, Kevin Kline, George Lazenby, Meat Loaf, Jennifer O'Neill, Michael Palin, Christopher Reeve, Cliff Richard, Jane Seymour, Helen Shaver, Mel Smith and John Travolta. The show was hosted by Stuart Hall, Les Dawson and Su Pollard. *It's A Knockout* was revived by Channel 5 (Five) in 1999 and hosted by Keith Chegwin, Lucy Alexander and Frank Bruno. It ran until 2001.

It's A Square World Comedy sketch show, written, created, and starring ex-Goon Michael Bentine. This show was a ground-breaking mix of scale models, special effects and location filming used to great comic effect. Memorable skits included, sinking the House of Commons with a Chinese Junk; discovering that the source of the Thames was a dripping tap; and sending BBC Television Centre into orbit with TV astronomer Patrick Moore. The most-famous recurring sketch was undoubtedly the imaginary flea-circus with Bentine giving a running commentary on the order of events. The programmes were enormously popular; a special edition, screened by the BBC on 19 April 1963, won the Golden Rose of Montreux that year; in 1962 Bentine won the Bafta award for best comedy performance. Other regular cast members included Dick Emery, Frank Thornton, Ronnie Barker, Clive Dunn, John Bluthal, Deryck Guyler, Benny Lee, Len Lowe, Leon Thau, Louis Mansi, Anthea Wyndham, Janette Rowselle, Freddie Earlie and Joe Gibbons. BBC 1960-64. The show transferred to ITV (1966-67) under the name *All Square*.

It's Dark Outside William Mervyn (DI Charles Rose), Keith Barron (DS Swift), John Carson (Anthony Brand), Anthony Ainley (DS Hunter), June Tobin (Alice), Veronica Strong

(Claire), John Stratton (Fred Blaine), Oliver Reed (Sebastian). Police drama series which became the second part of a trilogy featuring the acerbic Inspector Rose. Rose and his more pensive, and friendly, sidekick Swift are joined by barrister Anthony Brand and his journalist wife Alice. But this ensemble only lasted for one season and at its conclusion both the Brands and DS Swift departed for pastures new. Season two introduced DS Hunter, his girlfriend, Claire and her reporter friend, Fred Blaine. Playing the part of, Sebastian, a tearaway ringleader of a group of young juvenile delinquents, was a young Oliver Reed. The series theme song 'Where Are You Now (My Love)' became a chart topping hit for Jackie Trent in 1965. William Mervyn's character began to mellow throughout this series. ITV 1964-65. See also *The Odd Man* and *Mr Rose*.

It's Only TV... But I Like It Comedy celebrity panel game show about television, hosted by Jonathan Ross. Team captains Jack Dee (replaced by Phil Jupitus after 8 of the 32 episodes) and Julian Clary were each joined by two popular television celebrities every week and the teams battled against each other for points. BBC2 1999-2002.

ITV Independent Television was launched on 22 September 1955 under the auspices of the Independent Television Authority (ITA) to provide competition to the BBC. Often referred to as Channel 3 (partly to distinguish it from the BBC and partly because televisions were tuned to the station on the third button of the sets), since 1990 the channel is legally known as Channel 3. Unlike many of the TV channels in the United Kingdom, ITV is not owned by one single company, in fact it is presently in the hands of three companies: ITV plc, owners of twelve franchises in England, Wales, South Scotland, Isle of Man, the Channel Islands and the national breakfast franchise; STV Group plc owners of two franchises in North and Central Scotland; and UTV Media plc, the franchise for Northern Ireland. Since 1983, ITV has also included a national breakfast franchise for the period between 6:00 a.m. and 09:25 a.m., with the licence currently issued to ITV Breakfast Ltd. In July 2009, STV announced that it was withdrawing some networked programmes such as *The Bill, Doc Martin, Midsomer Murders, Poirot, Lewis* and a number of other high profile ITV network dramas from its schedules, instead preferring to concentrate on programming made within Scotland.

Ivanhoe Roger Moore (Sir Wilfrid of Ivanhoe, son of Sir Cedric of Rotherwood), Bruce Seton (King Richard), Andrew Keir (Prince John), John Pike (Bart), Robert Brown (Gurth). Deborah Cook adapted the writings of Sir Walter Scott. Set during the reign of King Richard I (aka Richard the Lionhearted). The Crusades have ended in disaster for the English king, who is believed dead - were that the case, Richard's brother, the ambitious and malevolent Prince John would become king, and strip the people of their rights and their land. Ivanhoe and his companions Bart and Gurth, ex-slaves that he freed from bondage to the sadistic and treacherous Sir Maurice of Melensford (Anthony Dawson), swear to uphold chivalry. The running plot of this series mostly concerns Prince John's various efforts to claim the British Crown and Ivanhoe's counter-moves, and his attempts to secure justice for the populace despite John's illicit rule. What makes this Anglo-American show hold up well, apart from lots of action, is the sheer amount of plot piled into each 30-minute segment of the 39 episodes. ITV 1958.

Ivor the Engine Cartoon series written by Oliver Postgate, drawn by Peter Firmin, and voiced by David Edwards, Anthony Jackson, Olwen Griffiths and Oliver Postgate. Ivor, a little green railway engine, was fired up by Idris the Dragon (Griffiths) who lived in Ivor's boiler. The engine driver was Jones the Steam (Postgate) and other characters included Owen the Signal and Dai Station the stationmaster who looked after Llaniog Station. Jones' great ambition was to sing in the choir like Evans the Song (Jackson). Then there was Eli the Baker, Mrs Porty, Mrs Griffiths, Mr Hughes the Gasworks, Mr Dinwiddy, Alice the Elephant (Postgate), Bani Moukerjee, Charlie Banger and Bluebell the Donkey. At the beginning of each episode viewers are told *Not very long ago, in the top left-hand corner of Wales, there was a railway. It wasn't a very long railway or a very important* railway, but it was called *The Merioneth and Llantisilly Rail Traction Company Limited*, and it was all there was. And in a shed, in a siding at the end of the railway, lives the Locomotive of the Merioneth and Llantisilly Rail Traction Company Limited, which was a long name for a little engine so his friends just called him Ivor. Oliver Postgate, the original narrator, repeated 'Pishdy Cuf' to emulate the sound of Ivor in motion. ITV 1959; 1962-63. The series transferred to the BBC between 1976 and 1979 with a selection of new stories.

Jack De Manio Precisely Born Giovanni Batista de Manio, 26 January 1914, of an Italian father and Polish mother living in Britain. Jack began life as a journalist but became one of the nation's most-loved radio presenters as host of the *Today* show between 1958 and 1971. His easy-going laidback style was almost as famous as his unfailing capacity for misreading the time on the studio clocks. In 1969 he was the first radio broadcaster to be permitted to interview Prince Charles and he was voted British Radio Personality of the Year in 1964 and 1971. Jack was given his own afternoon chat show in 1971 after leaving *Today* when the format was changed to accommodate two presenters. This show was hugely popular and gave a young Vivian Stanshall (of Bonzo Dog Doo-Dah Band fame) his first break as the in-house eccentric. Apart from some guest spots on *Woman's Hour* he retired in 1978 and died 28 October 1988. Radio 4 1971-78

Jack Docherty Show, The Jack Docherty was born in Edinburgh in 1962. He began as a comedy performer (see entry for *Absolutely*) but gradually moved into writing, his credits including *The News Huddlines, Spitting Image, Saturday Stayback, Alas Smith and Jones, The Lenny Henry Show, Max Headroom*, and *Mr Don & Mr George*. In 1997 he was part of the launch of Channel 5 becoming Britain's first five nights a week chat show host on *The Jack Docherty Show*. The show is also notable for featuring some of the first television work of writers Kevin Cecil and Andy Riley, Jesse Armstrong and Sam Bain, and writer/performers David Mitchell and Robert Webb. *Not The Jack Docherty Show*, broadcast when Docherty was on holiday, featured guest hosts including Phill Jupitus, Rich Hall, Melinda Messenger and Graham Norton. *Five* 1997-99

Jack the Ripper See *Second Verdict*

Jack Jackson Show, The Jack Jackson was born in Horsley, Derbyshire, 20 February 1906. He was the son of a Barnsley brass band conductor and he himself was a trumpeter for Ambrose, Jack Hylton and Jack Payne, before forming his own band in 1933 and becoming the resident in-house band at London's Dorchester Hotel (with Dancing In The Dark as his signature tune). The outbreak of war dispersed the musicians, and although they reformed after the war, Jackson retired as a bandleader in 1947 and turned to radio compering, both on Radio Luxembourg, whose Decca Records show he hosted, and the BBC Light Programme, where he launched *Record Round-Up* in 1948. The seminal Jackson style punctuated pop records with comedy clips from The Goons, Bob Newhart, Shelley Berman and others, and subverted the conventional record-spinning format with pre-recorded assemblages on tape, which featured quick cutting to comedy edits (later imitated so successfully by the likes of Kenny Everett and Harry Hill). *The Jack Jackson Show* transferred to television in the mid-1950s and his mix of music and chat (with regulars Joan Savage, Glen Mason and Dickie Valentine) made this one of the top ITV shows of the day. *Record Roundabout* was broadcast on both Radio 1 and 2 from the launch in 1967 until June 1968 and Jack was affectionately known as the 'daddy of all disc jockeys' during his brief spell (9 months) on Radio 1. He moved to Tenerife in 1960, where he had installed a radio studio in his house, to record his BBC radio shows but he moved back to the UK in 1973 as the climate contributed to health problems. He broadcast on Radio 2 between 1971 and 1977, but sadly died on 15 January 1978.

Jackanory Children's entertainment consisting of a celebrity reading a story in a daily 15-minute slot, usually over the course of a week. The programme's title came from the nursery rhyme *I'll tell you a story about Jack-a-Nory, And now my story's begun; I'll tell you another about Jack and his brother, And now my story's done*. The first story told was *Cap of Rushes* read by actor Lee Montague. Most prolific story tellers were comic actors Bernard Cribbins (111 appearances) and Kenneth Williams (69

appearances). In 1984, HRH Prince of Wales read his own *The Old Man of Lochnagar*. The introduction of the show utilised the same kaleidoscope image made famous in the opening of an earlier children's series, *Picture Book*. BBC 1/BBC 2 1965-96. The series was resurrected in November 2006 with John Sessions as its first storyteller. CBeebies began running a series of Jackanory Junior around the same time with a few more special effects and more animated narration.

Jam and Jerusalem Sue Johnston (Sal Vine), Pauline McLynn (Tip Haddem), Dawn French (Rosie Bales), Joanna Lumley (Delilah Stagg), Jennifer Saunders (Caroline Martin), Maggie Steed (Eileen Pike), David Mitchell (Dr. James Vine), Sally Phillips (Natasha 'Tash' Vine), Simon Farnaby (Samuel 'Spike' Pike), Doreen Mantle (Queenie), Salima Saxton (Yasmeen Vine), Patrick Barlow (Reverend Hillary), Rosie Cavaliero (Kate Bales), Suzy Aitchison (Susie), Nigel Lindsay (Marcus), Freya Edmondson (Freya Martin), Ella Edmondson (Ella Martin), Beattie Edmondson (Beattie Martin). Sitcom, written by Jennifer Saunders and Abigail Wilson, revolving around a Women's Guild in the fictional West Country town of Clatterford St. Mary. The title is a phrase often associated with the Women's Institute's member's propensity to make jam and sing the hymn Jerusalem. Jennifer Saunders' real life daughters, Freya, Ella and Beattie, played her daughters in the series. The theme tune is a version of The Kinks' *The Village Green Preservation Society*, sung by Kate Rusby. BBC1 2006-09.

Jamie at Home Jamie Oliver presented home-style recipes and gardening tips, with many ingredients coming from his substantial home garden. C4 2007. See also *The Naked Chef*.

Jamie Saves Our Bacon Jamie Oliver celebrates British pork and investigates why British pig farmers are disappearing. C4 2009. See also *The Naked Chef*.

Jamie's American Road Trip Another mix of culinary delights and social commentary as Jamie Oliver explores America. C4 2009. See also *The Naked Chef*.

Jamie's Chef Five years after Jamie Oliver's attempt to turn around the lives of a group of unemployed youngsters by training them to cook at new restaurant Fifteen, he now has 50 trainees who have graduated from the charitable scheme. This four-part series follows Jamie's mentoring of the winning trainee and his establishment of their own restaurant at The Cock, a pub near Braintree in Essex. The charitable Fifteen Foundation retained ownership of the property but provided a £125,000 loan for the winner, Aaron Craze, to refurbish the establishment. C4 2007. See also *The Naked Chef*.

Jamie's Fowl Dinners Having successfully taken on the Government regarding the appalling state of school dinners, Jamie Oliver tackled a new challenge: to make us aware of how the 950 million chickens a year produced in this country live and die before they end up on our plates. In this programme he hosts a gala dinner where, with the help of poultry farmers and experts such as Bill Oddie and Hugh Fearnley-Whittingstall, he uses demonstrations, films and interviews to highlight key aspects of chicken and egg production. C4 2008. See also *The Naked Chef*.

Jamie's Great Escape Jamie Oliver heads to Italy to escape and re-discover what inspired his love of food in the first place. In his clapped-out camper van, he travels the country in search of its gastronomic heart. C4 2007. See also *The Naked Chef*.

Jamie's Kitchen Five-part documentary series following Jamie Oliver's attempt to train a group of disadvantaged youths, who would - if they completed the course - be offered jobs at Jamie's new restaurant Fifteen. C4 2002. *Return to Jamie's Kitchen* followed in 2003. See also *The Naked Chef*.

Jamie's Ministry of Food Four-part series in which Jamie Oliver attempts to make Rotherham in South Yorkshire "the culinary capital of the United Kingdom". The series popularised the 'Pass It On' campaign whereby the local towns' people were taught one of a selection of recipes and passed it on to family members and friends. C4 2008. See also *The Naked Chef*.

Jamie's School Dinners In this four-part documentary series Jamie Oliver took responsibility for running the kitchen meals in Kidbrooke School, Greenwich, for a year. As a result of his criticisms of the meals and his campaign to improve them, the UK Government pledged to spend £280m on school dinners, spread over three years. C4 2005. Jamie returned to Kidbrooke the following year for a one-off progress report. See also *The Naked Chef*.

Jane Glynis Barber played the wartime cartoon character in the 1982 BBC2 television adaption.

Jane Eyre Ruth Wilson (Jane Eyre), Toby Stephens (Edward Fairfax Rochester), Lorraine Ashbourne (Mrs Fairfax), Pam Ferris (Grace Poole), Francesca Annis (Lady Ingram), Georgie Henley (Young Jane Eyre). Four-part television adaptation of Charlotte Bronte's novel about a young woman who becomes governess to the ward of Mr. Rochester, a brooding and enigmatic man. She falls in love with him. But what secrets lie in his past? BBC1 2006. The BBC also broadcast two other adaptations - a 1973 mini-series starring Sorcha Cusack as Jane Eyre, Juliet Waley as young Jane, Michael Jayston as Edward Rochester, Megs Jenkins as Mrs Fairfax and Stephanie Beacham as Blanche Ingram – and a 1956 six-part adaptation written by Ian Dallas with Daphne Slater as Jane Eyre and Stanley Baker as Mr Rochester.

Jason King Peter Wyngarde (Jason King), Ann Sharp (Nicola Harvester), Dennis Price (Sir Brian), Ronald Lacey (Ryland). Spin-off series from *Department S*, created by Monty Berman and Dennis Spooner. Jason King is a mystery novelist with a string of 'Mark Caine' books to his credit. He also indulges himself by solving real-life mysteries in a stylish, if slightly foppish manner. ITV 1971-72.

Jeeves and Wooster Stephen Fry (Reginald Jeeves), Hugh Laurie (Bertie Wooster). Although I have described the earlier Dennis Price and Ian Carmichael portrayals as definitive (see *The World of Wooster*), Fry and Laurie were at their finest as the super-efficient valet and his bumbling master. Broadcast on ITV 1990-93, and adapted by Clive Exton, the depictions would undoubtedly have made P. G. Woodhouse proud. The wonderful cast of characters included the likes of Gussie Fink Nottle, Oofy Prosser, Tuppy Glossop, Barmy Fotheringay Phipps, Madeline Bassett and Stiffy Byng; as well as the faithful aunts Agatha and Dahlia (many of these characters were played by different actors from series to series).

Jemima Shore Investigates Patricia Hodge played the TV Reporter, writer, sleuth and presenter of Megalith Television's *Jemima Shore Investigate*, in this 12-part adaptation of Lady Antonia Fraser's novels. ITV 1983. Jemima was first seen on screen in the ITV series *Armchair Theatre*. The 1978 episode, *Quiet as a Nun*, starred Maria Aitken as the super-sleuth.

Jeremy Kyle Show Born in Canning Town, London, 7 July 1965, Jeremy Kyle hosts this daytime talk show dealing with family and relationship issues, as well as taking a look at the every day conflicts that affect people's lives. Jeremy transferred the format of his popular radio show *Confessions* (on Capital FM) to television. Jeremy met his second wife, former model Carla Germaine, in 1999 whilst presenting the controversial BRMB radio show *Two Strangers and a Wedding*, where Carla won the Bride part of the show and married the unseen groom Greg Cordell, before swiftly divorcing and eventually marrying the talk-show host. The couple now have three children (as at July 2010) and one from a previous relationship of Carla's. ITV 2005-.

Jesus of Nazareth Robert Powell (Jesus as an adult), Immad Cohen (Jesus as a boy), Olivia Hussey (Virgin Mary), Yorgo Voyagis (Joseph), Anne Bancroft (Mary Magdalene), James Farentino (Simon Peter), Ian McShane (Judas Iscariot), Rod Steiger (Pontius Pilate), James Mason (Joseph of Arimathea), Peter Ustinov (Herod the Great), Michael York (John the Baptist), Stacy Keach (Barabbas), Laurence Olivier (Nicodemus), Valentina Cortese (Herodias), James Earl Jones (Balthazar), Donald Pleasance (Melchior), Ralph Richardson (Simeon), Fernando Rey (Gaspar), Isabel Mestres (Salome), Anthony Quinn (Caiaphas), Christopher Plummer (Herod Antipas), Stacy Keach (Barabbas). Lew Grade's breath-taking epic shot on location in Italy and Tunisia and directed by Franco Zeffirelli. ITV 1977.

Jeux Sans Frontières See *It's A Knockout*.

Jewel in the Crown, The Peggy Ashcroft (Barbie Batchelor), Geraldine James (Sarah Layton), Stuart Wilson (Major Clark), Tim Pigott-Smith (Ronald Merrick), Derrick Branche (Ahmed Kasim), Art Malik (Hari Kumar), Susan Wooldridge (Daphne Manners), Charles Dance (Sgt Guy Perron), Renee Goddard (Dr Anna Klaus), Zohra Segal (Lady Lili Chatterjee), Marne Maitland (Pandit Baba), Judy Parfitt (Mildred Layton), Wendy Morgan (Susan Layton/Bingham/Merrick), Rachel Kempson (Lady Ethel Manners), Fabia Drake (Mabel Layton), Rosemary Leach (Fenny Grace), Eric Porter (Count Dimitri Bronowsky), Jeremy Child (Robin White), Leslie Grantham (Signals sergeant), Warren Clarke (Cpl 'Sophie' Dixon), Bernard Horsfall (Major-General Rankin), Nicholas Le Prevost (Capt Nigel Rowan), Peter Jeffrey (Mr Peabody), Josephine Welcome (Mira). Paul Scott's epic four novels (adapted for television by Ken Taylor), known collectively as "The Raj Quartet", tell the extraordinary story of Daphne and Hari, of Ronald Merrick and Barbie Batchelor, the Layton family and Guy Perron, against the tumultuous background of the last years of British rule in India. It begins in 1942. The Japanese, having conquered Burma, are threatening to invade and Gandhi is calling on the British to leave India. In Mayapore, a young man, Hari Kumar, is arrested for the rape of hospital worker Daphne Manners thus starting off a chain of events binding English and Indians in a web of love, tragedy, and death. At the centre is Ronald Merrick, the sadistic District Superintendent of Police, a guardian of the British Empire of which India is 'The Jewel in the Crown'. ITV 1984.

Jigsaw Hosted by Adrian Hedley, Janet Ellis (later Julia Binstead in the guise of Dot) and "Jigg" - a giant floating orange puppet in the shape of a Jigsaw piece (voiced by John Leeson). *Jigsaw*, was a viewer participation programme, devised by Clive Doig, where the object each week was to identify a six-letter word. Each letter would be identified via a sketch of some variety. At the end of the programme, Mr Noseybonk (Adrian Hedley wearing a mask, tuxedo, and sporting a very, very long nose) would run around a park or some such location looking at different objects - the first letters of these prominent objects being the answer to the write-in competition. Other characters included the O-Men (Sylvester McCoy and David Rappaport), Wilf Lunn (who rather appropriately appeared as a mad inventor), Hector The Hedgehog, Biggum the Giant - all you ever saw of him was his sandal - and Pterry the Pterodactyl. BBC1 1979-85.

Jim Tavaré Show, The See entry in the comedy section.

Jim'll Fix It Sir James Wilson Vincent Savile was born in Leeds, 31 October 1926 and he died of pneumonia in Leeds on 29 October 2011. He started his radio career working as a Radio Luxembourg DJ between 1958 and 1967. Sir Jimmy had the distinction of being both the first and last presenter of *Top of the Pops*. Another distinction Jimmy holds is his professional wrestling record in which he lost his first 35 bouts! Sir Jimmy ran numerous marathons and even took part in the 1951 Tour of Britain cycle race. Another distinction is that Jimmy was the first civilian to finish the Royal Marine Commando 30-mile (48 km) Yomp. Jimmy, one of few celebrity members of Mensa, was awarded the OBE in 1971 and knighted in 1990. A pioneer of the two turntables method of playing music, Jimmy's other claim to fame in the early 1970s was series of public information films promoting the use of seatbelts, his famous slogan being "Clunk Click Every Trip". These television adverts led to a 1973 BBC1 Saturday evening chat show entitled *Clunk Click* which in 1974 featured the UK heats for the Eurovision Song Contest featuring Olivia Newton-John. When this series ended in 1975 it was immediately replaced by *Jim'll Fix It*, which became stock Saturday early evening viewing for almost 20 years. The simple premise was for viewers to write in to the show requesting their dreams to be made true. Jim would read out a selection of letters while sitting in his gadget-loaded armchair, sometimes in bright track-suit, often smoking a huge cigar, and always wearing loads of heavy jewellery. Nothing was too much trouble for Jim to fix it seemed and over the years he managed to fix it for children (and the occasional adult) to appear with pop bands, act in soap operas, become circus clowns, pilot Concorde, and interview prime ministers. At the end of each successful stunt Jim would hang a special medallion (inscribed with the words 'Jim Fixed It for Me') over the head of a proud recipient. The producer throughout the show's run was Roger Ordish, always referred to by Savile as

'Doctor Magic'. The closing theme tune: *Your letter was only the start of it, One letter, and now you're a part of it. Now you've done it—Jim has fixed it for you, And you and you... There must be something that you always want to do, The one thing that you always wanted to, Now you've done it—Jim has fixed it for you, And you and you and you.* BBC1 1975-94. A new series entitled *Jim'll Fix It Strikes Again* began in April 2007 on UKTV Gold, co-presented by Sir Jimmy and comedienne Mel Giedroyc. Shane Ritchie hosted a one-off Christmas special in 2011 by way of tribute to Jimmy Savile.

Jim's Inn Born in Norwich, 22 October 1918, Jimmy Hanley is possibly best remembered by film buffs as the new police recruit being taken through his paces by Jack Warner's avuncular PC George Dixon before young thug Dirk Bogarde kills the latter in the 1949 manhunt thriller *The Blue Lamp*, but to television viewers (of a certain age) Jim will always be remembered for this popular 'Admag' series. The *Jim's Inn* format revolved around a cosy village pub run by Jimmy and real-life (second) wife Maggie Hanley who, with their regulars - played by Roma Cresswell, John Sherlock, Jack Edwardes, Diane Watts, Dennis Bowen, Ken Howard and Victor Platt - discussed the merits (and prices) of various household products. Household names of the time such as Alma Cogan and Freddie Mills would also drop in to the local for some gentle banter. The Associated Rediffusion-produced series ran for some 300 live editions until Parliament in 1963 banned all advertising magazine programmes. Jimmy and Maggie continued their amiable-couple-with-good-advice characters in a series of TV commercials for Daz soap powder. Actress Jenny Hanley and politician Sir Jeremy Hanley are two of Jim's children by his first wife, actress Dinah Sheridan. ITV 1957-63.

Jo Maxi Irish teenage entertainment show, originally presented by Ray D'Arcy (b. 1 September 1964) and subsequently by Clíona Ní Bhuchalla, Antoinette Dawson and Geri Lawlor. *Jo Maxi* was broadcast each weeknight at 6 o'clock from the RTÉ Studios in Donnybrook. In 1993 *Jo Maxi* was revamped, doing away with the Jo Maxi brand, although the end credits still stated that it was a JMTV Production, and would also use the famous petrol pump logo. The new look *Jo Maxi* had a different show each weekday. Monday's was an arts review show called *Brash* presented by Niamh Walsh, Tuesday's was a chat show called *Hullabullu*, Wednesday's was a job/study guide called *Get a Life*, presented by Gemma Hill, Thursday's was a school's debate show called *Babel,* presented by Eileen O'Reilly and Friday's was an alternative pop music show called *Plastic Orange*, presented by Colin Murnane. In 1994 *Jo Maxi* was replaced by the Children's TV Show *Echo Island*. RTÉ Two 1988-93.

Joe 90 Children's animation series created by Gerry and Sylvia Anderson. Voices Len Jones (Joe McClaine/Joe 90), Rupert Davies (Professor Ian McClaine), David Healy (Commander Shane Weston), Keith Alexander (Sam Loover), Sylvia Anderson (Mrs Ada Harris). Joe McClaine's guardian is brilliant electronics engineer Professor Ian 'Mac' McClaine. Mac invents BIG RAT (Brain Impulse Galvanascope Record And Transfer) - A machine capable of transferring brain patterns, skills and experience from one person to another. Mac's friend Sam Loover is an operative from WIN (the World Intelligence Network) which is an organisation dedicated to maintaining world peace. Sam witnesses the BIGRAT in action when Mac tests the machine on Joe and immediately sees the potential. Nine-year-old Joe McClaine (alias Joe 90) begins to work for WIN using his father's invention and becomes their 'most special secret agent'. To download the skills necessary for each mission (which includes Joe assuming the role of air force pilot, astronaut, President of the World Bank, and rally driver among others), Joe sits on a special chair which is pneumatically elevated into the Rat Trap. The entry bars close and the trap begins to spin as the BIGRAT begins to work. Once the process is completed, the brainwave transfer only works when Joe puts on a pair of special glasses with built-in electrodes which connect to his temples. 30 episodes were made. ITV 1968-69.

John Browne's Body Peggy Mount (Virginia Browne), Naunton Wayne (Fitzroy), Trisha Mortimer (Kiki), Mark Kingston (Conroy), Zulema Dene (Felicity Gordon). Seven-part sitcom written by Rene Basilco. Virginia Browne inherits a half share in her late brother's private detective agency and gives up her

respectable job to become a 'gumshoe'. Notable for being the last screen performance of Naunton Wayne. ITV 1969.

Joker's Wild Celebrity panel game show hosted by comedy writer Barry Cryer, apart from one series broadcast in 1971 which was hosted by Michael Bentine. Two teams of comedians played for points by telling jokes on a subject chosen by the host. When a member of a team was telling a joke, a member of the other team could interrupt the joke by pressing the buzzer and finishing the joke to score bonus points for his/her team. Before the commercial break one of the comedians would be given one minute to get as many laughs as possible from the studio audience. The more laughs, the more points were scored. At the end of the show the team with the most points won a gag trophy of a jester carrying the Yorkshire Television chevron logo. Comedy panellists included: John Cleese, Rolf Harris, Les Dawson, Arthur Askey, Ted Rogers, Norman Collier, Chic Murray, Alfred Marks, Ted Ray, Ray Martine, Freddie Starr and Jack Douglas. ITV 1969-74.

Joking Apart Robert Bathurst (Mark Taylor), Tracie Bennett (Tracy Glazebrook), Fiona Gillies (Becky Johnson/Taylor), Paul Raffield (Robert Glazebrook), Paul-Mark Elliot (Trevor). Adult sitcom written by Steven Moffat (recent credits include *Dr Who*), looking at divorce from the viewpoint of standup comedian Mark Taylor. The series took place in two time frames: the present, with Mark trying to come to terms to life without Becky; and the past, viewed by Mark's reminiscences of their time together. These memories were usually sparked by a routine in his standup act, and caused his pain at her absence to grow even stronger. Becky, meanwhile, seemed quite capable of building herself a new life, and had a new partner, Trevor. Sympathising with Mark's plight but remaining on friendly, neutral terms with both him and Becky were couple Robert and Tracy, whose own relationship was rocky at times. The theme tune was Chris Rea's *Fool If You Think It's Over* sung by Kenny Craddock. BBC2 1993-95.

Jonathan Creek Alan Davies (Jonathan Creek), Caroline Quentin (Maddy Magellan 1997-2000), Stuart Milligan (Adam Klaus 1998-), Julia Sawalha (Carla Borrego 2001-04), Adrian Edmondson (Brendan Baxter 2003–04), Anthony Head (Adam Klaus 1997), Sheridan Smith (Joey Ross 2009-). Mystery series written by David Renwick. While Madeline Magellan, an investigative journalist, is writing a story about the murder of a famous artist she happens across a quiet but brilliant man named Jonathan Creek who makes a living inventing magical tricks for Adam Klaus. Maddy and Jonathan team up to solve the murder and again team up to solve near-impossible cases. After Caroline Quentin's departure in 2000, Julia Sawalha joined the cast the following year as new sidekick Carla Borrego, a theatrical agent turned television presenter. Guests stars, all in straight acting roles include: Bob Monkhouse, Griff Rhys Jones, Rik Mayall, Jack Dee, Bill Bailey, John Bird, Steven Berkoff, Geoffrey McGivern, John Bluthal, Kate Isitt, Sanjeev Bhaskar, Nigel Planer, Alistair McGowan, Colin Baker, Brian Murphy, Rebecca Front, Mary Tamm, Jim Bowen, Peter Davison, Maureen O'Brien, Lysette Anthony, Mark Caven, Lorelei King, Geoffrey Beevers, Annette Crosbie, Doreen Mantle, Charlie Brooks, Maureen Lipman, Paul Blackthorne and Jimmi Harkishin. Jonathan Ross, Michael Grade and Bamber Gascoigne have all appeared as themselves. The series ran on BBC1 for four series between 1997 and 2004 and then returned for a one-off special in 2009 and another in 2010. The programme won the BAFTA for Best Drama Series in 1998.

Jonny Briggs Richard Holian (Jonny Briggs), Jane Lowe (Mam Briggs), Leslie Schofield (Dad Briggs), Sue Devaney (Rita Briggs), Tommy Robinson (Albert Briggs), Jeremy Austin (Humphrey Briggs). Children's drama series developed by Valerie Georgeson and based on a book by Joan Eadington. The stories of little Jonny Briggs were first televised on Jackanory (read by Bernard Holley) and concerned Jonny's home life near Leeds with his mum, dad, sister Rita, elder brother Albert and his dog Razzle. BBC1 1986.

Jools Holland Hootenanny. See *Later... with Jools Holland*

Judge John Deed Martin Shaw (Judge John Deed), Jenny Seagrove (Jo Mills QC), Louisa Clein (Charlie Deed), Barbara Thorn (Rita 'Coop' Cooper), Christopher Cazenove (Row Colemore), Caroline Langrishe (Georgina 'George' Channing QC), Jemma Redgrave (Lady Francesca Rochester), Donald

Sinden (Sir Joseph Channing). Drama series produced and written by G. F. Newman. John Deed, a former crusading barrister with unorthodox methods loses none of his passion in pursuit of justice when promoted to the bench. Mimi, the dog in the series is a Spanish 'pinche ratonero' or ratting terrier. A very similar breed in England is the Potterdale terrier. BBC1 2001-07

Juke Box Jury A celebrity panel reviews new record releases. Presented by David Jacobs throughout its original run, the first panel consisted of Alma Cogan, Susan Stranks, Gary Miller and Pete Murray. Each panellist would vote the record either a 'hit' or a 'miss' and David would ring a bell or sound a klaxon depending on the verdict, at least one of the featured artists would appear from behind a hidden screen to add spice to the show. On Saturday 7 December 1963, the panel was made up of the four Beatles and on 4 July 1964, the panel, unusually, consisted of five members - The Rolling Stones. The final panel consisted of Pete Murray and Sue Stranks from the very first show, Lulu and Eric Sykes. The popular them tune *Hit and Miss* reached No 10 for the John Barry Seven in 1960. BBC1 1959-67. There were two attempts at revivals of *Juke Box Jury*. One in 1979 on BBC1, with Noel Edmonds in the chair, and one on BBC2, presented by Jools Holland (1989-90).

Juliet Bravo Stephanie Turner (Insp Jean Darblay), Anna Carteret (Insp Kate Longton), James Grout (Supt Hallam), David Ellison (Sgt Joseph Beck), Noel Collins (Sgt George Parrish). Created by Ian Kennedy Martin. Newly-promoted Inspector Jean Darblay takes charge of the police station in the fictional Lancashire town of Hartley. She is the first woman to be placed in charge of the station and initially there is considerable scepticism from the long-standing staff of Sergeants Joe Beck and George Parrish. After the second series, Jean Darblay left and was replaced by Kate Longton. BBC1 1980-85.

Junior Choice See *Children's Favourites*
Junior Criss Cross Quiz See *Criss Cross Quiz*.
Junior Mastermind See *Mastermind*
Junior Points of View See *Points of View*
Junior Police Five See *Police Five*
Junior Showtime Children's talent showcase presented by Bobbie Bennett. Recorded at the City Varieties Theatre in Leeds, many of the children based their acts around the old-time Music Hall. The show was produced by religious broadcasting supremo Jess 'The Bishop' Yates. Regulars included the Poole family (mainstays of *Stars on Sunday* which Jess Yates compered) and Bonnie Langford. The show also included a junior version of *The Black and White Minstrel Show* where the child performers would try to guess the answers to riddles posed by a similarly-attired and made-up Bobby Bennett as 'Mr. Interlocutor'. ITV 1969-74.

Just A Minute Long-running radio comedy panel game chaired since its inception by Nicholas Parsons. The object of the game is for the four celebrity panellists to talk for a minute on a given subject, "without repetition, hesitation or deviation". Created by Ian Messiter, as a variation of an old school punishment of his former history teacher who would test attention span by ordering pupils to repeat everything he had said in the previous minute without hesitation or repetition. The rules are loose but basically a panellist may score a point for making a correct challenge against a speaker although the speaker receives a point if the chairman deems the challenge incorrect. Comical interjections are often rewarded whether they be superfluous or not and the trend in recent years has been to make as many of these as possible. A player who makes a correct challenge takes over the subject for the remainder of the minute or until they themselves are successfully challenged, and the panellist speaking when the 60 seconds expires also scores a point. An extra point is awarded when a panellist speaks for the entire minute without being challenged. The regular panellists have been Clement Freud (1924-2009), Peter Jones (1920-2000), Derek Nimmo (1930-99), Kenneth Williams (1926-88) and Paul Merton. Other panellists have included Jeremy Beadle, Gyles Brandreth, Tim Brooke-Taylor, Janet Brown, Rob Brydon, Ian Carmichael, Peter Cook, Bernard Cribbins, Barry Cryer, Jack Dee, Hugh Dennis, Kenny Everett, Stephen Fry, Graeme Garden, Sheila Hancock, Tony Hawks, Kit Hesketh-Harvey, Thora Hird, Ian Hislop, Eddie Izzard, Brian Johnston, John Junkin, Helen Lederer, Sean Lock, Lee Mack, Alfred Marks, Aimi MacDonald, Alistair McGowan, David Mitchell, Warren Mitchell, Bob Monkhouse, Patrick Moore, Richard Murdoch, Ross Noble, Graham Norton, Dara Ó Briain, Michael Palin, Lance Percival, Sue Perkins, Caroline Quentin, Jan Ravens, Beryl Reid, Tim Rice, Wendy Richard, Kate Robbins, Willie Rushton, Prunella Scales, John Sergeant, Paul Sinha, Tony Slattery, Arthur Smith, Victor Spinetti, Richard Stilgoe, Elaine Stritch, Una Stubbs, Liza Tarbuck, Christopher Timothy, Sandi Toksvig, Barry Took, Tommy Trinder, Stanley Unwin, June Whitfield, Simon Williams, and Victoria Wood. BBC Radio 4 1967-

Just Good Friends Paul Nicholas (Vince Pinner), Jan Francis (Penny Warrender), Sylvia Kay (Daphne Warrender), John Ringham (Norman Warrender), Ann Lynn (Rita Pinner), Shaun Curry (Les Pinner), Adam French (Clifford Pinner), Charlotte Seely (Georgina Marshall). Sitcom, written by John Sullivan, concerning former lovers thrust back into awkward repeat relations. In the summer of 1976 Penny and Vince meet at a Rolling Stones concert in Hyde Park, London. After a stormy two-year relationship they plan to marry but, two days before the event, Vince gets a severe case of cold feet, hops on his motorbike and rides off into the sunset, leaving Penny broken-hearted. Five years later they meet again and find that the old attraction is still there. Vince works at Eddie Brown's Turf Accountants while Penny works for Mathews, Styles and Lieberman Advertising Agency. Although they insist on remaining 'just good friends', the old feelings quickly resurface and for the run of the series they conduct an on-off affair. Neither is helped in this venture by their respective parents, Penny's snobbish mother and unemployed father, and Vince's embarrassingly raucous mum and dad. They split for good in a 90 minute special but eventually wed in a second special. BBC1 1983-86.

Just The Two Of Us Light entertainment show pairing eight celebrities with eight internationally renowned singers, singing duets in a showdown complete with live band, a panel of judges and viewer voting to see who will be crowned *Just the Two of Us* champions. Hosting the event were real-life husband and wife presenting couple – Vernon Kay and Tess Daly. The judges were Trevor Nelson, Lulu, Cece Sammy and Stewart Copeland (replaced by Tito Jackson for Series 2). The first series winners were Russell Watson and Sian Reeves and the second series was won by Marti Pellow and Hannah Waterman. BBC1 2006-07.

Justice Margaret Lockwood (Harriet Peterson), John Stone (Dr Ian Moody), John Bryans (William Corletti), Philip Stone (Sir John Gallagher). Long-running legal drama written by James Mitchell. Harriet Peterson is a female barrister confronting the stuffy antiquated chauvinism of 'chambers'. ITV 1971-74

K9 and Company See *The Sarah Jane Adventures*

Kaleidoscope Based on the 1930s radio series Monday Night at Eight, the popular magazine show was transmitted live from the BBC's studios at Alexandra Palace. McDonald Hobley acted as the presenter, and it was initially produced by John Irwin. The programme had a variety of different features, including 'Collector's Corner', in which antiques expert Iris Brooke would show various items of interest; 'Word Play', a charades game performed by young actors and actresses from the Rank Organisation's "Company of Youth", also known as the "Charm School"; the 'Memory Man' (Leslie Welch), 'Puzzle Corner' with Ronnie Waldman (with viewers asked to spot the deliberate mistake) and 'Be Your Own Detective', a series of short thrillers designed to test the viewers' powers of observation, written by Mileson Horton in a similar style to his earlier series *Telecrime*. Anyone at home wishing to take part in the 'which year' tune medley competition had to place a copy of the Radio Times in their window by noon on broadcast day in order to be spotted and selected. There was also various comedy sketches – Tony Hancock had his first regular television role on the programme, appearing for four episodes in 1951 in the 'Fools Rush In' segment. Initially it was a thirty-minute show broadcast every other week, alternating with the early sitcom *Pinwright's*

Progress, but later in its run the running time increased to an hour. BBC 1946-53.

Karen Dunbar Show, The Following her success in *Chewin' The Fat*, Karen Dunbar (born in Ayr, 1 April 1971) was given her own award-winning sketch show. Sketches in this show included, A Russian Anne Robinson; a very twisted Shakira (song called "This is my arse - it's not yours, it's mine); Shoeless Josie the blonde drunk; Almost Angelic the cabaret duo from hell; Dr. Hambone; Mr Materson and Miss Dacey; Desperate Caroline; Taxi!; and Cliché Cops. BBC1 Scotland 2003-06.

Kate Phyllis Calvert (Kate Graham), Elizabeth Burger (Ellen Burwood), Penelope Keith (Wenda Padbury), Jack Hedley (Donald Killearn). Drama series. Kate works on a popular magazine as agony column writer 'Dear Monica'. Sometimes (in fact most times) she cannot help getting personally involved with the desperate who write to her. ITV 1970-72.

Kavanagh QC John Thaw (James Kavanagh QC), Geraldine James (Eleanor Harker QC), Lisa Harrow (Lizzie Kavanagh), Anna Chancellor (Julia Piper-Robinson), Valerie Redmond (Emma Taylor). Producer Chris Kelly (he of Food and Drink fame) admitted that the lead character was based on real-life defence barrister Michael Mansfield QC. ITV 1995-2001.

Keeping Up Appearances Patricia Routledge (Hyacinth Bucket), Geoffrey Hughes (Onslow), Clive Swift (Richard Bucket), Josephine Tewson (Elizabeth), David Griffin (Emmet Hawksworth), Judy Cornwell (Daisy), Shirley Stelfox (Rose - Series one), Mary Millar (Rose – Series 2-5), Anna Dawson (Violet), John Evitts (Bruce), George Webb (Daddy), Jeremy Gittins (Michael, the vicar). Sitcom created by Roy Clarke. Hyacinth Bucket (Hyacinth insists her name is pronounced 'Bouquet') is a snob. She devotes most of her energies to maintaining 'standards' and trying to impress 'influential' people. In the process, she frequently brings chaos into the lives of her friends, relatives and neighbours. Her long-suffering husband, Richard, keeps his head down and does his best to live with her domineering ways. Her next-door neighbour Elizabeth makes daily visits to the Bucket residence (in Blossom Avenue) for coffee. Elizabeth's brother Emmet is a less frequent (and much more reluctant) guest. Hyacinth has three sisters. Daisy lives in a council house with her slobbish husband Onslow (who drives an S-reg Cortina, complete with furry dice); Rose lives with Daisy and Onslow; Violet lives with her husband Bruce in a large detached house with "room for a swimming pool and a pony". BBC1 1990-95.

Keith Barret Show See *Marion and Geoff*.

Kennedys of Castleross, The Irish radio soap opera broadcast on Radio Éireann from 1955 to 1973 and originally sponsored by Fry-Cadbury. Each fifteen-minute episode was transmitted at lunchtime on Tuesdays and Thursdays, the cast including notable actors such as Marie Kean, T. P. McKenna, Vincent Dowling, Angela Newman, and Philip O'Flynn.

Kessler See *Secret Army*.

Kevin Bishop Show, The Kevin Bishop was born in Orpington, Greater London, 18 June 1980. This comedy sketch show stars the actor and comedian who found fame as a member of the *Star Stories* team. The sketches revolve around parodies of 'celebrity' as depicted in film and television and are written by Kevin Bishop and Lee Hupfield. Actors include David Cadji-Newby, Matthew Crosby, C J Davies, Alistair Griggs, Samantha Martin and Nico Tatarowicz. C4 2008-

Kevin the Gerbil See *Roland Rat*

Kevin Turvey See *A Kick Up the Eighties*

Kick Up the Eighties, A Comedy sketch show produced by BBC Scotland's comedy department. Richard Stilgoe was the anchor man between sketches that introduced a crop of new comic talent including Tracey Ullman, Ron Bain, Miriam Margolyes, Roger Sloman, Robbie Coltrane and Rik Mayall (under his alter ego of Kevin Turvey). A spin-off from the series was *Kevin Turvey - The Man Behind the Green Door* (1982). Robbie Coltrane took over as anchor man in series two. BBC2 1981; 1984

Kids Are All Right, The Game show hosted by John Barrowman. A team of four adults played a team of seven super smart kids in a series of rounds testing brainpower and mental agility. The first round was 'Instant Showdown'. Here, the adult team was given £5,000 with which to play the game. Taking turns, each adult played a three-question, head-to -head against a randomly selected Super Kid. The first to two points won. In the event the Super Kid won £1000 was knocked off the adult's total. Subsequent games included an against the clock video clip round 'Information Overload', plus 'Gridlocked' and 'Omission Impossible' before the final round 'Beat The Kids'. In this final round, the jackpot that the adults managed to accrue was up for grabs. Starting with the youngest child and working up, an adult had to answer a question against each Super Kid on the buzzer. If the adult won the point, the Super Kid was eliminated and vice versa. If an adult remained standing then the adults won, and took their jackpot, if not, they left with nothing. BBC1 2008.

Kids Say the Funniest Things Short-lived vehicle for the talents of Michael Barrymore in which he interviewed three very young children on stage in front of a studio audience, the children often being hyperactively-inclined to fidget and say typically outrageous things. ITV 1998.

King and Castle Derek Martin (Ronald King), Nigel Planer (David Castle), Terence Morgan (Dale Danbury). Drama series created by Ian Kennedy Martin in the vein of the more successful *Minder*. Ronald King is a bent copper whose dirty dealings are catching up with him, and who has to quit the Met before it quits him. David Castle is a gentle but tough aikido teacher and part-time genealogist, with debts to pay, a custody case to fight and no steady income. Thrown together by circumstance and desperation, these two join forces as King & Castle, Debt Collectors. From the East End to Wimbledon, the pair tread the fine line between law and disorder. ITV 1986-88.

King of the Ghetto Tim Roth (Matthew Long), Zia Mohyeddin (Timur Hussein), Gwyneth Strong (Sadie Deedes), Ian Dury (Sammy). Four-part drama series written by Farrukh Dhondy, about racial tensions in London's east end in the 1980s. BBC1 1986.

King Rollo Children's animation series first shown on the BBC in 1980 and based on the character created by David McKee. The title character is a child-like King who is always in need of advice and assistance from his friends, in particular, The Magician, Cook (a mother figure, who was arguably the real ruler of the kingdom), Queen Gwen, King Frank, and Rollo's wise cat, Hamlet. The thirteen episodes were narrated by Ray Brooks. See also *Watch With Mother*.

Kingdom Stephen Fry (Peter Kingdom), Hermione Norris (Beatrice Kingdom), Karl Davies (Lyle Anderson), Celia Imrie (Gloria Millington), Tony Slattery (Sidney Snell), Phyllida Law (Aunt Auriel), John Thomson (Nigel Pearson), Gerard Horan (DC Yelland), Kelly Campbell (Honor O'Sullivan), Lynsey De Paul (Sheila Larsen). Comedy drama series created by Simon Wheeler and Alan Whiting. Peter Kingdom is a Norfolk solicitor who is coping with family, colleagues, and the eccentric populace of Market Shipborough (real life Swaffham) who come to him for legal assistance. A continuous subplot involves the disappearance of Peter's brother Simon Kingdom (played by Dominic Mafham - although unseen with the exception of some photographs). Simon is found to be dead in Series three. ITV 2007-09

Kit Curran Radio Show Denis Lawson (Kit Curran), Brian Wilde (Roland Simpson). Sitcom written by Andy Hamilton and Guy Jenkin. Kit Curran is a top DJ working at a modest local commercial station Radio Newtown. Unfortunately, he is also a liar, a rogue, a con-man, greedy, self-obsessed and apathetic towards the listeners and staff alike. The radio station gets a new boss, Roland Simpson, with whom he clashes and by the second series (simply entitled Kit Curran) he is out of a job. Series 1 ITV 1984; Series 2 C4 1986.

Knight School Peter Jeffrey (Sir Hubert Grindcobbe), Stuart Rooker (Wally Scrope), Roger Lloyd Pack (Sir Baldwin de'Ath and Ben D'Izir), Joanna McCallum (Mistress Genevieve Gently), Mark Billingham (Scrubbe), Peter Cocks (Grockle), Blake Ritson (Sir Roger de Courcey), Amy Phillips (Lady Elizabeth de Gossard). Comedy drama series shown on Children's ITV written by Mark Billingham and Peter Cocks, who also starred in the series. Set in the Middle Ages, the action takes place at St Cuthbert's Academy, an exclusive school for young knights. The story begins with the school deciding to take a scholarship boy, Wally Scrope, a common but loveable dimwit. Wally battles for the affections of Lady Elizabeth de Gossard, head girl of the nearby St Catherine's School for Damsels, and he has a rival for her affections in the form of St Cuthbert's head boy and school bully Sir Roger de Courcey. ITV 1997-98.

Knock, The Malcolm Storry (Bill Adams), Mark Lewis Jones (David Ancrom), David Morrisey (Gerry Birch), Jack Ellis (Eddie Barton), Anthony Valentine (George Webster), Peter O'Brien (Glen Vaughan), Enzo Squillino Jnr (George Andreotti), Marston Bloom (Arnie Rheinhardt), Steve Toussaint (Barry Christie), Tracy Whitwell (Jo Chadwick), Alex Kingston (Katherine Roberts), Suzan Crowley (Nicki Lucas), Caroline Lee Johnson (Diane Ralston), Andrew Dunn (Kevin Butcher), Georgia Allen (Beverley Webster), Ian Burfield (Tommy Maddern), Eric Allan (David Archer). Drama concerning a team of customs officers working undercover to break smuggling rings. The music for the series was composed by Shadows drummer Brian Bennett. The series derived its name from the distinctive "Knock knock knock" command used over the radio to synchronise a raid. ITV 1994-2000.

Knock on Any Door Malcolm McDowell, Peter Vaughan , Billie Whitelaw, John Stride, Wendy Hiller, Jane Asher, Maurice Denham, Anna Quayle, John Bennett, Eileen Atkins, Jeremy Brett, George Sewell, Mervyn Johns, Peter Sallis. Anthology drama of 20 distinct stories, created and hosted by Ted Willis, with the premise that there is a story behind every door. ITV 1965-66.

Knowing Me, Knowing You Steve Coogan (Alan Partridge), Steve Brown (Glen Ponder). Spoof chat show spin-off from *The Day Today*. Catchphrase: Knowing Me Alan Partridge, Knowing you (Guest's name) aha!. BBC2 1994-95. See *I'm Alan Partridge*

Knowitalls Short-lived quiz show hosted by Gyles Brandreth. The show commences with two teams of 3 people shown locked away in separate rooms with Gyles saying in a voiceover: "Completely on their own. Two teams with no books, no phones and no Internet. They've been given today's subjects and just one hour to pool everything they know before they try to prove that they are today's Knowitalls." The quiz consists of the teams trying to impress three resident experts with their knowledge of the given subjects and thereby scoring points. Gyles dubbed the show "the quiz without questions". The resident experts included: Art & Literature (Natalie Haynes), Business & Politics (Adam Shaw), Entertainment (Colin Paterson), Food & Drink (Jay Rayner), History (Tessa Dunlop), Human Biology (Dr. Ayan Panja), Natural History (Chris Packham), Science (Greg Foot), Sport (Jim White) and Travel & Geography (Simon Calder). BBC2 2009.

Krôd Mändoon and the Flaming Sword of Fire Sean Maguire (Krôdford J. Mändoon), Matt Lucas (Chancellor Donold David Dongalor), India de Beaufort (Aneka), John Rhys-Davies (Grimshank), Steve Speirs (Loquasto), Kevin Hart (Zezelryck), Marques Ray (Bruce), Remie Purtill-Clarke ("Cute Girl"), James Murray (Ralph Longshaft), Alex MacQueen (Barnabus), Jonathan Slinger (Cyclops), Brad Johnson (Santu Mooseknuckle), James McDonnell (Gustav the Short and Curly). Roger Allam (General Arcadius) and Michael Gambon as the narrator. A British-American comedic sword and sorcery series created by Peter Knight. BBC2 2009

Krypton Factor, The Game showed billed as 'Britain's toughest quiz', testing contestant's physical and mental faculties. Four competitors took part in each heat, the established rounds being Mental Agility, Flight Simulator, Assault Course, Observation, Intelligence and General Knowledge. 10 points were awarded for first, 6 for second, 4 for third and 2 for fourth, except in the general knowledge round where points were awarded for each correct answer in 90 seconds on the buzzer. The presenter throughout the run was Gordon Burns, although he was joined by Penny Smith for the final series. The series was created by Jeremy Fox and originally produced by Stephen Leahy. Wayne Garvie (now a top BBC Executive) produced the final 'Gladiator -style' series which was plagued by technical problems, but for 18 years the Krypton Factor stood among the very best quiz shows, regularly drawing viewing audiences in excess of 10 million. Its distinctive staccato theme tune by the Art of Noise is as famous as the show itself. Ben Shephard hosted a revamped version of the show in 2009. Gone was the flight simulator but the assault course was tougher than ever. Aaron Burr, an odds setter for Ladbrokes, gained entry to the final as highest runner-up but went on to win the final by only losing the assault course round. A complete list of series winners follows: 1977 Harry Evans, 1978 Ken Wilmshurst, 1979 Peter Richardson, 1980 Philip Bradley, 1981 John McAllister, 1982 John Webley, 1983 Chris Topham, 1984 Paul Smith, 1985 Andrew Gillam, 1986 David Kemp, 1987 Marian Chanter, 1988 David Lee, 1989 Mike Berry, 1990 Duncan Heryett, 1991 Tony Hetherington, 1992 Andrew Craig, 1993 Tim Richardson, 1995 Andy Wilbur, 2009 Aaron Bell, 2010 Pete Thompson. Marion Chanter won the Champion of Champions edition and Ross King hosted a young person's series in 1988 and 1989. ITV 1977-95; 2009-

Kumars at No. 42, The Sanjeev Bhaskar (Sanjeev Kumar), Meera Syal (Sushila), Indira Joshi (Madhuri Kumar), Vincent Ebrahim (Ashwin Kumar). Comedy chat-show written by Sanjeev Bhaskar, Richard Pinto and Sharat Sardana. The premise of the part-sitcom, part-spoof is Sanjeev Kumar's desire to be the Asian Parkinson. A studio is set up in his home in Wembley and Sanjeev hosts the show with the help of mum Madhuri, dad Ashwin and Granny Sushila. Sanjeev asks a string of uneasy and somewhat inarticulate questions while the others interject with their own, Ashwin's more often than not cash-based and Granny's outrageously flirtatious. Madhuri is master of the put down line to her slightly overweight son. BBC2 2001-06

KYTV Angus Deayton (Mike Channel), Geoffrey Perkins (Mike Flex), Helen Atkinson Wood (Anna Daptor), Michael Fenton Stevens (Martin Brown). Sitcom written by Angus Deayton and Geoffrey Perkins. KYTV is a spoof on the problems associated with satellite television broadcasting. The fictional station is named after Sir Kenneth Yellowhammer. BBC2 1990-93. The series was a follow-up to the same team's Radio 4 series, *Radio Active*, in which the premise was the same albeit commercial radio stations being the subject of their parody.

Lab Rats Chris Addison (Doctor Alex Beenyman), Geoffrey McGivern (Professor John Mycroft), Jo Enright (Cara McIlvenny), Dan Tetsell (Brian Lalumaca), Selena Cadell (Dean Mieke Miedema), Helen Moon (Minty Clapper). Sitcom set in the Arnolfini, a research lab in St. Dunstan's University. Co-written by Chris Addison and Carl Cooper. BBC2 2008.

Lady Chatterley Joely Richardson (Lady Chatterley), Sean Bean (Mellors), James Wilby (Sir Clifford Chatterley), Shirley Anne Field (Mrs Bolton). Four-part adaptation of the famous D.H. Lawrence novel. Ken Russell not only wrote much of the screenplay and directed the series, but also starred in two episodes as Sir Michael Reid. BBC1 1993.

Ladykillers Joan Sims (Amelia Elizabeth Dyer), John Fraser (Dr 'Peter' Crippen), Hannah Gordon (Ethel Le Neve), Andrew Johns (Dr Bernard Spilsbury), John Justin (Mr Justice Scrutton). Robert Morley presented all fourteen episodes of this crime anthology depicting various infamous ladykillers. Andrew Johns as Dr Bernard Spilsbury was a common thread in several of the episodes as the pathologist and forensic expert. ITV 1980-81

Lame Ducks John Duttine (Brian Drake), Primi Townsend (Mrs Drake), Lorraine Chase (Angie), Brian Murphy (Ansell), Patric Turner (Tommy), Tony Millan (Maurice). Sitcom written by Peter J. Hammond. Brian Drake's life changes after being hit by a lorry on the way to work, and while recovering in hospital, is told his wife wants a divorce. On recovering, Brian decides to opt out of the rat race and use his share of the proceeds from selling their house to start afresh as a hermit. But things don't go according to plan. He is joined in his quest for a new life by Tommy, a reformed pyromaniac whom he met in the hospital, and on their way to their country cottage they pick up a hitch-hiker, Angie, a young woman who has drifted from relationship to relationship and seems to have no purpose in life. They in turn are joined by Maurice, another drifter whose peculiar ambition it is to 'ball-walk' (that is, walk on a ball) around the world, and who has left his job with the Post Office because they would not let him go to work on his ball. Ansell is the incompetent private detective sent by Brian's wife to track him down. BBC2 1984-85.

Lark Rise To Candleford Linda Bassett (Queenie Turrell), Claudie Blakley (Emma Timmins), Camille Coduri (Patty), Brendan Coyle (Robert Timmins), John Dagleish (Alf Arless), Phil Davis (Arthur Ashlow), Dawn French (Caroline Arless), Olivia Grant (Lady Adelaide Midwinter), Olivia Hallinan (Laura Timmins), Victoria Hamilton (Ruby 'Ruth' Pratt), Mark Heap (Thomas Brown), Oliver Jackson Cohen (Phillip), Karl Johnson (Twister Turrell), Sarah Lancashire as Adult Laura (Narrator), Stephen Marcus (Matthew Welby), Ben Miles (Sir Timothy Midwinter), Julia Sawalha (Dorcas Lane), Claire Skinner (Mrs Macey), Liz Smith (Zillah), Peter Vaughan (Reverend Ellison), Matilda Ziegler (Pearl 'Prudence' Pratt). Drama series based on Flora Thompson's trilogy of semi-autobiographical novels about the English countryside. Set in 19 century Oxfordshire, a young girl, Laura Timmins, moves to the local market town to begin an apprenticeship as a postmistress. BBC1 2008-11

Larkins, The David Kossoff (Alf Larkin), Peggy Mount (Ada Larkin), Shaun O'Riordan (Eddie Larkin), Ruth Trouncer (Joyce Rogers), Ronan O'Casey (Jeff Rogers), Barbara Mitchell (Hetty Prout), Charles Lloyd Pack (Vicar), Hugh Paddick (Major Osbert Rigby-Soames). Sitcom written by Fred Robinson. Alf Larkin is a cockney canteen-worker at the local plastics factory. His wife Ada is a well-meaning battleaxe who is not to be taken lightly and is disobeyed at your peril. They have a rather dim-witted son Eddie and a daughter Joyce, who is married to ex-G.I. Jeff Rogers. Jeff wrote cowboy stories for a comic, The Bullet, until being fired from the job. Barbara Mitchell played the typical nosey next-door neighbour Hetty Prout, her hair tied up in a cloth, borrowing and interfering in equal measure, and ever coo-eeing for a conversation over the garden fence. These characters formed the basis of every episode, with action usually taking place in the pub and at the Larkins' slum-like home, at 66 Sycamore Street, somewhere in the East End of London. ITV 1958-60, 1963-64.

Last Choir Standing Reality show presented by Myleene Klass and Nick Knowles with a panel of music experts consisting of singer Russell Watson, actress and singer Sharon D. Clarke and conductor Suzi Digby. The weekly competition ultimately crowned "The nations favourite choir". The ultimate winners were a Welsh male voice choir *Only Men Aloud!*. BBC1 2008

Last Man Standing Reality television show that featured six male athletes, all with different abilities, travelling around the world to take part in different tribal or traditional sports. Whoever outperformed the rest in the most challenges was declared the winner. Narrated by Richard Hammond, the series winner was Jason Bennett, a BMX racer and tree surgeon from Florida. Originally shown on BBC3 in 2007 but repeated on BBC2 in 2008. Ralf Little took over as narrator for the second series but this did not transfer across from BBC3.

Last of the Summer Wine Peter Sallis (Norman Clegg), Bill Owen (William 'Compo' Simmonite), Michael Bates (Cyril Blamire), Brian Wilde (Foggy Dewhurst), Michael Aldridge (Seymour Utterthwaite), Kathy Staff (Nora Batty), Jean Alexander (Auntie Wainwright), Joe Gladwin (Wally Batty), John Comer (Sid), Jane Freeman (Ivy), Jonathan Linsley (Crusher Milburn), Gordon Wharmby (Wesley Pegden), Thora Hird (Edie Pegden), Robert Fyfe (Howard), Jean Ferguson (Marina), Juliette Kaplan (Pearl), Sarah Thomas (Glenda), Mike Grady (Barry), Danny O'Dea (Eli), Stephen Lewis (Clem 'Smiler' Hemingway), Frank Thornton (Herbert 'Truly' Truelove), Brian Murphy (Alvin Smedley), Burt Kwouk ('Electrical' Entwistle), Russ Abbot (Luther 'Hobbo' Hobdyke), Tom Owen (Tom), Dora Bryan (Roz), Keith Clifford (Billy Hardcastle), Julie T. Wallace (Mrs Avery), Norman Wisdom (Billy Ingleton). Written by Roy Clarke and filmed in Holmfirth in Yorkshire. The longest-running sitcom in the world began as a one-off episode of the BBC's Comedy Playhouse programme in January, 1973. The tramp-like Compo (who lusted after Nora Batty) and lifelong Co-op furniture operative Clegg were principal characters from the beginning until the death of Bill Owen in 1999. The third member of the trio was originally Royal Signals sergeant Cyril Blamire (who was replaced by army sign-writer Foggy Dewhurst, who in turn was replaced by schoolteacher and inventor Seymour Utterthwaite and more recently by former policeman Truly Truelove). The current principal characters before the axe fell in 2010 were Clegg, Truelove, Entwistle, Hobbo and Smedley. BBC1 1973-2010

Last Place On Earth Martin Shaw (Captain R. F. Scott), Sverre Anker Ousdal (Roald Amundsen), Stephen Moore (Dr 'Bill' Wilson), Hugh Grant (Cherry-Garrard), Michael Maloney (Lt. 'Teddy' Evans), Richard Morant (Capt. 'Titus' Oates), Sylvester McCoy (Lt. 'Birdie' Bowers), Pat Roach (P.O. Evans), Bill Nighy (Cecil Meares), Max von Sydow (Fridtjof Nansen), Brian Dennehy (Frederick Cook), Richard Todd (Mr Barnes), Richard Wilson (Scott Keltie). Seven part serial, written by Trevor Griffiths, based on the book Scott and Amundsen by Roland Huntford. The series highlights the fierce rivalry between Scott and the Norwegian explorer, Roald Amundsen, in their 'race' to reach the South Pole. ITV 1985.

Late Late Breakfast Show, The Gameshow broadcast live on Saturday evenings and presented by Noel Edmonds with help from Mike Smith and John Peel. Among popular features were the Hit Squad hidden-camera segment and the 'Whirly Wheeler' stunts. Tragically, the series will always be remembered for the wrong reasons; it featured live stunts during shows, and there was some growing concern that they were becoming too dangerous and during one particular show in 1983, a stunt car driver was involved in a spectacular crash which clearly shocked the studio audience, viewers watching at home, and a horrified John Peel who was presenting this section of the show on location. The driver survived the crash but with fairly serious injuries. Worse was to come three years later when a volunteer for the 'Whirly Wheel' live stunt section, Michael Lush, was killed when a midweek rehearsal for a bungee jump/escapology stunt went wrong. BBC executives had no choice but to take the programme off the air. BBC1 1982-86.

Late Late Show, The When Telifís Éireann (later RTÉ when the radio network was added) was set up in 1961 one of its early shows was the Gay Byrne-hosted chat show *The Late Late Show*. The world's longest running chat show began on 6 July 1962 and remains the staple Friday evening viewing although Gay Byrne hosted his last show on 21 May 1999, handing over the reins to arch rival Pat Kenny (and then Ryan Tubridy in 2009). Gay had originally retired from the show at the end of the spring run in 1968 and the autumn season began with Frank Hall taking over at the helm, but the celebrated journalist looked ill at ease and by the following autumn season Gay had replaced him. The popular appeal of *The Late Late Show* is that it is live and that no one knows what is going to happen next. Guests are not publicised in advance and typically people with very opposing viewpoints are put on to see what will happen. One such instance was when an American writer with a book on enjoyable sex techniques was put up against a group of Hare Krishna devotees who preached sex for purely reproductive purposes! Two controversies established Gay Byrne and his show in the public consciousness, the first was the Bishop and the Nightie incident where a *Mr and Mrs*-style quiz took place on the show and a woman contestant admitted that she hadn't worn anything on her wedding night, a story which was greeted with laughter from the studio audience. The Bishop of Galway was watching and phoned Telifís Éireann to complain. This prompted council motions to condemn Gay Byrne and the television station for bringing 'filth' into Irish homes. The second also got councillors into a lather when a student described the same bishop as a 'moron' live on the show which prompted the well known anti semitic bishop MP Oliver J. Flanagan to memorably declare that there was "no sex in Ireland until the introduction of television". The show also made Byrne a star throughout the British Isles when it was shown on Channel 4 towards the end of his incumbency.

Late Show, The This series, originally hosted by Paul Morley, was built around a round-table discussion hosted by Clive James, but this format was dropped after the second season and it became more of a magazine-type programme covering everything from the arts to pop culture, although studio discussions remained an important part of its content. One such discussion featured an early performance by Lily Allen's father, Keith Allen as a foul-mouthed guest who derided everyone from the floor manager to the other guests. No one knows to this day whether this was a planned act of attention-seeking or a spontaneous fit of pique but it served to make the man very memorable by the late night viewers. The show often had themed weeks such as Irish Week, India Week and Italy Week, and occasionally gave the whole of the programme over to featuring one celebrity. A popular segment of the show was the musical interlude of live music presented by Jools Holland. This gave rise to a spin-off series *Later…With Jools Holland*. Presenters of *The Late Show* included Tracey MacLeod, Michael Ignatieff, Sarah Dunant, Waldemar Januszczak, Matthew Collings, Kirsty Wark, Francine Stock, Mark Lawson, Melvyn Bragg, Jeremy Isaacs and Fintan O'Toole. BBC2 1989-95.

Later with Jools Holland Widely respected showcase for live music of all varieties humourously linked by master musician Jools Holland, who also intermittently interviews various guests. The show, which began as a strand of *The Late Show*, is usually recorded on a Tuesday for Friday broadcast but occasionally a special live edition airs and the title reflects this. On other occasions a solitary act might be featured. The New Year's Eve edition is referred to as *Jools Holland's Hootenanny*. For the record Australian singer-songwriter Nick Cave has appeared more times than any other artist. BBC2 1992-. See also Jools Holland's entry in the biography section.

Law and Order: UK Bradley Walsh (D.S. Ronnie Brooks), Jamie Bamber (D.S. Matt Devlin), Harriet Walter (D.I. Natalie Chandler), Ben Daniels (Senior Crown Prosecutor James Steel), Freema Agyeman (Junior Crown Prosecutor Alesha Phillips), Bill Paterson (Director of CPS London George Castle). Adapted from the US series *Law & Order*, the first US drama television series to be adapted for British television. The series is based in London (and is in fact known as Law & Order: London on TV3 in Ireland) and follows its US counterpart in format, a typical episode focusing on the perpetration of a crime and the related police investigation in the first half, while the second half follows the efforts of the legal system to gain a conviction. ITV 2009-

Lead Balloon Sitcom about a disillusioned stand-up comedian, Rick Spleen, whose career has not gone to plan. Written by Jack Dee and Pete Sinclair. Jack Dee (Rick Spleen – real name Richard Shaw), Raquel Cassidy (Mel Spleen), Sean Power (Marty), Antonia Campbell-Hughes (Sam Spleen), Tony Gardner (Michael), Anna Crilly (Magda), Rasmus Hardiker (Ben). The six-episode first series was originally shown on BBC4 but soon repeated on BBC2 where it has remained into its fourth series. The show's theme tune is a cover of "One Way Road" performed by Paul Weller. BBC2 2006-

League of Gentlemen, The Sitcom, of sorts, written and performed by Mark Gatiss, Steve Pemberton and Reece Shearsmith (with Jeremy Dyson aiding the writing effort). Set in the fictional northern village of Royston Vasey, a picturesque spot populated by dangerous lunatics, social misfits, sinister grotesques and psychopaths. A sign reads 'Welcome to Royston Vasey. You'll Never Leave!' - an accurate prophesy, especially if your first port of call is the local shop. The husband and wife proprietors are serial killers Edward and Tubbs, who harbour a particular and deadly aversion to people who 'aren't local'. Upstairs, their monstrous son fills the air with beastly growls and howls of longing. Elsewhere, there is the butcher Hilary Briss, whose under-the-counter sales of 'special stuff' feeds the habits of certain carnivores in the village, especially those people in authority (Councilman Samuel Chignell being a regular customer). Then there's vet Matthew Chinnery, cursed with an uncanny ability to accidentally yet gruesomely slaughter any animals under his 'care'. There's job-restart officer Pauline, whose contempt for the unemployed is obvious and vindictive. Mrs Judee Levenson and her cleaning lady Iris Krell, taunt each other: Mrs Levenson with tales of her luxury lifestyle, Iris with lurid stories of her sex life. Al and Rich are the dominated sons of hideous, violent Pop, a Greek immigrant who has built a tiny news-stand empire. Stella and Charlie use their prospective son-in-law Tony as a pawn in their ongoing war of words. Then there's Barbara Dixon, the local minicab driver, midway through a sex change (from male to female) and more than willing to share the visceral details of his/her operations with passengers. The most normal of the residents is Les McQueen, one-time member of the progressive rock group Creme Brulée, now sadly reliving his past glories (which certainly do not seem that glorious) while

dreaming of renewed stardom. Although not local, the touring community theatre group, Legz Akimbo, with its dreadful stage productions, demonstrate enough angst to blend in perfectly, and another visitor is the German tour operator Herr Lipp, an oily individual who makes homosexual advances and mouths crude double entendres. Into this malevolent melting-pot arrives young Benjamin, who has arranged to meet a friend for a walking holiday in the area. Unfortunately, Benjamin's friend has met a sticky end at the hands of Tubbs and Edward, and Benjamin is forced to stay longer than planned with his aunt and uncle, Harvey and Val Denton, a toad-obsessed couple given to pathological cleaning bouts and living by petty, but unbreakable rules. Benjamin is virtually held prisoner in the Dentons' home, reeling from one humiliation to another and increasingly terrified by their daughters Chloe and Radcliffe, sinister twins who simultaneously speak the same lines and seem able to read minds. Another recurring strand is the plan to build a road through the town, and the murderous opposition towards it from Edward and Tubbs, and the propensity of the townsfolk to suffer nose-bleeds. *The League Of Gentlemen* rose to prominence as winners of the 1997 Perrier Award at the Edinburgh Fringe Festival, and the team were given their own series on BBC Radio 4 (six episodes, 6 November-11 December 1997), entitled *On The Town With The League Of Gentlemen*, an aural version of the subsequent TV show. This won a Sony Award, and the team, together with radio producer Sarah Smith, made the transition to the small screen with the same startlingly quick success. Royston Vasey is the real name of outrageous standup comedian Roy 'Chubby' Brown, who appeared occasionally in the second TV series as the town's foul-mouthed Mayor Vaughan. In the original radio series the town was named Spent. The series was filmed in the Derbyshire town of Hadfield. BBC2 1999-2002. Following numerous television awards including Baftas and the Golden Rose of Montreux, the four lads conquered the world of film in 2005 with *The League of Gentlemens Apocalypse*.

Lenny the Lion Show, The Ventriloquist Terry Hall and his famous feline puppet hosted this children's show which had a distinct musical bias. One of Lenny's endearing qualities was his inability to pwonounce his 'R's. Apart from the original series there was 'Lenny's Den' from 1959-61, and 'Pops and Lenny' from 1962-63 which featured an early appearance by *The Beatles*. BBC 1956-63.

Les Girls Debby Bishop (Jo-Ann), Rachel Fielding (Veronica), Janet McTeer (Susan), Sadie Frost (Amanda), Annie Lambert (Maggie), Arabella Weir (Polly), Gerard Horan (Mervyn). Seven-part comedy series written by Margaret Phelan and set in a modelling agency, Maggie's Models. ITV 1988.

Let Me Entertain You Daytime talent show based on the very popular US *Gong Show* whereby acts are voted off by the studio audience during their performance if not up to scratch. The acts, including one surprise one chosen in advance from the audience, attempt to last three minutes before 50 per cent of the audience vote them off. The daily winning act plus the best runner-up made it into the Friday final and the winner of that show into the Series Grand Final. Hosted by Brian Conley and Christine Bleakley, the show was originally 45 minutes in length but became 30 minutes for the second series although its tea-time slot of 4.30 was upgraded to a more prime time 6.30. Both series winners were 13-year-old singers, Matthew Crane and Lee Lambert respectively. BBC2 2006-07

Let Them Eat Cake Dawn French (Lisette), Jennifer Saunders (Colombine), Adrian Scarborough (Bouffant), Lucy Punch (Eveline), Alison Steadman (Madame de Plonge), Elizabeth Berrington (Marie Antoinette). Six-part sitcom written by Peter Learmouth. Set in the Palace of Versailles in 1782. Outside the gates, the peasants are almost revolting, whilst inside lives the truly revolting Columbine, the Comtesse De Vache. Aided by her faithful maid Lisette, Columbine skulks around the palace uncovering the dark secrets of her fellow nobles, always leaving her well prepared to out-do jealous rival Madame De Plonge and her innocent yet sharp-witted daughter Eveline. Meanwhile, Columbine's acid-tongued courtier, Bouffant, is charged with the difficult task of keeping her at the forefront of French fashion. BBC1 1999

Let There Be Love Paul Eddington (Timothy), Nanette Newman (Judy), Henry McGee (Dennis). Sitcom created by Johnnie Mortimer and Brian Cooke. Timothy Love is in partnership with Dennis Newberry, running a successful advertising agency. He is a confirmed bachelor until he meets Judy, a mother-of-three, who he eventually marries by the end of the first series. The humour stems from Timothy's lifestyle changes. ITV 1982-83.

Let's Talk See *Question Time*

Letter From America Alistair Cooke was born Alfred Cooke in Salford, England, 20 November 1908, he legally added the name "Alistair" at age 22. He was educated at Blackpool Grammar School and was awarded a scholarship to study at Jesus College, Cambridge, where he gained a first-class honours degree in English. As a graduate student, he went to Yale University and Harvard University in the United States for two years on a Commonwealth Fund Fellowship. In 1935, back in England, Cooke became a film critic for the BBC and London correspondent for NBC. Each week, he recorded a 15-minute talk for American listeners on life in Britain, under the series title of *London Letter*. Alistair returned to America in 1937, and became a naturalized citizen in 1941. Shortly after emigrating, he suggested to the BBC the idea of doing the *London Letter* in reverse i.e. a 15-minute talk for British listeners on life in America. A prototype, *Mainly About Manhattan*, was broadcast intermittently from 1938, but the idea was shelved with the outbreak of World War II in 1939. The first *American Letter* was broadcast on March 24, 1946; initially confirmed for only 13 instalments, the series finally came to an end 58 years and 2,869 instalments later on 2 March 2004. Along the way, it picked up a new name (changing from *American Letter* to *Letter From America* in 1950). It was broadcast not only in Britain (on BBC Radio 4) and in many other Commonwealth countries, but throughout the world by the BBC World Service. Alistair died at his home in New York City, 29 March 2004 (30 March UK time).

Lewis Kevin Whatley (DI Robbie Lewis), Laurence Fox (DS James Hathaway), Clare Holman (Dr Laura Hobson), Rebecca Front (Chief Supt Jean Innocent). Spin-off from *Inspector Morse* adapted by Stephen Churchett. Newly-promoted and newly-widowed Detective Inspector Lewis returns to Oxford following a two-year sabbatical in the British Virgin Isles. He now also has a new sidekick in ex-priest DS Hathaway and new boss in Chief Supt Innocent. ITV 2006-

Liars Anthology drama series shown under the ITV Television Playhouse banner. Four story-tellers Ian Ogilvy (Rupert), William Mervyn (Sir Gerald), Nyree Dawn-Porter (Hermione) and Isla Blair (Sarah). compete to tell the tallest tales. Some of the stories, written by Philip Mackie (who was also the producer) and Hugh Leonard were based on stories by Oscar Wilde, Saki, Guy de Maupassant, Lord Dunsany, William Sansom, Michael Arlen, Stacy Aumonier and Anatole France. Actors included Fabia Drake, Patrick Troughton, Wanda Ventham, Gerald Campion, Jack Woolgar, John Cater, Terence Alexander, Ursula Howells, Angela Thorne, Sheila Steafel, Richard Wattis, Maggie Jones, Roy Dotrice, Roy Marsden, Francis Matthews, Penelope Keith, David Langton, Frank Thornton and John Woodvine. The theme music for the series was composed and conducted by Armando Sciascia. ITV 1966

Life and Loves of a She Devil, The Julie T.Wallace (Ruth Patchett), Dennis Waterman (Bobbo Patchett), Patricia Hodge (Mary Fisher), Liz Smith (Mrs Fisher), Miriam Margolyes (Nurse Hopkins), Tom Baker (Father Ferguson). Adapted by Ted Whitehead from the novel by Fay Weldon. When Ruth discovers that her dull, accountant husband Bobbo has been having an affair with elegant novelist Mary Fisher she decides to exact her revenge. BBC2 1986.

Life and Times of Vivienne Vyle, The Jennifer Saunders (Vivienne Vyle), Miranda Richardson (Helena De' Wend – the producer), Conleth Hill (Jared), Jason Watkins (Dr Jonathan Fowler – the show's psychotherapist), Antonia Campbell-Hughes (Abigail Wilson – the runner), Helen Griffin (Carol – the floor manager), Dave Lamb (Des – the director), Lawry Lewin (Damien – the researcher), Christopher Ryan (Miriam), Brian Conley (Chris Connor). Sitcom about a daytime talk show, Vivienne Vyle Show. Written by Jennifer Saunders and Tanya Byron. Vivienne Vyle is a former weather presenter and worked on TV-am. Recurrent themes include Helena De Wend's child who only speaks Spanish as the nanny spends more time with him than his mother; Vivienne's possibly gay partner, Jared, who loves karaoke (particularly Shirley Bassey and show songs!); her PR adviser, the transsexual Miriam, who Jared has an intense dislike for, and Vivienne's rival talk show host, Chris Connor, who unlike Vyle has a good rapport with his audience. BBC2 2007

Life Begins Caroline Quentin (Maggie Mee), Ace Ryan (Becca Mee), Alexander Armstrong (Phil Mee), Elliot Henderson-Boyle (James Mee), Anne Reid (Brenda Thornhill), Frank Finlay (Eric Thornhill). Light-hearted drama series created by Mike Bullen. Maggie and Phil are a late-30s couple on summer holiday with their two teenage children. On their first morning away together, Phil announces he wants to move out. ITV 2004-06.

Life in Cold Blood Five-part nature documentary, the sixth and last of David Attenborough's specialised surveys following his major trilogy that began with Life on Earth. Each 50-minute episode was followed by *Under the Skin*, a 10-minute section that featured David interviewing the scientists whose work had led to the subject matter included in the main programme. BBC1 2008. See also *Animal, Vegetable, Mineral?, The Blue Planet, Life On Earth, The Living Planet, Natural World, Planet Earth, The Trials of Life.*

Life of Bliss, A George Cole (David Bliss), Sheila Sweet (Zoe Hunter), Colin Gordon (Tony Fellows), Isabel Dean (Anne Fellows), Frances Bennett (Pam Batten), Hugh Sinclair (Bob Batten). Sitcom written by Godfrey Harrison. David Bliss is an awkward, bumbling young man with a tendency to find himself in awkward situations. In the first series, the other main characters were David's girlfriend Zoe, his sister Anne and her husband Tony. In the second series, David moves to the seaside town of Havenville to stay with Bob Batten and his wife Pam. David's wire-haired fox-terrier (barked by Percy Edwards) was named Psyche. The programme was based on a long-running BBC radio series. BBC 1960-61.

Life of Riley, The Caroline Quentin (Maddy Riley), Neil Dudgeon (Jim Riley), Heather Craney (Alison Weaver), Lucinda Dryzek (Katy Riley), Taylor Fawcett (Danny Riley), Patrick Nolan (Ted Jackson), Ava and Neve Lamb (Rosie Riley), John Bell (Anthony Weaver), Jordan Clarke (Adam Weaver), Richard Lumsden (Roger Weaver). Sitcom created by Georgia Pritchett. Jim and Maddy are newly-weds. Jim has two children, teenagers Katie and Danny, from a previous relationship, whilst Maddy also has a young child, Ted from her previous marriage as well as baby Rosie with Jim. The plots concern the dysfunctional family's efforts to keep up with their neighbours, the Weavers. BBC1 2009-

Life On Earth Natural history series presented by David Attenborough and first broadcast on BBC2 in 1979. See *Life in Cold Blood*

Life On Mars John Simm (DI Sam Tyler), Philip Glenister (DCI Gene Hunt). Created by writers Tony Jordan, Matthew Graham and Ashley Pharoah, who also provided the majority of the scripts. The fourth writer on the first series was Chris Chibnall. The central character of this science fiction/police drama is Sam Tyler, who, after being hit by a car in 2006, finds himself somehow transported back to 1973. There, he is working for Manchester and Salford Police under Gene Hunt. As the story develops it becomes unclear whether Tyler really has travelled back in time, is in a coma in 2006 and imagining his experiences, or if he is from 1973 but mentally unstable. The concluding episode sees Sam jumping off a tower-block in 2006 and finally settling in the 1970s. BBC 1 2006-07 For the second series, episodes two and three had their debut showing on digital television channel BBC Four, immediately following the previous episode on BBC One. The Mars of the title refers to the Metropolitan Accountability And Reconciliation Strategy. See Also *Ashes To Ashes*.

Life With the Lyons American actors Ben Lyon (1901-79) and real-life wife Bebe Daniels (1901-71) gained great popularity when they made London their home during the Second World War and featured with comedian Vic Oliver in the hit radio series

Hi, Gang! (1940-49). *Life With The Lyons* followed (1951-61) and differed from other family sitcoms in that it was peopled by an actual family, with children Richard and Barbara Lyon playing themselves. The show transferred to BBC television in 1955 and, as with the radio version, Molly Weir was cast as the Lyons' housekeeper Aggie MacDonald and Doris Rogers was their nosey next-door neighbour Florrie Wainwright. Horace Percival was added to the cast as the nebulous Mr Wimple. Before switching to the small-screen there had been three cinema feature films, *Life With The Lyons* (1954) and *The Lyons In Paris* (1954), both directed by Val Guest for Hammer Films as well as the earlier *Hi, Gang!* movie in 1941. There was also a Life With The Lyons summer stage-play that ran in Blackpool and included a role for the up-and-coming young actress Diana Dors. After the BBC TV series the Lyons enjoyed three further outings on ITV, aired while the BBC radio series was still on air. These 32 new TV programmes depicted further sort of true-to-life mishaps and adventures that befell the Lyons, at the time described as Britain's best-loved clan. Indeed, such was the degree of accuracy that when, in real life, the Lyons moved home from Marble Arch to Holland Park, the third ITV series also had them in a new home, the studio sets matching reality as closely as possible, right down to colour schemes, decorations and furniture. As ever, Bebe was the brains in the husband-and-wife partnership, co-writing every show and acting as chief scriptwriter throughout. BBC 1955-56; ITV 1957-60.

Likely Lads, The James Bolam (Terry Collier), Bob Ferris (Rodney Bewes), Sheila Fearn (Audrey Collier- Terry's sister), Brigit Forsyth (Thelma Chambers/Ferris). Sitcom written by Dick Clement and Ian La Frenais. Terry and Bob have been friends since they were small children. Bob is the responsible one, doing his best to get on with his job and better himself. Terry is the irresponsible one, intent on living life to the full and forever getting himself into scrapes of one kind or another. At the end of the series the lads decide to join the army but Bob is turned down because of his flat feet. BBC2 1964-66. The lads were reunited seven years later for a second series *Whatever Happened to the Likely Lads?* In this follow-up series, Terry arrives home after demob to find that Bob is about to marry Thelma. The series concentrates on the changing relationship between the old pals. Bill Owen played Thelma's father George chambers in this series. The theme tune *What Happened To You?* was co-written by Ian La Frenais and Mike Hugg (ex-Manfred Mann). The latter had a minor hit in the UK in 1974 when he released a recording of it with a pop group called "The Highly Likely". A much-publicised falling out between the two stars has prevented further revivals. BBC1 1973-74.

Lillie Francesca Annis (Lillie Le Breton/Langtry), Anton Rodgers (Edward Langtry), Peter Egan (Oscar Wilde), Anthony Head (William Le Breton), Don Fellows (James Whistler), Denis Lill (Edward, Prince of Wales), John Justin (Prince Paul Esterhazy). Drama telling the story of the colourful life of actress Lillie Langtry. ITV 1978.

Linda Green Lisa Tarbuck (Linda Green). Comedy drama created by Paul Abbott. Linda is a northern lass with a modern outlook on life. Lisa Tarbuck's real-life father appeared in one episode as her Uncle Vic. BBC1 2001-02.

Lionel Nimrod's Inexplicable World Radio comedy series starring Stewart Lee and Richard Herring and narrated by Tom Baker in the guise of Lionel Nimrod, a parody of Leonard Nimoy in his role as host of the *In Search Of* documentaries. Contributors include Armando Iannucci and Rebecca Front. Much of the material was rehashed and used in the comedy duo's later television series, *Fist Of Fun*. BBC Radio 4 1992-93.

Lipstick on your Collar Giles Thomas (Private Francis), Ewan McGregor (Private Hopper), Louise Germaine (Sylvia Berry), Douglas Henshall (Corporal Berry), Peter Jeffrey (Colonel Bernwood), Clive Francis (Major Hedges), Roy Hudd (Harold Atterbow), Bernard Hill (Uncle Fred). Six-part mini-series written by Dennis Potter. During the Suez Crisis of 1956, two young Foreign Office clerks display little interest in the decline of the

British Empire. To their eyes, it can hardly compete with girls, rock music, and the intrigue of romantic entanglements. C4 1993.

Listen With Mother No other signature tune evokes the warmth and tenderness of childhood security as powerfully as the Berceuse from Faure's Dolly Suite. The time is a quarter to two. This is the BBC Light Programme for mothers and children at home. Are you ready for the music? When it stops, Catherine Edwards (later Julia Lang) will be here to speak to you. Ding-de-dong. Ding-de-dong, Ding, Ding! Are you sitting comfortably? Then I'll begin! So began Listen with Mother every afternoon at 1:45pm (just before Woman's Hour), a fifteen minute programme of stories, songs and nursery rhymes for children under five. The audience was over one million at its peak. With nursery rhymes set to music by Ann Driver and sung by George Dixon (a senior schools programme producer) and Eileen Browne, the songs were often unaccompanied. There cannot be many children who did not march up and down the hill with The Grand Old Duke of York. Daphne Oxenford and Dorothy Smith were very long-standing members of the team and read the stories on the programme for 21 and 26 years respectively. BBC Radio 1950-82. See *Watch With Mother.*

Little Big Time Children's entertainment show presented by Freddie Garrity. When pop group Freddie and the Dreamers came towards the end of their world fame, their lead singer turned to this combination of jokes, sketches, music and dance, with help from other band members Bernie Dwyer, Roy Crewsdon, Derek Quinn and Peter Birrell. The band split in 1970 but Garrity and Birrell remained together in the children's television show for a further four years. Recorded at Southampton University's Nuffield Theatre in front of 400 school-children, the most popular segment of the show was the serial pop opera Oliver in the Overworld (penned by Mike Hazelwood and Albert Hammond), portraying a world with no sky, just a painted tin-roof, ruled over by the Clockwork King (Philip Ray). It is a world where machines are born and the king's wife is aptly named Queen Necessity, the Mother of Invention, and their kingdom is aboard the 'Overmotive' train. Freddie enters this world to help his grandfather clock, Oliver, (Peter Birrell) retrieve his lost memory, and encounters the dastardly Undercog (Graham Haberfield). In subsequent series Freddie helps the king thwart the plans of sinister business tycoon The Mighty Dictaphone (Dave King) and his accomplice The Grim Gramophone (Blake Butler). In the final series the musical comedy theme returned and characters such as Stupid Nana (Peter Birrell) and Professor Frantic (Frankie Holmes) were introduced. The series theme tune was composed by Mitch Murray and Peter Callander. ITV 1968-74.

Little Britain Sketch show written and performed by Matt Lucas and David Walliams. First broadcast on BBC Radio 4 (2001-02) the show was transferred to television on the opening night of BBC3, broadcast simultaneously on BBC2. The premise of the comedy is an off-kilter look at various segments of British society, narrated by the booming voice of Tom Baker. Characters include Bubbles Devere (Lucas) - the overweight perpetual resident of the Hill Grange Health Spa in Trump, who, by series three is joined by her cockney ex-husband Roman (Rob Brydon) and new love rival, the dark and sultry morbidly obese Desiree (Walliams); Daffyd (Lucas) the committed 'homosexualist' who lives in the Welsh town of Llanddewi Brefi and flaunts his sexuality in a variety of rubber outfits, to the complete indifference of the villagers. He refuses to accept he's not the only 'gayer' in the village, and is outraged when fellow gays trespass on his patch but always has the sympathetic ear of barmaid Myfanwy (Ruth Jones); Dennis Waterman (Walliams) a pint-sized caricature of the great actor who is perennially visiting his agent Jeremy Rent and keeps turning down scripts to TV shows because he always wants to "star in it, write the feem toon, sing the feem toon"; Emily Howard and Florence a couple of transvestites who consider themselves real 'laydees' although Emily (Walliams) used to play left back for QPR, and Florence (Lucas) has a moustache!; Lou and Andy - Andy (Lucas) and his carer Lou Walliams). Lou selflessly dedicates his life to looking after wheelchair-bound Andy and Andy reciprocates by making things as difficult as possible for Lou. 'Yeah I know' is the inevitable reply from Andy to every pearl of wisdom uttered by Lou. What Lou doesn't know is that there's nothing wrong with Andy's legs, and whenever he turns his back, Andy's off out of his chair and gambolling about like a fat, balding, semi-naked spring lamb. Madame Tussaud's immortalised Lou and Andy in 2005; Mr Mann and Roy - Roy (Lucas) is a shopkeeper who tries everything he can to satisfy Mr Mann's (Walliams) bizarre requests, even going so far as to shout up the stairs to Margaret (who can't come down as she has no arms or legs). But when Roy comes up with the goods, Mr Mann isn't as pleased as you might expect; Marjorie Dawes the overbearing leader of weight loss support group Fatfighters. Every week, she mercilessly belittles and humiliates the group for being so fat, while all the time oblivious to her own size, and desperately trying to conceal her compulsive consumption of biscuits, crisps and any other junk she can get her hands on. Marjorie, the mother of George Dawes of Shooting Stars fame, is also racially prejudiced, constantly asking an Asian member of the club to repeat things 'say again'; Vicky Pollard (Lucas) a teenage chav delinquent, the sort you can see hanging around any number of off licences in Britain, trying to persuade people going inside to buy them 10 fags and a bottle of White Lightning. Whether nicking stuff from the supermarket or swapping her baby for a Westlife CD, Vicky reacts to any accusation with indignant outrage, 'yeah but, no but, yeah but' while filling you in on 'this fing wot you know nuffin about'; Sebastian and Michael - Clingy, bitchy and insanely jealous, Sebastian (Walliams) wants nothing more than to have the Prime Minister (Anthony Stewart Head) all to himself. The Blair-like Prime Minister tolerates Sebastian's erratic behaviour, but is largely oblivious to his aide's obsession. BBC2 2003-05; BBC1 2006

Little Robots Stop-motion animated children's series first broadcast on *CBeebies* in 2003, based on the eponymous book by Mike Brownlow. The show revolves around eleven Little Robots, each with his own distinct looks and personality. They were abandoned on a scrap heap in a junkyard until Tiny, the central figure of the story, fixed them. The robots then built a world of their own, using junk to build their houses, gadgets, plants and flowers, and even their own sun and moon. The centre of their world is the Nut And Bolt Tree, a big, metallic structure that serves as a home to Tiny. Other important features of their world are the Day-Night lever, which causes the sky to rotate 180 degrees, switching from night to day; and the junkyard, which constantly receives junk from the surface through a chute. The characters include: **Tiny(** voiced by Hayley Carmichael) - He is blue, has a red antenna on top of his head, and a red button on his belly, which serves to open the lid of his head where he stores his tools. He is also responsible for pulling the Day-Night lever at the right times. Tiny lives on the Nut And Bolt Tree, right next to the Day-Night lever. **Messy** - The robot dog who loves things dirty and messy. Scary teaches him tricks and makes shows with him, where he is known as "Messy, the Wonderhound". **Sporty** (voiced by Lenny Henry) - The strongest and fittest of all the robots, he is constantly running, playing games and sports, and never gets tired of making himself stronger and fitter. Sporty has his own, private gym with a trampoline and a conveyor belt. **Stretchy** (voiced by Jimmy Hibbert) - Very organised and efficient, he is in charge of sorting the junk that comes from the chute on the junkyard. He is blue and tall, and has a long, flexible neck. He lives in the junkyard, inside an abandoned radiator. **Rusty** (voiced by Morwenna Banks) - A feminine and sensitive Little Robot, she has a red dress made with rusty metal, and wears a funnel on top of her head. She lives in an old, rusty bucket, and she constantly has new ideas on how to improve and decorate it. She is very impulsive and accident prone, though, and tense situations or anything that causes her to get over-excited can make her overheat and release puffs of steam. She also has a notable, childish crush on Sporty. **Stripy** (voiced by Martin Clunes) - Big and made with coloured stripes of metal, he is practically the complete opposite of Sporty: moves and talks slowly, but he is a deep and introspective thinker, also a specialist in flowers and storytelling. His best friend is Teddy, his metallic teddy bear, and his favourite activities are taking care of his garden, telling stories to his friends and playing games that require little agility and lots of skill. **Noisy**

(voiced by Su Pollard) - Speaks loudly, has a trumpet for a nose, plays instruments, writes and sings songs, and loves whatever kind of noise she can produce. Her house is an old drum, with a xylophone-themed entryway. Her passion for loud music and noise can often be bothersome for her friends, but she is also a great entertainer. Her laughter is unforgettable. **Spotty** (voiced by Emma Chambers) - She's round, yellow, covered in coloured spots, wears specs, and can retract all her limbs and roll around like a ball for fast locomotion. She has a strong personality, likes rules and orders, and tends to give orders to her friends. Her dream is to be an artist. **Scary** (voiced by Mike Hayley) – He is purple and wears a black cape. Scary is a great actor with a Donald Sinden-esque voice, likes to scare his friends (though he's often not successful) and stage shows to entertain them. He has his own stage, which is also his house. **The Sparky Twins** (voiced by Mel Giedroyc and Sue Perkins) - They are debatably green or blue with red and yellow bellies. Sparky One and Sparky Two are almost identical twins who are full of energy, love dancing and doing practical jokes on other robots. Sparky One has a red spot on her belly and Sparky Two has a yellow spot on her belly. They are able to communicate over distances by exchanging electrical rays through the antennae on their heads, and their catch phrase is "Gimmie Three, Sparkee!" when they high-five. They live in a pair of speakers by an old record turntable.

Live and Kicking The long-running Saturday morning children's magazine originally hosted by Andi Peters and Emma Forbes filled the slot vacated by *Saturday Superstore* and maintained several of the features, including 'Run the Risk' (with Peter Simon and Shane Richie, later replaced by John Eccleston and then Bobby Davro) and the Trev and Simon slot (Trevor Neal and Simon Hickson) who introduced various game show items and took part in surreal sketches. From the second series two puppets joined the show. Leprechauns Mr Sage and Mr Onion (named in a viewer competition) were a mixture of hand puppetry and animatronics by Darryl Worbey, John Eccleston and Don Austen, the last two defecting from ITV's *What's Up Doc?*. In autumn 1996 Zoe Ball and Jamie Theakston replaced Andi and Emma and The Men In Trousers (Gez Foster, Ben Ward and Richard Webb) replaced Trev and Simon. Three years later Steve Wilson and Emma Ledden took over as hosts and the following year Ortis Deley, Trey Farley, Katy Hill (later replaced by Heather Suttie) and Sarah Cawood hosted a revamped format of the show. BBC1 1993-2001. *Live and Kicking* was replaced by *The Saturday Show*.

Live at the Apollo Originally titled *Jack Dee Live at the Apollo*, as the diminutive comedian hosted the first two series and the opening show of the third series. A recurring theme of the show was the segment where Jack's mobile phone number was given out to the theatre audience at the start of the show and a selection of the comments and jokes sent as text messages to the mobile are read out by the host at the end of the show. To date there have been six series from the Hammersmith Apollo. Guest hosts have included: Dara Ó Briain, Lenny Henry, Sean Lock, Lee Mack, Al Murray, Jimmy Carr, Jo Brand, Michael McIntyre, Russell Howard, Jason Manford, Rob Brydon, Alistair McGowan, Rhod Gilbert, Ed Byrne, Kevin Bridges and Stephen K Amos. BBC1 2004-

Live From Studio Five Daytime magazine show, hosted by Ian Wright, Melinda Messenger (later replaced by Jayne Middlemiss) and Kate Walsh, dealing with current celebrity news and gossip. *Five* 2009-

Liver Birds, The Polly James (Beryl Hennessey), Nerys Hughes (Sandra Hutchinson/Paynton), Pauline Collins (Dawn), Elizabeth Estensen (Carol Boswell), Mollie Sugden (Mrs Hutchinson), Ivan Beavis (Mr Hutchinson), John Nettles (Paul), Jonathan Lynn (Robert), Lucien Boswell (Michael Angelis), Eileen Kennally and Carmel McSharry (Mrs Boswell). Sitcom written by Carla Lane. Two young Liverpudlian girls share a bedsit in Huskisson Street and experience romantic, financial and family problems. For the first four episodes in 1969 Beryl and Dawn were flatmates but when the second series began in 1971 Sandra had replaced Dawn. At the end of series 4, Beryl left to marry Robert and was replaced by Carol. Other new characters introduced included Sandra's boyfriend Paul and Carol's brother Lucien and their mother who was the forerunner of Bread's Nellie Boswell. Following the series end in 1979 a brief revival was attempted in 1996 with the thrice-married Beryl now a lodger in Sandra's house. The title song was performed by The Scaffold. BBC1 1969-79; 1996.

Living Planet, The Natural history series presented by David Attenborough and first broadcast on BBC1 in 1984. See *Life in Cold Blood*

Livin' With Lucy Irish television programme presented by former air-hostess Lucy Kennedy (b. 21 April 1976, Sandycove, Co Dublin), the premise of the show being Lucy's trials and tribulations whilst spending a weekend living with a different celebrity each episode, analysing their daily lives and interviewing them in their own homes all the while with cameras filming in the background. RTÉ Two 2008-

Location, Location, Location When Phil Spencer is not running his successful Property Search company, Garrington Home Finders, with his business partner Kirstie Allsopp, he has, since 2001, co-presented, with Kirstie, the very popular Channel 4 property series' *Location, Location, Location, Relocation Relocation* and *Location Revisited*. Kirstie also hosts *The Property Chain* and *Kirstie's Homemade Home* for Channel 4.

Lock, Stock... Ralph Brown (Miami Vice - local gang lord who kills anyone who upsets him), Daniel Caltagirone (Moon - a chef, pervert and electronics expert), Del Synnott (Lee - a ladies man), Scott Maslen (Jamie - the fast talker), Shaun Parkes (Bacon - the ramrod), Christopher Adamson (Three Feet - enforcer working for Miami), Lisa Rogers (Tanya - who works as a dancer at Lapland). Off-shoot from the 1998 film *Lock, Stock and Two Smoking Barrels*. Written by Chris Baker and Andrew Day. A group of four friends (Bacon, Moon, Jamie and Lee) run The Lock, a pub in London, but their constant illegal wheeling and dealing gets them into more and more trouble, usually with the local gangland boss. C4 2000

Lollipop Peggy Mount (Maggie Robinson aka Lollipop), Hugh Lloyd (Reg Robinson aka Mr Mole). Sitcom written by Jimmy Perry about an unlikely pair of lovebirds. ITV 1971-72

London's Burning Mark Arden (Roland 'Vaseline' Cartwright), Glen Murphy (George Green), James Hazeldine (Mike 'Bayleaf' Wilson), Richard Walsh (Bert 'Sicknote' Quigley), Gerard Horan (Leslie 'Charisma' Appleby), Ben Onwukwe (Stuart 'Recall' Mackenzie), James Marcus (Station Officer Sidney Tate), Sean Blowers (Sub-Officer John Hallam), Treva Etienne (Tony Sanders), Rupert Baker (Malcolm Cross), Samantha Beckinsale (Kate Stevens), Liz Crowther (Alison Hemmings), Sharon Duce (Elaine Reeve). Drama series created by Jack Rosenthal, revolving around the Firefighters of Blue Watch B25, Blackwall. ITV 1988-2002.

Long Firm, The Mark Strong (Harry Starks), Derek Jacobi (Lord Edward 'Teddy' Thursby), Judy Parfitt (Lady Ruth Thursby), Damien Thomas (Tom Driberg), Joe Absolom (Tommy), Phil Daniels (Jimmy), Tracie Bennett (Judy Garland), Lena Headey (Ruby Ryder), Fiona Glascott (Janine). Michael Parkinson (as himself). Joe Penhall's four-part adaptation of Jake Arnott's critically acclaimed novel, The Long Firm, depicting the lives of characters who live, love and suffer through their association with the charismatic charms of sadistic homosexual gangster Harry Starks. BBC2 2004.

Long John Silver, The Adventures of Although an Australian production, included as a tribute to its British star. This was a 26-episode, half-hour series made for the English and American markets. Based on the Robert Louis Stevenson pirate character from his novel Treasure Island, and set at Porto Bello on the Spanish Main, the series featured English actor Robert Newton in the title role. Newton had previously played the same part in the 1950 Disney movie *Treasure Island*, which was the first total live-action motion picture made by the company, and reprised the role on film in *Long John Silver* (1954). The series was made in 1954 and 1955 but shown on ITV in 1957. Its cast also included Kit Taylor (Jim Hawkins), Connie Gilchrist (Purity Pinker), Rodney Taylor (Israel Hands), Henry Gilbert (Billy Bowledge), Lloyd Berrell (Mendoza), Grant Taylor (Patch), Harvey Adams (Governor Strong), Hans Stern (Reverend Monaster), Muriel Steinbeck (Governor's wife), Jean Wittle (Elizabeth, the Governor's daughter). See also *Treasure Island*.

Long Way Down Follow-on series from *Long Way Round*, in which are intrepid bikers, Ewan McGregor and Charley Boorman, undertook a motorcycle journey riding through 18 countries from John o' Groats in Scotland to Cape Town in South Africa via Europe and Africa starting on 12 May 2007 and finishing on 4 August 2007. The journey was almost frustrated by the detention of Boorman at Gatwick Airport after he made an inappropriate comment regarding bombs, and was detained for questioning by local police. BBC2 2007.

Long Way Round Television series documenting the 19,000-mile (31,000 km) journey of actors Ewan McGregor and Charley Boorman from London to New York on motorcycles, travelling eastwards through Europe and Asia, the long way round. The journey took place between 14 April and 29 July 2004 and visited twelve countries, starting in the UK, then passing through France, Belgium, Germany, the Czech Republic, Slovakia, Ukraine, Russia, Kazakhstan, Mongolia, USA and Canada, ending in New York. Ewan and Charley completed most of the journey riding BMW R1150GS Adventure all-terrain motorcycles. Cameraman Claudio von Planta rode a third BMW. Ewan and Charley were inspired by legendary motorcyclist Ted Simon's book *Jupiter's Travels*. They met up with Ted in Mongolia. The journey was used to bring attention to the humanitarian efforts of UNICEF. The theme Song 'Long Way Round' was written and performed by Kelly Jones lead singer of Stereophonics. The series spawned a best-selling book and DVD. Originally shown on Sky One in 2004 the seven-part series was repeated on BBC2 in 2007 and 2008. See also *Charley Boorman: Ireland to Sydney*.

Look Long-running natural history series presented by Peter Scott, founder of the Slimbridge Wildfowl Trust. The repeats were shown under the title *Look Again*. There was also a children's version that aired for the duration of the run. BBC1 1955-69.

Loose Women Lunchtime chat show originally anchored by Kaye Adams and Nadia Sawalha. The format is based around a panel of four women who gossip about random, sometimes topical issues and interview celebrities of both genders. Originally broadcast from the London Studios, after the second series in 2000, the show moved to Manchester and was briefly re-branded as *Live Talk*. In 2002, Loose Women returned for a third run, moving to Anglia's Studio 2 in Norwich but by series six in 2004, the show returned to The London Studios where it has remained. Jackie Brambles took her turn as anchor until the summer of 2009 whereupon the mainstays became Kate Thornton (replaced by Carol Vorderman in 2011) and Andrea McLean. Current panellists include Sherrie Hewson, Carol McGiffin, Lisa Maxwell, Jane McDonald, Denise Welch, Lynda Bellingham, Lesley Garrett and Zoe Tyler. Coleen Nolan bid a tearful farewell in July 2011 after eleven years as a loose woman. In the summer of 2009, ITV held a nationwide search for a female member of the public to appear as a panellist for five episodes. The winner was Rachel Agnew, who claimed in her audition tape to be the voice of "cashier number ... please" as heard in shops' queue systems. She first appeared as a panellist on Wednesday 8 July and was present for five shows in the run-up to the end of the series in August. ITV 1999-

Lord Peter Wimsey Ian Carmichael (Lord Peter Wimsey), Glyn Houston and Derek Newark (Bunter his manservant), Mark Eden (DCI Charles Parker). Dorothy L. Sayers' monocled sleuth was the scourge of all murderers in the 1920s and this series dramatised five of her novels, *Clouds Of Witness, The Unpleasantness at the Bellona Club, Murder Must Advertise, The Nine Tailors* and *Five Red Herrings*. BBC1 1972-75. Three more novels (*Strong Poison, Have His Carcase* and *Gaudy Night*) were dramatised on BBC2 in 1987 with Edward Petherbridge as Wimsey, Richard Morant as Bunter and David Quiller as Parker. Also appearing was Harriet Walter as Harriet Vane, Wimsey's crime-writer friend.

Lord Raingo Kenneth More (Sam Raingo), Janet Suzman (Delphine), Joss Ackland (Tom Hogarth), Joseph O'Conor (Andy Clyth), Diana Churchill (Adela). Four-part drama series based on the political novel of the same name by Arnold Bennett, based on the wartime dealings of Bennett's friend Lord Beaverbrook, published in 1926. Sam Raingo is a successful fiftyish millionaire business magnate with a wife and mistress. His life is stagnating and his health is not good and he has a yen to do something more with his life. The British government needs a propaganda machine to buoy up the hopes of the British people during the First World War. Both needs are fulfilled when Sam is offered, and accepts, the post and a peerage is thrown into the package. BBC 1966.

Lorna Doone Bill Travers (John Ridd), Jean Anderson (Mrs Ridd), Jane Merrow (Lorna Doone). 11-part mini-series based on R.D. Blackmore's classic tale. BBC 1963.

Lotus Eaters, The Ian Hendry (Erik Shepherd), Wanda Ventham (Ann Shepherd), Maurice Denham (Nestor Turton), Thorley Walters (Major Edward Woolley). Drama series created by Michael J. Bird. English couple Erik and Ann Shepherd, run a bar in Crete and as this compelling series progresses various secrets about their past, including the fact that they were involved with the secret service, are revealed. Series one is made up of nine individual plays with each character getting a lead role whilst series two is a traditional series and focuses on the Shepherd's espionage exploits. BBC2 1972-73.

Love and Mr Lewisham Brian Deacon (Mr George Lewisham), Carolyn Courage (Miss Ethel Henderson), Freddie Jones (Mr Chaffery), Jane Lapotaire (Miss Alice Heydinger). Four-part drama series based on a work of HG Wells. BBC1 1972.

Love for Lydia Mel Martin (Lydia Aspen), Jeremy Irons (Alex Sanderson), Rachel Kempson (Aunt Juliana), Sherrie Hewson (Nancy Holland), Christopher Blake (Edward Richardson), Beatrix Lehmann (Aunt Bertie), Ralph Arliss (Blackie Johnson), Peter Davison (Tom Holland), Michael Aldridge (Captain Rollo Aspen). Thirteen-part drama series written by George S. Davis and based on the H.E.Bates novel. Would-be writer Edward Richardson is in love with heiress Lydia Aspen and wants her all to himself. Lydia professes to be in love with him, but her first love is excitement. There are several other young men who vie with Richardson for Lydia's affection, and she sends mixed signals to them all, playing them off against each other, sometimes with dire results. At least that's the way Richardson sees things, but it's not the whole story! ITV 1977.

Love Hurts Adam Faith (Frank Carver), Zoe Wanamaker (Tessa Piggott), Jane Lapotaire (Rabbi Diane Warburg), Tony Selby (Max Taplow). Drama series created by Laurence Marks and Maurice Gran. When Tessa Piggott goes through a messy breakup (her married ex-lover and ex-boss leaves her for a younger mistress), she looks for a new job. Deciding to leave the rat-race, she finds herself a position in a charitable organization SEED (Society for Environmental and Ecological Development) with old college chum, Diane Warburg. Tessa finds a new boyfriend in Frank Carver, a roguish millionaire entrepreneur who is learning how to live with his college-age daughter. The course of Tessa and Frank's romance and the stories of their friends and families make up the episode plots. The theme song was performed by Peter Polycarpou. BBC1 1992-94.

Love Island See *Celebrity Love Island*.

Love Me Do Game Show hosted by Shane Richie in which three couples vie for the chance to wed. ITV 1997. This show actually began in 1996 under the title *The Shane Richie Experience*.

Love of Mike, The Michael Medwin (Mike Lane), Brian Wilde (Bob), Carmel McSharry (Biddy), George Roderick (George Smithers), Bernard Fox (Malcolm Danders). Sitcom, written by Gerald Kelsey and Dick Sharples, revolving around jazz musician Mike Lane and his convoluted love life. Brian Wilde left the series, and the role of Mike's flatmate, early on and was replaced by Bernard Fox. ITV 1960. Three of the cast from this, Medwin, Fox and Roderick, teamed up the following year for a spin-off series, *Three Live Wires* (1961), also starring Derek Benfield as Higgenbottom; and Deryck Guyler as Mr Farnum.

Love School Ben Kingsley (Rossetti), Kika Markham (Jane Morris), David Burke (William Morris), Kenneth Colley (Edward Burne-Jones), Patricia Quinn (Lizzie Siddall), Peter Egan (Millais), David Collings (John Ruskin), Bernard Lloyd (Holman Hunt), Malcolm Tierney (Ford Maddox-Brown). Six-episode drama series concerning the formation of the Pre-Raphaelite Brotherhood of painters. BBC2 1975.

Love Soup Michael Landes (Gil Raymond), Tamsin Greig (Alice Chenery), Sheridan Smith (Cleo Martin), Montserrat Lombard (Milly Russell), Owen Brenman (Lloyd Drewitt), Trudie Styler (Irene Andrews), Brian Protheroe (Bob Andrews), Mark Heap (Douglas McVitie), Amelia Curtis (Fae Maddison). Romantic comedy drama series with an adult theme, written by David Renwick and produced by Verity Lambert. The first series of six 60-minute episodes revolved around the relationship of Gil, an American comedy writer who has moved to England to write an episode of a new TV project called *Love Soup*, and Alice, the manageress of a perfume company in a London department store. Although the couple are clearly perfect for each other they are blissfully unaware of each other's existence. Michael Landes did not return for the second series and each episode now became a more stereotypical situation comedy format albeit of an adult nature. The length of each episode was shortened to 30 minutes for Series 2. The opening and closing jazz theme was *Alley Boogie* by Georgia White. Guest stars included Lee Montague, Lynda Bellingham, Sanjeev Bhaskar, Lucy Speed, Bill Bailey, Ronnie Corbett, Jan Ravens, Helen Lederer, Mackenzie Crook and Charlie Brooks. BBC1 2005 and 2008.

Love Story Umbrella title for a long-running weekly series of distinct 60-minute dramas based on themes of love and relationships. Actors involved in the 128 episodes include: John Hurt, Malcolm McDowell, Francesca Annis, Ian McShane, Vanessa Redgrave, Ann Todd, Helen Cherry, Roy Dotrice, Lynn Redgrave, Lee Montague, Leonard Rossiter, James Bolam, Dennis Waterman, Sydney Tafler, Eric Portman, Julia Foster, Michael Gambon, Susan Penhaligon, Robert Hardy, George Maharis, Eric Porter, Nyree Dawn Porter, Peter Bowles, Jack Hedley, Dudley Moore, Billie Whitelaw, Charles Gray, Brian Blessed, T.P. McKenna, Angharad Rees, Anton Rodgers, Elaine Paige, Frances Cuka, Penelope Keith, Leo McKern, Georgina Keyes, Gerald Harper, Ralph Bates, Michael Balfour, Miriam Karlin, Donald Houston, Bernard Lee, Warren Mitchell, John Standing, John Alderton, Michael Craig, Denholm Elliott, Ray Lonnen, Judy Parfitt, Beryl Reid, Anthony Valentine, Hannah Gordon, Felicity Kendal, Robert Lindsay, Richard O'Sullivan, Anna Massey, Patricia Brake, Michael Kitchen, Libby Morris, Clive Swift, James Villiers, Keith Barron, Gwen Watford, Patrick Macnee, Diana Coupland, Judy Cornwell, Cheryl Hall, Terence Alexander, Robin Bailey, Rodney Bewes, Derek Fowlds, John Junkin, Trevor Bannister, Johnny Briggs, Jeremy Kemp, Michele Dotrice, George Sewell, Mark Eden, Barry Foster, Bill Owen, Jane Asher, Wanda Ventham, Tessa Wyatt, Carmen Munroe, Peter Wyngarde, Brian Murphy, Sam Wanamaker, Fenella Fielding, Jean Kent, Marius Goring, John Gregson, Valerie French, Laurence Naismith, Alfred Burke, Simon Cadell, Warren Clarke, John Savident, Shirley Cheriton, Judy Cornwell, Barry Evans, Geoffrey Palmer, Windsor Davies, Bryan Pringle, Roy Barraclough, Rosemary Leach, Neville Buswell, Norman Bowler, Phyllis Calvert, Elizabeth Sellars, Alan Lake, Jennie Linden, Gwen Watford, Victor Platt, Peter Barkworth, Jane Merrow, Bella Emberg. ITV 1963-74.

Love Thy Neighbour Jack Smethurst (Eddie Booth), Kate Williams (Joan Booth), Rudolph Walker (Bill Reynolds), Nina Baden-Semper (Barbie Reynolds), Tommy Godfrey (Arthur), Keith Marsh (Jacko Jackson), Paul Luty (Nobby Garside). Sitcom written by Harry Driver and Vince Powell. Eddie Booth is a white trade-unionist who lives in ignorant bliss with his wife Joan in Maple Terrace until the day West Indian couple Bill and Barbie Reynolds move in next door. The women get on famously, but Eddie's loathsome racialism typified by his perpetual name-calling of "sambo" and "nignog" when referring to Bill is the catalyst for trouble. Much of the action is set in the Jubilee Social Club with Arthur and Jacko (Famous Saying: I'll 'ave 'alf) acting as referee as Eddie and Bill squabbled. Bill sometimes rose to the bait and called Eddie "White Honky" but he always came out on top, which probably saved the series from being more controversial than it already was. Stuart Gillies performed the theme song. ITV 1972-76.

Lovejoy Ian McShane (Lovejoy), Dudley Sutton (Tinker Dill), Chris Jury (Eric Catchpole), Phyllis Logan (Lady Jane Felsham), Diane Parish (Beth), Malcolm Tierney (Charlie Gimbert), Caroline Langrishe (Charlotte Cavendish). Drama series created by Ian La Frenais, based on the novels of Jonathan Gash. Lovejoy is a colourful East Anglian antique dealer who lives a somewhat hand-to-mouth life, despite being known as a 'divvie' - a man who knows in his bones the right and wrong of fine things. The Lovejoy Antiques team includes Tinker, his tweedy, beret-hatted friend, young Eric Catchpole, his apprentice (replaced by Beth in the fifth series), and Jane Felsham, a supportive aristocratic love interest (replaced as the love interest by auctioneer Charlotte Cavendish in the fifth series). Lovejoy's business rival Charlie Gimbert is both his landlord and a competitor for good buys of all kinds. The series used the technique known as 'breaking the fourth wall' whereby asides are made to camera to explain the plot scenario. Lovejoy's Morris Minor was affectionately known as Miriam. BBC1 1986-94.

Lovers, The Richard Beckinsale (Geoffrey Scrimgeor), Paula Wilcox (Beryl Battersby), Joan Scott (Mrs Battersby), Robin Nedwell (Roland Lomax). Sitcom created by Jack Rosenthal. A young Manchester couple, Beryl and Geoffrey (often called 'Geoffrey Bubbles Bon Bon' by Beryl) have been boyfriend and girlfriend for two years. Beryl dreams of marriage and a white wedding and is not prepared to engage in 'Percy Filth' (her name for the ultimate submission of the body). Geoffrey feels he is shirking his responsibility as a red-blooded male and so pursues his conjugal rights at every opportunity although he is secretly scared by the prospect. Beryl, too, has mixed feelings, and the two play a continual game of verbal sexual-cat-and-mouse that goes nowhere, but is as exhausting as the act itself. ITV 1970-71.

Lucky Dip Children's light entertainment show introduced by Muriel Young as part of the *Small Time* series. Fanny Craddock and her husband George had a regular spot in this series. ITV 1958.

Luna Patsy Kensit (Luna - series 1), Joanna Wyatt (Luna - series 2), Roy Macready (80H). Sci-fi comedy series written, produced and directed by former *Monkee*, Micky Dolenz. Set in a totalitarian society, with an almost unintelligible vocabulary of future-jargon. Everyone is cloned and have numbers instead of names. Luna was named after the Moon where she was born, and she was adopted by a family who all had nicknames to replace their numbers. Even the credits appear in "Teletalk", a futuristic jargon spoken by the characters; for example, "Phase Two" is used instead of "Part Two" and "High Grade Adminordinator" for "producer". ITV 1983-84

Lunchbox Daily sing-a-long show presented by Noele Gordon with Jerry Allen and his Trio providing the music. The show was eventually axed to make way for another Reg Watson production, *Crossroads*, and Noele was cast as the leading character of Meg Richardson. Another *Lunchbox* regular, guest singer John Bentley, was also to join the cast of *Crossroads* as Meg's husband Hugh Mortimer. ITV 1956-64.

Luther Idris Elba (Det Chief Insp John Luther), Ruth Wilson (Alice Morgan), Steven Mackintosh (Det Chief Insp Ian Reed), Indira Varma (Zoe Luther), Saskia Reeves (Det Supt Rose Teller), Warren Brown (Det Sgt Justin Ripley), Paul McGann (Mark North), Dermot Crowley (Det Chief Insp Martin Schenk). Police drama series written by Neil Cross. John Luther is an unconventional police officer who bends the rules on occasion but is saved from crossing certain boundaries by his conscience and high intellect. His marriage to Zoe is crumbling after a breakdown brought on by a traumatic case and his one salvation is his dedication to duty. The six-part series used the Columbo-style format of letting the viewer know who the murderer was from the outset. ITV 2010

Lytton's Diary Peter Bowles (Neville Lytton). Drama series created by Peter Bowles and Philip Broadley, and written by Ray Connolly. Incidents in the life of newspaper diarist, Neville Lytton, who works for The Daily News. ITV 1985-86.

Mackenzie Jack Galloway (Robert Mackenzie), Kara Wilson (Jean Mackenzie), Lynda Bellingham (Ruth Isaacs). Written by Andrea Newman. Beginning in 1955, the 12 episodes portray 19 turbulent years in the life of ambitious Scottish builder Robert Mackenzie. A young Tracey Ullman is seen as one of four actresses who played Ruth Isaacs' daughter, Lisa. BBC1 1980.

Made in Chelsea Reality soap set in the wealthy Chelsea district of London and often considered the 'Sloane' version of *The Only Way Is Essex*. The E4 show follows the lives of broker Spencer Matthews and his good friend singer/songwriter Catherine 'Caggie' Dunlop, musician Gabriella Ellis and her good friend Whiskey Mist' VIP host Ollie Locke, model Fredrik Ferrier, PR guru Hugo Taylor, make-up artist Milly Mackintosh, jewellery boutique owner Amber Atherton, investment front of house Alexandra 'Binky' Felstead, blogger Francesca Hull, student Rosie Fortescue, and IT and diamond entrepreneur Francis Boulle, who was listed in Tatler's Little Black Book of London's most eligible bachelors in 2008, 2009 and 2010. The first episode of the ongoing series premiered on 9 May 2011.

Maestro Clive Anderson presented this reality television show bringing eight diverse personalities together to compete for the chance to conduct the BBC Concert Orchestra in front of 40,000 people at BBC Proms in the Park. They were: drum'n'bass artist Goldie, Blur bassist Alex James, actress Jane Asher, newsreader Katie Derham, broadcaster Peter Snow, actor David Soul, comedian Sue Perkins and actor and comedian Bradley Walsh. Their mentors were: Brad Cohen, Jason Lai, Natalia Luis-Bassa, Matthew Rowe, Ivor Setterfield, Peter Stark, Sarah Tenant-Flowers and Christopher Warren-Green. The judges were: Sir Roger Norrington, who conducted the 2008 *Last Night of the Proms*, cellist and composer Zoë Martlew, conductor Simone Young and double bassist Dominic Seldis. In a very close final, ultimately judged by the viewing public, Sue Perkins narrowly beat Goldie for the honour of conducting Verdi's *The Sicilian Vespers*, Elgar's *Pomp and Circumstance No.4* and Mitch Leigh's *The Impossible Dream* from Man of La Mancha (sung by Lesley Garrett). BBC2 2008

Maggie and Her Julia McKenzie (Maggie Brooks), Irene Handl (Mrs P), Carmen Silvera (Miss Prosser), Anna Wing (Mrs Young). Light comedy sitcom written by Leonard Webb. The comedy revolves around the relationship between Maggie, a divorced school teacher living alone in a flat, and her nice but nosey neighbour, Mrs Perry (or 'Mrs P' as she was known to all and sundry long before Theo Paphitis coined the term to refer to his wife). Each episode saw Maggie embark tentatively on a new relationship, only for Mrs.P to either deliberately or unintentionally wreck it before it could get started. The pilot aired in 1976 and then two six-episode series followed. ITV 1976; 1978-79.

Magic Numbers Stephen Mulhern hosts the live gameshow in which one lucky viewer can win hundreds of thousands of pounds. Six magic numbers are generated in a series of entertaining, and sometimes bizarre ways, the numbers forming part of a phone number. Viewers enter by ringing a premium rate number if two of the magic numbers appear in the last six digits of their phone number, either landline or mobile. A series of general knowledge questions are asked for the finale and dependent on the number of correct answers an equal amount of boxes are opened some containing money deposited as a result of the correct answers and some either empty or containing one of three Xs which nullifies the winnings accrued. ITV 2010- See *Talking Telephone Numbers*

Magic Roundabout, The Originally a French series, written by Serge Danot, under the name *Le Manège Enchanté* (The Delightful Carousel), the BBC produced a version of the series using the original stop motion animation footage with new English-language scripts, written and performed by Eric Thompson with animation by Ivor Wood. Characters included Dougal (Pollux in the French version and based on the world-weary Tony Hancock character) a Skye Terrier; Zebedee (Zébulon) a jack-in-the-box; Brian (Ambroise) a snail; Ermintrude (Azalée) a cow, Dylan (Flappy; based on the great musician of the same name) a rabbit; and a 4-2-2 wheel-configured talking train. The two main human characters were Florence (Margote) a young girl; and Mr Rusty (le Père Pivoine) the operator of the roundabout. Other occasional humans included Uncle Hamish, Angus, Basil, Paul, Rosalie and Mr McHenry (an elderly man who rode a tricycle). At the end of each episode Zebedee invariably closed proceedings with the phrase "Time for bed". The iconic theme tune, by Alain Legrand, removed the vocals from the French version and increased the tempo of the tune while making it sound as if it were played on a fairground organ. BBC1 1965-77. Fifty-two additional episodes, not previously broadcast, were shown in 1991 on Channel 4's News Daily. Eric Thompson had died by this time, and the job of narrating them in a pastiche of Thompson's style went to actor Nigel Planer. A 2005 feature film, *The Magic Roundabout*, was the first computer-animated film to be made in the United Kingdom. The following year an American version of the film was released under the title of *Doogal* with many of the voice actors changed. The cast included (with British actor first if different from the US) Dougal / Doogal (Robbie Williams / Daniel Tay), Dylan (Bill Nighy / Jimmy Fallon), Zeebad (Tom Baker / Jon Stewart), Ermintrude (Joanna Lumley / Whoopi Goldberg), Brian (Jim Broadbent / William H. Macy), Train (Lee Evans / Chevy Chase), Narrator (Judi Dench), Florence (Kylie Minogue), Zebedee (Ian McKellen), Moose (Michael Angelis / Kevin Smith), Soldier Sam (Ray Winstone / Bill Hader), Coral (Daniella Loftus / Heidi Brook Myers).

Magnificent Evans, The Ronnie Barker (Plantagenet Evans), Dyfed Thomas (Home Rule O'Toole), Dickie Arnold (Willie), Myfanwy Talog (Bron), Sharon Morgan (Rachel). Sitcom written by Roy Clarke. Situated in deepest rural Wales, Evans, with his wide-brimmed hat and haughty presence, described himself as a 'genius, photographer and man of letters'. His long-time fiancée, Rachel, also doubled as his assistant and she had a full-time job steering his lusting eyes away from other women and back to his viewfinder. Only six episodes were made. BBC1 1984.

Magpie ITV's answer to Blue Peter was broadcast weekly from Thames TV's Teddington studios and began its run on 30 July 1968, which was Thames Television's first day of broadcasting. The original three presenters were Susan Stranks, Pete Brady, and Tony Bastable. David Jason reprised his role of Captain Fantastic (first seen on *Do Not Adjust Your Sets*) in a popular five-minute segment in the early days. After a successful first year it became a twice-weekly show featuring contemporary pop bands, sports items and serious news items. Bastable and Brady left the show in 1972 to be replaced by Mick Robertson and Douglas Rae. Jenny Hanley replaced Susan Stranks in 1974. This lineup remained until 1977, when Tommy Boyd replaced Rae. The show's mascot was Murgatroyd Magpie, and the theme tune (played by the Spencer Davis Group) was based around the old children's nursery rhyme "One for sorrow, Two for joy, Three for a Girl and Four for a boy, Five for Silver, Six for Gold, Seven is a secret never to be told, Eight's a wish and Nine's a kiss, Ten is a bird that you must not miss". ITV 1968-80.

Maid Marian and Her Merry Men Kate Lonergan (Maid Marian), Wayne Morris (Robin Hood), Tony Robinson (Sheriff of Nottingham), Danny John-Jules (Barrington), Howard Lew Lewis (Rabies), Mike Edmonds (Little Ron), Forbes Collins (King John), Mark Billingham (Gary), David Lloyd (Graeme). Created and written by Tony Robinson. Children's multi award-winning comedy series with a feminist spin on the Robin Hood legend. In this offering, Robin Hood (known as Robin of Islington) is an ineffectual wimp, whereas the formidable idealist Marian is the true leader of the resistance against the evil monarch King John. Marian terrorises the forest-dwelling peasants into following her commands as she plots to rob from the rich to feed the poor. But, courageous and capable though she is, her plans rarely turn out as she envisages, being derailed either by her naive idealism or the sheer incompetence of the mentally challenged nincompoops who comprise her Merry Men, including Rabies, Barrington (a Rastafarian) and the appropriately diminutive Little Ron. BBC1 1989-90; 1993-94.

Maigret Rupert Davies (Insp Jules Maigret), Ewen Solon (Lucas), Helen Shingler (Madame Henrietta Maigret). Belgian author Georges Simenon's French detective converted well to television and made a star of Davies. It is best-remembered for Ron Grainer's theme music (particularly the Paris street accordion) and the classic opening sequence of Maigret striking a match against a wall and the light flickering across his face as he lights his pipe. BBC 1960-63. Richard Harris took over the role for a 1988 Harlech television film and Michael Gambon for a 1992 ITV series.

Main Chance, The John Stride (David Main), Kate O'Mara (Julia Main), Anna Palk (Sarah Courtenay/Lady Radchester. Drama series created by Edmund Ward describing the story of a young successful Lawyer. ITV 1969-72; 1975.

Maisie Raine Pauline Quirke (DI Maisie Raine). Police drama following the exploits of Maisie Raine, the detective inspector of a plainclothes police unit. Maisie is as-tough-as-nails on the outside and in complete control professionally but her personal life is lacking stability. BBC1 1998-99.

Make Me A Supermodel The premise of the series was to find an undiscovered supermodel. From thousands of entrants the numbers were dwindled down to 12 finalists for the series-proper. Each week, a panel consisting of actress and model Rachel Hunter, agents Tandy Anderson and Sarah Leon, and international photographer Perou, dismissed one model until the winner was announced as sweet-natured student Alice Sinclair, who duly won the live catwalk show presented by Tess Daly and Dave Berry, and a contract with top UK modelling agency Select. A later documentary caught up with her after her first few months in the industry and also revisited some of the other memorable finalists. For the second series Dylan Jones, editor-in-chief of British GQ magazine, joined the judging panel and the competition included male models, the eventual winner being Albert Mordue. The live catwalk shows for series two were presented by Fearne Cotton on Fridays. *Five* 2005-06.

Making Out Margi Clarke (Queenie), Shirley Stelfox (Carol May), Tracie Bennett (Norma), Melanie Kilburn (Jill), Keith Allen (Rex), Brian Hibbard (Chunky), Gary Beadle (Simon), John Forgeham (Frankie), Don Henderson (Mr Beachcroft), Geoffrey Hughes (Dilk). Comedy drama series created by Franc Roddam and written by Debbie Horsfield. Set in a converted Manchester mill, the series mixed comedy and drama in its portrayal of the women who work on the factory floor at New Lyne Electronics, tackling the personal lives of the characters as well as wider issues of recession, redundancy and retrenchment as the factory goes through various crises and take-overs (the factory ultimately being known as Shangri-La Electronics). The music for the series was composed by New Order. BBC1 1989-91.

Mallens, The John Hallam (Thomas Mallen), John Duttine (Donald Radlet), Caroline Blakiston (Anna Brigmore), David Rintoul (Dick Mallen). Written by Jack Russell, based on Catherine Cookson's novels. Set in 19th century Northumberland, it follows the lively escapades of Thomas Mallen, who lives life to excess on his sprawling estate, High Banks Hall (filming actually took place in Dovedale, Derbyshire), despite the fact that he is seriously in debt to his banker. His son, who expects to inherit a fortune, is shocked to discover the truth, but then becomes part of an unfortunate turn of events. Donald Radlet is one of several illegitimate off-spring of Mallen from what basically boils down to rape. All of the offspring are identified by the white streak in their hair (The Mallen Streak). ITV 1979-80.

Man About the House Richard O'Sullivan (Robin Tripp), Paula Wilcox (Chrissy Plummer), Sally Thomsett (Jo), Brian Murphy (George Roper), Yootha Joyce (Mildred Roper), Dougie Fisher (Larry Simmons). Sitcom written by Johnnie Mortimer and Brian Cooke. Chrissy and Jo have a farewell party for their flatmate, who is moving out, now that she's engaged. The morning after the party, they find Robin in their bathtub, asleep. They need a new flatmate, and he needs a place to live, so it seems like a match made in heaven, and they invite him to move in. There's just one problem: Mr. and Mrs. Roper, the landlords who live downstairs! ITV 1973-76. Two spin-off series, *Robin's Nest* and *George and Mildred* followed.

Man Alive Long-running 50-minute documentary series, originally co-edited by Bill Morton and Desmond Wilcox (who doubled as the presenter). The theme often revolved around a topical concern, for instance the Northern Ireland problem, miner's strike, gay rights, healthcare; and endeavoured to find out what the man-on-the-street thought of these issues. Later presenters included Trevor Philpott, Esther Rantzen, John Pitman and Harold Williamson. The series was axed in 1982 by Will Wyatt, incoming Head of Documentaries, who replaced it with the more streamlined *Forty Minutes* BBC2 1965-82.

Man at the Top Kenneth Haigh (Joe Lampton). Drama series based on John Braine's novel, *Room at the Top*. A 1973 feature film of the same name followed the series. ITV 1970-72.

Man From Interpol, The Richard Wyler (Commander Anthony Smith), John Longden (Supt Mercer). Drama series following the exploits of an agent of the International Police Organisation. ITV 1960-61.

Man in a Suitcase Richard Bradford (McGill). A disgraced American CIA agent with only a gun and suitcase to his name begins to operate as a private detective, charging $500 per day plus expenses. ITV 1967-68.

Man in Room 17, The Richard Vernon (Edward Oldenshaw), Michael Aldridge (Ian Dimmock), Denholm Elliott (Imlac Defraits), Willoughby Goddard (Sir Geoffrey Norton). Criminologists working in an office (the room 17 of the title) near the Houses of Parliament (Dept of Social Research) help police solve rather difficult crimes. The novelty of the series was that Oldenshaw and his colleagues never needed to leave their office in order to resolve cases, preferring to spend their time playing the Japanese board game of Go. They simply provided their prognosis and left the police to do the cleaning up. Sir Anthony Hopkins made his first screen appearance in the episode, *A Minor Operation*, in 1965. ITV 1965-66. A spin-off series, *The Fellows (Late of Room 17)*, was broadcast on ITV in 1967. This series saw the pair relocated to All Saints College, Cambridge University, where they were appointed to the Peel Research Fellowship. Their research was "to investigate the general proposition that, in a period of rapid social change, the nature of crime (and therefore criminals) would change." Their research led them into encounters with gangland boss Alec Spindoe (Ray McAnally), who eventually ended up behind bars thanks (unknown to Spindoe) to psychological pressure from Oldenshaw. See also entry for *Spindoe*.

Man of the World Craig Stevens (Michael Strait), Tracy Reed (Maggie MacFarlane). Drama series created by Leslie Harris. A world-renowned photographer's international assignments lead him into investigating mysterious goings-on amongst the rich and famous. The series' theme music was by Henry Mancini. ITV 1962-63. See also *The Sentimental Agent*

Man O Man Prime-time version of the ITV show *God's Gift*. Hosted by Chris Tarrant, one of his co-hostesses in series 1 was Nell McAndrew (then working under the name Tracey McAndrew). Typical rounds included: Hunk in Trunks, Kissing, Dancing, Humour, Singing, True or False and Prince Charming. ITV 1996-99

Manageress, The Cherie Lunghi (Gabriella Benson), Camilla Power (young Gabriella), Warren Clarke (Martin Fisher), Mark McGann (Gary Halliwell), Stephen Tompkinson (Jim Wilson). When the wife of the Italian owner of a struggling second division football club is appointed club manager, the press and players are sceptical. C4 1989-90.

Manhunt Alfred Lynch (Jimmy Porter), Peter Barkworth (Vincent), Cyd Hayman (Nina), Maggie Fitzgibbon (Adelaide), Robert Hardy (Abwehr Sgt Gratz), Philip Madoc (Lutzig). Heroic Tales of French Resistance during WW2. Theme Tune: Beethoven's Fifth Symphony. ITV 1970.

Many Wives of Patrick, The Patrick Cargill (Patrick Woodford), Ursula Howells (Elizabeth Woodford), Elspet Gray (Nancy Grenville), Wendy Williams (Josephine Fabre), Bridget Armstrong (Laura Ryder), Lorna Dallas (Betsy Vanderhoof), Elizabeth Counsell (Helen Woodford), Robin Parkinson (Harold Randall), Wendy Padbury (Amanda Woodford), Julie Dawn Cole (Madeleine Woodford). Sitcom devised by William G Stewart, Patrick Cargill and Colin Frewin. Patrick Woodford, the proprietor of the Woodford Gallery Antiques Emporium in Bond Street, drives a yellow Rolls Royce and lives in luxury in Chester Square, Belgravia. He also has five living former wives, Elizabeth, Nancy, Laura, Betsy and Josephine; and present incumbent Helen; and nine children, Amanda and Madeleine appearing most prominently. Johnny Johnston wrote the theme music. ITV 1976-78.

Mapp & Lucia Prunella Scales (Elizabeth Mapp / Mapp-Flint), Geraldine McEwan (Emmeline 'Lucia' Lucas). A series based on the books by E. F. Benson as adapted by Gerald Savory. Set in the English countryside of the 1930s. The Mapp and Lucia of the title are two middle aged women who exist in a permanent state of one-upmanship with each other. Always trying to have the last word or to arrange the better garden party. Lucia, from Riseholme in the Cotswolds, decides to rent Elizabeth's house (Mallards) in the Sussex resort of Tilling-on-Sea and the battle soon commences. C4 1985-86.

March of the Peasants John Quilley (John Shandwick), Harold Jamieson (Earl of Salisbury), Gawn Grainger (King Richard II), Andre Van Gyseghem (Sir Martin Shandwick), Andrew Cruickshank (Sir William Walworth), Leo McKern (Josh Grober), Michael Godfrey (Black Ned), Michael Aldridge (Wat Tyler). Four-part historic children's series set in 1381, detailing events of the Peasant's Revolt. BBC 1952.

Marion and Geoff Rob Brydon (Keith Barret). Ten-minute comedic episodes written by Rob Brydon and Hugo Blick. Keith is a minicab driver who keeps a video diary in his cab and recalls happier days with wife Marion and children Rhys and Alun (his 'little smashers') but more painfully he describes the fateful barbecue whereupon his wife's affair with her boss Geoff is revealed. (the barbecue is given its own 50-minute special in 2001, *A Small Summer Part*, with Steve Coogan as Geoff and Tracy-Ann Oberman as Marion.). In the second series (now given a 30-minute slot) Keith is depicted as a chauffeur. BBC2 2000-03. *The Keith Barret Show* was a spin-off spoof chat show that aired on BBC2 in 2004.

Mark Saber Donald Gray (Mark Saber), Michael Balfour (Barny O'Keefe – Saber's assistant series 1), Neil Macallum (Pete Paulson - Saber's assistant series 2), Robert Arden (Bob Page - Saber's assistant series 3), Gordon Tanner (Larry Nelson - Saber's assistant series 4), Gary Thorne (Eddie Welles (Saber's assistant series 5), Diane Decker (Stevie - Saber's secretary), Theresa Thorne (Judy - Saber's secretary in the final series), Jennifer Jayne (Ann Somers - Saber's occasional love interest). The cases of a one-armed Scotland Yard detective turned private eye. In 1959 the series title was changed to *Saber of London*. The series was in fact a re-run of an American series, *The Vize*. ITV 1957-61.

Marriage Lines Richard Briars (George Starling), Prunella Scales (Kate Starling). Sitcom written by Richard Waring. Recently married George and Kate Starling live in a flat in Earl's Court, London. George is a lowly-paid clerk and Kate is now a housewife, although she was formerly his secretary. The humour is based around the newly-acquired domestic upheaval that wedlock sometimes brings. BBC1 1963-66.

Married Single Other Ralf Little (Clint), Miranda Raison (Abbey), Dean Lennox Kelly (Dickie), Amanda Abbington (Babs), Lucy Davis (Lillie), Shaun Dooley (Eddie), Tom Kane (Harry), Jack Scanlon (Joe), Gina Yashere (Flo), Leila Mimmack (Gina), Neil Bell (Mr Connelly), Oona Chaplin (Fabiana), Edward Franklin (Eros). Comedy drama created by Peter Souter, based on the lives of six people who are either married, single or other, all living in suburban Leeds. The title characters are Dickie and Babs (Married) Clint and Abbey (Single) and Lillie and Eddie (Other). The theme tune *Find My Way Back Home* is by Priscilla Ahn. ITV 2010

Marty Marty Feldman sketch show vehicle written by John Cleese, Tim Brooke-Taylor, Michael Palin, Terry Jones, Graham Chapman, Terry Gilliam, Peter Dickinson, Barry Took and Marty himself. Marty was joined by John Junkin, Tim Brooke-Taylor, Roland MacLeod and Mary Miller for many of the sketches. Famous sketches included Marty playing a gnome who goes to his bank to see about getting a mortgage on his toadstool and another where Marty plays a henpecked husband who makes repeated nocturnal assignations with beautiful girls right under his wife's nose! The first series won the Golden Rose Award at Montreux and the second series was retitled, *It's Marty*. BBC 1968-69. In 1971-72 Marty co-wrote and co-starred with Spike Milligan in *The Marty Feldman Comedy Machine* on ITV and in 1974 a short-lived BBC Sketch show *Marty Back Together Again*.

Mary Queen of Shops Mary Portas (b. 28 May 1960, Rickmansworth, Hertfordshire) is an English retail adviser. In each episode she is on a mission to help turn around the fortunes of struggling fashion boutiques in various locations in the UK. The third series in 2009 saw Mary turn her attention to charity shops and was renamed appropriately *Mary Queen of Charity Shops*. BBC 2 2007-10. Mary moved to Channel 4 in 2011, and created a new series *Mary Portas: Secret Shopper* which saw her using different disguises and secret filming to reveal bad customer service in UK shops. Her latest series for the channel, Mary Queen of Frocks was an observational documentary that followed Mary as she launched her own shop (*Mary & House of Fraser*) aimed at 40+ women with UK retailer House of Fraser. In May 2011, Mary was appointed by the UK Government to lead an independent review into the future of the high street. Her report, published on 13 December 2011, painted a bleak picture of town centre shops unless drastic action was taken.

Mary Whitehouse Experience, The Irreverent topical sketch show starring the double acts of Hugh Dennis & Steve Punt, and Rob Newman & David Baddiel. The series began on BBC Radio 1 in 1989 and contributors included Nick Hancock, Jo Brand, Jack Dee, Mark Thomas and Mark Hurst. The subsequent television series was along the lines of *The Idiot Weekly, Price 2d*, where topical themes of the day would be recreated in comedy sketch form. The show's most memorable sketch was History Today - a discussion programme presented by an unnamed elderly professor (Baddiel) and Professor F. J. Lewis, Emeritus Professor of History at All Souls College, Oxford (Newman). The programme begins as a conventional show but soon deteriorates into a puerile argument. This sketch spawned the show's most popular catchphrase "...That's you, that is". BBC Radio 1 1989-90; BBC2 1991-92.

Masterchef Annual knockout cookery contest. Three contestants take part each week and devise a menu to a limited budget which was then tasted and reviewed by presenter Loyd Grossman and a pair of celebrity guests. The amateur chefs would wait patiently while the judges 'deliberated, cogitated and digested'. Gary Rhodes took over from Grossman when the series transferred to BBC2 for a season in 2001. After four years the show was revived under the name of *Masterchef Goes Large* (although reverting back to its former name in 2008). In the new version, there are two permanent judges, John Torode and Gregg Wallace though neither addresses the viewer directly and the voiceover is performed by India Fisher. Masterchef winners: 1990 - Joan Bunting, 1991 - Sue Lawrence, 1992 - Vanessa Binns, 1993 - Derek Johns, 1994 - Gerry Goldwyre, 1995 - Marion Macfarlane, 1996 - Neil Haidar, 1997 - Julie Friend, 1999 - Lloyd Burgess, 2000 - Marjorie Lang, 2001 - Rosa Baden-Powell, 2005 - Thomasina Miers, 2006 - Peter Bayless, 2007 - Steven Wallis, 2008 - James Nathan, 2009 - Mat Follas, 2010 - Dhruv Baker, 2011 – Tim Anderson. BBC1 1990-2000; BBC2 2001; BBC1 2005- . *Junior Masterchef*, presented by Loyd Grossman throughout its run from 1994-2000 was for 10-15 year-olds and was revived in 2007 with Nadia Sawalha as host. Another spin-off is *Celebrity Masterchef* won by Matt Dawson (2006), Nadia Sawalha (2007), Liz McClarnon (2008), Jayne Middlemiss (2009), Lisa Faulkner (2010) and Phil Vickery (2011). *Masterchef the Professionals* began in 2008 with Greg Wallace and India Fisher reprising their roles but John Torode being replaced by Michel Roux Jr. *MasterChef: The Professionals* winners: 2008 - Derek Johnstone, 2009 - Steve Groves, 2010 – Claire Lara, 2011 – Ash Mair. In 2011, MasterChef Ireland, began on RTÉ Two, narrated by Lorraine Pilkington and judged by Dylan McGrath and Nick Munier.

Mastermind Iconic quiz show created by Bill Wright. The idea for the show came from Bill's experiences while held as a Prisoner of War during WWII. He was often asked for his "Name", "Rank" and "Number" (the only information he was obliged to give under the Geneva Convention). He decided to change this to "Name", "Occupation" and "Specialised Subject" for the show. To add to the military feel of the occasion a theme tune, aptly entitled Approaching Menace by Neil Richardson, was featured. The first-ever edition of *Mastermind* was recorded at Liverpool University and aired on BBC1 in 1972. The show was hosted by 43-year-old former journalist Magnus Magnusson, a formidable Scot of Icelandic parentage, who quickly became known as the doyen of all quizmasters and presided over affairs for the full 25-year run. The series was initially thought too high-brow for mainstream audiences and was given a late night slot. When it was tried in peak-time it clocked up such a huge audience that it remained there. Four contenders (occasionally five) were grilled for two minutes on the specialist subject of his or her choice, and then, in Round Two, for a further two minutes on their general knowledge. In later series the contenders would take their turn in reverse order according to their score in the specialist round. The production of the show was quite a logistical nightmare as the cathedrals, castles, town halls and places of learning used as venues all had their various recording problems to overcome. Producers included Bill Wright, Roger MacKay, Peter Massey, Penelope Cowell Doe, and David Mitchell. The main researcher was Dee Wallace. The full list of winners: Nancy Wilkinson (1972), Patricia Owen (1973), Elizabeth Horrocks (1974), John Hart (1975), Roger Pritchard (1976), Sir David Hunt (1977), Rosemary James (1978), Dr Philip Jenkins (1979), Fred Housego (1980), Leslie Grout (1981), No contest but Sir David Hunt won a 'champion of champions' competition of the previous ten years (1982), Christopher Hughes (1983), Margaret Harris (1984), Ian Meadows (1985), Jennifer Keaveney (1986), Dr Jeremy Bradbrooke (1987), David Beamish (1988), Mary-Elizabeth Raw (1989), David Edwards (1990), Stephen Allen (1991), Steve Williams (1992), Gavin Fuller (1993), George Davidson (1994), Kevin Ashman (1995), Richard Sturch (1996), Anne Ashurst (1997). The last programme was filmed at St Magnus Cathedral in Orkney. In 1979 Magnus hosted a special Mastermind International programme involving quiz show winners from around the world (including UK Mastermind champions David Hunt and Rosemary James), which was won by the Irish contender John Mulcahy. Following this, International Mastermind (hosted by Huw Evans) ran for five series from 1979-83. *Mastermind* was transferred to BBC Radio 4 between 1998 and 2000, hosted by Peter Snow. The three winners were Robert Gibson (1998), Christopher Carter (1999) and Stephen Follows (2000). In 2001, the television series was revived on The Discovery Channel, with well-known chat show host Clive Anderson as quizmaster, and a new interactive feature which allowed viewers at home to 'play along'. Former BBC host Magnus Magnusson presented the trophy to winner Michael Penrice. Mastermind soon returned to the BBC, this time on BBC2, for a Celebrity Special broadcast in 2002. July 2003 saw the first full series proper on the BBC in six years, with a new quizmaster - John Humphrys, best known as presenter of the Radio Four political and current affairs programme, *Today*. The first winner under the Humphrys' regime was Andy Page (2003) followed by Shaun Wallace, the first black winner (2004), Pat Gibson (2005), Geoff Thomas (2006), David Clark (2008), Nancy Dickman (2009), Jesse Honey (2010) and Ian Bayley (2011). In 2006 a Welsh-language version of Mastermind (*Mastermind Cymru*) was screened on S4C with Panorama presenter Betsan Powys as host. Emyr Rhys Jones was the first winner, Siôn Aled the second in 2007, Seren Jones the third in 2008 and Joseff Glyn Owen the fourth in 2009. In 2003 another spin-off *Junior Mastermind* began with Daniel Parker, Robin Geddes, Domhnall Ryan, Robert Stutter and David Verghese becoming the annual champions. One-off *Celebrity Mastermind* winners have included Jonathan Meades, Shaun Williamson, Bill Oddie, Stephen Fry, Edwina Currie, Matt Allwright, Steve Rider, Hugh Quarshie, Tom Ward, Jeremy Beadle, Monty Don, Graham Le Saux, Paul Ross, Iain Banks, Steven Pinder, Edward Stourton, Todd Carty, Iain Lee, Dave Spikey, Peter Serafinowicz, Jan Ravens, Steve Cram, Spoony and Kaye Adams. In August 2010 the first-ever Champion of Champions competition was held, 16 previous winners reliving their experience across four daily heats, the winners being invited back for the Friday final. The winner was Pat Gibson. In 2011, an Irish version of Mastermind began on TV3, hosted by Nora Owen, a former Irish Fine Gael politician. See also *Sports Mastermind*.

Match of the Day The long-running football showcase began on 22 August 1964 with a match between Liverpool and Arsenal in which Roger Hunt scored the first goal shown, his Liverpool team winning 3-2. Kenneth Wolstenholme was the chief commentator for many years and others have included David Coleman, Wally Barnes, John Motson, Barry Davies, Idwal Robling, Tony Gubba, Alan Parry, Gerald Sinstadt, Clive Tyldesley and Jon Champion. Presenters have included Kenneth Wolstenholme, David Coleman, Jimmy Hill, Bob Wilson, Des Lynam and, since 1999, Gary Lineker (with expert analysis from Alan Hansen and Mark Lawrenson). In April 2007 Jacqui Oatley made history by becoming the first female commentator on *Match of the Day*. The *Match of the Day* theme tune was composed for the show by Barry Stoller. The music that accompanies Match of the Day's Goal of the Month feature is an instrumental version of Ashes, by Embrace. BBC 1964-. In 2004, a spin-off program, Match of the Day 2, was launched on Sundays on BBC2, showing highlights of Sunday matches and further reaction to Saturday's action. It was presented by Adrian Chiles until 2010 when Colin Murray replaced him.

Material Girl Lenora Crichlow (Ali Redcliffe - a young up-and-coming fashion designer), Dervla Kirwan (Davina Bailey - the current hot designer who is protective of her position), Michael Landes (Marco Keriliak - Ali's business partner). Six-part drama series Set in the fashion world, inspired by the book *Fashion Babylon*. BBC1 2010.

Max and Paddy's Road To Nowhere. See *Peter Kay's Phoenix Nights*.

May to December Anton Rodgers (Alec Callender), Eve Matheson and Lesley Dunlop (Zoe Angell / Callender), Ashley Jensen (Rosie McConnachy). Sitcom written by Paul A. Mendelson. 53-year-old Alec Callendar, a Pinner solicitor who is a massive *Perry Mason* fan, meets and falls in love with Zoe Angell, a woman half his age. BBC1 1989-94.

Maybury Patrick Stewart (Dr Edward Roebuck), Yvonne Brewster (Sister Barbara Bowley), Michael Melia (Barry Donovan), Stuart Fox (Fred Tarkey), Shane Connaughton (Father Ryan), Kenneth Branagh (Robert Clyde Moffat), Floella Benjamin (Kayreen). Medical drama series, several episodes written by Anthony Minghella. Set in the psychiatric unit of Maybury General Hospital, the stories revolve around the case histories of Psychiatric Consultant Edward Roebuck. BBC2 1981-83.

Mayor of Casterbridge, The Alan Bates (Michael Henchard), Janet Maw (Elizabeth Jane Henchard), Jack Galloway (Donald Farfrae), Anna Massey (Lucetta Farfrae). Seven-part mini-series based on the classic Thomas Hardy novel. BBC1 1978.

McCallum John Hannah (Dr Iain McCallum), Gerard Murphy (DI Bracken), Suzanna Hamilton (Joanna Sparkes), Zara Turner (Dr Angela Moloney), Richard Moore (Sir/Professor Paddy Penfold), James Saxon (Dr Fuzzy Brightons), Richard O'Callaghan (Bobby Sykes), Alex Walkinshaw (DC Small), Hugo Speer (Dr Aidan Petit), Charlotte Randle (Clare Gilmore), Jason Barry (Rory O'Neil), Nathaniel Parker (Dr Dan Gallagher), Eva Pope (Dr Charley Fielding). Created by Stuart Hepburn. Forensic pathologist Dr. Iain McCallum, a working-class Scotsman, works in the morgue of St. Patrick's Hospital in London's East End. He and his colleagues find and interpret forensic evidence, using their skills to ensure that the guilty are punished and the innocent go free. After the second series McCallum and Moloney leave for California and are replaced by Dr Dan Gallagher and Dr Charley Fielding, although the name *McCallum* was kept. ITV 1995-98.

McFlannels, The First broadcast on 18 March 1939 on the Scottish Home Service, *The McFlannels* was a radio serial based on a working-class Glasgow family who all had surnames of different fabrics. Molly Weir played 'Poison' Ivy McTweed (who had a raucous laugh). Written by Helen W Pryde, *The McFlannels* was produced by Archie P Lee. For the best part of 20 years *The McFlannels* was staple Saturday evening entertainment before making the move to BBC Scottish television for a series in 1958. It starred real-life husband and wife Russell Hunter and Marjorie Thomson, plus Colette O'Neil and Clarke Tait. Rikki Fulton played his first prominent comedy role in the series as a Church of Scotland Minister, the Reverend David McCrepe.

Me and My Girl Richard O'Sullivan (Simon Harrap), Joanne Ridley (Samantha Harrap), Joan Sanderson (Nell Cresset), Tim Brooke-Taylor (Derek Yates). Sitcom created by Keith Leonard and John Kane, revolving around the relationship between Simon Harrap, an executive at the Eyecatchers Advertising Agency, in Covent Garden, and his teenage daughter, Samantha. The theme song was performed by Peter Skellern. ITV 1984-88.

Me Mammy Milo O'Shea (Bunjy Kennefick), Anna Manahan (Mrs Kennefick), Yootha Joyce (Miss Argyll), David Kelly (Cousin Enda), Ray McAnally (Father Patrick). Sitcom written by Hugh Leonard. The adventures of Irishman, Bunjy Kennefick, a top executive with a London company. His jet-set bachelor lifestyle of fast cars and faster women makes him the envy of his friends - until, that is, they meet his ever-present catholic mother. Her old-fashioned, traditional Irish morals, coupled with a devotion to her son's spiritual development, severely dent most of his more lecherous plans, especially where his regular girlfriend and secretary, the smouldering Miss Argyll, is concerned. BBC1 1969-71.

Me Too! Jane McCarry (Granny Murray), Rosemary Amoani (Dr Juno – owns a dog named Sampson), Donald Cameron (Mickey John - the school teacher), Matthew McVarish (Raymond - the train buffet car manager), Elaine McKenzie Ellis (Tina - the taxicab driver), Samantha Seager (Bobby - the bus cleaner), Ross Allan (Nurse Hendry), Chris McCausland (Rudi - the market trader), Joyce Galugbo (Chuck - Ferryboat band musician), Michelle Rodley (Louie - Ferryboat band musician). Drama series for four- to six-year-olds about the parallel lives of parents at work and their children who stay with warm-hearted minder Granny Murray. Part of the CBeebies diet of programmes. BBC2 2006-

Medics Tom Baker (Prof. Geoffrey Hoyt), Sue Johnston (Ruth Parry). Medical drama series focusing on the staff at the fictitious Henry Park Hospital. ITV 1990-95.

Meet the Huggetts Radio comedy series with Jack Warner as Joe Huggett and Kathleen Harrison as his wife, Ethel. It ran from 1953-61 and was a spin-off from the cinema's popular comedy drama of 1947, *Holiday Camp*, which had introduced the salt-of-the-earth Huggett Family.

Meet the Wife Thora Hird (Thora Blacklock), Freddie Frinton (Freddie Blacklock). Sitcom written by Ronald Wolfe and Ronald Chesney, stemming from a Comedy Playhouse Production called 'The Bed'. BBC1 1964-66.

Men Behaving Badly Martin Clunes (Gary Strang), Neil Morrissey (Tony Smart), Leslie Ash (Deborah), Caroline Quentin (Dorothy), Ian Lindsay (George), Valerie Minifie (Anthea). Sitcom written by Simon Nye. The first series featured Harry Enfield as Dermot but Neil Morrisey replaced him for Series 2. A pair of thirty-somethings, Gary and Tony cheerily indulge in their beer-swilling existence, talking out their fantasies - sexual and otherwise - and trying to avoid commitment or hard work by opening up another can or by heading off to their rooms for a spot of private pleasure with a top-shelf magazine. A glamorous blonde, Deborah, owns the flat above Gary's, and is well aware that Tony fancies her, but she usually decides that being single is preferable to being Tony's. Gary has an on-off girlfriend, Dorothy, a cynical hospital nurse who mostly loves Gary but would certainly like him more if his mental age advanced beyond 14. Usually embroiled in the lads' messy pranks, the girls despair over these male specimens but, perhaps sensing that they'd be no better off elsewhere, stay put and try to make the best of a bad situation. Gary owns a small security firm, where his colleagues are George and Anthea; Tony doesn't work. The status quo shifted for the 1997 series when Dorothy and Gary almost made it to the altar, and Tony finally eroded Deborah's resistance and became her boyfriend (a relationship that was already foundering by the 1997 Christmas special). The three-part series over Christmas 1998 brought the show to an end, with Gary closing down his business, Tony almost losing Deborah after taking a job as a postman - and turning into a bore in the process, and, most significantly, Dorothy giving birth to Gary's baby, whose name, was left in the melting pot. Although originally an ITV series, by Series 3 it was screened on BBC1. ITV 1992; BBC1 1994-98.

Menace Menace was a series of twenty-three plays running to seventy-five-minutes which found their basis in the aspects, perceptions and representations of menace in various settings in and around the villages, townships and cities of the United Kingdom. The cream of British acting talent took part in various episodes, notably Patricia Hodge in a play entitled, *Valentine* (1973), as Charmian – her very first screen role. BBC1 1970-73

Merlin Colin Morgan (Merlin), Prince / King Arthur Pendragon (Bradley James), Anthony Head (Uther Pendragon), Angel Coulby (Guinevere 'Gwen'), Katie McGrath (Morgana), Richard Wilson (Gaius), John Hurt (voice of the Great Dragon), Frank Finlay (Anhora), Michelle Ryan (Nimueh), Santiago Cabrera (Lancelot), Asa Butterfield (Mordred), Will Mellor (Valiant), Nathaniel Parker (Lord Agravaine), Colin Salmon (Aglain), Kenneth Cranham (Aulfric), Charles Dance (Aredian), Pauline Collins (Alice), Clive Russell (King Bayard), John Lynch (Balinor), Sarah Parish (Lady Catrina), Mackenzie Crook (Cedric / Cornelius Sigan), Tom Ellis (King Cenred), Katie Moore (Drea), Julian Rhind-Tutt (Edwin Muirden), Georgia King (Elena), Donald Sumpter (The Fisher King), Laura Donnelly (Freya), Michael Cronin (Geoffrey of Monmouth), Harry Melling (Gilli), Miriam Margolyes (Grunhilda), Eoin Macken (Sir Gwaine), Eve Myles (Lady Helen of Mora / Mary Collins), Caroline Faber (Hunith - Merlin's mother), Emilia Fox (Morgause), Adrian Lester (Myror), Mark Lewis Jones (King Olaf), Fintan McKeown (King Odin), Sean Francis (Sir Pellinor), Tom Hopper (Sir Percival), Holliday Grainger (Sophia), Karl Johnson (Taliesin), Cal Macaninch (Tauren), Rick English (Tristan De Bois the Black Knight - voiced by Christopher Fairbank), Georgia Moffett (Lady Vivian), Joe Dempsie (William), Alex Price (Sir William of Daira), Alice Patten (Ygraine Pendragon). Adventure series based loosely on the Arthurian legends but telling the story of Merlin in his youth. BBC1 2008-

Metal Mickey Ashley Knight (Ken Wilberforce), Irene Handl (Granny), Michael Stainton (Father), Georgina Melville (Mother), Lucinda Bateson (Haley), Lola Young (Janey), Gary Shail (Steve), Metal Mickey (voiced by Johnny Edward). Children's comedy written by Colin Bostock-Smith and produced by former Monkees legend Mickey Dolenz. Metal Mickey is a five-feet-tall rotund robot with red eyes, blue ears and a dazzling display of multi-coloured lights and buttons on his chest control-panel. He is the invention of Ken Wilberforce, a precocious science boffin who has assembled the automaton to assist with the household chores. But all is not well with the metallic man's workings and he just won't do what's expected of him. Mickey means well, but wreaks havoc and soon shows alarming tendencies towards summoning aliens, transporting people back in time and, worst of all, pop music. (He trundles around saying 'boogie boogie boogie' half the day and eating Atomic Thunderbusters (which had the appearance of lemon bonbons) the other half. The extended Wilberforce family - four children, parents and dear old Granny - are the victims of Mickey's antics. ITV 1980-83.

Michael McIntyre's Comedy Roadshow Stand-up comedy series hosted by comedian Michael McIntyre from different venues around the United Kingdom. Each one of the 12 episodes to-date have featured a routine from Michael, followed by three other comedians before the headline act; which have been: Rhod Gilbert, Jason Manford, Shappi Khorsandi, Sean Lock, Patrick Kielty, Al Murray, Kevin Bridges, Sarah Millican, John Bishop, Tommy Tiernan, Noel Fielding and Ardal O'Hanlon. BBC1 2009-

Mick and Montmerency See entry for Charlie Drake in the comedy section. ITV 1955-58.

Mickey Dunne Dinsdale Landen (Mickey Dunne). This 14-episode drama series made a star of Landen as the cockney chancer Mickey Dunne always on the lookout for the main chance. BBC1 1967.

Middlemarch Juliet Aubrey (Dorothea Brooke), Douglas Hodge (Dr Tertius Lydgate), Robert Hardy (Arthur Brooke), Peter Jeffrey (Bulstrode), Patrick Malahide (Rev. Edward Casaubon), Elizabeth Spriggs (Mrs. Cadwallader), Jacqueline Tong (Mrs Vincy), Michael Hordern (Peter Featherstone). Adapted from the George Eliot classic of the same name, the plot centers on the socially conscious, but naive Dorothea Brooke, whose disastrous match to the pedantic Rev. Edward Casaubon sets in motion a chain of events that will change the face of the fictional English town of Middlemarch forever. BBC1 1994.

Midnight Is A Place Simon Gipps-Kent (Lucas Bell), David Collings (Julian Oakapple), Maxine Gordon (Anne Marie), Erik Chitty (Gabriel Towzer), Ron Moody (Gudgeon). Drama series about two children who are the wards of a cantankerously unloving uncle who owns a rug factory that has brutal working conditions. Things take a turn for the worst when the Uncle, maddened by the fear of bill and tax collectors, sets fire to his own home to prevent its seizure and dies in the process. This leaves the children with no home or guardian. Now the two must struggle to survive on the streets of London. ITV 1977-78.

Midsomer Murders John Nettles (DCI Tom Barnaby), Daniel Casey (DS Gavin Troy), John Hopkins (DS Dan Scott), Jason Hughes (Detective Constable Ben Jones), Jane Wymark (Joyce Barnaby), Kirsty Dillon (DC Gail Stephens), Barry Jackson (Pathologist George Bullard), Laura Howard (Cully Barnaby), Neil Dudgeon (DCI John Barnaby), Toby Jones (Pathologist Dan Peterson). Based on the novels of Caroline Graham. Based in the town of Causton, a veteran DCI and his young sergeant investigate murders around the regional community of Midsomer (a fictional English county). Dan Scott replaced Sgt Troy as Barnaby's sidekick in the second episode of Series 7, shown early in 2004 and was himself replaced by DC Jones from the first episode of Series 9, in 2005. In early 2011 the series was involved in controversy when Brian True-May, the executive producer, was suspended for claiming that the show was "the last bastion of Englishness" and asserting that ethnic minorities had no place in the fictional village. ITV 1997-

Midweek BBC current affairs programme which replaced *24 Hours* in 1972 and was itself replaced by a revamped *Tonight* in 1975. BBC1 1972-75

Mighty Boosh, The Julian Barratt (Howard Moon), Noel Fielding (Vince Noir), Matt Berry (Dixon Bainbridge), Rich Fulcher (Bob Fossil), Michael Fielding (Naboo), Dave Brown (Naboo). Surreal sitcom written and performed by Barratt and Fielding. Two zookeepers, Howard and Vince, work at the Zooniverse, a rather run-down zoo, owned by Dixon Bainbridge and run by a frustrated militarian American Bob Fossil. The lads may end up in the Arctic tundra, Australian desert or dodging the grim reaper in Hell, but they always manage to get back to the zoo before the end of the show. *The Mighty Boosh* began as a stage show in 1998 and came to our screens via a six-episode 2001 Radio 4 series. A 2004 pilot episode and the series-proper was subsequently screened on BBC3 before transferring to BBC2 later in the year and running until 2007.

Mike Bassett: Manager Ricky Tomlinson (MikeBassett), Amanda Redman (Karine Bassett), Steve Edge (Doddsy), Adam Tedder (Laszlo Vig), Kobna Holdbrook-Smith (Carlton Dawes), Richard Bennett (Wrighty). Six-part comedy drama series created by John R. Smith and Rob Sprackling as a follow-up to the film *Mike Bassett: England Manager*. The plot continues after Mike took England to the semi-finals of the 2002 World Cup although his fortunes take a turn for the worse. The team fails to qualify for the 2004 European Championships and after an ignominious defeat by Liechtenstein, Mike is sacked. Three unproductive spells at Newcastle, Norwich and Colchester had Mike on the brink of retirement before he is offered the manager's job at his father's old club, Wirral County F.C. ITV 2005

Milkshake Channel 5 (Five) early morning programming strand, aimed at children 2 to 7 years old, broadcast on weekdays from 6am to 9am and on weekends from 7am to 10am since 1997. The original in-vision continuity presenters were Konnie Huq and Lucy Alexander. Former presenters were Eddie Matthews, Gavin Inskip, Dave Payne, Hannah Williams, Andrew McEwan and Kate McIntyre. Current presenters include Kemi Majeks, Beth Evans, Jen Pringle, Derek Moran, Amy Thompson and the main presenter Naomi Wilkinson. Current programmes include *The Adventures of Bottle Top Bill and His Best Friend Corky, Bert and Ernie's Great Adventures, Ben and Holly's Little Kingdom, Chiro and Friends, Ebb and Flo, Elmo's World, Family, Fifi and the Flowertots, Fireman Sam, Funky Valley, Gerald McBoing Boing, Hana's Helpline, Harry and His Bucket Full of DinosaursIgam Ogam, Little Lodgers, Little Princess, Make Way for Noddy, Milkshake! Musicbox, The Milkshake! Show, The*

Milky and Shake Show, Mio Mao, Mist: Sheepdog Tales, The Mr. Men Show, Olivia Peppa Pig, Pocoyo, Roary the Racing Car, Thomas and Friends and *The WotWots*. Past programmes include *A House That's Just Like Yours, Angels of Jarm, Anytime Tales, Babar, Bagpuss, Barney & Friends, Beachcomber Bay, Bear in the Big Blue House, Big School, Bird Bath, Captain Power and the Soldiers of the Future, Clangers, Collecting Things, Dappledown Farm, Demolition Dad, Dig and Dug With Daisy, Eric Carle Stories, Fat Dog Mendoza, Franklin, Franny's Feet, Funky Town, George Shrinks, Happy Monsters, Havakazoo, Hi-5, Ivor the Engine, Jane and the Dragon, Jay Jay the Jet Plane, Kablam, Knight Rider, The Loggerheads, Max Steel, Mr. Men and Little Miss, Miss Spider's Sunny Patch Friends, Muppet Babies, Noggin the Nog, Oswald, The Powerpuff Girls, PLAY, Redwall, Roobarb and Custard Too, Rolie Polie Olie, Round the Twist, Rupert Bear, Sailor Sid, Sandy and Mr Flapper, The Secret of Eel Island, The Singing Kettle, Softies, Stickin' Around, The Save-Ums, Tickle, Patch and Friends, Titch, The Adventures of Tintin, What-a-Mess, Where in the World is Carmen Sandiego?, Where on Earth is Carmen Sandiego?, Wimzie's House.*

Million Pound Drop Live, The Hosted by Davina McCall, this quiz show has aired every now and again since May 2010 and usually for approximately ten-day runs. Contestants start the game with a million pounds and risk money in £25,000 denominations on multiple-choice questions in order to stand a chance of answering the final even-chance jackpot question for the amount they have managed to keep hold of. C4 2010-

Mind of Mr. J.G. Reeder, The Hugh Burden (J.G. Reeder), Willoughby Goddard (Sir Jason Toovey), Mona Bruce (Mrs Houchin). Detective series based on the Edgar Wallace character. Mr JG Reeder is a shabbily dressed, diffident civil servant who prefers a cup of tea and a slice of seed cake to a shot of something stronger. Despite his outward appearance he is a master detective with a razor sharp brain. In fact his mind gives him great cause for sorrow. He has, he claims, a criminal mind which allows him insight into motive and method denied to other men. Reeder's boss, Sir Jason Toovey, is the head of the Department of Public Prosecutions. ITV 1969-71.

Mind Your Language Barry Evans (Jeremy Brown), Francoise Pascal (Danielle Favre), George Camiller (Giovanni Cupello), Pik-Sen-Lim (Chung Su-Lee), Dino Shafeek (Ali Nadim), Jamila Massey (Jamila Ranjha), Ricardo Montez (Juan Cervantes), Kevork Malikyan (Maximillian Papandrious), Gabor Vernon (Zoltan Szabo), Anna Bergman (Ingrid Svenson), Zara Nutley (Miss Courtney). Sitcom written by Vince Powell. Jeremy Brown is the teacher of an English evening class for foreign students whose ages ranged from twenties to pensionable. The comedy derived from misunderstandings, and with a class full of non-English speakers these were plentiful, whether Jeremy was protectively saving his students from trouble or finding himself the victim of their trivial pursuits. Problems also came courtesy of the frostily formidable college principal Miss Courtney, who, in best authoritarian sitcom style, always seemed to find Brown in compromising positions. ITV 1977-79; 1986.

Minder George Cole (Arthur Daly), Dennis Waterman (Terry McMann), Gary Webster (Ray Daley), Glynn Edwards (Dave), Patrick Malahide (DS Albert 'Charlie' Chisholm), Michael Povey (DC Jones), Peter Childs (Sgt Rycott). Comedy drama created by Leon Griffiths. Arthur Daly, a small-time conman, hires former boxer Terry McCann to be his minder, so Terry can protect him from other, small-time crooks. Arthur often hires Terry out to his dodgy associates, often putting the trusting minder in peril, and always exploiting him for all he is worth. The series was famous for its use of "Mockney", which sounded like Cockney slang but was made up by either George Cole or the scriptwriters. Some expressions became so well known they have since passed into the language, including "A nice little earner" (a profitable task), "'er indoors" (the wife), and "give him a little slap" (beat him up). In 1991 Gary Webster replaced Dennis Waterman in the role of Arthur's 'minder', playing Ray Daley, nephew of Arthur. The theme tune *I Could Be So Good For You* was sung by Dennis Waterman. ITV 1979-85; 1988-89; 1991-94. A short-lived *Five*

remake was shown in 2009 with Shane Richie taking over the George Cole role as Archie Daley, yet another nephew and Lex Shrapnel as Archie's 'minder' Jamie Cartwright. Glaswegian band, Attic Lights, supplied a version of the iconic theme tune.

Ministry of Mayhem CITV's successor to *SM:TV Live* was originally presented by Stephen Mulhern, Holly Willoughby and Michael Underwood, along with Ray Griffiths as "Ray", Peter Cocks as "The Doctor", and Laura Tilli and Jessica Tilli as "Tina and Gina" who supposedly answered phones. In January 2005 the show was renamed MoM and among its new characters were Scratch & Sniff (two hyenas played by Don Austen and John Eccleston) who were virtual recreations of their past characters-"Bro & Bro", the wolves, who they played on former Saturday Morning show *What's Up Doc?* between 1992 and 1995, and spin-off series *Wolf It* between 1993 and 1996. Scratch 'n' Sniff went on to present a comedy game show called *Scratch & Sniff's Den of Doom* for ITV in 2007. In January 2006 the Saturday morning show's name changed to *Holly and Stephen's Saturday Showdown*, reflecting the dual host's dominance since Michael Underwood's departure. ITV 2004-06.

Miranda Miranda Hart (Miranda), Patricia Hodge (Penny - Miranda's overbearing mother), Sarah Hadland (Stevie), Sally Phillips (Tilly), Katy Wix (Fanny), Tom Ellis (Gary), James Holmes (Clive – the waiter). Miranda is the proprietor of a joke shop run by her life-long friend Stevie Sutton. Tilly and Fanny are two old school friends who are more socially adept than Miranda. Gary Preston is the chef of the restaurant next door and also an old Uni friend of Miranda's whom she fancies. Much of the humour is based around the shop and the restaurant. BBC2 2009-See *Hyperdrive* and *Not Going Out*. See also Miranda's entry in the comedy section.

Misfit, The Ronald Fraser (Basil 'Badger' Allenby-Johnson), Simon Ward (Ted Allenby-Johnson), Susan Carpenter (Alicia Allenby-Johnson), Patrick Newell (Stanley Allenby-Johnson). Sitcom written by Roy Clarke. Badger returns from a colonial life in Malaya to an England he no longer recognises. ITV 1970-71.

Misleading Cases See A. P. Herbert's Misleading Cases

Miss Marple Joan Hickson (Miss Jane Marple), David Horovitz (DI/DCI Slack). The cases of Agatha Christie's celebrated female sleuth. BBC1 1984-92.

Mister Eleven Michelle Ryan (Saz), Sean Maguire (Dan), Adam Garcia (Alex), Denis Lawson (Len), Lynda Bellingham (Shirley), Olivia Coleman (Beth), Jocelyn Osorio (Alicia). Two-part romantic drama written by *Shameless* writer Amanda Coe. Award-winning actor Dev Patel had a minor role in the series, as a waiter. ITV 2009.

Mistress, The Felicity Kendall (Maxine), Jack Galloway and Peter McEnery (Luke Mansel), Jane Asher (Helen Mansel). Sitcom written by Carla Lane. Maxine manages a florist shop and is having an affair with Luke, whose wife, Helen, is unsuspecting. BBC2 1985-87.

Mistresses Sarah Parish (Katie Roden), Sharon Small (Trudi Malloy), Shelley Conn (Jessica Fraser), Orla Brady (Siobhan Dhillon). Drama series following the lives of four women and their involvement in an array of illicit and complex relationships. Written by Rachel Pole, Richard Warlow, Harriet Braun and Catrin Clarke. BBC1 2008-10

MIT: Murder Investigation Team Lindsey Coulson (DC Rosie MacManus), Steven Pacey (DCI Malcolm Savage), Samantha Spiro (DI Vivien Friend), Michael McKell (DS Trevor Hands0, Richard Hope (DS Danny Purvis), Meera Syal (DCI Anita Wishart), Will Mellor (DC Jed Griffiths), Vincenzo Pellegrino (Dr Fergus Gallagher), Diane Parish (DC Eva Sharpe). Spin-off from *The Bill* with regular cast members Lisa Maxwell (DI Samantha Nixon), Tony O'Callaghan (Sergeant Matthew Boyden), Nicola Alexis (PC Ruby Buxton) and Roberta Taylor (Inspector Gina Gold) making cameo appearances. ITV 2003-05

Mock The Week Topical panel game, hosted by Dara Ó Briain. Two teams of three (Frankie Boyle, Hugh Dennis and a guest panelist, against Russell Howard, Andy Parsons and a guest panellist) vie for points in the show often described as a cross between *Whose Line Is It Anyway*? and *Have I Got News For You*.

Rory Bremner was a regular panelist in Series 1 and 2. The show's theme music is "News of The World" by The Jam. BBC2 2005-

Mogul Ray Barrett (Peter Thornton), Geoffrey Keen (Brian Stead), Philip Latham (Willy Izard), Robert Hardy (Alec Stewart), Barry Foster (Robert Driscoll), Ronald Hines (Derek Prentice), Edward De Souza (Charles Grandmercy), Beryl Cooke (Miss Jenkins). Drama series created by John Elliot. Mogul International is a major oil company headed by managing director Brian Stead and his financial controller, Willy Izard. After the first series the action centred on the men in the field, principally, Peter Thornton and Alec Stewart. The title of the series was consequently changed to *The Troubleshooters* to reflect this move away from the boardroom dramas. BBC1 1965-72.

Moment of Truth Cilla Black hosted the show where each week, three families would get a chance to win fabulous prizes from Cilla's "Dream Directory". These would typically be cars, holidays, televisions and computers. Each member of the family would pick a prize that they wanted. However, to earn the prize, one member of the family, usually mum or dad but occasionally an older child, has to perform a very tricky task. They are given seven days to practice it, but when they arrive at the studio the next week they have one chance to get it right. ITV 1998-2001.

Monarch of the Glen Richard Briers (Hector Macdonald), Susan Hampshire (Molly MacDonald), Alastair Mackenzie (Archie MacDonald), Lloyd Owen (Paul Bowman-MacDonald), Lorraine Pilkington (Katrina Finlay), Alexander Morton (Golly Mackenzie), Julian Fellowes (Kilwillie), Angus Lennie (Badger). Drama series created by Michael Chaplin. Archie MacDonald, carving out a life for himself as a restaurateur in London, finds himself called back to his home in the Scottish Highlands to assume his role as The Laird of Glenbogle and attempts to get the 40,000-acre estate back on its feet. In 2003, Archie's half-brother Paul Bowman comes to Glenbogle, and becomes Laird of Glenbogle, whilst Archie and his new wife Lexie leave for New Zealand. BBC1 2000-05

Monarchy Presented by British academic David Starkey, charting the political and ideological history of the English monarchy (later British), from the Saxon period to modern times. C4 2004-07.

Monitor Arts magazine presented by Huw Weldon, who gave opportunities to a new generation of presenters and filmmakers, including Melvyn Bragg, Jonathan Miller, John Schlesinger, John Berger and Ken Russell. Russell contributed biopics of Elgar, Debussy, Rousseau and Bartok. Jonathan Miller took over as presenter for the final run. BBC1 1958-65.

Monocled Mutineer, The Paul McGann (Percy Toplis), Matthew Marsh (Charles Strange), Cherie Lunghi (Dorothy), Philip McGough (Woodhall), Nick Reding (Cruikshank). Drama series written by Alan Bleasdale (whose grandfather had died at Passchendaele) based on the novel by William Allison and John Fairley. The four-part drama tells the story of a World War One mutiny which took place at the Etaples Training Camp in northern France in 1917 on the eve of the Passchendaele battle. Following the mutiny the dashing Nottinghamshire miner Percy Toplis takes flight into the French hills, dressed as a British officer. He returns to England and embarks on a love affair with the beautiful young widow Dorothy, before being captured in the Lake District and 'executed' for his crimes by MI5 assassin Woodhall. The suggestion that deserters were executed by their own side (Cruikshank was shot for desertion) raised eyebrows in certain quarters. It remains uncertain how much of the story is factual. BBC1 1986.

Monsignor Renard John Thaw (Monsignor Augustine Renard), Joachim Paul Assböck (Unteroffizier Dieter Franz), John Axon (Sergeant Roger Duclos), Teresa Banham (Clara Baquet), Barbara Kellerman (Mme. Dufosse), Dominic Monaghan (Etienne Pierre Rollinger), Cheryl Campbell (Madeleine Claveau). Four-part mini-series set in the fictional village of St Jos-sur-Mer, close to Calais, focusing on the German occupation of France during WWII, through the eyes of a priest. ITV 2000

Monte Carlo Or Bust Three celebrity couples (Jack Dee and Ade Edmondson, in a VW camper van, Jodie Kidd and Julian Clary, in a Bentley convertible and Penny Smith and Rory McGrath, in a union jack bedecked Mini Cooper) hit the road on a mad-cap jaunt from London to Monte Carlo charged with collecting a total of three items that best represent the head, heart and stomach of each of the regions they pass through along the way. ITV 2010.

Monty Halls Born 5 November 1966, the former British Royal Marines officer graduated from the University of Plymouth with a First Class Honours degree in Marine Biology in 1999 and almost immediately became an explorer. On television he first became known when winning a Channel 4 series, *Superhuman*, in 2004. The following year he presented a nine-part TV series called *Great Ocean Adventures* for Channel 5. A second series of eight episodes was broadcast in 2007. He is best known for his BBC2 Great Escape series', *Monty Halls' Great Escape* (2009), *Monty Halls' Great Hebridean Escape* (2010) and *Monty Halls' Great Irish Escape* (2011) where he lived and worked in remote parts of the UK and Ireland with his dog and best friend Reuben.

Monty Python's Flying Circus Surreal sketches written by, and starring, Graham Chapman, John Cleese, Terry Gilliam, Eric Idle, Terry Jones and Michael Palin. Carol Cleveland supplied the glamour on occasion. Brought together by comedy writer Barry Took who had seen the various players in *At Last The 1948 Show*, *Do Not Adjust Your Set*, and *The Complete and Utter History of Britain*, the Python team had many strengths, mixing a goon-like surrealism with sharp and witty topical, and historical references, an understanding of continuity and symmetry, fantastic acting from the five main protagonists, and hilarious animations by Gilliam. Their seemingly aimless, stream-of-consciousness ideas and sketches were segued from one sketch to the next making it unnecessary to deliver the traditional punchline. Classic sketches include 'The Argument', wherein a man pays to argue; 'The Dead Parrot Sketch', where a dissatisfied customer seeks recompense from the pet-shop dealer who sold him a deceased Norwegian-blue; 'The Cheese Shop Sketch', where a man tries to buy cheese from a dedicated store that is nonetheless entirely devoid of the stuff (all three featuring Michael Palin and John Cleese), 'The Alan Whicker Sketch', where all five players impersonate the great roving reporter, and 'The Nudge-Nudge Sketch', where Eric Idle tries to sell naughty snaps to a straight-laced Terry Jones. The Four Yorkshiremen Sketch was in fact originally aired in *At Last The 1948 Show*. *Monty Python's Flying Circus* first aired on BBC1 between 5 October 1969 and 5 December 1974 in four series. The theme tune is *Liberty Bell March* by John Philip Sousa. See also individual entries in Comedy section.

Moody and Pegg Derek Waring (Roland Moody), Judy Cornwell (Daphne Pegg), Frances Bennett (Monica Bakewell), Tony Selby (Sid), Sheila Keith (Aunt Ethel), Peter Denyer (George), Adrienne Posta (Iris). Sitcom written by Donald Churchill and Julia Jones. Daphne Pegg walks out on her relationship with her boss in Bolton and relocates to London; newly divorced antiques dealer Roland Moody has also decided on a new start. What neither anticipates is that a shady estate agent has leased the same flat to both of them. ITV 1974-75

More Than Robbery Terence Morgan (Durbin), Helen Cherry (Norma Tredford). Six-part crime series with the two stars solving difficult cases. BBC 1958.

Morecambe and Wise Show See entry for Eric Morecambe in the comedy section.

Morgana Show, The Irreverent comedy sketch show written by Morgana Robinson (b. 21 June 1980) and James de Frond with additional material by Tom Davis and Terry Mynott who also act in some of the sketches. Other actors include Pippa Evans, Vas Blackwood, Paul Chan, Morgan Overton, Zack Morris and Ninette Finch. Morgana is seen as Cheryl Cole, Danni Minogue, Lady Gaga, Fearne Cotton, Boris Johnson and a host of fictional characters, notably Gilbert (see *The TNT Show*) and Madolynn (an alcoholic, seen-better-days Hollywood star). C4 2010-

Morgan's Boy Gareth Thomas (Morgan Thomas), Martyn Hesford (Lee Turner), Maxine Audley (Eileen Gregory). Eight-part drama series written by Alick Rowe. Lee Turner, a troubled boy from the big city goes to live with his Welsh hill farmer uncle Morgan, partly to escape trouble back home. The initial mutual hostility gives way to grudging respect on both sides, but external forces have other plans for both of them. BBC1 1984.

Morning Line, The Regular Saturday morning Channel 4 horse racing magazine with contributions from a panel of racing pundits including Mike Cattermole , Alastair Down, John Francome, Lesley Graham , Graham Goode , Richard Hoiles, Simon Holt,

Jim McGrath, John McCririck, Alice Plunkett, Emma Spencer, and Derek Thompson. Tanya Stevenson reports on the betting exchanges and bookmaker Barry Dennis has a weekly "Bismarck" (a favoured horse that he feels will sink without trace).

Mother Love Diana Rigg (Helena Vesey), James Wilby (Kit Vesey), David McCallum (Alex Vesey), Fiona Gillies (Angela), Isla Blair (Ruth). Four-part drama adaptation of Domini Taylor's novel by Andrew Davies. Helena Vesey loves her son, Kit, with an unnatural passion and when he announces his engagement to Angela, she begins a ruthless killing spree, disposing of anyone she sees as a barrier to her maternal love. Everyone and everything, from her ex-husband's (Alex) new wife (Ruth) to the family pet represents a target for this malicious and vengeful woman. Diana Rigg won a BAFTA for her role as the vengeful doting mother. BBC1 1989.

Mother Nature's Bloomers Roy Kinnear, Jean Boht, Colin Edwynn, Meg Johnson, Henry Livings. Surreal comedy series written by Leonard Barras in which the cast play various roles. BBC2 1979.

Motormouth Children's Saturday morning magazine mix of pop music, news reviews, games, phone-ins and cartoons which replaced *Get Fresh* and *No 73*. Presenters at various times included, Gaby Roslin, Neil Buchanan, Tony Gregory, Andrea Arnold, Julian Ballantyne, Caroline Hanson, Steve Johnson and Andy Crane. ITV 1988-92. *Motormouth* was succeeded by *What's Up Doc?*

Mountain Five hour-long episodes of Griff Rhys Jones travelling around Britain and scaling some of our greatest mountains. The five areas covered were, Snowdonia, North West Highlands, The Lakes, Central Scotland and the Pennines. BBC1 2007

Moviedrome Series where a cult movie was introduced and analysed before it was shown. Original presenter of *Moviedrome* was the so-called cult director Alex Cox, who strangely didn't choose the movies himself. In 1997 the show was reprised with movies chosen and introduced by Mark Cousins (known for his work at the Edinburgh Film Festival). BBC2 1988-94; 1997-2000.

Moving Wallpaper Ben Miller (Jonathan Pope), Sinead Keenan (Kelly Hawkins), Lucy Liemann (Samantha Phillips), Elizabeth Berrington (Mel Debrou), James Lance (Tom Warren), Dave Lamb (Carl Morris), Raquel Cassidy (Nancy Weeks), Sarah Hadland (Gillian McGovern), Alan Dale (Himself playing John), Kelly Brook (Herself playing Sam), Susie Amy (Herself playing Angela), Martine McCutcheon (Herself playing Susan), Jason Donovan (Himself playing Daniel), Hugo Speer (Himself playing Mark). Satirical comedy-drama series created by Tony Jordan and set in a TV production unit. The first of the two series concerned the production of a soap opera, *Echo Beach*, which actually followed in the slot after *Moving Wallpaper*. Following the axing of *Echo Beach* the second series was based around the production of a "zombie show" called *Renaissance*. The story revolves around manic producer, Jonathan Pope's attempts to hold together an assortment of egotistical writers and actors while simultaneously fighting off his ever-bitching boss. The title, "Moving Wallpaper", is a disparaging term applied to typically unimaginative TV shows portraying mindless images - as if staring at wallpaper! ITV 2008-09. See *Echo Beach*

Mr and Mrs Popular daytime gameshow where married couples were tested to see how much they knew about each other. The series was produced alternately by HTV and Border Television. Alan Taylor hosted the HTV show and Derek Batey those from Border. A Welsh language version, *Sion a Sian*, was the inspiration for the show. ITV 1969-88. The show was revived for cable television (UK Living) and entitled *The New Mr and Mrs* and was presented by Nino Firetto. In 1999 ITV again reprised the show with comedian Julian Clary presiding over a modern version where couples neither had to be married, nor indeed of different genders. Yet another ITV revamp took place in 2008. Hosted by Fern Britton and Phillip Schofield *All Star Mr & Mrs* consisted of three celebrities and their partners playing for a charity of their choice.

Mr Bean Rowan Atkinson's comic creation was written for television by Richard Curtis, Robin Driscoll and Atkinson himself. The opening credits show Mr. Bean being dropped from the heavens fully-grown promptly proving he has a complete ignorance of how to do the simplest of tasks. His classic symptom of dyspraxia gives him a certain innocence but makes him incredibly creative and he usually comes up with a solution to a problem that a smarter man would never think of. Driving around in a Mini with his faithful teddy bear, he also has a nasty habit of knocking over three-wheeled cars. In the rare moments of speech Mr Bean is seen to have a rather high-pitched staccato voice. The popularity of this series spawned a series of specials, cartoons and feature films. ITV 1990-95.

Mr Benn Children's animation series written and drawn by David McKee. The 13 episodes were narrated by Ray Brooks. Mr Benn lives at No. 52 Festive Road. He dresses as a regular city gent and pays irregular visits to a mysterious fancy dress shop, run by a mysterious fez-wearing shopkeeper. The changing room is more mysterious still, for once Mr Benn has put on one of the shopkeeper's costumes he finds himself stepping out into a fantasy land in which he is the star performer. Each time the land is different, in keeping with the costume Mr Benn has chosen and each time, problems are solved and situations sorted just before the shopkeeper mysteriously appears and directs Mr Benn through a magical portal, back to the changing room and the suburban world again. Was his experience for real? Mr Benn can't be sure, but after every adventure he always finds himself holding a memento from his trip. The 13 episodes were: The Red Knight, The Caveman, The Hunter, The Wizard, The Diver, The Cowboy, The Spaceman, The Clown, The Cook, The Zoo-Keeper, The Pirate, The Balloonist, The Magic Carpet. Originally shown as part of the *Watch With Mother* diet. BBC1 1972-73.

Mr Big Peter Jones (Eddie), Prunella Scales (Dolly), Ian Lavender (Ginger), Carol Hawkins (Norma), Ronald Fraser (Mr Oldenshaw). Peter Jones also wrote this popular comedy series that began in 1974 as a one-off Comedy Playhouse, before a further 13 episodes were commissioned in 1977. Eddie is a would-be mastermind who dreams of pulling off the ultimate crime, hence the theme song: "We're In The Money". He shares a house in East London with his wife and fellow thief 'Dolly'. BBC1 1974; 1977.

Mr Digby Darling Peter Jones (Roland Digby), Sheila Hancock (Thelma Teesdale). Sitcom written by Ken Hoare and Mike Sharland, reuniting Peter Jones and Sheila Hancock, two of the most popular characters from the hit sitcom *The Rag Trade*. Thelma Teesdale is the PA to Roland Digby, the PR manager for pesticide manufacturers Rid-O-Rat. She is totally devoted to him. From the time he arrives in the office in the morning until the time he leaves in the evening she caters for his every need; providing a cooked breakfast for him (in a stove hidden in his office filing cabinet), darning his socks and providing him with slippers so he can work in comfort. Thelma pulls out all the stops in the vain, and ultimately doomed, hope that he will respond to her advances. For Digby, the office becomes home-from-home and is a welcome escape from a domineering wife (the unseen Eleanor) and his three children. ITV 1969-71.

Mr Don and Mr George See *Absolutely*

Mr Majeika Stanley Baxter (Mr Majeika), Claire Sawyer (Melanie Brace-Girdle), Andrew Read (Thomas Grey), Roland MacLeod (Mr Potter), Pat Coombs (Flavia Jelley), Richard Murdoch (Worshipful Wizard), Fidelis Morgan (Bunty Brace-Girdle), Eve Ferret (Pam Bigmore), Christopher Ellison and Chris Mitchell (Ron Bigmore), Sanjiv Madan (Prince). Children's sitcom written by Jenny McDade, based on the Mr Majeika books of Humphrey Carpenter. Mr Majeika is an irrepressible wizard, sent to England (called 'Britland') from the planet Walpurgis by the Worshipful Wizard because he has failed his O-level sorcery exam for the seventeenth time. He drops into the sleepy village of Much Barty, finding a post at St Barty's School as Class Three's new form-teacher, where he quickly befriends two of the children, Melanie (daughter of Bunty Brace-Girdle, a busy-body local councillor) and Thomas (later replaced by an Asian boy, Prince).

Only they realise his ability to produce weird and wonderful sorcery. ITV 1988-90.

Mr Palfrey of Westminster Alec McCowen (Mr Palfrey), Caroline Blakiston (The Co-Ordinator), Clive Wood (Blair). 10-part spy drama. Mr. Palfrey is a meek and mild civil servant. He's also a spycatcher. Operating from a base in Westminster, his world embraces the shadowy halls of government, the offices and establishments in which enemies of the state and the unprincipled practitioners of internal politics lurk. His boss is the unnamed co-ordinator and his legwork is done by the vicious Blair. ITV 1984-85.

Mr Pastry Richard Hearne, an actor, acrobat and dancer invented this character, popular for over 20 yrs on television. See separate entry in the comedy section.

Mr Rose William Mervyn (Mr Rose), Donald Webster (John Halifax), Gillian Lewis (Drusilla Lamb), Jennifer Clulow (Jessica Dalton), Eric Woolfe (Robert Trent). Detective drama created by Philip Mackie. After receiving an inheritance from two maiden aunts, Charles Rose takes early retirement from the police force to live in a quiet little cottage in Eastbourne. Concentrating on writing his memoirs based on the many case papers that he had kept during his career on the force, he finds his past catching up with him. Mr Rose was soon on the scent of villainy once more although this time as a sleuth in civilian clothing. Aiding and abetting him in his Holmesian-like pursuits were his manservant, John Halifax, secretary Drusilla Lamb and, in the last series Jessica Dalton and Robert Trent. ITV 1967-68. See also *The Odd Man* and *It's Dark Outside*

Mrs Bradley Mysteries Diana Rigg (Mrs Adela Bradley), Neil Dudgeon (George Moody), Peter Davison (Insp Christmas). Detective drama series based on the novels of Gladys Mitchell. Thrice-divorced Mrs. Adela Bradley, along with her chauffeur George, solves mysteries in a variety of interesting places during the late 1920s. Following a 1998 pilot and four-episode first series, a second series was shown in 2003. In this series the 'tongue-in-chic' (sic) Bradley and sidekick George, crack cases at Mrs. B's old school, the circus, a haunted house, and the seaside resort where George's daughter is to marry a promising hotel clerk. Mrs. B. investigates with aplomb and frequent asides. At a performance of The Mikado, she complains: "Gilbert and Sullivan, I wish they'd never met." On a woman's change of hairstyle, she cautions: "Same old coiffure, husband secure. New style of hair, husband beware!" BBC1 2000; 2003.

Mrs Dale's Diary Long-running radio soap opera first broadcast on the Light Programme at 4pm on Monday 5 January 1948. The title character was Mary Dale (played by Ellis Powell until 1963 and then Jessie Matthews), a middle-class doctor's wife, who would begin each episode with a narrative along the lines of a diary entry. Mrs Dale lived with her husband Jim (played by Douglas Burbidge, James Dale and Charles Simon) and two children, Bob (played by Hugh Latimer, Leslie Heritage, Nicholas Parsons and Derek Hart) and Gwen (played by Virginia Hewitt, Joan Newell, Beryl Calder and Aline Waite), at Virginia Lodge in the Middlesex suburb of Parkwood Hill (later the stories were set in a town called Exton). Later in the series Bob and Gwen's spouses were Jenny (played by Julia Braddock, Shirley Dixon, Mary Steele and Sheila Sweet) and David Owen (played by Anthony James, Frank Partington, Gordon Morrison, John Spingett, Robin Lloyd and Lee Peters). Mrs. Dale's sister, Sally (played by Thelma Hughes and Margaret Ward), lived in Cheyne Walk, Chelsea, and ran a dress shop although she also had a country cottage complete with a housekeeper called Zenobia. There was also a char lady called Mrs. Morgan (played by Grace Allardyce) who subsequently married Mr. Maggs (played by Jack Howarth who later was to play Albert Tatlock in *Coronation Street*). Other characters included the grumpy neighbour Mrs Mountford (played by Vivienne Chatterton) who had a nervous companion called Miss Marchbanks and a parrot called Coco, along with a liking for chocolate cake; Mrs. Leathers who was a rather common Cockney (played by Hattie Jaques); Mrs. Freeman (or Mother-in-Law as Dr. Dale always used to call her - played by Courtney Hope and Dorothy Lane) who had a cat named Captain, and Monument the gardener (played by Charles Lamb). The scriptwriter for most of the run was Jonquil Anthony although she did collaborate with Ted Willis for much of the later series. The

series was the first to have an openly homosexual storyline when Sally's husband Richard Fulton was outed. Jonquil Antony based the character on Australian writer Patrick White. By the time the series ended on 25 April 1969, it had run for a total of 5531 episodes. The original theme music was played on the harp by Marie Goossens but this was updated by Ron Grainer when it was renamed *The Dales* in 1962, and favoured a flute melody. Comedians and caricaturists of the day picked up on Mrs Dale's catchphrase "I'm rather worried about Jim..." and rather aptly the last line of the last episode was "I shall always worry about Jim".

Mrs Merton and Malcolm Spin-off sitcom from *The Mrs Merton Show*. Craig Cash (Caroline's co-creator) played the child-like Malcolm (Mrs Merton's son) and Brian Murphy played pensioner Arthur Capstick. The sitcom highlighted the domestic life of the Mertons in Heaton Norris. BBC1 1999.

Mrs Merton Show, The Caroline Hook/Aherne (Mrs Dorothy Merton). Spoof chat-show hosted by the acerbically witted blue-rinsed bespectacled geriatric. BBC2 1995; BBC1 1996-98. See also separate entry in comedy section. The show produced a spin-off, *Mrs Merton and Malcolm*.

Mrs Thursday Kathleen Harrison (Alice Thursday), Hugh Manning (Richard B. Hunter). Comedy drama created by Ted Willis. A charlady inherits a fortune following the death of millionaire tycoon George Dunrich and is protected from unsavoury elements by the genial Richard Hunter. ITV 1966-67.

Much Binding in the Marsh BBC radio comedy show broadcast from 1944 to 1954, starring Kenneth Horne and Richard 'Stinker' Murdoch as senior staff in the fictional RAF station of Much Binding in the Marsh which eventually became a country club and finally a newspaper *The Weekly Bind*. Cast members included Sam Costa (famous for his catchphrase "Good morning Sir, was there something?"), Maurice Denham, Maureen Riscoe, Dora Bryan and Nicholas Parsons, all playing various characters. Musical interludes were provided by Stanley Black and the Dance Orchestra, and songs from Helen Hill. The show was briefly transferred to Radio Luxembourg between 1950 and 1951. The show was fondly remembered for its closing theme tune beginning "There's Much Binding in the Marsh…." before the ever-changing weekly topical lyrics along the lines of what had gone before in the show were comically performed.

Muck and Brass Mel Smith (Tom), Lindsay Duncan (Jean Torrode). Six-part drama following the determined fight of Tom Craig to reach the top of the property business in the fictional Midlands city of Slatterly. *Bullseye* host Jim Bowen made his acting debut in three episodes as Charles Sprowle, a crooked accountant. ITV 1982.

Muffin the Mule Muffin the Mule first appeared on television on 20 October 1946 on the BBC programme *Children's Hour*, presented by Annette Mills. The previously unnamed mule with the over-sized head was actually made 12 years earlier by Fred Tickner and was carefully stored, awaiting re-discovery and naming by Annette Mills, sister of actor John Mills. He quickly became a favourite with children across the nation and the BBC affectionately labelled him "the first ever star to be made by British Television". Muffin went from strength to strength, clumping around legs-a-kimbo on the piano top with Annette playing the music and Ann Hogarth standing on the piano to operate him from behind a partition. He initially used to perform alongside Crumpet the Clown but further sidekicks emerged as the shows went on, including a bossy penguin called Mr. Peregrine Esquire; a rather shy Louise the Lamb; Oswald the Ostrich (a slightly dim-witted bird inclined to "gape"); Willie the Worm; plus a genial minstrel puppet called Wally the Gog. There were many others including Peter the Pup; Poppy the Parrot; Grace the Giraffe; Hubert the Hippo; Katy the Kangaroo; Kirri the Kiwi; Monty the Monkey; Maurice and Doris the mice; Zebbie the Zebra; Sally the Sea-lion and Prudence and Primrose Kitten who were later rewarded with their own spin-off shows. BBC 1946-57. Muffin the Mule was revamped in September 2005 as part of the Cbeebies children's menu and immediately became one of the most popular programmes on children's television.

Multi-Coloured Swap Shop Saturday morning children's magazine show that subsequently regenerated more times than the good Doctor from Gallifrey. Hosted by Noel Edmonds and assisted by Maggie Philbin and Keith Chegwin, the running theme of the show was for children to have the facility to phone in to swap their belongings but the more popular parts of the show were the cartoons and pop music. The resident dinosaur was named Posh Paws and the unseen studio crane operator was Eric. BBC1 1976-82 (the show was simply called *Swap Shop* from 1980 onwards). In 1982 Mike Read took over the reins from Noel and the new revamped show was called *Saturday Superstore*.

Mumbai Calling Sanjeev Bhaskar (Kenny), Nitin Ganatra (Dev), Daisy Beaumont (Terri). Seven-part sitcom written by Sanjeev Bhaskar, Simon Blackwell, Colin Swash, Dan Gaster, Carl Carter, Tony Cooke, Nitin Ganatra and Allan McKeown. Kenny Gupta is a British-born Indian who is sent out to Mumbai to turn around Teknobable, a failing company being run by Dev Rajah - a manager more interested in chasing his female staff and using the centre for his own profitable side lines. The arrival of English business woman Terri Johnson, an assessor from London HQ, only adds to their problems. ITV 2009.

Murder Bag Raymond Francis (Det Supt. Tom Lockhart). The 'murder bag' of the title was the black forensic case shown in the opening sequence containing all manner of items to help Lockhart solve a murder. ITV 1957-59. See *Crime Sheet* and *No Hiding Place*.

Murder City Amanda Donohoe (DI Susan Alembic), Kris Marshall (DS Luke Stone), Geff Francis (DI Adrian Dumfries), Connor McIntyre (Frank Craven), Amber Agar (Dr. Anvar 'Annie' Parvez), Laura Main (DC Alison Bain), Tim Woodward (DCI Turner), Alexis Conran (Dr. Simon Dunne). Fast-moving detective drama sometimes stretching beyond the edge of credibility but always engrossing. ITV 2004-

Murder in Suburbia Caroline Catz (DI Kate 'Ash' Ashurst), Lisa Faulkner (DS Emma 'Scribbs' Scribbins), Jeremy Sheffield (DCI Sullivan), Glen Davies (Gallimore), Stuart Nurse (Dr. Weatherall). Detective drama series focusing on various murders in the fictional suburban England town of Middleford. ITV 2004-05.

Murder Most Famous Reality television show in which six celebrities faced the challenge of writing a crime fiction novel. The protagonists included *Gardeners' World* presenter Diarmuid Gavin, *Strictly Come Dancing* king Brendan Cole; one-time *Holby City* star Angela Griffin; ex-*Coronation Street* actress Sherrie Hewson; *Rogue Traders* host Matt Allwright; and former Sun editor Kelvin MacKenzie. Novelist Minette Walters was the judge and executioner. Sherrie Hewson was declared the winner. She won the opportunity to write her own crime fiction novel, published in 2009 by Pan Macmillan as one of their 'quick reads', part of the World Book Day celebrations. BBC 2 2008.

Murder Most Horrid Comedy anthology created by Paul Smith and starring Dawn French playing a different character in each episode (24 in all across four series), but one thing all the stories have in common is murder, and Dawn is always involved. Dawn's character either commits the crime, or in some unfortunately tragic but nevertheless still hilarious circumstances, she gets killed herself. BBC2 1991; 1994; 1996; 1999.

Murphy's Law James Nesbitt (DS Tommy Murphy). Drama series created by Colin Bateman. Murphy is a tough uncompromising undercover policeman whose family were taken hostage while in Northern Ireland. He was forced to make a choice; either carry a bomb and blow himself up in a local barracks, or have his daughter killed. He originally chose the first option but when he got to the barracks he couldn't go through with detonating a bomb that would kill two hundred people. When he got back to his house, he found that the terrorists had slit his daughter's throat while his wife had been forced to watch. He reflects on these events at intervals, and remarks that he received 'a nice medal' for 'saving' so many lives, but obviously still feels responsible for his daughter's death. BBC1 2001-07.

Music While You Work This daytime music programme was broadcast twice daily in the United Kingdom on the BBC General Forces Programme. It began in June 1940 during World War II to motivate production workers and consisted of a medley of non-stop popular music at an even tempo. For a period, a recorded version was rebroadcast in late evening for night-shift workers.

After the war, the broadcasts continued on the BBC Light Programme. The programme originally consisted of live orchestral performances of light music; pre-recorded material was introduced in 1963. It began and ended with *Calling All Workers* by Eric Coates. *Music While You Work* was discontinued in 1967 but revived for a week to mark the BBC's 60th anniversary in October 1982 and then as a regular part of Radio 2 from January 1983 to January 1984.

Mutual Friends Marc Warren (Martin Grantham), Alexander Armstrong (Patrick Turner), Alistair Petrie (Carl Cato), Keeley Hawes (Jen Grantham), Joshua Sarphie (Dan Grantham), Sarah Alexander (Liz), Claire Rushbrook (Leigh Cato), Emily Joyce (Sarah). Comedy drama series written by Richard Pinto and Anil Gupta. Martin has two best friends, Patrick and Carl, who couldn't be more different. One is an irresponsible, unreliable, feckless womaniser, and the other is dead! Martin also has a son, Dan, and is happily married to Jen. One day his best friend Carl throws himself under a train, setting off a disastrous sequence of events that will change Martin's life forever. Into this mess steps Patrick, a friend from way back. Patrick is everything Martin is not – glib, self-confident, popular and pathologically immature. He's the last person Martin needs in his life right now. Or is he? BBC1 2008.

My Big Fat Gypsy Wedding Series featuring the gypsy community in Britain today. Originally shown as a one-off documentary as part of the *Cutting Edge* series in February 2010, a further five episodes began in January 2011 under the series title *Big Fat Gypsy Weddings* and became the surprise hit of the winter's viewing with audience figures reaching eight million on occasion. The series has been criticised by the travelling community for misrepresenting them and at least one of the featured stars has subsequently admitted to playing-up to a stereotype for the cameras, however there has been no shortage of people coming forward to appear in subsequent series. C4 2010-

My Family Robert Lindsay (Ben Harper), Zoë Wanamaker (Susan Harper), Kris Marshall (Nick Harper), Daniela Denby-Ashe (Janey Harper), Gabriel Thomson (Michael Harper), Siobhan Hayes (Abi Harper), Keiron Self (Roger Bailey Jr), Rhodri Meilir (Alfie Butts), Rosemary Leach (Grace Riggs), Kevin Bishop (Stupid Brian), Tayler Marshall (Kenzo Harper), Penelope Wilton (Rosemary). Domestic comedy created by Fred Barron. Ben is a dentist who wishes that he'd become a doctor. He's married to the very organised and headstrong Susan, a tour guide who later works for an art gallery. They have three children Janey, a very self-centred young lady whose world revolves around high fashion and having a good time; Nick, a strange young man who can't hold down than a job for more than a day or two; and Michael, a computer genius with an interest in military matters. Young dentist Roger Bailey is a regular visitor to the Harper household in Chiswick. While Janey is away at Manchester University she becomes pregnant and later gives birth to Kenzo. The family is completed by Susan's niece Abi who, although gormless and clumsy, soon becomes the object of Roger's affections. BBC1 2000-

My Good Woman Leslie Crowther (Clive Gibbons), Sylvia Syms (Sylvia Gibbons), Keith Barron (Philip Broadmore), Glyn Houston (Bob Berris), Richard Wilson (Revd Martin Hooper). Sitcom following antiques dealer Clive Gibbons' tribulations as a charity widower, his wife, Sylvia, intent on supporting every good cause possible by means of jumble sales and auctions. ITV 1972-74.

My Hero Ardal O'Hanlon (George Sunday aka Thermoman), Emily Joyce (Janet Dawkins), Geraldine McNulty (Mrs Raven), Hugh Dennis (Dr Piers Crispin), Philip Whitchurch (Tyler), Lill Roughley (Ella Dawkins), Tim Wylton (Stanley Dawkins), Lou Hirsch (Arnie), Finlay Stroud (voice of Ollie). Sitcom concerning a mild-mannered shopkeeper, George Sunday, who, whenever danger threatens, changes into the superhero "Thermoman" and rushes off to save the world in a red and yellow lycra suit. George is really an alien from the planet Ultron and is 326-years-old. One day, Thermoman saves Janet Dawkins from certain death when she falls into the Grand Canyon. He tries to get to know her as George but things don't go to plan and he soon has to reveal to

Janet that he is really Thermoman. She accepts him anyway and the two end up living together. Eventually, they get married and after a six-day pregnancy Janet has a son (Ollie, who also has superpowers) and then a daughter. Janet works at a health centre for the egocentric Piers and alongside tactless receptionist Mrs Raven. Other characters include: Tyler (a Liverpudlian Ufologist), Arnie (George's fraudulent cousin, also from Ultron) and Janet's parents Stanley and Ella. James Dreyfus took over the role of Thermoman for the final series, on the premise that George loses his former human identity in a game of poker! BBC 1 2000-06.

My Kind of Music Game show hosted by Michael Barrymore. Three teams of two people competed over a series of rounds which showcased their musical knowledge and the singing ability of at least one of each pair of contestants. The second round questions were based around Michael's tour around the shopping malls of Britain "My Kind Of People" in which he invariably ended up singing along with one of the more humourous acts. The ultimate jackpot would be won by the identification of a fictional family of popstars, usually a father, mother, daughter and son. Paul Potts, who went on to win *Britain's Got Talent* appeared in one of the shows. ITV 1998-2002.

My Kind of People Michael Barrymore's tour of Britain's shopping malls in search of singing talent, which ranged from the sublime to the ridiculous. Susan Boyle was featured in one of the recordings. ITV 1995-2001.

My Place In The Sun See *A Place In The Sun*.

My Story In 2009, the BBC launched the 'My Story' competition to find the most remarkable true life stories in Britain. Altogether over 7,500 people sent in their stories and the 15 finalists were portrayed over five programmes, the winner having the chance to see their story become a published book. Presenters of the five shows included Maureen Lipman, Ronan Keating, Christine Bleakley, Jenny Colgan and George Alagiah. BBC1 2010.

My Wife Next Door John Alderton (George Bassett), Hannah Gordon (Suzy Bassett). Sitcom written by Richard Waring. A newly-divorced couple find themselves living next door to one another at Numbers 1 and 2 Copse Cottages, near Stoke Poges. The couple are clearly still in love but endeavour to maintain their independence. BBC1 1972.

Mystery and Imagination A British anthology series based on classic ghost stories and chillers from M. R. James, Edgar Allan Poe, Algernon Blackwood, Sheridan Le Fanu, Robert Louis Stevenson and others; later branching into feature-length teleplays of Dracula, Frankenstein and other famous novels. It was hosted by David Buck in the guise of Victorian adventurer Richard Beckett (who appeared in some of the stories). ITV 1966-70.

Naked Chef, The This was the first television series for celebrity chef James Trevor Oliver (born in Clavering, Essex, 27 May 1975). The title, devised by producer Patricia Llewellyn, was a reference to the simplicity of Oliver's recipes. *Oliver's Twist* (2002-) was a 52-episode spin-off from the series for airing outside the UK. Jamie is famous for his catchphrase "pukka", his Sainsbury adverts, his pop band, Scarlet Division, for which he plays drums, the unusual names of his two daughters Poppy Honey (born in March 2002) and Daisy Boo (born April 2003) by former model Juliette "Jools" Norton, and his pioneering efforts to bring change to the school meals system, chronicled in the series *Jamie's School Dinners*. BBC1 1998-99. See also *Jamie's American Road Show, Jamie's Great Escape, Jamie's Kitchen, Jamie's Chef, Jamie at home, Jamie's Fowl Dinners, Jamie's Ministry of Food* and *Jamie Saves Our Bacon*.

Naked Civil Servant, The John Hurt (Quentin Crisp). 90-minute dramatisation by Philip Mackie of Quentin Crisp's best-selling autobiography. It portrayed events in the life of an outspoken and overtly homosexual government employee and former art-school model from the 1920s to the mid-1970s. ITV 1975.

Naked Video Comedy sketch show written by, and starring, Gregor Fisher, Helen Lederer, Tony Roper, Andy Gray, Elaine C. Smith, Ron Bain, John Sparkes, Louise Beattie, Kate Donnelly and Jonathan Watson. The BBC Radio Scotland sketch comedy *Naked Radio* proved to be a popular part of the local schedule and was given a one-off airing by Radio 4 on 26 April 1982, and after further success on stage at the Edinburgh Festival Fringe, its producer Colin Gilbert managed to gain a national television slot on BBC2. Gregor Fisher's string-vested ne'er-do-well Rab C

Nesbitt was first unveiled to a national audience here, as was his other invention, the gormless Baldy Man (both subsequently given their own slots). Lederer performed her own monologues from a wine bar, and John Sparkes appeared as Welsh poet Siadwell (pronounced Shadwell). BBC2 1986-91.

Name That Toon Children's quiz show presented by Mark Speight, assisted by Marc Silk. In the first series, two teams of three from schools around the country battled it out to see who knew the most about cartoons. The winning team at the end of the series won a trip to Istanbul to see the Spice Girls in concert. The knockout element was dropped for the second series. ITV 1996-97

Name That Tune Musical quiz show originally hosted by Tom O'Connor (1983-84) and then Lionel Blair (1984-87). Two contestants would play four rounds **Melody Roulette** (sums of money decided by spinning a wheel and then naming a tune played by the resident orchestra), **Sing A Note** (Maggie Moone – originally Irish trio Sheeba – would sing more obscure parts of a song for the contestants to name the title), **Bid A Note** (where each contestant bid against each other to hear up to seven notes of a popular song played by Ronnie Price on the piano. This segment gave rise to the catchphrase "I'll name that tune in one" – usually meaning the contestant had guessed the song title from the clue given at the start of each bid), and **Golden Medley** (final buzzer round, featuring a succession of tunes from the orchestra and a 30-second countdown). The winner would then go on to play the prize tune and receive the jackpot accrued if they successfully named the tune. The series was almost a copy of the earlier *Spot the Tune* but in fact was first broadcast under the title *Name That Tune* as part of Tom O'Connor's variety show *Wednesday At Eight* between 1976 and 1978 which was rebranded as *London Night Out* (1978-83). ITV 1983-87. In 1997, the series was revived briefly on Channel 5 with Jools Holland as the host, and again in 2007 as part of *Vernon Kay's Gameshow Marathon* on ITV.

Nanny Wendy Craig (Barbara Gray / Taverner), Colin Douglas (Donald Gray), Patricia Hodge (Mrs Sackville), Anna Cropper (Mrs Rudd), David Burke (Sam Taverner). Drama series created by Wendy Craig, who submitted her proposal for the series to the BBC under the pseudonym Jonathan Marr because she was afraid that if her true identity was known, she would be dismissed as merely "an actress who thinks she can write". Nanny Barbara Gray looks after a series of children during war torn London. BBC1 1981-83.

Nathan Barley Nicholas Burns (Nathan Barley), Julian Barratt (Dan "Preacher Man" Ashcroft), Claire Keelan (Claire Ashcroft), Ben Whishaw (Pingu), Richard Ayoade (Ned Smanks), Spencer Brown (Rufus Onslatt), Rhys Thomas (Toby), Noel Fielding (Jones), David Hoyle aka "The Divine David" (Doug Rocket), Rupert Degas (Beer Gourd Man), Charlie Condou (Jonatton Yeah?). Sitcom written by Charlie Brooker and Chris Morris. Nathan Barley is a webmaster, guerrilla filmmaker, screenwriter, DJ and shit. Barley and his peers are often hired ahead of actual journalists, such as documentary film maker Claire Ashcroft, and her brother Dan, a jaded hack who, having written an article for his magazine entitled "The Rise of the Idiots", is disgusted to find that "the idiots" in question – Nathan and his contemporaries – have adopted him as their spiritual leader, failing to see that they are the very people he was criticising. Other recurring characters include the staff at Dan Ashcroft's magazine, *Sugar Ape*; chief editor Jonatton Yeah?, Ned Smanks and Rufus Onslatt, a pair of gormless graphic designers, Sasha the receptionist and the eccentric Doug Rocket, founder member of The Veryphonics (a parody of Dave Stewart of Eurythmics fame). C4 2005.

Nathaniel Titlark Bernard Miles (Nathaniel Titlark), Megs Jenkins (Series 1) and Maureen Pryor (Series 2) (Jessie Titlark). During the 1950s Bernard Miles created the rustic character Nathaniel Titlark who would tell outrageous stories "over the gate" and in 1956 this was developed into a TV sitcom featuring the country bumpkin of the title with his splendid way with words "They reckon that's the finest bit of sharp'nin' stone in 'ertfordshire. Mind you 'is old woman ain't no good; can't get no edge out of 'er" is a typical line. "I had a tidy good education", he claims; "I could read when I was 18- but, o' course, not to understand it" is another. BBC 1956-57.

National Lottery On 19 November 1994 the first-ever British National Lottery took place and was broadcast by the BBC in a show hosted by Noel Edmonds, assisted by Anthea Turner and Gordon Kennedy. Turner and Kennedy subsequently took over the hosting from the second week, visiting places of interest around the UK where the draw would take place (first venue was the Rhondda Heritage Park in South Wales) with a regular spot given to 'Mystic Meg' (real name Margaret Lake). Gordon Kennedy left the programme in summer 1995, and the draw gained a permanent home at BBC Television Centre. Anthea Turner left in summer 1996, to be replaced by Dale Winton (*In It To Win It*, 2002-), then Bob Monkhouse, Carol Smillie, Ulrika Jonsson (National Lottery Dreamworld), and by various one-off hosts during 1997. A Wednesday draw was added in early 1997, also hosted by Carol Smillie, and following a very similar format. At the same time, live coverage on radio transferred from Radio 1 to news station Radio 5. In 1998 the show became *The National Lottery: Big Ticket* and Anthea Turner returned as co-host with Patrick Kielty. The Lottery show has been seen in many guises since and presenters have included Terry Wogan, Bradley Walsh (*On Tour*), Brian Conley (*We've got Your Number*, 1999), Simon Mayo, and later, Philip Schofield (*Winning Lines*, 1999-2004), Eamonn Holmes (*Jet Set*, 2001-), Lulu and Terry Alderton (*Red Alert*,1999-2000), Des O'Connor and Suzi Perry (*On The Spot*, 2000), Ian Wright (*Wright Around the World*, 2003-05), Julian Clary (*Come and Have A Go If You Think You're Smart Enough*, 2005), Mark Durden-Smith (*Millionaire Manor*, 2005-06), Dermot O'Leary (Series 1 and 2) and Ben Shephard (Series 3 onwards) (*1 vs. 100*, 2006-), Jamie Theakston (*The People's Quiz*, 2007), Nick Knowles (*Who Dares Wins*, 2007, *Guesstimation*, 2008, and *Secret Fortune*, 2011), Tess Daly (*This Time Tomorrow*, 2008). Alan Dedicoat is the 'voice of the balls'. The Irish Lottery has followed a similar path although the current Saturday evening show on RTÉ 1, *The Winning Streak*, is the longest running lottery TV game show in Europe and regularly features among RTÉ's most popular programmes. In 2009, the National Lottery and TV3 began producing the Irish version of Deal Or No Deal, the first time a National Lottery game show has been produced outside RTÉ. As with *The Winning Streak*, the contestants become eligible by playing an associated scratch card game.

Nationwide News magazine covering current affairs, political discussion, consumer advice and light entertainment. The final BBC1 news bulletin from Alexandra Palace was read on the night of Friday 19 September 1969. Less than a fortnight earlier, Nationwide appeared for the first time - filling the early evening spot once occupied by *Tonight*. The aim was to exploit the BBC's powerful regional network - within a national framework. The programme began with a local news bulletin - before "going Nationwide", with Michael Barratt in the Lime Grove studio in London. Main presenters included Michael Barratt (1969-1977), Bob Wellings (1971-1980), Frank Bough (1972-1982), Sue Lawley (1973-1975, 1977-1983), Valerie Singleton (Consumer Unit 1973-1976 then main presenter 1976-1980), John Stapleton (Reporter 1975-1977 then main presenter 1977-1980), Hugh Scully (1980-1983), Sue Cook (1980-1983), Richard Kershaw (1980-1983), and David Dimbleby (1982). Regular features included Alan Titchmarsh's gardening tips, Richard Stilgoe performing a topical song, Susan Stranks taking a stroll down memory lane, and Des Lynam's sports round-up. BBC1 1969-83. See also *The One Show*.

Natural World The longest-running nature documentary series on British television began life as *The World About Us* on Sunday 3 December 1967, which also marked the first full evening of colour television in Britain. David Attenborough, at that time the Controller of BBC Two, commissioned the programme which became the first documentary series whose programmes ran to 50 minutes rather than the standard half-hour. This format has remained unchanged to the present day. The series title was altered to *The Natural World* in 1983 and then shortened to its current form in 2003. BBC2 1967-

Navy Lark, The Dennis Price (Lt Commander Price aka 'Number One' – Series 1), Leslie Phillips (Sub Lieutenant Phillips / Nato Rep / Naval Expenditure), Jon Pertwee (Chief Petty Officer Pertwee / Commander Weatherby / Vice-Admiral "Burbly" Burwasher / Vice Admiral Buttonshaw / The Master), Stephen Murray (Lt Commander Murray aka 'Number One' – Series 2-13), Richard Caldicot (Commander/ Captain 'Thunderguts' Povey), Ronnie Barker (Able Seaman Johnson / Lt Commander Stanton / Commander Bell / Lt Parfet / Lieutenant Queeg), Heather Chasen (Mrs. Ramona Povey / WRN Chasen / Lady Toddhunter-Brown / Rita Murray / Morpeth Goldstein / Natasha Snogitoff / Lady Quirk / Miss Simpkins / Lucy Doll), Tenniel Evans (Able Seaman / Leading Seaman Taffy Goldstein / Admiral Ffont-Bittocks / Sir Willoughby Toddhunter-Brown / Captain Hardcastle / Intelligence / The Sea Lord - Lord Quirk / Lt. Burkett / Shamus O'Ginsburg), Michael Bates (Able Seaman Ginger / Lt. Bates / Rear Admiral Ironbridge / Padre / Captain Ignatius Aloysius Atchison / Commander Shaw / Cuthbert Spinks / Pierre / Mr Proudfoot / Flag Lt Dingle / Lt Pike / Captain Atcherson / The Padre / Igor Astracarnovitch / Captain Come-up-from-the-ranks / Lt. Perregrin Pertwee / Nasa Colonel / Vice Admiral Ironbridge / Lt. Deacon / Gate Policeman), Judy Cornwell (WRN Cornwell), Janet Brown (WRN Brown / Mrs Crump), Laurie Wyman (Inspector Burt Tiddy / Ableseaman Tiddy / Captain Ormanroy). BBC Radio sitcom, produced by Alastair Scott Johnson and written by Laurie Wyman and George Evans, about life aboard a British Royal Navy frigate, HMS *Troutbridge*, based in HMNB Portsmouth, though in the first two series the ship and crew were stationed offshore at an unnamed location known simply as "The Island", which was later revealed to be owned by Lt Cdr Stanton. A typical episode consisted of the suave and sophisticated (and somewhat dim) Sub Lt Phillips, cunning Chief Petty Officer Pertwee and naive Lt. Murray attempting to extricate themselves from trouble they had created for themselves with the constant threat of being found out by their superior officer, Thunderguts Povey. Scenes frequently featured a string of eccentric characters, often played by Ronnie Barker and Tenniel Evans. The Republic of Potarneyland, a country situated somewhere on the Indian subcontinent, is featured in several episodes. *The Navy Lark* aired on the Light Programme (Radio 2 from 1967) between 1959 and 1976, across 13 series and 244 episodes. A feature film of the same name, based on the radio series, was made in 1959.

Nearest and Dearest Hylda Baker (Nellie Pledge), Jimmy Jewel (Eli Pledge), Madge Hindle (Lily), Edward Malin (Walter). Sitcom written by Vince Powell and Harry Driver. Upon the death of Joshua Pledge, a veteran pickle-magnate, his two unmarried middle-aged-plus children, Nellie and Eli, jointly inherit their father's assets: £9 17s 6d and Pledge's Purer Pickles Factory, with its decrepit ragbag staff, 12 tons of pickled onions, and stores of gherkins, cauliflower and beetroot. Endowed with the responsibility of keeping the concern afloat, the pair are hindered by the fact that they cannot abide each other's company - let alone the company they have to keep - and bicker constantly. Set in Colne, Lancashire, this North Country comedy worked well because of its strong scripts and the prowess of its two major stars, 4ft 10in battler Hylda Baker (Nellie), complete with her 'He knows, you know' catchphrase and armoury of double entendres and malapropisms, and veteran comic Jimmy Jewel, cast as a leering Lothario who inexplicably manages to pull all the blonde young beauties. Other characters include Nellie's cousin Lily and her bald-headed silent husband Walter who has a waterworks problem. The burning question is always 'has he been?' ITV 1968-73. See also *Not On your Nellie*.

Never Mind the Buzzcocks Pop music comedy quiz show with celebrity guest panellists. Presented by Mark Lamarr (replaced by Simon Amstell in 2006 and then various guest presenters from 2008) with regular team captains Sean Hughes (replaced by Bill Bailey in 2002 who himself was replaced by Noel Fielding in 2009) and Phil Jupitus. The title of the show is a play on the names of the Sex Pistols' *Never Mind the Bollocks* album, and punk band Buzzcocks. BBC2 1996-

Never Mind the Quality, Feel the Width John Bluthal (Emmanuel 'Manny' Cohen), Joe Lynch (Patrick Kelly). For 15 years, Irish-Catholic trousermaker Patrick Michael Kevin Aloysius Brendan Kelly has been working for Manny Cohen, a Jewish jacketmaker, in their back-street workroom in Whitechapel, in the East End of London. Then the two decide to combine forces and form a partnership, recognising that each requires the other's skill. Their religious differences provide the chief source of humour. ITV 1967-71.

Never the Twain Donald Sinden (Simon Peel), Windsor Davies (Oliver Smallbridge), Robin Kermode and Christopher Morris (David Peel), Julia Watson and Tacy Kneale (Lynn Smallbridge / Peel), Honor Blackman (Veronica Barton). Two antique dealers, with adjoining shops, are sworn enemies until the son of one marries the daughter of the other and they attempt to muster a relationship of convenience. ITV 1981-91.

New Avengers, The Joanna Lumley (Purdey), Gareth Hunt (Mike Gambit), Patrick MacNee (John Steed). ITV 1976-77. See *The Avengers*.

New Faces Talent show originally hosted by Derek Hobson. A variety of turns who had never appeared on television before were judged by a panel of talent spotters, usually a combination of celebrities and showbiz agents. They were marked out of 10 in various criteria with the highest scores moving on to semi-finals and finals. Regular judges included, in increasing scale of acerbity, Ed 'Stewpot' Stewart, Clifford Davis, Mickie Most, and the original 'Mr Nasty' Tony Hatch. The catchy theme tune *You're a Star, Superstar* was performed by Carl Wayne of The Move, its chorus being *You're a star, you're a star, lamé suit and a new guitar, And I know that you'll go far 'Cos you're a star.* Acts that were discovered on the show included Victoria Wood, Malandra Burrows, Les Dennis, Showaddywaddy, Lenny Henry, Jim Davidson, Roy Walker, and Marti Caine. The show was revived in 1986 and hosted by Marti Caine. It was set in a large theatre and the acts were judged from high up in a box, Nina Myscow reprising the Tony 'Hatchet' role but the audience ultimately deciding the result via a gigantic lightboard known as Spaghetti Junction, which lit up to a varying degree as the audience pushed buttons. The final was live and decided on by Marti going round all the ITV regions in a Eurovision Song contest style vote. ITV 1973-78; 1986-88. *New Faces* was also the title of a short-lived BBC talent show that began in the 1950s and was hosted by Irish comedian Dave Allen.

New Statesman, The Rik Mayall (Alan Beresford B'Stard), Terence Alexander (Sir Greville), Marsha Fitzalan (Sarah B'Stard), Michael Troughton (Piers Fletcher-Dervish), John Nettleton (Sir Stephen Baxter), Nick Stringer (Bob Crippen), Charles Gray (Roland Gidleigh-Park), Peter Sallis (Sidney Bliss), Steve Nallon (Mrs Thatcher), Johnny More (Neil Kinnock). Sitcom created by Laurence Marks and Maurice Gran. In May 1987, Alan Beresford B'Stard is elected - at the age of 31 - as the Conservative MP for the North Yorkshire constituency of Haltemprice. His majority of 26,738 is the largest in the House of Commons, a fact not unconnected to the head-on car crash involving his two principal election opponents, the Labour and SDP candidates, who were in hospital instead of on the hustings. To prevent the police from revealing that their cars had been tampered with, B'Stard promises to push through Parliament a bill enabling the boys in blue to pack pistols instead of truncheons. Thus lies the background to the vainglorious tenure of office of the most corrupt and obnoxious MP ever to grace the Commons. The theme music is the *Promenade* movement of Mussorgsky's *Pictures at an Exhibition*. ITV 1987-92.

New Tricks Amanda Redman (Sandra Pullman), Dennis Waterman (Ex-Det. Sgt. Gerry Standing), James Bolam (Ex-Det. Chief Insp. Jack Halford), Alun Armstrong (Ex-Det. Insp. Brian Lane), Susan Jameson (Esther Lane). New Tricks follows the antics of three retired cops recruited by Det. Superintendent Sandra Pullman to reinvestigate unsolved crimes as part of the Unsolved Crime and Open-Case Squad (UCOS). Dennis Waterman sings the theme tune "It's Alright", written by Mike Moran. BBC1 2003-

Newcomers, The Alan Browning (Ellis Cooper), Maggie Fitzgibbon (Vivienne Cooper), Judy Geeson (Maria Cooper), Gladys Henson (Gran Hamilton), Wendy Richard (Joyce Harker), Megs Jenkins (Mary Penrose), Beryl Cooke (Celia Stuart / Murray), Robin Bailey (Andrew Kerr), Jenny Agutter and Maggie Don (Kirsty Kerr), Conrad Phillips (Robert Malcolm), Jack Watling (Hugh Robertson), Deborah Watling (Julie Robertson). Twice-weekly soap opera created by Colin Morris, dealing with the subject of a London family, the Coopers, who moved to a housing estate in the fictional country town of Angleton. BBC1 1965-69.

News Richard Baker was the first newsreader to be heard on television, reading the BBC Television News on 5 July 1954. It was not until September 1955 that the first newsreader was seen on camera, Kenneth Kendall having the honour of being the first presenter to appear on television. Barbara Mandell was the first female news presenter when she read the ITV lunchtime news at noon, on the first full day of broadcasting, 23 September 1955. The first female BBC news presenter was Nan Winton, 20 June 1960. The first female newsreader on radio was Sheila Borrett on 21 August 1933. BBC newsreaders have included Michael Aspel, John Humphrys, John Simpson, Corbett Woodall, Bob Langley, John Edmunds, Richard Whitmore, Peter Woods, Andrew Harvey, Sue Lawley, Jan Leeming, Angela Rippon, Nicholas Witchell, Moira Stuart, Jill Dando, Huw Edwards, Sian Williams, Fiona Bruce and Sophie Raworth. ITV newsreaders have included Chris Chataway (the first), Reginald Bosanquet, Trevor McDonald, Pamela Armstrong, Fiona Armstrong, Carol Barnes and Tasmin Lucia Khan (nude pictures of her appeared in *The Sun* in August 2010). Tim Brinton, Martyn Lewis, Peter Sissons, Anna Ford and Julia Somerville have worked for both channels. Channel 5 news was launched by Kirsty Young in 1997. RTÉ news presenters have included Michael Murphy, Sharon Ní Bheoláin, Una O'Hagan, Aengus McGrianna, Mary Kennedy, Eileen Dunne, Bryan Dobson, Anne Doyle, Eamonn Lawlor, Áine Ní Fheinne, Kenn Hammond, John Finnerty, Anthony Murnane, Siún Nic Gearailt, Charles Mitchel, Maurice O'Doherty, Andy O'Mahony, and Seán Duignan. See also *News At Ten* and *Newsnight*.

News At Ten Introduced on 3rd July 1967, the ITN *News at Ten* broke new ground by introducing the dual newsreader system, which enabled late news items to be handed to the presenter who was not in vision at that moment, ready for insertion into the running order. It was scheduled to last just 13 weeks, but stayed on air for 32 years, finally ending (although returning on occasion between 2001 and 2004) on 5 March 1999. The original newscasters were Alastair Burnet and Andrew Gardner who were succeeded by such newscasting greats as Reginald Bosanquet, Gordon Honeycombe, Sandy Gall, Leonard Parkin, Ivor Mills, Peter Snow, Rory McPherson, Michael Nicholson, Alastair Stewart, John Suchet, Anna Ford, Jon Snow, Selina Scott, Nicholas Owen and Trevor McDonald, to mention but a few. In 1992, after 25 years, News at Ten dispensed with dual presentation, Trevor McDonald becoming the sole presenter. The theme music, composed by Johnny Pearson, is entitled *The Awakening*. The format was reintroduced for four nights a week in January 2008 with Sir Trevor McDonald as the co-presenter with Julie Etchingham and Mark Austin although he subsequently stood down later in the year. From 13 March 2009 the four nights was extended to include a Friday edition. Later in 2009 the famous opening graphic of Big Ben was dispensed with to make the programme less London-centric although the clock's distinctive chime remained.

News Huddlines, The See Roy Hudd's entry in the comedy section.

Newsnight News and current affairs programme originally presented by Peter Snow, Peter Hobday, Charles Wheeler and John Tusa, with Fran Morrison reading news bulletins and David Davies giving sport reports (later replaced by David Icke). Kirsty Wark, Jeremy Vine, Sue Cameron, John Simpson, James Cox, Huw Edwards, Gordon Brewer, Sarah Montague, Mark Urban, Martha Kearney, Gavin Esler and Emily Maitlis have all presented the programme more recently and undoubtedly the most famous presenter is Jeremy Paxman, a hard-hitting political interviewer. Perhaps the most memorable moment in the programme's history is when Paxman unsuccessfully pressed the then Home Secretary Michael Howard 14 times for an answer to the question, 'Did you threaten to overrule him?' referring to

Howard's dispute with Derek Lewis, the then Director General of the Prison Service. BBC2 1980-

Newsround News magazine aimed at the younger viewers. A six-week trial-run of *John Craven's Newsround* aired twice weekly from 4 April 1972, and by 1974 it was showing Monday to Thursday. After John left in 1989 the programme became known by its present title. Presenters have included, Richard Whitmore, Helen Rollason, Roger Finn, Krishnan Guru-Murthy, Julie Etchingham, Kate Sanderson, Lizo Mzimba, Adam Smyth, Rachel Horne, Adam Fleming, Lizzie Greenwood, Thalia Pellegrini, Laura Jones and Ellie Crisell. The current presenters are Sonali Shah and Ore Oduba with Ricky Boleto, Hayley Cutts and Leah Gooding assisting with reports. BBC 1972-

Nice Time Germaine Greer, Jonathan Routh, Kenny Everett and Sandra Gough starred in this wacky sketch show produced by future BBC Director-General John Birt. ITV 1968-69.

Nigel Slater See entry in miscellaneous section.

Night Fever Channel 5 celebrity karaoke programme hosted by Graham McPherson aka Suggs, with help from Will Mellor, Sara Cawood, Kieron Elliott and Danielle Nicholls. Also helping Suggs was Pop Monkey, who held the scores on cards in the shape of bananas and decided on the songs that would be sung on the show. Regular guest captains of the 'boys' and 'girls' teams included husband and wife pair Same Kane and Linda Lusardi. A popular regular guest was Shaun Williamson (Barry Evans on *Eastenders*) until the powers to be on *Eastenders* pulled the plug on his appearances. Channel 5 (now *Five*) 1997-2002.

Night Train to Surbiton Peter Jones (Matthew Pilbeam), Nicholas Parsons (Guy Bretherton). Six-part thriller series written by John T. Chapman. A quiet weekend away from the rat race for two businessmen turns out to be an adventure involving a disappearing corpse, a stolen briefcase and the plans of a devious arch-criminal. BBC 1965.

Nighty Night Julia Davis (Jill Tyrrell), Rebecca Front (Cathy), Angus Deayton (Don), Ruth Jones (Linda), Mark Gatiss (Glenn Bulb), Felicity Montagu (Sue Forks), Michael Fenton Stevens (Gordon Forks). Award-winning surreal comedy written by its star Julia Davis, first aired on BBC3 in 2004 before being shown on BBC1. Jill has a very unhealthy fascination with Don and will literally stop at nothing to attract his attention. The second series in 2005 was not as well-received as the first. Comedian Steve Coogan was an executive producer of the series.

1900 House, The As a social experiment, *The 1900 House* pitched a Somerset family (the Bowlers) back in time by asking them to live in an authentic Victorian home. The structure, standing at 50 Elliscombe Road, Charlton, appeared, from the outside, to be a typical London townhouse, but inside, it was quite a different story. All traces of the 20th century had been removed. The house had been fitted to appear and function just as it would have in the year 1900. There was no television, computer, or microwave oven. The Bowlers had to live without the benefit of central heating and electricity. The nine-part series followed the family's progress over the course of three months. C4 1999. See *The 1940s House*, and *The Edwardian Country House*.

1940s House, The Sequel to The 1900 House, this time concentrating on the Hymers from Yorkshire, living in a real house (17 Braemar Gardens, West Wickham, Kent) under wartime conditions. Their experience of rationing, blackouts, air-raids and day-to-day life was filmed and shown in the five-part series. C4 2001. See *The Edwardian Country House*

99p Challenge, The Spoof panel game written by Kevin Cecil, Andy Riley, Jon Holmes, and Tony Roche; originally broadcast on BBC Radio 4. Panellists are given silly tasks and are awarded pence for being funny. The player with the most money at the end of the show is given the chance to win 99p. The first series in 1998 was entitled, *King Stupid*, and was presented by William Vandyck. The subsequent four series, now renamed, 99p Challenge, were presented by Sue Perkins. Regular panellists include: Armando Iannucci, Simon Pegg, Peter Serafinowicz, Peter Baynham, Sue Perkins, Dave Green, Richard Herring, Mel Giedroyc, Sean Lock, Bill Bailey, Marcus Brigstocke, Miranda Hart, and Rob Rouse. BBC Radio 4 1998; 2000-04

99 – 1 Leslie Grantham (Mick Raynor), Robert Stephens (Commander Oakwood), Frances Tomelty (Commander Stone), Robert Carlyle (Detective Constable Trevor Prescott). Police drama series written by Barbara Cox, Peter Jukes and Terry Johnson. Maverick cop, Mick Raynor, infiltrates the interconnected networks of organized crime and corruption in Britain. His cover is close to the truth - a bent ex-policeman trying to get back at the force that abandoned him. In the first series he was answerable to Cmdr Oakwood and in the second series, the irrepressible Cmdr Stone. The series takes its title from the observation that police work is ninety-nine-per-cent boredom and one-per-cent terror. ITV 1994-95.

No Appointment Necessary Roy Kinnear (Alf Butler), Josephine Tewson (Penelope Marshall), Avril Angers (Beryl Armitage), Robert Dorning (Col. Marshall), Claire Faulconbridge (Sandra). Sitcom written by Peter Robinson and Hugh Stuckey. Alf Butler is a greengrocer who also has an 'interest' in a hairdressing salon. He has constant problems with the women who work for him. BBC1 1977.

No - That's Me Over Here! Ronnie Corbett (Ronnie), Rosemary Leach (Laura), Henry McGee (Henry), Jill Mai Meredith (Secretary), Ivor Dean (The Boss). Sitcom produced by Bill Hitchcock and Marty Feldman, with David Frost credited as executive producer (this term is sometimes given to an individual who ploughs money into the project but in this case Frost had the power to ensure a prime-time slot). Dressed sharply in his pin-striped suit, bowler hat, and with his briefcase, umbrella and copy of *The Times*, Ronnie commutes from suburbia into work each day on the train, together with his sniffy neighbour Henry who also works at the same place and vies for superiority. Laura is Ronnie's long-suffering wife. Barry Cryer, together with future Pythons Graham Chapman and Eric Idle, wrote the first series, Chapman and Cryer (along with Tim Brooke-Taylor) appearing in its final episode. Idle dropped out at this point and, after a second run, the programme lay dormant when Rediffusion lost its franchise. Two years later, however, LWT gave it another spin. ITV 1967-68; 1970. See also *Now Look Here* and its sequel *The Prince Of Denmark.*

No Hiding Place Raymond Francis (Det Chief Supt. Tom Lockhart), Johnny Briggs (Det Sgt Russell), Eric Lander (Det Sgt Harry Baxter). Police drama series with Raymond Francis reprising the role made famous in *Crimesheet* and *Murder Bag.* The enormous popularity of the series stemmed from the stiff-upper lipped Lockhart now having sidekicks in the guise of Sgt Baxter and then Sgt Russell whereas previously he had mostly worked alone. Eric Lander's portayal of Baxter was so popular he was given his own series, *Echo Four-Two.* The *No Hiding Place* theme tune performed by Ken Mackintosh and his Orchestra entered the charts in 1960. ITV 1959-67.

No Honestly John Alderton (Charles 'CD' Danby), Pauline Collins (Clara Burrell / Danby). Sitcom written by real-life man and wife Terence Brady and Charlotte Bingham (its two stars are also married in real-life). Charles Danby is an orphan-turned-actor of irregular employ who meets Clara - a debutante of ennobled parentage - at a Hampstead party. They begin a relationship and then marry. The premise of the series is that all of this took place ten years earlier, and each episode was seen in a flashback to those former, uncertain times, when the couple were not only younger but much more innocent. Consequently, each programme opened and closed with CD and Clara sitting together, in the present, talking directly to the viewer as they cast their minds back to bygone days. A decade on Clara has become a successful author of children's books about a character named Ollie the Otter and CD is a comic actor. The title song by Lynsey De Paul reached No 7 in the UK charts in 1974. ITV 1974-75. See also *Yes Honestly.*

No Place Like Home William Gaunt (Arthur Crabtree), Martin Clunes and Andrew Charleson (Nigel Crabtree) Patricia Garwood (Beryl), Stephen Watson (Paul Crabtree), Dee Sadler (Tracy Crabtree), Beverley Adams (Loraine Codd), Daniel Hill (Raymond Codd), Marcia Warren and Ann Penfold (Vera Botting), Michael Sharvell-Martin (Trevor Botting), Roger Martin

(Roger Duff). Sitcom written by Jon Watkins (later credited as John E. Watkins). When Arthur and Beryl Crabtree marry off their daughter Lorraine they are finally free of children, their three other offspring having already flown the nest. But their blissful liberty is short-lived because, almost immediately, financial and other crises cause Nigel, Tracy and Paul to move back home; soon afterwards, Lorraine has marital problems and she too returns. Her dolt of a husband, Raymond, desperate to patch things up, then becomes a regular visitor, as do the Crabtrees' neighbours Vera and Trevor Botting, so every last scrap of peace and tranquillity well and truly vanishes from Arthur and Beryl's lives. BBC1 1983-87.

No. 73 Sandi Toksvig (Ethel Davis), Andrea Arnold (Dawn Lodge), Nick Staverson (Harry Stern), Patrick Doyle (Percy Simmons), Neil Buchanan (Neil), Jeannie Crowther (Hazel Edwards), Richard Addison (Martin Edwards), Tony Aitken (Fred the Postman), Kim Goody (Kim), Nick Wilton (Tony Deal), Tony Hypolyte (Eazi), Kate Capstick (Maisie McConachie), Julian Callaghan (Jules), Nadia de Lemeny (Nadia), Richard Waites (Hamilton Dent). Children's Saturday morning light entertainment show. From the outside No. 73 looked like a tumbledown house, but once inside it was a different world. The house, in the south of England, was rented by an eccentric old lady called Ethel, who was like a fairy godmother to the children in the area. Each week she opened her door and was visited by superstars and famous personalities who provided a madcap spectacle of music, competitions and fun. Ethel was assisted in looking after her guests by her nephew Harry and her boyfriend Percy. Following Sandi Toksvig's departure in 1986 the show took on a different guise and a spin-off series, *Sunday at No. 73*, was added. The following year an outdoor wild west set was introduced and by 1988 the show's title had changed to *7T3* but proved disappointing and soon gave way to the more conventional *Motormouth*. ITV 1982-88.

Noah's Ark Anton Rodgers (Noah Kirby), Peter Wingfield (Tom Kirby), Angela Thorne (Val Kirby), Orla Brady (Clare Somers), Paul Warriner (Jake Henshaw). Drama series created by Johnny Byrne. Tom Kirby has resigned his job with a big company producing veterinary drugs. He has come home to the Worcestershire village of Melton but has no desire to join his father's veterinary practice. He and his father, Noah, are poles apart in their approach to medicine but the arrival of wildlife vet, Clare Somers, influences his decision to stay. ITV 1997-98.

Nobody's Perfect Elaine Stritch (Bill Hooper), Richard Griffiths (Sam Hooper), Kim Braden (Liz). Sitcom written by Elaine Stritch. Bill Hooper is a brash American woman living in London. She's married to a dowdy English doctor, Sam, who has a daughter, Liz, from his previous marriage. ITV 1980-82.

Noel's House Party Noel Edmonds, born Ilford, Essex, 22 December 1948, began his media career as a disc jockey on BBC Radio 1 in 1969 before becoming a mainstream television presenter beginning with *Top of the Pops* throughout the 1970s. This live Saturday evening light entertainment show was first broadcast on 23rd November 1991. The format grew out of the *Noel Edmonds Saturday Roadshow* (1988), but instead of changing locations it was regularly based at a stately home in the fictitious village of Crinkley Bottom. A popular feature was the 'Gotchas' where an unsuspecting celebrity would be the victim of an elaborate practical joke to test their patience to the full. Other regular features included 'Grab-a-Grand' (where a viewer would win time by answering a series of topical questions and a sports celebrity would then enter the Money Box which had wind blowing from underneath, into which Noel placed £1000 in bank notes, and try to grab as much of the money as possible within the allotted time), and NTV (where viewers would suddenly find themselves on television, via a microscopic camera installed in their living room. Celebrity victims included Chris Evans, Garry Bushell and Dale Winton). The show also gave us the pink and yellow blobbed creature, Mr Blobby, who became the real star of Noel's House Party, knocking Take That off the top of the charts to score the Christmas number one in 1993. Towards the end of its run the show ran out of ideas and viewing figures tumbled and it was eventually axed. BBC1 1991-99. See also *Multi-Coloured Swap Shop, Top of the Pops, The Late, Late Breakfast Show,*

Come Dancing, Juke Box Jury, National Lottery, Telly Addicts, Top Gear and *Deal or No Deal.*

Noggin the Nog See *The Saga of Noggin the Nog.*

North Square Philip Davis (Peter McLeish), Kevin McKidd (Billy Guthrie), Rupert Penry-Jones (Alex Hay), Dominic Rowan (Tom Mitford), James Murray (Johnny Boy), Helen McCrory (Rose Fitzgerald), Kim Vithana (Wendy de Souza), Ruth Millar (Morag Black), Victoria Smurfit (Dr Helen Ferryhough), Sasha Behar (Stevie Goode), Tony Monroe (Michael Marlowe), Murray Head (Judge Martin Bould). Drama series created by Peter Moffat and set around the practice of a Leeds Legal Chambers. The series was filmed in and around the real life Park Square, Leeds. C4 2000.

Northern Lights Robson Green (Colin Armstrong), Mark Benton (Howie Scott), Nicola Stephenson (Jackie), Sian Reeves (Pauline), Keith Clifford (Eric). Six-part comedy drama written by Jeff Pope and Bob Mills. Colin and Howie first came to our screens in *Christmas Lights* (ITV 2004, also written by Pope and Mills), a seasonal drama, featuring the two inseparable friends who worked for the same company and lived next door to one another and were married to sisters, Jackie and Pauline. Their affectionate rivalry, over who could have the best Christmas lights in the street, turning sour when Howie is promoted to a management position. Northern Lights is a light-hearted drama developing this typical male friendship and found the lads in all manner of improbable situations. The final episode highlights included an impromptu Karaoke duet of the great Madness hit *House of Fun*, followed swiftly by Howie being shot in the bottom by a deranged farmer. ITV 2006. Popular demand assured a further six-part series in 2007, now called *City Lights*. On a Saturday shopping trip in Manchester's city centre, the boys get into a row over a parking space with an aggressive stranger. They are forced to back off and with the incident soon forgotten they sneak off to the pub whilst their wives Jackie and Pauline are otherwise engaged. But when the mysterious stranger is gunned down in front of their eyes, the boys become the only witnesses to a vicious gangland execution and are subsequently informed that their own lives are in danger and they will have to join the Witness Protection Programme - leaving behind everything they know and starting new lives with their families in London. The girls are devastated and Colin (now known as Brad Shearer) is horrified when a search into their backgrounds throws up a guilty secret from his past which he'd thought long buried. To make matters worse Howie accidentally chooses 'Wayne Carr' as his new name! To complete the name changes Colin's wife Jackie is now known as Emily and Howie's wife as Nicole. Another Christmas special, *Clash of the Santas*, was broadcast in December 2008, Colin and Howie taking a trip to Lithuania to represent the UK in a Santa convention. Unfortunately the Scrooge-like Howie is picked as Santa, while true Christmas believer Colin is relegated to the role of cheerleading elf!

Not Going Out Lee Mack (Lee), Megan Dodds (Kate), Tim Vine (Tim), Sally Bretton (Lucy Adams), Katy Wix (Daisy), Timothy West (Geoffrey Adams), Deborah Grant (Wendy Adams), Miranda Hart (Barbara Pitreizkewadorski), Simon Dutton (Guy). Sitcom created by Lee Mack. Unburdened by ambition or drive, Lee drifts from one ill-advised job to another, living off the goodwill and generosity of his landlady, Kate, a clean-living Californian. Their easy-going, comfortable friendship is steadily moving into uncharted waters – a situation complicated by the fact that Lee's best mate, Tim is Kate's ex-boyfriend. Meanwhile, uptight accountant Tim struggles to get over his break-up with Kate and cope with her rapidly blossoming friendship with Lee. By the start of Series 2 Kate has gone back to America and the flat is bought by Tim's sister Lucy, a head hunter recently back from ten years abroad. BBC1 2006-

Not In Front Of The Children Wendy Craig (Jennifer Corner), Paul Daneman and Ronald Hines (Henry Corner), Roberta Tovey and Verina Greenlaw (Trudi Corner), Hugo Keith-Johnston (Robin Corner), Jill Riddick (Amanda Corner). Domestic sitcom created by Richard Waring, where Wendy Craig first perfected her harassed housewife persona subsequently seen in several other sitcoms. BBC1 1967-70. Richard Waring adapted 26 episodes of *Not In Front Of The Children* for broadcast by BBC Radio 4 between 30 September 1969 and 27 December 1970, with all of the television cast reprising their roles with the exception of Ronald Hines; Henry Corner being voiced by Francis Matthews.

Not On Your Nellie Hylda Baker (Nellie Pickersgill), Jack Douglas (Stanley Pickersgill), Wendy Richard (Doris). Sitcom written by Tom Brennand and Roy Bottomley. Wielding her boa, and mouthing more malapropisms per sentence than old Mrs Malaprop herself, Hylda Baker all but reprised the blunt, trussed-up, virginal northern-woman role she had played so well in *Nearest And Dearest* and in much of her stage career. Here she played the daughter of a London publican, who summoned her down from Bolton to Fulham to help out in his pub, The Brown Cow. ITV 1974-75.

Not Only But Also Peter Cook and Dudley Moore comedy revue. Three series were made although many of the shows were wiped by the BBC. Perhaps the most famous segment of the show were the so-called "Dagenham Dialogues" where the two raincoated stars would scoff their sandwiches and pontificate on the merits of Ruben's bottoms or discuss being harassed by Jane Russell (Dudley doing his best not to corpse at Peter's hilarious ad libs but failing miserably to the delight of both Peter and the viewers). The closing song, *Goodbye*, had many variations although invariably began *Now is the time to say goodbye (Goodbye), Now is the time to yield a sigh (Yield it, yield it), Now is the time to wend our way-eee, Until we meet again-eee, Some sunny day. Goodbye, goodbye, we're leaving you, skiddlydye. Goodbye, we wish a fond goodbye, fa-ta-ta-ta-ta, fa-ta-ta-ta. Goodbye, goodbye, we're leaving you, skiddlydum. Goodbye, we wish a fond goodbye, la-la-ta-ta-ta. La dah da, lah la la.* And a typical continuation would be [Spoken] *You know there comes a time in everyone's life when they must say goodbye. That time is now, and so with tears in either eye we say goodbye, as people have said throughout the years. We leave this mortal coil on which we strut and fret our weary ways, as Shakespeare put it, God bless him. What a wonderful old chap Shakespeare was, bald but sexy. Take that rhythm away with its wonderful melodies.*

Oh, goodbye they say. Goodbye, goodbye, we're leaving you goodbye, Goodbye, we wish you all .... a fond ...goodbyeeee. BBC 1965-66; 1970   See also Peter Cook entry in the comedy section.

Not So Much A Programme To give the show its full title, *Not so Much A Programme, More A Way Of Life*, was a satirical sketch show, a successor to the BBC's *That Was the Week That Was* (1962). It ran from November 1964 to April 1965. Picking up where they had left off on TW3, David Nathan and Dennis Potter continued as a sketch-writing team, although Potter dropped out before the end of the series. Produced by Ned Sherrin, the thrice-weekly show aired on Fridays, Saturdays and Sundays. Its most contentious sketch featured John Bird as President Jomo Kenyatta, which drew scathing criticism and an official complaint from the Kenyan High Commission. Another popular but sometimes controversial feature was a regular Sunday spot in which young actor Michael Crawford, as Byron, sounded off about aspects of British life: the National Health Service, religion, attitudes to sex and so on. (These sketches were written by Peter Lewis and Peter Dobereiner). Other contributors as actors and writers included David Frost (the main compere), poet and novelist P. J. Kavanagh (who supplied the links for early shows), Willie Rushton, Dougie Fisher, Eleanor Bron, Roy Hudd, John Fortune, and John Bird; the last four mentioned all making their television debuts. Guest writers included Jonathan Routh (he of *Candid Camera* fame), Kenneth Peacock Tynan (theatre critic who, on 13 November 1965, became the first man to use the word 'fuck' on British television), Galton & Simpson (erstwhile writers for Tony Hancock but now enjoying greater fame as writers of *Steptoe and Son*) and Labour politician Gerald Kaufman. Cleo Laine supplied the musical interlude. The programme lacked the sustained cutting-edge of TW3 and was replaced after one season by the Robert Robinson-fronted *BBC-3*.

Not The Nine O'Clock News Satirical sketch show created by radio producer John Lloyd and current affairs expert Sean Hardie. The series showcased the talents of Rowan Atkinson, Mel Smith, Pamela Stephenson and Chris Langham (replaced by Griff Rhys Jones in 1980). A typical episode packed sketches, songs and spoof news bulletins into a half-hour of deliriously unhinged comedy. The sketches were snappy and usually punchline-driven, but with a keenly observed satirical bent. A tight recording schedule ensured the jokes remained fiercely topical. The writers included Richard Curtis, David Renwick, Colin Bostock Smith, Howard Goodall, Douglas Adams, Guy Jenkin, Andy Hamilton, Jim Hitchmough and Clive Anderson. The title alluded to the fact that the programme aired at the same time as the BBC evening news slot. BBC2 1979-82.

Not With A Bang Stephen Rea (Colin Garrity), Mike Grady (Graham Wilkins), Josie Lawrence (Janet Wilkins), Ronald Pickup (Brian Appleyard). Seven-episode sitcom written by Tony Millan and Mike Walling. After *Tomorrow's World* presenter Judith Hann lets loose a deadly chemical on an unsuspecting world, the human race is wiped out except for four Britons who have somehow escaped the plague that killed everyone else. ITV 1990.

Now Look Here Ronnie Corbett (Ronnie), Rosemary Leach (Laura), Madge Ryan and Gillian Lind (Mother), Richard O'Sullivan (Keith), Henry McGee (Henry). Sitcom written by Graham Chapman and Barry Cryer, who had also scripted Corbett's earlier sitcom No - That's Me Over Here!, in which he was also married to a woman named Laura, also played by Rosemary Leach. The first series of *Now Look Here* cast Ronnie as a mother-dominated man (much like his role in Sorry!), desperate to find his own identity and shed the shackles of submissiveness. By the end of those seven episodes he had indeed found a soul-mate, Laura. By the start of the second series they had married and the format changed to reflect husband-and-wife storylines, split between domestic situations and Ronnie's insurance job. Gradually, the two premises began to merge, the fifth episode in the second series going as far as re-introducing Henry McGee from the earlier show, once again cast as Ronnie's aloof neighbour. BBC1 1971-73. See also *The Prince Of Denmark*.

Number 10 Denis Quilley (William Ewart Gladstone), Ian Richardson (James Ramsay MacDonald), John Stride (David Lloyd George), Bernard Archard (Duke of Wellington), David Langton (Herbert Henry Asquith), Richard Pasco (Benjamin Disraeli), Jeremy Brett (William Pitt the Younger). Anthology series depicting the lives of seven British Prime Ministers. The series is notable for the last screen performance of actress Celia Johnson as Mrs Gladstone. ITV 1983.

N.U.T.S. Comedy sketch show written by Alan Coren, Harry Lovelock, Geoff Rowley, Chris Emmett, Dave Evans (father of Lee), and Barry Took, the last three also starring in many of the items along with Claire Faulconbridge, Alan Freeman, Frederick Jaeger and Roy Kinnear. ITV 1976.

Odd Man, The Edwin Richfield (Steve Gardiner), Moultrie Kelsall (Chief Insp. Gordon), William Mervyn (Chief Insp. Rose), Keith Barron (DS Swift), Sarah Lawson (Judy Gardiner and Anne Braithwaite), Christopher Guinee (South). Police drama series created by Edward Boyd. *The Odd Man* followed five main characters : - theatrical agent and part time sleuth Steve Gardiner, his wife, Judy, the dour Chief Inspector Gordon, the amiable DS Swift and a mysterious villain named South, as they became enmeshed in a seedy world of crime and intrigue, which led to Judy's murder at the hands of South. Although each episode was written as a self-contained story the season had an overall thread as Steve Gardiner went in pursuit of his wife's killer. In season two CI Gordon made way for the rather unpleasant Chief Inspector Rose and actress Sarah Lawson returned, this time as Anne Braithwaite, the murdered girl's twin sister. ITV 1962-63. See also *It's Dark Outside* and *Mr Rose*.

Odd One In Game show in which celebrity teams try to spot the odd one in from a series of peculiar line-ups. Hosted by Bradley Walsh the Saturday evening show has two teams of two celebrities making decisions such as which one of five men has a false beard or which one of four people can do a handstand. The studio-audience play along too and the quickest highest-scoring person throughout the show plays a final game of Odd One In for

£5,000. Jason Manford and Peter Andre were the resident home team. Series two in 2011 was shown in the prime time Saturday evening slot and the studio-audience finale was dispensed with. ITV 2010-

Office, The Ricky Gervais (David Brent), Martin Freeman (Tim Canterbury), Mackenzie Crook (Gareth Keenan), Lucy Davis (Dawn Tinsley), Stirling Gallacher (Jennifer Taylor-Clarke), Robin Hooper (Malcolm), Sally Bretton (Donna), Ralph Ineson (Chris 'Finchy' Finch), Nicola Cotter (Karen Roper), Ewan MacIntosh (Keith), Patrick Baladi (Neil Godwin), Stacy Roca (Rachel), Rachel Isaac (Trudy). Sitcom written by Stephen Merchant and Ricky Gervais. The story of an office that faces closure when the company decides to downsize its branches. A BBC documentary film crew follow staff and the manager Brent to focus on how the ordinary British work place responds to change and business upheaval. In the first episode Jennifer Taylor Clark comes down from head office to warn of a merger between the Slough and Swindon branches of Wernham-Hogg paper merchants. The slough manager David Brent thinks he's the coolest, funniest, and most popular boss ever, so obviously is expecting to be named as boss of the new merged unit. Unfortunately, Brent is only a legend in his own mind and the job goes to Neil Godwin, the Swindon boss. Brent maintains his position as ramrod for the filming team and his whole working life is played out acutely aware of the cameras. This is his chance for the world to know what they have been missing as he shows his political biases, his stand-up comedy technique, and his incredible flair for song (He was formerly a member of Foregone Conclusion and wrote songs such as Spaceman, Free Love and the Princess Diana Song) and dance (Incidentally, the tune hummed by Brent during his legendary dance is the 70s hit Disco Inferno by The Trammps). Meanwhile, long-suffering Tim longs after Dawn the engaged receptionist and keeps himself sane by playing childish practical jokes on his insufferable, army-obsessed deskmate Gareth. Will the Slough office be closed? Will the BBC give Brent his own series? Will Tim and Dawn end up with each other? The theme song is Handbags and Gladrags written by Mike D'Abo and performed by Big George (aka George Webley). BBC2 2001-03.

OFI Sunday Entertainment series hosted by Chris Evans, its title initials standing for "Oh Flip Its" in a similar vein to Chris's earlier show *TFI Friday*, although again the 'F' was invariably referred to by all and sundry as another quite different F word. The programme was axed after five editions, critics accusing Chris of being self-indulgent in his choice of guests and general content of the show. ITV 2005.

Oh Boy! Britain's first total rock 'n' roll programme. Created by Jack Good, *Oh Boy!* was a madcap live show (from the Hackney Empire) where one song moved smoothly into another, where top recording artists sang together and separately, where older tunes mixed with the hit parade freely. The frenetic pace and high energy output suited minors and teens but the very real talent on parade also attracted the older audience. Good's featured artist was a young Cliff Richard (and his band the Shadows then known as The Drifters) but other regulars included Marty Wilde, Ronnie Carroll, Vince Eager, Don Lang, Lord Rockingham's XI (originally called Harry Robinson's Band before Good renamed them early in the series), Red Price, The Dallas Boys, Neville Taylor & The Cutters, Cherry Wainer, and The Vernons Girls. The comperes alternated between Tony Hall and Jimmy Henney. ITV 1958-59. The show was revived by ITV in 1979-80 with regulars, Alvin Stardust, Les Gray, Joe Brown and Shakin' Stevens.

Oh Brother! Derek Nimmo (Brother/Father Dominic), Felix Aylmer (Father Anselm). Derek Nimmo reprised his role of a bumbling stuttering cleric first seen in *All Gas and Gaiters*, albeit under a different identity. He was now a novice monk at Mountacres Priory but engaged in similar hilarious misunderstandings as his previous persona. BBC1 1968-70. A sequel, *Oh Father!*, aired on BBC1 in 1973 with the newly promoted Father Dominic leaving the Priory to become a curate.

Oh Father! See *Oh Brother!*

Oh Happy Band! Sitcom created by Jeremy Lloyd and David Croft. Harry Worth, whose character shares his name, starred as the leader of a brass-band in the small town of Nettlebridge. He

and his band find themselves at the forefront of a campaign against the proposed building of a nearby airport. The music for the series was provided by the Aldershot Brass Ensemble. BBC1 1980.

Oh in Colour Spike Milligan, John Bluthal, Eleanor Bron, Arthur Mullard, Rita Webb, Charlie Young Atom, Sheila Steafel. Surreal sketch show written by, and starring Spike Milligan. The six-episode series was originally designed to be the follow-up to Spike's *Q* series, with John Bluthal lending an equally helpful hand. As it turned out *Q* continued for several more series after this one finished. The quality was still very apparent and memorable sketches include Spike giving a Party Political Broadcast on behalf of the Tory party as an incoherent country yokel all the time playing with a perpetual motion ball-bearing device. BBC2 1970.

Oh No It's Selwyn Froggitt Bill Maynard (Selwyn Froggitt), Megs Jenkins (Mrs Froggitt), Robert Keegan (Maurice), Ray Mort (Ray), Richard Davies (Clive), Bill Dean (Jack), Harold Goodwin (Harry). Daytime finds the big bumbling Selwyn working as a labourer for the local council's Public Works department; by night he can be seen, a copy of *The Times* tucked under the sleeve of his donkey-jacket, down at the Scarsdale Working Men's Club And Institute where he drinks pints of 'cooking' and, as the result of a joke, he has been appointed concert secretary. Most of the show's humour was generated at two locations: here at the club, where Selwyn's well-intentioned problems are felt most keenly by the barman Ray and the drinking regulars Clive, Jack and Harry, and at home, where Selwyn exasperates his ever-loving mum and his brother Maurice. A thumbs-up cry of 'Magic' is Selwyn's always optimistic trademark. Alan Plater wrote the 1974 pilot (where incidentally Selwyn's surname was spelt Froggit) and the series proper although he bowed out after three seasons and the final series went out under the title 'Selwyn' and saw our hero leave Scarsdale to become Entertainments Officer at the Paradise Valley holiday camp on the Yorkshire coast. ITV 1974; 1976-77; 1978.

Oh, Doctor Beeching! Su Pollard (Ethel Schumann), Paul Shane (Jack Skinner), Jeffrey Holland (Cecil Parkin), Stephen Lewis (Harry Lambert), Julia Deakin (May Skinner), Barbara New (Vera Plumtree), Paul Aspden (Wilfred Schumann), Terry John (Percy), Ivor Roberts (Arnold), Perry Benson (Ralph), Lindsay Grimshaw (Gloria Skinner), Richard Spendlove (Mr Orkindale). In 1963 Doctor Beeching - commissioned by the government to recommend a course of action that would save the exchequer millions of pounds - called for the closure of 2128 stations in one sweep, and the ripping up of hundred of lines perceived to be uneconomic. The execution of his suggestions decimated the service, all but erasing the rural railways that served the less populous communities in Britain. Throughout 1963, virtually every town in Britain feared that it would lose its local service, and railway staff spent the year worrying about redundancy. This situation provided the background for *Oh, Doctor Beeching!*, a sitcom created and written by ensemble comedy maestro David Croft in collaboration with Richard Spendlove (who had worked on the railways for 30 years). The series was set at Hatley Station (real-life Arley, on the Severn Valley Railway). Jack Skinner, who sports a pronounced limp, is the acting stationmaster. He's an average man, not averse to the odd scam, but is delighted to have a beautiful wife, May, who runs the station buffet. Her looks and his insecurity make him prone to jealousy, however, and he always imagines that she is seeing other men. Jack and May live at the station with their daughter Gloria, who attends college. The other local residents and staff include ticket saleslady Ethel and her son, the odd-job man Wilfred (the product of Ethel's involvement with a US serviceman during the Second World War); Vera Plumtree, the widow of a respected train driver; signalman Harry Lambert who is sufficiently underworked to operate several sidelines from his signalbox, including hairdressing and selling fruit and vegetables; and train drivers/guards Arnold, Ralph and Percy. The arrival of the efficient and officious new stationmaster Cecil Parkin causes waves among the staff, however - especially May, who had a passionate affair with him before her marriage to Jack (according to the calendar it transpires that Cecil is Gloria's real father). BBC1 1996-97.

Old Grey Whistle Test Rock music showcase with a bias towards album releases rather than pop singles. The series title came from a 'tin pan alley' (music emporium in Denmark Street, London) phrase from years ago. When they got the first pressing of a record they would play it to people they called the old greys (grey-haired executives and grey-suited doormen). The ones they could remember and could whistle having heard it just once or twice had passed the old grey whistle test. The programme went out on BBC2, last thing on a Friday night, from a tiny studio on the fourth floor of Television centre. In the days before 24 hour television the station would close down at the end of the evening. This gave the last programme of the day some flexibility and this meant Whistle Test could last from anything between 25 and 90 minutes. The original presenters were Ian Whitcomb and Richard Williams but it was the bearded 'Whispering' Bob Harris, host for most of the 1970s and early 1980s that made the biggest impact. Other presenters in the 1980s included Anne Nightingale, Andy Kershaw, Mark Ellen, Richard Skinner, David Hepworth and Ro Newton. The budget for the show was famously small and David Bowie, for example, agreed to play three songs for £50 and John Lennon refused to accept his fee in cash, insisting that he should be rewarded instead with chocolate Bath Oliver biscuits! The titles sequence featured an animation of a man kicking a star. He was to become affectionately known as The Starkicker. The show's title music, with its distinctive harmonica, was a track called Stone Fox Chase by a Nashville band, Area code 615. In 1983 the the show's title became *Whistle Test*. BBC2 1971-88.

Old Guys, The Roger Lloyd-Pack (Tom Finnan), Clive Swift (Roy Bowden), Jane Asher (Sally), Katherine Parkinson (Amber), Justin Edwards (Steve), Cherie Lunghi (Barbara), Jeremy Clyde (Keith), Vincent Ebrahim (Rajan), Tessa Wyatt (Joanna). Sitcom written by Jesse Armstrong, Sam Bain and Simon Blackwell. Tom moves in with Roy after Roy's wife Penny deserts him. The two pensioners are fiercely stubborn and opinionated. Tom is slightly younger and describes their differences as "you're from the Macmillan age whilst I'm more Andy Warhol". Sally is the neighbour over the road whom they both fawn over. The theme tune is Ivor Cutler's *I'm Happy*, sung by the two co-stars for the second series. BBC1 2009-10

Old Men at the Zoo, The Stuart Wilson (Simon Carter), Marius Goring (Emile Englander), Andrew Cruickshank (Mr Sanderson), Toria Fuller (Martha Carter), Barry Stanton (Strawson), Robert Morley (Lord Godmanchester), Robert Urquhart (Sir Robert Falcon), John Phillips (Dr Charles Langley-Beard), Priscilla Morgan (Mrs Purrett), Maurice Denham (Dr Edwin Leacock), Shelagh Fraser (Diana Price), Jan Harvey (Harriet Leacock). Five-part adaptation of Angus Wilson's satirical novel by Troy Kennedy Martin about a zoo, which is plunged into a crisis when a giraffe escapes. BBC1 1983

Oliver Twist Bruce Prochnik (Oliver Twist), Max Adrian (Fagin), Carmel McSharry (Nancy), Peter Vaughan (Bill Sikes), John Carson (Monk), George Curzon (Mr Brownlow), Willoughby Goddard (Mr Bumble), Alan Rothwell (Charley Bates). 13-part adaptation of Dickens' classic tale. BBC 1962. A 1999 ITV four-part adaptation by Alan Bleasedale starred Sam Smith as Oliver Twist, Robert Lindsay as Fagin, Alex Crowley as the Artful Dodger, Keira Knightley as Rose Fleming, Marc Warren as Monks, and Andy Serkis as Bill Sikes. The series was controversial for not sticking too closely to Dicken's original story.

Omid Djalili Show, The Omid Djalili was born in Chelsea, to Iranian Bahá'í parents, 30 September 1965. He is one of Britain's most versatile performers. As a stand-up comedian he honed his skills at the Edinburgh Festival Fringe in 1995 in the guise of 'Short, Fat Kebab Shop Owner's Son' and soon developed an act based around being the world's only Iranian comedian. Omid's looks initially found him parts as a stereotypical Middle Eastern background character but it soon became evident in films such as *Gladiator, The Mummy, Mean Machine, Alien Autopsy, Spy Game, Sky Captain and the World of Tomorrow, Pirates of the Caribbean: At World's End, The Love Guru*, and *Sex and the City 2*, he is a fine character actor equally at home playing comic and

dramatic roles. *The Omid Djalili Show* saw two series. It was a mix of stand-up and sketches but with very original themes such as an hilarious minicab the musical sketch in which his ethnic drivers ultimately engage in a dance-off against the more traditional black cab drivers. BBC1 2007 and 2009.

Omnibus Long-running arts programme originally hosted by Henry Livings. Other presenters have included Richard Baker, Humphrey Burton, Barry Norman and Kirsty Wark. Subjects have included David Bowie (Cracked Actor), Dante Gabriel Rossetti (Ken Russell's offering entitled Dante's Inferno), and ballerina Darcey Bussell. Originally airing on BBC1 in 1967 it transferred to BBC2 towards the end of its run in 2001.

On Safari Wildlife programme presented by husband-and-wife team Armand and Michaela Denis, Belgian wildlife photographers. This popular series of quarter-hour programmes was later expanded to a half-hour and took them to different areas of Africa or South America, and could involve searches for a particular beast, such as the manatee, or profiles of a park or district with distinctive animal life. BBC 1957-66.

On the Braden Beat Consumer-affairs and light entertainment programme hosted by Bernard Braden with contributions from Peter Cook, Tim Brooke-Taylor and Jake Thackray. ITV 1962-67. See *Braden's Week*.

On the Buses Reg Varney (Stan Butler), Stephen Lewis (Inspector Cyril 'Blakey' Blake), Anna Karen (Olive Rudge), Michael Robbins (Arthur Rudge), Bob Grant (Jack Harper), Cicely Courtneidge and Doris Hare (Mrs Butler). Sitcom created by Ronald Chesney and Ronald Wolfe. The trials and tribulations of bus driver Stan and his conductor Jack who work for the London-based Luxton Bus Company, working the number 11 route to the cemetery gates. The lads shift usually consists of either chatting up the 'clippies' or working a fiddle, but their moustachioed boss, Inspector Blake, rules with an iron hand and an oft-spouted catchphrase of "I 'ate you Butler". Stan lives with his widowed mother, his dowdy sister, Olive, and her layabout husband, Arthur. ITV 1969-73. Three feature films followed and a spin-off series *Don't Drink the Water* (ITV 1974-75) which saw the character of Blakey moving into a retirement home in Spain with his spinster sister, Dorothy (Pat Coombs).

On the Hour See *The Day Today*.

On the Move Bob Hoskins (Alf), Donald Gee (Bert). Written by Barry Took, this award-winning series of 10-minute sketches involving removals men Alf and Bert who travel around Britain and remark on strange words in the English language, was made to stimulate interest in reading by the illiterate. BBC1 1975-76.

On the Up Dennis Waterman (Tony Carpenter), Sam Kelly (Sam), Joan Sims (Mrs Fiona Wembley), Judy Buxton (Ruth Carpenter), Jenna Russell (Maggie) and Pauline Letts (Mrs Carpenter). Sitcom written by Bob Larbey. Ardent Crystal Palace supporter Tony Carpenter, who has elevated a small taxi-cab company into a thriving executive car-hire business and made himself a millionaire in the process, has also managed to keep his East End sensibilities and outlook in spite of his wealth. He does, however, have a snobbish wife, Ruth, so lives in a big house in Esher, which requires a permanent staff. Tony's laid back attitude towards the staff has Ruth in fits. His 'we're-all-mates-together' perspective permits his secretary, Maggie, to procure a sharp line in backchat; the cook, Mrs Wembley, to works to her own agenda; and the butler, Sam, is just plain insolent. Dennis Waterman wrote and performed the programme's closing theme song. BBC1 1990-92.

On Thin Ice Documentary following a team consisting of Ben Fogle, James Cracknell, and Ed Coats (originally Johnny Lee Miller) in their epic race across Antarctica to the South Pole. Ben Fogle, born 3 November 1973, is the son of actress Julia Foster and broadcasting veterinary surgeon Bruce Fogle. BBC2 2009. See also *Cash in the Attic, Castaway 2000, One Man And His Dog*.

Once Upon a Time in the North Bernard Hill (Len Tollit), Christine Moore (Pat Tollit), Susan McArdle (Siobhan Tollit), Andrew Whyment (Sean Tollit), Bob Mason (Morris Tollit), Bryan Pringle (Mr Bebbington), Bill Stewart (Bob Carling).

Sitcom written by Tim Firth, involving the working-class Tollit family from the fictional Sutton Moor in Yorkshire. Each of the six episodes had titles beginning 'The time....' BBC1 1994.

One And Only, The Reality show that sought to find the UK's best tribute act. Presented by Graham Norton, the acts battled it out for the chance to perform on the grandest stage of them all, in Las Vegas, USA. Katy Setterfield as Dusty Springfield was crowned the winner. BBC1 2008

One By One Rob Heyland (Donald Turner), Peter Jeffrey (Maurice Webb). James Ellis (Paddy Reilly), Liz Smith (Gran Turner), Garfield Morgan (Howard Rundle), Jack Hedley (Peter Raymond), Peter Gilmore (Ben Bishop), Catherine Schell (Lady Ann). Based on the zoo vet series of autobiographical books by David Taylor. Over three series it showed ten years of Donald Turner's life as he struggled to make it as a wildlife vet, and his metamorphosis into the leading figure of wild animal surgery and healthcare. BBC1 1984-87.

One Foot in the Grave Richard Wilson (Victor Meldrew), Annette Crosbie (Margaret Meldrew), Angus Deayton (Patrick Trench), Janine Duvitski (Pippa Trench), Doreen Mantle (Mrs Jean Warboys), Owen Brennan (Mr Nick Swainey). Sitcom written by David Renwick. At the beginning of the first series Victor Meldrew is forced into taking early retirement from his job as a security guard, and tries to adjust to an unwanted life of leisure with his long-suffering wife Margaret. The Meldrews move from their demolished home at 37 Wingate Drive, to 19 Riverbank. On one side live bus-driver Pippa, her husband, Patrick, and their beloved dog, Denzil. On the other side live Mr Swainey and his invalid mother, Mrs Warboys, whose unseen husband, Chris, deserts her. Victor takes odd jobs, helps out with good causes and generally tries to make himself busy. All manner of wild coincidences, complex misunderstandings, bureaucratic inefficiencies and sheer, awesome bad luck conspire against him to which he can only exclaim 'I don't be-lieve it!'. A 1993 Christmas special was entitled *One Foot In The Algarve*, and only Christmas specials were made in 1996 and 1997. The 1997 special introduced the Meldrews' new neighbours Derek and Betty McVitie (played by Tim Brooke-Taylor and Marian McLoughlin), who moved into the house vacated by Patrick and Pippa. Then, after a gap of three years, the show returned for one final series (as did Patrick and Pippa). In the final episode Victor was the victim of a hit-and-run accident, the car driver (played by Hannah Gordon) later befriending Margaret - without, of course, revealing her guilty secret. The title song was written and performed by Eric Idle. The opening lyrics are: *They say I might as well face the truth, That I'm just too long in the tooth. Oh I'm an O.A.P. and weak-kneed, But I have not yet quite gone to seed. I may be over the hill now that I have retired, Fading away but I'm not yet expired. Clapped out, rundown, too old to save, One foot in the grave.* The closing lyrics are: *They say I might as well face the truth, That I'm just too long in the tooth. I've started to deteriorate, And now I've passed my own sell-by date. Oh I am no spring chicken it's true. I have to pop my teeth in to chew. And my old knees have started to knock. I've just got too many miles on the clock. So I'm a wrinkly, crinkly, set in my ways. It's true my body as seen better days. But give me half a chance and I can still misbehave. One foot in the grave. One foot in the grave. One foot in the grave.* BBC1 1990-97; 2000.

101 Ways to Leave a Gameshow Steve Jones, assisted by Nemone Metaxas, hosts the series where contestants are ejected in the most nerve-wracking, adrenaline-pumping means ever seen on television. The game sees eight contestants compete to be the winner of a £10,000 prize, by picking the right answers to general knowledge questions. Competitors who pick wrong answers are eliminated from the game in a variety of different ways, usually involving a large drop into a large pool; the final round via a trap door. As with its Endemol stablemate, *Total Wipeout*, the show is filmed at Endemol's facility in Buenos Aires, Argentina. BBC1 2010.

100% Three contestants answered 100 multiple-choice and True-or-False questions posed by an unseen questionmaster (Robin Houston). Every ten questions the category of the questions changed, but started and ended with general knowledge. (Originally it was general knowledge all the way through.) The person who scored closest to 100% pocketed £100 and could

return the next day. Contestant Ian Lygo had to be asked by the producers to step down as an undefeated champion after 75 victories in 1998, because the producers were worried that Ian's dominance on the show was affecting the ratings. The rules of the programme had to be changed especially to accommodate this extraordinary event. Ian also holds the highest score on an ordinary show (87%). Channel 5 (now *Five*) 1997-2001. Various spin-offs developed from the format, notably *100% Gold* for contestants over 50-years-old.

One Man And His Dog Sheep Dog Trials for the BBC Television Trophy. Hosted by Phil Drabble for 18 years with trials experts Eric Halsall, Ray Ollerenshaw and Gus Dermody supplying commentary. Robin Page took over from Phil in the mid 1990s until the series end in 1999. Clarissa Dickson Wright, Ben Fogle and Shauna Lowry have hosted the subsequent Christmas specials, recorded at Chatsworth House in Derbyshire. BBC2 1976-

One Show, The The curiously-named *The One Show*, first-aired in August 2006, as a modern-day spin-off of *Nationwide* with Adrian Chiles and Nadia Sawalha as the main presenters and Martin Lewis as consumer expert with Kate Humble as wildlife correspondent. In July 2007 Sawalha was replaced by Myleene Klass who in turn was replaced by Christine Bleakley the following month. Broadcast on weekdays at 7pm *The One Show* reporters have included Steve Backshall, Ellie Harrison, Joe Inglis and David Lindo as nature and wildlife reporters; Dan Snow and Neil Oliver as history reporters; Rav Wilding as crime reporter; Dominic Littlewood on consumer issues; Michael Mosley on health and science; and general reporters (and occasional presenters) Angellica Bell, Colin Jackson, Justin Rowlatt, John Sergeant, Lucy Siegle, Rajesh Mirchandani, Anna Adams, Matt Baker, Hardeep Singh Kohli, Carol Thatcher, Gabby Logan and Phil Tufnell. A revamp in August 2010 saw Jason Manford and Alex Jones become the regular presenters (Mon-Thursday) with Chris Evans presenting the Friday edition. Jason left after four months in the job and was initially replaced by guest presenters, Alexander Armstrong and Matt Allwright before Matt Baker was confirmed as regular presenter in January 2011. BBC1 2006-

One Summer David Morrissey (Billy Rizley), Spencer Leigh (Icky Higson), James Hazeldine (Kidder), Ian Davies (Rabbit). Two teenagers, Icky and Billy, grow tired of their life in Liverpool and decide to run away to North Wales. But it's not long before their past catches up with them. Five-part drama series notable for early screen appearances of Hollywood actors David Morrisey and Ian Hart (his last piece of work credited under his real name of Ian Davies). C4 1983.

One-Upmanship Richard Briers (Stephen Potter), Peter Jones (Gatling-Fenn), Frederick Jaeger (Cogg-Willoughby). Sitcom adapted by Barry Took from the famous Stephen Potter books. Richard Briers portrayed Stephen Potter, ex-B.B.C. broadcaster and college lecturer, and author of the spoof manuals 'Gamesmanship', 'Lifemanship', 'One-Upmanship', 'Supermanship', 'Anti-Woo' and 'The Complete Golf Gamesmanship'. What is 'One-Upmanship'? Well, nothing less than the art of getting one up on your opponents at all times. As Potter succinctly puts it: "The world is divided into two types of people - winners and losers, the one up and the one down. He who is not one-up is surely one-down'. BBC2 1976-78.

Onedin Line Peter Gilmore (Capt James Onedin), Brian Rawlinson and James Garbutt (Robert Onedin), Anne Stallybrass (Anne Webster / Onedin), Jane Seymour (Emma Callon/Fogarty), Jill Gascoigne (Letty Gaunt / Onedin), Michael Billington and Tom Adams (Daniel Fogarty), Jessica Benton (Elizabeth Onedin / Frazer / Lady Fogarty), Howard Lang (Captain Baines). James Onedin, a penniless sea captain with aspirations to greater things, returns from a voyage in 1860 and learns of the death of his shopkeeper father. The business goes to James' elder brother, Robert, and this spurs James on to make a success of his life. He marries Anne, the dowdy daughter of the late owner of the Charlotte Rhodes, his only motivation being to get his hands on the ship. James, a shrewd and often ruthless operator, soon builds up a fleet, assisted by the loyal Captain Baines. A sub-plot turned on James's flighty sister, Elizabeth, who became pregnant by Daniel Fogarty but instead married wealthy Albert Frazer, developer of steamship technology, a connection James soon turned to his own advantage. In a later series, Anne, whom James had come to love, died in childbirth, and he was torn between alternative replacement brides for a while, before settling for his daughter's governess, Letty Gaunt. Letty also died, and by the final series, James was onto his third wife, the exotic Margarita, and was by then a grandfather. The last series ended with the news of the death of Daniel Fogarty (whom Elizabeth had finally married after the death of her first husband). The series was created by Cyril Abraham. The opening credits of the series featured music from the ballet Spartacus by Aram Khachaturian. The programme set in the Liverpool Docks was recorded in Dartmouth, Devon. BBC1 1971-80.

Only Fools and Horses David Jason (Del Boy Trotter), Nicholas Lyndhurst (Rodney), Lennard Pearce (Grandad), Buster Merryfield (Uncle Albert), Tessa Peake-Jones (Raquel), Gwyneth Strong (Cassandra), Roger Lloyd Pack (Colin "Trigger" Ball), John Challis (Aubrey "Boycie" Boyce), Sue Holderness (Marlene). Sitcom written by John Sullivan. Derek 'Del Boy' Trotter is a gold jewellery-wearing, camel-hair coat-clad chancer, always looking to make a fast buck; with a never-ending supply of get-rich-quick schemes and an inner belief in his ability to sell anything to anyone. His brother is altogether more earnest. A tall, thin, worried individual, Rodney - or 'Rodders' as Del calls him when things are going well ('you plonker' when things are going less well) - looks upon all of Del's dealings with an air of pessimism, usually well-founded, yet he is always cajoled into going along with the capers. Academically, Rodney is much brighter than Del (he has two GCEs, Maths and Art) but lacks his elder brother's streetwise nous. The third member of the 'firm' was their Grandad, an indolent, scruffy man constantly moaning about his lot in life and rarely getting involved with hands-on work. When the actor Lennard Pearce died, John Sullivan didn't just replace him with another, he wrote Grandad's death into the plot, to face the issue of the family's loss in a touching yet comic way. Then, to keep the sturdy triangle of characters intact, he introduced Uncle Albert, a boastful ex-sea-dog who inveigles his way into the Trotters' lives, managing to stay with them - despite some early efforts to oust him - in their high-rise council flat at 368 Nelson Mandela House. Ultimately, Albert is accepted as an integral part of the team, mostly because of Del's unfailing sense of family loyalty and duty. Other characters include the suave villain Boycie and his vacuous wife Marlene, who is desperate to have a baby; the glum Denzil, who is often roped in on Del's schemes; the pub landlord, Mike (the pub being the Nag's Head); and, most memorably, Trigger, a long-faced, mentally-challenged roadsweeper who, throughout the entire run of the show, thinks that Rodney's name is Dave. The series also gave us the delightful expressions 'dipstick', 'plonker', 'luvverly jubberly' and 'this time next year we'll be millionaires'. As the series developed so did the characters and eventually both brothers married; Rodney to the bright Cassandra, and Del to Raquel, an aspiring actress who, when they met, was moonlighting as a stripogram. Eventually, Del and Raquel cemented their relationship with the birth of a baby, Damien (complete with music from The Omen whenever his name was mentioned). The show 'ended' in 1996 with three hour-long episodes that introduced Raquel's long-lost parents and culminated in a glorious triumph for Del and Rodney when an antique watch Del has had hanging around for years turns out to be a rarity of enormous historical value. It sells at auction for over £6m and the Trotters supposedly finish the show rich beyond even Del's wildest dreams. In 2001 it was announced that the show would return for two special episodes. The first materialised on Christmas Day 2001. Buster Merryfield had died since the previous broadcast (on 23 June 1999), as had Kenneth MacDonald, so their characters were written out - Uncle Albert was said to have died peacefully on the coast, publican Mike was ensconced in jail - but all the other regulars were back on board to find that, owing to some dodgy stock market dealings, the Trotters had lost their fortune. A second special appeared the following Christmas. Four images linger longest in the memory of this classic series. The first was when, while renovating a house, Rodney and Del Boy, with Grandad's assistance, cause a priceless crystal chandelier to smash to smithereens on the floor below. The second was a wonderful piece of physical comedy involving Del and Trigger in a yuppie wine bar; eyeing up a couple of girls, Del goes to lean on a bar flap which, unbeknownst to him, has just been raised, and with a perfect pratfall drops clean out of shot. The third was Del and Rodney attired in fancy dress as Batman and Robin running through the streets at the precise moment a crime was being committed. The final and perhaps most abiding memory is that of the dilapidated vehicle that served as the Trotters' company transport: an ancient yellow Reliant Robin three-wheeler bearing the legend that encapsulated Del's entire business philosophy, 'New York, Paris, Peckham'. The Only Fools and Horses themes were composed and sung by John Sullivan, the opening theme lyrics being: *Stick a pony in me pocket, I'll fetch the suitcase from the van. Cos if you want the best 'uns, but you don't ask questions, Then brother, I'm your man. 'Cos where it all comes from is a mystery, It's like the changin' of the seasons, and the tides of the sea. But here's the one that's drivin' me beserk, Why do only fools and horses work? La-la-la. La-lala-la. La-la-la. La-lala-la.* And the closing lyrics: *We've got some half price cracked ice and miles and miles of carpet tiles, T.V.s, deep freeze and David Bowie L.P.s, Ball games, gold chains, whatsnames, pictures frames and leather goods, And Trevor Francis track suits from a mush in Shepherds Bush, Bush, bush, bush, bush, bush, bush, bush ...No income tax, no V.A.T., no money back, no guarantee, Black or white, rich or poor, we'll cut prices at a stroke, God bless Hooky Street. Viva Hooky Street. Long live Hooky Street. C'est magnifique, Hooky Street, Magnifique, Hooky Street, Hooky Street.* BBC1 1981-93; 1996; 2001-02. A spin-off series *The Green Green Grass* began in 2005 with John Challis and Sue Holderness reprising their roles, and a 90-minute prequel, *Rock & Chips*, aired on 24 January 2010 with Nicholas Lyndhurst playing the part of local Peckham villain Freddie Robdal (Rodney's biological father) as his original character had only just been born (his mother naming him after actor Rod Taylor).

Only Way Is Essex, The BAFTA award-winning reality show based in Essex, depicting "real people in modified situations, saying unscripted lines but in a structured way." Narrated by Essex-girl Denise Van Outen, the show, usually referred to as TOWIE, starred former semi-professional footballer Mark Wright and his fiancée Lauren Goodger, nightclub manager Kirk Norcross, singer Jessica Wright, glamour model Samantha Faiers, wedding singer James Argent, fashion worker Lydia Rose Bright, student Harry Derbidge and Kirk's girlfriend Lauren Pope. Beautician Amy Childs, appeared in the first two series but left so that she could enter the *Celebrity Big Brother* house where she came fourth and subsequently starred in her own reality show *It's All About Amy* on Channel 5. Mark and Kirk left after the third series and raised their profiles by taking part in *I'm A Celebrity Get Me Out Of Here!* and *Celebrity Big Brother* respectively. The show, which is filmed just a few days in advance, debuted on ITV2 on 10 October 2010. The opening theme tune is *The Only Way is Up* by Yazz. In December 2011 the show's cast released a cover of the Wham! classic *Last Christmas*, which peaked at No 33 in the UK chart. *The Only Way Is Essex* will return in early 2012 for a fourth series. Gemma Collins and Chloe Sims will be promoted to the main cast from the 2011 Christmas Special, replacing Mark Wright and Kirk Norcross from the opening titles. See also *Made in Chelsea*

Only When I Laugh James Bolam (Roy Figgis), Peter Bowles (Archie Glover), Richard Wilson (Dr Gordon Thorpe), Christopher Strauli (Norman Binns), Derrick Branche (Staff Nurse Gupte). Sitcom written by Eric Chappell. Set in a ward of an NHS Hospital, the show chronicles the capers of three dressing-gown clad patients, who seem to be unwilling to leave. James Bolam utters the lyrics of the theme song: I'm H-A-P-P-Y, I'm H-A-P-P-Y, I know I am, I'm sure I am, I'm H-A-P-P-Y! ITV 1979-82.

OOglies Stop-action animated children's television sketch series produced by BBC Scotland as part of the CBBC menu. Most of the sketches involve household items with googly eyes, hence the show's title. The series was created and written by Nick Hopkin,

Tim Dann and Austin Low. Voices are provided by Tim Dann, Peter Dickson and Shelley Longworth. Each show begins with the announcement: "Attention all humans. The following stunts you are about to witness have been performed by trained OOglies. Under no circumstances should children or silly adults attempt to do any of the actions you see in the programme." Many of the sketches have comic-book violence as the punchline. Recurring characters include: The Battery Brothers, The Cheeky Carrots, The Cherry-aiders, The Chilli Peppers, The Duelling Toothbrushes, The Farty Pants, The Fruit Bunch and Devious Blender, Lonely Sprout, Mr and Miss Strawberry, The Playful Grapes and Melonhead, Racy Bacon and Mr Bun, Sal the Slice, Slippery Nana, Stunt Tomato, Sugar Cube, Zip Face and Pencil, and Zombie Vegetables. BBC1 2009

Open All Hours Ronnie Barker (Albert Arkwright), David Jason (Granville), Lynda Baron (Nurse Gladys Emmanuel), Kathy Staff (Mrs Blewitt), Stephanie Cole (Mrs Delphine Featherstone), Barbara Flynn (The Milk Woman), Maggie Ollerenshaw (Wavy Mavis). Sitcom written by Roy Clarke. First seen as part of *Seven Of One*, a series of Ronnie Barker pilots (aired in 1973 with Sheila Brennan as Nurse Gladys), Open All Hour's lead character was the stuttering, miserly, lustful shopkeeper Arkwright who opened before dawn and closed, reluctantly, after dusk. Granville, Arkwright's dreamer of a nephew, wiled away his hours as shop assistant and delivery boy (with trusty bicycle) sighing heavily, feeling that his life is slipping away without romance, foreign travel, glamour or experience. His unconsummated relationship with the milk woman, was a metaphor for all his missed opportunities. Arkwright himself lusts after the buxom nurse Gladys Emmanuel, who lives across the road but is tied in to caring for her aged mother. Alas, by the last episode, their relationship remained unrequited. Another star of the series was the shop's till, which grabbed the money with a speed and ferocity more commonly associated with a shark. Incidentally, the location of Arkwright's corner shop - Lister Avenue in Balby, Doncaster - has become a tourist landmark since the show began although the shop itself is now a unisex hairdressing salon called Beautique and under threat of demolition. BBC2 1973; 1976; BBC1 1981-82; 1985.

Open House Daytime magazine and chat show hosted by Gloria Hunniford. Channel 5 (now *Five*) 1998-2002. *Open House* was also the name of an Irish afternoon television show that was broadcast on RTÉ between 1998 and 2003. The magazine show was presented by Mary Kennedy and Marty Whelan with gardening tips from Dermot O'Neill. A short-lived discussion programme entitled *Open House* aired on BBC TV in 1964 and was presented by Gay Byrne, Peter Haigh and Robert Robinson.

Open House Kristian Digby fronted the programme offering prospective house buyers and sellers the chance to seal the deal in hours by arranging an open day where purchasers' bids must be submitted immediately. BBC1 2008. See *Too Buy or Not to Buy*.

Opportunity Knocks Talent show that began on Radio Luxembourg in the early 1950s and transferred to television soon after the introduction of ITV. Hughie Green presented the show throughout its 22-year ITV run. Each week a "clap-o-meter" was used to decide a winner in the studio but the viewing audience would ultimately decide who would return as winner on the next show. Multiple winners would return for an end of series final. One of the most famous winners in the 1960s was Tony Holland a muscle man who gyrated his stomach muscles to the tune of *Wheels Cha Cha*. Other notable acts who appeared included Mary Hopkin, Bonnie Langford, Les Dawson, Little and Large, Bobby Crush, Peters and Lee, Lena Zavaroni, Frank Carson and Freddie Starr. The series was revived by the BBC in 1987 with Bob Monkhouse as the host and his name preceding the original title. Les Dawson took over for the final series in 1990. The theme song for the BBC version was Kiki Dee's *Star*. ITV 1956-78; BBC1 1987-90.

Orchestra United Reality series made in association with Arts Council England and charting the creation of the Hallé Harmony Youth Orchestra, bringing together a diverse cross-section of young people from Manchester. The orchestra, conducted by James Lowe, ultimately performed a concert of classical music, in front of a paying audience of 2,400, at Manchester's Bridgewater Hall. C4 2010.

Orlando Sam Kydd (Orlando O'Connor), David Munro (Steve Morgan), Ben Kingsley (Peter Batterby). Spin-off from *Crane* sees the sea-faring right-hand man of Richard Crane return to London in pursuit of a murderer. ITV 1965-68.

'Orrible Johnny Vaughan (Paul 'Orrible' Clark), Ricky Grover (Sean Orlov), Clint Dyer (Noel), William Boyde (Tim), Lee Oakes (Lee), Angel Coulby (Shiv Clark), Di Botcher (Di Clark), Philip Madoc (Mervyn Rees). Sitcom written by Johnny Vaughan and Ed Allen. Mini-cab driver Paul Clark does a spot of 'driving' for local crime boss Mervyn Rees. The promise of a 'drink' leads him to believe that it won't be long before he has his foot on the first rung of the criminal ladder. The locals down the Fox and Hounds (stewarded by Tim who has a mysterious, possibly SAS past), particularly arch-rival Noel, are disbelieving of Paul's prowess as a master criminal despite him having some of the trimmings (for example an oversized friend and bodyguard Sean Orlov). Paul's homelife too lacks the gangsterbility factor and both his sister Shiv and her boyfriend Lee treat him with derision, and even his mum, Di (a merciless bailiff), struggles to take him seriously. An interesting footnote - All the Rees siblings are named after members of the Welsh grand slam winning rugby side of 1976. JJ after JJ Williams, JPR after JPR Williams and Gareth after Gareth Edwards. BBC2 2001. See Johnny Vaughan's entry in the biography section.

Osbournes, The Fly-on-the-wall documentary series looking at the home (a multi-million dollar Beverly Hills mansion) and family life of the dysfunctional Osbourne family, including former Black Sabbath frontman Ozzy Osbourne, his wife and manager Sharon, and their two children Jack and Kelly (elder daughter Aimee refused to appear). C4 2002-05.

OSS Ron Randell (Capt Frank Hawthorne), Lionel Murton (The Chief), Robert Gallico (Sgt O'Brien). Spy drama written by Paul Dudley concerning the Office of Strategic Services, the USA's forerunner of the CIA. Their top man is Frank Hawthorne (ably assisted by Sgt O'Brien), who work on the continent to expose foreign spies, rescue stranded operatives or mount sabotage missions. ITV 1957-58.

Other 'Arf, The Lorraine Chase (Lorraine Watts), John Standing (Charles Lattimer, MP), Patricia Hodge (Sybil Howarth), Steve Adler (Brian Sweeney), James Villiers (Lord Freddy Apthorpe). Sitcom based around the premise of an unlikely alliance between Cockney model Lorraine Watts and true-blue Tory MP Charles Latimer. ITV 1980-84.

OTT (Over The Top) Adult version of *Tiswas* with variations such as the three naked balloon dancers. Helen Atkinson-Wood and Alexei Sayle joined the regular cast of John Gorman, Lenny Henry, Chris Tarrant, and Bob Carolgees, all refugees from *Tiswas*. Sayle left midway through the series and was replaced by Bernard Manning. ITV 1982. A short-lived sequel, *Saturday Stayback*, also starring Chris Tarrant, was broadcast in 1983 and gave impressionist Phil Cool his screen debut.

Our Friends In The North Christopher Eccleston (Nicky Hutchinson), Daniel Craig (George 'Geordie' Peacock), Gina McKee (Mary Soulsby / Cox), Mark Strong (Terry 'Tosker' Cox), David Bradley (Eddie Wells), Peter Vaughan (Felix Hutchinson), Freda Dowie (Florrie Hutchinson), Alun Armstrong (Austin Donohue), Malcolm McDowell (Benny Barrett), Julian Fellowes (Claud Seabrook), Peter Jeffrey (Commissioner Sir Colin Blamire). Drama written by Peter Flannery. A nine-part series depicting the varying fortunes of four friends - Nicky, Geordie, Mary and Tosker - from the calm and optimistic times of the 1960s to the uncertainties of the 1990s. Taking nine pivotal years (1964, 1966, 1967, 1970, 1974, 1979, 1984, 1987, 1995) the personal lives of the characters become intertwined with the political struggles of their home town of Newcastle, and the capital, London. We also see the machinations behind the scenes that affect their lives, often for the worse: slum housing projects, police corruption, the rise of Thatcherism, political sleaze, and specific events like the 1984 Miners' Strike. BBC2 1996.

Our House Hattie Jacques (Georgina Ruddy), Charles Hawtrey (Simon Willow), Frederick Peisley (Herbert Keene), Leigh Madison (Marcia Hatton), Hylda Baker (Henrietta), Bernard Bresslaw (William Singer), Eugenie Cavanagh (Marina), Ina De La Haye (Mrs. Iliffe), Trader Faulkner (Stephen Hatton), Frank Pettingell (Captain Iliffe), Norman Rossington (Gordon Brent),

Joan Sims (Daisy Burke). Sitcom concerning a group of very different people who meet in an estate agent's office and decide to pool together their funds and buy a house large enough to accommodate them all. Characters include librarian Georgina Ruddy, council official Simon Willow, unemployable Daisy Burke, Yorkshire sea dog Captain Illiffe and his French musician wife, newlywed Hattons, bank clerk Herbert Keene and law student Gordon Brent. In the second series Henrietta, William Singer and Marina replaced the Iliffes, Daisy and Gordon. ITV 1960-61.

Our Man At St Mark's Leslie Phillips (Rev Andrew Parker), Donald Sinden (Rev Stephen Young), Joan Hickson (Mrs Peace), Anne Lawson (Anne Gibson), Harry Fowler (Harry 'The Yo-Yo' Danvers). Sitcom depicting the trials and tribulations of the vicar of St Marks Church in a small village called Felgate (real-life Denham Village, Bucks). With the aid of his stern but loyal housekeeper, Mrs Peace, and his girlfriend, Anne, he becomes involved in various episodes in the lives of his parishioners. After the first series, Leslie Phillips and Anne Lawson left and Donald Sinden became the new star of the show as the dog-loving Rev Stephen Young (Mr Robertson was the name of his Scottie dog) and Harry Fowler was brought in to play his young scooter-riding sexton Harry the Yo-Yo (so called because he was always bouncing in and out of jail). The final series, in which the programme was retitled *Our Man From St Mark's*, saw Reverend Young promoted to Archdeacon and moving away from the village to work in the cathedral city of Lynchester. (The cathedral location scenes were filmed in Lincoln). In this series Clive Morton played the bishop and Peter Vaughan, the Rev John Spencer. ITV 1963-66.

Our Mutual Friend Paul Daneman (John Rokesmith), Zena Walker (Miss Bella Wilfer), David McCallum (Eugene Wrayburn), Richard Leech ('Rogue' Riderhood), Richard Pearson (Nicodemus Boffin), Rachel Roberts (Lizzie Hexam). 12-part mini-series adaptation of the classic Dicken's tale. BBC 1958-59

Out of the Blue Orla Brady (D.S. Rebecca 'Becky' Bennett), Darrell D'Silva (D.C. Warren Allen), Neil Dudgeon (D.C. Marty Brazil), Stephen Billington (P.C. Alex Holder), Pauline Black (Dr. Innocent Adesigbin), John Hannah (D.S Frank 'Frankie' Drinkall), David Morrissey (D.S. Jim 'Lew' Llewyn), Nicola Stephenson (Lucy Shaw), John Duttine (D.I. Eric Temple). 12-episodes (across two series) were shown of this highly acclaimed drama series that follows the personal and professional lives of a group of detectives. BBC1 1995-96

Out of the Frying Pan The Series 2 *Restaurant* contestants James Knight Pacheco and Alasdair Hooper step out of the professional kitchen to test their skills in the real world, as event caterers. BBC2 2010

Out of this World British TV's first attempt at a science fiction anthology. Each one of 13 sixty-minute episodes was introduced by master of horror, Boris Karloff. The series featured dramatisations of short stories by popular fantasy writers such as Isaac Asimov, Philip K. Dick and Clifford Simak. Terry Nation adapted two scripts as well as writing 'Botony Bay,' in which a psychiatry student (William Gaunt) discovers that his patients are possessed by aliens. He kills one of them, and in a bitter twist, is committed to the same institution. The series also featured many familiar TV names such as Nigel Stock, Peter Wyngarde, Patrick Allen, Milo O'Shea and Paul Eddington. ITV 1962.

Out of Town Countryside programme introduced by Jack Hargreaves (1911-93) an author and television presenter famed for his love of outdoor pursuits and particularly nature and agricultural practices. *Out of Town* began as a regional programme on Southern Television from 1958 but was networked nationally throughout the 1960s on ITV. The theme song, performed by Max Bygraves began: *Say what you will, The countryside is still, The only place that I could settle down. Troubles there are, So much rarer.... Out of Town. Spring starts to spring, Robins start to sing, And Mother Nature wears her newest gown. What I'd give once, more to live right.......Out of town.*

Outnumbered Hugh Dennis (Pete), Claire Skinner (Sue) Daniel Roche (Ben), Tyger Drew-Honey (Jake), Ramona Marquez (Karen), Samantha Bond (Angela), David Ryall (Grandfather). Partly-improvised sitcom written by Andy Hamilton and Guy Jenkin. Pete, a history teacher, and his wife Sue, a part-time PA, are 'outnumbered' by their three demanding children, eleven-year-old Jake, seven-year-old Ben, and five-year-old Karen. The adult roles are scripted but actors are allowed to react naturally to the unscripted asides of the children. BBC1 2007-

Outside Edge Robert Daws (Roger Dervish), Brenda Blethyn (Miriam 'Mim' Dervish), Timothy Spall (Kevin Costello), Josie Lawrence (Maggie Costello). Sitcom written by Richard Harris. Roger Dervish is the pompous captain of a minor Sunday League cricket team. He plans his Brent Park Cricket Club campaigns like a military director, even wearing the club blazer at home. Chauvinistic and self-important, he speaks brusquely and patronisingly to Mim because, bereft of sensitivity, he knows no other way. Although he likes to think of himself as the driving force behind the team, it is his long-suffering wife that actually holds the whole thing together. Other characters include Roger's friend, Kevin Costello, a bit of a slob but a fine batsman. Kevin is married to the lovely Maggie, a very outgoing, affectionate woman. She adores Kevin and has a seemingly insatiable appetite for sex. Based on Richard Harris's stage play, which had previously been televised in 1982 (with Paul Eddington as Roger, Prunella Scales as Miriam, Jonathan Lynn as Kevin and Maureen Lipman as Maggie). ITV 1994-96.

Over the Rainbow Reality television show presented by Graham Norton, its aim, to find a Dorothy for a West End production of *The Wizard of Oz*. The judges were singer Charlotte Church, actors John Partridge and Sheila Hancock, and head judge Lord Andrew Lloyd Webber, who was also the co-producer of the new stage production. Danielle Hope was the eventual winner and "Dangerous Dave" won the role of "Toto" for the one-off Gala performance. BBC1 2010 (also broadcast on TV3 in Ireland). See also *How Do You Solve a Problem Like Maria?*, *Any Dream Will Do* and *I'd Do Anything*.

Oxbridge Blues Ian Charleson (Victor Geary -Oxbridge Blues), Rosalyn Landor (Wendy - Oxbridge Blues), Amanda Redman (Maxine - Oxbridge Blues), Michael Elphick (Curly Bonaventura - Oxbridge Blues), Malcolm Stoddard (Philip Geary - Oxbridge Blues; Michael - Similar Triangles), Kate Fahy (Eileen - Similar Triangles; Lizzie - Cheap Day), Ciaran Madden (Laura - Cheap Day; Rachel - Similar Triangles), Norman Rodway (Alec - Cheap Day; Narrator - Similar Triangles), Geoffrey Palmer (Fred - Cheap Day), Christopher Good (James - Cheap Day), Ben Kingsley (Geoff Craven - Sleeps Six), Diane Keen (Sherry Craven - Sleeps Six), Jeremy Child (Philip Witham - Sleeps Six), Jackie Smith-Wood (Lady Jane Witham - Sleeps Six), Susan Sarandon (Natalie - He'll See You Now), Barry Dennen (Dr. Stein - He'll See You Now), David Suchet (Colin - The Muse), Frances Tomelty (Angela Lane - The Muse), Carol Royle (Tory - That Was Tory; Ellen - The Muse), John Bird (Clive - That Was Tory), Joanna Lumley (GiGi - That Was Tory). Based on his own short stories, *The Glittering Prizes* author Frederic Raphael wrote this drama series featuring seven plays concerning Oxbridge graduates. BBC2 1984.

Packet of Three Off-beat comedy series written by and starring Frank Skinner (Frank), Jenny Éclair (Jenny) and Henry Normal (Henry), concerning the backstage shenanigans of the staff of the Crumpsall Palladium interspersed with three weekly stand up comedy acts. For the second series, retitled *Packing Them In*, Henry was replaced by Roger Mann (Reg) and Kevin Eldon (Boyle). C4 1991-92

Paddington Michael Bond's fictional creation was found at Paddington railway station in London by the Brown family. He was sitting on a suitcase with a note attached to his coat which read "Please look after this bear. Thank you." He arrived as a stowaway coming from "deepest, darkest Peru", sent by his Aunt Lucy. He tells them that his Peruvian name is "hard to pronounce", so the Browns decide to call him Paddington. They take him home to 32 Windsor Gardens near Portobello Road, and, narrated by actor Michael Hordern, the stories follow

Paddington's adventures and mishaps in England. BBC1 1976; 1979.

Palace, The Rupert Evans (King Richard IV), Jane Asher (Queen Charlotte), Sophie Winkleman (Princess Eleanor), Sebastian Armesto (Prince George), Roy Marsden (Sir Iain Ratalick), Zoe Telford (Abigail Thomas), David Harewood (Major Simon Brooks), Lorcan Cranitch (Jonty Roberts), Hugh Ross (Jeremy Robinson), John Ramm (Chief Superintendent Peter Bayfield), Huw Rhys (David Waverley), Owain Arthur (Jimmy Clacy), Kate O'Flynn (Ruby Riley), Russell Bright (Neil Haslam), Amit Shah (Vinny Ganatra), Fiona Button (Lucy Bedford), Nathalie Lunghi (Princess Isabelle), Shelley Conn (Miranda Hill), John Shrapnel (PM Edward Shaw), Heather Tobias (Anne Featherstone). A fictional account of a royal family living in England's Buckingham Palace. Created by Tom Grieves the story follows the British Royal Family in the aftermath of the death of King James III and the succession of his 24-year-old son, Richard IV. The series was filmed on location in Lithuania. ITV 2008.

Pallisers, The Susan Hampshire (Lady Glencora McCluskie/Palliser), Philip Latham (Plantagenet Palliser, MP), Donald Pickering (Dolly Longstaffe), Roger Livesey (Duke of St. Bungay), Moray Watson (Barrington Erle), Roland Culver (Duke of Omnium), Anna Massey (Laura Standish/Kennedy), Barry Justice (Burgo Fitzgerald), Anna Carteret (Lady Mabel Grex), Jeremy Irons (Frank Tregear), Anthony Andrews (Earl of Silverbridge), Derek Jacobi (Lord Fawn), Barbara Murray (Marie Goesler/Finn), Bryan Pringle (Mr Monk), Penelope Keith (Mrs Hittaway), Anthony Ainley (Rev Emilius), Martin Jarvis (Frank Greystock), Terence Alexander (Lord George), Robin Bailey (Mr Gresham), Peter Sallis (Mr Bonteen), June Whitfield (Mrs Bonteen), Jo Kendall (Adelaide Palliser), Jeremy Clyde (Gerard Maude), Stuart Wilson (Ferdinand Lopez), Clifford Rose (Quintus Slide), Lynne Frederick (Isabel Boncasson). 26-part adaptation of Anthony Trollope's six so-called 'political' novels (the protagonist eventually becomes Prime Minister). Politics and romantic intrigue surround the unlikely union of stolid MP Plantagenet Palliser and the vivacious heiress Lady Glencora, affecting the lives of their friends and family alike. BBC2 1974.

Panorama World's longest-running current affairs programme. First introduced by Max Robertson on 11 November 1953, it began as more of a magazine with Malcolm Muggeridge on hand to interview the famous. Denis Mathews was the art critic and Nancy Spain reviewed books whilst Lionel Hale discussed events in the theatre. After two years, Panorama was transformed to become a 'window on the world' and into the programme we know today by the arrival of Richard Dimbleby, originally aided by athlete Christopher Chataway and John Freeman. A famous April Fool's Day joke was played in 1957 when Panorama reported on a bumper spaghetti harvest in southern Switzerland. Television viewers saw Richard Dimbleby walking among trees growing spaghetti, while workers pulled the pasta off the trees and put it into baskets. When viewers called to ask how they could grow spaghetti plants, the BBC replied "place a sprig of spaghetti in a tin of tomato sauce and hope for the best." Lending the hoax credibility, was the fact that spaghetti was not a widely eaten food in Britain in the 1950s and was considered by many to be very exotic. When Richard retired in 1963 a succession of presenters and reporters, including Patrick Murphy, James Mossman, Robin Day, David Dimbleby, Alastair Burnet, Charles Wheeler, Fred Emery, Robert Kee, Betsan Powys and Alan Little have ensured style continuity. The present host is Jeremy Vine. Since 1971 the theme music has been an adaptation of Francis Lai's *Aujourd'Hui C'est Toi*. (Today It's You). Possibly the most famous Panorama programme of all was the 1995 interview of Diana, Princess of Wales by Martin Bashir, which occurred after her separation in which she talked frankly about her personal life. BBC1 1953-

Para Handy - Master Mariner Duncan Macrae (Peter 'Para Handy' McFarlane), John Grieve (Dan Macphail), Roddy McMillan (Dougie), Angus Lennie (Sunny Jim). Set in the lochs and channels of Western Scotland that Para Handy creator Neil Munro (initially using the pen-name Hugh Foulis in 1905 editions of the Glasgow Evening News) used in the original stories, this BBC Scotland production benefitted enormously from the filmed sequences, most of them directed by James MacTaggart. Duncan Ross updated the stories to contemporary times figuring that the trials and tribulations of a working life on the sea had changed little since the period in which the original tales were set. Para Handy was the wily skipper of the tiny Clyde steamer, *The Vital Spark*, delivering goods to remote communities. His crew consisted of Macphail the chief engineer, Dougie the mate, and Sunny Jim the cabin boy/cook. BBC1 1959-60. See also *The Vital Spark* and *The Tales of Para Handy*.

Paradise Club Leslie Grantham (Danny Kane), Don Henderson (Frank Kane). Drama created by Murray Smith. Two brothers, Frank and Danny Kane have drifted apart. Danny is a good-hearted London gangster while Frank, an ex-boxer, has become a priest who has a severe gambling addiction. Frank leaves the church after being falsely accused of stealing the collection money and subsequently inherits The Paradise Club (in Paradise Street, Rotherhithe) on the death of their mother. Frank returns to London to run the club with his brother and to also try and keep Danny on the straight and narrow. BBC1 1989-90.

Paradise Or Bust Take two 26-years-olds, a paradise island, a "tribe" of internet members and a dream of building an eco village – will it result in Paradise Or Bust? This unique observational documentary series followed the tears, tantrums and trials involved in getting such a business venture up and running and the relentless challenges it faced in its first year. With no experience and little money, the two young entrepreneurs – Ben Keene and Mark Bowness – set about making their vision a reality on a remote Fijian island called Vorovoro. Their objective was to build an eco-tourist village which would benefit nearby communities for generations to come. BBC2 2008.

Pardon My Genie Hugh Paddick and Arthur White (The Genie), Roy Barraclough (Mr Thomas Cobbledick), Ellis Jones (Hal Adden), Joe Dunlop (PC Appleby). Children's sitcom written by Bob Block and Larry Parker. Hal Adden, a young assistant in a hardware shop in the fictitious town of Widdimouth happens to be polishing up some watering cans when out pops a 4,000-year-old genie, keen to serve his new master. The only trouble is, his back's a bit stiff and well, what with one thing and another, his spells have a habit of going wrong. Other characters include, the shop owner, Mr Cobbledick; Hal's shaggy dog Fred; and the local bewildered bobby PC Appleby. In the second series the genie was played far more menacingly by Arthur White. ITV 1972-73.

Pardon The Expression Arthur Lowe (Leonard Swindley). Spin-off series from *Coronation Street* in which the former proprietor of Weatherfield's Gamma Garments boutique is now assistant branch manager of one of Dobson and Hawks' stores. Ben Kingsley made his screen debut in this series. ITV 1965-66. This series gave rise to another spin-off series Turn Out The Lights (1967) in which Swindley becomes an amateur ghostbuster.

Parent-Craft Janet Burnell (Mrs Pebble), Shirley Eaton (Anne Pebble), James Fox (Irving Pebble), William Mervyn (Mr Pebble), Robert Morley (R. Cressington-Tallboy). Six-part drama series notable for its all-star cast and the very first screen appearance of Shirley Eaton. BBC 1951.

Parents of the Band Jimmy Nail (Phil Parker), Peter Lossaso (Jack Parker), Nina Young (Marketa), Niky Wardley (Sandy Soutakis), David Barseghian (Eddie Soutakis), Lucinda Dryzek (Lucy Soutakis), Nicola Hughes (Carmen Cunningham), Colin McFarlane (Ashton Cunningham), Franz Drameh (Granville Cunningham), Michael Karim (Adi Kundra), Geoffrey McGivern (Kipper Hitchcock). Six-part comedy drama series created by Jimmy Nail and Tarquin Gotch and written by David Cummings, Dick Clement and Ian La Frenais. Phil is an ex rock-and-roller who was in an 80s band who were a one-hit-wonder with the song "I Cry". His son Jack is now a drummer in a teenage band and the plot revolves around the rivalry between the parents, each wanting to manage things their way. The theme music was composed by Jimmy Nail and Gary Kemp. BBC1 2008-09.

Parkinson Born in Cudworth, Yorkshire, 28 March 1935, Michael Parkinson began life as a newspaper journalist before breaking into broadcasting in the late 1960s. His chat-show, *Parkinson*, began in 1971 and he soon proved he was the natural successor to Eamonn Andrews as a good-humoured but incisive interviewer. For eleven years the show was the staple BBC Saturday night diet. 'Parky' left the BBC in 1982 to be co-founder and presenter on the ITV breakfast television station TV-am, where after many schedule upheavals he ended up presenting the

Sunday morning programme with his wife Mary (nee Heneghan). During this period Michael wrote a series of children's books called *The Woofits* about a family of anthropomorphic dog-like creatures in the fictional Yorkshire coal-mining village of Grimeworth. The books led to an ITV series (1981-82), which he narrated. He returned to the BBC in 1995 to present a series of retrospective shows, *Parkinson: The Interviews* featuring excerpts from *Parkinson*, eventually presenting a new, revived version of his chat show on BBC1 in 1998. Following a well-publicised slot dispute with BBC controller, Lorraine Heggessey, *Parkinson*, was 'poached' by ITV and from September 2004, Parkinson, aired on ITV for the first time. The last edition, *Parkinson: The Final Conversation*, was broadcast in December 2007.

Passion, The Joseph Mawle (Jesus), James Nesbitt (Pontius Pilate), Paul Nicholls (Judas), Ben Daniels (Caiaphas), Penelope Wilton (Mary), Denis Lawson (Annas), Paloma Baeza (Mary Magdalene), Darren Morfitt (Peter), Jamie Sives (John), Dean Lennox Kelly (James), Daniel Evans (Matthew), Tom Ellis (Philip), Eoin Geoghegan (Andrew), Eugene Wood (Bartholomew), Lewis Clay (Thomas), Stuart Kidd (Simon), Thomas Buchanan (James Alphaeus), Steve Morphew (Thaddeus), Stephen Graham (Barabbas), Vinette Robinson (Mina) and David Oyelowo (Joseph of Arimathea). Four-part drama written by Frank Deasy and shown in entirety on Easter Sunday 2008. The story is told from three points of view - the religious authorities, the Romans and Jesus. BBC 1 2008

Paul O'Grady Show, The Paul James Michael O'Grady was born in Birkenhead, Cheshire 14 June 1955. His alter-ego of Lilian May Veronica Savage was invented in 1977 and named after his mother's maiden name. Lily, a Liverpudlian prostitute, was based on several women who had influenced Paul's early life, notably his aunty Chris. When Paul's drag act first gained television exposure he always appeared in character and hosted several series of *Blankety Blank* as Lily. At the end of this series Paul began to take on work as himself, notably in the sitcom *Eyes Down*, and eventually retired the Lily Savage character in 2004 claiming he had "seen the light, taken the veil and packed herself off to a convent in France". Lily is however reported to be making a one-off comeback in Aladdin for the 2010/11 pantomime season. *The Paul O'Grady Show* began on ITV in 2004 and consisted of Paul reading viewers letters and engaging in some one-way badinage with his pet dogs Buster (a Shih Tzu / Bichon Frise cross) and Olga (a Cairn Terrier) until the first commercial break. Thereafter Paul would chat with invited guests and then play *Guess the Tune*, a phone-in-competition where Paul pretended to play tunes on his organ and the contestant had to guess them correctly to win up to £2000. The tune that Paul played leading into the game was "Sing As We Go", by Gracie Fields. When Paul defected to Channel 4 in 2006 the show was resurrected in the same 5pm slot and Paul's own television production company, Olga TV (named after one of the aforementioned dogs), took over production of the programme. The show became billed as *The New Paul O'Grady Show* and among other less than subtle changes *Guess the Tune* became *The Organ Game*. The series finally ended at Christmas 2009. ITV 2004-05; C4 2006-09. Paul returned to ITV in September 2010 to host a revamped version of the show entitled *Paul O'Grady Live* which aired at 9pm

Paul Temple Francis Matthews (Paul Temple), Ros Drinkwater (Steve Temple). Amateur sleuth created by Francis Durbridge (1912-98). The characters of Paul Temple and his, then, girlfriend Steve Trent, began their life in 1938, in a popular radio series, Paul originally being played by Hugh Morton and Steve by Bernadette Hodgson. The radio series ended in 1968 and by that time six other actors had played Temple; Carl Bernard (1941-42), Richard Williams (1944), Barry Morse (1945), Howard Marion Crawford (1946), Kim Peacock (1946-53) and Peter Coke (1954-68). The famous theme music for the series was "Coronation Scot" composed by Vivian Ellis (early serials featured a section from the 2nd movement of Rimsky-Korsakov's "Scheherazade" as the theme music). When the series transferred to television Francis Matthews (who had previously starred in a 1956

Durbridge BBC series *My Friend Charles*) took over the role at the request of Durbridge. Thirty-year-old Canadian-born novelist Temple now lived in a Chelsea apartment with his 25-year-old wife Steve. He drove a Rolls-Royce Silver Shadow Coupe and the success of his books meant he could travel the country for most of the year following his great passion as an amateur sleuth. Although this series was credited under the banner of *Francis Durbridge Presents: Paul Temple*, the master of suspense did not actually write any of the 52-episode television series, spread over four series. BBC1 1969-71.

Peak Practice Kevin Whatley (Dr Jack Kerruish), Amanda Burton (Dr Beth Glover/Kerruish), Simon Shepherd (Dr. Will Preston), Gary Mavers (Dr. Andrew Attwood), Saskia Wickham (Dr. Erica Matthews), Adrian Lukis (Dr. David Shearer), Haydn Gwynne (Dr. Joanna Graham), Joseph Millson (Dr. Sam Morgan), Gray O'Brien (Dr. Tom Deneley), Maggie O'Neill (Dr. Alex Redman), Jamie Bamber (Dr. Matt Kendal), Lynsey Baxter (Kate Turner), John Bowler (Mike Pullen), Joy Brook (Joanne Pearson), Sean Chapman (James Strickland), Esther Coles (Kim Beardsmore), Susannah Corbett (Kerri Davidson), Karl Davies (Nick Pullen), Hazel Ellerby (Chloe White), Christabel Fellowes (Leanne Shackleton), Regina Freedman (Liz Pullen), Fiona Gillies (Clare Shearer), Beth Goddard (Leanda Sharp), Deborah Grant (Carol Johnson), Julia Haworth (Julie Pullen), Sharon Hinds (Ellie Ndebala), James E. Kerr (Russ Skinner), Melanie Kilburn (Liz Pullen), Jacqueline Leonard (Sarah Preston), Thomas Lockyer (Dr. Nick Goodson), David Mallinson (Richard Turner), Margery Mason (Alice North), Victor McGuire (Shaun Carter), Shelagh McLeod (Kate Preston), Georgia Moffett (Nicki Davey), Siobhan O'Carroll (Bridgit Mellors), Paul Opacic (Mark Kershaw), Sarah Parish (Dawn Rudge), Richard Platt (James White), Eva Pope (Claire Brightwell), Shaun Prendergast (Trevor Sharp), Andrew Ray (Dr. John Reginald), Anne Reid (Rita Barrat), Veronica Roberts (Laura Elliott), Sukie Smith (Kirsty Attwood), Clive Swift (Norman Shorthose), Sylvia Syms (Isabel de Gines), Yolanda Vazquez (Clare Shearer), Ludmilla Vuli (Polly Stevens), Stuart Wells (Charlie Webster). Drama series created by Lucy Gannon. Dr Jack Kerruish has been running The Dry River Clinic in Africa. He moves back to England and eventually enters into a partnership with Dr. Will Preston and Dr. Beth Glover at The Beeches Surgery in the rural village of Cardale (real-life Crich), Derbyshire. In the third series Jack and Beth are married and return to Africa, being replaced at the surgery by Dr. Andrew Attwood and Dr. Erica Matthews. Further personnel changes occurred before the series was axed in 2002. ITV 1993-2002.

Pebble Mill At One The Pebble Mill studios have staged several BBC shows, most famously the *Pebble Mill at One* lunchtime chat show, which ran from 1972 to 1986. Bob Langley and Donny MacLeod were the original presenters. Other presenters and reporters included, Marion Foster, Anna Ford, Paul Coia, Magnus Magnusson, Josephine Buchan, Sarah Greene, Ross King, Jan Leeming, David Seymour, Alan Titchmarsh, Judi Spiers, Gloria Hunniford and Ross Kelly. During the February 1974 election campaign, the lunchtime news was extended from five minutes to 15. However the bulletin still began at 12.55pm. The result, of course, was that Pebble Mill at One actually went on air at 1.10pm. This anomaly meant the programme's title was temporarily changed to Pebble Mill and even when the show resumed its 1pm slot the new title remained until 1979 when it finally became Pebble Mill At One once more. Other items included in the format were gardening with Peter Seabrook, keep fit with Eileen Fowler, Collector's Corner with Arthur Negus, and cookery with Glyn Christian and Michael Smith. Five years after the show ended it was revived again for a further five-year run. BBC1 1972-86; 1991-96.

Peep Show David Mitchell (Mark Corrigan), Robert Webb (Jeremy Usbourne), Olivia Colman (Sophie Chapman), Matt King (Super Hans), Paterson Joseph (Alan Johnson), Neil Fitzmaurice (Jeff Heaney), Sophie Winkleman (Big Suze), Rachel Blanchard (Nancy), Isy Suttie (Dobby), Vera Filatova (Elena), Emily Bruni (Gail). Golden Rose-winning adult sitcom created by Andrew O'Connor, Jesse Armstrong and Sam Bain, following the domestic adventures of twentysomething south Croydon flatmates Mark and Jeremy. Mark is the sensible one, a professional brogue-wearer with a slightly disconcerting interest in World War Two. Jeremy is the loose cannon, a lazy waster with dodgy friends who dreams of becoming a musician but can never get his act together. The intimate thoughts of the two lads are made known to the viewer which lends itself to some very irreverent humour. C4 2003-

Pennies From Heaven Bob Hoskins (Arthur Parker), Cheryl Campbell (Eileen), Gemma Craven (Joan Parker), Hywel Bennett (Tom), Kenneth Colley (The Accordion Man), Freddie Jones (The Headmaster), Dave King (The Inspector), Nigel Havers (Conrad Baker). Dennis Potter's "play with music" tells the story of Arthur Parker, a rather cowardly and dishonest sheet-music salesman in 1930s Britain. Frustrated by his frigid wife and cynical shopkeepers, he looks to a desperate romance and his inner-life to reach the fantasy world of songs. The six-part serial gave playwright Dennis Potter his first popular success. Transforming his career, it would eventually lead to a lucrative spell working in Hollywood. BBC1 1978.

People Versus, The Game show originally hosted by Kirsty Young. In each round contestants were shown five questions from one of five specialist subjects. In Round One, each contestant had to attempt and answer correctly one of those five questions and if successful they carried on through subsequent rounds until ultimately answering all five questions of their last remaining subject. Each question was worth £5,000 and players could begin again if managing a clean run. Each player was also given three 'flips' which meant they could substitute any of the five given questions for another one. Also, if they had the cash, they could elect to 'buy' answers to questions at £10,000 a time. This was an inter-active game and viewers would supply some of the questions. If a contestant got their question wrong, they lost all money in that round and their seat in the game went to the person who set the question. Unfortunately for Dag Griffiths (one of Britain's leading quiz buffs) he was left stranded at the end of the first series and by the time the revamped version began the following year with new host Kaye Adams, the chance of winning a fortune had somewhat diminished. The new version had a much lower prize pool and also a version of David Briggs' 'Bong Game' where a recorded voice reads a sequence of numbers, representing an amount of money that increases in value by irregular amounts, for example: £1, £5, £20, £33, £70, £72, £200, £301, £600.... The recording ends, at an unpredictable point, with a "bong" sound. If the player shouts "stop" before the "bong", he or she wins the last sum of money mentioned. If the player waits too long and is interrupted by the "bong", he or she wins nothing. Contestants who shouted "stop" would then be played the rest of the tape to see how much more they could have won. In the People Versus version contestants could choose one of three sequences, one of which would permit the entire sum of money previously won to be retained before the bong was sounded. ITV 2000-02

People's Court, The Carol Smillie presented this British version of *Judge Judy* where real people argued their cases in a mock-court presided over alternately by Rhonda Anderson LLB and Jerome Lynch QC, the final verdict being decided by the viewing public. The resident court usher was Kevin Kelly. Filmed live at the Scottish Television studios in Glasgow from April 7th to May 20th 2005, this short-lived series was criticised for having two 'judges' who, unlike Judge Judith Sheindlin, had never presided over a real court and were ultimately too lenient with the 'litigants'. ITV 2005.

People's Quiz, The Shown in conjunction with BBC's Saturday evening National Lottery show and hosted by Jamie Theakston the quiz was given an X-Factor style format, the three question-masters (as opposed to judges) being Myleene Klass, Kate Garraway and William G. Stewart. The ultimate winner of the £200,700 prize was Stephanie Bruce. Theakston also hosted the companion show *The People's Quiz: Wildcard*. BBC1 2007

Peppa Pig Animated television series created by Neville Astley and Mark Baker. The show revolves around Peppa, an anthropomorphic female pig, and her family and friends; all of which are animals that display human traits. Peppa was voiced by Lily Snowden-Fine for the first series and then by Cecily Bloom

for the second in 2006. Nine-year-old Harley Bird (who won a children's BAFTA for her role) replaced Cecily for the third series in 2009. C5 2004-

Perfect Scoundrels Peter Bowles (Guy Buchanan), Bryan Murray (Harry Cassidy). Two con-men pool their talents in an effort for the big sting. The series was created by its two stars who had previously worked together on *The Irish RM*. ITV 1990-92.

Perfect Spy, A Peter Egan (Magnus Pym), Rüdiger Weigang (Axel), Jane Booker (Mary Pym), Ray McAnally (Rick Pym), Alan Howard (Jack Brotherhood), Sarah Badel (Baroness Weber). Seven-part adaptation of the novel by John le Carré. The story of Magnus Pym, from his childhood, strongly influenced by his multi-faceted father Rick who was a raconteur, con man, thief and black marketer, through his university days in Switzerland, where he is destined to meet the other person who will have the greatest influence in his life, Axel, a Czech refugee. As Pym enters his career in the British Secret Service, his relationship with Axel and the values he developed in childhood lead him down his own path of betrayal and loyalty. BBC1 1987.

Perfect World Paul Kaye (Bob Slay), Nina Wadia (Maggie), Derren Litten (Vaughan), Daniel Pertwee (Briony). Sitcom about a down-on-his-luck marketing manager, Bob Slay, of Gatehouse, a company that makes hygiene products. BBC2 2000-01.

Persuaders, The Tony Curtis (Danny Wilde), Roger Moore (Lord Brett Sinclair), Laurence Naismith (Judge Fulton). Created by Robert S. Baker and made by Lew Grade's ITC Entertainment as a vehicle for its two megastar actors. Lord Brett Sinclair and Danny Wilde, both millionaire international playboys, but from very different British and American backgrounds, are forced to team up to fight international crime by Judge Fulton who has a jail sentence hanging over their heads. Although the series lasted only 24 episodes (17 September 1971 – 25 February 1972) the quality of the performances were critically acclaimed around the world, the chemistry between Curtis and Moore enhancing the storylines greatly. The memorable theme tune was played by John Barry and his Orchestra and peaked at No 13 in the UK charts in December 1971. ITV 1971-72.

Peter Kay's Britain's Got the Pop Factor... and Possibly a New Celebrity Jesus Christ Soapstar Superstar Strictly on Ice Undoubtedly holding the record for the television show with the longest title, this spoof of reality television talent shows, is also up there with Sacha Baron Cohen's film *Borat: Cultural Learnings of America for Make Benefit Glorious Nation of Kazakhstan* as a title only true quiz buffs would ever remember, or perhaps want to! As well as being the title of the show, *Britain's Got the Pop Factor* is the title of the fictional series within the show, where *Celebrity Jesus Christ Soapstar Superstar Strictly on Ice* is the name of another talent show, to which the winner of *Britain's Got The Pop Factor* gains automatic entry. The programme was shown in the style of a live final talent show hosted by Cat Deeley and judged by Nicki Chapman, Pete Waterman and Neil Fox. The three category winners were Geraldine McQueen (Peter Kay), 2 Up 2 Down - a band in which the two women were wheelchair users (Jo Enright, Karl Lucas, David Hulston and Sian Foulkes) and R Wayne (Marc Pickering). Both 2 Up 2 Down and Geraldine (formerly a male named Gerry King) sang versions of the "Winner's Song", which was co-written by Peter Kay and Gary Barlow and reached No 2 in the UK Charts. Sir Paul McCartney made a cameo appearance as a mentor. Geraldine released *Once Upon a Christmas Song* as competition to Alex Burke's *Hallelujah* for that year's Christmas No 1 but alas failed miserably, only managing No 5 in the UK Charts. C4 2008.

Peter Kay's Phoenix Nights Peter Kay (Brian Potter and Max Bygraves), Dave Spikey (Jerry 'St Clair' Dignan), Neil Fitzmaurice (Ray Von), Janice Connolly (Holy Mary), Steve Edge (Alan Johnson), Toby Foster (Les), Bea Kelley (Marion), Archie Kelley (Kenny), Justin Moorhouse (Young Kenny), Patrick McGuinness (Paddy), Ted Robbins (Denzil 'Den' Perry), Sally Lindsay (Tracey Burns), Daniel Kitson (Spencer). Sitcom written by Peter Kay, Neil Fitzmaurice and Dave Spikey revolving around Bolton social club, the Phoenix. Its licensee is the bad-tempered, wheelchair-bound Brian Potter, whose struggles through mountains of difficulties - many of his own making - form the basis of the storylines. Brian is no stranger to club management but he has been dogged by bad luck - his first club flooded, his second burned down and then (at the end of the first series) the Phoenix went the same way, only to rise from the ashes in yet another tired new venture. Aiding Brian at the Phoenix are a motley staff: the compere/singer Jerry St Clair, the dangerously keen electrician / DJ Ray, the useless doormen Max and Paddy, the bar and cleaning staff Holy Mary and Marion, the gormless handyman Kenny and the musical twosome Alan and Les (Les Alanos). Potter's great rival is Den Perry, the owner of the Banana Grove club whom Brian believes torched his club. The series was a spin-off of a six-part fly-on-the-wall spoof collection narrated by Andrew Sachs entitled *That Peter Kay Thing* (C4 1999). The second series of *Peter Kay's Phoenix Nights* was simply entitled *Phoenix Nights*. C4 2001-02. After the second series Kay announced that the characters Max and Paddy (he played the former) would be given their own spin-off show. This was aired in 2004 as *Max and Paddy's Road To Nowhere*.

Peter Principle, The Jim Broadbent (Peter Duffley), Claire Skinner (Susan Harvey), Stephen Moore (Geoffrey Parkes), Tracy Keating (Brenda), David Schneider (Bradley Wilson), Daniel Flynn (David Edwards) Janette Legge (Iris) Sitcom concerning Peter Duffley, the inept manager of the Aldbridge branch of C&P (County and Provincial) Bank. The series title is an allusion to the so-called Peter Principle which states that everyone is promoted to their level of incompetence. Six episodes aired on BBC1 in 1997 followed by another six in 2000.

Peter Serafinowicz Show, The Sketch show starring the comedy actor / impressionist who had previously had supporting roles in *Black Books* and *Spaced*. Impressions include James Bond, Al Pacino, Elvis Presley, *The Beatles*, Simon Cowell and Charles Dickens! Other characters include the incompetent private investigator Brian Butterfield, Michael-6 – the robot chat show host who struggles to understand and solve the problems his guests bring onto the show - and *O News!* anchor man Kennedy St King. BBC2 2007. The six-episode series was followed by a one-off Christmas special in 2008.

Phoenix Nights See *Peter Kay's Phoenix Nights*

Picture Book Picture book was the fourth of the five regular programmes in the *Watch With Mother* slot (first airing in February 1955). It was originally presented by Patricia Driscoll (with stories read by Charles E. Stidwill) whose soft vocal tones "Do you think you could do this? - I am sure you could if you tried" inspired many a child on to early attempts at origami and other constructions. The pages of the book were turned to reveal various items for example, a way of making lanterns. Another page introduced Bizzy Lizzy, a wispy-haired little girl with a magic wishing flower on her dress. She was allowed four wishes by touching the flower but if she wished a fifth time all her wishes flew away. The Jolly Jack Tar sailors were a popular page, sometimes in search of the Talking Horse on strange lands such as Bottle Island (the moustachioed captain, Mr Mate, Jonathan the deck-hand and Ticky the monkey being possible inspirations for *Captain Pugwash*). A favourite game was played when the presenter would cover a tray of objects with a cloth, and then remove one and the young viewers had to guess which one had gone. Before the last page was turned, Sausage, a marionette dachshund would appear meaning it was time to put the book away. The kaleidoscope image at the beginning of the programme provided the inspiration for the introduction of *Jackanory* years later. Vera McKechnie took over the presentation when Patricia landed the role of Maid Marian in *The Adventures of Robin Hood*. BBC 1955-63.

Pie in the Sky Richard Griffiths (Henry Crabbe), Maggie Steed (Margaret Crabbe), Malcolm Sinclair (ACC Freddy Fisher). Drama series created by Andrew Payne. After 25 years loyal service, Henry Crabbe, an intelligent, sensible, mild-mannered man, desperately wants to retire from Barstock CID and devote his time and energy to his beloved restaurant, Pie In The Sky (situated in the fictional town of Middleton). However, Assistant Chief Constable Fisher won't allow him to take full retirement from the force as this would expose his own ineptitude to the unwelcome attention of his superiors. So, until Henry can solve

this invidious dilemma, he continues to work as ace detective and master chef. BBC1 1994-97.

Pigeon Street Children's animation series created by Alan Rogers and Peter Lang, first shown on the BBC in 1981. Characters on Pigeon Street included Clara the long distance lorry driver, her partner Hugo the chef, Mr Baskerville the detective, Mr Jupiter the astronomer, Mr Macadoo the petshop owner and two twins, Molly and Polly, who were only distinguishable by the letter M and P on their jumpers. The thirteen episodes were narrated by George Layton with additional voices by John Telfer. See also *Watch With Mother*.

Pig In The Middle Liza Goddard (Nellie Bligh), Dinsdale Landen and Terence Brady (Bartholomew 'Barty' Wade), Joanna Van Gyseghem (Susan Wade). Sitcom created by Terence Brady and Charlotte Bingham. The marriage of Barty and Susan Wade, no longer thirty-somethings, is proving something of a strain. He is the archetypal little boy turned civil servant who has never quite got around to growing up; she likes to maintain a certain middle-class standard, keeping house and husband trim; between them, they can reel off a list of mutual frustrations as tall as a church spire. Susan also likes to throw parties at their East Sheen (south-west London) home, and it is at one such gathering that Barty meets the easy-going, footloose and freely fanciable Nellie, for whom he falls hook, line and sinker, becoming the title's 'pig in the middle'. Despite Nellie's advances Barty does manage to keep their relationship on a platonic platform. Dinsdale Landen decided to leave after the first series, so writer Terence Brady took over the role of Barty for the remaining two series. ITV 1980-83.

Piglet Files, The Nicholas Lyndhurst (Peter Chapman), Clive Francis (Major Maurice Drummond), John Ringham (Major Andrew Maxwell), Serena Evans (Sarah Chapman). Sitcom written by Brian Leveson and Paul Minett. College lecturer Peter Chapman is recruited by MI5 (codename: Piglet) taking orders from Majors Drummond and Maxwell. Sarah is Peter's bemused wife. The theme music was composed by Rod Argent and Peter Van Hooke, and co-star Clive Francis drew the caricatures that featured in the title sequence. ITV 1990-92.

Pingwings, The Airing under the *Small Time* banner, The Pingwings was Oliver Postgate's first attempt at stop-frame puppet animation. Each story told of the adventures of a family of woolly penguins - Mr and Mrs Pingwing, children Paul and Penny and their tiny baby. The series was narrated by Postgate and Olwen Griffiths and the music was provided by Vernon Elliott. ITV 1962-63.

Pinky and Perky Created by Czech immigrants Jan and Vlasta Dalibor, the male twin pigs were as famous as The Beatles at the height of their fame. The string puppets had their own show throughout the 1960s but also appeared as guests on every variety show on the box. They made records (sometimes reviewed on Juke Box Jury), had their own TV station (the fictitious PPC TV) where they were joined by Horace Hare, The Whiskerley Sisters, Prunella Piglet, Morton Frog, Bertie Bonkers (a baby elephant), Vera Vixen, Conchita the cow, Basil Bloodhound, Ambrose Cat, and the all-bird group The Beakels. Their human straight-men included John Slater, Roger Moffat, Jimmy Thompson, Bryan Burdon and comedian Fred Emney for their television debut in 1957. The porcine couple were hardly distinguishable when attired in their sailor outfits but their usual mode of dress saw Pinky in red and Perky in blue (Perky wearing a red beret to aid black and white viewers). One of the nation's favourite pastimes in the 1960s was to play their favourite singles at a faster speed to simulate the high-pitched manic falsetto of the twin porkers. The multi-talented pigs were revived in the 1990s and had a Top 20 hit - Reet Petite. BBC/ITV 1957; 1960-68; ITV 1970-71.

Pinwright's Progress James Hayter (Mr J. Pinwright), Clarence Wright (Aubrey), Sara Gregory (Miss Doolittle), Daphne Maddox (Miss Peasbody), Doris Palmer (Mrs Sigsbee), Leonard Sharp (Ralph). Sitcom written by Rodney Hobson. Mr J. Pinwright is the proprietor of Macgillygally's Stores. He has a hated rival, and his staff only add to his problems by attempting to be helpful. Ralph, the messenger boy, is a deaf octogenarian. This is generally considered to be the world's first regular half-hour sitcom. The ten episodes, which aired fortnightly in alternation with Kaleidoscope, were broadcast live from the BBC studios at Alexandra Palace. BBC 1946-47

Pipkins See *Inigo Pipkin*.

Place By The Sea, A Holiday show presented by property guru Seetha Hallett, who helps more genuine house hunters fulfil their dream of escaping to the UK coast. C4 2005-

Place In The Sun, A Holiday home show hosted by various presenters although former estate agent Amanda Lamb is by far the most prolific. Other presenters have included Zilpah Hartley, Bella Crane, Fay Davies, Jasmine Harman, Jonnie Irwin, Simone Bienne and Victoria Hollingsworth. Each well-formatted episode highlights a couple looking at four selected properties in a particular area within a defined budget before deciding on what house they would like to purchase. *A Place in the Sun - Home or Away*, in which people view properties both in the UK and in a foreign country, is a spin-off series presented by Jasmine Harman and Jonnie Irwin. C4 2000- As with many Channel 4 holiday and property shows there are various spin-off series, *My Place In The Sun*, presented by Zilpah Hartley, is one such series that follows the aftermath of the purchases. See also *A Place By The Sea*.

Plane Makers, The Patrick Wymark (John Wilder), Barbara Murray and Ann Firbank (Pamela Wilder), Jack Watling (Don Henderson), Reginald Marsh (Arthur Sugden), Robert Urquhart (Henry Forbes), Peter Barkworth (Kenneth Bligh), Peter Jeffrey (James Cameron-Grant MP). Drama series set around the fictitious Scott Furlong aircraft factory and its 5,000 staff as they developed the innovative new Sovereign aircraft. After two series the programme was renamed *The Power Game* with John Wilder becoming very much the central character, leaving the aircraft industry to take up a position on the board of a bank and eventually receiving a knighthood. The series ended with the sudden death of its star (the father of actress Jane Wymark) in 1970. ITV 1963-65; 1965-69.

Planet Earth The most ambitious factual series ever commissioned by the BBC and a breathtaking exploration of our world. Each episode explores different aspects of Earth's formations including, mountains, seas, deserts, caves and rivers. Presented by David Attenborough and music by Sigur Rós. BBC1 2006 See *Life in Cold Blood*

Play Away Saturday afternoon programme known as the sister programme to *Play School*. It catered for slightly older children too and the presenters were basically the same as *Play School* with notable additions including, Anita Dobson, Julie Covington, Tony Robinson, Nerys Hughes and a young aspiring actor/musician named Jeremy Irons. The theme song was written by ex-Four Pennies vocalist Lionel Morton. BBC2 1971-84.

Play School At 11am on 21 April 1964, quite unintentionally, Play School became the first ever programme broadcast on BBC2. A grand opening for the channel had been planned for the night before, but was scuppered by a power failure. The pre-school age show was created by Joy Whitby and the first presenters were Gordon Rollings and Virginia Stride. Other presenters have included Brian Cant, Carol Chell, Chloe Ashcroft, Derek Griffiths, Eric Thompson, Phyllida Law, Floella Benjamin, Fred Harris, Carmen Munroe, Johnny Ball, Simon Davies, Kate Copstick, Julie Stevens, Toni Arthur, Colin Jeavons, Carole Ward, Wally Whyton and Stuart Bradley. The presenters were accompanied by a supporting cast of cuddly toys and dolls. The five regulars being: Big Ted and Little Ted; Humpty Dumpty; Jemima, a ragdoll with long red and white striped legs; Hamble, a rather dirty plastic doll (retired in 1986); and Poppy, a black doll who replaced Hamble in response to changing attitudes in society. A rocking horse named Dapple was also seen in some episodes, when a particular song or item suggested it. There were also real animals Katoo - a cockatoo, George and Peter - rabbits, a guinea pig named Elizabeth, Henry and Henrietta mice and two goldfish - Bit and Bot. Each episode began: 'Here is a house, here is a door, windows -- one, two, three, four. Ready to knock? Turn the lock. It's Play School'. The show began each day with a theme. Monday was useful box day, Tuesday dressing up day, Wednesday pets day, Thursday ideas day, and Friday science day. The high point of each episode was the video excursion into the outside world taken through one of three windows: the young viewers were invited to guess whether the round, square, or arched window would be chosen that day. A triangular window was added in 1983. Very often the film would be of a factory producing something such as buttons if it were the round window, walking sticks if the arched window and perhaps bars of chocolate if the rectangular window. The clue was always present in the shape of the subject and the shape of the window. The three window option lives on in the children's programme Tikkabilla (2002-), which borrows much from *Play School*. BBC2 1964-88. From 1971 to 1984, *Play School* also had a sister programme, called *Playaway*.

Play Your Cards Right Game show hosted by Bruce Forsyth. Two married couples attempt to answer survey questions asked to 100 people in a particular category, for example 'We surveyed 100 shopkeepers. How many said that they had overcharged a customer they did not like?' Brucie would then ask one couple to hazard a guess at the percentage and then ask the other couple if they thought it was higher or lower. The couples then proceed to turn over cards having to guess whether the card is higher or lower than the preceding one. The winning couple then go on to play a final game for big money or a car but now they are able to bet real money dependent on it being a good card or bad one. Several catchphrases were coined during the run, including, "What do points make? Prizes!", '"What a lovely audience! You're so much better than last week's." - the joke being that it was the same audience with whom Brucie had recorded a show an hour earlier, "Higher, lower, higher, lower", "You get nothing for a pair - not in this game", "It could still be a good night if you play your cards right", and "Don't touch the pack, we'll be right back!" Bruce would start each show with the instruction to his two hostesses "I'm the leader of the pack, which makes me such a lucky Jack, but here they are, they're so appealing, come on dollies do your dealing." The format was based on the *Card Sharks* format from the USA, created by Chester Feldman. ITV 1980-87; 1994-99; 2002.

Please Sir John Alderton (Bernard 'Privet' Hedges), Deryck Guyler (Norman Potter), Peter Cleall (Eric Duffy), Joan Sanderson (Doris Ewell), David Barry (Frankie Abbott), Richard Davies (Mr Price), Jill Kerman (Penny Wheeler/Hedges), Peter Denyer (Dennis Dunstable), Liz Gebhardt (Maureen Bullock), Penny Spencer and Carol Hawkins (Sharon Eversleigh), Malcolm McFee and Leon Vitali (Peter Craven), Erik Chitty (Mr 'Smithy' Smith), Noel Howlett (Mr Morris Cromwell). Sitcom written by John Esmonde and Bob Larbey. Bernard Hedges is a newly-qualified, idealistic young teacher working in a tough South London school, Fenn Street Secondary Modern. As the newest member of staff, he draws the short straw when he's put in charge of Class 5C, the most difficult group of children in the school. ITV 1968-72. Spin off Series: *The Fenn Street Gang*

Pobol y Cwm The longest-running television soap opera produced by the BBC. Pobol y Cwm (people of the valleys) was first transmitted on BBC Wales between 1974 and 1982 and then transferred to the Welsh language television station S4C when it opened in that year. It was briefly shown in the rest of the UK in 1994 on BBC2, with English subtitles. The series is set in the fictional village of Cwmderi, supposedly in the Carmarthen area. As in all good soaps the action centres around the local pub, the Deri Arms. Cast members have included Ioan Gruffudd, who played the part of Gareth Wyn Harries between 1987 and 1994, Michael Aspel, Gillian Elisa, Huw Garmon, Aneirin Hughes, Gwenno Saunders, Imogen Thomas and Rachel Thomas. **Present cast members as at the end of December 2011, include:** Gareth Lewis (Meic Pierce), Llewelyn Summerhayes (Gwern Monk), Nia Caron (Anita Pierce), Iwan Roberts (Kevin Powell), Richard Lynch (Garry Monk), Donna Edwards (Britt Monk), Arwel Davies (Eifion Rowlands), Arwyn Davies (Mark Jones), Elin Harries (Dani Jones nee Thomas), Osian-Wyn Rudge (Aaron Monk), Caryl Morgan (Esyllt 'Izzy' Evans), Owain Rhys Rudge (Wil Howarth), Mirain Alaw Jones (Lois Evans), Victoria Williams (Marian Rees - previously played by Buddug Williams), Madilyn Taylor (Catrin Morris), Catrin Powell (Cathryn "Cadno" Richards), Iestyn Cai Evans (Chester Morris), Bethan Ellis Owen (Ffion Roberts nee Llewelyn), Sharon Roberts (Gaynor Evans), Tonya Smith (Yvonne Evans), Lisa Victoria (Sheryl Hughes), Catrin Mara (Nesta Roberts), Llinor ap Gwynedd (Gwyneth Jones), Mark Flanagan (Huw 'Jinx Jenkins), Victoria Plucknett (Diane Ashurst nee Francis), Emyr Wyn (Dai 'Sgaffalde'

Ashurst), Jeremi Cockram (Siôn White), Rhys ap William (Cai Rossiter), Rhys Bidder (Macs White), Rhys Hartley (Huw White), Sera Cracroft (Eileen Markham), Aled Davies (Rhys Llywelyn), Gwyn Elfyn (Denzil Rees), Alex Harries (Scott Lewis), Justin Jones (Ieuan Griffiths), Nicholas McGaughey (Brandon Monk), Jonathan Nefydd (Colin Evans), Maria Pride (Debbie Collins), Dyfan Rees (Iolo White), Andrew Teilo (Hywel Llywelyn), Emily Tucker (Sioned Rees), Simon Watts (Gethin Thomas), Tomos West (Ricky Jones) and Siôn Ifan Williams (Liam Collins). **Recent departures include:** Darren Borst ("Dafyd Ap Bleddyn"), Huw Euron (Darren Howarth), Heledd Owen (Rhiannon Hughes), Iestyn Jones (Ieuan Griffiths), Helen Rosser Davies (Sara Francis), Rhys ap Hywel (Jason Francis), Alan H. Lloyd (Leighton White), Marged Esli (Nansi Furlong) and Elin Llwyd (Katie Edwards).

Pocoyo
Spanish pre-school animated television series about a four-year-old boy (born October 14th) who loves to wear blue and travel in his all-terrain Vamoosh machine. The series is adapted for UK audiences as part of the *Milkshake* menu on Five with Stephen Fry as narrator although it was first broadcast on CITV in 1997.
Podge and Rodge Show, The Irish chat show hosted by the popular puppets Podge and Rodge (aka Pádraig Judas O'Leprosy and Rodraig Spartacus O'Leprosy (b.1941), created and performed by Ciaran Morrison and Mick O'Hara. RTÉ Two 2006-10
Pointless Quiz show hosted by Alexander Armstrong. One hundred members of the public are given 100 seconds to recall answers of questions such as "name any top 40 single by David Bowie?" Studio contestants are then asked the same question and have to give the most obscure correct answer possible in order to proceed in the game – a pointless answer also boosting the jackpot fund by £250. Richard Osman assists the host by listing all the possible pointless answers by way of post mortem. BBC2 2009-
Points of View Originally hosted by Robert Robinson, *Points of View* was designed as an occasional five minute show to plug the gap between shows. It featured the letters of viewers offering criticism, witty observations, and occasional praise, on the television of recent weeks. Kenneth Robinson took over as host in 1965, though Robert Robinson took over again in 1969, before the show was dropped in 1971. The show returned in 1979 with Barry Took as host, and The Beatles' When I'm Sixty-Four as its theme tune (courtesy of the line "Send me a postcard, drop me a line, stating point of view"). Took was replaced by a succession of short-lived presenters including Tony Robinson, Alan Titchmarsh and Chris Serle, until Anne Robinson, and then Carol Vorderman, restored stability to the role of presenter. Between 1999 and 2008 the show was presented by Terry Wogan, and Jeremy Vine is the current host. BBC1 1961-71; 1979- Between 1963 and 1970 Robert Robinson (later replaced by Sarah Ward, Gaynor Morgan Rees and Cathy McGowan) presented a version designed for children's letters entitled *Junior Points of View*.
Poker Face Quiz Show hosted by Ant McPartlin and Declan Donnelly. Thirty six contestants played for a prize of £1million in the first series of seven shows aired on consecutive nights in July 2006. The first six shows acted as heats, the winner gaining £50,000 and a place in the Grand Final. Each heat began with an introduction of the players via "The Grilling" whereby each contestant supplied personal information which may or may not be true. The first of five rounds then commenced with eight questions worth £500 each. At the end of the round the six players had the option to fold and keep the money they had accrued or take a chance that someone else folded and kept them in the game. If no-one folded then the player with the lowest amount was eliminated and left with nothing. Subsequent rounds had five questions, Round 2 questions were worth £750 each and money was carried over from previous rounds. Round 3 questions were worth £1,000 each, Round 4 questions £1,250 and Round 5 questions £1,500. In the first-ever show Sarah Lang bluffed her way through to the final by telling her opponent, Oliver Holroyd-Pearce, that she was runner-up in the world quiz championships in Italy! It worked and Oliver folded although leading £16,500 to Sarah's £16,000. Sarah went on to win the £1million prize

although she was so far ahead no further bluffing was required. ITV 2006
Poldark Robin Ellis (Capt. Ross Poldark), Angharad Rees (Demelza Carne/Poldark), Clive Francis (Francis Poldark), Ralph Bates (George Warleggan), Jill Townsend (Elizabeth Chynoweth Poldark Warleggan), Nicholas Selby and Alan Tilvern (Nicholas Warleggan), Frank Middlemass (Charles Poldark), David Garfield (Jacka Hoblyn), Norma Streader (Verity Poldark), Paul Curran (Jud Paynter), John Blythe (Const. Vage), Mary Wimbush (Prudie Paynter), Tilly Tremayne (Ellen), Eric Dodson (Rev. Johns), Cynthia Grenville (Constance Bodrugan), John Baskcomb (Nathaniel 'Nat' Pearce), Judy Geeson (Caroline Penvenen/Enys), Richard Morant and Michael Cadman (Dr Dwight Enys), Kevin McNally (Drake Carne), Christopher Biggins (Revd Osborne Whitworth), Jane Wymark (Morwenna Chynoweth/Whitworth), Julie Dawn Cole (Rowella Chynoweth). The 29-episode series dramatised the original four novels which Winston Graham wrote at the end of World War II. Set in 18th-century Cornwall, the story begins with Ross Poldark returning home from the American War of Independence to restore Nampara, his father's ruined estate. The dashing Cornish squire also contends with local politics and a love triangle between himself, his less exciting cousin Francis Poldark and the aristocratic Elizabeth Chynoweth. Francis and Elizabeth are eventually married and Ross weds the engaging urchin Demelza after making her pregnant. BBC1 1975-77. The story was revived by HTV in 1996 in a two-hour sequel set ten years after the close of the BBC serial. John Bowe and Mel Martin took over the roles of Ross and Demelza in *Strangers From The Sea*.
Pole to Pole Michael Palin's sequel to *Around The World In 80 Days*. This time his journey took him from the North Pole to the South Pole, in as direct a route as possible, taking him through the eastern part of Africa. BBC1 1992.
Police, Camera, Action! Police video programme which was originally presented by Alistair Stewart until his second drink-driving conviction led to a temporary suspension in 2002 although he resumed his role with Adrian Simpson from 2007 until Gethin Jones took over in 2010. ITV 1994-
Police Five Produced in conjunction with New Scotland Yard, Police Five, as the title suggests, was a five-minute slot given over to appeals to the public for assistance in solving crimes, tracking down criminals and preventing future incidents. The programme concentrated on crimes in the London area mainly, although there were regional equivalents shown in various ITV areas. Shaw Taylor was the host throughout the run and he invariably signed off with the plea of 'Keep 'em peeled'. ITV 1962-90. *Junior Police Five* aired throughout the 1970s.
Police Surgeon See *The Avengers*
Pollyanna Elizabeth Archard (Pollyanna), Elaine Stritch (Aunt Polly), Paddy Frost (Nancy), Ray McAnally (John Pendleton), Robert Coleby (Timothy), Stephen Galloway (Jimmy Bean). Six-part adaptation of Eleanor H. Porter's eternally optimistic Pollyanna. BBC1 1973.
Pop Idol Talent show presented by Ant and Dec. The search for a new pop talent proved a popular format with viewers. Auditions were held at various venues around Britain and the final 50 were then split into five shows and the viewing public decided on a final ten contestants. Their verdict was helped by the panel of four judges, Simon Cowell (Head of A&R at RCA records), DJ Neil Fox, publicist Nicki Chapman and record producer Pete Waterman. Each week one artist would be eliminated until we were left with the eventual winner, Will Young, who narrowly beat Gareth Gates for the title of 'Pop Idol'. The other eight finalists were Darius Danesh (3rd), Zoe Birkett (4th), Hayley Evetts (5th), Rosie Ribbons (6th), Laura Doherty (7th), Aaron Bailey (8th), Jessica Garlick (9th), Korben (10th). A throat infection ruled out Rik Waller who was replaced in the final by the eventual third-placed contestant Darius Danesh. A second series was won by Michelle McManus and the other eleven finalists were Mark Rhodes (2nd), Sam Nixon (3rd), Chris Hide (4th), Susanne Manning (5th), Roxanne Cooper (6th), Andy Scott-Lee (7th), Kim Gee (8th), Marc Dillon (9th), Brian Ormond

(10th), Kirsty Crawford (11th), Leon McPherson (12th). A World Idol international television special was held in December 2003, featuring national first series Idol contest winners competing against each other; viewers worldwide voted Norwegian idol Kurt Nilsen the winner. ITV 2001-03.

Popstar to Operastar In the first series, eight pop stars, Darius Campbell (also known as Darius Danesh), Marcella Detroit, Alex James, Danny Jones, Kym Marsh, Bernie Nolan, Jimmy Osmond and Vanessa White, took up the challenge of being transformed into opera stars. Presented by Alan Titchmarsh and Myleene Klass with judges Katherine Jenkins, Rolando Villazón, Meat Loaf and Laurence Llewelyn-Bowen. The winner chosen by the viewing public was Darius. The second series saw Meat Loaf and Laurence Llewelyn-Bowen replaced by Vanessa-Mae and Simon Callow and the contestants were Midge Ure, Jocelyn Brown, Melody Thornton, Andy Bell, Joseph Washbourn, Claire Richards, Cheryl Baker and Joe McElderry, who narrowly beat Cheryl in the final. ITV 2010-.

Poppy Shakespeare Anna Maxwell Martin (N) and Naomie Harris (Poppy). 90-minute drama based on the novel of the same name about mental illness by Clare Allan, who herself spent ten years in a mental health institution. It tells the story of day patients at a mental health hospital. The central characters are Poppy Shakespeare, a new patient, and 'N', a long term patient. Poppy arrives at the hospital strongly asserting that she is sane and demanding that she is released from the program. To gain legal aid she must first prove she is sick so that she can get 'MAD money' i.e. state benefits. She is befriended by N, who helps her work the system. C4 2008.

Popstars This precursor to Pop Idol had the premise of forming a quintet by the same elimination process used so successfully, and lucratively, in later formats i.e. viewer voting. The judges were Nigel Lythgoe (a former Young Generation dancer), Nicki Chapman (publicist and manager) and Paul Adams (A&R Director of Polydor records). The final five Kym Marsh, Myleene Klass, Suzanne Shaw, Noel Sullivan and Danny Foster were named *Hear'Say* and had immediate success although eventually were disbanded. The five runners-up Jessica Taylor, Kevin Simms, Kelli Young, Tony Lundun and Michelle Heaton also formed a very successful band, *Liberty X*. ITV 2001. A follow-up series in 2002 *Popstars: The Rivals* split the girls and boys and two groups were formed an all-girl group (managed by Louis Walsh) and an all-boy group (managed by Pete Waterman). The race for the Christmas chart number one saw Walsh's *Girls Aloud* easily beating *One True Voice*, who quickly disbanded. The format was introduced originally in Australia with *Bardot* as the first winners.

Popworld Saturday morning music show originally presented by Miquita Oliver and Simon Amstell. *Popworld* was known for its witty, irreverent celebrity interviews, most famously (after Girls Aloud's Cheryl Cole (then Cheryl Tweedy), fresh from her court case involving an incident with a toilet attendant, being asked whether people were frightened to see her walk into the ladies?. Comic actor Leigh Francis made his mainstream television debut on this show as a character named Barry Gibson. Alex Zane and Alexa Chung took over presenting the programme in 2006. C4 2001-07.

Porridge Ronnie Barker (Norman Stanley Fletcher), Richard Beckinsale (Lennie Godber), Fulton MacKay (Mr MacKay), Peter Vaughan (Harry 'Groutie' Grout), David Jason (Blanco Webb), Brian Wilde (Mr Barrowclough), Patricia Brake (Ingrid Fletcher), Chris Biggins (Lukewarm), Maurice Denham (Judge Stephen Rawley), Tony Osoba (McLaren), Sam Kelly (Warren), Ronald Lacey (Harris), Brian Glover (Cyril Heslop), Ken Jones (Ives). Sitcom written by Dick Clement and Ian La Frenais. Set in the fictional HMP Slade in deepest Cumbria, the comedy character Fletcher was first seen in the second episode of Ronnie Barker's comedy showcase series *Seven Of One* (the first introduced the northern shopkeeper Arkwright, who went on to become a firm TV favourite in *Open All Hours*). Each episode of the subsequent series began with the noise of prison doors slamming shut and the ringing tones of a judge (voiced by Barker) sentencing the Muswell Hill-based old lag to prison for five years after summing up "Norman Stanley Fletcher, you have pleaded guilty to the charges brought by this court, and it is now my duty to pass

sentence. You are an habitual criminal who accepts arrest as an occupational hazard and presumably accepts imprisonment in the same casual manner". Fletcher shared a cell with naive Birmingham offender Lenny Godber and generally ran comic rings around the warders - notably strutting Scotsman Chief Officer MacKay and kindhearted warden Barrowclough -while earning the awe struck admiration of his fellow cons. These included Bunny Warren, gay cook Lukewarm, Black Scottish hardman McLaren and the simple Heslop. Slade Prison's Mr Big still ran his racket from within the prison and was played by the magnificent Peter Vaughan. David Jason also appeared on occasion as the brain-dead murderer Blanco. One of the most memorable comic scenes from the series saw 'Fletch' being examined by the prison doctor and determined to ensure soft duties by having flat feet recorded in his medical history. After managing to direct the conversation towards the subject of his flat feet at every opportunity Fletch is asked by the doctor "are you now or have you at any time been a practising homosexual?" "What? With these feet?" Fletch retorts. The scene continues in similar manner until the doc requests a urine sample. "Now you see those glasses over there, I want you to fill one for me," he orders. Fletcher's response: "What? From here?" BBC1 1974-77. A sequel *Going Straight* (BBC1 1978) saw Barker and Beckinsale reprise their roles on the outside (Godber begins to court Fletcher's daughter Ingrid) while Fletcher's teenage son Raymond was played by Nicholas Lyndhurst.

Porterhouse Blue David Jason (John Skullion), Ian Richardson (Sir Godber Evans), Griff Rhys Jones (Cornelius Carrington), John Sessions (Lionel Zipser), Willoughby Goddard (Professor Siblington), Charles Gray (Sir Cathcart D'eath), Barbara Jefford (Lady Mary Evans). Four-part adaptation of Tom Sharpe's comic novel by Malcolm Bradbury. In 1987 Britain, Porterhouse College Cambridge is an anachronism, its students uniformly male and (in the vast number of cases) privately educated. When the incumbent Master dies (from a stroke brought on by overeating) the government revenges itself on Porterhouse by appointing as his successor a former graduate, the politician Sir Godber Evans (Minister for Social Security). One of the tiny minority of state-school students the college has had forced on it over the years, Evans, the son of a butcher, returns to his alma mater determined, with the help of his wife, Lady Mary, to drag this bastion of privilege into the twentieth century. The elderly academic staff cease their bickering and close ranks against him, but the new Master finds his most implacable and unscrupulous opponent in Skullion, the college porter. A memorable scene was the sight of inflated condoms floating among the dreaming spires after Zipser filled them with gas and propelled them up his chimney to prevent Mrs Biggs from finding them. The title song *Dives in Omnia* (There's Money in Everything) was sung by a-cappella group *The Flying Pickets*. C4 1987.

Portrait of a Marriage Janet McTeer (Vita Sackville-West), Cathryn Harrison (Violet Keppel), David Haig (Harold Nicolson). Four-part mini-series set in 1918, detailing the real-life love affair between feminist writer Vita Sackville-West and novelist Violet Keppel against the backdrop of post-World War I England and opposition by Vita's politician husband Harold Nicolson. BBC1 1990.

Postman Pat Animated children's television series aimed at pre-school children, concerning the adventures of Pat Clifton, a postman in the fictional Yorkshire village of Greendale (inspired by the real valley of Longsleddale in the Lake District of Cumbria). The series was originally screened in 1981. John Cunliffe wrote the original treatment and scripts, and it was directed by animator Ivor Wood, who also worked on *The Magic Roundabout, Paddington Bear*, and *The Herbs*. Pat is the owner of a small black and white cat named Jess, who always travels with him. Other characters include his wife Sarah, six-year-old son Julian (the family living at Forge Cottage), Mrs Goggins, the postmistress, the bike-riding Miss Rebecca Hubbard, twins Katy and Tom Pottage, farmers George Lancaster and Alf Thompson (plus wife Dorothy), builder Ted Glen, Shepherd Peter Fogg, mobile shopkeeper Sam Waldron, lady doctor Sylvia Gilbertson, PC Selby, Major Forbes (who lives at Garner Hall), Granny Dryden and the vicar, Reverend Timms. Pat's red post-van bears the registration number PAT 1. The jaunty theme tune was a big hit for narrator Ken Barrie, and has enjoyed a revival as a mobile phone ring tone. The theme song has also been parodied for use mainly in school playgrounds. In June 2003, the Beast Banks post office in Kendal, the real-life inspiration for the Greendale post office, closed down due to lack of business. On 15 September 2004 a plaque was placed at the former post office to mark its role as the inspiration for the *Postman Pat* stories. In Scotland, *Postman Pat* is broadcast as "Pàdraig Post", in the Gaelic language, on BBC Scotland. However, it is still advertised in the programme schedules on the BBC Scotland website as "Postman Pat". From 2004 a new series of *Postman Pat* was produced and is shown as part of the Cbeebies transmission. BBC1 1981-82; 1991-92; 1995-97; 2004-

Pot Black Half-hour snooker programme which popularised the game as a television medium. Hosted by Alan Weeks (David Icke in the 1980s) and devised by 'Whispering' Ted Lowe (who also supplied commentary). It ran from 1969-86, the full list of winners being Ray Reardon (1969; 1979), John Spencer (1970-71; 1976), Eddie Charlton (1972-73; 1980), Graham Miles (1974-75), Perrie Mans (1977), Doug Mountjoy (1978; 1985), Cliff Thorburn (1981), Steve Davis (1982-83), Terry Griffiths (1984), Jimmy White (1986). A measure of the impact of the show was the fact that the viewing public gave two-time winner Graham Miles world champion status although he was only ever a journeyman pro. Pot Black's instantly recognisable theme tune was the ragtime classic Black And White Rag, composed by George Botsford and performed by Winifred Atwell. Pot Black was briefly revived in 1991 as *Pot Black: Timeframe*, introduced by Eamonn Holmes. A further one-off series, hosted by David Vine, reverted to the original format in 1993, Steve Davis winning his third *Pot Black* title. A *Masters Pot Black* was held in 1997, the winner being Joe Johnson. A one-day Pot Black tournament was held on October 29, 2005, hosted by Hazel Irvine and broadcast on the BBC sports programme *Grandstand*. The invitation event featured eight players, Ronnie O'Sullivan, Stephen Hendry, Stephen Maguire, Matthew Stevens, Paul Hunter, John Higgins, Jimmy White and Shaun Murphy, with Matthew Stevens beating Shaun Murphy in the final. BBC2 1969-86; 1991-93; 1997; BBC1 2005.

Pot The Question Snooker-based quiz show hosted by Stuart Hall with team captains Patrick Mower and Denis Law. BBC1 1984.

Potter Arthur Lowe (Redvers Potter) replaced by Robin Bailey when Arthur Lowe died between series. Sitcom written by Roy Clarke. Redvers Potter, the former managing director of Pottermints ('The Hotter Mints'), suddenly has time on his hands, a commuter no more and somewhat at a loose end in the leafy suburbs of south London. Rather than sit back and take it easy, Potter decides to lead a full life by making himself useful and wandering around 'assisting' people, whether or not they have asked for or require his help. A pedantic man with set ways and an outlook shaped by 50 years of reading The Daily Telegraph, Potter is permanently at odds with those he is trying to help and his presence usually exacerbates the situations. BBC1 1979-80; 1983.

Power Game, The See *The Plane Makers*

Practice, The John Fraser (Dr Lawrence Golding), Brigit Forsyth (Dr Judith Vincent), Tim Brierley (Dr David Armitage), Rob Edwards (Dr Chris Clark), Judith Barker (Pauline Kent), Eileen O'Brien (Carol Stansfield), Michelle Holmes (Susan Turner), Ronald Fraser (Dr Reginald Biddy). British Medical soap-opera set in Castlehume, a fictional suburb of Manchester. Dr Lawrence Golding was the senior GP and his assistants were Dr Judith Vincent and Dr David Armitage (replaced by Chris Clark in the second series). Originally a twice-weekly series but reduced to a single weekly episode in series two. ITV 1985-86.

Prank Patrol Children's programme hosted by Barney Harwood where young adults nominate their friends to play a prank on a la *Candid Camera*. The ten episodes were part of the CBBC menu and first shown in 2007.

Press Gang Julia Sawalha (Lynda Day), Dexter Fletcher (Spike Thomson), Lee Ross (Kenny Phillips), Kelda Holmes (Sarah Jackson), Clive Ward (Matt Kerr), Paul Reynolds (Colin

Mathews), Lucy Benjamin (Julie Craig), Gabrielle Anwar (Sam Black), Mmoloki Chrystie (Frazz Davies), Joanna Dukes (Tiddler), Charlie Creed-Miles (Danny McColl), Sadie Frost (Jennie Eliot), Ade Edmondson (Simon Knowles). Children's television comedy-drama based around the activities of a "children's newspaper" initially begun as a school project but in later series depicted as a commercial venture. Lynda Day was the tough editor-in-chief of the Junior Gazette, Kenny Phillips the deputy-editor, Spike Thompson the wise-cracking American chief reporter, and Colin Mathews the advertising manager. Julie Craig began as head of the graphics team but was then promoted to assistant editor, Sam Black replacing her as graphics boss. Sarah Jackson was the top writer, Frazz Davies supplied horoscopes. Forty-three episodes were filmed cinematically over five series and received a BAFTA award in 1991 for "Best Children's Entertainment/Drama". ITV 1989-93.

Preston Front Colin Buchanan (Dave Gadd 'Hodge'), Paul Haigh (Wayne Disley 'Eric'), Caroline Catz (Dawn Lomax), Adrian Hood (Tony Lloyd 'Lloydy'), Tony Marshall (Des Moyle 'Diesel'), Stephen Tompkinson (Simon Matlock 'Spock'), Alistair McGowan (replaced Tompkinson as Spock in 1995), Kate Gartside (Ally), David MacCreedy (Peter Polson), Keiran Flynn (Carl Rundle), Oliver Cotton (Declan), Susan Wooldridge and Carolyn Pickles (Jeanetta), Holly Grainger (Kirsty), Ozzie Yue (Mr. Wang), Angela Lonsdale (Mel), Nicky Henson (Greg Scarry). Comedy drama written by Tim Firth and entitled *All Quiet On The Preston Front* for its first series but became simply *Preston Front* thereafter. The comic everyday lives and mis-adventures of a group of friends most of whom belong to their local unit of the Territorial Army in Roker Bridge, Lancashire. Each episode stands perfectly well on its own, since each focuses on a different character and recaps of previous pertinent scenes are shown at the outset, but if there's one underlying storyline uniting every episode of *Preston Front*, it's Hodge's (his nickname a corruption of his middle names of Howard Roger) burgeoning relationship with the daughter he never knew he had. Here I Stand by the Milltown Brothers was the theme song. BBC1 1994-97.

Price is Right, The Game show based on contestants guessing the retail prices of featured prizes and other promotional products. Presenters: Leslie Crowther (1984-88) and Bruce Forsyth (1995-2001). Famous catchphrase was "Come on down!" When the show was revived in 1995 after a seven-year break, it aired under the name *Bruce's Price Is Right* and Emma Noble, the future wife of John Major's son (James) was one of the female models. Joe Pasquale hosted a weekday version of the show in 2006. ITV 1984-88; 1995-2001; 2006. Bob Warman hosted a 1989 Sky version entitled *The New Price Is Right*.

Pride and Prejudice Colin Firth (Fitzwilliam Darcy), Jennifer Ehle (Elizabeth Bennet), Alison Steadman (Mrs Bennet), Julia Sawalha (Lydia Bennet), Benjamin Whitrow (Mr Bennet), Barbara Leigh-Hunt (Lady Catherine), Susannah Harker (Jane Bennet). Andrew Davies wrote the screenplay for the mini-series based on Jane Austen's classic novel. BBC1 1995. An earlier six-part BBC mini-series was broadcast in 1952 with Thea Holme narrating the story as Jane Austen), Daphne Slater as Elizabeth Bennet, Peter Cushing as Darcy and Richard Johnson as Mr Wickham.

Prime Suspect Helen Mirren (DCI/Det. Supt. Jane Tennison), Tom Bell (DS Bill Otley), John Benfield (DCS Michael Kiernan), John Forgeham (DCI John Shefford), Craig Fairbrass (DI Frank Burkin), Jack Ellis (DI Tony Muddyman), Mossie Smith (WPC Maureen Havers), Zoe Wanamaker (Moyra Henson), John Bowe and Tim Woodward (George Marlow), Noel Dyson (Mrs. Tennison), Bryan Pringle (Felix Norman), Richard Hawley (DC/DI Richard Haskons), John McArdle (Det. Chief Supt. Ballinger), Oleg Menshikov (Milan Lukic), Ben Miles (DCI Simon Finch), Robert Pugh (DS Alun Simms), Clare Holman (Elizabeth Lukic), Mark Strong (Det. Chief Supt. Larry Hall), Liam Cunningham (Robert West), Velibor Topic (Zigic), Barnaby Kay (DC Michael Phillips), Tanya Moodie (DC Lorna Greaves), Frank Finlay (Arnold Tennison), Phoebe Nicholls (Shaw), Rad Lazar (Kasim), Serge Soric (Dr. Mulagu), Ingeborga Dapkunaite

(Jasmina). Seven series of the highly acclaimed multi-award-winning police drama series written by Lynda La Plante have aired, depicting the brilliant, methodical, resilient and complex personality of Jane Tennison and her struggle to overcome institutionalised sexism within the force and reconcile her professional responsibilities with her strained personal life. ITV 1991-96; 2003; 2006.

Prime Time *Prime Time* is the major news analysis, current affairs and politics programme broadcast on Radio Telifis Éireann in Ireland. It is currently presented by Miriam O'Callaghan and Mark Little. The veteran long-term presenter of the series, Brian Farrell, retired in 2004. Other previous presenters have included Olivia O'Leary and Eammon Lawlor. *Prime Time* is the successor of the hugely popular *Today Tonight* series. Initially, the programme went out on Thursday nights only, and was presented by people such as Olivia O'Leary, John Bowman and Pat Kenny. This was part of a shake-up of RTÉ's current affairs output, in which Brian Farrell presented a Sunday night programme (*Farrell*), and Tuesday nights saw a documentary strand (*Tuesday File*). However after a few years these programmes were re-integrated into *Prime Time*, which now follows an identical format to the *Today Tonight* programme it replaced.

Primeval Douglas Henshall (Nick), Hannah Spearritt (Abby), James Murray (Stephen), Andrew-Lee Potts (Connor), Lucy Brown (Claudia and Jennifer), Juliet Aubrey (Helen Cutter), Ben Miller (Sir James Peregrine Lester), Mark Wakeling (Captain Tom Ryan), Jason Flemyng (Danny Quinn), Ben Mansfield (Captain Becker), Ciarán McMenamin (Matt Anderson), Alexander Siddig (Philip Burton). Science fiction drama television series created by Adrian Hodges and Tim Haines and produced by Impossible Pictures. The series follows a team of scientists who investigate anomalies in time and deal with the ancient creatures that come through. The team of five is led by Nick Cutter, a palaeontologist determined to find his wife who disappeared while investigating a time anomaly in the Forest of Dean, Gloucestershire eight years previously. Professor Cutter is aided by zoologist Abby Maitland, lab technician Stephen Hart, dinosaur expert Connor Temple and Home Office official Claudia Brown (who disappears at the end of episode six and is replaced by an identical woman Jennifer Lewis). Stephen is killed at the end of the second series and Nick is killed by his wife, Helen in Series 3, Episode 3, after the ARC (Anomaly Research Centre) is attacked by Helen and her army of Cleaner replicas. Series 4 was preceded by five webisodes with new team leader Matt Anderson proving to be an enigmatic character. Other notable additions to the team are Jess Parker (Ruth Kearney), a coordinator for the field team and Philip Burton (Alexander Siddig) an entrepreneur funding the ARC in a public/private partnership with the government. Later in the series a group of time travellers arrive, including the mysterious Ethan Dobrowski (Jonathon Byrne), and Emily Merchant (Ruth Bradley), who is from the Victorian era. The fifth series of six episodes aired on *Watch* in May 2011. The closing theme song is *All Sparks* by Editors. ITV 2007-11

Prince and the Pauper, The Philip Sarson (Prince Edward), John Bowe (Earl of Hertford), Peter Jeffrey (Duke of Norfolk), Rupert Frazer (Sir Thomas Seymour), Elizabeth Ann O'Brien (Lady Elizabeth), Richenda Carey (Lady Milford), Sophia Myles (Lady Jane Grey), Jenny McCracken (Mother Canty), Lucy Speed (Nan Canty), Keith Michell (King Henry VIII). Six-part adaptation of the famed Mark Twain story. BBC1 1996.

Prince of Denmark Ronnie Corbett (Ronnie), Rosemary Leach (Laura), Roger Booth (Mr Yates), David Warwick (Steve). Sequel to *Now Look Here* also written by Graham Chapman and Barry Cryer. Ronnie leaves his job as an insurance salesman and begins a new career as a publican, assisted in his new role by his wife Laura. BBC1 1974. See also *No - That's Me Over Here!*

Prisoner, The Patrick McGoohan (The Prisoner - No. 6), Angelo Muscat (The Butler), Leo McKern (No. 2), Peter Wyngarde (No. 2), Patrick Cargill (No. 2), Anton Rodgers (No. 2), Eric Portman (No. 2), Jane Merrow (Alison aka No. 24). Seminal adventure series created by Patrick McGoohan and George Markstein. A high-ranking but un-named agent in the British Government resigns his post and leaves for a holiday. While packing he is gassed and is taken to a beautiful but deadly prison known only as "The Village" where people are taken, given a number to be called by and kept there for the rest of their lives if they don't tell No. 2 the required information. The agent is given the title of "No. 6" and the 17-episode series tells of his attempts to resist the plots of each No. 2 (who is replaced with another if an attempt on No. 6's information fails). Escape is almost impossible as the village has eyes everywhere and any attempts at fleeing are soon crushed (literally) by giant tracking balloons, known as rovers. The typical village day might consist of a game of human chess in the square, a penny-farthing ride, or a taxi trip in an automated buggy but for No. 6 it invariably consisted of a surreal battle of wits with his unknown captors. The piped blazers and repetitive greetings of "be seeing you" were reminiscent of a gentler time but the ever-present menace surrounding events made for a unique and thought-provoking series. In the final episode the face of No.1 was exposed as that of No. 6, although no further explanation was offered. Filmed in Portmeirion, North Wales (the Italian -style fantasy created by architect Sir Clough William-Ellis). ITV 1967-68. A six-part reinterpretation aired on ITV in 2010 with American actor James Caviezel as 6 (aka Michael) and Ian McKellen as 2 (aka Curtis). The mini-series was filmed in Swakopmund, Namibia.

Private Schulz Michael Elphick (Private Gerhard Schulz), Ian Richardson (Major Neuheim), Billie Whitelaw (Bertha Freyer), David Swift (Professor Bodelschwingh), Rula Lenska (Gertrude Steiner), Vernon Dobtcheff (Sturmer), Ken Campbell (Krauss), Ernest Clark (Count Von Fritsch). Comedy drama written by Jack Pulman. At the outbreak of war Schulz is released from Spandau jail where he has served a sentence for fraud. His aim is to sit out the war in a safe and anonymous job far from hostilities so applies for a role in the Postal Censorship department, so he can use his knowledge of five languages. Unfortunately, he is mistakenly recruited into SS Counter Espionage, headed by the deranged Major Neuheim. Schulz then parachutes into England with two million pounds in fivers - his mission, to spend them unobtrusively and return to the Fatherland. But things go wrong from the moment he enters an English pub and orders a coffee. BBC2 1981.

Probation Officer John Paul (Philip), David Davies (Jim), Honor Blackman (Iris), John Scott (Bert Bellman). Drama serial, chiefly written by Julian Bond, revolving around the work of three probation officers, Philip Main, Jim Blake and Iris Cope. Each episode was narrated in semi-documentary style and was based on real court cases. Notable for being the first hour-long series on ITV and also for the first screen appearance of John Hurt who appeared in two episodes in 1961 as Johnny Seton. ITV 1959-62.

Professionals, The Gordon Jackson (George Cowley), Lewis Collins (William Bodie), Martin Shaw (Ray Doyle). Drama series created by Brian Clemens. This series chronicled the lives of Bodie and Doyle, top agents for Britain's CI5 (Criminal Intelligence 5), and their controller, George Cowley. The mandate of CI5 was to fight terrorism and similar high-profile crimes. Cowley, a hard ex-MI5 operative, hand-picked each of his men. Bodie was a cynical ex-SAS paratrooper and former mercenary whose nature ran to controlled violence, while his partner, Doyle, came to CI5 from the regular police force, and was more of an open minded liberal. Their relationship was often rocky, but they were the top men in their field, and the ones to whom Cowley always assigned to the toughest cases. CI5 HQ was a constructed set within Teddington studios. ITV 1977-83.

Property Chain See *Location, Location, Location*.

Property Ladder Sarah Beeny offers invaluable property development and buying advice. The series underwent various revamps over the years not least of which was the programme title in 2009. To reflect the recession it became *Property Snakes and Ladders*. C4 2003-

Protectors, The Robert Vaughan (Harry Rule), Nyree Dawn Porter (Contessa di Contini), Tony Anholt (Paul Buchet), Yasuko Nagazami (Suki), Anthony Chinn (Chino). Adventure series created by Gerry Anderson. The Protectors of the title were Harry Rule, the Contessa di Contini and Paul Buchet, three freelance detective troubleshooters who ran an international crime fighting agency. Confusingly, Harry, (an American) was based in London and was the leader of the group. He had an Irish wolfhound named Gus and a martial-arts expert au pair named Suki. The English Contessa di Contini (formerly Lady Caroline Ogilvy) lived in Rome and, when she wasn't working with Harry, ran her own detective agency that specialized in exposing art frauds and recovering stolen art. She too had a martial-arts expert as an assistant/chauffeur. Paul Buchet, a Frenchman, worked out of Paris, and was the group's researcher and gadget specialist. Their adventures ranged from simple kidnapping to convoluted cases of international intrigue. The series theme tune *Avenues and Alleyways* by Tony Christie was a No 37 UK hit in 1973 and No 26 when re-released in 2005. The lyrics are: *Sleep like a baby, my little lady, Dream till the sunrise, creeps into your eyes. Dream till the sunrise, turns on the day. In the Avenues and Alleyways, while you sleep there's a whole world coming alive, Able and his brother, fighting one another, in and out of every dive. The Avenues and Alleyways, where the strong and the quick alone can survive, look around the jungle, see the rough and tumble, listen to a squealer cry, then a little later, in the morning paper, read about the way he died. Wake up my pretty, go to the city. Stay through the daytime, safe in the sunshine, stay till the daytime, turns into night. In the Avenues and Alleyways, where a mans gotta work out which side he's on, any way he chooses, chances are he loses, no one gets to live too long. The avenues and alleyways, where the soul of a man is easy to buy, everybody's wheeling, everybody's steeling, all the low are living high. Every city's got em, can we ever stop em, some of us are gonna try.* ITV 1972-74. A previous 1964 ITV series of the same name, starring Andrew Faulds as Ian Souter, Michael Atkinson as Robert Shoesmith and Ann Morrish as Heather Keys, followed a similar plot. The three crime fighters calling themselves SIS (Specialists In Security) and advertising their services in newspapers by asking potential clients to 'Call Welbeck 3269'.

Psychoville Steve Pemberton (Oscar Lomax/David Sowerbutts/George Aston), Reece Shearsmith (Maureen Sowerbutts/Brian/Mr Jelly), Dawn French (Joy Aston), Jason Tompkins (Robert Greenspan), David Smallbone (Martin),Nicholas Le Prevost (Graham), Daniel Kaluuya (Michael Fry), Adrian Scarborough (Mr Jolly), Daisy Haggard (Debbie), Eileen Atkins (Nurse Kenchington), Natalie Cassidy (Lorraine), Lisa Hammond (Kerry), Stacy Liu (Jennifer) and Alex Kelly (Karen Dalton). Comedy thriller series created by Reece Shearsmith and Steve Pemberton. The main characters are David Sowerbutts, a serial killer obsessed man-child who still lives with his mother Maureen; Mr. Jelly, an embittered one-handed children's entertainer; Oscar Lomax, a blind millionaire who collects Beanies; Joy Aston, a midwife who treats a practice doll as if it is her real child; and Robert Greenspan, a telekinetic panto dwarf in love with his Snow White. All five are connected by a mysterious blackmailer who has sent them a letter each, all of which contains the same message: "I know what you did…". BBC2 2009-11

Public Eye Alfred Burke (Frank Marker), Ray Smith (DI Firbank), Peter Childs (Ron Gash), Pauline Delaney (Helen Mortimer), John Grieve (Jim Hull). Atmospheric detective series created by Roger Marshall and Anthony Marriott. Alfred Burke was memorable as the world-weary, ageing, but sharp, and essentially honest central character of downtrodden private enquiry agent, Frank Marker. Working initially in London (series 1), then Birmingham (series 2 and three) and finally Brighton. Guided by his strong personal sense of what was 'right', Marker trod a thin line between the expectations of the forces of law and order on one side, and the inherent danger of dealing with the potentially violent and destructive elements of the underworld on the other, whilst retaining both his physical safety, and his innate integrity. The now lost final episode of the third season, 'Cross That Palm When We Come To It', culminated in Marker being sentenced to two and a half years in prison for a crime he didn't commit, and by the time he saw release at the beginning of season four in 1969, there had been drastic changes behind the scenes, as ABC had merged with Associated-Rediffusion to form a new production company, Thames, who went on to retain their franchise until 1992. The fifth series introduced John Grieve as Jim Hull, Marker's probation officer, and also saw the introduction of what was destined to become one of the shows most noteworthy characters, Detective Inspector Percy Firbank, who is always on the case of Marker, suspecting foul play at every turn. Other characters included Ron Gash, a fellow private detective who wants to form a partnership with Marker, and Marker's landlady, Helen Mortimer. ITV 1965-75.

Pursuers, The Louis Hayward (DI John Bollinger), Gaylord Cavallaro (DS Steve Wall). 39 episodes of this popular police drama were shown as part of an ITV late-night slot triple-bill of detective series. The two police officers patrolled the streets of London with their black German Shepherd dog named Ivan. ITV 1961-62.

Q Spike Milligan's comedy sketch show *Q* almost defies description. First aired in 1969 as *Q5* (- more series followed, oddly enough numbered *Q6*, *Q7*, *Q8* and *Q9*, although after *Q9* the BBC thought a change of title was required so what was to be Q10 became *There's A Lot Of It About*). Co-written with Neil Shand (with contributions from Andrew Marshall and David Renwick), the series' pipped Python to the post with their deliberate avoidance of punchlines, many of the sketches segueing into the next routine or simply being abandoned half way through. Spike would often make comic asides to the camera and even more often cause fellow actors John Bluthal and David Lodge to corpse (laugh uncontrollably). Some of the sketches appeared to be set-up as the show went along and were confusing but the sheer comic genius of Spike always guaranteed many laughs throughout each show. BBC2 1969; 1975; 1978-80; 1982.

QED Documentary series with a scientific bent, tackling both serious and light-hearted topics. The title stands for Quod Erat Demonstrandum (which was to be demonstrated). The editing team contained the future controller of BBC1 Lorraine Heggessey. BBC1 1982-98.

QI Comedy panel quiz hosted by Stephen Fry presiding over four panellists. First broadcast on BBC2 in 2003 with all the Series 1 questions having links to the letter A. The second series used the letter B as the initial theme, the third series the letter C, and the hope is to travel through the alphabet. The more witty, though usually wrong, answers are usually supplied by the one resident panellist Alan Davies. The QI of the title stands for 'Quite Interesting' and the theme music is by Howard Goodall, who has also doubled as a panellist. BBC2 2003-08; BBC1 2009-11; BBC2 2011-

Quatermass Nigel Kneale created sci-fi on British television with this classic series that pre-dated *A For Andromeda* and *Dr Who*. His 1950s Quatermass serials created the three main sci-fi plots still in use today. In the 1953 *Quatermass Experiment*, an Astronaut Victor Carroon (played by Duncan Lamont) returns from space and gradually turns into an alien. Professor Bernard Quatermass (played by Reginald Tate) of the British Rocket Group, tracks him down at Westminster Abbey and pleas for him to destroy himself to save the human race. In the 1955 series *Quatermass II*, the plot tells of an alien conspiracy that is taking over the British government, turning ordinary people into zombies, stopping at nothing to build their own breeding tank in a mysterious chemical factory. Professor Quatermass (now played by John Robinson as Reginald Tate died before filming commenced) is trying to perfect a dangerously unstable nuclear-powered rocket engine. After a disastrous test firing in Australia, his future son-in-law, Captain John Dillon (John Stone), draws the Professor's attention to a strange hollow meteorite which interrupts an Army Training exercise. They investigate, and discover a vast government production plant which has some connection with the meteorites. After coming in contact with the noxious gas contained inside the meteorites, Dillon is taken away by the plant's security guards. When Quatermass presses this issue with an old civil service acquaintance, he learns that the plant is supposedly making synthetic food. Both men learn that this is untrue, and that the true products of the plant will threaten the world itself. This was one of the most terrifying series ever shown on television, the combination of the dramatic opening music (*Mars, Bringer of War* from Gustav Holst's *The Planets* suite) and memorable scenes such as Ward (played by Derek Aylward) emerging from the Winnerden Flats plant covered in the corrosive black slime, or the last phone call of investigative journalist Hugh Conrad (played by Roger Delgado) struggling to hang on to his humanity, caused the BBC to issue a warning before each episode 'In our opinion it is not suitable for children or those who might have a nervous disposition'. Both the first two series were shown live from the BBC's Lime Grove Studios. The third series *Quatermass and the Pit* was as horrific as the previous two, although perhaps more subtly so. The professor was played this time by André Morell, the third actor to take the role. As in the previous stories, Quatermass was pitted against an extraterrestrial threat - in this case an ancient and hostile intelligence from Mars - in an exciting and intelligent story which mined mythology and folklore and carried serious political and philosophical ideas. The story begins with the discovery by workmen of a five-million-year-old skull in a deep pit. Further digging uncovers what appears to be an unexploded bomb - not an uncommon find more than a decade after the war. The professor gets involved when it becomes clear that the skull represents a previously unknown human relative, and that the 'bomb' is in fact an alien vessel. Although the Holst music of the previous two series was dropped in favour of a varied stock of dramatic themes, little was lost, and the stark horror conveyed by the military apprehension, made viewing compelling. BBC 1953; 1955; 1958-59. An ITV series aired in 1979 with John Mills playing the Professor but the impact of the original series was impossible to recreate.

Queenie's Castle Diana Dors (Queenie Shepherd). Sitcom created by Keith Waterhouse and Willis Hall. Queenie is a blunt northerner. She drinks light ale by the crate and rules the roost in her own 'castle' (a tower-block named Margaret Rose House, situated in the regally named Buckingham Flats). ITV 1970-72.

Question of Genius, A Weekday quiz show, hosted by Kirsty Wark, testing general knowledge, judgement and strategy. Eight contestants are whittled down to a solitary player via various rounds before the 'winner' attempts the ultimate 'Question of Genius', worth up to £5,000, on a specialist subject submitted before the show. The second series saw six contestants playing slightly revamped rounds, the jackpot dependent on how many questions were answered in the penultimate round, each question worth £1000. Daily champions returned the following day. BBC2 2009-10

Question of Sport, A Long-running sports celebrity quiz show hosted by David Vine (1970-78), David Coleman (1979-97) and Sue Barker (1998-). The show began life in 1968 as a BBC regional programme hosted by Stuart Hall before airing nationally in 1970. Two celebrity teams of three play each other over a series of sports-related rounds including 'Picture Round', 'What Happened Next?' and 'Mystery Celebrity' rounds. Although two of each team change each week, the captains are resident. Regular team captains: Cliff Morgan (1970-75), Henry Cooper (1970-79), Bobby Moore (1974), Bobby Charlton (1974-75), Freddie Trueman (1976-77), Brendan Foster (1977-79), Emlyn Hughes (1979-81; 1984-87), Gareth Edwards (1979-81), Bill Beaumont (1982-96), Willie Carson (1982-83), Ian Botham (1988-96), Ally McCoist (1996-2007), John Parrott (1996-2002), Frankie Dettori (2002-04), Matt Dawson (2004-present) and Phil Tufnell (2008-present). The guests for the very first show were Cliff Morgan, Lillian Board, Tom Finney, George Best, Henry Cooper and Ray Illingworth. Princess Anne joined the quiz for its 200th edition. One of the many highlights was Emlyn Hughes mistaking jump jockey John Reid for the aforementioned Princess Royal! BBC1 1970-

Question Time Long-running political debate programme originally hosted by Robin Day (1979-89), and then Peter Sissons (1989-93) and David Dimbleby (1994-present). The panels are drawn from significant figures in politics, industry, the media and entertainment. *Question Time* began on 25 September 1979, as a television version of the BBC Radio 4 question programme, *Any Questions?*. It originally had a panel of four guests, usually one member from each of the three major parties (Labour, the Conservatives, and the Liberal Democrats) and another public figure, for example non-governmental organisation directors, newspaper columnists, or religious leaders. In 1999, the panel was enlarged to five, with two non-partisan members. Questions are taken from the audience before the programme goes on air, and the chairman picks some to put to the panel. The panel do not get to see the questions before filming begins. In the Republic of Ireland, *Questions and Answers* is an RTÉ programme once presented by Olivia O'Leary, and currently chaired by Dr. John Bowman. It follows an almost identical format to *Question Time*. BBC Northern Ireland likewise has a similar format, *Let's Talk*, though this is only monthly and has greater audience interaction.

Questions and Answers See *Question Time*.

Quiz Ball Light-hearted soccer quiz. Two teams consisting of players and staff from a top flight football club and a celebrity supporter had a football match in the form of a general knowledge quiz. Teams chose whether to take four easy questions, three medium questions, two hard questions or one tough question to score a goal. The opposition could opt to take a tackle question a limited number of times in order to block the run, but a wrong answer meant conceding a goal. Whoever had the most goals at the end of the show was the winner. Originally hosted by David Vine and then subsequently by Barry Davies and Stuart Hall. BBC1 1966-72.

Rab C. Nesbit Gregor Fisher (Rab C. Nesbitt), Elaine C. Smith (Mary Nesbitt), Andrew Fairlie (Gash Nesbitt), Eric Cullen (Burney Nesbitt), Tony Roper (Jamesie Cotter), Barbara Rafferty (Ella Cotter). Sitcom written by Ian Pattison. Rab C. Nesbitt first gained national exposure in *Naked Video*, but graduated to his own show following a 1988 special, *Rab C Nesbitt's Seasonal Greet* (shown nationally in 1989). The perennially string-vested and head-banded Nesbitt, is a skiving, foul-mouthed, sexist drunkard, but he also has a philosophical streak which helps him through all the problems he brings on himself. Other characters included his wife Mary ('weak in a strong sort of way'), teenage sons Gash and Burney, devious drinking buddy Jamesie, and Jamesie's wife, the baby-craving Ella. The series ended in 1999 but returned to BBC2 for a Christmas special in 2008 and two further series have since been broadcast with Rab now converted to Christianity. BBC2 1988-99; 2008-

Raffles Anthony Valentine (A.J. Raffles), Christopher Strauli (Bunny Manders), Victor Carin (Insp. Mackenzie). Philip Mackie wrote the series based on the character created by Ernest William Hornung. Raffles is a gentleman of leisure and a top-rated cricketer, but he is also "the amateur Cracksman", an expert jewel thief. Alternately helped and hindered by his old friend, Bunny Manders, Raffles cuts a dashing swathe across Edwardian England, helping himself to the baubles of the very rich, sometimes playing amateur sleuth or crime fighter, and generally enjoying himself. Raffles was possibly the brother-in-law of Sherlock Holmes (suggested by author Philip Jose Farmer in his stories about the pair) as his creator EW Hornung married Constance Aimée Monica Doyle on 27 September 1893. This marriage made him the brother-in-law of Arthur Conan Doyle. ITV 1977. In 2001 the character was revived in a one-off BBC drama entitled *Gentleman Thief* which cast Nigel Havers as Raffles.

Rag Trade, The Peter Jones (Mr Harold Fenner), Reg Varney (Reg), Miriam Karlin (Paddy), Sheila Hancock (Carole), Esma Cannon (Little Lil), Barbara Windsor (Judy), Wanda Ventham (Shirley), Irene Handl (Reg's Mum). Sitcom written by Ronald Chesney and Ronald Wolfe. Set in the workshop of Fenner Fashions and focusing on a battle of wills between the management, Mr Fenner, and the workers, led by the trade union shop-steward, Paddy, who used any excuse to blow her whistle and bellow her catchphrase 'Everybody out!' Other characters included the foreman Reg, who had to appease both management and workers; Judy, Reg's love interest at the factory; Carole, the mischievous worker who caused Reg constant headaches; and the diminutive, eye-rolling Esma Cannon - grandly cast as Lilian Lavinia Lulu Swan but known to one and all as Lily or Little Lil - invariably stole the show with her fluttery antics. Irene Handl was cast as Reg's chatty mum, who came to work as Fenner's book-keeper for the third series. BBC 1961-63. ITV revived the series in 1977, only Peter Jones and Miriam Karlin reprising their previous roles. Christopher Beeny (Tony), Gillian Taylforth (Lyn) and Diane Langton (Kathy) were notable additions to the cast and Anna Karen reprised her On The Buses role of Olive now working as a mischievous machinist at Fenner's.

Rag, Tag and Bobtail The third addition to the *Watch With Mother* children's slot began in September 1953 and introduced some new friends for the very young with the hedgerow adventures of a trio of glove-puppet country animals. Louise Cochrane's delightful stories about a hedgehog (Rag), a mouse (Tag) and a rabbit (Bobtail), told by Charles E. Stidwell (and occasionally by David Enders or James Urquhart) were shown on Thursdays. Sometimes five baby rabbits would also appear with them. Although 26 episodes were made, the first two were never shown. Sam and Elizabeth Williams made the pictures and worked the puppets. BBC 1953-55

Railway Children, The Jenny Agutter (Roberta Faraday), Gillian Bailey (Phyllis Faraday), Ann Castle (Mother), Gordon Gostelow (Perks), Neil McDermott (Peter Faraday), Brian Hayes (Stationmaster), John Ringham (Dr Forrest). Seven-part dramatisation of Edith Nesbit's novel, Jenny Agutter later reprising her role in the 1970 film. BBC 1968. The BBC also serialised television versions in 1951 and 1957, the latter starring Anneke Wills as Roberta, Sandra Michaels as Phyllis and Jean Anderson as Mother.

Rainbow Children's pre-school series created by Pamela Lonsdale. Initially the series was to revolve around Rainbow the Bear, but by the time of the first episode, aired 16 October 1972, it centred around human presenter David Cook, Bungle Bear and strange oval-shaped puppet Zippy (named after the zip he had for a mouth and originally voice by Peter Hawkins), with interjections from glove puppets Sunshine and Moony and folk group Telltale. Within months the format was revised and Geoffrey Hayes became its long-time presenter, and Bungle and Zippy were joined by pink hippo George (voiced by Roy Skelton who also replaced Peter Hawkins as the voice of Zippy). Telltale were replaced with singing trio Charmian, Karl and Julian and then the more familiar Rod (Burton), Jane (Tucker) and Freddy (Marks), who eventually received their own spin-off series, 1981-85; 1989-91. Freddy Marks replaced none other than Matthew Corbett, of Sooty fame, in the trio. Zippo, Zippy's cousin, identical in appearance to Zippy, would make the occasional guest appearance. Originally portrayed as an eloquent Frenchman, but a later episode depicted him as an American-accented rapper with loud, flashy clothing. Dawn, the next-door neighbour, played by Dawn Bowden, who was introduced in the show's later years, first appeared in 1989. Although the original Rainbow died in 1992 with the non-renewal of Thames' franchise, it did come back in 1994 and 1995. This new show centred on the slightly-redesigned puppet characters (without a presenter) running a toy shop. A new character was introduced - Cleo the blue rabbit (voiced by Gillian Robic). This version of the show however, was short-lived. It came back again in 1996 and 1997 as a series of short 10-minute shows entitled *Rainbow Days* and hosted by Dale Superville. ITV 1972-97.

Raise the Roof Game show hosted by Bob Holness where one of six contestants could win a house. Bob began the show by introducing ERIC, the Electronic Random Inquisitor's Computer, on which the questions and answers appear. The first round consisted of seven "True" or "False" questions, the top three scorers progressing. The second round consisted of six questions and the two highest scorers again progressing to the final where they could bid a varying amount on a question depending on their degree of certainty. The final jackpot round saw the contestant having to answer four out of five questions correctly within a minute. This show seemed to open the floodgates for bigger and better prizes for quiz shows. ITV 1995-96

Ramsay's Kitchen Nightmares See Gordon Ramsay

Randall and Hopkirk (Deceased) Mike Pratt (Jeff Randall), Kenneth Cope (Marty Hopkirk), Annette Andre (Jeannie Hopkirk). Detective drama created by Dennis Spooner. Jeff Randall and Marty Hopkirk were private detective whose long-standing partnership came to an abrupt end when Marty is killed by a hit-and-run incident. Marty is soon back however....as a ghost!...to help solve his own murder. While he's doing this, he misses his chance to go to heaven, thanks to an ancient curse that states: "Before the sun shall rise, each ghost unto his grave must go. Cursed be the ghost who dares to stay and face the awful light of day." So Marty is stuck on Earth, as a white-suited spirit whom only Jeff can see, continuing their partnership and keeping tabs on his wife/widow, Jean. ITV 1969-70. BBC1 revived the series in 2001-02 with comic partnership Reeves and Mortimer playing Marty and Mike respectively. Charlie Higson and Paul Whitehouse wrote much of the script which ensured the humour of the original series was maintained. Tom Baker played Marty's guardian angel, Wyvern, and Emilia Fox played Jeannie.

Rapido Rapido was hosted by Antoine de Caunes and was the precursor of *Eurotrash* but focused more on reports from up and coming new bands. BBC2 1988-92.

Rastamouse Animated stop motion series aimed at children under six years of age and shown as part of the CBeebies menu. Created by Genevieve Webster and Michael De Souza, the series features an all-mouse reggae band — Rastamouse and Da Easy Crew — who hang out at the 'Nuff Song' recording studio in the fictional Mouseland. Rastamouse (voiced by Reggie Yates) sports traditional dreadlocks under his Rasta tam and rides a skateboard. His friend Scratchy (voiced by Sharon Duncan-Brewster) is dressed in a 1950s style balloon skirt with a ribbon bow on her head, and always wears roller skates. The contemporarily-styled Zoomer (voiced by William Vanderpuye) always wears roller blades. President Wensley Dale is voiced by Cornell John. The music for the series is composed by Andrew Kingslow and sung by Martin 'Sugar' Merchant, former singer in the rock/reggae band *Audioweb*. To-date 26 episodes have been broadcast. BBC 2011-

Rat Catchers, The Gerald Flood (Peregrine Pascale Smith), Philip Stone (Brigadier Davidson), Glyn Owen (Richard Hurst). Spy drama series concerning a secret Whitehall-based organisation (the Rat-catchers of the title). The three members of the team consisting of the Oxford educated managing director and international playboy Peregrine Smith, cold and calculating Brigadier Davidson and former Scotland Yard superintendent Richard Hurst. All are licensed to kill in their quest to protect the nation. ITV 1966-67.

Ready Steady Cook Cookery show originally hosted by Fern Britton (1994-2000) and now Ainsley Harriot (2000-present). Two top chefs have to create exciting new dishes from unexpected ingredients brought in by guests and battle it out against the clock, creating exciting dishes in 20 minutes from very few, and often very peculiar, ingredients. The teams are designated the red tomato or green pepper kitchen and the decision is decided by the studio audience. Guest chefs have included Lesley Waters, Brian Turner, Paul Rankin, Antony Worrall Thompson, Nick Nairn, James Tanner, Phil Vickery, James Martin, Kevin Woodford, Ross Burden, Mary Berry, Raymond Blanc, Jane Clarke, Jamie Oliver, Delia Smith, Gary Rhodes, Gino D'Acampo, Ed Baines, Alex Mackay, Garry Dawson, Lesley Waters, Richard Phillips, Maria Elia, Michael Barry and Tony Tobin. BBC2 1994-2010

Ready Steady Go "The weekend starts here" was announced every Friday evening. Cue psychedelic graphics and the catchy theme music (originally 'Wipeout' by The Surfaris but this was soon changed to '5-4-3-2-1' by Manfred Mann). Originally co-presented by Keith Fordyce (August 1963 to March 1965) and David Gell, who was replaced by Michael Aldred and then Cathy McGowan (1964 to December 1966). The first show on 9 August 1963 included Chris Barber (interview), Joyce Blair (in an interview, revealing she is the "Miss X" who recorded the single "I am Miss X"), Pat Boone (introducing a clip from his movie "The Main Attraction"), Billy Fury (singing "In Summer" and "Somebody Else's Girl"), Burl Ives (singing "Ugly Bug Ball" and also introducing a clip from "Summer Magic."), Joe Loss judging a dance contest, Brian Poole and The Tremeloes (singing "Twist And Shout" and "Do You Love Me"), Janette Scott (appearing as the week's guest DJ (she chooses Diane Ray's "Please Don't Talk to the Lifeguard"). ITV 1963-66.

Real McCoy, The Sketch series featuring an array of talented black comedy stars performing material aimed unashamedly at an across-the-board black audience. Actors included, Llewella Gideon, Curtis Walker, Ishmael Thomas, Collette Johnson, Perry Benson, Felix Dexter, Eddie Nestor, Kulvinder Ghir, Judith Jacob, Fraser Downie, Leon Black, Meera Syal, Robbie Gee, and Leo Chester. BBC2 1991-96.

Rebus Series 1 and 2: John Hannah (DI John Rebus), Sara Stewart (DCI Gill Templer), Gayanne Potter (DS Siobhan Clarke). Series 3 to 5: Ken Stott (DI John Rebus), Jennifer Black (DCS Gill Templer), Claire Price (DS Siobhan). Drama based on the Inspector Rebus novels by the Scottish author Ian Rankin set in and around Edinburgh. Four episodes were screened in the first two series and then a further ten, with a completely different cast, in Series 3 to 5. In actual fact the second episode of Series 2, *Mortal Causes*, due to be shown in September 2001 was postponed until November 2004 due to the 11 September 2001 attacks on the USA. ITV 2000-01; 2006-07

Record Breakers After twins Ross and Norris McWhirter had published a Book of world records, for Guinness, the BBC approached them with the idea of putting some of the best on television. The long-running show was thus conceived and more than 300 Guinness World Records were attempted over its near 30-year run. Originally hosted by Roy Castle along with the twins answering questions put to them by the studio audience. When Ross died his brother answered questions in a similar vein in his regular "Norris on the spot" feature. Fiona Kennedy assisted Roy for four series followed by Cheryl Baker, who joined Roy as co-host in 1987. When Roy died of lung cancer in 1994 Kriss Akabusi took over his mantle. Ron Reagan Jr, the son of the American President, joined the team in 1996. Other hosts have included Linford Christie, Jez Edwards, Fearne Cotton, Dilys Morgan, Julian Farino, Mark Curry, Dan Roland, Sally Gray and Kate Sanderson. The closing theme tune, performed by Roy Castle began: *Dedication oh, oh, dedication oh, oh , dedication, that's what you need. If you want to be the best, soar above the rest. Who-oh Dedication's what you need. If you want to be a record breaker, yeah.* BBC1 1972-2001.

Record Roundabout See *The Jack Jackson Show*.

Red or Black Game show presented by Ant & Dec. Broadcast over seven nights in September 2011, more than 100,000 contestants were whittled down during various stages and the live shows involved their ability to successfully choose the even chance of either red or black in order to advance further in the competition. The show's creator, Simon Cowell, was inspired by roulette and the story of Ashley Revell, who in 2004 had bet his entire life savings on "red" in a roulette game in Las Vegas. Unfortunately the show hit the headlines for the wrong reasons when the very first winner turned out to be a convicted criminal who was sentenced to five years for ABH. ITV 2011.

Red Dwarf Chris Barrie (Arnold Judas Rimmer, BSc, SSC), Craig Charles (Dave Lister), Danny John-Jules (Cat), Norman Lovett and Hattie Hayridge (Holly), David Ross and Robert Llewellyn (Kryten), Mac McDonald (Capt. Hollister), Clare Grogan and Chloe Annett (Kristine Kochanski). Sitcom created by Rob Grant and Doug Naylor. Three million years ago, a radiation leak killed the crew of the five-mile long, three-mile wide mining ship, Red Dwarf. The only survivor was Dave Lister, the chicken soup machine repairman. After coming out of suspended animation after 3,000,000 years he spends his time on the ship with a holographic projection of Arnold J. Rimmer (his dead bunkmate), Cat (a life-form that evolved from Dave's cat), Holly (the ship's senile computer only ever seen as a face on a screen), and Kryten (a service mechanoid). BBC2 1988-93; 1997-99. At Easter 2009, a three-episode production, *Red Dwarf: Back to Earth,* was screened by the digital channel Dave. A new series has recently been shot to air in 2012.

Redcap John Thaw got his first starring role as Sergeant John Mann of the Special Investigation Branch of the Royal Military Police (nicknamed a 'Redcap'), after being spotted by the producers in an episode of *The Avengers*. His forceful investigations concerned British troops accused of anything from rape, murder or simple desertion from places as far flung as Cyprus to Borneo, and many of the characteristics he portrayed (tough, no-nonsense) were re-employed when he became The Sweeney's Jack Reagan. ITV 1964-66. The series was remade by the BBC 2001-04 with Tamsin Outhwaite making it a female lead as Sgt Jo McDonagh.

Reggie Perrin See *The Fall and Rise of Reginald Perrin*

Reilly - Ace of Spies Sam Neill (Sidney Reilly), Peter Egan (Major Fothergill), Ian Charleson (Bruce Lockhart), Tom Bell (Dzerzhinsky), Norman Rodway (Cummings), David Burke (Stalin), Kenneth Cranham (Lenin), Leo McKern (Basil Zaharov), Donald Morley (Baldwin), David Suchet (Insp. Tsientsin). Spy drama written by Troy Kennedy Martin. Twelve-part mini-series based on Robin Bruce Lockhart's book that includes many of the Reilly legends (Sidney Reilly's real name was Sigmund Rosenblum), some of doubtful authenticity. Harry Rabinowitz adapted Dmitri Shostakovich's, *Fragments* from *The Gadfly*, Opus 97, as the sweeping theme music. ITV 1983.

Relocation, Relocation See *Location, Location, Location*.

Rentaghost Anthony Jackson (Fred Mumford), Michael Staniforth (Timothy Claypole), Edward Brayshaw (Harold Meaker), Michael Darbyshire (Hubert Davenport), John Dawson (Mr Mumford), Betty Alberge (Mrs Mumford), Ann Emery (Mrs Ethel Meaker), Jana Sheldon (Catastrophe Kate), Molly Weir (Hazel the McWitch), Christopher Biggins (Adam Painting), Sue Nicholls (Nadia Popov), Hal Dyer (Rose Perkins), Jeffrey Segal (Arthur Perkins), Aimi Macdonald (Susie Starlight), Paddie O'Neil (Queen Matilda), Lynda Marchal aka Lynda La Plante (Tamara Novek). Children's comedy drama series created by Bob Block. Fred Mumford returns from the spirit world and opens the agency Rentaghost, which offers ghosts and poltergeists for hire on a daily or weekly rental. He is helped (and hindered) in these plans by a fussy Victorian ghost, Davenport, and mischievous medieval poltergeist Claypole. Initially, Mumford enlists the additional support of his still-living parents, but things really take off when he links up with wheeler-dealer Mr Meaker, who becomes their agent. When Davenport and Mumford moved on, leaving Meaker and Claypole to run the show, other characters were brought in and began to share centre stage, notably Hazel the McWitch and, in later episodes, Nadia Popov (who sneezed whenever she was near flowers). The chaos the team wrought is reported via TV news bulletins. The constantly bemused neighbours are Rose and Arthur Perkins. The theme song was sung by Michael Staniforth. BBC1 1976-84.

Reporting Scotland BBC Scotland's national television news programme since 1968 and broadcasting from Pacific Quay, Glasgow since 2007. Mary Marquis was the main presenter until 1988 and the job is now held by Jackie Bird with frequent contributions from Sally Magnusson.

Restaurant, The Reality television series in which nine couples competed for the chance to set up a restaurant financially backed and personally supported by French chef Raymond Blanc. The winning couple were given their own restaurant to run, in Oxfordshire, near to Blanc's own Le Manoir aux Quat' Saisons. Winners of Series 1 were married couple Jeremy and Jane Hooper who opened their restaurant, Eight at the Thatch, in November 2007 in the Oxfordshire town of Thame. Sadly, the couple grew disenchanted with the project and left six months later. The format of the series was very similar to *The Apprentice* with Blanc signing off the "boardroom" grilling with 'I'm Closing Your Restaurant'. Narrated by Alex Jennings with Blanc's helpers including Sarah Willingham, David Moore, Lee Cash and John Lederer. For the second series the prize restaurant was in Marlow, Buckinghamshire and Barbara Flynn replaced Jennings as narrator. Michele English and Russell Clement were the winning couple. The third and final series was won by JJ Goodman and James Hopkins. BBC2 2007-09 A spin-off series, *The Restaurant: You're Fried!* (a play on *The Apprentice: You're Fired!*) aired on BBC Three after the main programme of the first series but was subsequently dropped. See also *Out of the Frying Pan*

Restoration Village Each week presenter Griff Rhys Jones and ruin detectives - architect Ptolemy Dean and surveyor Marianne Suhr - profiled three rural gems within a region of the UK and asked viewers to vote for which one should go through to the final. Seven finalists from around the country were then put forward for the ultimate public vote. A surprise eighth finalist also joined the line up (the runner-up that received the most viewer votes across the series). The series was a spin-off from the earlier *Restoration* series (first aired in 2003 with winners, The Old Grammar School, Saracen Head, Birmingham, and Victoria Baths, Manchester). The 21 historic properties (with winner in bold type) were: Massey's Folly, Alton, Hampshire; Watts Gallery, Compton, Surrey; Woodrolfe Granary, Tollesbury, Essex; Dawe's Twine Works, West Coker, Somerset; Newlyn Trinity Methodist Chapel, Newlyn, West Cornwall; Welcombe

Barton, Devon All Saints, Beckingham, Lincolnshire; **Chedham's Yard, Wellesbourne, Warwickshire**; Pennoyer's School, Pulham St Mary, Norfolk; Cromarty East Church, Black Isle, Scotland; Dennis Head Old Beacon, North Ronaldsay, Orkney; Greenlaw Town Hall, Berwickshire; Pembrey Court, Pembrey, Carmarthenshire; Pen Yr Orsedd Quarry, Nantlle, Caernarvon; The Prichard Jones Institute, Newborough, Anglesey ; Cushendun Former Parish Church, Cushendun, Co. Antrim; Gracehill Old Primary School, Ballymena; The White House, Belfast; Heugh Battery, Hartlepool; Higherford Mill, Higherford, Lancashire; Howsham Mill, North Yorkshire. The Live Final was on Sunday 17 September from the Weald and Downland Open Air Museum, near Chichester in Sussex. BBC2 2006

Return of the Saint Sequel to the very popular 1960s adventure series, *The Saint*. Ian Ogilvy played Simon Templar in much the same vein as Roger Moore although the show never reached the same level of popularity as its distinguished predecessor. ITV 1978-79.

Rev Tom Hollander (Adam Smallbone), Olivia Colman (Alex Smallbone), Steve Evets (Colin Lambert), Miles Jupp (Nigel McCall), Simon McBurney (Archdeacon Robert), Ellen Thomas (Adoha Onyeka), Darren Boyd (Darren Betts). Sitcom created by Tom Hollander and James Wood. The Revd Adam Smallbone is elevated from a small rural parish to the "socially disunited" St Saviour in the Marshes in East London. Adam is constantly challenged by the diversities of the needs of his congregation. BBC2 2010-11

Rex the Runt Surreal animated claymation children's series produced by Aardman Animations. The four main characters are plasticine dogs Vince (voiced by Steve Box, Vince uses short disjointed phrases and suffers from Random Pavarotti Disease. He is distinguished by his buck teeth and different sized eyes), Wendy (voiced by Elisabeth Hadley, Wendy wears a pink bow on her head), Bad Bob (voiced by Kevin Wrench for the first 13 episodes and Andy Jeffers for the last thirteen. Bob is a big couch potato who wears a black eye patch and often carries a large gun) and Rex (voiced by Andrew Franks first 13 episodes and Colin Rote for the last 13. Rex is a timid, irritable runt who often rescues the gang through his quick-wittedness. His favourite superhero is Rocket Raymond). Other characters include the moustachioed Doctor Dogg (voiced by Paul Merton, he tends to charge ten quid for his medical services), Arthur Dustcart (voiced by Arthur Smith, he tends to pong a bit), Mr Chittock (voiced by Steven Frost, he is the angry neighbour of Rex) and Stinky Basil (voiced by Antoine De Caunes, he is a smarmy French talent-spotter). Guest appearances were made by Mrs Mandelbrotska (voiced by Kathy Burke), Judith Poodle (Judith Chalmers), Johnny Saveloy (Bob Monkhouse), Mr Formal (Bob Holness), Melting Blob Man (Eddie Izzard), Constable Funnyname (Simon Day), Judge Pikelet (June Whitfield), Handsome Rex (Jonathan Ross), The Mouse (Phill Jupitus), Wayne (Tommy Cannon), Tiddles (Bobby Ball), Osvaldo Halitosis (Graham Norton), Mr Wangle (Stanley Unwin), Aunty Brenda (Pam Ayres) and Mrs Bloomers (Morwenna Banks). BBC2 1998-2001

Rhod Gilbert's Work Experience Welsh comedian Rhodri Gilbert (born Carmarthen, 18 October 1968) made his reputation telling stories based around the fictionalised village of Llanbobl (Located somewhere between Wrexham and Holyhead, just north of Newtown, Powys). In this four-part series Rhod tried his hand as a hairdresser, refuse collector, soldier and parent. BBC1 2010.

Rich Tea and Sympathy Patricia Hodge (Julia), Denis Quilley (George), Lionel Jeffries (Grandpa Rudge), Jean Alexander (Granny Trellis), Ray Lonnen (Steve Merrygrove), Anne Reid (Sally), Tracie Bennett (Nikki). Six-part drama series created by David Nobbs. A love story between two ill-matched characters - pompous biscuit factory owner George Rudge and feminist Julia Merrygrove. ITV 1991.

Richard & Judy Husband and wife team Richard Madeley (born Romford, 13 May 1956) and Judy Finnigan (born Newton Heath, Manchester, 16 May 1948) continued their daily magazine show after leaving *This Morning* in 2001. The show launched the Richard & Judy Book Club which ensured best-seller status for featured books. In 2007 the show was shrouded in controversy after it was announced that calls to the daily phone-in "You Say We Pay" were disregarded after the first ten minutes of the programme thereby defrauding later callers. C4 2001-08. See also *This Morning*.

Richard Arnold Show, The Friday morning magazine show which ran for five weeks in July and August 2007. Hosted by GMTV presenter Richard Arnold, allegedly after breakfast bosses bowed to pressure from the station's viewers, Ross King added reports from Hollywood and Debra Stephenson critiqued the latest television news. ITV 2007

Richard Hammond's 5 O'Clock Show See *5 O'Clock Show*

Richard the Lionheart Dermot Walsh (King Richard I, the Lionheart), Trader Faulkner (Prince John), Sheila Whittington (Queen Berengaria), Iain Gregory (Blondel), Robin Hunter (Sir Gilbert), Alan Hatwood (Sir Geoffrey), Francis De Wolfe (Leopold of France). When King Richard learns that his brother John is planning to take over the throne of England he returns from the crusades determined to put things to rights. All 39 episodes of this popular swashbuckler were directed by Ernest Morris and produced by Edward J. Danziger and Harry Lee Danziger (the Danziger Brothers). The "Richard the Lionheart" theme tune was written by Buddy Kaye and Philip Springer. ITV 1962-63

Right to Reply Channel 4's long-running equivalent to the BBC's Points of View although R2R critically discussed all channels after the first series. Presenters included Gus MacDonald, Linda Agran, Brian Hayes, Rory McGrath, Sheena McDonald and Roger Bolton. The show was axed in 2001 but after a seven year hiatus the channel aired a monthly soapbox programme, *The TV Show*. C4 1982-2001

Rings on Their Fingers Martin Jarvis (Oliver Pryde), Diane Keen (Sandy Bennett / Pryde), John Harvey (Gordon Bennett), Barbara Lott (Mrs Bennett). Sitcom written by Richard Waring. Oliver has been living with Sandy in his West Acton flat for six years but now she is beginning to get broody. By the end of the first series the couple are married and Sandy is soon pregnant. BBC1 1978-80.

Riordans, The After the success of *Tolka Row*, RTÉ produced their second Irish soap opera, set in the fictional townland of Leestown in County Kilkenny. Created by James Douglas, *The Riordans* featured ex-farmer Tom Riordan and his wife Mary, oldest son, Benjy and his brother Michael and sister Jude. Leading actors included: John Cowley (Tom Riordan), Moira Deady (Mary Riordan), Tom Hickey (Benjy Riordan), Chris O'Neill (Michael Riordan), Gabriel Byrne (Pat Barry), Tony Doyle (Father Sheehy), Annie Dalton (Minnie Brennan), Biddy White Lennon (Maggie Riordan). RTÉ 1965-79. See *Bracken*.

Ripping Yarns Series of spoofs in the style of Victorian/Edwardian *Boys' Own* books. Michael Palin starred as a different character in each programme and also shared the writing duties. Terry Jones co-wrote each episode but only appears in the 1976 pilot, *Tomkinson's Schooldays*, the only one of the episodes to be shot on video - the rest being shot on film. A full series began in 1977, the episodes entitled *The Testing Of Eric Olthwaite*, *Escape from Stalag Luft 112B*, *Murder At Moorstones Manor*, *Across The Andes By Frog* and *The Curse Of The Claw*. As the writers had wished, the production values were of a uniformly high standard, but this meant that the costs were significantly higher than normal for a comedy half-hour. For this reason, when Palin and Jones were planning a second series, the BBC decided they could afford only three more shows - a 1920s espionage thriller *Whinfrey's Last Case*, a football story *Golden Gordon* and a spoof of the overtly racist yarns that passed unchallenged in old schoolboy annuals, *Roger Of The Raj*. John Cleese made a silent but silly walk-on in *Golden Gordon*. BBC2 1976-79.

Rising Damp Leonard Rossiter (Rupert Rigsby), Richard Beckinsale (Alan Moore), Frances de la Tour (Miss Ruth Jones), Don Warrington (Philip Smith), Gay Rose (Brenda). Sitcom written by Eric Chappell based on his one-act play *The Banana Box* (in which the lead character was called Rooksby). Rigsby, the landlord of a rundown boarding-house in a northern university town, is obnoxious, bigoted, racist, lecherous, miserly, and interfering. All these traits are displayed to his three regular tenants, the lovelorn spinster Ruth Jones; the sexually inexperienced and generally immature medical student Alan; and the sage black student Philip, who never denied rumours that he was the son of a tribal chief. Miss Jones was the focus of Rigsby's sexual frustration (temporarily replaced by Brenda in series two) and although they had their moments his love remained unrequited, Miss Jones flirtatious tendencies being kindled more by Philip. Rigsby owned a cat named Vienna (often thought to be named after Rigsby's one night of passion in the Austrian capital as the cat had the same propensity to roam the streets late at night as the lady in question! ITV 1974-78.

Ritz, The Paul Rider (Chike), Andrew Dunn (Skodge), Andrew Livingstone (Kenny), Richard Ridings (Mad Mick), Julia Ford (Carol), Richard James Lewis (Eric), Kate Layden (Veronica), Shona Lindsay (Lisa). Six -part drama series written and co-directed by John Godber. Eric has sunk all his redundancy money into buying The Ritz disco, unaware that the previous owners lasted a mere five hours due to intimidation from the rival local disco-owner, Mad Mick and his entourage. Three bouncers Chike, Skodge, and Kenny, help to protect the club from Mick. The opening theme song was *Puttin' on the Ritz*. BBC2 1987.

Rivals of Sherlock Holmes, The Peter Vaughan (Horace Dorrington), Jeremy Irons (Nephew George), Derek Jacobi (William Drew), Ronald Fraser (Mr Horrocks), John Thaw (Lieutenant Holst), Catherine Schell (Maria Wolkonski), Michael Aldridge (Archduke Othmar), Nicola Pagett (Countess Nadja), Charles Gray (Eugene Valmont), Donald Sinden (Romney Pringle), Donald Pleasance (Carnacki), Ronald Hines (Jonathan Pryde), Michele Dotrice (Mary Higgins), John Neville (Dr Thorndyke), Terence Rigby (DS Bates), Roy Dotrice (Simon Carne), John Standing (Lord Amberley), Richard Beckinsale (Richard Frobisher), Robert Stephens (Max Carrados), John Carlisle (Stedman), Martin Jarvis (Philip Marsden), Sheila Gish (Mrs Chalmers), Denise Coffey (Miss Baines), Judy Geeson (Polly Burton), Robin Ellis (Charles Dallas), Carolyn Jones (Countess Tildi Leys), Mark Eden (Varley), Windsor Davies (Insp Illingworth), Peter Barkworth (Martin Hewett), Charles Lloyd Pack (Mr Neal), John Nettleton (Admiral Christador). Anthology of detective stories set in Victorian and Edwardian London. Based on Sir Hugh Greene's published anthology of stories of Sherlock Holmes' (fictional) contemporaries, although their creators were as real as Sir Arthur Conan Doyle. 2 x 13 episodes were shown with different production teams on each 50-minute episode. The actors involved, as can be gauged by the sample included above, contained the cream of British acting talent. ITV 1971; 1973.

River City Gordon Kennedy (Mac), Joyce Falconer (Roisin Henderson), Deirdre Davis (Eileen Donachie), Stefan Dennis (Dr. Marcus McKenzie), Barbara Rafferty (Shirley), Eric Barlow (Tommy Donachie), Ida Schuster (Lily Fraser), Duncan Duff (Lewis Cope), Paul Samson (Raymond Henderson), David Murray (Father Michael), Jason Pitt (Cormac O Sullivan), Ryan Fletcher (Vader), Jo Cameron Brown (Moria Henderson), Kari Corbett (Kirsty Henderson), Lorraine McIntosh (Alison Henderson), Allison McKenzie (Joanne Rossi), John Murtagh (George Henderson), Carmen Pieraccini (Kelly Marie Adams), Gilly Gilchrist (Archie Buchanan), Annmarie Fulton (Hazel Campbell), Daniel Healy (Drew), Maureen Carr (Theresa O'Hara), Una McLean (Molly O'Hara), Sandy Welch (Gordon Swan), Sam Robertson (Innes Maitland), Ewan Stewart (Daniel McKee), Frances Grey (Marianne McKee), Eileen McCallum (Liz Buchanan). Scottish soap opera created by Stephen Greenhorn, featuring the people who live and work in the fictional town of Shieldinch in Glasgow, particularly the local pub, The Tall Ship. First airing in 2002, and shown only on BBC1 Scotland on Tuesdays at 20:00 and Fridays at 20:30.

River, The David Essex (Davey Jackson), Katy Murphy (Sarah MacDonald), Shaun Scott (Tom Pike), Vilma Hollingbery (Aunty Betty), David Ryall (Colonel Danvers). Sitcom created by Michael Aitkens. Davey Jackson, a cockney wide-boy falls in love with nature during a spell in open prison and settles as a lock-keeper in rural Chumley-on-the-Water. But Davey's quiet life changes when he falls in love with the tactless but vulnerable

Sarah, a Scottish bargee who stays with him in his lock-keeper's cottage while her narrow-boat's broken propeller-shaft is repaired. BBC1 1988.

Rob Brydon Show, The Talk show hosted by comedian Rob Brydon, in which the regular format consists of one guest sitting on the sofa for a chat while another sings at the end of the show (as well as singing with Rob during their interview). A comedian also performs a short piece, with a short interview after by Rob. Before the show, Rob asks his Twitter fans to provide questions for his guests, which he then asks after the comedian performs. BBC2 2010- See *Gavin and Stacey, I'm Sorry I Haven't A Clue, Just A Minute, Little Britain, Marion and Geoff*, and *Would I Lie To You?* See also entry in the comedy section.

Robin Hood Patrick Troughton (Robin Hood), Josée Richard (Maid Marian), David Kossoff (Sheriff of Nottingham), Kenneth MacKintosh (Little John), Wensley Pithey (Friar Tuck), John Breslin (Alan Dale), Philip Guard (Will Scarlett), David Markham (King Richard I). Short lived six-episode BBC series of 1953.

Robin Hood Jonas Armstrong (Robin Hood), Lucy Griffiths (Maid Marian/Nightwatchman), Keith Allen (Vaisey, the Sheriff of Nottingham), Sam Troughton (Much), Gordon Kennedy (Little John), Richard Armitage (Sir Guy of Gisborne), Joe Armstrong (Allan A Dale), Harry Lloyd (Will Scarlett), Anjali Jay (Djaq), William Beck (Roy), David Harewood (Tuck), Lara Pulver (Isabella), Clive Standen (Archer), Joanne Froggatt (Kate), Toby Stephens (Prince John), Dean Lennox Kelly (Malcolm – Robin Hood's father). The first two series followed a fairly traditional path, although Allan A Dale became a Sheriff's informant for a time. At the end of Series 2 Gisborne murdered Robin's love, Maid Marian (Robin married Marian as she lay dying), and the third series began with the introduction of the warrior cleric, Tuck. Numerous twists ensued and the legendary outlaw who robbed from the rich and gave to the poor, was eventually discovered to be the half brother of Gisborne – Robin's father having an extra-marital relationship with Gisborne's mother, Ghislaine). After apparently killing the Sheriff of Nottingham, Gisborne joins Robin in search of their brother, Archer, the title of Sheriff of Nottingham being awarded to Gisborne's sister, Isabella. In the third series finale Vaisey returned from the dead and a spectacular battle is fought and although successful Robin succumbs to poison. BBC1 2006-09

Robin Hood, The Adventures of Richard Greene (Robin Hood), Bernadette O'Farrell & Patricia Driscoll (Lady Marian Fitzwalter), Archie Duncan & Rufus Cruikshank (Little John), Alexander Gauge (Friar Tuck), Alan Wheatley (Sheriff of Nottingham), Hubert Gregg, Brian Haines, Donald Pleasance (Prince John), Ronald Howard & Paul Eddington (Will Scarlett), Richard Coleman (Alan-a-Dale), Victor Woolf (Derwent), John Arnatt (Deputy Sheriff), Peter Asher, Richard O'Sullivan, Jonathan Bailey (Prince Arthur), Alfie Bass (Edgar / Lepidus). Theme tune by Edwin Astley was sung by Dick James. First aired on ITV 26 September 1955, the 143rd and last episode 'Trapped' being originally broadcast on 12 November 1960, although the series was staple Saturday tea-time diet throughout the 1960s. The series was shot at Nettlefold Studios, Walton-on-Thames, close to the historic Runnymede Meadow where King John signed the Magna Carta in 1215. This enabled the production to use authentic backgrounds among the English countryside which have remained unchanged for centuries. Rufus Cruickshank, a Scots actor, replaced Archie Duncan as Little John for about ten episodes of the series after an accident on the set. A heavy piece of scenery was about to fall on some children and Duncan pushed the kids out of the way. The set fell on him and broke his leg. He received a medal for his good deed. The lyrics to the theme song are as follows: *Robin Hood, Robin Hood, Robin Hood, riding through the glen. Robin Hood, Robin Hood, with his band of men. Feared by the bad, loved by the good. Robin Hood! Robin Hood! Robin Hood! He called the greatest archers to a tavern on the green. They vowed to help the people of the king. They handled all the trouble on the English country scene. And still found plenty of time to sing.*

Robin of Sherwood Michael Praed (Robin of Loxley), Jason Connery (Robert of Huntingdon), Clive Mantle (Little John), Ray Winstone (Will Scarlet), Judi Trott (Maid Marian), Phil Rose (Friar Tuck), Nickolas Grace (Sheriff of Nottingham), Peter Llewellyn-Williams (Much), John Rhys-Davies (King Richard I),

John Abineri (Herne the Hunter), Robert Addie (Guy of Gisborne). Robin of Loxley is chosen by the mystical Herne the Hunter to become his 'son' and champion the oppressed. Gathering a band of comrades around him he fights a guerilla campaign against their Norman dictators, particularly the Sheriff of Nottingham and his deputy, Guy de Gisburne. Loxley was succeeded by Robert of Huntingdon, renegade nobleman, for the final series. This retelling of the legend of Robin Hood introduces a strong fantasy element, with black magic. The theme music *Robin* (The Hooded Man) was performed by Clannad. ITV 1984-86.

Robin's Nest Richard O'Sullivan (Robin Tripp), Tessa Wyatt (Victoria Nicholls), Tony Britton (James Nicholls), David Kelly (Albert Riddle the one armed washer-up) Honor Blackman and Barbara Murray (Marion Nicholls). Written by Johnnie Mortimer and Brian Cooke. Spin-off sitcom from *Man About the House*, with Robin now living above his Fulham bistro 'Robin's Nest' with girlfriend (later wife) Vicky. ITV 1977-81.

Robinsons, The Martin Freeman (Ed Robinson), Hugh Bonneville (George Robinson), Abigail Cruttenden (Victoria Robinson), Richard Johnson (Hector Robinson), Anna Massey (Pam Robinson). Sitcom about a reinsurance actuary, Ed Robinson, who realises that reinsurance is not his passion and decides to rethink his life. BBC2 2005.

Robot Wars Gladiatorial contest putting home-made robots to the test. Each week groups of amateur inventors presented their radio-controlled objects of destruction with names such as Dreadnaught, Dead Metal, Sir Killalot, Cruella and Chaos 2. The programme was originally presented by Jeremy Clarkson with Philippa Forrester and commentary for the programme was provided by Jonathon Pierce. Each programme was divided into three segments: Gauntlet, Trial and Arena (the first two rounds being dropped from series three). Road Block was the winner of series one. Clarkson was replaced by Craig Charles after the first series, Julia Reed taking over from Philippa Forrester as assistant for series four (although Forrester returned for series five she was replaced by Jayne Middlemiss for the final series shown on Channel 5). BBC2 1998-2004; *Five* 2004-05

Rock Follies Charlotte Cornwell (Anna Wynd), Julie Covington (Devonia 'Dee' Rhoades), Rula Lenska (Nancy 'Q' Cunard de Longchamps, Derek Thompson (Harry Moon), Emlyn Price (Derek Huggin), Beth Porter (Kitty Schreiber), Sue Jones-Davies (Rox), Denis Lawson (Ken Church), Billy Murray (Spike). Drama written by Howard Schuman. The ups and downs of a fictional female rock band called the "Little Ladies" as they struggled for recognition and success. The spin-off album of music from the series entered the UK charts at number one - the first album since The Beatles to do so. A single, O.K.?, reached No. 10 in the UK charts (performed by the three leading actresses and Sue Jones-Davies).The songs were written by Andy Mackay, who was a founding member of Roxy Music. The show won a BAFTA award in 1976 but the second series, *Rock Follies of '77*, which also starred Bob Hoskins as Johnny Britten, was badly affected by industrial action at ITV which caused a six-month postponement and subsequent loss of impetus of a compelling series. ITV 1976-77.

Rock 'N' Roll Years Each episode charted the news for a particular year to a background of popular music of the day. The first year depicted was 1956 and the final programme illustrated the events of 1979. BBC1 1985-87. The 1980s were depicted in a 1994 series also shown on BBC1.

Rock Profile Spoof series written by and starring Matt Lucas and David Walliams, the first 13 episodes shown on the channel UK Play in 1999, and the second 13 episodes on BBC2 in 2000, where the first series was eventually repeated. The format was that Jamie Theakston would interview rock legends such as Ringo Starr, Kylie Minogue, Bono, Liam Gallagher (all portrayed by David), Elton John, George Harrison, Geri Halliwell, Paul McCartney and Gary Barlow (all portrayed by Matt). In 2009, a third series was recorded and subsequently made available on the internet for free viewing. Dermot O'Leary replaced Jamie Theakston as host.

Rock Rivals Michelle Collins (Karina Faith), Sean Gallagher (Mal Faith), Alison Newman (Lynette Hopkins), Gary Cooke (Vernon Fentor), Helen Modern (Sasha Reed), Lisa Dwan (Angel Islington), James Anderson (Pete Shepherd), Nicola Hughes (Sundae Gorgeous), Sophie Dawnay (Jinx Jones), Amy Garcia (Lucy Stone), Sol Heras (Luke Ellis), Holly Quin-Ankrah (Bethany Hopkins), Sammy Glenn (Dana Bigglesworth), Marcus O'Donovan (Jez Willard), Robert Sheehan (Addison Teller), Shane McDaid (Declan O'Brien), Kumar Kaneswaren (Caleb Coombs), Siva Kaneswaren (Carson Coombs), Adam Leese (Felix McGowan), Alice Henley (Ocean Faith) and Gerry McCann (Sam Winwood). Drama series, created by Maureen Chadwick and Ann McManus, following the lives, trial and tribulations of two celebrity judges on a *Pop Idol* style show as their marriage falls apart. The eight-part series was panned by the critics. ITV and TV3 Ireland - 2008

Rock School Rock Legend Gene Simmons (frontman of Kiss) took over the music class at boarding school Christ's Hospital in West Sussex, and transformed a class of classically trained 13-year-olds into junior rock gods, ultimately performing as support artists for Motorhead. The undoubted star of the first series was lead singer Josh 'The Emperor' Bell. The second series in 2006 saw Gene travel to a comprehensive in Lowestoft, Kirkley High School, to perform a similar transformation. The group's prize was to open for Judas Priest in front of 20,000 fans in Los Angeles. 15-year-old Chris Hardman fronted the band 'No Comment'. C4 2005-06

Rocket Man Robson Green (George Stevenson), Lucy Evans (Angela Stevenson), John Rhys Halliwell (Tom Stevenson), Charles Dale (Barney Scott), Alison Newman (Diane Scott), Janine Wood (Mary Hughes), Kay Bridgeman (Pam Tomlyn), Kai Owen (David 'Shiner' Owen), Dave Hill (Huw Masters), Philip Whitchurch (Lloyd Edwards). Six-part mini-series written by Alison Hume. Talented engineer George Stevenson immerses himself in the project of building a rocket to take his late wife's ashes to the stars. BBC1 2005

Rockliffe's Babies Ian Hogg (Det. Sergeant Rockliffe), Alphonsia Emmanuel (W.P.C. Janice Hargreaves), Susanna Shelling (W.P.C. Karen Walsh), Bill Champion (P.C. David Adams), John Blakey (P.C. Keith Chitty), Brett Fancy (P.C. Steve Hood), Joe McGann (P.C. Gerry O'Dowd), Martyn Ellis (P.C. Paul Georgiou), Malcolm Terris (Det Supt. Munro), Edward Wilson (Det. Insp. Charles Flight). Police drama created by Richard O'Keefe. DS Rockliffe is given the job of training seven new young recruits to the C.I.D., all fresh out of uniform. The third series was entitled *Rockcliffe's Folly*, and sees Rockliffe moving out of London and accepting a new appointment in Wessex. Co-stars include James Aubrey (Det. Insp. Derek Hoskins), Ian Brimble (Insp. Leslie Yaxley), Aaron Harris (DC Paul Whitmore), Carole Nimmons (Sgt. Rachel Osborne), Craig Nightingale (PC Guy Overton), Elizabeth Morton (WPC Hester Goswell), John Hartley (PC Alfred Duggan). BBC 1 1987-88.

Rod, Jane and Freddy See *Rainbow*

Roger and Val Have Just Got In Dawn French (Val Stephenson), Alfred Molina (Roger Stephenson). Sitcom written by Emma Kilcoyne, Beth Kilcoyne and Dawn French. The six episodes tell in real-time the everyday, seemingly trivial trials and tribulations faced by a middle-aged married couple. The bittersweet comedy, perhaps better suited to the captive audience of the stage, looks at how they get on in the first half an hour after walking through their front door and is more of a social comment than a laugh-a-minute joyride, pathos being the order of the day. BBC2 2010.

Roger Doesn't Live Here Anymore Jonathan Pryce (Roger Flower), Diane Fletcher (Emma Flower), Kate Fahy (Rose), Alice Berry (Arabella), Benjamin Taylor (Charles), Michael Elphick (Stanley). Six-part sitcom written by John Fortune. Roger Flower, an impoverished composer, is having an acrimonious divorce from his well-heeled wife, Emma. He has, however, found some consolation in the arms of Rose who finds an adulterous relationship a major turn on. In order to maintain their healthy sex-life she marries an all-in wrestler called Stanley on the morning of his divorce! BBC2 1981

Rogue Traders See *Watchdog*.

Roland Rat Television puppet character created, operated and voiced by David Claridge. Roland was introduced to TV-am viewers in 1983 and was largely responsible for expanding the audience from 100,000 to 1.8 million within two years. Roland drove a bright pink 1957 Ford Anglia (the ratmobile). He lived beneath King's Cross railway station and had an infant brother called Reggie, and a girlfriend: Glenis the Guinea Pig. His friends included dour Welsh technical whizz Errol the Hamster, and over-enthusiastic self-appointed "number one ratfan" Kevin the Gerbil. Under the name Roland Rat Superstar, Roland made three records, Rat Rapping (No 14 in 1983), Love Me Tender (No 32 in 1984) and No. 1 Rat Fan (No 72 in 1985). In 1985 he transferred to the BBC where he had a number of shows through the late 1980s, most notably *Roland Rat the Series*, a chat show supposedly set in Roland's sewer home, now converted into a high-tech media centre called the Ratcave. In a similar manner to *The Muppet Show* and its sequels, the show would intersperse the chat show segments with a storyline involving some sort of situation "behind the scenes". He also appeared in two spoof drama series, *Tales of the Rodent Sherlock Holmes*, in which he played Holmes with Kevin the Gerbil (who had a No 50 UK hit record with Summer Holiday in 1985) as Dr Watson, and *Ratman*, a Batman spoof with Kevin as his sidekick, "Pink Bucket Man". During Christmas 1985, British Telecom operated a free "ratphone" number on 0800 800 800. In the late 1990s he reappeared on Channel 5, in LA Rat, which featured Roland and his friends touring Los Angeles. Roland made another brief return in early 2003 as a guest presenter of CiTV. Roland made his final television appearance to-date on the puppet Christmas special of *The Weakest Link* in December 2007.

Roll Over Beethoven Liza Goddard (Belinda Purcell), Nigel Planer (Nigel Cochrane), Richard Vernon (Oliver Purcell), Emlyn Price (Marvin). Sitcom written by Laurence Marks and Maurice Gran. Nigel Cochrane, whose career as bass guitarist and lead singer with the heavy-metal band Graf Spee has given him superstar-status, quits at the age of 23 and moves into the Grange, a manor house in the quiet Surrey village of Churston Deckle to make solo music. The local piano-tutor, and church organ-player, Belinda Purcell, is asked to give Nigel keyboard lessons and romance blossoms. Belinda is the daughter of Oliver Purcell, a widower, retired school headmaster and writer of letters to *The Times*, now more interested in flower shows, a peaceful life and finding a man for his demure and unblemished daughter. Nigel does not fulfil his strict criteria for a future son-in-law. ITV 1985.

Romany Jones James Beck (Bert Jones), Jo Rowbottom (Betty Jones), Arthur Mullard (Wally Briggs), Queenie Watts (Lily Briggs), Jonathan Cecil (Jeremy Crichton-Jones), Gay Soper (Susan Crichton-Jones). Created by Ronald Chesney and Ronald Wolfe. Sitcom based around a run-down campsite. James Beck died after filming series two and the more up-market Crichton-Jones were introduced. ITV 1973-75. Arthur Mullard and Queenie Watts reprised their roles in a spin-off series *Yus My Dear*.

Rome Kevin McKidd (Lucius Vorenus), Kenneth Cranham (Pompey Magnus), Tobias Menzies (Marcus Junius Brutus), Ciaran Hinds (Gaius Julius Caesar), James Purefoy (Mark Antony), Indira Varma (Niobe), Rick Warden (Quintus Pompey), Lee Boardman (Timon), Ray Stevenson (Titus Pullo), Polly Walker (Atia of the Julii), Lindsay Duncan (Servilia of the Junii), Kerry Condon (Octavia of the Julii), David Bamber (Marcus Tullius Cicero), Max Pirkis (Gaius Octavian), Karl Johnson (Porcius Cato). Lavish historical drama with episodes directed by Michael Apted, Allen Coulter, Julian Farino, Jeremy Podeswa, Alan Poul, Mikael Salomon, Steve Shill, Alan Taylor, and Timothy Van Patten. The series begins in 52 BC, as Julius Caesar completes his conquest of Gaul after eight years of war, and prepares to return with his army to Rome. While Caesar's self-interested niece Atia and long-lost paramour Servilia anxiously await the general's return, ruling patricians despair that Caesar's homecoming will disrupt the status quo, and threaten the extravagant prosperity they've enjoyed at the expense of the lower class. In the Senate, old-guard leaders plot to undermine Caesar's influence by convincing his old friend, Pompey Magnus, that the general is a threat. Back at the front, two mismatched soldiers from Caesar's 13th Legion, Lucius Vorenus and Titus Pullo, are ordered into the wilds of Gaul to retrieve their legion's stolen standard, the unifying symbol of Caesar's legion, setting off a chain of circumstances that will entwine them in pivotal events of ancient Rome. As Caesar's legions move closer to Rome, allegiances are put to the test for soldiers and civilians - and the escalating tensions climax with a full-scale conflict destined to change history. BBC2 2005-07.

Roobarb Quirky cartoon that starred a green dog (Roobarb) and a pink cat (Custard). It was strange because of the way it looked - it shimmered. Created/written by Grange Calveley and produced/directed by Bob Godfrey (who later gave us *Henry's Cat*) on a tight budget using a cheap source of variously coloured marker-pens. Roobarb lived on his own, in a two-up two-down house. He wasn't overtly intelligent, but that didn't stop him thinking he was. He would come up with ideas that usually meant him going to his shed at the bottom of his garden in an attempt to make his invention become reality. This rarely happened. Custard lived next door to Roobarb. He liked to laze around on the fence watching Roobarb come up with his inventions. He would try to humiliate Roobarb with any chance he could and would normally be seen laughing the loudest at his misfortunes. The other members of the regular cast were the crow-like birds who acted as Roobarb's audience throughout his trials. All the characters of Roobarb were voiced by actor Richard Briers. BBC1 1974-75. All 30 original episodes were repeated in 2005 followed by 39 brand new stories with characters new and old.

Room at the Bottom Keith Barron (Kevin Hughes), James Bolam (Nesbitt Gunn), Richard Wilson (Chaplain Toby Duckworth). Sitcom written by John Antrobus and Ray Galton; based around the fictional television station, Megla TV. ITV 1986-88. This series was based on a short-lived 1960s ABC series of the same name with Lionel Jeffries in the role of Nesbitt Gunn. Both series and a further distinct 1960s series starring Kenny Lynch derived their names from the very successful 1959 film *Room at the Top*.

Room 101 Room 101 was the room in George Orwell's 1984 which contained "the worst thing in the world". The BBC took this concept and turned it into a radio show in 1992 (BBC Radio 5) before adapting the same format for television in 1994. The BBC's concept was for various celebrities to talk about things that they hate, the host deciding whether to banish the bêtes noires to Room 101 (originally along a conveyor belt and through a sliding door but in the Paul Merton era down a shaft by pulling a lever). The show was originally hosted by Nick Hancock (1994-98) and from 1999 by Paul Merton. Nick Hancock became Paul's first guest when he took over as host. BBC2 1994-2007. A revamped BBC1 series is scheduled for January 2012 with three guests choosing themed answers and host Frank Skinner deciding what goes in the room.

Ros na Rún Irish soap opera Ros na Rún (secrets of the woodland) began in 1995 on Irish language television channel TG4 and although it runs English subtitles it is the only soap in the world which is produced in the Irish language. The series is set in western County Galway.

Rosemary & Thyme Felicity Kendal (Rosemary Boxer) and Pam Ferris (Laura Thyme). Crime fiction series created by Tom Clegg and Brian Farnham. The eponymous heroes are gardeners cum detectives who solve various mysteries around the country, and also internationally on occasion, by use of their horticultural skills. ITV 2003-07

Rosie Paul Greenwood (PC Michael 'Rosie' Penrose), Frankie Jordan (Gillian Chislehurst), Tony Haygarth (PC Wilmot), Lorraine Peters (Auntie Ida), Allen Surtees (Uncle Norman), Maggie Jones (Glenda Chislehurst), Don McKillop (Bill Chislehurst), Avril Elgar and Patricia Kneale (Millie Penrose). Spin-off from *The Growing Pains of PC Penrose*. Writer Roy Clarke transferred Rosie to the coastal town of Ravensby on the premise his widowed mother is at death's door, but in fact the manipulative, mascara-laden Millie wants him back, because, as the show's theme music (co-written and sung by Rosie actor Paul Greenwood) indicates, he is her pride and joy, and she will never let him go. Rosie's Uncle Norman and Aunt Ida live with the Penroses' Uncle Norman, who is more supportive of Rosie, recognising the need for male-togetherness in their female-dominated world. Rosie's return to Ravensby delights his long-standing girlfriend Gillian, the daughter of affluent, disapproving parents Bill and Glenda. Gillian wants marriage but Rosie doesn't, and he constantly has to temper her enthusiasm. At the police station he strikes up a friendship with PC Wilmot, a man prone to adjusting his genitals in public. BBC1 1976-81.

Roughnecks Teresa Banham (Tessa Buckingham), Colum Convey (Ceefax), Paul Copley (Ian), James Cosmo (Tom), Liam Cunningham (Chris), Francesca Hunt (Hilary), Ashley Jensen (Heather), Bruce Jones (Terry), John McGlynn (Drew McAllister), Anne Raitt (Izzy), George Rossi (Kevin), Clive Russell (Archie), Ricky Tomlinson (Cinders), Hywel Simons (Wilf). Drama series created by Kieran Prendiville about the lives and loves of the crew of a North Sea oil-rig. BBC1 1994-95.

Round Britain Quiz Long-running panel game, originally hosted by Gilbert Harding and Lionel Hale, broadcast on BBC Radio 4 since 1947. Other chairmen have included Roy Plomley, Anthony Quinton, Gordon Clough, Nick Clarke and Tom Sutcliffe. Teams representing various regions around the UK play head-to-head battles, facing four multi-part questions with up to six points awarded at the chairman's discretion. The parts of the question generally have a common theme running throughout them, and a degree of lateral thought is necessary to score full marks. The chairman prompts teams and generally gives clues to teams to prevent long silences. Contestants have included Irene Thomas, John Julius Norwich, Fred Housego, Brian J. Ford, Patrick Hannan and Philippa Gregory.

Round The Horne Radio comedy programme created by Barry Took and Marty Feldman, transmitted on Sundays as the successor to *Beyond Our Ken*. Although there was only four series (due to Kenneth Horne's untimely death of a heart attack in February 1969 at the Bafta Awards ceremony at the Dorchester Hotel) as opposed to seven of its predecessor, and the cast was pretty much the same, this show captured the public's imagination in a time where radios were switched on in most homes on a Sunday, from Children's favourites in the morning through to The Clitheroe Kid and Billy Cotton Band Show while mum was cooking the Sunday roast, and Pick of the Pops in the evening. One of the most popular additions were the characters Julian and Sandy, featuring Hugh Paddick and Kenneth Williams as two outrageously camp out-of-work actors, speaking in the gay slang Polari, with Kenneth Horne as their unwitting comic foil. Other new characters included Dame Celia Molestrangler and Judy Coolibar, an aggressive Australian (both played by Betty Marsden), old English folk singer Rambling Syd Rumpo and J. Peasemold Gruntfuttock (both played by Kenneth Williams), Binkie Huckaback (Hugh Paddick - named after theatrical impresario Binkie Beaumont) and Seamus Android (Bill Pertwee's parody of Eamonn Andrews). BBC Light Programme/BBC Radio 2 1965-68

Royal, The See *Heartbeat*

Royal Bodyguard, The David Jason (Captain Guy Hubble), Geoffrey Whitehead (Colonel Dennis Whittington), Timothy Bentinck (Sir Edward Hastings), Tim Downie (Yates), David Walliams (Sir Ambrose, Surveyor of the Queen's Pictures). Sitcom written by Mark Bussell and Justin Sbresni. The inept Guy Hubble is assigned to car parking duties at 'the palace' until one day he rescues the Queen from a carriage accident. Guy becomes the Queen's trusted bodyguard much to the dismay of her more able staff. Although creating carnage all around him, Guy often comes up trumps in the end. BBC1 2011-

Royal Variety Performance The first Royal Variety Performance (known as the Royal Command Performance) took place on 1 July 1912 at the Palace Theatre, London. King George V and Queen Mary attended the lavish occasion; the theatre being decorated with three million roses which were draped around the auditorium and over the boxes. The performers included music hall stars Paul Cinquevalli, Vesta Tilley and the great Russian ballerina, Anna Pavlova. All profits from the show went to the Variety Artistes' Benevolent Fund (now called the Entertainment Artistes Benevolent Fund). Brinsworth House, a home for retired members of the entertainment profession and their dependants,

enjoys a good deal of funding from the annual extravaganza. Marie Lloyd, one of the most famous Music Hall artists of the time, did not appear because of a professional dispute. She held a rival performance in a nearby theatre, which she advertised was "by command of the British public". Since 1960 the show has been televised; initially by ITV for the first two years and then alternately with the BBC. When The Beatles topped the bill on 4 November 1963, John Lennon delivered the immortal line "For our last number I'd like to ask your help: Will the people in the cheaper seats clap your hands? And the rest of you, if you'll just rattle your jewellery ..."

Royle Family, The Caroline Aherne (Denise Royle/Best), Sue Johnston (Barbara Royle), Ricky Tomlinson (Jim Royle), Ralf Little (Antony Royle), Liz Smith (Norma Speakman), Craig Cash (Dave Best), Doreen Keogh (Mary Carroll), Peter Martin (Joe Carroll), Jessica Hynes nee Stevenson (Cheryl Carroll), Geoffrey Hughes ('Twiggy'), Sheridan Smith (Emma Kavanagh), Andrew Whyment (Darren Sinclair-Jones), Matthew Hughes and James Hughes (Baby David Best). Sitcom written by Caroline Aherne, Craig Cash, Henry Normal and Carmel Morgan. Set in a humble council house somewhere in Manchester; the camera position was usually fixed, rarely leaving the sitting room and never ever leaving the house. The 'couch potato' characters mostly sat, and sat, and sat, and their television was rarely switched off, providing a permanent background drone to the conversations. The dialogue, always humdrum, was occasionally interspersed with Jim's nose-picking interludes or his cry of 'my arse!'. The public identified with this caricature of the average working-class family and it won numerous awards in the late 1990s. The show's theme tune is "Half the World Away" by Oasis. BBC2 1998; BBC1 1999-2000. Since the series ended there has been a series of one-off specials, *The Queen of Sheeba* (2006), *The New Sofa* (2008) and *The Golden Eggcup* (2009), the last two being Christmas specials and the last one having scenes shot on location for the first time.

Ruddy Hell! It's Harry and Paul Harry Enfield and Paul Whitehouse were the eponymous stars of this sketch series with a gallery of completely new characters. There was Peskovitch the ever diving footballer, the Posh Scaffolders, the Fat Kids Jamie and Oliver, and Nelson Mandela as you have never seen him before. Other characters included Laurel and Hardy in Brokeback Mountain, The Greek Mr Bean, The Computer Billionaires and Bono and The Edge. Harry and Paul were joined by Morwenna Banks and newcomer Laura Solon. The second series, simply called Harry and Paul, again introduced new characters, the most memorable being Paul Whitehouse's portrayal of a multi-lingual football manager who manages to communicate his team talk to each individual player in a stereotypically perceived manner. The second series also reprised the ultra-clever surgeons Charles and Sheridan who manage to pontificate on all manner of intellectual subjects while performing the most intricate surgical operations. BBC2 2007-10

Rude Tube See entry for Alex Zane in miscellaneous section

Rumpole of the Bailey Leo McKern (Horace Rumpole), Patricia Hodge (Phyllida Trant/Erskine-Brown), Peter Bowles (Guthrie Featherstone), Bill Fraser (Justice Bullingham), Julian Curry (Claude Erskine-Brown), Moray Watson (George Frobisher), Peter Blythe (Samuel Ballard), Samantha Bond (1987) and Abigail McKern (1988-92) (Liz 'Mizz Liz' Probert), Richard Murdoch (Uncle Tom), Peggy Thorpe-Bates (1978-83) and Marion Mathie (1987-92) (Hilda Rumpole), David Yelland (Nick Rumpole). Legal drama written by John Mortimer that initially started out as a BBC Play for Today episode in 1975 before being serialised on ITV in 1978. Rumpole is a no-frills defence lawyer who tends to take on, and win, cases from working-class clients. Off duty he resides at 38 Froxbury Mansions and socialises at Pomeroy's wine-bar; particularly enjoying the house claret, Château Fleet Street. He has a propensity to refer to judges as 'old darling' and has a penchant for giving literary or historical nicknames to friends and foes. His wife Hilda's moniker, "She Who Must Be Obeyed," was originally applied to the title character of H. Rider Haggard's novel "She," while Phyllida Trant's nickname, "Portia," is from Shakespeare's "The Merchant of Venice." Samuel Ballard is dubbed "Soapy Sam" after Bishop Samuel Wilberforce (1805-73). BBC1 1975; ITV 1978-80; 1983; 1987-88; 1991-92.

Runaround General knowledge quiz show hosted by Cockney comedian Mike Reid. Mike would ask a question and then shout the word 'Go' and on this command, ten children ran to one of three podiums across the studio depending on what they thought the correct answer was. On the prompt of 'runaround' the children had the option to change their minds before the correct answer was revealed. Leslie Crowther and Stan Boardman replaced Reid in 1977 but Mike returned in 1978. ITV 1975-81.

Runaway Bay Carl Bradshaw (Inspector Grant), Eric Fried (Dion), Diana Eskell (Alex), Jeremy Lynch (Chan), Louis Mahoney (Jahman), Thomas M. Pollard (Satch), Andrew Fraser (Jojo), John Woodvine (M. Snotts). Anglo-French children's adventure series following a group of friends having adventures while living on the island of Martinique in the Caribbean. The character of Shuku was one of Naomie Harris's first television roles. ITV 1992-93.

Russell Harty Show Frederic Russell Harty was born in Blackburn, Lancashire, 5 September 1934. He got his first break in television in 1970 presenting the arts programme *Aquarius*. In 1973 he was given his own series *Russell Harty Plus* on ITV, which placed him against the BBC's *Parkinson*, conducting lengthy celebrity interviews. His endearing amateurish but knowledgeable style won him a dedicated audience. The show lasted until 1981. In 1983, Russell moved to the BBC with an early evening celebrity chatshow, which gained some notoriety when he was attacked by actress Grace Jones on live TV. This show was cancelled in 1985. Openly homosexual, his partner from the early 1980s was the novelist Jamie O'Neill. He died of AIDS related Hepatitis B, 8 June 1988.

Ruth Rendell Mysteries, The George Baker (DCI Reg Wexford), Christopher Ravenscroft (DI Mike Burden), Louie Ramsay (Dora Wexford), Ann Penfold (Jean Burden), Diane Keen (Jenny Ireland/Burden), Ken Kitson (DS Martin), John Burgess (Dr Crocker), Sean Pertwee, Robin Kermode and Matthew Mills (Sgt/DS Barry Vine). Detective Chief Inspector Wexford and his assistant Inspector Mike Burden investigate crimes in the Hampshire town of Kingsmarkham (Romsey was used for filming purposes). The extremely cultured Wexford first appeared in the 1964 novel *From Doon with Death* (dramatised in 1991) and, according to his creator Ruth Rendell, was "born at the age of 52". Most episodes foreground Wexford and Burden's domestic complications, with Burden's wife Jean appearing throughout the first series. By the beginning of series two, Burden is a widower, left alone to cope with his two young children, John and Emma. In series three he meets Jenny Ireland, his daughter's history teacher, and the two eventually marry. When TVS lost its franchise in 1992 Meridian revived the series, although Wexford rarely appeared in subsequent stories. George Baker wrote three scripts for the Wexford series, and one for the umbrella series, *The Ruth Rendell Mysteries* (Wexford did not appear in this one). After the death of his first wife, in 1993 Baker married Louie Ramsay, who plays his on-screen wife Dora. Former Shadows drummer Brian Bennett provided the music, including its memorably jaunty theme tune. ITV 1987-2000.

Rutland Weekend Television Sitcom-cum-sketch show starring Eric Idle as the programme controller of the financially stretched Rutland Weekend Television (RWT). The title - both a reference to Britain's smallest county, Rutland, which had disappeared in 1974 with the redrawing of boundaries, and a pun on the ITV Friday-Sunday franchise for the capital, London Weekend Television - was suggested by John Cleese, who, according to Idle, was paid £1 for his trouble. Neil Innes (a former member of the Bonzo Dog Doo-Dah Band), David Battley, Henry Woolf and Gwen Taylor helped perform the material and there were occasional guest star appearances, notably George Harrison in the 1975 Christmas special. Innes also provided comic songs which inspired a 1978 documentary-style spin-off, *The Rutles*. Idle co-directed, wrote and also appeared in the film - as the presenter and as the Paul McCartney-like Dirk McQuickly; Neil Innes was the John Lennon-like Ron Nasty; Rikki Fataar played the George Harrison-like Stig O'Hara; and John Halsey was the Ringo Starr-like drummer Barrington Womble, alias Barry Wom. George

Harrison, Michael Palin, Ron Wood, Mick Jagger, Paul Simon, John Belushi, Dan Aykroyd, Bill Murray and Gilda Radner were also in the cast, in cameo roles. The film was a triumph from the first frame to the last, and a resounding success not only for Idle but also for Innes, who provided a slew of spot-on Beatles song parodies, leading to a hit album and singles; a very-long-awaited sequel album was issued in 1996. (RWT had also generated spin-offs: the book *The Rutland Dirty Weekend Book* and the Innes album *The Rutland Weekend Songbook*.) BBC2 1975-76.

Saber of London See Mark Saber.

Sabotage Girls-only quiz show hosted by Maria McErlane. Three women attempted to earn points by answering questions on chosen subjects. When someone got a question correct, not only did they get points but they could also ask an opponent to put their hands on their head forcing them out of the next question. The woman with the most points got the chance to go on the next show if they could solve five picture puzzles in a minute. However the two losers could "sabotage" their efforts by answering questions correctly and thus removing these squares from play. C4 1994.

Saga of Noggin the Nog, The Children's animation series created by Peter Firmin and Oliver Postgate. The rather eerie opening music was punctuated by the narrator announcing even more eerily: 'In the lands of the North, where the Black Rocks stand guard against the cold sea, in the dark night that is very long, the Men of the Northlands sit by their great log fires and they tell a tale. And those tales were the stories of a kind and wise king and his people; they were the saga of Noggin the Nog'. The crown of Noggin, Prince of the Nogs is sought by his wicked uncle Nogbad the Bad who devises evil plots to threaten the safety of the kingdom, and sometimes the world, in order to force Noggin to give up his crown. In each saga Nogbad pursues his plot to the very brink of success with the aid of his gang of crows, but at the last moment he is foiled by some unexpected piece of luck, cleverness or lack of attention on the part of the Nogs. Noggin has a group of guards, led by Thor Nogson, and a group of friends and advisers including Olaf the Lofty (the court inventor) and Graculus (a big green bird). He and his Queen, Nooka (daughter of Nan of the Nooks!), live in a castle beside the sea with their young son and heir, Prince Knut. While Noggin is exceptionally brave and courageous, he is not too bright. Five Sagas of Noggin the Nog were made in black and white for the BBC between 1959 and 1965. In 1982, one of these, *Noggin and the Ice Dragon*, and a new one, *Noggin and the Pie*, were made in colour. BBC1 1959-65; 1982.

Sahara Michael Palin's 2002 offering for the BBC was a four-part series depicting his journey across the Sahara Desert beginning and ending in Gibraltar.

Sailor Ten-part documentary depicting the life of the 2,500 crew aboard HMS *Ark Royal*. The theme song was Rod Stewart's classic hit *Sailing*. BBC1 1976.

Sailor of Fortune Lorne Greene (Grant Mitchell), Rupert Davies (Alphonso), Jack MacGowran (Sean), Paul Carpenter (Johnny). Adventure series concerning Grant 'Mitch' Mitchell's adventures as skipper of a freighter, *The Shipwreck*, as he endeavours to make a living shipping cargo around the world while very often pausing to help out the locals with their problems. Michael Balfour replaced Rupert Davies as Alphonso the Italian ship's engineer for four episodes in 1957. ITV 1955-58.

Saint, The Roger Moore (Simon Templar alias The Saint), Ivor Dean (Insp. Claude Eustace Teal). Adventure series based on the Leslie Charteris James Bond-like character who drives a Volvo P1800S and is independently wealthy enough to pick and choose his work. He involves himself in international intrigue, often attracting the attention of Inspector Teal (originally played by Campbell Singer, who was replaced by Wensley Pithey and then Norman Pitt in Series Two before Ivor Dean made the role his own between 1963 and 1969) and a bevy of beautiful women. ITV 1962-69. See also *The Return of the Saint*.

Saints and Scroungers Dominic Littlewood follows the work of benefit fraud investigators as they track down, investigate and eventually prosecute benefit cheats. BBC1 2009

Sale of the Century Quiz in which the money won can be spent on bargain prizes. The original version was hosted by Nicholas Parsons and announced by John Benson, who delivered the memorable opening 'From Norwich...It's the Quiz of the Week!'. Produced by Anglia Television and shown on ITV weekly from 1971 to 1983, six 'instant bargains' would be offered throughout the show. Any of three players were allowed to buzz in and purchase the bargain, evaluating whether to store their accrued funds or spend some which may jeopardise the winning of the game. There were three distinct rounds of questioning, with the values rising appropriately (£1, £3, £5). The winner was the player with the highest accrued funds at the end of the game. This contestant had the opportunity to spend their winnings on a bargain or come back for a jackpot prize (usually a car). Peter Marshall hosted a revived version on Sky in the late 1980s and early 1990s and Keith Chegwin hosted a 1997 version shown on Challenge TV with Robin Houston as the announcer. Simon Cowell was a contestant on the show in 1990.

Salon, The Reality TV show where various members of the public (some famous) were invited daily to have treatments (mostly hair styles) in a studio-built beauty salon situated in the Trocadero in the West End of London. Viewers were also given an insight into the running and bickering of life in a professional salon with manager Paul Merritt (Adie Pheelan deputised for a short stint) and his team of trainees and employees. The show was most notable for bringing fame to Brazilian-born hairstylist Ricardo Ribeiro and introducing viewers to Ozzy Osbourne's nephew, Terry Longden. It aired on Channel 4, with daily live coverage on E4 at certain times. The show began in 2003 and ended in early 2004. Brian Dowling was the narrator of the last series. Some of the show's celebrity guests included Carrie Grant, Brigitte Nielsen and Michael Barrymore. The show was produced by Endemol who's other work includes *Big Brother* and *Celebrity Scissorhands*.

Sam Kevin Moreton (Sam aged 11 to 14), Mark McManus (Sam as an adult), Barbara Ewing (Dora), Jennifer Hilary (Sarah Corby / Wilson). Drama series set in the coalfields of Yorkshire in the inter-war period and written by John Finch. After his father sets sail to Canada with another woman 10-year-old Sam Wilson and his mother, Dora, are forced to settle in the small mining community of Skellerton. There young Sam's life revolves around his close relatives, grandfather, aunts and uncles all of whom face various hardships such as unemployment or poverty. By the age of 14 Sam is forced to earn a living by working down the mines, but eventually he rebels against his expected fate and runs away to sea. He eventually returns, takes a job in an engineering factory, marries Sarah Corby and settles down in the town of Golwick, although he never forgot his roots or the hardships he faced through the 1930s and 1940s. The young Sam is played by Kevin Moreton in series one whilst the grown-up Sam was played by future *Taggart* star Mark McManus in Series Two and Three. ITV 1973-75.

Sam and Mark's Guide to Dodging Disaster Sam Nixon (born 21 March 1986 in Barnsley), and Mark Rhodes (born 11 September 1981 in Walsall) finished 3rd and 2nd respectively behind *Pop Idol* winner Michelle McManus before teaming up to become a successful singing duo, their debut single, a cover of The Beatles' song "With a Little Help from My Friends" reaching No 1 in the UK Charts. The two lads remained together presenting various BBC shows and this CBBC show, first aired in 2009, involved the duo performing mimes by way of averting disaster in a series of unlikely situations although always with an educational content. Hugh Dennis provided the voice-over. See *Copycats*

Sam's Game Davina McCall (Sam), Ed Byrne (Alex), Tristan Gemmill (Phil), Tameka Empson (Marcia). Six-episode sitcom written by Paul Waite. Short-lived acting stint for Davina McCall. Four friends get involved in each others lives and loves, while renting flats in a large London house. Sam is big-hearted and gutsy, but underneath her confident exterior lies considerable angst. Alex is Sam's neurotic flatmate; Phil is Sam's flirtatious neighbour and Marcia is Sam's upstairs neighbour. Marcia is the waitress at their local café - a chronic gossip with big attitude. ITV 2001.

Sandbaggers, The Roy Marsden (Neil Burnside), Richard Vernon and Dennis Burgess ('C'), Diane Keen (Laura Dickens),

Ray Lonnen (Willie Caine), Michael Cashman (Mike Wallace), Elizabeth Bennett (Diane Lawler). Spy drama created by Ian MacKintosh. British version of *Mission Impossible*. The stories centred on the elite covert operations section of British Intelligence, the Special Intelligence Force (SIF), nicknamed the Sandbaggers, and their boss, Neil Burnside, himself a former Sandbagger but now having to battle more with British bureaucracy than with enemy agents. Burnside chose his agents from a small pool depending on their expertise handling anything from pickups to assassinations. The plot stresses the cerebral side of operations, and the ambiguity of the cold war. ITV 1978-80.

Sapphire and Steel Joanna Lumley (Sapphire), David McCallum (Steel), David Collings (Silver). Science fiction series created by P. J. Hammond. Each episode began "All irregularities will be handled by the forces controlling each dimension. Transuranic heavy elements may not be used where there is life. Medium atomic weights are available: Gold, Lead, Copper, Jet, Diamond, Radium, Sapphire, Silver and Steel. Sapphire and Steel have been assigned." The series gives the viewer very little information regarding the eponymous main characters, preferring instead to get straight into the events of the story itself. All that we are told is that Sapphire and Steel are 'elements' - beings from another dimension, who have been assigned by a higher power to prevent the fabric of time from being compromised. Time is a 'corridor', and creatures from the beginning and ends of time are constantly looking for ways to break into the present and cause chaos. These creatures seek weak spots in the fabric of time, often using anachronistic elements as triggers to break through. These triggers can be the reciting of nursery rhymes in an old house; the use of mirrors and old photographs; or the presence of a resentful ghost haunting a train station. Of the two agents, Sapphire is more gentle and diplomatic, while Steel is cold and calculating, caring little for the people caught up in the events that the two of them have been sent to correct, and choosing to be quite ruthless when it comes to rectifying the situation. Both agents have special powers to assist them in their duties: Sapphire can roll back time to a limited extent, is able to tell the age of objects by touching them, and has some telekinetic powers. Steel is able to freeze objects to near absolute zero - which he utilises to hold off the creatures attempting to break through from other dimensions - and, as suggested by his name, has immense physical strength. Together, both agents also share a telepathic link. ITV 1979-82.

Sarah and Hoppity Children's puppet series originally shown as part of the *Small Time* broadcasts but the 52 episodes were much repeated until the end of the 1960s. *Sara And Hoppity* was based on a series of books written by Roberta Leigh. Sara Brown was a typical young girl, whose parents run a hospital for toys. Her favourite toy was Hoppity, a clockwork doll which could be wound up to do his hippity-hop dance (Hoppity had one leg shorter than the other). Hoppity had been found in a Goblin Ring, and being a Goblin Toy was frequently naughty, getting Sara into all sorts of trouble. Sara was voiced by Ysanne Churchman and Hoppity by Ronnie Stevens. The puppeteers were Sally Bussell and Joan Garrick. The series theme song went thus: *Sara Brown has a toy as naughty can be, And he'll start to sing if you wind-up his key. He'll sing and he'll dance, all over the floor, And when he stands still then you wind him some more. Dear old Hoppity, naughty Hoppity, There is no toy more naughty than he, Dear old Hoppity, clever Hoppity, He sings 'Diddlee-Dum' and he sings 'Diddlee-Dee'.* ITV 1962-63.

Sarah Jane Adventures, The Spin-off from *Dr Who*, created by Russell T Davies as part of the CBBC schedule. Elisabeth Sladen (Sarah Jane Smith), Yasmin Paige (Maria Jackson), Thomas Knight (Luke Smith), Daniel Anthony (Clyde Langer), Anjli Mohindra (Rani Chandra), Alexander Armstrong (voice of Mr Smith, a computer), John Leeson (voice of K9). The spin-off was first mooted in 1981 when a pilot episode entitled *K9 and Company* aired on BBC1 but was never made into a series. BBC1 2007- A series entitled *K9* was made in 2009 and shown on *Five* although not part of the *Dr Who* franchise

Saturday Live Virtually anyone who was anyone on the current comedy scene appeared in *Saturday Live*. Turning up twice or more were Chris Barrie, Craig Charles, Cliff Hanger (Pete McCarthy, Rebecca Stevens, Tony Haase, Robin Driscoll), Dawn French and Jennifer Saunders, Nick Hancock and Neil Mullarkey, Jeremy Hardy, Lenny Henry, Helen Lederer and Andy de la Tour, while among those popping up once apiece were Rowan Atkinson with Angus Deayton, Morwenna Banks, Julian Clary (as the Joan Collins Fan Club), Robbie Coltrane, Josie Lawrence, Jenny Lecoat, Norman Lovett, Paul Merton, Nigel Planer, Steve Punt and Hugh Dennis, Kate Robbins, Timothy Spall and Emma Thompson. There were also spots for visiting American comics, including Abby Stein, Emo Philips, Charles Fleischer, Rita Rudner, Louie Anderson and Will Durst, while Steven Wright hosted one of the editions in the first series, as did Ben Elton, Tracey Ullman, Lenny Henry, Pamela Stephenson, Chris Barrie, Michael Barrymore, Hale and Pace, Fascinating Aida and Peter Cook. Stephen Fry and Hugh Laurie, who appeared in all 20 editions of the two full series, were another act to gain great strength from *Saturday Live*, but the biggest leap to fame was afforded to Harry Enfield, who began it as an unknown and shot to stardom by producing the first of his array of created characters: Stavros, the Greek immigrant who runs a kebab shop in Hackney, east London, and has, at best, a faltering command of the English language. (The character was based on a real kebab shop owner, Adam Athanaffiou, who had a shop in Well Street, Hackney, where Enfield had been lodging with his friend Paul Whitehouse). Enfield went on to become the star of Saturday Live's follow-on series *Friday Night Live* where he added the brilliantly drawn Loadsamoney (again, with much inspiration from Whitehouse) to his portfolio of characters. The show also featured comic duo Ade Edmondson and Rik Mayall in the controversial and eventually banned sketch "The Dangerous Brothers." C4 1985-87. ITV revived the concept in 1996 with Lee Hurst as host.

Saturday Night Armistice, The Late-night topical fun from Armando Iannucci, Peter Baynham and David Schneider. Recurring features included the travels of 'The Mr Tony Blair Puppet', a gonk caricature of the (then) Leader of the Opposition; 'Hunt The Old Woman', in which viewers were asked to phone in if they spotted the show's resident OAP inveigling herself on to other shows or into filmed news items; and 'The Miniaturised Area', a scaled-down set (complete with its own miniature Mr Tony Blair Puppet) from which the gang supposedly accessed the world's security cameras in order to see 'What Happened Next' after certain pieces of news footage ended. The third series introduced 'The Dummies', a set of five bland mannequins who, with the help of a professional PR company and wide TV exposure over the coming weeks, would be launched as a successful music group. From 1996 the series was retitled *The Friday Night Armistice*. BBC2 1995-98.

Saturday Show, The Children's television show which replaced Tiswas. Originally planned to be called "Big Daddy's Saturday Show" as the host of the pilot was wrestling star Big Daddy (born Shirley Crabtree 14 November 1930 d. 2 December 1997), but when the heavyweight presenter pulled out at short notice it was retitled *The Saturday Show*, and was presented by Isla St Clair and ex-*Magpie* host Tommy Boyd. Jeremy Beadle occasionally hosted the show and actor David Rappaport was a permanent fixture playing the character "Shades", as was soccer legend, Jimmy Greaves. The show was notable for broadcasting a computer programme live which viewers could record from their television and upload to a Spectrum. This was developed into the game 'Up for Grabs' where a contestant at home had to steer a robotic arm in the studio and pick up prizes from a rotating turntable. ITV 1982-84.

Saturday Show, The Replaced *Live and Kicking* as the BBC's Saturday morning magazine show for children. Hosted by Dani Behr and Joe Mace (replaced by Fearne Cotton and Simon Grant in its second year, and when Fearne left the following year she in turn was replaced by Angellica Bell and Jake Humphrey). Sophie McDonnell and Ortis Deley provided outside broadcasts for the final season. The most popular slot of the show was The Tiny and Mr Duck Show. Several spin-off shows followed as part of the CBeebies slot. BBC1 2001-05.

Saturday Special Children's variety show hosted by Peter Butterworth and his wife Janet Brown, and famous for developing the budding career of glove puppet Sooty, although Porterhouse the Parrot was the in-house puppet for much of the run. Tony Hart also made his television debut on this programme as an artist and illustrator. *Saturday Special* was broadcast on alternate Saturdays with *Whirligig*, a similar show that had started the year before and also starred Peter Butterworth. BBC 1951-53

Saturday Starship, The Saturday morning children's series hosted by Tommy Boyd and Bonnie Langford which replaced *The Saturday Show*. ITV 1984-85. See *Get Fresh*

Saturday Stayback See *OTT*

Saturday Superstore The follow-on show from *Swap Shop*. Hosted by Mike Read, Sarah Greene and Keith Chegwin. The premise of the show was that Mike was the general manager of a superstore and Sarah was the customer services manager and Cheggers was the salesman out and about in his delivery van. Other departments included, Sport - David Icke; News - John Craven and sundries with Vicky Licorish, Phillip Schofield, Philip Hodson, and Peter Simon. First opened on BBC1 on 2 October 1982, the store held its closing sale in April 1987 and was replaced by Going Live!

Sat'day While Sunday Sarah-Jane Gwillim (Charlotte), Malcolm McDowell (Frankie), Timothy Dalton (Peter), Roger McGough (Narrator). Seven two-part stories revolving around the relationship between three northern youngsters. ITV 1967.

Saxondale Steve Coogan (Tommy Saxondale), Ruth Jones (Magz), Rasmus Hardiker (Raymond), Morwenna Banks (Vicky). Sitcom written by Steve Coogan and Neil Maclennan. Tommy is an ex-roadie with anger management issues and a pest control business. Survivor of a hostile divorce, he now lives with his girlfriend Magz, proprietress of the anarchic T-shirt shop Smash the System. Tommy regards himself as a maverick and a free-thinker and takes every opportunity to impart his wisdom to his young assistant Raymond. And as well as Pharaoh ants, mice and occasionally moths, Tommy has to battle with snowboarders, pigeon-loving activists... and people who talk about property prices. Vicky, the receptionist who hands out the jobs for Tommy's Stealth Pest Control operation, takes banter to the next level, knowing exactly how to provoke instant frustration. BBC2 2006-07.

Scales of Justice, The A series of thirteen British B-movies produced between 1962 and 1967 for Anglo-Amalgamated at Merton Park Studios in London . Hosted by British crime writer Edgar Lustgarten, the 30-minute films featuring an assortment of criminal cases, and a galaxy of well-known British actors, were originally shown in cinemas but were then shown on ITV from 1968 onwards. The series derives its title from the symbolic scales held by the Statue of Justice which is situated above the dome of London's Central Criminal Court, The Old Bailey. In the opening narration she is described as having '...in her right hand, the Sword of Retribution, and in her left - The Scales of Justice". The concluding theme music, *Scales of Justice*, was played by The Tornados. See also entry for *Scotland Yard.*

Scarlet Pimpernel, The Adventures of the Marius Goring (Sir Percy Blakeney / The Scarlet Pimpernel), Stanley Van Beers (Chauvelin), Patrick Troughton (Sir Andrew Ffoulkes), Lucie Mannheim (Countess la Villiere), Anthony Newlands (Lord Richard Hastings), Alexander Gauge (Prince Regent). Based on the book by Baroness Orczy; the 18 episodes depict the adventures of the Scarlet Pimpernel, who hides behind his guise as a foppish English aristocrat but in reality is the elusive hero of the French Revolution. Peter O'Toole made his screen debut in the episode, *A Tale of Two Pigtails*, playing 'the first soldier'. ITV 1956. Richard E. Grant revived the role for a 1999 BBC1 series, with Martin Shaw playing his arch-enemy Chauvelin and Peter Jeffrey playing Marquis de Rochambeau in his last screen appearance before his death.

School's Out Danny Wallace quizzes three celebrities on what they learned at school. All the usual school curriculum subjects are covered, including a French oral examination by Virginie Hopstein. BBC1 2006-07

Scotland Yard A series of 39 films made at Merton Park Studios from 1953 to 1961 as cinema second features. Hosted by Edgar Lustgarten, *Scotland Yard* was retitled *Casebook*, slightly cut to a 25 minute running time and shown on ITV from 1962. Channel Four repeated much of the series with its original title *Scotland*

Yard in the 1980s, and Bravo screened the same episodes in the 1990s. From 1962 Edgar Lustgarten also hosted 13 courtroom dramas under the title, *Scales of Justice*, the series ending in 1967 when the studios closed. See also entry for *Scales of Justice*.

Scratchy & Co Saturday morning CITV show which replaced *What's Up Doc?* It starred Mark Speight as "Scratchy" and Elliot Henderson-Boyle as "Reg", the pair complete with solid rubber wigs and sky blue jackets marked with clouds. Other characters included Sedgely the penguin and Fathead the football. Gail Porter was the presenter for the final series. ITV 1995-98

Screen One Producer Kenith Trodd was part of a 1984 team brought together to study how the BBC should respond to Channel Four's pioneering efforts in making films for both television and theatrical release. The result was a transition from the earlier concept of studio-made plays, such as *Play for Today* and the introduction of the new BBC anthology film series, *Screen One* and *Screen Two*, with Trodd's supervision of the initial group of titles in 1985. Both series ran on BBC1 and BBC2 between 1985 and 2002.

Screen Test Children's Quiz consisting of a series of clips from popular films and then a test of observation and general knowledge. Michael Rodd, the long-time presenter (1969-78), is the uncle of artist "Scanner" (real name Robin Rimbaud), the techno-artist who used a telephone scanner to make music out of people's phone calls. Brian Trueman replaced Rodd between 1979 and 1983 and Mark Curry hosted the final series in 1984. The theme tune was *Marching There and Back* by Syd Dale. BBC1 1969-84.

Screen Two See Screen One

Scully Andrew Schofield (Francis 'Franny' Scully), Ray Kingsley ('Mooey' Morgan), Mark McGann (Mad Dog), Cathy Tyson (Joanna), Richard Burke (Snooty Dog), Lucinda Scrivener (Puppy Dog), Jean Boht (Gran), Kenny Dalglish (himself), Val Lilley (Mrs Scully), Judith Barker (Mrs Heath), Tom Georgeson (Isaiah), Gilly Coman (Marie Morgan), Peter Christian (Tony Scully), Tony Haygarth (Dracula), Jimmy Gallagher (Arthur Scully), Paula Jacobs (Florrie), Elvis Costello (Henry Scully). Seven-episode sitcom written by Alan Bleasdale. Hard-headed 15-year-old Scouser, Franny Scully, daydreams about being a hero for Liverpool Football Club. He attends school, but spends most of his time in a world of his own, running on to the Anfield pitch while the Kop sing 'one Franny Scully, there's only one Franny Scully'. Scully's idol - as he regularly informs the viewers via straight-to-camera asides - is the Reds' striker supreme Kenny Dalglish, who appears frequently in his visions. Scully's best mate is Mooey, a relentlessly cheerful school friend whose nickname is 'Bungalow Head' because people reckon 'he's got nothing upstairs'. Among the family characters are Gran, who guzzles pina coladas, train-obsessed brother Henry, who listens to railway recordings through headphones, and goody-goody brother Arthur. Elvis Costello, in a rare acting role, also wrote and performed the theme song "Turning the Town Red". C4 1984.

Sculptress, The Pauline Quirke (Olive Martin), Caroline Goodall (Rosaling Leigh), Lynda Rooke (Iris Fielding), Christopher Fulford (Hal Hawksley). Drama based on the novel by Minette Walters. Olive Martin a heavily overweight young woman is convicted of killing and butchering her mother and sister and sentenced to life imprisonment where she spends her time carving out human shapes from candles stolen from the prison chapel. Five years after her conviction, publisher Iris Fielding commissions author Rosalind Leigh to write a book about Olive's case. Roz begins to develop a relationship with Olive and is soon convinced of her innocence. With the help of restaurant owner and former policeman Hal Hawksley (he was the Det Sgt who discovered the crime and had since left the force due to trauma), she sets out to prove it and undo what she sees as a miscarriage of justice. However, all is not what is seems. BBC1 1996.

Sea of Souls Bill Paterson (Dr Douglas Monaghan), Dawn Steele (Justine McManus), Iain Robertson (Craig Stevenson), Archie Panjabi (Megan Sharma), Douglas Henshall (Robert Dunbar), Peter McDonald (Dr. Andrew Gemmill). Drama series based around Dr. Douglas Monaghan, who is the head of a parapsychology unit at the fictional Clyde University (real-life University of Strathclyde), in Glasgow, Scotland, and his team of 'ghost-hunters'. In the first series he is assisted by Megan Sharma and Dr. Andrew Gemmill, but these characters were replaced in the second series by Justine McManus and Craig Stevenson. Produced in-house by BBC Scotland, in association with Sony Pictures Television International, the series debuted on BBC1 in the UK in February 2004. A second series was shown from January 2005, with a third following in 2006/07. The programme was created by writer David Kane, who also wrote the entire first series.

Search for the Nile, The Kenneth Haigh (Sir Richard Francis Burton), John Quentin (John Hanning Speke), Barbara Leigh-Hunt (Isabel Arundell), Andre Van Gyseghem (Sir Roderick Murchison), Seth Adagala (Bombay), Michael Gough (David Livingstone), Ian McCulloch (Capt. James Grant), Norman Rossington (Samuel Baker). The Nile's source was the last great mystery for European explorers in the 19th century. The story of its discovery is one of heroism in the service of faith, greed, and obsession. This six-part mini-series narrated by James Mason depicts the trials and tribulations of the intrepid explorers of the world's longest river. BBC1 1971.

Second Thoughts James Bolam (Bill Macgregor), Lynda Bellingham (Faith Grayshot), Julia Sawalha (Hannah Grayshot), Mark Denham (Joe Grayshot), Belinda Lang (Liza Ferrari), Geoffrey Whitehead (Richard Smith). Comedy series based upon the real-life relationship of the writers, husband and wife team Jan Etherington and Gavin Petrie, two middle-aged divorcees from very different backgrounds trying to develop a relationship despite the pressures pulling it apart. It originally aired as a radio series on BBC Radio 4 broadcast between 1988 and 1992. ITV 1991-94. A spin-off series, *Faith in the Future*, was broadcast on ITV between 1995 and 1998, and continued the story of Faith and Hannah, a mother and daughter who were constantly bickering, both Lynda Bellingham and Julia Sawalha reprising their roles and Simon Pegg joining the cast as Jools.

Second Verdict Stratford Johns and Frank Windsor reprised for a final time their double-act as Detective Chief Superintendents Barlow and Watt, which began in the long-running series *Z Cars*. Created by Troy Kennedy Martin and Elwyn Jones, the six-part series in which classic criminal cases and unsolved crimes from history were re-appraised, included "The Lindbergh Kidnapping", "Who Killed the Princes in the Tower?", "Lizzie Borden" and "Who Burned the Reichstag?". The idea was developed after the 1973 series *Jack the Ripper* in which the two fictional detectives were drawn together to discuss possible solutions to the unsolved murders. BBC1 1976.

Seconds Out Robert Lindsay (Pete Dodds), Lee Montague (Tom Sprake), Ken Jones (Dave Locket), Leslie Ash (Hazel). Sitcom written by Bill MacIlwraith. Talented amateur boxer Pete Dodds turns pro under the guidance of manager Tom Sprake and trainer Dave Locket. He wins the British middleweight title and then fights for the European crown. Hazel is Pete's girlfriend. BBC1 1981-82.

Secret Army Jan Francis (Lisa Colbert; codename Yvette), Bernard Hepton (Albert Foiret), Angela Richards (Monique Duchamps), Clifford Rose (Sturmbahnführer Ludwig Kessler), Christopher Neame (Squadron Leader John Curtis), Stephen Yardley (Max Brocard), Marianne Stone (Lena van Broecken), Michael Byrne -series 2- / Ralph Bates -series 3- (Paul Vercors). Drama series created by Gerald Glaister and Wilfred Greatorex. The underground movement 'Lifeline' is showcased in *Secret Army*; specialising in smuggling trapped Allied serviceman ('evaders') back to Britain. The Belgian resistance group is led by Lisa Colbert, assisted by Albert Foiret, the owner of Le Candide, a Brussels restaurant in the Rue Deschanel which acts as their base. Other operatives include Monique, the mistress of Foiret; John Curtis, the RAF liaison officer, and Brocard, a pianist-cum-forger. Kessler is the cruel Gestapo leader. BBC1 1977-79. A 1981 spin-off, *Kessler,* saw the sadistic Gestapo leader resurface under the alias Manfred Dorf. The hugely popular *'Allo 'Allo* was a parody of *Secret Army*.

Secret Diary of Adrian Mole, Aged 13 ¾ Gian Sammarco (Adrian Mole), Stephen Moore (George Mole), Julie Walters (Pauline Mole), Lindsey Stagg (Pandora Braithwaite), Beryl Reid (Grandma Mole). Bill Fraser (Bert Baxter), Doris Hare (Queenie), Paul Greenwood (Mr Lucas). Sitcom based on the Sue Townsend novels. Adrian has a lot to contend with! His parents, George and Pauline, are perpetually on the verge of divorce, he volunteers to help the aged and gets stuck with a revolting old man, Bert Baxter, who treats him like a skivvy, he thinks he's an intellectual but still can't manage to do very well at school, the girl he likes, Pandora, starts going out with his best friend and the only person who seems on his side is his mad old grandma. The title song, Profoundly In Love With Pandora, was composed and sung by Ian Dury. ITV 1985. The second series in 1987 was entitled *The Growing Pains of Adrian Mole*, with Adrian now aged 15, and Lulu taking over the role of Pauline. A 2001 series on BBC1 *Adrian Mole: The Cappuccino Years* saw Adrian (Stephen Mangan) now in his thirties and living in London, where he works as an offal chef in a trendy Soho restaurant, Hoi Polloi. Divorced from a Nigerian wife, he has a five-year-old son, William (Harry Tomes), who lives with Adrian's parents, now reunited, in Ashby-de-la-Zouch. Pauline (Alison Steadman) is resentful and bored, husband George (Alun Armstrong) is bedridden with clinical depression emanating from long-term unemployment and impotence. Pandora (Helen Baxendale), meanwhile, with a university doctorate, has become a power-crazed Tory-in-disguise 'Blair babe', standing as the Labour candidate in Ashby-de-la-Zouch and duly winning her seat in the House of Commons.

Secret Millionaire, The Heart-warming reality television show in which millionaires go undercover into impoverished communities in order to find worthy causes they could help financially. Members of the community are usually told the cameras are present due to a documentary on the return of a former resident to a deprived neighbourhood. Millionaires featured in the first nine series include: Ben Way, John Elliott, Charan Gill, Paul Williams, Emma Harrison, Gill Fielding, Chek Whyte, Terry George, Mo Chaudry, David Pearl, Margaret Heffernan, James Benamor, Kavita Oberoi, Nick Leslau, Carl Hopkins, Daniel Smith, Hilary Devey, Gavin Wheeldon, Caroline Marsh, Kevin Morley, Gary Eastwood, Jennifer Cheyne, Jonathan Hick, Rob Lloyd, Martin Stamp, Rob Calcraft, Roisin Isaacs, Liz Jackson, Kevin Green, Dominic List, Tony Banks, Charlie Mullins, John Griffin, Dawn Gibbins, Paul Ragan, Jahan Abedi, Fil Adams-Mercer, David Jamilly, Chris Brown, Richard North, Marcelle Speller, Mark Pearson, Bradley Reback, Gordon McAlpine, Tom Mairs, Sean Gallagher, Simrin Choudhrie, Piers Linney, Lyn Cecil, Sue Stone, Aria Taheri, Adee Phelan, Ivan Massow, Edward Douglas-Miller, Lee Stafford, Dr Chai Patel, Mike Greene, Charles Allen and Mike Holland. C4 2006-

Secret Tourist, The Consumer travel series presented by Matt Allwright. Families go undercover to investigate holiday destinations. Matt also reconstructs popular scams on unsuspecting tourists abroad. BBC1 2010.

See Hear Weekly magazine programme for deaf and hard of hearing people presented entirely in British Sign Language and broadcast with voice-over and subtitles. Memnos Costi and Radha Manjeshwar are the current presenters. Former presenters include Martin Colville, Maggie Woolley, Clive Mason and Lara Crooks. The programme has been revamped several times during its run, the original slot being on Sundays, then moved to Saturdays, and since 2007, on Wednesdays at 1pm and now featuring topical areas of discussion often unrelated to the deaf community. BBC2 1981-

See It Saw It Children's game show, created by Clive Doig, about a King (played by Mark Speight) who ruled over the kingdom of "Much Jollity-On-The-Mirth". The studio audience of children would be asked an observation question by the King, which they would answer by climbing on board a giant see-saw. The majority answer would be indicated by which way the see-saw tipped. The show's main catchphrase was "See it?" asked by the king, to which the audience would shout back, "Saw it!" The series introduced actress and model Natasha Collins as the court jester 'See' (see entries for Mark Speight and Natasha Collins in the biography section). BBC1 1999-2001.

Seeing Sport Children's sports magazine show anchored by Peter West aided by a host of guest presenters. BBC1 1957-73.

See-Saw See *Watch With Mother*.

Selwyn See *Oh No It's Selwyn Froggitt*

Sense of Guilt, A Trevor Eve (Felix Cramer), Lisa Harrow (Helen Irving), Jim Carter (Richard Murray), Morag Hood (Elizabeth Cramer), Malgoscha Gebel (Inge Murray), Rudi Davies (Sally Hinde). Seven-part drama written by Andrea Newman. Family tensions are unearthed when a middle-aged writer has an affair with his friend's teenage daughter. BBC1 1990.

Sensitive Skin Joanna Lumley (Davina Jackson), Denis Lawson (Al Jackson), Nicholas Jones (Roger Dorkins), Oliver Cotton (Sam), James Lance (Orlando Jackson), Maggie Steed (Veronica Dorkins). Comedy series created by Hugo Blick. Al Jackson is a pundit for a broadsheet newspaper and is paid to find imperfection in everything, while his wife Davina works in an art gallery and is paid to make life more beautiful. But being 60 isn't simple – the couple's 30 year old son, Orlando refuses to acknowledge adulthood, and Davina's sister, Veronica, and her husband, Roger, intimidate the Jacksons with their confident and controlled grasp of life. BBC2 2005; 2007

Sentimental Agent, The Carlos Thompson (Carlos Varela), Burt Kwouk (Chin), Clemence Bettany (Miss Carter), Diana Rigg (Francy). Spin-off from *Man of the World*, the character of Carlos Varela first appearing in a November 1962 episode which became the title of this series. An Argentinian import-export agent based in London finds his business, Mercury International, takes him into criminal activity. Carlos Thompson was married to actress Lilli Palmer. ITV 1963.

September Song Michael Williams (Billy Balsam), Russ Abbot (Ted Fenwick), Michael Angelis (Arnie), Susan Brown (Cilla), Julie Peasgood (Roxy/Jenny), Diane Keen (Connie French), Diana Quick (Katherine Hillyard), Frank Windsor (Cyril Wendage). Drama written by Ken Blakeson. When his wife dies, Ted Fenwick, a gentle, sensitive schoolteacher, joins his friend Billy Balsam, a comedian, in Blackpool. Billy finds a job as a compere at a strip club, The Magic Cat, and meets exotic dancer, Cilla; Ted also finds unrequited love in the guise of Roxy, a stripper. In a second series, Ted takes Billy on a cruise to the Greek Islands as convalescense after Billy suffers a heart attack. Ted bumps into old flame Katherine Hillyard while Billy battles the bottle. The third and final series sees the action switched to Cromer, where Billy finds work as a pier comic and Ted continues an uneasy relationship with Katherine. The title of the series is from the song about the stages of love composed by Kurt Weill, with lyrics by Maxwell Anderson, introduced by Walter Huston in the 1938 Broadway musical *Knickerbocker Holiday*. ITV 1993-95. The series was first broadcast on BBC Radio 4 in 1991.

Sergeant Cork John Barrie (Sgt Cork), William Gaunt (Bob Marriott), Arnold Diamond (Det Joseph Bird), John Richmond (Supt Billy Nelson), Charles Morgan (Supt Rodway). Police drama written by Ted Willis. Set in London in the 1890s, Sergeant Cork works for the newly formed Criminal Investigation Department of the Metropolitan Police. Cork is shown as a man of vision and a passionate believer in modern techniques in criminology, constantly waging a one-man war with his superiors to achieve proper status and facilities for the CID. The 42 year-old Sergeant who comes from middle class parentage and lives a bachelor life in comfortable lodgings in London's Bayswater Road, is assisted by Bob Marriott, a 25 year-old ex public schoolboy and university graduate who got into the CID through his contacts. Although the two men are from different worlds, Cork has a fond admiration for Marriott who had pursued a career in detection to the despair of his family, who regarded the police with complete disgust. Conflict and opposition come in the form of Detective Joseph Bird who is representative of everything Cork dislikes. Servile to his superiors, bureaucratic and a narrow-minded man of the 'old school', this deeply religious, strong disciplinarian has mutual feelings towards Cork and his methods. However, Cork has another ally in Superintendent Billy Nelson, an ex-military man who doesn't always understand his Sergeant's methods but is always prepared to back him to the hilt. ITV 1963-66.

Seven Deadly Sins A septet of plays covering the traditional Seven Deadly Sins although which particular sin was not revealed to the viewer until the end of each episode. The most famous play was Joe Orton's *The Erpingham Camp*, a sharp-witted, maximum-velocity farce presenting a modern parable of revolution and retribution within the microcosm of an English leisure camp. Or in this case, forced leisure camp. ITV 1966. A follow-on septet of plays aired in 1967, *Seven Deadly Virtues*.

Seven Faces Of Jim Three series of sitcoms written by Frank Muir and Denis Norden and starring Jimmy Edwards, Ronnie Barker and June Whitfield. The first series aired as *The Seven Faces of Jim*, the second as *Six More Faces of Jim* and the third series as *More Faces of Jim*. In the first episode of Series 2 Jimmy and June reprised their roles as Mr Glum and Eth from *Take It From Here* with Ronnie Barker playing Ron Glum. BBC 1961-63

Seven of One Series of seven separate comedies starring Ronnie Barker the first two of which (*Open All Hours* and *Prisoner and Escort*) served as pilots for hit sitcoms *Open All Hours* and *Porridge*. Roy Castle co-starred in one of the episodes, *Another Fine Mess*, playing a Stan Laurel impersonator to Ronnie's Oliver Hardy. BBC1 1973

Seven Up Ground-breaking documentary film series (a spin-off from *World In Action*) that follows the lives of fourteen British people from the age of seven to adulthood. The fourteen subjects are of different races, genders, and socio-economic backgrounds. Every seven years, the documentarians reconnect with the individuals and catch up on their lives. The series began in 1964 on the ITV network and was directed at first by Paul Almond and subsequently taken over by Michael Apted, who had been a researcher on the first series and chose the original children with Gordon McDougall. The premise of the film was taken from the Jesuit motto "Give me a child until he is seven and I will give you the man", which is based on a quote by Francis Xavier. The 1998 programme was commissioned by BBC1, although still produced for them by Granada. The fourteen subjects are Bruce Balden (a teacher), Jackie Bassett (a divorcee), Symon Basterfield (the only black participant), Andrew Brackfield (a wealthy man), John Brisby (a lawyer who dropped out at 42 but returned for 49 Up), Peter Davies (another lawyer who dropped out of the series at 28), Susan Davis (a single-parent), Charles Furneaux (a television producer who dropped out of the programme at 21), Nicholas Hitchon (a physicist), Neil Hughes (often perceived as the most interesting one), Lynn Johnson (a librarian), Paul Kligerman (the Australian-based one), Suzanne Lusk (an upper-class housewife), and Tony Walker (a cockney taxi-driver-cum-actor). ITV 1964; 1970 (*Seven Plus Seven*); 1977 (*21 Up*); 1984 (*28 Up*); 1991 (*35 Up*); BBC2 1998 (*42 Up*); 2005 (*49 Up*); 2012 (*56 Up*).

71 Degrees North Reality show featuring 10 celebrities having to compete against each other, sometimes in teams, in order to reach their destination within the Arctic Circle. Along the way there were various immunity challenges. At the end of each episode, a celebrity was voted out by who received the most votes. The celebrities were Joe Absolom, Susie Amy, Andrew Castle, Diarmuid Gavin, Gavin Henson, Konnie Huq, Michelle Mone, Marcus Patric (winner), Shane Richie and Lauren Socha. The presenters were Kate Thornton and Gethin Jones. A second series was hosted by Paddy McGuinness and Charlotte Jackson with 12 celebrities taking part: Amy Williams, Angellica Bell, Brooke Kinsella, Charlie Dimmock, Martin Kemp, John Thomson, Lisa Maxwell, Nicky Clarke, Rav Wilding (Winner), Sean Maguire, Richard Arnold and John Barnes. ITV 2010-

7T3 See *No. 73*.

Sex Education Show, The Presented by journalist Anna Richardson, this six-part series set out to tackle the nation's sexual ignorance and reticence by capturing a wide range of different personal experiences of sexual issues and problems, as well as offering candid advice. The series was surrounded by controversy for showing explicit material before the 9pm watershed. C4 2008

Sexton Blake Laurence Payne (Sexton Blake), Roger Foss (Edward 'Tinker' Clark), Dorothea Phillips (Mrs Bardell), Ernest Clark (Insp. Cutts), Leonard Sachs (Insp. Van Steen). Children's detective drama featuring the illustrious sleuth, created in the 19th century by Harry Blyth (writing as Hal Meredeth). Sexton Blake was called the "prince of the penny dreadfuls" and "the office

boys' Sherlock Holmes." He first came to life on 20 December 1893 in the pages of *The Halfpenny Marvel* (first story entitled *The Missing Millionaire*) shortly after a certain Mr. Holmes had toppled off Reichenbach Falls. Blake's cases were stronger on action rather than deduction but there were parallels to be drawn with Conan Doyle's detective; substitute a cigar for Holmes' pipe, a landlady called Mrs. Bardell and his own Watson in the form of street-smart Tinker Carter (changed to Clark for the television series), who was not adverse to rolling his sleeves up and getting 'stuck in' whenever the fists were flying. Blake also had a pet dog, a bloodhound called Pedro. In the early stories Blake dashed about town on a bicycle but this was traded in for a white Rolls Royce nicknamed 'The Grey Panther' in later stories (and this series), set in the 1920s. Sexton Blake stories have subsequently been written by more than 200 authors. ITV 1967-71. Interestingly, Blake is one of three fictional super-sleuths residing in Baker Street, London; Sherlock Holmes and Dangermouse are the other two!.

Shabby Tiger Prunella Gee (Anna), John Nolan (Nick), Sharon Mughan (Rachel Rosing), John Sharp (Piggy White). Drama series written by Geoffrey Lancashire and Adele Rose based on Howard Spring's novel. Nick Faunt, a millionaire's son, takes up a bohemian lifestyle as an artist and meets Anna Fitzgerald, a wild flame-haired Irishwoman, who becomes his model and girlfriend. The seven-part series made a star of Prunella Gee, not least because of the nude scenes. To recreate 1930s Manchester, the production team built a city set around the tram museum at Crich, Derbyshire. ITV 1973.

Shades Dervla Kirwan (Maeve), Stephen Tompkinson (Mark). Six-part drama series written by Sian Evans. After their unexpected deaths, Maeve Sullivan and Mark Roberts find themselves still on Earth. They can interact with strangers but not those they once knew - and the living will forget anything that happened once the dead leave the scene. The series follows their attempts to set things right in the world after their deaths. BBC1 2001.

Shades of Greene Anthology series based on short stories written by the author Graham Greene, each hour-long episode dealing with issues such as guilt and the Catholic faith, as well as looking at life in general. Among many notable actors were John Gielgud, Leo McKern, Virginia McKenna, Paul Schofield, Denholm Elliott, Harry Andrews, Arthur Lowe and Roy Kinnear. ITV 1975-76.

Shadow Squad Rex Garner (Det Vic Steele), George Moon (Ginger Smart), Kathleen Boutall (Mrs Moggs), Peter Williams (DI Don Carter). Former Flying Squad detective Vic Steele sets up his own detective agency, Shadow Squad, ably assisted by his Cockney sidekick Ginger Smart, and on occasion by his char lady Mrs Moggs. After the first series of 26 episodes Rex Garner left and was replaced by Peter Williams for the remaining run. In total 175 thirty minute episodes were broadcast, the final episode finishing in bizarre manner with actors Moon and Williams dropping out of character and introducing themselves by their real names before walking off set. ITV 1957-59. A popular spin-off, *Skyport*, followed between 1959 and 1960, with Moon reprising his role of Ginger, who was now a security man. Edward Woodward, in an early television role appeared in several episodes in 1959.

Shameless The multi-award-winning comedy drama written by Paul Abbott and Danny Brocklehurst features the dysfunctional Gallagher family who live at 2 Windsor Gardens on Manchester's Chatsworth Estate. The cast has included: David Threlfall (Vernon Francis 'Frank' Gallagher), Anne-Marie Duff (Fiona Gallagher), Jody Latham (Phillip 'Lip' Gallagher), James McAvoy (Steve McBride), Gerard Kearns (Ian Gallagher), Maxine Peake (Veronica Ball née Fisher), Dean Lennox Kelly (Kev Ball), Maggie O'Neill (Sheila Jackson née Gallagher), Rebecca Atkinson (Karen Maguire née Jackson), Jack Deam (Marty Fisher), Gillian Kearney (Sue), Marjorie Yates (Carol Fisher), Rebecca Ryan (Debbie Gallagher), Samantha Siddall (Mandy Maguire), Tina Malone (Catherine Mary Joy "Mimi" Maguire née Murphy), Clyve Bonelle (Donny Maguire), John

Peat (Dicko), Marcus Hercules (Jimmy), Luke Tittensor (Carl Gallagher – Series 1), Elliott Tittensor (Carl Gallagher – Series 1 to present), Joseph Furnace (Liam Gallagher – Series 1 and 2), Johnny Bennett (Liam Gallagher – Series 3 to present), Kelli Hollis (Yvonne Karib, Lindsey Dawson (Jez), Lindzey Cocker (Zadie), James Peter Wells (Russell), Nichola Burley (Chloe), Nicky Evans (Shane Maguire), Chris Bisson (Kash Karib), Annabelle Apsion (Monica Gallagher), Ciaran Griffiths (Mickey Maguire), Aaron McCusker (Jamie Maguire), Alice Barry (Lillian Tyler), Sally Carman (Kelly-Marie Maguire), Qasim Akhtar (Chesney Karib), Joanna Higson (Maxine Donnelly), Warren Donnelly (PC Stan Waterman), Pauline McLynn (Libby Croker), Dystin Johnson (Norma Starkey), Philip Hill-Pearson (Bruce Donnelly), Sean Gilder (Paddy Maguire), Ben Batt (Joe Pritchard), Robbie Conway (Aidan Croker), Michael Taylor (Billy Tutton), Karen Bryson (Avril Powell nee Carson), Kira Martin (Letitia Powell), Emmanuel Ighodaro (Jackson Powell), Jill Halfpenny (Roxy Ball). C4 2004-.

Shane Frank Skinner (Shane), Elizabeth Berrington (Mertyl), Kelly Scott (Velma), Tony Bignell (Lenny), David Schneider (Bazza), Carli Norris (Sheila). Sitcom written by and starring Frank Skinner as a middle aged taxi driver coping with domestic strife. His wife, Mertyl, is a mature student who enjoys creative writing and amateur dramatics. Their children are daughter Velma, a seventeen year-old feminist, and son Lenny, a pre-pubescent child who, much to Mertyl's disappointment, shows signs of developing a similar sense of humour to Shane. Shane's best friend and boss is Bazza, with whom he spends much time down the pub. The barmaid at the pub is Sheila, whom Shane has a keen interest in. Seven episodes were shown but because of contractual problems the second series has never been shown. ITV 2004.

Shane Richie Experience, The See *Love Me Do*

Sharon and Elsie Brigit Forsyth (Elsie), Janette Beverley (Sharon), Bruce Montague (Roland Beecroft), John Landry (Stanley), Maggie Jones (Ivy), Gordon Rollings (Ike Hepworth), John Junkin (Tommy Wallace), Lee Daley (Elvis Wilkes). Sitcom written by Arline Whittaker. Elsie Beecroft works as a supervisor in the greetings cards and calendars printing firm of James Blake and son, based in Manchester. She believes that she is a cut above the rest but is shaken out of her complacency by the arrival of Sharon Wilkes, a young, punk school leaver, employed as the firm's new secretary. Elsie and Sharon have opposing views on almost everything, opinions formed by their respective ages and social backgrounds. Nevertheless, a friendship develops and both begin, albeit grudgingly, to see the other's point of view. Elsie soon comes to question the beliefs that she held firm, including such fundamentals as the nature of marriage, families and the work ethic. BBC1 1984-85.

Sharp End, The Gwen Taylor (Celia Forrest), James Cosmo (Carmichael), Philip Martin Brown (Andy Barras), Clare Kelly (Mrs Forrest), Rachel Egan (Wendy Forrest), Gaynor Faye (Crystal). Sitcom written by Roy Clarke. Celia Forrest inherits her father's dilapidated debt-collection agency. Neither her bereaved mother nor her stroppy teenage daughter, Wendy, believes that she can handle the task, and rival debt collector Andy Barras impresses upon her his belief that it is no job for a woman. But Celia is headstrong and determines to rise to the challenge. Taking on one of her debtors, the dyslexic Carmichael, as an assistant, she is soon out and about in the Yorkshire town of Rawthorne, in pursuance of those who fail to pay (leaving the office in the barely capable hands of a secretary, Crystal). The clashes and problems she encounters while doing so are almost outweighed by the quarrels she has with the fiery Carmichael, but gradually a grudging fondness grows between them. BBC1 1991.

Sharp Intake Of Breath, a David Jason (Peter Barnes), Jacqueline Clarke (Sheila Barnes). Sitcom created by Ronnie Taylor featuring Peter Barnes, a hapless Mr Average character, ever trying to beat officialdom and red tape. Sharing in his frustrations are his wife of seven years, Sheila, but against him are actors Richard Wilson and Alun Armstrong, the pair showing up each week in different jobsworth roles that defeat Jason's incompetent war against bureaucracy. ITV 1978-81

Sharpe Sean Bean (Lt/Capt/Major Richard Sharpe), Daragh O'Malley (Sgt Patrick Harper), Peter Postlethwaite (Obadiah Hakeswill), Philip Whitchurch (Frederickson), Caroline Langrishe (Lady Anne Camoynes), Liz Hurley (Isabella Farthingdale), Assumpta Serna (Teresa: 1st Mrs Sharpe), Abigail Cruttenden (Lady Jane Gibbons: 2nd Mrs Sharpe), Cecile Paoli (Lucille Dubert: 3rd Mrs Sharpe), Louise Germaine (Sally Clayton), Brian Cox (Hogan), Michael Cochrane (Sir Henry Simmerson), David Troughton and Hugh Fraser (Arthur Wellesley, Duke of Wellington), Paul Trussell (Tongue). Based on the novels of Bernard Cornwell concerning a rough-and-ready soldier who is promoted from the ranks after saving the life of the Duke of Wellington. The 14 films begin in 1809 and take the action right up to the Battle of Waterloo in 1815. Paul McGann was originally chosen to play Sharpe but a football injury forced the series to be recast. John Tams who played Hagman also co-wrote the Music. ITV 1993-97. In 2006, Sean Bean reprised his role in *Sharpe's Challenge*, a mini-series shot on location in Rajasthan, India. Two years after Wellington crushes Napoleon at Waterloo, dispatches from India tell of a local Maharaja, Khande Rao, who is threatening British interests there. Sharpe is sent to investigate on what turns out to be his most dangerous mission to date. When a beautiful general's daughter is kidnapped by the Indian warlord, the tension mounts, leaving Sharpe no option but to pursue the enemy right into its deadly lair. Deep in the heart of enemy territory he also has to keep at bay the beautiful but scheming Regent, Madhuvanthi (played by Padma Lakshmi), who is out to seduce him.

Shelley Hywel Bennett (James Shelley), Belinda Sinclair (Frances Smith/Shelley), Josephine Tewson (Edna Hawkins), Frederick Jaeger (Gordon Smith), Kenneth Cope (Forsyth), Sylvia Kay (Isobel Shelley), Warren Clarke (Paul), Rowena Cooper (Alice), Garfield Morgan (Desmond), Caroline Langrishe (Carol), Andrew Castell (Graham), Stephen Hoye (Phil), David Ryall (Ted Bishop). Sitcom created by Peter Tilbury. When the first series began, Shelley was a 28-year-old geography graduate, living on social security. He and his girlfriend, Fran had moved into a tiny bedsit in Pangloss Road, north London, where Shelley's verbal dexterity and jaded views failed to impress the stern landlady, Mrs Hawkins. Fran then became pregnant, they married, moved home and, at the end of the third series, Fran delivered unto Shelley a baby, Emma (named after Bennett's own real-life daughter). But not even the arrival of a dependant could imbue in Shelley a sense of responsibility and, at the start of the fifth series, Fran kicked him out, insisting that he shouldn't return until he had proved himself capable of looking after his wife and child. Shelley, of course, was unchangeable and, after moving in temporarily with his best man, Paul, the series appeared to have ended when Shelley went off to America. Four years on, the series was revived for what would become 32 new episodes entitled *The Return of Shelley*. As before, with Shelley unable to stick a job for long enough to gather any savings (he had, for a short while, worked at the Foreign Office and then gone into temping), he had to live in shared accommodation (actually, a neat way of providing the scriptwriters with a changing cast of characters). Mrs Hawkins was now off the scene but, in her place were Graham and Carol, upwardly mobile yuppies of the type that Shelley was unfamiliar with, having quit Britain before the dawn of Thatcher's Eighties. Back in Blighty after five years of teaching English - first in America and then the Arab Emirates - Shelley was quite unprepared for what had befallen his home country, a place where money was everything (and he, of course, had none) and where crime was on the increase - he was even mugged in one of the episodes. Now over 40 years old, Shelley had essentially the same views on life as before and, except for his landlords - in the final two series he lodged with the slightly kooky OAP widower Ted Bishop - he was truly alone. Fran and Emma, oft referred to and occasionally spoken to by phone, were now living in Canada. ITV 1979-84; 1988-92.

Sherlock Benedict Cumberbatch (Sherlock Holmes), Martin Freeman (Dr John Watson), Rupert Graves (DI Lestrade), Una Stubbs (Mrs Hudson), Louise Brealey (Molly Hooper), Vinette Robinson (Sgt Sally Donovan), Zoe Telford (Sarah), Phil Davis (Jeff), Paul Chequer (DI Dimmock), Gemma Chan (Soo Lin Yao), John Sessions (Kenny Prince), Haydn Gwynne (Miss Wenceslas). Drama series co-created by Steven Moffat (the present *Dr Who* writer) and Mark Gatiss (another *Dr Who* writer, who also plays

Holmes' brother Mycroft Holmes), based on Arthur Conan Doyle's Sherlock Holmes detective stories. BBC1 2010-

Sherlock Holmes Douglas Wilmer and Peter Cushing (Sherlock Holmes), Nigel Stock (Dr Watson). Long-running drama series based on the stories of Arthur Conan Doyle. Douglas Wilmer was replaced by Peter Cushing in the title role after the first series. BBC 1964-68.

Sherlock Holmes, The Adventures of Jeremy Brett (Sherlock Holmes), David Burke (Dr John Watson), Rosalie Williams (Mrs Hudson), Colin Jeavons (Inspector Lestrade), Charles Gray (Mycroft Holmes). Two series on ITV 1984-85 produced by Michael Cox. Two series of *The Return of Sherlock Holmes* (1986-88) produced by June Wyndham-Davies followed with Edward Hardwicke replacing David Burke as Watson. This cast stayed together for *The Casebook of Sherlock Holmes* (1991, produced by Michael Cox) and *The Memoirs of Sherlock Holmes* (1994, produced by June Wyndham-Davies) as well as two feature-length episodes also produced by Wyndham-Davies.

Shillingbury Tales Robin Nedwell (Peter Higgins), Diane Keen (Sally Higgins), Lionel Jeffries (Major Langton), Bernard Cribbins (Cuffy), Jack Douglas (Jake), Diana (Mrs Simpkins), Joe Black (Harvey), Nigel Lambert (Reverend Norris). Comedy drama written by Francis Essex and based on his one-off play, *The Shillingbury Blowers*, about an inept local brass band. Set in the fictional village of Shillingbury in Hertfordshire; Londoners Peter and Sally Higgins move to the idyllic English countryside to enjoy the ambience of fine thatched-roofed cottages, strawberry cream teas, oak-timbered pubs and a collection of eccentric locals, including grumpy farmer Jake, his sexy daughter Mandy, crafty tramp Cuffy, old busybody Mrs Simpkins, nosy postman Harvey and the twittering Reverend Norris. ITV 1981. *Cuffy*, was a 1983 spin-off series.

Shine On Harvey Moon Kenneth Cranham and Nicky Henson (Harvey Moon), Linda Robson (Maggie Moon/Lewis), Nigel Planer (Lou Lewis), Elizabeth Spriggs (Violet Moon 'Nan'), Pauline Quirke (Veronica), Maggie Steed (Rita Moon), Lee Whitlock (Stanley Moon), Leonard Fenton (Erich Gottlieb), Vincenzo Nicoli (Azzopardi), Fiona Victory (Harriet Wright), Suzanne Bertish (Frieda Gottlieb). Comedy Drama written by Laurence Marks and Maurice Gran. On 9 November 1945 Corporal Harvey Moon is demobilised after the end of World War Two and returns home to Hackney, east London, having served His Majesty's Forces in relative safety, as a stores clerk for the RAF in Bombay. Everyone believes him to be dead, killed in action, so plenty of goings-on have been going on in his absence - his wife Rita has been more than accommodating with American GIs; his 17-year-old daughter Maggie is going about with Harvey's RAF pal, the spiv Lou; his infant son Stanley is a street-wise and precocious pre-pubescent youngster; and his home has been bombed flat. This is all a mighty come-down for Harvey, who had built himself up nicely before the war, earning a steady wage as a professional footballer for Clapton Orient. Amid rationing and rubble, and as the calendar turns through to 1948, Harvey sets about rebuilding his life, his mum (Nan) providing the only real rock of support. Harvey is elected a local Labour councillor, begins a relationship with Stanley's school headmistress, Harriet Wright, and lives with Stanley and Nan in a prefab bungalow. Unfortunately, this too is blown up, by a hitherto unexploded wartime bomb, so he moves in as lodger with Erich Gottlieb and his sister Frieda. Nicky Henson took over the title role for the 1995 revival, in which the story had reached the 1950s. Maggie had married Lou (now called 'one-lung Lou' as he lost the other one); Stanley had grown up and been conscripted into the RAF; and Nan is bitterly opposed in general to the 'coloureds' that are 'invading Britain' and specifically opposed to Harvey's Jamaican friend Noah (Colin Salmon), who is lodging with them. As before, the episodes traced the changes in Britain - and British attitudes - after the war, reflecting the gloom but embracing the bright future engendered by the Festival Of Britain, the Queen's Coronation and BBC radio comedy. ITV 1982-85; 1995.

Shipmates Naval life in Devon went under the spotlight in this documentary featuring behind the scenes at Devonport Royal Naval base and in particular the frigate HMS *Chatham*'s six-month deployment in the Gulf and also her involvement in humanitarian operations after the Boxing Day tsunami in Sri Lanka. BBC1 2005

Shipwrecked Reality television series first airing in 2000. Originally presented by Kate Humble, the series followed the fortunes of a group of young British contestants who were left stranded in the Cook Islands to fend for themselves. The second series in 2001 followed a similar format but the third series in 2002 saw the location change to Fiji and the contestants, including Jeff Brazier the future partner of fellow reality tv star Jade Goody, being chosen from other English-speaking countries. After a lull of four years the show returned in 2006 with a substantially different format for its fourth series, entitled *Shipwrecked: Battle of the Islands*. The competitors were now split into two islands, both competing for a prize of £70,000. The two teams, the Sharks and the Tigers, lived on the previously uninhabited Pacific islands of Motoraku and Rapota respectively (both are part of the Cook Islands). The show was narrated by actor and voice-over artist, Craig Kelly of *Queer as Folk* fame. A new contestant arrived every week and spent half the week with one team and half the week with the other before deciding which team he or she would like to stay with. The team with the most members at the end of the show's five month run won the prize money. The Sharks ultimately won the series 15-14 but the Tigers reversed this result in 2007 and 2008 (prize money now increasing to £100,000) before the Sharks hit back to gain victory in the final series. C4 2000-02, 2006-09.

Shirley's World Shirley MacLaine (Shirley Logan), John Gregson (Dennis Croft), Nicky Henson (Beanie), Ron Moody (Matthew Quick). Anglo-American sitcom production revolving around a globe-trotting magazine writer-photographer and Dennis Croft, her London based editor. ITV 1971-72.

Shoebox Zoo Alan Cumming (Bruno the Bear), Rik Mayall (Edwin the Eagle), Siobhan Redmond (Ailsa the Adder), Bill Paterson (Storyteller), Vivien Endicott Douglas (Marnie McBride), Peter Mullan (Michael Scot), Simon Callow (Wolfgang the Wolf), David McKay (McTaggart), Jason Connery (Dad), Tony Donaldson (Toledo), Krystina Coates (Laura), Frances Low (Ms MacKay). Children's fantasy series originally shown as part of the CBBC menu. It is mostly live-action, but with CGI used for the animal figurines. Colorado-born eleven year old Marnie McBride is mourning the loss of her beloved mother as she settles into her new home in Scotland with her widowed father, who takes her to a run-down junk shop on her eleventh birthday. There, she is given a box of toy animals by a mysterious old man, which spring to life the next morning. She soon learns from these creatures that they are on an important quest to find an ancient book that holds a dark magical power within its pages, and need to find it before the evil shape shifter, Toledo does first. BBC 2004.

Shoestring Trevor Eve (Eddie Shoestring), Michael Medwin (Don Satchley), Liz Crowther (Sonia), Doran Godwin (Erica Bayliss). Detective drama created by Robert Banks Stewart and Richard Harris. The worlds of detecting and DJ-ing mixed in this drama about a West Country Private investigator with his own local radio show. Eddie Shoestring, a crime-solving former mental patient with a penchant for wearing pyjama jackets instead of shirts worked as a radio presenter on Radio West. He asked listeners to ring in with investigations he could pursue, mainly in the Bristol area. The 'private ear' would then report the outcome on air, although the names were changed to protect the innocent. Shoestring's talents ran to sketching and mimicry and when he was not driving around in his battered old red Ford Cortina estate he was languishing in his equally run-down houseboat for moments of inspiration, reflection and drinking bouts. After two very popular series Trevor Eve decided to return to the theatre and Robert Banks Stewart developed the character of Bergerac from his unused ideas for *Shoestring*. ITV 1979-80. Shortly after the series had finished, a real-life radio station of the same name was launched in Bristol.

Shooting Stars Spoof game show hosted by Vic Reeves (see entry in comedy section) and Bob Mortimer. The early series began with Vic and Bob singing "*Welcome to Shooting Stars, Welcome whoever you are, The guests have been greeted, The stars are now seated, So come along and let's start Shooting Stars*". They would then take their seats as chairmen and Graham Skidmore (of *Blind Date* fame) would introduce the celebrity guests with an unlikely career synopsis while a close-up camera scrutinised their every nose-hair. The two teams of three were captained by Mark Lamarr and Ulrika Jonsson and the scorer was Matt Lucas in the guise of oversized baby George Dawes. Rounds included 'True or False'; 'Impressions' (where Vic would sing a song in traditional club-singer style); 'Dove From Above' (Vic would begin by telling a dove related joke which would be met with about thirty seconds of silence, the sound of a funeral knell, tumbleweed blown across the stormy silence and then the resumption of the quiz as if nothing had happened. If they got a question wrong in this round they would hear this: "ERANU!" and Vic would also pull a funny face. If they pick the special category they would win a prize and be met with "OOVAVO" and another silly face); and the final 'Buzzer Round' where Vic and Bob would announce, "we really wanna see those fingers!" Other catchphrases and running jokes included, "What's the scores, George Dawes?" Vic rubbing his legs every time he saw a half-decent looking female and Vic and Bob smashing each other around the head with a frying pan every few minutes. The show was revived in 2002 with Will Self replacing Mark Lamarr and Donald Cox, the Sweaty Fox, replacing the Dove from Above. Yet another revival in 2009 saw a reversion back to the original format, the teams being led by Jack Dee and Ulrika Jonsson with former regular panelist Angelos Epithemiou (b. Daniel Renton Skinner, 25 January 1973, London; Dan is a member of the popular British five-man sketch troupe Dutch Elm Conservatoire along with Stephen Evans, Jim Field Smith, Rufus Jones, and Jordan Long) taking over as scorer for the 2010 series. BBC2 1995-97; 2002 and 2009-11. The 1993 pilot saw Jonathan Ross and Danny Baker as the team captains.

Show Called Fred, A Peter Sellers, Spike Milligan, Graham Stark, Kenneth Connor, Valentine Dyall, Patti Lewis, Max Geldray. Surreal comedy sketch show directed by Richard Lester. Following the six editions of *The Idiot Weekly, Price 2d* that finished only a month earlier, Spike Milligan and Peter Sellers returned with a further attempt to translate the surreal lunacy of *The Goon Show* to the small-screen. Again, only London-area viewers got to see it, and again the result was reasonably successful, creating a crazy visual style to match the bizarre audio antics that elevated the radio series above its contemporaries. Later still, in 1956, the team returned to TV for a third time with a direct descendant of this series, *Son Of Fred*. ITV 1956.

Show Me the Money Live afternoon gameshow presented by Louise Noel. The premise of the game was for five teams of three to make as much money as possible from an imaginary £100,000 on the Stock Market by the end of the series. Each team had a dedicated day of the week to show their imaginary portfolios and state what they were buying and selling. If a team ever had below £90,000 in their imaginary pot at the beginning of their show they were kicked off and a new team brought in to replace them. A financial expert, Tom Winnifrith, was on hand to give the teams advice with their portfolio. Before deciding on what they would buy or sell a Managing Director of a business listed on the Stock Exchange would come on and give a 60 second pitch to the team. Alice Beer presented three episodes while Louise was taken ill. C4 1999-2000. A show of the same name is currently broadcast on RTÉ1 with presenter Eddie Hobbs giving similar financial advice. This programme is also similar to the recent BBC2 series *Your Money Or Your Life*, presented by American finance guru Alvin Hall.

Shrink Rap Clinical psychologist and former comedienne Dr Pamela Stephenson presented this insight into famous celebrities as a sort of antidote to the conventional chat show. C4 2007-08

Silence, The Douglas Henshall (Jim), Dervla Kirwan (Maggie),Gina McKee (Anna), Hugh Bonneville (Chris), Genevieve Barr (Amelia), Harry Ferrier (Tom), Tom Kane (Joel),

Rebecca Oldfield (Sophie), Rod Hallett (Mac), David Westhead (Frank). Four-part thriller written by Fiona Seres concerning Amelia, a deaf teen who witnesses a policewoman's death. DCI Jim Edwards tackles the case while keeping Amelia's anonymity. BBC1 2010.

Silent Witness Amanda Burton (Dr/Professor Samantha 'Sam' Ryan, John McGlynn (DI Tom Adams), William Gaminara (Leo Dalton), Tom Ward (Dr Harry Cunningham), Emilia Fox (Nikki Alexander), Clare Higgins (DS Harriet Farmer). Drama series created by Nigel McCrery. The gruesome cases of a determined Belfast-born pathologist, Sam Ryan, 37, initially working out of Cambridge and then the University of London. Sam's personal life is prominent in the stories; her father was an RUC officer who was murdered by terrorists while her mother was a victim of Alzheimer's. Amanda Burton left in 2004 and Emilia Fox took over a starring role as a bright young archaeo-pathologist. Currently in its 14th series, the theme tune to *Silent Witness* is Silencium by John Harle. BBC1 1996-.

Silk Maxine Peake (Martha Costello), Rupert Penry-Jones (Clive Reader), Neil Stuke (Billy Lamb), Tom Hughes (Nick Slade), Natalie Dormer (Niamh Cranitch), Nina Sosanya (Kate Brockman). Legal drama series written by Peter Moffat, based on his experiences at the Bar. The series' title refers to the act of being appointed a Queen's Counsel, known as "taking silk". BBC1 2011

Silverville Moving series that followed the lives and loves of some of the 350 residents of a new retirement village, Lovat Fields, in Milton Keynes. BBC1 2009.

Simon and the Witch Elizabeth Spriggs (The Witch), Hugh Pollard (Simon), Joan Sims (Lady Fox-Custard), Nicola Stapleton (Sally), Naomie Harris (Joyce). Children's dramatisation of the books of Margaret Stuart Barry concerning the relationship between a real-life witch and her apprentice and friend, schoolboy Simon. The first of the stories (The Backwards Spell) was dramatised for Children's BBC in 1985 and shown as a one-off episode (called *Simon and the Witch*). In 1987, the books were made into a television series for Children's BBC consisting of 25 fifteen-minute episodes. The series is notable for an early appearance of actress/singer Nicola Stapleton in 1988 and the first screen appearance of film actress Naomie Harris in 1987. BBC 1985; 1987-88.

Simon Dee Born Carl Nicholas Henty-Dodd, Ottawa Canada, 1935; his family moved to the UK in 1948. He changed his name to Simon Dee and was recruited to DJ for Radio Caroline in time for their launch in March 1964. His was the first voice heard on the opening broadcast. Already a familiar face on ITV from appearances in Smith's Crisps commercials and *Top of the Pops*, his fame in the UK rapidly increased when in 1967 he was offered his own regular 30 minute BBC TV show *Dee Time*. Here he interviewed major TV, film and pop stars; his first show alone included Cat Stevens, Lance Percival and Jimi Hendrix! Broadcast on Saturday nights, the show's opening sequence featured Dee arriving at BBC Television Centre in an E-type Jag accompanied by a nubile blonde to the announcement "It's Siiiiiimon Dee!" (each show ended with Simon driving off with the same blonde). The show became a magnet for the celebrities of the era and at its height had a faithful following of 15 million viewers. Following newspaper revelations about his political opinions and an alleged previous conviction, the BBC did not renew his contract in 1969. The following year Simon moved to present a similar format show on ITV Saturday nights, *The Simon Dee Show*, which was short lived and his position in the media spotlight diminished. His fall from grace was completed by various spats with the law over unpaid debts and a much-publicised prison sentence. Simon initially signed on at Fulham Labour Exchange but soon found various employment including as a bus driver. Listeners to Radio 2 on Saturdays in 1988 heard Simon once again, presenting a new series titled *Sounds of the Sixties* for 13 weeks, later presented by Brian Matthew. An excellent presenter with real charisma, Simon's story is a famous showbusiness tragedy. He died in August 2009.

Sing It Back: Lyric Champion Hosted by Radio 1's JK and Joel, the series saw members of the public go head to head, singing missing lyrics from well-known songs. Paul Gambaccini was the resident pop expert and Nathan was the eventual winner. ITV 2007

Sing Something Simple Easy-listening music show first broadcast on the Light Programme (became Radio 2 in 1967) in 1959. The format would begin with the opening theme *Sing something simple As cares go by, Sing something simple Just you and I,* followed by the announcement "We invite you to Sing Something Simple, a collection of favourite songs, old and new, sung by The Adams Singers, accompanied by Jack Emblow." The theme would then continue *We'll sing the old songs like you used to do, We'll sing something simple for you, something for you.* Cliff Adams would then perform a piano solo, which he would introduce, after which his singers would continue with a selection of popular songs both modern and old. Cliff Adams was born in 1923 and was a former singer with the Stargazers, a popular vocal group on BBC radio throughout the 1950s with six top 20 hits. Cliff also composed for TV commercials including Fry's Turkish Delight, Cadbury's Milk Tray and Cadbury's Smash. The Cliff Adams singers were formed in 1954 and this series was heard on Sunday evenings until Cliff's death in 2001, a continuous run of 42 years.

Singing Detective, The Michael Gambon (Philip E.Marlow), Joanne Whalley (Nurse Mills/Carlotta), Patrick Malahide (Mark Binney/Mark Finney/Raymond Binney), Jim Carter (Mr Marlow), Alison Steadman (Beth Marlow/Lili), Lyndon Davies (Philip Marlow, aged 10), Janet Suzman (Nicola Marlow), Bill Paterson (Dr Gibbon), Janet Henfrey (Schoolteacher / Scarecrow), William Speakman (Mark Binney, aged 10). Reworking material from his first novel, *Hide and Seek* (1973), and folding this into a prismatic blend of semi-autobiographical details, popular music and 1940s film noir, Dennis Potter delivered a drama now regarded as a 20th-century masterwork. Detective novelist Philip Marlow suffers from the crippling disease of psoriatic arthropathy. Confined to a hospital bed on the Sherpa Tensing ward, Marlow mentally rewrites his early Chandleresque thriller, *The Singing Detective,* with himself in the title role, drifting into a surreal 1945 fantasy of spies and criminals, along with vivid memories of a childhood in the Forest of Dean. As past events and 1940s songs surface in his subconscious, Marlow's voyage of self-discovery provides a key to conquering his illness, while his noir-styled hallucinations evoke the Philip Marlowe of Chandler's *Murder, My Sweet* (1944), starring Dick Powell, who later became a "singing detective" on radio's *Richard Diamond, Private Detective* (1949), crooning to girlfriend Helen Asher at the end of each episode. BBC1 1986. The story was made into a 2003 film starring Robert Downey Jr and Mel Gibson.

Sink or Swim Peter Davison (Brian Webber), Sara Corper (Sonia), Ron Pember (Mike Connor), Briony McRoberts (Charlotte). Sitcom written by Alex Shearer. Brian Webber is a northerner who has ventured south to seek his fame and fortune but ends up living on a damp houseboat in London. He desperately wants to better himself but seems doomed to be unlucky; his girlfriend, Sonia, is an ecologically conscious vegetarian, a glum and earnest young woman involved in numerous causes. Into this far from perfect life arrives Brian's younger brother, Steve - an idle, cynical, loutish individual, obsessed with sex. Steve's presence embarrasses his older brother and alienates Sonia, who views him with derision. But blood is thicker than water and Brian tolerates his younger sibling, rediscovering aspects of his own character along the way. In the third and final series the two brothers moved out of their boat to Newcastle, where Brian enrols as a computer student and Steve remains unemployed. Sonia shares a flat with student Charlotte but Steve is an ever-present spirit. The theme music was by Ronnie Hazlehurst. BBC1 1980-82.

Sins, The Pete Postlethwaite (Len Green), Geraldine James (Gloria Green), Caroline Hayes (Charity Green), Billie Cook (Dolores Green), Frank Finlay (Uncle Irwin Green). Mini-series written by William Ivory. Len Green is a reformed bank robber. Now middle-aged, with an expensive house (bought with the proceeds of the robberies), and an attractive wife and four grown-up daughters to whom he is devoted, he resolves to change his lifestyle. This time he will "go straight". But having joined his Uncle Irwin in the family firm of undertakers, he is faced with many temptations. BBC1 2000.

Sion a Sian *Sion a Sian* was the original Welsh-speaking version of the programme which later became *Mr and Mrs* - first on Border TV then picked up nationally. Created by Roy Ward Dixon and made by HTV for S4C, it began in 1964 and initially ran until 1967 before returning in 1971 with presenter Dai Jones. I B Gruffudd took over in 1987; its final presenter being Ieuan Rhys (assisted by Gillian Elisa) between 1996 and 2003.

Sir Francis Drake Terence Morgan (Sir Francis Drake), Jean Kent (Queen Elizabeth), Michael Crawford (John Drake), Patrick McLoughlin (Trevelyan), Roger Delgado (Mendoza). Twenty-six episodes of the exploits of the Elizabethan swashbuckler popularised the great adventurer although his depiction was far from being historically accurate. A host of future stars made their television debuts, amongst them Michael Crawford as the good admiral's nephew, John Drake. The villain of the piece, the swarthy Spaniard Mendoza, was played by Roger Delgado, who would later star as the first incarnation of Doctor Who's nemesis, The Master. Guest stars included David McCallum, Susan Hampshire, Barry Foster, Nanette Newman and Warren Mitchell. The opening sequence showed Drake's famous ship the Golden Hind. ITV 1961-62.

Sir Lancelot, The Adventures of William Russell (Sir Lancelot du Lac), Jane Hylton (Queen Guinevere), Bruce Seton and Ronald Leigh-Hunt (King Arthur), Cyril Smith (Merlin), David Morrell (Sir Kay), Robert Scroggins (Brian). The first British series to be shot in colour and, using background information researched at Oxford University, featured accurate 14th Century settings, even though the legend of King Arthur and his Knights of the Round Table hailed from the 6th century. An Anglo-Saxon village with huts, sheep, goats and costumes was constructed at Nettlefold Studios for *The Adventures of Robin Hood* and used for this and most of the other ITC series. Outside location work was shot in Kent, where the company requisitioned Allington Castle, a fitting site for such activity since its long history included settlement by Ancient Britons, Romans and Saxons. The theme song was as follows: *Now listen to my story yes listen while I sing, of days of old in England when Arthur was the king, of Merlin the magician and Guinevere the queen and Lancelot the bravest knight the world has ever seen* (chorus) *In days of old, when knights were bold this stories told of Lancelot. He rode the wilds of England adventures for to seek, to rescue maidens in distress and help the poor and weak, if anyone oppressed you he'd be your champion, he fought a million battles and never lost a one* (chorus). ITV 1956-57.

Sir Prancelot, The Adventures of This animated tale originated from the same stable that produced *Captain Pugwash. The Adventures of Sir Prancelot* follows the exploits of the heroic but somewhat eccentric Sir Prancelot and his household as they set off for the Crusades to the Holy Land. The five minute adventures ran for 19 episodes and were created by John Ryan, who also designed the sets and adapted the scripts for a stereo record production. Peter Hawkins supplied the voices for all of the characters to be found in the series. Those characters included Sir Prancelot, the hero and the guardian of Sim and Sue; The Lady Hysteria, wife of Sir Prancelot who believes that "there is nothing like steel wool next to the skin"; Sim and Sue, the children, "a proper pair of little demons"; Master Girth, introduced as the Major Domo, a "mean old so and so" who administers the castle accounts; Serf Albert (Bert) and Serf Harold (Harry), two soldiers who are sent to carry out many plans; Pig William (or Pigwig), the Lady Hysteria's pet pig; Count Otto the Blot, (or Blotto) "a nasty piece of work"; Duke Uglio, "proper mean, real nasty"; and The Minstrel who happily narrates to us the enfolding adventures. BBC1 1972.

Sirens Rhys Thomas (Stuart Bayldon), Richard Madden (Ashley Greenwick), Kayvan Novak (Rachid Mansaur), Amy Beth Hayes (Sgt Maxine Fox), Ben Batt (Craig Scruton) Kobna Holdbrook-Smith (Ryan Bailey), Tuppence Middleton (Sarah), Robert Stone (Fat Carl). Six-part comedy-drama series about an ambulance service team, based on the book *Blood, Sweat & Tea* by Brian Kellett.

Six Dates With Barker Six one-off comedies, all set in different time periods and all starring Ronnie Barker, who also wrote the last one. The six were: 1937: *The Removals Person* (written by Hugh Leonard and was the inspiration for *Clarence*, although Ronnie's character name in this was Fred), 1899: *The Phantom Raspberry Blower of Old London Town* (Spike Milligan – later serialized in *The Two Ronnies*), 1970: *The Odd Job* (Bernard McKenna), 1915: *Lola* (Ken Hoare and Mike Sharland), 1971: *Come in and Lie Down* (John Cleese), 2774 AD: *All the World's a Stooge* (Ronnie Barker). ITV 1971

Six English Towns Alec Clifton-Taylor's first 'English Towns' series for BBC2 television was broadcast in 1978. The keen admirer of architecture guided the viewer through what he called the "pattern of English building" in small English towns of great character. Chichester, Richmond (in Yorkshire), Tewkesbury, Stamford, Totnes and Ludlow are covered alongside the presenter's historical and architectural comments on the buildings. There were two further series, *Six More English Towns*, concentrating on Warwick, Berwick-on-Tweed, Saffron Walden, Lewes, Bradford-on-Avon, and Beverley; and *Another Six English Towns*, concentrating on Cirencester, Whitby, Bury St Edmunds, Devizes, Sandwich and Durham, rounded off the trilogy. BBC2 1978; 1981; 1984.

Six Faces Kenneth More (Richard Drew), Zena Walker (Mary Drew), Kika Markham (Lucy Walters), Eve Pearce (Miss Haverford), Joss Ackland (Harry Mellor), Hildegard Neil (Helen Barlow). Six-part Drama series about businessman Richard Drew, who can present a different personality to everyone he meets. The story is told from the viewpoints of six people who come into contact with him. BBC1 1972.

Six-Five Special, The Up until 1957, a closed period of television between 6-7pm called the "Toddler's Truce" was in place. This was to enable parents to put their young children to bed and generally remind viewers that more adult programmes would begin broadcasting after the watershed. This was formally ended on Saturday 16 February 1957 at 6pm, when the BBC broadcast a five minute news bulletin, followed by a new programme aimed at young people featuring live music and a live audience. *Six-Five Special* was born and a small piece of television and Rock n' Roll history was made. Intended to run for only six weeks, the first show was presented by Pete Murray and co-producer Josephine Douglas and was played in and out by Kenny Baker and his Jazzmen. Michael Holliday contributed a couple of ballads and the Rock n' Roll was provided by Bobbie and Rudy and the King Brothers. Emerging double-act Mike and Bernie Winters provided the light interludes. Pete Murray introduced the very first Six-Five Special like this: "Welcome aboard the Six-Five Special. We've got almost a hundred cats jumping here, some real cool characters to give us the gas, so just get on with it and have a ball." Josephine Douglas then translated hip cat Murray's words for 1950s parents: "Well, I'm just a square it seems, but for all the other squares with us, roughly translated what Pete Murray said was: We've got some lively musicians and personalities mingling with us here, so just relax and catch the mood with us." Boxer Freddie Mills was later recruited to present a sports item featuring lesser known activities and a filmed feature was included such as bandleader Ray Anthony demonstrating the 'Bunny Hop'. The show developed a particularly strong association with Skiffle (Lonnie Donegan, Chas McDevitt and Willie McCormick all made regular appearances) and Tommy Steele (Britain's first native Rock n' Roller) was an early guest as was Vince Eager. The programme was able to influence record sales and The Diamonds' *'Little Darlin'* was an early beneficiary. Jim Dale, a singer who subsequently became the show's presenter, and Marty Wilde both benefited in their careers from the programme. There were also a string of *Six-Five Special* regulars such as the King Brothers, The Mudlarks and Don Lang who had recorded the immensely catchy theme tune. Studio guests included the likes of Jon Pertwee and Spike Milligan. The opening sequence showed a steam train whizzing down the track to Don Lang's lyrics thus: *Over the points, over the points, over the points, over the points, over the points, over the points, over the points. The 6.5 Special's steamin' down the line, The 6.5 Special's right on time.*

Coal in the boiler burnin' up'n bright, Rollin' and a-rockin' through the night, And my heart's a-beatin' 'cos I'll be meetin' The 6.5. Special at the station tonight. Hear the whistle blowin' 12 to the bar. See the lights a-glowin' bright as a star. Now the wheels a-slowin', it can't be far. Over the points, over the points, over the points, over the points. (guitar solo). The tune continued *The 6.5 Special better not be late, The 6.5 Special platform 8, The train starts a-brakin' hard as can be, The station is a-shakin' like a tree' And I won't be missin' that special kissin' When the 6.5 Special brings my baby to me*, although this was not heard during the opening sequence. Jack Good was the original Producer and Adam Faith made his debut on his way to stardom. BBC 1957-58.

Six Pairs of Pants Neil Mullarkey, Jessica Hynes nee Stevenson, Simon Pegg, Sally Phillips, Simon Schatzberger, Katy Carmichael. Short-lived sketch show included two Kiwi characters who had moved to the UK and worked behind various bars, the whole group as "Flatmates" and various spoof horror trailers. C4 1995.

Six Wives of Henry VI I I, The Keith Michell (Henry VIII), Annette Crosbie (Catherine of Aragon), Dorothy Tutin (Anne Boleyn), Anne Stallybrass (Jane Seymour), Elvi Hale (Anne of Cleves), Angela Pleasance (Catherine Howard), Rosalie Crutchley (Catherine Parr), Patrick Troughton (Duke of Norfolk), John Baskcomb (Cardinal Wolsey), Wolfe Morris (Thomas Cromwell), Bernard Hepton (Archbishop Thomas Cranmer), Anthony Quayle (narrator). Created by Maurice Cowan, the award-winning six-part costume drama told the story of England's most-famous king and the relationship with his six wives, one per episode. BBC2 1970.

Sixpenny Corner Patricia Dainton (Sally Norton), Howard Pays (Bill Norton), Robert Webber (Chas Norton), Betty Bowden (Doris Sharpe), Stuart Saunders (Uncle Fred), Olive Milbourne (Aunt Mabel), Shirley Mitchell (Yvonne Sharpe), Robert Desmond (Stan Norton), Bernard Fox (Tom Norton), Walter Horsbrugh (Mr Sharpe), Edward Judd (Denis Boyes), Elizabeth Gott (Mrs Boyes), Christine Pollon (Grete Edler), Jan Miller (Moira O'Shea), Michael Collins (Dr Tim O'Shea), John Charlesworth (Eddie Perkins), Elizabeth Frazer (Julie Perkins), Charles Ross (Phillip Collier), Vi Stevens (Rosie Chubb). Created by Hazel Adair and written by Jonquil Antony. This was Britain's first ever daily soap opera; shown on Independent Television in the UK, beginning on their second day of broadcast. It was about the life and love of a young couple, Bill and Sally Norton, running a garage together at Sixpenny Corner in the rural town of Springwood. ITV 1955-56.

$64,000 Dollar Question, The The British version of the popular American quiz show was based on the American radio show *Take It Or Leave It*, which had a jackpot prize of $64, which was arrived at by doubling-up from a dollar, the questions becoming progressively more difficult. First airing between 1956 and 1958 and hosted by Jerry Desmonde (actor Robin Bailey hosted a spinoff *64,000 Challenge* in 1957), the questions were worth multiples of sixpence per question with a top prize of £1,600 (later doubled to £3,200). Questions were guarded every week by actor Bruce Seton in his famous television role of Detective Fabian and the show was called *The 64,000 Question*. Bob Monkhouse hosted the revived version in the early 1990s and the jackpot prize was limited to £6,400. ITV 1956-58; 1990-93.

Sixty Minutes Short-lived news programme which replaced *Nationwide*. Presenters included Desmond Wilcox, Sally Magnusson, Nick Ross, Beverly Anderson and Sarah Kennedy. BBC1 1984.

Sketch Show, The Comedy sketch series featuring Lee Mack, Jim Tavaré, Tim Vine, Karen Taylor and Ronni Ancona (later replaced by Kitty Flanagan). All five of the cast contributed to the writing of the show and other contributions were made by Ricky Gervais, Matthew Hardy, Stephen Colledge and Daniel Maier, although none of these appeared on screen. ITV 2001-03

Ski Sunday Long-running BBC Sports television programme variously shown on BBC1 and BBC2. Presenters have included Ron Pickering, David Vine (1978-96), Hazel Irvine, Matt Chilton, Graham Bell and Ed Leigh. The iconic theme music to the programme is the first 30 seconds of *Pop Looks Bach* by Sam Fonteyn. BBC 1978-

Sky At Night The world's longest-running science programme began on BBC1 in 1957 and has been hosted by Patrick Moore throughout its run although cosmologist Chris Lintott hosted the show in July 2004 when Moore had a bout of food poisoning. The theme music is 'At The Castle Gate' from *Peléas et Mélisande* by Jean Sibelius.

Skylarks, The Anton Rodgers (Lt Gilmore RN), Roland Curram (Lt Copper), A.E. Matthews (Vice Admiral Sir Geoffrey Wiggin-Fanshawe KBE DSO DSC RN), Robert Chetwyn (Lt Stannard RN), William Mervyn (Capt. Crocker-Dobson DSO RN). Seafaring sitcom written by Trevor Peacock. BBC 1958.

Sky's The Limit, The Quiz show invented by Vic Hallums and hosted by Hughie Green with co-hosts Monica Rose and Katya Wyeth plus adjudicator Ann Meo. Contestants answered questions on geography with air miles their reward. The top prize was 21,000 miles and £600 spending money. ITV 1970-74. See *Double Your Money*

Slammer, The Children's comedy series starring Ted Robbins as the Governor of the fictional prison, HMP Slammer. Inmates perform variety acts to a young audience, who decide which act should be released at the end of each show by a clapometer. Warders include Mr Burgess (Ian Kirkby) and Governor's nephew Jeremy Gimbert (Lee Barnett). Resident lags include Peter Nokio (Dave Chapman) a poor ventriloquist who is serving time for crimes against showbiz, and Melvin Odoom playing a dancer of the same name whose act once went badly wrong in front of "none other than the Queen" at the Royal Variety Performance, resulting in him suffering from incurable stage-fright. The show is produced by Harry Batt and Steve Ryde (who also produced *Dick and Dom in da Bungalow*, hence the same supporting actors). BBC1 2006-

Slight Case Of, A Roy Kinnear (H A Wormsley), Joe Melia (Mr Poliansky). Spoofish sitcom written by Leon Griffiths. Seedy, disreputable private eye H A Wormsley solves the case at hand in each episode in spite of his ineptitude. BBC2 1965.

Slinger's Day See *Tripper's Day*

SM:TV Live CITV's most popular Saturday morning show. Presenters have included Des Clarke (2003), Stephen Mulhern (2003), Shavaughn Ruakere (2003), Tess Daly (2002-2003), Brian Dowling (2002-2003), Ian 'H' Watkins (2002), Claire Richards (2002), James W. Redmond (2002), Jonathan Wilkes (2002). Cat Deeley (1998-2002), Ant McPartlin (1998-2001), Declan Donnelly (1998-2001). First aired in August 1998 and originally hosted by Ant and Dec with Cat Deeley. Popular games included Wonky Donkey and the Pikachu game based on the Pokemon character. Following the departure of the comic duo the series bumbled along for two years but was eventually cancelled. The last ever episode on 27 December 2003 saw the return of Ant, Dec and Cat for final episodes of Challenge Ant, Secret of My Sucess and Chums. Brian, Tess & Shavaughn also joined Des Clarke for a last ever episode of Eminemmerdale. ITV 1998-2003.

Smack the Pony Comedy sketch show with a female slant on life. Written and performed by Doon Mackichan, Fiona Allen and Sally Phillips. The supporting cast (which became more prominent by the second series) included Miranda Hart, Sarah Alexander, Darren Boyd, Cavan Clerkin, Kevin Eldon, Tamzin Griffin, James Lance, Michael Wildman and Bruce Mackinnon. The show's catchy theme tune, *In The Middle of Nowhere* (originally a hit for Dusty Springfield), was sung by musical comedy star Jackie Clune. C4 1999-2002).

Small Time Beginning on the day after Independent Television's opening night in London on Thursday 22nd September 1955, *Small Time* was the generic name of the 15-minute slot for the under fives broadcast from 1955 to 1962 (the equivalent of today's Cbeebies). The show introduced some super series over the years including *The Adventures of Twizzle, Lucky Dip* and *Sarah and Hoppity*. Its presenters included Rolf Harris, Jimmy Hanley and Oliver Postgate. On Friday 16th October 1959 Patrick Boyle told the very first Tum story which was followed by Muriel Young talking to Pussy Cat Willum, a glove puppet devised and animated by Janet Nicholls. This started a regular slot by the popular feline puppet and over the years Pussy Cat Willum appeared with Liz

Shingler, Bert Weedon and Wally Whyton as well as Muriel in brief cameos before the main feature. Liverpudlian owl Ollie Beak, voiced by Wally Whyton, and Fred Barker, voiced by Ivan Owen were first seen on *Small Time*. In 1962 the name *Small Time* became *Tuesday Rendezvouz* and Pussy Cat Willum was replaced by Ollie Beak as the regular front owl, although little else changed.

Smart Children's television programme based on the subject of art. Part of the CBBC schedule, *SMart* has a similar format to *Take Hart* and *Hart Beat*. Presenters included Zoë Ball (1994-1996), Jay Burridge (1994-2003), Mark Speight (1994-2008), Josie D'Arby (1996-1998), Lizi Botham (1999-2004), Susan Ribeiro (2002), Kirsten O'Brien (1999-2009) and Mike Fischetti (2007-09). BBC1 1994-2009. Spin-off series have included *SMart on the Road* and *SMarteenies*. See *See It Saw It*

Smile Sunday morning children's magazine programme featuring celebrity guests, Presenters included Kirsten O'Brien, Barney Harwood, Reggie Yates, Fearne Cotton, Devin Griffin (credited as DJ Devstar), Rochelle Wiseman and Nev the Bear. Voiced by Ross Mullan, Nev was a small blue bear with part of his ear missing due to the cat under his bed - Bandit - trying to eat him. BBC2 2002-07

Smiley's People See *Tinker, Tailor, Soldier, Spy.*

So You Think You Can Dance Reality show seeking the UK's favourite dancer. Presented by Cat Deeley, the judges were Nigel Lythgoe, Arlene Phillips, Louise Redknapp and Sisco Gomez. The winner of Series 1 was Charlie Bruce, 19, from Leicester. BBC1 2010-

So You Think You've Got Troubles Warren Mitchell (Ivan Fox), James Ellis (Charley Adamson), Harry Towb (George Nathan). Six-part sitcom written by Laurence Marks and Maurice Gran. Ivan Fox, the Jewish manager of a north London pipe tobacco factory, is relocated to Belfast and is soon enmeshed in the religious battle between Catholic and Protestant. BBC1 1991.

Softly Softly Stratford Johns (Det Chief Supt Barlow), Frank Windsor (DCI/Det Supt/Det Chief Supt. John Watt), Norman Bowler (DS/DI/DCI Harry Hawkins), Terence Rigby (PC Henry Snow), Garfield Morgan (DC/Insp Gwyn Lewis), John Barron (Austin Gilbert), Warren Clarke (DS Stirling). Created by Elwyn Jones, a direct spin-off from *Z Cars*. First aired on BBC1 in 1966, the title changed to *Softly Softly - Task Force* in 1969 when Stratford Johns left to star in yet another spin-off *Barlow at Large* although he did team up again with Frank Windsor to reprise their roles in a 1973 Jack the Ripper investigation and a 1976 series *Second Verdict*, which looked at similar mysteries. *Softly Softly* was set at Thamesford Constabulary in Wyvern. Interestingly, although it was a spin-off from *Z Cars*, by the time it had its final series in 1976, the original show was still going strong.

Soldier, Soldier Jerome Flynn (L.Cpl/Cpl/Acting Sgt Paddy Garvey), Robson Green (Fusilier/L.Cpl Dave Tucker), David Haig (Major Tom Cadman), Cathryn Harrison (Laura Cadman), Holly Aird (Cpl/Sgt Nancy Thorpe/Garvey RMP), Sean Baker (CSM Chick Henwood), Robert Glenister (Colour Sgt Ian Anderson), Mark Aiken (Capt Andrew Beamish), Miles Anderson (Lt. Col Dan Fortune), Annabelle Apsion (Joy Wilton), Kate Ashfield (Cate Hobbs), William Ash (Jack Stubbs), Rakie Ayola (Bernie Roberts), Debra Beaumont (Sgt Sally Hawkins), Duncan Bell (Lt. Col Paul Philips), Fiona Bell (Angela McCleod), John Bowe (Lt. Col Ian Jennings), Philip Bowen (Lt. Col Mike Eastwood), Suzanne Burden (Sandra Radley), Michelle Butterly (Julie Oldroyd), James Callis (Major Tim Forrester), Angela Clarke (Colette Daly), Lucy Cohu (Major Jessica Bailey), James Cosmo (Lt. Col Philip Drysdale), Thomas Craig (Fusilier Jacko Barton), Danny Cunningham (Fusilier Andy Butcher), Biddy Hodson (2nd Lt Samantha Sheridan), Laura Howard (Deborah Osbourne/Briggs), Lee Ingleby (Kevin Fitzpatrick), Paterson Joseph (Fusilier Eddie Nelson), Melanie Kilburn (Carol Anderson), Jonathan Guy Lewis (Sgt Chris McCleod, Mo Sesay (Fusilier Michael 'Midnight' Rawlings), Simon Sherlock (Fusilier Mel Briggs), Tara Simpson (Sarah Stubbs), Alison Skilbeck (Dr Sarah Eastwood), Sarah Smart (Lucy Fitzpatrick), Rob Spendlove (CSM/RSM/Lt Michael Stubbs), Steve Truglia (Cpl Gray), Lesley

Vickerage (2nd Lt/Lt/Capt Kate Butler/Voce), Denise Welch (Marsha Stubbs), Tracy Whitwell (Kelly Deeley), Peter Wingfield (Lt Nick Pasco), Samantha Morton (Clare Anderson) – her first screen role. Drama created by Lucy Gannon, following the life of the officers and men of the King's Own Fusiliers regiment, during their home lives, training exercises and battles. Jerome Flynn and Robson Green left in 1995 to pursue a short-lived but highly successful pop career. ITV 1991-97.

Solo Felicity Kendal (Gemma Palmer), Stephen Moore (Danny), Elspet Gray (Mrs Palmer), Susan Bishop (Gloria), Michael Howe (Sebastian). Sitcom written by Carla Lane. Gemma Palmer decides to go it alone after discovering her boyfriend, Danny, is having an affair with her best friend, Gloria. BBC1 1981-82.

Some Mothers do 'Ave 'Em Michael Crawford (Frank Spencer), Michele Dotrice (Betty). Sitcom written by Raymond Allen. The everyday trials of the hapless beret-wearing Frank Spencer and his long-suffering wife Betty. In later episodes the world-weary couple had a daughter, Jessica (played by Jessica Forte). Various Frank Spencer catchphrases were spawned from the 22 episodes, such as "I've had a lot of ha-RASSments lately" and the long quivering "Oooh..." but interestingly despite comedians of the day (and almost every person in the country at some point) reciting the famous 'ooh Betty' catchphrase, this was never actually said by Frank. BBC1 1973-75; 1978.

Son of Fred See *A Show Called Fred*

Songs of Praise Television's longest-running religious programme. The first broadcast came from the Tabernacle Baptist Chapel, Cardiff. Presenters have included Cliff Michelmore, Debbie Thrower, Roger Royle, Gloria Hunniford, Sally Magnusson, Pam Rhodes, Hugh Scully, Stephanie Hughes, Aled Jones, Diane Louise Jordan, Deborah McAndrew, Harry Secombe, Alan Titchmarsh, Steve Chalke, Huw Edwards, Eamonn Holmes, Jonathan Edwards and Gavin Peacock. BBC1 1961-

Sooty Sooty was created by Harry Corbett (born in Bradford, 28 January 1918, died in Dorset 17 August 1989), who bought the puppet as a present for his son, Matthew Corbett, from a stall when he was on holiday in Blackpool in 1948. Harry gained his love of showbusiness as a piano player in the world famous Guiseley fish and chip restaurant owned by his mother's brother Harry Ramsden. Sooty, a small yellow bear with black ears, is mute to the audience but can communicate with his operator by apparently whispering in his ear. He first appeared on screen in 1952 on the BBC's *Talent Night*, and was adjudged the overall winner on the live finale and Sooty became instantly famous nationwide. Sooty and Harry then became regulars on the BBC children's show *Saturday Special* from 1952-55 before receiving their own show, *The Sooty Show*, which ran from 1955-67 on the BBC before transferring to ITV between 1967 and 1992, Matthew, taking over as stooge in 1975 after his father suffered a heart attack. Sooty's friends Sweep (a grey squeaking dog) and Soo (a panda) first appeared in 1957 and 1964 respectively. Soo won the Weakest Link Christmas special in December 2007. Other recurring characters include Kipper (a cat), Butch (another dog who occasionally plays the part of a villain), Ramsbottom (a snake), 'Enry the Robot (a robot), Cousin Scampi (another bear), Miki (a Brazilian cat) and Maggie Mouse (a mouse). Sooty plays the xylophone and keeps a wand with which he performs magic. This is accompanied by the catchphrase "Izzy wizzy, let's get busy!" Sooty is also known for his propensity to soak Matthew with his water pistol. Each show ended with Matthew carrying on Harry's tradition of uttering the immortal words "Bye bye everybody, bye bye". Sooty has rarely been off our screens since his birth on 19th July 1948 and when The Sooty Show ended in 1992 Sooty & Co began the following year on ITV and Matthew and Sooty were now found running a shop in Manchester. When Matthew retired in 1998 a new series, Sooty Heights, was aired between 1999 and 2000 presented by Richard Cadell and Liana Bridges. The final ITV offering came between 2001 and 2004 with Sooty, presented by Richard Cadell and Vicki Lee Taylor, although Sooty is frequently repeated on the CITV channel.

Sorcerer's Apprentice, The Children's television programme originally hosted by Barney Harwood. The first series aired on BBC1 and saw seven girls and seven boys given 18 days of training by professional magicians in order to become the Sorcerer's Apprentice. The Sorcerer was Maximillian Somerset III, and the two teachers were Sophie Evans and Tariq Knight. David Penn was a regular on *The Sorcerer's Apprentice Extra*, a follow-up programme broadcast the following day on BBC2. Ortis Deley took over as host in 2009 when the series began airing on BBC2. BBC 2008-09.

Sorry ! Ronnie Corbett (Timothy Lumsden), Barbara Lott (Mrs Phyllis Lumsden). Sitcom written by Ian Davidson and Peter Vincent. Timothy Lumsden, a 41-year-old librarian (ageing, eventually, to 48) is still tied to his mother's apron strings. BBC1 1981-82; 1985-88.

Sounds of the 60s Long-running BBC Radio 2 show with classic hits, requests and obscurities. Presented by Brian Matthew.

South Bank Show, The Sunday night arts programme which replaced *Aquarius* and presented throughout its run by Melvyn Bragg. The first programme, broadcast on Saturday 14 January 1978 (it soon changed to Sundays), highlighted the career of Paul McCartney. The theme music is an Andrew Lloyd Webber arrangement on the theme from Paganini's 24th Caprice, Variations 1-4 from the musical *Song and Dance*, performed by his brother, Julian Lloyd-Webber. ITV 1978-2010.

Space Cadets Spoof space travel reality television show presented by Johnny Vaughan and shown on Channel 4 between 7th and 16th December 2005. Nine young innocents (and three actors) suffered two weeks of intensive astronaut training believing they were in Star City, near Moscow, and labouring under the illusion that they were part of a real space mission and would be immortalised as the first British space tourists. In fact, the cadets had only travelled as far as a disused military base in Suffolk but the illusion was aided by Hollywood visual effects specialists, Wonderworks, whose credits include *The Day After Tomorrow* and *Apollo 13*. The mock space shuttle was built from a NASA blueprint. The event turned out to be something of a damp squib as the viewer had difficulty in believing in the 'contestants' who appeared to be chosen for their gullibility and lack of knowledge of space travel history. The joke could have been up at any point if any of the cadets had guessed the truth but as they were prepared to believe that the city of Minsk was named after Minsky the dog, an early space pioneer, this was highly unlikely.

Space Patrol Classic puppet series created and written by Roberta Leigh. In the year 2100, Space Patrol is the active unit of the United Galactic Organisation, a federation consisting of the planets Earth, Venus and Mars, keeping the peace between the worlds in a similar fashion to the United Nations of today. The series plotted the adventure aboard the patrol's lead ship, Galasphere 347, captained by Earthman Capt Larry Dart (voice of Dick Vosburgh), who was ably assisted by the logical and all-knowing Venusian, Slim (voice of Ronnie Stevens), and Gruff but loyal Martian, Husky (Stevens). Husky had a pet Gabblerdictum bird (voice of Libby Morris) who never stopped talking but often came up with results. Back at base the orders are given by Colonel Raeburn (voice of Murray Kash) and his secretary is the super-efficient blonde Venusian, Marla (Morris). 'On Venus there is no such thing as a dumb blonde'. The science officer is Professor Haggerty (Stevens) assisted by his daughter Cassiopea, known as Cassie (Morris). The puppeteers were Sally Bussell and Joan Garrick. ITV 1963-64.

Space: 1999 Martin Landau (Commander John Koenig), Barbara Bain (Dr Helena Russell), Barry Morse (Professor Victor Bergman), Tony Anholt (First Officer Tony Verdeschi), Nick Tate (Captain Alan Carter), Catherine Schell (Maya), voice of Barbara Kelly (Moonbase computer). Despite its American co-stars this science fiction series was a British co-production with Italy's RAI organisation, created by puppet masters Gerry and Sylvia Anderson. On 13 September 1999, the 311 inhabitants of Moonbase Alpha are stranded when the Moon is hurled from Earth's orbit into darkest space when nuclear waste is ignited by magnetic radiation. The Alphans are desperate to find a new home before their supplies run out and they encounter all manner of aliens during their journey. Maya from the planet Psychon is one such alien, with her chameleon powers she joins the crew and becomes a valued asset. ITV 1975-77.

Spaced Simon Pegg (Tim Bisley), Jessica Hynes nee Stevenson (Daisy Steiner), Julia Deakin (Marsha Klein), Mark Heap (Brian

Topp), Katy Carmichael (Twist Morgan), Nick Frost (Mike Watt), Anna Wilson-Jones (Sarah), Peter Serafinowicz (Duane Benzie), Bill Bailey (Bilbo Bagshot), Aida the Dog (Colin, a Miniature Schnauzer). Sitcom written by and starring Simon Pegg and Jessica Stevenson. Tim, an aspiring comic book artist, and Daisy, an aspiring writer, meet by chance in a cafe while both are flat-hunting. Despite barely knowing each other, they conspire to pose as a young "professional" couple in order to meet the requisites of an advertisement for a relatively cheap flat in the distinctive building at 23 Meteor Street, London, which is owned by the permanently sozzled landlady, Marsha Klein. Also living in the building is Brian, an eccentric conceptual artist. Frequent visitors include Tim's best friend, Mike and Daisy's best friend, Twist Morgan. Tim and Daisy repeatedly stress that they aren't a couple to everyone but Marsha, but despite this, romantic tension develops between them, particularly during the second series. Tim is a rather grumpy and quick to irritation at the slightest provocation, mostly because his girlfriend, Sarah broke his heart and dumped him after an affair with Tim's friend - Duane Benzie. He initially works as an assistant manager at a comic book shop, "Fantasy Bazaar", alongside its manager/owner, Bilbo Bagshot. Daisy owns a dog named Colin and has an innate knack for martial arts, although this is seldom called into use. Fourteen episodes (two series of seven episodes) were broadcast in 1999 and 2001on Channel 4.

Spatz Vas Blackwood (Dexter), Paul Michael (T.J. Strickland), Jonathan Copestake (Stanley), Joe Greco (Vince), Stephanie Charles (Debbie), Jennifer Calvert (Karen Hansson), Katy Murphy (Freddy), Samantha Womack (Toni), Denise Coffey (Mildred), Rhys Ifans (Dave). Sitcom based around the UK's only branch of fast-food chain, Spatz. Notable for Rhys Ifans first screen appearance. ITV 1990-92.

Speaker, The Reality television show which aimed to find the best young speaker, aged between 14 and 18, in the United Kingdom. Narrated by Jane Horrocks, the three judges were stand-up comedian Jo Brand, former American basketball player and political activist John Amaechi and Jeremy Stockwell. Duncan from Bristol was the eventual winner. BBC2 2009

Special Branch George Sewell (Det Chief Insp Alan Craven), Patrick Mower (Det Chief Insp Tom Haggerty), Derren Nesbitt (Det Insp Jordan), Wensley Pithey (Supt Eden), Fulton Mackay (Det Supt Inman), Paul Eddington (Strand). The first two series of this police drama featured the partnership of Eden and the snappily-dressed Jordan. When the series was revived Craven and Haggerty (who were also sartorially conscious) became the central characters. ITV 1969-70; 1973-74.

Spend, Spend, Spend Susan Littler (Vivian Nicholson), John Duttine (Keith Nicholson). True-life one-off drama written by Jack Rosenthal. When Viv Nicholson and her second husband Keith (a miner who tragically died prematurely in a road accident) won £152,319 on the pools in 1961 she famously announced she would "spend, spend, spend". By the time this *Play for Today* was broadcast, Viv was living on social security in the Yorkshire town of Castleford having been married five times. BBC1 1977.

Spender Jimmy Nail (DS Spender), Sammy Johnson (Stick), Paul Greenwood (Supt Yelland), Denise Welch (Frances). Police drama series created by Jimmy Nail and Ian La Frenais. Spender is a tough and fearless plain-clothes cop cleaning up the streets of London using somewhat unorthodox methods. Following a tragic incident, he's sent back to the North-East to his home-town of Newcastle-Upon-Tyne, and is re-united with old friends and haunting ghosts (including ex-wife Frances) from his untamed past. BBC1 1991-93.

Spin Star Daytime weekday quiz show hosted by Bradley Walsh based around five contestants and a five-reel slot machine called the Moneyspinner. The reels display question subjects, the names of the five contestants who will answer the questions, and cash amounts that are won if the questions are answered correctly. The contestants win the money for the contestant who has been there the longest, the Spin Star. Therefore each contestant was on the show for six episodes, five answering questions for someone else, then one where they are in charge of the Moneyspinner. ITV 2008

Spindoe Ray McAnally (Alec Spindoe), Richard Hurndall (Henry Mackleson), Rachel Herbert (Renata), Bryan Marshall (Det. Sgt. Peach), George Sewell (Scaliger). The character of London extortioner and gangland boss Alec Spindoe first appeared in several episodes of Granada TV's serial *The Fellows*. In that series, two university academics based in Cambridge solve crimes in the outside world by pure theory, without ever leaving their university buildings. Spindoe falls foul of one of these theories when he panics over a threatening letter, in truth sent to him by one of the Fellows in the hope that he will react exactly as he does. His panic leads him to set up a jewellery shop robbery, where he is caught and arrested. The following year, Spindoe returned in his own series, which depicted events after Spindoe's release from prison. The series, devised by Robin Chapman, portrays London gangland in a realistic and unsentimental light. *Spindoe* was an early directorial project for Cormac Newell, better known as Mike Newell, director of Four Weddings and a Funeral. ITV 1968. See also *Big Breadwinner Hog*.

Spitting Image Satirical puppet show created by Peter Fluck, Roger Law and Michael Lambie-Nairn. Impressionist's voices included Chris Barrie, Steve Nallon, Jan Ravens, Harry Enfield, Rory Bremner, Steve Coogan, Alistair McGowan, John Sessions, Hugh Dennis, Kate Robbins, Enn Reitel, Jon Glover and Jessica Martin. Memorable political depictions include Kenneth Baker as a slug, Norman Tebbitt as a skinhead and George Kaufman as Hannibal Lecter. The show always ended on a topical song and one such offering about the annual mass exodus to Benidorm by a stereotypical British sun-seeker The Chicken Song (a parody of Agadoo by Black Lace) became a 1986 chart-topper. With music by Philip Pope and lyrics by Naylor and Grant of Red Dwarf fame, the lead vocalists were Michael Fenton Stevens and Kate Robbins. Lyrics: *Its the time of year, Now that Spring is in the air, When those two wet gits with their girly curly hair. Make another song for moronic holidays, That nauseate-ate-ate, In a million different ways. From the shores of Spain, To the coast of Southern France, No matter where you hide, You just can't escape this dance. (chorus) Hold a chicken in the air, Stick a deckchair up your nose, Buy a jumbo jet, And then bury all your clothes. Paint your left knee green, Then extract your wisdom teeth, Form a string quartet, And pretend your name is Keith. Skin yourself alive, Learn to speak Arapahoe, Climb inside a dog, And behead an eskimo. Eat a Renault Four with salami in your ears, Casserole your gran, Disembowel yourself with spears. The disco is vibrating, The sound is loud and grating, Its truly nauseating, Let's do the dance again. Hold a chicken in the air, Stick a deckchair up your nose, Yes you'll hear this song in the holiday discos, And there's no escape in the clubs or in the bars, You would hear this song if you holidayed in Mars. Skin yourself alive, Learn to speak Arapahoe, Climb inside a dog, And behead an eskimo. Now you've heard it once, Your brain will spring a leak, And though you hate this song, You'll be humming it for weeks.* ITV 1984-96.

Spooks Matthew Macfadyen (Tom Quinn), Keeley Hawes (Zoe Reynolds), David Oyelowo (Danny Hunter), Peter Firth (Harry Pearce), Jenny Agutter (Tessa Phillips), Lisa Faulkner (Helen Flynn), Hugh Simon (Malcolm Wynn-Jones), Esther Hall (Ellie Simm), Heather Cave (Maisie Simm), Graeme Mearns (Jed Kelley), Rupert Penry-Jones (Adam Carter), Fiona Carter (Olga Sosnovska), Raza Jaffrey (Zafar Younis), Anna Chancellor (Juliet Shaw), Miranda Raison (Jo Portman), Shazad Latif (Tariq Masood), Sophia Myles (Beth Bailey), Max Brown (Dimitri Levendis), Richard Armitage (Lucas North), Nicola Walker (Ruth Evershed), Richard Johnson (Bernard Qualtrough). Secret agent drama written by David Wolstencroft, Simon Mirren and Howard Brenton. The title derives from a popular colloquialism for spies, as the series follows the work of a group of MI5 agents. BBC1 2002-

Spooner's Patch Ronald Fraser and Donald Churchill (Inspector Spooner), Peter Cleall (DC Bulsover), Norman Rossington (PC Goatman), Dermot Kelly (Kelly), Patricia Hayes (Mrs Cantaford), Harry Fowler (Jimmy the Con), John Lyons (PC Killick). Sitcom written by Johnny Speight and Ray Galton. Inspector Spooner is in charge of a small police station in Woodley, London. He's a vain, eccentric man who lives in a flat above the station. His methods of policing are rather unconvential and he's not averse to taking the odd "back-hander". A regular character in the final two series was the cantankerous traffic warden, Mrs Cantaford. Three actors played Spooner; Ian Bannen in the pilot-episode, Ronald Fraser for the first series and Donald Churchill for series two and three. William G Stewart was the producer. ITV 1979-82.

Sportsnight See *Sportsview.*

Sports Mastermind Des Lynam was the interrogator of this Spin-off series from *Mastermind* which followed the familiar format of two minutes grilling on specialist and general rounds. BBC2 2008.

Sports Report The iconic sports bulletin began on BBC Radio in January 1948 with Raymond Glendenning as its first presenter. A full list of other presenters include: 1955 Eamonn Andrews, 1964 Robin Marler, 1968 Peter Jones, 1970 Desmond Lynam, 1980 Mike Ingham, 1985 Renton Laidlaw, 1987 John Inverdale, 1994 Ian Payne and 1997 Mark Pougatch. The football results have been read out by the unmistakable voice of James Alexander Gordon since 1973. The distinctive theme tune "Out Of The Blue", was composed by Hubert Bath and played by the Central Band of the RAF. Mark Pougatch currently presents Sports Report (now called Sport on Five) most Fridays and Saturdays on BBC Radio Five Live.

Sportsview Peter Dimmock was the first host of the long-running midweek sport's magazine which featured Roger Bannister running the world's first four-minute mile on 6 May 1954 and also inspired the annual BBC Sports Review of the Year later that year. Later presenters included Brian Johnston and Frank Bough. Sportsview ran between 1954 and 1968 before changing its name to Sportsnight, with David Coleman taking over as the presenter (later presenters included Frank Bough, Des Lynam, Steve Rider, Tony Gubba, Ray Stubbs and Harry Carpenter). BBC 1 1968-97.

Spot the Tune Popular musical quiz game in which contestants had to spot the tune from just a few bars of a piece of music. Presenters included Ken Platt, Ted Ray, Jackie Rae and Pete Murray. ITV 1956-62. See *Name That Tune.*

Spread of the Eagle, The Robert Hardy (Coriolanus), Barry Jones (Julius Caesar), Keith Michell (Marc Antony), Mary Morris (Cleopatra), Peter Cushing (Cassius), Paul Eddington (Brutus), Peter Jeffrey (Sicinius Velutus). Mini-series depicting the Roman Shakespearean plays Corialanus, Julius Caesar and Antony and Cleopatra. BBC 1963.

Spring and Autumn Jimmy Jewel (Tommy Butler), Charlie Hawkins (Charlie Harris), Larry Martyn (Brian Reid), June Barry (Vera Reid), Jo Warne (Betty Harris). Comedy series written by Vince Powell and Harry Driver. Tommy, a retired railway worker, is forced to go and live with his daughter and her loquacious husband in their high-rise flat after his house is demolished by the local council. Tommy goes for a walk in the park, where he meets Charlie, a young Cockney tearaway being raised by his single mum. The old man becomes a father figure to the boy and soon they are to be seen fishing, walking and sharing their wildly differing views on life. The title of this 26-episode series is a nod to Charlie being in the Spring of his life while Tommy is in his Autumn. ITV 1972-76

Squirrels, The Bernard Hepton (Mr Fletcher), Ken Jones (Rex), Patsy Rowlands (Susan), Alan David (Harry), Ellis Jones (Burke), Karin MacCarthy (Carol). Sitcom written by Eric Chappell. Mr Fletcher attempts to keep order in an office full of shirkers. ITV 1974-77. See *Fiddlers Three.*

Staggering Stories of Ferdinand De Bargos, The Comedy based around the overdubbing of archive footage (mostly documentary) with comic dialogue of a strongly topical nature performed by gifted voice artists. 24 episodes were made, 22 of 20 minutes and two 1991 specials. The short 10-minute special *The Staggering Story Of Lime Grove*, utilising footage from the earliest days of British television, was presented as part of a day-long BBC2 tribute to its Lime Grove studio facility, upon its closure. The second special was the 30-minute *The Staggering Year of Ferdinand de Bargos*. The team included Enn Reitel, Jon Glover, Jim Broadbent, Kate Robbins, Susie Blake, Caroline Leddy, Joanna Brookes, Steve Steen, Ronni Ancona, Alistair McGowan, Arabella Weir, Ann Bryson, Peter Bland and Roger Blake. Kim

Fuller and Geoff Atkinson wrote much of the material. BBC2 1989-95.

Stake Out Children's hidden-camera game show that finds out how well kids know their mates. Presented by Peter Firman. Part of the CBBC schedule. BBC1 2008-
A quiz show of the same name, presented by Anthony Davis, aired for a short run on Challenge TV in 2001/02.

Stand Easy See entry for Charlie Chester in comedy section.

Stand Up Nigel Barton Keith Barron (Nigel Barton), Jack Woolgar (Harry Barton), Barbara Keogh (Mrs Taylor), Janet Henfrey (Miss Tillings), Valerie Gearon (Anne Barton), John Bailey (Jack Hay), Cyril Luckham (Archibald Lake). Drama written by Dennis Potter. Nigel leaves his working class home in a South Nottinghamshire mining village to take up his place at Oxford. He struggles to come to terms with the cultural distance he has travelled. Taking an increasingly active part in Oxford politics, Nigel delivers a "Paper Speech" at the Union against the motion that class no longer matters in Britain. After the debate, at a small buffet-supper in the president's office, Nigel is approached to contribute to a forthcoming BBC documentary on "Britain - A Land of Barriers". Back at home, the Barton family sit around the TV set to watch the programme as it is transmitted and the full extent of Nigel's apparent disloyalty to and betrayal of his background becomes clear. First broadcast on 8 December 1965 as part of *The Wednesday Play* series, a follow-on play, *Vote, Vote, Vote for Nigel Barton*, aired the following Wednesday to critical acclaim. BBC1 1965.

Star Maidens Lisa Harrow (Liz Becker), Christian Quadflieg (Rudi Schmidt), Christiane Krüger (Octavia), Derek Farr (Prof. Evans), Judy Geeson (Fulvia), Gareth Thomas (Shem), Dawn Addams (President Clara). Anglo-German Sci-Fi series created by Eric Paice. A planet from another solar system drifts into Earth's system and is detected by some Earth scientists who investigate. The surface of this planet is no longer habitable and the residents have moved to a high-tech underground city. The society is ruled by the women, who are all beautiful. Men are considered mentally inferior and are divided into two categories: the "adequately intelligent" who are selected by women to act as their personal domestics for household chores, and the remainder who are forced to perform menial labour under the supervision of female guards. ITV 1976

Star Stories Irreverent comedy parodying celebrities and their lifestyles. 'Victims' included David & Victoria Beckham, George Michael, Catherine Zeta-Jones, Guy Ritchie, Sadie Frost, Jennifer Aniston, Take That, Tom Cruise, Simon Cowell, Britney Spears, Elton John, Heather Mills, Peter Andre and Jordan, Kate Moss, and Bono. Actors included Tom Basden, Daisy Beaumont, Kevin Bishop, Fergus Craig, Steve Edge, Trevor Lock, Harry Peacock, Alex Woodhall and Thaila Zucchi. C4 2006-08.

Starr and Company William Sherwood (Joseph Starr), Pat Ann Key (Julia Starr), Barbara Cavan (Edith Starr), Nancy Nevinson (Megs Turner), Gillian Gale (Gwyneth Turner), Barry MacGregor (Hughie Turner), Philip Ray (Jim Turner), Brian McDermott (Tom Turner), Michael Murray (Robin Starr), Deirdre Day (Jane Starr), Arnold Ridley (Harry Crane), Patricia Mort (Mary Tennison), Katherine Parr (Rene Cremer). Short-lived soap opera based around Starr & Co, an engineering factory that makes shipping buoys, in Sullbridge, 50 miles from London. BBC 1958.

Stars and Garters Variety series that helped launch successful chart-topping careers for two of Britain's most popular singers, Kathy Kirby and Vince Hill. *Stars and Garters* gave the appearance of being set in a pub filled with real customers as they were entertained with a mixture of music and jokes. Hosted originally by Ray Martine and then co-hosted by the unlikely partnership of Jill Browne and Willie Rushton for its final run when its title became *The New Stars and Garters*. ITV 1963-66.

Stars In Their Eyes Reality show in which contestants impersonate a popular singer past or present. Presenters have included Leslie Crowther (1990-92), Matthew Kelly (1993-2004), Russ Abbot (one-off Elvis special), Davina McCall (celebrity specials) and Cat Deeley (2004-06). Series winners include 1990 Maxine Barrie as Shirley Bassey, 1991 Bernard Wenton as Nat "King" Cole, 1992 Amanda Normansell as Patsy Cline, 1993 Jacquii Cann as Alison Moyet, 1994 John Finch as Marti Pellow, 1995 Lee Griffiths as Bobby Darin, 1996 Paul Doody as Marti

Pellow, 1997 Faye Dempsey as Olivia Newton-John, 1998 Jason Searle as Neil Diamond, 1999 Ian Moor as Chris De Burgh, 2000 Garry Mullen as Freddie Mercury, 2000 Nicola Kirsch as Maria Callas (Millennium special show), 2001 Emma Wilkinson as Dusty Springfield, 2002 Stewart Duff as Elvis Presley, 2004 Charles Ngandwe as Paul Robeson, 2005 Gordon Hendricks as Elvis Presley. In 1999 Ian Moor as Chris De Burgh won a special Champion of Champions edition. Cat Deeley also presented *Stars In Their Eyes: Kids* since 2002. Winners: 2002 Charlotte Geffen as Eva Cassidy, 2003 Laura Jenkins as Connie Francis, 2004 Paul Kowperthwaite as Michael Jackson, 2006 Christopher Napier as George Formby . Numerous celebrity specials were also broadcast, one of the most memorable being Jarvis Cocker impersonating Rolf Harris – and winning! ITV 1990-2006

Stars On Sunday ITV's answer to *Songs of Praise* was a mixture of Biblical readings and hymns with regular celebrity guests such as Harry Secombe, James Mason, The Beverley Sisters, Gracie Fields, John Mills and Anna Neagle. Jess Yates was the presenter for the first five years of its run. Other presenters included Anthony Valentine, Robert Dougall, Cliff Michelmore, Wilfred Pickles, Moira Anderson and Gordon Jackson. ITV 1969-79.

State of Play David Morrissey (Stephen Collins, a Labour MP), John Simm (Cal McCaffrey, reporter and Stephen Collins' former campaign manager), Kelly Macdonald (Della Smith, reporter), Bill Nighy (Cameron Foster, editor of *The Herald*), Polly Walker (Anne Collins, wife of Stephen Collins), James McAvoy (Dan Foster, reporter), Philip Glenister (DCI William Bell), Marc Warren (Dominic Foy), James Laurenson (George Fergus, Energy Minister), Amelia Bullmore (Helen Preger, reporter). Six-part drama serial directed by David Yates and written by Paul Abbott, telling the story of a newspaper's investigation into the death of a young woman, and centres on the relationship between the leading journalist and his old friend, who is a Member of Parliament and the murdered woman's employer. BBC1 2003. The series was later adapted into a film in 2009.

Stay Lucky Dennis Waterman (Thomas Gynn), Jan Francis (Sally Hardcastle), Chris Jury (Kevin), Niall Toibin (Lively), Emma Wray (Pippa), Susan George (Samantha Mansfield), Rula Lenska (Isabel), Leslie Ash (Jo). Thomas Gynn, on the run from some shady underworld characters meets Sally Hardcastle and in no time is sharing a houseboat with her. By the third season Sally had left and was replaced as a love interest by Samantha Mansfield, administrator of the Yorkshire Industrial Museum. Susan George left the series somewhat under a cloud and Leslie Ash joined the cast in a similar role. ITV 1989-93.

Staying Alive Jessica Hynes nee Stevenson (Alice Timpson), Amanda Royle (Sue McPherson), Susannah Wise (Michaela Lennox). Drama series about a group of student nurses in a London hospital. ITV 1996-97.

Stella Street Spoof soap about the antics of a group of American and British celebrities who all happen to live on Stella Street, Surbiton (in reality Hartswood Road, Chiswick). The characters themselves were impressions of famous celebrities mainly played by John Sessions and Phil Cornwell (although supported by Sandra Cush and others). Unlikely scenarios were the order of the day (such as Roger Moore visiting David Bowie at Christmas to give him a face flannel for a present or Mick Jagger and Keith Richards running the local corner shop). Cornwell as Michael Caine often linked the sketches, talking to the camera in the style adopted in the 1966 film *Alfie*. Sessions and Cornwell also played non-celebrity roles including old-world housekeeper, and lifelong Stella Street resident Mrs Huggett, couple-from-hell Pam and Graham Slurry, dopey builder Dean Barraclough and the potentially murderous gardener Len. BBC2 1997-2001.

Steptoe and Son Harry H Corbett (Harold), Wilfred Brambell (Albert). The classic sitcom focusing on the love-hate relationship of a widower father and unmarried son who run a decrepit rag-and-bone business, was conceived as one of a Comedy Playhouse season of ten unrelated pieces by Ray Galton and Alan Simpson after Tony Hancock, whom they had served so ably, relinquished their services. The first of the playlets, *The Offer* (1962) was very well-received by the public and turned into a series. Its underlying theme of a son trying desperately to escape the clutches of his wily father imbued the series with a pathos and poignancy hitherto absent from the sitcom genre. It was decided to keep Harold's age hovering around 40, since they felt that, at this age, there was still a possibility, albeit a slight one, that he might somehow escape. As it was, viewers instantly recognised Harold's dilemma - home was a prison, work was a prison, and not only was escape difficult but to where would he run? Perennially short of money, life was hard, and much as Harold aspired to a greater degree of sophistication (not difficult, considering Albert's truly disgusting personal habits) and a long-term female relationship, he knew that his cunning father would always maintain his grip. As for Albert, he felt that he had done his bit, so was entitled to laze around their ramshackle west London home (Mews Cottage, Oil Drum Lane, Shepherd's Bush) and expect his son - and horse, Hercules - to cart home the spoils that 'totting' can bring. When he felt particularly threatened by an imminent Harold desertion he would immediately play his trump card and feign heart disease ("Harold, it's me heart"). The plight of the two desperate totters was never more graphically exposed than in an episode of 1972, Desperate Hours, in which two escaped convicts break into their home with a view to nicking the family silver. It soon becomes apparent that the old lags have a higher standard of living than the Steptoes who can't even raise a shilling for the meter between them. A touching scene where one of the thugs offers Harold a precious cigarette is testament to the genius of this comedy drama. By the end of the episode Harold is begging the couple to take him with them to a better life on the run! The much-loved theme tune *Old Ned*, was composed by Ron Grainer. BBC1 1962-65; 1970-74.

Stewart Lee's Comedy Vehicle Stewart Graham Lee (born 5 April 1968 in Shropshire) is an English stand-up comedian, writer and director probably best known for being one half of the 1990s comedy duo Lee and Herring. This stand-up and sketch show has a different theme each week (such as books, television and religion) and the supporting cast includes Simon Munnery, Kevin Eldon, Paul Putner and Peter Serafinowicz. The opening theme tune is *Tom Hark* by Elias & His Zig-Zag Jive Flutes. BBC2 2009-

Stig of the Dump *Stig of the Dump* is a children's novel (illustrated by Edward Ardizzone) written by Clive King, published in 1963. It has been twice adapted for television, in 1981 and in 2002. The 1981 ITV series starred Keith Jayne as Stig, a caveman who lives at the bottom of the old quarry close to his friend Barney's grandmother's house. Barney was played by Grant Warnock. The 2002 BBC series starred Robert Tannion as Stig (while Nick Ryan provided Stig's voice), Thomas Brodie-Sangster as Barney and Phyllida Law as Grandma Marjorie.

Still Game *Chewin' The Fat* spawned a sitcom spin-off, *Still Game*, focusing on two old-men characters from the show, Jack Jarvis and Victor McDade, performed by Ford Kiernan and Greg Hemphill respectively, who also wrote the episodes. Shown only on BBC1 Scotland (six episodes, 6 September-11 October 2002; nine episodes, 28 March-23 May 2003), it attracted very high ratings and only narrowly missed out on the coveted Golden Rose of Montreux prize in 2003.

Stingray Voices of Don Mason (Troy Tempest), Robert Easton (George 'Phones' Sheridan and Agent X20), Lois Maxwell (Atlanta Shore), Ray Barrett (Cmdr Sam Shore, Sub Lt Fisher, Titan). The year is 2065, and the world is united in peace. Mankind has conquered the stars, so attention turns to the exploration of the oceans. The vast, uncharted depths provide valuable minerals, but also hide new and mysterious alien races, not all of whom are entirely friendly. The Aquaphibians take offence to the surface dweller's forays into their undersea kingdom of Titanica. Titan, their ruler, assisted by his inept land-based agent X20, swears to invade the surface world in revenge. All that can stop him is the World Aquanaut Security Patrol - WASP, an organisation of fearless individuals dedicated to preserving world peace. Their key weapon in the fight against the Aquaphibians is Stingray, a futuristic, nuclear-powered submarine. Troy Tempest is its heroic captain, ably supported by his team at Marineville headquarters: George Lee Sheridan, Troy's co-pilot, nicknamed 'Phones' due to his expertise with the underwater Hydrophone communication system; Marina the subterranean mute daughter of Emperor Aphony from Pacifica (her pet seal was called Oink). She was enslaved by Titan, who has threatened to destroy her people if she ever speaks; Atlanta Shore, the commander's daughter and Marineville's assistant communications officer. She supervises the launch of Stingray. She loves Troy from afar, so has a friendly rivalry with Marina; Commander Sam Shore, the head of WASP, he was once involved in a submarine accident. He uses a special hoverchair to get around Marineville due to his injuries. Stingray was created by Gerry Anderson, who went on to create *Thunderbirds*. Originally shown in 1964, it was the first British television series to be filmed in colour although it was first transmitted in black and white, as colour TV didn't start until 1967 in Britain! The opening theme music was composed by Barry Gray and the action sequences saw Cmdr Shore utter the immortal words "Anything can happen in the next half-hour". The closing theme was 'Aquamarina' also by Barry Gray, the lyrics were thus*: Marina, Aqua Marina, What are these strange enchantments that start whenever you're near? Marina, Aqua Marina, Why can't you whisper the words my heart is longing to hear? Your magic to me, a beautiful mystery. I'm certain to fall 1 know, because you enthrall me so. Marina, Aqua Marina, Why don't you say, that you'll always stay, close to my heart.* ITV 1964-65.

Story Makers, The CBeebies offering first shown in 2002. At the stroke of midnight, three-year-old Jelly (a puppet with green sticking out hair voiced by Aliex Yuill) and seven-year-old Jackson (a pink porcupine-like puppet voiced by Nick Mercer), who live secretly in a library, come out and are joined by a guest presenter, one of the members of the Wordsworth family, who recites "The sun is down, the stars are bright, Story Makers come out at night". Items found in the library are then put into the top of the story machine and the three recite "Imagine, imagine, imagine a story!"; and the story machine produces a book containing a story based on the objects. The story is then acted out in live action or animation. As dawn breaks, the Story Makers take their leave with "Dawn is upon us, the morning is nigh, we've made our stories, so we bid you goodbye" and disappear, the story machine turning back into a computer, although the books produced overnight remain for the librarian and children to find when the library opens in the morning.

Story Parade Anthology series that became the first drama programme broadcast on BBC2 when the new channel began transmissions in April 1964. Script edited by Irene Shubik, the series was designed to dramatise various examples of "modern fictional writing," rather than showcase original works. The most popular episode was an adaptation of Isaac Asimov's *The Caves of Steel*, which was broadcast as the fifth story on 5th June, Peter Cushing taking the lead role of Elijah Baley. Another 1964 episode, *The Unknown Citizen*, is notable for the screen debut of Patrick Stewart. BBC2 1964-65

Strange Report, The Anthony Quayle (Adam Strange), Charles Lloyd Pack (Professor Marks). The adventures of a retired Home Office criminologist. Each episode began with the episode being given a 'report number'. Unusually, Strange arrived at the scene of the crimes in an unlicenced black taxi cab. ITV 1968-69.

Strange World of Gurney Slade, The Anthony Newley (Gurney Slade). Sitcom created by Anthony Newley and written by Sid Green and Dick Hills. From the opening scene which depicted a confused Slade sitting amid a squabbling family, apparently filming a soap opera, the viewer knew this was not going to be the usual sitcom fare. Suddenly Slade walked off the set and out of the studio. This was so realistic that the viewer's initial reaction was to suppose that it was Newley that had walked out, although it soon became apparent that this was a surreal and fantastic journey where they became privy to Slade's innermost thoughts and inanimate objects began to talk to him. Bernie Winters made several cameo appearances during the run, as did Dilys Laye. This was a truly groundbreaking six-episode sitcom which was ahead of its time in its plotless storyline but had elements of sheer genius. Newley plucked the title character's name from that of a Somerset village. The show's theme tune by composer Max Harris, was later used in the "animated clock" segments on the BBC children's show *Vision On*, the piano figure prominent in the

recording (which Newley would play air-piano to) was lifted from Mose Allison's song "Parchman Farm". ITV 1960.

Stranger on the Shore Jeanne le Bars (Marie-Hélène Ronsin), Amanda Grinling (Penelope Gough), Beatrix Mackey (Mrs. Gough), Richard Vernon (David Gough), Denis Gilmore (Paul 'Podger' Gough). Five-episode drama series written by Ruth Sheila Hodgson. A young French teenager, on her first trip to England as an au pair, lives with a family in Brighton, and faces the challenges of both language and culture shock. A teenage Wendy Richard made her television debut in one of the episodes. The series is also notable for its haunting title track, performed by Acker Bilk, which was released the month after the series aired and remained in the charts for the next 12 months, eventually becoming the UK's best-selling instrumental single of all time. BBC 1961. The series was followed the following year by a sequel, *Stranger in the City,* with the same writer and cast.

Strangers Don Henderson (Det Sgt/ DCI George Bulman), Frances Tomelty (WDC Linda Doran), Thorley Waters (William Dugdale), Mark McManus (Det Chief Supt Jack Lambie), Dennis Blanch (DC/DS Derek Willis). Spin-off series from *The XYY Man*, the title describing the relationship of police partners Bulman and Doran thrown together to patrol the streets of Manchester where the local officers are too well known to be effective. ITV 1978-82. See *Bulman.*

Strangers From The Sea See *Poldark.*

Street, The Jane Horrocks (Angela Quinn), Jim Broadbent (Stan McDermott), Sue Johnston (Brenda McDermott), Timothy Spall (Eddie McEvoy), Bob Hoskins (Paddy Gargan), Daniel Ryan (Arthur Quinn), Shaun Dooley (Peter Harper), Liz White (Eileen Harper), Lee Ingleby (Sean O'Neill), Christine Bottomley (Yvonne O'Neill), Alexandra Pearson (Katy Quinn), Dean McGonagle (Jamie Quinn), Katy Clayton (Joanne Harper), Penny Deakin (Nicky Harper), Joshua Thurston (Jimmy Harper), Eamonn Riley (PC Jones), Neil Dudgeon (Brian Peterson), Lindsey Coulson (Ann Peterson), Jody Latham (Billy Roberts), David Schofield (John Roberts), Jamiu Adebiyi (Ojo), Jodhi May (Jean), David Thewlis (Harry and Joe Jennerson), Will Mellor (Tom), Toby Kebbell (Paul Billerton), Liam Cunningham (Thomas Miller), Anna Friel (Dee Purnell), Jonas Armstrong (Private Nick Calshaw), Joseph Mawle (Kieran Corrigan), Stephen Graham (Shay Ryan), Maxine Peake (Madeleine), Ruth Jones (Sandra). Drama series written by, among others, Jimmy McGovern, who is also the co-executive producer with Andy Harries. Set in the North of England (filmed in Rock Street, Salford), each emotionally-powerful episode concentrates on a different house in the street. Each story is distinctive and individual but linked by community and shared experience. BBC1 2006-09.

Street That Cut Everything, The Documentary, billed as a social experiment, presented by BBC political editor Nick Robinson. Fifty residents of Beacon Avenue, Fulwood, Preston, Lancashire were persuaded to go without all council services for six weeks, and work together to run their own community with the aid of the Council Tax rebates they received for not having local authority services. During the period of the experiment, refuse was no longer collected, street lighting was switched off and other services provided by the local authority were withdrawn. To make life more difficult the programme arranged for the street to be daubed with graffiti, for items to be fly tipped, for dogs to foul pavements and for actors to pose as anti-social teenagers who the neighbours were required to deal with. The film's objective was to highlight issues regarding the cuts to public spending being implemented by the Conservative-led coalition government and the effects these might have on the provision of local services. The programme aired on BBC1 in two episodes on Monday 16 May 2011.

Street Doctor Reality show in which four GPs (Dr Jonty Heaversedge, Dr Barbara Murray, Dr Ayan Panja and Dr George Rae) took to the streets to diagnose, advise and treat people. BBC1 2007-08. A spin-off from the show called *Beach Doctor* was shown as part of *The One Show* in August 2007.

Streetmate Dating game show hosted by Davina McCall. Davina picked an eligible male or female from the street and then with their help, chose a suitable member of the opposite sex for a date. The couple then went on the date and reported back on its success or failure. C4 1998-2001. The show was revived on ITV2 in 2007 with Holly Willoughby as the new host.

Streets Ahead Sarah Beeny helped residents around Britain turn their roads into more desirable places to live. Sarah managed to get neighbours to work together making changes to anything seen from street level - front gardens, garages, curtains, trees - to help raise the ceiling price of their street. The residents had to commit to working four weekends and at least 100 hours to improving their street. In return, they received help and advice from Sarah and project manager David Flight. C4 2005.

Stressed Eric Joint British/American/New Zealand cartoon series revolving around Eric Feeble (voiced by Mark Heap), a middle class 40-year-old man who is perpetually stressed by life's machinations. Other characters include next door neighbours Mr and Mrs Perfect (voiced by Gordon Kennedy and Alison Steadman – her memorable catchphrase being "How art thou, Eric?"), their snobbish daughter Heather (voiced by Morwenna Banks who also voices Eric's daughter Claire), Eric's wife (voiced by Rebecca Front), Eric's boss, Paul Power (voiced by Geoffrey McGivern – his memorable catchphrase being "Double arseburgers, Eric!"), Eric's best friend, Doc (voiced by Paul Shearer) and Eric's secretary, Alison Scabie (voiced by Doon Mackichan). BBC2 1998-2000,

Strictly Come Dancing When Come Dancing ended its 45-year run in 1995 it left a great void for the hordes of ballroom dancing fans and the purists initially treated this re-vamped version with a certain amount of derision fearing a typically uncompetitive celebrity non-event. How wrong they were! The passion and craft of the professional dancers rubbed off on the celebs and the arduous training regime lent itself to high quality dance routines which captured the hearts of the viewing public from the start. Hosted by the multi-talented Bruce Forsyth and delightful Tess Daly, each show highlights a wide spectrum of sportspeople, actors and presenters attempting foxtrots, tangos, rumbas and sambas before being awarded marks out of ten by four professional dancers/choreographers i.e. Arlene Phillips, Bruno Tonioli, Craig Revel Horwood and Len Goodman. The judge's marks account for half the score and the other half is determined by the viewing public, the couple with the lowest combined score leaving the contest. Notable footloose non-winners worthy of praise include athletes Colin Jackson (series 3) and Denise Lewis (series 2), rugby player Matt Dawson (series 4), former Spice Girl Emma Bunton (series 4), television presenter Zoe Ball (series 3) and funny girl Pamela Stephenson (series 8) but not all the celebrities showed a natural flair for dance and the unco-ordinated stacatto steps of television presenter Quentin Willson and strained facial contortions of Countdown's Carol Vorderman in series 2 added an element of comic relief as did the laboured offerings of political journalist John Sergeant and former MP Ann Widdecombe. Series 1 was won by *Breakfast News* presenter Natasha Kaplinsky partnering Brendan Cole. Other winners include: Series 2 actress Jill Halfpenny & Darren Bennet; Series 3 cricketer Darren Gough & Lilia Kopylova; Series 4 cricketer Mark Ramprakash & Karen Hardy; Series 5 singer Alesha Dixon & Matthew Cutler; Series 6 actor Tom Chambers & Camilla Dallerup; Series 7 BBC sports presenter Chris Hollins & Ola Jordan; Series 8 actress Kara Tointon & Artem Chigvintsev; Series 9 McFly drummer Harry Judd & Aliona Vilani. Arlene Phillips was controversially dropped for the 7th series and replaced by Alesha Dixon while prima ballerina Darcy Bussell also appeared as a guest judge for the latter part of that series. First broadcast on BBC1 on Saturday evenings in 2004, the show has a weekday sister show on BBC2 (*Strictly Come Dancing - It Takes Two*) hosted by Claudia Winkleman until Zoe Ball replaced her for Series 9 with Claudia then hosting the main results show on the Sunday.

Strictly Dance Fever Graham Norton hosted this dance extravaganza which saw ten couples (from a starting field of thousands) taught a new dance routine each week from a variety of different dance styles in the hope of dancing away with the coveted prize of £50,000. Filling the spot between series of *Strictly Come Dancing* this popular series began in the spring of 2005, the first winners being Sadie Flower and Joseph Hall. Judges for the first series were Stacey Haynes, Arlene Phillips, Luca Tommassini and Jason Gardiner. Series two was won by Darrien Wright and Hollie Robertson; the judges being Stacey Haynes, Arlene Phillips, Wayne Sleep and Ben Richards. BBC1 2005-06

Strike It Lucky Game show hosted by Michael Barrymore in which contestants were required to dodge the "hotspots" by going "top, middle or bottom". Although the show was the usual formatted game show the unpredictability of its host, particularly during the opening 'meet the contestants' section, made it a classic series. ITV 1986-94. When the programme relaunched between 1996 and 1999 it offered increased prizes and changed its name to *Strike It Rich*.

Suburban Shootout Anna Chancellor (Camilla Diamond), Felicity Montagu, (Barbara Du Prez), Amelia Bullmore, (Joyce Hazeldine), Ralph Ineson, (Jeremy Hazeldine), Rachael Blake, (Hilary Davenport), Emma Kennedy, (Lillian Gordon-Moore), Cathryn Bradshaw (Margaret Littlefair), Lucy Robinson (Pam Draper). Surreal comedy drama series. In Little Stempington, the women don't kill time – they kill each other, with anything from Glock 9mm machine pistols to potato peelers if necessary. In fact, this sleepy English town is more South Central LA than Home Counties. Beneath the charity fundraising and mid-morning aerobic classes lies a secret, super-sexed, super-violent world. Industrial strength Viagra is grated into husbands' suppers, high doses of illegal HRT are smuggled in from Marseilles and every high street shop is at the mercy of a protection racket so fierce no one is prepared to stand in its way. Into this rural battlefield walk innocent Joyce Hazeldine and her policeman husband Jeremy, itching to find a stress-free life away from the high crime rate of the big city. As wife of the new local superintendent, Joyce soon becomes an unwilling pawn in the epic power struggle between two rival gangs, led by Camilla Diamond and Barbara Du Prez. *Five* 2006-07

Sugar Rush Olivia Hallinan (Kimberly Daniels), Lenora Crichlow (Maria 'Sugar' Sweet), Richard Lumsden (Nathan Daniels), Sara Stewart (Stella Daniels), Kurtis O'Brien (Matt Daniels), Sarah-Jane Potts (Saint), Neil Jackson (Dale), Andrew Garfield (Tom). Comedy drama series based on the Julie Burchill novel of the same name, revolving around the life of 15 year old lesbian, Kim Daniels, newly arrived in Brighton. The opening theme music was "One Way or Another" by Blondie. C4 2005-06.

Sunday Night at the London Palladium Long-running variety show that became a British institution in the 1950s and 1960s. The cream of British talent appeared during its run and, particularly in the early days, the top-of-the-bill act was often an American legend such as Judy Garland or Bob Hope. Dickie Henderson, Alfred Marks, Bob Monkhouse and Robert Morley initially took turns as host (usually on a four-week run basis) and Tommy Trinder became the first regular compere followed by Bruce Forsyth, Norman Vaughan, Jimmy Tarbuck and Des O'Connor. Other guest presenters included Hughie Green, Dave Allen, Roger Moore, Don Arrol and Arthur Haynes. The 60-minute show began with the high-kicking Tiller Girls followed by a bit of patter from the compere and then into the acts. Topo Gigio, the Italian mouse puppet, was one of the most-popular acts as were Danny Kaye, The Beatles and Norman Wisdom. After the first commercial break there would be a game of *Beat The Clock* where members of the audience would have to bounce balls into baskets or work a piece of wire around an electrical circuit without setting it off. The winner would have to unravel a well-known phrase on a velcro board to win a modest prize. After the second commercial break the star-turn would appear followed by the whole cast waving goodbye on a revolving stage behind giant letters of the show's title. The Orchestra was led by Eric Rogers, who served as the theatre music director for three years. Cyril Ornadel took over as musical director when Eric left and was later followed by Jack Parnell and his Orchestra. The famous theme tune was called *Startime* and was composed by Eric Rogers. Sometimes called *Val Parnell's Sunday Night at the London Palladium* (after its creator) the show ended in 1967 but was reprised in 1973 with Jim Dale as compere. ITV 1955-67; 1973-74.

Supercar The series that coined the phrase 'Supermarionation' (meaning the lip synchronisation of voices to the lip movements of the puppets). Mike Mercury (voiced by Graydon Gould), test pilot for Supercar a space-age vehicle designed and built by Professor Popkiss (voiced by George Murcell and Cyril Shaps) and Doctor Beaker (voiced by David Graham). This fabulous craft is automobile, aircraft, spaceship and submarine in one. Operating from their laboratory in Black Rock Nevada, Mercury and his young friend, Jimmy Gibson (voiced by Sylvia Anderson), and his pet monkey Mitch (David Graham) get up to various escapades often foiling the schemes of the villainous Masterspy (George Murcell and Cyril Shaps) and his companion Zarin (David Graham). Created by Gerry Anderson and Reg Hill. ITV 1961-62.

Supergran Gudrun Ure (Granny 'Supergran' Smith), Iain Cuthbertson (Scunner Campbell), Bill Shine (Inventor Black), Robert Austin (Insp Muggins), Alan Snell (Muscles), Brian Lewis (Dustin), Holly English (Edison), Terry Joyce (PC Leekie), Lee Marshall (Tub), Ian Towell (Willard). Children's comedy series written by Jenny McDade. A dear old lady is struck by a beam from a magic ray machine of Inventor Black's and is endowed with super powers. Supergran sets out on her 'flycycle' to defend the good folk of Chisleton against baddies, usually in the guise of The Scunner Campbell and his cronies. Based on the books by Forrest Wilson the series became hugely popular Sunday afternoon viewing. The theme tune was co-written by comedian Billy Connolly who also performed the song and had a No 32 hit with it. The lyrics were: *Stand back Superman, Iceman, Spiderman. Batman and Robin too. Don't wanna cause a fracas, but BA Baracas, have I got a match for you. She makes them look like a bunch of fairies. She's got more bottle than United Dairies. Hang about - Look out! For Supergran. You can take your heroes, your Robert De Niros too. They say Stallone is just another phoney. He couldn't lace his shoes. After her they're all big girl's blouses she's got more front than a row of houses. Hang about - Look out! For Supergran. She's a serious granny (Supergran!) A serious granny (Supergran!). She'll do things that you never saw your granny do Scunner Campbell: Is there nothing that she cannae do?* ITV 1985-87.

Supernanny Reality show featuring professional nanny Jo Frost, who attempts to help out parents with their child-rearing skills - her favoured method often involving the 'naughty-chair'. Narrators: Series 1 Anthony Green, Series 2-5 Nick Frost (although Mark Heap narrated the first three episodes of Series 2) and Series 6 onwards Bob Marsden. C4 2004-

Superstars, The Originally presented by David Vine, *Superstars* was an all-around sports competition that pitted elite athletes from different sports against one another in a series of athletic challenges resembling a decathlon. David Hemery, the 1968 Olympic champion in the 400 meter hurdles, won the first *British Superstars* in 1973. Lynn Davies, Keith Fielding, Brian Jacks, Des Drummond and Malcolm McDonald were other notable competitors. Pole vaulter Brian Hooper was the only British competitor to have won *World Superstars*, his triumph coming in 1982 in America. The series ended its first run in 1985 but in 2002, Sir Steven Redgrave, Gianluca Vialli and Dwight Yorke were among nine competitors who appeared in a one-off special for *Sport Relief*, with England rugby union star Austin Healey the eventual winner. The show's success prompted the return of a brand new series the following year, with a whole new generation of sports stars taking part, including footballer Dennis Wise, cricketer Henry Olonga, boxer Ricky Hatton and former world champion hurdler Colin Jackson. Track star Du'aine Ladejo eventually claimed victory in the men's final, while swimmer Zoe Baker and snowboarder Lesley McKenna came joint-first in the women's special. Du'aine retained his title in 2004 just pipping skier Alain Baxter, who reversed the placings in the 2005 final. The memorable theme music was composed by Johnny Pearson and titled *Heavy Action*. BBC1 1973-85; 2002-05. A team Superstars was shown on *Five* in 2008.

Superted Voices of Derek Griffiths (Superted), Jon Pertwee (Spottyman), Victor Spinetti (Texas Pete), Roy Kinnear (Bulk), Melvyn Hayes (Skeleton). Written by Robin Lyons and narrated by Peter Hawkins. Superted was created by Mike Young, and his wife, Maura, as a bedtime story for his young son, who was very afraid of the dark. Each episode began with the tale of how Superted came to life. He was a teddy bear found to be defective in the toy factory where he was made, and then disposed of into a storeroom in the basement. A Spottyman found him there and brought him to life with his "cosmic dust". He was later taken to Mother Nature and given magical powers that enabled him to fight evil. This evil invariably took the form of Texas Pete (An evil cowboy) and his gang; Bulk (an overweight, bumbling fool) and Skeleton (a live skeleton with pink slippers). *Superted* was a Welsh language animated television series that first aired on 1 November 1982 on the Welsh television channel S4C. Later dubbed into English, the series was picked up by the BBC and was first shown the following year. BBC1 1983-86. In 1990 a brief series *The Further Adventures of Superted* made for the American market and voiced by US actors, was also shown on BBC1.

Surgical Spirit Nichola McAuliffe (Dr Sheila Sabatini), Duncan Preston (Dr Jonathan Haslam). Sitcom created by Peter Learmouth. Sheila Sabatini is a hard-working surgeon at Gillies Hospital. She begins a relationship with her anaesthetist Jonathan Haslam and much of the comedy revolves around their domestic circumstances. ITV 1989-95.

Surprise, Surprise Surprising members of the public with long-held wishes and reuniting them with long-lost loved ones was the order of the day. The concept of the first series had been to film 'surprising' and often odd items of the type previously seen in *Game for a Laugh* - the format was not successful. However, the final item in the final show of the first series featured a successful 'surprise' reunion and executive producer Alan Boyd changed the format slightly, so all items in subsequent series involved 'surprises' rather than just being 'surprising'. Hosted by Cilla Black, produced by London Weekend Television. Christopher Biggins was the original co-host, a role later occupied by Bob Carolgees. In some series, Gordon Burns presented the "SearchLine" segment, which advertised information of missing people. Cilla introduced and closed each show by singing the theme song, written by Kate Robbins and often imitated by Cilla impersonators (Kate being the best Cilla impersonator of all), which began *The more the world is changing, the more it stays the same...* A different song was used for later series: "Reaching out! Holding hands, Reliving Memories... Life is Full, Full of Surprises...And the nicest surprise in my life, is you!" ITV 1984-2001.

Survival Long-running wildlife series created by Aubrey Buxton and narrated by Peter Scott (1909-89 - son of Arctic explorer Robert Falcon Scott) and David Bellamy. Originally consisted of 30 minute episodes but 60 minute specials became the order of the day often narrated by celebrities such as Sean Bean, Richard Briers, Rory Bremner, Ian Holm, Andrew Sachs, Brian Cox, Rolf Harris, Dennis Waterman, Rula Lenska, Toyah Willcox, Robert Powell, Tony Robinson, Diana Rigg and Gaby Roslin. ITV 1961-2001. Some of the almost a thousand editions have been repeated on Channel 4 in recent years and the name has been revived in 2010 with *Survival with Ray Mears* (born Kenley, Surrey 7 February 1964) on ITV, although the British woodsman is often in shot unlike the previous narrators.

Survivor Sixteen contestants were marooned on the island of Pulau Tiga and were split into two tribes. They completed in challenges and schemed against each other. The format was based on an earlier American format. Charlotte Hobrough won the first series. Despite the disappointing performance of the first series, ITV commissioned a second series with some changes. Presenters Mark Austin and John Leslie were replaced by Channel 4 cricket presenter Mark Nicholas. There were twelve contestants instead of sixteen and the show was scheduled in a later time slot. The second series was set in Panama, in the Bocas Del Toro area, not in the Pearl Islands, and Jonny Gibb won. The ratings remained low and the show was subsequently cancelled. ITV 2001-02.

Survivors Carolyn Seymour (Abby Grant), Ian McCulloch (Greg Preston), Lucy Fleming (Jenny Richards), Denis Lill (Charles Vaughan), Talfryn Thomas (Tom Price), Chris Tranchell (Paul Pitman), Michael Gover (Arthur Russell), Terry Scully and Hugh Walters (Vic Thatcher), Hana Maria Pravda (Emma Cohen), John Abineri (Hubert Goss), Gordon Salkilld (Jack Wood), Eileen

Helsby (Charmian Wentworth), John Hallet (Barney), Richard Heffer (Jimmy Garland), Myra Frances (Anne Tranter), Julie Neubert (Wendy), Stephen Dudley (John Millon), Tanya Ronder and Angie Stevens (Lizzie Willoughby), Brian Peck (Dave Long), Peter Duncan (Dave), Sally Osborn and Anna Pitt (Agnes), Lorna Lewis (Pet Simpson), Celia Gregory (Ruth Anderson), William Dysart (Alec Campbell), Edward Underdown (Frank Garner). Science fiction series created by Terry Nation. The survivors of a virus that has decimated the world's population struggle to rebuild civilization and establish a new world order. BBC1 1975-77. The series was remade in 2008 and broadcast on BBC1, with Julie Graham and Paterson Joseph taking over the leading roles of Abby Grant and Greg Preston respectively and Max Beesley playing Tom Price. Other actors included Freema Agyeman (Jenny Walsh), Zoe Tapper (Dr Anya Raczynski), Nikki Amuka-Bird (Samantha Willis) and Phillip Rhys (Al Sadiq).

Sutherland's Law Iain Cuthbertson played the Procurator Fiscal John Sutherland in a small Scottish town. The theme tune was *The Land of the Mountain and the Flood* by Hamish MacCunn. BBC1 1973-76

Swapheads Two contestants swapped specialist subjects at the start and then had two days to bone up, with the help of an outside expert and access to specialist books, CD-ROM and the Internet. They then faced ten questions, worth between one and ten points (the questions being rated in order of difficulty by the opponent), and the contestant with the most points won. Questionmaster Johnny Ball appeared as a disembodied head on a television screen. *Five* 2002. See *Don't Call Me Stupid.*

Sweeney, The John Thaw (Det Inspector Jack Regan), Dennis Waterman (Det Sgt George Carter). Drama series created by Ian Kennedy Martin focusing on two members of the Flying Squad, a branch of the Metropolitan Police specialising in tackling armed robbery and violent crime in London, operating under the watchful eye of DCI Frank Haskins (played by Garfield Morgan). George always referred to Regan as 'Guv' while on duty. A typical scene would see Jack and George breaking into a room with the villain in bed with his moll and offer the advice "get your trousers on – you're nicked" – at least that is the way that every impersonator of the day remembers it! The programme's title derives from Sweeney Todd, which is Cockney rhyming slang for 'Flying Squad'. The catchy theme tune was composed by Harry South. Two feature films, *Sweeney!* (1977) and *Sweeney 2* (1978) were made. ITV 1975-78. See *Armchair Theatre.*

Sweet Sixteen Penelope Keith (Helen Walker), Christopher Villiers (Peter Morgan), Joan Blackham (Jane), Mike Grady (Dr Ballantine), Matthew Solon (James Walker), Victor Spinetti (Ken Green). Sitcom written by Douglas Watkinson. Helen Walker is a 41-year-old businesswoman who runs a successful building firm, Carrington & Daughter. Her life is suddenly turned upside down when she falls in love with Peter Morgan, a man 16 years younger than herself. One series of six episodes were made. BBC1 1983.

Sword Of Freedom Edmund Purdom (Marco del Monte), Adrienne Corri (Angelica), Roland Bartrop (Sandro) Martin Benson (Duke de Medici), Kenneth Hyde (Machiavelli), Monica Stevenson (Francesca). Adventure series about a Florentine painter, Marco del Monte, who engages in a continual uprising against the evil Medici rulers, showing a high degree of swordsmanship in the process. ITV 1958-61.

Sykes After a five year hiatus Eric Sykes and Hattie Jacques reprised their roles as twins, now living two doors down from their previous abode at the end-of-terrace No 28 Sebastopol Terrace. Eric also wrote all the episodes which co-starred Richard Wattis and Deryck Guyler in their previous roles although when Wattis died in 1975 Joy Harrington took over as their neighbour Melanie Rumbelow. Also making occasional appearances was Joan Sims as the local baker Madge Kettlewell who had a love interest in Eric. One of the most memorable episodes from this era was *Stranger* (1972) with Peter Sellers playing old lag Tommy Grando who turns up at the Sykes residence with plans to marry Hattie. This was a remake of the 1961 episode Sykes and A Stranger (now shown in colour). Other remakes included *Sykes and A Dream* where Hattie experiences vivid dreams and *Sykes*

and A Bath where Eric manages to trap his big toe in the bath tap. The series ended when Hattie died in 1980. BBC1 1972-79. The inspiration for this series was a 1971 BBC1 sketch series starring Eric and Hattie, *Sykes and a Big, Big Show* with musical interludes by Ian Wallace. See also *Sykes and A* and Eric's entry in the comedy section

Sykes and A......... Iconic sitcom written by Eric Sykes, Johnny Speight, John Antrobus and Spike Milligan which first portrayed Eric Sykes and Hattie Jacques as the brother and sister living at Sebastopol Terrace, East Acton. Sixty episodes were made (including *Sykes and his Sister* - part of Christmas Night with the Stars broadcast on 25 December 1962) all having the prefix Sykes and A. Richard Wattis played neighbour Charles Brown for the first three series and Deryck Guyler played PC Wilfred 'Corky' Turnbull for Series 4-9). So convincing was the double act that many folk believed Eric and Hat were actually brother and sister in real life, some believing them to be married. BBC 1960-65. See also *Sykes* and Eric's entry in the comedy section

Taggart Mark McManus (Det Chief Insp Jim Taggart), Neil Duncan (Det Sgt Peter Livingstone), Iain Anderson (Jack McVitie). Long-running police drama created by Glenn Chandler and originally set and filmed in the area of Maryhill police station in Glasgow, Scotland. In 1987 the character of Mike Jardine (played by James MacPherson) was introduced, and when Neil Duncan left the series in 1989, his character was replaced by a new female sidekick, Jackie Reid (played by Blythe Duff). Jardine became the central character following McManus' death in 1994. When MacPherson left the series in 2002, his character was killed off, and replaced with DCI Matt Burke (played by Alex Norton). The series became more of an ensemble piece, following the addition of Colin McCredie as DC Stuart Fraser in 1994 and John Michie as DI Robbie Ross in 1998 although Burke remains a strong central character. The programme's theme music is *No Mean City* by Maggie Bell, formerly a member of Stone the Crows. Since the demise of *The Bill*, Taggart is the UK's longest continually running police drama series. ITV 1983-

Take Hart See *Vision On.*

Take It From Here Iconic radio comedy programme written by Frank Muir and Denis Norden and broadcast by the BBC between 1948 and 1960. Starring British comedian Jimmy Edwards and two Australian comic actors Joy Nichols and Dick Bentley, the series was born out of a 1947 radio series *Navy Mixture*, which gave a recently demobbed Edwards his first acting role. Initially the familiar characters were Dick Bentley's poet who always began his monologue with the strangulated cry "Oh Mavis!", and Joy's husky-voiced Miss Arundel, who interpreted every remark as a reference to her red-blooded fiancé, Gilbert. Wallas Eaton joined the crew for the second series and shows were typically divided into three spots: the opening 'stage patter', where issues such as Jim's waistline or Dick's cigarette advertising deal were discussed, a 'gimmick' sketch on a recent news event or a series of sketches on a particular topic (eg: country life, education or popular music) and finally a film parody. In 1950 a regular sketch *The Glums* was introduced and this had instant and lasting success. The premise of *The Glums* was the long engagement between Ron Glum and his long-term fiancée Eth. As a result of post-war austerity, long engagements were common in 1950s Britain. Each episode would start in the pub, with Mr Glum (played by Jimmy Edwards) telling the barman (played by Wallas Eaton) about the latest episode in the lives of Ron, Mr Glum's not-so-bright son (played by Dick Bentley), and Eth, a plain girl for whom Ron represented her only chance of marriage (played by Joy Nicholls, and from 1953 by June Whitfield). A short signature tune would herald a change of scene to the Glum's front room, where Ron and Eth would be sitting on the sofa. Eth would say, "Oh, Ron...!" — her catchphrase — and Ron would vacantly reply something like, "Yes, Eth?" and the week's story would begin in earnest. Singer Alma Cogan would contribute the housewifely noises of Mrs Glum, although she never had a speaking role as such in this part of the show. In 1959, Muir and Norden decided to move into writing for television, and the BBC brought in Barry Took and Eric Merriman to write the final season of TIFH. *The Glums* was revived for television in 1978 as part of *Bruce Forsyth's Big Night* programme and two series were later made by LWT with Ron Glum being played by Ian Lavender and Eth by Patricia Brake, while Edwards reprised the role of Pa Glum.

Take Me Robson Green (Jack Chambers), Beth Goddard (Kay Chambers), Daniel Webb (Doug Patton, as Danny Webb), Keith Barron (Don Chambers, Jack's father). A contemporary love story by Caleb Ranson. When Jack and his wife Kay leave their city apartment for an exclusive housing estate, they hope to save their ailing marriage. Hadleigh Corner is the rural idyll of their dreams and the newly-built house is the perfect symbol of their fresh start. At first, all is rosy; The villagers are warm and welcoming and the party invitations are flowing. Even their children seem more settled. But as Jack and Kay try to rebuild their relationship, they discover their new neighbours are anything but normal. ITV 2001.

Take Me Out Television dating game show, hosted by Paddy McGuinness. The format consists of a single man's attempt to impress thirty single women. Each woman has a light which she can turn off if she is unimpressed by the man. The man's aim is to convince as many women as possible to keep their lights on so that he can then choose from the women remaining the one that he wishes to take out on a date. If no lights are left on, then the man must leave the show without a date. The successful couples are taken on a date to Fernando's in Manchester (which is actually Club Bijou on Chapel Street), snippets of which is shown as part of the following week's show. Paddy's catchphrases include "No likey, no lightey" and "If you're turned off, turn off". ITV 2010-

Take The High Road Soap opera created by Don Houghton and produced by Scottish Television and set in the fictional village of Glendarroch (the real-life village of Luss on the banks of Loch Lomond) and the neighbouring parish of Auchtarne. It started in 1980 as an ITV daytime soap opera and was dropped by the British TV network in 1992. It continued to be produced by STV for a Scottish audience until it was cancelled in 2003. In 1995, its name was changed to just *High Road*. The soap was introduced as a replacement for *Garnock Way* which contained more or less all of the original characters of *High Road*. It, too, had spun off from an STV soap called *High Living*. There were a few themes in *High Road*, in line with stereotypical Scottish culture, namely, the idea of the rich female Laird who owned the town and the theme of religion which was always present. It also entertained the feeling that outsiders were simply not welcome into the small close knit community something which may up to a point exist in any small village. Perhaps one of the reasons it finally ended was the lack of continuity in plot-lines. The lead character Mrs Mack, for example, had been transformed from a traditional Presbyterian to some kind of party animal who enjoyed going to football matches. In a bid to stop the show going under, Andy Cameron, a well known Scottish comedian was introduced to the show. However, this move failed to attract younger viewers and the departure of the main younger characters such as the Mackays did not help. Although young relationships and characters were always present and bizarrely enough not always Scottish. Cast members in alphabetical order included: Iain Agnew (Bob Taylor), Joan Alcorn (Lorna Seton), Derek Anders (David Blair), Georgine Anderson (Joyce Cameron), Iain Andrew (Victor Kemp), Bill Armour (Hamish McNeil), Caroline Ashley (Fiona Cunningham / Ryder), Gary Bakewell (Mark Torrance), David Bannerman (Father Brendan), Ginni Barlow (Gladys Aitken / Lachlan), Frederick Bartman (Klaus Meier), Jonathan Battersby (Tom Clifton), Bridget Biagi (Helen Blair), Leigh Biagi (Beth Anderson), Norman Bird (Roger Primrose), Stewart Bishop (P.C. Graham McPhee), Ian Bleasdale (Joe Reilly), Freddie Boardley (Malky Wilson), Michael Browning (Sir John Ross-Gifford), Steven Brown (Donald Lachlan), James Bryce (Crawford - the headmaster), Trudy Bryce (Irene Lamont), Harriet Buchan (Miss Symonds), Jim Byars (Graeme B. Hogg), Juliet Cadzow (Sarah Lindsey), Doreen Cameron (Sadie McDonald), Robin Cameron (Eddie Ramsay), Walter Carr (Willie Stewart), Fiona Chalmers (Jean Kennedy), Jimmy Chisholm (Jimmy Blair), Cedar Chozam (Kalsang), Madeleine Christie (Lady William Ross-Gifford), Martin Cochrane (Alan McIntyre), Richard Conlon (Dr. Andy Sharpe), James Copeland (Jamie Stewart), James Cosmo (Alex Geddes), Carol Ann Crawford (Alison Lambert), Alan Cumming (Jim Hunter - wood-cutter), Patrick Daly (Father Joseph Houston), Marjorie Dalziel (Nan Anderson), Joyce Deans (Jennifer 'Fraser'), Brown Derby (Sir William Fleming), Donald Douglas (Peter Cunningham), Alan Dunbar (Donald Lachlan (as baby), Lucy Durham-Matthews (Kate Blair), Michael Elder (Dr. Alexander Wallace), Ewen Emery (Willie Gillespie), Catriona Evans (Sally McGann), Kern Falconer (Colin Begg), Jackie Farrell (Jockie McDonald), Jean Faulds (Jean McTaggart), Jeannie Fisher (Morag Stewart / Kerr), Lesley Fitz-Simons (Sheila Lamont / Ramsay), Bernard Gallagher (Lord Strathmorris), Jenni Giffen (Jean Semple), Jacqueline Gilbrook (Susan Duncan), Clive Graham (Douglas Dunbar), Richard Greenwood (Eric Ross-Gifford), Joseph Greig (Hugh Robbie), Sarah Gudgeon (Kitty McIvor), Gwyneth Guthrie (Mrs Mary Mack), Ingrid Hafner (Jane Steedman), Johanna Hargreaves (Sandra Blair), Mike Hayward (Alun Morgan), Vivien Heilbron (Kay Grant), Martin Heller (Mr. Cochrane - father of Marion), Bill Henderson (Ken Calder), Stuart Herd (Donald Lachlan), Stephen Hogan (Nick Stapleton), Gary Hollywood (Dominic), George Howell (Colin Young), Alan Hunter (Greg Ryder), Frederick Jaeger (Max Langemann), Charles Jamieson (Ruari Galbraith), Ray Jeffries (Dan Lamont), Tamara Kennedy (JoannaSimpson/Ross-Gifford), Paul Kermack (Archie Menzies), Anne Kidd (Moira Reilly), Teri Lally (Carol McKay/Wilson), Fay Lenore (Mrs. Russell - Sneddon's housekeeper), Jimmy Logan (Captain Robert Groves), Derek Lord (Davie Sneddon), Edith MacArthur (Elizabeth Cunningham), Gordon MacArthur (Michael Ross), James MacDonald (Sergeant Murray), Una MacNab (Hazel Young), Rose McBain (Frances Kay), Hazel McBride (Jackie Ogilvie), Eileen McCallum (Isabel Blair/Morgan), Bridget McCann (Heather McNeil), Ian McCulloch (Derek Conway), Joseph McFadden (Gary McDonald), Alan McHugh (PC Tony Piacentini), Ellen McIntosh (Lady Strathmorris), David McKail (Councillor Robert Watt), Gillian McNeill (Lynne McNeil), Lawrie McNicol (Harry Shaw), Micky McPherson (Scott Logan), Briony McRoberts (Sam Hagen), Janet Michael (Maisie Forbes), Julie Miller (Claire Millar/Kerr), Morgan Miller (Baby Sadie McDonald), Primrose Milligan (Mrs. Woods), Alec Monteath (Dougal Lachlan), Alexander Morton (Andy Semple), Joe Mullaney (Willie Gillespie), Chic Murray (Sojer Johnny), John Murtagh (Tam Logan), Anne Myatt (Mairi McNeil), Hector Nichol (Fraser Ramsay), Diana Olsson (Mrs. Galbraith), Glyn Owen (Paul Cassell), Ron Paterson (Sorry Watson), Stewart Preston (Sam Scanlon), Shonagh Price (Sarah McDonald), Lizzy Radford (Marion Cochrane), Peter Raffan (Mark Ritchie), Barbara Rafferty (Alice McEwan/Taylor), Hilary Reynolds (Kathleen Sneddon), Peter Richey (Drew Sneddon), Mary Riggans (Effie McInnes/McDonald), Natalie Robb (Trish McDonald), Beth Robens (Chrissie McAlpine), Andrew Robertson (Leslie Maxwell), Graeme Robertson (P.C. Douglas Kirk), Thelma Rogers (Lily Taylor), Muriel Romanes (Alice McEwan/Taylor), Sean Scanlan (Oggie Wilson), Michael Sheard (Nikki Zaharoff), Kevin Shearer (Donald Lachlan), Leon Sinden (George Carradine), Jay Smith (Peter Craig), John Stahl (Tom Kerr, 'Inverdarroch'), Ian Stewart (Jock Campbell), Irene Sunters (Maggie Ferguson), Judith Sweeney (Sally Shaw), William Tapley (Phineas ('Fin') North), James Telfer (Lecturer, Sheila Ramsay's lover), Marjorie Thompson (Grace Lachlan), Anne Marie Timoney (Judith Crombie), Robert Trotter (Obadiah Arthur Murdoch), Terry Vale (Victor Spinetti), Anita Vettesse (Louise Boyd), Ian Wallace (Robert Forsyth), Derek Waring (Harry Somers), Keith Warwick (Nigel Jenkins), Jan Waters (Lady Margaret Ross-Gifford), Kenneth Watson (Brian Blair), Amanda Whitehead (Emma Aitken), Frank Wylie (Fergus Jamieson), John Young (Reverend Ian McPherson), Paul Young (Reverend Gerald Parker).

Take Three Girls Angela Down (Avril), Liza Goddard (Victoria), Susan Jameson (Kate). Comedy drama series written by Charlotte Bingham, Terence Brady and Hugo Charteris following the lives of three girls, cello-playing Victoria, single mother Kate and Cockney art student Avril, sharing a flat in 'Swinging' London. For the second series, the characters of Kate and Avril were replaced by journalist Jenny and American psychology graduate Lulie (played by Carolyn Seymour and Barra Grant). The theme music *Light Flight,* by the British folk rock group Pentangle, was a British chart hit in 1970. BBC1 1969-71. A four-episode sequel *Take Three Women*, showing the original characters at a later stage in their lives, was shown on BBC2 in 1982.

Take Your Pick As with *Double Your Money*, the other very popular quiz show of the day, *Take Your Pick*, was adapted from an earlier Radio Luxembourg quiz of the same name. It aired shortly before *Double Your Money* in 1955 and was therefore the first British game show to offer cash prizes. Presented by New Zealand-born Michael Miles (1919-71), the show began with a "Yes-No Interlude" (in which contestants were required to answer a series of questions without using the words "yes" or "no" for one minute or be gonged off stage by po-faced Alec Dane). The second half of the show consisted of the genial but forceful host offering a sum of money to obtain a key from the successful contestants who scored highest in the "Yes-No Interlude". A box number would then be selected and opened and the contestant would receive the contents unless they had already accepted the offered amount. There was always a star prize and three booby prizes among the more usual washing machines and sets of golf clubs and the key to box No 13 was sometimes lucky and sometimes not so lucky. Bob Danvers-Walker was the announcer and Harold Smart the organist who played a well known jingle after the boxes were opened. When the series ended in 1968 Michael hosted a short-lived show of similar nature entitled *Wheel of Fortune* (not related to the gameshow highlighted below). Both Michael and Hughie Green often engaged in light-hearted references to the other during the introductions, often referring to each other as 'father'. The original series ran from 1955 to 1968 but was revived in 1992 with Des O'Connor as host John Sachs and Steve Jones as announcers and Jodie Wilson (later to become Des's wife), Gillian and Gail Blakeney, Sarah Matravers, Sasha Lawrence and Debbie Flett as hostesses. A one-off show hosted by Ant and Dec was broadcast in 2005 as part of their Gameshow Marathon. ITV 1955-68; 1992-98; 2005.

Takeover Bid Game show vehicle for Bruce Forsyth ably assisted by Claire Sutton. Each contestant had to answer Forsyth's Fact or Fib? to win up to 4 stars in order to proceed to the Crazy Cryptics round and ultimately to Star Spin to win the star prize (usually a holiday). Bruce would invariably try to kid the contestants by showing opposite emotions in response to the fact or fib answers, for instance "Aaaahhh - you're absolutely.....right!" or, "Ha ha! You're absolutely wrong!" Every one of the 28 shows began with Bruce attempting to throw his hat and umbrella onto a hat-stand, always failing miserably. BBC1 1990-91

Taking the Flak Martin Jarvis (David Bradburn), Bruce Mackinnon (Harry Chambers), Damian O'Hare (Rory Wallace), Rhashan Stone (Jeremy Morris), Lucy Chalkley (Samantha Cunninham Fleming), Doon Mackichan (Jane Thomason), Joanna Brookes (Margaret Hollis), Kobna Holdbrook-Smith (Joyful Sifuri). Comedy drama series created by Tira Shubart, Jon Rolph and Sandra Jones. Set in the fictional African republic of Karibu which unwittingly becomes the main front in a new superpower clash. A team of BBC journalists arrive from London to report on the war. BBC2 2009

Tales From Dickens Basil Rathbone (Ebenezer Scrooge), Robert Morley (Mr Micawber), Irene Handl (Mrs Micawber), Harry Fowler (Sam Weller), William Russell (David Copperfield), Martin Stephens (David Copperfield), Barbara Ogilvie (Peggotty), June Laverick (Dora Spenlow), John Salew (Pickwick). 14-episode drama series based on the works of Charles Dickens. Each episode was narrated by Fredric March. ITV 1958-59.

Tales of Para Handy, The Gregor Fisher (Para Handy), Rikki Fulton (Dan Macphail), Sean Scanlan (Dougie), Andrew Fairlie (Sunny Jim). An adaptation of the famous tales of Neil Munro's. This time, the stories were set in the 1930s, but otherwise the style was much the same as the earlier adventures. BBC1 1994-95. See also *Para Handy - Master Mariner* and *The Vital Spark*.

Tales Of The Riverbank Originally shown at 5pm in its own slot but moved as part of the *Watch With Mother* slot in 1963, this children's series featured real animals and related the adventures of two friends; Hammy (a hamster) and Roderick (a tiny white

rat). Both animals lived along a riverbank and shared adventures with their neighbours - a guinea pig, a raccoon, a squirrel, a chipmunk, a frog, a toad, and various weasels and skunks. The stars of the show were shown moving around in miniature boats, cars, balloons and airplanes and their homes were fully furnished with animal size furniture. The fifteen minute episodes were filmed at double the normal speed to allow the camera to slow down the movements of the animals. Narration for each story was provided by Johnny Morris. BBC 1960-64

Tales of The Unexpected Originally called *Roald Dahl's Tales of The Unexpected* each episode stood alone and had its own cast, and for two seasons each was introduced by Dahl himself from a fireside arm-chair. He took a back seat when most of the stories coming forward were based on the work of other writers, all sharing the common theme of having a sting in the tail. The series introduced by sinister fairground music playing over the gyrations of a silhouetted female siren was an instant hit and clocked up a total of 112 episodes. ITV 1979-88.

Talking Telephone Numbers Game show created by Steven Knight, Mike Whitehill and David Briggs. Originally hosted by Emma Forbes and Phillip Schofield, Emma was replaced by Claudia Winkleman for the final series. The convoluted format basically boiled down to celebrities and guests performing acts to find a way to generate a random number. When five numbers were revealed, viewers were invited to call in if these numbers matched the last five digits of their telephone number. Three questions were then asked and a jackpot of up to £25,000 was at stake. The series is probably more notable for the television debut of Charlotte Church (singing Pie Jesu) towards the end of its run. ITV 1994-97. See *Magic Numbers*.

Tandoori Nights Saeed Jaffrey (Jimmy Sharma), Tariq Yunus (Alaudin), Shelley King (Bubbly), Andrew Johnson (Noor), Zohra Sehgal (Gran), Rita Wolf (Asha), Roly Lamas (Gazloo), Badi Uzzaman (Rashid). Sitcom written by Farrukh Dhondy, Philip Martin, H.O. Nazareth, Barry Simner and Meera Syal. Jimmy Sharma is the owner of "Jewel in the Crown Tandoori Restaurant" in Brick Lane, East London. His rival is the restaurant across the street "The Far Pavilions", owned by one of his former waiters. C4 1985-87

Target Patrick Mower (Det Supt Steve Hackett). Mower had perfected his tough-guy persona as Cross in *Callan* but now portrayed an equally hard-hitting character in this drama series about a Hampshire regional crime squad. BBC1 1977-78.

Taxi Sid James (Sid Stone), Ray Brooks (Terry Mills), Bill Owen (Fred Cuddell). Comedy drama series created by Ted Willis. Sid and Terry are London cab drivers who share a room in a converted house. Fred was Sid's business partner in the first series but the original minor role of Terry came to the fore and by season two he was co-starring with Sid. The series was a great vehicle for the post-Hancock Sid James and introduced Ray Brooks as one of the finest young British actors in a role he was subsequently to make famous under various guises. BBC 1963-64.

Teachers Andrew Lincoln (Simon Casey - English), Adrian Bower (Brian Steadman – PE and Geography), Navin Chowdhry (Kurt McKenna - IT), Raquel Cassidy (Susan Gately - Psychology), Nina Sosanya (Jenny Paige - English), Tamzin Malleson (Penny Neville - English), James Lance (Matt Harvey - English), Shaun Evans (J P Keating – Modern Foreign Languages), Vicky Hall (Lindsay Pearce - Biology), Lee Williams (Ewan Doherty - English), Matthew Horne (Ben Birkett – Religious Education). Sitcom created by Tim Loane. The first three series were set in the fictional Summerdown Comprehensive, which merges with another school in the fourth series to form Wattkins School. The series was filmed at the former Merrywood school, and other locations around Bristol, England. C4 2001-04

TECX Rob Spendlove (Chris Tierney), Urbano Barberini (Fabio Cavalcanti), Ulrike Schwarz (Anna Holz), Jenny Agutter (Kate Milverton). Drama series revolving around a Brussels-based detective agency, owned by Kate Milverton, with English,

German, and Italian detectives all working together on international cases. ITV 1990.

Teenage Kicks Sitcom co-written by Ade Edmondson and Nigel Smith; originally a series on BBC Radio 2 between January 6 and February 10 2007 before transferring to television in 2008. Vernon (Edmondson) is a former front man for a punk rock band called "The Plague". After living off his wife for the last twenty years and spending most of his time in the pub, the two divorce, and Vernon is forced to move into a student flat occupied by his children Max (Ed Coleman) and Milly (Laura Aikman), as well as their flatmate David (Jonathan Chan-Pensley). Vernon believes that moving in with them will reignite his former youthful passions but his offspring merely find him an embarrassment and his best friend and former Plague member Bryan (Ben Elton) appears to have "Sold-out", now working as a deputy head teacher of a primary school and happily married. ITV 2008.

Telebugs, The One of animation studio Telemagination first big productions. The title characters were three cute-as-a-modem robots created by Professor Reginald Brainstain: CHIP (Co-Ordinated Hexadecimal Information Processor), SAMANTHA (Solar-Activated Micro Automated Non-InTerference-Hearing-Apparatus) and BUG (Binary Unmanned Gamma-camera). They were programmed to help people in need and had TV sets where their heads should be and a flying handy-cam 'dog' called MIC (Mobile Independent Camera) following them around. The Telebugs, and other characters, were voiced by Ron Moody and Suzy Westerby. ITV 1986.

Telegoons Short-lived but much-loved animated version of *The Goons*. Voiced by Harry Secombe, Peter Sellers and Spike Milligan and written by Eric Sykes, Spike Milligan and Larry Stephens, the series made use of archive radio programmes for its soundtrack although additional material was added. BBC 1963-64. See *The Goon Show*.

Teletubbies Tinky Winky (Dave Thompson), Dipsy (John Simmit), Laa-Laa (Nikky Smedley), Po (Pui Fan Lee). Created by Anne Wood and written by Andrew Davenport; the Teletubbies live in Teletubbyland with rabbits, talking flowers, a magic windmill and periscope-like voice-trumpets which surface to make announcements. Their home is the Tubbytronic Superdome, where they are looked after by a vacuum cleaner called Noo Noo. In descending order of size Tinky Winky is purple with a triangular aerial on his head. He is prone to falling over and became a gay icon due to his propensity to carry a handbag; Dipsy is green with a spike aerial protruding from the centre of his head. He is prone to sing 'Bptum, bptum, bptum, bptum'; Laa-Laa is yellow with a curly aerial and is constantly happy. She is the only female Teletubby; and Po is red with a loop aerial is excitable and prone to sing in Cantonese. All have Babygros on their stomachs which open to reveal televisions at certain times. Their diet consists of Tubby Custard and Tubby Toast. Also seen are a toy lion and a bear (voiced by Eric Sykes and Penelope Keith respectively). All is watched over by a baby framed in the corona of the sun. Toyah Wilcox provides the opening narration. Aimed at the under-five market as a learning tool (hence the repetitive nature of phrases and film) the series was often criticised by parents for teaching bad grammar but many experts felt that the formatting was an excellent introduction to life for pre-school children. The 1997 chart-topper 'Teletubbies Say Eh-Oh!' was a typical reference to the broken English of toddlers, Eh-Oh meaning Hello. The 335 episodes to date aired on BBC2 between 1997 and 2001 but are likely to be repeated for many more years.

Television Dancing Club The BBC's first effort in bringing dance music to our screens began on radio in 1941. Victor Marlborough Silvester, born Wembley, London, 25 February 1900, hosted this show, then known as *BBC Dance Club*. Silvester won the World Ballroom Championships in 1922 partnering Phyllis Clarke, and a few days later married Dorothy Newton. In 1935 Victor formed his own five-piece band, later enlarged and named Victor Silvester and his Ballroom Orchestra, whose first record, *You're Dancing on My Heart* (by Al Bryan and George M. Meyer) was to become his signature tune. In subsequent years he became indelibly associated with the catch-phrase "slow, slow, quick-quick-slow" – a rhythm of the slow foxtrot. Victor's band became resident when *BBC Dance Club* transferred to television

in 1948 as *Television Dancing Club*, and he also hosted for much of its run until first Patti Morgan and then Rosalie Ashley took over. Another leading dancer of the day Peggy Spencer, who was to later have such an influence on *Come Dancing* through her dance schools, was frequently featured dancing with her husband Frank. In 1958, Victor published his autobiography 'Dancing is My Life'. He died 14 August 1978. BBC 1948-64. See also *Come Dancing*.

Telford's Change Peter Barkworth (Mark Telford), Hannah Gordon (Sylvia Telford), Keith Barron (Tim Hart). Drama series produced by Mark Shivas; based around the mid-life crisis of international bank manager Mark Telford and the reluctance of his wife Sylvia to join him in a new life running a small bank in Dover; preferring to stay behind in London to form a relationship with Tim Hart. BBC1 1979

Telly Addicts Light-hearted but very competitive quiz show between two families of couch potatoes. Hosted by Noel Edmonds the format changed in 1994 when Charles Collingwood was recruited to make barbed comments while giving the scores and the BBC dropped the 'family' prerequisite so teams of four could be made up by work-mates and friends. BBC1 1985-98.

Tempo Originally hosted by the Earl of Harewood, *Tempo* was an arts programme put out as a response to the BBC's *Monitor*. Other presenters included Clive Goodwin, Leonard Maguire and David Mahlowe. Film director Mike Hodges directed and produced the programme between 1965 and 1966. ITV 1961-67.

Ten Mile Menu Filmed in different locations around the UK, two teams composed of a professional chef and a celebrity are set the task of creating a three-course menu that epitomises that day's location. Both teams set out from their kitchen, and must find the best local produce to create their meal from. However all their ingredients must be sourced from within a ten mile radius of the kitchen. Once the meals have been prepared, they are judged by a panel composed of local residents, who decide which is the winning team. The professional chefs were Jason Atherton, Paul Rankin, Ed Baines, Richard Corrigan, Galton Blackiston, Daniel Galmiche, Lawrence Keogh, James Tanner, Aldo Zilli and Oliver Rowe. The celebrities were Charley Boorman, Jenni Falconer, Ali Bastian, Ricky Groves, Sherrie Hewson, Rowland Rivron, Colin Jackson, Phil Tufnell, Linda Robson and Claire Sweeney. The voiceover was added by Caroline Quentin. ITV 2010.

10 O'Clock Live Satirical television series that took a light-hearted but cutting look at topical issues; presented by Charlie Brooker, Jimmy Carr, Lauren Laverne and David Mitchell. The series was commissioned following the success of Channel 4's *Alternative Election Night*, fronted by the same four presenters in May 2010. The show's theme tune was "Bernie" by The Jon Spencer Blues Explosion. C4 2011.

Tenko Stephanie Beacham (Rose Millar), Stephanie Cole (Dr Beatrice Mason), Bert Kwouk (Major Yamauchi), Ann Bell (Marion Jefferson), Renee Asherson (Sylvia Ashburton), Claire Oberman (Kate Norris), Jeananne Crowley (Nellie Keene), Jean Anderson (Joss Holbrook), Veronica Roberts (Dorothy Bennett), Louise Jameson (Blanche Simmons), Rosemary Martin (Verna Johnson), Nigel Harman (Timmy), Patricia Lawrence (Sister Ulrica), Elizabeth Chambers (Mrs Domenica Van Meyer). Drama series created by Lavinia Warner. Following the Japanese invasion of Singapore in 1942 the expatriate women of Britain and Holland are torn from their menfolk and imprisoned in makeshift holding camps. Tenko - meaning 'roll-call' in Japanese - tells the story of one such group of women. Appointed head of the women is Marion Jefferson, a colonel's wife. Around her are the likes of Rose Millar, a rape victim; Beatrice Mason, an uncompromising doctor; nurses Kate Norris and Nellie Keene; ageing academic Joss Holbrook and Dorothy Bennett, who, having lost her husband and child, turns to prostitution with the guards. Other characters include flighty Cockney Blanche Simmons and the contrasting Verna Johnson with her superior lady-like ways. The formidable Sister Ulrica is leader of the Dutch section and the deplorably selfish Mrs Van Meyer is another leading character. A young Nigel Harman makes his television debut in the series. BBC1 1981-84.

Terrahawks Childrens science fiction Supermacromation series created by Gerry Anderson. The Terrahawks were an elite troup of dare-devils who constantly saved the Earth from alien invasion in the year 2020. Headed by Dr Tiger Ninestein (voice of Jeremy Hitcher), the ninth clone of Austrian -American scientist Gerhard Stein, the Terrahawks consisted of ace pilot Capt Mary Falconer (voice of Denise Bryer); Lt Hawkeye (Jeremy Hitcher) an American with computer-aided vision; Lt Hiro (Jeremy Hitcher), the squad's computer expert; and Capt Kate Kestrel (Anne Ridler), a part-time pop singer. The team work out of Hawknest, a secret location in South America. Their main adversary is the cackling prune-faced android, Zelda (Denise Bryer), and her equally hideous allies from the planet Guk. These include her good-for-nothing son Yung Star (Ben Stevens) and her vindictive twin sister Cy-Star (Anne Ridler). Zelda aims to take over the planet with the use of her cuboid robots and other agents like Yuri the space bear and MOID (Master of Infinite Disguise). The Terrahawks in their Hawkwing spaceship are assisted by round robots called Zeroids, controlled while on Earth by Sgt Major Zero (Windsor Davies) and when in space by Space Sgt 101 (Ben Stevens). Hudson (Ben Stevens) the Rolls Royce was always at hand to create mischief. ITV 1983-86.

Terry and June Terry Scott (Terry Medford), June Whitfield (June Medford), Reginald Marsh (Sir Dennis Hodge), Rosemary Frankau (Beattie), Terence Alexander, Tim Barrett and John Quayle (Malcolm). A reworking of the *Happy Ever After* format with Terry and June just moved to Purley, south-east of London. Aunt Lucy and the mynah bird had disappeared, as had the occasionally visiting daughters. Terry and June now mixed with a friendly next-door neighbour, Beattie, Terry's chatty work colleague, Malcolm, and their gruff boss Sir Dennis Hodge. BBC1 1979-87

TFI Friday Light entertainment show, produced by Ginger Productions, written by Danny Baker and hosted by the founder of Ginger, Chris Evans, for the first 5 series; the 6th and final series being hosted by various guest presenters. Officially, the title stood for "Thank Four It's Friday", a play on the popular phrase "Thank God it's Friday", however the show was popularly known as "Thank Fuck It's Friday", as was clearly implied. Regular features included **Freak or Unique** - where five people would be waiting outside the studio, of whom three would be selected to show off a special if freakish talent. A running gag was the 'Incredibly Tall Old Lady' who would always be waiting outside the studio but was never nominated (mainly because she was clearly standing on a box!), **Baby Left Baby Right** where a small child was placed on a cushion and the guest was asked which way it might fall, **What Does The Fat Bloke Do?** Where an overweight man was asked about his occupation, before dancing and leaving!, and **Comment From The Cafe** where Rastafarian Cedric, the owner of a local café, pontificated on various topics in ham fashion. Cedric became famous for his catchphrase "Helloooooooooo!" The show's producer, Will MacDonald, would also feature heavily by demonstrating a trick that could be performed using items commonly found in a pub in the **Will: Pub Genius** spot as well as being the brunt of the running gag where everyone in the bar would point their fingers at him and chant 'Wiiilll' very demonstratively. The show's theme tune was Ron Grainer's theme from *Man in a Suitcase*. C4 1996-2000. See *Who Wants To Be A Millionaire?* and *OFI Sunday*.

T4 A scheduling slot, targeted at the 16-34 age group, on Channel 4 from about 09:00 until 14:00 Saturday and 17:00 on Sundays. It also airs on weekdays in the school holidays. *T4* began in 1998 and includes an annual summer festival, *T4 on the Beach*, in the resort of Weston-super-Mare, which includes top flight musical acts. *T4* presenters have included: Fran Lee (1998–99), Omar Gurnah (1998–99), Dermot O'Leary (1998–2001), Ben Shephard (1999–2000), Margherita Taylor (1999–2001), Vernon Kay (2000–05), June Sarpong (2000–07), MC Harvey (2003–04), Simon Amstell (2003–06), Anthony Crank (2004–05), Alex Zane (2007–08), Alexa Chung (2008–09), Dave Berry (2006–07), Steve Jones (2003-10) and Miquita Oliver (2006-10). Current presenters are: Rick Edwards (2007-), Jameela Jamil (2009-), Nick Grimshaw (2010-), Georgie Okell (2010-) and Matt Edmondson (2011-).

Thank Your Lucky Stars Saturday evening pop show originally presented by Keith Fordyce but always associated with its host of five years, Brian Matthews (replaced by Jim Dale for its final run). A popular segment of the show was 'spin-a-disc' a blatant steal from *Juke Box Jury* whereby a panel would vote on the merits of a latest release. It was this segment that gave us the 16-year-old office clerk Janice Nicholls in 1962. Her broad Black Country accent was memorable as she declared "oi'll give it foive" (a phrase that has remained in the public consciousness almost 50 years on.......well at least for the over-50s!). The programme was also famous for giving the world the first television look at The Beatles in February 1963. ITV 1961-66.

That Anthony Cotton Show Camp Corrie actor Anthony Cotton hosted this short-lived light, fluffy, upbeat, irreverent and gossipy daytime chat show. ITV 2007

That Mitchell and Webb Look Comedy sketch show starring David Mitchell and Robert Webb. Originally directed by David Kerr, who also directed Mitchell and Webb's previous television sketch show *The Mitchell and Webb Situation* (shown on Play UK in 2001), the third and fourth series are directed by Ben Gosling Fuller. Writers include Jesse Armstrong, James Bachman, Sam Bain, Olivia Colman, Toby Davies, Mark Evans, John Finnemore, Jason Hazeley, Simon Kane, David Mitchell, Joel Morris, Chris Pell, Jonathan Dryden Taylor and Robert Webb. The supporting cast includes James Bachman, Gus Brown, Abigail Burdess, Olivia Colman, Mark Evans, Sarah Hadland and Paterson Joseph. Sketches include: **Angel Summoner and BMX Bandit** - A pair of mismatched superheroes, one of whom can summon an awesomely powerful celestial horde while the other can only do stunts on his BMX.; **Chip and Pin** - Two separate pairs of entertainers, "Fish and Chip" and "Pin and Cushion". Chip (Mitchell) joins up with Pin (Webb) to form "Chip and Pin", with big plans for success. However, in the end they achieve no success at all, while Fish (Webb) and Cushion (Mitchell) end up teaming up and becoming famous. They even win the contract to star in advertisements for Chip and Pin!; **The Surprising Adventures of Sir Digby Chicken-Caesar** - Sir Digby (Webb) and his sidekick Ginger (Mitchell) believe that they are a pair of detectives in the style of Sherlock Holmes and Doctor Watson when in fact they are drunken tramps. They are so poor that they have to hum their own theme tune (Devil's Gallop), which is usually sung as the intrepid duo are escaping from a crime scene, and regularly fight each other for loose change. They believe that plots are constantly being hatched against them by their "nemesis" described as "some bastard who is presumably responsible". Henchmen of their nemesis turn up in the shape of the police or whoever stumbles in front of them. Sir Digby first appeared on radio in the show's precursor; *That Mitchell and Webb Sound* (Radio 4 2003-09) but was known then as Sir Digby Caesar-Salad; **Ted and Peter** - A pair of hard-drinking, chain-smoking snooker commentators who also first appeared on *That Mitchell and Webb Sound*. Ted Wilkes is played by David Mitchell and Peter DeCoursey by Robert Webb. **Colin and Ray** - Characters which first appear in series two, Colin (Webb) and Ray (Mitchell) are co-workers in the same office, although they have different jobs which tend to involve extraordinary plots. Colin works as a hostage negotiator, while Ray writes the plots to pornographic films; **Get Me Hennimore!** - A parody of classic sitcoms, each episode featuring Hennimore (Webb) being given an improbable task by his boss (Mitchell) which invariably ends in disaster due to Hennimore's often understandable confusion as the items and rooms he must not mix up actually look identical; and **Numberwang** - A parody of game shows, with a presenter played by Webb. BBC2 2006-

That Peter Kay Thing See Peter Kay's Phoenix Nights

That Uncertain Feeling Denis Lawson (John Aneurin Lewis), Sheila Gish (Mrs Gruffydd-Williams). Mini-series based on the Kingsley Amis novel about life and culture in a Welsh seaside town, in which a married librarian begins an affair with the bored wife of a local bigwig. The two stars began a relationship when meeting on set and eventually married. BBC2 1985

That Was The Week That Was Originally proposed to the BBC under the title *Saturday Night*, this late-night satirical review of current events (the first such show in Britain) built a huge audience, going from 3.5 million viewers on its opening night (November 24, 1962) to ten million by end of its first season (April 1963). The pilot was hosted by John Bird and David Frost took over for the show-proper. Other contributors included Willie Rushton, Bernard Levin, Roy Kinnear, Kenneth Cope, John Cleese and Lance Percival (who sang a topical calypso each week). Millicent Martin sang the theme song and a host of other topically written songs. Perhaps the most famous TW3 (as it was affectionately known) sketch, **What Is a Mum?** (aka "Mother's Day"), was written by Dennis Potter and David Nathan from an idea by Jack Rosenthal. "What Is a Mum?" depicted a housewife in terms of ad slogans: "She thinks every washday is a miracle. And since she adds the extra egg to everything except the bacon, she is probably constipated as well." TW3 would appear tame by today's standards but in the early 1960s it was groundbreakingly irreverent. The series was cancelled in late 1963, because, post-Profumo scandal, the General Election (which was not, in fact, held until October 1964) appeared to be in prospect and the show's bias was deemed unacceptable. BBC 1962-63.

That's Life Long-running consumer affairs programme conceived as a follow-up to *Braden's Week*. Esther Rantzen was promoted from reporter to host and immediately made the show her own. George Layton and Bob Wellings were Esther's original co-hosts and Cyril Fletcher joined in 1974, his 'odd odes' being an integral part of the diet of the show. Cyril also brought comic misprints to the attention of the public (a role later taken over by Mollie Sugden and Doc Cox). Richard Stilgoe provided topical songs (Victoria Wood also made regular appearances in this role) but it was Esther's ability to get the best out of the public in her 'out-and-about' jaunts that were the mainstay of the programme. All manner of oddities were portrayed including a talking dog who appeared to revel in reciting the word 'sausages' over and over. In 1984 the plight of two-year-old Ben Hardwicke was highlighted. Suffering from an incurable liver disease Ben died as organ donors were almost non-existent at this time. Marti Webb issued the Michael Jackson song Ben as part of the awareness campaign and it reached the top five in 1985. Other presenters of the show have included Kieran Prendiville, Glyn Worsnip, Paul Heiney, Chris Serle, Bill Buckley, Gavin Campbell, Michael Groth, Joanna Munro, John Gould, Maev Alexander, Kevin Devine, Scott Sherrin, Simon Fanshawe, Howard Leader, Adrian Mills and Grant Baynham. BBC1 1973-94.

That's My Boy Mollie Sugden (Ida Willis), Christopher Blake (Dr Robert Price). Sitcom written by Pam Valentine and Michael Ashton. Ida Willis takes residence as housekeeper to Dr Robert Price only to realise that the good doctor is her son given away for adoption at birth. ITV 1981-86. Comedian Jimmy Clitheroe also starred in a short-lived sitcom of the same name in 1963 where he played his famous naughty schoolboy role alongside Deryck Guyler and Gordon Rollings.

That's What I Call Television Saturday evening light entertainment show featuring a celebrity choosing clips of their favourite tv programmes of yesteryear. Hosted by Fern Britton the series often invited actors from classic bygone series to talk about their show's success. ITV 2009.

That's Your Funeral Bill Fraser (Basil Bulstrode), Raymond Huntley (Emanuel Holroyd), David Battley (Percy), Dave King (Charlie). Sitcom written by Peter Lewis revolving around a funeral parlour. A sort of forerunner of *In Loving Memory*. BBC1 1971. Bill Fraser reprised his role of funeral director Basil Bulstrode in a 1972 spin-off film.

Theatre Night Anthology series depicting classic plays including *Lady Windermere's Fan* (15 September 1985), *Trelawny of the Wells* (20 October 1985), *The Birthday Party* (21 June 1987), *The Master Builder* (15 May 1988), *The Rivals* (5 June 1988), *Arms and the Man* (16 April 1989), *The Winslow Boy* (30 April 1989), *Othello* (23 June 1990). BBC1 1985-90.

There's A Lot Of It About 1982 comedy sketch show - See *Q*

They Think It's All Over Comedy sports quiz that steals its title from the famous Kenneth Wolstenholme commentary just prior to Geoff Hurst scoring the fourth England goal in the 1966 World Cup final. Originally presented by Nick Hancock (replaced by Lee Mack in 2005), the two opposing captains were David Gower and Gary Lineker and resident comedians were Rory McGrath and Lee Hurst (later replaced by Jonathan Ross), each team of three being completed by a contemporary sports star. Phil Tuffnell and David Seaman replaced Gower and Lineker as team captains in 2003 and Ian Wright took over from David Seaman in 2004 whilst Boris Becker replaced Tufnell in 2005. BBC1 1995-2006

Thick Of It, The Satire based on the machinations of British governmental departments, first broadcast on BBC4 in 2005. Written and directed by Armando Iannucci, it stars Chris Langham and Peter Capaldi (Langham was replaced by Rebecca Front in series three after his much-publicised court case and subsequent imprisonment). The action is centred upon the fictitious Department of Social Affairs and Citizenship (formerly known as the Department of Social Affairs, prior to the reshuffle of episode five). Hugh Abbot (Langham) is a minister heading the department, who is continually trying to do his job, or rather look like he is doing his job, while under the watchful eye of Malcolm Tucker (Capaldi), Number 10's highly aggressive and domineering enforcer in the Alastair Campbell mode. Filmed with hand-held cameras to give it a mockumentary look and feel, the series has no laughter track and some of the dialogue is also improvised to add to the effect. The series transferred to BBC2 in 2006 and after repeats of the first two series a third series was broadcast in 2009 when Nicola Murray (Rebecca Front) replaced Hugh Abbot as minister. *In the Loop* was a 2009 spin-off film by the makers of the series, starring many members of the same cast, albeit in different roles.

Thicker Than Water Jean Kent (Aggie Plunkett), Roberta Rex (Vicki Eccles), Carolyn Moody (Janet Eccles), Jimmy Jewel (Jim Eccles), Jill Kerman (Carol Eccles). Sitcom written by Peter Robinson revolving around the troubled Eccles household. Freddie Frinton, who starred as Fred Holmes in the pilot show, died before the series started, and was replaced by Jimmy Jewel. BBC1 1968; 1969

Thin Blue Line, The Rowan Atkinson (Insp Raymond Fowler), Serena Evans (Sgt Patricia Dawkins), James Dreyfus (PC Kevin Goody), Mina Anwar (PC Maggie Habib), Rudolph Walker (PC Frank Gladstone), David Haig (DI Derek Grim), Kevin Allen (DC Kray), Mark Addy (DC Gary Boyle), Lucy Robinson (Mayoress Wickham). Sitcom written by Ben Elton centring around Gasforth police station. Insp. Fowler, the head of the station, is and old-fashioned, by-the-book policeman, scrupulously honest and totally dedicated both to the job in hand and to his team of uniformed officers. These comprise his desk sergeant, Patricia Dawkins, Fowler's girlfriend of 10 years standing; veteran of the force PC Gladstone, an unexcitable and rather pedestrian officer; the camp but hetero PC Goody; and Indian PC Maggie Habib, the level-headed, brightest one of the bunch. These uniformed officers clashed constantly with the other occupants of the station: the plain-clothed detectives, led by DI Grim. BBC1 1995-96.

Third Man, The Michael Rennie (Harry Lime), Jonathan Harris (Bradford Webster), Rupert Davies (Insp. Arthur Shillings), Naomi Chance (Janet). Although the series was based on characters in the novel *The Third Man* by Graham Greene and on the 1949 motion picture of the same name, the character of Harry Lime was vastly different. Harry was now an amateur sleuth travelling the globe to solve crimes while running various import/export businesses, specialising in art deals. He was assisted by his manservant Bradford Webster. Other regulars included a lady friend, Janet, and a policeman friend Arthur Shillings. The first 20 episodes were filmed at the Hollywood studios of 20th Century-Fox Film Corporation for the BBC and thereafter at Shepperton Studios, England. The series used the same popular theme tune (The Harry Lime Theme) from the feature film, played on the Zither by Anton Karas. BBC 1959-65.

This is England '86 Vicky McClure (Lol), Joe Gilgun (Woody), Andrew Shim (Milky), Thomas Turgoose (Shaun), Rosamund Hanson (Smell), Chanel Cresswell (Kelly), Danielle Watson (Trev), Andrew Ellis (Gadget), Michael Socha (Harvey), Perry Benson (Meggy), George Newton (Banjo), Johnny Harris (Mick), Hannah Walters (Trudy), Stephen Graham (Combo), Jo Hartley (Cynthia), Kriss Dosanjh (Mr Sandhu), Olivia Morgan (Bub), Jamie Taylor (Buloosweet), Joseph Dempsie (Higgy), Georgia May Foote (Gemma), Steve Brody (Richard), Rebecca Manley

(Babs). A four-episode spin-off of the film *This Is England*, set three years later, focusing on the mod revival scene instead of the skinhead subculture. Original director Shane Meadows helms the final two episodes and Tom Harper the first two. C4 2010.

This Is Your Life Long-running programme taking an intimate look at the life of someone with an interesting lifestyle, generally an established celebrity but sometimes focusing on deserving non-celebs. Eamonn Andrews was the host until his death in 1987 when he was replaced by Michael Aspel. Eamonn was in fact the first-ever victim, albeit as a makeshift stand-in, as Ralph Edwards, the presenter of the American version (which began in 1952) was originally chosen to host the inaugural show with Stanley Matthews as the target but unfortunately the footballing maestro caught wind of arrangements and so Eamonn was promoted from trainee presenter to the show's first star victim. Originally the show was transmitted live with Eamonn undergoing various elaborate disguises to get his target but several people refused to submit to the scrutiny, notably footballer Danny Blanchflower and novelist Richard Gordon (although he later relented), so the programme eventually lost some of its edge by being pre-recorded. BBC 1955-64; ITV 1969-94; BBC1 1994-2003. In 2007, Trevor McDonald surprised Simon Cowell in a one off special.

This Life Jack Davenport (Miles Stewart), Amita Dhiri (Djamila 'Milly' Nassim), Jason Hughes (Warren Jones), Andrew Lincoln (Edgar 'Egg' Cook), Daniela Nardini (Anna Forbes), Geoffrey Bateman (James Hooperman), David Mallinson (Michael O'Donnell), Cyril Nri (Graham Enamejowa), Ramon Tikaram (Ferdinand 'Ferdy' Garcia), Paul J. Medford (Paul), Greg Prentice (George), Charlotte Bicknell (Delilah), Steve John Shepherd (Jo), Gillian McCutcheon (the therapist). Drama series created by Amy Jenkins and Tony Garnett. The lifestyle of professional young Londoners, through the eyes of five housesharers, the slightly arrogant and homophobic ex public schoolboy, Miles; Milly, a hard-working perfectionist; Egg, Milly's somewhat sensitive boyfriend; the brash but witty Anna; and gay Welshman Warren, who although outwardly confident makes regular visits to a therapist. They reside at 13 Benjamin Street. Milly, Egg and Warren work at Moore, Spencer, Wright solicitors while Miles and Anna are court advocates. BBC2 1996-97.

This Morning Daytime magazine show hosted by Richard Madeley and Judy Finnegan between 1988 and 2001. The programme became synonymous with the husband and wife team to the extent that it was almost universally known as the Richard and Judy Show. When Richard and Judy departed the series in 2001, they were replaced by Coleen Nolan and Twiggy, with Fern Britton and John Leslie remaining as hosts on Fridays (a position that began in 1998). The show was presented by Fern Britton (between 1999 and 2009) and Phillip Schofield (2002 - present) with Ruth Langsford replacing Fern on Fridays and Eamonn Holmes filling in holiday gaps. In July 2009 Fern left the show and was replaced by Holly Willoughby in September 2009. Other presenters have included Caron Keating, Lorraine Kelly, Cat Deeley, Penny Smith and Gloria Hunniford. ITV 1988- See also *Richard & Judy*.

This Morning With Richard Not Judy Comedy series starring the double-act of Lee and Herring with much of the material rehashed from their earlier series *Fist of Fun* and *Lionel Nimrod's Inexplicable World*, albeit set in a chat show format. The title of the show was a satirical reference to ITV's *This Morning*. Kevin Eldon reprised two of his characters from *Fist of Fun*, Simon Quinlank the King of Hobbies and the false Rod Hull, jelly fanatic with a false arm and giant chin. Rod actually appeared in one episode shortly before he died. Other recurring themes were the talking orange (played by Paul Putner), When Insects Attack (A parody of the show *When Animals Attack!*, with a voice-over by Mark Gatiss in the guise of actor Greg Evigan), Trevor and Nathalie (A man with an extremely small face –actor Trevor Lock – and a woman called Nathalie would appear each episode in non-speaking roles as prop hands or extras), King or Queen of the Show, Pause for Thought for the Day (Kevin Eldon as the unusual priest), Roger Crowley the self-styled most evil man alive (played

by Roger Mann and based on notorious mystic Aleister Crowley) and Richard Herring's forlorn attempt to popularise the acronym of the show TMWRNJ in the style of Tiswas. BBC2 1998-99

This Week Long-running topical news magazine. Presenters included: Leslie Mitchell, René Cutforth, Michael Westmore, Ludovic Kennedy, Daniel Farson, Brian Connell, Alastair Burnet, Jonathan Dimbleby. Reporters included: Desmond Wilcox, James Cameron, Robert Kee, Jonathan Dimbleby, Llew Gardner, Bryan Gould and Jeremy Thorpe. ITV 1956-92. Between 1978 and 1986 the programme was entitled *TV Eye*.

Thomas and Sarah Spin-off of the award-winning historical drama *Upstairs Downstairs*, charting the lives, loves, and exploits of Thomas (John Alderton) the chauffeur and Sarah (Pauline Collins) the parlour maid as they try to strike it rich in Edwardian England after leaving the Bellamy household in 1910. ITV 1979.

Thomas the Tank Engine & Friends Children's series originally shown on ITV and narrated by Ringo Starr for the first two series between 1984 and 1986 and then Michael Angelis from Series 3 in 1991 to the present. The children's animation sticks faithfully to the Rev Wilbert Vere Awdry's classic stories of the 1940s. Star of the show is Thomas, the blue tank engine No 1. Joining Thomas on the fictional Island of Sodor (supposedly situated in the Irish Sea, between the Isle of Man and Barrow-in-Furness in Cumbria - in actual fact the Isle of Man constitutes the Church of England diocese of Sodor and Man) are Edward, another blue engine No 2; Henry, a green 3 engine; Gordon, a blue 4 engine; James the red mixed traffic engine No 5; Percy the green saddle tank engine No 6; Toby the brown tram engine No 7; Montague the green Great Western engine No 8 - affectionately known as duck because he waddles along; the twin black engines Donald (9) and Douglas (10); and Oliver the green No 11 engine. Thomas' carriages are Annie and Clarabel, and also seen are Daisy the diesel rail car, Diesel, a diesel engine, Terence the tractor, Harold the helicopter, Bertie the bus and another carriage named Henrietta. All operate under the instructions of Sir Topham Hat, better known as the Fat Controller, who, like all the human characters, is depicted as a static figurine. In 2003 the title became *Thomas and Friends* and the series is now broadcast on *Five*.

3@three The weekday magazine show is suitably entitled as it airs at 3pm and is hosted by three presenters permed from Fiona Phillips, Gloria Hunniford, Kelvin MacKenzie, Penny Smith, Carol Smillie, Andrea McLean and Mark Durden-Smith. ITV 2010.

Three Hungry Boys Hugh Fearnley Whittingstall challenged three marine biologists, Trevor, Thom and Tim, to live off the land in the islands off western Scotland, for a month without spending a single penny. C4 2010

Three In A Bed Reality show in which bed and breakfast owners throw open their doors and take turns to stay with one another - and pay what they consider fair for their stay. C4 2009- In Autumn 2010 the format changed from three to four couples and the series title became *Four In A Bed*.

Three Live Wires See *The Love of Mike*

Three Men In A Boat Griff Rhys Jones, Rory McGrath and Dara Ó Briain in an old wooden skiff re-traced the journey of Jerome K. Jerome from his book *Three Men in a Boat*. BBC2 2006. A follow-up two-parter, *Three Men In Another Boat*, shown in January 2008, saw the three amateur sailors sailing from London to the Isle of Wight in Griff's Undina to race against her sister ship, Josephine (both 45ft sloops, 50s vintage). Yet another follow-up two-parter, *Three Men in More Than One Boat*, shown in January 2009, saw the intrepid sailors in a variety of boats off the Cornwall coast culminating in a trip to the Scilly Isles and their ultimate destination atop the Bishop Rock Lighthouse. Subsequent series in what has become a brand include: *Three Men go to Ireland* (2009-10), *Three Men go to Scotland* (2010); and *Three Men go to Venice* (2011).

Three Of A Kind Comedy sketch show presented by Tracey Ullman, David Copperfield and Lenny Henry. BBC1 1981-83. A 1967 show of the same name was a showcase for the talents of Lulu, Mike Yarwood and Ray Fell.

3-2-1 Ted Rogers hosted the long-running quiz based on the Spanish *Uno, Dos, Tres*. Three married couples took part in the complex quiz, with even more complex cryptic clues. Resident comics Chris Emmet, Dougie Brown and Debbie Arnold were known as 'The Disrepertory Company' and the Brian Rogers' Connection was the supporting dance troupe. Ted Rogers' team of hostesses were known as 'The Gentle Secs'. The themed sketches would end with one of the protagonists reading out a clue by way of a riddle for the contestants to solve in order to gauge their prize. The couple remaining at the end had to unravel a final riddle, oft-repeated by Mr Rogers, to gauge their ultimate prize. The jackpot prize was usually a car and the booby-prize was a metal rubbish-bin, representing the show's robotic mascot Dusty Bin. ITV 1978-87.

Three Up, Two Down Michael Elphick (Sam Tyler), Angela Thorne (Daphne Trenchard), Lysette Anthony (Angie Tyler), Ray Burdis (Nick Tyler), Neil Stacy (Major Giles Bradshaw). Sitcom created by Richard Ommanney. With a new son on the horizon, Nick (a photographer) and Angie Tyler (a model) decide to install one of their parents as baby-sitter in their basement flat. Nick's working-class father, Sam, and Angie's upper crust mother Daphne, both accept the offer and are forced into an uneasy alliance as flat-mates. Sam, a cockney taxidermist, is enamoured with Daphne and after she has a disastrous dalliance with Giles Bradshaw, the Cheltenham-raised socialite finally embarks on a more harmonious relationship with Sam. BBC1 1985-89.

Through The Keyhole Game show in which a panel of celebrities have to try and work out who owns a particular house by dint of clues. David Frost was the in-studio presenter and Loyd Grossman (Catherine Gee took over in 2004) led the camera team through the various rooms of a celebrity house. For the final series in 2007 Lisa Snowdon conducted the European property tours while actress Stefanie Powers did likewise in America. ITV 1987-95; Sky1 1996; BBC1 1997-2007

Thunderbirds Childrens science fiction animation created by Gerry and Sylvia Anderson. A 21st century family runs a global rescue service (International Rescue) using advanced technology. Set in the year 2063 retired astronaut Jeff Tracy (voiced by Peter Dyneley) and his five sons frequently save the world, or at least part of it, from imminent disaster using a Pacific island base for launch of the Thunderbirds. Thunder Bird 1 Pilot Scott Tracy, the eldest brother voiced by Shane Rimmer (usually first at the scene because of its high speed capability), Thunder Bird 2 Pilot Virgil voiced by David Holliday and Jeremy Wilkin (pod carrier for Thunderbird 4 and any special equipment required), Thunder Bird 3 Pilot Alan voiced by Matt Zimmerman (rocket back up.) Alan also manned the Spacestation occasionally, Thunder Bird 4 Pilot Gordon voiced by David Graham (underwater machine which had great versatility), Thunder Bird 5 Pilot John voiced by Ray Barrett (the stationery space station). Jeff Tracy's staff include Kyrano (voiced by David Graham) an oriental manservant, and Tin-Tin (voiced by Christine Finn) an electronics expert and love-interest of Alan's. The London agent is Lady Penelope Creighton-Ward (voiced by Sylvia Anderson) and the chauffeur of her pink Rolls Royce (Reg No FAB 1) is Aloysius Parker (voiced by David Graham) (Penelope also has a luxury yacht : Reg No FAB 2). Incidentally FAB is also the call sign of the Thunderbirds. The evil Hood, half-brother of Kyrano, is the arch-rival of the Tracy clan. Living in a temple in the Thai jungle he often asserts mind-control over Kyrano. The gadget co-ordinator and creator of the Thunderbirds, aptly named Brains (voiced by David Graham), is a stammering bespectacled genius, real name Hiram Hackenbacker. The theme music was by Barry Gray. ITV 1965-66.

Tich and Quackers See entry in the comedy section for Ventriloquists.

Tikkabilla See *Play School* and *Cbeebies*

Till Death Us Do Part Warren Mitchell (Alf Garnett), Anthony Booth (Mike), Dandy Nichols (Else), Una Stubbs (Rita), Patricia Hayes (Min Reed), Alfie Bass (Bert Reed). Sitcom written by Johnny Speight. A bigoted East End docker, Alf Garnett, pontificates on the inequality of life, mainly while watching television with his down-trodden wife Else (referred to by Alf as 'silly old moo'), daughter Rita, and son-in-law Mike (often referred to by Alf as 'Shirley Temple' or 'scouse git'). Alf is racist and anti-Labour in every sense of the word. He adores the Queen and West Ham football club but hates foreigners and bureaucracy. Beginning as an episode of *Comedy Playhouse* in 1965, Warren Mitchell played Alf Ramsey in the pilot with Gretchen Franklin playing his wife. BBC1 1965-68; 1972-75; 1981. Between 1985 and 1992 the series was entitled *In Sickness And In Health* and Alf was joined by gay black home-help Winston (Eamonn Walker) as sparring partner. On the death of Dandy Nichols in 1986, Alf was attended by his neighbour Mrs Hollingbery (Carmel McSharry).

Time After Time Brian Conley (Kenny Conway), Georgia Allen (Donna Strachan), Samantha Beckinsale (Gillian Walcott), Richard Graham (Jake Brewer), Neil McCaul (Mr Tredwell), David Shane (Robbie Conway), Kate Williams (Ma Conway), Deddie Davies (Auntie Dot). Sitcom written by Paul Minett & Brian Leveson. Kenny Conway, a petty criminal from a family of petty criminals, resolves to go straight after his release from a spell in prison. The series was born out of a one-off comedy drama entitled Outside Chance in 1993 and a 13-episode series followed the following year. ITV 1993, 1994-95.

Time of My Life Mark Kingston (Ken Archer), Amanda Barrie (Joan Archer), Andrew Paul (Wayne Archer), Jean Kent (Mrs Wordsworth). Sitcom written by Jim Eldridge. Ken Archer is 49 years old and gainfully employed by the same company for 33 years. His life is turned upside-down when he is made redundant and on the same day returns home to hear his wife, Joan, scream as he opens the front door is: "Ken, I want a divorce!". It turns out she has been conducting a secret affair with her son's best friend, Stephen. Over the next five episodes Ken's luck worsens! BBC2 1980.

Time to Dance, A Ronald Pickup (Andrew Powell), Dervla Kirwan (Bernadette Kennedy), Geoffrey Beevers (Christopher Pearson), Joseph Crilly (Joe Kennedy), Jacqueline Leonard (Theresa Kennedy), David MacCreedy (David Kennedy), Rosemary McHale (Angela Powell). Three-part television adaptation of Melvyn Bragg's novel. A middle-aged English Banker, Andrew Powell, embarks on an affair with a teenage waif, Bernadette Kennedy, causing him grief at work and at home. The series was controversial for its explicit nudity and the BBC subsequently banned it from being repeated, much to the relief of Dervla Kirwan, who was not comfortable with some of its production, although undoubtedly a fine piece of work. BBC1 1992.

Time Team Long-running archaeology-based programme created by Tim Taylor and presented by actor Tony Robinson. The show features a team of specialists carrying out an archaeological dig in three days, with Robinson explaining the process in layman's terms. *Time Team* was developed from an earlier Channel 4 series *Time Signs*, first broadcast in 1991. Produced by Tim Taylor, it featured Mick Aston and Phil Harding, who both went on to appear on *Time Team*. There have been many companion shows during its run, including *Time Team Extra*, *History Hunters* and *Time Team Digs*. The series also features special episodes, often documentaries on history or archaeology, and live episodes. The team members have included: Robin Bush, Helen Geake, Carenza Lewis, Mick Aston, Guy de la Bédoyère, Francis Pryor, Phil Harding, Stewart Ainsworth, John Gater, Margaret Cox, Bettany Hughes, David S. Neal, Neil Holbrook, Philippa Walton, Sam Newton, Henry Chapman, and Victor Ambrus. C4 1994-

Timewatch Long-running television series showing documentaries on historical subjects, spanning all human history. Everything from Beatlemania to the Gunpowder Plot have been examined over the years. The Timewatch brandname is used as a banner title in the UK, but many of the individual documentaries can be found on US cable channels (like Discovery Times or The History Channel International) without the branding. Actor Michael Praed has been the most frequent narrator (56 episodes between 2003 and 2009). In 2010, Michael Palin narrated, *The Last Day of World War One*, telling the stories of the last soldiers to die in the First World War. BBC2 1981-

Tingha and Tucker Children's puppet show, the eponymous heroes being two koala bear puppets. Jean Morton, a continuity announcer on ATV, was sent the two koala stuffed toys in 1962 and took them on screen; they proved to be a big success. Before long puppets were made to replace the original toys, and The Tingha and Tucker Club was formed. The club itself attracted about 750,000 members until the Post Office and ATV couldn't cope with the volume of mail and had to close it. Thousands of children attended meetings of the club, where the secret sign would be exchanged. The programme varied in length between ten and twenty minutes, and through its heyday was on every weekday at the beginning of afternoon children's programes, with a special Sunday edition called *The Tree House Family* where Jean Morton read bible stories to the puppets. The Tingha and Tucker Club was killed off by Lew Grade when he bought the rights to Rupert Bear in 1970. The whereabouts of Tingha and Tucker are unknown; they were stolen from a store cupboard at ATV shortly after the series ended. ITV 1962-70.

Tinker Tailor Soldier Spy Alec Guinness (George Smiley), Bernard Hepton (Toby Esterhase), Beryl Reid (Connie Sachs), Patrick Stewart (Karla), Terence Rigby (Roy Bland), Michael Aldridge (Percy Alleline), Ian Richardson (Bill Haydon), Michael Jayston (Peter Guillam), Hywel Bennett (Ricki Tarr), George Sewell (Inspector Mendel), Ian Bannen (Jim Prideaux), Sian Phillips (Ann Smiley). Seven-part spy drama written by Arthur Hopcraft and based on the novel by John Le Carre. A British spycatcher George Smiley, is brought out of retirement in order to catch a mole (double-agent) that has infiltrated British Intelligence. The title of the series alludes to the codenames of those agents under suspicion i.e. Esterhase (Tinker), Bland (Tailor), Alleline (Soldier) and Haydon (Poor Man). BBC2 1979. Smiley was resurrected in the 1982 sequel *Smiley's People* this time having to cross swords again with his old Russian adversary Karla.

Tipping the Velvet Rachael Stirling (Nan Astley), Keeley Hawes (Kitty Butler), Anna Chancellor (Diana Lethaby), Jodhi May (Florence Banner), Hugh Bonneville (Ralph Banner), Johnny Vegas (Gully Sutherland), Alexei Sayle (Charles Frobisher), John Bowe (Walter Bliss), Sally Hawkins (Zena Blake). Dramatised from Sarah Waters' acclaimed debut novel and telling the story of Nancy Astley, a young girl who works as cook and waitress in her father's seaside restaurant in the 1890s - that is until she witnesses the extraordinary performance of a new-to-town male impersonator, Kitty Butler and begins to undergo a complete life transformation. Suddenly whipped up by her love affair with Kitty, she experiences both euphoria and deep disillusion as she embarks on a seven-year journey of self-discovery, finally realizing that a life of sensation just isn't enough. The phrase 'tipping the velvet' alludes to cunnilingus. BBC1 2002.

TISWAS Although ostensibly a children's show, the anarchic Tiswas format attracted a wide audience. Presenters included Chris Tarrant, John Asher, Trevor East, Sally James, Lenny Henry, John Gorman, Clive Webb, Sylvester McCoy, Frank Carson, Fogwell Flax, Peter Tomlinson, David Rappaport, Clive "Wizard" Webb, Joan Palmer, Den Boog, and Bob Carolgees & Spit the Dog. Basically, the show consisted of a studio full of grown adults throwing custard pies and buckets of water at each other while linking cartoons or sketches. Popular segments included The Phantom Flan Flinger, The Bucketeers (Tarrant, James, Gorman and Carolgees had a hit record with The Bucket of Water song) and The Cage (where people were subjected to regular dousings). The show's name Tiswas variously stood for Today Is Saturday, Wear A (or Watch And) Smile depending on who is telling the story. Following the departure of most of the main presenters at the end of the penultimate series, the final series team consisted of Sally James, Gordon Astley and Den Hegarty. ITV 1974-82. See *OTT*.

Titch and Quackers Children's show hosted by ventriloquist Ray Allen with his 'Titch' character (a small boy not remotely like Lord Charles) and his sidekick 'Quackers' the duck, operated by Tony Hart, who also supplied a drawing feature. For the most part, operating Quackers was a thankless task until Lulu appeared on the show one day and clasped 'Quackers' to her bosom - a most memorable moment for the then young Tony Hart. BBC 1963-70

Tittybangbang Comedy sketch show including an exhibitionist cleaning lady ('don't look at me!'); a team of quivering darters led by their twitching captain Paula; Maxine Bendix the plastic slapper who suffers from just a little bit of seepage; and frustrated bachelor Don Peacock who never quite fulfills his fantasies. They are joined by menopausal, near naked needle-pointers; a dysfunctional family who cannot enjoy any meal in peace; a fighting OAP and an entertainer with a very unique animal act. Written by Jill Parker and produced by Lisa Clark, *Tittybangbang* is performed by Lucy Montgomery, Debbie Chazen, Lorraine Cheshire, Shelley Longworth, Velile Tshabalala, Tony Way and Dominic Frisby. Originally airing on BBC3 in 2005 but repeated highlights shown on BBC2 in 2006.

TNT Show, The Late-night topical sketch and entertainment show hosted by young comedy newcomers Jack Whitehall and Holly Walsh. Regular features included: Jack Whitehall Investigates (where Jack gathers an audience of real people together who think they're on a real discussion show, although the guests are in fact all actors); Holly Walsh's Celebrity News (where Holly takes a fast paced, graphics-filled look at the latest celebrity news); Dictionary Corner (where Tom Allen presents new words that have just become part of the dictionary e.g. 'Shitney' - a pop singer who is no longer any good) and Gilbert's Special Report (where Gilbert - played by Morgana Robinson - and his crew all have disabilities, but that doesn't stop them interviewing celebrities. C4 2009- See *The Morgana Show*

To Buy Or Not To Buy Formatted reality television series. After introducing prospective buyers and their idea of an ideal home, including location, features and price range, each of two presenters selects a property they feel fits that ideal. A third property, the so-called 'wild card', may not fully fit this wish list, but is believed to be adequate by the presenters. Prospective buyers are then given the opportunity to inspect each property, discussing its merits with the presenters before guessing the property's price. They are then allowed to choose one property for an in-depth 'try before you buy' segment. Each episode concludes with a final conversation with the prospective buyers, asking them whether they are in fact interested in purchasing the property. The original presenters were Kristian Digby and Dominic Littlewood. Other presenters have included Melissa Porter, Simon O'Brien, Simon Rimmer, Jenny Powell, Ed Hall, Sarah Walker, Ian Blandford, Melinda Messenger, Sid Owen, Rani Price, Jonnie Irwin and Jonny Benarr. Kristian Digby (born in Torquay, 24 June 1977) and Ed Hall were the co-hosts before Kristian's death on 1 March 2010. BBC1 2003-

To Play the King See *House of Cards*

To Serve Them All My Days John Duttine (David Powlett-Jones), Nicholas Lyndhurst (R. A. I. Dobson), Frank Middlemas (Algy Herries), Susan Jameson (Christine Forster/Powlett-Jones), Patricia Lawrence (Ellie Herries), Alan MacNaughton (Ian Howarth), Belinda Lang (Beth Marwood/Powlett-Jones), Neil Stacy (T. S. Carter), John Welsh (Judy Cordwainer), Kim Braden (Julia Derbyshire), David King (Barnaby). Drama series written by Andrew Davies, based on the novel by R. F. Delderfield. Second Lieutenant David Powlett-Jones of the South Wales Borderers, the youngest son of a mining family from Pontnewydd, near Abergavenny, is invalided out of the army towards the end of World War I and becomes a teacher of Modern History and English at Banfylde School, on the fringe of Exmoor, Devon, where he is taken under the wing of headmaster, the Rev Algy Herries and the chain-smoking English teacher, Ian Howarth. The series charts the professional success of Powlett-Jones firstly as housemaster of Havelock's and ultimately as headmaster. David's life also has traumas and after his first wife Beth, and twin baby daughters Gracie and Joan, are killed in a car accident, he embarks on a fruitless relationship with Julia Derbyshire before eventually marrying Christine Forster, an equally headstrong socialist. The 13-part series was filmed at Milton Abbey School in Dorset. The music was by Kenyon Emrys-Roberts. BBC1 1980-81.

To The Manor Born Penelope Keith (Audrey Fforbes-Hamilton), Peter Bowles (Richard de Vere), Michael Bilton (Ned), Angela Thorne (Marjory Frobisher), John Rudling (Brabinger), Daphne Heard (Mrs Polouvicka). Sitcom created by Peter Spence. When Martin Fforbes-Hamilton dies, his wife, Audrey, is forced to sell Grantleigh Manor to cover the death-duties. Former costermonger, Richard de Vere, now head of supermarket chain Cavendish Foods, comes to the rescue and buys the property at auction for £876,000. Audrey is determined that the Nouveau Riche de Vere makes good on the property and moves in to one of the minor annexes, with her butler Brabinger, to keep an eye on him. Audrey's oldest friend Marjory is always at hand to lend a sympathetic ear as is Richard's Czech mother, Mrs Polouvicka; ultimately to good effect as Audrey marries Richard at the end of the final series. The series was filmed at Cricket St Thomas in Somerset. BBC1 1979-81. A radio version aired in 1997 with Penelope Keith reprising her role opposite Keith Barron's de Vere. Oddly enough the tv series was originally devised for radio although the pilot starring Bernard Braden as de Vere, never aired. 26 years after the series ended a one-off Christmas special was made in 2007 with Audrey and Richard celebrating their 25th wedding anniversary.

Today Today is Radio 4's flagship news and current affairs programme. It is widely considered the most significant news broadcast in the UK, and numbers among its listeners most of the country's politicians, opinion-formers and journalists. Number 10 Downing Street - the Prime Minister's residence - records the entire three-hour programme each day, and since its inception every Prime Minister has appeared on the programme from Harold Macmillan to David Cameron. Former presenter, the late Brian Redhead dubbed it "the newspaper of the airwaves", and said "If you want to drop a word in the ear of the nation, then this is the programme in which to do it." On Monday 28 October 1957 the first Today programme went out on the airwaves, presented by Alan Skempton and Raymond Baxter. Former presenters include such luminaries of British broadcasting as John Timpson, Brian Redhead, Barry Norman, Derek Cooper, Jenni Murray, Melvyn Bragg, Peter Hobday, John Shuttleworth and Jack De Manio. Even Des Lynam, later to become the BBC's sports anchor, had a short spell as a presenter before returning to sports broadcasting. In the 70s, the regular eight-minute religious slot became "Thought for the Day". It has evolved with the programme and today many faiths are represented, and its presenters have become familiar names across the nation. Broadcast weekdays 6-9am and Saturdays 7-9am, its recent presenters include John Humphrys, Sarah Montague, James Naughtie, Carolyn Quinn, Edward Stourton and Evan Davis; the first three being immortalised in egg cups with their faces depicted in order to raise funds for Children In Need. The present host, since 2009, is Justin Webb.

Today Tonight See *Prime Time*

Today with Des and Mel Monday to Friday lunchtime chat show hosted by TV veteran Des O' Connor and Melanie Sykes, a former model who is probably most famous for her part in a Boddingtons beer advert. The format proved an inspired pairing and the show had broad appeal, however the show was controversially axed in 2006 despite its popularity. ITV 2002-06.

Tolka Row The first Irish soap opera made by Raidió Teilifís Éireann (then called Telifís Éireann). The series was written by Maura Laverty, based on her 1951 play of the same name, and featured the Nolan family, who lived in the fictional Dublin housing estate of Tolka Row. RTÉ 1964-68.

Tom, Dick and Harriet Lionel Jeffries (Thomas Maddison), Ian Ogilvy (Richard Maddison), Brigit Forsyth (Harriet Maddison). Two series of six-episodes per series of this delightful sitcom were written by Brian Cooke and Johnnie Mortimer. After becoming a widower Thomas Maddison, heads off to London, where his son Richard lives with his wife Harriet, and systematically causes chaos for the well-manicured executives; him in advertising, her in magazine publishing. ITV 1982-83.

Tomorrow People, The Nicholas Young (John), Elizabeth Adare (Elizabeth 'Liz' M'Bundo), Peter Vaughan-Clarke (Stephen Jameson), Stephen Salmon (Kenny), Sammie Winmill (Carol), Philip Gilbert (Timus/Tikno/Voice of TIM), Dean Lawrence (Tyso Boswell), Michael Holloway (Michael Bell), Misako Koba (Hsui Tai), Nigel Rhodes (Andrew Forbes), Frances de Wolff and Roger Bizley (Jedekiah), Michael Standing (Ginge), Derek Crewe (Lefty). Children's science fiction series. The adventures of several teenagers who were the first to gain telepathic powers in the next stages of human evolution. 17-year-old John was the first 'homosuperion', empowered with ESP, telepathy and telekinesis and he helped others in the painful process of development known as 'breaking out'. Carol and Kenny soon join John to become

ambassadors for earth to the Galactic Empire. ITV 1973-79. The series creator Roger Price re-introduced the series between 1992-95 starring Kristian Schmid as Adam, Christian Tessier as Megabyte, Naomie Harris as Ami Jackson, Adam Pearce as Kevin, Kristen Ariza as Lisa and Peggy Mount, in her final screen role, as Mrs Butterworth.

Tomorrow's World Long-running science programme taking a weekly look at innovations and discoveries likely to change our lives. For the first twelve years of its life, *Tomorrow's World* was hosted by BBC commentator and ex-Spitfire pilot Raymond Baxter, with narration by Derek Cooper, the voice of Michael Apted's *7 Up* documentaries. Another popular presenter was James Burke. Coming from an academic, as opposed to Baxter's patrician, background, Burke, a former English teacher and interpreter at the Vatican, came to the BBC from Granada TV, and quickly made a name for himself anchoring the Beeb's coverage of major US and Soviet space launches. James cut a slightly eccentric, mad-haired figure next to his more restrained co-hosts. James left in 1974 and Raymond was joined by William Woollard, Judith Hann and Michael Rodd. On the retirement of Baxter a proliferation of presenters have included Anna Ford, Kieren Prenderville, Maggie Philbin, Su Ingle, Howard Stableford, Carol Vorderman, Shahnaz Pakravan, Vivienne Parry, Rebecca Stephens, Monty Don, Phillippa Forrester, Jez Nelson, Peter Snow, Craig Doyle, Anya Sitaram, Lindsey Fallow, Adam Hart-Davis and Roger Black. BBC1 1965-2002.

Tonight Daily current affairs programme presented by Cliff Michelmore. Notable reporters included, Trevor Philpott, Julian Pettifer, Magnus Magnusson, Alan Whicker, Derek Hart, Polly Elwes, and the hugely popular Fyfe Robertson. Robin Hall and Jimmie Macgregor were the resident folk singers. The host would end each show 'The next *Tonight* will be tomorrow night'. BBC 1957-65. *Tonight* was replaced by *24 Hours* but resurfaced in 1975 as replacement for *Midweek*, albeit a far more serious programme presented by Sue Lawley, Donald MacCormack, Denis Tuohy and John Simpson.

Tonight With Trevor McDonald Current affairs programme launched in 1999 as replacement for *World In Action*. A typically controversial edition from 2003 featured Martin Bashir interviewing Michael Jackson leading to the singer being charged for sexual molestation. ITV 1999-2007. The programme returned in January 2010 with Julie Etchingham as the new host and now entitled simply *Tonight*.

Tonight's the Night Saturday evening variety show hosted by all-round entertainer John Barrowman. Regular items include 'John Barrowman versus....' where the host takes part in some sort of challenge against another celebrity; amateur performers realizing their dream of appearing as a professional; and a top-of-the-bill star turn. BBC1 2009-

Too Posh To Wash See *How Clean Is Your House?*

Toonattik Children's TV slot airing on weekend mornings and presented by Jamie Rickers and Anna Williamson. Originally the show was a presentation of American cartoons previously shown on *Diggit* and *Up on the Roof* and this part of the show was subtitled Wakey Wakey. The presenters then appeared from 7.15am and introduced further cartoons and in-studio games. A current highlight is the battle between Jamie's 'pie boys' and Anna's 'pie girls'. The loser of the show, either the boys or the girls, will be given a pie in the face as a punishment. Each of the games is chosen randomly by spinning the 'Golden wheel of twizzle' and the player is determined by the 'Toonattik twizzler'. Viewers also have the chance to send in game suggestions which are pulled from a special chest named the 'challenge chest'. In May 2010, Jamie and Anna departed and the slot was immediately re-launched with out-of-vision presentation. From that point Toonattik also featured British cartoons. ITV 2005-

Top Gear The award-winning Motoring Magazine first aired on BBC2 in 1978 with Angela Rippon and Barrie Gill as presenters. Other hosts have included William Woolard, Noel Edmonds, Steve Berry, Andy Wilman, Kate Humble, Jason Barlow, Vicki Butler-Henderson, Jason Dawe, Sue Baker, Quentin Willson, Tiff Needell, Chris Goffey, Tony Mason, Janet Trewin, and Michele Newman. Jeremy Clarkson hosted the programme between 1989 and 1999 before devising a format change in 2002. It is now consistently the most watched show on BBC2 with 250 million viewers around the world, and won an International Emmy in 2005 (for best non-scripted entertainment show). Jeremy Clarkson's excellently-scripted programmes, enthusiasm, and humorous interplay with fellow presenters Richard Hammond and James May have given the show a universal appeal beyond the motoring anoraks it was originally designed for. For much of the original series' lifespan, Elton John's instrumental "Out Of The Blue" was played over the closing credits. The programme is filmed at Dunsfold Park, a former airfield in Surrey, where a custom race circuit was built and a large hangar is used for inside filming. Much speculation has taken place as to the identity of the show's stunt driver, The Stig. Perry McCarthy is known to have portrayed the character but was sacked after breaking cover and was last seen driving over a cliff during the 2003 season. His replacement, former SAS soldier Ben Collins, successfully defended a High Court action brought about by the BBC against the disclosure of his identity as The Stig, after it was made known that Collins was to publish his autobiography, *The Man In the White Suit*, in September 2010. Ben was immediately relieved of his duties as the stunt driver.

Top of the Form Launched on BBC Radio in 1948, the general knowledge school's quiz ran for 38 years and pitted two teams of pupils of varying ages in a national competition to decide the title 'Top of the Form'. Each school had to field a team of four, of different ages - under thirteen, under fourteen, under sixteen and under eighteen. Presenters included John Ellison, Robert MacDermott, Richard Dimbleby, Wynford Vaughan-Thomas, Lionel Gamlin, John Dunn and Bob Holness. The theme music was taken from "Marching Strings" by Marshall Ross popularised by Ray Martin and his Orchestra. The series transferred to BBC television between 1962 and 1975 under the name *Television Top of the Form* with presenters Geoffrey Wheeler and David Dimbleby, and questions supplied by Boswell Taylor. Other presenters included Paddy Feeny, Tim Gudgin and John Edmunds. An interesting fact is that Bob Holness began his career unseen as the first James Bond on radio in South Africa, where he'd emigrated after growing up in Kent and doing National Service. While working as a reporter he was chosen from thousands to take the role of the famous agent for an adaptation of *Moonraker*, the book having just been published in 1955.

Top of the Pops The long-running pop music show began on New Year's Day 1964 and focuses on the top-selling singles of the day, culminating in the number one single being played at the end of the show, following the chart rundown. Disc jockey Sir Jimmy Savile, presented the first show from a studio converted from a disused church in Manchester, the running-order being The Rolling Stones with "I Wanna Be Your Man"', Dusty Springfield with "I Only Want to be With You", the Dave Clark Five with "Glad All Over", The Hollies with "Stay", The Swinging Blue Jeans with "The Hippy Hippy Shake" and The Beatles with "I Want to Hold Your Hand", that week's number one. The first three years saw Sir Jimmy alternate as host with Alan Freeman, Pete Murray and David Jacobs. Between 1967 and 1991 the Radio 1 disc jockey presenters included Tony Blackburn, Noel Edmonds, Dave Lee Travis, Kenny Everett, Ed Stewart, Mike Read, David 'Kid' Jensen, Janice Long, John Peel, David Hamilton, Peter Powell, Simon Bates, Tommy Vance, Andy Peebles, Bruno Brookes, Gary Davies, Mike Smith, Nicky Campbell, Jakki Brambles, Mark Goodier, Richard Skinner, Steve Wright and Simon Mayo. In 1991 the format was changed and between October 1991 and January 1994 no Radio 1 DJs presented the show and the venue for recordings changed to BBC Elstree (in 1999 TOTP was recorded from provincial cities before returning to BBC Television Centre in 2001). When the Radio 1 DJ format was reintroduced regular presenters included Mark Radcliffe, Marc Riley, Zoe Ball and Jo Whiley, alternating with likes of Jamie Theakston, Jayne Middlemiss, Kate Thornton, Gail Porter, Richard Blackwood, Sarah Cawood, Lisa Snowdon, Richard Bacon, Tim Kash, Reggie Yates and Fearne Cotton. The show was traditionally shown on a Thursday night, but was moved to a Friday in 1996 and then a Sunday on 17 July 2005 at 7pm, when it also transferred to BBC2, presented by Fearne

Cotton and a series of guest presenters, notably Rufus Hound and Richard Bacon. Between 1967 and 1976 the show featured the tightly choreographed dance troupe Pan's People, Babs (now the wife of actor Robert Powell), Ruth, Dee-Dee, Louise, Andrea (and later Cherry and Sue), plus American choreographer Flick Colby. Ruby Flipper, Legs and Co, and finally Zoo, replaced them, before dance troupes made way for pop videos in 1983. Between 1994 and 2004, BBC2 broadcast TOTP2 which showed archive footage from as early as the 1960s of musicians on earlier Top of the Pops shows. Steve Wright wrote the factoid items of interest that were depicted over the tracks and did the voice-over links. The original theme music was an obscure swing track which ended with the voice-over "Yes it's No 1, Its Top of the Pops". A version of Led Zeppelin's "Whole Lotta Love" by C. C. S. was used as the show's theme tune for most of the 1970s, and also in a remixed version between 1998 and 2003, although ironically the band never performed on the show. In 1981 an original song 'Yellow Pearl' by Phil Lynott was commissioned as the new theme music. This was replaced in 1986 with "The Wizard", a composition by Paul Hardcastle. The final theme was a remixed version of the one used between 1991 and 1995, "Get Out Of That" composed by Tony Gibber. On the 20 June 2006 the BBC announced that the show was to be axed and the final show was recorded on 26 July and aired on 30 July 2006.

Top Of The World General knowledge quiz to find the brainiest person in the English-speaking world. Satellite links between Miami, Sydney and London enabled Eamonn Andrews to ask contestants about their own countries, each other's countries, a specialist subject and the rest of the world. The top prize was the 1924 Rolls Royce from the film *Chitty Chitty Bang Bang*. Jim Eccleson, a stalwart of the Merseyside Quiz Leagues was the eventual champion. ITV 1982.

Top Secret Life Of Edgar Briggs, The David Jason (Edgar Briggs), Barbara Angell (Jennifer Briggs), Elizabeth Counsell (Cathy), Noel Coleman (The Commander), Michael Stainton (Buxton), Mark Eden (Spencer). Sitcom written by Bernard McKenna and Richard Laing. With his trilby and pipe, Edgar Briggs was an inept counter-espionage agent, transferred to the Secret Intelligence Service (SIS) by dint of an administrative error. Other characters include, Jennifer, his devoted wife, Cathy, his assistant, fellow agents Buxton and Spencer, and his base commander. ITV 1974.

Torchwood Spin-off from *Dr Who*, created by Russell T Davies, but of a more adult nature. John Barrowman (Captain Jack Harkness), Eve Myles (Gwen Cooper), Burn Gorman (Owen Harper), Naoko Mori (Toshiko Sato), Gareth David Lloyd (Ianto Jones). As with the recent series of *Dr Who* the series is filmed in Cardiff but unlike *Dr Who* where Cardiff is a fictionalized London, the Torchwood base is actually set in the Welsh capital. The Torchwood underground base harbours aliens and alien technology. Its team of alien detectives operate with powers "beyond the police" in order to save the world from impending tragedies. Incidentally, Torchwood is an anagram of Doctor Who. The show has transitioned its broadcast channel every year since its inception, moving from BBC3 to BBC2 to BBC1, and acquiring US financing in its fourth series, shown in 2011 with American stars: Mekhi Phifer (Rex Matheson), Alexa Havins (Esther Drummond) and Bill Pullman (Oswald Danes) being added to the cast. BBC 2006-

Torchy the Battery Boy Puppet series written and created by Roberta Leigh with the voices of Olwyn Griffiths, Kenneth Connor, Jill Raymond and Patricia Somerset. Torchy, a battery toy (with a bulb on his forehead), with the help of Mr. Bumble-Drop, a kind old Earthman, was rocketed to Topsy-Turvy Land - "a wonderful twinkling star where toys could walk and animals could talk; where the fields were full of lollipops, and cream buns grew on trees." There, Torchy lived in Frutown with friends, Pom Pom a toy poodle, who was Torchy's closest friend, Flopsy the rag doll, Ena the kindly old hyena, Pilliwig the toy clown, Sparky the baby dragon, Squish the space boy and Pongo the rag pirate. King Dithers ruled this land, with a little help from Torchy, and he lived in the Orange Peel Palace with his animal aides. All the toys in

Topsy-Turvy land were those who had been mistreated or neglected down on Earth. But once they were just as alive as human beings on Earth, and walked and talked and ate and lived as we do. ITV 1958.

Total Wipeout Game show hosted by Richard Hammond and Amanda Byram in which contestants compete in a series of water-based challenges in an attempt to win £10,000. Although the assault course is filmed in Argentina for insurance purposes, Richard provides his voice-overs from a studio in Britain, while, Amanda interviews the contestants prior to their attempts and continues to shout encouragement (sometimes laughter) as they make their way through the course. Various celebrity versions have also been recorded. BBC1 2009-

Totally Saturday Short-lived audience participation show hosted by Graham Norton and assisted by Stuart Hall. BBC1 2009

Tots TV Now shown as part of the CBeebies schedule the original series of 276 episodes was shown on Children's ITV between 1993 and 1998. It featured three ragdoll friends: Tilly, a French girl, with red hair, who spoke in basic French, Tom, a blue haired dark boy with glasses, and Tiny, the youngest Tot, who had green hair. The series was written by Robin Stevens and Andrew Davenport who also played the characters Tom and Tiny in the show; Tilly being played by Claire Carre. A typical show would see the Tots have an adventure which often involved them helping out a young child. This also sometimes involved them using a magic sack which they always took with them, Tiny always carried it and Tilly always operated it. When asked to help it would always produce a single item to help them in the situation. Other characters included a small dog named Furry Boo and a donkey simply referred to as donkey.

Touch of Frost, A David Jason (DI William Edward 'Jack' Frost), Bruce Alexander (Supt. Norman Mullett), John Lyons (DS George Toolan), James McKenna (Sgt. Don Brady), Arthur White (PC Ernest 'Ernie' Trigg), David Gooderson (Derek Simpkins, Pathologist), Lindy Whiteford (Shirley Fisher), Matt Bardock (DC/DS Clive Barnard), Susannah Doyle (DS Liz Maud), Ian Driver (PC Ken Jordan), Nigel Harrison (DCI Jim Peters), Paul Jesson (DS Dorridge), Tristan Maguire (Mr. Bagshaw), Neil Phillips (DCI Jim Allen), Christopher Rickwood (PC Keith Stringer), Bill Stewart (Sandy Longford, 'Denton Evening News' Reporter), Tricia Thorns (Miss Grey, Simpkins' Secretary). Based on the character created by R. D. Wingfield. Detective Inspector William Frost, known as Jack to everyone but his wife, is an experienced and dedicated copper given to clashing with his superiors, mainly represented in the series by Superintendent Norman "Horn-rimmed Harry" Mullett. The two have highly incompatible personalities. Mullett is an ambitious buttoned-down by-the-book administrator, and Frost is a down-to-earth "street copper". Nonetheless, they appreciate each other's professional abilities. Frost has a cavalier approach to the rules, thinking nothing of breaking into a suspect's property without a warrant. He can also be rude and aggressive and has a tendency to become emotionally involved in his cases, but he does produce the goods. Many also regard him as a hero because he was once shot while on duty, for which he was awarded the George Cross, however Frost himself is modest about this, regarding himself as unworthy of the honour. The reality is that he was depressed and drunk at the time and approached the armed man out of recklessness, not caring whether he lived or died. ITV 1992-2010

Tracy Beaker, The Story Of Dani Harmer (Tracy Beaker), Lisa Coleman (Cam Lawson), Sophie Borja (Roxy), Jack Edwards (Marco). Based on the stories by Jacqueline Susan and illustrations by Nick Sharratt. Tracy Beaker is a 10 year old child, who was placed in a children's home, aptly referred to as the 'Dumping Ground'. Tracy makes new friends along the way, and causes mischief where ever she goes. In the later series, Cam Lawson and new husband Gary adopt Tracy. Part of the CBBC menu. BBC1 2002-06. Dani reprised her role in the 2010 BAFTA-winning spin-off *Tracy Beaker Returns*. The ongoing series depicts the newly-divorced Cam and Tracy living in a new house. Tracy is a slightly older girl now and working as a care-worker.

Traffik Bill Paterson (Jack Lithgow), Julia Ormond (Caroline Lithgow), Lindsay Duncan (Helen Rosshalde), Fritz Müller-Scherz (Ulli), George Kukura (Karl Rosshalde), Jamal Shah (Fazal), Talat Hussain (Tariq Butt). Six-part drama series written by Simon Moore; its three stories, about the illegal drug trade, are interwoven, with strands told from the perspectives of Pakistani growers, German dealers, and British users. The BAFTA winning mini-series gave us the first screen appearance of Julia Ormond, as the drug-addicted of the Home Office minister, Jack Lithgow. C4 1989.

Trainer Mark Greenstreet (Mike Hardy), Susannah York (Rachel Ware), David McCallum (John Grey), Floyd Bevan (Nick Peters), Neil Nisbet (Danny Foster), Audrey Jenkinson (Mo Ratcliffe), Des McAleer (Joe Hogan), Marcus D'Amico (David Ware), Nigel Davenport (James Brant), Patrick Ryecart (Hugo Latimer), Kenneth Farrington (Jack Ross), John Bowe (Robert Firman), Emma Harbour (Emma Carter), Angharad Rees (Caroline Farrell), Joanna McCallum (Toni Mountford), Jeremy Sinden (Freddie Farrell). Drama series set in the world of horse racing. Filming took place in and around the village of Compton near Newbury, and centred on aspiring horse trainer, Mike Hardy. Other major characters included local gambler John Grey and widow Rachel Ware. The theme song, "More to Life", written by Simon May and Mike Read, was performed by Cliff Richard. From a trivia aspect Joanna McCallum is not related to David McCallum, in fact she is the daughter of actress Googie Withers. BBC1 1991-92.

Trapped Children's adventure game show. Six children must work together to escape from a Gothic fairytale tower. However, one of them is a saboteur and cannot be trusted. Part of the CBBC menu since 2007.

Treacle People, The Children's animation first shown as part of the CITV menu and repeated on Channel 4 in 2009. Written by Brian and Jonathan Trueman and developed for Television by Iain Russell and Mike Furness, the 26 episodes broadcast across two series were based in a fictionalized version of the Northern English village of Sabden, in Pendle – treacle country! The two main characters, Wizzle and Rosie, concentrate their efforts in reopening the once prosperous Mitton Treacle Mining Co. Voices of all the characters were Alec Bregonzi, Caroline Bernstein, Jim McManus, Glynn Mills and Jim Norton. The title song was rather aptly entitled *Sticky*. ITV 1995-97.

Treasure Hunt Helicopter 'skyrunner' Anneka Rice races against the clock to find directions to treasure at locations worked out by studio guests from cryptic clues. The action/adventure series was hosted in the studio by Kenneth Kendall throughout its original run although Annabel Croft replaced Anneka Rice for the final series in 1989. Adjudicators in the studio were Anne Meo (1983), Annette Lynton (1984) and Wincey Willis (1985-89). C4 1983-89. *Treasure Hunt* was revived by BBC2 in 2002 with Dermot Murnaghan as studio presenter and Suzi Perry as the 'sky runner'.

Treasure Island Bernard Miles (Long John Silver), Valentine Dyall (Dr Livesey), John Quayle (Jim Hawkins), Raymond Rollett (Squire Trelawney), Derek Birch (Captain Smollett), Douglas Blackwell (Israel Hands), Peter Jones (Black Dog), Toke Townley (Ben Gunn), Brian Haines (Narrator). Seven-part drama series based on Robert Louis Stevenson's book. BBC 1951. See also *The Adventures of Long John Silver*.

Tree House Family, The See *Tingha and Tucker*.

Trials of Life, The David Attenborough's third part of his epic wildlife documentary series which began with *Life On Earth* and continued with *The Living Planet*. The 12-part examination of animal behaviour focuses on the struggle for survival of the planet's many species. BBC1 1990. See *Life in Cold Blood*

Triangle Kate O'Mara (Katherine Laker), Michael Craig (John Anderson), Larry Lamb (Matt Taylor), Nigel Stock (Wally James), Tony Anholt (Nick Stevens), Diana Coupland (Marion Terson), Dawn Addams (Mrs Landers), Sandra Dickinson (Penny Warrender), George Baker (David West). Drama aboard a North Sea ferry created by Bill Sellars. The twice-weekly soap followed the passengers and crew of a Triangles Line ferry (named from its route between Felixstowe-Gothenburg-Rotterdam). The initial focus was on the appointment of the new chief purser Katherine Laker whose first scantily-dressed shot sunbathing on deck was one of few highlights of the three-year run. BBC1 1981-83.

Tribe Former Royal Marine instructor Bruce Parry (born 17 March 1969, Hythe, Hampshire) first appeared on television in 2002 in an episode of BBC1's *Extreme Lives* series entitled

"Cannibals and Crampons". In his second offering he visited several remote African and Asian tribes in the Himalayas, Ethiopia, West Papua, Gabon and Mongolia, spending a month living and interacting with each society. BBC2 2005-07. See also *Amazon with Bruce Parry*.

Trigger Happy TV Hidden camera television show, created, produced by and starring Dom Joly. Typical sketches include Joly answering a very large mobile phone and shouting at the top of his voice (normally in quiet locations), a chef chasing an actor in a large rat costume out of a restaurant, and two actors dressed as masked Mexican wrestlers getting into a spontaneous fight in a grocery store. Other scenes include people dressed as animals breaking into a fight and the progress of various costumed pedestrians (such as a snail and an old man) across a zebra crossing in London. Joly also often dressed as a Cub Scout, a Swiss person with bad English, a burglar, or a park attendant. The show did not use canned laughter but instead played instrumental and sometimes sad music to highlight pathos or irony. C4 2000-01. See also *World Shut Your Mouth*

Trinny & Susannah Undress... Fashion gurus Trinny Woodall (born Sarah-Jane Woodall, 8 February 1964) and Susannah Constantine (born 3 June 1962) attempted to rekindle the spark in relationships soured by lack of personal style. ITV 2006-07. See also *What Not To Wear* and *Trinny & Susan Undress the Nation*.

Trinny & Susannah Undress the Nation Fashion advisors Trinny Woodall and Susannah Constantine explored some of the major fashion problems in Britain. The series was famous for stunts including Susannah being transformed into a 70-year-old to look at how people dress for their age and a very controversial one where Trinny, Susannah and 100 women gave the East Sussex pagan symbol, the Long Man of Wilmington, a temporary female form by adding pigtails, breasts and hips. The women created the effect by lying down in white boiler suits to make different shapes. ITV 2007-08. See also *What Not To Wear* and *Trinny & Susan Undress...*

Trip, The Steve Coogan (Steve), Rob Brydon (Rob), Claire Keelan (Emma), Margo Stilley (Mischa), Rebecca Johnson (Sally). The series stars Steve Coogan and Rob Brydon as fictionalised versions of themselves (a continuation of their performances in the Michael Winterbottom-directed *A Cock and Bull Story*) undertaking a restaurant tour of northern England. The series is a largely improvised sitcom in which Coogan plays a food critic for the *Observer* who is joined on a working road trip by his friend, Rob, who fills in at the last minute when Coogan's romantic relationship falls apart. BBC2 2010. The series was also edited into a feature film which premiered at the Toronto International Film festival in September 2010 and is set for release in the US by IFC Films in 2011.

Tripper's Day Leonard Rossiter (Norman Tripper) Sitcom created by Brian Cooke. Norman Tripper, the manager of the Supafare Supermarket, is a fan of American detective series and runs his store with military precision. Leonard died after series one and the show was recast with Bruce Forsyth in the lead role of Cecil Slinger for two further series, its title becoming *Slinger's Day*. ITV 1984; 1986-87.

Trisha Born in London in December 1957, Trisha Goddard began her broadcasting career in Australia as the presenter of *Play School*. In 1998 after returning to Britain she became the host of ITV's new flagship daytime chat show, *Trisha*, produced by Anglia Television. In September, 2004 she left ITV to join *Five* in a new programme, *Trisha Goddard*, which made its TV debut on 24 January 2005. The programme, in similar style to her old show, focused on relationships, families in crisis and reunions. The show was produced by Town House Productions and ended in 2009. In March 2008, it was revealed that Trisha had breast cancer, although she is now in remission.

Trivial Pursuit Game show hosted by Rory McGrath, based on the general knowledge board game. BBC1 1990. A show of the same name was broadcast on the Family Channel (1993-94) hosted by Tony Slattery.

Troubleshooters, The See *Mogul.*

True Dare Kiss Pooky Quesnel (Nita McKinnon), Lorraine Ashbourne (Beth Sweeney), Paul Hilton (Dennis Tyler), Paul McGann (Nash McKinnon), Dervla Kirwan (Phil Tyler), Esther Hall (Alice Tyler), Brendan Coyle (Kaz Sweeney), Ciarán McMenamin (Bryce Waghorn). Drama series created by Debbie Horsfield. Set in Manchester, the plot concerns the reunion of four sisters and a brother following the death of their estranged father, unravelling the truth and hidden secrets of the past. BBC1 2007.

Trumpton Spin off series from *Camberwick Green* but the action moved from Pippin Fort to the larger town of Trumpton. Captain Flack's local firemen : Hugh, Pugh, Barney McGrew, Cuthbert, Dibble and Grubb. Some of the Camberwick Green characters remained but new ones included Miss Lovelace and her yapping dogs, Mrs Cobbit, Mr Platt, the Town Clerk, and Mr Troop. Each episode began with the Trumpton clock and ended with a fire brigade band concert in the park. First broadcast on BBC1 in 1967 and narrated by Brian Cant, the 13 episodes were frequently repeated and spawned a spin-off *Chigley*.

Tube, The Live Friday night music show with edge and attitude presented by former Squeeze keyboard player Jools Holland and the late Paula Yates. The show was devised by Malcolm Gerrie and Andrea Wonfor, who called it *The Tube* because of the Perspex tunnel entrance to their office. *The Tube* was broadcast live from Tyne Tees Studio 5 in Newcastle and was an instant hit with young viewers. Apart from the lasting effect the show had on the British music scene, comedy regularly made up 30% of the show, with Vic Reeves making his TV debut on *The Tube* with a spoof of *Celebrity Squares*. Controversy was never far away during the five-year run and Paula once used the f-word and received a stern warning, while Jools was suspended for swearing during a trailer - calling it "a groovy little fucker". Other presenters included Leslie Ash, Muriel Gray and Gary James. C4 1982-87.

Tubridy Tonight Irish Saturday night chat show presented by broadcaster, writer and songwriter Ryan Tubridy (b. 28 May 1973, Dublin). Ryan went on to host *The Late Late Show* at the series end. RTÉ One 2004-09.

Tucker's Luck Spin-off from *Grange Hill* starring Todd Carty as Peter "Tucker" Jenkins, the leading character of the school soap for the first four years of its run. Also created by Phil Redmond, the series followed the fortunes of Tucker and his old schoolfriends Alan and Tommy. Other cast members included George Armstrong (Alan Humphries), Paul McCarthy (Tommy Watson), Elaine Lordan (Michelle Passmore), Peter McNamara (Ralph Passmore), Steven Brown (Brains) and Michelle Herbert (Trisha Yates). BBC1 1983-85.

Tudors, The Jonathan Rhys Meyers (King Henry VIII), Peter O'Toole (Pope Paul III), Natalie Dormer (Anne Boleyn), Henry Cavill (Charles Brandon), Maria Doyle Kennedy (Katherine of Aragon), James Frain (Thomas Cromwell), Nick Dunning (Thomas Boleyn), Jeremy Northam (Thomas More), Jamie Thomas King (Thomas Wyatt), Anita Briem (Jane Seymour), Hans Matheson (Thomas Cranmer), Sam Neill (Cardinal Thomas Wolsey), Callum Blue (Anthony Knivert), Henry Czerny (Duke of Norfolk), Kristen Holden-Ried (William Compton), Gabrielle Anwar (Margaret Tudor), Joely Richardson (Catherine Parr). Historical fiction series written by Michael Hirst, loosely based upon the early reign of English monarch Henry VIII. The series is a joint production between Reveille Eire (Ireland), Working Title Films (UK) and the Canadian Broadcasting Corporation, and is filmed in Ireland. BBC2 2007-10

Tuesday File See *Prime Time*

Tuesday Rendezvous See *Small Time* and *The Five O'Clock Club*.

Turn Out The Lights See *Pardon the Expression*

Tutti Frutti Robbie Coltrane (Danny McGlone), Emma Thompson (Suzie Kettles), Maurice Roeves (Vincent Diver), Richard Wilson (Eddie Clockerty), Janis Toner (Katy Murphy), Stuart McGugan (Bomba MacAteer), Ron Donachie (Dennis Sproul), Jake D'Arcy (Fud O'Donnell). Six-part comedy drama series written by John Byrne. The Majestics, a Scottish rock band, are about to embark on their "Silver Jubilee" tour when their lead singer, Big Jazza McGlone collapses and dies. The group talk Big Jazza's younger brother, Danny into joining the band as their new lead singer. BBC1 1987.

TV Eye See *This Week*.

TV Heaven, Telly Hell Comedy show presented by Sean Lock on a format similar to *Room 101*, with special guests discussing their likes and dislikes of items on the television. The show also saw itself as a sealed knot to television, and allowed the guest to reconstruct any moment in television history in the way they wanted it happen. C4 2006-07

TV Show, The Krishnan Guru-Murthy presents a monthly live discussion programme in which members of the public debate what they have enjoyed and disliked on television over the previous month. C4 2008- See *Right to Reply*

24 Hour Call See *Emergency Ward 10*

24 Hours Current affairs programme which replaced *Tonight*, its presenters included Cliff Michelmore, Kenneth Allsop, Ian Trethowan, Michael Barrett, Robert McKenzie, David Dimbleby and Ludovic Kennedy. Reporters included Michael Parkinson, Fyfe Robertson, Leonard Parkin, Robin Day, Julian Pettifer, Denis Tuohy and Linda Blandford. BBC1 1965-72. See *Midweek*.

Twenty Questions Radio quiz show, where a panellist had 20 tries to identify a word or phrase which was either animal, vegetable, mineral or abstract. Simply subtitled 'a radio parlour game' this quiz series was first broadcast in March 1947. It was originally chaired by Stewart MacPherson, and later by Gilbert Harding and eventually by Kenneth Horne. The idea was that a panel was invited to identify objects by asking only twenty questions with only a yes or no as the required response. Regular panellists in the 1950s included Richard Dimbleby, Anona Winn, Joy Adamson, Daphne Padel and Jack Train. Norman Hackforth was, for many years, the 'Mystery Voice' who informed the audience of the next object to be guessed, in a whisper close to the microphone, so that the panel could not hear. Mike Meehan produced the programme. The final edition on BBC Radio 4 was broadcast in 1976. The phrase Animal, Vegetable or Mineral was taken from the "Major-General's Song," a piece from the Gilbert and Sullivan opera The Pirates of Penzance."I am the very model of a modern Major-General, I've information vegetable, animal, and mineral, I know the kings of England, and I quote the fights historical". The format was briefly used again on BBC Radio 4 in the 1990s for a single season hosted by Jeremy Beadle.

Twice a Fortnight Comedy sketch series starring Terry Jones, Michael Palin, Graeme Garden, Bill Oddie, Jonathan Lynn and Tony Buffery, the first four also writing for all ten episodes. BBC1 1967

Twizzle, The Adventures of Twizzle was a boy doll who wore a Wee-Willy Winkie hat and ran away from a toy shop. He teamed up with Footso, a little black cat with big paws and together they built Stray Town, where all the stray toys in the world could go and live in peace, safe from a world where their young owners pulled them about and treated them badly. Twizzle was so called for his ability to extend, or rather 'cri.. crick" his arms and legs in a rather noisy fashion, and be tall as a lamp post, or even taller! Twizzle's pride and joy was his brick-red breakdown van, which he got off his garage mechanic friend in exchange for a sprite sportscar, given to him by a doll he had saved from a burning house. Two of the most popular regulars were Jiffy the Broomstick Man, and Chawky the white-faced Golliwog. Other characters included Polly Moppet, Candy Floss the momma doll, who couldn't say "momma", and Bouncy the ball who'd lost his bounce. Twizzle was Gerry Anderson's first directorial contribution to British television. Dennis Bryer was the voice of Twizzle and all the puppets were made by Joy Laurey except for Footso which was made by Christine Glanville. Joy and Christine along with Murray Clark were the puppet operators. Roberta Leigh was the creator and writer. The lyrics to the theme song (written by Barry Gray) are as follows: *My hair is red. My hat is green. I'm a lovely toy. The nicest one you've ever seen. Watch me jump for joy. Cri-crick, cri-crick. Watch me as I grow. Cri-crick, cri-crick. Watch me as I grow. I'm a very special boy, Twizzle. A very extra clever toy, Twizzle. I've got a very special trick just wait and see. When I start to go cri-crick, I'm taller than a tree. I can make my arms long if I Twizzle. I can make my legs long if I Twizzle. When I walk along, the road and see a wall. Oh, I just*

start to crick, myself I just start to crick, myself until I'm tall. I'm a very special toy, Twizzle. An extra special twizzly toy, Twizzle. Sometime I can make myself so wee and small. Sometime I can twizzle till I'm very, very tall. ITV 1957-58

Two Fat Ladies Cookery-cum-travel show featuring Clarissa Dickson Wright and Jennifer Paterson. Clarissa was born in London on 28 June 1947 and Christened Clarissa Theresa Philomena Aileen Mary Josephine Agnes Elsie Trilby Louise Esmerelda Dickson Wright. Her father, Arthur, was a surgeon to the Royal Family and her cousin is actor and comedian Alexander Armstrong. Clarissa was formerly a barrister and has the distinction of being the youngest-ever woman to be called to the Bar. Jennifer Mary Paterson was also born in London (3 April 1928) where she was formerly a cook for the Ugandan legation. A devout Roman Catholic, Jennifer's uncle was Monsignor Canon Anthony Bartlett, the Gentiluomo to Cardinal Basil Hume. Jennifer died of lung cancer, 10 August 1999. The premise of the show was for the two well-proportioned ladies to travel around the country on a combination motorcycle, Jennifer steering the Triumph Thunderbird motorcycle (Reg No. N88TFL) while Clarissa rode in the Watsonian GP-700 "doublewide" sidecar, stopping off at various destinations to prepare large meals for organized gatherings. BBC2 1996-99 See *The Hairy Bikers*.

Two In Clover Sid James (Sid Turner), Victor Spinetti (Vic˜ Evans). Sitcom written by Vince Powell and Harry Driver. A pair of stressed-out City insurance-clerks retreat to the country village of Fletchley, in their Morris-Minor, intent on turning over new leaves. They buy a smallholding, Clover Farm, and soon became bogged down in all manner of farm life, not knowing how to manage chickens, pigs, sheep and cows. ITV 1969-70

Two of Us, The Nicholas Lyndhurst (Ashley Phillips), Janet Dibley (Elaine). Sitcom written by Alex Shearer. Computer-programmer Ashley and Elaine, are an unmarried couple living together, but not in domestic bliss. Ashley's grandad, Perce, was originally played by former Dr Who actor Patrick Troughton, who died during filming and was replaced by Tenniel Evans. ITV 1986-90.

2 Point 4 Children Belinda Lang (Bill Porter), Gary Olsen (Ben Porter), John Pickard (David Porter), Clare Woodgate (Jenny Porter - series 1 & 2), Clare Buckfield (Jenny Porter - series 3 - 8), Patricia Brake (Tina - Series 1), Sandra Dickinson (Tina - Series 2 - 8), Roger Lloyd Pack (Jake 'The Klingon' Klinger), Liz Smith (Aunts Bette and Belle), Barbara Lott (Aunt Pearl). Sitcom created by Andrew Marshall. On the surface, the Porters are a normal family. They live at 142 Chepstow Road, Chiswick, the title of the series is the national average family size, although the .4 alludes in this case to the fact that the husband/father is still a bit of a child himself. The family consists of central-heating engineer Ben; his wife, catering worker Bill; and their teenage children David and Jenny. Other regular characters include Ben's sister Tina and his arch rival, Jake The Klingon. All are unexceptional in themselves although the situations in which the family find themselves are anything but. Bad luck, strange occurrences and poor judgement all conspire to turn the Porters' world topsy-turvy. BBC1 1991-99.

Two Ronnies, The Comedy entertainment courtesy of Ronnie Barker and Ronnie Corbett. Each show opened with the two Ronnies sitting behind desks reading terribly corny but nonetheless very funny spoof news items. A series of sketches would follow, the most lauded being the famous 'Four Candles' sketch where Ronnie B, in the guise of a local farmer, attempts to purchase various items from a hardware store from an exasperated Ronnie C who feels the man is being purposely evasive. A musical interlude by a 'special' guest would usually occur midway through proceedings followed by filmed episodic sketches that were serialised throughout different series. These adventures usually cast the recurring private detectives Charley Farley (Corbett) and Piggy Malone (Barker) - or variations on the characters - and were written by Ronnie B under the pseudonym Gerald Wiley. Another popular serialisation was The Phantom Raspberry Blower of Old London Town, written by Spike Milligan. Next came the 'Ronnie in the chair' solo spot for Corbett, in which he delivered a rambling comedy monologue that, while straying wildly from the original subject, always managed to get back on course at the finish (these interludes were written by Spike Mullins). The penultimate item in the show was usually a richly humorous musical spoof in which the Ronnies danced, marched, paraded or pretended to be musicians while delivering a comedy lyric; and the closing item in every show was a further selection of spoof news items, back at the desks, which would end with Corbett bidding the audience 'goodnight from me', to which Barker would add 'and it's goodnight from him'. BBC1 1971-87. See also individual entries in comedy section.

Two Thousand Acres of Sky Paul Kaye (Kenny Marsh), Michelle Collins (Abby Wallace), Michael Carter (Douglas Raeburn), Philip Dowling (Alfie Wallace), Charlotte Graham (Charley Wallace), Ashley Jensen (Angie Raeburn). Light-hearted drama series set on the fictional island of Ronansay (actually a Scottish coastal village called Port Logan in Dumfries and Galloway. The harbour scenes are actually filmed in Portpatrick, just outside Port Logan). Single mother Abby Wallace has spent her whole life on a rundown estate in East London and has never realised her dreams of leaving and making a better future for herself and her two children, Alfie and Charlotte. When she walks out of the latest in a long line of dead end jobs to deal with Alfie's bullying problem (he's the bully), she knows it is time to do something. Abby spots an ad for a job on the remote Scottish island of Ronansay which seems to promise the way of life she dreams of, but there's a problem: it specifies a married couple and Abby is a single parent. Abby persuades Kenny, her childhood friend and neighbour and a perpetually aspiring musician, to pose as her husband, at least for the interview on Ronansay. BBC1 2001-03.

Two's Company Elaine Stritch (Dorothy McNab), Donald Sinden (Robert Hiller). Sitcom based around the relationship between a brash American author living in London, and her staid British butler. ITV 1975-79. A later American version starred Peter Cook as the butler and Mimi Kennedy as his mistress.

Tycoon Peter Jones, a leading British businessman, used his extensive experience, acumen and money, to help seven entrepreneurs achieve their dreams. Elizabeth, Iain, Lauren, Helen & Cathy, Justin and Tom were the budding tycoons. The series' original prime-time spot was put back an hour due to apparent disappointing viewing figures. Iain, 29, from Portsmouth was eventually crowned series winner for his mini-helicopter business. ITV 2007.

UFO Ed Bishop (Commander Edward Straker), George Sewell (Colonel Alec Freeman), Peter Gordeno (Peter Karlin), Gabrielle Drake (Lt Gay Ellis), Michael Billington (Colonel Paul Foster), Wanda Ventham (Colonel Virginia Lake). Science fiction series created by Gerry and Sylvia Anderson. In the year 1980 the Earth is threatened by an alien race which kidnap and kill humans and use them for body parts. A highly secret military organisation is set up in the hope of defending the Earth from this alien threat. This organisation is named SHADO (Supreme Headquarters Alien Defence Organisation) and operates from a secret location beneath the Harlington-Straker film studios just outside London. SHADO is headed by Commander Ed Straker, a former United States Air Force Colonel who poses as the studio's chief executive. SHADO has a variety of high-tech hardware and vehicles at its disposal to implement a layered defence of Earth. Early warning of alien attack came from SID (Space Intruder Detector), a computerised tracking satellite that constantly scans for UFO incursions into the solar system. The forward line of defence is MoonBase from which the three female-piloted Lunar Interceptor spacecraft with nuclear missiles are launched. The second line of defense includes SkyDiver, a submarine mated with the submersible, undersea-launched Sky One interceptor aircraft which would attack UFOs in earth atmosphere. The last line of defence were ground units including the armed, tank-like SHADO Mobiles, fitted with caterpillar tracks. Special effects, as in all Anderson's marionette shows, were supervised by Derek Meddings. The distinctive pulsing electronic whine of the alien ships were actually produced by series composer Barry Gray on an Ondes Martenot. Captured aliens were almost human in appearance but breathed a green oxygenated liquid, which was believed to cushion their bodies against the extreme acceleration

of interstellar flight. To protect their eyes from the liquid the aliens wore opaque contact lenses with small pinholes for vision. After the autopsy of the body of a captured alien it was discovered that the body is, in fact, human, the assumption being that the aliens were controlling the dead bodies of abducted humans. The show's opening sequence began by showing the image of the removal of one of these lenses from an obviously real eye with a pair of forceps. ITV 1970-73.

Ultimate Force Ross Kemp (Sgt Henno Garvie), Jamie Draven (Jamie Dow), Jamie Bamber (Lt 'Totsy' Doheny), Miles Anderson (Colonel Dempsey), Heather Peace (Becca Gallagher). Drama series co-devised by decorated former SAS soldier Chris Ryan and Rob Heyland, concerning the 22 Regiment of the SAS, under the command of Colonel Dempsey and his junior officer Totsy Doheny. Red Troop leader Henno Garvie is the tough no-nonsense veteran who constantly reminds the men not to let emotion affect their performance. In series three, Becca Gallagher becomes the first female member of the elite force. ITV 2002-05

Ultra Quiz The famous Japanese game show with extreme tasks and forfeits was adapted for the UK by Jeremy Fox. 24 episodes were filmed over three series, the first having the highest budget. It featured Michael Aspel in a television studio and Jonathan King and Sally James in various locations around the world. Series 2 was presented by Sir David Frost with Willie Rushton assisting on location and Series 3 by Stu Francis and Sara Hollamby. In series 1, 2000 contestants lined up on Brighton Beach and were whittled down to just 200 by means of a number of either/or questions. The lucky few then boarded a cross-channel Ferry to France, and given a quiz to do, the top 50 progressing to the elimination stage while the losers went home. The top prize for the winner was £10,000 in newly-minted £1 coins. ITV 1983-85

Unanimous Interesting game show hosted by Alex Humes in which nine contestants were holed up in a mock-up bunker with only one decision to make. Which one of them should pocket the ultimate prize of £1 million. The show was recorded in real time but shown as weekly episodes. At the end of each show the nine contestants nominated each other, but not themselves, in an effort to make a unanimous decision on who receives the bounty. A further vote was then taken on who they wanted out of the game and thus ineligible to receive the prize although this person was allowed to stay in the bunker as a stalking-horse to influence the vote, and indeed vote themselves. An interesting twist was added after episode two when a countdown clock was introduced with the warning that every second that goes by without a unanimous decision a pound would be deducted from the jackpot. The ultimate winner was twenty-one-year-old mum Sian who pocketed £106,562. C4 2006

Unbreakable Reality television show presented by Benedict Allen. Eight people so driven to compete that they would stand in front of exploding bombs, walk through piranha-infested waters and breathe in CS gas for nothing more than pride. The series was heavily criticized for crossing the fine line between entertainment and sadism. The show's motto was 'Pain is glory, pain is pride, pain is great to watch'. Of the eight original contestants Frazer Herald, Angus Morrison and Matthew Taylor all remained 'unbreakable'. *Five* 2008.

Under the Same Sun A series of ten stories from various countries of the world enacted by Ailsa Berk, Howard Goorney, Roman Stefanski, Tessa Worsley, Melanie Parr, and Clive Duncan. James Hayter was the narrator. ITV 1978-1980.

Undercover Boss Reality series where each week a senior executive of a company works undercover in order to probe how the company really works and identify how it can be improved, as well as rewarding its hard working staff. C4 2009-

United! David Lodge (Gerry Barford), Bryan Marshall (Jack Birkett), George Layton (Jimmy Stokes), Stephen Yardley (Kenny Craig), Harold Goodwin (Horace Martin), Robin Wentworth (Ted Dawson), Arnold Peters (Frank Sibley), Arthur Pentelow (Dan Davis), Ronald Allen (Mark Wilson), Tony Caunter (Dick Mitchell). Drama series created by Brian Hayles. Airing on Mondays and Wednesday evenings *United!* was the BBC's attempt to break the stranglehold *Coronation Street* had on viewing figures. Focusing on struggling second division football side Brentwich United just as its new manager Gerry Barford took over. After a year Mark Wilson replaced him as team manager. Most prominent members of the club were its captain and main striker Jack Birkett, goalkeeper Kenny Craig, striker Jimmy Stokes, trainer Horace Martin and chairman Ted Dawson. BBC1 1965-67.

University Challenge Long-running quiz for teams of four students, each team drawn from one university. Based on the US format College Bowl by Don Reid, the series was hosted by Bamber Gascoigne for its first 25-year run. All eight contestants individually attempt to buzz in to answer the "Starter For Ten", for their team; however, an incorrect interruption merits a five-point deduction. The team producing a correct answer then attempt to answer three more questions as a team, upon a different common theme, for five points per correct answer. Winning teams were invited back the following week to attempt to another two victories in order to make the end of series knockout finals. The first-ever contest took place between the universities of Reading and Leeds. Famous former contestants include, Stephen Fry, Clive James, Sebastian Faulkes, David Aaronovitch, Miriam Margolyes, Julian Fellowes, John Simpson, David Starkey, Malcolm Rifkind and David Mellor. When the show was revived in 1994, Jeremy Paxman took over as questionmaster and the format was changed to winning teams and highest runners-up progressing to the next knockout round. The theme music is called College Boy composed by Derek New and the current version is performed by the Balanescu Quartet. The voice-over announcers were Jim Pope (1963-2002) and Roger Tilling (2002-). Series winners:1963 Leicester; 1965 New College, Oxford; 1966 Oriel College, Oxford;1967 Sussex; 1968 Keele; 1969 Sussex; 1970 Churchill College, Cambridge; 1971 Sidney Sussex College, Cambridge; 1972 University College, Oxford; 1973 Fitzwilliam College, Cambridge; 1974 Trinity College, Cambridge; 1975 Keble College, Oxford; 1976 University College, Oxford; 1977 Durham; 1978 Sidney Sussex College, Cambridge; 1979 Bradford; 1980 Merton College, Oxford; 1981 Queen's University, Belfast; 1982 St. Andrews; 1983 Dundee; 1984 Open University; 1986 Jesus College, Oxford; 1987 Keble College, Oxford;1995 Trinity College, Cambridge; 1996 Imperial College, London; 1997 Magdalen College, Oxford; 1998 Magdalen College, Oxford; 1999 Open University; 2000 Durham; 2001 Imperial College, London; 2002 Somerville College, Oxford; 2003 Birkbeck College, London; 2004 Magdalen College, Oxford; 2005 Corpus Christi College, Oxford; 2006 University of Manchester; 2007 University of Warwick; 2008 Christ Church, Oxford; 2009 University of Manchester; 2010 Emmanuel College, Cambridge; 2011 Magdalen College, Oxford. Corpus Christi, Oxford were originally the winners of the 2009 event, but were subsequently disqualified for "breaking the series rules" by fielding an ineligible contestant, Sam Kay, 22, who was no longer a student midway through the series. ITV 1962-87; BBC2 1994-. In 2002, a special 40th anniversary series of University Challenge, invited many series-winning teams, and in a few cases losing finalists, to have a champion of champions showdown. The series aired as *University Challenge Reunited*, and the winners were the 1978 team of Sidney Sussex College, Cambridge. *University Challenge - The Professionals*, first aired in 2003, the Inland Revenue being the first winners. Subsequent winners were the British Library (2004) and the Privy Council Office (2005).

Up on the Roof Children's TV show which replaced *Diggin' It* and was presented by Jamie Rickers. Cartoons included Poke'mon, Power Rangers, Spiderman and Teenage Mutant Ninja Turtles. ITV 2002-05. See also *Toonattik*.

Up Pompeii! Frankie Howerd (Lurcio). Sitcom created by Talbot Rothwell and based on *A Funny Thing Happened On The Way To The Forum*, in which Frankie Howerd had played two roles (Prologus and Pseudolus) during its highly successful London stage run from October 1963. Lurcio was the slave for Ludicrus, a government senator, and his busty wife Ammonia, and every episode embroiled him in senate intrigue and danger. *Up Pompeii!* was a purpose-built vehicle for Frankie Howerd's distinctive stage-honed comedic style, giving him every opportunity to share confidences with the audience (both in the Shepherd's Bush studio and at home) via constant asides, usually commenting on the

improbability of the plot and the standard of the acting or writing. In so doing, he constantly stepped in and out of both his character and the time-frame. Thirteen 30-minute episodes were made, in two series (March – May and September – October 1970). In addition there was a pilot episode (1969) and two special episodes entitled *Further Up Pompeii*, one in 1975 and the other in 1991. BBC1 1969; 1970; 1975; 1991. *Whoops Baghdad* was a 1973 spin-off series and several feature films and television specials followed.

Up the Elephant and Round the Castle Jim Davidson (Jim London), Anita Dobson (Lois Tight), John Bardon (Ernie London), Sue Nichols (Wanda Pickles), Brian Capron (Tosh Carey). Sitcom vehicle for stand-up comic Jim Davidson. Jim London, an out of work 'Jack The Lad' from the East End of London, falls on his feet when his Aunt Minnie dies and leaves him a Victorian terraced house (17 Railway Terrace) in the Elephant And Castle area of South London. Jim quickly finds that being a homeowner isn't always a bed of roses. He has a squatter upstairs and a bunch of rather dodgy neighbours. ITV 1983-85. The character was reprised by Jim in *Home James*.

Up the Junction Geraldine Sherman (Rube), Carol White (Sylvie), Vickery Turner (Eileen), Michael Standing (Terry), Tony Selby (Dave), Rita Webb (Mrs Hardy). Controversial play tackling the previously taboo subject of abortion. Based on the 1963 novel written by Nell Dunn depicting contemporary life in the industrial slums of Battersea, this powerful drama, directed by Ken Loach, was shown under *The Wednesday Play* banner. BBC1 1965.

Upchat Line, The John Alderton (Mike Upchat). Sitcom written by Keith Waterhouse. Mike Upchat was not the real name of the 'hero' of the series, and the viewer never found out what it was. 'Upchat' used the pseudonym, and a variety of vocations to wile his way into a woman's bed, preferably for the night as he lived out of a left-luggage locker at Marylebone Station! The second series aired as *The Upchat Connection* and was set in Australia, the original 'Upchat' having passed on his name to a new Mike Upchat (now played by Robin Nedwell). ITV 1977-78.

Upper Crusts, The Margaret Leighton (Lady Seacroft), Charles Gray (Lord Seacroft), Lalla Ward (Davina Seacroft), Martin Neil (Gareth Seacroft). Six-part sitcom written by Willis Hall and Keith Waterhouse. An aristocratic couple without any money, have to leave their stately home to live in a council house. ITV 1973.

Upper Hand, The Joe McGann (Charlie Burrows), Diana Weston (Caroline Wheatley), Honor Blackman (Laura West), Kellie Bright (Joanna Burrows), William Puttock (Tom Wheatley), Nicky Henson (Michael Wheatley). Sitcom concerning the exploits of former footballer Charlie Burrows who is taken on as live-in housekeeper to attractive executive Caroline Wheatley, mother of seven-year-old Tom, and estranged wife of Michael, a wildlife film-maker. Other characters include Joanna, the 11-year-old daughter of Charlie, and Laura, the man-eating mother of Caroline. ITV 1990-96.

Upstairs Downstairs Gordon Jackson (Mr Angus Hudson), Angela Baddeley (Mrs Kate Bridges/Hudson), Jean Marsh (Rose Buck), David Langton (Lord Richard Bellamy), Rachel Gurney (Lady Marjorie Southwold Bellamy), Simon Williams (Capt James Bellamy), Nicola Pagett (Elizabeth Bellamy/Kirbridge), Lesley-Anne Down (Georgina Worsley), Jacqueline Tong (Daisy Peel), Christopher Beeny (Edward Barnes), Pauline Collins (Sarah Moffat/Delice/Clemence Dumas) John Alderton (Thomas Watkins), Hannah Gordon (Lady Virginia Hamilton Bellamy), Ian Ogilvy (Lawrence Kirbridge), Anthony Andrews (Lord Robert Stockbridge / Marquis of Stockbridge), Joan Benham (Lady Prudence Fairfax), Gareth Hunt (Frederick Norton), Jenny Tomasin (Ruby Finch). The series, created by Jean Marsh and Eileen Atkins, follows the lives of both the family and the servants in the London townhouse at 165 Eaton Place, Belgravia. Richard Bellamy, the head of the household, is a member of Parliament, and his wife a member of the titled aristocracy. Below stairs, Hudson, the Scottish butler directs and guides the other servants about their tasks and (sometimes) their proper place. Real-life events from 1903-1930 are incorporated into the stories of the Bellamy household, including their loss of wealth in the

1929 Wall Streeet Crash and the subsequent suicide of James Bellamy. ITV 1971-75. See also *Thomas and Sarah*

Vacant Lot See *Bootsie and Snudge.*

Van Der Valk Barry Foster (Simon 'Piet' van der Valk), Susan Travers (Arlette van der Valk), Michael Latimer (Insp Johnny Kroon). Police drama depicting the exploits of a Dutch detective in Amsterdam. Based on the books of Nicolas Freeling. The theme tune, *Eye Level* composed by Jack Trombey and performed by the Simon Park Orchestra, topped the UK charts in 1973. ITV 1972-73; 1977; 1991-92.

Vanishing Man, The Neil Morrisey (Nick Cameron) Six-part science fiction series created by Linda Agran and Anthony Horowitz concerning an air-freight pilot who is convicted of a crime he does not commit and volunteers to take part in the 'Gyges Experiment' not realising the end result is invisibility whenever he gets wet! ITV 1998.

Variety Bandbox Radio variety show transmitted on the Light Programme (later became BBC Radio2). First broadcast in 1941, presented by Philip Slessor, the show became the staple diet for the listening public on a Sunday evening for the next decade. Comedian Derek Roy later hosted Variety Bandbox, and in this period the talent show made famous the likes of Michael Bentine, Jimmy Edwards, Tony Hancock, Alfred Marks, Morecambe and Wise, Harry Secombe, Graham Stark, Arthur English (who played the resident comedian and Prince of The Wide Boys. His catchphrase: 'Play the music, Open the cage!'), Max Wall, Bill Kerr, Reg Dixon, Frankie Howerd and Harry Worth. Eric Sykes began his scriptwriting career as a writer on the show. A series within a series called 'Blessem Hall' was broadcast every other week from March 1950 as part of the show. Peter Sellers played Major Manoeuvre the Manager, Giuseppe Chipolata the Waiter and Erbert Perks the Night Porter whilst Miriam Karlin played Mrs. Bucket the Benevolent Char, Mrs. Snitchlepuffle a guest and refugee and the "refained" Receptionist.

Vault, The At the start of each show, contestants (seven in series one, eight in series two and nine in series three) tried to guess the four-digit combination to The Vault, which contained jackpot money, starting at £100,000 and increasing by a further £100,000 every week it remained unopened. The four contestants who guessed the closest to the actual vault combination became players, and the other four became brokers, who could offer answers to questions in return for cash that players earned in the question rounds. In the final round, 10 home brokers were also on hand to offer their answers for similar cash rewards, which they negotiated with the player. After the first round, which consisted of the four players being given three minutes to answer 10 general knowledge questions correctly, and the two highest scoring players going through to the semi-final, came the final round, which saw the player with the highest amount of money trying to unlock the vault by answering a further ten questions correctly. If they reached the ninth question and answered that correctly, the clock would be stopped and the player would be given three categories for their last question. If they answered that correctly, then they had the knowledge to unlock the Vault and would win the jackpot contained within it. If the Vault was not opened by the studio contestant at the end of their final two minute round, then the same Vault jackpot was offered to someone watching at home, selected randomly by the computer from all the people who had registered over the past week. The lucky selected viewer had to answer six questions in 60 seconds, two of which had already been asked in the show. If they succeeded, the viewer would win the jackpot themselves. If they didn't, £100,000 was added to the jackpot for next week's show. In Series Three, the jackpot rolled over for nine weeks consecutively and reached £1 Million. Karen Shand, a home viewer in Series Three, answered the six questions correctly within the time limit and won one million pounds, which earned *The Vault* the record for being the first quiz show in Britain to give away £1 million live on national television (*TFI Friday* was partly recorded and not a quiz show). The show was hosted by Davina McCall (Series 1), Melanie Sykes (Series 2) and Gabby Logan (Series 3) who had stood in for Melanie previously when she was on maternity leave. ITV 2002-04

Vera Brenda Blethyn (DCI Vera Stanhope), David Leon (DS Joe Ashworth), Wunmi Mosaku (DC Holly Lawson), Paul Ritter (Billy Cartwright), Jon Morrison (DC Kenny Lockhart), Georg Nikoloff (Scipper). Police drama series written by Paul Rutman, based on the works of crime author Ann Cleeves. ITV 2011

Very British Coup, A Ray McAnally (Harry Perkins). Three-part drama written by Alan Plater (based on the novel of the same name by Chris Mullins, who had been elected Labour MP for Sunderland a year before the series aired) concerning a born-and-bred steelworker who works his way up the ladder to become prime minister. C4 1998.

Very Merry Widow, The Moira Lister (Jacqueline Villiers), Sally Thomsett (Jennifer Villiers), Donald Hewlett (Freddie Phillipson), Molly Urquhart (Mrs Frayle). Sitcom written by Alan Melville. Jacqui Villiers, whose husband Charles has drowned off Cape Finisterre after borrowing the yacht (and the wife) of a friend, Lord Carroway. To make matters worse, Jacqui has been left with Charles' debts, some £22,000 worth! In order to pay them she embarks upon a determined quest to raise cash, taking a variety of jobs along the way to keep the wolf from the door, and stay in her London mews flat. She also takes in a lodger, Freddie Phillipson. Jacqui is helped in her ventures by her teenage daughter Jennifer. BBC1 1967-69.

Very Peculiar Practice, A Peter Davison (Dr Stephen Daker), David Troughton (Dr Bob Buzzard), Barbara Flynn (Dr Rose Marie), Graham Crowden (Dr Jock McCannon), Amanda Hillwood (Lyn Turtle), Michael J.Shannon (Jack B.Daniels), Takashi Kawahara (Chen Sung Yau), Joanna Kanska (Dr Grete Grotowska). Drama series written by Andrew Davies. Set in the surreal world of Lowlands University, where brilliant doctor, but disastrous human being, Stephen Daker arrives from a broken marriage with a phobia of being touched. Daker discovers his boss, Dr Jock Macannon, is a drunk, his colleagues are a radical lesbian and a squash-obsessed fascist, and he's being haunted by nuns. Some degree of sanity comes in the form of police student Lyn Tuttle and Daker's mathematician flatmate Chen Sung Yau. They offer humanity when he gets caught in the crossfire between Bob Buzzard and Rose Marie, and when the outside world of government cuts and investment threaten the medical centre. Series two features Daker replacing Jock as the head of the medical centre and falling for the charms of Polish art historian Grete Grotowska. This time conflict comes in the form of the new vice-chancellor, right-wing American Jack B Daniels. BBC2 1986-88.

Very Social Secretary, A Bernard Hill (David Blunkett), Robert Lindsay (Tony Blair), Doon Mackichan (Cherie Blair), Sara Stewart (Carole Caplin), Alex Jennings (Alastair Campbell), Stuart McQuarrie (Boris Johnson). Light-hearted drama written by Alastair Beaton. Although played a little tongue-in-cheek, the fictionalised account of the demise of David Blunkett as a Cabinet Minister was considered quite cruel by many critics. It premiered as the centrepiece of the opening night of the new UK television channel "More4" in 2005. C4 2005.

Vet, The Suzanne Burden (Jennifer Holt), Richard Hawley (Chris Lennox), Gabrielle Cowburn (Laura Sinclair), Neil McKinven (Murray Wilson), Diana Kent (Patricia Lennox), Tom Brodie (Steven Holt), Hugh Bonneville (Alan Sinclair), Samantha Morton (Amanda Mulholland). 13-part drama series filmed in Cornwall and variously written by Andy de la Tour, Amanda Coe, Bernard Dempsey, Emily Brigdon, Alick Rowe and Tony Etchells. BBC1 1995.

Vicar Of Dibley, The Dawn French (Geraldine Granger), Gary Waldhorn (David Horton), James Fleet (Hugo Horton), Emma Chambers (Alice Tinker / Horton), Liz Smith (Letitia Cropley), John Bluthal (Frank Pickle), Trevor Peacock (Jim Trott), Roger Lloyd Pack (Owen Newitt), Clive Mantle (Simon Horton). Sitcom written by Richard Curtis and Paul Mayhew-Archer. Following the death of their ancient vicar, Pottle, during the middle of a service, the villagers of Dibley prepare for a suitable replacement, hoping that the new man is young and enthusiastic enough to stir the locals from their apathy and single-figure church attendances. What they get is Geraldine Granger, a chocaholic, radical reverend who, by nature of her gender alone, bemuses the local parish council and in particular its head figure, local squire David Horton, who takes steps to have her replaced. Geraldine's optimistic outlook and obvious enthusiasm prove popular with the wacky villagers, however, and David is forced reluctantly to accept her appointment, forming a working friendship although often disagreeing fundamentally on policy or method. Other characters include Horton's son, the hapless Hugo; the vague parish clerk, Frank; the incomprehensible Jim Trott ('no, no, no, no no, no......yes'); the straight-talking land worker Owen; and the elderly flower-arranger Letitia. The other main player was the verger, Alice Tinker, a staggeringly naive, off-beam young woman who went on to become engaged to Hugo, much to the distress of his father, and eventually married. Each episode would end with Geraldine trying to explain a risqué joke to Alice, invariably to no avail. The character of Geraldine was reputedly inspired by real-life Reverend Joy Carroll of Streatham, south London. Dervla Kirwan reprised her role of Assumpta Fitzgerald in a March 1997 episode, *Ballykissdibley*. BBC1 1994-2000. Six Christmas and Comic Relief specials followed between 2004-07

Vice, The Ken Stott (DI Pat Chappel), Caroline Catz (P.C. Cheryl Hutchins), Anna Chancellor (Dr Christina Weir), David Harewood (Sgt/DI Joe Robinson), Marc Warren (PC Dougie Raymond), Garry Cooper (Supt. Jeff Callard), Rosie Marcel (P.C. Kirsty Morgan), Victoria Shalet (Sarah Farrell), Tim Pigott-Smith (DS Frank Vickers). Drama series created by Barry Simner and Rob Pursey. Veteran Inspector Chappel heads up the Metropolitan vice squad as he and his team investigate prostitution and pornography in the London sex trade. Rock band Portishead provided the theme music for the series. ITV 1999-2003.

Victoria Wood As Seen On TV Comedy sketch series written by and starring comedienne Victoria Wood, with Julie Walters, Celia Imrie, Duncan Preston, Susie Blake and Patricia Routledge. A regular segment was *Acorn Antiques*, which was turned into a musical by Wood, opening in 2005. The series was also famous for its musical performances by Wood including her most well-known number, The Ballad of Barry and Freda ("Let's Do It"). BBC2 1985-87. See also entry for *Wood and Walters* and Victoria Wood's entry in the comedy section.

Village Hall Anthology series with each episode a different story set in a village hall. Actors who appeared in the 14 episodes include Ron Moody, Bernard Hill, Richard Griffiths, Liz Smith, Bernard Hepton, Dilys Laye, Lewis Collins, Colin Welland, Sydney Tafler, Zoë Wanamaker, Gerald Flood, Sue Nicholls, Joan Hickson, Anton Rodgers. ITV 1974.

Vincent Ray Winstone (Vincent), Suranne Jones (Beth), Joe Absolom (Robert), Ian Puleston-Davies (John), Angel Coulby (Gillian), Philip Glenister (DCI David Driscoll), Eva Pope (Cathy). Crime drama series written by Stephen Butchard following workaholic private detective Vincent Gallagher and his colleagues, including an attractive female sidekick. ITV 2005-06.

Vision On Conceived by BBC producers Ursula Eason and Patrick Dowling, Vision On replaced a monthly series called For Deaf Children, which had begun in 1952, and was intended to reflect changes in the education of deaf children, placing an emphasis upon communication and interaction rather than image-based storytelling alone. The main presenter was Pat Keysell, who had combined an acting career with teaching deaf children. Keysell was usually the only presenter to address the audience directly (she signed for those who could not hear). Pat's co-host was graphic artist Tony Hart, who encouraged viewers to send in their paintings to the *Vision On* gallery, which showed viewers' paintings in sequence in the middle of the programme. Other presenters at various times included Ben Benison, and Sylvester McCoy, both of whom specialized in mime in the series, and Wilf Makepeace Lunn, who appeared as an eccentric inventor of equally eccentric machines. David Cleveland appeared in filmed sequences as "the Prof". Despite changes in presenter, Tony Hart remained the mainstay of the show throughout its run. BBC 1964-76. Tony Hart took the gallery concept to a spin-off art series, *Take Hart* (1977-83) and later *Hart Beat* (1984-93). Many episodes of *Vision On* featured short animations produced by the Aardman Animations team, who went on to animate the claymation character Morph in *Take Hart* and produced the

Wallace & Gromit films. *Vision On*'s last producer, Clive Doig took its visual style on to his later series' *Jigsaw* and *Eureka.*

Vital Spark, The Roddy McMillan (Peter 'Para Handy' McFarlane), John Grieve (Dan Macphail), Walter Carr (Dougie), Alex McAvoy (Sunny Jim). Further adventures of the Scottish salts, again shot in authentic locations and featuring some of the same crew from the earlier TV series *Para Handy - Master Mariner,* including producer Pharic Maclaren and actors John Grieve (cast once again as Dan Macphail) and Roddy McMillan (now promoted from Dougie, the mate, to skipper Para Handy). After a successful pilot in the Comedy Playhouse strand, a series arrived the following year. BBC1 1965-67. See also *The Tales of Para Handy.*

Waggoners' Walk Daily soap opera which began on BBC Radio 2 on 28 April 1969 as a replacement for BBC Radio 4's *Mrs Dale's Diary*. It had much more gritty storylines and sought to capture the tensions of the swinging sixties with its rebellious youth culture. It featured three young women, Tracey, Lynn and Barbara sharing a flat in Hampstead. One had an illegitimate child and married a homosexual (who later 'reformed'), another's marriage broke up and the third lived in sin. *Waggoner's Walk* threw itself into social problems such as abortion, child custody, hypothermia, murder, and by the end, alien invasion! By 1974 it had an audience of four million listeners which was much higher than *The Archers*. The plots became a little daft towards the end and it was eventually axed as part of a money-saving plan, the final broadcast airing on 30 May 1980. When the BBC brought the series to an end, thousands of listeners thought they would never know whether the 30-years younger Sophie Richmond accepted George Underdown's proposal of marriage... Or why Peter Tyson had a mysterious package of money through the post... Or what were Shirley Edwards' chances of continuing to evade Maurice Gill's advances. After *Waggoners' Walk* ended, a novel was published, *Waggoners Walk - The Story Continues...,* written by Terry James, one of the show's scriptwriters, and all these questions were answered.

Waiting For God Stephanie Cole (Diana Trent), Graham Crowden (Tom Ballard), Daniel Hill (Harvey Baines). Sitcom written by Michael Aitkens. Diana Trent is a resident of the Bayview Retirement Home, Bournemouth. With the aid of fellow resident Tom Ballard, she spends much of her time finding new ways to make life difficult for Harvey Baines, the manager of Bayview. BBC1 1990-94.

Waking the Dead Trevor Eve (DCI Peter Boyd), Sue Johnston (Dr Grace Foley), Claire Goose (DC Amelia 'Mel' Silver), Holly Aird (Dr Frankie Wharton), Will Johnson (DS Spencer Johnson), Simon Kunz (DAC Ralph Christie), Esther Hall (Felix Gibson), Félicité Du Jeu (Stella Goodman). DCI Boyd, the head of the new Cold Case Squad, set up to investigate the Metropolitan Police's backlog of unresolved crimes, hunts a killer who murdered a schoolgirl five years earlier. The killer contacts him saying he's abducted another girl. Could exhuming the murderer's first victim provide vital clues? Aided by criminal psychologist Grace Foley, Boyd uses new technology to identify the murderer. BBC1 2000-05.

Walk on the Wild Side Comedy sketch show involving the overdubbing of voiceovers to natural history footage. Jason Manford, Jon Richardson, Isy Suttie and Gavin Webster write the series as well as providing voiceovers. The writing team is completed by Alex Horne, Alistair Griggs and Ian Manford. Regular voiceover artists include Sarah Millican, Rhod Gilbert, Pal Aron, Steve Edge, Harriet Carmichael and Jason Byrne. Guest voiceovers have been provided by Stephen Fry, Rolf Harris, Barbara Windsor, Richard E. Grant, Tom Jones, Ozzy and Sharon Osbourne, John Goodman, Dom Joly, Al Murray, John Humphrys and Michael Mcintyre. BBC1 2009-

Walking With Dinosaurs Six-part natural history series narrated by Kenneth Branagh and directed by Tim Haines. Broadcast on BBC1 in 1999, *Walking with Dinosaurs* sets out to create the most accurate portrayal of prehistoric animals ever seen on the screen. Combining fact and informed speculation with cutting-edge computer graphics and animatronics effects, the series took two years to make. *Walking With Beasts* was the 2001 sequel and featured actors for the first time. *Walking With Monsters* was a 2005 prequel to *Walking with Dinosaurs*. Among other spin-offs from the series was *Walking with Cavemen* (2003) although this series was not directed by Haines.

Wallander Kenneth Branagh (Kurt Wallander), Sarah Smart (Anne-Britt Hoglun), Tom Beard (Svedberg), Richard McCabe (Nyberg), Sadie Shimmin (Lisa Holgersson), Jeany Spark (Linda Wallender), David Warner (Povel Wallender), Polly Hemingway (Gertrude Wallender) and Tom Hiddleston (Martinsson). BAFTA Award-winning television drama series adapted by Richard Cottan and Richard McBrien from Henning Mankell's Kurt Wallander novels. The series was set in and filmed in the fictional police inspector's hometown of Ystad, Sweden. The theme tune is "Nostalgia" by Emily Barker. BBC1 2008-11

Walrus and the Carpenter, The Hugh Griffith (Luther Flannery), Felix Aylmer (Gascoigne Quilt), Hazel Hughes (Luther's Daughter). Six-part sitcom written by Marty Feldman and Barry Took, the humour created by the unlikely friendship of two mismatched men. It originated from a one-off comedy Playhouse episode in 1963, BBC 1963; 1965.

War Game, The Drama documentary depicting the effects of nuclear war on Britain. Written, directed, and produced by Peter Watkins for the BBC's *The Wednesday Play* anthology series. The film won the Academy Award for Best Documentary Feature in 1966, although remained unshown in full on British television until 1985 because of its sensitive content. Michael Aspel and Peter Graham are the two commentators on the fictional Soviet attack. BBC1 1965

Warship Donald Burton (Commander Mark Nialls), Graeme Eton (Lieutenant Wakelin), Richard Warwick (Lieutenant Parry), Malcolm Terris (Commander 'Murky' Murton), Michael Cochrane (Lieutenant Palfrey RM), James Leith (Lieutenant Tagg), Anthony Ainley (Phillip Tashing), Struan Rodger (Sub-Lieutenant Penn), Peter Davison (Constable Munk), Colin Rix (LMA Milner), Lewis Collins (Lieutenant / Seaman Steele), Anthony Webb (AB Radcliffe), William Lucas (Captain Herrick), Prunella Ransome (Zoe Carter), Wei Wei Wong (Lily Tan). Military soap opera devised by serving Naval officer Ian Mackintosh and series producer Anthony Coburn. The series took as its central premise the lives and duties of those serving on board *HMS Hero* (No. F42, actually real-life frigate *HMS Phoebe*) and was designed to reflect the changing nature of the British Navy in the early 1970s. The series focused on patrols in the east Mediterranean and far east. BBC1 1973-77.

Watch With Mother The sister programme of *Listen with Mother* began in 1953 and was the brainchild of Freda Lingstrom, who became Head of Children's Television at the BBC. It became hugely popular by 1955 when its daily format was established as Monday: *Picture Book*, Tuesday: *Andy Pandy*, Wednesday: *The Flowerpot Men*, Thursday: *Rag, Tag and Bobtail*, Friday: *The Woodentops*. Later additions in the 1960s included *Tales of the Riverbank, Camberwick Green, Pogle's Wood, Joe, Trumpton, The Herbs, Bizzy Lizzy, Chigley* and *Mary, Mungo and Midge*; and in the 1970s *Mr Benn, Bagpuss, Fingerbobs, Barnaby, Bod* and *The Mister Men*. By 1980 the umbrella name of *Watch With Mother* had disappeared and was replaced by *See-Saw*, although many of the programmes remained the same, additions included *King Rollo*, and *Bric-A-Brac, Postman Pat, Bertha, Pigeon Street* and *Pie in the Sky*. In the Autumn of 1987 the *See-Saw* series was moved across to BBC2 and took a 1.20pm or 1.25pm lunchtime slot only. One of the last programmes to be shown with a *See-Saw* banner in the Radio Times of December 1988 was *The Adventures Of Spot*. From 1989 the slot was now placed under the Children's BBC banner and hosted a new range of programmes such as *Greenclaws, Joshua Jones, The Brollys, Philomena's Cat*, and *PC Pinkerton*. BBC 1953-1988.

Watchdog Consumer-affairs programme. *Watchdog* began in 1980 as a weekly slot on BBC One's teatime news magazine programme, *Nationwide*, and was presented by Hugh Scully. It was given its own programme slot five years later. Presenters have included Nick Ross, Lynn Faulds Wood, John Stapleton, Anne Robinson (current), Alice Beer, Charlotte Hudson, Nicky Campbell, Julia Bradbury, Kate Sanderson, Paul Heiney, Saima Mohsin, Anita Rani (current) and Matt Allwright (current). *Rogue*

Traders, a BBC1 show presented by Matt Allwright (with Dan Penteado) where unscrupulous door-to-door tradesmen and salesmen are secretly filmed, began in 2001 and was incorporated into *Watchdog* in 2009. BBC1 1985-

Watching Paul Bown (Malcolm Stoneway), Liza Tarbuck (Pamela Wilson / Lynch), Emma Wray (Brenda Wilson), Patsy Byrne (Mrs Marjorie Stoneway), Al T Kossy (Harold), Bill Moores (Cedric), Perry Fenwick (Terry Milton), Philip Fox (Sidney Clough), John Bowler (David Lynch), Liz Crowther (Susan Roberts), Dave Dutton (Oswald), Russell Boulter (Chris), Elizabeth Morton (Lucinda Davis/Stoneway), Noreen Kershaw (Mrs Joyce Wilson). Sitcom written by Jim Hitchmough and set in Merseyside. Brenda and Pamela Wilson are sisters whose idea of fun is to go out to their local pub, The Grapes, and watch men, trying to guess their backgrounds, how old they are, what religion and what job they have. Into the pub walks Malcolm Stoneway, a watcher of a different kind: he's a keen ornithologist. Unaware of this, Brenda manoeuvres him into asking her out, and for their first date he collects her in his motorcycle (a 1939 Norton 500) and 1936 sidecar and heads out into the country with his binoculars. She hates every minute of it, thinking of him as 'a 14-carat wimp'. And yet, against all odds, a relationship develops. ITV 1987-93.

Waterfront Beat John Ashton (Chief Supt Don Henderson), Geoffrey Leesley (Det. Supt. Frank Mathews), Rupert Frazer (Supt Peter Fallows), Brian McCardle (PC Ronnie Barker), Philip Middlemiss (PC Barry Smith), Jane Hazelgrove (WPC Madeline Forest), Tommy Boyle (Denny Hagland). Following extensive research into the structure of the Merseyside Police Force, Phil Redmond devised *Waterfront Beat* as a drama serial which gave a fresh and realistic look at the practice of modern policing in the UK. Concentrating on a non-metropolitan force coming to terms with the reorganisation of its city division. BBC1 1990-91.

Waterloo Road Current cast members include: Chelsee Healey (Janeece Bryant), Darcey Isa (Lauren Andrews), Philip Martin Brown (Grantly Budgen), Jason Done (Tom Clarkson), Shannon Flynn (Emily James), Reece Douglas (Denzil Kelly), William Rush (Josh Stevenson), Katie McGlynn (Jodie 'Scout' Allen), Alec Newman (Michael Byrne), George Sampson (Kyle Stack), Mark Benton (Daniel Chalk), Alex Walkinshaw (Jez Diamond), Georgia Henshaw (Madi Diamond), Jaye Jacobs (Sian Diamond), Lee Abbate (Zack Diamond), Hope Katana (Rhona Mansfield), Millie Katana (Shona Mansfield), Sarah Hadland (Linda Radleigh), Jack McMullen (Finn Sharkey), Naveed Choudhry (Tariq Siddiqui), Aryana Ramkhalawon (Trudi Siddiqui), Kane Tomlinson-Weaver (Harley Taylor), Kaya Moore (Phoenix Taylor), Chris Geere (Matt Wilding). **Former cast members include**: Jason Merrells (Jack Rimmer), Jason Done (Tom Clarkson), Jeff Merchant (Brian Vaisey), Judith Barker (Estelle Cooper), Jill Halfpenny (Izzie Redpath), Jamie Glover (Andrew Treneman), Angela Griffin (Kim Campbell), Lauren Drummond (Mika Grainger), Katie Griffiths (Chlo Grainger), Denise Welch (Steph Haydock), Rhea Bailey (Yasmin Deardon), Rebecca Ryan (Vicki MacDonald), John McArdle (Oliver Mead), Elizabeth Berrington (Ruby Fry), Elaine Symons (Rose Kelly), Holly Kenny (Sambuca Kelly), William Ash (Christopher Mead), Ayesha Gwilt (Amy Porter), Tina O'Brien (Bex Fisher), Martin Kemp (Mr Burley), Amanda Burton (Karen Fisher), Neil Morrissey (Eddie Lawson), Eva Pope (Rachel Mason), Robson Green (Rob Scotcher), Debra Stephenson (Naomi Scotcher), John Thomson (Nelson Smith), Tim Healy (Dave Miller), Sarah-Jane Potts (Jo Lipsett). Waterloo Road Comprehensive is on the scrap heap. It lurks near the bottom of every league table there is. Its despondent teachers have given up trying to make a difference as they struggle to cope with their own personal problems as well as their nightmare day jobs. When the headmaster has a nervous breakdown, Jack Rimmer (followed by Rachel Mason and Karen Fisher) is reluctantly thrown into the hot seat. He recruits optimistic, educational zealot Andrew Treneman (followed as deputy head by Eddie Lawson and Christopher Mead) who wants to give up his comfortable private school job to bring the benefits of his elite educational experience to Waterloo Road. Together with feisty Guidance Head Kim Campbell the three teachers set out to turn around the fortunes of Waterloo Road. Michael Byrne is the current head teacher and Sian Diamond his deputy. The school used for the fictional Waterloo Road is situated in the heart of a housing estate in Rochdale. The title music is by Mark Hinton Stewart. BBC1 2006-

Waybuloo Cbeebies animation and human production created by Dan Good and Absolutely Cuckoo. Set in the land of Nara and having remarkable similarities to the earlier teletubbies the program makers describe it as "...a philosophy for a happy life, and like nothing children will have ever seen before". The main characters are four Piplings, 3D CGI animated creatures with large heads and eyes, placed on a filmed background, with the second half of each twenty-minute show featuring human children. Nok Tok is a bear with a blue body with slightly tanned skin; De Li is a cat with a pink body and blue eyes, slightly pointed ears on top of her head and a tail with a white tip. She wears a flower on top of her head; Lau Lau is a rabbit with a lilac coloured body and green eyes, extremely long ears and a puff tail; Yojojo is a monkey with an amber coloured body, blue eyes, rounded ears and four thick hairs rising above his right ear which flop over to his left like a comb-over. He is often seen hiding in a log with his long tail showing. To-date there have been 100 episodes made over two series. BBC2 2009-

Way We Were, The Nostalgic look back at British way of life through the eyes of people's youth and with the help of archive footage. The incidental theme music is called Tenderness composed by husband and wife team Clair Marlo and Alexander Baker. ITV 2008

We Are the Champions Peter Charlton produced and Ron Pickering hosted the long-running inter-school series of athletic events including running, jumping, throwing, swimming and a mini-assault course. A special edition for disabled youngsters was held in 1987 and the show-proper ended later that year. A series of one-off specials were held in the 1990s and following Ron's untimely death, Gary Lineker, and then Linford Christie, took over towards the end of its run. BBC1 1973-95.

We'll Meet Again Susannah York (Dr Helen Dereham), Michael Shannon (Major James Kiley), Patrick O'Connell (Jack Blair), Lynne Pearson (Rosie Blair), James Saxon (Sgt Elmer Jones), Lou Hirsch (Sgt Hymie Stutz). 13-part romantic drama series created by David Butler and set during WWII. ITV 1982.

Weakest Link, The Anne Robinson irreverently hosts the quiz show where knowledge does not necessarily convert to success as the contestants themselves vote off the 'weakest link', who then has the ignominy of the 'walk of shame'. At its peak the show was hugely popular but declining viewing figures saw it stuck in an early afternoon slot. BBC1 2000- The series is due to end in 2012 when Anne Robinson's contract is ended.

Weather Weather forecasts were first broadcast in Britain by BBC Radio from 26 March 1923. The world's first television weather forecast was broadcast by the BBC on 20 November 1936 at 4.01pm, an anonymous hand sketched in the isobars on a weather chart, while an off-screen voice provided the forecast. Regular forecasts on the BBC began on 29 July 1949. George Cowling became Britain's first weatherman to be seen on camera on 11 January 1954 when he presented the forecast from the BBC's Lime Grove Studios. Barbara Edwards became the BBC's, and Britain's, first female weather presenter in January 1974. Other BBC forecasters include, Bert Foord, Jack Scott (who was also a weatherman on Thames TV between 1983 and 1988), Graham Parker, Keith Best, Michael Fish, Ian McCaskill, Jim Bacon, John Kettley, Bernard Davey, Suzanne Charlton, Peter Cockroft, Rob McElwee, Penny Tranter, Richard Edgar, Philip Avery, Helen Young, Peter Gibbs, David Lee, Isobel Lang, David Braine, Sarah Wilmshurst, Darren Bett, Helen Willetts, Bill Giles, Francis Wilson, Carol Kirkwood, Matt Taylor, Liam Dutton, Chris Fawkes, Alex Deakin and Tomasz Schafernaker (who was in the news in 2007 for describing the Outer Hebrides as "nowheresville" and again in 2010 for giving News 24's Simon McCoy the finger gesture during a live link). ITV began its own national weather forecasts in 1989 with Ulrika Jonsson presenting it for Breakfast TV. Other presenters include, Alex Hill, Sian Lloyd, Trish Williamson, Martyn Davies, Laura Greene, Fiona Farrell, John Hammond, Clare Nasir, Chrissie Reidy, Lucy

Verasamy, Andrea McLean, Robin Lermitte and Kirsty McCabe (who previously worked for the BBC). Ireland's first TV weather-person was George Callaghan, who presented the inaugural forecast on the new RTE television channel in January 1962. George, one of a team of six which included Seamus Miller, Michael Gilligan, Paddy MacHugh, Charles Daly and Denis Fitzgerald, kept TV weather forecasts rolling during the 1960s; Miller, Gilligan and Daly, alas, all died relatively young and the others are now honourably retired. The 1980s saw the first arrival of a woman on the TV weather scene, Evelyn Murphy, who has now progressed to become an expert on marine meteorology. Since Evelyn's debut, the TV team has always been a mixed one, comprising at various times familiar names like Gerald Fleming, Aidan Nulty, Evelyn Cusack, John Doyle, Michael Cleary, Brendan McWilliams, Gerry Scully and Joan Blackburn.

Weaver's Green Created by Peter and Betty Lambda, this short-lived soap opera is notable for being one of the first television programmes to be shot on location using videotape and outside broadcast equipment, rather than film, as had usually been the case for non-studio shooting up until this point. The series dealt with life in a small country town and provided an early TV role for Kate O'Mara as a student vet, a far cry from her later TV bitch characters. The village of Heydon, north of Reepham was used for the main outside filming, and County School railway station was also used for some scenes. The excellent cast included Eric Flynn, Megs Jenkins, Grant Taylor, Georgina Ward, Richard Coleman, Susan Field, Vanessa Forsyth, John Glyn-Jones, Maurice Kaufmann, John Moulder Brown, Wendy Richard, Gerald Young, Brian Cant, Edward Underdown, Susan George, and Marjie Lawrence who starred as Hazel Westcott in all 49 episodes. ITV 1966.

Weekend World Sunday lunchtime political programme, originally presented by John Torode, Mary Holland, and Peter Jay (who became the solo presenter within six months). When Jay left to take up his appointment as British ambassador to the USA in 1977, he was replaced by former Labour MP Brian Walden (1977-86). Former Tory MP Matthew Parris took over for the final two years. The guitar-heavy theme music was Nantucket Sleighride by American rock band, Mountain. ITV 1972-88.

Wednesday Play Anthology series of British television plays which ran on BBC1 from October 1964 to May 1970. See separate entries for Cathy Come Home, Stand Up Nigel Barton, Up the Junction and The War Game

Weirdsister College See entry for The Worst Witch

Wexford See The Ruth Rendell Mysteries.

Whack-O! Jimmy Edwards (Prof James Edwards), Arthur Howard and Julian Orchard (Mr Oliver Pettigrew), Kenneth Cope (Mr F. D. Price Whittaker), Peter Glaze (Mr R. P. Trench), Brian Rawlinson (Mr Proctor), Norman Bird (Mr S. A. Smallpiece). Sitcom written by Frank Muir and Denis Norden. Professor James Edwards, MA, is headmaster of Chiselbury School and rules over pupils with an iron cane! His deputy-head, Mr Pettigrew, is altogether a different proposition and has a far more sympathetic nature. BBC 1956-60. Jimmy reprised his role in a 1971-72 series in which Pettigrew was played by Julian Orchard.

What in the World Quiz, The Science-based panel show hosted by Marcus Brigstocke. Two teams headed by comedians Lee Hurst and Dominic Holland went head to head over four rounds of questions and challenges based on science, nature, technology, and human achievement, covering such diverse topics as poisonous plants, sailing stones and light refraction. Each team captain was joined by a non-famous scientist, who brought in something to show the viewer by way of explaining what they do. Five 2008-09

What Not To Wear Makeover television show presented by Trinny Woodall and Susannah Constantine. The show began on BBC2 but later moved to BBC1. Lisa Butcher and Mica Paris took over as presenters of the show for the final two series. Every episode features an "ambush" style confrontation and makeover of a man or (more often) a woman who has been nominated by their friends as particularly unfashionable. The subject has their current fashion sense evaluated. The presenters take particular regard to the subject's body-shape and self-image (with the help of a 360 degree mirror cabinet) and determine what will work best for them. The subject is then given £2,000 to go shopping for a new wardrobe, which is supposed to be in accordance with the advice they have been given. Although they are free to spend how they wish, they are spied upon and counselled on the ways of fashion by the show's two hosts. BBC2 2001-03; BBC1 2004-07. See also *Trinny & Susan Undress…*

What the Ancients Did For Us A series of popular history programmes presented by keen cyclist, scientist and historian Adam Hart-Davis. Born in Henley-on-Thames, 4 July 1943, Hart-Davis is a direct descendant of King William IV and his mistress Dorothea Jordan and is therefore fifth cousin once removed of Queen Elizabeth II, second cousin once removed of the British Prime Minister David Cameron and first cousin once removed of the historian John Julius Norwich. The first series exploring the ancients, in 2000, was entitled *What the Romans did for Us* (a reference to the John Cleese character in *Monty Python's Life of Brian*) and subsequent series explored the Victorians (2001), Tudors (2002) and Stuarts (2002). The 2003 offering, *What the Industrial Revolution Did for Us*, was presented by Dan Cruickshank. *What the Ancients Did For Us* was broadcast in 2005 and again presented by Adam Hart-Davis with contributions from Hermione Cockburn, Jamie Darling, Amani Zain and Marty Jopson. Each episode examined the impact of ancient civilizations on modern society. BBC2 2000-05.

What the Papers Say Although *The Sky At Night* is often cited as the longest-running British television programme, in fact, *What the Papers Say* began a year earlier and was in fact the holder of that title until it ended its run on television in 2008 (It was reintroduced on BBC Radio 4 in 2010 prior to the General Election). The format, consisting of readings from the previous week's newspapers, linked by a studio presenter, had remained unchanged for more than half a century. Actors reading the excerpts from the papers, out of vision, included Peter Wheeler, Daphne Oxenford, Ray Moore and Barrie Hesketh. The show has always been made by Granada Television, the longest-running broadcasting company in the UK other than the BBC, and was the last surviving programme from the company's original line-up in 1956. For the first 26 years of its run the programme appeared on ITV. The first programme, on November 5th 1956, was presented by Brian Inglis, deputy editor of *The Spectator*; the following week Kingsley Martin, editor of *The New Statesman*, presented the programme thus beginning the tradition of rotating journalists as host although Brian Inglis became an ever-present for some years making almost 200 appearances in total. In 1969 the programme was briefly relaunched as *The Papers*, with Stuart Hall, of the Open University, as the first presenter. This version of the programme lasted for only 10 weeks and it then reverted to its original title. Originally the programme ran for 25 minutes, later dropping to 20. The show moved from ITV to Channel Four when the latter launched in 1982, but was dropped in 1989, to be taken up by BBC2 where it remained, broadcast on Saturday afternoons, with a running time of 10 minutes (15 minutes initially). The theme music was originally *The Procession of the Sardar*, by Mikhail Ippolitov-Ivanov, the 10 programmes entitled *The Papers* used the Gershwin *Piano Concerto in F*, and when the programme reverted to its original title, it was replaced by the distinctive Allegro Non Troppo, the 5th movement of Malcolm Arnold's Second Set of English Dances Opus 33. ITV 1956-82; C4 1982-89; BBC2 1990-2008

Whatever Happened to the Likely Lads? See *The Likely Lads*.

What's My Line Game show where a celebrity panel endeavoured to guess contestant's occupations simply by watching them 'sign in' and perform a short mime of their chosen profession. A series of questions would then be asked, the answers only requiring a 'yes' or 'no'. If ten 'nos' are recorded the contestant has beaten the panel and wins a certificate. A popular midway round was the 'mystery celebrity' who would appear to huge audience recognition, but a blindfolded panel. Much disguising of voice was usually the order of the day. Eamonn Andrews was the first presenter, the original panel being Isobel Barnett, David Nixon, Gilbert Harding, and Barbara Kelly. BBC1 1951-63. When the show was revived on BBC2 in 1973-74 David Jacobs replaced Eamonn Andrews as presenter. The show was revived for a third

time on ITV in 1984 with Eamonn again taking over proceeding until his death in 1987, when Penelope Keith took over until 1988 and then Angela Rippon for the remaining two years of its run. A final revival was made by Meridian TV (1994-96) with Emma Forbes in the chair.

What's Up Doc? Saturday morning children's magazine show which replaced *Motormouth*. Presented by Andy Crane, Yvette Fielding and Pat Sharp, the programme was designed to promote Warner Bros products and Looney Tunes animated shorts were the order of the day. The show also featured a vast array of characters including Simon Perry, Colin, Wooly, Billy Box, Baljit, Pasty the Worm, Mister Spanky, Naughty Torty, Gaston, Sam Sam and most memorably Bro & Bro the Wolves (worked by puppeteers Don Austen and John Eccleston who had a spin-off show, *Wolf It*). Such was the popularity of Austen and Eccleston that when they defected to the BBC's Saturday Morning show *Live & Kicking* to star as a couple of leprechaun brothers in 1995 ratings dropped and the show was cancelled. ITV 1992-95.

Wheel of Fortune Game show where contestants were required to guess well-known phrases by selecting a letter of the alphabet after spinning a wheel to make points towards the ultimate winning target. Presenters included Nicky Campbell (1988-96), Bradley Walsh (1997), John Leslie (1998-2000) and Paul Hendy (2001). Hostesses included Carol Smillie (1988-94) and Jenny Powell (1995-2000). Scottish Television for ITV 1988-2001. See *Take Your Pick*

Wheeltappers' and Shunters Social Club Variety show hosted by Bernard Manning from the fictitious club. Concert chairman was Colin Crompton who was forever interrupting the host with comical announcements in the manner of a real northern social club. The title of the show derives from two specialist railway occupations. ITV 1974-77.

When the Boat Comes In James Bolam (Jack Ford), Susan Jameson (Jessie Seaton / Ashton), James Garbutt (Bill Seaton), Madelaine Newton (Dolly Headley / Ford), John Nightingale (Tom Seaton), Basil Henson (Sir Horatio Manners). Sgt Jack Ford returns home to Gallowshields in the North East of England, embittered after the end of World War One, and is determined to make something of his life. He meets teacher Jessie Seaton, falls in love, and plays a pivotal part in the fortunes of her and her family after becoming a bigwig in the unions. Jack ends up losing Jessie when he gets Sir Horatio's maid Dolly pregnant and marries her, albeit for a short while (she would later get a divorce from Jack and marry Tom.) The series ended in 1977 but four years later was back, with Jack newly-returned from America having got into trouble with gangsters there thanks to his bootlegging activities. It was now the mid 1930s and Jack found himself persuaded by Jessie and her brother Billy to get involved in the Spanish Civil War, running guns to the anti government forces; again, mainly motivated by money, Jack agrees but this ends up having tragic consequences for him. The series ends with Jack being killed in an ambush, dying in Jessie's arms. The popular theme tune (written by David Fanshawe and sung by Alex Glasson) went thus: *Come here, maw little Jacky, Now aw've smoked mi backy, Let's hev a bit o' cracky, Till the boat comes in. Dance ti' thy daddy, sing ti' thy mammy, Dance ti' thy daddy, ti' thy mammy sing; Thou shall hev a fishy on a little dishy, Thou shall hev a fishy when the boat comes in.* BBC1 1976-7; 1981.

Where the Heart Is Pam Ferris (Margaret 'Peggy' Snow), Sarah Lancashire (Ruth Goddard), Tony Haygarth (Vic Snow), Thomas Craig (Simon Goddard), William Ash and Jason Done (Stephen Snow), Jessica Baglow (Lucy Snow), Melanie Kilburn (Sandra Harrison), Lesley Dunlop (Anna Kirkwall), Leslie Ash (Karen Buckley), Philip Middlemiss (David Buckley), Danny Seward (Joe Beresford), Brian Capron (Ozias Harding), Keith Barron (Alan Boothe), Alex Carter (Craig Harrison), Shobna Gulati (Nisha Clayton), Denise van Outen (Kim Blakeney), Tom Chadbon (Dr. Kenworthy), Shirley Anne Field (Linda), Keith David (Moses Whitecotten), Marsha Thomason and Paulette Williams (Jacqui Richards / Snow). Drama series created by Ashley Pharoah and Vicky Featherstone. The original series concerned the story of two sisters-in-law working as district nurses in the Yorkshire town of Skelthwaite. Kind-hearted and sympathetic 48-year-old Peggy Snow is the wife of Vic and mother of teenage son Stephen and younger daughter Lucy. Ruth, the wife of Peggy's calculating brother Simon, is about to give birth to their first child, Alfie, as the series opens. Simon owns the toilet paper company where Vic works. Action developed over the years to focus on the human stories rather than the medical issues, the Skelthwaite Arms figuring prominently among members of the Skelthwaite Skorpions rugby league team who love the odd pint of Chapstons. Paddy McAloon of the band Prefab Sprout wrote and performed the theme song. ITV 1997-2006

Whicker's World Alan Donald Whicker. Born in Cairo, Egypt, 2 August 1925. He attended Haberdashers' Aske's School, London, and served as captain in the Devonshire Regiment during World War II. Following a stint as a newspaper war correspondent in Korea, Alan became a radio broadcaster before joining BBC television in 1957, presenting nightly film reports from around the world for *Tonight*. *Whicker's World*, initially a compilation of his *Tonight* reports, began on the BBC in 1959 and helped to launch Yorkshire Television. For the next 35 years Alan was hardly off our screens with a proliferation of news, current affairs and travel series including, *Whicker Down Under* (1961), *Whicker on Top of the World*! (1962), *Whicker in Sweden* (1963), *Whicker in the Heart of Texas* (1963), *Whicker Down Mexico Way* (1963), *Whicker's World* (1965-67), *Whicker's New World* (1969), *Whicker in Europe* (1969), *Whicker's Walkabout* (1970), *World of Whicker* (1971), *Whicker's Orient* (1972), *Whicker Within a Woman's World* (1972), *Whicker Way Out West* (1973), *Whicker's South Seas* (1973), *Whicker's World* (1974-77), *Whicker's World - Down Under* (1976), *Whicker's World: US* (1977), *Whicker's World: India* (1978), *Whicker's World: Indonesia* (1979), *Whicker's World: California* (1980), *Whicker's World Aboard the Orient Express* (1982), *Whicker!* (1984), *Whicker's World - Living with Uncle Sam* (1985), *Whicker's World - Living with Waltzing Matilda* (1987-88), *Whicker's World - Hong Kong* (1990), *Whicker's World - A Taste of Spain* (1992), *Whicker's Miss World* (1993), *Whicker's World Aboard the Real Orient Express* (1994) and *Whicker's War* (2004).

Whiplash Peter Graves (Christopher Cobb). Western series. American Chris Cobb arrives in Fury Creek, Australia, in the 1850s to establish Cobb & Co, the country's first stagecoach service and meets a varied assortment of cowboys and outlaws on his travels. The series had a memorable title tune sung by Frank Ifield, truncated by the sound of a whiplash it went as follows: *Whiplash, Whiplash, Whiplash, Whiplash. In 1851 the Great Australian gold rush. The only law a gun, the only shelter wildbush. Whiplash, Whiplash. The Mulga woods and deserts, the stage thunders by. From Sydney to Camden and on to Gundagai. Whiplash, Whiplash.* ITV 1960-61.

Whirligig See *Saturday Special*

Whistle Test See *The Old Grey Whistle Test*.

White Heather Club, The *The White Heather Club* took up the baton from *Draw in Your Chair* and made Andy Stewart (born Glasgow 1933, died Arbroath 1993) an international star. Stewart presented and sang in the Scottish country dance music show, which, at its peak, drew in an audience of 10 million people. This very Scottish image, awash with kilts and fiddles, is one which the rest of the network took to be a true representation of Scotland! First televised on 7 May 1958, tenor Robert Wilson was supposed to present the first ever edition but unforeseen circumstances led to Andy Stewart stepping in at the last minute. Although Wilson subsequently fulfilled his contractual term Andy soon returned to make the show his own. The ever-popular Robin Hall and Jimmie Macgregor were the resident folk singers (splitting their time between this show and *Tonight*) and all the top Scottish acts, including Jimmy Logan, Chic Murray, Jimmy Shand and Moira Anderson were featured. BBC1 1958-68.

White Hunter Rhodes Reason (John A. Hunter). Filmed at Twickenham Studios and Beaconsfield Studios, London, England, with location scenes filmed in Africa. Adventure series based on the true-life exploits of John A. Hunter, author of the books, African Safari and Hunter's Tracks. 39 episodes of this hugely popular series, aired across three series, depicting game hunter cum detective John Hunter. ITV 1958-60.

Whites Alan Davies (Roland White), Darren Boyd (Bib Spears), Stephen Wight (Skoose), Katherine Parkinson (Caroline), Isy Suttie (Kiki), Maggie Steed (Celia), Amit Shah (Axel), Matt King (Melvin), Oliver Lansley (Robin). Sitcom written by Matt King and Oliver Lansley. Set in the kitchen of a country house hotel, Whites follows the trials and tribulations of head chef Roland and his long suffering sous chef Bib. Having been on the brink of success 15 years ago, Roland has since lost the sparkle and drive needed to win a long-coveted Michelin star. He can cook with the best of them when he puts his mind to it, but laziness gets the better of him, much to the annoyance of restaurant manager Caroline. Bib, meanwhile, is under pressure and hasn't spent time with his wife for months. It doesn't help that Skoose the apprentice chef, has zero respect for him or that quirky waitress Kiki is a little dimwitted, having once taken an order for an eggless omelette. BBC2 2010-

Whittle Game show hosted by comedian Tim Vine. An audience of 100 people were 'whittled' down to a single winner by a series of general knowledge questions. When the field was reduced to 10 players correct answers would now earn ten pounds. Incorrect answers led to elimination from the game and for comic effect, the eliminated contestants were punished by being made to wear a "Whittle mask" - in bright yellow with a large purple W on it. There were up to four questions in the second half, the last one of which may be timed, aiming to find a single winner, who earned a guaranteed £250. The end game consisted of the winner trying to place four items in the correct sequence to double their money, however, if they failed, all the audience members who got the correct sequence and typed it into their keypads within 15 seconds split the second £250 between them. Channel 5 (now *Five*) 1997-98. See also *Everybody's Equal*.

Who Dares Sings! Karaoke challenge hosted by Denise Van Outen and Ben Shephard. 100 members of the studio audience took centre stage and belted out chart-topping hits before being randomly selected by a computer named SAM (Sound Analysis Machine) to compete for a jackpot prize of £50,000. ITV 2008

Who Dares, Wins Comedy sketch show featuring Jimmy Mulville, Rory McGrath, Philip Pope, Julia Hills and Tony Robinson. The opening title sequence showed a man staggering home from the pub to get to the television in time for the programme. The series established Mulville's Hat Trick Productions as a producer of comedy material for Channel 4. Possibly the most famous sketch was Tony Robinson's appearance as the emperor (as in The Emperor's New Clothes), and appearing on stage totally naked and is then shown hanging around in following sketches (and the following show), still naked, seemingly not knowing what to do with himself. C4 1984-88.

Who Do You Do? Showcase for established and up-and-coming impressionists. Featured artists included Peter Goodwright, Margo Henderson, Janet Brown, Paul Melba, Johnny More, Russ Abbot, Dustin Gee, Jerry Stevens, Little and Large, Aiden J Harvey, Les Dennis and Michael Barrymore. The series confirmed the arrival of Freddie Starr as a major British entertainer with his imitations of everyone from Max Wall to Tarzan by way of Mick Jagger, Elvis Presley, Norman Wisdom, the wrestler Adrian Street, Tom Jones and scores of others. ITV 1972-76. In 1975 the show was renamed *New Who Do you Do?* and in 1976 *Now Who Do you Do?*. The show was revived by Central TV for a 30-week run from 23 June 1995, screened in the Midlands but not networked.

Who Do You Think You Are? In each episode of this documentary series, a celebrity goes on a journey to trace their family tree. Celebrities featured have included: Bill Oddie, Amanda Redman, Sue Johnston, Jeremy Clarkson, Ian Hislop, Moira Stuart, Alan Cumming, David Baddiel, Lesley Garrett, Meera Syal, Vic Reeves, Jeremy Paxman, Sheila Hancock, Stephen Fry, Julian Clary, Jane Horrocks, Dervla Kirwan, Gurinder Chadha, Barbara Windsor, Robert Lindsay, Colin Jackson, David Tennant, David Dickinson, Nigella Lawson, Jeremy Irons, Julia Sawalha, Nicky Campbell, Natasha Kaplinsky, John Hurt, Griff Rhys Jones, Carol Vorderman, Alistair McGowan, Graham Norton, Sir Matthew Pinsent, Patsy Kensit, Boris Johnson, Jerry Springer, Esther Rantzen, Ainsley Harriott, David Suchet, Jodie Kidd, Laurence Llewelyn-Bowen, Rory Bremner, Fiona Bruce, Rick Stein, Zoë Wanamaker, Bruce Forsyth and Kevin Whately. Actor David Morrissey narrated

Series 1 & 2 on BBC2 and actor Mark Strong has provided the narration since 2006. BBC2 2004-06, BBC1 2006-

Who Is Sylvia? Charlie Drake (Charles Rameses), Kathleen Byron (Mrs. Proudpiece). Seven-episode sitcom written by Donald Churchill and Charlie Drake. In each episode Charlie would visit a marriage bureau looking for the love of his life but was always thwarted. The title character was never actually seen. The title tune was sung by Charlie and described his search, ending poignantly with "…..*Sylvia – where are you*" ITV 1967. See Charlie Drake's entry in the comedy section.

Who Wants To Be A Millionaire? Quiz show devised by David Briggs and hosted by Chris Tarrant. Ten contestants answer a 'Fastest Finger' question in order to earn the right to sit in the hot seat to play for up to £1 million. The contestant must answer 15 multiple-choice questions correctly in a row to win the jackpot. The contestant may quit at any time and keep their earnings. For each question, they are shown the question and four possible answers in advance before deciding whether to play on or not. If they do decide to offer an answer, it must be correct to stay in the game. At any point, the contestant may use up one (or more) of their three "lifelines". These are: "50:50" - two of the three incorrect answers are removed (invariably the two you knew it couldn't be, although Chris informs the audience it is a random selection!); "Phone a friend" - the contestants may speak to a friend or relative on the phone for 30 seconds to discuss the question; "Ask the audience" - the audience votes with their keypads on their choice of answer (unfortunately 92 per cent of the audience gave the wrong answer when i appeared on the show!). The question increments were £100, £200, £300, £500, £1,000, £2,000, £4,000, £8,000, £16,000, £32,000, £64,000, £125,000, £250,000, £500,000, £1,000,000 but in August 2007 became: £500, £1,000, £2,000, £5,000, £10,000, £20,000, £50,000, £75,000, £150,000, £250,000, £500,000, £1,000,000 (an audition process was also introduced at this time in an attempt to dissuade syndicates from circumventing the 'random' selection of phone-in application rules). The first millionaire winner was Judith Keppel on 20 November 2000 (Clare Barwick was Britain's first-ever quiz show millionaire on the Virgin Radio Breakfast show on 17 December 1999 and Ian Woodley became Britain's first-ever television quiz millionaire a week later on 24 December during Chris Evans' Channel 4 *TFI Friday* entertainment show in a slot called Someone's GOING to be a Millionaire). Other millionaire winners include, David Edwards (21 April 2001) Robert Brydges (9 September 2001), Pat Gibson (24 April 2004) and Ingram Wilcox (23 September 2006). The show is known to have asked at least one erroneous question. In the episode aired on March 8th 1999 Tony Kennedy, a warehouseman from Blackpool, was asked the following question for £64,000: "Theoretically, what is the minimum number of strokes with which a tennis player can win a set?" Tony answered B: 24 and Tarrant informed him it was the correct answer and he went on to win £125,000 by answering the next question correctly. The correct answer should have been A: 12 because you could serve twelve aces to win games 1, 3 and 5, then your opponent could double-fault twelve times, so you win games 2, 4 and 6 without hitting a shot and hence win the set after twelve shots. Tony was allowed to keep his winnings. On 7 April 2003, three people who tried to defraud the television quiz show out of its £1 million top prize were found guilty of deception at Southwark Crown Court. Major Charles Ingram and his wife, Diana, were sentenced to 18 months in prison, suspended for two years. Each was fined £15,000 and ordered to pay £10,000 costs. Their accomplice, Tecwen Whittock, whose 19 strategic coughs steered the Royal Engineers major to the jackpot win during September 2001, was sentenced to 12 months in prison, also suspended for two years, fined £10,000 and ordered to pay £7,500 costs. The much-lauded music, which runs almost continuously throughout the whole show, was written by Keith and Matthew Strachan. In 2010 further changes were made to the format and fastest finger was done away with altogether and the early rounds were timed. A fourth lifeline was also introduced whereby contestants had the chance to flip one of the questions at the £50,000 level. ITV 1988-. The Irish version (which first aired on RTE in October 2000) was hosted by Gay Byrne and had a jackpot of a million euros. It ended in 2002.

Whodunnit? Long-running panel show written by Lance Percival and Jeremy Lloyd, in which a celebrity panel had to work out who perpetrated a dastardly murder after watching a short murder-mystery enactment. The panellists were allowed to interview the cast afterwards and only the murderer was allowed to lie. The 1972 broadcast pilot was hosted by Shaw Taylor and the two panellists were Edward Woodward and Frank Windsor, all three connected to very popular detective series. For the first series of six episodes in 1973 Woodward took the chair and from then onwards Jon Pertwee hosted the final five series of 43 episodes with three (sometimes four) guest panellists including at various times, Woodward, Patrick Mower, Anouska Hempel, William Franklyn, Jackie Collins, Rodney Bewes, Reginald Bosanquet, Billie Whitelaw, Kingsley Amis, Dawn Addams, Aimi MacDonald, Diana Dors, Dilys Laye, Terry Scott, Honor Blackman, Leslie Crowther, Sheila Hancock, Stratford Johns, Magnus Pyke, Gareth Hunt, Norman Bowler and Julie Ege. ITV 1972-78.

Whole Nineteen Yards, The The first gameshow in Britain to be filmed in high definition. Presented by Vernon Kay and Caroline Flack the game consists of a series of rounds to whittle four contestants down to one, each round consisting of a physical challenge of some sort and always commencing with the contestant having to answer a general knowledge question. The final round is played for a jackpot of up to £100,000 and becomes more general knowledge-based as the winner merely needs to be fit enough to scamper down a nineteen yards-long grid to press the buzzer when knowing an answer. If five out of five questions are answered successfully then the jackpot is won. Glenn Hugill is the announcer and commentates on events for viewers at home. The title of the show is a pun on the popular saying 'the whole nine yards'. ITV 2010

Whoops Baghdad! Frankie Howerd (Ali Oopla). An Arabian Nights-style variation on *Up Pompeii!*. BBC1 1973.

Whoops! Apocalypse Barry Morse (Johnny Cyclops), Richard Griffiths (Premier Dubienkin), Ed Bishop (Jay Garrick), Alexei Sayle (Commissar Solzhenitsyn), Peter Jones (Kevin Pork), John Cleese (Lacrobat), John Barron (The Deacon), Geoffrey Palmer (Dave), Richard Davies (Brian), Bruce Montague (Shah Mashiq Rassim). Sitcom written by Andrew Marshall and David Renwick. The balance of world power is held by the leaders of Russia (the ageing Dubienkin) and the United States (President Johnny Cyclops, a former screen actor who is recently lobotomised). In the middle of the pair is the idiotic British PM, Kevin Pork, aided by his Foreign Secretary (Dave) and Chancellor of the Exchequer (Brian). Also fogging the picture is the mad master-of-disguise Lacrobat - the world's most hunted international terrorist and nuclear-bomb-stealer - and, perhaps most frighteningly of all, the Deacon, the fanatical, God-fearing American security adviser. All the while, the Shah of Iran has been deposed and secret Western attempts to restore his brother to power fail to amount to much (at one point, he is stuck on a cross-channel ferry). Disastrously, in the final episode, a Quark nuclear bomb accidentally destroys Israel, sending the planet cascading towards the Third World War and nuclear holocaust. ITV 1982.

Whose Baby? Game show devised by Eamonn Andrews. A celebrity panel meets the child of a well-known person, and guess who their parents are. The original host for series one and two in 1973 was magician David Nixon and the two regular panelists were singer/disc jockey Jimmy Young and actor Richard Coleman, who were joined by a guest panelist. Penny Meredith was David's assistant. Roy Castle took over as host for the third series in 1977, assisted by Belinda Mayne. The regular panelists were Jon Pertwee, Sylvia Syms and Terry Wogan. The fourth series onwards, in 1984, was hosted by comedian Bernie Winters, assisted by Sarah Hollamby and the ever-present Schnorbitz the St Bernard dog. The panelists changed from week to week. ITV 1973; 1977, 1984-88.

Whose Line Is It Anyway? Comedy game show wherein host Clive Anderson challenged four actors and comedians to improvise sketches based only on a word or notion he, or the audience, would suggest to them. Originally a BBC Radio 4 programme that aired in early 1988, it quickly emulated its success when transferred to television. Typical rounds included two players acting out a scene given by Clive who would buzz in and instruct the players to suddenly act it out in style of his choosing, from a pool of ideas the audience has shouted out; 'Party Quirks', whereby one player hosted a party and the other three joined one by one but had a quirk that members of the audience had written down beforehand. The host of the party had to work out what the quirks were. Clive dished out the points randomly, but whoever 'won' had the rather dubious honour of reading out the credits in a style of Clive's choosing. Regular guests included Greg Proops, Colin Mochrie, Ryan Styles, John Sessions, Stephen Fry, Josie Lawrence, Tony Slattery, Paul Merton, Sandi Toksvig, Mike McShane and Caroline Quentin. Music was supplied by Richard Vranch at the piano. C4 1988-2000

Why Don't You...? Children's entertainment show initially billed in Radio Times as Wdyjsoytsagadslbi? Standing for Why don't you just switch off your television set and go and do something less boring instead? Various groups of kids eg. The Belfast Gang, The Birmingham Gang (A young Ant McPartlin was one of the Newcastle Gang) would arrive every school holidays to suggest things which might be less boring than watching TV. If the programme had actually succeeded of course then it wouldn't have had an audience. The long-running show changed its format on a regular basis. BBC1 1973-95.

Widow of Bath, The John Justin (Hugh Everton), Barbara Murray (Lucy Bath). Nothing to do with Chaucer at all but rather a six-part drama based on the novel of Margot Bennett and starring the husband and wife team of Justin and Murray. BBC 1959.

Widows Ann Mitchell (Dolly Rawlins), Fiona Hendley (Shirley Miller), Maureen O'Farrell (Linda Pirelli), Eva Mottley (Bella O'Reilly), Maurice O'Connell (Harry Rawlins), Terry Stuart (Terry Miller), Michael John Paliotti (Joe Perelli), David Calder (DI Resnick), Christopher Ellison (Tony Fisher), Jeffrey Chiswick (Arnie Fisher), Kate Williams (Audrey Withey). Crime drama series written by Lynda La Plante. Four women carry out their late husbands' planned armoured-car robbery. When Harry Rawlins is killed in an attempted hold-up, his wife, Dolly, inherits his plans for future robberies and recruits Shirley and Linda (whose husbands, Terry and Jo, were killed alongside Rawlins) and black stripper Bella O'Reilly (whose husband had died of a drugs overdose). Major obstacles in their way include the Fisher brothers (sworn enemies of Rawlins) and DI Resnick, a suspicious policeman. At the end of the first series the girls fly off to Rio with suitcase-loads of cash. In the sequel, *Widows 2*, shown two years later, Harry is shown to be alive, having faked his own death, and now wants the money that he feels is rightly his. Debby Bishop took over the role of Bella for the sequel, after Eva Mottley had died from a drugs overdose. In a second sequel, *She's Out*, Dolly is released after an eight-year jail term and has various unsavoury characters after her hidden stash. ITV 1983; 1985; 1995.

Wife Swap Reality television programme whereby two families, usually from very different social classes, swap wives for two weeks. The women try to fill their counterpart's role, usually not succeeding particularly well. The adopted family also tries to cope with the change. Each wife leaves a house manual which explains their role in the family and the duties they hold. During the first week of the swap, they attempt to keep up with the demands set by their new lifestyle and in the second week, the roles are reversed with the family having to abide by the rules set by the new wife. At the end, the women meet for the first time and along with their husbands, discuss how they feel about the two weeks. This often descends into personal insults and has degenerated into violence on at least one occasion. C4 2003-09 A further programme *Wife Swap: the Aftermath* followed each episode on E4 (originally presented by Jacqui Joseph and then Ed Hall)

Wild At Heart Stephen Tompkinson (Danny Trevanion), Amanda Holden (Sarah Trevanion), Lucy-Jo Hudson (Rosie Trevanion), Luke Ward-Wilkinson (Evan Trevanion), Rafaella Hutchinson (Olivia Trevanion), Deon Stewardson (Anders Du

Plessis aka Doop), Nomsa Xaba (Nomsa Nguni), Hayley Mills (Caroline), Jessie Wallace (Amy Kriel), Olivia Scott-Taylor (Olivia Adams \ Trevanion), Cal MacAninch (Rowan Collins), Dawn Steele (Alice Collins), Thapelo Mokoena (Cedric Fatani), Juliet Mills (Georgina Black). Drama series, created by Ashley Pharoah, about a Bristol-based vet and his family relocating to start a game park in South Africa. ITV 2006-

Wild West Dawn French (Mary Trewednack), Catherine Tate (Angela Phillips), David Bradley (Old Jake), Stewart Wright (PC Alan Allen), Sean Foley (Jeff), Robin Weaver (Holly - second series), Anne-Marie Duff (Holly - first series), Richard Mylan (Harry), Bill Bailey (Doug). Sitcom created by Simon Nye, set in the Cornish town of St Gweep (actual Portloe). Most of the plots revolve around the understated lesbian general store owners, Mary and Angela. Other characters include: Holly, owner of the local witchcraft centre; Harry, a young hippy; Old Jake, who runs the local boat tour; Jeff , a swinger and sexual deviant who owns the local pub with his deaf wife Daphne; and PC Allen (Wright), the bumbling policeman who becomes Mary's major romantic interest in series 2. BBC1 2002-04.

Wild Wild Women Barbara Windsor (Millie), Paul Whitsun-Jones (Mr Harcourt – the boss), Pat Coombs (Daisy), Ken Platt (Albert – the foreman), Toni Palmer (Ruby), Jessie Robins (Blossom), Daphne Heard (Ginny), Anna Karen (Maude), Joan Sanderson (Mrs Harcourt). Sitcom written by Ronald Chesney and Ronald Wolfe, who also wrote the very similar themed but vastly more successful *The Rag Trade*. The six-episode series was set in Edwardian times so the factory girls were not allowed to strike, so no whistles and certainly no cries of "everybody out". BBC1 1969

William Tell, The Adventures of Conrad Phillips (William Tell), Jennifer Jayne (Hedda), Willoughby Goddard (Landburgher Gessler), Richard Rogers (Walter Tell), Nigel Greene (Fertog aka The Bear), John Howard Davies (Bruno / Karl). Set in fourteenth century Switzerland in a town called Altdorf. Tell's legendary act of marksmanship, shooting an apple off his son's head, was relived in episode one *The Emperor's Hat* (broadcast on ITV 15 September 1958) but thereafter the stories bore little resemblance to the Johann von Schiller classic wherein the hero ambushes and kills the tyrannical Gessler. Willoughby Goddard played the thoroughly perfidious and corpulent Austrian Governor who, to capture and kill Tell, used every dirty trick conceivable, including assassins disguised as resistance heroes and kidnapping Tell's beautiful wife, Hedda, but Tell, although humiliating Gessler in almost every episode, always fell short of assassination. The 39th and final episode, *Undercover*, was broadcast 15 June 1959. The opening credits began with the blowing of a huge alpenhorn followed by the re-enactment of the aforementioned crossbow scene with Rossini's *William Tell Overture* performed by David Whitfield's rousing *Come away, come away with William Tell. Come away, for the land he loved so welll. What a day, what a day, when the apple fell, for Tell and Switzerland.* The series was shot at Nettlefold Studios, Walton-on-Thames, and the mountain scenes at Snowdonia.

Willo the Wisp Created by Nick Spargo, originally for an educational cartoon for British Gas in 1975, explaining the way the gas network works in the UK. A series was produced comprising 26 five-minute episodes, with all characters voiced by Kenneth Williams. *Willo the Wisp* (based on the North European folklore legend of Will-o'the-Wisp – being the ghost lights sometimes seen on marshes), was the narrator in the programmes, with the main characters being a fairy named Mavis Cruet and Evil Edna - a witch, who takes the form of a talking television set. Other characters included Arthur (a caterpillar), Carwash (a cat who acts like Noël Coward), The Moog (a dog), The Beast (a prince that Evil Edna transformed into a hairy beast, and Twit (a little bird). All episodes were set in Doyley Woods, Oxfordshire. BBC1 1981. In 2005, Bobbie Spargo (daughter of Nick Spargo) created a second series of *Willo the Wisp* for the "Playhouse Disney UK" channel, with scripts written by Jamie Rix, and all characters voiced by James Dreyfus.

Win, Lose or Draw Game show based on members of teams drawing clues to well-known phrases or titles, being awarded points if the rest of the team guess the correct answer. Hosts: Allan Stewart, Danny Baker, Shane Richie, Bob Mills, Lisa

Tarbuck (adult version with team captains Sue Perkins and Ed Hall), Darren Day (Junior version). In 1996 a contestant named Michael Pennington appeared and first told the world of his intention to become a comedian, as Johnny Vegas. ITV 1988-2004.

Win My Wage Daily weekday game show hosted by Nick Hancock in which a contestant attempts to pick out the panellist with the highest salary in order to win it. The salaries are known but not who earns them. When the panellists are whittled down to three the contestant must make their selection of who they believe is the highest earner remaining. To give them more of a chance at this final stage they can be informed of the three jobs but not of course who does them. The price for this extra information is half the salary shown. C4 2007

Wind in the Willows, The Children's animation series based on Kenneth Grahame's 1908 novel. The actors reprised their roles from the 1983 film of the same name. Voices were Michael Hordern (Badger), David Jason (Toad), Peter Sallis (Rat), Richard Pearson (Mole). ITV 1984-87. Following the fourth series an hour-long feature, *A Tale of Two Toads*, aired in 1989, and a further series of 13 episodes was aired in 1990 under the title *Oh! Mr Toad*.

Wink To Me Only Beryl Reid (Irene 'Rene' Jelliot), Hugh Paddick (Sydney Jelliot). Six-episode sitcom concerning the strange and somewhat surreal events in the life of long-married couple Rene and Sydney Jelliot. The series was a spin-off from "View by Appointment," an episode of the BBC anthology Comedy Playhouse. BBC1 1969

Winner Takes All Popular quiz show where semi-final contestants began with fifty points and answered a series of five questions, wagering between five and fifty of their accumulated total on their ability to select the correct answer from the five displayed. Each answer was associated with a set of odds, between 2-1 and 5-1 and the outsider at 10-1. The two highest-scoring semi-finalists played each other in the final for real money at the end of the show (the two players in the second semi-final always had the advantage of knowing the value of the final question if they were sharp-minded as the odds necessarily had to be weighted equally throughout the two matches). The winner of each show had the choice to return and play the highest scorer of the following week's two matches but if unsuccessful would forfeit half of their accrued winnings. The original host of the series was Jimmy Tarbuck with the show's creator Geoffrey Wheeler being the unseen question-master. Geoffrey took over as host for the final series. ITV 1975-87. Challenge TV revived the format in a daily slot in 1996 with Bobby Davro as host.

Winning Widows The "winning widows" of this sitcom were middle-aged sisters Martha (Peggy Mount) and Mildred (Avice Landone). Having outlived three husbands apiece, Martha and Mildred decided to move in together, selecting a small but uncomfortable London house. While Martha, hardened by her marital experiences, was quarrelsome and vindictive, timid Mildred was still looking for romance, albeit usually in the wrong places. ITV 1961-62

Winston Churchill - The Wilderness Years Robert Hardy (Winston Churchill), Sian Phillips (Clementine Churchill), Peter Barkworth (Stanley Baldwin), Eric Porter (Neville Chamberlain), Edward Woodward (Samuel Hoare). Eight-part dramatisation of Churchill's period of political exile during the 1930s. ITV 1981.

Wipeout Game show originally in a prime time slot and hosted by Paul Daniels. A screen of sixteen possible answers to a question such as "Which of these words describe female attributes?") was shown - eleven were correct. Each one of three contestants had to choose at least one answer from the board. If they managed to avoid a Wipeout, they could continue picking answers for as long as they wished, until they either hit a Wipeout and lose their entire score, or passed control to the next player, thereby protecting their score until their next turn. The two contestants with the highest score at the end of Round 1 went on to play in the Wipeout Auction. From 12 options, players bid on how many correct answers they could pick out (up to the maximum of eight), for instance "Name the eight actors who have played Dr Who?".

Hitting a wipeout allowed the opponent to steal the frame if they could find just one correct answer. Winning two frames got you through to the final. The finalist had to select six correct answers from the 12 options offered within 60 seconds and were free to deselect wrong answers time-permitting. Bob Monkhouse took over as host after a year's break in 1998 and the show was given a daytime slot. BBC1 1994-2002

Wish Me Luck Jane Asher (Faith Ashley), Michael J. Jackson (Kit Vanston), Kate Buffery (Liz Grainger), Jane Snowden (Emily Whitbread aka Adele), Julian Glover (Colonel James Cadogan), Lynn Farleigh (Vivien Ashton), Felicity Montagu (Nicole Dissard), Catherine Schell (Virginia Mitchell aka Dominique), Warren Clarke (Colonel Werner Krieger). Drama series created by Lavinia Warner and Jill Hyem, about the exploits of British women agents during the Second World War. ITV 1988-90.

Within These Walls Googie Withers (Faye Boswell), Katharine Blake (Helen Forrester), Sarah Lawson (Susan Marshall). Prison drama series set in HMP Stone Park. Faye Boswell was replaced as prisoner governess after two series by Helen Forrester, who was herself replaced for the final series by Susan Marshall. ITV 1974-78.

Without Walls A generic title for a series of periodic stark and candid Channel 4 interviews, the most famous of which was Melvyn Bragg interviewing a dying Dennis Potter in 1994 while the great playwright was forced to sip liquid morphine from a wine glass to stave off the effects of pancreatic cancer.

Wogan Terence Wogan was born in Limerick, 3 August 1938. After leaving Crescent College Terry initially went into banking before joining Radio Telefis Eireann as a newsreader / announcer. After two years of interviewing and presenting documentary features, Terry moved to light entertainment as a disc jockey and host of television quiz and variety shows. His first regular BBC Radio show was *Midday Spin* and, when Radio 1 started (in 1967), he presented *Late Night Extra* for two years, flying over from Dublin every week. In 1969 he stood in for Jimmy Young and later that year was given his own daily show on Radio 1 and 2. In April 1972 he took over the 7.00-9.30am morning show on Radio 2 and his first stinted ended in 1984. Terry's extensive television credits include his live chat show series *Wogan* which he presented three times a week for seven years on BBC1 (1985-92), *Song For Europe, The Eurovision Song Contest, Lunchtime With Wogan, Come Dancing, Celebrity Squares, New Faces* and *Blankety Blank*. More recently Terry has presented *Wogan's Island, Do The Right Thing, Auntie's Bloomers, Auntie's Sporting Bloomers, the National Lottery Live* and *Wogan's Web*. Terry's name is synonymous with *Children In Need* and he has hosted the annual BBC charity night every year since its inception in 1980. In 1993 Terry rejoined Radio 2 to present *Wake Up To Wogan* and won the 1994 Sony Radio Award for the Best Breakfast Show. In 2005 he was awarded Radio Broadcaster of the Year at the Broadcasting Press Guild awards. Terry was awarded an honorary OBE in the 1997 New Year's Honours List, and in June 2005 was awarded an honorary knighthood. In 2006 his radio show became the most popular on the radio with regular listeners in excess of eight million. Due to the cynical voting of many of the Eurovision nations Terry announced, after more than 30 years, he would no longer supply the whimsical voiceover and Graham Norton replaced him for the 2009 contest. Terry finally bid farewell to his TOGS (Terry's Old Geezers and Gals) on Friday 19 December 2009, after 27 years hosting the Radio 2 breakfast show. Anthony Newley's classic *The Party's Over* was Sir Tel's final record choice. Chris Evans took over the slot in January 2010 while Terry returned to host a Sunday morning show the following month.

Wogan's Perfect Recall Game show in which four contestants have a chance to win £100,000 if they can answer 20 questions inside a minute. Terry Wogan hosts the quiz show where the same 20 answers are given for each of four rounds but the questions change each time. The final jackpot run gives the contestant the option to answer from 11, up to 20, questions in order to win increasing amounts of money. The catch is that the nominated score has to be achieved, for instance if 14 answers are nominated for a possible prize of £2,500 then 13 answers wins nothing and more than 14 correct answers would only win £2,500. C4 2008-

Woman of Substance, A Deborah Kerr (Emma Harte), Jenny Seagrove (Young Emma Harte), George Baker (Bruce McGill), Gayle Hunnicutt (Olivia Wainwright), Megs Jenkins (Mrs Turner), John Mills (Henry Rossiter), Barry Morse (Murgatroyd), Liam Neeson (Blackie O'Neill), Miranda Richardson (Paula McGill Amory). Mini-series adaptation of Barbara Taylor Bradford's novel, charting the life of Emma Harte, from kitchen maid at the beginning of the 20th Century, to respected business woman and Grandmother in the 1980s. C4 1985.

Woman's Hour Created by Norman Collins and originally presented by Alan Ivimey, the magazine programme was originally broadcast on the BBC's Light Programme (now called Radio 2) from its inception on 7 October 1946, but transferred to Radio 4 in 1973. The format has changed little over the years and consists of 45 minutes of topical reports, usually with a female slant, followed by a 15-minute drama serial, although prior to 1998 this segment was taken up by readings. Presenters have included Olive Shapley, Jean Metcalfe, Marjorie Anderson, Sue MacGregor, Martha Kearney, Sheila McClennon, Carolyn Quinn, Jane Little and Ritula Shah. The present host, since 1987, is Jenni Murray. Guest presenters have included Oona King and Amanda Platell. On 1 January 2005, the show became *Man's Hour* for one day and was presented by Channel 4 News anchor Jon Snow. On 18 July 2010, after 64 years of *Woman's Hour*, the BBC began broadcasting a full series called *Men's Hour* on BBC Radio 5 presented by Tim Samuels.

Wombles, The Children's animation series narrated by Bernard Cribbins. The Wombles were created by Elisabeth Beresford (once married to broadcaster Max Robertson) in 1968. Great Uncle Bulgaria is the oldest, wisest womble. Apparently the young wombles choose their names by sticking pins in an atlas, apart from Bungo who chose his completely randomly. The Wombles' names were Wellington (scientifically-inclined), Orinoco (overweight shirker), Tobermory (engineer and craftsman), Tomsk (athlete), Madame Cholet (the cook) and Miss Adelaide (the schoolmistress). The series was brought to the small screen in 1973 with animation by Ivor Wood. Mike Batt performed the theme song, *The Wombling Song*, which rose to No 4 in the UK Charts in January 1974 (Batt brought the song out under the name The Wombles and was contracted to always appear as Orinoco so was never seen. He had several further hits under this name). The lyrics, which summed up the premise of the show, were as follows: *Underground, Overground, Wombling Free, The Wombles of Wimbledon Common are we. Making good use of the things that we find, Things that the everyday folks leave behind. Uncle Bulgaria, He can remember the days when he wasn't behind The Times, With his map of the World. Pick up the papers and take them to Tobermory! Wombles are organized, work as a team. Wombles are tidy and Wombles are clean. Underground, Overground, wombling free, The Wombles of Wimbledon Common are we! People don't notice us, they never see, Under their noses a Womble may be. We womble by night and we womble by day, Looking for litter to trundle away. We're so incredibly, utterly devious, Making the most of everything. Even bottles and tins. Pick up the pieces and make them into something new, Is what we do!* The Wombles were resurrected in 1990 for two one-off stories and again in 1998 when four new Wombles were introduced, Stepney (a Cockney), Obidos (a pan piper from Brazil), Shansi (from China) and the skateboarding Alderney (a distant relative of Great Uncle Bulgaria who lives in a tree-house on the Common). BBC1 1973-75; 1990-91; 1998-99.

Wonders of the Solar System Professor Brian Cox visited the most extreme locations on Earth to explain how the laws of physics carved natural wonders across the solar system. BBC2 2010. Following the initial five-episode series a further four were broadcast on BBC2 in 2011 under the title Wonders of the Universe, in which Brian considers the nature of time, how living things are composed, gravity and light. Following complaints from viewers that the background music was too loud to comprehend Cox's narration, the BBC remixed the sound for all the episodes.

Wood and Walters Sketch show starring Julie Walters and Victoria Wood, who also wrote the series. Regular contributors

included John Dowie, Rik Mayall, Michael Angelis, Roger Brierley, Jill Summers, and Duncan Preston. A regular item entitled "Dotty's Slot" featured Julie Walters performing a witty monologue as middle-classed housewife, Dotty. A pilot was broadcast in 1981 and six further episodes the following year, although never attaining the popularity of their subsequent collaboration in *Victoria wood As Seen On TV*. ITV 1981; 1982.

Woodentops, The First broadcast in December 1955, completing the daily *Watch With Mother* quintet of programmes as the Friday offering. Characters included Daddy and Mummy Woodentop, their twin children Jenny and Willy, Baby Woodentop, Mrs Scrubbit, Sam the man who helped out in the garden, Buttercup the Cow, and the ever-popular Spotty the mischievous dog (described as 'the biggest spotty dog you ever did see'), famed for his strange bark and mechanical movements. Each episode ended with the cast waving goodbye over the closing credits. Audrey Atterbury, Molly Gibson and Gordon Murray pulled the strings. Voices by Eileen Browne, Josephina Ray and Peter Hawkins. Scripts and music by Maria Bird. The Woodentop's Theme music was the *Cowkeeper's Tune* from Two Norwegian Melodies, Op. 63, by Edvard Grieg. BBC 1955-58.

Woof! Liza Goddard (Mrs Jessop), Adam Roper (Rex Thomas), Sebastian Mahjouri (Jim Walters), Edward Fidoe (Eric Banks), Sarah Smart (Rachel Hobbs), Lionel Jeffries (Grandad), Leslie Grantham (Garrett). Long running Children's TV series telling stories and adventures of a young schoolboy who gains the power of transforming himself into a dog. Based on the book by Allan Ahlberg, the rather aptly named Edward Fidoe played Eric Banks, the boy who turned into a dog (played by Pippin), from 1989-93. Only Eric's best friend knows about his ability and helps him protect the secret from the boy's parents, the school headmaster Mr. Blocker and also from their friend and their school-teacher Miss Jessop. From Series Six which began airing in 1993, the episodes featured the adventures of Rex Thomas who had inherited the same power as Edward. Lionel Jeffries guest-starred as Rex's Grandfather in 1993. Stephen Fry appeared in one episode, as a cartoonist whose work is disrupted by Grandad and Rex. The ninth and final series, consisting of seven episodes, aired in 1997 and featured Jim Walters as the metamorphing schoolboy. The three generations were used to facilitate the credibility of the actors as schoolboys - all with Miss Jessop linking them. ITV 1989-97.

Woofits, The See *Parkinson*.

Word, The Late-night live music and chat show which was moved from its original slot of 6pm to 11pm due to its adult content. One of the more memorable segments was 'The Hopefuls' which began the trend of ordinary members of the public proving they would do almost anything to appear on television. Presenters included, Terry Christian, Amanda de Cadanet, Kate Puckrik, Mark Lamarr, Dani Behr, Huffty, Jasmine Dottiwala and Andrew Connor. Pop superstars Oasis made their television debut on the programme. C4 1990-95.

Worker, The Iconic sit-com invariably beginning with Charlie Drake standing in the queue at the Weybridge labour exchange awaiting the attentions of the exasperated Mr Pugh (Henry Magee) who would inevitably become so frustrated (not least by Charlie's propensity to mispronounce his name Mr Poo), he would grab Charlie by the lapels and haul him up over the counter whereupon Charlie would give a sideways glance at the camera and immediately win over his audience as the downtrodden good-intentioned little man being bullied by the establishment. Mr Pugh would ultimately send him off to yet another disastrous situation (Charlie had 980 jobs in 20 years) which ensured a speedy return to the queue. In the first series the labour exchange clerk was Mr Whittaker (played by Percy Herbert). With what proved to be his last regular spot on television, in the variety show *Bruce Forsyth's Big Night* (ITV, 1978), Charlie reprised *The Worker* format in a series of ten-minute sketches. The title song, performed by Charlie went as follows: *I wakes up every morning at half past eight, I'm always punctual never never late. With a nice cup of tea, a little toast and jam, I toddles off to work cos i'm a working man.* ITV 1965-70. See Charlie Drake's entry in the comedy section.

Worker's Playtime Iconic radio variety programme transmitted by the BBC between 1941 and 1964. Originally intended as a morale-booster for industrial workers in Britain during World War II, the programme was broadcast at lunchtime, three times a week, live from a different factory canteen "somewhere in Britain", initially on the BBC Home Service (now Radio 4) and, from 1957, on the Light Programme (now Radio 2). For all its 23 years each show concluded with the words from the show's producer, Bill Gates "Good luck, all workers!" or more usually just plain "Good Luck". Throughout World War II, Ernest Bevin, the Minister of Labour and National Service, would appear on these shows from time to time to congratulate the workers and exhort them to greater efforts. Many famous variety, vocal and comedy artists appeared over the years such as Charlie Chester, Peter Sellers, Tony Hancock, Frankie Howerd, Ann Shelton, Betty Driver, Eve Boswell, Dorothy Squires, Julie Andrews, Morecambe and Wise, Peter Cavanagh, Janet Brown, Bob Monkhouse, Peter Goodwright, Percy Edwards, Ken Dodd, Ken Platt, Elsie and Doris Waters and many, many more.

World About Us, The See *Natural World*

World At One, The Broadcast on weekdays from 1.00 - 1.30pm, *The World at One* is Britain's leading political radio programme. Martha Kearney became its first female presenter in April 2007. Shaun Ley presents *The World at One* on Fridays and its sister programme *The World This Weekend* on Sundays. Former presenters include Bill Hardcastle, William Davis, Sir Robin Day, James Naughtie and Nick Clarke. BBC Home Service (became Radio 4 in 1967) 1965-

World at War World War Two history documentary researched by Noble Frankland, produced by Jeremy Isaacs and narrated in suitably gravitas fashion by Laurence Olivier. Carl Davis' portentous main title theme and score underlines the grand scale of the enterprise. The original 26 episodes were supplemented three years later by six special programmes containing footage edited out of the original series (now narrated by Eric Porter), bringing the total running time to a truly epic 32 hours. ITV 1973-74.

World In Action Long-running hard-hitting current affairs programme often highlighting topical issues of the day. The show launched the first *Seven Up!* programme in 1964. The theme tune is called "Jam for World in Action" by Jonathon Weston. *World in Action*'s demise in favour of the more populist *Tonight with Trevor McDonald* was criticised by some as part of a "dumbing-down" strategy. ITV 1963-98.

World of Beachcomber, The Spike Milligan (Dr Strabismus), Ann Lancaster, Frank Thornton, Clive Dunn, Sir Michael Redgrave, Julian Orchard, Hattie Jacques, Patricia Hayes, Leon Thau, Sheila Steafel, Arthur Mullard. Surreal television comedy show, written by Spike Milligan, Barry Took, John Junkin and Neil Shand, inspired by the Beachcomber column in the Daily Express newspaper. The show, like the column, consisted of a series of unrelated pieces of humour. Links between the items were provided by Spike Milligan, in the guise of Dr Strabismus, dressed in a smoking jacket and cap, as in the cartoon logo above the newspaper column. The regular contributors, in various guises, are listed above but many of the leading comedy actors of the day made cameo appearances. Regular skits included the spoof commercials for "Snibbo", usually a washing soap with a tendency to remove stains, buttons and skin, and, with a sung jingle, "Threadgold's Thorough-grip Garterettes". Another memorable sketch was the 'Readings from the lists of Huntingdonshire Cabmen', whereupon Michael Redgrave solemnly walked to a lectern, donned his reading glasses and read the names, in alphabetical order, with great seriousness, as one might read the names of the dead at a war memorial. This was a variation on a theme performed before and since by Joyce Grenfell and Rowan Atkinson sketch in which the school register is read out in a humorous and theatrical manner. Probably the most famous sketches were those set in the courtroom of Mr Justice Cocklecarrot, played by Clive Dunn, and his Twelve Red-Bearded Dwarves for jurors. BBC2 1968-69.

World of His Own Roy Kinnear (Stanley Blake), Anne Cunningham (Helen Blake). Sitcom written by Dave Freeman as a vehicle for the burgeoning talent of Roy Kinnear. Stanley was a gormless under-achiever who frequently escaped his humdrum experience by imagining a more exciting existence. BBC 1964-65.

World of Sport ITV's answer to *Grandstand* was hosted by Eamonn Andrews (1965-68) and then Dickie Davies for the duration of its run. Featured sports (with presenters and commentators) included Athletics (Adrian Metcalfe), Boxing (Reg Gutteridge), Football (Brian Moore, Jimmy Hill, Jimmy Greaves and Ian St John), Darts Tony Green), Horse Racing (John Rickman, Raleigh Gilbert, Brough Scott, Graham Goode), Snooker (John Pulman), Wrestling (Kent Walton). Freddie Trueman and Ian Wooldridge were specialist contributors during Eamonn Andrews' tenure. ITV 1965-85.

World of Wooster, The Ian Carmichael (Bertie Wooster), Dennis Price (Jeeves), Fabia Drake (Aunt Agatha), Derek Nimmo (Bingo Little), Tracy Reed (Bobbie Wickham), Eleanor Summerfield (Aunt Dahlia), Paul Whitsun-Jones (Sir Roderick Glossop). This hugely popular BBC1 sitcom first aired on Sunday 30 May 1965 and the 20th and final episode aired on Friday 17 November 1967. The natural persuasions of Price and Carmichael made them the definitive Jeeves and Wooster and their portrayals were highly-praised by P. G. Wodehouse, who created the odd couple. Wooster's timeless world was populated by rich, idle gentlemen, dreamy but determined women, irate fathers and fearsome aunts. Plots revolved around star-crossed romances, white lies that grew into complex misunderstandings, assumed identities and the quest for the sort of lazy life an eligible chap born on the right side of town, could reasonably expect. Locations for these excitements were Bertie's London pad, in Berkeley Street, Mayfair; the country estates of various relatives and friends; and the Drones Club, drinking and dining hole of the upper classes. Dashingly dressed, with a monocle firmly held in the eye, Bertie often turned up at such venues only to discover that he was accidentally engaged to a deb he scarcely knew; he then had to frantically avoid their fathers or homicidal ex-boyfriends; worse still, he had to face his awesome aunts. Wooster's ultra-competent man-servant Jeeves invariably saved the day through a piece of razor-sharp thinking and a dazzlingly intricate scheme, which not only extricated his master but also managed to effect the path of true love for the characters who really should be engaged. Interestingly, there was no mention of Jeeves' forename in the series as Wodehouse had not yet given him one. It was not until the 1971 *Much Obliged Jeeves* (US: *Jeeves and the Tie That Binds*) that it was exposed as Reginald. See also *Jeeves and Wooster*.

World Shut Your Mouth Dom Joly's follow-up series to the successful *Trigger Happy TV* was another hidden-camera offering albeit on a slightly different theme. As with his previous work, the programme had an emphasis on surrealism, with sketches such as a spying gnome, nerds taunting skaters and Joly dressing up in aluminium foil like a superhero. Unlike *Trigger Happy TV* many of the sketches were filmed on international locations. At the end of each show when the credits had finished rolling, a credit is given to "The Gund Corporation". The name Gund is a pseudonym used by Dom whenever he is lying or when a character requires an identity. Danny Wallace appeared in some sketches. BBC1 2005.

World's End Short lived soap opera created by Ted Whitehead and set around the 'Mulberry' public house, Chelsea. Michael Angelis (Danny), Barbara Angell (Connie), Gillian Barge (Antonia), Paul Brooke (Lord Arvin), Helen Bush (Angela), Harry Fowler (Andy), Peter Harlowe (Jonathan), Daniel Holender (Tim), Bradley Lavelle (Space), Victor Lucas (Stewart), Tom Marshall (Jack), Catherine Neilson (Lynn), Ellen Pollock (Dodie), Toby Salaman (Barney), Pam Scotcher (Camille), Neville Smith (Robin), Primi Townsend (Nicola), Brian Vaughan (Brahms). The series was pulled after only 13 episodes were shown. BBC1 1981.

Worst Witch, The Georgina Sherrington (Mildred Hubble), Felicity Jones - series 1 and Katie Allen - series 2 & 3 (Ethel Hallow), Emma Jayne Brown (Maud Moonshine), Jessica Fox (Enid Nightshade), Kate Duchêne (Miss Constance Hardbroom), Claire Porter (Miss Imogen Drill), Una Stubbs (Miss Davina Bat), Polly James (Miss Lavinia Crotchet). CITV series based on *The*

Worst Witch books by Jill Murphy, revolving around a group of young witches at Miss Cackle's Academy for Witches. Eastender's actress Lacey Turner made her television debut as Maddie Stevenson in the 1999 episode, *The Dragon's Hoard*. ITV 1998-2001. A series spin-off, *Weirdsister College*, aired for a short run in 2001/02

Worzel Gummidge Jon Pertwee (Worzel Gummidge), Una Stubbs (Aunt Sally), Geoffrey Bayldon (The Crowman), Lorraine Chase (Dolly Clothes-Peg), Joan Sims (Mrs Bloomsbury-Barton), Barbara Windsor (Saucy Nancy), Jeremy Austin (John Peters), Charlotte Coleman (Sue Peters), Mike Berry (Mr Peters), Megs Jenkins (Mrs Braithwaite), Norman Bird (Mr Braithwaite), Michael Ripper (Mr Shepherd), Norman Mitchell (PC Parsons). Written by Keith Waterhouse and Willis Hall from an adaption of Barbara Euphan Todd's novels. Worzel Gummidge, the mischievous turnip headed scarecrow from Ten Acre Field at Scatterbrook Farm, was the friend of young John and Sue Peters who had just moved to the countryside with their dad (having recently lost their mum). Worzel transformed their lives with his clumsy antics and good-natured humour. The Crowman was Worzel's creator and Aunt Sally was Worzel's horrid and reluctant skittle doll girlfriend. Worzel also fell for Saucy Nancy (a ship's figurehead) and flirted with a tailor's dummy called Dolly Clothes-Peg. ITV 1979-81. Television's first Worzel Gummidge was Frank Atkinson, who played the part in the 1953 BBC series *Worzel Gummidge Turns Detective*.

Would I Lie To You? Comedy panel game originally presented by Angus Deayton with regular team captains comedians David Mitchell and Lee Mack. Two celebrity guests join each of the team captains and compete head-to-head with each player revealing incredible facts about themselves for the consideration of the opposing team to decide whether the story is true or false. Rob Brydon took over as presenter for the third series in 2009. BBC1 2007-

Wycliffe Jack Shepherd (Det Supt Charles Wycliffe), Helen Masters (Det Insp Lucy Lane), Jimmy Yuill (Det Insp Doug Kersey), Sharon Duce (Supt Le Page). Police drama based on the novels of W. J. Burley focusing on a Penzance-based police force. ITV 1993-98.

X Factor, The Pop music reality show consisting of a series of filmed auditions around the British Isles and a Saturday night live knockout competition. Designed as a replacement for *Pop Idol*, the talent is divided into three groups 18-24s, over 24s and groups. Each group is mentored by pop experts, originally Louis Walsh, Sharon Osbourne and Simon Cowell. The series has varying elements to it. Initially the auditions highlight the good, the bad and the downright ugly but as the live shows progress and the field is whittled down, the focus is more on the talent. Voice-overs are provided by Peter Dickson and Enn Reitel. The winners to-date are Steve Brookstein (2004), Shayne Ward (2005), Leona Lewis (2006), Leon Jackson (2007), Alexandra Burke (2008), Joe McElderry (2009), Matt Cardle (2010) and Little Mix (2011 - the first group to win). G4 from the first series carved out a promising career before splitting in 2006. A celebrity edition in 2006 was won by actress Lucy Benjamin. In 2007 Dermot O'Leary replaced Kate Thornton as presenter and Dannii Minogue joined the three regular mentors the categories becoming, girls, boys, groups and over 25s. Cheryl Cole replaced Sharon Osbourne for the 2008 series onwards. For the 2011 series, Simon, Cheryl and Dannii were replaced by Gary Barlow, Kelly Rowland and Tulisa Contostavlos, leaving Louis as the only original judge. *The Xtra Factor* is a companion show that airs on digital channel ITV2 and TV3 Ireland on Saturday nights and was hosted by Ben Shephard (2004-06), Fearne Cotton (2007), Holly Willoughby (2008–09), Konnie Huq (2010) and Caroline Flack and Olly Murs (2011–). ITV 2004-

X Marks The Spot Radio panel game consisting of three celebrities attempting to identify four places around the UK, as well as answer a supplementary question set in those locations. The four locations joined up to form a giant X on the map. Where the two lines crossed, a treasure was metaphorically hidden. The panel had to identify the treasure using up to four lines of a riddle gained by answering the supplementary question correctly. The show was created by John Higgs and hosted by comedian and author Pete McCarthy until his death in October 2004, when

writer and broadcaster David Stafford took over. BBC Radio 4 1998-2006.

XYY Man, The Stephen Yardley (William 'Spider' Scott), Don Henderson (Det Sgt George Bulman). Spider Scott had an extra 'Y' chromosome which appeared to give him a liking for dangerous pursuits, sometimes criminal. Based on the books of Kenneth Royce, the series aired on ITV 1976-77 and spawned *Strangers* and *Bulman*.

Year in Provence, A John Thaw (Peter Mayle), Lindsay Duncan (Annie Mayle). Peter Mayle's *A Year In Provence* was a best-selling book in 1989, and the BBC filmed a version of it for a 12-part mini-series. Advertising executive Peter Mayle and his accountant wife, Annie, pull up the pegs and move to a farmhouse in the Luberon where Peter at first attempts to write a novel but then realises his own struggles with a foreign way of life are a far more interesting subject to put into print. BBC1 1993.

Yes Honestly Donal Donnelly (Matthew Browne), Liza Goddard (Lily Pond / Browne). Sitcom written by Terence Brady and Charlotte Bingham as a sequel to *No Honestly*. Again, the episodes followed the course of the relationship of the leading protagonists from first meeting - when unsuccessful music composer Matthew (affectionately known as Matt), who has little if any time for women, hires Lily Pond (a beautiful witty woman of Russian ancestry) as his typist - through to marriage. There were two series; Georgie Fame wrote and sang the theme tune for the first, also turning up in two episodes, as pop singer Clive Powell (his real name) and as himself. Lynsey de Paul wrote and performed the theme music for the second series. ITV 1976-77.

Yes Minister / Prime Minister Paul Eddington (Jim Hacker PC, MP, BDc (Econ)), Nigel Hawthorne (Sir Humphrey Appleby), Derek Fowlds (Bernard Wooley), Diana Hoddinott (Annie Hacker), John Nettleton (Sir Arnold Robinson). Sitcom created by Antony Jay and Jonathan Lynn. *Yes Minister* started airing in 1980 on BBC2. It consisted of three series, each with seven episodes. The story focuses around three main characters: Jim Hacker MP, Sir Humphrey Appleby and Bernard Woolley. It starts off with the political party of Jim Hacker (not mentioned originally but later revealed as a Tory) that has won the elections and forms a new government. Jim gets appointed Minister for the Department of Administrative Affairs. He has to work with his Permanent Under-Secretary Sir Humphrey Appleby. The interests of both are very different. Jim has to make sure he remains popular among the electorate and that he carries out cabinet policy. Sir Humphrey however is interested in securing and possibly extending the position of his department in terms of staffing and budget. These interests clash on numerous occasions. Bernard Woolley is positioned between the two. Bernard is Jim Hacker's Principal Private Secretary. Although he is most of the time sympathetic to Jim's plans, he is also a civil servant and has loyalties to the civil service and Sir Humphrey. In 1984, almost two years after the last episode, the BBC aired a one-hour long Christmas episode of Yes Minister. In this episode Sir Humphrey moves up the civil service hierarchy to become Cabinet Secretary. Jim Hacker enters in a fight for party leadership and finally achieves what he always dreamt of, Prime Minister of Great Britain. In 1986 the BBC started a new series, *Yes Prime Minister*. It consisted of two series each with eight episodes. The characters are still the same but the ambitions and surrounding have changed a bit. Jim Hacker as Prime Minister now wants to have his name written in the history books as a great statesman. Sir Humphrey as Cabinet Secretary now has a broader responsibility to maintain the power and position of the whole civil service, as well as his own. Bernard Woolley is still the Principal Private Secretary to Jim Hacker and he remains loyal to both sides. Both Antony Jay and Nigel Hawthorne were subsequently knighted following this series. BBC2 1980-84; 1986-88.

You Bet! Game show where members of the public attempted a range of weird and wacky stunts, sometimes physical but always 'mental'! 100 members of the audience bet on whether they think the outcome will be successful. Four (later three) celebs also try to guess the correct outcome, thus earning points (which are later turned into pounds for charity) as well as avoiding the all-important celebrity forfeit, usually performed at the start of the following week's programme. Presenters included Bruce Forsyth

(1988-90), Matthew Kelly (1991-95) and Darren Day (with the help of Diane Youdale, 1996). ITV 1988-96.

You Rang M'Lord Paul Shane (Alf Stokes), Su Pollard (Ivy Teesdale), Jeffrey Holland (James Twelvetrees), Barbara Windsor (Myrtle), Donald Hewlett (Lord George Meldrum), Michael Knowles (Hon. Teddy Meldrum). Sitcom written by Jimmy Perry and David Croft. In the trenches during the First World War, two foot-soldiers come upon the unconscious figure of an officer. Assuming him to be dead, one of them, Alf, attempts to rob the man, much to the disgust of his comrade, the steadfast James. When they realise that he is alive they carry him to safety, and the officer, the Honourable Teddy Meldrum, tells them that he is forever in their debt. Nearly ten years later, we find that Meldrum has repaid said debt to James who is now serving as head of the household to Teddy's brother Lord Meldrum, a factory-owning aristocrat. Following the death of a butler, shifty Alf Stokes reappears on the scene too, claiming his side of the deal; he is duly appointed, much against the wishes of James, who remembers all too well Alf's criminal tendencies. At the same time, Alf arranges for a new parlour maid, Ivy, to join the staff. Unbeknown to the others, Ivy is really Alf's daughter and is ensconced in the house to (sometimes unwillingly) help her father swindle the Meldrums out of their money. The title song, written by Jimmy Perry and Roy Moore, was sung by Paul Shane and Bob Monkhouse. BBC1 1990-93.

Young At Heart John Mills (Albert Collyer), Megs Jenkins (Ethel Collyer), David Neilson (Norman Charlton), Carol Leader (Barbara Charlton). Rare excursion into television situation comedy for film actor John mills. Written by Vince Powell. Albert Collyer is about to retire after fifty years working in a Stoke-On-Trent pottery. He boasts to all and sundry he expects to get a golden handshake but instead all he receives from the manager (Geoffrey Palmer) is a carriage clock and a thank you. With time weighing heavily on his hands, he looks around for other interests, but other than football, the pub, and meddling in the lives of his neighbours the Charltons, has none. He's also a bit of a miser, forever moaning about rising prices and the smallness of his pension, and his wife Ethel finds him a right pain now that he is home all day. ITV 1980-82.

Young Ones, The Rik Mayall (Rick), Nigel Planer (Neil), Ade Edmondson (Vyvyan), Christopher Ryan (Mike), Alexei Sayle (Jerzy Balowski...and his family). Sitcom written by Ben Elton, Rik Mayall and Lise Mayer. This series depicted a house-share from hell, with four anarchic, lazy, dysfunctional students living on the breadline and hating and abusing one another. Rick was the unlikely Cliff Richard fan who owned a pet hamster known as SPG (Special Patrol Group), Vyvyan, the mad, fearless, self-abusing, heavy-metal-loving lunatic punk, Neil, the brainless, hippy character, and Mike, who appeared the most normal of the four but was obviously seriously disturbed by normal standards. The 12-episode series also had regular appearances by Alexei Sayle as their landlord and guest appearances by Keith Allen, Mark Arden, Helen Atkinson Wood, Jim Barclay, Chris Barrie, Arnold Brown, Robbie Coltrane, Lee Cornes, Andy de la Tour, Ben Elton, Dawn French, Stephen Frost, Stephen Fry, Gareth Hale, Lenny Henry, Griff Rhys Jones, Terry Jones, Hugh Laurie, Helen Lederer, Norman Lovett, Pauline Melville, Paul Merton, Norman Pace, Daniel Peacock, David Rappaport, Tony Robinson, Jennifer Saunders, Mel Smith and Emma Thompson. The show also had musical guests - a first for a sitcom - whose appearances somehow had to be accommodated within the story. In the final episode, 'Summer Holiday', the main characters were killed off when their double-decker bus exploded after tumbling over a cliff. Despite their untimely end, the team have occasionally reappeared, usually at fund-raising events and most memorably when singing along with Cliff Richard to 'Living Doll', a charity release that became a number-one hit single in April 1986. And in July 1984 Nigel Planer stepped out, solo, as neil (sic) to release a hippy-dippy cover version of Traffic's 'Hole In My Shoe', which peaked at the same number on the singles chart, two, as the original had done 17 years earlier. A memorable saying from the

series was "For Cliff's Sake" (Cliff being interpolated Instead of God). BBC2 1982-84.

You're A Star An Irish singing contest created by Screentime ShinAwiL and Radio Telefís Éireann. Presented by Ray D'Arcy (Series 1-3), Derek Mooney (Series 4), Keith Duffy (Series 5) and Brian Ormond (Series 6), the show was broadcast live from The Helix theatre in Dublin. Originally designed to select the Irish Eurovision entry this idea was dropped in 2005. Judges included Linda Martin, singer and Eurovision winner (Series 1, 2, 4 and 5), Brendan O'Connor, journalist (Series 4, 5 and 6), Phil Coulter, songwriter (Series 1 and 2), Thomas Black, producer (Series 4 and 5), Kerry Katona, singer (Series 1), Darren Smith, producer (Series 1), Louis Walsh, band manager (Series 2), Barbara Galvin (Series 3), Dave Fanning, DJ (Series 3), Hazel Kaneswaran, model (Series 3), Michelle Heaton, singer (Series 6) and Keith Duffy, singer and actor (Series 6). Winners: Mickey Joe Harte (2003), Chris Doran (2004), Donna and Joseph McCaul (2005), Lucia Evans (2006), David O'Connor (2007) and Leanne Moore (2008). RTÉ 1 2002-08. See *The All Ireland Talent Show*

You're Only Young Twice During the 1970s, British television fans were treated to two different sitcoms bearing the title *You're Only Young Twice*, both of which used a retirement home as a comedy backdrop. The second, and more successful, of these two programs was set in Paradise Lodge, an old ladies home where the irrepressible Flora Petty (Peggy Mount) invariably led the other tenants into all sorts of mischief. The other principal characters were Flora's loyal "lieutenant" Cissy Lupin (Pat Coombs), humourless nursing home matron Miss Milton (Charmian May), and Miss Milton's equally dour assistant Miss Finch (Georgina Moon). Thirty-one half-hour episodes and two hour-long specials were broadcast. Written by Pam Valentine and Michael Ashton. ITV 1977-81. Incidentally, the other series of the same name was set in Twilight Lodge and followed almost exactly the same plot. It starred Liam Redmond, Adrienne Corri, Peter Copley, George Woodbridge, Leslie Dwyer, Vic Wise, and Carmen Munroe. Written by Jack Trevor Story. ITV 1971.

Your Money Or Your Life See *Show Me The Money*

You've Been Framed Home video bloopers sent in by the public that gave rise to several spin-off series. Presenters include Jeremy Beadle (1990-97), Lisa Riley (1998-2002), Jonathan Wilkes (2003-04) and Harry Hill (2004-).

Yus My Dear Spin-off series from *Romany Jones*. Arthur Mullard (Wally Briggs), Queenie Watts (Lily Briggs), Mike Reid (Benny Briggs). The Briggs are now situated in a council house with Wally taking a job as a bricklayer. ITV 1976.

Z Cars Stratford Johns (Det Chief Insp Barlow), Frank Windsor (Det Sgt/Det Chief Supt. John Watt), Brian Blessed (PC William 'Fancy' Smith), Joseph Brady (PC John 'Jock' Weir), James Ellis (PC/Sgt/Insp. Herbert 'Bert' Lynch), Jeremy Kemp (PC Bob Steele), Terence Edmond (PC Ian Sweet), Colin Welland (PC David Graham), Leonard Rossiter (Det Insp Bamber), John Slater (Det Sgt Tom Stone), Alison Steadman (WPC Bayliss), Stephen Yardley (PC Alex May), Geoffrey Hayes (DC Scatliff), Geoffrey Whitehead (DS Miller), Nicholas Smith (PC Yates), George Sewell (DI Brogan), Joss Ackland (DI Todd), John Woodvine (DI Alan Witty), Derek Waring (DI Neil Goss), Tommy Boyle (DI Maddan), Sharon Duce (WPC Cameron), John Barrie (Sam Hudson). Created by Troy Kennedy Martin, the classic police series was one of the longest-running crime shows ever, at 14 series and 667 episodes. It was grittily realistic for its time. Set in Newtown, a fictitious town to the north of Liverpool. At the spearhead of operations were the four police constables: "Jock" Weir, "Fancy" Smith, Bob Steele and Bert Lynch. They occupied the two radio crime cars Z-Victor 1 and Z-Victor 2, from which the series gained its title. Supervising operations via a VHF radio operator in the station, and securing prosecutions in the interrogation room, were Detective Sergeant Watt and the formidable Detective Inspector Barlow. Watched by nearly 14 million viewers in its first season, *Z Cars* rapidly captured the public imagination, and the leading characters became household names. Though in later seasons new characters might be brought in as replacements and the crime cars up-dated, the same basic formula applied. Bert Lynch, played by James Ellis, remained throughout the programme's run. Promoted to station sergeant in 1966 he was still in place at the desk when the doors were finally closed down on the cars in 1978. The long-running C.I.D. series *Softly-Softly* (1966-75) was a direct spin-off from *Z Cars*, achieved by promoting Barlow to the rank of chief inspector, transferring him to a regional crime squad and replacing the squad car with a dog-handling unit. The *Z-Cars* theme tune was arranged by Fritz Spiegl from the traditional folk song *Johnny Todd*. BBC1 1962-78.

Zodiac Game, The Short-lived game show based on astrological signs hosted by Tom O'Connor with assistance from Russell Grant in the second series. ITV 1984-85.

Zoo Gang, The John Mills (Tommy Devon - codename: Elephant), Brian Keith (Stephen Halliday - Fox), Barry Morse (Alec Marlowe - Tiger), Lili Palmer (Manouche Roget - Leopard), Michael Petrovitch (Lt Georges Roget), Seretta Wilson (Jill Burton). Adventure series created by Paul Gallico. Four former French Resistance fighters reunite 30 years after the end of the war to maintain law and order on the French Riviera. The theme music was performed by Paul and Linda McCartney. ITV 1974.

Zoo Time Desmond Morris, helped by various animal experts and zoo staff, hosted the programme from 'The Den', an outside broadcast unit situated behind the Bird House at Regent's Park Zoo, London. Desmond's live commentary and animal information linked relatively static camera shots of the various parts of the zoo. Occasional editions were broadcast live from Whipsnade Zoo in Bedfordshire. After a short break the programme relocated to Chester Zoo from July 1967, in order to justify Granada's 'From the North' tag as the 1968 ITV franchise renewals loomed. Granada newsman Chris Kelly assumed presenting duties. Presenters were Desmond Morris (1956-66), Chris Kelly (1967-68) and Harry Watt (who assisted Morris from 1960). The theme tune was from Prokofiev's *Peter and the Wolf*. Desmond Morris, the former curator of mammals at London Zoo, left the programme in 1966 to write his best-selling *The Naked Ape*. ITV 1956-68.

Beauty Pageants

The most revered beauty pageant in the United Kingdom and Ireland remains the Miss World contest. Created by Eric Morley in 1951 and first televised by the BBC in 1959, at its height in the 1960s and 70s it attracted up to 30 million viewers and was usually the top-rated show of the year. With five winners representing the UK and one from Ireland, the home countries top the board of most number of wins, although India and Venezuela have both managed five victories to-date. A mixture of apathy and political correctness has meant a decline in popularity in Britain and Ireland and since Eric Morley's death in 2000 the pageant has not been televised on any British terrestrial channel, although still attracting vast television audiences around the world.

Eric's wife Julia Morley is now the president of the Miss World Organization and whereas previously the winner of Miss United Kingdom would go forward to the Miss World competition as a representative of the four constituent countries, since 1999 Scotland and Wales have entered separately and England and Northern Ireland followed suit in 2000. Unfortunately this meant that Zöe Salmon missed out in 1999 as Nicola Willoughby represented the UK at Miss World, having won the final competed-for Miss UK title.

Since 2000 the highest ranking competitor at Miss World, of the four constituent countries, is then presented with the title and crown of Miss United Kingdom and competes at the Miss International pageant the following year. Since the inception of the new qualifying rules the highest-placed UK entry has been Juliet-Jane Horne (later a contestant on *Make Me A Supermodel*), who placed 3rd in Miss World in 2001.

The other major change during Julia's leadership has been to promote the personality and talents of the girls rather than merely their beauty and there are now several sub-events held within the main competition.

London was for many years the home of the Miss World pageant but since the 1990s it has been held in several other countries and more recently seems to have found a fairly regular home in China.

The following table is a list of all United Kingdom representatives at Miss World
(the Miss United Kingdom conferee is shown in brackets)

	Miss England	Miss Scotland	Miss Wales	Miss Northern Ireland
1999	Nicola Willoughby	Stephanie Norrie	Clare Daniel	Zöe Salmon
2000	Michelle Walker	Michelle Watson (UK)	Sophie Kate Cahill	Julie Lee-Ann Martin
2001	Sally Kettle	Juliet-Jane Horne (UK)	Charlotte Faicheney	Angela McCarthy
2002	Danielle Luan	Paula Murphy	Michelle Bush	Gayle Williamson (UK)
2003	Jackie Turner	Nicola Jolly (UK)	Imogen Thomas	Diana Sayers
2004	Danielle Lloyd	Lois Weatherup	Amy Guy (UK)	Kirsty Stewart
2005	Hammasa Kohistani	Aisling Friel	Claire Evans	Lucy Evangelista (UK)
2006	Eleanor Glynn	Nicola McLean (UK)	Sarah Fleming	Catherine Jean Milligan
2007	Georgia Horsley	Nieve Jennings (UK)	Kelly Pesticcio	Melissa Patton
2008	Laura Coleman	Stephanie Willemse	Chloe-Beth Morgan (UK)	Judith Wilson
2009	Katrina Hodge	Katharine Brown (UK)	Lucy Whitehouse	Cherie Gardiner
2010	Jessica Linley	Nicola Mimnagh (UK)	Courtenay Hamilton	Lori Moore
2011	Alize Lily Mounter (UK)	Jennifer Reoch	Sara Manchipp	Finola Guinnane

The **Miss England** competition is open to females aged 17–24 years living in England and holding a British passport. The first winner, in 1928, was Nonni Shields and other high profile winners include Beverley Isherwood in 1978, who appeared as a scorer on *Countdown* and *It's A Knockout*; Carolyn Seaward in 1979, who was runner-up in both Miss Universe and Miss World and appeared as a Bond Girl in *Octopussy*; Hammasa Kohistani in 2005, born in Uzbekistan, the first Muslim winner of the crown; and Rachel Christie in 2009, who is the niece of former Olympic sprint champion Linford Christie. Rachel relinquished her crown in favour of Lance Corporal Katrina Hodge after being arrested on suspicion of assaulting Miss Manchester Sara Beverley Jones at a Manchester nightclub.

The **Miss Scotland** competition is open to females aged 18–24 years living in Scotland and holding a British passport. High profile winners include Nicci Jolly in 2003, who went on to become a television presenter, newspaper columnist and contestant on *Celebrity Fear Factor*.

The **Miss Northern Ireland** competition is open to females aged 17–24 years living in Northern Ireland and holding a valid Northern Ireland passport. The first winner in 1980 was Geraldine McGrory. High profile winners include Zoe Salmon in 1999 (who beat future *Big Brother* contestant Orlaith McAllister into 2nd), who went on to become a *Blue Peter* presenter and host of numerous other television shows.

The **Miss Wales** competition is open to unmarried and childless females aged 16–24 years living in Wales and holding a British passport. The first winner in 1952 was Betty Geary and high profile winners include Rosemarie Frankland (1943-2000) who won the title in 1961 and subsequently became the first British woman to win the Miss World competition, representing the United Kingdom; Helen Morgan, who emulated Rosemarie's feats in 1974 but was forced to resign four days later, upon the disclosure that she had an

18 month old son; Sian Adey-Jones in 1976, who became a Page 3 Girl in *The Sun* and Bond Girl in *A View To A Kill*; Imogen Thomas in 2003, who became a *Big Brother* contestant in 2006 and later appeared on *Celebrity Coach Trip* partnered with her friend Bianca Gascoigne; and Amy Guy in 2004, who subsequently appeared as Siren, in the revived version of *Gladiators* on Sky.

The first **Miss United Kingdom** winner was Eileen Sheridan in 1958. Eileen also won Miss Great Britain in 1960 but is probably best known for being a friend of the notorious Kray family. High profile winners include Ann Sidney in 1964, who subsequently became the first English woman to win the Miss World title and carved out a media career for a few years aided by her illicit relationship with entertainer Bruce Forsyth; Lesley Langley in 1965, who became the second English woman to become Miss World; Sarah-Jane Hutt in 1983, who became the third English woman to become Miss World and the second from Dorset (she was from Poole whilst Lesley Langley was from Weymouth); and Kirsty Roper in 1988, who subsequently married Swiss billionaire Ernesto Bertarelli and went on to co-write "Black Coffee", a number one hit for All Saints in 2000.

The **Miss Great Britain** beauty pageant is different from all the others previously mentioned inasmuch as it is not a qualifying competition for any other crown. Originating in 1945 (Lydia Read being the first winner) and held in the seaside resort of Morecambe between 1956 and 1989, the 2010 competition was held at the new Grand Pier in Western Super Mare.
High profile winners include Violet Pretty in 1950 (see entry for Anne Heywood in the cinema section); Leila Williams in 1957, who became the first *Blue Peter* presenter the following year; Debbie Greenwood in 1984, who became a television presenter and is the wife of Scottish presenter Paul Coia; Leilani Dowding in 1998 (see entry in miscellaneous section); and Gemma Garrett in 2007, who became the official face of the Formula One British Grand Prix at Silverstone, had a small role in the 2008 film *Direct Contact* and then stood unsuccessfully as a candidate in the Crewe and Nantwich by-election on 22 May 2008, representing the "Beauties for Britain" party and later the Haltemprice and Howden by-election following the resignation of its MP, David Davis, this time representing the "Miss Great Britain Party". Danielle Lloyd, the Miss England winner in 2004, won the Miss Great Britain title in 2006 but was stripped of her title (see entry in miscellaneous section) and replaced by Preeti Desai, who originally only placed fifth in the competition but was elected Miss Great Britain 2006 by the British public in a poll of readers of *The Sun*. Danielle was reinstated in 2010.

The **Miss Ireland** competition is open to unmarried and childless females aged 17–24 who are at least 5ft 7ins (1.7m) in height and are citizens of the Irish Republic, either by birth or naturalisation. The first winner in 1947 was Violet Nolan and the event became a permanent annual competition in 1952 when the winners qualified to enter the Miss World pageant.
High profile winners include Michelle Rocca, who became the wife of Arsenal and Ireland footballer John Devine and later, the wife of Van Morrison (in between also being engaged to Cathal Ryan, son of Tony Ryan the co-founded of Ryanair); Amanda Brunker, who became a journalist for the Irish *Sunday World* newspaper; Pamela Flood, who became a popular televison presenter; and Rosanna Davison, the daughter of singer Chris de Burgh, who went on to become the only Irish winner of Miss World in 2003.
Charlotte Delamere, in 1969, and actress and artist Nuala Holloway, in 1974, were also Miss Ireland representatives in other international pageants but not Miss World.

Miss Ireland Winners

1947 Violet Nolan	1987 Adrienne Rock
1952 Eithne Dunne	1988 Collette [Colette] Jackson
1953 Mary Murphy	1989 Barbara Ann Curran
1954 Connie Rodgers	1990 Siobhan McClafferty
1955 Evelyn Foley	1991 Amanda Brunker
1956 Amy Kelly	1992 Sharon Ellis
1957 Nessa Welsh	1993 Pamela Flood
1958 Susan Riddell	1994 Anna Maria McCarthy
1959 Ann Fitzpatrick	1995 Joanne Black
1960 Irene Ruth Kane	1996 Niamh Marie Redmond
1961 Olive Ursula White	1997 Andrea Roche
1962 Muriel O'Hanlon	1998 Vivienne Doyle
1963 Joan Power	1999 Emir-Maria Holohan Doyle
1964 Mairead Cullen	2000 Yvonne Ellard
1965 Gladys Anne Waller	2001 Catrina Supple
1966 Helen McMahon	2002 Lynda Duffy
1967 Gemma McNabb	2003 Rosanna Davison
1968 June MacMahon	2004 Natasha Nic Gairbheith
1969 Hilary Clarke	2005 Aoife Mary Cogan
1970 Mary Elizabeth McKinley	2006 Sarah Morrissey
1971 June Glover	2007 Bláthnaid McKenna
1972 Pauline Theresa Fitzsimons	2008 Sinéad Noonan
1973 Yvonne Costelloe	2009 Laura Patterson
1974 Julie Ann Farnham	2010 Emma Waldron
1975 Elaine Rosemary O'Hara	2011 Holly Carpenter
1976 Jakki Moore	
1977 Loraine Bernadette Enriquez	
1978 Lorraine Marion O'Conner	
1979 Maura McMenamim	
1980 Michelle Rocca	
1981 Geraldine Mary McGrory	
1982 Roberta Brown	
1983 Patricia 'Trish' Nolan	
1984 Olivia Tracey	
1985 Anne Marie Gannon	
1986 Rosemary Elizabeth Thompson	

This section includes biographies of all those people that do not fit neatly into my main categories of film, radio and television, comedy and popular music.

Adebibe, Karima Born 14 February 1985, Bethnal Green, London. The 5' 8½" (1.74 m) tall model has a Moroccan father and Irish mother. A former secretary, Karima, had a small role as a sacrificial maiden in the 2004 film *Alien vs. Predator*. On her 21st birthday she became the 8th model to take up the role of Lara Croft in the popular video game series *Tomb Raider*, following Nathalie Cook (1996-97), Rhona Mitra (1997-98), Vanessa Demouy (1998), Nell McAndrew (1998-99), Lara Weller (1999-2000), Lucy Clarkson (2000-02) and Jill de Jong (2002-04). Karima, whose costume was based on the updated version of Lara Croft in *Legend*, was the first model Eidos allowed to portray Lara outside posing for photography, and to prepare herself for the role and the subsequent promotion she trained in areas the character was expected to excel in such as combat, motorcycling, elocution, and conduct. Perhaps it was fitting that Karima took over the role on her birthday as St Valentine's Day is also Lara's birthday! Gymnast Alison Carroll succeeded Karima in 2008. In 2009 Karima appeared in the independent film, *Frontier Blues* and in 2011 a small role as the Shush Club Maitre D in *Sherlock Holmes: A Game of Shadows*. She has had an on/off relationship with radio and television presenter George Lamb for several years.

Allsopp, Kirstie Born 31 August 1971, Hampstead, London. Television presenter best known for the Channel 4 property programmes: *Location, Location, Location; Relocation, Relocation; Location Revisited; The Property Chain; Kirstie's Homemade Home* and *Kirstie's Handmade Britain;* the first three of which were co-presented with Phil Spencer. The Honourable Kirstie Allsopp is the daughter of Charles Henry Allsopp, 6th Baron Hindlip and former chairman of Christie's, and the interior designer Fiona Victoria Jean Atherley McGowan. Kirstie has two sons, Bay Atlas (b. 29 July 2006) and Oscar Hercules (b. 21 August 2008) with her partner, property tycoon Ben Anderson.

Atkinson, Gemma Born Gemma Louise Atkinson, 16 November 1984, Bury, Greater Manchester. Actress and model. Her first major acting role was playing Lisa Hunter in *Hollyoaks* from 2001 to 2005. She later appeared in a spin-off series *Hollyoaks: Let Loose* (2005) for E4 with Marcus Patric (who played Ben Davies), in which their characters started a new life together in Chester. She also appeared in another spin-off *Hollyoaks: In the City* in 2006. She made her debut video game appearance in *Command & Conquer: Red Alert 3* (2008) in the role of Lt. Eva McKenna, which she reprised in *Command & Conquer Red Alert 3: Uprising* (2009). Gemma made a brief appearance in a 2009 episode of *The Bill* where she played Ria Crossley, the girlfriend of a drug dealer. She has appeared as a contestant on *I'm A Celebrity... Get Me Out of Here!*, *Celebrity Weakest Link*, *Celebrity Mastermind*, *Celebrity Masterchef*, *All Star Family Fortunes* and *Soapstar Superstar*, where she reached the final four with impressive vocals. In 2006, the 5' 9" (1.75 m) tall actress had a breast enlargement, taking her bra size to a striking 34E. She is now a glamour model in high demand and has appeared semi-nude in numerous men's magazines including *Arena, FHM, Loaded, Maxim, Zoo* and *Nuts*. Gemma is also well known for her charity runs which have raised money for breast cancer awareness. In 2009, she appeared in the British independent film *Boogie Woogie* and a horror film *13Hrs* and in 2010 she played the small role of Karen in the UK gangster film *Baseline*. She also went on tour with *Calendar Girls* in early 2010, playing Elaine. Her recent projects include appearances in the films *The Sweet Shop* (2010 - as Katie Powell), *How to Stop Being a Loser* (2011 - as Hannah) and *Airborne* (2012 - as Harriett) and in August 2011 she began a short stint as Tamzin, a paramedic, in BBC 1's *Casualty* medical programme. She once dated Manchester United's Cristiano Ronaldo and is reported to have given up the chance to see him play so that her parents, who are both hardcore United fans, could go to the match. Gemma adopted a chimpanzee with her then-partner, Marcus Bent. The Chimpanzee is called Bryan. The decision came after Gemma watched Channel 5 show *Monkey Life*. She is currently dating Liam Richards who appeared on the 2008 series of *Britain's Got Talent*.

Bailey, Laura Born 6 August 1972, London. Laura studied English at the University of Southampton and graduated with a 1st class Honours degree in English Literature. She began working behind the bar at the Chelsea Arts Club before being scouted when she was 21-years-old on the Kings Road in London and then becoming well known for her short relationship with Richard Gere. After signing up to the Independent Talent Group, the 5'8" (1.73cm) model became the face of the new *Jaguar X Type* from its launch in 2001. Laura appeared in a promotional campaign for Marks and Spencer in 2005 and later that year posed nude in the book *4 Inches* featuring female celebrities wearing nothing but Cartier jewellery and shoes by designer Jimmy Choo – all proceeds going to the Elton John AIDS Foundation. Laura's long-time partner is film mogul Eric Fellner and they have two children: a son, Luc, and a daughter, Lola Tiger. Having spent much of her childhood at Brasenose College, Oxford, where her father taught, she announced in 2009 that she had been considering training to become a teacher although more recently she has been putting her writing talents to good effect on behalf of *Vogue*, penning an online fashion-based blog.

Banks, Morwenna Born 14 January 1964, Flushing, Cornwall. Very much an unsung heroine of comedy, Morwenna is not a household name, or face, but ever since she made her television debut in *The Lenny Henry Show* in 1985, her comedy impressions and characterizations have been consistently good. Best-known as the schoolgirl who sat on the edge of a desk in *Absolutely*, Morwenna is also an accomplished straight actress on both sides of the Atlantic and has appeared as The Keeper of the Rules in the American TV series *Sabrina, the Teenage Witch*, and played Anthea Stonem in the E4 teen drama *Skins* between 2007 and 2010. In 1995, Morwenna became only the third non-US cast member on *Saturday Night Live*, although she subsequently left after four episodes. At the turn of the Millennium she wrote, produced and appeared in the British ensemble film *The Announcement* (2000). She has lived with comedian David Baddiel for more than a decade and they have two children, Dolly Loveday (b. 2001) and Ezra Beckett (b. 2004), both born in Westminster, London. See also entries in the television section for *Absolutely, Little Robots, Rex the Runt, Ruddy Hell! It's Harry and Paul, Saturday Live, Saxondale,* and *Stressed Eric*.

Bashy See entry for Ashley Thomas

Beckham, David Born David Robert Joseph Beckham, 2 May 1975, Leytonstone, London. Footballer, advertising brand and fashion icon. As at the end of December 2011, David has received 115 caps for England (only surpassed by Peter Shilton's 125) and scored 17 goals. The 6' (1.83m) midfielder and master of the set-piece captained England from 2000-06 across 59 matches. His ten-year career with Manchester United produced 265 appearances and 65 goals, the club winning the Premier League title six times, the FA Cup twice, and the UEFA Champions League in 1999. David left Manchester United to sign for Real Madrid in 2003, where he remained for four seasons, clinching the La Liga championship in his final year with the club. During his time there he made 116 appearances and scored 13 goals, sporting the No 23 shirt as his talisman. In 2007, David signed for the Major League Soccer club Los Angeles Galaxy, and has thus far made 75 appearances and scored 11 goals. During this period he has had loan spells with Italian club AC Milan in 2009 and 2010, making 29 appearances and scoring two goals. David proposed to Victoria Adams on 24 January 1998 in a restaurant in Cheshunt, Hertfordshire and married the singer and fashion designer at Luttrellstown Castle, nr Dublin, on 4 July 1999, the wedding and reception being paid for by an exclusive deal with *OK!* Magazine. David and Victoria have four children, sons Brooklyn Joseph (b. 4 March 1999, London, but famously conceived in Brooklyn, New York), Romeo James (b. 1 September 2002, London), and Cruz David (b. 20 February 2005, Madrid); and a daughter, Harper Seven (b. 10 July 2011, Los Angeles). The Beckhams' daughter is believed to be named after a Disney character her three brothers adore - called Harper Finkle. Both Brooklyn and Romeo's godfather is Elton John and their godmother is Elizabeth Hurley. David was voted the BBC Sports Personality of the Year for 2001 and awarded an OBE for services to football on 13 June 2003. David is undoubtedly the most famous footballer in the world. His success was not instant however. During the 1998 World Cup, he received a red card in England's match against Argentina, after kicking Diego Simeone in the calf whilst lying on the floor. This sending off was a defining moment in his career and although it was not the last red card he was to receive it certainly made him a more responsible player. Away from football, "Posh and Becks" have become media royalty, their home in Hertfordshire, being unofficially dubbed Beckingham Palace, although their current main residence is an Italian villa in Beverly Hills, California. David's career has been such that Victoria refers to him affectionately as "Golden Balls". He has launched fragrances and clothes lines, endorsed all manner of products, gained sponsorships, raised huge amounts for charity and generally raised his profile to the extent that his footballing career has become secondary to the extra-curricular projects he is involved with. On screen, David appeared in the 2005 film *Goal!: The Dream Begins* (lookalike Andy Harmer played him in *Bend It Like Beckham*) and in the sequel *Goal! 2: Living the Dream* (2007). Famous for his numerous tattoos, which include a black-and-white image of Christ drawn on his right side and an angel with the text 'In the face of adversity' on his right shoulder; he also has the names of his wife and first three children inscribed - with undoubtedly a plot already chosen for the inscription of his baby daughter.

Beckwith, Tamara Born 17 April 1970, London. Tamara is the daughter of property tycoon Peter Beckwith. Tamara attended Cheltenham Ladies' College but dropped out in 1987 to have her first child, Anouska Poppy Pearl; the father, William Gerhauser, was an American marine and son of Bill Gerhauser, Finance Director of the *Playboy* empire. The so-called *It-Girl* began to appear in glossy celebrity magazines such as *OK!* and *Hello!* often as a partner-in-crime of fellow socialite Tara Palmer-Tomkinson (see separate entry). For the past 15 years Tamara has made a string of television appearances in programmes such as *Daddy's Girl* (1996), *Shooting Stars* (1996), *An Audience With the Spice Girls* (1997), *Casting Couch* (1999), *Trigger Happy TV* (2000), *An Audience with Kylie Minogue* (2001), *Loose Women* (2003), *Loose Lips* (2003), *The Wright Stuff* (2003), *Celebrities Under Pressure* (2004), *I'm Famous and Frightened* (2004), *Richard and Judy* (2003-05), *Dancing on Ice* (2006), *Celebair* (2008) and *Come Dine With Me* (2008). She has also appeared in two films, *Tunnel of Love* (1997 – as 'woman in car') and *An Ideal Husband* (1998 – as Margaret Marchmont). As a presenter she has worked for *MTV* and *VH-1*. Tamara also designs a range of jewellery for *QVC*. After dating Sylvester Stallone and Charlie Sheen, Tamara was engaged to Sharon Stone's brother, Michael, but after that relationship ended she married Giorgio Veroni on 27th August 2007 in Venice; having met the construction industry heir at the Monaco Grand Prix. On the 28th of January 2009 Tamara and Giorgio welcomed the newest addition to their family, Violet Angiolina Rose.

Best, Calum Born Calum Milan Best, 6 February 1981, San Jose, California. Calum is the son of football legend George Best and his first wife, Angie. His middle name is after his godfather, Milan Mandarić, his father's lifelong friend, and the present chairman of Sheffield Wednesday. Calum is the cousin of English actress Samantha Janus. Not possessing his father's sporting prowess, Calum has carved out a career as a fashion model and television personality. He came to public attention in 2005 when he featured in ITV1's *Celebrity Love Island*. He appeared again in the 2006 series and was ultimately victorious. In September 2006, he appeared in the ITV2 series *Calum, Fran and Dangerous Danan*, in which he travelled from Texas to Los Angeles on America's U.S. Route 66 with fellow *Love Island* contestants Paul Danan and Fran Cosgrave. After the series aired Calum gave his name to a men's fragrance produced by Jigsaw. Around this time he played himself in the final episode of ITV1's cult drama series *Footballers' Wives*. Despite his television appearances, Calum is better known for his playboy lifestyle which has gained him column inches in tabloid newspapers and celebrity magazines. He has reportedly dated models Kate Moss, Agyness Deyn, Amy Green and Gemma Atkinson as well as actress Lindsay Lohan. Calum has a daughter, Amelia Grace Hogan (b. 19 December 2006, London), as the result of a one-night-stand with model Lorna Hogan. In 2008, Calum appeared on RTÉ's *Livin' With Lucy* and later that year he featured in MTV's *Totally Calum Best,* which featured his attempts to remain celibate for fifty days. More recently Calum has filled in for Ian Wright on *Live from Studio Five* on January 8, 2010 and later that year appeared as a celebrity on *All Star Family Fortunes* opposite actress Denise Welch and her family.

Best, George Born 22 May 1946, Belfast, Northern Ireland. Iconic footballer who popularized the game amongst the non-sports-loving public, particularly women. As a footballer George was a speedy winger with outrageous dribbling skills, bravery, balance and positional nous – even in a Manchester United team including Denis Law and Bobby Charlton, George was considered the star player and is thought by many good judges to be as good as there ever was at his peak. George hit the headlines when he scored two goals in a European Cup quarter-final match against Benfica in 1966. Because of his Beatle-crop haircut, the Portuguese media dubbed him "O Quinto Beatle" (the fifth Beatle) and his flair, good looks and extravagant celebrity lifestyle made him a media darling, with appearances on chat-shows and pop shows such as *Top of the Pops*. In 1968, the year United won the European Cup, George was named European Footballer of the Year. This accolade was undoubtedly the highpoint of his career but the drink problem he had subdued began to rise to the surface. George opened two nightclubs in Manchester, in the late 1960s, Oscar's and the more famous Slack Alice's (which later became 42nd Street Nightclub). He also owned fashion boutiques, in partnership with Mike Summerbee of Manchester City. George's first professional match for United was against West Bromwich Albion in 1963. at age 17. He scored his first goal in a match against Burnley. His last competitive game for Manchester United was on 1 January 1974 against Queens Park Rangers at Loftus Road. In total George made 470 appearances for Manchester United in all competitions from 1963 to 1974, and scored 179 goals (including six in one game against fourth division Northampton Town in 1970). After a brief spell with South African side Jewish Guild (1974) George signed for Fulham and played 42 games over two seasons and scored eight goals in a memorable partnership with Rodney Marsh; in one famous game the two deciding to tackle each other just for the enjoyment of the crowd. In 1979 he made his debut for Hibernian. The club was struggling to fill the ground, topping 8,000 fans, until George appeared. Over 20,000 fans turned up to watch his first home match. Other appearances include: Dunstable Town, 5 scoring 0 (1974-75), Stockport County, 3 scoring 2 goals (1975-76), Cork Celtic, 3 scoring 0 goals (1975-76), LA Aztecs, 23 scoring 15 goals (1976) and after leaving Fulham 32 more games scoring 12 goals (1977-78), Fort Lauderdale Strikers, 28 scoring 6 goals (1978-79), Hibernian, 17 scoring 3 goals (1979-81), San Jose Earthquakes, 56 scoring 21 goals (1980-81), Bournemouth, 5 scoring 0 goals (1982-83), Brisbane Lions, 4 scoring 0 goals (1983) as well as guest appearances for Hong Kong First Division teams Sea Bees and Rangers (1982) and Newry Lions (1983) before finally hanging up his boots. He was capped 37 times for Northern Ireland, scoring nine goals. Of his nine international goals four were scored against Cyprus and one each against Albania, England, Scotland, Switzerland and Turkey. After George's playing career was over he began a lucrative spell as after dinner speaker and raconteur although becoming increasingly erratic and unreliable. In September 1990, George appeared on an edition of BBC chat show *Wogan* in which he was clearly drunk and swore, at one point repeatedly saying to the host, "Terry, I like screwing". Although he had a successful liver transplant at King College Hospital in London, he continued to drink and eventually died on 25 November 2005 in London. George was married twice, to Angela MacDonald-Janes (b. 26 July 1952, Southend on Sea, Essex) between 1978 and 1986 and Alex Pursey (b. 29 January 1972, London) between 1995 and 2004. George had a son, Calum (see separate entry) by his first wife and is reported to have had two daughters by other women. His niece by marriage is actress Samantha Janus, who is the daughter of his first wife's brother. In 2004, his second wife appeared as a contestant on the reality television programme *I'm a Celebrity... Get Me Out of Here!* George's legacy includes Belfast City Airport being renamed George Best Belfast City Airport in 2006. George was also famous for his memorable quotes such as "I spent a lot of money on booze, birds and fast cars. The rest I just squandered" and "I used to go missing a lot... Miss Canada, Miss United Kingdom, Miss World". Perhaps the most famous story George told was when a room service waiter brought him more bottles of champagne and there was George in bed with two stunning models, his bed strewn with £20 notes. The waiter looked at George and said – "Mr Best where did it all go wrong".

Boateng, Ozwald Born 22 February 1967, Muswell Hill, North London. Fashion designer of Ghanaian descent; his style inspired by his father's immaculate suits. Ozwald began studying computing at Southgate College, aged 16, but ultimately graduated in fashion and design after being introduced to cutting and designing by his then girlfriend. Fresh out of his teens, Ozwald sold his first collection to a menswear shop in Covent Garden and the proceeds from this eventually allowed him to open his first studio in Portobello Road in 1991. This busy area of the Notting Hill district of The Royal Borough of Kensington and Chelsea proved lucrative, and punters, attracted by the famous weekend market, spent freely. In 1994, Ozwald staged his first catwalk presentation during Paris Fashion Week, the first tailor to stage a catwalk show in Paris. Mentored by Tommy Nutter (see separate entry), the success of the Paris show enabled Ozwald to open a boutique on Vigo Street, on the south end of Savile Row, in 1995. Since 2008, Ozwald's flagship store stands at No. 30 Savile Row (the former premises of Anderson and Sheppard), on the corner of Savile Row and Clifford Street. Although making his name with bespoke fashion accessories, Ozwald has diversified in recent years and has had successful collaborations with French fashion house Givenchy, private banking house, Coutts (The Coutts 'World Credit Card' appears in Ozwald's trademark imperial purple) and Virgin Atlantic (for whom he designed their critically-acclaimed upper class amenity kits). Ozwald has also designed for films such as *Hannibal, Lock Stock and Two Smoking Barrels, Tomorrow Never Dies, Sex and the City, Ugly Betty, Eastern Promises, Gangster Number One, Alfie, Assault on Precinct 13, The Matrix, Miami Vice, Oceans 13,* and *Rush Hour 3.*

Botham, Ian Born Ian Terence Botham, 24 November 1955, Heswall, Cheshire. Aggressive right-hand batsman and right-arm medium-fast bowler for Somerset, Worcestershire, Durham, Queensland and England from 1974 to 1993. England's outstanding post-war all-round cricketer. In his 102 Tests, he took an English record 383 wickets @ 28.40 (27 times taking five wickets in an innings), scored 5,200 runs @ 33.54 including 14 centuries (highest score 208 v India, The Oval 1982) and held 120 catches, an English record he shares with Colin Cowdrey. In 1979-80 he took 13 for 106 and scored 114 v India in Bombay; the first player to score a century and take ten wickets in the same Test, and later became the first to score 3,000 runs and take 300 wickets in Tests. Against Australia in 1981, his famous 149 n.o. helped England to an unlikely victory at Headingley, and at Old Trafford, Manchester he hit 118 with 13 fours and six sixes. In his career, he totalled 19,399 runs @ 33.97 (with 38 centuries), took 1,172 wickets @ 27.22 and held 354 catches. He hit a world record number of sixes in an English season (80 in 1985) and once scored 100 in 52 minutes (v Warwickshire in 1982). He also made 11 Football League appearances for Scunthorpe United (including four as substitute) between 1979-80 and 1984-85. Since retiring from cricket Ian has been a prodigious fundraiser for charitable causes, undertaking a total of 12 long-distance charity walks. His

first, in 1985, was a 900-mile trek from John o' Groats to Land's End; inspired by a visit to Taunton's Musgrove Park Hospital children's ward and learning that some of the children had only weeks to live. Since then, his efforts have raised more than £12 million for charity, with Leukaemia Research among the many causes to benefit. Ian married Kathryn Waller in 1976 and they have two daughters Becky and Sarah, and a son Liam (b. August 1977), a talented cricketer and rugby player but now a commentator for Sky Sports.

Bowery, Leigh Born 26 March 1961, Sunshine, Victoria, Australia. Although not strictly British, neither born nor bred, Leigh was an integral part of the British pop culture scene throughout the 1980s and into the 1990s. Based in London from 1980, Leigh was a performance artist, club promoter, actor, pop star, model and fashion designer, who influenced Alexander McQueen, Lucian Freud, Vivienne Westwood, Boy George, Antony and the Johnsons, John Galliano, and the Scissor Sisters, to name but a few. Leigh was a large man, in the mould of Boy George, but carried off a distinctive look like no other; his white-faced multi-spectacled visage with its exuberant over-use of mascara and lipstick becoming an iconic look. In January 1985, Leigh opened the poly-sexual disco club, Taboo (a sort of British version of Studio 54, only even more cutting edge. The Thursday night spectacular gave its name to the Boy George-inspired stage musical which opened at the Venue Theatre in London's West End on 29 January 2002). By 1987 Taboo was over, AIDS and hard drugs causing the death of Leigh's best friend and erstwhile lover Trojan, and also the infamous Taboo 'door whore' Marc Valtier. Leigh also contracted AIDS at this time but carried on working as an occasional living sculpture, a nude model for Lucian Freud and a design consultant for Rifat Ozbek. In 1993, Leigh formed the art rock pop band *Minty* with Richard Torry, Nicola Bateman and Matthew Glammore. Their single *Useless Man* was a minor hit in Holland. Later that year he also formed the band *Raw Sewage* with leading clubbers Sheila Tequila and Stella Stein. They performed nude with their faces blacked up, wearing 18" platforms and pubic wigs. Although Leigh always described himself as gay he married his longtime friend Nicola Bateman on 13 May 1994, in Tower Hamlets, London, seven months before his death from AIDS-related illness at the Middlesex Hospital, London, on New Year's Eve 1994. Among his last requests was that his middle name be unknown.

Branson, Richard Born Richard Charles Nicholas Branson, 18 July 1950, Blackheath, London. Although suffering from dyslexia, which blighted his academic career, Richard's first business venture, aged 16, was a magazine entitled, *The Student.* This was a huge success and he soon diversified into discounted records, trading under his now familiar brand name of Virgin. In 1972 he co-founded Virgin Records with Nik Powell (b. 4 November 1950, Gt Kingshill, Buckinghamshire) the second husband of singer Sandie Shaw and currently director of the National Film and Television School and deputy chairman of the European Film Academy. The chart-topping *Tubular Bells* (1973) was Virgin Records' first release and this enabled the label to sign such diverse bands as *The Sex Pistols* and *Culture Club.* In 1982, Richard made a rare excursion into record production with the novelty record *Baa, Baa, Black Sheep,* by *Singing Sheep* in association with Doug McLean and Grace McDonald. The record consisted of a herd of sheep baaing along to a drum machine and reached No 42 in the UK charts. Richard had formed Virgin Atlantic Airways in 1984, but had to sell the Virgin record label to EMI in 1992 for £500 million, in order to keep the airline solvent. He did maintain an interest in the music industry for some years after, founding V2 Records in 1996. Among his many business interests are Virgin Trains (launched in 1993), Virgin Galactic (a space tourism company founded in 2004) and Virgin Racing (a Formula One racing team launched in 2009 as Manor Grand Prix and now known as Marussia Virgin Racing – after the Russian sports car company). This last business venture is typical of Richard's brand ethic and it is somewhat unclear as to the exact control he asserts on many of the Virgin-named companies. He launched Virgin Mobile in 1999 but subsequently sold it to UK cable TV, broadband, and telephone company NTL/NTL:Telewest (now Virgin Media) for almost £1 billion in 2006. Known to be a fair employer, when he won £500,000 by way of compensation for a "dirty tricks" campaign by British Airways Richard divided the spoils among his staff. Richard is currently the 5th richest person in the United Kingdom and 254th in the world according to Forbes' 2011 list of billionaires, with an approximate net worth of £2.58 billion (US$4.2 billion). He is the eldest of four siblings; his sister Vanessa (b. 1959, Surrey) and her husband Robert Devereux being the owners of the Inner Hebridean island of Eilean Shona. He also has a brother, Tom, and sister, Andrea. Richard was married to Kristen Tomassi in 1972 but divorced her in 1979 after falling in love with Joan Templeman, with whom he has a daughter Holly (b. 1981) and son Sam (b. 1985). Their eldest daughter, Clare Sarah, died in 1979 when she was just four days old. The couple eventually married in 1989 at Necker Island, a 74-acre (30 ha) island in the British Virgin Islands belonging to Richard (itself making the news in August 2011 after actress Kate Winslet was among 20 guests forced to flee the Caribbean island as lightning during Hurricane Irene set it ablaze). Richard's autobiography, *Losing My Virginity*, was published in 1998. His much-publicised leisure pursuits include several attempts at the fastest Atlantic Ocean crossing, in 1986 beating the record by two hours in his "Virgin Atlantic Challenger II" alongside sailing expert Daniel McCarthy. The following year his 2,300,000 cubic feet (65,000 m3), hot air balloon "Virgin Atlantic Flyer" became the first to cross the Atlantic. Between 1995 and 1998, Richard teamed up with adventurers, Per Lindstrand (b. 1948) and Steve Fossett (b. 1944; d. 2007) in an unsuccessful exercise to circumnavigate the globe by balloon. Richard has also played himself in several TV and film productions, been parodied on *The Simpsons*, and even had a cameo role in the Bollywood film, *London Dreams* (2009). On 30 March 2000, Richard was knighted at Buckingham Palace by HRH The Prince of Wales.

Brook, Kelly Born Kelly Ann Parsons, 23 November 1979, Rochester, Kent. Model, actress and television presenter. Kelly attended school in Rochester before studying at the Italia Conti stage school in London for three years. Her modelling career began aged 16 after winning a beauty competition that her mother entered her in. This success enabled her to work on a range of advertising campaigns, including Foster's Lager, Renault Megane, Walkers Crisps and Bravissimo, who specialise in bras and lingerie for large-breasted women. This attracted the editorial team of the *Daily Star* tabloid, where she became a Page Three girl. Kelly went on to feature in magazines such as *GQ*, *Loaded* and *FHM*. Her mainstream television presenting breakthrough came in January 1999 when she was chosen to replace Denise van Outen as the female half of *The Big Breakfast* hosting team, alongside Johnny Vaughan. She left the show in July 1999. 2005 saw her host the reality television program *Celebrity Love Island* for ITV and also top the 'FHM 100 Sexiest Women in the World' list. In 2006, Kelly introduced her own range of swimwear and lingerie at New Look stores. The 5'8" (1.73cm) model took part in BBC1's *Strictly Come Dancing* in 2007, where her professional partner was Brendan Cole. She withdrew however in week nine due to the death of her father from cancer. January 2009 saw her join the third series of *Britain's Got Talent* as a fourth judge, but she subsequently left, the producers deciding that the four-judge format was "too complicated". She has starred in a few films but nothing major to date although she made a short appearance as Lyle's girlfriend in the 2003 film *The Italian Job* and a slightly longer one in *Piranha 3D* (2009 – as Danni Arslow). On television Kelly has played Victoria Hardwick, the girlfriend of Lex Luthor in four episodes of the television series *Smallville* and more recently appeared as Jemima in an episode of *Skins* (2011). In November 2009 she began playing Celia (aka Miss September) in *Calendar Girls* at the Noel Coward Theatre. Kelly dated English actor Jason Statham for seven years before splitting in 2004. She met her next boyfriend, actor Billy Zane whilst filming thriller *Survival Island* in Greece in 2004. They were engaged to be married but Kelly postponed the wedding upon the death of her father. The couple later split and she subsequently dated Wasps and England rugby union player Danny Cipriani from September 2008 to June 2010. Kelly has been dating former Scottish international rugby union player Thom Evans since December 2010. Thom is a cousin of radio and television presenter, Chris Evans. On 16 March 2011, Kelly announced via her Twitter account that she and Thom were expecting a baby girl. Tragically, on 9 May 2011, she suffered a miscarriage.

Butcher, Lisa Born 1 January 1971, London. English fashion model and television presenter. At just 15 she won *Elle's* Face of 1987 and impressively her first job after finishing school was for Ralph Lauren in New York. Lisa has also modelled for Max Factor, Yves Saint Laurent, John Galliano and Vidal Sassoon. Royal photographer Norman Parkinson called her the "Face of the '90s", and she appeared on the covers of magazines including *Vogue, Elle* and *Marie Claire*. Lisa has been the face of Hardy Amies since 2003 and is also the face for Long Tall Sally. A highly talented individual, she has her own jewellery design, The Eden Collection. Lisa first appeared on television presenting *The Big Breakfast* with Chris Evans but really came to prominence in this field for hosting Living TV's *Britain's Next Top Model*. Lisa and her friend Mica Paris took over from Trinny Woodall and Susannah Constantine in 2006 as the presenters of BBC1's *What Not to Wear*. The 6' (1.83 m) model has been married twice, to chef Marco Pierre White (with Albert Roux as best man) for a few weeks in 1992 and then Chilean polo player Gabriel Donoso, who fathered her two children, Olivia and Amber, before passing away due to injuries sustained in a match. Subsequent boyfriends have included actor Jeremy Northam, entrepreneur Damian Aspinall, actor Jonathan Rhys Meyers and 24 year old toyboy socialite Jacobi Anstruther-Gough-Calthorpe.

Campbell, Naomi Born 22 May 1970, Streatham, London. English supermodel of Jamaican decent. Her mother, Valerie is a former ballet dancer who travelled across Europe with the dance troupe Fantastica. Naomi was cast as a pupil to appear in a music video for Bob Marley's song *Is This Love?* when just 7, and at the age of 10, she was accepted into the Italia Conti Academy stage school, where she emulated her mother by studying ballet. Naomi was spotted at age 15 at a shopping arcade at Covent Gardens, signing with Elite Model Management and later appearing on the cover of *Elle*. In August 1988, she appeared on the cover of *Vogue* Paris (and later for *Vogue* UK and *Time* magazine) as that publication's first black cover girl, with backing from her friend and mentor, Yves St. Laurent. She famously starred in George Michael's music video *Freedom! '90*, with Linda Evangelista, Christy Turlington, Cindy Crawford and Tatjana Patitz. In 1991, she appeared on Vanilla Ice's single *Cool as Ice*. In 1992, Naomi appeared in Madonna's music video for *Erotica*, which featured filmed footage for the book *Sex*. She has also appeared in videos for artists including Michael Jackson, Nelly, Jay-Z, P Diddy, The Notorious B.I.G, Macy Gray, Prince and Usher. The high point of her career was in the late 1980s when she was part of the so-called 'Trinity' of models (alongside Christy Turlington and Linda Evangelista) dubbed supermodels and early 1990s, when she was part of the so-called Big Six (with Cindy Crawford, Claudia Schiffer and Kate Moss added to the existing Trinity members). Her 1994 novel *Swan* (ghostwritten by Caroline Upcher) told the tale of a supermodel being blackmailed over dark secrets in her past. Later in 1994, Naomi released an album, *babywoman*, named after designer Rifat Ozbek's nickname for her. Although a critical and commercial flop, the album spawned the single *Love and Tears*, which reached No. 40 in the UK charts. In 1995, she and fellow models Claudia Schiffer and Elle Macpherson invested in an ill-fated chain of restaurants called the Fashion Café. At this time she attempted an acting career gaining small roles in *Miami Rhapsody* (1995) and Spike Lee's *Girl 6* (1996), as well as a recurring role on the second season of *New York Undercover*, as Simone Jeffers. Since 1997, the 5'9" (1.75 m) beauty has all but retired from the catwalk (partly because of magazines such as *Time* declaring the end of the supermodel era, partly because of advancing years and partly because her reputation as being high maintenance and confrontational meant bookings became less frequent) and has been involved in charitable ventures with the likes of Nelson Mandela and has also participated in Fashion Relief, raising over a million dollars for Hurricane Katrina victims. In 1999, Naomi entered rehab after a five-year addiction to cocaine. Later in the year she founded the Design House of Naomi Campbell and has thus far created seven fragrances for women including Cat Deluxe and Mystery. In 2000, Naomi pleaded guilty in Toronto to assaulting her personal assistant Georgina Galanis with a cell phone. Numerous cases of assault have been filed throughout the first decade of the new Millennium, perhaps the most famous in Britain being her arrest inside Heathrow's Terminal 5 in 2008 on suspicion of assaulting a police officer after one of her bags had been lost. She was sentenced to 200 hours of community service. Naomi received further media attention in 2009 after allegedly describing the fashion industry as "racist." She was quoted as saying "You know, the American president may be black, but as a black woman, I am still an exception in this business. I always have to work harder to be treated equally." Naomi has made cameo appearances in films and television programmes including *Ali G Indahouse*, *Absolutely Fabulous* and *Ugly Betty* and still struts the catwalk on occasion. Ex boyfriends include Mike Tyson, Robert De Niro, Eric Clapton, Adam Clayton, Flavio Briatore and Usher. She is reported to be dating Russian real estate entrepreneur Vladislav Doronin, sometimes referred to as Russia's Donald Trump. In August 2010, Naomi made a highly-publicised appearance at a war crimes trial against former Liberian president Charles Taylor at the Special Court for Sierra Leone in The Hague. She was called to give evidence on a "blood diamond" she allegedly received from Taylor during a Nelson Mandela Children's Fund function in 1997. She testified that she was given "dirty-looking" stones late at night by two unidentified men, and claimed she did not know the diamonds had originated from Taylor until being told so the next morning by a fellow attendee, actress Mia Farrow.

Childs, Amy Born 7 June 1990, Barking & Dagenham, Essex. Amy is best-known for her love of spray tans, all things pink and for inventing the vajazzle (the adornment and decoration of the pubic region) on the ITV2 semi-reality show *The Only Way is Essex* (2010). A trained beautician, Amy has done well for a girl with chronic dyslexia who left school with just one GCSE (a B in French). After leaving *TOWIE* she finished fourth in *Celebrity Big Brother* 2011. Amy has her own clothing line and her own tan and false eyelash range. She also now has her own TV show, *All About Amy*, on Channel 5 and her own beauty slot on ITV's *This Morning*. Like her heroine, Katie Price, she is not averse to a bit of ghost-writing and puts her name to a column in *New!* magazine. Amy recently split up with her stockbroker boyfriend Joe Hurlock after nine months of dating. In July 2011, Amy was named Personality of the Year at the National Reality TV Awards.

Chung, Alexa Born 5 November 1983, Privett, Hampshire. Television presenter and fashion model. Alexa began her professional career as a cover girl for teen magazines such as *Elle Girl* and *CosmoGIRL!* and appeared in adverts for products including Fanta, Sony Ericsson, Sunsilk and Tampax. In April 2006, she became the co-host of the Saturday morning magazine show *Popworld*, alongside former MTV presenter Alex Zane, and immediately showed a flair for the irreverent style of interview the show was famed for. Despite a less-than-spectacular ratings success as co-host of topical satire show *Get A Grip* in April 2007, Alexa's star has continued to shine ever brighter, turning up on numerous digital channels and occasionally on mainstream television, notably as presenter of Channel 4's early morning music programme *Freshly Squeezed* and as the roving reporter in *Gok's Fashion Fix*. At present, she is the face of Lacoste's "Joy of Pink" fragrance and Superga's Italian sneakers. At the British Fashion Awards 2011, Alexa won the British Style Award, which was voted for by the public. She appeared in a dress by Christopher Kane. From October 2007 until July 2011 she was in a relationship with Alex Turner of the *Arctic Monkeys*. She has recently been dating *Hurts* frontman Theo Hutchcraft. See also entries in the television section for *Get A Grip*, *Popworld*, and *T4*.

Cipriani, Danny Born Daniel Jerome Cipriani, 2 November 1987, Roehampton, London. Danny has a Trinidadian father and English mother. A fine all-round sportsman while at Whitgift School in Croydon, Danny was on the books of Queens Park Rangers as a junior and also played schoolboy cricket for Berkshire and Oxfordshire and was invited to join Surrey County Cricket Club as a batsman. He also played squash at county level

before joining Rosslyn Park and immediately showing the promise that was to develop into a fine, if somewhat chequered rugby union career as a nifty fly-half/full-back with London Wasps and England. Danny's England debut was due to be against Scotland in the Six Nations Championship on 8 March 2008 but two days before the match he was axed from the squad due to "inappropriate behaviour" after being photographed leaving a London nightclub at 12.30am. Controversy has never been far away from both his sporting and personal life ever since. The following weekend he made his debut against Ireland and was the star of England's 33-10 victory (converting all of his goal kicks) although again courting trouble by swearing during the post-match BBC interview. On 6 October 2008 Danny was involved in a fracas with international team-mate Josh Lewsey and was left nursing a bloody nose and cut lip. Injuries plus in-and-out form then frustrated Danny's career and his high-profile relationship with model Kelly Brook raised concerns to his commitment. He joined the Melbourne Rebels in late 2010 and made his debut for them in early 2011 although his off the field activities have again contributed to an unsettled future. In October 2011 it was reported he spent the night with Katie Price, after her break up with Argentinian model Leandro Penna, much to the chagrin of Imogen Thomas who considered herself to be Danny's current girlfriend.

Clarke, John Cooper Born 25 January 1949, Salford. The best-known performance poet of his day, John was at the height of his powers during the punk era when his Bob Dylan looks and deadpan delivery became the template for all those that followed, including comedy performers such as Jack Dee, Craig Charles and John Hegley (b. 1 October 1953, London) who took over the mantle of Britain's favourite cutting edge performance poet when John went into decline throughout the 1980s due to heroin addiction. Three of John's poems are currently on the GCSE syllabus. He has also had one Top 40 hit record, *Gimmix! Play Loud* (No 39 in 1979) and one charting LP, *Snap Crackle and Bop* (No 26 in 1980) and inspired several pop acts, notably The Arctic Monkeys, and in particular Alex Turner. The revival of the punk phenomenon has seen John gigging again all over the UK. In 1979, John joined actors' union Equity, under the name Lenny Siberia and is currently working on a film idea with Plan B. He has also been working closely with Nottingham's Click Films to make a documentary, *Evidently John Cooper Clarke*, about his life which will be shown on BBC4 in Spring 2012. John's voice can currently be heard tempting you to buy pizza in the new Dominos advert. He is no stranger to television adverts, starring in the 1988 Honey Monster ads for Sugar Puffs. John had a brief unsuccessful marriage but now lives with his partner, Evie, in Colchester, Essex. They have a daughter, Stella (b. 1994).

Clement, Jessica-Jane Born 24 February 1985, Sheffield, South Yorkshire. The glamour model and actress studied Performing Arts and Psychology at The Sheffield College before going on to study at the Dartington College of Arts. She first came to public attention in 2006 as one of the presenters of the BBC3 programme *The Real Hustle*; demonstrating how confidence tricks and distraction scams are performed on an unsuspecting public. The show is currently filming its 12th series. Her acting roles have included Cindi Marshall in Sky TV's *Dream Team* for (2005-07), the Jade Dragon escort in the film *Moussaka & Chips* (2005) and Danny Dyer's character's (Neil) girlfriend in the horror comedy *Doghouse* (2009). She has also appeared in the long-running hospital drama, *Casualty*. In November 2008, Jessica-Jane took part in the third series of *Celebrity Scissorhands* and she is currently in a relationship with the show's professional hairdresser Lee Stafford (see separate entry). In November 2011, she took part in the eleventh series of ITV's reality television show *I'm a Celebrity...Get Me Out of Here!*.

Clifford, Max Born Maxwell Frank Clifford, 6 April 1943, Kingston upon Thames, London. From a humble background, Clifford left school aged 15 with no qualifications and after a brief stint working at Ely's department store began his working life as an editorial assistant on the *Eagle* comic. After taking redundancy he trained as a journalist with South London Press. He next joined the EMI press office in 1962 which led to a job at Chris Hutchins'

PR agency. In 1970, he left Hutchins and started his own PR agency, Max Clifford Associates. He became known to the British public in 1986 after concocting a story to promote Freddie Starr (see entry in comedy section). Max has been courting controversy ever since. Among many stories he spun for maximum financial gain was the 1989 *News of the World* headline "CALL GIRL WORKS IN COMMONS" after it was discovered Pamela Bordes (who was simultaneously dating arms dealer Adnan Khashoggi, *Sunday Times* editor Andrew Neil, *The Observer* editor Donald Trelford and junior minister Colin Moynihan) had a House of Commons security pass arranged by MPs David Shaw and Henry Bellingham. In July 2000, the equally controversial boss of Harrods, Mohamed Al-Fayed retained Clifford in an effort to attain a more positive image after it had been tarnished following the "Cash for questions" scandal where he purportedly paid politician Neil Hamilton for asking questions in the House of Commons on his behalf. On 10 August 2001, Neil and Christine Hamilton were arrested by police investigating an alleged rape. The investigation against them was dropped when it became apparent that the accusations were entirely false. In June 2003, the woman who had fabricated the accusation, Nadine Milroy-Sloan, was imprisoned for attempting to pervert the course of justice. In February 2005, Clifford, who had acted for Milroy-Sloan, paid an undisclosed sum in damages to settle for the 2001 rape allegations, although he himself did not face any criminal charges over the case. However, the judge in the case pointed out that Clifford had offered the offender £80,000 in connection with the claims! Max has never been averse to using his 'skills' for his own political ends, having famously invented the story, which made the front page of *The Sun*, that David Mellor, the then Secretary of State for National Heritage, made love in Chelsea F.C. football kit. Whatever one thinks of a man who earns his living by manipulating the media and concocting stories which can have a devastating effect on the lives of the innocent, there is no doubt that he is one of the shrewdest operators acting within the law of the land.

Cole, Lily Born Lily Luahana Cole, 19 May 1988, Torquay, Devon. The 5' 10½" (1.79 m) tall red-head attended the St Marylebone church school for girls before achieving 'A's in her A-level examinations in English, Politics, Drama, History, and Philosophy & Ethics at Latymer Upper School. This is a fantastic accomplishment considering her modelling career began at the age of fourteen. Lily was initially reluctant, but eventually signed on with agency Storm Models and gained her big break in 2003 with photographer Steven Meisel who was captivated by her long limbs, porcelain skin and fiery red hair. Since then, Lily has worked with many of the industries most noted photographers. In November 2004, at the British Fashion Awards, she was named 'Model of the Year' and has since featured in many well known fashion magazines and advertising campaigns. Notable appearances include Vogue and Marks and Spencer. In October 2009, Lily signed to model for cosmetics company Rimmel London and subsequently became the exclusive face of the M&S Limited Collection. Lily has also completed several nude photo-shoots which have caused mixed reception. Not content with modelling, Lily made her film debut, as Polly the Geek, in *St. Trinian's* (2007). Other films include: *Rage* (2009 - as Lettuce Leaf) and *There Be Dragons* (2011 - as Aline). She landed her first leading role in the 2009 film *The Imaginarium of Doctor Parnassus* where she played Valentina. In February 2010, Lily was voted the fourth "sexiest redhead of all time", after Florence Welch, Prince Harry of Wales, and Nicola Roberts in a poll conducted by the *Daily Mirror*. Despite her modelling and acting successes she is very focused on academia, recently studying at King's College, Cambridge, reading History of Art. Having commenced in the Michaelmas term, 2008, she gained a first in her examinations at the end of her first two years. Lily was in a relationship with actor Enrique Murciano, star of American television series *Without a Trace*, between August 2008 and February 2011 and has recently rekindled her relationship with actor Jude Law, whom she briefly dated in the past. In May 2011, Lily appeared in *The Curse of the Black Spot*, the third episode of the sixth series of *Doctor Who*. In March 2012, The Body Shop launched its Beauty With Heart campaign, making Lily the company's first ambassador. Her recent films include: *There Be*

Dragons (2011), *The Moth Diaries* (2011) and the upcoming *Snow White & the Huntsman* (2012 - as Greta).

Coleman, Jenna-Louise Born 27 April 1986, Blackpool, Lancashire. Actress, famous for playing the part of lesbian Jasmine Thomas in *Emmerdale* between 2005 and 2009 and tough-girl Lindsay James in *Waterloo Road* in 2009. After a period of unemployment she made her big screen debut in *Captain America: The First Avenger* (2011 - as Connie) but her profile is likely to be raised in 2012 by virtue of a starring role as cockney Annie Desmond in the four-part ITV blockbuster, *Titanic*, and by landing the role of Dr Who's next companion for the seventh series of the revived sci-fi drama.

Collins, Natasha Born 7 July 1976, London. Actress and model who made her debut on television in the children's television series *See It Saw It* in 1999. A serious car accident, in 2000, left her with seizures that curtailed her career. Natasha was the fiancée of fellow *See It Saw It* presenter Mark Speight (see separate entry). On 3 January 2008, police were called to the couple's North West London home, where Natasha was found dead in the bath. Mark was arrested on suspicion of murder and supplying class A drugs but charges were later dropped. On 2 April 2008, the coroner recorded a verdict of death by misadventure after Natasha was found with scalds covering about 60% of her body and a "very significant amount of cocaine in her system at the time". Mark subsequently went missing and was found hanged in a deserted annexe of London's Paddington railway station on 13 April 2008, six days after he had died.

Corden, James Born James Kimberley Corden, 22 August 1978, Hillingdon, London. Whilst at school James fostered the idea of becoming a pop star and forming his own boy band. This short-lived venture made his mind up that it was an actor's life for him and his first professional gig, aged 18, was in a stage production of *Martin Guerre*. After minor television roles, including a memorable advert for *Tango*, he starred as an overweight bullied young lad in ITV's *Fat Friends* (a role that was close to his heart having had real-life experience of bullying which kept him away from school for long periods). This part led him to gain the role of Timms in the original London stage production of Alan Bennett's play *The History Boys* where he befriended actor Dominic Cooper and shared a home with him until meeting his then girlfriend, actress Sheridan Smith. James then teamed up with his *Fat Friends* co-star Ruth Jones to co-write the BBC3 sitcom *Gavin and Stacey* and his role of Smithy soon became one of the great television comic characterisations. He immediately formed a great friendship with co-star Mathew Horne and the two became as inseparable off-screen as on. By 2009, James was an ever-present TV personality but unfortunately his personal relationships began to break down and by his own admission began to suffer from the age-old 'showbusiness disease' of ego. The ill-fated BBC3 sketch show *Horne and Corden* was panned by the critics and eventually the two friends went their separate ways. At the same time James split from Sheridan although the year was not a complete disaster as the highlight of *Comic Relief* was probably James (as Smithy) giving the England football team a motivational talking-to. In June 2010, James was embroiled in a televised argument with actor Sir Patrick Stewart whilst hosting the *Glamour Women of the Year Awards* in central London. Although the spat saw neither man in a good light James began to look at himself in more reflective tones and almost immediately began to practise greater humility. James is now happier than ever after becoming a dad when fiancée Julia Carey gave birth to baby Max in March 2011. Recently he has written his autobiography *Can I Have Your Attention Please?*, has been treading the boards in the play *One Man, Two Guvnors* in London's West End and continues to host the Sky One comedy/sports panel show *A League of Their Own* alongside team captains Andrew Flintoff and Jamie Redknapp. As well as theatre and television work, James has worked prolifically in film, making his feature film debut, as Tonka, in the Shane Meadows' film *Twenty Four Seven* (1997). Other films include, *Whatever Happened to Harold Smith?* (1999), *All or Nothing* (2002), *Heartlands* (2002), *Cruise of the Gods* (2002), *Pierrepoint* (2005), *Heroes and Villains* (2006), *The History Boys* (2006), *Starter for 10* (2006 - as Tone), *How to Lose Friends & Alienate People* (2008), *Lesbian Vampire Killers* (2009 - as Fletch), *Telstar* (2009), *The Boat That Rocked* (2009), *Planet 51* (2009),

Gulliver's Travels (2010 - as Jinks), *Animals United* (2010 - voice of Billy the Meerkat) and *The Three Musketeers* (2011 - as Planchet). He has also played the role of Craig Owens in two recent series of *Doctor Who*. See also entries in the television section for *Fat Friends*, and *Gavin and Stacey*.

Cotton, Fearne Born 3 September 1981, Northwood, London. Broadcaster who began her career, aged 16, presenting *GMTV* children's programme's *The Disney Club* and later *Diggit, Draw Your Own Toons*, and *Mouse*. Fearne has eleven tattoos over her body, the most notable of which is a fern leaf, covering her right hip up to her rib cage. Fearne currently presents BBC Radio 1's weekday mid-morning programme, taking over from long-time host Jo Whiley. See also entries in the television section for *The Billy Cotton Band Show, Celebrity Juice, Celebrity Love Island, Diggit, Finger Tips, Holly & Fearne Go Dating, Make Me A Supermodel, The Morgana Show, Record Breakers, The Saturday Show, Smile, Top of the Pops*, and *The X Factor*.

Cowell, Simon Born Simon Phillip Cowell, 7 October 1959, Lambeth, London. Simon was brought up in Elstree, Hertfordshire so was never very far away from showbusiness. His father was an executive at the recording giant EMI Music Publishing and managed to get Simon a job in the mail room. A hard-earned apprenticeship followed in music publishing with little success until he teamed up with Iain Burton, the manager of choreographer Arlene Phillips and founder of the independent record label Fanfare Records. Simon worked with Iain for eight good years, Sinitta being their flagship artist with a string of chart hits beginning with *So Macho* (No 2, March 1986). By 1989 Fanfare's parent, Public Company, found itself in financial difficulties and Fanfare was placed in the hands of the Bertelsmann Music Group with an in-debt Cowell now, famously, forced to move back in with his parents. Later that year, he became an A&R consultant for BMG. In 1990, in order to swell his ailing coffers Simon made his television debut as a contestant on the Sky One version of *Sale of the Century*, hosted by Peter Marshall. Unfortunately, despite winning his first show, he returned to be beaten in his next and he ended up winning only £20 worth of kitchen utensils for his trouble. Back to his day job, Simon signed up a number of chart-topping acts throughout the 1990s including Westlife and Robson and Jerome as well as novelty acts such as Zig and Zag and the Mighty Morphin Power Rangers, all recording on the RCA label. Simon was given the role of judge on the first series of *Pop Idol* in 2001 and made an immediate impact with his acerbic one-liners apparently coached by publicist Max Clifford. Simon subsequently became a judge on the first season of *American Idol* in 2002 and later that year he set up the Syco Music label, which later became part of Columbia Records and Sony BMG Music Entertainment, to facilitate an outlet for the proliferation of reality show talent he inherited via the various national and international televised competitions he was now controlling. Simon continues to produce money-making talent-orientated series on both sides of the Atlantic and his fame is such that he has appeared as a guest voice in an episode of *Family Guy* ("Lois Kills Stewie") in which he tells Stewie that his singing is so awful that he should be dead, and two episodes of *The Simpsons* ("Smart and Smarter" and "Judge Me Tender"), in the first of which he gets beaten up by Homer Simpson while criticising Homer's punches. Despite constant media speculation as to his sexuality, Simon is known to have had a close relationship with Sinitta in the 1990s, television presenter Terri Seymour (2002-08) and in February 2010 became engaged to make up artist Mezhgan Hussainy, whom he met on the set of *American Idol*. In January 2011 Simon announced that he and Mezhgan hadn't seen each other for a month, were on a break, and he would perhaps never get married. Simon's autobiography, published in 2003, is appropriately titled *I Don't Mean to be Rude, but....* See also entries in the television section for *Britain's Got Talent, Grease Is the Word: Live, The Peter Serafinowicz Show, Pop Idol, Sale of the Century, Star Stories, This Is Your Life,* and *The X Factor.*

Craig-Martin, Michael See Damien Hirst

Dahl, Sophie Born Sophie Holloway, 15 September 1977, London. Author and former model. Her father is the actor Julian Holloway and her mother, the writer Tessa Dahl. Her paternal grandfather was actor Stanley Holloway but perhaps more famously, her maternal grandparents were the author Roald Dahl and the actress Patricia Neal. Interestingly Patricia Neal and Stanley Holloway each co-starred alongside Audrey Hepburn, the former in *Breakfast at Tiffany's* (1961) and the latter in *My Fair Lady* (1964). Sophie was expelled from school but shortly after was discovered by Isabella Blow, joining the Storm Model Agency. Magazines she later featured in included *Elle, Harper's Bazaar, Marie Claire* and *Vogue*. Sophie became better known in 2000 after she appeared in an advertisement naked on a black satin background for Yves Saint-Laurent's perfume brand Opium. Due to its controversy, it was later removed from UK billboards. She was also a contributing editor at *Men's Vogue*, prior to its closure in 2008 and is currently a regular columnist for *British Vogue*. Sophie was the first plus size model to make a global impact although ironically she has shed considerable weight since retiring from modelling. A talented author, Sophie has written four books: *The Man With the Dancing Eyes* (2003), *Playing with the Grown-Ups* (2008) and the cook-books, *Miss Dahl's Voluptuous Delights* (2009) and *From Season To Season* (2011). In early 2010, her six-part cookery series, *The Delicious Miss Dahl*, was broadcast on BBC 2. Sophie once dated Mick Jagger but married singer and pianist Jamie Cullum (b. 20 August 1979) at Westminster Abbey on 9 January 2010. People often comment on their height difference. Sophie is 5' 11" (1.80m) and Jamie 5' 5" (1.65m). Their daughter, Lyra, was born on 2 March 2011.

Daly, Tess Born Helen Elizabeth Daly, 27 April 1971, Stockport, Greater Manchester. Tess grew up in Birch Vale, near New Mills, Derbyshire. Originally a model, in 1990 she appeared in two *Duran Duran* videos for the songs *Serious* and *Violence of Summer*, both from the album *Liberty*. She also appeared in the 1992 video for *The Beloved* entitled *Sweet Harmony* where she appeared to be naked. Tess made her first television appearance in 2000, when she hosted the 'Find Me A Model' competition on Channel 4's *The Big Breakfast*. She is best known today for co-hosting *Strictly Come Dancing*. Tess is also the face of lingerie company La Senza in the UK. She married Vernon Kay (see separate entry) on 12 September 2003, at St Mary's Catholic Church in Horwich, Bolton. They have two children, Phoebe Elizabeth Kay (b. 7 October 2004) and Amber Isabella Kay (b. 30 May 2009), both born in London. See also entries in the television section for *Just The Two Of Us, Make Me A Supermodel, National Lottery, SM:TV Live,* and *Strictly Come Dancing*

Deeley, Cat Born Catherine Elizabeth Deeley, 23 October 1976, Sutton Coldfield, Birmingham. Cat was signed to the Storm modelling agency as a teenager and by the time she was eighteen worked as a fashion model. After a stint as a presenter on MTV she teamed up with Ant & Dec to co-host *SMTV Live*. On radio she worked at Capital FM alongside Edith Bowman with whom she had previously worked at MTV. In 2006, she began hosting the second season of American reality show *So You Think You Can Dance*, and the following year she presented the UK coverage of the sixth season of *American Idol* for ITV2. Cat's promotional career includes being the face of Pantene shampoo in the UK, since 2008. See also entries in the television section for *Fame Academy, Peter Kay's Britain's Got the Pop Factor... and Possibly a New Celebrity Jesus Christ Soapstar Superstar Strictly on Ice, SM:TV Live, So You Think You Can Dance, Stars In Their Eyes,* and *This Morning.*

Degg, Jackie Born 20 February 1978, Stone, Staffordshire. Model and actress. Jackie studied dance as a child, beginning in ballet and progressing to disco and rock and roll competition dancing. After leaving school she became a hairdresser, managing her own salon (in Walsall) by the age of 20. After winning the inaugural *Max Power* magazine babes competition in 1999 she became a *Sun* Page 3 girl, her short stature – 5' 3" (1.60 m) – precluding her from the catwalk. In 2001, she was voted "greatest ever Page 3 girl". She subsequently won the Page 3 model charity special edition of *The Weakest Link* beating Leilani Dowding in the final with her winnings going to the RSPCA. During a break from topless modelling, Jakki appeared, as Missy, in the American film *Eurotrip* (2004) and also played the lead in the short film *Remember My Dream*. She returned to Page 3 of *The Sun* in August 2006. Jakki once dated Blackburn Rovers and England footballer David Dunn.

Deyn, Agyness Born Laura Hollins, 16 February 1983, Littleborough, Greater Manchester. Model, actress and singer. Agyness attended All Saints RC High School, as well as Bacup and Rawtenstall Grammar School before attending Sixth Form in Waterfoot, Rossendale. She later attended college in Hull, studying drama and music. Even at an early age she had an eye for style having had short hair since she was 13 and a 'skinhead' by 17 (a style she reverted back to in 2010). Agyness's best friend is fashion designer Henry Holland (b. 26 May 1983, Ramsbottom, Greater Manchester), with whom she was walking in Kentish Town when she was spotted by SELECT model management (she is now with Models 1). Her name was supposedly coined after she consulted her mother's friend, a numerology expert who advised her of the most 'fortuitous' way to spell the name 'Agnes'. It was thought it would further her modelling career. In 1999, she won the Rossendale Free Press "Face of '99" competition, aged just 16. By November 2006, the 5'8" (1.73 m) tall model was on the cover of *Vogue* Italia and, in June 2007, British *Vogue* and then, in 2008, *Time* magazine. Agyness has also appeared in advertisements for Anna Sui, Blugirl by Blumarine, Burberry, Cacharel, Gianfranco Ferré, Moussy, Maison Gilfy, Shiseido, Shiatzy Chen, Giorgio Armani, Mulberry, Paul Smith, Reebok and Vivienne Westwood. She is currently the face of the new fragrance, The Beat, by Burberry, Gold by Giles Deacon at New Look (replacing Drew Barrymore), Jean Paul Gautier's fragrance Ma Dame, Shiseido (replacing Angelina Jolie), and House of Holland. In June 2009, the Daily Mirror reported that she had quit modelling to spend more time with her boyfriend and to pursue an acting career. A talented individual, she provided vocals for the single *Who* by Five O'Clock Heroes, was once a member of a band called Lucky Knitwear and also appeared, as Aphrodite, in the 2010 film *Clash of the Titans*. Her love of music extends to her choice of boyfriends, having dated Josh Hubbard of *The Paddingtons*, Albert Hammond, Jr. of *The Strokes*, Miles Kane from *The Last Shadow Puppets* and *Rascals*, and Alex Greenwald of *Phantom Planet*

Dowding, Leilani Born 30 January 1980, Bournemouth, Dorset. English Page Three girl and glamour model with dark sultry looks. Brought up in Bournemouth, Leilani excelled at school, earning eleven GCSEs and three A-levels (2 'A's and 1 'B'). Her big break came while studying for an economics degree at Royal Holloway, University of London, in Surrey when she entered and won the 1998 Miss Great Britain competition. This success enabled her to become the first woman of Asian descent (she has a Filipino mother Zena, and British father Chris) to represent Britain in Miss Universe. She made the difficult decision to give up her studies in order to pursue a full-time modelling career. Ironically it was as a Page Three girl in *The Sun* newspaper where she became a household name, ironic as she had been bullied at school for having small breasts. Leilani's younger sister Melanie was also a model and they have posed together for topless shoots. Leilani has been a guest on various television shows including *The Big Breakfast*, a Page 3 episode of *The Weakest Link* for charity (where she lost in the final to her friend Jakki Degg) and *This Morning*. She has appeared as an actress in *Dream Team* and *Mile High* and has also enjoyed a season in pantomime as Tiger Lilly in *Peter Pan*. A caring individual, she has travelled to many war-torn areas on morale-boosting trips for British soldiers. In 2008, the 5'6" (1.68m) model became engaged to pizza restaurant chain millionaire Richie Palmer, following his divorce from actress Raquel Welch.

Dowling, Brian Born Brian Patrick Robert Dowling, 13 June 1978, Rathangan, Co Kildare. The Irish television presenter was working as a flight attendant for Ryanair before winning the second series of *Big Brother* in 2001, having only told his parents he was gay two weeks before entering the house. Brian is one of few lasting success stories from the reality TV show having worked consistently throughout the past decade on both Irish and British television. Recently he guest presented *Live From Studio*

Five alongside Kate Walsh and is currently the presenter of the C5 version of *Big Brother*. See also entries in the television section for *Big Brother, Fáilte Towers, Hell's Kitchen, The Salon*, and *SM:TV Live*.

Downes, Katie See entry for *Arctic Monkeys* in the pop biography section.

Du Beke, Anton Born Anthony Paul Beke, 20 July 1966, Sevenoaks, Kent. From the age of fourteen Anton set out his stall to be a dancer, his Hungarian father and Spanish mother giving him rich support. He studied Ballet, Contemporary, Jazz and modern theatre dance. Anton was also a junior boxer and played county football. On leaving school he worked as a salesman to finance his ballroom career. He naturally favoured the Foxtrot; its classy, stylish and romantic lilt bringing out all the traits of his Hollywood idol, Fred Astaire. In 1997 he met Erin Boag and within a year of forming their partnership they won the New Zealand Championships, retaining their title the following year. Anton and Erin turned professional in 2002 and placed 3rd in the UK in their first professional competition in Blackpool. The couple were chosen in 2004 to star in the first series of the BBC1 television show *Strictly Come Dancing* and are the only professional couple to have appeared in every series to date. Known for his impeccable dress, charm and wit, Anton is a natural in front of the camera and has become a celebrity in his own right, presenting the BBC cookery show *Step Up to the Plate* and serving as a captain and, from series 2, the host of the game show *Hole in the Wall*.

Ellison, Jennifer Born Jennifer Lesley Ellison, 30 May 1983, Liverpool. Actress, glamour model, television personality, dancer and singer. Jennifer studied dance from the age of three and later attended the Elizabeth Hill School of Dancing in St. Helens, Merseyside. She initially chose to pursue a professional career in dance, successfully auditioning for the Royal Ballet Lower School, but eventually having to leave, her large bust ruining her chances of becoming a classical ballerina. The 5' 7" (1.69cm) dancer rose to fame as an actress in 1998, playing Emily Shadwick in *Brookside*, leaving in 2003 to pursue a career in music and film. Her first single, *Baby I Don't Care*, released in June 2003, reached No 6 in the UK charts and her second single, *Bye Bye Boy* reached No 13 the following year (both songs reaching No 8 in the Irish charts). Jennifer made her film debut as Meg Giry in the 2004 film adaptation of *The Phantom of the Opera*. Her only other film role to-date has been as Tracey in *The Cottage* (2008). The success of her first film landed her the role of Roxie Hart in the London West End theatre version of the musical *Chicago* in 2004, at the Adelphi Theatre. On television, she has appeared in episodes of *The Brief, Hotel Babylon, New Street Law* and *The Commander* and was victorious in the first series of *Hell's Kitchen* (2004) under the watchful eye of Gordon Ramsay. Jennifer has also had a successful modelling career, her long blonde hair, stunning looks and curvaceous body having been displayed on numerous magazine covers. Liverpool FC fans may remember Jennifer as a former girlfriend of Steven Gerrard in the early years of the new Millennium. Jennifer married boxer, Robbie Tickle, in Mauritius on 10 October 2009. The couple have one child, a baby boy named Bobby (b. 4 February 2010, Liverpool). Jennifer recently lost five stone to take part in the TV series *Dancing on Ice* and she came fourth, partnering Daniel Whiston.

Emin, Tracey Born Tracey Karima Emin, 3 July 1963, Croydon, Greater London. Artist associated with the Young British Artists movement. Brought up in Margate, Tracey has a twin brother, Paul (now an unemployed carpenter). She had a traumatic early life, with her Turkish-Cypriot father supporting another household, and in her early teens Tracey experienced a rape that was to define her outlook and work. Tracey studied fashion at Medway College of Design (1980–82) and began a relationship with Billy Childish (b. Steven John Hamper, 1 December 1959, Chatham, Kent) becoming associated with The Medway Poets (Miriam Carney, Rob Earl, Bill Lewis, Sexton Ming, Charles Thomson, Childish and Emin among others). Childish had a similarly harrowing upbringing to Tracey and it was during their four-year relationship that their confessional artistic styles came to the fore. After studying at Maidstone Art College, Tracey moved to London to study at the Royal College of Art, where she obtained an MA in painting. In 1993, she opened 'The Shop' with fellow artist Sarah Lucas (b. 1962, Holloway, London). From these premises at 103 Bethnal Green Road they sold their individual works, including T-shirts and ash trays with Damien Hirst's picture stuck to the bottom. The celebrated art dealer Jay Jopling (b. 1963) became her dealer at this time and the following year she had her first solo show, *My Major Retrospective*, at the White Cube Gallery, London. 1997 turned out to be Tracey's breakthrough year. Her work *Everyone I Have Ever Slept With 1963–1995*, a blue tent appliquéd with names, was shown at Charles Saatchi's *Sensation* exhibition held at the Royal Academy in London (the work was destroyed in the 2004 Momart, Leyton, London warehouse fire). Later in 1997, Tracey gained considerable media attention after appearing seemingly drunk and disorderly on a live Channel 4 TV discussion programme (actor Keith Allen made a similarly memorable TV debut on such a programme). In 1999, Tracey was shortlisted for the Turner Prize for her controversial work *My Bed*, which was exhibited at the Tate Gallery in 1998. Although she didn't win, *My Bed*, with its bedsheets stained with bodily secretions and the surrounding floor displaying condoms and a pair of knickers with menstrual period stains, caused quite a stir. More publicity was raised when two performance artists, Yuan Chai and Jian Jun Xi, jumped on the bed with bare torsos and had a pillow fight, calling their performance *Two Naked Men Jump Into Tracey's Bed*. Like all serious artists, Tracey's work has developed and she has gone through phases of inspiration. Her early success was with monoprints such as *From The Week Of Hell '94* (1995), *Ripped Up* (1995), *Fuck You Eddy* (1995), *Sad Shower in New York* (1995) and *Poor Love* (1999). Her installation pieces cemented her fame at the turn of the new Millennium and her photographic work includes the iconic self portraits taken inside her famous beach hut, *The Last Thing I Said To You Is Don't Leave Me Here I* (2000) and *The Last Thing I Said To You Is Don't Leave Me Here II* (2000). In recent years she has become quite a prolific painter although losing nothing of her shock value, typical paintings include: *Purple Virgin* (2004) an acrylic watercolour series of purple brush strokes depicting her naked open legs, *Asleep Alone With Legs Open* (2005), *Reincarnation* (2005) and *Masturbating* (2006), all exhibited at her 2007 Venice Biennale show. In February 2005, Tracey's first public artwork, a bronze sculpture commissioned by the BBC, went on display outside the Oratory, adjacent to Liverpool Cathedral. It consists of a small bird perched on a tall bronze pole, and is designed so that the bird seems to disappear when viewed from the front. Her most recent public work is a neon artwork sign reading "More Passion"; installed outside the Terracotta Room at Number 10 Downing Street in August 2011. On a personal note, Tracey was made a Royal Academician in March 2007 and was also the inspiration for the so-called Stuckism art movement. Stuckism is an international art movement founded in 1999 by Billy Childish and Charles Thomson to promote figurative painting in opposition to conceptual art. The name "Stuckism" was coined in January 1999 by Charles Thomson in response to a poem read to him several times by Billy Childish. In it, Childish recites that his former girlfriend, Tracey Emin had said he was "stuck! stuck! stuck!" with his art, poetry and music. Tracey has recently appeared on *Who Do You Think You Are?*

Evans, Chris Born Christopher James Evans, 1 April 1966, Warrington, Cheshire. Radio and television presenter. After having several unusual jobs such as private detective and Tarzanogram, Chris began his broadcasting career at Manchester Piccadilly Radio in 1983, as an assistant to Timmy Mallett. After working at several other regional radio stations, Chris moved to Radio 1 in 1992, replacing Phillip Schofield in the Sunday afternoon slot, his after dinner show being aptly named, *Too Much Gravy*. Later that year he presented Channel 4's *The Big Breakfast*, with co-host Gaby Roslin and his unique zany random style made him an instant success. After forming his own television production company, Ginger Productions (named after his hair colour), his first major programme was the iconic, *Don't Forget Your Toothbrush*. In April 1995, Chris began hosting the Radio 1 Breakfast Show but a series of fall outs with management saw him leaving in 1997 to join Virgin Radio, eventually buying the station for £85m. In March 2000 Chris agreed the sale of Ginger Media Group to SMG plc for £225m, making him one of the highest-paid performers in the UK at that time. The following year, Chris was sacked by Virgin after a high-profile "18-hour bender" and Chris set up a radio and television production company, UMTV. After a few years out of the public eye Chris returned to the BBC as a Radio 2 presenter, eventually taking over the breakfast show from Sir Terry Wogan in January 2010. In January 2011, Chris presented the Channel 4 reality show *Famous and Fearless*, in which eight celebrities, four boys and four girls, took part in a series of mainly motorised arena challenges. The contestants were Rufus Hound, Charley Boorman, Sam Branson, Jonah Lomu, Jenny Frost, Kacey Ainsworth, Sarah Jayne Dunn and Dame Kelly Holmes. Holmes won the girls'; Boorman won the boys' and the show outright. Chris has been married three times, to television presenter Carol McGiffin (1991-98), actress and singer Billie Piper (2001–07) and professional golfer Natasha Shishmanian (2007–present). He has a son, Noah Nicholas Martin (b. 10 February 2009, London) and a daughter, Jade (b. 1986), by former fiancée Alison Ward. He and Natasha are expecting their second child in 2012. See also entries in the television section for *The Big Breakfast, Don't Forget Your Toothbrush, Noel's House Party, OFI Sunday, The One Show, TFI Friday, Who Wants To Be A Millionaire?* and *Wogan*.

Flack, Caroline Born Caroline Louise Flack, 9 November 1980, London. Raised in Norfolk, Caroline had a variety of jobs, including working in the local pork factory, before studying drama and dance and setting her sights on a television career. After a brief stint as a magician's assistant she made her screen debut in the television film *Is Harry on the Boat?* (2001) as an unnamed blonde. Caroline got her big break playing "Michael Jackson's" girlfriend on *Bo' Selecta!*, then becoming a co-presenter on the Saturday-morning show *TMi*. In 2008 she joined Ian Wright as a co-host on *Gladiators*, then became the host of *I'm A Celebrity... Get Me Out Of Here! Now!* Caroline is a keen poker player, her interest in the game beginning in 2004 when she hosted the televised *European Poker Tour*. In 2011, she began co-presenting the eighth series of *The Xtra Factor* alongside Olly Murs. Caroline has been erroneously linked to several famous people, including Prince Harry, but is currently happily single although she was dating *One Direction*'s 17-year-old singer Harry Styles until recently. See also entries in the television section for *Bo' Selecta!, Escape From Scorpion Island, I'm a Celebrity Get Me Out Of Here, The X Factor*, and *The Whole Nineteen Yards*.

Fox, Samantha Born Samantha Karen Fox, 15 April 1966, London. Former glamour model and pop star. Sam enrolled in the Anna Scher Theatre School, aged five, and her first television appearance came in 1976, in a BBC play entitled *No Way Out*. However it was as a model she became a household name in the 1980s. With parental consent, her first *Sun* Page Three photograph was published under the headline "Sam, 16, Quits A-Levels for Ooh-Levels". Her 36D breasts were famously insured for a quarter of a million pounds after she won *The Sun's* Page Three Girl of the Year award for three consecutive years between 1984 and 1986. The 5' 1" (1.55 m) model retired from Page Three in 1986 to concentrate on a musical career; her biggest chart hit, in March 1986, being the single *Touch Me* which peaked at No 3 in both the UK and Irish charts. Her other two top ten UK singles were *Do Ya Do Ya (Wanna Please Me)* - No 10 in June 1986 (not released in Ireland) and *Nothing's Gonna Stop Me Now*, No 8 in May 1987 (No 5 in Ireland). Sam's only other top twenty hit, *I Only Wanna Be with You*, reached No 16 in the UK charts in January 1989 but reached No 9 in Ireland. In 1989, Sam co-presented the BRIT Awards with Mick Fleetwood, which became notorious for turning into a farce; Sam blaming the failing of the autocue for her shambolic performance. From 1991, Sam's music career became less commercially successful after leaving Jive, although she continued to perform and make records. In the mid-1990s she made a brief comeback as a topless model, making a one-off appearance in *The Sun* to promote Page Three's 25th anniversary week and appearing in the October 1996 issue of *Playboy* magazine. In February 2003, she made a statement about her personal life declaring the gay relationship with her manager Myra Stratton. This came as a shock to many of her fans. In 2008, Sam and Myra took part in *Celebrity Wife Swap*, exchanging with Freddie Starr and his wife Donna. In November 2009, she took part in ITV's *I'm a Celebrity, Get Me Out of Here* being voted out on the 16th day. In July 2010, she took part in a celebrity episode of *Come Dine With Me*, appearing with Calum Best, Janice Dickinson & Jeff Brazier. Sam's previous lovers include Peter Foster (notorious for promoting a diet tea product that was eventually revealed as a scam, and 'Cheriegate' where he helped Cherie Blair, wife of the then British prime minister Tony Blair, buy properties in Bristol) and Paul Stanley, the singer and rhythm guitarist from the band *KISS*.

Francis, Leigh Born Leigh Szaak Francis, 30 April 1973, Leeds, West Yorkshire. Sharing the same John Noel Management team as Dermot O'Leary, Davina McCall and Russell Brand, it was inevitable that the comedy impressionist shot to fame as a regular pundit on the various *Big Brother* supplement shows. Leigh remained in the character of Avid Merrion, the *Big Brother* super-fan with a permanent neck disability, in all his television appearances until appearing on the *Frank Skinner Show* as himself in 2004. Since 2006 Leigh has conducted interviews and presented television shows in the guise of Keith Lemon, a sort of Alan Partridge character with permanent right hand/wrist injury. Leigh married beauty therapist Jill Carter in 2003 and the couple have a daughter, Matilda (b. 2009). See also entries in the television section for *Bo' Selecta!*, *Celebrity Juice*, and *Popworld*.

Galliano, John Born John Charles Galliano, 28 November 1960, British overseas territory of Gibraltar, the son of a Gibraltarian father and Spanish mother who moved to England when John was six-years-old to settle in South London. After graduating from Central Saint Martins College of Art and Design in 1984 with a first class honours degree in fashion design, John made an immediate impact with his first collection, *Les Incroyables* (inspired by the French Revolution), which was bought by the London fashion boutique Browns. Although finding himself bankrupt by 1990, he moved to Paris and the following year designed the costumes for Kylie Minogue's *Let's Get to It Tour* and this increased his profile. Prominent Paris backers came on board and several top fashion houses worked for him for reduced fees to glean the mutual benefits. In July 1995, John was appointed chief designer of Givenchy, becoming the first British designer to head a French *haute couture* house. In late 1996, John became head of Christian Dior and remained there for the next 15 years until being suspended on 25 February 2011, following his arrest over an alleged anti-Semitic outburst in a Paris bar. On 8 September 2011, he was found guilty of making anti-Semitic remarks and sentenced to pay a total of €6,000 (US$8,400) in suspended fines after a French court found him guilty of giving public insults on account of race. John's long-term boyfriend is style consultant Alexis Roche. John has been British Designer of the Year four times (1987, 1994, 1995 and 1997 - when he shared the award with Alexander McQueen, his successor at Givenchy). In 2001 he was awarded the CBE and in 2009, the French Legion of Honour.

Gandy, David Born David James Gandy, 19 February 1980, Billericay, Essex. After David graduated from the University Of Gloucestershire in 2001, friends secretly entered him for a male model competition on Richard and Judy's *This Morning* show which he won, landing a contract with top agency Select Model Management. After signing to Public Image Worldwide and spending several years learning the trade David gained his big break when Domenico Dolce and Stefano Gabbana selected him to front their campaign for the new fragrance Light Blue Pour Homme, the accompanying advert receiving 11million online hits and seeing a 50 ft poster of him grace Times Square. David is Britain's No 1 male model and in June 2009, *Forbes Magazine* ranked him as the world's third most successful male model, behind Canadian Matt Gordon and American Sean O'Pry. David writes a blog for *Vogue* where he discusses his modelling and interests such as his love for cars. He was in a relationship with Mollie King of *The Saturdays* between April 2011 and February 2012.

Gascoigne, Paul Born Paul John Gascoigne, 27 May 1967, Dunston, Gateshead, Tyne & Wear. Gifted footballer who played for Newcastle United 1985-88, Tottenham Hotspur 1988-92 (signed for £2m), Lazio 1992-95 (signed for £5.5m), Rangers 1995-98 (signed for £4.3m), Middlesbrough 1998-2000 (signed for £3.45m), Everton 2000-02, Burnley 2002, and Gansu Tianma (China) 2002-03. In July 2004, he was signed by League Two side Boston United as player-coach, but only made five appearances and scored no goals before leaving three months later. He then became manager of Kettering Town in October 2005 but his tenure lasted just 39 days; the club's owner sacking him for an alleged drinking problem. His footballing honours include: FA Cup 1991 (with Tottenham Hotspur); Scottish League Championship 1996, 1997 (with Rangers); Scottish Cup 1996 (with Rangers); Scottish League Cup 1997 (with Rangers). International caps (for England): 57, 10 goals. Known as 'Gazza'. A brilliant midfielder who was let down by a temperament which endeared and infuriated in equal measure. At the height of his fame in 1990 Gazza reached No 2 in the UK Charts with *Fog on the Tyne*, a collaborative cover with *Lindisfarne*. He also had a small Christmas hit that year with *Geordie Boys (Gazza Rap)* which reached No 31. Gazza had an addictive personality from a young age and after becoming a fruit machine addict as a teenager then turned to drink once his playing career was curtailed through injury. He married his childhood sweetheart, Sheryl Failes (b. 24 September 1965) in 1996 but was divorced two years later. They have a son, Regan Paul Gascoigne (b. 1996, Hatfield, Hertfordshire) and Gazza adopted Sheryl's two children from her first marriage; one of which is reality TV star Bianca Gascoigne (b. 28 October 1986). In 2004 he published his autobiography *Gazza: My Story*, written with Hunter Davies. He published a follow-up book *Being Gazza: Tackling My Demons* in 2006. In recent years, Paul's wellbeing has been questionable. On 9 July 2010, he appeared at the scene of the tense stand-off between the police and Britain's most wanted man Raoul Moat, claiming to be a friend of the fugitive and bragging that he had brought him 'a can of lager, some chicken, fishing rod, a Newcastle shirt and a dressing gown'. Later that month he entered rehab for the ninth time. In 2011, Paul has made a concerted effort to sort out his problems although his millionaire's lifestyle is but a distant memory.

Ghadie, Samia Born Samia Maxine Ghadie, 13 July 1982, Eccles, Salford. Actress. Samia is best known as Maria Connor in ITV's *Coronation Street*, however, her career started at the age of 11, when she appeared in an episode of *Cracker*. Samia also made appearances on television in *Children's Ward*, *Heartbeat*, *Doctors* and *Life Force* and made her film debut, as Sara, in *There's Only One Jimmy Grimble* (2000) before gaining the part of Maria in *Corrie* in 2000, beating off Suzanne Shaw and Kimberley Walsh for the role. Samia has appeared in several reality shows, notably, *Celebrity Who Wants to Be a Millionaire?;* where she and Jennie McAlpine won £50,000 for charity and *Celebrity Stars in Their Eyes*, as Holly Valance, which she went on to win. On 10 September 2005 Samia married property developer Matthew Smith and worked under her married name for the next five years. On 19 October 2009, Samia gave birth to a baby girl called Freya. She and her husband announced that they have separated by mutual agreement on 4 January 2011. Samia is currently in a relationship with her former on-screen *Corrie* boyfriend Will Thorp.

Goody, Jade Born Jade Cerisa Lorraine Goody, 5 June 1981, Bermondsey, London. Television personality. Daughter of Andrew Robert Goody and Jackiey Budden. Jade's parents split when she was two years old, her father later dying of a drug overdose at the age of 42. The Jade Goody phenomenon began in 2002 when she walked into Channel 4's *Big Brother* house for Series 3 as an unknown dental technician but by the time of her death, less than seven years later, she had two autobiographies published. On the original show she became a media target instantly mainly due to her apparent lack of general knowledge; believing Rio de Janeiro to be the name of a person and referring to East Anglia as 'East Angular' and thinking it to be overseas. The other memorable Jade moments were the under-the-sheets activity with fellow housemate Peter James "PJ" Ellis (b. 10 August 1979, Birmingham) and her ending up naked on the sofa after playing strip poker. Jade ultimately finished fourth. On leaving the BB house, Jade appeared regularly in the tabloids and gossip-oriented women's magazines such as *Heat* and *OK!*. In 2005, she starred in Living TV's *Jade's Salon*, a reality show featuring the opening of Jade's first business "Ugly's". During this period Jade had a short relationship with footballer Ryan Amoo. The following year Jade starred in another reality show for Living, *Just Jade*, which amongst other things followed her preparations for the 2006 London Marathon, in which she failed to finish, completing 21 miles before collapsing and being taken to hospital for what turned out to be an overnight stay. Her comment afterwards was; "I don't really understand miles. I didn't actually know how far it was going to be". She raised £550 for the NSPCC. Other Living TV shows that Jade starred in that year include *Jade's Shape Challenge* and *Jade's P.A.*, in which one of her devoted fans were given the chance to become her personal assistant. In January 2007, Jade signed up for *Celebrity Big Brother 5* and entered the house along with her mum and boyfriend Jack Tweed. Whilst in the house, Jade was vilified in the press for being the ringleader of a triumvirate of girls (see also entry for Danielle Lloyd) who verbally abused Indian actress Shilpa Shetty, the show receiving almost 50,000 complaints about the incident. When Jade was eventually up for eviction against Shilpa she received an astounding 82% of the vote. To her credit, when Jade was evicted she made several public apologies and explained that the references to the Bollywood star as 'Shilpa Fuckawalla' and 'Shilpa Poppadom' were not intentionally racist. In 2008, Jade was asked to appear in India's version of *Big Brother*; *Bigg Boss*. Two days into the show however, she was informed that she had cervical cancer. She left the show immediately and flew back home to England. In October of the same year, Jade opened her second beauty salon "Homme Fatel". By now, Jade's cancer was reported to be 'advanced and life threatening' and she died in the early hours of Mothering Sunday 22 March 2009. Jade left two children, both from a previous relationship with fellow reality television star Jeff Brazier, Bobby Jack Brazier (b. June 2003) and Freddie Brazier (b. September 2004) and both born in Harlow. Jade married on-off boyfriend Jack Tweed (b. 9 June 1987, Waltham Forest, London) a month before she died, on 22 February 2009 at Down Hall country house near Hatfield Heath, Essex. She wore a £3,500 Manuel Mota dress, given to her by Harrods owner Mohamed Al Fayed. The couple signed an exclusive £700,000 deal with *OK!* magazine for photographs of the ceremony. Jack was granted an exemption to his curfew for the night of 22/23 February. On 3 March 2009, he was convicted of common assault for attacking a taxi driver in May 2008. At Harlow Magistrates Court, on 14 April 2009, he was sentenced to 12 weeks imprisonment, of which he served six. Jade was buried in her wedding dress along with two photographs, one of each of her two boys. Jade's legacy includes two autobiographies: *Jade: My Autobiography* (2006) and *Jade: Catch a Falling Star* (2008) plus two fragrances: Shh (2006) and Controversial (2009). Although Jade has often been ridiculed in the same way as Katie Price as the epitome of someone who is merely famous for being famous, the fact that the length of this biography exceeds many others in this book tells a tale of someone who captured the public's imagination for better or for worse.

Hamilton, Lewis Born Lewis Carl Davidson Hamilton, 7 January 1985, Stevenage, Hertfordshire. Lewis is a mixed-race sportsman, his mother being white and his father, Anthony, a black Brit whose parents emigrated from Grenada to the United Kingdom in the 1950s. Lewis was named after American sprinter Carl Lewis. He began his racing career, aged 8, after his father bought him a go-kart as a Christmas present two years earlier. At the age of ten he approached McLaren F1 team boss Ron Dennis for an autograph, and told him, "Hi. I'm Lewis Hamilton. I won the British Championship and one day I want to be racing your cars." Dennis wrote in his autograph book, "Phone me in nine years, we'll sort something out then." Ron actually signed him three years later and Lewis became the youngest ever driver to secure a contract which later resulted in an F1 drive. After a glittering career in Formula 3 and GP2, Lewis began his F1 career in 2007, partnering Fernando Alonso at McLaren. He made his debut at the Australian Grand Prix, qualifying fourth and finishing third in the race. Lewis gained both his first pole position and first victory of his F1 career in the Canadian Grand Prix at Montreal and subsequently ended his first season as runner-up to Kimi Räikkönen in the world drivers' championship. The following year, Lewis won a thrilling championship by one point from Felipe Massa. Despite neither the Brazilian nor the Briton vying for the championship since 2008, their relationship has been prickly to say the least and during the 2011 season they had several on track incidents although ultimately ending the season with a hug. Lewis has dated Nicole Scherzinger, the lead singer of the American girl band *Pussycat Dolls*, since 2007 although their relationship has been an off-on one recently. He was awarded an MBE by the Queen in the 2009 New Year Honours. Lewis' half-brother Nicolas signed with Total Control Racing to start a racing career in the 2011 Renault Clio Cup, an outstanding achievement for a lad with cerebral palsy.

Hamilton, Richard Born 24 February 1922, Pimlico, London. Richard was often described as the founder of Pop Art. Modern art, he wrote, should be "Popular, Transient, Expendable, Low-cost, Mass-produced, Young, Witty, Sexy, Gimmicky, Glamorous, Big Business." His 1956 collage *Just What Is It That Makes Today's Homes So Different, So Appealing?* not only introduced the word "pop" into art (emblazoned on the bodybuilder's phallic lollipop) but also originated the use of such iconic images as the television; the Warner Bros billboard; the comic poster; the packaged ham and the Ford logo. Richard had a huge influence on pop music and while teaching art in Newcastle his pupils included *Roxy Music* founder Bryan Ferry and Ferry's visual collaborator Nicholas De Ville. His series of prints depicting Mick Jagger's arrest on drugs charges in the late 1960s and early 1970s epitomised Andy Warhol's technique of multiple reproductions. He also designed the cover for the 1968 double album *The Beatles*. The plain white sleeve led to its becoming known universally as *The White Album*. Richard was much more than a mere pop artist, he was an innovator who worked with "found objects", and as painter, typographist, collagist, printmaker, graphic designer, digital image manipulator, screen printer, photographer – and more recently as software programmer and computer builder. Richard married Terry O'Reilly in 1947; they had a son and a daughter. In 1962 Terry was killed in a car crash. His second wife, whom he married in 1991, was painter Rita Donagh. Appointed Companion of Honour in 2000, Richard died 13 September 2011. Damien Hirst referred to him as "the greatest".

Hamnett, Katharine Born 16 August 1947, Gravesend, Kent. Katharine is a fashion designer best known for her political t-shirts as worn in the 1980s by pop groups *Wham!*, *Queen* and *Frankie Goes to Hollywood* in various videos. Models such as Naomi Campbell have also appeared in Hamnett shirts bearing the slogans "USE A CONDOM" and "PEACE". Her most famous slogan is "CHOOSE LIFE" which was originally directed at drug abuse and suicide but has more recently been used by the pro-life movement to encourage a choice against abortion.

Harries, Lauren Born James Charles Harries in 1978, Surrey. The precocious ten-year-old proprietor of an antiques business in Cardiff, first came to public attention on the *Wogan* show in 1988 where, in his lisping upper-class accent, he spoke about his business and all manner of other adult things, including the state of the economy. Young James appeared oblivious to the fact that while some were intrigued by his in depth knowledge of worldly matters, others scoffed at his arrogant and condescending manner. By the age of 14 James had published a book, *Rags to Riches*, which explained how to make money from jumble sales. As time went on it became clear that James' knowledge was far more superficial than thought previously. His family, who home-tutored him, were involved in a number of scandals and court cases and all went quiet in the Harries' household until the turn of the new Millennium when James quite mysteriously re-emerged as a 23-year-old woman, Lauren Charlotte Harries under the media-charge of the ubiquitous Max Clifford. For the past 10 years Lauren has picked up scraps of television work, the latest being as a 'fashion' consultant for the latest series of *Big Brother* on Five.

Hayes, Chanelle Born Chanelle Jade Sinclair, 11 November 1987, Styal, Cheshire. Television personality, singer and glamour model. Born in Styal Prison, Chanelle's life began sadly when her mother, Andrea Sinclair, a 32-year-old drug addict and street prostitute, was murdered by a client when Chanelle was five months old. Chanelle was adopted and raised in Wakefield, West Yorkshire by Christine and Harry Hayes. She became famous in 2007, after appearing on the eighth series of *Big Brother*. She was tested by Big Brother and had one of the highest IQs in the house, scoring 114, to the surprise of many! Chanelle's spell on the show was particularly talked about due to her relationship with another contestant, Ziggy Lichman, while in the house. The relationship didn't last long once the series was over. Since *Big Brother*, Chanelle has enjoyed some success as a glamour model, regularly appearing in magazines such as *Nuts*. She has also designed and launched her own perfume called *Mwah*. A lover of music, Chanelle was signed by Eminence Records and in May 2008 released a single entitled *I Want It* which peaked at No 63 in the UK charts (No 33 in Ireland). The following year Chanelle had a tempestuous relationship with Middlesbrough footballer Matthew Bates and on 6 August 2009, she was rushed to hospital after attempting suicide by taking an overdose of paracetamol and red wine following a heated argument with him. Despite their relationship being long over, Chanelle gave birth to Matthew's son, Blakely Hayes-Bates, on 20 July 2010, around the time she had a short relationship with Jack Tweed. In 2011 she opened a cake making business in Wakefield.

Hazell, Keeley Born Keeley Rebecca Hazell, 18 September 1986, Lewisham, London. Actress and former Page 3 Girl. Keeley left school at the age of 16 to work as a hairdresser and it was there that her work colleagues persuaded her to do some modelling. She took part in The *Daily Star*'s "Search for a Beach Babe" contest and won but at 17, she was not old enough to pose on Page 3, so began studying at Lewisham College instead. The following year she entered *The Sun*'s Page 3 Idol competition and won that too, her reward being a one-year exclusive glamour modelling contract with the newspaper. The 5' 6¼" (1.68 m) model with a stunning natural 32F-24-36 figure, was regularly featured in lad mags such as *Nuts* and *Zoo*. Very popular with the men, she finished in the top three of *FHM*'s Sexiest Women from 2006-2008. Keeley is also known for being a supporter of breast cancer awareness campaigns and PETA (People for the Ethical Treatment of Animals). Recently, Keeley has been taking acting lessons in America and starred in the film short *Venus & the Sun* (2010) and the feature length *Like Crazy* (2011 - as Sabrina). Keeley once made a private sex tape while on vacation with her then-boyfriend Lloyd Miller in the Canary Islands and was horrified when it appeared in the public domain. She has kept her private life very private ever since although is known to be currently dating television presenter Steve Jones.

Hirst, Damien Born Damien Steven Hirst, 7 June 1965, Bristol. Growing up in Leeds, Damien was a typically rebellious youth of the punk era who was not particularly academically gifted, although he did manage an "E" grade in his Art A-Level which eventually led him to study at Leeds College of Art. Between 1986 and 1989 he studied at Goldsmiths, University of London (under the tutelage of Michael Craig-Martin RA, b. 28 August 1941, Dublin, - famous for his iconic work *An Oak Tree*, which consists of a glass of water standing on a shelf with a text explanation as to why it is an oak tree). In July 1988, in his second year at Goldsmiths, Damien organised an independent student exhibition, *Freeze*, in a disused Port of London Authority administrative block in London's Docklands; his own contribution being a cluster of cardboard boxes painted with household paint. Two years later Charles Saatchi bought Damien's first major "animal" installation, *A Thousand Years*, consisting of a large glass case containing maggots and flies feeding off a rotting cow's head. In 1992, at the Young British Artists exhibition at the Saatchi Gallery in North London, Damien exhibited *The Physical Impossibility of Death in the Mind of Someone Living*, which consisted of a 14-foot (4.3 m) tiger shark preserved in formaldehyde in a glass display case. The shark, which had been caught by a commissioned fisherman in Australia for the price of £6,000, sold for £50,000 (the buyer, Charles Saatchi, eventually selling it to American collector Steve Cohen, for £6.5 million). Damien's first major international presentation was in the Venice Biennale in 1993 with the work, *Mother and Child Divided*, a cow and a calf cut into sections and exhibited in a series of separate vitrines. The following year he exhibited *Away from the Flock*, at the Serpentine Gallery. This piece, consisting of a sheep in a tank of formaldehyde, was damaged by Mark Bridger, a 35 year old artist from Oxford, who walked in to the gallery and poured black ink into the tank, and retitled the work Black Sheep. Bridger was subsequently prosecuted and given two years' probation and the sculpture was restored at a cost of £1,000. In 1995 Damien won the Turner Prize and later that year he directed the video for the *Blur* song *Country House*. In 1997, his autobiography and art book, *I Want To Spend the Rest of My Life Everywhere, with Everyone, One to One, Always, Forever, Now*, was published. His next project was the formation of *Fat Les*, with Keith Allen and Alex James; their debut hit, *Vindaloo* (an anthem for the 1998 World Cup) reaching No 2 in the UK Charts and their 2000 follow-up *Jerusalem Fat Les* (which peaked at No 10) being adopted as the official England football song for the European Championships. Throughout the new Millennium, Damien's work has appreciated and in June 2007 his *Lullaby Spring* (a 3 metre-wide steel cabinet with 6,136 pills) sold for $19.2m to Sheikh Hamad bin Khalifa Al-Thani, the Emir of Qatar. The following September, he sold a complete show, *Beautiful Inside My Head Forever*, at Sotheby's for £111m ($198m) breaking the record for a one-artist auction. Estimated to have wealth in excess of £200m, in 2007 he created *For the Love of God*, a platinum human skull adorned with 8,601 diamonds weighing a total of 1,106.18 carats. Approximately £15m worth of diamonds were used and a price tag of £50m asked for. Damien is currently restoring the Grade I listed Toddington Manor, near Cheltenham, where he intends to eventually house his complete private art collection. Away from the art world, Damien once formed a partnership with chef Marco Pierre White in the restaurant "Quo Vadis", but in 1999 Marco accused Damien of plagiarising his own work, *Rising Sun*, with the similar *Butterflies On Mars*, eventually exchanging the Hirst work (on display in Quo Vadis) with his own. This was the first of several such claims against the artist. Damien lives with his Californian girlfriend, Maia Norman, in Devon and has three sons, Connor Ojala, (b. 1995, Kensington and Chelsea, London), Cassius Atticus (b. 2000, North Devon) and Cyrus Joe (b. 2005, Westminster, London).

Houghton, Chantelle Born Chantelle Vivien Houghton, 21 August 1983, Wickford, Essex. Glamour model and reality show contestant. Hoping to follow in the footsteps of her idol Katie Price, she entered a *Daily Star* competition to find a Page Three girl and although she didn't win she appeared once and began to gain exposure. Portraying Paris Hilton, she worked for a while in a look-alike agency and also appeared as a Soccerette model on Sky TV's *Soccer AM* show. After previously being a standby on *Big Brother* 6, Chantelle became known to the public following her appearance as a 'non-celebrity' housemate in *Celebrity Big Brother* 2006. In order to remain in the house, she had to pretend to be the lead singer of a fictional girl-group, *Kandy Floss*, and sing her 'biggest hit' *I Want It Right Now*. She succeeded and better still, went on to win the show. During the series, Chantelle forged a close friendship with *Ordinary Boys'* lead singer, Samuel Preston. After the show, the two dated for a while before getting married on 25 August 2006 at Dartmouth House in Mayfair, London. The couple divorced in November 2007. Chantelle has presented *The Paul O'Grady Show* and also had her own post *Big Brother* show called *Chantelle: Living the Dream*. Chantelle re-entered the *Big Brother* house for *Ultimate Big Brother*, following the conclusion of *Big Brother* 2010, to signal the end of *Big Brother* on Channel 4. The producers also booked her ex-husband Preston for the show and this led to false rumours that they might get together again. She continues to make television appearances and like her idol, had a breast enlargement. After her marriage breakdown, she briefly dated footballer Jermain Defoe and *Crimewatch* presenter Rav Wilding. Chantelle is currently engaged to mixed martial artist Alex Reid (b. 21 July 1975,

Aldershot, Hampshire) who uses the nickname *The Reidernator* (see also Katie Price).

Huntington-Whiteley, Rosie Born Rosie Alice Huntington-Whiteley, 18 April 1987, Plymouth, Devon. Model and actress. Brought up on her parent's country farm, Rosie was discovered by Profile Model Management in 2003, while studying at Tavistock College, Devon. Her first professional gig soon followed, posing for a Levi's commercial. The 5' 9" (1.75 m) beauty hit the big time in 2006 when she began modelling for American lingerie and beauty products brand Victoria's Secret (in 2010 becoming one of their top models, known as Victoria's Secret Angels) and its sub brand PINK. Rosie remained relatively unknown in the fashion world until 2008, when she replaced Agyness Deyn for Burberry's fall/winter campaign alongside actor Sam Riley. After gaining her first British *Vogue* cover in November 2008, Rosie has hardly been off the front covers of magazines such as *Harper's Bazaar*, *GQ* (formerly Gentlemen's Quarterly), *Maxim* and *FHM*. In 2010, she posed nude for the Pirelli Calendar, photographed by Terry Richardson, and in March 2011, she gained her first solo British *Vogue* cover. Since then her star has shone ever brighter and she was voted No. 1 in *Maxim*'s Hot 100 list and *FHM*'s World's Sexiest Woman 2011 poll. In July 2011 she appeared on the front cover of the UK editions of *Elle* and *GQ*. Rosie made her film debut, in the leading female role of Carly Spencer, in *Transformers: Dark of the Moon* (2011), after Megan Fox pulled out just before the start of filming. Her previous relationships include Tyrone Wood (son of *Rolling Stone* Ronnie Wood) and French actor Olivier Martinez but since April 2010, she has been in a relationship with English actor Jason Statham.

Jenkins, Katherine Born 29 June 1980, Neath, South Wales to Selwyn John and Susan Jenkins. Her father was 23 years older than her mother and had two daughters from his first marriage, neither of which Katherine has met but saw for the first time pictured in the *Daily Mail*. Her father died, of cancer, when she was 15-years-old and this had a profound effect on both Katherine's and her sister Laura's life. By the time Katherine won a scholarship to study at the Royal Academy of Music, aged 17, she was already an experienced chorister and pianist. Whilst studying in London a man in his mid-thirties unsuccessfully tried to rape Katherine and in the end settled for the contents of her purse. After working as a singing teacher, tour guide on the London Eye and as a model, Katherine became the *Face of Wales* 2000. She first came to national attention when she sang at Westminster Cathedral honouring Pope John Paul II's silver jubilee in October 2003. The Welsh mezzo-soprano signed a £1million contract with *Universal* and began making albums in 2004; all seven studio albums to-date reaching No 1 in the classical charts. A major crossover artist, Katherine's albums have also been successful in the UK album charts; the list, with peak position, and date, in brackets, as follows: *Premiere* (No 31 - 2004), *Second Nature* (No 16 - 2004), *Living a Dream* (No 4 - 2005), *Serenade* (No 5 - 2006), *Rejoice* (No 3 - 2007), *Sacred Arias* (No 5 - 2008). Her seventh album, *Believe* (No 6 – 2009). Her latest studio album, *Daydream*, was released in October 2011 by *Warner Brothers* and has so far attained a No 6 position in the UK album charts. Katherine has not had a top ten album in the Irish charts nor has she had a single in the UK charts. In 2007 she co-starred in *Viva la Diva*, an operatic ballet, alongside prima ballerina Darcey Bussell. On television Katherine has made a cameo appearance in two episodes of *Emmerdale* and also been a judge and mentor in the ITV reality show *Popstar to Operastar* (see entry in the television section). Her autobiography, *Time to Say Hello*, was released on 28 January 2008. Katherine's four-year relationship with TV presenter Gethin Jones (see separate entry) ended in December 2011. Katherine has adopted a raunchier image of late in an effort to make a breakthrough in the USA. After denying ever taking drugs in an interview with Piers Morgan in 2007 she later phoned him up to admit taking ecstasy and cocaine although making it clear she would never do so in the future.

Joly, Dom Born Dominic John Romulus Joly, 15 November 1967, Beirut, Lebanon. Dom was born of British parents and on returning to Britain was educated at The Dragon preparatory school in Oxford, Haileybury public school, near Hertford, and the School of Oriental and African Studies in London. His early career as a political researcher for the *New Statesman* and *Roth's Parliamentary Profiles* led him to work on the BBC political programme *Around Westminster*. After being recruited to work as a producer on ITN's political discussion programme *House to House*, on Channel 4, Dom went on to work for *The Mark Thomas Comedy Product*, mainly due to his political knowledge. He then created his own show for the Paramount Comedy Channel called *War of the Flea*. Dom is best known for *Trigger Happy TV*, which was first broadcast as part of the *Comedy Lab* output. His BBC3 spoof chatshow, *This is Dom Joly* (2003), was less successful. In similar vein to the earlier Ricky Gervais effort, Dom played an appallingly egotistical media character who had the same name as him, thereby confusing a lot of the audience as to what was real and what wasn't. In 2005, Dom starred in a one-off documentary as part of a series on Sky One, *Dom Joly's Excellent Adventure*, which involved him travelling back to Beirut for the first time since he left in the late 1980s, and embarking on a road trip through the Syrian Desert to find a cave in which he had scrawled his name in as a child, that he re-discovered after much searching. His next project for Sky One was a critically acclaimed spoof travel series supposedly investigating attitudes to alcohol around the world, entitled *Dom Joly's Happy Hour*. More recently Dom came fourth in the 10th series of *I'm a Celebrity* and is currently writing columns for several newspapers. In his private life, Dom was once the singer in an Indie band called *Hang David* and several years later stood in the 1997 UK general election as part of the Teddy Bear Alliance, changing his name to Edward 'Teddy' Bear (a reference to Winnie-the-Pooh). He stood in Kensington and Chelsea against Alan Clark. Hiring out hundreds of teddy bear costumes, he staged mock protests at Westminster and came fifth out of nine candidates, receiving 218 votes (0.6%). Dom is married to Canadian graphic designer Stacey MacDougall. The couple have a daughter, Parker (b. 2000) and son Jackson (b. 2004). See also entries in the television section for *Comedy Lab*, *I'm a Celebrity Get Me Out Of Here*, *Trigger Happy TV*, *Walk on the Wild Side*, and *World Shut Your Mouth*.

Jones, Gethin Born Gethin Clifford Jones, 12 February 1978, Cardiff, Wales. With Welsh as his first language, Gethin joined S4C in 2001 as a presenter of *Popty* (the Welsh equivalent of *Top of the Pops*). The following year he began a three-year run as presenter of the S4C children's entertainment show *Uned 5* (Unit 5) and in 2004, as part of a challenge on the show, he learned how to fly a plane and eventually gained his pilot's licence. This experience was the perfect grounding for *Blue Peter* and Gethin became the 31st presenter in 2005, assuming the dare-devil role previously occupied by the likes of John Noakes and Peter Duncan. In 2007. Gethin came third in Series 5 of *Strictly Come Dancing*, partnering Camilla Dallerup. An ever-present on television these days, Gethin has hosted game shows such as *Sell Me The Answer* (2009-10) on Sky1 and appeared as a Cyberman in a 2006 episode of *Doctor Who* and as a Dalek operator in a 2008 episode. He also guest-starred as himself in *The Sarah Jane Adventures* pilot *Invasion of the Bane* (2007). Gethin recently become engaged to Katherine Jenkins (see separate entry) but their relationship ended amicably in December 2011. See also entries in the television section for *Blue Peter*, *Holding Out For A Hero*, *Police, Camera, Action!* and *71 Degrees North*.

Jones, Steve Born Stephen Ashton Jones, 16 March 1977, Rhondda, near Cardiff, South Wales. Beginning his professional career as a printer, Steve then became a Versace model for *Esquire*, before moving into presenting, making his television debut on the Welsh TV show, *The Pop Factory* (TPF), co-presenting with Liz Fuller between 2003 and 2008. His first exposure in England was as one of the regular presenters (along with Vernon Kay and June Sarpong) of *T4 Pop Beach*. In 2008 Steve made his acting debut in the comedy film short, *The Trevor Ending Story*; later that year making his feature debut as Jem in the romantic comedy *Angus, Thongs and Full-Frontal Snogging*.

In February 2009 he made his BBC1 debut, hosting *Let's Dance for Comic Relief* with Claudia Winkleman, a role he has reprised in subsequent years; Alex Jones becoming his co-host in 2012. In 2011, Steve was the host of the first season of *The X Factor USA*. He has been romantically linked to many high-profile celebrities including Fearne Cotton, Sky Sports presenter Georgie Thompson (the ex of Declan Donnelly), Pamela Anderson, Hayden Panettiere and Halle Berry. Steve's current girlfriend is Keeley Hazell (see separate entry and entries in the television section for *As Seen On TV, 101 Ways to Leave a Gameshow,* and *T4*).

Kay, Vernon Born Vernon Charles Kay, 28 April 1974, Bolton, Greater Manchester. Radio and television presenter best known for being a staunch Bolton Wanderers fan and the husband of Tess Daly (see separate entry). In February 2010, Vernon admitted to exchanging racy text messages with glamour model Rhian Sugden, after they had met in a Bolton nightclub. He is also a keen American football fan and plays on occasion for the London Warriors. See also entries in the television section for *Beat the Star, Family Fortunes, For One Night Only, Fully Booked, HeadJam, Just The Two Of Us, Name That Tune, T4,* and *The Whole Nineteen Yards*

Laverne, Lauren Born Lauren Cecilia Gofton, 28 April 1978, Sunderland. Radio DJ, television presenter, author, comedienne and singer. In 1994, while at college studying for her A Levels, Lauren formed a punk band called *Kenickie* with her brother Peter (taking the stage names Lauren Laverne and Johnny X) and friends Marie Nixon (stage name Marie du Santiago) and Emma Jackson (stage name Emmy-Kate Montrose). The band had limited success in the UK Singles Chart, their highest position being No 24 with the single *In Your Car*, which opened *Top of the Pops* on the 10 January 1997 edition. Their debut album *At The Club*, peaked at No 9 in the UK Albums Chart in May 1997. After *Kenickie* split in 1998 Lauren released a solo EP, and also sang on the 2000 *Mint Royale* single, *Don't Falter*, which reached No 15 in the UK chart. Lauren was also an uncredited vocalist on *The Divine Comedy's* 2004 single *Come Home Billy Bird* which reached No 25 in the UK chart. For the next three years Lauren presented various radio shows on radio station Xfm, most notably the breakfast show, before quitting in April 2007. She also moved into television, where her witty outlook on life gained her guest spots on *Have I Got News For You* and early episodes of music quiz *Never Mind the Buzzcocks*. The successful transition to television saw Lauren land her own weekly spot on Channel 4 music show *Planet Pop* and become co-presenter, with Myleene Klass, of ITV music programme *cd:uk* in 2005, and subsequently led her to hosting duties on Channel 4's music show *Transmission* with Steve Jones in 2006 and 2007. She was lead host of BBC 2's *The Culture Show* between 2006 and 2010 and has her own daily radio show on BBC 6 Music, as well as occasionally deputising for holidaying presenters on BBC Radio 2. She also co-hosts Channel 4 show, *10 O'Clock Live*, with David Mitchell, Jimmy Carr and Charlie Brooker. In 2010, she published her first novel *Candypop – Candy and the Broken Biscuits*, about rock chick Candy Caine, 15, on her journey to the world's biggest music festival, Glastonbury. Lauren married television producer and DJ Graeme Fisher in August 2005.

Lloyd, Danielle Born 16 December 1983, Liverpool. Glamour model and reality show contestant. The winner of Miss England 2004, she became famous after being stripped of her Miss Great Britain 2006 title after posing for nude pictures in *Playboy* magazine. Although reinstated in 2010, the title was also considered controversial following Danielle's alleged relationship with one of the competition's judges, footballer Teddy Sheringham, who she subsequently dated for a year. The 5' 8" (1.73 m) beauty queen has had her 32AA breasts increased by surgery three times, and is presently a striking 32DD. In 2007, Danielle was offered a place on *Celebrity Big Brother*. It was here however that she hit a career low point when along with Jade Goody and Jo O'Meara, was accused of using bullying tactics and making racist comments directed against the Indian actress Shilpa Shetty. In May 2007, Danielle attended a Shilpa Shetty movie premiere at Leicester Square where the two hugged and kissed on the red carpet in front of fans. Danielle later apologised for her behaviour and said she would learn from mistakes made. She surprised many in 2008, by participating in, and winning £8,950

on a Glamour Models Special of *The Weakest Link*. In 2010, Danielle appeared in a Celebrity edition of *Total Wipeout* aired on the BBC, in which she cleared all the rounds and impressively, went on to win the entire competition. She raised £10,000 for the charity Guiding Light/The Lantern Project. Danielle made her film debut, as Annette, in *Cut* (2010) which was mainly filmed in the Peak District of Derbyshire and was notable for having more than an hour of the film shot in one continuous take. Danielle may be considered most famous for her string of relationships with notable footballers including the already mentioned Teddy Sheringham, Marcus Bent and Jermain Defoe. She did buck the trend by briefly becoming engaged to pop-star DJ Ironik. Since December 2009, Danielle has been engaged to Wolverhampton Wanderers midfielder Jamie O'Hara and the couple have two children, Archie O'Hara (b. 11 July 2010) and Harry James O'Hara (b. 13 July 2011).

Lowe, Daisy Born Daisy Rebecca Lowe, 27 January 1989, London, the only child of singer/songwriter turned textile and fashion designer Pearl Lowe (b. 7 April 1970, Wimbledon) and the lead singer of British rock group *Bush*, Gavin Rossdale (b. 30 October 1965, Kilburn, London). Daisy was the result of a brief relationship - her mother more famously being the partner of *Supergrass* drummer Danny Goffey and her father more famously being the husband of American singer Gwen Stefani since 2002 (and before that the boyfriend of Marilyn, Boy George's old flame). Daisy had a brief relationship with record producer Mark Ronson and an 18-month romance with actor Matt Smith which ended in November 2011 - although there has since been much newspaper speculation of a reconciliation with the *Dr Who* star.

Lucas, Sarah See Tracey Emin

Lusardi, Linda Born 18 September 1958, Palmers Green, London. Page 3 Girl and actress. Linda began her topless modelling career as a Page Three girl in 1976, and the following year appeared nude in the February edition of *Mayfair* magazine and the November edition of *Fiesta*. The 5' 5" (1.65 m) model also posed nude for the cover of *Penthouse* in 1985. In 1988, Linda gained two small film roles in *Olympus Force: The Key* (as Suzie) and *Consuming Passions* (as a French beauty). After a long period out of the limelight, Linda took part in the reality game show *The Games* in 2004 where she showed impressive sprinting skills beating women years younger than herself. Back in the public's imagination, Linda was voted *The Sun* readers Best Page 3 Girl Ever in 2005. As a television actress, Linda was recruited for ten episodes of *The Bill* to play detective Don Beech's estranged girlfriend Maggie Lyons in one of the drama's biggest-ever story lines. She joined the cast of *Emmerdale* in 2007 as Carrie Nicholls, an ex of Tom King and mother of his secret child, Scarlet. She left the show the following year. Her lead stage roles include Eliza Doolittle in *Pygmalion* and Shirley in *Funny Peculiar*. She has also appeared in *Not Now Darling* and the musical *Happy as a Sandbag*. Presenting credits include her own fitness slot on GMTV and being a regular guest presenter on *Wish You Were Here*. In early 2008, Linda joined the new series of ITV's *Dancing On Ice*, partnering professional skater, Daniel Whiston. Linda had to catch up with her fellow skaters after falling and breaking a bone in her foot during her first hour on the ice and eventually finished a creditable sixth. Later in the year she took part in, and won, the Channel 4 show *Celebrity Come Dine With Me*. Linda is a regular pantomime actress, starring with her husband (and former Brookside actor) Sam Kane (b. 1968) in *Snow White and the Seven Dwarfs* each Christmas. The couple have two children together: Lucy Anne (b. 1996) and Jack Francis (b. 1999).

McCall, Davina Born Davina Lucy Pascale McCall, 16 October 1967, Wimbledon, London, of a French mother and British father. Davina inherited some of her mother's 'wild child' nature and as a youth dabbled in drugs and also suffered from anorexia. She began her professional life as a singing waitress and once dated family friend Eric Clapton. In 1992 she had a career switch and began presenting *Ray Cokes' Most Wanted* on MTV Europe. The following year she became the female voice dubber on the first series of Channel 4's *Eurotrash* and has been an ever-present on our screens ever since. Apart from her numerous terrestrial television appearances she has also co-hosted the first two series of the Sky TV show *Prickly Heat* (1998-2000) with Julian Clary and currently hosts the dance talent show *Got To Dance* on Sky1. Davina's career has had highs and lows, including her ill-fated prime-time BBC 1 chat show, *Davina*, which was axed in April 2006 after viewing-figures plummeted across its short run. She has been married twice, to Andrew Leggett (1997-99) and the presenter of Pet Rescue Matthew Robertson (2000-present). The couple have three children; daughters Holly Willow (b. 22 September 2001) and Tilly Pippy (b. 23 September 2003), and son, Chester Micky (b. 14 September 2006). See also entries in the television section for *Big Brother, The Biggest Loser, Don't Try This at Home, Eurotrash, God's Gift, The Million Pound Drop Live, Sam's Game, Stars In Their Eyes, Streetmate,* and *The Vault.*

McIlroy, Rory Born 4 May 1989, Holywood, Co. Down, Northern Ireland. After a successful amateur career, topping the World Amateur Golf Ranking as a 17-year-old in 2007, Rory turned professional later that year and made an immediate impact. He had his first win on the European Tour in 2009 and represented Europe in the 2010 Ryder Cup. On 19 June 2011, he won his first major, the U.S. Open, by eight shots with a record score of 16-under-par, to become the youngest winner since Bobby Jones in 1923. At the end of 2011 he lay second in the world rankings behind Ryder Cup teammate Luke Donald but after winning the Honda classic in March 2012 briefly held the No 1 spot before Luke snatched it back a fortnight later. Rory is currently in a relationship with the Danish tennis player Caroline Wozniacki.

McQueen, Alexander Born Lee Alexander McQueen, 17 March 1969, Lewisham, London. It became clear where Alexander's talent lay from a very young age when he designed dresses for his three sisters. After serving his apprenticeship as a bespoke tailor on Savile Row, firstly with Anderson & Sheppard and then with Gieves & Hawkes, he travelled to Milan to work for the then up-and-coming young fashion designer, Romeo Gigli. On returning to London in 1994 he received his masters degree in fashion design, from Central Saint Martins College of Art and Design, and his graduation collection was bought by fashion magazine editor Isabella Blow (see separate entry). Alexander was chief designer at Givenchy from 1996 to 2001 and became known for reviving the trend for low-rise jeans in his "Dante" collection show, with Kate Moss and others modelling the "bumsters". After leaving Givenchy to found his own label he was now described as the *l'enfant terrible* or occasionally as "the hooligan of English fashion", known for his spectacular but unconventional runway shows such as his recreation of a shipwreck (2003), human chess game (2005) and Widows of Culloden (2006) which featured a life-sized hologram of Kate Moss adorned in yards of shimmering fabric. Alexander has been British Designer of the Year three times outright (1996, 2001 and 2003) and in 1997 he shared the award with John Galliano, his predecessor at Givenchy. In 2000 he 'married' George Forsyth, a documentary filmmaker, but the relationship ended the following year. Alexander was found hanged at his home on Green Street, London W1, on 11 February 2010, nine days after the death of his mother, Joyce, 75, from cancer.

Marsh, Jodie Born Jodie Louisa Marsh, 23 December 1978, Brentwood, Essex. Glamour model and reality show contestant. Jodie first came to prominence in 2002 after appearing in the reality TV programme *Essex Wives*. The 5' 2'' (1.56m) glamour model went on to appear topless in many lad mags and tabloid newspapers, including *The Sun*'s Page 3, and early in her career became involved in a fierce rivalry with Katie "Jordan" Price. Jodie, who interestingly has a brother named Jordan, made much of the fact that unlike her more famous rival, her breasts were real. In addition to glamour modelling, Jodie has taken part in numerous reality television shows, including *The Games* and perhaps most notably *Celebrity Big Brother*, in which she clashed with many of the house-mates and became the first to be voted out. Jodie's next venture was the reality series, *Totally Jodie Marsh: Who'll Take Her Up the Aisle?* - the man who got the job being an ex of Katie Price's, Matt Peacock, although Jodie later admitted that the wedding wasn't genuine. In 2005, Jodie

published her autobiography *Keeping It Real* where she mentioned relationships with various celebrities and also her previously unknown academic prowess. In fact, Jodie left school with 11 GCSEs (all A and B grades) and three A Levels. Her ex-boyfriends include Fran Cosgrave, Calum Best, Antony Costa, Kian Egan and ex-Blazin' Squad singer and *Celebrity Big Brother* 2005 runner-up Kenzie (born James Victor MacKenzie, 6 January 1986, Chingford, London). In October 2008, Jodie began dating a woman, known as Nina, a hairdresser. More recently she has become involved in body building and a tabloid picture of her deeply-tanned muscular physique caused much debate in October 2011.

Minchin, Tim Born Timothy David Minchin, 7 October 1975, Northampton. Tim was born in the UK to Australian parents and grew up in Perth, Western Australia. He attended the University of Western Australia and graduated with a Bachelor of Arts in English and Theatre, and in 1998 completed an Advanced Diploma in Contemporary Music at the Western Australian Academy of Performing Arts. Tim began his professional life composing music for documentaries and theatre. In 2000 he wrote and starred in the musical *Pop* at the Blue Room Theatre in Perth. The following year he released a CD entitled *Sit* with his band *Timmy the Dog*. In 2002 he moved to Melbourne and began to perform a mixture of satirical songs and more serious pop songs eventually concentrating more on the comedy aspect. Tim's act can be described as a cross between Victoria Wood and Bill Bailey; his long-haired Goth look and clever song lyrics always demanding the full attention of his audience. Tim received the Perrier Comedy Award for Best Newcomer for his 2005 show, *Darkside* and followed this up in 2006 with his critically acclaimed *So Rock* show. His subsequent shows have included *So Live* (2007), *So F**king Rock Live* (2008), *Ready for This?* (2009) and *Tim Minchin and the Heritage Orchestra* (2010) all available on DVD. He also co-wrote a musical version of Roald Dahl's novel *Matilda* with Dennis Kelly for the Royal Shakespeare Company. Although better known in Australia, Tim is rapidly becoming a huge star in Britain thanks to his *Live at the O2* show in 2010 and his show-stealing performance at the 2011 Royal Variety Performance singing *The Three Minute Song*. As an actor Tim has appeared in several Aussie dramas and two films, *Two Fists, One Heart* (2008 - as Tom) and *The Lost Thing* (2010 - voice of the boy). He currently lives in London with his wife, Sarah and their two children, Violet and Caspar.

Mone, Michelle Born 7 October 1971, Glasgow, Scotland. Model and businesswoman. In August 1999, Michelle launched her Ultimo bras at Selfridges department store in London and the success was immediate. The following year she won the prestigious *World Young Business Achiever Award*. Now, one of the most successful female businesswomen in Britain, Michelle has made numerous guest appearances on television in shows such as *Loose Women, The Apprentice* and *I'm A Celebrity Get Me Out of Here NOW!* In January 2010, Michelle was awarded an OBE for her contribution to business. Until recently she lived on the outskirts of Glasgow with her husband Michael and their three children: Rebecca 19; Declan, 15; and Bethany 11. On the 27 December 2011, lawyers announced the couple's formal separation. Michelle runs MJM International with 45-year-old Michael and the curvaceous tycoon is reported to have lost several stone in order to strip for promotional photos.

Moss, Kate Born Katherine Ann Moss, 16 January 1974, Addiscombe, nr Croydon, London. Model and Fashion Designer. Kate attended the local Riddlesdown school but left with no qualifications to speak of. She was discovered in 1988 at JFK Airport, New York, by Sarah Doukas, the founder of Storm Model Management. Two years later, black-and-white photographs appeared of her in the British magazine *The Face*, in a photo shoot entitled "The Third Summer of Love". Although not known for her curvaceous, tall figure like her counterparts, Kate, at 5 ft 6 in (1.68 m), nevertheless became one of the most successful supermodels of the 1990s. Her zero size waif appearance became the face of the so-called heroin chic look in 1993 when she was involved with a highly publicised campaign for Calvin Klein. Campaigns with Gucci, Dolce & Gabbana, Louis Vuitton, Versace, Chanel, Dior and Yves Saint-Laurent followed. Kate has also been featured in fashion spreads in most of the major fashion magazines including *Vanity Fair, Vogue* and *W.* 2005 saw a decline in her popularity and a number of lost contracts due to her cocaine addiction, although by the following year she was earning more than ever. In 2007, with estimated earnings of $9 million, she was the second highest paid model in the world, ironically behind Brazilian model Gisele Bündchen who is often credited with ending the heroin chic era of modelling. Nowadays Kate is better known as an international fashion icon and clothes designer, particularly known for her work at the Topshop chain. She has recently designed a range of handbags for luxury goods house Longchamp and also released several fragrances. Outside of the fashion industry, her accolades include appearing in various music videos, playing Maid Marian in the 1999 short film, *Blackadder: Back & Forth* and lots of charity work. In 2008, Mark Quinn, designed a 50 kg (110 lb) 100% gold hollow statue of Kate, entitled *Siren,* which was shown as part of a British Museum exhibition. The piece cost £1.5m ($2.8m) to produce. Kate has a daughter, Lila Grace Moss (b. 29 September 2002) with former *Dazed & Confused* editor Jefferson Hack. During the 1990s, she had a courtship with Johnny Depp but the relationship that dominated the headlines was with Pete Doherty. They finally split after a series of rows and Kate became engaged to *Kills* guitarist, Jamie Hince, in 2008, eventually marrying him on 1 July 2011 at St Peter's Church, Southrop in Gloucestershire. Kate wore a dress by John Galliano.

Moyles, Chris Born 22 February 1974, Leeds. Broadcaster, author and DJ. Whilst still at school, Chris began presenting on WBHS (Wakefield's Broadcast to Hospitals Service), a voluntary staffed hospital radio station in the West Yorkshire city. His next stints were on Aire FM and RTL Luxembourg, until the station closed in 1992. In 1996, he joined the London independent station Capital FM, hosting the Friday & Saturday evening show titled 'The Late Bit', before leaving after clashing with fellow DJ 'Doctor' Neil Fox. Prior to this Chris had been dismissed from local station *The Pulse of West Yorkshire* when he'd made some offhand remarks about the previous presenter. Clearly, his controversial nature was difficult to tame, but, he persevered and joined BBC Radio 1 in 1997. Chris has presented *The Chris Moyles Show* on Radio 1 since 2004 (replacing Sara Cox who moved to his afternoon slot), where he is ably assisted by Comedy Dave (b. David Lloyd Vitty, 24 April 1974, Hong Kong). Ironically, he succeeded in overtaking Johnny Vaughan's Capital FM show to take the position of the capital's most listened-to youth breakfast show. On 7 September 2009, Chris became Radio 1's longest serving breakfast presenter, breaking the record previously set by Tony Blackburn. In October 2004, *The Chris Moyles Show* team replaced U2's *Vertigo* at No 1 in the UK Official Download Chart with their download-only charity song *Dogz Don't Kill People (Wabbitz Do),* under the name *Mouldie Lookin' Stain.* The song was a spoof of *Guns Don't Kill People Rappers Do* by *Goldie Lookin' Chain* (itself a spoof rap song) and proceeds went to *Comic Relief.* Famous for his parody songs, the aptly-titled *The Parody Album* (2009) reached No 17 in the UK Album Charts. In 2006, Chris appeared on the ITV show *The X Factor: Battle Of The Stars,* where he showed fine vocal talent before being voted out of the show in the semi-final. In 2007, the rugby league team Featherstone Rovers named their Post Office Road ground after Chris, although it is now known as the Bigfellas Stadium. Since 2009, Chris has presented the Channel 4 show, *Chris Moyles' Quiz Night.* In March 2011, Chris and Comedy Dave broke the Guinness World Record for Worldwide Longest Marathon Radio DJ (Team). They totalled 52 consecutive hours on air and raised £2,622,421 for *Comic Relief.*

Norton, Graham See entry in the television section for *The Graham Norton Show*

Nutter, Tommy Born 17 April 1943, Barmouth, Merioneth, Wales. Tailor, famous for reinventing the Savile Row suit in the 1960s. After studying tailoring at the Tailor and Cutter Academy, Tommy joined traditional tailors Donaldson, Williamson & Ward in 1962 and learned his trade thoroughly. In 1969, he joined up with Edward Sexton, to open Nutters of Savile Row, at No 35a Savile Row. They were financially backed by Cilla Black and her husband Bobby Willis, amongst others. Tommy began designing for the Hardy Amies range and became an instant success; his clients numbering the likes of Mick Jagger and Bianca Jagger as well as Elton John. Tommy himself was most proud of the fact that he dressed all but George Harrison for the cover of *The Beatles'* album *Abbey Road* in 1969. In the 1980s, he described his suits as a "cross between the big-shouldered *Miami Vice* look and the authentic Savile Row." On film his most famous creation was the clothing of The Joker worn by Jack Nicholson in the 1989 film *Batman.* Tommy died on 17 August 1992 at Cromwell Hospital, London, from an Aids-related illness.

O'Brien, Tina Born Christine Michelle O'Brien, 7 August 1983, Rusholme, Manchester. Actress. Daughter of Tina and Steven O'Brien. Tina left secondary school with nine GCSEs. Her acting career began in 1997 when she appeared as Claire in ITV's *Children's Ward.* She then appeared in *The Cops* (1998) and *Clocking Off* (2000), playing the on-screen sister of actor Jack P. Shepherd who later became her on-screen brother David in *Coronation Street.* In 1999 she replaced Lyndsay King as Sarah Platt in *Corrie.* The character of Sarah won her a National Television Award for Best Newcomer. In April 2007, Tina announced that she would be leaving the soap and her first role after was playing Cinderella in a Manchester Opera House pantomime. Her first Television role post-*Corrie* was in the ITV police drama *Blue Murder,* filmed whilst four months pregnant, in which, she played a character called Amy Kirkland. More recently Tina has been starring in the sixth series of BBC school drama *Waterloo Road* as Bex Fisher, the eldest daughter of the new headmistress Karen Fisher. She also took part in the 2010 series of *Strictly Come Dancing,* being eliminated in the 5th week. Tina had been in a relationship with Ryan Thomas, her husband in *Coronation Street,* since 2003. On 26 October 2008, Tina gave birth to their first child, a daughter; Scarlett Jacqueline Thomas. Tina and Ryan split in 2009. Tina's latest role is as Chloe Trent in *Casualty.*

O'Connor, Erin Born 9 February 1978, Brownhills, nr Walsall, West Midlands. Model who Karl Lagerfeld has described as "one of the best models in the world." On a school trip to the Birmingham Clothes Show she was spotted by a scout. Her first published pictures were by Juergen Teller for a 1996 issue of *i-D.* She was described as "freak chic" - but went on to model for most of the luxury brands, top photographers, always *couture* and, since 2005, has been one of the faces of Marks & Spencer. One of Britain's best paid models, her big break came during a shoot in Brazil, with photographer David Sims and hairdresser Guido, when she decided to get her hair cut off. In 2008, the 6' (1.83m) model with dark brown hair and hazel coloured eyes, launched the haircare line *model.me* for Toni & Guy, alongside Jamelia and Helena Christensen. Since she split up with the television presenter Jamie Theakston, Erin has been dating author, Dan Stewart, who she met at the Glastonbury music festival. In March 2011, her personal assistant Michelle Know-Brown, 46, who was employed by the face of M&S to look after her diary and day-to-day expenses from an office at Erin's Camberwell home, was convicted of defrauding Erin over a three year period between April 2007 and March 2010.

Osbourne, Jack Born Jack Joseph Osbourne, 8 November 1985, St John's Wood, London. Best known as the son of Ozzy and Sharon and brother of Aimee and Kelly Osbourne. Jack had a difficult childhood being diagnosed with a form of dyslexia, aged 8, and two years later being diagnosed with attention-deficit disorder and ending up in Park Century School for special needs where he was prescribed Ritalin for his ADD. Despite these difficulties Jack started work as an A&R scout for Epic Records. His big break came in 2002 when the reality TV show, *The Osbournes,* began airing on MTV and Jack made a cameo appearance in the film *Austin Powers in Goldmember* (2002). The following year he was admitted to a child psychiatric ward for an addiction to the opium-derivative OxyContin and then while depressed he attempted suicide by taking absinthe, a cocktail of prescription pills, and cutting his hands with shards of glass. After rehabilitation he made another film cameo, in *New York Minute* (2004) before co-hosting the ITV2 show, *Celebrity Wrestling: Bring It On!* (2005) and subsequently developing an interest in dangerous sports. *Jack Osbourne: Adrenaline Junkie* was then commissioned by the channel and ran for five series over four years. In October 2011, Jack announced he is expecting his first child with his fiancée, Lisa Stelly. Among his numerous tattoos are a smiley face on each knee (his father, Ozzy, having the same tattoo) and the name "Kelly" on his inner left wrist (his sister, Kelly, having one that says "Jack").

Palmer-Tomkinson, Tara Born 23 December 1971, Hampshire. Tara grew up on her parents' estate in Dummer, Hampshire, and was educated at Sherborne School for Girls in Dorset. Her father once represented his country at the Winter Olympics in the skiing event. A skilled pianist and budding poet, Tara left school with three A-levels (a B and two Cs in English, art and ancient history). She is the younger sister of Santa Montefiore. The socialite and celebrated 'It-girl' has made numerous appearances on television as reality contestant, chat show guest, panellist and presenter, including: *Shooting Stars, Top Gear, The Frank Skinner Show, Blind Date, Celebrities Under Pressure, This Morning, Friday Night with Jonathan Ross, The Sharon Osbourne Show, Comic Relief Does Fame Academy, Ant & Dec's Saturday Night Takeaway, 8 Out of 10 Cats, Hell's Kitchen, Big Brother's Little Brother, Animals Do the Funniest Things* (as presenter), *Loose Women, Would I Lie to You?, John Bishop's Britain, Footballers' Wives, Whatever Happened to the Wild Child?* and *I'm a Celebrity, Get Me Out of Here!* She has also appeared on the reality show *Cold Turkey*, which followed her attempts to quit smoking with Sophie Anderton. TPT, as she is sometimes known, has also made two brief film appearances, in *Mad Cows* (1999 – as herself) and *An Ideal Husband* (2000 – as Olivia Basildon) and written columns for *The Sunday Times, The Spectator, The Mail on Sunday, GQ, Eve, Harpers and Queen, Tatler, Instyle* and *The Observer*. In September 2007 her book *The Naughty Girl's Guide to Life*, co-authored with Sharon Marshall, was released and in October 2010 her first novel, *Inheritance*, was published. In 1999, Tara was treated at the Meadows clinic in Arizona for cocaine addiction, and in 2006, she underwent cosmetic surgery to have her septum nasi rebuilt after it collapsed due to her former £400-a-day coke habit. Now in full recovery, Tara is actively involved with several drug rehabilitation charities.

Pascale, Lorraine See entry in the television section for *Baking Made Easy*.

Perry, Grayson Born 24 March 1960, Chelmsford, Essex. After taking an art foundation course at Braintree College, Grayson studied for a BA in fine art at Portsmouth Polytechnic, graduating in 1982. By this time he was already estranged from his family, mainly due to his propensity for dressing up as a woman when going out. For a while he lived with milliner Stephen Jones (b. 31st May 1957, Wirral, Cheshire) and pop star Boy George, the three of them competing to see who could wear the most outrageous outfits to Blitz, a New Romantic nightclub in Covent Garden, owned by Steve Strange. Over the next 20 years Grayson carved out a career in ceramics culminating in being awarded the Turner Prize in 2003, attending the award ceremony dressed as his alter-ego - Claire. An autobiographical account of his formative years, *Portrait of the Artist as a Young Girl* (co-written with Wendy Jones), was published in 2006. Grayson married psychotherapist Philippa Fairclough in 1992 and the couple had a daughter, Flo, later that year. He is chiefly known for his beautiful ceramic vases (often depicting depraved sexual imagery), multi-coloured motorbikes, teddy bear fetish, model aeroplanes, and of course - Claire.

Pinder, Lucy Born Lucy Katherine Pinder, 20 December 1983, Winchester, Hampshire. Glamour model and magazine columnist. In the summer of 2003, Lucy was spotted by freelance photographer Lee Earle while sunbathing on Bournemouth beach which led to her signing a professional modelling contract with the *Daily Star*. At the beginning of her career the 5' 5'' (1.65m) brown-eyed model was regularly featured with Michelle Marsh and since then has been photographed with former *Big Brother* housemates Saskia Howard-Clarke and Chanelle Hayes. Lucy is particularly associated with *Nuts* magazine where she currently runs a weekly advice column entitled "The Truth About Women." After four years of posing semi-nude, Lucy finally revealed her

nipples in *Nuts* in 2007. Later that year, Lucy appeared as a contestant on a "Wags and Glamour Girls" edition of the *Weakest Link*, where she was voted off before reaching the final. In 2009, she appeared in the sixth series of *Celebrity Big Brother*, where she revealed that she is "a bit of a Tory bird" and that 'thick' people irritate her. On Day 8, she was the first housemate to be voted out. Lucy has appeared as a celebrity Soccerette on *Soccer AM* where she wore her beloved Southampton jersey and answered questions on football and modelling. An intelligent girl, Lucy has 11 GCSEs and two A-levels and was destined for university before her modelling career took off. Her breasts are a striking 32E cup size. Lucy has been dating her boyfriend Daniel Hooper, a carpenter, since her career took off.

Portas, Mary See entry in the television section for *Mary Queen of Shops*

Price, Katie Born Katrina Amy Alexandria Alexis Infield, 22 May 1978, Brighton, East Sussex. Glamour model, television personality, magazine columnist, published author and businesswoman. Katie took the surname Price after her mother remarried following the split from her biological father when she was a child. She began her professional career as a topless Page 3 Model with *The Sun* and this coincided with a change of working name to Jordan. The 5' 5'' (1.65m) model's much-publicised breast enlargements have seen her swell from a 32B to a 32G cup size (although now reduced to a 32C), and her earning facility has mirrored this increase. Katie made several special appearances in *Playboy* magazine and began to take television roles, initially as guest presenter on the *Big Breakfast* and then playing herself in an episode of the Sky football drama series *Dream Team* (she later played herself again in *Footballer's Wives*). During the 2001 British General Election, Katie ran as a candidate in Stretford and Urmston, winning 713 votes. Her campaign slogan was 'For a Bigger and Betta Future'. As part of her election campaign she promised free breast implants and a ban on parking tickets. On 27 May 2002, she gave birth to a baby boy, whom she named Harvey Daniel; choosing the name Harvey after her grandfather, and Daniel after her brother. Harvey's father is the footballer Dwight Yorke. Harvey was born with a condition known as septo-optic dysplasia, meaning that his optic nerve hasn't developed correctly. Katie's television career took off in 2004 after making an appearance in the reality TV series *I'm a Celebrity... Get Me Out of Here!* where she met her future husband, the singer, Peter Andre (they married at Highclere Castle, Hampshire, in September 2005). The couple later featured in the TV shows *When Jordan Met Peter* (ITV), *Jordan & Peter: Laid Bare* (ITV2), *Jordan & Peter: Marriage and Mayhem* (ITV2), and the *Katie & Peter* series, including *Katie & Peter: The Next Chapter* (ITV2) and *Katie & Peter: The Baby Diaries*. A further series aired in August/September 2009 called *What Katie Did Next*, which showed Katie's life after her split and eventual divorce from Peter earlier in the year. Also a keen singer, Katie was one of the acts competing for the right to represent the United Kingdom at the Eurovision Song Contest 2005, singing a song titled *Not Just Anybody*, however, she lost the public vote, coming in second place in the pre-selection show *Making Your Mind Up*, behind Javine. Katie gave birth by Caesarean section to her second child, a 5lb 13oz boy named Junior Savva Andreas, on 13 June 2005. Katie and Peter released an album of duets on 27 November 2006 titled *A Whole New World* with all proceeds going to their chosen charities. On 29 June 2007 Katie gave birth to her third child, a daughter named Princess Tiáamii. To-date, Katie has published four autobiographies: *Being Jordan* (2004), *Jordan: A Whole New World* (2006), *Pushed to the Limit* (2008) and *You Only Live Once* (2010) plus six novels: *Angel* (2006), *Crystal* (2007), *Angel Uncovered* (2008), *Sapphire* (2009), *Paradise* (2010) and *The Comeback Girl* (2011). She openly admits these books were ghostwritten by Rebecca Farnworth. Katie Price's *Perfect Ponies*, a series of children's books, were released by Random House in 2007. Katie and Peter hosted their own chat show in the autumn of 2007, *Katie and Peter: Unleashed*, on ITV2. Katie continues to write a regular advice column in *OK!* Magazine. On 15 November 2009, she made a return visit to *I'm a Celebrity... Get Me Out Of Here!* and whilst in the jungle, the public repeatedly voted for her to undertake each and every "Bush Tucker Trial" challenge. After it had been announced that she had been selected for her seventh consecutive trial, Katie quit the show a week after her arrival. Katie has had brief relationships with many celebrities and sports stars including footballers Teddy Sheringham and Dwight Yorke, singers Dane Bowers and Gareth Gates, and the TV Gladiator 'Ace' (real name Warren Furman). She married MMA cage fighter and *Celebrity Big Brother* winner, Alex Reid, on 2 February 2010 in a private ceremony in Las Vegas at the chapel of the Wynn Hotel, although according to US officials their wedding was not legal. A keen horse rider from an early age, she now has her own clothing range – Katie Price Equestrian. In January 2011 she announced the break-up of her marriage and started divorce proceedings; her decree nisi finally granted on 20 March 2012. Most recently, Katie dated Argentine model Leandro Penna between March and October 2011. Her most recent TV show was *Signed By Katie Price*, giving wannabes a chance to emulate her. The winner was nineteen-year-old Amy Willerton. Katie currently writes a column in the Sunday edition of *The Sun*. In 2012 she was voted the Foxy Bingo.com Celebrity Mum of the Year for the second time having first won the title in 2007.

Reade, Sophie Born Sophie Victoria Reade, 18 May 1989, Nantwich, Cheshire. Glamour model and reality show contestant. Already a glamour model, Sophie shot to fame during the *Big Brother* 2009 series. She changed her name by deed poll to Dogface in order to become a housemate and had a romantic relationship with Kris in the House. On Day 72 as a special prize, she legally changed her name back to Sophie. She went on to win the series and has since returned to topless modelling, most frequently appearing in *Nuts* magazine. In April 2010, the *Daily Star* reported that the 30GG stunner is desperate to upgrade to 30HH. In early 2011, Sophie revealed her former boyfriend, Manchester City and Italy footballer Mario Balotelli, cheated on her the previous New Year's Eve.

Ridley, Emma Born 10 May 1972, Hampstead, London. The so-called wild child of the London set is the younger sister of actress Joanne Ridley (b. 23 March 1970, London). A Disney child star who got her Equity card aged four, Emma co-starred alongside Anthony Franciosa and Carroll Baker in Jackie Collin's first novel turned movie, *The World is Full of Married Men* (1979), playing their child, Lucy. Adding another feature film to her credits at the tender age of eight, Emma played Sophie Peters in one of the well-known Hammer House of Horrors film productions, *The House That Bled To Death* (1980), and five years later appeared as Ozma in *Return to Oz* (1985), the unofficial Disney sequel to the Wizard of Oz (1939). A talented young dancer, Emma was with the Royal Ballet School from the age of six, but dropped out when she went off the rails and travelled to Las Vegas, aged 15, to marry the 30-year-old actor Robert Poreno. The 1987 marriage lasted two years. In 1992 she moved to America and in 1997 she again married a much older man, Philip Ehrlich, and although they had a son, Otto Ridley-Ehrlich (b. 1996), the marriage lasted little more than a year. Emma married her third husband, David Tyler, in 1999 and the couple have a son, Elim Tyler (b. 2000) and daughter, Isis Tyler (b. 2002). In the summer of 2011 the couple had an acrimonious split with Emma appearing in court, accused of slapping her husband while a dispute arose over the ownership of her Californian Goddess Fitness Dance studio. Earlier in the year, born-again Christian Emma appeared in the Channel 4 series, *Celebrity Five Go To..* and finished a creditable third despite pushing non-swimmer Russell Grant into a Turkish swimming pool. Emma's bubbly unpredictable personality and keen sense of fun has attracted several media opportunities and she is currently in talks concerning a reality show about her life and Goddess Fitness.

Ronson, Mark Born Mark Daniel Ronson, 4 September 1975, St John's Wood, London. Brought up in Conservative Judaism, his family name was originally Aaronson. Mark is the nephew of property tycoon Gerald Ronson and is related to British Conservative politicians Sir Malcolm Rifkind and Leon Brittan, as well as Odeon Cinemas founder Oscar Deutsch. He has younger twin sisters, Charlotte Ronson (b. 7 August 1977), a fashion designer, and Samantha Ronson, a singer and DJ. After his parents broke up, his mother married *Foreigner* guitarist Mick Jones and had two children, Alexander and Annabelle. Mark also has three other half-siblings, David, Henrietta, and Joshua, through his father's remarriage to model Michele First. Mark made his name as a DJ on the New York club scene in 1993, and six years later was featured in an ad in a recording studio wearing Tommy Hilfiger denim for a campaign for the fashion company. Mark used this exposure as a springboard to produce music, his first success being the title track of Nikka Costa's 2001 album, *Everybody Got Their Something*. Mark subsequently signed a record contract with Elektra Records. His first album, *Here Comes the Fuzz*, was released in 2003, and Mark not only wrote the songs but also made the beats and played guitar, keyboards, and bass. The album featured such diverse artistes as Mos Def, Jack White, Sean Paul, Nikka Costa, Nappy Roots and Rivers Cuomo. The best known song from the album, *Ooh Wee*, samples *Sunny* by Boney M and features Nate Dogg, Ghostface Killah, Trife Da God, and Saigon and peaked at No 15 in the UK chart in November 2003. In 2004, Mark formed his own record label, Allido Records, and the first artist he signed was rapper Saigon. He has produced songs for Macy Gray, Rhymefest, Christina Aguilera, Amy Winehouse, Lily Allen, and Robbie Williams amongst many others. In 2007, Mark released a cover of The Smiths' track *Stop Me If You Think You've Heard This One Before* under the title *Stop Me*, featuring singer Daniel Merriweather. This song reached No 2 in the UK singles charts. He has had three other top-ten hits, *Oh My God* (ft Lily Allen - No 8 in 2007), *Valerie* (ft Amy Winehouse - No 2 in 2007) and *Bang Bang Bang* (ft MNDR & Q-Tip - No 6 in 2010). Although his first album only reached No 70 in the charts, his two subsequent releases, *Version* (2007) and *Record Collection* (2010) both reached No 2 in the UK Album Charts. In 2008, he won his first Brit for 'Best Male Solo Artist'. After a broken engagement to Quincy Jones's daughter, actress/singer Rashida Jones and brief dalliances with Daisy Lowe (see separate entry) and drummer Tennessee Thomas he married French actress and singer Joséphine de La Baume on 3 September 2011.

Rooney, Wayne Born 24 October 1985, Croxteth, Liverpool. Wayne was a precocious young talent who scored 72 goals in one season for Liverpool Schoolboys and 99 goals in one season for Copplehouse boys' club in the local Walton and Kirkdale junior league. He grew up supporting Everton, and in particular Duncan Ferguson. On the field Wayne can play as an attacking midfielder or more potently as a striker. He played for Everton between 2002 and 2004 before joining Manchester United for the start of the 2004/05 season for a transfer fee of £25.6m. Wayne became the youngest footballer to play for England when he earned his first cap in a friendly against Australia on 12 February 2003, aged 17 (Theo Walcott subsequently broke Wayne's record by 36 days in May 2006) and also became youngest goalscorer for England at the tender age of 17 years and 317 days when scoring against Macedonia in a World Cup qualifier in 2003. An outstanding club player, Wayne has not always excelled on the international scene and after a disappointing draw against Algeria in the 2010 World Cup in South Africa, the England players were booed off the pitch by supporters, to which Wayne reacted by commenting on camera as he walked off "Nice to see your home fans boo you, that's loyalty, for fuck's sake!" In his two seasons with Everton he scored 17 goals and as at November 2011 he has scored 158 goals for Manchester United and 28 for England (73 caps). Wayne married Coleen McLoughlin on 12 June 2008 after six years of dating, during which he openly admitted visiting prostitutes. The couple have a son, Kai Wayne Rooney (b. 2 November 2009). Wayne has a tattoo of the words *Just Enough Education to Perform*, the title of an album by his favourite band, the Stereophonics. In June 2011, he visited the Harley Street Hair Clinic and had a hair transplant.

Savile, Jimmy See entry for *Jim'll Fix It* in the television section

Self, Will Born William Woodard Self, 26 September 1961, London. Despite his Oxford education and middle-class upbringing Will has always seen himself as the voice of the proletariat and indeed this confused juxtaposition is enhanced by his young history of self-harming and drug addiction. After a short career as a cartoonist for the *New Statesman* and as a stand-up comedian, he became known for his satirical, grotesque, and absurd writing style transcending the classes but at the same time sometimes alienating his intended market. His short stories include: *The Quantity Theory of Insanity* (1991), *Grey Area* (1994), *Design Faults in the Volvo 760 Turbo* (1998), *Tough, Tough Toys for Tough, Tough Boys* (1998), *Dr. Mukti and Other Tales of Woe* (2004), *Liver: A Fictional Organ with a Surface Anatomy of Four Lobes* (2008) and *The Undivided Self: Selected Stories* (2010). He has also written an illustrated novella, *The Sweet Smell of Psychosis* (1996). Will has also carved out something of a television career with regular appearances on *Question Time* and *Have I Got New For You.*

Sergeant, Emma Born in 1959, London. The daughter of Sir Patrick Sergeant, the millionaire financial journalist, she chose, at 16, to abandon a smart private education at Channing School in north London to enter the state system at Camden High School for Girls, where she started painting as a hobby. During a holiday in 1976, a chance encounter with a member of the Cobbold brewing family led to a commission to paint pub signs, and she decided that a hobby could be a career. Emma attended Camberwell School of Arts & Crafts from 1978-79. While still a 21-year-old student (now studying at The Slade School of Fine Art) she astonished the art world by scooping the National Portrait Gallery Portrait Prize for artists under 40. During her time at the Slade, Emma won a national portrait gallery competition and was commissioned to paint Lord David Cecil and Lord Laurence Olivier. In 1985, Emma packed herself off to Afghanistan and became a war artist, in aid of UNICEF. At this time she was dating former Pakistan cricketer, Imran Khan. Soon after their relationship ended she married a young banker, Riccardo Pavoncelli, but the marriage was short-lived. In 1994 Emma was commissioned to paint a portrait of H.R.H. The Duke of York, which is on display at The National Portrait Gallery. In 1995, Emma travelled with H.R.H. The Prince of Wales as his official artist during his tour to Egypt and Morocco and the following year accompanied him to various Central Asian Republics. In 2001 Emma married New York-born historian Count Adam Stefan Zamoyski (b. 11 January 1949).

Shepherd, Jack P. Born Jack Peter Shepherd, 14 January 1988, Pudsey, Leeds. Actor. Jack uses his middle initial as there is already a well-known British actor named Jack Shepherd. He made his debut as Spencer Bone in the television film *Put Out More Fags* in 1999 but is best known as David Platt on ITV's *Coronation Street*; a role that he has played since April 2000, taking over from Thomas Ormson. Although fully committed to *Corrie*, he has performed in local Yorkshire theatre in *West Side Story* and *Oliver!* Jack has won two awards whilst playing the role of David Platt; Inside Soap Awards-Best Bad Boy Award and, British Soap Awards-Best Villain. Jack and girlfriend make-up artist Lauren Shippey, who have been together since the age of 14, announced on 1 July 2008 that they were due to be parents. On 13 February 2009, Lauren gave birth to a baby girl; Nyla Rae. Jack and Lauren announced their engagement in April 2011 just three months after Sammy Milewski, 25, gave birth to Jack's lovechild, a boy named Grayson, following a one-night stand in April 2010.

Simons, Rita Born Rita Joanne Simons, 10 March 1977, Whipps Cross, Leytonstone. Actress and singer. Rita is the daughter of Derek Shaw, the former chairman of Preston North End FC. Her mother is the sister of Lord Sugar's wife, Ann. Rita's parents divorced several years ago. In 1998, Rita was a member of *Tantrum*, a band whose other members included Duncan James (later of *Blue*) and Zachary Lichman (of *Big Brother* fame). In 2000 she was in a band called *Girls@Play* - a sort of female village people - her particular character being a mechanic. They released two singles: *Airhead* (12 February 2001) and *Respectable* (1 October 2001). She then appeared in *Dream Team* and *Mile High* and also presented on Nickelodeon. Rita became Roxy Mitchell in BBC's *EastEnders* on 11 May 2007. She married hairdresser Theo Silveston in August 2006. They have twin daughters, Jaimee and Maiya (b. April 2006).

Slater, Nigel Born 9 April 1958, Wolverhampton, West Midlands. Nigel gained an OND in catering at Worcester Technical College in 1976 before working in restaurants and hotels and eventually becoming a food writer for *Marie Claire* magazine in 1988. After the success of his bestselling book *The 30-Minute Cook* (1994) he hosted the Channel 4 series *Nigel Slater's Real Food Show.* He returned to television in 2006 hosting the chat/food show *A Taste of My Life* for the BBC. In 2009 he presented the six part series *Simple Suppers* on BBC1 and a second series the following year. His other successful books include: *Eating for England: The Delights & Eccentricities of the British at Table,* and an autobiography *Toast: The Story of A Boy's Hunger,* which described his family relationships and his confused sexuality.

Smith, Paul Born 5 July 1946, Beeston, Nottinghamshire. A promising junior cyclist, Paul suffered an horrific accident which caused him to concentrate fully on a career in the fashion industry. Eventually joining Lincroft Kilgour in Savile Row, Paul's designs began to become fashionable among celebrities, including footballer George Best. In partnership with his future wife, Pauline Denyer, who was an RCA fashion graduate, he opened his first shop 10 Byard Lane, Nottingham in 1970. By 1976 he showed his first menswear collection in Paris, under his own label. He gradually expanded the retail business, being the first fashion brand to open on Floral Street at Covent Garden in 1979, where his shop offered an eclectic combination of clothes and 'finds' for men which reflected his own magpie personality. In 1998 he opened his flagship shop in Notting Hill and later that year showed his first women's collection at London Fashion Week. Today Paul has shops around the world and is particularly popular in Japan. In 2000 he was knighted by the Queen.

Snowdon, Lisa Born Lisa Marie Snowdon, 23 January 1972, Welwyn Garden City, Hertfordshire. Model, Television and Radio Presenter. Lisa moved to London as a teenager to attend the Italia Conti Academy of Theatre Arts, alongside Naomi Campbell. She was spotted by a Premier Model Management agent at age 19 while pole-dancing in a London nightclub and went on to do cover shots for *Vogue, Marie Claire, Cosmopolitan,* and *Elle,* before becoming the face for Gucci. Taking over from Lisa Butcher, she was the host of the reality television show *Britain's Next Top Model* from 2006 until 2009. During this time, Lisa had a very successful appearance on BBC's *Strictly Come Dancing* in 2008 where she partnered Brendan Cole. Despite two perfect scores of 40 in the final, she finished in third place to the surprise of many viewers. Since 2007, the 5' 10'' (1.78m) model with a 34F-24-35 figure, has been a co-presenter of *Through the Keyhole* with Sir David Frost on BBC One and has also been a guest panellist on *Loose Women.* She is perhaps best known however for presenting the breakfast show on the London station 95.8 Capital FM with Johnny Vaughan. In 2005, Lisa became an ambassador for the breast cancer care charity and later participated in a charity celebrity edition of *The Apprentice.* Lisa was the envy of many women having dated George Clooney from 2000-05 but more recent boyfriends include Queens Park Rangers football striker Jay Bothroyd and fellow model Aaron Turner. Her most recent modelling assignments include being one of the models for the Marks & Spencer autumn 2010 campaign.

Speight, Mark Born Mark Warwick Fordham Speight, 6 August 1965, Seisdon, Staffordshire. Television presenter best known for presenting the long-running BBC children's art programme *SMart* and the ITV Saturday morning show *Scratchy & Co.* He also hosted the series *Beat the Cyborgs, See It Saw It* and *SMarteenies.* In January 2008, Mark discovered the body of his fiancée and former *See It Saw It* colleague Natasha Collins (see separate entry) in the bath of their London flat. He was originally arrested in connection with the death after openly admitting both he and Natasha had taken cocaine, sleeping pills, wine and vodka, but he was later released without charge. On 28 February 2008 Mark announced he was quitting the programme *SMart*, because the "tragic loss" of Collins had left him unable to continue with the show. On 8 April 2008, he was reported missing by family and friends after failing to attend a meeting the previous day after being dropped off at Wood Green tube station, London in the morning. He was last seen that afternoon boarding a Bakerloo line train. On 13 April 2008 his body was found hanged on the roof of

MacMillan House next to London's Paddington railway station. He was thought to have died on 7 April 2008.

Stafford, Lee Born 17 October 1966, Leigh-on-Sea, Essex. Lee opened his first salon, *The House That Hair Built*, in 1984 and first came to public attention when winning the title of Men's British Hairdresser of the Year in 1997. After opening his second salon in Wardour Street, London, W1, he launched his own range of award-winning haircare products. In November 2006 he began the first series of *Celebrity Scissorhands* which propelled him to superstardom. In November 2011 he appeared on the ninth series of *The Secret Millionaire* and in the same month his girlfriend Jessica-Jane Clement (see separate entry) appeared on *I'm A Celebrity...Get Me Out of Here!* See also entries in the television section for *Celebrity Scissorhands* and *The Secret Millionaire*.

Stewart, Kimberly Born Kimberly Alana Stewart, 21 August 1979, Holmby Hills, Los Angeles, California. Socialite, model and designer. Daughter of rock star Rod Stewart and model Alana Stewart. Kimberly always wanted to follow in her mother's footsteps and after attending a modelling school she was snapped up by Tommy Hilfiger Co. In 2005-06 she became the face of Antz Pantz, an Australian underwear line. Also in 2006 she became the, 'Daughter of Rock' face of Blend jeans. Kimberly also has her own range of clothing, Pinky Star Fish. In spring 2007 she became the face of Specsavers and Ultimo Lingerie. Kimberly's television career consists of appearances in *Undeclared* (2002 - as Amanda Haythe), *The Osbournes, E! True Hollywood Story, Celebrities Uncensored* (2003), *Cribs* (2004) and *The Insider* (2005). In 2007 Kimberley's own reality TV show, *Living with Kimberly Stewart*, aired in the UK. The series followed Kimberly as she chose two flatmates to stay in her London apartment. Kimberly has a tattoo which originally read *Daddy's Little Girl*. The tattoo has been modified several times. When she first started a relationship with Cisco Adler, the tattoo was modified to say *Daddy's Little Girl Loves Cisco,* but once the relationship ended it was again modified to *Daddy's Little Girl Loves Disco*. It currently reads *Daddy's Little Girl Loves Discounts*. Kimberly had breast implants after graduating modelling school but, when she later had them removed, she signed them and sent them to Jack Osbourne, who hung them on his bedroom wall. In 2005, Kimberly became engaged to Talan Torriero, one of the stars of the MTV reality show *Laguna Beach* - after knowing him just a few weeks. At the time, he was 19 and she was 26. The couple called off their engagement less than two weeks after announcing it. On 17 November 2006 Kimberly's health was said to be in question after her father told a UK tabloid that she was being treated for liver damage due to excess alcohol consumption. By now fully recovered, on 11 April 2011, Benicio del Toro's publicist announced that Kimberly was pregnant with his child, although the two were not a couple. Kimberly subsequently gave birth to a daughter, Delilah Genoveva Stewart Del Toro (b. 21 August 2011); Rod Stewart's first grandchild.

Strange, Steve Born Steven John Harington, 28 May 1959, Newbridge, South Wales. British pop singer and club promoter who came from a broken home and left Newbridge Comprehensive School with an O level, in Art. He headed for London, aged 17, and joined forces with Rusty Egan. Together they hosted and Deejayed at the Blitz nightclub in London. Afterwards, the pair ran the Camden Palace nightclub. However, arguments with the financial backers of the venture, the pair decided to get out. They went on to The Playground, another nightclub, but this venture wasn't as successful. Steve then became part of the band, *The Moors Murderers*. They released one song, *Free Hindley* and performed several gigs before finally splitting in the first half of 1978. Later that same year, Steve briefly became part of a band called *The Photons* before forming *Visage* with Rusty Egan and Midge Ure. Their first single was released in 1979, but *Tar* failed to chart. In December 1980 their second single, *Fade to Grey*, reached No 8 in the UK chart but by 1985, after releasing several other top twenty singles, the band decided to split. Steven has made it clear in various tabloids that he has shared relationships with both men, and women. He struggled for many years to overcome his addiction to heroin and eventually had a nervous breakdown. Arrested for shoplifting, Steven was given a three month suspended sentence. The British media tore him to pieces. In 2002, Steven's autobiography,

Blitzed! was published. In it, he talks about his heroin addiction, his sexuality, his nervous breakdown and, how he's trying to rebuild his life. On 14 February 2008, Steven appeared in episode two of the BBCs 80s series, *Ashes to Ashes*, starring Philip Glennister. He played himself performing Visage's *Fade to Grey*.

Sugar, Alan Born Alan Michael Sugar, 24 March 1947, Hackney, London. As a child Alan made pocket money by boiling and selling beetroot from a stall before progressing to selling car aerials and electrical goods out of a van he had bought with his savings of £100. By 1968 he had founded the electronics company Amstrad, the name being an acronym of his initials Alan Michael Sugar Trading. Over the next forty years, Alan became a leading trader of commercial computers. In 2007 BSkyB bought Amstrad for approximately £125m and although initially remaining as chairman he left the board in 2008 to concentrate on his other businesses. Alan is of course best known to the general public as the autocratic boss in the BBC reality series *The Apprentice*. Away from business Alan is a keen cyclist and aviator (he is a qualified pilot with over 30 years experience). He was also chairman of Tottenham Hotspur FC from 1991 to 2001. Knighted in 2000 for services to business, in 2009 he became the government's "Enterprise Champion" a non-political office (although he was subsequently created Baron Sugar, of Clapton in the London Borough of Hackney). Alan married Ann Simons (the aunt of actress Rita Simons) on 28 April 1968; they have two sons and a daughter. With an estimated fortune of £770m (US$1.14 billion), Lord Sugar was ranked 89th in the Sunday Times Rich List 2011

Thomas, Ashley Born 4 February 1985, Chiswick, West London. Actor and rapper better known by his stage name Bashy. A product of the BRIT School for performing Arts, Bashy initially worked as a postman and then a bus driver while trying to carve out a musical career. He rose to prominence in 2007 with the release of his controversial recording, *Black Boys*, which although not having chart success, became a relevant statement amid a country suffering from recession and rioting. He was subsequently invited to perform at the Love Music Hate Racism Rally in 2008 at Victoria Park, to a crowd of 100,000. Bashy composed the theme music for the film *Adulthood* (2008) and then released his debut album, *Catch Me If You Can*, on 1 June 2009, the track *Kidulthood to Adulthood* becoming the best known. He made his acting debut in Mo Ali's *Shank* (2010) and then played Smoothy in Noel Clarke's *4.3.2.1* (2010).

Thompson, Daley Born Francis Morgan Ayódélé Thompson, 30 July 1958, Notting Hill, London, the son of a Nigerian father and Scottish mother. Daley is undoubtedly one of the world's finest-ever athletes having dominated the decathlon from the late 1970s to the late 1980s. As a junior athlete he set a British record of 6,685 points in 1974 and although the then Crawley-based Essex Beagle only managed a lowly 18th position in the Montreal Olympics of 1976 his talent was self-evident. Daley could have represented Great Britain at several events from 100 metres up to 400 metres and was a fine pole-vaulter and the very best British long-jumper. In 1977 he won the European Junior Decathlon Championship and the following year became Commonwealth Champion in Edmonton, Canada. Daley was beaten at the European Championships but was not to lose another decathlon for nine years. In May 1980 he set a world record 8,622 points and then won the first of his Olympic titles. Following this victory he gained lucrative sponsorship deals with Adidas and Lucozade. In 1982 Daley broke his own world record at the European Championships in Athens and then again at the Commonwealth Games in Brisbane. In 1983 he won gold at the first World Athletics Championships and was also awarded the OBE. In 1984 Daley won his second Olympic title in a fierce duel with the giant Jurgen Hingsen and although his points tally of 8,797 was initially adjudged to be one point shy of the world record, the new scoring tables introduced in 1985, and implemented retrospectively, showed the new adjusted total to be 8,847 and a new world record. In 1986 he won both the Commonwealth gold in Edinburgh and the European gold in Stuttgart. Injury now prevented Daley training effectively and he was beaten into fourth place in the 1987 World Championships and had the same result at the Seoul Olympics of 1988. Daley attempted to make the 1992 Olympic team but retired after the 100 metre sprint at the trials.

He was voted the greatest British athlete of the 20th Century by viewers of a Channel 4 show *The Greatest*. In the 1990s Daley played professional football for Mansfield Town and Stevenage Borough F.C., and then worked as fitness coach for Wimbledon F.C. and Luton Town football clubs. He also took part in motorsport, entering the Ford Credit Fiesta Challenge Championship in 1994. Daley was a natural showman who you either loved or loathed. His irreverent personality was glimpsed when he refused to carry the English flag at the opening ceremony of the 1982 Commonwealth Games and again two years later when he whistled the British national anthem after receiving his Olympic gold medal. He won the BBC Sports Personality of the Year award in 1982 and during his acceptance speech at the live broadcast of the programme uttered an obscenity, which caused adverse media comment. Daley has three children with ex-wife Trish Quinlan and two with present partner Lisa.

Titmuss, Abi Born Abigail Evelyn Titmuss, 8 February 1976, Ruskington, Lincolnshire. Glamour model, television personality and actress. Abi, then a staff nurse at London's University College Hospital, met TV presenter John Leslie at a party in a pub on the Fulham Road in 1998 and the pair soon started dating. She supported her boyfriend during his high-profile rape trial in which he was acquitted in July 2003. However, the pair soon broke up and their careers moved in opposite directions. After doing some reporting on the television show, *Richard and Judy*, Abi undertook a series of interviews promoting her naughtier side aided by a sex tape allegedly involving her and Leslie. This made her an obvious candidate to present on pornographic channel Television X and she also authored an erotic novel published by Black Lace. Abi soon became a regular feature in *FHM, Nuts, Zoo Weekly, Loaded, GQ* and *Maxim* magazines, and also appeared topless in several tabloid newspapers. Her other television work includes training as a chef on the 2004 series of *Hell's Kitchen*, and in 2005, appearing on ITV1's *Celebrity Love Island*, where she began a relationship *with* footballer Lee Sharpe. After announcing a break from glamour modelling, Abi took a short course at the Central School of Speech and Drama, making her West End acting debut in March 2006 playing a prostitute with a multiple personality disorder in *Two Way Mirror* by Arthur Miller, at the Courtyard Theatre, Kings Cross. She returned to glamour modelling with a new *Nuts* shoot in April 2009 but remains keen on developing an acting career (in November 2009, she appeared in Shakespeare's *Macbeth*, playing the character of Lady Macbeth). On 18 February 2012, she played the role of Tara Edmonds in an episode of BBC TV's *Casualty*. Abi has been linked to a number of celebrities but confirmed ex-boyfriends include comedian David Walliams and actor Marc Warren.

Tong, Pete Born 30 July 1960, Dartford, Kent. Educated at King's School, Rochester, Pete was a drummer in his formative years before becoming a DJ, aged 15. Gaining experience in various aspects of the music industry, Pete worked as a writer for *Blues & Soul Magazine* for four years before joining London Records in 1983, as an A&R manager. He had by now already made his debut on radio at Europe's first soul station, Radio Invicta 92.4fm. After a brief stint at BBC Radio Medway Pete made his first appearance on Radio 1 in 1981, hosting a 15 minute feature on Peter Powell's show before landing the prestigious gig of *The Essential Selection*, a pre-chart show on a Sunday afternoon. In 1991 the show moved to Friday evenings and since 2006 is known as *Pete Tong: The Official Start To The Weekend*. For all his fame as a disc jockey Pete will always be identified with the phrase "It's all gone Pete Tong", which has become accepted rhyming slang for "wrong". The phrase was coined by Paul Oakenfold (co-writer of the *Big Brother* theme) in late 1987 in an article about Acid House called 'Bermondsey Goes Balearic' for Terry Farley and Pete Heller's *Boys Own* Fanzine.

Turner, Lacey Born Lacey Amelia Turner, 28 March 1988, Hendon, London. When she turned ten, Lacey began an education at the Sylvia Young Theatre School but, left after only a year. She attended a local all girls' school and took singing and acting classes outside of school. In November 2004 her dream to appear on BBC's *Eastenders* came to fruition. Originally auditioning for the part of Demi Miller, she was surprised when she was offered the part of the mouthy, trouble-making Stacey Slater. Lacey has won more British Soap Awards than any other actor in any soap, and, at the age of 17, she was the youngest person to ever win Best Actress, an award she went on to win four times. After leaving *Eastenders* in 2010, Lacey appeared in the BBC3 supernatural drama series, *Being Human* as Lia Sharman. It was confirmed on the 21st December 2011 that she shall take on the leading role of Ellie a character who claims to see ghosts and spirits in the second series of the Sky Living series, *Bedlam*. Lacey has two sisters, Daisy (b.1990), a model and actress who has recently begun a stint in *Hollyoaks* as Jenny, and Lily (b. 2001) who has appeared in *Eastenders*, as Shenice. See also entry in the television section for *Eastenders* and *The Worst Witch*.

Twiggy Born Leslie Hornby, 19 September 1949, Neasden, London. Model, actress, and singer, now known by her married name of Lawson. Twiggy was arguably the first international supermodel and a fashion icon of the 1960s and 70s. The 5' 6" (1.68m) model weighed a mere 6½ stone (41 kg, 91 lbs) at the height of her fame in the mid-1960s and had a 31-22-32 figure, her short blonde hair and prominent dark eyelashes giving her an androgynous sex appeal which was sometimes referred to as pixie. The *Daily Express* dubbed her "The Face of 1966" and by the following year she had graced the covers of many of the best-known international magazines, guided by her then boyfriend, hairdresser Justin de Villeneuve (b. Nigel Davies). After the first stint of her modelling career, Twiggy went on to become a successful actress in film, stage and television, beginning her acting career by starring as Polly Browne in Ken Russell's film *The Boyfriend* (1971), for which she won two Golden Globe awards; Most Promising Newcomer and Best Actress in a Musical. Other films include: *The Blues Brothers* (1980), *The Doctor and the Devils* (1985), *Club Paradise* (1986), *Madame Sousatzka* (1988), *Istanbul* (1989), *Edge of Seventeen* (1998 - as Marlene Dichtrich) and *Woundings* (1998). Twiggy has also recorded several albums, encompassing a variety of styles including pop, rock, disco, country and show tunes. Her successful recordings have earned her two silver discs, two chart albums (*Twiggy* UK No 33 in 1976 and *Please Get My Name Right* UK No 35 in 1977) and the hit single *Here I Go Again* (UK No 17 in 1976). In 1977, Twiggy married actor Michael Witney, whom she starred opposite in the 1974 suspense film, *W*. They had one daughter, Carly (b. 1978). The marriage ended tragically with Michael's sudden death from a heart-attack in 1983. Twiggy has been married to actor Leigh Lawson since 1988. Since 2005 she has been part of the phenomenally successful Marks & Spencer advertising campaign alongside Myleene Klass, Erin O'Connor and Lily Cole. She has also been a guest judge on top US reality show *America's Next Top Model* opposite the shows creator Tyra Banks and stood in for Richard and Judy as presenter of the popular weekday magazine show, *This Morning*.

Vettriano, Jack Born Jack Hoggan, 17 November 1951, Methil, Fife, Scotland. Whilst working as an apprentice mining engineer, Jack took up painting when a girlfriend bought him a set of watercolours for his 21st birthday. He was 36 before he displayed his work in public and after some good early sales he moved to Edinburgh and changed his name to Vettriano (adding an 'a' to his mother's maiden name). His most famous piece is his 1992 work *The Singing Butler*, which portrays a couple dancing elegantly during a storm while a butler and maid protect them from the elements with umbrellas. In April 2004 the original canvas of this painting sold at auction for £744,500 although the reproductions on posters and postcards have earned him far more. This picture is typical of his film noir style, often depicting romantic or nude themes. To cap an excellent year, Jack was awarded an OBE for Services to the Visual Arts. In 2008, Jack painted a portrait of the Queen's granddaughter Zara Phillips MBE as part of a charity fund-raising project for Sport Relief. In November 2011 his self-portrait, *The Weight*, was displayed at the Scottish National Portrait Gallery.

Wan, Gok See entry in television section for *Gok's Fashion Fix*

Westwood, Vivienne Born Vivienne Isabel Swire, 8 April 1941, Tintwistle, Derbyshire. After studying at the Harrow School of Art, Vivienne became a primary school teacher, supplementing her income by creating her own jewellery line and selling it at the Portobello Road market. In 1962 she married Derek Westwood and had a son, Ben (b. 1963) but by 1965 she was divorced and living with Malcolm McLaren (see entry in pop section) with whom she also had a son, Joseph Ferdinand Corré (b. 30 November 1967) who is best known for co-founding the British lingerie company *Agent Provocateur* in 1994. In 1971 Vivienne and Malcolm rented the back part of a shop at 430 King's Road and named it *Let it Rock,* their big break coming with the commission to make costumes for the film *That'll Be the Day* (1973). After a short-lived change of name to *Too Fast Too Live, Too Young To Die,* the shop became known as *Sex* and sold a mixture of fetish and biker gear. Both Glen Matlock (founder member of the McLaren-managed band *The Sex Pistols*) and original punk model and actress Jordan (b. Pamela Rooke, 23 June 1955, Seaford, East Sussex) worked at *Sex* and by the mid-1970s, the look that became punk had its origin at the shop. In 1976 the shop again changed its name, to *Seditionaries,* and Vivienne began to use tartan accessories with safety pins, razors and silver phalluses. In 1981, Vivienne held her first catwalk show and chose the pirates theme which was already made fashionable by another of Malcolm's protégés, Adam Ant. Subsequent themes included Savage (from the ethnic dresses she sold at her London shop, *Nostalgia of Mud*), Buffalo Girls (Bolivian women's dresses with bras worn on the outside, Witches (the Haitian Voodoo look), Hypnosis (featuring sportswear fabrics) and Clint Eastwood (with shoes designed by Patrick Cox). In 1984, Vivienne introduced the Mini Crini, an idea that was taken up by Versace and Lacroix. Between 1988 and 1992 (The Pagan Years) she introduced clothes slashed in the style of the Middle Ages but also experimented with a classic tailored look and platform shoes. In 1991 Vivienne won the British Designer of the Year award for the second time running and the following year was awarded the OBE. The period from 1993 to 1999 she called "Anglomania" and was notable for the bustle and her present period is referred to as "Exploration". Some of Vivienne's designs from this period were featured in the 2008 film adaptation of the award winning television series *Sex and the City.* In 2006 Vivienne was created a DBE but, unlike her award ceremony fourteen years earlier when she arrived at Buckingham Palace knicker-less, she was on this occasion fully under-garmented. Vivienne has been married to her former fashion student, Austrian-born Andreas Kronthaler, since 1992.

Whiley, Jo Born 4 July 1965, Northampton. Disc jockey and television presenter. Jo began her broadcasting career at BBC Radio Sussex before gaining a job as a researcher at BBC Radio 4; eventually becoming a presenter on the departure of Terry Christian and Gary Crowley. Jo transferred to BBC Radio 1 in September 1993, co-hosting (with Steve Lamacq) a weekday evening show, *The Evening Session.* In 1995 Jo and Steve began co-hosting *Top of the Pops* and between 1996 and 1998 Jo became sole presenter, alternating with Jayne Middlemiss and her friend Zoe Ball. In July 2009, Jo published her autobiography, *My World in Motion.* In April 2011 she switched to BBC Radio 2 in a move that cynics blasted as "ageist". More recently Jo has joined Sky TV to present *The Jo Whiley Show* focusing on the latest stories in the pop world. Jo has been married to pop group manager Steve Morton since 1991 and they have two daughters, India and Coco Lux, and two sons, Jude and Cassius.

White, Marco Pierre Born 11 December 1961, Leeds, West Yorkshire, to an English father and Italian mother. Marco studied under the Roux brothers at Le Gavroche (Albert Roux describing him as "my little bunny") before moving to work for Raymond Blanc at Le Manoir aux Quat' Saisons, a hotel-restaurant in Great Milton, Oxfordshire. In 1987, Marco opened Harveys at Wandsworth Common, London, and in successive years won Michelin stars before becoming chef-patron of The Restaurant Marco Pierre White in the dining room at the Hyde Park Hotel (now Mandarin Oriental) and gaining his third Michelin star aged 33, in the process becoming the youngest chef ever to be so honoured. Marco next moved to the Oak Room at Le Meridien Piccadilly. He has trained some of the most famous contemporary chefs, including Gordon Ramsay, Eric Chavot, Heston Blumenthal, Bryn Williams and Matt Tebbutt. In 1999, Marco retired from the kitchen and gave back his stars, explaining that they meant little to him as he had come to realise that he knew more than the judges. He did however remain in the catering business and became a restaurateur. Marco has been married three times, to Alex McArthur (1988–90), Lisa Butcher (1992 – see separate entry) and Matilde Conjero (2000–present). He is usually chauffeured around by his Japanese assistant, Mr Ishii. See also entries in the television section for *Chefs, Gordon Ramsay* and *Hell's Kitchen.*

Whitehall, Jack Born Jack Peter Benedict Whitehall, 7 July 1988, Westminster, London. Spiky-haired comedian and television presenter. With an actress mother and a theatrical agent father it was almost inevitable that Jack would enter show business. His father Michael John Whitehall (author of the memoir, *Shark-Infested Waters*) represented the likes of Dame Judi Dench, Colin Firth, Daniel Day-Lewis and Stewart Granger in his day and one of Jack's godparents is actor Nigel Havers. Jack attended The Harrodian School in Barnes, London, where he was a contemporary of *Twilight Saga* star Robert Pattinson - a fact that he has built into a very funny comic routine based around his mother's (Hilary) fixation with R-Pattz. In 2007, Jack was a finalist in *So You Think You're Funny?* the annual stand-up comedy competition for new acts held every August at The Gilded Balloon during the Edinburgh Festival Fringe. Since then he has appeared on numerous television panel shows to showcase his comedic talents and in 2010 made the bill of The Royal Variety Performance. Although Jack's star is on the up his career to-date has not been without controversy. In September 2009, during his *Nearly Rebellious* show, he was accused of stealing Stewart Lee's comic routine dealing with the subject of life after walking in space, and in June 2010, a photograph of him appeared in the *News of the World,* purportedly showing him in possession of cocaine in Manchester. Despite this setback Jack's popular Channel 4 series, *The TNT Show* (see TV section) has been commissioned for a second series and his 2011 semi-scripted Fringe show, *Back Chat* (where he was joined on stage by his father) played to packed audiences. His six-part Channel 4 series *Hit The Road Jack,* began airing on 20 March 2012, following Jack on a comedy tour of the country.

Whitmore, Laura Born 4 May 1985, Bray, County Wicklow, Ireland. After studying journalism at Dublin City University and Boston University in America, Laura worked as a researcher on award winning *Lunchtime with Eamon Keane* for Irish radio station Newstalk. She first came to public attention in 2008, battling it out against other contestants to become the face of MTV News in MTV Europe. Currently, she hosts news bulletins for MTV in Ireland, the UK and pan-European MTV channels. The stunning blonde presenter gained a wider audience when taking over from Caroline Flack as host of *I'm a Celebrity...Get Me Out of Here! NOW!* on ITV2 in November 2011. Laura has her own clothing range, *A Wear,* in Ireland. Since January 2011 she has been dating Danny O' Reilly, lead singer of Irish rock band *The Coronas,* and son of famous Irish folk singer Mary Black (b. 22 May 1955, Dublin).

Zane, Alex Born Faris Alexander Albayaty, 3 March 1979, Leeds, West Yorkshire. After a year studying Medicine at University College London, Alex switched his attention to Media and Communications at Goldsmiths College. Even before beginning his degree course Alex had made the final of an open-mic competition, *So You Think You're Funny,* aged 18, and he subsequently presented *The Alex Zane Show* on UCL's student radio station Rare FM. After working for several commercial radio stations, in 2006 he was signed by Channel 4 as a television presenter. In February 2008, Alex hosted the pilot of *Rude Tube,* A C4 programme (and occasional E4 series hosted by Matt Kirshen) listing the top 50 original videos on YouTube. The pilot drew 2.5 million viewers when aired in the Friday primetime slot and has become an ongoing success, being shown periodically when the list is updated. In 2010 Alex performed at the Edinburgh Festival with his stand-up show, *Just One More Thing...* As a writer he has produced comedy material for *The Eleven O'Clock Show* (C4), *Smack the Pony* (C4), *Brain Candy* (BBC3), and *The Sketch Show* (ITV1). As an actor he has had a small role in *Dawn* of the Dead (2004) and also in the 2005 films *Deuce Bigalow: European Gigolo*, *Land of the Dead* and *The League of Gentlemen's Apocalypse*. The long-haired irreverent comedy performer is also the film reviewer for *The Sun*. See also entries in

the television section for *Balls of Steel*, *Celebrity Scissorhands*, *Popworld*, and *T4*

Zucchi, Thaila See entry in the pop section for allSTARS*

Famous British Car and Motorbike Manufacturers

AC - Founded by the Weller brothers of West Norwood, London, at the turn of the twentieth century. The name of the company was derived from the 648 cc single-cylinder air-cooled three-wheeled 'Auto Carrier' delivery trucks produced between 1904 and 1914.The company built its reputation after the Hurlock family bought AC Cars in 1930, initially by developing its AC Six sports cars and after the Second World War by making invalid carriages for the NHS from the Thames Ditton headquarters in Surrey. The AC Ace, designed by John Tojeiro, was produced in 1953 originally with its own AC engine from earlier models but from 1956 with Bristol's 130bhp 2-Litre firecracker which produced a top speed of 115mph and an acceleration of 0-60mph in 9 seconds. When Bristol stopped making this engine in 1961, AC adopted Ford's Zephyr 'six' engine for the final two years of the life of the two-seater open-topped aluminium sports car. The AC Cobra was developed in 1961 at the behest of Texan millionaire Carroll Shelby, a former racing driver who was keen to have a car capable of beating any Ferrari. Based on the Ace design, but with a Ford V8 engine, the Shelby Cobra was produced at Thames Ditton and shipped over to California. Other popular models include the AC Sociable (1907-14), AC Ten (1913-16), AC 12 hp (1920-27), AC 2-Litre (1947-58), AC Petite (1952-58), AC Aceca (1954-63), AC Greyhound (1959-63), AC Frua (1965-73) and AC ME3000 (1979-85). The Hurlock family sold the company in 1986 to William West who immediately passed on the rights to Brian Angliss who developed a new AC Ace before finally selling out to Alan Lubinsky in 1996. The latest AC model is the Mark VI, introduced in April 2009 at the Top Marques car show in Monaco. It is the first AC not to be built in England (manufactured by Gullwing GmbH in Heyda, Germany), the first to use a V8 engine not manufactured by Ford, the first to be available in a coupé version that was not designed specifically for racing and the first version to feature gullwing doors in its coupé form.

AJS - Founded in 1909 as A. J. Stevens Ltd by the four sons of motorcycle engineer Joe Stevens. Initially the company was set up to promote Albert John 'Jack' Stevens' entry into the recently inaugurated Isle of Man TT albeit riding a Wearwell motorcycle fitted with a Stevens side-valve single-cylinder engine. Factory premises were found in Retreat Street, Wolverhampton, and their first 300cc AJS appeared at the Motor Cycle Show in 1910. Although Jack Stevens gave his name to the company it was very much a Stevens family concern with Harry the managing director, George the commercial manager, Joe Jr the innovations manager and Jack the production manager. A popular 349cc machine was developed by 1914 and this bike scooped all the top places in the Junior Isle of Man TT race that year. The company also produced a less popular 800 cc (6 hp) V-twin at this time. After the war the 349cc machine was revamped with the side-valve engine being replaced by a new overhead-valve that produced 10bhp and this machine began to dominate the TT races with Howard Davies finishing first in the 1921 Senior TT, two minutes and three seconds ahead of the runner-up, Freddie Dixon on his 500cc 'Indian'. This was the first time a 350 cc motorcycle had won the Senior race. The 1922 design became the classic 350cc AJS, known as the 'Big Port' because of its large-diameter exhaust port and pipe (initially 1 5/8 inches), although the company produced models ranging from 250 to 1,000 cc. By 1931 the company hit financial trouble due to recession and their latest model, AJS S3 V-twin, a 496 cc transverse V-twin tourer with shaft primary drive and alloy cylinder heads was slow to sell. AJS tried to diversify into car production and even buses and coaches but although it held 117 world motorcycle records the company became bankrupt

later that year, the motorcycle assets being taken over by the Collier brothers' Matchless company and production was moved to Plumstead. The AJS name was kept alive under various badges and with varying degrees of success. In 1939, a water-cooled and supercharged version of the 495 cc AJS V4 was built to compete against the supercharged BMWs then dominating racing and this became the first bike to lap the Ulster Grand Prix course at over 100 mph, with a top end speed of 135 mph. In 1949 Leslie Graham won the inaugural GP World Championship riding a 500cc AJS Porcupine. This bike was originally designed to be supercharged (forced induction of an internal combustion engine creating more oxygen to support combustion than would be available in a naturally-aspirated engine) but the rules banned supercharging in 1946 and the bike was modified accordingly. AJS was acquired by the Norton Villiers Group in 1966 and although initially continuing with producing road bikes, AJS scramblers were produced between 1968 and 1974 in 250 (aka Y4), 370 (aka Y5 or Stormer) and 410cc engine sizes, Vic Eastwood being an ever-present winner of televised races on his 250cc AJS on a Saturday afternoon. In 1974, Norton Villiers sold the AJS rights to former racer and designer Fluff Brown who moved the business to Goodworth Clatford near Andover. AJS Motorcycles Ltd is still going strong today, specialising in smaller bikes such as the AJS Regal Raptor (available in 50, 125 and 250cc).

Alvis - Founded in 1919 by T. G. John, a manufacturer of stationary engines and motor scooters, the Alvis 10/30, designed by Geoffrey de Freville, was the first production model to bear the famous inverted red triangle logo. The most famous models were the TD21, produced in 1958, and its two derivatives, ironically the last of the produce of the factory in Coventry before it concentrated on military vehicles in 1967. The TD21 was developed from the TC21/100 (popularly known as the Grey Lady) which had a top speed of 100 mph due to its 100bhp 3-Litre straight-six engine. The TD21 adopted a Swiss design by Hermann Graber and was a two-door four-seater saloon with a top speed of 110mph thanks to a 120bhp engine. A popular convertible was also available. The TE21 first hit the road in 1963 and featured four headlamps and was available with power steering and automatic transmission. The TF21 was the last of the line featured a triple carb and 150bhp engine giving a top speed of 120 mph. Other popular models included the Speed 20 (1932-36), Firefly 12 (1933-34), Crested Eagle (1933-40), Firebird (1935-36), Speed 25 (1936-40) an, Silver Crest (1937-40). In the 1930s Alvis produced quality aircraft engines such as the Alcides, Leonides, Maeonides and Pelides. Its military vehicles include the Saladin FV601, Saracen FV603, Stalwart FV620, Scorpion FV101, Stormer FV4333 and Salamander 6x6 Crash Tender. The Alvis Register is a club dedicated to all things related to the vintage Alvis motor cars (1920 to 1932).

Ariel – The first Ariel cycles were in fact penny farthings and the company, founded by James Starling in the 1860s in Birmingham didn't produce its first motorcycle until 1901. The company also produced cars from 1902 until 1916. Early motorcycle models included the Ariel 3hp and the Ariel 4hp with a White and Poppe engine. After WWI the company hired Val Page as designer and Edward Turner as technician and together they produced the Square Four (sometimes known as the Squariel) and the Ariel Red Hunter singles. The company was liquidated in 1932 but then restarted as a smaller venture with a rationalised model structure. During WWII the company adapted the Square Four for military use as the Ariel W/NG. The company was absorbed into BSA in

1944 and produced the Ariel KG & KH (Fieldmaster) and in 1954 the Ariel FH (Huntmaster) with a BSA A10 engine. Later popular models included the 250cc Ariel Leader and Ariel Arrow and the rather less successful 50cc BSA Beagle engined Ariel Pixie, an attempt to enter the motorcycle market at the bottom rung, a position successfully filled by the Honda 50. The last Ariel badged model was the three-wheeled 50cc Ariel 3 before the name was dropped in 1969.

Armstrong – Founded in 1980 in Bolton, Lancashire after the acquisition of the Cotton company. It produced the MT500, a machine designed to be simple and rugged and primarily used by the military. The MT500 had a Rotax engine and was used by the British Army during the Falklands War. The company withdrew from production in 1987 and the line was transferred to Harley-Davidson.

Aston Martin - Founded in Kensington, London, in 1914 by Lionel Martin and Robert Bamford. The 'Aston' part of the company's name derives from a Buckinghamshire hill at Aston Clinton, a popular venue for uphill races. The Aston Martin logo is a webbed wing-shaped design with the company name displayed in green. Prior to the Second World War its halcyon days were between 1926 and 1937 when Augustus 'Bert' Bertelli was the technical director of Aston Martin, and the designer of all Aston Martin cars during this period, including the 1½ litre 'T-type', the 'International, the 'Le Mans', the 'MKII' its racing derivative the 'Ulster, and the 2 litre 15/98 and its racing derivative the 'Speed Model'. Headquarters were now moved to the former Whitehead Aircraft Limited works in Feltham, Middlesex. During this period the famous 'Buzzbox' overhead cam 4 cylinder engine was developed by Bertelli and Bill Renwick using Renwick's patented combustion chamber design. Yorkshire engineering tycoon David Brown bought Aston Martin in 1947 for £20,000 and soon after purchased Lagonda for £55,000 with the intent of implementing Lagonda's six-cylinder twin overhead camshaft engine (designed by W. O. Bentley) into Aston Martin's Atom chassis. The Aston Martin DB2 was the eventual result. The car went on sale in 1950 at £1,920 and customers could opt for coupé or convertible, two-seaters panelled in aluminium and a gearlever mounted on the floor or steering column. Two racing derivative Aston Martin DB2 Vantages entered Le Mans in 1950 and being production models themselves were driven to the track and finished in 5th and 6th places. The iconic DB5 was launched in 1963, costing £4,249 and had a top speed of 150 mph. Made in aluminium over a tubular frame, the DB5 was a subtle upgrade of the DB4 produced in 1958 but was immediately recognisable by its faired-in headlights. Popularised by the 1964 James Bond film *Goldfinger*, the actual production model did not have ejector seats or a bullet-proof raisable back shield but a Christmas toy model of that year had all these features. In 1965 the DB5 was replaced by the DB6 and the Short Chassis Volante which was a hybrid of the two cars. Introduced at the 1965 London Motor Show, the DB6, with its improved aerodynamics, was notable as the first model engineered following a factory move from Feltham to Newport Pagnell. The Duke of Edinburgh famously bought Prince Charles a DB6 Volante for his 21st birthday and this car remains in the ownership of the heir to the throne, although now converted to run on eco-friendly bio-fuel, including surplus wine! The DBS, first produced in 1967, was a GT version of the DB6 with sleeker design and vastly superior handling. It was shown several times in the film *On Her Majesty's Secret Service* and was the car in which Bond's wife, Tracy, was shot at the end of the film. David Brown sold the company in 1972 but despite the oil crisis at this time Aston Martin managed to keep afloat mainly due to the DB6 upgrade, the Aston Martin V8, an eight-cylinder two-door coupe designed by Polish automobile engineer Tadek Marek, which became the company's dominant output throughout the 1970s and 1980s, although an upgrade became available in 1977 (the V8 Vantage - hailed as Britain's first 'super' car due to it's top speed of 170mph) and 1986 (the V8 Zagato - powered by a 430bhp V8 engine with twin-choke Weber carburettors giving a top speed of 186 mph). The Aston Martin Vanquish, a grand tourer designed by Ian Callum in 2001, became the company's flagship vehicle

after featuring in the 2002 Bond film *Die Another Day*. When Ford ended its 20-year ownership of Aston Martin in 2007 car-making was shifted entirely to Gaydon in Warwickshire although Newport Pagnell still sites Aston Martin's service and restoration hub. Current models include the V8 Vantage, V8 Vantage Roadster, V12 Vantage, DB9, DB9 Volante, DBS V12, DBS Volante and the Rapide. Jeremy Clarkson eulogised over the V12 Vantage in a memorable finale of the autumn 2009 series of BBC2's *Top Gear*. The model incorporates many of the best bits from earlier models with an added carbon fibre bonnet and boot giving a weight of a mere 1,680kg, top speed of 190mph and sprint to 60mph from standstill in 4.1sec. A rear airflow diffuser and an adjustable rear aerofoil make handling a dream - the only drawback is the £135,000 retail price!

Austin - Founded at Longbridge, a suburb of Birmingham, in 1905 by Herbert Austin, the former guiding light at Wolseley. The company grew throughout the First World War, as the demand for army trucks and ambulances increased, and became one of the biggest in Britain by 1920 when the payroll count was in excess of 22,000. However, partly due to the Government's 1920 Motor Car Act, which penalised large-engined cars like Austin's 20hp, and partly due to the decline in demand for military vehicles, the company hit hard times. Austin decided to 'motorise the common man' with a small economic car he designed at his palatial home of Lickey Grange with the help of a young draughtsman called Stanley Edge, and in 1922 the first Austin Seven was produced with a launch price of £165, which was soon lowered when production soared. Although this car had the same name as a 1909 model it was a vastly different car from that short-lived single cylinder sluggard. The 1922 version offered four seats, brakes on all four wheels and a top speed of 40 mph from its four-cylinder 747cc engine. This car made all other British small cars obsolete and the rights were sold worldwide with BMW producing them under licence as the 'Dixi', and the French and American markets selling them as the Rosengart and Bantam respectively. Even the first Datsun (the 1932 type 10) was a rip-off of the Austin Seven. By the time of its discontinuation in 1939 more than 302,000 Austin Sevens had been produced and used '7s' virtually created the second-hand car market. A series of post war saloons were produced in rapid succession including the A40 Devon (1947-52), A40 Dorset (1947-52), A70 Hampshire (1948-50), A70 Hereford (1950-54), A40 Somerset (1952-54), Austin Cambridge (sold as A40, A50, A55, and A60 between 1954 and 1969 as cars and 1971 as light commercials) and Austin Westminster (sold as A90, A95, A99, A105, and A110 during the same time span as the Cambridge but as replacement for the Hereford as opposed to the Somerset. The A30 was introduced in 1951 as the "New Austin Seven", it was Austin's answer to the Morris Minor. At launch the car cost approximately £520, undercutting the Minor by 20 per cent. It was the first Austin built without a separate chassis. In 1956 the car was upgraded from a 803cc engine to a 948cc engine and renamed A35 and although both models were discontinued in 1959 the A35 Countryman Estate lasted until 1962 and the A35 Vans until 1968. At £1,064 in 1953, the Austin Healey 100 became the world's cheapest 100mph sports car (hence its name) and in 1959 the car was renamed the Austin-Healey 3000 (after its 2.9-Litre engine). Another sports model worthy of mention here is the Austin-Healey Sprite, affectionately known as the 'Frogeye' because of its headlights being prominently mounted on top of the bonnet. Unfortunately this aspect of its design was done away with for its final production run in 1971 and much of the character went with it. Austin-Healey produced cars until 1972 when the 20-year agreement between Healey and Austin came to an end. Donald Healey actually left the company in 1968 to join Jenson Motors and became their chairman in 1972.
The Austin 1100 was marketed in 1963 as part of the ADO16 (Austin Drawing Office project number 16) designed by Sir Alec Issigonis with fluid suspension system designed by Dr Alex Moulton. The 1,098cc version of the BMC A-Series engine was first marketed a year earlier as the Morris 1100. The Austin 1300 followed in 1967 and both models were consistently the nation's best-selling model range from the mid 1960s until the Allegro manufactured by British Leyland under the Austin name supplanted both models from 1973 until 1983. The Allegro sold

only 667,000 during this decade, far short of the millions of the 1100/1300 and this was perceived as a constant reminder of all that was wrong with Leyland's attitude to the buying public, from misguided design to uneven quality. In 1980 BL finally sat up and took notice of their European rivals and produced the Austin Metro. Launched as the Austin miniMetro, the car was an instant success with its hatchback design, roomy interior and nimble road handling. During its 18-year lifespan, the Metro was rebranded as Austin Metro, MG Metro and Rover Metro. It was re-badged as the Rover 100 series in 1994. There were also van versions known as the Morris Metro and later, Metrovan. The Austin Motor Company was merged in 1952 into the British Motor Corporation Ltd. The BMC was the predecessor of British Leyland. In 1986 it was renamed as the Rover Group, later to become MG Rover Group, which went into administration in 2005, bringing an end to mass car production by British owned manufacturers—with MG becoming part of China's Nanjing Automobile, which currently owns the Austin trademark.

Bentley – Founded by Walter Owen Bentley in 1919 it has a winged "B" badge. Bentley already had a reputation as an aero-engine manufacturer. With production based in Cricklewood, the first Bentley – which was to become the world famous Bentley 3 Litre - was sold in September 1921. By 1924 Bentley already had a win at the Le Mans 24-Hour race and had built a reputation for both strength and reliability. The weight and size of the Bentley led rival Ettore Bugatti to call it "the fastest lorry in the world". The "Bentley Boys", who included Woolf Barnato, a diamond millionaire who had bailed the company out, Sammy Davis, and Sir Henry Birkin helped Bentley gain successive Le Mans victories between 1927 and 1930 driving the Bentley 3 Litre Sport, Bentley 4.5 Litre (the Blower Bentley) and the 6.5 Litre Speed Six. Bentley was taken over by Rolls-Royce in 1931 and the production was moved from Cricklewood to Derby. The "new" firm produced the 3.5 Litre in 1933, which was largely a Rolls-Royce variant but was well-received nonetheless. Production moved to Crewe after World War II and in 1952 the Bentley R-Type Continental was released. Only 208 were built between 1952 and 1955 with a rolling chassis delivered to a coachbuilder of choice (usually H. J. Mulliner). Other 1950s and 1960s Bentleys such as the S-Type saw an increasing tendency towards Bentley models being merely a Rolls-Royce with a different grill and badge. The S-Series was a rebadged Silver Cloud and the T-Series was a rebadged Silver Shadow. Financial problems for Rolls-Royce Motors created in the early 1970s and eventually both Rolls-Royce and Bentley were bought by Vickers in 1980. The main models produced under the new set-up, which saw more differentiation from Rolls-Royce, were the Bentley Mulsanne (named after the Mulsanne Straight at Le Mans) which was manufactured, with variants such as the Turbo and "S", until 1992 and the Bentley Continental R (1991-2002). The company was bought by Volkswagen in 1998. The Bentley State Limousine was presented to the Queen on the occasion of her Golden Jubilee in 2002. The Bentley Continental GT, a two-door coupé was released in 2003, to replace the previous Rolls-Royce-based Continental R and T. A variant, the Bentley Continental Flying Spur was introduced in 2005. The high-end luxury Bentley Mulsanne was unveiled in 2009 to replace the Arnage (1998-2009).

Bond – Founded by Lawrie Bond in Preston, Lancashire in 1948, it changed its name from Sharps Commercials to Bond Cars Ltd in 1965. The first model produced was the Bond Minicar, a three-wheeler powered by a 122 cc single cylinder 2 stroke engine which was increased to 197cc in 1950. As a three-wheeler it could be driven on a motorcycle license and, although it had no reverse gear it could turn within its own body-length. It went through many variants during the 1950s including van and estate versions, and there were models "A" to "G", the last being introduced in 1961. The firm produced the four-wheel Equipe sports car from 1963 to 1970, which was based on a Triumph Herald chassis. The Bond 875 three-wheeler was produced from 1965 using a Hillman

Imp engine. A van version of the 875 was known as the Ranger. The company's best known model was the Tom Karen designed Bond Bug which was commissioned after the firm had been purchased by Reliant in 1970. The Bug was a wedge-shaped three-wheeler microcar, with a lift-up canopy and plastic side screens instead of conventional doors and based on the Reliant Regal chassis. Noted for its bright orange colour scheme, it was sold with two different four-cylinder engines, 701 cc and 748 cc and could reach 78 mph. The Bug was produced from 1970 to 1974.

Bristol – Bristol Cars was created in 1945 as a division of the Bristol Aeroplane Company (BAC) which had created the Bristol Blenheim and the Bristol Beaufighter, as a means of utilising the surplus workforce which had been employed on war work and also to benefit from assets acquired from BMW as reparations. The first model produced was the Bristol 400 Saloon aimed at the quality car market. It was heavily based on pre-war BMW designs and until 1961 all Bristol cars used evolutions of the 6-cylinder BMW-derived engine. The asking price of the 1948 Bristol 401 Saloon was 3 times that of the equivalent Jaguar and barely covered its costs. In contrast to the 400 the new model, and its sister the 402 Cabriolet, was based on Italian styling and was aerodynamically tested by the aeroplane division. A sports car, the 450, was produced in 1953 to compete in the Le Mans 24 Hour race, winning its class in 1954 and 1955. The car was scrapped following the 1955 Le Mans disaster and Bristol withdrew from racing. Bristol Cars separated from BAC in 1960 and after this all were Bristol models were fitted with Chrysler V8 engines. The first such model was the Bristol 407. The 411 was released in 1970 and had the reputation of being "the fastest true four-seater touring car" with a top speed of 143 mph. The Model 412 was introduced in 1975 and had the Bristol Beaufighter and Bristol Beaufort as later variants. It was in production until the mid-1990s. Introduced alongside the 412 and still in production is the Bristol 603 with its variants the Britannia, Brigand and Blenheim. In 1999 Bristol revealed the Fighter project, a gull-winged supercar boasting a Chrysler V10 engine and released the car in 2004. A turbocharged version, the Fighter T, was introduced in 2006.

Brough and Brough Superior – Brough Motorcycles were founded in 1908 in Nottingham by William E Brough and concentrated on producing single and v-twin engined models. This company lasted until 1926. In 1919 William's son George decided to branch out on his own and set up his own factory in Nottingham. After he heard his son was calling his models Brough Superior, William is quoted as saying "I suppose that makes mine the Brough Inferior". The Brough Superior machines were custom built, were described as the "Rolls-Royce of motorcycles" and priced accordingly. The top model was the SS100, of which fewer than 400 were made between 1924 and 1940. The SS stood for Super Sports and the 100 meant the bike was guaranteed to reach 100 mph. The specification of the SS100 was changed constantly through listening to customer suggestions, with a result that very few SS100s were identical. Various speed records were broken riding SS100s during the 1930s. Other models included the SS80 and the SS680. Infamously T.E. Lawrence (Lawrence of Arabia) was fatally injured whilst riding one of his many SS100s (this one nicknamed by him "George VII") near Wareham, Dorset in May 1935. A new model known as the Dream was revealed in 1938 but never reached production after the factory was turned over to war work and no further motorcycles were produced.

BSA - in June 1861 the Birmingham Small Arms Company was formed and in 1863 a factory was built at Small Heath. By 1880, the market for guns had declined and the company started to make bicycles and tricycles. Its first motorcycle was produced in 1903 and the BSA 3 hp, the first wholly BSA motorcycle, was displayed in 1910. The 770cc BSA Twin was introduced in 1921 and another early popular model was the 500cc S27 (introduced in

1927) and known as the Sloper. By WWII the company consisted of 67 factories and produced 126,000 M20 motorcycles during the war. BSA had already acquired Ariel and Sunbeam and the purchase of Triumph in 1951 made the BSA Group the largest producer of motorcycles in the world. The company produced the B32GS Gold Star in 1948 and the model went through various versions until production ended in 1963. It proved very successful in both versions for trials and for touring. The four-stroke unit construction C15 was manufactured between 1958 and 1967, when it was replaced by the C25 Barracuda. Jeff Smith won the 500cc World Moto-Cross Championship on a BSA C15T 'Trials Cat' in both 1964 and 1965. Based on a "repatriated" German design, one of the most popular models was the lightweight Bantam, which was in production from 1948 until 1971 in various guises. The BSA Golden Flash A10 was launched in 1949 and other versions of the A10 such as the Super Flash, Road Rocket and the Super Rocket appeared until production was halted in 1961. Models appearing in the 1960s included the BSA A65S Spitfire and the A75R Rocket Three. Intense competition from Germany and Japan meant that in 1972 BSA was absorbed into Manganese Bronze in a rescue plan initiated by the DOI. Several abortive attempts to rescue the Norton, BSA and Triumph motorcycle factories failed and Norton's Wolverhampton factory together with BSA's Small Heath were closed. A BSA company survived producing lightweight bikes mainly for the Third World including the popular BSA Bushman. In 1991 BSA Group was formed and purchased Norton Spares, becoming BSA Regal Group in 1994. Now based in Southampton, this company specialises in hand built and limited edition models.

Caterham – Having been a Lotus 7 dealer during the 1960s, when in 1973 Lotus announced its intention to discontinue the model, Graham Nearn, the founder of Caterham Cars, purchased the rights to continue its manufacture. The production of Lotus 7 Series 4 was short-lived and a switch to Series 3 was made in 1974 with the cars becoming known as Caterham Sevens. In 1984 Caterham offered a Starter Kit to enable enthusiasts to build their own Seven. In 1987 the production moved from Caterham to Dartford. The firm offers variants of the original Seven such as the Classic, Roadsport and Superlight, plus the more radically modified CSR. A Superlight R500 briefly held the world record for production car 0–60 mph times (at 3.4 seconds). A two-seater sports car, the Caterham 21, was introduced in 1994 to celebrate 21 years of Caterham Cars manufacture of the Lotus Seven. It is also based on the Seven and only 48 were ever made. The Nearn family sold Caterham Cars in 2005 to a consortium of former Lotus managers.

Cotton – Having patented a triangulated frame design in 1914, Francis Willoughby Cotton founded the firm in Gloucester in 1918. The early machines became popular following success in the IOM TT's in the 1920s. The famous "coTTon" badge inspired by Stanley Woods IOM TT win in 1923. During the 1930s the firm offered a range of models with JAP, Villiers and Blackburne engines. The original firm went bankrupt in 1940. A new company was formed at the old factory in the 1950s and some road racing success followed in Britain in the early 1960s. The company finally ceased to exist in 1980.

Coventry-Eagle – The firm began as bicycle manufacturer Hotchkiss, Mayo & Meek but changed its name to Coventry-Eagle in 1897. One model was the luxurious Flying 8, first produced in 1923 but other models were more utilitarian and used a variety of engine manufacturers including JAP, Matchless and Villiers. Dual seat, partially enclosed Pullman models were featured in the late 1930s. In 1937 the company offered the Matchless powered N25 Flying 250, N35 Flying 350 and N50 Flying N500, but the onset of World War II saw the end of motorcycle production.

Daimler Motor Company – Based in Coventry and founded in 1896 by Frederick Simms as the first company in Britain specifically to make cars. It had no link with the German Daimler Motoren Gesellschaft. The first Daimler took to the roads in 1897. In 1902, King Edward VII ordered his 22HP for Ascot Week, he honoured the Daimler Company with a Royal Warrant. In 1910 the company became part of BSA. And during World War I the company produced engines for the first tanks plus lorries and aircraft engines. During the 1920s Daimler had seven basic models including the V12 Double Six. Daimler/BSA bought the Lanchester Motor Company in 1931. By the mid-1930s models included the Daimler Fifteen, Daimler Twenty and a Straight 8. During World War II Daimler developed a four-wheel drive scout car known as the Dingo and an armoured car capable of climbing a 1:2 gradient. Post-war Daimler also manufactured the Ferret Scout Car. Daimler's image was regarded as rather stuffy in the post-war world but in 1954 the company introduced the Conquest Roadster sports car. Under the management of Jack Sangster and designer Edward Turner the company produced the Daimler SP250 (originally known as the Dart) and the Majestic Major. In 1960 the Daimler name was acquired by Jaguar Cars. The Daimler V8 engine and Jaguar MK 2 body were married to produce the successful Daimler 2.5 Litre V8. Apart from the Daimler DS420, most Daimlers produced after this period were rebadged or re-engineered Jaguar models. In 1989 Ford Motor Company took over Jaguar and with it the right to use the Daimler name. In 1992, Daimler stopped production of the DS420 Limousine, the only model that was not just a re-badged Jaguar. In 1996 the Ford Motor Company took over Jaguar and with it the right to use the Daimler name and by 2006 the use of the Daimler brand was limited to one model, the Daimler Super Eight. In 2008 Tata Motors of India acquired Jaguar Land Rover and with them the Daimler brand.

DeLorean – the DeLorean Motor Company (DMC) was founded by John DeLorean in Detroit, Michigan in 1975. Having received an offer from Northern Ireland's Industrial Development Board a factory was built in Dunmurry, a suburb of Belfast, with the production line opening in 1981. It produced just one model — the distinctive stainless steel DeLorean DMC-12 sports car featuring gull-wing doors. Unfortunately not enough units were sold to make the company a going concern and DMC collapsed in 1982, taking with it 2,500 jobs. The DeLorean DMC-12 was back in the public eye in 1985 when Doc Brown built his into a time machine with the benefit of his flux capacitor in the *Back to the Future* film trilogy.

Douglas – Founded by brothers William and Edward Douglas in Kingswood, Bristol, the firm began manufacturing motorcycles, mainly flat-twins, in 1907 and supplied the British army during World War I. Its most popular models were the Endeavour, produced in 1934, and the Drangonfly, its last model from 1955. The firm had success producing models for dirt track racing and also gained victories in TT racing. The company was bought by The Westinghouse Brake and Signal Company Ltd and production of motorcycles ended in 1957.

Excelsior – It began manufacturing motorcycles in 1896, making Excelsior possibly Britain's first motorcycle maker. Originally based in Coventry, the firm moved to Birmingham in 1921. Known as Bayliss, Thomas and Co, the company changed its name to Excelsior in 1910. It was taken over by R Walker & Sons in 1919, which led to the move to Tyseley, Birmingham. Excelsior specialized in small-capacity machines and won success in 1933 IOM TT with the 250cc Mechanical Marvel. The Marvel was replaced by the Excelsior Manxman in 1935. During World War II the company manufactured a single-seat motorcycle known as the Welbike devised for use by Special Operations Executive (SOE). A 98cc Villiers two stroke was mounted horizontally and the seat and handlebars folded into an airdrop container. In the end, it was not much used by the SOE, and some were used by paratroopers at Arnhem during Operation Market Garden. Later models included 250 cc Viking and Talisman but production ceased in the early 1960s.

Ford of Britain – The first Ford factory outside the United States was opened in Trafford Park, Manchester in 1911 in order to build the Model T and by the end of 1913 Ford was Britain's largest motor manufacturer. The first moving assembly line was installed in 1914 and during World War I Model T ambulances and service vehicles were produced. The peak year of Model T output was 1920 and it continued in production until August 1927. Production of the Model A began in Manchester in 1928 but production was transferred to a new plant beside the Thames at Dagenham in 1931. Poor sales of the Model A in the UK led to the development of the first Ford designed specifically for the British motorist – the Model Y, which was priced at an all-time low £100. The Model Y was later revamped into the Ford Popular and Ford Anglia. The Ford 7Y replaced the Model Y in 1937 and a slight facelift saw it become the Ford Anglia in 1939 – which went through four versions whilst the name remained in production until the late 1960s. A similar lifecycle was enjoyed by the similar Ford Prefect which was produced from 1939 to 1961. The third budget car in the range was the Ford Popular. The three models in the Ford Zephyr range – the Ford Consul, The Ford Zephyr and the Ford Zephyr Zodiac – appeared in the early 1950s, with the last two being in production until the early 1970s. The Zodiac was the top of the range and boasted some "American" type styling including whitewall tyres. The Consul Classic was introduced in 1961 and was soon joined by the Ford Capri, Ford Corsair and the top-selling mid-sized Ford Cortina which was sold in five distinct series until 1982. Ford opened a new production plant in Halewood, Liverpool in 1963 to build the small family Anglia 105E saloon. The Ford Corsair, Ford Escort and Ford Orion were all built at Halewood before the plant was turned over to produce Jaguar models in the early 2000s. Ford of Britain was merged with Ford Germany in 1967 to form Ford of Europe. In 1968 the first new model rolled-out in England for the new company was the Ford Escort, which was the Ford Anglia replacement and this was followed by the Ford Capri sporting coupe in 1969. The Zephyr/Zodiac was replaced by the Ford Granada in 1972 which was manufactured at Dagenham until 1976 when production was switched to Germany. In 1982 the company replaced the Ford Cortina as the popular "sales fleet" car with the Ford Sierra, produced at Dagenham until 1993. The Ford Fiesta was also manufactured at Dagenham, although the chief production plant for the model was in Spain. It was decided not to re-tool the plant for the new version of the Fiesta in 2002 and the plant became dedicated solely to Ford engine manufacture.

Francis-Barnett – Founded in Coventry in 1919 by Gordon Francis and Arthur Barnett, the company specialised in lightweight Villiers powered roadsters. Its best known machine was possibly the Cruiser which was produced in 1933 and featured some weatherproofing fairings and guards. The company's attempt at a more luxurious model, the Pullman 10, proved a failure. Apart from these two models, Francis-Barnett had a tradition of naming its machines after birds – Merlin, Kestrel and Falcon lines being produced. The company was taken over by Associated Motor Cycles in 1947 and later combined with James, eventually closing for business in 1966.

Greeves – Originally set-up by Bert Greeves to produce invalid carriages and known as Invacar, from 1952 it began producing motorcycles mainly for the trials and off-road market, including the 20T. Road bikes included the Fleetwing - initially with a British Anzani engine and later a Villiers engine - and the later Fleetmaster, Sports Twin and Sports Single, Sportsman and Silverstone. By the 1960s the firm had developed its own engines and gearbox. The scramblers achieved considerable success over the years, with models such as the Hawkstone (1950s), and the Moto-Cross and Challenger (1960s). More success was achieved in Trials with the Scottish model and in 1967 the Anglian was introduced. The original company closed in the early 1970s but a new Greeves company was begun in the early 2000s concentrating on trials machines, including a new version of the Anglian.

Hesketh – Begun in the early 1980s by Lord Hesketh in a very short-lived attempt to revive the British motorcycle industry, the first model produced was the V-twin V1000 in 1982. Due mainly to technical problems and unreliability fewer than 150 were sold

before the firm was forced into receivership. An adaptation known as the Vampire was produced, primarily for the export market, but again failed to grab the public's attention with the result that the company closed.

Hillman – Founded by William Hillman as a bicycle maker in Coventry. Hillman's designer for the first car produced in 1907 was Louis Coatalen and the car was the 24hp Hillman-Coatalen. Coatalen then left to join Singer. In 1913 the firm introduced the Hillman 9hp, which was its most popular to date. The Hillman 11 was produced from 1915 until 1926 when the Hillman 14 was introduced into the model range. By this point the day-to-day running of the firm was in the hands of John Black and Spencer Wilks. In 1928 Hillman was taken over by Humber and then by the Rootes Group in 1931. The Hillman Minx, versions of which remained in production until 1966, was introduced in 1932. A larger version, the Hillman Super Minx, was in production from 1961 to 1965 and a small estate version known as the Husky was manufactured in the 1950s. The Hillman Imp was produced at Linwood in Scotland from 1963 until 1976. The Rootes company was acquired by Chrysler in the 1967. A new Hillman model, the Hunter (1966-1979), was introduced and joined by the Hillman Avenger in 1970 but was rebadged as a Chrysler in 1976. The rights to the Hillman marque are now owned by Peugeot which acquired Chrysler Europe in 1979.

Humber – Founded by Thomas Humber in 1868 in Sheffield as a bicycle maker. By 1889 the company had factories in Nottingham, Beeston, Wolverhampton and Coventry. The Beeston built Voiturette, designed by Louis Coatelan, appeared in 1901. The Humberette was introduced in 1903 and car production moved completely to Coventry in 1908 when the Beeston factory closed. By this time Louis Coatelan had moved on to Hillman. A new air-cooled 8hp v-twin version of the Humberette appeared in 1913. During the 1920s the model range included the successful Humber 9/20hp, Humber 14/40hp and Humber 20/55hp models. The Great Depression, as with many British motor companies, saw the firm in difficulties which led to the merger with Hillman and then the swallowing of both companies by the Rootes Group in the early 1930s. A revised model range saw the introduction of the Humber 16/50hp and the Humber Snipe. Other models produced in the 1930s included the Humber Pullman, Humber 12, Humber 16, Humber Imperial and the Humber Super Snipe. The Pullman was produced until 1954 and the Imperial until 1967. The Super Snipe, which was produced from 1938 to 1967 is possibly best known as providing Field Marshall Montgomery with staff cars nicknamed "Old Faithful" and "Victory". During World War II the firm manufactured the Humber Command Car and the Humber Scout Car and later developed an armoured personnel carrier which was used by the British Army until the 1970s. Post-war models included the Humber Hawk (1945-1967). The company was acquired by Chrysler in 1964 and the last model issued under the Humber name was the Humber Sceptre, which remained in production until 1976.

Invicta – Founded in 1925 by former racing driver Albert Noel Campbell Macklin, who had previously attempted car manufacture with Eric-Campbell and the Silver Hawk. Financed by Oliver Lyle of Tate & Lyle, the first model was 2.5 Litre with a Meadows engine and this was joined in the late 1920s by 3 Litre and 4.5 Litre machines with Macklin's aim being to marry the luxury of Rolls-Royce with the performance of Bentley. Unfortunately the financial crisis of the period hit the firm hard and, despite wins in rallies and trials, the company had ceased production by the mid-1930s. The marquee was revived in the immediate post-War period with the production of the Black Prince by W G Watson, who had worked on the original cars. It was in production from 1946 to 1950. Yet another new Invicta, the S1, powered by a Ford V8, has been in production since 2004 by the Invicta Car Company based in Chippenham, Wiltshire.

Jaguar – Jaguar was founded in Blackpool by William Lyons in the 1920s, although it was originally known as the Swallow

Sidecar Company. An early model was a remodelled Austin 7 which was followed by "SS" sports cars and the company changed its name to SS Cars in 1934. However, given the unfortunate connotation of those initials during the 1930s and 1940s by the end of World War II the company name was changed again, this time to Jaguar Cars Ltd. The production line had also been moved from Blackpool to Coventry. The 2.5 Litre SS Jaguar saloon powered by a 20hp Standard engine appeared in 1935 together with the sporty SS 90 – with a top speed of 90mph - and SS 100. A 1.5 Litre and a 3.5 Litre were also added to the range in the late 1930s. The 1948 Earl's Court Motor Show saw the introduction of both the Jaguar Mark V saloon and the highly successful and very stylish XK120 sports car which featured the Jaguar twin-camshaft straight-six XK engine and a top speed of 120mph. The XK120 was produced from 1948 until 1954 and was succeeded by the XK140 and XK150 during the rest of the 1950s. Saloon models produced at the same time were the large Mark VII, Mark VIII and Mark IX, and the smaller Mark I (not an official model name) and Mark II (as driven on TV by Inspector Morse), with both saloons and sports cars fulfilling the sales slogan of "Space, Pace and Grace". The racing versions of the sports cars, the C Type (Competition Type) and D Type had considerable success, with a Jaguar XK-120C winning Le Mans in 1951, a C Type winning in 1953 and a D Type victorious from 1955 to 1957. 1961 saw the appearance of the sleek and iconic Jaguar E Type, described by an American journalist back in those non-PC days as "the greatest crumpet-catcher known to man". The E Type went through many versions before it was withdrawn in 1974. The company introduced the Jaguar XJ6 luxury saloon in 1968 which featured power assisted steering and twin fuel tanks and in 1972 it was joined by the XJ12 which was powered by a 5.3 Litre V12 engine. The XJ6 went through to further updates (Series II and III) until 1986, when it was replaced by the XJ40 and in 1995 it was restyled, to be followed by the XJ8 and the latest XJ in 2009. The replacement for the E-Type was the XJ-S (1975-1996) and the current sports car or Grand Tourer models in the range, including convertibles, are designated XK, with a second generation version introduced in 2007. In 1960 Jaguar acquired Daimler and in the 1960s merged with the British Motor Corporation (BMC) to form British Motor Holdings (BMH) and later the British Leyland Motor Corporation and in 1975 British Leyland. In 1984 Jaguar was floated as a separate company but was bought by Ford in 1989 and in 1999 it became, along with at that time Aston Martin and later Land Rover, part of Ford's Premier Automotive Group. Ford sold both Jaguar and Land Rover to Tata Motors of India in 2008. In 1999 Ford bought Stewart GP and rebranded it as Jaguar Racing from the 2000 GP season. The team was sold to Red Bull Racing at the end of the 2004 GP season.

James – Founded by Harry James, this Birmingham based cycle company branched out into motorcycle production in 1902 with the Model B. The company began making two-strokes in 1913 and during the 1920s and 1930s produced a variety of Villiers and James powered machines. During World War II they produced the ML (Military Lightweight) motorcycle which was designed to be dropped from aircraft to add to troop mobility after operations such as the D-Day Landings. In the immediate post-war period the company was hampered by supply problems and only produced an adaptation of the ML and the 98cc Autocycle. The company was bought by AMC (Associated Motor Cycles – see also Matchless) in the early 1950s but continued to produce models such as the Comet, Captain, Commodore and also a scooter. Production ceased in 1966.

JAP – The initials J.A.P. stand for John Alfred Prestwich, a precision engineering firm based in Tottenham, London. JAP produced its own motorcycles for a short time between 1904 and 1908 but then concentrated on supplying its engines to many other British marques, including Brough Superior and Royal Enfield. In the 1930s JAP began designing speedway bike frames and the design – powered by JAP and later Villiers badged engines - dominated the sport in Britain until the late 1950s. The company was taken over by Villiers in the 1940s and disappeared as a name in the 1960s.

Jensen – The company was founded in the 1934 by brothers Alan and Richard Jensen, who took over the business of W J Smith & Sons in West Bromwich. Having completed a commission from Clark Gable to provide bodywork for a Ford V8 chassis, the firm completed a deal with Ford to produce similar Jensen-Fords. The first all Jensen model was the open tourer White Lady which appeared in 1936. At the same time the Jensens were providing commercial vehicle bodywork and they produced their first lorry in 1939 – the JNSN. After spending World War II adapting military vehicles and tanks, the company introduced the PW luxury saloon and then concluded a deal with Austin for the supply of Sheerline engines. The original Jensen Interceptor was introduced in 1950 and produced until 1957 and was then the fibre-glass bodied Jensen 541. The innovative four-wheel drive FF (Ferguson Formula) version of the CV-8 was included in the model range from 1966 to 1971. The most famous Jensen, the Interceptor with its Italian styled bodywork and glass domed tailgate was produced from 1966 until 1976 and bore no relation to the previous model of that name. A lucrative agreement with Austin to supply Austin Healey 100 bodies ended in the late 1960s and was replaced by the commercially unsuccessful Jensen-Healey, which was produced from 1972 until 1975. However, the company's financial difficulties meant that in 1976 it was sold to a holding company – Britcar Holdings – and production ceased. Various attempts to revive the Interceptor were usually short-lived although the production of a completely new Jensen – the S-V8 – took place between 1998 and 2002 by Creative Design Limited.

Jowett – The Jowett Motor Manufacturing Company was founded in Bradford by brothers Benjamin and William Jowett and began making cars in 1906, going into full production in 1910 with a 6.48hp two-seater model. A 7hp "Short Two" was introduced in 1919 and the ruggedness of the model was shown when two Jowett's pulling trailers crossed Africa from the West Coast to the Red Sea in 1926 in less than two months. The 7hp "Long" Kestrel saloon was produced between 1930 and 1936 and to this was added the Jowett Ten (10hp) and the Jowett Eight by the end of the 1930s. The company changed its image after World War II when it introduced the aerodynamically styled Jowett Javelin which also featured torsion-bar suspension and rack-and-pinion steering. As well as being a family car it also managed a class win in the 1949 Monte Carlo Rally. The other new model was the Jowett Jupiter, a sports car built from 1950 to 1954 and powered by a Jowett 1486cc flat four pushrod engine. The Jupiter gained class victories at Le Mans in 1950, 1951 and 1952, the final win with a Jupiter R1. Unfortunately the Javelin proved unreliable in the long-term and the company began to run into difficulties which led to the cessation of production in 1954.

Lagonda – The company was founded by former opera singer Wilbur Gunn and he named it after a river near his home town of Springfield, Ohio in the United States. The firm progressed from making motorcycles, through three-wheelers and onto making cars by 1907. An early model won a reliability trial from Moscow to St Petersburg in 1910 and boosted exports to Russia in the pre-war period. Models in 1913 included a 6 cylinder 30hp machine and a lighter car known as the 11.1. After World War I the 11.1 continued to be produced alongside a longer wheel-based 1420cc 11.9. Wilbur Gunn died in 1920. The 12/24 appeared in the early 1920s and the sporty 4 Litre 14/60 was produced from 1925 along with the 2 Litre Speed. The Lagonda 16/80 featured a 2 Litre 6-cylinder Crossley engine when it appeared in 1932 and it was joined during the early 1930s by the Lagonda M45R Rapide, the Rapier and a 3.5 Litre model. Unfortunately the company had overstretched itself and went into Receivership in 1935. It was bought by Alan Good, who scrapped all the existing models in favour of the new LG45, utilizing the M45 Rapide engine and designed by W O Bentley, the company's new chief designer. Other new models were the LG6 and the V12, both introduced in 1938. The V12, also designed by Bentley is possibly the most admired of all the Lagonda models, although the then Transport Minister is said to have been affronted by the resemblance of the car's horn fairings to parts of female anatomy when he saw the car on display at the 1937 Earl's Court Motor Show. The Lagonda 2.6

Litre was in development during World War II but was not introduced until 1948 by which time Lagonda and Aston Martin had been bought and merged by David Brown. The production line was transferred from the original Staines site founded by Gunn to Feltham. W O Bentley left the firm at the same time. The 2.6 Litre was replaced by a Lagonda 3 Litre in 1953, in two-door, four-door and convertible models. In 1955 all production moved from Feltham to Newport Pagnell in Buckinghamshire. The only "Lagonda" produced in the 1960s was the 4 Litre Rapide, but this was virtually an Aston Martin DB4. A V8 Lagonda was produced in 1974 but only seven were made. Then in 1976 the Aston Martin Lagonda appeared, and proved popular amongst the wealthier members of society, with a production run of over 600 by 1990. Since 1990 many four-door Aston Martin models have been badged as Lagonda.

Lanchester – Founded in Birmingham in the 1890s by aviation pioneer and scientist Frederick William Lanchester, the company may, in 1895, have produced the first British four-wheeled petrol driven motor car, although the firm did not go into production for the public until 1900 with the Lanchester Ten. Frederick's brothers George and Frank were involved in the company. Having built the car from "first principles" it featured a single-cylinder air-cooled engine and a lever or tiller rather than a steering wheel. A twin-cylinder engine was fitted in 1897 and by 1904 a four-cylinder 20hp model (Lanchester Twenty) was introduced with again a novel design with the engine and gearbox mounted between the front seats, being mid-engined with practically no bonnet but plenty of space for passengers, especially in the back seats. Lanchester's were noted for these innovations and differences from the more "standardised" machines of their competitors. However, "different" doesn't always sell and by 1908 a steering wheel was introduced as an option together with more conventional pedals and gear lever. A 6hp machine was introduced in 1906 and by 1911 the range was updated and renamed to the Lanchester 25hp and Lanchester 38hp. The chassis of the latter was then used as the basis for an armoured car during World War I. Frederick left the company in 1913 and in the post-war years and the 1920s, with George Lanchester as chief engineer and designer, the model range took on a more conventional "long-bonnet" appearance and included the 40hp (Lanchester Forty), the smaller 21hp (Lanchester Twenty-One), which became the Lanchester Twenty-Three in 1926, and later the straight eight 30hp (Lanchester Thirty). As with so many other British marques, the Depression curtailed the company's ability to sell its models, especially those at the more luxury end of the market, and in 1931 the firm was bought by BSA and merged with Daimler. Production was moved to Coventry. During the 1930s a new model, the Eighteen, appeared together with the Ten, which was a version of the BSA 10. The last pre-war model was the Lanchester Fourteen Roadrider, introduced in 1937. After World War II the only non-Daimler/BSA equivalent model produced was the LD10, which ran from 1946 until 1951 and by the mid-1950s the Lanchester had disappeared as a separately badged marque.

Land Rover and Range Rover – The first Land Rover was based on the successful Willy's Jeep which had been a ubiquitous all-terrain vehicle during World War II. The Land Rover was designed by the Wilkes Brothers, Maurice and Spencer, in 1947 and was manufactured by the Rover Company. Post-war shortages of steel led to the bodywork being made from an alloy of 93% aluminium – in plentiful supply from aircraft manufacture – and 7% magnesium, known as Birmabright. For its first production run the Series 1 was only available in Avro Green colour in order to take advantage of more war surplus. With its reputation for ruggedness, ease of maintenance – they were designed to be field-serviced - and general longevity the Land Rover proved popular with the military – the British Army use the 300TDi version – and in the Developing World, with more than 50% of all Series I vehicles being for export. Series II was introduced in 1958 to be followed by Series III in 1971. In the intervening period Rover had become part of Leyland Motors Ltd (later British Leyland). Land Rover Ltd was formed in 1978 as a separate subsidiary of British Leyland. The Land Rover 90 and 110 were introduced in 1983 to replace the Series I to III and were in 1990 re-designated as Land Rover Defender after the Land Rover Discovery was brought into the model range in 1989. The current Land Rover models are therefore the Defender, the Discovery 4 (fourth generation of the model), and the Freelander 2, which was introduced in 1997 and a new model produced from 2006. The Range Rover was introduced in a basic utility vehicle form in 1970, with vinyl seats and a plastic dashboard for ease of cleaning but the model was later "upgraded" with power-steering, carpets, leather seats and wooden trim. Originally only two-door, a four-door model was introduced in 1981, with the two-door model discontinued in 1984. The original Range Rover was re-designated as the Range Rover Classic when the second generation model was introduced in 1994 and was finally discontinued in 1996. The third generation and increasingly up-market Range Rover was added to the model range in 2002. Meanwhile the Land Rover company had gone through a few ownership changes. In 1994 the Rover Group was taken over by BMW and then in 2000 the Rover Group was broken up and BMW sold Land Rover to Ford. In 2008 Ford sold Land Rover (and Jaguar) to Tata Motors of India.

London Taxi – the iconic London taxi – the "black cab" – has been through various versions and manufacturers over the many years since the original (horse drawn) Hackney Carriage, when, in 1834 (for Hansom Cabs), rules stated that there should be enough rear headroom to accommodate a gentleman wearing a top hat. Alongside models produced by Beardsmore – originally from Glasgow – the major manufacturer of cabs was Austin who began producing them in the late 1920s in conjunction with Mann and Overton. The models came with various body shells, including the "low loader" introduced in 1934. In 1948 the Austin FX3 was produced, a three door model with a luggage space next to the driver. This became the first of the iconic "black cab" designs. The FX3 was replaced in 1958 by the four-door Austin FX4. It was built in conjunction with Mann and Overton and Carbodies, most usually with a diesel engine and automatic transmission. The chassis production was moved from Longbridge initially to Adderley Par and then in 1971 to Carbodies in Coventry, who eventually bought the production rights from Austin in 1982 In 1989 it was fitted with a Nissan TD27 diesel engine and renamed the Fairway LT1. London Taxis International (LTI) was formed in 1984 by Manganese Bronze Ltd, the owner of both Carbodies and Mann and Overton. In 1997 LTI introduced the TX1 as the replacement for the ancient FX4. This was itself superseded by the LTII in 2002 and the TX4 in 2007. A majority share of Manganese Bronze Ltd was bought by Geely Automobile Holdings Ltd of China in 2007, with manufacture moved to Shanghai and from 2010 knock-down TX4 kits being re-exported to Britain for assembly.

Lotus – Lotus was founded as the Lotus Engineering Company by Anthony Colin Bruce Chapman (always known as Colin) in 1952 with the help of a loan of £50 from his girlfriend. He had already built 2 trials cars and 1 circuit racer (later renamed the Mark 1, 2 and 3 Lotus). The firm's first production car, built in Hornsey, was the Mark 6 Lotus,, a racer. In 1954 Team Lotus was formed and immediately found success with the Mark 8 Lotus. The Mark 9 and Mark 10 models also appeared in 1955 and were followed by the Lotus Eleven (the first of the more "traditional" Lotus naming pattern) in 1956, which went on to track success including class wins at Le Mans. The Lotus Seven sports car appeared in 1957 and was in production until 1973 (see Caterham above). The Lotus (Type 14) Elite was launched at the 1957 London Motor Show and featured glass-fibre monocoque bodywork. In 1957 the Lotus 12 was Colin Chapman's first foray into single-seater racing and was followed by the similarly front-engined Lotus 16. In 1959 the factory was moved from Hornsey to Cheshunt. Chapman produced the mid-engined Lotus 18 in

1960 and this proved a breakthrough for Team Lotus as Stirling Moss (driving for the Rob Walker Racing Team) gained a victory at Monaco, repeating the feat in 1961. The next generation Type 21 gave Team Lotus a first win of its own when it was driven to victory at Watkins Glen in 1961 by Innes Ireland. The Type 25 with its revolutionary fully stressed monocoque chassis design was driven Jim Clark to four wins in the 1962 F1 World Championship season and in 1963 Clark won seven grand prix to win not only the driver's championship for himself but also the International Cup for F1 Manufacturers for Team Lotus. This feat was repeated in 1965 with Clark driving the Lotus Type 33 and in the same year he won the Indianapolis 500 driving a Lotus Ford. In the road-going market the Lotus Elite was replaced by the successful Lotus Elan in 1962. The Elan featured a steel backbone and a glass-fibre bodyshell, together with pop-up headlights. The longer wheelbase Elan +2 was introduced in 1967 and was produced until 1975. The Elan went out of production in 1973. Production moved to Hethel in Norfolk in 1966 and the two-door mid-engined GT coupe Lotus Europa was produced there until 1975. On the track 1968 was a very mixed year for Team Lotus with Jim Clark being killed driving a Lotus 48 whilst Graham Hill won the F1 World Championship driving the Lotus 49 and gave the team another Constructor's title. Team Lotus went on to win 3 more driver's championships - 1970 (Jochen Rindt – killed at Monza during the season), 1972 (Emerson Fittipaldi) and 1978 (Mario Andretti) – plus an additional constructer's title in 1973. In road car manufacture, the Lotus Elan Sprint was introduced in 1970 followed by the company's first four-seater, the Lotus 2+2 Elite in 1974. In 1975 the Lotus Europa was replaced by the wedge-shaped Lotus Esprit, styled by designer Giorgetto Giugiaro, most famous for being driven underwater by James Bond in "The Spy Who Loved Me". The Lotus Eclat, introduced alongside the Esprit at the 1975 Paris Motor Show, was essentially a fastback Elite. The Lotus Esprit Turbo was launched in 1980 and the Esprit itself was being constantly updated, including re-designs in 1987 and 1993. It went out of production in 2003 with a new Lotus Esprit model slated to appear in 2013. The Lotus Eclat was replaced by the Lotus 2+2 Excel in 1982 but that year also saw the death of Colin Chapman at the age of 54. In 1986 General Motors acquired a 100% share of Group Lotus plc., and a new front-wheel drive model Lotus Elan was launched at the London Motorfair in 1989 thanks to new investment. In 1993, GM sold the company to ACBN. Holdings S.A. of Luxembourg, a company controlled by Italian businessman Romano Artioli, who also owned Bugatti Automobili SpA. Team Lotus withdrew from F1 at the end of the 1994 season. The highly successful Lotus Elise (named after Atioli's granddaughter) was introduced in 1995 and produced from 1996. An 80% majority shareholding was acquired Malaysian car company Perusahaan Otomobil Nasional Bhd (Proton) and this became 100% in 2002. In 2000 Lotus launched the Exige, styled on the sport version of the Elise and the Series 2 Exige appeared in 2004. The Lotus Evora, a mid-engined 2+2 was unveiled in 2008, The current Lotus road model range is the Lotus Elise, the Lotus Exige, the Lotus Exige S, and the Lotus Evora. A Malaysian based Lotus team returned to F1 as Lotus Racing in 2010 (rebranded as Team Lotus in 2011 and then changed to Caterham F1 Team at the end of 2011) and Lotus Cars took a stake in the Renault F1 team in 2011, becoming Lotus Renault GP for the 2012 season.

Marcos – Founded in 1959 in Luton, Bedfordshire by Jem Marsh and Frank Costin, who constructed the name from the first letters of their surnames. The first Marcos cars sported gullwing doors and used a wood laminated body and chassis, resulting in a light weight combined with 1 or 1.5 Litre Ford engines. Frank Costin left the company in 1961 and the design task was handed to Dennis and Peter Adams. In 1963 the company moved to Bradford on Avon in Wiltshire. The Marcos 1800 GT was unveiled at the Earl's Court Motor Show of 1963 and proved an instant hit with its long bonnet and short tail. The wooden chassis was replaced with one made of steel in 1969. The Mini Marcos, which had a fibreglass shell and mini components appeared in 1966. It proved a good seller for the firm and also fared well in races, with a Mini Marcos being the only British car to finish at Le Mans in 1966. The company moved production to Westbury

but after the failure of the four-seater Marcos Mantis in 1970 and unsold export stock the company fell into financial problems and went into liquidation in the early 1970s. Jem Marsh reacquired the rights to the cars and name in 1976. He eventually re-launched the marque with the Marcos V6 Coupe in 1981, which was sold in component form. In the mid-1980s the Marcos Mantula Coupe and the Marcos Mantula Spyder appeared and the Mini Marcos was re-launched in 1991 as the Mark V. A home-build variant of the Mantula, the Martina, was introduced in 1991, using Ford Cortina components. The all-new Marcos Mantara was unveiled at the 1992 NEC Motor Show. The following year the Marcos GT LM (Le Mans) race cars were launched with engine variations resulting in the LM400, LM500 and LM600, and the proved quite successful. A new Marcos Mantis, powered by a Ford V8 engine, appeared in 1996 and a Rover V8 engined version with a re-styled bodywork known as the Mantaray was introduced in 1998. In the early 2000s the race car production moved to Eurotech in Holland and in 2001 the road car operation in Westbury went into receivership with the rights, tooling etc. purchased by Marcos Heritage. The new Marcasite TS250, based on the Mantaray, appeared in 2002 to be followed by the TS500 the next year. Production was then moved to Prodrive in Kenilworth, Warwickshire and the Chevrolet V8 powered TSO was announced. The company folded yet again in 2007.

Matchless - the firm was founded in 1899 in Plumstead, London by H H Collier and his sons Charlie and Harry. Charlie won the inaugural IOM TT in 1907 and Harry won in 1909 with Charlie repeating his win in 1910. Matchless made mostly singles, but they also made v-twins and a v-four. In the early 1930s the Silver Arrow and the Silver Hawk were introduced. The firm bought AJS from the Stevens brothers in 1931 to become Associated Motor Cycles (AMC), a firm which would eventually also absorb Norton. During the World War II, Matchless manufactured the G3 and the G3L models, the latter which featured the adoption of the "Teledraulic" front fork for the Allies. The company's best known models were probably the G80, which was produced between 1949 and 1966, and the G12 (Deluxe, CS and CSR models - 1959 to 1966). AMC collapsed in 1967.

McLaren - The company was established as a motor racing team by Bruce McLaren in 1963. Since then the F1 team have won 8 F1 Constructors' Championships (1974, 1984, 1985, 1988, 1989, 1990, 1991, and 1998) and 12 F1 Drivers' Championships (Emerson Fittipaldi (1974), James Hunt (1976), Niki Lauda (1984), Alain Prost (1985, 1986 and 1989), Ayrton Senna (1988, 1990 and 1991), Mika Hakkinen (1998 and 1999), and Lewis Hamilton (2008)). The racing team has also had some success at Indianapolis and in Can-Am sports car racing. The first attempt to be a road car was the McLaren M6GT which was fitted with a Chevrolet V-8 engine producing 400 bhp. A super-car before that term was really applied, Bruce McLaren used the prototype M6GT as his personal road car for 6 months. However, the project was shelved after his untimely death in June 1970. McLaren would not attempt to produce another street-legal car for over twenty years. McLaren Cars was established in 1989 and is now known as McLaren Automotive. The McLaren F1 was designed by Gordon Murray and ex-Lotus stylist Peter Stevens, was launched in Monte Carlo in 1993 and proved to be one of the fastest production cars ever produced. It featured a complete carbon fibre composite monocoque, active aerodynamics and butterfly doors. The seating plan was unique, with the driver in a central position with the driver's seat in the middle, ahead of the fuel tank and the engine, with a passenger seat slightly behind and on either side. It was powered by a BMW V12 engine. Priced at £634,500, only 64 were built between 1993 and 1998. Five F1 LMs (LM for Le Mans) and three F1 GT variants were built. The next roadcar was the Mercedes-Benz SLR McLaren which was produced between 2003 and 2010 at the McLaren Technology Centre in Woking, Surrey, with an intended production run of 3,500. SLR stands for "Sport, Leicht, Rennsport" (sport, light, racing) and the car was made of carbon-fibre composite and powered by a Mercedes-AMG V8 engine. Further variants of the SLR were the 722 Edition, named after the racing number of Stirling Moss's 1955 Mille Miglia winning Mercedes-Benz 300

SLR, the SLR Roadster convertible, and the SLR Stirling Moss. The latest McLaren road car, the MP4-12C, was unveiled in 2010 and is due to go into full production in 2011. Like the McLaren F1, it is wholly designed and built within McLaren Automotive. It is a mid-engined two-seater with a carbon-fibre composite body and is powered by a McLaren M838T 3.8-litre V8 twin-turbo engine.

MG – MG, which stands for Morris Garages, produced the first car in the mid-1920s, a medium saloon with the designation MG 14/28 based on a Morris Oxford chassis and which was in production until 1927. At this point the owner of the company was Cecil Kimber the manager of a Morris cars dealership in Oxford. The MG Car Company was established in 1928 and, with William Morris himself as the main shareholder, the production line was moved to a new location in Abingdon, Oxfordshire in 1929. The first MG Midget (the M Type) was introduced the same year, a sportier version of the Morris Minor. More Midget Types (C, D, J and P) sports cars appeared in the early 1930s and in 1936 the first of the T-Types, the TA, was produced. The TB appeared in 1939 and, after a break for World War II the very popular MG Midget TC was introduced in 1945. In 1935 the company became part of the Nuffield Organisation when Morris himself sold the company to Morris Motors. Cecil Kimber was killed in a rail crash at Kings Cross Station in February 1945. The TC was superseded by the TD in 1950 and then by the very successful TF in 1953. The company then became part of the British Motor Corporation (BMC) from 1952 until 1967, then for a short time part of British Motor Holdings until in 1968 it merged with the Leyland Motor Corporation to become the British Leyland Motor Corporation (British Leyland from 1975). For much of this period MGs, apart from the small sports cars, were merely MG badge-engineered versions of other marques in the group. However, in the sports car range the MGA was released in 1955 to be followed by the larger, more comfortable and more powerful MGB in 1962 and the MGB GT in 1965. A new Midget, based on the Austin-Healey Sprite was introduced in 1961. The MGB GT V8 was launched in 1973 but the Abingdon plant was closed in 1980 and in the following decade MGs such as the MG Metro, MG Maestro and MG Montego were high performance versions of standard Austin-Rover saloons. Ownership passed to BMW in 1994, with the MGF introduced in 1995 and then onto the MG Rover Group in 2000. The early 2000s saw the introduction of sports models based on existing Rover saloons – the MG ZR (Rover 25), the MG ZS (Rover 45) and the MG ZT (Rover 75). In 2005 the rights to the MG brand were bought by the Nanjing Automobile Group. A further merger with the Shanghai Automotive Industry Corporation (SAIC) in 2007 transferred the MG brand and the Longbridge factory to SAIC. The MG TF was manufactured at Longbridge from 2008 to 2010 and new models the MG 6 family saloon and the MG 3 supermini are due to be built at the factory from 2011.

Morgan – Unlike most British car manufacturers the Morgan Motor Company remains in the hands of the family who formed it in 1910. It was founded in Malvern Link by H F S Morgan and the first car produced was the Morgan Runabout, a single seat three-wheeler with a JAP engine. A two-seater version was quickly introduced and sports versions were successful in both speed and reliability trials in the pre-War period. After World War I the range remained much the same until 1932 when the F Series of three-wheelers was introduced which included the F-4, the F-2 and the F-Super. The company's first four-wheeler, the Morgan 4/4 came into production in 1936 and has been in the Morgan model range virtually ever since. A larger and more powerful version of the 4/4, the Morgan Plus 4 (+4) appeared in 1950 and was produced until 1969, then revived in 1985 until 2000, and came back yet again in 2005. A phase II Morgan 4/4 arrived in 1955. The Morgan Plus 8 (+8), powered by a Rover V8 engine, was produced from 1969 until 2004 when it was replaced by the Morgan Roadster. The Morgan Aero 8 was unveiled at the Geneva Motor Show in 2000 and the extravagantly contoured

Morgan AeroMax Coupe was introduced at the same show in 2005. The latest model to join the range, in 2010, is the Morgan Aero Supersports.

Morris – The first Morris car – the two-seater Morris Oxford "Bullnose" (short for "Bulletnose") - was produced in 1913 and was an amalgam of a White and Poppe engine, Sankey wheels and Raworth bodywork. It was built by William Morris, a bicycle manufacturer in Cowley, Oxford. The Oxford was produced until 1926, when it was replaced by a new model with an 1802cc engine. In 1915 it had been joined by the larger 1496cc engined Morris Cowley, which was in production for twenty years. A price cutting policy during the 1920s saw the company gain a major share of the UK market. In 1927 Morris bought Wolseley and used one of that company's 847cc engines to power its new 1928 model – the Morris Minor. This version of the Minor was replaced in 1934 by the best-selling Morris Eight. Morris, Wolseley, Riley and MG were formed into the Nuffield Organisation – William Morris having become Lord Nuffield in 1934. The Morris Ten, along with the Morris Eight was still produced after World War II and then the Ten was replaced by a new Morris Oxford and the Eight was replaced in 1948 by the iconic Morris Minor designed by Alec Issigonis. The new Minor stayed in production until 1971 in various versions including the Morris Minor 1000 and the Morris Traveller and was the first British car to sell over a million units. The Nuffield Organisation merged with its rival Austin in 1952 to form the British Motor Corporation (BMC). In the 1960s a version of the mini was sold as the Morris Mini Minor and further models included the Morris Mini Moke, the Morris 1100 and the Morris 1300. 1968 saw the emergence of the British Leyland from the take-over of BMC by the Leyland Motor Corporation to become the British Leyland Motor Corporation (British Leyland from 1975). The final two models released with the Morris badge were the Morris Marina (1971-1980) and the Morris Ital (1980-1984), the latter being basically a Marina after a facelift.

Noble – Founded in Barwell, Leicestershire by Lee Noble in 1999 with the aim of producing high-speed sports cars. The first model, the two-door, two-seat convertible Noble M10 was replaced by the Noble M12 in 2000. The M12 is powered by a Ford Duratec V6 and variants include the M12 GTO-3R and the track version the M400. Development of the Noble M14 was sidelined in favour of the Noble M15 but this too is yet to appear in production. The company was bought by Peter Dawson in 2006 and Lee Noble left the firm in 2008. The latest model is the Noble M600.

Norton - the Norton factory was established in 1902 by James Landsdowne Norton at Bracebridge Street, Birmingham. Rem Fowler rode a privately entered Norton to win the very first IOM TT in 1907. The Brooklands Special (BS) was the world's first production racing bike and was sold with a certificate confirming it had exceeded 75mph. The first factory success in the TT came in 1924. The development of their overhead camshaft engine made them a dominant marque during the 1930s, taking both the senior and junior TTs in every year bar 2 in the years between 1931 and 1938. The Norton CS1 (CS stands for camshaft) was originally designed for the TT but a replica road bike was also produced from 1928 to 1939. Other models of this period included the Models 18, 19, 20 and 22. The Norton 16H was produced from 1911 until 1954 and it was supplied in very large numbers to the Allies during World War II when it was designated WD16H (WD meaning War Department). The "featherbed" frame on such models as the Norton Manx helped Norton to remain competitive in the immediate post war years. Norton's World riders champions were 350cc Duke 1951 and 1952; 500cc Duke 1951; sidecar Oliver 1949 - 1951 and 1953, Cyril Smith 1952. Norton was World Manufacturers champion: 350cc 1951 and 1952; 500cc 1950, 1951 and 1952; sidecar 1949 – 1953, but withdrew from road racing in 1955. The Dominator Model 7 was produced from 1948 with its featherbed framed replacements including the

Dominator 88 and Dominator 77. The company was taken over by Associated Motorcycles Limited in 1953 (who also owned AJS and Matchless) and production was moved to South London. The company was restructured as Norton Villiers in 1966 and produced the Norton Commando from 1967 (the Mk1 750cc). The company was liquidated in the late 1970s.

OK and OK-Supreme – OK was founded in 1882 as bicycle manufacturers in Birmingham by Ernie Humphries and Charles Dawes. They produced a two-stroke motorcycle using a Precision engine in 1911. In 1926 Humphries left the company and formed a new marque – OK-Supreme. In 1928 riders of OK-Supreme machines swept the board in the IOM Lightweight TT. In 1931 the Lighthouse model appeared, so named because of the little inspection window in the cam tower. Other models included the series known as the Flying Clouds. The factory was turned over to war production in 1939 and no further motorcycles were produced.

Panther – Panther Westwinds was a small production output bespoke luxury car marque founded by Robert Jankel in 1972 with the first model being the roadster Panther J.72 styled on the Jaguar SS100. It was joined by the Panther de Ville in 1974, which like the J.72 very much appealed to people in the film and music industry. The Panther Rio was a Triumph Dolomite finished to "Rolls-Royce standards". The fibre-glass bodied Panther Lima was produced from 1976 to 1982. Unfortunately the company collapsed after only eight years and was acquired by the Korean SsangYong Motor Company who eventually moved production from near the Brooklands circuit in Surrey to Harlow in Essex. The company produced the Panther Kallista, which replaced the Panther Lima and in 1989 announced the mid-engined Panther Solo. All production ceased in 1990.

Reliant – Founded in Tamworth in the early 1930s by T L Williams and began by building the Raleigh Safety Seven three-wheeled van under license. Reliant's own cars appeared in the immediate pre-War period and in 1952 the four-seat Reliant Regal was introduced. By the time the Mark III Regal was released in 1956 it featured completely glass-fibre bodywork, which became standard for Reliant models. The final version of the Reliant Regal was the Reliant Supervan III – as used by Trotters Independent Traders in *Only Fools and Horses*. The successor to the Regal was the Reliant Robin, which was launched in November 1973. It was powered by a 750cc engine which was upgraded in 1975 to an 850cc engine. The Robin was itself replaced by the Reliant Rialto in 1981 but the Robin name was resurrected in 1989 as a hatchback. A new Robin model was produced from 1999 until 2001 when the company manufactured a final 65 high-spec (including leather trim) Special Edition Robins (the Robin 65) as a tribute to 65 years of 3-wheeler production. A short run of Robins were produced under license by B&N Plastics in 2002. Reliant also built what were basically four-wheel versions of the Regal and Robin known as the Reliant Rebel (from 1964 to 1973) and Reliant Kitten (from 1975 to 1982) respectively. The Reliant Fox two-door utility vehicle based on the Reliant Kitten was manufactured in the 1980s. In addition to these quite utilitarian models the company also produced sports cars such as the Reliant Sabre and Reliant Sabre Six in the early 1960s and then the best known, the Reliant Scimitar which was built in various versions from 1964 to 1995. Famously, HRH Princess Anne owned a Reliant Scimitar GTE (Grand Touring Estate). Reliant ceased motor manufacture in 2002.

Rex (Rex-Acme) – Rex was founded by the Williamson brothers in Coventry in 1899. The first motorcycles – singles and twins - were built from 1904 and featured some innovatory features and used both in-house built engines and those supplied by Blackburne. Models included the Light Rex and a 349 cc two stroke and 940 cc V twins. The founders were fired in 1911 and in 1919 an amalgamation with the Acme company led to the company becoming Rex-Acme in 1922. During the 1920s the range of machines included 15 models from 172cc to 746cc capacity. In 1932 the company was taken over by side-car

manufacturers Mills-Fullford and they ceased motorcycle manufacture in 1933.

Riley – Originally begun by William Riley as a bicycle manufacturer in the 1890s in Coventry and its first four-wheeler was a single-cylinder voiturette built by William's young son Percy in 1899. In 1903 Percy and his brothers formed the Riley Engine Company because his father had insisted his company was only to make bicycles. One of Percy's innovations was the mechanically operated inlet valve. The first Riley production car was introduced in 1906 and a more powerful model appeared in 1908. In the late 1920s Percy Riley designed his highly successful Riley Nine with a Riley engine, and it was used as a basis for many variants including the Riley Nine Monaco, and the racer Riley Brooklands. The Nine was replaced with a 1.5 Litre engine in the late 1930s which was used in such models as the Riley Sprite, Riley Lynx, and also for some models of the Kestrel, Falcon, Merlin and Adelphi. Another new engine, a 2½-litre four-cylinder known as the Big Four was also fitted in Kestrel and Adelphi bodies. Financial problems and the unsuccessful Autovia model saw the company swallowed by the Nuffield Organisation in 1938. After World War II the company produced the RM-Series of models including the saloon RMA saloon (later replaced by the RME), the larger RMB (later replaced by the RMF), the RMC roadster and the RMD coupè. All featured a swallow-tail body. The merger of Nuffield and Austin as the British Motor Corporation in the early 1950s saw many Riley models which were merely badge-engineered Austin, Morris or Wolseley models. The 1953 Riley Pathfinder still featured the Big Four but was later sold with a different engine as a Wolseley 6/90. Production of cars carrying the Riley name ceased in 1969 by which time the range included the Riley Elf (a mini and also badged as the Wolseley Hornet) and the Kestrel (an Austin 1100).

Rolls-Royce – Rolls-Royce was formed by a partnership in March 1906 between Manchester based businessman Henry Royce, who had built his first car, the Royce 10, in 1904 and Charles Stewart Rolls, the owner of C S Rolls & Co, a car dealership in Fulham, London specialising in selling cars from overseas. Rolls wanted to distribute an English made car and met with Royce in May 1904. Having road-tested the Royce 10 he decided this was the car he had been looking for. Rolls instructed Royce to produce cars which were comfortable, reliable and elegant and the first models included beautifully engineered two, three, four and six cylinder cars. In 1907 Royce produced the famous six-cylinder 40/50hp Silver Ghost which remained in production until 1925. Following the success of the Silver Ghost Rolls-Royce opened a factory in Derby in 1908. In July 1910 Henry Rolls was killed in an air crash at Hengistbury Airfield, Bournemouth during a flying display, becoming the first Briton to be killed in an aeronautical accident. Shortly afterwards ill-health sent Henry Royce into semi-retirement in Sussex for the next twenty years. The Rolls-Royce 20hp was launched in 1922. The New Phantom (or Phantom I) replaced the Silver Ghost in 1925, to be followed by the Phantom II in 1929 and the V12 powered Phantom III in 1936. Bentley were taken over by Rolls-Royce in 1931 and Henry Royce died in 1933. A new factory was built in Crewe, originally to handle the production of aero-engines during World War II and this became the home of Rolls-Royce Limited in 1946. The first model produced after the war at the Crewe factory was the Rolls-Royce Silver Wraith. This was the last Rolls-Royce model to be delivered in "chassis only" form. This and previous models had been supplied to coachwork builders such as Hooper, Barker and Park Ward. The Rolls-Royce Silver Dawn (1949-1955), originally for export only, was therefore the first model to be offered with a factory built body. The very exclusive Rolls-Royce Phantom IV was supplied only to royalty and heads of state, with only 18 ever made. The Rolls-Royce Silver Cloud was introduced in 1955, with a steel body designed by J P Blatchley and the V8 Phantom V appeared in 1959. The Silver Shadow was produced from 1965 to 1980 and featured a monocoque chassis. The company was nationalised in 1971 and then in 1973 the motor car manufacturing arm of was hived off into Rolls-Royce Motors whilst the aero and marine engine divisions remained in public ownership – they were finally privatised in 1987. The 1970s saw the appearance of the Rolls-Royce Corniche and the Rolls-Royce Camargue, both of which benefitted from coachwork built by Mulliner Park Ward and the latter being designed at Pininfarina making it the first post-War Rolls-Royce not to be designed in-house. Rolls-Royce was bought by Vickers in 1980 the same year that the Silver Spirit was launched, to be joined by the longer wheelbase Silver Spur. The Silver Spirit was the first model to feature a retractable version of the *Spirit of Ecstasy* bonnet ornament. The Silver Spur was replaced by the Silver Seraph in 1998 and was the last Rolls-Royce model to be built at Crewe and, following the acquisition of the company by BMW, Rolls-Royce Motor Cars Ltd became a BMW Group subsidiary. The Silver Seraph (1998-2002) was powered by a 5.4 Litre BMW V12 engine. The assembly plant and HQ was moved to Goodwood, West Sussex. The Rolls-Royce Corniche V (2000-2002) shared some of its styling with the Silver Seraph but was powered by a V8 engine. Three models in the Phantom family have been introduced in the 2000s – the Phantom, was launched in 2003; the convertible Phantom Drophead Coupé (convertible) was introduced in 2007; and the Phantom Coupé joined the family in 2008. The latest model is the Rolls-Royce Ghost.

Rover – The company was originally founded by John Kemp Stanley in the mid-1880s in order to make bicycles. Stanley died in 1901, a few years before the company expanded into motor car production. Early models included the Rover 10/12 and Rover 16/20. Owen Clegg became designer in 1911, and although his stint at the company was short-lived, by 1913 had reduced a plethora of short-run production models to just a single model, the Rover Twelve. This model continued in production after World War I, when it was joined by the small Rover Eight. The Twelve was replaced by the Fourteen in the mid-1920s and the Eight was replaced by the Rover Nine at around the same time. By the end of the 1930s the range of large, solid models included new versions of the Twelve and Fourteen, plus the Rover Ten and Rover Sixteen (known collectively as the P1 – for Project1 - series). P2 included revised versions of the P1 range and the P3 range, introduced in 1948, consisted of the Rover 60 and the Rover 75. The P4 Series of four and six cylinder cars – the Rover 60, 75, 80, 90, 100 and 105 – formed the firm's range of dependable cars designed to be driven by members of the professions throughout the 1950s and into the early 1960s. The more upmarket 3 Litre P5 model was produced from 1958 and the 3.5 Litre Rover P5B powered by a Buick-derived V8 engine arrived in 1967. The final "P" designation was the P6 range – the 2 Litre Rover 2000, the 2.2 Litre Rover 2200 and the 3.5 Litre Rover 3500 – were produced from 1963 until 1976, the Rover 2000 having been the first European Car of the Year in 1964. The company was absorbed into the Leyland Motor Corporation (later British Leyland) in 1967. The Rover SD1 (Specialist Division Number 1 of British Leyland – including both Rover and Triumph) was designed to replace both the Rover P6 range and the Triumph 2000. The models in the SD1 range were the Rover 2000, 2300, 2400, 2600, 3500 and the Rover Vitesse. The Rover 3500 was particularly well received and won the European Car of the Year 1977 award although its sales subsequently suffered through inconsistent build quality. The Austin Rover Group came into being in 1981 effectively to be the mass-market arm of British Leyland and saw the end of the Triumph, Morris, Riley and Wolseley marques. In 1984, as part of a collaboration with Honda, the Rover 200 series was launched. The Rover 200 was effectively a Honda Ballade clone, and the Rover 800 series of executive cars which was introduced in 1986 had the same floor plan as the Honda Legend but continued the SD1 styling. As with the SD1 the series was well received but suffered because of supply problems. The result was that the main model promoted by the company was the Honda V6 powered Rover 825 in preference to the BL M16 powered models, where the engine was in short supply. The Austin Rover Group became the Rover Group in 1986 and two years later it was bought by British Aerospace. However, the rationale behind new Rover models remained virtually unchanged with the Rover 400 being based on the Honda

Concerto saloon and the Rover 600 (1993-1999) evolved around the mechanics of the Honda Accord. By the time BAe sold Rover to BMW in 1994 the range of models included the 200, 400, 600 and 800. The replacement for the 600 and 800 models, the Rover 75 was finally unveiled at the NEC Motor Show in 1998. However, in 2000 BMW sold Rover to Phoenix Venture Holdings (the Phoenix Consortium) who renamed it as MG Rover Group. The overall deal meant that Rover was dismembered, with the mini staying at BMW, Land Rover going to Ford, and Rover (with the Rover 25, 45 and 75 and the MGF models) being taken by Phoenix. However, BMW retained the ownership of the Rover brand and only licensed it to the MG Rover Group. Launched in 1999, the Rover 25 and 45 were face-lifted versions of the Rover 200 and 400 respectively. The MG Rover Group went under in 2005. The Rover brand name then passed to Ford as per an agreement made in 2000 when it bought Land Rover and by 2008 it was owned by Tata Motors of India.

Royal Enfield – Founded as the Eadie Manufacturing Company by Albert Eadie and Robert Walker Smith in Redditch in the early 1890s and became the Enfield Cycling Company in 1897. After building tricycles and quadri-cycles they produced basic motorcycles with Minerva engines in the early 1900s. Pre World War I, Enfield produced a series of V-twins with in-house, JAP and Motosacoche engines and during the war they supplied the British army, including a sidecar version mounted with a Vickers machine-gun. Post-war saw the development of a 976cc V-twin specifically designed for sidecar use. By the late 1920s the road range had adopted saddle tanks and centre-spring forks and included a JAP engine four-stroke. During the 1930s the Bullet and J models included a range of 250cc, 350cc and 500cc four-stroke singles. During World War II Royal Enfield once again produced military machines, including the Flying Flea, a 125cc two-stroke designed to be used by airborne troop after it had been dropped in a parachute fitted tube cage. The 350cc Bullet was also used by dispatch riders. The post –war period saw the introduction of trials and road versions of the 350cc Bullet. Other new models in the 1950s included the Meteors (500cc), Super Meteors (600cc) and Constellations (700cc) twins. Royal Enfield also produced a number of 250cc machines including the popular Crusader series. A variant of the Crusader was the four-stroke single Continental GT, which was introduced in 1966. A 700cc Interceptor was introduced in the early 1960s, mainly for the US market. Royal Enfield was taken over by Norton Villiers in 1967 with the Redditch factory ceasing production and the Bradford-on-Avon factory closing in 1970. However, Enfield machines continue to be made in India by Royal Enfield (India), based in Chennai.

Rudge-Whitworth – With the sales motto "Rudge it, don't trudge it", the company was formed in Coventry by the amalgamation of two bicycle manufacturers and produced its first innovative machines from 1911 onwards. The Rudge Multigear – with a variable gear capable of 21 positions – was introduced in 1912 and in 1914 Cyril Pullin won the Senior IOM TT riding one. The multigear was eventually replaced by a 4-speed gearbox which appeared in the Rudge Four, introduced in the early 1920s. Inn 1928 the firm's sales manager won the Ulster GP, which led to the launch of the Rudge Ulster. Rudge machines won both the Junior and Senior IOM TTs in 1930 and its first 250cc and 350cc road machines were introduced in 1931. In the mid-1930s Rudge was bought by EMI and production was moved to Hayes, Middlesex. The Hayes factory was turned over to making radar equipment in 1939 and the Rudge name was sold to Raleigh.

Scott – Founded by Arthur Scott in Shipley, Yorkshire. The first few machines were produced by Jowett in Bradford before Scott set up his own factory in 1910. He was a pioneer of the two-stroke engine and his early models also featured innovations such as a kick start and a foot change two-speed gearbox. Scott machines won the Senior IOM TT in both 1912 and 1913. After World War I Arthur Scott left the company to develop the three-wheeled Scott Sociable, based on a design for a military machine-gun carrier he had tried to develop during the war. He died in 1923 without returning to the company. The firm's most famous and popular machines appeared in the early 1920s. These were the water cooled two-stroke parallel twin Squirrel (1922) followed by the Super Squirrel (1925), Sports Squirrel and Flying Squirrel (1926). In 1950 the company went into liquidation and the rights to the name were bought by the Birmingham based Aerco Company and in 1956 they began producing what are known as the Birimingham Scotts.

Singer – The company was founded by George Singer in Coventry in 1875 in order to make bicycles. Having built motorcycles from 1901, the firm built its first four-wheeler in 1905 which had a 3 cylinder 1400cc engine and was made under licence from Lea-Francis. A year later an all-Singer designed car was produced. The Singer Ten was introduced in 1911 and continued in production throughout the 1920s, joined later in that decade by the Singer Junior, a light alternative to the rather heavy Ten. The four-door sedan Airstream was introduced in 1934 but was a sales failure. A move into racing with the Singer Le Mans in the mid-1930s proved to be financially risky. The Singer Roadster appeared in 1939 but production was curtailed until the end of World War II. The Hunter was introduced in 1954 as a restyled version of 1948s SM1500 but by this time the company was in difficulties and in 1956 it was bought by Rootes Brothers. After that new models included the Singer Gazelle, which was a variant of the Hillman Minx, and both the Vogue and the Chamois, were also re-modelled Hillmans. The Singer name had disappeared by the 1970s.

Standard – Founded in Coventry in 1903 by Reginald Walter Maudslay. The first car had a single-cylinder engine but by 1906 the 16/20 hp tourer was being produced. In the 1920s the range of tourers was joined by saloons and some models were named after towns such as 'Canley' (the location of the factory) and 'Kenilworth'. During the 1930s the company was known for its competitively priced cars such as the Standard Nine and Standard Ten. In the latter part of the decade the Standard Flying range of semi streamlined cars was introduced and included the Flying Eight, Flying Ten and Flying Twelve. During World War II the company produced an armoured car known as the Beaverette (the name being inspired(!) by Lord Beaverbrook). The Standard Eight and Standard Twelve were revived in the immediate post-War period and the company also bought the Triumph Motor Company in 1945. There was a one-model policy from 1948 to 1953 with the introduction of the 2 Litre Standard Vanguard. It was styled by Walter Belgrove, who had been instructed to look at as many American sedans as possible before arriving at his design for a British car with a distinctive sloped back. This Vanguard Phase I was replaced in 1953 by the more conventionally styled notchback Phase II and in 1955 by the all-new Phase III. There were later variants such as the Sportsman, Ensign, Vanguard Vignale and Vanguard Six. The Standard Eight was revived in 1953, the Standard Ten returned in 1954 and in 1957 the Standard Pennant with prominent tail fins was introduced. The company also produced commercial vans such as the Standard Atlas and the Standard Atlas Major. The Standard-Triumph company was taken over in 1960 by Leyland Motors Ltd. The final Standard cars were produced in 1963.

Sunbeam (cars) – The John Marston firm (see Sunbeam motorcycles below) began making motorcars for sale to the public in the early 1900s including badge-engineered French Berliets. The Sunbeam Motor Car Company was created as a separate entity in 1905 and in 1909 Louis Coatalen joined as chief designer. The new cars were produced using in-house parts rather than out-sourced and Coatalen oversaw the introduction of the Sunbeam 14/20, 16/20 and the 12/16. Sunbeams also gained success in racing in the pre-World War I period. This racing success carried on after the war and Sunbeam cars were also involved in setting speed records. Sunbeam joined with Talbot and Darracq to form Sunbeam-Talbot-Darracq (STD) in 1920. Models introduced in this period include the Sunbeam 14/40 in two-seater or four-seater versions, which replaced the Fourteen, the 20/60, the 12/30 and in 1924 the advanced Sunbeam 3-Litre Super Sports. During the 1920s Sunbeam cars were well-known

for setting land speed records. In 1924 Malcolm Campbell drove his Sunbeam Blue Bird to set the Flying Mile record at Pendine Sands, breaking his own record in 1925. Henry Segrave then set the land speed record in his Sunbeam Tiger (known as "Ladybird") on Southport beach in 1926. Segrave regained his record in 1927 when he drove the Sunbeam aero-engine powered 1000hp Sunbeam Mystery (also known as 'the Slug') at the Daytona Beach Road Course. In the early 1930s models included the Sunbeam Twenty, the Sunbeam Twenty-Five and, the final machine produced at Wolverhampton, the Sunbeam Dawn. Unfortunately by the mid-1930s the company was in severe financial difficulties and in 1934 Sunbeam Motor Cars was purchased by the Rootes Group, which had already picked up Talbot. The Sunbeam and Talbot brands were combined as Sunbeam-Talbot. The Sunbeam-Talbot Ten and the Sunbeam-Talbot Two Litre were produced both pre and post World War II but the Sunbeam-Talbot Three Litre and Sunbeam-Talbot Four Litre (based on the Humber Snipe and Humber Super Snipe) were only produced until 1939. Production was moved to Ryton, Warwickshire in 1946 and the first new Sunbeam-Talbots – the Sunbeam-Talbot 80 and Sunbeam-Talbot 90 – rolled out in 1948. By the time the Mark III of the 90 was introduced in 1954 the Talbot part of the name had been dropped. The Sunbeam Alpine and Sunbeam Rapier were added to the range in the later 1950s, with both becoming successful rally cars, and both were produced well into the 1960s with various upgrades. The sporty Sunbeam Tiger was introduced in 1964 and it was joined by the small Sunbeam Imp Sport (based on the Hillman Imp) and the Sunbeam Stiletto (with a Hillman Imp Californian body-shell). The Sunbeam Rapier and the Sunbeam Rapier Fastback were produced from 1967 until 1976. Chrysler bought into Rootes in the early 1960s and by 1970 the Rootes Group became Chrysler UK. Production was moved to Linwood in Scotland. During the 1970s the Talbot Sunbeam Lotus (see Talbot below) appeared but with the closure of Linwood in 1981 the Sunbeam marque finally disappeared.

Sunbeam (motorcycles) – John Marston founded Sunbeam in the 1860s and began making high-quality bicycles. He rather reluctantly entered motorcycle manufacture as late as 1912 with a 350cc single featuring a fully enclosed drive chain as seen on Sunbeam bicycles. Sunbeam's won the IOM Senior TT in 1920 and 1922. In 1924 the company renamed its models from Model 1 to Model 11 but by 1931 the range was reduced to only four models. In 1937, the Sunbeam motorcycle trademark was sold to Associated Motor Cycles Ltd (AMC), which continued to make motorcycles until 1939 and in 1943 AMC sold the Sunbeam name to BSA. The Redditch built Sunbeam S7, S7 Deluxe and S8 were designed by Erling Poppe. Unfortunately they failed to revive Sunbeam Cycles enough to prevent production ceasing in the mid-1950s.

Talbot – Financed in 1903 by the 20th Earl of Shrewsbury, Charles Chetwynd-Talbot and Adolphe Clement, the original company was intended to sell imported French Clement-Bayard cars. From 1905 the cars were branded Clement-Talbot and the all-British Talbot 16hp model was manufactured in a factory in Kensington. During World War I the company made ambulances and in 1919 it was taken over by the Paris based, but British controlled, Darracq company in 1919 and in 1920 this joint company amalgamated with the Sunbeam company to form Sunbeam-Talbot-Darracq (STD) Motors. The chief designer was Georges Roesch, who had joined Talbot in 1916, and during the early 1920s he worked under the Sunbeam engineer Louis Coatalen. Roesch designed the Talbot 14/45 which made its first appearance in 1926 was later known as the Talbot 105. The 105 was also a successful racer, especially at Brooklands for the Fox & Nicholl team. The 20/70 (or Talbot 70) was introduced at the 1930 London Motor Show. However, STD failed commercially and was taken over by the Rootes Group in 1935. In Britain the Sunbeam and Talbot brands were combined as Sunbeam-Talbot with the Talbot name disappearing in 1955. Rootes was taken over by Chrysler in 1967 and then in 1978 Chrysler Europe was bought by Peugeot, who decided to resurrect the Talbot brand and all Chrysler (and Hillman or Simca badged) products became

Talbots including the Avenger, Alpine, Horizon and Sunbeam. The Talbot Sunbeam Lotus was successful in rally sport in the early 1980s, with Henri Toivonen winning the RAC Rally in 1980. The only completely "new" Talbots produced was the three-door hatchback Talbot Samba and the short-lived executive Talbot Tagora. However, neither of these was manufactured in England. The Talbot brand ceased, at least for the present, in 1992.

Triumph (cars) - Founded by Siegfried Bettmann and Mauritz Schulte, both originally from Nuremberg in 1888 in Coventry to make pedal cycles. The company produced its first motorcycle in 1902 (see below) but it was not until 1923, having acquired the Dawson Car Company, that the first motorcar, the 1.4 Litre Triumph 10/20. The popular Triumph Super 7 appeared in 1928 and was followed in the 1930s by the Triumph Super 8 and Triumph Super 9 by which time the firm was known as the Triumph Motor Company. The sporting Triumph Gloria range using both Coventry Climax and in-house built engines was also introduced in the 1930s and in 1937 this range was joined by the elegant Triumph Dolomite. However, the firm was in financial difficulties and went into receivership in 1939. It was purchased by T W Ward but World War II saw a halt to production and then the destruction of the factory in a bombing raid. The company was then bought by Standard Motor Company in 1945. The first cars built under the new ownership were the elegant Triumph 1800 and 2000 Saloons and Roadsters. The TV detective Bergerac drove a burgundy 1947 Triumph Roadster around Jersey. Also produced were the large Triumph Renown and the smaller Triumph Mayflower saloons both of which had aluminium bodywork because of the post-war shortage of steel. The 2-Litre TR2 sports car made its first appearance in 1952 and was succeeded during the 1950s by the TR3 and TR3A. By the end of the 1950s the Triumph name was considered more saleable than Standard and so the Standard Eight was replaced in 1959 by the Triumph Herald, which featured styling by Giovanni Michelotti. Standard Triumph was bought by Leyland Motors in 1960. The Triumph Vitesse was introduced in 1962 and was a 6-cylinder performance version of the Herald. Michelotti also had a hand in styling other Triumph favourites such as the TR4, the small and sporty Triumph Spitfire, the mid-sized Triumph 2000 and the luxury sport Triumph Stag. More TR models followed in the 1960s – TR4A, TR5 and the most successful of all the range, the TR6 in 1969. The relatively unsuccessful Triumph 1300, 1500 and Triumph Toledo were replaced by the Triumph Dolomite which was launched at the London Motor Show in October 1971. The wedge shaped Triumph TR7 – produced under the Rover Triumph brand - appeared in 1975 and was followed by the similarly designed but more powerful TR8 in 1978, although the majority of this model was exported to North America. The TR7 seems to have been a bit of a poison chalice as it was successively manufactured at BL plants which then closed in the late 1970s and early 1980s - Speke, Liverpool; Canley, Coventry, which also produced the Triumph Dolomite and the Triumph Spitfire 1500; and finally the Solihull plant, which was turned over completely to Land Rover. The final car bearing the Triumph name was the Acclaim, effectively a rebadged Honda Ballade and built at Cowley, Oxford. Production of the Acclaim finished in 1984 when it was replaced by the Rover 200.

Triumph (motorcycles) - Founded by Siegfried Bettmann and Mauritz Schulte, both originally from Nuremberg in 1888 in Coventry to make pedal cycles. Produced its first motorcycle in 1902, with a Minerva engine but by 1905 it had produced a completely in-house model. An early example was the 500cc Model H which was produced from 1914 to 1924 and featured a three-speed gearbox, clutch and kick-starter. They were supplied to the British Army during World War I and gained the nickname of the "Trusty Triumph". During the 1920s the popular 500cc Model P was produced but in 1936 the company was sold to Jack Sangster, the owner of Ariel. He revamped the model range and renamed the 250cc, 350cc and 500cc machines as Tiger 70, 80 and 90. In 1937 the Speed Twin, an all-new parallel-twin 500cc

machine was introduced and proved to be a turning point in Triumph's fortunes. The sporty Tiger 100, the TR5 Trophy and 650cc Thunderbird also proved successful, the latter gaining some notoriety as the model ridden by Marlon Brando in *The Wild One* (1953). After the bombing of Coventry, production had moved to Meriden in 1942 and in 1951 the company was sold to BSA. Lightweight models such as the T15 Terrier and T20 Tiger Cub were produced in the early 1950s. The highly successful Triumph T120 Bonneville was produced in 1959, based on the existing Tiger 110. The Triumph T150 Trident (an equivalent to the BSA Rocket 3) first appeared in 1968 with one particular bike becoming famous - "Slippery Sam", a production class Trident prepared by Les Williams which won consecutive production TT races at the Isle of Man five years running from 1971 through 1975. Later triple models were the Triumph X-75 Hurricane (1972) and the T160 (1975). In 1972 the company was merged with Norton Villiers (itself the remains of Associated Motor Cycles, which had gone bust in 1966) to become Norton Villiers Triumph. The Triumph factory at Meriden closed in 1973 despite a workers sit-in and the company finally went into liquidation in 1983. It was resurrected under John Bloor in 1990 with a new factory at Hinckley and a series of models including the Speed Triple and the Thunderbird Legend TT. In July 2011 Triumph announced it was to rival the Royal Enfield Bullet by launching several models customised for the Indian market.

TVR – The company was founded in Layton, Blackpool as Trevcar Motors in 1947 by Trevor Wilkinson mainly as a repairing and selling operation. TVR Engineering (with its name derived from TreVoR) began with a couple of hand built models. In 1955 an American enthusiast, Ray Saidel, asked TVR Engineering to provide him with a racing chassis and a Coventry Climax engine. The resulting car was known as the Jomar, derived from the names of Saidel's two children (JOanna and MARc). Saidel marketed a Jomar MK2 and a Jomar Coupe in 1959. Meanwhile TVR Engineering had become TVR but a change of financial backing saw another name change to Layton Sports Cars Ltd, at which point Saidel also ditched his dealership and severely squeezed export prospects. In 1959 Grantura Engineering was set up to supply components and body shells, with Layton handling the final assembly and it was at this point that production really began with the TVR Mark I (also known as the Grantura), which featured a body made of GRP (glass fibre-reinforced plastic) and a multi-tubular chassis. The Grantura went through various upgrades and differing engine offerings during the early 1960s with the Grantura (Mark) II, IIa and III in the range, with the Mark III offering a new chassis and body shell. The final variant was the Grantura 1800S in 1966. The TVR Griffith 200 made its first appearance in 1963 and was designed because an American car repair shop owner had unsuccessfully tried fitting a Ford V8 into a Grantura belonging to a client. A new chassis was designed and a car with great performance but not so great reliability emerged. It was superseded by the TVR Griffith 400 in 1964. However, at around this time Trevor Wilkinson left the company and in 1965 Martin Lilley bought what was then called Grantura Engineering, renamed it TVR Engineering and together with his father Arthur ran the company until 1981, turning it into a more structured car manufacturer. Models such as the Tuscan (replacing the Grantura) and the Vixen (replacing the Griffith) were introduced under this new regime during the late 1960s. The M-Series (the M stands for Martin – a seeming trait of this company in general – appeared in the 1970s. The M-Series was launched at the 1971 Motor Show replete with reclining nude models but managed to rise above the tabloid hype to become a respected British sports car range, including the TVR 3000M Turbo – the UKs first production turbo-charged car. Variants such as the hatchback TVR Taimar and the convertible TVR 3000S were introduced from 1976 onwards. A radical redesign saw the angular styling of the wedge-shaped TVR Tasmin (named after a friend of Martin Lilley) introduced in 1980. However, the company was in financial difficulty and was bought by Peter Wheeler in 1981. The Tasmin name was quietly dropped in the

1980s and saw the new model range, still based on "the wedge", powered by the Rover V8. The TVR S-Series was introduced in 1986 with a more rounded design and powered by a Ford Cologne V6. The early 1990s saw the Speed Eight, a new two-seater Griffith and the Chimaera added to the model range. A new in-house TVR engine, the 4.2 Litre AJP was developed by Al Melling, John Ravenscroft and Peter Wheeler and its derivative, the Speed Six, featured in the new models introduced between 1996 and 2004 – TVR Cerbera, TVR Tamora, TVR T350, a new TVR Tuscan, TVR Sagaris and TVR Typhon. In 2004 the company was bought by Nikolai Smolenski, a young Russian entrepreneur and the firm has yet to produce a new model.

Vauxhall – The company was founded in 1857 by Alexander Wilson in Vauxhall, London for the purpose of building pumps and marine engines. The first Vauxhall motorcar appeared in 1903, a tiller-steered model. Production was moved to Luton, Bedfordshire in 1905. The Vauxhall Y-Type was developed into the successful A-Type production model which was made between 1908 and 1914. Another pre-World War I Vauxhall - the C10-Type – was known as the Prince Henry after a 1910 Prince Henry of Prussia Trials Race in which some of the machines competed. The Vauxhall D-Type was based on the C-Type and was supplied to the British military during World War I as a staff car. Production of the sporty 30/98 Vauxhall E-Type spanned the war but by 1925 the now struggling company was bought by General Motors. The American influence could be seen in the Vauxhall Cadet which was unveiled at the 1930 Motor Show and by 1932 it had become the first British car to boast micromesh gears. The 1930s also saw the introduction of the four-door saloon Vauxhall Ten-Four, which featured another innovation in Britain in having unitary construction. It was produced from 1937 until 1946 but unfortunately there was a gap for World War II when the factory was turned over to the production of the Churchill tank. The post war period saw the launch of the six-cylinder Vauxhall Velox, which had a production run which only ended in the mid-1960s, and the four-cylinder Vauxhall Wyvern which shared its body-shell. The Velox was replaced by the Vauxhall Cresta PA, featuring white-wall tyres and tailfins in 1957 and at the same time the Wyvern bowed out in favour of the short-lived Vauxhall Victor. A new manufacturing plant was opened at Ellesmere Port in Cheshire in the early 1960s. Vauxhall introduced its first small family car, the popular Vauxhall Viva, in 1963 and its three versions, the HA, HB and HC stayed in production until 1979. The two-door coupe Vauxhall Firenza was produced from 1970 until 1975. In the smaller car range the Vauxhall Chevette appeared in 1975, initially as a three-door hatchback and later in two, three and four-door saloon versions. It was replaced in 1984 by the Spanish-built Vauxhall Nova. The very successful Vauxhall Cavalier, based on the Opel Ascona and, in its third incarnation, on the Opel Vectra, was produced from 1975 until 1995. The Vauxhall Astra, eventually to become a very popular hot hatchback, was launched in 1980. In 1985 the Mark II version of the Astra, together with its "sister" Opel Kadett, was voted European Car of the Year. General Motors inaugurated GM Europe in 1986. The Vauxhall Vectra replaced the Cavalier in 1995, with the Vectra B being the last model made in Luton before it was closed for car production in 2001, with some production moved to Ellesmere Port. New Vauxhall/Opel models are produced in various countries in Europe – Vauxhall Corsa (Spain); Vauxhall Astra (UK – Ellesmere Port, and elsewhere); Vauxhall Zafira (Germany); Vauxhall Agila (Hungary); Vauxhall Meriva (Spain); Vauxhall Antara (Russia); and the Vauxhall Insignia (Germany). General Motors filed for Chapter 11 bankruptcy in 2009 and Opel and Vauxhall were at that point due to be sold to the Canadian company Magna. However, the deal was called off in November 2009 and the two companies remain part of General Motors.

Velocette - The firm of Veloce Ltd was founded in Hall Green, Birmingham in 1904 by German immigrant Johannes Gutgemann, who subsequently anglicised his name to John Goodman. His sons Percy and Eugene and his grandsons Bertie and Peter were all involved in both testing and racing the firms' machines. The first motorcycle produced in 1905 and a smaller version of the 1911 VMC was produced in 1913 and was called the "Velocette". This name was eventually applied to all the machines produced by the company. The Model K was introduced in 1925, the first Velocette with an in-house designed engine and by the mid-1930s the range included the KSS, the KTT and the KTP. Velocettes had a great deal of success at the IOM TTs of the late 1920s, 1930s and 1940s. The KTT model became the private racers "mount of choice" in the 350cc class. The company had World Riders Champions: 350cc Frith 1949, Foster 1950 and also won World Manufacturers titles: 350cc 1949 and 1950. The bikes had a distinctive black and gold colour scheme and a distinctive fish-tail silencer. During the 1950s the high-performance sports bikes the 500cc Venom and 350cc Viper appeared and led to variants such as the Venom Clubman and the Venom Thruxton (1965). Other more unusual models included the Viceroy, a 250cc scooter, and the 150cc four-stroke, water cooled LE (standing for Little Engine) which was sold to police forces from 1951 and came to be known as the "Noddy bike". Along with many other British manufacturers the firm ran into problems in the late 1960s and the factory was closed on 5 February 1971.

Vincent-HRD – Founded when Philip Vincent bought HRD in 1928, with production in Stevenage, Hertfordshire. In 1928 the first Vincent-HRD motorcycle used a JAP single-cylinder engine in a Vincent-designed cantilever frame. Rudge engines were also used but by 1936 the use of in-house engines was preferred. The 1937 range included the 998cc Vincent Rapide, the first Vincent v-twin, with a frame incorporating an innovative cantilever rear suspension. After World War II the Series B Rapide appeared with a shortened wheel-base and in 1948 the Series C Black Shadow and Black Lightning were introduced. The Black Lightning was advertised as "The World's Fastest Standard Motorcycle" and indeed one was used in 1948 to raise the motorcycle speed record to 150.313 mph on Bonneville Salt Flats and further records were set over the next seven years. The final series of models produced were the Black Knight (an upgraded Rapide) and the Black Prince (an upgraded Shadow). Other models included the single-cylinder Meteor and Comet. The expensive models failed to sell in large enough numbers to save the company from closure in December 1955.

Wolseley – The first Wolseley car was built in 1897 by Herbert Austin who worked for Frederick Wolseley's Wolseley Sheep Shearing Company Ltd. However, this and the next few examples were not production models. The Wolseley Motor Company was founded in 1901 and Austin left shortly after the purchase of the Siddeley Autocar Company and the appointment of John Siddeley (later Baron Kenilworth) as manager of Wolseley-Siddeley. Siddeley resigned in 1910 and the company reverted to the Wolseley Motor Company in 1914. In the early 1920s the firm produced the Wolseley 10 and Wolseley 15 and opened a prestigious show-room next to the Ritz Hotel in London (now the Wolseley Restaurant which opened in 2003). However, financial problems saw the firm collapse under the burden of its debts and in 1927 it was purchased by William Morris. From this point on the Wolseley marquee became a victim of badge-engineering with models based on Morris designs such as the 1930 Wolseley Hornet based on the Morris Minor. Other models in the range included the Wolseley Wasp and the Wolseley 10/40. In 1938 Morris, Wolseley, Riley and MG were formed into the Nuffield Organisation which merged with its rival Austin in 1952 to form the British Motor Corporation (BMC). Production had moved to Cowley in Oxford in 1949. Throughout the 1950s to the 1970s the Wolseley marque shared common bodywork with MG and Riley models such as the Wolseley Hornet - Riley Elf, the Wolseley 15/50 – MG Magnette, and the Wolseley 16/60 – Austin A60. The Wolseley badge finally disappeared in the mid-1970s.

Celebrity Mums and Dads of the Year

The Celebrity Mum and Dad of the Year is voted by members of the public on the website of the sponsoring company. The votes submitted have sometimes topped 30,000.

The award ceremonies usually take place in a London hotel although on occasion the winner has not been available to attend and so has been presented with the trophy at another venue. The Mum of the Year award is presented just before Mother's Day and similarly the Dad of the Year is presented in June, just prior to Father's Day. The original sponsor's of the 'Mums' was Quality Street but when their four-year support ended there have been various sponsors. In 2007 Tesco Magazine began their own version of the award. Stacey Solomon was axed a month before her tenure ended as it was revealed she had been smoking whilst seven months pregnant.

Although there has been continuity in the mum's award since its inauguration in 2002, the men's award has been more sporadic and since its inception in 2003 has not been awarded in 2006, 2008 and 2009.

Celebrity Mums of the Year

2002 Kerry Katona (sponsored by Quality Street)
2003 Melinda Messenger (sponsored by Quality Street)
2004 Ulrika Jonsson (sponsored by Quality Street)
2005 Kerry Katona (sponsored by Quality Street)
2006 Sharon Osbourne (sponsored by Freemans of London)
2007 Katie Price (aka Jordan) (sponsored by Grattan)
    Fiona Phillips (sponsored by Tesco Magazine)
2008 Suzanne Shaw (sponsored by La Redoute)
    Kym Marsh (sponsored by Tesco Magazine)
2009 Kym Marsh (sponsored by Bounty.com)
    Nell McAndrew (sponsored by Tesco Magazine)
2010 Holly Willoughby (sponsored by Bounty.com)
    Tana Ramsay (sponsored by Tesco Magazine)
2011 Stacey Solomon (sponsored by Foxy Bingo.com)
    Sally Dynevor (sponsored by Tesco Magazine)
2012 Gabby Logan (sponsored by Tesco Magazine)
    Katie Price (aka Jordan) (sponsored by Foxy Bingo.com)

Celebrity Dads of the Year

2003 Bryan McFadden (sponsored by Epson)
2004 Jono Coleman and Tommy Walsh (sponsored by Epson)
2005 Anthony Worrall Thompson (sponsored by Epson)
2007 Andrew 'Freddie' Flintoff (sponsored by Virgin Money)
2010 Peter Andre (sponsored by Bounty.com)
2011 Peter Andre (sponsored by Premier Inn)

Comics, Cartoon Strips, and Magazines

Alex Alex is a cartoon strip created by Charles Peattie (artist) and Russell Taylor (writer). It first appeared in the newly-launched *London Daily News* in February 1987 but transferred to *The Independent* after the collapse of the 'News' in July 1987. In 1992 it found its present home at the *Daily Telegraph*. Unlike many cartoon strips it is written in real time, hence, 27-year-old investment banker Alex Masterley married Penny soon after the launch of the strip and had a son, Christopher, two years later. Alex and Penny are now middle-aged and Christopher celebrated his 21st birthday in 2010. Alex's co-worker at the Docklands-based Megabank is Clive Reed, who lives with his girlfriend Bridget. Clive was once favoured by the boss, Rupert Sterling, but has long since fallen from his pedestal having proven to be inferior to the status-obsessed Alex in every aspect of the job. Alex's former employer Mr Hardcastle employs Megabank for a lot of his financial work. He is the stereotypical gruff down-to-earth Northern boss of a manufacturing company. Other recurring characters include Greg Masterley (a reporter and Alex's brother), Vince (a nouveau riche cockney money broker from the dealing floor at Megabank), Faberge (a lapdancer that Clive meets surreptitiously outside work), and Carolyn (Alex's client and mistress of the past four years). The most common format is a four-panel strip involving a conversation between Alex and another character which tends to lead the reader up a certain path only for the final caption to unleash a cunning spin on all that was said previously. On occasion a two-panel format might show a similar scene with the second panel having a subtle change of dialogue to give comic effect. The humour revolving around the yuppie world of high finance, has a distinct topical edge and calls for a high degree of research. Actor Robert Bathurst played Alex in a 2007 play staged at the Arts Theatre, London, and subsequently embarked on an international tour of the play in 2008, beginning in Melbourne and eventually ending back in London.

Andy Capp Andy Capp was created by cartoonist Reg Smythe (1917–1998) and first appeared in the *Daily Mirror* in August 1957, originally as a single-panel cartoon, later expanding to four panels but more recently varying between two and three. Reg based the characters of Andy and his wife Florrie on his working-class parents, his mother actually sharing the name of the strip's heroine. Reg was born and bred in Hartlepool, as was Andy, but there the similarity ends. Andy has never been known to hold down a job and relies on hand-outs from Flo (Andy refers to her as 'pet') to subsidise his hobbies of pigeon-fancying, fishing, the horses, darts and snooker (his trusty cue, Deliilah, known to be the source of a little extra on occasions). Andy also engages in more physical activities from time to time but whether it be football, cricket or rugby, he invariably ends up in a punch up. The Capps live at 37 Durham Street, scene of much of the action, when Flo is not out charring and Andy is not down the pub. Percy Ritson the rent collector also spends a lot of his time at the Capp's residence! Andy has never made any great concession to the PC world although he has given up smoking and prefers to engage in marriage guidance nowadays rather than taking on Flo in one-on-one combat. He still religiously wears his green plaid cap, pulled down over his eyes, on all occasions. Next door neighbours, Chalkie and Ruby White, are long-standing friends and share many of the same values as the Capps although Chalkie has been known to hold down a job at various times. Other recurring characters include Jackie the barman, the vicar, Nancy (Andy's pet whippet), Polly (Flo's sister who is never seen) and Flo's mum, who is also never seen and is referred to as 'missus' by Andy. After Reg Smythe died the strip was initially uncredited but since November 2004 has been ascribed to Roger Mahoney (artist) and Roger Kettle (writer). Attempts at bringing Andy into the three dimensional world have had mixed success. In 1981 a stage musical with songs by Alan Price and Trevor Peacock, starring Tom Courtenay as Andy and Val McLane as Florrie, had a short run at London's Aldwych Theatre, and in 1988 a six-part television drama with James Bolam as the eponymous hero was panned by critics for portraying northern stereotypes. There has also been two loose offshoots of the strip. When the children's comic *Buster* was launched in 1960, Buster was originally billed as Buster, son of Andy Capp. The *Daily Mirror* also runs the *Mandy* comic strip, which was originally called *Mandy Capp* although the exact relationship has never been developed or explained. In June 2007 a 5ft 8in bronze statue of Andy Capp, designed by Shrewsbury sculptor Jane Robbins, was erected in Hartlepool.

Beano *The Beano* is a children's comic, published by Dundee-based publisher D.C. Thomson & Co (founded by David Coupar Thomson in 1905), first appearing on 30 July 1938. Although *The Dandy* was first published in 1937, *The Beano* can be said to be the most prolific British weekly comic, since *The Dandy* became a fortnightly comic between 2007 and 2010 and fell behind *The Beano*'s number of issues. *The Beano* is currently edited by Alan Digby, who also edits the *BeanoMAX*, a monthly version of *The Beano* for older readers. Nick Park guest-edited the 70th anniversary issue dated 2 August 2008. The present strips include Dennis and Gnasher, Billy Whizz, Minnie the Minx, Ball Boy, Calamity James, The Numskulls, Ratz, The Bash Street Kids, Robbie Rebel, Fred's Bed, Ivy the Terrible, Little Plum, The 3 Bears, and Roger the Dodger. **Dennis the Menace** was created by cartoonist David Law (1908-71) and first appeared in issue No 452, dated 17 March 1951, and is the longest-running strip in the comic. Dennis was promoted from the back cover to replace Biffo the Bear as the front cover strip in issue No 1678, dated 14 September 1974, although an additional '60 second Dennis' strip is currently displayed on the back inside cover also. Originally billed as Dennis the Menace 'The World's Naughtiest Boy', Dennis's particular brand of menace is usually unleashed against an unsuspecting public or members of "the softies", Bertie Blenkinsop and Algernon "Spotty" Perkins, but in particular Walter. Justice was formerly seen to be done by the corporal use of a slipper by Dennis's dad but in recent years more ingenious methods have been adopted to ensure Dennis gets his comeuppance. In the 31 August 1968 issue, Dennis found a scruffy looking Abyssinian wire-haired tripe hounddog on the street while on his way to the dog show at the local town hall. Gnasher soon became Dennis's partner in crime and the strip's title was eventually changed to "Dennis the Menace & Gnasher" on 29 July 1970 (now shortened to Dennis and Gnasher). In May 1979 Dennis's pet pig, Rasher, made his first appearance and in 1987 Dennis's spider, Dasher, debuted, although unlike Gnasher and Rasher was never lucky enough to have his own spin-off cartoon strip. Dennis' baby sister, Bea, was born in issue No 2931, dated 19 September 1998. Bea, who has a pet dog named Gnipper, was voted naughtiest baby in Beanotown when she was only a week old. Although Dennis is still kitted out in his trademark red and black hooped jersey and short black trousers his outward disposition has changed over the years from a constant scowling demeanour to a more playful, smiley mien. **Minnie the Minx** was created and originally drawn by Leo Baxendale. She made her debut in issue No 596, dated 19 December 1953. Minnie is a female version of Dennis, right down to the red and black hooped jersey and the propensity towards mayhem. Minnie has a cat called Chester, who is forever taunting bitter rival, Bonzo, a dog from number 12. Other characters in the strip include PC Justin Thyme, Soppy Susan and Fatty Fudge. **Roger the Dodger** was created and originally drawn by Ken Reid. He first appeared in issue 561, dated 18 April 1953. Roger spends his life escaping chores by enacting previously written dodges, referring to them by their number in the respective book. Roger's friends include Crafty Colin and Sneaky Pete and his arch-enemy is a bully named Cruncher Kerr, who owns a dog called Muncher, who is an equally bitter rival to Roger's cat – Dodge Cat. Roger dresses in the

same red and black as Dennis and Minnie, although he sports checks rather than hoops. **The Bash Street Kids** was created by Leo Baxendale under the title When the Bell Rings, and debuted in issue No 604, dated 13 February 1954. It became The Bash Street Kids in 1956, portraying the ten children of Class 2B of Bash Street School, Beanotown, where the teacher and headmaster still wear mortar boards and gowns and pupils sit at wooden desks with inkwells. The children are Daniel 'Danny' Deathshead Morgan, the accredited leader who wears a black and white skull and cross bones sweater and black and red hoped cap; Percival Proudfoot Plugsey, better known as Plug (an aesthetically-challenged over-sized beanpole with protruding top lip and two large front teeth); John 'Smiffy' Smith, a good-natured simpleton with savant tendencies and distinguishable by his yellow jumper; 'Erbert, a bespectacled, slightly overweight boy; Fatty, not as tall as Plug but with much larger girth fashioned by his propensity for food; Sidney, the spikey-haired animal lover who forms part of the 'terrible twins' with his sister, Toots, a tomboy and only girl in the gang; Spotty, a short boy who often wears a long tie. Originally known as Jasper, he is proud of his 976 black spots which seem to adorn mostly his face, his legs being distinguishable by them; Wilfrid, a shy boy distinguishable by his green jersey worn all the way up to his nose. Wilfrid's egg-shaped body appears to be without a neck to speak of, on the rare occasions he has taken off his jersey his vest also stretches to his nose; and Cuthbert Cringeworthy, the brightest child in the class and teacher's pet, therefore on the periphery of being a full gang member. Other characters include, Teacher (his proper name of Algernon is never used), The headmaster (Headward Headington-Hail, alternatively known as Chocilus Bicius), Mrs Teacher, Winston the cat (who is a rather plump black and white mischievous moggy who wears the same hat as the janitor, Techno the science teacher, Olive the school cook, and The Blob Street Kids (schoolchildren from a nearby posh school who individually have a direct nemesis among their less posh rivals). **Billy Whizz** was created by Malcolm Judge and first appeared in issue 1139, dated 16 May 1964, when it replaced The Country Cuzzins. Billed as 'the world's fastest boy', Billy not only runs fast but in fact does everything fast (such as solving billion piece jigsaws in the blink of an eye). Billy's younger brother, Alfie, originally ran faster than Billy but in recent years has been portrayed as a mischievous baby, Billy himself developing from a quite normal-looking boy in red top and black pants into a super-hero-type character with protruding eyes. **Ivy the Terrible** was created by Robert Nixon and first appeared in issue 2233, dated 4 May 1985. Dressed in red boiler suit and yellow undershirt, the tousled pig-tailed Ivy originally aspired to be the toughest Beano character but after Nixon's death in 2002 Trevor Metcalfe took over and gave Ivy a more mischievous imp-like personality. Tony O'Donnell took over the following year and Ivy reverted back to her darker persona. In August 2008, the strip was merged with the strip Bea and renamed Bea and Ivy for a short while but in October 2010, new single page strips of Ivy started appearing in the comic, drawn by Diego Jourdan Pereira. After a change of editor in February 2011, Ivy was dropped for a few months but returned in May of that year. **Little Plum** was created by Leo Baxendale under the working title of Booster, and debuted in issue No 586, dated 10 October 1953. When Leo left The Beano in 1962, Robert Nixon took over the strip for a short time before Ron Spencer became the regular artist. The strip was discontinued in 1986 but reappeared periodically; its last regular spot beginning in issue No 3566, dated 1 January 2001, drawn by Hunt Emerson. The eponymous hero and his friends Chiefy, Pimple and Hole-in-um-Head are members of the "Smellyfoot" American Indian tribe, who spend much of their time clashing with their rivals the "Puttyfoot" tribe. Other characters include Dr Kildeer (the tribal medicine-man), Treaclefoot (Plum's faithful horse) and Pudding Bison (a 'marvelous' creature who eats anything – and also features in spin-off strips Baby Face Finlayson and The Three Bears). **Calamity James** was created by Tom Paterson and first appeared in issue No 2311, dated 1 November 1986, as replacement for Biffo the Bear and Little Plum, which had both been reduced to a half page by this time. Calamity James is billed as 'the world's unluckiest boy' and sports a red shirt with a large No 13 depicted on the front. James has a friendly pet called Alexander Lemming. The strip has many subtle and not so subtle visual jokes. Various themes recur; notably the "Little Squelchy Things" which appear in a wide variety of guises and the oddly named buildings. **The 3 Bears** was created by Leo Baxendale and debuted in issue No 881, dated 6 June 1959. Bob McGrath drew the strip for most of its first run, originally disappearing from the comic after issue 2253, dated 21 September 1985. The strip returned in 1988 and has had periods of discontinuation ever since. It is presently drawn by Mike Pearse. Ma and Pa Bear and their young son Teddy (later called Ted) are lazy and gluttonous, and live in a cave upon a hill. Early storylines revolved around their attempts to steal "grub" from the local storekeeper Hank (who often shot at the Three Bears with his blunderbuss for trying to rob him). More recent stories have featured the mischievous pranks of Teddy and his friends on the local Indian reservation. **Lord Snooty** was created by Dudley D. Watkins and first appeared in issue No 1, dated 30 July 1938. The eponymous character was Lord Marmaduke, Earl of Bunkerton, known to his friends as Snooty. Regular characters included Snooty's guardian Aunt Matilda, mischievous identical twins Snitch and Snatch, the pugilistically-inclined Scrapper Smith, Rosie, a short blonde girl who loves to cook, the greedy, overweight Big Fat Joe, Swanky Lanky Liz, Professor Screwtop the inventor and Thomas, an indecisive boy, whose hair was shaped like a question mark. The bitter rivals of Snooty and Friends were The Gasworks Gang. Although the strip has been long discontinued it did make a re-appearance under the name Lord Snooty the Third for a 2008 edition. **Biffo the Bear** was created by Dudley D. Watkins and made its debut (on the front cover) in issue No 327, dated 24 January 24 1948. Biffo remained on the front cover until issue No 1677, dated 7 September 1974, and was drawn by David Sutherland after the sudden death of Watkins in 1969. The strip was discontinued after issue No 2310, dated 25 October 1986 although Biffo has made guest returns in other strips from time to time.

Beau Peep Comic strip published in the *Daily Star*, from its launch on 2 November 1978. Written by Roger Kettle and illustrated by Andrew Christine, the strip focuses on the misadventures of the short, mustachioed, bespectacled Bert Peep, who joins the French Foreign Legion in the deserts of North Africa to escape his shrewish wife Doris. Other characters include: Dennis Pratt (Beau's dim-witted best friend who has a brother named Hector and a sister named Mavis), The Nomad (an unnamed nomadic Arab who is sometimes known as "Bobby Brains", the desert whiz kid". He is Bert's sworn enemy), Honest Abdul (a travelling salesman in the desert who sells all manner of dodgy goods), Sergeant Bidet (Bert's immediate superior who sends him on the occasional suicide mission), Egon (the bad-tempered and unhygienic fort cook), Mad Pierre (a bullying bruiser who generally vents his considerable anger on Bert), Colonel Escargot (The highly eccentric – downright mad - fort commander), Vera of the Seven Veils (an exotic belly dancer and stripper at the local saloon, whom Dennis is madly in love with), Hamish (a stereotypical Scotsman), Sopwith (Bert's camel) and The Vultures (A father-son duo with a yawning generation gap). The strip was dropped in December 1997 and as a result the circulation dropped, but when reintroduced in March 1999 sales increased substantially. Reprints of the strip have been featured in the *Sunday Express* and *People* and currently appear in the *Sunday Mail* and the *Daily Star Sunday*.

Beezer The broadsheet-sized first issue of *The Beezer* appeared on 21st January 1956. The strips included, Ginger, Pop Dick and Harry, Baby Crockett, The Banana Bunch and The Numskulls. Other early strips included: Colonel Blink, The Voyage Of The Bushwhacker, Mick On The Moon, Lone Wolfe, Nosey Parker, Nero And Zero, Calamity Jane, The Hillys And The Billys, Big Ed The Heavyweight Chump, Charlie Chick Up to Every Trick, Mumbo and Jumbo, The Pair From The Jungle, Smart Alice She Knows All The Answers, Shorty The Happy Little Chappy and The Kings Of Castaway Island. In 1981 the comic was reduced to A4 and in 1990 amalgamated with *The Topper* and ran for three more years, the final issue dated 21 August 1993. **Ginger** was created by Dudley Watkins, who drew the strip until his death in 1969. The adventures of the carrot-topped schoolboy were depicted on the cover of the *Beezer* for the first five years and after a five year break returned to its rightful place until the strip ended when the *Beezer* merged with the *Topper* in 1990. Like Ginger, **Pop, Dick and Harry** also appeared for the full duration of the Beezer's run. Dick and Harry were twins although not identical, Dick sporting blonde hair and Harry, black (in a Jedward style). Their rather overweight father was the victim of much of their scheming. The strip was drawn by Tom Bannister until 1981 and then by Peter Moonie (1981–87) and Brian Walker (1987–90). **Baby Crockett** was drawn by Bill Ritchie for much of its run. It also appeared throughout the run of the *Beezer* but also for the three years the comic merged with the *Topper*. The character was supposedly a baby version of Davy Crockett. Another strip that appeared from 1956 until 1993 was **The Banana Bunch**. Drawn by Leo Baxendale, members of the gang variously included Brainy, Dopey, Lanky, Titch, Fatty, Cookie, Thatch, and Sis. **Colonel Blink** debuted in November 1958, drawn by Tom Bannister. The character was a sort of British Mr Magoo, his shortsightedness being the basis of the plot lines. Among his long suffering stooges were his auntie, Rover the dog, and his neighbour, Cartwright. After the merger of the Beezer and Topper, the strip was retitled *Blinky*, the main character being the nephew of the colonel. This strip was later transferred to the *Dandy*. **The Numskulls** was a very popular strip throughout most of the run of the comic. Drawn by Malcolm Judge - Brainy (controlled the brain), Blinky (controlled the eyes), Radar (originally called Luggy; controlled the ears), Snitch (originally called Nosey; controlled the nose) and Cruncher (replaced Alf & Fred and controlled the mouth). Originally they lived inside a man's head but when the comic amalgamated with the *Topper* the man was replaced by a boy, Edd Case. More recently the strip has transferred to *The Beano*.

Boy's Own *The Boy's Own Paper* was aimed at young and teenage boys and its first issue was dated 19 January 1879. Published by the Religious Tract Society as a means to encourage young children to read and also to introduce Christian morals during their formative years, the paper was published weekly until November 1913, when it became a monthly. Each year's issues were bound together and sold as the *Boy's Own Annual,* eventually ceasing after the 1940-41 edition due to wartime paper rationing. A smaller annual was later published as the *Boy's Own Companion* (1959-63), changing its title to *Boy's Own Annual II* from 1964 until its demise in 1976. Typical content of the paper might include adventure stories, notes on how to practice nature study, sports and games, puzzles, and essay competitions. Famous contributors included cricket legend W.G. Grace, writers Arthur Conan Doyle, Jules Verne and R.M. Ballantyne plus the founder of the Boy Scout Movement, Robert Baden-Powell. Edward Whymper, the first man to climb the Matterhorn in 1865, contributed engravings (including the masthead). Perhaps because of its middle-class persuasions, by 1967 the paper's sales diminished and BPC Publishing

Ltd, who had been publishing it since 1965, discontinued production.

Bunty Published by D.C. Thomson, Bunty was the older sister of *Mandy* and designed for girls under the age of fourteen. The first issue, dated 18th January 1958, came with a free gift of a 'Ladybird' ring. Strips included The Four Marys, Uncle Tom's Cabin, Girl of the Islands, Bimbo and her Baby, Dancing Life of Moira Kent, Parachute Nurse, and Pocahontas. Later strips included: Bella the Bookworm, Lydia and the Little People, Boyfriend from Blupo, Toots, Sharon's Stone, Superstitious Cindy, Mighty Mo, Margie the Swimming Marvel, Laurel and the Talking Doll, Wonderful Wanda, When Harry Dumped Sally, and many others. The back page originally displayed a cut-out doll and paper clothes but this eventually gave way to a wall-poster. The final issue of *Bunty* was dated 17 February 2001. **The Four Marys** was drawn by artist Barrie Mitchell and ran throughout the life of the comic. It featured four young teenagers who lived in a girls-only boarding school, St. Elmo's, in Elmbury.

Buster *Buster* was a children's comic published by IPC Magazines Ltd (later Fleetway); first appearing on 28 May 1960. The eponymous hero invariably appeared on the front cover, originally billed as Buster: Son of Andy Capp. Like his more famous father, Buster wore the same cloth cap which was only removed in the very last strip, dated 4 May 2000, when he was revealed to have a hairstyle like Dennis the Menace. By the mid-1960s all reference to Buster being the son of Andy Capp ceased although his mother continued to be drawn as Florrie. Numerous comics merged with Buster over the years but one popular strip (which ran from 20 July 1964 to 15 June 1974) was The Astounding Adventures of Charlie Peace, loosely based on the real-life nineteenth-century murderer and burglar of the same name, although the comic strip portrayed him far more sympathetically than he probably deserved.

Cloggies *The Cloggies, an Everyday Saga in the Life of Clog Dancing Folk*, to give it its full title, was a cartoon strip by Bill Tidy that ran in the satirical magazine *Private Eye* from 1967 to 1981, and later in the radio magazine *The Listener* from 1985 to 1986. As with his more famous Fosdyke Saga, Tidy satirised northern British male culture, against a backdrop of the scurrilous delights of Lancashire clog-dancing. The Cloggies team consisted of Stan (the captain who was later ennobled as Lord Stan of Blagdon), Albert (second boot; known for his false teeth), Neville (third boot; known for his trilby and glasses), Arnold (fourth boot), Ted (fifth boot; known for his grey socks), Wally (sixth boot, later deceased and replaced by the bearded Norman). An unsavoury local resident was Reg Thrumper, the "Blagdon Amateur Rapist".

Dandy *The Dandy* is a children's comic, published by Dundee-based publisher D.C. Thomson & Co, first appearing on 4 December 1937 as *The Dandy Comic*. It was published weekly until 6 September 1941, when wartime paper shortages forced it to switch to fortnightly, alternating with *The Beano*. It returned to its weekly schedule on 30 July 1949. From 17 July 1950, the magazine changed its name to *The Dandy*. After issue No 3282, dated 16 October 2004, the comic changed its content to reflect a more television-oriented style and it also began to be printed on glossy magazine paper instead of newsprint. Between August 2007 and October 2010 the comic was rebranded *Dandy Xtreme*, a fortnightly comic-magazine hybrid. The first *Dandy Xtreme* had Bart Simpson on its cover. From issue No 3508, dated 27 October 2010, *The Dandy* returned as a weekly comic and ditched the 'Xtreme' from the title although maintaining its glossy style and topical television elements. Recent strips include old favourites Desperate Dan and Korky the Cat, Harry Hill's Real-Life Adventures in TV Land, Mr Meecher the Uncool Teacher, Davina McCaw, George vs Dragon,

Disaster Chef, Bananaman, 101 Ways to Use a Meerkat, The Arena of Awesome, Little Celebs, and Boo. **Desperate Dan** was created by Dudley D. Watkins and made its debut in the first issue in 1937. When Watkins died in 1969 his past strips were repeated until 1983 when new strips were drawn by Peter Davidson for a few issues before Ken H. Harrison took over as regular artist. In 1984 Dan was promoted to the front cover, replacing Korky who had been there since the first edition. From issue No 2985, dated 6 February 1999, Cuddles and Dimples replaced Dan on the front cover, although by the following year Dan had resumed his rightful place. Jamie Smart took over drawing and writing the strip, now seen on the back cover, in April 2008. Dan is a wild west character living in Cactusville with his Aunt Aggie. He is sometimes billed as 'the world's strongest man' his strength acquired from devouring huge portions of his favourite cow pie, complete with horns and tail. Dan's character has changed from an initial mean hombre to a more sympathetic law-abiding citizen over the years. Other characters in the strip have included his nephew, Danny, niece, Katey, and girlfriend Little Bear, although she disappeared with the 2007 *Dandy* re-launch, when Dan's artwork style changed to a more basic but still recognizable depiction. **Korky the Cat** was created by James Crichton and appeared on the front cover from the first issue until usurped by Desperate Dan in 1984, although Keyhole Kate relegated Korky to the inside for issue No 294, dated 9 June 1945. Originally a mute character, Korky began speaking in issue No 149, dated 5 October 1940, his opening words being "Let's ask the butcher for some sausages!". The 1950s saw the introduction of his 'Kits', Nip, Lip, and Rip. Crichton drew the strip until issue No 1051, dated 13 January 1962, when Charles Grigg took over from issue No 1052 until issue No 2116, dated 12 June 1982. Subsequent artists have included David Gudgeon (1982-86) and Robert Nixon (1986-99). Korky's final appearance was to be in issue 3294, dated 8 January 2005, however he returned from issue 3338, dated 19 November 2005, this time being drawn by Andrew Painter on computer. Although dropped during the *Dandy Xtreme* period, Korky reappeared on October 27, 2010 when *The Dandy* was relaunched, with Phil Corbett taking over as the Korky artist. Corbett's depiction is that of a short squat cat with blue and white fur, green bulging eyes and red nose, a far cry from the original black and white stand-up human-type animal of the Crichton era. **Winker Watson** was created by Eric Roberts and first appeared in issue No 1010, dated 1 April 1961. The date of April Fools was perhaps fitting as Winker, a pupil of the Third Form of Greytowers Boarding School, was known as the "wangler" of the school, constantly playing tricks and avoiding unpleasant school activities, much to the chagrin of his teacher Mr Clarence Creep. His character was certainly similar to that of *The Beano's* Roger the Dodger in the early days and he too wore red and black pants and top, albeit the other way around. Later strips had Winker attired in short black pants and bright red blazer. Winker's best pal was Tim Trott and the third member of his regular group was his other friend Sandy. Terry Bave took over as artist after Eric Roberts' death in 1982 and Stephen White took over in 2002 until the strip was dropped in 2007.

Eagle The *Eagle* was founded by Marcus Morris, an Anglican vicar from Lancashire. Its first edition, published by Hulton Press, was released on 14 April 1950. The weekly comic with the distinctive Eagle logo, was published on Fridays, and although priced at a relatively high 3d sold 900,000 copies of its first issue. Featured in colour on the front cover was the comic's most iconic strip, Dan Dare, Pilot of the Future, created by Frank Hampson, who had previously collaborated with Morris on *The Anvil*, a parish magazine which had such luminary contributors as C. S. Lewis and Harold Macmillan. On the back page was a religious story about Saint Paul. Other popular stories included Riders of the Range, Cavendish Brown, Harris Tweed, Jack o' Lantern, Storm Nelson, Luck of the Legion and PC 49. Each issue also featured a centre-spread full-colour cutaway illustration of a piece of machinery—the first detailed the inner workings of a British Rail 18000 locomotive. By 1960 both Morris and Hampson had left and sales steadily plummeted throughout the 1960s, the comic eventually being subsumed by its rival, *Lion*; the last issue selling on 26 April 1969. Eagle was relaunched by IPC Magazines in 1982 and ran for more than 500 issues, before being dropped by its publisher in 1994. **Dan Dare** was set in the late 1990s. His full title was Colonel Daniel McGregor Dare, chief pilot of the Interplanet Space Fleet. His spaceship was the *Anastasia*. Dan was born in Manchester, England, in 1967 and educated at Rossall School. He upheld Christian virtues and never lied or broke his word. His uniform was light green and his cap badge was a vertical, antique rocketship in a circle with one five-pointed star on either side. Dan's batman was the rather plump Albert Fitzwilliam Digby from Wigan. It was after Digby's Aunt Anastasia that Dan named his spaceship. Other characters included: Sir Hubert Guest (the Controller of the Space Fleet), Professor Jocelyn Mabel Peabody (the brains behind many of the team's most inventive plans), pilots Hank Hogan and Pierre Lafayette (stereotypically American and French; Pierre was primarily a pilot, Hank more a mechanic), Sondar the Treen (a reptilian inhabitant of northern Venus), Christopher 'Flamer' Spry (a freckle-faced student at 'Astral' space academy, who accompanies Dan on many later missions), Lex O'Malley (a bearded Irish submarine commander, who also accompanies Dan on later missions) and of course The Mekon (the super-intelligent ruler of the Treens and Dan's arch-enemy. He invariably escaped at the end of each story to return with an even more inventive scheme for the conquest of Earth). Illustrator Frank Hampson also wrote the first stories, which would often be long and elaborate and would unfold over a period of anything up to a year. Arthur C Clarke was a notable advisor for early plot lines which involved Dan making the first successful flight to Venus. The Reverend Chad Varah, who founded The Samaritans in 1953, wrote some early stories notably "Marooned on Mercury" (1952). In 1962 the strip was removed from the front to the inside of the comic, in black and white, and was drawn by Keith Watson. Over the remaining years the strip varied in format and quality, eventually returning to the front page in colour, until it ended in 1967 with Dan retiring to become Space Fleet controller. In 1977, Dan Dare appeared again in the first issue of *2000 AD* (26 February 1977). The first instalment, scripted by Ken Armstrong and Pat Mills, had the character revived from suspended animation after two hundred years to find himself in a different world. The Mekon also survived but otherwise the cast was different. In 1982 *Eagle* was re-launched, with Dan Dare again its flagship strip, the new character being the great-great-great-grandson of the original hero. In 2008 *Virgin Comics* published a seven-issue Dan Dare mini-series written by Garth Ennis, with art by Gary Erskine.

FHM The lad mag began publication in 1985 under the name *For Him* and changed its title to *FHM* in 1994, although the full *For Him Magazine* continues to be printed on the spine of each issue. The monthly magazine has been published by Bauer Media Group since February 2008. The international mag publishes an annual *FHM* 100 Sexiest Women in the World. The full list of winners with age in brackets follows: 1995 Claudia Schiffer (25), 1996 Gillian Anderson (28), 1997 Teri Hatcher (33), 1998 Jenny McCarthy (26), 1999 Sarah Michelle Gellar (22), 2000 Jennifer Lopez (31), 2001 Jennifer Lopez (32), 2002 Anna Kournikova (22), 2003 Halle Berry (37), 2004 Britney Spears (23), 2005 Kelly Brook (25), 2006 Keira Knightley (21), 2007 Jessica Alba (26), 2008 Megan Fox (22), 2009 Cheryl Cole (25), 2010 Cheryl Cole (26), 2011 Rosie Huntington-Whiteley (24).

Fosdyke Saga The Fosdyke Saga was a comic strip by cartoonist Bill Tidy, published in the *Daily Mirror* from March 1971 to February 1985. Full of typical northern humour, the strip was a parody of The Forsyte Saga and told the story of Roger Ditchley, the prodigal son of tripe magnate, Old Ben Ditchley, who was deliberately disinherited by his father in favour of Jos Fosdyke. Roger, blinded by rage, seeks to regain his rightful inheritance over the next twelve years. His wicked plans are always thwarted as he enlists the most inept allies and twisted methods to attain his goal.

Fred Basset Comic strip created by Scottish cartoonist Alex Graham featuring a male basset hound, first published in the *Daily Mail* on 8 July 1963. The strip has since been syndicated around the world, Fred being known as Wurzel in Germany, Lillo in Italy, Lorang in Norway, Laban in Sweden and Retu in Finland. After Alex Graham died, on 3 December 1991, Michael Martin took over the strip.

Gambols *The Gambols* is a comic strip created by Barry Appleby and first published in the *Daily Express* on 6th March 1950. George and Gaye Gambol are a happily married, suburban, middle class couple with no children. The humour revolves around George's misadventures, usually whilst pursuing DIY projects. Occasionally, George's nephew and niece (cousins - respectively Flivver and Miggy), come to visit. Barry Appleby was the illustrator of the strip and his wife, Doris (Dobs) was credited as the writer until her death in 1985 from which time Barry took over both jobs. When Barry died in 1996 the strip was taken over by Roger Mahoney until it moved to the *Mail on Sunday* in 1999.

Garth *Garth* was a comic strip created by Steve Dowling and debuting in the *Daily Mirror* on 24 July 24 1943. Fifteen-year-old John Allard took over the strip after 59 adventures but relinquished the artist role in favour of Frank Bellamy in 1971, although he remained the writer. When Bellamy died in 1976 the drawing was handed over to Martin Asbury for the last 21 years until the strip ended on 22 March 1997. Garth himself was a tall blond hero with amazing strength. He battled various villains throughout the world across many time frames. Recently the strip has appeared on the *Daily Mirror* website, drawn by Huw J. Davies, and a run of reprints appeared in the newspaper from Monday 21 February 2011.

Girls Own *The Girl's Own Paper* was the counterpart of *Boys Own* and catered for girls and young women. Also published by the Religious Tract Society (which later became Lutterworth Press), the first edition appeared on 3 January 1890. In October 1929, the title became *Girl's Own Paper and Woman's Magazine* but in 1930 the *Woman's Magazine* became a separate publication. In December 1947 the name was changed to *Girl's Own Paper and Heiress* and from 1951, until its demise in 1956, it was called *Heiress incorporating the Girl's Own Paper*. Typical content might include poetry, music, short stories, reader's letters, information on serious careers for girls and advice on style and dress. Contributors included famous children's writers such as Noel Streatfeild, Sarah Doudney, Rosa N. Carey, Angela Brazil, Lucy Maud Montgomery, Richmal Crompton and Baroness Orczy.

Heat British entertainment magazine launched in February 1999 by German company Bauer Media Group; its original editor being Barry McIlheney. In 2000, Mark Frith (b. 1970, Sheffield) took over as editor and during his eight-year tenancy the magazine became one of the best-selling in the UK. *Heat* contains celebrity news, gossip, fashion, movie and music reviews, TV listings and celebrity interviews. It particularly concentrates on reality TV stars, having in the past gone in for saturation coverage of *Big Brother*, although it remains to be seen whether the magazine offers the same facility for the Channel 5 series, launched in 2011 although the early series have been featured prominently. The current editor is Lucie Cave, previously better known for ghost-writing the autobiographies of Jade Goody and Abi Titmus.

Hello! Weekly magazine first published in 1988 by Eduardo Sánchez Junco, as a sister paper to his Spanish magazine *¡HOLA!* (launched in 1944). *Hello!* (often stylised as *HELLO!*) specialises in celebrity news, human-interest stories and blanket coverage of royalty. The magazine has a reputation for positive coverage of celebrities and has therefore secured many exclusives, including the births of Brad Pitt and Angelina Jolie's children Shiloh, Vivienne and Knox, and the wedding of Tom Cruise and Katie Holmes. However, the magazine has also found itself in breach of rival's exclusivity, most famously in 2003 when Catherine Zeta Jones and Michael Douglas sued *Hello!* for publishing unauthorised photographs of their wedding and the couple received £14,600. *OK!,* who had an exclusive contract for pictures of the wedding, also sued *Hello!* and were awarded £1,033,156 in damages.

Hot Press Fortnightly music and political magazine founded in Dublin in 1977. The magazine has been edited throughout its run by Niall Stokes. *Hot Press* covers all the major international music events, as well as Irish festivals such as Oxegen, Electric Picnic, Live at the Marquee, Cois Fharraige and Heineken Green Energy.

Jackie Weekly magazine for girls, published by D. C. Thomson. The first issue of Jackie was published on 11 January 1964 and it soon became the best-selling teen magazine in Britain with average sales in excess of half a million per week. *Jackie* contained a mix of fashion and beauty tips, gossip, reader's true life experiences, short stories and comic strips. Another popular section was the "Cathy and Claire" problem page which received hundreds of letters every week. The centre pages invariably contained a pull-out poster of a pop or film star. Nina Myskow, who made a name for herself as "the bitch on the box" when a judge on the television talent show *New Faces*, was the first female editor of *Jackie*, having worked on the magazine for some years prior to that appointment. After the NHS made the contraceptive pill free on prescription in 1974, Nina introduced a "Dear Doctor" column, which covered what were termed as "below the waist issues". Sales declined throughout the 1980s and by its last issue, dated 3 July 1993, had fallen below 50,000.

Jane *Jane* was a comic strip created and drawn by Norman Pett, debuting in the *Daily Mirror* on 5 December 1932. Originally entitled *Jane's Journal - Or the Diary of a Bright Young Thing*, the strip featured the misadventures of Jane Gay, who somehow or other always seemed to lose much of her clothing whilst going about her daily business, often accompanied by her pet dachshund, Fritz. Jane was initially modelled on Pett's wife Mary until 1940 when Chrystabel Leighton-Porter (1913-2000) took over and began a music hall striptease-act based on the Jane character which toured army bases around the country and boosted morale considerably. In 1949 Chrystabel starred in a popular film, *The Adventures of Jane*, based on the Jane character. The original strip ended on 10 October 1959 with Jane settling down with charmer Georgie, although there have been several revivals since. A television series was made by the BBC in the early 1980s, starring Glynis Barber in the title role.

Kerrang! Weekly rock music magazine published by the Bauer Media Group; its name deriving from the sound made when playing a power chord on an electric guitar. *Kerrang!* was launched on 7 June 1981; Angus Young of AC/DC appearing on its first cover.

Loaded *Loaded* was founded in 1994 by Mick Bunnage, Tim Southwell and James Brown as a magazine for men. Considered to be the original lad mag, its motto is "For men who should know better". In the early days the magazine unashamedly exalted so-called bad boys such as Liam Gallagher, Oliver Reed, Paul Gascoigne and Vinnie Jones. IPC Media sold *Loaded* to Vitality Publishing in 2010 and since then it has maintained its market share by including more varied fare.

Look Glossy high street fashion and celebrity weekly magazine launched in February 2007, primarily aimed at young women. Edited by Ali Hall, it features current and affordable fashion, high street shopping advice, celebrity style and news, and real life stories.

Magnet *The Magnet* was a boys' weekly story paper published by Amalgamated Press which ran for 1683 issues between 1908 and 1940. Each issue contained a long story about the boys of the fictional public school, Greyfriars, located somewhere in Kent. Charles Hamilton (1876-1961) wrote the stories under the pseudonym Frank Richards. Although there was no star character in the early years of the stories it became apparent that Billy Bunter (aka the Fat Owl of the Remove) provoked most interest among readers and he became the focal point of the Greyfriars stories. Billy's family consisted of sister, Bessie, a pupil at the nearby Cliff House Girls School; younger brother Sammy, who was in the second form at Greyfriars; his somewhat stern father, Mr Samuel Bunter who worked as a stockbroker and was invariably heard complaining about income tax and school fees; and his kindly mother, Mrs Amelia Bunter, who only appeared in seven stories. After the demise of the paper, Bunter appeared in several other comics, notably *TV Comic*. Charles Hamilton wrote many strips for *The Magnet*, all under pen-names, for example St Jim's (as Martin Clifford), Rookwood (as Owen Conquest), Herlock Sholmes (as Peter Todd) and The Rio Kid (as Ralph Redway). The various eras of *The Magnet* are generally divided as to the colour of its cover i.e. Red (1908–15), Blue and White (1915–22), Blue and Orange (1922–37) and Salmon Pink (1937–40).

Maxim International men's magazine best known for depicting semi-nude actresses, singers, and models. Launched in the UK in 1995, on 23 April 2009 Dennis Publishing announced the conclusion of the printed edition of *Maxim* in the UK, though the website for the UK version will remain. Each year since 2000 the magazine has released the Maxim Hot 100, a list that features the 100 hottest woman of that year. The winners and their corresponding ages and the year in which the magazine was released follow: 2000 Estella Warren (22), 2001 Jessica Alba (20), 2002 Jennifer Garner (30), 2003 Christina Aguilera (23), 2004 Jessica Simpson (24), 2005 Eva Longoria (30), 2006 Eva Longoria (31), 2007 Lindsay Lohan (21), 2008 Marisa Miller (30), 2009 Olivia Wilde (25), 2010 Katy Perry (26), 2011 Rosie Huntington-Whiteley (24).

Modesty Blaise Comic strip which debuted in the London *Evening Standard* on 13 May 1963. Created by writer Peter O'Donnell and artist Jim Holdaway, the eponymous heroine escaped from a Greek displaced person camp in 1945 and befriended Lob, a Jewish Hungarian scholar from Budapest. Lob educated the child and gave her the name Modesty (Blaise she added herself later, after Merlin's tutor from the Arthurian legends). Lob died when Modesty was 12 years old and in 1953, his ward took over a criminal gang in Tangier from Henri Louche and expanded it to international status as "The Network". Modesty's right-hand man was Willie Garvin, a tall handsome British ex-Foreign Legion member, skilled in the art of Thai boxing. Although other members of The Network would call Modesty "Mam'selle", Willie always referred to her as 'Princess'. Modesty obtained British nationality by marrying, and quickly divorcing, Englishman

James Turner in Beirut. Her largely ill-gotten gains brought her a penthouse in London overlooking Hyde Park, and also a villa in Tangier and a cottage two miles from Benildon, Wiltshire. Having a distinctly moralistic disposition, Modesty was recruited by Sir Gerald Tarrant, a high-ranking official of the British Secret Service, and eventually used her combat skills to fight injustice, her preferred weapons included a kongo (also called a yawara stick), Colt .32 and Mab Brevete, while Willie's weapon of choice was a throwing knife, of which he usually carried two. The final Modesty Blaise strip ran in the *Evening Standard* on 11 April 2001. The strip inspired several films, 15 novels, radio and television broadcasts and numerous reprints in various comics.

Mojo Monthly music magazine published by the Bauer Media Group, focusing on classic rock music; the first issue, published on 15 October 1993, depicted Bob Dylan and John Lennon on the cover. In 2004 it introduced the Mojo Honours list, an awards ceremony which is a mixture of readers' and critics' awards.

NME The *New Musical Express* has been published weekly since March 1952. It started as a music newspaper, and gradually moved toward a magazine format during the 1980s, changing from newsprint in 1998. It was the first British paper to include a singles chart, in the 14 November 1952 edition. In 2000 *NME* absorbed another IPC music paper *Melody Maker* (founded in 1926). In October 2006 *NME* launched a short-lived Irish version of the magazine called *NME Ireland*. Current editor, Krissi Murison, became NME's first female editor in September 2009.

NOW Weekly entertainment magazine launched in late 1996, published by IPC Media Limited. Edited by Sally Eyden, the magazine has a circulation in excess of 300,000 and bills itself as "The UK's best-loved celebrity magazine".

Nuts Weekly lad mag founded in 2004 by IPC Media, currently edited by Dominic Smith. Published every Tuesday, its marketing slogan is "Women, don't expect any help on a Tuesday". Although aimed at much the same demographic as *Zoo*, and indeed containing similar content, *Nuts* has a larger circulation.

OK! Celebrity gossip magazine first published in April 1993 as a monthly magazine, before becoming a weekly paper in 2006. Owned by Richard Desmond, *OK!* was the best-selling celebrity weekly until superseded by Bauer Media's *Closer* in 2009. Released on Tuesdays, *OK!* currently costs £1.45 and contains two inner mags, *Hot Stars* and *OK! USA*. Best-known for its celebrity wedding coverage which include: Melanie Brown and Jimmy Gulzar (September 1998), Kym Marsh and Jack Ryder (August 2002), Jordan and Peter Andre (October 2005), Christina Aguilera and Jordan Bratman (November 2005), Cheryl Tweedy and Ashley Cole (July 2006), Kerry Katona and Mark Croft (February 2007), Alex Curran and Steven Gerrard (June 2007), Toni Poole and John Terry (June 2007), Eva Longoria and Tony Parker (July 2007), Holly Willoughby and Dan Baldwin (August 2007), Natasha Hamilton and Riad Erraji (November 2007), Coleen McLoughlin and Wayne Rooney (June 2008), Jade Goody and Jack Tweed (February 2009), Patsy Kensit and Jeremy Healy (April 2009), Jodi Albert and Kian Egan (May 2009), Samantha Janus and Mark Womack (May 2009) and Hilary Duff and Mike Comrie (August 2010). The magazine sparked controversy in March 2009 when it published an 'Official Tribute Issue' for Jade Goody with the front-page captions 'In Loving Memory' and '1981-2009', even though Jade was still alive at the time of going to press. Brand extensions include *OK! TV*, an early evening magazine programme, broadcast on Channel 5, presented by Kate Walsh and Matt Johnson, and *OK! Insider*, a weekly vidcast, written and presented by

Layla Anna-Lee. See also entry for *Hello!* concerning the marriage of Catherine Zeta Jones and Michael Douglas.

Oz Originally published in Sydney, Australia in 1963, the irreverent psychedelic satirical magazine was first published in the UK in 1967 by Australians Jim Anderson, Martin Sharp and Richard Neville, who remained the central editor throughout the magazine's life. Contributors included feminist broadcaster and writer Germaine Greer, artist and filmmaker Philippe Mora, photographer Robert Whitaker, journalist Lillian Roxon, and cartoonist Michael Leunig. Felix Dennis, who later launched *Maxim* in the UK, replaced Martin Sharp as a partner in 1969. In May 1970 the three members of the editorial team allowed schoolchildren to edit issue No 28 and the resultant magazine included a cover depicting naked women touching themselves provocatively and a highly sexualised Rupert Bear parody within its covers. This set the scene for the famous *Oz* obscenity trial of 1971 in which Dennis and Anderson were represented by lawyer and writer John Mortimer (creator of the *Rumpole of the Bailey* series). Neville chose to represent himself having had experience in doing so during the earlier Australian version obscenity trial. The trial brought the magazine to the attention of John Lennon and Yoko Ono who joined the protest march against the prosecution and organised the recording of "God Save Us" (originally entitled "God Save Oz") by the makeshift group Elastic Oz Band to raise funds and gain publicity. At the committal hearing, Neville, Dennis and Anderson appeared wearing rented schoolgirl costumes which probably didn't help their cause. At the end of the original trial the "Oz Three" were found not guilty on a conspiracy charge, but were convicted of two lesser offences and sentenced to imprisonment; Felix Dennis being given a lighter sentence as the judge, Justice Michael Argyle, considered that he was "very much less intelligent" than Neville and Anderson. Shortly after the verdicts were handed down they were taken to prison and their heads shaved, which caused an even greater stir on top of the already considerable outcry surrounding the trial and verdict. At the appeal trial (where the defendants appeared wearing long wigs) it was found that Justice Argyle had grossly misdirected the jury on numerous occasions and the convictions were overturned. Despite the initial boost in circulation created by the case sales of *Oz* soon dropped below break even and the last issue, No 48, was published in November 1973.

Perishers The Perishers was a comic strip created and written by Maurice Dodd (1922-2005), debuting in the *Daily Mirror* on 19 October 1959. Originally drawn by Dennis Collins until his retirement in 1983, after which Dodd took over the dual roles. After Dodd's death the strip continued with several weeks' backlog of strips and some reprints until 10 June 2006. The story is set in the fictional south London borough of Croynge (the name deriving from Croydon and Penge). The main characters included: **Wellington** (a thoughtful orphan boy who in the early days of the strip lived in a concrete pipe section in a builder's yard but in 1966 moved into a small railway station that had become victim of the Beeching Axe. Wellington, who shared a birthday – 25 October – with his creator Maurice Dodd, supported himself by selling hand-made wooden buggies), **Boot** (Wellington's white Old English Sheepdog who was given to flights of fancy and was convinced that he was in fact an 18th century English lord enchanted into a dog by a gypsy wench. Boot's mother was named "Cherry Blossom."), **Marlon** (a slow-witted boy who dreamt of becoming a brain surgeon or a sewer worker, and whose invention of the 2.5cm-thick ketchup sandwich often resulted in a huge dollop of ketchup hitting whoever happened to be standing nearby, **Maisie** (a tomboy-ish girl with a crush on Marlon) and **Baby**

Grumpling (Maisie's younger brother with a mischievous streak).

Private Eye Fortnightly British satirical and current affairs magazine, currently edited by Ian Hislop. Since it was founded by Andrew Osmond in October 1961, the magazine has distinguished itself from other titles with its unique combination of humorous cartoons and satire with hard-hitting journalism which has been examined in the libel courts on numerous occasions. *Private Eye* was initially edited by Christopher Booker and designed by Willie Rushton, who also drew cartoons for it. Richard Ingrams took over as editor at issue 40 in 1963 and when financial assistance was needed Peter Cook gained a majority shareholding on the proceeds of his very successful night club The Establishment. Richard vacated the editor's chair in 1986 (launching *The Oldie* in 1992, a monthly magazine he still edits) with Ian Hislop taking over. Before he relinquished his duties, Ingrams and John Wells found great success writing fictional letters from Denis Thatcher to Bill Deedes in the Dear Bill column, mocking Margaret Thatcher's husband as an amiable, golf-playing drunk. The column was collected in a series of books and became a play in which Wells played the fictional Denis, a character who became inextricably blurred with the real historical figure as portrayed in the media. In the early days of the magazine, Paul Foot (1937-2004) wrote on politics, local government and corruption as did Nigel Dempster (1941-2007) although when Dempster subsequently fell out with the editor he was invariably referred to in the mag as 'Nigel Pratt-Dumpster'. During this initial vicennial period Gerald Scarfe (b. 1936) drew caricatures of public figures. Celebrated poet Christopher Logue was another long-time contributor, providing a column of "True Stories" featuring cuttings from the national press. Some of the contributors to the magazine are media figures who write anonymously, often under humorous pseudonyms. A financial column at the back of *Private Eye* ("In the City", written by Michael Gillard) has found a popular readership since a number of financial scandals have been exposed there. The first half of the magazine has a number of recurring in-jokes and convoluted references, often decipherable only to those who have read the magazine for several years. These in-jokes include references to controversies or legal ambiguities in a subtle euphemistic code, such as replacing "drunk" with "tired and emotional", or using the phrase "Ugandan discussions" to denote illicit sexual exploits; and more obvious parodies utilising easily-recognisable stereotypes, such as the lampooning of Conservative MPs viewed to be particularly old-fashioned and bigoted as "Sir Bufton Tufton". The second half of the issue tends to contain more parody and cutting humour, presented in a more confrontational style. Public figures are referred to under pseudonyms some of the more famous being: Queen Elizabeth II (Brenda), Prince of Wales (Brian), Duke of Edinburgh (Keith), Princess Margaret (Yvonne), Diana, Princess of Wales (Cheryl), Jeffrey Archer (Lord Archhole), Margaret Beckett (Rosa Klebb), Mohamed Al-Fayed (The Phoney Pharaoh), Richard Branson (Beardie), Derek Jameson (Sid Yobbo), Piers Morgan (Piers Moron), Andrew Neil (Brillo Pad), Lady Antonia Fraser (Lady Magnesia Freelove) and Sir Paul McCartney (Sir Spigismond Topes). Newspaper have also been given nicknames i.e. The Grauniad (*Guardian*), The Torygraph (*Telegraph*), The Absurder (*Observer*), Daily Sexpress (*Express*), The Sindie (*Independent on Sunday*) and The Moron (*Mirror*). Among its recent popular cartoon strips is Dave Snooty – drawn in the style of *The Beano* - it parodies David Cameron as "Dave Snooty" (a reference to the *Beano* character "Lord Snooty"), involved in public schoolboy-type behaviour with members of his cabinet. Regular columns include: **Commentatorballs** (previously known as Colemanballs) which describes verbal gaffes of broadcasters; **Wikipedia Whispers** which reports cases of personalities apparently editing their own Wikipedia entries to make them more positive; **Rotten Boroughs** a column reporting dubious practices and corruption in local government; **Nooks & Corners** containing architectural criticism - founded by Sir John Betjeman and currently written by architectural historian Gavin Stamp using the name 'Piloti'; **Curse of Gnome** in which targets of *Private Eye* who have responded in return are mocked when they suffer a misfortune; **Brussels Sprouts** depicting the foibles of the European Union and its parliament; and **Ad Nauseam** describing the excesses, plagiarism and creative failings of the advertising industry. See also entry for The Cloggies.

Punch *Punch, or the London Charivari* (named as tribute to the Paris satirical magazine *Le Charivari*) was a weekly satirical magazine established on 17 July 1841 by engraver Ebenezer Landells and journalist Henry Mayhew, who co-edited the magazine with Mark Lemon (b. 30 November 1809, London; d. 23 May 1870, Crawley, West Sussex). The iconic masthead depicting the glove puppet, Punchinello, of Punch and Judy, was a dual reference to the anarchic nature of its content and also referred to a joke made early on by Mark Lemon, that "punch is nothing without lemon". In December 1842 the magazine was sold to publishers Bradbury and Evans. Artists and writers who published in *Punch* in the early days were known as "The Punch Brotherhood" and included John Leech, Richard Doyle, John Tenniel, Charles Keene, Harry Furniss, Linley Sambourne, Francis Carruthers Gould, Phil May, and Charles Dickens, who joined Bradbury and Evans after leaving Chapman and Hall in 1843. *Punch* authors and artists also contributed to another Bradbury and Evans literary magazine called *Once A Week*, created in response to Dickens' departure from *Household Words*. *Punch* gave birth to several phrases, including the 'Crystal Palace', the 'Curate's egg' (first seen in an 1895 cartoon) and the word 'cartoon' itself, when used in the sense of a humorous illustration. Several British humour classics were first serialised in *Punch*, such as the *Diary of a Nobody* and *1066 and All That*. Circulation of *Punch* peaked during the 1940s at 175,000 but declined thereafter, finally closing in 1992, although revived briefly in 1996 (bought as a hobbyhorse by Egyptian businessman Mohamed Al-Fayed) before closing permanently in 2002.

Q Monthly up-market music magazine founded by Mark Ellen and David Hepworth in October 1986. The magazine is famous for its annual awards, which commenced in 1990, and for rating albums from one to five stars; the rating an album receives is often added to media advertising for the album in the UK and Ireland. It also compiles a list of approximately eight albums, which it classes as the best new releases of the previous three months. The magazine is also famous for compiling lists such as "The 100 Greatest albums". Other features include: the **Spine Line** where readers attempt to work out what the message on the spine has to do with the contents of the mag; the **Q50**, wherein the magazine lists the top 50 essential tracks of the month; **Cash for Questions**, in which a famous artiste(s) answers question sent in by readers - who win £25 if their question is printed; **Ten Commandments** in which a particular singer creates their very individualistic ten commandments by which to live; and **Rewind**, in which the reader is taken back in time through the history of music via archive issues of *Q*. The magazine is published by the Bauer Media Group and the current editor is Paul Rees.

Rover See entry for *The Wizard* and also entry for *The Victor*.

Rupert Bear Comic strip character created by the English artist Mary Tourtel, first appearing in the *Daily Express* on 8 November 1920. Alfred Bestall was the author and illustrator of *Rupert Bear* from 1935 to 1974. Rupert is a white bear who lives with his parents in a house in Nutwood. He invariably wears a red jumper and bright yellow checked trousers, with matching yellow scarf. Rupert's friends include Bill Badger, Edward Trunk and Willie the mouse, Pong-Ping the Pekingese, Algy Pug, Podgy Pig, Ming the dragon, Raggety, a woodland troll-creature made from twigs, and the kindly Wise Old Goat. The human characters include: the Professor (who lives in a castle with his servant), Tiger Lily (a Chinese girl) and less frequently occurring characters such as Sailor Sam, Captain Binnacle and Rollo, the Gypsy boy. The Rupert strip is unusual inasmuch as it is produced in the original form of strip with illustrations accompanying text, as opposed to text being incorporated into the art through the use of speech bubbles. The strip has inspired books, films, television programmes and videogames. Rupert also appeared in Paul McCartney's 1984 music video "We All Stand Together" and his subsequent animated video, "Rupert and the Frog Song".

Smash! Weekly comic that ran for 257 issues, between 5 February 1966 and 3 April 1971 and published originally by Odhams Press and subsequently by IPC Magazines Ltd. Part of the *Power Comics* range, on 14 September 1968, with issue 137, it merged with *Pow!* (which had previously absorbed *Wham!*). On 2 November 1968, with issue 144, it merged with *Fantastic* (which had previously absorbed *Terrific*), to become *Smash and Pow* incorporating *Fantastic*. The comic was a mix of American super hero strips such as the Incredible Hulk and Fantastic Four plus a host of humorous strips drawn by Leo Baxendale, notably Eagle-Eye Junior Spy, The Man from BUNGLE, Bad Penny, and The Nervs, which was a busier format of The Numskulls, the aforementioned Nervs inhabiting a schoolboy called Fatty. The most memorable strip was Grimly Feendish (alias The Rottenest Crook in the World). Transferred from Wham!, the aim of the super-villain was world domination which he attempted to achieve using various monsters and outrageous plot devices such as exploding treacle.

Spectator *The Spectator* is a weekly political and high cultural magazine founded by Robert Stephen Rintoul on 6 July 1828 and currently owned by twins David and Frederick Barclay, who also own *The Daily Telegraph* and The Ritz Hotel in Piccadilly. It is a distinct magazine from the 18th century journal of the same name (see *The Tatler*). Editorship of *The Spectator* has often been part of a route to high office in the Conservative Party; past editors include Iain Macleod, Ian Gilmour and Nigel Lawson, all of whom became Cabinet ministers and Boris Johnson, the current Mayor of London. The current editor is Fraser Nelson.

Striker Comic strip created by Pete Nash, featuring in *The Sun* between 1985 and 2009. The plots revolve around Nick Jarvis' football career, firstly with Thamesford (at one time managed by rock star Rod Stewart) and then as player-manager with Warbury Warriors (a club that Nick helped out of the Conference to ultimately win the Champions League - beating Chelsea 2-1 in the final) during which time Nick briefly played for an Australian club, but had his playing career curtailed after having his leg bitten off by a shark. The strip began in black and white format, moving to colour in 1990 and being relaunched as Striker VR in a 3D rendered format in 1998 and the following year being renamed Striker 3D. In 2003, *Striker* broke away from *The Sun* (replacing Striker with its own 3D football strip named The Premier) and became its own magazine. This proved an unsuccessful venture and Striker returned to *The Sun* in October 2005. The final strip appeared in *The Sun* on Friday 18 September 2009, following which it experienced a short revival in the British magazine *Nuts* between January and October 2010.

Sugar Monthly magazine launched in October 1994 as a rival to *Just Seventeen* (a weekly magazine that ran from October 1983 to April 2004) targeting the teenage girl market. The magazine featured advice on relationships, body image and female health issues. It also included in-depth coverage of fashion, celebrities, and real-life stories concerning teenagers. Boys were not neglected and a free lad

mag was included. The magazine became defunct in March 2011 although the *Sugar* website still exists.

Tatler Several British journals and magazines have used the name, *The Tatler*. The original literary and society journal was founded by Richard Steele in 1709 under the nom de plume "Isaac Bickerstaff, Esquire", his spec was to cover the news and gossip heard in London coffeehouses. In its first incarnation, it was published three times a week. The original Tatler was published for only two years, from 12 April 1709 to 2 January 1711. Contributors included MP Joseph Addison and satirist Jonathan Swift (who also wrote under the pen name of Isaac Bickerstaff). Two months after the final edition, Steele and Joseph Addison co-founded the short-lived *The Spectator* magazine (distinct from the present day magazine). Although several attempts were made to revive *The Tatler* it was not until 3 July 1901 that the modern magazine was founded by Clement Shorter, who had published *The Sphere* the year before. Nowadays the monthly magazine, edited by Kate Reardon, covers newsworthy and gently satirical content as well as fashion and high class celebrity news. One of *Tatler's* most famous features is the annual Little Black Book, a compilation of the 100 most eligible below-thirty-somethings in London, generally made up of an assortment of heirs, aristocrats and European royalty.

Tiger Whilst sci-fi fans were lapping up the adventures of Dan Dare in the *Eagle*, IPC recognised that there was still a market for a sports-based comic. The first issue of *Tiger* appeared on 11 September 1954 with a free gift of a 'Space Gun Novelty'. Stories featured Roy Of The Rovers, The Speedster From Bleakmoor, The Mascot Of Bad Luck, Bulldog Bryant's Amazon Adventure, Tales Of Whitestoke School, Is Knowall Right Or Wrong?, Young Hurricane, Captives In The Fort Of Doom, Will Strongbow, The Two-Wheeled Whirlwind and Dodger Caine - The Lad With A Wheeze Up His Sleeve. Later strips included: Billy's Boots', Nipper, Hot Shot Hamish, Johnny Cougar, Martin's Marvellous Mini, and Skid Solo. Tiger survived for 1555 issues and incorporated a number of titles including *Champion* (1955), *Comet* (1959), *Hurricane* (1965), *Jag* (1969), *Scorcher* (1974) and *Speed* (1980) before being incorporated itself into the *Eagle* in 1985. The most famous story in *Tiger* was **Roy of the Rovers** who in the first issue was playing as centre forward for the Milston Youth Club team but being watched by Melchester Rover's scout Alf Leeds. The coloured cover of *Tiger* number one showed Roy Race scoring the first goal of many for Tiger readers but the last for Milston Youth Club. Alf was impressed and Roy was given a chance in the Melchester juniors on the back page. Roy was on his way to the longest career in football strips and most probably in football history. Roy was the invention of a writer called Frank S. Pepper who was also the creator of Captain Condor, an Amalgamated Press (Amalgamated press became IPC in 1969) attempt to rival Dan Dare. Pepper, who used the pen name Stewart Colwyn, conceptualised the story to be that of an ordinary, humble lad that readers would identify with and who would be signed by a great team and eventually become a star. The original artist was Joe Colquhoun. In September 1976 Roy was given his own comic, *Roy of the Rovers*, a spin-off from *Tiger and Scorcher* and also its sister paper. In a glittering career, Roy played for Melchester Rovers 1954-83, 1984-93; Walford Rovers (1983-84) and England. After being shot in 1982 he missed the 1986 World Cup finals after being kidnapped in Basran. His left foot was amputated following a helicopter crash in 1993 but he remains the club manager.

Topper The first issue of D.C. Thomson's *The Topper*, dated 17 February 1953, introduced Mickey the Monkey on its all-colour front cover. The cheerful simian was ably assisted by

Mickey's friend Polly the Parrot, and went on to make 1074 front cover appearances before settling down inside the covers, Send for Kelly replacing it. That strip was replaced by Danny's Tranny in 1975, and then Tricky Dicky in 1979. Beryl the Peril took over on 24 May 1986, and remained there until the merger with *The Beezer* on 15 September 1990. Originally a broadsheet (A3) *The Topper* was reduced to A4 in 1980. The most famous strip was **Beryl the Peril**, created by David Law. Beryl was designed to be the female equivalent of Law's other creation, *The Beano*'s Dennis the Menace (Minnie the Minx was created later in 1953). Wearing a red top underneath a black dress and sporting long pigtails with red ribbons, Beryl was the scourge of neighbours, parents and school teachers. Beryl was the flagship strip throughout the run of the comic and the amalgamation as *The Beezer and Topper* (1990-93), although by then she was sporting a blue and white striped jumper underneath a red dress. Since 1993 Beryl has made regular appearances in *The Dandy*.

TV Comic The first issue of *TV Comic*, dated 9 November 1951, had Muffin the Mule on the cover. The weekly comic was a mix of full colour gloss and black-and-white strips based on television shows of the day, although not exclusively so. The adventures of Mr Pastry figured prominently in the early years, as did Larry the Lamb, Sooty, Coco the Clown, Noddy and Lenny the Lion. Into the 1960s the strips were aimed at slightly older children and stories included Gerry Anderson fare such as Four Feather Falls, Supercar and Fireball XL5 as well as classic American stories such as The Lone Ranger. Other popular strips in the 1960s included, The Avengers (from Issue No 720), Dr Who (from Issue No 674), Space Patrol, Bootsie and Snudge, and The Telegoons. Ken Dodd and his Diddy Men were a long-running favourite, often adorning the cover. Non-TV strips included the American strip Beetle Bailey, TV Terrors (Cuthbert, Buttons and Monica plus their nemesis Hoppit), Arthur! and The Bakers' Dozen. TV Comic absorbed *TV Land* and *TV Express* in 1962, *TV Action* (formerly *Countdown*) in 1973, *Tom and Jerry Weekly* in 1974 (Tom and Jerry already featured in TV Comic) and *Target* in 1978. For issue No 1292, in 1976, it was relaunched as *Mighty TV Comic* and switched to a tabloid format, although reverting to an A4 format by issue No 1377. The 1697th and final issue of *TV Comic* was dated 29 June 1984.

2000 AD Science fiction-based comic, first published by IPC Magazines on 26 February 1977 and famous for its Judge Dredd strip. In 2000, the computer games company, Rebellion Developments, bought the comic from the IPC subsidiary, Fleetway Publications, and introduced several characters from the comic to the games market, notably Judge Dredd and Rogue Trooper. An ongoing joke is that the editor of *2000 AD* is Tharg the Mighty, a green extraterrestrial from Betelgeuse who terms his readers "Earthlets". American law enforcement officer, Judge Joseph Dredd, made his first appearance in the second issue of the comic and is the magazine's longest running character. Dredd and his fellow judges operate in the violent futuristic Mega-City One where summary punishment is often carried out. He was created by writer John Wagner and artist Carlos Ezquerra. Other successful strips in 2000 AD include Harlem Heroes (about a team of black aeroball players, inspired by the popularity during the 1970s of basketball greats, the Harlem Globetrotters), Robo Hunter (The hero, Sam Slade, being a private detective specialising in robot-related cases), Shakara (featuring a host of bizarre aliens using fantastically advanced technology), Caballistics, Inc (concerning the ghost-busting "Department Q", a division of the Ministry of Defence), The Red Seas (featuring Captain Jack Dancer and the crew of his ship the Red Wench).and Dan Dare (which transferred from the *Eagle* and featured between 1977-79).

Uncut Monthly magazine, launched in May 1997, targeting men aged 25-45, focusing primarily on music but also featuring books and films. In May 2006, the magazine dropped its book content and also severely reduced its film content. Published by IPC Media, it has been edited throughout its run by Allan Jones, former editor of *Melody Maker*.

Victor *Victor* No 1 appeared on 25 February 1961, complete with free super squirt ring, and lasted until 21 November 1992. The *Victor* had numerous war and sport related stories and a number of humorous stories including 'Cecil the Stone-age Scrapper' which told the story of Pete Pringle who found a stone-age man frozen in a block of ice. Pete thawed out the man, named him Cecil and taught him to box! Associated with the comic was the annually published *The Victor Book for Boys* (1964-94). The first issue of the comic saw the appearance of **I Flew with Braddock**, the story of fictional war hero, Sergeant - Pilot Matt Braddock whose wartime exploits had won him the Victoria Cross and Bar amongst many other medals. With the aid of pictures, the *Victor* brought to life his story as told by his flight navigator, Sergeant George Bourne. The story of Matt Braddock had originally first appeared in *The Rover* No 1414 (2nd August 1952) as a text story. Although highly decorated for his valiant deeds, Braddock was only interested in getting on with the war and winning it. Braddock was portrayed as a man-of-the-people, excelling in pub sports, particularly darts. The use of Rover text stories continued with **The Tough of the Track** in serial form. First appearing in Rover in 1949, Alf Tupper, as he was better known, was a welder's apprentice who loved to run. The character was created by Bill Blaine and written by Gilbert Lawford Dalton (as were the Braddock stories). When transferring to the Victor, in 1962, Pete Sutherland became the illustrator. A working-class hero, Alf lived with his Aunt Meg in Anchor Alley, Greystone, and would often go running in odd running shoes which he would buy out of his meagre earnings. His prowess at running soon made itself apparent when he won the mile for Greyshire in the Inter Counties Contest at the White City, on a diet of fish and chips. A good all-round athlete with the physique of a shot-putter and stamina of a marathon runner, Alf's catchphrase was "I ran 'em all!". He was last heard of in 1992 when he was in training for the Barcelona Olympics. Other popular strips included **Gorgeous Gus** who was in actuality the Earl of Boote, the owner of Redburn Rovers football club. He was nicknamed "Gorgeous Gus" by the fans because of his aristocratic airs and graces. For example, he would sit on the sidelines during games, attended to by his faithful butler Jenkins; **Joe Bones the Human Fly** a young soldier in the British Army during the Second World War who was also a talented climber. Joe was sent on commando missions by Government agent Lord Plimpton (referred to by Joe as "The Guv") that involved climbing all manner of impossible obstacles; and **Morgyn the Mighty** the world's strongest man who in the first storyline is the sole survivor of the shipwrecked schooner *Hebrides*, stranded on Black Island. He uses his strength and talents to fight wild beasts and become master of the island. Morgyn began life in the first issue of *The Beano* and transferred to *The Rover* in 1951 before becoming a permanent fixture in *The Victor* in 1962.

Viz *Viz* was launched in December 1979 from the bedroom of Chris Donald in his parents' Jesmond home, just north of the centre of Newcastle upon Tyne. Initially he was helped by his brother Simon and friend Jim Brownlow. The first 12-page issue was produced as a fanzine for a local record label and went on sale locally for 20p (30p to students!) and the run of 150 copies sold out within hours. As sales steadily increased, Brownlow left and freelance artists Graham Dury and Simon Thorp joined the team; the Donald brothers, plus Graham and Simon forming the nucleus of *Viz* for the next decade. In 1985, a deal was signed with *Virgin Books* to publish the comic nationally every other month. In 1987, the Virgin director responsible for *Viz*, John Brown, set up his own publishing company to handle *Viz*. Sales exceeded a million by the end of 1989, making *Viz* one of the biggest-selling magazines in the country. By the turn of the new millennium sales had settled at approximately 200,000 and Chris Donald had resigned as editor and passed control to a team consisting of his brother, Simon, Dury, Thorp plus Davey Jones and Alex Collier. In June 2001, *Viz* was acquired by I Feel Good (IFG), a company belonging to ex-Loaded editor James Brown, and increased in frequency to ten times a year. In 2003, it changed hands again when IFG were bought out by Dennis Publishing. Simon Donald subsequently left and the editorial team was bolstered by contributions from Robin Halstead, Jason Hazeley, Joel Morris and Alex Morris, the authors of *The Framley Examiner* (the spoof book depicting a town where nothing much happens - actually based upon the town of Chelmsford), and by James MacDougall and Christina Martin. Sales of the comic are currently around the 75,000 mark and its price is £3.20. The style of *Viz* is to parody extant British comics such as *The Beano* and *The Dandy*, albeit using incongruous, often crude, language. Viz also sends up tabloid newspapers and satirises current events and politicians and is usually referred to as an 'alternative' comic. The three best known strips are **The Fat Slags** Sandra Burke and Tracey Tunstall, known universally as San and Tray, who made their debut in 1989; **Roger Mellie** ("The Man on the Telly") the foul-mouthed television presenter who works for both the fictional Fulchester Television (FTV) and the BBC. Roger's catchphrase is "Hello, good evening and bollocks!" and **Billy the Fish** who despite being born half man, half fish, has managed to have a long and successful career as goalkeeper for Fulchester Utd FC. Other regular strips have included: Nobby's Piles, Johnny Fartpants, Buster Gonad, Sid the Sexist, Sweary Mary, Cockney Wanker, and Finbarr Saunders and his Double Entendres.

Which? The Consumers' Association is a product-testing and campaigning charity founded in 1957 by Michael Young. Its monthly magazine, *Which?* was first published from a converted garage in Bethnal Green, London in October 1957. It maintains its integrity by not accepting advertising and everything bought for testing is paid for at full price. *Which?* is funded entirely by its subscribers and has no shareholders. It is one of the most powerful non-governmental organisations in the UK and has statutory powers under the *Unfair Terms in Consumer Contracts Regulations 1999* to seek an injunction to restrain the use of an unfair contract term by a trader against consumers. It also communicates regularly with the Office of Fair Trading. *Which?* publishes the annual *Good Food Guide*, plus several self-help books such as *Giving and Inheriting, Divorce and Splitting Up, Be your own Financial Advisor, The Pension Handbook*, and *Working for yourself*. The *Which?* tagline is "Independent expert advice you can trust" and it is the largest consumer organisation in the UK, with more than 1 million subscribers.

Wizard *The Wizard,* published by D. C. Thomson & Co, was launched as a weekly text comic on 22 September 1922. It was merged with *The Rover* (which was launched on 4 March 1922) in September 1963, becoming *Rover and Wizard*, and renamed *The Rover* in August 1969. *The Wizard* was relaunched on 14 February 1970, and continued until 10 June 1978, by which time 1,970 issues had been produced. **Wilson the Wonder Athlete** first appeared in issue No 1029, dated 24 July 1943. Written by Gilbert Lawford Dalton using the pen name W S K Webb, William Wilson (born in the village of Stayling in Yorkshire) was indeed a wonder athlete who frankly was in a different league to Alf Tupper. The first adventure found William joining a race from out of the crowd and managing to run a three-minute mile! Although his stories were initially told in prose in *The Wizard*, a subsequent move to the comic papers *The Hornet* and *Hotspur* saw the character depicted in comic strip form. **Wolf of Kabul** better known as Second Lieutenant William Sampson was an agent of the British Intelligence Corps on the Northwest Frontier. Disguised as a native, he was armed only with two knives, while his Oriental sidekick, Chung, made devastating use of a cricket bat which he called "clicky-ba". The series reappeared in comic format in issue 102 of *The Hotspur* in 1961, and ran there until 1975.

Zoo Weekly lad mag, launched on 29 January 2004 by the Bauer Media Group and currently priced at £1.80. *ZOO* features comedy news, sports commentary, girls, jokes, an entertainments guide, fashion, and a very popular section of reader's pictures sent in because of their rude or comic content. Regular features include "The Week In Boobs", "Real Girls of the Year", "In Bed With..." and "Camera Flash".

Pipe Smokers of the Year

For nigh on 40 years this award was presented by the Pipe & Pipe Tobacco Trade Association (formerly known as The Pipesmokers' Council) to an individual who had made conspicuous their love of the briar, meerschaum, calabash or clay, in the year prior to their award. The Association's only criterion was that the victor must be British, famous, real and alive. This necessarily precluded the likes of Joseph Stalin, Albert Einstein, Sherlock Holmes and Popeye from being recipients of the much-coveted golden pipe, but from those filling the qualification criteria the list of winners remains a veritable pantheon of pipe-smoking gods.

The term pipesmoker is used loosely within the definition as at least one of the winners, flat green bowler David Bryant, did not in fact 'smoke' his pipe at all but simply placed it in his mouth and chewed on the mouthpiece as a prop to aid concentration. Indeed several other winners laid dubious claim to being honoured. Rupert Davies and Jeremy Brett for instance won their awards for portrayals of pipesmoking fictional detectives Jules Maigret and Sherlock Holmes and even Harold Wilson, who was honoured twice, his second award in 1976 being inscribed as 'Pipeman of the Decade', was not a true aficionado of the shag and briar but only sought to portray the character of an avuncular statesman in public while privately puffing on large Havanas.

The Tobacco Advertising and Promotion Act 2002, banning tobacco advertising and promotion caused the inevitable discontinuation of the award ceremony, the last being held at the Savoy in 2003 and won by Stephen Fry who claims to have taken up the pleasures of the pipe as a teenager whilst teaching in his gap year. Stephen felt it helped the staff to differentiate him from the pupils and also gave him the mien of someone with extreme mental acuity.

The following is a complete list of winners, all household names with the possible exception of Richard Dunhill, the grandson of tobacco magnate Alfred Dunhill.

1964 Rupert Davies (actor)
1985 Jimmy Greaves (footballer)
1965 Harold Wilson (politician)
1986 David Bryant (bowler)

1966 Andrew Cruikshank (actor)
1987 Barry Norman (television presenter)
1967 Warren Mitchell (actor)
1988 Ian Botham (cricketer)

1968 Peter Cushing (actor)
1989 Jeremy Brett (actor)
1969 Jack Hargreaves (television presenter)
1990 Laurence Marks (scriptwriter)
1970 Eric Morecambe (comedian)
1991 John Harvey-Jones (industrialist)
1971 Lord Shinwell (politician)
1992 Tony Benn (politician)
1973 Frank Muir (comedy writer)
1993 Rod Hull (comedian)
1974 Fred Trueman (cricketer)
1994 Ranulph Fiennes (adventurer)
1975 Campbell Adamson (industrialist)
1995 Jethro (comedian)
1976 Harold Wilson (politician)
1996 Colin Davis (conductor)

1977 Brian Barnes (golfer)
1997 Malcolm Bradbury (writer)
1978 Magnus Magnusson (television presenter)
1998 Willie John McBride (rugby player)
1979 J. B. Priestley (novelist)
1999 Trevor Baylis (inventor)
1980 Edward Fox (actor)
2000 Joss Ackland (actor)
1981 James Galway (flautist)
2001 Russ Abbot (comedian)
1982 Dave Lee Travis (radio DJ)
2002 Richard Dunhill (businessman)
1983 Patrick Moore (television presenter)
2003 Stephen Fry (actor)
1984 Henry Cooper (boxer)

Rear of the Year

Created by publicity consultant Anthony Edwards and currently sponsored by Wizard Jeans, the light-hearted award is given to someone in the public eye who is considered to have a notable posterior. Initially presented as a one-off accolade to Barbara Windsor for her outstanding cheekiness in several Carry On films, the award was made an annual event in 1981 and has remained so apart from three dormant years.

In 1986 the award ceremony at Olympia was won by Michael Barrymore, the first male recipient, and 1991 saw Marina Ogilvy, the daughter of Princess Alexandra, become the first royal recipient. From 1997 the awards have been presented annually to both sexes. The event has for the last four years been held in June at London's Dorchester Hotel in Park Lane.

The full list of winners with their age at time of victory following in brackets:

1976 — Barbara Windsor (39)
1981 — Felicity Kendal (34)
1982 — Suzi Quatro (31)
1983 — Lulu (34)
1984 — Elaine Paige (36)
1985 — Lynsey De Paul (34)
1986 — Anneka Rice (27) and Michael Barrymore (34)
1987 — Anita Dobson (38)
1988 — Su Pollard (38)
1991 — Marina Ogilvy (25)
1992 — Ulrika Jonsson (25)
1993 — Sarah Lancashire (29)
1994 — Mandy Smith (24) and Richard Fairbrass (41)
1995 — No competition
1996 — Tracy Shaw (23)
1997 — Melinda Messenger (26) and Gary Barlow (26)

1998 — Carol Smillie (26) and Frank Skinner (41)
1999 — Denise van Outen (25) and Robbie Williams (25)
2000 — Jane Danson (21) and Graham Norton (37)
2001 — Claire Sweeney (30) and John Altman (39)
2002 — Charlotte Church (16) and Scott Wright (27)
2003 — Natasha Hamilton (21) and Ronan Keating (26)
2004 — Alex Best (32) and Aled Haydn Jones (28)
2005 — Nell McAndrew (31) and Will Young (26)
2006 — Javine Hylton (24) and Ian Wright (42)
2007 — Siân Lloyd (49) and Lee Mead (26)
2008 — Jennifer Ellison (25) and Ryan Thomas (24)
2009 — Rachel Stevens (31) and Russell Watson (42)
2010 — Fiona Bruce (46) and Ricky Whittle (28)
2011 — Carol Vorderman (50) and Anton du Beke (44)